Capt. Tjader

MANUAL FOR COURTS-MARTIAL UNITED STATES (2008 EDITION)

The 2008 Edition of the MCM is a complete revision of the 2005 MCM incorporating all Executive Orders (EO) through 28 Sep 07 (EO 12473 promulgating the 1984 MCM; EO 12484, 15 Nov 84; EO 12550, 19 Feb 86; EO 12586, 3 Mar 87; EO 12708, 23 Mar 90; EO 12767, 27 Jun 91; EO 12888, 23 Dec 93; EO 12936, 10 Nov 94; EO 12960, 12 May 95; EO 13086, 27 May 98; EO 13140, 6 Oct 99; EO 13262, 11 Apr 02; EO 13365, 3 Dec 04; EO 13387, 14 Oct 05; EO 13430, 18 Apr 07; EO 13447, 28 Sep 07). Copies of each Executive Order can be found in Appendix 25.

PREFACE

The Manual for Courts-Martial (MCM), United States (2008 Edition) updates the MCM, (2005 Edition). It is a complete reprinting and incorporates the MCM (2005 Edition), the 2005 amendments to the MCM Rules for Courts-Martial, Military Rules of Evidence, and Punitive Articles made by the President in Executive Order (EO) 13387, 14 October 2005, the 2007 amendments contained in EO 13430, 18 April 2007, and the further 2007 amendments contained in EO 13447, 28 September 2007. The EOs referenced above can be found at Appendix 25 of this MCM. This edition also contains amendments to the UCMJ made by the National Defense Authorization Acts for Fiscal Years 2006 and 2007. Some of the significant changes from the MCM (2005 Edition) are summarized and listed below. This summary is for quick reference only and should not be relied upon or cited by practitioners in lieu of the actual provisions of the MCM that have been amended.

Rules for Courts-Martial (R.C.M.) in Part II of the MCM:

• R.C.M. 103(2) and R.C.M. 201(f)(1)(A)(iii)(b) changed the wording of rules requiring convening authorities to act affirmatively to refer a capital punishment eligible offense for trial as a capital case.

• R.C.M. 201(e)(2)(B), (e)(2)(C), (e)(3) and (e)(4), in their amended form, preclude commanders of joint organizations from trying service members not assigned to their joint command. The revision also clarified that implementing regulations of the accused's service apply when trial is conducted under a joint command, and that members and counsel from different services may be detailed to a court-martial convened by a joint commander.

• R.C.M. 501(a) expressly requires 12 members and a military judge in all capital cases unless 12 members are not reasonably available because of military exigencies or physical conditions.

• R.C.M. 503(b)(3) and (c)(3) clarify that a military judge and/or counsel from any service may be detailed to a court-martial convened by a joint or combatant commander.

• R.C.M. 504(b)(2)(A) and (b)(2)(B) clarify that a joint command or task force is ordinarily considered to be separate or detached and that the general court-martial convening authority of a joint command determines whether or not a unit is separate or detached.

• R.C.M. 703(b)(1) authorizes the presiding military judge in a court-martial to allow any witness to testify on interlocutory questions by remote means (e.g. VTC) or similar technology if practical difficulties in producing the witness on balance outweigh the significance of the witness' personal appearance. This authorization does not apply to trial sessions on the merits of the case when either party objects to the remote testimony.

• R.C.M. 804 and 805 allow the military judge to hold Article 39(a) sessions via remote means, so long as the accused has counsel physically present at his location. Service regulations are required to implement this change.

• R.C.M. 804 was also amended to clarify the procedures and requirements for allowing the presiding military judge to authorize the use of remote live testimony of a child. The change specifically applies to situations where remote testimony is warranted to protect the child from the traumatic experience of testifying in person at trial in front of the accused. It also clarifies the procedures and requirements for the limited circumstances in which the presiding military judge may authorize the accused to be absent from the courtroom for the limited purpose of a child's testimony.

• R.C.M. 912(f)(4) states that when a challenge for cause against a member has been denied, the successful use of a peremptory challenge against that same member by either party precludes further consideration of that excused member upon appellate or other review.

• R.C.M. 916 conforms to the Article 120, UCMJ, amendments regarding the defense of mistake of fact as to age in the prosecution of sexual offenses with a child and mistake of fact as to consent applicable to the offenses of rape, aggravated sexual assault, aggravated sexual contact and abusive sexual contact.

• R.C.M. 920 references the applicability of the R.C.M. 916 changes to the issue of mistake of fact as to consent and age.

• R.C.M. 1004, regarding capital cases, was amended to add as an aggravating factor that murder was committed while the accused was engaged in the commission or attempted commission of rape or other specified sex offenses under the amended Article 120, UCMJ.

• R.C.M. 1004(b) now requires the convening authority to include a special instruction in the referral block of the charge sheet if a case is to be tried as a capital case.

• R.C.M. 1103A contains new rules and procedures for sealed exhibits.

• R.C.M. 1204 sets forth the process by which courts-martial cases with sentences requiring the approval of the President (capital cases) are transmitted by The Judge Advocate General of the Military Department through the Secretary concerned, and then through the Secretary of Defense before being transmitted to the President. The amendment requires the Secretary of Defense to make a recommendation.

Military Rules of Evidence (MRE) in Part III of the MCM:

• MRE 412, "Sex offense cases; relevance of alleged victim's sexual behavior or sexual predisposition," was amended to define and include "sexual offenses" covered by the protections of the rule and amends the procedures to be used in determining admissibility.

• MRE 503 regarding the privilege attached to communications to clergy, was amended to define persons who qualify as covered "clergyman's assistants."

• MRE 504, regarding the husband-wife privilege, was amended to define the term "child of either," for which the privilege would not apply when one spouse is charged with an offense against such child. The new definition also includes a child who is under the permanent or temporary physical custody of one of the spouses, regardless of a legal parent-child relationship, and defines the term "temporary physical custody."

Punitive articles contained in Part IV of the MCM:

• Paragraph 14, Article 90, Assaulting or Willfully Disobeying Superior Commissioned Officer. A new definition subparagraph was added clarifying that the lawfulness of an order is a question of law to be determined by a military judge.

• Paragraph 43, Article 118, Murder, was amended to add offenses from the new Article 120 to the list of offenses which, if committed and during which the victim is killed, constitute murder.

• Paragraph 44a, Article 119a, Death or Injury to an Unborn Child. The change provided guidance to further implement the offense of causing the death or injury to an unborn child, as established by the Unborn Victims of Violence Act of 2004 (Public Law 108-212).

• Paragraph 45, Article 120, was amended and consolidated numerous paragraphs throughout the Punitive Articles into a single paragraph (Article) addressing sexual offenses, titled: "Rape, Sexual Assault, and other Sexual Misconduct." New offenses constituting degrees of sexual assault offenses were added. Text, explanation, elements of offenses, lesser offenses, maximum punishments, and sample specifications were provided for each enumerated sexual offense under paragraph 45, Article 120.

• Paragraph 45a, Article 120a, Stalking. The change added and implemented a new offense for stalking, with a maximum punishment for each offense consisting of a dishonorable discharge, forfeiture of all pay and allowances, and confinement for 3 years.

• Paragraph 50, Article 124, Maiming, was amended to increase the maximum punishment to confinement from 7 years to 20 years.

• Paragraph 54, Article 128, Assault, was amended to differentiate aggravated assault offenses committed against a child under the age of 16 and increase the maximum punishment in these cases.

• Paragraph 63, Article 134, Assault-Indecent. This offense was removed as it was subsumed into the new Article 120 provision.

• Paragraph 68a, Article 134, Child Endangerment, was added to the list of enumerated Article 134 offenses and addresses offenses committed by the accused who has a duty of care to a child under the age of 16. It requires that the accused endangered the child's mental or physical health, safety, or welfare through design or culpable negligence, provides definitions of the terms used, and establishes a hierarchy of maximum punishments depending on the manner and type of harm committed.

• Paragraph 87, Article 134, Indecent Acts or Liberties with a Child. This offense was removed as it was subsumed into the new Article 120 provision.

• Paragraph 88, Article 134, Indecent Exposure. This offense was removed as it was subsumed into the new Article 120 provision.

• Paragraph 90, Article 134, Indecent Acts with Another. This offense was removed as it was subsumed into the new Article 120 provision.

• Paragraph 97, Article 134, Pandering and Prostitution. The amendments added a new offense of patronizing a prostitute.

• Paragraph 109, Article 134, Threat or Hoax: Bomb. The amendments broadened the offense beyond threats involving explosives, to now include weapons of mass destruction, biological or chemical agents, substances, or weapons or hazardous material.

<u>Other UCMJ Articles contained in Appendix 2 of the MCM</u>:

• Article 2(a)(10) was amended to apply jurisdiction to persons serving with or accompanying an armed force in the field in time of declared war or contingency operation.

• Articles 8, 22, 46, 47, 49, 58, and 88 were amended to remove the obsolete reference to "Territory" of the United States.

• Article 39 was amended to allow for Article 39(a) sessions to be held with the accused present via audiovisual technology (such as videoteleconferencing) so long as the accused has counsel present at the accused's location. This amendment requires service regulations for implementation.

• Article 43 was amended to list offenses punishable by death to which the statute of limitations does not apply; It also extended the statute of limitations for child abuse offenses to the life of the child victim or five years from the date of the offense, whichever is later.

• Articles 1, 6, 15, 88, and 46, as well as other portions of the MCM were amended to change references to the Coast Guard as being part of the Department of Transportation to reflect the Coast Guard being under the Department of Homeland Security.

JOINT SERVICE COMMITTEE
ON MILITARY JUSTICE

CONTENTS

Page

SECTION III EXCLUSIONARY RULES AND RELATED MATTERS CONCERNING SELF-INCRIMINATION, SEARCH AND SEIZURE, AND EYEWITNESS IDENTIFICATION

Appendices

PART I
PREAMBLE

1. Sources of military jurisdiction

The sources of military jurisdiction include the Constitution and international law. International law includes the law of war.

2. Exercise of military jurisdiction

(a) *Kinds.* Military jurisdiction is exercised by:

(1) A government in the exercise of that branch of the municipal law which regulates its military establishment. (Military law).

(2) A government temporarily governing the civil population within its territory or a portion of its territory through its military forces as necessity may require. (Martial law).

(3) A belligerent occupying enemy territory. (Military government).

(4) A government with respect to offenses against the law of war.

(b) *Agencies.* The agencies through which military jurisdiction is exercised include:

(1) Courts-martial for the trial of offenses against military law and, in the case of general courts-martial, of persons who by the law of war are subject to trial by military tribunals. *See* Parts II, III, and IV of this Manual for rules governing courts-martial.

(2) Military commissions and provost courts for the trial of cases within their respective jurisdictions. Subject to any applicable rule of international law or to any regulations prescribed by the President or by other competent authority, military commissions and provost courts shall be guided by the appropriate principles of law and rules of procedures and evidence prescribed for courts-martial.

(3) Courts of inquiry for the investigation of any matter referred to such court by competent authority. *See* Article 135. The Secretary concerned may prescribe regulations governing courts of inquiry.

(4) Nonjudicial punishment proceedings of a commander under Article 15. *See* Part V of this Manual.

3. Nature and purpose of military law

Military law consists of the statutes governing the military establishment and regulations issued thereunder, the constitutional powers of the President and regulations issued thereunder, and the inherent authority of military commanders. Military law includes jurisdiction exercised by courts-martial and the jurisdiction exercised by commanders with respect to nonjudicial punishment. The purpose of military law is to promote justice, to assist in maintaining good order and discipline in the armed forces, to promote efficiency and effectiveness in the military establishment, and thereby to strengthen the national security of the United States.

4. Structure and application of the Manual for Courts-Martial

The Manual for Courts-Martial shall consist of this Preamble, the Rules for Courts-Martial, the Military Rules of Evidence, the Punitive Articles, and Nonjudicial Punishment Procedures (Part I–V). This Manual shall be applied consistent with the purpose of military law.

The Manual shall be identified as "Manual for Courts-Martial, United States (2007 edition)." Any amendments to the Manual made by Executive Order shall be identified as "2006" Amendments to the Manual for Courts-Martial, United States, "2006" being the year the Executive Order was signed.

The Department of Defense Joint Service Committee (JSC) on Military Justice reviews the Manual for Courts-Martial and proposes amendments to the Department of Defense for consideration by the President on an annual basis. In conducting its annual review, the JSC is guided by DoD Directive 5500.17, "The Roles and Responsibilities of the Joint Service Committee (JSC) on Military Justice." DoD Directive 5500.17 includes provisions allowing public participation in the annual review process.

Discussion

The Department of Defense, in conjunction with the Department of Homeland Security, has published supplementary materials to accompany the Manual for Courts-Martial. These materials consist of a Discussion (accompanying the Preamble, the Rules for Courts-Martial, and the Punitive Articles), an Analysis, and various appendices. These supplementary materials do not constitute the official views of the Department of Defense, the Department of Homeland Security, the Department of Justice, the military departments, the United States Court of Appeals for the Armed Forces, or any other authority of the Government of the United States, and they do not constitute rules. Cf., for example, 5 U.S.C.§ 551 (1982). The supplementary materials do not create rights or responsibilities that are binding on any person, party, or other entity (including any authority of the Government of the

United States whether or not included in the definition of "agency" in 5 U.S.C. §551(1)). Failure to comply with matter set forth in the supplementary materials does not, of itself, constitute error, although these materials may refer to requirements in the rules set forth in the Executive Order or established by other legal authorities (for example, binding judicial precedents applicable to courts-martial) which are based on sources of authority independent of the supplementary materials.

The 1995 amendment to paragraph 4 of the Preamble is intended to eliminate the practice of identifying the Manual for Courts-Martial, United States, by a particular year. As long as the Manual was published in its entirety sporadically (*e.g.*, 1917, 1921, 1928, 1949, 1951, 1969 and 1984), with amendments to it published piecemeal, it was logical to identify the Manual by the calendar year of publication, with periodic amendments identified as "Changes" to the Manual. The more frequent publication of a new edition of the Manual, however, means that it is more appropriately identified by the calendar year of edition. Amendments made in a particular calendar year will be identified by publishing the relevant Executive order containing those amendments in its entirety in a Manual appendix.

The amendment to paragraph 4 of the Preamble is intended to address the possibility of more frequent amendments to the Manual and the arrival of the 21st century. In the event that multiple editions of the Manual are published in the same year, the numbering and lettering of the edition should match that of the most recent Executive Order included in the publication.

Part II - R.C.M.

Part II - R.C.M.

PART II
RULES FOR COURTS–MARTIAL

CHAPTER I. GENERAL PROVISIONS

Rule 101. Scope, title

(a) *In general.* These rules govern the procedures and punishments in all courts-martial and, whenever expressly provided, preliminary, supplementary, and appellate procedures and activities.

(b) *Title.* These rules may be known and cited as the Rules for Courts-Martial (R.C.M.).

Rule 102. Purpose and construction

(a) *Purpose.* These rules are intended to provide for the just determination of every proceeding relating to trial by court-martial.

(b) *Construction.* These rules shall be construed to secure simplicity in procedure, fairness in administration, and the elimination of unjustifiable expense and delay.

Rule 103. Definitions and rules of construction

The following definitions and rules of construction apply throughout this Manual, unless otherwise expressly provided.

(1) "Article" refers to articles of the Uniform Code of Military Justice unless the context indicates otherwise.

(2) "Capital case" means a general court-martial to which a capital offense has been referred with an instruction that the case be treated as capital, and, in the case of a rehearing or new or other trial, for which offense death remains an authorized punishment under R.C.M. 810(d).

(3) "Capital offense" means an offense for which death is an authorized punishment under the code and Part IV of this Manual or under the law of war.

(4) "Code" refers to the Uniform Code of Military Justice, unless the context indicates otherwise.

Discussion

The Uniform Code of Military Justice is set forth at Appendix 2.

---

(5) "Commander" means a commissioned officer in command or an officer in charge except in Part V or unless the context indicates otherwise.

(6) "Convening authority" includes a commissioned officer in command for the time being and successors in command.

Discussion

See R.C.M. 504 concerning who may convene courts-martial.

---

(7) "Copy" means an accurate reproduction, however made. Whenever necessary and feasible, a copy may be made by handwriting.

(8) "Court-martial" includes, depending on the context:

(A) The military judge and members of a general or special court-martial;

(B) The military judge when a session of a general or special court-martial is conducted without members under Article 39(a);

(C) The military judge when a request for trial by military judge alone has been approved under R.C.M. 903;

(D) The members of a special court-martial when a military judge has not been detailed; or

(E) The summary court-martial officer.

(9) "Days." When a period of time is expressed in a number of days, the period shall be in calendar days, unless otherwise specified. Unless otherwise specified, the date on which the period begins shall not count, but the date on which the period ends shall count as one day.

(10) "Detail" means to order a person to perform a specific temporary duty, unless the context indicates otherwise.

(11) "Explosive" means gunpowders, powders used for blasting, all forms of high explosives, blasting materials, fuzes (other than electrical circuit breakers), detonators, and other detonating agents, smokeless powders, any explosive bomb, grenade, missile, or similar device, and any incendiary bomb or grenade, fire bomb, or similar device, and any other compound, mixture, or device which is an explosive within the meaning of 18 U.S.C. § 232(5) or 844(j).

(12) "Firearm" means any weapon which is de-

signed to or may be readily converted to expel any projectile by the action of an explosive.

(13) "Joint" in connection with military organization connotes activities, operations, organizations, and the like in which elements of more than one military service of the same nation participate.

(14) "Members." The members of a court-martial are the voting members detailed by the convening authority.

(15) "Military judge" means the presiding officer of a general or special court-martial detailed in accordance with Article 26. Except as otherwise expressly provided, in the context of a summary court-martial "military judge" includes the summary court-martial officer or in the context of a special court-martial without a military judge, the president. Unless otherwise indicated in the context, "the military judge" means the military judge detailed to the court-martial to which charges in a case have been referred for trial.

(16) "Party." Party, in the context of parties to a court-martial, means:

(A) The accused and any defense or associate or assistant defense counsel and agents of the defense counsel when acting on behalf of the accused with respect to the court-martial in question; and

(B) Any trial or assistant trial counsel representing the United States, and agents of the trial counsel when acting on behalf of the trial counsel with respect to the court-martial in question.

(17) "Staff judge advocate" means a judge advocate so designated in Army, Air Force, or Marine Corps, and means the principal legal advisor of a command in the Navy and Coast Guard who is a judge advocate.

(18) "*sua sponte*" means that the person involved acts on that person's initiative, without the need for a request, motion, or application.

(19) "War, time of." For purpose of R.C.M. 1004(c)(6) and of implementing the applicable paragraphs of Parts IV and V of this Manual only, "time of war" means a period of war declared by Congress or the factual determination by the President that the existence of hostilities warrants a finding that a "time of war" exists for purposes of R.C.M. 1004(c)(6) and Parts IV and V of this Manual.

(20) The definitions and rules of construction in 1 U.S.C. §§ 1 through 5 and in 10 U.S.C. §§ 101 and 801.

Discussion

1 U.S.C. §§ 1 through 5, 10 U.S.C. § 101, and 10 U.S.C. § 801 (Article 1) are set forth below.

1 U.S.C. § 1. Words denoting number, gender, and so forth.

In determining the meaning of any Act of Congress, unless the context indicates otherwise—

words importing the singular include and apply to several persons, parties, or things; words importing the plural include the singular;

words importing the masculine gender include the feminine as well;

words used in the present tense include the future as well as the present;

the words "insane" and "insane person" and "lunatic" shall include every idiot, lunatic, insane person, and person non compos mentis; the words "person" and "whoever" include corporations, companies, associations, firms, partnerships, societies, and joint stock companies, as well as individuals;

"officer" includes any person authorized by law to perform the duties of the office;

"signature" or "subscription" includes a mark when the person making the same intended it as such;

"oath" includes affirmation, and "sworn" includes affirmed;

"writing" includes printing and typewriting and reproductions of visual symbols by photographing, multigraphing, mimeographing, manifolding, or otherwise.

§ 2. "County" as including "parish," and so forth.

The word "county" includes a parish, or any other equivalent subdivision of a State or Territory of the United States.

§ 3. "Vessel" as including all means of water transportation.

The word "vessel" includes every description of watercraft or other artificial contrivance used or capable of being used, as a means of transportation on water.

§ 4. "Vehicle" as including all means of land transportation.

The word "vehicle" includes every description of carriage or other artificial contrivance used or capable of being used, as a means of transportation on land.

§ 5. "Company" or "association" as including successors and assigns.

The word "company" or "association", when used in reference to a corporation, shall be deemed to embrace the words "successors and assigns of such company or association", in like manner as if these last-named words, or words of similar import, were expressed.

10 U.S.C. § 101. *Definitions*

In addition to the definitions in sections 1-5 of title 1, the following definitions apply in this title:

(1) "United States", in a geographic sense, means the States and the District of Columbia.

(2) Except as provided in section 101(1) of title 32 for laws relating to the militia, the National Guard, the Army National Guard of the United States, and the Air National Guard of the United States, "Territory" means any Territory organized after this title is enacted, so long as it remains a Territory.

(3) "Possessions" includes the Virgin Islands, the Canal Zone, Guam, American Samoa, and the Guano islands, so long as

they remain possessions, but does not include any Territory or Commonwealth.

(4) "Armed forces" means the Army, Navy, Air Force, Marine Corps, and Coast Guard.

(5) "Department", when used with respect to a military department, means the executive part of the department and all field headquarters, forces, reserve components, installations, activities, and functions under the control or supervision of the Secretary of the department. When used with respect to the Department of Defense, it means the executive part of the department, including the executive parts of the military departments, and all field headquarters, forces, reserve components, installations, activities, and functions under the control or supervision of the Secretary of Defense, including those of the military departments.

(6) "Executive part of the department" means the executive part of the Department of the Army, Department of the Navy, or Department of the Air Force, as the case may be, at the seat of government.

(7) "Military departments" means the Department of the Army, the Department of the Navy, and the Department of the Air Force.

(8) "Secretary concerned" means—

(A) the Secretary of the Army, with respect to matters concerning the Army;

(B) the Secretary of the Navy, with respect to matters concerning the Navy, the Marine Corps, and the Coast Guard when it is operating as a service in the Navy;

(C) the Secretary of the Air Force, with respect to matters concerning the Air Force; and

(D) the Secretary of Homeland Security, with respect to matters concerning the Coast Guard when it is not operating as a service in the Navy.

(9) "National Guard" means the Army National Guard and the Air National Guard.

(10) "Army National Guard" means that part of the organized militia of the several States and Territories, Puerto Rico, and the Canal Zone, and the District of Columbia, active and inactive, that—

(A) is a land force;

(B) is trained, and has its officers appointed, under the sixteenth clause of section 8, article 1, of the Constitution;

(C) is organized, armed, and equipped wholly or partly at Federal expense; and

(D) is federally recognized.

(11) "Army National Guard of the United States" means the reserve component of the Army all of whose members are members of the Army National Guard.

(12) "Air National Guard" means that part of the organized militia of the several States and Territories, Puerto Rico, the Canal Zone, and the District of Columbia, active and inactive, that—

(A) is an air force;

(B) is trained, and has its officers appointed, under the sixteenth clause of section 8, article 1, of the Constitution;

(C) is organized, armed, and equipped wholly or partly at Federal expense; and

(D) is federally recognized.

(13) "Air National Guard of the United States" means the reserve component of the Air Force all of whose members are members of the Air National Guard.

(14) "Officer" means commissioned or warrant officer.

(15) "Commissioned officer" includes a commissioned warrant officer.

(16) "Warrant officer" means a person who holds a commission or warrant in a warrant officer grade.

(17) "Enlisted member" means a person in an enlisted grade.

(18) "Grade" means a step or degree, in a graduated scale of office or military rank that is established and designated as a grade by law or regulation.

(19) "Rank" means the order of precedence among members of the armed forces.

[Definitions established in clauses (18) and (19) post-date the enactment of the code and, as a result, differ from usage of the same terms in the code and current and prior Manual provisions. *See* Articles 1(5) and 25(d)(1); R.C.M. 1003(c)(2); paragraphs 13c(1), 83c(2), and 84c, Part IV, MCM, 1984. MCM 1951 referred to officer personnel by 'rank' and enlisted personnel by "grade." *See* paragraphs 4c, 16b, 126d, 126i, and 168, MCM, 1951. "Rank" as defined in 10 U.S.C. § 101, clause (19) above, refers to the MCM, 1951 provision regarding "lineal precedence, numbers, and seniority." Paragraph 126i, MCM, 1951; *see also* paragraph 126i, MCM, 1969 (Rev). Except where lineal position or seniority is clearly intended, rank, as commonly and traditionally used, and grade refer to the current definition of "grade."]

(20) "Rating" means the name (such as "boatswain's mate") prescribed for members of an armed force in an occupational field. "Rate" means the name (such as "chief boatswain's mate") prescribed for members in the same rating or other category who are in the same grade (such as chief petty officer or seaman apprentice).

[Note: The definitions in clauses (3), (15), (18)-(21), (23)-(30), and (31)-(33) reflect the adoption of terminology which, though undefined in the source statutes restated in this title, represents the closest practicable approximation of the ways in which the terms defined have been most commonly used. A choice has been made where established uses conflict.]

(21) "Authorized strength" means the largest number of members authorized to be in an armed force, a component, a branch, a grade, or any other category of the armed forces.

(22) "Active duty" means full-time duty in the active military service of the United States. It includes full-time training duty, annual training duty, and attendance, while in the active military service, at a school designated as a service school by law or by the Secretary of the military department concerned.

(23) "Active duty for a period of more than 30 days" means active duty under a call or order that does not specify a period of 30 days or less.

(24) "Active service" means service on active duty.

(25) "Active status" means the status of a reserve commissioned officer, other than a commissioned warrant officer, who is not in the inactive Army National Guard or inactive Air National Guard, on an inactive status list, or in the Retired Reserve.

(26) "Supplies" includes material, equipment, and stores of all kinds.

(27) "Pay" includes basic pay, special pay, retainer pay, incentive pay, retired pay, and equivalent pay, but does not include allowances.

(28) "Shall" is used in an imperative sense.

(29) "May" is used in a permissive sense. The words

"no person may . . ." mean that no person is required, authorized, or permitted to do the act prescribed.

(30) "Includes" means "includes but is not limited to."

(31) "Inactive-duty training" means—

(A) duty prescribed for Reserves by the Secretary concerned under section 206 of title 37 or any other provision of law; and

(B) special additional duties authorized for Reserves by an authority designated by the Secretary concerned and performed by them on a voluntary basis in connection with the prescribed training or maintenance activities of the units to which they are assigned.

It includes those duties when performed by Reserves in their status as members of the National Guard.

(32) "Spouse" means husband or wife, as the case may be.

(33) "Regular", with respect to an enlistment, appointment, grade, or office, means enlistment, appointment, grade, or office in a regular component of an armed force.

(34) "Reserve", with respect to an enlistment, appointment, grade, or office, means enlistment, appointment, grade, or office held as a Reserve of an armed force.

(35) "Original", with respect to the appointment of a member of the armed forces in a regular or reserve component, refers to his most recent appointment in the component that is neither a promotion nor a demotion.

(36) Repealed.

(37) "Active-duty list" means a single list for the Army, Navy, Air Force or Marine Corps (required to be maintained under section 620 of this title) which contains the names of all officers of that armed force, other than officers described in section 641 of this title, who are serving on active duty.

(38) "Medical officer" means an officer of the Medical Corps of the Army, an officer of the Medical Corps of the Navy, or an officer in the Air Force designated as a medical officer.

(39) "Dental officer" means an officer of the Dental Corps of the Army, an officer of the Dental Corps of the Navy, or an officer of the Air Force designated as a dental officer.

(40) "General officer" means an officer of the Army, Air Force, or Marine Corps serving in or having the grade of general, lieutenant general, major general, or brigadier general.

(41) "Flag officer" means an officer of the Navy or Coast Guard serving in or having the grade of admiral, vice admiral, rear admiral, or commodore.

10 U.S.C. § 801. *Article 1. Definitions* In this chapter:

(1) "Judge Advocate General" means, severally, the Judge Advocates General of the Army, Navy, and Air Force and, except when the Coast Guard is operating as a service in the Navy, an official designated to serve as Judge Advocate General of the Coast Guard by the Secretary of Homeland Security. [NOTE: The Secretary of Homeland Security has designated the Chief Counsel, U.S. Coast Guard, to serve as the Judge Advocate General of the Coast Guard.].

(2) The Navy, the Marine Corps, and the Coast Guard when it is operating as a service in the Navy, shall be considered as one armed force.

(3) "Commanding officer" includes only commissioned officers.

(4) "Officer in charge" means a member of the Navy, the Marine Corps, or the Coast Guard designated as such by appropriate authority.

(5) "Superior commissioned officer" means a commissioned officer superior in rank or command.

(6) "Cadet" means a cadet of the United States Military Academy, the United States Air Force Academy, or the United States Coast Guard Academy.

(7) "Midshipman" means a midshipman of the United States Naval Academy and any other midshipman on active duty in the naval service.

(8) "Military" refers to any or all of the armed forces.

(9) "Accuser" means a person who signs and swears to charges, any person who directs that charges nominally be signed and sworn to by another, and any other person who has an interest other than an official interest in the prosecution of the accused.

(10) "Military judge" means an official of a general or special court-martial detailed in accordance with section 826 of this title (article 26). [*See also* R.C.M. 103(15).]

(11) "Law specialist" means a commissioned officer of the Coast Guard designated for special duty (law).

(12) "Legal officer" means any commissioned officer of the Navy, Marine Corps, or Coast Guard designated to perform legal duties for a command.

(13) "Judge Advocate" means—

(A) an officer of the Judge Advocate General's Corps of the Army or Navy;

(B) an officer of the Air Force or the Marine Corps who is designated as a judge advocate; or

(C) an officer of the Coast Guard who is designated as a law specialist.

(14) "Classified information" (A) means any information or material that has been determined by an official of the United States pursuant to law, an Executive Order, or regulation to require protection against unauthorized disclosure for reasons of national security, and (B) any restricted data, as defined in section 2014(y) of title 42, United States Code.

(15) "National security" means the national defense and foreign relations of the United States.

Rule 104. Unlawful command influence

(a) *General prohibitions.*

(1) *Convening authorities and commanders.* No convening authority or commander may censure, reprimand, or admonish a court-martial or other military tribunal or any member, military judge, or counsel thereof, with respect to the findings or sentence adjudged by the court-martial or tribunal, or with respect to any other exercise of the functions of the court-martial or tribunal or such persons in the conduct of the proceedings.

(2) *All persons subject to the code.* No person subject to the code may attempt to coerce or, by any unauthorized means, influence the action of a court-martial or any other military tribunal or any member

thereof, in reaching the findings or sentence in any case or the action of any convening, approving, or reviewing authority with respect to such authority's judicial acts.

(3) *Exceptions.*

(A) *Instructions.* Subsections (a)(1) and (2) of the rule do not prohibit general instructional or informational courses in military justice if such courses are designed solely for the purpose of instructing personnel of a command in the substantive and procedural aspects of courts-martial.

(B) *Court-martial statements.* Subsections (a)(1) and (2) of this rule do not prohibit statements and instructions given in open session by the military judge or counsel.

(C) *Professional supervision.* Subsections (a)(1) and (2) of this rule do not prohibit action by the Judge Advocate General concerned under R.C.M. 109.

(D) *Offense.* Subsection (a)(1) and (2) of this rule do not prohibit appropriate action against a person for an offense committed while detailed as a military judge, counsel, or member of a court-martial, or while serving as individual counsel.

(b) *Prohibitions concerning evaluations.*

(1) *Evaluation of member or defense counsel.* In the preparation of an effectiveness, fitness, or efficiency report or any other report or document used in whole or in part for the purpose of determining whether a member of the armed forces is qualified to be advanced in grade, or in determining the assignment or transfer of a member of the armed forces, or in determining whether a member of the armed forces should be retained on active duty, no person subject to the code may:

(A) Consider or evaluate the performance of duty of any such person as a member of a court-martial; or

(B) Give a less favorable rating or evaluation of any defense counsel because of the zeal with which such counsel represented any accused.

(2) *Evaluation of military judge.*

(A) *General courts-martial.* Unless the general court-martial was convened by the President or the Secretary concerned, neither the convening authority nor any member of the convening authority's staff may prepare or review any report concerning the effectiveness, fitness, or efficiency of the military judge detailed to a general court-martial, which relates to the performance of duty as a military judge.

(B) *Special courts-martial.* The convening authority may not prepare or review any report concerning the effectiveness, fitness, or efficiency of a military judge detailed to a special court-martial which relates to the performance of duty as a military judge. When the military judge is normally rated or the military judge's report is reviewed by the convening authority, the manner in which such military judge will be rated or evaluated upon the performance of duty as a military judge may be as prescribed in regulations of the Secretary concerned which shall ensure the absence of any command influence in the rating or evaluation of the military judge's judicial performance.

Discussion

See paragraph 22 of Part IV concerning prosecuting violations of Article 37 under Article 98.

Rule 105. Direct communications: convening authorities and staff judge advocates; among staff judge advocates

(a) *Convening authorities and staff judge advocates.* Convening authorities shall at all times communicate directly with their staff judge advocates in matters relating to the administration of military justice.

(b) *Among staff judge advocates and with the Judge Advocate General.* The staff judge advocate of any command is entitled to communicate directly with the staff judge advocate of a superior or subordinate command, or with the Judge Advocate General.

Discussion

See R.C.M. 103(17) for a definition of staff judge advocate.

Rule 106. Delivery of military offenders to civilian authorities

Under such regulations as the Secretary concerned may prescribe, a member of the armed forces accused of an offense against civilian authority may be delivered, upon request, to the civilian authority for trial. A member may be placed in restraint by military authorities for this purpose only upon receipt of a duly issued warrant for the apprehension of the member or upon receipt of information establishing probable cause that the member committed an offense, and upon reasonable belief that such restraint is necessary. Such restraint may continue only for such time as is reasonably necessary to effect the delivery.

Discussion

See R.C.M. 1113(d)(2)(A)(ii) for the effect of such delivery on the execution of a court-martial sentence.

Rule 107. Dismissed officer's right to request trial by court-martial

If a commissioned officer of any armed force is dismissed by order of the President under 10 U.S.C. § 1161(a)(3), that officer may apply for trial by general court-martial within a reasonable time.

Discussion

See Article 4 for the procedures to be followed. *See also* Article 75(c).

Rule 108. Rules of court

The Judge Advocate General concerned and persons designated by the Judge Advocate General may make rules of court not inconsistent with these rules for the conduct of court-martial proceedings. Such rules shall be disseminated in accordance with procedures prescribed by the Judge Advocate General concerned or a person to whom this authority has been delegated. Noncompliance with such procedures shall not affect the validity of any rule of court with respect to a party who has received actual and timely notice of the rule or who has not been prejudiced under Article 59 by the absence of such notice. Copies of all rules of court issued under this rule shall be forwarded to the Judge Advocate General concerned.

Rule 109. Professional supervision of military judges and counsel

(a) *In general.* Each Judge Advocate General is responsible for the professional supervision and discipline of military trial and appellate military judges, judge advocates, and other lawyers who practice in proceedings governed by the code and this Manual. To discharge this responsibility each Judge Advocate General may prescribe rules of professional conduct not inconsistent with this rule or this Manual. Rules of professional conduct promulgated pursuant to this rule may include sanctions for violations of such rules. Sanctions may include but are not limited to indefinite suspension from practice in courts-martial and in the Courts of Criminal Appeals. Such suspensions may only be imposed by the Judge Advocate General of the armed service of such courts. Prior to imposing any discipline under this rule, the subject of the proposed action must be provided notice and an opportunity to be heard. The Judge Advocate General concerned may upon good cause shown modify or revoke suspension. Procedures to investigate complaints against military trial judges and appellate military judges are contained in subsection (c) of this rule.

(b) *Action after suspension or disbarment.* When a Judge Advocate General suspends a person from practice or the Court of Appeals for the Armed Forces disbars a person, any Judge Advocate General may suspend that person from practice upon written notice and opportunity to be heard in writing.

(c) *Investigation of judges.*

(1) *In general.* These rules and procedures promulgated pursuant to Article 6a are established to investigate and dispose of charges, allegations, or information pertaining to the fitness of a military trial judge or appellate military judge to perform the duties of the judge's office.

(2) *Policy.* Allegations of judicial misconduct or unfitness shall be investigated pursuant to the procedures of this rule and appropriate action shall be taken. Judicial misconduct includes any act or omission that may serve to demonstrate unfitness for further duty as a judge, including, but not limited to violations of applicable ethical standards.

Discussion

The term "unfitness" should be construed broadly, including, for example, matters relating to the incompetence, impartiality, and misconduct of the judge. Erroneous decisions of a judge are not subject to investigation under this rule. Challenges to these decisions are more appropriately left to the appellate process.

---

(3) *Complaints.* Complaints concerning a military trial judge or appellate military judge will be forwarded to the Judge Advocate General of the service concerned or to a person designated by the Judge

Advocate General concerned to receive such complaints.

Discussion

Complaints need not be made in any specific form, but if possible complaints should be made under oath. Complaints may be made by judges, lawyers, a party, court personnel, members of the general public or members of the military community. Reports in the news media relating to the conduct of a judge may also form the basis of a complaint.

An individual designated to receive complaints under this subsection should have judicial experience. The chief trial judge of a service may be designated to receive complaints against military trial judges.

---

(4) *Initial action upon receipt of a complaint.* Upon receipt, a complaint will be screened by the Judge Advocate General concerned or by the individual designated in subsection (c)(3) of this rule to receive complaints. An initial inquiry is necessary if the complaint, taken as true, would constitute judicial misconduct or unfitness for further service as a judge. Prior to the commencement of an initial inquiry, the Judge Advocate General concerned shall be notified that a complaint has been filed and that an initial inquiry will be conducted. The Judge Advocate General concerned may temporarily suspend the subject of a complaint from performing judicial duties pending the outcome of any inquiry or investigation conducted pursuant to this rule. Such inquiries or investigations shall be conducted with reasonable promptness.

Discussion

Complaints under this subsection will be treated with confidentiality. Confidentiality protects the subject judge and the judiciary when a complaint is not substantiated. Confidentiality also encourages the reporting of allegations of judicial misconduct or unfitness and permits complaints to be screened with the full cooperation of others.

Complaints containing allegations of criminality should be referred to the appropriate criminal investigative agency in accordance with Appendix 3 of this Manual.

---

(5) *Initial inquiry.*

(A) *In general.* An initial inquiry is necessary to determine if the complaint is substantiated. A complaint is substantiated upon finding that it is more likely than not that the subject judge has engaged in judicial misconduct or is otherwise unfit for further service as a judge.

(B) *Responsibility to conduct initial inquiry.* The Judge Advocate General concerned, or the person designated to receive complaints under subsection (c)(3) of this rule will conduct or order an initial inquiry. The individual designated to conduct the inquiry should, if practicable, be senior to the subject of the complaint. If the subject of the complaint is a military trial judge, the individual designated to conduct the initial inquiry should, if practicable, be a military trial judge or an individual with experience as a military trial judge. If the subject of the complaint is an appellate military judge, the individual designated to conduct the inquiry should, if practicable, have experience as an appellate military judge.

Discussion

To avoid the type of conflict prohibited in Article 66(g), the Judge Advocate General's designee should not ordinarily be a member of the same Court of Criminal Appeals as the subject of the complaint. If practicable, a former appellate military judge should be designated.

(C) *Due process.* During the initial inquiry, the subject of the complaint will, at a minimum, be given notice and an opportunity to be heard.

(D) *Action following the initial inquiry.* If the complaint is not substantiated pursuant to subsection (c)(5)(A) of this rule, the complaint shall be dismissed as unfounded. If the complaint is substantiated, minor professional disciplinary action may be taken or the complaint may be forwarded, with findings and recommendations, to the Judge Advocate General concerned. Minor professional disciplinary action is defined as counseling or the issuance of an oral or written admonition or reprimand. The Judge Advocate General concerned will be notified prior to taking minor professional disciplinary action or dismissing a complaint as unfounded.

(6) *Action by the Judge Advocate General.*

(A) *In general.* The Judge Advocates General are responsible for the professional supervision and discipline of military trial and appellate military judges under their jurisdiction. Upon receipt of findings and recommendations required by subsection (c)(5) of this rule the Judge Advocate General concerned will take appropriate action.

(B) *Appropriate actions.* The Judge Advocate General concerned may dismiss the complaint, order an additional inquiry, appoint an ethics commission to consider the complaint, refer the matter to another appropriate investigative agency or take appropriate professional disciplinary action pursuant to the rules of professional conduct prescribed by the Judge Advocate General under subsection (a) of this rule. Any decision of the Judge Advocate General, under this rule, is final and is not subject to appeal.

Discussion

The discretionary reassignment of military trial judges or appellate military judges to meet the needs of the service is not professional disciplinary action.

(C) *Standard of proof.* Prior to taking professional disciplinary action, other than minor disciplinary action as defined in subsection (c)(5) of this rule, the Judge Advocate General concerned shall find, in writing, that the subject of the complaint engaged in judicial misconduct or is otherwise unfit for continued service as a military judge, and that such misconduct or unfitness is established by clear and convincing evidence.

(D) *Due process.* Prior to taking final action on the complaint, the Judge Advocate General concerned will ensure that the subject of the complaint is, at a minimum, given notice and an opportunity to be heard.

(7) *The Ethics Commission.*

(A) *Membership.* If appointed pursuant to subsection (c)(6)(B) of this rule, an ethics commission shall consist of at least three members.
If the subject of the complaint is a military trial judge, the commission should include one or more military trial judges or individuals with experience as a military trial judge. If the subject of the complaint is an appellate military judge, the commission should include one or more individuals with experience as an appellate military judge. Members of the commission should, if practicable, be senior to the subject of the complaint.

(B) *Duties.* The commission will perform those duties assigned by the Judge Advocate General concerned. Normally, the commission will provide an opinion as to whether the subject's acts or omissions constitute judicial misconduct or unfitness. If the commission determines that the affected judge engaged in judicial misconduct or is unfit for continued judicial service, the commission may be required to recommend an appropriate disposition to The Judge Advocate General concerned.

Discussion

The Judge Advocate General concerned may appoint an ad hoc or a standing commission.

---

(8) *Rules of procedure.* The Secretary of Defense or the Secretary of the service concerned may establish additional procedures consistent with this rule and Article 6a.

CHAPTER II. JURISDICTION

Rule 201. Jurisdiction in general

(a) *Nature of courts-martial jurisdiction.*

(1) The jurisdiction of courts-martial is entirely penal or disciplinary.

Discussion

"Jurisdiction" means the power to hear a case and to render a legally competent decision. A court-martial has no power to adjudge civil remedies. For example, a court-martial may not adjudge the payment of damages, collect private debts, order the return of property, or order a criminal forfeiture of seized property. A summary court-martial appointed under 10 U.S.C. §§ 4712 or 9712 to dispose of the effects of a deceased person is not affected by these Rules or this Manual.

---

(2) The code applies in all places.

Discussion

Except insofar as required by the Constitution, the code, or the Manual, jurisdiction of courts-martial does not depend on where the offense was committed.

The code applies in all places (Article 5), but its application may be limited by the service-connection doctrine. The location of an offense is often of major importance in the application of this doctrine. *See* R.C.M. 203 and discussion. Article 2(a)(11) and (12) establishes court-martial jurisdiction only in certain places. *See* R.C.M. 202.

---

(3) The jurisdiction of a court-martial with respect to offenses under the code is not affected by the place where the court-martial sits. The jurisdiction of a court-martial with respect to military government or the law of war is not affected by the place where the court-martial sits except as otherwise expressly required by this Manual or applicable rule of international law.

Discussion

In addition to the power to try persons for offenses under the code, general courts-martial have power to try certain persons for violations of the law of war and for crimes or offenses against the law of the territory occupied as an incident of war or belligerency whenever the local civil authority is superseded in whole or part by the military authority of the occupying power. *See* R.C.M. 201(f)(1)(B). In cases where a person is tried by general court-martial for offenses against the law of an occupied territory, the court-martial normally sits in the country where the offense is committed, and must do so under certain circumstances. *See* Articles 4, 64, and 66, Geneva Convention Relative to the Protection of Civilian Persons in Time of War, August 12, 1949, arts. 4, 64, and 66, 6 U.S.T. 3516, 3559-60 T.I.A.S. No. 3365.

(b) *Requisites of court-martial jurisdiction.* A court-martial always has jurisdiction to determine whether it has jurisdiction. Otherwise for a court-martial to have jurisdiction:

(1) The court-martial must be convened by an official empowered to convene it;

Discussion

See R.C.M. 504; 1302.

---

(2) The court-martial must be composed in accordance with these rules with respect to number and qualifications of its personnel. As used here "personnel" includes only the military judge, the members, and the summary court-martial;

Discussion

See R.C.M. 501-504; 1301.

---

(3) Each charge before the court-martial must be referred to it by competent authority;

Discussion

See R.C.M. 601.

---

(4) The accused must be a person subject to court-martial jurisdiction; and

Discussion

See R.C.M. 202.

---

(5) The offense must be subject to court-martial jurisdiction.

Discussion

See R.C.M. 203.

The judgment of a court-martial without jurisdiction is void and is entitled to no legal effect. *See* R.C.M. 907(b)(2)(C)(iv). *But see* R.C.M. 810(d) concerning the effect of certain decisions by courts-martial without jurisdiction.

(c) *Contempt.* A court-martial may punish for contempt any person who uses any menacing word, sign, or gesture in its presence, or who disturbs its proceedings by any riot or disorder. The punishment may not exceed confinement for 30 days or a fine of $100, or both.

Discussion

See R.C.M. 809 for procedures and standards for contempt proceedings.

(d) *Exclusive and nonexclusive jurisdiction.*

(1) Courts-martial have exclusive jurisdiction of purely military offenses.

(2) An act or omission which violates both the code and local criminal law, foreign or domestic, may be tried by a court-martial, or by a proper civilian tribunal, foreign or domestic, or, subject to R.C.M. 907(b)(2)(C) and regulations of the Secretary concerned, by both.

(3) Where an act or omission is subject to trial by court-martial and by one or more civil tribunals, foreign or domestic, the determination which nation, state, or agency will exercise jurisdiction is a matter for the nations, states, and agencies concerned, and is not a right of the suspect or accused.

Discussion

In the case of an act or omission which violates the code and a criminal law of a State, the United States, or both, the determination which agency shall exercise jurisdiction should normally be made through consultation or prior agreement between appropriate military officials (ordinarily the staff judge advocate) and appropriate civilian authorities (United States Attorney, or equivalent). *See also* Memorandum of Understanding Between Departments of Justice and Defense Relating to the Investigation and Prosecution of Crimes Over Which the Two Departments Have Concurrent Jurisdiction at Appendix 3.

Under the Constitution, a person may not be tried for the same misconduct by both a court-martial and another federal court. *See* R.C.M. 907(b)(2)(C). Although it is constitutionally permissible to try a person by court-martial and by a State court for the same act, as a matter of policy a person who is pending trial or has been tried by a State court should not ordinarily be tried by court-martial for the same act. Overseas, international agreements might preclude trial by one state of a person acquitted or finally convicted of a given act by the other state.

Under international law, a friendly foreign nation has jurisdiction to punish offenses committed within its borders by members of a visiting force, unless expressly or impliedly consents to relinquish its jurisdiction to the visiting sovereign. The procedures and standards for determining which nation will exercise jurisdiction are normally established by treaty. *See*, for example, NATO Status of Forces Agreement, June 19, 1951, 4 U.S.T. 1792, T.I.A.S. No. 2846. As a matter of policy, efforts should be made to maximize the exercise of court-martial jurisdiction over persons subject to the code to the extent possible under applicable agreements.

See R.C.M. 106 concerning delivery of offenders to civilian authorities.

See also R.C.M. 201(g) concerning the jurisdiction of other military tribunals.

(e) *Reciprocal jurisdiction.*

(1) Each armed force has court-martial jurisdiction over all persons subject to the code.

(2)(A) A commander of a unified or specified combatant command may convene courts-martial over members of any of the armed forces.

(B) So much of the authority vested in the President under Article 22(a)(9) to empower any commanding officer of a joint command or joint task force to convene courts-martial is delegated to the Secretary of Defense, and such a commanding officer may convene general courts-martial for the trial of members of any of the armed forces assigned or attached to a combatant command or joint command.

(C) A commander who is empowered to convene a court-martial under subsections (e)(2)(A) or (e)(2)(B) of this rule may expressly authorize a commanding officer of a subordinate joint command or subordinate joint task force who is authorized to convene special and summary courts-martial to convene such courts-martial for the trial of members of other armed forces assigned or attached to a joint command or joint task force, under regulations which the superior command may prescribe.

(3) A member of one armed force may be tried by a court-martial convened by a member of another armed force, using the implementing regulations and procedures prescribed by the Secretary concerned of the military service of the accused, when:

(A) The court-martial is convened by a commander authorized to convene courts-martial under subsection (e)(2) of this rule; or

(B) The accused cannot be delivered to the armed force of which the accused is a member without manifest injury to the armed forces.

An accused should not ordinarily be tried by a court-martial convened by a member of a different armed force except when the circumstances described in (A) or (B) exist. However, failure to comply with this policy does not affect an otherwise valid referral.

(4) Nothing in this rule prohibits detailing to a court-martial a military judge, member, or counsel who is a member of an armed force different from that of the accused or the convening authority, or both.

(5) In all cases, departmental review after that by the officer with authority to convene a general court-martial for the command which held the trial, where that review is required by the code, shall be carried out by the department that includes the armed force of which the accused is a member.

(6) When there is a disagreement between the Secretaries of two military departments or between the Secretary of a military department and the commander of a unified or specified combatant command or other joint command or joint task force as to which organization should exercise jurisdiction over a particular case or class of cases, the Secretary of Defense or an official acting under the authority of the Secretary of Defense shall designate which organization will exercise jurisdiction.

(7) Except as provided in subsections (5) and (6) or as otherwise directed by the President or Secretary of Defense, whenever action under this Manual is required or authorized to be taken by a person superior to—

(A) a commander of a unified or specified combatant command or;

(B) a commander of any other joint command or joint task force that is not part of a unified or specified combatant command, the matter shall be referred to the Secretary of the armed force of which the accused is a member. The Secretary may convene a court-martial, take other appropriate action, or, subject to R.C.M. 504(c), refer the matter to any person authorized to convene a court-martial of the accused.

Discussion

As to the authority to convene courts-martial, see R.C.M. 504. "Manifest injury" does not mean minor inconvenience or expense. Examples of manifest injury include direct and substantial effect on morale, discipline, or military operations, substantial expense or delay, or loss of essential witnesses.

As to the composition of a court-martial for the trial of an accused who is a member of another armed force, *see* R.C.M. 503(a)(3) Discussion. Cases involving two or more accused who are members of different armed forces should not be referred to a court-martial for a common trial.

(f) *Types of courts-martial.*

(1) *General courts-martial.*

(A) *Cases under the code.*

(i) Except as otherwise expressly provided, general courts-martial may try any person subject to the code for any offense made punishable under the code. General courts-martial also may try any person for a violation of Article 83, 104, or 106.

(ii) Upon a finding of guilty of an offense made punishable by the code, general courts-martial may, within limits prescribed by this Manual, adjudge any punishment authorized under R.C.M. 1003.

(iii) Notwithstanding any other rule, the death penalty may not be adjudged if:

(a) Not specifically authorized for the offense by the code and Part IV of this Manual; or

(b) The case has not been referred with a special instruction that the case is to be tried as capital.

(B) *Cases under the law of war.*

(i) General courts-martial may try any person who by the law of war is subject to trial by military tribunal for any crime or offense against:

(a) The law of war; or

(b) The law of the territory occupied as an incident of war or belligerency whenever the local civil authority is superseded in whole or part by the military authority of the occupying power. The law of the occupied territory includes the local criminal law as adopted or modified by competent authority, and the proclamations, ordinances, regulations, or orders promulgated by competent authority of the occupying power.

Discussion

Subsection (f)(1)(B)(i)*(b)* is an exercise of the power of military government.

(ii) When a general court-martial exercises jurisdiction under the law of war, it may adjudge any punishment permitted by the law of war.

Discussion

Certain limitations on the discretion of military tribunals to adjudge punishment under the law of war are prescribed in international conventions. *See*, for example, Geneva Convention Relative to the Protection of Civilian Persons in Time of War, Aug. 12, 1949, art. 68, 6 U.S.T. 3516, T.I.A.S. No. 3365.

(C) *Limitations in judge alone cases.* A general court-martial composed only of a military judge does not have jurisdiction to try any person for any offense for which the death penalty may be adjudged unless the case has been referred to trial as noncapital.

(2) *Special courts-martial.*

(A) *In general.* Except as otherwise expressly provided, special courts-martial may try any person subject to the code for any noncapital offense made punishable by the code and, as provided in this rule, for capital offenses.

(B) *Punishments.*

(i) Upon a finding of guilty, special courts-martial may adjudge, under limitations prescribed by this Manual, any punishment authorized under R.C.M. 1003 except death, dishonorable discharge, dismissal, confinement for more than 1 year, hard labor without confinement for more than 3 months, forfeiture of pay exceeding two-thirds pay per month, or any forfeiture of pay for more than 1 year.

(ii) A bad-conduct discharge, confinement for more than six months, or forfeiture of pay for more than six months, may not be adjudged by a special court-martial unless:

(a) Counsel qualified under Article 27(b) is detailed to represent the accused; and

(b) A military judge is detailed to the trial, except in a case in which a military judge could not be detailed because of physical conditions or military exigencies. Physical conditions or military exigencies, as the terms are here used, may exist under rare circumstances, such as on an isolated ship on the high seas or in a unit in an inaccessible area, provided compelling reasons exist why trial must be held at that time and at that place. Mere inconvenience does not constitute a physical condition or military exigency and does not excuse a failure to detail a military judge. If a military judge cannot be detailed because of physical conditions or military exigencies, a bad-conduct discharge, confinement for more than six months, or forfeiture of pay for more than six months, may be adjudged provided the other conditions have been met. In that event, however, the convening authority shall, prior to trial, make a written statement explaining why a military judge could not be obtained. This statement shall be appended to the record of trial and shall set forth in detail the reasons why a military judge could not be detailed, and why the trial had to be held at that time and place.

Discussion

See R.C.M. 503 concerning detailing the military judge and counsel.

The requirement for counsel is satisfied when counsel qualified under Article 27(b), and not otherwise disqualified, has been detailed and made available, even though the accused may not choose to cooperate with, or use the services of, such detailed counsel.

The physical condition or military exigency exception to the requirement for a military judge does not apply to the requirement for detailing counsel qualified under Article 27(b).

See also R.C.M. 1103(c) concerning the requirements for a record of trial in special courts-martial.

(C) *Capital offenses*

(i) A capital offense for which there is prescribed a mandatory punishment beyond the punitive power of a special court-martial shall not be referred to such a court-martial.

(ii) An officer exercising general court-martial jurisdiction over the command which includes the accused may permit any capital offense other than one described in subsection (f)(2)(C)(i) of this rule to be referred to a special court-martial for trial.

(iii) The Secretary concerned may authorize, by regulation, officers exercising special court-martial jurisdiction to refer capital offenses, other than those described in subsection (f)(2)(C)(i) of this rule, to trial by special court-martial without first obtaining the consent of the officer exercising general court-martial jurisdiction over the command.

Discussion

See R.C.M. 103(3) for a definition of capital offenses.

---

(3) *Summary courts-martial. See* R.C.M. 1301(c) and (d)(1).

(g) *Concurrent jurisdiction of other military tribunals.* The provisions of the code and this Manual conferring jurisdiction upon courts-martial do not deprive military commissions, provost courts, or other military tribunals of concurrent jurisdiction with respect to offenders or offenses that by statute or by the law of war may be tried by military commissions, provost courts, or other military tribunals.

Discussion

See Articles 104 and 106 for some instances of concurrent jurisdiction.

Rule 202. Persons subject to the jurisdiction of courts-martial

(a) *In general.* Courts-martial may try any person when authorized to do so under the code.

Discussion

(1) *Authority under the code.* Article 2 lists classes of persons who are subject to the code. These include active duty personnel (Article 2(a)(1)); cadets, aviation cadets, and midshipmen (Article 2(a)(2)); certain retired personnel (Article 2(a)(4) and (5)); members of Reserve components not on active duty under some circumstances (Article 2(a)(3) and (6)); persons in the custody of the armed forces serving a sentence imposed by court-martial (Article 2(a)(7)); and, under some circumstances, specified categories of civilians (Article 2(a)(8), (9), (10), (11), and (12); *see* subsection (3) and (4) of this discussion). In addition, certain persons whose status as members of the armed forces or as persons otherwise subject to the code apparently has ended may, nevertheless, be amendable to trial by court-martial. *See* Article 3, 4, and 73. A person need not be subject to the code to be subject to trial by court-martial under Articles 83, 104, or 106. *See also* Article 48 and R.C.M. 809 concerning who may be subject to the contempt powers of a court-martial.

(2) *Active duty personnel.* Court-martial jurisdiction is most commonly exercised over active duty personnel. In general, a person becomes subject to court-martial jurisdiction upon enlistment in or induction into the armed forces, acceptance of a commission, or entry onto active duty pursuant to orders. Court-martial jurisdiction over active duty personnel ordinarily ends on delivery of a discharge certificate or its equivalent to the person concerned issued pursuant to competent orders. Orders transferring a person to the inactive reserve are the equivalent of a discharge certificate for purposes of jurisdiction.

These are several important qualifications and exceptions to these general guidelines.

(A) *Inception of court-martial jurisdiction over active duty personnel.*

(i) *Enlistment.* "The voluntary enlistment of any person who has the capacity to understand the significance of enlisting in the armed forces shall be valid for purposes of jurisdiction under [Article 2(a)] and a change of status from civilian to member of the armed forces shall be effective upon taking the oath of enlistment." Article 2(b). A person who is, at the time of enlistment, insane, intoxicated, or under the age of 17 does not have the capacity to enlist by law. No court-martial jurisdiction over such a person may exist as long as the incapacity continues. If the incapacity ceases to exist, a "constructive enlistment" may result under Article 2(c). *See* discussion of "constructive enlistment" below. Similarly, if the enlistment was involuntary, court-martial jurisdiction will exist only when the coercion is removed and a "constructive enlistment" under Article 2(c) is established.

Persons age 17 (but not yet 18) may not enlist without parental consent. A parent or guardian may, within 90 days of its inception, terminate the enlistment of a 17-year-old who enlisted without parental consent, if the person has not yet reached the age of 18. 10 U.S.C. § 1170. *See also* DOD Directive 1332.14 and service regulations for specific rules on separation of persons 17 years of age on the basis of a parental request. Absent effective action by a parent or guardian to terminate such an enlistment, court-martial jurisdiction exists over the person. An application by a parent for release does not deprive a court-martial of jurisdiction to try a person for offenses committed before action is completed on such an application.

Even if a person lacked capacity to understand the effect of enlistment or did not enlist voluntarily, a "constructive enlistment" may be established under Article 2(c), which provides:

Notwithstanding any other provision of law, a person serving with an armed force who—

(1) submitted voluntary to military authority;

(2) met the mental competency and minimum age qualifications of sections 504 and 505 of this title at the time of voluntary submission to military authority [that is, not insane, intoxicated, or under the age of 17]

(3) received military pay or allowances; and

(4) performed military duties;

is subject to [the code] until such person's active service has been terminated in accordance with law or regulations promulgated by the Secretary concerned.

Even if a person never underwent an enlistment or induction proceeding of any kind, court-martial jurisdiction could be established under this provision.

(ii) *Induction.* Court-martial jurisdiction does not extend to a draftee until: the draftee has completed an induction ceremony which was in substantial compliance with the requirements prescribed by statute and regulations; the draftee by conduct after an apparent induction, has waived objection to substantive defects in it; or a "constructive enlistment" under Article 2(c) exists.

The fact that a person was improperly inducted (for example, because of incorrect classification or erroneous denial of exemption) does not of itself negate court-martial jurisdiction. When a person has made timely and persistent efforts to correct such an error, court-martial jurisdiction may be defeated if improper induction is found, depending on all the circumstances of the case.

(iii) *Call to active duty.* A member of a reserve component may be called or ordered to active duty for a variety of reasons, including training, service in time of war or national emergency, discipline, or as a result of failure to participate satisfactorily in unit activities.

When a person is ordered to active duty for failure to satisfactorily participate in unit activities, the order must substantially comply with procedures prescribed by regulations, to the extent due process requires, for court-martial jurisdiction to exist. Generally, the person must be given notice of the activation and the reasons therefor, and an opportunity to object to the activation. A person waives the right to contest involuntary activation by failure to exercise this right within a reasonable time after notice of the right to do so.

(B) *Termination of jurisdiction over active duty personnel.* As indicated above, the delivery of a valid discharge certificate or its equivalent ordinarily serves to terminate court-martial jurisdiction.

(i) *Effect of completion of term of service.* Completion of an enlistment or term of service does not by itself terminate court-martial jurisdiction. An original term of enlistment may be adjusted for a variety of reasons, such as making up time lost for unauthorized absence. Even after such adjustments are considered, court-martial jurisdiction normally continues past the time of scheduled separation until a discharge certificate or its equivalent is delivered or until the Government fails to act within a reasonable time after the person objects to continued retention.

As indicated in subsection (c) of this rule, servicemembers may be retained past their scheduled time of separation, over protest, by action with a view to trial while they are still subject to the code. Thus, if action with a view to trial is initiated before discharge or the effective terminal date of self-executing orders, a person may be retained beyond the date that the period of service would otherwise have expired or the terminal date of such orders.

(ii) *Effect of discharge and reenlistment.* For offenses occurring on or after 23 October 1992, under the 1992 Amendment to Article 3(a), a person who reenlists following a discharge may be tried for offenses committed during the earlier term of service. For offenses occurring prior to 23 October 1992, a person who reenlists following a discharge may be tried for offenses committed during the earlier term of service only if the offense was punishable by confinement for five (5) years or more and could not be tried in the courts of the United States or of a State, a Territory, or the District of Columbia. However, *see* (iii)(a) below.

(iii) *Exceptions.* There are several exceptions to the general principle that court-martial jurisdiction terminates on discharge or its equivalent.

(a) A person who was subject to the code at the time an offense was committed may be tried by court-martial for that offense despite a later discharge or other termination of that status if:

(1) For offenses occurring on or after 23 October 1992, the person is, at the time of the court-martial, subject to the code, by reentry into the armed forces or otherwise. *See* Article 3(a) as amended by the National Defense Authorization Act for Fiscal Year 1993, Pub.L. No. 102-484, 106 Stat. 2315, 2505 (1992);

(2) For offenses occurring before 23 October 1992,

(A) The offense is one for which a court-martial may adjudge confinement for five (5) or more years;

(B) The person cannot be tried in the courts of the United States or of a State, Territory, or the District of Columbia; and

(C) The person is, at the time of the court-martial, subject to the code, by reentry into the armed forces or otherwise. *See* Article 3(a) prior to the 1992 amendment.

(b) A person who was subject to the code at the time the offense was committed is subject to trial by court-martial despite a later discharge if—

(1) The discharge was issued before the end of the accused's term of enlistment for the purpose of reenlisting;

(2) The person remains, at the time of the court-martial, subject to the code; and

(3) The reenlistment occurred after 26 July 1982.

(c) Persons in the custody of the armed forces serving a sentence imposed by a court-martial remain subject to the code and court-martial jurisdiction. A prisoner who has received a discharge and who remains in the custody of an armed force may be tried for an offense committed while a member of the armed forces and before the execution of the discharge as well as for offenses committed after it.

(d) A person discharged from the armed forces who is later charged with having fraudulently obtained that discharge is, subject to the statute of limitations, subject to trial by court-martial on that charge, and is after apprehension subject to the code while in the custody of the armed forces for trial. Upon conviction of that charge such a person is subject to trial by court-martial for any offenses under the code committed before the fraudulent discharge.

(e) No person who has deserted from the armed forces is relieved from court-martial jurisdiction by a separation from any later period of service.

(f) When a person's discharge or other separation does not interrupt the status as a person belonging to the general category of persons subject to the code, court-martial jurisdiction over that person does not end. For example, when an officer holding a commission in a Reserve component of an armed force is discharged from that commission while on active duty because of acceptance of a commission in a Regular component of that armed force, without an interval between the periods of service under the two commissions, that officer's military status does not end. There is merely a change in personnel status from temporary to permanent officer, and court-martial jurisdiction over an offense committed before the discharge is not affected.

(3) *Public Health Service and National Oceanic and Atmospheric Administration.* Members of the Public Health Service and the National Oceanic and Atmospheric Administration become subject to the code when assigned to and serving with the armed forces.

(4) *Limitations on jurisdiction over civilians.* Court-martial jurisdiction over civilians under the code is limited by judicial decisions. The exercise of jurisdiction under Article 2(a)(11) in peacetime has been held unconstitutional by the Supreme Court of the United States. Article 2(a)(10) has also been limited. Before initiating court-martial proceedings against a civilian, relevant statutes and decisions should be carefully examined.

(5) *Members of a Reserve Component.* Members of a reserve component in federal service on active duty, as well as those in federal service on inactive-duty training, are subject to the code. Moreover, members of a reserve component are amenable to the jurisdiction of courts-martial notwithstanding the termination of a period of such duty. *See* R.C.M. 204.

(b) *Offenses under the law of war.* Nothing in this rule limits the power of general courts-martial to try persons under the law of war. *See* R.C.M. 201(f)(1)(B).

(c) *Attachment of jurisdiction over the person.*

(1) *In general.* Court-martial jurisdiction attaches over a person when action with a view to trial of that person is taken. Once court-martial jurisdiction over a person attaches, such jurisdiction shall continue for all purposes of trial, sentence, and punishment, notwithstanding the expiration of that person's term of service or other period in which that person was subject to the code or trial by court-martial. When jurisdiction attaches over a servicemember on active duty, the servicemember may be held on active duty over objection pending disposition of any offense for which held and shall remain subject to the code during the entire period.

Discussion

Court-martial jurisdiction exists to try a person as long as that person occupies a status as a person subject to the code. *See also* Article 104 and 106. Thus, a servicemember is subject to court-martial jurisdiction until lawfully discharged or, when the servicemember's term of service has expired, the government fails to act within a reasonable time on objection by the servicemember to continued retention.

Court-martial jurisdiction attaches over a person upon action with a view to trial. Once court-martial jurisdiction attaches, it continues throughout the trial and appellate process, and for purposes of punishment.

If jurisdiction has attached before the effective terminal date of self-executing orders, the person may be held for trial by court-martial beyond the effective terminal date.

---

(2) *Procedure.* Actions by which court-martial jurisdiction attaches include: apprehension; imposition of restraint, such as restriction, arrest, or confinement; and preferral of charges.

Rule 203. Jurisdiction over the offense

To the extent permitted by the Constitution, courts-martial may try any offense under the code and, in the case of general courts-martial, the law of war.

Discussion

(a) *In general.* Courts-martial have power to try any offense under the code except when prohibited from so doing by the Constitution. The rule enunciated in *Solorio v. United States*, 483 U.S. 435 (1987) is that jurisdiction of courts-martial depends solely on the accused's status as a person subject to the Uniform Code of Military Justice, and not on the "service-connection" of the offense charged.

(b) *Pleading and proof.* Normally, the inclusion of the accused's rank or grade will be sufficient to plead the service status of the accused. Ordinarily, no allegation of the accused's armed force or unit is necessary for military members on active duty. *See* R.C.M. 307 regarding required specificity of pleadings.

Rule 204. Jurisdiction over certain reserve component personnel

(a) *Service regulations.* The Secretary concerned shall prescribe regulations setting forth rules and procedures for the exercise of court-martial jurisdiction and nonjudicial punishment authority over reserve component personnel under Article 2(a)(3) and 2(d), subject to the limitations of this Manual and the UCMJ.

Discussion

Such regulations should describe procedures for ordering a reservist to active duty for disciplinary action, for the preferral, investigation, forwarding, and referral of charges, designation of convening authorities and commanders authorized to conduct nonjudicial punishment proceedings, and for other appropriate purposes.

See definitions in R.C.M. 103 (Discussion). *See* paragraph 5e and f, Part V, concerning limitations on nonjudicial punishments imposed on reservists while on inactive-duty training.

Members of the Army National Guard and the Air National Guard are subject to Federal court-martial jurisdiction only when the offense concerned is committed while the member is in Federal service.

(b) *Courts-Martial*

(1) *General and special court-martial proceedings.* A member of a reserve component must be on active duty prior to arraignment at a general or special court-martial. A member ordered to active duty pursuant to Article 2(d) may be retained on active duty to serve any adjudged confinement or other restriction on liberty if the order to active duty was approved in accordance with Article 2(d)(5), but such member may not be retained on active duty pursuant to Article 2(d) after service of the confinement or other restriction on liberty. All punishments remaining unserved at the time the member is released from active duty may be carried over to subsequent periods of inactive-duty training or active duty.

Discussion

An accused ordered to active duty pursuant to Article 2(d) may be retained on active duty after service of the punishment if permitted by other authority. For example, an accused who commits another offense while on active duty ordered pursuant to Article 2(d) may be retained on active duty pursuant to R.C.M. 202(c)(1).

(2) *Summary courts-martial.* A member of a reserve component may be tried by summary court-martial either while on active duty or inactive-duty training. A summary court-martial conducted during inactive-duty training may be in session only during normal periods of such training. The accused may not be held beyond such periods of training for trial or service or any punishment. All punishments remaining unserved at the end of a period of active duty or the end of any normal period of inactive duty training may be carried over to subsequent periods of inactive-duty training or active duty.

Discussion

A "normal period" of inactive-duty training does not include periods which are scheduled solely for the purpose of conducting court-martial proceedings.

(c) *Applicability.* This subsection is not applicable when a member is held on active duty pursuant to R.C.M. 202(c).

(d) *Changes in type of service.* A member of a reserve component at the time disciplinary action is initiated, who is alleged to have committed an offense while on active duty or inactive-duty training, is subject to court-martial jurisdiction without regard to any change between active and reserve service or within different categories of reserve service subsequent to commission of the offense. This subsection does not apply to a person whose military status was completely terminated after commission of an offense.

Discussion

A member of a regular or reserve component remains subject to court-martial jurisdiction after leaving active duty for offenses committed prior to such termination of active duty if the member retains military status in a reserve component without having been discharged from all obligations of military service.

See R.C.M. 202(a), Discussion, paragraph (2)(B)(ii) and (iii) regarding the jurisdictional effect of a discharge from military service. A "complete termination" of military status refers to a discharge relieving the servicemember of any further military service. It does not include a discharge conditioned upon acceptance of further military service.

CHAPTER III. INITIATION OF CHARGES; APPREHENSION; PRETRIAL RESTRAINT; RELATED MATTERS

Rule 301. Report of offense

(a) *Who may report.* Any person may report an offense subject to trial by court-martial.

(b) *To whom reports conveyed for disposition.* Ordinarily, any military authority who receives a report of an offense shall forward as soon as practicable the report and any accompanying information to the immediate commander of the suspect. Competent authority superior to that commander may direct otherwise.

Discussion

Any military authority may receive a report of an offense. Typically such reports are made to law enforcement or investigative personnel, or to appropriate persons in the chain of command. A report may be made by any means, and no particular format is required. When a person who is not a law enforcement official receives a report of an offense, that person should forward the report to the immediate commander of the suspect unless that person believes it would be more appropriate to notify law enforcement or investigative authorities.

If the suspect is unidentified, the military authority who receives the report should refer it to a law enforcement or investigative agency.

Upon receipt of a report, the immediate commander of a suspect should refer to R.C.M. 306 (Initial disposition). *See also* R.C.M. 302 (Apprehension); R.C.M. 303 (Preliminary inquiry); R.C.M. 304, 305 (Pretrial restraint, confinement).

Rule 302. Apprehension

(a) *Definition and scope.*

(1) *Definition.* Apprehension is the taking of a person into custody.

Discussion

Apprehension is the equivalent of "arrest" in civilian terminology. (In military terminology, "arrest" is a form of restraint. *See* Article 9; R.C.M. 304.) *See* subsection (c) of this rule concerning the bases for apprehension. An apprehension is not required in every case; the fact that an accused was never apprehended does not affect the jurisdiction of a court-martial to try the accused. However, *see* R.C.M. 202(c) concerning attachment of jurisdiction.

An apprehension is different from detention of a person for investigative purposes, although each involves the exercise of government control over the freedom of movement of a person. An apprehension must be based on probable cause, and the custody initiated in an apprehension may continue until proper authority is notified and acts under R.C.M. 304 or 305. An investigative detention may be made on less than probable cause (*see* Mil. R. Evid. 314(f)), and normally involves a relatively short period of custody. Furthermore, an extensive search of the person is not authorized incident to an investigative detention, as it is with an apprehension. *See* Mil. R. Evid. 314(f) and (g). This rule does not affect any seizure of the person less severe than apprehension.

Evidence obtained as the result of an apprehension which is in violation of this rule may be challenged under Mil. R. Evid. 311(c)(1). Evidence obtained as the result of an unlawful civilian arrest may be challenged under Mil. R. Evid. 311(c)(1), (2).

---

(2) *Scope.* This rule applies only to apprehensions made by persons authorized to do so under subsection (b) of this rule with respect to offenses subject to trial by court-martial. Nothing in this rule limits the authority of federal law enforcement officials to apprehend persons, whether or not subject to trial by court-martial, to the extent permitted by applicable enabling statutes and other law.

Discussion

R.C.M. 302 does not affect the authority of any official to detain, arrest, or apprehend persons not subject to trial under the code. The rule does not apply to actions taken by any person in a private capacity.

Several federal agencies have broad powers to apprehend persons for violations of federal laws, including the Uniform Code of Military Justice. For example, agents of the Federal Bureau of Investigation, United States Marshals, and agents of the Secret Service may apprehend persons for any offenses committed in their presence and for felonies. 18 U.S.C. §§ 3052, 3053, 3056. Other agencies have apprehension powers include the General Services Administration, 40 U.S.C. § 318 and the Veterans Administration, 38 U.S.C. § 218. The extent to which such agencies become involved in the apprehension of persons subject to trial by courts-martial may depend on the statutory authority of the agency and the agency's formal or informal relationships with the Department of Defense.

(b) *Who may apprehend.* The following officials may apprehend any person subject to trial by court-martial:

(1) *Military law enforcement officials.* Security police, military police, master at arms personnel, members of the shore patrol, and persons designated by proper authorities to perform military criminal investigative, guard, or police duties, whether subject to the code or not, when in each of the foregoing instances, the official making the apprehension is in the execution of law enforcement duties;

Discussion

Whenever enlisted persons, including police and guards, and civilian police and guards apprehend any commissioned or warrant officer, such persons should make an immediate report to the commissioned officer to whom the apprehending person is responsible.

The phrase "persons designated by proper authority to perform military criminal investigative, guard or police duties" includes special agents of the Defense Criminal Investigative Service.

---

(2) *Commissioned, warrant, petty, and noncommissioned officers.* All commissioned, warrant, petty, and noncommissioned officers on active duty or inactive duty training;

Discussion

Noncommissioned and petty officers not otherwise performing law enforcement duties should not apprehend a commissioned officer unless directed to do so by a commissioned officer or in order to prevent disgrace to the service or the escape of one who has committed a serious offense.

---

(3) *Civilians authorized to apprehend deserters.* Under Article 8, any civilian officer having authority to apprehend offenders under laws of the United States or of a State, Territory, Commonwealth, or possession, or the District of Columbia, when the apprehension is of a deserter from the armed forces.

Discussion

The code specifically provides that any civil officer, whether of a State, Territory, district, or of the United States may apprehend any deserter.However, this authority does not permit state and local law enforcement officers to apprehend persons for other violations of the code. *See* Article 8.

(c) *Grounds for apprehension.* A person subject to the code or trial thereunder may be apprehended for an offense triable by court-martial upon probable cause to apprehend. Probable cause to apprehend exists when there are reasonable grounds to believe that an offense has been or is being committed and the person to be apprehended committed or is committing it. Persons authorized to apprehend under subsection (b)(2) of this rule may also apprehend persons subject to the code who take part in quarrels, frays, or disorders, wherever they occur.

Discussion

"Reasonable grounds" means that there must be the kind of reliable information that a reasonable, prudent person would rely on which makes it more likely than not that something is true. A mere suspicion is not enough but proof which would support a conviction is not necessary. A person who determines probable cause may rely on the reports of others.

(d) *How an apprehension may be made.*

(1) *In general.* An apprehension is made by clearly notifying the person to be apprehended that person is in custody. This notice should be given orally or in writing, but it may be implied by the circumstances.

(2) *Warrants.* Neither warrants nor any other authorization shall be required for an apprehension under these rules except as required in subsection (e)(2) of this rule.

(3) *Use of force.* Any person authorized under these rules to make an apprehension may use such force and means as reasonably necessary under the circumstances to effect the apprehension.

Discussion

In addition to any other action required by law or regulation or proper military officials, any person making an apprehension under these rules should: maintain custody of the person apprehended; and inform as promptly as possible the immediate commander of the person apprehended, or any official higher in the chain of command of the person apprehended if it is impractical to inform the immediate commander.

(e) *Where an apprehension may be made.*

(1) *In general.* An apprehension may be made at any place, except as provided in subsection (e)(2) of this rule.

(2) *Private dwellings.* A private dwelling includes dwellings, on or off a military installation, such as single family houses, duplexes, and apartments. The quarters may be owned, leased, or rented by the residents, or assigned, and may be occupied on a temporary or permanent basis. "Private dwelling" does not include the following, whether or not subdivided into individual units: living areas in military barracks, vessels, aircraft, vehicles, tents, bunkers, field encampments, and similar places. No person may enter a private dwelling for the purpose of making an apprehension under these rules unless:

(A) Pursuant to consent under Mil. R. Evid. 314(e) of 316(d)(2);

(B) Under exigent circumstances described in Mil. R. Evid. 315(g) or 316(d)(4)(B);

(C) In the case of a private dwelling which is military property or under military control, or nonmilitary property in a foreign country.

(i) if the person to be apprehended is a resident of the private dwelling, there exists, at the time of the entry, reason to believe that the person to be apprehended is present in the dwelling, and the apprehension has been authorized by an official listed in Mil. R. Evid. 315(d) upon a determination that probable cause to apprehend the person exists; or

(ii) if the person to be apprehended is not a resident of the private dwelling, the entry has been authorized by an official listed in Mil. R. Evid. 315(d) upon a determination that probable cause exists to apprehend the person and to believe that the person to be apprehended is or will be present at the time of the entry;

(D) In the case of a private dwelling not included in subsection (e)(2)(C) of this rule,

(i) if the person to be apprehended is a resident of the private dwelling, there exists at the time of the entry, reason to believe that the person to be apprehended is present and the apprehension is authorized by an arrest warrant issued by competent civilian authority; or

(ii) if the person to be apprehended is not a resident of the private dwelling, the apprehension is authorized by an arrest warrant and the entry is authorized by a search warrant, each issued by competent civilian authority.

A person who is not a resident of the private dwelling entered may not challenge the legality of an apprehension of that person on the basis of failure to secure a warrant or authorization to enter that dwelling, or on the basis of the sufficiency of such a warrant or authorization. Nothing in this subsection ((e)(2)) affects the legality of an apprehension which is incident to otherwise lawful presence in a private dwelling.

Discussion

For example, if law enforcement officials enter a private dwelling pursuant to a valid search warrant or search authorization, they may apprehend persons therein if grounds for an apprehension exist. This subsection is not intended to be an independent grant of authority to execute civilian arrest or search warrants. The authority must derive from an appropriate Federal or state procedure. *See e.g.* Fed. R. Crim. P. 41 and 28 C.F.R. 60.1.

Rule 303. Preliminary inquiry into reported offenses

Upon receipt of information that a member of the command is accused or suspected of committing an offense or offenses triable by court-martial, the immediate commander shall make or cause to be made a preliminary inquiry into the charges or suspected offenses.

Discussion

The preliminary inquiry is usually informal. It may be an examination of the charges and an investigative report or other summary of expected evidence. In other cases a more extensive investigation may be necessary. Although the commander may conduct the investigation personally or with members of the command, in serious or complex cases the commander should consider whether to seek the assistance of law enforcement personnel in conducting any inquiry or further investigation. The inquiry should gather all reasonably available evidence bearing on guilt or innocence and any evidence relating to aggravation, extenuation, or mitigation.

The Military Rules of Evidence should be consulted when conducting interrogations (*see* Mil. R. Evid. 301-306), searches (*see* Mil. R. Evid. 311-317), and eyewitness identifications (*see* Mil. R. Evid. 321).

If the offense is one for which the Department of Justice has investigative responsibilities, appropriate coordination should be made under the Memorandum of Understanding, *see* Appendix 3, and any implementing regulations.

If it appears that any witness may not be available for later proceedings in the case, this should be brought to the attention of appropriate authorities. *See also* R.C.M. 702 (depositions).

A person who is an accuser (*see* Article 1(9)) is disqualified from convening a general or special court-martial in that case. R.C.M. 504(c)(1). Therefore, when the immediate commander is a general or special court-martial convening authority, the preliminary inquiry should be conducted by another officer of the command. That officer may be informed that charges may be preferred if the officer determines that preferral is warranted.

Rule 304. Pretrial restraint

(a) *Types of pretrial restraint.* Pretrial restraint is moral or physical restraint on a person's liberty which is imposed before and during disposition of offenses. Pretrial restraint may consist of conditions on liberty, restriction in lieu of arrest, arrest, or confinement.

(1) *Conditions on liberty.* Conditions on liberty are imposed by orders directing a person to do or

refrain from doing specified acts. Such conditions may be imposed in conjunction with other forms of restraint or separately.

(2) *Restriction in lieu of arrest.* Restriction in lieu of arrest is the restraint of a person by oral or written orders directing the person to remain within specified limits; a restricted person shall, unless otherwise directed, perform full military duties while restricted.

(3) *Arrest.* Arrest is the restraint of a person by oral or written order not imposed as punishment, directing the person to remain within specified limits; a person in the status of arrest may not be required to perform full military duties such as commanding or supervising personnel, serving as guard, or bearing arms. The status of arrest automatically ends when the person is placed, by the authority who ordered the arrest or a superior authority, on duty inconsistent with the status of arrest, but this shall not prevent requiring the person arrested to do ordinary cleaning or policing, or to take part in routine training and duties.

(4) *Confinement.* Pretrial confinement is physical restraint, imposed by order of competent authority, depriving a person of freedom pending disposition of offenses. *See* R.C.M. 305.

Discussion

Conditions on liberty include orders to report periodically to a specified official, orders not to go to a certain place (such as the scene of the alleged offense), and orders not to associate with specified persons (such as the alleged victim or potential witnesses). Conditions on liberty must not hinder pretrial preparation, however. Thus, when such conditions are imposed, they must by sufficiently flexible to permit pretrial preparation.

Restriction in lieu of arrest is a less severe restraint on liberty than is arrest. Arrest includes suspension from performing full military duties and the limits of arrest are normally narrower than those of restriction in lieu of arrest. The actual nature of the restraint imposed, and not the characterization of it by the officer imposing it, will determine whether it is technically an arrest or restriction in lieu of arrest.

Breach of arrest or restriction in lieu of arrest or violation of conditions on liberty are offenses under the code. *See* paragraphs 16, 19, and 102, Part IV. When such an offense occurs, it may warrant appropriate action such as nonjudicial punishment or court-martial. *See* R.C.M. 306. In addition, such a breach or violation may provide a basis for the imposition of a more severe form of restraint.

R.C.M. 707(a) requires that the accused be brought to trial within 120 days of preferral of charges or imposition of restraint under R.C.M. 304(a)(2)-(4).

(b) *Who may order pretrial restraint.*

(1) *Of civilians and officers.* Only a commanding officer to whose authority the civilian or officer is subject may order pretrial restraint of that civilian or officer.

Discussion

Civilians may be restrained under these rules only when they are subject to trial by court-martial. *See* R.C.M. 202.

---

(2) *Of enlisted persons.* Any commissioned officer may order pretrial restraint of any enlisted person.

(3) *Delegation of authority.* The authority to order pretrial restraint of civilians and commissioned and warrant officers may not be delegated. A commanding officer may delegate to warrant, petty, and noncommissioned officers authority to order pretrial restraint of enlisted persons of the commanding officer's command or subject to the authority of that commanding officer.

(4) *Authority to withhold.* A superior competent authority may withhold from a subordinate the authority to order pretrial restraint.

(c) *When a person may be restrained.* No person may be ordered into restraint before trial except for probable cause. Probable cause to order pretrial restraint exists when there is a reasonable belief that:

(1) An offense triable by court-martial has been committed;

(2) The person to be restrained committed it; and

(3) The restraint ordered is required by the circumstances.

Discussion

The decision whether to impose pretrial restraint, and, if so, what type or types, should be made on a case-by-case basis. The factors listed in the Discussion of R.C.M. 305(h)(2)(B) should be considered. The restraint should not be more rigorous than the circumstances require to ensure the presence of the person restrained or to prevent foreseeable serious criminal misconduct.

Restraint is not required in every case. The absence of pretrial restraint does not affect the jurisdiction of a court-martial. However, *see* R.C.M. 202(c) concerning attachment of jurisdiction. *See* R.C.M. 305 concerning the standards and procedures governing pretrial confinement.

(d) *Procedures for ordering pretrial restraint.* Pretrial restraint other than confinement is imposed by notifying the person orally or in writing of the restraint, including its terms or limits. The order to an enlisted person shall be delivered personally by the authority who issues it or through other persons subject to the code. The order to an officer or a civilian shall be delivered personally by the authority who issues it or by another commissioned officer. Pretrial confinement is imposed pursuant to orders by a competent authority by the delivery of a person to a place of confinement.

(e) *Notice of basis for restraint.* When a person is placed under restraint, the person shall be informed of the nature of the offense which is the basis for such restraint.

Discussion

See R.C.M. 305(e) concerning additional information which must be given to a person who is confined. If the person ordering the restrain is not the commander of the person restrained, that officer should be notified.

(f) *Punishment prohibited.* Pretrial restraint is not punishment and shall not be used as such. No person who is restrained pending trial may be subjected to punishment or penalty for the offense which is the basis for that restraint. Prisoners being held for trial shall not be required to undergo punitive duty hours or training, perform punitive labor, or wear special uniforms prescribed only for post-trial prisoners. This rule does not prohibit minor punishment during pretrial confinement for infractions of the rules of the place of confinement. Prisoners shall be afforded facilities and treatment under regulations of the Secretary concerned.

Discussion

Offenses under the code by a person under restraint may be disposed of in the same manner as any other offenses.

(g) *Release.* Except as otherwise provided in R.C.M. 305, a person may be released from pretrial restraint by a person authorized to impose it. Pretrial restraint shall terminate when a sentence is adjudged, the accused is acquitted of all charges, or all charges are dismissed.

Discussion

Pretrial restraint may be imposed (or reimposed) if charges are to be reinstated or of a rehearing or "other" trial is to be ordered.

(h) *Administrative restraint.* Nothing in this rule prohibits limitations on a servicemember imposed for operational or other military purposes independent of military justice, including administrative hold or medical reasons.

Discussion

See also R.C.M. 306.

Rule 305. Pretrial confinement

(a) *In general.* Pretrial confinement is physical restraint, imposed by order of competent authority, depriving a person of freedom pending disposition of charges.

Discussion

No member of the armed forces may be placed in confinement in immediate association with enemy prisoners or other foreign nationals not members of the armed forces of the United States. Article 12. However, if members of the armed forces of the United States are separated from prisoners of the other categories mentioned, they may be confined in the same confinement facilities.

(b) *Who may be confined.* Any person who is subject to trial by court-martial may be confined if the requirements of this rule are met.

Discussion

See R.C.M. 201 and 202 and the discussions therein concerning persons who are subject to trial by courts-martial.

(c) *Who may order confinement. See* R.C.M. 304(b).

Discussion

"No provost marshal, commander of a guard, or master at arms may refuse to receive or keep any prisoner committed to his charge by a commissioned officer of the armed forces, when the committing officer furnishes a statement, signed by him, of the offense charged against the prisoner." Article 11(a).

(d) *When a person may be confined.* No person may be ordered into pretrial confinement except for probable cause. Probable cause to order pretrial confinement exists when there is a reasonable belief that:

(1) An offense triable by court-martial has been committed;

(2) The person confined committed it; and

(3) Confinement is required by the circumstances.

Discussion

The person who directs confinement should consider the matters discussed under subsection (h)(2)(B) of this rule before ordering confinement. However, the person who initially orders confinement is not required to make a detailed analysis of the necessity for confinement. It is often not possible to review a person's background and character or even the details of an offense before physically detaining the person. For example, until additional information can be secured, it may be necessary to confine a person apprehended in the course of a violent crime.

"[W]hen charged only with an offense normally tried by summary court-martial, [an accused] shall not ordinarily be paced in confinement." Article 10.

Confinement should be distinguished from custody. Custody is restraint which is imposed by apprehension and which may be, but is not necessarily, physical. Custody may be imposed by anyone authorized to apprehend (*see* R.C.M. 302(b)), and may continue until a proper authority under R.C.M. 304(B) is notified and takes action. Thus, a person who has been apprehended could be physically restrained, but this would not be pretrial confinement in the sense of this rule until a person authorized to do so under R.C.M. 304(b) directed confinement.

(e) *Advice to the accused upon confinement.* Each person confined shall be promptly informed of:

(1) The nature of the offenses for which held;

(2) The right to remain silent and that any statement made by the person may be used against the person;

(3) The right to retain civilian counsel at no expense to the United States, and the right to request assignment of military counsel; and

(4) The procedures by which pretrial confinement will be reviewed.

(f) *Military counsel.* If requested by the prisoner and such request is made known to military authorities, military counsel shall be provided to the prisoner before the initial review under subsection (i) of this rule or within 72 hours of such a request being first communicated to military authorities, whichever occurs first. Counsel may be assigned for the limited purpose of representing the accused only during the pretrial confinement proceedings before charges are referred. If assignment is made for this limited purpose, the prisoner shall be so informed. Unless otherwise provided by regulations of the Secretary concerned, a prisoner does not have a right under this rule to have military counsel of the prisoner's own selection.

(g) *Who may direct release from confinement.* Any commander of a prisoner, an officer appointed under regulations of the Secretary concerned to conduct the review under subsection (i) and/or (j) of this rule, or, once charges have been referred, a military judge detailed to the court-martial to which the charges against the accused have been referred, may direct release from pretrial confinement. For purposes of this subsection, "any commander" includes the immediate or higher commander of the prisoner and the commander of the installation on which the confinement facility is located.

(h) *Notification and action by commander.*

(1) *Report.* Unless the commander of the prisoner ordered the pretrial confinement, the commissioned, warrant, noncommissioned, or petty officer into whose charge the prisoner was committed shall, within 24 hours after that commitment, cause a report to be made to the commander that shall contain the name of the prisoner, the offenses charged against the prisoner, and the name of the person who ordered or authorized confinement.

Discussion

This report may be made by any means. Ordinarily, the immediate commander of the prisoner should be notified. In unusual cases any commander to whose authority the prisoner is subject, such as the commander of the confinement facility, may be notified. In the latter case, the commander so notified must ensure compliance with subsection (h)(2) of this rule.

---

(2) *Action by commander.*

(A) *Decision.* Not later than 72 hours after the commander's ordering of a prisoner into pretrial confinement or, after receipt of a report that a member of the commander's unit or organization has been confined, whichever situation is applicable, the commander shall decide whether pretrial confinement will continue. A commander's compliance with this subsection may also satisfy the 48-hour probable cause determination of subsection R.C.M. 305(i)(1) below, provided the commander is a neutral and detached officer and acts within 48 hours of the imposition of confinement under military control. Nothing in subsections R.C.M. 305(d), R.C.M.

305(i)(1), or this subsection prevents a neutral and detached commander from completing the 48-hour probable cause determination and the 72-hour commander's decision immediately after an accused is ordered into pretrial confinement.

(B) *Requirements for confinement.* The commander shall direct the prisoner's release from pretrial confinement unless the commander believes upon probable cause, that is, upon reasonable grounds, that:

(i) An offense triable by a court-martial has been committed;

(ii) The prisoner committed it; and

(iii) Confinement is necessary because it is foreseeable that:

(a) The prisoner will not appear at trial, pretrial hearing, or investigation, or

(b) The prisoner will engage in serious criminal misconduct; and

(iv) Less severe forms of restraint are inadequate.

Serious criminal misconduct includes intimidation of witnesses or other obstruction of justice, serious injury of others, or other offenses which pose a serious threat to the safety of the community or to the effectiveness, morale, discipline, readiness, or safety of the command, or to the national security of the United States. As used in this rule, "national security" means the national defense and foreign relations of the United States and specifically includes: a military or defense advantage over any foreign nation or group of nations; a favorable foreign relations position; or a defense posture capable of successfully resisting hostile or destructive action from within or without, overt or covert.

Discussion

A person should not be confined as a mere matter of convenience or expedience.

Some of the factors which should be considered under this subsection are:

(1) The nature and circumstances of the offenses charged or suspected, including extenuating circumstances;

(2) The weight of the evidence against the accused;

(3) The accused's ties to the locale, including family, off-duty employment, financial resources, and length of residence;

(4) The accused's character and mental condition;

(5) The accused's service record, including any record of previous misconduct;

(6) The accused's record of appearance at or flight from other pretrial investigations, trials, and similar proceedings; and

(7) The likelihood that the accused can and will commit further serious criminal misconduct if allowed to remain at liberty.

Although the Military Rules of Evidence are not applicable, the commander should judge the reliability of the information available. Before relying on the reports of others, the commander must have a reasonable belief that the information is believable and has a factual basis. The information may be received orally or in writing. Information need not be received under oath, but an oath may add to its reliability. A commander may examine the prisoner's personnel records, police records, and may consider the recommendations of others.

Less serious forms of restraint must always be considered before pretrial confinement may be approved. Thus the commander should consider whether the prisoner could be safely returned to the prisoner's unit, at liberty or under restriction, arrest, or conditions on liberty. *See* R.C.M. 304.

(C) *72-hour memorandum.* If continued pretrial confinement is approved, the commander shall prepare a written memorandum that states the reasons for the conclusion that the requirements for confinement in subsection (h)(2)(B) of this rule have been met. This memorandum may include hearsay and may incorporate by reference other documents, such as witness statements, investigative reports, or official records. This memorandum shall be forwarded to the 7-day reviewing officer under subsection (i)(2) of this rule. If such a memorandum was prepared by the commander before ordering confinement, a second memorandum need not be prepared; however, additional information may be added to the memorandum at any time.

(i) *Procedures for review of pretrial confinement.*

(1) *48-hour probable cause determination.* Review of the adequacy of probable cause to continue pretrial confinement shall be made by a neutral and detached officer within 48 hours of imposition of confinement under military control. If the prisoner is apprehended by civilian authorities and remains in civilian custody at the request of military authorities, reasonable efforts will be made to bring the prisoner under military control in a timely fashion.

(2) *7-day review of pretrial confinement.* Within 7 days of the imposition of confinement, a neutral and detached officer appointed in accordance with regulations prescribed by the Secretary concerned shall review the probable cause determination and necessity for continued pretrial confinement. In calculating the number of days of confinement for purposes of this rule, the initial date of confinement

under military control shall count as one day and the date of the review shall also count as one day.

(A) *Nature of the 7-day review.*

(i) *Matters considered.* The review under this subsection shall include a review of the memorandum submitted by the prisoner's commander under subsection (h)(2)(C) of this rule. Additional written matters may be considered, including any submitted by the accused. The prisoner and the prisoner's counsel, if any, shall be allowed to appear before the 7-day reviewing officer and make a statement, if practicable. A representative of the command may also appear before the reviewing officer to make a statement.

(ii) *Rules of evidence.* Except for Mil. R. Evid., Section V (Privileges) and Mil. R. Evid. 302 and 305, the Military Rules of Evidence shall not apply to the matters considered.

(iii) *Standard of proof.* The requirements for confinement under subsection (h)(2)(B) of this rule must be proved by a preponderance of the evidence.

(B) *Extension of time limit.* The 7-day reviewing officer may, for good cause, extend the time limit for completion of the review to 10 days after the imposition of pretrial confinement.

(C) *Action by 7-day reviewing officer.* Upon completion of review, the reviewing officer shall approve continued confinement or order immediate release.

(D) *Memorandum.* The 7-day reviewing officer's conclusions, including the factual findings on which they are based, shall be set forth in a written memorandum. A copy of the memorandum and of all documents considered by the 7-day reviewing officer shall be maintained in accordance with regulations prescribed by the Secretary concerned and provided to the accused or the Government on request.

(E) *Reconsideration of approval of continued confinement.* The 7-day reviewing officer shall upon request, and after notice to the parties, reconsider the decision to confine the prisoner based upon any significant information not previously considered.

(j) *Review by military judge.* Once the charges for which the accused has been confined are referred to trial, the military judge shall review the propriety of pretrial confinement upon motion for appropriate relief.

(1) *Release.* The military judge shall order release from pretrial confinement only if:

(A) The 7-day reviewing officer's decision was an abuse of discretion, and there is not sufficient information presented to the military judge justifying continuation of pretrial confinement under subsection (h)(2)(B) of this rule;

(B) Information not presented to the 7-day reviewing officer establishes that the prisoner should be released under subsection (h)(2)(B) of this rule; or

(C) The provisions of subsection (i)(1) or (2) of this rule have not been complied with and information presented to the military judge does not establish sufficient grounds for continued confinement under subsection (h)(2)(B) of this rule.

(2) *Credit.* The military judge shall order administrative credit under subsection (k) of this rule for any pretrial confinement served as a result of an abuse of discretion or failure to comply with the provisions of subsections (f), (h), or (i) of this rule.

(k) *Remedy.* The remedy for noncompliance with subsections (f), (h), (i), or (j) of this rule shall be an administrative credit against the sentence adjudged for any confinement served as the result of such noncompliance. Such credit shall be computed at the rate of 1 day credit for each day of confinement served as a result of such noncompliance. The military judge may order additional credit for each day of pretrial confinement that involves an abuse of discretion or unusually harsh circumstances. This credit is to be applied in addition to any other credit the accused may be entitled as a result of pretrial confinement served. This credit shall be applied first against any confinement adjudged. If no confinement is adjudged, or if the confinement adjudged is insufficient to offset all the credit to which the accused is entitled, the credit shall be applied against hard labor without confinement, restriction, fine, and forfeiture of pay, in that order, using the conversion formula under R.C.M. 1003(b)(6) and (7). For purposes of this subsection, 1 day of confinement shall be equal to 1 day of total forfeiture or a like amount of fine. The credit shall not be applied against any other form of punishment.

(l) *Confinement after release.* No person whose release from pretrial confinement has been directed by a person authorized in subsection (g) of this rule may be confined again before completion of trial except upon the discovery, after the order of release, of evidence or of misconduct which, either alone or in conjunction with all other available evidence, justifies confinement.

Discussion

See R.C.M. 304(b) concerning who may order confinement.

(m) *Exceptions.*

(1) *Operational necessity.* The Secretary of Defense may suspend application of subsections (e)(2) and (3), (f), (h)(2)(A) and (C), and (i) of this rule to specific units or in specified areas when operational requirements of such units or in such areas would make application of such provisions impracticable.

(2) *At sea.* Subsections (e)(2) and (3), (f), (h)(2)(C), and (i) of this rule shall not apply in the case of a person on board a vessel at sea. In such situations, confinement on board the vessel at sea may continue only until the person can be transferred to a confinement facility ashore. Such transfer shall be accomplished at the earliest opportunity permitted by the operational requirements and mission of the vessel. Upon such transfer the memorandum required by subsection (h)(2)(C) of this rule shall be transmitted to the reviewing officer under subsection (i) of this rule and shall include an explanation of any delay in the transfer.

Discussion

Under this subsection the standards for confinement remain the same (although the circumstances giving rise to the exception could bear on the application of those standards). Also, pretrial confinement remains subject to judicial review. The prisoner's commander still must determine whether confinement will continue under subsection (h)(2)(B) of this rule. The suspension of subsection (h)(2)(A) of this rule removes the 72-hour requirement since in a combat environment, the commander may not be available to comply with it. The commander must make the pretrial confinement decision as soon as reasonably possible, however. (This provision is not suspended under subsection (2) since the commander of a vessel is always available.)

Rule 306. Initial disposition

(a) *Who may dispose of offenses.* Each commander has discretion to dispose of offenses by members of that command. Ordinarily the immediate commander of a person accused or suspected of committing an offense triable by court-martial initially determines how to dispose of that offense. A superior commander may withhold the authority to dispose of offenses in individual cases, types of cases, or generally. A superior commander may not limit the discretion of a subordinate commander to act on cases over which authority has not been withheld.

Discussion

Each commander in the chain of command has independent, yet overlapping discretion to dispose of offenses within the limits of that officer's authority. Normally, in keeping with the policy in subsection (b) of this rule, the initial disposition decision is made by the official at the lowest echelon with the power to make it. A decision by a commander ordinarily does not bar a different disposition by a superior authority. *See* R.C.M. 401(c); 601(f). Once charges are referred to a court-martial by a convening authority competent to do so, they may be withdrawn from that court-martial only in accordance with R.C.M. 604.

See Appendix 3 with respect to offenses for which coordination with the Department of Justice is required.

(b) *Policy.* Allegations of offenses should be disposed of in a timely manner at the lowest appropriate level of disposition listed in subsection (c) of this rule.

Discussion

The disposition decision is one of the most important and difficult decisions facing a commander. Many factors must be taken into consideration and balanced, including, to the extent practicable, the nature of the offenses, any mitigating or extenuating circumstances, the character and military service of the accused, any recommendations made by subordinate commanders, the interest of justice, military exigencies, and the effect of the decision on the accused and the command. The goal should be a disposition that is warranted, appropriate, and fair.

In deciding how an offense should be disposed of, factors the commander should consider, to the extent they are known, include:

(A) the character and military service of the accused;

(B) the nature of and circumstances surrounding the offense and the extent of the harm caused by the offense, including the offense's effect on morale, health, safety, welfare, and discipline;

(C) appropriateness of the authorized punishment to the particular accused or offense;

(D) possible improper motives of the accuser;

(E) reluctance of the victim or others to testify;

(F) cooperation of the accused in the apprehension or conviction of others;

(G) availability and likelihood of prosecution of the same or similar and related charges against the accused by another jurisdiction;

(H) availability and admissibility of evidence;

(I) existence of jurisdiction over the accused and the offense; and

(J) likely issues.

(c) *How offenses may be disposed of.* Within the limits of the commander's authority, a commander may take the actions set forth in this subsection to initially dispose of a charge or suspected offense.

Discussion

Prompt disposition of charges is essential. *See* R.C.M. 707 (speedy trial requirements).

Before determining an appropriate disposition, a commander should ensure that a preliminary inquiry under R.C.M. 303 has been conducted. If charges have not already been preferred, the commander may, if appropriate, prefer them and dispose of them under this rule. *But see* R.C.M. 601 (c) regarding disqualification of an accuser.

If charges have been preferred, the commander should ensure that the accused has been notified in accordance with R.C.M. 308, and that charges are in proper form. *See* R.C.M. 307. Each commander who forwards or disposes of charges may make minor changes therein. *See* R.C.M. 603(a) and (b). If major changes are necessary, the affected charge should be preferred anew. *See* R.C.M. 603(d).

When charges are brought against two or more accused with a view to a joint or common trial, *see* R.C.M. 307(c)(5); 601(e)(3). If it appears that the accused may lack mental capacity to stand trial or may not have been mentally responsible at the times of the offenses, *see* R.C.M. 706; 909; 916(k).

---

(1) *No action.* A commander may decide to take no action on an offense. If charges have been preferred, they may be dismissed.

Discussion

A decision to take no action or dismissal of charges at this stage does not bar later disposition of the offenses under subsection (c)(2) through (5) of this rule.

See R.C.M. 401(a) concerning who may dismiss charges, and R.C.M. 401(c)(1) concerning dismissal of charges.

When a decision is made to take no action, the accused should be informed.

---

(2) *Administrative action.* A commander may take or initiate administrative action, in addition to or instead of other action taken under this rule, subject to regulations of the Secretary concerned. Administrative actions include corrective measures such as counseling, admonition, reprimand, exhortation, disapproval, criticism, censure, reproach, rebuke, extra military instruction, or the administrative withholding of privileges, or any combination of the above.

Discussion

Other administrative measures, which are subject to regulations of the Secretary concerned, include matters related to efficiency reports, academic reports, and other ratings; rehabilitation and reassignment; career field reclassification; administrative reduction for inefficiency; bar to reenlistment; personnel reliability program reclassification; security classification changes; pecuniary liability for negligence or misconduct; and administrative separation.

---

(3) *Nonjudicial punishment.* A commander may consider the matter pursuant to Article 15, nonjudicial punishment. *See* Part V.

(4) *Disposition of charges.* Charges may be disposed of in accordance with R.C.M. 401.

Discussion

If charges have not been preferred, they may be preferred. *See* R.C.M. 307 concerning preferral of charges. However, *see* R.C.M. 601(c) concerning disqualification of an accuser.

Charges may be disposed of by dismissing them, forwarding them to another commander for disposition, or referring them to a summary, special, or general court-martial. Before charges may be referred to a general court-martial, compliance with R.C.M. 405 and 406 is necessary. Therefore, if appropriate, an investigation under R.C.M. 405 may be directed. Additional guidance on these matters is found in R.C.M. 401-407.

---

(5) *Forwarding for disposition.* A commander may forward a matter concerning an offense, or charges, to a superior or subordinate authority for disposition.

Discussion

The immediate commander may lack authority to take action which that commander believes is an appropriate disposition. In such cases, the matter should be forwarded to a superior officer with a recommendation as to disposition. *See also* R.C.M. 401(c)(2) concerning forwarding charges. If allegations are forwarded to a higher authority for disposition, because of lack of authority or otherwise, the disposition decision becomes a matter within the discretion of the higher authority.

A matter may be forwarded for other reasons, such as for investigation of allegations and preferral of charges, if warranted (*see* R.C.M. 303; 307), or so that a subordinate can dispose of the matter.

(d) *National security matters.* If a commander not authorized to convene general courts-martial finds that an offense warrants trial by court-martial, but believes that trial would be detrimental to the prosecution of a war or harmful to national security, the matter shall be forwarded to the general court-martial convening authority for action under R.C.M. 407(b).

Rule 307. Preferral of charges

(a) *Who may prefer charges.* Any person subject to the code may prefer charges.

Discussion

No person may be ordered to prefer charges to which that person is unable to make truthfully the required oath. *See* Article 30(a) and subsection (b) of this rule. A person who has been the accuser or nominal accuser (*see* Article 1(9)) may not also serve as the convening authority of a general or special court-martial to which the charges are later referred. *See* Articles 22(b) and 23(b); R.C.M. 601; however, *see* R.C.M. 1302(b) (summary court-martial convening authority is not disqualified by being the accuser). A person authorized to dispose of offenses (*see* R.C.M. 306(a); 401–404 and 407) should not be ordered to prefer charges when this would disqualify that person from exercising that persons's authority or would improperly restrict that person's discretion to act on the case. *See* R.C.M. 104 and 504(c).

Charges may be preferred against a person subject to trial by court-martial at any time but should be preferred without unnecessary delay. *See* the statute of limitations prescribed by Article 43. Preferral of charges should not be unnecessarily delayed. When a good reason exists—as when a person is permitted to continue a course of conduct so that a ringleader or other conspirators may also be discovered or when a suspected counterfeiter goes uncharged until guilty knowledge becomes apparent—a reasonable delay is permissible. However, *see* R.C.M. 707 concerning speedy trial requirements.

(b) *How charges are preferred; oath.* A person who prefers charges must:

(1) Sign the charges and specifications under oath before a commissioned officer of the armed forces authorized to administer oaths; and

(2) State that the signer has personal knowledge of or has investigated the matters set forth in the charges and specifications and that they are true in fact to the best of that person's knowledge and belief.

Discussion

See Article 136 for authority to administer oaths. The following form may be used to administer the oath:

"You (swear) (affirm) that you are a person subject to the Uniform Code of Military Justice, that you have personal knowledge of or have investigated the matters set forth in the foregoing charge(s) and specification(s), and that the same are true in fact to the best of your knowledge and belief. (So help you God.)"

The accuser's belief may be based upon reports of others in whole or in part.

(c) *How to allege offenses.*

(1) *In general.* The format of charge and specification is used to allege violations of the code.

Discussion

See Appendix 4 for a sample of a Charge Sheet (DD Form 458).

---

(2) *Charge.* A charge states the article of the code, law of war, or local penal law of an occupied territory which the accused is alleged to have violated.

Discussion

The particular subdivision of an article of the code (for example, Article 118(1)) should not be included in the charge. When there are numerous infractions of the same article, there will be only one charge, but several specifications thereunder. There may also be several charges, but each must allege a violation of a different article of the code. For violations of the law of war, *see* (D) below.

(A) *Numbering charges.* If there is only one charge, it is not numbered. When there is more than one charge, each charge is numbered by a Roman numeral.

(B) *Additional charges.* Charges preferred after others have been preferred are labeled "additional charges" and are also numbered with Roman numerals, beginning with "I" if there is more than one additional charge. These ordinarily relate to offenses not known at the time or committed after the original charges were preferred. Additional charges do not require a separate trial if incorporated in the trial of the original charges before arraignment. *See* R.C.M. 601(e)(2).

(C) *Preemption.* An offense specifically defined by Articles 81 through 132 may not be alleged as a violation of Article 134. *See* paragraph 60c(5)(a) of Part IV. *But see* subsection (d) of this rule.

(D) *Charges under the law of war.* In the case of a person subject to trial by general court-martial for violations of the law of war (*see* Article 18), the charge should be: "Violation of the Law of War"; or "Violation of __________, __________" referring to the local penal law of the occupied territory. *See* R.C.M. 201(f)(1)(B). *But see* subsection (d) of this rule. Ordinarily persons subject to the code should be charged with a specific violation of the code rather than a violation of the law of war.

---

(3) *Specification.* A specification is a plain, concise, and definite statement of the essential facts constituting the offense charged. A specification is sufficient if it alleges every element of the charged

offense expressly or by necessary implication. Except for aggravating factors under R.C.M 1003(d) and R.C.M. 1004, facts that increase the maximum authorized punishment must be alleged in order to permit the possible increased punishment. No particular format is required.

Discussion

How to draft specifications.

(A) *Sample specifications.* Before drafting a specification, the drafter should read the pertinent provisions of Part IV, where the elements of proof of various offenses and forms for specifications appear.

(B) *Numbering specifications.* If there is only one specification under a charge it is not numbered. When there is more than one specification under any charge, the specifications are numbered in Arabic numerals. The term "additional" is not used in connection with the specifications under an additional charge.

(C) *Name and description of the accused.*

(i) *Name.* The specification should state the accused's full name: first name, middle name or initial, last name. If the accused is known by more than one name, the name acknowledged by the accused should be used. If there is no such acknowledgment, the name believed to be the true name should be listed first, followed by all known aliases. For example: Seaman John P. Smith, U.S. Navy, alias Lt. Robert R. Brown, U.S. Navy.

(ii) *Military association.* The specification should state the accused's rank or grade. If the rank or grade of the accused has changed since the date of an alleged offense, and the change is pertinent to the offense charged, the accused should be identified by the present rank or grade followed by rank or grade on the date of the alleged offense. For example: In that Seaman ____________, then Seaman Apprentice ______, etc.

(iii) *Social security number or service number.* The social security number or service number of an accused should not be stated in the specification.

(iv) *Basis of personal jurisdiction.*

(a) *Military members on active duty.* Ordinarily, no allegation of the accused's armed force or unit or organization is necessary for military members on active duty.

(b) *Persons subject to the code under Article 2(a), subsections (3) through (12), or subject to trial by court-martial under Articles 3 or 4.* The specification should describe the accused's armed force, unit or organization, position, or status which will indicate the basis of jurisdiction. For example: John Jones, (a person employed by and serving with the U.S. Army in the field in time of war) (a person convicted of having obtained a fraudulent discharge), etc.

(D) *Date and time of offense*

(i) *In general.* The date of the commission of the offense charged should be stated in the specification with sufficient precision to identify the offense and enable the accused to understand what particular act or omission to defend against.

(ii) *Use of "on or about."* In alleging the date of the offense it is proper to allege it as "on or about" a specified day.

(iii) *Hour.* The exact hour of the offense is ordinarily not alleged except in certain absence offenses. When the exact time is alleged, the 24-hour clock should be used. The use of "at or about" is proper.

(iv) *Extended periods.* When the acts specified extend(s) over a considerable period of time it is proper to allege it (or them) as having occurred, for example, "from about 15 June 1983 to about 4 November 1983," or "did on divers occasions between 15 June 1983 and 4 November 1983."

(E) *Place of offense.* The place of the commission of the offense charged should be stated in the specification with sufficient precision to identify the offense and enable the accused to understand the particular act or omission to defend against. In alleging the place of the offense, it is proper to allege it as "at or near" a certain place if the exact place is uncertain.

(F) *Subject-matter jurisdiction allegations.* Pleading the accused's rank or grade along with the proper elements of the offense normally will be sufficient to establish subject-matter jurisdiction.

(G) *Description of offense.*

(i) *Elements.* The elements of the offense must be alleged, either expressly or by necessary implication. If a specific intent, knowledge, or state of mind is an element of the offense, it must be alleged.

(ii) *Words indicating criminality.* If the alleged act is not itself an offense but is made an offense either by applicable statute (including Articles 133 and 134), or regulation or custom having the effect of law, then words indicating criminality such as "wrongfully," "unlawfully," or "without authority" (depending upon the nature of the offense) should be used to describe the accused's acts.

(iii) *Specificity.* The specification should be sufficiently specific to inform the accused of the conduct charged, to enable the accused to prepare a defense, and to protect the accused against double jeopardy. Only those facts that make the accused's conduct criminal ordinarily should be alleged. Specific evidence supporting the allegations ordinarily should not be included in the specifications.

(iv) *Duplicitousness.* One specification should not allege more than one offense, either conjunctively (the accused "lost and destroyed") or alternatively (the accused "lost or destroyed"). However, if two acts or a series of acts constitute one offense, they may be alleged conjunctively. *See* R.C.M. 906(b)(5).

(H) *Other considerations in drafting specifications.*

(i) *Principals.* All principals are charged as if each was the perpetrator. *See* paragraph 1 of Part IV for a discussion of principals.

(ii) *Victim.* In the case of an offense against the person or property of a person, the first name, middle initial and last name of such person should be alleged, if known. If the name of the victim is unknown, a general physical description may be used. If this cannot be done, the victim may be described as "a person whose name is unknown." Military rank or grade should be alleged, and must be alleged if an element of the offense, as in an allegation of disobedience of the command of a superior officer. If the person has no military position, it may otherwise be necessary to allege the status as in an allegation of using provoking words toward a person subject to the code. *See* paragraph 42 of Part IV.

(iii) *Property.* In describing property generic terms should be used, such as "a watch" or "a knife," and descriptive details such as make, model, color, and serial number should ordinarily be omitted. In some instances, however, details may be essential to the offense, so they must be alleged. For example: the length of a knife blade may be important when alleging a violation of general regulation prohibiting carrying a knife with a blade that exceeds a certain length.

(iv) *Value.* When the value of property or other amount determines the maximum punishment which may be adjudged for an offense, the value or amount should be alleged, for in such a case increased punishments that are contingent upon value may not be adjudged unless there is an allegation, as well as proof, of a value which will support the punishment. If several articles of different kinds are the subject of the offense, the value of each article should be stated followed by a statement of the aggregate value. Exact value should be stated, if known. For ease of proof an allegation may be "of a value not less than ________." If only an approximate value is known, it may be alleged as "of a value of about ________." If the value of an item is unknown but obviously minimal, the term "of some value" may be used. These principles apply to allegations of amounts.

(v) *Documents.* When documents other than regulations or orders must be alleged (for example, bad checks in violation of Article 123a), the document may be set forth verbatim (including photocopies and similar reproductions) or may be described, in which case the description must be sufficient to inform the accused of the offense charged.

(vi) *Orders.*

(a) *General orders.* A specification alleging a violation of a general order or regulation (Article 92(1)) must clearly identify the specific order or regulation allegedly violated. The general order or regulation should be cited by its identifying title or number, section or paragraph, and date. It is not necessary to recite the text of the general order or regulation verbatim.

(b) *Other orders.* If the order allegedly violated is an "other lawful order" (Article 92(2)), it should be set forth verbatim or described in the specification. When the order is oral, *see* (vii) below.

(c) *Negating exceptions.* If the order contains exceptions, it is not necessary that the specification contain a specific allegation negating the exceptions. However, words of criminality may be required if the alleged act is not necessarily criminal. *See* subsection (G)(ii) of this discussion.

(vii) *Oral statements.* When alleging oral statements the phrase "or words to that effect" should be added.

(viii) *Joint offense.* In the case of a joint offense each accused may be charged separately as if each accused acted alone or all may be charged together in a single specification. For example:

(a) If Doe and Roe are joint perpetrators of an offense and it is intended to charge and try both at the same trial, they should be charged in a single specification as follows:

"In that Doe and Roe, acting jointly and pursuant to a common intent, did. . . ."

(b) If it is intended that Roe will be tried alone or that Roe will be tried with Doe at a common trial, Roe may be charged in the same manner as if Roe alone had committed the offense. However, to show in the specification that Doe was a joint actor with Roe, even though Doe is not to be tried with Roe, Roe may be charged as follows:

"In that Roe did, in conjunction with Doe, ..."

(ix) *Matters in aggravation.* Matters in aggravation that do not increase the maximum authorized punishment ordinarily should not be alleged in the specification. Prior convictions need not be alleged in the specification to permit increased punishment. Aggravating factors in capital cases should not be alleged in the specification. Notice of such factors is normally provided in accordance with R.C.M. 1004(b)(1).

(x) *Abbreviations.* Commonly used and understood abbreviations may be used, particularly abbreviations for ranks, grades, units and organizations, components, and geographic or political entities, such as the names of states or countries.

---

(4) *Multiple offenses.* Charges and specifications alleging all known offenses by an accused may be preferred at the same time. Each specification shall state only one offense. What is substantially one transaction should not be made the basis for an unreasonable multiplication of charges against one person.

Discussion

See R.C.M. 906(b)(12) and 1003(c)(1)(C). For example, a person should not be charged with both failure to report for a routine scheduled duty, such as reveille, and with absence without leave if the failure to report occurred during the period for which the accused is charged with absence without leave. There are times, however, when sufficient doubt as to the facts or the law exists to warrant making one transaction the basis for charging two or more offenses. In no case should both an offense and a lesser included offense thereof be separately charged.

See also R.C.M. 601(e)(2) concerning referral of several offenses.

---

(5) *Multiple offenders.* A specification may name more than one person as an accused if each person so named is believed by the accuser to be a principal in the offense which is the subject of the specification.

Discussion

See also R.C.M. 601(e)(3) concerning joinder of accused.

A joint offense is one committed by two or more persons acting together with a common intent. Principals may be charged jointly with the commission of the same offense, but an accessory after the fact cannot be charged jointly with the principal whom the accused is alleged to have received, comforted, or assisted. Offenders are properly joined only if there is a common unlawful design or purpose; the mere fact that several persons happen to have committed the same kinds of offenses at the time, although material as tending to show concert of purpose, does not necessarily establish this. The fact that several persons happen to have absented themselves without leave at about the same time will not, in the absence of evidence indicating a joint design, purpose, or plan justify joining them in one specification, for they may merely have been availing themselves of the same opportunity. In joint offenses the participants may be separately or jointly charged. However, if the participants are members of different armed forces, they must be charged separately because their trials must be separately reviewed. The preparation of joint charges is discussed in subsection (c)(3) Discussion (H) (viii)*(a)* of this rule. The advantage of a joint charge is that all accused will be tried at one trial, thereby saving time, labor, and expense. This must be weighed against the possible unfairness to the accused which may result if their defenses are inconsistent or antagonistic. An accused cannot be called as a witness except upon that accused's own request. If the testimony of an accomplice is necessary, the accomplice should not be tried jointly with those against whom the accomplice is expected to testify. *See also* Mil. R. Evid. 306.

See R.C.M. 603 concerning amending specifications.

See R.C.M. 906(b)(5) and (6) concerning motions to amend specifications and bills of particulars.

(d) *Harmless error in citation.* Error in or omission of the designation of the article of the code or other statute, law of war, or regulation violated shall not be ground for dismissal of a charge or reversal of a conviction if the error or omission did not prejudicially mislead the accused.

Rule 308. Notification to accused of charges

(a) *Immediate commander.* The immediate commander of the accused shall cause the accused to be informed of the charges preferred against the accused, and the name of the person who preferred the charges and of any person who ordered the charges to be preferred, if known, as soon as practicable.

Discussion

When notice is given, a certificate to that effect on the Charge Sheet should be completed. *See* Appendix 4.

(b) *Commanders at higher echelons.* When the accused has not been informed of the charges, commanders at higher echelons to whom the preferred charges are forwarded shall cause the accused to be informed of the matters required under subsection (a) of this rule as soon as practicable.

(c) *Remedy.* The sole remedy for violation of this rule is a continuance or recess of sufficient length to permit the accused to adequately prepare a defense, and no relief shall be granted upon a failure to comply with this rule unless the accused demonstrates that the accused has been hindered in the preparation of a defense.

CHAPTER IV. FORWARDING AND DISPOSITION OF CHARGES

Rule 401. Forwarding and disposition of charges in general

(a) *Who may dispose of charges.* Only persons authorized to convene courts-martial or to administer nonjudicial punishment under Article 15 may dispose of charges. A superior competent authority may withhold the authority of a subordinate to dispose of charges in individual cases, types of cases, or generally.

Discussion

See R.C.M. 504 as to who may convene courts-martial and paragraph 2 of Part V as to who may administer nonjudicial punishment. If the power to convene courts-martial and to administer nonjudicial punishment has been withheld, a commander may not dispose of charges under this rule.

Ordinarily charges should be forwarded to the accused's immediate commander for initial consideration as to disposition. Each commander has independent discretion to determine how charges will be disposed of, except to the extent that the commander's authority has been withheld by superior competent authority. *See also* R.C.M. 104.

Each commander who forwards or disposes of charges may make minor changes therein. *See* R.C.M. 603(a) and (b). If major changes are necessary, the affected charge should be preferred anew. *See* R.C.M. 603(d). If a commander is an accuser (*see* Article 1(9); 307(a)) that commander is ineligible to refer such charges to a general or special court-martial. *See* R.C.M. 601(c). However, see R.C.M. 1302(b) (accuser may refer charges to a summary court-martial).

(b) *Prompt determination.* When a commander with authority to dispose of charges receives charges, that commander shall promptly determine what disposition will be made in the interest of justice and discipline.

Discussion

In determining what level of disposition is appropriate, *see* R.C.M. 306(b) and (c). When charges are brought against two or more accused with a view to a joint or common trial, *see* R.C.M. 307(c)(5); 601(e)(3). If it appears that the accused may lack mental capacity to stand trial or may not have been mentally responsible at the times of the offenses, *see* R.C.M. 706; 909; 916(k).

As to the rules concerning speedy trial, *see* R.C.M. 707. *See also* Articles 10; 30; 33; 98.

Before determining an appropriate disposition, a commander who receives charges should ensure that: (1) a preliminary inquiry under R.C.M. 303 has been conducted; (2) the accused has been notified in accordance with R.C.M. 308; and (3) the charges are in proper form.

(c) *How charges may be disposed of.* Unless the authority to do so has been limited or withheld by superior competent authority, a commander may dispose of charges by dismissing any or all of them, forwarding any or all of them to another commander for disposition, or referring any or all of them to a court-martial which the commander is empowered to convene. Charges should be disposed of in accordance with the policy in R.C.M. 306(b).

Discussion

A commander may dispose of charges individually or collectively. If charges are referred to a court-martial, ordinarily all known charges should be referred to a single court-martial.

See Appendix 3 when the charges may involve matters in which the Department of Justice has an interest.

---

(1) *Dismissal.* When a commander dismisses charges further disposition under R.C.M. 306(c) of the offenses is not barred.

Discussion

Charges are ordinarily dismissed by lining out and initialing the deleted specifications or otherwise recording that a specification is dismissed. When all charges and specifications are dismissed, the accuser and the accused ordinarily should be informed.

A charge should be dismissed when it fails to state an offense, when it is unsupported by available evidence, or when there are other sound reasons why trial by court-martial is not appropriate. Before dismissing charges because trial would be detrimental to the prosecution of a war or harmful to national security, *see* R.C.M. 401(d); 407(b).

If the accused has already refused nonjudicial punishment, charges should not be dismissed with a view to offering nonjudicial punishment unless the accused has indicated willingness to accept nonjudicial punishment if again offered. The decision whether to dismiss charges in such circumstances is within the sole discretion of the commander concerned.

Charges may be amended in accordance with R.C.M. 603.

It is appropriate to dismiss a charge and prefer another charge anew when, for example, the original charge failed to state an offense, or was so defective that a major amendment was required (*see* R.C.M. 603(d)), or did not adequately reflect the nature or seriousness of the offense.

See R.C.M. 907(b)(2)(C) concerning the effect of dismissing charges after the court-martial has begun.

---

(2) *Forwarding charges.*

(A) *Forwarding to a superior commander.* When charges are forwarded to a superior commander for disposition, the forwarding commander shall make a personal recommendation as to disposition. If the forwarding commander is disqualified from acting as convening authority in the case, the basis for the disqualification shall be noted.

Discussion

A commander's recommendation is within that commander's sole discretion. No authority may direct a commander to make a specific recommendation as to disposition.

When charges are forwarded to a superior commander with a view to trial by general or special court-martial, they should be forwarded by a letter of transmittal or indorsement. To the extent practicable without unduly delaying forwarding the charges, the letter should include or carry as inclosures: a summary of the available evidence relating to each offense; evidence of previous convictions and nonjudicial punishments of the accused; an indication that the accused has been offered and refused nonjudicial punishment, if applicable; and any other matters required by superior authority or deemed appropriate by the forwarding commander. Other matters which may be appropriate include information concerning the accused's background and character of military service, and a description of any unusual circumstances in the case. The summary of evidence should include available witness statements, documentary evidence, and exhibits. When practicable, copies of signed statements of the witnesses should be forwarded, as should copies of any investigative or laboratory reports. Forwarding charges should not be delayed, however, solely to obtain such statements or reports when it otherwise appears that sufficient evidence to warrant trial is or will be available in time for trial. If because of the bulk of documents or exhibits, it is impracticable to forward them with the letter of transmittal, they should be properly preserved and should be referred to in the letter of transmittal.

When it appears that any witness may not be available for later proceedings in the case or that a deposition may be appropriate, that matter should be brought to the attention of the convening authority promptly and should be noted in the letter of transmittal.

When charges are forwarded with a view to disposition other than trial by general or special court-martial, they should be accompanied by sufficient information to enable the authority receiving them to dispose of them without further investigation.

(B) *Other cases.* When charges are forwarded to a commander who is not a superior of the forwarding commander, no recommendation as to disposition may be made.

Discussion

Except when directed to forward charges, a subordinate commander may not be required to take any specific action to dispose of charges. *See* R.C.M. 104. *See also* paragraph 1d(2) of Part V. When appropriate, charges may be sent or returned to a subordinate commander for compliance with procedural requirements. *See*, for example, R.C.M. 303 (preliminary inquiry); R.C.M. 308 (notification to accused of charges).

---

(3) *Referral of charges. See* R.C.M. 403, 404, 407, 601.

(d) *National security matters.* If a commander who is not a general court-martial convening authority finds that the charges warrant trial by court-martial but believes that trial would probably be detrimental to the prosecution of a war or harmful to national security, the charges shall be forwarded to the officer exercising general court-martial convening authority.

Discussion

See R.C.M. 407(b).

Rule 402. Action by commander not authorized to convene courts-martial

When in receipt of charges, a commander authorized to administer nonjudicial punishment but not authorized to convene courts-martial may:

(1) Dismiss any charges; or

Discussion

See R.C.M. 401(c)(1) concerning dismissal of charges, the effect of dismissal, and options for further action.

---

(2) Forward them to a superior commander for disposition.

Discussion

See R.C.M. 401(c)(2) for additional guidance concerning forwarding charges. *See generally* R.C.M. 303 (preliminary inquiry); 308 (notification to accused of charges) concerning other duties of the immediate commander when in receipt of charges.

When the immediate commander is authorized to convene courts-martial, *see* R.C.M. 403, 404, or 407, as appropriate.

Rule 403. Action by commander exercising summary court-martial jurisdiction

(a) *Recording receipt.* Immediately upon receipt of sworn charges, an officer exercising summary court-martial jurisdiction over the command shall cause the hour and date of receipt to be entered on the charge sheet.

Discussion

See Article 24 and R.C.M. 1302(a) concerning who may exercise summary court-martial jurisdiction.

The entry indicating receipt is important because it stops the running of the statute of limitations. *See* Article 43; R.C.M. 907(b)(2)(B). Charges may be preferred and forwarded to an officer exercising summary court-martial jurisdiction over the command to stop the running of the statute of limitations even though the accused is absent without authority.

(b) *Disposition.* When in receipt of charges a commander exercising summary court-martial jurisdiction may:

(1) Dismiss any charges;

Discussion

See R.C.M. 401(c)(1) concerning dismissal of charges, the effect of dismissing charges, and options for further action.

---

(2) Forward charges (or, after dismissing charges, the matter) to a subordinate commander for disposition;

Discussion

See R.C.M. 401(c)(2)(B) concerning forwarding charges to a subordinate. When appropriate, charges may be forwarded to a subordinate even if the subordinate previously considered them.

---

(3) Forward any charges to a superior commander for disposition;

Discussion

See R.C.M. 401(c)(2)(A) for guidance concerning forwarding charges to a superior.

---

(4) Subject to R.C.M. 601(d), refer charges to a summary court-martial for trial; or

Discussion

See R.C.M. 1302(c) concerning referral of charges to a summary court-martial.

---

(5) Unless otherwise prescribed by the Secretary concerned, direct a pretrial investigation under R.C.M. 405, and, if appropriate, forward the report of investigation with the charges to a superior commander for disposition.

Discussion

An investigation should be directed when it appears that the charges are of such a serious nature that trial by general court-martial may be warranted. *See* R.C.M. 405. If an investigation of the subject matter already has been conducted, *see* R.C.M. 405(b).

Rule 404. Action by commander exercising special court-martial jurisdiction

When in receipt of charges, a commander exercising special court-martial jurisdiction may:

(a) Dismiss any charges;

Discussion

See R.C.M. 401(c)(1) concerning dismissal of charges, the effect of dismissing charges, and options for further action.

(b) Forward charges (or, after dismissing charges, the matter) to a subordinate commander for disposition;

Discussion

See R.C.M. 401(c)(2)(B) concerning forwarding charges to a subordinate. When appropriate, charges may be forwarded to a subordinate even if that subordinate previously considered them.

(c) Forward any charges to a superior commander for disposition;

Discussion

See R.C.M. 401(c)(2)(A) for guidance concerning forwarding charges to a superior.

(d) Subject to R.C.M. 601(d), refer charges to a summary court-martial or to a special court-martial for trial; or

Discussion

See Article 23 and R.C.M. 504(b)(2) concerning who may convene special courts-martial.

See R.C.M. 601 concerning referral of charges to a special court-martial. *See* R.C.M. 1302(c) concerning referral of charges to a summary court-martial.

(e) Unless otherwise prescribed by the Secretary concerned, direct a pretrial investigation under R.C.M. 405, and, if appropriate, forward the report of investigation with the charges to a superior commander for disposition.

Discussion

An investigation should be directed when it appears that the charges are of such a serious nature that trial by general court-martial may be warranted. *See* R.C.M. 405. If an investigation of the subject matter already has been conducted, *see* R.C.M. 405(b).

Rule 405. Pretrial investigation

(a) *In general.* Except as provided in subsection (k) of this rule, no charge or specification may be referred to a general court-martial for trial until a thorough and impartial investigation of all the matters set forth therein has been made in substantial compliance with this rule. Failure to comply with this rule shall have no effect if the charges are not referred to a general court-martial.

Discussion

The primary purpose of the investigation required by Article 32 and this rule is to inquire into the truth of the matters set forth in the charges, the form of the charges, and to secure information on which to determine what disposition should be made of the case. The investigation also serves as a means of discovery. The function of the investigation is to ascertain and impartially weigh all available facts in arriving at conclusions and recommendations, not to perfect a case against the accused. The investigation should be limited to the issues raised by the charges and necessary to proper disposition of the case. The investigation is not limited to examination of the witnesses and evidence mentioned in the accompanying allied papers. *See* subsection (e) of this rule. Recommendations of the investigating officer are advisory.

If at any time after an investigation under this rule the charges are changed to allege a more serious or essentially different offense, further investigation should be directed with respect to the new or different matters alleged.

Failure to comply substantially with the requirements of Article 32, which failure prejudices the accused, may result in delay in disposition of the case or disapproval of the proceedings. *See* R.C.M. 905(b)(1) and 906(b)(3) concerning motions for appropriate relief relating to the pretrial investigation.

The accused may waive the pretrial investigation. *See* subsection (k) of this rule. In such case, no investigation need be held. The commander authorized to direct the investigation may direct that it be conducted notwithstanding the waiver.

(b) *Earlier investigation.* If an investigation of the subject matter of an offense has been conducted before the accused is charged with an offense, and the accused was present at the investigation and afforded the rights to counsel, cross-examination, and presentation of evidence required by this rule, no further investigation is required unless demanded by the accused to recall witnesses for further cross-examination and to offer new evidence.

Discussion

An earlier investigation includes courts of inquiry and similar investigations which meet the requirements of this subsection.

(c) *Who may direct investigation.* Unless prohibited by regulations of the Secretary concerned, an investigation may be directed under this rule by any court-martial convening authority. That authority may also give procedural instructions not inconsistent with these rules.

(d) *Personnel.*

(1) *Investigating officer.* The commander directing an investigation under this rule shall detail a commissioned officer not the accuser, as investigating officer, who shall conduct the investigation and make a report of conclusions and recommendations. The investigating officer is disqualified to act later in the same case in any other capacity.

Discussion

The investigating officer should be an officer in the grade of major or lieutenant commander or higher or one with legal training. The investigating officer may seek legal advice concerning the investigating officer's responsibilities from an impartial source, but may not obtain such advice from counsel for any party.

(2) *Defense counsel.*

(A) *Detailed counsel.* Except as provided in subsection (d)(2)(B) of this rule, military counsel certified in accordance with Article 27(b) shall be detailed to represent the accused.

(B) *Individual military counsel.* The accused may request to be represented by individual military counsel. Such requests shall be acted on in accordance with R.C.M. 506(b). When the accused is represented by individual military counsel, counsel detailed to represent the accused shall ordinarily be excused, unless the authority who detailed the defense counsel, as a matter of discretion, approves a request by the accused for retention of detailed counsel. The investigating officer shall forward any request by the accused for individual military counsel to the commander who directed the investigation. That commander shall follow the procedures in R.C.M. 506(b).

(C) *Civilian counsel.* The accused may be represented by civilian counsel at no expense to the United States. Upon request, the accused is entitled to a reasonable time to obtain civilian counsel and to have such counsel present for the investigation. However, the investigation shall not be unduly delayed for this purpose. Representation by civilian counsel shall not limit the rights to military counsel under subsections (d)(2)(A) and (B) of this rule.

Discussion

See R.C.M. 502(d)(6) concerning the duties of defense counsel.

(3) *Others.* The commander who directed the investigation may also, as a matter of discretion, detail or request an appropriate authority to detail:

(A) Counsel to represent the United States;

(B) A reporter; and

(C) An interpreter.

(e) *Scope of investigation.* The investigating officer shall inquire into the truth and form of the charges, and such other matters as may be necessary to make a recommendation as to the disposition of the charges. If evidence adduced during the investigation indicates that the accused committed an uncharged offense, the investigating officer may investigate the subject matter of such offense and make a recommendation as to its disposition, without the accused first having been charged with the offense. The accused's rights under subsection (f) are the same with regard to investigation of both charged and uncharged offenses.

Discussion

The investigation may properly include such inquiry into issues raised directly by the charges as is necessary to make an appropriate recommendation. For example, inquiry into the legality of a search or the admissibility of a confession may be appropriate. However, the investigating officer is not required to rule on the admissibility of evidence and need not consider such matters except as the investigating officer deems necessary to an informed recommendation. When the investigating officer is aware that evidence may not be admissible, this should be noted in the report. *See also* subsection (i) of this rule.

In investigating uncharged misconduct identified during the pretrial investigation, the investigating officer will inform the accused of the general nature of each uncharged offense investigated, and otherwise afford the accused the same opportunity for representation, cross examination, and presentation afforded during the investigation of any charge offense.

(f) *Rights of the accused.* At any pretrial investigation under this rule the accused shall have the right to:

(1) Be informed of the charges under investigation;

(2) Be informed of the identity of the accuser;

(3) Except in circumstances described in R.C.M. 804(b)(2), be present throughout the taking of evidence;

(4) Be represented by counsel;

(5) Be informed of the witnesses and other evidence then known to the investigating officer;

(6) Be informed of the purpose of the investigation;

(7) Be informed of the right against self-incrimination under Article 31;

(8) Cross-examine witnesses who are produced under subsection (g) of this rule;

(9) Have witnesses produced as provided for in subsection (g) of this rule;

(10) Have evidence, including documents or physical evidence, within the control of military authorities produced as provided under subsection (g) of this rule;

(11) Present anything in defense, extenuation, or mitigation for consideration by the investigating officer; and

(12) Make a statement in any form.

(g) *Production of witnesses and evidence; alternatives.*

(1) *In general.*

(A) *Witnesses.* Except as provided in subsection (g)(4)(A) of this rule, any witness whose testimony would be relevant to the investigation and not cumulative, shall be produced if reasonably available. This includes witnesses requested by the accused, if the request is timely. A witness is "reasonably available" when the witness is located within 100 miles of the situs of the investigation and the significance of the testimony and personal appearance of the witness outweighs the difficulty, expense, delay, and effect on military operations of obtaining the witness' appearance. A witness who is unavailable under Mil. R. Evid. 804(a)(1)-(6), is not "reasonably available."

Discussion

A witness located beyond the 100-mile limit is not *per se* unavailable. To determine if a witness beyond 100 miles is reasonably available, the significance of the witness' live testimony must be balanced against the relative difficulty and expense of obtaining the witness' presence at the hearing.

(B) *Evidence.* Subject to Mil. R. Evid., Section V, evidence, including documents or physical evidence, which is under the control of the Government and which is relevant to the investigation and not cumulative, shall be produced if reasonably available. Such evidence includes evidence requested by the accused, if the request is timely. As soon as practicable after receipt of a request by the accused for information which may be protected under Mil. R. Evid. 505 or 506, the investigating officer shall notify the person who is authorized to issue a protective order under subsection (g)(6) of this rule, and the convening authority, if different. Evidence is reasonably available if its significance outweighs the difficulty, expense, delay, and effect on military operations of obtaining the evidence.

Discussion

In preparing for the investigation, the investigating officer should consider what evidence will be necessary to prepare a thorough and impartial investigation. The investigating officer should consider, as to potential witnesses, whether their personal appearance will be necessary. Generally, personal appearance is preferred, but the investigating officer should consider whether, in light of the probable importance of a witness' testimony, an alternative to testimony under subsection (g)(4)(A) of this rule would be sufficient.

After making a preliminary determination of what witnesses will be produced and other evidence considered, the investigating officer should notify the defense and inquire whether it requests the production of other witnesses or evidence. In addition to witnesses for the defense, the defense may request production of witnesses whose testimony would favor the prosecution.

Once it is determined what witnesses the investigating officer intends to call it must be determined whether each witness is reasonably available. That determination is a balancing test. The more important the testimony of the witness, the greater the difficulty, expense, delay, or effect on military operations must be to permit nonproduction. For example, the temporary absence of a witness on leave for 10 days would normally justify using an alternative to that witness' personal appearance if the sole reason for the witness' testimony was to impeach the credibility of another witness by reputation evidence, or to establish a mitigating character trait of the accused. On the other hand, if the same witness was the only eyewitness to the offense, personal appearance would be required if the defense requested it and the witness is otherwise reasonably available. The time and place of the investigation may be changed if reasonably necessary to permit the appearance of a witness. Similar considerations apply to the production of evidence.

If the production of witnesses or evidence would entail substantial costs or delay, the investigating officer should inform the commander who directed the investigation.

The provision in (B), requiring the investigating officer to notify the appropriate authorities of requests by the accused for information privileged under Mil. R. Evid. 505 or 506, is for the purpose of placing the appropriate authority on notice that an order, as authorized under subparagraph(g)(6), may be required to protect whatever information the government may decide to release to the accused.

---

(2) *Determination of reasonable availability.*

(A) *Military witnesses.* The investigating officer shall make an initial determination whether a military witness is reasonably available. If the investigating officer decides that the witness is not reasonably available, the investigating officer shall inform the parties. Otherwise, the immediate commander of the witness shall be requested to make the witness available. A determination by the immediate commander that the witness is not reasonably available is not subject to appeal by the accused but may be reviewed by the military judge under R.C.M. 906(b)(3).

Discussion

The investigating officer may discuss factors affecting reasonable availability with the immediate commander of the requested witness and with others. If the immediate commander determined that the witness is not reasonably available, the reasons for that determination should be provided to the investigating officer.

(B) *Civilian witnesses.* The investigating officer shall decide whether a civilian witness is reasonably available to appear as a witness.

Discussion

The investigating officer should initially determine whether a civilian witness is reasonably available without regard to whether the witness is willing to appear. If the investigating officer determines that a civilian witness is apparently reasonably available, the witness should be invited to attend and when appropriate, informed that necessary expenses will be paid.

If the witness refuses to testify, the witness is not reasonably available because civilian witnesses may not be compelled to attend a pretrial investigation. Under subsection (g)(3) of this rule, civilian witnesses may be paid for travel and associated expenses to testify at a pretrial investigation. Except for use in support of the deposition of a witness under Article 49, UCMJ, and ordered pursuant to R.C.M. 702(b), the investigating officer and any government representative to an Article 32, UCMJ, proceeding does not possess authority to issue a subpoena to compel against his or her will a civilian witness to appear and provide testimony or documents.

(C) *Evidence.* The investigating officer shall make an initial determination whether evidence is reasonably available. If the investigating officer decides that it is not reasonably available, the investigating officer shall inform the parties. Otherwise, the custodian of the evidence shall be requested to provide the evidence. A determination by the custodian that the evidence is not reasonably available is not subject to appeal by the accused, but may be reviewed by the military judge under R.C.M. 906(b)(3).

Discussion

The investigating officer may discuss factors affecting reasonable availability with the custodian and with others. If the custodian determines that the evidence is not reasonably available, the reasons for that determination should be provided to the investigating officer.

(D) *Action when witness or evidence is not reasonably available.* If the defense objects to a determination that a witness or evidence is not reasonably available, the investigating officer shall include a statement of the reasons for the determination in the report of investigation.

(3) *Witness expenses.* Transportation expenses and a per diem allowance may be paid to civilians requested to testify in connection with an investigation under this rule according to regulations prescribed by the Secretary of a Department.

Discussion

See Department of Defense Joint Travel Regulations, Vol 2, paragraphs C3054, C6000.

---

(4) *Alternatives to testimony.*

(A) Unless the defense objects, an investigating officer may consider, regardless of the availability of the witness:

(i) Sworn statements;

(ii) Statements under oath taken by telephone, radio, or similar means providing each party the opportunity to question the witness under circumstances by which the investigating officer may reasonably conclude that the witness' identity is as claimed;

(iii) Prior testimony under oath;

(iv) Depositions;

(v) Stipulations of fact or expected testimony;

(vi) Unsworn statements; and

(vii) Offers of proof of expected testimony of that witness.

(B) The investigating officer may consider, over objection of the defense, when the witness is not reasonably available:

(i) Sworn statements;

(ii) Statements under oath taken by telephone, radio, or similar means providing each party the opportunity to question the witness under circumstances by which the investigating officer may reasonably conclude that the witness' identity is a claimed;

(iii) Prior testimony under oath; and

(iv) Deposition of that witness; and

(v) In time of war, unsworn statements.

(5) *Alternatives to evidence.*

(A) Unless the defense objects, an investigating officer may consider, regardless of the availability of the evidence:

(i) Testimony describing the evidence;

(ii) An authenticated copy, photograph, or reproduction of similar accuracy of the evidence;

(iii) An alternative to testimony, when permitted under subsection (g)(4)(B) of this rule, in which the evidence is described;

(iv) A stipulation of fact, document's contents, or expected testimony;

(v) An unsworn statement describing the evidence; or

(vi) An offer of proof concerning pertinent characteristics of the evidence.

(B) The investigating officer may consider, over objection of the defense, when the evidence is not reasonably available:

(i) Testimony describing the evidence;

(ii) An authenticated copy, photograph, or reproduction of similar accuracy of the evidence; or

(iii) An alternative to testimony, when permitted under subsection (g)(4)(B) of this rule, in which the evidence is described.

(6) *Protective order for release of privileged information.* If, prior to referral, the Government agrees to disclose to the accused information to which the protections afforded by Mil. R. Evid. 505 or 506 may apply, the convening authority, or other person designated by regulation of the Secretary of the service concerned, may enter an appropriate protective order, in writing, to guard against the compromise of information disclosed to the accused. The terms of any such protective order may include prohibiting the disclosure of the information except as authorized by the authority issuing the protective order, as well as those terms specified by Mil. R. Evid. 505(g)(1)(B) through (F) or 506(g)(2) through (5).

(h) *Procedure.*

(1) *Presentation of evidence.*

(A) *Testimony.* All testimony shall be taken under oath, except that the accused may make an unsworn statement. The defense shall be given wide latitude in cross-examining witnesses.

Discussion

The following oath may be given to witnesses:

"Do you (swear) (affirm) that the evidence you give shall be the truth, the whole truth, and nothing but the truth (, so help you God)?"

The investigating officer is required to include in the report of the investigation a summary of the substance of all testimony. *See* subsection (j)(2)(B) of this rule. After the hearing, the investigating officer should, whenever possible, reduce the substance of the testimony of each witness to writing and, unless it would unduly delay completion of the investigation, have each witness sign and swear to the truth of the respective summaries. The following oath may be given to a witness in such cases:

"You (swear) (affirm) that this statement is the truth, the whole truth, and nothing but the truth (, so help you God)?"

If the accused testifies, the investigating officer may invite but not require the accused to swear to the truth of a summary of that testimony. If substantially verbatim notes of a testimony or recordings of testimony were taken during the investigation, they should be preserved until the end of trial.

If it appears that material witnesses for either side will not be available at the time anticipated for trial, the investigating officer should notify the commander who directed the investigation so that depositions may be taken if necessary.

If during the investigation any witness subject to the code is suspected of an offense under the code, the investigating officer should comply with the warning requirements of Mil. R. Evid. 305(c), (d), and, if necessary, (e).

(B) *Other evidence.* The investigating officer shall inform the parties what other evidence will be considered. The parties shall be permitted to examine all other evidence considered by the investigating officer.

(C) *Defense evidence.* The defense shall have full opportunity to present any matters in defense, extenuation, or mitigation.

(2) *Objections.* Any objection alleging failure to comply with this rule, except subsection (j), shall be made to the investigating officer promptly upon discovery of the alleged error. The investigating officer shall not be required to rule on any objection. An objection shall be noted in the report of investigation if a party so requests. The investigating officer may require a party to file any objection in writing.

Discussion

See also subsection (k) of this rule.

Although the investigating officer is not required to rule on objections, the investigating officer may take corrective action in response to an objection as to matters relating to the conduct of the proceedings when the investigating officer believes such action is appropriate.

If an objection raises a substantial question about a matter within the authority of the commander who directed the investigation (for example, whether the investigating officer was properly appointed) the investigating officer should promptly inform the commander who directed the investigation.

---

(3) *Access by spectators.* Access by spectators to all or part of the proceeding may be restricted or foreclosed in the discretion of the commander who directed the investigation or the investigating officer.

Discussion

Article 32 investigations are public hearings and should remain open to the public whenever possible. When an overriding interest exists that outweighs the value of an open investigation, the hearing may be closed to spectators. Any closure must be narrowly tailored to achieve the overriding interest that justified the closure. Commanders or investigating officers must conclude that no lesser methods short of closing the Article 32 can be used to protect the overriding interest in the case. Commanders or investigating officers must conduct a case-by-case, witness-by-witness, circumstance-by-circumstance analysis of whether closure is necessary. If a commander or investigating officer believes closing the Article 32 investigation is necessary, the commander or investigating officer must make specific findings of fact in writing that support the closure. The written findings of fact must be included in the Article 32 investigating officer's report. Examples of overriding interests may include: preventing psychological harm or trauma to a child witness or an alleged victim of a sexual crime, protecting the safety of a witness or alleged victim, protecting classified material, and receiving evidence where a witness is incapable of testifying in an open setting.

---

(4) *Presence of accused.* The further progress of the taking of evidence shall not be prevented and the accused shall be considered to have waived the right to be present, whenever the accused:

(A) After being notified of the time and place of the proceeding is voluntarily absent (whether or not informed by the investigating officer of the obligation to be present); or

(B) After being warned by the investigating officer that disruptive conduct will cause removal from the proceeding, persists in conduct which is such as to justify exclusion from the proceeding.

(i) *Military Rules of Evidence.* The Military Rules of Evidence—other than Mil. R. Evid. 301, 302, 303, 305, 412 and Section V—shall not apply in pretrial investigations under this rule.

Discussion

The investigating officer should exercise reasonable control over the scope of the inquiry. *See* subsection (e) of this rule. An investigating officer may consider any evidence, even if that evidence would not be admissible at trial. However, *see* subsection (g)(4) of this rule as to limitations on the ways in which testimony may be presented.

Certain rules relating to the form of testimony which may be considered by the investigating officer appear in subsection (g) of this rule.

(j) *Report of investigation.*

(1) *In general.* The investigating officer shall make a timely written report of the investigation to the commander who directed the investigation.

Discussion

If practicable, the charges and the report of investigation should be forwarded to the general court-martial convening authority within 8 days after an accused is ordered into arrest or confinement. Article 33.

---

(2) *Contents.* The report of investigation shall include:

(A) A statement of names and organizations or addresses of defense counsel and whether defense counsel was present throughout the taking of evidence, or if not present the reason why;

(B) The substance of the testimony taken on both sides, including any stipulated testimony;

(C) Any other statements, documents, or matters considered by the investigating officer, or recitals of the substance or nature of such evidence;

(D) A statement of any reasonable grounds for belief that the accused was not mentally responsible for the offense or was not competent to participate in the defense during the investigation;

Discussion

See R.C.M. 909 (mental capacity); 916(k) (mental responsibility).

(E) A statement whether the essential witnesses will be available at the time anticipated for trial and the reasons why any essential witness may not then be available;

(F) An explanation of any delays in the investigation;

(G) The investigating officer's conclusion whether the charges and specifications are in proper form;

(H) The investigating officer's conclusion whether reasonable grounds exist to believe that the accused committed the offenses alleged; and

(I) The recommendations of the investigating officer, including disposition.

Discussion

For example, the investigating officer may recommend that the charges and specifications be amended or that additional charges be preferred. *See* R.C.M. 306 and 401 concerning other possible dispositions.

See Appendix 5 for a sample of the Investigating Officer's Report (DD Form 457).

---

(3) *Distribution of the report.* The investigating officer shall cause the report to be delivered to the commander who directed the investigation. That commander shall promptly cause a copy of the report to be delivered to each accused.

(4) *Objections.* Any objection to the report shall be made to the commander who directed the investigation within 5 days of its receipt by the accused. This subsection does not prohibit a convening au-

thority from referring the charges or taking other action within the 5-day period.

(k) *Waiver.* The accused may waive an investigation under this rule. In addition, failure to make a timely objection under this rule, including an objection to the report, shall constitute waiver of the objection. Relief from the waiver may be granted by the investigating officer, the commander who directed the investigation, the convening authority, or the military judge, as appropriate, for good cause shown.

Discussion

See also R.C.M. 905(b)(1); 906(b)(3).

If the report fails to include reference to objections which were made under subsection (h)(2) of this rule, failure to object to the report will constitute waiver of such objections in the absence of good cause for relief from the waiver.

The commander who receives an objection may direct that the investigation be reopened or take other action, as appropriate.

Even if the accused made a timely objection to failure to produce a witness, a defense request for a deposition may be necessary to preserve the issue for later review.

Rule 406. Pretrial advice

(a) *In general.* Before any charge may be referred for trial by a general court-martial, it shall be referred to the staff judge advocate of the convening authority for consideration and advice.

Discussion

A pretrial advice need not be prepared in cases referred to special or summary courts-martial. A convening authority may, however, seek the advice of a lawyer before referring charges to such a court-martial. When charges have been withdrawn from a general court-martial (*see* R.C.M. 604) or when a mistrial has been declared in a general court-martial (*see* R.C.M. 915), supplementary advice is necessary before the charges may be referred to another general court-martial.

The staff judge advocate may make changes in the charges and specifications in accordance with R.C.M. 603.

(b) *Contents.* The advice of the staff judge advocate shall include a written and signed statement which sets forth that person's:

(1) Conclusion with respect to whether each specification alleges an offense under the code;

(2) Conclusion with respect to whether the allegation of each offense is warranted by the evidence indicated in the report of investigation (if there is such a report);

(3) Conclusion with respect to whether a court-martial would have jurisdiction over the accused and the offense; and

(4) Recommendation of the action to be taken by the convening authority.

Discussion

The staff judge advocate is personally responsible for the pretrial advice and must make an independent and informed appraisal of the charges and evidence in order to render the advice. Another person may prepare the advice, but the staff judge advocate is, unless disqualified, responsible for it and must sign it personally. Grounds for disqualification in a case include previous action in that case as investigating officer, military judge, trial counsel, defense counsel, or member.

The advice need not set forth the underlying analysis or rationale for its conclusions. Ordinarily, the charge sheet, forwarding letter, endorsements, and report of investigation are forwarded with the pretrial advice. In addition, the pretrial advice should include when appropriate: a brief summary of the evidence; discussion of significant aggravating, extenuating, or mitigating factors; any recommendations for disposition of the case by commanders or others who have forwarded the charges; and the recommendation of the Article 32 investigating officer. However, there is no legal requirement to include such information, and failure to do so is not error.

Whatever matters are included in the advice, whether or not they are required, should be accurate. Information which is incorrect or so incomplete as to be misleading may result in a determination that the advice is defective, necessitating appropriate relief. *See* R.C.M. 905(b)(1);906(b)(3).

The standard of proof to be applied in R.C.M. 406(b)(2) is probable cause. *See* R.C.M. 601(d)(1). Defects in the pretrial advice are not jurisdictional and are raised by pretrial motion. *See* R.C.M.905(b)(1) and its Discussion.

(c) *Distribution.* A copy of the advice of the staff judge advocate shall be provided to the defense if charges are referred to trial by general court-martial.

Rule 407. Action by commander exercising general court-martial jurisdiction

(a) *Disposition.* When in receipt of charges, a commander exercising general court-martial jurisdiction may:

(1) Dismiss any charges;

Discussion

See R.C.M. 401(c)(1) concerning dismissal of charges and the effect of dismissing charges.

(2) Forward charges (or, after dismissing charges,

the matter) to a subordinate commander for disposition;

Discussion

See R.C.M. 401(c)(2)(B) concerning forwarding charges to a subordinate.

A subordinate commander may not be required to take any specific action or to dispose of charges. *See* R.C.M. 104. *See also* paragraph 1d(2) of Part V. When appropriate, charges may be sent or returned to a subordinate commander for compliance with procedural requirements. *See*, for example, R.C.M. 303 (preliminary inquiry); R.C.M. 308 (notification to accused of charges).

---

(3) Forward any charges to a superior commander for disposition;

Discussion

See R.C.M. 401 (c)(2)(A) for guidance concerning forwarding charges to a superior.

---

(4) Refer charges to a summary court-martial or a special court-martial for trial;

Discussion

See R.C.M. 601; 1302(c).

---

(5) Unless otherwise prescribed by the Secretary concerned, direct a pretrial investigation under R.C.M. 405, after which additional action under this rule may be taken;

Discussion

An investigation should be directed when it appears the charges are of such a serious nature that trial by general court-martial may be warranted. *See* R.C.M. 405. If an investigation of the subject matter already has been conducted. *See* R.C.M. 405(b).

---

(6) Subject to R.C.M. 601(d), refer charges to a general court-martial.

Discussion

See Article 22 and R.C.M. 504(b)(1)concerning who may exercise general court-martial jurisdiction.

See R.C.M. 601 concerning referral of charges. *See* R.C.M. 306 and 401 concerning other dispositions.

(b) *National security matters.* When in receipt of charges the trial of which the commander exercising general court-martial jurisdiction finds would probably be inimical to the prosecution of a war or harmful to national security, that commander, unless otherwise prescribed by regulations of the Secretary concerned, shall determine whether trial is warranted and, if so, whether the security considerations involved are paramount to trial. As the commander finds appropriate, the commander may dismiss the charges, authorize trial of them, or forward them to a superior authority.

Discussion

In time of war, charges may be forwarded to the Secretary concerned for disposition under Article 43(e). Under Article 43(e), the Secretary may take action suspending the statute of limitations in time of war.

CHAPTER V. COURT-MARTIAL COMPOSITION AND PERSONNEL; CONVENING COURTS-MARTIAL

Rule 501. Composition and personnel of courts-martial

(a) *Composition of courts-martial.*

(1) *General courts-martial.*

(A) Except in capital cases, general courts-martial shall consist of a military judge and not less than five members, or of the military judge alone if requested and approved under R.C.M. 903.

(B) In all capital cases, general courts-martial shall consist of a military judge and no fewer than 12 members, unless 12 members are not reasonably available because of physical conditions or military exigencies. If 12 members are not reasonably available, the convening authority shall detail the next lesser number of reasonably available members under 12, but in no event fewer than five. In such a case, the convening authority shall state in the convening order the reasons why 12 members are not reasonably available.

(2) *Special courts-martial.* Special courts-martial shall consist of:

(A) Not less than three members;

(B) A military judge and not less than three members; or

(C) A military judge alone if a military judge is detailed and if requested and approved under R.C.M. 903.

Discussion

See R.C.M. 1301(a) concerning composition of summary courts-martial.

(b) *Counsel in general and special courts-martial.* Military trial and defense counsel shall be detailed to general and special courts-martial. Assistant trial and associate or assistant defense counsel may be detailed.

(c) *Other personnel.* Other personnel, such as reporters, interpreters, bailiffs, clerks, escorts, and orderlies, may be detailed or employed as appropriate but need not be detailed by the convening authority personally.

Discussion

The convening authority may direct that a reporter not be used in special courts-martial. Regulations of the Secretary concerned may also require or restrict the use of reporters in special courts-martial.

Rule 502. Qualifications and duties of personnel of courts-martial

(a) *Members.*

(1) *Qualifications.* The members detailed to a court-martial shall be those persons who in the opinion of the convening authority are best qualified for the duty by reason of their age, education, training, experience, length of service, and judicial temperament. Each member shall be on active duty with the armed forces and shall be:

(A) A commissioned officer;

(B) A warrant officer, except when the accused is a commissioned officer; or

(C) An enlisted person if the accused is an enlisted person and has made a timely request under R.C.M. 503(a)(2).

Discussion

Retired members of any Regular component and members of Reserve components of the armed forces are eligible to serve as members if they are on active duty.

Members of the National Oceanic and Atmospheric Administration and of the Public Health Service are eligible to serve as members when assigned to and serving with an armed force. The Public Health Service includes both commissioned and warrant officers. The National Oceanic and Atmospheric Administration includes only commissioned officers.

(2) *Duties.* The members of a court-martial shall determine whether the accused is proved guilty and, if necessary, adjudge a proper sentence, based on the evidence and in accordance with the instructions of the military judge. Each member has an equal voice and vote with other members in deliberating upon and deciding all matters submitted to them, except as otherwise specifically provided in these rules. No member may use rank or position to influence another member. No member of a court-martial may have access to or use in any open or closed session this Manual, reports of decided cases, or any other reference material, except the president of a special

court-martial without a military judge may use such materials in open session.

Discussion

Members should avoid any conduct or communication with the military judge, witnesses, or other trial personnel during the trial which might present an appearance of partiality. Except as provided in these rules, members should not discuss any part of a case with anyone until the matter is submitted to them for determination. Members should not on their own visit or conduct a view of the scene of the crime and should not investigate or gather evidence of the offense. Members should not form an opinion on any matter in connection with a case until that matter has been submitted to them for determination.

(b) *President.*

(1) *Qualifications.* The president of a court-martial shall be the detailed member senior in rank then serving.

(2) *Duties.* The president shall have the same duties as the other members and shall also:

(A) Preside over closed sessions of the members of the court-martial during their deliberations;

(B) Speak for the members of the court-martial when announcing the decision of the members or requesting instructions from the military judge; and

(C) In a special court-martial without a military judge, perform the duties assigned by this Manual to the military judge except as otherwise expressly provided.

(c) *Qualifications of military judge.* A military judge shall be a commissioned officer of the armed forces who is a member of the bar of a Federal court or a member of the bar of the highest court of a State and who is certified to be qualified for duty as a military judge by the Judge Advocate General of the armed force of which such military judge is a member. In addition, the military judge of a general court-martial shall be designated for such duties by the Judge Advocate General or the Judge Advocate General's designee, certified to be qualified for duty as a military judge of a general court-martial, and assigned and directly responsible to the Judge Advocate General or the Judge Advocate General's designee. The Secretary concerned may prescribe additional qualifications for military judges in special courts-martial. As used in this subsection "military judge" does not include the president of a special court-martial without a military judge.

Discussion

See R.C.M. 801 for description of some of the general duties of the military judge.

Military judges assigned as general court-martial judges may perform duties in addition to the primary duty of judge of a general court-martial only when such duties are assigned or approved by the Judge Advocate General, or a designee, of the service of which the military judge is a member. Similar restrictions on other duties which a military judge in special courts-martial may perform may be prescribed in regulations of the Secretary concerned.

(d) *Counsel.*

(1) *Certified counsel required.* Only persons certified under Article 27(b) as competent to perform duties as counsel in courts-martial by the Judge Advocate General of the armed force of which the counsel is a member may be detailed as defense counsel or associate defense counsel in general or special courts-martial or as trial counsel in general courts-martial.

Discussion

To be certified by the Judge Advocate General concerned under Article 27(b), a person must be a member of the bar of a Federal court or the highest court of a State. The Judge Advocate General concerned may establish additional requirements for certification.

When the accused has individual military or civilian defense counsel, the detailed counsel is "associate counsel" unless excused from the case. *See* R.C.M. 506(b)(3).

---

(2) *Other military counsel.* Any commissioned officer may be detailed as trial counsel in special courts-martial, or as assistant trial counsel or assistant defense counsel in general or special courts-martial. The Secretary concerned may establish additional qualifications for such counsel.

(3) *Qualifications of individual military and civilian defense counsel.* Individual military or civilian defense counsel who represents an accused in a court-martial shall be:

(A) A member of the bar of a Federal court or of the bar of the highest court of a State; or

(B) If not a member of such a bar, a lawyer who is authorized by a recognized licensing authority to practice law and is found by the military judge to be qualified to represent the accused upon a showing to the satisfaction of the military judge that the counsel has appropriate training and familiarity with the general principles of criminal law which apply in a court-martial.

Discussion

In making such a determination—particularly in the case of civilian defense counsel who are members only of a foreign bar—the military judge also should inquire into:

(i) the availability of the counsel at times at which sessions of the court-martial have been scheduled;

(ii) whether the accused wants the counsel to appear with military defense counsel;

(iii) the familiarity of the counsel with spoken English;

(iv) practical alternatives for discipline of the counsel in the event of misconduct;

(v) whether foreign witnesses are expected to testify with whom the counsel may more readily communicate than might military counsel; and

(vi) whether ethnic or other similarity between the accused and the counsel may facilitate communication and confidence between the accused and civilian defense counsel.

---

(4) *Disqualifications.* No person shall act as trial counsel or assistant trial counsel or, except when expressly requested by the accused, as defense counsel or associate or assistant defense counsel in any case in which that person is or has been:

(A) The accuser;

(B) An investigating officer;

(C) A military judge; or

(D) A member.

No person who has acted as counsel for a party may serve as counsel for an opposing party in the same case.

Discussion

In the absence of evidence to the contrary, it is presumed that a person who, between referral and trial of a case, has been detailed as counsel for any party to the court-martial to which the case has been referred, has acted in that capacity.

---

(5) *Duties of trial and assistant trial counsel.* The trial counsel shall prosecute cases on behalf of the United States and shall cause the record of trial of such cases to be prepared. Under the supervision of trial counsel an assistant trial counsel may perform any act or duty which trial counsel may perform under law, regulation, or custom of the service.

Discussion

(A) *General duties before trial.* Immediately upon receipt of referred charges, trial counsel should cause a copy of the charges to be served upon accused. *See* R.C.M. 602.

Trial counsel should: examine the charge sheet and allied papers for completeness and correctness; correct (and initial) minor errors or obvious mistakes in the charges but may not without authority make any substantial changes (*see* R.C.M. 603); and assure that the information about the accused on the charge sheet and any evidence of previous convictions are accurate.

(B) *Relationship with convening authority.* Trial counsel should: report to the convening authority any substantial irregularity in the convening orders, charges, or allied papers; report an actual or anticipated reduction of the number of members below quorum to the convening authority; bring to the attention of the convening authority any case in which trial counsel finds trial inadvisable for lack of evidence or other reasons.

(C) *Relations with the accused and defense counsel.* Trial counsel must communicate with a represented accused only through the accused's defense counsel. However, *see* R.C.M. 602. Trial counsel may not attempt to induce an accused to plead guilty or surrender other important rights.

(D) *Preparation for trial.* Trial counsel should: ensure that a suitable room, a reporter (if authorized), and necessary equipment and supplies are provided for the court-martial; obtain copies of the charges and specifications and convening orders for each member and all personnel of the court-martial; give timely notice to the members, other parties, other personnel of the court-martial, and witnesses for the prosecution and (if known) defense of the date, time, place, and uniform of the meetings of the court-martial; ensure that any person having custody of the accused is also informed; comply with applicable discovery rules (*see* R.C.M. 701); prepare to make a prompt, full, and orderly presentation of the evidence at trial; consider the elements of proof of each offense charged, the burden of proof of guilt and the burdens of proof on motions which may be anticipated, and the Military Rules of Evidence; secure for use at trial such legal texts as may be available and necessary to sustain the prosecution's contentions; arrange for the presence of witnesses and evidence in accordance with R.C.M. 703; prepare to make an opening statement of the prosecution's case (*see* R.C.M. 913); prepare to conduct the examination and cross-examination of witnesses; and prepare to make final argument on the findings and, if necessary, on sentencing (*see* R.C.M. 919; 1001(g)).

(E) *Trial.* Trial counsel should bring to the attention of the military judge any substantial irregularity in the proceedings. Trial counsel should not allude to or disclose to the members any evidence not yet admitted or reasonably expected to be admitted in evidence or intimate, transmit, or purport to transmit to the military judge or members the views of the convening authority or others as to the guilt or innocence of the accused, an appropriate sentence, or any other matter within the discretion of the court-martial.

(F) *Post-trial duties.* Trial counsel must promptly provide written notice of the findings and sentence adjudged to the convening authority or a designee, the accused's immediate commander, and (if applicable) the officer in charge of the confinement facility (*see* R.C.M. 1101(a)), and supervise the preparation, authentication, and distribution of copies of the record as required by these rules and regulations of the Secretary concerned (*see* R.C.M. 1103; 1104).

(G) *Assistant trial counsel.* An assistant trial counsel may act in that capacity only under the supervision of the detailed trial counsel. Responsibility for trial of a case may not devolve to an assistant not qualified to serve as trial counsel. Unless the contrary appears, all acts of an assistant trial counsel are presumed to have been done by the direction of the trial counsel. An assistant trial counsel may not act in the absence of trial counsel at trial in a general court-martial unless the assistant has the qualifications required of a trial counsel. *See* R.C.M. 805(c).

---

(6) *Duties of defense and associate or assistant defense counsel.* Defense counsel shall represent the accused in matters under the code and these rules arising from the offenses of which the accused is then suspected or charged. Under the supervision of the defense counsel an associate or assistant defense counsel may perform any act or duty which a defense counsel may perform under law, regulation, or custom of the service.

Discussion

(A) *Initial advice by military defense counsel.* Defense counsel should promptly explain to the accused the general duties of the defense counsel and inform the accused of the rights to request individual military counsel of the accused's own selection, and of the effect of such a request, and to retain civilian counsel. If the accused wants to request individual military counsel, the defense counsel should immediately inform the convening authority through trial counsel and, if the request is approved, serve as associate counsel if the accused requests and the convening authority permits. Unless the accused directs otherwise, military counsel will begin preparation of the defense immediately after being detailed without waiting for approval of a request for individual military counsel or retention of civilian counsel. *See R.C.M. 506.*

(B) *General duties of defense counsel.* Defense counsel must: guard the interests of the accused zealously within the bounds of the law without regard to personal opinion as to the guilt of the accused; disclose to the accused any interest defense counsel may have in connection with the case, any disqualification, and any other matter which might influence the accused in the selection of counsel; represent the accused with undivided fidelity and may not disclose the accused's secrets or confidences except as the accused may authorize (*see also* Mil. R. Evid. 502). A defense counsel designated to represent two or more co-accused in a joint or common trial or in allied cases must be particularly alert to conflicting interests of those accused. Defense counsel should bring such matters to the attention of the military judge so that the accused's understanding and choice may be made a matter of record. *See* R.C.M. 901(d)(4)(D).

Defense counsel must explain to the accused: the elections available as to composition of the court-martial and assist the accused to make any request necessary to effect the election (*see* R.C.M. 903); the right to plead guilty or not guilty and the meaning and effect of a plea of guilty; the rights to introduce evidence, to testify or remain silent, and to assert any available defense; and the rights to present evidence during sentencing and the rights of the accused to testify under oath, make an unsworn statement, and have counsel make a statement on behalf of the accused. These explanations must be made regardless of the intentions of the accused as to testifying and pleading.

Defense counsel should try to obtain complete knowledge of the facts of the case before advising the accused, and should give the accused a candid opinion of the merits of the case.

(C) *Preparation for trial.* Defense counsel may have the assistance of trial counsel in obtaining the presence of witnesses and evidence for the defense. *See* R.C.M. 703.

Defense counsel should consider the elements of proof of the offenses alleged and the pertinent rules of evidence to ensure that evidence that the defense plans to introduce is admissible and to be prepared to object to inadmissible evidence offered by the prosecution.

Defense counsel should: prepare to make an opening statement of the defense case (*see* R.C.M. 913(b)); and prepare to examine and cross-examine witnesses, and to make final argument on the findings and, if necessary, on sentencing (*see* R.C.M. 919; 1001(g)).

(D) *Trial.* Defense counsel should represent and protect the interests of the accused at trial.

When a trial proceeds in the absence of the accused, defense counsel must continue to represent the accused.

(E) *Post-trial duties.*

(i) *Deferment of confinement.* If the accused is sentenced to confinement, the defense counsel must explain to the accused the right to request the convening authority to defer service of the sentence to confinement and assist the accused in making such a request if the accused chooses to make one. *See* R.C.M. 1101(c).

(ii) *Examination of the record; appellate brief.* The defense counsel should in any case examine the record for accuracy and note any errors in it. This notice may be forwarded for attachment to the record. *See* R.C.M. 1103(b)(3)(C). *See* also R.C.M. 1103(i)(1)(B).

(iii) *Submission of matters.* If the accused is convicted, the defense counsel may submit to the convening authority matters for the latter's consideration in deciding whether to approve the sentence or to disapprove any findings. *See* R.C.M. 1105. Defense counsel should discuss with the accused the right to submit matters to the convening authority and the powers of the convening authority in taking action on the case. Defense counsel may also submit a brief of any matters counsel believes should be considered on further review.

(iv) *Appellate rights.* Defense counsel must explain to the accused the rights to appellate review that apply in the case, and advise the accused concerning the exercise of those rights. If the case is subject to review by the Court of Criminal Appeals, defense counsel should explain the powers of that court and advise the accused of the right to be represented by counsel before it. *See* R.C.M. 1202 and 1203. Defense counsel should also explain the possibility of further review by the Court of Appeals for the Armed Forces and the Supreme Court. *See* R.C.M. 1204 and 1205. If the case may be examined in the office of the Judge Advocate General under Article 69(a), defense counsel should explain the nature of such review to the accused. *See* R.C.M. 1201(b)(1). Defense counsel must explain the consequences of waiver of appellate review, when applicable, and, if the accused elects to waive appellate review, defense counsel will assist in preparing the waiver. *See* R.C.M. 1110. If the accused waives appellate review, or if it is not available, defense counsel should explain that the case will be reviewed by a judge advocate and should submit any appropriate matters for consideration by the judge advocate. *See* R.C.M. 1112. The accused should be advised of the right to apply to the Judge Advocate General for relief under Article 69(b) when such review is available. *See* R.C.M. 1201(b)(3).

(v) *Examination of post-trial recommendation.* When the post-trial recommendation is served on defense counsel, defense counsel should examine it and reply promptly in writing, noting any errors or omissions. Failure to note defects in the recommendation waives them. *See* R.C.M. 1106(f).

(F) *Associate or assistant defense counsel.* Associate or assistant counsel may act in that capacity only under the supervision and by the general direction of the defense counsel. A detailed defense counsel becomes associate defense counsel when the accused has individual military or civilian counsel and detailed counsel is not excused. Although associate counsel acts under the general supervision of the defense counsel, associate defense counsel may act without such supervision when circumstances require. *See*, for example, R.C.M. 805(c). An assistant defense counsel may do this only if such counsel has the qualifications to act as defense counsel. Responsibility for trial of a case may not devolve upon an assistant who is not qualified to serve as defense counsel. An assistant defense counsel may not act in the absence of the defense counsel at trial unless the assistant has the qualifications required of a defense counsel. *See also* R.C.M. 805. Unless the contrary appears, all acts of an assistant or associate defense counsel are presumed to have been done under the supervision of the defense counsel.

(e) *Interpreters, reporters, escorts, bailiffs, clerks, and guards.*

(1) *Qualifications.* The qualifications of interpreters and reporters may be prescribed by the Secretary concerned. Any person who is not disqualified under subsection (e)(2) of this rule may serve as escort, bailiff, clerk, or orderly, subject to removal by the military judge.

(2) *Disqualifications.* In addition to any disqualifications which may be prescribed by the Secretary concerned, no person shall act as interpreter, reporter, escort, bailiff, clerk, or orderly in any case in which that person is or has been in the same case:

(A) The accuser;

(B) A witness;

(C) An investigating officer;

(D) Counsel for any party; or

(E) A member of the court-martial or of any earlier court-martial of which the trial is a rehearing or new or other trial.

(3) *Duties.* In addition to such other duties as the Secretary concerned may prescribe, the following persons may perform the following duties.

(A) *Interpreters.* Interpreters shall interpret for the court-martial or for an accused who does not speak or understand English.

Discussion

The accused also may retain an unofficial interpreter without expense to the United States.

(B) *Reporters.* Reporters shall record the proceedings and testimony and shall transcribe them so as to comply with the requirements for the record of trial as prescribed in these rules.

(C) *Others.* Other personnel detailed for the assistance of the court-martial shall have such duties as may be imposed by the military judge.

(4) *Payment of reporters, interpreters.* The Secretary concerned may prescribe regulations for the payment of allowances, expenses, per diem, and compensation of reporters and interpreters.

Discussion

See R.C.M. 807 regarding oaths for reporters, interpreters, and escorts.

(f) *Action upon discovery of disqualification or lack of qualifications.* Any person who discovers that a person detailed to a court-martial is disqualified or lacks the qualifications specified by this rule shall cause a report of the matter to be made before the court-martial is first in session to the convening authority or, if discovered later, to the military judge.

Rule 503. Detailing members, military judge, and counsel

(a) *Members.*

(1) *In general.* The convening authority shall detail qualified persons as members for courts-martial.

Discussion

The following persons are subject to challenge under R.C.M. 912(f) and should not be detailed as members: any person who is, in the same case, an accuser, witness, investigating officer, or counsel for any party; any person who, in the case of a new trial, other trial, or rehearing, was a member of any court-martial which previously heard the case; any person who is junior to the accused, unless this is unavoidable; an enlisted member from the same unit as the accused; any person who is in arrest or confinement.

---

(2) *Enlisted members.* An enlisted accused may,

before assembly, request orally on the record or in writing that enlisted persons serve as members of the general or special court-martial to which that accused's case has been or will be referred. If such a request is made, an enlisted accused may not be tried by a court-martial the membership of which does not include enlisted members in a number comprising at least one-third of the total number of members unless eligible enlisted members cannot be obtained because of physical conditions or military exigencies. If the appropriate number of enlisted members cannot be obtained, the court-martial may be assembled, and the trial may proceed without them, but the convening authority shall make a detailed written explanation why enlisted members could not be obtained which must be appended to the record of trial.

Discussion

When such a request is made, the convening authority should:

(1) Detail an appropriate number of enlisted members to the court-martial and, if appropriate, relieve an appropriate number of commissioned or warrant officers previously detailed;

(2) Withdraw the charges from the court-martial to which they were originally referred and refer them to a court-martial which includes the proper proportion of enlisted members; or

(3) Advise the court-martial before which the charges are then pending to proceed in the absence of enlisted members if eligible enlisted members cannot be detailed because of physical conditions or military exigencies.

See also R.C.M. 1103(b)(2)(D)(iii).

---

(3) *Members from another command or armed force.* A convening authority may detail as members of general and special courts-martial persons under that convening authority's command or made available by their commander, even if those persons are members of an armed force different from that of the convening authority or accused.

Discussion

Concurrence of the proper commander may be oral and need not be shown by the record of trial.

Members should ordinarily be of the same armed force as the accused. When a court-martial composed of members of different armed forces is selected, at least a majority of the members should be of the same armed force as the accused unless exigent circumstances make it impractical to do so without manifest injury to the service.

(b) *Military judge.*

(1) *By whom detailed.* The military judge shall be detailed, in accordance with regulations of the Secretary concerned, by a person assigned as a military judge and directly responsible to the Judge Advocate General or the Judge Advocate General's designee. The authority to detail military judges may be delegated to persons assigned as military judges. If authority to detail military judges has been delegated to a military judge, that military judge may detail himself or herself as military judge for a court-martial.

(2) *Record of detail.* The order detailing a military judge shall be reduced to writing and included in the record of trial or announced orally on the record at the court-martial. The writing or announcement shall indicate by whom the military judge was detailed. The Secretary concerned may require that the order be reduced to writing.

(3) *Military judge from a different armed force.* A military judge from one armed force may be detailed to a court-martial convened in a different armed force, a combatant command or joint command when permitted by the Judge Advocate General of the armed force of which the military judge is a member. The Judge Advocate General may delegate authority to make military judges available for this purpose.

(c) *Counsel.*

(1) *By whom detailed.* Trial and defense counsel, assistant trial and defense counsel, and associate defense counsel shall be detailed in accordance with regulations of the Secretary concerned. If authority to detail counsel has been delegated to a person, that person may detail himself or herself as counsel for a court-martial.

(2) *Record of detail.* The order detailing a counsel shall be reduced to writing and included in the record of trial or announced orally on the record at the court-martial. The writing or announcement shall indicate by whom the counsel was detailed. The Secretary concerned may require that the order be reduced to writing.

(3) *Counsel from a different armed force.* A person from one armed force may be detailed to serve as counsel in a court-martial in a different armed force, a combatant command or joint command when permitted by the Judge Advocate General of the armed force of which the counsel is a member.

The Judge Advocate General may delegate authority to make persons available for this purpose.

Rule 504. Convening courts-martial

(a) *In general.* A court-martial is created by a convening order of the convening authority.

(b) *Who may convene courts-martial.*

(1) *General courts-martial.* Unless otherwise limited by superior competent authority, general courts-martial may be convened by persons occupying positions designated in Article 22(a) and by any commander designated by the Secretary concerned or empowered by the President.

Discussion

The authority to convene courts-martial is independent of rank and is retained as long as the convening authority remains a commander in one of the designated positions. The rule by which command devolves are found in regulations of the Secretary concerned.

(2) *Special courts-martial.* Unless otherwise limited by superior competent authority, special courts-martial may be convened by persons occupying positions designated in Article 23(a) and by commanders designated by the Secretary concerned.

Discussion

See the discussion of subsection (b)(1) of this rule. Persons authorized to convene general courts-martial may also convene special courts-martial.

(A) *Definition.* For purposes of Articles 23 and 24, a command or unit is "separate or detached" when isolated or removed from the immediate disciplinary control of a superior in such manner as to make its commander the person held by superior commanders primarily responsible for discipline. "Separate or detached" is used in a disciplinary sense and not necessarily in a tactical or physical sense. A subordinate joint command or joint task force is ordinarily considered to be "separate or detached."

Discussion

The power of a commander of a separate or detached unit to convene courts-martial, like that of any other commander, may be limited by superior competent authority.

(B) *Determination.* If a commander is in doubt whether the command is separate or detached, the matter shall be determined:

(i) In the Army or the Air Force, by the officer exercising general court-martial jurisdiction over the command; or

(ii) In the Naval Service or Coast Guard, by the flag or general officer in command or the senior officer present who designated the detachment; or

(iii) In a combatant command or joint command, by the officer exercising general court-martial jurisdiction over the command.

(3) *Summary courts-martial. See* R.C.M. 1302(a).

Discussion

See the discussion under subsection (b)(1) of this rule.

(4) *Delegation prohibited.* The power to convene courts-martial may not be delegated.

(c) *Disqualification.*

(1) *Accuser.* An accuser may not convene a general or special court-martial for the trial of the person accused.

Discussion

See also Article 1(9); 307(a); 601(c). However, *see* R.C.M. 1302(b) (accuser may convene a summary court-martial).

(2) *Other.* A convening authority junior in rank to an accuser may not convene a general or special court-martial for the trial of the accused unless that convening authority is superior in command to the accuser. A convening authority junior in command to an accuser may not convene a general or special court-martial for the trial of the accused.

(3) *Action when disqualified.* When a commander who would otherwise convene a general or special court-martial is disqualified in a case, the charges shall be forwarded to a superior competent authority for disposition. That authority may personally dispose of the charges or forward the charges to another convening authority who is superior in rank to the accuser, or, if in the same chain of command, who is superior in command to the accuser.

Discussion

See also R.C.M. 401(c).

(d) *Convening orders.*

(1) *General and special courts-martial.* A convening order for a general or special court-martial shall designate the type of court-martial and detail the members and may designate where the court-martial will meet. If the convening authority has been designated by the Secretary concerned, the convening order shall so state.

Discussion

See Appendix 6 for a suggested format for a convening order.

(2) *Summary courts-martial.* A convening order for a summary court-martial shall designate that it is a summary court-martial and detail the summary court-martial, and may designate where the court-martial will meet. If the convening authority has been designated by the Secretary concerned, the convening order shall so state.

Discussion

See also R.C.M. 1302(c).

(3) *Additional matters.* Additional matters to be included in convening orders may be prescribed by the Secretary concerned.

(e) *Place.* The convening authority shall ensure that an appropriate location and facilities for courts-martial are provided.

Rule 505. Changes of members, military judge, and counsel

(a) *In general.* Subject to this rule, the members, military judge, and counsel may be changed by an authority competent to detail such persons. Members also may be excused as provided in subsections (c)(1)(B)(ii) and (c)(2)(A) of this rule.

Discussion

Changes of the members of the court-martial should be kept to a minimum. If extensive changes are necessary and no session of the court-martial has begun, it may be appropriate to withdraw the charges from one court-martial and refer them to another. *See* R.C.M. 604.

(b) *Procedure.* When new persons are added as members or counsel or when substitutions are made as to any members or counsel or the military judge, such persons shall be detailed in accordance with R.C.M. 503. An order changing the members of the court-martial, except one which excuses members without replacement, shall be reduced to writing before authentication of the record of trial.

Discussion

When members or counsel have been excused and the excusal is not reduced to writing, the excusal should be announced on the record. A member who has been temporarily excused need not be formally reappointed to the court-martial.

(c) *Changes of members.*

(1) *Before assembly.*

(A) *By convening authority.* Before the court-martial is assembled, the convening authority may change the members of the court-martial without showing cause.

(B) *By convening authority's delegate.*

(i) *Delegation.* The convening authority may delegate, under regulations of the Secretary concerned, authority to excuse individual members to the staff judge advocate or legal officer or other principal assistant to the convening authority.

(ii) *Limitations.* Before the court-martial is assembled, the convening authority's delegate may excuse members without cause shown; however, no more than one-third of the total number of members detailed by the convening authority may be excused by the convening authority's delegate in any one court-martial. After assembly the convening authority's delegate may not excuse members.

(2) *After assembly.*

(A) *Excusal.* After assembly no member may be excused, except:

(i) By the convening authority for good cause shown on the record;

(ii) By the military judge for good cause shown on the record; or

(iii) As a result of challenge under R.C.M. 912.

(B) *New members.* New members may be detailed after assembly only when, as a result of excusals under subsection (c)(2)(A) of this rule, the number of members of the court-martial is reduced below a quorum, or the number of enlisted members, when the accused has made a timely written request for enlisted members, is reduced below one-third of the total membership.

(d) *Changes of detailed counsel.*

(1) *Trial counsel.* An authority competent to detail trial counsel may change the trial counsel and any assistant trial counsel at any time without showing cause.

(2) *Defense counsel.*

(A) *Before formation of attorney-client relationship.* Before an attorney-client relationship has been formed between the accused and detailed defense counsel or associate or assistant defense counsel, an authority competent to detail defense counsel may excuse or change such counsel without showing cause.

(B) *After formation of attorney-client relationship.* After an attorney-client relationship has been formed between the accused and detailed defense counsel or associate or assistant defense counsel, an authority competent to detail such counsel may excuse or change such counsel only:

(i) Under R.C.M. 506(b)(3);

(ii) Upon request of the accused or application for withdrawal by such counsel under R.C.M. 506(c); or

(iii) For other good cause shown on the record.

(e) *Change of military judge.*

(1) *Before assembly.* Before the court-martial is assembled, the military judge may be changed by an authority competent to detail the military judge, without cause shown on the record.

(2) *After assembly.* After the court-martial is assembled, the military judge may be changed by an authority competent to detail the military judge only when, as a result of disqualification under R.C.M. 902 or for good cause shown, the previously detailed military judge is unable to proceed.

(f) *Good cause.* For purposes of this rule, "good cause" includes physical disability, military exigency, and other extraordinary circumstances which render the member, counsel, or military judge unable to proceed with the court-martial within a reasonable time. "Good cause" does not include temporary inconveniences which are incident to normal conditions of military life.

Rule 506. Accused's rights to counsel

(a) *In general.* The accused has the right to be represented before a general or special court-martial by civilian counsel if provided at no expense to the Government, and either by the military counsel detailed under Article 27 or military counsel of the accused's own selection, if reasonably available. The accused is not entitled to be represented by more than one military counsel.

Discussion

See R.C.M. 502(d)(3) as to qualifications of civilian counsel or individual military counsel.

(b) *Individual military counsel.*

(1) *Reasonably available.* Subject to this subsection, the Secretary concerned shall define "reasonably available." While so assigned, the following persons are not reasonably available to serve as individual military counsel because of the nature of their duties or positions:

(A) A general or flag officer;

(B) A trial or appellate military judge;

(C) A trial counsel;

(D) An appellate defense or government counsel;

(E) A principal legal advisor to a command, organization, or agency and, when such command, organization, or agency has general court-martial jurisdiction, the principal assistant of such an advisor;

(F) An instructor or student at a service school or academy:

(G) A student at a college or university;

(H) A member of the staff of the Judge Advocate General of the Army, Navy, or Air Force, the Chief Counsel of the Coast Guard, or the Director, Judge Advocate Division, Headquarters, Marine Corps.

The Secretary concerned may determine other persons to be not reasonably available because of the nature or responsibilities of their assignments, geolineart considerations, exigent circumstances, or military necessity. A person who is a member of an armed force different from that of which the accused is a member shall be reasonably available to serve as individual military counsel for such accused to the same extent as that person is available to serve as individual military counsel for an accused in the same armed force as the person requested. The Secretary concerned may prescribe circumstances under which exceptions may be made to the prohibitions in this subsection when merited by the existence of an attorney-client relationship regarding matters relating to a charge in question. However, if the attorney-client relationship arose solely because the counsel represented the accused on review under Article 70, this exception shall not apply.

(2) *Procedure.* Subject to this subsection, the Secretary concerned shall prescribe procedures for determining whether a requested person is "reasonably available" to act as individual military counsel. Requests for an individual military counsel shall be made by the accused or the detailed defense counsel through the trial counsel to the convening authority. If the requested person is among those not reasonably available under subsection (b)(1) of this rule or under regulations of the Secretary concerned, the convening authority shall deny the request and notify the accused, unless the accused asserts that there is an existing attorney-client relationship regarding a charge in question or that the person requested will not, at the time of the trial or investigation for which requested, be among those so listed as not reasonably available. If the accused's request makes such a claim, or if the person is not among those so listed as not reasonably available, the convening authority shall forward the request to the commander or head of the organization, activity, or agency to which the requested person is assigned. That authority shall make an administrative determination whether the requested person is reasonably available in accordance with the procedure prescribed by the Secretary concerned. This determination is a matter within the sole discretion of that authority. An adverse determination may be reviewed upon request of the accused through that authority to the next higher commander or level of supervision, but no administrative review may be made which requires action at the departmental or higher level.

(3) *Excusal of detailed counsel.* If the accused is represented by individual military counsel, detailed defense counsel shall normally be excused. The authority who detailed the defense counsel, as a matter of discretion, may approve a request from the accused that detailed defense counsel shall act as associate counsel. The action of the authority who detailed the counsel is subject to review only for abuse of discretion.

Discussion

A request under subsection (b)(3) should be considered in light of the general statutory policy that the accused is not entitled to be represented by more than one military counsel. Among the factors that may be considered in the exercise of discretion are the seriousness of the case, retention of civilian defense counsel, complexity of legal or factual issues, and the detail of additional trial counsel.

See R.C.M. 905(b)(6) and 960(b)(2) as to motions concerning denial of a request for individual military counsel or retention of detailed counsel as associate counsel.

(c) *Excusal or withdrawal.* Except as otherwise provided in R.C.M. 505(d)(2) and subsection (b)(3) of this rule, defense counsel may be excused only with the express consent of the accused, or by the military judge upon application for withdrawal by the defense counsel for good cause shown.

(d) *Waiver.* The accused may expressly waive the right to be represented by counsel and may thereafter conduct the defense personally. Such waiver shall be accepted by the military judge only if the military judge finds that the accused is competent to understand the disadvantages of self-representation and that the waiver is voluntary and understanding. The military judge may require that a defense counsel remain present even if the accused waives counsel and conducts the defense personally. The right of the accused to conduct the defense personally may be revoked if the accused is disruptive or fails to follow basic rules of decorum and procedure.

(e) *Nonlawyer present.* Subject to the discretion of the military judge, the accused may have present and seated at the counsel table for purpose of consultation persons not qualified to serve as counsel under R.C.M. 502.

Discussion

See also Mil. R. Evid. 615 if the person is a potential witness in the case.

CHAPTER VI. REFERRAL, SERVICE, AMENDMENT, AND WITHDRAWAL OF CHARGES

Rule 601. Referral

(a) *In general.* Referral is the order of a convening authority that charges against an accused will be tried by a specified court-martial.

Discussion

Referral of charges requires three elements: a convening authority who is authorized to convene the court-martial and is not disqualified (*see* R.C.M. 601(b) and (c)); preferred charges which have been received by the convening authority for disposition (*see* R.C.M. 307 as to preferral of charges and Chapter IV as to disposition); and a court-martial convened by that convening authority or a predecessor (*see* R.C.M. 504).

If trial would be warranted but would be detrimental to the prosecution of a war or inimical to national security, *see* R.C.M. 401(d) and 407(b).

(b) *Who may refer.* Any convening authority may refer charges to a court-martial convened by that convening authority or a predecessor, unless the power to do so has been withheld by superior competent authority.

Discussion

See R.C.M. 306(a), 403, 404, 407, and 504.

The convening authority may be of any command, including a command different from that of the accused, but as a practical matter the accused must be subject to the orders of the convening authority or otherwise under the convening authority's control to assure the appearance of the accused at trial. The convening authority's power over the accused may be based upon agreements between the commanders concerned.

(c) *Disqualification.* An accuser may not refer charges to a general or special court-martial.

Discussion

Convening authorities are not disqualified from referring charges by prior participation in the same case except when they have acted as accuser. For a definition of "accuser," *see* Article 1(9). A convening authority who is disqualified may forward the charges and allied papers for disposition by competent authority superior in rank or command. *See* R.C.M. 401(c) concerning actions which the superior may take.

See R.C.M. 1302 for rules relating to convening summary courts-martial.

(d) *When charges may be referred.*

(1) *Basis for referral.* If the convening authority finds or is advised by a judge advocate that there are reasonable grounds to believe that an offense triable by a court-martial has been committed and that the accused committed it, and that the specification alleges an offense, the convening authority may refer it. The finding may be based on hearsay in whole or in part. The convening authority or judge advocate may consider information from any source and shall not be limited to the information reviewed by any previous authority, but a case may not be referred to a general court-martial except in compliance with subsection (d)(2) of this rule. The convening authority or judge advocate shall not be required before charges are referred to resolve legal issues, including objections to evidence, which may arise at trial.

Discussion

For a discussion of selection among alternative dispositions, *see* R.C.M. 306. The convening authority is not obliged to refer all charges which the evidence might support. The convening authority should consider the options and considerations under R.C.M. 306 in exercising the discretion to refer.

---

(2) *General courts-martial.* The convening authority may not refer a specification under a charge to a general court-martial unless—

(A) There has been substantial compliance with the pretrial investigation requirements of R.C.M. 405; and

(B) The convening authority has received the advice of the staff judge advocate required under R.C.M. 406. These requirements may be waived by the accused.

Discussion

See R.C.M. 201(f)(2)(C) concerning limitations on referral of capital offenses to special courts-martial. *See* R.C.M. 103(3) for the definition of a capital offense.

See R.C.M. 1301(c) concerning limitations on the referral of certain cases to summary courts-martial.

(e) *How charges shall be referred.*

(1) *Order, instructions.* Referral shall be by the personal order of the convening authority. The con-

vening authority may include proper instructions in the order.

Discussion

Referral is ordinarily evidenced by an indorsement on the charge sheet. Although the indorsement should be completed on all copies of the charge sheet, only the original must be signed. The signature may be that of a person acting by the order or direction of the convening authority. In such a case the signature element must reflect the signer's authority.

If, for any reason, charges are referred to a court-martial different from that to which they were originally referred, the new referral is ordinarily made by a new indorsement attached to the original charge sheet. The previous indorsement should be lined out and initialed by the person signing the new referral. The original indorsement should not be obliterated. *See also* R.C.M. 604.

If the only officer present in a command refers the charges to a summary court-martial and serves as the summary court-martial under R.C.M. 1302, the indorsement should be completed with the additional comments, "only officer present in the command."

The convening authority may instruct that the charges against the accused be tried with certain other charges against the accused. *See* subsection (2) below.

The convening authority may instruct that charges against one accused be referred for joint or common trial with another accused. *See* subsection (3) below.

The convening authority shall indicate that the case is to be tried as a capital case by including a special instruction in the referral block of the charge sheet. Failure to include this special instruction at the time of the referral shall not bar the convening authority from later adding the required special instruction, provided that the convening authority has otherwise complied with the applicable notice requirements. If the accused demonstrates specific prejudice from such failure to include the special instruction, a continuance or a recess is an adequate remedy.

The convening authority should acknowledge by an instruction that a bad-conduct discharge, confinement for more than six months, or forfeiture of pay for more than six months, may not be adjudged when the prerequisites under Article 19 will not be met. *See* R.C.M. 201(f)(2)(B)(ii). For example, this instruction may be given when a court reporter is not detailed.

Any special instructions must be stated in the referral indorsement.

When the charges have been referred to a court-martial, the indorsed charge sheet and allied papers should be promptly transmitted to the trial counsel.

---

(2) *Joinder of offenses.* In the discretion of the convening authority, two or more offenses charged against an accused may be referred to the same court-martial for trial, whether serious or minor offenses or both, regardless whether related. Additional charges may be joined with other charges for a single trial at any time before arraignment if all necessary procedural requirements concerning the additional charges have been complied with. After arraignment of the accused upon charges, no additional charges may be referred to the same trial without consent of the accused.

Discussion

Ordinarily all known charges should be referred to a single court-martial.

---

(3) *Joinder of accused.* Allegations against two or more accused may be referred for joint trial if the accused are alleged to have participated in the same act or transaction or in the same series of acts or transactions constituting an offense or offenses. Such accused may be charged in one or more specifications together or separately, and every accused need not be charged in each specification. Related allegations against two or more accused which may be proved by substantially the same evidence may be referred to a common trial.

Discussion

A joint offense is one committed by two or more persons acting together with a common intent. Joint offenses may be referred for joint trial, along with all related offenses against each of the accused. A common trial may be used when the evidence of several offenses committed by several accused separately is essentially the same, even though the offenses were not jointly committed. *See* R.C.M. 307(c)(5) Discussion. Convening authorities should consider that joint and common trials may be complicated by procedural and evidentiary rules.

(f) *Superior convening authorities.* Except as otherwise provided in these rules, a superior competent authority may cause charges, whether or not referred, to be transmitted to the authority for further consideration, including, if appropriate, referral.

Rule 602. Service of charges

The trial counsel detailed to the court-martial to which charges have been referred for trial shall cause to be served upon each accused a copy of the charge sheet. In time of peace, no person may, over objection, be brought to trial—including an Article 39(a) session—before a general court-martial within a period of five days after service of charges, or before a special court-martial within a period of three days after service of charges. In computing these periods, the date of service of charges and the date of trial are excluded; holidays and Sundays are included.

Discussion

Trial counsel should comply with this rule immediately upon receipt of the charges. Whenever after service the charges are amended or changed the trial counsel must give notice of the changes to the defense counsel. Whenever such amendments or changes add a new party, a new offense, or substantially new allegations, the charge sheet so amended or changed must be served anew. *See also* R.C.M. 603.

Service may be made only upon the accused; substitute service upon defense counsel is insufficient. The trial counsel should promptly inform the defense counsel when charges have been served.

If the accused has questions when served with charges, the accused should be told to discuss the matter with defense counsel.

Rule 603. Changes to charges and specifications

(a) *Minor changes defined.* Minor changes in charges and specifications are any except those which add a party, offenses, or substantial matter not fairly included in those previously preferred, or which are likely to mislead the accused as to the offenses charged.

Discussion

Minor changes include those necessary to correct inartfully drafted or redundant specifications; to correct a misnaming of the accused; to allege the proper article; or to correct other slight errors. Minor charges also include those which reduce the seriousness of an offense, as when the value of an allegedly stolen item in a larceny specification is reduced, or when a desertion specification is amended to allege only unauthorized absence.

(b) *Minor changes before arraignment.* Any person forwarding, acting upon, or prosecuting charges on behalf of the United States except an investigating officer appointed under R.C.M. 405 may make minor changes to charges or specifications before arraignment.

Discussion

Charges forwarded or referred for trial should be free from defects of form and substance. Minor errors may be corrected and the charge may be redrafted without being sworn anew by the accuser. Other changes should be signed and sworn to by an accuser. All changes in the charges should be initialed by the person who makes them. A trial counsel acting under this provision ordinarily should consult with the convening authority before making any changes which, even though minor, change the nature or seriousness of the offense.

(c) *Minor changes after arraignment.* After arraignment the military judge may, upon motion, permit minor changes in the charges and specifications at any time before findings are announced if no substantial right of the accused is prejudiced.

(d) *Major changes.* Changes or amendments to charges or specifications other than minor changes may not be made over the objection of the accused unless the charge or specification affected is preferred anew.

Discussion

If there has been a major change or amendment over the accused's objection to a charge already referred, a new referral is necessary. Similarly, in the case of a general court-martial, a new investigation under R.C.M. 405 will be necessary if the charge as amended or changed was not covered in the prior investigation. If the substance of the charge or specification as amended or changed has not been referred or, in the case of a general court-martial, investigated, a new referral and, if appropriate, investigation are necessary. When charges are re-referred, they must be served anew under R.C.M. 602.

Rule 604. Withdrawal of charges

(a) *Withdrawal.* The convening authority or a superior competent authority may for any reason cause any charges or specifications to be withdrawn from a court-martial at any time before findings are announced.

Discussion

Charges which are withdrawn from a court-martial should be dismissed (*see* R.C.M. 401(c)(1)) unless it is intended to refer them anew promptly or to forward them to another authority for disposition.

Charges should not be withdrawn from a court-martial arbitrarily or unfairly to an accused. *See also* subsection (b) of this rule.

Some or all charges and specifications may be withdrawn. In a joint or common trial the withdrawal may be limited to charges against one or some of the accused.

Charges which have been properly referred to a court-martial may be withdrawn only by the direction of the convening authority or a superior competent authority in the exercise of that officer's independent judgment. When directed to do so by the convening authority or a superior competent authority, trial counsel may withdraw charges or specifications by lining out the affected charges or specifications, renumbering remaining charges or specifications as necessary, and initialing the changes. Charges and specifications withdrawn before commencement of trial will not be brought to the attention of the members. When charges or specifications are withdrawn after they have come to the attention of the members, the military judge must instruct them that the withdrawn charges or specifications may not be considered for any reason.

(b) *Referral of withdrawn charges.* Charges which have been withdrawn from a court-martial may be referred to another court-martial unless the withdrawal was for an improper reason. Charges withdrawn after the introduction of evidence on the general issue of guilt may be referred to another court-martial only if the withdrawal was necessitated by urgent and unforeseen military necessity.

Discussion

See also R.C.M. 915 (Mistrial).

When charges which have been withdrawn from a court-martial are referred to another court-martial, the reasons for the withdrawal and later referral should be included in the record of the later court-martial, if the later referral is more onerous to the accused. Therefore, if further prosecution is contemplated at the time of the withdrawal, the reasons for the withdrawal should be included in or attached to the record of the earlier proceeding.

Improper reasons for withdrawal include an intent to interfere with the free exercise by the accused of constitutional or codal rights, or with the impartiality of a court-martial. A withdrawal is improper if it was not directed personally and independently by the convening authority or by a superior competent authority.

Whether the reason for a withdrawal is proper, for purposes of the propriety of a later referral, depends in part on the stage in the proceedings at which the withdrawal takes place. Before arraignment, there are many reasons for a withdrawal which will not preclude another referral. These include receipt of additional charges, absence of the accused, reconsideration by the convening authority or by a superior competent authority of the seriousness of the offenses, questions concerning the mental capacity of the accused, and routine duty rotation of the personnel constituting the court-martial. Charges withdrawn after arraignment may be referred to another court-martial under some circumstances. For example, it is permissible to refer charges which were withdrawn pursuant to a pretrial agreement if the accused fails to fulfill the terms of the agreement. *See* R.C.M. 705. Charges withdrawn after some evidence on the general issue of guilty is introduced may be re-referred only under the narrow circumstances described in the rule.

CHAPTER VII. PRETRIAL MATTERS

Rule 701. Discovery

(a) *Disclosure by the trial counsel.* Except as otherwise provided in subsections (f) and (g)(2) of this rule, the trial counsel shall provide the following information or matters to the defense—

(1) *Papers accompanying charges; convening orders; statements.* As soon as practicable after service of charges under R.C.M. 602, the trial counsel shall provide the defense with copies of, or, if extraordinary circumstances make it impracticable to provide copies, permit the defense to inspect:

(A) Any paper which accompanied the charges when they were referred to the court-martial, including papers sent with charges upon a rehearing or new trial;

(B) The convening order and any amending orders; and

(C) Any sworn or signed statement relating to an offense charged in the case which is in the possession of the trial counsel.

(2) *Documents, tangible objects, reports.* After service of charges, upon request of the defense, the Government shall permit the defense to inspect:

(A) Any books, papers, documents, photographs, tangible objects, buildings, or places, or copies of portions thereof, which are within the possession, custody, or control of military authorities, and which are material to the preparation of the defense or are intended for use by the trial counsel as evidence in the prosecution case-in-chief at trial, or were obtained from or belong to the accused; and

(B) Any results or reports of physical or mental examinations, and of scientific tests or experiments, or copies thereof, which are within the possession, custody, or control of military authorities, the existence of which is known or by the exercise of due diligence may become known to the trial counsel, and which are material to the preparation of the defense or are intended for use by the trial counsel as evidence in the prosecution case-in-chief at trial.

Discussion

For specific rules concerning certain mental examinations of the accused or third party patients, *see* R.C.M. 701(f), R.C.M. 706, Mil. R. Evid. 302 and Mil. R. Evid. 513.

(3) *Witnesses.* Before the beginning of trial on the merits the trial counsel shall notify the defense of the names and addresses of the witnesses the trial counsel intends to call:

(A) In the prosecution case-in-chief; and

(B) To rebut a defense of alibi, innocent ingestion, or lack of mental responsibility, when trial counsel has received timely notice under subsection (b)(1) or (2) of this rule.

Discussion

Such notice should be in writing except when impracticable.

(4) *Prior convictions of accused offered on the merits.* Before arraignment the trial counsel shall notify the defense of any records of prior civilian or court-martial convictions of the accused of which the trial counsel is aware and which the trial counsel may offer on the merits for any purpose, including impeachment, and shall permit the defense to inspect such records when they are in the trial counsel's possession.

(5) *Information to be offered at sentencing.* Upon request of the defense the trial counsel shall:

(A) Permit the defense to inspect such written material as will be presented by the prosecution at the presentencing proceedings; and

(B) Notify the defense of the names and addresses of the witnesses the trial counsel intends to call at the presentencing proceedings under R.C.M. 1001(b).

(6) *Evidence favorable to the defense.* The trial counsel shall, as soon as practicable, disclose to the defense the existence of evidence known to the trial counsel which reasonably tends to:

(A) Negate the guilt of the accused of an offense charged;

(B) Reduce the degree of guilt of the accused of an offense charged; or

(C) Reduce the punishment.

Discussion

In addition to the matters required to be disclosed under subsection (a) of this rule, the Government is required to notify the defense of or provide to the defense certain information under other rules. Mil. R. Evid. 506 covers the disclosure of unclassified information which is under the control of the Government. Mil. R. Evid. 505 covers disclosure of classified information.

Other R.C.M. and Mil. R. Evid. concern disclosure of other specific matters. *See* R.C.M. 308 (identification of accuser), 405 (report of Article 32 investigation), 706(c)(3)(B) (mental examination of accused), 914 (production of certain statements), and 1004(b)(1) (aggravating circumstances in capital cases); Mil. R. Evid. 301(c)(2) (notice of immunity or leniency to witnesses), 302 (mental examination of accused), 304(d)(1) (statements by accused), 311(d)(1) (evidence seized from accused), 321(c)(1) (evidence based on lineups), 507 (identity of informants), 612 (memoranda used to refresh recollection), and 613(a) (prior inconsistent statements).

Requirements for notice of intent to use certain evidence are found in: Mil. R. Evid. 201A(b) (judicial notice of foreign law), 301(c)(2) (immunized witnesses), 304(d)(2) (notice of intent to use undisclosed confessions), 304(f) (testimony of accused for limited purpose on confession), 311(d)(2)(B) (notice of intent to use undisclosed evidence seized), 311(f) (testimony of accused for limited purpose on seizures), 321(c)(2)(B) (notice of intent to use undisclosed line-up evidence), 321(e) (testimony of accused for limited purpose of line-ups), 412(c)(1) and (2) (intent of defense to use evidence of sexual misconduct by a victim); 505(h) (intent to disclose classified information), 506(h) (intent to disclose privilege government information), and 609(b) (intent to impeach with conviction over 10 years old).

(b) *Disclosure by the defense.* Except as otherwise provided in subsections (f) and (g)(2) of this rule, the defense shall provide the following information to the trial counsel—

(1) *Names of witnesses and statements.*

(A) Before the beginning of trial on the merits, the defense shall notify the trial counsel of the names and addresses of all witnesses, other than the accused, whom the defense intends to call during the defense case in chief, and provide all sworn or signed statements known by the defense to have been made by such witnesses in connection with the case.

(B) Upon request of the trial counsel, the defense shall also

(i) Provide the trial counsel with the names and addresses of any witnesses whom the defense intends to call at the presentencing proceedings under R.C.M. 1001(c); and

(ii) Permit the trial counsel to inspect any written material that will be presented by the defense at the presentencing proceeding.

Discussion

Such notice shall be in writing except when impracticable. *See* R.C.M. 701(f) for statements that would not be subject to disclosure.

---

(2) *Notice of certain defenses.* The defense shall notify the trial counsel before the beginning of trial on the merits of its intent to offer the defense of alibi, innocent ingestion, or lack of mental responsibility, or its intent to introduce expert testimony as to the accused's mental condition. Such notice by the defense shall disclose, in the case of an alibi defense, the place or places at which the defense claims the accused to have been at the time of the alleged offense, and, in the case of an innocent ingestion defense, the place or places where, and the circumstances under which the defense claims the accused innocently ingested the substance in question, and the names and addresses of the witnesses upon whom the accused intends to rely to establish any such defenses.

Discussion

Such notice should be in writing except when impracticable. *See* R.C.M. 916(k) concerning the defense of lack of mental responsibility. *See* R.C.M. 706 concerning inquiries into the mental responsibility of the accused. *See* Mil. R. Evid. 302 concerning statements by the accused during such inquiries. If the defense needs more detail as to the time, date, or place of the offense to comply with this rule, it should request a bill of particulars. *See* R.C.M. 906(b)(6).

---

(3) *Documents and tangible objects.* If the defense requests disclosure under subsection (a)(2)(A) of this rule, upon compliance with such request by the Government, the defense, on request of the trial counsel, shall permit the trial counsel to inspect books, papers, documents, photographs, tangible objects, or copies or portions thereof, which are within the possession, custody, or control of the defense and which the defense intends to introduce as evidence in the defense case-in-chief at trial.

(4) *Reports of examination and tests.* If the defense requests disclosure under subsection (a)(2)(B) of this rule, upon compliance with such request by the Government, the defense, on request of trial counsel, shall (except as provided in R.C.M. 706, Mil. R. Evid. 302, and Mil. R. Evid. 513) permit the trial counsel to inspect any results or reports of physical or mental examinations and of scientific tests or experiments made in connection with the particular case, or copies thereof, that are within the

possession, custody, or control of the defense that the defense intends to introduce as evidence in the defense case-in-chief at trial or that were prepared by a witness whom the defense intends to call at trial when the results or reports relate to that witness' testimony.

(5) *Inadmissibility of withdrawn defense.* If an intention to rely upon a defense under subsection (b)(2) of this rule is withdrawn, evidence of such intention and disclosures by the accused or defense counsel made in connection with such intention is not, in any court-martial, admissible against the accused who gave notice of the intention.

Discussion

In addition to the matters covered in subsection (b) of this rule, defense counsel is required to give notice or disclose evidence under certain Military Rules of Evidence: Mil. R. Evid. 201A(b) (judicial notice of foreign law), 304(f) (testimony by the accused for a limited purpose in relation to a confession), 311(b) (same, search), 321(e) (same, lineup), 412(c)(1) and (2) (intent to offer evidence of sexual misconduct by a victim), 505(h) (intent to disclose classified information), 506(h) (intent to disclose privileged government information), 609(b) (intent to impeach a witness with a conviction older than 10 years), 612(2) (writing used to refresh recollection), and 613(a) (prior inconsistent statements).

(c) *Failure to call witness.* The fact that a witness' name is on a list of expected or intended witnesses provided to an opposing party, whether required by this rule or not, shall not be ground for comment upon a failure to call the witness.

(d) *Continuing duty to disclose.* If, before or during the court-martial, a party discovers additional evidence or material previously requested or required to be produced, which is subject to discovery or inspection under this rule, that party shall promptly notify the other party or the military judge of the existence of the additional evidence or material.

(e) *Access to witnesses and evidence.* Each party shall have adequate opportunity to prepare its case and equal opportunity to interview witnesses and inspect evidence. No party may unreasonably impede the access of another party to a witness or evidence.

Discussion

Convening authorities, commanders and members of their immediate staffs should make no statement, oral or written, and take no action which could reasonably be understood to discourage or prevent witnesses from testifying truthfully before a court-martial, or as a threat of retribution for such testimony.

(f) *Information not subject to disclosure.* Nothing in this rule shall be construed to require the disclosure of information protected from disclosure by the Military Rules of Evidence. Nothing in this rule shall require the disclosure or production of notes, memoranda, or similar working papers prepared by counsel and counsel's assistants and representatives.

(g) *Regulation of discovery.*

(1) *Time, place, and manner.* The military judge may, consistent with this rule, specify the time, place, and manner of making discovery and may prescribe such terms and conditions as are just.

(2) *Protective and modifying orders.* Upon a sufficient showing the military judge may at any time order that the discovery or inspection be denied, restricted, or deferred, or make such other order as is appropriate. Upon motion by a party, the military judge may permit the party to make such showing, in whole or in part, in writing to be inspected only by the military judge. If the military judge grants relief after such an ex parte showing, the entire text of the party's statement shall be sealed and attached to the record of trial as an appellate exhibit. Such material may be examined by reviewing authorities in closed proceedings for the purpose of reviewing the determination of the military judge.

(3) *Failure to comply.* If at any time during the court-martial it is brought to the attention of the military judge that a party has failed to comply with this rule, the military judge may take one or more of the following actions:

(A) Order the party to permit discovery;

(B) Grant a continuance;

(C) Prohibit the party from introducing evidence, calling a witness, or raising a defense not disclosed; and

(D) Enter such other order as is just under the circumstances. This rule shall not limit the right of the accused to testify in the accused's behalf.

Discussion

Factors to be considered in determining whether to grant an exception to exclusion under subsection (3)(C) include: the extent of disadvantage that resulted from a failure to disclose; the reason for the failure to disclose; the extent to which later events mitigated the disadvantage caused by the failure to disclose; and any other relevant factors.

The sanction of excluding the testimony of a defense witness should be used only upon finding that the defense counsel's failure to comply with this rule was willful and motivated by a desire to obtain a tactical advantage or to conceal a plan to present fabricated testimony. Moreover, the sanction of excluding the testimony of a defense witness should only be used if alternative sanctions could not have minimized the prejudice to the Government. Before imposing this sanction, the military judge must weigh the defendant's right to compulsory process against the countervailing public interests, including (1) the integrity of the adversary process; (2) the interest in the fair and efficient administration of military justice; and (3) the potential prejudice to the truth-determining function of the trial process.

Procedures governing refusal to disclose classified information are in Mil. R. Evid. 505. Procedures governing refusal to disclose other government information are in Mil. R. Evid. 506. Procedures governing refusal to disclose an informant's identity are in Mil. R. Evid. 507.

(h) *Inspect.* As used in this rule "inspect" includes the right to photograph and copy.

Rule 702. Depositions

(a) *In general.* A deposition may be ordered whenever, after preferral of charges, due to exceptional circumstances of the case it is in the interest of justice that the testimony of a prospective witness be taken and preserved for use at an investigation under Article 32 or a court-martial.

Discussion

A deposition is the out-of-court testimony of a witness under oath in response to questions by the parties, which is reduced to writing or recorded on videotape or audiotape or similar material. A deposition taken on oral examination is an oral deposition, and a deposition taken on written interrogatories is a written deposition. Written interrogatories are questions, prepared by the prosecution, defense, or both, which are reduced to writing before submission to a witness whose testimony is to be taken by deposition. The answers, reduced to writing and properly sworn to, constitute the deposition testimony of the witness.

Note that under subsection (i) of this rule a deposition may be taken by agreement of the parties without necessity of an order.

A deposition may be taken to preserve the testimony of a witness who is likely to be unavailable at the investigation under Article 32 (*see* R.C.M. 405(g)) or at the time of trial (*see* R.C.M. 703(b)). Part of all of a deposition, so far as otherwise admissible under the Military Rules of Evidence, may be used on the merits or on an interlocutory question as substantive evidence if the witness is unavailable under Mil. R. Evid. 804(a) except that a deposition may be admitted in a capital case only upon offer by the defense. *See* Mil. R. Evid. 804(b)(1). In any case, a deposition may be used by any party for the purpose of contradicting or impeaching the testimony of the deponent as a witness. *See* Mil. R. Evid. 613. If only a part of a deposition is offered in evidence by a party, an adverse party may require the proponent to offer all which is relevant to the part offered, and any party may offer other parts. *See* Mil. R. Evid. 106.

A deposition which is transcribed is ordinarily read to the court-martial by the party offering it. *See also* subsection (g)(3) of this rule. The transcript of a deposition may not be inspected by the members. Objections may be made to testimony in a written deposition in the same way that they would be if the testimony were offered through the personal appearance of a witness.

Part or all of a deposition so far as otherwise admissible under the Military Rules of Evidence may be used in presentencing proceedings as substantive evidence as provided in R.C.M. 1001.

DD Form 456 (Interrogatories and Deposition) may be used in conjunction with this rule.

(b) *Who may order.* A convening authority who has the charges for disposition or, after referral, the convening authority or the military judge may order that a deposition be taken on request of a party.

(c) *Request to take deposition.*

(1) *Submission of request.* At any time after charges have been preferred, any party may request in writing that a deposition be taken.

Discussion

A copy of the request and any accompanying papers ordinarily should be served on the other parties when the request is submitted.

(2) *Contents of request.* A request for a deposition shall include:

(A) The name and address of the person whose deposition is requested, or, if the name of the person is unknown, a description of the office or position of the person;

(B) A statement of the matters on which the person is to be examined;

(C) A statement of the reasons for taking the deposition; and

(D) Whether an oral or written deposition is requested.

(3) *Action on request.*

(A) *In general.* A request for a deposition may be denied only for good cause.

Discussion

Good cause for denial includes: failure to state a proper ground for taking a deposition; failure to show the probable relevance of the witness' testimony, or that the witness' testimony would be unnecessary. The fact that the witness is or will be available for trial is good cause for denial in the absence of unusual circumstances, such as improper denial of a witness request at an Article 32 hearing, unavailability of an essential witness at an Article 32 hearing, or when the Government has improperly impeded defense access to a witness.

(B) *Written deposition.* A request for a written deposition may not be approved without the consent of the opposing party except when the deposition is ordered solely in lieu of producing a witness for sentencing under R.C.M. 1001 and the authority ordering the deposition determines that the interests of the parties and the court-martial can be adequately served by a written deposition.

Discussion

A request for an oral deposition may be approved without the consent of the opposing party.

(C) *Notification of decision.* The authority who acts on the request shall promptly inform the requesting party of the action on the request and, if the request is denied, the reasons for denial.

(D) *Waiver.* Failure to review before the military judge a request for a deposition denied by a convening authority waives further consideration of the request.

(d) *Action when request is approved.*

(1) *Detail of deposition officer.* When a request for a deposition is approved, the convening authority shall detail an officer to serve as deposition officer or request an appropriate civil officer to serve as deposition officer.

Discussion

See Article 49(c).

When a deposition will be at a point distant from the command, an appropriate authority may be requested to make available an officer to serve as deposition officer.

(2) *Assignment of counsel.* If charges have not yet been referred to a court-martial when a request to take a deposition is approved, the convening authority who directed the taking of the deposition shall ensure that counsel qualified as required under R.C.M. 502(d) are assigned to represent each party.

Discussion

The counsel who represents the accused at a deposition ordinarily will form an attorney-client relationship with the accused which will continue through a later court-martial. *See* R.C.M. 506.

If the accused has formed an attorney-client relationship with military counsel concerning the charges in question, ordinarily that counsel should be appointed to represent the accused.

(3) *Instructions.* The convening authority may give instructions not inconsistent with this rule to the deposition officer.

Discussion

Such instruction may include the time and place for taking the deposition.

(e) *Notice.* The party at whose request a deposition is to be taken shall give to every other party reasonable written notice of the time and place for taking the deposition and the name and address of each person to be examined. On motion of a party upon whom the notice is served the deposition officer may for cause shown extend or shorten the time or change the place for taking the deposition, consistent with any instructions from the convening authority.

(f) *Duties of the deposition officer.* In accordance with this rule, and subject to any instructions under subsection (d)(3) of this rule, the deposition officer shall:

(1) Arrange a time and place for taking the deposition and, in the case of an oral deposition, notify the party who requested the deposition accordingly;

(2) Arrange for the presence of any witness whose deposition is to be taken in accordance with the procedures for production of witnesses and evidence under R.C.M. 703(e);

(3) Maintain order during the deposition and protect the parties and witnesses from annoyance, embarrassment, or oppression;

(4) Administer the oath to each witness, the reporter, and interpreter, if any;

(5) In the case of a written deposition, ask the questions submitted by counsel to the witness;

(6) Cause the proceedings to be recorded so that a verbatim record is made or may be prepared;

(7) Record, but not rule upon, objections or motions and the testimony to which they relate;

(8) Authenticate the record of the deposition and

forward it to the authority who ordered the deposition; and

(9) Report to the convening authority any substantial irregularity in the proceeding.

Discussion

When any unusual problem, such as improper conduct by counsel or a witness, prevents an orderly and fair proceeding, the deposition officer should adjourn the proceedings and inform the convening authority.

The authority who ordered the deposition should forward copies to the parties.

(g) *Procedure.*

(1) *Oral depositions.*

(A) *Rights of accused.* At an oral deposition, the accused shall have the rights to:

(i) Be present except when: *(a)* the accused, absent good cause shown, fails to appear after notice of time and place of the deposition; *(b)* the accused is disruptive within the meaning of R.C.M. 804(b)(2); or *(c)* the deposition is ordered in lieu of production of a witness on sentencing under R.C.M. 1001 and the authority ordering the deposition determines that the interests of the parties and the court-martial can be served adequately by an oral deposition without the presence of the accused; and

(ii) Be represented by counsel as provided in R.C.M. 506.

(B) *Examination of witnesses.* Each witness giving an oral deposition shall be examined under oath. The scope and manner of examination and cross-examination shall be such as would be allowed in the trial itself. The Government shall make available to each accused for examination and use at the taking of the deposition any statement of the witness which is in the possession of the United States and to which the accused would be entitled at the trial.

Discussion

As to objections, *see* subsections (f)(7) and (h) of this rule. As to production of prior statements of witnesses, *see* R.C.M. 914; Mil. R. Evid. 612, 613.

A sample oath for a deposition follows.

"You (swear) (affirm) that the evidence you give shall be the truth, the whole truth, and nothing but the truth (so help you God)?"

---

(2) *Written depositions.*

(A) *Rights of accused.* The accused shall have the right to be represented by counsel as provided in R.C.M. 506 for the purpose of taking a written deposition, except when the deposition is taken for use at a summary court-martial.

(B) *Presence of parties.* No party has a right to be present at a written deposition.

(C) *Submission of interrogatories to opponent.* The party requesting a written deposition shall submit to opposing counsel a list of written questions to be asked of the witness. Opposing counsel may examine the questions and shall be allowed a reasonable time to prepare cross-interrogatories and objections, if any.

Discussion

The interrogatories and cross-interrogatories should be sent to the deposition officer by the party who requested the deposition. *See* subsection (h)(3) of this rule concerning objections.

(D) *Examination of witnesses.* The deposition officer shall swear the witness, read each question presented by the parties to the witness, and record each response. The testimony of the witness shall be recorded on videotape, audiotape, or similar material or shall be transcribed. When the testimony is transcribed, the deposition shall, except when impracticable, be submitted to the witness for examination. The deposition officer may enter additional matters then stated by the witness under oath. The deposition shall be signed by the witness if the witness is available. If the deposition is not signed by the witness, the deposition officer shall record the reason. The certificate of authentication shall then be executed.

(3) *How recorded.* In the discretion of the authority who ordered the deposition, a deposition may be recorded by a reporter or by other means including videotape, audiotape, or sound film. In the discretion of the military judge, depositions recorded by videotape, audiotape, or sound film may be played for the court-martial or may be transcribed and read to the court-martial.

Discussion

A deposition read in evidence or one that is played during a court-martial, is recorded and transcribed by the reporter in the same way as any other testimony. The deposition need not be included in the record of trial.

(h) *Objections.*

(1) *In general.* A failure to object prior to the deposition to the taking of the deposition on grounds which may be corrected if the objection is made prior to the deposition waives such objection.

(2) *Oral depositions.* Objections to questions, testimony, or evidence at an oral deposition and the grounds for such objection shall be stated at the time of taking such deposition. If an objection relates to a matter which could have been corrected if the objection had been made during the deposition, the objection is waived if not made at the deposition.

Discussion

A party may show that an objection was made during the deposition but not recorded, but, in the absence of such evidence, the transcript of the deposition governs.

(3) *Written depositions.* Objections to any question in written interrogatories shall be served on the party who proposed the question before the interrogatories are sent to the deposition officer or the objection is waived. Objections to answers in a written deposition may be made at trial.

(i) *Deposition by agreement not precluded.*

(1) *Taking deposition.* Nothing in this rule shall preclude the taking of a deposition without cost to the United States, orally or upon written questions, by agreement of the parties.

(2) *Use of deposition.* Subject to Article 49, nothing in this rule shall preclude the use of a deposition at the court-martial by agreement of the parties unless the military judge forbids its use for good cause.

Rule 703. Production of witnesses and evidence

(a) *In general.* The prosecution and defense and the court-martial shall have equal opportunity to obtain witnesses and evidence, including the benefit of compulsory process.

Discussion

See also R.C.M. 801(c) concerning the opportunity of the court-martial to obtain witnesses and evidence.

(b) *Right to witnesses.*

(1) *On the merits or on interlocutory questions.* Each party is entitled to the production of any witness whose testimony on a matter in issue on the merits or on an interlocutory question would be relevant and necessary. With the consent of both the accused and Government, the military judge may authorize any witness to testify via remote means. Over a party's objection, the military judge may authorize any witness to testify on interlocutory questions via remote means or similar technology if the practical difficulties of producing the witness outweigh the significance of the witness' personal appearance (although such testimony will not be admissible over the accused's objection as evidence on the ultimate issue of guilt). Factors to be considered include, but are not limited to, the costs of producing the witness; the timing of the request for production of the witness; the potential delay in the interlocutory proceeding that may be caused by the production of the witness; the willingness of the witness to testify in person; the likelihood of significant interference with military operational deployment, mission accomplishment, or essential training; and, for child witnesses, the traumatic effect of providing in-court testimony.

Discussion

See Mil. R. Evid. 401 concerning relevance.

Relevant testimony is necessary when it is not cumulative and when it would contribute to a party's presentation of the case in some positive way on a matter in issue. A matter is not in issue when it is stipulated as a fact.

The procedures for receiving testimony via remote means and the definition thereof are contained in R.C.M. 914B. An issue may arise as both an interlocutory question and a question that bears on the ultimate issue of guilt. See R.C.M. 801(e)(5). In such circumstances, this rule authorizes the admission of testimony by remote means or similar technology over the accused's objection only as evidence on the interlocutory question. In most instances, testimony taken over a party's objection will not be admissible as evidence on the question that bears on the ultimate issue of guilt; however, there may be certain limited circumstances where the testimony is admissible on the ultimate issue of guilt. Such determinations must be made based upon the relevant rules of evidence.

(2) *On sentencing.* Each party is entitled to the

production of a witness whose testimony on sentencing is required under R.C.M. 1001(e).

(3) *Unavailable witness.* Notwithstanding subsections (b)(1) and (2) of this rule, a party is not entitled to the presence of a witness who is unavailable within the meaning of Mil. R. Evid. 804(a). However, if the testimony of a witness who is unavailable is of such central importance to an issue that it is essential to a fair trial, and if there is no adequate substitute for such testimony, the military judge shall grant a continuance or other relief in order to attempt to secure the witness' presence or shall abate the proceedings, unless the unavailability of the witness is the fault of or could have been prevented by the requesting party.

(c) *Determining which witness will be produced.*

(1) *Witnesses for the prosecution.* The trial counsel shall obtain the presence of witnesses whose testimony the trial counsel considers relevant and necessary for the prosecution.

(2) *Witnesses for the defense.*

(A) *Request.* The defense shall submit to the trial counsel a written list of witnesses whose production by the Government the defense requests.

(B) *Contents of request.*

(i) *Witnesses on merits or interlocutory questions.* A list of witnesses whose testimony the defense considers relevant and necessary on the merits or on an interlocutory question shall include the name, telephone number, if known, and address or location of the witness such that the witness can be found upon the exercise of due diligence and a synopsis of the expected testimony sufficient to show its relevance and necessity.

(ii) *Witnesses on sentencing.* A list of witnesses wanted for presentencing proceedings shall include the name, telephone number, if known, and address or location of the witness such that the witness can be found upon the exercise of due diligence, a synopsis of the testimony that it is expected the witness will give, and the reasons why the witness' personal appearance will be necessary under the standards set forth in R.C.M. 1001(e).

(C) *Time of request.* A list of witnesses under this subsection shall be submitted in time reasonably to allow production of each witness on the date when the witness' presence will be necessary. The military judge may set a specific date by which such lists must be submitted. Failure to submit the name of a witness in a timely manner shall permit denial of a motion for production of the witness, but relief from such denial may be granted for good cause shown.

(D) *Determination.* The trial counsel shall arrange for the presence of any witness listed by the defense unless the trial counsel contends that the witness' production is not required under this rule. If the trial counsel contends that the witness' production is not required by this rule, the matter may be submitted to the military judge. If the military judge grants a motion for a witness, the trial counsel shall produce the witness or the proceedings shall be abated.

Discussion

When significant or unusual costs would be involved in producing witnesses, the trial counsel should inform the convening authority, as the convening authority may elect to dispose of the matter by means other than a court-martial. *See* R.C.M. 906(b)(7). *See also* R.C.M. 905(j).

(d) *Employment of expert witnesses.* When the employment at Government expense of an expert is considered necessary by a party, the party shall, in advance of employment of the expert, and with notice to the opposing party, submit a request to the convening authority to authorize the employment and to fix the compensation for the expert. The request shall include a complete statement of reasons why employment of the expert is necessary and the estimated cost of employment. A request denied by the convening authority may be renewed before the military judge who shall determine whether the testimony of the expert is relevant and necessary, and, if so, whether the Government has provided or will provide an adequate substitute. If the military judge grants a motion for employment of an expert or finds that the Government is required to provide a substitute, the proceedings shall be abated if the Government fails to comply with the ruling. In the absence of advance authorization, an expert witness may not be paid fees other than those to which entitled under subsection (e)(2)(D) of this rule.

Discussion

See Mil. R. Evid. 702, 706.

(e) *Procedures for production of witnesses.*

(1) *Military witnesses.* The attendance of a military witness may be obtained by notifying the commander of the witness of the time, place, and date the witness' presence is required and requesting the commander to issue any necessary orders to the witness.

Discussion

When military witnesses are located near the court-martial, their presence can usually be obtained through informal coordination with them and their commander. If the witness is not near the court-martial and attendance would involve travel at government expense, or if informal coordination is inadequate, the appropriate superior should be requested to issue the necessary order.

If practicable, a request for the attendance of a military witness should be made so that the witness will have at least 48 hours notice before starting to travel to attend the court-martial.

The attendance of persons not on active duty should be obtained in the manner prescribed in subsection (e)(2) of this rule.

---

(2) *Civilian witnesses—subpoena.*

(A) *In general.* The presence of witnesses not on active duty may be obtained by subpoena.

Discussion

A subpoena is not necessary if the witness appears voluntarily at no expense to the United States.

Civilian employees of the Department of Defense may be directed by appropriate authorities to appear as witnesses in courts-martial as an incident of their employment. Appropriate travel orders may be issued for this purpose.

A subpoena may not be used to compel a civilian to travel outside the United States and its territories.

A witness must be subject to United States jurisdiction to be subject to a subpoena. Foreign nationals in a foreign country are not subject to subpoena. Their presence may be obtained through cooperation of the host nation.

(B) *Contents.* A subpoena shall state the command by which the proceeding is directed, and the title, if any, of the proceeding. A subpoena shall command each person to whom it is directed to attend and give testimony at the time and place specified therein. A subpoena may also command the person to whom it is directed to produce books, papers, documents or other objects designated therein at the proceeding or at an earlier time for inspection by the parties.

Discussion

A subpoena may not be used to compel a witness to appear at an examination or interview before trial, but a subpoena may be used to obtain witnesses for a deposition or a court of inquiry.

A subpoena normally is prepared, signed, and issued in duplicate on the official forms. *See* Appendix 7 for an example of a Subpoena with certificate of service (DD Form 453) and a Travel Order (DD Form 453-1).

(C) *Who may issue.* A subpoena may be issued by the summary court-martial or trial counsel of a special or general court-martial to secure witnesses or evidence for that court-martial. A subpoena may also be issued by the president of a court of inquiry or by an officer detailed to take a deposition to secure witnesses or evidence for those proceedings respectively.

(D) *Service.* A subpoena may be served by the person authorized by this rule to issue it, a United States marshal, or any other person who is not less than 18 years of age. Service shall be made by delivering a copy of the subpoena to the person named and by tendering to the person named travel orders and fees as may be prescribed by the Secretary concerned.

Discussion

See Department of Defense Pay and Entitlements Manual.

If practicable, a subpoena should be issued in time to permit service at least 24 hours before the time the witness will have to travel to comply with the subpoena.

Informal service. Unless formal service is advisable, the person who issued the subpoena may mail it to the witness in duplicate, enclosing a postage-paid envelope bearing a return address, with the request that the witness sign the acceptance of service on the copy and return it in the envelope provided. The return envelope should be addressed to the person who issued the subpoena. The person who issued the subpoena should include with it a statement to the effect that the rights of the witness to fees and mileage will not be impaired by voluntary compliance with the request and that a voucher for fees and mileage will be delivered to the witness promptly on being discharged from attendance.

Formal service. Formal service is advisable whenever it is anticipated that the witness will not comply voluntarily with the subpoena. Appropriate fees and mileage must be paid or tendered. *See* Article 47. If formal service is advisable, the person who issued the subpoena must assure timely and economical service. That person may do so by serving the subpoena personally when the witness is in the vicinity. When the witness is not in the vicinity, the subpoena may be sent in duplicate to the commander of a military installation near the witness. Such commanders should give prompt and effective assistance, issuing travel orders for their personnel to serve the subpoena when necessary.

Service should ordinarily be made by a person subject to the code. The duplicate copy of the subpoena must have entered upon it proof of service as indicated on the form and must be promptly returned to the person who issued the subpoena. If service cannot be made, the person who issued the subpoena must be informed promptly. A stamped, addressed envelope should be provided for these purposes.

(E) *Place of service.*

(i) *In general.* A subpoena requiring the attendance of a witness at a deposition, court-martial, or court of inquiry may be served at any place within the United States, it Territories, Commonwealths, or possessions.

(ii) *Foreign territory.* In foreign territory, the attendance of civilian witnesses may be obtained in accordance with existing agreements or, in the absence of agreements, with principles of international law.

(iii) *Occupied territory.* In occupied enemy territory, the appropriate commander may compel the attendance of civilian witnesses located within the occupied territory.

(F) *Relief.* If a person subpoenaed requests relief on grounds that compliance is unreasonable or oppressive, the convening authority or, after referral, the military judge may direct that the subpoena be modified or withdrawn if appropriate.

(G) *Neglect or refusal to appear.*

(i) *Issuance of warrant of attachment.* The military judge or, if there is no military judge, the convening authority may, in accordance with this rule, issue a warrant of attachment to compel the attendance of a witness or production of documents.

Discussion

A warrant of attachment (DD Form 454) may be used when necessary to compel a witness to appear or produce evidence under this rule. A warrant of attachment is a legal order addressed to an official directing that official to have the person named in the order brought before a court.

Subpoenas issued under R.C.M. 703 are Federal process and a person not subject to the code may be prosecuted in a Federal civilian court under Article 47 for failure to comply with a subpoena issued in compliance with this rule and formally served.

Failing to comply with such a subpoena is a felony offense, and may result in a fine or imprisonment, or both, at the discretion of the district court. The different purposes of the warrant of attachment and criminal complaint under Article 47 should be borne in mind. The warrant of attachment, available without the intervention of civilian judicial proceedings, has as its purpose the obtaining of the witness' presence, testimony, or documents. The criminal complaint, prosecuted through the civilian Federal courts, has as its purpose punishment for failing to comply with process issued by military authority. It serves to vindicate the military interest in obtaining compliance with its lawful process.

(ii) *Requirements.* A warrant of attachment may be issued only upon probable cause to believe that the witness was duly served with a subpoena, that the subpoena was issued in accordance with these rules, that appropriate fees and mileage were tendered to the witness, that the witness is material, that the witness refused or willfully neglected to appear at the time and place specified on the subpoena, and that no valid excuse reasonably appears for the witness' failure to appear.

(iii) *Form.* A warrant of attachment shall be written. All documents in support of the warrant of attachment shall be attached to the warrant, together with the charge sheet and convening orders.

(iv) *Execution.* A warrant of attachment may be executed by a United States marshal or such other person who is not less than 18 years of age as the authority issuing the warrant may direct. Only such nondeadly force as may be necessary to bring the witness before the court-martial or other proceeding may be used to execute the warrant. A witness attached under this rule shall be brought before the court-martial or proceeding without delay and shall testify as soon as practicable and be released.

Discussion

In executing a warrant of attachment, no more force than necessary to bring the witness to the court-martial, deposition, or court of inquiry may be used.

(v) *Definition.* For purposes of subsection (e)(2)(G) of this rule "military judge" does not include a summary court-martial or the president of a special court-martial without a military judge.

(f) *Right to evidence.*

(1) *In general.* Each party is entitled to the production of evidence which is relevant and necessary.

Discussion

See Mil. R. Evid. 401 concerning relevance.

Relevant evidence is necessary when it is not cumulative and when it would contribute to a party's presentation of the case in some positive way on a matter in issue. A matter is not in issue when it is stipulated as a fact.

As to the discovery and introduction of classified or other

government information, *see* Mil. R. Evid. 505 and 506.

---

(2) *Unavailable evidence.* Notwithstanding subsection (f)(1) of this rule, a party is not entitled to the production of evidence which is destroyed, lost, or otherwise not subject to compulsory process. However, if such evidence is of such central importance to an issue that it is essential to a fair trial, and if there is no adequate substitute for such evidence, the military judge shall grant a continuance or other relief in order to attempt to produce the evidence or shall abate the proceedings, unless the unavailability of the evidence is the fault of or could have been prevented by the requesting party.

(3) *Determining what evidence will be produced.* The procedures in subsection (c) of this rule shall apply to a determination of what evidence will be produced, except that any defense request for the production of evidence shall list the items of evidence to be produced and shall include a description of each item sufficient to show its relevance and necessity, a statement where it can be obtained, and, if known, the name, address, and telephone number of the custodian of the evidence.

(4) *Procedures for production of evidence.*

(A) *Evidence under the control of the Government.* Evidence under the control of the Government may be obtained by notifying the custodian of the evidence of the time, place, and date the evidence is required and requesting the custodian to send or deliver the evidence.

(B) *Evidence not under the control of the Government.* Evidence not under the control of the Government may be obtained by subpoena issued in accordance with subsection (e)(2) of this rule.

(C) *Relief.* If the person having custody of evidence requests relief on grounds that compliance with the subpoena or order of production is unreasonable or oppressive, the convening authority or, after referral, the military judge may direct that the subpoena or order of production be withdrawn or modified. Subject to Mil. R. Evid. 505 and 506, the military judge may direct that the evidence be submitted to the military judge for an in camera inspection in order to determine whether such relief should be granted.

Rule 704. Immunity

(a) *Types of immunity.* Two types of immunity may be granted under this rule.

(1) *Transactional immunity.* A person may be granted transactional immunity from trial by court-martial for one or more offenses under the code.

(2) *Testimonial immunity.* A person may be granted immunity from the use of testimony, statements, and any information directly or indirectly derived from such testimony or statements by that person in a later court-martial.

Discussion

"Testimonial" immunity is also called "use" immunity.

Immunity ordinarily should be granted only when testimony or other information from the person is necessary to the public interest, including the needs of good order and discipline, and when the person has refused or is likely to refuse to testify or provide other information on the basis of the privilege against self-incrimination.

Testimonial immunity is preferred because it does not bar prosecution of the person for the offenses about which testimony or information is given under the grant of immunity.

In any trial of a person granted testimonial immunity after the testimony or information is given, the Government must meet a heavy burden to show that it has not used in any way for the prosecution of that person the person's statements, testimony, or information derived from them. In many cases this burden makes difficult a later prosecution of such a person for any offense that was the subject of that person's testimony or statements. Therefore, if it is intended to prosecute a person to whom testimonial immunity has been or will be granted for offenses about which that person may testify or make statements, it may be necessary to try that person before the testimony or statements are given.

(b) *Scope.* Nothing in this rule bars:

(1) A later court-martial for perjury, false swearing, making a false official statement, or failure to comply with an order to testify; or

(2) Use in a court-martial under subsection (b)(1) of this rule of testimony or statements derived from such testimony or statements.

(c) *Authority to grant immunity.* Only a general court-martial convening authority may grant immunity, and may do so only in accordance with this rule.

Discussion

Only general court-martial convening authorities are authorized to grant immunity. However, in some circumstances, when a person testifies or makes statements pursuant to a promise of immunity, or a similar promise, by a person with apparent authority to make it, such testimony or statements and evidence derived from them may be inadmissible in a later trial. Under some circumstances a promise of immunity by someone other than a general court-martial convening authority may bar prosecution altogether. Persons not authorized to grant immunity should exercise care when dealing with accused or suspects to avoid inadvertently causing statements to be inadmissible or prosecution to be barred.

A convening authority who grants immunity to a prosecution witness in a court-martial may be disqualified from taking post-trial action in the case under some circumstances.

---

(1) *Persons subject to the code.* A general court-martial convening authority may grant immunity to any person subject to the code. However, a general court-martial convening authority may grant immunity to a person subject to the code extending to a prosecution in a United States District Court only when specifically authorized to do so by the Attorney General of the United States or other authority designated under 18 U.S.C. § 6004.

Discussion

When testimony or a statement for which a person subject to the code may be granted immunity may relate to an offense for which that person could be prosecuted in a United States District Court, immunity should not be granted without prior coordination with the Department of Justice. Ordinarily coordination with the local United States Attorney is appropriate. Unless the Department of Justice indicates it has no interest in the case, authorization for the grant of immunity should be sought from the Attorney General. A request for such authorization should be forwarded through the office of the Judge Advocate General concerned. Service regulations may provide additional guidance. Even if the Department of Justice expresses no interest in the case, authorization by the Attorney General for the grant of immunity may be necessary to compel the person to testify or make a statement if such testimony or statement would make the person liable for a Federal civilian offense.

---

(2) *Persons not subject to the code.* A general court-martial convening authority may grant immunity to persons not subject to the code only when specifically authorized to do so by the Attorney General of the United States or other authority designated under 18 U.S.C. § 6004.

Discussion

See the discussion under subsection (c)(1) of this rule concerning forwarding a request for authorization to grant immunity to the Attorney General.

---

(3) *Other limitations.* The authority to grant immunity under this rule may not be delegated. The authority to grant immunity may be limited by superior authority.

Discussion

Department of Defense Directive 1355.1 (21 July 1981) provides: "A proposed grant of immunity in a case involving espionage, subversion, aiding the enemy, sabotage, spying, or violation of rules or statutes concerning classified information or the foreign relations of the United States, shall be forwarded to the General Counsel of the Department of Defense for the purpose of consultation with the Department of Justice. The General Counsel shall obtain the view of other appropriate elements of the Department of defense in furtherance of such consultation."

(d) *Procedure.* A grant of immunity shall be written and signed by the convening authority who issues it. The grant shall include a statement of the authority under which it is made and shall identify the matters to which it extends.

Discussion

A person who has received a valid grant of immunity from a proper authority may be ordered to testify. In addition, a servicemember who has received a valid grant of immunity may be ordered to answer questions by investigators or counsel pursuant to that grant. *See* Mil. R. Evid. 301(c). A person who refuses to testify despite a valid grant of immunity may be prosecuted for such refusal. Persons subject to the code may be charged under Article 134. *See* paragraph 108, Part IV. A grant of immunity removes the right to refuse to testify or make a statement on self-incrimination grounds. It does not, however, remove other privileges against disclosure of information. *See* Mil. R. Evid., Section V.

An immunity order or grant must not specify the contents of the testimony it is expected the witness will give.

When immunity is granted to a prosecution witness, the accused must be notified in accordance with Mil. R. Evid. 301(c)(2).

(e) *Decision to grant immunity.* Unless limited by superior competent authority, the decision to grant immunity is a matter within the sole discretion of the appropriate general court-martial convening authority. However, if a defense request to immunize a witness has been denied, the military judge may, upon motion by the defense, grant appropriate relief directing that either an appropriate convening authority grant testimonial immunity to a defense witness or, as to the affected charges and specifications, the proceedings against the accused be abated, upon findings that:

(1) The witness intends to invoke the right

against self-incrimination to the extent permitted by law if called to testify; and

(2) The Government has engaged in discriminatory use of immunity to obtain a tactical advantage, or the Government, through its own overreaching, has forced the witness to invoke the privilege against self-incrimination; and

(3) The witness' testimony is material, clearly exculpatory, not cumulative, not obtainable from any other source and does more than merely affect the credibility of other witnesses.

Rule 705. Pretrial agreements

(a) *In general.* Subject to such limitations as the Secretary concerned may prescribe, an accused and the convening authority may enter into a pretrial agreement in accordance with this rule.

Discussion

The authority of convening authorities to refer cases to trial and approve pretrial agreements extends only to trials by courts-martial. To ensure that such actions do not preclude appropriate action by Federal civilian authorities in cases likely to be prosecuted in the United States district courts, convening authorities shall ensure that appropriate consultation under the "Memorandum of Understanding Between the Departments of Justice and Defense Relating to the Investigation and Prosecution of Crimes Over Which the Two Departments Have Concurrent Jurisdiction " has taken place prior to trial by court-martial or approval of a pretrial agreement in cases where such consultation is required. *See* Appendix 3.

(b) *Nature of agreement.* A pretrial agreement may include:

(1) A promise by the accused to plead guilty to, or to enter a confessional stipulation as to one or more charges and specifications, and to fulfill such additional terms or conditions which may be included in the agreement and which are not prohibited under this rule; and

(2) A promise by the convening authority to do one or more of the following:

(A) Refer the charges to a certain type of court-martial;

(B) Refer a capital offense as noncapital;

(C) Withdraw one or more charges or specifications from the court-martial;

Discussion

A convening authority may withdraw certain specifications and/or charges from a court-martial and dismiss them if the accused fulfills the accused's promises in the agreement. Except when jeopardy has attached (*see* R.C.M. 907(b)(2)(C)), such withdrawal and dismissal does not bar later reinstitution of the charges by the same or a different convening authority. A judicial determination that the accused breached the pretrial agreement is not required prior to reinstitution of withdrawn or dismissed specifications and/or charges. If the defense moves to dismiss the reinstituted specifications and/or charges on the grounds that the government remains bound by the terms of the pretrial agreement, the government will be required to prove, by a preponderance of the evidence, that the accused has breached the terms of the pretrial agreement. If the agreement is intended to grant immunity to an accused, *see* R.C.M. 704.

(D) Have the trial counsel present no evidence as to one or more specifications or portions thereof; and

(E) Take specified action on the sentence adjudged by the court-martial.

Discussion

For example, the convening authority may agree to approve no sentence in excess of a specified maximum, to suspend all or part of a sentence, to defer confinement, or to mitigate certain forms of punishment into less severe forms.

(c) *Terms and conditions.*

(1) *Prohibited terms or conditions.*

(A) *Not voluntary.* A term or condition in a pretrial agreement shall not be enforced if the accused did not freely and voluntarily agree to it.

(B) *Deprivation of certain rights.* A term or condition in a pretrial agreement shall not be enforced if it deprives the accused of: the right to counsel; the right to due process; the right to challenge the jurisdiction of the court-martial; the right to a speedy trial; the right to complete sentencing proceedings; the complete and effective exercise of post-trial and appellate rights.

Discussion

A pretrial agreement provision which prohibits the accused from making certain pretrial motions (*see* R.C.M. 905–907) may be improper.

---

(2) *Permissible terms or conditions.* Subject to subsection (c)(1)(A) of this rule, subsection (c)(1)(B) of this rule does not prohibit either party from proposing the following additional conditions:

(A) A promise to enter into a stipulation of fact

concerning offenses to which a plea of guilty or as to which a confessional stipulation will be entered;

(B) A promise to testify as a witness in the trial of another person;

Discussion

See R.C.M. 704(a)(2) concerning testimonial immunity. Only a general court-martial convening authority may grant immunity.

(C) A promise to provide restitution;

(D) A promise to conform the accused's conduct to certain conditions of probation before action by the convening authority as well as during any period of suspension of the sentence, provided that the requirements of R.C.M. 1109 must be complied with before an alleged violation of such terms may relieve the convening authority of the obligation to fulfill the agreement; and

(E) A promise to waive procedural requirements such as the Article 32 investigation, the right to trial by court-martial composed of members or the right to request trial by military judge alone, or the opportunity to obtain the personal appearance of witnesses at sentencing proceedings.

(d) *Procedure.*

(1) *Negotiation.* Pretrial agreement negotiations may be initiated by the accused, defense counsel, trial counsel, the staff judge advocate, convening authority, or their duly authorized representatives. Either the defense or the government may propose any term or condition not prohibited by law or public policy. Government representatives shall negotiate with defense counsel unless the accused has waived the right to counsel.

(2) *Formal submission.* After negotiation, if any, under subsection (d)(1) of this rule, if the accused elects to propose a pretrial agreement, the defense shall submit a written offer. All terms, conditions, and promises between the parties shall be written. The proposed agreement shall be signed by the accused and defense counsel, if any. If the agreement contains any specified action on the adjudged sentence, such action shall be set forth on a page separate from the other portions of the agreement.

Discussion

The first part of the agreement ordinarily contains an offer to plead guilty and a description of the offenses to which the offer extends. It must also contain a complete and accurate statement of any other agreed terms or conditions. For example, if the convening authority agrees to withdraw certain specifications, or if the accused agrees to waive the right to an Article 32 investigation, this should be stated. The written agreement should contain a statement by the accused that the accused enters it freely and voluntarily and may contain a statement that the accused has been advised of certain rights in connection with the agreement.

---

(3) *Acceptance.* The convening authority may either accept or reject an offer of the accused to enter into a pretrial agreement or may propose by counteroffer any terms or conditions not prohibited by law or public policy. The decision whether to accept or reject an offer is within the sole discretion of the convening authority. When the convening authority has accepted a pretrial agreement, the agreement shall be signed by the convening authority or by a person, such as the staff judge advocate or trial counsel, who has been authorized by the convening authority to sign.

Discussion

The convening authority should consult with the staff judge advocate or trial counsel before acting on an offer to enter into a pretrial agreement.

---

(4) *Withdrawal.*

(A) *By accused.* The accused may withdraw from a pretrial agreement at any time; however, the accused may withdraw a plea of guilty or a confessional stipulation entered pursuant to a pretrial agreement only as provided in R.C.M. 910(h) or 811(d), respectively.

(B) *By convening authority.* The convening authority may withdraw from a pretrial agreement at any time before the accused begins performance of promises contained in the agreement, upon the failure by the accused to fulfill any material promise or condition in the agreement, when inquiry by the military judge discloses a disagreement as to a material term in the agreement, or if findings are set aside because a plea of guilty entered pursuant to the agreement is held improvident on appellate review.

(e) *Nondisclosure of existence of agreement.* Except in a special court-martial without a military judge, no member of a court-martial shall be informed of the existence of a pretrial agreement. In addition, except as provided in Mil. R. Evid. 410, the fact that an accused offered to enter into a pretrial agreement, and any statements made by an accused in connection therewith, whether during negotiations or during a providence inquiry, shall not be otherwise disclosed to the members.

Discussion

See also R.C.M. 910(f) (plea agreement inquiry).

Rule 706. Inquiry into the mental capacity or mental responsibility of the accused

(a) *Initial action.* If it appears to any commander who considers the disposition of charges, or to any investigating officer, trial counsel, defense counsel, military judge, or member that there is reason to believe that the accused lacked mental responsibility for any offense charged or lacks capacity to stand trial, that fact and the basis of the belief or observation shall be transmitted through appropriate channels to the officer authorized to order an inquiry into the mental condition of the accused. The submission may be accompanied by an application for a mental examination under this rule.

Discussion

See R.C.M. 909 concerning the capacity of the accused to stand trial and R.C.M. 916(k) concerning mental responsibility of the accused.

(b) *Ordering an inquiry.*

(1) *Before referral.* Before referral of charges, an inquiry into the mental capacity or mental responsibility of the accused may be ordered by the convening authority before whom the charges are pending for disposition.

(2) *After referral.* After referral of charges, an inquiry into the mental capacity or mental responsibility of the accused may be ordered by the military judge. The convening authority may order such an inquiry after referral of charges but before beginning of the first session of the court-martial (including any Article 39(a) session) when the military judge is not reasonably available. The military judge may order a mental examination of the accused regardless of any earlier determination by the convening authority.

(c) *Inquiry.*

(1) *By whom conducted.* When a mental examination is ordered under subsection (b) of this rule, the matter shall be referred to a board consisting of one or more persons. Each member of the board shall be either a physician or a clinical psychologist. Normally, at least one member of the board shall be either a psychiatrist or a clinical psychologist. The board shall report as to the mental capacity or mental responsibility or both of the accused.

(2) *Matters in inquiry.* When a mental examination is ordered under this rule, the order shall contain the reasons for doubting the mental capacity or mental responsibility, or both, of the accused, or other reasons for requesting the examination. In addition to other requirements, the order shall require the board to make separate and distinct findings as to each of the following questions:

(A) At the time of the alleged criminal conduct, did the accused have a severe mental disease or defect? (The term "severe mental disease or defect" does not include an abnormality manifested only by repeated criminal or otherwise antisocial conduct, or minor disorders such as nonpsychotic behavior disorders and personality defects.)

(B) What is the clinical psychiatric diagnosis?

(C) Was the accused, at the time of the alleged criminal conduct and as a result of such severe mental disease or defect, unable to appreciate the nature and quality or wrongfulness of his or her conduct?

(D) Is the accused presently suffering from a mental disease or defect rendering the accused unable to understand the nature of the proceedings against the accused or to conduct or cooperate intelligently in the defense?

Other appropriate questions may also be included.

(3) *Directions to board.* In addition to the requirements specified in subsection (c)(2) of this rule, the order to the board shall specify:

(A) That upon completion of the board's investigation, a statement consisting only of the board's ultimate conclusions as to all questions specified in the order shall be submitted to the officer ordering the examination, the accused's commanding officer, the investigating officer, if any, appointed pursuant to Article 32 and to all counsel in the case, the convening authority, and, after referral, to the military judge;

(B) That the full report of the board may be released by the board or other medical personnel only to other medical personnel for medical purposes, unless otherwise authorized by the convening authority or, after referral of charges, by the military judge, except that a copy of the full report shall be furnished to the defense and, upon request, to the commanding officer of the accused; and

(C) That neither the contents of the full report nor any matter considered by the board during its investigation shall be released by the board or other medical personnel to any person not authorized to receive the full report, except pursuant to an order by the military judge.

Discussion

Based on the report, further action in the case may be suspended, the charges may be dismissed by the convening authority, administrative action may be taken to discharge the accused from the service or, subject to Mil. R. Evid. 302, the charges may be tried by court-martial.

---

(4) *Additional examinations.* Additional examinations may be directed under this rule at any stage of the proceedings as circumstances may require.

(5) *Disclosure to trial counsel.* No person, other than the defense counsel, accused, or, after referral of charges, the military judge may disclose to the trial counsel any statement made by the accused to the board or any evidence derived from such statement.

Discussion

See Mil. R. Evid. 302.

Rule 707. Speedy trial

(a) *In general.* The accused shall be brought to trial within 120 days after the earlier of:

(1) Preferral of charges;

Discussion

Delay from the time of an offense to preferral of charges or the imposition of pretrial restraint is not considered for speedy trial purposes. *See also* Article 43 (statute of limitations). In some circumstances such delay may prejudice the accused and may result in dismissal of the charges or other relief. Offenses ordinarily should be disposed of promptly to serve the interests of good order and discipline. Priority shall be given to persons in arrest or confinement.

---

(2) The imposition of restraint under R.C.M. 304(a)(2)–(4); or

(3) Entry on active duty under R.C.M. 204.

(b) *Accountability.*

(1) *In general.* The date of preferral of charges, the date on which pretrial restraint under R.C.M. 304 (a)(2)-(4) is imposed, or the date of entry on active duty under R.C.M. 204 shall not count for purpose of computing time under subsection (a) of this rule. The date on which the accused is brought to trial shall count. The accused is brought to trial within the meaning of this rule at the time of arraignment under R.C.M. 904.

(2) *Multiple Charges.* When charges are preferred at different times, accountability for each charge shall be determined from the appropriate date under subsection (a) of this rule for that charge.

(3) *Events which affect time periods.*

(A) *Dismissal or mistrial.* If charges are dismissed, or if a mistrial is granted, a new 120-day time period under this rule shall begin on the date of dismissal or mistrial for cases in which there is no repreferral and cases in which the accused is in pretrial restraint. In all other cases, a new 120-day time period under the rule shall begin on the earlier of

(i) the date of repreferral;

(ii) the date of imposition of restraint under R.C.M. 304(a)(2)–(4).

(B) *Release from restraint.* If the accused is released from pretrial restraint for a significant period, the 120-day time period under this rule shall begin on the earlier of

(i) the date of preferral of charges;

(ii) the date on which restraint under R.C.M. 304(a) (2)-(4) is reimposed; or

(iii) the date of entry on active duty under R.C.M. 204.

(C) *Government appeals.* If notice of appeal under R.C.M. 908 is filed, a new 120-day time period under this rule shall begin, for all charges neither proceeded on nor severed under R.C.M. 908(b)(4), on the date of notice to the parties under R.C.M. 908(b)(8) or 908(c)(3), unless it is determined that the appeal was filed solely for the purpose of delay with the knowledge that it was totally frivolous and without merit. After the decision of the Court of Criminal Appeals under R.C.M. 908, if there is a further appeal to the Court of Appeals for the Armed Forces or, subsequently, to the Supreme Court, a new 120-day time period under this rule shall begin on the date the parties are notified of the final decision of the Court of Appeals for the Armed Forces, or, if appropriate, the Supreme Court.

(D) *Rehearings.* If a rehearing is ordered or authorized by an appellate court, a new 120-day time period under this rule shall begin on the date that the responsible convening authority receives the record of trial and the opinion authorizing or directing a rehearing. An accused is brought to trial within the meaning of this rule at the time of arraignment under R.C.M. 904 or, if arraignment is not required (such as in the case of a sentence-only rehearing), at the time of the first session under R.C.M. 803.

(E) *Commitment of the incompetent accused.* If the accused is committed to the custody of the Attorney General for hospitalization as provided in R.C.M. 909(f), all periods of such commitment shall be excluded when determining whether the period in subsection (a) of this rule has run. If, at the end of the period of commitment, the accused is returned to the custody of the general court-martial convening authority, a new 120-day time period under this rule shall begin on the date of such return to custody.

(c) *Excludable delay.* All periods of time during which appellate courts have issued stays in the proceedings, or the accused is absent without authority, or the accused is hospitalized due to incompetence, or is otherwise in the custody of the Attorney General, shall be excluded when determining whether the period in subsection (a) of this rule has run. All other pretrial delays approved by a military judge or the convening authority shall be similarly excluded.

(1) *Procedure.* Prior to referral, all requests for pretrial delay, together with supporting reasons, will be submitted to the convening authority or, if authorized under regulations prescribed by the Secretary concerned, to a military judge for resolution. After referral, such requests for pretrial delay will be submitted to the military judge for resolution.

Discussion

The decision to grant or deny a reasonable delay is a matter within the sole discretion of the convening authority or a military judge. This decision should be based on the facts and circumstances then and there existing. Reasons to grant a delay might, for example, include the need for: time to enable counsel to prepare for trial in complex cases; time to allow examination into the mental capacity of the accused; time to process a member of the reserve component to active duty for disciplinary action; time to complete other proceedings related to the case; time requested by the defense; time to secure the availability of the accused, substantial witnesses, or other evidence; time to obtain appropriate security clearances for access to classified information or time to declassify evidence; or additional time for other good cause.

Pretrial delays should not be granted ex parte, and when practicable, the decision granting the delay, together with supporting reasons and the dates covering the delay, should be reduced to writing.

Prior to referral, the convening authority may delegate the authority to grant continuances to an Article 32 investigating officer.

---

(2) *Motions.* Upon accused's timely motion to a military judge under R.C.M. 905 for speedy trial relief, counsel should provide the court a chronology detailing the processing of the case. This chronology should be made a part of the appellate record.

(d) *Remedy.* A failure to comply with this rule will result in dismissal of the affected charges, or, in a sentence-only rehearing, sentence relief as appropriate.

(1) *Dismissal.* Dismissal will be with or without prejudice to the government's right to reinstitute court-martial proceedings against the accused for the same offense at a later date. The charges must be dismissed with prejudice where the accused has been deprived of his or her constitutional right to a speedy trial. In determining whether to dismiss charges with or without prejudice, the court shall consider, among others, each of the following factors: the seriousness of the offense; the facts and circumstances of the case that lead to dismissal; the impact of a re-prosecution on the administration of justice; and any prejudice to the accused resulting from the denial of a speedy trial.

(2) *Sentence relief.* In determining whether or how much sentence relief is appropriate, the military judge shall consider, among others, each of the following factors: the length of the delay, the reasons for the delay, the accused's demand for speedy trial, and any prejudice to the accused from the delay. Any sentence relief granted will be applied against the sentence approved by the convening authority.

Discussion

See subsection (c)(1) and the accompanying Discussion concerning reasons for delay and procedures for parties to request delay.

(e) *Waiver.* Except as provided in R.C.M. 910(a)(2), a plea of guilty which results in a finding of guilty waives any speedy trial issue as to that offense.

Discussion

Speedy trial issues may also be waived by a failure to raise the issue at trial. *See* R.C.M. 905(e) and 907(b)(2).

CHAPTER VIII. TRIAL PROCEDURE GENERALLY

Rule 801. Military judge's responsibilities; other matters

(a) *Responsibilities of military judge.* The military judge is the presiding officer in a court-martial.

Discussion

The military judge is responsible for ensuring that court-martial proceedings are conducted in a fair and orderly manner, without unnecessary delay or waste of time or resources. Unless otherwise specified, the president of a special court-martial without a military judge has the same authority and responsibility as a military judge. *See* R.C.M. 502(b)(2).

The military judge shall:

(1) Determine the time and uniform for each session of a court-martial;

Discussion

The military judge should consult with counsel concerning the scheduling of sessions and the uniform to be worn. The military judge recesses or adjourns the court-martial as appropriate. Subject to R.C.M. 504(d)(1), the military judge may also determine the place of trial. *See also* R.C.M. 906(b)(11).

---

(2) Ensure that the dignity and decorum of the proceedings are maintained;

Discussion

See also R.C.M. 804 and 806. Courts-martial should be conducted in an atmosphere which is conducive to calm and detached deliberation and determination of the issues presented and which reflects the seriousness of the proceedings.

---

(3) Subject to the code and this Manual, exercise reasonable control over the proceedings to promote the purposes of these rules and this Manual;

Discussion

See R.C.M. 102. The military judge may, within the framework established by the code and this Manual, prescribe the manner and order in which the proceedings may take place. Thus, the military judge may determine: when, and in what order, motions will be litigated (*see* R.C.M. 905); the manner in which voir dire will be conducted and challenges made (*see* R.C.M. 902(d) and 912); the order in which witnesses may testify (*see* R.C.M. 913; Mil. R. Evid. 611); the order in which the parties may argue on a motion or objection; and the time limits for argument (*see* R.C.M. 905; 919; 1001(g)).

The military judge should prevent unnecessary waste of time and promote the ascertainment of truth, but must avoid undue interference with the parties' presentations or the appearance of partiality. The parties are entitled to a reasonable opportunity to properly present and support their contentions on any relevant matter.

---

(4) Subject to subsection (e) of this rule, rule on all interlocutory questions and all questions of law raised during the court-martial; and

(5) Instruct the members on questions of law and procedure which may arise.

Discussion

The military judge instructs the members concerning findings (*see* R.C.M. 920) and sentence (*see* R.C.M. 1005), and when otherwise appropriate. For example, preliminary instructions to the members concerning their duties and the duties of other trial participants and other matters are normally appropriate. *See* R.C.M. 913. Other instructions (for example, instructions on the limited purpose for which evidence has been introduced, *see* Mil. R. Evid. 105) may be given whenever the need arises.

(b) *Rules of court; contempt.* The military judge may:

(1) Subject to R.C.M. 108, promulgate and enforce rules of court.

(2) Subject to R.C.M. 809, exercise contempt power.

(c) *Obtaining evidence.* The court-martial may act to obtain evidence in addition to that presented by the parties. The right of the members to have additional evidence obtained is subject to an interlocutory ruling by the military judge.

Discussion

The members may request and the military judge may require that a witness be recalled, or that a new witness be summoned, or other evidence produced. The members or military judge may direct trial counsel to make an inquiry along certain lines to discover and produce additional evidence. *See* also Mil. R. Evid. 614. In taking such action, the court-martial must not depart from an impartial role.

(d) *Uncharged offenses.* If during the trial there is evidence that the accused may be guilty of an untried offense not alleged in any specification before the court-martial, the court-martial shall proceed with the trial of the offense charged.

Discussion

A report of the matter may be made to the convening authority after trial. If charges are preferred for an offense indicated by the evidence referred to in this subsection, no member of the court-martial who participated in the first trial should sit in any later trial. Such a member would ordinarily be subject to a challenge for cause. *See* R.C.M. 912. *See also* Mil. R. Evid. 105 concerning instructing the members on evidence of uncharged misconduct.

(e) *Interlocutory questions and questions of law.* For purposes of this subsection "military judge" does not include the president of a special court-martial without a military judge.

(1) *Rulings by the military judge.*

(A) *Finality of rulings.* Any ruling by the military judge upon a question of law, including a motion for a finding of not guilty, or upon any interlocutory question is final.

(B) *Changing a ruling.* The military judge may change a ruling made by that or another military judge in the case except a previously granted motion for a finding of not guilty, at any time during the trial.

(C) *Article 39(a) sessions.* When required by this Manual or otherwise deemed appropriate by the military judge, interlocutory questions or questions of law shall be presented and decided at sessions held without members under R.C.M. 803.

Discussion

Sessions without members are appropriate for interlocutory questions, questions of law, and instructions. *See also* Mil. R. Evid. 103; 304; 311; 321. Such sessions should be used to the extent possible consistent with the orderly, expeditious progress of the proceedings.

---

(2) *Ruling by the president of a special court-martial without a military judge.*

(A) *Questions of law.* Any ruling by the president of a special court-martial without a military judge on any question of law other than a motion for a finding of not guilty is final.

(B) *Questions of fact.* Any ruling by the president of a special court-martial without a military judge on any interlocutory question of fact, including a factual issue of mental capacity of the accused, or on a motion for a finding of not guilty, is final unless objected to by a member.

(C) *Changing a ruling.* The president of a special court-martial without a military judge may change a ruling made by that or another president in the case except a previously granted motion for a finding of not guilty, at any time during the trial.

(D) *Presence of members.* Except as provided in R.C.M. 505 and 912, all members will be present at all sessions of a special court-martial without a military judge, including sessions at which questions of law or interlocutory questions are litigated. However, the president of a special court-martial without a military judge may examine an offered item of real or documentary evidence before ruling on its admissibility without exposing it to other members.

(3) *Procedures for rulings by the president of a special court-martial without a military judge which are subject to objection by a member.*

(A) *Determination.* The president of a special court-martial without a military judge shall determine whether a ruling is subject to objection.

(B) *Instructions.* When a ruling by the president of a special court-martial without a military judge is subject to objection, the president shall so advise the members and shall give such instructions on the issue as may be necessary to enable the members to understand the issue and the legal standards by which they will determine it if objection is made.

(C) *Voting.* When a member objects to a ruling by the president of a special court-martial without a military judge which is subject to objection, the court-martial shall be closed, and the members shall vote orally, beginning with the junior in rank, and the question shall be decided by a majority vote. A tie vote on a motion for a finding of not guilty is a determination against the accused. A tie vote on any other question is a determination in favor of the accused.

(D) *Consultation.* The president of a special court-martial without a military judge may close the court-martial and consult with other members before ruling on a matter, when such ruling is subject to the objection of any member.

(4) *Standard of proof.* Questions of fact in an interlocutory question shall be determined by a preponderance of the evidence, unless otherwise stated in this Manual. In the absence of a rule in this Manual assigning the burden of persuasion, the party

making the motion or raising the objection shall bear the burden of persuasion.

Discussion

A ruling on an interlocutory question should be preceded by any necessary inquiry into the pertinent facts and law. For example, the party making the objection, motion, or request may be required to furnish evidence or legal authority in support of the contention. An interlocutory issue may have a different standard of proof. *See*, for example, Mil. R. Evid. 314(e)(5), which requires consent for a search to be proved by clear and convincing evidence.

Most of the common motions are discussed in specific rules in this Manual, and the burden of persuasion is assigned therein. The prosecution usually bears the burden of persuasion (*see* Mil. R. Evid. 304(e); 311(e); *see also* R.C.M. 905 through 907) once an issue has been raised. What "raises" an issue may vary with the issue. Some issues may be raised by a timely motion or objection. *See*, for example, Mil. R. Evid. 304(e). Others may not be raised until the defense has made an offer of proof or presented evidence in support of its position. *See*, for example, Mil. R. Evid. 311(g)(2). The rules in this Manual and relevant decisions should be consulted when a question arises as to whether an issue is raised, as well as which side has the burden of persuasion. The military judge or president of a special court-martial may require a party to clarify a motion or objection or to make an offer of proof, regardless of the burden of persuasion, when it appears that the motion or objection is vague, inapposite, irrelevant, or spurious.

---

(5) *Scope.* Subsection (e) of this rule applies to the disposition of questions of law and interlocutory questions arising during trial except the question whether a challenge should be sustained.

Discussion

Questions of law and interlocutory questions include all issues which arise during trial other than the findings (that is, guilty or not guilty), sentence, and administrative matters such as declaring recesses and adjournments. A question may be both interlocutory and a question of law. Challenges are specifically covered in R.C.M. 902 and 912.

Questions of the applicability of a rule of law to an undisputed set of facts are normally questions of law. Similarly, the legality of an act is normally a question of law. For example, the legality of an order when disobedience of an order is charged, the legality of restraint when there is a prosecution for breach of arrest, or the sufficiency of warnings before interrogation are normally questions of law. It is possible, however, for such questions to be decided solely upon some factual issue, in which case they would be questions of fact. For example, the question of what warnings, if any, were given by an interrogator to a suspect would be a factual question.

A question is interlocutory unless the ruling on it would finally decide whether the accused is guilty. Questions which may determine the ultimate issue of guilt are not interlocutory. An issue may arise as both an interlocutory question and a question which may determine the ultimate issue of guilt. An issued is not purely interlocutory if an accused raises a defense or objection and the disputed facts involved determine the ultimate question of guilt. For example, if during a trial for desertion the accused moves to dismiss for lack or jurisdiction and presents some evidence that the accused is not a member of an armed force, the accused's status as a military person may determine the ultimate question of guilt because status is an element of the offense. If the motion is denied, the disputed facts must be resolved by each member in deliberation upon the findings. (The accused's status as a servicemember would have to be proved by a preponderance of the evidence to uphold jurisdiction, *see* R.C.M. 907, but beyond a reasonable doubt to permit a finding of guilty.) If, on the other hand, the accused was charged with larceny and presented the same evidence as to military status, the evidence would bear only upon amenability to trial and the issue would be disposed of solely as an interlocutory question.

Interlocutory questions may be questions of fact or questions of law. This distinction is important because the president of a special court-martial without a military judge rules finally on interlocutory questions of law, but not on interlocutory questions of fact. On interlocutory questions of fact the president of a special court-martial without a military judge rules subject to the objection of any other member. On mixed questions of fact and law, rulings by the president are subject to objection by any member to the extent that the issue of fact can be isolated and considered separately.

(f) *Rulings on record.* All sessions involving rulings or instructions made or given by the military judge or the president of a special court-martial without a military judge shall be made a part of the record. All rulings and instructions shall be made or given in open session in the presence of the parties and the members, except as otherwise may be determined in the discretion of the military judge. For purposes of this subsection [R.C.M. 801(f)] "military judge" does not include the president of a special court-martial without a military judge.

Discussion

See R.C.M. 808 and 1103 concerning preparation of the record of trial.

(g) *Effect of failure to raise defenses or objections.* Failure by a party to raise defenses or objections or to make requests or motions which must be made at the time set by this Manual or by the military judge under authority of this Manual, or prior to any extension thereof made by the military judge, shall constitute waiver thereof, but the military judge for good cause shown may grant relief from the waiver.

Rule 802. Conferences

(a) *In general.* After referral, the military judge may, upon request of any party or *sua sponte*, order one or more conferences with the parties to consider such matters as will promote a fair and expeditious trial.

Discussion

Conferences between the military judge and counsel may be held when necessary before or during trial. The purpose of such conference is to inform the military judge of anticipated issues and to expeditiously resolve matters on which the parties can agree, not to litigate or decide contested issues. *See* subsection (c) below. No party may be compelled to resolve any matter at a conference.

A conference may be appropriate in order to resolve scheduling difficulties, so that witnesses and members are not unnecessarily inconvenienced. Matters which will ultimately be in the military judge's discretion, such as conduct of voir dire, seating arrangements in the courtroom, or procedures when there are multiple accused may be resolved at a conference. Conferences may be used to advise the military judge of issues or problems, such as unusual motions or objections, which are likely to arise during trial.

Occasionally it may be appropriate to resolve certain issues, in addition to routine or administrative matters, if this can be done with the consent of the parties. For example, a request for a witness which, if litigated and approved at trial, would delay the proceedings and cause expense or inconvenience, might be resolved at a conference. Note, however, that this could only be done by an agreement of the parties and not by a binding ruling of the military judge. Such a resolution must be included in the record. *See* subsection (b) below.

A military judge may not participate in negotiations relating to pleas. *See* R.C.M. 705 and Mil. R. Evid. 410.

No place or method is prescribed for conducting a conference. A conference may be conducted by remote means or similar technology consistent with the definition in R.C.M. 914B.

(b) *Matters on record.* Conferences need not be made part of the record, but matters agreed upon at a conference shall be included in the record orally or in writing. Failure of a party to object at trial to failure to comply with this subsection shall waive this requirement.

(c) *Rights of parties.* No party may be prevented under this rule from presenting evidence or from making any argument, objection, or motion at trial.

(d) *Accused's presence.* The presence of the accused is neither required nor prohibited at a conference.

Discussion

Normally the defense counsel may be presumed to speak for the accused.

(e) *Admission.* No admissions made by the accused or defense counsel at a conference shall be used against the accused unless the admissions are reduced to writing and signed by the accused and defense counsel.

(f) *Limitations.* This rule shall not be invoked in the case of an accused who is not represented by counsel, or in special court-martial without a military judge.

Rule 803. Court-martial sessions without members under Article 39(a)

A military judge who has been detailed to the court-martial may, under Article 39(a), after service of charges, call the court-martial into session without the presence of members. Such sessions may be held before and after assembly of the court-martial, and when authorized in these rules, after adjournment and before action by the convening authority. All such sessions are a part of the trial and shall be conducted in the presence of the accused, defense counsel, and trial counsel, in accordance with R.C.M. 804 and 805, and shall be made a part of the record. For purposes of this rule "military judge" does not include the president of a special court-martial without a military judge.

Discussion

The purpose of Article 39(a) is "to give statutory sanction to pretrial and other hearings without the presence of the members concerning those matters which are amenable to disposition on either a tentative or final basis by the military judge." The military judge and members may, and ordinarily should, call the court-martial into session without members to ascertain the accused's understanding of the right to counsel, the right to request trial by military judge alone, or when applicable, enlisted members, and the accused's choices with respect to these matters; dispose of interlocutory matters; hear objections and motions; rule upon other matters that may legally be ruled upon by the military judge, such as admitting evidence; and perform other procedural functions which do not require the presence of members. *See*, for example, R.C.M. 901–910. The military judge may, if permitted by regulations of the Secretary concerned, hold the arraignment, receive pleas, and enter findings of guilty upon an accepted plea of guilty.

Evidence may be admitted and process, including a subpoena, may be issued to compel attendance of witnesses and production of evidence at such sessions. *See* R.C.M. 703.

Article 39(a) authorizes sessions only after charges have been referred to trial and served on the accused, but the accused has an absolute right to object, in time of peace, to any session until the period prescribed by Article 35 has run.

See R.C.M. 804 concerning waiver by the accused of the right to be present. *See also* R.C.M. 802 concerning conferences.

Rule 804. Presence of the accused at trial proceedings

(a) *Presence required.* The accused shall be present at the arraignment, the time of the plea, every stage of the trial including sessions conducted under Article 39(a), voir dire and challenges of members, the return of the findings, sentencing proceedings, and post-trial sessions, if any, except as otherwise provided by this rule.

(b) *Presence by remote means.* If authorized by the regulations of the Secretary concerned, the military judge may order the use of audiovisual technology, such as videoteleconferencing technology, between the parties and the military judge for purposes of Article 39(a) sessions. Use of such audiovisual technology will satisfy the "presence" requirement of the accused only when the accused has a defense counsel physically present at his location. Such technology may include two or more remote sites as long as all parties can see and hear each other.

(c) *Continued presence not required.* The further progress of the trial to and including the return of the findings and, if necessary, determination of a sentence shall not be prevented and the accused shall be considered to have waived the right to be present whenever an accused, initially present:

(1) Is voluntarily absent after arraignment (whether or not informed by the military judge of the obligation to remain during the trial); or

(2) After being warned by the military judge that disruptive conduct will cause the accused to be removed from the courtroom, persists in conduct which is such as to justify exclusion from the courtroom.

Discussion

Express waiver. The accused may expressly waive the right to be present at trial proceedings. There is no right to be absent, however, and the accused may be required to be present over objection. Thus, an accused cannot frustrate efforts to identify the accused at trial by waiving the right to be present. The right to be present is so fundamental, and the Government's interest in the attendance of the accused so substantial, that the accused should be permitted to waive the right to be present only for good cause, and only after the military judge explains to the accused the right, and the consequences of foregoing it, and secures the accused's personal consent to proceeding without the accused.

Voluntary absence. In any case the accused may forfeit the right to be present by being voluntarily absent after arraignment.

"Voluntary absence" means voluntary absence from trial. For an absence from court-martial proceedings to be voluntary, the accused must have known of the scheduled proceedings and intentionally missed them. For example, although an accused servicemember might voluntarily be absent without authority, this would not justify proceeding with a court-martial in the accused's absence unless the accused was aware that the court-martial would be held during the period of the absence.

An accused who is in military custody or otherwise subject to military control at the time of trial or other proceeding may not properly be absent from the trial or proceeding without securing the permission of the military judge on the record.

The prosecution has the burden to establish by a preponderance of the evidence that the accused's absence from trial is voluntary. Voluntariness may not be presumed, but it may be inferred, depending on the circumstances. For example, it may be inferred, in the absence of evidence to the contrary, that an accused who was present when the trial recessed and who knew when the proceedings were scheduled to resume, but who nonetheless is not present when court reconvenes at the designated time, is absent voluntarily.

Where there is some evidence that an accused who is absent for a hearing or trial may lack mental capacity to stand trial, capacity to voluntarily waive the right to be present for trial must be shown. *See* R.C.M. 909.

Subsection (1) authorizes but does not require trial to proceed in the absence of the accused upon the accused's voluntary absence. When an accused is absent from trial after arraignment, a continuance or a recess may be appropriate, depending on all the circumstances.

Presence of the accused by remote means does not require the consent of the accused.

Removal for disruption. Trial may proceed without the presence of an accused who has disrupted the proceedings, but only after at least one warning by the military judge that such behavior may result in removal from the courtroom. In order to justify removal from the proceedings, the accused's behavior should be of such a nature as to materially interfere with the conduct of the proceedings.

The military judge should consider alternatives to removal of a disruptive accused. Such alternatives include physical restraint (such as binding, shackling, and gagging) of the accused, or physically segregating the accused in the courtroom. Such alternatives need not be tried before removing a disruptive accused under subsection (2). Removal may be preferable to such an alternative as binding and gagging, which can be an affront to the dignity and decorum of the proceedings.

Disruptive behavior of the accused may also constitute contempt. *See* R.C.M. 809. When the accused is removed from the courtroom for disruptive behavior, the military judge should—

(A) Afford the accused and defense counsel ample opportunity to consult throughout the proceedings. To this end, the accused should be held or otherwise required to remain in the vicinity of the trial, and frequent recesses permitted to allow counsel to confer with the accused.

(B) Take such additional steps as may be reasonably practicable to enable the accused to be informed about the proceedings. Although not required, technological aids, such as closed-circuit television or audio transmissions, may be used for this purpose.

(C) Afford the accused a continuing opportunity to return to the courtroom upon assurance of good behavior. To this end, the accused should be brought to the courtroom at appropriate intervals, and offered the opportunity to remain upon good behavior.

(D) Ensure that the reasons for removal appear in the record.

(d) *Voluntary absence for limited purpose of child testimony.*

(1) *Election by accused.* Following a determination by the military judge that remote live testimony of a child is appropriate pursuant to Mil. R. Evid. 611(d)(3), the accused may elect to voluntarily absent himself from the courtroom in order to preclude the use of procedures described in R.C.M. 914A.

(2) *Procedure.* The accused's absence will be conditional upon his being able to view the witness' testimony from a remote location. Normally, transmission of the testimony will include a system that will transmit the accused's image and voice into the courtroom from a remote location as well as transmission of the child's testimony from the courtroom to the accused's location. A one-way transmission may be used if deemed necessary by the military judge. The accused will also be provided private, contemporaneous communication with his counsel. The procedures described herein shall be employed unless the accused has made a knowing and affirmative waiver of these procedures.

(3) *Effect on accused's rights generally.* An election by the accused to be absent pursuant to subsection (c)(1) shall not otherwise affect the accused's right to be present at the remainder of the trial in accordance with this rule.

(e) *Appearance and security of accused.*

(1) *Appearance.* The accused shall be properly attired in the uniform or dress prescribed by the military judge. An accused servicemember shall wear the insignia of grade and may wear any decorations, emblems, or ribbons to which entitled. The accused and defense counsel are responsible for ensuring that the accused is properly attired; however, upon request, the accused's commander shall render such assistance as may be reasonably necessary to ensure that the accused is properly attired.

Discussion

This subsection recognizes the right, as well as the obligation, of an accused servicemember to present a good military appearance at trial. An accused servicemember who refuses to present a proper military appearance before a court-martial may be compelled to do so.

---

(2) *Custody.* Responsibility for maintaining custody or control of an accused before and during trial may be assigned, subject to R.C.M. 304 and 305, and subsection (c)(3) of this rule, under such regulations as the Secretary concerned may prescribe.

(3) *Restraint.* Physical restraint shall not be imposed on the accused during open sessions of the court-martial unless prescribed by the military judge.

Rule 805. Presence of military judge, members, and counsel

(a) *Military judge.* No court-martial proceeding, except the deliberations of the members, may take place in the absence of the military judge, if detailed. If authorized by regulations of the Secretary concerned, for purposes of Article 39(a) sessions solely, the presence of the military judge at Article 39(a) sessions may be satisfied by the use of audiovisual technology, such as videoteleconferencing technology.

(b) *Members.* Unless trial is by military judge alone pursuant to a request by the accused, no court-martial proceeding may take place in the absence of any detailed member except: Article 39(a) sessions under R.C.M. 803; examination of members under R.C.M. 912(d); when the member has been excused under R.C.M. 505 or 912(f); or as otherwise provided in R.C.M. 1102. No general court-martial proceeding requiring the presence of members may be conducted unless at least five members are present, or in capital cases, at least 12 members are present except as provided in R.C.M. 501(a)(1)(B), where 12 members are not reasonably available because of physical conditions or military exigencies. No special court-martial proceeding requiring the presence of members may be conducted unless at least three members are present except as provided in R.C.M. 912(h). Except as provided in R.C.M. 503(a)(2), when an enlisted accused has requested enlisted members, no proceeding requiring the presence of members may be conducted unless at least one-third of the members actually sitting on the court-martial are enlisted persons.

(c) *Counsel.* As long as at least one qualified counsel for each party is present, other counsel for each party may be absent from a court-martial session. An assistant counsel who lacks the qualifications necessary to serve as counsel for a party may not act at a session in the absence of such qualified counsel. If authorized by regulations of the Secretary concerned, for purposes of Article 39(a) sessions solely, the presence of counsel at Article 39(a) sessions may be satisfied by the use of audiovisual technology, such as videoteleconferencing technology. At least one qualified defense counsel shall be physically present with the accused.

Discussion

See R.C.M. 504(d) concerning qualifications of counsel.

Ordinarily, no court-martial proceeding should take place if any defense or assistant defense counsel is absent unless the accused expressly consents to the absence. The military judge may, however proceed in the absence of one or more defense counsel, without the consent of the accused, if the military judge finds that, under the circumstances, a continuance is not warranted and that the accused's right to be adequately represented would not be impaired.

See R.C.M. 502(d)(6) and 505(d)(2) concerning withdrawal or substitution of counsel. *See* R.C.M. 506(d) concerning the right of the accused to proceed without counsel.

(d) *Effect of replacement of member or military judge.*

(1) *Members.* When after presentation of evidence on the merits has begun, a new member is detailed under R.C.M. 505(c)(2)(B), trial may not proceed unless the testimony and evidence previously admitted on the merits, if recorded verbatim, is read to the new member, or, if not recorded verbatim, and in the absence of a stipulation as to such testimony and evidence, the trial proceeds as if no evidence has been presented.

Discussion

At a rehearing, the trier of fact is not bound by the sentence previously adjudged or approved. The members should not be advised of the sentence limitation under this rule. *See* R.C.M. 1005(e)(1). An appropriate sentence on a retried or reheard offense should be adjudged without regard to any credit to which the accused may be entitled. *See* R.C.M. 103(2) and R.C.M. 103(3) as to when a rehearing may be a capital case.

---

(2) *Military judge.* When, after the presentation of evidence on the merits has begun in trial before military judge alone, a new military judge is detailed under R.C.M. 505(e)(2) trial may not proceed unless the accused requests, and the military judge approves, trial by military judge alone, and a verbatim record of the testimony and evidence or a stipulation thereof is read to the military judge, or the trial proceeds as if no evidence had been presented.

Rule 806. Public trial

(a) *In general.* Except as otherwise provided in this rule, courts-martial shall be open to the public. For purposes of this rule, "public" includes members of both the military and civilian communities.

Discussion

Because of the requirement for public trials, courts-martial must be conducted in facilities which can accommodate a reasonable number of spectators. Military exigencies may occasionally make attendance at courts-martial difficult or impracticable, as, for example, when a court-martial is conducted on a ship at sea or in a unit in a combat zone. This does not violate this rule. However, such exigencies should not be manipulated to prevent attendance at a court-martial. The requirements of this rule may be met even though only servicemembers are able to attend a court-martial. Although not required, servicemembers should be encouraged to attend courts-martial.

When public access to a court-martial is limited for some reason, including lack of space, special care must be taken to avoid arbitrary exclusion of specific groups or persons. This may include allocating a reasonable number of seats to members of the press and to relatives of the accused, and establishing procedures for entering and exiting from the courtroom. *See also* subsection (b) below. There is no requirement that there actually be spectators at a court-martial.

The fact that a trial is conducted with members does not make it a public trial.

(b) *Control of spectators and closure.*

(1) *Control of spectators.* In order to maintain the dignity and decorum of the proceedings or for other good cause, the military judge may reasonably limit the number of spectators in, and the means of access to, the courtroom, and exclude specific persons from the courtroom. When excluding specific persons, the military judge must make findings on the record establishing the reason for the exclusion, the basis for the military judge's belief that exclusion is necessary, and that the exclusion is as narrowly tailored as possible.

Discussion

The military judge must ensure that the dignity and decorum of the proceedings are maintained and that the other rights and interests of the parties and society are protected. Public access to a session may be limited, specific persons excluded from the courtroom, and, under unusual circumstances, a session may be closed.

Exclusion of specific persons, if unreasonable under the circumstances, may violate the accused's right to a public trial, even though other spectators remain. Whenever specific persons or some members of the public are excluded, exclusion must be limited in time and scope to the minimum extent necessary to achieve the purpose for which it is ordered. Prevention of overcrowding or noise may justify limiting access to the courtroom. Disruptive or distracting appearance or conduct may justify excluding specific persons. Specific persons may be excluded when necessary to protect witnesses from harm or intimidation. Access may be reduced when no other means is available to relieve a witness' inability to testify due to embarrassment or extreme nervousness. Witnesses will ordinarily be excluded from the courtroom so that they cannot hear the testimony of other witnesses. *See* Mil. R. Evid. 615.

(2) *Closure.* Courts-martial shall be open to the public unless (1) there is a substantial probability that an overriding interest will be prejudiced if the proceedings remain open; (2) closure is no broader than necessary to protect the overriding interest; (3) reasonable alternatives to closure were considered and found inadequate; and (4) the military judge makes case-specific findings on the record justifying closure.

Discussion

The military judge is responsible for protecting both the accused's right to, and the public's interest in, a public trial. A court-martial session is "closed" when no member of the public is permitted to attend. A court-martial is not "closed" merely because the exclusion of certain individuals results in there being no spectators present, as long as the exclusion is not so broad as to effectively bar everyone who might attend the sessions and is put into place for a proper purpose.

A session may be closed over the objection of the accused or the public upon meeting the constitutional standard set forth in this Rule. *See also* Mil. R. Evid. 412(c), 505(i), and 513(e)(2).

The accused may waive his right to a public trial. The fact that the prosecution and defense jointly seek to have a session closed does not, however, automatically justify closure, for the public has a right in attending courts-martial. Opening trials to public scrutiny reduces the chance of arbitrary and capricious decisions and enhances public confidence in the court-martial process.

The most likely reason for a defense request to close court-martial proceedings is to minimize the potentially adverse effect of publicity on the trial. For example, a pretrial Article 39(a) hearing at which the admissibility of a confession will be litigated may, under some circumstances, be closed, in accordance with this Rule, in order to prevent disclosure to the public (and hence to potential members) of the very evidence that may be excluded. When such publicity may be a problem, a session should be closed only as a last resort.

There are alternative means of protecting the proceedings from harmful effects of publicity, including a thorough *voir dire* (*see* R.C.M. 912), and, if necessary, a continuance to allow the harmful effects of publicity to dissipate (*see* R.C.M. 906(b)(1)). Alternatives that may occasionally be appropriate and are usually preferable to closing a session include: directing members not to read, listen to, or watch any accounts concerning the case; issuing a protective order (*see* R.C.M. 806(d)); selecting members from recent arrivals in the command, or from outside the immediate area (*see* R.C.M.503(a)(3)); changing the place of trial (*see* R.C.M.906(b)(11)); or sequestering the members.

(c) *Photography and broadcasting prohibited.* Video and audio recording and the taking of photographs—except for the purpose of preparing the record of trial—in the courtroom during the proceedings and radio or television broadcasting of proceedings from the courtroom shall not be permitted. However, the military judge may, as a matter of discretion permit contemporaneous closed-circuit video or audio transmission to permit viewing or hearing by an accused removed under R.C.M. 804 or by spectators when courtroom facilities are inadequate to accommodate a reasonable number of spectators.

(d) *Protective orders.* The military judge may, upon request of any party or *sua sponte*, issue an appropriate protective order, in writing, to prevent parties and witnesses from making extrajudicial statements that present a substantial likelihood of material prejudice to a fair trial by impartial members. For purposes of this subsection, "military judge" does not include the president of a special court-martial without a military judge.

Discussion

A protective order may proscribe extrajudicial statements by counsel, parties, and witnesses that might divulge prejudicial matter not of public record in the case. Other appropriate matters may also be addressed by such a protective order. Before issuing a protective order, the military judge must consider whether other available remedies would effectively mitigate the adverse effects that any publicity might create, and consider such an order's likely effectiveness in ensuring an impartial court-martial panel. A military judge should not issue a protective order without first providing notice to the parties and an opportunity to be heard. The military judge must state on the record the reasons for issuing the protective order. If the reasons for issuing the order change, the military judge may reconsider the continued necessity for a protective order.

Rule 807. Oaths

(a) *Definition.* "Oath" includes "affirmation."

Discussion

An affirmation is the same as an oath, except in an affirmation the words "so help you God" are omitted.

(b) *Oaths in courts-martial.*

(1) *Who must be sworn.*

(A) *Court-martial personnel.* The military judge, members of a general or special court-martial, trial counsel, assistant trial counsel, defense counsel, associate defense counsel, assistant defense counsel, reporter, interpreter, and escort shall take an oath to perform their duties faithfully. For purposes of this rule, "defense counsel," "associate defense counsel," and "assistant defense counsel," include detailed and individual military and civilian counsel.

Discussion

Article 42(a) provides that regulations of the Secretary concerned shall prescribed: the form of the oath; the time and place of the taking thereof; the manner of recording it; and whether the oath shall be taken for all cases in which the duties are to be performed or in each case separately. In the case of certified legal personnel (Article 26(b); Article 27(b)) these regulations may provide for the administration of an oath on a one-time basis. *See also* R.C.M. 813 and 901 concerning the point in the proceedings at which it is ordinarily determined whether the required oaths have been taken or are then administered.

(B) *Witnesses.* Each witness before a court-martial shall be examined on oath.

Discussion

See R.C.M. 307 concerning the requirement for an oath in preferral of charges. *See* R.C.M. 405 and 702 concerning the requirements for an oath in Article 32 investigations and depositions.

An accused making an unsworn statement is not a "witness." *See* R.C.M. 1001(c)(2)(C).

---

(2) *Procedure for administering oaths.* Any procedure which appeals to the conscience of the person to whom the oath is administered and which binds that person to speak the truth, or, in the case of one other than a witness, properly to perform certain duties, is sufficient.

Discussion

When the oath is administered in a session to the military judge, members, or any counsel, all persons in the courtroom should stand. In those rare circumstances in which the trial counsel testifies as a witness, the military judge administers the oath.

Unless otherwise prescribed by the Secretary concerned the forms below may be used, as appropriate, to administer an oath.

(A) *Oath for military judge.* When the military judge is not previously sworn, the trial counsel will administer the following oath to the military judge:

"Do you (swear) (affirm) that you will faithfully and impartially perform, according to your conscience and the laws applicable to trial by court-martial, all the duties incumbent upon you as military judge of this court-martial (, so help you God)?"

(B) *Oath for members.* The following oath, as appropriate, will be administered to the members by the trial counsel:

"Do you (swear) (affirm) that you will answer truthfully the questions concerning whether you should serve as a member of this court-martial; that you will faithfully and impartially try, according to the evidence, your conscience, and the laws applicable to trial by court-martial, the case of the accused now before this court; and that you will not disclose or discover the vote or opinion of any particular member of the court (upon a challenge or) upon the findings or sentence unless required to do so in due course of law (, so help you God)?"

(C) *Oaths for counsel.* When counsel for either side, including any associate or assistant, is not previously sworn the following oath, as appropriate, will be administered by the military judge:

"Do you (swear) (affirm) that you will faithfully perform all the duties of (trial) (assistant trial) (defense)(associate defense) (assistant defense) counsel in the case now in hearing (, so help you God)?"

(D) *Oath for reporter.* The trial counsel will administer the following oath to every reporter of a court-martial who has not been previously sworn:

"Do you (swear) (affirm) that you will faithfully perform the duties of reporter to this court-martial (, so help you God)?"

(E) *Oath for interpreter.* The trial counsel or the summary court-martial shall administer the following oath to every interpreter in the trial of any case before a court-martial:

"Do you (swear) (affirm) that in the case now in hearing you will interpret truly the testimony you are called upon to interpret (, so help you God)?"

(F) *Oath for witnesses.* The trial counsel or the summary court-martial will administer the following oath to each witness before the witness first testifies in a case:

"Do you (swear) (affirm) that the evidence you shall give in the case now in hearing shall be the truth, the whole truth, and nothing but the truth (, so help you God)?"

(G) *Oath for escort.* The escort on views or inspections by the court-martial will, before serving, take the following oath, which will be administered by the trial counsel:

"Do you (swear) (affirm) that you will escort the court-martial and will well and truly point out to them (the place in which the offense charged in this case is alleged to have been committed) (__________); and that you will not speak to the members concerning (the alleged offense) (__________), except to describe (the place aforesaid) (__________) (, so help you God)?"

See Article 136 concerning persons authorized to administer oaths.

Rule 808. Record of trial

The trial counsel of a general or special court-martial shall take such action as may be necessary to ensure that a record which will meet the requirements of R.C.M. 1103 can be prepared.

Discussion

Except in a special court-martial not authorized to adjudge a bad-conduct discharge, confinement for more than six months, or forfeiture of pay for more than six months, the trial counsel should ensure that a qualified court reporter is detailed to the court-martial. Trial counsel should also ensure that all exhibits and other documents relating to the case are properly maintained for later inclusion in the record. *See also* R.C.M. 1103(j) as to the use of videotapes, audiotapes, and similar recordings for the record of trial. Because of the potential requirement for a verbatim transcript, all proceedings, including sidebar conferences, arguments, and rulings and instructions by the military judge, should be recorded.

Where there is recorder failure or loss of court reporter's notes, the record should be reconstructed as completely as possible. *See also* R.C.M. 1103(f). If the interruption is discovered during trial, the military judge should summarize or reconstruct the portion of the proceedings which has not been recorded and then proceed anew and repeat the proceedings from the point where the interruption began.

See R.C.M. 1305 concerning the record of trial in summary courts-martial.

See DD Forms 490 (Record of Trial), 491 (Summarized Record of Trial), and 491–1 (Summarized Record of Trial-Article 39(a) Session).

Rule 809. Contempt proceedings

(a) *In general.* Courts-martial may exercise contempt power under Article 48.

Discussion

Article 48 provides: "A court-martial, provost court, or military commission may punish for contempt any person who uses any menacing word, sign, or gesture in its presence, or who disturbs its proceedings by any riot or disorder. The punishment may not exceed confinement for 30 days or a fine of $100, or both."

Article 48 makes punishable "direct" contempt, that is, contempt which is committed in the presence of the court-martial or its immediate proximity. "Presence" includes those places outside the courtroom itself, such as waiting areas, deliberation room, and other places set aside for the use of the court-martial while it is in session. A "direct" contempt may be actually seen or heard by the court-martial, in which case it may be punished summarily. *See* subsection (b)(1) below. A "direct" contempt may also be a contempt not actually observed by the court-martial, for example, when an unseen person makes loud noises, whether inside or outside the courtroom, which impede the orderly progress of the proceedings. In such a case the procedures for punishing for contempt are more extensive. *See* subsection (b)(2) below.

The words "any person," as used in Article 48, include all persons, whether or not subject to military law, except the military judge, members, and foreign nationals outside the territorial limits of the United States who are not subject to the code.

Each contempt may be separately punished.

A person subject to the code who commits contempt may be tried by court-martial or otherwise disciplined for such misconduct in addition to or instead of punishment for contempt. The military judge may order the offender removed whether or not contempt proceedings are held. In some cases it may be appropriate to warn a person whose conduct is improper that persistence therein may result in removal or punishment for contempt. *See* R.C.M. 804, 806.

The military judge may issue orders when appropriate to ensure the orderly progress of the trial. Violation of such orders is not punishable under Article 48, but may be prosecuted as a violation of Article 90 or 92. *See also* Article 98.

Refusal to appear or to testify is not punishable under Article 48. Persons not subject to military law having been duly subpoenaed, may be prosecuted in Federal civilian court under Article 47 for neglect or refusal to appear or refusal to qualify as a witness or to testify or to produce evidence. Persons subject to the code may be punished under Article 134 for such offenses. *See* paragraph 108, Part IV.

A summary court-martial may punish for contempt.

(b) *Method of disposition.*

(1) *Summary disposition.* When conduct constituting contempt is directly witnessed by the court-martial, the conduct may be punished summarily.

(2) *Disposition upon notice and hearing.* When the conduct apparently constituting contempt is not directly witnessed by the court-martial, the alleged offender shall be brought before the court-martial and informed orally or in writing of the alleged contempt. The alleged offender shall be given a reasonable opportunity to present evidence, including calling witnesses. The alleged offender shall have the right to be represented by counsel and shall be so advised. The contempt must be proved beyond a reasonable doubt before it may be punished.

(c) *Procedure.* The military judge shall in all cases determine whether to punish for contempt and, if so, what the punishment shall be. The military judge shall also determine when during the court-martial the contempt proceedings shall be conducted; however, if the court-martial is composed of members, the military judge shall conduct the contempt proceedings outside the members' presence. The military judge may punish summarily under subsection (b)(1) only if the military judge recites the facts for the record and states that they were directly witnessed by the military judge in the actual presence of the court-martial. Otherwise, the provisions of subsection (b)(2) shall apply.

(d) *Record; review.* A record of the contempt proceedings shall be part of the record of the court-martial during which it occurred. If the person was held in contempt, then a separate record of the contempt proceedings shall be prepared and forwarded to the convening authority for review. The convening authority may approve or disapprove all or part of the sentence. The action of the convening authority is not subject to further review or appeal.

(e) *Sentence.* A sentence of confinement pursuant to a finding of contempt shall begin to run when it is adjudged unless deferred, suspended, or disapproved by the convening authority. The place of confinement for a civilian or military person who is held in contempt and is to be punished by confinement shall be designated by the convening authority. A fine does not become effective until ordered executed by the convening authority. The military judge may delay announcing the sentence after a finding of contempt to permit the person involved to continue to participate in the proceedings.

Discussion

The immediate commander of the person held in contempt, or, in the case of a civilian, the convening authority should be notified immediately so that the necessary action on the sentence may be taken. *See* R.C.M. 1101.

(f) *Informing person held in contempt.* The person held in contempt shall be informed by the convening authority in writing of the holding and sentence, if any, of the court-martial and of the action of the convening authority upon the sentence.

Discussion

Copies of this communication should be furnished to such other persons including the immediate commander of the offender as may be concerned with the execution of the punishment. A copy shall be included with the record of both the trial and the contempt proceeding.

Rule 810. Procedures for rehearings, new trials, and other trials

(a) *In general.*

(1) *Rehearings in full and new or other trials.* In rehearings which require findings on all charges and specifications referred to a court-martial and in new or other trials, the procedure shall be the same as in an original trial except as otherwise provided in this rule.

(2) *Rehearings on sentence only.* In a rehearing on sentence only, the procedure shall be the same as in an original trial, except that the portion of the procedure which ordinarily occurs after challenges and through and including the findings is omitted, and except as otherwise provided in this rule.

(A) *Contents of the record.* The contents of the record of the original trial consisting of evidence properly admitted on the merits relating to each offense of which the accused stands convicted but not sentenced may be established by any party whether or not testimony so read is otherwise admissible under Mil. R. Evid. 804(b)(1) and whether or not it was given through an interpreter.

Discussion

Matters excluded from the record of the original trial on the merits or improperly admitted on the merits must not be brought to the attention of the members as a part of the original record of trial.

(B) *Plea.* The accused at a rehearing only on sentence may not withdraw any plea of guilty upon which findings of guilty are based. However, if such a plea is found to be improvident, the rehearing shall be suspended and the matter reported to the authority ordering the rehearing.

(3) *Combined rehearings.* When a rehearing on sentence is combined with a trial on the merits of one or more specifications referred to the court-martial, whether or not such specifications are being tried for the first time or reheard, the trial will proceed first on the merits, without reference to the offenses being reheard on sentence only. After findings on the merits are announced, the members, if any, shall be advised of the offenses on which the

rehearing on sentence has been directed. Additional challenges for cause may be permitted, and the sentencing procedure shall be the same as at an original trial, except as otherwise provided in this rule. A single sentence shall be adjudged for all offenses.

(b) *Composition.*

(1) *Members.* No member of the court-martial which previously heard the case may sit as a member of the court-martial at any rehearing, new trial, or other trial of the same case.

(2) *Military judge.* The military judge at a rehearing may be the same military judge who presided over a previous trial of the same case. The existence or absence of a request for trial by military judge alone at a previous hearing shall have no effect on the composition of a court-martial on rehearing.

(3) *Accused's election.* The accused at a rehearing or new or other trial shall have the same right to request enlisted members or trial by military judge alone as the accused would have at an original trial.

Discussion

See R.C.M. 902; 903.

(c) *Examination of record of former proceedings.* No member may, upon a rehearing or upon a new or other trial, examine the record of any former proceedings in the same case except:

(1) When permitted to do so by the military judge after such matters have been received in evidence; or

(2) That the president of a special court-martial without a military judge may examine that part of the record of former proceedings which relates to errors committed at the former proceedings when necessary to decide the admissibility of offered evidence or other questions of law, and such a part of the record may be read to the members when necessary for them to consider a matter subject to objection by any member.

Discussion

See R.C.M. 801(e)(2).

When a rehearing is ordered, the trial counsel should be provided a record of the former proceedings, accompanying documents, and any decision or review relating to the case, as well as a statement of the reason for the rehearing.

(d) *Sentence limitations.*

(1) *In general.* Sentences at rehearings, new trials, or other trials shall be adjudged within the limitations set forth in R.C.M. 1003. Except as otherwise provided in subsection (d)(2) of this rule, offenses on which a rehearing, new trial, or other trial has been ordered shall not be the basis for an approved sentence in excess of or more severe than the sentence ultimately approved by the convening or higher authority following the previous trial or hearing, unless the sentence prescribed for the offense is mandatory. When a rehearing or sentencing is combined with trial on new charges, the maximum punishment that may be approved by the convening authority shall be the maximum punishment under R.C.M. 1003 for the offenses being reheard as limited above, plus the total maximum punishment under R.C.M. 1003 for any new charges of which the accused has been found guilty. In the case of an "other trial" no sentence limitations apply if the original trial was invalid because a summary or special court-martial improperly tried an offense involving a mandatory punishment or one otherwise considered capital.

Discussion

At a rehearing, the trier of fact is not bound by the sentence previously adjudged or approved. The members should not be advised of the sentence limitation under this rule. See R.C.M. 1005(e)(1). An appropriate sentence on a retried or reheard offense should be adjudged without regard to any credit to which the accused may be entitled. See R.C.M. 103(2) and R.C.M. 103(3) as to when a rehearing may be a capital case.

---

(2) *Pretrial agreement.* If, after the earlier court-martial, the sentence was approved in accordance with a pretrial agreement and at the rehearing the accused fails to comply with the pretrial agreement, by failing to enter a plea of guilty or otherwise, the approved sentence resulting at a rehearing of the affected charges and specifications may include any otherwise lawful punishment not in excess of or more serious than lawfully adjudged at the earlier court-martial.

(e) *Definition.* "Other trial" means another trial of a case in which the original proceedings were declared invalid because of lack of jurisdiction or failure of a charge to state an offense.

Rule 811. Stipulations

(a) *In general.* The parties may make an oral or written stipulation to any fact, the contents of a document, or the expected testimony of a witness.

(b) *Authority to reject.* The military judge may, in the interest of justice, decline to accept a stipulation.

Discussion

Although the decision to stipulate should ordinarily be left to the parties, the military judge should not accept a stipulation if there is any doubt of the accused's or any other party's understanding of the nature and effect of the stipulation. The military judge should also refuse to accept a stipulation which is unclear or ambiguous. A stipulation of fact which amounts to a complete defense to any offense charged should not be accepted nor, if a plea of not guilty is outstanding, should one which practically amounts to a confession, except as described in the discussion under subsection (c) of this rule. If a stipulation is rejected, the parties may be entitled to a continuance.

(c) *Requirements.* Before accepting a stipulation in evidence, the military judge must be satisfied that the parties consent to its admission.

Discussion

Ordinarily, before accepting any stipulation the military judge should inquire to ensure that the accused understands the right not to stipulate, understands the stipulation, and consents to it.

If the stipulation practically amounts to a confession to an offense to which a not guilty plea is outstanding, it may not be accepted unless the military judge ascertains: (A) from the accused that the accused understands the right not to stipulate and that the stipulation will not be accepted without the accused's consent; that the accused understands the contents and effect of the stipulation; that a factual basis exists for the stipulation; and that the accused, after consulting with counsel, consents to the stipulation; and (B) from the accused and counsel for each party whether there are any agreements between the parties in connection with the stipulation, and, if so, what the terms of such agreements are.

A stipulation practically amounts to a confession when it is the equivalent of a guilty plea, that is, when it establishes, directly or by reasonable inference, every element of a charged offense and when the defense does not present evidence to contest any potential remaining issue of the merits. Thus, a stipulation which tends to establish, by reasonable inference, every element of a charged offense does not practically amount to a confession if the defense contests an issue going to guilt which is not foreclosed by the stipulation. For example, a stipulation of fact that contraband drugs were discovered in a vehicle owned by the accused would normally practically amount to a confession if no other evidence were presented on the issue, but would not if the defense presented evidence to show that the accused was unaware of the presence of the drugs. Whenever a stipulation establishes the elements of a charged offense, the military judge should conduct an inquiry as described above.

If, during an inquiry into a confessional stipulation the military judge discovers that there is a pretrial agreement, the military judge must conduct an inquiry into the pretrial agreement. *See* R.C.M. 910(f). *See also* R.C.M. 705.

(d) *Withdrawal.* A party may withdraw from an agreement to stipulate or from a stipulation at any time before a stipulation is accepted; the stipulation may not then be accepted. After a stipulation has been accepted a party may withdraw from it only if permitted to do so in the discretion of the military judge.

Discussion

If a party withdraws from an agreement to stipulate or from a stipulation, before or after it has been accepted, the opposing party may be entitled to a continuance to obtain proof of the matters which were to have been stipulated.

If a party is permitted to withdraw from a stipulation previously accepted, the stipulation must be disregarded by the court-martial, and an instruction to that effect should be given.

(e) *Effect of stipulation.* Unless properly withdrawn or ordered stricken from the record, a stipulation of fact that has been accepted is binding on the court-martial and may not be contradicted by the parties thereto. The contends of a stipulation of expected testimony or of a document's contents may be attacked, contradicted, or explained in the same way as if the witness had actually so testified or the document had been actually admitted. The fact that the parties so stipulated does not admit the truth of the indicated testimony or document's contents, nor does it add anything to the evidentiary nature of the testimony or document. The Military Rules of Evidence apply to the contents of stipulations.

(f) *Procedure.* When offered, a written stipulation shall be presented to the military judge and shall be included in the record whether accepted or not. Once accepted, a written stipulation of expected testimony shall be read to the members, if any, but shall not be presented to them; a written stipulation of fact or of a document's contents may be read to the members, if any, presented to them, or both. Once accepted, an oral stipulation shall be announced to the members, if any.

Rule 812. Joint and common trials

In joint trials and in common trials, each accused shall be accorded the rights and privileges as if tried separately.

Discussion

See R.C.M. 307(c)(5) concerning preparing charges and specifications for joint trials. *See* R.C.M. 601(e)(3) concerning referral of charges for joint or common trials, and the distinction between the two. *See* R.C.M. 906(b)(9) concerning motions to sever and other appropriate motions in joint or common trials.

In a joint or common trial, each accused may be represented by separate counsel, make challenges for cause, make peremptory challenges (*see* R.C.M. 912), cross-examine witnesses, elect whether to testify, introduce evidence, request that the membership of the court include enlisted persons, if an enlisted accused, and, if a military judge has been detailed, request trial by military judge alone.

Where different elections are made (and, when necessary, approved) as to court-martial composition a severance is necessary. Thus, if one co-accused elects to be tried by a court-martial composed of officers, and a second requests that enlisted members be detailed to the court, and a third submits a request for trial by military judge alone, which request is approved, three separate trials must be conducted.

In a joint or common trial, evidence which is admissible against only one or some of the joint or several accused may be considered only against the accused concerned. For example, when a stipulation is accepted which was made by only one or some of the accused, the stipulation does not apply to those accused who did not join it. *See also* Mil. R. Evid. 306. In such instances the members must be instructed that the stipulation or evidence may be considered only with respect to the accused with respect to whom it is accepted.

Rule 813. Announcing personnel of the court-martial and accused

(a) *Opening sessions.* When the court-martial is called to order for the first time in a case, the military judge shall ensure that the following is announced:

(1) The order, including any amendment, by which the court-martial is convened;

(2) The name, rank, and unit or address of the accused;

(3) The name and rank of the military judge, if one has been detailed;

(4) The names and ranks of the members, if any, who are present;

(5) The names and ranks of members who are absent, if presence of members is required;

(6) The names and ranks (if any) of counsel who are present;

(7) The names and ranks (if any) of counsel who are absent; and

(8) The name and rank (if any) of any detailed court reporter.

(b) *Later proceedings.* When the court-martial is called to order after a recess or adjournment or after it has been closed for any reason, the military judge shall ensure that the record reflects whether all parties and members who were present at the time of the adjournment or recess, or at the time the court-martial closed, are present.

(c) *Additions, replacement, and absences of personnel.* Whenever there is a replacement of the military judge, any member, or counsel, either through the appearance of new personnel or personnel previously absent or through the absence of personnel previously present, the military judge shall ensure the record reflects the change and the reason for it.

CHAPTER IX. TRIAL PROCEDURES THROUGH FINDINGS

Rule 901. Opening session

(a) *Call to order.* A court-martial is in session when the military judge so declares.

Discussion

The military judge should examine the charge sheet, convening order, and any amending orders before calling the initial session to order.

Article 35 provides that in time of peace, no proceedings, including Article 39(a) sessions, may be conducted over the accused's objection until five days have elapsed from the service of charges on the accused in the case of a general court-martial. The period is three days for a special court-martial. In computing these periods, the date of service and the date of the proceedings are excluded. Holidays and Sundays are not excluded. Failure to object waives the right to the waiting period, but if it appears that the waiting period has not elapsed, the military judge should bring this to the attention of the defense and secure an affirmative waiver on the record.

(b) *Announcement of parties.* After the court-martial is called to order, the presence or absence of the parties, military judge, and members shall be announced.

Discussion

If the orders detailing the military judge and counsel have not been reduced to writing, an oral announcement of such detailing is required. *See* R.C.M. 503(b) and (c).

(c) *Swearing reporter and interpreter.* After the personnel have been accounted for as required in subsection (b) of this rule, the trial counsel shall announce whether the reporter and interpreter, if any is present, have been properly sworn. If not sworn, the reporter and interpreter, if any, shall be sworn.

Discussion

See R.C.M. 807 concerning the oath to be administered to a court reporter or interpreter. If a reporter or interpreter is replaced at any time during trial, this should be noted for the record, and the procedures in this subsection should be repeated.

(d) *Counsel.*

(1) *Trial counsel.* The trial counsel shall announce the legal qualifications and status as to oaths of the members of the prosecution and whether any member of the prosecution has acted in any manner which might tend to disqualify that counsel.

(2) *Defense counsel.* The detailed defense counsel shall announce the legal qualifications and status as to oaths of the detailed members of the defense and whether any member of the defense has acted in any manner which might tend to disqualify that counsel. Any defense counsel not detailed shall state that counsel's legal qualifications, and whether that counsel has acted in any manner which might tend to disqualify the counsel.

(3) *Disqualification.* If it appears that any counsel may be disqualified, the military judge shall decide the matter and take appropriate action.

Discussion

Counsel may be disqualified because of lack of necessary qualifications, or because of duties or actions which are inconsistent with the role of counsel. *See* R.C.M. 502(d) concerning qualifications of counsel.

If it appears that any counsel may be disqualified, the military judge should conduct an inquiry or hearing. If any detailed counsel is disqualified, the appropriate authority should be informed. If any defense counsel is disqualified, the accused should be so informed.

If the disqualification of trial or defense counsel is one which the accused may waive, the accused should be so informed by the military judge, and given the opportunity to decide whether to waive the disqualification. In the case of defense counsel, if the disqualification is not waivable or if the accused elects not to waive the disqualification, the accused should be informed of the choices available and given the opportunity to exercise such options.

If any counsel is disqualified, the military judge should ensure that the accused is not prejudiced by any actions of the disqualified counsel or any break in representation of the accused.

Disqualification of counsel is not a jurisdictional defect; such error must be tested for prejudice.

If the membership of the prosecution or defense changes at any time during the proceedings, the procedures in this subsection should be repeated as to the new counsel. In addition, the military judge should ascertain on the record whether the accused objects to a change of defense counsel. *See* R.C.M. 505(d)(2) and 506(c).

---

(4) *Inquiry.* The military judge shall, in open session:

(A) Inform the accused of the rights to be represented by military counsel detailed to the defense; or by individual military counsel requested by the accused, if such military counsel is reasonably available; and by civilian counsel, either alone or in association with military counsel, if such civilian counsel is provided at no expense to the United States;

(B) Inform the accused that, if afforded individual military counsel, the accused may request retention of detailed counsel as associate counsel, which request may be granted or denied in the sole discretion of the authority who detailed the counsel;

(C) Ascertain from the accused whether the accused understands these rights;

(D) Promptly inquire, whenever two or more accused in a joint or common trial are represented by the same detailed or individual military or civilian counsel, or by civilian counsel who are associated in the practice of law, with respect to such joint representation and shall personally advise each accused of the right to effective assistance of counsel, including separate representation. Unless it appears that there is good cause to believe no conflict of interest is likely to arise, the military judge shall take appropriate measures to protect each accused's right to counsel; and

Discussion

Whenever it appears that any defense counsel may face a conflict of interest, the military judge should inquire into the matter, advise the accused of the right to effective assistance of counsel, and ascertain the accused's choice of counsel. When defense counsel is aware of a potential conflict of interest, counsel should discuss the matter with the accused. If the accused elects to waive such conflict, counsel should inform the military judge of the matter at an Article 39(a) session so that an appropriate record can be made.

(E) Ascertain from the accused by whom the accused chooses to be represented.

(5) *Unsworn counsel.* The military judge shall administer the oath to any counsel not sworn.

Discussion

See R.C.M. 807.

(e) *Presence of members.* In cases in which a military judge has been detailed, the procedures described in R.C.M. 901 through 903, 904 when authorized by the Secretary concerned, and 905 through 910 shall be conducted without members present in accordance with R.C.M. 803.

Rule 902. Disqualification of military judge

(a) *In general.* Except as provided in subsection (e) of this rule, a military judge shall disqualify himself or herself in any proceeding in which that military judge's impartiality might reasonably be questioned.

(b) *Specific grounds.* A military judge shall also disqualify himself or herself in the following circumstances:

(1) Where the military judge has a personal bias or prejudice concerning a party or personal knowledge of disputed evidentiary facts concerning the proceeding.

(2) Where the military judge has acted as counsel, investigating officer, legal officer, staff judge advocate, or convening authority as to any offense charged or in the same case generally.

(3) Where the military judge has been or will be a witness in the same case, is the accuser, has forwarded charges in the case with a personal recommendation as to disposition, or, except in the performance of duties as military judge in a previous trial of the same or a related case, has expressed an opinion concerning the guilt or innocence of the accused.

(4) Where the military judge is not eligible to act because the military judge is not qualified under R.C.M. 502(c) or not detailed under R.C.M. 503(b).

(5) Where the military judge, the military judge's spouse, or a person within the third degree of relationship to either of them or a spouse of such person:

(A) Is a party to the proceeding;

(B) Is known by the military judge to have an interest, financial or otherwise, that could be substantially affected by the outcome of the proceeding; or

(C) Is to the military judge's knowledge likely to be a material witness in the proceeding.

Discussion

A military judge should inform himself or herself about his or her financial interests, and make a reasonable effort to inform himself or herself about the financial interests of his or her spouse and minor children living in his or her household.

(c) *Definitions.* For the purposes of this rule the following words or phrases shall have the meaning indicated—

(1) "Proceeding" includes pretrial, trial, post-trial, appellate review, or other stages of litigation.

(2) The "degree of relationship" is calculated according to the civil law system.

Discussion

Relatives within the third degree of relationship are children, grandchildren, great grandchildren, parents, grandparents, great grandparents, brothers, sisters, uncles, aunts, nephews, and nieces.

---

(3) "Military judge" does not include the president of a special court-martial without a military judge.

(d) *Procedure.*

(1) The military judge shall, upon motion of any party or *sua sponte*, decide whether the military judge is disqualified.

Discussion

There is no peremptory challenge against a military judge. A military judge should carefully consider whether any of the grounds for disqualification in this rule exist in each case. The military judge should broadly construe grounds for challenge but should not step down from a case unnecessarily.

Possible grounds for disqualification should be raised at the earliest reasonable opportunity. They may be raised at any time, and an earlier adverse ruling does not bar later consideration of the same issue, as, for example, when additional evidence is discovered.

---

(2) Each party shall be permitted to question the military judge and to present evidence regarding a possible ground for disqualification before the military judge decides the matter.

Discussion

Nothing in this rule prohibits the military judge from reasonably limiting the presentation of evidence, the scope of questioning, and argument on the subject so as to ensure that only matters material to the central issue of the military judge's possible disqualification are considered, thereby, preventing the proceedings from becoming a forum for unfounded opinion, speculation or innuendo.

---

(3) Except as provided under subsection (e) of this rule, if the military judge rules that the military judge is disqualified, the military judge shall recuse himself or herself.

(e) *Waiver.* No military judge shall accept from the parties to the proceeding a waiver of any ground for disqualification enumerated in subsection (b) of this rule. Where the ground for disqualification arises only under subsection (a) of this rule, waiver may be accepted provided it is preceded by a full disclosure on the record of the basis for disqualification.

Rule 903. Accused's elections on composition of court-martial

(a) *Time of elections.*

(1) *Request for enlisted members.* Before the end of the initial Article 39(a) session or, in the absence of such a session, before assembly, the military judge shall ascertain, as applicable, whether an enlisted accused elects to be tried by a court-martial including enlisted members. The military judge may, as a matter of discretion, permit the accused to defer requesting enlisted members until any time before assembly, which time may be determined by the military judge.

(2) *Request for trial by military judge alone.* Before the end of the initial Article 39(a) session, or, in the absence of such a session, before assembly, the military judge shall ascertain, as applicable, whether in a noncapital case, the accused requests trial by the military judge alone. The accused may defer requesting trial by military judge alone until any time before assembly.

Discussion

Only an enlisted accused may request that enlisted members be detailed to a court-martial. Trial by military judge alone is not permitted in capital cases (*see* R.C.M. 201(f)(1)(C)) or in special courts-martial in which no military judge has been detailed.

(b) *Form of election.*

(1) *Request for enlisted members.* A request for the membership of the court-martial to include enlisted persons shall be in writing and signed by the accused or shall be made orally on the record.

(2) *Request for trial by military judge alone.* A request for trial by military judge alone shall be in writing and signed by the accused or shall be made orally on the record.

(c) *Action on election.*

(1) *Request for enlisted members.* Upon notice of a timely request for enlisted members by an enlisted accused, the convening authority shall detail enlisted members to the court-martial in accordance with R.C.M. 503 or prepare a detailed written statement explaining why physical conditions or military exi-

gencies prevented this. The trial of the general issue shall not proceed until this is done.

(2) *Request for military judge alone.* Upon receipt of a timely request for trial by military judge alone the military judge shall:

(A) Ascertain whether the accused has consulted with defense counsel and has been informed of the identity of the military judge and of the right to trial by members; and

Discussion

Ordinarily the military judge should inquire personally of the accused to ensure that the accused's waiver of the right to trial by members is knowing and understanding. Failure to do so is not error, however, where such knowledge and understanding otherwise appear on the record.

DD Form 1722 (Request for Trial Before Military Judge Alone (Art.16, UCMJ)) should normally be used for the purpose of requesting trial by military judge alone under this rule, if a written request is used.

(B) Approve or disapprove the request, in the military judge's discretion.

Discussion

A timely request for trial by military judge alone should be granted unless there is substantial reason why, in the interest of justice, the military judge should not sit as factfinder. The military judge may hear arguments from counsel before acting on the request. The basis for denial of a request must be made a matter of record.

---

(3) *Other.* In the absence of a request for enlisted members or a request for trial by military judge alone, trial shall be by a court-martial composed of officers.

Discussion

Ordinarily if no request for enlisted members or trial by military judge alone is submitted, the military judge should inquire whether such a request will be made (*see* subsection (a)(1) of this rule) unless these elections are not available to the accused.

(d) *Right to withdraw request.*

(1) *Enlisted members.* A request for enlisted members may be withdrawn by the accused as a matter of right any time before the end of the initial Article 39(a) session, or, in the absence of such a session, before assembly.

(2) *Military judge.* A request for trial by military judge alone may be withdrawn by the accused as a matter of right any time before it is approved, or even after approval, if there is a change of the military judge.

Discussion

Withdrawal of a request for enlisted members or trial by military judge alone should be shown in the record.

(e) *Untimely requests.* Failure to request, or failure to withdraw a request for enlisted members or trial by military judge alone in a timely manner shall waive the right to submit or to withdraw such a request. However, the military judge may until the beginning of the introduction of evidence on the merits, as a matter of discretion, approve an untimely request or withdrawal of a request.

Discussion

In exercising discretion whether to approve an untimely request or withdrawal of a request, the military judge should balance the reason for the request (for example, whether it is a mere change of tactics or results from a substantial change of circumstances) against any expense, delay, or inconvenience which would result from granting the request.

(f) *Scope.* For purposes of this rule, "military judge" does not include the president of a special court-martial without a military judge.

Rule 904. Arraignment

Arraignment shall be conducted in a court-martial session and shall consist of reading the charges and specifications to the accused and calling on the accused to plead. The accused may waive the reading.

Discussion

Arraignment is complete when the accused is called upon to plead; the entry of pleas is not part of the arraignment.

When authorized by regulations of the Secretary concerned, the arraignment should be conducted at an Article 39(a) session when a military judge has been detailed. The accused may not be arraigned at a conference under R.C.M. 802.

Once the accused has been arraigned, no additional charges against that accused may be referred to that court-martial for trial with the previously referred charges. *See* R.C.M. 601(e)(2).

The defense should be asked whether it has any motions to make before pleas are entered. Some motions ordinarily must be made before a plea is entered. *See* R.C.M. 905(b).

Rule 905. Motions generally

(a) *Definitions and form.* A motion is an application to the military judge for particular relief. Motions may be oral or, at the discretion of the military judge, written. A motion shall state the grounds upon which it is made and shall set forth the ruling or relief sought. The substance of a motion, not its form or designation, shall control.

Discussion

Motions may be motions to suppress [(*see* R.C.M. 905(b)(3))]; motions for appropriate relief (*see* R.C.M. 906); motions to dismiss (*see* R.C.M. 907); or motions for findings of not guilty (*see* R.C.M. 917).

(b) *Pretrial motions.* Any defense, objection, or request which is capable of determination without the trial of the general issue of guilt may be raised before trial. The following must be raised before a plea is entered:

(1) Defenses or objections based on defects (other than jurisdictional defects) in the preferral, forwarding, investigation, or referral of charges;

Discussion

Such nonjurisdictional defects include unsworn charges, inadequate Article 32 investigation, and inadequate pretrial advice. *See* R.C.M. 307; 401–407; 601–604.

---

(2) Defenses or objections based on defects in the charges and specifications (other than any failure to show jurisdiction or to charge an offense, which objections shall be resolved by the military judge at any time during the pendency of the proceedings);

Discussion

See R.C.M. 307; 906(b)(3).

---

(3) Motions to suppress evidence;

Discussion

Mil. R. Evid. 304(d), 311(d), and 321(c) deal with the admissibility of confessions and admissions, evidence obtained from unlawful searches and seizures, and eyewitness identification, respectively. Questions concerning the admissibility of evidence on other grounds may be raised by objection at trial or by motions *in limine*. *See* R.C.M. 906(b)(13); Mil. R. Evid. 103(c); 104(a) and (c).

---

(4) Motions for discovery under R.C.M. 701 or for production of witnesses or evidence;

Discussion

See also R.C.M. 703; 1001(e).

---

(5) Motions for severance of charges or accused; or

Discussion

See R.C.M. 812; 906(b)(9) and (10).

---

(6) Objections based on denial of request for individual military counsel or for retention of detailed defense counsel when individual military counsel has been granted.

Discussion

See R.C.M. 506(b); 906(b)(2).

(c) *Burden of proof.*

(1) *Standard.* Unless otherwise provided in this Manual, the burden of proof on any factual issue the resolution of which is necessary to decide a motion shall be by a preponderance of the evidence.

Discussion

See Mil. R. Evid. 104(a) concerning the applicability of the Military Rules of Evidence to certain preliminary questions.

---

(2) *Assignment.*

(A) Except as otherwise provided in this Manual the burden of persuasion on any factual issue the resolution of which is necessary to decide a motion shall be on the moving party.

Discussion

See, for example, subsection (c)(2)(B) of this rule, R.C.M. 908 and Mil. R. Evid. 304(e), 311(e), and 321(d) for provisions specifically assigning the burden of proof.

(B) In the case of a motion to dismiss for lack of jurisdiction, denial of the right to speedy trial under R.C.M. 707, or the running of the statute of limitations, the burden of persuasion shall be upon the prosecution.

(d) *Ruling on motions.* A motion made before pleas are entered shall be determined before pleas are entered unless, if otherwise not prohibited by this Manual, the military judge for good cause orders that determination be deferred until trial of the general issue or after findings, but no such determination shall be deferred if a party's right to review or appeal is adversely affected. Where factual issues are involved in determining a motion, the military judge shall state the essential findings on the record.

Discussion

When trial cannot proceed further as the result of dismissal or other rulings on motions, the court-martial should adjourn and a record of the proceedings should be prepared for the convening authority. *See* R.C.M. 908(b)(4) regarding automatic stay of certain rulings and orders subject to appeal under that rule. Notwithstanding the dismissal of some specifications, trial may proceed in the normal manner as long as one or more charges and specifications remain. The promulgating orders should reflect the action taken by the court-martial on each charge and specification, including any which were dismissed by the military judge on a motion. *See* R.C.M. 1114.

(e) *Effect of failure to raise defenses or objections.* Failure by a party to raise defenses or objections or to make motions or requests which must be made before pleas are entered under subsection (b) of this rule shall constitute waiver. The military judge for good cause shown may grant relief from the waiver. Other motions, requests, defenses, or objections, except lack of jurisdiction or failure of a charge to allege an offense, must be raised before the court-martial is adjourned for that case and, unless otherwise provided in this Manual, failure to do so shall constitute waiver.

Discussion

See also R.C.M. 910(j) concerning matters waived by a plea of guilty.

(f) *Reconsideration.* On request of any party or *sua sponte*, the military judge may, prior to authentication of the record of trial, reconsider any ruling, other than one amounting to a finding of not guilty, made by the military judge.

Discussion

Subsection (f) permits the military judge to reconsider any ruling that affects the legal sufficiency of any finding of guilt or the sentence. *See* R.C.M. 917(d) for the standard to be used to determine the legal sufficiency of evidence. *See also* R.C.M. 1102 concerning procedures for post-trial reconsideration. Different standards may apply depending on the nature of the ruling. *See United States v. Scaff*, 29 M.J. 60 (C.M.A. 1989).

(g) *Effect of final determinations.* Any matter put in issue and finally determined by a court-martial, reviewing authority, or appellate court which had jurisdiction to determine the matter may not be disputed by the United States in any other court-martial of the same accused, except that, when the offenses charged at one court-martial did not arise out of the same transaction as those charged at the court-martial at which the determination was made, a determination of law and the application of law to the facts may be disputed by the United States. This rule also shall apply to matters which were put in issue and finally determined in any other judicial proceeding in which the accused and the United States or a Federal governmental unit were parties.

Discussion

See also R.C.M. 907(b)(2)(C). Whether a matter has been finally determined in another judicial proceeding with jurisdiction to decide it, and whether such determination binds the United States in another proceeding are interlocutory questions. *See* R.C.M. 801(e). It does not matter whether the earlier proceeding ended in an acquittal, conviction, or otherwise, as long as the determination is final. Except for a ruling which is, or amounts to, a finding of not guilty, a ruling ordinarily is not final until action on the court-martial is completed. *See* Article 76; R.C.M. 1209. The accused is not bound in a court-martial by rulings in another court-martial. *But see* Article 3(b); R.C.M. 202.

The determination must have been made by a court-martial, reviewing authority, or appellate court, or by another judicial body, such as a United States court. A pretrial determination by a convening authority is not a final determination under this rule, although some decisions by a convening authority may bind the Government under other rules. *See*, for example, R.C.M. 601, 604, 704, 705.

The United States is bound by a final determination by a court of competent jurisdiction even if the earlier determination is erroneous, except when the offenses charged at the second proceeding arose out of a different transaction from those charged at the first and the ruling at the first proceeding was based on an incorrect determination of law.

A final determination in one case may be the basis for a motion to dismiss or a motion for appropriate relief in another case, depending on the circumstances. The nature of the earlier determination and the grounds for it will determine its effect in other proceedings.

Examples:

(1) The military judge dismissed a charge for lack of personal jurisdiction, on grounds that the accused was only 16 years old at the time of enlistment and when the offenses occurred. At a second court-martial of the same accused for a different offense, the determination in the first case would require dismissal of the new charge unless the prosecution could show that since that determination the accused had effected a valid enlistment or constructive enlistment. *See* R.C.M. 202. Note, however, that if the initial ruling had been based on an error of law (for example, if the military judge had ruled the enlistment invalid because the accused was 18 at the time of enlistment) this would not require dismissal in the second court-martial for a different offense.

(2) The accused was tried in United States district court for assault on a Federal officer. The accused defended solely on the basis of alibi and was acquitted. The accused is then charged in a court-martial with assault on a different person at the same time and place as the assault on a Federal officer was alleged to have occurred. The acquittal of the accused in Federal district court would bar conviction of the accused in the court-martial. In cases of this nature, the facts of the first trial must be examined to determine whether the finding of the first trial is logically inconsistent with guilt in the second case.

(3) At a court-martial for larceny, the military judge excluded evidence of a statement made by the accused relating to the larceny and other uncharged offenses because the statement was obtained by coercion. At a second court-martial for an unrelated offense, the statement excluded at the first trial would be inadmissible, based on the earlier ruling, if the first case had become final. If the earlier ruling had been based on an incorrect interpretation of law, however, the issue of admissibility could be litigated anew at the second proceeding.

(4) At a court-martial for absence without authority, the charge and specification were dismissed for failure to state an offense. At a later court-martial for the same offense, the earlier dismissal would be grounds for dismissing the same charge and specification, but would not bar further proceedings on a new specification not containing the same defect as the original specification.

(h) *Written motions.* Written motions may be submitted to the military judge after referral and when appropriate they may be supported by affidavits, with service and opportunity to reply to the opposing party. Such motions may be disposed of before arraignment and without a session. Upon request, either party is entitled to an Article 39(a) session to present oral argument or have an evidentiary hearing concerning the disposition of written motions.

(i) *Service.* Written motions shall be served on all other parties. Unless otherwise directed by the military judge, the service shall be made upon counsel for each party.

(j) *Application to convening authority.* Except as otherwise provided in this Manual, any matters which may be resolved upon motion without trial of the general issue of guilt may be submitted by a party to the convening authority before trial for decision. Submission of such matter to the convening authority is not, except as otherwise provided in this Manual, required, and is, in any event, without prejudice to the renewal of the issue by timely motion before the military judge.

(k) *Production of statements on motion to suppress.* Except as provided in this subsection, R.C.M. 914 shall apply at a hearing on a motion to suppress evidence under subsection (b)(3) of this rule. For purposes of this subsection, a law enforcement officer shall be deemed a witness called by the Government, and upon a claim of privilege the military judge shall excise portions of the statement containing privileged matter.

Rule 906. Motions for appropriate relief

(a) *In general.* A motion for appropriate relief is a request for a ruling to cure a defect which deprives a party of a right or hinders a party from preparing for trial or presenting its case.

(b) *Grounds for appropriate relief.* The following may be requested by motion for appropriate relief. This list is not exclusive.

(1) *Continuances.* A continuance may be granted only by the military judge.

Discussion

The military judge should, upon a showing of reasonable cause, grant a continuance to any party for as long and as often as is just. Article 40. Whether a request for a continuance should be granted is a matter within the discretion of the military judge. Reasons for a continuance may include: insufficient opportunity to prepare for trial; unavailability of an essential witness; the interest of Government in the order of trial of related cases; and illness of an accused, counsel, military judge, or member. *See also* R.C.M. 602; 803.

---

(2) Record of denial of individual military counsel or of denial of request to retain detailed counsel when a request for individual military counsel was granted. If a request for military counsel was denied, which denial was upheld on appeal (if available) or if a request to retain detailed counsel was denied when the accused is represented by individual military counsel, and if the accused so requests, the military judge shall ensure that a record of the mat-

ter is included in the record of trial, and may make findings. The trial counsel may request a continuance to inform the convening authority of those findings. The military judge may not dismiss the charges or otherwise effectively prevent further proceedings based on this issue. However, the military judge may grant reasonable continuances until the requested military counsel can be made available if the unavailability results from temporary conditions or if the decision of unavailability is in the process of review in administrative channels.

(3) Correction of defects in the Article 32 investigation or pretrial advice.

Discussion

See R.C.M. 405; 406. If the motion is granted, the military judge should ordinarily grant a continuance so the defect may be corrected.

---

(4) *Amendment of charges or specifications.* A charge or specifications. A charge or specification may not be amended over the accused's objection unless the amendment is minor within the meaning of R.C.M. 603(a).

Discussion

See also R.C.M. 307.

An amendment may be appropriate when a specification is unclear, redundant, inartfully drafted, misnames an accused, or is laid under the wrong article. A specification may be amended by striking surplusage, or substituting or adding new language. Surplusage may include irrelevant or redundant details or aggravating circumstances which are not necessary to enhance the maximum authorized punishment or to explain the essential facts of the offense. When a specification is amended after the accused has entered a plea to it, the accused should be asked to plead anew to the amended specification. A bill of particulars (*see* subsection (b)(6) of this rule) may also be used when a specification is indefinite or ambiguous.

If a specification, although stating an offense, is so defective that the accused appears to have been misled, the accused should be given a continuance upon request, or, in an appropriate case (*see* R.C.M. 907(b)(3)), the specification may be dismissed.

---

(5) Severance of a duplicitous specification into two or more specifications.

Discussion

Each specification may state only one offense. R.C.M. 307(c)(4). A duplicitous specification is one which alleges two or more separate offenses. Lesser included offenses (*see* Part IV, paragraph 2) are not separate, nor is a continuing offense involving several separate acts. The sole remedy for a duplicitous specification is severance of the specification into two or more specifications, each of which alleges a separate offense contained in the duplicitous specification. However, if the duplicitousness is combined with or results in other defects, such as misleading the accused, other remedies may be appropriate. *See* subsection (b)(3) of this rule. *See also* R.C.M. 907(B)(3).

---

(6) *Bill of particulars.* A bill of particulars may be amended at any time, subject to such conditions as justice permits.

Discussion

The purposes of a bill of particulars are to inform the accused of the nature of the charge with sufficient precision to enable the accused to prepare for trial, to avoid or minimize the danger of surprise at the time of trial, and to enable the accused to plead the acquittal or conviction in bar of another prosecution for the same offense when the specification itself is too vague and indefinite for such purposes.

A bill of particulars should not be used to conduct discovery of the Government's theory of a case, to force detailed disclosure of acts underlying a charge, or to restrict the Government's proof at trial.

A bill of particulars need not be sworn because it is not part of the specification. A bill of particulars cannot be used to repair a specification which is otherwise not legally sufficient.

---

(7) Discovery and production of evidence and witnesses.

Discussion

See R.C.M. 701 concerning discovery. *See* R.C.M. 703, 914 and 1001(e) concerning production of evidence and witnesses.

---

(8) Relief from pretrial confinement in violation of R.C.M. 305.

Discussion

See R.C.M. 305(j).

---

(9) Severance of multiple accused, if it appears that an accused or the Government is prejudiced by a joint or common trial. In a common trial, a severance shall be granted whenever any accused, other than the moving accused, faces charges unrelated to those charged against the moving accused.

Discussion

A motion for severance is a request that one or more accused against whom charges have been referred to a joint or common trial be tried separately. Such a request should be liberally considered in a common trial, and should be granted if good cause is shown. For example, a severance is ordinarily appropriate when: the moving party wishes to use the testimony of one or more of the coaccused or the spouse of a coaccused; a defense of a coaccused is antagonistic to the moving party; or evidence as to any other accused will improperly prejudice the moving accused.

If a severance is granted by the military judge, the military judge will decide which accused will be tried first. *See* R.C.M. 801(a)(1). In the case of joint charges, the military judge will direct an appropriate amendment of the charges and specifications.

See also R.C.M. 307(c)(5); 601(e)(3); 604; 812.

---

(10) Severance of offenses, but only to prevent manifest injustice.

Discussion

Ordinarily, all known charges should be tried at a single court-martial. Joinder of minor and major offenses, or of unrelated offenses is not alone a sufficient ground to sever offenses. For example, when an essential witness as to one offense is unavailable, it might be appropriate to sever that offense to prevent violation of the accused's right to a speedy trial.

---

(11) *Change of place of trial.* The place of trial may be changed when necessary to prevent prejudice to the rights of the accused or for the convenience of the Government if the rights of the accused are not prejudiced thereby.

Discussion

A change of the place of trial may be necessary when there exists in the place where the court-martial is pending so great a prejudice against the accused that the accused cannot obtain a fair and impartial trial there, or to obtain compulsory process over an essential witness.

When it is necessary to change the place of trial, the choice of places to which the court-martial will be transferred will be left to the convening authority, as long as the choice is not inconsistent with the ruling of the military judge.

---

(12) Determination of multiplicity of offenses for sentencing purposes.

Discussion

See R.C.M. 1003 concerning determination of the maximum punishment. *See also* R.C.M. 907(b)(3)(B) concerning dismissal of charges on grounds of multiplicity.

A ruling on this motion ordinarily should be deferred until after findings are entered.

---

(13) Preliminary ruling on admissibility of evidence.

Discussion

See Mil. R. Evid. 104(c)

A request for a preliminary ruling on admissibility is a request that certain matters which are ordinarily decided during trial of the general issue be resolved before they arise, outside the presence of members. The purpose of such a motion is to avoid the prejudice which may result from bringing inadmissible matters to the attention of court members.

Whether to rule on an evidentiary question before it arises during trial is a matter within the discretion of the military judge. *But see* R.C.M. 905(b)(3) and (d); and Mil. R. Evid. 304(e)(2); 311(e)(2); 321(d)(2). Reviewability of preliminary rulings will be controlled by the Supreme Court's decision in *Luce v. United States*, 469 U.S. 38 (1984).

---

(14) Motions relating to mental capacity or responsibility of the accused.

Discussion

See R.C.M. 706, 909, and 916(k) regarding procedures and standards concerning the mental capacity or responsibility of the accused.

Rule 907. Motions to dismiss

(a) *In general.* A motion to dismiss is a request to terminate further proceedings as to one or more charges and specifications on grounds capable of resolution without trial of the general issue of guilt.

Discussion

Dismissal of a specification terminates the proceeding with respect to that specification unless the decision to dismiss is reconsidered and reversed by the military judge. *See* R.C.M. 905(f). Dismissal of a specification on grounds stated in subsection (b)(1) or (b)(3)(A) below does not ordinarily bar a later court-martial for the same offense if the grounds for dismissal no longer exist. *See also* R.C.M. 905(g) and subsection (b)(2) below.

See R.C.M. 916 concerning defenses.

(b) *Grounds for dismissal.* Grounds for dismissal include the following—

(1) *Nonwaivable grounds.* A charge or specification shall be dismissed at any stage of the proceedings if:

(A) The court-martial lacks jurisdiction to try the accused for the offense; or

Discussion

See R.C.M. 201-203.

(B) The specification fails to state an offense.

Discussion

See R.C.M. 307(c)

---

(2) *Waivable grounds.* A charge or specification shall be dismissed upon motion made by the accused before the final adjournment of the court-martial in that case if:

(A) Dismissal is required under R.C.M. 707;

(B) The statute of limitations (Article 43) has run, provided that, if it appears that the accused is unaware of the right to assert the statute of limitations in bar of trial, the military judge shall inform the accused of this right;

Discussion

Except for certain offenses for which there is either: no limitation as to time; or child abuse offenses for which a time limitation has been enacted and applies that is based upon the life of a child abuse victim, *see* Article 43(a) and (b)(2) , a person charged with an offense under the code may not be tried by court-martial over objection if sworn charges have not been received by the officer exercising summary court-martial jurisdiction over the command within five years. *See* Article 43(b). This period may be tolled (Article 43(c) and (d)), extended (Article 43(e) and (g)), or suspended (Article 43(f)) under certain circumstances. The prosecution bears the burden of proving that the statute of limitations has been tolled, extended, or suspended if it appears that is has run.

Some offenses are continuing offenses and any period of the offense occurring within the statute of limitations is not barred. Absence without leave, desertion, and fraudulent enlistment are not continuing offenses and are committed, respectively, on the day the person goes absent, deserts, or first receives pay or allowances under the enlistment.

When computing the statute of limitations, periods in which the accused was fleeing from justice or periods when the accused was absent without leave or in desertion are excluded. The military judge must determine by a preponderance, as an interlocutory matter, whether the accused was absent without authority or fleeing from justice. It would not be necessary that the accused be charged with the absence offense. In cases where the accused is charged with both an absence offense and a non-absence offense, but is found not guilty of the absence offense, the military judge would reconsider, by a preponderance, his or her prior determination whether that period of time is excludable.

If sworn charges have been received by an officer exercising summary court-martial jurisdiction over the command within the period of the statute, minor amendments (*see* R.C.M. 603(a)) may be made in the specification after the statute of limitations has run. However, if new charges are drafted or a major amendment made (*see* R.C.M. 603(d)) after the statute of limitations has run, prosecution is barred. The date of receipt of sworn charges is excluded when computing the appropriate statutory period. The date of the offense is included in the computation of the elapsed time. Article 43(g) allows the government time to reinstate charges dismissed as defective or insufficient for any cause. The government would have up to six months to reinstate the charges if the original period of limitations has expired or will expire within six months of the dismissal.

In some cases, the issue whether the statute of limitations has run will depend on the findings on the general issue of guilt. For example, where the date of an offense is in dispute, a finding by the court-martial that the offense occurred at an earlier time may affect a determination as to the running of the statute of limitations.

When the statute of limitations has run as to a lesser included offense, but not as to the charged offense, *see* R.C.M. 920(e)(2) with regard to instructions on the lesser offense.

(C) The accused has previously been tried by court-martial or federal civilian court for the same offense, provided that:

(i) No court-martial proceeding is a trial in the sense of this rule unless presentation of evidence on the general issue of guilt has begun;

(ii) No court-martial proceeding which has been terminated under R.C.M. 604(b) or R.C.M. 915 shall bar later prosecution for the same offense or offenses, if so provided in those rules;

(iii) No court-martial proceeding in which an accused has been found guilty of any charge or specification is a trial in the sense of this rule until the finding of guilty has become final after review of the case has been fully completed; and

(iv) No court-martial proceeding which lacked jurisdiction to try the accused for the offense is a trial in the sense of this rule.

(D) Prosecution is barred by:

(i) A pardon issued by the President;

Discussion

A pardon may grant individual or general amnesty.

(ii) Immunity from prosecution granted by a person authorized to do so;

Discussion

See R.C.M. 704.

(iii) Constructive condonation of desertion established by unconditional restoration to duty without trial of a deserter by a general court-martial convening authority who knew of the desertion; or

(iv) Prior punishment under Articles 13 or 15 for the same offense, if that offense was minor.

Discussion

See Articles 13 and 15(f). *See* paragraph 1e of Part V for a definition of "minor" offenses.

---

(3) *Permissible grounds.* A specification may be dismissed upon timely motion by the accused if:

(A) The specification is so defective that it substantially misled the accused, and the military judge finds that, in the interest of justice, trial should proceed on remaining charges and specifications without undue delay; or

(B) The specification is multiplicious with another specification, is unnecessary to enable the prosecution to meet the exigencies of proof through trial, review, and appellate action, and should be dismissed in the interest of justice.

Discussion

A specification is multiplicious with another if it alleges the same offense, or an offense necessarily included in the other. A specification may also be multiplicious with another if they describe substantially the same misconduct in two different ways. For example, assault and disorderly conduct may be multiplicious if the disorderly conduct consists solely of the assault. *See also* R.C.M. 1003(c)(1)(C).

Ordinarily, a specification should not be dismissed for multiplicity before trial unless it clearly alleges the same offense, or one necessarily included therein, as is alleged in another specification. It may be appropriate to dismiss the less serious of any multiplicious specifications after findings have been reached. Due consideration must be given, however, to possible post-trial or appellate action with regard to the remaining specification.

Rule 908. Appeal by the United States

(a) *In general.* In a trial by a court-martial over which a military judge presides and in which a punitive discharge may be adjudged, the United States may appeal an order or ruling that terminates the proceedings with respect to a charge or specification, or excludes evidence that is substantial proof of a fact material in the proceedings, or directs the disclosure of classified information, or that imposes sanctions for nondisclosure of classified information. The United States may also appeal a refusal by the military judge to issue a protective order sought by the United States to prevent the disclosure of classified information or to enforce such an order that has previously been issued by the appropriate authority. However, the United States may not appeal an order or ruling that is, or amounts to, a finding of not guilty with respect to the charge or specification.

(b) *Procedure.*

(1) *Delay.* After an order or ruling which may be subject to an appeal by the United States, the court-martial may not proceed, except as to matters unaffected by the ruling or order, if the trial counsel requests a delay to determine whether to file notice of appeal under this rule. Trial counsel is entitled to no more than 72 hours under this subsection.

(2) *Decision to appeal.* The decision whether to file notice of appeal under this rule shall be made within 72 hours of the ruling or order to be appealed. If the Secretary concerned so prescribes, the trial counsel shall not file notice of appeal unless authorized to do so by a person designated by the Secretary concerned.

(3) *Notice of appeal.* If the United States elects to appeal, the trial counsel shall provide the military judge with written notice to this effect not later than 72 hours after the ruling or order. Such notice shall identify the ruling or order to be appealed and the charges and specifications affected. Trial counsel shall certify that the appeal is not taken for the purpose of delay and (if the order or ruling appealed is one which excludes evidence) that the evidence excluded is substantial proof of a fact material in the proceeding.

(4) *Effect on the court-martial.* Upon written notice to the military judge under subsection (b)(3) of this rule, the ruling or order that is the subject of the appeal is automatically stayed and no session of the court-martial may proceed pending disposition by the Court of Criminal Appeals of the appeal, except that solely as to charges and specifications not affected by the ruling or order:

(A) Motions may be litigated, in the discretion of the military judge, at any point in the proceedings;

(B) When trial on the merits has not begun,

(i) a severance may be granted upon request of all the parties;

(ii) a severance may be granted upon request

of the accused and when appropriate under R.C.M. 906(b)(10); or

(C) When trial on the merits has begun but has not been completed, a party may, on that party's request and in the discretion of the military judge, present further evidence on the merits.

(5) *Record.* Upon written notice to the military judge under subsection (b)(3) of this rule, trial counsel shall cause a record of the proceedings to be prepared. Such record shall be verbatim and complete to the extent necessary to resolve the issues appealed. R.C.M. 1103(g), (h), and (i) shall apply and the record shall be authenticated in accordance with R.C.M. 1104(a). The military judge or the Court of Criminal Appeals may direct that additional parts of the proceeding be included in the record; R.C.M. 1104(d) shall not apply to such additions.

(6) *Forwarding.* Upon written notice to the military judge under subsection (b)(3) of this rule, trial counsel shall promptly and by expeditious means forward the appeal to a representative of the Government designated by the Judge Advocate General. The matter forwarded shall include: a statement of the issues appealed; the record of the proceedings or, if preparation of the record has not been completed, a summary of the evidence; and such other matters as the Secretary concerned may prescribe. The person designated by the Judge Advocate General shall promptly decide whether to file the appeal with the Court of Criminal Appeals and notify the trial counsel of that decision.

(7) *Appeal filed.* If the United States elects to file an appeal, it shall be filed directly with the Court of Criminal Appeals, in accordance with the rules of that court.

(8) *Appeal not filed.* If the United States elects not to file an appeal, trial counsel promptly shall notify the military judge and the other parties.

(9) *Pretrial confinement of accused pending appeal.* If an accused is in pretrial confinement at the time the United States files notice of its intent to appeal under subsection (3) above, the commander, in determining whether the accused should be confined pending the outcome of an appeal by the United States, should consider the same factors which would authorize the imposition of pretrial confinement under R.C.M. 305(h)(2)(B).

(c) *Appellate proceedings.*

(1) *Appellate counsel.* The parties shall be represented before appellate courts in proceedings under this rule as provided in R.C.M. 1202. Appellate Government counsel shall diligently prosecute an appeal under this rule.

(2) *Court of Criminal Appeals.* An appeal under Article 62 shall, whenever practicable, have priority over all other proceedings before the Court of Criminal Appeals. In determining an appeal under Article 62, the Court of Criminal Appeals may take action only with respect to matters of law.

(3) *Action following decision of Court of Criminal Appeals.* After the Court of Criminal Appeals has decided any appeal under Article 62, the accused may petition for review by the Court of Appeals for the Armed Forces, or the Judge Advocate General may certify a question to the Court of Appeals for the Armed Forces. The parties shall be notified of the decision of the Court of Criminal Appeals promptly. If the decision is adverse to the accused, the accused shall be notified of the decision and of the right to petition the Court of Appeals for the Armed Forces for review within 60 days orally on the record at the court-martial or in accordance with R.C.M. 1203(d). If the accused is notified orally on the record, trial counsel shall forward by expeditious means a certificate that the accused was so notified to the Judge Advocate General, who shall forward a copy to the clerk of the Court of Appeals for the Armed Forces when required by the Court. If the decision by the Court of Criminal Appeals permits it, the court-martial may proceed as to the affected charges and specifications pending further review by the Court of Appeals for the Armed Forces or the Supreme Court, unless either court orders the proceedings stayed. Unless the case is reviewed by the Court of Appeals for the Armed Forces, it shall be returned to the military judge or the convening authority for appropriate action in accordance with the decision of the Court of Criminal Appeals. If the case is reviewed by the Court of Appeals for the Armed Forces, R.C.M. 1204 and 1205 shall apply.

(d) *Military judge.* For purposes of this rule, "military judge" does not include the president of a special court-martial without a military judge.

Rule 909. Capacity of the accused to stand trial by court-martial

(a) *In general.* No person may be brought to trial by court-martial if that person is presently suffering from a mental disease or defect rendering him or her mentally incompetent to the extent that he or she is unable to understand the nature of the proceedings against them or to conduct or cooperate intelligently in the defense of the case.

Discussion

See also R.C.M. 916(k).

(b) *Presumption of capacity.* A person is presumed to have the capacity to stand trial unless the contrary is established.

(c) *Determination before referral.* If an inquiry pursuant to R.C.M. 706 conducted before referral concludes that an accused is suffering from a mental disease or defect that renders him or her mentally incompetent to stand trial, the convening authority before whom the charges are pending for disposition may disagree with the conclusion and take any action authorized under R.C.M. 401, including referral of the charges to trial. If that convening authority concurs with the conclusion, he or she shall forward the charges to the general court-martial convening authority. If, upon receipt of the charges, the general court-martial convening authority similarly concurs, then he or she shall commit the accused to the custody of the Attorney General. If the general court-martial convening authority does not concur, that authority may take any action that he or she deems appropriate in accordance with R.C.M. 407, including referral of the charges to trial.

(d) *Determination after referral.* After referral, the military judge may conduct a hearing to determine the mental capacity of the accused, either *sua sponte* or upon request of either party. If an inquiry pursuant to R.C.M. 706 conducted before or after referral concludes that an accused is suffering from a mental disease or defect that renders him or her mentally incompetent to stand trial, the military judge shall conduct a hearing to determine the mental capacity of the accused. Any such hearing shall be conducted in accordance with paragraph (e) of this rule.

(e) *Incompetence determination hearing.*

(1) *Nature of issue.* The mental capacity of the accused is an interlocutory question of fact.

(2) *Standard.* Trial may proceed unless it is established by a preponderance of the evidence that the accused is presently suffering from a mental disease or defect rendering him or her mentally incompetent to the extent that he or she is unable to understand the nature of the proceedings or to conduct or cooperate intelligently in the defense of the case. In making this determination, the military judge is not bound by the rules of evidence except with respect to privileges.

(3) If the military judge finds the accused is incompetent to stand trial, the judge shall report this finding to the general court-martial convening authority, who shall commit the accused to the custody of the Attorney General

(f) *Hospitalization of the accused.* An accused who is found incompetent to stand trial under this rule shall be hospitalized by the Attorney General as provided in section 4241(d) of title 18, United States Code. If notified that the accused has recovered to such an extent that he or she is able to understand the nature of the proceedings and to conduct or cooperate intelligently in the defense of the case, then the general court-martial convening authority shall promptly take custody of the accused. If, at the end of the period of hospitalization, the accused's mental condition has not so improved, action shall be taken in accordance with section 4246 of title 18, United States Code.

Discussion

Under section 4241(d) of title 18, the initial period of hospitalization for an incompetent accused shall not exceed four months. However, in determining whether there is a substantial probability the accused will attain the capacity to permit the trial to proceed in the foreseeable future, the accused may be hospitalized for an additional reasonable period of time. This additional period of time ends either when the accused's mental condition is improved so that trial may proceed, or when the pending charges against the accused are dismissed. If charges are dismissed solely due to the accused's mental condition, the accused is subject to hospitalization as provided in section 4246 of title 18.

(g) *Excludable delay.* All periods of commitment shall be excluded as provided by R.C.M. 707(c). The 120-day time period under R.C.M. 707 shall begin anew on the date the general court-martial convening authority takes custody of the accused at the end of any period of commitment.

Rule 910. Pleas

(a) *Alternatives.*

(1) *In general.* An accused may plead as follows: guilty; not guilty to an offense as charged, but guilty of a named lesser included offense; guilty with ex-

ceptions, with or without substitutions, not guilty of the exceptions, but guilty of the substitutions, if any; or, not guilty. A plea of guilty may not be received as to an offense for which the death penalty may be adjudged by the court-martial.

Discussion

See paragraph 2, Part IV, concerning lesser included offenses. When the plea is to a named lesser included offense without the use of exceptions and substitutions, the defense counsel should provide a written revised specification accurately reflecting the plea and request that the revised specification be included in the record as an appellate exhibit. A plea of guilty to a lesser included offense does not bar the prosecution from proceeding on the offense as charged. *See* also subsection (g) of this rule.

A plea of guilty does not prevent the introduction of evidence, either in support of the factual basis for the plea, or, after findings are entered, in aggravation. *See* R.C.M. 1001(b)(4).

---

(2) *Conditional pleas.* With the approval of the military judge and the consent of the Government, an accused may enter a conditional plea of guilty, reserving the right, on further review or appeal, to review of the adverse determination of any specified pretrial motion. If the accused prevails on further review or appeal, the accused shall be allowed to withdraw the plea of guilty. The Secretary concerned may prescribe who may consent for Government; unless otherwise prescribed by the Secretary concerned, the trial counsel may consent on behalf of the Government.

(b) *Refusal to plead; irregular plea.* If an accused fails or refuses to plead, or makes an irregular plea, the military judge shall enter a plea of not guilty for the accused.

Discussion

An irregular plea includes pleas such as guilty without criminality or guilty to a charge but not guilty to all specifications thereunder. When a plea is ambiguous, the military judge should have it clarified before proceeding further.

(c) *Advice to accused.* Before accepting a plea of guilty, the military judge shall address the accused personally and inform the accused of, and determine that the accused understands, the following:

(1) The nature of the offense to which the plea is offered, the mandatory minimum penalty, if any, provided by law, and the maximum possible penalty provided by law;

Discussion

The elements of each offense to which the accused has pleaded guilty should be described to the accused. *See also* subsection (e) of this rule.

---

(2) In a general or special court-martial, if the accused is not represented by counsel, that the accused has the right to be represented by counsel at every stage of the proceedings;

Discussion

In a general or special court-martial, if the accused is not represented by counsel, a plea of guilty should not be accepted.

---

(3) That the accused has the right to plead not guilty or to persist in that plea if already made, and that the accused has the right to be tried by a court-martial, and that at such trial the accused has the right to confront and cross-examine witnesses against the accused, and the right against self-incrimination;

(4) That if the accused pleads guilty, there will not be a trial of any kind as to those offenses to which the accused has so pleaded, so that by pleading guilty the accused waives the rights described in subsection (c)(3) of this Rule; and

(5) That if the accused pleads guilty, the military judge will question the accused about the offenses to which the accused has pleaded guilty, and, if the accused answers these questions under oath, on the record, and in the presence of counsel, the accused's answers may later be used against the accused in a prosecution for perjury or false statement.

Discussion

The advice in subsection (5) is inapplicable in a court-martial in which the accused is not represented by counsel.

(d) *Ensuring that the plea is voluntary.* The military judge shall not accept a plea of guilty without first, by addressing the accused personally, determining that the plea is voluntary and not the result of force or threats or of promises apart from a plea agreement under R.C.M. 705. The military judge shall also inquire whether the accused's willingness to plead guilty results from prior discussions between the convening authority, a representative of the convening authority, or trial counsel, and the accused or defense counsel.

(e) *Determining accuracy of plea.* The military judge shall not accept a plea of guilty without making such inquiry of the accused as shall satisfy the military judge that there is a factual basis for the plea. The accused shall be questioned under oath about the offenses.

Discussion

A plea of guilty must be in accord with the truth. Before the plea is accepted, the accused must admit every element of the offense(s) to which the accused pleaded guilty. Ordinarily, the elements should be explained to the accused. If any potential defense is raised by the accused's account of the offense or by other matter presented to the military judge, the military judge should explain such a defense to the accused and should not accept the plea unless the accused admits facts which negate the defense. If the statute of limitations would otherwise bar trial for the offense, the military judge should not accept a plea of guilty to it without an affirmative waiver by the accused. *See* R.C.M. 907(b)(2)(B).

The accused need not describe from personal recollection all the circumstances necessary to establish a factual basis for the plea. Nevertheless the accused must be convinced of, and able to describe all the facts necessary to establish guilt. For example, an accused may be unable to recall certain events in an offense, but may still be able to adequately describe the offense based on witness statements or similar sources which the accused believes to be true.

The accused should remain at the counsel table during questioning by the military judge.

(f) *Plea agreement inquiry.*

(1) *In general.* A plea agreement may not be accepted if it does not comply with R.C.M. 705.

(2) *Notice.* The parties shall inform the military judge if a plea agreement exists.

Discussion

The military judge should ask whether a plea agreement exists. *See* subsection (d) of this rule. Even if the military judge fails to so inquire or the accused answers incorrectly, counsel have an obligation to bring any agreements or understandings in connection with the plea to the attention of the military judge.

---

(3) *Disclosure.* If a plea agreement exists, the military judge shall require disclosure of the entire agreement before the plea is accepted, provided that in trial before military judge alone the military judge ordinarily shall not examine any sentence limitation contained in the agreement until after the sentence of the court-martial has been announced.

(4) *Inquiry.* The military judge shall inquire to ensure:

(A) That the accused understands the agreement; and

(B) That the parties agree to the terms of the agreement.

Discussion

If the plea agreement contains any unclear or ambiguous terms, the military judge should obtain clarification from the parties. If there is doubt about the accused's understanding of any terms in the agreement, the military judge should explain those terms to the accused.

(g) *Findings.* Findings based on a plea of guilty may be entered immediately upon acceptance of the plea at an Article 39(a) session unless:

(1) Such action is not permitted by regulations of the Secretary concerned;

(2) The plea is to a lesser included offense and the prosecution intends to proceed to trial on the offense as charged; or

(3) Trial is by a special court-martial without a military judge, in which case the president of the court-martial may enter findings based on the pleas without a formal vote except when subsection (g)(2) of this rule applies.

Discussion

If the accused has pleaded guilty to some offenses but not to others, the military judge should ordinarily defer informing the members of the offenses to which the accused has pleaded guilty until after findings on the remaining offenses have been entered. *See* R.C.M. 913(a), Discussion and R.C.M. 920(e), Discussion, paragraph 3.

(h) *Later action.*

(1) *Withdrawal by the accused.* If after acceptance of the plea but before the sentence is announced the accused requests to withdraw a plea of guilty and substitute a plea of not guilty or a plea of guilty to a lesser included offense, the military judge may as a matter of discretion permit the accused to do so.

(2) *Statements by accused inconsistent with plea.* If after findings but before the sentence is announced the accused makes a statement to the court-

martial, in testimony or otherwise, or presents evidence which is inconsistent with a plea of guilty on which a finding is based, the military judge shall inquire into the providence of the plea. If, following such inquiry, it appears that the accused entered the plea improvidently or through lack of understanding of its meaning and effect a plea of not guilty shall be entered as to the affected charges and specifications.

Discussion

When the accused withdraws a previously accepted plea for guilty or a plea of guilty is set aside, counsel should be given a reasonable time to prepare to proceed. In a trial by military judge alone, recusal of the military judge or disapproval of the request for trial by military judge alone will ordinarily be necessary when a plea is rejected or withdrawn after findings; in trial with members, a mistrial will ordinarily be necessary.

---

(3) *Pretrial agreement inquiry.* After sentence is announced the military judge shall inquire into any parts of a pretrial agreement which were not previously examined by the military judge. If the military judge determines that the accused does not understand the material terms of the agreement, or that the parties disagree as to such terms, the military judge shall conform, with the consent of the Government, the agreement to the accused's understanding or permit the accused to withdraw the plea.

Discussion

See subsection (f)(3) of this rule.

(i) *Record of proceedings.* A verbatim record of the guilty plea proceedings shall be made in cases in which a verbatim record is required under R.C.M. 1103. In other special courts-martial, a summary of the explanation and replies shall be included in the record of trial. As to summary courts-martial, *see* R.C.M. 1305.

(j) *Waiver.* Except as provided in subsection (a)(2) of this rule, a plea of guilty which results in a finding of guilty waives any objection, whether or not previously raised, insofar as the objection relates to the factual issue of guilt of the offense(s) to which the plea was made.

Rule 911. Assembly of the court-martial

The military judge shall announce the assembly of the court-martial.

Discussion

When trial is by a court-martial with members, the court-martial is ordinarily assembled immediately after the members are sworn. The members are ordinarily sworn at the first session at which they appear, as soon as all parties and personnel have been announced. The members are seated with the president, who is the senior member, in the center, and the other members alternately to the president's right and left according to rank. If the rank of a member is changed, or if the membership of the court-martial changes, the members should be reseated accordingly.

When trial is by military judge alone, the court-martial is ordinarily assembled immediately following approval of the request for trial by military judge alone.

Assembly of the court-martial is significant because it marks the point after which: substitution of the members and military judge may no longer take place without good cause (*see* Article 29; R.C.M. 505; 902; 912); the accused may no longer, as a matter of right, request trial by military judge alone or withdraw such a request previously approved (*see* Article 16; R.C.M. 903(a)(2)(d)); and the accused may no longer request, even with the permission of the military judge, or withdraw from a request for, enlisted members (*see* Article 25(c)(1); R.C.M. 903(a)(1)(d)).

Rule 912. Challenge of selection of members; examination and challenges of members

(a) *Pretrial matters.*

(1) *Questionnaires.* Before trial the trial counsel may, and shall upon request of the defense counsel, submit to each member written questions requesting the following information:

(A) Date of birth;

(B) Sex;

(C) Race;

(D) Marital status and sex, age, and number of dependents;

(E) Home of record;

(F) Civilian and military education, including, when available, major areas of study, name of school or institution, years of education, and degrees received;

(G) Current unit to which assigned;

(H) Past duty assignments;

(I) Awards and decorations received;

(J) Date of rank; and

(K) Whether the member has acted as accuser,

counsel, investigating officer, convening authority, or legal officer or staff judge advocate for the convening authority in the case, or has forwarded the charges with a recommendation as to disposition.

Additional information may be requested with the approval of the military judge. Each member's responses to the questions shall be written and signed by the member.

Discussion

Using questionnaires before trial may expedite voir dire and may permit more informed exercise of challenges.

If the questionnaire is marked or admitted as an exhibit at the court-martial it must be attached to or included in the record of trial. *See* R.C.M. 1103(b)(2)(D)(iv) and (b)(3)(B).

---

(2) *Other materials.* A copy of any written materials considered by the convening authority in selecting the members detailed to the court-martial shall be provided to any party upon request, except that such materials pertaining solely to persons who were not selected for detail as members need not be provided unless the military judge, for good cause, so directs.

(b) *Challenge of selection of members.*

(1) *Motion.* Before the examination of members under subsection (d) of this rule begins, or at the next session after a party discovered or could have discovered by the exercise of diligence, the grounds therefor, whichever is earlier, that party may move to stay the proceedings on the ground that members were selected improperly.

Discussion

See R.C.M. 502(a) and 503(a) concerning selection of members. Members are also improperly selected when, for example, a certain group or class is arbitrarily excluded from consideration as members.

---

(2) *Procedure.* Upon a motion under subsection (b)(1) of this rule containing an offer of proof of matters which, if true, would constitute improper selection of members, the moving party shall be entitled to present evidence, including any written materials considered by the convening authority in selecting the members. Any other party may also present evidence on the matter. If the military judge determines that the members have been selected improperly, the military judge shall stay any proceedings requiring the presence of members until members are properly selected.

(3) *Waiver.* Failure to make a timely motion under this subsection shall waive the improper selection unless it constitutes a violation of R.C.M. 501(a), 502(a)(1), or 503(a)(2).

(c) *Stating grounds for challenge.* The trial counsel shall state any ground for challenge for cause against any member of which the trial counsel is aware.

(d) *Examination of members.* The military judge may permit the parties to conduct the examination of members or may personally conduct the examination. In the latter event the military judge shall permit the parties to supplement the examination by such further inquiry as the military judge deems proper or the military judge shall submit to the members such additional questions by the parties as the military judge deems proper. A member may be questioned outside the presence of other members when the military judge so directs.

Discussion

Examination of the members is called "voir dire." If the members have not already been placed under oath for the purpose of voir dire (*see* R.C.M. 807(b)(2) Discussion (B)), they should be sworn before they are questioned.

The opportunity for voir dire should be used to obtain information for the intelligent exercise of challenges; counsel should not purposely use voir dire to present factual matter which will not be admissible or to argue the case.

The nature and scope of the examination of members is within the discretion of the military judge. Members may be questioned individually or collectively. Ordinarily, the military judge should permit counsel to personally question the members. Trial counsel ordinarily conducts an inquiry before the defense. Whether trial counsel will question all the members before the defense begins or whether some other procedure will be followed depends on the circumstances. For example, when members are questioned individually outside the presence of other members, each party would ordinarily complete questioning that member before another member is questioned. The military judge and each party may conduct additional questioning, after initial questioning by a party, as necessary.

Ordinarily the members should be asked whether they are aware of any ground for challenge against them. This may expedite further questioning. The members should be cautioned, however, not to disclose information in the presence of other members which might disqualify them.

(e) *Evidence.* Any party may present evidence relating to whether grounds for challenge exist against a member.

(f) *Challenges and removal for cause.*

(1) *Grounds.* A member shall be excused for cause whenever it appears that the member:

(A) Is not competent to serve as a member under Article 25(a), (b), or (c);

(B) Has not been properly detailed as a member of the court-martial;

(C) Is an accuser as to any offense charged;

(D) Will be a witness in the court-martial;

(E) Has acted as counsel for any party as to any offense charged;

(F) Has been an investigating officer as to any offense charged;

(G) Has acted in the same case as convening authority or as the legal officer or staff judge advocate to the convening authority;

(H) Will act in the same case as reviewing authority or as the legal officer or staff judge advocate to the reviewing authority;

(I) Has forwarded charges in the case with a personal recommendation as to disposition;

(J) Upon a rehearing or new or other trial of the case, was a member of the court-martial which heard the case before;

(K) Is junior to the accused in grade or rank, unless it is established that this could not be avoided;

(L) Is in arrest or confinement;

(M) Has informed or expressed a definite opinion as to the guilt or innocence of the accused as to any offense charged;

(N) Should not sit as a member in the interest of having the court-martial free from substantial doubt as to legality, fairness, and impartiality.

Discussion

Examples of matters which may be grounds for challenge under subsection (N) are that the member: has a direct personal interest in the result of the trial; is closely related to the accused, a counsel, or a witness in the case; has participated as a member or counsel in the trial of a closely related case; has a decidedly friendly or hostile attitude toward a party; or has an inelastic opinion concerning an appropriate sentence for the offenses charged.

---

(2) *When made.*

(A) *Upon completion of examination.* Upon completion of any examination under subsection (d) of this rule and the presentation of evidence, if any, on the matter, each party shall state any challenges for cause it elects to make.

(B) *Other times.* A challenge for cause may be made at any other time during trial when it becomes apparent that a ground for challenge may exist. Such examination of the member and presentation of evidence as may be necessary may be made in order to resolve the matter.

(3) *Procedure.* Each party shall be permitted to make challenges outside the presence of the members. The party making a challenge shall state the grounds for it. Ordinarily the trial counsel shall enter any challenges for cause before the defense counsel. The military judge shall rule finally on each challenge. When a challenge for cause is granted, the member concerned shall be excused. The burden of establishing that grounds for a challenge exist is upon the party making the challenge. A member successfully challenged shall be excused.

(4) *Waiver.* The grounds for challenge in subsection (f)(1)(A) of this rule may not be waived except that membership of enlisted members in the same unit as the accused may be waived. Membership of enlisted members in the same unit as the accused and any other ground for challenge is waived if the party knew of or could have discovered by the exercise of diligence the ground for challenge and failed to raise it in a timely manner. Notwithstanding the absence of a challenge or waiver of a challenge by the parties, the military judge may, in the interest of justice, excuse a member against whom a challenge for cause would lie. When a challenge for cause has been denied the successful use of a peremptory challenge by either party, excusing the challenged member from further participation in the court-martial, shall preclude further consideration of the challenge of that excused member upon later review. Further, failure by the challenging party to exercise a peremptory challenge against any member shall constitute waiver of further consideration of the challenge upon later review.

Discussion

See also Mil. R. Evid. 606(b) when a member may be a witness.

(g) *Peremptory challenges.*

(1) *Procedure.* Each party may challenge one member peremptorily. Any member so challenged

shall be excused. No party may be required to exercise a peremptory challenge before the examination of members and determination of any challenges for cause has been completed. Ordinarily the trial counsel shall enter any peremptory challenge before the defense.

Discussion

Generally, no reason is necessary for a peremptory challenge. *But see Batson v. Kentucky* 476 U.S. 79 (1986); *United States v. Curtis*, 33 M.J. 101 (C.M.A. 1991), *cert. denied*, 112 S.Ct. 1177 (1992); *United States v. Moore*, 28 M.J. 366 (C.M.A. 1989); *United States v. Santiago-Davilla*, 26 M.J. 380 (C.M.A. 1988).

(2) *Waiver.* Failure to exercise a peremptory challenge when properly called upon to do so shall waive the right to make such a challenge. The military judge may, for good cause shown, grant relief from the waiver, but a peremptory challenge may not be made after the presentation of evidence before the members has begun. However, nothing in this subsection shall bar the exercise of a previously unexercised peremptory challenge against a member newly detailed under R.C.M. 505(c)(2)(B), even if presentation of evidence on the merits has begun.

Discussion

When the membership of the court-martial has been reduced below a quorum (*see* R.C.M. 501) or, when enlisted members have been requested, the fraction of enlisted members has been reduced below one-third, the proceedings should be adjourned and the convening authority notified so that new members may be detailed. *See* R.C.M. 505. *See also* R.C.M. 805(d) concerning other procedures when new members are detailed.

(h) *Special courts-martial without a military judge.* In a special court-martial without a military judge, the procedures in this rule shall apply, except that challenges shall be made in the presence of the members and a ruling on any challenge for cause shall be decided by a majority vote of the members upon secret written ballot in closed session. The challenged member shall not be present at the closed session at which the challenge is decided. A tie vote on a challenge disqualifies the member challenged. Before closing, the president shall give such instructions as may be necessary to resolve the challenge. Each challenge shall be decided separately, and all unexcused members except the challenged member shall participate. When only three members are present and one is challenged, the remaining two may decide the challenge. When the president is challenged, the next senior member shall act as president for purposes of deciding the challenge.

(i) *Definitions.*

(1) *Military judge.* For purpose of this rule, "military judge" does not include the president of a special court-martial without a military judge.

(2) *Witness.* For purposes of this rule, "witness" includes one who testifies at a court-martial and anyone whose declaration is received in evidence for any purpose, including written declarations made by affidavit or otherwise.

Discussion

For example, a person who by certificate has attested or otherwise authenticated an official record or other writing introduced in evidence is a witness.

(3) *Investigating officer.* For purposes of this rule, "investigating officer" includes any person who has investigated charges under R.C.M. 405 and any person who as counsel for a member of a court of inquiry, or otherwise personally has conducted an investigation of the general matter involving the offenses charged.

Rule 913. Presentation of the case on the merits

(a) *Preliminary instructions.* The military judge may give such preliminary instructions as may be appropriate. If mixed pleas have been entered, the military judge should ordinarily defer informing the members of the offenses to which the accused pleaded guilty until after the findings on the remaining contested offenses have been entered.

Discussion

Preliminary instructions may include a description of the duties of members, procedures to be followed in the court-martial, and other appropriate matters.

Exceptions to the rule requiring the military judge to defer informing the members of an accused's prior pleas of guilty include cases in which the accused has specifically requested, on the record, that the military judge instruct the members of the prior pleas of guilty and cases in which a plea of guilty was to a lesser included offense within the contested offense charged in the specification. *See* R.C.M. 910(g), Discussion and R.C.M. 920(e), Discussion, paragraph 3.

(b) *Opening statements.* Each party may make one opening statement to the court-martial before presentation of evidence has begun. The defense may elect to make its statement after the prosecution has rested, before the presentation of evidence for the defense. The military judge may, as a matter of discretion, permit the parties to address the court-martial at other times.

Discussion

Counsel should confine their remarks to evidence they expect to be offered which they believe in good faith will be available and admissible and a brief statement of the issues in the case.

(c) *Presentation of evidence.* Each party shall have full opportunity to present evidence.

(1) *Order of presentation.* Ordinarily the following sequence shall be followed:

(A) Presentation of evidence for the prosecution;

(B) Presentation of evidence for the defense;

(C) Presentation of prosecution evidence in rebuttal;

(D) Presentation of defense evidence in surrebuttal;

(E) Additional rebuttal evidence in the discretion of the military judge; and

(F) Presentation of evidence requested by the military judge or members.

Discussion

See R.C.M. 801(a) and Mil. R. Evid. 611 concerning control by the military judge over the order of proceedings.

---

(2) *Taking testimony.* The testimony of witnesses shall be taken orally in open session, unless otherwise provided in this Manual.

Discussion

Each witness must testify under oath. *See* R.C.M. 807(b)(1)(B); Mil. R. Evid. 603. After a witness is sworn, the witness should be identified for the record (full name, rank, and unit, if military, or full name and address, if civilian). The party calling the witness conducts direct examination of the witness, followed by cross-examination of the witness by the opposing party. Redirect and re-cross-examination are conducted as necessary, followed by any questioning by the military judge and members. *See* Mil. R. Evid. 611; 614.

All documentary and real evidence (except marks or wounds on a person's body) should be marked for identification when first referred to in the proceedings and should be included in the record of trial whether admitted in evidence or not. *See* R.C.M. 1103(b)(2)(C), (c). "Real evidence" include physical objects, such as clothing, weapons, and marks or wounds on a person's body. If it is impracticable to attach an item of real evidence to the record, the item should be clearly and accurately described by testimony, photographs, or other means so that it may be considered on review. Similarly, when documentary evidence is used, if the document cannot be attached to the record (as in the case of an original official record or a large map), a legible copy or accurate extract should be included in the record. When a witness points to or otherwise refers to certain parts of a map, photograph, diagram, chart, or other exhibit, the place to which the witness pointed or referred should be clearly identified for the record, either by marking the exhibit or by an accurate description of the witness' actions with regard to the exhibit.

---

(3) *Views and inspections.* The military judge may, as a matter of discretion, permit the court-martial to view or inspect premises or a place or an article or object. Such a view or inspection shall take place only in the presence of all parties, the members (if any), and the military judge. A person familiar with the scene may be designated by the military judge to escort the court-martial. Such person shall perform the duties of escort under oath. The escort shall not testify, but may point out particular features prescribed by the military judge. Any statement made at the view or inspection by the escort, a party, the military judge, or any member shall be made part of the record.

Discussion

A view or inspection should be permitted only in extraordinary circumstances. The fact that a view or inspection has been made does not necessarily preclude the introduction in evidence of photographs, diagrams, maps, or sketches of the place or item viewed, if these are otherwise admissible.

---

(4) *Evidence subject to exclusion.* When offered evidence would be subject to exclusion upon objection, the military judge may, as a matter of discretion, bring the matter to the attention of the parties and may, in the interest of justice, exclude the evidence without an objection by a party.

Discussion

The military judge should not exclude evidence which is not objected to by a party except in extraordinary circumstances. Counsel should be permitted to try the case and present the evidence without unnecessary interference by the military judge. *See also* Mil. R. Evid. 103.

---

(5) *Reopening case.* The military judge may, as a matter of discretion, permit a party to reopen its case after it has rested.

Rule 914. Production of statements of witnesses

(a) *Motion for production.* After a witness other than the accused has testified on direct examination, the military judge, on motion of a party who did not call the witness, shall order the party who called the witness to produce, for examination and use by the moving party, any statement of the witness that relates to the subject matter concerning which the witness has testified, and that is:

(1) In the case of a witness called by the trial counsel, in the possession of the United States; or

(2) In the case of a witness called by the defense, in the possession of the accused or defense counsel.

Discussion

See also R.C.M. 701 (Discovery).

Counsel should anticipate legitimate demands for statements under this and similar rules and avoid delays in the proceedings by voluntary disclosure before arraignment.

This rule does not apply to investigations under Article 32.

As to procedures for certain government information as to which a privilege is asserted, *see* Mil. R. Evid. 505; 506.

(b) *Production of entire statement.* If the entire contents of the statement relate to the subject matter concerning which the witness has testified, the military judge shall order that the statement be delivered to the moving party.

(c) *Production of excised statement.* If the party who called the witness claims that the statement contains matter that does not relate to the subject matter concerning which the witness has testified, the military judge shall order that it be delivered to the military judge. Upon inspection, the military judge shall excise the portions of the statement that do not relate to the subject matter concerning which the witness has testified, and shall order that the statement, with such material excised, be delivered to the moving party. Any portion of a statement that is withheld from an accused over objection shall be preserved by the trial counsel, and, in the event of a conviction, shall be made available to the reviewing authorities for the purpose of determining the correctness of the decision to excise the portion of the statement.

(d) *Recess for examination of the statement.* Upon delivery of the statement to the moving party, the military judge may recess the trial for the examination of the statement and preparation for its use in the trial.

(e) *Remedy for failure to produce statement.* If the other party elects not to comply with an order to deliver a statement to the moving party, the military judge shall order that the testimony of the witness be disregarded by the trier of fact and that the trial proceed, or, if it is the trial counsel who elects not to comply, shall declare a mistrial if required in the interest of justice.

(f) *Definition.* As used in this rule, a "statement" of a witness means:

(1) A written statement made by the witness that is signed or otherwise adopted or approved by the witness;

(2) A substantially verbatim recital of an oral statement made by the witness that is recorded contemporaneously with the making of the oral statement and contained in a stenolineart, mechanical, electrical, or other recording or a transcription thereof; or

(3) A statement, however taken or recorded, or a transcription thereof, made by the witness to a Federal grand jury.

Rule 914A. Use of remote live testimony of a child

(a) *General procedures.* A child shall be allowed to testify out of the presence of the accused after the military judge has determined that the requirements of Mil. R. Evid. 611(d)(3) have been satisfied. The procedure used to take such testimony will be determined by the military judge based upon the exigencies of the situation. At a minimum, the following procedures shall be observed:

(1) The witness shall testify from a remote location outside the courtroom;

(2) Attendance at the remote location shall be limited to the child, counsel for each side (not including an accused pro se), equipment operators, and other persons, such as an attendant for the child,

whose presence is deemed necessary by the military judge;

(3) Sufficient monitors shall be placed in the courtroom to allow viewing and hearing of the testimony by the military judge, the accused, the members, the court reporter and the public;

(4) The voice of the military judge shall be transmitted into the remote location to allow control of the proceedings; and

(5) The accused shall be permitted private, contemporaneous communication with his counsel.

(b) *Definition.* As used in this rule, "remote live testimony" includes, but is not limited to, testimony by videoteleconference, closed circuit television, or similar technology.

(c) *Prohibitions.* The procedures described above shall not be used where the accused elects to absent himself from the courtroom pursuant to R.C.M. 804(c).

Discussion

For purposes of this rule, unlike R.C.M. 914B, remote means or similar technology does not include receiving testimony by telephone where the parties cannot see and hear each other.

Rule 914B. Use of remote testimony

(a) *General procedures.* The military judge shall determine the procedures used to take testimony via remote means. At a minimum, all parties shall be able to hear each other, those in attendance at the remote site shall be identified, and the accused shall be permitted private, contemporaneous communication with his counsel.

(b) *Definition.* As used in this rule, testimony via "remote means" includes, but is not limited to, testimony by videoteleconference, closed circuit television, telephone, or similar technology.

Discussion

This rule applies for all witness testimony other than child witness testimony specifically covered by M.R.E. 611(d) and R.C.M. 914A. When utilizing testimony via remote means, military justice practitioners are encouraged to consult the procedure used in *In re San Juan Dupont Plaza Hotel Fire Litigation*, 129 F.R.D. 424 (D.P.R. 1989) and to read *United States v. Gigante*, 166 F.3d 75 (2d Cir. 1999), cert. denied, 528 U.S. 1114 (2000).

Rule 915. Mistrial

(a) *In general.* The military judge may, as a matter of discretion, declare a mistrial when such action is manifestly necessary in the interest of justice because of circumstances arising during the proceedings which cast substantial doubt upon the fairness of the proceedings. A mistrial may be declared as to some or all charges, and as to the entire proceedings or as to only the proceedings after findings.

Discussion

The power to grant a mistrial should be used with great caution, under urgent circumstances, and for plain and obvious reasons. As examples, a mistrial may be appropriate when inadmissible matters so prejudicial that a curative instruction would be inadequate are brought to the attention of the members or when members engage in prejudicial misconduct. Also a mistrial is appropriate when the proceedings must be terminated because of a legal defect, such as a jurisdictional defect, which can be cured; for example, when the referral is jurisdictionally defective. *See also* R.C.M. 905(g) concerning the effect of rulings in one proceeding on later proceedings.

(b) *Procedure.* On motion for a mistrial or when it otherwise appears that grounds for a mistrial may exist, the military judge shall inquire into the views of the parties on the matter and then decide the matter as an interlocutory question.

Discussion

Except in a special court-martial without a military judge, the hearing on a mistrial should be conducted out of the presence of the members.

(c) *Effect of declaration of mistrial.*

(1) *Withdrawal of charges.* A declaration of a mistrial shall have the effect of withdrawing the affected charges and specifications from the court-martial.

Discussion

Upon declaration of a mistrial, the affected charges are returned to the convening authority who may refer them anew or otherwise dispose of them. *See* R.C.M. 401-407.

---

(2) *Further proceedings.* A declaration of a mistrial shall not prevent trial by another court-martial on the affected charges and specifications except when the mistrial was declared after jeopardy attached and before findings, and the declaration was:

(A) An abuse of discretion and without the consent of the defense; or

(B) The direct result of intentional prosecutorial misconduct designed to necessitate a mistrial.

Rule 916. Defenses

(a) *In general.* As used in this rule, "defenses" includes any special defense which, although not denying that the accused committed the objective acts constituting the offense charged, denies, wholly or partially, criminal responsibility for those acts.

Discussion

Special defenses are also called "affirmative defenses."

"Alibi" and "good character" are not special defenses, as they operate to deny that the accused committed one or more of the acts constituting the offense. As to evidence of the accused's good character, *see* Mil. R. Evid. 404(a)(1). *See* R.C.M. 701(b)(1) concerning notice of alibi.

(b) *Burden of proof.*

(1) *General rule.* Except as listed below in paragraphs (2), (3), and (4), the prosecution shall have the burden of proving beyond a reasonable doubt that the defense did not exist.

(2) *Lack of mental responsibility.* The accused has the burden of proving the defense of lack of mental responsibility by clear and convincing evidence.

(3) *Mistake of fact as to age.* In the defense of mistake of fact as to age as described in Part IV, para. 45a(o)(2) in a prosecution of a sexual offense with a child under Article 120, the accused has the burden of proving mistake of fact as to age by a preponderance of the evidence. After the accused meets his or her burden, the prosecution shall have the burden of proving beyond a reasonable doubt that the defense did not exist.

(4) *Mistake of fact as to consent.* In the defense of mistake of fact as to consent in Article 120(a), rape, Article 120(c), aggravated sexual assault, Article 120(e), aggravated sexual contact, and Article 120(h), abusive sexual contact, the accused has the burden of proving mistake of fact as to consent by a preponderance of the evidence. After the defense meets its burden, the prosecution shall have the burden of proving beyond a reasonable doubt that the defense did not exist.

Discussion

A defense may be raised by evidence presented by the defense, the prosecution, or the court-martial. For example, in a prosecution for assault, testimony by prosecution witnesses that the victim brandished a weapon toward the accused may raise a defense of self-defense. *See* subsection (e) below. More than one defense may be raised as to a particular offense. The defenses need not necessarily be consistent.

See R.C.M. 920(e)(3) concerning instructions on defenses.

(c) *Justification.* A death, injury, or other act caused or done in the proper performance of a legal duty is justified and not unlawful.

Discussion

The duty may be imposed by statute, regulation, or order. For example, the use of force by a law enforcement officer when reasonably necessary in the proper execution of a lawful apprehension is justified because the duty to apprehend is imposed by lawful authority. Also, killing an enemy combatant in battle is justified.

(d) *Obedience to orders.* It is a defense to any offense that the accused was acting pursuant to orders unless the accused knew the orders to be unlawful or a person of ordinary sense and understanding would have known the orders to be unlawful.

Discussion

Ordinarily the lawfulness of an order is finally decided by the military judge. *See* R.C.M. 801(e). An exception might exist when the sole issue is whether the person who gave the order in fact occupied a certain position at the time.

An act performed pursuant to a lawful order is justified. *See* subsection (c) of this rule. An act performed pursuant to an unlawful order is excused unless the accused knew it to be unlawful or a person of ordinary sense and understanding would have known it to be unlawful.

(e) *Self-defense.*

(1) *Homicide or assault cases involving deadly force.* It is a defense to a homicide, assault involving deadly force, or battery involving deadly force that the accused:

(A) Apprehended, on reasonable grounds, that death or grievous bodily harm was about to be inflicted wrongfully on the accused; and

(B) Believed that the force the accused used

was necessary for protection against death or grievous bodily harm.

Discussion

The words "involving deadly force" described the factual circumstances of the case, not specific assault offenses. If the accused is charged with simple assault, battery or any form of aggravated assault, or if simple assault, battery or any form of aggravated assault is in issue as a lesser included offense, the accused may rely on this subsection if the test specified in subsections (A) and (B) is satisfied.

The test for the first element of self-defense is objective. Thus, the accused's apprehension of death or grievous bodily harm must have been one which a reasonable, prudent person would have held under the circumstances. Because this test is objective, such matters as intoxication or emotional instability of the accused are irrelevant. On the other hand, such matters as the relative height, weight, and general build of the accused and the alleged victim, and the possibility of safe retreat are ordinarily among the circumstances which should be considered in determining the reasonableness of the apprehension of death or grievous bodily harm.

The test for the second element is entirely subjective. The accused is not objectively limited to the use of reasonable force. Accordingly, such matters as the accused's emotional control, education, and intelligence are relevant in determining the accused's actual belief as to the force necessary to repel the attack.

See also Mil. R. Evid. 404(a)(2) as to evidence concerning the character of the victim.

---

(2) *Certain aggravated assault cases.* It is a defense to assault with a dangerous weapon or means likely to produce death or grievous bodily harm that the accused:

(A) Apprehended, on reasonable grounds, that bodily harm was about to be inflicted wrongfully on the accused; and

(B) In order to deter the assailant, offered but did not actually apply or attempt to apply such means or force as would be likely to cause death or grievous bodily harm.

Discussion

The principles in the discussion of subsection (e)(1) of this rule concerning reasonableness of the apprehension of bodily harm apply here.

If, as a result of the accused's offer of a means or force likely to produce grievous bodily harm, the victim was killed or injured unintentionally by the accused, this aspect of self-defense may operate in conjunction with the defense of accident (*see* subsection (f) of this rule) to excuse the accused's acts. The death or injury must have been an unintended and unexpected result of the accused's exercise of the right of self-defense.

---

(3) *Other assaults.* It is a defense to any assault punishable under Article 90, 91, or 128 and not listed in subsections (e)(1) or (2) of this rule that the accused:

(A) Apprehended, upon reasonable grounds, that bodily harm was about to be inflicted wrongfully on the accused; and

(B) Believed that the force that accused used was necessary for protection against bodily harm, provided that the force used by the accused was less than force reasonably likely to produce death or grievous bodily harm.

Discussion

The principles in the discussion under subsection (e)(1) apply here.

If, in using only such force as the accused was entitled to use under this aspect of self-defense, death or serious injury to the victim results, this aspect of self-defense may operate in conjunction with the defense of accident (*see* subsection (f) of this rule) to excuse the accused's acts. The death or serious injury must have been an unintended and unexpected result of the accused's proper exercise of the right of self-defense.

---

(4) *Loss of right to self-defense.* The right to self-defense is lost and the defenses described in subsections (e)(1), (2), and (3) of this rule shall not apply if the accused was an aggressor, engaged in mutual combat, or provoked the attack which gave rise to the apprehension, unless the accused had withdrawn in good faith after the aggression, combat, or provocation and before the offense alleged occurred.

Discussion

A person does not become an aggressor or provocateur merely because that person approaches another to seek an interview, even if the approach is not made in a friendly manner. For example, one may approach another and demand an explanation of offensive words or redress of a complaint. If the approach is made in a nonviolent manner, the right to self-defense is not lost.

Failure to retreat, when retreat is possible, does not deprive the accused of the right to self-defense if the accused was lawfully present. The availability of avenues of retreat is one factor which may be considered in addressing the reasonableness of the accused's apprehension of bodily harm and the sincerity of the accused's belief that the force used was necessary for self-protection.

---

(5) *Defense of another.* The principles of self-defense under subsection (e)(1) through (4) of this rule apply to defense of another. It is a defense to homicide, attempted homicide, assault with intent to kill,

or any assault under Article 90, 91, or 128 that the accused acted in defense of another, provided that the accused may not use more force than the person defended was lawfully entitled to use under the circumstances.

Discussion

The accused acts at the accused's peril when defending another. Thus, if the accused goes to the aid of an apparent assault victim, the accused is guilty of any assault the accused commits on the apparent assailant if, unbeknownst to the accused, the apparent victim was in fact the aggressor and not entitled to use self-defense.

(f) *Accident.* A death, injury, or other event which occurs as the unintentional and unexpected result of doing a lawful act in a lawful manner is an accident and excusable.

Discussion

The defense of accident is not available when the act which caused the death, injury, or event was a negligent act.

(g) *Entrapment.* It is a defense that the criminal design or suggestion to commit the offense originated in the Government and the accused had no predisposition to commit the offense.

Discussion

The "Government" includes agents of the Government and persons cooperating with them (for example, informants). The fact that persons acting for the Government merely afford opportunities or facilities for the commission of the offense does not constitute entrapment. Entrapment occurs only when the criminal conduct is the product of the creative activity of law enforcement officials.

When the defense of entrapment is raised, evidence of uncharged misconduct by the accused of a nature similar to that charged is admissible to show predisposition. *See* Mil. R. Evid. 404(b).

(h) *Coercion or duress.* It is a defense to any offense except killing an innocent person that the accused's participation in the offense was caused by a reasonable apprehension that the accused or another innocent person would be immediately killed or would immediately suffer serious bodily injury if the accused did not commit the act. The apprehension must reasonably continue throughout the commission of the act. If the accused has any reasonable opportunity to avoid committing the act without subjecting the accused or another innocent person to the harm threatened, this defense shall not apply.

Discussion

The immediacy of the harm necessary may vary with the circumstances. For example, a threat to kill a person's wife the next day may be immediate if the person has no opportunity to contact law enforcement officials or otherwise protect the intended victim or avoid committing the offense before then.

(i) *Inability.* It is a defense to refusal or failure to perform a duty that the accused was, through no fault of the accused, not physically or financially able to perform the duty.

Discussion

The test of inability is objective in nature. The accused's opinion that a physical impairment prevented performance of the duty will not suffice unless the opinion is reasonable under all the circumstances.

If the physical or financial inability of the accused occurred through the accused's own fault or design, it is not a defense. For example, if the accused, having knowledge of an order to get a haircut, spends money on other nonessential items, the accused's inability to pay for the haircut would not be a defense.

(j) *Ignorance or mistake of fact.*

(1) *Generally.* Except as otherwise provided in this subsection, it is a defense to an offense that the accused held, as a result of ignorance or mistake, an incorrect belief of the true circumstances such that, if the circumstances were as the accused believed them, the accused would not be guilty of the offense. If the ignorance or mistake goes to an element requiring premeditation, specific intent, willfulness, or knowledge of a particular fact, the ignorance or mistake need only have existed in the mind of the accused. If the ignorance or mistake goes to any other element requiring only general intent or knowledge, the ignorance or mistake must have existed in the mind of the accused and must have been reasonable under all the circumstances. However, if the accused's knowledge or intent is immaterial as to an element, then ignorance or mistake is not a defense.

(2) *Child Sexual Offenses.* It is a defense to a prosecution for Article 120(d), aggravated sexual assault of a child, Article 120(f), aggravated sexual abuse of a child, Article 120(i), abusive sexual contact with a child, or Article 120 (j), indecent liberty

with a child that, at the time of the offense, the child was at least 12 years of age, and the accused reasonably believed the person was at least 16 years of age. The accused must prove this defense by a preponderance of the evidence.

Discussion

Examples of ignorance or mistake which need only exist in fact include: ignorance of the fact that the person assaulted was an officer; belief that property allegedly stolen belonged to the accused; belief that a controlled substance was really sugar.

Examples of ignorance or mistake which must be reasonable as well as actual include: belief that the accused charged with unauthorized absence had permission to go; belief that the accused had a medical "profile" excusing shaving as otherwise required by regulation. Some offenses require special standards of conduct (*see*, for example, paragraph 68, Part IV, Dishonorable failure to maintain sufficient funds); the element of reasonableness must be applied in accordance with the standards imposed by such offenses.

Examples of offenses in which the accused's intent or knowledge is immaterial include: rape of a child, aggravated sexual contact with a child, or indecent liberty with a child (if the victim is under 12 years of age, knowledge or belief as to age is immaterial). However, such ignorance or mistake may be relevant in extenuation and mitigation.

See subsection (l)(1) of this rule concerning ignorance or mistake of law. The statutory text of Article 120(r) specifically limits the affirmative defense for mistake of fact as to consent to Article 120(a) (Rape), Article 120(c) (Aggravated sexual assault), Article 120(e) (Aggravated sexual contact), and Article 120(h) (Abusive sexual contact). For all other offenses under Article 120, consent is not an issue and mistake of fact as to consent is not an affirmative defense.

---

(3) *Sexual offenses.* It is an affirmative defense to a prosecution for Article 120(a), rape, Article 120(c), aggravated sexual assault, Article 120(e), aggravated sexual contact, and Article 120(h), abusive sexual contact that the accused held, as a result of ignorance or mistake, an incorrect belief that the other person engaging in the sexual conduct consented. The ignorance or mistake must have existed in the mind of the accused and must have been reasonable under all the circumstances. To be reasonable the ignorance or mistake must have been based on information, or lack of it, which would indicate to a reasonable person that the other person consented. Additionally, the ignorance or mistake cannot be based on the negligent failure to discover the true facts. Negligence is the absence of due care. Due care is what a reasonably careful person would do under the same or similar circumstances. The accused's state of intoxication, if any, at the time of the offense is not relevant to mistake of fact. A mistaken belief that the other person consented must be that which a reasonably careful, ordinary, prudent, sober adult would have had under the circumstances at the time of the offense.

(k) *Lack of mental responsibility.*

(1) *Lack of mental responsibility.* It is an affirmative defense to any offense that, at the time of the commission of the acts constituting the offense, the accused, as a result of a severe mental disease or defect, was unable to appreciate the nature and quality or the wrongfulness of his or her acts. Mental disease or defect does not otherwise constitute a defense.

Discussion

See R.C.M. 706 concerning sanity inquiries; R.C.M. 909 concerning the capacity of the accused to stand trial; and R.C.M. 1102A concerning any post-trial hearing for an accused found not guilty only by reason of lack of mental responsibility.

---

(2) *Partial mental responsibility.* A mental condition not amounting to a lack of mental responsibility under subsection (k)(1) of this rule is not an affirmative defense.

Discussion

Evidence of a mental condition not amounting to a lack of mental responsibility may be admissible as to whether the accused entertained a state of mind necessary to be proven as an element of the offense. The defense must notify the trial counsel before the beginning of trial on the merits if the defense intends to introduce expert testimony as to the accused's mental condition. *See* R.C.M. 701(b)(2).

---

(3) *Procedure.*

(A) *Presumption.* The accused is presumed to have been mentally responsible at the time of the alleged offense. This presumption continues until the accused establishes, by clear and convincing evidence, that he or she was not mentally responsible at the time of the alleged offense.

Discussion

The accused is presumed to be mentally responsible, and this presumption continues throughout the proceedings unless the finder of fact determines that the accused has proven lack of mental responsibility by clear and convincing evidence. *See* subsection (b) of this rule.

(B) *Inquiry.* If a question is raised concerning the mental responsibility of the accused, the military judge shall rule finally whether to direct an inquiry under R.C.M. 706. In a special court-martial without a military judge, the president shall rule finally except to the extent that the question is one of fact, in which case the president rules subject to objection by any member.

Discussion

See R.C.M. 801(e)(3) for the procedures for voting on rulings of the president of a special court-martial without a military judge.

If an inquiry is directed, priority should be given to it.

(C) *Determination.* The issue of mental responsibility shall not be considered as an interlocutory question.

(l) *Not defenses generally.*

(1) *Ignorance or mistake of law.* Ignorance or mistake of law, including general orders or regulations, ordinarily is not a defense.

Discussion

For example, ignorance that it is a crime to possess marijuana is not a defense to wrongful possession of marijuana.

Ignorance or mistake of law may be a defense in some limited circumstances. If the accused, because of a mistake as to a separate nonpenal law, lacks the criminal intent or state of mind necessary to establish guilt, this may be a defense. For example, if the accused, under mistaken belief that the accused is entitled to take an item under property law, takes an item, this mistake of law (as to the accused's legal right) would, if genuine, be a defense to larceny. On the other hand, if the accused disobeyed an order, under the actual but mistaken belief that the order was unlawful, this would not be a defense because the accused's mistake was as to the order itself, and not as to a separate nonpenal law. Also, mistake of law may be a defense when the mistake results from reliance on the decision or pronouncement of an authorized public official or agency. For example, if an accused, acting on the advice of an official responsible for administering benefits that the accused is entitled to those benefits, applies for and receives those benefits, the accused may have a defense even though the accused was not legally eligible for the benefits. On the other hand, reliance on the advice of counsel that a certain course of conduct is legal is not, of itself, a defense.

(2) *Voluntary intoxication.* Voluntary intoxication, whether caused by alcohol or drugs, is not a defense. However, evidence of any degree of voluntary intoxication may be introduced for the purpose of raising a reasonable doubt as to the existence of actual knowledge, specific intent, willfulness, or a premeditated design to kill, if actual knowledge, specific intent, willfulness, or premeditated design to kill is an element of the offense.

Discussion

Intoxication may reduce premeditated murder to unpremeditated murder, but it will not reduce murder to manslaughter or any other lesser offense. *See* paragraph 43c(2)(c), Part IV.

Although voluntary intoxication is not a defense, evidence of voluntary intoxication may be admitted in extenuation.

Rule 917. Motion for a finding of not guilty

(a) *In general.* The military judge, on motion by the accused or *sua sponte*, shall enter a finding of not guilty of one or more offenses charged after the evidence on either side is closed and before findings on the general issue of guilt are announced if the evidence is insufficient to sustain a conviction of the offense affected. If a motion for a finding of not guilty at the close of the prosecution's case is denied, the defense may offer evidence on that offense without having reserved the right to do so.

(b) *Form of motion.* The motion shall specifically indicate wherein the evidence is insufficient.

(c) *Procedure.* Before ruling on a motion for a finding of not guilty, whether made by counsel or *sua sponte*, the military judge shall give each party an opportunity to be heard on the matter.

Discussion

The military judge ordinarily should permit the trial counsel to reopen the case as to the insufficiency specified in the motion.

See R.C.M. 801(e)(2) and (3) for additional procedures to be followed in a special court-martial without a military judge. *See* R.C.M. 1102(b)(2) for the military judge's authority, upon motion or sua sponte, to enter finding of not guilty after findings but prior to authentication of the record.

(d) *Standard.* A motion for a finding of not guilty shall be granted only in the absence of some evidence which, together with all reasonable inferences and applicable presumptions, could reasonably tend to establish every essential element of an offense charged. The evidence shall be viewed in the light most favorable to the prosecution, without an evaluation of the credibility of witnesses.

(e) *Motion as to greater offense.* A motion for a finding of not guilty may be granted as to part of a specification and, if appropriate, the corresponding charge, as long as a lesser offense charged is alleged in the portion of the specification as to which the motion is not granted. In such cases, the military judge shall announce that a finding of not guilty has been granted as to specified language in the specification and, if appropriate, corresponding charge. In cases before members, the military judge shall instruct the members accordingly, so that any findings later announced will not be inconsistent with the granting of the motion.

(f) *Effect of ruling.* A ruling granting a motion for a finding of not guilty is final when announced and may not be reconsidered. Such a ruling is a finding of not guilty of the affected specification, or affected portion thereof, and, when appropriate, of the corresponding charge. A ruling denying a motion for a finding of not guilty may be reconsidered at any time prior to authentication of the record of trial.

(g) *Effect of denial on review.* If all the evidence admitted before findings, regardless by whom offered, is sufficient to sustain findings of guilty, the findings need not be set aside upon review solely because the motion for finding of not guilty should have been granted upon the state of the evidence when it was made.

Rule 918. Findings

(a) *General findings.* The general findings of a court-martial state whether the accused is guilty of each offense charged. If two or more accused are tried together, separate findings as to each shall be made.

(1) *As to a specification.* General findings as to a specification may be: guilty; not guilty of an offense as charged, but guilty of a named lesser included offense; guilty with exceptions, with or without substitutions, not guilty of the exceptions, but guilty of the substitutions, if any; not guilty only by reason of lack of mental responsibility; or, not guilty. Exceptions and substitutions may not be used to substantially change the nature of the offense or to increase the seriousness of the offense or the maximum punishment for it.

Discussion

Exceptions and substitutions. One or more words or figures may be excepted from a specification and, when necessary, others substituted, if the remaining language of the specification, with or without substitutions, states an offense by the accused which is punishable by court-martial. Changing the date or place of the offense may, but does not necessarily, change the nature or identity of an offense.

If A and B are joint accused and A is convicted but B is acquitted of the offense charged, A should be found guilty be excepting the name of B from the specification as well as any other words indicating the offense was a joint one.

Lesser included offenses. If the evidence fails to prove the offense charged but does prove an offense necessarily included in the offense charged, the factfinder may find the accused not guilty of the offense charged but guilty of a named lesser offense, which is included in the offense charged, without the use of exceptions and substitutions. Ordinarily an attempt is a lesser included offense even if the evidence establishes that the offense charged was consummated. *See* Part IV concerning lesser included offenses.

Offenses arising from the same act or transaction. The accused may be found guilty of two or more offenses arising from the same act or transaction, whether or not the offenses are separately punishable. *But see* R.C.M. 906(b)(12); 907(b)(3)(B); 1003(c)(1)(C).

---

(2) *As to a charge.* General findings as to a charge may be: guilty; not guilty, but guilty of a violation of Article ______; not guilty only by reason of lack of mental responsibility; or not guilty.

Discussion

Where there are two or more specifications under one charge, conviction of any of those specifications requires a finding of guilty of the corresponding charge. Under such circumstances any findings of not guilty as to the other specifications do not affect that charge. If the accused is found guilty of one specification and of a lesser included offense prohibited by a different Article as to another specification under the same charge, the findings as to the corresponding charge should be: Of the Charge as the specification 1: Guilty; as to specification 2; not guilty, but guilty of a violation of Article ______.

An attempt should be found as a violation of Article 80 unless the attempt is punishable under Articles 85, 94, 100, 104, or 128, in which case it should be found as a violation of that Article.

A court-martial may not find an offense as a violation of an article under which it was not charged solely for the purpose of increasing the authorized punishment or for the purpose of adjudging less than the prescribed mandatory punishment.

(b) *Special findings.* In a trial by court-martial composed of military judge alone, the military judge shall make special findings upon request by any party. Special findings may be requested only as to matters of fact reasonably in issue as to an offense and need be made only as to offenses of which the accused was found guilty. Special findings may be requested at any time before general findings are announced. Only one set of special findings may be requested by a party in a case. If the request is for findings on specific matters, the military judge may require that the request be written. Special findings may be entered orally on the record at the court-martial or in writing during or after the court-martial, but in any event shall be made before authentication and included in the record of trial.

Discussion

Special findings ordinarily include findings as to the elements of the offenses of which the accused has been found guilty, and any affirmative defense relating thereto.

See also R.C.M. 905(d); Mil. R. Evid. 304(d)(4); 311(d)(4); 321(f) concerning other findings to be made by the military judge.

Members may not make special findings.

(c) *Basis of findings.* Findings may be based on direct or circumstantial evidence. Only matters properly before the court-martial on the merits of the case may be considered. A finding of guilty of any offense may be reached only when the factfinder is satisfied that guilt has been proved beyond a reasonable doubt.

Discussion

Direct evidence is evidence which tends directly to prove or disprove a fact in issue (for example, an element of the offense charged). Circumstantial evidence is evidence which tends directly to prove not a fact in issue but some other fact or circumstance from which, either alone or together with other facts or circumstances, one may reasonably infer the existence or non-existence of a fact in issue. There is no general rule for determining or comparing the weight to be given to direct or circumstantial evidence.

A reasonable doubt is a doubt based on reason and common sense. A reasonable doubt is not mere conjecture; it is an honest, conscientious doubt suggested by the evidence, or lack of it, in the case. An absolute or mathematical certainty is not required. The rule as to reasonable doubt extends to every element of the offense. It is not necessary that each particular fact advanced by the prosecution which is not an element be proved beyond a reasonable doubt.

The factfinder should consider the inherent probability or improbability of the evidence, using common sense and knowledge of human nature, and should weigh the credibility of witnesses. A fact finder may properly believe one witness and disbelieve others whose testimony conflicts with that of the one. A factfinder may believe part of the testimony of a witness and disbelieve other parts.

Findings of guilty may not be based solely on the testimony of a witness other than the accused which is self-contradictory, unless the contradiction is adequately explained by the witness. Even if apparently credible and corroborated, the testimony of an accomplice should be considered with great caution.

Rule 919. Argument by counsel on findings

(a) *In general.* After the closing of evidence, trial counsel shall be permitted to open the argument. The defense counsel shall be permitted to reply. Trial counsel shall then be permitted to reply in rebuttal.

(b) *Contents.* Arguments may properly include reasonable comment on the evidence in the case, including inferences to be drawn therefrom, in support of a party's theory of the case.

Discussion

The military judge may exercise reasonable control over argument. *See* R.C.M. 801(a)(3).

Argument may include comment about the testimony, conduct, motives, interests, and biases of witnesses to the extent supported by the evidence. Counsel should not express a personnel belief or opinion as to the truth or falsity of any testimony or evidence or the guilt or innocence of the accused, nor should counsel make arguments calculated to inflame passions or prejudices. In argument counsel may treat the testimony of witnesses as conclusively establishing the facts related by the witnesses. Counsel may not cite legal authorities or the facts of other cases when arguing to members on findings.

Trial counsel may not comment on the accused's exercise of the right against self-incrimination or the right to counsel. *See* Mil. R. Evid. 512. Trial counsel may not argue that the prosecution's evidence is unrebutted if the only rebuttal could come from the accused. When the accused is on trial for several offenses and testifies only as to some of the offenses, trial counsel may not comment on the accused's failure to testify as to the others. When the accused testifies on the merits regarding an offense charged, trial counsel may comment on the accused's failure in that testimony to deny or explain specific incriminating facts that the evidence for the prosecution tends to establish regarding that offense.

Trial counsel may not comment on the failure of the defense to call witnesses or of the accused to testify at the Article 32 investigation or upon the probable effect of the court-martial's findings on relations between the military and civilian communities.

The rebuttal argument of trial counsel is generally limited to matters argued by the defense. If trial counsel is permitted to introduce new matter in closing argument, the defense should be allowed to reply in rebuttal. However, this will not preclude trial counsel from presenting a final argument.

(c) *Waiver of objection to improper argument.* Failure to object to improper argument before the military judge begins to instruct the members on findings shall constitute waiver of the objection.

Discussion

If an objection that an argument is improper is sustained, the military judge should immediately instruct the members that the argument was improper and that they must disregard it. In extraordinary cases improper argument may require a mistrial. *See* R.C.M. 915. The military judge should be alert to improper argument and take appropriate action when necessary.

Rule 920. Instructions on findings

(a) *In general.* The military judge shall give the members appropriate instructions on findings.

Discussion

Instructions consist of a statement of the issues in the case and an explanation of the legal standards and procedural requirements by which the members will determine findings. Instructions should be tailored to fit the circumstances of the case, and should fairly and adequately cover the issues presented.

(b) *When given.* Instructions on findings shall be given before or after arguments by counsel, or at both times, and before the members close to deliberate on findings, but the military judge may, upon request of the members, any party, or *sua sponte*, give additional instructions at a later time.

Discussion

After members have reached a finding on a specification, instructions may not be given on an offense included therein which was not described in an earlier instruction unless the finding is illegal. This is true even if the finding has not been announced. When instructions are to be given is a matter within the sole discretion of the military trial judge.

(c) *Requests for instructions.* At the close of the evidence or at such other time as the military judge may permit, any party may request that the military judge instruct the members on the law as set forth in the request. The military judge may require the requested instruction to be written. Each party shall be given the opportunity to be heard on any proposed instruction on findings before it is given. The military judge shall inform the parties of the proposed action on such requests before their closing arguments.

Discussion

Requests for and objections to instructions should be resolved at an Article 39(a) session. *But see* R.C.M 801(e)(3); 803.

If an issue has been raised, ordinarily the military judge must instruct on the issue when requested to do so. The military judge is not required to give the specific instruction requested by counsel, however, as long as the issue is adequately covered in the instructions.

The military judge should not identify the source of any instruction when addressing the members.

All written requests for instructions should be marked as appellate exhibits, whether or not they are given.

(d) *How given.* Instructions on findings shall be given orally on the record in the presence of all parties and the members. Written copies of the instructions, or, unless a party objects, portions of them, may also be given to the members for their use during deliberations.

Discussion

A copy of any written instructions delivered to the members should be marked as an appellate exhibit.

(e) *Required instructions.* Instructions on findings shall include:

(1) A description of the elements of each offense charged, unless findings on such offenses are unnecessary because they have been entered pursuant to a plea of guilty;

(2) A description of the elements of each lesser included offense in issue, unless trial of a lesser included offense is barred by the statute of limitations (Article 43) and the accused refuses to waive the bar;

(3) A description of any special defense under R.C.M. 916 in issue;

(4) A direction that only matters properly before the court-martial may be considered;

(5) A charge that—

(A) The accused must be presumed to be innocent until the accused's guilt is established by legal and competent evidence beyond reasonable doubt;

(B) In the case being considered, if there is a reasonable doubt as to the guilt of the accused, the doubt must be resolved in favor of the accused and the accused must be acquitted;

(C) If, when a lesser included offense is in issue, there is a reasonable doubt as to the degree of guilt of the accused, the finding must be in a lower degree as to which there is not reasonable doubt; and

(D) The burden of proof to establish the guilt of the accused is upon the Government. [When the issue of lack of mental responsibility is raised, add: The burden of proving the defense of lack of mental responsibility by clear and convincing evidence is upon the accused. When the issue of mistake of fact under R.C.M. 916(j)(2) or (j)(3) is raised, add: The accused has the burden of proving the defense of mistake of fact as to consent or age by a preponderance of the evidence.]

(6) Directions on the procedures under R.C.M. 921 for deliberations and voting; and

(7) Such other explanations, descriptions, or directions as may be necessary and which are properly requested by a party or which the military judge determines, *sua sponte*, should be given.

Discussion

A matter is "in issue" when some evidence, without regard to its source or credibility, has been admitted upon which members might rely if they choose. An instruction on a lesser included offense is proper when an element from the charged offense which distinguishes thatoffense from the lesser offense is in dispute.

See R.C.M. 918(c) and discussion as to reasonable doubt and other matters relating to the basis for findings which may be the subject of an instruction.

Other matters which may be the subject of instruction in appropriate cases included: inferences (*see* the explanations in Part IV concerning inferences relating to specific offenses); the limited purpose for which evidence was admitted (regardless of whether such evidence was offered by the prosecution of defense) (*see* Mil. R. Evid. 105); the effect of character evidence (*see* Mil. R. Evid. 404; 405); the effect of judicial notice (*see* Mil. R. Evid. 201, 201A); the weight to be given a pretrial statement (*see* Mil. R. Evid. 340(e)); the effect of stipulations (*see* R.C.M. 811); that, when a guilty plea to a lesser included offense has been accepted, the members should accept as proved the matters admitted by the plea, but must determine whether the remaining elements are established; that a plea of guilty to one offense may not be the basis for inferring the existence of a fact or element of another offense; the absence of the accused from trial should not be held against the accused; and that no adverse inferences may be drawn from an accused's failure to testify (*see* Mil. R. Evid. 301(g)).

The military judge may summarize and comment upon evidence in the case in instructions. In doing so, the military judge should present an accurate, fair, and dispassionate statement of what the evidence shows; not depart from an impartial role; not assume as true the existence or nonexistence of a fact in issue when the evidence is conflicting or disputed, or when there is no evidence to support the matter; and make clear that the members must exercise their independent judgment as to the facts.

(f) *Waiver.* Failure to object to an instruction or to omission of an instruction before the members close to deliberate constitutes waiver of the objection in the absence of plain error. The military judge may require the party objecting to specify of what respect the instructions given were improper. The parties shall be given the opportunity to be heard on any objection outside the presence of the members.

Rule 921. Deliberations and voting on findings

(a) *In general.* After the military judge instructs the members on findings, the members shall deliberate and vote in a closed session. Only the members shall be present during deliberations and voting. Superiority in rank shall not be used in any manner in an attempt to control the independence of members in the exercise of their judgment.

(b) *Deliberations.* Deliberations properly include full and free discussion of the merits of the case. Unless otherwise directed by the military judge, members may take with them in deliberations their notes, if any, any exhibits admitted in evidence, and any written instructions. Members may request that the court-martial be reopened and that portions of the record be read to them or additional evidence introduced. The military judge may, in the exercise of discretion, grant such request.

(c) *Voting.*

(1) *Secret ballot.* Voting on the findings for each charge and specification shall be by secret written ballot. All members present shall vote.

(2) *Numbers of votes required to convict.*

(A) *Death penalty mandatory.* A finding of guilty of an offense for which the death penalty is mandatory results only if all members present vote for a finding of guilty.

Discussion

Article 106 is the only offense under the code for which the death penalty is mandatory.

(B) *Other offenses.* As to any offense for which the death penalty is not mandatory, a finding of guilty results only if at least two-thirds of the members present vote for a finding of guilty.

Discussion

In computing the number of votes required to convict, any fraction of a vote is rounded up to the next whole number. For example, if there are five members, the concurrence of at least four would be required to convict. The military judge should instruct the members on the specific number of votes required to convict.

---

(3) *Acquittal.* If fewer than two-thirds of the members present vote for a finding of guilty—or, when the death penalty is mandatory, if fewer than all the members present vote for a finding of guilty—a finding of not guilty has resulted as to the charge or specification on which the vote was taken.

(4) *Not guilty only by reason of lack of mental responsibility.* When the defense of lack of mental responsibility is in issue under R.C.M. 916(k)(1), the members shall first vote on whether the prosecution has proven the elements of the offense beyond a reasonable doubt. If at least two-thirds of the members present (all members for offenses where the death penalty is mandatory) vote for a finding of guilty, then the members shall vote on whether the accused has proven lack of mental responsibility. If a majority of the members present concur that the accused has proven lack of mental responsibility by clear and convincing evidence, a finding of not guilty only by reason of lack of mental responsibility results. If the vote on lack of mental responsibility does not result in a finding of not guilty only by reason of lack of mental responsibility, then the defense of lack of mental responsibility has been rejected and the finding of guilty stands.

Discussion

If lack of mental responsibility is in issue with regard to more than one specification, the members should determine the issue of lack of mental responsibility on each specification separately.

---

(5) *Included offenses.* Members shall not vote on a lesser included offense unless a finding of not guilty of the offense charged has been reached. If a finding of not guilty of an offense charged has been reached the members shall vote on each included offense on which they have been instructed, in order of severity beginning with the most severe. The members shall continue the vote on each included offense on which they have been instructed until a finding of guilty results or findings of not guilty have been reached as to each such offense.

(6) *Procedure for voting.*

(A) *Order.* Each specification shall be voted on separately before the corresponding charge. The order of voting on several specifications under a charge or on several charges shall be determined by the president unless a majority of the members object.

(B) *Counting votes.* The junior member shall collect the ballots and count the votes. The president shall check the count and inform the other members of the result.

Discussion

Once findings have been reached, they may be reconsidered only in accordance with R.C.M. 924.

(d) *Action after findings are reached.* After the members have reached findings on each charge and specification before them, the court-martial shall be opened and the president shall inform the military judge that findings have been reached. The military judge may, in the presence of the parties, examine any writing which the president intends to read to announce the findings and may assist the members in putting the findings in proper form. Neither that writing nor any oral or written clarification or discussion concerning it shall constitute announcement of the findings.

Discussion

Ordinarily a findings worksheet should be provided to the members as an aid to putting the findings in proper form. *See* Appendix 10 for a format for findings. If the military judge examines any writing by the members or otherwise assists them to put findings in proper form, this must be done in an open session and counsel should be given the opportunity to examine such a writing and to be heard on any instructions the military judge may give. *See* Article 39(b).

The president should not disclose any specific number of votes for or against any finding.

Rule 922. Announcement of findings

(a) *In general.* Findings shall be announced in the presence of all parties promptly after they have been determined.

Discussion

See Appendix 10. A finding of an offense about which no instructions were given is not proper.

(b) *Findings by members.* The president shall announce the findings by the members.

(1) If a finding is based on a plea of guilty, the president shall so state.

(2) In a capital case, if a finding of guilty is unanimous with respect to a capital offense, the president shall so state. This provision shall not apply during reconsideration under R.C.M. 924(a) of a finding of guilty previously announced in open court unless the prior finding was announced as unanimous.

Discussion

If the findings announced are ambiguous, the military judge should seek clarification. *See also* R.C.M. 924. A nonunanimous finding of guilty as to a capital offense may be reconsidered, but not for the purpose of rendering a unanimous verdict in order to authorize a capital sentencing proceeding. The president shall not make a statement regarding unanimity with respect to reconsideration of findings as to an offense in which the prior findings were not unanimous.

(c) *Findings by military judge.* The military judge shall announce the findings when trial is by military judge alone or when findings may be entered upon R.C.M. 910(g).

(d) *Erroneous announcement.* If an error was made in the announcement of the findings of the court-martial, the error may be corrected by a new announcement in accordance with this rule. The error must be discovered and the new announcement made before the final adjournment of the court-martial in the case.

Discussion

See R.C.M. 1102 concerning the action to be taken if the error in the announcement is discovered after final adjournment.

(e) *Polling prohibited.* Except as provided in Mil. R. Evid. 606, members may not be questioned about their deliberations and voting.

Rule 923. Impeachment of findings

Findings which are proper on their face may be impeached only when extraneous prejudicial information was improperly brought to the attention of a member, outside influence was improperly brought to bear upon any member, or unlawful command influence was brought to bear upon any member.

Discussion

Deliberations of the members ordinarily are not subject to disclosure. *See* Mil. R. Evid. 606. Unsound reasoning by a member, misconception of the evidence, or misapplication of the law is not a proper basis for challenging the findings. However, when a showing of a ground for impeaching the verdict has been made, members may be questioned about such a ground. The military judge determines, as an interlocutory matter, whether such an inquiry will be conducted and whether a finding has been impeached.

Rule 924. Reconsideration of findings

(a) *Time for reconsideration.* Members may reconsider any finding reached by them before such finding is announced in open session.

(b) *Procedure.* Any member may propose that a finding be reconsidered. If such a proposal is made in a timely manner the question whether to reconsider shall be determined in closed session by secret written ballot. Any finding of not guilty shall be reconsidered if a majority vote for reconsideration. Any finding of guilty shall be reconsidered if more than one-third of the members vote for reconsideration. When the death penalty is mandatory, a request by any member for reconsideration of a guilty finding requires reconsideration. Any finding of not guilty only by reason of lack of mental responsibility shall be reconsidered on the issue of the finding of guilty of the elements if more than one-third of the members vote for reconsideration, and on the issue of mental responsibility if a majority vote for reconsideration. If a vote to reconsider a finding succeeds, the procedures in R.C.M. 921 shall apply.

Discussion

After the initial secret ballot vote on a finding in closed session, no other vote may be taken on that finding unless a vote to reconsider succeeds.

(c) *Military judge sitting alone.* In trial by military judge alone, the military judge may reconsider any finding of guilty at any time before announcement of sentence and may reconsider the issue of the finding of guilty of the elements in a finding of not guilty only by reason of lack of mental responsibility at any time before announcement of sentence or authentication of the record of trial in the case of a complete acquittal.

CHAPTER X. SENTENCING

Rule 1001. Presentencing procedure

(a) *In general.*

(1) *Procedure.* After findings of guilty have been announced, the prosecution and defense may present matter pursuant to this rule to aid the court-martial in determining an appropriate sentence. Such matter shall ordinarily be presented in the following sequence—

(A) Presentation by trial counsel of:

(i) service data relating to the accused taken from the charge sheet;

(ii) personal data relating to the accused and of the character of the accused's prior service as reflected in the personnel records of the accused;

(iii) evidence of prior convictions, military or civilian;

(iv) evidence of aggravation; and

(v) evidence of rehabilitative potential.

(B) Presentation by the defense of evidence in extenuation or mitigation or both.

(C) Rebuttal.

(D) Argument by the trial counsel on sentence.

(E) Argument by the defense counsel on sentence.

(F) Rebuttal arguments in the discretion of the military judge.

(2) *Adjudging sentence.* A sentence shall be adjudged in all cases without unreasonable delay.

(3) *Advice and inquiry.* The military judge shall personally inform the accused of the right to present matters in extenuation and mitigation, including the right to make a sworn or unsworn statement or to remain silent, and shall ask whether the accused chooses to exercise those rights.

(b) *Matter to be presented by the prosecution.*

(1) *Service data from the charge sheet.* Trial counsel shall inform the court-martial of the data on the charge sheet relating to the pay and service of the accused and the duration and nature of any pretrial restraint. In the discretion of the military judge, this may be done by reading the material from the charge sheet or by giving the court-martial a written statement of such matter. If the defense objects to the data as being materially inaccurate or incomplete, or containing specified objectionable matter, the military judge shall determine the issue. Objections not asserted are waived.

(2) *Personal data and character of prior service of the accused.* Under regulations of the Secretary concerned, trial counsel may obtain and introduce from the personnel records of the accused evidence of the accused's marital status; number of dependents, if any; and character of prior service. Such evidence includes copies of reports reflecting the past military efficiency, conduct, performance, and history of the accused and evidence of any disciplinary actions including punishments under Article 15.

"Personnel records of the accused" includes any records made or maintained in accordance with departmental regulations that reflect the past military efficiency, conduct, performance, and history of the accused. If the accused objects to a particular document as inaccurate or incomplete in a specified respect, or as containing matter that is not admissible under the Military Rules of Evidence, the matter shall be determined by the military judge. Objections not asserted are waived.

(3) *Evidence of prior convictions of the accused.*

(A) *In general.* The trial counsel may introduce evidence of military or civilian convictions of the accused. For purposes of this rule, there is a "conviction" in a court-martial case when a sentence has been adjudged. In a civilian case, a "conviction" includes any disposition following an initial judicial determination or assumption of guilt, such as when guilt has been established by guilty plea, trial, or plea of nolo contendere, regardless of the subsequent disposition, sentencing procedure, or final judgment. However, a "civilian conviction" does not include a diversion from the judicial process without a finding or admission of guilt; expunged convictions; juvenile adjudications; minor traffic violations; foreign convictions; tribal court convictions; or convictions reversed, vacated, invalidated or pardoned because of errors of law or because of subsequently discovered evidence exonerating the accused.

Discussion

A vacation of a suspended sentence (*see* R.C.M. 1109) is not a conviction and is not admissible as such, but may be admissible under subsection (b)(2) of this rule as reflective of the character of the prior service of the accused.

Whether a civilian conviction is admissible is left to the discretion of the military judge. As stated in the rule, a civilian "conviction" includes any disposition following an initial judicial determination or assumption of guilt regardless of the sentencing procedure and the final judgment following probation or other sentence. Therefore, convictions may be admissible regardless of whether a court ultimately suspended judgment upon discharge of the accused following probation, permitted withdrawal of the guilty plea, or applies some other form of alternative sentencing. Additionally, the term "conviction" need not be taken to mean a final judgment of conviction and sentence.

(B) *Pendency of appeal.* The pendency of an appeal therefrom does not render evidence of a conviction inadmissible except that a conviction by summary court-martial or special court-martial without a military judge may not be used for purposes of this rule until review has been completed pursuant to Article 64 or Article 66, if applicable. Evidence of the pendency of an appeal is admissible.

(C) *Method of proof.* Previous convictions may be proved by any evidence admissible under the Military Rules of Evidence.

Discussion

Normally, previous convictions may be proved by use of the personnel records of the accused, by the record of the conviction, or by the order promulgating the result of trial. *See* DD Form 493 (Extract of Military Records of Previous Convictions).

---

(4) *Evidence in aggravation.* The trial counsel may present evidence as to any aggravating circumstances directly relating to or resulting from the offenses of which the accused has been found guilty. Evidence in aggravation includes, but is not limited to, evidence of financial, social, psychological, and medical impact on or cost to any person or entity who was the victim of an offense committed by the accused and evidence of significant adverse impact on the mission, discipline, or efficiency of the command directly and immediately resulting from the accused's offense. In addition, evidence in aggravation may include evidence that the accused intentionally selected any victim or any property as the object of the offense because of the actual or perceived race, color, religion, national origin, ethnicity, gender, disability, or sexual orientation of any person. Except in capital cases a written or oral deposition taken in accordance with R.C.M. 702 is admissible in aggravation.

Discussion

See also R.C.M. 1004 concerning aggravating circumstances in capital cases.

---

(5) *Evidence of rehabilitative potential.* Rehabilitative potential refers to the accused's potential to be restored, through vocational, correctional, or therapeutic training or other corrective measures to a useful and constructive place in society.

(A) *In general.* The trial counsel may present, by testimony or oral deposition in accordance with R.C.M. 702(g)(1), evidence in the form of opinions concerning the accused's previous performance as a servicemember and potential for rehabilitation.

(B) *Foundation for opinion.* The witness or deponent providing opinion evidence regarding the accused's rehabilitative potential must possess sufficient information and knowledge about the accused to offer a rationally-based opinion that is helpful to the sentencing authority. Relevant information and knowledge include, but are not limited to, information and knowledge about the accused's character, performance of duty, moral fiber, determination to be rehabilitated, and nature and severity of the offense or offenses.

Discussion

See generally Mil. R. Evid. 701, Opinion testimony by lay witnesses. *See also* Mil. R. Evid. 703, Bases of opinion testimony by experts, if the witness or deponent is testifying as an expert. The types of information and knowledge reflected in this subparagraph are illustrative only.

(C) *Bases for opinion.* An opinion regarding the accused's rehabilitative potential must be based upon relevant information and knowledge possessed by the witness or deponent, and must relate to the accused's personal circumstances. The opinion of the witness or deponent regarding the severity or nature of the accused's offense or offenses may not serve as the principal basis for an opinion of the accused's rehabilitative potential.

(D) *Scope of opinion.* An opinion offered under this rule is limited to whether the accused has rehabilitative potential and to the magnitude or quality of any such potential. A witness may not offer an opinion regarding the appropriateness of a punitive discharge or whether the accused should be returned to the accused's unit.

Discussion

On direct examination, a witness or deponent may respond affirmatively or negatively regarding whether the accused has rehabilitative potential. The witness or deponent may also opine succinctly regarding the magnitude or quality of the accused rehabilitative potential; for example, the witness or deponent may opine that the accused has "great" or "little" rehabilitative potential. The witness or deponent, however, generally may not further elaborate on the accused's rehabilitative potential, such as describing the particular reasons for forming the opinion.

(E) *Cross-examination.* On cross-examination, inquiry is permitted into relevant and specific instances of conduct.

(F) *Redirect.* Notwithstanding any other provision in this rule, the scope of opinion testimony permitted on redirect may be expanded, depending upon the nature and scope of the cross-examination.

Discussion

For example, on redirect a witness or deponent may testify regarding specific instances of conduct when the cross-examination of the witness or deponent concerned specific instances of misconduct. Similarly, for example, on redirect a witness or deponent may offer an opinion on matters beyond the scope of the accused's rehabilitative potential if an opinion about such matters was elicited during cross-examination of the witness or deponent and is otherwise admissible.

(c) *Matter to be presented by the defense.*

(1) *In general.* The defense may present matters in rebuttal of any material presented by the prosecution and may present matters in extenuation and mitigation regardless whether the defense offered evidence before findings.

(A) *Matter in extenuation.* Matter in extenuation of an offense serves to explain the circumstances surrounding the commission of an offense, including those reasons for committing the offense which do not constitute a legal justification or excuse.

(B) *Matter in mitigation.* Matter in mitigation of an offense is introduced to lessen the punishment to be adjudged by the court-martial, or to furnish grounds for a recommendation of clemency. It includes the fact that nonjudicial punishment under Article 15 has been imposed for an offense growing out of the same act or omission that constitutes the offense of which the accused has been found guilty, particular acts of good conduct or bravery and evidence of the reputation or record of the accused in the service for efficiency, fidelity, subordination, temperance, courage, or any other trait that is desirable in a servicemember.

(2) *Statement by the accused.*

(A) *In general.* The accused may testify, make an unsworn statement, or both in extenuation, in mitigation or to rebut matters presented by the prosecution, or for all three purposes whether or not the accused testified prior to findings. The accused may limit such testimony or statement to any one or more of the specifications of which the accused has been found guilty. This subsection does not permit the filing of an affidavit of the accused.

(B) *Testimony of the accused.* The accused may give sworn oral testimony under this paragraph and shall be subject to cross-examination concerning it by the trial counsel or examination on it by the court-martial, or both.

(C) *Unsworn statement.* The accused may make an unsworn statement and may not be cross-examined by the trial counsel upon it or examined upon it by the court-martial. The prosecution may, however, rebut any statements of facts therein. The unsworn statement may be oral, written, or both, and may be made by the accused, by counsel, or both.

Discussion

An unsworn statement ordinarily should not include what is properly argument, but inclusion of such matter by the accused when personally making an oral statement normally should not be grounds for stopping the statement.

---

(3) *Rules of evidence relaxed.* The military judge may, with respect to matters in extenuation or mitigation or both, relax the rules of evidence. This may include admitting letters, affidavits, certificates of military and civil officers, and other writings of similar authenticity and reliability.

(d) *Rebuttal and surrebuttal.* The prosecution may rebut matters presented by the defense. The defense in surrebuttal may then rebut any rebuttal offered by the prosecution. Rebuttal and surrebuttal may continue, in the discretion of the military judge. If the Military Rules of Evidence were relaxed under subsection (c)(3) of this rule, they may be relaxed during rebuttal and surrebuttal to the same degree.

(e) *Production of witnesses.*

(1) *In general.* During the presentence proceedings, there shall be much greater latitude than on the merits to receive information by means other than testimony presented through the personal appearance of witnesses. Whether a witness shall be produced to testify during presentence proceedings is a matter within the discretion of the military judge, subject to the limitations in subsection (e)(2) of this rule.

Discussion

See R.C.M. 703 concerning the procedures for production of witnesses.

---

(2) *Limitations.* A witness may be produced to testify during presentence proceedings through a subpoena or travel orders at Government expense only if—

(A) The testimony expected to be offered by the witness is necessary for consideration of a matter of substantial significance to a determination of an appropriate sentence, including evidence necessary to resolve an alleged inaccuracy or dispute as to a material fact;

(B) The weight or credibility of the testimony is of substantial significance to the determination of an appropriate sentence;

(C) The other party refuses to enter into a stipulation of fact containing the matters to which the witness is expected to testify, except in an extraordinary case when such a stipulation of fact would be an insufficient substitute for the testimony;

(D) Other forms of evidence, such as oral depositions, written interrogatories, former testimony, or testimony by remote means would not be sufficient to meet the needs of the court-martial in the determination of an appropriate sentence; and

(E) The significance of the personal appearance of the witness to the determination of an appropriate sentence, when balanced against the practical difficulties of producing the witness, favors production of the witness. Factors to be considered include the costs of producing the witness, the timing of the request for production of the witness, the potential delay in the presentencing proceeding that may be caused by the production of the witness, and the likelihood of significant interference with military operational deployment, mission accomplishment, or essential training.

Discussion

The procedures for receiving testimony via remote means and the definition thereof are contained in R.C.M. 914B.

(f) *Additional matters to be considered.* In addition to matters introduced under this rule, the court-martial may consider—

(1) That a plea of guilty is a mitigating factor; and

(2) Any evidence properly introduced on the merits before findings, including:

(A) Evidence of other offenses or acts of misconduct even if introduced for a limited purpose; and

(B) Evidence relating to any mental impairment or deficiency of the accused.

Discussion

The fact that the accused is of low intelligence or that, because of a mental or neurological condition the accused's ability to adhere to the right is diminished, may be extenuating. On the other hand, in determining the severity of a sentence, the court-martial may consider evidence tending to show that an accused has little regard for the rights of others.

(g) *Argument.* After introduction of matters relating to sentence under this rule, counsel for the prosecution and defense may argue for an appropriate sentence. Trial counsel may not in argument purport to speak for the convening authority or any higher authority, or refer to the views of such authorities or any policy directive relative to punishment or to any punishment or quantum of punishment greater than that court-martial may adjudge. Trial counsel may, however, recommend a specific lawful sentence and may also refer to generally accepted sentencing philosophies, including rehabilitation of the accused, general deterrence, specific deterrence of misconduct by the accused, and social retribution. Failure to object to improper argument before the military judge begins to instruct the members on sentencing shall constitute waiver of the objection.

Rule 1002. Sentence determination

Subject to limitations in this Manual, the sentence

to be adjudged is a matter within the discretion of the court-martial; except when a mandatory minimum sentence is prescribed by the code, a court-martial may adjudge any punishment authorized in this Manual, including the maximum punishment or any lesser punishment, or may adjudge a sentence of no punishment.

Discussion

See R.C.M. 1003 concerning authorized punishments and limitations on punishments. *See also* R.C.M. 1004 in capital cases.

Rule 1003. Punishments

(a) *In general.* Subject to the limitations in this Manual, the punishments authorized in this rule may be adjudged in the case of any person found guilty of an offense by a court-martial.

Discussion

"Any person" includes officers, enlisted persons, person in custody of the armed forces serving a sentence imposed by a court-martial, and, insofar as the punishments are applicable, any other person subject to the code. *See* R.C.M. 202.

(b) *Authorized punishments.* Subject to the limitations in this Manual, a court-martial may adjudge only the following punishments:

(1) *Reprimand.* A court-martial shall not specify the terms or wording of a reprimand. A reprimand, if approved, shall be issued, in writing, by the convening authority;

Discussion

A reprimand adjudged by a court-martial is a punitive censure.

---

(2) *Forfeiture of pay and allowances.* Unless a total forfeiture is adjudged, a sentence to forfeiture shall state the exact amount in whole dollars to be forfeited each month and the number of months the forfeitures will last.

Allowances shall be subject to forfeiture only when the sentence includes forfeiture of all pay and allowances. The maximum authorized amount of a partial forfeiture shall be determined by using the basic pay, retired pay, or retainer pay, as applicable, or, in the case of reserve component personnel on inactive-duty, compensation for periods of inactive-duty training, authorized by the cumulative years of service of the accused, and, if no confinement is adjudged, any sea or hardship duty pay. If the sentence also includes reduction in grade, expressly or by operation of law, the maximum forfeiture shall be based on the grade to which the accused is reduced.

Discussion

A forfeiture deprives the accused of the amount of pay (and allowances) specified as it accrues. Forfeitures accrue to the United States.

Forfeitures of pay and allowances adjudged as part of a court-martial sentence, or occurring by operation of Article 58b are effective 14 days after the sentence is adjudged or when the sentence is approved by the convening authority, whichever is earlier.

"Basic pay" does not include pay for special qualifications, such as diving pay, or incentive pay such as flying, parachuting, or duty on board a submarine.

Forfeiture of pay and allowances under Article 58b is not a part of the sentence, but is an administrative result thereof.

At general courts-martial, if both a punitive discharge and confinement are adjudged, then the operation of Article 58b results in total forfeiture of pay and allowances during that period of confinement. If only confinement is adjudged, then if that confinement exceeds six months, the operation of Article 58b results in total forfeiture of pay and allowances during that period of confinement. If only a punitive discharge is adjudged, Article 58b has no effect on pay and allowances. A death sentence results in total forfeiture of pay and allowances.

At a special court-martial, if a bad-conduct discharge and confinement are adjudged, then the operation of Article 58b results in a forfeiture of two-thirds of pay only (not allowances) during that period of confinement. If only confinement is adjudged, and that confinement exceeds six months, then the operation of Article 58b results in a forfeiture of two-thirds of pay only (not allowances) during the period of confinement. If only a bad conduct discharge is adjudged, Article 58b has no effect on pay.

If the sentence, as approved by the convening authority or other competent authority, does not result in forfeitures by the operation of Article 58b, then only adjudged forfeitures are effective.

Article 58b has no effect on summary courts-martial.

---

(3) *Fine.* Any court-martial may adjudge a fine in lieu of or in addition to forfeitures. Special and summary courts-martial may not adjudge any fine or combination of fine and forfeitures in excess of the total amount of forfeitures that may be adjudged in that case. In order to enforce collection, a fine may be accompanied by a provision in the sentence that, in the event the fine is not paid, the person fined shall, in addition to any period of confinement adjudged, be further confined until a fixed period considered an equivalent punishment to the fine has

expired. The total period of confinement so adjudged shall not exceed the jurisdictional limitations of the court-martial;

Discussion

A fine is in the nature of a judgement and, when ordered executed, makes the accused immediately liable to the United States for the entire amount of money specified in the sentence. A fine normally should not be adjudged against a member of the armed forces unless the accused was unjustly enriched as a result of the offense of which convicted. Ordinarily, a fine, rather than a forfeiture, is the proper monetary penalty to be adjudged against a civilian subject to military law.

See R.C.M. 1113(d)(3) concerning imposition of confinement when the accused fails to pay a fine.

Where the sentence adjudged at a special court-martial includes a fine, see R.C.M. 1107(d)(5) for limitations on convening authority action on the sentence.

---

(4) *Reduction in pay grade.* Except as provided in R.C.M. 1301(d), a court-martial may sentence an enlisted member to be reduced to the lowest or any intermediate pay grade;

Discussion

Reduction under Article 58a is not a part of the sentence but is an administrative result thereof.

---

(5) *Restriction to specified limits.* Restriction may be adjudged for no more than 2 months for each month of authorized confinement and in no case for more than 2 months. Confinement and restriction may be adjudged in the same case, but they may not together exceed the maximum authorized period of confinement, calculating the equivalency at the rate specified in this subsection;

Discussion

Restriction does not exempt the person on whom it is imposed from any military duty. Restriction and hard labor without confinement may be adjudged in the same case provided they do not exceed the maximum limits for each. *See* subsection (c)(1)(A)(ii) of this rule. The sentence adjudged should specify the limits of the restriction.

---

(6) *Hard labor without confinement.* Hard labor without confinement may be adjudged for no more than 1-1/2 months for each month of authorized confinement and in no case for more than three months. Hard labor without confinement may be adjudged only in the cases of enlisted members. The court-martial shall not specify the hard labor to be performed. Confinement and hard labor without confinement may be adjudged in the same case, but they may not together exceed the maximum authorized period of confinement, calculating the equivalency at the rate specified in this subsection.

Discussion

Hard labor without confinement is performed in addition to other regular duties and does not excuse or relieve a person from performing regular duties. Ordinarily, the immediate commander of the accused will designate the amount and character of the labor to be performed. Upon completion of the daily assignment, the accused should be permitted to take leave or liberty to which entitled.

See R.C.M. 1301(d) concerning limitations on hard labor without confinement in summary courts-martial.

---

(7) *Confinement.* The place of confinement shall not be designated by the court-martial. When confinement for life is authorized, it may be with or without eligibility for parole. A court-martial shall not adjudge a sentence to solitary confinement or to confinement without hard labor;

Discussion

The authority executing a sentence to confinement may require hard labor whether or not the words "at hard labor" are included in the sentence. *See* Article 58(b). To promote uniformity, the words "at hard labor" should be omitted in a sentence to confinement.

---

(8) *Punitive separation.* A court-martial may not adjudge an administrative separation from the service. There are three types of punitive separation.

(A) *Dismissal.* Dismissal applies only to commissioned officers, commissioned warrant officers, cadets, and midshipmen and may be adjudged only by a general court-martial. Regardless of the maximum punishment specified for an offense in Part IV of this Manual, a dismissal may be adjudged for any offense of which a commissioned officer, commissioned warrant officer, cadet, or midshipman has been found guilty;

(B) *Dishonorable discharge.* A dishonorable discharge applies only to enlisted persons and warrant officers who are not commissioned and may be adjudged only by a general court-martial. Regardless of the maximum punishment specified for an offense in Part IV of this Manual, a dishonorable discharge may be adjudged for any offense of which a warrant officer who is not commissioned has been found guilty. A dishonorable discharge should be reserved for those who should be separated under conditions of dishonor, after having been convicted of offenses usually recognized in civilian jurisdictions as felonies, or of offenses of a military nature requiring severe punishment; and

Discussion

See also subsection (d)(1) of this rule regarding when a dishonorable discharge is authorized as an additional punishment.

See Article 56a.

(C) *Bad conduct discharge.* A bad-conduct discharge applies only to enlisted persons and may be adjudged by a general court-martial and by a special court-martial which has met the requirements of R.C.M. 201(f)(2)(B). A bad-conduct discharge is less severe than a dishonorable discharge and is designed as a punishment for bad-conduct rather than as a punishment for serious offenses of either a civilian or military nature. It is also appropriate for an accused who has been convicted repeatedly of minor offenses and whose punitive separation appears to be necessary;

Discussion

See also subsections (d)(2) and (3) of this rule regarding when a bad-conduct discharge is authorized as an additional punishment.

---

(9) *Death.* Death may be adjudged only in accordance with R.C.M. 1004; and

(10) *Punishments under the law of war.* In cases tried under the law of war, a general court-martial may adjudge any punishment not prohibited by the law of war.

(c) *Limits on punishments.*

(1) *Based on offenses.*

(A) *Offenses listed in Part IV.*

(i) *Maximum punishment.* The maximum limits for the authorized punishments of confinement, forfeitures and punitive discharge (if any) are set forth for each offense listed in Part IV of this Manual. These limitations are for each separate offense, not for each charge. When a dishonorable discharge is authorized, a bad-conduct discharge is also authorized.

(ii) *Other punishments.* Except as otherwise specifically provided in this Manual, the types of punishments listed in subsections (b)(1), (3), (4), (5), (6) and (7) of this rule may be adjudged in addition to or instead of confinement, forfeitures, a punitive discharge (if authorized), and death (if authorized).

(B) *Offenses not listed Part IV.*

(i) *Included or related offenses.* For an offense not listed in Part IV of this Manual which is included in or closely related to an offense listed therein the maximum punishment shall be that of the offense listed; however if an offense not listed is included in a listed offense, and is closely related to another or is equally closely related to two or more listed offenses, the maximum punishment shall be the same as the least severe of the listed offenses.

(ii) *Not included or related offenses.* An offense not listed in Part IV and not included in or closely related to any offense listed therein is punishable as authorized by the United States Code, or as authorized by the custom of the service. When the United States Code provides for confinement for a specified period or not more than a specified period the maximum punishment by court-martial shall include confinement for that period. If the period is 1 year or longer, the maximum punishment by court-martial also includes a dishonorable discharge and forfeiture of all pay and allowances; if 6 months or more, a bad-conduct discharge and forfeiture of all pay and allowances; if less than 6 months, forfeiture of two-thirds pay per month for the authorized period of confinement.

(C) *Multiplicity.* When the accused is found guilty of two or more offenses, the maximum authorized punishment may be imposed for each separate offense. Except as provided in paragraph 5 of Part IV, offenses are not separate if each does not require proof of an element not required to prove the other. If the offenses are not separate, the maximum punishment for those offenses shall be the maximum authorized punishment for the offense carrying the greatest maximum punishment.

Discussion

See also R.C.M. 906(b)(12);907(b)(3)(B).

The basis of the concept of multiplicity in sentencing is that an accused may not be punished twice for what is, in effect, one offense. Offenses arising out of the same act or transaction may be multiplicious for sentencing depending on the evidence. No single test or formula has been developed which will resolve the question of multiplicity.

The following tests have been used for determining whether

offenses are separate. Offenses are not separate if one is included in the other or unless each requires proof of an element not required to prove the other. For example, if an accused is found guilty of escape from confinement (*see* paragraph 19, Part IV) and desertion (*see* paragraph 9, Part IV) which both arose out of the same act or transaction, the offenses would be separate because intent to remain permanently absent is not an element of escape from confinement and a freeing from restraint is not an element of desertion. However, if the accused had been found guilty of unauthorized absence instead of desertion, the offenses would not be separate because unauthorized absence does not require proof of any element not also required to prove escape.

Even if each offense requires proof of an element not required to prove the other, they may not be separately punishable if the offenses were committed as the result of a single impulse or intent. For example, if an accused found guilty of larceny (*see* paragraph 46, Part IV) and of unlawfully opening mail matter (*see* paragraph 93, Part IV) opened the mail bag for the purpose of stealing money in a letter in the bag, the offenses would not be separately punishable. Also, if there was a unity of time and the existence of a connected chain of events, the offenses may not be separately punishable, depending on all the circumstances, even if each required proof of a different element.

---

(2) *Based on rank of accused.*

(A) *Commissioned or warrant officers, cadets, and midshipmen.*

(i) A commissioned or warrant officer or a cadet, or midshipman may not be reduced in grade by any court-martial. However, in time of war or national emergency the Secretary concerned, or such Under Secretary or Assistant Secretary as may be designated by the Secretary concerned, may commute a sentence of dismissal to reduction to any enlisted grade.

(ii) Only a general court-martial may sentence a commissioned or warrant officer or a cadet, or midshipman to confinement.

(iii) A commissioned or warrant officer or a cadet or midshipman may not be sentenced to hard labor without confinement.

(iv) Only a general court-martial, upon conviction of any offense in violation of the Code, may sentence a commissioned or warrant officer or a cadet or midshipman to be separated from the service with a punitive separation. In the case of commissioned officers, cadets, midshipmen, and commissioned warrant officers, the separation shall be by dismissal. In the case of all other warrant officers, the separation shall by dishonorable discharge.

(B) *Enlisted persons. See* subsection (b)(9) of this rule and R.C.M. 1301(d).

(3) *Based on reserve status in certain circumstances.*

(A) *Restriction on liberty.* A member of a reserve component whose order to active duty is approved pursuant to Article 2(d)(5) may be required to serve any adjudged restriction on liberty during that period of active duty. Other members of a reserve component ordered to active duty pursuant to Article 2(d)(1) or tried by summary court-martial while on inactive duty training may not—

(i) by sentenced to confinement; or

(ii) be required to serve a court-martial punishment consisting of any other restriction on liberty except during subsequent periods of inactive-duty training or active duty.

(B) *Forfeiture.* A sentence to forfeiture of pay of a member not retained on active duty after completion of disciplinary proceedings may be collected from active duty and inactive-duty training pay during subsequent periods of duty.

Discussion

For application of this subsection, *see* R.C.M. 204. At the conclusion of nonjudicial punishment proceedings or final adjournment of the court-martial, the reserve component member who was ordered to active duty for the purpose of conducting disciplinary proceedings should be released from active duty within one working day unless the order to active duty was approved by the Secretary concerned and confinement or other restriction on liberty was adjudged. Unserved punishments may be carried over to subsequent periods of inactive-duty training or active duty.

---

(4) *Based on other rules.* The maximum limits on punishments in this rule may be further limited by other Rules of Courts-martial.

Discussion

The maximum punishment may be limited by: the jurisdictional limits of the court-martial (*see* R.C.M. 201(f) and 1301(d)); the nature of the proceedings (*see* R.C.M. 810(d) (sentence limitations in rehearings, new trials, and other trials)); and by instructions by a convening authority (*see* R.C.M. 601(e)(1)). *See also* R.C.M. 1107(d)(4) concerning limits on the maximum punishment which may be approved depending on the nature of the record.

(d) *Circumstances permitting increased punishments.*

(1) *Three or more convictions.* If an accused is found guilty of an offense or offenses for none of which a dishonorable discharge is otherwise authorized, proof of three or more previous convictions adjudged by a court-martial during the year next preceding the commission of any offense of which the accused stands convicted shall authorize a dishonorable discharge and forfeiture of all pay and allowances and, if the confinement otherwise authorized is less than 1 year, confinement for 1 year. In computing the 1-year period preceding the commission of any offense, periods of unauthorized absence shall be excluded. For purposes of this subsection, the court-martial convictions must be final.

(2) *Two or more convictions.* If an accused is found guilty of an offense or offenses for none of which a dishonorable or bad-conduct discharge is otherwise authorized, proof of two or more previous convictions adjudged by a court-martial during the 3 years next preceding the commission of any offense of which the accused stands convicted shall authorize a bad-conduct discharge and forfeiture of all pay and allowances and, if the confinement otherwise authorized is less than 3 months, confinement for 3 months. In computing the 3 year period preceding the commission of any offense, periods of unauthorized absence shall be excluded. For purposes of this subsection the court-martial convictions must be final.

(3) *Two or more offenses.* If an accused is found guilty of two or more offenses for none of which a dishonorable or bad-conduct discharge is otherwise authorized, the fact that the authorized confinement for these offenses totals 6 months or more shall, in addition, authorize a bad-conduct discharge and forfeiture of all pay and allowances.

Discussion

All of these increased punishments are subject to all other limitations on punishments set forth elsewhere in this rule. Convictions by summary court-martial may not be used to increase the maximum punishment under this rule. However they may be admitted and considered under R.C.M. 1001.

Rule 1004. Capital cases

(a) *In general.* Death may be adjudged only when:

(1) Death is expressly authorized under Part IV of this Manual for an offense of which the accused has been found guilty or is authorized under the law of war for an offense of which the accused has been found guilty under the law of war; and

(2) The accused was convicted of such an offense by the concurrence of all the members of the court-martial present at the time the vote was taken; and

(3) The requirements of subsections (b) and (c) of this rule have been met.

(b) *Procedure.* In addition to the provisions in R.C.M. 1001, the following procedures shall apply in capital cases—

(1) *Notice.*

(A) *Referral.* The convening authority shall indicate that the case is to be tried as a capital case by including a special instruction in the referral block of the charge sheet. Failure to include this special instruction at the time of the referral shall not bar the convening authority from later adding the required special instruction, provided:

(i) that the convening authority has otherwise complied with the notice requirement of subsection (B); and

(ii) that if the accused demonstrates specific prejudice from such failure to include the special instruction, a continuance or a recess is an adequate remedy.

(B) *Arraignment.* Before arraignment, trial counsel shall give the defense written notice of which aggravating factors under subsection (c) of this rule the prosecution intends to prove. Failure to provide timely notice under this subsection of any aggravating factors under subsection (c) of this rule shall not bar later notice and proof of such additional aggravating factors unless the accused demonstrates specific prejudice from such failure and that a continuance or a recess is not an adequate remedy.

(2) *Evidence of aggravating factors.* Trial counsel may present evidence in accordance with R.C.M. 1001(b)(4) tending to establish one or more of the aggravating factors in subsection (c) of this rule.

Discussion

See also subsection (b)(5) of this rule.

(3) *Evidence in extenuation and mitigation.* The accused shall be given broad latitude to present evidence in extenuation and mitigation.

Discussion

See R.C.M. 1001(c).

(4) *Necessary findings.* Death may not be adjudged unless—

(A) The members find that at least one of the aggravating factors under subsection (c) existed;

(B) Notice of such factor was provided in accordance with paragraph (1) of this subsection and all members concur in the finding with respect to such factor; and

(C) All members concur that any extenuating or mitigating circumstances are substantially outweighed by any aggravating circumstances admissible under R.C.M. 1001(b)(4), including the factors under subsection (c) of this rule.

(5) *Basis for findings.* The findings in subsection (b)(4) of this rule may be based on evidence introduced before or after findings under R.C.M. 921, or both.

(6) *Instructions.* In addition to the instructions required under R.C.M. 1005, the military judge shall instruct the members of such aggravating factors under subsection (c) of this rule as may be in issue in the case, and on the requirements and procedures under subsections (b)(4), (5), (7), and (8) of this rule. The military judge shall instruct the members that they must consider all evidence in extenuation and mitigation before they may adjudge death.

(7) *Voting.* In closed session, before voting on a sentence, the members shall vote by secret written ballot separately on each aggravating factor under subsection (c) of this rule on which they have been instructed. Death may not be adjudged unless all members concur in a finding of the existence of at least one such aggravating factor. After voting on all the aggravating factors on which they have been instructed, the members shall vote on a sentence in accordance with R.C.M. 1006.

(8) *Announcement.* If death is adjudged, the president shall, in addition to complying with R.C.M. 1007, announce which aggravating factors under subsection (c) of this rule were found by the members.

(c) *Aggravating factors.* Death may be adjudged only if the members find, beyond a reasonable doubt, one or more of the following aggravating factors:

(1) That the offense was committed before or in the presence of the enemy, except that this factor shall not apply in the case of a violation of Article 118 or 120;

Discussion

See paragraph 23, Part IV, for a definition of "before or in the presence of the enemy."

(2) That in committing the offense the accused—

(A) Knowingly created a grave risk of substantial damage to the national security of the United States; or

(B) Knowingly created a grave risk of substantial damage to a mission, system, or function of the United States, provided that this subparagraph shall apply only if substantial damage to the national security of the United States would have resulted had the intended damage been effected;

(3) That the offense caused substantial damage to the national security of the United States, whether or not the accused intended such damage, except that this factor shall not apply in case of a violation of Article 118 or 120;

(4) That the offense was committed in such a way or under circumstances that the life of one or more persons other than the victim was unlawfully and substantially endangered, except that this factor shall not apply to a violation of Articles 104, 106a, or 120;

(5) That the accused committed the offense with the intent to avoid hazardous duty;

(6) That, only in the case of a violation of Article 118 or 120, the offense was committed in time of war and in territory in which the United States or an ally of the United States was then an occupying power or in which the armed forces of the United States were then engaged in active hostilities;

(7) That, only in the case of a violation of Article 118(1):

(A) The accused was serving a sentence of confinement for 30 years or more or for life at the time of the murder;

(B) The murder was committed: while the accused was engaged in the commission or attempted commission of any robbery, rape, rape of a child, aggravated sexual assault, aggravated sexual assault of a child, aggravated sexual contact, aggravated sexual abuse of a child, aggravated sexual contact with a child, aggravated arson, sodomy, burglary, kidnapping, mutiny, sedition, or piracy of an aircraft or vessel; or while the accused was engaged in the commission or attempted commission of any offense involving the wrongful distribution, manufacture, or introduction or possession, with intent to distribute, of a controlled substance; or, while the accused was engaged in flight or attempted flight after the commission or attempted commission of any such offense.

(C) The murder was committed for the purpose of receiving money or a thing of value;

(D) The accused procured another by means of compulsion, coercion, or a promise of an advantage, a service, or a thing of value to commit the murder;

(E) The murder was committed with the intent to avoid or to prevent lawful apprehension or effect an escape from custody or confinement;

(F) The victim was the President of the United States, the President-elect, the Vice President, or, if there was no Vice President, the officer in the order of succession to the office of President of the United States, the Vice-President-elect, or any individual who is acting as President under the Constitution and laws of the United States, any Member of Congress (including a Delegate to, or Resident Commissioner in, the Congress) or Member-of-Congress elect, justice or judge of the United States, a chief of state or head of government (or the political equivalent) of a foreign nation, or a foreign official (as such term is defined in section 1116(b)(3)(A) of title 18, United States Code), if the official was on official business at the time of the offense and was in the United States or in a place described in Mil. R. Evid.315(c)(2), 315(c)(3);

(G) The accused then knew that the victim was any of the following persons in the execution of office: a commissioned, warrant, noncommissioned, or petty officer of the armed services of the United States; a member of any law enforcement or security activity or agency, military or civilian, including correctional custody personnel; or any firefighter;

(H) The murder was committed with intent to obstruct justice;

(I) The murder was preceded by the intentional infliction of substantial physical harm or prolonged, substantial mental or physical pain and suffering to the victim. For purposes of this section, "substantial physical harm" means fractures or dislocated bones, deep cuts, torn members of the body, serious damage to internal organs, or other serious bodily injuries. The term "substantial physical harm" does not mean minor injuries, such as a black eye or bloody nose. The term "substantial mental or physical pain or suffering" is accorded its common meaning and includes torture.

(J) The accused has been found guilty in the same case of another violation of Article 118;

(K) The victim of the murder was under 15 years of age.

(8) That only in the case of a violation of Article 118(4), the accused was the actual perpetrator of the killing or was a principal whose participation in the burglary, sodomy, rape, rape of a child, aggravated sexual assault, aggravated sexual assault of a child, aggravated sexual contact, aggravated sexual abuse of a child, aggravated sexual contact with a child, robbery, or aggravated arson was major and who manifested a reckless indifference for human life.

Discussion

Conduct amounts to "reckless indifference" when it evinces a wanton disregard of consequences under circumstances involving grave danger to the life of another, although no harm is necessarily intended. The accused must have had actual knowledge of the grave danger to others or knowledge of circumstances that would cause a reasonable person to realize the highly dangerous character of such conduct. In determining whether participation in the offense was major, the accused's presence at the scene and the extent to which the accused aided, abetted, assisted, encouraged, or advised the other participants should be considered. *See United States v. Berg*, 31 M.J. 38 (C.M.A. 1990); *United States v. McMonagle* 38 M.J. 53 (C.M.A. 1993).

---

(9) That, only in the case of a violation of Article 120:

(A) The victim was under the age of 12; or

(B) The accused maimed or attempted to kill the victim;

(10) That, only in the case of a violation of the law of war, death is authorized under the law of war for the offense;

(11) That, only in the case of a violation of Article 104 or 106a:

(A) The accused has been convicted of another offense involving espionage or treason for which either a sentence of death or imprisonment for life was authorized by statute; or

(B) That in committing the offense, the accused knowingly created a grave risk of death to a person other than the individual who was the victim.

For purposes of this rule, "national security" means the national defense and foreign relations of the United States and specifically includes: a military or defense advantage over any foreign nation or group of nations; a favorable foreign relations position; or a defense posture capable of successfully resisting hostile or destructive action from within or without.

Discussion

Examples of substantial damage of the national security of the United States include: impeding the performance of a combat mission or operation; impeding the performance of an important mission in a hostile fire or imminent danger pay area (*see* 37 U.S.C. § 310(a)); and disclosing military plans, capabilities, or intelligence such as to jeopardize any combat mission or operation of the armed services of the United States or its allies or to materially aid an enemy of the United States.

(d) *Spying.* If the accused has been found guilty of spying under Article 106, subsections (a)(2), (b), and (c) of this rule and R.C.M. 1006 and 1007 shall not apply. Sentencing proceedings in accordance with R.C.M. 1001 shall be conducted, but the military judge shall announce that by operation of law a sentence of death has been adjudged.

(e) *Other penalties.* Except for a violation of Article 106, when death is an authorized punishment for an offense, all other punishments authorized under R.C.M. 1003 are also authorized for that offense, including confinement for life, with or without eligibility for parole, and may be adjudged in lieu of the death penalty, subject to limitations specifically prescribed in this Manual. A sentence of death includes a dishonorable discharge or dismissal as appropriate. Confinement is a necessary incident of a sentence of death, but not a part of it.

Discussion

A sentence of death may not be ordered executed until approved by the President. *See* R.C.M. 1207. A sentence to death which has been finally ordered executed will be carried out in the manner prescribed by the Secretary concerned. *See* R.C.M. 1113(d)(1).

Rule 1005. Instructions on sentence

(a) *In general.* The military judge shall give the members appropriate instructions on sentence.

Discussion

Instructions should be tailored to the facts and circumstances of the individual case.

(b) *When given.* Instructions on sentence shall be given after arguments by counsel and before the members close to deliberate on sentence, but the military judge may, upon request of the members, any party, or *sua sponte*, give additional instructions at a later time.

(c) *Requests for instructions.* After presentation of matters relating to sentence or at such other time as the military judge may permit, any party may request that the military judge instruct the members on the law as set forth in the request. The military judge may require the requested instruction to be written. Each party shall be given the opportunity to be heard on any proposed instruction on sentence before it is given. The military judge shall inform the parties of the proposed action on such requests before their closing arguments on sentence.

Discussion

Requests for and objections to instructions should be resolved at an Article 39(a) session. *But see* R.C.M. 801(e)(1)(C); 803.

The military judge is not required to give the specific instruction requested by counsel if the matter is adequately covered in the instructions.

The military judge should not identify the source of any instruction when addressing the members.

All written requests for instructions should be marked as appellate exhibits, whether or not they are given.

(d) *How given.* Instructions on sentence shall be given orally on the record in the presence of all parties and the members. Written copies of the instructions, or unless a party objects, portions of them, may also be given to the members for their use during deliberations.

Discussion

A copy of any written instructions delivered to the members should be marked as an appellate exhibit.

(e) *Required instructions.* Instructions on sentence shall include:

(1) A statement of the maximum authorized punishment that may be adjudged and of the mandatory minimum punishment, if any;

Discussion

The maximum punishment that may be adjudged is the lowest of the total permitted by the applicable paragraph(s) in Part IV for each separate offense of which the accused was convicted (*see also* R.C.M. 1003 concerning additional limits on punishments and additional punishments which may be adjudged) or the jurisdictional limit of the court-martial (*see* R.C.M. 201(f) and R.C.M. 1301(d)). *See also* Discussion to R.C.M. 810(d). The military judge may upon request or when otherwise appropriate instruct on lesser punishments. *See* R.C.M. 1003. If an additional punishment is authorized under R.C.M. 1003(d), the members must be informed of the basis for the increased punishment.

A carefully drafted sentence worksheet ordinarily should be used and should include reference to all authorized punishments in the case.

---

(2) A statement of the effect any sentence announced including a punitive discharge and confinement, or confinement in excess of six months, will have on the accused's entitlement to pay and allowances;

(3) A statement of the procedures for deliberation and voting on the sentence set out in R.C.M. 1006;

Discussion

See also R.C.M. 1004 concerning additional instructions required in capital cases.

---

(4) A statement informing the members that they are solely responsible for selecting an appropriate sentence and may not rely on the possibility of any mitigating action by the convening or higher authority; and

Discussion

See also R.C.M. 1002.

---

(5) A statement that the members should consider all matters in extenuation, mitigation, and aggravation, whether introduced before or after findings, and matters introduced under R.C.M. 1001(b)(1), (2), (3) and (5).

Discussion

For example, tailored instructions on sentencing should bring attention to the reputation or record of the accused in the service for good conduct, efficiency, fidelity, courage, bravery, or other traits of good character, and any pretrial restraint imposed on the accused.

(f) *Waiver.* Failure to object to an instruction or to omission of an instruction before the members close to deliberate on the sentence constitutes waiver of the objection in the absence of plain error. The military judge may require the party objecting to specify in what respect the instructions were improper. The parties shall be given the opportunity to be heard on any objection outside the presence of the members.

Rule 1006. Deliberations and voting on sentence

(a) *In general.* The members shall deliberate and vote after the military judge instructs the members on sentence. Only the members shall be present during deliberations and voting. Superiority in rank shall not be used in any manner to control the independence of members in the exercise of their judgment.

(b) *Deliberations.* Deliberations may properly include full and free discussion of the sentence to be imposed in the case. Unless otherwise directed by the military judge, members may take with them in deliberations their notes, if any, any exhibits admitted in evidence, and any written instructions. Members may request that the court-martial be reopened and that portions of the record be read to them or additional evidence introduced. The military judge may, in the exercise of discretion, grant such requests.

(c) *Proposal of sentences.* Any member may propose a sentence. Each proposal shall be in writing and shall contain the complete sentence proposed. The junior member shall collect the proposed sentences and submit them to the president.

Discussion

A proposal should state completely each kind and, where appropriate, amount of authorized punishment proposed by that member. For example, a proposal of confinement for life would state whether it is with or without eligibility for parole. *See* R.C.M.1003(b).

(d) *Voting.*

(1) *Duty of members.* Each member has the duty to vote for a proper sentence for the offenses of which the court-martial found the accused guilty, regardless of the member's vote or opinion as to the guilt of the accused.

(2) *Secret ballot.* Proposed sentences shall be voted on by secret written ballot.

(3) *Procedure.*

(A) *Order.* All members shall vote on each proposed sentence in its entirety beginning with the least severe and continuing, as necessary, with the next least severe, until a sentence is adopted by the concurrence of the number of members required under subsection (d)(4) of this rule. The process of proposing sentences and voting on them may be repeated as necessary until a sentence is adopted.

(B) *Counting votes.* The junior member shall collect the ballots and count the votes. The president shall check the count and inform the other members of the result.

Discussion

A sentence adopted by the required number of members may be reconsidered only in accordance with R.C.M. 1009.

(4) *Number of votes required.*

(A) *Death.* A sentence which includes death may be adjudged only if all members present vote for that sentence.

Discussion

See R.C.M. 1004.

(B) *Confinement for life, with or without eligibility for parole, or more than 10 years.* A sentence that includes confinement for life, with or without eligibility for parole, or more than 10 years may be adjudged only if at least three-fourths of the members present vote for that sentence.

(C) *Other.* A sentence other than those described in subsection (d)(4)(A) or (B) of this rule may be adjudged only if at least two-thirds of the members present vote for that sentence.

Discussion

In computing the number of votes required to adopt a sentence, any fraction of a vote is rounded up to the next whole number. For example, if there are seven members, at least six would have to concur to impose a sentence requiring a three-fourths vote, while at least five would have to concur to impose a sentence requiring a two-thirds vote.

(5) *Mandatory sentence.* When a mandatory minimum is prescribed under Article 118 the members shall vote on a sentence in accordance with this rule.

(6) *Effect of failure to agree.* If the required number of members do not agree on a sentence after a reasonable effort to do so, a mistrial may be declared as to the sentence and the case shall be returned to the convening authority, who may order a rehearing on sentence only or order that a sentence of no punishment be imposed.

(e) *Action after a sentence is reached.* After the members have agreed upon a sentence, the court-martial shall be opened and the president shall inform the military judge that a sentence has been reached. The military judge may, in the presence of the parties, examine any writing which the president intends to read to announce the sentence and may assist the members in putting the sentence in proper form. Neither that writing nor any oral or written clarification or discussion concerning it shall constitute announcement of the sentence.

Discussion

Ordinarily a sentence worksheet should be provided to the members as an aid to putting the sentence in proper form. *See* Appendix 11 for a format for forms of sentences. If a sentence worksheet has been provided, the military judge should examine it before the president announces the sentence. If the military judge intends to instruct the members after such examination, counsel should be permitted to examine the worksheet and to be heard on any instructions the military judge may give.

The president should not disclose any specific number of votes for or against any sentence.

If the sentence is ambiguous or apparently illegal, *see* R.C.M. 1009.

Rule 1007. Announcement of sentence

(a) *In general.* The sentence shall be announced by the president or, in a court-martial composed of a military judge alone, by the military judge, in the presence of all parties promptly after it has been determined.

Discussion

See Appendix 11.

An element of a sentence adjudged by members about which no instructions were given and which is not listed on a sentence worksheet is not proper.

(b) *Erroneous announcement.* If the announced sentence is not the one actually determined by the court-martial, the error may be corrected by a new announcement made before the record of trial is authenticated and forwarded to the convening authority. This action shall not constitute reconsideration of the sentence. If the court-martial has been adjourned before the error is discovered, the military judge may call the court-martial into session to correct the announcement.

Discussion

For procedures governing reconsideration of the sentence, *see* R.C.M. 1009. *See also* R.C.M. 1102 concerning the action to be taken if the error in the announcement is discovered after the record is authenticated and forwarded to the convening authority.

(c) *Polling prohibited.* Except as provided in Mil. R. Evid. 606, members may not otherwise be questioned about their deliberations and voting.

Rule 1008. Impeachment of sentence

A sentence which is proper on its face may be impeached only when extraneous prejudicial information was improperly brought to the attention of a member, outside influence was improperly brought to bear upon any member, or unlawful command influence was brought to bear upon any member.

Discussion

See R.C.M. 923 Discussion concerning impeachment of findings.

Rule 1009. Reconsideration of sentence

(a) *Reconsideration.* Subject to this rule, a sentence may be reconsidered at any time before such sentence is announced in open session of the court.

(b) *Exceptions.*

(1) If the sentence announced in open session was less than the mandatory minimum prescribed for an offense of which the accused has been found guilty, the court that announced the sentence may reconsider such sentence upon reconsideration in accordance with subsection (e) of this rule.

(2) If the sentence announced in open session exceeds the maximum permissible punishment for the offense or the jurisdictional limitation of the court-martial, the sentence may be reconsidered after announcement in accordance with subsection (e) of this rule.

(c) *Clarification of sentence.* A sentence may be clarified at any time prior to action of the convening authority on the case.

(1) *Sentence adjudged by the military judge.* When a sentence adjudged by the military judge is ambiguous, the military judge shall call a session for clarification as soon as practical after the ambiguity is discovered.

(2) *Sentence adjudged by members.* When a sentence adjudged by members is ambiguous, the military judge shall bring the matter to the attention of the members if the matter is discovered before the court-martial is adjourned. If the matter is discovered after adjournment, the military judge may call a session for clarification by the members who adjudged the sentence as soon as practical after the ambiguity is discovered.

(d) *Action by the convening authority.* When a sentence adjudged by the court-martial is ambiguous, the convening authority may return the matter to the court-martial for clarification. When a sentence adjudged by the court-martial is apparently illegal, the convening authority may return the matter to the court-martial for reconsideration or may approve a sentence no more severe than the legal, unambiguous portions of the adjudged sentence.

(e) *Reconsideration procedure.* Any member of the court-martial may propose that a sentence reached by the members be reconsidered.

(1) *Instructions.* When a sentence has been reached by members and reconsideration has been initiated, the military judge shall instruct the members on the procedure for reconsideration.

(2) *Voting.* The members shall vote by secret written ballot in closed session whether to reconsider a sentence already reached by them.

(3) *Number of votes required.*

(A) *With a view to increasing.* Subject to subsection (b) of this rule, members may reconsider a sentence with a view of increasing it only if at least a majority vote for reconsideration.

(B) *With a view to decreasing.* Members may reconsider a sentence with a view to decreasing it only if:

(i) In the case of a sentence which includes death, at least one member votes to reconsider;

(ii) In the case of a sentence which includes confinement for life, with or without eligibility for parole, or more than 10 years, more than one-fourth of the members vote to reconsider; or;

(iii) In the case of any other sentence, more than one-third of the members vote to reconsider.

Discussion

After a sentence has been adopted by secret ballot vote in closed session, no other vote may be taken on the sentence unless a vote to reconsider succeeds.

For example, if six of nine (two-thirds) members adopt a sentence, a vote of at least five would be necessary to reconsider to increase it; four would have to vote to reconsider in order to decrease it. If seven of nine (three-fourths) members is required to adopt a sentence, a vote of at least five would be necessary to reconsider to increase it, while three would be necessary to reconsider to decrease it.

(4) *Successful vote.* If a vote to reconsider a sentence succeeds, the procedures in R.C.M. 1006 shall apply.

Rule 1010. Notice concerning post-trial and appellate rights

In each general and special court-martial, prior to adjournment, the military judge shall ensure that the defense counsel has informed the accused orally and in writing of:

(a) The right to submit matters to the convening authority to consider before taking action;

(b) The right to appellate review, as applicable, and the effect of waiver or withdrawal of such right;

(c) The right to apply for relief from the Judge Advocate General if the case is neither reviewed by a Court of Criminal Appeals nor reviewed by the Judge Advocate General under R.C.M. 1201(b)(1); and

(d) The right to the advice and assistance of counsel in the exercise of the foregoing rights or any decision to waive them.

The written advice to the accused concerning post-trial and appellate rights shall be signed by the accused and the defense counsel and inserted in the record of trial as an appellate exhibit.

Discussion

The post-trial duties of the defense counsel concerning the appellate rights of the accused are set forth in paragraph (E)(iv) of the Discussion accompanying R.C.M. 502(d)(6). The defense counsel shall explain the appellate rights to the accused and prepare the written document of such advisement prior to or during trial.

Rule 1011. Adjournment

The military judge may adjourn the court-martial at the end of the trial of an accused or proceed to trial of other cases referred to that court-martial. Such an adjournment may be for a definite or indefinite period.

Discussion

A court-martial and its personnel have certain powers and responsibilities following the trial. *See*, for example, R.C.M. 502(d)(5) Discussion (F); 502(d)(6) Discussion (E); 808; 1007; 1009; Chapter XI.

CHAPTER XI. POST-TRIAL PROCEDURE

Rule 1101. Report of result of trial; post-trial restraint; deferment of confinement, forfeitures and reduction in grade; waiver of Article 58b forfeitures

(a) *Report of the result of trial.* After final adjournment of the court-martial in a case, the trial counsel shall promptly notify the accused's immediate commander, the convening authority or the convening authority's designee, and, if appropriate, the officer in charge of the confinement facility of the findings and sentence.

(b) *Post-trial confinement.*

(1) *In general.* An accused may be placed in post-trial confinement if the sentence adjudged by the court-martial includes death or confinement.

(2) *Who may order confinement.* Unless limited by superior authority, a commander of the accused may order the accused into post-trial confinement when post-trial confinement is authorized under subsection (b)(1) of this rule. A commander authorized to order post-trial confinement under this subsection may delegate this authority to the trial counsel.

Discussion

The commander may release the accused, order confinement, or order other appropriate restraint. Regardless whether the accused is ordered into confinement, a sentence to confinement begins to run on the date it is adjudged unless it is deferred under subsection (c) of this rule. *See* Article 57.

(3) *Confinement on other grounds.* Nothing in this rule shall prohibit confinement of a person after a court-martial on proper grounds other than the offenses for which the accused was tried at the court-martial.

Discussion

See R.C.M. 304, 305, and paragraph 5b(2), Part V, for other grounds for confinement.

(c) *Deferment of confinement, forfeitures or reduction in grade.*

(1) *In general.* Deferment of a sentence to confinement, forfeitures, or reduction in grade is a postponement of the running of the sentence.

Discussion

Deferment is not suspension of the sentence or a form of clemency.

(2) *Who may defer.* The convening authority or, if the accused is no longer in the convening authority's jurisdiction, the officer exercising general court-martial jurisdiction over the command to which the accused is assigned, may, upon written application of the accused, at any time after the adjournment of the court-martial, defer the accused's service of a sentence to confinement, forfeitures, or reduction in grade that has not been ordered executed.

(3) *Action on deferment request.* The authority acting on the deferment request may, in that authority's discretion, defer service of a sentence to confinement, forfeitures, or reduction in grade. The accused shall have the burden of showing that the interests of the accused and the community in deferral outweigh the community's interests in imposition of the punishment on its effective date. Factors that the authority acting on a deferment request may consider in determining whether to grant the deferment request include, where applicable: the probability of the accused's flight; the probability of the accused's commission of other offenses, intimidation of witnesses, or interference with the administration of justice; the nature of the offenses (including the effect on the victim) of which the accused was convicted; the sentence adjudged; the command's immediate need for the accused; the effect of deferment on good order and discipline in the command; the accused's character, mental condition, family situation, and service record. The decision of the authority acting on the deferment request shall be subject to judicial review only for abuse of discretion. The action of the authority acting on the deferment request shall be in writing and a copy shall be provided to the accused.

Discussion

The deferment request and the action on the request must be attached to the record of trial. *See* R.C.M. 1103(b)(3)(D). If the request for deferment is denied, the basis for the denial should be in writing and attached to the record of trial.

(4) *Orders.* The action granting deferment shall be

reported in the convening authority's action under R.C.M. 1107(f)(4)(E) and shall include the date of the action on the request when it occurs prior to or concurrently with the action. Action granting deferment after the convening authority's action under R.C.M. 1107 shall be reported in orders under R.C.M. 1114 and included in the record of trial.

(5) *Restraint when deferment is granted.* When deferment of confinement is granted, no form of restraint or other limitation on the accused's liberty may be ordered as a substitute form of punishment. An accused may, however, be restricted to specified limits or conditions may be placed on the accused's liberty during the period of deferment for any other proper reason, including a ground for restraint under R.C.M. 304.

(6) *End of deferment.* Deferment of a sentence to confinement, forfeitures, or reduction in grade ends when:

(A) The convening authority takes action under R.C.M. 1107, unless the convening authority specifies in the action that service of confinement after the action is deferred;

(B) The confinement, forfeitures, or reduction in grade are suspended;

(C) The deferment expires by its own terms; or

(D) The deferment is otherwise rescinded in accordance with subsection (c)(7) of this rule. Deferment of confinement may not continue after the conviction is final under R.C.M. 1209.

Discussion

When the sentence is ordered executed, forfeitures or reduction in grade may be suspended, but may not be deferred; deferral of confinement may continue after action in accordance with R.C.M. 1107. A form of punishment cannot be both deferred and suspended at the same time. When deferment of confinement, forfeitures, or reduction in grade ends, the sentence to confinement, forfeitures, or reduction in grade begins to run or resumes running, as appropriate. When the convening authority has specified in the action that confinement will be deferred after the action, the deferment may not be terminated, except under subsections (6)(B), (C), or (D), until the conviction is final under R.C.M. 1209.

See R.C.M. 1203 for deferment of a sentence to confinement pending review under Article 67(a)(2).

---

(7) *Rescission of deferment.*

(A) *Who may rescind.* The authority who granted the deferment or, if the accused is no longer within that authority's jurisdiction, the officer exercising general court-martial jurisdiction over the command to which the accused is assigned, may rescind the deferment.

(B) *Action.* Deferment of confinement, forfeitures, or reduction in grade may be rescinded when additional information is presented to a proper authority which, when considered with all other information in the case, that authority finds, in that authority's discretion, is grounds for denial of deferment under subsection (c)(3) of this rule. The accused shall promptly be informed of the basis for the rescission and of the right to submit written matters in the accused's behalf and to request that the rescission be reconsidered. However, the accused may be required to serve the sentence to confinement, forfeitures, or reduction in grade pending this action.

(C) *Execution.* When deferment of confinement is rescinded after the convening authority's action under R.C.M. 1107, the confinement may be ordered executed. However, no such order to rescind a deferment of confinement may be issued within 7 days of notice of the rescission of a deferment of confinement to the accused under subsection (c)(7)(B) of this rule, to afford the accused an opportunity to respond. The authority rescinding the deferment may extend this period for good cause shown. The accused shall be credited with any confinement actually served during this period.

(D) *Orders.* Rescission of a deferment before or concurrently with the initial action in the case shall be reported in the action under R.C.M. 1107(f)(4)(E), which action shall include the dates of the granting of the deferment and the rescission. Rescission of a deferment of confinement after the convening authority's action shall be reported in supplementary orders in accordance with R.C.M. 1114 and shall state whether the approved period of confinement is to be executed or whether all or part of it is to be suspended.

Discussion

See Appendix 16 for forms.

(d) *Waiving forfeitures resulting from a sentence to confinement to provide for dependent support.*

(1) With respect to forfeiture of pay and allowances resulting only by operation of law and not adjudged by the court, the convening authority may

waive, for a period not to exceed six months, all or part of the forfeitures for the purpose of providing support to the accused's dependent(s). The convening authority may waive and direct payment of any such forfeitures when they become effective by operation of Article 57(a).

(2) Factors that may be considered by the convening authority in determining the amount of forfeitures, if any, to be waived include, but are not limited to, the length of the accused's confinement, the number and age(s) of the accused's family members, whether the accused requested waiver, any debts owed by the accused, the ability of the accused's family members to find employment, and the availability of transitional compensation for abused dependents permitted under 10 U.S.C. 1059.

(3) For the purposes of this Rule, a "dependent" means any person qualifying as a "dependent" under 37 U.S.C. 401.

Discussion

Forfeitures resulting by operation of law, rather than those adjudged as part of a sentence, may be waived for six months or for the duration of the period of confinement, whichever is less. The waived forfeitures are paid as support to dependent(s) designated by the convening authority. When directing waiver and payment, the convening authority should identify by name the dependent(s) to whom the payments will be made and state the number of months for which the waiver and payment shall apply. In cases where the amount to be waived and paid is less than the jurisdictional limit of the court, the monthly dollar amount of the waiver and payment should be stated.

Rule 1102. Post-trial sessions

(a) *In general.* Post-trial sessions may be proceedings in revision or Article 39(a) sessions. Such sessions may be directed by the military judge or the convening authority in accordance with this rule.

(b) *Purpose.*

(1) *Proceedings in revision.* Proceedings in revision may be directed to correct an apparent error, omission, or improper or inconsistent action by the court-martial, which can be rectified by reopening the proceedings without material prejudice to the accused.

Discussion

Because the action at a proceeding in revision is corrective, a proceeding in revision may not be conducted for the purpose of presenting additional evidence.

Examples when a proceeding in revision is appropriate include: correction of an ambiguous or apparently illegal action by the court-martial; inquiry into the terms of a pretrial agreement; and inquiry to establish the accused's awareness of certain rights.

See also R.C.M. 1104(d) concerning correction of the record by certificate of correction.

---

(2) *Article 39(a) sessions.* An Article 39(a) session under this rule may be called, upon motion of either party or *sua sponte* by the military judge, for the purpose of inquiring into, and, when appropriate, resolving any matter that arises after trial and that substantially affects the legal sufficiency of any findings of guilty or the sentence. The military judge may also call an Article 39(a) session, upon motion of either party or sua sponte, to reconsider any trial ruling that substantially affects the legal sufficiency of any findings of guilty or the sentence. The military judge may, *sua sponte*, at any time prior to authentication of the record of trial, enter a finding of not guilty of one or more offenses charged, or may enter a finding of not guilty of a part of a specification as long as a lesser offense charged is alleged in the remaining portion of the specification. Prior to entering such a finding or findings, the military judge shall give each party an opportunity to be heard on the matter in a post-trial Article 39(a) session.

Discussion

For example, an Article 39(a) session may be called to permit a military judge to reconsider a trial ruling, or to examine allegations of misconduct by a counsel, a member, or a witness. *See* R.C.M. 917(d) for the standard to be used to determine the legal sufficiency of evidence.

(c) *Matters not subject to post-trial sessions.* Post-trial session may not be directed:

(1) For reconsideration of a finding of not guilty of any specification, or a ruling which amounts to a finding of not guilty;

(2) For reconsideration of a finding of not guilty of any charge, unless the record shows a finding of guilty under a specification laid under that charge, which sufficiently alleges a violation of some article of the code; or

(3) For increasing the severity of the sentence

unless the sentence prescribed for the offense is mandatory.

(d) *When directed.* The military judge may direct a post-trial session any time before the record is authenticated. The convening authority may direct a post-trial session any time before the convening authority takes initial action on the case or at such later time as the convening authority is authorized to do so by a reviewing authority.

(e) *Procedure.*

(1) *Personnel.* The requirements of R.C.M. 505 and 805 shall apply at post-trial sessions except that—

(A) For a proceeding in revision, if trial was before members and the matter subject to the proceeding in revision requires the presence of members:

(i) The absence of any members does not invalidate the proceedings if, in the case of a general court-martial, at least five members are present, or, in the case of a special court-martial, at least three members are present; and

(ii) A different military judge may be detailed, subject to R.C.M. 502(c) and 902, if the military judge who presided at the earlier proceedings is not reasonably available.

(B) For an Article 39(a) session, a different military judge may be detailed, subject to R.C.M. 502(c) and 902, for good cause.

(2) *Action.* The military judge shall take such action as may be appropriate, including appropriate instructions when members are present. The members may deliberate in closed session, if necessary, to determine what corrective action, if any, to take. Prior to the military judge *sua sponte* entering a finding of not guilty of one or more offenses charged or entering a finding of not guilty of a part of a specification as long as a lesser offense charged is alleged in the remaining portion of the specification, the military judge shall give each party an opportunity to be heard on the matter.

(3) *Record.* All post-trial sessions, except any deliberations by the members, shall be held in open session. The record of the post-trial sessions shall be prepared, authenticated, and served in accordance with R.C.M. 1103 and 1104 and shall be included in the record of the prior proceedings.

Rule 1102A. Post-trial hearing for person found not guilty only by reason of lack of mental responsibility

(a) *In general.* The military judge shall conduct a hearing not later than forty days following the finding that an accused is not guilty only by reason of a lack of mental responsibility.

(b) *Psychiatric or psychological examination and report.* Prior to the hearing, the military judge or convening authority shall order a psychiatric or psychological examination of the accused, with the resulting psychiatric or psychological report transmitted to the military judge for use in the post-trial hearing.

(c) *Post-trial hearing.*

(1) The accused shall be represented by defense counsel and shall have the opportunity to testify, present evidence, call witnesses on his or her behalf, and to confront and cross-examine witnesses who appear at the hearing.

(2) The military judge is not bound by the rules of evidence except with respect to privileges.

(3) An accused found not guilty only by reason of a lack of mental responsibility of an offense involving bodily injury to another, or serious damage to the property of another, or involving a substantial risk of such injury or damage, has the burden of proving by clear and convincing evidence that his or her release would not create a substantial risk of bodily injury to another person or serious damage to property of another due to a present mental disease or defect. With respect to any other offense, the accused has the burden of such proof by a preponderance of the evidence.

(4) If, after the hearing, the military judge finds the accused has satisfied the standard specified in subsection (3) of this section, the military judge shall inform the general court-martial convening authority of this result and the accused shall be released. If, however, the military judge finds after the hearing that the accused has not satisfied the standard specified in subsection (3) of this section, then the military judge shall inform the general court-martial convening authority of this result and that authority may commit the accused to the custody of the Attorney General.

Rule 1103. Preparation of record of trial

(a) *In general.* Each general, special, and summary

court-martial shall keep a separate record of the proceedings in each case brought before it.

(b) *General courts-martial.*

(1) *Responsibility for preparation.* The trial counsel shall:

(A) Under the direction of the military judge, cause the record of trial to be prepared; and

(B) Under regulations prescribed by the Secretary concerned, cause to be retained stenolineart or other notes or mechanical or electronic recordings from which the record of trial was prepared.

(2) *Contents.*

(A) *In general.* The record of trial in each general court-martial shall be separate, complete, and independent of any other document.

(B) *Verbatim transcript required.* Except as otherwise provided in subsection (j) of this rule, the record of trial shall include a verbatim written transcript of all sessions except sessions closed for deliberations and voting when:

(i) Any part of the sentence adjudged exceeds six months confinement, forfeiture of pay greater than two-thirds pay per month, or any forfeiture of pay for more than six months or other punishments that may be adjudged by a special court-martial; or

(ii) A bad-conduct discharge has been adjudged.

Discussion

A verbatim transcript includes: all proceedings including sidebar conferences, arguments of counsel, and rulings and instructions by the military judge; matter which the military judge orders stricken from the record or disregarded; and when a record is amended in revision proceedings (*see* R.C.M. 1102), the part of the original record changed and the changes made, without physical alteration of the original record. Conferences under R.C.M. 802 need not be recorded, but matters agreed upon at such conferences must be included in the record. If testimony is given through an interpreter, a verbatim transcript must so reflect.

(C) *Verbatim transcript not required.* If a verbatim transcript is not required under subsection (b)(2)(B) of this rule, a summarized report of the proceedings may be prepared instead of a verbatim transcript.

Discussion

See also R.C.M. 910(i) concerning guilty plea inquiries.

(D) *Other matters.* In addition to the matter required under subsection (b)(2)(B) or (b)(2)(C) of this rule, a complete record shall include:

(i) The original charge sheet or a duplicate;

(ii) A copy of the convening order and any amending order(s);

(iii) The request, if any, for trial by military judge alone, or that the membership of the court-martial include enlisted persons, and, when applicable, any statement by the convening authority required under R.C.M. 201(f)(2)(B)(ii) or 503(a)(2);

(iv) The original dated, signed action by the convening authority; and

(v) Exhibits, or, with the permission of the military judge, copies, photographs, or descriptions of any exhibits which were received in evidence and any appellate exhibits.

(3) *Matters attached to the record.* The following matters shall be attached to the record:

(A) If not used as exhibits—

(i) The report of investigation under Article 32, if any;

(ii) The staff judge advocate's pretrial advice under Article 34, if any;

(iii) If the trial was a rehearing or new or other trial of the case, the record of the former hearing(s); and

(iv) Written special findings, if any, by the military judge.

(B) Exhibits or, with the permission of the military judge, copies, photographs, or descriptions of any exhibits which were marked for and referred to on the record but not received in evidence;

(C) Any matter filed by the accused under R.C.M. 1105, or any written waiver of the right to submit such matter;

(D) Any deferment request and the action on it;

(E) Explanation for any substitute authentication under R.C.M. 1104(a)(2)(B);

(F) Explanation for any failure to serve the record of trial on the accused under R.C.M. 1104(b);

(G) The post-trial recommendation of the staff judge advocate or legal officer and proof of service on defense counsel in accordance with R.C.M. 1106(f)(1);

(H) Any response by defense counsel to the post-trial review;

(I) Recommendations and other papers relative to clemency;

(J) Any statement why it is impracticable for the convening authority to act;

(K) Conditions of suspension, if any, and proof of service on probationer under R.C.M. 1108;

(L) Any waiver or withdrawal of appellate review under R.C.M. 1110; and

(M) Records of any proceedings in connection with vacation of suspension under R.C.M. 1109.

(c) *Special courts-martial.*

(1) *Involving a bad-conduct discharge, confinement for more than six months, or forfeiture of pay for more than six months.* The requirements of subsections (b)(1), (b)(2)(A), (b)(2)(B), (b)(2)(D), and (b)(3) of this rule shall apply in a special court-martial in which a bad-conduct discharge, confinement for more than six months, or forfeiture of pay for more than six months, has been adjudged.

(2) *All other special courts-martial.* If the special court-martial resulted in findings of guilty but a bad-conduct discharge, confinement for more than six months, or forfeiture of pay for more than six months, was not adjudged, the requirements of subsections (b)(1), (b)(2)(D), and (b)(3)(A)-(F) and (I)-(M) of this rule shall apply.

(d) *Summary courts-martial.* The summary court-martial record of trial shall be prepared as prescribed in R.C.M. 1305.

(e) *Acquittal; courts-martial resulting in findings of not guilty only by reason of lack of mental responsibility; termination prior to findings.* Notwithstanding subsections (b), (c), and (d) of this rule, if proceedings resulted in an acquittal of all charges and specifications or in a finding of not guilty only by reason of lack of mental responsibility of all charges and specifications, or if the proceedings were terminated by withdrawal, mistrial, or dismissal before findings, the record may consist of the original charge sheet, a copy of the convening order and amending orders (if any), and sufficient information to establish jurisdiction over the accused and the offenses (if not shown on the charge sheet). The convening authority or higher authority may prescribe additional requirements.

Discussion

The notes or recordings of court-martial proceedings described in this subsection should be retained if reinstitution and re-referral of the affected charges is likely or when they may be necessary for the trial of another accused in a related case. *See* R.C.M. 905(g) and 914.

(f) *Loss of notes or recordings of the proceedings.* If, because of loss of recordings or notes, or other reasons, a verbatim transcript cannot be prepared when required by subsection (b)(2)(B) or (c)(1) of this rule, a record which meets the requirements of subsection (b)(2)(C) of this rule shall be prepared, and the convening authority may:

(1) Approve only so much of the sentence that could be adjudged by a special court-martial, except that a bad-conduct discharge, confinement for more than six months, or forfeiture of two-thirds pay per month for more than six months, may not be approved; or

(2) Direct a rehearing as to any offense of which the accused was found guilty if the finding is supported by the summary of the evidence contained in the record, provided that the convening authority may not approve any sentence imposed at such a rehearing more severe than or in excess of that adjudged by the earlier court-martial.

(g) *Copies of the record of trial.*

(1) *General and special courts-martial.*

(A) *In general.* In general and special courts-martial which require a verbatim transcript under subsections (b) or (c) of this rule and are subject to a review by a Court of Criminal Appeals under Article 66, the trial counsel shall cause to be prepared an original and four copies of the record of trial. In all other general and special courts-martial the trial counsel shall cause to be prepared an original and one copy of the record of trial.

Discussion

In a joint or common trial an additional copy of the record must be prepared for each accused. *See* R.C.M. 1104(b).

(B) *Additional copies.* The convening or higher authority may direct that additional copies of the record of trial of any general or special court-martial be prepared.

(2) *Summary courts-martial.* Copies of the summary court-martial record of trial shall be prepared as prescribed in R.C.M. 1305(b).

(h) *Security classification.* If the record of trial contains matter which must be classified under applicable security regulations, the trial counsel shall cause a proper security classification to be assigned to the record of trial and on each page thereof on which classified material appears.

Discussion

See R.C.M. 1104(b)(1)(D) concerning the disposition of records of trial requiring security protection.

(i) *Examination and correction before authentication.*

(1) *General and special courts-martial.*

(A) *Examination and correction by trial counsel.* In general and special courts-martial, the trial counsel shall examine the record of trial before authentication and cause those changes to be made which are necessary to report the proceedings accurately. The trial counsel shall not change the record after authentication.

Discussion

The trial counsel may personally correct and initial the necessary changes or, if major changes are necessary, direct the reporter to rewrite the entire record or the portion of the record which is defective.

The trial counsel must ensure that the reporter makes a true, complete, and accurate record of the proceedings such that the record will meet the applicable requirements of this rule.

(B) *Examination by defense counsel.* Except when unreasonable delay will result, the trial counsel shall permit the defense counsel to examine the record before authentication.

Discussion

If the defense counsel discovers errors or omissions in the record, the defense counsel may suggest to the trial counsel appropriate changes to make the record accurate, forward for attachment to the record under Article 38(c) any objections to the record, or bring any suggestions for correction of the record to the attention of the person who authenticates the record.

The defense counsel should be granted reasonable access to the reporter's notes and tapes to facilitate the examination of the record.

A suitable notation that the defense counsel has examined the record should be made on the authentication page. *See* Appendix 13 or 14 for sample forms.

---

(2) *Summary courts-martial.* The summary court-martial shall examine and correct the summary court-martial record of trial as prescribed in R.C.M. 1305(a).

(j) *Videotape and similar records.*

(1) *Recording proceedings.* If authorized by regulations of the Secretary concerned, general and special courts-martial may be recorded by videotape, audiotape, or similar material from which sound and visual images may be reproduced to accurately depict the entire court-martial. Such means of recording may be used in lieu of recording by a qualified court reporter, when one is required, subject to this rule.

(2) *Preparation of written record.* When the court-martial, or any part of it, is recorded by videotape, audiotape, or similar material under subsection (j)(1) of this rule, a written transcript or summary as required in subsection (b)(2)(A), (b)(2)(B), (b)(2)(C), or (c) of this rule, as appropriate, shall be prepared in accordance with this rule and R.C.M. 1104 before the record is forwarded under R.C.M. 1104(e), unless military exigencies prevent transcription.

(3) *Military exigency.* If military exigency prevents preparation of a written transcript or summary, as required, and when the court-martial has been recorded by videotape, audiotape, or similar material under subsection (j)(1) of this rule, the videotape, audiotape, or similar material, together with the matters in subsections (b)(2)(D) and (b)(3) of this rule shall be authenticated and forwarded in accordance with R.C.M. 1104, provided that in such case the convening authority shall cause to be attached to the record a statement of the reasons why a written record could not be prepared, and provided further that in such case the defense counsel shall be given reasonable opportunity to listen to or to view and listen to the recording whenever defense counsel is otherwise entitled to examine the record under these rules. Subsection (g) of this rule shall not apply in case of military exigency under this subsection.

(4) *Further review.*

(A) *Cases reviewed by the Court of Criminal*

Appeals. Before review, if any, by a Court of Criminal Appeals of a case in which the record includes an authenticated recording prepared under subsection (j)(3) of this rule, a complete written transcript shall be prepared and certified as accurate in accordance with regulations of the Secretary concerned. The authenticated recording shall be retained for examination by appellate authorities.

(B) *Cases not reviewed by the Court of Criminal Appeals.* In cases in which the record includes an authenticated recording prepared under subsection (j)(3) of this rule, a written record shall be prepared under such circumstances as the Secretary concerned may prescribe.

(5) *Accused's copy.* When a record includes an authenticated recording under subsection (j)(3) of this rule, the Government shall, in order to comply with R.C.M. 1104(b):

(A) Provide the accused with a duplicate copy of the videotape, audiotape, or similar matter and copies of any written contents of and attachments to the record, and give the accused reasonable opportunity to use such viewing equipment as is necessary to listen to or view and listen to the recording; or

(B) With the written consent of the accused, defer service of the record until a written record is prepared under subsection (4) of this rule.

Rule 1103A. Sealed exhibits and proceedings.

(a) *In general.* If the record of trial contains exhibits, proceedings, or other matter ordered sealed by the military judge, the trial counsel shall cause such materials to be sealed so as to prevent indiscriminate viewing or disclosure. Trial counsel shall ensure that such materials are properly marked, including an annotation that the material was sealed by order of the military judge, and inserted at the appropriate place in the original record of trial. Copies of the record shall contain appropriate annotations that matters were sealed by order of the military judge and have been inserted in the original record of trial. This Rule shall be implemented in a manner consistent with Executive Order 12958, as amended, concerning classified national security information.

(b) *Examination of sealed exhibits and proceedings.* Except as provided in the following subsections to this rule, sealed exhibits may not be examined.

(1) *Examination of sealed matters.* For the purpose of this rule, "examination" includes reading, viewing, photocopying, photographing, disclosing, or manipulating the documents in any way.

(2) *Prior to authentication.* Prior to authentication of the record by the military judge, sealed materials may not be examined in the absence of an order from the military judge based on good cause shown.

(3) *Authentication through action.* After authentication and prior to disposition of the record of trial pursuant to Rule for Courts-Martial 1111, sealed materials may not be examined in the absence of an order from the military judge upon a showing of good cause at a post-trial Article 39a session directed by the Convening Authority.

(4) *Reviewing and appellate authorities.*

(A) Reviewing and appellate authorities may examine sealed matters when those authorities determine that such action is reasonably necessary to a proper fulfillment of their responsibilities under the Uniform Code of Military Justice, the Manual for Courts-Martial, governing directives, instructions, regulations, applicable rules for practice and procedure, or rules of professional responsibility.

(B) Reviewing and appellate authorities shall not, however, disclose sealed matter or information in the absence of:

(i) Prior authorization of the Judge Advocate General in the case of review under Rule for Courts-Martial 1201(b); or

(ii) Prior authorization of the appellate court before which a case is pending review under Rules for Courts-Martial 1203 and 1204.

(C) In those cases in which review is sought or pending before the United States Supreme Court, authorization to disclose sealed materials or information shall be obtained under that Court's rules of practice and procedure.

(D) The authorizing officials in paragraph (B)(ii) above may place conditions on authorized disclosures in order to minimize the disclosure.

(E) For purposes of this rule, reviewing and appellate authorities are limited to:

(i) Judge advocates reviewing records pursuant to Rule for Courts-Martial 1112;

(ii) Officers and attorneys in the office of the Judge Advocate General reviewing records pursuant to Rule for Courts-Martial 1201(b);

(iii) Appellate government counsel;

(iv) Appellate defense counsel;

(v) Appellate judges of the Courts of Criminal Appeals and their professional staffs;

(vi) The judges of the United States Court of Appeals for the Armed Forces and their professional staffs;

(vii) The Justices of the United States Supreme Court and their professional staffs; and

(viii) Any other court of competent jurisdiction.

Rule 1104. Records of trial: Authentication; service; loss; correction; forwarding

(a) *Authentication.*

(1) *In general.* A record is authenticated by the signature of a person specified in this rule who thereby declares that the record accurately reports the proceedings. No person may be required to authenticate a record of trial if that person is not satisfied that it accurately reports the proceedings.

(2) *General and special courts-martial.*

(A) *Authentication by the military judge.* In special courts-martial in which a bad-conduct discharge, confinement for more than six months, or forfeiture of pay for more than six months, has been adjudged and in general courts-martial, except as provided in subsection (a)(2)(B) of this rule, the military judge present at the end of the proceedings shall authenticate the record of trial, or that portion over which the military judge presided. If more than one military judge presided over the proceedings, each military judge shall authenticate the record of the proceedings over which that military judge presided, except as provided in subsection (a)(2)(B) of this rule. The record of trial of special courts-martial in which a bad-conduct discharge, confinement for more than six months, or forfeiture of pay for more than six months, was not adjudged shall be authenticated in accordance with regulations of the Secretary concerned.

(B) *Substitute authentication.* If the military judge cannot authenticate the record of trial because of the military judge's death, disability, or absence, the trial counsel present at the end of the proceedings shall authenticate the record of trial. If the trial counsel cannot authenticate the record of trial because of the trial counsel's death, disability, or absence, a member shall authenticate the record of trial. In a court-martial composed of a military judge alone, or as to sessions without members, the court reporter shall authenticate the record of trial when this duty would fall upon a member under this subsection. A person authorized to authenticate a record under this subsection may authenticate the record only as to those proceedings at which that person was present.

Discussion

See Appendix 13 or 14 for sample forms.

Substitute authentication is authorized only in emergencies. A brief, temporary absence of the military judge from the situs of the preparation of the record of trial does not justify a substitute authentication. Prolonged absence, including permanent change of station, ordinarily justifies substitute authentication.

The person who authenticates the record of trial instead of the military judge should attach to the record of trial an explanation for the substitute authentication. *See* R.C.M. 1103(b)(3) (E).

---

(3) *Summary courts-martial.* The summary court-martial shall authenticate the summary court-martial record of trial as prescribed in R.C.M. 1305(a).

(b) *Service.*

(1) *General and special courts-martial.*

(A) *Service of record of trial on accused.* In each general and special court-martial, except as provided in subsection (b)(1)(C) or (D) of this rule, the trial counsel shall cause a copy of the record of trial to be served on the accused as soon as the record of trial is authenticated.

(B) *Proof of service of record of trial on accused.* The trial counsel shall cause the accused's receipt for the copy of the record of trial to be attached to the original record of trial. If it is impracticable to secure a receipt from the accused before the original record of trial is forwarded to the convening authority, the trial counsel shall prepare a certificate indicating that a copy of the record of trial has been transmitted to the accused, including the means of transmission and the address, and cause the certificate to be attached to the original record of trial. In such a case the accused's receipt shall be forwarded to the convening authority as soon as it is obtained.

(C) *Substitute service.* If it is impracticable to serve the record of trial on the accused because of the transfer of the accused to a distant place, the unauthorized absence of the accused, or military exigency, or if the accused so requests on the record at the court-martial or in writing, the accused's copy of the record shall be forwarded to the accused's defense counsel, if any. Trial counsel shall attach a statement to the record explaining why the accused was not served personally. If the accused has more than one counsel, R.C.M. 1106(f)(2) shall apply. If the accused has no counsel and if the accused is absent without authority, the trial counsel shall prepare an explanation for the failure to serve the record. The explanation and the accused's copy of the record shall be forwarded with the original record. The accused shall be provided with a copy of the record as soon as practicable.

Discussion

See Appendix 13 or 14 for sample forms.

(D) *Classified information.*

(i) *Forwarding to convening authority.* If the copy of the record of trial prepared for the accused contains classified information, the trial counsel, unless directed otherwise by the convening authority, shall forward the accused's copy to the convening authority, before it is served on the accused.

(ii) *Responsibility of the convening authority.* The convening authority shall:

(a) cause any classified information to be deleted or withdrawn from the accused's copy of the record of trial;

(b) cause a certificate indicating that classified information has been deleted or withdrawn to be attached to the record of trial; and

(c) cause the expurgated copy of the record of trial and the attached certificate regarding classified information to be served on the accused as provided in subsections (b)(1)(A) and (B) of this rule except that the accused's receipt shall show that the accused has received an expurgated copy of the record of trial.

(iii) *Contents of certificate.* The certificate regarding deleted or withdrawn classified information shall indicate:

(a) that the original record of trial may be inspected in the Office of the Judge Advocate General concerned under such regulations as the Secretary concerned may prescribe;

(b) the pages of the record of trial from which matter has been deleted;

(c) the pages of the record of trial which have been entirely deleted; and

(d) the exhibits which have been withdrawn.

Discussion

See R.C.M. 1103(h) concerning classified information.

---

(2) *Summary courts-martial.* The summary court-martial record of trial shall be disposed of as provided in R.C.M. 1305(d). Subsection (b)(1)(D) of this rule shall apply if classified information is included in the record of trial of a summary court-martial.

(c) *Loss of record.* If the authenticated record of trial is lost or destroyed, the trial counsel shall, if practicable, cause another record of trial to be prepared for authentication. The new record of trial shall become the record of trial in the case if the requirements of R.C.M. 1103 and this rule are met.

(d) *Correction of record after authentication; certificate of correction.*

(1) *In general.* A record of trial found to be incomplete or defective after authentication may be corrected to make it accurate. A record of trial may be returned to the convening authority by superior competent authority for correction under this rule.

Discussion

The record of trial is corrected with a certificate of correction.

See Appendix 13 or 14 for a form for a certificate of correction. A certificate of correction may be used only to make the record of trial correspond to the actual proceedings. If the members were not sworn, for example, the error cannot be cured by a certificate of correction. If the members were sworn but the record did not so reflect, the record could be corrected.

---

(2) *Procedure.* An authenticated record of trial believed to be incomplete or defective may be returned to the military judge or summary court-martial for a certificate of correction. The military judge or summary court-martial shall give notice of the proposed correction to all parties and permit them to examine and respond to the proposed correction before authenticating the certificate of correction. All parties shall be given reasonable access to any original reporter's notes or tapes of the proceedings.

Discussion

The type of opportunity to respond depends on the nature and scope of the proposed correction. In many instances an adequate opportunity can be provided by allowing the respective parties to present affidavits and other documentary evidence to the person authenticating the certificate of correction or by a conference telephone call among the authenticating person, the parties, and the reporter. In other instances, an evidentiary hearing with witnesses may be required. The accused need not be present at any hearing on a certificate of correction.

---

(3) *Authentication of certificate of correction; service on the accused.* The certificate of correction shall be authenticated as provided in subsection (a) of this rule and a copy served on the accused as provided in subsection (b) of this rule. The certificate of correction and the accused's receipt for the certificate of correction shall be attached to each copy of the record of trial required to be prepared under R.C.M. 1103(g).

(e) *Forwarding.* After every court-martial, including a rehearing and new and other trials, the authenticated record shall be forwarded to the convening authority for initial review and action, provided that in case of a special court-martial in which a bad-conduct discharge or confinement for one year was adjudged or a general court-martial, the convening authority shall refer the record to the staff judge advocate or legal officer for recommendation under R.C.M. 1106 before the convening authority takes action.

Rule 1105. Matters submitted by the accused

(a) *In general.* After a sentence is adjudged in any court-martial, the accused may submit matters to the convening authority in accordance with this rule.

(b) *Matters which may be submitted.*

(1) The accused may submit to the convening authority any matters that may reasonably tend to affect the convening authority's decision whether to disapprove any findings of guilty or to approve the sentence. The convening authority is only required to consider written submissions.

(2) Submissions are not subject to the Military Rules of Evidence and may include:

(A) Allegations of errors affecting the legality of the findings or sentence;

(B) Portions or summaries of the record and copies of documentary evidence offered or introduced at trial;

(C) Matters in mitigation which were not available for consideration at the court-martial; and

Discussion

For example, post-trial conduct of the accused, such as providing restitution to the victim or exemplary behavior, might be appropriate.

(D) Clemency recommendations by any member, the military judge, or any other person. The defense may ask any person for such a recommendation.

Discussion

A clemency recommendation should state reasons for the recommendation and should specifically indicate the amount and character of the clemency recommended.

A clemency recommendation by a member should not disclose the vote or opinion of any member expressed in deliberations. Except as provided in R.C.M. 923 and 1008 and Mil. R. Evid. 606(b), a clemency recommendation does not impeach the findings or the sentence. If the sentencing authority makes a clemency recommendation in conjunction with the announced sentence, *see* R.C.M. 1106(d)(3)(B).

Although only written submissions must be considered, the convening authority may consider any submission by the accused, including, but not limited to, videotapes, photographs, and oral presentations.

(c) *Time periods.*

(1) *General and special courts-martial.* After a general or special court-martial, the accused may submit matters under this rule within the later of 10 days after a copy of the authenticated record of trial or, if applicable, the recommendation of the staff judge advocate or legal officer, or an addendum to the recommendation containing new matter is served on the accused. If, within the 10-day period, the accused shows that additional time is required for the accused to submit such matters, the convening authority or that authority's staff judge advocate may, for good cause, extend the 10-day period for not more than 20 additional days; however, only the convening authority may deny a request for such an extension.

(2) *Summary courts-martial.* After a summary court-martial, the accused may submit matters under this rule within 7 days after the sentence is announced. If the accused shows that additional time is required for the accused to submit such comments, the convening authority may, for good cause, extend

the period in which comments may be submitted for up to 20 additional days.

(3) *Post-trial sessions.* A post-trial session under R.C.M. 1102 shall have no effect on the running of any time period in this rule, except when such session results in the announcement of a new sentence, in which case the period shall run from that announcement.

(4) *Good cause.* For purposes of this rule, good cause for an extension ordinarily does not include the need for securing matters which could reasonably have been presented at the court-martial.

(d) *Waiver.*

(1) *Failure to submit matters.* Failure to submit matters within the time prescribed by this rule shall be deemed a waiver of the right to submit such matters.

(2) *Submission of matters.* Submission of any matters under this rule shall be deemed a waiver of the right to submit additional matters unless the right to submit additional matters within the prescribed time limits is expressly reserved in writing.

(3) *Written waiver.* The accused may expressly waive, in writing, the right to submit matters under this rule. Once filed, such waiver may not be revoked.

(4) *Absence of accused.* If, as a result of the unauthorized absence of the accused, the record cannot be served on the accused in accordance with R.C.M. 1104(b)(1) and if the accused has no counsel to receive the record, the accused shall be deemed to have waived the right to submit matters under this rule within the time limit which begins upon service on the accused of the record of trial.

Discussion

The accused is not required to raise objections to the trial proceedings in order to preserve them for later review.

Rule 1106. Recommendation of the staff judge advocate or legal officer

(a) *In general.* Before the convening authority takes action under R.C.M. 1107 on a record of trial by general court-martial or a record of trial by special court-martial that includes a sentence to a bad-conduct discharge or confinement for one year, that convening authority's staff judge advocate or legal officer shall, except as provided in subsection (c) of this rule, forward to the convening authority a recommendation under this rule.

(b) *Disqualification.* No person who has acted as member, military judge, trial counsel, assistant trial counsel, defense counsel, associate or assistant defense counsel, or investigating officer in any case may later act as a staff judge advocate or legal officer to any reviewing or convening authority in the same case.

Discussion

The staff judge advocate or legal officer may also be ineligible when, for example, the staff judge advocate or legal officer; served as the defense counsel in a companion case; testified as to a contested matter (unless the testimony is clearly uncontroverted); has other than an official interest in the same case; or must review that officer's own pretrial action (such as the pretrial advice under Article 34; *see* R.C.M. 406) when the sufficiency or correctness of the earlier action has been placed in issue.

(c) *When the convening authority has no staff judge advocate.*

(1) *When the convening authority does not have a staff judge advocate or legal officer or that person is disqualified.* If the convening authority does not have a staff judge advocate or legal officer, or if the person serving in that capacity is disqualified under subsection (b) of this rule or otherwise, the convening authority shall:

(A) Request the assignment of another staff judge advocate or legal officer to prepare a recommendation under this rule; or

(B) Forward the record for action to any officer exercising general court-martial jurisdiction as provided in R.C.M. 1107(a).

(2) *When the convening authority has a legal officer but wants the recommendation of a staff judge advocate.* If the convening authority has a legal officer but no staff judge advocate, the convening authority may, as a matter of discretion, request designation of a staff judge advocate to prepare the recommendation.

(d) *Form and content of recommendation.*

(1) The purpose of the recommendation of the staff judge advocate or legal officer is to assist the convening authority to decide what action to take on the sentence in the exercise of command prerogative. The staff judge advocate or legal officer shall

use the record of trial in the preparation of the recommendation.

(2) *Form.* The recommendation of the staff judge advocate or legal officer shall be a concise written communication.

(3) *Required contents.* Except as provided in subsection (e) of this rule, the recommendation of the staff judge advocate or legal officer shall include concise information as to:

(A) The findings and sentence adjudged by the court-martial;

(B) A recommendation for clemency by the sentencing authority, made in conjunction with the announced sentence;

Discussion

The recommendation required by this rule need not include information regarding other recommendations for clemency. *See* R.C.M. 1105(b)(4), which pertains to clemency recommendations that may be submitted by the accused to the convening authority.

(C) A summary of the accused's service record, to include length and character of service, awards and decorations received, and any records of nonjudicial punishment and previous convictions;

(D) A statement of the nature and duration of any pretrial restraint;

(E) If there is a pretrial agreement, a statement of any action the convening authority is obligated to take under the agreement or a statement of the reasons why the convening authority is not obligated to take specific action under the agreement; and

(F) A specific recommendation as to the action to be taken by the convening authority on the sentence.

(4) *Legal errors.* The staff judge advocate or legal officer is not required to examine the record for legal errors. However, when the recommendation is prepared by a staff judge advocate, the staff judge advocate shall state whether, in the staff judge advocate's opinion, corrective action on the findings or sentence should be taken when an allegation of legal error is raised in matters submitted under R.C.M. 1105 or when otherwise deemed appropriate by the staff judge advocate. The response may consist of a statement of agreement or disagreement with the matter raised by the accused. An analysis or rationale for the staff judge advocate's statement, if any, concerning legal errors is not required.

(5) *Optional matters.* The recommendation of the staff judge advocate or legal officer may include, in addition to matters included under subsections (d)(3) and (4) of this rule, any additional matters deemed appropriate by the staff judge advocate or legal officer. Such matter may include matters outside the record.

Discussion

See R.C.M. 1107(b)(3)(B)(iii) if matters adverse to the accused from outside the record are included.

(6) *Effect of error.* In case of error in the recommendation not otherwise waived under subsection (f)(6) of this rule, appropriate corrective action shall be taken by appellate authorities without returning the case for further action by a convening authority.

(e) *No findings of guilty; findings of not guilty only by reason of lack of mental responsibility.* If the proceedings resulted in an acquittal or in a finding of not guilty only by reason of lack of mental responsibility of all charges and specifications, or if, after the trial began, the proceedings were terminated without findings and no further action is contemplated, a recommendation under this rule is not required.

(f) *Service of recommendation on defense counsel and accused; defense response.*

(1) *Service of recommendation on defense counsel and accused.* Before forwarding the recommendation and the record of trial to the convening authority for action under R.C.M. 1107, the staff judge advocate or legal officer shall cause a copy of the recommendation to be served on counsel for the accused. A separate copy will be served on the accused. If it is impracticable to serve the recommendation on the accused for reasons including but not limited to the transfer of the accused to a distant place, the unauthorized absence of the accused, or military exigency, or if the accused so requests on the record at the court-martial or in writing, the accused's copy shall be forwarded to the accused's defense counsel. A statement shall be attached to the record explaining why the accused was not served personally.

Discussion

The method of service and the form of the proof of service are not prescribed and may be by any appropriate means. *See* R.C.M. 1103(b)(3)(G). For example, a certificate of service, attached to the record of trial, would be appropriate when the accused is served personally.

(2) *Counsel for the accused.* The accused may, at trial or in writing to the staff judge advocate or legal officer before the recommendation has been served under this rule, designate which counsel (detailed, individual military, or civilian) will be served with the recommendation. In the absence of such designation, the staff judge advocate or legal officer shall cause the recommendation to be served in the following order of precedence, as applicable, on: (1) civilian counsel; (2) individual military counsel; or (3) detailed defense counsel. If the accused has not retained civilian counsel and the detailed defense counsel and individual military counsel, if any, have been relieved or are not reasonably available to represent the accused, substitute military counsel to represent the accused shall be detailed by an appropriate authority. Substitute counsel shall enter into an attorney-client relationship with the accused before examining the recommendation and preparing any response.

Discussion

When the accused is represented by more than one counsel, the military judge should inquire of the accused and counsel before the end of the court-martial as to who will act for the accused under this rule.

(3) *Record of trial.* The staff judge advocate or legal officer shall, upon request of counsel for the accused served with the recommendation, provide that counsel with a copy of the record of trial for use while preparing the response to the recommendation.

(4) *Response.* Counsel for the accused may submit, in writing, corrections or rebuttal to any matter in the recommendation believed to be erroneous, inadequate, or misleading, and may comment on any other matter.

Discussion

See also R.C.M. 1105.

(5) *Time period.* Counsel for the accused shall be given 10 days from service of the record of trial under R.C.M. 1104(b) or receipt of the recommendation, whichever is later, in which to submit comments on the recommendation. The convening authority may, for good cause, extend the period in which comments may be submitted for up to 20 additional days.

(6) *Waiver.* Failure of counsel for the accused to comment on any matter in the recommendation or matters attached to the recommendation in a timely manner shall waive later claim of error with regard to such matter in the absence of plain error.

Discussion

The accused is not required to raise objections to the trial proceedings in order to preserve them for later review.

(7) *New matter in addendum to recommendation.* The staff judge advocate or legal officer may supplement the recommendation after the accused and counsel for the accused have been served with the recommendation and given an opportunity to comment. When new matter is introduced after the accused and counsel for the accused have examined the recommendation, however, the accused and counsel for the accused must be served with the new matter and given 10 days from service of the addendum in which to submit comments. Substitute service of the accused's copy of the addendum upon counsel for the accused is permitted in accordance with the procedures outlined in subparagraph (f)(1) of this rule.

Discussion

"New matter" includes discussion of the effect of new decisions on issues in the case, matter from outside the record of trial, and issues not previously discussed. "New matter" does not ordinarily include any discussion by the staff judge advocate or legal officer of the correctness of the initial defense comments on the recommendation. The method of service and the form of the proof of service are not prescribed and may be by any appropriate means. *See* R.C.M. 1103(b)(3)(G). For example, a certificate of service, attached to the record of trial, would be appropriate when the accused is served personally.

Rule 1107. Action by convening authority

(a) *Who may take action.* The convening authority shall take action on the sentence and, in the discretion of the convening authority, the findings, unless it is impracticable. If it is impracticable for the convening authority to act, the convening authority shall, in accordance with such regulations as the Secretary concerned may prescribe, forward the case to an officer exercising general court-martial jurisdiction who may take action under this rule.

Discussion

The convening authority may not delegate the function of taking action on the findings or sentence. The convening authority who convened the court-martial may take action on the case regardless whether the accused is a member of or present in the convening authority's command.

It would be impracticable for the convening authority to take initial action when, for example, a command has been decommissioned or inactivated before the convening authority's action; when a command has been alerted for immediate overseas movement; or when the convening authority is disqualified because the convening authority has other than an official interest in the case or because a member of the court-martial which tried the accused later became the convening authority.

If the convening authority forwards the case to an officer exercising general court-martial jurisdiction for initial review and action, the record should include a statement of the reasons why the convening authority did not act.

(b) *General considerations.*

(1) *Discretion of convening authority.* The action to be taken on the findings and sentence is within the sole discretion of the convening authority. Determining what action to take on the findings and sentence of a court-martial is a matter of command prerogative. The convening authority is not required to review the case for legal errors or factual sufficiency.

Discussion

The action is taken in the interests of justice, discipline, mission requirements, clemency, and other appropriate reasons. If errors are noticed by the convening authority, the convening authority may take corrective action under this rule.

---

(2) *When action may be taken.* The convening authority may take action only after the applicable time periods under R.C.M. 1105(c) have expired or the accused has waived the right to present matters under R.C.M. 1105(d), whichever is earlier, subject to regulations of the Secretary concerned.

(3) *Matters considered.*

(A) *Required matters.* Before taking action, the convening authority shall consider:

(i) The result of trial;

Discussion

See R.C.M. 1101(a).

(ii) The recommendation of the staff judge advocate or legal officer under R.C.M. 1106, if applicable; and

(iii) Any matters submitted by the accused under R.C.M. 1105 or, if applicable, R.C.M. 1106(f).

(B) *Additional matters.* Before taking action the convening authority may consider:

(i) The record of trial;

(ii) The personnel records of the accused; and

(iii) Such other matters as the convening authority deems appropriate. However, if the convening authority considers matters adverse to the accused from outside the record, with knowledge of which the accused is not chargeable, the accused shall be notified and given an opportunity to rebut.

(4) *When proceedings resulted in finding of not guilty or not guilty only by reason of lack of mental responsibility, or there was a ruling amounting to a finding of not guilty.* The convening authority shall not take action disapproving a finding of not guilty, a finding of not guilty only by reason of lack of mental responsibility, or a ruling amounting to a finding of not guilty. When an accused is found not guilty only by reason of lack of mental responsibility, the convening authority, however, shall commit the accused to a suitable facility pending a hearing and disposition in accordance with R.C.M. 1102A.

Discussion

Commitment of the accused to the custody of the Attorney General for hospitalization is discretionary.

---

(5) *Action when accused lacks mental capacity.* The convening authority may not approve a sentence while the accused lacks mental capacity to understand and to conduct or cooperate intelligently in the post-trial proceedings. In the absence of substantial evidence to the contrary, the accused is presumed to have the capacity to understand and to conduct or cooperate intelligently in the post-trial proceedings. If a substantial question is raised as to the requisite

mental capacity of the accused, the convening authority may direct an examination of the accused in accordance with R.C.M. 706 before deciding whether the accused lacks mental capacity, but the examination may be limited to determining the accused's present capacity to understand and cooperate in the post-trial proceedings. The convening authority may approve the sentence unless it is established, by a preponderance of the evidence—including matters outside the record of trial—that the accused does not have the requisite mental capacity. Nothing in this subsection shall prohibit the convening authority from disapproving the findings of guilty and sentence.

(c) *Action on findings.* Action on the findings is not required. However, the convening authority may, in the convening authority's sole discretion:

(1) Change a finding of guilty to a charge or specification to a finding of guilty to an offense that is a lesser included offense of the offense stated in the charge or specification; or

(2) Set aside any finding of guilty and—

(A) Dismiss the specification and, if appropriate, the charge, or

(B) Direct a rehearing in accordance with subsection (e) of this rule.

Discussion

The convening authority may for any reason or no reason disapprove a finding of guilty or approve a finding of guilty only of a lesser offense. However, *see* subsection (e) of this rule if a rehearing is ordered. The convening authority is not required to review the findings for legal or factual sufficiency and is not required to explain a decision to order or not to order a rehearing, except as provided in subsection (e) of this rule. The power to order a rehearing, or to take other corrective action on the findings, is designed solely to provide an expeditious means to correct errors that are identified in the course of exercising discretion under the rule.

(d) *Action on the sentence.*

(1) *In general.* The convening authority may for any or no reason disapprove a legal sentence in whole or in part, mitigate the sentence, and change a punishment to one of a different nature as long as the severity of the punishment is not increased. The convening or higher authority may not increase the punishment imposed by a court-martial. The approval or disapproval shall be explicitly stated.

Discussion

A sentence adjudged by a court-martial may be approved if it was within the jurisdiction of the court-martial to adjudge (*see* R.C.M. 201(f)) and did not exceed the maximum limits prescribed in Part IV and Chapter X of this Part for the offense(s) of which the accused legally has been found guilty.

When mitigating forfeitures, the duration and amounts of forfeiture may be changed as long as the total amount forfeited is not increased and neither the amount nor duration of the forfeitures exceeds the jurisdiction of the court-martial. When mitigating confinement or hard labor without confinement, the convening authority should use the equivalencies at R.C.M. 1003(b)(6) and (7), as appropriate. One form of punishment may be changed to a less severe punishment of a different nature, as long as the changed punishment is one that the court-martial could have adjudged. For example, a bad-conduct discharge adjudged by a special court-martial could be changed to confinement for up to one year (but not vice versa). A pretrial agreement may also affect what punishments may be changed by the convening authority.

See also R.C.M. 810(d) concerning sentence limitations upon a rehearing or new or other trial.

---

(2) *Determining what sentence should be approved.* The convening authority shall approve that sentence which is warranted by the circumstances of the offense and appropriate for the accused. When the court-martial has adjudged a mandatory punishment, the convening authority may nevertheless approve a lesser sentence.

Discussion

In determining what sentence should be approved the convening authority should consider all relevant factors including the possibility of rehabilitation, the deterrent effect of the sentence, and all matters relating to clemency, such as pretrial confinement. *See also* R.C.M. 1001 through 1004.

When an accused is not serving confinement, the accused should not be deprived of more than two-thirds pay for any month as a result of one or more sentences by court-martial and other stoppages or involuntary deductions, unless requested by the accused. Since court-martial forfeitures constitute a loss of entitlement of the pay concerned, they take precedence over all debts.

---

(3) *Deferring service of a sentence to confinement.*

(A) In a case in which a court-martial sentences an accused referred to in subsection (B), below, to confinement, the convening authority may defer service of a sentence to confinement by a court-martial, without the consent of the accused, until after the accused has been permanently released to the armed forces by a state or foreign country.

(B) Subsection (A) applies to an accused who, while in custody of a state or foreign country, is temporarily returned by that state or foreign country to the armed forces for trial by court-martial; and after the court-martial, is returned to that state or foreign country under the authority of a mutual agreement or treaty, as the case may be.

(C) As used in subsection (d)(3), the term "state" means a state of the United States, the District of Columbia, a territory, and a possession of the United States.

Discussion

The convening authority's decision to postpone service of a court-martial sentence to confinement normally should be reflected in the action.

---

(4) *Limitations on sentence based on record of trial.* If the record of trial does not meet the requirements of R.C.M. 1103(b)(2)(B) or (c)(1), the convening authority may not approve a sentence in excess of that which may be adjudged by a special court-martial, or one that includes a bad-conduct discharge, confinement for more than six months, forfeiture of pay exceeding two-thirds pay per month, or any forfeiture of pay for more than six months.

Discussion

See also R.C.M. 1103(f).

---

(5) *Limitations on sentence of a special court-martial where a fine has been adjudged.* A convening authority may not approve in its entirety a sentence adjudged at a special court-martial when, if approved, the cumulative impact of the fine and forfeitures, whether adjudged or by operation of Article 58b, would exceed the jurisdictional maximum dollar amount of forfeitures that may be adjudged at that court-martial.

(e) *Ordering rehearing or other trial.*

(1) *Rehearing.*

(A) *In general.* Subject to subsections (e)(1)(B) through (e)(1)(E) of this rule, the convening authority may in the convening authority's discretion order a rehearing. A rehearing may be ordered as to some or all offenses of which findings of guilty were entered and the sentence, or as to sentence only.

Discussion

A rehearing may be appropriate when an error substantially affecting the findings or sentence is noticed by the convening authority. The severity of the findings or the sentence of the original court-martial may not be increased at a rehearing unless the sentence prescribed for the offense is mandatory. *See* R.C.M. 810(d). If the accused is placed under restraint pending a rehearing, *see* R.C.M. 304; 305.

(B) *When the convening authority may order a rehearing.* The convening authority may order a rehearing:

(i) When taking action on the court-martial under this rule;

(ii) In cases subject to review by the Court of Criminal Appeals, before the case is forwarded under R.C.M. 1111(a)(1) or (b)(1), but only as to any sentence which was approved or findings of guilty which were not disapproved in any earlier action. In such a case, a supplemental action disapproving the sentence and some or all of the findings, as appropriate, shall be taken; or

(iii) *When authorized to do so by superior competent authority.* If the convening authority finds a rehearing as to any offenses impracticable, the convening authority may dismiss those specifications and, when appropriate, charges.

Discussion

A sentence rehearing, rather than a reassessment, may be more appropriate in cases where a significant part of the government's case has been dismissed. The convening authority may not take any actions inconsistent with directives of superior competent authority. Where that directive is unclear, appropriate clarification should be sought from the authority issuing the original directive.

(iv) *Sentence reassessment.* If a superior authority has approved some of the findings of guilty and has authorized a rehearing as to other offenses and the sentence, the convening authority may, unless otherwise directed, reassess the sentence based on the approved findings of guilty and dismiss the remaining charges. Reassessment is appropriate only where the convening authority determines that the accused's sentence would have been at least of a certain magnitude had the prejudicial error not been committed and the reassessed sentence is appropriate in relation to the affirmed findings of guilty.

(C) *Limitations.*

(i) *Sentence approved.* A rehearing shall not

be ordered if, in the same action, a sentence is approved.

(ii) *Lack of sufficient evidence.* A rehearing may not be ordered as to findings of guilty when there is a lack of sufficient evidence in the record to support the findings of guilty of the offense charged or of any lesser included offense. A rehearing may be ordered, however, if the proof of guilt consisted of inadmissible evidence for which there is available an admissible substitute. A rehearing may be ordered as to any lesser offense included in an offense of which the accused was found guilty, provided there is sufficient evidence in the record to support the lesser included offense.

Discussion

For example, if proof of absence without leave was by improperly authenticated documentary evidence admitted over the objection of the defense, the convening authority may disapprove the findings of guilty and sentence and order a rehearing if there is reason to believe that properly authenticated documentary evidence or other admissible evidence of guilt will be available at the rehearing. On the other hand, if no proof of unauthorized absence was introduced at trial, a rehearing may not be ordered.

(iii) *Rehearing on sentence only.* A rehearing on sentence only shall not be referred to a different kind of court-martial from that which made the original findings. If the convening authority determines a rehearing on sentence is impracticable, the convening authority may approve a sentence of no punishment without conducting a rehearing.

(D) *Additional charges.* Additional charges may be referred for trial together with charges as to which a rehearing has been directed.

(E) *Lesser included offenses.* If at a previous trial the accused was convicted of a lesser included offense, a rehearing may be ordered only as to that included offense or as to an offense included in that found. If, however, a rehearing is ordered improperly on the original offense charged and the accused is convicted of that offense at the rehearing, the finding as to the lesser included offense of which the accused was convicted at the original trial may nevertheless be approved.

(2) *"Other" trial.* The convening or higher authority may order an "other" trial if the original proceedings were invalid because of lack of jurisdiction or failure of a specification to state an offense. The authority ordering an "other" trial shall state in the action the basis for declaring the proceedings invalid.

(f) *Contents of action and related matters.*

(1) *In general.* The convening authority shall state in writing and insert in the record of trial the convening authority's decision as to the sentence, whether any findings of guilty are disapproved, and orders as to further disposition. The action shall be signed personally by the convening authority. The convening authority's authority to sign shall appear below the signature.

Discussion

See Appendix 16 for forms.

---

(2) *Modification of initial action.* The convening authority may recall and modify any action taken by that convening authority at any time before it has been published or before the accused has been officially notified. The convening authority may also recall and modify any action at any time prior to forwarding the record for review, as long as the modification does not result in action less favorable to the accused than the earlier action. In addition, in any special court-martial, the convening authority may recall and correct an illegal, erroneous, incomplete, or ambiguous action at any time before completion of review under R.C.M. 1112, as long as the correction does not result in action less favorable to the accused than the earlier action. When so directed by a higher reviewing authority or the Judge Advocate General, the convening authority shall modify any incomplete, ambiguous, void, or inaccurate action noted in review of the record of trial under Article 64, 66, 67, or examination of the record of trial under Article 69. The convening authority shall personally sign any supplementary or corrective action.

Discussion

For purposes of this rule, a record is considered to have been forwarded for review when the convening authority has either delivered it in person or has entrusted it for delivery to a third party over whom the convening authority exercises no lawful control (*e.g.*, the United States Postal Service).

---

(3) *Findings of guilty.* If any findings of guilty are disapproved, the action shall so state. If a rehearing is not ordered, the affected charges and specifica-

tions shall be dismissed by the convening authority in the action. If a rehearing or other trial is directed, the reasons for the disapproval shall be set forth in the action.

Discussion

If a rehearing or other trial is not directed, the reasons for disapproval need not be stated in the action, but they may be when appropriate. It may be appropriate to state them when the reasons may affect administrative disposition of the accused; for example, when the finding is disapproved because of the lack of mental responsibility of the accused or the running of the statute of limitations.

No express action is necessary to approve findings of guilty. *See* subsection (c) of this rule.

---

(4) *Action on sentence.*

(A) *In general.* The action shall state whether the sentence adjudged by the court-martial is approved. If only part of the sentence is approved, the action shall state which parts are approved. A rehearing may not be directed if any sentence is approved.

Discussion

See Appendix 16 for forms.

See R.C.M. 1108 concerning suspension of sentences.

See R.C.M. 1113 concerning execution of sentences.

(B) *Execution; suspension.* The action shall indicate, when appropriate, whether an approved sentence is to be executed or whether the execution of all or any part of the sentence is to be suspended. No reasons need be stated.

(C) *Place of confinement.* If the convening authority orders a sentence of confinement into execution, the convening authority shall designate the place of confinement in the action, unless otherwise prescribed by the Secretary concerned. If a sentence of confinement is ordered into execution after the initial action of the convening authority, the authority ordering the execution shall designate the place of confinement unless otherwise prescribed by the Secretary concerned.

Discussion

See R.C.M. 1113(d)(2)(C) concerning the place of confinement.

(D) *Custody or confinement pending appellate review; capital cases.* When a record of trial involves an approved sentence to death, the convening authority shall, unless any approved sentence of confinement has been ordered into execution and a place of confinement designated, provide in the action for the temporary custody or confinement of the accused pending final disposition of the case on appellate review.

(E) *Deferment of service of sentence to confinement.* Whenever the service of the sentence to confinement is deferred by the convening authority under R.C.M. 1101(c) before or concurrently with the initial action in the case, the action shall include the date on which the deferment became effective. The reason for the deferment need not be stated in the action.

(F) *Credit for illegal pretrial confinement.* When the military judge has directed that the accused receive credit under R.C.M. 305(k), the convening authority shall so direct in the action.

(G) *Reprimand.* The convening authority shall include in the action any reprimand which the convening authority has ordered executed.

Discussion

See R.C.M. 1003(b)(1) concerning reprimands.

---

(5) *Action on rehearing or new or other trial.*

(A) *Rehearing or other trial.* In acting on a rehearing or other trial the convening authority shall be subject to the sentence limitations prescribed in R.C.M. 810(d). Except when a rehearing or other trial is combined with a trial on additional offenses and except as otherwise provided in R.C.M. 810(d), if any part of the original sentence was suspended and the suspension was not properly vacated before the order directing the rehearing, the convening authority shall take the necessary suspension action to prevent an increase in the same type of punishment as was previously suspended. The convening authority may approve a sentence adjudged upon a rehearing or other trial regardless whether any kind or amount of the punishment adjudged at the former trial has been served or executed. However, in computing the term or amount of punishment to be actually served or executed under the new sentence, the accused shall be credited with any kind or amount of the former sentence included within the new sentence that was served or executed before the time it was disapproved or set aside. The convening authority shall, if any part of a sentence adjudged upon a rehearing or other trial is approved, direct in the action that any part or amount of the former sentence served or executed between the date it was adjudged and the date it was disapproved or set aside shall be credited to the accused. If, in the action on the record of a rehearing, the convening authority disapproves the findings of guilty of all charges and specifications which were tried at the former hearing and that part of the sentence which was based on these findings, the convening authority shall, unless a further rehearing is ordered, provide in the action that all rights, privileges, and property affected by any executed portion of the sentence adjudged at the former hearing shall be restored. The convening authority shall take the same restorative action if a court-martial at a rehearing acquits the accused of all charges and specifications which were tried at the former hearing.

(B) *New trial.* The action of the convening authority on a new trial shall, insofar as practicable, conform to the rules prescribed for rehearings and other trials in subsection (f)(5)(A) of this rule.

Discussion

See R.C.M. 810 for procedures at other trials.

In approving a sentence not in excess of or more severe than one previously approved (*see* R.C.M. 810(d)), a convening authority is prohibited from approving a punitive discharge more severe than one formerly approved, e.g., a convening authority is prohibited from approving a dishonorable discharge if a bad conduct discharge had formerly been approved. Otherwise, in approving a sentence not in excess of or more severe than one previously imposed, a convening authority is not limited to approving the same or lesser type of "other punishments" formerly approved.

(g) *Incomplete, ambiguous, or erroneous action.* When the action of the convening or of a higher authority is incomplete, ambiguous, or contains clerical error, the authority who took the incomplete, ambiguous, or erroneous action may be instructed by an authority acting under Article 64, 66, 67, or 69 to withdraw the original action and substitute a corrected action.

(h) *Service on accused.* A copy of the convening authority's action shall be served on the accused or on defense counsel. If the action is served on defense counsel, defense counsel shall, by expeditious means, provide the accused with a copy.

Discussion

If the promulgating order is prepared promptly, service of it will satisfy subsection (h).

Rule 1108. Suspension of execution of sentence; remission

(a) *In general.* Suspension of a sentence grants the accused a probationary period during which the suspended part of an approved sentence is not executed, and upon the accused's successful completion of which the suspended part of the sentence shall be remitted. Remission cancels the unexecuted part of a sentence to which it applies.

(b) *Who may suspend and remit.* The convening authority may, after approving the sentence, suspend the execution of all or any part of the sentence of a court-martial, except for a sentence of death. The general court-martial convening authority over the accused at the time of the court-martial may, when taking the action under R.C.M. 1112(f), suspend or remit any part of the sentence. The Secretary concerned and, when designated by the Secretary concerned, any Under Secretary, Assistant Secretary, Judge Advocate General, or commanding officer may suspend or remit any part or amount of the unexecuted part of any sentence other than a sentence approved by the President or a sentence of confinement for life without eligibility for parole that has been ordered executed. The Secretary concerned may, however, suspend or remit the unexecuted part of a sentence of confinement for life without eligibility for parole only after the service of a period of confinement of not less than 20 years. The commander of the accused who has the authority to convene a court-martial of the kind that adjudged the sentence may suspend or remit any part of the unexecuted part of any sentence by summary court-martial or of any sentence by special court-martial that does not include a bad-conduct discharge regardless of whether the person acting has previously approved the sentence. The "unexecuted part of any sentence" is that part that has been approved and ordered executed but that has not actually been carried out.

Discussion

See R.C.M. 1113 (execution of sentences); R.C.M. 1201 (action by the Judge Advocate General); R.C.M. 1206 (powers and responsibilities of the Secretary).

The military judge and members of courts-martial may not suspend sentences.

(c) *Conditions of suspension.* The authority who suspends the execution of the sentence of a court-martial shall:

(1) Specify in writing the conditions of the suspension;

(2) Cause a copy of the conditions of the suspension to be served on the probationer; and

(3) Cause a receipt to be secured from the probationer for service of the conditions of the suspension.

Unless otherwise stated, an action suspending a sentence includes as a condition that the probationer not violate any punitive article of the code.

(d) *Limitations on suspension.* Suspension shall be for a stated period or until the occurrence of an anticipated future event. The period shall not be unreasonably long. The Secretary concerned may further limit by regulations the period for which the execution of a sentence may be suspended. The convening authority shall provide in the action that unless the suspension is sooner vacated, the expiration of the period of suspension shall remit the suspended portion of the sentence. An appropriate authority may, before the expiration of the period of suspension, remit any part of the sentence, including a part which has been suspended; reduce the period of suspension; or, subject to R.C.M. 1109, vacate the suspension in whole or in part.

(e) *Termination of suspension by remission.* Expiration of the period provided in the action suspending a sentence or part of a sentence shall remit the suspended portion unless the suspension is sooner vacated. Death or separation which terminates status as a person subject to the code shall result in remission of the suspended portion of the sentence.

Discussion

See R.C.M. 1109(b)(4) concerning interruption of the period of suspension.

Rule 1109. Vacation of suspension of sentence

(a) *In general.* Suspension of execution of the sentence of a court-martial may be vacated for violation of the conditions of the suspension as provided in this rule.

(b) *Timeliness.*

(1) *Violation of conditions.* Vacation shall be based on a violation of the conditions of suspension which occurs within the period of suspension.

(2) *Vacation proceedings.* Vacation proceedings under this rule shall be completed within a reasonable time.

(3) *Order vacating the suspension.* The order vacating the suspension shall be issued before the expiration of the period of suspension.

Discussion

The order vacating a suspended sentence must be issued before the end of suspension even though, in certain cases, it may not be effective as an order of execution of the suspended sentence until the completion of appellate review or action by the President or the Secretary concerned. *See* R.C.M. 1113 concerning execution of sentences.

(4) *Interruptions to the period of suspension.* Unauthorized absence of the probationer or the commencement of proceedings under this rule to vacate suspension interrupts the running of the period of suspension.

(c) *Confinement of probationer pending vacation proceedings.*

(1) *In general.* A probationer under a suspended sentence to confinement may be confined pending action under subsection (d)(2) of this rule, in accordance with the procedures in this subsection.

(2) *Who may order confinement.* Any person who may order pretrial restraint under R.C.M. 304(b) may order confinement of a probationer under a suspended sentence to confinement.

(3) *Basis for confinement.* A probationer under a suspended sentence to confinement may be ordered into confinement upon probable cause to believe the probationer violated any conditions of the suspension.

Discussion

A determination that confinement is necessary to ensure the presence of the probationer or to prevent further misconduct is not required.

If the violation of the conditions also constitutes an offense under the code for which trial by court-martial is considered, an appropriate form of pretrial restraint may be imposed as an alternative to confinement under this rule. *See* R.C.M. 304 and 305.

---

(4) *Review of confinement.* Unless proceedings under subsection (d)(1), (e), (f), or (g) of this rule are completed within 7 days of imposition of confinement of the probationer (not including any delays requested by probationer), a preliminary hearing shall be conducted by a neutral and detached officer appointed in accordance with regulations of the Secretary concerned.

(A) *Rights of accused.* Before the preliminary hearing, the accused shall be notified in writing of:

(i) The time, place, and purpose of the hearing, including the alleged violation(s) of the conditions of suspension;

(ii) The right to be present at the hearing;

(iii) The right to be represented at the hearing by civilian counsel provided by the probationer or, upon request, by military counsel detailed for this purpose; and

(iv) The opportunity to be heard, to present witnesses who are reasonably available and other evidence, and the right to confront and cross-examine adverse witnesses unless the hearing officer determines that this would subject these witnesses to risk or harm. For purposes of this subsection, a witness is not reasonably available if the witness requires reimbursement by the United States for cost incurred in appearing, cannot appear without unduly delaying the proceedings or, if a military witness, cannot be excused from other important duties.

(B) *Rules of evidence.* Except for Mil. R. Evid. Section V (Privileges) and Mil. R. Evid. 302 and 305, the Military Rules of Evidence shall not apply to matters considered at the preliminary hearing under this rule.

(C) *Decision.* The hearing officer shall determine whether there is probable cause to believe that the probationer violated the conditions of the probationer's suspension. If the hearing officer determines that probable cause is lacking, the hearing officer shall issue a written order directing that the probationer released from confinement. If the hearing officer determines that there is probable cause to believe that the probationer violated the conditions of suspension, the hearing officer shall set forth in a written memorandum, detailing therein the evidence relied upon and reasons for making the decision. The hearing officer shall forward the original memorandum or release order to the probationer's commander and forward a copy to the probationer and the officer in charge of the confinement facility.

(d) *Vacation of suspended general court-martial sentence.*

(1) *Action by officer having special court-martial jurisdiction over probationer.*

(A) *In general.* Before vacation of the suspension of any general court-martial sentence, the officer having special court-martial jurisdiction over the probationer shall personally hold a hearing on the alleged violation of the conditions of suspension. If there is no officer having special court-martial jurisdiction over the probationer who is subordinate to the officer having general court-martial jurisdiction over the probationer, the officer exercising general court-martial jurisdiction over the probationer shall personally hold a hearing under subsection (d)(1) of this rule. In such cases, subsection (d)(1)(D) of this rule shall not apply.

(B) *Notice to probationer.* Before the hearing, the officer conducting the hearing shall cause the probationer to be notified in writing of:

(i) The time, place, and purpose of the hearing;

(ii) The right to be present at the hearing;

(iii) The alleged violation(s) of the conditions of suspension and the evidence expected to be relied on;

(iv) The right to be represented at the hearing by civilian counsel provided by the probationer or, upon request, by military counsel detailed for this purpose; and

(v) The opportunity to be heard, to present witnesses and other evidence, and the right to confront and cross-examine adverse witnesses unless the hearing officer determines that there is good cause for not allowing confrontation and cross-examination.

Discussion

The notice should be provided sufficiently in advance of the hearing to permit adequate preparation.

(C) *Hearing.* The procedure for the vacation hearing shall follow that prescribed in R.C.M. 405(g), (h)(1), and (i).

(D) *Record and recommendation.* The officer who conducts the vacation proceeding shall make a summarized record of the proceeding and forward the record and that officer's written recommendation concerning vacation to the officer exercising general court-martial jurisdiction over the probationer.

(E) *Release from confinement.* If the special court-martial convening authority finds there is not probable cause to believe that the probationer violated the conditions of the suspension, the special court-martial convening authority shall order the release of the probationer from any confinement ordered under subsection (c) of this rule. The special court-martial convening authority shall, in any event, forward the record and recommendation under subsection (d)(1)(D) of this rule.

Discussion

See Appendix 18 for a sample of a Report of Proceedings to Vacate Suspension of a General Court-Martial Sentence under Article 72, UCMJ, and R.C.M. 1109 (DD Form 455).

(2) *Action by officer exercising general court-martial jurisdiction over probationer.*

(A) *In general.* The officer exercising general court-martial jurisdiction over the probationer shall review the record produced by and the recommendation of the officer exercising special court-martial jurisdiction over the probationer, decide whether the probationer violated a condition of suspension, and, if so, decide whether to vacate the suspended sentence. If the officer exercising general court-martial jurisdiction decides to vacate the suspended sentence, that officer shall prepare a written statement of the evidence relied on and the reasons for vacating the suspended sentence.

(B) *Execution.* Any unexecuted part of a suspended sentence ordered vacated under this rule shall, subject to R.C.M. 1113(c), be ordered executed.

(e) *Vacation of a suspended special court-martial sentence wherein a bad-conduct discharge or confinement for one year was not adjudged.*

(1) *In general.* Before vacating the suspension of a special court-martial punishment that does not include a bad-conduct discharge or confinement for one year, the special court-martial convening authority for the command in which the probationer is serving or assigned shall cause a hearing to be held on the alleged violation(s) of the conditions of suspension.

(2) *Notice to probationer.* The person conducting the hearing shall notify the probationer, in writing, before the hearing of the rights specified in subsection (d)(1)(B) of this rule.

(3) *Hearing.* The procedure for the vacation hearing shall follow that prescribed in R.C.M. 405(g), (h)(1), and (i).

(4) *Authority to vacate suspension.* The special court-martial convening authority for the command in which the probationer is serving or assigned shall have the authority to vacate any punishment that the officer has the authority to order executed.

(5) *Record and recommendation.* If the hearing is not held by the commander with authority to vacate the suspension, the person who conducts the hearing shall make a summarized record of the hearing and forward the record and that officer's written recommendation concerning vacation to the commander with authority to vacate the suspension.

(6) *Decision.* The special court-martial convening authority shall review the record produced by and the recommendation of the person who conducted the vacation proceeding, decide whether the probationer violated a condition of suspension, and, if so, decide whether to vacate the suspended sentence. If the officer exercising jurisdiction decides to vacate the suspended sentence, that officer shall prepare a written statement of the evidence relied on and the reasons for vacating the suspended sentence.

(7) *Execution.* Any unexecuted part of a suspended sentence ordered vacated under this subsection shall be ordered executed.

(f) *Vacation of a suspended special court-martial sentence that includes a bad-conduct discharge or confinement for one year.*

(1) The procedure for the vacation of a suspended approved bad-conduct discharge or of any suspended portion of an approved sentence to confinement for

one year, shall follow that set forth in subsection (d) of this rule.

(2) The procedure for the vacation of a suspension of any lesser special court-martial punishment shall follow that set forth in subsection (e) of this rule.

Discussion

An officer exercising special court-martial jurisdiction may vacate any suspended punishments other than an approved suspended bad-conduct discharge or any suspended portion of an approved sentence to confinement for one year, regardless of whether they are contained in the same sentence as the bad-conduct discharge or confinement for one year. See Appendix 18 for a sample of a Report of Proceedings to Vacate Suspension of a Special Court-Martial Sentence including a bad-conduct discharge or confinement for one year under Article 72, UCMJ, and R.C.M. 1109 (DD Form 455).

(g) *Vacation of a suspended summary court-martial sentence.*

(1) Before vacation of the suspension of a summary court-martial sentence, the summary court-martial convening authority for the command in which the probationer is serving or assigned shall cause a hearing to be held on the alleged violation(s) of the conditions of suspension.

(2) *Notice to probationer.* The person conducting the hearing shall notify the probationer before the hearing of the rights specified in subsections (d)(1)(B)(i), (ii), (iii), and (v) of this rule.

(3) *Hearing.* The procedure for the vacation hearing shall follow that prescribed in R.C.M. 405(g), (h)(1), and (i).

(4) *Authority to vacate suspension.* The summary court-martial convening authority for the command in which the probationer is serving or assigned shall have the authority to vacate any punishment that the officer had the authority to order executed.

(5) *Record and recommendation.* If the hearing is not held by the commander with authority to vacate the suspension, the person who conducts the vacation proceeding shall make a summarized record of the proceeding and forward the record and that officer's written recommendation concerning vacation to the commander with authority to vacate the suspension.

(6) *Decision.* A commander with authority to vacate the suspension shall review the record produced by and the recommendation of the person who conducted the vacation proceeding, decide whether the probationer violated a condition of suspension, and, if so, decide whether to vacate the suspended sentence. If the officer exercising jurisdiction decides to vacate the suspended sentence, that officer shall prepare a written statement of the evidence relied on and the reasons for vacating the suspended sentence.

(7) *Execution.* Any unexecuted part of a suspended sentence ordered vacated under this subsection shall be ordered executed.

Rule 1110. Waiver or withdrawal of appellate review

(a) *In general.* After any general court-martial, except one in which the approved sentence includes death, and after any special court-martial in which the approved sentence includes a bad-conduct discharge or confinement for one year, the accused may waive or withdraw appellate review.

Discussion

Appellate review is not available for special courts-martial in which a bad-conduct discharge or confinement for one year was not adjudged or approved or for summary courts-martial. Cases not subject to appellate review, or in which appellate review is waived or withdrawn, are reviewed by a judge advocate under R.C.M. 1112. Such cases may also be submitted to the Judge Advocate General for review. *See* R.C.M. 1201(b)(3). Appellate review is mandatory when the approved sentence includes death.

(b) *Right to counsel.*

(1) *In general.* The accused shall have the right to consult with counsel qualified under R.C.M. 502(d)(1) before submitting a waiver or withdrawal of appellate review.

(2) *Waiver.*

(A) *Counsel who represented the accused at the court-martial.* The accused shall have the right to consult with any civilian, individual military, or detailed counsel who represented the accused at the court-martial concerning whether to waive appellate review unless such counsel has been excused under R.C.M. 505(d)(2)(B).

(B) *Associate counsel.* If counsel who represented the accused at the court-martial has not been excused but is not immediately available to consult with the accused, because of physical separation or other reasons, associate defense counsel shall be detailed to the accused upon request by the accused. Such counsel shall communicate with counsel who represented the accused at the court-martial, and shall advise the accused concerning whether to waive appellate review.

(C) *Substitute counsel.* If counsel who represented the accused at the court-martial has been excused under R.C.M. 505(d)(2)(B), substitute defense counsel shall be detailed to advise the accused concerning waiver of appellate rights.

(3) *Withdrawal.*

(A) *Appellate defense counsel.* If the accused is represented by appellate defense counsel, the accused shall have the right to consult with such counsel concerning whether to withdraw the appeal.

(B) *Associate defense counsel.* If the accused is represented by appellate defense counsel, and such counsel is not immediately available to consult with the accused, because of physical separation or other reasons, associate defense counsel shall be detailed to the accused, upon request by the accused. Such counsel shall communicate with appellate defense counsel and shall advise the accused whether to withdraw the appeal.

(C) *No counsel.* If appellate defense counsel has not been assigned to the accused, defense counsel shall be detailed for the accused. Such counsel shall advise the accused concerning whether to withdraw the appeal. If practicable, counsel who represented the accused at the court-martial shall be detailed.

(4) *Civilian counsel.* Whether or not the accused was represented by civilian counsel at the court-martial, the accused may consult with civilian counsel, at no expense to the United States, concerning whether to waive or withdraw appellate review.

(5) *Record of trial.* Any defense counsel with whom the accused consults under this rule shall be given reasonable opportunity to examine the record of trial.

Discussion

Ordinarily counsel may use the accused's copy of the record. If this is not possible, as when the accused and counsel are physically separated, another copy should be made available to counsel.

---

(6) *Consult.* The right to consult with counsel, as used in this rule, does not require communication in the presence of one another.

(c) *Compulsion, coercion, inducement prohibited.* No person may compel, coerce, or induce an accused by force, promises of clemency, or otherwise to waive or withdraw appellate review.

(d) *Form of waiver or withdrawal.* A waiver or withdrawal of appellate review shall:

(1) Be written;

(2) State that the accused and defense counsel have discussed the accused's right to appellate review and the effect of waiver or withdrawal of appellate review and that the accused understands these matters;

(3) State that the waiver or withdrawal is submitted voluntarily; and

(4) Be signed by the accused and by defense counsel.

Discussion

See Appendix 19 (DD Form 2330) or Appendix 20 (DD Form 2331) for samples of forms.

(e) *To whom submitted.*

(1) *Waiver.* A waiver of appellate review shall be filed with the convening authority. The waiver shall be attached to the record of trial.

(2) *Withdrawal.* A withdrawal of appellate review may be filed with the authority exercising general court-martial jurisdiction over the accused, who shall promptly forward it to the Judge Advocate General, or directly with the Judge Advocate General.

(f) *Time limit.*

(1) *Waiver.* The accused may sign a waiver of appellate review at any time after the sentence is announced. The waiver must be filed within 10 days after the accused or defense counsel is served with a copy of the action under R.C.M. 1107(h). Upon written application of the accused, the convening authority may extend this period for good cause, for not more than 30 days.

(2) *Withdrawal.* The accused may file withdrawal from appellate review at any time before such review is completed.

(g) *Effect of waiver or withdrawal; substantial compliance required.*

(1) *In general.* A waiver or withdrawal of appellate review under this rule shall bar review by the Judge Advocate General under R.C.M. 1201(b)(1) and by the Court of Criminal Appeals. Once submit-

ted, a waiver or withdrawal in compliance with this rule may not be revoked.

(2) *Waiver.* If the accused files a timely waiver of appellate review in accordance with this rule, the record shall be forwarded for review by a judge advocate under R.C.M. 1112.

(3) *Withdrawal.* Action on a withdrawal of appellate review shall be carried out in accordance with procedures established by the Judge Advocate General, or if the case is pending before a Court of Criminal Appeals, in accordance with the rules of such court. If the appeal is withdrawn, the Judge Advocate General shall forward the record to an appropriate authority for compliance with R.C.M. 1112.

(4) *Substantial compliance required.* A purported waiver or withdrawal of an appeal which does not substantially comply with this rule shall have no effect.

Rule 1111. Disposition of the record of trial after action

(a) *General courts-martial.*

(1) *Cases forwarded to the Judge Advocate General.* A record of trial by general court-martial and the convening authority's action shall be sent directly to the Judge Advocate General concerned if the approved sentence includes death or if the accused has not waived review under R.C.M. 1110. Unless otherwise prescribed by regulations of the Secretary concerned, 10 copies of the order promulgating the result of trial as to each accused shall be forwarded with the original record of trial. Two additional copies of the record of trial shall accompany the original record if the approved sentence includes death or if it includes dismissal of an officer, cadet, or midshipman, dishonorable or bad-conduct discharge, or confinement for one year or more and the accused has not waived appellate review.

(2) *Cases forwarded to a judge advocate.* A record of trial by general court-martial and the convening authority's action shall be sent directly to a judge advocate for review under R.C.M. 1112 if the sentence does not include death and if the accused has waived appellate review under R.C.M. 1110. Unless otherwise prescribed by the Secretary concerned, 4 copies of the order promulgating the result of trial shall be forwarded with the original record of trial.

(b) *Special courts-martial.*

(1) *Cases including an approved bad-conduct discharge or confinement for one year.* If the approved sentence of a special court-martial includes a bad-conduct discharge or confinement for one year, the record shall be disposed of as provided in subsection (a) of this rule.

(2) *Other cases.* The record of trial by a special court-martial in which the approved sentence does not include a bad-conduct discharge or confinement for one year shall be forwarded directly to a judge advocate for review under R.C.M. 1112. Four copies of the order promulgating the result of trial shall be forwarded with the record of trial, unless otherwise prescribed by regulations of the Secretary concerned.

(c) *Summary courts-martial.* The convening authority shall dispose of a record of trial by summary court-martial as provided by R.C.M. 1306.

Discussion

See DD Form 494 (Court-Martial Data Sheet).

Rule 1112. Review by a judge advocate

(a) *In general.* Except as provided in subsection (b) of this rule, under regulations of the Secretary concerned, a judge advocate shall review:

(1) Each general court-martial in which the accused has waived or withdrawn appellate review under R.C.M. 1110.

(2) Each special court-martial in which the accused has waived or withdrawn appellate review under R.C.M. 1110 or in which the approved sentence does not include a bad-conduct discharge or confinement for one year; and

(3) Each summary court-martial.

(b) *Exception.* If the accused was found not guilty or not guilty only by reason of lack of mental responsibility of all offenses or if the convening authority disapproved all findings of guilty, no review under this rule is required.

(c) *Disqualification.* No person may review a case under this rule if that person has acted in the same case as an accuser, investigating officer, member of the court-martial, military judge, or counsel, or has otherwise acted on behalf of the prosecution or defense.

(d) *Form and content of review.* The judge advocate's review shall be in writing and shall contain the following:

(1) Conclusions as to whether—

(A) The court-martial had jurisdiction over the accused and each offense as to which there is a finding of guilty which has not been disapproved;

(B) Each specification as to which there is a finding of guilty which has not been disapproved stated an offense; and

(C) The sentence was legal;

(2) A response to each allegation of error made in writing by the accused. Such allegations may be filed under R.C.M. 1105, 1106(f), or directly with the judge advocate who reviews the case; and

(3) If the case is sent for action to the officer exercising general court-martial jurisdiction under subsection (e) of this rule, a recommendation as to the appropriate action to be taken and an opinion as to whether corrective action is required as a matter of law.

Copies of the judge advocate's review under this rule shall be attached to the original and all copies of the record of trial. A copy of the review shall be forwarded to the accused.

(e) *Forwarding to officer exercising general court-martial jurisdiction.* In cases reviewed under subsection (a) of this rule, the record of trial shall be sent for action to the officer exercising general court-martial convening authority over the accused at the time the court-martial was held (or to that officer's successor) when:

(1) The judge advocate who reviewed the case recommends corrective action;

(2) The sentence approved by the convening authority includes dismissal, a dishonorable or bad-conduct discharge, or confinement for more than 6 months; or

(3) Such action is otherwise required by regulations of the Secretary concerned.

(f) *Action by officer exercising general court-martial jurisdiction.*

(1) *Action.* The officer exercising general court-martial jurisdiction who receives a record under subsection (e) of this rule may—

(A) Disapprove or approve the findings or sentence in whole or in part;

(B) Remit, commute, or suspend the sentence in whole or in part;

(C) Except where the evidence was insufficient at the trial to support the findings, order a rehearing on the findings, on the sentence, or on both; or

(D) Dismiss the charges.

Discussion

See R.C.M. 1113 concerning when the officer exercising general court-martial jurisdiction may order parts of the sentence executed. *See* R.C.M. 1114 concerning orders promulgating the action of the officer exercising general court-martial jurisdiction. *See also* Appendix 16 (Forms for actions) and Appendix 17 (Forms for court-martial orders).

---

(2) *Rehearing.* If the officer exercising general court-martial jurisdiction orders a rehearing, but the convening authority finds a rehearing impracticable, the convening authority shall dismiss the charges.

(3) *Notification.* After the officer exercising general court-martial jurisdiction has taken action, the accused shall be notified of the action and the accused shall be provided with a copy of the judge advocate's review.

(g) *Forwarding following review under this rule.*

(1) *Records forwarded to the Judge Advocate General.* If the judge advocate who reviews the case under this rule states that corrective action is required as a matter of law, and the officer exercising general court-martial jurisdiction does not take action that is at least as favorable to the accused as that recommended by the judge advocate, the record of trial and the action thereon shall be forwarded to the Judge Advocate General concerned for review under R.C.M. 1201(b)(2).

(2) *Sentence including dismissal.* If the approved sentence includes dismissal, the record shall be forwarded to the Secretary concerned.

Discussion

A dismissal may not be ordered executed until approved by the Secretary or the Secretary's designee. *See* R.C.M. 1206.

---

(3) *Other records.* Records reviewed under this rule which are not forwarded under subsection (g)(1) of this rule shall be disposed of as prescribed by the Secretary concerned.

Discussion

A dismissal may not be ordered executed until approved by the Secretary or the Secretary's designee under R.C.M. 1206.

Rule 1113. Execution of sentences

(a) *In general.* No sentence of a court-martial may be executed unless it has been approved by the convening authority.

Discussion

An order executing the sentence directs that the sentence be carried out. Except as provided in subsections (d)(2), (3), and (5) of this rule, no part of a sentence may be carried out until it is ordered executed.

(b) *Punishments which the convening authority may order executed in the initial action.* Except as provided in subsection (c) of this rule, the convening authority may order all or part of the sentence of a court-martial executed when the convening authority takes initial action under R.C.M. 1107.

(c) *Punishments which the convening authority may not order executed in the initial action.*

(1) *Dishonorable or a bad-conduct discharge.* Except as may otherwise be prescribed by the Secretary concerned, a dishonorable or a bad-conduct discharge may be ordered executed only by:

(A) The officer who reviews the case under R.C.M. 1112(f), as part of the action approving the sentence, except when that action must be forwarded under R.C.M. 1112(g)(1); or

(B) The officer then exercising general court-martial jurisdiction over the accused.

A dishonorable or bad-conduct discharge may be ordered executed only after a final judgment within the meaning of R.C.M. 1209 has been rendered in the case. If on the date of final judgment a servicemember is not on appellate leave and more than 6 months have elapsed since approval of the sentence by the convening authority, before a dishonorable or a bad-conduct discharge may be executed, the officer exercising general court-martial jurisdiction over the servicemember shall consider the advice of that officer's staff judge advocate as to whether retention of the servicemember would be in the best interest of the service. Such advice shall include the findings and sentence as finally approved, the nature and character of duty since approval of the sentence by the convening authority, and a recommendation whether the discharge should be executed.

(2) *Dismissal of a commissioned officer, cadet, or midshipman.* Dismissal of a commissioned officer, cadet, or midshipman may be approved and ordered executed only by the Secretary concerned or such Under Secretary or Assistant Secretary as the Secretary concerned may designate.

Discussion

See R.C.M. 1206(a) concerning approval by the Secretary.

(3) *Sentences extending to death.* A punishment of death may be ordered executed only by the President.

Discussion

See R.C.M. 1207 concerning approval by the President.

(d) *Other considerations concerning the execution of certain sentences.*

(1) *Death.*

(A) *Manner carried out.* A sentence to death which has been finally ordered executed shall be carried out in the manner prescribed by the Secretary concerned.

(B) *Action when accused lacks mental capacity.* An accused lacking the mental capacity to understand the punishment to be suffered or the reason for imposition of the death sentence may not be put to death during any period when such incapacity exists. The accused is presumed to have such mental capacity. If a substantial question is raised as to whether the accused lacks capacity, the convening authority then exercising general court-martial jurisdiction over the accused shall order a hearing on the question. A military judge, counsel for the government, and counsel for the accused shall be detailed. The convening authority shall direct an examination of the accused in accordance with R.C.M. 706, but the examination may be limited to determining whether the accused understands the punishment to be suffered and the reason therefore. The military judge shall consider all evidence presented, including evidence provided by the accused. The accused has the burden of proving such lack of capacity by a preponderance of the evidence. The military judge shall make findings of fact, which will then be forwarded to the convening authority ordering the hearing. If the accused is found to lack capacity, the convening authority shall stay the execution until the accused regains appropriate capacity.

Discussion

A verbatim transcript of the hearing should accompany the findings of fact.

---

(2) *Confinement.*

(A) *Effective date of confinement.* Any period of confinement included in the sentence of a court-martial begins to run from the date the sentence is adjudged by the court-martial, but the following shall be excluded in computing the service of the term of confinement:

(i) Periods during which the sentence to confinement is suspended or deferred;

(ii) Periods during which the accused is in custody of civilian authorities under Article 14 from the time of the delivery to the return to military custody, if the accused was convicted in the civilian court;

(iii) Periods during which the accused is in custody of civilian or foreign authorities after the convening authority, pursuant to Article 57(e), has postponed the service of a sentence to confinement.

Discussion

The convening authority's decision to postpone service of a court-martial sentence to confinement normally should be reflected in the action.

(iv) Periods during which the accused has escaped or is absent without authority, or is absent under a parole which proper authority has later revoked, or is erroneously released from confinement through misrepresentation or fraud on the part of the prisoner, or is erroneously released from confinement upon the prisoner's petition for a writ of habeas corpus under a court order which is later reversed; and

(v) Periods during which another sentence by court-martial to confinement is being served. When a prisoner serving a court-martial sentence to confinement is later convicted by a court-martial of another offense and sentenced to confinement, the later sentence interrupts the running of the earlier sentence. Any unremitted remaining portion of the earlier sentence will be served after the later sentence is fully executed.

(B) *Nature of the confinement.* The omission of "hard labor" from any sentence of a court-martial which has adjudged confinement shall not prohibit the authority who orders the sentence executed from requiring hard labor as part of the punishment.

(C) *Place of confinement.* The authority who orders a sentence to confinement into execution shall designate the place of confinement under regulations prescribed by the Secretary concerned, unless otherwise prescribed by the Secretary concerned. Under such regulations as the Secretary concerned may prescribe, a sentence to confinement adjudged by a court-martial or other military tribunal, regardless whether the sentence includes a punitive discharge or dismissal and regardless whether the punitive discharge or dismissal has been executed, may be ordered to be served in any place of confinement under the control of any of the armed forces or in any penal or correctional institution under the control of the United States or which the United States may be allowed to use. Persons so confined in a penal or correctional institution not under the control of one of the armed forces are subject to the same discipline and treatment as persons confined or committed by the courts of the United States or of the State, Territory, District of Columbia, or place in which the institution is situated. When the service of a sentence to confinement has been deferred and the deferment is later rescinded, the convening authority shall designate the place of confinement in the initial action on the sentence or in the order rescinding the deferment. No member of the armed forces may be placed in confinement in immediate association with enemy prisoners or other foreign nationals not members of the armed forces. The Secretary concerned may prescribe regulations governing the place and conditions of confinement.

Discussion

See R.C.M. 1101(c) concerning deferment of a sentence to confinement.

---

(3) *Confinement in lieu of fine.* Confinement may not be executed for failure to pay a fine if the accused demonstrates that the accused has made good faith efforts to pay but cannot because of in-

digency, unless the authority considering imposition of confinement determines, after giving the accused notice and opportunity to be heard, that there is no other punishment adequate to meet the Government's interest in appropriate punishment.

(4) *Restriction; hard labor without confinement.* When restriction and hard labor without confinement are included in the same sentence, they shall, unless one is suspended, be executed concurrently.

(5) *More than one sentence.* If at the time forfeitures may be ordered executed, the accused is already serving a sentence to forfeitures by another court-martial, the authority taking action may order that the later forfeitures will be executed when the earlier sentence to forfeitures is completed.

Rule 1114. Promulgating orders

(a) *In general.*

(1) *Scope of rule.* Unless otherwise prescribed by the Secretary concerned, orders promulgating the result of trial and the actions of the convening or higher authorities on the record shall be prepared, issued, and distributed as prescribed in this rule.

(2) *Purpose.* A promulgating order publishes the result of the court-martial and the convening authority's action and any later action taken on the case.

(3) *Summary courts-martial.* An order promulgating the result of a trial by summary court-martial need not be issued.

Discussion

See R.C.M. 1306(b)(2) concerning summary courts-martial.

(b) *By whom issued.*

(1) *Initial orders.* The order promulgating the result of trial and the initial action of the convening authority shall be issued by the convening authority.

(2) *Orders issued after the initial action.* Any action taken on the case subsequent to the initial action shall be promulgated in supplementary orders. The subsequent action and the supplementary order may be the same document if signed personally by the appropriate convening or higher authority.

(A) *When the President or the Secretary concerned has taken final action.* General court-martial orders publishing the final result in cases in which the President or the Secretary concerned has taken final action shall be promulgated as prescribed by regulations of the Secretary concerned.

(B) *Other cases.* In cases other than those in subsection (b)(2)(A) of this rule, the final action may be promulgated by an appropriate convening authority.

(c) *Contents.*

(1) *In general.* The order promulgating the initial action shall set forth: the type of court-martial and the command by which it was convened; the charges and specifications, or a summary thereof, on which the accused was arraigned; the accused's pleas; the findings or other disposition of each charge and specification; the sentence, if any; and the action of the convening authority, or a summary thereof. Supplementary orders shall recite, verbatim, the action or order of the appropriate authority, or a summary thereof.

(2) *Dates.* A promulgating order shall bear the date of the initial action, if any, of the convening authority. An order promulgating an acquittal, a court-martial terminated before findings, a court-martial resulting in a finding of not guilty only by reason of lack of mental responsibility of all charges and specifications, or action on the findings or sentence taken after the initial action of the convening authority shall bear the date of its publication. A promulgating order shall state the date the sentence was adjudged, the date on which the acquittal was announced, or the date on which the proceedings were otherwise terminated.

Discussion

See Appendix 17 for sample forms for promulgating orders.

(3) *Order promulgated regardless of the result of trial or nature of the action.* An order promulgating the result of trial by general or special court-martial shall be issued regardless of the result and regardless of the action of the convening or higher authorities.

(d) *Orders containing classified information.* When an order contains information which must be classified, only the order retained in the unit files and those copies which accompany the record of trial shall be complete and contain the classified information. The order shall be assigned the appropriate security classification. Asterisks shall be substituted for the classified information in the other copies of the order.

(e) *Authentication.* The promulgating order shall be authenticated by the signature of the convening or other competent authority acting on the case, or a person acting under the direction of such authority. A promulgating order prepared in compliance with this rule shall be presumed authentic.

(f) *Distribution.* Promulgating orders shall be distributed as provided in regulations of the Secretary concerned.

CHAPTER XII. APPEALS AND REVIEW

Rule 1201. Action by the Judge Advocate General

(a) *Cases required to be referred to a Court of Criminal Appeals.* The Judge Advocate General shall refer to a Court of Criminal Appeals the record in each trial by court-martial:

(1) In which the sentence, as approved, extends to death; or

(2) In which—

(A) The sentence, as approved, extends to dismissal of a commissioned officer, cadet, or midshipman, dishonorable or bad-conduct discharge, or confinement for 1 year or longer; and

(B) The accused has not waived or withdrawn appellate review.

Discussion

See R.C.M. 1110 concerning waiver or withdrawal of appellate review.

See also subsection (b)(1) of this rule concerning cases reviewed by the Judge Advocate General which may be referred to a Court of Criminal Appeals.

See R.C.M. 1203 concerning review by the Court of Criminal Appeals and the powers and responsibilities of the Judge Advocate General after such review. *See* R.C.M. 1202 concerning appellate counsel.

(b) *Cases reviewed by the Judge Advocate General.*

(1) *Mandatory examination of certain general courts-martial.* Except when the accused has waived the right to appellate review or withdrawn such review, the record of trial by a general court-martial in which there has been a finding of guilty and a sentence, the appellate review of which is not provided for in subsection (a) of this rule, shall be examined in the office of the Judge Advocate General. If any part of the findings or sentence is found unsupported in law, or if reassessment of the sentence is appropriate, the Judge Advocate General may modify or set aside the findings or sentence or both. If the Judge Advocate General so directs, the record shall be reviewed by a Court of Criminal Appeals in accordance with R.C.M. 1203. If the case is forwarded to a Court of Criminal Appeals, the accused shall be informed and shall have the rights under R.C.M. 1202(b)(2).

Discussion

A case forwarded to a Court of Criminal Appeals under this subsection is subject to review by the Court of Appeals for the Armed Forces upon petition by the accused under Article 67(a)(3) or when certified by the Judge Advocate General under Article 67(a)(2).

---

(2) *Mandatory review of cases forwarded under R.C.M. 1112(g)(1).* The Judge Advocate General shall review each case forwarded under R.C.M. 1112(g)(1). On such review, the Judge Advocate General may vacate or modify, in whole or part, the findings or sentence, or both, of a court-martial on the ground of newly discovered evidence, fraud on the court-martial, lack of jurisdiction over the accused or the offense, error prejudicial to the substantial rights of the accused, or the appropriateness of the sentence.

(3) *Review by the Judge Advocate General after final review.*

(A) *In general.* Notwithstanding R.C.M. 1209, the Judge Advocate General may, *sua sponte* or upon application of the accused or a person with authority to act for the accused, vacate or modify, in whole or in part, the findings, sentence, or both of a court-martial which has been finally reviewed, but has not been reviewed either by a Court of Criminal Appeals or by the Judge Advocate General under subsection (b)(1) of this rule, on the ground of newly discovered evidence, fraud on the court-martial, lack of jurisdiction over the accused or the offense, error prejudicial to the substantial rights of the accused, or the appropriateness of the sentence.

Discussion

See R.C.M. 1210 concerning petition for new trial. Review of a case by a Judge Advocate General under this subsection is not part of appellate review within the meaning of Article 76 or R.C.M. 1209.

Review of a finding of not guilty only by reason of lack of mental responsibility under this rule may not extend to the determination of lack of mental responsibility. Thus, modification of a finding of not guilty only by reason of lack of mental responsibility under this rule is limited to changing the finding to not guilty or not guilty only by reason of lack of mental responsibility of a lesser included offense.

(B) *Procedure.* Each Judge Advocate General shall provide procedures for considering all cases properly submitted under subsection (b)(3) of this rule and may prescribe the manner by which an application for relief under subsection (b)(3) of this rule may be made and, if submitted by a person other than the accused, may require that the applicant show authority to act on behalf of the accused.

Discussion

See R.C.M. 1114 concerning orders promulgating action under this rule.

(C) *Time limits on applications.* Any application for review by the Judge Advocate General under Article 69 must be made on or before the last day of the two year period beginning on the date the sentence is approved by the convening authority or the date the findings are announced for cases which do not proceed to sentencing, unless the accused establishes good cause for failure to file within that time.

(4) *Rehearing.* If the Judge Advocate General sets aside the findings or sentence, the Judge Advocate General may, except when the setting aside is based on lack of sufficient evidence in the record to support the findings, order a rehearing. If the Judge Advocate General sets aside the findings and sentence and does not order a rehearing, the Judge Advocate General shall order that the charges be dismissed. If the Judge Advocate General orders a rehearing but the convening authority finds a rehearing impractical, the convening authority shall dismiss the charges.

(c) *Remission and suspension.* The Judge Advocate General may, when so authorized by the Secretary concerned under Article 74, at any time remit or suspend the unexecuted part of any sentence, other than a sentence approved by the President.

Rule 1202. Appellate counsel

(a) *In general.* The Judge Advocate General concerned shall detail one or more commissioned officers as appellate Government counsel and one or more commissioned officers as appellate defense counsel who are qualified under Article 27(b)(1).

(b) *Duties.*

(1) *Appellate Government counsel.* Appellate Government counsel shall represent the United States before the Court of Criminal Appeals or the United States Court of Appeals for the Armed Forces when directed to do so by the Judge Advocate General concerned. Appellate Government counsel may represent the United States before the United States Supreme Court when requested to do so by the Attorney General.

(2) *Appellate defense counsel.* Appellate defense counsel shall represent the accused before the Court of Criminal Appeals, the Court of Appeals for the Armed Forces, or the Supreme Court when the accused is a party in the case before such court and:

(A) The accused requests to be represented by appellate defense counsel;

(B) The United States is represented by counsel; or

(C) The Judge Advocate General has sent the case to the United States Court of Appeals for the Armed Forces. Appellate defense counsel is authorized to communicate directly with the accused. The accused is a party in the case when named as a party in pleadings before the court or, even if not so named, when the military judge is named as respondent in a petition by the Government for extraordinary relief from a ruling in favor of the accused at trial.

Discussion

For a discussion of the duties of the trial defense counsel concerning post-trial and appellate matters, *see* R.C.M. 502(d)(6) Discussion (E). Appellate defense counsel may communicate with trial defense counsel concerning the case. *See also* Mil. R. Evid. 502 (privileges).

If all or part of the findings and sentence are affirmed by the Court of Criminal Appeals, appellate defense counsel should advise the accused whether the accused should petition for further review in the United States Court of Appeals for the Armed Forces and concerning which issues should be raised.

The accused may be represented by civilian counsel before the Court of Criminal Appeals, the Court of Appeals for the Armed Forces, and the Supreme Court. Such counsel will not be provided at the expense of the United States. Civilian counsel may represent the accused before these courts in addition to or instead of military counsel.

If, after any decision of the Court of Appeals for the Armed Forces, the accused may apply for a writ of certiorari (*see* R.C.M. 1205), appellate defense counsel should advise the accused whether to apply for review by the Supreme Court and which issues might be raised. If authorized to do so by the accused, appellate defense counsel may prepare and file a petition for a writ of certiorari on behalf of the accused.

The accused has no right to select appellate defense counsel. Under some circumstances, however, the accused may be entitled to request that the detailed appellate defense counsel be replaced by another appellate defense counsel.

See also R.C.M. 1204(b)(1) concerning detailing counsel with respect to the right to petition the Court of Appeals for the Armed Forces for review.

Rule 1203. Review by a Court of Criminal Appeals

(a) *In general.* Each Judge Advocate General shall establish a Court of Criminal Appeals composed of appellate military judges.

Discussion

See Article 66 concerning the composition of the Courts of Criminal Appeals, the qualifications of appellate military judges, the grounds for their ineligibility, and restrictions upon the official relationship of the members of the court to other members. Uniform rules of court for the Courts of Criminal Appeals prescribed by the Judge Advocates General.

(b) *Cases reviewed by a Court of Criminal Appeals.* A Court of Criminal Appeals shall review cases referred to it by the Judge Advocate General under R.C.M. 1201(a) or (b)(1).

Discussion

See R.C.M. 1110 concerning withdrawal of a case pending before a Court of Criminal Appeals.

See R.C.M. 908 concerning procedures for interlocutory appeals by the Government.

In cases referred to it under R.C.M. 1201, a Court of Criminal Appeals may act only with respect to the findings and sentence as approved by proper authority. It may affirm only such findings of guilty or such part of a finding of guilty as includes an included offense, as it finds correct in law and fact and determines on the basis of the entire record should be approved. A Court of Criminal Appeals has generally the same powers as the convening authority to modify a sentence (*see* R.C.M. 1107), but it may not suspend all or part of a sentence. However, it may reduce the period of a suspension prescribed by a convening authority. It may not defer service of a sentence to confinement. (*see* R.C.M. 1101(c)). It may, however, review a decision by a convening authority concerning deferral, to determine whether that decision was an abuse of the convening authority's discretion.

In considering the record of a case referred to it under R.C.M. 1201, a Court of Criminal Appeals may weigh the evidence, judge the credibility of witnesses, and determine controverted questions of fact, recognizing that the court-martial saw and heard the evidence. A finding or sentence of a court-martial may not be held incorrect on the ground of an error of law unless the error materially prejudices the substantial rights of the accused. Article 59(a).

If a Court of Criminal Appeals sets aside any findings of guilty or the sentence, it may, except as to findings set aside for lack of sufficient evidence in the record to support the findings, order an appropriate type of rehearing or reassess the sentence as appropriate. *See* R.C.M. 810 concerning rehearings. If the Court of Criminal Appeals sets aside all the findings and the sentence and does not order a rehearing, it must order the charges dismissed. *See* Articles 59(a) and 66.

A Court of Criminal Appeals may on petition for extraordinary relief issue all writs necessary or appropriate in aid of its jurisdiction and agreeable to the usages and principles of law. Any party may petition a Court of Criminal Appeals for extraordinary relief.

(c) *Action on cases reviewed by a Court of Criminal Appeals.*

(1) *Forwarding by the Judge Advocate General to the Court of Appeals for the Armed Forces.* The Judge Advocate General may forward the decision of the Court of Criminal Appeals to the Court of Appeals for the Armed Forces for review with respect to any matter of law. In such a case, the Judge Advocate General shall cause a copy of the decision of the Court of Criminal Appeals and the order forwarding the case to be served on the accused and on appellate defense counsel. While a review of a forwarded case is pending, the Secretary concerned may defer further service of a sentence to confinement that has been ordered executed in such a case.

(2) *Action when sentence is set aside.* In a case reviewed by it under this rule in which the Court of Criminal Appeals has set aside the sentence and which is not forwarded to the Court of Appeals for the Armed Forces under subsection (c)(1) of this rule, the Judge Advocate General shall instruct an appropriate convening authority to take action in accordance with the decision of the Court of Criminal Appeals. If the Court of Criminal Appeals has ordered a rehearing, the record shall be sent to an appropriate convening authority. If that convening authority finds a rehearing impracticable that convening authority may dismiss the charges.

Discussion

If charges are dismissed, *see* R.C.M. 1208 concerning restoration of rights, privileges, and property. *See* R.C.M. 1114 concerning promulgating orders.

(3) *Action when sentence is affirmed in whole or part.*

(A) *Sentence requiring approval by the Presi-*

dent. If the Court of Criminal Appeals affirms any sentence which includes death, the Judge Advocate General shall transmit the record of trial and the decision of the Court of Criminal Appeals directly to the Court of Appeals for the Armed Forces when any period for reconsideration provided by the rules of the Courts of Criminal Appeals has expired.

(B) *Other cases.* If the Court of Criminal Appeals affirms any sentence other than one which includes death, the Judge Advocate General shall cause a copy of the decision of the Court of Criminal Appeals to be served on the accused in accordance with subsection (d) of this rule.

(4) *Remission or suspension.* If the Judge Advocate General believes that a sentence as affirmed by the Court of Criminal Appeals, other than one which includes death, should be remitted or suspended in whole or part, the Judge Advocate General may, before taking action under subsections (c)(1) or (3) of this rule, transmit the record of trial and the decision of the Court of Criminal Appeals to the secretary concerned with a recommendation for action under Article 74 or may take such action as may be authorized by the Secretary concerned under Article 74(a).

Discussion

See R.C.M. 1201(c); 1206.

---

(5) *Action when accused lacks mental capacity.* An appellate authority may not affirm the proceedings while the accused lacks mental capacity to understand and to conduct or cooperate intelligently in the appellate proceedings. In the absence of substantial evidence to the contrary, the accused is presumed to have the capacity to understand and to conduct or cooperate intelligently in the appellate proceedings. If a substantial question is raised as to the requisite mental capacity of the accused, the appellate authority may direct that the record be forwarded to an appropriate authority for an examination of the accused in accordance with R.C.M. 706, but the examination may be limited to determining the accused's present capacity to understand and cooperate in the appellate proceedings. The order of the appellate authority will instruct the appropriate authority as to permissible actions that may be taken to dispose of the matter. If the record is thereafter returned to the appellate authority, the appellate authority may affirm part or all of the findings or sentence unless it is established, by a preponderance of the evidence—including matters outside the record of trial—that the accused does not have the requisite mental capacity. If the accused does not have the requisite mental capacity, the appellate authority shall stay the proceedings until the accused regains appropriate capacity, or take other appropriate action. Nothing in this subsection shall prohibit the appellate authority from making a determination in favor of the accused which will result in the setting aside of a conviction.

(d) *Notification to accused.*

(1) *Notification of decision.* The accused shall be notified of the decision of the Court of Criminal Appeals in accordance with regulations of the Secretary concerned.

Discussion

The accused may be notified personally, or a copy of the decision may be sent, after service on appellate counsel of record, if any, by first class certified mail to the accused at an address provided by the accused or, if no such address has been provided by the accused, at the latest address listed for the accused in the accused's official service record.

If the Judge Advocate General has forwarded the case to the Court of Appeals for the Armed Forces, the accused should be so notified. *See* subsection (c)(1) of this rule.

---

(2) *Notification of right to petition the Court of Appeals for the Armed Forces for review.* If the accused has the right to petition the Court of Appeals for the Armed Forces for review, the accused shall be provided with a copy of the decision of the Court of Criminal Appeals bearing an endorsement notifying the accused of this right. The endorsement shall inform the accused that such a petition:

(A) May be filed only within 60 days from the time the accused was in fact notified of the decision of the Court of Criminal Appeals or the mailed copy of the decision was postmarked, whichever is earlier; and

(B) May be forwarded through the officer immediately exercising general court-martial jurisdiction over the accused and through the appropriate Judge Advocate General or filed directly with the Court of Appeals for the Armed Forces.

Discussion

See Article 67(c).

See also R.C.M. 1204(b).

The accused may petition the Court of Appeals for the Armed Forces for review, as to any matter of law, of any decision of the Court of Criminal Appeals except: (1) a case which was referred to the Court of Criminal Appeals by the Judge Advocate General under R.C.M. 1201(b)(1); (2) a case in which the Court of Criminal Appeals has set aside the sentence; and (3) a case in which the sentence includes death (because review by the Court of Appeals for the Armed Forces is mandatory).

The placing of a petition for review in proper military channels divests the Court of Criminal Appeals of jurisdiction over the case, and jurisdiction is thereby conferred on the Court of Appeals for the Armed Forces. *See* R.C.M. 1113 concerning action to be taken if the accused does not file or the Court of Appeals for the Armed Forces denies a petition for review.

---

(3) *Receipt by the accused—disposition.* When the accused has the right to petition the Court of Appeals for the Armed Forces for review, the receipt of the accused for the copy of the decision of the Court of Criminal Appeals, a certificate of service on the accused, or the postal receipt for delivery of certified mail shall be transmitted in duplicate by expeditious means to the appropriate Judge Advocate General. If the accused is personally served, the receipt or certificate of service shall show the date of service. The Judge Advocate General shall forward one copy of the receipt, certificate, or postal receipt to the clerk of the Court of Appeals for the Armed Forces when required by the court.

(e) *Cases not reviewed by the Court of Appeals for the Armed Forces.* If the decision of the Court of Criminal Appeals is not subject to review by the Court of Appeals for the Armed Forces, or if the Judge Advocate General has not forwarded the case to the Court of Appeals for the Armed Forces and the accused has not filed or the Court of Appeals for the Armed Forces has denied a petition for review, the Judge Advocate General shall—

(1) If the sentence affirmed by the Court of Criminal Appeals includes a dismissal, transmit the record, the decision of the Court of Criminal Appeals, and the Judge Advocate General's recommendation to the Secretary concerned for action under R.C.M. 1206; or

(2) If the sentence affirmed by the Court of Criminal Appeals does not include a dismissal, notify the convening authority, the officer exercising general court-martial jurisdiction over the accused, or the Secretary concerned, as appropriate, who, subject to R.C.M. 1113(c)(1), may order into execution any unexecuted sentence affirmed by the Court of Criminal Appeals or take other action, as authorized.

Discussion

See R.C.M. 1113, 1206, and Article 74(a) concerning the authority of the Secretary and others to take action.

(f) *Scope.* Except as otherwise expressly provided in this rule, this rule does not apply to appeals by the Government under R.C.M. 908.

Rule 1204. Review by the Court of Appeals for the Armed Forces

(a) *Cases reviewed by the Court of Appeals for the Armed Forces.* Under such rules as it may prescribe, the Court of Appeals for the Armed Forces shall review the record in all cases:

(1) In which the sentence, as affirmed by a Court of Criminal Appeals, extends to death;

(2) Reviewed by a Court of Criminal Appeals which the Judge Advocate General orders sent to the Court of Appeals for the Armed Forces for review; and

(3) Reviewed by a Court of Criminal Appeals, except those referred to it by the Judge Advocate General under R.C.M. 1201(b)(1), in which, upon petition by the accused and on good cause shown, the Court of Appeals for the Armed Forces has granted a review.

Discussion

See Article 67(a) concerning the composition of the Court of Appeals for the Armed Forces. In any case reviewed by it, the Court of Appeals for the Armed Forces may act only with respect to the findings and sentence as approved by the convening authority and as affirmed or set aside as incorrect in law by the Court of Criminal Appeals. *See* Article 67(d) and (e). The rules of practice and procedure before the Court of Appeals for the Armed Forces are published in the Military Justice Reporter.

The Court of Appeals for the Armed Forces may entertain petitions for extraordinary relief and may issue all writs necessary or appropriate in aid of its jurisdiction and agreeable to the usages and principles of law. Any party may petition the Court of Appeals for the Armed Forces for extraordinary relief. However, in the interest of judicial economy, such petitions usually should be filed with and adjudicated before the appropriate Court of Criminal Appeals prior to submission to the Court of Appeals for the Armed Forces.

(b) *Petition by the accused for review by the Court of Appeals for the Armed Forces.*

(1) *Counsel.* When the accused is notified of the right to forward a petition for review by the Court of Appeals for the Armed Forces, if requested by the accused, associate counsel qualified under R.C.M. 502(d)(1) shall be detailed to advise and assist the accused in connection with preparing a petition for further appellate review.

Discussion

If reasonably available, the counsel who conducted the defense at trial may perform these duties. The counsel detailed to represent the accused should communicate with the appellate defense counsel representing the accused. *See* R.C.M. 1202.

---

(2) *Forwarding petition.* The accused shall file any petition for review by the Court of Appeals for the Armed Forces under subsection (a)(3) of this rule directly with the Court of Appeals for the Armed Forces.

Discussion

See Article 67(c) and R.C.M. 1203(d)(2) concerning notifying the accused of the right to petition the Court of Appeals for the Armed Forces for review and the time limits for submitting a petition. *See also* the rules of the Court of Appeals for the Armed Forces concerning when the time for filing a petition begins to run and when a petition is now timely.

(c) *Action on decision by the Court of Appeals for the Armed Forces.*

(1) *In general.* After it has acted on a case, the Court of Appeals for the Armed Forces may direct the Judge Advocate General to return the record to the Court of Criminal Appeals for further proceedings in accordance with the decision of the court. Otherwise, unless the decision is subject to review by the Supreme Court, or there is to be further action by the President or the Secretary concerned, the Judge Advocate General shall instruct the convening authority to take action in accordance with that decision. If the Court has ordered a rehearing, but the convening authority to whom the record is transmitted finds a rehearing impracticable, the convening authority may dismiss the charges.

Discussion

See R.C.M. 1114 concerning final orders in the case. *See also* R.C.M. 1206 and Article 74(a).

---

(2) *Sentence requiring approval of the President.*

(A) If the Court of Appeals for the Armed Forces has affirmed a sentence that must be approved by the President before it may be executed, the Judge Advocate General shall transmit the record of trial, the decision of the Court of Criminal Appeals, the decision of the Court of Appeals for the Armed Forces, and the recommendation of the Judge Advocate General to the Secretary concerned.

(B) If the Secretary concerned is the Secretary of a military department, the Secretary concerned shall forward the material received under paragraph (A) to the Secretary of Defense, together with the recommendation of the Secretary concerned. The Secretary of Defense shall forward the material, with the recommendation of the Secretary concerned and the recommendation of the Secretary of Defense, to the President for the action of the President.

(C) If the Secretary concerned is the Secretary of Homeland Security, the Secretary concerned shall forward the material received under paragraph (A) to the President, together with the recommendation of the Secretary concerned, for the action of the President.

Discussion

See Article 71(a) and R.C.M. 1207.

---

(3) *Sentence requiring approval of the Secretary concerned.* If the Court of Appeals for the Armed Forces has affirmed a sentence which requires approval of the Secretary concerned before it may be executed, the Judge Advocate General shall follow the procedure in R.C.M. 1203(e)(1).

Discussion

See Article 71(b) and R.C.M. 1206.

---

(4) *Decision subject to review by the Supreme Court.* If the decision of the Court of Appeals for the Armed Forces is subject to review by the Supreme Court, the Judge Advocate General shall take no action under subsections (c)(1), (2), or (3) of this rule until: (A) the time for filing a petition for a writ of certiorari with the Supreme Court has expired; or (B) the Supreme Court has denied any petitions for writ of certiorari filed in the case. After (A) or (B) has occurred, the Judge Advocate General

shall take action under subsection (c)(1), (2), or (3). If the Supreme Court grants a writ of certiorari, the Judge Advocate General shall take action under R.C.M. 1205(b).

Rule 1205. Review by the Supreme Court

(a) *Cases subject to review by the Supreme Court.* Under 28 U.S.C. § 1259 and Article 67(h), decisions of the Court of Appeals for the Armed Forces may be reviewed by the Supreme Court by writ of certiorari in the following cases:

(1) Cases reviewed by the Court of Appeals for the Armed Forces under Article 67(b)(1);

(2) Cases certified to the Court of Appeals for the Armed Forces by the Judge Advocate General under Article 67(b)(2);

(3) Cases in which the Court of Appeals for the Armed Forces granted a petition for review under Article 67(b)(3); and

(4) Cases other than those described in subsections (a)(1), (2), and (3) of this rule in which the Court of Appeals for the Armed Forces granted relief.

The Supreme Court may not review by writ of certiorari any action of the Court of Appeals for the Armed Forces in refusing to grant a petition for review.

(b) *Action by the Supreme Court.* After the Supreme Court has taken action, other than denial of a petition for writ of certiorari, in any case, the Judge Advocate General shall, unless the case is returned to the Court of Appeals for the Armed Forces for further proceedings, forward the case to the President or the Secretary concerned in accordance with R.C.M. 1204(c)(2) or (3) when appropriate, or instruct the convening authority to take action in accordance with the decision.

Rule 1206. Powers and responsibilities of the Secretary

(a) *Sentences requiring approval by the Secretary.* No part of a sentence extending to dismissal of a commissioned officer, cadet, or midshipman may be executed until approved by the Secretary concerned or such Under Secretary or Assistant Secretary as may be designated by the Secretary.

Discussion

See Article 71(b).

(b) *Remission and suspension.*

(1) *In general.* The Secretary concerned and, when designated by the Secretary concerned, any Under Secretary, Assistant Secretary, Judge Advocate General, or commander may remit or suspend any part or amount of the unexecuted part of any sentence, including all uncollected forfeitures, other than a sentence approved by the President.

(2) *Substitution of discharge.* The Secretary concerned may, for good cause, substitute an administrative discharge for a discharge or dismissal executed in accordance with the sentence of a court-martial.

(3) *Sentence commuted by the President.* When the President has commuted a death sentence to a lesser punishment, the Secretary concerned may remit or suspend any remaining part or amount of the unexecuted portion of the sentence of a person convicted by a military tribunal under the Secretary's jurisdiction.

Rule 1207. Sentences requiring approval by the President

No part of a court-martial sentence extending to death may be executed until approved by the President.

Discussion

See Article 71(a). *See also* R.C.M. 1203 and 1204 concerning review by the Court of Criminal Appeals and Court of Appeals for the Armed Forces in capital cases.

Rule 1208. Restoration

(a) *New trial.* All rights, privileges, and property affected by an executed portion of a court-martial sentence—except an executed dismissal or discharge—which has not again been adjudged upon a new trial or which, after the new trial, has not been sustained upon the action of any reviewing authority, shall be restored. So much of the findings and so much of the sentence adjudged at the earlier trial shall be set aside as may be required by the findings and sentence at the new trial. Ordinarily, action taken under this subsection shall be announced in the court-martial order promulgating the final results of the proceedings.

Discussion

See Article 75(b) and (c) concerning the action to be taken on an executed dismissal or discharge which is not imposed at a new trial.

(b) *Other cases.* In cases other than those in subsection (a) of this rule, all rights, privileges, and property affected by an executed part of a court-martial sentence which has been set aside or disapproved by any competent authority shall be restored unless a new trial, other trial, or rehearing is ordered and such executed part is included in a sentence imposed at the new trial, other trial, or rehearing. Ordinarily, any restoration shall be announced in the court-martial order promulgating the final results of the proceedings.

Discussion

See R.C.M. 1114 concerning promulgating orders.

Rule 1209. Finality of courts-martial

(a) *When a conviction is final.* A court-martial conviction is final when:

(1) Review is completed by a Court of Criminal Appeals and—

(A) The accused does not file a timely petition for review by the Court of Appeals for the Armed Forces and the case is not otherwise under review by that court;

(B) A petition for review is denied or otherwise rejected by the Court of Appeals for the Armed Forces; or

(C) Review is completed in accordance with the judgment of the Court of Appeals for the Armed Forces and—

(i) A petition for a writ of certiorari is not filed within the time limits prescribed by the Supreme Court,

(ii) A petition for writ of certiorari is denied or otherwise rejected by the Supreme Court, or

(iii) Review is otherwise completed in accordance with the judgment of the Supreme Court; or

Discussion

See R.C.M. 1201, 1203, 1204, and 1205 concerning cases subject to review by a Court of Criminal Appeals, the Court of Appeals for the Armed Forces, and the Supreme Court. *See also* R.C.M. 1110.

---

(2) In cases not reviewed by a Court of Criminal Appeals—

(A) The findings and sentence have been found legally sufficient by a judge advocate and, when action by such officer is required, have been approved by the officer exercising general court-martial jurisdiction over the accused at the time the court-martial was convened (or that officer's successor); or

(B) The findings and sentence have been affirmed by the Judge Advocate General when review by the Judge Advocate General is required under R.C.M. 1112(g)(1) or 1201(b)(1).

(b) *Effect of finality.* The appellate review of records of trial provided by the code, the proceedings, findings, and sentences of courts-martial as approved, reviewed, or affirmed as required by the code, and all dismissals and discharges carried into execution under sentences by courts-martial following approval, review, or affirmation as required by the code, are final and conclusive. Orders publishing the proceedings of courts-martial and all action taken pursuant to those proceedings are binding upon all departments, courts, agencies, and officers of the United States, subject only to action upon a petition for a new trial under Article 73, to action by the Judge Advocate General under Article 69(b), to action by the Secretary concerned as provided in Article 74, and the authority of the President.

Rule 1210. New trial

(a) *In general.* At any time within 2 years after approval by the convening authority of a court-martial sentence, the accused may petition the Judge Advocate General for a new trial on the ground of newly discovered evidence or fraud on the court-martial. A petition may not be submitted after the death of the accused. A petition for a new trial of the facts may not be submitted on the basis of newly discovered evidence when the petitioner was found guilty of the relevant offense pursuant to a guilty plea.

(b) *Who may petition.* A petition for a new trial may

be submitted by the accused personally, or by accused's counsel, regardless whether the accused has been separated from the service.

(c) *Form of petition.* A petition for a new trial shall be written and shall be signed under oath or affirmation by the accused, by a person possessing the power of attorney of the accused for that purpose, or by a person with the authorization of an appropriate court to sign the petition as the representative of the accused. The petition shall contain the following information, or an explanation why such matters are not included:

(1) The name, service number, and current address of the accused;

(2) The date and location of the trial;

(3) The type of court-martial and the title or position of the convening authority;

(4) The request for the new trial;

(5) The sentence or a description thereof as approved or affirmed, with any later reduction thereof by clemency or otherwise;

(6) A brief description of any finding or sentence believed to be unjust;

(7) A full statement of the newly discovered evidence or fraud on the court-martial which is relied upon for the remedy sought;

(8) Affidavits pertinent to the matters in subsection (c)(6) of this rule; and

(9) The affidavit of each person whom the accused expects to present as a witness in the event of a new trial. Each such affidavit should set forth briefly the relevant facts within the personal knowledge of the witness.

(d) *Effect of petition.* The submission of a petition for a new trial does not stay the execution of a sentence.

(e) *Who may act on petition.* If the accused's case is pending before a Court of Criminal Appeals or the Court of Appeals for the Armed Forces, the Judge Advocate General shall refer the petition to the appropriate court for action. Otherwise, the Judge Advocate General of the armed force which reviewed the previous trial shall act on the petition, except that petitions submitted by persons who, at the time of trial and sentence from which the petitioner seeks relief, were members of the Coast Guard, and who, and who were members of the Coast Guard at the time the petition is submitted, shall be acted on in the Department in which the Coast Guard is serving at the time the petition is so submitted.

(f) *Grounds for new trial.*

(1) *In general.* A new trial may be granted only on grounds of newly discovered evidence or fraud on the court-martial.

(2) *Newly discovered evidence.* A new trial shall not be granted on the grounds of newly discovered evidence unless the petition shows that:

(A) The evidence was discovered after the trial;

(B) The evidence is not such that it would have been discovered by the petitioner at the time of trial in the exercise of due diligence; and

(C) The newly discovered evidence, if considered by a court-martial in the light of all other pertinent evidence, would probably produce a substantially more favorable result for the accused.

(3) *Fraud on court-martial.* No fraud on the court-martial warrants a new trial unless it had a substantial contributing effect on a finding of guilty or the sentence adjudged.

Discussion

Examples of fraud on a court-martial which may warrant granting a new trial are: confessed or proved perjury in testimony or forgery of documentary evidence which clearly had a substantial contributing effect on a finding of guilty and without which there probably would not have been a finding of guilty of the offense; willful concealment by the prosecution from the defense of evidence favorable to the defense which, if presented to the court-martial, would probably have resulted in a finding of not guilty; and willful concealment of a material ground for challenge of the military judge or any member or of the disqualification of counsel or the convening authority, when the basis for challenge or disqualification was not known to the defense at the time of trial (*see* R.C.M. 912).

(g) *Action on the petition.*

(1) *In general.* The authority considering the petition may cause such additional investigation to be made and such additional information to be secured as that authority believes appropriate. Upon written request, and in its discretion, the authority considering the petition may permit oral argument on the matter.

(2) *Courts of Criminal Appeals; Court of Appeals for the Armed Forces.* The Courts of Criminal Appeals and the Court of Appeals for the Armed

Forces shall act on a petition for a new trial in accordance with their respective rules.

(3) *The Judge Advocates General.* When a petition is considered by the Judge Advocate General, any hearing may be before the Judge Advocate General or before an officer or officers designated by the Judge Advocate General. If the Judge Advocate General believes meritorious grounds for relief under Article 74 have been established but that a new trial is not appropriate, the Judge Advocate General may act under Article 74 if authorized to do so, or transmit the petition and related papers to the Secretary concerned with a recommendation. The Judge Advocate General may also, in cases which have been finally reviewed but have not been reviewed by a Court of Criminal Appeals, act under Article 69.

Discussion

See also R.C.M. 1201(b)(3).

(h) *Action when new trial is granted.*

(1) *Forwarding to convening authority.* When a petition for a new trial is granted, the Judge Advocate General shall select and forward the case to a convening authority for disposition.

(2) *Charges at new trial.* At a new trial, the accused may not be tried for any offense of which the accused was found not guilty or upon which the accused was not tried at the earlier court-martial.

Discussion

See also R.C.M. 810 concerning additional special rules which apply at a new trial. In other respects a new trial is conducted like any other court-martial.

(3) *Action by convening authority.* The convening authority's action on the record of a new trial is the same as in other courts-martial.

(4) *Disposition of record.* The disposition of the record of a new trial is the same as for other courts-martial.

(5) *Court-martial orders.* Court-martial orders promulgating the final action taken as a result of a new trial, including any restoration of rights, privileges, and property, shall be promulgated in accordance with R.C.M. 1114.

Discussion

See Article 75 and R.C.M. 1208 concerning restoration of rights when the executed portion of a sentence is not sustained in a new trial or action following it.

(6) *Action by persons charged with execution of the sentence.* Persons charged with the administrative duty of executing a sentence adjudged upon a new trial after it has been ordered executed shall credit the accused with any executed portion or amount of the original sentence included in the new sentence in computing the term or amount of punishment actually to be executed pursuant to the sentence.

CHAPTER XIII. SUMMARY COURTS-MARTIAL

Rule 1301. Summary courts-martial generally

(a) *Composition.* A summary court-martial is composed of one commissioned officer on active duty. Unless otherwise prescribed by the Secretary concerned a summary court-martial shall be of the same armed force as the accused. Summary courts-martial shall be conducted in accordance with the regulations of the military service to which the accused belongs. Whenever practicable, a summary court-martial should be an officer whose grade is not below lieutenant of the Navy or Coast Guard or captain of the Army, Air Force, or Marine Corps. When only one commissioned officer is present with a command or detachment, that officer shall be the summary court-martial of that command or detachment. When more than one commissioned officer is present with a command or detachment, the convening authority may not be the summary court-martial of that command or detachment.

(b) *Function.* The function of the summary court-martial is to promptly adjudicate minor offenses under a simple procedure. The summary court-martial shall thoroughly and impartially inquire into both sides of the matter and shall ensure that the interests of both the Government and the accused are safeguarded and that justice is done. A summary court-martial may seek advice from a judge advocate or legal officer on questions of law, but the summary court-martial may not seek advice from any person on factual conclusions which should be drawn from evidence or the sentence which should be imposed, as the summary court-martial has the independent duty to make these determinations.

Discussion

For a definition of "minor offenses," *see* paragraph 1e, Part V.

(c) *Jurisdiction.* Subject to Chapter II, summary courts-martial have the power to try persons subject to the code, except commissioned officers, warrant officers, cadets, aviation cadets, and midshipmen, for any noncapital offense made punishable by the code.

Discussion

See R.C.M. 103(3) for a definition of capital offenses.

(d) *Punishments.*

(1) *Limitations—amount.* Subject to R.C.M. 1003, summary courts-martial may adjudge any punishment not forbidden by the code except death, dismissal, dishonorable or bad-conduct discharge, confinement for more than 1 month, hard labor without confinement for more than 45 days, restriction to specified limits for more than 2 months, or forfeiture of more than two-thirds of 1 month's pay.

Discussion

The maximum penalty which can be adjudged in a summary court-martial is confinement for 30 days, forfeiture of two-thirds pay per month for one month, and reduction to the lowest pay grade. *See* subsection (2) below for additional limits on enlisted persons serving in pay grades above the fourth enlisted pay grade.

A summary court-martial may not suspend all or part of a sentence, although the summary court-martial may recommend to the convening authority that all or part of a sentence be suspended. If a sentence includes both reduction in grade and forfeitures, the maximum forfeiture is calculated at the reduced pay grade. *See also* R.C.M. 1003 concerning other punishments which may be adjudged, the effects of certain types of punishment, and combination of certain types of punishment. The summary court-martial should ascertain the effect of Article 58a in that armed force.

---

(2) *Limitations—pay grade.* In the case of enlisted members above the fourth enlisted pay grade, summary courts-martial may not adjudge confinement, hard labor without confinement, or reduction except to the next pay grade.

Discussion

The provisions of this subsection apply to an accused in the fifth enlisted pay grade who is reduced to the fourth enlisted pay grade by the summary court-martial.

(e) *Counsel.* The accused at a summary court-martial does not have the right to counsel. If the accused has civilian counsel provided by the accused and qualified under R.C.M. 502(d)(3), that counsel shall be permitted to represent the accused at the summary court-martial if such appearance will not unreasonably delay the proceedings and if military exigencies do not preclude it.

Discussion

Neither the Constitution nor any statute establishes any right to counsel at summary courts-martial. Therefore, it is not error to deny an accused the opportunity to be represented by counsel at a summary court-martial. However, appearance of counsel is not prohibited. The detailing authority may, as a matter of discretion, detail, or otherwise make available, a military attorney to represent the accused at a summary court-martial.

(f) *Power to obtain witnesses and evidence.* A summary court-martial may obtain evidence pursuant to R.C.M. 703.

Discussion

The summary court-martial must obtain witnesses for the prosecution and the defense pursuant to the standards in R.C.M. 703. The summary court-martial rules on any request by the accused for witnesses or evidence in accordance with the procedure in R.C.M. 703(c) and (f).

(g) *Secretarial limitations.* The Secretary concerned may prescribe procedural or other rules for summary courts-martial not inconsistent with this Manual or the code.

Rule 1302. Convening a summary court-martial

(a) *Who may convene summary courts-martial.* Unless limited by competent authority summary courts-martial may be convened by:

(1) Any person who may convene a general or special court-martial;

(2) The commander of a detached company or other detachment of the Army;

(3) The commander of a detached squadron or other detachment of the Air Force;

(4) The commander or officer in charge of any other command when empowered by the Secretary concerned; or

(5) A superior competent authority to any of the above.

(b) *When convening authority is accuser.* If the convening authority or the summary court-martial is the accuser, it is discretionary with the convening authority whether to forward the charges to a superior authority with a recommendation to convene the summary court-martial. If the convening authority or the summary court-martial is the accuser, the jurisdiction of the summary court-martial is not affected.

(c) *Procedure.* After the requirements of Chapters III and IV of this Part have been satisfied, summary courts-martial shall be convened in accordance with R.C.M. 504(d)(2). The convening order may be by notation signed by the convening authority on the charge sheet. Charges shall be referred to summary courts-martial in accordance with R.C.M. 601.

Discussion

When the convening authority is the summary court-martial because the convening authority is the only commissioned officer present with the command or detachment, *see* R.C.M. 1301(a), that fact should be noted on the charge sheet.

Rule 1303. Right to object to trial by summary court-martial

No person who objects thereto before arraignment may be tried by summary court-martial even if that person also refused punishment under Article 15 and demanded trial by court-martial for the same offenses.

Discussion

If the accused objects to trial by summary court-martial, the convening authority may dispose of the case in accordance with R.C.M. 401.

Rule 1304. Trial procedure

(a) *Pretrial duties.*

(1) *Examination of file.* The summary court-martial shall carefully examine the charge sheet, allied papers, and immediately available personnel records of the accused before trial.

Discussion

"Personnel records" are those personnel records of the accused which are maintained locally and are immediately available. "Allied papers" in a summary court-martial include convening orders, investigative reports, correspondence relating to the case, and witness statements.

---

(2) *Report of irregularity.* The summary court-martial shall report to the convening authority any

substantial irregularity in the charge sheet, allied papers, or personnel records.

Discussion

The summary court-martial should examine the charge sheet, allied papers, and personnel records to ensure that they are complete and free from errors or omissions which might affect admissibility. The summary court-martial should check the charges and specifications to ensure that each alleges personal jurisdiction over the accused (*see* R.C.M. 202) and an offense under the code (*see* R.C.M. 203 and Part IV). Substantial defects or errors in the charges and specifications must be reported to the convening authority, since such defects cannot be corrected except by preferring and referring the affected charge and specification anew in proper form. A defect or error is substantial if correcting it would state an offense not otherwise stated, or include an offense, person, or matter not fairly included in the specification as preferred. *See* subsection (3) below concerning minor errors.

---

(3) *Correction and amendment.* The summary court-martial may, subject to R.C.M. 603, correct errors on the charge sheet and amend charges and specifications. Any such corrections or amendments shall be initialed.

(b) *Summary court-martial procedure.*

Discussion

A sample guide is at Appendix 9. The summary court-martial should review and become familiar with the guide used before proceeding.

---

(1) *Preliminary proceeding.* After complying with R.C.M. 1304(a), the summary court-martial shall hold a preliminary proceeding during which the accused shall be given a copy of the charge sheet and informed of the following:

(A) The general nature of the charges;

(B) The fact that the charges have been referred to a summary court-martial for trial and the date of referral;

(C) The identity of the convening authority;

(D) The name(s) of the accuser(s);

(E) The names of the witnesses who could be called to testify and any documents or physical evidence which the summary court-martial expects to introduce into evidence;

(F) The accused's right to inspect the allied papers and immediately available personnel records;

(G) That during the trial the summary court-martial will not consider any matters, including statements previously made by the accused to the officer detailed as summary court-martial unless admitted in accordance with the Military Rules of Evidence;

(H) The accused's right to plead not guilty or guilty;

(I) The accused's right to cross-examine witnesses and have the summary court-martial cross-examine witnesses on behalf of the accused;

(J) The accused's right to call witnesses and produce evidence with the assistance of the summary court-martial as necessary;

(K) The accused's right to testify on the merits, or to remain silent with the assurance that no adverse inference will be drawn by the summary court-martial from such silence;

(L) If any findings of guilty are announced, the accused's rights to remain silent, to make an unsworn statement, oral or written or both, and to testify, and to introduce evidence in extenuation or mitigation;

(M) The maximum sentence which the summary court-martial may adjudge if the accused is found guilty of the offense or offenses alleged; and

(N) The accused's right to object to trial by summary court-martial.

(2) *Trial proceeding.*

(A) *Objection to trial.* The summary court-martial shall give the accused a reasonable period of time to decide whether to object to trial by summary court-martial. The summary court-martial shall thereafter record the response. If the accused objects to trial by summary court-martial, the summary court-martial shall return the charge sheet, allied papers, and personnel records to the convening authority. If the accused fails to object to trial by summary court-martial, trial shall proceed.

(B) *Arraignment.* After complying with R.C.M. 1304(b)(1) and (2)(A), the summary court-martial shall read and show the charges and specifications to the accused and, if necessary, explain them. The accused may waive the reading of the charges. The summary court-martial shall then ask the accused to plead to each specification and charge.

(C) *Motions.* Before receiving pleas the summary court-martial shall allow the accused to make motions to dismiss or for other relief. The summary court-martial shall take action on behalf of the accused, if requested by the accused, or if it appears necessary in the interests of justice.

(D) *Pleas.*

(i) *Not guilty pleas.* When a not guilty plea is entered, the summary court-martial shall proceed to trial.

(ii) *Guilty pleas.* If the accused pleads guilty to any offense, the summary court-martial shall comply with R.C.M. 910.

(iii) *Rejected guilty pleas.* If the summary court-martial is in doubt that the accused's pleas of guilty are voluntarily and understandingly made, or if at any time during the trial any matter inconsistent with pleas of guilty arises, which inconsistency cannot be resolved, the summary court-martial shall enter not guilty pleas as to the affected charges and specifications.

(iv) *No plea.* If the accused refuses to plead, the summary court-martial shall enter not guilty pleas.

(v) *Changed pleas.* The accused may change any plea at any time before findings are announced. The accused may change pleas from guilty to not guilty after findings are announced only for good cause.

(E) *Presentation of evidence.*

(i) The Military Rules of Evidence (Part III) apply to summary courts-martial.

(ii) The summary court-martial shall arrange for the attendance of necessary witnesses for the prosecution and defense, including those requested by the accused.

Discussion

See R.C.M. 703. Ordinarily witnesses should be excluded from the courtroom until called to testify. *See* Mil. R. Evid. 615.

(iii) Witnesses for the prosecution shall be called first and examined under oath. The accused shall be permitted to cross-examine these witnesses. The summary court-martial shall aid the accused in cross-examination if such assistance is requested or appears necessary in the interests of justice. The witnesses for the accused shall then be called and similarly examined under oath.

(iv) The summary court-martial shall obtain evidence which tends to disprove the accused's guilt or establishes extenuating circumstances.

Discussion

See R.C.M. 703 and 1001.

(F) *Findings and sentence.*

(i) The summary court-martial shall apply the principles in R.C.M. 918 in determining the findings. The summary court-martial shall announce the findings to the accused in open session.

(ii) The summary court-martial shall follow the procedures in R.C.M. 1001 and apply the principles in the remainder of Chapter X in determining a sentence. The summary court-martial shall announce the sentence to the accused in open session.

(iii) If the sentence includes confinement, the summary court-martial shall advise the accused of the right to apply to the convening authority for deferment of the service of the confinement.

(iv) If the accused is found guilty, the summary court-martial shall advise the accused of the rights under R.C.M. 1306(a) and (d) after the sentence is announced.

(v) The summary court-martial shall, as soon as practicable, inform the convening authority of the findings, sentence, recommendations, if any, for suspension of the sentence, and any deferment request.

(vi) If the sentence includes confinement, the summary court-martial shall cause the delivery of the accused to the accused's commanding officer or the commanding officer's designee.

Discussion

If the accused's immediate commanding officer is not the convening authority, the summary court-martial should ensure that the immediate commanding officer is informed of the findings, sentence, and any recommendations pertaining thereto. *See* R.C.M. 1101 concerning post-trial confinement.

Rule 1305. Record of trial

(a) *In general.* The record of trial of a summary court-martial shall be prepared as prescribed in subsection (b) of this rule. The convening or higher authority may prescribe additional requirements for the record of trial.

Discussion

See Appendix 15 for a sample of a Record of Trial by Summary Court-Martial (DD Form 2329).

Any petition submitted under R.C.M. 1306(a) should be appended to the record of trial.

(b) *Contents.* The summary court-martial shall prepare an original and at least two copies of the record of trial, which shall include:

(1) The pleas, findings, and sentence, and if the accused was represented by counsel at the summary court-martial, a notation to that effect;

(2) The fact that the accused was advised of the matters set forth in R.C.M. 1304(b)(1);

(3) If the summary court-martial is the convening authority, a notation to that effect.

(c) *Authentication.* The summary court-martial shall authenticate the record by signing the original record of trial.

Discussion

"Authentication" means attesting that the record accurately reports the proceedings. *See* R.C.M. 1104(a).

(d) *Forwarding copies of the record.*

(1) *Accused's copy.*

(A) *Service.* The summary court-martial shall cause a copy of the record of trial to be served on the accused as soon as it is authenticated.

(B) *Receipt.* The summary court-martial shall cause the accused's receipt for the copy of the record of trial to be obtained and attached to the original record of trial or shall attach to the original record of trial a certificate that the accused was served a copy of the record. If the record of trial was not served on the accused personally, the summary court-martial shall attach a statement explaining how and when such service was accomplished. If the accused was represented by counsel, such counsel may be served with the record of trial.

(C) *Classified information.* If classified information is included in the record of trial of a summary court-martial, R.C.M. 1104(b)(1)(D) shall apply.

(2) *Forwarding to the convening authority.* The original and one copy of the record of trial shall be forwarded to the convening authority after compliance with subsection (d)(1) of this rule.

(3) *Further disposition.* After compliance with R.C.M. 1306(b) and (c), the record of trial shall be disposed of under regulations prescribed by the Secretary concerned.

Rule 1306. Post-trial procedure

(a) *Matters submitted by the accused.* After a sentence is adjudged, the accused may submit written matters to the convening authority in accordance with R.C.M. 1105.

(b) *Convening authority's action.*

(1) *Who shall act.* Except as provided herein, the convening authority shall take action in accordance with R.C.M. 1107. The convening authority shall not take action before the period prescribed in R.C.M. 1105(c)(2) has expired, unless the right to submit matters has been waived under R.C.M. 1105(d).

(2) *Action.* The action of the convening authority shall be shown on all copies of the record of trial except that provided the accused if the accused has retained that copy. An order promulgating the result of a trial by summary court-martial need not be issued. A copy of the action shall be forwarded to the accused.

(3) *Signature.* The action on the original record of trial shall be signed by the convening authority. The convening authority's action on other copies of the record of trial shall either be signed by the convening authority or be prepared and certified as true copies of the original.

(4) *Subsequent action.* Any action taken on a summary court-martial after the initial action by the convening authority shall be in writing, signed by the authority taking the action, and promulgated in appropriate orders.

Discussion

See R.C.M. 1114 concerning promulgating orders.

(c) *Review by a judge advocate.* Unless otherwise prescribed by regulations of the Secretary concerned, the original record of the summary court-martial shall be reviewed by a judge advocate in accordance with R.C.M. 1112.

(d) *Review by the Judge Advocate General.* The accused may request review of a final conviction by summary court-martial by the Judge Advocate General in accordance with R.C.M. 1201(b)(3).

Part III - M.R.E.

Part III - M.R.E.

PART III
MILITARY RULES OF EVIDENCE

SECTION I
GENERAL PROVISIONS

Rule 101. Scope

(a) *Applicability.* These rules are applicable in courts-martial, including summary courts-martial, to the extent and with the exceptions stated in Mil. R. Evid. 1101.

(b) *Secondary Sources.* If not otherwise prescribed in this Manual or these rules, and insofar as practicable and not inconsistent with or contrary to the code or this Manual, courts-martial shall apply:

(1) First, the rules of evidence generally recognized in the trial of criminal cases in the United States district courts; and

(2) Second, when not inconsistent with subdivision(b)(1), the rules of evidence at common law.

(c) *Rule of construction.* Except as otherwise provided in these rules, the term "military judge" includes the president of a special court-martial without a military judge and a summary court-martial officer.

Rule 102. Purpose and construction

These rules shall be construed to secure fairness in administration, elimination of unjustifiable expense and delay, and promotion of growth and development of the law of evidence to the end that the truth may be ascertained and proceedings justly determined.

Rule 103. Ruling on evidence

(a) *Effect of erroneous ruling.* Error may not be predicated upon a ruling which admits or excludes evidence unless the ruling materially prejudices a substantial right of a party, and

(1) *Objection.* In case the ruling is one admitting evidence, a timely objection or motion to strike appears of record, stating the specific ground of objection, if the specific ground was not apparent from the context; or

(2) *Offer of proof.* In case the ruling is one excluding evidence, the substance of the evidence was made known to the military judge by offer or was apparent from the context within which questions were asked. Once the military judge makes a definitive ruling on the record admitting or excluding evidence, either at or before trial, a party need not renew an objection or offer of proof to preserve a claim of error for appeal. The standard provided in this subdivision does not apply to errors involving requirements imposed by the Constitution of the United States as applied to members of the armed forces except insofar as the error arises under these rules and this subdivision provides a standard that is more advantageous to the accused than the constitutional standard.

(b) *Record of offer and ruling.* The military judge may add any other or further statement which shows the character of the evidence, the form in which it was offered, the objection made, and the ruling thereon. The military judge may direct the making of an offer in question and answer form.

(c) *Hearing of members.* In a court-martial composed of a military judge and members, proceedings shall be conducted, to the extent practicable, so as to prevent inadmissible evidence from being suggested to the members by any means, such as making statements or offers of proof or asking questions in the hearing of the members.

(d) *Plain error.* Nothing in this rule precludes taking notice of plain errors that materially prejudice substantial rights although they were not brought to the attention of the military judge.

Rule 104. Preliminary questions

(a) *Questions of admissibility generally.* Preliminary questions concerning the qualification of a person to be a witness, the existence of a privilege, the admissibility of evidence, an application for a continuance, or the availability of a witness shall be determined by the military judge. In making these determinations the military judge is not bound by the rules of evidence except those with respect to privileges.

(b) *Relevancy conditioned on fact.* When the relevancy of evidence depends upon the fulfillment of a condition of fact, the military judge shall admit it upon, or subject to, the introduction of evidence sufficient to support a finding of the fulfillment of the condition. A ruling on the sufficiency of evidence to support a finding of fulfillment of a condition of fact is the sole responsibility of the military judge, except where these rules or this Manual provide expressly to the contrary.

(c) *Hearing of members.* Except in cases tried before a special court-martial without a military judge, hearings on the admissibility of statements of an accused under Mil. R. Evid. 301–306 shall in all cases be conducted out of the hearing of the members. Hearings on other preliminary matters shall be so conducted when the interests of justice require or, when an accused is a witness, if the accused so requests.

(d) *Testimony by accused.* The accused does not, by testifying upon a preliminary matter, become subject to cross-examination as to other issues in the case.

(e) *Weight and credibility.* This rule does not limit the right of a party to introduce before the members evidence relevant to weight or credibility.

Rule 105. Limited admissibility

When evidence which is admissible as to one party or for one purpose but not admissible as to another party or for another purpose is admitted, the military judge, upon request, shall restrict the evidence to its proper scope and instruct the members accordingly.

Rule 106. Remainder of or related writings or recorded statements

When a writing or recorded statement or part thereof is introduced by a party, an adverse party may require that party at that time to introduce any other part or any other writing or recorded statement which ought in fairness to be considered contemporaneously with it.

SECTION II

JUDICIAL NOTICE

Rule 201. Judicial notice of adjudicative facts

(a) *Scope of rule.* This rule governs only judicial notice of adjudicative facts.

(b) *Kinds of facts.* A judicially noticed fact must be one not subject to reasonable dispute in that it is either (1) generally known universally, locally, or in the area pertinent to the event or (2) capable of accurate and ready determination by resort to sources whose accuracy cannot reasonably be questioned.

(c) *When discretionary.* The military judge may take judicial notice, whether requested or not. The parties shall be informed in open court when, without being requested, the military judge takes judicial notice of an adjudicative fact essential to establishing an element of the case.

(d) *When mandatory.* The military judge shall take judicial notice if requested by a party and supplied with the necessary information.

(e) *Opportunity to be heard.* A party is entitled upon timely request to an opportunity to be heard as to the propriety of taking judicial notice and the tenor of the matter noticed. In the absence of prior notification, the request may be made after judicial notice has been taken.

(f) *Time of taking notice.* Judicial notice may be taken at any stage of the proceeding.

(g) *Instructing members.* The military judge shall instruct the members that they may, but are not required to, accept as conclusive any matter judicially noticed.

Rule 201A. Judicial notice of law

(a) *Domestic law.* The military judge may take judicial notice of domestic law. Insofar as a domestic law is a fact that is of consequence to the determination of the action, the procedural requirements of Mil. R. Evid. 201—except Mil. R. Evid. 201(g)—apply.

(b) *Foreign law.* A party who intends to raise an issue concerning the law of a foreign country shall give reasonable written notice. The military judge, in determining foreign law, may consider any relevant material or source including testimony whether or not submitted by a party or admissible under these rules. Such a determination shall be treated as a ruling on a question of law.

SECTION III

EXCLUSIONARY RULES AND RELATED MATTERS CONCERNING SELF-INCRIMINATION, SEARCH AND SEIZURE, AND EYEWITNESS IDENTIFICATION

Rule 301. Privilege concerning compulsory self-incrimination

(a) *General rule.* The privileges against self-incrimination provided by the Fifth Amendment to the Constitution of the United States and Article 31 are applicable only to evidence of a testimonial or communicative nature. The privilege most beneficial to the individual asserting the privilege shall be applied.

(b) *Standing.*

(1) *In general.* The privilege of a witness to refuse to respond to a question the answer to which may tend to incriminate the witness is a personal one that the witness may exercise or waive at the discretion of the witness.

(2) *Judicial advice.* If a witness who is apparently uninformed of the privileges under this rule appears likely to incriminate himself or herself, the military judge should advise the witness of the right to decline to make any answer that might tend to incriminate the witness and that any self-incriminating answer the witness might make can later be used as evidence against the witness. Counsel for any party or for the witness may request the military judge to so advise a witness provided that such a request is made out of the hearing of the witness and, except in a special court-martial without a military judge, the members. Failure to so advise a witness does not make the testimony of the witness inadmissible.

(c) *Exercise of the privilege.* If a witness states that the answer to a question may tend to incriminate him or her, the witness may not be required to answer unless facts and circumstances are such that no answer the witness might make to the question could have the effect of tending to incriminate the witness or that the witness has, with respect to the question, waived the privilege against self-incrimination. A witness may not assert the privilege if the witness is not subject to criminal penalty as a result of an answer by reason of immunity, running of the statute of limitations, or similar reason.

(1) *Immunity generally.* The minimum grant of immunity adequate to overcome the privilege is that which under either R.C.M. 704 or other proper authority provides that neither the testimony of the witness nor any evidence obtained from that testimony may be used against the witness at any subsequent trial other than in a prosecution for perjury, false swearing, the making of a false official statement, or failure to comply with an order to testify after the military judge has ruled that the privilege may not be asserted by reason of immunity.

(2) *Notification of immunity or leniency.* When a prosecution witness before a court-martial has been granted immunity or leniency in exchange for testimony, the grant shall be reduced to writing and shall be served on the accused prior to arraignment or within a reasonable time before the witness testifies. If notification is not made as required by this rule, the military judge may grant a continuance until notification is made, prohibit or strike the testimony of the witness, or enter such other order as may be required.

(d) *Waiver by a witness.* A witness who answers a question without having asserted the privilege against self-incrimination and thereby admits a self-incriminating fact may be required to disclose all information relevant to that fact except when there is a real danger of further self-incrimination. This limited waiver of the privilege applies only at the trial in which the answer is given, does not extend to a rehearing or new or other trial, and is subject to Mil. R. Evid. 608(b).

(e) *Waiver by the accused.* When an accused testifies voluntarily as a witness, the accused thereby waives the privilege against self-incrimination with respect to the matters concerning which he or she so testifies. If the accused is on trial for two or more offenses and on direct examination testifies concerning the issue of guilt or innocence as to only one or some of the offenses, the accused may not be cross-examined as to guilt or innocence with respect to the other offenses unless the cross-examination is relevant to an offense concerning which the accused has testified. This waiver is subject to Mil. R. Evid. 608(b).

(f) *Effect of claiming the privilege.*

(1) *Generally.* The fact that a witness has asserted the privilege against self-incrimination in refusing to answer a question cannot be considered as raising any inference unfavorable to either the accused or the government.

(2) *On cross-examination.* If a witness asserts the privilege against self-incrimination on cross-examination, the military judge, upon motion, may strike the direct testimony of the witness in whole or in part, unless the matters to which the witness refuses to testify are purely collateral.

(3) *Pretrial.* The fact that the accused during official questioning and in exercise of rights under the Fifth Amendment to the Constitution of the United States or Article 31, remained silent, refused to answer a certain question, requested counsel, or requested that the questioning be terminated is inadmissible against the accused.

(g) *Instructions.* When the accused does not testify at trial, defense counsel may request that the members of the court be instructed to disregard that fact and not to draw any adverse inference from it. Defense counsel may request that the members not be so instructed. Defense counsel's election shall be binding upon the military judge except that the military judge may give the instruction when the instruction is necessary in the interests of justice.

Rule 302. Privilege concerning mental examination of an accused

(a) *General rule.* The accused has a privilege to prevent any statement made by the accused at a mental examination ordered under R.C.M. 706 and any derivative evidence obtained through use of such a statement from being received into evidence against the accused on the issue of guilt or innocence or during sentencing proceedings. This privilege may be claimed by the accused notwithstanding the fact that the accused may have been warned of the rights provided by Mil. R. Evid. 305 at the examination.

(b) *Exceptions.*

(1) There is no privilege under this rule when the accused first introduces into evidence such statements or derivative evidence.

(2) An expert witness for the prosecution may testify as to the reasons for the expert's conclusions and the reasons therefor as to the mental state of the accused if expert testimony offered by the defense as to the mental condition of the accused has been received in evidence, but such testimony may not extend to statements of the accused except as provided in (1).

(c) *Release of evidence.* If the defense offers expert testimony concerning the mental condition of the accused, the military judge, upon motion, shall order the release to the prosecution of the full contents, other than any statements made by the accused, of any report prepared pursuant to R.C.M. 706. If the defense offers statements made by the accused at such examination, the military judge may upon motion order the disclosure of such statements made by the accused and contained in the report as may be necessary in the interests of justice.

(d) *Noncompliance by the accused.* The military judge may prohibit an accused who refuses to cooperate in a mental examination authorized under R.C.M. 706 from presenting any expert medical testimony as to any issue that would have been the subject of the mental examination.

(e) *Procedure.* The privilege in this rule may be claimed by the accused only under the procedure set forth in Mil. R. Evid. 304 for an objection or a motion to suppress.

Rule 303. Degrading questions

No person may be compelled to make a statement or produce evidence before any military tribunal if the statement or evidence is not material to the issue and may tend to degrade that person.

Rule 304. Confessions and admissions

(a) *General rule.* Except as provided in subsection (b), an involuntary statement or any derivative evidence therefrom may not be received in evidence against an accused who made the statement if the accused makes a timely motion to suppress or an objection to the evidence under this rule.

(b) *Exceptions.*

(1) Where the statement is involuntary only in terms of noncompliance with the requirements of Mil. R. Evid. 305(c) or 305(f), or the requirements concerning counsel under Mil. R. Evid. 305(d), 305(e), and 305(g), this rule does not prohibit use of the statement to impeach by contradiction the in-court testimony of the accused or the use of such statement in a later prosecution against the accused for perjury, false swearing, or the making of a false official statement.

(2) Evidence that was obtained as a result of an involuntary statement may be used when the evidence would have been obtained even if the involuntary statement had not been made.

(3) *Derivative evidence.* Evidence that is challenged under this rule as derivative evidence may be admitted against the accused if the military judge finds by a preponderance of the evidence that the statement was made voluntarily, that the evidence was not obtained by use of the statement, or that the

evidence would have been obtained even if the statement had not been made.

(c) *Definitions.* As used in these rules:

(1) *Confession.* A "confession" is an acknowledgment of guilt.

(2) *Admission.* An "admission" is a self-incriminating statement fallingshort of an acknowledgment of guilt, even if it was intended by its maker to be exculpatory.

(3) *Involuntary.* A statement is "involuntary" if it is obtained in violation of the self-incrimination privilege or due process clause of the Fifth Amendment to the Constitution of the United States, Article 31, or through the use of coercion, unlawful influence, or unlawful inducement.

(d) *Procedure.*

(1) *Disclosure.* Prior to arraignment, the prosecution shall disclose to the defense the contents of all statements, oral or written, made by the accused that are relevant to the case, known to the trial counsel, and within the control of the armed forces.

(2) *Motions and objections.*

(A) Motions to suppress or objections under this rule or Mil. R. Evid. 302 or 305 to statements that have been disclosed shall be made by the defense prior to submission of a plea. In the absence of such motion or objection, the defense may not raise the issue at a later time except as permitted by the military judge for good cause shown. Failure to so move or object constitutes a waiver of the objection.

(B) If the prosecution intends to offer against the accused a statement made by the accused that was not disclosed prior to arraignment, the prosecution shall provide timely notice to the military judge and to counsel for the accused. The defense may enter an objection at that time and the military judge may make such orders as are required in the interests of justice.

(C) If evidence is disclosed as derivative evidence under this subdivision prior to arraignment, any motion to suppress or objection under this rule or Mil. R. Evid. 302 or 305 shall be made in accordance with the procedure for challenging a statement under (A). If such evidence has not been so disclosed prior to arraignment, the requirements of (B) apply.

(3) *Specificity.* The military judge may require the defense to specify the grounds upon which the defense moves to suppress or object to evidence. If defense counsel, despite the exercise of due diligence, has been unable to interview adequately those persons involved in the taking of a statement, the military judge may make any order required in the interests of justice, including authorization for the defense to make a general motion to suppress or general objection.

(4) *Rulings.* A motion to suppress or an objection to evidence made prior to plea shall be ruled upon prior to plea unless the military judge, for good cause, orders that it be deferred for determination at trial, but no such determination shall be deferred if a party's right to appeal the ruling is affected adversely. Where factual issues are involved in ruling upon such motion or objection, the military judge shall state essential findings of fact on the record.

(5) *Effect of guilty plea.* Except as otherwise expressly provided in R.C.M. 910(a)(2), a plea of guilty to an offense that results in a finding of guilty waives all privileges against self-incrimination and all motions and objections under this rule with respect to that offense regardless of whether raised prior to plea.

(e) *Burden of proof.* When an appropriate motion or objection has been made by the defense under this rule, the prosecution has the burden of establishing the admissibility of the evidence. When a specific motion or objection has been required under subdivision (d)(3), the burden on the prosecution extends only to the grounds upon which the defense moved to suppress or object to the evidence.

(1) *In general.* The military judge must find by a preponderance of the evidence that a statement by the accused was made voluntarily before it may be received into evidence. When trial is by a special court-martial without a military judge, a determination by the president of the court that a statement was made voluntarily is subject to objection by any member of the court. When such objection is made, it shall be resolved pursuant to R.C.M. 801(e)(3)(C).

(2) *Weight of the evidence.* If a statement is admitted into evidence, the military judge shall permit the defense to present relevant evidence with respect to the voluntariness of the statement and shall instruct the members to give such weight to the statement as it deserves under all the circumstances. When trial is by military judge without members, the military judge shall determine the appropriate weight to give the statement.

(3) *Derivative evidence.* Evidence that is challenged under this rule as derivative evidence may be admitted against the accused if the military judge finds by a preponderance of the evidence that the statement was made voluntarily, that the evidence was not obtained by use of the statement, or that the evidence would have been obtained even if the statement had not been made.

(f) *Defense evidence.* The defense may present evidence relevant to the admissibility of evidence as to which there has been an objection or motion to suppress under this rule. An accused may testify for the limited purpose of denying that the accused made the statement or that the statement was made voluntarily. Prior to the introduction of such testimony by the accused, the defense shall inform the military judge that the testimony is offered under this subdivision. When the accused testifies under this subdivision, the accused may be cross-examined only as to the matter on which he or she testifies. Nothing said by the accused on either direct or cross-examination may be used against the accused for any purpose other than in a prosecution for perjury, false swearing, or the making of a false official statement.

(g) *Corroboration.* An admission or a confession of the accused may be considered as evidence against the accused on the question of guilt or innocence only if independent evidence, either direct or circumstantial, has been introduced that corroborates the essential facts admitted to justify sufficiently an inference of their truth. Other uncorroborated confessions or admissions of the accused that would themselves require corroboration may not be used to supply this independent evidence. If the independent evidence raises an inference of the truth of some but not all of the essential facts admitted, then the confession or admission may be considered as evidence against the accused only with respect to those essential facts stated in the confession or admission that are corroborated by the independent evidence. Corroboration is not required for a statement made by the accused before the court by which the accused is being tried, for statements made prior to or contemporaneously with the act, or for statements offered under a rule of evidence other than that pertaining to the admissibility of admissions or confessions.

(1) *Quantum of evidence needed.* The independent evidence necessary to establish corroboration need not be sufficient of itself to establish beyond a reasonable doubt the truth of facts stated in the admission or confession. The independent evidence need raise only an inference of the truth of the essential facts admitted. The amount and type of evidence introduced as corroboration is a factor to be considered by the trier of fact in determining the weight, if any, to be given to the admission or confession.

(2) *Procedure.* The military judge alone shall determine when adequate evidence of corroboration has been received. Corroborating evidence usually is to be introduced before the admission or confession is introduced but the military judge may admit evidence subject to later corroboration.

(h) *Miscellaneous.*

(1) *Oral statements.* A voluntary oral confession or admission of the accused may be proved by the testimony of anyone who heard the accused make it, even if it was reduced to writing and the writing is not accounted for.

(2) *Completeness.* If only part of an alleged admission or confession is introduced against the accused, the defense, by cross-examination or otherwise, may introduce the remaining portions of the statement.

(3) *Certain admissions by silence.* A person's failure to deny an accusation of wrongdoing concerning an offense for which at the time of the alleged failure the person was under official investigation or was in confinement, arrest, or custody does not support an inference of an admission of the truth of the accusation.

(4) *Refusal to obey order to submit body substance.* If an accused refuses a lawful order to submit for chemical analysis a sample of his or her blood, breath, urine or other body substance, evidence of such refusal may be admitted into evidence on:

(A) A charge of violating an order to submit such a sample; or

(B) Any other charge on which the results of the chemical analysis would have been admissible.

Rule 305. Warnings about rights

(a) *General rule.* A statement obtained in violation of this rule is involuntary and shall be treated under Mil. R. Evid. 304.

(b) *Definitions.* As used in this rule:

(1) *Person subject to the code.* A "person subject to the code" includes a person acting as a knowing

agent of a military unit or of a person subject to the code.

(2) *Interrogation.* "Interrogation" includes any formal or informal questioning in which an incriminating response either is sought or is a reasonable consequence of such questioning.

(c) *Warnings concerning the accusation, right to remain silent, and use of statements.* A person subject to the code who is required to give warnings under Article 31 may not interrogate or request any statement from an accused or a person suspected of an offense without first:

(1) informing the accused or suspect of the nature of the accusation;

(2) advising the accused or suspect that the accused or suspect has the right to remain silent; and

(3) advising the accused or suspect that any statement made may be used as evidence against the accused or suspect in a trial by court-martial.

(d) *Counsel rights and warnings.*

(1) *General rule.* When evidence of a testimonial or communicative nature within the meaning of the Fifth Amendment to the Constitution of the United States either is sought or is a reasonable consequence of an interrogation, an accused or a person suspected of an offense is entitled to consult with counsel as provided by paragraph (2) of this subdivision, to have such counsel present at the interrogation, and to be warned of these rights prior to the interrogation if—

(A) The interrogation is conducted by a person subject to the code who is required to give warnings under Article 31 and the accused or suspect is in custody, could reasonably believe himself or herself to be in custody, or is otherwise deprived of his or her freedom of action in any significant way; or

(B) The interrogation is conducted by a person subject to the code acting in a law enforcement capacity, or the agent of such a person, the interrogation is conducted subsequent to the preferral of charges, and the interrogation concerns the offenses or matters that were the subject of the preferral of the charges.

(2) *Counsel.* When a person entitled to counsel under this rule requests counsel, a judge advocate or an individual certified in accordance with Article 27(b) shall be provided by the United States at no expense to the person and without regard to the person's indigency or lack thereof before the interrogation may proceed. In addition to counsel supplied by the United States, the person may retain civilian counsel at no expense to the United States. Unless otherwise provided by regulations of the Secretary concerned, an accused or suspect does not have a right under this rule to have military counsel of his or her own selection.

(e) *Presence of Counsel.*

(1) *Custodial interrogation.* Absent a valid waiver of counsel under subdivision (g)(2)(B), when an accused or person suspected of an offense is subjected to custodial interrogation under circumstances described under subdivision (d)(1)(A) of this rule, and the accused or suspect requests counsel, counsel must be present before any subsequent custodial interrogation may proceed.

(2) *Post-preferral interrogation.* Absent a valid waiver of counsel under subdivision (g)(2)(C), when an accused or person suspected of an offense is subjected to interrogation under circumstances described in subdivision (d)(1)(B) of this rule, and the accused or suspect either requests counsel or has an appointed or retained counsel, counsel must be present before any subsequent interrogation concerning that offense may proceed.

(f) *Exercise of rights.*

(1) *The privilege against self-incrimination.* If a person chooses to exercise the privilege against self-incrimination under this rule, questioning must cease immediately.

(2) *The right to counsel.* If a person subjected to interrogation under the circumstances described in subdivision (d)(1) of this rule chooses to exercise the right to counsel, questioning must cease until counsel is present.

(g) *Waiver.*

(1) *General rule.* After receiving applicable warnings under this rule, a person may waive the rights described therein and in Mil. R. Evid. 301 and make a statement. The waiver must be made freely, knowingly, and intelligently. A written waiver is not required. The accused or suspect must acknowledge affirmatively that he or she understands the rights involved, affirmatively decline the right to counsel and affirmatively consent to making a statement.

(2) *Counsel.*

(A) If the right to counsel in subdivision (d) is applicable and the accused or suspect does not decline affirmatively the right to counsel, the prosecution must demonstrate by a preponderance of the evidence that the individual waived the right to counsel.

(B) If an accused or suspect interrogated under circumstances described in subdivision (d)(1)(A) requests counsel, any subsequent waiver of the right to counsel obtained during a custodial interrogation concerning the same or different offenses is invalid unless the prosecution can demonstrate by a preponderance of the evidence that—

(i) the accused or suspect initiated the communication leading to the waiver; or

(ii) the accused or suspect has not continuously had his or her freedom restricted by confinement, or other means, during the period between the request for counsel and the subsequent waiver.

(C) If an accused or suspect interrogated under circumstances described in subdivision (d)(1)(B) requests counsel, any subsequent waiver of the right to counsel obtained during an interrogation concerning the same offenses is invalid unless the prosecution can demonstrate by a preponderance of the evidence that the accused or suspect initiated the communication leading to the waiver.

(h) *Nonmilitary interrogations.*

(1) *General rule.* When a person subject to the code is interrogated by an official or agent of the United States, of the District of Columbia, or of a State, Commonwealth, or possession of the United States, or any political subdivision of such a State, Commonwealth, or possession, and such official or agent is not required to give warning under subdivision (c), the person's entitlement to rights warnings and the validity of any waiver of applicable rights shall be determined by the principles of law generally recognized in the trial of criminal cases in the United States district courts involving similar interrogations.

(2) *Foreign interrogations.* Neither warnings under subdivisions (c) or (d), nor notice to counsel under subdivision (e) are required during an interrogation conducted abroad by officials of a foreign government or their agents unless such interrogation is conducted, instigated, or participated in by military personnel or their agents or by those officials or agents listed in subdivision (h)(1). A statement obtained during such an interrogation is involuntary within the meaning of Mil. R. Evid. 304(b)(3) if it is obtained through the use of coercion, unlawful influence, or unlawful inducement. An interrogation is not "participated in" by military personnel or their agents or by the officials or agents listed in subdivision (h)(1) merely because such a person was present at an interrogation conducted in a foreign nation by officials of a foreign government or their agents, or because such a person acted as an interpreter or took steps to mitigate damage to property or physical harm during the foreign interrogation.

Rule 306. Statements by one of several accused

When two or more accused are tried at the same trial, evidence of a statement made by one of them which is admissible only against him or her or only against some but not all of the accused may not be received in evidence unless all references inculpating an accused against whom the statement is inadmissible are deleted effectively or the maker of the statement is subject to cross-examination.

Rule 311. Evidence obtained from unlawful searches and seizures

(a) *General rule.* Evidence obtained as a result of an unlawful search or seizure made by a person acting in a governmental capacity is inadmissible against the accused if:

(1) *Objection.* The accused makes a timely motion to suppress or an objection to the evidence under this rule; and

(2) *Adequate interest.* The accused had a reasonable expectation of privacy in the person, place or property searched; the accused had a legitimate interest in the property or evidence seized when challenging a seizure; or the accused would otherwise have grounds to object to the search or seizure under the Constitution of the United States as applied to members of the armed forces.

(b) *Exceptions.*

(1) Evidence that was obtained as a result of an unlawful search or seizure may be used to impeach by contradiction the in-court testimony of the accused.

(2) Evidence that was obtained as a result of an unlawful search or seizure may be used when the evidence would have been obtained even if such unlawful search or seizure had not been made.

(3) Evidence that was obtained as a result of an unlawful search or seizure may be used if:

(A) The search or seizure resulted from an authorization to search, seize or apprehend issued by an individual competent to issue the authorization under Mil. R. Evid. 315(d) or from a search warrant or arrest warrant issued by competent civilian authority;

(B) The individual issuing the authorization or warrant had a substantial basis for determining the existence of probable cause; and

(C) The officials seeking and executing the authorization or warrant reasonably and with good faith relied on the issuance of the authorization or warrant. Good faith shall be determined on an objective standard.

(c) *Nature of search or seizure.* A search or seizure is "unlawful" if it was conducted, instigated, or participated in by:

(1) *Military personnel.* Military personnel or their agents and was in violation of the Constitution of the United States as applied to members of the armed forces, an Act of Congress applicable to trials by court-martial that requires exclusion of evidence obtained in violation thereof, or Mil. R. Evid. 312–317;

(2) *Other officials.* Other officials or agents of the United States, of the District of Columbia, or of a State, Commonwealth, or possession of the United States or any political subdivision of such a State, Commonwealth, or possession and was in violation of the Constitution of the United States, or is unlawful under the principles of law generally applied in the trial of criminal cases in the United States district courts involving a similar search or seizure; or

(3) *Officials of a foreign government.* Officials of a foreign government or their agents and was obtained as a result of a foreign search or seizure which subjected the accused to gross and brutal maltreatment. A search or seizure is not "participated in" merely because a person is present at a search or seizure conducted in a foreign nation by officials of a foreign government or their agents, or because a person acted as an interpreter or took steps to mitigate damage to property or physical harm during the foreign search or seizure.

(d) *Motions to suppress and objections.*

(1) *Disclosure.* Prior to arraignment, the prosecution shall disclose to the defense all evidence seized from the person or property of the accused, or believed to be owned by the accused, that it intends to offer into evidence against the accused at trial.

(2) *Motion or objection.*

(A) When evidence has been disclosed under subdivision (d)(1), any motion to suppress or objection under this rule shall be made by the defense prior to submission of a plea. In the absence of such motion or objection, the defense may not raise the issue at a later time except as permitted by the military judge for good cause shown. Failure to so move or object constitutes a waiver of the motion or objection.

(B) If the prosecution intends to offer evidence seized from the person or property of the accused that was not disclosed prior to arraignment, the prosecution shall provide timely notice to the military judge and to counsel for the accused. The defense may enter an objection at that time and the military judge may make such orders as are required in the interest of justice.

(C) If evidence is disclosed as derivative evidence under this subdivision prior to arraignment, any motion to suppress or objection under this rule shall be made in accordance with the procedure for challenging evidence under (A). If such evidence has not been so disclosed prior to arraignment, the requirements of (B) apply.

(3) *Specificity.* The military judge may require the defense to specify the grounds upon which the defense moves to suppress or object to evidence. If defense counsel, despite the exercise of due diligence, has been unable to interview adequately those persons involved in the search or seizure, the military judge may enter any order required by the interests of justice, including authorization for the defense to make a general motion to suppress or a general objection.

(4) *Rulings.* A motion to suppress or an objection to evidence made prior to plea shall be ruled upon prior to plea unless the military judge, for good cause, orders that it be deferred for determination at the trial of the general issue or until after findings, but no such determination shall be deferred if a party's right to appeal the ruling is affected adversely. Where factual issues are involved in ruling upon such motion or objection, the military judge shall state essential findings of fact on the record.

(e) *Burden of proof.*

(1) *In general.* When an appropriate motion or objection has been made by the defense under subdivision (d), the prosecution has the burden of proving by a preponderance of the evidence that the evidence was not obtained as a result of an unlawful search or seizure, that the evidence would have been obtained even if the unlawful search or seizure had not been made, or that the evidence was obtained by officials who reasonably and with good faith relied on the issuance of an authorization to search, seize, or apprehend or a search warrant or an arrest warrant.

(2) *Derivative evidence.* Evidence that is challenged under this rule as derivative evidence may be admitted against the accused if the military judge finds by a preponderance of the evidence that the evidence was not obtained as a result of an unlawful search or seizure, that the evidence ultimately would have been obtained by lawful means even if the unlawful search or seizure had not been made, or that the evidence was obtained by officials who reasonably and with good faith relied on the issuance of an authorization to search, seize or apprehend or a search warrant or an arrest warrant. Notwithstanding other provisions of this Rule, an apprehension made in a dwelling in a manner that violates R.C.M. 302 (d)(2) and (e) does not preclude the admission into evidence of a statement of an individual apprehended provided (1) that the apprehension was based on probable cause, (2) that the statement was made subsequent to the apprehension at a location outside the dwelling, and (3) that the statement was otherwise in compliance with these rules.

(3) *Specific motions or objections.* When a specific motion or objection has been required under subdivision (d)(3), the burden on the prosecution extends only to the grounds upon which the defense moved to suppress or object to the evidence.

(f) *Defense evidence.* The defense may present evidence relevant to the admissibility of evidence as to which there has been an appropriate motion or objection under this rule. An accused may testify for the limited purpose of contesting the legality of the search or seizure giving rise to the challenged evidence. Prior to the introduction of such testimony by the accused, the defense shall inform the military judge that the testimony is offered under this subdivision. When the accused testifies under this subdivision, the accused may be cross-examined only as to the matter on which he or she testifies. Nothing said by the accused on either direct or cross-examination may be used against the accused for any purpose other than in a prosecution for perjury, false swearing, or the making of a false official statement.

(g) *Scope of motions and objections challenging probable cause.*

(1) *Generally.* If the defense challenges evidence seized pursuant to a search warrant or search authorization on the grounds that the warrant or authorization was not based upon probable cause, the evidence relevant to the motion is limited to evidence concerning the information actually presented to or otherwise known by the authorizing officer, except as provided in paragraph (2).

(2) *False statements.* If the defense makes a substantial preliminary showing that a government agent included a false statement knowingly and intentionally or with reckless disregard for the truth in the information presented to the authorizing officer, and if the allegedly false statement is necessary to the finding of probable cause, the defense, upon request, shall be entitled to a hearing. At the hearing, the defense has the burden of establishing by a preponderance of the evidence the allegation of knowing and intentional falsity or reckless disregard for the truth. If the defense meets its burden, the prosecution has the burden of proving by a preponderance of the evidence, with the false information set aside, that the remaining information presented to the authorizing officer is sufficient to establish probable cause. If the prosecution does not meet its burden, the objection or motion shall be granted unless the search is otherwise lawful under these rules.

(h) *Objections to evidence seized unlawfully.* If a defense motion or objection under this rule is sustained in whole or in part, the members may not be informed of that fact except insofar as the military judge must instruct the members to disregard evidence.

(i) *Effect of guilty plea.* Except as otherwise expressly provided in R.C.M. 910(a)(2), a plea of guilty to an offense that results in a finding of guilty waives all issues under the Fourth Amendment to the Constitution of the United States and Mil. R. Evid. 311-317 with respect to the offense whether or not raised prior to plea.

Rule 312. Body views and intrusions

(a) *General rule.* Evidence obtained from body views and intrusions conducted in accordance with this rule is admissible at trial when relevant and not otherwise inadmissible under these rules.

(b) *Visual examination of the body.*

(1) *Consensual.* Visual examination of the unclothed body may be made with the consent of the individual subject to the inspection in accordance with Mil. R. Evid. 314(e).

(2) *Involuntary.* An involuntary display of the unclothed body, including a visual examination of body cavities, may be required only if conducted in reasonable fashion and authorized under the following provisions of the Military Rules of Evidence: inspections and inventories under Mil. R. Evid. 313; searches under Mil. R. Evid. 314(b) and 314(c) if there is a reasonable suspicion that weapons, contraband, or evidence of crime is concealed on the body of the person to be searched; searches within jails and similar facilities under Mil. R. Evid. 314(h) if reasonably necessary to maintain the security of the institution or its personnel; searches incident to lawful apprehension under Mil. R. Evid. 314(g); emergency searches under Mil. R. Evid. 314(i); and probable cause searches under Mil. R. Evid. 315. An examination of the unclothed body under this rule should be conducted whenever practicable by a person of the same sex as that of the person being examined; provided, however, that failure to comply with this requirement does not make an examination an unlawful search within the meaning of Mil. R. Evid. 311.

(c) *Intrusion into body cavities.* A reasonable nonconsensual physical intrusion into the mouth, nose, and ears may be made when a visual examination of the body under subdivision (b) is permissible. Nonconsensual intrusions into other body cavities may be made:

(1) *For purposes of seizure.* When there is a clear indication that weapons, contraband, or other evidence or crime is present, to remove weapons, contraband, or evidence of crime discovered under subdivisions (b) and (c)(2) of this rule or under Mil. R. Evid. 316(d)(4)(C) if such intrusion is made in a reasonable fashion by a person with appropriate medical qualifications; or

(2) *For purposes of search.* To search for weapons, contraband, or evidence of crime if authorized by a search warrant or search authorization under Mil. R. Evid. 315 and conducted by a person with appropriate medical qualifications.

Notwithstanding this rule, a search under Mil. R. Evid. 314(h) may be made without a search warrant or authorization if such search is based on a reasonable suspicion that the individual is concealing weapons, contraband, or evidence of crime.

(d) *Extraction of body fluids.* Nonconsensual extraction of body fluids, including blood and urine, may be made from the body of an individual pursuant to a search warrant or a search authorization under Mil. R. Evid. 315. Nonconsensual extraction of body fluids may be made without such warrant or authorization, notwithstanding Mil. R. Evid. 315(g), only when there is clear indication that evidence of crime will be found and that there is reason to believe that the delay that would result if a warrant or authorization were sought could result in the destruction of the evidence. Involuntary extraction of body fluids under this rule must be done in a reasonable fashion by a person with appropriate medical qualifications.

(e) *Other intrusive searches.* Nonconsensual intrusive searches of the body made to locate or obtain weapons, contraband, or evidence of crime and not within the scope of subdivisions (b) or (c) may be made only upon search warrant or search authorization under Mil. R. Evid. 315 and only if such search is conducted in a reasonable fashion by a person with appropriate medical qualifications and does not endanger the health of the person to be searched. Compelling a person to ingest substances for the purposes of locating the property described above or to compel the bodily elimination of such property is a search within the meaning of this section. Notwithstanding this rule, a person who is neither a suspect nor an accused may not be compelled to submit to an intrusive search of the body for the sole purpose of obtaining evidence of crime.

(f) *Intrusions for valid medical purposes.* Nothing in this rule shall be deemed to interfere with the lawful authority of the armed forces to take whatever action may be necessary to preserve the health of a servicemember. Evidence or contraband obtained from an examination or intrusion conducted for a valid medical purpose may be seized and is not evidence obtained from an unlawful search or seizure within the meaning of Mil. R. Evid. 311.

(g) *Medical qualifications.* The Secretary concerned may prescribe appropriate medical qualifications for persons who conduct searches and seizures under this rule.

Rule 313. Inspections and inventories in the armed forces

(a) *General rule.* Evidence obtained from inspections and inventories in the armed forces conducted in accordance with this rule is admissible at trial when relevant and not otherwise inadmissible under these rules.

(b) *Inspections.* An "inspection" is an examination of the whole or part of a unit, organization, installation, vessel, aircraft, or vehicle, including an examination conducted at entrance and exit points, conducted as an incident of command the primary purpose of which is to determine and to ensure the security, military fitness, or good order and discipline of the unit, organization, installation, vessel, aircraft, or vehicle. An inspection may include but is not limited to an examination to determine and to ensure that any or all of the following requirements are met: that the command is properly equipped, functioning properly, maintaining proper standards of readiness, sea or airworthiness, sanitation and cleanliness, and that personnel are present, fit, and ready for duty. An inspection also includes an examination to locate and confiscate unlawful weapons and other contraband. An order to produce body fluids, such as urine, is permissible in accordance with this rule. An examination made for the primary purpose of obtaining evidence for use in a trial by court-martial or in other disciplinary proceedings is not an inspection within the meaning of this rule. If a purpose of an examination is to locate weapons or contraband, and if: (1) the examination was directed immediately following a report of a specific offense in the unit, organization, installation, vessel, aircraft, or vehicle and was not previously scheduled; (2) specific individuals are selected for examination; or (3) persons examined are subjected to substantially different intrusions during the same examination, the prosecution must prove by clear and convincing evidence that the examination was an inspection within the meaning of this rule. Inspections shall be conducted in a reasonable fashion and shall comply with Mil. R. Evid. 312, if applicable. Inspections may utilize any reasonable natural or technological aid and may be conducted with or without notice to those inspected. Unlawful weapons, contraband, or other evidence of crime located during an inspection may be seized.

(c) *Inventories.* Unlawful weapons, contraband, or other evidence of crime discovered in the process of an inventory, the primary purpose of which is administrative in nature, may be seized. Inventories shall be conducted in a reasonable fashion and shall comply with Mil. R. Evid. 312, if applicable. An examination made for the primary purpose of obtaining evidence for use in a trial by court-martial or in other disciplinary proceedings is not an inventory within the meaning of this rule.

Rule 314. Searches not requiring probable cause

(a) *General rule.* Evidence obtained from reasonable searches not requiring probable cause conducted pursuant to this rule is admissible at trial when relevant and not otherwise inadmissible under these rules.

(b) *Border searches.* Border searches for customs or immigration purposes may be conducted when authorized by Act of Congress.

(c) *Searches upon entry to or exit from United States installations, aircraft, and vessels abroad.* In addition to the authority to conduct inspections under Mil. R. Evid. 313(b), a commander of a United States military installation, enclave, or aircraft on foreign soil, or in foreign or international airspace, or a United States vessel in foreign or international waters, may authorize appropriate personnel to search persons or the property of such persons upon entry to or exit from the installation, enclave, aircraft, or vessel to ensure the security, military fitness, or good order and discipline of the command. Such searches may not be conducted at a time or in a manner contrary to an express provision of a treaty or agreement to which the United States is a party. Failure to comply with a treaty or agreement, however, does not render a search unlawful within the meaning of Mil. R. Evid. 311. A search made for the primary purpose of obtaining evidence for use in a trial by court-martial or other disciplinary proceeding is not authorized by this subdivision.

(d) *Searches of government property.* Government property may be searched under this rule unless the person to whom the property is issued or assigned has a reasonable expectation of privacy therein at the time of the search. Under normal circumstances, a person does not have a reasonable expectation of privacy in government property that is not issued for personal use. Wall or floor lockers in living quarters issued for the purpose of storing personal possessions normally are issued for personal use; but the determination as to whether a person has a reasonable expectation of privacy in government property issued for personal use depends on the facts and circumstances at the time of the search.

(e) *Consent searches.*

(1) *General rule.* Searches may be conducted of any person or property with lawful consent.

(2) *Who may consent.* A person may consent to a search of his or her person or property, or both, unless control over such property has been given to another. A person may grant consent to search property when the person exercises control over that property.

(3) *Scope of consent.* Consent may be limited in any way by the person granting consent, including limitations in terms of time, place, or property and may be withdrawn at any time.

(4) *Voluntariness.* To be valid, consent must be given voluntarily. Voluntariness is a question to be determined from all the circumstances. Although a person's knowledge of the right to refuse to give consent is a factor to be considered in determining voluntariness, the prosecution is not required to demonstrate such knowledge as a prerequisite to establishing a voluntary consent. Mere submission to the color of authority of personnel performing law enforcement duties or acquiescence in an announced or indicated purpose to search is not a voluntary consent.

(5) *Burden of proof.* Consent must be shown by clear and convincing evidence. The fact that a person was in custody while granting consent is a factor to be considered in determining the voluntariness of consent, but it does not affect the burden of proof.

(f) *Searches incident to a lawful stop.*

(1) *Stops.* A person authorized to apprehend under R.C.M. 302(b) and others performing law enforcement duties may stop another person temporarily when the person making the stop has information or observes unusual conduct that leads him or her reasonably to conclude in light of his or her experience that criminal activity may be afoot. The purpose of the stop must be investigatory in nature.

(2) *Frisks.* When a lawful stop is performed, the person stopped may be frisked for weapons when that person is reasonably believed to be armed and presently dangerous. Contraband or evidence located in the process of a lawful frisk may be seized.

(3) *Motor vehicles.* When a person lawfully stopped is the driver or a passenger in a motor vehicle, the passenger compartment of the vehicle may be searched for weapons if the official who made the stop has a reasonable belief that the person stopped is dangerous and that the person stopped may gain immediate control of a weapon.

(g) *Searches incident to a lawful apprehension.*

(1) *General rule.* A person who has been lawfully apprehended may be searched.

(2) *Search for weapons and destructible evidence.* A search may be conducted for weapons or destructible evidence, in the area within the immediate control of a person who has been apprehended. The area within the person's "immediate control" is the area which the individual searching could reasonably believe that the person apprehended could reach with a sudden movement to obtain such property; provided, that the passenger compartment of an automobile, and containers within the passenger compartment may be searched as a contemporaneous incident of the apprehension of an occupant of the automobile, regardless whether the person apprehended has been removed from the vehicle.

(3) *Examination for other persons.*

(A) When an apprehension takes place at a location in which other persons might be present who might endanger those conducting the apprehension and others in the area of the apprehension, a reasonable examination may be made of the general area in which such other persons might be located. A reasonable examination under this rule is permitted if the apprehending officials have a reasonable suspicion based on specific and articulable facts that the area to be examined harbors an individual posing a danger to those in the area of the apprehension.

(B) Apprehending officials may, incident to apprehension, as a precautionary matter and without probable cause or reasonable suspicion, look in closets and other spaces immediately adjoining the place of apprehension from which an attack could be immediately launched.

(h) *Searches within jails, confinement facilities, or similar facilities.* Searches within jails, confinement facilities, or similar facilities may be authorized by persons with authority over the institution.

(i) *Emergency searches to save life or for related purposes.* In emergency circumstances to save life or for a related purpose, a search may be conducted of persons or property in a good faith effort to render immediate medical aid, to obtain information that will assist in the rendering of such aid, or to prevent immediate or ongoing personal injury.

(j) *Searches of open fields or woodlands.* A search of open fields or woodlands is not an unlawful search within the meaning of Mil. R. Evid. 311.

(k) *Other searches.* A search of a type not otherwise included in this rule and not requiring probable cause under Mil. R. Evid. 315 may be conducted when permissible under the Constitution of the United States as applied to members of the armed forces.

Rule 315. Probable cause searches

(a) *General rule.* Evidence obtained from searches requiring probable cause conducted in accordance with this rule is admissible at trial when relevant and not otherwise inadmissible under these rules.

(b) *Definitions.* As used in these rules:

(1) *Authorization to search.* An "authorization to search" is an express permission, written or oral, issued by competent military authority to search a person or an area for specified property or evidence or for a specific person and to seize such property, evidence, or person. It may contain an order directing subordinate personnel to conduct a search in a specified manner.

(2) *Search warrant.* A "search warrant" is an express permission to search and seize issued by competent civilian authority.

(c) *Scope of authorization.* A search authorization may be issued under this rule for a search of:

(1) *Persons.* The person of anyone subject to military law or the law of war wherever found;

(2) *Military property.* Military property of the United States or of nonappropriated fund activities of an armed force of the United States wherever located;

(3) *Persons and property within military control.* Persons or property situated on or in a military installation, encampment, vessel, aircraft, vehicle, or any other location under military control, wherever located; or

(4) *Nonmilitary property within a foreign country.*

(A) Property owned, used, occupied by, or in the possession of an agency of the United States other than the Department of Defense when situated in a foreign country. A search of such property may not be conducted without the concurrence of an appropriate representative of the agency concerned. Failure to obtain such concurrence, however, does not render a search unlawful within the meaning of Mil. R. Evid. 311.

(B) Other property situated in a foreign country. If the United States is a party to a treaty or agreement that governs a search in a foreign country, the search shall be conducted in accordance with the treaty or agreement. If there is no treaty or agreement, concurrence should be obtained from an appropriate representative of the foreign country with respect to a search under paragraph (4)(B) of this subdivision. Failure to obtain such concurrence or noncompliance with a treaty or agreement, however, does not render a search unlawful within the meaning of Mil. R. Evid. 311.

(d) *Power to authorize.* Authorization to search pursuant to this rule may be granted by an impartial individual in the following categories:

(1) *Commander.* A commander or other person serving in a position designated by the Secretary concerned as either a position analogous to an officer in charge or a position of command, who has control over the place where the property or person to be searched is situated or found, or, if that place is not under military control, having control over persons subject to military law or the law of war; or

(2) *Military judge.* A military judge or magistrate if authorized under regulations prescribed by the Secretary of Defense or the Secretary concerned. An otherwise impartial authorizing official does not lose the character merely because he or she is present at the scene of a search or is otherwise readily available to persons who may seek the issuance of a search authorization; nor does such an official lose impartial character merely because the official previously and impartially authorized investigative activities when such previous authorization is similar in intent or function to a pretrial authorization made by the United States district courts.

(e) *Power to search.* Any commissioned officer, warrant officer, petty officer, noncommissioned officer, and, when in the execution of guard or police duties, any criminal investigator, member of the Air Force security police, military police, or shore patrol, or person designated by proper authority to perform guard or police duties, or any agent of any such person, may conduct or authorize a search when a search authorization has been granted under this rule or a search would otherwise be proper under subdivision (g).

(f) *Basis for Search authorizations.*

(1) *Probable cause requirement.* A search authorization issued under this rule must be based upon probable cause.

(2) *Probable cause determination.* Probable cause to search exists when there is a reasonable belief that the person, property, or evidence sought is located in the place or on the person to be searched. A search authorization may be based upon hearsay evidence in whole or in part. A determination of probable cause under this rule shall be based upon any or all of the following:

(A) Written statements communicated to the authorizing officer;

(B) Oral statements communicated to the authorizing official in person, via telephone, or by other appropriate means of communication; or

(C) Such information as may be known by the authorizing official that would not preclude the officer from acting in an impartial fashion. The Secretary of Defense or the Secretary concerned may prescribe additional requirements.

(g) *Exigencies.* A search warrant or search authorization is not required under this rule for a search based on probable cause when:

(1) *Insufficient time.* There is a reasonable belief that the delay necessary to obtain a search warrant or search authorization would result in the removal, destruction, or concealment of the property or evidence sought;

(2) *Lack of communications.* There is a reasonable military operational necessity that is reasonably believed to prohibit or prevent communication with a person empowered to grant a search warrant or authorization and there is a reasonable belief that the delay necessary to obtain a search warrant or search authorization would result in the removal, destruction, or concealment of the property or evidence sought;

(3) *Search of operable vehicle.* An operable vehicle is to be searched, except in the circumstances where a search warrant or authorization is required by the Constitution of the United States, this Manual, or these rules; or

(4) *Not required by the Constitution.* A search warrant or authorization is not otherwise required by the Constitution of the United States as applied to members of the armed forces. For purpose of this rule, a vehicle is "operable" unless a reasonable person would have known at the time of search that the vehicle was not functional for purposes of transportation.

(h) *Execution.*

(1) *Notice.* If the person whose property is to be searched is present during a search conducted pursuant to a search authorization granted under this rule, the person conducting the search should when possible notify him or her of the act of authorization and the general substance of the authorization. Such notice may be made prior to or contemporaneously with the search. Failure to provide such notice does not make a search unlawful within the meaning of Mil. R. Evid. 311.

(2) *Inventory.* Under regulations prescribed by the Secretary concerned, and with such exceptions as may be authorized by the Secretary, an inventory of the property seized shall be made at the time of a seizure under this rule or as soon as practicable thereafter. At an appropriate time, a copy of the inventory shall be given to a person from whose possession or premises the property was taken. Failure to make an inventory, furnish a copy thereof, or otherwise comply with this paragraph does not render a search or seizure unlawful within the meaning of Mil. R. Evid. 311.

(3) *Foreign searches.* Execution of a search authorization outside the United States and within the jurisdiction of a foreign nation should be in conformity with existing agreements between the United States and the foreign nation. Noncompliance with such an agreement does not make an otherwise lawful search unlawful.

(4) *Search warrants.* Any civilian or military criminal investigator authorized to request search warrants pursuant to applicable law or regulation is authorized to serve and execute search warrants. The

execution of a search warrant affects admissibility only insofar as exclusion of evidence is required by the Constitution of the United States or an applicable Act of Congress.

Rule 316. Seizures

(a) *General rule.* Evidence obtained from seizures conducted in accordance with this rule is admissible at trial if the evidence was not obtained as a result of an unlawful search and if the evidence is relevant and not otherwise inadmissible under these rules.

(b) *Seizure of property.* Probable cause to seize property or evidence exists when there is a reasonable belief that the property or evidence is an unlawful weapon, contraband, evidence of crime, or might be used to resist apprehension or to escape.

(c) *Apprehension.* Apprehension is governed by R.C.M. 302.

(d) *Seizure of property or evidence.*

(1) *Abandoned property.* Abandoned property may be seized without probable cause and without a search warrant or search authorization. Such seizure may be made by any person.

(2) *Consent.* Property or evidence may be seized with consent consistent with the requirements applicable to consensual searches under Mil. R. Evid. 314.

(3) *Government property.* Government property may be seized without probable cause and without a search warrant or search authorization by any person listed in subdivision (e), unless the person to whom the property is issued or assigned has a reasonable expectation of privacy therein, as provided in Mil. R. Evid. 314(d), at the time of the seizure.

(4) *Other property.* Property or evidence not included in paragraph (1)-(3) may be seized for use in evidence by any person listed in subdivision (e) if:

(A) *Authorization.* The person is authorized to seize the property or evidence by a search warrant or a search authorization under Mil. R. Evid. 315;

(B) *Exigent circumstances.* The person has probable cause to seize the property or evidence and under Mil. R. Evid. 315(g) a search warrant or search authorization is not required; or

(C) *Plain view.* The person while in the course of otherwise lawful activity observes in a reasonable fashion property or evidence that the person has probable cause to seize.

(5) *Temporary detention.* Nothing in this rule shall prohibit temporary detention of property on less than probable cause when authorized under the Constitution of the United States.

(e) *Power to seize.* Any commissioned officer, warrant officer, petty officer, noncommissioned officer, and, when in the execution of guard or police duties, any criminal investigator, member of the Air Force security police, military police, or shore patrol, or individual designated by proper authority to perform guard or police duties, or any agent of any such person, may seize property pursuant to this rule.

(f) *Other seizures.* A seizure of a type not otherwise included in this rule may be made when permissible under the Constitution of the United States as applied to members of the armed forces.

Rule 317. Interception of wire and oral communications

(a) *General rule.* Wire or oral communications constitute evidence obtained as a result of an unlawful search or seizure within the meaning of Mil. R. Evid. 311 when such evidence must be excluded under the Fourth Amendment to the Constitution of the United States as applied to members of the armed forces or if such evidence must be excluded under a statute applicable to members of the armed forces.

(b) *Authorization for judicial applications in the United States.* Under 18 U.S.C. § 2516(1), the Attorney General, or any Assistant Attorney General specially designated by the Attorney General may authorize an application to a federal judge of competent jurisdiction for, and such judge may grant in conformity with 18 U.S.C. § 2518, an order authorizing or approving the interception of wire or oral communications by the Department of Defense, the Department of Homeland Security, or any Military Department for purposes of obtaining evidence concerning the offenses enumerated in 18 U.S.C. § 2516(1), to the extent such offenses are punishable under the Uniform Code of Military Justice.

(c) *Regulations.* Notwithstanding any other provision of these rules, members of the armed forces or their agents may not intercept wire or oral communications for law enforcement purposes unless such interception:

(1) takes place in the United States and is authorized under subdivision (b);

(2) takes place outside the United States and is authorized under regulations issued by the Secretary of Defense or the Secretary concerned; or

(3) is authorized under regulations issued by the Secretary of Defense or the Secretary concerned and is not unlawful under 18 U.S.C. § 2511.

Rule 321. Eyewitness identification

(a) *General rule.*

(1) *Admissibility.* Testimony concerning a relevant out of court identification by any person is admissible, subject to an appropriate objection under this rule, if such testimony is otherwise admissible under these rules. The witness making the identification and any person who has observed the previous identification may testify concerning it. When in testimony a witness identifies the accused as being, or not being, a participant in an offense or makes any other relevant identification concerning a person in the courtroom, evidence that on a previous occasion the witness made a similar identification is admissible to corroborate the witness' testimony as to identity even if the credibility of the witness has not been attacked directly, subject to appropriate objection under this rule.

(2) *Exclusionary rule.* An identification of the accused as being a participant in an offense, whether such identification is made at the trial or otherwise, is inadmissible against the accused if:

(A) The accused makes a timely motion to suppress or an objection to the evidence under this rule and if the identification is the result of an unlawful lineup or other unlawful identification process conducted by the United States or other domestic authorities; or

(B) Exclusion of the evidence is required by the due process clause of the Fifth Amendment to the Constitution of the United States as applied to members of the armed forces. Evidence other than an identification of the accused that is obtained as a result of the unlawful lineup or unlawful identification process is inadmissible against the accused if the accused makes a timely motion to suppress or an objection to the evidence under this rule and if exclusion of the evidence is required under the Constitution of the United States as applied to members of the armed forces.

(b) *Definition of "unlawful".*

(1) *Lineups and other identification processes.* A lineup or other identification process is "unlawful" if the identification is unreliable. An identification is unreliable if the lineup or other identification process, under the circumstances, is so suggestive as to create a substantial likelihood of misidentification.

(2) *Lineups: right to counsel.* A lineup is "unlawful" if it is conducted in violation of the following rights to counsel:

(A) *Military lineups.* An accused or suspect is entitled to counsel if, after preferral of charges or imposition of pretrial restraint under R.C.M. 304 for the offense under investigation, the accused is subjected by persons subject to the code or their agents to a lineup for the purpose of identification. When a person entitled to counsel under this rule requests counsel, a judge advocate or a person certified in accordance with Article 27(b) shall be provided by the United States at no expense to the accused or suspect and without regard to indigency or lack thereof before the lineup may proceed. The accused or suspect may waive the rights provided in this rule if the waiver is freely, knowingly, and intelligently made.

(B) *Nonmilitary lineups.* When a person subject to the code is subjected to a lineup for purposes of identification by an official or agent of the United States, of the District of Columbia, or of a State, Commonwealth, or possession of the United States, or any political subdivision of such a State, Commonwealth, or possession, and the provisions of paragraph (A) do not apply, the person's entitlement to counsel and the validity of any waiver of applicable rights shall be determined by the principles of law generally recognized in the trial of criminal cases in the United States district courts involving similar lineups.

(c) *Motions to suppress and objections.*

(1) *Disclosure.* Prior to arraignment, the prosecution shall disclose to the defense all evidence of a prior identification of the accused as a lineup or other identification process that it intends to offer into evidence against the accused at trial.

(2) *Motion or objection.*

(A) When such evidence has been disclosed, any motion to suppress or objection under this rule shall be made by the defense prior to submission of a plea. In the absence of such motion or objection, the defense may not raise the issue at a later time except as permitted by the military judge for good cause shown. Failure to so move constitutes a waiver of the motion or objection.

(B) If the prosecution intends to offer such evidence and the evidence was not disclosed prior to arraignment, the prosecution shall provide timely notice to the military judge and counsel for the accused. The defense may enter an objection at that time and the military judge may make such orders as are required in the interests of justice.

(C) If evidence is disclosed as derivative evidence under this subdivision prior to arraignment, any motion to suppress or objection under this rule shall be made in accordance with the procedure for challenging evidence under (A). If such evidence has not been so disclosed prior to arraignment, the requirements of (B) apply.

(3) *Specificity.* The military judge may require the defense to specify the grounds upon which the defense moves to suppress or object to evidence. If defense counsel, despite the exercise of due diligence, has been unable to interview adequately those persons involved in the lineup or other identification process, the military judge may enter any order required by the interests of justice, including authorization for the defense to make a general motion to suppress or a general objection.

(d) *Burden of proof.* When a specific motion or objection has been required under subdivision (c)(3), the burden on the prosecution extends only to the grounds upon which the defense moved to suppress or object to the evidence. When an appropriate objection under this rule has been made by the defense, the issue shall be determined by the military judge as follows:

(1) *Right to counsel.* When an objection raises the right to presence of counsel under this rule, the prosecution must prove by a preponderance of the evidence that counsel was present at the lineup or that the accused, having been advised of the right to the presence of counsel, voluntarily and intelligently waived that right prior to the lineup. When the military judge determines that an identification is the result of a lineup conducted without the presence of counsel or an appropriate waiver, any later identification by one present at such unlawful lineup is also a result thereof unless the military judge determines that the contrary has been shown by clear and convincing evidence.

(2) *Unreliable identification.* When an objection raises the issue of an unreliable identification, the prosecution must prove by a preponderance of the evidence that the identification was reliable under the circumstances; provided, however, that if the military judge finds the evidence of identification inadmissible under this subdivision, a later identification may be admitted if the prosecution proves by clear and convincing evidence that the later identification is not the result of the inadmissible identification.

(e) *Defense evidence.* The defense may present evidence relevant to the issue of the admissibility of evidence as to which there has been an appropriate motion or objection under this rule. An accused may testify for the limited purpose of contesting the legality of the lineup or identification process giving rise to the challenged evidence. Prior to the introduction of such testimony by the accused, the defense shall inform the military judge that the testimony is offered under this subdivision. When the accused testifies under this subdivision, the accused may be cross-examined only as to the matter on which he or she testifies. Nothing said by the accused on either direct or cross-examination may be used against the accused for any purpose other than in a prosecution for perjury, false swearing, or the making of a false official statement.

(f) *Rulings.* A motion to suppress or an objection to evidence made prior to plea under this rule shall be ruled upon prior to plea unless the military judge, for good cause, orders that it be deferred for determination at the trial of the general issue or until after findings, but no such determination shall be deferred if a party's right to appeal the ruling is affected adversely. Where factual issues are involved in ruling upon such motion or objection, the military judge shall state his or her essential findings of fact on the record.

(g) *Effect of guilty pleas.* Except as otherwise expressly provided in R.C.M. 910(a)(2), a plea of guilty to an offense that results in a finding of guilty waives all issues under this rule with respect to that offense whether or not raised prior to the plea.

SECTION IV
RELEVANCY AND ITS LIMITS

Rule 401. Definition of "relevant evidence"

"Relevant evidence" means evidence having any

tendency to make the existence of any fact that is of consequence to the determination of the action more probable or less probable than it would be without the evidence.

Rule 402. Relevant evidence general admissible; irrelevant evidence inadmissible

All relevant evidence is admissible, except as otherwise provided by the Constitution of the United States as applied to members of the armed forces, the code, these rules, this Manual, or any Act of Congress applicable to members of the armed forces. Evidence which is not relevant is not admissible.

Rule 403. Exclusion of relevant evidence on grounds of prejudice, confusion, or waste of time

Although relevant, evidence may be excluded if its probative value is substantially outweighed by the danger of unfair prejudice, confusion of the issues, or misleading the members, or by considerations of undue delay, waste of time, or needless presentation of cumulative evidence.

Rule 404. Character evidence not admissible to prove conduct; exceptions; other crimes

(a) *Character evidence generally.* Evidence of a person's character or a trait of character is not admissible for the purpose of proving action in conformity therewith on a particular occasion, except:

(1) *Character of the accused.* Evidence of a pertinent trait of character offered by an accused, or by the prosecution to rebut the same, or if evidence of a pertinent trait of character of the alleged victim of the crime is offered by an accused and admitted under Mil. R. Evid. 404(a)(2), evidence of the same trait of character, if relevant, of the accused offered by the prosecution;

(2) *Character of alleged victim* Evidence of a pertinent trait of character of the alleged victim of the crime offered by an accused, or by the prosecution to rebut the same, or evidence of a character trait of peacefulness of the alleged victim offered by the prosecution in a homicide or assault case to rebut evidence that the alleged victim was an aggressor;

(3) *Character of witness.* Evidence of the character of a witness, as provided in Mil. R. Evid. 607, 608, and 609.

(b) *Other crimes, wrongs, or acts.* Evidence of other crimes, wrongs, or acts is not admissible to prove the character of a person in order to show action in conformity therewith. It may, however, be admissible for other purposes, such as proof of motive, opportunity, intent, preparation, plan, knowledge, identity, or absence of mistake or accident, provided, that upon request by the accused, the prosecution shall provide reasonable notice in advance of trial, or during trial if the military judge excuses pretrial notice on good cause shown, of the general nature of any such evidence it intends to introduce at trial.

Rule 405. Methods of proving character

(a) *Reputation or opinion.* In all cases in which evidence of character or a trait of character of a person is admissible, proof may be made by testimony as to reputation or by testimony in the form of an opinion. On cross-examination, inquiry is allowable into relevant specific instances of conduct.

(b) *Specific instances of conduct.* In cases in which character or a trait of character of a person is an essential element of an offense or defense, proof may also be made of specific instances of the person's conduct.

(c) *Affidavits.* The defense may introduce affidavits or other written statements of persons other than the accused concerning the character of the accused. If the defense introduces affidavits or other written statements under this subdivision, the prosecution may, in rebuttal, also introduce affidavits or other written statements regarding the character of the accused. Evidence of this type may be introduced by the defense or prosecution only if, aside from being contained in an affidavit or other written statement, it would otherwise be admissible under these rules.

(d) *Definitions.* "Reputation" means the estimation in which a person generally is held in the community in which the person lives or pursues a business or profession. "Community" in the armed forces includes a post, camp, ship, station, or other military organization regardless of size.

Rule 406. Habit; routine practice

Evidence of the habit of a person or of the routine practice of an organization, whether corroborated or not and regardless of the presence of eyewitnesses, is relevant to prove that the conduct of the person or organization on a particular occasion was in conformity with the habit or routine practice.

Rule 407. Subsequent remedial measures

When, after an injury or harm allegedly caused by an event, measures are taken that, if taken previously, would have made the injury or harm less likely to occur, evidence of the subsequent measures is not admissible to prove negligence, culpable conduct, a defect in a product, a defect in a product's design, or a need for a warning or instruction. This rule does not require the exclusion of evidence of subsequent measures when offered for another purpose, such as proving ownership, control, or feasibility of precautionary measures, if controverted, or impeachment.

Rule 408. Compromise and offer to compromise

Evidence of (1) furnishing or offering or promising to furnish, or (2) accepting or offering or promising to accept, a valuable consideration in compromising or attempting to compromise a claim which was disputed as to either validity or amount, is not admissible to prove liability for or invalidity of the claim or its amount. Evidence of conduct or statements made in compromise negotiations is likewise not admissible. This rule does not require the exclusion of any evidence otherwise discoverable merely because it is presented in the course of compromise negotiations. This rule also does not require exclusion when the evidence is offered for another purpose, such as proving bias or prejudice of a witness, negating a contention of undue delay, or proving an effort to obstruct a criminal investigation or prosecution.

Rule 409. Payment of medical and similar expenses

Evidence of furnishing or offering or promising to pay medical, hospital, or similar expenses occasioned by an injury is not admissible to prove liability for the injury.

Rule 410. Inadmissibility of pleas, plea discussions, and related statements

(a) *In general.* Except as otherwise provided in this rule, evidence of the following is not admissible in any court-martial proceeding against the accused who made the plea or was a participant in the plea discussions:

(1) a plea of guilty which was later withdrawn;

(2) a plea of nolo contendere;

(3) any statement made in the course of any judicial inquiry regarding either of the foregoing pleas; or

(4) any statement made in the course of plea discussions with the convening authority, staff judge advocate, trial counsel or other counsel for the Government which do not result in a plea of guilty or which result in a plea of guilty later withdrawn. However, such a statement is admissible (i) in any proceeding where in another statement made in the course of the same plea or plea discussions has been introduced and the statement ought in fairness be considered contemporaneously with it, or (ii) in a court-martial proceedings for perjury or false statement if the statement was made by the accused under oath, on the record and in the presence of counsel.

(b) *Definitions.* A "statement made in the course of plea discussions" includes a statement made by the accused solely for the purpose of requesting disposition under an authorized procedure for administrative action in lieu of trial by court-martial; "on the record" includes the written statement submitted by the accused in furtherance of such request.

Rule 411. Liability insurance

Evidence that a person was or was not insured against liability is not admissible upon the issue whether the person acted negligently or otherwise wrongfully. This rule does not require the exclusion of evidence of insurance against liability when offered for another purpose, such as proof of agency, ownership, or control, or bias or prejudice of a witness.

Rule 412. Sex offense cases; relevance of alleged victim's sexual behavior or sexual predisposition

(a) *Evidence generally inadmissible.* The following evidence is not admissible in any proceeding involving an alleged sexual offense except as provided in subdivisions (b) and (c):

(1) Evidence offered to prove that any alleged victim engaged in other sexual behavior.

(2) Evidence offered to prove any alleged victim's sexual predisposition.

(b) *Exceptions.*

(1) In a proceeding, the following evidence is admissible, if otherwise admissible under these rules:

(A) evidence of specific instances of sexual behavior by the alleged victim offered to prove that a person other than the accused was the source of semen, injury, or other physical evidence;

(B) evidence of specific instances of sexual behavior by the alleged victim with respect to the person accused of the sexual misconduct offered by the accused to prove consent or by the prosecution; and

(C) evidence the exclusion of which would violate the constitutional rights of the accused.

(c) *Procedure to determine admissibility.*

(1) A party intending to offer evidence under subsection (b) must—

(A) file a written motion at least 5 days prior to entry of pleas specifically describing the evidence and stating the purpose for which it is offered unless the military judge, for good cause shown, requires a different time for filing or permits filing during trial; and

(B) serve the motion on the opposing party and the military judge and notify the alleged victim or, when appropriate, the alleged victim's guardian or representative.

(2) Before admitting evidence under this rule, the military judge must conduct a hearing, which shall be closed. At this hearing, the parties may call witnesses, including the alleged victim, and offer relevant evidence. The alleged victim must be afforded a reasonable opportunity to attend and be heard. In a case before a court-martial composed of a military judge and members, the military judge shall conduct the hearing outside the presence of the members pursuant to Article 39(a). The motion, related papers, and the record of the hearing must be sealed and remain under seal unless the court orders otherwise.

(3) If the military judge determines on the basis of the hearing described in paragraph (2) of this subsection that the evidence that the accused seeks to offer is relevant for a purpose under subsection (b) and that the probative value of such evidence outweighs the danger of unfair prejudice to the alleged victim's privacy, such evidence shall be admissible under this rule to the extent an order made by the military judge specifies evidence that may be offered and areas with respect to which the alleged victim may be examined or cross-examined. Such evidence is still subject to challenge under Mil. R. Evid. 403.

(d) For purposes of this rule, the term "sexual offense" includes any sexual misconduct punishable under the Uniform Code of Military Justice, federal law or state law. "Sexual behavior" includes any sexual behavior not encompassed by the alleged offense. The term "sexual predisposition" refers to an alleged victim's mode of dress, speech, or lifestyle that does not directly refer to sexual activities or thoughts but that may have a sexual connotation for the factfinder.

(e) A "nonconsensual sexual offense" is a sexual offense in which consent by the victim is an affirmative defense or in which the lack of consent is an element of the offense. This term includes rape, forcible sodomy, assault with intent to commit rape or forcible sodomy, indecent assault, and attempts to commit such offenses.

Rule 413. Evidence of similar crimes in sexual assault cases

(a) In a court-martial in which the accused is charged with an offense of sexual assault, evidence of the accused's commission of one or more offenses of sexual assault is admissible and may be considered for its bearing on any matter to which it is relevant.

(b) In a court-martial in which the Government intends to offer evidence under this rule, the Government shall disclose the evidence to the accused, including statements of witnesses or a summary of the substance of any testimony that is expected to be offered, at least 5 days before the scheduled date of trial, or at such later time as the military judge may allow for good cause.

(c) This rule shall not be construed to limit the admission or consideration of evidence under any other rule.

(d) For purposes of this rule, "offenses of sexual assault" means an offense punishable under the Uniform Code of Military Justice, or a crime under Federal law or the law of a State that involved—

(1) any sexual act or sexual contact, without consent, proscribed by the Uniform Code of Military Justice, Federal law, or the law of a State;

(2) contact, without consent of the victim, between any part of the accused's body, or an object held or controlled by the accused, and the genitals or anus of another person;

(3) contact, without consent of the victim, between the genitals or anus of the accused and any part of another person's body;

(4) deriving sexual pleasure or gratification from the infliction of death, bodily injury, or physical pain on another person; or

(5) an attempt or conspiracy to engage in conduct described in paragraphs (1) through (4).

(e) For purposes of this rule, the term "sexual act" means:

(1) contact between the penis and the vulva or the penis and the anus, and for purposes of this rule, contact occurs upon penetration, however slight, of the penis into the vulva or anus;

(2) contact between the mouth and the penis, the mouth and the vulva, or the mouth and the anus;

(3) the penetration, however slight, of the anal or genital opening of another by a hand or finger or by any object, with an intent to abuse, humiliate, harass, degrade, or arouse or gratify the sexual desire of any person; or

(4) the intentional touching, not through the clothing, of the genitalia of another person who has not attained the age of 16 years, with an intent to abuse, humiliate, harass, degrade, or arouse or gratify the sexual desire of any person.

(f) For purposes of this rule, the term "sexual contact" means the intentional touching, either directly or through clothing, of the genitalia, anus, groin, breast, inner thigh, or buttocks of any person with an intent to abuse, humiliate, harass, degrade, or arouse or gratify the sexual desire of any person.

(g) For purposes of this rule, the term "State" includes a State of the United States, the District of Columbia, Puerto Rico, Guam, the Virgin Islands, and any other territory or possession of the United States.

Rule 414. Evidence of similar crimes in child molestation cases

(a) In a court-martial in which the accused is charged with an offense of child molestation, evidence of the accused's commission of one or more offenses of child molestation is admissible and may be considered for its bearing on any matter to which it is relevant.

(b) In a court-martial in which the Government intends to offer evidence under this rule, the Government shall disclose the evidence to the accused, including statements of witnesses or a summary of the substance of any testimony that is expected to be offered, at least 5 days before the scheduled date of trial or at such later time as the military judge may allow for good cause.

(c) This rule shall not be construed to limit the admission or consideration of evidence under any other rule.

(d) For purposes of this rule, "child" means a person below the age of sixteen, and "offense of child molestation" means an offense punishable under the Uniform Code of Military Justice, or a crime under Federal law or the law of a State that involved—

(1) any sexual act or sexual contact with a child proscribed by the Uniform Code of Military Justice, Federal law, or the law of a State;

(2) any sexually explicit conduct with children proscribed by the Uniform Code of Military Justice, Federal law, or the law of a State;

(3) contact between any part of the accused's body, or an object controlled or held by the accused, and the genitals or anus of a child;

(4) contact between the genitals or anus of the accused and any part of the body of a child;

(5) deriving sexual pleasure or gratification from the infliction of death, bodily injury, or physical pain on a child; or

(6) an attempt or conspiracy to engage in conduct described in paragraphs (1) through (5) of this subdivision.

(e) For purposes of this rule, the term "sexual act" means:

(1) contact between the penis and the vulva or the penis and the anus, and for purposes of this rule, contact occurs upon penetration, however slight, of the penis into the vulva or anus;

(2) contact between the mouth and the penis, the mouth and the vulva, or the mouth and the anus;

(3) the penetration, however slight, of the anal or genital opening of another by a hand or finger or by any object, with an intent to abuse, humiliate, harass, degrade, or arouse or gratify the sexual desire of any person; or

(4) the intentional touching, not through the clothing, of the genitalia of another person who has not attained the age of 16 years, with an intent to abuse, humiliate, harass, degrade, or arouse or gratify the sexual desire of any person.

(f) For purposes of this rule, the term "sexual contact" means the intentional touching, either directly or through clothing, of the genitalia, anus, groin, breast, inner thigh, or buttocks of any person with an intent to abuse, humiliate, harass, degrade, or arouse or gratify the sexual desire of any person.

(g) For purposes of this rule, the term "sexually explicit conduct" means actual or simulated:

(1) sexual intercourse, including genital-genital, oral-genital, anal-genital, or oral-anal, whether between person of the same or opposite sex;

(2) bestiality;

(3) masturbation;

(4) sadistic or masochistic abuse; or

(5) lascivious exhibition of the genitals or pubic area of any person.

(h) For purposes of this rule, the term "State" includes a State of the United States, the District of Columbia, Puerto Rico, Guam, the Virgin Islands, and any other territory or possession of the United States.

SECTION V

PRIVILEGES

Rule 501. General rule

(a) A person may not claim a privilege with respect to any matter except as required by or provided for in:

(1) The Constitution of the United States as applied to members of the armed forces;

(2) An Act of Congress applicable to trials by courts-martial;

(3) These rules or this Manual; or

(4) The principles of common law generally recognized in the trial of criminal cases in the United States district courts pursuant to rule 501 of the Federal Rules of Evidence insofar as the application of such principles in trials by courts-martial is practicable and not contrary to or inconsistent with the code, these rules, or this Manual.

(b) A claim of privilege includes, but is not limited to, the assertion by any person of a privilege to:

(1) Refuse to be a witness;

(2) Refuse to disclose any matter;

(3) Refuse to produce any object or writing; or

(4) Prevent another from being a witness or disclosing any matter or producing any object or writing.

(c) The term "person" includes an appropriate representative of the Federal Government, a State, or political subdivision thereof, or any other entity claiming to be the holder of a privilege.

(d) Notwithstanding any other provision of these rules, information not otherwise privileged does not become privileged on the basis that it was acquired by a medical officer or civilian physician in a professional capacity.

Rule 502. Lawyer-client privilege

(a) *General rule of privilege.* A client has a privilege to refuse to disclose and to prevent any other person from disclosing confidential communications made for the purpose of facilitating the rendition of professional legal services to the client, (1) between the client or the client's representative and the lawyer or the lawyer's representative, (2) between the lawyer and the lawyer's representative, (3) by the client or the client's lawyer to a lawyer representing another in a matter of common interest, (4) between representatives of the client or between the client and a representative of the client, or (5) between lawyers representing the client.

(b) *Definitions.* As used in this rule:

(1) A "client" is a person, public officer, corporation, association, organization, or other entity, either public or private, who receives professional legal services from a lawyer, or who consults a lawyer with a view to obtaining professional legal services from the lawyer.

(2) A "lawyer" is a person authorized, or reasonably believed by the client to be authorized, to practice law; or a member of the armed forces detailed, assigned, or otherwise provided to represent a per-

son in a court-martial case or in any military investigation or proceeding. The term "lawyer" does not include a member of the armed forces serving in a capacity other than as a judge advocate, legal officer, or law specialist as defined in Article 1, unless the member: (a) is detailed, assigned, or otherwise provided to represent a person in a court-martial case or in any military investigation or proceeding; (b) is authorized by the armed forces, or reasonably believed by the client to be authorized, to render professional legal services to members of the armed forces; or (c) is authorized to practice law and renders professional legal services during off-duty employment.

(3) A "representative" of a lawyer is a person employed by or assigned to assist a lawyer in providing professional legal services.

(4) A communication is "confidential" if not intended to be disclosed to third persons other than those to whom disclosure is in furtherance of the rendition of professional legal services to the client or those reasonably necessary for the transmission of the communication.

(c) *Who may claim the privilege.* The privilege may be claimed by the client, the guardian or conservator of the client, the personal representative of a deceased client, or the successor, trustee, or similar representative of a corporation, association, or other organization, whether or not in existence. The lawyer or the lawyer's representative who received the communication may claim the privilege on behalf of the client. The authority of the lawyer to do so is presumed in the absence of evidence to the contrary.

(d) *Exceptions.* There is no privilege under this rule under the following circumstances:

(1) *Crime or fraud.* If the communication clearly contemplated the future commission of a fraud or crime or if services of the lawyer were sought or obtained to enable or aid anyone to commit or plan to commit what the client knew or reasonably should have known to be a crime or fraud;

(2) *Claimants through same deceased client.* As to a communication relevant to an issue between parties who claim through the same deceased client, regardless of whether the claims are by testate or intestate succession or by inter vivos transaction;

(3) *Breach of duty by lawyer or client.* As to a communication relevant to an issue of breach of duty by the lawyer to the client or by the client to the lawyer;

(4) *Document attested by lawyer.* As to a communication relevant to an issue concerning an attested document to which the lawyer is an attesting witness; or

(5) *Joint clients.* As to a communication relevant to a matter of common interest between two or more clients if the communication was made by any of them to a lawyer retained or consulted in common, when offered in an action between any of the clients.

Rule 503. Communications to clergy

(a) *General rule of privilege.* A person has a privilege to refuse to disclose and to prevent another from disclosing a confidential communication by the person to a clergyman or to a clergyman's assistant, if such communication is made either as a formal act of religion or as a matter of conscience.

(b) *Definitions.* As used in this rule:

(1) A "clergyman" is a minister, priest, rabbi, chaplain, or other similar functionary of a religious organization, or an individual reasonably believed to be so by the person consulting the clergyman.

(2) A "clergyman's assistant" is a person employed by or assigned to assist a clergyman in his capacity as a spiritual advisor.

(3) A communication is "confidential" if made to a clergyman in the clergyman's capacity as a spiritual adviser or to a clergyman's assistant in the assistant's official capacity and is not intended to be disclosed to third persons other than those to whom disclosure is in furtherance of the purpose of the communication or to those reasonably necessary for the transmission of the communication.

(c) *Who may claim the privilege.* The privilege may be claimed by the person, by the guardian, or conservator, or by a personal representative if the person is deceased. The clergyman or clergyman's assistant who received the communication may claim the privilege on behalf of the person. The authority of the clergyman or clergyman's assistant to do so is presumed in the absence of evidence to the contrary.

Rule 504. Husband-wife privilege

(a) *Spousal incapacity.* A person has a privilege to refuse to testify against his or her spouse.

(b) *Confidential communication made during marriage.*

(1) *General rule of privilege.* A person has a privilege during and after the marital relationship to refuse to disclose, and to prevent another from disclosing, any confidential communication made to the spouse of the person while they were husband and wife and not separated as provided by law.

(2) *Definition.* A communication is "confidential" if made privately by any person to the spouse of the person and is not intended to be disclosed to third persons other than those reasonably necessary for transmission of the communication.

(3) *Who may claim the privilege.* The privilege may be claimed by the spouse who made the communication or by the other spouse on his or her behalf. The authority of the latter spouse to do so is presumed in the absence of evidence of a waiver. The privilege will not prevent disclosure of the communication at the request of the spouse to whom the communication was made if that spouse is an accused regardless of whether the spouse who made the communication objects to its disclosure.

(c) *Exceptions.*

(1) *Spousal incapacity only.* There is no privilege under subdivision (a) when, at the time the testimony of one of the parties to the marriage is to be introduced in evidence against the other party, the parties are divorced or the marriage has been annulled.

(2) *Spousal incapacity and confidential communications.* There is no privilege under subdivisions (a) or (b):

(A) In proceedings in which one spouse is charged with a crime against the person or property of the other spouse or a child of either, or with a crime against the person or property of a third person committed in the course of committing a crime against the other spouse;

(B) When the marital relationship was entered into with no intention of the parties to live together as spouses, but only for the purpose of using the purported marital relationship as a sham, and with respect to the privilege in subdivision (a), the relationship remains a sham at the time the testimony or statement of one of the parties is to be introduced against the other; or with respect to the privilege in subdivision (b), the relationship was a sham at the time of the communication; or

(C) In proceedings in which a spouse is charged, in accordance with Article 133 or 134, with importing the other spouse as an alien for prostitution or other immoral purpose in violation of 8 U.S.C. § 1328; with transporting the other spouse in interstate commerce for immoral purposes or other offense in violation of 18 U.S.C. §§ 2421–2424; or with violation of such other similar statutes under which such privilege may not be claimed in the trial of criminal cases in the United States district courts.

(d) *Definitions.* As used in this rule:

(1) The term "a child of either" includes not only a biological child, adopted child, or ward of one of the spouses but also includes a child who is under the permanent or temporary physical custody of one of the spouses, regardless of the existence of a legal parent-child relationship. For purposes of this rule only, a child is: (i) an individual under the age of 18; or (ii) an individual with a mental handicap who functions under the age of 18.

(2) The term "temporary physical custody" includes instances where a parent entrusts his or her child with another. There is no minimum amount of time necessary to establish temporary physical custody nor must there be a written agreement. Rather, the focus is on the parent's agreement with another for assuming parental responsibility for the child. For example, temporary physical custody may include instances where a parent entrusts another with the care of their child for recurring care or during absences due to temporary duty or deployments.

Rule 505. Classified information

(a) *General rule of privilege.* Classified information is privileged from disclosure if disclosure would be detrimental to the national security. As with other rules of privilege this rule applies to all stages of the proceedings.

(b) *Definitions.* As used in this rule:

(1) *Classified information.* "Classified information" means any information or material that has been determined by the United States Government pursuant to an executive order, statute, or regulations, to require protection against unauthorized dis-

closure for reasons of national security, and any restricted data, as defined in 42 U.S.C. § 2014(y).

(2) *National security.* "National security" means the national defense and foreign relations of the United States.

(c) *Who may claim the privilege.* The privilege may be claimed by the head of the executive or military department or government agency concerned based on a finding that the information is properly classified and that disclosure would be detrimental to the national security. A person who may claim the privilege may authorize a witness or trial counsel to claim the privilege on his or her behalf. The authority of the witness or trial counsel to do so is presumed in the absence of evidence to the contrary.

(d) *Action prior to referral of charges.* Prior to referral of charges, the convening authority shall respond in writing to a request by the accused for classified information if the privilege in this rule is claimed for such information. The convening authority may:

(1) Delete specified items of classified information from documents made available to the accused;

(2) Substitute a portion or summary of the information for such classified documents;

(3) Substitute a statement admitting relevant facts that the classified information would tend to prove;

(4) Provide the document subject to conditions that will guard against the compromise of the information disclosed to the accused; or

(5) Withhold disclosure if actions under (1) through (4) cannot be taken without causing identifiable damage to the national security.

Any objection by the accused to withholding of information or to the conditions of disclosure shall be raised through a motion for appropriate relief at a pretrial session.

(e) *Pretrial session.* At any time after referral of charges and prior to arraignment, any party may move for a session under Article 39(a) to consider matters relating to classified information that may arise in connection with the trial. Following such motion or *sua sponte*, the military judge promptly shall hold a session under Article 39(a) to establish the timing of requests for discovery, the provision of notice under subdivision (h), and the initiation of the procedure under subdivision (i). In addition, the military judge may consider any other matters that relate to classified information or that may promote a fair and expeditious trial.

(f) *Action after referral of charges.* If a claim of privilege has been made under this rule with respect to classified information that apparently contains evidence that is relevant and necessary to an element of the offense or a legally cognizable defense and is otherwise admissible in evidence in the court-martial proceeding, the matter shall be reported to the convening authority. The convening authority may:

(1) institute action to obtain the classified information for the use by the military judge in making a determination under subdivision (i);

(2) dismiss the charges;

(3) dismiss the charges or specifications or both to which the information relates; or

(4) take such other action as may be required in the interests of justice.

If, after a reasonable period of time, the information is not provided to the military judge in circumstances where proceeding with the case without such information would materially prejudice a substantial right of the accused, the military judge shall dismiss the charges or specifications or both to which the classified information relates.

(g) *Disclosure of classified information to the accused.*

(1) *Protective order.* If the Government agrees to disclose classified information to the accused, the military judge, at the request of the Government, shall enter an appropriate protective order to guard against the compromise of the information disclosed to the accused. The terms of any such protective order may include provisions:

(A) Prohibiting the disclosure of the information except as authorized by the military judge;

(B) Requiring storage of material in a manner appropriate for the level of classification assigned to the documents to be disclosed;

(C) Requiring controlled access to the material during normal business hours and at other times upon reasonable notice;

(D) All persons requiring security clearances shall cooperate with investigatory personnel in any investigations which are necessary to obtain a security clearance.

(E) Requiring the maintenance of logs regarding access by all persons authorized by the military judge to have access to the classified information in connection with the preparation of the defense;

(F) Regulating the making and handling of notes taken from material containing classified information; or

(G) Requesting the convening authority to authorize the assignment of government security personnel and the provision of government storage facilities.

(2) *Limited disclosure.* The military judge, upon motion of the Government, shall authorize (A) the deletion of specified items of classified information from documents to be made available to the defendant, (B) the substitution of a portion or summary of the information for such classified documents, or (C) the substitution of a statement admitting relevant facts that the classified information would tend to prove, unless the military judge determines that disclosure of the classified information itself is necessary to enable the accused to prepare for trial. The Government's motion and any materials submitted in support thereof shall, upon request of the Government, be considered by the military judge *in camera* and shall not be disclosed to the accused.

(3) *Disclosure at trial of certain statements previously made by a witness.*

(A) *Scope.* After a witness called by the Government has testified on direct examination, the military judge, on motion of the accused, may order production of statements in the possession of the United States under R.C.M. 914. This provision does not preclude discovery or assertion of a privilege otherwise authorized under these rules or this Manual.

(B) *Closed session.* If the privilege in this rule is invoked during consideration of a motion under R.C.M. 914, the Government may deliver such statement for the inspection only by the military judge *in camera* and may provide the military judge with an affidavit identifying the portions of the statement that are classified and the basis for the classification assigned. If the military judge finds that disclosure of any portion of the statement identified by the Government as classified could reasonably be expected to cause damage to the national security in the degree required to warrant classification under the applicable executive order, statute, or regulation and that such portion of the statement is consistent with the witness' testimony, the military judge shall excise the portion from the statement. With such material excised, the military judge shall then direct delivery of such statement to the accused for use by the accused. If the military judge finds that such portion of the statement is inconsistent with the witness' testimony, the Government may move for a proceeding under subdivision (i).

(4) *Record of trial.* If, under this subdivision, any information is withheld from the accused, the accused objects to such withholding, and the trial is continued to an adjudication of guilt of the accused, the entire unaltered text of the relevant documents as well as the Government's motion and any materials submitted in support thereof shall be sealed and attached to the record of trial as an appellate exhibit. Such material shall be made available to reviewing authorities in closed proceedings for the purpose of reviewing the determination of the military judge.

(h) *Notice of the accused's intention to disclose classified information.*

(1) *Notice by the accused.* If the accused reasonably expects to disclose or to cause the disclosure of classified information in any manner in connection with a court-martial proceeding, the accused shall notify the trial counsel in writing of such intention and file a copy of such notice with the military judge. Such notice shall be given within the time specified by the military judge under subdivision (e) or, if no time has been specified, prior to arraignment of the accused.

(2) *Continuing duty to notify.* Whenever the accused learns of classified information not covered by a notice under (1) that the accused reasonably expects to disclose at any such proceeding, the accused shall notify the trial counsel and the military judge in writing as soon as possible thereafter.

(3) *Content of notice.* The notice required by this subdivision shall include a brief description of the classified information. The description, to be sufficient, must be more than a mere general statement of the areas about which evidence may be introduced. The accused must state, with particularity, which items of classified information he reasonably expects will be revealed by his defense.

(4) *Prohibition against disclosure.* The accused may not disclose any information known or believed to be classified until notice has been given under this subdivision and until the Government has been

afforded a reasonable opportunity to seek a determination under subdivision (i).

(5) *Failure to comply.* If the accused fails to comply with the requirements of this subdivision, the military judge may preclude disclosure of any classified information not made the subject of notification and may prohibit the examination by the accused of any witness with respect to any such information.

(i) *In camera proceedings for cases involving classified information.*

(1) *Definition.* For purposes of this subdivision, an "*in camera proceeding*" is a session under Article 39(a) from which the public is excluded.

(2) *Motion for in camera proceeding.* Within the time specified by the military judge for the filing of a motion under this rule, the Government may move for an *in camera* proceeding concerning the use at any proceeding of any classified information. Thereafter, either prior to or during trial, the military judge for good cause shown or otherwise upon a claim of privilege under this rule may grant the Government leave to move for an *in camera* proceeding concerning the use of additional classified information.

(3) *Demonstration of national security nature of the information.* In order to obtain an *in camera* proceeding under this rule, the Government shall submit the classified information and an affidavit *ex parte* for examination by the military judge only. The affidavit shall demonstrate that disclosure of the information reasonably could be expected to cause damage to the national security in the degree required to warrant classification under the applicable executive order, statute, or regulation.

(4) *In camera proceeding.*

(A) *Procedure.* Upon finding that the Government has met the standard set forth in subdivision (i)(3) with respect to some or all of the classified information at issue, the military judge shall conduct an *in camera* proceeding. Prior to the *in camera* proceeding, the Government shall provide the accused with notice of the information that will be at issue. This notice shall identify the classified information that will be at issue whenever that information previously has been made available to the accused in connection with proceedings in the same case. The Government may describe the information by generic category, in such form as the military judge may approve, rather than identifying the classified information when the Government has not previously made the information available to the accused in connection with pretrial proceedings. Following briefing and argument by the parties in the *in camera* proceeding the military judge shall determine whether the information may be disclosed at the court-martial proceeding. Where the Government's motion under this subdivision is filed prior to the proceeding at which disclosure is sought, the military judge shall rule prior to the commencement of the relevant proceeding.

(B) *Standard.* Classified information is not subject to disclosure under this subdivision unless the information is relevant and necessary to an element of the offense or a legally cognizable defense and is otherwise admissible in evidence. In presentencing proceedings, relevant and material classified information pertaining to the appropriateness of, or the appropriate degree of, punishment shall be admitted only if no unclassified version of such information is available.

(C) *Ruling.* Unless the military judge makes a written determination that the information meets the standard set forth in (B), the information may not be disclosed or otherwise elicited at a court-martial proceeding. The record of the *in camera* proceeding shall be sealed and attached to the record of trial as an appellate exhibit. The accused may seek reconsideration of the determination prior to or during trial.

(D) *Alternatives to full disclosure.* If the military judge makes a determination under this subdivision that would permit disclosure of the information or if the Government elects not to contest the relevance, necessity, and admissibility of any classified information, the Government may proffer a statement admitting for purposes of the proceeding any relevant facts such information would tend to prove or may submit a portion of summary to be used in lieu of the information. The military judge shall order that such statement, portion, or summary by used by the accused in place of the classified information unless the military judge finds that use of the classified information itself is necessary to afford the accused a fair trial.

(E) *Sanctions.* If the military judge determines that alternatives to full disclosure may not be used and the Government continues to object to disclosure of the information, the military judge shall issue any order that the interests of justice require. Such an order may include an order:

(i) striking or precluding all or part of the testimony of a witness;

(ii) declaring a mistrial;

(iii) finding against the Government on any issue as to which the evidence is relevant and material to the defense;

(iv) dismissing the charges, with or without prejudice; or

(v) dismissing the charges or specifications or both to which the information relates.

Any such order shall permit the Government to avoid the sanction for nondisclosure by permitting the accused to disclose the information at the pertinent court-martial proceeding.

(j) *Introduction of classified information.*

(1) *Classification status.* Writings, recordings, and photographs containing classified information may be admitted into evidence without change in their classification status.

(2) *Precautions by the military judge.* In order to prevent unnecessary disclosure of classified information, the military judge may order admission into evidence of only part of a writing, recording, or photograph or may order admission into evidence of the whole writing, recording, or photograph with excision of some or all of the classified information contained therein.

(3) *Contents of writing, recording, or photograph.* The military judge may permit proof of the contents of a writing, recording, or photograph that contains classified information without requiring introduction into evidence of the original or a duplicate.

(4) *Taking of testimony.* During the examination of a witness, the Government may object to any question or line of inquiry that may require the witness to disclose classified information not previously found to be relevant and necessary to the defense. Following such an objection, the military judge shall take such suitable action to determine whether the response is admissible as will safeguard against the compromise of any classified information. Such action may include requiring the Government to provide the military judge with a proffer or the witness' response to the question or line of inquiry and requiring the accused to provide the military judge with a proffer of the nature of the information the accused seeks to elicit.

(5) *Closed session.* The military judge may exclude the public during that portion of the presentation of evidence that discloses classified information.

(6) *Record of trial.* The record of trial with respect to any classified matter will be prepared under R.C.M. 1103(h) and 1104(b)(1)(D).

(k) *Security procedures to safeguard against compromise of classified information disclosed to courts-martial.* The Secretary of Defense may prescribe security procedures for protection against the compromise of classified information submitted to courts-martial and appellate authorities.

Rule 506. Government information other than classified information

(a) *General rule of privilege.* Except where disclosure is required by an Act of Congress, government information is privileged from disclosure if disclosure would be detrimental to the public interest.

(b) *Scope.* "Government information" includes official communication and documents and other information within the custody or control of the Federal Government. This rule does not apply to classified information (Mil. R. Evid. 505) or to the identity of an informant (Mil. R. Evid. 507).

(c) *Who may claim the privilege.* The privilege may be claimed by the head of the executive or military department or government agency concerned. The privilege for records and information of the Inspector General may be claimed by the immediate superior of the inspector general officer responsible for creation of the records or information, the Inspector General, or any other superior authority. A person who may claim the privilege may authorize a witness or the trial counsel to claim the privilege on his or her behalf. The authority of a witness or the trial counsel to do so is presumed in the absence of evidence to the contrary.

(d) *Action prior to referral of charges.* Prior to referral of charges, the Government shall respond in writing to a request for government information if the privilege in this rule is claimed for such information. The Government shall:

(1) delete specified items of government information claimed to be privileged from documents made available to the accused;

(2) substitute a portion or summary of the information for such documents;

(3) substitute a statement admitting relevant facts that the government information would tend to prove;

(4) provide the document subject to conditions similar to those set forth in subdivision (g) of this rule; or

(5) withhold disclosure if actions under (1) through (4) cannot be taken without causing identifiable damage to the public interest.

(e) *Pretrial session.* At any time after referral of charges and prior to arraignment, any party may move for a session under Article 39(a) to consider matters relating to government information that may arise in connection with the trial. Following such motion, or *sua sponte*, the military judge promptly shall hold a pretrial session under Article 39(a) to establish the timing of requests for discovery, the provision of notice under subdivision (h), and the initiation of the procedure under subdivision (i). In addition, the military judge may consider any other matters that relate to government information or that may promote a fair and expeditious trial.

(f) *Action after motion for disclosure of information.* After referral of charges, if the defense moves for disclosure of government information for which a claim of privilege has been made under this rule, the matter shall be reported to the convening authority. The convening authority may:

(1) institute action to obtain the information for use by the military judge in making a determination under subdivision (i);

(2) dismiss the charges;

(3) dismiss the charges or specifications or both to which the information relates; or

(4) take other action as may be required in the interests of justice.

If, after a reasonable period of time, the information is not provided to the military judge, the military judge shall dismiss the charges or specifications or both to which the information relates.

(g) *Disclosure of government information to the accused.* If the Government agrees to disclose government information to the accused subsequent to a claim of privilege under this rule, the military judge, at the request of the Government, shall enter an appropriate protective order to guard against the compromise of the information disclosed to the accused. The terms of any such protective order may include provisions:

(1) Prohibiting the disclosure of the information except as authorized by the military judge;

(2) Requiring storage of the material in a manner appropriate for the nature of the material to be disclosed; upon reasonable notice;

(3) Requiring controlled access to the material during normal business hours and at other times upon reasonable notice;

(4) Requiring the maintenance of logs recording access by persons authorized by the military judge to have access to the government information in connection with the preparation of the defense;

(5) Regulating the making and handling of notes taken from material containing government information; or

(6) Requesting the convening authority to authorize the assignment of government security personnel and the provision of government storage facilities.

(h) *Prohibition against disclosure.* The accused may not disclose any information known or believed to be subject to a claim of privilege under this rule unless the military judge authorizes such disclosure.

(i) *In camera proceedings.*

(1) *Definition.* For the purpose of this subdivision, an "*in camera proceeding*" is a session under Article 39(a) from which the public is excluded.

(2) *Motion for in camera proceeding.* Within the time specified by the military judge for the filing of a motion under this rule, the Government may move for an *in camera* proceeding concerning the use at any proceeding of any government information that may be subject to a claim of privilege. Thereafter, either prior to or during trial, the military judge for good cause shown or otherwise upon a claim of privilege may grant the Government leave to move for an *in camera* proceeding concerning the use of additional government information.

(3) *Demonstration of public interest nature of the information.* In order to obtain an *in camera* proceeding under this rule, the Government shall demonstrate, through the submission of affidavits and information for examination only by the military judge, that disclosure of the information reasonably could be expected to cause identifiable damage to the public interest.

(4) *In camera proceeding.*

(A) *Finding of identifiable damage.* Upon finding that the disclosure of some or all of the information submitted by the Government under subsection (i)(3) reasonably could be expected to cause identifiable damage to the public interest, the military judge shall conduct an *in camera* proceeding.

(B) *Disclosure of the information to the defense.* Subject to subdivision (F), below, the Government shall disclose government information for which a claim of privilege has been made to the accused, for the limited purpose of litigating, *in camera*, the admissibility of the information at trial. The military judge shall enter an appropriate protective order to the accused and all other appropriate trial participants concerning the disclosure of the information according to subsection (g), above. The accused shall not disclose any information provided under this subsection unless, and until, such information has been admitted into evidence by the military judge. In the *in camera* proceeding, both parties shall have the opportunity to brief and argue the admissibility of the government information at trial.

(C) *Standard.* Government information is subject to disclosure at the court-martial proceeding under this subsection if the party making the request demonstrates a specific need for information containing evidence that is relevant to the guilt or innocence or to punishment of the accused, and is otherwise admissible in the court-martial proceeding.

(D) *Ruling.* No information may be disclosed at the court-martial proceeding or otherwise unless the military judge makes a written determination that the information is subject to disclosure under the standard set forth in subsection (C), above. The military judge will specify in writing any information that he or she determines is subject to disclosure. The record of the *in camera* proceeding shall be sealed and attached to the record of trial as an appellate exhibit. The accused may seek reconsideration of the determination prior to or during trial.

(E) *Alternatives to full disclosure.* If the military judge makes a determination under this subsection that the information is subject to disclosure, or if the Government elects not to contest the relevance, necessity, and admissibility of the government information, the Government may proffer a statement admitting for purposes of the court-martial any relevant facts such information would tend to prove or may submit a portion or summary to be used in lieu of the information. The military judge shall order that such statement, portion, summary, or some other form of information which the military judge finds to be consistent with the interests of justice, be used by the accused in place of the government information, unless the military judge finds that use of the government information itself is necessary to afford the accused a fair trial.

(F) *Sanctions.* Government information may not be disclosed over the Government's objection. If the Government continues to object to disclosure of the information following rulings by the military judge, the military judge shall issue any order that the interests of justice require. Such an order may include:

(i) striking or precluding all or part of the testimony of a witness;

(ii) declaring a mistrial;

(iii) finding against the Government on any issue as to which the evidence is relevant and necessary to the defense;

(iv) dismissing the charges, with or without prejudice; or

(v) dismissing the charges or specifications or both to which the information relates.

(j) *Appeals of orders and rulings.* In a court-martial in which a punitive discharge may be adjudged, the Government may appeal an order or ruling of the military judge that terminates the proceedings with respect to a charge or specification, directs the disclosure of government information, or imposes sanctions for nondisclosure of government information. The government may also appeal an order or ruling in which the military judge refuses to issue a protective order sought by the United States to prevent the disclosure of government information, or to enforce such an order previously issued by appropriate authority. The Government may not appeal an order or ruling that is, or amounts to, a finding of not guilty with respect to the charge or specification.

(k) *Introduction of government information subject to a claim of privilege.*

(1) *Precautions by military judge.* In order to prevent unnecessary disclosure of government information after there has been a claim of privilege under this rule, the military judge may order admission into evidence of only part of a writing, recording, or photograph or may order admission into evidence of the whole writing, recording, or photograph with

excision of some or all of the government information contained therein.

(2) *Contents of writing, recording, or photograph.* The military judge may permit proof of the contents of a writing, recording, or photograph that contains government information that is the subject of a claim of privilege under this rule without requiring introduction into evidence of the original or a duplicate.

(3) *Taking of testimony.* During examination of a witness, the prosecution may object to any question or line of inquiry that may require the witness to disclose government information not previously found relevant and necessary to the defense if such information has been or is reasonably likely to be the subject of a claim of privilege under this rule. Following such an objection, the military judge shall take such suitable action to determine whether the response is admissible as will safeguard against the compromise of any government information. Such action may include requiring the Government to provide the military judge with a proffer of the witness' response to the question or line of inquiry and requiring the accused to provide the military judge with a proffer of the nature of the information the accused seeks to elicit.

(l) *Procedures to safeguard against compromise of government information disclosed to courts-martial.* The Secretary of Defense may prescribe procedures for protection against the compromise of government information submitted to courts-martial and appellate authorities after a claim of privilege.

Rule 507. Identity of informant

(a) *Rule of privilege.* The United States or a State or subdivision thereof has a privilege to refuse to disclose the identity of an informant. An "informant" is a person who has furnished information relating to or assisting in an investigation of a possible violation of law to a person whose official duties include the discovery, investigation, or prosecution of crime. Unless otherwise privileged under these rules, the communications of an informant are not privileged except to the extent necessary to prevent the disclosure of the informant's identity.

(b) *Who may claim the privilege.* The privilege may be claimed by an appropriate representative of the United States, regardless of whether information was furnished to an officer of the United States or a State or subdivision thereof. The privilege may be claimed by an appropriate representative of a State or subdivision if the information was furnished to an officer thereof, except the privilege shall not be allowed if the prosecution objects.

(c) *Exceptions.*

(1) *Voluntary disclosures; informant as witness.* No privilege exists under this rule: (A) if the identity of the informant has been disclosed to those who would have cause to resent the communication by a holder of the privilege or by the informant's own action; or (B) if the informant appears as a witness for the prosecution.

(2) *Testimony on the issue of guilt or innocence.* If a claim of privilege has been made under this rule, the military judge shall, upon motion by the accused, determine whether disclosure of the identity of the informant is necessary to the accused's defense on the issue of guilt or innocence. Whether such a necessity exists will depend on the particular circumstances of each case, taking into consideration the offense charged, the possible defense, the possible significance of the informant's testimony, and other relevant factors. If it appears from the evidence in the case or from other showing by a party that an informant may be able to give testimony necessary to the accused's defense on the issue of guilt or innocence, the military judge may make any order required by the interests of justice.

(3) *Legality of obtaining evidence.* If a claim of privilege has been made under this rule with respect to a motion under Mil. R. Evid. 311, the military judge shall, upon motion of the accused, determine whether disclosure of the identity of the informant is required by the Constitution of the United States as applied to members of the armed forces. In making this determination, the military judge may make any order required by the interests of justice.

(d) *Procedures.* If a claim of privilege has been made under this rule, the military judge may make any order required by the interests of justice. If the military judge determines that disclosure of the identity of the informant is required under the standards set forth in this rule, and the prosecution elects not to disclose the identity of the informant, the matter shall be reported to the convening authority. The convening authority may institute action to secure disclosure of the identity of the informant, terminate the proceedings, or take such other action as may be appropriate under the circumstances. If, after a reasonable period of time disclosure is not made, the military judge, *sua sponte* or upon motion of either counsel and after a hearing if requested by either party, may dismiss the charge or specifications or both to which the information regarding the informant would relate if the military judge determines that further proceedings would materially prejudice a substantial right of the accused.

Rule 508. Political vote

A person has a privilege to refuse to disclose the tenor of the person's vote at a political election conducted by secret ballot unless the vote was cast illegally.

Rule 509. Deliberations of courts and juries

Except as provided in Mil. R. Evid. 606, the deliberations of courts and grand and petit juries are privileged to the extent that such matters are privileged in trial of criminal cases in the United States district courts, but the results of the deliberations are not privileged.

Rule 510. Waiver of privilege by voluntary disclosure

(a) A person upon whom these rules confer a privilege against disclosure of a confidential matter or communication waives the privilege if the person or the person's predecessor while holder of the privilege voluntarily discloses or consents to disclosure of any significant part of the matter or communication under such circumstances that it would be inappropriate to allow the claim of privilege. This rule does not apply if the disclosure is itself a privileged communication.

(b) Unless testifying voluntarily concerning a privileged matter or communication, an accused who testifies in his or her own behalf or a person who testifies under a grant or promise of immunity does not, merely by reason of testifying, waive a privilege to which he or she may be entitled pertaining to the confidential matter or communication.

Rule 511. Privileged matter disclosed under compulsion or without opportunity to claim privilege

(a) Evidence of a statement or other disclosure of privileged matter is not admissible against the holder of the privilege if disclosure was compelled erroneously or was made without an opportunity for the holder of the privilege to claim the privilege.

(b) The telephonic transmission of information otherwise privileged under these rules does not affect its privileged character. Use of electronic means of communication other than the telephone for transmission of information otherwise privileged under these rules does not affect the privileged character of such information if use of such means of communication is necessary and in furtherance of the communication.

Rule 512. Comment upon or inference from claim of privilege; instruction

(a) *Comment or inference not permitted.*

(1) The claim of a privilege by the accused whether in the present proceeding or upon a prior occasion is not a proper subject of comment by the military judge or counsel for any party. No inference may be drawn therefrom.

(2) The claim of a privilege by a person other than the accused whether in the present proceeding or upon a prior occasion normally is not a proper subject of comment by the military judge or counsel for any party. An adverse inference may not be drawn therefrom except when determined by the military judge to be required by the interests of justice.

(b) *Claiming privilege without knowledge of members.* In a trial before a court-martial with members, proceedings shall be conducted, to the extent practicable, so as to facilitate the making of claims of privilege without the knowledge of the members. This subdivision does not apply to a special court-martial without a military judge.

(c) *Instruction.* Upon request, any party against whom the members might draw an adverse inference from a claim of privilege is entitled to an instruction that no inference may be drawn therefrom except as provided in subdivision (a)(2).

Rule 513. Psychotherapist-patient privilege

(a) *General rule of privilege.* A patient has a privilege to refuse to disclose and to prevent any other person from disclosing a confidential communication made between the patient and a psychotherapist or an assistant to the psychotherapist, in a case arising under the UCMJ, if such communication was made for the purpose of facilitating diagnosis or treatment of the patient's mental or emotional condition.

(b) *Definitions.* As used in this rule of evidence:

(1) A "patient" is a person who consults with or is examined or interviewed by a psychotherapist for purposes of advice, diagnosis, or treatment of a mental or emotional condition.

(2) A "psychotherapist" is a psychiatrist, clinical psychologist, or clinical social worker who is licensed in any state, territory, possession, the District of Columbia or Puerto Rico to perform professional services as such, or who holds credentials to provide such services from any military health care facility, or is a person reasonably believed by the patient to have such license or credentials.

(3) An "assistant to a psychotherapist" is a person directed by or assigned to assist a psychotherapist in providing professional services, or is reasonably believed by the patient to be such.

(4) A communication is "confidential" if not intended to be disclosed to third persons other than those to whom disclosure is in furtherance of the rendition of professional services to the patient or those reasonably necessary for such transmission of the communication.

(5) "Evidence of a patient's records or communications" is testimony of a psychotherapist, or assistant to the same, or patient records that pertain to communications by a patient to a psychotherapist, or assistant to the same for the purposes of diagnosis or treatment of the patient's mental or emotional condition.

(c) *Who may claim the privilege.* The privilege may be claimed by the patient or the guardian or conservator of the patient. A person who may claim the privilege may authorize trial counsel or defense counsel to claim the privilege on his or her behalf. The psychotherapist or assistant to the psychotherapist who received the communication may claim the privilege on behalf of the patient. The authority of such a psychotherapist, assistant, guardian, or conservator to so assert the privilege is presumed in the absence of evidence to the contrary.

(d) *Exceptions.* There is no privilege under this rule:

(1) when the patient is dead;

(2) when the communication is evidence of spouse abuse, child abuse, or neglect or in a proceeding in which one spouse is charged with a crime against the person of the other spouse or a child of either spouse;

(3) when federal law, state law, or service regulation imposes a duty to report information contained in a communication;

(4) when a psychotherapist or assistant to a psychotherapist believes that a patient's mental or emotional condition makes the patient a danger to any person, including the patient;

(5) if the communication clearly contemplated the future commission of a fraud or crime or if the services of the psychotherapist are sought or obtained to enable or aid anyone to commit or plan to commit what the patient knew or reasonably should have known to be a crime or fraud;

(6) when necessary to ensure the safety and security of military personnel, military dependents, military property, classified information, or the accomplishment of a military mission;

(7) when an accused offers statements or other evidence concerning his mental condition in defense, extenuation, or mitigation, under circumstances not covered by R.C.M. 706 or Mil. R. Evid. 302. In such situations, the military judge may, upon motion, order disclosure of any statement made by the accused to a psychotherapist as may be necessary in the interests of justice; or

(8) when admission or disclosure of a communication is constitutionally required.

(e) *Procedure to determine admissibility of patient records or communications.*

(1) In any case in which the production or admission of records or communications of a patient other than the accused is a matter in dispute, a party may seek an interlocutory ruling by the military judge. In order to obtain such a ruling, the party shall:

(A) file a written motion at least 5 days prior to entry of pleas specifically describing the evidence and stating the purpose for which it is sought or offered, or objected to, unless the military judge, for good cause shown, requires a different time for filing or permits filing during trial; and

(B) serve the motion on the opposing party, the military judge and, if practical, notify the patient or the patient's guardian, conservator, or representative that the motion has been filed and that the patient has an opportunity to be heard as set forth in subparagraph (e)(2).

(2) Before ordering the production or admission

of evidence of a patient's records or communication, the military judge shall conduct a hearing. Upon the motion of counsel for either party and upon good cause shown, the military judge may order the hearing closed. At the hearing, the parties may call witnesses, including the patient, and offer other relevant evidence. The patient shall be afforded a reasonable opportunity to attend the hearing and be heard at the patient's own expense unless the patient has been otherwise subpoenaed or ordered to appear at the hearing. However, the proceedings shall not be unduly delayed for this purpose. In a case before a court-martial composed of a military judge and members, the military judge shall conduct the hearing outside the presence of the members.

(3) The military judge shall examine the evidence or a proffer thereof *in camera*, if such examination is necessary to rule on the motion.

(4) To prevent unnecessary disclosure of evidence of a patient's records or communications, the military judge may issue protective orders or may admit only portions of the evidence.

(5) The motion, related papers, and the record of the hearing shall be sealed and shall remain under seal unless the military judge or an appellate court orders otherwise.

SECTION VI

WITNESSES

Rule 601. General rule of competency

Every person is competent to be a witness except as otherwise provided in these rules.

Rule 602. Lack of personal knowledge

A witness may not testify to a matter unless evidence is introduced sufficient to support a finding that the witness has personal knowledge of the matter. Evidence to prove personal knowledge may, but need not, consist of the testimony of the witness. This rule is subject to the provisions of Mil. R. Evid. 703, relating to opinion testimony by expert witnesses.

Rule 603. Oath or affirmation

Before testifying, every witness shall be required to declare that the witness will testify truthfully, by oath or affirmation administered in a form calculated to awaken the witness's conscience and impress the witness's mind with the duty to do so.

Rule 604. Interpreters

An interpreter is subject to the provisions of these rules relating to qualifications as an expert and the administration of an oath or affirmation that the interpreter will make a true translation.

Rule 605. Competency of military judge as witness

(a) The military judge presiding at the court-martial may not testify in that court-martial as a witness. No objection need be made to preserve the point.

(b) This rule does not preclude the military judge from placing on the record matters concerning docketing of the case.

Rule 606. Competency of court member as witness

(a) *At the court-martial.* A member of the court-martial may not testify as a witness before the other members in the trial of the case in which the member is sitting. If the member is called to testify, the opposing party, except in a special court-martial without a military judge, shall be afforded an opportunity to object out of the presence of the members.

(b) *Inquiry into validity of findings or sentence.* Upon an inquiry into the validity of the findings or sentence, a member may not testify as to any matter or statement occurring during the course of the deliberations of the members of the court-martial or, to the effect of anything upon the member's or any other member's mind or emotions as influencing the member to assent to or dissent from the findings or sentence or concerning the member's mental process in connection therewith, except that a member may testify on the question whether extraneous prejudicial information was improperly brought to the attention of the members of the court-martial, whether any outside influence was improperly brought to bear upon any member, or whether there was unlawful command influence. Nor may the member's affidavit or evidence of any statement by the member concerning a matter about which the member would be precluded from testifying be received for these purposes.

Rule 607. Who may impeach

The credibility of a witness may be attacked by any party, including the party calling the witness.

Rule 608. Evidence of character, conduct, and bias of witness

(a) *Opinion and reputation evidence of character.* The credibility of a witness may be attacked or supported by evidence in the form of opinion or reputation, but subject to these limitations: (1) the evidence may refer only to character for truthfulness or untruthfulness, and (2) evidence of truthful character is admissible only after the character of the witness for truthfulness has been attacked by opinion or reputation evidence or otherwise.

(b) *Specific instances of conduct.* Specific instances of the conduct of a witness, for the purpose of attacking or supporting the witness' character for truthfulness, other than conviction of crime as provided in Mil. R. Evid. 609, may not be proved by extrinsic evidence. They may, however, in the discretion of the military judge, if probative of truthfulness or untruthfulness, be inquired into on cross-examination of the witness (1) concerning character of the witness for truthfulness or untruthfulness, or (2) concerning the character for truthfulness or untruthfulness of another witness as to which character the witness being cross-examined has testified. The giving of testimony, whether by an accused or by another witness, does not operate as a waiver of the privilege against self-incrimination when examined with respect to matters that relate only to character for truthfulness.

(c) *Evidence of bias.* Bias, prejudice, or any motive to misrepresent may be shown to impeach the witness either by examination of the witness or by evidence otherwise adduced.

Rule 609. Impeachment by evidence of conviction of crime

(a) *General rule.* For the purpose of attacking the credibility of a witness, (1) evidence that a witness other than the accused has been convicted of a crime shall be admitted, subject to Mil. R. Evid. 403, if the crime was punishable by death, dishonorable discharge, or imprisonment in excess of one year under the law under which the witness was convicted, and evidence that an accused has been convicted of such a crime shall be admitted if the military judge determines that the probative value of admitting this evidence outweighs its prejudicial effect to the accused; and (2) evidence that any witness has been convicted of a crime shall be admitted if it involved dishonesty or false statement, regardless of the punishment. In determining whether a crime tried by court-martial was punishable by death, dishonorable discharge, or imprisonment in excess of one year, the maximum punishment prescribed by the President under Article 56 at the time of the conviction applies without regard to whether the case was tried by general, special, or summary court-martial.

(b) *Time limit.* Evidence of a conviction under this rule is not admissible if a period of more than ten years has elapsed since the date of the conviction or of the release of the witness from the confinement imposed for that conviction, whichever is the later date, unless the court determines, in the interests of justice, that the probative value of the conviction supported by specific facts and circumstances substantially outweighs its prejudicial effect. However, evidence of a conviction more than ten years old as calculated herein, is not admissible unless the proponent gives to the adverse party sufficient advance written notice of intent to use such evidence to provide the adverse party with a fair opportunity to contest the use of such evidence.

(c) *Effect of pardon, annulment, or certificate of rehabilitation.* Evidence of a conviction is not admissible under this rule if (1) the conviction has been the subject of a pardon, annulment, certificate of rehabilitation, or other equivalent procedure based on a finding of the rehabilitation of the person convicted, and that person has not been convicted of a subsequent crime which was punishable by death, dishonorable discharge, or imprisonment in excess of one year, or (2) the conviction has been the subject of a pardon, annulment, or other equivalent procedure based on a finding of innocence.

(d) *Juvenile adjudications.* Evidence of juvenile adjudications is generally not admissible under this rule. The military judge, however, may allow evidence of a juvenile adjudication of a witness other than the accused if conviction of the offense would be admissible to attack the credibility of an adult and the military judge is satisfied that admission in evidence is necessary for a fair determination of the issue of guilt or innocence.

(e) *Pendency of appeal.* The pendency of an appeal therefrom does not render evidence of a conviction inadmissible except that a conviction by summary court-martial or special court-martial without a military judge may not be used for purposes of impeachment until review has been completed pursuant to Article 64 or Article 66 if applicable. Evidence of the pendency of an appeal is admissible.

(f) *Definition.* For purposes of this rule, there is a "conviction" in a court-martial case when a sentence has been adjudged.

Rule 610. Religious beliefs or opinions

Evidence of the beliefs or opinions of a witness on matters of religion is not admissible for the purpose of showing that by reason of their nature the credibility of the witness is impaired or enhanced.

Rule 611. Mode and order of interrogation and presentation

(a) *Control by the military judge.* The military judge shall exercise reasonable control over the mode and order of interrogating witnesses and presenting evidence so as to (1) make the interrogation and presentation effective for the ascertainment of the truth, (2) avoid needless consumption of time, and (3) protect witnesses from harassment or undue embarrassment.

(b) *Scope of cross-examination.* Cross-examination should be limited to the subject matter of the direct examination and matters affecting the credibility of the witness. The military judge may, in the exercise of discretion, permit inquiry into additional matters as if on direct examination.

(c) *Leading questions.* Leading questions should not be used on the direct examination of a witness except as may be necessary to develop the testimony of the witness. Ordinarily leading questions should be permitted on cross-examination. When a party calls a hostile witness or a witness identified with an adverse party, interrogation may be by leading questions.

(d) *Remote live testimony of a child.*

(1) In a case involving abuse of a child or domestic violence, the military judge shall, subject to the requirements of subsection (3) of this rule, allow a child victim or witness to testify from an area outside the courtroom as prescribed in R.C.M. 914A.

(2) The term "child" means a person who is under the age of 16 at the time of his or her testimony. The term "abuse of a child" means the physical or mental injury, sexual abuse or exploitation, or negligent treatment of a child. The term "exploitation" means child pornography or child prostitution. The term "negligent treatment" means the failure to provide, for reasons other than poverty, adequate food, clothing, shelter, or medical care so as to endanger seriously the physical health of the child. The term "domestic violence" means an offense that has as an element the use, attempted use, or threatened use of physical force against a person and is committed by a current or former spouse, parent, or guardian of the victim; by a person with whom the victim shares a child in common; by a person who is cohabiting with or has cohabited with the victim as a spouse, parent, or guardian; or by a person similarly situated to a spouse, parent, or guardian of the victim.

(3) Remote live testimony will be used only where the military judge makes a finding on the record that a child is unable to testify in open court in the presence of the accused, for any of the following reasons:

(A) The child is unable to testify because of fear;

(B) There is substantial likelihood, established by expert testimony, that the child would suffer emotional trauma from testifying;

(C) The child suffers from a mental or other infirmity; or

(D) Conduct by an accused or defense counsel causes thechild to be unable to continue testifying.

(4) Remote live testimony of a child shall not be utilized where the accused elects to absent himself from the courtroom in accordance with R.C.M. 804(c).

Rule 612. Writing used to refresh memory

If a witness uses a writing to refresh his or her memory for the purpose of testifying, either

(1) while testifying, or

(2) before testifying, if the military judge determines it is necessary in the interests of justice, an adverse party is entitled to have the writing produced at the hearing, to inspect it, to cross-examine the witness thereon, and to introduce in evidence those portions which relate to the testimony of the witness. If it is claimed that the writing contains privileged information or matters not related to the

subject matter of the testimony, the military judge shall examine the writing *in camera*, excise any privileged information or portions not so related, and order delivery of the remainder to the party entitled thereto. Any portion withheld over objections shall be attached to the record of trial as an appellate exhibit. If a writing is not produced or delivered pursuant to order under this rule, the military judge shall make any order justice requires, except that when the prosecution elects not to comply, the order shall be one striking the testimony or, if in discretion of the military judge it is determined that the interests of justice so required, declaring a mistrial. This rule does not preclude disclosure of information required to be disclosed under other provisions of these rules or this Manual.

Rule 613. Prior statements of witnesses

(a) *Examining witness concerning prior statement.* In examining a witness concerning a prior statement made by the witness, whether written or not, the statement need not be shown nor its contents disclosed to him at that time, but on request the same shall be shown or disclosed to opposing counsel.

(b) *Extrinsic evidence of prior inconsistent statement of witness.* Extrinsic evidence of a prior inconsistent statement by a witness is not admissible unless the witness is afforded an opportunity to explain or deny the same and the opposite party is afforded an opportunity to interrogate the witness thereon, or the interests of justice otherwise require. This provision does not apply to admissions of a party-opponent as defined in Mil. R. Evid. 801(d)(2).

Rule 614. Calling and interrogation of witnesses by the court-martial

(a) *Calling by the court-martial.* The military judge may, *sua sponte*, or at the request of the members or the suggestion of a party, call witnesses, and all parties are entitled to cross-examine witnesses thus called. When the members wish to call or recall a witness, the military judge shall determine whether it is appropriate to do so under these rules or this Manual.

(b) *Interrogation by the court-martial.* The military judge or members may interrogate witnesses, whether called by the military judge, the members, or a party. Members shall submit their questions to the military judge in writing so that a ruling may be made on the propriety of the questions or the course of questioning and so that questions may be asked on behalf of the court by the military judge in a form acceptable to the military judge. When a witness who has not testified previously is called by the military judge or the members, the military judge may conduct the direct examination or may assign the responsibility to counsel for any party.

(c) *Objections.* Objections to the calling of witnesses by the military judge or the members or to the interrogation by the military judge or the members may be made at the time or at the next available opportunity when the members are not present.

Rule 615. Exclusion of witnesses

At the request of the prosecution or defense the military judge shall order witnesses excluded so that they cannot hear the testimony of other witnesses, and the military judge may make the order *sua sponte*. This rule does not authorize exclusion of (1) the accused, or (2) a member of an armed service or an employee of the United States designated as representative of the United States by the trial counsel, or (3) a person whose presence is shown by a party to be essential to the presentation of the party's case, or (4) a person authorized by statute to be present at courts-martial, or (5) any victim of an offense from the trial of an accused for that offense because such victim may testify or present any information in relation to the sentence or that offense during the presentencing proceedings.

SECTION VII
OPINIONS AND EXPERT TESTIMONY

Rule 701. Opinion testimony by lay witnesses

If the witness is not testifying as an expert, the witness' testimony in the form of opinions or inferences is limited to those opinions or inferences that are (a) rationally based on the perception of the witness, (b) helpful to a clear understanding of the witness' testimony or the determination of a fact in issue, and (c) not based in scientific, technical, or other specialized knowledge within the scope of Rule 702.

Rule 702. Testimony by experts

If scientific, technical, or other specialized knowledge will assist the trier of fact to understand the evidence or to determine a fact in issue, a witness qualified as an expert by knowledge, skill, experience, training, or education may testify thereto in the form of an opinion or otherwise if (1) the testimony is based upon sufficient facts or data, (2) the testimony is the product of reliable principles and methods, and (3) the witness has applied the principles and methods reliably to the facts of the case.

Rule 703. Bases of opinion testimony by experts

The facts or data in the particular case upon which an expert bases an opinion or inference may be those perceived by or made known to the expert, at or before the hearing. If of a type reasonably relied upon by experts in the particular field in forming opinions or inferences upon the subject, the facts or data need not be admissible in evidence in order for the opinion or inference to be admitted. Facts or data that are otherwise inadmissible shall not be disclosed to the members by the proponent of the opinion or inference unless the military judge determines that their probative value in assisting the members to evaluate the expert's opinion substantially outweighs their prejudicial effect.

Rule 704. Opinion on ultimate issue

Testimony in the form of an opinion or inference otherwise admissible is not objectionable because it embraces an ultimate issue to be decided by the trier of fact.

Rule 705. Disclosure of facts or data underlying expert opinion

The expert may testify in terms of opinion or inference and give the expert's reasons therefor without prior disclosure of the underlying facts or data, unless the military judge requires otherwise. The expert may in any event be required to disclose the underlying facts or data on cross-examination.

Rule 706. Court appointed experts

(a) *Appointment and compensation.* The trial counsel, the defense counsel, and the court-martial have equal opportunity to obtain expert witnesses under Article 46. The employment and compensation of expert witnesses is governed by R.C.M. 703.

(b) *Disclosure of employment.* In the exercise of discretion, the military judge may authorize disclosure to the members of the fact that the military judge called an expert witness.

(c) *Accused's experts of own selection.* Nothing in this rule limits the accused in calling expert witnesses of the accused's own selection and at the accused's own expense.

Rule 707. Polygraph Examinations

(a) Notwithstanding any other provision of law, the results of a polygraph examination, the opinion of a polygraph examiner, or any reference to an offer to take, failure to take, or taking of a polygraph examination, shall not be admitted into evidence.

(b) Nothing in this section is intended to exclude from evidence statements made during a polygraph examination which are otherwise admissible.

SECTION VIII

HEARSAY

Rule 801. Definitions

The following definitions apply under this section:

(a) *Statement.* A "statement" is (1) an oral or written assertion or(2) nonverbal conduct of a person, if it is intended by the person as an assertion.

(b) *Declarant.* A "declarant" is a person who makes a statement.

(c) *Hearsay.* "Hearsay" is a statement, other than the one made by the declarant while testifying at the trial or hearing, offered in evidence to prove the truth of the matter asserted.

(d) *Statements which are not hearsay.* A statement is not hearsay if:

(1) *Prior statement by witness.* The declarant testifies at the trial or hearing and is subject to cross-examination concerning the statement, and the statement is (A) inconsistent with the declarant's testimony, and was given under oath subject to the penalty of perjury at a trial, hearing, or other proceeding, or in a deposition, or (B) consistent with the declarant's testimony and is offered to rebut an express or implied charge against the declarant of recent fabrication or improper influence or motive, or (C) one of

identification of a person made after perceiving the person; or

(2) *Admission by party-opponent.* The statement is offered against a party and is (A) the party's own statement in either the party's individual or representative capacity, or (B) a statement of which the party has manifested the party's adoption or belief in its truth, or (C) a statement by a person authorized by the party to make a statement concerning the subject, or (D) a statement by the party's agent or servant concerning a matter within the scope of the agency or employment of the agent or servant, made during the existence of the relationship, or (E) a statement by a co-conspirator of a party during the course and in furtherance of the conspiracy. The contents of the statement shall be considered but are not alone sufficient to establish the declarant's authority under subdivision (C), the agency or employment relationship and the scope thereof under subdivision (D), or the existence of the conspiracy and the participation therein of the declarant and the party against whom the statement is offered under subdivision (E).

Rule 802. Hearsay rule

Hearsay is not admissible except as provided by these rules or by any Act of Congress applicable in trials by court-martial.

Rule 803. Hearsay exceptions; availability of declarant immaterial

The following are not excluded by the hearsay rule, even though the declarant is available as a witness:

(1) *Present sense impression.* A statement describing or explaining an event or condition made while declarant was perceiving the event or condition or immediately thereafter.

(2) *Excited utterance.* A statement relating to a startling event or condition made while the declarant was under the stress of excitement caused by the event or condition.

(3) *Then existing mental, emotional, or physical condition.* A statement of the declarant's then existing state of mind, emotion, sensation, or physical condition (such as intent, plan, motive, design, mental feeling, pain, and bodily health), but not including a statement of memory or belief to prove the fact remembered or believed unless it relates to the execution, revocation, identification, or terms of declarant's will.

(4) *Statements for purposes of medical diagnosis or treatment.* Statements made for purposes of medical diagnosis or treatment and describing medical history, or past or present symptoms, pain, or sensations, or the inception or general character of the cause or external source thereof insofar as reasonably pertinent to diagnosis or treatment.

(5) *Recorded recollection.* A memorandum or record concerning a matter about which a witness once had knowledge but now has insufficient recollection to enable the witness to testify fully and accurately, shown to have been made or adopted by the witness when the matter was fresh in the witness' memory and to reflect that knowledge correctly. If admitted, the memorandum or record may be read into evidence, but may not itself be received as an exhibit unless offered by an adverse party.

(6) *Records of regularly conducted activity.* A memorandum, report, record, or data compilation, in any form, of acts, events, conditions, opinions, or diagnoses, made at or near the time by, or from information transmitted by, a person with knowledge, if kept in the course of a regularly conducted business activity, and if it was the regular practice of that business activity to make the memorandum, report, record, or data compilation, all as shown by the testimony of the custodian or other qualified witness, or by certification that complies with Mil. R. Evid. 902(11) or any other statute permitting certification in a criminal proceeding in a court of the United States, unless the source of the information or the method or circumstances of preparation indicate a lack of trustworthiness. The term "business" as used in this paragraph includes the armed forces, a business, institution, association, profession, occupation, and calling of every kind, whether or not conducted for profit. Among those memoranda, reports, records, or data compilations normally admissible pursuant to this paragraph are enlistment papers, physical examination papers, outline-figure and fingerprint cards, forensic laboratory reports, chain of custody documents, morning reports and other personnel accountability documents, service records, officer and enlisted qualification records, logs, unit personnel diaries, individual equipment records, daily strength records of prisoners, and rosters of prisoners.

(7) *Absence of entry in records kept in accordance*

with the provisions of paragraph (6). Evidence that a matter is not included in the memoranda, reports, records, or data compilations, in any form, kept in accordance with the provisions of paragraph (6), to prove the nonoccurrence or nonexistence of the matter, if the matter was of a kind of which a memorandum, report, record, or data compilation was regularly made and preserved, unless the sources of information or other circumstances indicate lack of trustworthiness.

(8) *Public records and reports.* Records, reports, statements, or data compilations, in any form, of public office or agencies, setting forth (A) the activities of the office or agency, or (B) matters observed pursuant to duty imposed by law as to which matters there was a duty to report, excluding, however, matters observed by police officers and other personnel acting in a law enforcement capacity, or (C) against the government, factual findings resulting from an investigation made pursuant to authority granted by law, unless the sources of information or other circumstances indicate lack of trustworthiness. Notwithstanding (B), the following are admissible under this paragraph as a record of a fact or event if made by a person within the scope of the person's official duties and those duties included a duty to know or to ascertain through appropriate and trustworthy channels of information the truth of the fact or event and to record such fact or event: enlistment papers, physical examination papers, outline figure and fingerprint cards, forensic laboratory reports, chain of custody documents, morning reports and other personnel accountability documents, service records, officer and enlisted qualification records, records of court-martial convictions, logs, unit personnel diaries, individual equipment records, guard reports, daily strength records of prisoners, and rosters of prisoners.

(9) *Records of vital statistics.* Records or data compilations, in any form, of births, fetal deaths, deaths, or marriages, if the report thereof was made to a public office pursuant to requirements of law.

(10) *Absence of public record or entry.* To prove the absence of a record, report, statement, or data compilation in any form, or the nonoccurrence or nonexistence of a matter of which a record, report, statement, or data compilation, in any form, was regularly made and preserved by a public office or agency, evidence in the form of a certification in accordance with Mil. R. Evid. 902, or testimony, that diligent search failed to disclose the record, report, statement, or data compilation, or entry.

(11) *Records of religious organizations.* Statements of births, marriages, divorces, deaths, legitimacy, ancestry, relationship by blood or marriage, or other similar facts of personal or family history contained in a regularly kept record of a religious organization.

(12) *Marriage, baptismal, and similar certificates.* Statements of fact obtained in a certificate that the maker performed a marriage or other ceremony or administered a sacrament, made by a clergyman, public official, or other person authorized by the rules or practices of a religious organization or by law to perform the act certified, and purporting to have been issued at the time of the act or within a time thereafter.

(13) *Family records.* Statements of facts concerning personal or family history contained in family Bibles, genealogies, charts, engravings on rings, inscription on family portraits, engravings on urns, crypts, or tombstones, or the like.

(14) *Records of documents affecting an interest in property.* The record of a document purporting to establish or affect an interest in property, as proof of the content of the original recorded document and its execution and delivery by each person by whom it purports to have been executed, if the record is a record of a public office and an applicable statute authorizes the recording of documents of the kind in that office.

(15) *Statements in documents affecting an interest in property.* A statement contained in a document purporting to establish or affect an interest in property if the matter stated was relevant to the purpose of the document, unless dealings with the property since the document was made have been inconsistent with the truth of the statement or the purport of the document.

(16) *Statements in ancient documents.* Statements in a document in existence twenty years or more the authenticity of which is established.

(17) *Market reports, commercial publications.* Market quotations, tabulations, directories, lists (including government price lists), or other published compilations generally used and relied upon by the public or by persons in particular occupations.

(18) *Learned treatises.* To the extent called to the attention of an expert witness upon cross-examination or relied upon by the expert in direct examina-

tion, statements contained in published treatises, periodicals, or pamphlets on a subject of history, medicine or other science or art, established as a reliable authority by the testimony or admission of the witness or by other expert testimony or by judicial notice. If admitted, the statements may be read into evidence but may not be received as exhibits.

(19) *Reputation concerning personal or family history.* Reputation among members of the person's family by blood, adoption, or marriage, or among the person's associates, or in the community, concerning the person's birth, adoption, marriage, divorce, death, legitimacy, relationship by blood, adoption, or marriage, ancestry, or other similar fact of the person's personal or family history.

(20) *Reputation concerning boundaries or general history.* Reputation in a community, arising before the controversy, as to boundaries of or customs affecting lands in the community, and reputation as to events of general history important to the community or State or nation in which located.

(21) *Reputation as to character.* Reputation of a person's character among the person's associates or in the community.

(22) *Judgment of previous conviction.* Evidence of a final judgment, entered after a trial or upon a plea of guilty (but not upon a plea of nolo contendere), adjudging a person guilty of a crime punishable by death, dishonorable discharge, or imprisonment in excess of one year, to prove any fact essential to sustain the judgment, but not including, when offered by the Government for purposes other than impeachment, judgments against persons other than the accused. The pendency of an appeal may be shown but does not affect admissibility. In determining whether a crime tried by court-martial was punishable by death, dishonorable discharge, or imprisonment in excess of one year, the maximum punishment prescribed by the President under Article 56 at the time of the conviction applies without regard to whether the case was tried by general, special, or summary court-martial.

(23) *Judgment as to personal, family or general history, or boundaries.* Judgments as proof of matters of personal, family, or general history, or boundaries essential to the judgment, if the same would be provable by evidence of reputation.

(24) *Other exceptions.* [Transferred to M.R.E. 807]

Rule 804. Hearsay exceptions; declarant unavailable

(a) *Definitions of unavailability.* "Unavailability as a witness" includes situations in which the declarant—

(1) is exempted by ruling of the military judge on the ground of privilege from testifying concerning the subject matter of the declarant's statement; or

(2) persists in refusing to testify concerning the subject matter of the declarant's statement despite an order of the military judge to do so; or

(3) testifies to a lack of memory of the subject matter of the declarant's statement; or

(4) is unable to be present or to testify at the hearing because of death or then existing physical or mental illness or infirmity; or

(5) is absent from the hearing and the proponent of the declarant's statement has been unable to procure the declarant's attendance (or in the case of a hearsay exception under subdivision (b)(2), (3), or (4), the declarant's attendance or testimony) by process or other reasonable means; or

(6) is unavailable within the meaning of Article 49(d)(2).

A declarant is not unavailable as a witness if the declarant's exemption, refusal, claim of lack of memory, inability, or absence is due to the procurement or wrongdoing of the proponent of the declarant's statement for the purpose of preventing the witness from attending or testifying.

(b) *Hearsay exceptions.* The following are not excluded by the hearsay rule if the declarant is unavailable as a witness.

(1) *Former testimony.* Testimony given as a witness at another hearing of the same or different proceeding, or in a deposition taken in compliance with law in the course of the same or another proceeding, if the party against whom the testimony is now offered had an opportunity and similar motive to develop the testimony by direct, cross, or redirect examination. A record of testimony given before courts-martial, courts of inquiry, military commissions, other military tribunals, and before proceedings pursuant to or equivalent to those required by Article 32 is admissible under this subdivision if such a record is a verbatim record. This paragraph is subject to the limitations set forth in Articles 49 and 50.

(2) *Statement under belief of impending death.* In a prosecution for homicide or for any offense result-

ing in the death of the alleged victim, a statement made by a declarant while believing that the declarant's death was imminent, concerning the cause or circumstances of what the declarant believed to be the declarant's impending death.

(3) *Statement against interest.* A statement which was at the time of its making so far contrary to the declarant's pecuniary or proprietary interest, or so far tended to subject the declarant to civil or criminal liability, or to render invalid a claim by the declarant against another, that a reasonable person in the position of the declarant would not have made the statement unless the person believed it to be true. A statement tending to expose the declarant to criminal liability and offered to exculpate the accused is not admissible unless corroborating circumstances clearly indicate the trustworthiness of the statement.

(4) *Statement of personal or family history.* (A) A statement concerning the declarant's own birth, adoption, marriage, divorce, legitimacy, relationship by blood, adoption, or marriage, ancestry, or other similar fact of personal or family history, even though declarant had no means of acquiring personal knowledge of the matter stated; or (B) a statement concerning the foregoing matters, and death also, of another person, if the declarant was related to the other by blood, adoption, or marriage or was so intimately associated with the other's family as to be likely to have accurate information concerning the matter declared.

(5) *Other exceptions.* [Transferred to M.R.E. 807]

(6) *Forfeiture by wrongdoing.* A statement offered against a party that has engaged or acquiesced in wrongdoing that was intended to, and did, procure the unavailability of the declarant as a witness.

Rule 805. Hearsay within hearsay

Hearsay included within hearsay is not excluded under the hearsay rule if each part of the combined statements conforms with an exception to the hearsay rule provided in these rules.

Rule 806. Attacking and supporting credibility of declarant

When a hearsay statement, or a statement defined in Mil. R. Evid. 801(d)(2)(C), (D), or (E), has been admitted in evidence, the credibility of the declarant may be attacked, and if attacked may be supported, by any evidence which would be admissible for those purposes if declarant had testified as a witness. Evidence of a statement or conduct by the declarant at any time, inconsistent with the declarant's hearsay statement, is not subject to any requirement that the declarant may have been afforded an opportunity to deny or explain. If the party against whom a hearsay statement has been admitted calls the declarant as a witness, the party is entitled to examine the declarant on the statement as if under cross-examination.

Rule 807. Residual exception.

A statement not specifically covered by Rule 803 or 804 but having equivalent circumstantial guarantees of trustworthiness, is not excluded by the hearsay rule, if the court determines that (A) the statement is offered as evidence of a material fact; (B) the statement is more probative on the point for which it is offered than other evidence which the proponent can procure through reasonable efforts; and (C) the general purposes of these rules and the interests of justice will best be served by admission of the statement into evidence. However, a statement may not be admitted under this exception unless the proponent of it makes known to the adverse party sufficiently in advance of the trial or hearing to provide the adverse party with a fair opportunity to prepare to meet it, the proponent's intention to offer the statement and the particulars of it, including the name and address of the declarant.

SECTION IX
AUTHENTICATION AND IDENTIFICATION

Rule 901. Requirement of authentication or identification

(a) *General provision.* The requirement of authentication or identification as a condition precedent to admissibility is satisfied by evidence sufficient to support a finding that the matter in question is what its proponent claims.

(b) *Illustrations.* By way of illustration only, and not by way of limitation, the following are examples of authentication or identification conforming with the requirements of this rule:

(1) *Testimony of witness with knowledge.* Testimony that a matter is what it is claimed to be.

(2) *Nonexpert opinion on handwriting.* Nonexpert

opinion as to the genuineness of handwriting, based upon familiarity not acquired for purposes of the litigation.

(3) *Comparison by trier or expert witness.* Comparison by the trier of fact or by expert witnesses with specimens which have been authenticated.

(4) *Distinctive characteristics and the like.* Appearance, contents, substance, internal patterns, or other distinctive characteristics, taken in conjunction with circumstances.

(5) *Voice identification.* Identification of a voice, whether heard firsthand or through mechanical or electronic transmission or recording, by opinion based upon hearing the voice at any time under circumstances connecting it with the alleged speaker.

(6) *Telephone conversations.* Telephone conversations, by evidence that a call was made to the number assigned at the time by the telephone company to a particular persons or business, if (A) in the case of a person, circumstances, including self-identification, show the person answering to be the one called, or (B) in the case of a business, the call was made to a place of business and the conversation related to business reasonably transacted over the telephone.

(7) *Public records or reports.* Evidence that a writing authorized by law to be recorded or filed and in fact recorded or filed in a public office, or a purported public record, report, statement, or data compilation, in any form, is from the public office where items of this nature are kept.

(8) *Ancient documents or data compilation.* Evidence that a document or data compilation, in any form, (A) is in such condition as to create no suspicion concerning its authenticity, (B) was in place where it, if authentic, would likely be, and (C) has been in existence 20 years or more at the time it is offered.

(9) *Process or system.* Evidence describing a process or system used to produce a result and showing that the process or system produces an accurate result.

(10) *Methods provided by statute or rule.* Any method of authentication or identification provided by Act of Congress, by rules prescribed by the Supreme Court pursuant to statutory authority, or by applicable regulations prescribed pursuant to statutory authority.

Rule 902. Self-authentication

Extrinsic evidence of authenticity as a condition precedent to admissibility is not required with respect to the following:

(1) *Domestic public documents under seal.* A document bearing a seal purporting to be that of the United States, or any State, district, Commonwealth, territory, or insular possession thereof, or the Panama Canal Zone, or the Trust Territory of the Pacific Islands, or a political subdivision, department, officer, or agency thereof, and a signature purporting to be an attestation or execution.

(2) *Domestic public documents not under seal.* A document purporting to bear the signature in the official capacity of an officer or employee of any entity included in paragraph (1) hereof, having no seal, if a public officer having a seal and having official duties in the district or political subdivision of the officer or employee certifies under seal that the signer has the official capacity and that the signature is genuine.

(3) *Foreign public documents.* A document purporting to be executed or attested in an official capacity by a person authorized by the laws of a foreign country to make the execution or attestation, and accompanied by a final certification as to the genuineness of the signature and official position (A) of the executing or attesting person, or (B) of any foreign official whose certificate of genuineness of signature and official position relates to the execution or attestation or is in a chain of certificates of genuineness of signature and official position relating to the execution of attestation. A final certification may be made by a secretary of embassy or legation, consul general, consul, vice consul, or consular agent of the United States, or a diplomatic or consular official of the foreign country assigned or accredited to the United States. If reasonable opportunity has been given to all parties to investigate the authenticity and accuracy of official documents, the court may, for good cause shown, order that they be treated as presumptively authentic without final certification or permit them to be evidenced by an attested summary with or without final certification.

(4) *Certified copies of public records.* A copy of an official record or report of entry therein, or of a document authorized by law to be recorded or filed

and actually recorded or filed in a public office, including data compilations in any form, certified as correct by the custodian or other person authorized to make the certification, by certificate complying with paragraphs (1), (2), or (3) of this rule or complying with any Act of Congress, rule prescribed by the Supreme Court pursuant to statutory authority, or an applicable regulation prescribed pursuant to statutory authority.

(4a) *Documents or records of the United States accompanied by attesting certificates.* Documents or records kept under the authority of the United States by any department, bureau, agency, office, or court thereof when attached to or accompanied by an attesting certificate of the custodian of the document or record without further authentication.

(5) *Official publications.* Books, pamphlets, or other publications purporting to be issued by public authority.

(6) *Newspapers and periodicals.* Printed material purporting to be newspapers or periodicals.

(7) *Trade inscriptions and the like.* Inscriptions, signs, tags or labels purporting to have been affixed in the course of business and indicating ownership, control, or origin.

(8) *Acknowledged documents.* Documents accompanied by a certificate of acknowledgment executed in the manner provided by law by a notary public or other officer authorized by law to take acknowledgments.

(9) *Commercial paper and related documents.* Commercial paper, signatures thereon, and documents relating thereto to the extent provided by general commercial law.

(10) *Presumptions under Acts of Congress and regulations.* Any signature, document, or other matter declared by Act of Congress or by applicable regulation prescribed pursuant to statutory authority to be presumptively or *prima facie* genuine or authentic.

(11) *Certified domestic records of regularly conducted activity.* The original or a duplicate of a domestic record of regularly conducted activity that would be admissible under Mil. R. Evid. 803(6) if accompanied by a written declaration of its custodian or other qualified person, in a manner complying with any Act of Congress or rule prescribed by the Supreme Court pursuant to statutory authority, certifying that the record (A) was made at or near the time of the occurrence of the matters set forth by, or from information transmitted by, a person with knowledge of those matters; (B) was kept in the course of the regularly conducted activity; and (C) was made by the regularly conducted activity as a regular practice. A party intending to offer a record into evidence under this paragraph must provide written notice of that intention to all adverse parties, and must make the record and declaration available for inspection sufficiently in advance of their offer into evidence to provide an adverse party with a fair opportunity to challenge them.

Rule 903. Subscribing witness' testimony unnecessary

The testimony of a subscribing witness is not necessary to authenticate a writing unless required by the laws of the jurisdiction whose laws govern the validity of the writing.

SECTION X
CONTENTS OF WRITINGS, RECORDINGS, AND PHOTOGRAPHS

Rule 1001. Definitions

For purposes of this section the following definitions are applicable:

(1) *Writings and recordings.* "Writings" and "recordings" consist of letters, words, or numbers, or their equivalent, set down by handwriting, typewriting, printing, photostating, photographing, magnetic impulse, mechanical or electronic recording, or other form of data compilation.

(2) *Photographs.* "Photographs" include still photographs, X-ray films, video tapes, and motion pictures.

(3) *Original.* An "original" of a writing or recording is the writing or recording itself or any counterpart intended to have the same effect by a person executing or issuing it. An "original" of a photograph includes the negative or any print therefrom. If data are stored in a computer or similar device, any printout or other output readable by sight, shown to reflect the data accurately, is an "original."

(4) *Duplicate.* A "duplicate" is a counterpart produced by the same impression as the original, or from the same matrix, or by means of photography, including enlargements and miniatures, or by mechanical or electronic rerecording, or by chemical

reproduction, or by other equivalent techniques which accurately reproduce the original.

Rule 1002. Requirement of an original

To prove the content of a writing, recording, or photograph, the original writing, recording, or photograph is required, except as otherwise provided in these rules, this Manual, or by Act of Congress.

Rule 1003. Admissibility of duplicates

A duplicate is admissible to the same extent as an original unless (1) a genuine question is raised as to the authenticity of the original or (2) in the circumstances it would be unfair to admit the duplicate in lieu of the original.

Rule 1004. Admissibility of other evidence of contents

The original is not required, and other evidence of the contents of a writing, recording, or photograph is admissible if:

(1) *Originals lost or destroyed.* All originals are lost or have been destroyed, unless the proponent lost or destroyed them in bad faith; or

(2) *Original not obtainable.* No original can be obtained by any available judicial process or procedure; or

(3) *Original in possession of opponent.* At a time when an original was under the control of the party against whom offered, the party was put on notice, by the pleadings or otherwise, that the contents would be a subject of proof at the hearing, and the party does not produce the original at the hearing; or

(4) *Collateral matters.* The writing, recording, or photograph is not closely related to a controlling issue.

Rule 1005. Public records

The contents of an official record, or of a document authorized to be recorded or filed and actually recorded or filed, including data compilations in any form, if otherwise admissible, may be proved by copy, certified as correct or attested to in accordance with Mil. R. Evid. 902 or testified to be correct by a witness who has compared it with the original. If a copy which complies with the foregoing cannot be obtained by the exercise of reasonable diligence, then other evidence of the contents may be given.

Rule 1006. Summaries

The contents of voluminous writings, recordings, or photographs which cannot conveniently be examined in court may be presented in the form of a chart, summary, or calculation. The originals, or duplicates, shall be made available for examination or copying, or both, by other parties at reasonable time and place. The military judge may order that they be produced in court.

Rule 1007. Testimony or written admission of party

Contents of writings, recordings, or photographs may be proved by the testimony or deposition of the party against whom offered or by the party's written admission, without accounting for the nonproduction of the original.

Rule 1008. Functions of military judge and members

When the admissibility of other evidence of contents of writings, recordings, or photographs under these rules depends upon the fulfillment of a condition of fact, the question whether the condition has been fulfilled is ordinarily for the military judge to determine in accordance with the provisions of Mil. R. Evid. 104. However, when an issue is raised (a) whether the asserted writing ever existed, or (b) whether another writing, recording, or photograph produced at trial is the original, or (c) whether other evidence of contents correctly reflects the contents, the issue is for the trier of fact to determine as in the case of other issues of fact.

SECTION XI
MISCELLANEOUS RULES

Rule 1101. Applicability of rules

(a) *Rules applicable.* Except as otherwise provided in this Manual, these rules apply generally to all courts-martial, including summary courts-martial; to proceedings pursuant to Article 39(a); to limited factfinding proceedings ordered on review; to proceedings in revision; and to contempt proceedings except those in which the judge may act summarily.

(b) *Rules of privilege.* The rules with respect to privileges in Section III and V apply at all stages of all actions, cases, and proceedings.

(c) *Rules relaxed.* The application of these rules may be relaxed in sentencing proceedings as provided under R.C.M. 1001 and otherwise as provided in this Manual.

(d) *Rules inapplicable.* These rules (other than with respect to privileges and Mil. R. Evid. 412) do not apply in investigative hearings pursuant to Article 32; proceedings for vacation of suspension of sentence pursuant to Article 72; proceedings for search authorizations; proceedings involving pretrial restraint; and in other proceedings authorized under the code or this Manual and not listed in subdivision (a).

Rule 1102. Amendments.

(a) Amendments to the Federal Rules of Evidence shall apply to the Military Rules of Evidence 18 months after the effective date of such amendments, unless action to the contrary is taken by the President.

(b) *Rules Determined Not To Apply.* The President has determined that the following Federal Rules of Evidence do not apply to the Military Rules of Evidence: Rules 301, 302, 415, and 902(12).

Rule 1103. Title

These rules may be known and cited as the Military Rules of Evidence.

Part IV
Punitive Articles

Part IV
Punitive Articles

PART IV
PUNITIVE ARTICLES
(Statutory text of each Article is in bold)

Discussion

Paragraphs 1 and 2 discuss the two articles of the code that are located in the punitive article subchapter of the code, but which are not punitive as such: Article 77, principals; and Article 79, lesser included offenses.

R.C.M. 307 prescribes rules for preferral of charges. The discussion under that rule explains how to allege violations under the code using the format of charge and specification.

Beginning with paragraph 3, the punitive articles of the code are discussed using the following sequence:

a. Text of the article
b. Elements of the offense or offenses
c. Explanation
d. Lesser included offenses
e. Maximum punishment
f. Sample specifications

The term "elements," as used in Part IV, includes both the statutory elements of the offense and any aggravating factors listed under the President's authority which increases the maximum permissible punishment when specified aggravating factors are pleaded and proven.

The prescriptions of maximum punishments in subparagraph e of each paragraph of this part must be read in conjunction with R.C.M. 1003, which prescribes additional punishments that may be available and additional limitations on punishments. The sample specifications provided in subparagraph f of each paragraph in this part are guides. The specifications may be varied in form and content as necessary. *See* R.C.M. 307 for additional guidance.

---

1. Article 77—Principals

a. *Text of statute.* **Any person punishable under this chapter who—**

(1) **commits an offense punishable by this chapter, or aids, abets, counsels, commands, or procures its commission; or**

(2) **causes an act to be done which if directly performed by him would be punishable by this chapter; is a principal.**

b. *Explanation.*

(1) *Purpose.* Article 77 does not define an offense. Its purpose is to make clear that a person need not personally perform the acts necessary to constitute an offense to be guilty of it. A person who aids, abets, counsels, commands, or procures the commission of an offense, or who causes an act to be done which, if done by that person directly, would be an offense is equally guilty of the offense as one who commits it directly, and may be punished to the same extent.

Article 77 eliminates the common law distinctions between principal in the first degree ("perpetrator"); principal in the second degree (one who aids, counsels, commands, or encourages the commission of an offense and who is present at the scene of the crime—commonly known as an "aider and abettor"); and accessory before the fact (one who aids, counsels, commands, or encourages the commission of an offense and who is not present at the scene of the crime). All of these are now "principals."

(2) *Who may be liable for an offense.*

(a) *Perpetrator.* A perpetrator is one who actually commits the offense, either by the perpetrator's own hand, or by causing an offense to be committed by knowingly or intentionally inducing or setting in motion acts by an animate or inanimate agency or instrumentality which result in the commission of an offense. For example, a person who knowingly conceals contraband drugs in an automobile, and then induces another person, who is unaware and has no reason to know of the presence of drugs, to drive the automobile onto a military installation, is, although not present in the automobile, guilty of wrongful introduction of drugs onto a military installation. (On these facts, the driver would be guilty of no crime.) Similarly, if, upon orders of a superior, a soldier shot a person who appeared to the soldier to be an enemy, but was known to the superior as a friend, the superior would be guilty of murder (but the soldier would be guilty of no offense).

(b) *Other Parties.* If one is not a perpetrator, to be guilty of an offense committed by the perpetrator, the person must:

(i) Assist, encourage, advise, instigate, counsel, command, or procure another to commit, or assist, encourage, advise, counsel, or command another in the commission of the offense; and

(ii) Share in the criminal purpose of design.

One who, without knowledge of the criminal venture or plan, unwittingly encourages or renders assistance to another in the commission of an offense is not guilty of a crime. *See* the parentheticals in the examples in paragraph 1b(2)(a) above. In some circumstances, inaction may make one liable as a party, where there is a duty to act. If a person (for example, a security guard) has a duty to interfere in the commission of an offense, but does not interfere, that person is a party to the crime *if* such a noninterference is intended to and does operate as an aid or encouragement to the actual perpetrator.

(3) *Presence.*

(a) *Not necessary.* Presence at the scene of the crime is not necessary to make one a party to the crime and liable as a principal. For example, one who, knowing that person intends to shoot another person and intending that such an assault be carried out, provides the person with a pistol, is guilty of assault when the offense is committed, even though not present at the scene.

(b) *Not sufficient.* Mere presence at the scene of a crime does not make one a principal unless the requirements of paragraph 1b(2)(a) or (b) have been met.

(4) *Parties whose intent differs from the perpetrator's.* When an offense charged requires proof of a specific intent or particular state of mind as an element, the evidence must prove that the accused had that intent or state of mind, whether the accused is charged as a perpetrator or an "other party" to crime. It is possible for a party to have a state of mind more or less culpable than the perpetrator of the offense. In such a case, the party may be guilty of a more or less serious offense than that committed by the perpetrator. For example, when a homicide is committed, the perpetrator may act in the heat of sudden passion caused by adequate provocation and be guilty of manslaughter, while the party who, without such passion, hands the perpetrator a weapon and encourages the perpetrator to kill the victim, would be guilty of murder. On the other hand, if a party assists a perpetrator in an assault on a person who, known only to the perpetrator, is an officer, the party would be guilty only of assault, while the perpetrator would be guilty of assault on an officer.

(5) *Responsibility for other crimes.* A principal may be convicted of crimes committed by another principal if such crimes are likely to result as a natural and probable consequence of the criminal venture or design. For example, the accused who is a party to a burglary is guilty as a principal not only of the offense of burglary, but also, if the perpetrator kills an occupant in the course of the burglary, of murder. (*see also* paragraph 5 concerning liability for offenses committed by co-conspirators.)

(6) *Principals independently liable.* One may be a principal, even if the perpetrator is not identified or prosecuted, or is acquitted.

(7) *Withdrawal.* A person may withdraw from a common venture or design and avoid liability for any offenses committed after the withdrawal. To be effective, the withdrawal must meet the following requirements:

(a) It must occur before the offense is committed;

(b) The assistance, encouragement, advice, instigation, counsel, command, or procurement given by the person must be effectively countermanded or negated; and

(c) The withdrawal must be clearly communicated to the would-be perpetrators or to appropriate law enforcement authorities in time for the perpetrators to abandon the plan or for law enforcement authorities to prevent the offense.

2. Article 78—Accessory after the fact

a. *Text of statute.* **Any person subject to this chapter who, knowing that an offense punishable by this chapter has been committed, receives, comforts, or assists the offender in order to hinder or prevent his apprehension, trial, or punishment shall be punished as a court-martial may direct.**

b. *Elements.*

(1) That an offense punishable by the code was committed by a certain person;

(2) That the accused knew that this person had committed such offense;

(3) That thereafter the accused received, comforted, or assisted the offender; and

(4) That the accused did so for the purpose of hindering or preventing the apprehension, trial, or punishment of the offender.

c. *Explanation.*

(1) *In general.* The assistance given a principal by an accessory after the fact is not limited to assistance designed to effect the escape or concealment of the principal, but also includes acts performed to conceal the commission of the offense by the principal (for example, by concealing evidence of the offense).

(2) *Failure to report offense.* The mere failure to

report a known offense will not make one an accessory after the fact. Such failure may violate a general order or regulation, however, and thus constitute an offense under Article 92. *See* paragraph 16. If the offense involved is a serious offense, failure to report it may constitute the offense of misprision of a serious offense, under Article 134. *See* paragraph 95.

(3) *Offense punishable by the code.* The term "offense punishable by this chapter" in the text of the article means any offense described in the code.

(4) *Status of principal.* The principal who committed the offense in question need not be subject to the code, but the offense committed must be punishable by the code.

(5) *Conviction or acquittal of principal.* The prosecution must prove that a principal committed the offense to which the accused is allegedly an accessory after the fact. However, evidence of the conviction or acquittal of the principal in a separate trial is not admissible to show that the principal did or did not commit the offense. Furthermore, an accused may be convicted as an accessory after the fact despite the acquittal in a separate trial of the principal whom the accused allegedly comforted, received, or assisted.

(6) *Accessory after the fact not a lesser included offense.* The offense of being an accessory after the fact is not a lesser included offense of the primary offense.

(7) *Actual knowledge.* Actual knowledge is required but may be proved by circumstantial evidence.

d. *Lesser included offense.* Article 80- attempts

e. *Maximum punishment.* Any person subject to the code who is found guilty as an accessory after the fact to an offense punishable by the code shall be subject to the maximum punishment authorized for the principal offense, except that in no case shall the death penalty nor more than one-half of the maximum confinement authorized for that offense be adjudged, nor shall the period of confinement exceed 10 years in any case, including offenses for which life imprisonment may be adjudged.

f. *Sample specification.*

In that ______ (personal jurisdiction data), knowing that (at/on board—location), on or about ______ 20 ______ committed an offense punishable by the Uniform Code of Military Justice, to wit: ______, did, (at/on board—location) (subject-matter jurisdiction data, if required), on or about ______ 20 ___, in order to (hinder) (prevent) the (apprehension) (trial) (punishment) of the said ______, (receive) (comfort) (assist) the said ______ by ______.

3. Article 79—Conviction of lesser included offenses

a. *Text of statute.* **An accused may be found guilty of an offense necessarily included in the offense charged or of an attempt to commit either the offense charged or an offense necessarily included therein.**

b. *Explanation.*

(1) *In general.* A lesser offense is included in a charged offense when the specification contains allegations which either expressly or by fair implication put the accused on notice to be prepared to defend against it in addition to the offense specifically charged. This requirement of notice may be met when:

(a) All of the elements of the lesser offense are included in the greater offense, and the common elements are identical (for example, larceny as a lesser included offense of robbery);

(b) All of the elements of the lesser offense are included in the greater offense, but one or more elements is legally less serious (for example, housebreaking as a lesser included offense of burglary); or

(c) All of the elements of the lesser offense are included and necessary parts of the greater offense, but the mental element is legally less serious (for example, wrongful appropriation as a lesser included offense of larceny).

The notice requirement may also be met, depending on the allegations in the specification, even though an included offense requires proof of an element not required in the offense charged. For example, assault with a dangerous weapon may be included in a robbery.

(2) *Multiple lesser included offenses.* When the offense charged is a compound offense comprising two or more included offenses, an accused may be found guilty of any or all of the offenses included in the offense charged. For example, robbery includes both larceny and assault. Therefore, in a proper case, a court-martial may find an accused not guilty of

robbery, but guilty of wrongful appropriation and assault.

(3) *Findings of guilty to a lesser included offense.* A court-martial may find an accused not guilty of the offense charged, but guilty of a lesser included offense by the process of exception and substitution. The court-martial may except (that is, delete) the words in the specification that pertain to the offense charged and, if necessary, substitute language appropriate to the lesser included offense. For example, the accused is charged with murder in violation of Article 118, but found guilty of voluntary manslaughter in violation of Article 119. Such a finding may be worded as follows:

(4) *Specific lesser included offenses.* Specific lesser included offenses, if any, are listed for each offense discussed in this Part, but the lists are not all-inclusive.

4. Article 80—Attempts

a. *Text of statute.*

(a) **An act, done with specific intent to commit an offense under this chapter, amounting to more than mere preparation and tending, even though failing, to effect its commission, is an attempt to commit that offense.**

(b) **Any person subject to this chapter who attempts to commit any offense punishable by this chapter shall be punished as a court-martial may direct, unless otherwise specifically prescribed.**

(c) **Any person subject to this chapter may be convicted of an attempt to commit an offense although it appears on the trial that the offense was consummated.**

b. *Elements.*

(1) That the accused did a certain overt act;

(2) That the act was done with the specific intent to commit a certain offense under the code;

(3) That the act amounted to more than mere preparation; and

(4) That the act apparently tended to effect the commission of the intended offense.

c. *Explanation.*

(1) *In general.* To constitute an attempt there must be a specific intent to commit the offense accompanied by an overt act which directly tends to accomplish the unlawful purpose.

(2) *More than preparation.* Preparation consists of devising or arranging the means or measures necessary for the commission of the offense. The overt act required goes beyond preparatory steps and is a direct movement toward the commission of the offense. For example, a purchase of matches with the intent to burn a haystack is not an attempt to commit arson, but it is an attempt to commit arson to applying a burning match to a haystack, even if no fire results. The overt act need not be the last act essential to the consummation of the offense. For example, an accused could commit an overt act, and then voluntarily decide not to go through with the intended offense. An attempt would nevertheless have been committed, for the combination of a specific intent to commit an offense, plus the commission of an overt act directly tending to accomplish it, constitutes the offense of attempt. Failure to complete the offense, whatever the cause, is not a defense.

(3) *Factual impossibility.* A person who purposely engages in conduct which would constitute the offense if the attendant circumstances were as that person believed them to be is guilty of an attempt. For example, if A, without justification or excuse and with intent to kill B, points a gun at B and pulls the trigger, A is guilty of attempt to murder, even though, unknown to A, the gun is defective and will not fire. Similarly, a person who reaches into the pocket of another with the intent to steal that person's billfold is guilty of an attempt to commit larceny, even though the pocket is empty.

(4) *Voluntary abandonment.* It is a defense to an attempt offense that the person voluntarily and completely abandoned the intended crime, solely because of the person's own sense that it was wrong, prior to the completion of the crime. The voluntary abandonment defense is not allowed if the abandonment results, in whole or in part, from other reasons, for example, the person feared detection or apprehension, decided to await a better opportunity for success, was unable to complete the crime, or encountered unanticipated difficulties or unexpected resistance. A person who is entitled to the defense of voluntary abandonment may nonetheless be guilty of a lesser included, completed offense. For example, a person who voluntarily abandoned an attempted armed robbery may nonetheless be guilty of assault with a dangerous weapon.

(5) *Solicitation.* Soliciting another to commit an

offense does not constitute an attempt. *See* paragraph 6 for a discussion of article 82, solicitation.

(6) *Attempts not under Article 80.* While most attempts should be charged under Article 80, the following attempts are specifically addressed by some other article, and should be charged accordingly:

(a) Article 85—desertion

(b) Article 94—mutiny or sedition.

(c) Article 100—subordinate compelling

(d) Article 104—aiding the enemy

(e) Article 106a—espionage

(f) Article 119a-attempting to kill an unborn child

(g) Article 128—assault

(7) *Regulations.* An attempt to commit conduct which would violate a lawful general order or regulation under Article 92 (*see* paragraph 16) should be charged under Article 80. It is not necessary in such cases to prove that the accused intended to violate the order or regulation, but it must be proved that the accused intended to commit the prohibited conduct.

d. *Lesser included offenses.* If the accused is charged with an attempt under Article 80, and the offense attempted has a lesser included offense, then the offense of attempting to commit the lesser included offense would ordinarily be a lesser included offense to the charge of attempt. For example, if an accused was charged with attempted larceny, the offense of attempted wrongful appropriation would be a lesser included offense, although it, like the attempted larceny, would be a violation of Article 80.

e. *Maximum punishment.* Any person subject to the code who is found guilty of an attempt under Article 80 to commit any offense punishable by the code shall be subject to the same maximum punishment authorized for the commission of the offense attempted, except that in no case shall the death penalty be adjudged, nor shall any mandatory minimum punishment provisions apply; and in no case, other than attempted murder, shall confinement exceeding 20 years be adjudged.

f. *Sample specification.*

In that ________ (personal jurisdiction data) did, (at/on board—location) (subject-matter jurisdiction data, if required), on or about ________ 20 ____, attempt to (describe offense with sufficient detail to include expressly or by necessary implication every element).

5. Article 81—Conspiracy

a. *Text of statute.* **Any person subject to this chapter who conspires with any other person to commit an offense under this chapter shall, if one or more of the conspirators does an act to effect the object of the conspiracy, be punished as a court-martial may direct.**

b. *Elements.*

(1) That the accused entered into an agreement with one or more persons to commit an offense under the code; and

(2) That, while the agreement continued to exist, and while the accused remained a party to the agreement, the accused or at least one of the co-conspirators performed an overt act for the purpose of bringing about the object of the conspiracy.

c. *Explanation.*

(1) *Co-conspirators.* Two or more persons are required in order to have a conspiracy. Knowledge of the identity of co-conspirators and their particular connection with the criminal purpose need not be established. The accused must be subject to the code, but the other co-conspirators need not be. A person may be guilty of conspiracy although incapable of committing the intended offense. For example, a bedridden conspirator may knowingly furnish the car to be used in a robbery. The joining of another conspirator after the conspiracy has been established does not create a new conspiracy or affect the status of the other conspirators. However, the conspirator who joined an existing conspiracy can be convicted of this offense only if, at or after the time of joining the conspiracy, an overt act in furtherance of the object of the agreement is committed.

(2) *Agreement.* The agreement in a conspiracy need not be in any particular form or manifested in any formal words. It is sufficient if the minds of the parties arrive at a common understanding to accomplish the object of the conspiracy, and this may be shown by the conduct of the parties. The agreement need not state the means by which the conspiracy is to be accomplished or what part each conspirator is to play.

(3) *Object of the agreement.* The object of the

agreement must, at least in part, involve the commission of one or more offenses under the code. An agreement to commit several offenses is ordinarily but a single conspiracy. Some offenses require two or more culpable actors acting in concert. There can be no conspiracy where the agreement exists only between the persons necessary to commit such an offense. Examples include dueling, bigamy, incest, adultery, and bribery.

(4) *Overt act.*

(a) The overt act must be independent of the agreement to commit the offense; must take place at the time of or after the agreement; must be done by one or more of the conspirators, but not necessarily the accused; and must be done to effectuate the object of the agreement.

(b) The overt act need not be in itself criminal, but it must be a manifestation that the agreement is being executed. Although committing the intended offense may constitute the overt act, it is not essential that the object offense be committed. Any overt act is enough, no matter how preliminary or preparatory in nature, as long as it is a manifestation that the agreement is being executed.

(c) An overt act by one conspirator becomes the act of all without any new agreement specifically directed to that act and each conspirator is equally guilty even though each does not participate in, or have knowledge of, all of the details of the execution of the conspiracy.

(5) *Liability for offenses.* Each conspirator is liable for all offenses committed pursuant to the conspiracy by any of the co-conspirators while the conspiracy continues and the person remains a party to it.

(6) *Withdrawal.* A party to the conspiracy who abandons or withdraws from the agreement to commit the offense before the commission of an overt act by any conspirator is not guilty of conspiracy. An effective withdrawal or abandonment must consist of affirmative conduct which is wholly inconsistent with adherence to the unlawful agreement and which shows that the party has severed all connection with the conspiracy. A conspirator who effectively abandons or withdraws from the conspiracy after the performance of an overt act by one of the conspirators remains guilty of conspiracy and of any offenses committed pursuant to the conspiracy up to the time of the abandonment or withdrawal. However, a person who has abandoned or withdrawn from the conspiracy is not liable for offenses committed thereafter by the remaining conspirators. The withdrawal of a conspirator from the conspiracy does not affect the status of the remaining members.

(7) *Factual impossibility.* It is not a defense that the means adopted by the conspirators to achieve their object, if apparently adapted to that end, were actually not capable of success, or that the conspirators were not physically able to accomplish their intended object.

(8) *Conspiracy as a separate offense.* A conspiracy to commit an offense is a separate and distinct offense from the offense which is the object of the conspiracy, and both the conspiracy and the consummated offense which was its object may be charged, tried, and punished. The commission of the intended offense may also constitute the overt act which is an element of the conspiracy to commit that offense.

(9) *Special conspiracies under Article 134.* The United States Code prohibits conspiracies to commit certain specific offenses which do not require an overt act. These conspiracies should be charged under Article 134. Examples include conspiracies to impede or injure any Federal officer in the discharge of duties under 18 U.S.C. § 372, conspiracies against civil rights under 18 U.S.C. § 241, and certain drug conspiracies under 21 U.S.C. § 846. *See* paragraph 60c(4)(c)(ii).

d. *Lesser included offense.* Article 80—attempts

e. *Maximum punishment.* Any person subject to the code who is found guilty of conspiracy shall be subject to the maximum punishment authorized for the offense which is the object of the conspiracy, except that in no case shall the death penalty be imposed.

f. *Sample specification.*

In that ______ (personal jurisdiction data), did, (at/on board—location) (subject-matter jurisdiction data, if required), on or about ______ 20 ___, conspire with ______ (and ______) to commit an offense under the Uniform Code of Military Justice, to wit: (larceny of ______, of a value of (about) $ ______, the property of ______), and in order to effect the object of the conspiracy the said ______ (and ______) did ______.

6. Article 82—Solicitation

a. *Text of statute.*

(a) **Any person subject to this chapter who solicits or advises another or other to desert in violation of section 885 of this title (Article 85) or mutiny in violation of section 894 of this title (Article 94) shall, if the offense solicited or advised is attempted or committed, be punished with the punishment provided for the commission of the offense, but, if the offense solicited or advised is not committed or attempted, he shall be punished as a court-martial may direct.**

(b) **Any person subject to this chapter who solicits or advises another or others to commit an act of misbehavior before the enemy in violation of section 899 of this title (Article 99) or sedition in violation of section 894 of this title (Article 94) shall, if the offense solicited or advised is committed, be punished with the punishment provided for the commission of the offense, but, if the offense solicited or advised is not committed, he shall be punished as a court-martial may direct.**

b. *Elements.*

(1) That the accused solicited or advised a certain person or persons to commit any of the four offenses named in Article 82; and

(2) That the accused did so with the intent that the offense actually be committed.

[Note: If the offense solicited or advised was attempted or committed, add the following element]

(3) That the offense solicited or advised was (committed) (attempted) as the proximate result of the solicitation.

c. *Explanation.*

(1) *Instantaneous offense.* The offense is complete when a solicitation is made or advice is given with the specific wrongful intent to influence another or others to commit any of the four offenses named in Article 82. It is not necessary that the person or persons solicited or advised agree to or act upon the solicitation or advice.

(2) *Form of solicitation.* Solicitation may be by means other than word of mouth or writing. Any act or conduct which reasonably may be construed as a serious request or advice to commit one of the four offenses named in Article 82 may constitute solicitation. It is not necessary that the accused act alone in the solicitation or in the advising; the accused may act through other persons in committing this offense.

(3) *Solicitations in violation of Article 134.* Solicitation to commit offenses other than violations of the four offenses named in Article 82 may be charged as violations of Article 134. *See* paragraph 105. However, some offenses require, as an element of proof, some act of solicitation by the accused. These offenses are separate and distinct from solicitations under Articles 82 and 134. When the accused's act of solicitation constitutes, by itself, a separate offense, the accused should be charged with that separate, distinct offense—for example, pandering (*see* paragraph 97) and obstruction of justice (*see* paragraph 96) in violation of Article 134.

d. *Lesser included offense.* Article 80—attempts

e. *Maximum punishment.* If the offense solicited or advised is committed or (in the case of soliciting desertion or mutiny) attempted, then the accused shall be punished with the punishment provided for the commission of the offense solicited or advised. If the offense solicited or advised is not committed or (in the case of soliciting desertion or mutiny) attempted, then the following punishment may be imposed:

(1) To desert—Dishonorable discharge, forfeiture of all pay and allowances, and confinement for 3 years.

(2) To mutiny—Dishonorable discharge, forfeiture of all pay and allowances, and confinement for 10 years.

(3) To commit an act of misbehavior before the enemy—Dishonorable discharge, forfeiture of all pay and allowances, and confinement for 10 years.

(4) To commit an act of sedition—Dishonorable discharge, forfeiture of all pay and allowances, and confinement for 10 years.

f. *Sample specifications.*

(1) *For soliciting desertion (Article 85) or mutiny (Article 94).*

In that ________ (personal jurisdiction data), did, (at/on board—location), on or about ________ 20 ________, (a time of war) by (here state the manner and form of solicitation or advice), (solicit) (advise) ________ (and ________) to (desert in violation of Article 85) (mutiny in violation of Article 94)

[*Note: If the offense solicited or advised is attempted*

or committed, add the following at the end of the specification:]

and, as a result of such (solicitation) (advice), the offense (solicited) (advised) was, on or about ________, 20 ________, (at/on board—location), (attempted) (committed) by ________ (and ________).

(2) *For soliciting an act of misbehavior before the enemy (Article 99) or sedition (Article 94).*

In that ________ (personal jurisdiction data) did, (at/on board—location), on or about ________ 20 ____, (a time of war) by (here state the manner and form of solicitation or advice), (solicit) (advise), ________ (and ________) to commit (an act of misbehavior before the enemy in violation of Article 99) (sedition in violation of Article 94)

[*Note: If the offense solicited or advised is committed, add the following at the end of the specification:*]

and, as a result of such (solicitation) (advice), the offense (solicited) (advised) was, on or about ________ 20 ________, (at/on board—location), committed by ________ (and ________).

7. Article 83—Fraudulent enlistment, appointment, or separation

a. *Text of statute.*

Any person who—

(1) procures his own enlistment or appointment in the armed forces by knowingly false representation or deliberate concealment as to his qualifications for that enlistment or appointment and receives pay or allowances thereunder; or

(2) procures his own separation from the armed forces by knowingly false representation or deliberate concealment as to his eligibility for that separation;

shall be punished as a court-martial may direct.

b. *Elements.*

(1) *Fraudulent enlistment or appointment.*

(a) That the accused was enlisted or appointed in an armed force;

(b) That the accused knowingly misrepresented or deliberately concealed a certain material fact or facts regarding qualifications of the accused for enlistment or appointment;

(c) That the accused's enlistment or appointment was obtained or procured by that knowingly false representation or deliberate concealment; and

(d) That under this enlistment or appointment that accused received pay or allowances or both.

(2) *Fraudulent separation.*

(a) That the accused was separated from an armed force;

(b) That the accused knowingly misrepresented or deliberately concealed a certain material fact or facts about the accused's eligibility for separation; and

(c) That the accused's separation was obtained or procured by that knowingly false representation or deliberate concealment.

c. *Explanation.*

(1) *In general.* A fraudulent enlistment, appointment, or separation is one procured by either a knowingly false representation as to any of the qualifications prescribed by law, regulation, or orders for the specific enlistment, appointment, or separation, or a deliberate concealment as to any of those disqualifications. Matters that may be material to an enlistment, appointment, or separation include any information used by the recruiting, appointing, or separating officer in reaching a decision as to enlistment, appointment, or separation in any particular case, and any information that normally would have been so considered had it been provided to that officer.

(2) *Receipt of pay or allowances.* A member of the armed forces who enlists or accepts an appointment without being regularly separated from a prior enlistment or appointment should be charged under Article 83 only if that member has received pay or allowances under the fraudulent enlistment or appointment. Acceptance of food, clothing, shelter, or transportation from the government constitutes receipt of allowances. However, whatever is furnished the accused while in custody, confinement, arrest, or other restraint pending trial for fraudulent enlistment or appointment is not considered an allowance. The receipt of pay or allowances may be proved by circumstantial evidence.

(3) *One offense.* One who procures one's own enlistment, appointment, or separation by several

misrepresentations or concealment as to qualifications for the one enlistment, appointment, or separation so procured, commits only one offense under Article 83.

d. *Lesser included offense.* Article 80—attempts

e. *Maximum punishment.*

(1) *Fraudulent enlistment or appointment.* Dishonorable discharge, forfeiture of all pay and allowances, and confinement for 2 years.

(2) *Fraudulent separation.* Dishonorable discharge, forfeiture of all pay and allowances, and confinement for 5 years.

f. *Sample specifications.*

(1) *For fraudulent enlistment or appointment.*

In that ______ (personal jurisdiction data), did, (at/on board—location), on or about ______ 20 ______, by means of (knowingly false representations that (here state the fact or facts material to qualification for enlistment or appointment which were represented), when in fact (here state the true fact of facts)) (deliberate concealment of the fact that (here state the fact or facts disqualifying the accused for enlistment or appointment which were concealed)), procure himself/herself to be (enlisted as a ______) (appointed as a ______) in the (here state the armed force in which the accused procured the enlistment or appointment), and did thereafter, (at/on board—location), receive (pay) (allowances) (pay and allowances) under the enlistment) (appointment) so procured.

(2) *For fraudulent separation.*

In that ______ (personal jurisdiction data), did, (at/on board—location), on or about ______ 20 ______, by means of (knowingly false representations that (here state the fact or facts material to eligibility for separation which were represented), when in fact (here state the true fact or facts)) (deliberate concealment of the fact that (here state the fact or facts concealed which made the accused ineligible for separation)), procure himself/herself to be separated from the (here state the armed force from which the accused procured his/her separation).

8. Article 84—Effecting unlawful enlistment, appointment, or separation

a. *Text of statute.* **Any person subject to this chapter who effects an enlistment or appointment in or a separation from the armed forces of any person who is known to him to be ineligible for that enlistment, appointment, or separation because it is prohibited by law, regulation, or order shall be punished as a court-martial may direct.**

b. *Elements.*

(1) That the accused effected the enlistment, appointment, or separation of the person named;

(2) That this person was ineligible for this enlistment, appointment, or separation because it was prohibited by law, regulation, or order; and

(3) That the accused knew of the ineligibility at the time of the enlistment, appointment, or separation.

c. *Explanation.* It must be proved that the enlistment, appointment, or separation was prohibited by law, regulation, or order when effected and that the accused then knew that the person enlisted, appointed, or separated was ineligible for the enlistment, appointment, or separation.

d. *Lesser included offense.* Article 80—attempts

e. *Maximum punishment.* Dishonorable discharge, forfeiture of all pay and allowances, and confinement for 5 years.

f. *Sample specification.*

In that ______ (personal jurisdiction data), did, (at/on board—location), on or about ______ 20 ______, effect (the (enlistment) (appointment) of ______ as a ______ in (here state the armed force in which the person was enlisted or appointed)) (the separation of ______ from (here state the armed force from which the person was separated)), then well knowing that the said ______ was ineligible for such (enlistment) (appointment) (separation) because (here state facts whereby the enlistment, appointment, or separation was prohibited by law, regulation, or order).

9. Article 85—Desertion

a. *Text of statute.*

(a) **Any member of the armed forces who—**

(1) **without authority goes or remains absent from his unit, organization, or place of duty with intent to remain away therefrom permanently;**

(2) **quits his unit, organization, or place of duty with intent to avoid hazardous duty or to shirk important service; or**

(3) **without being regularly separated from one of the armed forces enlists or accepts an appointment in the same or another one of the armed forces without fully disclosing the fact that he has not been regularly separated, or enters any foreign armed service except when authorized by the United States**
[Note: This provision has been held not to state a separate offense by the United States Court of Military Appeals in *United States v. Huff*, 7 U.S.C.M.A. 247, 22 C.M.R. 37 (1956)]; is guilty of desertion.

(b) **Any commissioned officer of the armed forces who, after tender of his resignation and before notice of its acceptance, quits his post or proper duties without leave and with intent to remain away therefrom permanently is guilty of desertion.**

(c) **Any person found guilty of desertion or attempt to desert shall be punished, if the offense is committed in time of war, by death or such other punishment as a court-martial may direct, but if the desertion or attempt to desert occurs at any other time, by such punishment, other than death, as a court-martial may direct.**

b. *Elements.*

(1) *Desertion with intent to remain away permanently.*

(a) That the accused absented himself or herself from his or her unit, organization, or place of duty;

(b) That such absence was without authority;

(c) That the accused, at the time the absence began or at some time during the absence, intended to remain away from his or her unit, organization, or place of duty permanently; and

(d) That the accused remained absent until the date alleged.

[Note: If the absence was terminated by apprehension, add the following element]

(e) That the accused's absence was terminated by apprehension.

(2) *Desertion with intent to avoid hazardous duty or to shirk important service.*

(a) That the accused quit his or her unit, organization, or other place of duty;

(b) That the accused did so with the intent to avoid a certain duty or shirk a certain service;

(c) That the duty to be performed was hazardous or the service important;

(d) That the accused knew that he or she would be required for such duty or service; and

(e) That the accused remained absent until the date alleged.

(3) *Desertion before notice of acceptance of resignation.*

(a) That the accused was a commissioned officer of an armed force of the United States, and had tendered his or her resignation;

(b) That before he or she received notice of the acceptance of the resignation, the accused quit his or her post or proper duties;

(c) That the accused did so with the intent to remain away permanently from his or her post or proper duties; and

(d) That the accused remained absent until the date alleged.

[Note: If the absence was terminated by apprehension, add the following element]

(e) That the accused's absence was terminated by apprehension.

(4) *Attempted desertion.*

(a) That the accused did a certain overt act;

(b) That the act was done with the specific intent to desert;

(c) That the act amounted to more than mere preparation; and

(d) That the act apparently tended to effect the commission of the offense of desertion.

c. *Explanation.*

(1) *Desertion with intent to remain away permanently.*

(a) *In general.* Desertion with intent to remain away permanently is complete when the person absents himself or herself without authority from his or her unit, organization, or place of duty, with the intent to remain away therefrom permanently. A prompt repentance and return, while material in extenuation, is no defense. It is not necessary that the person be absent entirely from military jurisdiction and control.

(b) *Absence without authority* —inception, duration, termination. *See* paragraph 10c.

(c) *Intent to remain away permanently.*

(i) The intent to remain away permanently

from the unit, organization, or place of duty may be formed any time during the unauthorized absence. The intent need not exist throughout the absence, or for any particular period of time, as long as it exists at some time during the absence.

(ii) The accused must have intended to remain away permanently from the unit, organization, or place of duty. When the accused had such an intent, it is no defense that the accused also intended to report for duty elsewhere, or to enlist or accept an appointment in the same or a different armed force.

(iii) The intent to remain away permanently may be established by circumstantial evidence. Among the circumstances from which an inference may be drawn that an accused intended to remain absent permanently or; that the period of absence was lengthy; that the accused attempted to, or did, dispose of uniforms or other military property; that the accused purchased a ticket for a distant point or was arrested, apprehended, or surrendered a considerable distance from the accused's station; that the accused could have conveniently surrendered to military control but did not; that the accused was dissatisfied with the accused's unit, ship, or with military service; that the accused made remarks indicating an intention to desert; that the accused was under charges or had escaped from confinement at the time of the absence; that the accused made preparations indicative of an intent not to return (for example, financial arrangements); or that the accused enlisted or accepted an appointment in the same or another armed force without disclosing the fact that the accused had not been regularly separated, or entered any foreign armed service without being authorized by the United States. On the other hand, the following are included in the circumstances which may tend to negate an inference that the accused intended to remain away permanently: previous long and excellent service; that the accused left valuable personal property in the unit or on the ship; or that the accused was under the influence of alcohol or drugs during the absence. These lists are illustrative only.

(iv) Entries on documents, such as personnel accountability records, which administratively refer to an accused as a "deserter" are not evidence of intent to desert.

(v) Proof of, or a plea of guilty to, an unauthorized absence, even of extended duration, does not, without more, prove guilt of desertion.

(d) *Effect of enlistment or appointment in the same or a different armed force.* Article 85a(3) does not state a separate offense. Rather, it is a rule of evidence by which the prosecution may prove intent to remain away permanently. Proof of an enlistment or acceptance of an appointment in a service without disclosing a preexisting duty status in the same or a different service provides the basis from which an inference of intent to permanently remain away from the earlier unit, organization, or place of duty may be drawn. Furthermore, if a person, without being regularly separated from one of the armed forces, enlists or accepts an appointment in the same or another armed force, the person's presence in the military service under such an enlistment or appointment is not a return to military control and does not terminate any desertion or absence without authority from the earlier unit or organization, unless the facts of the earlier period of service are known to military authorities. If a person, while in desertion, enlists or accepts an appointment in the same or another armed force, and deserts while serving the enlistment or appointment, the person may be tried and convicted for each desertion.

(2) *Quitting unit, organization, or place of duty with intent to avoid hazardous duty or to shirk important service.*

(a) *Hazardous duty or important service.* "Hazardous duty" or "important service" may include service such as duty in a combat or other dangerous area; embarkation for certain foreign or sea duty; movement to a port of embarkation for that purpose; entrainment for duty on the border or coast in time of war or threatened invasion or other disturbances; strike or riot duty; or employment in aid of the civil power in, for example, protecting property, or quelling or preventing disorder in times of great public disaster. Such services as drill, target practice, maneuvers, and practice marches are not ordinarily "hazardous duty or important service." Whether a duty is hazardous or a service is important depends upon the circumstances of the particular case, and is a question of fact for the court-martial to decide.

(b) *Quits.* "Quits" in Article 85 means "goes absent without authority."

(c) *Actual knowledge.* Article 85 *a*(2) requires proof that the accused actually knew of the hazardous duty or important service. Actual knowledge may be proved by circumstantial evidence.

(3) *Attempting to desert.* Once the attempt is made, the fact that the person desists, voluntarily or otherwise, does not cancel the offense. The offense is complete, for example, if the person, intending to desert, hides in an empty freight car on a military reservation, intending to escape by being taken away in the car. Entering the car with the intent to desert is the overt act. For a more detailed discussion of attempts, *see* paragraph 4. For an explanation concerning intent to remain away permanently, *see* subparagraph 9c(1)(c).

(4) *Prisoner with executed punitive discharge.* A prisoner whose dismissal or dishonorable or bad-conduct discharge has been executed is not a "member of the armed forces" within the meaning of Articles 85 or 86, although the prisoner may still be subject to military law under Article 2(*a*)(7). If the facts warrant, such a prisoner could be charged with escape from confinement under Article 95 or an offense under Article 134.

d. *Lesser included offense.* Article 86—absence without leave

e. *Maximum punishment.*

(1) *Completed or attempted desertion with intent to avoid hazardous duty or to shirk important service.* Dishonorable discharge, forfeiture of all pay and allowances, and confinement for 5 years.

(2) *Other cases of completed or attempted desertion.*

(a) *Terminated by apprehension.* Dishonorable discharge, forfeiture of all pay and allowances, and confinement for 3 years.

(b) *Terminated otherwise.* Dishonorable discharge, forfeiture of all pay and allowances, and confinement for 2 years.

(3) *In time of war.* Death or such other punishment as a court-martial may direct.

f. *Sample specifications.*

(1) *Desertion with intent to remain away permanently.*

In that ______ (personal jurisdiction data), did, on or about ______ 20 ____, (a time of war) without authority and with intent to remain away therefrom permanently, absent himself/herself from his/her (unit) (organization) (place of duty), to wit: ______, located at (______), and did remain so absent in desertion until (he/she was apprehended) on or about ______ 20 ____.

(2) *Desertion with intent to avoid hazardous duty or shirk important service.*

In that ______ (personal jurisdiction data), did, on or about ______ 20 ____, (a time of war) with intent to (avoid hazardous duty) (shirk important service), namely: ______, quit his/her (unit) (organization) (place of duty), to wit: ______, located at (______), and did remain so absent in desertion until on or about ______ 20 ____.

(3) *Desertion prior to acceptance of resignation.*

In that ______ (personal jurisdiction data) having tendered his/her resignation and prior to due notice of the acceptance of the same, did, on or about ______ 20 ____, (a time of war) without leave and with intent to remain away therefrom permanently, quit his/her (post) (proper duties), to wit: ______, and did remain so absent in desertion until (he/she was apprehended) on or about ______ 20 ____.

(4) *Attempted desertion.*

In that ______ (personal jurisdiction data), did (at/on board-location), on or about ______ 20 ____, (a time of war) attempt to (absent himself/herself from his/her (unit) (organization) (place of duty) to wit: ______, without authority and with intent to remain away therefrom permanently) (quit his/her (unit) (organization) (place of duty), to wit: ______, located at ______, with intent to (avoid hazardous duty) (shirk important service) namely ______) (______).

10. Article 86—Absence without leave

a. *Text of statute.* **Any member of the armed forces who, without authority—**

(1) **fails to go to his appointed place of duty at the time prescribed;**

(2) **goes from that place; or**

(3) **absents himself or remains absent from his unit, organization, or place of duty at which he is required to be at the time prescribed; shall be punished as a court-martial may direct.**

b. *Elements.*

(1) *Failure to go to appointed place of duty.*

(a) That a certain authority appointed a certain time and place of duty for the accused;

(b) That the accused knew of that time and place; and

(c) That the accused, without authority, failed to go to the appointed place of duty at the time prescribed.

(2) *Going from appointed place of duty.*

(a) That a certain authority appointed a certain time and place of duty for the accused;

(b) That the accused knew of that time and place; and

(c) That the accused, without authority, went from the appointed place of duty after having reported at such place.

(3) *Absence from unit, organization, or place of duty.*

(a) That the accused absented himself or herself from his or her unit, organization, or place of duty at which he or she was required to be;

(b) That the absence was without authority from anyone competent to give him or her leave; and

(c) That the absence was for a certain period of time. [Note: if the absence was terminated by apprehension, add the following element]

(d) That the absence was terminated by apprehension.

(4) *Abandoning watch or guard.*

(a) That the accused was a member of a guard, watch, or duty;

(b) That the accused absented himself or herself from his or her guard, watch, or duty section;

(c) That absence of the accused was without authority; and

[Note: If the absence was with intent to abandon the accused's guard, watch, or duty section, add the following element]

(d) That the accused intended to abandon his or her guard, watch, or duty section.

(5) *Absence from unit, organization, or place of duty with intent to avoid maneuvers or field exercises.*

(a) That the accused absented himself or herself from his or her unit, organization, or place of duty at which he or she was required to be;

(b) That the absence of the accused was without authority;

(c) That the absence was for a certain period of time;

(d) That the accused knew that the absence would occur during a part of a period of maneuvers or field exercises; and

(e) That the accused intended to avoid all or part of a period of maneuvers or field exercises.

c. *Explanation.*

(1) *In general.* This article is designed to cover every case not elsewhere provided for in which any member of the armed forces is through the member's own fault not at the place where the member is required to be at a prescribed time. It is not necessary that the person be absent entirely from military jurisdiction and control. The first part of this article—relating to the appointed place of duty—applies whether the place is appointed as a rendezvous for several or for one only.

(2) *Actual knowledge.* The offenses of failure to go to and going from appointed place of duty require proof that the accused actually knew of the appointed time and place of duty. The offense of absence from unit, organization, or place of duty with intent to avoid maneuvers or field exercises requires proof that the accused actually knew that the absence would occur during a part of a period of maneuvers or field exercises. Actual knowledge may be proved by circumstantial evidence.

(3) *Intent.* Specific intent is not an element of unauthorized absence. Specific intent is an element for certain aggravated unauthorized absences.

(4) *Aggravated forms of unauthorized absence.* There are variations of unauthorized absence under Article 86(3) which are more serious because of aggravating circumstances such as duration of the absence, a special type of duty from which the accused absents himself or herself, and a particular specific intent which accompanies the absence. These circumstances are not essential elements of a violation of Article 86. They simply constitute special matters in aggravation. The following are aggravated unauthorized absences:

(a) Unauthorized absence for more than 3 days (duration).

(b) Unauthorized absence for more than 30 days (duration).

(c) Unauthorized absence from a guard, watch, or duty (special type of duty).

(d) Unauthorized absence from guard, watch,

or duty section with the intent to abandon it (special type of duty and specific intent).

(e) Unauthorized absence with the intent to avoid maneuvers or field exercises (special type of duty and specific intent).

(5) *Control by civilian authorities.* A member of the armed forces turned over to the civilian authorities upon request under Article 14 (*see* R.C.M. 106) is not absent without leave while held by them under that delivery. When a member of the armed forces, being absent with leave, or absent without leave, is held, tried, and acquitted by civilian authorities, the member's status as absent with leave, or absent without leave, is not thereby changed, regardless how long held. The fact that a member of the armed forces is convicted by the civilian authorities, or adjudicated to be a juvenile offender, or the case is "diverted" out of the regular criminal process for a probationary period does not excuse any unauthorized absence, because the member's inability to return was the result of willful misconduct. If a member is released by the civilian authorities without trial, and was on authorized leave at the time of arrest or detention, the member may be found guilty of unauthorized absence only if it is proved that the member actually committed the offense for which detained, thus establishing that the absence was the result of the member's own misconduct.

(6) *Inability to return.* The status of absence without leave is not changed by an inability to return through sickness, lack of transportation facilities, or other disabilities. But the fact that all or part of a period of unauthorized absence was in a sense enforced or involuntary is a factor in extenuation and should be given due weight when considering the initial disposition of the offense. When, however, a person on authorized leave, without fault, is unable to return at the expiration thereof, that person has not committed the offense of absence without leave.

(7) *Determining the unit or organization of an accused.* A person undergoing transfer between activities is ordinarily considered to be attached to the activity to which ordered to report. A person on temporary additional duty continues as a member of the regularly assigned unit and if the person is absent from the temporary duty assignment, the person becomes absent without leave from both units, and may be charged with being absent without leave from either unit.

(8) *Duration.* Unauthorized absence under Article 86(3) is an instantaneous offense. It is complete at the instant an accused absents himself or herself without authority. Duration of the absence is a matter in aggravation for the purpose of increasing the maximum punishment authorized for the offense. Even if the duration of the absence is not over 3 days, it is ordinarily alleged in an Article 86(3) specification. If the duration is not alleged or if alleged but not proved, an accused can be convicted of and punished for only 1 day of unauthorized absence.

(9) *Computation of duration.* In computing the duration of an unauthorized absence, any one continuous period of absence found that totals not more than 24 hours is counted as 1 day; any such period that totals more than 24 hours and not more than 48 hours is counted as 2 days, and so on. The hours of departure and return on different dates are assumed to be the same if not alleged and proved. For example, if an accused is found guilty of unauthorized absence from 0600 hours, 4 April, to 1000 hours, 7 April of the same year (76 hours), the maximum punishment would be based on an absence of 4 days. However, if the accused is found guilty simply of unauthorized absence from 4 April to 7 April, the maximum punishment would be based on an absence of 3 days.

(10) *Termination—methods of return to military control.*

(a) *Surrender to military authority.* A surrender occurs when a person presents himself or herself to any military authority, whether or not a member of the same armed force, notifies that authority of his or her unauthorized absence status, and submits or demonstrates a willingness to submit to military control. Such a surrender terminates the unauthorized absence.

(b) *Apprehension by military authority.* Apprehension by military authority of a known absentee terminates an unauthorized absence.

(c) *Delivery to military authority.* Delivery of a known absentee by anyone to military authority terminates the unauthorized absence.

(d) *Apprehension by civilian authorities at the request of the military.* When an absentee is taken into custody by civilian authorities at the request of military authorities, the absence is terminated.

(e) *Apprehension by civilian authorities with-*

out prior military request. When an absentee is in the hands of civilian authorities for other reasons and these authorities make the absentee available for return to military control, the absence is terminated when the military authorities are informed of the absentee's availability.

(11) *Findings of more than one absence under one specification.* An accused may properly be found guilty of two or more separate unauthorized absences under one specification, provided that each absence is included within the period alleged in the specification and provided that the accused was not misled. If an accused is found guilty of two or more unauthorized absences under a single specification, the maximum authorized punishment shall not exceed that authorized if the accused had been found guilty as charged in the specification.

d. *Lesser included offense.* Article 80—attempts

e. *Maximum punishment.*

(1) *Failing to go to, or going from, the appointed place of duty.* Confinement for 1 month and forfeiture of two-thirds pay per month for 1 month.

(2) *Absence from unit, organization, or other place of duty.*

(a) For not more than 3 days. Confinement for 1 month and forfeiture of two-thirds pay per month for 1 month.

(b) For more than 3 days but not more than 30 days. Confinement for 6 months and forfeiture of two-thirds pay per month for 6months.

(c) For more than 30 days. Dishonorable discharge, forfeiture of all pay and allowances, and confinement for 1 year.

(d) For more than 30 days and terminated by apprehension. Dishonorable discharge, forfeiture of all pay and allowances, and confinement for 18 months.

(3) *From guard or watch.* Confinement for 3 months and forfeiture of two-thirds pay per month for 3 months.

(4) *From guard or watch with intent to abandon.* Bad-conduct discharge, forfeiture of all pay and allowances, and confinement for 6 months.

(5) *With intent to avoid maneuvers or field exercises.* Bad-conduct discharge, forfeiture of all pay and allowances, and confinement for 6 months.

f. *Sample specifications.*

(1) *Failing to go or leaving place of duty.* In that ______ (personal jurisdiction data), did (at/on board—location), on or about ______ 20 ______, without authority, (fail to go at the time prescribed to) (go from) his/her appointed place of duty, to wit: (here set forth the appointed place of duty).

(2) *Absence from unit, organization, or place of duty.* In that ______ (personal jurisdiction data), did, on or about ______ 20 ______, without authority, absent himself/herself from his/her (unit) (organization) (place of duty at which he/she was required to be), to wit: ______, located at ______, and did remain so absent until (he/she was apprehended) on or about ______ 20 ______.

(3) *Absence from unit, organization, or place of duty with intent to avoid maneuvers or field exercises.* In that ______ (personal jurisdiction data), did, on or about ______ 20 ______, without authority and with intent to avoid (maneuvers) (field exercises), absent himself/herself from his/her (unit) (organization) (place of duty at which he/she was required to be), to wit: ______ located at (______), and did remain so absent until on or about ______ 20 ______.

(4) *Abandoning watch or guard.* In that ______ (personal jurisdiction data), being a member of the ______ (guard) (watch) (duty section), did, (at/on board-location), on or about ______ 20 ______, without authority, go from his/her (guard) (watch) (duty section) (with intent to abandon the same).

11. Article 87—Missing movement

a. *Text of statute.*

Any person subject to this chapter who through neglect or design misses the movement of a ship, aircraft, or unit with which he is required in the course of duty to move shall be punished as a court-martial may direct.

b. *Elements.*

(1) That the accused was required in the course of duty to move with a ship, aircraft or unit;

(2) That the accused knew of the prospective movement of the ship, aircraft or unit;

(3) That the accused missed the movement of the ship, aircraft or unit; and

(4) That the accused missed the movement through design or neglect.

c. *Explanation.*

(1) *Movement.* "Movement" as used in Article 87 includes a move, transfer, or shift of a ship, aircraft, or unit involving a substantial distance and period of time. Whether a particular movement is substantial is a question to be determined by the court-martial considering all the circumstances. Changes which do not constitute a "movement" include practice marches of a short duration with a return to the point of departure, and minor changes in location of ships, aircraft, or units, as when a ship is shifted from one berth to another in the same shipyard or harbor or when a unit is moved from one barracks to another on the same post.

(2) *Mode of movement.*

(a) *Unit.* If a person is required in the course of duty to move with a unit, the mode of travel is not important, whether it be military or commercial, and includes travel by ship, train, aircraft, truck, bus, or walking. The word "unit" is not limited to any specific technical category such as those listed in a table of organization and equipment, but also includes units which are created before the movement with the intention that they have organizational continuity upon arrival at their destination regardless of their technical designation, and units intended to be disbanded upon arrival at their destination.

(b) *Ship, aircraft.* If a person is assigned as a crew member or is ordered to move as a passenger aboard a particular ship or aircraft, military or chartered, then missing the particular sailing or flight is essential to establish the offense of missing movement.

(3) *Design.* "Design" means on purpose, intentionally, or according to plan and requires specific intent to miss the movement.

(4) *Neglect.* "Neglect" means the omission to take such measures as are appropriate under the circumstances to assure presence with a ship, aircraft, or unit at the time of a scheduled movement, or doing some act without giving attention to its probable consequences in connection with the prospective movement, such as a departure from the vicinity of the prospective movement to such a distance as would make it likely that one could not return in time for the movement.

(5) *Actual knowledge.* In order to be guilty of the offense, the accused must have actually known of the prospective movement that was missed. Knowledge of the exact hour or even of the exact date of the scheduled movement is not required. It is sufficient if the approximate date was known by the accused as long as there is a causal connection between the conduct of the accused and the missing of the scheduled movement. Knowledge may be proved by circumstantial evidence.

(6) *Proof of absence.* That the accused actually missed the movement may be proved by documentary evidence, as by a proper entry in a log or a morning report. This fact may also be proved by the testimony of personnel of the ship, aircraft, or unit (or by other evidence) that the movement occurred at a certain time, together with evidence that the accused was physically elsewhere at that time.

d. *Lesser included offenses.*

(1) *Design.*

(a) Article 87—missing movement through neglect

(b) Article 86—absence without authority

(c) Article 80—attempts

(2) *Neglect.* Article 86—absence without authority

e. *Maximum punishment.*

(1) *Design.* Dishonorable discharge, forfeiture of all pay and allowances, and confinement for 2 years.

(2) *Neglect.* Bad-conduct discharge, forfeiture of all pay and allowances, and confinement for 1 year.

f. *Sample specification.*

In that ________ (personal jurisdiction data), did, (at/on board—location), on or about ________ 20 ________, through (neglect) (design) miss the movement of (Aircraft No. ________) (Flight ________) (the USS ________) (Company A, 1st Battalion, 7th Infantry) (________) with which he/she was required in the course of duty to move.

12. Article 88—Contempt toward officials

a. *Text of statute.*

Any commissioned officer who uses contemptuous words against the President, the Vice President, Congress, the Secretary of Defense, the Secretary of a military department, the Secretary of Homeland Security, or the Governor or legislature of any State, Territory, Commonwealth, or possession in which he is on duty or present shall be punished as a court-martial may direct.

b. *Elements.*

(1) That the accused was a commissioned officer of the United States armed forces;

(2) That the accused used certain words against an official or legislature named in the article;

(3) That by an act of the accused these words came to the knowledge of a person other than the accused; and

(4) That the words used were contemptuous, either in themselves or by virtue of the circumstances under which they were used.

[Note: If the words were against a Governor or legislature, add the following element]

(5) That the accused was then present in the State, Territory, Commonwealth, or possession of the Governor or legislature concerned.

c. *Explanation.* The official or legislature against whom the words are used must be occupying one of the offices or be one of the legislatures named in Article 88 at the time of the offense. Neither "Congress" nor "legislature" includes its members individually. "Governor" does not include "lieutenant governor." It is immaterial whether the words are used against the official in an official or private capacity. If not personally contemptuous, adverse criticism of one of the officials or legislatures named in the article in the course of a political discussion, even though emphatically expressed, may not be charged as a violation of the article. Similarly, expressions of opinion made in a purely private conversation should not ordinarily be charged. Giving broad circulation to a written publication containing contemptuous words of the kind made punishable by this article, or the utterance of contemptuous words of this kind in the presence of military subordinates, aggravates the offense. The truth or falsity of the statements is immaterial.

d. *Lesser included offense.* Article 80—attempts

e. *Maximum punishment.* Dismissal, forfeiture of all pay and allowances, and confinement for 1 year.

f. *Sample specification.*

In that ________ (personal jurisdiction data), did, (at/on board—location), on or about ________ 20 ________, [use (orally and publicly) (________) the following contemptuous words] [in a contemptuous manner, use (orally and publicly) (________) the following words] against the [(President) (Vice President) (Congress) (Secretary of ________)] [(Governor) (legislature) of the (State of ________) (Territory of ________) (________), a (State) (Territory) (________) in which he/she, the said ________, was then (on duty), (present)], to wit: "________," or words to that effect.

13. Article 89—Disrespect toward a superior commissioned officer

a. *Text of statute.*

Any person subject to this chapter who behaves with disrespect toward his superior commissioned officer shall be punished as a court-martial may direct.

b. *Elements.*

(1) That the accused did or omitted certain acts or used certain language to or concerning a certain commissioned officer;

(2) That such behavior or language was directed toward that officer;

(3) That the officer toward whom the acts, omissions, or words were directed was the superior commissioned officer of the accused;

(4) That the accused then knew that the commissioned officer toward whom the acts, omissions, or words were directed was the accused's superior commissioned officer; and

(5) That, under the circumstances, the behavior or language was disrespectful to that commissioned officer.

c. *Explanation.*

(1) *Superior commissioned officer.*

(a) *Accused and victim in same armed force.* If the accused and the victim are in the same armed force, the victim is a "superior commissioned officer" of the accused when either superior in rank or command to the accused; however, the victim is not a "superior commissioned officer" of the accused if the victim is inferior in command, even though superior in rank.

(b) *Accused and victim in different armed forces.* If the accused and the victim are in different armed forces, the victim is a "superior commissioned officer" of the accused when the victim is a commissioned officer and superior in the chain of command over the accused or when the victim, not a medical officer or a chaplain, is senior in grade to the accused and both are detained by a hostile entity so that recourse to the normal chain of command is prevented. The victim is not a "superior commissioned officer" of the accused merely because the victim is superior in grade to the accused.

(c) *Execution of office.* It is not necessary that the "superior commissioned officer" be in the execution of office at the time of the disrespectful behavior.

(2) *Knowledge.* If the accused did not know that the person against whom the acts or words were directed was the accused's superior commissioned officer, the accused may not be convicted of a violation of this article. Knowledge may be proved by circumstantial evidence.

(3) *Disrespect.* Disrespectful behavior is that which detracts from the respect due the authority and person of a superior commissioned officer. It may consist of acts or language, however expressed, and it is immaterial whether they refer to the superior as an officer or as a private individual. Disrespect by words may be conveyed by abusive epithets or other contemptuous or denunciatory language. Truth is no defense. Disrespect by acts includes neglecting the customary salute, or showing a marked disdain, indifference, insolence, impertinence, undue familiarity, or other rudeness in the presence of the superior officer.

(4) *Presence.* It is not essential that the disrespectful behavior be in the presence of the superior, but ordinarily one should not be held accountable under this article for what was said or done in a purely private conversation.

(5) *Special defense—unprotected victim.* A superior commissioned officer whose conduct in relation to the accused under all the circumstances departs substantially from the required standards appropriate to that officer's rank or position under similar circumstances loses the protection of this article. That accused may not be convicted of being disrespectful to the officer who has so lost the entitlement to respect protected by Article 89.

d. *Lesser included offenses.*

(1) Article 117—provoking speeches or gestures

(2) Article 80—attempts

e. *Maximum punishment.* Bad-conduct discharge, forfeiture of all pay and allowances, and confinement for 1 year.

f. *Sample specification.*

In that __________ (personal jurisdiction data), did, (at/on board—location), on or about __________ 20 __________, behave himself/herself with disrespect toward __________, his/her superior commissioned officer, then known by the said __________ to be his/her superior commissioned officer, by (saying to him/her "__________," or words to that effect) (contemptuously turning from and leaving him/her while he/she, the said __________, was talking to him/her, the said __________) (__________).

14. Article 90—Assaulting or willfully disobeying superior commissioned officer

a. *Text of statute.* **Any person subject to this chapter who—**

(1) **strikes his superior commissioned officer or draws or lifts up any weapon or offers any violence against him while he is in the execution of his office; or**

(2) **willfully disobeys a lawful command of his superior commissioned officer;**

shall be punished, if the offense is committed in time of war, by death or such other punishment as a court-martial may direct, and if the offense is committed at any other time, by such punishment, other than death, as a court-martial may direct.

b. *Elements.*

(1) *Striking or assaulting superior commissioned officer.*

(a) That the accused struck, drew, or lifted up a weapon against, or offered violence against, a certain commissioned officer;

(b) That the officer was the superior commissioned officer of the accused;

(c) That the accused then knew that the officer was the accused's superior commissioned officer; and

(d) That the superior commissioned officer was then in the execution of office.

(2) *Disobeying superior commissioned officer.*

(a) That the accused received a lawful command from a certain commissioned officer;

(b) That this officer was the superior commissioned officer of the accused;

(c) That the accused then knew that this officer was the accused's superior commissioned officer; and

(d) That the accused willfully disobeyed the lawful command.

c. *Explanation.*

(1) *Striking or assaulting superior commissioned officer.*

(a) *Definitions.*

(i) *Superior commissioned officer.* The definitions in paragraph 13c(1)(*a*) and(*b*) apply here and in subparagraph c(2).

(ii) *Strikes.* "Strikes" means an intentional blow, and includes any offensive touching of the person of an officer, however slight.

(iii) *Draws or lifts up any weapon against.* The phrase "draws or lifts up any weapon against" covers any simple assault committed in the manner stated. The drawing of any weapon in an aggressive manner or the raising or brandishing of the same in a threatening manner in the presence of and at the superior is the sort of act proscribed. The raising in a threatening manner of a firearm, whether or not loaded, of a club, or of anything by which a serious blow or injury could be given is included in "lifts up."

(iv) *Offers any violence against.* The phrase "offers any violence against" includes any form of battery or of mere assault not embraced in the preceding more specific terms "strikes" and "draws or lifts up." If not executed, the violence must be physically attempted or menaced. A mere threatening in words is not an offering of violence in the sense of this article.

(b) *Execution of office.* An officer is in the execution of office when engaged in any act or service required or authorized by treaty, statute, regulation, the order of a superior, or military usage. In general, any striking or use of violence against any superior officer by a person over whom it is the duty of that officer to maintain discipline at the time, would be striking or using violence against the officer in the execution of office. The commanding officer on board a ship or the commanding officer of a unit in the field is generally considered to be on duty at all times.

(c) *Knowledge.* If the accused did not know the officer was the accused's superior commissioned officer, the accused may not be convicted of this offense. Knowledge may be proved by circumstantial evidence.

(d) *Defenses.* In a prosecution for striking or assaulting a superior commissioned officer in violation of this article, it is a defense that the accused acted in the proper discharge of some duty, or that the victim behaved in a manner toward the accused such as to lose the protection of this article (*see* paragraph 13c(5)). For example, if the victim initiated an unlawful attack on the accused, this would deprive the victim of the protection of this article, and, in addition, could excuse any lesser included offense of assault as done in self-defense, depending on the circumstances (*see* paragraph 54c; R.C.M. 916(*e*)).

(2) *Disobeying superior commissioned officer.*

(a) *Lawfulness of the order.*

(i) *Inference of lawfulness.* An order requiring the performance of a military duty or act may be inferred to be lawful and it is disobeyed at the peril of the subordinate. This inference does not apply to a patently illegal order, such as one that directs the commission of a crime.

(ii) *Determination of lawfulness.* The lawfulness of an order is a question of law to be determined by the military judge.

(iii) *Authority of issuing officer.* The commissioned officer issuing the order must have authority to give such an order. Authorization may be based on law, regulation, or custom of the service.

(iv) *Relationship to military duty.* The order must relate to military duty, which includes all activities reasonably necessary to accomplish a military mission, or safeguard or promote the morale, discipline, and usefulness of members of a command and directly connected with the maintenance of good order in the service. The order may not, without such a valid military purpose, interfere with private rights or personal affairs. However, the dictates of a person's conscience, religion, or personal philosophy cannot justify or excuse the disobedience of an otherwise lawful order. Disobedience of an order which has for its sole object the attainment of some private end, or which is given for the sole purpose of increasing the penalty for an offense which it is expected the accused may commit, is not punishable under this article.

(v) *Relationship to statutory or constitutional rights.* The order must not conflict with the statutory or constitutional rights of the person receiving the order.

(b) *Personal nature of the order.* The order

must be directed specifically to the subordinate. Violations of regulations, standing orders or directives, or failure to perform previously established duties are not punishable under this article, but may violate Article 92.

(c) *Form and transmission of the order.* As long as the order is understandable, the form of the order is immaterial, as is the method by which it is transmitted to the accused.

(d) *Specificity of the order.* The order must be a specific mandate to do or not to do a specific act. An exhortation to "obey the law" or to perform one's military duty does not constitute an order under this article.

(e) *Knowledge.* The accused must have actual knowledge of the order and of the fact that the person issuing the order was the accused's superior commissioned officer. Actual knowledge may be proved by circumstantial evidence.

(f) *Nature of the disobedience.* "Willful disobedience" is an intentional defiance of authority. Failure to comply with an order through heedlessness, remissness, or forgetfulness is not a violation of this article but may violate Article 92.

(g) *Time for compliance.* When an order requires immediate compliance, an accused's declared intent not to obey and the failure to make any move to comply constitutes disobedience. If an order does not indicate the time within which it is to be complied with, either expressly or by implication, then a reasonable delay in compliance does not violate this article. If an order requires performance in the future, an accused's present statement of intention to disobey the order does not constitute disobedience of that order, although carrying out that intention may.

(3) *Civilians and discharged prisoners.* A discharged prisoner or other civilian subject to military law (*see* Article 2) and under the command of a commissioned officer is subject to the provisions of this article.

d. *Lesser included offenses.*

(1) *Striking superior commissioned officer in execution of office.*

(a) Article 90—drawing or lifting up a weapon or offering violence to superior commissioned officer in execution of office

(b) Article 128—assault; assault consummated by a battery; assault with a dangerous weapon

(c) Article 128—assault or assault consummated by a battery upon commissioned officer not in the execution of office

(d) Article 80—attempts

(2) *Drawing or lifting up a weapon or offering violence to superior commissioned officer in execution of office.*

(a) Article 128—assault, assault with dangerous weapon

(b) Article 128—assault upon a commissioned officer not in the execution of office

(c) Article 80—attempts

(3) Willfully disobeying lawful order of superior commissioned officer.

(a) Article 92—failure to obey lawful order

(b) Article 89—disrespect to superior commissioned officer

(c) Article 80—attempts

e. *Maximum punishment.*

(1) *Striking, drawing, or lifting up any weapon or offering any violence to superior commissioned officer in the execution of office.* Dishonorable discharge, forfeiture of all pay and allowances, and confinement for 10 years.

(2) *Willfully disobeying a lawful order of superior commissioned officer.* Dishonorable discharge, forfeiture of all pay and allowances, and confinement for 5 years.

(3) *In time of war.* Death or such other punishment as a court-martial may direct.

f. *Sample specifications.*

(1) *Striking superior commissioned officer.*

In that ________ (personal jurisdiction data), did, (at/on board—location) (subject-matter jurisdiction data, if required), on or about ________ 20 ____, (a time of war) strike ________, his/her superior commissioned officer, then known by the said ________ to be his/her superior commissioned officer, who was then in the execution of his/her office, (in) (on) the ________ with (*a*) (his/her) ________.

(2) *Drawing or lifting up a weapon against superior commissioned officer.*

In that ________ (personal jurisdiction data), did, (at/on board—location) (subject-matter jurisdiction data, if required), on or about ________ 20 ____, (a time of war) (draw) lift up) a weapon, to wit: a ________, against , his/her superior commissioned officer, then known by the said to be his/her superior commissioned officer, who was then in the execution of his/her office.

(3) *Offering violence to superior commissioned officer.*

In that (personal jurisdiction data), did, (at/on board—location) (subject-matter jurisdiction data, if required), on or about 20 , (a time of war) offer violence against , his/her superior commissioned officer, then known by the said- to be his/her superior commissioned officer, who was then in the execution of his/her office, by .

(4) *Willful disobedience of superior commissioned officer.*

In that (personal jurisdiction data), having received a lawful command from , his/her superior commissioned officer, then known by the said to be his/her superior commissioned officer, to , or words to that effect, did, (at/on board—location), on or about 20 , willfully disobey the same.

15. Article 91—Insubordinate conduct toward warrant officer, noncommissioned officer, or petty officer

a. *Text of statute.* **Any warrant officer or enlisted member who—**

(1) **strikes or assaults a warrant officer, noncommissioned officer, or petty officer, while that officer is in the execution of his office;**

(2) **willfully disobeys the lawful order of a warrant officer, noncommissioned officer, or petty officer; or**

(3) **treats with contempt or is disrespectful in language or deportment toward a warrant officer, noncommissioned officer, or petty officer while that officer is in the execution of his office; shall be punished as a court-martial may direct.**

b. *Elements.*

(1) *Striking or assaulting warrant, noncommissioned, or petty officer.*

(a) That the accused was a warrant officer or enlisted member;

(b) That the accused struck or assaulted a certain warrant, noncommissioned, or petty officer;

(c) That the striking or assault was committed while the victim was in the execution of office; and

(d) That the accused then knew that the person struck or assaulted was a warrant, noncommissioned, or petty officer.

[Note: If the victim was the superior noncommissioned or petty officer of the accused, add the following elements]

(e) That the victim was the superior noncommissioned, or petty officer of the accused; and

(f) That the accused then knew that the person struck or assaulted was the accused's superior noncommissioned, or petty officer.

(2) *Disobeying a warrant, noncommissioned, or petty officer.*

(a) That the accused was a warrant officer or enlisted member;

(b) That the accused received a certain lawful order from a certain warrant, noncommissioned, or petty officer;

(c) That the accused then knew that the person giving the order was a warrant, noncommissioned, or petty officer;

(d) That the accused had a duty to obey the order; and

(e) That the accused willfully disobeyed the order.

(3) *Treating with contempt or being disrespectful in language or deportment toward a warrant, noncommissioned, or petty officer.*

(a) That the accused was a warrant officer or enlisted member;

(b) That the accused did or omitted certain acts, or used certain language;

(c) That such behavior or language was used toward and within sight or hearing of a certain warrant, noncommissioned, or petty officer;

(d) That the accused then knew that the person toward whom the behavior or language was directed was a warrant, noncommissioned, or petty officer;

(e) That the victim was then in the execution of office; and

(f) That under the circumstances the accused, by such behavior or language, treated with contempt or was disrespectful to said warrant, noncommissioned, or petty officer.

[Note: If the victim was the superior noncommissioned, or petty officer of the accused, add the following elements]

(g) That the victim was the superior noncommissioned, or petty officer of the accused; and

(h) That the accused then knew that the person toward whom the behavior or language was directed was the accused's superior noncommissioned, or petty officer.

c. *Explanation.*

(1) *In general.* Article 91 has the same general objects with respect to warrant, noncommissioned, and petty officers as Articles 89 and 90 have with respect to commissioned officers, namely, to ensure obedience to their lawful orders, and to protect them from violence, insult, or disrespect. Unlike Articles 89 and 90, however, this article does not require a superior-subordinate relationship as an element of any of the offenses denounced. This article does not protect an acting noncommissioned officer or acting petty officer, nor does it protect military police or members of the shore patrol who are not warrant, noncommissioned, or petty officers.

(2) *Knowledge.* All of the offenses prohibited by Article 91 require that the accused have actual knowledge that the victim was a warrant, noncommissioned, or petty officer. Actual knowledge may be proved by circumstantial evidence.

(3) *Striking or assaulting a warrant, noncommissioned, or petty officer.* For a discussion of "strikes" and "in the execution of office," *see* paragraph 14c. For a discussion of "assault," see paragraph 54c. An assault by a prisoner who has been discharged from the service, or by any other civilian subject to military law, upon a warrant, noncommissioned, or petty officer should be charged under Article 128 or 134.

(4) *Disobeying a warrant, noncommissioned, or petty officer. See* paragraph 14c(2) for a discussion of lawfulness, personal nature, form, transmission, and specificity of the order, nature of the disobedience, and time for compliance with the order.

(5) *Treating with contempt or being disrespectful in language or deportment toward a warrant, noncommissioned, or petty officer.* "Toward" requires that the behavior and language be within the sight or hearing of the warrant, noncommissioned, or petty officer concerned. For a discussion of "in the execution of his office," *see* paragraph 14c. For a discussion of disrespect, *see* paragraph 13c.

d. *Lesser included offenses.*

(1) *Striking or assaulting warrant, noncommissioned, or petty officer in the execution of office.*

(a) Article 128—assault; assault consummated by a battery; assault with a dangerous weapon

(b) Article 128—assault upon warrant, noncommissioned, or petty officer not in the execution of office

(c) Article 80—attempts

(2) *Disobeying a warrant, noncommissioned, or petty officer.*

(a) Article 92—failure to obey a lawful order

(b) Article 80—attempts

(3) *Treating with contempt or being disrespectful in language or deportment toward warrant, noncommissioned, or petty officer in the execution of office.*

(a) Article 117—using provoking or reproachful speech

(b) Article 80—attempts

e. *Maximum punishment.*

(1) *Striking or assaulting warrant officer.* Dishonorable discharge, forfeiture of all pay and allowances, and confinement for 5 years.

(2) *Striking or assaulting superior noncommissioned or petty officer.* Dishonorable discharge, forfeiture of all pay and allowances, and confinement for 3 years.

(3) *Striking or assaulting other noncommissioned or petty officer.* Dishonorable discharge, forfeiture of all pay and allowances, and confinement for 1 year.

(4) *Willfully disobeying the lawful order of a warrant officer.* Dishonorable discharge, forfeiture of all pay and allowances, and confinement for 2 years.

(5) *Willfully disobeying the lawful order of a noncommissioned or petty officer.* Bad-conduct discharge, forfeiture of all pay and allowances, and confinement for 1 year.

(6) *Contempt or disrespect to warrant officer.* Bad-conduct discharge, forfeiture of all pay and allowances, and confinement for 9 months.

(7) *Contempt or disrespect to superior noncommissioned or petty officer.* Bad-conduct discharge, forfeiture of all pay and allowances, and confinement for 6 months.

(8) *Contempt or disrespect to other noncommissioned or petty officer.* Forfeiture of two-thirds pay per month for 3 months, and confinement for 3 months.

f. *Sample specifications.*

(1) *Striking or assaulting warrant, noncommissioned, or petty officer.*

In that ______ (personal jurisdiction data), did, (at/on board—location) (subject-matter jurisdiction data, if required), on or about ______ 20 ___, (strike) (assault) ______, a ______ officer, then known to the said ______ to be a (superior) ______ officer who was then in the execution of his/her office, by ______ him/her (in) (on) (the ______) with (*a*) ______ (his/her) ______.

(2) *Willful disobedience of warrant, noncommissioned, or petty officer.*

In that ______ (personal jurisdiction data), having received a lawful order from ______, a ______ officer, then known by the said ______ to be a ______ officer, to ______, an order which it was his/her duty to obey, did (at/on board— location), on or about ______ 20 ___, willfully disobey the same.

(3) *Contempt or disrespect toward warrant, noncommissioned, or petty officer.*

In that ______ (personal jurisdiction data) (at/on board—location), on or about ______ 20 ______, [did treat with contempt] [was disrespectful in (language) (deportment) toward] ______, a ______ officer, then known by the said ______ to be a (superior) ______ officer, who was then in the execution of his/her office, by (saying to him/her, "______," or words to that effect) (spitting at his/her feet) (______)

16. Article 92—Failure to obey order or regulation

a. *Text of statute.* **Any person subject to this chapter who—**

(1) **violates or fails to obey any lawful general order or regulation;**

(2) **having knowledge of any other lawful order issued by a member of the armed forces, which it is his duty to obey, fails to obey the order; or**

(3) **is derelict in the performance of his duties; shall be punished as a court-martial may direct.**

b. *Elements.*

(1) *Violation of or failure to obey a lawful general order or regulation.*

(a) That there was in effect a certain lawful general order or regulation;

(b) That the accused had a duty to obey it; and

(c) That the accused violated or failed to obey the order or regulation.

(2) *Failure to obey other lawful order.*

(a) That a member of the armed forces issued a certain lawful order;

(b) That the accused had knowledge of the order;

(c) That the accused had a duty to obey the order; and

(d) That the accused failed to obey the order.

(3) *Dereliction in the performance of duties.*

(a) That the accused had certain duties;

(b) That the accused knew or reasonably should have known of the duties; and

(c) That the accused was (willfully) (through neglect or culpable inefficiency) derelict in the performance of those duties.

c. *Explanation.*

(1) *Violation of or failure to obey a lawful general order or regulation.*

(a) *Authority to issue general orders and regulations.* General orders or regulations are those orders or regulations generally applicable to an armed force which are properly published by the President or the Secretary of Defense, of Homeland Security, or of a military department, and those orders or regulations generally applicable to the command of the officer issuing them throughout the command or a particular subdivision thereof which are issued by:

(i) an officer having general court-martial jurisdiction;

(ii) a general or flag officer in command; or

(iii) a commander superior to (i) or (ii).

(b) *Effect of change of command on validity of order.* A general order or regulation issued by a commander with authority under Article 92(1) retains its character as a general order or regulation when another officer takes command, until it expires by its own terms or is rescinded by separate action, even if it is issued by an officer who is a general or flag officer in command and command is assumed by another officer who is not a general or flag officer.

(c) *Lawfulness.* A general order or regulation is lawful unless it is contrary to the Constitution, the laws of the United States, or lawful superior orders or for some other reason is beyond the authority of the official issuing it. *See* the discussion of lawfulness in paragraph 14c(2)(a).

(d) *Knowledge.* Knowledge of a general order or regulation need not be alleged or proved, as knowledge is not an element of this offense and a lack of knowledge does not constitute a defense.

(e) *Enforceability.* Not all provisions in general orders or regulations can be enforced under Article 92(1). Regulations which only supply general guidelines or advice for conducting military functions may not be enforceable under Article 92(1).

(2) *Violation of or failure to obey other lawful order.*

(a) *Scope.* Article 92(2) includes all other lawful orders which may be issued by a member of the armed forces, violations of which are not chargeable under Article 90, 91, or 92(1). It includes the violation of written regulations which are not general regulations. *See also* subparagraph (1)(e) above as applicable.

(b) *Knowledge.* In order to be guilty of this offense, a person must have had actual knowledge of the order or regulation. Knowledge of the order may be proved by circumstantial evidence.

(c) *Duty to obey order.*

(i) *From a superior.* A member of one armed force who is senior in rank to a member of another armed force is the superior of that member with authority to issue orders which that member has a duty to obey under the same circumstances as a commissioned officer of one armed force is the superior commissioned officer of a member of another armed force for the purposes of Articles 89 and 90. *See* paragraph 13c(1).

(ii) *From one not a superior.* Failure to obey the lawful order of one not a superior is an offense under Article 92(2), provided the accused had a duty to obey the order, such as one issued by a sentinel or a member of the armed forces police. *See* paragraph 15b(2) if the order was issued by a warrant, noncommissioned, or petty officer in the execution of office.

(3) *Dereliction in the performance of duties.*

(a) *Duty.* A duty may be imposed by treaty, statute, regulation, lawful order, standard operating procedure, or custom of the service.

(b) *Knowledge.* Actual knowledge of duties may be proved by circumstantial evidence. Actual knowledge need not be shown if the individual reasonably should have known of the duties. This may be demonstrated by regulations, training or operating manuals, customs of the service, academic literature or testimony, testimony of persons who have held similar or superior positions, or similar evidence.

(c) *Derelict.* A person is derelict in the performance of duties when that person willfully or negligently fails to perform that person's duties or when that person performs them in a culpably inefficient manner. "Willfully" means intentionally. It refers to the doing of an act knowingly and purposely, specifically intending the natural and probable consequences of the act. "Negligently" means an act or omission of a person who is under a duty to use due care which exhibits a lack of that degree of care which a reasonably prudent person would have exercised under the same or similar circumstances. "Culpable inefficiency" is inefficiency for which there is no reasonable or just excuse.

(d) *Ineptitude.* A person is not derelict in the performance of duties if the failure to perform those duties is caused by ineptitude rather than by willfulness, negligence, or culpable inefficiency, and may not be charged under this article, or otherwise punished. For example, a recruit who has tried earnestly during rifle training and throughout record firing is not derelict in the performance of duties if the recruit fails to qualify with the weapon.

d. *Lesser included offense.* Article 80—attempts

e. *Maximum punishment.*

(1) *Violation or failure to obey lawful general order or regulation.* Dishonorable discharge, forfeiture of all pay and allowances, and confinement for 2 years.

(2) *Violation of failure to obey other lawful order.* Bad-conduct discharge, forfeiture of all pay and allowances, and confinement for 6 months.

[Note: For (1) and (2), above, the punishment set

forth does not apply in the following cases: if in the absence of the order or regulation which was violated or not obeyed the accused would on the same facts be subject to conviction for another specific offense for which a lesser punishment is prescribed; or if the violation or failure to obey is a breach of restraint imposed as a result of an order. In these instances, the maximum punishment is that specifically prescribed elsewhere for that particular offense.]

(3) *Dereliction in the performance of duties.*

(A) *Through neglect or culpable inefficiency.* Forfeiture of two-thirds pay per month for 3 months and confinement for 3 months.

(B) *Willful.* Bad-conduct discharge, forfeiture of all pay and allowances, and confinement for 6 months.

f. *Sample specifications.*

(1) *Violation or failure to obey lawful general order or regulation.*

In that ________ (personal jurisdiction data), did, (at/on board—location) (subject-matter jurisdiction data, if required), on or about ________ 20 ___, (violate) (fail to obey) a lawful general (order) (regulation), to wit: (paragraph ________, (Army) (Air Force) Regulation ________, dated ________ 20 ___) (Article ________, U.S. Navy Regulations, dated ________ 20 ________) (General Order No. ________, U.S. Navy, dated ________ 20 ___) (________), by (wrongfully) ________.

(2) *Violation or failure to obey other lawful written order.*

In that ________ (personal jurisdiction data), having knowledge of a lawful order issued by ________, to wit: (paragraph ________, (________ the Combat Group Regulation No. ________) (USS ________, Regulationtion ________), dated ________) (________), an order which it was his/her duty to obey, did, (at/on board—location) (subject-matter jurisdiction data, if required), on or about ________ 20 ________, fail to obey the same by (wrongfully) ________.

(3) *Failure to obey other lawful order.*

In that ________, (personal jurisdiction data) having knowledge of a lawful order issued by ________ (to submit to certain medical treatment) (to ________) (not to ________) (________), an order which it was his/her duty to obey, did (at/on board—location) (subject-matter jurisdiction data, if required), on or about ________ 20 ________, fail to obey the same (by (wrongfully) ________.)

(4) *Dereliction in the performance of duties.*

In that ________, (personal jurisdiction data), who (knew) (should have known) of his/her duties (at/on board—location) (subject-matter jurisdiction data, if required), (on or about ________ 20 ___) (from about ________ 20 ________ to about ________ 20 ___), was derelict in the performance of those duties in that he/she (negligently) (willfully) (by culpable inefficiency) failed ________, as it was his/her duty to do.

17. Article 93—Cruelty and maltreatment

a. *Text of statute.*

Any person subject to this chapter who is guilty of cruelty toward, or oppression or maltreatment of, any person subject to his orders shall be punished as a court-martial may direct.

b. *Elements.*

(1) That a certain person was subject to the orders of the accused; and

(2) That the accused was cruel toward, or oppressed, or maltreated that person.

c. *Explanation.*

(1) *Nature of victim.* "Any person subject to his orders" means not only those persons under the direct or immediate command of the accused but extends to all persons, subject to the code or not, who by reason of some duty are required to obey the lawful orders of the accused, regardless whether the accused is in the direct chain of command over the person.

(2) *Nature of act.* The cruelty, oppression, or maltreatment, although not necessarily physical, must be measured by an objective standard. Assault, improper punishment, and sexual harassment may constitute this offense. Sexual harassment includes influencing, offering to influence, or threatening the career, pay, or job of another person in exchange for sexual favors, and deliberate or repeated offensive comments or gestures of a sexual nature. The imposition of necessary or proper duties and the exaction of their performance does not constitute this offense

even though the duties are arduous or hazardous or both.

d. *Lesser included offense.* Article 80—attempts

e. *Maximum punishment.* Dishonorable discharge, forfeiture of all pay and allowances, and confinement for 1 year.

f. *Sample specification.*

In that ______ (personal jurisdiction data), (at/on board—location) (subject-matter jurisdiction data, if required), on or about ______ 20 ___, (was cruel toward) (did (oppress) (maltreat)) ______, a person subject to his/her orders, by (kicking him/her in the stomach) (confining him/her for twenty-four hours without water) (______).

18. Article 94—Mutiny and sedition

a. *Text of statute.*

Any person subject to this chapter who—

(1) **with intent to usurp or override lawful military authority, refuse, in concert with any other person, to obey orders or otherwise do his duty or creates any violence or disturbance is guilty of mutiny;**

(2) **with intent to cause the overthrow or destruction of lawful civil authority, creates, in concert with any other person, revolt, violence, or other disturbance against that authority is guilty of sedition;**

(3) **fails to do his utmost to prevent and suppress a mutiny or sedition being committed in his presence, or fails to take all reasonable means to inform his superior commissioned officer or commanding officer of a mutiny or sedition which he knows or has reason to believe is taking place, is guilty of a failure to suppress or report a mutiny or sedition.**

(b) **A person who is found guilty of attempted mutiny, mutiny, sedition, or failure to suppress or report a mutiny or sedition shall be punished by death or such other punishment as a court-martial may direct.**

b. *Elements.*

(1) *Mutiny by creating violence or disturbance.*

(a) That the accused created violence or a disturbance; and

(b) That the accused created this violence or disturbance with intent to usurp or override lawful military authority.

(2) *Mutiny by refusing to obey orders or perform duty.*

(a) That the accused refused to obey orders or otherwise do the accused's duty;

(b) That the accused in refusing to obey orders or perform duty acted in concert with another person or persons; and

(c) That the accused did so with intent to usurp or override lawful military authority.

(3) *Sedition.*

(a) That the accused created revolt, violence, or disturbance against lawful civil authority;

(b) That the accused acted in concert with another person or persons; and

(c) That the accused did so with the intent to cause the overthrow or destruction of that authority.

(4) *Failure to prevent and suppress a mutiny or sedition.*

(a) That an offense of mutiny or sedition was committed in the presence of the accused; and

(b) That the accused failed to do the accused's utmost to prevent and suppress the mutiny or sedition.

(5) *Failure to report a mutiny or sedition.*

(a) That an offense of mutiny or sedition occurred;

(b) That the accused knew or had reason to believe that the offense was taking place; and

(c) That the accused failed to take all reasonable means to inform the accused's superior commissioned officer or commander of the offense.

(6) *Attempted mutiny.*

(a) That the accused committed a certain overt act;

(b) That the act was done with specific intent to commit the offense of mutiny;

(c) That the act amounted to more than mere preparation; and

(d) That the act apparently tended to effect the commission of the offense of mutiny.

c. *Explanation.*

(1) *Mutiny.* Article 94(*a*)(1) defines two types of mutiny, both requiring an intent to usurp or override military authority.

(a) *Mutiny by creating violence or disturbance.*

Mutiny by creating violence or disturbance may be committed by one person acting alone or by more than one acting together.

(b) *Mutiny by refusing to obey orders or perform duties.* Mutiny by refusing to obey orders or perform duties requires collective insubordination and necessarily includes some combination of two or more persons in resisting lawful military authority. This concert of insubordination need not be preconceived, nor is it necessary that the insubordination be active or violent. It may consist simply of a persistent and concerted refusal or omission to obey orders, or to do duty, with an insubordinate intent, that is, with an intent to usurp or override lawful military authority. The intent may be declared in words or inferred from acts, omissions, or surrounding circumstances.

(2) *Sedition.* Sedition requires a concert of action in resistance to civil authority. This differs from mutiny by creating violence or disturbance. *See* subparagraph c(1)(*a*) above.

(3) *Failure to prevent and suppress a mutiny or sedition.* "Utmost" means taking those measures to prevent and suppress a mutiny or sedition which may properly be called for by the circumstances, including the rank, responsibilities, or employment of the person concerned. "Utmost" includes the use of such force, including deadly force, as may be reasonably necessary under the circumstances to prevent and suppress a mutiny or sedition.

(4) *Failure to report a mutiny or sedition.* Failure to "take all reasonable means to inform" includes failure to take the most expeditious means available. When the circumstances known to the accused would have caused a reasonable person in similar circumstances to believe that a mutiny or sedition was occurring, this may establish that the accused had such "reason to believe" that mutiny or sedition was occurring. Failure to report an impending mutiny or sedition is not an offense in violation of Article 94. *But see* paragraph 16c(3) (dereliction of duty).

(5) *Attempted mutiny.* For a discussion of attempts, see paragraph 4.

d. *Lesser included offenses.*

(1) *Mutiny by creating violence or disturbance.*

(a) Article 90—assault on commissioned officer

(b) Article 91—assault on warrant, noncommissioned, or petty officer

(c) Article 94—attempted mutiny

(d) Article 116—riot; breach of peace

(e) Article 128—assault

(f) Article 134—disorderly conduct

(2) *Mutiny by refusing to obey orders or perform duties.*

(a) Article 90—willful disobedience of commissioned officer

(b) Article 91—willful disobedience of warrant, noncommissioned, or petty officer

(c) Article 92—failure to obey lawful order

(d) Article 94—attempted mutiny

(3) *Sedition.*

(a) Article 116—riot; breach of peace

(b) Article 128—assault

(c) Article 134—disorderly conduct

(d) Article 80—attempts

e. *Maximum punishment.* For all offenses under Article 94, death or such other punishment as a court-martial may direct.

f. *Sample specifications.*

(1) *Mutiny by creating violence or disturbance.*

In that __________ (personal jurisdiction data), with intent to (usurp) (override) (usurp and override) lawful military authority, did, (at/on board—location) (subject-matter jurisdiction data, if required), on or about __________ 20 ____, create (violence) (a disturbance) by (attacking the officers of the said ship) (barricading himself/herself in Barracks T7, firing his/her rifle at __________, and exhorting other persons to join him/her in defiance of __________) (__________).

(2) *Mutiny by refusing to obey orders or perform duties.*

In that __________ (personal jurisdiction data), with intent to (usurp) (override) (usurp and override) lawful military authority, did, (at/on board— location) on or about __________ 20 ____, refuse, in concert with __________ (and __________) (others whose names are unknown), to (obey the orders of __________ to __________) (perform his/her duty as __________).

(3) *Sedition.*

In that __________ (personal jurisdiction data),

with intent to cause the (overthrow) (destruction) (overthrow and destruction) of lawful civil authority, to wit: ________, did, (at/on board—location) (subject-matter jurisdiction data, if required), on or about ________ 20 ____, in concert with (________) and (________) (others whose names are unknown), create (revolt) (violence) (a disturbance) against such authority by (entering the Town Hall of ________ and destroying property and records therein) (marching upon and compelling the surrender of the police of ________) (________).

(4) *Failure to prevent and suppress a mutiny or sedition.*

In that ________ (personal jurisdiction data), did, (at/on board—location) (subject-matter jurisdiction data, if required), on or about ________ 20 ____, fail to do his/her utmost to prevent and suppress a (mutiny) (sedition) among the (soldiers) (sailors) (airmen) (marines) (________) of ________, which (mutiny) (sedition) was being committed in his/her presence, in that (he/she took no means to compel the dispersal of the assembly) (he/she made no effort to assist ________ who was attempting to quell the mutiny) (________).

(5) *Failure to report a mutiny or sedition.*

In that ________ (personal jurisdiction data), did, (at/on board—location) (subject-matter jurisdiction data, if required), on or about ________ 20 ____, fail to take all reasonable means to inform his/her superior commissioned officer or his/her commander of a (mutiny) (sedition) among the (soldiers) (sailors) (airmen) (marines) (________) of ________, which (mutiny) (sedition) he/she, the said ________ (knew) (had reason to believe) was taking place.

(6) *Attempted mutiny.*

In that ________ (personal jurisdiction data), with intent to (usurp) (override) (usurp and override) lawful military authority, did, (at/on board— location) (subject-matter jurisdiction data, if required), on or about ________ 20 ____, attempt to (create (violence) (a disturbance) by ________) (________).

19. Article 95—Resistance, flight, breach of arrest, and escape

a. *Text of statute.*

Any person subject to this chapter who—

(1) resists apprehension; (2) flees from apprehension; (3) breaks arrest; or (4) escapes from custody or confinement;

shall be punished as a court-martial may direct.

b. *Elements.*

(1) *Resisting apprehension.*

(a) That a certain person attempted to apprehend the accused;

(b) That said person was authorized to apprehend the accused; and

(c) That the accused actively resisted the apprehension.

(2) *Flight from apprehension.*

(a) That a certain person attempted to apprehend the accused;

(b) That said person was authorized to apprehend the accused; and

(c) That the accused fled from the apprehension.

(3) *Breaking arrest.*

(a) That a certain person ordered the accused into arrest;

(b) That said person was authorized to order the accused into arrest; and

(c) That the accused went beyond the limits of arrest before being released from that arrest by proper authority.

(4) *Escape from custody.*

(a) That a certain person apprehended the accused;

(b) That said person was authorized to apprehend the accused; and

(c) That the accused freed himself or herself from custody before being released by proper authority.

(5) *Escape from confinement.*

(a) That a certain person ordered the accused into confinement;

(b) That said person was authorized to order the accused into confinement; and

(c) That the accused freed himself or herself from confinement before being released by proper authority. [Note: If the escape was post-trial confinement, add the following element]

(d) That the confinement was the result of a court-martial conviction.

c. *Explanation.*

(1) *Resisting apprehension.*

(a) *Apprehension.* Apprehension is the taking of a person into custody. *See* R.C.M. 302.

(b) *Authority to apprehend. See* R.C.M. 302(*b*) concerning who may apprehend. Whether the status of a person authorized that person to apprehend the accused is a question of law to be decided by the military judge. Whether the person who attempted to make an apprehension had such a status is a question of fact to be decided by the factfinder.

(c) *Nature of the resistance.* The resistance must be active, such as assaulting the person attempting to apprehend. Mere words of opposition, argument, or abuse, and attempts to escape from custody after the apprehension is complete, do not constitute the offense of resisting apprehension although they may constitute other offenses.

(d) *Mistake.* It is a defense that the accused held a reasonable belief that the person attempting to apprehend did not have authority to do so. However, the accused's belief at the time that no basis exists for the apprehension is not a defense.

(e) *Illegal apprehension.* A person may not be convicted of resisting apprehension if the attempted apprehension is illegal, but may be convicted of other offenses, such as assault, depending on all the circumstances. An attempted apprehension by a person authorized to apprehend is presumed to be legal in the absence of evidence to the contrary. Ordinarily the legality of an apprehension is a question of law to be decided by the military judge.

(2) *Flight from apprehension.* The flight must be active, such as running or driving away.

(3) *Breaking arrest.*

(a) *Arrest.* There are two types of arrest: pretrial arrest under Article 9 (*see* R.C.M. 304) and arrest under Article 15 (*see* paragraph 5c.(3), Part V, MCM). This article prohibits breaking any arrest.

(b) *Authority to order arrest. See* R.C.M. 304(b) and paragraphs 2 and 5b, Part V, MCM concerning authority to order arrest.

(c) *Nature of restraint imposed by arrest.* In arrest, the restraint is moral restraint imposed by orders fixing the limits of arrest.

(d) *Breaking.* Breaking arrest is committed when the person in arrest infringes the limits set by orders. The reason for the infringement is immaterial. For example, innocence of the offense with respect to which an arrest may have been imposed is not a defense.

(e) *Illegal arrest.* A person may not be convicted of breaking arrest if the arrest is illegal. An arrest ordered by one authorized to do so is presumed to be legal in the absence of some evidence to the contrary. Ordinarily, the legality of an arrest is a question of law to be decided by the military judge.

(4) *Escape from custody.*

(a) *Custody.* "Custody" is restraint of free locomotion imposed by lawful apprehension. The restraint may be physical or, once there has been a submission to apprehension or a forcible taking into custody, it may consist of control exercised in the presence of the prisoner by official acts or orders. Custody is temporary restraint intended to continue until other restraint (arrest, restriction, confinement) is imposed or the person is released.

(b) *Authority to apprehend. See* subparagraph (1)(*b*) above.

(c) *Escape.* For a discussion of escape, *see* subparagraph c(5)(*c*), below.

(d) *Illegal custody.* A person may not be convicted of this offense if the custody was illegal. An apprehension effected by one authorized to apprehend is presumed to be lawful in the absence of evidence to the contrary. Ordinarily, the legality of an apprehension is a question of law to be decided by the military judge.

(e) *Correctional custody. See* paragraph 70.

(5) *Escape from confinement.*

(a) *Confinement.* Confinement is physical restraint imposed under R.C.M. 305, 1101, or paragraph 5b, Part V, MCM. For purposes of the element of post-trial confinement (subparagraph b(5)(d), above) and increased punishment therefrom (subparagraph e(4), below), the confinement must have been imposed pursuant to an adjudged sentence of a court-martial and not as a result of pretrial restraint or nonjudicial punishment.

(b) *Authority to order confinement. See* R.C.M. 304(*b*); 1101; and paragraphs 2 and 5b, Part V, MCM concerning who may order confinement.

(c) *Escape.* An escape may be either with or

without force or artifice, and either with or without the consent of the custodian. However, where a prisoner is released by one with apparent authority to do so, the prisoner may not be convicted of escape from confinement. *See also* paragraph 20c(1)(b). Any completed casting off of the restraint of confinement, before release by proper authority, is an escape, and lack of effectiveness of the restraint imposed is immaterial. An escape is not complete until the prisoner is momentarily free from the restraint. If the movement toward escape is opposed, or before it is completed, an immediate pursuit follows, there is no escape until opposition is overcome or pursuit is eluded.

(d) *Status when temporarily outside confinement facility.* A prisoner who is temporarily escorted outside a confinement facility for a work detail or other reason by a guard, who has both the duty and means to prevent that prisoner from escaping, remains in confinement.

(e) *Legality of confinement.* A person may not be convicted of escape from confinement if the confinement is illegal. Confinement ordered by one authorized to do so is presumed to be lawful in the absence of evidence to the contrary. Ordinarily, the legality of confinement is a question of law to be decided by the military judge.

d. *Lesser included offenses.*

(1) *Resisting apprehension.* Article 128—assault; assault consummated by a battery

(2) *Breaking arrest.*

(a) Article 134—breaking restriction

(b) Article 80—attempts

(3) *Escape from custody.* Article 80—attempts

(4) *Escape from confinement.* Article 80—attempts

e. *Maximum punishment.*

(1) *Resisting apprehension.* Bad-conduct discharge, forfeiture of all pay and allowances, and confinement for 1 year.

(2) *Flight from apprehension.* Bad-conduct discharge, forfeiture of all pay and allowances, and confinement for 1 year.

(3) *Breaking arrest.* Bad-conduct discharge, forfeiture of all pay and allowances, and confinement for 6 months.

(4) *Escape from custody, pretrial confinement, or confinement on bread and water or diminished rations imposed pursuant to Article 15.* Dishonorable discharge, forfeiture of all pay and allowances, and confinement for 1 year.

(5) *Escape from post-trial confinement.* Dishonorable discharge, forfeiture of all pay and allowances, and confinement for 5 years.

f. *Sample specifications.*

(1) *Resisting apprehension.*

In that ______ (personal jurisdiction data), did, (at/on board—location) (subject-matter jurisdiction data, if required), on or about ______ 20 ___, resist being apprehended by ______, (an armed force policeman) (______), a person authorized to apprehend the accused.

(2) *Flight from apprehension.*

In that ______ (personal jurisdiction data), did, (at/on board—location) (subject-matter jurisdiction data, if required), on or about ______ 20 ___, flee apprehension by ______, (an armed force policeman) (______), a person authorized to apprehend the accused.

(3) *Breaking arrest.*

In that ______ (personal jurisdiction data), having been placed in arrest (in quarters) (in his/her company area) (______) by a person authorized to order the accused into arrest, did, (at/on board—location) on or about ______ 20 ______, break said arrest.

(4) *Escape from custody.*

In that ______ (personal jurisdiction data), did, (at/on board—location) (subject-matter jurisdiction data, if required), on or about ______ 20 ___, escape from the custody of ______, a person authorized to apprehend the accused.

(5) *Escape from confinement.*

In that ______ (personal jurisdiction data), having been placed in (post-trial) confinement in (place of confinement), by a person authorized to order said accused into confinement did, (at/on board—location) (subject-matter jurisdiction data, if required), on or about ______ 20 ___, escape from confinement.

20. Article 96—Releasing prisoner without proper authority

a. *Text of statute.*

Any person subject to this chapter who, without proper authority, releases any prisoner committed to his charge, or who through neglect or design suffers any such prisoner to escape, shall be punished as a court-martial may direct, whether or not the prisoner was committed in strict compliance with law.

b. *Elements.*

(1) *Releasing a prisoner without proper authority.*

(a) That a certain prisoner was committed to the charge of the accused; and

(b) That the accused released the prisoner without proper authority.

(2) *Suffering a prisoner to escape through neglect.*

(a) That a certain prisoner was committed to the charge of the accused;

(b) That the prisoner escaped;

(c) That the accused did not take such care to prevent the escape as a reasonably careful person, acting in the capacity in which the accused was acting, would have taken in the same or similar circumstances; and

(d) That the escape was the proximate result of the neglect.

(3) *Suffering a prisoner to escape through design.*

(a) That a certain prisoner was committed to the charge of the accused;

(b) That the design of the accused was to suffer the escape of that prisoner; and

(c) That the prisoner escaped as a result of the carrying out of the design of the accused.

c. *Explanation.*

(1) *Releasing a prisoner without proper authority.*

(a) *Prisoner.* "Prisoner" includes a civilian or military person who has been confined.

(b) *Release.* The release of a prisoner is removal of restraint by the custodian rather than by the prisoner.

(c) *Authority to release. See* R.C.M. 305(*g*) as to who may release pretrial prisoners. Normally, the lowest authority competent to order release of a post-trial prisoner is the commander who convened the court-martial which sentenced the prisoner or the officer exercising general court-martial jurisdiction over the prisoner. *See also* R.C.M. 1101.

(d) *Committed.* Once a prisoner has been confined, the prisoner has been "committed" in the sense of Article 96, and only a competent authority (*see* subparagraph (*c*)) may order release, regardless of failure to follow procedures prescribed by the code, this Manual, or other law.

(2) *Suffering a prisoner to escape through neglect.*

(a) *Suffer.* "Suffer" means to allow or permit; not to forbid or hinder.

(b) *Neglect.* "Neglect" is a relative term. It is the absence of conduct which would have been taken by a reasonably careful person in the same or similar circumstances.

(c) *Escape.* Escape is defined in paragraph 19c(4)(*c*).

(d) *Status of prisoner after escape not a defense.* After escape, the fact that a prisoner returns, is captured, killed, or otherwise dies is not a defense.

(3) *Suffering a prisoner to escape through design.* An escape is suffered through design when it is intended. Such intent may be inferred from conduct so wantonly devoid of care that the only reasonable inference which may be drawn is that the escape was contemplated as a probable result.

d. *Lesser included offenses.*

(1) *Releasing a prisoner without proper authority.* Article 80—attempts

(2) *Suffering a prisoner to escape through neglect.* None

(3) *Suffering a prisoner to escape through design.*

(a) Article 96—suffering a prisoner to escape through neglect

(b) Article 80—attempts

e. *Maximum punishment.*

(1) *Releasing a prisoner without proper authority.* Dishonorable discharge, forfeiture of all pay and allowances, and confinement for 2 years.

(2) *Suffering a prisoner to escape through neglect.* Bad-conduct discharge, forfeiture of all pay and allowances, and confinement for 1 year.

(3) *Suffering a prisoner to escape through design.*

Dishonorable discharge, forfeiture of all pay and allowances, and confinement for 2 years.

f. *Sample specifications.*

(1) *Releasing a prisoner without proper authority.*

In that ______ (personal jurisdiction data), did, (at/on board—location), on or about ______ 20 ______, without proper authority, release ______, a prisoner committed to his/her charge.

(2) *Suffering a prisoner to escape through neglect or design.*

In that ______ (personal jurisdiction data), did, (at/on board—location), on or about ______ 20 ______, through (neglect) (design), suffer ______, a prisoner committed to his/her charge, to escape.

21. Article 97—Unlawful detention

a. *Text of statute.*

Any person subject to this chapter who, except as provided by law, apprehends, arrests, or confines any person shall be punished as a court-martial may direct.

b. *Elements.*

(1) That the accused apprehended, arrested, or confined a certain person; and

(2) That the accused unlawfully exercised the accused's authority to do so.

c. *Explanation.*

(1) *Scope.* This article prohibits improper acts by those empowered by the code to arrest, apprehend, or confine. *See* Articles 7 and 9; R.C.M. 302, 304, 305, and 1101, and paragraphs 2 and 5b, Part V. It does not apply to private acts of false imprisonment or unlawful restraint of another's freedom of movement by one not acting under such a delegation of authority under the code.

(2) *No force required.* The apprehension, arrest, or confinement must be against the will of the person restrained, but force is not required.

(3) *Defense.* A reasonable belief held by the person imposing restraint that it is lawful is a defense.

d. *Lesser included offense.* Article 80—attempts

e. *Maximum punishment.* Dishonorable discharge, forfeiture of all pay and allowances, and confinement for 3 years.

f. *Sample specification.* In that ______ (personal jurisdiction data), did, (at/on board—location), on or about ______ 20 ______, unlawfully (apprehend ______) (place ______ in arrest) (confine ______ in ______).

22. Article 98—Noncompliance with procedural rules

a. *Text of statute.*

Any person subject to this chapter who—

(1) **is responsible for unnecessary delay in the disposition of any case of a person accused of an offense under this chapter; or**

(2) **Knowingly and intentionally fails to enforce or comply with any provision of this chapter regulating the proceedings before, during, or after trial of an accused; shall be punished as a court-martial may direct.**

b. *Elements.*

(1) *Unnecessary delay in disposing of case.*

(a) That the accused was charged with a certain duty in connection with the disposition of a case of a person accused of an offense under the code;

(b) That the accused knew that the accused was charged with this duty;

(c) That delay occurred in the disposition of the case;

(d) That the accused was responsible for the delay; and

(e) That, under the circumstances, the delay was unnecessary.

(2) *Knowingly and intentionally failing to enforce or comply with provisions of the code.*

(a) That the accused failed to enforce or comply with a certain provision of the code regulating a proceeding before, during, or after a trial;

(b) That the accused had the duty of enforcing or complying with that provision of the code;

(c) That the accused knew that the accused was charged with this duty; and

(d) That the accused's failure to enforce or comply with that provision was intentional.

c. *Explanation.*

(1) *Unnecessary delay in disposing of case.* The purpose of section (1) of Article 98 is to ensure expeditious disposition of cases of persons accused of offenses under the code. A person may be respon-

sible for delay in the disposition of a case only when that person's duties require action with respect to the disposition of that case.

(2) *Knowingly and intentionally failing to enforce or comply with provisions of the code.* Section (2) of Article 98 does not apply to errors made in good faith before, during, or after trial. It is designed to punish intentional failure to enforce or comply with the provisions of the code regulating the proceedings before, during, and after trial. Unlawful command influence under Article 37 may be prosecuted under this Article. *See also* Article 31 and R.C.M. 104.

d. *Lesser included offense.* Article 80—attempts

e. *Maximum punishment.*

(1) *Unnecessary delay in disposing of case.* Bad-conduct discharge, forfeiture of all pay and allowances, and confinement for 6 months.

(2) *Knowingly and intentionally failing to enforce or comply with provisions of the code.* Dishonorable discharge, forfeiture of all pay and allowances, and confinement for 5 years.

f. *Sample specifications.*

(1) *Unnecessary delay in disposing of case.*

In that ________ (personal jurisdiction data), being charged with the duty of ((investigating) (taking immediate steps to determine the proper disposition of) charges preferred against ________, a person accused of an offense under the Uniform Code of Military Justice) (________), was, (at/on board—location), on or about ________ 20 ___, responsible for unnecessary delay in (investigating said charges) (determining the proper disposition of said charges (________), in that he/she (did ________) (failed to ________) (________).

(2) *Knowingly and intentionally failing to enforce or comply with provisions of the code.*

In that ________ (personal jurisdiction data), being charged with the duty of ________, did, (at/on board—location), on or about ________ 20 ___, knowingly and intentionally fail to (enforce) (comply with) Article ________, Uniform Code of Military Justice, in that he/she ________.

23. Article 99—Misbehavior before the enemy

a. *Text of statute.*

Any member of the armed forces who before or in the presence of the enemy—

(1) **runs away;**

(2) **shamefully abandons, surrenders, or delivers up any command, unit, place, or military property which it is his duty to defend;**

(3) **through disobedience, neglect, or intentional misconduct endangers the safety of any such command, unit, place, or military property;**

(4) **casts away his arms or ammunition;**

(5) **is guilty of cowardly conduct;**

(6) **quits his place of duty to plunder or pillage;**

(7) **causes false alarms in any command, unit, or place under control of the armed forces;**

(8) **willfully fails to do his utmost to encounter, engage, capture, or destroy any enemy troops, combatants, vessels, aircraft, or any other thing, which it is his duty so to encounter, engage, capture, or destroy; or**

(9) **does not afford all practicable relief and assistance to any troops, combatants, vessels, or aircraft of the armed forces belonging to the United States or their allies when engaged in battle; shall be punished by death or such other punishment as a court-martial may direct.**

b. *Elements.*

(1) *Running away.*

(a) That the accused was before or in the presence of the enemy;

(b) That the accused misbehaved by running away; and

(c) That the accused intended to avoid actual or impending combat with the enemy by running away.

(2) *Shamefully abandoning, surrendering, or delivering up command.*

(a) That the accused was charged by orders or circumstances with the duty to defend a certain command, unit, place, ship, or military property;

(b) That, without justification, the accused shamefully abandoned, surrendered, or delivered up that command, unit, place, ship, or military property; and

(c) That this act occurred while the accused was before or in the presence of the enemy.

(3) *Endangering safety of a command, unit, place, ship, or military property.*

(a) That it was the duty of the accused to defend a certain command, unit, place, ship, or certain military property;

(b) That the accused committed certain disobedience, neglect, or intentional misconduct;

(c) That the accused thereby endangered the safety of the command, unit, place, ship, or military property; and

(d) That this act occurred while the accused was before or in the presence of the enemy.

(4) *Casting away arms or ammunition.*

(a) That the accused was before or in the presence of the enemy; and

(b) That the accused cast away certain arms or ammunition.

(5) *Cowardly conduct.*

(a) That the accused committed an act of cowardice;

(b) That this conduct occurred while the accused was before or in the presence of the enemy; and

(c) That this conduct was the result of fear.

(6) *Quitting place of duty to plunder or pillage.*

(a) That the accused was before or in the presence of the enemy;

(b) That the accused quit the accused's place of duty; and

(c) That the accused's intention in quitting was to plunder or pillage public or private property.

(7) *Causing false alarms.*

(a) That an alarm was caused in a certain command, unit, or place under control of the armed forces of the United States;

(b) That the accused caused the alarm;

(c) That the alarm was caused without any reasonable or sufficient justification or excuse; and

(d) That this act occurred while the accused was before or in the presence of the enemy.

(8) *Willfully failing to do utmost to encounter enemy.*

(a) That the accused was serving before or in the presence of the enemy;

(b) That the accused had a duty to encounter, engage, capture, or destroy certain enemy troops, combatants, vessels, aircraft, or a certain other thing; and

(c) That the accused willfully failed to do the utmost to perform that duty.

(9) *Failing to afford relief and assistance.*

(a) That certain troops, combatants, vessels, or aircraft of the armed forces belonging to the United States or an ally of the United States were engaged in battle and required relief and assistance;

(b) That the accused was in a position and able to render relief and assistance to these troops, combatants, vessels, or aircraft, without jeopardy to the accused's mission;

(c) That the accused failed to afford all practicable relief and assistance; and

(d) That, at the time, the accused was before or in the presence of the enemy.

c. *Explanation.*

(1) *Running away.*

(a) *Running away.* "Running away" means an unauthorized departure to avoid actual or impending combat. It need not, however, be the result of fear, and there is no requirement that the accused literally run.

(b) *Enemy.* "Enemy" includes organized forces of the enemy in time of war, any hostile body that our forces may be opposing, such as a rebellious mob or a band of renegades, and includes civilians as well as members of military organizations. "Enemy" is not restricted to the enemy government or its armed forces. All the citizens of one belligerent are enemies of the government and all the citizens of the other.

(c) *Before the enemy.* Whether a person is "before the enemy" is a question of tactical relation, not distance. For example, a member of an antiaircraft gun crew charged with opposing anticipated attack from the air, or a member of a unit about to move into combat may be before the enemy although miles from the enemy lines. On the other hand, an organization some distance from the front or immediate area of combat which is not a part of a tactical operation then going on or in immediate prospect is not "before or in the presence of the enemy" within the meaning of this article.

(2) *Shamefully abandoning, surrendering, or delivering up of command.*

(a) *Scope.* This provision concerns primarily commanders chargeable with responsibility for defending a command, unit, place, ship or military property. Abandonment by a subordinate would ordinarily be charged as running away.

(b) *Shameful.* Surrender or abandonment without justification is shameful within the meaning of this article.

(c) *Surrender; deliver up.* "Surrender" and "deliver up" are synonymous for the purposes of this article.

(d) *Justification.* Surrender or abandonment of a command, unit, place, ship, or military property by a person charged with its can be justified only by the utmost necessity or extremity.

(3) *Endangering safety of a command, unit, place, ship, or military property.*

(a) *Neglect.* "Neglect" is the absence of conduct which would have been taken by a reasonably careful person in the same or similar circumstances.

(b) *Intentional misconduct.* "Intentional misconduct" does not include a mere error in judgment.

(4) *Casting away arms or ammunition.* Self-explanatory.

(5) *Cowardly conduct.*

(a) *Cowardice.* "Cowardice" is misbehavior motivated by fear.

(b) *Fear.* Fear is a natural feeling of apprehension when going into battle. The mere display of apprehension does not constitute this offense.

(c) *Nature of offense.* Refusal or abandonment of a performance of duty before or in the presence of the enemy as a result of fear constitutes this offense.

(d) *Defense.* Genuine and extreme illness, not generated by cowardice, is a defense.

(6) *Quitting place of duty to plunder or pillage.*

(a) *Place of duty.* "Place of duty" includes any place of duty, whether permanent or temporary, fixed or mobile.

(b) *Plunder or pillage.* "Plunder or pillage" means to seize or appropriate public or private property unlawfully.

(c) *Nature of offense.* The essence of this offense is quitting the place of duty with intent to plunder or pillage. Merely quitting with that purpose is sufficient, even if the intended misconduct is not done.

(7) *Causing false alarms.* This provision covers spreading of false or disturbing rumors or reports, as well as the false giving of established alarm signals.

(8) *Willfully failing to do utmost to encounter enemy.* Willfully refusing a lawful order to go on a combat patrol may violate this provision.

(9) *Failing to afford relief and assistance.*

(a) *All practicable relief and assistance.* "All practicable relief and assistance" means all relief and assistance which should be afforded within the limitations imposed upon a person by reason of that person's own specific tasks or mission.

(b) *Nature of offense.* This offense is limited to a failure to afford relief and assistance to forces "engaged in battle."

d. *Lesser included offenses.*

(1) *Running away.*

(a) Article 85—desertion with intent to avoid hazardous or important service

(b) Article 86—absence without authority; going from appointed place of duty

(c) Article 80—attempts

(2) *Shamefully abandoning, surrendering, or delivering up command.* Article 80—attempts

(3) *Endangering safety of a command, unit, place, ship, or military property.*

(a) *Through disobedience of order.* Article 92—failure to obey lawful order

(b) Article 80—attempts

(4) *Casting away arms or ammunition.*

(a) Article 108—military property of the United States—loss, damage, destruction, or wrongful disposition.

(b) Article 80—attempts

(5) *Cowardly conduct.*

(a) Article 85—desertion with intent to avoid hazardous duty or important service

(b) Article 86—absence without authority

(c) Article 99—running away

(d) Article 80—attempts

(6) *Quitting place of duty to plunder or pillage.*

(a) Article 86(2)—going from appointed place of duty

(b) Article 80—attempts

(7) *Causing false alarms.* Article 80—attempts

(8) *Willfully failing to do utmost to encounter enemy.* Article 80—attempts

(9) *Failing to afford relief and assistance.* Article 80—attempts

e. *Maximum punishment.* All offenses under Article 99. Death or such other punishment as a court-martial may direct.

f. *Sample specifications.*

(1) *Running away.*

In that ______ (personal jurisdiction data), did, (at/on board—location), on or about ______ 20 ______, (before) (in the presence of) the enemy, run away (from his/her company) (and hide) (______), (and did not return until after the engagement had been concluded) (______).

(2) *Shamefully abandoning, surrendering, or delivering up command.*

In that ______ (personal jurisdiction data), did, (at/on board—location), on or about ______ 20 ______, (before) (in the presence of) the enemy, shamefully (abandon) (surrender) (deliver up) ______, which it was his/her duty to defend.

(3) *Endangering safety of a command, unit, place, ship, or military property.*

In that ______ (personal jurisdiction data), did, (at/on board—location), on or about ______ 20 ______, (before) (in the presence of) the enemy, endanger the safety of ______, which it was his/her duty to defend, by (disobeying an order from ______ to engage the enemy)(neglecting his/her duty as a sentinel by engaging in a card game while on his/her post) (intentional misconduct in that he/she became drunk and fired flares, thus revealing the location of his/her unit) (______).

(4) *Casting away arms or ammunition.*

In that ______ (personal jurisdiction data), did, (at/on board—location), on or about ______ 20 ______, (before) (in the presence of) the enemy, cast away his/her (rifle) (ammunition) (______).

(5) *Cowardly conduct.*

In that ______ (personal jurisdiction data), (at/on board—location), on or about ______ 20 ______, (before) (in the presence of) the enemy, was guilty of cowardly conduct as a result of fear, in that ______.

(6) *Quitting place of duty to plunder or pillage.*

In that ______ (personal jurisdiction data), did, (at/on board— location), on or about ______ 20 ______, (before) (in the presence of) the enemy, quit his/her place of duty for the purpose of (plundering) (pillaging) (plundering and pillaging).

(7) *Causing false alarms.*

In that ______ (personal jurisdiction data), did, (at/on board—location), on or about ______ 20 ______, (before) (in the presence of) the enemy, cause a false alarm in (Fort ______) (the said ship) (the camp) (______) by (needlessly and without authority (causing the call to arms to be sounded) (sounding the general alarm)) (______).

(8) *Willfully failing to do utmost to encounter enemy.*

In that ______ (personal jurisdiction data), being (before) (in the presence of) the enemy, did, (at/on board—location), on or about ______ 20 ______, by, (ordering his/her troops to halt their advance) (______), willfully fail to do his/her utmost to (encounter) (engage) (capture) (destroy), as it was his/her duty to do, (certain enemy troops which were in retreat) (______).

(9) *Failing to afford relief and assistance.*

In that ______ (personal jurisdiction data), did, (at/on board—location), on or about ______ 20 ______, (before) (in the presence of) the enemy, fail to afford all practicable relief and assistance to (the USS ______, which was engaged in battle and had run aground, in that he/she failed to take her in tow) (certain troops of the ground forces of ______, which were engaged in battle and were pinned down by enemy fire, in that he/she failed to furnish air cover) (______) as he/she properly should have done.

24. Article 100—Subordinate compelling surrender

a. *Text of statute.*

Any person subject to this chapter who compels or attempts to compel the commander of any place, vessel, aircraft, or other military property, or of any body of members of the armed forces,

to give it up to an enemy or to abandon it, or who strikes the colors or flag to an enemy without proper authority, shall be punished by death or such other punishment as a court-martial may direct.

b. *Elements.*

(1) *Compelling surrender.*

(a) That a certain person was in command of a certain place, vessel, aircraft, or other military property or of a body of members of the armed forces;

(b) That the accused did an overt act which was intended to and did compel that commander to give it up to the enemy or abandon it; and

(c) That the place, vessel, aircraft, or other military property or body of members of the armed forces was actually given up to the enemy or abandoned.

(2) *Attempting to compel surrender.*

(a) That a certain person was in command of a certain place, vessel, aircraft, or other military property or of a body of members of the armed forces;

(b) That the accused did a certain overt act;

(c) That the act was done with the intent to compel that commander to give up to the enemy or abandon the place, vessel, aircraft, or other military property or body of members of the armed forces;

(d) That the act amounted to more than mere preparation; and

(e) That the act apparently tended to bring about the compelling of surrender or abandonment.

(3) *Striking the colors or flag.*

(a) That there was an offer of surrender to an enemy;

(b) That this offer was made by striking the colors or flag to the enemy or in some other manner;

(c) That the accused made or was responsible for the offer; and

(d) That the accused did not have proper authority to make the offer.

c. *Explanation.*

(1) *Compelling surrender.*

(a) *Nature of offense.* The offenses under this article are similar to mutiny or attempted mutiny designed to bring about surrender or abandonment. Unlike some cases of mutiny, however, concert of action is not an essential element of the offenses under this article. The offense is not complete until the place, military property, or command is actually abandoned or given up to the enemy.

(b) *Surrender.* "Surrender" and "to give it up to an enemy" are synonymous.

(c) *Acts required.* The surrender or abandonment must be compelled or attempted to be compelled by acts rather than words.

(2) *Attempting to compel surrender.* The offense of attempting to compel a surrender or abandonment does not require actual abandonment or surrender, but there must be some act done with this purpose in view, even if it does not accomplish the purpose.

(3) *Striking the colors or flag.*

(a) *In general.* To "strike the colors or flag" is to haul down the colors or flag in the face of the enemy or to make any other offer of surrender. It is traditional wording for an act of surrender.

(b) *Nature of offense.* The offense is committed when one assumes the authority to surrender a military force or position when not authorized to do so either by competent authority or by the necessities of battle. If continued battle has become fruitless and it is impossible to communicate with higher authority, those facts will constitute proper authority to surrender. The offense may be committed whenever there is sufficient contact with the enemy to give the opportunity of making an offer of surrender and it is not necessary that an engagement with the enemy be in progress. It is unnecessary to prove that the offer was received by the enemy or that it was rejected or accepted. The sending of an emissary charged with making the offer or surrender is an act sufficient to prove the offer, even though the emissary does not reach the enemy.

(4) *Enemy.* For a discussion of "enemy," *see* paragraph 23c(1)(*b*).

d. *Lesser included offense.* Striking the colors or flag. Article 80— attempts

e. *Maximum punishment.* All offenses under Article 100. Death or such other punishment as a court-martial may direct.

f. *Sample specifications.*

(1) *Compelling surrender or attempting to compel surrender.*

In that ________ (personal jurisdiction data), did, (at/on—board location), on or about ________ 20 ________, (attempt to) compel ________, the commander of __________, (to give up to the enemy) (to abandon) said __________, by __________.

(2) *Striking the colors or flag.*

In that __________ (personal jurisdiction data), did, (at/on board—location), on or about __________ 20 ____, without proper authority, offer to surrender to the enemy by (striking the (colors)(flag)) (__________).

25. Article 101—Improper use of countersign

a. *Text of statute.*

Any person subject to this chapter who in time of war discloses the parole or countersign to any person not entitled to receive it or who gives to another who is entitled to receive and use the parole or countersign a different parole or countersign from that which, to his knowledge, he was authorized and required to give, shall be punished by death or such other punishment as a court-martial may direct.

b. *Elements.*

(1) *Disclosing the parole or countersign to one not entitled to receive it.*

(a) That, in time of war, the accused disclosed the parole or countersign to a person, identified or unidentified; and

(b) That this person was not entitled to receive it.

(2) *Giving a parole or countersign different from that authorized.*

(a) That, in time of war, the accused knew that the accused was authorized and required to give a certain parole or countersign; and

(b) That the accused gave to a person entitled to receive and use this parole or countersign a different parole or countersign from that which the accused was authorized and required to give.

c. *Explanation.*

(1) *Countersign.* A countersign is a word, signal, or procedure given from the principal headquarters of a command to aid guards and sentinels in their scrutiny of persons who apply to pass the lines. It consists of a secret challenge and a password, signal, or procedure.

(2) *Parole.* A parole is a word used as a check on the countersign; it is given only to those who are entitled to inspect guards and to commanders of guards.

(3) *Who may receive countersign.* The class of persons entitled to receive the countersign or parole will expand and contract under the varying circumstances of war. Who these persons are will be determined largely, in any particular case, by the general or special orders under which the accused was acting. Before disclosing such a word, a person subject to military law must determine at that person's peril that the recipient is a person authorized to receive it.

(4) *Intent, motive, negligence, mistake, ignorance not defense.* The accused's intent or motive in disclosing the countersign or parole is immaterial to the issue of guilt, as is the fact that the disclosure was negligent or inadvertent. It is no defense that the accused did not know that the person to whom the countersign or parole was given was not entitled to receive it.

(5) *How accused received countersign or parole.* It is immaterial whether the accused had received the countersign or parole in the regular course of duty or whether it was obtained in some other way.

(6) *In time of war. See* R.C.M. 103(19).

d. *Lesser included offense.* Article 80—attempts

e. *Maximum punishment.* Death or such other punishment as a court-martial may direct.

f. *Sample specifications.*

(1) *Disclosing the parole or countersign to one not entitled to receive it.*

In that __________ (personal jurisdiction data), did, (at/on board—location), on or about __________ 20 ____, a time of war, disclose the (parole)(countersign), to wit: __________, to __________, a person who was not entitled to receive it.

(2) *Giving a parole or countersign different from that authorized.*

In that __________ (personal jurisdiction data), did, (at/on board—location), on or about __________ 20 ____, a time of war, give to __________, a person entitled to receive and use the (parole)(countersign), a (parole) (countersign), namely: __________ which was different from that which, to his/her knowledge, he/she was authorized and required to give, to wit: __________.

26. Article 102—Forcing a safeguard

a. *Text of statute.*

Any person subject to this chapter who forces a safeguard shall suffer death or such other pun-

ishment as a court-martial may direct.

b. *Elements.*

(1) that a safeguard had been issued or posted for the protection of a certain person or persons, place, or property;

(2) That the accused knew or should have known of the safeguard; and

(3) That the accused forced the safeguard.

c. *Explanation.*

(1) *Safeguard.* A safeguard is a detachment, guard, or detail posted by a commander for the protection of persons, places, or property of the enemy, or of a neutral affected by the relationship of belligerent forces in their prosecution of war or during circumstances amounting to a state of belligerency. The term also includes a written order left by a commander with an enemy subject or posted upon enemy property for the protection of that person or property. A safeguard is not a device adopted by a belligerent to protect its own property or nationals or to ensure order within its own forces, even if those forces are in a theater of combat operations, and the posting of guards or of off-limits signs does not establish a safeguard unless a commander takes those actions to protect enemy or neutral persons or property. The effect of a safeguard is to pledge the honor of the nation that the person or property shall be respected by the national armed forces.

(2) *Forcing a safeguard.* "Forcing a safeguard" means to perform an act or acts in violation of the protection of the safeguard.

(3) *Nature of offense.* Any trespass on the protection of the safeguard will constitute an offense under this article, whether the safeguard was imposed in time of war or in circumstances amounting to a state of belligerency short of a formal state of war.

(4) *Knowledge.* Actual knowledge of the safeguard is not required. It is sufficient if an accused should have known of the existence of the safeguard.

d. *Lesser included offense.* Article 80—attempts

e. *Maximum punishment.* Death or such other punishment as a court-martial may direct.

f. *Sample specification.* In that __________ (personal jurisdiction data), did, (at/on board—location), on or about ________ 20 ________, force a safeguard, (known by him/her to have been placed over the premises occupied by __________ at __________ by (overwhelming the guard posted for the protection of the same) (__________)) (__________).

27. Article 103—Captured or abandoned property

a. *Text of statute.*

(a) **All persons subject to this chapter shall secure all public property taken from the enemy for the service of the United States, and shall give notice and turn over to the proper authority without delay all captured or abandoned property in their possession, custody, or control.**

(b) **Any person subject to this chapter who—**

(1) **fails to carry out the duties prescribed in subsection (*a*);**

(2) **buys, sells, trades, or in any way deals in or disposes of captured or abandoned property, whereby he receives or expects any profit, benefit, or advantage to himself or another directly or indirectly connected with himself; or**

(3) **engages in looting or pillaging; shall be punished as a court-martial may direct.**

b. *Elements.*

(1) *Failing to secure public property taken from the enemy.*

(a) That certain public property was taken from the enemy;

(b) That this property was of a certain value; and

(c) That the accused failed to do what was reasonable under the circumstances to secure this property for the service of the United States.

(2) *Failing to report and turn over captured or abandoned property.*

(a) That certain captured or abandoned public or private property came into the possession, custody, or control of the accused;

(b) That this property was of a certain value; and

(c) That the accused failed to give notice of its receipt and failed to turn over to proper authority, without delay, the captured or abandoned public or private property.

(3) *Dealing in captured or abandoned property.*

(a) That the accused bought, sold, traded, or

otherwise dealt in or disposed of certain public or private captured or abandoned property;

(b) That this property was of certain value; and

(c) That by so doing the accused received or expected some profit, benefit, or advantage to the accused or to a certain person or persons connected directly or indirectly with the accused.

(4) *Looting or pillaging.*

(a) That the accused engaged in looting, pillaging, or looting and pillaging by unlawfully seizing or appropriating certain public or private property;

(b) That this property was located in enemy or occupied territory, or that it was on board a seized or captured vessel; and

(c) That this property was:

(i) left behind, owned by, or in the custody of the enemy, an occupied state, an inhabitant of an occupied state, or a person under the protection of the enemy or occupied state, or who, immediately prior to the occupation of the place where the act occurred, was under the protection of the enemy or occupied state; or

(ii) part of the equipment of a seized or captured vessel; or

(iii) owned by, or in the custody of the officers, crew, or passengers on board a seized or captured vessel.

c. *Explanation.*

(1) *Failing to secure public property taken from the enemy.*

(a) *Nature of property.* Unlike the remaining offenses under this article, failing to secure public property taken from the enemy involves only public property. Immediately upon its capture from the enemy public property becomes the property of the United States. Neither the person who takes it nor any other person has any private right in this property.

(b) *Nature of duty.* Every person subject to military law has an immediate duty to take such steps as are reasonably within that person's power to secure public property for the service of the United States and to protect it from destruction or loss.

(2) *Failing to report and turn over captured or abandoned property.*

(a) *Reports.* Reports of receipt of captured or abandoned property are to be made directly or through such channels as are required by current regulations, orders, or the customs of the service.

(b) *Proper authority.* "Proper authority" is any authority competent to order disposition of the property in question.

(3) *Dealing in captured or abandoned property.* "Disposed of" includes destruction or abandonment.

(4) *Looting or pillaging.* "Looting or pillaging" means unlawfully seizing or appropriating property which is located in enemy or occupied territory.

(5) *Enemy.* For a discussion of "enemy," see paragraph 23c(1)(b).

d. *Lesser included offense.* Article 80—attempts

e. *Maximum punishment.*

(1) *Failing to secure public property taken from the enemy; failing to secure, give notice and turn over, selling, or otherwise wrongfully dealing in or disposing of captured or abandoned property:*

(a) of a value of $500.00 or less. Bad-conduct discharge, forfeiture of all pay and allowances, and confinement for 6 months.

(b) of a value of more than $500.00 or any firearm or explosive. Dishonorable discharge, forfeiture of all pay and allowances, and confinement for 5 years.

(2) *Looting or pillaging.* Any punishment, other than death, that a court-martial may direct. *See* R.C.M. 1003.

f. *Sample specifications.*

(1) *Failing to secure public property taken from the enemy.*

In that ________ (personal jurisdiction data), did, (at/on board—location), on or about ________ 20 ____, fail to secure for the service of the United States certain public property taken from the enemy, to wit: ________, of a value of (about) $________.

(2) *Failing to report and turn over captured or abandoned property.*

In that ________ (personal jurisdiction data), did, (at/on board—location), on or about ________ 20 ____, fail to give notice and turn over to proper authority without delay certain (captured) (abandoned) property which had come into his/her (possession) (custody) (control), to wit: ________, of a value of (about), $________.

(3) *Dealing in captured or abandoned property.*

In that ______ (personal jurisdiction data), did, (at/on board—location), on or about ______ 20 ___, (buy) (sell) (trade) (deal in) (dispose of) (______) certain (captured) (abandoned) property, to wit: ______, (a firearm) (an explosive), of a value of (about) $______, thereby (receiving) (expecting) a (profit) (benefit) (advantage) to (himself/herself) (______, his/her accomplice) (______, his/her brother) (______).

(4) *Looting or pillaging.*

In that ______ (personal jurisdiction data), did, (at/on board—location), on or about ______ 20 ___, engage in (looting) (pillage) (looting and pillaging) by unlawfully (seizing) (appropriating) ______, (property which had been left behind) (the property of ______), (an inhabitant of ______) (______)).

28. Article 104—Aiding the enemy

a. *Text of statute.*

Any person who—

(1) **aids, or attempts to aid, the enemy with arms, ammunition, supplies, money, or other things; or**

(2) **without proper authority, knowingly harbors or protects or gives intelligence to or communicates or corresponds with or holds any intercourse with the enemy, either directly or indirectly; shall suffer death or such other punishment as a court-martial or military commission may direct.**

b. *Elements.*

(1) *Aiding the enemy.*

(a) That the accused aided the enemy; and

(b) That the accused did so with certain arms, ammunition, supplies, money, or other things.

(2) *Attempting to aid the enemy.*

(a) That the accused did a certain overt act;

(b) That the act was done with the intent to aid the enemy with certain arms, ammunition, supplies, money, or other things;

(c) That the act amounted to more than mere preparation; and

(d) That the act apparently tended to bring about the offense of aiding the enemy with certain arms, ammunition, supplies, money, or other things.

(3) *Harboring or protecting the enemy.*

(a) That the accused, without proper authority, harbored or protected a person;

(b) That the person so harbored or protected was the enemy; and

(c) That the accused knew that the person so harbored or protected was an enemy.

(4) *Giving intelligence to the enemy.*

(a) That the accused, without proper authority, knowingly gave intelligence information to the enemy; and

(b) That the intelligence information was true, or implied the truth, at least in part.

(5) *Communicating with the enemy.*

(a) That the accused, without proper authority, communicated, corresponded, or held intercourse with the enemy, and;

(b) That the accused knew that the accused was communicating, corresponding, or holding intercourse with the enemy.

c. *Explanation.*

(1) *Scope of Article 104.* This article denounces offenses by all persons whether or not otherwise subject to military law. Offenders may be tried by court-martial or by military commission.

(2) *Enemy.* For a discussion of "enemy," *see* paragraph 23c(1)(*b*).

(3) *Aiding or attempting to aid the enemy.* It is not a violation of this article to furnish prisoners of war subsistence, quarters, and other comforts or aid to which they are lawfully entitled.

(4) *Harboring or protecting the enemy.*

(a) *Nature of offense.* An enemy is harbored or protected when, without proper authority, that enemy is shielded, either physically or by use of any artifice, aid, or representation from any injury or misfortune which in the chance of war may occur.

(b) *Knowledge.* Actual knowledge is required, but may be proved by circumstantial evidence.

(5) *Giving intelligence to the enemy.*

(a) *Nature of offense.* Giving intelligence to the enemy is a particular case of corresponding with the enemy made more serious by the fact that the communication contains intelligence that may be useful to the enemy for any of the many reasons that make information valuable to belligerents. This intelligence may be conveyed by direct or indirect means.

(b) *Intelligence.* "Intelligence" imports that the information conveyed is true or implies the truth, at least in part.

(c) *Knowledge.* Actual knowledge is required but may be proved by circumstantial evidence.

(6) *Communicating with the enemy.*

(a) *Nature of the offense.* No unauthorized communication, correspondence, or intercourse with the enemy is permissible. The intent, content, and method of the communication, correspondence, or intercourse are immaterial. No response or receipt by the enemy is required. The offense is complete the moment the communication, correspondence, or intercourse issues from the accused. The communication, correspondence, or intercourse may be conveyed directly or indirectly. A prisoner of war may violate this Article by engaging in unauthorized communications with the enemy. *See also* paragraph 29c(3).

(b) *Knowledge.* Actual knowledge is required but may be proved by circumstantial evidence.

(c) *Citizens of neutral powers.* Citizens of neutral powers resident in or visiting invaded or occupied territory can claim no immunity from the customary laws of war relating to communication with the enemy.

d. *Lesser included offense.* For harboring or protecting the enemy, giving intelligence to the enemy, or communicating with the enemy. Article 80—attempts

e. *Maximum punishment.* Death or such other punishment as a court-martial or military commission may direct.

f. *Sample specifications.*

(1) *Aiding or attempting to aid the enemy.*

In that ______ (personal jurisdiction data), did, (at/on board—location), on or about ______ 20___, (attempt to) aid the enemy with (arms) (ammunition) (supplies) (money) (______), by (furnishing and delivering to ______, members of the enemy's armed forces ______) (______).

(2) *Harboring or protecting the enemy.*

In that ______ (personal jurisdiction data), did, (at/on board—location), on or about ______ 20___, without proper authority, knowingly (harbor) (protect) ______, an enemy, by (concealing the said ______ in his/her house) (______).

(3) *Giving intelligence to the enemy.*

In that ______ (personal jurisdiction data), did, (at/on board—location), on or about ______ 20___, without proper authority, knowingly give intelligence to the enemy, by (informing a patrol of the enemy's forces of the whereabouts of a military patrol of the United States forces) (______).

(4) *Communicating with the enemy.*

In that ______ (personal jurisdiction data), did, (at/on board—location), on or about ______ 20___, without proper authority, knowingly (communicate with) (correspond with) (hold intercourse with) the enemy (by writing and transmitting secretly through the lines to one ______, whom he/she, the said ______, knew to be (an officer of the enemy's armed forces)(______) a communication in words and figures substantially as follows, to wit: ______)) ((indirectly by publishing in ______, a newspaper published at ______, a communication in words and figures as follows, to wit: ______, which communication was intended to reach the enemy))((______)).

29. Article 105—Misconduct as a prisoner

a. *Text of statute.*

Any person subject to this chapter who, while in the hands of the enemy in time of war—

(1) for the purpose of securing favorable treatment by his captors acts without proper authority in a manner contrary to law, custom, or regulation, to the detriment of others of whatever nationality held by the enemy as civilian or military prisoners; or

(2) while in a position of authority over such persons maltreats them without justifiable cause; shall be punished as a court-martial may direct.

b. *Elements.*

(1) *Acting without authority to the detriment of another for the purpose of securing favorable treatment.*

(a) That without proper authority the accused

acted in a manner contrary to law, custom, or regulation;

(b) That the act was committed while the accused was in the hands of the enemy in time of war;

(c) That the act was done for the purpose of securing favorable treatment of the accused by the captors; and

(d) That other prisoners held by the enemy, either military or civilian, suffered some detriment because of the accused's act.

(2) *Maltreating prisoners while in a position of authority.*

(a) That the accused maltreated a prisoner held by the enemy;

(b) That the act occurred while the accused was in the hands of the enemy in time of war;

(c) That the accused held a position of authority over the person maltreated; and

(d) That the act was without justifiable cause.

c. *Explanation.*

(1) *Enemy.* For a discussion of "enemy," *see* paragraph 23c(1)(*b*).

(2) *In time of war. See* R.C.M. 103(19).

(3) *Acting without authority to the detriment of another for the purpose of securing favorable treatment.*

(a) *Nature of offense.* Unauthorized conduct by a prisoner of war must be intended to result in improvement by the enemy of the accused's condition and must operate to the detriment of other prisoners either by way of closer confinement, reduced rations, physical punishment, or other harm. Examples of this conduct include reporting plans of escape being prepared by others or reporting secret food caches, equipment, or arms. The conduct of the prisoner must be contrary to law, custom, or regulation.

(b) *Escape.* Escape from the enemy is authorized by custom. An escape or escape attempt which results in closer confinement or other measures against fellow prisoners still in the hands of the enemy is not an offense under this article.

(4) *Maltreating prisoners while in a position of authority.*

(a) *Authority.* The source of authority is not material. It may arise from the military rank of the accused or—despite service regulations or customs to the contrary—designation by the captor authorities, or voluntary election or selection by other prisoners for their self-government.

(b) *Maltreatment.* The maltreatment must be real, although not necessarily physical, and it must be without justifiable cause. Abuse of an inferior by inflammatory and derogatory words may, through mental anguish, constitute this offense.

d. *Lesser included offense.* Article 80—attempts

e. *Maximum punishment.* Any punishment other than death that a court-martial may direct. *See* R.C.M. 1003.

f. *Sample specifications.*

(1) *Acting without authority to the detriment of another for the purpose of securing favorable treatment.*

In that ________ (personal jurisdiction data), while in the hands of the enemy, did, (at/on board—location) on or about ________ 20____, a time of war, without proper authority and for the purpose of securing favorable treatment by his/her captors, (report to the commander of Camp ________ the preparations by ________, a prisoner at said camp, to escape, as a result of which report the said ________ was placed in solitary confinement) (________).

(2) *Maltreating prisoner while in a position of authority.*

In that ________ (personal jurisdiction data), did, (at/on board—location), on or about ________ 20____, a time of ward, while in the hands, of the enemy and in a position of authority over ________, a prisoner at ________, as (officer in charge of prisoners at ________) (________), maltreat the said ________ by (depriving him/her of ________)(________), without justifiable cause.

30. Article 106—Spies

a. *Text of statute.*

Any person who in time of war is found lurking as a spy or acting as a spy in or about any place, vessel, or aircraft, within the control or jurisdiction of any of the armed forces, or in or about any shipyard, any manufacturing or industrial plant, or any other place or institution engaged in work in aid of the prosecution of the war by the United States, or elsewhere, shall be tried by a general court-martial or by a military

commission and on conviction shall be punished by death.

b. *Elements.*

(1) That the accused was found in, about, or in and about a certain place, vessel, or aircraft within the control or jurisdiction of an armed force of the United States, or a shipyard, manufacturing or industrial plant, or other place or institution engaged in work in aid of the prosecution of the war by the United States, or elsewhere;

(2) That the accused was lurking, acting clandestinely or under false pretenses;

(3) That the accused was collecting or attempting to collect certain information;

(4) That the accused did so with the intent to convey this information to the enemy; and

(5) That this was done in time of war.

c. *Explanation.*

(1) *In time of war. See* R.C.M. 103(19).

(2) *Enemy.* For a discussion of "enemy,"*see* paragraph 23c(1)(*b*).

(3) *Scope of offense.* The words "any person" bring within the jurisdiction of general courts-martial and military commissions all persons of whatever nationality or status who commit spying.

(4) *Nature of offense.* A person can be a spy only when, acting clandestinely or under false pretenses, that person obtains or seeks to obtain information with the intent to convey it to a hostile party. It is not essential that the accused obtain the information sought or that it be communicated. The offense is complete with lurking or acting clandestinely or under false pretenses with intent to accomplish these objects.

(5) *Intent.* It is necessary to prove an intent to convey information to the enemy. This intent may be inferred from evidence of a deceptive insinuation of the accused among our forces, but evidence that the person had come within the lines for a comparatively innocent purpose, as to visit family or to reach friendly lines by assuming a disguise, is admissible to rebut this inference.

(6) *Persons not included under "spying".*

(a) Members of a military organization not wearing a disguise, dispatch drivers, whether members of a military organization or civilians, and persons in ships or aircraft who carry out their missions openly and who have penetrated enemy lines are not spies because, while they may have resorted to concealment, they have not acted under false pretenses.

(b) A spy who, after rejoining the armed forces to which the spy belongs, is later captured by the enemy incurs no responsibility for previous acts of espionage.

(c) A person living in occupied territory who, without lurking, or acting clandestinely or under false pretenses, merely reports what is seen or heard through agents to the enemy may be charged under Article 104 with giving intelligence to or communicating with the enemy, but may not be charged under this article as being a spy.

d. *Lesser included offenses.* None.

e. *Mandatory punishment.* Death

f. *Sample specification.* In that __________ (personal jurisdiction data), was, (at/on board—location), on or about ________ 20 ________, a time of war, found (lurking) (acting) as a spy (in) (about) (in and about) __________, (a (fortification) (port) (base) (vessel) (aircraft) (__________) within the (control)(jurisdiction) (control and jurisdiction) of an armed force of the United States, to wit:__________) (a (shipyard) (manufacturing plant) (industrial plant) (__________) engaged in work in aid of the prosecution of the war by the United States) (__________), for the purpose of (collecting) (attempting to collect) information in regard to the ((numbers) (resources) (operations) (__________) of the armed forces of the United States) ((military production) (__________) of the United States) (__________), with intent to impart the same to the enemy.

30a. Article 106a—Espionage

a. *Text of statute.*

(a)(1) **Any person subject to this chapter who, with intent or reason to believe that it is to be used to the injury of the United States or to the advantage of a foreign nation, communicates, delivers, or transmits, or attempts to communicate, deliver, or transmit, to any entity described in paragraph (2), either directly or indirectly, anything described in paragraph (3) shall be punished as a court-martial may direct, except that if the accused is found guilty of an offense that directly concerns (A) nuclear weaponry, military spacecraft or satellites, early warning systems, or other means of defense or retaliation against**

large scale attack, (B) war plans, (C) communications intelligence or cryptolineart information, or (D) any other major weapons system or major element of defense strategy, the accused shall be punished by death or such other punishment as a court-martial may direct.

(2) **An entity referred to in paragraph (1) is—**

(A) **a foreign government;**

(B) **a faction or party or military or naval force within a foreign country, whether recognized or unrecognized by the United States; or**

(C) **a representative, officer, agent, employee, subject, or citizen of such a government, faction, party, or force.**

(3) **A thing referred to in paragraph (1) is a document, writing, code book, signal book, sketch, photograph, photolineart negative, blueprint, plan, map, model, note, instrument, appliance, or information relating to the national defense.**

(b)(1) **No person may be sentenced by court-martial to suffer death for an offense under this section (article) unless—**

(A) **the members of the court-martial unanimously find at least one of the aggravating factors set out in subsection (c); and**

(B) **the members unanimously determine that any extenuating or mitigating circumstances are substantially outweighed by any aggravating circumstances, including the aggravating factors set out under subsection (c).**

(2) **Findings under this subsection may be based on—**

(A) **evidence introduced on the issue of guilt or innocence;**

(B) **evidence introduced during the sentencing proceeding; or**

(C) **all such evidence.**

(3) **The accused shall be given broad latitude to present matters in extenuation and mitigation.**

(c) **A sentence of death may be adjudged by a court-martial for an offense under this section (article) only if the members unanimously find, beyond a reasonable doubt, one or more of the following aggravating factors:**

(1) **The accused has been convicted of another offense involving espionage or treason for which either a sentence of death or imprisonment for life was authorized by statute.**

(2) **In the commission of the offense, the accused knowingly created a grave risk of substantial damage to the national security.**

(3) **In the commission of the offense, the accused knowingly created a grave risk of death to another person.**

(4) **Any other factor that may be prescribed by the President by regulations under section 836 of this title (Article 36).**

b. *Elements.*

(1) *Espionage.*

(a) That the accused communicated, delivered, or transmitted any document, writing, code book, signal book, sketch, photograph, photolineart negative, blueprint, plan, map, model, note, instrument, appliance, or information relating to the national defense;

(b) That this matter was communicated, delivered, or transmitted to any foreign government, or to any faction or party or military or naval force within a foreign country, whether recognized or unrecognized by the United States, or to any representative, officer, agent, employee, subject or citizen thereof, either directly or indirectly; and

(c) That the accused did so with intent or reason to believe that such matter would be used to the injury of the United States or to the advantage of a foreign nation.

(2) *Attempted espionage.*

(a) That the accused did a certain overt act;

(b) That the act was done with the intent to commit the offense of espionage;

(c) That the act amounted to more than mere preparation; and

(d) That the act apparently tended to bring about the offense of espionage.

(3) *Espionage as a capital offense.*

(a) That the accused committed espionage or attempted espionage; and

(b) That the offense directly concerned (1) nuclear weaponry, military spacecraft or satellites, early warning systems, or other means of defense or retaliation against large scale attack, (2) war plans, (3) communications intelligence or cryptolineart information, or (4) any other major weapons system or major element of defense strategy.

c. *Explanation.*

(1) *Intent.* "Intent or reason to believe" that the information "is to be used to the injury of the United States or to the advantage of a foreign nation" means that the accused acted in bad faith and without lawful authority with respect to information that is not lawfully accessible to the public.

(2) *National defense information.* "Instrument, appliance, or information relating to the national defense" includes the full range of modern technology and matter that may be developed in the future, including chemical or biological agents, computer technology, and other matter related to the national defense.

(3) *Espionage as a capital offense.* Capital punishment is authorized if the government alleges and proves that the offense directly concerned (1) nuclear weaponry, military spacecraft or satellites, early warning systems, or other means of defense or retaliation against large scale attack, (2) war plans, (3) communications intelligence or cryptolineart information, or (4) any other major weapons system or major element of defense strategy. *See* R.C.M. 1004 concerning sentencing proceedings in capital cases.

d. *Lesser included offense.* Although no lesser included offenses are set forth in the Code, federal civilian offenses on this matter may be incorporated through the third clause of Article 134.

e. *Maximum punishment.*

(1) *Espionage as a capital offense.* Death or such other punishment as a court-martial may direct. *See* R.C.M. 1003.

(2) *Espionage or attempted espionage.* Any punishment, other than death, that a court-martial may direct. *See* R.C.M. 1003.

f. *Sample specification.*

In that ______ (personal jurisdiction data), did, (at/on board—location), on or about ______ 20 ___, with intent or reason to believe it would be used to the injury of the United States or to the advantage of ______, a foreign nation, (attempt to) (communicate) (deliver) (transmit) ______ (description of item), (a document) (a writing) (a code book) (a sketch) (a photograph) (a photolineart negative) (a blueprint) (a plan) (a map) (a model) (a note) (an instrument) (an appliance) (information) relating to the national defense, ((which directly concerned (nuclear weaponry) (military spacecraft) (military satellites) (early warning systems) (______, a means of defense or retaliation against a large scale attack) (war plans) (communications intelligence) (cryptolineart information) (______, a major weapons system) (______, a major element of defense strategy)) to ______ ((a representative of) (an officer of) (an agent of) (an employee of) (a subject of) (a citizen of)) ((a foreign government) (a faction within a foreign country) (a party within a foreign country) (a military force within a foreign country) (a naval force within a foreign country)) (indirectly by ______).

31. Article 107—False official statements

a. *Text of statute.*

Any person subject to this chapter who, with intent to deceive, signs any false record, return, regulation, order, or other official document, knowing it to be false, or makes any other false official statement knowing it to be false, shall be punished as a court-martial may direct.

b. *Elements.*

(1) That the accused signed a certain official document or made a certain official statement;

(2) That the document or statement was false in certain particulars;

(3) That the accused knew it to be false at the time of signing it or making it; and

(4) That the false document or statement was made with the intent to deceive.

c. *Explanation.*

(1) *Official documents and statements.* Official documents and official statements include all documents and statements made in the line of duty.

(2) *Status of victim of the deception.* The rank of any person intended to be deceived is immaterial if that person was authorized in the execution of a particular duty to require or receive the statement or document from the accused. The government may be the victim of this offense.

(3) *Intent to deceive.* The false representation must be made with the intent to deceive. It is not necessary that the false statement be material to the issue inquiry. If, however, the falsity is in respect to a material matter, it may be considered as some evidence of the intent to deceive, while immateriality may tend to show an absence of this intent.

(4) *Material gain.* The expectation of material gain is not an element of this offense. Such expectation or lack of it, however, is circumstantial evidence bearing on the element of intent to deceive.

(5) *Knowledge that the document or statement was false.* The false representation must be one which the accused actually knew was false. Actual knowledge may be proved by circumstantial evidence. An honest, although erroneous, belief that a statement made is true, is a defense.

d. *Lesser included offense.* Article 80—attempts

e. *Maximum punishment.* Dishonorable discharge, forfeiture of all pay and allowances, and confinement for 5 years.

f. *Sample specification.* In that ________ (personal jurisdiction data), did, (at/on board—location), (subject-matter jurisdiction data, if required), on or about ________ 20____, with intent to deceive, (sign an official (record) (return) (________), to wit: ________) (make to ________, an official statement, to wit: ________), which (record) (return) (statement) (________) was (totally false) (false in that ________), and was then known by the said ________ to be so false.

32. Article 108—Military property of the United States—sale, loss, damage, destruction, or wrongful disposition

a. *Text of statute.*

Any person subject to this chapter who, without proper authority—

(1) sells or otherwise disposes of;

(2) willfully or through neglect damages, destroys, or loses; or

(3) willfully or through neglect suffers to be lost, damaged, destroyed, sold, or wrongfully disposed of, any military property of the United States, shall be punished as a court-martial may direct.

b. *Elements.*

(1) *Selling or otherwise disposing of military property.*

(a) That the accused sold or otherwise disposed of certain property (which was a firearm or explosive);

(b) That the sale or disposition was without proper authority;

(c) That the property was military property of the United States; and

(d) That the property was of a certain value.

(2) *Damaging, destroying, or losing military property.*

(a) That the accused, without proper authority, damaged or destroyed certain property in a certain way, or lost certain property;

(b) That the property was military property of the United States;

(c) That the damage, destruction, or loss was willfully caused by the accused or was the result of neglect by the accused; and

(d) That the property was of a certain value or the damage was of a certain amount.

(3) *Suffering military property to be lost, damaged, destroyed, sold, or wrongfully disposed of.*

(a) That certain property (which was a firearm or explosive) was lost, damaged, destroyed, sold, or wrongfully disposed of;

(b) That the property was military property of the United States;

(c) That the loss, damage, destruction, sale, or wrongful disposition was suffered by the accused, without proper authority, through a certain omission of duty by the accused;

(d) That the omission was willful or negligent; and

(e) That the property was of a certain value or the damage was of a certain amount.

c. *Explanation.*

(1) *Military property.* Military property is all property, real or personal, owned, held, or used by one of the armed forces of the United States. If is immaterial whether the property sold, disposed, destroyed, lost, or damaged had been issued to the accused, to someone else, or even issued at all. If it is proved by either direct or circumstantial evidence that items of individual issue were issued to the accused, it may be inferred, depending on all the evidence, that the damage, destruction, or loss proved was due to the neglect of the accused. Retail merchandise of service exchange stores is not military property under this article.

(2) *Suffering military property to be lost, damaged, destroyed, sold, or wrongfully disposed of.* "To suffer" means to allow or permit. The willful or negligent sufferance specified by this article in-

cludes: deliberate violation or intentional disregard of some specific law, regulation, or order; reckless or unwarranted personal use of the property; causing or allowing it to remain exposed to the weather, insecurely housed, or not guarded; permitting it to be consumed, wasted, or injured by other persons; or loaning it to a person, known to be irresponsible, by whom it is damaged.

(3) *Value and damage.* In the case of loss, destruction, sale, or wrongful disposition, the value of the property controls the maximum punishment which may be adjudged. In the case of damage, the amount of damage controls. As a general rule, the amount of damage is the estimated or actual cost of repair by the government agency normally employed in such work, or the cost of replacement, as shown by government price lists or otherwise, whichever is less.

d. *Lesser included offenses.*

(1) *Sale or disposition of military property.*

(a) Article 80—attempts

(b) Article 134—sale or disposition of non-military government property

(2) *Willfully damaging military property.*

(a) Article 108—damaging military property through neglect

(b) Article 109—willfully damaging non-military property

(c) Article 80—attempts

(3) *Willfully suffering military property to be damaged.*

(a) Article 108—through neglect suffering military property to be damaged

(b) Article 80—attempts

(4) *Willfully destroying military property.*

(a) Article 108—through neglect destroying military property

(b) Article 109—willfully destroying non-military property

(c) Article 108—willfully damaging military property

(d) Article 109—willfully damaging non-military property

(e) Article 108—through neglect damaging military property

(f) Article 80—attempts

(5) *Willfully suffering military property to be destroyed.*

(a) Article 108—through neglect suffering military property to be destroyed

(b) Article 108—willfully suffering military property to be damaged

(c) Article 108—through neglect suffering military property to be damaged

(d) Article 80—attempts

(6) *Willfully losing military property.*

(a) Article 108—through neglect, losing military property

(b) Article 80—attempts

(7) *Willfully suffering military property to be lost.*

(a) Article 108—through neglect, suffering military property to be lost

(b) Article 80—attempts

(8) *Willfully suffering military property to be sold.*

(a) Article 108—through neglect, suffering military property to be sold

(b) Article 80—attempts

(9) *Willfully suffering military property to be wrongfully disposed of.*

(a) Article 108—through neglect, suffering military property to be wrongfully disposed of in the manner alleged

(b) Article 80—attempts

e. *Maximum punishment.*

(1) *Selling or otherwise disposing of military property.*

(a) *Of a value of $500.00 or less.* Bad-conduct discharge, forfeiture of all pay and allowance, and confinement for 1 year.

(b) *Of a value of more than $500.00 or any firearm or explosive.* Dishonorable discharge, forfeiture of all pay and allowances, and confinement for 10 years.

(2) *Through neglect damaging, destroying, or losing, or through neglect suffering to be lost, damaged, destroyed, sold, or wrongfully disposed of, military property.*

(a) *Of a value or damage of $500.00 or less.* Confinement for 6 months, and forfeiture of two-thirds pay per month for 6 months.

(b) *Of a value or damage of more than*

$500.00. Bad-conduct discharge, forfeiture of all pay and allowances, and confinement for 1 year.

(3) *Willfully damaging, destroying, or losing, or willfully suffering to be lost, damaged, destroyed, sold, or wrongfully disposed of, military property.*

(a) *Of a value or damage of $500.00 or less.* Bad-conduct discharge, forfeiture of all pay and allowances, and confinement for 1 year.

(b) *Of a value or damage of more than $500.00, or of any firearm or explosive.* Dishonorable discharge, forfeiture of all pay and allowances, and confinement for 10 years.

f. *Sample specifications.*

(1) *Selling or disposing of military property.*

In that ________ (personal jurisdiction data), did, (at/on board—location) (subject-matter jurisdiction data, if required), on or about ________ 20 ____, without proper authority, (sell to ________) (dispose of by ________) ________, ((a firearm) (an explosive)) of a value of (about) $ ________, military property of the United States.

(2) *Damaging, destroying, or losing military property.*

In that ________ (personal jurisdiction data), did, (at/on board—location) (subject-matter jurisdiction data, if required), on or about ________ 20 ____, without proper authority, ((willfully) (through neglect)) ((damage by ________) (destroy by ________)) (lose)) ________ (of a value of (about) $ ________,) military property of the United States (the amount of said damage being in the sum of (about) $ ________).

(3) *Suffering military property to be lost, damaged, destroyed, sold, or wrongfully disposed of.*

In that ________ (personal jurisdiction data), did, (at/on board—location) (subject-matter jurisdiction data, if required), on or about ________ 20 ____, without proper authority, (willfully) (through neglect) suffer ________, ((a firearm) (an explosive)) (of a value of (about) $ ________) military property of the United States, to be (lost) (damaged by ________) (destroyed by ________) (sold to ________) (wrongfully disposed of by ________) (the amount of said damage being in the sum of (about $ ________).

33. Article 109—Property other than military property of the United States—waste, spoilage, or destruction

a. *Text of statute.*

Any person subject to this chapter who willfully or recklessly wastes, spoils, or otherwise willfully and wrongfully destroys or damages any property other than military property of the United States shall be punished as a court-martial may direct.

b. *Elements.*

(1) *Wasting or spoiling of non-military property.*

(a) That the accused willfully or recklessly wasted or spoiled certain real property in a certain manner;

(b) That the property was that of another person; and

(c) That the property was of a certain value.

(2) *Destroying or damaging non-military property.*

(a) That the accused willfully and wrongfully destroyed or damaged certain personal property in a certain manner;

(b) That the property was that of another person; and

(c) That the property was of a certain value or the damage was of a certain amount.

c. *Explanation.*

(1) *Wasting or spoiling non-military property.* This portion of Article 109 proscribes willful or reckless waste or spoliation of the real property of another. The terms "wastes" and "spoils" as used in this article refer to such wrongful acts of voluntary destruction of or permanent damage to real property as burning down buildings, burning piers, tearing down fences, or cutting down trees. This destruction in punishable whether done willfully, that is intentionally, or recklessly, that is through a culpable disregard of the foreseeable consequences of some voluntary act.

(2) *Destroying or damaging non-military property.* This portion of Article 109 proscribes the willful and wrongful destruction or damage of the personal property of another. To be destroyed, the property need not be completely demolished or annihilated, but must be sufficiently injured to be useless for its intended purpose. Damage consists of any physical injury to the property. To constitute an offense under

this section, the destruction or damage of the property must have been willful and wrongful. As used in this section "willfully" means intentionally and "wrongfully" means contrary to law, regulation, lawful order, or custom. Willfulness may be proved by circumstantial evidence, such as the manner in which the acts were done.

(3) *Value and damage.* In the case of destruction, the value of the property destroyed controls the maximum punishment which may be adjudged. In the case of damage, the amount of the damage controls. As a general rule, the amount of damage is the estimated or actual cost of repair by artisans employed in this work who are available to the community wherein the owner resides, or the replacement cost, whichever is less. *See also* paragraph 46c(1)(*g*).

d. *Lesser included offense.* Article 80—attempts

e. *Maximum punishment.* Wasting, spoiling, destroying, or damaging any property other than military property of the United States of a value or damage.

(1) *Of $500.00 or less.* Bad-conduct discharge, forfeiture of all pay and allowances, and confinement for 1 year.

(2) *Of more than $500.00.* Dishonorable discharge, forfeiture of all pay and allowances, and confinement for 5 years.

f. *Sample specification.*

In that __________ (personal jurisdiction data), did, (at/on board—location) (subject-matter jurisdiction data, if required), on or about __________ 20____, ((willfully) recklessly) waste) ((willfully) (recklessly) spoil) (willfully and wrongfully (destroy) (damage) by ________) ____________, (of a value of (about) $__________) (the amount of said damage being in the sum of (about $__________), the property of __________.

34. Article 110—Improper hazarding of vessel

a. *Text of statute.*

(a) **Any person subject to this chapter who willfully and wrongfully hazards or suffers to be hazarded any vessel of the armed forces shall suffer death or such other punishment as a court-martial may direct.**

(b) **Any person subject to this chapter who negligently hazards or suffers to be hazarded any vessel of the armed forces shall be punished as a court-martial may direct.**

b. *Elements.*

(1) That a vessel of the armed forces was hazarded in a certain manner; and

(2) That the accused by certain acts or omissions, willfully and wrongfully, or negligently, caused or suffered the vessel to be hazarded.

c. *Explanation.*

(1) *Hazard.* "Hazard" means to put in danger of loss or injury. Actual damage to, or loss of, a vessel of the armed forces by collision, stranding, running upon a shoal or a rock, or by any other cause, is conclusive evidence that the vessel was hazarded but not of the fact of culpability on the part of any particular person. "Stranded" means run aground so that the vessel is fast for a time. If the vessel "touches and goes," she is not stranded; if she "touches and sticks," she is. A shoal is a sand, mud, or gravel bank or bar that makes the water shallow.

(2) *Willfully and wrongfully.* As used in this article, "willfully" means intentionally and "wrongfully" means contrary to law, regulation, lawful order, or custom.

(3) *Negligence.* "Negligence" as used in this article means the failure to exercise the care, prudence, or attention to duties, which the interests of the government require a prudent and reasonable person to exercise under the circumstances. This negligence may consist of the omission to do something the prudent and reasonable person would have done, or the doing of something which such a person would not have done under the circumstances. No person is relieved of culpability who fails to perform such duties as are imposed by the general responsibilities of that person's grade or rank, or by the customs of the service for the safety and protection of vessels of the armed forces, simply because these duties are not specifically enumerated in a regulation or order. However, a mere error in judgment that a reasonably able person might have committed under the same circumstances does not constitute an offense under this article.

(4) *Suffer.* "To suffer" means to allow or permit. A ship is willfully suffered to be hazarded by one who, although not in direct control of the vessel, knows a danger to be imminent but takes no steps to prevent it, as by a plotting officer of a ship under

way who fails to report to the officer of the deck a radar target which is observed to be on a collision course with, and dangerously close to, the ship. A suffering through neglect implies an omission to take such measures as were appropriate under the circumstances to prevent a foreseeable danger.

d. *Lesser included offenses.*

(1) *Willfully and wrongfully hazarding a vessel.*

(a) Article 110—negligently hazarding a vessel

(b) Article 80—attempts

(2) *Willfully and wrongfully suffering a vessel to be hazarded.*

(a) Article 110—negligently suffering a vessel to be hazarded

(b) Article 80—attempts

e. *Maximum punishment.* Hazarding or suffering to be hazarded any vessel of the armed forces:

(1) *Willfully and wrongfully.* Death or such other punishment as a court-martial may direct.

(2) *Negligently.* Dishonorable discharge, forfeiture of all pay and allowances, and confinement for 2 years.

f. *Sample specifications.*

(1) *Hazarding or suffering to be hazarded any vessel, willfully and wrongfully.*

In that ______ (personal jurisdiction data), did, on ______ 20___, while serving as ______ aboard the ______ in the vicinity of ______, willfully and wrongfully (hazard the said vessel) (suffer the said vessel to be hazarded) by (causing the said vessel to collide with ______) (allowing the said vessel to run aground) (______).

(2) *Hazarding of vessel, negligently.*

(a) *Example 1.*

In that ______ (personal jurisdiction data), on ______ 20___, while serving in command of the ______, making entrance to (Boston Harbor), did negligently hazard the said vessel by failing and neglecting to maintain or cause to be maintained an accurate running plot of the true position of said vessel while making said approach, as a result of which neglect the said ______, at or about ______, hours on the day aforesaid, became stranded in the vicinity of (Channel Buoy Number Three).

(b) *Example 2.*

In that ______ (personal jurisdiction data), on ______ 20___, while serving as navigator of the ______, cruising on special service in the ______ Ocean off the coast of ______, notwithstanding the fact that at about midnight, ______ 20 ______, the northeast point of ______ Island bore abeam and was about six miles distant, the said ship being then under way and making a speed of about ten knots, and well knowing the position of the said ship at the time stated, and that the charts of the locality were unreliable and the currents thereabouts uncertain, did then and there negligently hazard the said vessel by failing and neglecting to exercise proper care and attention in navigating said ship while approaching ______ Island, in that he/she neglected and failed to lay a course that would carry said ship clear of the last aforesaid island, and to change the course in due time to avoid disaster; and the said ship, as a result of said negligence on the part of said ______, ran upon a rock off the southwest coast of ______ Island, at about ______ hours, ______, 20___, in consequence of which the said ______ was lost.

(c) *Example 3.*

In that ______ (personal jurisdiction data), on ______ 20___, while serving as navigator of the ______ and well knowing that at about sunset of said day the said ship had nearly run her estimated distance from the ______ position, obtained and plotted by him/her, to the position of ______, and well knowing the difficulty of sighting ______, from a safe distance after sunset, did then and there negligently hazard the said vessel by failing and neglecting to advise his/her commanding officer to lay a safe course for said ship to the northward before continuing on a westerly course, as it was the duty of said ______ to do; in consequence of which the said ship was, at about ______ hours on the day above mentioned, run upon ______ bank in the ______ Sea, about latitude ______ degrees, ______ minutes, north, and longitude ______ degrees, ______ minutes, west, and seriously injured.

(3) *Suffering a vessel to be hazarded, negligently.*

In that ______ (personal jurisdiction data), while serving as combat intelligence center officer on board the ______, making passage from Boston to Philadelphia, and having, between ________ and ________ hours on ________, 20____, been duly informed of decreasing radar ranges and constant radar bearing indicating that the said ________ was upon a collision course approaching a radar target, did then and there negligently suffer the said vessel to be hazarded by failing and neglecting to report said collision course with said radar target to the officer of the deck, as it was his/her duty to do, and he/she, the said ________, through negligence, did cause the said ________ to collide with the ________ at or about ________ hours on said date, with resultant damage to both vessels.

35. Article 111–Drunken or reckless operation of vehicle, aircraft, or vessel

a. *Text of statute.*

(a) Any person subject to this chapter who—

(1) operates or physically controls any vehicle, aircraft, or vessel in a reckless or wanton manner or while impaired by a substance described in section 912a(b) of this title (Article 112a(b)); or

(2) operates or is in actual physical control of any vehicle, aircraft, or vessel while drunk or when the alcohol concentration in the person's blood or breath is equal to or exceeds the applicable limit under subsection (b), shall be punished as a court-martial may direct.

(b)(1) For purposes of subsection (a), the applicable limit on the alcohol concentration in a person's blood or breath is as follows:

(A) In the case of the operation or control of a vehicle, aircraft, or vessel in the United States, such limit is the lesser of—

(i) the blood alcohol content limit under the law of the State in which the conduct occurred, except as may be provided under paragraph (2) for conduct on a military installation that is in more than one State; or

(ii) the blood alcohol content limit specified in paragraph (3).

(B) In the case of the operation or control of a vehicle, aircraft, or vessel outside the United States, the applicable blood alcohol content limit is the blood alcohol content limit specified in paragraph (3) or such lower limit as the Secretary of Defense may by regulation prescribe.

(2) In the case of a military installation that is in more than one State, if those States have different blood alcohol content limits under their respective State laws, the Secretary may select one such blood alcohol content limit to apply uniformly on that installation.

(3) For purposes of paragraph (1), the blood alcohol content limit with respect to alcohol concentration in a person's blood is 0.10 grams of alcohol per 100 milliliters of blood and with respect to alcohol concentration in a person's breath is 0.10 grams of alcohol per 210 liters of breath, as shown by chemical analysis.

(4) In this subsection:

(A) The term "blood alcohol content limit" means the amount of alcohol concentration in a person's blood or breath at which operation or control of a vehicle, aircraft, or vessel is prohibited.

(B) The term "United States" includes the District of Columbia, the Commonwealth of Puerto Rico, the Virgin Islands, Guam, and American Samoa and the term "State" includes each of those jurisdictions.

b. *Elements.*

(1) That the accused was operating or in physical control of a vehicle, aircraft, or vessel; and

(2) That while operating or in physical control of a vehicle, aircraft, or vessel, the accused:

(a) did so in a wanton or reckless manner, or

(b) was drunk or impaired, or

(c) the alcohol concentration in the accused's blood or breath equaled to or exceeded the applicable limit under subparagraph (b) of paragraph 35a. [NOTE: If injury resulted add the following element]

(3) That the accused thereby caused the vehicle, aircraft, or vessel to injure a person.

c. *Explanation.*

(1) *Vehicle. See* 1 U.S.C. § 4.

(2) *Vessel. See.* 1 U.S.C. § 3.

(3) *Aircraft.* Any contrivance used or designed for transportation in the air.

(4) *Operates.* Operating a vehicle, aircraft, or vessel includes not only driving or guiding a vehicle, aircraft or vessel while it is in motion, either in person or through the agency of another, but also setting of its motive power in action or the manipu-

lation of its controls so as to cause the particular vehicle, aircraft or vessel to move.

(5) *Physical control and actual physical control.* These terms as used in the statute are synonymous. They describe the present capability and power to dominate, direct or regulate the vehicle, vessel, or aircraft, either in person or through the agency of another, regardless of whether such vehicle, aircraft, or vessel is operated. For example, the intoxicated person seated behind the steering wheel of a vehicle with the keys of the vehicle in or near the ignition but with the engine not turned on could be deemed in actual physical control of that vehicle. However, the person asleep in the back seat with the keys in his or her pocket would not be deemed in actual physical control. Physical control necessarily encompasses operation.

(6) *Drunk or impaired.* "Drunk" and "impaired" mean any intoxication which is sufficient to impair the rational and full exercise of the mental or physical faculties. The term drunk is used in relation to intoxication by alcohol. The term impaired is used in relation to intoxication by a substance described in Article 112(a), Uniform Code of Military Justice.

(7) *Reckless.* The operation or physical control of a vehicle, vessel, or aircraft is "reckless" when it exhibits a culpable disregard of foreseeable consequences to others from the act or omission involved. Recklessness is not determined solely by reason of the happening of an injury, or the invasion of the rights of another, nor by proof alone of excessive speed or erratic operation, but all these factors may be admissible and relevant as bearing upon the ultimate question: whether, under all the circumstances, the accused's manner of operation or physical control of the vehicle, vessel, or aircraft was of that heedless nature which made it actually or imminently dangerous to the occupants, or to the rights or safety of others. It is operating or physically controlling a vehicle, vessel, or aircraft with such a high degree of negligence that if death were caused, the accused would have committed involuntary manslaughter, at least. The nature of the conditions in which the vehicle, vessel, or aircraft is operated or controlled, the time of day or night, the proximity and number of other vehicles, vessels, or aircraft and the condition of the vehicle, vessel, or aircraft, are often matters of importance in the proof of an offense charged under this article and, where they are of importance, may properly be alleged.

(8) *Wanton.* "Wanton" includes "reckless", but in describing the operation or physical control of a vehicle, vessel, or aircraft "wanton" may, in a proper case, connote willfulness, or a disregard of probable consequences, and thus describe a more aggravated offense.

(9) *Causation.* The accused's drunken or reckless driving must be a proximate cause of injury for the accused to be guilty of drunken or reckless driving resulting in personal injury. To be proximate, the accused's actions need not be the sole cause of the injury, nor must they be the immediate cause of the injury, that is, the latest in time and space preceding the injury. A contributing cause is deemed proximate only if it plays a material role in the victim's injury.

(10) *Separate offenses.* While the same course of conduct may constitute violations of both subsections (1) and (2) of the Article, e.g., both drunken and reckless operation or physical control, this article proscribes the conduct described in both subsections as separate offenses, which may be charged separately. However, as recklessness is a relative matter, evidence of all the surrounding circumstances that made the operation dangerous, whether alleged or not, may be admissible. Thus, on a charge of reckless driving, for example, evidence of drunkenness might be admissible as establishing one aspect of the recklessness, and evidence that the vehicle exceeded a safe speed, at a relevant prior point and time, might be admissible as corroborating other evidence of the specific recklessness charged. Similarly, on a charge of drunken driving, relevant evidence of recklessness might have probative value as corroborating other proof of drunkenness.

d. *Lesser included offense.*

(1) Reckless or wanton or impaired operation or physical control of a vessel. Article 110—improper hazarding of a vessel.

(2) Drunken operation of a vehicle, vessel, or aircraft while drunk or with a blood or breath alcohol concentration in violation of the described per se standard.

(a) Article 110—improper hazarding of a vessel

(b) Article 112—drunk on duty

(c) Article 134—drunk on station

e. *Maximum punishment.*

(1) *Resulting in personal injury.* Dishonorable

discharge, forfeiture of all pay and allowances, and confinement for 18 months.

(2) *No personal injury involved.* Bad-conduct discharge, forfeiture of all pay and allowances, and confinement for 6 months.

f. *Sample specification.*

In that ________ (personal jurisdiction data), did (at/on board required), on or about 20____, (in the motor pool area) (near the Officer's Club) (at the intersection of ________ and ________) (while in the Gulf of Mexico) (while in flight over North America) physically control [a vehicle, to wit: (a truck) (a passenger car)(______)] [an aircraft, to wit: (an AH-64 helicopter)(an F-14A fighter)(a KC-135 tanker)(________)] [a vessel, to wit: (the aircraft carrier USS ________) (the Coast Guard Cutter)(________)], [while drunk] [while impaired by ______] [while the alcohol concentration in his (blood)(breath) was, as shown by chemical analysis, equal to or exceeded (.10)(____) grams of alcohol per (100 milliliters of blood)(210 liters of breath), which is the limit under (cite applicable State law)(cite applicable statute or regulation)] [in a (reckless) (wanton) manner by (attempting to pass another vehicle on a sharp curve)(by ordering that the aircraft be flown below the authorized altitude)] [and did thereby cause said (vehicle)(aircraft)-(vessel) to (strike and)(injure ________)].

36. Article 112—Drunk on duty

a. *Text of statute.*

Any person subject to this chapter other than sentinel or look-out, who is found drunk on duty, shall be punished as a court-martial may direct.

b. *Elements.*

(1) That the accused was on a certain duty; and

(2) That the accused was found drunk while on this duty.

c. *Explanation.*

(1) *Drunk. See* paragraph 35c(6).

(2) *Duty.* "Duty" as used in this article means military duty. Every duty which an officer or enlisted person may legally be required by superior authority to execute is necessarily a military duty. Within the meaning of this article, when in the actual exercise of command, the commander of a post, or of a command, or of a detachment in the field is constantly on duty, as is the commanding officer on board a ship. In the case of other officers or enlisted persons, "on duty" relates to duties or routine or detail, in garrison, at a station, or in the field, and does not relate to those periods when, no duty being required of them by orders or regulations, officers and enlisted persons occupy the status of leisure known as "off duty" or "on liberty." In a region of active hostilities, the circumstances are often such that all members of a command may properly be considered as being continuously on duty within the meaning of this article. So also, an officer of the day and members of the guard, or of the watch, are on duty during their entire tour within the meaning of this article.

(3) *Nature of offense.* It is necessary that the accused be found drunk while actually on the duty alleged, and the fact the accused became drunk before going on duty, although material in extenuation, does not affect the question of guilt. If, however, the accused does not undertake the responsibility or enter upon the duty at all, the accused's conduct does not fall within the terms of this article, nor does that of a person who absents himself or herself from duty and is found drunk while so absent. Included within the article is drunkenness while on duty of an anticipatory nature such as that of an aircraft crew ordered to stand by for flight duty, or of an enlisted person ordered to stand by for guard duty.

(4) *Defenses.* If the accused is known by superior authorities to be drunk at the time a duty is assigned, and the accused is thereafter allowed to assume that duty anyway, or if the drunkenness results from an accidental over dosage administered for medicinal purposes, the accused will have a defense to this offense. *But see* paragraph 76 (incapacitation for duty).

d. *Lesser included offense.* Article 134—drunk on station

e. *Maximum punishment.* Bad-conduct discharge, forfeiture of all pay and allowances, and confinement for 9 months.

f. *Sample specification.*

In that ________ (personal jurisdiction data), was, (at/on board—location), on or about ________ 20________, found drunk while on duty as ________.

37. Article 112a—Wrongful use, possession, etc., of controlled substances

a. *Text of statute.*

(a) **Any person subject to this chapter who wrongfully uses, possesses, manufactures, distributes, imports into the customs territory of the United States, exports from the United States, or introduces into an installation, vessel, vehicle, or aircraft used by or under the control of the armed forces a substance described in subsection (b) shall be punished as a court-martial may direct.**

(b) **The substances referred to in subsection (a) are the following:**

(1) **opium, heroin, cocaine, amphetamine, lysergic acid diethylamide, methamphetamine, phencyclidine, barbituric acid, and marijuana, and any compound or derivative of any such substance.**

(2) **Any substance not specified in clause (1) that is listed on a schedule of controlled substances prescribed by the President for the purposes of this article.**

(3) **Any other substance not specified in clause (1) or contained on a list prescribed by the President under clause (2) that is listed in Schedules I through V of section 202 of the Controlled Substances Act (21 U.S.C. 812).**

b. *Elements.*

(1) *Wrongful possession of controlled substance.*

(a) That the accused possessed a certain amount of a controlled substance; and

(b) That the possession by the accused was wrongful.

(2) *Wrongful use of controlled substance.*

(a) That the accused used a controlled substance; and

(b) That the use by the accused was wrongful.

(3) *Wrongful distribution of controlled substance.*

(a) That the accused distributed a certain amount of a controlled substance; and

(b) That the distribution by the accused was wrongful.

(4) *Wrongful introduction of a controlled substance.*

(a) That the accused introduced onto a vessel, aircraft, vehicle, or installation used by the armed forces or under the control of the armed forces a certain amount of a controlled substance; and

(b) That the introduction was wrongful.

(5) *Wrongful manufacture of a controlled substance.*

(a) That the accused manufactured a certain amount of a controlled substance; and

(b) That the manufacture was wrongful.

(6) *Wrongful possession, manufacture, or introduction of a controlled substance with intent to distribute.*

(a) That the accused (possessed) (manufactured) (introduced) a certain amount of a controlled substance;

(b) That the (possession) (manufacture) (introduction) was wrongful; and

(c) That the (possession) (manufacture) (introduction) was with the intent to distribute.

(7) *Wrongful importation or exportation of a controlled substance.*

(a) That the accused (imported into the customs territory of) (exported from) the United States a certain amount of a controlled substance; and

(b) That the (importation) (exportation) was wrongful. [Note: When any of the aggravating circumstances listed in subparagraph e is alleged, it must be listed as an element.]

c. *Explanation.*

(1) *Controlled substance.* "Controlled substance" means amphetamine, cocaine, heroin, lysergic acid diethylamide, marijuana, methamphetamine, opium, phencyclidine, and barbituric acid, including phenobarbital and secobarbital. "Controlled substance" also means any substance which is included in Schedules I through V established by the Controlled Substances Act of 1970 (21 U.S.C. 812).

(2) *Possess.* "Possess" means to exercise control of something. Possession may be direct physical custody like holding an item in one's hand, or it may be constructive, as in the case of a person who hides an item in a locker or car to which that person may return to retrieve it. Possession must be knowing and conscious. Possession inherently includes the power or authority to preclude control by others. It is possible, however, for more than one person to possess an item simultaneously, as when several people share control of an item. An accused may not be convicted of possession of a controlled substance

if the accused did not know that the substance was present under the accused's control. Awareness of the presence of a controlled substance may be inferred from circumstantial evidence.

(3) *Distribute.* "Distribute" means to deliver to the possession of another. "Deliver" means the actual, constructive, or attempted transfer of an item, whether or not there exists an agency relationship.

(4) *Manufacture.* "Manufacture" means the production, preparation, propagation, compounding, or processing of a drug or other substance, either directly or indirectly or by extraction from substances of natural origin, or independently by means of chemical synthesis or by a combination of extraction and chemical synthesis, and includes any packaging or repackaging of such substance or labeling or relabeling of its container. "Production," as used in this subparagraph, includes the planting, cultivating, growing, or harvesting of a drug or other substance.

(5) *Wrongfulness.* To be punishable under Article 112a, possession, use, distribution, introduction, or manufacture of a controlled substance must be wrongful. Possession, use, distribution, introduction, or manufacture of a controlled substance is wrongful if it is without legal justification or authorization. Possession, distribution, introduction, or manufacture of a controlled substance is not wrongful if such act or acts are: (A) done pursuant to legitimate law enforcement activities (for example, an informant who receives drugs as part of an undercover operation is not in wrongful possession); (B) done by authorized personnel in the performance of medical duties; or (C) without knowledge of the contraband nature of the substance (for example, a person who possesses cocaine, but actually believes it to be sugar, is not guilty of wrongful possession of cocaine). Possession, use, distribution, introduction, or manufacture of a controlled substance may be inferred to be wrongful in the absence of evidence to the contrary. The burden of going forward with evidence with respect to any such exception in any court-martial or other proceeding under the code shall be upon the person claiming its benefit. If such an issue is raised by the evidence presented, then the burden of proof is upon the United States to establish that the use, possession, distribution, manufacture, or introduction was wrongful.

(6) *Intent to distribute.* Intent to distribute may be inferred from circumstantial evidence. Examples of evidence which may tend to support an inference of intent to distribute are: possession of a quantity of substance in excess of that which one would be likely to have for personal use; market value of the substance; the manner in which the substance is packaged; and that the accused is not a user of the substance. On the other hand, evidence that the accused is addicted to or is a heavy user of the substance may tend to negate an inference of intent to distribute.

(7) *Certain amount.* When a specific amount of a controlled substance is believed to have been possessed, distributed, introduced, or manufactured by an accused, the specific amount should ordinarily be alleged in the specification. It is not necessary to allege a specific amount, however, and a specification is sufficient if it alleges that an accused possessed, distributed, introduced, or manufactured "some," "traces of," or "an unknown quantity of" a controlled substance.

(8) *Missile launch facility.* A "missile launch facility" includes the place from which missiles are fired and launch control facilities from which the launch of a missile is initiated or controlled after launch.

(9) *Customs territory of the United States.* "Customs territory of the United States" includes only the States, the District of Columbia, and Puerto Rico.

(10) *Use.* "Use" means to inject, ingest, inhale, or otherwise introduce into the human body, any controlled substance. Knowledge of the presence of the controlled substance is a required component of use. Knowledge of the presence of the controlled substance may be inferred from the presence of the controlled substance in the accused's body or from other circumstantial evidence. This permissive inference may be legally sufficient to satisfy the government's burden of proof as to knowledge.

(11) *Deliberate ignorance.* An accused who consciously avoids knowledge of the presence of a controlled substance or the contraband nature of the substance is subject to the same criminal liability as one who has actual knowledge.

d. *Lesser included offenses.*

(1) *Wrongful possession of controlled substance.* Article 80—attempts

(2) *Wrongful use of controlled substance.*

(a) Article 112a—wrongful possession of controlled substance

(b) Article 80—attempts

(3) *Wrongful distribution of controlled substance.* Article 80—attempts

(4) *Wrongful manufacture of controlled substance.*

(a) Article 112a—wrongful possession of controlled substance

(b) Article 80—attempts

(5) *Wrongful introduction of controlled substance.*

(a) Article 112a—wrongful possession of controlled substance

(b) Article 80—attempts

(6) *Wrongful possession, manufacture, or introduction of a controlled substance with intent to distribute.*

(a) Article 112a—wrongful possession, manufacture, or introduction of controlled substance

(b) Article 80—attempts

(7) *Wrongful importation or exportation of a controlled substance.* Article 80—attempts

e. *Maximum punishments.*

(1) *Wrongful use, possession, manufacture, or introduction of controlled substance.*

(a) *Amphetamine, cocaine, heroin, lysergic acid diethylamide, marijuana (except possession of less than 30 grams or use of marijuana), methamphetamine, opium, phencyclidine, secobarbital, and Schedule I, II, III controlled substances.* Dishonorable discharge, forfeiture of all pay and allowances, and confinement 5 years.

(b) *Marijuana (possession of less than 30 grams or use), phenobarbital, and Schedule IV and V controlled substances.* Dishonorable discharge, forfeiture of all pay and allowances, and confinement for 2 years.

(2) *Wrongful distribution, possession, manufacture, or introduction of controlled substance with intent to distribute, or wrongful importation or exportation of a controlled substance.*

(a) *Amphetamine, cocaine, heroin, lysergic acid diethylamide, marijuana, methamphetamine, opium, phencyclidine, secobarbital, and Schedule I, II, and III controlled substances.* Dishonorable discharge, forfeiture of all pay and allowances, and confinement for 15 years.

(b) *Phenobarbital and Schedule IV and V controlled substances.* Dishonorable discharge, forfeiture of all pay and allowances, and confinement for 10 years.

When any offense under paragraph 37 is committed; while the accused is on duty as a sentinel or lookout; on board a vessel or aircraft used by or under the control of the armed forces; in or at a missile launch facility used by or under the control of the armed forces; while receiving special pay under 37 U.S.C. § 310; in time of war; or in a confinement facility used by or under the control of the armed forces, the maximum period of confinement authorized for such offense shall be increased by 5 years.

f. *Sample specifications.*

(1) *Wrongful possession, manufacture, or distribution of controlled substance.*

In that ______ (personal jurisdiction data) did, (at/on board—location) (subject-matter jurisdiction data, if required), on or about ______, 20 ___, wrongfully (possess) (distribute) (manufacture) ______ (grams) (ounces) (pounds)(______) of ______ (a schedule (______) controlled substance), (with the intent to distribute the said controlled substance) (while on duty as a sentinel or lookout) (while (on board a vessel/aircraft) (in or at a missile launch facility) used by the armed forces or under the control of the armed forces, to wit: ______) (while receiving special pay under 37 U.S.C. § 310) (during time of war).

(2) *Wrongful use of controlled substance.*

In that ______ (personal jurisdiction data), did, (at/on board—location) (subject-matter jurisdiction data, if required), on or about ______, 20 ___, wrongfully use ______ (a Schedule ______ controlled substance) (while on duty as a sentinel or lookout) (while (on board a vessel/aircraft) (in or at a missile launch facility) used by the armed forces or under the control of the armed forces, to wit: ______) (while receiving special pay under 37 U.S.C. § 310) (during time of war).

(3) *Wrongful introduction of controlled substance.*

In that ______ (personal jurisdiction data) did, (at/on board—location) on or about ______, 20 ___, wrongfully introduce ______ (grams) (ounces) (pounds) (______) of ______ (a Schedule (______) controlled substance) onto a vessel, aircraft, vehicle, or installation used by the armed forces or under control of the armed forces, to wit: ________ (with the intent to distribute the said controlled substance) (while on duty as a sentinel or lookout) (while receiving special pay under 37 U.S.C. § 310) (during a time of war).

(4) *Wrongful importation or exportation of controlled substance.*

In that ________ (personal jurisdiction data) did, (at/on board—location) on or about ________, 20____, wrongfully (import) (export) ________ (grams) (ounces) (pounds) (________) of ________ (a Schedule (________) controlled substance) (into the customs territory of) (from) the United States (while on board a vessel/aircraft used by the armed forces or under the control of the armed forces, to wit: ________) (during time of war).

38. Article 113—Misbehavior of sentinel or lookout

a. *Text of statute.*

Any sentinel or look-out who is found drunk or sleeping upon his post, or leaves it before he is regularly relieved, shall be punished, if the offense is committed in time of war, by death or such other punishment as a court-martial may direct, but if the offense is committed at any other time, by such punishment other than death as a court-martial may direct.

b. *Elements.*

(1) That the accused was posted or on post as a sentinel or lookout;

(2) That the accused was found drunk while on post, was found sleeping while on post, or left post before being regularly relieved.

[Note: If the offense was committed in time of war or while the accused was receiving special pay under 37 U.S.C. § 310, add the following element]

(3) That the offense was committed (in time of war) (while the accused was receiving special pay under 37 U.S.C. § 310).

c. *Explanation.*

(1) *In general.* This article defines three kinds of misbehavior committed by sentinels or lookouts: being found drunk or sleeping upon post, or leaving it before being regularly relieved. This article does not include an officer or enlisted person of the guard, or of a ship's watch, not posted or performing the duties of a sentinel or lookout, nor does it include a person whose duties as a watchman or attendant do not require constant alertness.

(2) *Post.* "Post" is the area where the sentinel or lookout is required to be for the performance of duties. It is not limited by an imaginary line, but includes, according to orders or circumstances, such surrounding area as may be necessary for the proper performance of the duties for which the sentinel or lookout was posted. The offense of leaving post is not committed when a sentinel or lookout goes an immaterial distance from the post, unless it is such a distance that the ability to fully perform the duty for which posted is impaired.

(3) *On post.* A sentinel or lookout becomes "on post" after having been given a lawful order to go "on post" as a sentinel or lookout and being formally or informally posted. The fact that a sentinel or lookout is not posted in the regular way is not a defense. It is sufficient, for example, if the sentinel or lookout has taken the post in accordance with proper instruction, whether or not formally given. A sentinel or lookout is on post within the meaning of the article not only when at a post physically defined, as is ordinarily the case in garrison or aboard ship, but also, for example, when stationed in observation against the approach of an enemy, or detailed to use any equipment designed to locate friend, foe, or possible danger, or at a designated place to maintain internal discipline, or to guard stores, or to guard prisoners while in confinement or at work.

(4) *Sentinel or lookout.* A sentinel or a lookout is a person whose duties include the requirement to maintain constant alertness, be vigilant, and remain awake, in order to observe for the possible approach of the enemy, or to guard persons, property, or a place and to sound the alert, if necessary.

(5) *Drunk.* For an explanation of "drunk," *see* paragraph 35c(3).

(6) *Sleeping.* As used in this article, "sleeping" is that condition of insentience which is sufficient sensibly to impair the full exercise of the mental and physical faculties of a sentinel or lookout. It is not necessary to show that the accused was in a wholly comatose condition. The fact that the accused's sleeping resulted from a physical incapacity caused by disease or accident is an affirmative defense. *See* R.C.M. 916(i).

d. *Lesser included offenses.*

(1) *Drunk on post.*

(a) Article 112—drunk on duty

(b) Article 92—dereliction of duty

(c) Article 134—drunk on station

(d) Article 134—drunk in uniform in a public place

(2) *Sleeping on post.*

(a) Article 92—dereliction of duty

(b) Article 134—loitering or wrongfully sitting down on post

(3) *Leaving post.*

(a) Article 92—dereliction of duty

(b) Article 86—going from appointed place of duty

e. *Maximum punishment.*

(1) *In time of war.* Death or such other punishment as a court-martial may direct.

(2) *While receiving special pay under 37 U.S.C. § 310.* Dishonorable discharge, forfeiture of all pay and allowances, and confinement for 10 years.

(3) *In all other places.* Dishonorable discharge, forfeiture of all pay and allowances, and confinement for 1 year.

f. *Sample specification.*

In that ______ (personal jurisdiction data), on or about ______ 20__ (a time of war) (at/on board—location), (while receiving special pay under 37 U.S.C. § 310), being (posted) (on post) as a (sentinel) (lookout) at (warehouse no. 7) (post no. 11) (for radar observation) (______) (was found (drunk) (sleeping) upon his/her post) (did leave his/her post before he/she was regularly relieved).

39. Article 114—Dueling

a. *Text of statute.*

Any person subject to this chapter who fights or promotes, or is concerned in or connives at fighting a duel, or who, having knowledge of a challenge sent or about to be sent, fails to report the fact promptly to the proper authority, shall be punished as a court-martial may direct.

b. *Elements.*

(1) *Dueling.*

(a) That the accused fought another person with deadly weapons;

(b) That the combat was for private reasons; and

(c) That the combat was by prior agreement.

(2) *Promoting a duel.*

(a) That the accused promoted a duel between certain persons; and

(b) That the accused did so in a certain manner.

(3) *Conniving at fighting a duel.*

(a) That certain persons intended to and were about to engage in a duel;

(b) That the accused had knowledge of the planned duel; and

(c) That the accused connived at the fighting of the duel in a certain manner.

(4) *Failure to report a duel.*

(a) That a challenge to fight a duel had been sent or was about to be sent;

(b) That the accused had knowledge of this challenge; and

(c) That the accused failed to report this fact promptly to proper authority.

c. *Explanation.*

(1) *Duel.* A duel is combat between two persons for private reasons fought with deadly weapons by prior agreement.

(2) *Promoting a duel.* Urging or taunting another to challenge or to accept a challenge to duel, acting as a second or as carrier of a challenge or acceptance, or otherwise furthering or contributing to the fighting of a duel are examples of promoting a duel.

(3) *Conniving at fighting a duel.* Anyone who has knowledge that steps are being taken or have been taken toward arranging or fighting a duel and who fails to take reasonable preventive action thereby connives at the fighting of a duel.

d. *Lesser included offense.* Article 80—attempts

e. *Maximum punishment.* For all Article 114 offenses: dishonorable discharge, forfeiture of all pay and allowances, and confinement for 1 year.

f. *Sample specifications.*

(1) *Dueling.*

In that ______ (personal jurisdiction data) (and ______), did, (at/on board—location) (subject-matter jurisdiction data, if required), on or about ______ 20______, fight a duel (with ________), using as weapons therefor (pistols) (swords) (________).

(2) *Promoting a duel.*

In that ________ (personal jurisdiction data), did, (at/on board—location) (subject-matter jurisdiction data, if required), on or about ________ 20 ____, promote a duel between ________ and ________ by (telling said ________ he/she would be a coward if he/she failed to challenge said ________ to a duel) (knowingly carrying from said ________ to said ________ a challenge to fight a duel).

(3) *Conniving at fighting a duel.*

In that ________ (personal jurisdiction data), having knowledge that ________ and ________ were about to engage in a duel, did (at/on board—location) (subject-matter jurisdiction data, if required), on or about ________ 20 ____, connive at the fighting of said duel by (failing to take reasonable preventive action) (________).

(4) *Failure to report a duel.*

In that ________ (personal jurisdiction data), having knowledge that a challenge to fight a duel (had been sent) (was about to be sent) by ________ to ________, did, (at/on board—location) (subject-matter jurisdiction data, if required), on or about ________ 20 ____ fail to report that fact promptly to the proper authority.

40. Article 115—Malingering

a. *Text of statute.*

Any person subject to this chapter who for the purpose of avoiding work, duty, or service ”—

(1) **feigns illness, physical disablement, mental lapse or derangement; or**

(2) **intentionally inflicts self-injury; shallbe punished as a court-martial may direct.**

b. *Elements.*

(1) That the accused was assigned to, or was aware of prospective assignment to, or availability for, the performance of work, duty, or service;

(2) That the accused feigned illness, physical disablement, mental lapse or derangement, or intentionally inflicted injury upon himself or herself; and

(3) That the accused's purpose or intent in doing so was to avoid the work, duty, or service.

[Note: If the offense was committed in time of war or in a hostile fire pay zone, add the following element]

(4) That the offense was committed (in time of war) (in a hostile fire pay zone).

c. *Explanation.*

(1) *Nature of offense.* The essence of this offense is the design to avoid performance of any work, duty, or service which may properly or normally be expected of one in the military service. Whether to avoid all duty, or only a particular job, it is the purpose to shirk which characterizes the offense. Hence, the nature or permanency of a self-inflicted injury is not material on the question of guilt, nor is the seriousness of a physical or mental disability which is a sham. Evidence of the extent of the self-inflicted injury or feigned disability may, however, be relevant as a factor indicating the presence or absence of the purpose.

(2) *How injury inflicted.* The injury may be inflicted by nonviolent as well as by violent means and may be accomplished by any act or omission which produces, prolongs, or aggravates any sickness or disability. Thus, voluntary starvation which results in debility is a self-inflicted injury and when done for the purpose of avoiding work, duty, or service constitutes a violation of this article.

d. *Lesser included offenses.*

(1) Article 134—self-injury without intent to avoid service

(2) Article 80—attempts

e. *Maximum punishment.*

(1) *Feigning illness, physical disablement, mental lapse, or derangement.* Dishonorable discharge, forfeiture of all pay and allowances, and confinement for 1 year.

(2) *Feigning illness, physical disablement, mental lapse, or derangement in a hostile fire pay zone or in time of war.* Dishonorable discharge, forfeiture of all pay and allowances, and confinement for 3 years.

(3) *Intentional self-inflicted injury.* Dishonorable discharge, forfeiture of all pay and allowances, and confinement for 5 years.

(4) *Intentional self-inflicted injury in a hostile fire pay zone or in time of war.* Dishonorable discharge, forfeiture of all pay and allowances, and confinement for 10 years.

f. *Sample specification.*

In that ________ (personal jurisdiction data),

did, (at/on board—location) (in a hostile fire pay zone) (subject-matter jurisdiction data, if required) (on or about ______ 20 ______) (from about ______ 20 ____ to about ______ 20 ____), (a time of war) for the purpose of avoiding (his/her duty as officer of the day) (his/her duty as aircraft mechanic) (work in the mess hall) (service as an enlisted person) (______) (feign (a headache) (a sore back) (illness) (mental lapse) (mental derangement) (______)) (intentionally injure himself/herself by ______).

41. Article 116—Riot or breach of peace

a. *Text of statute.*

Any person subject to this chapter who causes or participates in any riot or breach of the peace shall be punished as a court-martial may direct.

b. *Elements.*

(1) *Riot.*

(a) That the accused was a member of an assembly of three or more persons;

(b) That the accused and at least two other members of this group mutually intended to assist one another against anyone who might oppose them in doing an act for some private purpose;

(c) That the group or some of its members, in furtherance of such purpose, unlawfully committed a tumultuous disturbance of the peace in a violent or turbulent manner; and

(d) That these acts terrorized the public in general in that they caused or were intended to cause public alarm or terror.

(2) *Breach of the peace.*

(a) That the accused caused or participated in a certain act of a violent or turbulent nature; and

(b) That the peace was thereby unlawfully disturbed.

c. *Explanation.*

(1) *Riot.* "Riot" is a tumultuous disturbance of the peace by three or more persons assembled together in furtherance of a common purpose to execute some enterprise of a private nature by concerted action against anyone who might oppose them, committed in such a violent and turbulent manner as to cause or be calculated to cause public terror. The gravamen of the offense of riot is terrorization of the public. It is immaterial whether the act intended was lawful. Furthermore, it is not necessary that the common purpose be determined before the assembly. It is sufficient if the assembly begins to execute in a tumultuous manner a common purpose formed after it assembled.

(2) *Breach of the peace.* A "breach of the peace" is an unlawful disturbance of the peace by an outward demonstration of a violent or turbulent nature. The acts or conduct contemplated by this article are those which disturb the public tranquility or impinge upon the peace and good order to which the community is entitled. Engaging in an affray and unlawful discharge of firearms in a public street are examples of conduct which may constitute a breach of the peace. Loud speech and unruly conduct may also constitute a breach of the peace by the speaker. A speaker may also by guilty of causing a breach of the peace if the speaker uses language which can reasonably be expected to produce a violent or turbulent response and a breach of the peace results. The fact that the words are true or used under provocation is not a defense, nor is tumultuous conduct excusable because incited by others.

(3) *Community and public.* "Community" and "public" include a military organization, post, camp, ship, aircraft, or station.

d. *Lesser included offenses.*

(1) *Riot.*

(a) Article 116—breach of the peace

(b) Article 134—disorderly conduct

(c) Article 80—attempts

(2) *Breach of the peace.*

(a) Article 134—disorderly conduct

(b) Article 80—attempts

e. *Maximum punishment.*

(1) *Riot.* Dishonorable discharge, forfeiture of all pay and allowances, and confinement for 10 years.

(2) *Breach of the peace.* Confinement for 6 months and forfeiture of two-thirds pay per month for 6 months.

f. *Sample specifications.*

(1) *Riot.*

In that ______ (personal jurisdiction data), did, (at/on board—location) (subject-matter jurisdiction data, if required), on or about ______ 20 ____, (cause) (participate in) a riot by unlawfully assembling with ______ (and ______) (and) (others to the number of about ______ whose names are unknown) for the purpose of (resisting the police of ______) (assaulting passers-by) (______), and in furtherance of said purpose did (fight with said police) (assault certain persons, to wit: ______) (______), to the terror and disturbance of ______.

(2) *Breach of the peace.*

In that ______ (personal jurisdiction data), did, (at/on board—location) (subject-matter jurisdiction data, if required), on or about ______ 20 ______, (cause) (participate in) a breach of the peace by (wrongfully engaging in a fist fight in the dayroom with ______) (using the following provoking language (toward ______), to wit: "______," or words to that effect) (wrongfully shouting and singing in a public place, to wit: ______) (______).

42. Article 117—Provoking speeches or gestures

a. *Text of statute.*

Any person subject to this chapter who uses provoking or reproachful words or gestures towards any other person subject to this chapter shall be punished as a court-martial may direct.

b. *Elements.*

(1) That the accused wrongfully used words or gestures toward a certain person;

(2) That the words or gestures used were provoking or reproachful; and

(3) That the person toward whom the words or gestures were used was a person subject to the code.

c. *Explanation.*

(1) *In general.* As used in this article, "provoking" and "reproachful" describe those words or gestures which are used in the presence of the person to whom they are directed and which a reasonable person would expect to induce a breach of the peace under the circumstances. These words and gestures do not include reprimands, censures, reproofs and the like which may properly be administered in the interests of training, efficiency, or discipline in the armed forces.

(2) *Knowledge.* It is not necessary that the accused have knowledge that the person toward whom the words or gestures are directed is a person subject to the code.

d. *Lesser included offenses.* Article 80—attempts

e. *Maximum punishment.* Confinement for 6 months and forfeiture of two-thirds pay per month for 6 months.

f. *Sample specification.*

In that ______ (personal jurisdiction data), did, (at/on board—location) (subject-matter jurisdiction data, if required), on or about ______ 20 ______, wrongfully use (provoking) (reproachful) (words, to wit; "______:" or words to that effect) (and) (gestures, to wit: ______) towards (Sergeant ______, U.S. Air Force) (______).

43. Article 118—Murder

a. *Text of statute.*

Any person subject to this chapter who, without justification or excuse, unlawfully kills a human being, when he—

(1) **has a premeditated design to kill;**

(2) **intends to kill or inflict great bodily harm;**

(3) **is engaged in an act that is inherently dangerous to another and evinces a wanton disregard of human life; or**

(4) **is engaged in the perpetration or attempted perpetration of burglary, sodomy, rape, rape of a child, aggravated sexual assault, aggravated sexual assault of a child, aggravated sexual contact, aggravated sexual abuse of a child, aggravated sexual contact with a child, robbery or aggravated arson; is guilty of murder, and shall suffer such punishment as a court-martial may direct, except that if found guilty under clause (1) or (4), he shall suffer death or imprisonment for life as a court-martial may direct.**

b. *Elements.*

(1) *Premeditated murder.*

(a) That a certain named or described person is dead;

(b) That the death resulted from the act or omission of the accused;

(c) That the killing was unlawful; and

(d) That, at the time of the killing, the accused had a premeditated design to kill.

(2) *Intent to kill or inflict great bodily harm.*

(a) That a certain named or described person is dead;

(b) That the death resulted from the act or omission of the accused;

(c) That the killing was unlawful; and

(d) That, at the time of the killing, the accused had the intent to kill or inflict great bodily harm upon a person.

(3) *Act inherently dangerous to another.*

(a) That a certain named or described person is dead;

(b) That the death resulted from the intentional act of the accused;

(c) That this act was inherently dangerous to another and showed a wanton disregard for human life;

(d) That the accused knew that death or great bodily harm was a probable consequence of the act; and

(e) That the killing was unlawful.

(4) *During certain offenses.*

(a) That a certain named or described person is dead;

(b) That the death resulted from the act or omission of the accused;

(c) That the killing was unlawful; and

(d) That, at the time of the killing, the accused was engaged in the perpetration or attempted perpetration of burglary, sodomy, rape, rape of a child, aggravated sexual assault, aggravated sexual assault of a child, aggravated sexual contact, aggravated sexual abuse of a child, aggravated sexual contact with a child, robbery, or aggravated arson.

c. *Explanation.*

(1) *In general.* Killing a human being is unlawful when done without justification or excuse. *See* R.C.M. 916. Whether an unlawful killing constitutes murder or a lesser offense depends upon the circumstances. The offense is committed at the place of the act or omission although the victim may have died elsewhere. Whether death occurs at the time of the accused's act or omission, or at some time thereafter, it must have followed from an injury received by the victim which resulted from the act or omission.

(2) *Premeditated murder.*

(a) *Premeditation.* A murder is not premeditated unless the thought of taking life was consciously conceived and the act or omission by which it was taken was intended. Premeditated murder is murder committed after the formation of a specific intent to kill someone and consideration of the act intended. It is not necessary that the intention to kill have been entertained for any particular or considerable length of time. When a fixed purpose to kill has been deliberately formed, it is immaterial how soon afterwards it is put into execution. The existence of premeditation may be inferred from the circumstances.

(b) *Transferred premeditation.* When an accused with a premeditated design attempted to unlawfully kill a certain person, but, by mistake or inadvertence, killed another person, the accused is still criminally responsible for a premeditated murder, because the premeditated design to kill is transferred from the intended victim to the actual victim.

(c) *Intoxication.* Voluntary intoxication (*see* R.C.M. 916(*l*)(2)) not amounting to legal insanity may reduce premeditated murder (Article 118(1)) to unpremeditated murder (Article 118(2) or (3)) but it does not reduce either premeditated murder or unpremeditated murder to manslaughter (Article 119) or any other lesser offense.

(3) *Intent to kill or inflict great bodily harm.*

(a) *Intent.* An unlawful killing without premeditation is also murder when the accused had either an intent to kill or inflict great bodily harm. It may be inferred that a person intends the natural and probable consequences of an act purposely done. Hence, if a person does an intentional act likely to result in death or great bodily injury, it may be inferred that death or great bodily injury was intended. The intent need not be directed toward the person killed, or exist for any particular time before commission of the act, or have previously existed at all. It is sufficient that it existed at the time of the act or omission (except if death is inflicted in the heat of a sudden passion caused by adequate provocation— *see* paragraph 44). For example, a person committing housebreaking who strikes and kills the householder attempting to prevent flight can be guilty of murder even if the householder was not seen until the moment before striking the fatal blow.

(b) *Great bodily harm.* "Great bodily harm" means serious injury; it does not include minor injuries such as a black eye or a bloody nose, but it does include fractured or dislocated bones, deep cuts, torn members of the body, serious damage to internal organs, and other serious bodily injuries. It is synonymous with the term "grievous bodily harm."

(c) *Intoxication.* Voluntary intoxication not amounting to legal insanity does not reduce unpremeditated murder to manslaughter (Article 119) or any other lesser offense.

(4) *Act inherently dangerous to others.*

(a) *Wanton disregard of human life.* Intentionally engaging in an act inherently dangerous to another—although without an intent to cause the death of or great bodily harm to any particular person, or even with a wish that death will not be caused—may also constitute murder if the act shows wanton disregard of human life. Such disregard is characterized by heedlessness of the probable consequences of the act or omission, or indifference to the likelihood of death or great bodily harm. Examples include throwing a live grenade toward another in jest or flying an aircraft very low over one or more persons to cause alarm.

(b) *Knowledge.* The accused must know that death or great bodily harm was a probable consequence of the inherently dangerous act. Such knowledge may be proved by circumstantial evidence.

(5) *During certain offenses.*

(a) *In general.* The commission or attempted commission of any of the offenses listed in Article 118(4) is likely to result in homicide, and when an unlawful killing occurs as a consequence of the perpetration or attempted perpetration of one of these offenses, the killing is murder. Under these circumstances it is not a defense that the killing was unintended or accidental.

(b) *Separate offenses.* The perpetration or attempted perpetration of the burglary, sodomy, rape, robbery, or aggravated arson may be charged separately from the homicide.

d. *Lesser included offenses.*

(1) *Premeditated murder and murder during certain offenses.* Article 118(2) and (3)—murder

(2) *All murders under Article 118.*

(a) Article 119—involuntary manslaughter

(b) Article 128—assault; assault consummated by a battery; aggravated assault

(c) Article 134—negligent homicide

(3) *Murder as defined in Article 118(1), (2), and (4).*

(a) Article 80—attempts

(b) Article 119—voluntary manslaughter

(c) Article 134—assault with intent to commit murder

(d) Article 134—assault with intent to commit voluntary manslaughter

e. *Maximum punishment.*

(1) Article 118(1) or (4)—death. Mandatory minimum—imprisonment for life with eligibility for parole.

(2) Article 118(2) or (3)—such punishment other than death as a court-martial may direct.

f. *Sample specification.*

In that ______ (personal jurisdiction data), did, (at/on board—location) (subject-matter jurisdiction data, if required), on or about ______ 20 ___, (with premeditation) (while (perpetrating) (attempting to perpetrate) ______) murder ______ by means of (shooting him/her with a rifle) (______).

44. Article 119—Manslaughter

a. *Text of statute.*

(a) **Any person subject to this chapter who, with an intent to kill or inflict great bodily harm, unlawfully kills a human being in the heat of sudden passion caused by adequate provocation is guilty of voluntary manslaughter and shall be punished as a court-martial may direct.**

(b) **Any person subject to this chapter who, without an intent to kill or inflict great bodily harm, unlawfully kills a human being—**

(1) **by culpable negligence; or**

(2) **while perpetrating or attempting to perpetrate an offense, other than those named in clause (4) of section 918 of this title (article 118), directly affecting the person; is guilty of involuntary manslaughter and shall be punished as a court-martial may direct.**

b. *Elements.*

(1) *Voluntary manslaughter.*

(a) That a certain named or described person is dead;

(b) That the death resulted from the act or omission of the accused;

(c) That the killing was unlawful; and

(d) That, at the time of the killing, the accused had the intent to kill or inflict great bodily harm upon the person killed.

(2) *Involuntary manslaughter.*

(a) That a certain named or described person is dead;

(b) That the death resulted from the act or omission of the accused;

(c) That the killing was unlawful; and

(d) That this act or omission of the accused constituted culpable negligence, or occurred while the accused was perpetrating or attempting to perpetrate an offense directly affecting the person other than burglary, sodomy, rape, rape of a child, aggravated sexual assault, aggravated sexual assault of a child, aggravated sexual contact, aggravated sexual abuse of a child, aggravated sexual contact with a child, robbery, or aggravated arson.

c. *Explanation.*

(1) *Voluntary manslaughter.*

(a) *Nature of offense.* An unlawful killing, although done with an intent to kill or inflict great bodily harm, is not murder but voluntary manslaughter if committed in the heat of sudden passion caused by adequate provocation. Heat of passion may result from fear or rage. A person may be provoked to such an extent that in the heat of sudden passion caused by the provocation, although not in necessary defense of life or to prevent bodily harm, a fatal blow may be struck before self-control has returned. Although adequate provocation does not excuse the homicide, it does preclude conviction of murder.

(b) *Nature of provocation.* The provocation must be adequate to excite uncontrollable passion in a reasonable person, and the act of killing must be committed under and because of the passion. However, the provocation must not be sought or induced as an excuse for killing or doing harm. If, judged by the standard of a reasonable person, sufficient cooling time elapses between the provocation and the killing, the offense is murder, even if the accused's passion persists. Examples of acts which may, depending on the circumstances, constitute adequate provocation are the unlawful infliction of great bodily harm, unlawful imprisonment, and the sight by one spouse of an act of adultery committed by the other spouse. Insulting or abusive words or gestures, a slight blow with the hand or fist, and trespass or other injury to property are not, standing alone, adequate provocation.

(2) *Involuntary manslaughter.*

(a) *Culpable negligence.*

(i) *Nature of culpable negligence.* Culpable negligence is a degree of carelessness greater than simple negligence. It is a negligent act or omission accompanied by a culpable disregard for the foreseeable consequences to others of that act or omission. Thus, the basis of a charge of involuntary manslaughter may be a negligent act or omission which, when viewed in the light of human experience, might foreseeably result in the death of another, even though death would not necessarily be a natural and probable consequence of the act or omission. Acts which may amount to culpable negligence include negligently conducting target practice so that the bullets go in the direction of an inhabited house within range; pointing a pistol in jest at another and pulling the trigger, believing, but without taking reasonable precautions to ascertain, that it would not be dangerous; and carelessly leaving poisons or dangerous drugs where they may endanger life.

(ii) *Legal duty required.* When there is no legal duty to act there can be no neglect. Thus, when a stranger makes no effort to save a drowning person, or a person allows a beggar to freeze or starve to death, no crime is committed.

(b) *Offense directly affecting the person.* An "offense directly affecting the person" means one affecting some particular person as distinguished from an offense affecting society in general. Among offenses directly affecting the person are the various types of assault, battery, false imprisonment, voluntary engagement in an affray, and maiming.

d. *Lesser included offenses.*

(1) *Voluntary manslaughter.*

(a) Article 119—involuntary manslaughter

(b) Article 128—assault; assault consummated by a battery; aggravated assault

(c) Article 134—assault with intent to commit voluntary manslaughter

(d) Article 134—negligent homicide

(e) Article 80—attempts

(2) *Involuntary manslaughter.*

(a) Article 128—assault; assault consummated by a battery

(b) Article 134—negligent homicide

e. *Maximum punishment.*

(1) *Voluntary manslaughter.* Dishonorable discharge, forfeiture of all pay and allowances, and confinement for 15 years.

(2) *Involuntary manslaughter.* Dishonorable discharge, forfeiture of all pay and allowances, and confinement for 10 years.

f. *Sample specifications.*

(1) *Voluntary manslaughter.*

In that __________ (personal jurisdiction data), did, (at/on board—location) (subject-matter jurisdiction data, if required), on or about __________ 20 ____, willfully and unlawfully kill __________ by __________ him/her (in) (on) the __________ with a __________.

(2) *Involuntary manslaughter.*

In that __________ (personal jurisdiction data), did, (at/on board—location) (subject-matter jurisdiction data, if required), on or about __________ 20 ____, (by culpable negligence) (while (perpetrating) (attempting to perpetrate) an offense directly affecting the person of __________, to wit: (maiming) (a battery) (__________)) unlawfully kill __________ by __________ him/her (in) (on) the __________ with a __________.

44a. Article 119a.--Death or injury of an unborn child

a. *Text of statute.*

(a)(1) **Any person subject to this chapter who engages in conduct that violates any of the provisions of law listed in subsection (b) and thereby causes the death of, or bodily injury (as defined in section 1365 of title 18) to, a child, who is in utero at the time the conduct takes place, is guilty of a separate offense under this section and shall, upon conviction, be punished by such punishment, other than death, as a court-martial may direct, which shall be consistent with the punishments prescribed by the President for that conduct had that injury or death occurred to the unborn child's mother.**

(2) **An offense under this section does not require proof that—**

(i) **the person engaging in the conduct had knowledge or should have had knowledge that the victim of the underlying offense was pregnant; or**

(ii) **the accused intended to cause the death of, or bodily injury to, the unborn child.**

(3) **If the person engaging in the conduct thereby intentionally kills or attempts to kill the unborn child, that person shall, instead of being punished under paragraph (1), be punished as provided under sections 880, 918, and 919(a) of this title (articles 80, 118, and 119(a)) for intentionally killing or attempting to kill a human being.**

(4) **Notwithstanding any other provision of law, the death penalty shall not be imposed for an offense under this section.**

(b) **The provisions referred to in subsection (a) are sections 918, 919(a), 919(b)(2), 920(a), 922, 924, 926, and 928 of this title (articles 118, 119(a), 119(b)(2), 120(a), 122, 124, 126, and 128).**

(c) **Nothing in this section shall be construed to permit the prosecution—**

(1) **of any person authorized by state or federal law to perform abortions for conduct relating to an abortion for which the consent of the pregnant woman, or a person authorized by law to act on her behalf, has been obtained or for which such consent is implied by law;**

(2) **of any person for any medical treatment of the pregnant woman or her unborn child; or**

(3) **of any woman with respect to her unborn child.**

(d) **As used in this section, the term "unborn child" means a child in utero, and the term "child in utero" or "child, who is in utero" means a member of the species homo sapiens, at any stage of development, who is carried in the womb.**

b. *Elements.*

(1) *Injuring an unborn child.*

(a) That the accused was engaged in the [(murder (article 118)), (voluntary manslaughter (article 119(a))), (involuntary manslaughter (article 119(b)(2))), (rape (article 120)), (robbery (article 122)), (maiming (article 124)), (assault (article 128)), of] or [burning or setting afire, as arson (article 126), of (a dwelling inhabited by) (a structure or property (known to be occupied by) (belonging to))] a woman;

(b) That the woman was then pregnant; and

(c) That the accused thereby caused bodily injury to the unborn child of that woman.

(2) *Killing an unborn child.*

(a) That the accused was engaged in the [(murder (article 118)), (voluntary manslaughter (article 119(a))), (involuntary manslaughter (article 119(b)(2))), (rape (article 120)), (robbery (article 122)), (maiming (article 124)), (assault (article 128)), of] or [burning or setting afire, as arson (article 126), of (a dwelling inhabited by) (a structure or property known to (be occupied by) (belong to))] a woman;

(b) That the woman was then pregnant; and

(c) That the accused thereby caused the death of the unborn child of that woman.

(3) *Attempting to kill an unborn child.*

(a) That the accused was engaged in the [(murder (article 118)), (voluntary manslaughter (article 119(a))), (involuntary manslaughter (article 119(b)(2))), (rape (article 120)), (robbery (article 122)), (maiming (article 124)), (assault (article 128)), of] or [burning or setting afire, as arson (article 126), of (a dwelling inhabited by) (a structure or property (known to be occupied by) (belonging to))] a woman;

(b) That the woman was then pregnant; and

(c) That the accused thereby intended and attempted to kill the unborn child of that woman.

(4) *Intentionally killing an unborn child.*

(a) That the accused was engaged in the [(murder (article 118)), (voluntary manslaughter (article 119(a))), (involuntary manslaughter (article 119(b)(2))), (rape (article 120)), (robbery (article 122)), (maiming (article 124)), (assault (article 128)), of] or [burning or setting afire, as arson (article 126), of (a dwelling inhabited by) (a structure or property (known to be occupied by) (belonging to))] a woman;

(b) That the woman was then pregnant; and

(c) That the accused thereby intentionally killed the unborn child of that woman.

c. *Explanation.*

(1) *Nature of offense.* This article makes it a separate, punishable crime to cause the death of or bodily injury to an unborn child while engaged in arson (article 126, UCMJ); murder (article 118, UCMJ); voluntary manslaughter (article 119(a), UCMJ); involuntary manslaughter (article 119(b)(2), UCMJ); rape (article 120(a), UCMJ); robbery (article 122, UCMJ); maiming (article 124, UCMJ); or assault (article 128, UCMJ) against a pregnant woman. For all underlying offenses, except arson, this article requires that the victim of the underlying offense be the pregnant mother. For purposes of arson, the pregnant mother must have some nexus to the arson such that she sustained some "bodily injury" due to the arson. For the purposes of this article the term "woman" means a female of any age. This article does not permit the prosecution of any—

(a) person for conduct relating to an abortion for which the consent of the pregnant woman, or a person authorized by law to act on her behalf, has been obtained or for which such consent is implied by law;

(b) person for any medical treatment of the pregnant woman or her unborn child; or

(c) woman with respect to her unborn child.

(2) The offenses of "injuring an unborn child" and "killing an unborn child" do not require proof that—

(a) the person engaging in the conduct (the accused) had knowledge or should have had knowledge that the victim of the underlying offense was pregnant; or

(b) the accused intended to cause the death of, or bodily injury to, the unborn child.

(3) The offense of "attempting to kill an unborn child" requires that the accused intended by his conduct to cause the death of the unborn child (See paragraph b(3)(c) above).

(4) *Bodily injury.* For the purpose of this offense, the term "bodily injury" is that which is provided by section 1365 of title 18, to wit: a cut, abrasion, bruise, burn, or disfigurement; physical pain; illness; impairment of the function of a bodily member, organ, or mental faculty; or any other injury to the body, no matter how temporary.

(5) *Unborn child.* "Unborn child" means a child in utero or a member of the species homo sapiens who is carried in the womb, at any stage of development, from conception to birth.

d. *Lesser included offenses.*

(1) *Killing an unborn child.* Article 119a — injuring an unborn child

(2) *Intentionally killing an unborn child.*

(a) Article 119a — killing an unborn child

(b) Article 119a — injuring an unborn child

(c) Article 119a — attempts (attempting to kill an unborn child)

e. *Maximum punishment.*
The maximum punishment for (1) Injuring an unborn child; (2) Killing an unborn child; (3) Attempting to kill an unborn child; or (4) Intentionally killing an unborn child is such punishment, other than death, as a court-martial may direct, but shall be consistent with the punishment had the bodily injury, death, attempt to kill, or intentional killing occurred to the unborn child's mother.

f. *Sample specifications.*

(1) *Injuring an unborn child.*

In that ________ (personal jurisdiction data), did (at/on board—location), (subject-matter jurisdiction data, if required), on or about ________ 20 ____, cause bodily injury to the unborn child of , a pregnant woman, by engaging in the [(murder) (voluntary manslaughter) (involuntary manslaughter) (rape) (robbery) (maiming) (assault) of] [(burning) (setting afire) of (a dwelling inhabited by) (a structure or property known to (be occupied by) (belong to))] that woman.

(2) *Killing an unborn child.*

In that ________ (personal jurisdiction data), did (at/on board—location), (subject-matter jurisdiction data, if required), on or about ________ 20 ____, cause the death of the unborn child of , a pregnant woman, by engaging in the [(murder) (voluntary manslaughter) (involuntary manslaughter) (rape) (robbery) (maiming) (assault) of] [(burning) (setting afire) of (a dwelling inhabited by) (a structure or property known to (be occupied by) (belong to))] that woman.

(3) *Attempting to kill an unborn child.*

In that ________ (personal jurisdiction data), did (at/on board—location), (subject-matter jurisdiction data, if required), on or about ________ 20 ____, attempt to kill the unborn child of , a pregnant woman, by engaging in the [(murder) (voluntary manslaughter) (involuntary manslaughter) (rape) (robbery) (maiming) (assault) of] [(burning) (setting afire) of (a dwelling inhabited by) (a structure or property known to (be occupied by) (belong to))] that woman.

(4) *Intentionally killing an unborn child.*

In that ________ (personal jurisdiction data), did (at/on board—location), (subject-matter jurisdiction data, if required), on or about ________ 20 ____, intentionally kill the unborn child of , a pregnant woman, by engaging in the [(murder) (voluntary manslaughter) (involuntary manslaughter) (rape) (robbery) (maiming) (assault) of] [(burning) (setting afire) of (a dwelling inhabited by) (a structure or property known to (be occupied by) (belong to))] that woman.

45. Article 120—Rape, sexual assault, and other sexual misconduct

a. *Text of statute.*

(a) *Rape.* **Any person subject to this chapter who causes another person of any age to engage in a sexual act by—**

(1) **using force against that other person;**

(2) **causing grievous bodily harm to any person;**

(3) **threatening or placing that other person in fear that any person will be subjected to death, grievous bodily harm, or kidnapping;**

(4) **rendering another person unconscious; or**

(5) **administering to another person by force or threat of force, or without the knowledge or permission of that person, a drug, intoxicant, or other similar substance and thereby substantially impairs the ability of that other person to appraise or control conduct; is guilty of rape and shall be punished as a court-martial may direct.**

(b) *Rape of a child.* **Any person subject to this chapter who—**

(1) **engages in a sexual act with a child who has not attained the age of 12 years; or**

(2) **engages in a sexual act under the circumstances described in subsection (a) with a child who has attained the age of 12 years; is guilty of rape of a child and shall be punished as a court-martial may direct.**

(c) *Aggravated sexual assault.* **Any person subject to this chapter who—**

(1) **causes another person of any age to engage in a sexual act by—**

(A) **threatening or placing that other person in fear (other than by threatening or placing that other person in fear that any person will be** subjected to death, grievous bodily harm, or kidnapping); or

(B) causing bodily harm; or

(2) engages in a sexual act with another person of any age if that other person is substantially incapacitated or substantially incapable of—

(A) appraising the nature of the sexual act;

(B) declining participation in the sexual act; or

(C) communicating unwillingness to engage in the sexual act; is guilty of aggravated sexual assault and shall be punished as a court-martial may direct.

(d) *Aggravated sexual assault of a child.* Any person subject to this chapter who engages in a sexual act with a child who has attained the age of 12 years is guilty of aggravated sexual assault of a child and shall be punished as a court-martial may direct.

(e) *Aggravated sexual contact.* Any person subject to this chapter who engages in or causes sexual contact with or by another person, if to do so would violate subsection (a) (rape) had the sexual contact been a sexual act, is guilty of aggravated sexual contact and shall be punished as a court-martial may direct.

(f) *Aggravated sexual abuse of a child.* Any person subject to this chapter who engages in a lewd act with a child is guilty of aggravated sexual abuse of a child and shall be punished as a court-martial may direct.

(g) *Aggravated sexual contact with a child.* Any person subject to this chapter who engages in or causes sexual contact with or by another person, if to do so would violate subsection (b) (rape of a child) had the sexual contact been a sexual act, is guilty of aggravated sexual contact with a child and shall be punished as a court-martial may direct.

(h) *Abusive sexual contact.* Any person subject to this chapter who engages in or causes sexual contact with or by another person, if to do so would violate subsection (c) (aggravated sexual assault) had the sexual contact been a sexual act, is guilty of abusive sexual contact and shall be punished as a court-martial may direct.

(i) *Abusive sexual contact with a child.* Any person subject to this chapter who engages in or causes sexual contact with or by another person, if to do so would violate subsection (d) (aggravated sexual assault of a child) had the sexual contact been a sexual act, is guilty of abusive sexual contact with a child and shall be punished as a court-martial may direct.

(j) *Indecent liberty with a child.* Any person subject to this chapter who engages in indecent liberty in the physical presence of a child—

(1) with the intent to arouse, appeal to, or gratify the sexual desire of any person; or

(2) with the intent to abuse, humiliate, or degrade any person; is guilty of indecent liberty with a child and shall be punished as a court-martial may direct.

(k) *Indecent act.* Any person subject to this chapter who engages in indecent conduct is guilty of an indecent act and shall be punished as a court-martial may direct.

(l) *Forcible pandering.* Any person subject to this chapter who compels another person to engage in an act of prostitution with another person to be directed to said person is guilty of forcible pandering and shall be punished as a court-martial may direct.

(m) *Wrongful sexual contact.* Any person subject to this chapter who, without legal justification or lawful authorization, engages in sexual contact with another person without that other person's permission is guilty of wrongful sexual contact and shall be punished as a court-martial may direct.

(n) *Indecent exposure.* Any person subject to this chapter who intentionally exposes, in an indecent manner, in any place where the conduct involved may reasonably be expected to be viewed by people other than members of the actor's family or household, the genitalia, anus, buttocks, or female areola or nipple is guilty of indecent exposure and shall be punished as a court-martial may direct.

(o) *Age of child.*

(1) *Twelve years.* In a prosecution under subsection (b) (rape of a child), subsection (g) (aggravated sexual contact with a child), or subsection (j) (indecent liberty with a child), it need not be proven that the accused knew that the other person engaging in the sexual act, contact, or liberty

had not attained the age of 12 years. It is not an affirmative defense that the accused reasonably believed that the child had attained the age of 12 years.

(2) *Sixteen years.* In a prosecution under subsection (d) (aggravated sexual assault of a child), subsection (f) (aggravated sexual abuse of a child), subsection (i) (abusive sexual contact with a child), or subsection (j) (indecent liberty with a child), it need not be proven that the accused knew that the other person engaging in the sexual act, contact, or liberty had not attained the age of 16 years. Unlike in paragraph (1), however, it is an affirmative defense that the accused reasonably believed that the child had attained the age of 16 years.

(p) *Proof of threat.* In a prosecution under this section, in proving that the accused made a threat, it need not be proven that the accused actually intended to carry out the threat.

(q) *Marriage.*

(1) *In general.* In a prosecution under paragraph (2) of subsection (c) (aggravated sexual assault), or under subsection (d) (aggravated sexual assault of a child), subsection (f) (aggravated sexual abuse of a child), subsection (i) (abusive sexual contact with a child), subsection (j) (indecent liberty with a child), subsection (m) (wrongful sexual contact), or subsection (n) (indecent exposure), it is an affirmative defense that the accused and the other person when they engaged in the sexual act, sexual contact, or sexual conduct were married to each other.

(2) *Definition.* For purposes of this subsection, a marriage is a relationship, recognized by the laws of a competent State or foreign jurisdiction, between the accused and the other person as spouses. A marriage exists until it is dissolved in accordance with the laws of a competent State or foreign jurisdiction.

(3) *Exception.* Paragraph (1) shall not apply if the accused's intent at the time of the sexual conduct is to abuse, humiliate, or degrade any person.

(r) *Consent and mistake of fact as to consent.* Lack of permission is an element of the offense in subsection (m) (wrongful sexual contact). Consent and mistake of fact as to consent are not an issue, or an affirmative defense, in a prosecution under any other subsection, except they are an affirmative defense for the sexual conduct in issue in a prosecution under subsection (a) (rape), subsection (c) (aggravated sexual assault), subsection (e) (aggravated sexual contact), and subsection (h) (abusive sexual contact).

(s) *Other affirmative defenses not precluded.* The enumeration in this section of some affirmative defenses shall not be construed as excluding the existence of others.

(t) *Definitions.* In this section:

(1) *Sexual act.* The term "sexual act" means—

(A) contact between the penis and the vulva, and for purposes of this subparagraph contact involving the penis occurs upon penetration, however slight; or

(B) the penetration, however slight, of the genital opening of another by a hand or finger or by any object, with an intent to abuse, humiliate, harass, or degrade any person or to arouse or gratify the sexual desire of any person.

(2) *Sexual contact.* The term "sexual contact" means the intentional touching, either directly or through the clothing, of the genitalia, anus, groin, breast, inner thigh, or buttocks of another person, or intentionally causing another person to touch, either directly or through the clothing, the genitalia, anus, groin, breast, inner thigh, or buttocks of any person, with an intent to abuse, humiliate, or degrade any person or to arouse or gratify the sexual desire of any person.

(3) *Grievous bodily harm.* The term "grievous bodily harm" means serious bodily injury. It includes fractured or dislocated bones, deep cuts, torn members of the body, serious damage to internal organs, and other severe bodily injuries. It does not include minor injuries such as a black eye or a bloody nose. It is the same level of injury as in section 928 (article 128) of this chapter, and a lesser degree of injury than in section 2246(4) of title 18.

(4) *Dangerous weapon or object.* The term "dangerous weapon or object" means—

(A) any firearm, loaded or not, and whether operable or not;

(B) any other weapon, device, instrument, material, or substance, whether animate or inanimate, that in the manner it is used, or is intended to be used, is known to be capable of producing death or grievous bodily harm; or

(C) any object fashioned or utilized in such a manner as to lead the victim under the circumstances to reasonably believe it to be capable of producing death or grievous bodily harm.

(5) *Force.* The term "force" means action to compel submission of another or to overcome or prevent another's resistance by—

(A) the use or display of a dangerous weapon or object;

(B) the suggestion of possession of a dangerous weapon or object that is used in a manner to cause another to believe it is a dangerous weapon or object; or

(C) physical violence, strength, power, or restraint applied to another person, sufficient that the other person could not avoid or escape the sexual conduct.

(6) *Threatening or placing that other person in fear.* The term "threatening or placing that other person in fear" under paragraph (3) of subsection (a) (rape), or under subsection (e) (aggravated sexual contact), means a communication or action that is of sufficient consequence to cause a reasonable fear that non-compliance will result in the victim or another person being subjected to death, grievous bodily harm, or kidnapping.

(7) *Threatening or placing that other person in fear.*

(A) *In general.* The term "threatening or placing that other person in fear" under paragraph (1)(A) of subsection (c) (aggravated sexual assault), or under subsection (h) (abusive sexual contact), means a communication or action that is of sufficient consequence to cause a reasonable fear that non-compliance will result in the victim or another being subjected to a lesser degree of harm than death, grievous bodily harm, or kidnapping.

(B) *Inclusions.* Such lesser degree of harm includes—

(i) physical injury to another person or to another person's property; or

(ii) a threat—

(I) to accuse any person of a crime;

(II) to expose a secret or publicize an asserted fact, whether true or false, tending to subject some person to hatred, contempt, or ridicule; or

(III) through the use or abuse of military position, rank, or authority, to affect or threaten to affect, either positively or negatively, the military career of some person.

(8) *Bodily harm.* The term "bodily harm" means any offensive touching of another, however slight.

(9) *Child.* The term "child" means any person who has not attained the age of 16 years.

(10) *Lewd act.* The term "lewd act" means—

(A) the intentional touching, not through the clothing, of the genitalia of another person, with an intent to abuse, humiliate, or degrade any person, or to arouse or gratify the sexual desire of any person; or

(B) intentionally causing another person to touch, not through the clothing, the genitalia of any person with an intent to abuse, humiliate or degrade any person, or to arouse or gratify the sexual desire of any person.

(11) *Indecent liberty.* The term "indecent liberty" means indecent conduct, but physical contact is not required. It includes one who with the requisite intent exposes one's genitalia, anus, buttocks, or female areola or nipple to a child. An indecent liberty may consist of communication of indecent language as long as the communication is made in the physical presence of the child. If words designed to excite sexual desire are spoken to a child, or a child is exposed to or involved in sexual conduct, it is an indecent liberty; the child's consent is not relevant.

(12) *Indecent conduct.* The term "indecent conduct" means that form of immorality relating to sexual impurity that is grossly vulgar, obscene, and repugnant to common propriety, and tends to excite sexual desire or deprave morals with respect to sexual relations. Indecent conduct includes observing, or making a videotape, photograph, motion picture, print, negative, slide, or other mechanically, electronically, or chemically reproduced visual material, without another person's consent, and contrary to that other person's reasonable expectation of privacy, of—

(A) that other person's genitalia, anus, or buttocks, or (if that other person is female) that person's areola or nipple; or

(B) **that other person while that other person is engaged in a sexual act, sodomy (under section 925 (article 125) of this chapter), or sexual contact.**

(13) *Act of prostitution.* **The term "act of prostitution" means a sexual act, sexual contact, or lewd act for the purpose of receiving money or other compensation.**

(14) *Consent.* **The term "consent" means words or overt acts indicating a freely given agreement to the sexual conduct at issue by a competent person. An expression of lack of consent through words or conduct means there is no consent. Lack of verbal or physical resistance or submission resulting from the accused's use of force, threat of force, or placing another person in fear does not constitute consent. A current or previous dating relationship by itself or the manner of dress of the person involved with the accused in the sexual conduct at issue shall not constitute consent. A person cannot consent to sexual activity if—**

(A) **under 16 years of age; or**

(B) **substantially incapable of—**

(i) **appraising the nature of the sexual conduct at issue due to—**

(I) **mental impairment or unconsciousness resulting from consumption of alcohol, drugs, a similar substance, or otherwise; or**

(II) **mental disease or defect that renders the person unable to understand the nature of the sexual conduct at issue;**

(ii) **physically declining participation in the sexual conduct at issue; or**

(iii) **physically communicating unwillingness to engage in the sexual conduct at issue.**

(15) *Mistake of fact as to consent.* **The term "mistake of fact as to consent" means the accused held, as a result of ignorance or mistake, an incorrect belief that the other person engaging in the sexual conduct consented. The ignorance or mistake must have existed in the mind of the accused and must have been reasonable under all the circumstances. To be reasonable, the ignorance or mistake must have been based on information, or lack of it, that would indicate to a reasonable person that the other person consented. Additionally, the ignorance or mistake cannot be based on the negligent failure to discover the true facts. Negligence is the absence of due care. Due care is what a reasonably careful person would do under the same or similar circumstances. The accused's state of intoxication, if any, at the time of the offense is not relevant to mistake of fact. A mistaken belief that the other person consented must be that which a reasonably careful, ordinary, prudent, sober adult would have had under the circumstances at the time of the offense.**

(16) *Affirmative defense.* **The term "affirmative defense" means any special defense that, although not denying that the accused committed the objective acts constituting the offense charged, denies, wholly, or partially, criminal responsibility for those acts. The accused has the burden of proving the affirmative defense by a preponderance of evidence. After the defense meets this burden, the prosecution shall have the burden of proving beyond a reasonable doubt that the affirmative defense did not exist.**

b. *Elements.*

(1) *Rape.*

(a) *Rape by using force.*

(i) That the accused caused another person, who is of any age, to engage in a sexual act by using force against that other person.

(b) *Rape by causing grievous bodily harm.*

(i) That the accused caused another person, who is of any age, to engage in a sexual act by causing grievous bodily harm to any person.

(c) *Rape by using threats or placing in fear.*

(i) That the accused caused another person, who is of any age, to engage in a sexual act by threatening or placing that other person in fear that any person will be subjected to death, grievous bodily harm, or kidnapping.

(d) *Rape by rendering another unconscious.*

(i) That the accused caused another person, who is of any age, to engage in a sexual act by rendering that other person unconscious.

(e) *Rape by administration of drug, intoxicant, or other similar substance.*

(i) That the accused caused another person, who is of any age, to engage in a sexual act by administering to that other person a drug, intoxicant, or other similar substance;

(ii) That the accused administered the drug,

intoxicant or other similar substance by force or threat of force or without the knowledge or permission of that other person; and

(iii) That, as a result, that other person's ability to appraise or control conduct was substantially impaired.

(2) *Rape of a child.*

(a) *Rape of a child who has not attained the age of 12 years.*

(i) That the accused engaged in a sexual act with a child; and

(ii) That at the time of the sexual act the child had not attained the age of twelve years.

(b) *Rape of a child who has attained the age of 12 years but has not attained the age of 16 years by using force.*

(i) That the accused engaged in a sexual act with a child;

(ii) That at the time of the sexual act the child had attained the age of 12 years but had not attained the age of 16 years; and

(iii) That the accused did so by using force against that child.

(c) *Rape of a child who has attained the age of 12 years but has not attained the age of 16 years by causing grievous bodily harm.*

(i) That the accused engaged in a sexual act with a child;

(ii) That at the time of the sexual act the child had attained the age of 12 years but had not attained the age of 16 years; and

(iii) That the accused did so by causing grievous bodily harm to any person.

(d) *Rape of a child who has attained the age of 12 years but has not attained the age of 16 years by using threats or placing in fear.*

(i) That the accused engaged in a sexual act with a child;

(ii) That at the time of the sexual act the child had attained the age of 12 years but had not attained the age of 16 years; and

(iii) That the accused did so by threatening or placing that child in fear that any person will be subjected to death, grievous bodily harm, or kidnapping.

(e) *Rape of a child who has attained the age of 12 years but has not attained the age of 16 years by rendering that child unconscious.*

(i) That the accused engaged in a sexual act with a child;

(ii) That at the time of the sexual act the child had attained the age of 12 years but had not attained the age of 16 years; and

(iii) That the accused did so by rendering that child unconscious.

(f) *Rape of a child who has attained the age of 12 years but has not attained the age of 16 years by administration of drug, intoxicant, or other similar substance.*

(i) That the accused engaged in a sexual act with a child;

(ii) That at the time of the sexual act the child had attained the age of 12 years but had not attained the age of 16 years; and

(iii)(a) That the accused did so by administering to that child a drug, intoxicant, or other similar substance;

(b) That the accused administered the drug, intoxicant, or other similar substance by force or threat of force or without the knowledge or permission of that child; and

(c) That, as a result, that child's ability to appraise or control conduct was substantially impaired.

(3) *Aggravated sexual assault.*

(a) *Aggravated sexual assault by using threats or placing in fear.*

(i) That the accused caused another person, who is of any age, to engage in a sexual act; and

(ii) That the accused did so by threatening or placing that other person in fear that any person would be subjected to bodily harm or other harm (other than by threatening or placing that other person in fear that any person would be subjected to death, grievous bodily harm, or kidnapping).

(b) *Aggravated sexual assault by causing bodily harm.*

(i) That the accused caused another person, who is of any age, to engage in a sexual act; and

(ii) That the accused did so by causing bodily harm to another person.

(c) *Aggravated sexual assault upon a person substantially incapacitated or substantially incapa-*

ble of appraising the act, declining participation, or communicating unwillingness.

(i) That the accused engaged in a sexual act with another person, who is of any age; and

(Note: add one of the following elements)

(ii) That the other person was substantially incapacitated;

(iii) That the other person was substantially incapable of appraising the nature of the sexual act;

(iv) That the other person was substantially incapable of declining participation in the sexual act; or

(v) That the other person was substantially incapable of communicating unwillingness to engage in the sexual act.

(4) *Aggravated sexual assault of a child who has attained the age of 12 years but has not attained the age of 16 years.*

(a) That the accused engaged in a sexual act with a child; and

(b) That at the time of the sexual act the child had attained the age of 12 years but had not attained the age of 16 years.

(5) *Aggravated sexual contact.*

(a) *Aggravated sexual contact by using force.*

(i)(a) That the accused engaged in sexual contact with another person; or

(b) That the accused caused sexual contact with or by another person; and

(ii) That the accused did so by using force against that other person.

(b) *Aggravated sexual contact by causing grievous bodily harm.*

(i)(a) That the accused engaged in sexual contact with another person; or

(b) That the accused caused sexual contact with or by another person; and

(ii) That the accused did so by causing grievous bodily harm to any person.

(c) *Aggravated sexual contact by using threats or placing in fear.*

(i)(a) That the accused engaged in sexual contact with another person; or

(b) That the accused caused sexual contact with or by another person; and

(ii) That the accused did so by threatening or placing that other person in fear that any person will be subjected to death, grievous bodily harm, or kidnapping.

(d) *Aggravated sexual contact by rendering another unconscious.*

(i)(a) That the accused engaged in sexual contact with another person; or

(b) That the accused caused sexual contact with or by another person; and

(ii) That the accused did so by rendering that other person unconscious.

(e) *Aggravated sexual contact by administration of drug, intoxicant, or other similar substance.*

(i)(a) That the accused engaged in sexual contact with another person; or

(b) That the accused caused sexual contact with or by another person; and

(ii)(a) That the accused did so by administering to that other person a drug, intoxicant, or other similar substance;

(b) That the accused administered the drug, intoxicant, or other similar substance by force or threat of force or without the knowledge or permission of that other person; and

(c) That, as a result, that other person's ability to appraise or control conduct was substantially impaired.

(6) *Aggravated sexual abuse of a child.*

(a) That the accused engaged in a lewd act; and

(b) That the act was committed with a child who has not attained the age of 16 years.

(7) *Aggravated Sexual Contact with a Child.*

(a) *Aggravated sexual contact with a child who has not attained the age of 12 years.*

(i)(a) That the accused engaged in sexual contact with a child; or

(b) That the accused caused sexual contact with or by a child or by another person with a child; and

(ii) That at the time of the sexual contact the child had not attained the age of twelve years.

(b) *Aggravated sexual contact with a child who has attained the age of 12 years but has not attained the age of 16 years by using force.*

(i)(a) That the accused engaged in sexual contact with a child; or

(b) That the accused caused sexual contact

with or by a child or by another person with a child; and

(ii) That at the time of the sexual contact the child had attained the age of 12 years but had not attained the age of 16 years; and

(iii) That the accused did so by using force against that child.

(c) *Aggravated sexual contact with a child who has attained the age of 12 years but has not attained the age of 16 years by causing grievous bodily harm.*

(i)(a) That the accused engaged in sexual contact with a child; or

(b) That the accused caused sexual contact with or by a child or by another person with a child; and

(ii) That at the time of the sexual contact the child had attained the age of 12 years but had not attained the age of 16 years; and

(iii) That the accused did so by causing grievous bodily harm to any person.

(d) *Aggravated sexual contact with a child who has attained the age of 12 years but has not attained the age of 16 years by using threats or placing in fear.*

(i)(a) That the accused engaged in sexual contact with a child; or

(b) That the accused caused sexual contact with or by a child or by another person with a child; and

(ii) That at the time of the sexual contact the child had attained the age of 12 years but had not attained the age of 16 years; and

(iii) That the accused did so by threatening or placing that child or that other person in fear that any person will be subjected to death, grievous bodily harm, or kidnapping.

(e) *Aggravated sexual contact with a child who has attained the age of 12 years but has not attained the age of 16 years by rendering another or that child unconscious.*

(i)(a) That the accused engaged in sexual contact with a child; or

(b) That the accused caused sexual contact with or by a child or by another person with a child; and

(ii) That at the time of the sexual contact the child had attained the age of 12 years but had not attained the age of 16 years; and

(iii) That the accused did so by rendering that child or that other person unconscious.

(f) *Aggravated sexual contact with a child who has attained the age of 12 years but has not attained the age of 16 years by administration of drug, intoxicant, or other similar substance.*

(i)(a) That the accused engaged in sexual contact with a child; or

(b) That the accused caused sexual contact with or by a child or by another person with a child; and

(ii) That at the time of the sexual contact the child had attained the age of 12 years but had not attained the age of 16 years; and

(iii)(a) That the accused did so by administering to that child or that other person a drug, intoxicant, or other similar substance;

(b) That the accused administered the drug, intoxicant, or other similar substance by force or threat of force or without the knowledge or permission of that child or that other person; and

(c) That, as a result, that child's or that other person's ability to appraise or control conduct was substantially impaired.

(8) *Abusive sexual contact.*

(a) *Abusive sexual contact by using threats or placing in fear.*

(i)(a) That the accused engaged in sexual contact with another person; or

(b) That the accused caused sexual contact with or by another person; and

(ii) That the accused did so by threatening or placing that other person in fear that any person would be subjected to bodily harm or other harm (other than by threatening or placing that other person in fear that any person would be subjected to death, grievous bodily harm, or kidnapping).

(b) *Abusive sexual contact by causing bodily harm.*

(i)(a) That the accused engaged in sexual contact with another person; or

(b) That the accused caused sexual contact with or by another person; and

(ii) That the accused did so by causing bodily harm to another person.

(c) *Abusive sexual contact upon a person sub-*

stantially incapacitated or substantially incapable of appraising the act, declining participation, or communicating unwillingness.

(i)(a) That the accused engaged in sexual contact with another person; or

(b) That the accused caused sexual contact with or by another person; and

(Note: add one of the following elements)

(ii) That the other person was substantially incapacitated;

(iii) That the other person was substantially incapable of appraising the nature of the sexual contact;

(iv) That the other person was substantially incapable of declining participation in the sexual contact; or

(v) That the other person was substantially incapable of communicating unwillingness to engage in the sexual contact.

(9) *Abusive sexual contact with a child.*

(i)(a) That the accused engaged in sexual contact with a child; or

(b) That the accused caused sexual contact with or by a child or by another person with a child; and

(ii) That at the time of the sexual contact the child had attained the age of 12 years but had not attained the age of 16 years.

(10) *Indecent liberty with a child.*

(a) That the accused committed a certain act or communication;

(b) That the act or communication was indecent;

(c) That the accused committed the act or communication in the physical presence of a certain child;

(d) That the child was under 16 years of age; and

(e) That the accused committed the act or communication with the intent to:

(i) arouse, appeal to, or gratify the sexual desires of any person; or

(ii) abuse, humiliate, or degrade any person.

(11) *Indecent act.*

(a) That the accused engaged in certain conduct; and

(b) That the conduct was indecent conduct.

(12) *Forcible pandering.*

(a) That the accused compelled a certain person to engage in an act of prostitution; and

(b) That the accused directed another person to said person, who then engaged in an act of prostitution.

(13) *Wrongful sexual contact.*

(a) That the accused had sexual contact with another person;

(b) That the accused did so without that other person's permission; and

(c) That the accused had no legal justification or lawful authorization for that sexual contact.

(14) *Indecent exposure.*

(a) That the accused exposed his or her genitalia, anus, buttocks, or female areola or nipple;

(b) That the accused's exposure was in an indecent manner;

(c) That the exposure occurred in a place where the conduct involved could reasonably be expected to be viewed by people other than the accused's family or household; and

(d) That the exposure was intentional.

c. *Explanation.*

(1) *Definitions.* The terms are defined in Paragraph 45a.(t), supra.

(2) *Character of victim.* See Mil. R. Evid. 412 concerning rules of evidence relating to the character of the victim of an alleged sexual offense.

(3) *Indecent.* In conduct cases, "indecent" generally signifies that form of immorality relating to sexual impurity that is not only grossly vulgar, obscene, and repugnant to common propriety, but also tends to excite lust and deprave the morals with respect to sexual relations. Language is indecent if it tends reasonably to corrupt morals or incite libidinous thoughts. The language must violate community standards.

d. *Lesser included offenses.* The following lesser included offenses are based on internal cross-references provided in the statutory text of Article 120. See subsection (e) for a further listing of possible lesser included offenses.

(1) *Rape.*

(a) Article 120—Aggravated sexual contact

(b) Article 134—Assault with intent to commit rape

(c) Article 128—Aggravated assault; Assault; Assault consummated by a battery

(d) Article 80—Attempts

(2) *Rape of a child.*

(a) Article 120—Aggravated sexual contact with a child; Indecent act

(b) Article 134—Assault with intent to commit rape

(c) Article 128—Aggravated assault; Assault; Assault consummated by a battery; Assault consummated by a battery upon a child under 16

(d) Article 80—Attempts

(3) *Aggravated sexual assault.*

(a) Article 120—Abusive sexual contact

(b) Article 128—Aggravated assault; Assault; Assault consummated by a battery

(c) Article 80—Attempts

(4) *Aggravated sexual assault of a child.*

(a) Article 120—Abusive sexual contact with a child; Indecent act

(b) Article 128—Aggravated assault; Assault; Assault consummated by a battery; Assault consummated by a battery upon a child under 16

(c) Article 80—Attempts

(5) *Aggravated sexual contact.*

(a) Article 128—Aggravated assault; Assault; Assault consummated by a battery

(b) Article 80—Attempts

(6) *Aggravated sexual abuse of a child.*

(a) Article 120—Indecent act

(b) Article 128—Assault; Assault consummated by a battery; Assault consummated by a battery upon a child under 16

(c) Article 80—Attempts

(7) *Aggravated sexual contact with a child.*

(a) Article 120—Indecent act

(b) Article 128—Assault; Assault consummated by a battery; Assault consummated by a battery upon a child under 16

(c) Article 80—Attempts

(8) *Abusive sexual contact.*

(a) Article 128—Assault; Assault consummated by a battery

(b) Article 80—Attempts

(9) *Abusive sexual contact with a child.*

(a) Article 120—Indecent act

(b) Article 128—Assault; Assault consummated by a battery; Assault consummated by a battery upon a child under 16

(c) Article 80—Attempts

(10) *Indecent liberty with a child.*

(a) Article 120—Indecent act

(b) Article 80—Attempts

(11) *Indecent act.* Article 80—Attempts

(12) *Forcible pandering.* Article 80—Attempts

(13) *Wrongful sexual contact* Article 80—Attempts

(14) *Indecent exposure.* Article 80—Attempts

e. *Additional lesser included offenses.* Depending on the factual circumstances in each case, to include the type of act and level of force involved, the following offenses may be considered lesser included in addition to those offenses listed in subsection d. (See subsection (d) for a listing of the offenses that are specifically cross-referenced within the statutory text of Article 120.) The elements of the proposed lesser included offense should be compared with the elements of the greater offense to determine if the elements of the lesser offense are derivative of the greater offense and vice versa. See Appendix 23 for further explanation of lesser included offenses.

(1)(a) *Rape by using force.* Article 120—Indecent act; Wrongful sexual contact

(1)(b) *Rape by causing grievous bodily harm.* Article 120—Aggravated sexual assault by causing bodily harm; Abusive sexual contact by causing bodily harm; Indecent act; Wrongful sexual contact

(1)(c) *Rape by using threats or placing in fear.* Article 120—Aggravated sexual assault by using threats or placing in fear; Abusive sexual contact by using threats or placing in fear; Indecent act; Wrongful sexual contact

(1)(d) *Rape by rendering another unconscious.* Article 120—Aggravated sexual assault upon a person substantially incapacitated; Abusive sexual contact upon a person substantially incapacitated; Indecent act; Wrongful sexual contact

(1)(e) *Rape by administration of drug, intoxicant, or other similar substance.* Article 120—Aggravated sexual assault upon a person substantially incapacitated; Abusive sexual contact upon a person substantially incapacitated; Indecent act; Wrongful sexual contact

(2)(a) - (f) *Rape of a child who has not attained 12 years; Rape of a child who has attained the age of 12 years but has not attained the age of 16 years.* Article 120—Aggravated sexual assault of a child; Aggravated sexual abuse of a child; Abusive sexual contact with a child; Indecent liberty with a child; Wrongful sexual contact

(3) *Aggravated sexual assault.* Article 120—Wrongful sexual contact; Indecent act

(4) *Aggravated sexual assault of a child.* Article 120—Aggravated sexual abuse of a child; Indecent liberty with a child; Wrongful sexual contact

(5)(a) *Aggravated sexual contact by force.* Article 120—Indecent act; Wrongful sexual contact

(5)(b) *Aggravated sexual contact by causing grievous bodily harm.* Article 120—Abusive sexual contact by causing bodily harm; Indecent act; Wrongful sexual contact

(5)(c) *Aggravated sexual contact by using threats or placing in fear.* Article 120—Abusive sexual contact by using threats or placing in fear; Indecent act; Wrongful sexual contact

(5)(d) *Aggravated sexual contact by rendering another unconscious.* Article 120—Abusive sexual contact upon a person substantially incapacitated; Indecent act; Wrongful sexual contact

(5)(e) *Aggravated sexual contact by administration of drug, intoxicant, or other similar substance.* Article 120—Abusive sexual contact upon a person substantially incapacitated; Indecent act; Wrongful sexual contact

(6) *Aggravated sexual abuse of a child.* Article 120—Aggravated sexual contact with a child; Aggravated sexual abuse of a child; Indecent liberty with a child; Wrongful sexual contact

(7) *Aggravated sexual contact with a child.* Article 120—Abusive sexual contact with a child; Indecent liberty with a child; Wrongful sexual contact

(8) *Abusive sexual contact.* Article 120—Wrongful sexual contact; Indecent act

(9) *Abusive sexual contact with a child.* Article 120—Indecent liberty with a child; Wrongful sexual contact

(10) *Indecent liberty with a child.* Article 120—Wrongful sexual contact

f. *Maximum punishment.*

(1) *Rape and rape of a child.* Death or such other punishment as a court martial may direct.

(2) *Aggravated sexual assault.* Dishonorable discharge, forfeiture of all pay and allowances, and confinement for 30 years.

(3) *Aggravated sexual assault of a child who has attained the age of 12 years but has not attained the age of 16 years, aggravated sexual abuse of a child, aggravated sexual contact, and aggravated sexual contact with a child.* Dishonorable discharge, forfeiture of all pay and allowances, and confinement for 20 years.

(4) *Abusive sexual contact with a child and indecent liberty with a child.* Dishonorable discharge, forfeiture of all pay and allowances, and confinement for 15 years.

(5) *Abusive sexual contact.* Dishonorable discharge, forfeiture of all pay and allowances, and confinement for 7 years.

(6) *Indecent act or forcible pandering.* Dishonorable discharge, forfeiture of all pay and allowances, and confinement for 5 years.

(7) *Wrongful sexual contact or indecent exposure.* Dishonorable discharge, forfeiture of all pay and allowances, and confinement for 1 year.

g. *Sample specifications.*

(1) *Rape.*

(a) *Rape by using force.*

(i) *Rape by use or display of dangerous weapon or object.* In that ______ (personal jurisdiction data), did (at/on board-location) (subject-matter jurisdiction data, if required), on or about ______ 20 ___, cause ______ to engage in a sexual act, to wit: ______, by (using a dangerous weapon or object, to wit: ______ against (him)(her)) (displaying a dangerous weapon or object, to wit: ______ to (him)(her)).

(ii) *Rape by suggestion of possession of dangerous weapon or object.* In that ______ (-personal jurisdiction data), did (at/on board-location) (subject-matter jurisdiction data, if required), on or about ______ 20 ___, cause ______ to engage in a sexual act, to wit: ______, by the suggestion of possession of a dangerous weapon or an object that was used in a manner to cause (him-)(her) to believe it was a dangerous weapon or object.

(iii) *Rape by using physical violence, strength, power, or restraint to any person.* In that ______ (personal jurisdiction data), did (at/on board-location) (subject-matter jurisdiction data, if required), on or about ____ 20 ____, cause ____ to engage in a sexual act, to wit: ____, by using (physical violence) (strength) (power) (restraint applied to ____), sufficient that (he)(she) could not avoid or escape the sexual conduct.

(b) *Rape by causing grievous bodily harm.* In that ____ (personal jurisdiction data), did (at/on board-location) (subject-matter jurisdiction data, if required), on or about ____ 20 ____, cause ____ to engage in a sexual act, to wit: ____, by causing grievous bodily harm upon (him)(her)(____), to wit: a (broken leg-)(deep cut)(fractured skull)(____).

(c) *Rape by using threats or placing in fear.* In that ____ (personal jurisdiction data), did (at/on board-location) (subject-matter jurisdiction data, if required), on or about ____ 20 ____, cause ____ to engage in a sexual act, to wit: ____, by [threatening] [placing (him-)(her) in fear] that (he)(she) (____) will be subjected to (death)(grievous bodily harm) (kidnapping) by ____.

(d) *Rape by rendering another unconscious.* In that ____ (personal jurisdiction data), did (at/on board-location) (subject-matter jurisdiction data, if required), on or about ____ 20 ____, cause ____ to engage in a sexual act, to wit: ____, by rendering (him)(her) unconscious.

(e) *Rape by administration of drug, intoxicant, or other similar substance.* In that ____ (personal jurisdiction data), did (at/on board-location) (subject-matter jurisdiction data, if required), on or about ____ 20 ____, cause ____ to engage in a sexual act, to wit: ____, by administering to (him)(her) a drug, intoxicant, or other similar substance, (by force) (by threat of force) (without (his)(her) knowledge or permission), and thereby substantially impaired (his)(her) ability to [(appraise) (control)][(his) (her)] conduct.

(2) *Rape of a child.*

(a) *Rape of a child who has not attained the age of 12 years.* In that ____ (personal jurisdiction data), did (at/on board-location) (subject-matter jurisdiction data, if required), on or about ____ 20 ____, engage in a sexual act, to wit: ____ with ____, a child who had not attained the age of 12 years.

(b) *Rape of a child who has attained the age of 12 years but has not attained the age of 16 years by using force.*

(i) *Rape of a child who has attained the age of 12 years but has not attained the age of 16 years by use or display of dangerous weapon or object.* In that ____ (personal jurisdiction data), did (at/on board-location) (subject-matter jurisdiction data, if required), on or about ____ 20 ____, engage in a sexual act, to wit: ____, with ____, a child who had attained the age of 12 years, but had not attained the age of 16 years, by (using a dangerous weapon or object, to wit: ____ against (him)(her)) (displaying a dangerous weapon or object, to wit: ____ to (him)(her)).

(ii) *Rape of a child who has attained the age of 12 years but has not attained the age of 16 years by suggestion of possession of dangerous weapon or object.* In that ____ (personal jurisdiction data), did (at/on board-location) (subject-matter jurisdiction data, if required), on or about ____ 20 ____, engage in a sexual act, to wit: ____, with ____, a child who had attained the age of 12 years, but had not attained the age of 16 years, by the suggestion of possession of a dangerous weapon or an object that was used in a manner to cause (him)(her) to believe it was a dangerous weapon or object.

(iii) *Rape of a child who has attained the age of 12 years but has not attained the age of 16 years by using physical violence, strength, power, or restraint to any person.* In that ____ (personal jurisdiction data), did (at/on board-location) (subject-matter jurisdiction data, if required), on or about ____ 20 ____, engage in a sexual act, to wit: ____ with ____, a child who had attained the age of 12 years, but had not attained the age of 16 years, by using (physical violence) (strength) (power) (restraint applied to ____) sufficient that (he)(she) could not avoid or escape the sexual conduct.

(c) *Rape of a child who has attained the age of 12 years but has not attained the age of 16 years by causing grievous bodily harm.* In that ____ (personal jurisdiction data), did (at/on board-location) (subject-matter jurisdiction data, if required), on or about ____ 20 ____, engage in a sexual act, to wit: ____, with ____, a child who had attained the age of 12 years, but had not attained the age of

16 years, by causing grievous bodily harm upon (him)(her)( ), to wit: a (broken leg)(deep cut)(fractured skull)( ).

(d) *Rape of a child who has attained the age of 12 years but has not attained the age of 16 years by using threats or placing in fear.* In that (personal jurisdiction data), did (at/on board-location) (subject-matter jurisdiction data, if required), on or about 20 , engage in a sexual act, to wit: , with , a child who had attained the age of 12 years, but had not attained the age of 16 years, by [threatening] [placing (him)(her) in fear] that (he)(she) ( ) would be subjected to (death)(grievous bodily harm) (kidnapping) by .

(e) *Rape of a child who has attained the age of 12 years but has not attained the age of 16 years by rendering that child unconscious.* In that (personal jurisdiction data), did (at/on board-location) (subject-matter jurisdiction data, if required), on or about 20 , engage in a sexual act, to wit: , with , a child who had attained the age of 12 years, but had not attained the age of 16 years, by rendering (him)(her) unconscious.

(f) *Rape of a child who has attained the age of 12 years but has not attained the age of 16 years by administration of drug, intoxicant, or other similar substance.* In that (personal jurisdiction data), did (at/on board-location) (subject-matter jurisdiction data, if required), on or about 20 , engage in a sexual act, to wit: ,with , a child who had attained the age of 12 years, but had not attained the age of 16 years, by administering to (him)(her) a drug, intoxicant, or other similar substance (by force) (by threat of force) (without (his)(her) knowledge or permission), and thereby substantially impaired (his)(her) ability to [(appraise)(control)][(his)(her)] conduct.

(3) *Aggravated sexual assault.*

(a) *Aggravated sexual assault by using threats or placing in fear.* In that (personal jurisdiction data), did (at/on board-location) (subject-matter jurisdiction data, if required), on or about 20 , cause to engage in a sexual act, to wit: , by [threatening] [placing(him)(her) in fear of] [(physical injury to) (injury to 's property)(accusation of crime)(exposition of secret)(abuse of military position)( )].

(b) *Aggravated sexual assault by causing bodily harm.* In that (personal jurisdiction data), did (at/on board-location) (subject-matter jurisdiction data, if required), on or about 20 , cause to engage in a sexual act, to wit: , by causing bodily harm upon (him)(her)( ), to wit: .

(c) *Aggravated sexual assault upon a person substantially incapacitated or substantially incapable of appraising the act, declining participation, or communicating unwillingness.* In that (personal jurisdiction data), did (at/on board-location) (subject-matter jurisdiction data, if required), on or about 20 , engage in a sexual act, to wit: with , who was (substantially incapacitated) [substantially incapable of (appraising the nature of the sexual act)(declining participation in the sexual act) (communicating unwillingness to engage in the sexual act)].

(4) *Aggravated sexual assault of a child who has attained the age of 12 years but has not attained the age of 16 years.* In that (personal jurisdiction data), did (at/on board-location) (subject-matter jurisdiction data, if required), on or about 20 , engage in a sexual act, to wit: with , who had attained the age of 12 years, but had not attained the age of 16 years.

(5) *Aggravated sexual contact.*

(a) *Aggravated sexual contact by using force.*

(i) *Aggravated sexual contact by use or display of dangerous weapon or object.* In that (personal jurisdiction data), did (at/on board-location) (subject-matter jurisdiction data, if required), on or about 20 , [(engage in sexual contact, to wit: with) (cause to engage in sexual contact, to wit: , with) (cause sexual contact with or by , to wit:)] by (using a dangerous weapon or object, to wit: against (him)(her)) (displaying a dangerous weapon or object, to wit: to (him)(her)).

(ii) *Aggravated sexual contact by suggestion of possession of dangerous weapon or object.* In that (personal jurisdiction data), did (at/on board-location) (subject-matter jurisdiction data, if required), on or about 20 , [(engage in sexual contact, to wit: with-)(cause to engage in sexual contact, to wit: , with) (cause sexual contact with or by , to wit:)] by the suggestion of possession of a dangerous weapon or an object that was used in a manner to cause (him)(her)( ) to believe it was a dangerous weapon or object.

(iii) *Aggravated sexual contact by using physical violence, strength, power, or restraint to any person.* In that (personal jurisdiction data), did (at/on board-location) (subject-matter jurisdiction data, if required), on or about 20 , [(engage in sexual contact, to wit: with)(cause to engage in sexual contact, to wit: , with) (cause sexual contact with or by , to wit:)] by using (physical violence) (strength) (power) (restraint applied to), sufficient that (he)(she)( ) could not avoid or escape the sexual conduct.

(b) *Aggravated sexual contact by causing grievous bodily harm.* In that (personal jurisdiction data), did (at/on board-location) (subject-matter jurisdiction data, if required), on or about 20 , [(engage in sexual contact, to wit: with)(cause to engage in sexual contact, to wit: , with) (cause sexual contact with or by , to wit:)] by causing grievous bodily harm upon (him)(her)( ), to wit: a (broken leg)(deep cut)(fractured skull)( ).

(c) *Aggravated sexual contact by using threats or placing in fear.* In that (personal jurisdiction data), did (at/on board-location) (subject-matter jurisdiction data, if required), on or about 20 , [(engage in sexual contact, to wit: with)(cause to engage in sexual contact, to wit: , with) (cause sexual contact with or by , to wit:)] by (threatening (him)(her)( )] [(placing(him)(her)( ) in fear] that (he)(she)( ) will be subjected to (death)(grievous bodily harm)(kidnapping) by .

(d) *Aggravated sexual contact by rendering another unconscious.* In that (personal jurisdiction data), did (at/on board-location) (subject-matter jurisdiction data, if required), on or about 20 , [(engage in sexual contact, to wit: with)(cause to engage in sexual contact, to wit: , with) (cause sexual contact with or by , to wit:)] by rendering (him)(her)( ) unconscious.

(e) *Aggravated sexual contact by administration of drug, intoxicant, or other similar substance.* In that (personal jurisdiction data), did (at/on board-location) (subject-matter jurisdiction data, if required), on or about 20 , [(engage in sexual contact, to wit: with)(cause to engage in sexual contact, to wit: , with) (cause sexual contact with or by , to wit:)] by administering to (him)(her)( ) a drug, intoxicant, or other similar substance, (by force) (by threat of force) (without (his)(her)( ) knowledge or permission), and thereby substantially impaired (his)(her)( ) ability to [(appraise) (control)] [(his) (her)] conduct.

(6) *Aggravated sexual abuse of a child.* In that (personal jurisdiction data), did (at/on board-location) (subject-matter jurisdiction data, if required), on or about 20 , engage in a lewd act, to wit: with , a child who had not attained the age of 16 years.

(7) *Aggravated sexual contact with a child.*

(a) *Aggravated sexual contact with a child who has not attained the —age of 12 years.* In that (personal jurisdiction data), did (at/on board-location) (subject-matter jurisdiction data, if required), on or about 20 , [(engage in sexual contact, to wit: with , a child who had not attained the age of 12 years)(cause to engage in sexual contact, to wit: , with , a child who had not attained the age of 12 years) (cause sexual contact with or by , a child who had not attained the age of 12 years, to wit:)].

(b) *Aggravated sexual contact with a child who has attained the age of 12 years but has not attained the age of 16 years by using force.*

(i) *Aggravated sexual contact with a child who has attained the age of 12 years but has not attained the age of 16 years by use or display of dangerous weapon or object.* In that (personal jurisdiction data), did (at/on board-location) (subject-matter jurisdiction data, if required), on or about 20 , [(engage in sexual contact, to wit: with , a child who had attained the age of 12 years, but had not attained the age of 16 years)(cause to engage in sexual contact, to wit: , with , a child who had attained the age of 12 years, but had not attained the age of 16 years) (cause sexual contact with or by , a child who had attained the age of 12 years, but had not attained the age of 16 years, to wit:)] by (using a dangerous weapon or object, to wit: ______ against (him)(her)(______)) (displaying a dangerous weapon or object, to wit: ______ to (him)(her)(______)).

(ii) *Aggravated sexual contact with a child who has attained the age of 12 years but has not attained the age of 16 years by suggestion of possession of dangerous weapon or object.* In that ______ (personal jurisdiction data), did (at/on board-location) (subject-matter jurisdiction data, if required), on or about ______ 20 ______, [(engage in sexual contact, to wit: ______ with ______, a child who had attained the age of 12 years, but had not attained the age of 16 years)(cause ______ to engage in sexual contact, to wit: ______, with ______, a child who had attained the age of 12 years, but had not attained the age of 16 years) (cause sexual contact with or by ______, a child who had attained the age of 12 years, but had not attained the age of 16 years, to wit: ______)] by the suggestion of possession of a dangerous weapon or an object that was used in a manner to cause (him)(her)(______) to believe it was a dangerous weapon or object.

(iii) *Aggravated sexual contact with a child who has attained the age of 12 years but has not attained the age of 16 years by using physical violence, strength, power, or restraint to any person.* In that ______ (personal jurisdiction data), did (at/on board-location) (subject-matter jurisdiction data, if required), on or about ______ 20 ______, [(engage in sexual contact, to wit: ______ with ______, a child who had attained the age of 12 years, but had not attained the age of 16 years)(cause ______ to engage in sexual contact, to wit: ______, with ______, a child who had attained the age of 12 years, but had not attained the age of 16 years) (cause sexual contact with or by ______, a child who had not attained the age of 12 years, but had not attained the age of 16 years, to wit: ______)] by using (physical violence) (strength) (power) (restraint applied to ______) sufficient that (he)(she)(______) could not avoid or escape the sexual conduct.

(c) *Aggravated sexual contact with a child who has attained the age of 12 years but has not attained the age of 16 years by causing grievous bodily harm.* In that ______ (personal jurisdiction data), did (at/on board-location) (subject-matter jurisdiction data, if required), on or about ______ 20 ______, [(engage in sexual contact, to wit: ______ with ______, a child who had attained the age of 12 years, but had not attained the age of 16 years)(cause ______ to engage in sexual contact, to wit: ______, with ______, a child who had attained the age of 12 years, but had not attained the age of 16 years) (cause sexual contact with or by ______, a child who had attained the age of 12 years, but had not attained the age of 16 years, to wit: ______)] by causing grievous bodily harm upon (him)(her)(______), to wit: a (broken leg)(deep cut)(fractured skull)(______).

(d) *Aggravated sexual contact with a child who has attained the age of 12 years but has not attained the age of 16 years by using threats or placing in fear.* In that ______ (personal jurisdiction data), did (at/on board-location) (subject-matter jurisdiction data, if required), on or about ______ 20 ______, [(engage in sexual contact, to wit: ______ with ______, a child who had attained the age of 12 years, but had not attained the age of 16 years)(cause ______ to engage in sexual contact, to wit: ______, with ______, a child who had attained the age of 12 years, but had not attained the age of 16 years) (cause sexual contact with or by ______, a child who had attained the age of 12 years, but had not attained the age of 16 years, to wit: ______)] by [threatening] [placing (him)(her)(______) in fear] that (he)(she)(______) will be subjected to (death) (grievous bodily harm)(kidnapping) by ______.

(e) *Aggravated sexual contact with a child who has attained the age of 12 years but has not attained the age of 16 years by rendering that child or another unconscious.* In that ______ (personal jurisdiction data), did (at/on board-location) (subject-matter jurisdiction data, if required), on or about ______ 20 ______, [(engage in sexual contact, to wit: ______ with ______, a child who had attained the age of 12 years, but had not attained the age of 16 years)(cause ______ to engage in sexual contact, to wit: ______, with ______, a child who had attained the age of 12 years, but had not attained the age of 16 years) (cause sexual contact with or by ______, a child who had attained the age of 12 years, but had not attained the age of 16 years, to wit: ______)] by rendering (him)(her)(______) unconscious.

(f) *Aggravated sexual contact with a child who has attained the age of 12 years but has not attained the age of 16 years by administration of drug, intoxicant, or other similar substance.* In that ______ (personal jurisdiction data), did (at/on board-location) (subject-matter jurisdiction data, if required), on or about ______ 20 ______, [(engage in sexual contact, to wit: with , a child who had attained the age of 12 years but had not attained the age of 16 years)(cause to engage in sexual contact, to wit: , with , a child who had attained the age of 12 years but had not attained the age of 16 years) (cause sexual contact with or by , a child who had attained the age of 12 years but had not attained the age of 16 years, to wit:)] by administering to (him)(her)( ) a drug, intoxicant, or other similar substance (by force) (by threat of force) (without (his)(her)( ) knowledge or permission), and thereby substantially impaired (his)(her)( ) ability to [(appraise) (control)] [(his) (her)] conduct.

(8) *Abusive sexual contact.*

(a) *Abusive sexual contact by using threats or placing in fear.* In that (personal jurisdiction data), did (at/on board-location) (subject-matter jurisdiction data, if required), on or about 20 , [(engage in sexual contact, to wit: with) (cause to engage in sexual contact, to wit: , with) (cause sexual contact with or by , to wit:)] by (threatening) (placing (him)(her)( ) in fear of)] (physical injury to)(injury to 's property)(accusation of crime)(exposition of secret)(abuse of military position)( )].

(b) *Abusive sexual contact by causing bodily harm.* In that (personal jurisdiction data), did (at/on board-location) (subject-matter jurisdiction data, if required), on or about 20 , [(engage in sexual contact, to wit: with) (cause to engage in sexual contact, to wit: , with) (cause sexual contact with or by , to wit:)] by causing bodily harm upon (him)(her)( ), to wit: ( ).

(c) *Abusive sexual contact by engaging in a sexual act with a person substantially incapacitated or substantially incapable of appraising the act, declining participation, or substantially incapable of communicating unwillingness.* In that (-personal jurisdiction data), did (at/on board-location) (subject-matter jurisdiction data, if required), on or about 20 , [(engage in sexual contact, to wit: with) (cause to engage in sexual contact, to wit: , with) (cause sexual contact with or by , to wit:)] while (he)(she)( ) was [substantially incapacitated] [substantially incapable of (appraising the nature of the sexual contact) (declining participation in the sexual contact) (communicating unwillingness to engage in the sexual contact)].

(9) *Abusive sexual contact with a child.* In that (personal jurisdiction data), did (at/on board-location) (subject-matter jurisdiction data, if required), on or about 20 , [(engage in sexual contact, to wit: with , a child who had attained the age of 12 years but had not attained the age of 16 years)(cause to engage in sexual contact, to wit: , with , a child who had attained the age of 12 years but had not attained the age of 16 years) (cause sexual contact with or by , a child who had attained the age of 12 years but had not attained the age of 16 years, to wit:)].

(10) *Indecent liberties with a child.* In that (personal jurisdiction data), did, (at/on board-location) (subject-matter jurisdiction data, if required), on or about 20 ,(take indecent liberties) (engage in indecent conduct) in the physical presence of , a (female) (male) under 16 years of age, by (communicating the words: to wit:) (exposing one's private parts, to wit:) ( ), with the intent to [(arouse) (appeal to) (gratify) the (sexual desire) of the (or)] [(abuse)(humiliate)(degrade)].

(11) *Indecent act.* In that (personal jurisdiction data), did (at/on board-location) (subject-matter jurisdiction data, if required), on or about 20 ,wrongfully commit indecent conduct, to wit .

(12) *Forcible pandering.* In that (personal jurisdiction data), did (at/on board-location), (subject-matter jurisdiction data, if required), on or about 20 , compel to engage in [(a sexual act)(sexual contact) (lewd act), to wit:] for the purpose of receiving money or other compensation with (a) person(s) to be directed to (him)(her) by the said .

(13) *Wrongful sexual contact.* In that (personal jurisdiction data), did (at/on board-location), (subject-matter jurisdiction data, if required), on or about 20 , engage in sexual contact with , to wit: , and such sexual contact was without legal justification or lawful authorization and without the permission of .

(14) *Indecent exposure.* In that (personal jurisdiction data), did (at/on board-location), (subject-matter jurisdiction data, if required), on or about 20 , intentionally (expose in an

indecent manner (his) (her) (_____) (_____) while (at the barracks window) (in a public place) (________)."

45a. Article 120a—Stalking

a. *Text of statute.*

(a) **Any person subject to this section:**

(1) **who wrongfully engages in a course of conduct directed at a specific person that would cause a reasonable person to fear death or bodily harm, including sexual assault, to himself or herself or a member of his or her immediate family;**

(2) **who has knowledge, or should have knowledge, that the specific person will be placed in reasonable fear of death or bodily harm, including sexual assault, to himself or herself or a member of his or her immediate family; and**

(3) **whose acts induce reasonable fear in the specific person of death or bodily harm, including sexual assault, to himself or herself or to a member of his or her immediate family; is guilty of stalking and shall be punished as a court-martial may direct.**

(b) **In this section:**

(1) **The term "course of conduct" means:**

(A) **a repeated maintenance of visual or physical proximity to a specific person; or**

(B) **a repeated conveyance of verbal threat, written threats, or threats implied by conduct, or a combination of such threats, directed at or towards a specific person.**

(2) **The term "repeated," with respect to conduct, means two or more occasions of such conduct.**

(3) **The term "immediate family," in the case of a specific person, means a spouse, parent, child, or sibling of the person, or any other family member, relative, or intimate partner of the person who regularly resides in the household of the person or who within the six months preceding the commencement of the course of conduct regularly resided in the household of the person.**

b. *Elements.*

(1) That the accused wrongfully engaged in a course of conduct directed at a specific person that would cause a reasonable person to fear death or bodily harm to himself or herself or a member of his or her immediate family;

(2) That the accused had knowledge, or should have had knowledge, that the specific person would be placed in reasonable fear of death or bodily harm to himself or herself or a member of his or her immediate family; and

(3) That the accused's acts induced reasonable fear in the specific person of death or bodily harm to himself or herself or to a member of his or her immediate family.

c. *Explanation.* See Paragraph 54.c(1)(a) for an explanation of "bodily harm".

d. *Lesser included offenses.* Article 80 — attempts.

e. *Maximum punishment.* Dishonorable discharge, forfeiture of all pay and allowances, and confinement for 3 years.

f. *Sample Specification.*

In that _____ (personal jurisdiction data), who (knew)(should have known) that _____ would be placed in reasonable fear of (death)(bodily harm) to (himself) (herself) (_____, a member of his or her immediate family) did (at/on board -- location) (subject-matter jurisdiction data, if required), (on or about _____ 20 _____)(from about _____ to about _____ 20 _____), wrongfully engage in a course of conduct directed at _____, to wit: __________ thereby inducing in _____, a reasonable fear of (death)(bodily harm) to (himself)(herself) (_____, a member of his or her immediate family)."

46. Article 121—Larceny and wrongful appropriation

a. *Text of statute.*

(a) **Any person subject to this chapter who wrongfully takes, obtains, or withholds, by any means, from the possession of the owner or of any other person any money, personal property, or article of value of any kind—**

(1) **with intent permanently to deprive or defraud another person of the use and benefit of property or to appropriate it to his own use or the use of any person other than the owner, steals that property and is guilty of larceny; or**

(2) **with intent temporarily to deprive or defraud another person of the use and benefit of property or to appropriate it to his own use or the use of any person other than the owner, is guilty of wrongful appropriation.**

(b) **Any person found guilty of larceny or**

wrongful appropriation shall be punished as a court-martial may direct.

b. *Elements.*

(1) *Larceny.*

(a) That the accused wrongfully took, obtained, or withheld certain property from the possession of the owner or of any other person;

(b) That the property belonged to a certain person;

(c) That the property was of a certain value, or of some value; and

(d) That the taking, obtaining, or withholding by the accused was with the intent permanently to deprive or defraud another person of the use and benefit of the property or permanently to appropriate the property for the use of the accused or for any person other than the owner.

[Note: If the property is alleged to be military property, as defined in paragraph 32c(1), add the following element]

(e) That the property was military property.

(2) *Wrongful appropriation.*

(a) That the accused wrongfully took, obtained, or withheld certain property from the possession of the owner or of any other person;

(b) That the property belonged to a certain person;

(c) That the property was of a certain value, or of some value; and

(d) That the taking, obtaining, or withholding by the accused was with the intent temporarily to deprive or defraud another person of the use and benefit of the property or temporarily to appropriate the property for the use of the accused or for any person other than the owner.

c. *Explanation.*

(1) *Larceny.*

(a) *In general.* A wrongful taking with intent permanently to deprive includes the common law offense of larceny; a wrongful obtaining with intent permanently to defraud includes the offense formerly known as obtaining by false pretense; and a wrongful withholding with intent permanently to appropriate includes the offense formerly known as embezzlement. Any of the various types of larceny under Article 121 may be charged and proved under a specification alleging that the accused "did steal" the property in question.

(b) *Taking, obtaining, or withholding.* There must be a taking, obtaining, or withholding of the property by the thief. For instance, there is no taking if the property is connected to a building by a chain and the property has not been disconnected from the building; property is not "obtained" by merely acquiring title thereto without exercising some possessory control over it. As a general rule, however, any movement of the property or any exercise of dominion over it is sufficient if accompanied by the requisite intent. Thus, if an accused enticed another's horse into the accused's stable without touching the animal, or procured a railroad company to deliver another's trunk by changing the check on it, or obtained the delivery of another's goods to a person or place designated by the accused, or had the funds of another transferred to the accused's bank account, the accused is guilty of larceny if the other elements of the offense have been proved. A person may "obtain" the property of another by acquiring possession without title, and one who already has possession of the property of another may "obtain" it by later acquiring title to it. A "withholding" may arise as a result of a failure to return, account for, or deliver property to its owner when a return, accounting, or delivery is due, even if the owner has made no demand for the property, or it may arise as a result of devoting property to a use not authorized by its owner. Generally, this is so whether the person withholding the property acquired it lawfully or unlawfully. *See* subparagraph c(1)(f) below. However, acts which constitute the offense of unlawfully receiving, buying, or concealing stolen property or of being an accessory after the fact are not included within the meaning of "withholds." Therefore, neither a receiver of stolen property nor an accessory after the fact can be convicted of larceny on that basis alone. The taking, obtaining, or withholding must be of specific property. A debtor does not withhold specific property from the possession of a creditor by failing or refusing to pay a debt, for the relationship of debtor and creditor does not give the creditor a possessory right in any specific money or other property of the debtor.

(c) *Ownership of the property.*

(i) *In general.* Article 121 requires that the taking, obtaining, or withholding be from the possession of the owner or of any other person. Care, custody, management, and control are among the definitions of possession.

(ii) *Owner.* "Owner" refers to the person who, at the time of the taking, obtaining, or withholding, had the superior right to possession of the property in the light of all conflicting interests therein which may be involved in the particular case. For instance, an organization is the true owner of its funds as against the custodian of the funds charged with the larceny thereof.

(iii) *Any other person.* "Any other person" means any person—even a person who has stolen the property—who has possession or a greater right to possession than the accused. In pleading a violation of this article, the ownership of the property may be alleged to have been in any person, other than the accused, who at the time of the theft was a general owner or a special owner thereof. A general owner of property is a person who has title to it, whether or not that person has possession of it; a special owner, such as a borrower or hirer, is one who does not have title but who does have possession, or the right of possession, of the property.

(iv) *Person.* "Person," as used in referring to one from whose possession property has been taken, obtained, or withheld, and to any owner of property, includes (in addition to a natural person) a government, a corporation, an association, an organization, and an estate. Such a person need not be a legal entity.

(d) *Wrongfulness of the taking, obtaining, or withholding.* The taking, obtaining, or withholding of the property must be wrongful. As a general rule, a taking or withholding of property from the possession of another is wrongful if done without the consent of the other, and an obtaining of property from the possession of another is wrongful if the obtaining is by false pretense. However, such an act is not wrongful if it is authorized by law or apparently lawful superior orders, or, generally, if done by a person who has a right to the possession of the property either equal to or greater than the right of one from whose possession the property is taken, obtained, or withheld. An owner of property who takes or withholds it from the possession of another, without the consent of the other, or who obtains it therefrom by false pretense, does so wrongfully if the other has a superior right—such as a lien—to possession of the property. A person who takes, obtains, or withholds property as the agent of another has the same rights and liabilities as does the principal, but may not be charged with a guilty knowledge or intent of the principal which that person does not share.

(e) *False pretense.* With respect to obtaining property by false pretense, the false pretense may be made by means of any act, word, symbol, or token. The pretense must be in fact false when made and when the property is obtained, and it must be knowingly false in the sense that it is made without a belief in its truth. A false pretense is a false representation of past or existing fact. In addition to other kinds of facts, the fact falsely represented by a person may be that person's or another's power, authority, or intention. Thus, a false representation by a person that person presently intends to perform a certain act in the future is a false representation of an existing fact—the intention—and thus a false pretense. Although the pretense need not be the sole cause inducing the owner to part with the property, it must be an effective and intentional cause of the obtaining. A false representation made after the property was obtained will not result in a violation of Article 121. A larceny is committed when a person obtains the property of another by false pretense and with intent to steal, even though the owner neither intended nor was requested to part with title to the property. Thus, a person who gets another's watch by pretending that it will be borrowed briefly and then returned, but who really intends to sell it, is guilty of larceny.

(f) *Intent.*

(i) *In general.* The offense of larceny requires that the taking, obtaining, or withholding by the thief be accompanied by an intent permanently to deprive or defraud another of the use and benefit of property or permanently to appropriate the property to the thief's own use or the use of any person other than the owner. These intents are collectively called an intent to steal. Although a person gets property by a taking or obtaining which was not wrongful or which was without a concurrent intent to steal, a larceny is nevertheless committed if an intent to steal is formed after the taking or obtaining and the property is wrongfully withheld with that intent. For example, if a person rents another's vehicle, later decides to keep it permanently, and then either fails to return it at the appointed time or uses it for a purpose not authorized by the terms of the rental, larceny has been committed, even though at the time the vehicle was rented, the person intended to return it after using it according to the agreement.

(ii) *Inference of intent.* An intent to steal may be proved by circumstantial evidence. Thus, if a person secretly takes property, hides it, and denies knowing anything about it, an intent to steal may be inferred; if the property was taken openly and returned, this would tend to negate such an intent. Proof of sale of the property may show an intent to steal, and therefore, evidence of such a sale may be introduced to support a charge of larceny. An intent to steal may be inferred from a wrongful and intentional dealing with the property of another in a manner likely to cause that person to suffer a permanent loss thereof.

(iii) *Special situations.*

(A) *Motive does not negate intent.* The accused's purpose in taking an item ordinarily is irrelevant to the accused's guilt as long as the accused had the intent required under subparagraph c(1)(f)(i) above. For example, if the accused wrongfully took property as a "joke" or "to teach the owner a lesson" this would not be a defense, although if the accused intended to return the property, the accused would be guilty of wrongful appropriation, not larceny. When a person takes property intending only to return it to its lawful owner, as when stolen property is taken from a thief in order to return it to its owner, larceny or wrongful appropriation is not committed.

(B) *Intent to pay for or replace property not a defense.* An intent to pay for or replace the stolen property is not a defense, even if that intent existed at the time of the theft. If, however, the accused takes money or a negotiable instrument having no special value above its face value, with the intent to return an equivalent amount of money, the offense of larceny is not committed although wrongful appropriation may be.

(C) *Return of property not a defense.* Once a larceny is committed, a return of the property or payment for it is no defense. *See* subparagraph c(2) below when the taking, obtaining, or withholding is with the intent to return.

(g) *Value.*

(i) *In general.* Value is a question of fact to be determined on the basis of all of the evidence admitted.

(ii) *Government property.* When the stolen property is an item issued or procured from Government sources, the price listed in an official publication for that property at the time of the theft is admissible as evidence of its value. *See* Mil. R. Evid. 803(17). However, the stolen item must be shown to have been, at the time of the theft, in the condition upon which the value indicated in the official price list is based. The price listed in the official publication is not conclusive as to the value of the item, and other evidence may be admitted on the question of its condition and value.

(iii) *Other property.* As a general rule, the value of other stolen property is its legitimate market value at the time and place of the theft. If this property, because of its character or the place where it was stolen, had no legitimate market value at the time and place of the theft or if that value cannot readily be ascertained, its value may be determined by its legitimate market value in the United States at the time of the theft, or by its replacement cost at that time, whichever is less. Market value may be established by proof of the recent purchase price paid for the article in the legitimate market involved or by testimony or other admissible evidence from any person who is familiar through training or experience with the market value in question. The owner of the property may testify as to its market value if familiar with its quality and condition. The fact that the owner is not an expert of the market value of the property goes only to the weight to be given that testimony, and not to its admissibility. *See* Mil. R. Evid. 701. When the character of the property clearly appears in evidence—for instance, when it is exhibited to the court-martial—the court-martial, from its own experience, may infer that it has some value. If as a matter of common knowledge the property is obviously of a value substantially in excess of $500.00, the court-martial may find a value of more than $500.00. Writings representing value may be considered to have the value—even though contingent—which they represented at the time of the theft.

(iv) *Limited interest in property.* If an owner of property or someone acting in the owner's behalf steals it from a person who has a superior, but limited, interest in the property, such as a lien, the value for punishment purposes shall be that of the limited interest.

(h) *Miscellaneous considerations.*

(i) *Lost property.* A taking or withholding of lost property by the finder is larceny if accompanied by an intent to steal and if a clue to the identity of the general or special owner, or through which such identity may be traced, is furnished by the character, location, or marketing of the property, or by other circumstances.

(ii) *Multiple article larceny.* When a larceny of several articles is committed at substantially the same time and place, it is a single larceny even though the articles belong to different persons. Thus, if a thief steals a suitcase containing the property of several persons or goes into a room and takes property belonging to various persons, there is but one larceny, which should be alleged in but one specification.

(iii) *Special kinds of property which may also be the subject of larceny.* Included in property which may be the subject of larceny is property which is taken, obtained, or withheld by severing it from real estate and writings which represent value such as commercial paper.

(iv) *Services.* Theft of services may not be charged under this paragraph, but *see* paragraph 78.

(vi) *Credit, Debit, and Electronic Transactions.* Wrongfully engaging in a credit, debit, or electronic transaction to obtain goods or money is an obtaining-type larceny by false pretense. Such use to obtain goods is usually a larceny of those goods from the merchant offering them. Such use to obtain money or a negotiable instrument (e.g., withdrawing cash from an automated teller or a cash advance from a bank) is usually a larceny of money from the entity presenting the money or a negotiable instrument. For the purpose of this section, the term æcredit, debit, or electronic transactionÆ includes the use of an instrument or device, whether known as a credit card, debit card, automated teller machine (ATM) card or by any other name, including access devices such as code, account number, electronic serial number or personal identification number, issued for the use in obtaining money, goods, or anything else of value.

(2) *Wrongful appropriation.*

(a) *In general.* Wrongful appropriation requires an intent to temporarily—as opposed to permanently—deprive the owner of the use and benefit of, or appropriate to the use of another, the property wrongfully taken, withheld, or obtained. In all other respects wrongful appropriation and larceny are identical.

(b) *Examples.* Wrongful appropriation includes: taking another's automobile without permission or lawful authority with intent to drive it a short distance and then return it or cause it to be returned to the owner; obtaining a service weapon by falsely pretending to be about to go on guard duty with intent to use it on a hunting trip and later return it; and while driving a government vehicle on a mission to deliver supplies, withholding the vehicle from government service by deviating from the assigned route without authority, to visit a friend in a nearby town and later restore the vehicle to its lawful use. An inadvertent exercise of control over the property of another will not result in wrongful appropriation. For example, a person who fails to return a borrowed boat at the time agreed upon because the boat inadvertently went aground is not guilty of this offense.

d. *Lesser included offenses.*

(1) *Larceny.*

(a) Article 121—wrongful appropriation

(b) Article 80—attempts

(2) *Larceny of military property.*

(a) Article 121—wrongful appropriation

(b) Article 121—larceny of property other than military property

(c) Article 80—attempts

(3) *Wrongful appropriation.* Article 80—attempts

e. *Maximum punishment.*

(1) *Larceny.*

(a) *Military property of a value of $500 or less.* Bad-conduct discharge, forfeiture of all pay and allowances, and confinement for 1 year.

(b) *Property other than military property of a value of $500 or less.* Bad-conduct discharge, forfeiture of all pay and allowances, and confinement for 6 months.

(c) *Military property of a value of more than $500 or of any military motor vehicle, aircraft, vessel, firearm, or explosive.* Dishonorable discharge, forfeiture of all pay and allowances, and confinement for 10 years.

(d) *Property other than military property of a value of more than $500 or any motor vehicle, aircraft, vessel, firearm, or explosive not included in subparagraph e(1)(c).* Dishonorable discharge, forfeiture of all pay and allowances, and confinement for five years.

(2) *Wrongful appropriation.*

(a) *Of a value of $500.00 or less.* Confinement for 3 months, and forfeiture of two-thirds pay per month for 3 months.

(b) *Of a value of more than $500.00.* Bad-conduct discharge, forfeiture of all pay and allowances, and confinement for 6 months.

(c) *Of any motor vehicle, aircraft, vessel, firearm, or explosive.* Dishonorable discharge, forfeiture of all pay and allowances, and confinement for 2 years.

f. *Sample specifications.*

(1) *Larceny.*

In that ______ (personal jurisdiction data), did, (at/on board—location) (subject-matter jurisdiction data, if required), on or about ______ 20 __, steal ______, (military property), of a value of (about) $______, the property of ______.

(2) *Wrongful appropriation.*

In that ______ (personal jurisdiction data), did, (at/on board—location) (subject matter jurisdiction data, if required), on or about ______ 20 __, wrongfully appropriate ______, of a value of (about) $______, the property of ______.

47. Article 122—Robbery

a. *Text of statute.*

Any person subject to this chapter who with intent to steal takes anything of value from the person or in the presence of another, against his will, by means of force or violence or fear of immediate or future injury to his person or property or to the person or property of a relative or member of his family or of anyone in his company at the time of the robbery, is guilty of robbery and shall be punished as a court-martial may direct.

b. *Elements.*

(1) That the accused wrongfully took certain property from the person or from the possession and in the presence of a person named or described;

(2) That the taking was against the will of that person;

(3) That the taking was by means of force, violence, or force and violence, or putting the person in fear of immediate or future injury to that person, a relative, a member of the person's family, anyone accompanying the person at the time of the robbery, the person's property, or the property of a relative, family member, or anyone accompanying the person at the time of the robbery;

(4) That the property belonged to a person named or described;

(5) That the property was of a certain or of some value; and

(6) That the taking of the property by the accused was with the intent permanently to deprive the person robbed of the use and benefit of the property. [Note: If the robbery was committed with a firearm, add the following element]

(7) That the means of force or violence or of putting the person in fear was a firearm.

c. *Explanation.*

(1) *Taking in the presence of the victim.* It is not necessary that the property taken be located within any certain distance of the victim. If persons enter a house and force the owner by threats to disclose the hiding place of valuables in an adjoining room, and, leaving the owner tied, go into that room and steal the valuables, they have committed robbery.

(2) *Force or violence.* For a robbery to be committed by force or violence, there must be actual force or violence to the person, preceding or accompanying the taking against the person's will, and it is immaterial that there is no fear engendered in the victim. Any amount of force is enough to constitute robbery if the force overcomes the actual resistance of the person robbed, puts the person in such a position that no resistance is made, or suffices to overcome the resistance offered by a chain or other fastening by which the article is attached to the person. The offense is not robbery if an article is merely snatched from the hand of another or a pocket is picked by stealth, no other force is used, and the owner is not put in fear. But if resistance is overcome in snatching the article, there is sufficient violence, as when an earring is torn from a person's ear. There is sufficient violence when a person's attention is diverted by being jostled by a confederate of a pickpocket, who is thus enabled to steal the person's watch, even though the person had no knowledge of the act; or when a person is knocked insensible and that person's pockets rifled; or when a guard steals property from the person of a prisoner in the guard's charge after handcuffing the prisoner on the pretext of preventing escape.

(3) *Fear.* For a robbery to be committed by putting the victim in fear, there need be no actual force or violence, but there must be a demonstration of force or menace by which the victim is placed in such fear that the victim is warranted in making no resistance. The fear must be a reasonable apprehension of present or future injury, and the taking must occur while the apprehension exists. The injury apprehended may be death or bodily injury to the person or to a relative or family member, or to anyone in the person's company at the time, or it may be the destruction of the person's habitation or other property or that of a relative or family member or anyone in the person's company at the time of sufficient gravity to warrant giving up the property demanded by the assailant.

(4) *Larceny by taking.* Robbery includes "taking with intent to steal"; hence, a larceny by taking is an integral part of a charge of robbery and must be proved at the trial. *See* paragraph 46c(1).

(5) *Multiple-victim robberies.* Robberies of different persons at the same time and place are separate offenses and each such robbery should be alleged in a separate specification.

d. *Lesser included offenses.*

(1) Article 121—larceny

(2) Article 121—wrongful appropriation

(3) Article 128—assault; assault consummated by a battery

(4) Article 128—assault with a dangerous weapon

(5) Article 128—assault intentionally inflicting grievous bodily harm

(6) Article 134—assault with intent to rob

(7) Article 80—attempts

[Note: More than one lesser included offense may be found in an appropriate case because robbery is a compound offense. For example, a person may be found not guilty of robbery but guilty of wrongful appropriation and assault.]

e. *Maximum punishment.*

(1) *When committed with a firearm.* Dishonorable discharge, forfeiture of all pay and allowances, and confinement for 15 years.

(2) *Other cases.* Dishonorable discharge, forfeiture of all pay and allowances, and confinement for 10 years.

f. *Sample specifications.*

In that ________ (personal jurisdiction data), did, (at/on board—location) (subject-matter jurisdiction data, if required), on or about ________ 20 ____, by means of (force) (violence) (force and violence) (and) (putting him/her in fear) (with a firearm) steal from the (person) (presence) of ________, against his/her will, (a watch) (________) of value of (about) $________, the property of ________.

48. Article 123—Forgery

a. *Text of statute.*

Any person subject to this chapter who, with intent to defraud—

(1) **falsely makes or alters any signature to, or any part of, any writing which would, if genuine, apparently impose a legal liability on another or change his legal right or liability to his prejudice; or**

(2) **utters, offers, issues, or transfers such a writing, known by him to be so made or altered; is guilty of forgery and shall be punished as a court-martial may direct.**

b. *Elements.*

(1) *Forgery—making or altering.*

(a) That the accused falsely made or altered a certain signature or writing;

(b) That the signature or writing was of a nature which would, if genuine, apparently impose a legal liability on another or change another's legal rights or liabilities to that person's prejudice; and

(c) That the false making or altering was with the intent to defraud.

(2) *Forgery—uttering.*

(a) That a certain signature or writing was falsely made or altered;

(b) That the signature or writing was of a nature which would, if genuine, apparently impose a legal liability on another or change another's legal rights or liabilities to that person's prejudice;

(c) That the accused uttered, offered, issued, or transferred the signature or writing;

(d) That at such time the accused knew that the signature or writing had been falsely made or altered; and

(e) That the uttering, offering, issuing or transferring was with the intent to defraud.

c. *Explanation.*

(1) *In general.* Forgery may be committed either by falsely making a writing or by knowingly uttering a falsely made writing. There are three elements common to both aspects of forgery: a writing falsely made or altered; and apparent capability of the writing as falsely made or altered to impose a legal liability on another or to change another's legal rights or liabilities to that person's prejudice; and an intent to defraud.

(2) *False.* "False" refers not to the contents of the writing or to the facts stated therein but to the making or altering of it. Hence, forgery is not committed by the genuine making of a false instrument even when made with intent to defraud. A person who, with intent to defraud, signs that person's own signature as the maker of a check drawn on a bank in which that person does not have money or credit does not commit forgery. Although the check falsely represents the existence of the account, it is what it purports to be, a check drawn by the actual maker, and therefore it is not falsely made. *See*, however, paragraph 49. Likewise, if a person makes a false signature of another to an instrument, but adds the word "by" with that person's own signature thus indicating authority to sign, the offense is not forgery even if no such authority exists. False recitals of fact in a genuine document, as an aircraft flight report which is "padded" by the one preparing it, do not make the writing a forgery. *But see* paragraph 31 concerning false official statements.

(3) *Signatures.* Signing the name of another to an instrument having apparent legal efficacy without authority and with intent to defraud is forgery as the signature is falsely made. The distinction is that in this case the falsely made signature purports to be the act of one other than the actual signer. Likewise, a forgery may be committed by a person signing that person's own name to an instrument. For example, when a check payable to the order of a certain person comes into the hands of another of the same name, forgery is committed if, knowing the check to be another's, that person indorses it with that person's own name intending to defraud. Forgery may also be committed by signing a fictitious name, as when Roe makes a check payable to Roe and signs it with a fictitious name—Doe—as drawer.

(4) *Nature of writing.* The writing must be one which would, if genuine, apparently impose a legal liability on another, as a check or promissory note, or change that person's legal rights or liabilities to that person's prejudice, as a receipt. Some other instruments which may be the subject of forgery are orders for the delivery of money or goods, railroad tickets, and military orders directing travel. A writing falsely "made" includes an instrument that may be partially or entirely printed, engraved, written with a pencil, or made by photography or other device. A writing may be falsely "made" by materially altering an existing writing, by filling in a paper signed in blank, or by signing an instrument already written. With respect to the apparent legal efficacy of the writing falsely made or altered, the writing must appear either on its face or from extrinsic facts to impose a legal liability on another, or to change a legal right or liability the prejudice of another. If under all the circumstances the instrument has neither real nor apparent legal efficacy, there is no forgery. Thus, the false making with intent to defraud of an instrument affirmatively invalid on its face is not forgery nor is the false making or altering, with intent to defraud, of a writing which could not impose a legal liability, as a mere letter of introduction. However, the false making of another's signature on an instrument with intent to defraud is forgery, even if there is no resemblance to the genuine signature and the name is misspelled.

(5) *Intent to defraud. See* paragraph 49c(14). The intent to defraud need not be directed toward anyone in particular nor be for the advantage of the offender. If is immaterial that nobody was actually defrauded, or that no further step was made toward carrying out the intent to defraud other than the false making or altering of a writing.

(6) *Alteration.* The alteration must effect a material change in the legal tenor of the writing. Thus, an alteration which apparently increases, diminishes, or discharges any obligation is material. Examples of material alterations in the case of a promissory note are changing the date, amount, or place of payment. If a genuine writing has been delivered to the accused and while in the accused's possession is later found to be altered, it may be inferred that the writing was altered by the accused.

(7) *Uttering. See* paragraph 49c(4).

d. *Lesser included offense.* Article 80—attempts

e. *Maximum punishment.* Dishonorable discharge, forfeiture of all pay and allowances, and confinement for 5 years.

f. *Sample specifications.*

(1) *Forgery—making or altering.*

In that ________ (personal jurisdiction data), did, (at/on board—location) (subject-matter jurisdiction data, if required), on or about ________ 20 ____, with intent to defraud, falsely[make (in its entirety) (the signature of ________ as an indorsement to) (the signature of ________ to) (________) a certain (check) (writing) (________) in the following words and figures, to wit: ________] [alter a certain (check) (writing) (________) in the following words and figures, to wit: ________, by (adding thereto ________) (________)], which said (check) (writing) (________) would, if genuine, apparently operate to the legal harm of another[*and which- ________ (could be) (was) used to the legal harm of ________, in that ________].

[*Note: This allegation should be used when the document specified is not one which by its nature would clearly operate to the legal prejudice of another—for example, an insurance application. The manner in which the document could be or was used to prejudice the legal rights of another should be alleged in the last blank.]

(2) *Forgery—uttering.*

In that ________ (personal jurisdiction data), did, (at/on board—location) (subject-matter jurisdiction data, if required), on or about ________ 20 ____, with intent to defraud, (utter) (offer) (issue) (transfer) a certain (check) (writing) (________) in the following words and figures, to wit: ________, a writing which would, if genuine, apparently operate to the legal harm of another, (which said (check) (writing) (________)) (the signature to which said (check) (writing) (________)) (________) was, as he/she, the said ________, then well knew, falsely (made) (altered) (*and which ________ (could be) (was) used to the legal harm of ________, in that ________). [*Note: *See* the note following (1), above]

49. Article 123a—Making, drawing, or uttering check, draft, or order without sufficient funds

a. *Text of statute.*

Any person subject to this chapter who—

(1) **for the procurement of any article or thing of value, with intent to defraud; or**

(2) **for the payment of any past due obligation, or for any other purpose, with intent to deceive; makes, draws, utters, or delivers any check, draft, or order for the payment of money upon any bank or other depository, knowing at the time that the maker or drawer has not or will not have sufficient funds in, or credit with, the bank or other depository for the payment of that check, draft, or order in full upon its presentment, shall be punished as a court-martial may direct. The making, drawing, uttering, or delivering by a maker or drawer of a check, draft, or order, payment of which is refused by the drawee because of insufficient funds of the maker or drawer in the drawee's possession or control, is prima facie evidence of his intent to defraud or deceive and of his knowledge of insufficient funds in, or credit with, that bank or other depository, unless the maker or drawer pays the holder the amount due within five days after receiving notice, orally or in writing, that the check, draft, or order was not paid on presentment. In this section, the word "credit" means an arrangement or understanding, express or implied, with the bank or other depository for the payment of that check, draft, or order.**

b. *Elements.*

(1) *For the procurement of any article or thing of value, with intent to defraud.*

(a) That the accused made, drew, uttered, or delivered a check, draft, or order for the payment of money payable to a named person or organization;

(b) That the accused did so for the purpose of procuring an article or thing of value;

(c) That the act was committed with intent to defraud; and

(d) That at the time of making, drawing, uttering, or delivery of the instrument the accused knew that the accused or the maker or drawer had not or would not have sufficient funds in, or credit with, the bank or other depository for the payment thereof upon presentment.

(2) *For the payment of any past due obligation, or for any other purpose, with intent to deceive.*

(a) That the accused made, drew, uttered, or delivered a check, draft, or order for the payment of money payable to a named person or organization;

(b) That the accused did so for the purpose or purported purpose of effecting the payment of a past due obligation or for some other purpose;

(c) That the act was committed with intent to deceive; and

(d) That at the time of making, drawing, uttering, or delivering of the instrument, the accused knew that the accused or the maker or drawer had not or would not have sufficient funds in, or credit with, the bank or other depository for the payment thereof upon presentment.

c. *Explanation.*

(1) *Written instruments.* The written instruments covered by this article include any check, draft (including share drafts), or order for the payment of money drawn upon any bank or other depository, whether or not the drawer bank or depository is actually in existence. It may be inferred that every check, draft, or order carries with it a representation that the instrument will be paid in full by the bank or other depository upon presentment by a holder when due.

(2) *Bank or other depository.* "Bank or other depository" includes any business regularly but not necessarily exclusively engaged in public banking activities.

(3) *Making or drawing.* "Making" and "drawing" are synonymous and refer to the act of writing and signing the instrument.

(4) *Uttering or delivering.* "Uttering" and "delivering" have similar meanings. Both mean transferring the instrument to another, but "uttering" has the additional meaning of offering to transfer. A person need not personally be the maker or drawer of an instrument in order to violate this article if that person utters or delivers it. For example, if a person holds a check which that person knows is worthless, and utters or delivers the check to another, that person may be guilty of an offense under this article despite the fact that the person did not personally draw the check.

(5) *For the procurement.* "For the procurement" means for the purpose of obtaining any article or thing of value. It is not necessary that an article or thing of value actually be obtained, and the purpose of the obtaining may be for the accused's own use or benefit or for the use or benefit of another.

(6) *For the payment.* "For the payment" means for the purpose or purported purpose of satisfying in whole or in part any past due obligation. Payment need not be legally effected.

(7) *For any other purpose.* "For any other purpose" includes all purposes other than the payment of a past due obligation or the procurement of any article or thing of value. For example, it includes paying or purporting to pay an obligation which is not yet past due. The check, draft, or order, whether made or negotiated for the procurement of an article or thing of value or for the payment of a past due obligation or for some other purpose, need not be intended or represented as payable immediately. For example, the making of a postdated check, delivered at the time of entering into an installment purchase contract and intended as payment for a future installment, would, if made with the requisite intent and knowledge, be a violation of this article.

(8) *Article or thing of value.* "Article or thing of value" extends to every kind of right or interest in property, or derived from contract, including interests and rights which are intangible or contingent or which mature in the future.

(9) *Past due obligation.* A "past due obligation" is an obligation to pay money, which obligation has legally matured before making, drawing, uttering, or delivering the instrument.

(10) *Knowledge.* The accused must have knowledge, at the time the accused makes, draws, utters, or delivers the instrument, that the maker or drawer, whether the accused or another, has not or will not have sufficient funds in, or credit with, the bank or other depository for the payment of the instrument in full upon its presentment. Such knowledge may be proved by circumstantial evidence.

(11) *Sufficient funds.* "Sufficient funds" refers to a condition in which the account balance of the maker or drawer in the bank or other depository at the time of the presentment of the instrument for payment is not less than the face amount of the instrument and has not been rendered unavailable for payment by garnishment, attachment, or other legal procedures.

(12) *Credit.* "Credit" means an arrangement or understanding, express or implied, with the bank or other depository for the payment of the check, draft, or order. An absence of credit includes those situations in which an accused writes a check on a nonexistent bank or on a bank in which the accused has no account.

(13) *Upon its presentment.* "Upon its presentment" refers to the time the demand for payment is made upon presentation of the instrument to the bank or other depository on which it was drawn.

(14) *Intent to defraud.* "Intent to defraud" means an intent to obtain, through a misrepresentation, an article or thing of value and to apply it to one's own use and benefit or to the use and benefit of another, either permanently or temporarily.

(15) *Intent to deceive.* "Intent to deceive" means an intent to mislead, cheat, or trick another by means of a misrepresentation made for the purpose of gaining an advantage for oneself or for a third person, or of bringing about a disadvantage to the interests of the person to whom the representation was made or to interests represented by that person.

(16) *The relationship of time and intent.* Under this article, two times are involved: (a) when the accused makes, draws, utters, or delivers the instrument; and (b) when the instrument is presented to the bank or other depository for payment. With respect to (a), the accused must possess the requisite intent and must know that the maker or drawer does not have or will not have sufficient funds in, or credit with, the bank or the depository for payment of the instrument in full upon its presentment when due. With respect to (b), if it can otherwise be shown that the accused possessed the requisite intent and knowledge at the time the accused made, drew, uttered, or delivered the instrument, neither proof of presentment nor refusal of payment is necessary, as when the instrument is one drawn on a nonexistent bank.

(17) *Statutory rule of evidence.* The provision of this article with respect to establishing prima facie evidence of knowledge and intent by proof of notice and nonpayment within 5 days is a statutory rule of evidence. The failure of an accused who is a maker or drawer to pay the holder the amount due within 5 days after receiving either oral or written notice from the holder of a check, draft, or order, or from any other person having knowledge that such check, draft, or order was returned unpaid because of insufficient funds, is prima facie evidence (a) that the accused had the intent to defraud or deceive as alleged; and (b) that the accused knew at the time the accused made, drew, uttered, or delivered the check, draft, or order that the accused did not have or would not have sufficient funds in, or credit with, the bank or other depository for the payment of such check, draft, or order upon its presentment for payment. Prima facie evidence is that evidence from which the accused's intent to defraud or deceive and the accused's knowledge of insufficient funds in or credit with the bank or other depository may be inferred, depending on all the circumstances. The failure to give notice referred to in the article, or payment by the accused, maker, or drawer to the holder of the amount due within 5 days after such notice has been given, precludes the prosecution from using the statutory rule of evidence but does not preclude conviction of this offense if all the elements are otherwise proved.

(18) *Affirmative defense.* Honest mistake is an affirmative defense to offenses under this article. *See* R.C.M. 916(j).

d. *Lesser included offenses.*

(1) Article 134—making, drawing, uttering or delivering a check, draft, or order, and thereafter wrongfully and dishonorably failing to maintain sufficient funds

(2) Article 80—attempts

e. *Maximum punishment.*

(1) *For the procurement of any article or thing of value, with intent to defraud, in the face amount of:*

(a) *$500.00 or less.* Bad-conduct discharge, forfeiture of all pay and allowances, and confinement for 6 months.

(b) *More than $500.00.* Dishonorable discharge, forfeiture of all pay and allowances, and confinement for 5 years.

(2) *For the payment of any past due obligation, or for any other purpose, with intent to deceive.* Bad-conduct discharge, forfeiture of all pay and allowances, and confinement for 6 months.

f. *Sample specifications.*

(1) *For the procurement of any article or thing of value, with intent to defraud.*

In that ________ (personal jurisdiction data), did, (at/on board—location) (subject-matter jurisdiction data, if required), on or about ________ 20 ____, with intent to defraud and for the procurement of (lawful currency) (and) (________ (an article) (a thing) of value), wrongfully and unlawfully ((make (draw)) (utter) (deliver) to ________,) a certain (check) (draft) (money order) upon the (________ Bank) (________ depository) in words and figures as follows, to wit: ________, then knowing that (he/she)

(__________), the (maker) (drawer) thereof, did not or would not have sufficient funds in or credit with such (bank) (depository) for the payment of the said (check) (draft) (order) in full upon its presentment.

(2) *For the payment of any past due obligation, or for any other purpose, with intent to deceive.*

In that __________ (personal jurisdiction data), did, (at/on board—location) (subject-matter jurisdiction data, if required), on or about __________ 20 ____, with intent to deceive and for the payment of a past due obligation, to wit: __________ (for the purpose of __________) wrongfully and unlawfully ((make) (draw)) (utter) (deliver) to __________, a certain (check) (draft) (money order) for the payment of money upon (__________ Bank) (__________ depository), in words and figures as follows, to wit: __________, then knowing that (he/she) (__________), the (maker) (drawer) thereof, did not or would not have sufficient funds in or credit with such (bank) (depository) for the payment of the said (check) (draft) (order) in full upon its presentment.

50. Article 124—Maiming

a. *Text of statute.*

Any person subject to this chapter who, with intent to injure, disfigure, or disable, inflicts upon the person of another an injury which—

(1) seriously disfigures his person by any mutilation thereof;

(2) destroys or disables any member or organ of his body; or

(3) seriously diminishes his physical vigor by the injury of any member or organ; is guilty of maiming and shall be punished as a court-martial may direct.

b. *Elements.*

(1) That the accused inflicted a certain injury upon a certain person;

(2) That this injury seriously disfigured the person's body, destroyed or disabled an organ or member, or seriously diminished the person's physical vigor by the injury to an organ or member; and

(3) That the accused inflicted this injury with an intent to cause some injury to a person.

c. *Explanation.*

(1) *Nature of offense.* It is maiming to put out a person's eye, to cut off a hand, foot, or finger, or to knock out a tooth, as these injuries destroy or disable those members or organs. It is also maiming to injure an internal organ so as to seriously diminish the physical vigor of a person. Likewise, it is maiming to cut off an ear or to scar a face with acid, as these injuries seriously disfigure a person. A disfigurement need not mutilate any entire member to come within the article, or be of any particular type, but must be such as to impair perceptibly and materially the victim's comeliness. The disfigurement, diminishment of vigor, or destruction or disablement of any member or organ must be a serious injury of a substantially permanent nature. However, the offense is complete if such an injury is inflicted even though there is a possibility that the victim may eventually recover the use of the member or organ, or that the disfigurement may be cured by surgery.

(2) *Means of inflicting injury.* To prove the offense it is not necessary to prove the specific means by which the injury was inflicted. However, such evidence may be considered on the question of intent.

(3) *Intent.* Maiming requires a specific intent to injure generally but not a specific intent to maim. Thus, one commits the offense who intends only a slight injury, if in fact there is infliction of an injury of the type specified in this article. Infliction of the type of injuries specified in this article upon the person of another may support an inference of the intent to injure, disfigure, or disable.

(4) *Defenses.* If the injury is done under circumstances which would justify or excuse homicide, the offense of maiming is not committed. *See* R.C.M. 916.

d. *Lesser included offenses.*

(1) Article 128—assault; assault consummated by a battery

(2) Article 128—assault with a dangerous weapon

(3) Article 128—assault intentionally inflicting grievous bodily harm

(4) Article 80—attempts

e. *Maximum punishment.* Dishonorable discharge, forfeiture of all pay and allowances, and confinement for 20 years.

f. *Sample specification.*

In that __________ (personal jurisdiction data), did, (at/on board—location) (subject-matter jurisdiction data, if required) on or about ______ 20 ____, maim ______ by (crushing his/her foot with a sledge hammer) (______).

51. Article 125—Sodomy

a. *Text of statute.*

(a) **Any person subject to this chapter who engages in unnatural carnal copulation with another person of the same or opposite sex or with an animal is guilty of sodomy. Penetration, however slight, is sufficient to complete the offense.**

(b) **Any person found guilty of sodomy shall by punished as a court-martial may direct.**

b. *Elements.*

(1) That the accused engaged in unnatural carnal copulation with a certain other person or with an animal.

(Note: Add any of the following as applicable)

(2) That the act was done with a child under the age of 12.

(3) That the act was done with a child who had attained the age of 12 but was under the age of 16.

(4) That the act was done by force and without the consent of the other person.

c. *Explanation.* It is unnatural carnal copulation for a person to take into that person's mouth or anus the sexual organ of another person or of an animal; or to place that person's sexual organ in the mouth or anus of another person or of an animal; or to have carnal copulation in any opening of the body, except the sexual parts, with another person; or to have carnal copulation with an animal.

d. *Lesser included offenses.*

(1) *With a child under the age of 16.*

(a) Article 125—forcible sodomy (and offenses included therein; *see* subparagraph (2) below)

(b) Article 80—attempts

(2) *Forcible sodomy.*

(a) Article 125—sodomy (and offenses included therein; *see* subparagraph (3) below)

(b) Article 134—assault with intent to commit sodomy

(c) Article 80—attempts.

(3) *Sodomy.* Article 80—attempts

(Note: Consider lesser included offenses under Art. 120, depending on the factual circumstances in each case.)

e. *Maximum punishment.*

(1) *By force and without consent.* Dishonorable discharge, forfeiture of all pay and allowances, and confinement for life without eligibility for parole.

(2) *With a child who, at the time of the offense, has attained the age of 12 but is under the age of 16 years.* Dishonorable discharge, forfeiture of all pay and allowances, and confinement for 20 years.

(3) *With a child under the age of 12 years at the time of the offense.* Dishonorable discharge, forfeiture of all pay and allowances, and confinement for life without eligibility for parole.

(4) *Other cases.* Dishonorable discharge, forfeiture of all pay and allowances, and confinement for 5 years.

f. *Sample specification.*

In that ______ (personal jurisdiction data), did, (at/on board—location) (subject-matter jurisdiction data, if required), on or about ______ 20 ____, commit sodomy with ______, (a child under the age of 12) (a child who had attained the age of 12 but was under the age of 16) (by force and without the consent of the said ______).

52. Article 126—Arson

a. *Text of statute.*

(a) **Any person subject to this chapter who willfully and maliciously burns or sets on fire an inhabited dwelling, or any other structure, movable or immovable, wherein to the knowledge of the offender there is at the time a human being, is guilty of aggravated arson and shall be punished as a court-martial may direct.**

(b) **Any person subject to this chapter who willfully and maliciously burns or sets fire to the property of another, except as provided in subsection (a), is guilty of simple arson and shall be punished as a court-martial may direct.**

b. *Elements.*

(1) *Aggravated arson.*

(a) *Inhabited dwelling.*

(i) That the accused burned or set on fire an inhabited dwelling;

(ii) That this dwelling belonged to a certain person and was of a certain value; and

(iii) That the act was willful and malicious.

(b) *Structure.*

(i) That the accused burned or set on fire a certain structure;

(ii) That the act was willful and malicious;

(iii) That there was a human being in the structure at the time;

(iv) That the accused knew that there was a human being in the structure at the time; and

(v) That this structure belonged to a certain person and was of a certain value.

(2) *Simple arson.*

(a) That the accused burned or set fire to certain property of another;

(b) That the property was of a certain value; and

(c) That the act was willful and malicious.

c. *Explanation.*

(1) *In general.* In aggravated arson, danger to human life is the essential element; in simple arson, it is injury to the property of another. In either case, it is immaterial that no one is, in fact, injured. It must be shown that the accused set the fire willfully and maliciously, that is, not merely by negligence or accident.

(2) *Aggravated arson.*

(a) *Inhabited dwelling.* An inhabited dwelling includes the outbuildings that form part of the cluster of buildings used as a residence. A shop or store is not an inhabited dwelling unless occupied as such, nor is a house that has never been occupied or which has been temporarily abandoned. A person may be guilty of aggravated arson of the person's dwelling, whether as owner or tenant.

(b) *Structure.* Aggravated arson may also be committed by burning or setting on fire any other structure, movable or immovable, such as a theater, church, boat, trailer, tent, auditorium, or any other sort of shelter or edifice, whether public or private, when the offender knows that there is a human being inside at the time. It may be that the offender had this knowledge when the nature of the structure—as a department store or theater during hours of business, or other circumstances—are shown to have been such that a reasonable person would have known that a human being was inside at the time.

(c) *Damage to property.* It is not necessary that the dwelling or structure be consumed or materially injured; it is enough if fire is actually communicated to any part thereof. Any actual burning or charring is sufficient, but a mere scorching or discoloration by heat is not.

(d) *Value and ownership of property.* For the offense of aggravated arson, the value and ownership of the dwelling or other structure are immaterial, but should ordinarily be alleged and proved to permit the finding in an appropriate case of the included offense of simple arson.

(3) *Simple arson.* "Simple arson" is the willful and malicious burning or setting fire to the property of another under circumstances not amounting to aggravated arson. The offense includes burning or setting fire to real or personal property of someone other than the offender. *See also* paragraph 67 (Burning with intent to defraud).

d. *Lesser included offenses.*

(1) *Aggravated arson.*

(a) Article 126—simple arson

(b) Article 80—attempts

(2) *Simple arson.* Article 80—attempts

e. *Maximum punishment.*

(1) *Aggravated arson.* Dishonorable discharge, forfeiture of all pay and allowances, and confinement for 20 years.

(2) *Simple arson, where the property is—*

(a) *Of a value of $500.00 or less.* Dishonorable discharge, forfeiture of all pay and allowances, and confinement for 1 year.

(b) *Of a value of more than $500.00.* Dishonorable discharge, forfeiture of all pay and allowances, and confinement for 5 years.

f. *Sample specifications.*

(1) *Aggravated arson.*

(a) *Inhabited dwelling.*

In that ______ (personal jurisdiction data), did, (at/on board—location) (subject-matter jurisdiction data, if required), on or about ______ 20 __, willfully and maliciously (burn) (set on fire) an inhabited dwelling, to wit: (the residence of ______) (______), (the property of ______) of a value of (about) $______.

(b) *Structure.*

In that ______ (personal jurisdiction data), did, (at/on board—location) (subject-matter jurisdiction data, if required), on or ______ 20 __, willfully and maliciously (burn) (set on fire), knowing that a human being was therein at the time, (the Post

Theater) (________, the property of ______________), of a value of (about) $________.

(2) *Simple arson.*
In that _________ (personal jurisdiction data), did, (at/on board— location) (subject-matter jurisdiction data, if required), on or about _________ 20____, willfully and maliciously (burn) (set fire to) (an automobile)(______________), the property of _________, of a value of (about) $________.

53. Article 127—Extortion

a. *Text of statute.*

Any person subject to this chapter who communicates threats to another person with the intention thereby to obtain anything of value or any acquittance, advantage, or immunity is guilty of extortion and shall be punished as a court-martial may direct.

b. *Elements.*

(1) That the accused communicated a certain threat to another; and

(2) That the accused intended to unlawfully obtain something of value, or any acquittance, advantage, or immunity.

c. *Explanation.*

(1) *In general.* Extortion is complete upon communication of the threat with the requisite intent. The actual or probable success of the extortion need not be proved.

(2) *Threat.* A threat may be communicated by any means but must be received by the intended victim. The threat may be: a threat to do any unlawful injury to the person or property of the person threatened or to any member of that person's family or any other person held dear to that person; a threat to accuse the person threatened, or any member of that persons's family or any other person held dear to that person, of any crime; a threat to expose or impute any deformity or disgrace to the person threatened or to any member of that person's family or any other person held dear to that person; a threat to expose any secret affecting the person threatened or any member of that person's family or any other person held dear to that person; or a threat to do any other harm.

(3) *Acquittance.* An "acquittance" is a release or discharge from an obligation.

(4) *Advantage or immunity.* Unless it is clear from the circumstances, the advantage or immunity sought should be described in the specification. An intent to make a person do an act against that person's will is not, by itself, sufficient to constitute extortion.

d. *Lesser included offenses.*

(1) Article 134—communicating a threat

(2) Article 80—attempts

e. *Maximum punishment.* Dishonorable discharge, forfeiture of all pay and allowances, and confinement for 3 years.

f. *Sample specification.*
In that _________ (personal jurisdiction data), did, (at/on board—location) (subject-matter jurisdiction data, if required), on or about _________ 20____, with intent unlawfully to obtain (something of value) (an acquittance) (an advantage, to wit _________) (an immunity, to wit ____________), communicate to _________ a threat to (here describe the threat).

54. Article 128—Assault

a. *Text of statute.*

(a) **Any person subject to this chapter who attempts or offers with unlawful force or violence to do bodily harm to another person, whether or not the attempt or offer is consummated, is guilty of assault and shall be punished as a court-martial may direct.**

(b) **Any person subject to this chapter who—**

(1) **commits an assault with a dangerous weapon or other means or force likely to produce death or grievous bodily harm; or**

(2) **commits an assault and intentionally inflicts grievous bodily harm with or without a weapon; is guilty of aggravated assault and shall be punished as a court-martial may direct.**

b. *Elements.*

(1) *Simple assault.*

(a) That the accused attempted or offered to do bodily harm to a certain person; and

(b) That the attempt or offer was done with unlawful force or violence.

(2) *Assault consummated by a battery.*

(a) That the accused did bodily harm to a certain person; and

(b) That the bodily harm was done with unlawful force or violence.

(3) *Assaults permitting increased punishment based on status of victim.*

(a) *Assault upon a commissioned, warrant, noncommissioned, or petty officer.*

(i) That the accused attempted to do, offered to do, or did bodily harm to a certain person;

(ii) That the attempt, offer, or bodily harm was done with unlawful force or violence;

(iii) That the person was a commissioned, warrant, noncommissioned, or petty officer; and

(iv) That the accused then knew that the person was a commissioned, warrant, noncommissioned, or petty officer.

(b) *Assault upon a sentinel or lookout in the execution of duty, or upon a person in the execution of law enforcement duties.*

(i) That the accused attempted to do, offered to do, or did bodily harm to a certain person;

(ii) That the attempt, offer, or bodily harm was done with unlawful force or violence;

(iii) That the person was a sentinel or lookout in the execution of duty or was a person who then had and was in the execution of security police, military police, shore patrol, master at arms, or other military or civilian law enforcement duties; and

(iv) That the accused then knew that the person was a sentinel or lookout in the execution of duty or was a person who then had and was in the execution of security police, military police, shore patrol, master at arms, or other military or civilian law enforcement duties.

(c) *Assault consummated by a battery upon a child under 16 years.*

(i) That the accused did bodily harm to a certain person;

(ii) That the bodily harm was done with unlawful force or violence; and

(iii) That the person was then a child under the age of 16 years.

(4) *Aggravated assault.*

(a) *Assault with a dangerous weapon or other means of force likely to produce death or grievous bodily harm.*

(i) That the accused attempted to do, offered to do, or did bodily harm to a certain person;

(ii) That the accused did so with a certain weapon, means, or force;

(iii) That the attempt, offer, or bodily harm was done with unlawful force or violence; and

(iv) That the weapon, means, or force was used in a manner likely to produce death or grievous bodily harm.

(Note: Add any of the following as applicable)

(v) That the weapon was a loaded firearm.

(vi) That the person was a child under the age of 16 years.

(b) *Assault in which grievous bodily harm is intentionally inflicted.*

(i) That the accused assaulted a certain person;

(ii) That grievous bodily harm was thereby inflicted upon such person;

(iii) That the grievous bodily harm was done with unlawful force or violence; and

(iv) That the accused, at the time, had the specific intent to inflict grievous bodily harm.

(Note: Add any of the following as applicable)

(v) That the injury was inflicted with a loaded firearm.

(vi) That the person was a child under the age of 16 years.

c. *Explanation.*

(1) *Simple assault.*

(a) *Definition of assault.* An "assault" is an attempt or offer with unlawful force or violence to do bodily harm to another, whether or not the attempt or offer is consummated. It must be done without legal justification or excuse and without the lawful consent of the person affected. "Bodily harm" means any offensive touching of another, however slight.

(b) *Difference between "attempt" and "offer" type assaults.*

(i) *Attempt type assault.* An "attempt" type assault requires a specific intent to inflict bodily harm, and an overt act—that is, an act that amounts to more than mere preparation and apparently tends to effect the intended bodily harm. An attempt type assault may be committed even though the victim had no knowledge of the incident at the time.

(ii) *Offer type assault.* An "offer" type assault is an unlawful demonstration of violence, either by an intentional or by a culpably negligent act or omission, which creates in the mind of another a reasonable apprehension of receiving immediate bodily harm. Specific intent to inflict bodily harm is not required.

(iii) *Examples.*

(A) If Doe swings a fist at Roe's head intending to hit Roe but misses, Doe has committed an attempt type assault, whether or not Roe is aware of the attempt.

(B) If Doe swings a fist in the direct of Roe's head either intentionally or as a result of culpable negligence, and Roe sees the blow coming and is thereby put in apprehension of being struck, Doe has committed an offer type assault whether or not Doe intended to hit Roe.

(C) If Doe swings at Roe's head, intending to hit it, and Roe sees the blow coming and is thereby put in apprehension of being struck, Doe has committed both on offer and an attempt type assault.

(D) If Doe swings at Roe's head simply to frighten Roe, not intending to hit Roe, and Roe does not see the blow and is not placed in fear, then no assault of any type has been committed.

(c) *Situations not amounting to assault.*

(i) *Mere preparation.* Preparation not amounting to an overt act, such as picking up a stone without any attempt or offer to throw it, does not constitute an assault.

(ii) *Threatening words.* The use of threatening words alone does not constitute an assault. However, if the threatening words are accompanied by a menacing act or gesture, there may be an assault, since the combination constitutes a demonstration of violence.

(iii) *Circumstances negating intent to harm.* If the circumstances known to the person menaced clearly negate an intent to do bodily harm there is no assault. Thus, if a person accompanies an apparent attempt to strike another by an unequivocal announcement in some form of an intention not to strike, there is no assault. For example, if Doe raises a stick and shakes it at Roe within striking distance saying, "If you weren't an old man, I would knock you down," Doe has committed no assault. However, an offer to inflict bodily injury upon another instantly if that person does not comply with a demand which the assailant has no lawful right to make is an assault. Thus, if Doe points a pistol at Roe and says, "If you don't hand over your watch, I will shoot you," Doe has committed an assault upon Roe. *See also* paragraph 47 (robbery) of this part.

(d) *Situations not constituting defenses to assault.*

(i) *Assault attempt fails.* It is not a defense to a charge of assault that for some reason unknown to the assailant, an assault attempt was bound to fail. Thus, if a person loads a rifle with what is believed to be a good cartridge and, pointing it at another, pulls the trigger, that person may be guilty of assault although the cartridge was defective and did not fire. Likewise, if a person in a house shoots through the roof at a place where a policeman is believed to be, that person may be guilty of assault even though the policeman is at another place on the roof.

(ii) *Retreating victim.* An assault is complete if there is a demonstration of violence and an apparent ability to inflict bodily injury causing the person at whom it was directed to reasonably apprehend that unless the person retreats bodily harm will be inflicted. This is true even though the victim retreated and was never within actual striking distance of the assailant. There must, however, be an apparent present ability to inflict the injury. Thus, to aim a pistol at a person at such a distance that it clearly could not injure would not be an assault.

(2) *Battery.*

(a) *In general.* A "battery" is an assault in which the attempt or offer to do bodily harm is consummated by the infliction of that harm.

(b) *Application of force.* The force applied in a battery may have been directly or indirectly applied. Thus, a battery can be committed by inflicting bodily injury on a person through striking the horse on which the person is mounted causing the horse to throw the person, as well as by striking the person directly.

(c) *Examples of battery.* It may be a battery to spit on another, push a third person against another, set a dog at another which bites the person, cut another's clothes while the person is wearing them though without touching or intending to touch the person, shoot a person, cause a person to take poison, or drive an automobile into a person. A person who, although excused in using force, uses more force than is required, commits a battery. Throwing an object into a crowd may be a battery on anyone whom the object hits.

(d) *Situations not constituting battery.* If bodily

harm is inflicted unintentionally and without culpable negligence, there is no battery. It is also not a battery to touch another to attract the other's attention or to prevent injury.

(3) *Assaults permitting increased punishment based on status of victims.*

(a) *Assault upon a commissioned, warrant, noncommissioned, or petty officer.* The maximum punishment is increased when assault is committed upon a commissioned officer of the armed forces of the United States, or of a friendly foreign power, or upon a warrant, noncommissioned, or petty officer of the armed forces of the United States. Knowledge of the status of the victim is an essential element of the offense and may be proved by circumstantial evidence. It is not necessary that the victim be superior in rank or command to the accused, that the victim be in the same armed force, or that the victim be in the execution of office at the time of the assault.

(b) *Assault upon a sentinel or lookout in the execution of duty, or upon a person in the execution of law enforcement duties.* The maximum punishment is increased when assault is committed upon a sentinel or lookout in the execution of duty or upon a person who was then performing security police, military police, shore patrol, master at arms, or other military or civilian law enforcement duties. Knowledge of the status of the victim is an essential element of this offense and may be proved by circumstantial evidence. *See* paragraph 38c(4) for the definition of "sentinel or lookout."

(c) *Assault consummated by a battery upon a child under 16 years of age.* The maximum punishment is increased when assault consummated by a battery is committed upon a child under 16 years of age. Knowledge that the person assaulted was under 16 years of age is not an element of this offense.

(4) *Aggravated assault.*

(a) *Assault with a dangerous weapon or other means or force likely to produce death or grievous bodily harm.*

(i) *Dangerous weapon.* A weapon is dangerous when used in a manner likely to produce death or grievous bodily harm.

(ii) *Other means or force.* The phrase "other means or force" may include any means or instrumentality not normally considered a weapon. When the natural and probable consequence of a particular use of any means or force would be death or grievous bodily harm, it may be inferred that the means or force is "likely" to produce that result. The use to which a certain kind of instrument is ordinarily put is irrelevant to the question of its method of employment in a particular case. Thus, a bottle, beer glass, a rock, a bunk adaptor, a piece of pipe, a piece of wood, boiling water, drugs, or a rifle butt may be used in a manner likely to inflict death or grievous bodily harm. On the other hand, an unloaded pistol, when presented as a firearm and not as a bludgeon, is not a dangerous weapon or a means of force likely to produce grievous bodily harm, whether or not the assailant knew it was unloaded.

(iii) *Grievous bodily harm.* "Grievous bodily harm" means serious bodily injury. It does not include minor injuries, such as a black eye or a bloody nose, but does include fractured or dislocated bones, deep cuts, torn members of the body, serious damage to internal organs, and other serious bodily injuries.

(iv) *Death or injury not required.* It is not necessary that death or grievous bodily harm be actually inflicted to prove assault with a dangerous weapon or means likely to produce grievous bodily harm.

(v) *When committed upon a child under 16 years of age.* The maximum punishment is increased when aggravated assault with a dangerous weapon or means likely to produce death or grievous bodily harm is inflicted upon a child under 16 years of age. Knowledge that the person assaulted was under the age of 16 years is not an element of the offense.

(b) *Assault in which grievous bodily harm is intentionally inflicted.*

(i) *In general.* It must be proved that the accused specifically intended to and did inflict grievous bodily harm. Culpable negligence will not suffice.

(ii) *Proving intent.* Specific intent may be proved by circumstantial evidence. When grievous bodily harm has been inflicted by means of intentionally using force in a manner likely to achieve that result, it may be inferred that grievous bodily harm was intended. On the other hand, that inference might not be drawn if a person struck another with a fist in a sidewalk fight even if the victim fell so that the victim's head hit the curbstone and a skull fracture resulted. It is possible, however, to commit this kind of aggravated assault with the fists, as when the victim is held by one of several assailants while the others beat the victim with their fists and break a nose, jaw, or rib.

(iii) *Grievous bodily harm. See* subparagraph (4)(a)(iii).

(iv) *When committed on a child under 16 years of age.* The maximum punishment is increased when aggravated assault with intentional infliction of grievous bodily harm is inflicted upon a child under 16 years of age. Knowledge that the person assaulted was under the age of 16 years is not an element of the offense.

d. *Lesser included offenses.*

(1) *Simple assault.* None

(2) *Assault consummated by a battery.* Article 128—simple assault

(3) *Assault upon a commissioned, warrant, noncommissioned, or petty officer.* Article 128—simple assault; assault consummated by a battery

(4) *Assault upon a sentinel or lookout in the execution of duty, or upon a person in the execution of police duties.* Article 128—simple assault; assault consummated by a battery

(5) *Assault consummated by a battery upon a child under 16 years.* Article 128—simple assault; assault consummated by a battery

(6) *Assault with a dangerous weapon or other means or force likely to produce death or grievous bodily harm.* Article 128—simple assault; assault consummated by a battery; (when committed upon a child under the age of 16 years; assault consummated by a battery upon a child under the age of 16 years).

(7) *Assault in which grievous bodily harm is intentionally inflicted.* Article 128—simple assault; assault consummated by a battery; assault with a dangerous weapon; (when committed upon a child under the age of 16 years -- assault consummated by a battery upon a child under the age of 16 years).

e. *Maximum punishment.*

(1) *Simple assault.*

(A) *Generally.* Confinement for 3 months and forfeiture of two-thirds pay per month for 3 months.

(B) *When committed with an unloaded firearm.* Dishonorable discharge, forfeiture of all pay and allowances, and confinement for 3 years.

(2) *Assault consummated by a battery.* Bad conduct discharge, forfeiture of all pay and allowances, and confinement for 6 months.

(3) *Assault upon a commissioned officer of the armed forces of the United States or of a friendly foreign power, not in the execution of office.* Dishonorable discharge, forfeiture of all pay and allowances, and confinement for 3 years.

(4) *Assault upon a warrant officer, not in the execution of office.* Dishonorable discharge, forfeiture of all pay and allowances, and confinement for 18 months.

(5) *Assault upon a noncommissioned or petty officer, not in the execution of office.* Bad-conduct discharge, forfeiture of all pay and allowances, and confinement for 6 months.

(6) *Assault upon a sentinel or lookout in the execution of duty, or upon any person who, in the execution of office, is performing security police, military police, shore patrol, master at arms, or other military or civilian law enforcement duties.* Dishonorable discharge, forfeiture of all pay and allowances, and confinement for 3 years.

(7) *Assault consummated by a battery upon a child under 16 years.* Dishonorable discharge, forfeiture of all pay and allowances, and confinement for 2 years.

(8) *Aggravated assault with a dangerous weapon or other means of force likely to produce death or grievous bodily harm.*

(a) *When committed with a loaded firearm.* Dishonorable discharge, forfeiture of all pay and allowances, and confinement for 8 years.

(b) *Aggravated assault with a dangerous weapon or other means of force likely to produce death or grievous bodily harm when committed upon a child under the age of 16 years.* Dishonorable discharge, total forfeitures, and confinement for 5 years.

(c) *Other cases.* Dishonorable discharge, forfeiture of all pay and allowances, and confinement for 3 years.

(9) *Aggravated assault in which grievous bodily harm is intentionally inflicted.*

(a) *When the injury is inflicted with a loaded firearm.* Dishonorable discharge, forfeiture of all pay and allowances, and confinement for 10 years.

(b) *Aggravated assault in which grievous bodily harm is intentionally inflicted when committed upon a child under the age of 16 years.* Dishonorable discharge, total forfeitures, and confinement for 8 years.

(c) *Other cases.* Dishonorable discharge, forfeiture of all pay and allowances, and confinement for 5 years.

f. *Sample specifications.*

(1) *Simple assault.*

In that ______ (personal jurisdiction data), did, (at/on board—location), (subject-matter jurisdiction data, if required), on or about ______ 20 ___, assault ______ by (striking at him/her with a ______) (______).

(2) *Assault consummated by a battery.*

In that ______ (personal jurisdiction data), did, (at/on board—location) (subject-matter jurisdiction data, if required), on or about ______ 20 ___, unlawfully (strike) (______) ______ (on) (in) the ______ with ______.

(3) *Assault upon a commissioned officer.*

In that ______ (personal jurisdiction data), did, (at/on board—location) (subject-matter jurisdiction data, if required), on or about ______ 20 ___, assault ______, who then was and was then known by the accused to be a commissioned officer of (______, a friendly foreign power) (the United States(Army) (Navy) (Marine Corps) (Air Force) (Coast Guard)) by ______.

(4) *Assault upon a warrant, noncommissioned, or petty officer.*

In that ______ (personal jurisdiction data), did, (at/on board—location) (subject-matter jurisdiction data, if required), on or about ______ 20 ___, assault ______, who then was and was then known by the accused to be a (warrant) (noncommissioned) (petty) officer of the United States (Army) (Navy) (Marine Corps) (Air Force) (Coast Guard), by ______.

(5) *Assault upon a sentinel or lookout.*

In that ______ (personal jurisdiction data), did, (at/on board—location) (subject-matter jurisdiction data, if required), on or about ______ 20 ___, assault ______, who then was and was then known by the accused to be a (sentinel) (lookout) in the execution of his/her duty, ((in) (on) the ______) by ______.

(6) *Assault upon a person in the execution of law enforcement duties.*

In that ______ (personal jurisdiction data), did, (at/on board—location) (subject-matter jurisdiction data, if required), on or about ______ 20 ___, assault ______, who then was and was then known by the accused to be a person then having and in the execution of (Air Force security police) (military police) (shore patrol) (master at arms) ((military) (civilian) law enforcement)) duties, by ______.

(7) *Assault consummated by a battery upon a child under 16 years.*

In that ______ (personal jurisdiction data), did, (at/on board—location) (subject-matter jurisdiction data, if required), on or about ______ 20 ___, unlawfully (strike) (______) ______ a child under the age of 16 years, (in) (on) the ______ with ______.

(8) *Assault, aggravated—with a dangerous weapon, means or force.*

In that ______ (personal jurisdiction data), did, (at/on board-location)(subject matter jurisdiction data, if required), on or about ______ 20 ___, commit an assault upon ______ (a child under the age of 16 years) by (shooting)(pointing)(striking)(cutting) (___) (at him/her)(him/her) (in-)(on)(the ___) with (a dangerous weapon)(a (means)(force) likely to produce death or grievous bodily harm), to wit: a (loaded firearm)(pickax)(bayonet)(club)(___).

(9) *Assault, aggravated—inflicting grievous bodily harm.*

In that ______ (personal jurisdiction data), did, (at/on board-location)(subject matter jurisdiction data, if required), on or about ______ 20 ___, commit an assault upon ___ (a child under the age of 16 years) by (shooting)(striking)(cutting)(___) (him/her)(on) the ______ with a (loaded firearm)(club)(rock)(brick)(___) and did thereby intentionally inflict grievous bodily harm upon him/her, to wit: a (broken leg)(deep cut)(fractured skull)(___).

55. Article 129—Burglary

a. *Text of statute.*

Any person subject to this chapter who, with intent to commit an offense punishable under sections 918-928 of this title (articles 118-128), breaks and enters, in the nighttime, the dwelling house of another, is guilty of burglary and shall be punished as a court-martial may direct.

b. *Elements.*

(1) That the accused unlawfully broke and entered the dwelling house of another;

(2) That both the breaking and entering were done in the nighttime; and

(3) That the breaking and entering were done with the intent to commit an offense punishable under Article 118 through 128, except Article 123a.

c. *Explanation.*

(1) *In general.* "Burglary" is the breaking and entering in the nighttime of the dwelling house of another, with intent to commit an offense punishable under Articles 118 through 128, except 123a. In addition, an intent to commit an offense which, although not covered by Article 118 through 128, necessarily includes an offense within one of these articles, satisfies the intent element of this article. This includes, for example, assaults punishable under Article 134 which necessarily include simple assault under Article 128.

(2) *Breaking.* There must be a breaking, actual or constructive. Merely to enter through a hole left in the wall or roof or through an open window or door will not constitute a breaking; but if a person moves any obstruction to entry of the house without which movement the person could not have entered, the person has committed a "breaking." Opening a closed door or window or other similar fixture, opening wider a door or window already partly open but insufficient for the entry, or cutting out the glass of a window or the netting of a screen is a sufficient breaking. The breaking of an inner door by one who has entered the house without breaking, or by a person lawfully within the house who has no authority to enter the particular room, is a sufficient breaking, but unless such a breaking is followed by an entry into the particular room with the requisite intent, burglary is not committed. There is a constructive breaking when the entry is gained by a trick, such as concealing oneself in a box; under false pretense, such as impersonating a gas or telephone inspector; by intimidating the occupants through violence or threats into opening the door; through collusion with a confederate, an occupant of the house; or by descending a chimney, even if only a partial descent is made and no room is entered.

(3) *Entry.* An entry must be effected before the offense is complete, but the entry of any part of the body, even a finger, is sufficient. Insertion into the house of a tool or other instrument is also a sufficient entry, unless the insertion is solely to facilitate the breaking or entry.

(4) *Nighttime.* Both the breaking and entry must be in the nighttime. "Nighttime" is the period between sunset and sunrise when there is not sufficient daylight to discern a person's face.

(5) *Dwelling house of another.* To constitute burglary the house must be the dwelling house of another. "Dwelling house" includes outbuildings within the common inclosure, farmyard, or cluster of buildings used as a residence. Such an area is the "curtilage." A store is not a dwelling house unless part of, or also used as, a dwelling house, as when the occupant uses another part of the same building as a dwelling, or when the store in habitually slept in by family members or employees. The house must be used as a dwelling at the time of the breaking and entering. It is not necessary that anyone actually be in it at the time of the breaking and entering, but if the house has never been occupied at all or has been left without any intention of returning, it is not a dwelling house. Separate dwellings within the same building, such as a barracks room, apartment, or a room in a hotel, are subjects of burglary by other residents or guests, and in general by the owner of the building. A tent is not a subject of burglary.

(6) *Intent to commit offense.* Both the breaking and entry must be done with the intent to commit in the house an offense punishable under Articles 118 through 128, except 123a. If, after the breaking and entering, the accused commits one or more of these offenses, it may be inferred that the accused intended to commit the offense or offenses at the time of the breaking and entering. If the evidence warrants, the intended offense may be separately charged. It is immaterial whether the offense intended is committed or even attempted. If the offense is intended, it is no defense that its commission was impossible.

(7) *Separate offense.* If the evidence warrants, the intended offense in the burglary specification may be separately charged.

d. *Lesser included offenses.*

(1) Article 130—housebreaking

(2) Article 134—unlawful entry

(3) Article 80—attempts

e. *Maximum punishment.* Dishonorable discharge,

forfeiture of all pay and allowances, and confinement for 10 years.

f. *Sample specification.*

In that ________ (personal jurisdiction data), did, at ________, (subject-matter jurisdiction data, if required), on or about ________ 20 ____, in the nighttime, unlawfully break and enter the (dwelling house) (________ within the curtilage) of ________, with intent to commit (murder) (larceny) (________) therein.

56. Article 130—Housebreaking

a. *Text of statute.*

Any person subject to this chapter who unlawfully enters the building or structure of another with intent to commit a criminal offense therein is guilty of housebreaking and shall be punished as a court-martial may direct.

b. *Elements.*

(1) That the accused unlawfully entered a certain building or structure of a certain other person; and

(2) That the unlawful entry was made with the intent to commit a criminal offense therein.

c. *Explanation.*

(1) *Scope of offense.* The offense of housebreaking is broader than burglary in that the place entered is not required to be a dwelling house; it is not necessary that the place be occupied; it is not essential that there be a breaking; the entry may be either in the night or in the daytime; and the intent need not be to commit one of the offenses made punishable under Articles 118 through 128.

(2) *Intent.* The intent to commit some criminal offense is an essential element of housebreaking and must be alleged and proved to support a conviction of this offense. If, after the entry the accused committed a criminal offense inside the building or structure, it may be inferred that the accused intended to commit that offense at the time of the entry.

(3) *Criminal offense.* Any act or omission which is punishable by courts-martial, except an act or omission constituting a purely military offense, is a "criminal offense."

(4) *Building, structure.* "Building" includes a room, shop, store, office, or apartment in a building. "Structure" refers only to those structures which are in the nature of a building or dwelling. Examples of these structures are a stateroom, hold, or other compartment of a vessel, an inhabitable trailer, an inclosed truck or freight car, a tent, and a houseboat. It is not necessary that the building or structure be in use at the time of the entry.

(5) *Entry. See* paragraph 55c(3).

(6) *Separate offense.* If the evidence warrants, the intended offense in the housebreaking specification may be separately charged.

d. *Lesser included offenses.*

(1) Article 134—unlawful entry

(2) Article 80—attempts

e. *Maximum punishment.* Dishonorable discharge, forfeiture of all pay and allowances, and confinement for 5 years.

f. *Sample specification.*

In that ________, (personal jurisdiction data), did, (at/on board—location) (subject-matter jurisdiction data, if required), on or about ________ 20 ____, unlawfully enter a (dwelling) (room) (bank) (store) (warehouse) (shop) (tent) (stateroom) (________), the property of ________, with intent to commit a criminal offense, to wit: ________, therein.

57. Article 131—Perjury

a. *Text of statute.*

Any person subject to this chapter who in a judicial proceeding or in a course of justice willfully and corruptly—

(1) **upon a lawful oath or in any form allowed by law to be substituted for an oath, gives any false testimony material to the issue or matter of inquiry; or**

(2) **in any declaration, certificate, verification, or statement under penalty of perjury as permitted under section 1746 of title 28, United States Code, subscribes any false statement material to the issue or matter of inquiry; is guilty of perjury and shall be punished as a court-martial may direct.**

b. *Elements.*

(1) *Giving false testimony.*

(a) That the accused took an oath or affirmation in a certain judicial proceeding or course of justice;

(b) That the oath or affirmation was administered to the accused in a matter in which an oath or affirmation was required or authorized by law;

(c) That the oath or affirmation was administered by a person having authority to do so;

(d) That upon the oath or affirmation that accused willfully gave certain testimony;

(e) That the testimony was material;

(f) That the testimony was false; and

(g) That the accused did not then believe the testimony to be true.

(2) *Subscribing false statement.*

(a) That the accused subscribed a certain statement in a judicial proceeding or course of justice;

(b) That in the declaration, certification, verification, or statement under penalty of perjury, the accused declared, certified, verified, or stated the truth of that certain statement;

(c) That the accused willfully subscribed the statement;

(d) That the statement was material;

(e) That the statement was false; and

(f) That the accused did not then believe the statement to be true.

c. *Explanation.*

(1) *In general.* "Judicial proceeding" includes a trial by court-martial and "course of justice" includes an investigation conducted under Article 32. If the accused is charged with having committed perjury before a court-martial, it must be shown that the court-martial was duly constituted.

(2) *Giving false testimony.*

(a) *Nature.* The testimony must be false and must be willfully and corruptly given; that is, it must be proved that the accused gave the false testimony willfully and did not believe it to be true. A witness may commit perjury by testifying to the truth of a matter when in fact the witness knows nothing about it at all or is not sure about it, whether the thing is true or false in fact. A witness may also commit perjury in testifying falsely as to a belief, remembrance, or impression, or as to a judgment or opinion. It is no defense that the witness voluntarily appeared, that the witness was incompetent as a witness, or that the testimony was given in response to questions that the witness could have declined to answer.

(b) *Material matter.* The false testimony must be with respect to a material matter, but that matter need not be the main issue in the case. Thus, perjury may be committed by giving false testimony with respect to the credibility of a material witness or in an affidavit in support of a request for a continuance, as well as by giving false testimony with respect to a fact from which a legitimate inference may be drawn as to the existence or nonexistence of a fact in issue.

(c) *Proof.* The falsity of the allegedly perjured statement cannot be proved by circumstantial evidence alone, except with respect to matters which by their nature are not susceptible of direct proof. The falsity of the statement cannot be proved by the testimony of a single witness unless that testimony directly contradicts the statement and is corroborated by other evidence either direct or circumstantial, tending to prove the falsity of the statement. However, documentary evidence directly disproving the truth of the statement charged to have been perjured need not be corroborated if: the document is an official record shown to have been well known to the accused at the time the oath was taken; or the documentary evidence originated from the accused—or had in any manner been recognized by the accused as containing the truth—before the allegedly perjured statement was made.

(d) *Oath.* The oath must be one recognized or authorized by law and must be duly administered by one authorized to administer it. When a form of oath has been prescribed, a literal following of that form is not essential; it is sufficient if the oath administered conforms in substance to the prescribed form. "Oath" includes an affirmation when the latter is authorized in lieu of an oath.

(e) *Belief of accused.* The fact that the accused did not believe the statement to be true may be proved by testimony of one witness without corroboration or by circumstantial evidence.

(3) *Subscribing false statement. See* subparagraphs (1) and (2), above, as applicable. Section 1746 of title 28, United States Code, provides for subscribing to the truth of a document by signing it expressly subject to the penalty for perjury. The signing must take place in a judicial proceeding or course of justice—for example, if a witness signs under penalty of perjury summarized testimony given at an Article 32 investigation. It is not required that the document be sworn before a third party. Section 1746 does not change the requirement that a deposition be given under oath or alter the situation where an oath is required to be taken before a specific person.

d. *Lesser included offense.* Article 80—attempts.

e. *Maximum punishment.* Dishonorable discharge, forfeiture of all pay and allowances, and confinement for 5 years.

f. *Sample specifications.*

(1) *Giving false testimony.*

In that ________ (personal jurisdiction data), having taken a lawful (oath) (affirmation) in a (trial by ________ court-martial of ________) (trial by a court of competent jurisdiction, to wit: ________ of ________) (deposition for use in a trial by ________ of ________) (________) that he/she would (testify) (depose) truly, did, (at/on board—location) (subject-matter jurisdiction data, if required), on or about ________ 20____, willfully, corruptly, and contrary to such (oath) (affirmation), (testify) (depose) falsely in substance that ________, which (testimony) (deposition) was upon a material matter and which he/she did not then believe to be true.

(2) *Subscribing false statement.*

In that ________ (personal jurisdiction data), did (at/on board—location) (subject-matter jurisdiction data, if required), on or about ________ 20____, in a (judicial proceeding) (course of justice), and in a (declaration) (certification) (verification) (statement) under penalty of perjury pursuant to section 1746 of title 28, United States Code, willfully and corruptly subscribed a false statement material to the (issue) (matter of inquiry), to wit: ________, which statement was false in that ________, and which statement he/she did not then believe to be true.

58. Article 132—Frauds against the United States

a. *Text of statute.*

Any person subject to this chapter—

(1) **who, knowing it to be false or fraudulent—**

(a) **makes any claim against the United States or any officer thereof; or**

(b) **presents to any person in the civil or military service thereof, for approval or payment, any claim against the United States or any officer thereof;**

(2) **who, for the purpose of obtaining the approval, allowance, or payment of any claim against the United States or any officer thereof—**

(a) **makes or uses any writing or other paper knowing it to contain any false or fraudulent statements;**

(b) **makes any oath to any fact or to any writing or other paper knowing the oath to be false; or**

(c) **forges or counterfeits any signature upon any writing or other paper, or uses any such signature knowing it to be forged or counterfeited;**

(3) **who, having charge, possession, custody, or control of any money, or other property of the United States, furnished or intended for the armed forces thereof, knowingly delivers to any person having authority to receive it, any amount thereof less than that for which he receives a certificate or receipt; or**

(4) **who, being authorized to make or deliver any paper certifying the receipt of any property of the United States furnished or intended for the armed forces thereof, makes or delivers to any person such writing without having full knowledge of the truth of the statements therein contained and with intent to defraud the United States; shall, upon conviction, be punished as a court-martial may direct.**

b. *Elements.*

(1) *Making a false or fraudulent claim.*

(a) That the accused made a certain claim against the United States or an officer thereof;

(b) That the claim was false or fraudulent in certain particulars; and

(c) That the accused then knew that the claim was false or fraudulent in these particulars.

(2) *Presenting for approval or payment a false or fraudulent claim.*

(a) That the accused presented for approval or payment to a certain person in the civil or military service of the United States having authority to approve or pay it a certain claim against the United States or an officer thereof;

(b) That the claim was false or fraudulent in certain particulars; and

(c) That the accused then knew that the claim was false or fraudulent in these particulars.

(3) *Making or using a false writing or other paper in connection with claims.*

(a) That the accused made or used a certain writing or other paper;

(b) That certain material statements in the writing or other paper were false or fraudulent;

(c) That the accused then knew the statements were false or fraudulent; and

(d) That the act of the accused was for the purpose of obtaining the approval, allowance, or payment of a certain claim or claims against the United States or an officer thereof.

(4) *False oath in connection with claims.*

(a) That the accused made an oath to a certain fact or to a certain writing or other paper;

(b) That the oath was false in certain particulars;

(c) That the accused then knew it was false; and

(d) That the act was for the purpose of obtaining the approval, allowance, or payment of a certain claim or claims against the United States or an officer thereof.

(5) *Forgery of signature in connection with claims.*

(a) That the accused forged or counterfeited the signature of a certain person on a certain writing or other paper; and

(b) That the act was for the purpose of obtaining the approval, allowance, or payment of a certain claim against the United States or an officer thereof.

(6) *Using forged signature in connection with claims.*

(a) That the accused used the forged or counterfeited signature of a certain person;

(b) That the accused then knew that the signature was forged or counterfeited; and

(c) That the act was for the purpose of obtaining the approval, allowance, or payment of a certain claim against the United States or an officer thereof.

(7) *Delivering less than amount called for by receipt.*

(a) That the accused had charge, possession, custody, or control of certain money or property of the United States furnished or intended for the armed forces thereof;

(b) That the accused obtained a certificate or receipt for a certain amount or quantity of that money or property;

(c) That for the certificate or receipt the accused knowingly delivered to a certain person having authority to receive it an amount or quantity of money or property less than the amount or quantity thereof specified in the certificate or receipt; and

(d) That the undelivered money or property was of a certain value.

(8) *Making or delivering receipt without having full knowledge that it is true.*

(a) That the accused was authorized to make or deliver a paper certifying the receipt from a certain person of certain property of the United States furnished or intended for the armed forces thereof;

(b) That the accused made or delivered to that person a certificate or receipt;

(c) That the accused made or delivered the certificate without having full knowledge of the truth of a certain material statement or statements therein;

(d) That the act was done with intent to defraud the United States; and

(e) That the property certified as being received was of a certain value.

c. *Explanation.*

(1) *Making a false or fraudulent claim.*

(a) *Claim.* A "claim" is a demand for a transfer of ownership of money or property and does not include requisitions for the mere use of property. This article applies only to claims against the United States or any officer thereof as such, and not to claims against an officer of the United States in that officer's private capacity.

(b) *Making a claim.* Making a claim is a distinct act from presenting it. A claim may be made in one place and presented in another. The mere writing of a paper in the form of a claim, without any further act to cause the paper to become a demand against the United States or an officer thereof, does not constitute making a claim. However, any act placing the claim in official channels constitutes making a claim, even if that act does not amount to presenting a claim. It is not necessary that the claim be allowed or paid or that it be made by the person to be benefited by the allowance or payment. *See* also subparagraph (2), below.

(c) *Knowledge.* The claim must be made with knowledge of its fictitious or dishonest character.

This article does not proscribe claims, however groundless they may be, that the maker believes to be valid, or claims that are merely made negligently or without ordinary prudence.

(2) *Presenting for approval or payment a false or fraudulent claim.*

(a) *False and fraudulent.* False and fraudulent claims include not only those containing some material false statement, but also claims which the claimant knows to have been paid or for some other reason the claimant knows the claimant is not authorized to present or upon which the claimant knows the claimant has no right to collect.

(b) *Presenting a claim.* The claim must be presented, directly or indirectly, to some person having authority to pay it. The person to whom the claim is presented may be identified by position or authority to approve the claim, and need not be identified by name in the specification. A false claim may be tacitly presented, as when a person who knows that there is no entitlement to certain pay accepts it nevertheless without disclosing a disqualification, even though the person may not have made any representation of entitlement to the pay. For example, a person cashing a pay check which includes an amount for a dependency allowance, knowing at the time that the entitlement no longer exists because of a change in that dependency status, has tacitly presented a false claim. *See also* subparagraph (1), above.

(3) *Making or using a false writing or other paper in connection with claims.* The false or fraudulent statement must be material, that is, it must have a tendency to mislead governmental officials in their consideration or investigation of the claim. The offense of making a writing or other paper known to contain a false or fraudulent statement for the purpose of obtaining the approval, allowance, or payment of a claim is complete when the writing or paper is made for that purpose, whether or not any use of the paper has been attempted and whether or not the claim has been presented. *See also* the explanation in subparagraph (1) and (2), above.

(4) *False oath in connection with claims. See* subparagraphs (1) and (2), above.

(5) *Forgery of signature in connection with claims.* Any fraudulent making of the signature of another is forging or counterfeiting, whether or not an attempt is made to imitate the handwriting. *See* paragraph 48(c) and subparagraph (1) and (2), above.

(6) *Delivering less than amount called for by receipt.* It is immaterial by what means—whether deceit, collusion, or otherwise—the accused effected the transaction, or what was the accused's purpose.

(7) *Making or delivering receipt without having full knowledge that it is true.* When an officer or other person subject to military law is authorized to make or deliver any paper certifying the receipt of any property of the United States furnished or intended for the armed forces thereof, and a receipt or other paper is presented for signature stating that a certain amount of supplies has been furnished by a certain contractor, it is that person's duty before signing the paper to know that the full amount of supplies therein stated to have been furnished has in fact been furnished, and that the statements contained in the paper are true. If the person signs the paper with intent to defraud the United States and without that knowledge, that person is guilty of a violation of this section of the article. If the person signs the paper with knowledge that the full amount was not received, it may be inferred that the person intended to defraud the United States.

d. *Lesser included offense.* Article 80—attempts

e. *Maximum punishment.*

(1) Article 132(1) and (2). Dishonorable discharge, forfeiture of all pay and allowances, and confinement for 5 years.

(2) Article 132(3) and (4).

(a) *When amount is $500.00 or less.* Bad-conduct discharge, forfeiture of all pay and allowances, and confinement for 6 months.

(b) *When amount is over $500.00.* Dishonorable discharge, forfeiture of all pay and allowances, and confinement for 5 years.

f. *Sample specifications.*

(1) *Making false claim.*

In that ______ (personal jurisdiction data), did, (at/on board—location) (subject-matter jurisdiction data, if required), on or about ______ 20 ___, (by preparing (a voucher) (______) for presentation for approval or payment) (______), make a claim against the (United States) (finance officer at ______) (______) in the amount of $______ for (private property alleged to have been (lost) (destroyed) in the military service) (______), which claim was (false) (fraudulent) (false and fraudulent) in the amount of $ in that and was then known by the said to be (false) (fraudulent) (false and fraudulent).

(2) *Presenting false claim.*
In that (personal jurisdiction data), did, (at/on board—location) (subject-matter jurisdiction data, if required), on or about 20 , by presenting (a voucher)( ) to , an officer of the United States duly authorized to (approve) (pay) (approve and pay) such claim, present for (approval) (payment) (approval and payment) a claim against the (United States) (finance officer at) ( ) in the amount of $ for (services alleged to have been rendered to the United States by during) ( ), which claim was (false) (fraudulent) (false and fraudulent) in the amount of $ in that , and was then known by the said to be (false) (fraudulent) (false and fraudulent).

(3) *Making or using false writing.*
In that (personal jurisdiction data), for the purpose of obtaining the (approval) (allowance) (payment) (approval, allowance, and payment), of a claim against the United States in the amount of $, did (at/on board— location) (subject-matter jurisdiction data, if required), on or about 20 , (make) (use) (make and use) a certain (writing) (paper), to wit: , which said (writing) (paper), as he/she, the said , then knew, contained a statement that , which statement was (false) (fraudulent) (false and fraudulent) in that , and was then known by the said to be (false) (fraudulent) (false and fraudulent).

(4) *Making false oath.*
In that (personal jurisdiction data), for the purpose of obtaining the (approval) (allowance) (payment) (approval, allowance, and payment) of a claim against the United States, did, (at/on board—location) (subject-matter jurisdiction data, if required), on or about 20 , make an oath (to the fact that) (to a certain (writing) (paper), to wit: , to the effect that), which said oath was false in that , and was then known by the said to be false.

(5) *Forging or counterfeiting signature.*
In that (personal jurisdiction data), for the purpose of obtaining the (approval) (allowance) (payment) (approval, allowance, and payment) of a claim against the United States, did (at/on board—location) (subject-matter jurisdiction data, if required), on or about 20 , (forge) (counterfeit) (forge and counterfeit) the signature of upon a in words and figures as follows: .

(6) *Using forged signature.*
In that , for the purpose of obtaining the (approval) (allowance) (payment) (approval, allowance, and payment) of a claim against the United States, did, (at/on board—location) (subject-matter jurisdiction data, if required), on or about 20 , use the signature of on a certain (writing) (paper), to wit: , then knowing such signature to be (forged) (counterfeited) (forged and counterfeited).

(7) *Paying amount less than called for by receipt.*
In that (personal jurisdiction data), having (charge) (possession) (custody) (control) of (money) ( ) of the United States, (furnished) (intended) (furnished and intended) for the armed forces thereof, did, (at/on board—location) (subject-matter jurisdiction data, if required), on or about 20 , knowingly deliver to , the said having authority to receive the same, (an amount) ( ), which, as he/she, , then knew, was ($) ( ) less than the (amount) ( ) for which he/she received a (certificate) (receipt) from the said .

(8) *Making receipt without knowledge of the facts.*
In that (personal jurisdiction data), being authorized to (make) (deliver) (make and deliver) a paper certifying the receipt of property of the United States (furnished) (intended) (furnished and intended) for the armed forces thereof, did, (at/on board—location) (subject-matter jurisdiction data, if required), on or about 20 , without having full knowledge of the statement therein contained and with intent to defraud the United States, (make) (deliver) (make and deliver) to , such a writing, in words and figures as fol-

lows: __________, the property therein certified as received being of a value of about $__________.

59. Article 133—Conduct unbecoming an officer and gentleman

a. *Text of statute.*

Any commissioned officer, cadet, or midshipman who is convicted of conduct unbecoming an officer and a gentleman shall be punished as a court-martial may direct.

b. *Elements.*

(1) That the accused did or omitted to do certain acts; and

(2) That, under the circumstances, these acts or omissions constituted conduct unbecoming an officer and gentleman.

c. *Explanation.*

(1) *Gentleman.* As used in this article, "gentleman" includes both male and female commissioned officers, cadets, and midshipmen.

(2) *Nature of offense.* Conduct violative of this article is action or behavior in an official capacity which, in dishonoring or disgracing the person as an officer, seriously compromises the officer's character as a gentleman, or action or behavior in an unofficial or private capacity which, in dishonoring or disgracing the officer personally, seriously compromises the person's standing as an officer. There are certain moral attributes common to the ideal officer and the perfect gentleman, a lack of which is indicated by acts of dishonesty, unfair dealing, indecency, indecorum, lawlessness, injustice, or cruelty. Not everyone is or can be expected to meet unrealistically high moral standards, but there is a limit of tolerance based on customs of the service and military necessity below which the personal standards of an officer, cadet, or midshipman cannot fall without seriously compromising the person's standing as an officer, cadet, or midshipman or the person's character as a gentleman. This article prohibits conduct by a commissioned officer, cadet, or midshipman which, taking all the circumstances into consideration, is thus compromising. This article includes acts made punishable by any other article, provided these acts amount to conduct unbecoming an officer and a gentleman. Thus, a commissioned officer who steals property violates both this article and Article 121. Whenever the offense charged is the same as a specific offense set forth in this Manual, the elements of proof are the same as those set forth in the paragraph which treats that specific offense, with the additional requirement that the act or omission constitutes conduct unbecoming an officer and gentleman.

(3) *Examples of offenses.* Instances of violation of this article include knowingly making a false official statement; dishonorable failure to pay a debt; cheating on an exam; opening and reading a letter of another without authority; using insulting or defamatory language to another officer in that officer's presence or about that officer to other military persons; being drunk and disorderly in a public place; public association with known prostitutes; committing or attempting to commit a crime involving moral turpitude; and failing without good cause to support the officer's family.

d. *Lesser included offense.* Article 80—attempts

e. *Maximum punishment.* Dismissal, forfeiture of all pay and allowances, and confinement for a period not in excess of that authorized for the most analogous offense for which a punishment is prescribed in this Manual, or, if none is prescribed, for 1 year.

f. *Sample specifications.*

(1) *Copying or using examination paper.*

In that __________ (personal jurisdiction data), did, (at/on board—location), on or about __________ 20 __________, while undergoing a written examination on the subject of __________, wrongfully and dishonorably (receive) (request) unauthorized aid by ((using) (copying) the examination paper of __________)) (__________).

(2) *Drunk or disorderly.*

In that __________ (personal jurisdiction data), was, (at/on board—location), on or about __________ 20 __________, in a public place, to wit: __________, (drunk) (disorderly) (drunk and disorderly) while in uniform, to the disgrace of the armed forces.

60. Article 134—General article

a. *Text of statute.*

Though not specifically mentioned in this chapter, all disorders and neglects to the prejudice of good order and discipline in the armed forces, all conduct of a nature to bring discredit upon the armed forces, and crimes and offenses not capital, of which persons subject to this chapter may

be guilty, shall be taken cognizance of by a general, special, or summary court-martial, according to the nature and degree of the offense, and shall be punished at the discretion of that court.

b. *Elements.* The proof required for conviction of an offense under Article 134 depends upon the nature of the misconduct charged. If the conduct is punished as a crime or offense not capital, the proof must establish every element of the crime or offense as required by the applicable law. If the conduct is punished as a disorder or neglect to the prejudice of good order and discipline in the armed forces, or of a nature to bring discredit upon the armed forces, then the following proof is required:

(1) That the accused did or failed to do certain acts; and

(2) That, under the circumstances, the accused's conduct was to the prejudice of good order and discipline in the armed forces or was of a nature to bring discredit upon the armed forces.

c. *Explanation.*

(1) *In general.* Article 134 makes punishable acts in three categories of offenses not specifically covered in any other article of the code. These are referred to as "clauses 1, 2, and 3" of Article 134. Clause 1 offenses involve disorders and neglects to the prejudice of good order and discipline in the armed forces. Clause 2 offenses involve conduct of a nature to bring discredit upon the armed forces. Clause 3 offenses involve noncapital crimes or offenses which violate Federal law including law made applicable through the Federal Assimilative Crimes Act, *see* subsection (4) below. If any conduct of this nature is specifically made punishable by another article of the code, it must be charged as a violation of that article. *See* subparagraph (5)(a) below. However, *see* paragraph 59 *c* for offenses committed by commissioned officers, cadets, and midshipmen.

(2) *Disorders and neglects to the prejudice of good order and discipline in the armed forces (clause 1).*

(a) *To the prejudice of good order and discipline.* "To the prejudice of good order and discipline" refers only to acts directly prejudicial to good order and discipline and not to acts which are prejudicial only in a remote or indirect sense. Almost any irregular or improper act on the part of a member of the military service could be regarded as prejudicial in some indirect or remote sense; however, this article does not include these distant effects. It is confined to cases in which the prejudice is reasonably direct and palpable. An act in violation of a local civil law or of a foreign law may be punished if it constitutes a disorder or neglect to the prejudice of good order and discipline in the armed forces. However, *see* R.C.M. 203 concerning subject-matter jurisdiction.

(b) *Breach of custom of the service.* A breach of a custom of the service may result in a violation of clause 1 of Article 134. In its legal sense, "custom" means more than a method of procedure or a mode of conduct or behavior which is merely of frequent or usual occurrence. Custom arises out of long established practices which by common usage have attained the force of law in the military or other community affected by them. No custom may be contrary to existing law or regulation. A custom which has not been adopted by existing statute or regulation ceases to exist when its observance has been generally abandoned. Many customs of the service are now set forth in regulations of the various armed forces. Violations of these customs should be charged under Article 92 as violations of the regulations in which they appear if the regulation is punitive. *See* paragraph 16c.

(3) *Conduct of a nature to bring discredit upon the armed forces (clause 2).* "Discredit" means to injure the reputation of. This clause of Article 134 makes punishable conduct which has a tendency to bring the service into disrepute or which tends to lower it in public esteem. Acts in violation of a local civil law or a foreign law may be punished if they are of a nature to bring discredit upon the armed forces. However, *see* R.C.M. 203 concerning subject-matter jurisdiction.

(4) *Crimes and offenses not capital (clause 3).*

(a) *In general.* State and foreign laws are not included within the crimes and offenses not capital referred to in this clause of Article 134 and violations thereof may not be prosecuted as such except when State law becomes Federal law of local application under section 13 of title 18 of the United States Code (Federal Assimilative Crimes Act— *see* subparagraph (4)(c) below). For the purpose of court-martial jurisdiction, the laws which may be applied under clause 3 of Article 134 are divided into two groups: crimes and offenses of unlimited application (crimes which are punishable regardless where they may be committed), and crimes and offenses of local application (crimes which are punishable only if committed in areas of federal jurisdiction).

(b) *Crimes and offenses of unlimited application.* Certain noncapital crimes and offenses prohibited by the United States Code are made applicable under clause 3 of Article 134 to all persons subject to the code regardless where the wrongful act or omission occurred. Examples include: counterfeiting (18 U.S.C. § 471), and various frauds against the Government not covered by Article 132.

(c) *Crimes and offenses of local application.*

(i) *In general.* A person subject to the code may not be punished under clause 3 of Article 134 for an offense that occurred in a place where the law in question did not apply. For example, a person may not be punished under clause 3 of Article 134 when the act occurred in a foreign country merely because that act would have been an offense under the United States Code had the act occurred in the United States. Regardless where committed, such an act might be punishable under clauses 1 or 2 of Article 134. There are two types of congressional enactments of local application: specific federal statutes (defining particular crimes), and a general federal statute, the Federal Assimilative Crimes Act (which adopts certain state criminal laws).

(ii) *Federal Assimilative Crimes Act (18 U.S.C. § 13).* The Federal Assimilative Crimes Act is an adoption by Congress of state criminal laws for areas of exclusive or concurrent federal jurisdiction, provided federal criminal law, including the UCMJ, has not defined an applicable offense for the misconduct committed. The Act applies to state laws validly existing at the time of the offense without regard to when these laws were enacted, whether before or after passage of the Act, and whether before or after the acquisition of the land where the offense was committed. For example, if a person committed an act on a military installation in the United States at a certain location over which the United States had either exclusive or concurrent jurisdiction, and it was not an offense specifically defined by federal law (including the UCMJ), that person could be punished for that act by a court-martial if it was a violation of a noncapital offense under the law of the State where the military installation was located. This is possible because the Act adopts the criminal law of the state wherein the military installation is located and applies it as though it were federal law. The text of the Act is as follows: Whoever within or upon any of the places now existing or hereafter reserved or acquired as provided in section 7 of this title, is guilty of any act or omission which, although not made punishable by any enactment of Congress, would be punishable if committed or omitted within the jurisdiction of the State, Territory, Possession, or District in which such place is situated, by the laws thereof in force at the time of such act or omission, shall be guilty of a like offense and subject to a like punishment.

(5) *Limitations on Article 134.*

(a) *Preemption doctrine.* The preemption doctrine prohibits application of Article 134 to conduct covered by Articles 80 through 132. For example, larceny is covered in Article 121, and if an element of that offense is lacking—for example, intent—there can be no larceny or larceny-type offense, either under Article 121 or, because of preemption, under Article 134. Article 134 cannot be used to create a new kind of larceny offense, one without the required intent, where Congress has already set the minimum requirements for such an offense in Article 121.

(b) *Capital offense.* A capital offense may not be tried under Article 134.

(6) *Drafting specifications for Article 134 offenses.*

(a) *In general.* A specification alleging a violation of Article 134 need not expressly allege that the conduct was "a disorder or neglect," that it was "of a nature to bring discredit upon the armed forces," or that it constituted "a crime or offense not capital." The same conduct may constitute a disorder or neglect to the prejudice of good order and discipline in the armed forces and at the same time be of a nature to bring discredit upon the armed forces.

(b) *Specifications under clause 3.* When alleging a clause 3 violation, each element of the federal or assimilated statute must be alleged expressly or by necessary implication. In addition, the federal or assimilated statute should be identified.

(c) *Specifications for clause 1 or 2 offenses not listed.* If conduct by an accused does not fall under any of the listed offenses for violations of Article 134 in this Manual (paragraphs 61 through 113 of this Part) a specification not listed in this Manual may be used to allege the offense.

61. Article 134—(Abusing public animal)

a. *Text of statute. See* paragraph 60.

b. *Elements.*

(1) That the accused wrongfully abused a certain public animal; and

(2) That, under the circumstances, the conduct of the accused was to the prejudice of good order and discipline in the armed forces or was of a nature to bring discredit upon the armed forces.

c. *Explanation.* A public animal is any animal owned or used by the United States; and animal owned or used by a local or State government in the United States, its territories or possessions; or any wild animal located on any public lands in the United States, its territories or possessions. This would include, for example, drug detector dogs used by the government.

d. *Lesser included offenses.* Article 80—attempts

e. *Maximum punishment.* Confinement for 3 months and forfeiture of two-thirds pay per month for 3 months.

f. *Sample specification.*

In that __________ (personal jurisdiction data), did (at/on board—location) (subject-matter jurisdiction data, if required), on or about __________ 20____, wrongfully (kick a public drug detector dog in the nose) (__________).

62. Article 134—(Adultery)

a. *Text of statute. See* paragraph 60.

b. *Elements.*

(1) That the accused wrongfully had sexual intercourse with a certain person;

(2) That, at the time, the accused or the other person was married to someone else; and

(3) That, under the circumstances, the conduct of the accused was to the prejudice of good order and discipline in the armed forces or was of a nature to bring discredit upon the armed forces.

c. *Explanation.*

(1) *Nature of offense.* Adultery is clearly unacceptable conduct, and it reflects adversely on the service record of the military member.

(2) *Conduct prejudicial to good order and discipline or of a nature to bring discredit upon the armed forces.* To constitute an offense under the UCMJ, the adulterous conduct must either be directly prejudicial to good order and discipline or service discrediting. Adulterous conduct that is directly prejudicial includes conduct that has an obvious, and measurably divisive effect on unit or organization discipline, morale, or cohesion, or is clearly detrimental to the authority or stature of or respect toward a servicemember. Adultery may also be service discrediting, even though the conduct is only indirectly or remotely prejudicial to good order and discipline. Discredit means to injure the reputation of the armed forces and includes adulterous conduct that has a tendency, because of its open or notorious nature, to bring the service into disrepute, make it subject to public ridicule, or lower it in public esteem. While adulterous conduct that is private and discreet in nature may not be service discrediting by this standard, under the circumstances, it may be determined to be conduct prejudicial to good order and discipline. Commanders should consider all relevant circumstances, including but not limited to the following factors, when determining whether adulterous acts are prejudicial to good order and discipline or are of a nature to bring discredit upon the armed forces:

(a) The accused's marital status, military rank, grade, or position;

(b) The co-actor's marital status, military rank, grade, and position, or relationship to the armed forces;

(c) The military status of the accused's spouse or the spouse of co-actor, or their relationship to the armed forces;

(d) The impact, if any, of the adulterous relationship on the ability of the accused, the co-actor, or the spouse of either to perform their duties in support of the armed forces;

(e) The misuse, if any, of government time and resources to facilitate the commission of the conduct;

(f) Whether the conduct persisted despite counseling or orders to desist; the flagrancy of the conduct, such as whether any notoriety ensued; and whether the adulterous act was accompanied by other violations of the UCMJ;

(g) The negative impact of the conduct on the units or organizations of the accused, the co-actor or the spouse of either of them, such as a detrimental effect on unit or organization morale, teamwork, and efficiency;

(h) Whether the accused or co-actor was legally separated; and

(i) Whether the adulterous misconduct involves an ongoing or recent relationship or is remote in time.

(3) *Marriage.* A marriage exists until it is dissolved in accordance with the laws of a competent state or foreign jurisdiction.

(4) *Mistake of fact.* A defense of mistake of fact exists if the accused had an honest and reasonable belief either that the accused and the co-actor were both unmarried, or that they were lawfully married to each other. If this defense is raised by the evidence, then the burden of proof is upon the United States to establish that the accused's belief was unreasonable or not honest.

d. *Lesser included offense.* Article 80—attempts

e. *Maximum punishment.* Dishonorable discharge, forfeiture of all pay and allowances, and confinement for 1 year.

f. *Sample specification.*

In that ______ (personal jurisdiction data), (a married man/a married woman), did, (at/on board—location) (subject-matter jurisdiction data, if required), on or about ____ 20 ____, wrongfully have sexual intercourse with ____, a (married) (woman/man) not (his wife) (her husband).

63. Deleted – see Appendix 27.

64. Article 134—(Assault—with intent to commit murder, voluntary manslaughter, rape, robbery, sodomy, arson, burglary, or housebreaking)

a. *Text of statute. See* paragraph 60.

b. *Elements.*

(1) That the accused assaulted a certain person;

(2) That, at the time of the assault, the accused intended to kill (as required for murder or voluntary manslaughter) or intended to commit rape, robbery, sodomy, arson, burglary, or housebreaking; and

(3) That, under the circumstances, the conduct of the accused was to the prejudice of good order and discipline in the armed forces or was of a nature to bring discredit upon the armed forces.

c. *Explanation.*

(1) *In general.* An assault with intent to commit any of the offenses mentioned above is not necessarily the equivalent of an attempt to commit the intended offense, for an assault can be committed with intent to commit an offense without achieving that proximity to consummation of an intended offense which is essential to an attempt. *See* paragraph 4.

(2) *Assault with intent to murder.* Assault with intent to commit murder is assault with specific intent to kill. Actual infliction of injury is not necessary. To constitute an assault with intent to murder with a firearm, it is not necessary that the weapon be discharged. When the intent to kill exists, the fact that for some unknown reason the actual consummation of the murder by the means employed is impossible is not a defense if the means are apparently adapted to the end in view. The intent to kill need not be directed against the person assaulted if the assault is committed with intent to kill some person. For example, if a person, intending to kill Jones, shoots Smith, mistaking Smith for Jones, that person is guilty of assaulting Smith with intent to murder. If a person fires into a group with intent to kill anyone in the group, that person is guilty of and assault with intent to murder each member of the group.

(3) *Assault with intent to commit voluntary manslaughter.* Assault with intent to commit voluntary manslaughter is an assault committed with a specific intent to kill under such circumstances that, if death resulted therefrom, the offense of voluntary manslaughter would have been committed. There can be no assault with intent to commit involuntary manslaughter, for it is not a crime capable of being intentionally committed.

(4) *Assault with intent to commit rape.* In assault with intent to commit rape, the accused must have intended to complete the offense. Any lesser intent will not suffice. No actual touching is necessary, but indecent advances and importunities, however earnest, not accompanied by such an intent, do not constitute this offense, nor do mere preparations to rape not amounting to an assault. Once an assault with intent to commit rape is made, it is no defense that the accused voluntarily desisted.

(5) *Assault with intent to rob.* For assault with intent to rob, the fact that the accused intended to take money and that the person the accused intended to rob had none is not a defense.

(6) *Assault with intent to commit sodomy.* Assault with intent to commit sodomy is an assault against a human being and must be committed with a specific

intent to commit sodomy. Any lesser intent, or different intent, will not suffice.

d. *Lesser included offenses.*

(1) *Assault with intent to murder.*

(a) Article 128—assault; assault consummated by a battery; assault with a dangerous weapon; assault intentionally inflicting grievous bodily harm

(b) Article 134—assault with intent to commit voluntary manslaughter; willful or careless discharge of a firearm

(2) *Assault with intent to commit voluntary manslaughter.*

(a) Article 128—assault; assault consummated by a battery; assault with a dangerous weapon; assault intentionally inflicting grievous bodily harm

(b) Article 134—willful or careless discharge of a firearm

(3) *Assault with intent to commit rape or sodomy.* Article 128—assault; assault consummated by a battery; assault with a dangerous weapon

(4) *Assault with intent to commit burglary.*

(a) Article 128—assault; assault consummated by a battery; assault with a dangerous weapon

(b) Article 134—assault with intent to commit housebreaking

(5) *Assault with intent to commit robbery, arson, or housebreaking.* Article 128—assault; assault consummated by a battery; assault with a dangerous weapon

e. *Maximum punishment.*

(1) *Assault with intent to commit murder or rape.* Dishonorable discharge, forfeiture of all pay and allowances, and confinement for 20 years.

(2) *Assault with intent to commit voluntary manslaughter, robbery, sodomy, arson, or burglary.* Dishonorable discharge, forfeiture of all pay and allowances, and confinement for 10 years.

(3) *Assault with intent to commit housebreaking.* Dishonorable discharge, forfeiture of all pay and allowances, and confinement for 5 years.

f. *Sample specification.*

In that ______ (personal jurisdiction data), did, (at/on board—location) (subject-matter jurisdiction data, if required), on or about ______ 20 ___, with intent to commit (murder) (voluntary manslaughter) (rape) (robbery) (sodomy) (arson) (burglary) (housebreaking), commit an assault upon ______ by ______.

65. Article 134—(Bigamy)

a. *Text of statute. See* paragraph 60.

b. *Elements.*

(1) That the accused had a living lawful spouse;

(2) That while having such spouse the accused wrongfully married another person; and

(3) That, under the circumstances, the conduct of the accused was to the prejudice of good order and discipline in the armed forces or was of a nature to bring discredit upon the armed forces.

c. *Explanation.* Bigamy is contracting another marriage by one who already has a living lawful spouse. If a prior marriage was void, it will have created no status of "lawful spouse." However, if it was only voidable and has not been voided by a competent court, this is no defense. A belief that a prior marriage has been terminated by divorce, death of the other spouse, or otherwise, constitutes a defense only if the belief was reasonable. *See* R.C.M. 916(j)(1).

d. *Lesser included offense.* Article 80—attempts

e. *Maximum punishment.* Dishonorable discharge, forfeiture of all pay and allowances, and confinement for 2 years.

f. *Sample specification.*

In that ______ (personal jurisdiction data), did, at ______, (subject-matter jurisdiction data, if required), on or about ______ 20 ___, wrongfully marry ______, having at the time of his/her said marriage to ______ a lawful wife/husband then living, to wit: ______.

66. Article 134—(Bribery and graft)

a. *Text of statute. See* paragraph 60.

b. *Elements.*

(1) *Asking, accepting, or receiving.*

(a) That the accused wrongfully asked, accepted, or received a thing of value from a certain person or organization;

(b) That the accused then occupied a certain official position or had certain official duties;

(c) That the accused asked, accepted, or received this thing of value (with the intent to have the accused's decision or action influenced with respect to a certain matter)* (as compensation for or in recognition of services rendered, to be rendered, or both, by the accused in relation to a certain matter)**;

(d) That this certain matter was an official matter in which the United States was and is interested; and

(e) That, under the circumstances, the conduct of the accused was to the prejudice of good order and discipline in the armed forces or was of a nature to bring discredit upon the armed forces.

(*Note: This element is required for bribery.)

(**Note: This element is required for graft.)

(2) *Promising, offering, or giving.*

(a) That the accused wrongfully promised, offered, or gave a thing of value to a certain person;

(b) That this person then occupied a certain official position or had certain official duties;

(c) That this thing of value was promised, offered, or given (with the intent to influence the decision or action of this person)* (as compensation for or in recognition of services rendered, to be rendered, or both, by this person in relation to a certain matter)**;

(d) That this matter was an official matter in which the United States was and is interested; and

(e) That, under the circumstances, the conduct of the accused was to the prejudice of good order and discipline in the armed forces or was of a nature to bring discredit upon the armed forces.

(*Note: This element is required for bribery.)

(**Note: This element is required for graft.)

c. *Explanation.* Bribery requires an intent to influence or be influenced in an official matter; graft does not. Graft involves compensation for services performed in an official matter when no compensation is due.

d. *Lesser included offenses.*

(1) *Bribery.* Article 134—graft

(2) *Bribery and graft.* Article 80—attempts

e. *Maximum punishment.*

(1) *Bribery.* Dishonorable discharge, forfeiture of all pay and allowances, and confinement for 5 years.

(2) *Graft.* Dishonorable discharge, forfeiture of all pay and allowances, and confinement for 3 years.

f. *Sample specifications.*

(1) *Asking, accepting, or receiving.*

In that ______ (personal jurisdiction data), being at the time (a contracting officer for ______) (the personnel officer of ______) (______), did, (at/on board—location) (subject-matter jurisdiction data, if required), on or about ______ 20 ______, wrongfully (ask) (accept) (receive) from ______, (a contracting company) engaged in ______ (______), (the sum of $______) (______, of a value of (about) $______) (______), (with intent to have his/her (decision) (action) influenced with respect to*) ((as compensation for) (in recognition of)) service (rendered) (to be rendered) (rendered and to be rendered) by him/her the said ______ in relation to**) an official matter in which the United States was and is interested, to wit: (the purchasing of military supplies from ______) (the transfer of ______ to duty with (______) (______).

(*Note: This language should be used to allege bribery.) (**Note: This language should be used to allege graft.)

(2) *Promising, offering, or giving.*

In that ______ (personal jurisdiction data), did (at/on board—location) (subject-matter jurisdiction data, if required), on or about ______ 20 ______, wrongfully (promise) (offer) (give) to ______, (his/her commanding officer) (the claims officer of ______) (______), (the sum of $______) (______, of a value of (about $______) (______, (with intent to influence the (decision) (action) of the said ______ with respect to*) ((as compensation for) (in recognition of)) services (rendered) (to be rendered) (rendered and to be rendered) by the said ______ in relation to**) an official matter in which the United States was and is interested, to wit: (the granting of leave to ______) (the processing of a claim against the United States in favor of ______) (______).

(*Note: This language should be used to allege bribery.) (**Note: This language should be used to allege graft.)

67. Article 134—(Burning with intent to defraud)

a. *Text of statute. See* paragraph 60.

b. *Elements.*

(1) That the accused willfully and maliciously burned or set fire to certain property owned by a certain person or organization;

(2) That such burning or setting on fire was with

the intent to defraud a certain person or organization; and

(3) That, under the circumstances, the conduct of the accused was to the prejudice of good order and discipline in the armed forces or was of a nature to bring discredit upon the armed forces.

c. *Explanation. See* paragraph 49c(14) for a discussion of "intent to defraud."

d. *Lesser included offense.* Article 80—attempts

e. *Maximum punishment.* Dishonorable discharge, forfeiture of all pay and allowances, and confinement for 10 years.

f. *Sample specification.*
In that ________ (personal jurisdiction data), did, (at/on board—location) (subject-matter jurisdiction data, if required), on or about ________ 20___, willfully and maliciously (burn) (set fire to) (a dwelling) (a barn) (an automobile), the property of ____________, with intent to defraud (the insurer thereof, to wit: ________) (________).

68. Article 134—(Check, worthless, making and uttering—by dishonorably failing to maintain funds)

a. *Text of statute. See* paragraph 60.

b. *Elements.*

(1) That the accused made and uttered a certain check;

(2) That the check was made and uttered for the purchase of a certain thing, in payment of a debt, or for a certain purpose;

(3) That the accused subsequently failed to place or maintain sufficient funds in or credit with the drawee bank for payment of the check in full upon its presentment for payment;

(4) That this failure was dishonorable; and

(5) That, under the circumstances, the conduct of the accused was to the prejudice of good order and discipline in the armed forces or was of a nature to bring discredit upon the armed forces.

c. *Explanation.* This offense differs from an Article 123a offense (paragraph 49) in that there need be no intent to defraud or deceive at the time of making, drawing, uttering, or delivery, and that the accused need not know at that time that the accused did not or would not have sufficient funds for payment. The gist of the offense lies in the conduct of the accused after uttering the instrument. Mere negligence in maintaining one's bank balance is insufficient for this offense, for the accused's conduct must reflect bad faith or gross indifference in this regard. As in the offense of dishonorable failure to pay debts (*see* paragraph 71), dishonorable conduct of the accused is necessary, and the other principles discussed in paragraph 71 also apply here.

d. *Lesser included offenses.* None.

e. *Maximum punishment.* Bad-conduct discharge, forfeiture of all pay and allowances, and confinement for 6 months.

f. *Sample specification.*
In that ________ (personal jurisdiction data), did, (at/on board—location) (subject-matter jurisdiction data, if required), on or about ________ 20___, make and utter to ________ a certain check, in words and figures as follows, to wit: ________, (for the purchase of ____________) (in payment of a debt) (for the purpose of ________), and did thereafter dishonorably fail to (place) (maintain) sufficient funds in the ________ Bank for payment of such check in full upon its presentment for payment.

68a. Article 134—(Child endangerment)

a. *Text of statute.* See paragraph 60.

b. *Elements.*

(1) That the accused had a duty for the care of a certain child;

(2) That the child was under the age of 16 years;

(3) That the accused endangered the child's mental or physical health, safety, or welfare through design or culpable negligence; and

(4) That, under the circumstances, the conduct of the accused was to the prejudice of good order and discipline in the armed forces or was of a nature to bring discredit upon the armed forces.

c. *Explanation.*

(1) *In general.* This offense is intended to prohibit and therefore deter child endangerment through design or culpable negligence.

(2) *Design.* Design means on purpose, intentionally, or according to plan and requires specific intent to endanger the child.

(3) *Culpable negligence.* Culpable negligence is a degree of carelessness greater than simple negligence. It is a negligent act or omission accompanied

by a culpable disregard for the foreseeable consequences to others of that act or omission. In the context of this offense, culpable negligence may include acts that, when viewed in the light of human experience, might foreseeably result in harm to a child, even though such harm would not necessarily be the natural and probable consequences of such acts. In this regard, the age and maturity of the child, the conditions surrounding the neglectful conduct, the proximity of assistance available, the nature of the environment in which the child may have been left, the provisions made for care of the child, and the location of the parent or adult responsible for the child relative to the location of the child, among others, may be considered in determining whether the conduct constituted culpable negligence.

(4) *Harm.* Actual physical or mental harm to the child is not required. The offense requires that the accused's actions reasonably could have caused physical or mental harm or suffering. However, if the accused's conduct does cause actual physical or mental harm, the potential maximum punishment increases. See Paragraph 54(c)(4)(a)(iii) for an explanation of "grievous bodily harm".

(5) *Endanger.* "Endanger" means to subject one to a reasonable probability of harm.

(6) *Age of victim as a factor.* While this offense may be committed against any child under 16, the age of the victim is a factor in the culpable negligence determination. Leaving a teenager alone for an evening may not be culpable (or even simple) negligence; leaving an infant or toddler for the same period might constitute culpable negligence. On the other hand, leaving a teenager without supervision for an extended period while the accused was on temporary duty outside commuting distance might constitute culpable negligence.

(7) *Duty required.* The duty of care is determined by the totality of the circumstances and may be established by statute, regulation, legal parent-child relationship, mutual agreement, or assumption of control or custody by affirmative act. When there is no duty of care of a child, there is no offense under this paragraph. Thus, there is no offense when a stranger makes no effort to feed a starving child or an individual/neighbor not charged with the care of a child does not prevent the child from running and playing in the street.

d. *Lesser included offenses.*

(1) *Child Endangerment by Design.* Article 134-Child endangerment by culpable negligence

(2) *Article 80—Attempts*

e. *Maximum punishment.*

(1) *Endangerment by design resulting in grievous bodily harm.* Dishonorable discharge, forfeiture of all pay and allowances, and confinement for 8 years.

(2) *Endangerment by design resulting in harm.* Dishonorable discharge, forfeiture of all pay and allowances, and confinement for 5 years.

(3) *Other cases by design.* Dishonorable discharge, forfeiture of all pay and allowances and confinement for 4 years.

(4) *Endangerment by culpable negligence resulting in grievous bodily harm.* Dishonorable discharge, forfeiture of all pay and allowances, and confinement for 3 years.

(5) *Endangerment by culpable negligence resulting in harm.* Bad-conduct discharge, forfeiture of all pay and allowances, and confinement for 2 years.

(6) *Other cases by culpable negligence.* Bad-conduct discharge, forfeiture of all pay and allowances, and confinement for 1 year.

f. *Sample specification.*

(1) *Resulting in grievous bodily harm.* In that ____ (personal jurisdiction data),(at/on board-location) (subject matter jurisdiction data, if required) on or about ____, 20 ____, had a duty for the care of ____, a child under the age of 16 years and did endanger the (mental health) (physical health)(safety)(welfare) of said ____, by (leaving the said ____ unattended in his quarters for over ____ hours/days with no adult present in the home) (by failing to obtain medical care for the said ____'s diabetic condition) (____), and that such conduct (was by design)(constituted culpable negligence)(which resulted in grievous bodily harm, to wit:) (broken leg)(deep cut)(fractured skull)(____).

(2) *Resulting in harm.* In that ____ (personal jurisdiction data),(at/on board-location) (subject matter jurisdiction data, if required) on or about ____, 20 ____, had a duty for the care of ____, a child under the age of 16 years, and did endanger the (mental health) (physical health)(safety)(welfare) of said ____, by (leaving the said ____ unattended in his quarters for over ____ hours/days with no adult present in the home) (by failing to obtain medical care for the said ____'s diabetic condition) (____), and that such conduct (was by design)(constituted

culpable negligence) (which resulted in (harm, to wit:) (a black eye)(bloody nose)(minor cut)(____).

(3) *Other cases.* In that ____ (personal jurisdiction data),(at/on board-location) (subject matter jurisdiction data, if required) on or about ____, 20 ____, was responsible for the care of ____, a child under the age of 16 years, and did endanger the (mental health) (physical health)(safety)(welfare) of said ____, by (leaving the said ____ unattended in his quarters for over ____ hours/days with no adult present in the home) (by failing to obtain medical care for the said ____'s diabetic condition) (____), and that such conduct (was by design)(constituted culpable negligence).

69. Article 134—(Cohabitation, wrongful)

a. *Text of statute. See* paragraph 60.

b. *Elements.*

(1) That, during a certain period of time, the accused and another person openly and publicly lived together as husband and wife, holding themselves out as such;

(2) That the other person was not the spouse of the accused;

(3) That, under the circumstances, the conduct of the accused was to the prejudice of good order and discipline in the armed forces or was of a nature to bring discredit upon the armed forces.

c. *Explanation.* This offense differs from adultery (*see* paragraph 62) in that it is not necessary to prove that one of the partners was married or that sexual intercourse took place. Public knowledge of the wrongfulness of the relationship is not required, but the partners must behave in a manner, as exhibited by conduct or language, that leads others to believe that a martial relationship exists.

d. *Lesser included offense.* Article 80—attempts

e. *Maximum punishment.* Confinement for 4 months and forfeiture of two-thirds pay per month for 4 months.

f. *Sample specification.*

In that ____ (personal jurisdiction data), did, (at/on board—location) (subject-matter jurisdiction data, if required), from about ____ 20 ____, to about 20 ____, wrongfully cohabit with ____, (a woman not his wife) (a man not her husband).

70. Article 134—(Correctional custody—offenses against)

a. *Text of statute. See* paragraph 60.

b. *Elements.*

(1) *Escape from correctional custody.*

(a) That the accused was placed in correctional custody by a person authorized to do so;

(b) That, while in such correctional custody, the accused was under physical restraint;

(c) That the accused freed himself or herself from the physical restraint of this correctional custody before being released therefrom by proper authority; and

(d) That, under the circumstances, the conduct of the accused was to the prejudice of good order and discipline in the armed forces or was of a nature to bring discredit upon the armed forces.

(2) *Breach of correctional custody.*

(a) That the accused was placed in correctional custody by a person authorized to do so;

(b) That, while in correctional custody, a certain restraint was imposed upon the accused;

(c) That the accused went beyond the limits of the restraint imposed before having been released from the correctional custody or relieved of the restraint by proper authority; and

(d) That, under the circumstances, the conduct of the accused was to the prejudice of good order and discipline in the armed forces or was of a nature to bring discredit upon the armed forces.

c. *Explanation.*

(1) *Escape from correctional custody.* Escape from correctional custody is the act of a person undergoing the punishment of correctional custody pursuant to Article 15, who, before being set at liberty by proper authority, casts off any physical restraint imposed by the custodian or by the place or conditions of custody.

(2) *Breach of correctional custody.* Breach of restraint during correctional custody is the act of a person undergoing the punishment who, in the absence of physical restraint imposed by a custodian or by the place or conditions of custody, breaches any form of restraint imposed during this period.

(3) *Authority to impose correctional custody. See* Part V concerning who may impose correctional custody. Whether the status of a person authorized that person to impose correctional custody is a ques-

tion of law to be decided by the military judge. Whether the person who imposed correctional custody had such a status is a question of fact to be decided by the factfinder.

d. *Lesser included offense.* Article 80—attempts

e. *Maximum punishment.*

(1) *Escape from correctional custody.* Dishonorable discharge, forfeiture of all pay and allowances, and confinement for 1 year.

(2) *Breach of correctional custody.* Bad-conduct discharge, forfeiture of all pay and allowances, and confinement for 6 months.

f. *Sample specifications.*

(1) *Escape from correctional custody.*

In that ________ (personal jurisdiction data), while undergoing the punishment of correctional custody imposed by a person authorized to do so, did, (at/on board—location), on or about ________ 20 ____, escape from correctional custody.

(2) *Breach of correctional custody.*

In that ________ (personal jurisdiction data), while duly undergoing the punishment of correctional custody imposed by a person authorized to do so, did, (at/on board—location), on or about ________ 20 ____, breach the restraint imposed thereunder by ________.

71. Article 134—(Debt, dishonorably failing to pay)

a. *Text of statute. See* paragraph 60.

b. *Elements.*

(1) That the accused was indebted to a certain person or entity in a certain sum;

(2) That this debt became due and payable on or about a certain date;

(3) That while the debt was still due and payable the accused dishonorably failed to pay this debt; and

(4) That, under the circumstances, the conduct of the accused was to the prejudice of good order and discipline in the armed forces or was of a nature to bring discredit upon the armed forces.

c. *Explanation.* More than negligence in nonpayment is necessary. The failure to pay must be characterized by deceit, evasion, false promises, or other distinctly culpable circumstances indicating a deliberate nonpayment or grossly indifferent attitude toward one's just obligations. For a debt to form the basis of this offense, the accused must not have had a defense, or an equivalent offset or counterclaim, either in fact or according to the accused's belief, at the time alleged. The offense should not be charged if there was a genuine dispute between the parties as to the facts or law relating to the debt which would affect the obligation of the accused to pay. The offense is not committed if the creditor or creditors involved are satisfied with the conduct of the debtor with respect to payment. The length of the period of nonpayment and any denial of indebtedness which the accused may have made may tend to prove that the accused's conduct was dishonorable, but the court-martial may convict only if it finds from all of the evidence that the conduct was in fact dishonorable.

d. *Lesser included offenses.* None.

e. *Maximum punishment.* Bad-conduct discharge, forfeiture of all pay and allowances, and confinement for 6 months.

f. *Sample specification.*

In that ________ (personal jurisdiction data), being indebted to ________ in the sum of $________ for ________, which amount became due and payable (on) (about) (on or about) ________ 20 ____, did (at/on board—location)(subject-matter jurisdiction data, if required), from ________ 20 ____, to ________ 20 ____, dishonorably fail to pay said debt.

72. Article 134—(Disloyal statements)

a. *Text of statute. See* paragraph 60.

b. *Elements.*

(1) That the accused made a certain statement;

(2) That the statement was communicated to another person;

(3) That the statement was disloyal to the United States;

(4) That the statement was made with the intent to promote disloyalty or disaffection toward the United States by any member of the armed forces or to interfere with or impair the loyalty to the United States or good order and discipline of any member of the armed forces; and

(5) That, under the circumstances, the conduct of the accused was to the prejudice of good order and

discipline in the armed forces or was of a nature to bring discredit upon the armed forces.

c. *Explanation.* Certain disloyal statements by military personnel may not constitute an offense under 18 U.S.C. §§ 2385, 2387, and 2388, but may, under the circumstances, be punishable under this article. Examples include praising the enemy, attacking the war aims of the United States, or denouncing our form of government with the intent to promote disloyalty or disaffection among members of the armed services. A declaration of personal belief can amount to a disloyal statement if it disavows allegiance owed to the United States by the declarant. The disloyalty involved for this offense must be to the United States as a political entity and not merely to a department or other agency that is a part of its administration.

d. *Lesser included offense.* Article 80—attempts

e. *Maximum punishment.* Dishonorable discharge, forfeiture of all pay and allowances, and confinement for 3 years.

f. *Sample specification.*

In that ______ (personal jurisdiction data), did, (at/on board—location), on or about ______ 20 ______, with intent to (promote (disloyalty) (disaffection) (disloyalty and disaffection)) ((interfere with) (impair) the (loyalty) (good order and discipline)) of any member of the armed forces of the United States communicate to ______, the following statement, to wit: "______," or words to that effect, which statement was disloyal to the United States.

73. Article 134—(Disorderly conduct, drunkenness)

a. *Text of statute. See* paragraph 60.

b. *Elements.*

(1) That the accused was drunk, disorderly, or drunk and disorderly on board ship or in some other place; and

(2) That, under the circumstances, the conduct of the accused was to the prejudice of good order and discipline in the armed forces or was of a nature to bring discredit upon the armed forces.

c. *Explanation.*

(1) *Drunkenness. See* paragraph 35c(6) for a discussion of intoxication.

(2) *Disorderly.* Disorderly conduct is conduct of such a nature as to affect the peace and quiet of persons who may witness it and who may be disturbed or provoked to resentment thereby. It includes conduct that endangers public morals or outrages public decency and any disturbance of a contentious or turbulent character.

(3) *Service discrediting.* Unlike most offenses under Article 134, "conduct of a nature to bring discredit upon the armed forces" must be included in the specification and proved in order to authorized the higher maximum punishment when the offense is service discrediting.

d. *Lesser included offense.* Article 80—attempts

e. *Maximum punishment.*

(1) *Disorderly conduct.*

(a) *Under such circumstances as to bring discredit upon the military service.* Confinement for 4 months and forfeiture of two-thirds pay per month for 4 months.

(b) *Other cases.* Confinement for 1 month and forfeiture of two-thirds pay per month for 1 month.

(2) *Drunkenness.*

(a) *Aboard ship or under such circumstances as to bring discredit upon the military service.* Confinement for 3 months and forfeiture of two-thirds pay per month for 3 months.

(b) *Other cases.* Confinement for 1 month and forfeiture of two-thirds pay per month for 1 month.

(3) *Drunk and disorderly.*

(a) *Aboard ship.* Bad-conduct discharge, forfeiture of all pay and allowances, and confinement for 6 months.

(b) *Under such circumstances as to bring discredit upon the military service.* Confinement for 6 months and forfeiture of two-thirds pay per month for 6 months.

(c) *Other cases.* Confinement for 3 months and forfeiture of two-thirds pay per month for 3 months.

f. *Sample specification.*

In that ______ (personal jurisdiction data), was, (at/on board—location) (subject-matter jurisdiction data, if required), on or about ______ 20 ______, (drunk) (disorderly) (drunk and disorderly) (which conduct was of a nature to bring discredit upon the armed forces).

74. Article 134—(Drinking liquor with prisoner)

a. *Text of statute. See* paragraph 60.

b. *Elements.*

(1) That the accused was a sentinel or in another assignment in charge of a prisoner;

(2) That, while in such capacity, the accused unlawfully drank intoxicating liquor with a prisoner;

(3) That the prisoner was under the charge of the accused;

(4) That the accused knew that the prisoner was a prisoner under the accused's charge; and

(5) That, under the circumstances, the conduct of the accused was to the prejudice of good order and discipline in the armed forces or was of a nature to bring discredit upon the armed forces.

c. *Explanation.*

(1) *Prisoner.* A "prisoner" is a person who is in confinement or custody imposed under R.C.M. 302, 304, or 305, or under sentence of a court-martial who has not been set free by proper authority.

(2) *Liquor.* For the purposes of this offense, "liquor" includes any alcoholic beverage.

d. *Lesser included offense.* Article 80—attempts

e. *Maximum punishment.* Confinement for 3 months and forfeiture of two-thirds pay per month for 3 months.

f. *Sample specification.*

In that ______ (personal jurisdiction data), a (sentinel) (______) in charge of prisoners, did, (at/on board—location), on or about 20____, unlawfully drink intoxicating liquor with ______, a prisoner under his/her charge.

75. Article 134—(Drunk prisoner)

a. *Text of statute. See* paragraph 60.

b. *Elements.*

(1) That the accused was a prisoner;

(2) That while in such status the accused was found drunk; and

(3) That, under the circumstances, the conduct of the accused was to the prejudice of good order and discipline in the armed forces or was of a nature to bring discredit upon the armed forces.

c. *Explanation.*

(1) *Prisoner. See* paragraph 74c(1).

(2) *Drunk. See* paragraph 35c(6) for a discussion of intoxication.

d. *Lesser included offenses.* None.

e. *Maximum punishment.* Confinement for 3 months and forfeiture of two-thirds pay per month for 3 months.

f. *Sample specification.*

In that ______ (personal jurisdiction data), a prisoner, was (at/on board— location), on or about ______ 20____, found drunk.

76. Article 134—(Drunkenness—incapacitation for performance of duties through prior wrongful indulgence in intoxicating liquor or any drug)

a. *Text of statute. See* paragraph 60.

b. *Elements.*

(1) That the accused had certain duties to perform;

(2) That the accused was incapacitated for the proper performance of such duties;

(3) That such incapacitation was the result of previous wrongful indulgence in intoxicating liquor or any drug; and

(4) That, under the circumstances, the conduct of the accused was to the prejudice of good order and discipline in the armed forces or was of a nature to bring discredit upon the armed forces.

c. *Explanation.*

(1) *Liquor. See* paragraph 74c(2).

(2) *Incapacitated.* Incapacitated means unfit or unable to perform properly. A person is "unfit" to perform duties if at the time the duties are to commence, the person is drunk, even though physically able to perform the duties. Illness resulting from previous overindulgence is an example of being "unable" to perform duties. For a discussion of "drunk" *see* paragraph 35*c*(6).

(3) *Affirmative defense.* The accused's lack of knowledge of the duties assigned is an affirmative defense to this offense.

d. *Lesser included offense.* Article 80—attempts

e. *Maximum punishment.* Confinement for 3 months and forfeiture of two-thirds pay per month for 3 months.

f. *Sample specification.*

In that ______ (personal jurisdiction data),

was, (at/on board—location), on or about 20 , as a result of wrongful previous overindulgence in intoxicating liquor or drugs incapacitated for the proper performance of his/her duties.

77. Article 134—(False or unauthorized pass offenses)

a. *Text of statute. See* paragraph 60.

b. *Elements.*

(1) *Wrongful making, altering, counterfeiting, or tampering with a military or official pass, permit, discharge certificate, or identification card.*

(a) That the accused wrongfully and falsely made, altered, counterfeited, or tampered with a certain military or official pass, permit, discharge certificate, or identification card; and

(b) That, under the circumstances, the conduct of the accused was to the prejudice of good order and discipline in the armed forces or was of a nature to bring discredit upon the armed forces.

(2) *Wrongful sale, gift, loan, or disposition of a military or official pass, permit, discharge certificate, or identification card.*

(a) That the accused wrongfully sold, gave, loaned, or disposed of a certain military or official pass, permit, discharge certificate, or identification card;

(b) That the pass, permit, discharge certificate, or identification card was false or unauthorized;

(c) That the accused then knew that the pass, permit, discharge certificate, or identification card was false or unauthorized; and

(d) That, under the circumstances, the conduct of the accused was to the prejudice of good order and discipline in the armed forces or was of a nature to bring discredit upon the armed forces.

(3) *Wrongful use or possession of a false or unauthorized military or official pass, permit, discharge certificate, or identification card.*

(a) That the accused wrongfully used or possessed a certain military or official pass, permit, discharge certificate, or identification card;

(b) That the pass, permit, discharge certificate, or identification card was false or unauthorized;

(c) That the accused then knew that the pass, permit, discharge certificate, or identification card was false or unauthorized; and

(d) That, under the circumstances, the conduct of the accused was to the prejudice of good order and discipline in the armed forces or was of a nature to bring discredit upon the armed forces.

[Note: When there is intent to defraud or deceive, add the following element after (c) above: That the accused used or possessed the pass, permit, discharge certificate, or identification card with an intent to defraud or deceive.]

c. *Explanation.*

(1) *In general.* "Military or official pass, permit, discharge certificate, or identification card" includes, as well as the more usual forms of these documents, all documents issued by any governmental agency for the purpose of identification and copies thereof.

(2) *Intent to defraud or deceive. See* paragraph 49c(14) and (15).

d. *Lesser included offenses.*

(1) *Wrongful use or possession of false or unauthorized military or official pass, permit, discharge certificate, or identification card, with the intent to defraud or deceive.* Article 134—same offenses, except without the intent to defraud or deceive.

(2) *All false or unauthorized pass offenses.* Article 80—attempts

e. *Maximum punishment.*

(1) *Possessing or using with intent to defraud or deceive, or making, altering, counterfeiting, tampering with, or selling.* Dishonorable discharge, forfeiture of all pay and allowances, and confinement for 3 years.

(2) *All other cases.* Bad-conduct discharge, forfeiture of all pay and allowances, and confinement for 6 months.

f. *Sample specifications.*

(1) *Wrongful making, altering, counterfeiting, or tampering with military or official pass, permit, discharge certificate, or identification card.* In that (personal jurisdiction data), did, (at/on board—location) (subject-matter jurisdiction data, if required), on or about 20 , wrongfully and falsely (make) (forge) (alter by) (counterfeit) (tamper with by) (a certain instrument purporting to be) (a) (an) (another's) (naval) (military) (official) (pass) (permit) (discharge certificate) (identification

card) (________) in words and figures as follows: ________.

(2) *Wrongful sale, gift, loan, or disposition of a military or official pass, permit, discharge certificate, or identification card.*

In that ________ (personal jurisdiction data), did, (at/on board—location) (subject-matter jurisdiction data, if required), on or about ________ 20 ____, wrongfully (sell to ________) (give to ________) (loan to ________) (dispose of by ________) (a certain instrument purporting to be) (a) (an) (another's) (naval) (military) (official) (pass) (permit)(discharge certificate) (identification card) (________) in words and figures as follows: ________, he/she, the said ________, then well knowing the same to be (false) (unauthorized).

(3) *Wrongful use or possession of a false or unauthorized military or official pass, permit, discharge certificate, or identification card.*

In that ________ (personal jurisdiction data), did (at/on board—location) (subject-matter jurisdiction data, if required), on or about ________ 20 ____, wrongfully (use) (possess) (with intent to (defraud) (deceive)) (a certain instrument purporting to be) (a) (an) (another's) (naval) (military) (official) (pass) (permit) (discharge certificate) (identification card) (________), he/she, the said ________, then well knowing the same to be (false) (unauthorized).

78. Article 134—(False pretenses, obtaining services under)

a. *Text of statute. See* paragraph 60.

b. *Elements.*

(1) That the accused wrongfully obtained certain services;

(2) That the obtaining was done by using false pretenses;

(3) That the accused then knew of the falsity of the pretenses;

(4) That the obtaining was with intent to defraud;

(5) That the services were of a certain value; and

(6) That, under the circumstances, the conduct of the accused was to the prejudice of good order and discipline in the armed forces or was of a nature to bring discredit upon the armed forces.

c. *Explanation.* This offense is similar to the offenses of larceny and wrongful appropriation by false pretenses, except that the object of the obtaining is services (for example, telephone service) rather than money, personal property, or articles of value of any kind as under Article 121. *See* paragraph 46c. *See* paragraph 49c(14) for a definition of "intent to defraud."

d. *Lesser included offense.* Article 80—attempts

e. *Maximum punishment.* Obtaining services under false pretenses.

(1) *Of a value of $500.00 or less.* Bad-conduct discharge, forfeiture of all pay and allowances, and confinement for 6 months.

(2) *Of a value of more than $500.00.* Dishonorable discharge, forfeiture of all pay and allowances, and confinement for 5 years.

f. *Sample specification.*

In that ________ (personal jurisdiction data), did, (at/on board—location) (subject-matter jurisdiction data, if required), on or about ________ 20 ____, with intent to defraud, falsely pretend to ________ that ________, then knowing that the pretenses were false, and by means thereof did wrongfully obtain from ________ services, of a value of (about) $ ________, to wit: ________.

79. Article 134—(False swearing)

a. *Text of statute. See* paragraph 60.

b. *Elements.*

(1) That the accused took an oath or equivalent;

(2) That the oath or equivalent was administered to the accused in a matter in which such oath or equivalent was required or authorized by law;

(3) That the oath or equivalent was administered by a person having authority to do so;

(4) That upon this oath or equivalent the accused made or subscribed a certain statement;

(5) That the statement was false;

(6) That the accused did not then believe the statement to be true; and

(7) That, under the circumstances, the conduct of the accused was to the prejudice of good order and discipline in the armed forces or was of a nature to bring discredit upon the armed forces.

c. *Explanation.*

(1) *Nature of offense.* False swearing is the mak-

ing under a lawful oath or equivalent of any false statement, oral or written, not believing the statement to be true. It does not include such statements made in a judicial proceeding or course of justice, as these are under Article 131, perjury (*see* paragraph 57). Unlike a false official statement under Article 107 (*see* paragraph 31) there is no requirement that the statement be made with an intent to deceive or that the statement be official. *See* paragraphs 57c(1), c(2)(*c*) and c(2) (*e*) concerning "judicial proceeding or course of justice," proof of the falsity, and the belief of the accused, respectively.

(2) *Oath. See* Article 136 and R.C.M. 807 as to the authority to administer oaths, and *see* Section IX of Part III (Military Rules of Evidence) concerning proof of the signatures of persons authorized to administer oaths. An oath includes an affirmation when authorized in lieu of an oath.

d. *Lesser included offense.* Article 80—attempts

e. *Maximum punishment.* Dishonorable discharge, forfeiture of all pay and allowances, and confinement for 3 years.

f. *Sample specification.*

In that ________ (personal jurisdiction data), did, (at/on board—location) (subject-matter jurisdiction data, if required), on or about ________ 20 ____, (in an affidavit) (in ________), wrongfully and unlawfully (make) (subscribe) under lawful (oath) (affirmation) a false statement in substance as follows: ________, which statement he/she did not then believe to be true.

80. Article 134—(Firearm, discharging—through negligence)

a. *Text of statute. See* paragraph 60.

b. *Elements.*

(1) That the accused discharged a firearm;

(2) That such discharge was caused by the negligence of the accused; and

(3) That, under the circumstances, the conduct of the accused was to the prejudice of good order and discipline in the armed forces or was of a nature to bring discredit upon the armed forces.

c. *Explanation.* For a discussion of negligence,*see* paragraph 85c(2).

d. *Lesser included offenses.* None

e. *Maximum punishment.* Confinement for 3 months and forfeiture of two-thirds pay per month for 3 months.

f. *Sample specification.*

In that ________ (personal jurisdiction data), did, (at/on board—location) (subject-matter jurisdiction data, if required), on or about ________ 20 ____, through negligence, discharge a (service rifle) (________) in the (squadron) (tent) (barracks) (________) of ________.

81. Article 134—(Firearm, discharging—willfully, under such circumstances as to endanger human life)

a. *Text of statute. See* paragraph 60.

b. *Elements.*

(1) That the accused discharged a firearm;

(2) That the discharge was willful and wrongful;

(3) That the discharge was under circumstances such as to endanger human life; and

(4) That, under the circumstances, the conduct of the accused was to the prejudice of good order and discipline in the armed forces or was of a nature to bring discredit upon the armed forces.

c. *Explanation.* "Under circumstances such as to endanger human life" refers to a reasonable potentiality for harm to human beings in general. The test is not whether the life was in fact endangered but whether, considering the circumstances surrounding the wrongful discharge of the weapon, the act was unsafe to human life in general.

d. *Lesser included offenses.*

(1) Article 134—firearm, discharging—through negligence

(2) Article 80—attempts

e. *Maximum punishment.* Dishonorable discharge, forfeiture of all pay and allowances, and confinement for 1 year.

f. *Sample specification.*

In that ________ (personal jurisdiction data), did, (at/on board—location) (subject-matter jurisdiction data, if required), on or about ________ 20 ____, wrongfully and willfully discharge a firearm, to wit: ________, (in the mess hall of ________) (________), under circumstances such as to endanger human life.

82. Article 134—(Fleeing scene of accident)

a. *Text of statute. See* paragraph 60.

b. *Elements.*

(1) *Driver.*

(a) That the accused was the driver of a vehicle;

(b) That while the accused was driving the vehicle was involved in an accident;

(c) That the accused knew that the vehicle had been in an accident;

(d) That the accused left the scene of the accident without (providing assistance to the victim who had been struck (and injured) by the said vehicle) or (providing identification);

(e) That such leaving was wrongful; and

(f) That, under the circumstances, the conduct of the accused was to the prejudice of good order and discipline in the armed forces or was of a nature to bring discredit upon the armed forces.

(2) *Senior passenger.*

(a) That the accused was a passenger in a vehicle which was involved in an accident;

(b) That the accused knew that said vehicle had been in an accident;

(c) That the accused was the superior commissioned or noncommissioned officer of the driver, or commander of the vehicle, and wrongfully and unlawfully ordered, caused, or permitted the driver to leave the scene of the accident without (providing assistance to the victim who had been struck (and injured) by the said vehicle) (or) (providing identification); and

(d) That, under the circumstances, the conduct of the accused was to the prejudice of good order and discipline in the armed forces or was of a nature to bring discredit upon the armed forces.

c. *Explanation.*

(1) *Nature of offense.* This offense covers "hit and run" situations where there is damage to property other than the driver's vehicle or injury to someone other than the driver or a passenger in the driver's vehicle. It also covers accidents caused by the accused, even if the accused's vehicle does not contact other people, vehicles, or property.

(2) *Knowledge.* Actual knowledge that an accident has occurred is an essential element of this offense. Actual knowledge may be proved by circumstantial evidence.

(3) *Passenger.* A passenger other than a senior passenger may also be liable under this paragraph. *See* paragraph 1 of this Part.

d. *Lesser included offense.* Article 80—attempts

e. *Maximum punishment.* Bad-conduct discharge, forfeiture of all pay and allowances, and confinement for 6 months.

f. *Sample specification.*

In that ________ (personal jurisdiction data), (the driver of) (a passenger in*) (the senior officer/noncommissioned officer in) (________ in) a vehicle at the time of an accident in which said vehicle was involved, and having knowledge of said accident, did, at ________ (-subject-matter jurisdiction data, if required), on or about ________ 20___ (wrongfully leave) (by ________, assist the driver of the said vehicle in wrongfully leaving*) (wrongfully order, cause, or permit the driver to leave) the scene of the accident without (providing assistance to ________, who had been struck (and injured) by the said vehicle) (making his/her (the driver's) identity known). [Note: This language should be used when the accused was a passenger and is charged as a principal. *See* paragraph 1 of this part.]

83. Article 134—(Fraternization)

a. *Text of statute. See* paragraph 60.

b. *Elements.*

(1) That the accused was a commissioned or warrant officer;

(2) That the accused fraternized on terms of military equality with one or more certain enlisted member(s) in a certain manner;

(3) That the accused then knew the person(s) to be (an) enlisted member(s);

(4) That such fraternization violated the custom of the accused's service that officers shall not fraternize with enlisted members on terms of military equality; and

(5) That, under the circumstances, the conduct of the accused was to the prejudice of good order and discipline in the armed forces or was of a nature to bring discredit upon the armed forces.

c. *Explanation.*

(1) *In general.* The gist of this offense is a viola-

tion of the custom of the armed forces against fraternization. Not all contact or association between officers and enlisted persons is an offense. Whether the contact or association in question is an offense depends on the surrounding circumstances. Factors to be considered include whether the conduct has compromised the chain of command, resulted in the appearance of partiality, or otherwise undermined good order, discipline, authority, or morale. The acts and circumstances must be such as to lead a reasonable person experienced in the problems of military leadership to conclude that the good order and discipline of the armed forces has been prejudiced by their tendency to compromise the respect of enlisted persons for the professionalism, integrity, and obligations of an officer.

(2) *Regulations.* Regulations, directives, and orders may also govern conduct between officer and enlisted personnel on both a service-wide and a local basis. Relationships between enlisted persons of different ranks, or between officers of different ranks may be similarly covered. Violations of such regulations, directives, or orders may be punishable under Article 92. *See* paragraph 16.

d. *Lesser included offense.* Article 80—attempts

e. *Maximum punishment.* Dismissal, forfeiture of all pay and allowances, and confinement for 2 years.

f. *Sample specification.*

In that ________ (personal jurisdiction data), did, (at/on board—location), on or about ________, 20 ___, knowingly fraternize with ________, an enlisted person, on terms of military equality, to wit: ____________, in violation of the custom of (the Naval Service of the United States) (the United States Army) (the United States Air Force) (the United States Coast Guard) that officers shall not fraternize with enlisted persons on terms of military equality.

84. Article 134—(Gambling with subordinate)

a. *Text of statute. See* paragraph 60.

b. *Elements.*

(1) That the accused gambled with a certain servicemember;

(2) That the accused was then a noncommissioned or petty officer;

(3) That the servicemember was not then a noncommissioned or petty officer and was subordinate to the accused;

(4) That the accused knew that the servicemember was not then a noncommissioned or petty officer and was subordinate to the accused; and

(5) That, under the circumstances, the conduct of the accused was to the prejudice of good order and discipline in the armed forces or was of a nature to bring discredit upon the armed forces.

c. *Explanation.* This offense can only be committed by a noncommissioned or petty officer gambling with an enlisted person of less than noncommissioned or petty officer rank. Gambling by an officer with an enlisted person may be a violation of Article 133. *See also* paragraph 83.

d. *Lesser included offense.* Article 80—attempts

e. *Maximum punishment.* Confinement for 3 months and forfeiture of two-thirds pay per month for 3 months.

f. *Sample specification.*

In that ____________ (personal jurisdiction data), did (at/on board—location) (subject-matter jurisdiction data, if required), on or about ________ 20 ___, gamble with ________, then knowing that the said ________ was not a noncommissioned or petty officer and was subordinate to the said ________.

85. Article 134—(Homicide, negligent)

a. *Text of statute. See* paragraph 60.

b. *Elements.*

(1) That a certain person is dead;

(2) That this death resulted from the act or failure to act of the accused;

(3) That the killing by the accused was unlawful;

(4) That the act or failure to act of the accused which caused the death amounted to simple negligence; and

(5) That, under the circumstances, the conduct of the accused was to the prejudice of good order and discipline in the armed forces or was of a nature to bring discredit upon the armed forces.

c. *Explanation.*

(1) *Nature of offense.* Negligent homicide is any unlawful homicide which is the result of simple negligence. An intent to kill or injure is not required.

(2) *Simple negligence.* Simple negligence is the

absence of due care, that is, an act or omission of a person who is under a duty to use due care which exhibits a lack of that degree of care of the safety of others which a reasonably careful person would have exercised under the same or similar circumstances. Simple negligence is a lesser degree of carelessness than culpable negligence. *See* paragraph 44c(2)(*a*).

d. *Lesser included offenses.* None

e. *Maximum punishment.* Dishonorable discharge, forfeiture of all pay and allowances, and confinement for 3 years.

f. *Sample specification.*

In that ____ (personal jurisdiction data), did, (at/on board—location) (subject-matter jurisdiction data, if required), on or about ____ 20 ____, unlawfully kill ____, (by negligently ____ the said ____ (in) (on) the ____ with a ____) (by driving a (motor vehicle) (____) against the said ____ in a negligent manner) (____).

86. Article 134—(Impersonating a commissioned, warrant, noncommissioned, or petty officer, or an agent or official)

a. *Text of statute. See* paragraph 60.

b. *Elements.*

(1) That the accused impersonated a commissioned, warrant, noncommissioned, or petty officer, or an agent of superior authority of one of the armed forces of the United States, or an official of a certain government, in a certain manner;

(2) That the impersonation was wrongful and willful; and

(3) That, under the circumstances, the conduct of the accused was to the prejudice of good order and discipline in the armed forces or was of a nature to bring discredit upon the armed forces.

[Note 1: If intent to defraud is in issue, add the following additional element after (2), above: That the accused did so with the intent to defraud a certain person or organization in a certain manner;].

[Note 2: If the accused is charged with impersonating an official of a certain government without an intent to defraud, use the following additional element after (2) above: That the accused committed one or more acts which exercised or asserted the authority of the office the accused claimed to have;].

c. *Explanation.*

(1) *Nature of offense.* Impersonation does not depend upon the accused deriving a benefit from the deception or upon some third party being misled, although this is an aggravating factor.

(2) *Willfulness.* "Willful" means with the knowledge that one is falsely holding one's self out as such.

(3) *Intent to defraud. See* paragraph 49c(14).

d. *Lesser included offense.* Article 80—attempts

e. *Maximum punishment.* Impersonating a commissioned, warrant, noncommissioned, or petty officer, or an agent or official.

(1) *With intent to defraud.* Dishonorable discharge, forfeiture of all pay and allowances, and confinement for 3 years.

(2) *All other cases.* Bad-conduct discharge, forfeiture of all pay and allowances, and confinement for 6 months.

f. *Sample specification.*

In that ____ (personal jurisdiction data), did, (at/on board—location) (subject-matter jurisdiction data, if required), on or about ____ 20 ____, wrongfully and willfully impersonate (a (commissioned officer) (warrant officer) (noncommissioned officer) (petty officer) (agent of superior authority) of the (Army) (Navy) (Marine Corps) (Air Force) (Coast Guard)) (an official of the Government of ____) by (publicly wearing the uniform and insignia of rank of a (lieutenant of the ____) (____)) (showing the credentials of ____) (____) (with intent to defraud ____ by ____*) (and (exercised) (asserted) the authority of ____ by ____**).

(**See* subsection b note 1.)

(***See* subsection b note 2.)

87. Deleted – see Appendix 27.

88. Deleted – see Appendix 27.

89. Article 134—(Indecent language)

a. *Text of statute. See* paragraph 60.

b. *Elements.*

(1) That the accused orally or in writing communicated to another person certain language;

(2) That such language was indecent; and

(3) That, under the circumstances, the conduct of the accused was to the prejudice of good order and

discipline in the armed forces or was of a nature to bring discredit upon the armed forces.

[Note: In appropriate cases add the following element after element (1): That the person to whom the language was communicated was a child under the age of 16.]

c. *Explanation.* "Indecent" language is that which is grossly offensive to modesty, decency, or propriety, or shocks the moral sense, because of its vulgar, filthy, or disgusting nature, or its tendency to incite lustful thought. Language is indecent if it tends reasonably to corrupt morals or incite libidinous thoughts. The language must violate community standards. *See* paragraph 45 if the communication was made in the physical presence of a child.

d. *Lesser included offenses.*

(1) Article 117—provoking speeches

(2) Article 80—attempts

e. *Maximum punishment.* Indecent or insulting language.

(1) *Communicated to any child under the age of 16 years.* Dishonorable discharge, forfeiture of all pay and allowances, and confinement for 2 years.

(2) *Other cases.* Bad-conduct discharge; forfeiture of all pay and allowances, and confinement for 6 months.

f. *Sample specification.*

In that _______ (personal jurisdiction data), did (at/on board—location) (subject-matter jurisdiction data, if required), on or about _______ 20 ____, (orally) (in writing) communicate to _______, (a child under the age of 16 years), certain indecent language, to wit: _______.

90. Deleted – see Appendix 27.

91. Article 134—(Jumping from vessel into the water)

a. *Text of statute. See* paragraph 60.

b. *Elements.*

(1) That the accused jumped from a vessel in use by the armed forces into the water;

(2) That such act by the accused was wrongful and intentional; and

(3) That, under the circumstances, the conduct of the accused was to the prejudice of good order and discipline in the armed forces or was of a nature to bring discredit upon the armed forces.

c. *Explanation.* "In use by" means any vessel operated by or under the control of the armed forces. This offense may be committed at sea, at anchor, or in port.

d. *Lesser included offense.* Article 80—attempts

e. *Maximum punishment.* Bad-conduct discharge, forfeiture of all pay and allowances, and confinement for 6 months.

f. *Sample specification.*

In that _______ (personal jurisdiction data), did, on board _______, at (location), on or about _______ 20 ____, wrongfully and intentionally jump from _______, a vessel in use by the armed forces, into the (sea) (lake) (river).

92. Article 134—(Kidnapping)

a. *Text of statute. See* paragraph 60.

b. *Elements.*

(1) That the accused seized, confined, inveigled, decoyed, or carried away a certain person;

(2) That the accused then held such person against that person's will;

(3) That the accused did so willfully and wrongfully; and

(4) That, under the circumstances, the conduct of the accused was to the prejudice of good order and discipline in the armed forces or was of a nature to bring discredit upon the armed forces.

c. *Explanation.*

(1) *Inveigle, decoy.* "Inveigle" means to lure, lead astray, or entice by false representations or other deceitful means. For example, a person who entices another to ride in a car with a false promise to take the person to a certain destination has inveigled the passenger into the car. "Decoy" means to entice or lure by means of some fraud, trick, or temptation. For example, one who lures a child into a trap with candy has decoyed the child.

(2) *Held.* "Held" means detained. The holding must be more than a momentary or incidental detention. For example, a robber who holds the victim at gunpoint while the victim hands over a wallet, or a rapist who throws his victim to the ground, does not, by such acts, commit kidnapping. On the other hand, if, before or after such robbery or rape, the victim is involuntarily transported some substantial distance,

as from a housing area to a remote area of the base or post, this may be kidnapping, in addition to robbery or rape.

(3) *Against the will.* "Against that person's will" means that the victim was held involuntarily. The involuntary nature of the detention may result from force, mental or physical coercion, or from other means, including false representations. If the victim is incapable of having a recognizable will, as in the case of a very young child or a mentally incompetent person, the holding must be against the will of the victim's parents or legal guardian. Evidence of the availability or nonavailability to the victim of means of exit or escape is relevant to the voluntariness of the detention, as is evidence of threats or force, or lack thereof, by the accused to detain the victim.

(4) *Willfully.* The accused must have specifically intended to hold the victim against the victim's will to be guilty of kidnapping. An accidental detention will not suffice. The holding need not have been for financial or personal gain or for any other particular purpose. It may be an aggravating circumstance that the kidnapping was for ransom, however. *See* R.C.M. 1001(b)(4).

(5) *Wrongfully.* "Wrongfully" means without justification or excuse. For example, a law enforcement official may justifiably apprehend and detain, by force if necessary (*see* R.C.M. 302(d)(3)), a person reasonably believed to have committed an offense. An official who unlawfully uses the official's authority to apprehend someone is not guilty of kidnapping, but may be guilty of unlawful detention. *See* paragraph 21. It is not wrongful under this paragraph and therefore not kidnapping for a parent or legal guardian to seize and hold that parent's or legal guardian's minor child.

d. *Lesser included offense.* Article 80—attempts

e. *Maximum punishment.* Dishonorable discharge, forfeiture of all pay and allowances, and confinement for life without eligibility for parole.

f. *Sample specification.*

In that ________, (personal jurisdiction data), did, (at/on board—location) (subject-matter jurisdiction data, if required), on or about ________ 20 ____, willfully and wrongfully (seize) (confine) (inveigle) (decoy) (carry away) and hold ________ (a minor whose parent or legal guardian the accused was not) (a person not a minor) against his/her will.

93. Article 134—(Mail: taking, opening, secreting, destroying, or stealing)

a. *Text of statute. See* paragraph 60.

b. *Elements.*

(1) *Taking.*

(a) That the accused took certain mail matter;

(b) That such taking was wrongful;

(c) That the mail matter was taken by the accused before it was delivered to or received by the addressee;

(d) That such taking was with the intent to obstruct the correspondence or pry into the business or secrets of any person or organization; and

(e) That, under the circumstances, the conduct of the accused was to the prejudice of good order and discipline in the armed forces or was of a nature to bring discredit upon the armed forces.

(2) *Opening, secreting, destroying, or stealing.*

(a) That the accused opened, secreted, destroyed, or stole certain mail matter;

(b) That such opening, secreting, destroying, or stealing was wrongful;

(c) That the mail matter was opened, secreted, destroyed, or stolen by the accused before it was delivered to or received by the addressee; and

(d) That, under the circumstances, the conduct of the accused was to the prejudice of good order and discipline in the armed forces or was of a nature to bring discredit upon the armed forces.

c. *Explanation.* These offenses are intended to protect the mail and mail system. "Mail matter" means any matter deposited in a postal system of any government or any authorized depository thereof or in official mail channels of the United States or an agency thereof including the armed forces. The value of the mail matter is not an element. *See* paragraph 46c(1) concerning "steal."

d. *Lesser included offenses.*

(1) Article 121—larceny; wrongful appropriation

(2) Article 80—attempts

e. *Maximum punishment.* Dishonorable discharge, forfeiture of all pay and allowances, and confinement for 5 years.

f. *Sample specifications.*

(1) *Taking.*

In that ______ (personal jurisdiction data), did, (at/on board—location) (subject-matter jurisdiction data, if required), on or about ______ 20 ______, wrongfully take certain mail matter, to wit: (a) (letter(s)) (postal card(s)) (package(s)), addressed to ______, (out of the (______ Post Office ______) (orderly room of ______) (unit mail box of ______) (______)) (from ______) before (it) (they) (was) (were) (delivered) (actually received) (to) (by) the (addressee) with intent to (obstruct the correspondence) (pry into the (business) (secrets)) of ______.

(2) *Opening, secreting, destroying, or stealing.*

In that ______ (personal jurisdiction data), did, (at/on board—location) (subject-matter jurisdiction data, if required), on or about ______ 20 ______, (wrongfully (open) (secret) (destroy)) (steal) certain mail matter, to wit: (a) (letter(s)) (postal card(s)) (package(s)) addressed to ______, which said (letter(s)) (______) (was) (were) then (in the fice ______) (orderly room of ______) (unit mail box of ______) (custody of ______) (______)) (had previously been committed to ______, (a representative of ______,) (an official agency for the transmission of communications)) before said (letter(s)) (______) (was) (were) (delivered) (actually received) (to) (by) the (addressee).

94. Article 134—(Mails: depositing or causing to be deposited obscene matters in)

a. *Text of statute. See* paragraph 60.

b. *Elements.*

(1) That the accused deposited or caused to be deposited in the mails certain matter for mailing and delivery;

(2) That the act was done wrongfully and knowingly;

(3) That the matter was obscene; and

(4) That, under the circumstances, the conduct of the accused was to the prejudice of good order and discipline in the armed forces or was of a nature to bring discredit upon the armed forces.

c. *Explanation.* Whether something is obscene is a question of fact. "Obscene" is synonymous with "indecent" as the latter is defined in paragraph 89c. The matter must violate community standards of decency or obscenity and must go beyond customary limits of expression. "Knowingly" means the accused deposited the material with knowledge of its nature.

d. *Lesser included offense.* Article 80—attempts

e. *Maximum punishment.* Dishonorable discharge, forfeiture of all pay and allowances, and confinement for 5 years.

f. *Sample specification.*

In that ______ (personal jurisdiction data), did, (at/on board—location) (subject-matter jurisdiction data, if required), on or about ______ 20 ______, wrongfully and knowingly (deposit) (cause to be deposited) in the (United States) (______) mails, for mailing and delivery a (letter) (picture) (______) (containing) (portraying) (suggesting) (______) certain obscene matters, to wit: ______.

95. Article 134—(Misprision of serious offense)

a. *Text of statute. See* paragraph 60.

b. *Elements.*

(1) That a certain serious offense was committed by a certain person;

(2) That the accused knew that the said person had committed the serious offense;

(3) That, thereafter, the accused concealed the serious offense and failed to make it known to civilian or military authorities as soon as possible;

(4) That the concealing was wrongful; and

(5) That, under the circumstances, the conduct of the accused was to the prejudice of good order and discipline in the armed forces or was of a nature to bring discredit upon the armed forces.

c. *Explanation.*

(1) *In general.* Misprision of a serious offense is the offense of concealing a serious offense committed by another but without such previous concert with or subsequent assistance to the principal as would make the accused an accessory. *See* paragraph 3. An intent to benefit the principal is not necessary to this offense.

(2) *Serious offense.* For purposes of this paragraph, a "serious offense" is any offense punishable under the authority of the code by death or by confinement for a term exceeding 1 year.

(3) *Positive act of concealment.* A mere failure or refusal to disclose the serious offense without some positive act of concealment does not make one guilty of this offense. Making a false entry in an account book for the purpose of concealing a theft committed by another is an example of a positive act of concealment.

d. *Lesser included offense.* Article 80—attempts

e. *Maximum punishment.* Dishonorable discharge, forfeiture of all pay and allowances, and confinement for 3 years.

f. *Sample specification.*

In that ________ (personal jurisdiction data), having knowledge that ________ had actually committed a serious offense to wit: (the murder of ________) (________), did, (at/on board—location) (subject-matter jurisdiction data, if required from about ________ 20 __, to about ________ 20 __, wrongfully conceal such serious offense by ________ and fail to make the same known to the civil or military authorities as soon as possible.

96. Article 134—(Obstructing justice)

a. *Text of statute. See* paragraph 60.

b. *Elements.*

(1) That the accused wrongfully did a certain act;

(2) That the accused did so in the case of a certain person against whom the accused had reason to believe there were or would be criminal proceedings pending;

(3) That the act was done with the intent to influence, impede, or otherwise obstruct the due administration of justice; and

(4) That, under the circumstances, the conduct of the accused was to the prejudice of good order and discipline in the armed forces or was of a nature to bring discredit upon the armed forces.

c. *Explanation.* This offense may be based on conduct that occurred before preferral of charges. Actual obstruction of justice is not an element of this offense. For purposes of this paragraph "criminal proceedings" includes nonjudicial punishment proceedings under Part V of this Manual. Examples of obstruction of justice include wrongfully influencing, intimidating, impeding, or injuring a witness, a person acting on charges under this chapter, an investigating officer under R.C.M. 406, or a party; and by means of bribery, intimidation, misrepresentation, or force or threat of force delaying or preventing communication of information relating to a violation of any criminal statute of the United States to a person authorized by a department, agency, or armed force of the United States to conduct or engage in investigations or prosecutions of such offenses; or endeavoring to do so. *See also* paragraph 22 and Article 37.

d. *Lesser included offenses.* None.

e. *Maximum punishment.* Dishonorable discharge, forfeiture of all pay and allowances, and confinement for 5 years.

f. *Sample specification.*

In that ________ (personal jurisdiction data), did, (at/on board—location) (subject-matter jurisdiction data, if required), on or about ________ 20 __, wrongfully (endeavor to) (impede (a trial by court-martial) (an investigation) (________)) [influence the actions of ________, (a trial counsel of the court-martial) (a defense counsel of the court-martial) (an officer responsible for making a recommendation concerning disposition of charges) (________)] [(influence) (alter) the testimony of ________ as a witness before a (court-martial) (an investigating officer) (________)] in the case of ________ by [(promising) (offering) (giving) to the said ________, (the sum of $________) (________, of a value of about $________)] [communicating to the said ________ a threat to ________] [________], (if) (unless) he/she, the said ________, would [recommend dismissal of the charges against said ________] [(wrongfully refuse to testify) (testify falsely concerning ________) (________)] [(at such trial) (before such investigating officer)] [________].

96a. Art 134 (Wrongful interference with an adverse administrative proceeding)

a. *Text of statute. See* paragraph 60.

b. *Elements.*

(1) That the accused wrongfully did a certain act;

(2) That the accused did so in the case of a cer-

tain person against whom the accused had reason to believe there was or would be an adverse administrative proceeding pending;

(3) That the act was done with the intent to influence, impede, or obstruct the conduct of such administrative proceeding, or otherwise obstruct the due administration of justice;

(4) That under the circumstances, the conduct of the accused was to the prejudice of good order and discipline in the armed forces or was of a nature to bring discredit upon the armed forces.

c. *Explanation.* For purposes of this paragraph "adverse administrative proceeding" includes any administrative proceeding or action, initiated against a servicemember, that could lead to discharge, loss of special or incentive pay, administrative reduction in grade, loss of a security clearance, bar to reenlistment, or reclassification. Examples of wrongful interference include wrongfully influencing, intimidating, impeding, or injuring a witness, an investigator, or other person acting on an adverse administrative action; by means of bribery, intimidation, misrepresentation, or force or threat of force delaying or preventing communication of information relating to such administrative proceeding; and, the wrongful destruction or concealment of information relevant to such adverse administrative proceeding.

d. *Lesser included offenses.* None.

e. *Maximum punishment.* Dishonorable discharge, forfeiture of all pay and allowances, and confinement for 5 years.

f. *Sample specification.*

In that ______ (personal jurisdiction data), did (at/on board-location) (subject-matter jurisdiction data, if required), on or about ______ 20 ___, (wrongfully endeavor to) [impede (an adverse administrative proceeding) (an investigation) (______)] [influence the actions of ______, (an officer responsible for making a recommendation concerning the adverse administrative action)(an individual responsible for making a decision concerning an adverse administrative proceeding) (an individual responsible for processing an adverse administrative proceeding)(______)] [(influence)(alter) the testimony of ______ a witness before (a board established to consider an administrative proceeding or elimination) (an investigating officer)(______)] in the case of ______, by](promising) (offering) (giving) to the said ______, (the sum of $ ______) (______, of a value of about $ ______)] [communicating to the said ______ a threat to ______] [______], (if) (unless) the said ______, would [recommend dismissal of the action against said ______] [(wrongfully refuse to testify) (testify falsely concerning ______) (______)] [(at such administrative proceeding) (before such investigating officer) (before such administrative board)] [______].

97. Article 134—(Pandering and prostitution)

a. *Text of statute. See* paragraph 60.

b. *Elements.*

(1) *Prostitution.*

(a) That the accused had sexual intercourse with another person not the accused's spouse;

(b) That the accused did so for the purpose of receiving money or other compensation;

(c) That this act was wrongful; and

(d) That, under the circumstances, the conduct of the accused was to the prejudice of good order and discipline in the armed forces or was of a nature to bring discredit upon the armed forces.

(2) *Patronizing a prostitute.*

(a) That the accused had sexual intercourse with another person not the accused's spouse;

(b) That the accused compelled, induced, enticed, or procured such person to engage in an act of sexual intercourse in exchange for money or other compensation; and

(c) That this act was wrongful; and

(d) That, under the circumstances, the conduct of the accused was to the prejudice of good order and discipline in the armed forces or was of a nature to bring discredit upon the armed forces.

(3) *Pandering by inducing, enticing, or procuring act of prostitution.*

(a) That the accused induced, enticed, or procured a certain person to engage in an act of sexual intercourse for hire and reward with a person to be directed to said person by the accused;

(b) That this inducing, enticing, or procuring was wrongful;

(c) That, under the circumstances, the conduct of the accused was to the prejudice of good order and discipline in the armed forces or was of a nature to bring discredit upon the armed forces.

(4) *Pandering by arranging or receiving consideration for arranging for sexual intercourse or sodomy.*

(a) That the accused arranged for, or received valuable consideration for arranging for, a certain person to engage in sexual intercourse or sodomy with another person;

(b) That the arranging (and receipt of consideration) was wrongful; and

(c) That, under the circumstances, the conduct of the accused was to the prejudice of good order and discipline in the armed forces or was of a nature to bring discredit upon the armed forces.

c. *Explanation.* Prostitution may be committed by males or females. Sodomy for money or compensation is not included in subparagraph b(1). Sodomy may be charged under paragraph 51. Evidence that sodomy was for money or compensation may be a matter in aggravation. *See* R.C.M. 1001(b)(4).

d. *Lesser included offense.* Article 80—attempts

e. *Maximum punishment.*

(1) *Prostitution and patronizing a prostitute.* Dishonorable discharge, forfeiture of all pay and allowances, and confinement for 1 year.

(2) *Pandering.* Dishonorable discharge, forfeiture of all pay and allowances, and confinement for 5 years.

f. *Sample specifications.*

(1) *Prostitution.*

In that ________ (personal jurisdiction data), did, (at/on board-location) (subject-matter jurisdiction data, if required), on or about ____ 20 ___, wrongfully engage in (an act) (acts) of sexual intercourse with __________, a person not his/her spouse, for the purpose of receiving (money) (________).

(2) *Patronizing a prostitute.*

In that ________ (personal jurisdiction data), did, (at/on board location) (subject-matter jurisdiction data, if required), on or about ____ 20 ___, wrongfully (compel) (induce) (entice) (procure) ____, a person not his/her spouse, to engage in (an act) (acts) of sexual intercourse with the accused in exchange for (money) ( ).

(3) *Inducing, enticing, or procuring act of prostitution.*

In that ________ (personal jurisdiction data), did (at/on board-location) (subject-matter jurisdiction data, if required), on or about ____ 20 ___, wrongfully (induce)(entice)(procure) ____ to engage in (an act)(acts) of (sexual intercourse for hire and reward) with persons to be directed to him/her by the said ________.

(4) *Arranging, or receiving consideration for arranging for sexual intercourse or sodomy.*

In that ________ (personal jurisdiction data), did, (at/on board-location) (subject-matter jurisdiction data, if required), on or about ____ 20 ___, wrongfully (arrange for) (receive valuable consideration, to wit: ____ on account of arranging for-) ____ to engage in (an act) (acts) of (sexual intercourse) (sodomy) with ________.

97a. Article 134—(Parole, Violation of)

a. *Text of statute. See* paragraph 60.

b. *Elements.*

(1) That the accused was a prisoner as the result of a court-martial conviction or other criminal proceeding;

(2) That the accused was on parole;

(3) That there were certain conditions of parole that the parolee was bound to obey;

(4) That the accused violated the conditions of parole by doing an act or failing to do an act; and

(5) That, under the circumstances, the conduct of the accused was to the prejudice of good order and discipline in the armed forces or was of a nature to bring discredit upon the armed forces

c. *Explanation.*

(1) "Prisoner" refers only to those in confinement resulting from conviction at a court-martial or other criminal proceeding.

(2) 'Parole' is defined as "word of honor." A prisoner on parole, or parolee, has agreed to adhere to a parole plan and conditions of parole. A "parole plan" is a written or oral agreement made by the prisoner prior to parole to do or refrain from doing certain acts or activities. A parole plan may include a residence requirement stating where and with whom a parolee will live, and a requirement that the prisoner have an offer of guaranteed employment. "Conditions of parole" include the parole plan and other reasonable and appropriate conditions of pa-

role, such as paying restitution, beginning or continuing treatment for alcohol or drug abuse, or paying a fine ordered executed as part of the prisoner's court-martial sentence. In return for giving his or her "word of honor" to abide by a parole plan and conditions of parole, the prisoner is granted parole.

d. *Lesser included offense.* Article 80—attempts

e. *Maximum punishment.* Bad-conduct discharge, confinement for 6 months, and forfeiture of two-thirds pay per month for 6 months.

f. *Sample specifications.*

In that __________ (personal jurisdiction data), a prisoner on parole, did, (at/on board—location), on or about __________ 20 ______, violate the conditions of his/her parole by __________ .

98. Article 134—(Perjury: subornation of)

a. *Text of statute. See* paragraph 60.

b. *Elements.*

(1) That the accused induced and procured a certain person to take an oath or its equivalent and to falsely testify, depose, or state upon such oath or its equivalent concerning a certain matter;

(2) That the oath or its equivalent was administered to said person in a matter in which an oath or its equivalent was required or authorized by law;

(3) That the oath or its equivalent was administered by a person having authority to do so;

(4) That upon the oath or its equivalent said person willfully made or subscribed a certain statement;

(5) That the statement was material;

(6) That the statement was false;

(7) That the accused and the said person did not then believe that the statement was true; and

(8) That, under the circumstances, the conduct of the accused was to the prejudice of good order and discipline in the armed forces or was of a nature to bring discredit upon the armed forces.

c. *Explanation. See* paragraph 57c for applicable principles. "Induce and procure" means to influence, persuade, or cause.

d. *Lesser included offense.* Article 80—attempts

e. *Maximum punishment.* Dishonorable discharge, forfeiture of all pay and allowances, and confinement for 5 years.

f. *Sample specification.*

In that __________ (personal jurisdiction data), did, (at/on board—location) (subject-matter jurisdiction data, if required), on or about __________ 20 ______, procure __________ to commit perjury by inducing him/her, the said __________, to take a lawful (oath) (affirmation) in a (trial by court-martial of __________) (trial by a court of competent jurisdiction, to wit: __________ of __________) (deposition for use in a trial by __________ of __________) (__________) that he/she, the said __________, would (testify) (depose) (__________) truly, and to (testify) (depose) (__________) willfully, corruptly, and contrary to such (oath) (affirmation) in substance that __________, which (testimony) (deposition) (__________) was upon a material matter and which the accused and the said __________ did not then believe to be true.

99. Article 134—(Public record: altering, concealing, removing, mutilating, obliterating, or destroying)

a. *Text of statute. See* paragraph 60.

b. *Elements.*

(1) That the accused altered, concealed, removed, mutilated, obliterated, destroyed, or took with the intent to alter, conceal, remove, mutilate, obliterate, or destroy, a certain public record;

(2) That the act of the accused was willful and unlawful; and

(3) That, under the circumstances, the conduct of the accused was to the prejudice of good order and discipline in the armed forces or was of a nature to bring discredit upon the armed forces.

c. *Explanation.* "Public records" include records, reports, statements, or data compilations, in any form, of public offices or agencies, setting forth the activities of the office or agency, or matters observed pursuant to duty imposed by law as to which matters there was a duty to report. "Public records" includes classified matters.

d. *Lesser included offense.* Article 80—attempts

e. *Maximum punishment.* Dishonorable discharge, forfeiture of all pay and allowances, and confinement for 3 years.

f. *Sample specification.*

In that ______ (personal jurisdiction data), did, (at/on board—location) (subject-matter jurisdiction data, if required), on or about ______ 20 ___, willfully and unlawfully ((alter) (conceal) (remove) (mutilate) (obliterate) (destroy)) (take with intent to (alter)(conceal) (remove) (mutilate) (obliterate) (destroy)) a public record, to wit: ______.

100. Article 134—(Quarantine: medical, breaking)

a. *Text of statute. See* paragraph 60.

b. *Elements.*

(1) That a certain person ordered the accused into medical quarantine;

(2) That the person was authorized to order the accused into medical quarantine;

(3) That the accused knew of this medical quarantine and the limits thereof;

(4) That the accused went beyond the limits of the medical quarantine before being released therefrom by proper authority; and

(5) That, under the circumstances, the conduct of the accused was to the prejudice of good order and discipline in the armed forces or was of a nature to bring discredit upon the armed forces.

c. *Explanation.* None.

d. *Lesser included offenses.*

(1) Article 134—breaking restriction

(2) Article 80—attempts

e. *Maximum punishment.* Confinement for 6 months and forfeiture of two-thirds pay per month for 6 months.

f. *Sample specification.*

In that ______ (personal jurisdiction data) having been placed in medical quarantine by a person authorized to order the accused into medical quarantine, did, (at/on board—location) (subject-matter jurisdiction data, if required), on or about ______ 20 ___, break said medical quarantine.

100a. Article 134—(Reckless endangerment)

a. *Text of statute. See* paragraph 60.

b. *Elements.*

(1) That the accused did engage in conduct;

(2) That the conduct was wrongful and reckless or wanton;

(3) That the conduct was likely to produce death or grievous bodily harm to another person; and

(4) That, under the circumstances, the conduct of the accused was to the prejudice of good order and discipline in the armed forces or was of a nature to bring discredit upon the armed forces.

c. *Explanation.*

(1) *In general.* This offense is intended to prohibit and therefore deter reckless or wanton conduct that wrongfully creates a substantial risk of death or grievous bodily harm to others.

(2) *Wrongfulness.* Conduct is wrongful when it is without legal justification or excuse.

(3) *Recklessness.* "Reckless" conduct is conduct that exhibits a culpable disregard of foreseeable consequences to others from the act or omission involved. The accused need not intentionally cause a resulting harm or know that his conduct is substantially certain to cause that result. The ultimate question is whether, under all the circumstances, the accused's conduct was of that heedless nature that made it actually or imminently dangerous to the rights or safety of others.

(4) *Wantonness.* "Wanton" includes "Reckless" but may connote willfulness, or a disregard of probable consequences, and thus describe a more aggravated offense.

(5) *Likely to produce.* When the natural or probable consequence of particular conduct would be death or grievous bodily harm, it may be inferred that the conduct is "likely" to produce that result. *See* paragraph 54c(4)(a)(ii).

(6) *Grievous bodily harm.* "Grievous bodily harm" means serious bodily injury. It does not include minor injuries, such as a black eye or a bloody nose, but does include fractured or dislocated bones, deep cuts, torn members of the body, serious damage to internal organs, and other serious bodily injuries.

(7) *Death or injury not required.* It is not necessary that death or grievous bodily harm be actually inflicted to prove reckless endangerment.

d. *Lesser included offenses.* None.

e. *Maximum punishment.* Bad-conduct discharge, forfeiture of all pay and allowances, and confinement for 1 year.

f. *Sample specification.*

In that ______ (personal jurisdiction data), did, (at/on board—location) (subject-matter jurisdiction data, if required), on or about ______ 20 ___, wrongfully and (recklessly) (wantonly) engage in conduct, to wit: (describe conduct), conduct likely to cause death or grievous bodily harm to ______.

101. Article 134—(Requesting commission of an offense)

Paragraph 101 was deleted pursuant to Executive Order 12708.

102. Article 134—(Restriction, breaking)

a. *Text of statute. See* paragraph 60.

b. *Elements.*

(1) That a certain person ordered the accused to be restricted to certain limits;

(2) That said person was authorized to order said restriction;

(3) That the accused knew of the restriction and the limits thereof;

(4) That the accused went beyond the limits of the restriction before being released therefrom by proper authority; and

(5) That, under the circumstances, the conduct of the accused was to the prejudice of good order and discipline in the armed forces or was of a nature to bring discredit upon the armed forces.

c. *Explanation.* Restriction is the moral restraint of a person imposed by an order directing a person to remain within certain specified limits. "Restriction" includes restriction under R.C.M. 304(*a*) (2), restriction resulting from imposition of either nonjudicial punishment (*see* Part V) or the sentence of a court-martial (*see* R.C.M. 1003(*b*) (6)), and administrative restriction in the interest of training, operations, security, or safety.

d. *Lesser included offenses.* Article 80—attempts

e. *Maximum punishment.* Confinement for 1 month and forfeiture of two-thirds pay per month for 1 month.

f. *Sample specification.*

In that ______ (personal jurisdiction data), having been restricted to the limits of ______, by a person authorized to do so, did, (at/on board—location), on or about ______ 20 ___, break said restriction.

103. Article 134—(Seizure: destruction, removal, or disposal of property to prevent)

a. *Text of statute. See* paragraph 60.

b. *Elements.*

(1) That one or more persons authorized to make searches and seizures were seizing, about to seize, or endeavoring to seize certain property;

(2) That the accused destroyed, removed, or otherwise disposed of that property with intent to prevent the seizure thereof;

(3) That the accused then knew that person(s) authorized to make searches were seizing, about to seize, or endeavoring to seize the property; and

(4) That, under the circumstances, the conduct of the accused was to the prejudice of good order and discipline in the armed forces or was of a nature to bring discredit upon the armed forces.

c. *Explanation. See* Mil. R. Evid. 316(*e*) concerning military personnel who may make seizures. It is not a defense that a search or seizure was technically defective.

d. *Lesser included offense.* Article 80—attempts

e. *Maximum punishment.* Dishonorable discharge, forfeiture of all pay and allowances, and confinement for 1 year.

f. *Sample specification.*

In that ______ (personal jurisdiction data), did, (at/on board—location) (subject matter jurisdiction data, if required), on or about ______ 20 ___, with intent to prevent its seizure, (destroy) (remove) (dispose of) ______, property which, as ______ then knew, (a) person(s) authorized to make searches and seizures were (seizing) (about to seize) (endeavoring to seize).

103a. Article 134—(Self-injury without intent to avoid service)

a. *Text of statute. See* paragraph 60.

b. *Elements.*

(1) That the accused intentionally inflicted injury upon himself or herself;

(2) That, under the circumstances, the conduct of the accused was to the prejudice of good order and

discipline in the armed forces or was of a nature to bring discredit upon the armed forces.
[Note: If the offense was committed in time of war or in a hostile fire pay zone, add the following element]

(3) That the offense was committed (in time of war) (in a hostile fire pay zone).

c. *Explanation.*

(1) *Nature of offense.* This offense differs from malingering (see paragraph 40) in that for this offense, the accused need not have harbored a design to avoid performance of any work, duty, or service which may properly or normally be expected of one in the military service. This offense is characterized by intentional self-injury under such circumstances as prejudice good order and discipline or discredit the armed forces. It is not required that the accused be unable to perform duties, or that the accused actually be absent from his or her place of duty as a result of the injury. For example, the accused may inflict the injury while on leave or pass. The circumstances and extent of injury, however, are relevant to a determination that the accused's conduct was prejudicial to good order and discipline, or service-discrediting.

(2) *How injury inflicted.* The injury may be inflicted by nonviolent as well as by violent means and may be accomplished by any act or omission that produces, prolongs, or aggravates a sickness or disability. Thus, voluntary starvation that results in a debility is a self-inflicted injury. Similarly, the injury may be inflicted by another at the accused's request.

d. *Lesser included offense.* Article 80—attempts

e. *Maximum punishment.*

(1) *Intentional self-inflicted injury.* Dishonorable discharge, forfeiture of all pay and allowances, and confinement for 2 years.

(2) *Intentional self-inflicted injury in time of war or in a hostile fire pay zone.* Dishonorable discharge, forfeiture of all pay and allowances, and confinement for 5 years.

f. *Sample specification.*

In that ______ (personal jurisdiction data), did, (at/on board—location) (in a hostile fire pay zone) on or about ______ 20 ___, (a time of war,) intentionally injure himself/herself by ______ (nature and circumstances of injury).

104. Article 134—(Sentinel or lookout: offenses against or by)

a. *Text of statute. See* paragraph 60.

b. *Elements.*

(1) *Disrespect to a sentinel or lookout.*

(a) That a certain person was a sentinel or lookout;

(b) That the accused knew that said person was a sentinel or lookout;

(c) That the accused used certain disrespectful language or behaved in a certain disrespectful manner;

(d) That such language or behavior was wrongful;

(e) That such language or behavior was directed toward and within the sight or hearing of the sentinel or lookout;

(f) That said person was at the time in the execution of duties as a sentinel or lookout; and

(g) That, under the circumstances, the conduct of the accused was to the prejudice of good order and discipline in the armed forces or was of a nature to bring discredit upon the armed forces.

(2) *Loitering or wrongfully sitting on post by a sentinel or lookout.*

(a) That the accused was posted as a sentinel or lookout;

(b) That while so posted, the accused loitered or wrongfully sat down on post; and

(c) That, under the circumstances, the conduct of the accused was to the prejudice of good order and discipline in the armed forces or was of a nature to bring discredit upon the armed forces.
[Note: If the offense was committed in time of war or while the accused was receiving special pay under 37 U.S.C. § 310, add the following element after element (a): That the accused was so posted (in time of war) (while receiving special pay under 37 U.S.C. § 310).]

c. *Explanation.*

(1) *Disrespect.* For a discussion of "disrespect, "*see* paragraph 13c(3).

(2) *Loitering or wrongfully sitting on post.*

(a) *In general.* The discussion set forth in paragraph 38c applies to loitering or sitting down while posted as a sentinel or lookout as well.

(b) *Loiter.* "Loiter" means to stand around, to move about slowly, to linger, or to lag behind when that conduct is in violation of known instructions or accompanied by a failure to give complete attention to duty.

d. *Lesser included offenses.*

(1) *Disrespect to a sentinel or lookout.* Article 80—attempts

(2) *Loitering or wrongfully sitting on post by a sentinel or lookout.* Article 80—attempts

e. *Maximum punishment.*

(1) *Disrespect to a sentinel or lookout.* Confinement for 3 months and forfeiture of two-thirds pay per month for 3 months.

(2) *Loitering or wrongfully sitting on post by a sentinel or lookout.*

(a) *In time of war or while receiving special pay under 37 U.S.C. § 310.* Dishonorable discharge, forfeiture of all pay and allowances, and confinement for 2 years.

(b) *Other cases.* Bad-conduct discharge, forfeiture of all pay and allowances, and confinement for 6 months.

f. *Sample specifications.*

(1) *Disrespect to a sentinel or lookout.*

In that ______ (personal jurisdiction data), did, (at/on board—location), on or about ______ 20 ___, then knowing that ______ was a sentinel or lookout, (wrongfully use the following disrespectful language "______," or words to that effect, to ______) (wrongfully behave in a disrespectful manner toward ______, by ______) a (sentinel) (lookout) in the execution of his/her duty.

(2) *Loitering or wrongfully sitting down on post by a sentinel or lookout.*

In that ______ (personal jurisdiction data), while posted as a (sentinel) (lookout), did, (at/on board—location) (while receiving special pay under 37 U.S.C. § 310) on or about ______ 20 ___, (a time of war) (loiter) (wrongfully sit down) on his/her post.

105. Article 134—(Soliciting another to commit an offense)

a. *Text of statute. See* paragraph 60.

b. *Elements.*

(1) That the accused solicited or advised a certain person or persons to commit a certain offense under the code other than one of the four offenses named in Article 82;

(2) That the accused did so with the intent that the offense actually be committed; and

(3) That, under the circumstances, the conduct of the accused was to the prejudice of good order and discipline in the armed forces or was a nature to bring discredit upon the armed forces.

c. *Explanation. See* paragraph 6c. If the offense solicited was actually committed, *see also* paragraph 1.

d. *Lesser included offenses.* Article 80 —attempts.

e. *Maximum punishment.* Any person subject to the code who is found guilty of soliciting or advising another person to commit an offense which, if committed by one subject to the code, would be punishable under the code, shall be subject to the maximum punishment authorized for the offense solicited or advised, except that in no case shall the death penalty be imposed nor shall the period of confinement in any case, including offenses for which life imprisonment may be adjudged, exceed 5 years. However, any person subject to the code who is found guilty of soliciting or advising another person to commit the offense of espionage (Article 106a) shall be subject to any punishment, other than death, that a court-martial may direct.

f. *Sample specification.*

In that ______ (personal jurisdiction data), did, (at/on board—location) (subject-matter jurisdiction data, if required), on or about ______ 20 ___, wrongfully (solicit) (advise) ______ (to disobey a general regulation, to wit: ______) (to steal ______, of a value of (about) $______, the property of ______) (to ______), by ______.

106. Article 134—(Stolen property: knowingly receiving, buying, concealing)

a. *Text of statute. See* paragraph 60.

b. *Elements.*

(1) That the accused wrongfully received, bought, or concealed certain property of some value;

(2) That the property belonged to another person;

(3) That the property had been stolen;

(4) That the accused then knew that the property had been stolen; and

(5) That, under the circumstances, the conduct of the accused was to the prejudice of good order and discipline in the armed forces or was of a nature to bring discredit upon the armed forces.

c. *Explanation.*

(1) *In general.* The actual thief is not criminally liable for receiving the property stolen; however a principal to the larceny (*see* paragraph 1), when not the actual thief, may be found guilty of knowingly receiving the stolen property but may not be found guilty of both the larceny and receiving the property.

(2) *Knowledge.* Actual knowledge that the property was stolen is required. Knowledge may be proved by circumstantial evidence.

(3) *Wrongfulness.* Receiving stolen property is wrongful if it is without justification or excuse. For example, it would not be wrongful for a person to receive stolen property for the purpose of returning it to its rightful owner, or for a law enforcement officer to seize it as evidence.

d. *Lesser included offense.* Article 80—attempts

e. *Maximum punishment.* Stolen property, knowingly receiving, buying, or concealing.

(1) *Of a value of $500.00 or less.* Bad-conduct discharge, forfeiture of all pay and allowances, and confinement for 6 months.

(2) *Of a value of more than $500.00.* Dishonorable discharge, forfeiture of all pay and allowances, and confinement for 3 years.

f. *Sample specification.*

In that ______ (personal jurisdiction data), did, (at/on board—location) (subject-matter jurisdiction data, if required), on or about ______ 20 ___, wrongfully (receive) (buy) (conceal) ______, of a value of (about) $______, the property of ______, which property, as he/she, the said ______, then knew, had been stolen.

107. Article 134—(Straggling)

a. *Text of statute. See* paragraph 60.

b. *Elements.*

(1) That the accused, while accompanying the accuse's organization on a march, maneuvers, or similar exercise, straggled;

(2) That the straggling was wrongful; and

(3) That, under the circumstances, the conduct of the accused was to the prejudice of good order and discipline in the armed forces or was of a nature to bring discredit upon the armed forces.

c. *Explanation.* "Straggle" means to wander away, to stray, to become separated from, or to lag or linger behind.

d. *Lesser included offense.* Article 80—attempts

e. *Maximum punishment.* Confinement for 3 months and forfeiture of two-thirds pay per month for 3 months.

f. *Sample specification.*

In that ______ (personal jurisdiction data), did, at ______, on or about ______ 20 ___, while accompanying his/her organization on (a march) (maneuvers) (______), wrongfully straggle.

108. Article 134—(Testify: wrongful refusal)

a. *Text of statute. See* paragraph 60.

b. *Elements.*

(1) That the accused was in the presence of a court-martial, board of officer(s), military commission, court of inquiry, an officer conducting an investigation under Article 32, or an officer taking a deposition, of or for the United States, at which a certain person was presiding;

(2) That the said person presiding directed the accused to qualify as a witness or, having so qualified, to answer a certain question;

(3) That the accused refused to qualify as a witness or answer said question;

(4) That the refusal was wrongful; and

(5) That, under the circumstances, the conduct of the accused was to the prejudice of good order and discipline in the armed forces or was of a nature to bring discredit upon the armed forces.

c. *Explanation.* To "qualify as a witness" means that the witness declares that the witness will testify truthfully. *See* R.C.M. 807; Mil. R. Evid. 603. A good faith but legally mistaken belief in the right to remain silent does not constitute a defense to a charge of wrongful to testify. *See also* Mil. R. Evid. 301 and Section V.

d. *Lesser included offenses.* None.

e. *Maximum punishment.* Dishonorable discharge, forfeiture of all pay and allowances, and confinement for 5 years.

f. *Sample specification.*

In that ________ (personal jurisdiction data), being in the presence of (a) (an) ((general) (special) (summary) court-martial) (board of officer(s)) (military commission) (court of inquiry) (officer conducting an investigation under Article 32, Uniform Code of Military Justice) (officer taking a deposition) (________) (of) (for) the United States, of which ________ was (military judge) (president), (________), (and having been directed by the said ________ to qualify as a witness) (and having qualified as a witness and having been directed by the said ________ to answer the following question(s) put to him/her as a witness, "________"), did, (at/on board—location), on or about ________ 20____, wrongfully refuse (to qualify as a witness) (to answer said question(s)).

109. Article 134—(Threat or hoax designed or intended to cause panic or public fear)

a. *Text of statute.* See paragraph 60.

b. *Elements.*

(1) *Threat.*

(a) That the accused communicated certain language;

(b) That the information communicated amounted to a threat;

(c) That the harm threatened was to be done by means of an explosive; weapon of mass destruction; biological or chemical agent, substance, or weapon; or hazardous material;

(d) That the communication was wrongful; and

(e) That, under the circumstances, the conduct of the accused was to the prejudice of good order and discipline in the armed forces or was of a nature to bring discredit upon the armed forces.

(2) *Hoax.*

(a) That the accused communicated or conveyed certain information;

(b) That the information communicated or conveyed concerned an attempt being made or to be made by means of an explosive; weapon of mass destruction; biological or chemical agent, substance, or weapon; or hazardous material, to unlawfully kill, injure, or intimidate a person or to unlawfully damage or destroy certain property;

(c) That the information communicated or conveyed by the accused was false and that the accused then knew it to be false;

(d) That the communication of the information by the accused was malicious; and

(e) That, under the circumstances, the conduct of the accused was to the prejudice of good order and discipline in the armed forces or was of a nature to bring discredit upon the armed forces.

c. *Explanation.*

(1) *Threat.* A "threat" means an expressed present determination or intent to kill, injure, or intimidate a person or to damage or destroy certain property presently or in the future. Proof that the accused actually intended to kill, injure, intimidate, damage, or destroy is not required.

(2) *Explosive.* "Explosive" means gunpowder, powders used for blasting, all forms of high explosives, blasting materials, fuses (other than electrical circuit breakers), detonators, and other detonating agents, smokeless powders, any explosive bomb, grenade, missile, or similar device, and any incendiary bomb or grenade, fire bomb, or similar device, and any other explosive compound, mixture, or similar material.

(3) *Weapon of mass destruction.* A weapon of mass destruction means any device, explosive or otherwise, that is intended, or has the capability, to cause death or serious bodily injury to a significant number of people through the release, dissemination, or impact of: toxic or poisonous chemicals, or their precursors; a disease organism; or radiation or radioactivity.

(4) *Biological agent.* The term "biological agent" means any micro-organism (including bacteria, viruses, fungi, rickettsiac, or protozoa), pathogen, or infectious substance, and any naturally occurring, bioengineered, or synthesized component of any such micro-organism, pathogen, or infectious substance, whatever its origin or method of production, that is capable of causing—

(a) death, disease, or other biological malfunction in a human, an animal, a plant, or another living organism;

(b) deterioration of food, water, equipment, supplies, or materials of any kind; or

(c) deleterious alteration of the environment.

(5) *Chemical agent, substance, or weapon.* A chemical agent, substance, or weapon refers to a toxic chemical and its precursors or a munition or device, specifically designed to cause death or other harm through toxic properties of those chemicals that would be released as a result of the employment of such munition or device, and any equipment specifically designed for use directly in connection with the employment of such munitions or devices.

(6) *Hazardous material.* A substance or material (including explosive, radioactive material, etiologic agent, flammable or combustible liquid or solid, poison, oxidizing or corrosive material, and compressed gas, or mixture thereof) or a group or class of material designated as hazardous by the Secretary of Transportation.

(7) *Malicious.* A communication is "malicious" if the accused believed that the information would probably interfere with the peaceful use of the building, vehicle, aircraft, or other property concerned, or would cause fear or concern to one or more persons.

d. *Lesser included offenses.*

(1) *Threat.*

(a) Article 134—communicating a threat

(b) Article 80—attempts

(c) Article 128—assault

(2) *Hoax.* Article 80—attempts

e. *Maximum punishment.* Dishonorable discharge, forfeitures of all pay and allowances, and confinement for 10 years.

f. *Sample specifications.*

(1) *Threat.*

In that ________ (personal jurisdiction data) did, (at/on board--location) on or about ________ 20 ____, wrongfully communicate certain information, to wit: ________, which language constituted a threat to harm a person or property by means of a(n) [explosive; weapon of mass destruction; biological agent, substance, or weapon; chemical agent, substance, or weapon; and/or (a) hazardous material(s)].

(2) *Hoax.*

In that ________ (personal jurisdiction data) did, (at/on board--location), on or about ________ 20 ____, maliciously (communicate) (convey) certain information concerning an attempt being made or to be made to unlawfully [(kill) (injure) (intimidate) ________] [(damage) (destroy) ________] by means of a(n) [explosive; weapon of mass destruction; biological agent, substance, or weapon; chemical agent, substance, or weapon; and/or (a) hazardous material(s)], to wit: ________, which information was false and which the accused then knew to be false.

110. Article 134—(Threat, communicating)

a. *Text of statute. See* paragraph 60.

b. *Elements.*

(1) That the accused communicated certain language expressing a present determination or intent to wrongfully injure the person, property, or reputation of another person, presently or in the future;

(2) That the communication was made known to that person or to a third person;

(3) That the communication was wrongful; and

(4) That, under the circumstances, the conduct of the accused was to the prejudice of good order and discipline in the armed forces or was of a nature to bring discredit upon the armed forces.

c. *Explanation.* To establish the threat it is not necessary that the accused actually intended to do the injury threatened. However, a declaration made under circumstances which reveal it to be in jest or for an innocent or legitimate purpose, or which contradict the expressed intent to commit the act, does not constitute this offense. Nor is the offense committed by the mere statement of intent to commit an unlawful act not involving injury to another. *See also* paragraph 109 concerning bomb threat.

d. *Lesser included offenses.*

(1) Article 117—provoking speeches or gestures

(2) Article 80—attempts

e. *Maximum punishment.* Dishonorable discharge, forfeiture of all pay and allowances, and confinement for 3 years.

f. *Sample specification.*

In that ________ (personal jurisdiction data), did, (at/on board—location) (subject-matter jurisdiction data, if required), on or about ________ 20 ____, wrongfully communicate to ________ a threat (injure ________ by ________) (accuse ______ of having committed the offense of ______) (______).

111. Article 134—(Unlawful entry)

a. *Text of statute. See* paragraph 60.

b. *Elements.*

(1) That the accused entered the real property of another or certain personal property of another which amounts to a structure usually used for habitation or storage;

(2) That such entry was unlawful; and

(3) That, under the circumstances, the conduct of the accused was to the prejudice of good order and discipline in the armed forces or was of a nature to bring discredit upon the armed forces.

c. *Explanation. See* paragraph 55 for a discussion of "entry." An entry is "unlawful" if made without the consent of any person authorized to consent to entry or without other lawful authority. No specific intent or breaking is required for this offense. *See* paragraph 56 for a discussion of housebreaking. The property protected against unlawful entry includes real property and the sort of personal property which amounts to a structure usually used for habitation or storage. It would usually not include an aircraft, automobile, tracked vehicle, or a person's locker, even though used for storage purposes. However, depending on the circumstances, an intrusion into such property may be prejudicial to good order and discipline.

d. *Lesser included offense.* Article 80—attempts

e. *Maximum punishment.* Bad-conduct discharge, forfeiture of all pay and allowances, and confinement for 6 months.

f. *Sample specification.*

In that ______ (personal jurisdiction data), did, (at/on board—location) (subject-matter jurisdiction data, if required), on or about ______ 20 ___, unlawfully enter the (dwelling house) (garage) (warehouse) (tent) (vegetable garden) (orchard) (stateroom) (______) of ______.

112. Article 134—(Weapon: concealed, carrying)

a. *Text of statute. See* paragraph 60.

b. *Elements.*

(1) That the accused carried a certain weapon concealed on or about the accused's person;

(2) That the carrying was unlawful;

(3) That the weapon was a dangerous weapon; and

(4) That, under the circumstances, the conduct of the accused was to the prejudice of good order and discipline in the armed forces or was of a nature to bring discredit upon the armed forces.

c. *Explanation.*

(1) *Concealed weapon.* A weapon is concealed when it is carried by a person and intentionally covered or kept from sight.

(2) *Dangerous weapon.* For purposes of this paragraph, a weapon is dangerous if it was specifically designed for the purpose of doing grievous bodily harm, or it was used or intended to be used by the accused to do grievous bodily harm.

(3) *On or about.* "On or about" means the weapon was carried on the accused's person or was within the immediate reach of the accused.

d. *Lesser included offense.* Article 80—attempts

e. *Maximum punishment.* Bad-conduct discharge, forfeiture of all pay and allowances, and confinement for 1 year.

f. *Sample specification.*

In that ______ (personal jurisdiction data), did, (at/on board—location) (subject-matter jurisdiction data, if required), on or about ______ 20 ___, unlawfully carry on or about his/her person a concealed weapon, to wit: a ______.

113. Article 134—(Wearing unauthorized insignia, decoration, badge, ribbon, device, or lapel button)

a. *Text of statute. See* paragraph 60.

b. *Elements.*

(1) That the accused wore a certain insignia, decoration, badge, ribbon, device, or lapel button upon the accused's uniform or civilian clothing;

(2) That the accused was not authorized to wear the item;

(3) That the wearing was wrongful; and

(4) That, under the circumstances, the conduct of the accused was to the prejudice of good order and

discipline in the armed forces or was of a nature to bring discredit upon the armed forces.

c. *Explanation.* None.

d. *Lesser included offense.* Article 80—attempts

e. *Maximum punishment.* Bad-conduct discharge, forfeiture of all pay and allowances, and confinement for 6 months.

f. *Sample specification.*

In that ______ (personal jurisdiction data), did, (at/on board—location), on or about ______ 20 ______, wrongfully and without authority wear upon his/her (uniform) (civilian clothing) (the insignia or grade of a (master sergeant of ______) (chief gunner's mate of ______)) (Combat Infantryman Badge) (the Distinguished Service Cross) (the ribbon representing the Silver Star) (the lapel button representing the Legion of Merit) (______).

PART V
NONJUDICIAL PUNISHMENT PROCEDURE

1. General

a. *Authority.* Nonjudicial punishment in the United States Armed Forces is authorized by Article 15.

b. *Nature.* Nonjudicial punishment is a disciplinary measure more serious than the administrative corrective measures discussed in paragraph 1g, but less serious than trial by court-martial.

c. *Purpose.* Nonjudicial punishment provides commanders with an essential and prompt means of maintaining good order and discipline and also promotes positive behavior changes in servicemembers without the stigma of a court-martial conviction.

d. *Policy.*

(1) *Commander's responsibility.* Commanders are responsible for good order and discipline in their commands. Generally, discipline can be maintained through effective leadership including, when necessary, administrative corrective measures. Nonjudicial punishment is ordinarily appropriate when administrative corrective measures are inadequate due to the nature of the minor offense or the record of the servicemember, unless it is clear that only trial by court-martial will meet the needs of justice and discipline. Nonjudicial punishment shall be considered on an individual basis. Commanders considering nonjudicial punishment should consider the nature of the offense, the record of the servicemember, the needs for good order and discipline, and the effect of nonjudicial punishment on the servicemember and the servicemember's record.

(2) *Commander's discretion.* A commander who is considering a case for disposition under Article 15 will exercise personal discretion in evaluating each case, both as to whether nonjudicial punishment is appropriate, and, if so, as to the nature and amount of punishment appropriate. No superior may direct that a subordinate authority impose nonjudicial punishment in a particular case, issue regulations, orders, or "guides" which suggest to subordinate authorities that certain categories of minor offenses be disposed of by nonjudicial punishment instead of by court-martial or administrative corrective measures, or that predetermined kinds or amounts of punishments be imposed for certain classifications of offenses that the subordinate considers appropriate for disposition by nonjudicial punishment.

(3) *Commander's suspension authority.* Commanders should consider suspending all or part of any punishment selected under Article 15, particularly in the case of first offenders or when significant extenuating or mitigating matters are present. Suspension provides an incentive to the offender and gives an opportunity to the commander to evaluate the offender during the period of suspension.

e. *Minor offenses.* Nonjudicial punishment may be imposed for acts or omissions that are minor offenses under the punitive articles (*see* Part IV). Whether an offense is minor depends on several factors: the nature of the offense and the circumstances surrounding its commission; the offender's age, rank, duty assignment, record and experience; and the maximum sentence imposable for the offense if tried by general court-martial. Ordinarily, a minor offense is an offense which the maximum sentence imposable would not include a dishonorable discharge or confinement for longer than 1 year if tried by general court-martial. The decision whether an offense is "minor" is a matter of discretion for the commander imposing nonjudicial punishment, but nonjudicial punishment for an offense other than a minor offense (even though thought by the commander to be minor) is not a bar to trial by court-martial for the same offense. *See* R.C.M. 907(b)(2)(D)(iv). However, the accused may show at trial that nonjudicial punishment was imposed, and if the accused does so, this fact must be considered in determining an appropriate sentence. *See* Article 15(f); R.C.M. 1001(c)(1)(B).

f. *Limitations on nonjudicial punishment.*

(1) *Double punishment prohibited.* When nonjudicial punishment has been imposed for an offense, punishment may not again be imposed for the same offense under Article 15. *But see* paragraph 1e concerning trial by court-martial.

(2) *Increase in punishment prohibited.* Once nonjudicial punishment has been imposed, it may not be increased, upon appeal or otherwise.

(3) *Multiple punishment prohibited.* When a commander determines that nonjudicial punishment is appropriate for a particular servicemember, all known offenses determined to be appropriate for disposition by nonjudicial punishment and ready to be considered at that time, including all such offenses arising from a single incident or course of conduct,

shall ordinarily be considered together, and not made the basis for multiple punishments.

(4) *Statute of limitations.* Except as provided in Article 43(d), nonjudicial punishment may not be imposed for offenses which were committed more than 2 years before the date of imposition. *See* Article 43(c).

(5) *Civilian courts.* Nonjudicial punishment may not be imposed for an offense tried by a court which derives its authority from the United States. Nonjudicial punishment may not be imposed for an offense tried by a State or foreign court unless authorized by regulations of the Secretary concerned.

g. *Relationship of nonjudicial punishment to administrative corrective measures.* Article 15 and Part V of this Manual do not apply to include, or limit use of administrative corrective measures that promote efficiency and good order and discipline such as counseling, admonitions, reprimands, exhortations, disapprovals, criticisms, censures, reproofs, rebukes, extra military instruction, and administrative withholding of privileges. *See also* R.C.M. 306. Administrative corrective measures are not punishment, and they may be used for acts or omissions which are not offenses under the code and for acts or omissions which are offenses under the code.

h. *Applicable standards.* Unless otherwise provided, the service regulations and procedures of the service member shall apply.

i. *Effect of errors.* Failure to comply with any of the procedural provisions of Part V of this Manual shall not invalidate a punishment imposed under Article 15, unless the error materially prejudiced a substantial right of the servicemember on whom the punishment was imposed.

2. Who may impose nonjudicial punishment

The following persons may serve as a nonjudicial punishment authority for the purposes of administering nonjudicial punishment proceedings under this Part:

a. *Commander.* As provided by regulations of the Secretary concerned, a commander may impose nonjudicial punishment upon any military personnel of that command. "Commander" means a commissioned or warrant officer who, by virtue of rank and assignment, exercises primary command authority over a military organization or prescribed territorial area, which under pertinent official directives is recognized as a "command." "Commander" includes a commander of a joint command. Subject to subparagraph 1d(2) and any regulations of the Secretary concerned, the authority of a commander to impose nonjudicial punishment as to certain types of offenses, certain categories of persons, or in specific cases, or to impose certain types of punishment, may be limited or withheld by a superior commander or by the Secretary concerned.

b. *Officer in charge.* If authorized by regulations of the Secretary concerned, an officer in charge may impose nonjudicial punishment upon enlisted persons assigned to that unit.

c. *Principal assistant.* If authorized by regulations of the Secretary concerned, a commander exercising general court-martial jurisdiction or an officer of general or flag rank in command may delegate that commander's powers under Article 15 to a principal assistant. The Secretary concerned may define "principal assistant."

3. Right to demand trial

Except in the case of a person attached to or embarked in a vessel, punishment may not be imposed under Article 15 upon any member of the armed forces who has, before the imposition of nonjudicial punishment, demanded trial by court-martial in lieu of nonjudicial punishment. This right may also be granted to a person attached to or embarked in a vessel if so authorized by regulations of the Secretary concerned. A person is "attached to" or "embarked in" a vessel if, at the time nonjudicial punishment is imposed, that person is assigned or attached to the vessel, is on board for passage, or is assigned or attached to an embarked staff, unit, detachment, squadron, team, air group, or other regularly organized body.

4. Procedure

a. *Notice.* If, after a preliminary inquiry (*see* R.C.M. 303), the nonjudicial punishment authority determines that disposition by nonjudicial punishment proceedings is appropriate (*see* R.C.M. 306: paragraph 1 of this Part), the nonjudicial punishment authority shall cause the servicemember to be notified. The notice shall include:

(1) a statement that the nonjudicial punishment

authority is considering the imposition of nonjudicial punishment;

(2) a statement describing the alleged offenses—including the article of the code—which the member is alleged to have committed;

(3) a brief summary of the information upon which the allegations are based or a statement that the member may, upon request, examine available statements and evidence;

(4) a statement of the rights that will be accorded to the servicemember under subparagraphs 4c(1) and (2) of this Part;

(5) unless the right to demand trial is not applicable (*see* paragraph 3 of this Part), a statement that the member may demand trial by court-martial in lieu of nonjudicial punishment, a statement of the maximum punishment which the nonjudicial punishment authority may impose by nonjudicial punishment; a statement that, if trial by court-martial is demanded, charges could be referred for trial by summary, special, or general court-martial; that the member may not be tried by summary court-martial over the member's objection; and that at a special or general court-martial the member has the right to be represented by counsel.

b. *Decision by servicemember.*

(1) *Demand for trial by court-martial.* If the servicemember demands trial by court-martial (when this right is applicable), the nonjudicial proceedings shall be terminated. It is within the discretion of the commander whether to forward or refer charges for trial by court-martial (*see* R.C.M. 306; 307; 401–407) in such a case, but in no event may nonjudicial punishment be imposed for the offenses affected unless the demand is voluntarily withdrawn.

(2) *No demand for trial by court-martial.* If the servicemember does not demand trial by court-martial within a reasonable time after notice under paragraph 4a of this Part, or if the right to demand trial by court-martial is not applicable, the nonjudicial punishment authority may proceed under paragraph 4c of this Part.

c. *Nonjudicial punishment accepted.*

(1) *Personal appearance requested; procedure.* Before nonjudicial punishment may be imposed, the servicemember shall be entitled to appear personally before the nonjudicial punishment authority who offered nonjudicial punishment, except when appearance is prevented by the unavailability of the nonjudicial punishment authority or by extraordinary circumstances, in which case the servicemember shall be entitled to appear before a person designated by the nonjudicial punishment authority who shall prepare a written summary of any proceedings before that person and forward it and any written matter submitted by the servicemember to the nonjudicial punishment authority. If the servicemember requests personal appearance, the servicemember shall be entitled to:

(A) Be informed in accordance with Article 31(b);

(B) Be accompanied by a spokesperson provided or arranged for by the member unless the punishment to be imposed will not exceed extra duty for 14 days, restriction for 14 days, and an oral reprimand. Such a spokesperson need not be qualified under R.C.M. 502(d); such spokesperson is not entitled to travel or similar expenses, and the proceedings need not be delayed to permit the presence of a spokesperson; the spokesperson may speak for the servicemember, but may not question witnesses except as the nonjudicial punishment authority may allow as a matter of discretion;

(C) Be informed orally or in writing of the information against the servicemember and relating to the offenses alleged;

(D) Be allowed to examine documents or physical objects against the member which the nonjudicial punishment authority has examined in connection with the case and on which the nonjudicial punishment authority intends to rely in deciding whether and how much nonjudicial punishment to impose;

(E) Present matters in defense, extenuation, and mitigation orally, or in writing, or both;

(F) Have present witnesses, including those adverse to the servicemember, upon request if their statements will be relevant and they are reasonably available. For purposes of this subparagraph, a witness is not reasonably available if the witness requires reimbursement by the United States for any cost incurred in appearing, cannot appear without unduly delaying the proceedings, or, if a military witness, cannot be excused from other important duties;

(G) Have the proceeding open to the public unless the nonjudicial punishment authority determines that the proceeding should be closed for good cause, such as military exigencies or security interests, or unless the punishment to be imposed will not exceed extra duty for 14 days, restriction for 14 days, and an oral reprimand; however, nothing in this subparagraph requires special arrangements to be made to facilitate access to the proceeding.

(2) *Personal appearance waived; procedure.* Subject to the approval of the nonjudicial punishment authority, the servicemember may request not to appear personally under subparagraph 4c(1) of this Part. If such request is granted, the servicemember may submit written matters for consideration by the nonjudicial punishment authority before such authority's decision under subparagraph 4c(4) of this Part. The servicemember shall be informed of the right to remain silent and that matters submitted may be used against the member in a trial by court-martial.

(3) *Evidence.* The Military Rules of Evidence (Part III), other than with respect to privileges, do not apply at nonjudicial punishment proceedings. Any relevant matter may be considered, after compliance with subparagraphs 4c(1)(C) and (D) of this Part.

(4) *Decision.* After considering all relevant matters presented, if the nonjudicial punishment authority—

(A) Does not conclude that the servicemember committed the offenses alleged, the nonjudicial punishment authority shall so inform the member and terminate the proceedings;

(B) Concludes that the servicemember committed one or more of the offenses alleged, the nonjudicial punishment authority shall:

(i) so inform the servicemember;

(ii) inform the servicemember of the punishment imposed; and

(iii) inform the servicemember of the right to appeal (*see* paragraph 7 of this Part).

d. *Nonjudicial punishment based on record of court of inquiry or other investigative body.* Nonjudicial punishment may be based on the record of a court of inquiry or other investigative body, in which proceeding the member was accorded the rights of a party. No additional proceeding under subparagraph 4c(1) of this Part is required. The servicemember shall be informed in writing that nonjudicial punishment is being considered based on the record of the proceedings in question, and given the opportunity, if applicable, to refuse nonjudicial punishment. If the servicemember does not demand trial by court-martial or has no option, the servicemember may submit, in writing, any matter in defense, extenuation, or mitigation, to the officer considering imposing nonjudicial punishment, for consideration by that officer to determine whether the member committed the offenses in question, and, if so, to determine an appropriate punishment.

5. Punishments

a. *General limitations.* The Secretary concerned may limit the power granted by Article 15 with respect to the kind and amount of the punishment authorized. Subject to paragraphs 1 and 4 of this Part and to regulations of the Secretary concerned, the kinds and amounts of punishment authorized by Article 15(b) may be imposed upon servicemembers as provided in this paragraph.

b. *Authorized maximum punishments.* In addition to or in lieu of admonition or reprimand, the following disciplinary punishments subject to the limitation of paragraph 5d of this Part, may be imposed upon servicemembers:

(1) *Upon commissioned officers and warrant officers—*

(A) By any commanding officer—restriction to specified limits, with or without suspension from duty for not more than 30 consecutive days;

(B) If imposed by an officer exercising general court-martial jurisdiction, an officer of general or flag rank in command, or a principal assistant as defined in paragraph 2c of this Part—

(i) arrest in quarters for not more than 30 consecutive days;

(ii) forfeiture of not more than one-half of one month's pay per month for 2 months;

(iii) restriction to specified limits, with or without suspension from duty, for not more than 60 consecutive days;

(2) *Upon other military personnel of the command—*

(A) By any nonjudicial punishment authority—

(i) if imposed upon a person attached to or embarked in a vessel, confinement on bread and water or diminished rations for not more than 3 consecutive days;

(ii) correctional custody for not more than 7 consecutive days;

(iii) forfeiture of not more than 7 days' pay;

(iv) reduction to the next inferior grade, if the grade from which demoted is within the promotion authority of the officer imposing the reduction or any officer subordinate to the one who imposes the reduction;

(v) extra duties, including fatigue or other duties, for not more than 14 consecutive days;

(vi) restriction to specified limits, with or without suspension from duty, for not more than 14 consecutive days;

(B) If imposed by a commanding officer of the grade of major or lieutenant commander or above or a principal assistant as defined in paragraph 2c of this Part—

(i) if imposed upon a person attached to or embarked in a vessel, confinement on bread and water or diminished rations for not more than 3 consecutive days;

(ii) correctional custody for not more than 30 consecutive days;

(iii) forfeiture of not more than one-half of 1 month's pay per month for 2 months;

(iv) reduction to the lowest or any intermediate pay grade, if the grade from which demoted is within the promotion authority of the officer imposing the reduction or any officer subordinate to the one who imposes the reduction, but enlisted members in pay grades above E-4 may not be reduced more than one pay grade, except that during time of war or national emergency this category of persons may be reduced two grades if the Secretary concerned determines that circumstances require the removal of this limitation;

(v) extra duties, including fatigue or other duties, for not more than 45 consecutive days;

(vi) restriction to specified limits, with or without suspension from duty, for not more than 60 consecutive days.

c. *Nature of punishment.*

(1) *Admonition and reprimand.* Admonition and reprimand are two forms of censure intended to express adverse reflection upon or criticism of a person's conduct. A reprimand is a more severe form of censure than an admonition. When imposed as nonjudicial punishment, the admonition or reprimand is considered to be punitive, unlike the nonpunitive admonition and reprimand provided for in paragraph 1g of this Part. In the case of commissioned officers and warrant officers, admonitions and reprimands given as nonjudicial punishment must be administered in writing. In other cases, unless otherwise prescribed by the Secretary concerned, they may be administered either orally or in writing.

(2) *Restriction.* Restriction is the least severe form of deprivation of liberty. Restriction involves moral rather than physical restraint. The severity of this type of restraint depends on its duration and the geolineartal limits specified when the punishment is imposed. A person undergoing restriction may be required to report to a designated place at specified times if reasonably necessary to ensure that the punishment is being properly executed. Unless otherwise specified by the nonjudicial punishment authority, a person in restriction may be required to perform any military duty.

(3) *Arrest in quarters.* As in the case of restriction, the restraint involved in arrest in quarters is enforced by a moral obligation rather than by physical means. This punishment may be imposed only on officers. An officer undergoing this punishment may be required to perform those duties prescribed by the Secretary concerned. However, an officer so punished is required to remain within that officer's quarters during the period of punishment unless the limits of arrest are otherwise extended by appropriate authority. The quarters of an officer may consist of a military residence, whether a tent, stateroom, or other quarters assigned, or a private residence when government quarters have not been provided.

(4) *Correctional custody.* Correctional custody is the physical restraint of a person during duty or nonduty hours, or both, imposed as a punishment under Article 15, and may include extra duties, fatigue duties, or hard labor as an incident of correctional custody. A person may be required to serve correctional custody in a confinement facility, but if practicable, not in immediate association with persons awaiting trial or held in confinement pursuant to trial by court-martial. A person undergoing correctional custody may be required to perform those regular military duties, extra duties, fatigue duties, and hard labor which may be assigned by the authority charged with the administration of the punishment. The conditions under which correctional custody is served shall be prescribed by the Secre-

tary concerned. In addition, the Secretary concerned may limit the categories of enlisted members upon whom correctional custody may be imposed. The authority competent to order the release of a person from orrectional custody shall be as designated by the Secretary concerned.

(5) *Confinement on bread and water or diminished rations.* Confinement on bread and water or diminished rations involves confinement in places where the person so confined may communicate only with authorized personnel. The ration to be furnished a person undergoing a punishment of confinement on bread and water or diminished rations is that specified by the authority charged with the administration of the punishment, but the ration may not consist solely of bread and water unless this punishment has been specifically imposed. When punishment of confinement on bread and water or diminished rations is imposed, a signed certificate of a medical officer containing an opinion that no serious injury to the health of the person to be confined will be caused by that punishment, must be obtained before the punishment is executed. The categories of enlisted personnel upon whom this type of punishment may be imposed may be limited by the Secretary concerned.

(6) *Extra duties.* Extra duties involve the performance of duties in addition to those normally assigned to the person undergoing the punishment. Extra duties may include fatigue duties. Military duties of any kind may be assigned as extra duty. However, no extra duty may be imposed which constitutes a known safety or health hazard to the member or which constitutes cruel or unusual punishment or which is not sanctioned by customs of the service concerned. Extra duties assigned as punishment of noncommissioned officers, petty officers, or any other enlisted persons of equivalent grades or positions designated by the Secretary concerned, should not be of a kind which demeans their grades or positions.

(7) *Reduction in grade.* Reduction in grade is one of the most severe forms of nonjudicial punishment and it should be used with discretion. As used in Article 15, the phrase "if the grade from which demoted is within the promotion authority of the officer imposing the reduction or any officer subordinate to the one who imposes the reduction" does not refer to the authority to promote the person concerned but to the general authority to promote to the grade held by the person to be punished.

(8) *Forfeiture of pay.* Forfeiture means a permanent loss of entitlement to the pay forfeited. "Pay," as used with respect to forfeiture of pay under Article 15, refers to the basic pay of the person or, in the case of reserve component personnel on inactive-duty, compensation for periods of inactive-duty training, plus any sea or hardship duty pay. "Basic pay" includes no element of pay other than the basic pay fixed by statute for the grade and length of service of the person concerned and does not include special pay for a special qualification, incentive pay for the performance of hazardous duties, proficiency pay, subsistence and quarters allowances, and similar types of compensation. If the punishment includes both reduction, whether or not suspended, and forfeiture of pay, the forfeiture must be based on the grade to which reduced. The amount to be forfeited will be expressed in whole dollar amounts only and not in a number of day's pay or fractions of monthly pay. If the forfeiture is to be applied for more than 1 month, the amount to be forfeited per month and the number of months should be stated. Forfeiture of pay may not extend to any pay accrued before the date of its imposition.

d. *Limitations on combination of punishments.*

(1) Arrest in quarters may not be imposed in combination with restriction;

(2) Confinement on bread and water or diminished rations may not be imposed in combination with correctional custody, extra duties, or restriction;

(3) Correctional custody may not be imposed in combination with restriction or extra duties;

(4) Restriction and extra duties may be combined to run concurrently, but the combination may not exceed the maximum imposable for extra duties;

(5) Subject to the limits in subparagraphs d(1) through (4) all authorized punishments may be imposed in a single case in the maximum amounts.

e. *Punishments imposed on reserve component personnel while on inactive-duty training.* When a punishment under Article 15 amounting to a deprivation of liberty (for example, restriction, correctional custody, extra duties, or arrest in quarters) is imposed on a member of a reserve component during a period of inactive-duty training, the punishment may be served during one or both of the following:

(1) a normal period of inactive-duty training; or

(2) a subsequent period of active duty (not including a period of active duty under Article 2(d)(1), unless such active duty was approved by the Secretary concerned).

Unserved punishments may be carried over to subsequent periods of inactive-duty training or active duty. A sentence to forfeiture of pay may be collected from active duty and inactive-duty training pay during subsequent periods of duty.

f. *Punishments imposed on reserve component personnel when ordered to active duty for disciplinary purposes.* When a punishment under Article 15 is imposed on a member of a reserve component during a period of active duty to which the reservist was ordered pursuant to R.C.M. 204 and which constitutes a deprivation of liberty (for example, restriction, correctional custody, extra duties, or arrest in quarters), the punishment may be served during any or all of the following:

(1) that period of active duty to which the reservist was ordered pursuant to Article 2(d), but only where the order to active duty was approved by the Secretary concerned;

(2) a subsequent normal period of inactive-duty training; or

(3) a subsequent period of active duty (not including a period of active duty pursuant to R.C.M. 204 which was not approved by the Secretary concerned).

Unserved punishments may be carried over to subsequent periods of inactive-duty training or active duty. A sentence to forfeiture of pay may be collected from active duty and inactive-duty training pay during subsequent periods of duty.

g. *Effective date and execution of punishments.* Reduction and forfeiture of pay, if unsuspended, take effect on the date the commander imposes the punishments. Other punishments, if unsuspended, will take effect and be carried into execution as prescribed by the Secretary concerned.

6. Suspension, mitigation, remission, and setting aside

a. *Suspension.* The nonjudicial punishment authority who imposes nonjudicial punishment, the commander who imposes nonjudicial punishment, or a successor in command over the person punished, may, at any time, suspend any part or amount of the unexecuted punishment imposed and may suspend a reduction in grade or a forfeiture, whether or not executed, subject to the following rules:

(1) An executed punishment of reduction or forfeiture of pay may be suspended only within a period of 4 months after the date of execution.

(2) Suspension of a punishment may not be for a period longer than 6 months from the date of the suspension, and the expiration of the current enlistment or term of service of the servicemember involved automatically terminates the period of suspension.

(3) Unless the suspension is sooner vacated, suspended portions of the punishment are remitted, without further action, upon the termination of the period of suspension.

(4) Unless otherwise stated, an action suspending a punishment includes a condition that the servicemember not violate any punitive article of the code. The nonjudicial punishment authority may specify in writing additional conditions of the suspension.

(5) A suspension may be vacated by any nonjudicial punishment authority or commander competent to impose upon the servicemember concerned punishment of the kind and amount involved in the vacation of suspension. Vacation of suspension may be based only on a violation of the conditions of suspension which occurs within the period of suspension. Before a suspension may be vacated, the servicemember ordinarily shall be notified and given an opportunity to respond. Although a hearing is not required to vacate a suspension, if the punishment is of the kind set forth in Article 15(e)(1)-(7), the servicemember should, unless impracticable, be given an opportunity to appear before the officer authorized to vacate suspension of the punishment to present any matters in defense, extenuation, or mitigation of the violation on which the vacation action is to be based. Vacation of a suspended nonjudicial punishment is not itself nonjudicial punishment, and additional action to impose nonjudicial punishment for a violation of a punitive article of the code upon which the vacation action is based is not precluded thereby.

b. *Mitigation.* Mitigation is a reduction in either the quantity or quality of a punishment, its general nature remaining the same. Mitigation is appropriate when the offender's later good conduct merits a reduction in the punishment, or when it is determined that the punishment imposed was disproportionate.

The nonjudicial punishment authority who imposes nonjudicial punishment, the commander who imposes nonjudicial punishment, or a successor in command may, at any time, mitigate any part or amount of the unexecuted portion of the punishment imposed. The nonjudicial punishment authority who imposes nonjudicial punishment, the commander who imposes nonjudicial punishment, or a successor in command may also mitigate reduction in grade, whether executed or unexecuted, to forfeiture of pay, but the amount of the forfeiture may not be greater than the amount that could have been imposed by the officer who initially imposed the nonjudicial punishment. Reduction in grade may be mitigated to forfeiture of pay only within 4 months after the date of execution.

When mitigating—

(1) Arrest in quarters to restriction;

(2) Confinement on bread and water or diminished rations to correctional custody;

(3) Correctional custody or confinement on bread and water or diminished rations to extra duties or restriction, or both; or

(4) Extra duties to restriction, the mitigated punishment may not be for a greater period than the punishment mitigated. As restriction is the least severe form of deprivation of liberty, it may not be mitigated to a lesser period of another form of deprivation of liberty, as that would mean an increase in the quality of the punishment.

c. *Remission.* Remission is an action whereby any portion of the unexecuted punishment is cancelled. Remission is appropriate under the same circumstances as mitigation. The nonjudicial punishment authority who imposes punishment, the commander who imposes nonjudicial punishment, or a successor in command may, at any time, remit any part or amount of the unexecuted portion of the punishment imposed. The expiration of the current enlistment or term of service of the servicemember automatically remits any unexecuted punishment imposed under Article 15.

d. *Setting aside.* Setting aside is an action whereby the punishment or any part or amount thereof, whether executed or unexecuted, is set aside and any property, privileges, or rights affected by the portion of the punishment set aside are restored. The nonjudicial punishment authority who imposed punishment, the commander who imposes nonjudicial punishment, or a successor in command may set aside punishment. The power to set aside punishments and restore rights, privileges, and property affected by the executed portion of a punishment should ordinarily be exercised only when the authority considering the case believes that, under all circumstances of the case, the punishment has resulted in clear injustice. Also, the power to set aside an executed punishment should ordinarily be exercised only within a reasonable time after the punishment has been executed. In this connection, 4 months is a reasonable time in the absence of unusual circumstances.

7. Appeals

a. *In general.* Any servicemember punished under Article 15 who considers the punishment to be unjust or disproportionate to the offense may appeal through the proper channels to the next superior authority.

b. *Who may act on appeal.* A "superior authority," as prescribed by the Secretary concerned, may act on an appeal. When punishment has been imposed under delegation of a commander's authority to administer nonjudicial punishment (*see* paragraph 2c of this Part), the appeal may not be directed to the commander who delegated the authority.

c. *Format of appeal.* Appeals shall be in writing and may include the appellant's reasons for regarding the punishment as unjust or disproportionate.

d. *Time limit.* An appeal shall be submitted within 5 days of imposition of punishment, or the right to appeal shall be waived in the absence of good cause shown. A servicemember who has appealed may be required to undergo any punishment imposed while the appeal is pending, except that if action is not taken on the appeal within 5 days after the appeal was submitted, and if the servicemember so requests, any unexecuted punishment involving restraint or extra duty shall be stayed until action on the appeal is taken.

e. *Legal review.* Before acting on an appeal from any punishment of the kind set forth in Article 15(e)(1)-(7), the authority who is to act on the appeal shall refer the case to a judge advocate or to a lawyer of the Department of Homeland Security for consideration and advice, and may so refer the case upon appeal from any punishment imposed under Article 15. When the case is referred, the judge advocate or lawyer is not limited to an examination of any written matter comprising the record of proceedings and may make any inquiries and examine any additional matter deemed necessary.

f. *Action by superior authority.*

(1) *In general.* In acting on an appeal, the superior authority may exercise the same power with respect to the punishment imposed as may be exercised under Article 15(d) and paragraph 6 of this Part by the officer who imposed the punishment. The superior authority may take such action even if no appeal has been filed.

(2) *Matters considered.* When reviewing the action of an officer who imposed nonjudicial punishment, the superior authority may consider the record of the proceedings, any matters submitted by the servicemember, any matters considered during the legal review, if any, and any other appropriate matters.

(3) *Additional proceedings.* If the superior authority sets aside a nonjudicial punishment due to a procedural error, that authority may authorize additional proceedings under Article 15, to be conducted by the officer who imposed the nonjudicial punishment, the commander, or a successor in command, for the same offenses involved in the original proceedings. Any punishment imposed as a result of these additional proceedings may be no more severe than that originally imposed.

(4) *Notification.* Upon completion of action by the superior authority, the servicemember upon whom punishment was imposed shall be promptly notified of the result.

(5) *Delegation to principal assistant.* If authorized by regulation of the Secretary concerned a superior authority who is a commander exercising general court-martial jurisdiction, or is an officer of general or flag rank in command, may delegate the power under Article 15(e) and this paragraph to a principal assistant.

8. Records of nonjudicial punishment

The content, format, use, and disposition of records of nonjudicial punishment may be prescribed by regulations of the Secretary concerned.

APPENDIX 1
CONSTITUTION OF THE UNITED STATES—1787

We the People of the United States, in Order to form a more perfect Union, establish Justice, insure domestic Tranquility, provide for the common defence, promote the general Welfare, and secure the Blessings of Liberty to ourselves and our Posterity, do ordain and establish this Constitution of the United States of America.

ARTICLE I

Section 1. All legislative Powers herein granted shall be vested in a Congress of the United States, which shall consist of a Senate and a House of Representatives.

Section 2. The House of Representatives shall be composed of Members chosen every second year by the people of the several states, and the Electors in each State shall have the Qualifications requisite for Electors of the most numerous Branch of the State Legislature.

No person shall be a Representative who shall not have attained to the Age of twenty-five Years, and been seven Years a Citizen of the United States, and who shall not, when elected, be an Inhabitant of that State in which he shall be chosen.

[1] Representative and direct Taxes shall be apportioned among the several States which may be included within this Union, according to their respective Numbers, which shall be determined by adding to the whole Number of free Persons, including those bound to Service for a Term of Years, and excluding Indians not taxed, three fifths of all other Persons. The actual Enumeration shall be made within three Years after the first Meeting of the Congress of the United States, and within every subsequent Term of ten Years in such Manner as they shall by Law direct. The Number of Representative shall not exceed one for every thirty Thousand, but each state shall have at Least one Representative; and until such enumeration shall be made, the state of New Hampshire shall be entitled to choose three, Massachusetts eight, Rhode Island and Providence Plantations one, Connecticut five, New York six, New Jersey four, Pennsylvania eight, Delaware one, Maryland six, Virginia ten, North Carolina five, South Carolina five, and Georgia three.

When vacancies happen in the Representation from any state, the Executive Authority thereof shall issue Writs of Election to fill such Vacancies.

The House of Representatives shall choose the Speaker and other officers; and shall have the sole power of Impeachment.

Section 3. [2] The Senate of the United States shall be composed of two Senators from each State chosen by the Legislature thereof, for six Years and each Senator shall have one Vote.

Immediately after they shall be assembled in Consequence of the first Election, they shall be divided as equally as may be into three Classes. The Seats of the Senators of the first Class shall be vacated at the Expiration of the second Year, of the second Class at the Expiration of the fourth Year, and of the third Class at the Expiration of the sixth Year, so that one third may be chosen every second Year; and if Vacancies happen by Resignation, or otherwise during the Recess of the Legislature of any State, the Executive thereof may make temporary Appointments until the next Meeting of the Legislature, which shall then fill such Vacancies.

No person shall be a Senator who shall not have attained to the Age of thirty Years, and been nine Years a Citizen of the United States, who shall not, when elected, be an Inhabitant of that State for which he shall be chosen.

The Vice-President of the United States shall be President of the Senate, but shall have no Vote unless they be equally divided.

The Senate shall choose their other Officers, and also a President pro tempore, in the Absence of the Vice-President, or when he shall exercise the Office of President of the United States.

The Senate shall have the sole Power to try all Impeachments. When sitting for that Purpose, they shall be on Oath or Affirmation. When the President of the United States is tried, the Chief Justice shall preside: And no Person shall be convicted without the Concurrence of two-thirds of the Members present.

Judgement in Cases of Impeachment shall not extend further than to removal from Office and disqualification to hold and enjoy any Office of honor, Trust or Profit under the United States; but the Party convicted shall nevertheless be liable and subject to Indictment, Trial, Judgment and Punishment, according to Law.

Section 4. The Times, Places and Manner of holding Elections for Senators and Representatives, shall be prescribed in each State by the Legislature thereof: but the Congress may at any time by Law make or alter such Regulations, except as to the Places of choosing Senators.

[3] The Congress shall assemble at least once in every Year, and such Meeting shall be on the first Monday in December, unless they shall by Law appoint a different Day.

Section 5. Each House shall be the Judge of the Elections, Returns and Qualifications of its own Members, and a Majority of each shall constitute a Quorum to do Business; but a smaller Number may adjourn from day to day, and may be authorized to compel the Attendance of absent Members, in such Manner, and under such Penalties as each House may provide.

Each House may determine the Rules of its Proceedings, punish its Members for disorderly Behaviour, and with the Concurrence of two-thirds, expel a Member.

Each House shall keep a Journal of its Proceedings, and from time to time publish the same, excepting such Parts as may in their Judgment require Secrecy; and the Yeas and Nays of the Members either House on any question shall, at the Desire of one fifth of those Present be entered on the Journal.

Neither House, during the Session of Congress shall, without the Consent of the other, adjourn for more than three days, nor to any other Place than that in which the two Houses shall be sitting.

---

[1] This clause has been affected by the 14th and 16th amendments.

[2] This section has been affected by the 17th amendment

[3] This clause has been affected by the 20th amendment

Section 6. The Senators and Representatives shall receive a Compensation for their Services, to be ascertained by Law, and paid out of the Treasury of the United States. They shall in all Cases, except Treason, Felony and Breach of the Peace, be privileged from Arrest during their Attendance at the Session of their respective Houses, and in going to and returning from the same; and for any Speech or Debate in either House, they shall not be questioned in any other Place.

No Senator or Representative shall, during the Time for which he is elected, be appointed to any Civil Office under the Authority of the United States, which shall have been created, or the Emoluments whereof shall have been increased during such time; and no Person holding any Office under the United States, shall be a Member of either House during his Continuance in Office.

Section 7. All Bills for raising Revenue shall originate in the House of Representatives; but the Senate may propose or concur with Amendments as on other Bills.

Every Bill which shall have passed the House of Representatives and the Senate, shall, before it become a Law, be presented to the President of the United States; if he approve he shall sign it, but if not he shall return it, with his Objections to that House in which it shall have originated, who shall enter the Objections at large on their Journal, and proceed to reconsider it. If after such Reconsideration two-thirds of that House shall agree to pass the Bill, it shall be sent, together with the Objections, to the other House, by which is shall likewise be reconsidered, and if approved by two-thirds of that House, it shall become a Law. But in all such Cases the Votes of Both Houses shall be determined by Yeas and Nays, and the Names of the Persons voting for and against the Bill shall be entered on the Journal of each House respectively. If any Bill shall not be returned by the President within ten Days (Sundays excepted) after it shall have been presented to him, the Same shall be a Law, in like Manner as if he had signed it, unless the Congress by their Adjournment prevent its Return, in which Case it shall not be a Law.

Every Order, Resolution, or Vote to which the Concurrence of the Senate and House of Representative may be necessary (except on a question of Adjournment) shall be presented to the President of the United States; and before the Same shall take Effect, shall be approved by him,or being disapproved by him, shall be repassed by two thirds of the Senate and House of Representatives, according to the Rules and Limitations prescribed in the Case of a Bill.

Section 8. The Congress shall have Power To lay and collect Taxes, Duties, Imposts and Excises, to pay the Debts and provide for the common Defence and general Welfare of the United States; but all Duties, Imposts and Excises shall be uniform throughout the United States.

To borrow Money on the credit of the United States; To regulate Commerce with foreign Nations, and among the several States, and with the Indian Tribes;

To establish an uniform rule of Naturalization, and uniform Laws on the subject of Bankruptcies throughout the United States;

To coin Money, regulate the Value thereof, and of foreign coin, and fix the Standard of Weights and Measures;

To provide for the Punishment of counterfeiting the Securities and current Coin of the United States;

To establish Post Offices and post Roads;

To promote the Progress of Science and useful Arts, by securing for limited Times to Authors and Inventors the exclusive Right to their respective Writings and Discoveries;

To constitute Tribunals inferior to the supreme Court;

To define and punish Piracies and Felonies committed on the high Seas, and Offenses against the Law of Nations;

To declare War, grant Letters of Marque and Reprisal, and make Rules concerning Captures on Land and Water;

To raise and support Armies, but no Appropriation of Money to that use shall be for a longer Term than two Years;

To provide and maintain a Navy;

To make Rules for the Government and Regulation of the land and naval Forces;

To provide for calling forth the Militia to execute the Laws of the Union, suppress Insurrections and repel Invasions.;

To provide for organizing, arming, and disciplining, the Militia, and for governing such Part of them as may be employed in the Service of the United States, reserving to the States respectively, the Appointment of the Officers, and the Authority of training the Militia according to the discipline prescribed by Congress;

To exercise exclusive Legislation in all Cases whatsoever, over such District (not exceeding ten Miles square) as may, by Cession of particular States, and the Acceptance of Congress,become the Seat of the Government of the United States, and to exercise like Authority over all Places purchased by the Consent of the Legislature of the States in which the Same shall be, for the Erection of Forts, Magazines, Arsenals, dock-Yards, and other needful Buildings; And

To make all Laws which shall be necessary and proper for carrying into Execution the foregoing Powers, and all other Powers vested by the Constitution in the Government of the United States, or in any Department or Officer thereof.

Section 9. The Migration or Importation of such Persons as any of the States now existing shall think proper to admit, shall not be prohibited by the Congress prior to the Year one thousand eight hundred and eight, but a Tax or duty may be imposed on such Importation, not exceeding ten dollars for each Person.

Privilege of the Writ of Habeas Corpus shall not be suspended, unless when in Cases of Rebellion or Invasion the public Safety require it.

No Bill of Attainder or ex post facto Law shall be passed.

No Capitation, or other direct, Tax shall be laid, unless in Proportion to the Census or Enumeration herein before directed to be taken.

No Tax or Duty shall be laid on Articles exported from any State.

No Preference shall be given by any Regulation of Commerce or Revenue to the Ports of one State over those of another: nor shall Vessels bound to, or from, one State, be obliged to enter, clear, or pay Duties in another.

No Money shall be drawn from the Treasury, but in Consequence of Appropriations made by Law; and a regular Statement and Account of the Receipts and Expenditures of all public Money shall be published from time to time.

No Title of Nobility shall be granted by the United States: And no Person holding any Office of Profit or Trust under them, shall, without the Consent of the Congress, accept of any present,

Emolument, Office, or Title, of any kind whatever, from any King, Prince, or foreign State.

Section 10. No State shall enter into any Treaty, Alliance, or Confederation; grant Letters of Marque and Reprisal; coin Money; emit Bills of Credit; make any Thing but gold and silver Coin a Tender in Payment of Debts; pass any Bill of Attainder, ex post facto Law, or Law impairing the Obligation of Contracts, or grant any Title of Nobility.

No State shall, without the Consent of the Congress, lay any Imposts or Duties on Imports or Exports, except what may be absolutely necessary for executing its inspection Laws; and the net Produce of all Duties and Imports, laid by any State on Imports or Exports, shall be for the Use of the Treasury of the United States; all such Laws shall be subject to the Revision and Control of the Congress.

No State shall, without the Consent of Congress, lay any Duty of Tonnage, keep Troops, or Ships of War in time of Peace, enter into any Agreement or Compact with another State, or with a foreign Power, or engage in War, unless actually invaded, or in such imminent Danger as will not admit of delay.

ARTICLE II

Section 1. The executive Power shall be vested in a President of the United States and, together with the Vice President,chosen for the same Term, be elected as follows.

Each State shall appoint, in such Manner as the Legislature thereof may direct, a Number of Electors, equal to the whole Number of Senators and Representatives to which the State may be entitled in the Congress: but no Senator or Representative, or Person holding an Office of Trust or Profit under the United States, shall be appointed an Elector.

[4] The Electors shall meet in their respective States, and vote by Ballot for two Persons, of whom one at least shall not be an Inhabitant of the same State with themselves. And they shall make a List of all the Persons voted for, and of the Number of Votes for each; which List they shall sign and certify, and transmit sealed to the Seat of the Government of the United States, directed to the President of the Senate. The President of the Senate shall, in the Presence of the Senate and House of Representatives, open all the Certificates, and the Votes shall then be counted. The Person having the greatest Number of Votes shall be the President, if such Number be a Majority of the whole Number of Electors appointed; and if there be more than one who have such Majority, and have an equal Number of Electors appointed; and if there be more than one who have such Majority, and have an equal Number of Votes, then the House of Representatives shall immediately choose by Ballot one of them for President; and if no Person have a Majority, then from the five highest on the List the said House shall in like Manner choose the President. But in choosing the President, the Votes shall be taken by States, the Representation from each State having one Vote; a quorum for this Purpose shall consist of a Member or Members from two thirds of the States, and a Majority of all the states shall be necessary to a choice. In every case, after the Choice of the President, the Person having the greatest Number of Votes of the Electors shall be the Vice President. But if there should remain two or more who have equal Votes, the Senate shall choose from them by Ballot the Vice President.

The Congress may determine the Time of the choosing the Electors, and the Day on which they shall give their Votes; which Day shall be the same throughout the United States.

No Person except a natural born Citizen, or a Citizen of the United States, at the time of the Adoption of this Constitution, shall be eligible to the Office of President;neither shall any Person be eligible to that Office who shall not have attained to the Age of thirty five Years, and been fourteen Years a Resident within the United States.

In Case of the Removal of the President from Office, or his Death, Resignation, or Inability to discharge the Powers and Duties of the said Office, the Same shall devolve on the Vice President, and the Congress may by Law provide for the Case of Removal, Death, Resignation or Inability, both of the President and Vice President, declaring what Officer shall then act as President, and such Officer shall act accordingly, until the Disability be removed, or a President be elected.

The President shall, at stated Times, receive for his Services,a Compensation, which shall neither be increased nor diminished during the Period for which he shall have been elected, and he shall not receive within a Period any other Emolument from the United States, or any of them.

Before he enter on the Execution of his Office, he shall take the following Oath or Affirmation: "I do solemnly swear (or affirm) that I will faithfully execute the Office of President of the United States, and will to the best of my Ability, preserve, protect and defend the Constitution of the United States. "

Section 2. The President shall be Commander in Chief of the Army and Navy of the United States, and of the Militia of the several States, when called into the actual Service of the United States; he may require the Opinion, in writing of the principal Officer in each of the executive Departments, upon any Subject relating to the Duties of their respective Offices, and he shall have power to grant Reprieves and Pardons for Offenses against the United States, except in Cases of Impeachment.

He shall have Power, by and with the Advice and Consent of the Senate, to make Treaties, provided two thirds of the Senators present concur; and he shall nominate, and by and with the Advice and Consent of the Senate, shall appoint Ambassadors, other public Ministers and Consuls, Judges of the supreme Court, and all other Officers of the United States, whose Appointments are not herein otherwise provided for, and which shall be established by Law. But the Congress may by law vest the Appointment of such inferior Officers, as they think proper, in the President alone, in the Courts of Law, or in the Heads of Departments.

The President shall have Power to fill up all Vacancies that may happen during the Recess of the Senate, by granting Commissions which shall expire at the End of their Session.

Section 3. He shall from time to time give to the Congress Information of the State of the Union, and recommend to their Consideration such Measures as he shall judge necessary and expedient; he may, on extraordinary Occasions, convene both Houses, or either of them, and in Case of Disagreement between

[4] This clause has been affected by the 12th amendment.

them, with Respect to the Time of Adjournment, he may adjourn them to such Time as he shall think proper; he shall receive Ambassadors and other public Ministers; he shall take Care that the Laws be faithfully executed, and shall Commission all the Officers of the United States.

Section 4. The President, Vice President and all civil Officers of the United States, shall be removed from Office on Impeachment for, and Conviction of, Treason, Bribery, or other high Crimes and Misdemeanors.

ARTICLE III

Section 1. The judicial Power of the United States shall be vested in one Supreme Court, and in such inferior courts as the Congress may from time to time ordain and establish. The Judges, both of the Supreme and inferior Courts, shall hold their Offices during good Behavior, and shall, at stated Times, receive for their Services a Compensation which shall not be diminished during their Continuance in Office.

Section 2. The judicial Power shall extend to all Cases, in Law and Equity, arising under this Constitution, the Laws of the United States, and Treaties made, or which shall be made, under their Authority; to all Cases affecting Ambassadors, other public Ministers, and Consuls; to all Cases of admiralty and maritime Jurisdiction; to Controversies to which the United States shall be a Party; to Controversies between two or more States, between a State and Citizens of another State, between Citizens of different States, between Citizens of the same State claiming Lands under Grants of different States, and between a State or the Citizens thereof, and foreign States, Citizens, or Subjects.

In all Cases affecting Ambassadors, other public Ministers and Consuls, and those in which a State shall be a Party, the Supreme Court shall have original Jurisdiction. In all the other Cases before mentioned, the Supreme Court shall have appellate Jurisdiction, both as to Law and Fact, with such Exceptions and under such Regulations as the Congress shall make.

The Trial of all Crimes, except in Cases of Impeachment,shall be by Jury; and such Trial shall be held in the State where the said Crimes shall have been committed; but when not committed within any State the Trial shall be at such Place or Places as the Congress may by Law have directed.

Section 3. Treason against the United States shall consist only in levying War against them, or in adhering to their Enemies, giving them Aid and Comfort. No Person shall be convicted of Treason unless on the Testimony of two Witnesses to the same overt Act, or on Confession in open Court.

The Congress shall have Power to declare the Punishment of Treason, but no Attainder of Treason shall work Corruption of Blood, or Forfeiture except during the Life of the Person attained.

ARTICLE IV

Section 1. Full Faith and Credit shall be given in each State to the public Act, Records, and judicial Proceedings of every other State. And the Congress may, by general Laws, prescribe the Manner in which such Acts, Records, and Proceedings shall be proved, and the Effect thereof.

Section 2. The Citizens of each State shall be entitled to all Privileges and Immunities of Citizens in the several States.

A Person charged in any State with Treason, Felony, or other Crime, who shall flee from Justice, and be found in another State, shall, on Demand of the executive Authority of the State from which he fled, be delivered up, to be removed to the State having Jurisdiction of the Crime.

No Person held to Service or Labor in one State, under the Laws thereof, escaping into another, shall, in Consequence of any Law or Regulation therein, be discharged from such Service or Labor, but shall be delivered up on Claim of the Party to whom such Service or Labor may be due.

Section 3. New States may be admitted by the Congress into this Union; but no new State shall be formed or erected within the Jurisdiction of any other State, nor any State be formed by the Junction of two or more States, or Parts of States, without the Consent of the Legislatures of the States concerned as well as of the Congress.

The Congress shall have Power to dispose of and make all needful Rules and Regulations respecting the Territory or other Property belonging to the United States; and nothing in this Constitution shall be so construed as to Prejudice any Claims of the United States, or of any particular State.

Section 4. The United States shall guarantee to every State in this Union a Republican Form of Government, and shall protect each of them against Invasion; and on Application of the Legislature, or of the Executive (when the Legislature cannot be convened), against domestic Violence.

ARTICLE V

The Congress, whenever two thirds of both House shall deem it necessary, shall propose Amendments to this Constitution, or, on the Application of the Legislatures of two thirds of the several States, shall call a Convention for proposing Amendments, which, in either Case, shall be valid, to all intents and Purposes, as Part of this Constitution, when ratified by the Legislatures of three fourths of the several States, or by Conventions in three fourths thereof, as the one or the other Mode of Ratification may be proposed by the Congress; Provided that no Amendment which may be made prior to the Year One thousand eight hundred and eight shall in any Manner affect the first and fourth Clauses in the Ninth Section of the first Article; and that no State, without its Consent, shall be deprived of its equal Suffrage in the Senate.

ARTICLE VI

All Debts contracted and Engagements entered into,before the Adoption of this Constitution, shall be as valid against the United States under this Constitution, as under the Confederation.

This Constitution, and the Laws of the United States which shall be made in Pursuance thereof, and all Treaties made,or which shall be made, under the Authority of the United States, shall be the supreme Law of the Land; and the Judges in every State shall be bound thereby, Anything in the Constitution or Laws of any State to the Contrary notwithstanding.

The Senators and Representatives before mentioned, and the Members of the several State Legislatures, and all executive and judicial Officers, both of the United States and of the several States, shall be bound, by Oath or Affirmation, to support this

Constitution; but no religious Test shall ever be required as a Qualification to any Office or public Trust under the United States.

ARTICLE VII

The Ratification of the Conventions of nine States shall be sufficient for the Establishment of this Constitution between the States so ratifying the Same.

Articles in Addition to, and Amendment of, the Constitution of the United States of America, Proposed by Congress, and Ratified by the Legislatures of the Several States Pursuant to the Fifth Article of the Original Constitution

AMENDMENT I

Congress shall make no law respecting an establishment of religion, or prohibiting the free exercise thereof; or abridging the freedom of speech, or of the press; or the right of the people peaceably to assemble, and to petition the Government for a redress of grievances.

AMENDMENT II

A well-regulated Militia being necessary to the security of a free State, the right of the people to keep and bear Arms, shall not be infringed.

AMENDMENT III

No Soldier shall, in time of peace, be quartered in any house, without the consent of the Owner; nor in time of war, but in a manner to be prescribed by law.

AMENDMENT IV

The right of the people to be secure in their persons, houses, papers, and effects, against unreasonable searches and seizures, shall not be violated; and no Warrants shall issue, but upon probable cause, supported by Oath or affirmation, and particularly describing the place to be searched and the persons or things to be seized.

AMENDMENT V

No person shall be held to answer for a capital, or otherwise infamous, crime, unless on a presentment or indictment of a Grand Jury, except in cases arising in the land or naval forces, or in the Militia, when in actual service, in time of War, or public danger; nor shall any person be subject, for the same offence, to be twice put in jeopardy of life or limb; nor shall be compelled in any criminal case to be a witness against himself nor be deprived of life, liberty, or property, without due process of law; nor shall private property be taken for public use, without just compensation.

AMENDMENT VI

In all criminal prosecutions, the accused shall enjoy the right to a speedy and public trial, by an impartial jury of the State and district wherein the crime shall have been committed, which district shall have been previously ascertained by law; and to be informed of the nature and cause of the accusation; to be confronted with the witnesses against him; to have compulsory process for obtaining witnesses in his favor; and to have the Assistance of Counsel for his defence.

AMENDMENT VII

In Suits at common law, where the value in controversy shall exceed twenty dollars, the right of trial by jury shall be preserved; and no fact, tried by a jury, shall be otherwise reexamined in any Court of the United States than according to the rules of the common law.

AMENDMENT VIII

Excessive bail shall not be required, nor excessive fines imposed, nor cruel and unusual punishment inflicted.

AMENDMENT IX

The enumeration in the Constitution of certain rights shall not be construed to deny or disparage others retained by the people.

AMENDMENT X

The powers not delegated to the United States by the Constitution, nor prohibited by it to the States, are reserved to the States respectively or to the people.

AMENDMENT XI

The Judicial power of the United States shall not be construed to extend to any suit in law or equity, commenced or prosecuted against one of the United States by Citizens of another State or by Citizens or Subjects of any Foreign State.

AMENDMENT XII

The Electors shall meet in their respective States, and vote by ballot for President and Vice-President, one of whom, at least, shall not be an inhabitant of the same State with themselves; they shall name in their ballots the person voted for as President, and in distinct ballots the person voted for as Vice-President; and they shall make distinct lists of all persons voted for as President, and of all persons voted for as Vice-President, and of the number of votes for each, which lists they shall sign, and certify, and transmit, sealed, to the seat of the government of the United States, directed to the President of the Senate; the President of the Senate shall, in the presence of the Senate and the House of Representatives, open all the certificates, and the votes shall then be counted; the person having the greatest number of votes for President shall be the President, if such number be a majority of the whole number of Electors appointed; and if no person have such a majority, then, from the persons having the highest numbers, not exceeding three, on the list of those voted for a President, the House of Representatives shall choose immediately, by ballot, the President. But in choosing the President, the votes shall be taken by States, the representation from each State having one vote; a quorum for this purpose shall consist of a member or members from two-thirds of the States, and a majority of all the States shall be necessary to a choice. And if the House of Representatives shall not choose a President, whenever the right of choice shall devolve upon them, before the fourth day of March next following, the Vice-President shall act as President, as in case of death, or other constitutional disability of the President. The person having the greatest number of votes as Vice-President, shall be the Vice-President, if such number be a majority of the whole number of Electors appointed; and if no person have a majority, then, from the two highest numbers on the list, the Senate shall choose the Vice-President; a quorum for the purpose shall consist of two-thirds of the whole number of Senators; a majority of the whole number shall be necessary to a choice. But no person constitutionally ineligible to the office of President shall be eligible to that of Vice-President of the United States.

AMENDMENT XIII

Section 1. Neither slavery nor involuntary servitude, except as a punishment for crime, whereof the party shall have been duly convicted, shall exist within the United States, or any place subject to their jurisdiction.

Section 2. Congress shall have power to enforce this article by appropriate legislation.

AMENDMENT XIV

Section 1. All persons born or naturalized in the United States, and subject to the jurisdiction thereof, are citizens of the United States and of the State wherein they reside. No State shall make or enforce any law which shall abridge the privileges or immunities of citizens of the United States; nor shall any State deprive any person of life, liberty, or property, without due process of law, nor deny any person within its jurisdiction the equal protection of the laws.

Section 2. Representatives shall be apportioned among the several States according to their respective numbers, counting the whole number of persons in each State, excluding Indians not taxed. But when the right to vote at any election for the choice of electors for President and Vice-President of the United States, Representatives in Congress, the Executive and Judicial officers of a State, or the members of the Legislature thereof, is denied to any of the male inhabitants of such State, being twenty one years of age, and citizens of the United States, or in any way abridged, except for participation in rebellion or other crime, the basis of representation therein shall be reduced in the proportion which the number of such male citizens shall bear to the whole number of male citizens twenty one years of age in such State.

Section 3. No person shall be a Senator or Representative in Congress, or elector of President and Vice President, or hold any office, civil or military, under the United States, or under any State, who, having previously taken an oath, as a Member of Congress, or as an officer of the United States, or as a member of any State legislature, or as an executive or judicial officer of any State, to support the Constitution of the United States, shall have engaged in insurrection or rebellion against the same, or given aid or comfort to the enemies thereof. But Congress may, by a vote of two thirds of each House, remove such disability.

Section 4. The validity of the public debt of the United States, authorized by law, including debts incurred for payment of pensions and bounties for services in suppressing insurrection or rebellion, shall not be questioned. But neither the United States nor any State shall assume or pay any debt or obligation incurred in aid of insurrection or rebellion against the United States, or any claim for the loss or emancipation of any slave; but all such debts, obligations, and claims shall be held illegal and void.

Section 5. The Congress shall have power to enforce, by appropriate legislation, the provisions of this article.

AMENDMENT XV

Section 1. The right of citizens of the United States to vote shall not be denied or abridged by the United States or by any State on account of race, color, or previous condition of servitude.

Section 2. The Congress shall have power to enforce this article by appropriate legislation.

AMENDMENT XVI

The Congress shall have power to lay and collect taxes on incomes, from whatever source derived, without apportionment among the several States and without regard to any census or enumeration.

AMENDMENT XVII

The Senate of the United States shall be composed of two Senators from each State, elected by the people thereof, for six years; and each Senator shall have one vote. The electors in each State shall have the qualifications requisite for electors of the most numerous branch of the State legislatures.

When vacancies happen in the representation of any State in the Senate, the executive authority of such State shall issue writs of election to fill such vacancies: Provided, That the legislature of any State may empower the executive thereof to make temporary appointment until the people fill the vacancies by election as the legislature may direct.

This amendment shall not be so construed as to affect the election or term of any Senator chosen before it becomes valid as part of the Constitution.

AMENDMENT XVIII

5

Section 1. After one year from the ratification of this article the manufacture, sale or transportation of intoxicating liquors within, the importation thereof into, or the exportation thereof from the United States and all territory subject to the jurisdiction thereof for beverage purposes is hereby prohibited.

Section 2. The Congress and the several States shall have concurrent power to enforce this article by appropriate legislation.

Section 3. This article shall be inoperative unless it shall have been ratified as an amendment to the Constitution by the legislatures of the several States, as provided in the Constitution, within seven years of the date of the submission hereof to the States by Congress.

[5] This article was replaced by the 21st amendment

AMENDMENT XIX

The right of citizens of the United States to vote shall not be denied or abridged by the United States or by any State on account of sex.

Congress shall have power to enforce this article by appropriate legislation.

AMENDMENT XX

Section 1. The terms of the President and Vice President shall end at noon on the 20th day of January, and the terms of Senators and Representatives at noon on the 3d day of January, of the years in which such terms would have ended if this article had not been ratified; and the terms of their successors shall then begin.

Section 2. The Congress shall assemble at least once in every year, and such meeting shall begin at noon on the 3d day of January, unless they shall by law appoint a different day.

Section 3. If, at the time fixed for the beginning of the term of the President, the President-elect shall have died, the Vice President-elect shall become President. If a President shall not have been chosen before the time fixed for the beginning of his term, or if the President-elect shall have failed to qualify, then the Vice President-elect shall act as President until a President shall have qualified; and the Congress may by law provide for the case wherein neither a President-elect nor a Vice President-elect shall have qualified, declaring who shall then act as President, or the manner in which one who is to act shall be selected, and such person shall act accordingly until a President or Vice President shall have qualified.

Section 4. The Congress may by law provide for the case of the death of any of the persons from whom the House of Representatives may choose a President whenever the right of choice shall have devolved upon them, and for the case of the death of any of the persons from whom the Senate may choose a Vice President whenever the right of choice shall have devolved upon them.

Section 5. Sections 1 and 2 shall take effect on the 15th day of October following the ratification of this article.

Section 6. This article shall be inoperative unless it shall have been ratified as an amendment to the Constitution by three fourths of the several States within seven years from the date of its submission.

AMENDMENT XXI

Section 1. The eighteenth article of amendment to the Constitution of the United States is hereby repealed.

Section 2. The transportation or importation into any State, Territory, or possession of the United States for delivery or use therein of intoxicating liquors, in violation of the laws thereof, is hereby prohibited.

Section 3. This article shall be inoperative unless it shall have been ratified as an amendment to the Constitution by conventions in the several States, as provided in the Constitution, within seven years from the date of the submission hereof to the States by the Congress.

AMENDMENT XXII

Section 1. No person shall be elected to the office of the President more than twice, and no person who has held the office of President, or acted as President, for more than two years of a term to which some other person was elected President shall be elected to the office of the President more than once. But this Article shall not apply to any person holding the office of President when this Article was proposed by the Congress, and shall not prevent any person who may be holding the office of President, or acting as President, during the term within which his Article becomes operative from holding the office of President or acting as President during the remainder of such term.

Section 2. This article shall be inoperative unless it shall have been ratified as an amendment to the Constitution by the legislatures of three-fourths of the several States within seven years from the date of its submission to the States by the Congress.

AMENDMENT XXIII

Section 1. The District constituting the seat of Government of the United States shall appoint in such manner as the Congress may direct:

A number of electors of President and Vice President equal to the whole number of Senators and Representative in Congress to which the District would be entitled if it were a State, but in no event more than the least populous State; they shall be considered, for the purposes of the election of President and Vice President, to be electors appointed by a State; and they shall meet in the District and perform such duties as provided by the twelfth article of amendment.

Section 2. The Congress shall have power to enforce this article by appropriate legislation.

AMENDMENT XXIV

Section 1. The right of citizens of the United States to vote in any primary or other election for President or Vice President, for electors for President or Vice President, or for Senator or Representative in Congress, shall not be denied or abridged by the United States or any State by reason of failure to pay any poll tax or other tax.

Section 2. The Congress shall have power to enforce this article by appropriate legislation.

AMENDMENT XXV

Section 1. In case of the removal of the President from office or of his death or resignation, the Vice President shall become President.

Section 2. Whenever there is a vacancy in the office of the Vice President, the President shall nominate a Vice President who shall take office upon confirmation by a majority vote of both Houses of Congress.

Section 3. Whenever the President transmits to the President pro tempore of the Senate and the Speakers of the House of Representatives his written declaration that he is unable to discharge the powers and duties of his office, and until he transmits to them a written declaration to the contrary, such powers and duties shall be discharged by the Vice President as Acting President.

Section 4. Whenever the Vice President and a majority of either the principal officers of the Executive departments or of such other body as Congress may by law provide, transmit to the President pro tempore of the Senate and the Speaker of the House of Representatives their written declaration that the President is unable to discharge the powers and duties of his office, the Vice President shall immediately assume the powers and duties of the office as Acting President.

Thereafter, when the President transmits to the President pro tempore of the Senate and the Speaker of the House of Representatives his written declaration that no inability exists, he shall resume the powers and duties of his office unless the Vice President and a majority of either principal officers of the executive department or of such other body as Congress may by law provide, transmit within four days to the President pro tempore of the Senate and the Speaker of the House of Representatives their written declaration that the President is unable to discharge the powers and duties of his office. Thereupon Congress shall decide the issue, assembling within forty eight hours for that purpose if not in session. If the Congress, within twenty one days after Congress is required to assemble, determines by two thirds vote of both Houses that the President is unable to discharge the powers and duties of his office, the Vice President shall continue to discharge the same as Acting President; otherwise, the President shall resume the powers and duties of his office.

AMENDMENT XXVI

Section 1. The right of citizens of the United States, who are eighteen years of age or older, to vote shall not be denied or abridged by the United States or by any State on account of age.

Section 2. The Congress shall have the power to enforce this article by appropriate legislation.

AMENDMENT XXVII

No law, varying the compensation for the services of the Senators and Representatives, shall take effect, until an election of Representatives shall have intervened.

U.C.M.J.

U.C.M.J.

APPENDIX 2
UNIFORM CODE OF MILITARY JUSTICE

CHAPTER 47. UNIFORM CODE OF MILITARY JUSTICE

SUBCHAPTER 1. GENERAL PROVISIONS

§ 801. Art. 1. Definitions

In this chapter—

(1) The term "Judge Advocate General " means, severally, the Judge Advocates General of the Army, Navy, and Air Force and, except when the Coast Guard is operating as a service in the Navy, the General Counsel of the Department of Homeland Security.

(2) The Navy, the Marine Corps, and the Coast Guard when it is operating as a service in the Navy, shall be considered as one armed force.

(3) The term "commanding officer " includes only commissioned officers.

(4) The term "officer in charge " means a member of the Navy, the Marine Corps, or the Coast Guard designated as such by appropriate authority.

(5) The term "superior commissioned officer " means a commissioned officer superior in rank or command.

(6) The term "cadet" means a cadet of the United States Military Academy, the United States Air Force Academy, or the United States Coast Guard Academy.

(7) The term "midshipman" means a midshipman of the United States Naval Academy and any other midshipman on active duty in the naval service.

(8) The term "military" refers to any or all of the armed forces.

(9) The term "accuser" means a person who signs and swears to charges, any person who directs that charges nominally be signed and sworn to by another, and any other person who has an interest other than an official interest in the prosecution of the accused.

(10) The term "military judge" means an official of a general or special court-martial detailed in accordance with section 826 of this title (article 26).

(11) The term "law specialist " means a commissioned officer of the Coast Guard designated for special duty (law).

(12) The term "legal officer " means any commissioned officer of the Navy, Marine Corps, or Coast Guard designated to perform legal duties for a command.

(13) The term "judge advocate" means—

(A) an officer of the Judge Advocate General's Corps of the Army or the Navy;

(B) an officer of the Air Force or the Marine Corps who is designated as a judge advocate; or

(C) an officer of the Coast Guard who is designated as a law specialist.

(14) The term "record" , when used in connection with the proceedings of a court-martial, means -

(A) an official written transcript, written summary, or other writing relating to the proceedings; or

(B) an official audiotape, videotape, or similar material from which sound, or sound and visual images, depicting the proceedings may be reproduced.

(15) The term "classified information" means—

(A) any information or material that has been determined by an official of the United States pursuant to law, an Executive order, or regulation to require protection against unauthorized disclosure for reasons of national security, and

(B) any restricted data, as defined in section 11(y) of the Atomic Energy Act of 1954 (42 U.S.C. 2014(y)).

(16) The term "national security" means the national defense and foreign relations of the United States.

§ 802. Art. 2. Persons subject to this chapter

(a) The following persons are subject to this chapter:

(1) Members of a regular component of the armed forces, including those awaiting discharge after expiration of their terms of enlistment; volunteers from the time of their muster or acceptance into the armed forces; inductees from the time of their actual induction into the armed forces; and other persons lawfully called or ordered into, or to duty in or for training in, the armed forces, from the dates when they are required by the terms of the call or order to obey it.

(2) Cadets, aviation cadets, and midshipmen.

(3) Members of a reserve component while on inactive-duty training, but in the case of members of the Army National Guard of the United States or the Air National Guard of the United States only when in Federal service.

(4) Retired members of a regular component of the armed forces who are entitled to pay.

(5) Retired members of a reserve component who are receiving hospitalization from an armed force.

(6) Members of the Fleet Reserve and Fleet Marine Corps Reserve.

(7) Persons in custody of the armed forces serving a sentence imposed by a court-martial.

(8) Members of the National Oceanic and Atmospheric Administration, Public Health Service, and other organizations, when assigned to and serving with the armed forces.

(9) Prisoners of war in custody of the armed forces.

(10) In time of declared war or contingency operation, persons serving with or accompanying an armed force in the field.

(11) Subject to any treaty or agreement to which the United States is or may be a party or to any accepted rule of international law, persons serving with, employed by, or accompanying the armed forces outside the United States and outside the Commonwealth of Puerto Rico, Guam, and the Virgin Islands.

(12) Subject to any treaty or agreement to which the United States is or may be a party or to any accepted rule of international law, persons within an area leased by or otherwise reserved or acquired for the use of the United States which is under the control of the Secretary concerned and which is outside the United States and outside the Canal Zone, the Commonwealth of Puerto Rico, Guam, and the Virgin Islands.

(b) The voluntary enlistment of any person who has the capacity to understand the significance of enlisting in the armed forces shall be valid for purposes of jurisdiction under subsection (a) and a change of status from civilian to member of the armed forces shall be effective upon the taking of the oath of enlistment.

(c) Notwithstanding any other provision of law, a person serving with an armed force who—

(1) submitted voluntarily to military authority;

(2) met the mental competence and minimum age qualifications of sections 504 and 505 of this title at the time of voluntary submission to military authority;

(3) received military pay or allowances; and

(4) performed military duties;

is subject to this chapter until such person's active service has been terminated in accordance with law or regulations promulgated by the Secretary concerned.

(d)(1) A member of a reserve component who is not on active duty and who is made the subject of proceedings under section 81 (article 15) or section 830 (article 30) with respect to an offense against this chapter may be ordered to active duty involuntarily for the purpose of

(A) investigation under section 832 of this title (article 32);

(B) trial by court-martial; or

(C) nonjudicial punishment under section 815 of this title (article 15).

(2) A member of a reserve component may not be ordered to active duty under paragraph (1) except with respect to an offense committed while the member was

(A) on active duty; or

(B) on inactive-duty training, but in the case of members of the Army National Guard of the United States or the Air National Guard of the United States only when in Federal service.

(3) Authority to order a member to active duty under paragraph (1) shall be exercised under regulations prescribed by the President.

(4) A member may be ordered to active duty under paragraph (1) only by a person empowered to convene general courts-martial in a regular component of the armed forces.

(5) A member ordered to active duty under paragraph (1), unless the order to active duty was approved by the Secretary concerned, may not

(A) be sentenced to confinement; or

(B) be required to serve a punishment consisting of any restriction on liberty during a period other than a period of inactive-duty training or active duty (other than active duty ordered under paragraph (l)).

(e) The provisions of this section are subject to section 876(d)(2) of this title (article 76b(d)(2).

§ 803. Art. 3. Jurisdiction to try certain personnel

(a) Subject to section 843 of this title (article 43), a person who is in a status in which the person is subject to this chapter and who committed an offense against this chapter while formerly in a status in which the person was subject to this chapter is not relieved from amenability to the jurisdiction of this chapter for that offense by reason of a termination of that person's former status.

(b) Each person discharged from the armed forces who is later charged with having fraudulently obtained his discharge is, subject to section 843 of this title (article 43), subject to trial by court-martial on that charge and is after apprehension subject to this chapter while in the custody of the armed forces for that trial. Upon conviction of that charge he is subject to trial by court-martial for all offenses under this chapter committed before the fraudulent discharge.

(c) No person who has deserted from the armed forces may be relieved from amenability to the jurisdiction of this chapter by virtue of a separation from any later period of service.

(d) A member of a reserve component who is subject to this chapter is not, by virtue of the termination of a period of active duty or inactive-duty training, relieved from amenability to the jurisdiction of this chapter for an offense against this chapter committed during such period of active duty or inactive-duty training.

§ 804. Art. 4. Dismissed officer's right to trial by court-martial

(a) If any commissioned officer, dismissed by order of the President, makes a written application for trial by court-martial setting forth, under oath, that he has been wrongfully dismissed, the President, as soon as practicable, shall convene a general court-martial to try that officer on the charges on which he was dismissed. A court-martial so convened has jurisdiction to try the dismissed officer on those charges, and he shall be considered to have waived the right to plead any statute of limitations applicable to any offense with which he is charged. The court-martial may, as part of its sentence, adjudge the affirmance of the dismissal, but if the court-martial acquits the accused or if the sentence adjudged, as finally approved or affirmed, does not include dismissal or death, the Secretary concerned shall substitute for the dismissal ordered by the President a form of discharge authorized for administrative issue.

(b) If the President fails to convene a general court-martial within six months from the preparation of an application for trial under this article, the Secretary concerned shall substitute for the dismissal order by the President a form of discharge authorized for administrative issue.

(c) If a discharge is substituted for a dismissal under this article, the President alone may reappoint the officer to such commissioned grade and with such rank as, in the opinion of the President, that former officer would have attained had he not been dismissed. The reappointment of such a former officer shall be without regard to the existence of a vacancy and shall affect the promotion status of other officers only insofar as the President may direct. All time between the dismissal and the reappointment shall be considered as actual service for all purposes, including the right to pay and allowances.

(d) If an officer is discharged from any armed force by administrative action or is dropped from the rolls by order of the President, he has no right to trial under this article.

§ 805. Art. 5. Territorial applicability of this chapter

This chapter applies in all places.

§ 806. Art. 6. Judge Advocates and legal officers

(a) The assignment for duty of judge advocates of the Army, Navy, Air Force, and Coast Guard shall be made upon the recommendation of the Judge Advocate General of the armed force of which they are members. The assignment for duty of judge advocates of the Marine Corps shall be made by direction of the Commandant of the Marine Corps. The Judge Advocate General or senior members of his staff shall make frequent inspection in the field in supervision of the administration of military justice.

(b) Convening authorities shall at all times communicate directly with their staff judge advocates or legal officers in matters relating to the administration of military justice; and the staff judge advocate or legal officer of any command is entitled to communicate directly with the staff judge advocate or legal officer of a superior or subordinate command, or with the Judge Advocate General.

(c) No person who has acted as member, military judge, trial counsel, assistant trial counsel, defense counsel, assistant defense counsel, or investigating officer in any case may later act as a staff judge advocate or legal officer to any reviewing authority upon the same case.

(d)(1) A judge advocate who is assigned or detailed to perform the functions of a civil office in the Government of the United States under section 973(b)(2)(B) of this title may perform such duties as may be requested by the agency concerned, including representation of the United States in civil and criminal cases.

(2) The Secretary of Defense, and the Secretary of Homeland Security with respect to the Coast Guard when it is not operating as a service in the Navy, shall prescribe regulations providing that reimbursement may be a condition of assistance by judge advocates assigned or detailed under section 973(b)(2)(B) of this title.

§ 806a. Art. 6a. Investigation and disposition of matters pertaining to the fitness of military judges

(a) The President shall prescribe procedures for the investigation and disposition of charges, allegations, or information pertaining to the fitness of a military judge or military appellate judge to perform the duties of the judge's position. To the extent practicable, the procedures shall be uniform for all armed forces.

(b) The President shall transmit a copy of the procedures prescribed pursuant to this section to the Committees on Armed Services of the Senate and the House of Representatives.

SUBCHAPTER II. APPREHENSION AND RESTRAINT

§ 807. Art. 7. Apprehension

(a) Apprehension is the taking of a person into custody.

(b) Any person authorized under regulations governing the armed forces to apprehend persons subject to this chapter or to trial thereunder may do so upon reasonable belief that an offense has been committed and that the person apprehended committed it.

(c) Commissioned officers, warrant officers, petty officers, and noncommissioned officers have authority to quell quarrels, frays and disorders among persons subject to this chapter and to apprehend persons subject to this chapter who take part therein.

§ 808. Art. 8. Apprehension of deserters

Any civil officer having authority to apprehend offenders under the laws of the United States or of a State, Commonwealth, or possession, or the District of Columbia may summarily apprehend a deserter from the armed forces and deliver him into the custody of those forces.

§ 809. Art. 9. Imposition of restraint

(a) Arrest is the restraint of a person by an order, not imposed as a punishment for an offense, directing him to remain within certain specified limits. Confinement is the physical restraint of a person.

(b) An enlisted member may be ordered into arrest or confinement by any commissioned officer by an order, oral or written, delivered in person or through other persons subject to this chapter. A commanding officer may authorize warrant officers, petty officers, or noncommissioned officers to order enlisted members of his command or subject to his authority into arrest or confinement.

(c) A commissioned officer, a warrant officer, or a civilian subject to this chapter or to trial thereunder may be ordered into arrest or confinement only by a commanding officer to whose authority he is subject, by an order, oral or written, delivered in person or by another commissioned officer. The authority to order such persons into arrest or confinement may not be delegated.

(d) No person may be ordered into arrest or confinement except for probable cause.

(e) Nothing in this article limits the authority of persons authorized to apprehend offenders to secure the custody of an alleged offender until proper authority may be notified.

§ 810. Art. 10. Restraint of persons charged with offenses

Any person subject to this chapter charged with an offense under this chapter shall be ordered into arrest or confinement, as circumstances may require; but when charged only with an offense normally tried by a summary court-martial, he shall not ordinarily be placed in confinement. When any person subject to this chapter is placed in arrest or confinement prior to trial, immediate steps shall be taken to inform him of the specific wrong of which he is accused and to try him or to dismiss the charges and release him.

§ 811. Art. 11. Reports and receiving of prisoners

(a) No provost marshal, commander or a guard, or master at arms may refuse to receive or keep any prisoner committed to his charge by a commissioned officer of the armed forces, when the committing officer furnishes a statement, signed by him, of the offense charged against the prisoner.

(b) Every commander of a guard or master at arms to whose charge a prisoner is committed shall, within twenty-four hours after that commitment or as soon as he is relieved from guard, report to the commanding officer the name of the prisoner, the offense charged against him, and the name of the person who ordered or authorized the commitment.

§ 812. Art. 12. Confinement with enemy prisoners prohibited

No member of the armed forces may be placed in confinement in immediate association with enemy prisoners or other foreign nationals not members of the armed forces.

§ 813. Art. 13. Punishment prohibited before trial

No person, while being held for trial, may be subjected to punishment or penalty other than arrest or confinement upon the charges pending against him, nor shall the arrest or confinement imposed upon him be any more rigorous than the circumstances required to insure his presence, but he may be subjected to minor punishment during that period for infractions of discipline.

§ 814. Art. 14. Delivery of offenders to civil authorities

(a) Under such regulations as the Secretary concerned may prescribe, a member of the armed forces accused of an offense against civil authority may be delivered, upon request, to the civil authority for trial.

(b) When delivery under this article is made to any civil authority of a person undergoing sentence of a court-martial, the delivery, if followed by conviction in a civil tribunal, interrupts the execution of the sentence of the court-martial, and the offender after having answered to the civil authorities for his offense shall, upon the request of competent military authority, be returned to military custody for the completion of his sentence.

SUBCHAPTER III. NON-JUDICIAL PUNISHMENT

§ 815. Art. 15. Commanding Officer's non-judicial punishment

(a) Under such regulations as the President may prescribe, and under such additional regulations as may be prescribed by the Secretary concerned, limitations may be placed on the powers granted by this article with respect to the kind and amount of punishment authorized, the categories of commanding officers and warrant officers exercising command authorized to exercise those powers, the applicability of this article to an accused who demands trial by court-martial, and the kinds of courts-martial to which the case may be referred upon such a demand. However, except in the case of a member attached to or embarked in a vessel, punishment may not be imposed upon any member of the armed forces under this article if the member has, before the imposition of such punishment, demanded trial by court-martial in lieu of such punishment. Under similar regulations, rules may be prescribed with respect to the suspension of punishments authorized hereunder. If authorized by regulations of the Secretary concerned, a commanding officer exercising general court-martial jurisdiction or an officer of general or flag rank in command may delegate his powers under this article to a principal assistant.

(b) Subject to subsection (a) any commanding officer may, in addition to or in lieu of admonition or reprimand, impose one or more of the following disciplinary punishments for minor offenses without the intervention of a court-martial—

(1) upon officers of his command

(A) restriction to certain specified limits, with or without suspension from duty, for not more than 30 consecutive days;

(B) if imposed by an officer exercising general court-martial jurisdiction or an officer of general or flag rank in command

(i) arrest in quarters for not more than 30 consecutive days;

(ii) forfeiture of not more than one-half of one month's pay per month for two months;

(iii) restriction to certain specified limits, with or without suspension from duty, for not more than 60 consecutive days;

(iv) detention of not more than one-half of one month's pay per month for three months;

(2) upon other personnel of his command—

(A) if imposed upon a person attached to or embarked in a vessel, confinement on bread and water or diminished rations for not more than three consecutive days;

(B) correctional custody for not more than seven consecutive days;

(C) forfeiture of not more than seven days' pay;

(D) reduction to the next inferior pay grade, if the grade from which demoted is within the promotion authority of the officer imposing the reduction or any officer subordinate to the one who imposes the reduction;

(E) extra duties, including fatigue or other duties, for not more than 14 consecutive days;

(F) restriction to certain specified limits, with or without suspension from duty, for not more than 14 consecutive days;

(G) detention of not more than 14 days' pay;

(H) if imposed by an officer of the grade of major or lieutenant commander, or above

(i) the punishment authorized under clause (A);

(ii) correctional custody for not more than 30 consecutive days;

(iii) forfeiture of not more than one-half of one month's pay per month for two months;

(iv) reduction to the lowest or any intermediate pay grade, if the grade from which demoted is within the promotion authority of the officer imposing the reduction or any officer subordinate to the one who imposes the reduction, but an enlisted member in a pay grade above E4 may not be reduced more than two pay grades;

(v) extra duties, including fatigue or other duties, for not more than 45 consecutive days;

(vi) restriction to certain specified limits, with or without suspension from duty, for not more than 60 consecutive days;

(vii) detention of not more than one-half of one month's pay per month for three months.

Detention of pay shall be for a stated period of not more than one year but if the offender's term of service expires earlier, the detention shall terminate upon that expiration. No two or more of the punishments of arrest in quarters, confinement on bread and water or diminished rations, correctional custody, extra duties, and restriction may be combined to run consecutively in the maximum amount imposable for each. Whenever any of those punishments are combined to run consecutively, there must be an apportionment. In addition, forfeiture of pay may not be combined with detention of pay without an apportionment. For the purpose of this subsection, "correctional custody" is the physical restraint of a person during duty or nonduty hours and may include extra duties, fatigue duties, or hard labor. If practicable, correctional custody will not be served in immediate association with persons awaiting trial or held in confinement pursuant to trial by court-martial.

(c) An officer in charge may impose upon enlisted members assigned to the unit of which he is in charge such of the punishments authorized under subsection (b)(2)(A)-(G) as the Secretary concerned may specifically prescribe by regulation.

(d) The officer who imposes the punishment authorized in subsection (b), or his successor in command, may, at any time, suspend probationally any part or amount of the unexecuted punishment imposed and may suspend probationally a reduction in grade or a forfeiture imposed under subsection (b), whether or not executed. In addition, he may, at any time, remit or mitigate any part or amount of the unexecuted punishment imposed and may set aside in whole or in part the punishment, whether executed or unexecuted, and restore all rights, privileges and property affected. He may also mitigate reduction in grade to forfeiture or detention of pay. When mitigating—

(1) arrest in quarters to restriction;

(2) confinement on bread and water or diminished rations to correctional custody;

(3) correctional custody or confinement on bread and water or diminished rations to extra duties or restriction, or both; or

(4) extra duties to restriction; the mitigated punishment shall not be for a greater period than the punishment mitigated.When mitigating forfeiture of pay to detention of pay, the amount of the detention shall not be greater than the amount of the forfeiture. When mitigating reduction in grade to forfeiture or detention of pay, the amount of the forfeiture or detention shall not be greater than the amount that could have been imposed initially under this article by the officer who imposed the punishment mitigated.

(e) A person punished under this article who considers his punishment unjust or disproportionate to the offense may, through the proper channel, appeal to the next superior authority. The appeal shall be promptly forwarded and decided, but the person punished may in the meantime be required to undergo the punishment adjudged. The superior authority may exercise the same powers with respect to the punishment imposed as may be exercised under subsection (d) by the officer who imposed the punishment.Before acting on an appeal from a punishment of -

(1) arrest in quarters for more than seven days;

(2) correctional custody for more than seven days;

(3) forfeiture of more than seven days' pay;

(4) reduction of one or more pay grades from the fourth or a higher pay grade;

(5) extra duties for more than 14 days;

(6) restriction for more than 14 days; or

(7) detention of more than 14 days' pay;

the authority who is to act on the appeal shall refer the case to a judge advocate or a lawyer of the Department of Homeland Security for consideration and advice, and may so refer the case upon appeal from any punishment imposed under subsection (b).

(f) The imposition and enforcement of disciplinary punishment under this article for any act or omission is not a bar to trial by court-martial for a serious crime or offense growing out of the same act or omission, and not properly punishable under this article; but the fact that a disciplinary punishment has been enforced may be shown by the accused upon trial, and when so shown shall be considered in determining the measure of punishment to be adjudged in the event of a finding of guilty.

(g) The Secretary concerned may, by regulation, prescribe the form of records to be kept of proceedings under this article and may also prescribe that certain categories of those proceedings shall be in writing.

SUBCHAPTER IV. COURT-MARTIAL JURISDICTION

§ 816. Art. 16. Courts-martial classified

The three kinds of courts-martial in each of the armed forces are—

(1) general courts-martial, consisting of—

(A) a military judge and not less than five members or, in a case in which the accused may be sentenced to a penalty of death, the number of members determined under section 825a of this title (article 25a); or

(B) only a military judge, if before the court is assembled the accused, knowing the identity of the military judge and after consultation with defense counsel, requests orally on the record or in writing a court composed only of a military judge and the military judge approves;

(2) special courts-martial, consisting of—

(A) not less than three members; or

(B) a military judge and not less than three members; or

(C) only a military judge, if one has been detailed to the court, and the accused under the same conditions as those prescribed in clause (1)(B) so requests; and

(3) summary courts-martial, consisting of one commissioned officer.

§ 817. Art. 17. Jurisdiction of courts-martial in general

(a) Each armed force has court-martial jurisdiction over all persons subject to this chapter. The exercise of jurisdiction by one armed force over personnel of another armed force shall be in accordance with regulations prescribed by the President.

(b) In all cases, departmental review after that by the officer with authority to convene a general court-martial for the command which held the trial, where that review is required under this chapter, shall be carried out by the department that includes the armed force of which the accused is a member.

§ 818. Art. 18. Jurisdiction of general courts-martial

Subject to section 817 of this title (article 17), general courts-martial have jurisdiction to try persons subject to this chapter for any offense made punishable by this chapter and may, under such limitations as the President may prescribe, adjudge any punishment not forbidden by this chapter, including the penalty of death when specifically authorized by this chapter. General courts-martial also have jurisdiction to try any person who by the law of war is subject to trial by a military tribunal and may adjudge any punishment permitted by the law of war. However, a general court-martial of the kind specified in section 816(1)(B) of this title (article 16(1)(B)) shall not have jurisdiction to try any person for any offense for which the death penalty may be adjudged unless the case has been previously referred to trial as a noncapital case.

§ 819. Art. 19. Jurisdiction of special courts-martial

Subject to section 817 of this title (article 17), special courts-martial have jurisdiction to try persons subject to this chapter for any noncapital offense made punishable by this chapter and, under such regulations as the President may prescribe, for capital offenses. Special courts-martial may, under such limitations as the President may prescribe, adjudge any punishment not forbidden by this chapter except death, dishonorable discharge, dismissal, confinement for more than one year, hard labor without confinement for more than three months, forfeiture of pay exceeding two-thirds pay per month, or forfeiture of pay for more than one year. A bad-conduct discharge, confinement for more than six months, or forfeiture of pay for more than six months may not be adjudged unless a complete record of the proceedings and testimony has been made, counsel having the qualifications prescribed under section 827(b) of this title (article 27(b)) was detailed to represent the accused, and a military judge was detailed to the trial, except in any case in which a military judge could not be detailed to the trial because of physical conditions or military exigencies. In any such case in which a military judge was not detailed to the trial, the convening authority shall make a detailed written statement, to be appended to the record, stating the reason or reasons a military judge could not be detailed.

§ 820. Art. 20. Jurisdiction of summary courts-martial

Subject to section 817 of this title (article 17), summary courts-martial have jurisdiction to try persons subject to this chapter, except officers, cadets, aviation cadets, and midshipmen, for any noncapital offense made punishable by this chapter. No person with respect to whom summary courts-martial have jurisdiction may be brought to trial before a summary court-martial if he objects thereto. If objection to trial by summary court-martial is made by an accused, trial may be ordered by special or general court-martial as may be appropriate. Summary courts-martial may, under such limitations as the President may prescribe, adjudge any punishment not forbidden by this chapter except death, dismissal, dishonorable or bad-conduct discharge, confinement for more than one month, hard labor without confinement for more than 45 days, restriction to specified limits for more than two months, or forfeiture of more than two-thirds of one month's pay.

§ 821. Art. 21. Jurisdiction of courts-martial not exclusive

The provisions of this chapter conferring jurisdiction upon courts-martial do not deprive military commissions, provost courts, or other military tribunals of concurrent jurisdiction with respect to offenders or offenses that by statute or by the law of war may be tried by military commissions, provost courts, or other military tribunals.

SUBCHAPTER V. COMPOSITION OF COURTS-MARTIAL

§ 822. Art. 22. Who may convene general courts-martial

(a) General courts-martial may be convened by—

(1) the President of the United States;

(2) the Secretary of Defense;

(3) the commanding officer of a unified or specified combatant command;

(4) the Secretary concerned;

(5) the commanding officer of an Army Group, an Army, an Army Corps, a division, a separate brigade, or a corresponding unit of the Army or Marine Corps;

(6) the commander in chief of a fleet; the commanding officer of a naval station or larger shore activity of the Navy beyond the United States;

(7) the commanding officer of an air command, an air force, an air division, or a separate wing of the Air Force or Marine Corps;

(8) any other commanding officer designated by the Secretary concerned; or

(9) any other commanding officer in any of the armed forces when empowered by the President.

(b) If any such commanding officer is an accuser, the court shall be convened by superior competent authority, and may in any case be convened by such authority if considered desirable by him.

§ 823. Art. 23. Who may convene special courts-martial

(a) Special courts-martial may be convened by—

(1) any person who may convene a general court-martial;

(2) the commanding officer of a district, garrison, fort, camp, station, Air Force base, auxiliary air field, or other place where members of the Army or the Air Force are on duty;

(3) the commanding officer of a brigade, regiment, detached battalion, or corresponding unit of the Army;

(4) the commanding officer of a wing, group, or separate squadron of the Air Force;

(5) the commanding officer of any naval or Coast Guard vessel, shipyard, base, or station; the commanding officer of any Marine brigade, regiment, detached battalion, or corresponding unit; the commanding officer of any Marine barracks, wing, group, separate squadron, station, base, auxiliary air field, or other place where members of the Marine Corps are on duty;

(6) the commanding officer of any separate or detached command or group of detached units of any of the armed forces placed under a single commander for this purpose; or

(7) the commanding officer or officer in charge of any other command when empowered by the Secretary concerned.

(b) If any such officer is an accuser, the court shall be convened by superior competent authority, and may in any case be convened by such authority if considered advisable by him.

§ 824. Art. 24. Who may convene summary courts-martial

(a) Summary courts-martial may be convened by—

(1) any person who may convene a general or special court-martial;

(2) the commanding officer of a detached company or other detachment of the Army;

(3) the commanding officer of a detached squadron or other detachment of the Air Force; or

(4) the commanding officer or officer in charge of any other command when empowered by the Secretary concerned.

(b) When only one commissioned officer is present with a command or detachment he shall be the summary court-martial of that command or detachment and shall hear and determine all summary court-martial cases brought before him. Summary courts-martial may, however, be convened in any case by superior competent authority when considered desirable by him.

§ 825. Art. 25. Who may serve on courts-martial

(a) Any commissioned officer on active duty is eligible to serve on all courts-martial for the trial of any person who may lawfully be brought before such courts for trial.

(b) Any warrant officer on active duty is eligible to serve on general and special courts-martial for the trial of any person, other than a commissioned officer, who may lawfully be brought before such courts for trial.

(c)(1) Any enlisted member of an armed force on active duty who is not a member of the same unit as the accused is eligible to serve on general and special courts-martial for the trial of any enlisted member of an armed force who may lawfully be brought before such courts for trial, but he shall serve as a member of a court only if, before the conclusion of a session called by the military judge under section 839(a) of this title (article 39(a)) prior to trial or, in the absence of such a session, before the court is assembled for the trial of the accused, the accused personally has requested orally on the record or in writing that enlisted members serve on it. After such a request, the accused may not be tried by a general or special court-martial the membership of which does not include enlisted members in a number comprising at least one-third of the total membership of the court, unless eligible enlisted members cannot be obtained on account of physical conditions or military exigencies. If such members cannot be obtained, the court may be assembled and the trial held without them, but the convening authority shall make a detailed written statement, to be appended to the record, stating why they could not be obtained.

(2) In this article, "unit" means any regularly organized body as defined by the Secretary concerned, but in no case may it be a body larger than a company, squadron, ship's crew, or body corresponding to one of them.

(d)(1) When it can be avoided, no member of an armed force may be tried by a court-martial any member of which is junior to him in rank or grade.

(2) When convening a court-martial, the convening authority shall detail as members thereof such members of the armed forces as, in his opinion, are best qualified for the duty by reason of age, education, training, experience, length of service, and judicial temperament. No member of an armed force is eligible to serve as a member of a general or special court-martial when he is the accuser or a witness for the prosecution or has acted as investigating officer or as counsel in the same case.

(e) Before a court-martial is assembled for the trial of a case, the convening authority may excuse a member of the court from participating in the case. Under such regulations as the Secretary concerned may prescribe, the convening authority may delegate his authority under this subsection to his staff judge advocate or legal officer or to any other principal assistant.

§ 825a. Art. 25a. Number of members in capital cases

In a case in which the accused may be sentenced to a penalty of death, the number of members shall be not less than 12, unless 12 members are not reasonably available because of physical conditions or military exigencies, in which case the convening authority shall specify a lesser number of members not less than five, and the court may be assembled and the trial held with not less than the number of members so specified. In such a case, the convening authority shall make a detailed written statement, to be appended to the record, stating why a greater number of members were not reasonably available.

§ 826. Art. 26. Military judge of a general or special court-martial

(a) A military judge shall be detailed to each general court-martial. Subject to regulations of the Secretary concerned, a military judge may be detailed to any special court-martial. The Secretary concerned shall prescribe regulations providing for the manner in which military judges are detailed for such courts-martial and for the persons who are authorized to detail military judges for such courts-martial. The military judge shall preside over each open session of the court-martial to which he has been detailed.

(b) A military judge shall be a commissioned officer of the armed forces who is a member of the bar of a Federal court or a member of the bar of the highest court of a State and who is certified to be qualified for duty as a military judge by the Judge Advocate General of the armed force of which such military judge is a member.

(c) The military judge of a general court-martial shall be designated by the Judge Advocate General, or his designee, of the armed force of which the military judge is a member for detail in accordance with regulations prescribed under subsection (a). Unless the court-martial was convened by the President or the Secretary concerned, neither the convening authority nor any member of his staff shall prepare or review any report concerning the effectiveness, fitness, or efficiency of the military judge so detailed, which relates to his performance of duty as a military judge. A commissioned officer who is certified to be qualified for duty as a military judge of a general court-martial may perform such duties only when he is assigned and directly responsible to the Judge Advocate General, or his designee, of the armed force of which the military judge is a member and may perform duties of a judicial or nonjudicial nature other than those relating to his primary duty as a military judge of a general court-martial when such duties are assigned to him by or with the approval of that Judge Advocate General or his designee.

(d) No person is eligible to act as military judge in a case if he is the accuser or a witness for the prosecution or has acted as investigating officer or a counsel in the same case.

(e) The military judge of a court-martial may not consult with the members of the court except in the presence of the accused, trial counsel, and defense counsel, nor may he vote with the members of the court.

§ 827. Art. 27. Detail of trial counsel and defense counsel

(a)

(1) Trial counsel and defense counsel shall be detailed for each general and special court-martial. Assistant trial counsel and assistant and associate defense counsel may be detailed for each general and special court-martial. The Secretary concerned shall prescribe regulations providing for the manner in which counsel are detailed for such courts-martial and for the persons who are authorized to detail counsel for such courts-martial.

(2) No person who has acted as investigating officer, military judge, or court member in any case may act later as trial counsel, assistant trial counsel, or, unless expressly requested by the accused, as defense counsel or assistant or associate defense counsel in the same case. No person who has acted for the prosecution may act later in the same case for the defense, nor may any person who has acted for the defense act later in the same case for the prosecution.

(b) Trial counsel or defense counsel detailed for a general court-martial—

(1) must be a judge advocate who is a graduate of an accredited law school or is a member of the bar of a Federal court or of the highest court of a State; or must be a member of the bar of a Federal court or of the highest court of a State; and

(2) must be certified as competent to perform such duties by the Judge Advocate General of the armed force of which he is a member.

(c) In the case of a special court-martial—

(1) the accused shall be afforded the opportunity to be represented at the trial by counsel having the qualifications prescribed under section 827(b) of this title (article 27(b)) unless counsel having such qualifications cannot be obtained on account of physical conditions or military exigencies. If counsel having such qualifications cannot be obtained, the court may be convened and the trial held but the convening authority shall make a detailed written statement, to be appended to the record, stating why counsel with such qualifications could not be obtained;

(2) if the trial counsel is qualified to act as counsel before a general court-martial, the defense counsel detailed by the convening authority must be a person similarly qualified; and

(3) if the trial counsel is a judge advocate or a member of the bar of a Federal court or the highest court of a State, the defense counsel detailed by the convening authority must be one of the foregoing.

§ 828. Art. 28. Detail or employment of reporters and Interpreters

Under such regulations as the Secretary concerned may prescribe, the convening authority of a court-martial, military commission, or court of inquiry shall detail or employ qualified court reporters, who shall record the proceedings of and testimony taken before that court or commission. Under like regulations the convening authority of a court-martial, military commission, or court of inquiry may detail or employ interpreters who shall interpret for the court or commission.

§ 829. Art. 29. Absent and additional members

(a) No member of a general or special court-martial may be absent or excused after the court has been assembled for the trial of the accused unless excused as a result of a challenge, excused by the military judge for physical disability or other good cause, or excused by order of the convening authority for good cause.

(b) Whenever a general court-martial, other than a general court-martial composed of a military judge only, is reduced below five members, the trial may not proceed unless the convening authority details new members sufficient in number to provide not less than five members. The trial may proceed with the new members present after the recorded evidence previously introduced before the members of the court has been read to the court in the presence of the military judge, the accused, and counsel for both sides.

(c) Whenever a special court-martial, other than a special court-martial composed of a military judge only, is reduced below three members, the trial may not proceed unless the convening authority details new members sufficient in number to provide not less than three members. The trial shall proceed with the new members present as if no evidence had previously been introduced at the trial, unless a verbatim record of the evidence previously introduced before the members of the court or a stipulation thereof is read to the court in the presence of the military judge, if any, the accused and counsel for both sides.

(d) If the military judge of a court-martial composed of a military judge only is unable to proceed with the trial because of physical disability, as a result of a challenge, or for other good cause, the trial shall proceed, subject to any applicable conditions of section 8 16(1)(B) or (2)(C) of this title (article 16(1)(B) or (2)(C)), after the detail of a new military judge as if no evidence had previously been introduced, unless a verbatim record of the evidence previously introduced or a stipulation thereof is read in court in the presence of the new military judge, the accused, and counsel for both sides.

SUBCHAPTER VI. PRE-TRIAL PROCEDURE

§ 830. Art. 30. Charges and specifications

(a) Charges and specifications shall be signed by a person subject to this chapter under oath before a commissioned officer of the armed forces authorized to administer oaths and shall state—

(1) that the signer has personal knowledge of, or has investigated, the matters set forth therein; and

(2) that they are true in fact to the best of his knowledge and belief.

(b) Upon the preferring of charges, the proper authority shall take immediate steps to determine what disposition should be made thereof in the interest of justice and discipline, and the person accused shall be informed of the charges against him as soon as practicable.

§ 831. Art. 31. Compulsory self-incrimination prohibited

(a) No person subject to this chapter may compel any person to incriminate himself or to answer any question the answer to which may tend to incriminate him.

(b) No person subject to this chapter may interrogate, or request any statement from an accused or a person suspected of an offense without first informing him of the nature of the accusation and advising him that he does not have to make any statement regarding the offense of which he is accused or suspected and that any statement made by him may be used as evidence against him in a trial by court-martial.

(c) No person subject to this chapter may compel any person to make a statement or produce evidence before any military tribunal if the statement or evidence is not material to the issue and may tend to degrade him.

(d) No statement obtained from any person in violation of this article, or through the use of coercion, unlawful influence, or unlawful inducement may be received in evidence against him in a trial by court-martial.

§ 832. Art. 32. Investigation

(a) No charge or specification may be referred to a general court-martial for trial until a thorough and impartial investigation of all the matters set forth therein has been made. This investigation shall include inquiry as to the truth of the matter set forth in the charges, consideration of the form of charges, and a recommendation as to the disposition which should be made of the case in the interest of justice and discipline.

(b) The accused shall be advised of the charges against him and of his right to be represented at that investigation by counsel. The accused has the right to be represented at that investigation as provided in section 838 of this title (article 38) and in regulations prescribed under that section. At that investigation full opportunity shall be given to the accused to cross-examine witnesses against him if they are available and to present anything he may desire in his own behalf, either in defense or mitigation, and the investigation officer shall examine available witnesses requested by the accused. If the charges are forwarded after the investigation, they shall be accompanied by a statement of the substance of the testimony taken on both sides and a copy thereof shall be given to the accused.

(c) If an investigation of the subject matter of an offense has been conducted before the accused is charged with the offense, and if the accused was present at the investigation and afforded the opportunities for representation, cross-examination, and presentation prescribed in subsection (b), no further investigation of that charge is necessary under this article unless it is demanded by the accused after he is informed of the charge. A demand for further investigation entitles the accused to recall witnesses for further cross-examination and to offer any new evidence in his own behalf.

(d) If evidence adduced in an investigation under this article indicates that the accused committed an uncharged offense, the investigating officer may investigate the subject matter of that offense without the accused having first been charged with the offense if the accused—

(1) is present at the investigation;

(2) is informed of the nature of each uncharged offense investigated; and

(3) is afforded the opportunities for representation, cross-examination, and presentation prescribed in subsection (b).

(e) The requirements of this article are binding on all persons administering this chapter but failure to follow them does not constitute jurisdictional error.

§ 833. Art. 33. Forwarding of charges

When a person is held for trial by general court-martial the commanding officer shall, within eight days after the accused is ordered into arrest or confinement, if practicable, forward the charges, together with the Investigation and allied papers, to the officer exercising general court-martial jurisdiction. If that is not practicable, he shall report in writing to that officer the reasons for delay.

§ 834. Art. 34. Advice of staff judge advocate and reference for trial

(a) Before directing the trial of any charge by general court-martial, the convening authority shall refer it to his staff judge advocate for consideration and advice. The convening authority may not refer a specification under a charge to a general court-martial for trial unless he has been advised in writing by the staff judge advocate that—

(1) the specification alleges an offense under this chapter;

(2) the specification is warranted by the evidence indicated in the report of investigation under section 832 of this title (article 32) (if there is such a report); and

(3) a court-martial would have jurisdiction over the accused and the offense.

(b) The advice of the staff judge advocate under subsection (a) with respect to a specification under a charge shall include a written and signed statement by the staff judge advocate

(1) expressing his conclusions with respect to each matter set forth in subsection (a); and

(2) recommending action that the convening authority take regarding the specification.

If the specification is referred for trial, the recommendation of the staff judge advocate shall accompany the specification.

(c) If the charges or specifications are not formally correct or do not conform to the substance of the evidence contained in the report of the investigating officer, formal corrections, and such changes in the charges and specifications as are needed to make them conform to the evidence, may be made.

§ 835. Art. 35. Service of charges

The trial counsel to whom court-martial charges are referred for trial shall cause to be served upon the accused a copy of the charges upon which trial is to be had. In time of peace no person may, against his objection, be brought to trial or be required to participate by himself or counsel in a session called by the military judge under section 839(a) of this title (article 39(a)), in a general court-martial case within a period of five days after the service of charges upon him or in a special court-martial within a period of three days after the service of the charges upon him.

SUBCHAPTER VII. TRIAL PROCEDURE

§ 836. Art. 36. President may prescribe rules

(a) Pretrial, trial, and post-trial procedures, including modes of proof, for cases arising under this chapter triable in courts-martial, military commissions and other military tribunals, and procedures for courts of inquiry, may be prescribed by the President by regulations which shall, so far as he considers practicable, apply the principles of law and the rules of evidence generally recognized in the trial of criminal cases in the United States district courts, but which may not be contrary to or inconsistent with this chapter.

(b) All rules and regulations made under this article shall be uniform insofar as practicable.

§ 837. Art. 37. Unlawfully influencing action of court

(a) No authority convening a general, special, or summary court-martial, nor any other commanding officer, may censure, reprimand, or admonish the court or any member, military judge, or counsel thereof, with respect to the findings or sentence adjudged by the court, or with respect to any other exercises of its or his functions in the conduct of the proceedings. No person subject to this chapter may attempt to coerce or, by any unauthorized means, influence the action of a court-martial or any other military tribunal or any member thereof, in reaching the findings or sentence in any case, or the action of any convening, approving, or reviewing authority with respect to his judicial acts. The foregoing provisions of the subsection shall not apply with respect to (1) general instructional or informational courses in military justice if such courses are designed solely for the purpose of instructing members of a command in the substantive and procedural aspects of courts-martial, or (2) to statements and instructions given in open court by the military judge, president of a special court-martial, or counsel.

(b) In the preparation of an effectiveness, fitness, or efficiency report or any other report or document used in whole or in part for the purpose of determining whether a member of the armed forces is qualified to be advanced, in grade, or in determining the assignment or transfer of a member of the armed forces or in determining whether a member of the armed forces should be retained on active duty, no person subject to this chapter may, in preparing any such report (1) consider or evaluate the performance of duty of any such member of a court-martial, or (2) give a less favorable rating or evaluation of any member of the armed forces because of the zeal with which such member, as counsel, represented any accused before a court-martial.

§ 838. Art. 38. Duties of trial counsel and defense counsel

(a) The trial counsel of a general or special court-martial shall prosecute in the name of the United States, and shall, under the direction of the court, prepare the record of the proceedings.

(b)(1) The accused has the right to be represented in his defense before a general or special court-martial or at an investigation under section 832 of this title (article 32) as provided in this subsection.

(2) The accused may be represented by civilian counsel if provided by him.

(3) The accused may be represented—

(A) by military counsel detailed under section 827 of this title (article 27); or

(B) by military counsel of his own selection if that counsel is reasonably available (as determined under regulations prescribed under paragraph (7)).

(4) If the accused is represented by civilian counsel, military counsel detailed or selected under paragraph (3) shall act as associate counsel unless excused at the request of the accused.

(5) Except as provided under paragraph (6), if the accused is represented by military counsel of his own selection under paragraph (3)(B), any military counsel detailed under paragraph (3)(A) shall be excused.

(6) The accused is not entitled to be represented by more than one military counsel. However, the person authorized under regulations prescribed under section 827 of this title (article 27) to detail counsel in his sole discretion—

(A) may detail additional military counsel as assistant defense counsel; and

(B) if the accused is represented by military counsel of his own selection under paragraph (3)(B), may approve a request from the accused that military counsel detailed under paragraph (3)(A) act as associate defense counsel.

(7) The Secretary concerned shall, by regulation, define "reasonably available" for the purpose of paragraph (3)(B) and establish procedures for determining whether the military counsel selected by an accused under that paragraph is reasonably available. Such regulations may not prescribe any limitation based on the reasonable availability of counsel solely on the grounds that the counsel selected by the accused is from an armed force other than the armed force of which the accused is a member. To the maximum extent practicable, such regulations shall establish uniform policies among the armed forces while recognizing the differences in the circumstances and needs of the various armed forces. The Secretary concerned shall submit copies of regulations prescribed under this paragraph to the Committees on Armed Services of the Senate and House of Representatives.

(c) In any court-martial proceeding resulting in a conviction, the defense counsel—

(1) may forward for attachment to the record of proceedings a brief of such matters as he determines should be considered in behalf of the accused on review (including any objection to the contents of the record which he considers appropriate);

(2) may assist the accused in the submission of any matter under section 860 of this title (article 60); and

(3) may take other action authorized by this chapter.

(d) An assistant trial counsel of a general court-martial may, under the direction of the trial counsel or when he is qualified to be a trial counsel as required by section 827 of this title (article 27), perform any duty imposed by law, regulation, or the custom of the service upon the trial counsel of the court. An assistant trial counsel of a special court-martial may perform any duty of the trial counsel.

(e) An assistant defense counsel of a general or special court-martial may, under the direction of the defense counsel or when he is qualified to be the defense counsel as required by section 827 of this title (article 27), perform any duty imposed by law, regulation, or the custom of the service upon counsel for the accused.

§ 839. Art. 39. Sessions

(a) At any time after the service of charges which have been referred for trial to a court-martial composed of a military judge and members, the military judge may, subject to section 835 of this title (article 35), call the court into session without the presence of the members for the purpose of—

(1) hearing and determining motions raising defenses or objections which are capable of determination without trial of the issues raised by a plea of not guilty;

(2) hearing and ruling upon any matter which may be ruled upon by the military judge under this chapter, whether or not the matter is appropriate for later consideration or decision by the members of the court;

(3) if permitted by regulations of the Secretary concerned, holding the arraignment and receiving the pleas of the accused; and

(b) performing any other procedural function which may be performed by the military judge under this chapter or under rules prescribed pursuant to section 836 of this title (article 36) and which does not require the presence of the members of the court. Proceedings under subsection (a) shall be conducted in the presence of the accused, the defense counsel, and the trial counsel and shall be made a part of the record. These proceedings may be conducted notwithstanding the number of members of the court and without regard to section 829 of this title (article 29). If authorized by regulations of the Secretary concerned, and if at least one defense counsel is physically in the presence of the accused, the presence required by this subsection may otherwise be established by audiovisual technology (such as videoteleconferencing technology).

(c) When the members of a court-martial deliberate or vote, only the members may be present. All other proceedings, including any other consultation of the members of the court with counsel or the military judge, shall be made a part of the record and shall be in the presence of the accused, the defense counsel, the trial counsel, and in cases in which a military judge has been detailed to the court, the military judge.

§ 840. Art. 40. Continuances

The military judge or a court-martial without a military judge may, for reasonable cause, grant a continuance to any party for such time, and as often, as may appear to be just.

§ 841. Art. 41. Challenges

(a)(1) The military judge and members of a general or special court-martial may be challenged by the accused or the trial counsel for cause stated to the court. The military judge, or, if none, the court, shall determine the relevance and validity of challenges for cause, and may not receive a challenge to more than one person at a time. Challenges by the trial counsel shall ordinarily be presented and decided before those by the accused are offered.

(2) If exercise of a challenge for cause reduces the court below the minimum number of members required by section 816 of this title (article 16), all parties shall (notwithstanding section 829 of this title (article 29)) either exercise or waive any challenge for cause then apparent against the remaining members of the court before additional members are detailed to the court. However, peremptory challenges shall not be exercised at that time.

(b)(1) Each accused and the trial counsel are entitled initially to one peremptory challenge of the members of the court. The military judge may not be challenged except for cause.

(2) If exercise of a peremptory challenge reduces the court below the minimum number of members required by section 816 of this title (article 16), the parties shall (notwithstanding section 829 of this title (article 29)) either exercise or waive any remaining peremptory challenge (not previously waived) against the remaining members of the court before additional members are detailed to the court.

(c) Whenever additional members are detailed to the court, and after any challenges for cause against such additional members are presented and decided, each accused and the trial counsel are entitled to one peremptory challenge against members not previously subject to peremptory challenge.

(As amended Nov. 5, 1990, Pub.L. 101–510, Div. A, Title V, § 541(b)–(d), 104 Stat. 1565.)

§ 842. Art. 42. Oaths

(a) Before performing their respective duties, military judges, members of general and special courts-martial, trial counsel, assistant trial counsel, defense counsel, assistant or associate defense counsel, reporters, and interpreters shall take an oath to perform their duties faithfully. The form of the oath, the time and place of the taking thereof, the manner of recording the same, and whether the oath shall be taken for all cases in which these duties are to be performed or for a particular case, shall be as prescribed in regulations of the Secretary concerned. These regulations may provide that an oath to perform faithfully duties as a military judge, trial counsel, assistant trial counsel, defense counsel, or assistant or associate defense counsel may be taken at any time by any judge advocate or other person certified to be qualified or competent for the duty, and if such an oath is taken it need not again be taken at the time the judge advocate, or other person is detailed to that duty.

(b) Each witness before a court-martial shall be examined on oath.

§ 843. Art. 43. Statute of limitations

(a) A person charged with absence without leave or missing movement in time of war, with murder, rape, or rape of a child, or with any other offense punishable by death, may be tried and punished at any time without limitation.

(b)(1) Except as otherwise provided in this section (article), a person charged with an offense is not liable to be tried by court-martial if the offense was committed more than five years before the receipt of sworn charges and specifications by an officer exercising summary court-martial jurisdiction over the command.

(2)(A) A person charged with having committed a child abuse offense against a child is liable to be tried by court-martial if the sworn charges and specifications are received during the life of the child or within five years after the date on which the offense was committed, whichever provides a longer period, by an officer exercising summary court-martial jurisdiction with respect to that person.

(B) In subparagraph (A), the term "child abuse offense" means an act that involves abuse of a person who has not attained the age of 16 years and constitutes any of the following offenses:

(i) Any offense in violation of section 920 of this title (article 120).

(ii) Maiming in violation of section 924 of this title (article 124).

(iii) Sodomy in violation of section 925 of this title (article 125).

(iv) Aggravated assault or assault consummated by a battery in violation of section 928 of this title (article 128).

(v) Kidnapping; indecent assault; assault with intent to commit murder, voluntary manslaughter, rape, or sodomy, or indecent acts or liberties with a child in violation of section 934 of this title (article 134).

(C) In subparagraph (A), the term 'child abuse offense' includes an act that involves abuse of a person who has not attained the age of 18 years and would constitute an offense under chapter 110 or 117, or under section 1591, of title 18.

(3) A person charged with an offense is not liable to be punished under section 815 of this title (article 15) if the offense was committed more than two years before the imposition of punishment.

(c) Periods in which the accused is absent without authority or fleeing from justice shall be excluded in computing the period of limitation prescribed in this section (article).

(d) Periods in which the accused was absent from territory in which the United States has the authority to apprehend him, or in the custody of civil authorities, or in the hands of the enemy, shall be excluded in computing the period of limitation prescribed in this article.

(e) For an offense the trial of which in time of war is certified to the President by the Secretary concerned to be detrimental to the prosecution of the war or inimical to the national security, the period of limitation prescribed in this article is extended to six months after the termination of hostilities as proclaimed by the President or by a joint resolution of Congress.

(f) When the United States is at war, the running of any statute of limitations applicable to any offense under this chapter—

(1) involving fraud or attempted fraud against the United States or any agency thereof in any manner, whether by conspiracy or not;

(2) committed in connection with the acquisition, care, handling, custody, control, or disposition of any real or personal property of the United States; or

(3) committed in connection with the negotiation, procurement, award, performance, payment, interim financing, cancellation, or other termination or settlement, of any contract, subcontract, or purchase order which is connected with or related to the prosecution of the war, or with any disposition of termination inventory by any war contractor or Government agency;

is suspended until three years after the termination of hostilities as proclaimed by the President or by a joint resolution of Congress.

(g)(1) If charges or specifications are dismissed as defective or insufficient for any cause and the period prescribed by the applicable statute of limitations—

(A) has expired; or

(B) will expire within 180 days after the date of dismissal of the charges and specifications, trial and punishment under new charges and specifications are not barred by the statute of limitations if the conditions specified in paragraph (2) are met.

(2) The conditions referred to in paragraph (1) are that the new charges and specifications must—

(A) be received by an officer exercising summary court-martial jurisdiction over the command within 180 days after the dismissal of the charges or specifications; and

(B) allege the same acts or omissions that were alleged in the dismissed charges or specifications (or allege acts or omissions that were included in the dismissed charges or specifications).

§ 844. Art. 44. Former jeopardy

(a) No person may, without his consent, be tried a second time for the same offense.

(b) No proceeding in which an accused has been found guilty by court-martial upon any charge or specification is a trial in the sense of this article until the finding of guilty has become final after review of the case has been fully completed.

(c) A proceeding which, after the introduction of evidence but before a finding, is dismissed or terminated by the convening authority or on motion of the prosecution for failure of available evidence or witnesses without any fault of the accused is a trial in the sense of this article.

§ 845. Art. 45. Pleas of the accused

(a) If an accused after arraignment makes an irregular pleading, or after a plea of guilty sets up matter inconsistent with the plea, or if it appears that he has entered the plea of guilty improvidently or through lack of understanding of its meaning and effect, or if he fails or refuses to plead, a plea of not guilty shall be entered in the record, and the court shall proceed as though he had pleaded not guilty.

(b) A plea of guilty by the accused may not be received to any charge or specification alleging an offense for which the death penalty may be adjudged. With respect to any other charge or specification to which a plea of guilty has been made by the accused and accepted by the military judge or by a court-martial without a military judge, a finding of guilty of the charge or specification may, if permitted by regulations of the Secretary concerned, be entered immediately without vote. This finding shall constitute the finding of the court unless the plea of guilty is withdrawn prior to announcement of the sentence, in which event the proceedings shall continue as though the accused had pleaded not guilty.

§ 846. Art. 46. Opportunity to obtain witnesses and other evidence

The trial counsel, the defense counsel, and the court-martial shall have equal opportunity to obtain witnesses and other evidence in accordance with such regulations as the President may prescribe. Process issued in court-martial cases to compel witnesses to appear and testify and to compel the production of other evidence shall be similar to that which courts of the United States having criminal jurisdiction may lawfully issue and shall run to any part of the United States, or the Commonwealths and possessions.

§ 847. Art. 47. Refusal to appear or testify

(a) Any person not subject to this chapter who—

(1) has been duly subpoenaed to appear as a witness before a court-martial, military commission, court of inquiry, or any other military court or board, or before any military or civil officer designated to take a deposition to be read in evidence before such a court, commission, or board;

(2) has been duly paid or tendered the fees and mileage of a witness at the rates allowed to witnesses attending the courts of the United States; and

(3) willfully neglects or refuses to appear, or refuses to qualify as a witness or to testify or to produce any evidence which that person may have been legally subpoenaed to produce;

is guilty of an offense against the United States.

(b) Any person who commits an offense named in subsection (a) shall be tried on indictment or information in a United States district court or in a court of original criminal jurisdiction in any of the Commonwealths or possessions of the United States, and jurisdiction is conferred upon those courts for that purpose. Upon conviction, such a person shall be fined or imprisoned, or both, at the court's discretion.

(c) The United States attorney or the officer prosecuting for the United States in any such court of original criminal jurisdiction shall, upon the certification of the facts to him by the military court, commission, court of inquiry, or board, file an information against and prosecute any person violating this article.

(d) The fees and mileage of witnesses shall be advanced or paid out of the appropriations for the compensation of witnesses.

§ 848. Art. 48. Contempts

A court-martial, provost court, or military commission may punish for contempt any person who uses any menacing word, sign, or gesture in its presence, or who disturbs its proceedings by any riot or disorder. The punishment may not exceed confinement for 30 days or a fine of $100, or both.

§ 849. Art. 49. Depositions

(a) At any time after charges have been signed as provided in section 830 of this title (article 30), any party may take oral or written depositions unless the military judge or court-martial without a military judge hearing the case or, if the case is not being heard, an authority competent to convene a court-martial for the trial of those charges forbids it for good cause. If a deposition is to be taken before charges are referred for trial, such an authority may designate commissioned officers to represent the prosecution and the defense and may authorize those officers to take the deposition of any witness.

(b) The party at whose instance a deposition is to be taken shall give to every other party reasonable written notice of the time and place for taking the deposition.

(c) Depositions may be taken before and authenticated by any military or civil officer authorized by the laws of the United States or by the laws of the place where the deposition is taken to administer oaths.

(d) A duly authenticated deposition taken upon reasonable notice to the other parties, so far as otherwise admissible under the rules of evidence, may be read in evidence or, in the case of audiotape, videotape, or similar material, may be played in evidence before any military court or commission in any case not capital, or in any proceeding before a court of inquiry or military board, if it appears

(1) that the witness resides or is beyond the State, Commonwealth, or District of Columbia in which the court, commission, or board is ordered to sit, or beyond 100 miles from the place of trial or hearing;

(2) that the witness by reason of death, age, sickness, bodily infirmity, imprisonment, military necessity, nonamenability to process, or other reasonable cause, is unable or refuses to appear and testify in person at the place of trial or hearing; or

(3) that the present whereabouts of the witness is unknown.

(e) Subject to subsection (d), testimony by deposition may be presented by the defense in capital cases.

(f) Subject to subsection (d), a deposition may be read in evidence or, in the case of audiotape, videotape, or similar material, may be played in evidence in any case in which the death penalty is authorized but is not mandatory, whenever the convening authority directs that the case be treated as not capital, and in such a case a sentence of death may not be adjudged by the court-martial.

§ 850. Art. 50. Admissibility of records of courts of inquiry

(a) In any case not capital and not extending to the dismissal of a commissioned officer, the sworn testimony, contained in the duly authenticated record of proceedings of a court of inquiry, of a person whose oral testimony cannot be obtained, may, if otherwise admissible under the rules of evidence, be read in evidence by any party before a court-martial or military commission if the accused was a party before the court of inquiry and if the same issue was involved or if the accused consents to the introduction of such evidence.

(b) Such testimony may be read in evidence only by the defense in capital cases or cases extending to the dismissal of a commissioned officer.

(c) Such testimony may also be read in evidence before a court of inquiry or a military board.

§ 850a. Art. 50a. Defense of lack of mental responsibility

(a) It is an affirmative defense in a trial by court-martial that, at the time of the commission of the acts constituting the offense, the accused, as a result of a severe mental disease or defect, was unable to appreciate the nature and quality or the wrongfulness of the acts. Mental disease or defect does not otherwise constitute a defense.

(b) The accused has the burden of proving the defense of lack of mental responsibility by clear and convincing evidence.

(c) Whenever lack of mental responsibility of the accused with respect to an offense is properly at issue, the military judge, or the president of a court-martial without a military judge, shall instruct the members of the court as to the defense of lack of mental responsibility under this section and shall charge them to find the accused—

(1) guilty;

(2) not guilty; or

(3) not guilty only by reason of lack of mental responsibility.

(d) Subsection (c) does not apply to a court-martial composed of a military judge only. In the case of a court-martial composed of a military judge only, whenever lack of mental responsibility of the accused with respect to an offense is properly at issue, the military judge shall find the accused—

(1) guilty;

(2) not guilty; or

(3) not guilty only by reason of lack of mental responsibility.

(e) Notwithstanding the provisions of section 852 of this title (article 52), the accused shall be found not guilty only by reason of lack of mental responsibility if—

(1) a majority of the members of the court-martial present at the time the vote is taken determines that the defense of lack of mental responsibility has been established; or

(2) in the case of court-martial composed of a military judge only, the military judge determines that the defense of lack of mental responsibility has been established.

§ 851. Art. 51. Voting and rulings

(a) Voting by members of a general or special court-martial on the findings and on the sentence, and by members of a court-martial without a military judge upon questions of challenge, shall be by secret written ballot. The junior member of the court shall count the votes. The count shall be checked by the president, who shall forthwith announce the result of the ballot to the members of the court.

(b) The military judge and, except for questions of challenge, the president of a court-martial without a military judge shall rule upon all questions of law and all interlocutory questions arising during the proceedings. Any such ruling made by the military judge upon any question of law or any interlocutory question other than the factual issue of mental responsibility of the accused, or by the president of a court-martial without a military Judge upon any question of law other than a motion for a finding of not guilty, is final and constitutes the ruling of the court. However, the military judge or the president of a court-martial without a military judge may change his ruling at any time during the trial. Unless the ruling is final, if any member objects thereto, the court shall be cleared and closed and the question decided by a voice vote as provided in section 852 of this title (article 52), beginning with the junior in rank.

(c) Before a vote is taken on the findings, the military judge or the president of a court-martial without a military judge shall, in the presence of the accused and counsel, instruct the members of the court as to the elements of the offense and charge them—

(1) that the accused must be presumed to be innocent until his guilt is established by legal and competent evidence beyond reasonable doubt;

(2) that in the case being considered, if there is a reasonable doubt as to the guilt of the accused, the doubt must be resolved in favor of the accused and he must be acquitted;

(3) that, if there is reasonable doubt as to the degree of guilt, the finding must be in a lower degree as to which there is no reasonable doubt; and

(4) that the burden of proof to establish the guilt of the accused beyond reasonable doubt is upon the United States.

(d) Subsections (a), (b), and (c) do not apply to a court-martial composed of a military judge only. The military judge of such a court-martial shall determine all questions of law and fact arising during the proceedings and, if the accused is convicted, adjudge an appropriate sentence. The military judge of such a court-martial shall make a general finding and shall in addition on request find the facts specially. If an opinion or memorandum of decision is filed, it will be sufficient if the findings of fact appear therein.

§ 852. Art. 52. Number of votes required

(a)(1) No person may be convicted of an offense for which the death penalty is made mandatory by law, except by the concurrence of all the members of the court-martial present at the time the vote is taken.

(2) No person may be convicted of any other offense, except as provided in section 845(b) of this title (article 45(b)) or by the concurrence of two-thirds of the members present at the time the vote is taken.

(b)(1) No person may be sentenced to suffer death, except by the concurrence of all the members of the court-martial present at the time the vote is taken and for an offense in this chapter expressly made punishable by death.

(2) No person may be sentenced to life imprisonment or to confinement for more than ten years, except by the concurrence of three-fourths of the members present at the time the vote is taken.

(3) All other sentences shall be determined by the concurrence of two-thirds of the members present at the time the vote is taken.

(c) All other questions to be decided by the members of a general or special court-martial shall be determined by a majority vote, but a determination to reconsider a finding of guilty or to reconsider a sentence, with a view toward decreasing it, may be made by any lesser vote which indicates that the reconsideration is not opposed by the number of votes required for that finding or sentence. A tie vote on a challenge disqualifies the member challenged. A tie vote on a motion for a finding of not guilty or on a motion relating to the question of the accused's sanity is a determination against the accused. A tie vote on any other question is a determination in favor of the accused.

§ 853. Art. 53. Court to announce action

A court-martial shall announce its findings and sentence to the parties as soon as determined.

§ 854. Art. 54. Record of trial

(a) Each general court-martial shall keep a separate record of the proceedings in each case brought before it, and the record shall be authenticated by the signature of the military judge. If the record cannot be authenticated by the military judge by reason of his death, disability, or absence, it shall be authenticated by the signature of the trial counsel or by that of a member if the trial counsel is unable to authenticate it by reason of his death, disability, or absence. In a court-martial consisting of only a military judge the record shall be authenticated by the court reporter under the same conditions which would impose such a duty on a member under the subsection.

(b) Each special and summary court-martial shall keep a separate record of the proceedings in each case, and the record shall be authenticated in the manner required by such regulations as the President may prescribe.

(c)(1) A complete record of the proceedings and testimony shall be prepared—

(A) in each general court-martial case in which the sentence adjudged includes death, a dismissal, a discharge, or (if the sentence adjudged does not include a discharge) any other punishment which exceeds that which may otherwise be adjudged by a special court-martial; and

(B) in each special court-martial case in which the sentence adjudged includes a bad-conduct discharge, confinement for more than six months, or forfeiture of pay for more than six months.

(2) In all other court-martial cases, the record shall contain such matters as may be prescribed by regulations of the President.

(d) A copy of the record of the proceedings of each general and special court-martial shall be given to the accused as soon as it is authenticated.

SUBCHAPTER VIII. SENTENCES

§ 855. Art. 55. Cruel and unusual punishments prohibited

Punishment by flogging, or by branding, marking, or tattooing on the body, or any other cruel or unusual punishment, may not be adjudged by a court-martial or inflicted upon any person subject to this chapter. The use of irons, single or double, except for the purpose of safe custody, is prohibited.

§ 856. Art. 56. Maximum limits

The punishment which a court-martial may direct for an offense may not exceed such limits as the President may prescribe for that offense.

§ 856a. Art. 56a. Sentence of confinement for life without eligibility for parole

(a) For any offense for which a sentence of confinement for life may be adjudged, a court-martial may adjudge a sentence of confinement for life without eligibility for parole.

(b) An accused who is sentenced to confinement for life without eligibility for parole shall be confined for the remainder of the accused's life unless—

(1) the sentence is set aside or otherwise modified as a result of—

(A) action taken by the convening authority, the Secretary concerned, or another person authorized to act under section 860 of this title (article 60); or

(B) any other action taken during post-trial procedure and review under any other provision of subchapter IX;

(2) the sentence is set aside or otherwise modified as a result of action taken by a Court of Criminal Appeals, the Court of Appeals for the Armed Forces, or the Supreme Court; or

(3) the accused is pardoned.

§ 857. Art. 57. Effective date of sentences

(a)

(1) Any forfeiture of pay or allowances or reduction in grade that is included in a sentence of a court-martial takes effect on the earlier of—

(A) the date that is 14 days after the date on which the sentence is adjudged; or

(B) the date on which the sentence is approved by the convening authority.

(2) On application by an accused, the convening authority may defer a forfeiture of pay or allowances or reduction in grade that would otherwise become effective under paragraph (1)(A) until the date on which the sentence is approved by the convening authority. Such a deferment may be rescinded at any time by the convening authority.

(3) A forfeiture of pay and allowances shall be applicable to pay and allowances accruing on and after the date on which the sentence takes effect.

(4) In this subsection, the term "convening authority ", with respect to a sentence of a court-martial, means any person authorized to act on the sentence under section 860 of this title (article 60).

(b) Any period of confinement included in a sentence of a court-martial begins to run from the date the sentence is adjudged by the court-martial, but periods during which the sentence to confinement is suspended or deferred shall be excluded in computing the service of the term of confinement.

(c) All other sentences of courts-martial are effective on the date ordered executed.

§ 857a. Art. 57a. Deferment of sentences

(a) On application by an accused who is under sentence to confinement that has not been ordered executed, the convening authority or, if the accused is no longer under his jurisdiction, the officer exercising general court-martial jurisdiction over the command to which the accused is currently assigned, may in his sole discretion defer service of the sentence to confinement. The deferment shall terminate when the sentence is ordered executed. The deferment may be rescinded at any time by the officer who granted it or, if the accused is no longer under his jurisdiction, by the officer exercising general court-martial jurisdiction over the command to which the accused is currently assigned.

(b)

(1) In any case in which a court-martial sentences a person referred to in paragraph (2) to confinement, the convening authority may defer the service of the sentence to confinement, without the consent of that person, until after the person has been permanently released to the armed forces by a state or foreign country referred to in that paragraph.

(2) Paragraph (1) applies to a person subject to this chapter who—

(A) While in the custody of a state or foreign country is temporarily returned by that state or foreign country to the armed forces for trial by court-martial; and

(B) After the court-martial, is returned to that state or foreign country under the authority of a mutual agreement or treaty, as the case may be.

(3) In this subsection, the term "state " means a state of the United States, the District of Columbia, a territory, or a possession of the United States.

(c) In any case in which a court-martial sentences a person to confinement and the sentence to confinement has been ordered executed, but in which review of the case under section 867(a)(2) of this title (article 67(a)(2)) is pending, the Secretary concerned may defer further service of sentence to confinement while that review is pending.

§ 858. Art. 58. Execution of confinement

(a) Under such instructions as the Secretary concerned may prescribe, a sentence of confinement adjudged by a court-martial or other military tribunal, whether or not the sentence includes discharge or dismissal, and whether or not the discharge or dismissal has been executed, may be carried into execution by confinement in any place of confinement under the control of any of the armed forces or in any penal or correctional institution under the control of the United States, or which the United States may be allowed to use. Persons so confined in a penal or correctional institution not under the control of one of the armed forces are subject to the same discipline and treatment as persons confined or committed by the courts of the United States or of the State, District of Columbia, or place in which the institution is situated.

(b) The omission of the words "hard labor " from any sentence of a court-martial adjudging confinement does not deprive the authority executing that sentence of the power to require hard labor as a part of the punishment.

§ 858a. Art. 58a. Sentences: reduction in enlisted grade upon approval

(a) Unless otherwise provided in regulations to be prescribed by the Secretary concerned, a court-martial sentence of an enlisted member in a pay grade above E–1, as approved by the convening authority, that includes—

(1) a dishonorable or bad-conduct discharge;

(2) confinement; or

(3) hard labor without confinement;

reduces that member to pay grade E-1, effective on the date of that approval.

(b) If the sentence of a member who is reduced in pay grade under subsection (a) is set aside or disapproved, or, as finally approved, does not include any punishment named in subsection (a)(l), (2), or (3), the rights and privileges of which he was deprived because of that reduction shall be restored to him and he is entitled to the pay and allowances to which he would have been entitled for the period the reduction was in effect, had he not been so reduced.

§ 858b. Art. 58b. Sentences: forfeiture of pay and allowances during confinement

(a)

(1) A court-martial sentence described in paragraph (2) shall result in the forfeiture of pay, or of pay and allowances, due that member during any period of confinement or parole. The forfeiture pursuant to this section shall take effect on the date determined under section 857(a) of this title (article 57(a)) and may be deferred as provided in that section. The pay and allowances forfeited, in the case of a general court-martial, shall be all pay and allowances due that member during such period and, in the case of a special court-martial, shall be two-thirds of all pay due that member during such period.

(2) A sentence covered by this section is any sentence that includes—

(A) confinement for more than six months or death; or

(B) confinement for six months or less and a dishonorable or bad-conduct discharge or dismissal.

(b) In a case involving an accused who has dependents, the convening authority or other person acting under section 860 of this title (article 60) may waive any or all of the forfeitures of pay and allowances required by subsection (a) for a period not to exceed six months. Any amount of pay or allowances that, except for a waiver under this subsection, would be forfeited shall be paid, as the convening authority or other person taking action directs, to the dependents of the accused.

(c) If the sentence of a member who forfeits pay and allowances under subsection (a) is set aside or disapproved or, as finally approved, does not provide for a punishment referred to in subsection (a)(2), the member shall be paid the pay and allowances which the member would have been paid, except for the forfeiture, for the period which the forfeiture was in effect.

SUBCHAPTER IX. POST-TRIAL PROCEDURE AND REVIEW OF COURTS-MARTIAL

§ 859. Art. 59. Error of law; lesser included offense

(a) A finding or sentence of court-martial may not be held incorrect on the ground of an error of law unless the error materially prejudices the substantial rights of the accused.

(b) Any reviewing authority with the power to approve or affirm a finding of guilty may approve or affirm, instead, so much of the finding as includes a lesser included offense.

§ 860. Art. 60. Action by the Convening authority

(a) The findings and sentence of a court-martial shall be reported promptly to the convening authority after the announcement of the sentence. Any such submission shall be in writing.

(b)(1) The accused may submit to the convening authority matters for consideration by the convening authority with respect to the findings and the sentence. Any such submissions shall be in writing. Except in a summary court-martial case, such a submission shall be made within 10 days after the accused has been given an authenticated record of trial and, if applicable, the recommendation of the staff judge advocate or legal officer under subsection (d). In a summary court-martial case, such a submission shall be made within seven days after the sentence is announced.

(2) If the accused shows that additional time is required for the accused to submit such matters, the convening authority or other person taking action under this section, for good cause, may extend the applicable period under paragraph (1) for not more than an additional 20 days.

(3) In a summary court-martial case, the accused shall be promptly provided a copy of the record of trial for use in preparing a submission authorized by paragraph (1).

(4) The accused may waive his right to make a submission to the convening authority under paragraph (1). Such a waiver must be made in writing and may not be revoked. For the purposes of subsection (c)(2), the time within which the accused may make a submission under this subsection shall be deemed to have expired upon the submission of such a waiver to the convening authority.

(c)(1) The authority under this section to modify the findings and sentence of a court-martial is a matter of command prerogative involving the sole discretion of the convening authority. Under regulations of the Secretary concerned, a commissioned officer commanding for the time being, a successor in command, or any person exercising general court-martial jurisdiction may act under this section in place of the convening authority.

(2) Action on the sentence of a court-martial shall be taken by the convening authority or by another person authorized to act under this section. Subject to regulations of the Secretary concerned, such action may be taken only after consideration of any matters submitted by the accused under subsection (b) or after the time for submitting such matters expires, whichever is earlier. The convening authority or other person taking such action, in his sole discretion, may approve, disapprove, commute, or suspend the sentence in whole or in part.

(3) Action on the findings of a court-martial by the convening authority or other person acting on the sentence is not required. However, such person, in his sole discretion, may—

(A) dismiss any charge or specification by setting aside a finding of guilty thereto; or

(B) change a finding of guilty to a charge or specification to a finding of guilty to an offense that is a lesser included offense of the offense stated in the charge or specification.

(d) Before acting under this section on any general court-martial case or any special court-martial case that includes a bad-conduct discharge, the convening authority or other person taking action under this section shall obtain and consider the written recommendation of his staff judge advocate or legal officer. The convening authority or other person taking action under this section shall refer the record of trial to his staff judge advocate or legal officer, and the staff judge advocate or legal officer shall use such record in the preparation of his recommendation. The recommendation of the staff judge advocate or legal officer shall include such matters as the President may prescribe by regulation and shall be served on the accused, who may submit any matter in response under subsection (b). Failure to object in the response to the recommendation or to any matter attached to the recommendation waives the right to object thereto.

(e)(1) The convening authority or other person taking action under this section, in his sole discretion, may order a proceeding in revision or a rehearing.

(2) A proceeding in revision may be ordered if there is an apparent error or omission in the record or if the record shows improper or inconsistent action by a court-martial with respect to the findings or sentence that can be rectified without material prejudice to the substantial rights of the accused. In no case, however, may a proceeding in revision—

(A) reconsider a finding of not guilty of any specification or a ruling which amounts to a finding of not guilty;

(B) reconsider a finding of not guilty of any charge, unless there has been a finding of guilty under a specification laid under that charge, which sufficiently alleges a violation of some article of this chapter; or

(C) increase the severity of some article of the sentence unless the sentence prescribed for the offense is mandatory.

(3) A rehearing may be ordered by the convening authority or other person taking action under this section if he disapproves the findings and sentence and states the reasons for disapproval of the findings. If such person disapproves the findings and sentence and does not order a rehearing, he shall dismiss the charges. A rehearing as to the findings may not be ordered where there is a lack of sufficient evidence in the record to support the findings. A

rehearing as to the sentence may be ordered if the convening authority or other person taking action under this subsection disapproves the sentence.

§ 861. Art. 61. Waiver or withdrawal of appeal

(a) In each case subject to appellate review under section 866 or 869(a) of this title (article 66 or 69(a)), except a case in which the sentence as approved under section 860(c) of this title (article 60(c)) includes death, the accused may file with the convening authority a statement expressly waiving the right of the accused to such review. Such a waiver shall be signed by both the accused and by defense counsel and must be filed within 10 days after the action under section 860(c) of this title (article 60(c)) is served on the accused or on defense counsel. The convening authority or other person taking such action, for good cause, may extend the period for such filing by not more than 30 days.

(b) Except in a case in which the sentence as approved under section 860(c) of this title (article 60(c)) includes death, the accused may withdraw an appeal at any time.

(c) A waiver of the right to appellate review or the withdrawal of an appeal under this section bars review under section 866 or 869(a) of this title (article 66 or 69(a)).

§ 862. Art. 62. Appeal by the United States

(a)

(1) In a trial by court-martial in which a military judge presides and in which a punitive discharge may be adjudged, the United States may appeal the following (other than an order or ruling that is, or that amounts to, a finding of not guilty with respect to the charge or specification):

(A) An order or ruling of the military judge which terminates the proceedings with respect to a charge or specification.

(B) An order or ruling which excludes evidence that is substantial proof of a fact material in the proceeding.

(C) An order or ruling which directs the disclosure of classified information.

(D) An order or ruling which imposes sanctions for nondisclosure of classified information.

(E) A refusal of the military judge to issue a protective order sought by the United States to prevent the disclosure of classified information.

(F) A refusal by the military judge to enforce an order described in subparagraph (E) that has previously been issued by appropriate authority.

(2) An appeal of an order or ruling may not be taken unless the trial counsel provides the military judge with written notice of appeal from the order or ruling within 72 hours of the order or ruling. Such notice shall include a certification by the trial counsel that the appeal is not taken for the purpose of delay and (if the order or ruling appealed is one which excludes evidence) that the evidence excluded is substantial proof of a fact material in the proceeding.

(3) An appeal under this section shall be diligently prosecuted by appellate Government counsel.

(b) An appeal under this section shall be forwarded by a means prescribed under regulations of the President directly to the Court of Criminal Appeals and shall, whenever practicable, have priority over all other proceedings before that court. In ruling on an appeal under this section, the Court of Criminal Appeals may act only with respect to matters of law, notwithstanding section 866(c) of this title (article 66(c)).

(c) Any period of delay resulting from an appeal under this section shall be excluded in deciding any issue regarding denial of a speedy trial unless an appropriate authority determines that the appeal was filed solely for the purpose of delay with the knowledge that it was totally frivolous and without merit.

§ 863. Art. 63. Rehearings

Each rehearing under this chapter shall take place before a court-martial composed of members not members of the court-martial which first heard the case. Upon a rehearing the accused may not be tried for any offense of which he was found not guilty by the first court-martial, and no sentence in excess of or more severe than the original sentence may be approved, unless the sentence is based upon a finding of guilty of an offense not considered upon the merits in the original proceedings, or unless the sentence prescribed for the offense is mandatory. If the sentence approved after the first court-martial was in accordance with a pretrial agreement and the accused at the rehearing changes his plea with respect to the charges or specifications upon which the pretrial agreement was based, or otherwise does not comply with the pretrial agreement, the approved sentence as to those charges or specifications may include any punishment not in excess of that lawfully adjudged at the first court-martial.

§ 864. Art. 64. Review by a judge advocate

(a) Each case in which there has been a finding of guilty that is not reviewed under section 866 or 869(a) of this title (article 66 or 69(a)) shall be reviewed by a judge advocate under regulations of the Secretary concerned. A judge advocate may not review a case under this subsection if he has acted in the same case as an accuser, investigating officer, member of the court, military judge, or counsel or has otherwise acted on behalf of the prosecution or defense. The judge advocate's review shall be in writing and shall contain the following:

(1) Conclusions as to whether—

(A) the court had jurisdiction over the accused and the offense;

(B) the charge and specification stated an offense; and

(C) the sentence was within the limits prescribed as a matter of law.

(2) A response to each allegation of error made in writing by the accused.

(3) If the case is sent for action under subsection (b), a recommendation as to the appropriate action to be taken and an opinion as to whether corrective action is required as a matter of law.

(b) The record of trial and related documents in each case reviewed under subsection (a) shall be sent for action to the person exercising general court-martial jurisdiction over the accused at the time the court was convened (or to that person's successor in command) if—

(1) the judge advocate who reviewed the case recommends corrective action;

(2) the sentence approved under section 860(c) of this title (article 60(c)) extends to dismissal, a bad-conduct or dishonorable discharge, or confinement for more than six months; or

(3) such action is otherwise required by regulations of the Secretary concerned.

(c)(1) The person to whom the record of trial and related documents are sent under subsection (b) may—

(A) disapprove or approve the findings or sentence, in whole or in part;

(B) remit, commute, or suspend the sentence in whole or in part;

(C) except where the evidence was insufficient at the trial to support the findings, order a rehearing on the findings, on the sentence, or on both; or

(D) dismiss the charges.

(2) If a rehearing is ordered but the convening authority finds a rehearing impracticable, he shall dismiss the charges.

(3) If the opinion of the judge advocate in the judge advocate's review under subsection (a) is that corrective action is required as a matter of law and if the person required to take action under subsection (b) does not take action that is at least as favorable to the accused as that recommended by the judge advocate, the record of trial and action thereon shall be sent to Judge Advocate General for review under section 869(b) of this title (article 69(b)).

§ 865. Art. 65. Disposition of records

(a) In a case subject to appellate review under section 866 or 869(a) of this title (article 66 or 69(a)) in which the right to such review is not waived, or an appeal is not withdrawn, under section 861 of this title (article 61), the record of trial and action thereon shall be transmitted to the Judge Advocate General for appropriate action.

(b) Except as otherwise required by this chapter, all other records of trial and related documents shall be transmitted and disposed of as the Secretary concerned may prescribe by regulation.

§ 866. Art. 66. Review by Court of Criminal Appeals

(a) Each Judge Advocate General shall establish a Court of Criminal Appeals which shall be composed of one or more panels, and each such panel shall be composed of not less than three appellate military judges. For the purpose of reviewing court-martial cases, the court may sit in panels or as a whole in accordance with rules prescribed under subsection (f). Any decision of a panel may be reconsidered by the court sitting as a whole in accordance with such rules. Appellate military judges who are assigned to a Court of Criminal Appeals may be commissioned officers or civilians, each of whom must be a member of a bar of a Federal court or the highest court of a State. The Judge Advocate General shall designate as chief judge one of the appellate military judges of the Court of Criminal Appeals established by him. The chief judge shall determinate on which panels of the court the appellate judges assigned to the court will serve and which military judge assigned to the court will act as the senior judge on each panel.

(b) The Judge Advocate General shall refer to a Court of Criminal Appeals the record in each case of trial by court-martial—

(1) in which the sentence, as approved, extends to death, dismissal of a commissioned officer, cadet, or midshipman, dishonorable or bad-conduct discharge, or confinement for one year or more; and

(2) except in the case of a sentence extending to death, the right to appellate review has not been waived or an appeal has not been withdrawn under section 861 of this title (article 61).

(c) In a case referred to it, the Court of Criminal Appeals may act only with respect to the findings and sentence as approved by the convening authority. It may affirm only such findings of guilty and the sentence or such part or amount of the sentence, as it finds correct in law and fact and determines, on the basis of the entire record, should be approved. In considering the record, it may weigh the evidence, judge the credibility of witnesses, and determine controverted questions of fact, recognizing that the trial court saw and heard the witnesses.

(d) If the Court of Criminal Appeals sets aside the findings and sentence, it may, except where the setting aside is based on lack of sufficient evidence in the record to support the findings, order a rehearing. If it sets aside the findings and sentence and does not order a rehearing, it shall order that the charges be dismissed.

(e) The Judge Advocate General shall, unless there is to be further action by the President, the Secretary concerned, the Court of Appeals for the Armed Forces, or the Supreme Court, instruct the convening authority to take action in accordance with the decision of the Court of Criminal Appeals. If the Court of Criminal Appeals has ordered a rehearing but the convening authority finds a rehearing impracticable, he may dismiss the charges.

(f) The Judge Advocates General shall prescribe uniform rules of procedure for Courts of Criminal Appeals and shall meet periodically to formulate policies and procedure in regard to review of court-martial cases in the office of the Judge Advocates General and by Courts of Criminal Appeals.

(g) No member of a Court of Criminal Appeals shall be required, or on his own initiative be permitted, to prepare, approve, disapprove, review, or submit, with respect to any other member of the same or another Court of Criminal Appeals, an effectiveness, fitness, or efficiency report, or any other report documents used in whole or in part for the purpose of determining whether a member of the armed forces is qualified to be advanced in grade, or in determining the assignment or transfer of a member of the armed forces, or in determining whether a member of the armed forces shall be retained on active duty.

(h) No member of a Court of Criminal Appeals shall be eligible to review the record of any trial if such member served as investigating officer in the case or served as a member of the court-martial before which such trial was conducted, or served as military judge, trial or defense counsel, or reviewing officer of such trial.

§ 867. Art. 67. Review by the Court of Appeals for the Armed Forces

(a) The Court of Appeals for the Armed Forces shall review the record in—

(1) all cases in which the sentence, as affirmed by a Court of Criminal Appeals, extends to death;

(2) all cases reviewed by a Court of Criminal Appeals which the Judge Advocate General orders sent to the Court of Appeals for the Armed Forces for review; and

(3) all cases reviewed by a Court of Criminal Appeals in which, upon petition of the accused and on good cause shown, the Court of Appeals for the Armed Forces has granted a review.

(b) The accused may petition the Court of Appeals for the Armed Forces for review of a decision of a Court of Criminal Appeals within 60 days from the earlier of—

(1) the date on which the accused is notified of the decision of the Court of Criminal Appeals; or

(2) the date on which a copy of the decision of the Court of Criminal Appeals, after being served on appellate counsel of record for the accused (if any), is deposited in the United States mails for delivery by first class certified mail to the accused at an address provided by the accused or, if no such address has been provided by the accused, at the latest address listed for the accused in his official service record. The Court of Appeals for the Armed Forces shall act upon such a petition promptly in accordance with the rules of the court.

(c) In any case reviewed by it, the Court of Appeals for the Armed Forces may act only with respect to the findings and sentence as approved by the convening authority and as affirmed or set aside as incorrect in law by the Court of Criminal Appeals. In a case which the Judge Advocate General orders sent to the Court of Appeals for the Armed Forces, that action need be taken only with respect to the issues raised by him. In a case reviewed upon petition of the accused, that action need be taken only with respect to issues specified in the grant of review. The Court of Appeals for the Armed Forces shall take action only with respect to matters of law.

(d) If the Court of Appeals for the Armed Forces sets aside the findings and sentence, it may, except where the setting aside is based on lack of sufficient evidence in the record to support the findings, order a rehearing. If it sets aside the findings and sentence and does not order a rehearing, it shall order that the charges be dismissed.

(e) After it has acted on a case, the Court of Appeals for the Armed Forces may direct the Judge Advocate General to return the record to the Court of Criminal Appeals for further review in accordance with the decision of the court. Otherwise, unless there is to be further action by the President or the Secretary concerned, the Judge Advocate General shall instruct the convening authority to take action in accordance with that decision. If the court has ordered a rehearing, but the convening authority finds a rehearing impracticable, he may dismiss the charges.

§ 867a. Art. 67a. Review by the Supreme Court

(a) Decisions of the United States Court of Appeals for the Armed Forces are subject to review by the Supreme Court by writ of certiorari as provided in section 1259 of title 28. The Supreme Court may not review by a writ of certiorari under this section any action of the Court of Appeals for the Armed Forces in refusing to grant a petition for review.

(b) The accused may petition the Supreme Court for a writ of certiorari without prepayment of fees and costs or security therefor and without filing the affidavit required by section 1915(a) of title 28.

§ 868. Art. 68. Branch offices

The Secretary concerned may direct the Judge Advocate General to establish a branch office with any command. The branch office shall be under an Assistant Judge Advocate General who, with the consent of the Judge Advocate General, may establish a Court of Criminal Appeals with one or more panels. That Assistant Judge Advocate General and any Court of Criminal Appeals established by him may perform for that command under the general supervision of the Judge Advocate General, the respective duties which the Judge Advocate General and a Court of Criminal Appeals established by the Judge Advocate General would otherwise be required to perform as to all cases involving sentences not requiring approval by the President.

§ 869. Art. 69. Review in the office of the Judge Advocate General

(a) The record of trial in each general court-martial that is not otherwise reviewed under section 866 of this title (article 66) shall be examined in the office of the Judge Advocate General if there is a finding of guilty and the accused does not waive or withdraw his right to appellate review under section 861 of this title (article 61). If any part of the findings or sentence is found to be unsupported in law or if reassessment of the sentence is appropriate, the Judge Advocate General may modify or set aside the findings or sentence or both.

(b) The findings or sentence, or both, in a court-martial case not reviewed under subsection (a) or under section 866 of this title (article 66) may be modified or set aside, in whole or in part, by the Judge Advocate General on the ground of newly discovered evidence, fraud on the court, lack of jurisdiction over the accused or the offense, error prejudicial to the substantial rights of the accused, or the appropriateness of the sentence. If such a case is considered upon application of the accused, the application must be filed in the office of the Judge Advocate General by the accused on or before the last day of the two-year period beginning on the date the sentence is approved under section 860(c) of this title (article 60(c)), unless the accused establishes good cause for failure to file within that time.

(c) If the Judge Advocate General sets aside the findings or sentence, he may, except when the setting aside is based on lack of sufficient evidence in the record to support the findings, order a rehearing. If he sets aside the findings and sentence and does not order a rehearing, he shall order that the charges be dismissed. If the Judge Advocate General orders a rehearing but the convening authority finds a rehearing impractical, the convening authority shall dismiss the charges.

(d) A Court of Criminal Appeals may review, under section 866 of this title (article 66)—

(1) any court-martial case which (A) is subject to action by the Judge Advocate General under this section, and (B) is sent to the Court of Criminal Appeals by order of the Judge Advocate General; and,

(2) any action taken by the Judge Advocate General under this section in such case.

(e) Notwithstanding section 866 of this title (article 66), in any case reviewed by a Court of Criminal Appeals under this section, the Court may take action only with respect to matters of law.

§ 870. Art. 70. Appellate counsel

(a) The Judge Advocate General shall detail in his office one or more commissioned officers as appellate Government counsel, and one or more commissioned officers as appellate defense counsel, who are qualified under section 827(b)(l) of this title (article 27(b)(l)).

(b) Appellate Government counsel shall represent the United States before the Court of Criminal Appeals or the Court of Appeals for the Armed Forces when directed to do so by the Judge Advocate General. Appellate Government counsel may represent the United States before the Supreme Court in cases arising under this chapter when requested to do so by the Attorney General.

(c) Appellate defense counsel shall represent the accused before the Court of Criminal Appeals, the Court of Appeals for the Armed Forces, or the Supreme Court—

(1) when requested by the accused;

(2) when the United States is represented by counsel; or

(3) when the Judge Advocate General has sent the case to the Court of Appeals for the Armed Forces.

(d) The accused has the right to be represented before the Court of Criminal Appeals, the Court of Appeals for the Armed Forces, or the Supreme Court by civilian counsel if provided by him.

(e) Military appellate counsel shall also perform such other functions in connection with the review of court-martial cases as the Judge Advocate General directs.

§ 871. Art. 71. Execution of sentence; suspension of sentence

(a) If the sentence of the court-martial extends to death, that part of the sentence providing for death may not be executed until approved by the President. In such a case, the President may commute, remit, or suspend the sentence, or any part thereof, as he sees fit. That part of the sentence providing for death may not be suspended.

(b) If in the case of a commissioned officer, cadet, or midshipman, the sentence of a court-martial extends to dismissal, that part of the sentence providing for dismissal may not be executed until approved by the Secretary concerned or such Under Secretary or Assistant Secretary as may be designated by the Secretary concerned. In such a case, the Secretary, Under Secretary or Assistant Secretary, as the case may be, may commute, remit, or suspend the sentence, or any part of the sentence, as he sees fit. In time of war or national emergency he may commute a sentence of dismissal to reduction to any enlisted grade. A person so reduced may be required to serve for the duration of the war or emergency and six months thereafter.

(c)(1) If a sentence extends to death, dismissal, or a dishonorable or bad-conduct discharge and if the right of the accused to appellate review is not waived, and an appeal is not withdrawn, under section 861 of this title (article 61), that part of the sentence extending to death, dismissal, or a dishonorable or bad-conduct discharge may not be executed until there is a final judgment as to the legality of the proceedings (and with respect to death or dismissal, approval under subsection (a) or (b), as appropriate). A judgment as to legality of the proceedings is final in such cases when review is completed by a Court of Criminal Appeals and—

(A) the time for the accused to file a petition for review by the Court of Appeals for the Armed Forces has expired and the accused has not filed a timely petition for such review and the case is not otherwise under review by that Court;

(B) such a petition is rejected by the Court of Appeals for the Armed Forces; or

(C) review is completed in accordance with the judgment of the Court of Appeals for the Armed Forces and—

(i) a petition for a writ of certiorari is not filed within the time limits prescribed by the Supreme Court;

(ii) such a petition is rejected by the Supreme Court; or

(iii) review is otherwise completed in accordance with the judgment of the Supreme Court.

(2) If a sentence extends to dismissal or a dishonorable or bad-conduct discharge and if the right of the accused to appellate review is waived, or an appeal is withdrawn, under section 861 of this title (article 61), that part of the sentence extending to dismissal or a bad-conduct or dishonorable discharge may not be executed until review of the case by a judge advocate (and any action of that review) under section 864 of this title (article 64) is completed. Any other part of a court-martial sentence may be ordered executed by the convening authority or other person acting on the case under section 860 of this title (article 60) when approved by him under that section.

(d) The convening authority or other person acting on the case under section 860 of this title (article 60) may suspend the execution of any sentence or part thereof, except a death sentence.

§ 872. Art. 72. Vacation of suspension

(a) Before the vacation of the suspension of a special court-martial sentence which as approved includes a bad-conduct discharge, or of any general court-martial sentence, the officer having special court-martial jurisdiction over the probationer shall hold a hearing on the alleged violation of probation. The probationer shall be represented at the hearing by counsel if he so desires.

(b) The record of the hearing and the recommendation of the officer having special court-martial jurisdiction shall be sent for action to the officer exercising general court-martial jurisdiction over the probationer. If he vacates the suspension, any unexecuted part of the sentence, except a dismissal, shall be executed, subject to applicable restrictions in section 871(c) of this title (article 71(c)). The vacation of the suspension of a dismissal is not effective until approved by the Secretary concerned.

(c) The suspension of any other sentence may be vacated by any authority competent to convene, for the command in which the accused is serving or assigned, a court of the kind that imposed the sentence.

§ 873. Art. 73. Petition for a new trial

At any time within two years after approval by the convening authority of a court-martial sentence, the accused may petition the

Judge Advocate General for a new trial on the grounds of newly discovered evidence or fraud on the court. If the accused's case is pending before a Court of Criminal Appeals or before the Court of Appeals for the Armed Forces, the Judge Advocate General shall refer the petition to the appropriate court for action. Otherwise the Judge Advocate General shall act upon the petition.

§ 874. Art. 74. Remission and suspension

(a) The Secretary concerned and, when designated by him, any Under Secretary, Assistant Secretary, Judge Advocate General, or commanding officer may remit or suspend any part or amount of the unexecuted part of any sentence, including all uncollected forfeitures other than a sentence approved by the President. However, in the case of a sentence of confinement for life without eligibility for parole, after the sentence is ordered executed, the authority of the Secretary concerned under the preceding sentence (1) may not be delegated, and (2) may be exercised only after the service of a period of confinement of not less than 20 years.

(b) The Secretary concerned may, for good cause, substitute an administrative form of discharge for a discharge or dismissal executed in accordance with the sentence of a court-martial.

§ 875. Art. 75. Restoration

(a) Under such regulations as the President may prescribe, all rights, privileges, and property affected by an executed part of a court-martial sentence which has been set aside or disapproved, except an executed dismissal or discharge, shall be restored unless a new trial or rehearing is ordered and such executed part is included in a sentence imposed upon the new trial or rehearing.

(b) If a previously executed sentence of dishonorable or bad-conduct discharge is not imposed on a new trial, the Secretary concerned shall substitute therefor a form of discharge authorized for administrative issuance unless the accused is to serve out the remainder of this enlistment.

(c) If a previously executed sentence of dismissal is not imposed on a new trial, the Secretary concerned shall substitute therefor a form of discharge authorized for administrative issue, and the commissioned officer dismissed by the sentence may be reappointed by the President alone to such commissioned grade and with such rank as in the opinion of the President that former officer would have attained had he not been dismissed. The reappointment of such a former officer shall be without regard to the existence of a vacancy and shall affect the promotion status of other officers only insofar as the President may direct. All time between the dismissal and the reappointment shall be considered as actual service for all purposes, including the right to pay and allowances.

§ 876. Art. 76. Finality of proceedings, findings, and sentences

The appellate review of records of trial provided by this chapter, the proceedings, findings, and sentences of courts-martial as approved, reviewed, or affirmed as required by this chapter, and all dismissals and discharges carried into execution under sentences by courts-martial following approval, review, or affirmation as required by this chapter, are final and conclusive. Orders publishing the proceedings of courts-martial and all action taken pursuant to those proceedings are binding upon all departments, courts, agencies, and officers of the United States, subject only to action upon a petition for a new trial as provided in section 873 of this title (article 73) and to action by the Secretary concerned as provided in section 874 of this title (article 74), and the authority of the President.

§ 876a. Art. 76a. Leave required to be taken pending review of certain court-martial convictions

Under regulations prescribed by the Secretary concerned, an accused who has been sentenced by a court-martial may be required to take leave pending completion of action under this subchapter if the sentence, as approved under section 860 of this title (article 60), includes an unsuspended dismissal or an unsuspended dishonorable or bad-conduct discharge. The accused may be required to begin such leave on the date on which the sentence is approved under section 860 of this title (article 60) or at any time after such date, and such leave may be continued until the date which action under this subchapter is completed or may be terminated at any earlier time.

§ 876b. Art. 76b. Lack of mental capacity or mental responsibility: commitment of accused for examination and treatment

(a) Persons incompetent to stand trial—

(1) In the case of a person determined under this chapter to be presently suffering from a mental disease or defect rendering the person mentally incompetent to the extent that the person is unable to understand the nature of the proceedings against that person or to conduct or cooperate intelligently in the defense of the case, the general court-martial convening authority for that person shall commit the person to the custody of the Attorney General.

(2) The Attorney General shall take action in accordance with section 4241(d) of title 18.

(3) If at the end of the period for hospitalization provided for in section 4241(d) of title 18, it is determined that the committed person's mental condition has not so improved as to permit the trial to proceed, action shall be taken in accordance with section 4246 of such title.

(4)

(A) When the director of a facility in which a person is hospitalized pursuant to paragraph (2) determines that the person has recovered to such an extent that the person is able to understand the nature of the proceedings against the person and to conduct or cooperate intelligently in the defense of the case, the director shall promptly transmit a notification of that determination to the Attorney General and to the general court-martial convening authority for the person. The director shall send a copy of the notification to the person's counsel.

(B) Upon receipt of a notification, the general court-martial convening authority shall promptly take custody of the person unless the person covered by the notification is no longer subject to this chapter. If the person is no longer subject to this chapter, the Attorney General shall take any action within the authority of the Attorney General that the Attorney General considers appropriate regarding the person.

(C) The director of the facility may retain custody of the person for not more than 30 days after transmitting the notifications required by subparagraph (A).

(5) In the application of section 4246 of title 18 to a case under this subsection, references to the court that ordered the commitment of a person, and to the clerk of such court, shall be deemed to refer to the general court-martial convening authority for that person. However, if the person is no longer subject to this chapter at a time relevant to the application of such section to the person, the United States district court for the district where the person is hospitalized or otherwise may be found shall be considered as the court that ordered the commitment of the person.

(b) Persons found not guilty by reason of lack of mental responsibility—

(1) If a person is found by a court-martial not guilty only by reason of lack of mental responsibility, the person shall be committed to a suitable facility until the person is eligible for release in accordance with this section.

(2) The court-martial shall conduct a hearing on the mental condition in accordance with subsection (c) of section 4243 of title 18. Subsections (b) and (d) of that section shall apply with respect to the hearing.

(3) A report of the results of the hearing shall be made to the general court-martial convening authority for the person.

(4) If the court-martial fails to find by the standard specified in subsection (d) of section 4243 of title 18 that the person's release would not create a substantial risk of bodily injury to another person or serious damage of property of another due to a present mental disease or defect—

(A) the general court-martial convening authority may commit the person to the custody of the Attorney General; and

(B) the Attorney General shall take action in accordance with subsection (e) of section 4243 of title 18.

(5) Subsections (f), (g), and (h) of section 4243 of title 18 shall apply in the case of a person hospitalized pursuant to paragraph (4)(B), except that the United States district court for the district where the person is hospitalized shall be considered as the court that ordered the person's commitment.

(c) General provisions—

(1) Except as otherwise provided in this subsection and subsection (d)(1), the provisions of section 4247 of title 18 apply in the administration of this section.

(2) In the application of section 4247(d) of title 18 to hearings conducted by a court-martial under this section or by (or by order of) a general court-martial convening authority under this section, the reference in that section to section 3006A of such title does not apply.

(d) Applicability—

(1) The provisions of chapter 313 of title 18 referred to in this section apply according to the provisions of this section notwithstanding section 4247(j) of title 18.

(2) If the status of a person as described in section 802 of this title (article 2) terminates while the person is, pursuant to this section, in the custody of the Attorney General, hospitalized, or on conditional release under a prescribed regimen of medical, psychiatric, or psychological care or treatment, the provisions of this section establishing requirements and procedures regarding a person no longer subject to this chapter shall continue to apply to that person notwithstanding the change of status.

SUBCHAPTER X. PUNITIVE ARTICLES

§ 877. Art. 77. Principals

Any person punishable under this chapter who

(1) commits an offense punishable by this chapter, or aids, abets, counsels, commands, or procures its commission; or

(2) causes an act to be done which if directly performed by him would be punishable by this chapter; is a principal.

§ 878. Art. 78. Accessory after the fact

Any person subject to this chapter who, knowing that an offense punishable by this chapter has been committed, receives, comforts, or assists the offender in order to hinder or prevent his apprehension, trial, or punishment shall be punished as a court-martial may direct.

§ 879. Art. 79. Conviction of lesser included offense

An accused may be found guilty of an offense necessarily included in the offense charged or of an attempt to commit either the offense charged or an offense necessarily included therein.

§ 880. Art. 80. Attempts

(a) An act, done with specific intent to commit an offense under this chapter, amounting to more than mere preparation and tending, even though failing, to effect its commission, is an attempt to commit that offense.

(b) Any person subject to this chapter who attempts to commit any offense punishable by this chapter shall be punished as a court-martial may direct, unless otherwise specifically prescribed.

(c) Any person subject to this chapter may be convicted of an attempt to commit an offense although it appears on the trial that the offense was consummated.

§ 881. Art. 81. Conspiracy

Any person subject to this chapter who conspires with any other person to commit an offense under this chapter shall. if one or more of the conspirators does an act to effect the object of the conspiracy, be punished as a court-martial may direct.

§ 882. Art. 82. Solicitation

(a) Any person subject to this chapter who solicits or advises another or others to desert in violation of section 885 of this title (article 85) or mutiny in violation of section 894 of this title (article 94) shall, if the offense solicited or advised is attempted or committed, be punished with the punishment provided for the commission of the offense, but, if the offense solicited or advised is not committed or attempted, he shall be punished as a court-martial may direct.

(b) Any person subject to this chapter who solicits or advises another or others to commit an act of misbehavior before the enemy in violation of section 899 of this title (article 99) or sedition in violation of section 894 of this title (article 94) shall, if the offense solicited or advised is committed, be punished with the punishment provided for the commission of the offense, but, if the offense solicited or advised is not committed, he shall be punished as a court-martial may direct.

§ 883. Art. 83. Fraudulent enlistment, appointment, or separation

Any person who—

(1) procures his own enlistment or appointment in the armed forces by knowingly false representation or deliberate concealment as to his qualifications for the enlistment or appointment and receives pay or allowances thereunder; or

(2) procures his own separation from the armed forces by knowingly false representation or deliberate concealment as to his eligibility for that separation; shall be punished as a court-martial may direct.

§ 884. Art. 84. Unlawful enlistment, appointment, or separation

Any person subject to this chapter who effects an enlistment or appointment in or a separation from the armed forces of any person who is known to him to be ineligible for that enlistment, appointment, or separation because it is prohibited by law, regulation, or order shall be punished as a court-martial may direct.

§ 885. Art. 85. Desertion

(a) Any member of the armed forces who—

(1) without authority goes or remains absent from his unit, organization, or place of duty with intent to remain away therefrom permanently;

(2) quits his unit, organization, or place of duty with intent to avoid hazardous duty or to shirk important service; or

(3) without being regularly separated from one of the armed forces enlists or accepts an appointment in the same or another one of the armed forces without fully disclosing the fact that he has not been regularly separated, or enters any foreign armed service except when authorized by the United States; is guilty of desertion.

(b) Any commissioned officer of the armed forces who, after tender of his resignation and before notice of its acceptance, quits his post or proper duties without leave and with intent to remain away therefrom permanently is guilty of desertion.

(c) Any person found guilty of desertion or attempt to desert shall be punished, if the offense is committed in time of war, by death or such other punishment as a court-martial may direct, but if the desertion or attempt to desert occurs at any other time, by such punishment, other than death, as a court-martial may direct.

§ 886. Art. 86. Absence without leave

Any member of the armed forces who, without authority—

(1) fails to go to his appointed place of duty at the time prescribed;

(2) goes from that place; or

(3) absents himself or remains absent from his unit, organization, or place of duty at which he is required to be at the time prescribed; shall be punished as a court-martial may direct.

§ 887. Art. 87. Missing movement

Any person subject to this chapter who through neglect or design misses the movement of a ship, aircraft, or unit with which he is required in the course of duty to move shall be punished as a court-martial may direct.

§ 888. Art. 88. Contempt toward officials

Any commissioned officer who uses contemptuous words against the President, the Vice President, Congress, the Secretary of Defense, the Secretary of a military department, the Secretary of Homeland Security, or the Governor or legislature of any State, Commonwealth, or possession in which he is on duty or present shall be punished as a court-martial may direct.

§ 889. Art. 89. Disrespect toward superior commissioned officer

Any person subject to this chapter who behaves with disrespect toward his superior commissioned officer shall be punished as a court-martial may direct.

§ 890. Art. 90. Assaulting or willfully disobeying superior commissioned officer

Any person subject to this chapter who—

(1) strikes his superior commissioned officer or draws or lifts up any weapon or offers any violence against him while he is in the execution of his office; or

(2) willfully disobeys a lawful command of his superior commissioned officer;

shall be punished, if the offense is committed in time of war, by death or such other punishment as a court-martial may direct, and if the offense is committed at any other time, by such punishment, other than death, as a court-martial may direct.

§ 891. Art. 91. Insubordinate conduct toward warrant officer, noncommissioned officer, or petty officer

Any warrant officer or enlisted member who

(1) strikes or assaults a warrant officer, noncommissioned officer, or petty officer, while that officer is in the execution of his office;

(2) willfully disobeys the lawful order of a warrant officer, noncommissioned officer, or petty officer; or

(3) treats with contempt or is disrespectful in language or deportment toward a warrant officer, noncommissioned officer, or petty officer while that officer is in the execution of his office;

shall be punished as a court-martial may direct.

§ 892. Art. 92. Failure to obey order or regulation

Any person subject to this chapter who—

(1) violates or fails to obey any lawful general order or regulation;

(2) having knowledge of any other lawful order issued by a member of the armed forces, which it is his duty to obey, fails to obey the order; or

(3) is derelict in the performance of his duties; shall be punished as a court-martial may direct.

§ 893. Art. 93. Cruelty and maltreatment

Any person subject to this chapter who is guilty of cruelty toward, or oppression or maltreatment of, any person subject to his orders shall be punished as a court-martial may direct.

§ 894. Art. 94. Mutiny or sedition

(a) Any person subject to this chapter who—

(1) with intent to usurp or override lawful military authority, refuses, in concert with any other person, to obey orders or otherwise do his duty or creates any violence or disturbance is guilty of mutiny;

(2) with intent to cause the overthrow or destruction of lawful civil authority, creates, in concert with any other person, revolt, violence, or other disturbance against that authority is guilty of sedition;

(3) fails to do his utmost to prevent and suppress a mutiny or sedition being committed in his presence, or fails to take all reasonable means to inform his superior commissioned officer or commanding officer of a mutiny or sedition which he knows or has reason to believe is taking place, is guilty of a failure to suppress or report a mutiny or sedition.

(b) A person who is found guilty of attempted mutiny, mutiny, sedition, or failure to suppress or report a mutiny or sedition shall be punished by death or such other punishment as a court-martial may direct.

§ 895. Art. 95. Resistance, flight, breach of arrest, and escape

Any person subject to this chapter who—

(1) resists apprehension;

(2) flees from apprehension;

(3) breaks arrest; or

(4) escapes from custody or confinement;

shall be punished as a court-martial may direct.

§ 896. Art. 96. Releasing prisoner without proper authority

Any person subject to this chapter who, without proper authority, releases any prisoner committed to his charge, or who through neglect or design suffers any such prisoner to escape, shall be punished as a court-martial may direct, whether or not the prisoner was committed in strict compliance with law.

§ 897. Art. 97. Unlawful detention

Any person subject to this chapter who, except as provided by law, apprehends, arrests, or confines any person shall be punished as a court-martial may direct.

§ 898. Art. 98. Noncompliance with procedural rules

Any person subject to this chapter who—

(1) is responsible for unnecessary delay in the disposition of any case of a person accused of an offense under this chapter;or

(2) knowingly and intentionally fails to enforce or comply with any provision of this chapter regulating the proceedings before, during, or after trial of an accused;
shall be punished as a court-martial may direct.

§ 899. Art. 99. Misbehavior before the enemy

Any person subject to this chapter who before or in the presence of the enemy—

(1) runs away;

(2) shamefully abandons, surrenders, or delivers up any command, unit, place, or military property which it is his duty to defend;

(3) through disobedience, neglect, or intentional misconduct endangers the safety of any such command, unit, place, or military property;

(4) casts away his arms or ammunition;

(5) is guilty of cowardly conduct;

(6) quits his place of duty to plunder or pillage;

(7) causes false alarms in any command, unit, or place under control of the armed forces;

(8) willfully fails to do his utmost to encounter, engage, capture, or destroy any enemy troops, combatants, vessels, aircraft, or any other thing, which it is his duty so to encounter, engage, capture, or destroy; or

(9) does not afford all practicable relief and assistance to any troops, combatants, vessels, or aircraft of the armed forces belonging to the United States or their allies when engaged in battle;
shall be punished by death or such other punishment as a court-martial may direct.

§ 900. Art. 100. Subordinate compelling surrender

Any person subject to this chapter who compels or attempts to compel the commander of any place, vessel, aircraft, or other military property, or of any body of members of the armed forces, to give it up to an enemy or to abandon it, or who strikes the colors or flag to any enemy without proper authority, shall be punished by death or such other punishment as a court-martial may direct.

§ 901. Art. 101. Improper use of countersign

Any person subject to this chapter who in time of war discloses the parole or countersign to any person not entitled to receive it or who gives to another who is entitled to receive and use the parole or countersign a different parole or countersign from that which, to his knowledge, he was authorized and required to give, shall be punished by death or such other punishment as a court-martial may direct.

§ 902. Art. 102. Forcing a safeguard

Any person subject to this chapter who forces a safeguard shall suffer death or such other punishment as a court-martial may direct.

§ 903. Art. 103. Captured or abandoned property

(a) All persons subject to this chapter shall secure all public property taken from the enemy for the service of the United States, and shall give notice and turn over to the proper authority without delay all captured or abandoned property in their possession, custody, or control.

(b) Any person subject to this chapter who—

(1) fails to carry out the duties prescribed in subsection (a);

(2) buys, sells, trades, or in any way deals in or disposes of captured or abandoned property, whereby he receives or expects any profit, benefit, or advantage to himself or another directly or indirectly connected with himself; or

(3) engages in looting or pillaging;
shall be punished as a court-martial may direct.

§ 904. Art. 104. Aiding the enemy

Any person who—

(1) aids, or attempts to aid, the enemy with arms, ammunition, supplies, money, or other things; or

(2) without proper authority, knowingly harbors or protects or gives intelligence to or communicates or corresponds with or holds any intercourse with the enemy, either directly or indirectly;
shall suffer death or such other punishment as a court-martial or military commission may direct.

§ 905. Art. 105. Misconduct as prisoner

Any person subject to this chapter who, while in the hands of the enemy in time of war—

(1) for the purpose of securing favorable treatment by his captors acts without proper authority in a manner contrary to law, custom, or regulation, to the detriment of others of whatever nationality held by the enemy as civilian or military prisoners; or

(2) while in a position of authority over such persons maltreat them without justifiable cause;
shall be punished as a court-martial may direct.

§ 906. Art. 106. Spies

Any person who in time of war is found lurking as a spy or acting as a spy in or about any place, vessel, or aircraft, within the control or jurisdiction of any of the armed forces, or in or about any shipyard, any manufacturing or industrial plant, or any other place or institution engaged in work in aid of the prosecution of the war by the United States, or elsewhere, shall be tried by a general court-martial or by a military commission and on conviction shall be punished by death.

§ 906a. Art. 106a. Espionage

(a)(1) Any person subject to this chapter who, with intent or reason to believe that it is to be used to the injury of the United States or to the advantage of a foreign nation, communicates, delivers, or transmits, or attempts to communicate, deliver, or transmit, to any entity described in paragraph (2), either directly or indirectly, any thing described in paragraph (3) shall be punished as a court-martial may direct, except that if the accused is found guilty of an offense that directly concerns (A) nuclear weaponry, military spacecraft or satellites, early warning systems, or other means of defense or retaliation against large scale attack, (B) war plans, (C) communications intelligence or cryptolineart information, or (D) any other major weapons system or major element of defense strategy, the accused shall be punished by death or such other punishment as a court-martial may direct.

(2) An entity referred to in paragraph (1) is—

(A) a foreign government;

(B) a faction or party or military or naval force within a foreign country, whether recognized or unrecognized by the United States; or

(C) a representative, officer, agent, employee, subject, or citizen of such a government, faction, party, or force.

(3) A thing referred to in paragraph (1) is a document, writing, code book, signal book, sketch, photograph, photolineart negative, blueprint, plan, map, model, note, instrument, appliance, or information relating to the national defense.

(b)(1) No person may be sentenced by court-martial to suffer death for an offense under this section (article) unless—

(A) the members of the court-martial unanimously find at least one of the aggravating factors set out in subsection (c); and

(B) the members unanimously determine that any extenuating or mitigating circumstances are substantially outweighed by any aggravating circumstances, including the aggravating factors set out under subsection (c).

(2) Findings under this subsection may be based on—

(A) evidence introduced on the issue of guilt or innocence;

(B) evidence introduced during the sentencing proceeding; or

(C) all such evidence.

(3) The accused shall be given broad latitude to present matters in extenuation and mitigation.

(c) A sentence of death may be adjudged by a court-martial for an offense under this section (article) only if the members unanimously find, beyond a reasonable doubt, one or more of the following aggravating factors:

(1) The accused has been convicted of another offense involving espionage or treason for which either a sentence of death or imprisonment for life was authorized by statute.

(2) In the commission of the offense, the accused knowingly created a grave risk of substantial damage to the national security.

(3) In the commission of the offense, the accused knowingly created a grave risk of death to another person.

(4) Any other factor that may be prescribed by the President by regulations under section 836 of this title (Article 36).

§ 907. Art. 107. False official statements

Any person subject to this chapter who, with intent to deceive, signs any false record, return, regulation, order, or other official document, knowing it to be false, or makes any other false official statement knowing it to be false, shall be punished as a court-martial may direct.

§ 908. Art. 108. Military property of United States—Loss, damage, destruction, or wrongful disposition

Any person subject to this chapter who, without proper authority—

(1) sells or otherwise disposes of;

(2) willfully or through neglect damages, destroys, or loses; or

(3) willfully or through neglect suffers to be lost, damaged, sold, or wrongfully disposed of;

any military property of the United States, shall be punished as a court-martial may direct.

§ 909. Art. 109. Property other than military property of United States - Waste, spoilage, or destruction

Any person subject to this chapter who willfully or recklessly wastes, spoils, or otherwise willfully and wrongfully destroys or damages any property other than military property of the United States shall be punished as a court-martial may direct.

§ 910. Art. 110. Improper hazarding of vessel

(a) Any person subject to this chapter who willfully and wrongfully hazards or suffers to be hazarded any vessel of the armed forces shall suffer death or such punishment as a court-martial may direct.

(b) Any person subject to this chapter who negligently hazards or suffers to be hazarded any vessel of the armed forces shall be punished as a court-martial may direct.

§ 911. Art. 111. Drunken or reckless operation of a vehicle, aircraft, or vessel

(a) Any person subject to this chapter who—

(1) operates or physically controls any vehicle, aircraft, or vessel in a reckless or wanton manner or while impaired by a substance described in section 912a(b) of this title (article 112a(b)), or

(2) operates or is in actual physical control of any vehicle, aircraft, or vessel while drunk or when the alcohol concentration in the person's blood or breath is equal to or exceeds the applicable limit under subsection (b), shall be punished as a court-martial may direct.

(b)(1) For purposes of subsection (a), the applicable limit on the alcohol concentration in a person's blood or breath is as follows:

(A) In the case of the operation or control of a vehicle, aircraft, or vessel in the United States, such limit is the lesser of—

(i) the blood alcohol content limit under the law of the State in which the conduct occurred, except as may be provided under paragraph (2) for conduct on a military installation that is in more than one State; or

(ii) the blood alcohol content limit specified in paragraph (3).

(B) In the case of the operation or control of a vehicle,

aircraft, or vessel outside the United States, the applicable blood alcohol content limit is the blood alcohol content limit specified in paragraph (3) or such lower limit as the Secretary of Defense may by regulation prescribe.

(2) In the case of a military installation that is in more than one State, if those States have different blood alcohol content limits under their respective State laws, the Secretary may select one such blood alcohol content limit to apply uniformly on that installation.

(3) For purposes of paragraph (1), the blood alcohol content limit with respect to alcohol concentration in a person's blood is 0.10 grams of alcohol per 100 milliliters of blood and with respect to alcohol concentration in a person's breath is 0.10 grams of alcohol per 210 liters of breath, as shown by chemical analysis.

(4) In this subsection:

(A) The term "blood alcohol content limit" means the amount of alcohol concentration in a person's blood or breath at which operation or control of a vehicle, aircraft, or vessel is prohibited.

(B) The term "United States" includes the District of Columbia, the Commonwealth of Puerto Rico, the Virgin Islands, Guam, and American Samoa and the term "State" includes each of those jurisdictions.

§ 912. Art. 112. Drunk on duty

Any person subject to this chapter other than a sentinel or lookout, who is found drunk on duty, shall be punished as a court-martial may direct.

§ 912a. Art 112a. Wrongful use, possession, etc., of controlled substances

(a) Any person subject to this chapter who wrongfully uses, possesses, manufactures, distributes, imports into the customs territory of the United States, exports from the United States, or introduces into an installation, vessel, vehicle, or aircraft used by or under the control of the armed forces a substance described in subsection (b) shall be punished as a court-martial may direct.

(b) The substances referred to in subsection (a) are the following:

(1) Opium, heroin, cocaine, amphetamine, lysergic acid diethylamide, methamphetamine, phencyclidine, barbituric acid, and marijuana and any compound or derivative of any such substance.

(2) Any substance not specified in clause (1) that is listed on a schedule of controlled substances prescribed by the President for the purposes of this article.

(3) Any other substance not specified in clause (1) or contained on a list prescribed by the President under clause (2) that is listed in schedules I through V of section 202 of the Controlled Substances Act (21 U.S.C. 812).

§ 913. Art. 113. Misbehavior of sentinel

Any sentinel or lookout who is found drunk or sleeping upon his post or leaves it before being regularly relieved, shall be punished, if the offense is committed in time of war, by death or such other punishment as a court-martial may direct, but if the offense is at any other time, by such punishment other than death as a court-martial may direct.

§ 914. Art 114. Dueling

Any person subject to this chapter who fights or promotes, or is concerned in or connives at fighting a duel, or who, having knowledge of a challenge sent or about to be sent, fails to report the fact promptly to the proper authority, shall be punished as a court-martial may direct.

§ 915. Art. 115. Malingering

Any person subject to this chapter who for the purpose of avoiding work, duty, or service—

(1) feigns illness, physical disablement, mental lapse, or derangement; or

(2) intentionally inflicts self-injury;

shall be punished as a court-martial may direct.

§ 916. Art 116. Riot or breach of peace

Any person subject to this chapter who causes or participates in any riot or breach of the peace shall be punished as a court-martial may direct.

§ 917. Art. 117. Provoking speeches or gestures

Any person subject to this chapter who uses provoking or reproachful words or gestures towards any other person subject to this chapter shall be punished as a court-martial may direct.

§ 918. Art. 118. Murder

Any person subject to this chapter who, without justification or excuse, unlawfully kills a human being, when he—

(1) has a premeditated design to kill;

(2) intends to kill or inflict great bodily harm;

(3) is engaged in an act that is inherently dangerous to another and evinces a wanton disregard of human life; or

(4) is engaged in the perpetration or attempted perpetration of burglary, sodomy, rape, rape of a child, aggravated sexual assault, aggravated sexual assault of a child, aggravated sexual contact, aggravated sexual abuse of a child, aggravated sexual contact with a child, robbery, or aggravated arson; is guilty of murder, and shall suffer such punishment as a court-martial may direct, except that if found guilty under clause (1) or (4), he shall suffer death or imprisonment for life as a court-martial may direct.

§ 919. Art. 119. Manslaughter

(a) Any person subject to this chapter who, with an intent to kill or inflict great bodily harm, unlawfully kills a human being in the heat of sudden passion caused by adequate provocation is guilty of voluntary manslaughter and shall be punished as a court-martial may direct.

(b) Any person subject to this chapter who, without an intent to kill or inflict great bodily harm, unlawfully kills a human being -

(1) by culpable negligence; or

(2) while perpetrating or attempting to perpetrate an offense, other than those named in clause (4) of section 918 of this title (article 118), directly affecting the person;

is guilty of involuntary manslaughter and shall be punished as a court-martial may direct.

§ 919a. Art. 119a. Death or injury of an unborn child

(a)(1) Any person subject to this chapter who engages in conduct that violates any of the provisions of law listed in subsection (b) and thereby causes the death of, or bodily injury (as defined in section 1365 of title 18) to, a child, who is in utero at the time the conduct takes place, is guilty of a separate offense under this section and shall, upon conviction, be punished by such punishment, other than death, as a court-martial may direct, which shall be consistent with the punishments prescribed by the President for that conduct had that injury or death occurred to the unborn child's mother.

(2) An offense under this section does not require proof that—

(i) the person engaging in the conduct had knowledge or should have had knowledge that the victim of the underlying offense was pregnant; or

(ii) the accused intended to cause the death of, or bodily injury to, the unborn child.

(3) If the person engaging in the conduct thereby intentionally kills or attempts to kill the unborn child, that person shall, instead of being punished under paragraph (1), be punished as provided under sections 880, 918, and 919(a) of this title (articles 80, 118, and 119(a)) for intentionally killing or attempting to kill a human being.

(4) Notwithstanding any other provision of law, the death penalty shall not be imposed for an offense under this section.

(b) The provisions referred to in subsection (a) are sections 918, 919(a), 919(b)(2), 920(a), 922, 924, 926, and 928 of this title (articles 118, 119(a), 119(b)(2), 120(a), 122, 124, 126, and 128).

(c) Nothing in this section shall be construed to permit the prosecution—

(1) of any person for conduct relating to an abortion for which the consent of the pregnant woman, or a person authorized by law to act on her behalf, has been obtained or for which such consent is implied by law;

(2) of any person for any medical treatment of the pregnant woman or her unborn child; or

(3) of any woman with respect to her unborn child.

(d) In this section, the term "unborn child" means a child in utero, and the term "child in utero" or "child, who is in utero" means a member of the species homo sapiens, at any stage of development, who is carried in the womb.

§ 920. Art. 120. Rape, sexual assault, and other sexual misconduct

(a) *Rape.* Any person subject to this chapter who causes another person of any age to engage in a sexual act by—

(1) using force against that other person;

(2) causing grievous bodily harm to any person;

(3) threatening or placing that other person in fear that any person will be subjected to death, grievous bodily harm, or kidnaping;

(4) rendering another person unconscious; or

(5) administering to another person by force or threat of force, or without the knowledge or permission of that person, a drug, intoxicant, or other similar substance and thereby substantially impairs the ability of that other person to appraise or control conduct; is guilty of rape and shall be punished as a court-martial may direct.

(b) *Rape of a Child.* Any person subject to this chapter who—

(1) engages in a sexual act with a child who has not attained the age of 12 years; or

(2) engages in a sexual act under the circumstances described in subsection (a) with a child who has attained the age of 12 years; is guilty of rape of a child and shall be punished as a court-martial may direct.

(c) *Aggravated Sexual Assault.* Any person subject to this chapter who—

(1) causes another person of any age to engage in a sexual act by—

(A) threatening or placing that other person in fear (other than by threatening or placing that other person in fear that any person will be subjected to death, grievous bodily harm, or kidnapping); or

(B) causing bodily harm; or

(2) engages in a sexual act with another person of any age if that other person is substantially incapacitated or substantially incapable of—

(A) appraising the nature of the sexual act;

(B) declining participation in the sexual act; or

(C) communicating unwillingness to engage in the sexual act; is guilty of aggravated sexual assault and shall be punished as a court-martial may direct.

(d) *Aggravated Sexual Assault of a Child.* Any person subject to this chapter who engages in a sexual act with a child who has attained the age of 12 years is guilty of aggravated sexual assault of a child and shall be punished as a court-martial may direct.

(e) *Aggravated Sexual Contact.* Any person subject to this chapter who engages in or causes sexual contact with or by another person, if to do so would violate subsection (a) (rape) had the sexual contact been a sexual act, is guilty of aggravated sexual contact and shall be punished as a court-martial may direct.

(f) *Aggravated Sexual Abuse of a Child.* Any person subject to this chapter who engages in a lewd act with a child is guilty of aggravated sexual abuse of a child and shall be punished as a court-martial may direct.

(g) *Aggravated Sexual Contact With a Child.* Any person subject to this chapter who engages in or causes sexual contact with or by another person, if to do so would violate subsection (b) (rape of a child) had the sexual contact been a sexual act, is guilty of aggravated sexual contact with a child and shall be punished as a court-martial may direct.

(h) *Abusive Sexual Contact.* Any person subject to this chapter who engages in or causes sexual contact with or by another person, if to do so would violate subsection (c) (aggravated sexual assault) had the sexual contact been a sexual act, is guilty of abusive sexual contact and shall be punished as a court-martial may direct.

(i) *Abusive Sexual Contact With a Child.* Any person subject to this chapter who engages in or causes sexual contact with or by another person, if to do so would violate subsection (d) (aggravated sexual assault of a child) had the sexual contact been a sexual act, is guilty of abusive sexual contact with a child and shall be punished as a court-martial may direct.

(j) *Indecent Liberty With a Child.* Any person subject to this chapter who engages in indecent liberty in the physical presence of a child—

(1) with the intent to arouse, appeal to, or gratify the sexual desire of any person; or

(2) with the intent to abuse, humiliate, or degrade any person; is guilty of indecent liberty with a child and shall be punished as a court-martial may direct.

(k) *Indecent Act.* Any person subject to this chapter who engages in indecent conduct is guilty of an indecent act and shall be punished as a court-martial may direct.

(l) *Forcible Pandering.* Any person subject to this chapter who compels another person to engage in an act of prostitution with another person to be directed to said person is guilty of forcible pandering and shall be punished as a court-martial may direct.

(m) *Wrongful Sexual Contact.* Any person subject to this chapter who, without legal justification or lawful authorization, engages in sexual contact with another person without that other person's permission is guilty of wrongful sexual contact and shall be punished as a court-martial may direct.

(n) *Indecent Exposure.* Any person subject to this chapter who intentionally exposes, in an indecent manner, in any place where the conduct involved may reasonably be expected to be viewed by people other than members of the actor's family or household, the genitalia, anus, buttocks, or female areola or nipple is guilty of indecent exposure and shall by punished as a court-martial may direct.

(o) *Age of Child.*

(1) *Twelve years.* In a prosecution under subsection (b) (rape of a child), subsection (g) (aggravated sexual contact with a child), or subsection (j) (indecent liberty with a child), it need not be proven that the accused knew that the other person engaging in the sexual act, contact, or liberty had not attained the age of 12 years. It is not an affirmative defense that the accused reasonably believed that the child had attained the age of 12 years.

(2) *Sixteen years.* In a prosecution under subsection (d) (aggravated sexual assault of a child), subsection (f) (aggravated sexual abuse of a child), subsection (i) (abusive sexual contact with a child), or subsection (j) (indecent liberty with a child), it need not be proven that the accused knew that the other person engaging in the sexual act, contact, or liberty had not attained the age of 16 years. Unlike in paragraph (1), however, it is an affirmative defense that the accused reasonably believed that the child had attained the age of 16 years.

(p) *Proof of Threat.* In a prosecution under this section, in proving that the accused made a threat, it need not be proven that the accused actually intended to carry out the threat.

(q) *Marriage.*

(1) *In general.* In a prosecution under paragraph (2) of subsection (c) (aggravated sexual assault), or under subsection (d) (aggravated sexual assault of a child), subsection (f) (aggravated sexual abuse of a child), subsection (i) (abusive sexual contact with a child), subsection (j) (indecent liberty with a child), subsection (m) (wrongful sexual contact), or subsection (n) (indecent exposure), it is an affirmative defense that the accused and the other person when they engaged in the sexual act, sexual contact, or sexual conduct are married to each other.

(2) *Definition.* For purposes of this subsection, a marriage is a relationship, recognized by the laws of a competent State or foreign jurisdiction, between the accused and the other person as spouses. A marriage exists until it is dissolved in accordance with the laws of a competent State or foreign jurisdiction.

(3) *Exception.* Paragraph (1) shall not apply if the accused's intent at the time of the sexual conduct is to abuse, humiliate, or degrade any person.

(r) *Consent and Mistake of Fact as to Consent.* Lack of permission is an element of the offense in subsection (m) (wrongful sexual contact). Consent and mistake of fact as to consent are not an issue, or an affirmative defense, in a prosecution under any other subsection, except they are an affirmative defense for the sexual conduct in issue in a prosecution under subsection (a) (rape), subsection (c) (aggravated sexual assault), subsection (e) (aggravated sexual contact), and subsection (h) (abusive sexual contact).

(s) *Other Affirmative Defenses not Precluded.* The enumeration in this section of some affirmative defenses shall not be construed as excluding the existence of others.

(t) *Definitions.* In this section:

(1) *Sexual act.* The term 'sexual act' means—

(A) contact between the penis and the vulva, and for purposes of this subparagraph contact involving the penis occurs upon penetration, however slight; or

(B) the penetration, however slight, of the genital opening of another by a hand or finger or by any object, with an intent to abuse, humiliate, harass, or degrade any person or to arouse or gratify the sexual desire of any person.

(2) *Sexual contact.* The term 'sexual contact' means the intentional touching, either directly or through the clothing, of the genitalia, anus, groin, breast, inner thigh, or buttocks of another person, or intentionally causing another person to touch, either directly or through the clothing, the genitalia, anus, groin, breast, inner thigh, or buttocks of any person, with an intent to abuse, humiliate, or degrade any person or to arouse or gratify the sexual desire of any person.

(3) *Grievous bodily harm.* The term 'grievous bodily harm' means serious bodily injury. It includes fractured or dislocated bones, deep cuts, torn members of the body, serious damage to internal organs, and other severe bodily injuries. It does not include minor injuries such as a black eye or a bloody nose. It is the same level of injury as in section 928 (article 128) of this chapter, and a lesser degree of injury than in section 2246(4) of title 18.

(4) *Dangerous weapon or object.* The term 'dangerous weapon or object' means—

(A) any firearm, loaded or not, and whether operable or not;

(B) any other weapon, device, instrument, material, or substance, whether animate or inanimate, that in the manner it is used, or is intended to be used, is known to be capable of producing death or grievous bodily harm; or

(C) any object fashioned or utilized in such a manner as to

lead the victim under the circumstances to reasonably believe it to be capable of producing death or grievous bodily harm.

(5) *Force.* The term 'force' means action to compel submission of another or to overcome or prevent another's resistance by—

(A) the use or display of a dangerous weapon or object;

(B) the suggestion of possession of a dangerous weapon or object that is used in a manner to cause another to believe it is a dangerous weapon or object; or

(C) physical violence, strength, power, or restraint applied to another person, sufficient that the other person could not avoid or escape the sexual conduct.

(6) *Threatening or placing that other person in fear.* The term 'threatening or placing that other person in fear' under paragraph (3) of subsection (a) (rape), or under subsection (e) (aggravated sexual contact), means a communication or action that is of sufficient consequence to cause a reasonable fear that non-compliance will result in the victim or another person being subjected to death, grievous bodily harm, or kidnapping.

(7) *Threatening or placing that other person in fear.*

(A) *In general.* The term 'threatening or placing that other person in fear' under paragraph (1)(A) of subsection (c) (aggravated sexual assault), or under subsection (h) (abusive sexual contact), means a communication or action that is of sufficient consequence to cause a reasonable fear that non-compliance will result in the victim or another being subjected to a lesser degree of harm than death, grievous bodily harm, or kidnapping.

(B) *Inclusions.* Such lesser degree of harm includes—

(i) physical injury to another person or to another person's property; or

(ii) a threat—

(I) to accuse any person of a crime;

(II) to expose a secret or publicize an asserted fact, whether true or false, tending to subject some person to hatred, contempt or ridicule; or

(III) through the use or abuse of military position, rank, or authority, to affect or threaten to affect, either positively or negatively, the military career of some person.

(8) *Bodily harm.* The term 'bodily harm' means any offensive touching of another, however slight.

(9) *Child.* The term 'child' means any person who has not attained the age of 16 years.

(10) *Lewd act.* The term 'lewd act' means—

(A) the intentional touching, not through the clothing, of the genitalia of another person, with an intent to abuse, humiliate, or degrade any person, or to arouse or gratify the sexual desire of any person; or

(B) intentionally causing another person to touch, not through the clothing, the genitalia of any person with an intent to abuse, humiliate or degrade any person, or to arouse or gratify the sexual desire of any person.

(11) *Indecent liberty.* The term 'indecent liberty' means indecent conduct, but physical contact is not required. It includes one who with the requisite intent exposes one's genitalia, anus, buttocks, or female areola or nipple to a child. An indecent liberty may consist of communication of indecent language as long as the communication is made in the physical presence of the child. If words designed to excite sexual desire are spoken to a child, or a child is exposed to or involved in sexual conduct, it is an indecent liberty; the child's consent is not relevant.

(12) *Indecent conduct.* The term 'indecent conduct' means that form of immorality relating to sexual impurity which is grossly vulgar, obscene, and repugnant to common propriety, and tends to excite sexual desire or deprave morals with respect to sexual relations. Indecent conduct includes observing, or making a videotape, photograph, motion picture, print, negative, slide, or other mechanically, electronically, or chemically reproduced visual material, without another person's consent, and contrary to that other person's reasonable expectation of privacy, of—

(A) that other person's genitalia, anus, or buttocks, or (if that other person is female) that person's areola or nipple; or

(B) that other person while that other person is engaged in a sexual act, sodomy (under section 925 (article 125)), or sexual contact.

(13) *Act of prostitution.* The term 'act of prostitution' means a sexual act, sexual contact, or lewd act for the purpose of receiving money or other compensation.

(14) *Consent.* The term 'consent' means words or overt acts indicating a freely given agreement to the sexual conduct at issue by a competent person. An expression of lack of consent through words or conduct means there is no consent. Lack of verbal or physical resistance or submission resulting from the accused's use of force, threat of force, or placing another person in fear does not constitute consent. A current or previous dating relationship by itself or the manner of dress of the person involved with the accused in the sexual conduct at issue shall not constitute consent. A person cannot consent to sexual activity if—

(A) under 16 years of age; or

(B) substantially incapable of—

(i) appraising the nature of the sexual conduct at issue due to—

(I) mental impairment or unconsciousness resulting from consumption of alcohol, drugs, a similar substance, or otherwise; or

(II) mental disease or defect which renders the person unable to understand the nature of the sexual conduct at issue;

(ii) physically declining participation in the sexual conduct at issue; or

(iii) physically communicating unwillingness to engage in the sexual conduct at issue.

(15) *Mistake of fact as to consent.* The term 'mistake of fact as to consent' means the accused held, as a result of ignorance or mistake, an incorrect belief that the other person engaging in the sexual conduct consented. The ignorance or mistake must have existed in the mind of the accused and must have been reasonable under all the circumstances. To be reasonable the ignorance or mistake must have been based on information, or lack of it, which would indicate to a reasonable person that the other person consented. Additionally, the ignorance or mistake cannot be based on the negligent failure to discover the true facts. Negligence is the absence of due care. Due care is what a reasonably careful person would do under the same or similar circumstances. The accused's state of intoxication, if any, at the time of the offense is not

relevant to mistake of fact. A mistaken belief that the other person consented must be that which a reasonably careful, ordinary, prudent, sober adult would have had under the circumstances at the time of the offense.

(16) *Affirmative defense.* The term 'affirmative defense' means any special defense which, although not denying that the accused committed the objective acts constituting the offense charged, denies, wholly, or partially, criminal responsibility for those acts. The accused has the burden of proving the affirmative defense by a preponderance of evidence. After the defense meets this burden, the prosecution shall have the burden of proving beyond a reasonable doubt that the affirmative defense did not exist.

§ 920a. Art. 120a. Stalking

(a) Any person subject to this section—

(1) who wrongfully engages in a course of conduct directed at a specific person that would cause a reasonable person to fear death or bodily harm, including sexual assault, to himself or herself or a member of his or her immediate family;

(2) who has knowledge, or should have knowledge, that the specific person will be placed in reasonable fear of death or bodily harm, including sexual assault, to himself or herself or a member of his or her immediate family; and

(3) whose acts induce reasonable fear in the specific person of death or bodily harm, including sexual assault, to himself or herself or to a member of his or her immediate family; is guilty of stalking and shall be punished as a court-martial may direct.

(b) In this section:

(1) The term 'course of conduct' means—

(A) a repeated maintenance of visual or physical proximity to a specific person; or

(B) a repeated conveyance of verbal threat, written threats, or threats implied by conduct, or a combination of such threats, directed at or toward a specific person.

(2) The term 'repeated', with respect to conduct, means two or more occasions of such conduct;

(3) The term 'immediate family', in the case of a specific person, means a spouse, parent, child, or sibling of the person, or any other family member, relative, or intimate partner of the person who regularly resides in the household of the person or who within the six months preceding the commencement of the course of conduct regularly resided in the household of the person.

§ 921. Art. 121. Larceny and wrongful appropriation

(a) Any person subject to this chapter who wrongfully takes, obtains, or withholds, by any means, from the possession of the owner or of any other person any money, personal property, or article of value of any kind—

(1) with intent permanently to deprive or defraud another person of the use and benefit of property or to appropriate it to his own use or the use of any person other than the owner, steals that property and is guilty of larceny; or

(2) with intent temporarily to deprive or defraud another person of the use and benefit of property or to appropriate it to his own use or the use of any person other than the owner, is guilty of wrongful appropriation.

(b) Any person found guilty of larceny or wrongful appropriation shall be punished as a court-martial may direct.

§ 922. Art. 122. Robbery

Any person subject to this chapter who with intent to steal takes anything of value from the person or in the presence of another, against his will, by means of force or violence or fear of immediate or future injury to his person or property or to the person or property of a relative or member of his family or of anyone in his company at the time of the robbery, is guilty of robbery and shall be punished as a court-martial may direct.

§ 923. Art. 123. Forgery

Any person subject to this chapter who, with intent to defraud—

(1) falsely makes or alters any signature, to, or any part of, any writing which would, if genuine, apparently impose a legal liability on another or change his legal right or liability to his prejudice; or

(2) utters, offers, issues, or transfers such a writing, known by him to be so made or altered;

is guilty of forgery and shall be punished as a court-martial may direct.

§ 923a. Art. 123a. Making, drawing, or uttering check, draft, or order without sufficient funds

Any person subject to this chapter who—

(1) for the procurement of any article or thing of value, with intent to defraud; or

(2) for the payment of any past due obligation, or for any other purpose, with intent to deceive;

makes, draws, utters, or delivers any check, draft, or order for the payment of money upon any bank or other depository, knowing at the time that the maker or drawer has not or will not have sufficient funds in, or credit with, the bank or other depository for the payment of that check, draft, or order in full upon its presentment, shall be punished as a court-martial may direct. The making, drawing, uttering, or delivering by a maker or drawer of a check, draft, or order, payment of which is refused by the drawee because of insufficient funds of the maker or drawer in the drawee's possession or control, is prima facie evidence of his intent to defraud or deceive and of his knowledge of insufficient funds in, or credit with, that bank or other depository, unless the maker or drawer pays the holder the amount due within five days after receiving notice, orally or in writing, that the check, draft, or order was not paid on presentment. In this section, the word "credit" means an arrangement or understanding, express or implied, with the bank or other depository for the payment of that check, draft, or order.

§ 924. Art. 124. Maiming

Any person subject to this chapter who, with intent to injure, disfigure, or disable, inflicts upon the person of another an injury which

(1) seriously disfigures his person by a mutilation thereof;

(2) destroys or disables any member or organ of his body; or

(3) seriously diminishes his physical vigor by the injury of any member or organ;

is guilty of maiming and shall be punished as a court-martial may direct.

§ 925. Art. 125. Sodomy

(a) Any person subject to this chapter who engages in unnatural carnal copulation with another person of the same or opposite sex or with an animal is guilty of sodomy. Penetration, however slight, is sufficient to complete the offense.

(b) Any person found guilty of sodomy shall be punished as a court-martial may direct.

§ 926. Art. 126. Arson

(a) Any person subject to this chapter who willfully and maliciously burns or sets on fire an inhabited dwelling, or any other structure, movable or immovable, wherein to the knowledge of the offender there is at the time a human being, is guilty of aggravated arson and shall be punished as court-martial may direct.

(b) Any person subject to this chapter who willfully and maliciously burns or sets fire to the property of another, except as provided in subsection (a), is guilty of simple arson and shall be punished as a court-martial may direct.

§ 927. Art. 127. Extortion

Any person subject to this chapter who communicates threats to another person with the intention thereby to obtain anything of value or any acquittance, advantage, or immunity is guilty of extortion and shall be punished as a court-martial may direct.

§ 928. Art. 128. Assault

(a) Any person subject to this chapter who attempts or offers with unlawful force or violence to do bodily harm to another person, whether or not the attempt or offer is consummated, is guilty of assault and shall be punished as a court-martial may direct.

(b) Any person subject to this chapter who—

(1) commits an assault with a dangerous weapon or other means or force likely to produce death or grievous bodily harm; or

(2) commits an assault and intentionally inflicts grievous bodily harm with or without a weapon;

is guilty of aggravated assault and shall be punished as a court-martial may direct.

§ 929. Art. 129. Burglary

Any person subject to this chapter who, with intent to commit an offense punishable under section 918–928 of this title (article 118–128), breaks and enters, in the nighttime, the dwelling house of another, is guilty of burglary and shall be punished as a court-martial may direct.

§ 930. Art. 130. Housebreaking

Any person subject to this chapter who unlawfully enters the building or structure of another with intent to commit a criminal offense therein is guilty of housebreaking and shall be punished as a court-martial may direct.

§ 931. Art. 131. Perjury

Any person subject to this chapter who in a judicial proceeding or in a course of justice willfully and corruptly—

(1) upon a lawful oath or in any form allowed by law to be substituted for an oath, gives any false testimony material to the issue or matter of inquiry; or

(2) in any declaration, certificate, verification, or statement under penalty or perjury as permitted under section 1746 of title 28, United States Code, subscribes any false statement material to the issue or matter of inquiry;

is guilty of perjury and shall be punished as a court-martial may direct.

§ 932. Art. 132. Frauds against the United States

Any person subject to this chapter—

(1) who, knowing it to be false or fraudulent—

(A) makes any claim against the United States or any officer thereof; or

(B) presents to any person in the civil or military service thereof, for approval or payment, any claim against the United States or any officer thereof;

(2) who, for the purpose of obtaining the approval, allowance, or payment of any claim against the United States or any officer thereof—

(A) makes or uses any writing or other paper knowing it to contain any false or fraudulent statements;

(B) makes any oath to any fact or to any writing or other paper knowing the oath to be false; or

(C) forges or counterfeits any signature upon any writing or other paper, or uses any such signature knowing it to be forged or counterfeited;

(3) who, having charge, possession, custody, or control of any money, or other property of the United States, furnished or intended for the armed forces thereof, knowingly delivers to any person having authority to receive it, any amount thereof less than that for which he receives a certificate or receipt; or

(4) who, being authorized to make or deliver any paper certifying the receipt of any property of the United States furnished or intended for the armed forces thereof, makes or delivers to any person such writing without having full knowledge of the truth of the statements therein contained and with intent to defraud the United States;

shall, upon conviction, be punished as a court-martial may direct.

§ 933. Art. 133. Conduct unbecoming an officer and a gentleman

Any commissioned officer, cadet, or midshipman who is convicted of conduct unbecoming an officer and a gentleman shall be punished as a court-martial may direct.

§ 934. Art. 134. General article

Though not specifically mentioned in this chapter, all disorders and neglects to the prejudice of good order and discipline in the armed forces, all conduct of a nature to bring discredit upon the armed forces, and crimes and offenses not capital, of which persons subject to this chapter may be guilty, shall be taken cognizance of by a general, special, or summary court-martial, according to the nature and degree of the offense, and shall be punished at the discretion of that court.

SUBCHAPTER XI. MISCELLANEOUS PROVISIONS

§ 935. Art. 135. Courts of inquiry

(a) Courts of inquiry to investigate any matter may be convened by any person authorized to convene a general court-martial or by any other person designated by the Secretary concerned for that purpose, whether or not the persons involved have requested such an inquiry.

(b) A court of inquiry consists of three or more commissioned officers. For each court of inquiry the convening authority shall also appoint counsel for the court.

(c) Any person subject to this chapter whose conduct is subject to inquiry shall be designated as a party. Any person subject to this chapter or employed by the Department of Defense who has a direct interest in the subject of inquiry has the right to be designated as a party upon request to the court. Any person designated as a party shall be given due notice and has the right to be present, to be represented by counsel, to cross-examine witnesses, and to introduce evidence.

(d) Members of a court of inquiry may be challenged by a party, but only for cause stated to the court.

(e) The members, counsel, the reporter, and interpreters of courts of inquiry shall take an oath to faithfully perform their duties.

(f) Witnesses may be summoned to appear and testify and be examined before courts of inquiry, as provided for courts-martial.

(g) Courts of inquiry shall make findings of fact but may not express opinions or make recommendations unless required to do so by the convening authority.

(h) Each court of inquiry shall keep a record of its proceedings, which shall be authenticated by the signatures of the president and counsel for the court and forwarded to the convening authority. If the record cannot be authenticated by the president, it shall be signed by a member in lieu of the president. If the record cannot be authenticated by the counsel for the court, it shall be signed by a member in lieu of the counsel.

§ 936. Art. 136. Authority to administer oaths and to act as notary

(a) The following persons on active duty or performing inactive-duty training may administer oaths for the purposes of military administration, including military justice:

(1) All judge advocates.

(2) All summary courts-martial.

(3) All adjutants, assistant adjutants, acting adjutants, and personnel adjutants.

(4) All commanding officers of the Navy, Marine Corps, and Coast Guard.

(5) All staff judge advocates and legal officers, and acting or assistant staff judge advocates and legal officers.

(6) All other persons designated by regulations of the armed forces or by statute.

(b) The following persons on active duty or performing inactive-duty training may administer oaths necessary in the performance of their duties:

(1) The president, military judge, trial counsel, and assistant trial counsel for all general and special courts-martial.

(2) The president and the counsel for the court of any court of inquiry.

(3) All officers designated to take a deposition.

(4) All persons detailed to conduct an investigation.

(5) All recruiting officers.

(6) All other persons designated by regulations of the armed forces or by statute.

§ 937. Art. 137. Articles to be explained

(a)(1) The sections of this title (articles of the Uniform Code of Military Justice) specified in paragraph (3) shall be carefully explained to each enlisted member at the time of (or within fourteen days after)—

(A) the member's initial entrance on active duty; or

(B) the member's initial entrance into a duty status with a reserve component.

(2) Such sections (articles) shall be explained again—

(A) after the member has completed six months of active duty or, in the case of a member of a reserve component, after the member has completed basic or recruit training; and

(B) at the time when the member reenlists.

(3) This subsection applies with respect to sections 802, 803, 807–815, 825, 827, 831, 837, 838, 855,877–934, and 937–939 of this title(articles 2, 3, 7–15, 25, 27, 31, 37, 38, 55, 77–134, and 137–139).

(b) The text of the Uniform Code of Military Justice and of the regulations prescribed by the President under such Code shall be made available to a member on active duty or to a member of a reserve component, upon request by the member, for the member's personal examination.

§ 938. Art. 138. Complaints of wrongs

Any member of the armed forces who believes himself wronged by his commanding officer, and who, upon due application to that commanding officer, is refused redress, may complain to any superior commissioned officer, who shall forward the complaint to the officer exercising general court-martial jurisdiction over the officer against whom it is made. The officer exercising general court-martial jurisdiction shall examine into the complaint and take proper measures for redressing the wrong complained of; and he shall, as soon as possible, send to the Secretary concerned a true statement of that complaint, with the proceedings had thereon.

§ 939. Art. 139. Redress of injuries to property

(a) Whenever complaint is made to any commanding officer that willful damage has been done to the property of any person or that his property has been wrongfully taken by members of the armed forces, he may, under such regulations as the Secretary concerned may prescribe, convene a board to investigate the complaint. The board shall consist of from one to three commissioned officers and, for the purpose of that investigation, it has power to summon witnesses and examine them upon oath, to receive depositions or other documentary evidence, and to assess the damages sustained against the responsible parties. The assessment of damages made by the board is subject to the approval of the commanding officer, and in the amount approved by him shall be charged against the pay of the offenders. The order of the commanding officer directing charges herein authorized is conclusive on any disbursing officer for the payment by him to the injured parties of the damages as assessed and approved.

(b) If the offenders cannot be ascertained, but the organization or detachment to which they belong is known, charges totaling the amount of damages assessed and approved may be made in such proportion as may be considered just upon the individual members thereof who are shown to have been present at the scene at the time the damages complained of were inflicted, as determined by the approved findings of the board.

§ 940. Art. 140. Delegation by the President

The President may delegate any authority vested in him under this chapter, and provide for the subdelegation of any such authority.

SUBCHAPTER XII. UNITED STATES COURT OF APPEALS FOR THE ARMED FORCES

§ 941. Art. 141. Status

There is a court of record known as the United States Court of Appeals for the Armed Forces. The court is established under article I of the Constitution. The court is located for administrative purposes only in the Department of Defense.

§ 942. Art. 142. Judges

(a) *Number.* The United States Court of Appeals for the Armed Forces consists of five judges.

(b) *Appointment; qualification.*

(1) Each judge of the court shall be appointed from civilian life by the President, by and with the advice and consent of the Senate, for a specified term determined under paragraph (2). A judge may serve as a senior judge as provided in subsection (e).

(2) The term of a judge shall expire as follows:

(A) In the case of a judge who is appointed after March 31 and before October 1 of any year, the term shall expire on September 30 of the year in which the fifteenth anniversary of the appointment occurs.

(B) In the case of a judge who is appointed after September 30 of any year and before April 1 of the following year, the term shall expire fifteen years after such September 30.

(3) Not more than three of the judges of the court may be appointed from the same political party, and no person may be appointed to be a judge of the court unless the person is a member of the bar of a Federal court or the highest court of a State.

(4) For purposes of appointment of judges to the court, a person retired from the armed forces after 20 or more years of active service (whether or not such person is on the retired list) shall not be considered to be in civilian life.

(c) *Removal.* Judges of the court may be removed from office by the President, upon notice and hearing, for—

(1) neglect of duty;

(2) misconduct; or

(3) mental or physical disability.

A judge may not be removed by the President for any other cause.

(d) *Pay and allowances.* Each judge of the court is entitled to the same salary and travel allowances as are, and from time to time may be, provided for judges of the United States Court of Appeals.

(e) *Senior judges.*

(1)(A) A former judge of the court who is receiving retired pay or an annuity under section 945 of this title (article 145) or under subchapter III of chapter 83 or chapter 84 of title 5 shall be a senior judge. The chief judge of the court may call upon an individual who is a senior judge of the court under this subparagraph, with the consent of the senior judge, to perform judicial duties with the court—

(i) during a period a judge of the court is unable to perform his duties because of illness or other disability;

(ii) during a period in which a position of judge of the court is vacant; or

(iii) in any case in which a judge of the court recuses himself.

(B) If, at the time the term of a judge expires, no successor to that judge has been appointed, the chief judge of the court may call upon that judge (with the judge's consent) to continue to perform judicial duties with the court until the vacancy is filled. A judge who, upon the expiration of the judge's term, continues to perform judicial duties with the court without a break in service under this subparagraph shall be a senior judge while such service continues.

(2) A senior judge shall be paid for each day on which he

performs judicial duties with the court an amount equal to the daily equivalent of the annual rate of pay provided for a judge of the court. Such pay shall be in lieu of retired pay and in lieu of an annuity under section 945 of this title (Article 145), subchapter III of chapter 83 or subchapter II of chapter 84 of title 5, or any other retirement system for employees of the Federal Government.

(3) A senior judge, while performing duties referred to in paragraph (2), shall be provided with such office space and staff assistance as the chief judge considers appropriate and shall be entitled to the per diem, travel allowances, and other allowances provided for judges of the court.

(4) A senior judge shall be considered to be an officer or employee of the United States with respect to his status as a senior judge, but only during periods the senior judge is performing duties referred to in paragraph (2). For the purposes of section 205 of title 18, a senior judge shall be considered to be a special Government employee during such periods. Any provision of law that prohibits or limits the political or business activities of an employee of the United States shall apply to a senior judge only during such periods.

(5) The court shall prescribe rules for the use and conduct of senior judges of the court. The chief judge of the court shall transmit such rules, and any amendments to such rules, to the Committees on Armed Services of the Senate and the House of Representatives not later than 15 days after the issuance of such rules or amendments, as the case may be.

(6) For purposes of subchapter III of chapter 83 of title 5 (relating to the Civil Service Retirement and Disability System) and chapter 84 of such title (relating to the Federal Employees' Retirement System) and for purposes of any other Federal Government retirement system for employees of the Federal Government—

(A) a period during which a senior judge performs duties referred to in paragraph (1) shall not be considered creditable service;

(B) no amount shall be withheld from the pay of a senior judge as a retirement contribution under section 8334, 8343, 8422, or 8432 of title 5 or under other such retirement system for any period during which the senior judge performs duties referred to in paragraph (1);

(C) no contribution shall be made by the Federal Government to any retirement system with respect to a senior judge for any period during which the senior judge performs duties referred to in paragraph (1); and

(D) a senior judge shall not be considered to be a reemployed annuitant for any period during which the senior judge performs duties referred to in paragraph (1).

(f) *Service of article III judges.*

(1) The Chief Justice of the United States, upon the request of the chief judge of the court, may designate a judge of a United States Court of Appeals or of a United States District Court to perform the duties of judge of the United States Court of Appeals for the Armed Forces—

(A) during a period a judge of the court is unable to perform his duties because of illness or other disability; or

(B) in any case in which a judge of the court recuses himself; or

(C) during a period when there is a vacancy on the court and in the opinion of the chief judge of the court such a designation is necessary for the proper dispatch of the business of the court.

(2) The chief judge of the court may not request that a designation be made under paragraph (1) unless the chief judge has determined that no person is available to perform judicial duties with the court as a senior judge under subsection (e).

(3) A designation under paragraph (1) may be made only with the consent of the designated judge and the concurrence of the chief judge of the court of appeals or district court concerned.

(4) Per diem, travel allowances, and other allowances paid to the designated judge in connection with the performance of duties for the court shall be paid from funds available for the payment of per diem and such allowances for judges of the court.

(g) *Effect of vacancy on court.* A vacancy on the court does not impair the right of the remaining judges to exercise the powers of the court.

§ 943. Art. 143. Organization and employees

(a) *Chief judge.*

(1) The chief judge of the United States Court of Appeals for the Armed Forces shall be the judge of the court in regular active service who is senior in commission among the judges of the court who—

(A) have served for one or more years as judges of the court; and

(B) have not previously served as chief judge.

(2) In any case in which there is no judge of the court in regular active service who has served as a judge of the court for at least one year, the judge of the court in regular active service who is senior in commission and has not served previously as chief judge shall act as the chief judge.

(3) Except as provided in paragraph (4), a judge of the court shall serve as the chief judge under paragraph (1) for a term of five years. If no other judge is eligible under paragraph (1) to serve as chief judge upon the expiration of that term, the chief judge shall continue to serve as chief judge until another judge becomes eligible under that paragraph to serve as chief judge.

(4)(A) The term of a chief judge shall be terminated before the end of five years if—

(i) The chief judge leaves regular active service as a judge of the court; or

(ii) The chief judge notifies the other judges of the court in writing that such judge desires to be relieved of his duties as chief judge.

(B) The effective date of a termination of the term under subparagraph (A) shall be the date on which the chief judge leaves regular active service or the date of the notification under subparagraph (A)(ii), as the case may be.

(5) If a chief judge is temporarily unable to perform his duties as achief judge, the duties shall be performed by the judge of the court in active service who is present, able, and qualified to act, and is next in precedence.

(b) *Precedence of judges.* The chief judge of the court shall have precedence and preside at any session that he attends. The other judges shall have precedence and preside according to the seniority of their original commissions. Judges whose commissions bear the same date shall have precedence according to seniority in age.

(c) *Status of Certain positions.*

(1) Attorney positions of employment under the Court of Appeals for the Armed Forces are excepted from the competitive service. A position of employment under the court that is provided primarily for the service of one judge of the court, reports directly to the judge, and is a position of a confidential character is excepted from the competitive service. Appointments to positions referred to in the preceding sentences shall be made by the court, without the concurrence of any other officer or employee of the executive branch, in the same manner as appointments are made to other executive branch positions of a confidential or policy-determining character for which it is not practicable to examine or to hold a competitive examination. Such positions shall not be counted as positions of that character for purposes of any limitation on the number of positions of that character provided in law.

(2) In making appointments to the positions described in paragraph (1), preference shall be given, among equally qualified persons, to persons who are preference eligibles (as defined in section 2108(3) of title 5).

§ 944. Art. 144. Procedure

The United States Court of Appeals for the Armed Forces may prescribe its rules of procedure and may determine the number of judges required to constitute a quorum.

§ 945. Art. 145. Annuities for judges and survivors

(a) *Retirement annuities for judges.*

(1) A person who has completed a term of service for which he was appointed as a judge of the United States Court of Appeals for the Armed Forces is eligible for an annuity under this section upon separation from civilian service in the Federal Government. A person who continues service with the court as a senior judge under section 943(e)(1)(B) of this title (art. 143(e)(1)(B)) upon the expiration of the judge's term shall be considered to have been separated from civilian service in the Federal Government only upon the termination of that continuous service.

(2) A person who is eligible for any annuity under this section shall be paid that annuity if, at the time he becomes eligible to receive that annuity, he elects to receive that annuity in lieu of any other annuity for which he may be eligible at the time of such election (whether an immediate or a deferred annuity) under subchapter III of chapter 83 or subchapter II of chapter 84 of title 5 or any other retirement system for civilian employees of the Federal Government. Such an election may not be revoked.

(3)(A) The Secretary of Defense shall notify the Director of the Office of Personnel Management whenever an election under paragraph (2) is made affecting any right or interest under subchapter III of chapter 83 or subchapter 11 of chapter 85 of title 5 based on service as a judge of the United States Court of Appeals for the Armed Forces.

(B) Upon receiving any notification under subparagraph (A) in the case of a person making an election under (2), the Director shall determine the amount of the person's lump-sum credit under subchapter 111 of chapter 83 or subchapter II of chapter 84 of title 5, as applicable, and shall request the Secretary of the Treasury to transfer such amount from the Civil Service Retirement and Disability Fund to the Department of Defense Military Retirement Fund. The Secretary of the Treasury shall make any transfer so requested.

(C) In determining the amount of a lump-sum credit under section 8331(8) of title 5 for purposes of this paragraph -

(i) interest shall be computed using the rates under section 8334(e)(3) of such title; and

(ii) the completion of 5 years of civilian service (or longer) shall not be a basis for excluding interest.

(b) *Amount of annuity.* The annuity payable under this section to a person who makes an election under subsection (a)(2) is 80 percent of the rate of pay for a judge in active service on the United States Court of Appeals for the Armed Forces as of the date on which the person is separated from civilian service.

(c) *Relation to thrift savings plan.* Nothing in this section affects any right of any person to participate in the thrift savings plan under section 8351 of title 5 of subchapter III of chapter 84 of such title.

(d) *Survivor annuities.* The Secretary of Defense shall prescribe by regulation a program to provide annuities for survivors and former spouses of persons receiving annuities under this section by reason of elections made by such persons under subsection (a)(2). That program shall, to the maximum extent practicable, provide benefits and establish terms and conditions that are similar to those provided under survivor and former spouse annuity programs under other retirement systems for civilian employees of the Federal Government. The program may include provisions for the reduction in the annuity paid the person as a condition for the survivor annuity. An election by a judge (including a senior judge) or former judge to receive an annuity under this section terminates any right or interest which any other individual may have to a survivor annuity under any other retirement system for civilian employees of the Federal Government based on the service of that judge or former judge as a civilian officer or employee of the Federal Government (except with respect to an election under subsection (g)(1)(B)).

(e) *Cost-of-living increases.* The Secretary of Defense shall periodically increase annuities and survivor annuities paid under this section in order to take account of changes in the cost of living. The Secretary shall prescribe by regulation procedures for increases in annuities under this section. Such system shall, to the maximum extent appropriate, provide cost-of-living adjustments that are similar to those that are provided under other retirement systems for civilian employees of the Federal Government.

(f) *Dual compensation.* A person who is receiving an annuity under this section by reason of service as a judge of the court and who is appointed to a position in the Federal Government shall, during the period of such person's service in such position, be entitled to receive only the annuity under this section or the pay for that position, whichever is higher.

(g) *Election of judicial retirement benefits.*

(1) A person who is receiving an annuity under this section by reason of service as a judge of the court and who later is appointed as a justice or judge of the United States to hold office during good behavior and who retires from that office, or from regular active service in that office, shall be paid either—

(A) the annuity under this section, or

(B) the annuity or salary to which he is entitled by reason of his service as such a justice or judge of the United States, as determined by an election by that person at the time of his retirement from the office, or from regular active service in the office, of justice or judge of the United States. Such an election may not be revoked.

(2) An election by a person to be paid an annuity or salary pursuant to paragraph (1)(B) terminates (A) any election previously made by such person to provide a survivor annuity pursuant to subsection (d), and (B) any right of any other individual to receive a survivor annuity pursuant to subsection (d) on the basis of the service of that person.

(h) *Source of payment of annuities.* Annuities and survivor annuities paid under this section shall be paid out of the Department of Defense Military Retirement Fund.

(i) *Eligibility to elect between retirement systems.*

(1) This subsection applies with respect to any person who—

(A) prior to being appointed as a judge of the United States Court of Appeals for the Armed Forces, performed civilian service of a type making such person subject to the Civil Service Retirement System; and

(B) would be eligible to make an election under section 301(a)(2) of the Federal Employees' Retirement System Act of 1986, by virtue of being appointed as such a judge, but for the fact that such person has not had a break in service of a sufficient duration to be considered someone who is being reemployed by the Federal Government.

(2) Any person with respect to whom this subsection applies shall be eligible to make an election under section 301(a)(2) of the Federal Employees' Retirement System Act of 1986 to the same extent and in the same manner (including subject to the condition set forth in section 301(d) of such Act) as if such person's appointment constituted reemployment with the Federal Government.

(Added Pub.L. 101–189, Div. A, Title XIII, § 1301(c), Nov. 29, 1989, 103 Stat. 1572, and amended Pub.L. 102–190, Div. A, Title X, § 1061(b)(1)(C), Dec. 5, 1991, 105 Stat. 1474; Pub.L. 102–484, Div. A, Title X, §§ 1052(11), 1062(a)(1), Oct. 23, 1992, 106 Stat. 2499, 2504.)

§ 946. Art. 146. Code committee

(a) *Annual survey.* A committee shall meet at least annually and shall make an annual comprehensive survey of the operation of this chapter.

(b) *Composition of committee.* The committee shall consist of—

(1) the judges of the United States Court of Appeals for the Armed Forces;

(2) the Judge Advocates General of the Army, Navy, and Air Force, the Chief Counsel of the Coast Guard, and the Staff Judge Advocate to the Commandant of the Marine Corps; and

(3) two members of the public appointed by the Secretary of Defense.

(c) *Reports.*

(1) After each such survey, the committee shall submit a report—

(A) to the Committees on Armed Services of the Senate and House of Representatives; and

(B) to the Secretary of Defense, the Secretaries of the military departments, and the Secretary of Homeland Security.

(2) Each report under paragraph (1) shall include the following:

(A) Information on the number and status of pending cases.

(B) Any recommendation of the committee relating to—

(i) uniformity of policies as to sentences;

(ii) amendments to this chapter; and

(iii) any other matter the committee considers appropriate.

(d) *Qualifications and terms of appointed members.* Each member of the committee appointed by the Secretary of Defense under subsection (b)(3) shall be a recognized authority in military justice or criminal law. Each such member shall be appointed for a term of three years.

(e) *Applicability of Federal Advisory Committee Act.* The Federal Advisory Committee Act (5 U.S.C.App. 1) shall not apply to the committee.

APPENDIX 3
DoD Directive 5525.7

Department of Defense DIRECTIVE

January 22, 1985
NUMBER 5525.7

GC/IG, DoD

SUBJECT:

Implementation of the Memorandum of Understanding Between the Department of Justice and the Department of Defense Relating to the Investigation and Prosecution of Certain Crimes

References:

(a) DoD Directive 1355.1, "Relationships with the Department of Justice on Grants of Immunity and the Investigation and Prosecution of Certain ~Crimes," July 21, 1981 (hereby canceled)

(b) Memorandum of Understanding Between the Department Relating to the Investigation and Prosecution of Certain Crimes, August 1984

(c) Title 18, United State Code

(d) Title 10, United States Code, Sections 801-940 (Articles 1-140), "Uniform Code of Military Justice (UCMJ)"

(e) Manual for Courts-Martial, United States, 1984 (R.C.M. 704)

A. REISSUANCE AND PURPOSE

This Directive reissues reference (a), updates policy and procedures, assigns responsibilities, and implements the 1984 Memorandum of Understanding (MOU) between the Department of Justice (DoJ) and the Department of Defense (DoD).

B. APPLICABILITY

This Directive applies to the Office of the Secretary of Defense, the Military Departments, the Office of Inspector General, DoD, the Organization of the Joint Chiefs of Staff, the Defense Agencies, and Unified and Specified Commands (hereafter referred to collectively as "DoD Components"). The term "DoD criminal investigative organizations," as used herein, refers collectively to the United States Army Criminal Investigation Command (USACIDC); Naval Investigative Service (NIS); U.S. Air Force Office of Special Investigations (AFOSI), and Defense Criminal Investigative Service (DCIS), Office of the Inspector General, DoD.

C. POLICY

It is DoD policy to maintain effective working relationships with the DoJ in the investigation and prosecution of crimes involving the programs, operations, or personnel of the Department of Defense.

D. PROCEDURES

With respect to inquiries for which the DoJ has assumed investigative responsibility based on the MOU, DoD investigative agencies should seek to participate jointly with DoJ investigative agencies whenever the inquiries relate to the programs, operations, or personnel of the Department of Defense. This applies to cases referred to the Federal Bureau of Investigation (FBI) under paragraph C.1.a. of the attached MOU (*see* enclosure 1) as well as to those cases for which a DoJ investigative agency is assigned primary investigative responsibility by a DoJ prosecutor. DoD components shall comply with the terms of the MOU and DoD Supplemental Guidance (*see* enclosure 1).

E. RESPONSIBILITIES

1. *The Inspector General, Department of Defense* (IG, DoD), shall:

a. Establish procedures to implement the investigative policies set forth in this Directive.

b. Monitor compliance by DoD criminal investigative organizations to the terms of the MOU.

c. Provide specific guidance regarding investigative matters, as appropriate.

2. *The General Counsel, Department of Defense,* shall:

a. Establish procedures to implement the prosecutive policies set forth in this Directive.

b. Monitor compliance by the DoD Components regarding the prosecutive aspects of the MOU.

c. Provide specific guidance, as appropriate.

d. Modify the DoD Supplemental Guidance at enclosure 1, with the concurrence of the IG, DoD, after requesting comments from affected DoD Components.

3. The *Secretaries of the Military Departments* shall establish procedures to implement the policies set forth in this Directive.

F. EFFECTIVE DATE AND IMPLEMENTATION

This Directive is effective immediately. The Military Departments shall forward two copies of implementing documents to the Inspector General, Department of Defense, within 90 days. Other DoD Components shall disseminate this Directive to appropriate personnel.

Signed by William H. Taft, IV
Deputy Secretary of Defense

Enclosure—1
Memorandum of Understanding Between the Departments of Justice And Defense Relating to the Investigation and Prosecution of Certain Crimes

MEMORANDUM OF UNDERSTANDING BETWEEN THE DEPARTMENTS OF JUSTICE AND DEFENSE

This enclosure contains the verbatim text of the 1984 Memorandum of Understanding Between the Departments of Justice and Defense Relating to the Investigation and Prosecution of Certain Crimes (reference (b)). Matter that is identified as "DoD Supplemental Guidance" has been added by the Department of Defense. DoD Components shall comply with the MOU and the DoD Supplemental Guidance.

MEMORANDUM OR UNDERSTANDING BETWEEN THE DEPARTMENTS OF JUSTICE AND DEFENSE RELATING TO THE INVESTIGATION AND PROSECUTION OF CERTAIN CRIMES

A. PURPOSE, SCOPE AND AUTHORITY

This Memorandum of Understanding (MOU) establishes policy for the Department of Justice and the Department of Defense with regard to the investigation and prosecution of criminal matters over which the two Departments have jurisdiction. This memorandum is not intended to confer any rights, benefits, privileges or form of due process procedure upon individuals, associations, corporations or other persons or entities.

This Memorandum applies to all components and personnel of the Department of Justice and the Department of Defense. The statutory bases for the Department of Defense and the Department of Justice investigation and prosecution responsibilities include, but are not limited to:

1. Department of Justice: Titles 18, 21 and 28 of the United States Code; and

2. Department of Defense: The Uniform Code of Military Justice, Title 10, United States Code, Sections 801-940; the Inspector General Act of 1978, Title 5 United States Code, Appendix 3; and Title 5 United States Code, Section 301.

B. POLICY

The Department of Justice has primary responsibility for enforcement of federal laws in the United States District Courts. The Department of Defense has responsibility for the integrity of its programs, operations and installations and for the discipline of the Armed Forces. Prompt administrative actions and completion of investigations within the two (2) year statute of limitations under the Uniform Code of Military Justice require the Department of Defense to assume an important role in federal criminal investigations. To encourage joint and coordinated investigative efforts, in appropriate cases where the Department of Justice assumes investigative responsibility for a matter relating to the Department of Defense, it should share information and conduct the inquiry jointly with the interested Department of Defense investigative agency.

It is neither feasible nor desirable to establish inflexible rules regarding the responsibilities of the Department of Defense and the Department of Justice as to each matter over which they may have concurrent interest. Informal arrangements and agreements within the spirit of this MOU are permissible with respect to specific crimes or investigations.

C. INVESTIGATIVE AND PROSECUTIVE JURISDICTION

1. *CRIMES ARISING FROM THE DEPARTMENT OF DEFENSE OPERATIONS*

a. *Corruption Involving the Department of Defense Personnel* The Department of Defense investigative agencies will refer to the FBI on receipt all significant allegations of bribery and conflict of interest involving military or civilian personnel of the Department of Defense. In all corruption matters the subject of a referral to the FBI, the Department of Defense shall obtain the concurrence of the Department of Justice prosecutor or the FBI before initiating any independent investigation preliminary to any action under the Uniform code of Military Justice. If the Department of Defense is not satisfied with the initial determination, the matter will be reviewed by the Criminal Division of the Department of Justice.

The FBI will notify the referring agency promptly regarding whether they accept the referred matters for investigation. The FBI will attempt to make such decision in one (1) working day of receipt in such matters.

DoD Supplemental Guidance

A. Certain bribery and conflict of interest allegations (also referred to as "corruption" offenses in the MOU) are to be referred immediately to the FBI.

B. For the purposes of this section, bribery and conflict of interest allegations are those which would, if proven, violate 18 U.S.C., Sections 201, 203, 205, 208, 209, or 219 (reference (c)).

C. Under paragraph C.1.a., DoD criminal investigative organizations shall refer to the FBI those "significant" allegations of bribery and conflict of interest that implicate directly military or civilian personnel of the Department of Defense, including allegations of bribery or conflict of interest that arise during the course of an ongoing investigation.

1. All bribery and conflict of interest allegations against present, retired, or former General or Flag officers and civilians in grade GS-16 and above, the Senior Executive Service and the Executive Level will be considered "significant" for purposes of referral to the FBI.

2. In cases not covered by subsection C.1., above, the determination of whether the matter is "significant" for purposes of referral to the FBI should be made in light of the following factors: sensitivity of the DoD program, involved, amount of money in the alleged bribe, number of DoD personnel implicated, impact on the affected DoD program, and with respect to military personnel, whether the matter normally would be handled under the Uniform Code of Military Justice (reference (d)). Bribery and conflicts of interest allegations warranting consideration of Federal prosecution, which were not referred to the FBI based on the application of these guidelines and not otherwise disposed of under reference (d), will be developed and brought to the attention of the Department of Justice through the "conference" mechanism described in paragraph C.1.b. of the MOU(reference (b)).

D. Bribery and conflict of interest allegations when military or DoD civilian personnel are not subjects of the investigation are not covered by the referral requirement of paragraph C.1.a of reference (b). Matters in which the suspects are solely DoD contractors and their subcontractors, such as commercial bribery between a DoD subcontractor and a DoD prime contractor, do not require referral upon receipt to the FBI. The "conference" procedure described in paragraph C.1.b. of reference (b) shall be used in these types of cases.

E. Bribery and conflict of interest allegations that arise from events occurring outside the United States, its territories, and possessions, and requiring investigation outside the United States, its territories, and possessions need not be referred to the FBI.

b. *Frauds Against the Department of Defense and Theft and Embezzlement of Government Property* The Department of Justice and the Department of Defense have investigative responsibility for frauds against the Department of Defense and theft and embezzlement of Government property from the Department of Defense. The Department of Defense will investigate frauds against the Department of Defense and theft of government property from the Department of Defense. Whenever a Department of Defense investigative agency identifies a matter which, if developed by investigation, would warrant federal prosecution, it will confer with the United States Attorney or the Criminal Division, the Department of Justice, and the FBI field office. At the time of this initial conference, criminal investigative responsibility will be determined by the Department of Justice in consultation with the Department of Defense.

DoD Supplemental Guidance

A. Unlike paragraph C.1.a. of the MOU (reference (b)), paragraph C.1.b. does not have an automatic referral requirement. Under paragraph C.1.b., DoD criminal investigative organizations shall confer with the appropriate federal prosecutor and the FBI on matters which, if developed by investigation, would warrant Federal prosecution. This "conference" serves to define the respective roles of DoD criminal investigative organizations and the FBI on a case-by-case basis. Generally, when a conference is warranted, the DoD criminal investigative organization shall arrange to meet with the prosecutor and shall provide notice to the FBI that such meeting is being held. Separate conferences with both the prosecutor and the FBI normally are not necessary.

B. When investigations are brought to the attention of the Defense Procurement Fraud Unit (DPFU), such contact will satisfy the "conference" requirements of paragraph C.1.b. (reference (b)) as to both the prosecutor and the FBI.

C. Mere receipt by DoD criminal investigative organizations of raw allegations of fraud or theft does not require conferences with the DoJ and the FBI. Sufficient evidence should be developed before the conference to allow the prosecutor to make an informed judgment as to the merits of a case dependent upon further investigation. However, DoD criminal investigative organizations should avoid delay in scheduling such conferences, particularly in complex fraud cases, because an early judgment by a prosecutor can be of assistance in focusing the investigation on those matters that most likely will result in criminal prosecution.

2. *CRIMES COMMITTED ON MILITARY INSTALLATIONS*

a. *Subject(s) can be Tried by Court-Martial or are Unknown* Crimes (other than those covered by paragraph C.1.) committed on a military installation will be investigated by the Department of Defense investigative agency concerned and, when committed by a person subject to the Uniform Code of Military Justice, prosecuted by the Military Department concerned. The Department of Defense will provide immediate notice to the Department of Justice of significant cases in which an individual subject/victim is other than a military member or dependent thereof.

b. *One or More Subjects cannot be Tried by Court-Martial* When a crime (other than those covered by paragraph C.1.) has occurred on a military installation and there is reasonable basis to believe that it has been committed by a person or persons, some or all of whom are not subject to the Uniform Code of Military Justice, the Department of Defense investigative agency will provide immediate notice of the matter to the appropriate Department of Justice investigative agency unless the Department of Justice has relieved the Department of Defense of the reporting requirement for that type or class of crime.

DoD Supplemental Guidance

A. Subsection C.2. of the MOU (reference (b)) addresses crimes committed on a military installation other than those listed in paragraphs C.1.a. (bribery and conflict of interest) and C.1.b. (fraud, theft, and embezzlement against the Government).

B. Unlike paragraph C.1.a. of reference (b), which requires "referral" to the FBI of certain cases, and paragraph C.1.b., which requires "conferences" with respect to certain cases, subsection C.2. requires only that "notice" be given to DoJ of certain cases. Relief from the reporting requirement of subsection C.2. may be granted by the local U.S. attorney as to types or classes of cases.

C. For purposes of paragraph C.2.a. (when the subjects can be tried by court-martial or are unknown), an allegation is "significant" for purposes of required notice to the DoJ only if the offense falls within the prosecutorial guidelines of the local U.S. attorney. Notice should be given in other cases when the DoD Component believes that Federal prosecution is warranted or otherwise determines that the case may attract significant public attention.

3. *CRIMES COMMITTED OUTSIDE MILITARY INSTALLATIONS BY PERSONS WHO CAN BE TRIED BY COURT-MARTIAL*

a. *Offense is Normally Tried by Court-Martial* Crimes (other than those covered by paragraph C.1.) committed outside a military installation by persons subject to the Uniform Code of Military Justice which, normally, are tried by court-martial will be investigated and prosecuted by the Department of Defense. The Department of Defense will provide immediate notice of significant cases to the appropriate Department of Justice investigative agency. The Department of Defense will provide immediate notice in all cases where one or more subjects is not under military jurisdiction unless the Department of Justice has relieved the Department of Defense of the reporting requirement for that type or class of crime.

DoD Supplemental Guidance

For purposes of this paragraph, an allegation is "significant" for purposes of required notice to the DoJ only if the offense falls within prosecutorial guidelines of the local U.S. attorney. Notice should be given in other cases when the DoD Component believes that Federal prosecution is warranted, or otherwise determines that the case may attract significant public attention.

b. *Crimes Related to Scheduled Military Activities* Crimes related to scheduled Military activities outside of a military installation, such as organized maneuvers in which persons subject to the Uniform Code of Military Justice are suspects, shall be treated as if committed on a military installation for purposes of this Memorandum. The FBI or other Department of Justice investigative agency may assume jurisdiction with the concurrence of the United States Attorney or the Criminal Division, Department of Justice.

c. *Offense is not Normally Tried by Court-Martial* When there are reasonable grounds to believe that a Federal crime (other than those covered by paragraph C.1.) normally not tried by court-martial, has been committed outside a military installation by a person subject to the Uniform Code of Military Justice, the Department of Defense investigative agency will immediately refer the case to the appropriate Department of Justice investigative agency unless the Department of Justice has relieved the Department of Defense of the reporting requirement for that type or class of crime.

D. REFERRALS AND INVESTIGATIVE ASSISTANCE

1. *REFERRALS* Referrals, notices, reports, requests and the general transfer of information under this Memorandum normally should be between the FBI or other Department of Justice investigative agency and the appropriate Department of Defense investigative agency at the field level.

If a Department of Justice investigative agency does not accept a referred matter and the referring Department of Defense investigative agency then, or subsequently, believes that evidence exists supporting prosecution before civilian courts, the Department of Defense agency may present the case to the United States Attorney or the Criminal Division, Department of Justice, for review.

2. *INVESTIGATIVE ASSISTANCE* In cases where a Department of Defense or Department of Justice investigative agency has primary responsibility and it requires limited assistance to pursue outstanding leads, the investigative agency requiring assistance will promptly advise the appropriate investigative agency in the other Department and, to the extent authorized by law and regulations, the requested assistance should be provided without assuming responsibility for the investigation.

E. PROSECUTION OF CASES

1. With the concurrence of the Department of Defense, the Department of Justice will designate such Department of Defense attorneys as it deems desirable to be Special Assistant United States Attorneys for use where the effective prosecution of cases may be facilitated by the Department of Defense attorneys.

2. The Department of Justice will institute civil actions expeditiously in United States District Courts whenever appropriate to recover monies lost as a result of crimes against the Department of Defense; the Department of Defense will provide appropriate assistance to facilitate such actions.

3. The Department of Justice prosecutors will solicit the views of the Department of Defense prior to initiating action against an individual subject to the Uniform Code of Military Justice.

4. The Department of Justice will solicit the views of the Department of Defense with regard to its Department of Defense-related cases and investigations in order to effectively coordinate the use of civil, criminal and administrative remedies.

DoD Supplemental Guidance

Prosecution of Cases and Grants of Immunity

A. The authority of court-martial convening authorities to refer cases to trial, approve pretrial agreements, and issue grants of immunity under the UCMJ (reference (d)) extends only to trials by court-martial. In order to ensure that such actions do not preclude appropriate action by Federal civilian authorities in cases likely to be prosecuted in the U.S. district courts, court-martial convening authorities shall ensure that appropriate consultation as required by this enclosure has taken place before trial by court-martial, approval of a pretrial agreement, or issuance of a grant of immunity in cases when such consultation is required.

B. Only a general court-martial convening authority may grant immunity under the UCMJ (reference (d)), and may do so only in accordance with R.C.M. 704 (reference (e)).

1. Under reference (d), there are two types of immunity in the military justice system:

a. A person may be granted transactional immunity from trial by court-martial for one or more offenses under reference (d).

b. A person may be granted testimonial immunity, which is immunity from the use of testimony, statements, and any information directly or indirectly derived from such testimony or statements by that person in a later court-martial.

2. Before a grant of immunity under reference (d), the general court-martial convening authority shall ensure that there has been appropriate consultation with the DoJ with respect to offenses in which consultation is required by this enclosure.

3. A proposed grant of immunity in a case involving espionage, subversion, aiding the enemy, sabotage, spying, or violation of rules or statutes concerning classified information or the foreign relations of the United States shall be forwarded to the General Counsel of the Department of Defense for the purpose of consultation with the DoJ. The General Counsel shall obtain the views of other appropriate elements of the Department of Defense in furtherance of such consultation.

C. The authority of court-martial convening authorities extends only to grants of immunity from action under reference (d). Only the Attorney General or other authority designated under 18 U.S.C. Secs. 6001-6005 (reference (c)) may authorize action to obtain a grant of immunity with respect to trials in the U.S. district courts.

F. MISCELLANEOUS MATTERS

1. *THE DEPARTMENT OF DEFENSE ADMINISTRATIVE ACTIONS* Nothing in this Memorandum limits the Department of Defense investigations conducted in support of administrative actions to be taken by the Department of Defense. However, the Department of Defense investigative agencies will coordinate all such investigations with the appropriate Department of Justice prosecutive agency and obtain the concurrence of the Department of Justice prosecutor or the Department of Justice investigative agency prior to conducting any administrative investigation during the pendency of the criminal investigation or prosecution.

2. *SPECIAL UNIFORM CODE OF MILITARY JUSTICE FACTORS* In situations where an individual subject to the Uniform Code of Military Justice is a suspect in any crime for which a Department of Justice investigative agency has assumed jurisdiction, if a Department of Defense investigative agency believes that the crime involves special factors relating to the administration and discipline of the Armed Forces that would justify its investigation, the Department of Defense investigative agency will advise the appropriate Department of Justice investigative agency or the Department of Justice prosecuting authorities of these factors. Investigation of such a crime may be undertaken by the appropriate Department of Defense investigative agency with the concurrence of the Department of Justice.

3. *ORGANIZED CRIME* The Department of Defense investigative agencies will provide to the FBI all information collected during the normal course of agency operations pertaining to the element generally known as "organized crime " including both traditional (La Cosa Nostra) and nontraditional organizations whether or not the matter is considered prosecutable. The FBI should be notified of any investigation involving any element of organized crime and may assume jurisdiction of the same.

4. *DEPARTMENT OF JUSTICE NOTIFICATIONS TO DEPARTMENT OF DEFENSE INVESTIGATIVE AGENCIES*

a. The Department of Justice investigative agencies will promptly notify the appropriate Department of Defense investigative agency of the initiation of the Department of Defense related investigations which are predicated on other than a Department of Defense referral except in those rare instances where notification might endanger agents or adversely affect the investigation. The Department of Justice investigative agencies will also notify the Department of Defense of all allegations of the Department of Defense related crime where investigation is not initiated by the Department of Justice.

b. Upon request, the Department of Justice investigative agencies will provide timely status reports on all investigations relating to the Department of Defense unless the circumstances indicate such reporting would be inappropriate.

c. The Department of Justice investigative agencies will promptly furnish investigative results at the conclusion of an investigation and advise as to the nature of judicial action, if any, taken or contemplated.

d. If judicial or administrative action is being considered by the Department of Defense, the Department of Justice will, upon written request, provide existing detailed investigative data and documents (less any federal grand jury material, disclosure of which would be prohibited by Rule 6(e), Federal Rules of Criminal Procedure), as well as agent testimony for use in judicial or administrative proceedings, consistent with Department of Justice and other federal regulations. The ultimate use of the information shall be subject to the concurrence of the federal prosecutor during the pendency of any related investigation or prosecution.

5. *TECHNICAL ASSISTANCE*

a. The Department of Justice will provide to the Department of Defense all technical services normally available to federal investigative agencies.

b. The Department of Defense will provide assistance to the Department of Justice in matters not relating to the Department of Defense as permitted by law and implementing regulations.

6. *JOINT INVESTIGATIONS*

a. To the extent authorized by law, the Department of Justice investigative agencies and the Department of Defense investigative agencies may agree to enter into joint investigative endeavors, including undercover operations, in appropriate circumstances. However, all such investigations will be subject to Department of Justice guidelines.

b. The Department of Defense, in the conduct of any investigation that might lead to prosecution in Federal District Court, will conduct the investigation consistent with any Department of Justice guidelines. The Department of Justice shall provide copies of all relevant guidelines and their revisions.

DoD Supplemental Guidance

When DoD procedures concerning apprehension, search and seizure, interrogation, eyewitnesses, or identification differ from those of DoJ, DoD procedures will be used, unless the DoJ prosecutor has directed that DoJ procedures be used instead. DoD criminal investigators should bring to the attention of the DoJ prosecutor, as appropriate, situations when use of DoJ procedures might impede or preclude prosecution under the UCMJ (reference (d)).

7. *APPREHENSION OF SUSPECTS* To the extent authorized by law, the Department of Justice and the Department of Defense will each promptly deliver or make available to the other suspects, accused individuals and witnesses where authority to investigate the crimes involved is lodged in the other Department. This MOU neither expands nor limits the authority of either Department to perform apprehensions, searches, seizures, or custodial interrogations.

G. EXCEPTION

This Memorandum shall not affect the investigative authority now fixed by the 1979 "Agreement Governing the Conduct of the Defense Department Counter intelligence Activities in Conjunction with the Federal Bureau of Investigation" and the 1983 Memorandum of Understanding between the Department of Defense, the Department of Justice and the FBI concerning "Use of Federal Military Force in Domestic Terrorist Incidents."

APPENDIX 3.1

MEMORANDUM OF UNDERSTANDING BETWEEN THE DEPARTMENTS OF JUSTICE AND TRANSPORTATION (COAST GUARD) RELATING TO THE INVESTIGATIONS AND PROSECUTION OF CRIMES OVER WHICH THE TWO DEPARTMENTS HAVE CONCURRENT JURISDICTION.

Whereas, certain crimes committed by Coast Guard personnel subject to the Uniform Code of Military Justice may be prosecuted by Coast Guard tribunals under the Code or by civilian authorities in the Federal Courts; and

Whereas, it is recognized that although the administration and discipline of the Coast Guard requires that certain types of crimes committed by its personnel be investigated by that service and prosecuted before Coast Guard military tribunals other types of crimes committed by such military personnel should be investigated by civil authorities and prosecuted before civil tribunals; and

Whereas, it is recognized that it is not feasible to impose inflexible rules to determine the respective responsibility of the civilian and Coast Guard military authorities as to each crime over which they may have concurrent jurisdiction and that informal arrangements and agreements may be necessary with respect to specific crimes or investigations; and

Whereas, agreement between the Department of Justice and the Department of Transportation (Coast Guard) as to the general areas in which they will investigate and prosecute crimes to which both civil and military jurisdiction attach will, nevertheless, tend to make the investigation and prosecution of crimes more expeditious and efficient and give appropriate effect to the policies of civil government and the requirements of the United States Coast Guard;

It is hereby agreed and understood between the Department of Justice and the Department of Transportation (Coast Guard) as follows:

1. *Crimes committed on military installations (including aircraft and vessels).* Except as hereinafter indicated, all crimes committed on a military installation by Coast Guard personnel subject to the Uniform Code of Military Justice shall be investigated and prosecuted by the Coast Guard if the Coast Guard makes a determination that there is a reasonable likelihood that only Coast Guard personnel subject to the Uniform Code of Military justice are involved in such crimes as principles or accessories, and except in extraordinary cases, that there is no victim other than persons who are subject to the Uniform Code of Military Justice or who are bona fide dependents or members of a household of military or civilian personnel residing on the installation. Unless such a determination is made, the Coast Guard shall promptly advise the Federal Bureau of Investigation of any crime committed on a military installation if such crime is within the investigative authority of the Federal Bureau of Investigation. The Federal Bureau of Investigation shall investigate any serious crime of which it has been so advised for the purpose of prosecution in the civil courts unless the Department of Justice determines that investigation and prosecution may be conducted more efficiently and expeditiously by the Coast Guard. Even if the determination provided for in the first sentence of this paragraph is made by the Coast Guard, it shall promptly advise the Federal Bureau of Investigation of any crime committed on a military installation in which there is a victim who is not subject to the Uniform Code of Military Justice or a bona fide dependent or member of the household of military or civilian personnel residing on the installation and that the Coast Guard is investigating the crime because it has been determined to be extraordinary. The Coast Guard shall promptly advise the Federal Bureau of Investigation whenever the crime, except in minor offenses, involves fraud against the government, misappropriation, robbery, or theft of government property of funds, or is of a similar nature. All such crimes shall be investigated by the Coast Guard unless it receives prompt advise that the Department of Justice has determined that the crime should be investigated by the Federal Bureau of Investigation and that the Federal Bureau of Investigation will undertake the investigation for the purpose of prosecution in the civil courts.

2. *Crimes committed outside of military installations.* Except as hereinafter indicated, all crimes committed outside of military installations, which fall within the investigative jurisdiction of the Federal Bureau of Investigation and in which there is involved as a suspect an individual subject to the Uniform Code of Military Justice, shall be investigated by the Federal Bureau of Investigation for the purpose of prosecution in civil courts, unless the

Department of Justice determines that investigation and prosecution may be conducted more efficiently and expeditiously by other authorities. All such crimes which come first to the attention of Coast Guard authorities shall be referred promptly by them to the Federal Bureau of Investigation, unless relieved of this requirement by the Federal Bureau of Investigation as to particular types or classes of crime. However, whenever Coast Guard military personnel are engaged in scheduled military activities outside of military installations such as organized maneuvers or organized movement, the provisions of paragraph 1 above shall apply, unless persons not subject to the Uniform Code of Military Justice are involved as principals, accessories or victims.

If, however, there is involved as a suspect or as an accused in any crime committed outside of a military installation and falling within the investigative authority of the Federal Bureau of Investigation, an individual who is subject to the Uniform Code of Military Justice and if the Coast Guard authorities believe that the crime involves special factors relating to the administration and discipline of the Coast Guard which would justify investigation by them for the purpose of prosecution before a Coast Guard military tribunal, they shall promptly advise the Federal Bureau of Investigation of the crime and indicate their views on the matter. Investigation of such a crime may be undertaken by the Coast Guard military authorities if the Department of Justice agrees.

3. *Transfer of investigative authority.* An investigative body of the Coast Guard which has initiated an investigation pursuant to paragraphs 1 and 2 hereof, shall have exclusive investigative authority and may proceed therewith to prosecution. If, however, any Coast Guard investigative body comes to the view that effectuation of those paragraphs requires the transfer of investigative authority over a crime, investigation of which has already been initiated by that or by any other investigative body, it shall promptly advise the other interested investigative body of its views. By agreement between the Departments of Justice and Transportation (Coast ~Guard),~ investigative authority may then be transferred.

4. *Administrative action.* Exercise of exclusive investigative authority by the Federal Bureau of Investigation pursuant to this agreement shall not preclude Coast Guard military authorities from making inquiries for the purpose of administrative action related to the crime being investigated. The Federal Bureau of Investigation will make the results of its investigations available to Coast Guard military authorities for use in connection with such action.

Whenever possible, decisions with respect to the application in particular cases of the provisions of this Memorandum of Understanding will be made at the local level, that is, between the Special Agent in Charge of the local office of the Federal Bureau of Investigation and the local Coast Guard military commander.

5. *Surrender of suspects.* To the extent of the legal authority conferred upon them, the Department of Justice and Coast Guard military authorities will each deliver to the other promptly suspects and accused individuals if authority to investigate the crimes in which such accused individuals and suspects are involved is lodged in the other by paragraphs 1 and 2 hereof.

Nothing in this memorandum shall prevent the Coast Guard from prompt arrest and detention of any person subject to the Uniform Code of Military Justice whenever there is knowledge or reasonable basis to believe that such a person has committed an offense in violation of such code and detaining such person until he is delivered to the Federal Bureau of Investigation if such action is required pursuant to this memorandum.

APPROVED:

/s/ Ramsey Clark	/s/ Alan S. Boyd
Ramsey Clark	Alan S. Boyd
Attorney General	Secretary of Transportation
Date: 9 October 1967	Date: 24 October 1967

APPENDIX 4
Charge Sheet (DD FORM 458)

CHARGE SHEET

I. PERSONAL DATA

1. NAME OF ACCUSED *(Last, First, Middle Initial)*	2. SSN	3. GRADE OR RANK	4. PAY GRADE
James, Reuben J.	111-11-1111	PFC	E-3

5. UNIT OR ORGANIZATION	6. CURRENT SERVICE a. INITIAL DATE	b. TERM
Co A, 1st Battalion, 61st Inf. Bde., Fort Blank, MO	1 April 2006	3 years

7. PAY PER MONTH a. BASIC	b. SEA/FOREIGN DUTY	c. TOTAL	8. NATURE OF RESTRAINT OF ACCUSED	9. DATE(S) IMPOSED
1,534.00	0.00	1,534.00	Restriction	1 August 2007

II. CHARGES AND SPECIFICATIONS

10. CHARGE: I **VIOLATION OF THE UCMJ, ARTICLE** 86

SPECIFICATION:

In that Private First Class Reuben J. James, U.S. Army, Company A, 1st Battalion, 61st Infantry Brigade, Fort Blank, Missouri, did, on or about 15 July 2007, without authority, absent himself from his unit, to wit: Company A, 1st Battalion, 61st Infantry Brigade, located at Fort Blank, Missouri, and did remain so absent until on or about 30 July 2007.

Charge II: Violation of the UCMJ, Article 112a

In that Private First Class Reuben J. James, U.S. Army, Company A, 1st Battalion, 61st Infantry Brigade, Fort Blank, Missouri, did, on or about 12 July 2007, wrongfully possess 10 grams of marijuana.

III. PREFERRAL

11a. NAME OF ACCUSER *(Last, First, Middle Initial)*	b. GRADE	c. ORGANIZATION OF ACCUSER
Richards, Jonathan E.	CPT	Co A, 1st Bn, 61st Inf Bdc

d. SIGNATURE OF ACCUSER	e. DATE *(YYYYMMDD)*
Jonathan E. Richards	1 AUG 07

AFFIDAVIT: Before me, the undersigned, authorized by law to administer oath in cases of this character, personally appeared the above named accuser this 1st day of August, 2007, and signed the foregoing charges and specifications under oath that he/she is a person subject to the Uniform Code of Military Justice and that he/she either haspersonal knowledge of or has investigated the matters set forth therein and that the same are true to the best of his/her knowledge and belief.

Will M. Wilson	1st Bn, 61st Inf Bdc
Typed Name of Officer	*Organization of Officer*
CPT	Adjutant
Grade	*Official Capacity to Administer Oath (See R.C.M. 307(b)_ must be commissioned officer)*
Will M Wilson	
Signature	

DD FORM 458, MAY 2000 PREVIOUS EDITION IS OBSOLETE.

12.
On 2 August , 2007 , the accused was informed of the charges against him/her and of the name(s) of the accuser(s) known to me *(See R.C.M. 308(a)). (See R.C.M. 308 if notification cannot be made.)*

Jonathan E. Richards — *Typed Name of Immediate Commander*

Co A, 1st Bn, 61st Inf Bde — *Organization of Immediate Commander*

O-3/CPT — *Grade*

Jonathan E. Richards — *Signature*

IV. RECEIPT BY SUMMARY COURT-MARTIAL CONVENING AUTHORITY

13.
The sworn charges were received at 1100 hours, 2 August , 2007 at 1st Bn, 61st Inf Bde *Designation of Command or Officer Exercising Summary Court-Martial Jurisdiction (See R.C.M. 403)*.

FOR THE [1] COMMANDER

Will M. Wilson — *Typed Name of Officer*

Adjutant — *Official Capacity of Officer Signing*

CPT — *Grade*

Will M. Wilson — *Signature*

V. REFERRAL; SERVICE OF CHARGES

14a. DESIGNATION OF COMMAND OF CONVENING AUTHORITY	b. PLACE	c. DATE *(YYYYMMDD)*
61st Infantry Brigade	Fort Blank, Missouri	2 August 2007

Referred for trial to the special court-martial convened by CMCO number 12 dated ,

1 August , 2007 , subject to the following instructions: [2]

None.

~~By~~ ______ *Command or Order* ~~of~~ ______

Carl E. Nevens — *Typed Name of Officer*

Commander, 61st Infantry Brigade — *Official Capacity of Officer Signing*

O-6/COL — *Grade*

Carl E. Nevens — *Signature*

15.
On 8 August , 2007 , I (caused to be) served a copy hereof on (each of) the above named accused.

Hamilton Burger — *Typed Name of Trial Counsel*

CPT, JAGC — *Grade or Rank of Trial Counsel*

Hamilton Burger — *Signature*

FOOTNOTES: 1 - When an appropriate commander signs personally, inapplicable words are stricken.
2 - See R.C.M. 601(e) concerning instructions. If none, so state.

DD FORM 458 (BACK), MAY 2000

APPENDIX 5
Investigating Officer Report (DD FORM 457)

INVESTIGATING OFFICER'S REPORT
(Of Charges Under Article 32, UCMJ and R.C.M. 405, Manual for Courts-Martial)

1a. FROM: *(Name of Investigating Officer - Last, First, MI)*	b. GRADE	c. ORGANIZATION	d. DATE OF REPORT
Adamson, Adam A.	O-4	1st Bn, 61st Inf Bde	1 Sep 07

2a. TO: *(Name of Officer who directed the investigation - Last, First, MI)*	b. TITLE	c. ORGANIZATION
Harrison, Barry A.	Commanding Officer	1st Bn, 61st Inf Bde, Fort Custer, Texas

3a. NAME OF ACCUSED *(Last, First, MI)*	b. GRADE	c. SSN	d. ORGANIZATION	e. DATE OF CHARGES
Benton, Ben B.	E-3	111-11-1111	Co A, 1st Bn, 61st Inf Bde	24 Aug 07

(Check appropriate answer)	YES	NO
4. IN ACCORDANCE WITH ARTICLE 32, UCMJ, AND R.C.M. 405, MANUAL FOR COURTS-MARTIAL, I HAVE INVESTIGATED THE CHARGES APPENDED HERETO (Exhibit 1)	X	
5. THE ACCUSED WAS REPRESENTED BY COUNSEL (If not, see 9 below)	X	
6. COUNSEL WHO REPRESENTED THE ACCUSED WAS QUALIFIED UNDER R.C.M. 405(d) (2), 502(d)	X	

7a. NAME OF DEFENSE COUNSEL *(Last, First, MI)*	b. GRADE	8a. NAME OF ASSISTANT DEFENSE COUNSEL *(If any)*	b. GRADE
Carlson, Carlos C.	O-3		

c. ORGANIZATION *(If appropriate)*	c. ORGANIZATION *(If appropriate)*
TDS w/Duty Fort Custer, Texas	
d. ADDRESS *(If appropriate)*	d. ADDRESS *(If appropriate)*

9. *(To be signed by accused if accused waives counsel. If accused does not sign, investigating officer will explain in detail in Item 21.)*

a. PLACE	b. DATE

I HAVE BEEN INFORMED OF MY RIGHT TO BE REPRESENTED IN THIS INVESTIGATION BY COUNSEL, INCLUDING MY RIGHT TO CIVILIAN OR MILITARY COUNSEL OF MY CHOICE IF REASONABLY AVAILABLE. I WAIVE MY RIGHT TO COUNSEL IN THIS INVESTIGATION.

c. SIGNATURE OF ACCUSED

10. AT THE BEGINNING OF THE INVESTIGATION I INFORMED THE ACCUSED OF: *(Check appropriate answer)*	YES	NO
a. THE CHARGE(S) UNDER INVESTIGATION	X	
b. THE IDENTITY OF THE ACCUSER	X	
c. THE RIGHT AGAINST SELF-INCRIMINATION UNDER ARTICLE 31	X	
d. THE PURPOSE OF THE INVESTIGATION	X	
e. THE RIGHT TO BE PRESENT THROUGHOUT THE TAKING OF EVIDENCE	X	
f. THE WITNESSES AND OTHER EVIDENCE KNOWN TO ME WHICH I EXPECTED TO PRESENT	X	
g. THE RIGHT TO CROSS-EXAMINE WITNESSES	X	
h. THE RIGHT TO HAVE AVAILABLE WITNESSES AND EVIDENCE PRESENTED	X	
i. THE RIGHT TO PRESENT ANYTHING IN DEFENSE, EXTENUATION, OR MITIGATION	X	
j. THE RIGHT TO MAKE A SWORN OR UNSWORN STATEMENT, ORALLY OR IN WRITING	X	
11a. THE ACCUSED AND ACCUSED'S COUNSEL WERE PRESENT THROUGHOUT THE PRESENTATION OF EVIDENCE *(If the accused or counsel were absent during any part of the presentation of evidence, complete b below.)*	X	

b. STATE THE CIRCUMSTANCES AND DESCRIBE THE PROCEEDINGS CONDUCTED IN THE ABSENCE OF ACCUSED OR COUNSEL

NOTE: If additional space is required for any item, enter the additional material in Item 21 or on a separate sheet. Identify such material with the proper numerical and, if appropriate, lettered heading *(Example: "7c".)* **Securely attach any additional sheets to the form and add a note in the appropriate item of the form: "See additional sheet."**

DD Form 457, AUG 84 (EG) EDITION OF OCT 69 IS OBSOLETE. Designed using Perform Pro, WHS/DIOR, Oct 94

12a. THE FOLLOWING WITNESSES TESTIFIED UNDER OATH: *(Check appropriate answer)*				
NAME *(Last, First, MI)*	GRADE *(If any)*	ORGANIZATION/ADDRESS *(Whichever is appropriate)*	YES	NO
Dodd, Donald D.	O-3	Co A, 1st Bn, 61st Inf Bde	x	
Evanston, Evan E.	E-5	Co A, 1st Bn, 61st Inf Bde	x	
Forman, Fred F.	E-7	400th MP Co	x	
b. THE SUBSTANCE OF THE TESTIMONY OF THESE WITNESSES HAS BEEN REDUCED TO WRITING AND IS ATTACHED.			x	

13a. THE FOLLOWING STATEMENTS, DOCUMENTS, OR MATTERS WERE CONSIDERED; THE ACCUSED WAS PERMITTED TO EXAMINE EACH.			
DESCRIPTION OF ITEM	LOCATION OF ORIGINAL *(If not attached)*		
CID Lab Report (fingerprint analysis)	CID, Bldg 10, Fort Custer, Texas	x	
Statement of Greg Greggson	CID, Bldg 10, Fort Custer, Texas	x	
b. EACH ITEM CONSIDERED, OR A COPY OR RECITAL OF THE SUBSTANCE OR NATURE THEREOF, IS ATTACHED		x	
14. THERE ARE GROUNDS TO BELIEVE THAT THE ACCUSED WAS NOT MENTALLY RESPONSIBLE FOR THE OFFENSE(S) OR NOT COMPETENT TO PARTICIPATE IN THE DEFENSE. *(See R.C.M. 909, 916(k).)*		x	
15. THE DEFENSE DID REQUEST OBJECTIONS TO BE NOTED IN THIS REPORT *(If Yes, specify in Item 21 below.)*		x	
16. ALL ESSENTIAL WITNESSES WILL BE AVAILABLE IN THE EVENT OF TRIAL		x	
17. THE CHARGES AND SPECIFICATIONS ARE IN PROPER FORM		x	
18. REASONABLE GROUNDS EXIST TO BELIEVE THAT THE ACCUSED COMMITTED THE OFFENSE(S) ALLEGED		x	
19. I AM NOT AWARE OF ANY GROUNDS WHICH WOULD DISQUALIFY ME FROM ACTING AS INVESTIGATING OFFICER. *(See R.C.M. 405(d) (1).*		x	

20. I RECOMMEND:
a. TRIAL BY ☐ SUMMARY ☐ SPECIAL ☒ GENERAL COURT-MARTIAL
b. ☐ OTHER *(Specify in Item 21 below)*

21. REMARKS *(Include, as necessary, explanation for any delays in the investigation, and explanation for any "no" answers above.)*

Examples of other matter that may be discussed here:

1. Discussion of evidence, credibility of witnesses, and sufficiency of proof.
2. Recommendations to dismiss charges or specifications.
3. Statement of any anticipated offenses or of any anticipated difficulties in proving any specification for which trial is recommended.
4. Any other matter which should be known to the convening authority or subsequent reviewing authorities.

22a. TYPED NAME OF INVESTIGATING OFFICER	b. GRADE	c. ORGANIZATION
Adam A. Adamson	O-4	1st Bn, 61st Inf Bde
d. SIGNATURE OF INVESTIGATING OFFICER: Adam A. Adamson		e. DATE: 1 Sep 07

DD Form 457 Reverse, AUG 84

APPENDIX 6
FORMS FOR ORDERS CONVENING COURTS-MARTIAL

a. General and special court-martial convening orders

(1) Convening orders.

[Note 1. *See* R.C.M. 504(d)]

(Date) ______________

(Designation of command of officer convening court-martial)

[Pursuant to (para. ________ General Order No. ________, Department of the ______________, ________) (SECNAV ltr ser ________ of ________) a] (A) (general) (special) court-martial is convened with the following members (and shall meet at ________, unless otherwise directed):

(Captain) (Colonel)

____

(Commander) (Lieutenant Colonel)

____

(Lieutenant Commander) (Major)

____

(Lieutenant) (Captain)

____

(Lieutenant, j.g.) (First Lieutenant)

____

[Note 2. The name, rank, and position of the convening authority should be shown. The order may be authenticated by the signature of the convening authority or a person acting under the direction of the convening authority.]

[Note 3. The language in brackets or parentheses in the foregoing samples should be used when appropriate. The Secretary concerned may prescribe additional requirements for convening orders. *See* R.C.M. 504(d)(3). Service regulations should be consulted when preparing convening orders.]

[Note 4. When a new court-martial is convened to replace one in existence, the following should be added below the names of the personnel of the court-martial and before the authentication line:]

All cases referred to the (general) (special) court-martial convened by order no. ________ this (headquarters) (ship) (______________), dated ______________, in which the proceedings have not begun, will be brought to trial before the court-martial hereby convened.

(2) Order amending convening orders.

[Note 5. The same heading and authentication used on convening order should be used on amending orders.]

[Note 6. A succession of amending orders may result in error. Care should be used in amending convening orders.]

(a) Adding members.

[Note 7. Members may be added in specific cases or for all cases.]

The following members are detailed to the (general) (special) court-martial convened by order no. ________, this (headquarters) (ship) (________), dated ________ ________ (for the trial of ________ only).

(b) Replacing members.

[Note 8. Members may be replaced in specific cases or for all cases.]

(Captain) (Colonel) ________, is detailed as a member of the (general) (special) court-martial convened by order no. ________, this (headquarters) (ship) (________), dated ________, relieved (for the case of ________ only).

b. Summary court-martial convening orders

(Date) ________

(Designation of command of officer convening court-martial)

[Pursuant to (para. ________, General Order No. ________, Department of the ________, ________,) (SECNAV ltr ser ________ of ________,)] (Lieutenant Commander) (Major) ________ is detailed a summary court-martial (and shall sit at ________, unless otherwise directed).

[Note 9. The name, rank, and position of the convening authority should be shown. The order may be authenticated by the signature of the convening authority or a person acting under the direction of the convening authority.]

[Note 10. The summary court-martial convening order may be a separate page or a notation on the charge sheet. *See* R.C.M. 504(d)(2) and 1302(c).]

APPENDIX 7
Subpoena (DD FORM 453)

SUBPOENA

The President of the United States, to Mr. James E. Kinsella.
(Name and Title of Person being Subpoenaed)

You are hereby summoned and required to appear on the 1st day of October, 2007, at 9 o'clock A.M., at Bldg 13, Fort Sunny, CO, (before ______________________
(Place of Proceeding) *(Name and Title of Deposition Officer)*
designated to take your deposition) (a general court-martial of the United States) (a court of inquiry), appointed by General Court-Martial Convening Order No. 3, dated 1 September,
(Identification of Convening Order or Convening Authority)
2007, to testify as a witness in the matter of United States v. Packer
(Name of Case)
(and bring with you ______________________).
(Specific Identification of Documents or Other Evidence)

Failure to appear and testify is punishable by a fine of not more than $500 or imprisonment for a period not more than six months, or both. (10 U.S.C. § 847). Failure to appear may also result in your being taken into custody and brought before the court-martial (______________) under a Warrant of Attachment (DD Form 454). Manual for Courts-Martial R.C.M. 703(e)(2)(G).

Bring this subpoena with you and do not depart from the proceeding without proper permission.

Subscribed at Fort Sunny, CO this 2nd day of September, 2007.

____
(Signature (See R.C.M. 703 (e)(2)(C))

The witness is requested to sign one copy of this subpoena and to return the signed copy to the person serving the subpoena.

I hereby accept service of the above subpoena. ______________________
Signature of Witness

NOTE: If the witness does not sign, complete the following:

Personally appeared before me, the undersigned authority, ______________________,
who, being first duly sworn according to law, deposes and says that at __________, __________,
__________, he personally delivered to ______________________ in person a duplicate of this subpoena.

______________ *Grade* ______________________ *Signature*

Subscribed and sworn to before me at ______________________, this ________ day of
______________________, ________.

______________ *Grade*

______________ *Official Status* ______________________ *Signature*

DD FORM 453, MAY 2000 PREVIOUS EDITION IS OBSOLETE.

TRAVEL ORDER

Payment of travel allowances is authorized pursuant to 10 U.S.C. § 847 and 28 U.S.C. § 1821. You should travel from Atlanta, Georgia ______ in sufficient time to arrive at Fort Sunny, CO ______ on the date and at the time specified. You will be paid fees and expenses for attendance at the specified hearing and travel directly to and from that place. You may travel by ☐ rail, ☐ commercial or military aircraft, ☐ bus, or ☐ privately owned automobile.

You ☐ have ☐ have not been given a "Government Transportation Request" to exchange for commercial tickets. No mileage will be paid for any transportation provided by the Government in kind or by Government Transportation Request. If a Government Transportation Request is not given to you and you travel by commercial carrier at personal expense, reimbursement for your cost of transportation will be limited to:

a. The least costly regularly scheduled air service between the points involved; or

b. The cost of the rail fare and a lower berth, or the lowest first-class rail accommodation available at the time reservations were made; or

c. Actual cost of commercial bus fare.

If you travel by private automobile, you will be reimbursed at the rate of *(twenty cents $.20)* ______ a mile, plus the cost of necessary parking fees, bridge, ferry, and other highway tolls incurred while traveling under this travel order. The total reimbursement will be limited to the cost of travel by the usual mode of common carrier, including per diem. Receipts and ticket stubs will be required to support your claim for cost of transportation and subsistence for each item in excess of *($15.00)* ______.

☐ You will be traveling to a high-cost area.

The travel regulations designate certain cities as high cost areas. Because your attendance requires travel to one of these cities, you will be authorized an actual expense allowance instead of a per diem allowance. You will be reimbursed for the actual expenses incurred, not to exceed the maximum amount prescribed for the city involved. The expenses may include lodgings; meals, tips to waiters, bellboys, maids, porters; personal laundry, pressing and dry-cleaning; local transportation *(including usual tips)* between places of lodging and duty; and other necessary expenses. You must itemize your daily actual expenses on your claim and receipts for lodging and any items over *($15.00)* ______ are required.

☐ You will not be traveling to a high-cost area.

Because you are not traveling to a high-cost area, you will be entitled to a per diem allowance to cover your expenses for lodging, meals, and incidentals. While traveling and attending the specified hearing within the continental United States, you will be authorized a per diem equal to the daily average you pay for lodging, plus *($23.00)* ______ per day for meals and incidentals, rounded off to the next dollar. If the resulting amount is more than the maximum per diem allowable, which is *($50.00)* ______, then you will be reimbursed only the maximum per diem authorized. You are required to state on your reimbursement claim that the per diem claimed is based on the average cost to you for lodging while on required travel within the continental United States during the period covered by the claim. Receipts are required for lodging. The per diem allowance for travel overseas is based on rates set by the Department of State or by the Department of Defense, and you will be reimbursed the amount specified for the particular overseas area involved.

You are entitled to an attendance fee of *($30.00)* ______ per day under 28 U.S.C. § 1821.

Address any inquiries regarding the matter to: CPT Will M. Willson, Office of the Staff Judge Advocate, Fort Sunny, CO Telephone: (303) 555-5151

This is travel order number XX1111-5551111-XX, dated 2 September 2007,
issued by *(headquarters)* Fort Sunny, CO.
TDN. Accounting Citation xxxx1111xx.

FOR THE COMMANDER

M. Mueller, CPT, USA, Trial Counsel	John R. Ledger, LTC, FC, USA, Disbursing Officer
Typed Name of Approving Official	*Typed Name of Authenticating Official*
______	______
Signature of Approving Official	*Signature of Authenticating Official*

DD FORM 453-1, AUG 84

Reset

APPENDIX 8
GUIDE FOR GENERAL AND SPECIAL COURTS-MARTIAL

[Note 1. This guide outlines the sequence of events ordinarily followed in general and special courts-martial, and suggests ways to conduct various procedures prescribed in the Rules for Courts-Martial. The guide is not mandatory; it is intended solely as an aid to users of the Manual for Courts-Martial.]

Section I. Opening Session Through Pleas

[Note 2. *See* R.C.M. 901–911.]

[Note 3. When a military judge has been detailed, the proceedings outlined in this section will be conducted at an Article 39(a) session. *See* R.C.M. 901(e). In special courts-martial without a military judge, these procedures should be followed in general; the president of a special court-martial without a military judge should also carefully examine pertinent Rules for Courts-Martial.]

Sessions called to order

MJ: This Article 39(a) session is called to order. (Be seated.)

Convening orders and referral of charges

TC: The court-martial is convened by (general) (special) court-martial convening order(s) number ________, (HQ ________) (USS ________) (________), (as amended by ________) copies of which have been furnished to the military judge, counsel, and the accused, (and to the reporter for insertion at this point in the record) (and which will be inserted at this point in the record). (Copies of any written orders detailing the military judge and counsel will be inserted at this point in the record.)

[Note 4. When detailed, the reporter records all proceedings verbatim. *See* R.C.M. 502(e)(3)(B), 808, and 1103. The reporter should account for the parties to the trial and keep a record of the hour and date of each opening and closing of the session, whether a recess, adjournment, or otherwise, for insertion in the record. *See* R.C.M. 813(b) ad 1103. *See also* Appendices 13 and 14.]

[Note 5. The military judge should examine the convening order and any amending orders.]

TC: The charges have been properly referred to this court-martial for trial and were served on the accused on ________.

[Note 6. In time of peace, if less than 5 days have elapsed since service of the charges in a general court-martial (3 days in case of a special court-martial), the military judge should inquire whether the accused objects to proceeding. If the accused objects, the military judge must grant a continuance. *See* R.C.M. 901(a).]

TC: (The following corrections are noted on the convening orders: ________).

[Note 7. Only minor changes, such as typolineartal errors or changes of grade due to promotion, may be made. Any correction which affects the identity of the individual concerned must be made by an amending or correcting order.]

Accounting for parties

[Note 8. *See* R.C.M. 813.]

TC: The accused and the following persons detailed to this court-martial are present: ________. The members and the following persons detailed to this court-martial are absent: ________.

Reporter detailed

[Note 9. When a reporter is detailed, the following announcement will be made. *See* R.C.M. 813(a)(8).]

TC: ________ has been detailed reporter for this court-martial and (has previously been sworn) (will now be sworn).

[Note 10. *See* R.C.M. 807(b)(2) Discussion (D) concerning the oath to be administered the reporter.]

Detail of trial counsel

TC: ((I) (All members of the prosecution) have been detailed to this court-martial by ________.)

Qualifications of

TC: (I am) (All members of the prosecution are) Prosecution qualified and certified under Article 27(b) and sworn under Article 42(a). (________.)

TC: (I have not) (No member of the prosecution has) acted in any manner which might tend to disqualify (me) (him) (or) (her) in this court-martial (________.)

Detail of defense counsel

DC: ((I) (All detailed members of the defense) have been detailed to this court-martial by ________.)

Qualifications of defense

DC: (All detailed members of the defense are) (I Counsel am) qualified and certified under Article 27(b) and sworn under Article 42(a). (________.)

DC: (I have not) (No member of the defense has) acted in any manner which might tend to disqualify (me) (him) (or) (her) in this court-martial. (________.)

Qualifications of individual counsel when present

IDC: My qualifications are ________. I have not acted in any manner which might tend to disqualify me in this court-martial.

[Note 11. If it appears that any counsel may be disqualified, the military judge must decide the matter and take appropriate action. *See* R.C.M. 901(d)(3).]

Rights to counsel

[Note 12. *See* R.C.M. 506.]

MJ: ________, you have the right to be represented in this court-martial by ________ (and ________), your detailed defense counsel, or you may be represented by military counsel of your own selection, if the counsel you request is reasonably available. If you are represented by military counsel of your own selection, you would lose the right to have ________ (and ________), your detailed counsel, continue to help in your defense. However, you may request that ________ (and ________, or one of them), your detailed counsel, continue to act as associate counsel with the military counsel you select, and ________, the detailing authority, may approve such a request. Do you understand?

ACC: ________.

MJ: In addition, you have the right to be represented by civilian counsel, at no expense to the United States. Civilian counsel may represent you alone or along with your military counsel. Do you understand?

[Note 13. If two or more accused in a joint or common trial are represented by the same counsel, or by civilian counsel who are associated in the practice of law, the military judge must inquire into the matter. *See* R.C.M. 901(d)(4)(D).]

MJ: Do you have any questions about your rights to counsel?

ACC: ______.

MJ: Who do you want to represent you?

ACC: ______.

[Note 14. If appropriate, the court-martial should be continued to permit the accused to obtain individual military or civilian counsel.]

MJ: Counsel for the parties have the necessary qualifications, and have been sworn (except ______, who will now be sworn.)

MJ: I have been detailed to this court-martial by ______.

[Note 15. *See* R.C.M. 807(b)(2) Discussion (C) concerning the oath to be administered to counsel.]

General nature of charges

TC: The general nature of the charge(s) in this case is ______. The charge(s) were preferred by ______, forwarded with recommendations as to disposition by ______ (, and investigated by ______). (______ is also an accuser in this case.)

Challenge of military judge

[Note 16. *See* R.C.M. 902.]

TC: Your honor, are you aware of any matter which may be a ground for challenge against you?

MJ: (I am aware of none.) (______.)

TC: (The Government has no challenge for cause against the military judge.) (______.)

DC: (The defense has no challenge for cause against the military judge.) (______.)

Accused's elections on composition of court-martial

[Note 17. *See* R.C.M. 903. *See also* R.C.M. 501(a) and 503(b).]

MJ: ______, do you understand that you have the right to be tried by a court-martial composed of members (including, if you request in writing, at least one-third enlisted persons) and that, if you are found guilty of any offense, those members would determine a sentence?

ACC: ______.

MJ: Do you also understand that you may request in writing or orally here in the court-martial trial before me alone, and that if I approve such a request, there will be no members and I alone will decide whether you are guilty and, if I find you guilty, determine a sentence?

ACC: ______.

MJ: Have you discussed these choices with your counsel?

ACC: ______.

MJ: By which type of court-martial do you choose to be tried?

ACC: ______.

[Note 18. *See* R.C.M. 903(a) concerning whether the accused may defer a decision on composition of court-martial.]

[Note 19. If the accused chooses trial by court-martial composed of members proceed to arraignment below. Any request for enlisted members will be marked as an Appellate Exhibit and inserted in the record of trial. *See* R.C.M. 1103(b)(2)(D)(iii). In a special court-martial without a military judge, the members should be sworn, and the challenge procedure conducted at this point. *See* Notes 38–17 below.]

Election to be tried by military judge alone

[Note 20. A request for trial by military judge alone must be written and signed by the accused and should identify the military judge by name or it may be made orally on the record. A written request will he marked as an Appellate Exhibit and inserted in the record of trial. *See* R.C.M. 1103(b)(2)(D)(iii).]

MJ: (I have Appellate Exhibit ______, a request for trial before me alone.) (I am (Colonel) (Captain) (______ ______.) ______. Have you discussed this request and the rights I just described with your counsel?

ACC: ______.

MJ: If I approve your request for trial by me alone you give up your right to trial by a court-martial composed of members (including, if you requested, enlisted members). Do you wish to request trial before me alone?

ACC: ______.

MJ: (Your request is approved. The court-martial is assembled.) (Your request is disapproved because ______.)

[Note 21. *See* R.C.M. 903(c)(2)(B) concerning approval or disapproval. *See* R.C.M. 911 concerning assembly of the court-martial.]

Arraignment

[Note 22. *See* R.C.M. 904.]

MJ: The accused will now be arraigned.

TC: All parties and the military judge have been furnished a copy of the charges and specifications. Does the accused want them read?

DC: The accused (waives reading of the charges) (wants the charges read).

MJ: (The reading may be omitted.)

TC: (______.)

TC: The charges are signed by ______, a person subject to the code, as accuser; are properly sworn to before a commissioned officer of the armed forces authorized to administer oaths, and are properly referred to this court-martial for trial by ______, the convening authority.

MJ: ______, how do you plead? Before receiving your pleas, I advise you that any motions to dismiss any charge or to grant other relief should be made at this time.

[Note 23. *See* R.C.M. 801(e), 905–907 concerning motions. *See* R.C.M. 908 if the Government elects to appeal a ruling adverse to it.]

DC: The defense has (no) (the following) motion(s). (__________.)

[Note 24. After any motions are disposed of pleas are ordinarily entered. *See* R.C.M. 910.]

DC: __________ pleads __________.

[Note 25. If the accused enters any pleas of guilty proceed with the remainder of section I. If no pleas of guilty are entered, proceed to section II if trial is before members, or section III if trial is before military judge alone.]

[Note 26. If trial is before members in a contested case, the military judge should examine the copy of the charge(s) to be provided the members, discuss any preliminary instructions with the parties, and determine whether other matters should be addressed before the Article 39(a) session is ended.]

Guilty plea inquiry

[Note 27. *See* R.C.M. 910(c), (d), (e), and (f). If a conditional guilty plea is entered, *see* R.C.M. 910(a)(2).]

Introduction

MJ: __________, your plea of guilty will not be accepted unless you understand its meaning and effect. I am going to discuss your plea of guilty with you now. If you have any questions, please say so. Do you understand?

ACC: __________.

MJ: A plea of guilty is the strongest form of proof known to the law. On your plea alone, without receiving any evidence, this court-martial could find you guilty of the offense(s) to which you are pleading guilty. Your plea will not be accepted unless you understand that by pleading guilty you admit every element of each offense and you are pleading guilty because you really are guilty. If you do not believe that you are guilty, you should not plead guilty for any reason. You have the right to plead not guilty and place the burden upon the prosecution to prove your guilt. Do you understand that?

ACC: __________.

Waiver of rights

MJ: By your plea of guilty you waive, or in other words, you give up certain important rights. (You give up these rights only as to the offense(s) to which you have pleaded guilty. You keep them as to the offense(s) to which you have pleaded not guilty). The rights you give up are: First, the right against self-incrimination, that is the right to say nothing at all about (this) (these) offense(s). Second, the right to a trial of the facts by the court-martial, that is, the right to have this court-martial decide whether or not you are guilty based on evidence presented by the prosecution and, if you chose to do so, by the defense. Third, the right to be confronted by the witnesses against you, that is to see and hear the witnesses against you here in the court-martial and to have them cross-examined, and to call witnesses in your behalf. Do you understand these rights?

ACC: __________.

MJ: If you plead guilty, there will not be a trial of any kind as to the offense(s) to which you are pleading guilty, so by pleading guilty you give up the rights I have just described. Do you understand that?

ACC: ______.

Maximum penalty

MJ: Defense counsel, what advice have you given ______ as to the maximum punishment for the offense(s) to which the accused pleaded guilty?

DC: ______.

MJ: Trial counsel, do you agree with that?

TC: ______.

[Note 28. If there is a question as to the maximum punishment, the military judge must resolve it. If the maximum punishment may be subject to further dispute, the military judge should advise the accused of the alternative possibilities and determine whether this affects the accused's decision to plead guilty.]

MJ: ______, by your plea of guilty this court-martial could sentence you to the maximum authorized punishment, which is ______. Do you understand that?

ACC: ______.

MJ: Do you feel you have had enough time to discuss your case with your counsel, ______?

ACC: ______.

MJ: ______, do you feel that you have had enough time to discuss the case with your client?

DC: ______.

MJ: ______, are you satisfied with ______ (and ______), your defense counsel, and do you believe (his) (her) (their) advice has been in your best interest?

ACC: ______.

MJ: Are you pleading guilty voluntarily?

ACC: ______.

MJ: Has anyone tried to force you to plead guilty?

ACC: ______.

Factual basis for plea

[Note 29. The accused will be placed under oath at this point. *See* R.C.M. 910(e). The military judge may inquire whether there is a stipulation in connection with the plea, and may inquire into the stipulation at this point. *See* R.C.M. 811.]

MJ: In a moment, you will be placed under oath and we will discuss the facts of your case. If what you say is not true, your statements may be used against you in a prosecution for perjury or false statement. Do you understand?

ACC: ______.

TC: Do you (swear) (affirm) that the statements you are about to make shall be the truth, the whole truth, and nothing but the truth (so help you God)?

ACC: ________.

MJ: I am going to explain the elements of the offense(s) to which you have entered pleas of guilty. By "elements" I mean the facts which the Government would have to prove by evidence beyond a reasonable doubt before you could be found guilty if you pleaded not guilty. When I state each of these elements ask yourself if it is true, and whether you want to admit that its true. Then be ready to talk about these facts with me.

MJ: Please look at your copy of the charges and specifications. You have pleaded guilty to Charge ________, Specification ________, a violation of Article ________ of the Uniform Code of Military Justice. The elements of that offense are ________.

[Note 30. *See* subparagraph b of the appropriate paragraph in Part IV. The description of the elements should be tailored to the allegations in the specification. Legal terms should be explained.]

MJ: Do you understand those elements?

ACC: ________.

MJ: Do the elements correctly describe what you did?

ACC: ________.

Accused's description of offense(s)

[Note 31. The military judge should elicit from the accused facts supporting the guilty plea by questioning the accused about the offense(s). The questioning should develop the accused's description of the offense(s) and establish the existence of each element of the offense(s). The military judge should be alert to discrepancies in the accused's description or between the accused's description and any stipulation. If the accused's discussion or other information discloses a possible defense, the military judge must inquire into the matter, and may not accept the plea if a possible defense exists. The military judge should explain to the accused the elements of a defense when the accused's description raises the possibility of one. The foregoing inquiry should be repeated as to each offense to which the accused has pleaded guilty.]

Identification of accused

MJ: Do you admit that you are ________, the accused in this case?

ACC: ________.

Jurisdiction

MJ: On (date of earliest offense) ________, were you a member of the United States (Army) (Navy) (Air Force) (Marine Corps) (Coast Guard) on active duty, and have you remained on active duty since then?

ACC: ________.

[Note 32. The military judge should determine whether jurisdiction might be affected by a post-offense reenlistment.]

Pretrial agreement

MJ: Is there a pretrial agreement in this case?

TC or DC: ________.

[Note 33. If the answer is yes proceed to note 35; if the answer is no, proceed as follows.]

MJ: ______ are you pleading guilty because of any promise by the Government that you will receive a sentence reduction or other benefit from the Government if you plead guilty?

ACC: ______.

[Note 34. If the answer is no, proceed to acceptance of the plea. If the answer is yes, the military judge should determine from the accused and counsel whether any agreement exists. If so, the plea agreement inquiry should continue. If not, then the military judge should clarify any misunderstanding the accused may have, and ascertain whether the accused still wants to plead guilty. Once any issue is resolved, if the accused maintains the plea of guilty, proceed to acceptance of the plea.]

[Note 35. If there is a pretrial agreement, the military judge must: (l) ensure that the entire agreement is presented, provided that in trial by military judge alone the military judge ordinarily will not examine any sentence limitation at this point; (2) ensure that the agreement complies with R.C.M. 705; and (3) inquire to ensure that the accused understands the agreement and that the parties agree to it. *See* R.C.M. 910(f). If the agreement contains any ambiguous or unclear terms, the military judge should obtain clarification from the parties.]

[Note 36. The agreement should be marked as an Appellate Exhibit. If the agreement contains a sentence limitation and trial is before military judge alone, the sentence limitation should be marked as a separate Appellate Exhibit, if possible.]

[Note 37. The language below is generally appropriate when trial is before military judge alone. It should be modified when trial is before members.]

MJ: ______, I have here Appellate Exhibit ______, which is part of a pretrial agreement between you and ______, the convening authority. Is this your signature which appears (on the bottom of page ______), (______) and did you read this part of the agreement?

ACC: ______.

MJ: Did you also read and sign Appellate Exhibit ______, which is the second part of the agreement?

ACC: ______.

MJ: Do you believe that you fully understand the agreement?

ACC: ______.

MJ: I don't know, and I don't want to know at this time the sentence limitation you have agreed to. However, I want you to read that part of the agreement over to yourself once again.

MJ: [After accused has done so.] Without saying what it is, do you understand the maximum punishment the convening authority may approve?

ACC: ______.

MJ: In a pretrial agreement, you agree to enter a plea of guilty to (some of) the charge(s) and specification(s), and, in return, the convening authority agrees to (approve no sentence greater than that listed in Appellate Exhibit ______, which you have just read) (______________). [In addition, (you have agreed to testify against ______________) (______) (the convening authority has agreed to withdraw Charge ______ and its specification) (______). Do you understand that?

ACC: ______.

MJ: If the sentence adjudged by this court-martial is greater than the one provided in the agreement, the convening authority would have to reduce the sentence to one no more severe than the one in your agreement. On the other hand, if the sentence adjudged by this court-martial is less than the one in your agreement, the convening authority cannot increase the sentence adjudged. Do you understand that?

ACC: ______.

[Note 38. The military judge should discuss the agreement with the accused, and explain any terms which the accused may not understand. If the accused does not understand a term, or if the parties disagree as to a term, the agreement should not be accepted unless the matter is clarified to the satisfaction of the parties. If there are any illegal terms, the agreement must be modified in accordance with R.C.M. 705. The trial counsel should be granted a recess on request to secure the assent of the convening authority to any material modification in the agreement.]

MJ: ______ is this agreement, Appellate Exhibit(s) ______________ (and ______) the entire agreement between you and the convening authority? In other words, is it correct that there are no other agreements or promises in this case?

ACC: ______.

MJ: Do counsel agree?

TC: ______.

DC: ______.

MJ: ______, do you understand your pretrial agreement?

ACC: ______.

MJ: Do counsel disagree with my explanation or interpretation of the agreement in any respect?

TC: ______.

DC: ______.

MJ: (To DC), did the offer to make a pretrial agreement originate with the defense?

DC: ______.

MJ: ______ are you entering this agreement freely and voluntarily?

AC: ________.

MJ: Has anyone tried to force you to enter this agreement?

ACC: ________.

MJ: Have you fully discussed this agreement with your counsel, and are you satisfied that (his) (her) advice is in your best interest?

ACC: ________.

MJ: ________, although you believe you are guilty, you have a legal and a moral right to plead not guilty and to require the Government to prove its case against you, if it can, by legal and competent evidence beyond a reasonable doubt. If you were to plead not guilty, then you would be presumed under the law to be not guilty, and only by introducing evidence and proving your guilt beyond a reasonable doubt can the Government overcome that presumption. Do you understand?

ACC: ________.

MJ: Do you have any questions about your plea of guilty, your pretrial agreement, or anything we have discussed?

ACC: ________.

Acceptance of guilty plea

MJ: Do you still want to plead guilty?

ACC: ________.

MJ: I find that the accused has knowingly, intelligently, and consciously waived (his) (her) rights against self-incrimination, to a trial of the facts by a court-martial, and to be confronted by the witnesses against (him) (her); that the accused is, in fact guilty; and (his) (her) plea of guilty is accepted.

MJ: ________, you may request to withdraw your plea of guilty any time before the sentence is announced in your case and if you have a good reason for your request, I will grant it. Do you understand?

ACC: ________.

Announcement of findings based on a guilty plea

[Note 39. Findings of guilty may, and ordinarily should, be entered at this point *except* when: (1) not permitted by regulations of the Secretary concerned; or (2) the plea is to a lesser included offense and the prosecution intends to proceed to trial on the offense as charged. *See* R.C.M. 910(g)(1) and (2). *See also* R.C.M. 910(g)(3) in special courts-martial without a military judge. In trials before military judge alone, when some offenses are to be contested, the military judge may elect to defer entry of any findings until the end of trial on the merits.]

[Note 40. *See* R.C.M. 922 and Appendix 10 concerning forms of findings.]

MJ: ________, in accordance with your plea(s) of guilty, this court-martial finds you (of all charges and specifications) (of Specification ________ of Charge ________ and Charge ________): Guilty.

[Note 41. If trial is before members, and no offenses remain to be contested on the merits, this may be an appropriate point for the military judge to inform the accused of the rights to allocution under R.C.M. 1001(a)(3). *See* Note 88 below. In addition, other issues relating to the information or evidence to be introduced on sentencing should ordinarily be resolved at this point. If other offenses remain to be contested, the military judge should consider, and solicit the views of the parties, whether to inform the members only of the offenses to which the accused pleaded not guilty. The copy of the charges presented to the members should reflect this decision. *See also* Note 26.]

Section II. Trial With Members; Preliminary Session

[Note 42. The following procedure is suggested for a trial with members after completion of the Article 39(a) session.

Before calling the court-martial to order, the military judge should examine the convening order and any amending orders and ensure that all members required to be present are present. Witnesses should be excluded from the courtroom except when they testify.

When the court-martial is ready to proceed the military judge should direct the bailiff, if any, or the trial counsel to call the members. Whenever the members enter the courtroom, all persons present except the military judge and reporter should rise.

The members are seated alternatively to the right and left of the president according to rank.]

MJ: The court-martial will come to order. You may be seated.

TC: This court-martial is convened by (general) (special) court-martial convening order number ______ (HQ ______) (USS ______) (______), as amended by ______), a copy of which has been furnished to each member.

TC: The accused and the following persons named in the convening orders are present: ______.

TC: The following persons named in the convening orders are absent: ______.

[Note 43. Persons who have been relieved (viced) by written orders need not he mentioned. The reason for any other absences should be stated.]

TC: The prosecution is ready to proceed with the trial in the case of United States v. ______ (who is present).

Oath of members

MJ: The members will now be sworn.

TC: All persons please rise.

"Do you [name(s) of member(s)] (swear) (affirm) that you will answer truthfully the questions concerning whether you should serve as a member of this court-martial; that you will faithfully and impartially try, according to the evidence, your conscience, and the laws applicable to trials by court-martial, the case of the accused now before this court; and that you will not disclose or discover the vote or opinion of any particular member of the court-martial (upon a challenge or) upon the findings or sentence unless required to do so in due course of law, (so help you God)?"

Each member: I do.

Assembly/preliminary instructions

MJ: Be seated please. The court-martial is assembled.

[Note 44. *See* R.C.M. 911 concerning assembly.]

[Note 45. At this point, the military judge may give the members preliminary instructions. These may include instructions on the general nature of the member's duties (*see* R.C.M. 502(a)(2) and Discussion, 922, 1006), the duties of the military judge (*see* R.C.M. 801, 920, 1005; Mil. R. Evid. 103). and the duties of counsel (*see* R.C.M. 502(d)(5) and (6)); on voir dire and possible grounds for challenge (*see* R.C.M. 912); on the procedures for questioning witnesses (*see* Mil. R. Evid. 611, 614); on taking notes; and such other matters as may be appropriate. The military judge may elect to defer giving instructions on some of these matters until after voir dire, or until another appropriate point in the proceedings.]

General nature of charges

[Note 46. Trial counsel should distribute copies of the charges and specifications to the members.]

TC: The general nature of the charge(s) in this case (is) (are) __________. The charge(s) were preferred by __________; forwarded with recommendations as to disposition by __________; (and investigated by __________.)

Challenges

TC: The records of this case disclose (no grounds for challenge) (grounds for challenge of __________, on the following grounds __________.)

TC: If any member is aware of any matter which may be a ground for challenge by any party, the member should so state.

[Note 47. In case of a negative response, trial counsel should announce "Apparently not."]

[Note 48. The military judge and, if permitted by the military judge, counsel may examine the members on voir dire. *See* R.C.M. 912(d) and Discussion. The parties may present evidence relating to challenges for cause. *See* R.C.M. 912(e). Upon completion of voir dire and taking evidence, if any, the parties will be called upon to enter challenges for cause. Ordinarily trial counsel enters challenges for cause before defense counsel. After any challenges for cause, the parties may be called upon to enter peremptory challenges. Ordinarily trial counsel enters a peremptory challenge before the defense. The parties must be permitted to enter challenges outside the presence of members. *See* R.C.M. 912(f) and (g). In special courts-martial without a military judge, *see* R.C.M. 912(h).]

[Note 49. If any members are successfully challenged, they should be excused in open session in the presence of the parties. The record should indicate that they withdrew from the courtroom. The members who remain after challenges should be reseated according to rank, as necessary.]

[Note 50. The military judge should ensure that a quorum remains, and, if the court-martial is composed with enlisted persons, that at least one-third of the remaining members are enlisted persons. *See* R.C.M. 912(g)(2) Discussion.]

[Note 51. If the members have not yet been informed of the plea(s), this should now be done.]

MJ: Members of the court-martial, at an earlier session the accused was arraigned and entered the following pleas: ________ .

[Note 52. In a special court-martial without a military judge, the accused should now be arraigned. *See* Notes 22–39.]

[Note 53. If the military judge entered findings based on pleas of guilty and no offenses remain to be contested, the military judge should give the following instruction and proceed to SECTION IV, below.]

MJ: I accepted the accused's pleas of guilty and entered findings of guilty as to (the) (all) Charge(s) (________) and Specification(s) (________) and ________). Therefore, we will now proceed to determine a sentence in the case.

[Note 54. If the accused pleaded guilty to some offenses, but others remain to be contested, and the members have been informed of the offenses to which the accused pleaded guilty, the military judge should instruct as follows.]

MJ: Members, you will not be required to reach findings regarding Charge (________) and Specification(s) (________) (and ________) (and ________). Findings will be required, however, as to Charge (________) and Specification(s) (________) (and ________) (and ________), to which the accused has pleaded not guilty. You may not consider the fact that the accused pleaded guilty to (one) (some) offense(s) in any way in deciding whether the accused is guilty of the offense(s) to which (he) (she) has pleaded not guilty.

[Note 55. If the accused has pleaded guilty to a lesser included offense and the prosecution intends to prove the greater offense, the military judge should instruct as follows.]

MJ: The accused's plea of guilty to the lesser included offense of ________ admits some of the elements of the offense charged in (the) Specification (________) of (the) Charge (________). These elements are, therefore, established by the accused's plea without need of further proof. However, the accused's plea of guilty to this lesser included offense provides no basis for a finding of guilty as charged, because there still remains in issue the elements of ________ . No inference of guilt of such remaining elements may be drawn from the accused's plea. Before the accused may be found guilty of the offense charged, the prosecution must prove the remaining element(s) beyond a reasonable doubt.

[Note 56. The military judge may give such additional preliminary instructions as may be appropriate at this point.]

SECTION III. TRIAL

[Note 57. *See* R.C.M. 913.]

MJ: Will the prosecution make an opening statement?

TC: (No) (Yes. ________ .)

MJ: Will the defense make an opening statement?

DC: (No) (The defense will make its statement after the prosecution has rested.) (Yes. __________.)

TC: The prosecution calls as its first witness __________.

Oath of witness

[Note 58. *See* R.C.M. 807.]

TC: Do you (swear) (affirm) that the evidence you give in the case now in hearing shall be the truth, the whole truth, and nothing but the truth, (so help you God)?

WIT: __________.

Preliminary questions

TC: (Are you (*state name, grade, organization, station, and armed force) (state name and address, if civilian*)?) (Please state your name (grade, organization, station, and armed force) (and address).

WIT: __________.

[Note 59. The address of witnesses should be omitted in appropriate cases, as where it might endanger the witness.]

[Note 60. Except when an identification is inappropriate (e.g., when the witness is a laboratory technician) or where a foundation must be laid, Trial Counsel ordinarily should ask the witness to identify the accused.]

TC: Do you know the accused?

WIT: __________.

[Note 61. If the witness answers affirmatively:]

TC: Please point to the accused and state (his) (her) name.

WIT: __________.

TC: Let the record show that the witness pointed to the accused when stating (his) (her) name.

Testimony

[Note 62. Trial counsel should now conduct direct examination of the witness. *See* Mil. R. Evid. 611.]

TC: No further questions.

MJ: __________, you may cross-examine.

[Note 63. Defense counsel may cross-examine the witness.]

DC: No (further) questions.

[Note 64. The parties should be permitted to conduct such redirect and recross-examination as may reasonably be necessary. *See* Mil. R. Evid. 611. After the parties have completed their questioning, the military judge and members may ask additional questions. *See* Mil. R. Evid. 614. The members should be instructed on the procedures for questioning. Each member's questions will be collected by the bailiff, if any, or trial counsel, marked as an Appellate Exhibit, examined by counsel for each side, and given to the military judge. If there are any objections, they should be raised at an Article 39(a) session or at a side-bar conference.]

[Note 65. After questioning of a witness is completed, the military judge should determine whether the witness will be excused temporarily or permanently. The military judge should advise the witness as follows.]

MJ: ________ thank you. You are (temporarily) excused. (Please wait (in the waiting room) (________)). (You are free to go.) As long as this trial continues, do not discuss your testimony or knowledge of the case with anyone except counsel. If anyone else tries to talk to you about the case, stop them and report the matter to one of the counsel.

[Note 66. The witness will withdraw from the courtroom. *See* Mil. R. Evid. 615.]

TC: The prosecution calls as its next witness ________.

[Note 67. Trial counsel continues to present the prosecution case. If exhibits were admitted at an Article 39(a) session, trial counsel may, with the permission of the military judge, read or present the evidence to the court-martial.]

Recess, adjournment, or Article 39(a) session

[Note 68. In the event of a recess, continuance, adjournment, or Article 39(a) session the military judge should announce when the court-martial will reconvene, and should instruct or remind the members not to discuss the case with anyone, not to consult legal references, and to avoid exposure to matters relating to the case.]

Reopening

[Note 69. When the court-martial is reopened, the following announcement is appropriate.]

MJ: The court-martial will come to order.

TC: The members, the parties, and the military judge are all present.

Prosecution rests

TC: The prosecution rests.

[Note 70. A motion for a finding of not guilty may be raised at this point. *See* R.C.M. 917. Any such motion should be made outside the presence of the members. If a motion is made in the presence of members, and is denied, the military judge should instruct the members that the military judge applies a different standard in ruling on the motion than they must apply in reaching their findings, and that the denial must have no effect on their deliberations and findings.]

Presentation of evidence by defense

[Note 71. Defense counsel may make an opening statement if one was not made previously.]

DC: The defense calls as its first witness ________.

[Note 72. Trial counsel administers the oath to each witness. Defense counsel conducts direct examination, and trial counsel cross-examination of each witness. Redirect and recross-examination may be conducted as appropriate. The military judge and members may question each witness. *See note* 64.]

[Note 73. Defense counsel continues to present the defense case. If exhibits were admitted at an Article 39(a) session, defense counsel may, with the permission of the military judge, read or present the evidence to the court-martial.]

DC: The defense rests.

Rebuttal and surrebuttal

[Note 74. The parties may present evidence in rebuttal and surrebuttal. *See* R.C.M. 913(c)(l). After the parties complete their presentations, additional evidence may be presented when the military judge so directs. *See* R.C.M. 801(c), 913(c)(l)(F).]

[Note 75. When a witness is recalled, the following is appropriate.]

TC: Are you the same ________ who testified earlier in this court-martial?

WIT: I am.

TC: You are reminded that you are still under oath.

[Note 76. If trial is by military judge alone, counsel should be permitted to make closing arguments. *See* R.C.M. 919. After arguments, proceed to announcement of findings.]

Out of court hearing on findings instructions

[Note 77. Ordinarily the military judge will conducts Article 39(a) session to discuss findings instructions and examine the findings worksheet. *See* R.C.M. 920,921(d). If such instructions are discussed at a conference, *see* R.C.M. 802.]

Closing arguments

[Note 78. *See* R.C.M. 919.]

TC: ______.

DC: ______.

TC: ______.

Instructions

[Note 79. *See* R.C.M. 920.]

MJ: ______.

MJ: Does any member have any questions concerning these instructions?

MEMBERS: ______

MJ: Do counsel have any objections to these instructions not previously raised?

TC: ______.

DC: ______.

[Note 80. *See* R.C.M. 920(f).]

[Note 81. Any exhibits which the members are to consider should be given to the president before the court-martial closes.]

Closing

MJ: The court-martial is closed.

[Note 82. While the members are deliberating, the military judge may take up certain matters which may arise if the accused is found guilty of any offense. The admissibility of evidence during sentencing proceedings and advice to the accused about allocution rights may be considered at an Article 39(a) session at this point. *See* R.C.M. 1001. *See* Note 88 below concerning allocution advice.]

After findings reached

MJ: The court-martial will come to order.

TC: All parties and members and the military judge are present.

MJ: (To president) ______ have the members reached findings?

PRES: ______

MJ: Are the findings on Appellate Exhibit ______?

PRES: Yes.

MJ: Would (the bailiff) (trial counsel), without examining it please bring me Appellate Exhibit ______?

MJ: I have examined Appellate Exhibit ______. It appears to be in proper form. Please return it to the president.

[Note 83. *See* R.C.M. 921(d) concerning a findings worksheet, and the procedure to be followed if any problems are indicated. *See* R.C.M. 924 if reconsideration of a finding may be necessary.]

Announcement of findings

MJ: ______, would you and your counsel stand up please (and approach the president).

MJ: ______, announce the findings please.

PRES: ______, this court-martial finds you ______.

MJ: Please be seated.

[Note 84. If the accused is found not guilty of all charges and specifications, the court-martial is ordinarily adjourned at this point.]

SECTION IV. PRESENTENCING PROCEDURE

[Note 85. If the accused pleaded guilty to some specifications and the members have not yet been informed of these, the members should now be given copies of these specifications and be informed of the accused's plea to them. *See* text following Note 51.]

Data from charge sheet

[Note 86. *See* R.C.M. 1001(b)(1).]

MJ: The court-martial will now hear the data concerning the accused shown on the charge sheet.

TC: ______.

Matters presented by prosecution

MJ: Does the prosecution have other matters to present?

[Note 87. The prosecution may present certain matters from the accused's personnel records, evidence of previous convictions, evidence in aggravation, and evidence of rehabilitative potential. *See* R.C.M. 1001(b)(2) through (5).]

TC: The prosecution has nothing further.

Matters presented by defense

[Note 88. If the accused has not previously been advised in accordance with R.C.M. 1001(a)(3), such advice should now be given. In trial before members, this advice should be given at an Article 39(a) session.]

MJ: ______, you have the right to present matters in extenuation and mitigation, that is, matters about the offense(s) or yourself which you want the court-martial to consider in deciding a sentence. Included in your right to present evidence are the rights you have to testify under oath, to make an unsworn statement, or to remain silent. If you testify, you may be cross-examined by the trial counsel and questioned by me (and the members). If you decide to make an unsworn statement you may not be cross-examined by trial counsel or questioned by me (or the members). You may make an unsworn statement orally or in writing, personally, or through your counsel, or you may use a combination of these ways. If you decide to exercise your right to remain silent, that cannot be held against you in any way. Do you understand your rights?

ACC: ______.

MJ: Which of these rights do you want to exercise?

ACC: __________.

[Note 89. The defense may present matters in rebuttal and extenuation and mitigation. *See* R.C.M. 1001(c).]

DC: The defense has nothing further.

Rebuttal

[Note 90. The parties may present additional matters in rebuttal, as appropriate. *See* R.C.M. 1001(a)(l)(C).]

Out of court hearing on sentencing instructions

[Note 91. If trial is by military judge alone, counsel should be permitted to make arguments on sentencing. After arguments proceed to announcement of the sentence.]

[Note 92. Ordinarily the military judge will conduct an Article 39(a) session to discuss sentencing instructions and examine the sentence worksheet. *See* R.C.M. 1005. If such instructions are discussed at a conference, *see* R.C.M. 802.]

Closing arguments

[Note 93. *See* R.C.M. 1001(g).]

TC: __________.

DC: __________.

Instructions

[Note 94. *See* R.C.M. 1005.]

MJ: __________.

MJ: Does any member have any questions concerning these instructions?

MEMBERS: __________.

MJ: Do counsel have any objections concerning these instructions not previously raised?

TC: __________.

DC: __________.

[Note 95. *See* R.C.M. 1005(f).]

[Note 96. Any exhibits which the members are to consider should be given to the president before the court-martial closes.]

Closing

MJ: The court-martial is closed.

After sentence reached

MJ: The court-martial will come to order.

TC: All parties and members and the military judge are present.

MJ: (To president) __________, have the members reached a sentence?

PRES: __________.

MJ: Is the sentence on Appellate Exhibit __________?

PRES: Yes.

MJ: Would (the bailiff) (trial counsel), without examining it, please bring me Appellate Exhibit ________.

MJ: I have examined Appellate Exhibit ________. It appears to be in proper form. Please return it to the president.

[Note 97. *See* R.C.M. 1006(e) concerning a sentence worksheet, and the procedure to be followed if any problems are indicated. *See* R.C.M. 1009 if reconsideration of the sentence may be necessary.]

Announcement of sentence

MJ: ________, would you and your counsel stand up please (and approach the president).

MJ: ________, would you announce the sentence please.

PRES: ________, this court-martial sentences you to: ________.

MJ: Please be seated.

[Note 98. In trial before members, ordinarily the members should be excused at this point. If no other matters remain to be considered, the court-martial should be adjourned. If there are additional matters to be considered (e.g., punishment limitation in a pretrial agreement in a trial by military judge alone, *see* R.C.M. 910(f)(3) or, if the accused was represented by more than one counsel, which counsel will prepare any response to the post-trial review) these matters should be addressed before the court-martial is adjourned.]

Advice of post-trial and appellate rights

[Note 99. The military judge must advise the accused of the accused's post-trial and appellate rights. *See* R.C.M. 1010.]

MJ: ________, I will explain to you your post-trial and appellate rights.

MJ: After the record of trial is prepared in your case, ________ the convening authority will act on your case. The convening authority can approve the sentence (adjudged) (provided in your pretrial agreement), or (he) (she) can approve a lesser sentence or disapprove the sentence entirely. The convening authority cannot increase the sentence. The convening authority can also disapprove (some or all of) the findings of guilty. The convening authority is not required to review the case for legal errors, but may take action to correct legal errors. Do you understand?

ACC: ________.

Advice in GCMs and SPCMs in which BCD or confinement for one year is adjudged

[Note 100. In cases subject to review by a Court of Criminal Appeals, the following advice should be given. In other cases proceed to Note 101 or 102 as appropriate.]

MJ: __________, I will now advise you of your post-trial and appellate rights. Remember that in exercising these rights you have the right to the advice and assistance of military counsel provided free of charge or civilian counsel provided at your own expense.

You have the right to submit any matters you wish the convening authority to consider in deciding whether to approve all, part, or any of the findings and sentence in your case. Such matters must be submitted within 10 days after you or your counsel receive a copy of the record of trial and the recommendation of the (staff judge advocate) (legal officer).

If the convening authority approves the discharge or confinement at hard labor for a year or more, your case will be reviewed by a Court of Criminal Appeals.

After the Court of Criminal Appeals completes its review, you may request that your case be reviewed by the Court of Appeals for the Armed Forces; if your case is reviewed by that Court, you may request review by the United States Supreme Court.

You also have the right to give up review by the Court of Criminal Appeals, or to withdraw your case from appellate review at any time before such review is completed.

If you give up your right to review by the Court of Criminal Appeals or later withdraw your case from appellate review.

(a) That decision is final and you cannot change your mind later.

(b) Your case will be reviewed by a military lawyer for legal error. It will also be sent to the (general court-martial*) convening authority for final action.

(*Use only for special court-martial.)

(c) Within 2 years after final action is taken on your case, you may request The Judge Advocate General to take corrective action.

ACC: __________.

MJ: The court-martial is adjourned.

GCM subject to review under Article 69

[Note 101. In general courts-martial subject to review under Article 69, the following advice should be given. In other cases, proceed to Note 102.]

MJ: __________, I will now advise you of your post-trial and appellate rights. Remember that in exercising these rights you have the right to the advice and assistance of military counsel provided free of charge or civilian counsel provided at your own expense.

You have the right to submit any matters you wish the convening authority to consider in deciding whether to approve all, part, or any of the findings and sentence in your case. Such matters must be submitted within 10 days after you or your counsel receive a copy of the record of trial and the recommendation of the (staff judge advocate) (legal officer). If the convening authority approves any part of your sentence, your case will be examined in the Office of The Judge Advocate General for any legal errors and to determine whether your sentence is fair. The Judge Advocate General may take corrective action, if appropriate. You also have the right to give up examination by The Judge Advocate General or to withdraw your case from such examination at any time before such examination is completed. If you give up your right to examination by The Judge Advocate General or later withdraw your case from such examination:

(a) That decision is final and you cannot change your mind later.

(b) Your case will be reviewed by a military lawyer for legal error. It will also be sent to the convening authority for final action.

(c) Within 2 years after action is taken on your case, you may request The Judge Advocate General to take corrective action.

ACC: __________.

MJ: The court-martial is adjourned.

SPCM not involving a BCD or confinement for one year

[Note 102. In special courts-martial not involving BCD or confinement for one year, the following advice should be given.]

MJ: __________, I will now advise you of your post-trial and appellate rights. Remember that in exercising these rights, you have the right to the advice and assistance of military counsel provided free of charge or civilian counsel provided at your own expense. You have the right to submit any matters you wish the convening authority to consider in deciding whether to approve all, part, or any of the findings and sentence in your case. Such matters must be submitted within 10 days after you or your counsel receive a copy of the record of trial. If the convening authority approves any part of the findings or sentence, your case will be reviewed by a military lawyer for legal error. It may be sent to the general court-martial convening authority for final action on any recommendation by the lawyer for corrective action. Within 2 years after final action is taken on your case, you may request The Judge Advocate General to take corrective action. Do you have any questions?

ACC: __________.

MJ: The court-martial is adjourned.

APPENDIX 9
GUIDE FOR SUMMARY COURTS-MARTIAL

[General Note to SCM: It is not the purpose of this guide to answer all questions which may arise during a trial. When this guide, chapter 13 of the Rules for Courts-Martial, and other legal materials available fail to provide sufficient information concerning law or procedure, the summary court-martial should seek advice on these matters from a judge advocate. *See* R.C.M. 1301(b). If the accused has obtained, or wishes to obtain, defense counsel, *see* R.C.M. 1301(e). The SCM should examine the format for record of trial at appendix 15. It may be useful as a checklist during the proceedings to ensure proper preparation after trial. The SCM should become familiar with this guide before using it. Instructions for the SCM are contained in brackets, and should not be read aloud. Language in parentheses reflects optional or alternative language. The SCM should read the appropriate language aloud.]

Preliminary Proceeding

Identity of SCM

SCM: I am ________. I have been detailed to conduct a summary court-martial (by Summary Court-Martial Convening Order (Number ________), Headquarters, ________, dated [*see*convening order]).

Referral of charges to trial

Charges against you have been referred to me for trial by summary court-martial by ([*name and title of convening authority*]) on ([*date of referral*]) [*see* block IV on page 2 of charge sheet].

[Note 1. Hand copy of charge sheet to the accused.]

Providing the accused with charge sheet

I suggest that you keep this copy of the charge sheet and refer to it during the trial. The charges are signed by [*see* first name at top of page 2 of charge sheet], a person subject to the Uniform Code of Military Justice, as accuser, and are properly sworn to before a commissioned officer of the armed forces authorized to administer oaths. (________ ordered the charges to be preferred.) The charges allege, in general, violation of Article ________, in that you ________ - (and Article ________, in that you ________). I am now going to tell you about certain rights you have in this trial. You should carefully consider each explanation because you will soon have to decide whether to object to trial by summary court-martial. Until I have completed my explanation, do not say anything except to answer the specific questions which I ask you. Do you understand that?

ACC: ________.

Duties of SCM

SCM: As summary court-martial it is my duty to obtain and examine all the evidence concerning any offense(s) to which you plead not guilty, and to thoroughly and impartially inquire into both sides of the matter. I will call witnesses for the prosecution and question them, and I will help you in cross-examining those witnesses. I will help you obtain evidence and present the defense. This means that one of my duties is to help you present your side of the case. You may also represent yourself, and if you do, it is my duty to help you. You are presumed to be innocent until your guilt has been proved by legal and competent evidence beyond a reasonable doubt. If you are found guilty of an offense, it is also my duty to consider matters which might affect the sentence, and then to adjudge an appropriate sentence. Do you understand that?

	ACC:	______.
Right to object to SCM	SCM:	You have the absolute right to object to trial by summary court-martial. If you object the appropriate authority will decide how to dispose of the case. The charges may be referred to a special or general court-martial, or they may be dismissed, or the offenses charged may be disposed of by (nonjudicial punishment [if not previously offered and refused] or) administrative measures.[*See* R.C.M. 306.] Do you understand that?
	ACC:	______.
Right to inspect allied papers and personnel records.	SCM:	You may inspect the allied papers and personnel records [Hand those documents which are available to the accused for examination in your presence.] (You may also inspect [*identify personnel records or other documents which are not present*] which are located at ______. You may have time to examine these if you wish.)
Witnesses/other evidence for the government	SCM:	The following witnesses will probably appear and testify against you: ______. The following documents and physical evidence will probably be introduced: ______.
Right to cross-examine		After these witnesses have testified in response to my questions, you may cross-examine them. If you prefer, I will do this for you after you inform me of the matters about which you want the witness to be questioned. Do you understand that?
	ACC:	______.
Right to present evidence	SCM:	You also have the right to call witnesses and present other evidence. This evidence may concern any or all of the charges. (I have arranged to have the following witnesses for you present at the trial.) I will arrange for the attendance of other witnesses and the production of other evidence requested by you. I will help you in any way possible. Do you understand that?
	ACC:	______.
Evidence to be considered	SCM:	In deciding this case, I will consider only evidence introduced during the trial. I will not consider any other information, including any statements you have made to me, which is not introduced in accordance with the Military Rules of Evidence during the court-martial. Do you understand that?
	ACC:	______.
Right to remain silent	SCM:	You have the absolute right during this trial to choose not to testify and to say nothing at all about the offense(s) with which you are charged. If you do not testify, I will not hold it against you in any way. I will not consider it as an admission that you are guilty. If you remain silent, I am not permitted to question you about the offense(s).

Right to testify concerning the offense(s)

However, if you choose, you may be sworn and testify as a witness concerning the offense(s) charged against you. If you do that, I will consider your testimony just like the testimony of any other witness.

[Note 2. Use the following if there is only one specification.]

If one specification

If you decide to testify concerning the offense, you can be questioned by me about the whole subject of the offense. Do you understand that?

ACC: ______.

[Note 3. Use the following if there is more than one specification.]

If more than one specification

SCM: If you decide to testify, you may limit your testimony to any particular offense charged against you and not testify concerning any other offense(s) charged against you. If you do this, I may question you about the whole subject of the offense about which you testify, but I may not question you about any offense(s) concerning which you do not testify. Do you understand that?

ACC: ______.

Right to testify, remain silent or make an unsworn statement in extenuation and mitigation

SCM: In addition, if you are found guilty of an offense, you will have the right to testify under oath concerning matters regarding an appropriate sentence. You may, however, remain silent, and I will not hold your silence against you in any way. You may, if you wish, make an unsworn statement about such matters. This statement may be oral, in writing, or both. If you testify, I may cross-examine you. If you make an unsworn statement, however, I am not permitted to question you about it, but I may receive evidence to contradict anything contained in the statement. Do you understand that?

ACC: ______.

Maximum punishment

SCM: If I find you guilty (of the offense) (of any of the offenses charged), the maximum sentence which I am authorized to impose is:

[Note 4. For an accused of a pay grade of E–4 or below, proceed as follows.]

E-4 and below

(1) reduction to lowest enlisted pay grade; and

(2) forfeiture of two-thirds of 1 month's pay; and

(3) confinement for 1 month.

[Note 5. For an accused of a pay grade above E–4, proceed as follows.]

E-5 and above

(1) reduction to the next inferior pay grade; and

(2) forfeiture of two-thirds of 1 month's pay; and

(3) restriction to specified limits for 2 months.

SCM: Do you understand the maximum punishment which this court-martial is authorized to adjudge?

ACC: ________.

Plea options

SCM: You may plead not guilty or guilty to each offense with which you are charged. You have an absolute right to plead not guilty and to require that your guilt be proved beyond a reasonable doubt before you can be found guilty. You have the right to plead not guilty even if you believe you are guilty. Do you understand that?

ACC: ________.

SCM: If you believe you are guilty of an offense, you may, but are not required to, plead guilty to that offense. If you plead guilty to an offense, you are admitting that you committed that offense, and this court-martial could find you guilty of that offense without hearing any evidence, and could sentence you to the maximum penalty I explained to you before. Do you understand that?

ACC: ________.

Lesser included offenses

SCM: [Examine the list of lesser included offenses under each punitive article alleged to have been violated. *See* Part IV. If a lesser included offense may be in issue, give the following advice.] You may plead not guilty to Charge ________, Specification ________, as it now reads, but plead guilty to the offense of ________, which is included in the offense charged. Of course, you are not required to do this. If you do, then I can find you guilty of this lesser offense without hearing evidence on it. Furthermore, I could still hear evidence on the greater offense for purposes of deciding whether you are guilty of it. Do you understand that?

ACC: ________.

SCM: Do you need more time to consider whether to object to trial by summary court-martial or to prepare for trial?

ACC: ________.

SCM: [If time is requested or otherwise appropriate.] We will convene the court-martial at ________. When we convene, I will ask you whether you object to trial by summary court-martial. If you do not object, I will then ask for your pleas to the charge(s) and specification(s), and for you to make any motions you may have.

Trial Proceedings

Convene

SCM: This summary court-martial is now in session.

Objection/consent to trial by SCM

SCM: Do you object to trial by summary court-martial?

ACC: ________.

Entries on record of trial

[Note 6. If there is an objection, adjourn the court-martial and return the file to the convening authority. If the accused does not object, proceed as follows. The accused may be asked to initial the notation on the record of trial that the accused did or did not object to trial by summary court-martial. This is not required, however.]

Readings of the charges

SCM: Look at the charge sheet.Have you read the charge(s) and specification(s)?

ACC: ______.

SCM: Do you want me to read them to you?

ACC: [If accused requests, read the charge(s) and specification(s).]

Arraignment

SCM: How do you plead? Before you answer that question, if you have any motion to dismiss (the) (any) charge or specification, or for other relief, you should make it now.

ACC: ______.

Motions

[Note 7. If the accused makes a motion to dismiss or to grant other relief, or such a motion is raised by the summary court-martial, do not proceed with the trial until the motions have been decided. *See* R.C.M. 905–907, and R.C.M. 1304(b)(2)(c). After any motions have been disposed of and if termination of the trial has not resulted, have the accused enter pleas and proceed as indicated below.]

Pleas

ACC: I plead: ______.

[Note 8. If the accused refuses to plead to any offense charged, enter pleas of not guilty. If the accused refuses to enter any plea, evidence must be presented to establish that the accused is the person named in the specification(s) and is subject to court-martial jurisdiction. *See* R.C.M. 202, 1301(c)]

[Note 9. If the accused pleads not guilty to all offenses charged, proceed to the section entitled "Procedures-Not Guilty Pleas."]

[Note 10. If the accused pleads guilty to one or more offenses, proceed as follows.]

Procedures-guilty pleas

SCM: I will now explain the meaning and effect of your pleas, and question you so that I can be sure you understand. Refer to the charge(s) and specification(s). I will not accept your pleas of guilty unless you understand their meaning and effect. You are legally and morally entitled to plead not guilty even though you believe you are guilty, and to require that your guilt be proved beyond a reasonable doubt. A plea of guilty is the strongest form of proof known to the law. On your pleas of guilty alone, without receiving any evidence, I can find you guilty of the offense(s) to which you have pleaded guilty. I will not accept your pleas unless you realize that by your pleas you admit every element of the offense(s) to which you have pleaded guilty, and that you are pleading guilty because you really are guilty. If you are not convinced that you are in fact guilty, you should not allow anything to influence you to plead guilty. Do you understand that?

ACC: ______.

SCM: Do you have any questions?

ACC: ______.

SCM: By your pleas of guilty you give up three very important rights. (You keep these rights with respect to any offense(s) to which you have pleaded not guilty.) The rights which you give up when you plead guilty are:

First, the right against self-incrimination. This means you give up the right to say nothing at all about (this) (these) offense(s) to which you have pleaded guilty. In a few minutes I will ask you questions about (this) (these) offense(s), and you will have to answer my questions for me to accept your pleas of guilty.

Second, the right to a trial of the facts by this court-martial. This means you give up the right to have me decide whether you are guilty based upon the evidence which would be presented.

Third, the right to be confronted by and to cross-examine any witnesses against you. This means you give up the right to have any witnesses against you appear, be sworn and testify, and to cross-examine them under oath.

Do you understand these rights?

ACC: ________.

SCM: Do you understand that by pleading guilty you give up these rights?

ACC: ________.

SCM: On your pleas of guilty alone you could be sentenced to ________.

[Note 11. Re-read the appropriate sentencing section at notes 4 or 5 above unless the summary court-martial is a rehearing or new or other trial, in which case *see* R.C.M. 810(d).]

Do you have any questions about the sentence which could be imposed as a result of your pleas of guilty?

ACC: ________.

SCM: Has anyone made any threat or tried in any other way to force you to plead guilty?

ACC: ________.

Pretrial agreement

SCM: Are you pleading guilty because of any promises or understandings between you and the convening authority or anyone else?

ACC: ________.

[Note 12. If the accused answers yes, the summary court-martial must inquire into the terms of such promises or understandings in accordance with R.C.M. 910. *See* Appendix 8, Note 35 through acceptance of plea.]

[Note 13. If the accused has pleaded guilty to a lesser included offense, also ask the following question.]

Effect of guilty pleas to lesser included offenses

SCM: Do you understand that your pleas of guilty to the lesser included offense of ________ confess all the elements of the offense charged except ________, and that no proof is necessary to establish those elements admitted by your pleas?

ACC: ________.

SCM: The following elements state what would have to be proved beyond a reasonable doubt before the court-martial could find you guilty if you had pleaded not guilty. As I read each of these elements to you, ask yourself whether each is true and whether you want to admit that each is true, and then be prepared to discuss each of these elements with me when I have finished.

The elements of the offense(s) which your pleas of guilty admit are ________.

[Note 14. Read the elements of the offense(s) from the appropriate punitive article in Part IV. This advice should be specific as to names, dates, places, amounts, and acts.]

Do you understand each of the elements of the offense(s)?

ACC: ________.

SCM: Do you believe, and admit, that taken together these elements correctly describe what you did?

ACC: ________.

[Note 15. The summary court-martial should now question the accused about the circumstances of the offense(s) to which the accused has pleaded guilty. The accused will he placed under oath for this purpose. *See* oath below. The purpose of these questions is to develop the circumstances in the accused's own words, so that the summary court-martial may determine whether each element of the offense(s) is established.]

Oath to accused for guilty plea inquiry

SCM: Do you (swear) (affirm) that the statements you are about to make shall be the truth, the whole truth, and nothing but the truth (so help you God)?

ACC: ________.

SCM: Do you have any questions about the meaning and effect of your pleas of guilty?

ACC: ________.

SCM: Do you believe that you understand the meaning and effect of your pleas of guilty?

ACC: ________.

Determination of providence of pleas of guilty

[Note 16. Pleas of guilty may not be accepted unless the summary court-martial finds that they are made voluntarily and with understanding of their meaning and effect, and that the accused has knowingly, intelligently, and consciously waived the rights against self-incrimination, to a trial of the facts by a court-martial, and to be confronted by the witnesses. Pleas of guilty may be improvident when the accused makes statements at any time during the trial which indicate that there may be a defense to the offense(s), or which are otherwise inconsistent with an admission of guilt. If the accused makes such statements and persists in them after questioning, then the summary court-martial must reject the accused's guilty pleas and enter pleas of not guilty for the accused. Turn to the section entitled "Procedures-Not Guilty Pleas" and continue as indicated. If (the) (any of the) accused's pleas of guilty are found provident, the summary court-martial should announce findings as follows.]

Acceptance of guilty pleas

SCM: I find that the pleas of guilty are made voluntarily and with understanding of their meaning and effect. I further specifically find that you have knowingly, intelligently, and consciously waived your rights against self-incrimination, to a trial of the facts by a court-martial, and to be confronted by the witnesses against you. Accordingly, I find the pleas are provident, and I accept them. However, you may ask to take back your guilty pleas at any time before the sentence is announced. If you have a sound reason for your request, I will grant it. Do you understand that?

ACC: __________.

If any not guilty pleas remain

[Note 17. If no pleas of not guilty remain, go to note 26. If the accused has changed pleas of guilty to not guilty, if the summary court-martial has entered pleas of not guilty to any charge(s) and specification(s), or if the accused has pleaded not guilty to any of the offenses or pleaded guilty to a lesser included offense, proceed as follows.]

Witnesses for the accused

SCM: If there are witnesses you would like to call to testify for you, give me the name, rank, and organization or address of each, and the reason you think they should be here, and I will arrange to have them present if their testimony would be material. Do you want to call witnesses?

ACC: __________.

[Note 18. The summary court-martial should estimate the length of the case and arrange for the attendance of witnesses. The prosecution evidence should be presented before evidence for the defense.]

Calling witnesses

SCM: I call as a witness __________.

Witness oath

SCM: [To the witness, both standing] Raise your right hand.

Do you swear (or affirm) that the evidence you shall give in the case now in hearing shall be the truth, the whole truth, and nothing but the truth (, so help you God)? [Do not use the phrase, "so help you God," if the witness prefers to affirm.]

WIT: __________.

SCM: Be seated. State your full name, rank, organization, and armed force ([or if a civilian witness] full name, address, and occupation).

WIT: __________.

[Note 19. The summary court-martial should question each witness concerning the alleged offense(s). After direct examination of each witness, the accused must be given an opportunity to cross-examine. If the accused declines to cross-examine the witness, the summary court-martial should ask any questions that it feels the accused should have asked. If cross-examination occurs, the summary court-martial may ask questions on redirect examination and the accused may ask further questions in recross-examination.]

[Note 20. After each witness has testified, instruct the witness as follows.]

SCM: Do not discuss this case with anyone except the accused, counsel, or myself until after the trial is over. Should anyone else attempt to discuss this case with you, refuse to do so and report the attempt to me immediately. Do you understand that?

WIT: ________.

SCM: [To the witness]You are excused.

Recalling witnesses

[Note 21. Witnesses may be recalled if necessary. A witness who is recalled is still under oath and should be so reminded.]

[Note 22. After all witnesses against the accused have been called and any other evidence has been presented, the summary court-martial will announce the following.]

SCM: That completes the evidence against you. I will now consider the evidence in your favor.

Presentation of defense case

[Note 23. Witnesses for the accused should now be called to testify and other evidence should be presented. Before the defense case is terminated the summary court-martial should ask the accused if there are other matters the accused wants presented. If the accused has not testified, the summary court-martial should remind the accused of the right to testify or to remain silent.]

Closing argument

SCM: I have now heard all of the evidence. You may make an argument on this evidence before I decide whether you are guilty or not guilty.

Deliberations on findings

[Note 24. The court-martial should normally close for deliberations. If the summary court-martial decides to close, proceed as follows.]

SCM: The court-martial is closed so that I may review the evidence. Wait outside the courtroom until I recall you.

[Note 25. The summary court-martial should review the evidence and applicable law. It must acquit the accused unless it is convinced beyond a reasonable doubt by the evidence it has received in court in the presence of the accused that each element of the alleged offense(s) has been proved beyond a reasonable doubt. *See* R.C.M. 918. It may not consider any facts which were not admitted into evidence, such as a confession or admission of the accused which was excluded because it was taken in violation of Mil. R. Evid. 304. The summary court-martial may find the accused guilty of only the offense(s) charged, a lesser included offense, or of an offense which does not change the identity of an offense charged or a lesser included offense thereof.]

Announcing the findings

[Note 26. The summary court-martial should recall the accused, who will stand before the court-martial when findings are announced. All findings including any findings of guilty resulting from guilty pleas, should be announced at this time. The following forms should be used in announcing findings.]

Not guilty of all offenses

SCM: I find you of (the) (all) Charge(s) and Specification(s): Not Guilty.

Guilty of all offenses

I find you of (the) (all) Charge(s) and Specification(s): Guilty.

Guilty of some but not all offenses

I find you of (the) Specification (________) of (the) Charge (________): Not Guilty; of (the) Specification (________) of (the) Charge (________): Guilty; of (the) Charge (________): Guilty.

Guilty of lesser included offense or with exceptions and substitutions

I find you of (the Specification (________) of (the) Charge (________): Guilty, except the words ________ - and ________; (substituting therefor, respectively, the words ________ and ________;) of the excepted words: Not Guilty; (of the substituted words: Guilty;) of the Charge: (Guilty) (Not Guilty, but Guilty of a violation of Article ________, UCMJ, a lesser included offense).

Entry of findings

[Note 27. The summary court-martial shall note all findings on the record of trial.]

Procedure if total acquittal

[Note 28. If the accused has been found not guilty of all charges and specifications, adjourn the court-martial, excuse the accused, complete the record of trial, and return the charge sheet, personnel records, allied papers, and record of trial to the convening authority.]

Procedure if any findings of guilty

[Note 29. If the accused has been found guilty of any offense, proceed as follows.]

Presentence procedure

SCM: I will now receive information in order to decide on an appropriate sentence. Look at the information concerning you on the front page of the charge sheet. Is it correct?

[Note 30. If the accused alleges that any of the information is incorrect, the summary court-martial must determine whether it is correct and correct the charge sheet, if necessary.]

[Note 31. Evidence from the accused's personnel records, including evidence favorable to the accused, should now be received in accordance with R.C.M. 1001(b)(2). These records should be shown to the accused.]

SCM: Do you know any reason why I should not consider these?

ACC: ______.

[Note 32. The summary court-martial shall resolve objections under R.C.M. 1002(b)(2) and the Military Rules of Evidence and then proceed as follows. *See also* R.C.M. 1001(b)(3), (4), and (5) concerning other evidence which may be introduced.]

Extenuation and mitigation

SCM: In addition to the information already admitted which is favorable to you, and which I will consider, you may call witnesses who are reasonably available, you may present evidence, and you may make a statement. This information may be to explain the circumstances of the offense(s), including any reasons for committing the offense(s), and to lessen the punishment for the offense(s) regardless of the circumstances. You may show particular acts of good conduct or bravery, and evidence of your reputation in the service for efficiency, fidelity, obedience, temperance, courage, or any other trait desirable in a good servicemember. You may call available witnesses or you may use letters, affidavits, certificates of military and civil officers, or other similar writings. If you introduce such matters, I may receive written evidence for the purpose of contradicting the matters you presented. If you want me to get some military records that you would otherwise be unable to obtain, give me a list of these documents. If you intend to introduce letters, affidavits, or other documents, but you do not have them, tell me so that I can help you get them. Do you understand that?

ACC: ______.

Rights of accused to testify, remain silent, and make an unsworn statement

SCM: I informed you earlier of your right to testify under oath, to remain silent, and to make an unsworn statement about these matters.

SCM: Do you understand these rights?

ACC: ______.

SCM: Do you wish to call witnesses or introduce anything in writing?

ACC: ______.

[Note 33. If the accused wants the summary court-martial to obtain evidence, arrange to have the evidence produced as soon as practicable.]

[Note 34. The summary court-martial should now receive evidence favorable to the accused. If the accused does not produce evidence, the summary court-martial may do so if there are matters favorable to the accused which should be presented.]

SCM: Do you wish to testify or make an unsworn statement?

ACC: ________.

Questions concerning pleas of guilty

[Note 35. If as a result of matters received on sentencing, including the accused's testimony or an unsworn statement, any matter is disclosed which is inconsistent with the pleas of guilty, the summary court-martial must immediately inform the accused and resolve the matter. *See* Note 16.]

Argument on sentence

SCM: You may make an argument on an appropriate sentence.

ACC: ________.

Deliberations prior to announcing sentence

[Note 36. After receiving all matters relevant to sentencing, the summary court-martial should normally close for deliberations. If the summary court-martial decides to close, proceed as follows.]

Closing the court-martial

SCM: This court-martial is closed for determination of the sentence. Wait outside the courtroom until I recall you.

[Note 37. *See* Appendix 11 concerning proper form of sentence. Once the summary court-martial has determined the sentence, it should reconvene the court-martial and announce the sentence as follows.]

Announcement of sentence

SCM: Please rise. I sentence you to ________.

[Note 38. If the sentence includes confinement, advise the accused as follows.]

SCM: You have the right to request in writing that [name of convening authority] defer your sentence to confinement. Deferment is not a form of clemency and is not the same as suspension of a sentence. It merely postpones the running of a sentence to confinement.

[Note 39. Whether or not the sentence includes confinement, advise the accused as follows.]

SCM: You have the right to submit in writing a petition or statement to the convening authority. This statement may include any matters you feel the convening authority should consider, a request for clemency, or both. This statement must be submitted within 7 days, unless you request and convening authority approves an extension of up to 20 days. After the convening authority takes action, your case will be reviewed by a judge advocate for legal error. You may suggest, in writing, legal errors for the judge advocate to consider. If, after final action has been taken in your case, you believe that there has been a legal error, you may request review of your case by The Judge Advocate General of ________. Do you understand these rights?

ACC: ________.

Adjourning the court-martial

SCM: This court-martial is adjourned.

Entry on charge sheet

[Note 40. Record the sentence in the record of trial, inform the convening authority of the findings, recommendations for suspension, if any, and any deferment request. If the sentence includes confinement, arrange for the delivery of the accused to the accused's commander, or someone designated by the commander, for appropriate action. Ensure that the commander is informed of the sentence. Complete the record of trial and forward to the convening authority.]

APPENDIX 10
FORMS OF FINDINGS

a. *Announcement of findings*

*See*R.C.M. 922.

In announcing the findings the president or, in cases tried by military judge alone, the military judge should announce:

"(Name of accused), this court-martial finds you ______________."

The findings should now be announced following one of the forms in b below, or any necessary modification or combination thereof.

b. *Forms*

[Note: The following may, in combination with the format for announcing the findings in a above, be used as a format for a findings worksheet, appropriately tailored for the specific case.]

Forms of Findings

I. Acquittal of all Charges

Of all Specifications and Charges: Not Guilty

II. Findings of Not Guilty only by Reason of Lack of Mental Responsibility

Of (the) Specification (_______) of (the) Charge (_______) and of (the) Charge (_______): Not Guilty only by Reason of Lack of Mental Responsibility

III. Conviction of all Charges

Of all Specifications and Charges: Guilty

IV. Conviction of all Specifications of some Charges

Of all Specification(s) of Charge I: Guilty

Of Charge I: Guilty

Of all Specification(s) of Charge II: Not Guilty

Of Charge II: Not Guilty

V. Conviction of some Specifications of a Charge

Of Specification(s) _______ of Charge I: Guilty

Of Specification(s) _______ of Charge I: Not Guilty

Of Charge I: Guilty

VI. Conviction by exceptions

Of (the) Specification (_______) of Charge I: Guilty except the words "______________";

Of the excepted words: Not Guilty

Of Charge I: (Guilty) (Not Guilty, but Guilty of a violation of Article _______)

VII. Conviction by exceptions and substitutions

Of (the) Specification (_______) of Charge I: Guilty except the words "_______," substituting therefor the words "_______";

Of the excepted words: Not Guilty

Of the substituted words: Guilty

Of Charge I: (Guilty) (Not Guilty, but Guilty of a violation of Article _________)

VIII. Conviction under one Charge of offenses under different Articles

Of Specification 1 of (the) Charge (_______): Guilty, of Specification 2 of (the) Charge (_______): Guilty, except the words "______________."

Of (the) Charge (_______), as to Specification 1: Guilty, as to Specification 2: Not Guilty, but Guilty of a violation of Article _______.

APPENDIX 11
FORMS OF SENTENCES

a. *Announcement of sentence*

See R.C.M. 1007.

In announcing the sentence, the president or, in cases tried by military judge alone, the military judge should announce:

"(Name of accused), this court-martial sentences you ________."

The sentence should now be announced following one of the forms contained in *b* below, or any necessary modification or combination thereof. Each of the forms of punishment prescribed in *b* are separate, that is, the adjudging of one form of punishment is not contingent upon any other punishment also being adjudged. The forms in *c*, however, may be combined and modified so long as the punishments adjudged is not forbidden by the code and does not exceed the maximum authorized by this Manual (*see* R.C.M. 1003 and Part IV) in the particular case being tried. In announcing a sentence consisting of combined punishments, the president or military judge may, for example, state:

"To be dishonorably discharged from the service, to be confined for one year, to forfeit all pay and allowances, and to be reduced to Private, E–1;" or

"To be discharged from the service with a bad-conduct discharge, to be confined for six months, and to forfeit $35.00 pay per month for six months;" or

"To be dismissed from the service, to be confined for one year, and to forfeit all pay and allowances;" or

"To perform hard labor without confinement for one month and to forfeit $25.00 pay per month for one month."

b. *Single punishment forms*

[Note: The following may, in combination with the format for announcing the sentence in *a* above, be used as a format for a sentence worksheet, appropriately tailored for the specific case.]

1. To no punishment

Reprimand

2. To be reprimanded.

Forfeitures, Etc.

3. To forfeit $________ pay per month for ________ (months) (years).

4. To forfeit all pay and allowances.

5. To pay the United States a fine of $________ (and to serve (additional) confinement of ________ (days) (months) (years) if the fine is not paid).

Reduction of Enlisted Personnel

6. To be reduced to ________.

Restraint and Hard Labor

7. To be restricted to the limits of________ for (days) (months).

8. To perform hard labor without confinement for ________ (days) (months).

9. To be confined for ________ (days) (months) (years) (the length of your natural life with eligibility) (the length of your natural life without eligibility for parole).

10. To be confined on (bread and water) (diminished rations) for ________ days.

Punitive Discharge

11. To be discharged from the service with a bad-conduct discharge (Enlisted Personnel only).

12. To be dishonorably discharged from the service (Enlisted Personnel and Noncommissioned Warrant Officers only).

13. To be dismissed from the service (Commissioned Officers, Commissioned Warrant Officers, Cadets, and Midshipmen only).

Death

14. To be put to death.

[Note: A court-martial has no authority to suspend a sentence or any part of a sentence.]

Maximum Punishment

Maximum Punishment

APPENDIX 12
MAXIMUM PUNISHMENT CHART

This chart was compiled for convenience purposes only and is not the authority for specific punishments. *See* Part IV and R.C.M. 1003 for specific limits and additional information concerning maximum punishments.

Article	*Offense*	*Discharge*	*Confinement*	*Forfeitures*
77	Principals (*see* Part IV, Para. 1 and pertinent offenses)			
78	Accessory after the fact (*see* Part IV, Para. 3.e.)			
79	Lesser included offenses (*see* Part IV, Para. 2 and pertinent offenses)			
80	Attempts (*see* Part IV, Para. 4.e.)			
81	Conspiracy (*see* Part IV, Para. 5.e.)			
82	Solicitation			
	If solicited offense committed, or attempted, *see* Part IV, Para. 6.e.			
	If solicited offense not committed:			
	Solicitation to desert[1]	DD, BCD	3 yrs.[1]	Total
	Solicitation to mutiny[1]	DD, BCD	10 yrs.[1]	Total
	Solicitation to commit act of misbehavior before enemy[1]	DD, BCD	10 yrs.[1]	Total
	Solicitation to commit act of sedition [1]	DD, BCD	10 yrs.[1]	Total
83	Fraudulent enlistment, appointment	DD, BCD	2 yrs.	Total
	Fraudulent separation	DD, BCD	5 yrs.	Total
84	Effecting unlawful enlistment, appointment, separation	DD, BCD	5 yrs.	Total
85	Desertion			
	In time of war	Death, DD, BCD	Life[4]	Total
	Intent to avoid hazardous duty, shirk important service [1]	DD, BCD	5 yrs.[1]	Total
	Other cases			
	Terminated by apprehension	DD, BCD	3 yrs.[1]	Total
	Otherwise terminated	DD, BCD	2 yrs.[1]	Total
86	Absence without leave, etc.			
	Failure to go, going from place of duty	None	1 mo.	2/3 1 mo.
	Absence from unit, organization, etc.			
	Not more than 3 days	None	1 mo.	2/3 1 mo.
	More than 3, not more than 30 days	None	6 mos.	2/3 6 mos.
	More than 30 days	DD, BCD	1 yr.	Total
	More than 30 days and terminated by apprehension	DD, BCD	1 yr., 6 mos.	Total
	Absence from guard or watch	None	3 mos.	2/3 3 mos.
	Absence from guard or watch with intent to abandon	BCD	6 mos.	Total
	Absence with intent to avoid maneuvers, field exercises	BCD	6 mos.	Total
87	Missing movement			
	Through design	DD, BCD	2 yrs.	Total
	Through neglect	BCD	1 yr.	Total
88	Contempt toward officials	Dismissal	1 yr.	Total
89	Disrespect toward superior commissioned officer	BCD	1 yr.	Total
90	Assaulting, willfully disobeying superior commissioned officer			
	In time of war	Death, DD, BCD	Life[4]	Total
	Striking, drawing or lifting up any weapon or offering any violence toward superior commissioned officer execution of duty[1]	DD, BCD	10 yrs.[1]	Total
	Willfully disobeying lawful order of superior commissioned officer[1]	DD, BCD	5 yrs.[1]	Total
91	Insubordinate conduct toward warrant, noncommissioned, petty officer			
	Striking or assaulting:			
	Warrant officer	DD, BCD	5 yrs.	Total
	Superior noncommissioned officer	DD, BCD	3 yrs.	Total
	Other noncommissioned or petty officer	DD, BCD	1 yr.	Total
	Willfully disobeying:			
	Warrant officer	DD, BCD	2 yrs.	Total
	Noncommissioned or petty officer	BCD	1 yr.	Total
	Contempt, disrespect toward:			
	Warrant Officer	BCD	9 mos.	Total
	Superior noncommissioned or petty officer	BCD	6 mos.	Total
	Other noncommissioned or petty officer	None	3 mos.	2/3 3 mos.

This chart was compiled for convenience purposes only and is not the authority for specific punishments. *See* Part IV and R.C.M. 1003 for specific limits and additional information concerning maximum punishments.

Article	*Offense*	*Discharge*	*Confinement*	*Forfeitures*
92	Failure to obey order, regulation			
	Violation, failure to obey general order or regulation [2]	DD, BCD	2 yrs.	Total
	Violation, failure to obey other order [2]	BCD	6 mos.	Total
	Dereliction in performance of duties			
	Through neglect, culpable inefficiency	None	3 mos.	2/3 3 mos.
	Willful	BCD	6 mos.	Total
93	Cruelty, maltreatment of subordinates	DD, BCD	1 yr.	Total
94	Mutiny & sedition	Death, DD, BCD	Life[4]	Total
95	Resisting apprehension, flight, breach of arrest, escape			
	Resisting apprehension	BCD	1 yr.	Total
	Flight from apprehension	BCD	1 yr.	Total
	Breaking arrest	BCD	6 mos.	Total
	Escape from custody, pretrial confinement, or confinement on bread and water or diminished rations	DD, BCD	1 yr.	Total
	Escape from post-trial confinement	DD, BCD	5 yrs.	Total
96	Releasing prisoner without proper authority	DD, BCD	2 yrs.	Total
	Suffering prisoner to escape through neglect	BCD	1 yr.	Total
	Suffering prisoner to escape through design	DD, BCD	2 yrs.	Total
97	Unlawful detention	DD, BCD	3 yrs.	Total
98	Noncompliance with procedural rules, etc.			
	Unnecessary delay in disposition of case	BCD	6 mos.	Total
	Knowingly, intentionally failing to comply, enforce code	DD, BCD	5 yrs.	Total
99	Misbehavior before enemy	Death, DD, BCD	Life[4]	Total
100	Subordinate compelling surrender	Death, DD, BCD	Life[4]	Total
101	Improper use of countersign	Death, DD, BCD	Life[4]	Total
102	Forcing safeguard	Death, DD, BCD	Life[4]	Total
103	Captured, abandoned property; failure to secure, etc.			
	Of value of $500.00 or less	BCD	6 mos.	Total
	Of value of more than $500.00	DD, BCD	5 yrs.	Total
	Any firearm or explosive	DD, BCD	5 yrs.	Total
	Looting, pillaging	DD, BCD	Life[4]	Total
104	Aiding the enemy	Death, DD, BCD	Life[4]	Total
105	Misconduct as prisoner	DD, BCD	Life[4]	Total
106	Spying	Mandatory Death, DD, BCD	Not applicable	Total
106a	Espionage			
	Cases listed in Art. 106a(a)(l)(A)–(D)	Death, DD, BCD	Life[4]	Total
	Other cases	DD, BCD	Life[4]	Total
107	False official statements	DD, BCD	5 yrs.	Total
108	Military property; loss, damage, destruction, disposition			
	Selling, otherwise disposing			
	Of value of $500.00 or less	BCD	1 yr.	Total
	Of value of more than $500.00	DD, BCD	10 yrs.	Total
	Any firearm, explosive or incendiary device	DD, BCD	10 yrs.	Total
	Damaging, destroying, losing or suffering to be lost, damaged, destroyed, sold, or wrongfully disposed:			
	Through neglect, of a value of:			
	$500.00 or less	None	6 mos.	2/3 6 mos.
	More than $500.00	BCD	1 yr.	Total
	Willfully, of a value of			
	$500.00 or less	BCD	1 yr.	Total
	More than $500.00	DD, BCD	10 yrs.	Total
	Any firearm, explosive, or incendiary device	DD, BCD	10 yrs.	Total

This chart was compiled for convenience purposes only and is not the authority for specific punishments. *See* Part IV and R.C.M. 1003 for specific limits and additional information concerning maximum punishments.

Article	*Offense*	*Discharge*	*Confinement*	*Forfeitures*
109	Property other than military property of U.S.: loss, damage, destruction, disposition:			
	Wasting, spoiling, destroying, or damaging property of a value of:			
	$500.00 or less	BCD	1 yr.	Total
	More than $500.00	DD, BCD	5 yrs.	Total
110	Hazarding a vessel			
	Willfully and wrongfully	Death, DD, BCD	Life[4]	Total
	Negligently	DD, BCD	2 yrs.	Total
111	Drunken driving			
	Resulting in personal injury	DD, BCD	1 yr., 6 mos.	Total
	Other cases	BCD	6 mos.	Total
112	Drunk on duty	BCD	9 mos.	Total
112a	Wrongful use, possession, etc. of controlled substances [3]			
	Wrongful use, possession, manufacture, or introduction of:			
	Amphetamine, cocaine, heroin, lysergic acid diethylamide, marijuana (except possession of less than 30 grams or use), methamphetamine, opium, phencyclidine, secobarbital, and Schedule I, II, and III controlled substances	DD, BCD	5 yrs.	Total
	Marijuana (possession of less than 30 grams or use), phenobarbital, and Schedule IV and V controlled substances	DD, BCD	2 yrs.	Total
	Wrongful distribution of, or, with intent to distribute, wrongful possession, manufacture, introduction, or wrongful importation of or exportation of:			
	Amphetamine, cocaine, heroin, lysergic acid diethylamide, marijuana, methamphetamine, opium, phencyclidine, secobarbital, and Schedule I, II, and III controlled substances	DD, BCD	15 yrs.	Total
	Phenobarbital and Schedule IV and V controlled substances	DD, BCD	10 yrs.	Total
113	Misbehavior of sentinel or lookout			
	In time of war	Death, DD, BCD	Life[4]	Total
	In other time:			
	While receiving special pay under 37 U.S.C. 310	DD, BCD	10 yrs.	Total
	Other places	DD, BCD	1 yr.	Total
114	Dueling	DD, BCD	1 yr.	Total
115	Malingering			
	Feigning illness, etc.			
	In time of war, or while receiving special pay under 37 U.S.C. 310	DD, BCD	3 yrs.	Total
	Other	DD, BCD	1 yr.	Total
	Intentional self-inflicted injury			
	In time of war, or while receiving special pay under 37 U.S.C. 310	DD, BCD	10 yrs.	Total
	Other	DD, BCD	5 yrs.	Total
116	Riot	DD, BCD	10 yrs.	Total
	Breach of peace	None	6 mos.	2/3 6 mos.
117	Provoking speech, gestures	None	6 mos.	2/3 6 mos.
118	Murder			
	Article 118(1) or (4)	Death, mandatory minimum life with parole, DD, BCD	Life[4]	Total
	Article 118(2) or (3)	DD, BCD	Life[4]	Total
119	Manslaughter			
	Voluntary	DD, BCD	15 yrs.	Total
	Involuntary	DD, BCD	10 yrs.	Total
119a	Death or injury to an Unborn Child (*see* Part IV, Para. 44a.(a)(1))			

This chart was compiled for convenience purposes only and is not the authority for specific punishments. *See* Part IV and R.C.M. 1003 for specific limits and additional information concerning maximum punishments.

Article	*Offense*	*Discharge*	*Confinement*	*Forfeitures*
	Injuring or killing an unborn child	Such punishment, other than death, as a court-martial may direct, but such punishment shall be consistent with the punishment had the bodily injury or death occurred to the unborn child's mother.		
	Attempting to kill an unborn child	Such punishment, other than death, as a court-martial may direct, but such punishment shall be consistent with the punishment had the attempt been made to kill the unborn child's mother.		
	Intentional killing of an unborn child	Such punishment, other than death, as a court-martial may direct, but such punishment shall be consistent with the punishment had the death occurred to the unborn child's mother.		
120	Rape and Rape of a Child	Death, DD, BCD	Life	Total
	Aggravated Sexual Assault	DD, BCD	30 yrs	Total
	Aggravated Sexual Assault of a Child	DD, BCD	20 yrs	Total
	Aggravated Sexual Abuse of a Child	DD, BCD	20 yrs	Total
	Aggravated Sexual Contact	DD, BCD	20 yrs	Total
	Aggravated Sexual Contact with a Child	DD, BCD	20 yrs	Total
	Abusive Sexual Contact with a Child	DD, BCD	15 yrs	Total
	Indecent Liberty with a Child	DD, BCD	15 yrs	Total
	Abusive Sexual Contact	DD, BCD	7 yrs	Total
	Indecent Act	DD, BCD	5 yrs	Total
	Forcible Pandering	DD, BCD	5 yrs	Total
	Wrongful Sexual Contact	DD, BCD	1 yr	Total
	Indecent Exposure	DD, BCD	1 yr	Total
120a	Stalking	DD, BCD	3 yrs	Total
121	Larceny			
	Of military property of a value of $500.00 or less	BCD	1 yr.	Total
	Of property other than military property of a value of $500.00 or less	BCD	6 mos.	Total
	Of military property of a value of more than $500.00 or of any military motor vehicle, aircraft, vessel, firearm, or explosive	DD, BCD	10 yrs.	Total
	Of property other than military property of a value of more than $500.00 or any motor vehicle, aircraft, vessel, firearm, or explosive	DD, BCD	5 yrs.	Total
	Wrongful appropriation			
	Of value of $500.00 or less	None	3 mos.	2/3 3 mos.
	Of value of more than $500.00	BCD	6 mos.	Total
	Of any motor vehicle, aircraft, vessel, firearm, or explosive	DD, BCD	2 yrs.	Total
122	Robbery			
	Committed with a firearm	DD, BCD	15 yrs.	Total
	Other cases	DD, BCD	10 yrs.	Total
123	Forgery	DD, BCD	5 yrs.	Total

This chart was compiled for convenience purposes only and is not the authority for specific punishments. *See* Part IV and R.C.M. 1003 for specific limits and additional information concerning maximum punishments.

Article	*Offense*	*Discharge*	*Confinement*	*Forfeitures*
123a	Checks, etc., insufficient funds, intent to deceive			
	To procure anything of value of:			
	$500.00 or less	BCD	6 mos.	Total
	More than $500.00	DD, BCD	5 yrs.	Total
	For payment of past due obligation, and other cases	BCD	6 mos.	Total
124	Maiming	DD, BCD	20 yrs	Total
125	Sodomy			
	By force and without consent	DD, BCD	Life[4]	Total
	With child under age of 16 years and at least 12	DD, BCD	20 yrs.	Total
	With child under the age of 12	DD, BCD	Life[4]	Total
	Other cases	DD, BCD	5 yrs.	Total
126	Arson			
	Aggravated	DD, BCD	20 yrs.	Total
	Other cases, where property value is:			
	$500.00 or less	DD, BCD	1 yr.	Total
	More than $500.00	DD, BCD	5 yrs.	Total
127	Extortion	DD, BCD	3 yrs.	Total
128	Assaults			
	Simple Assault:			
	Generally	None	3 mos.	2/3 3 mos.
	With an unloaded firearm	DD, BCD	3 yrs.	Total
	Assault consummated by battery	BCD	6 mos.	Total
	Assault upon commissioned officer of U.S. or friendly power not in execution of office	DD, BCD	3 yrs.	Total
	Assault upon warrant officer, not in execution of office	DD, BCD	1 yr., 6 mos.	Total
	Assault upon noncommissioned or petty officer not in execution of office	BCD	6 mos.	Total
	Assault upon, in execution of office, person serving as sentinel, lookout, security policeman, military policeman, shore patrol, master at arms, or civil law enforcement	DD, BCD	3 yrs.	Total
	Assault consummated by battery upon child under age of 16 years	DD, BCD	2 yrs.	Total
	Assault with dangerous weapon or means likely to produce grievous bodily harm or death:			
	Committed with loaded firearm	DD, BCD	8 yrs.	Total
	Other cases	DD, BCD	3 yrs.	Total
	Assault in which grievous bodily harm is intentionally inflicted:			
	With a loaded firearm	DD, BCD	10 yrs.	Total
	Other cases	DD, BCD	5 yrs.	Total
	Aggravated assault with a dangerous weapon or other means of force to produce death or grievous bodily harm when committed upon a child under the age of 16 years	DD, BCD	5 yrs	Total
	Aggravated assault in which grievous bodily harm is intentionally inflicted when committed upon a child under the age of 16 years	DD, BCD	8 yrs	Total
129	Burglary	DD, BCD	10 yrs.	Total
130	Housebreaking	DD, BCD	5 yrs.	Total
131	Perjury	DD, BCD	5 yrs.	Total
132	Frauds against the United States			
	Offenses under article 132(1) or (2)	DD, BCD	5 yrs.	Total
	Offenses under article 132(3) or (4)			
	$500.00 or less	BCD	6 mos.	Total
	More than $500.00	DD, BCD	5 yrs.	Total
133	Conduct unbecoming officer (*see* Part IV, para. 59e)	Dismissal	1 yr. or as prescribed	Total
134	Abusing public animal	None	3 mos.	2/3 3 mos.
	Adultery	DD, BCD	1 yr.	Total
	Assault			
	With intent to commit murder or rape	DD, BCD	20 yrs.	Total

This chart was compiled for convenience purposes only and is not the authority for specific punishments. *See* Part IV and R.C.M. 1003 for specific limits and additional information concerning maximum punishments.

Article	*Offense*	*Discharge*	*Confinement*	*Forfeitures*
	With intent to commit voluntary manslaughter, robbery, sodomy, arson, or burglary	DD, BCD	10 yrs.	Total
	With intent to commit housebreaking	DD, BCD	5 yrs.	Total
	Bigamy	DD, BCD	2 yrs.	Total
	Bribery	DD, BCD	5 yrs.	Total
	Graft	DD, BCD	3 yrs.	Total
	Burning with intent to defraud	DD, BCD	10 yrs.	Total
	Check, worthless, making and uttering—by dishonorably failing to maintain funds	BCD	6 mos.	Total
	Child Endangerment:			
	Endangerment by design resulting in grievous bodily harm	DD, BCD	8 yrs	Total
	Endangerment by design resulting in harm	DD, BCD	5 yrs	Total
	Other cases by design	DD, BCD	4 yrs	Total
	Endangerment by culpable negligence resulting in grievous bodily harm	DD, BCD	3 yrs	Total
	Endangerment by culpable negligence resulting in harm	BCD	2 yrs	Total
	Other cases by culpable negligence	BCD	1 yr	Total
	Cohabitation, wrongful	None	4 mos.	2/3 4 mos.
	Correctional custody, escape from	DD, BCD	1 yr.	Total
	Correctional custody, breach of	BCD	6 mos.	Total
	Debt, dishonorably failing to pay	BCD	6 mos.	Total
	Disloyal statements	DD, BCD	3 yrs.	Total
	Disorderly conduct			
	Under such circumstances as to bring discredit	None	4 mos.	2/3 4 mos.
	Other cases	None	1 mo.	2/3 1 mo.
	Drunkenness			
	Aboard ship or under such circumstances as to bring discredit	None	3 mos.	2/3 3 mos.
	Other cases	None	1 mo.	2/3 1 mo.
	Drunk and disorderly			
	Aboard ship	BCD	6 mos.	Total
	Under such circumstances as to bring discredit	None	6 mos.	2/3 6 mos.
	Other cases	None	3 mos.	2/3 3 mos.
	Drinking liquor with prisoner	None	3 mos.	2/3 3 mos.
	Drunk prisoner	None	3 mos.	2/3 3 mos.
	Drunkenness—incapacitating oneself for performance of duties through prior indulgence in intoxicating liquor or drugs	None	3 mos.	2/3 3 mos.
	Endangerment, reckless	BCD	1 yr.	Total
	False or unauthorized pass offenses			
	Possessing or using with intent to defraud or deceive, or making, altering, counterfeiting, tampering with, or selling	DD, BCD	3 yrs.	Total
	All other cases	BCD	6 mos.	Total
	False pretenses, obtaining services under			
	Of a value of $500.00 or less	BCD	6 mos.	Total
	Of a value of more than $500.00	DD, BCD	5 yrs.	Total
	False swearing	DD, BCD	3 yrs.	Total
	Firearm, discharging—through negligence	None	3 mos.	2/3 3 mos.
	Firearm, discharging—willfully, under such circumstances as to endanger human life	DD, BCD	1 yr.	Total
	Fleeing scene of accident	BCD	6 mos.	Total
	Fraternization	Dismissal	2 yrs.	Total
	Gambling with subordinates	None	3 mos.	2/3 3 mos.
	Homicide, negligent	DD, BCD	3 yrs.	Total
	Impersonation			
	With intent to defraud	DD, BCD	3 yrs.	Total
	All other cases	BCD	6 mos.	Total
	Indecent language			
	Communicated to child under 16 yrs	DD, BCD	2 yrs.	Total
	Other cases	BCD	6 mos.	Total
	Jumping from vessel into the water	BCD	6 mos.	Total
	Kidnapping	DD, BCD	Life[4]	Total
	Mail, taking, opening, secreting, destroying, or stealing	DD, BCD	5 yrs.	Total

This chart was compiled for convenience purposes only and is not the authority for specific punishments. *See* Part IV and R.C.M. 1003 for specific limits and additional information concerning maximum punishments.

Article	*Offense*	*Discharge*	*Confinement*	*Forfeitures*
	Mails, depositing or causing to be deposited obscene matters in	DD, BCD	5 yrs.	Total
	Misprision of serious offense	DD, BCD	3 yrs.	Total
	Obstructing justice	DD, BCD	5 yrs.	Total
	Wrongful interference with an adverse administrative proceeding	DD, BCD	5 yrs.	Total
	Pandering	DD, BCD	5 yrs.	Total
	Prostitution and patronizing a prostitute	DD, BCD	1 yr.	Total
	Parole, violation of	BCD	6 mos.	2/3 6 mos.
	Perjury, subornation of	DD, BCD	5 yrs.	Total
	Public record, altering, concealing, removing, mutilating, obliterating, or destroying	DD, BCD	3 yrs.	Total
	Quarantine, breaking	None	6 mos.	2/3 6 mos.
	Reckless endangerment	BCD	1 yr.	Total
	Restriction, breaking	None	1 mo.	2/3 1 mo.
	Seizure, destruction, removal, or disposal of property to prevent	DD, BCD	1 yr.	Total
	Self-injury without intent to avoid service			
	In time of war, or in a hostile fire pay zone	DD	5 yrs.	Total
	Other	DD	2 yrs.	Total
	Sentinel, lookout			
	Disrespect to	None	3 mos.	2/3 3 mos.
	Loitering or wrongfully sitting on post by			
	In time of war or while receiving special pay	DD, BCD	2 yrs.	Total
	Other cases	BCD	6 mos.	Total
	Soliciting another to commit an offense (*see* Part IV, para. 105e)			
134				
	Of a value of $500.00 or less	BCD	6 mos.	Total
	Of a value of more than $500.00	DD, BCD	3 yrs.	Total
	Straggling	None	3 mos.	2/3 3 mos.
	Testify, wrongfully refusing to	DD, BCD	5 yrs.	Total
	Threat, bomb, or hoax	DD, BCD	5 yrs.	Total
	Threat, communicating	DD, BCD	3 yrs.	Total
	Unlawful entry	BCD	6 mos.	Total
	Weapon, concealed, carrying	BCD	1 yr.	Total
	Wearing unauthorized insignia, decoration, badge, ribbon, device, or lapel button	BCD	6 mos.	Total

Notes:

1. Suspended in time of war.

2. *See* paragraph 16e(1) & (2) Note, Part IV

3. When any offense under paragraph 37, Part IV, is committed: while the accused is on duty as a sentinel or lookout; on board a vessel or aircraft used by or under the control of the armed forces; in or at a missile launch facility used by or under the control of the armed forces; while receiving special pay under 37 U.S.C. sec. 310; in time of war; or in a confinement facility used by or under the control of the armed forces, the maximum period of confinement authorized for such offense shall be increased by 5 years.

4. With or without eligibility for parole.

APPENDIX 13
GUIDE FOR PREPARATION OF RECORD OF TRIAL BY GENERAL COURT-MARTIAL AND BY SPECIAL COURT-MARTIAL WHEN A VERBATIM RECORD IS NOT REQUIRED

a. *Record of trial*

If a verbatim record is not required (*see* R.C.M. 1103(h)(2)(C) and (c)(2)), a summarized report of testimony, objections, and other proceedings is permitted. In the event of an acquittal of all charges and specifications, or termination of the proceedings prior to findings by withdrawal, mistrial, or dismissal, the record may be further summarized and need only contain sufficient information to establish lawful jurisdiction over the accused and the offenses. *See* R.C.M. 1103(e).

This appendix is to be used as a general guide; the actual record may depart from it as appropriate. The manner of summarizing several items of procedure is shown in Appendix 14 *a*.

Note. All pen and ink changes to the transcribed record of trial shall be initialed. All pages in the transcribed record of trial shall be numbered consecutively, beginning with "1." The page number shall be centered on the page 1/2 inch from the bottom. A margin of 1 1/2 inches, or more as necessary, will be left at the top to permit binding. A one-inch margin will be left on the bottom of the page and on the left side of each page. The left margin will be increased as necessary in the event that left-hand binding is used rather than top binding. If left-hand binding is used, the top margin should be decreased to one-inch. Words on the margins of this appendix are not part of the form of record. All records of trial should begin as follows:

Title

RECORD OF TRIAL
of

____
(Name-last, first, middle initial) (SSN) (Grade)

____
(Organization and armed force) (Station or ship)

by

____ COURT-MARTIAL

Convened by ____
(Title of convening authority)

____
(Command of convening authority)

Tried at

______________________ on ______________________
(Place or places of trial) (Date or dates of trial)

COPIES OF RECORD

Copies of record

________ copy of record furnished the accused as per attached certificate or receipt. ________ copy(ies) of record forwarded herewith.

RECEIPT FOR COPY OF RECORD

Receipt for record

I hereby acknowledge receipt of a copy of the above-described record of trial, delivered to me at ________ this ________ day of ________.

(Signature of accused or defense counsel)

(Name of accused or defense counsel)

Note. *See* R.C.M. 1104(b)(1) concerning service of record on the accused or defense Counsel.

CERTIFICATE

________ ________.

(Place) (Date)

Certificate in lieu of receipt

I certify that on this day delivery of a copy of the above-described record of trial was made to the accused, ________ at ________, by
(Name of accused) (Place of delivery)

____

(Means of effecting delivery, i.e., mail messenger, etc.)
and that the receipt of the accused had not been received on the date this record was forwarded to the convening authority. The receipt of the accused will be forwarded as soon as it is received.
(Signature of trial counsel)
(Name of trial counsel)

Note. If accused's defense counsel receives the record, the trial counsel must attach an explanation to the record. *See* R.C.M. 1104(b)(1)(C). The following format may be used:

The accused's defense counsel was served the accused's copy of the record because (the accused so requested in a written request, which is attached) (the accused so requested on the record at the court-martial) (the accused was transferred to ________) (the accused is absent without authority) (________).
(Signature of trial counsel)
(Name of trial counsel)

Note. If the accused cannot be served and has no counsel to receive the record, an explanation for failure to serve the record will be attached to the record. *See* R.C.M. 1104(b)(l)(C). The following format may be used:

The accused was not served a copy of this record because the accused (is absent without authority) (________) Accused has no defense counsel to receive the record because (defense counsel has been excused under R.C.M.505(d)(2)(B)) (________.)
(Signature of trial counsel)
(Name of trial counsel)

Article 39(a) session

PROCEEDINGS OF A ________ COURT-MARTIAL ARTICLE 39(a) SESSION. The summarized record of an Article 39(a) session should proceed as follows:

Note. If trial was before a special court-martial without a military judge, there will have been no Article 39(a) session. However, generally the same sequence will be followed except as noted below. In special courts-martial without a military judge, substitute "president" for "military judge" when it appears, and "court-martial" for "Article 39(a) session."

Convening orders

The military judge called the Article 39(a) session to order (at) (on [nb) A] board) ________, at ________ hours, ________________, pursuant to the following orders:

Note. Here insert a copy of the convening orders and copies of any amending orders. Any written orders detailing the military judge and counsel will be attached.Any request of an enlisted accused for enlisted members will be inserted immediately following the convening orders, together with any declaration of the nonavailability of such enlisted persons. Any written request for trial by the military judge alone will also be inserted at this point. *See* R.C.M. 503(a)(2), 903.

Time of session

Note. The reporter should note and record the time and date of the beginning and ending of each session of the court-martial. For example:

The session was called to order at ________ hours, ________________.

The session (adjourned) (recessed) at ________ hours, ________________.

PERSONS PRESENT

Military judge, counsel members present and absent

Note. Here list the names of the military judge, counsel, accused, and members if present.

PERSONS ABSENT

Note. The names of the members need not be listed if members are not present. The absence of other detailed persons should be noted. The record should include any reasons given for the absence of detailed persons. If the accused was questioned about the absence of any detailed defense counsel, this inquiry should be summarized at the point in the record at which such inquiry occurred.

Accused and defense counsel present

The accused and the following (detailed defense counsel and associate or assistant defense counsel) (civilian or individual military counsel) were present:

Swearing reporter; interpreter

The following detailed (reporter) (and) (interpreter) (was) (were) (had previously been) sworn:

Note. Applicable only when a reporter or interpreter is used.

Qualification of trial counsel

The trial counsel announced the legal qualifications and status as to oaths of all members of the prosecution (and that (he) (she) (they) had been detailed by ________).

Prior participation of trial counsel

The trial counsel further stated that no member of the prosecution had acted in a manner which might tend to disqualify (him) (her) except as indicated below.

Note. If a member of the prosecution is unqualified or disqualified under R.C.M. 502(d) that will be shown, together with the action taken under R.C.M. 901(d). Any inquiry or hearing into the matter should be summarized.

Qualification of defense counsel

The detailed defense counsel announced the legal qualifications and status as to oaths of all members of the defense (and) that he (and ________________) had been detailed by ________.)

Note. Legal qualifications of any civilian or individual military counsel will be shown.

Prior participation of defense counsel

The defense counsel stated that no member of the defense had acted in a manner which might tend to disqualify (him) (her) except as indicated below.

Note. If a member of the defense is unqualified or disqualified under R.C.M. 502(d), the record will show that fact and the action taken under R.C.M. 901(d). Any inquiry or hearing into the matter should be summarized.

Inquiry concerning Article 38(b)

The military judge informed the accused of the rights concerning counsel as set forth in Article 38(b) and R.C.M. 901(d).
The accused responded that he/she understood the rights with respect to counsel, and that he/she chose to be defended by ________.

Personnel sworn

The military judge and the personnel of the prosecution and defense who were not previously sworn in accordance with Article 42(a) were sworn. The prosecution and each accused were extended the right to challenge the military judge for cause.

Challenge: military judge

The military judge was (not) challenged for cause (by ________) (on the ground that ________).

Note. The record should show the grounds for the challenge, a summary of evidence presented, if any, and the action taken.

Request for trial by military judge alone

The military judge ascertained that the accused had been advised of his right to request trial by the military judge alone and that the accused did (not) desire to submit such a request.

Note. If the accused requests trial by the military judge alone, any written request will be included in the record. The action on the request, whether oral or written, should be indicated as follows:

After ascertaining that the accused had consulted with defense counsel and had been informed of the identity of the military judge and of the right to trial by members, the military judge (approved) (disapproved) the accused's request for trial by military judge alone.

Note. If the military judge announced at this point that the court-martial was assembled, the record should so reflect. If assembly was announced at a different point it should be so shown in the record.

Note. If the military judge disapproved the accused's request, this fact and any reasons given for the disapproval should be summarized.

Note. If the accused did not submit, or the military judge disapproved, a request for trial by military judge alone, and if the accused is an enlisted person, the following should be included:

Request for enlisted members

The trial counsel announced that the accused had (not) made a request in writing that the membership of the court-martial include enlisted persons. The defense counsel announced that the accused had been advised of the right to request enlisted members and that the accused did (not) want to request enlisted members.

Note. If the accused did request enlisted members, the written request will be included in the record.

Convening authority identified

(*Name, rank, and organization of convening authority*) convened the court-martial and referred the charges and specifications to it.

Note. In a special court-martial without a military judge, ordinarily the examination and challenges of members would occur at this point. The format used below for examination and challenges may be inserted here as appropriate.

Arraignment

The accused was arraigned on the following charges and specifications:

Note. Here insert the original charge sheet. If there are not enough copies of the charge sheet to insert in each copy of the record, copy verbatim from the charge sheet the charges and specifications, and the name of the accuser, the affidavit, and the reference to the court-martial for trial.

Motions

Note. If any motions were made at arraignment, the substance of the motion, a summary of any evidence presented concerning it, and the military judge's ruling will be included in the record. Motions or objections made at other times in the court-martial should be similarly treated at a point in the record corresponding to when they were raised.

Pleas

The accused pleaded as follows:
To all the Specifications and Charges: (Not Guilty) (Guilty)
To Specification 1 of Charge I: (Not Guilty) (Guilty)
To Specification 2 of Charge I: (Not Guilty) (Guilty)
To Charge I: (Not Guilty) (Guilty)
etc.

Note. If the accused pleads guilty the plea inquiry should be summarized. The following may be used as a guide.

Guilty plea inquiry

The military judge inquired into the providence of the accused's pleas of guilty. The military judge informed the accused of: the right to counsel [if the accused had no counsel]; of the right to plead not guilty and to be tried by court-martial and that at such court-martial the accused would have the right to confront and cross-examine witnesses against the accused and the right against self-incrimination; that by pleading guilty the accused waived the rights to trial of the offense(s), to confront and cross-examine witnesses, and against self-incrimination; and that the military judge would question the accused, under oath, about the offense(s) to which the accused pleaded guilty and that if the accused answered those questions under oath, on the record, and in the presence of counsel, the accused's answers could be used against the accused in a prosecution for perjury or false statement. The accused stated that he/she understood these rights.The military judge questioned the accused and determined that the plea(s) of guilty (was) (were) voluntary and not the result of force or threats or of promises (other than those in the pretrial agreement). The military judge informed the accused of the elements of the offense(s) and the maximum punishment which could be imposed for (this) (these) offense(s). The accused stated that he/she understood.
The military judge asked the accused about the offense(s) to which the accused pleaded guilty. Under oath the accused stated as follows:

Note. Here summarize the accused's description of the offense(s).

The military judge ascertained that there was (not) a pretrial agreement in the case.

Note. If there was a pretrial agreement, the military judges's inquiry into it should be summarized. The following may be used as a guide:

The pretrial agreement was marked as Appellate Exhibit(s) ________. (The military judge did not examine Appellate Exhibit ________ at this time.) The military judge inquired and ensured that the accused understood the agreement and that the parties agreed to its terms.

Note. If there was a question or dispute as to the meaning of any term in the agreement, the resolution of that matter should be described.

Note. If the accused entered a conditional guilty plea (*see* R.C.M. 910(a)(2)), this will be included in the record.

The military judge found the accused's pleas of guilty provident and accepted them.

Note. If findings were entered (*see* R.C.M. 910(g)) on any charges and specifications at this point, the record should so reflect. *See* FINDINGS below for format.

Note. If the accused pleaded not guilty to any charge(s) and specification(s) which were not dismissed or withdrawn, in trial before military judge alone, proceed with PRESENTATION OF PROSECUTION CASE. If the accused pleaded guilty to all charge(s) and specification(s) in trial before military judge alone, proceed with SENTENCING PROCEEDINGS below. If trial was before members proceed with INITIAL SESSION WITH MEMBERS below.

Note. If the court-martial recessed, closed, or adjourned, or if an Article 39(a) session terminated and a session of the court-martial begins, the record should indicate the time of the recess, closing, or adjournment, and the time of reopening, using the following formats:

For example:
The Article 39(a) session terminated at ________ hours, ________. The court-martial (recessed) (adjourned) (closed) at ________ hours, ________.

Note. Whenever the court-martial reopens after a recess or adjournment, or after being closed, the record should indicate whether any party, member, or the military judge previously present was absent, or, if not previously present, was now present. Persons present for the first time should be identified by name. For example:

The military judge and all parties previously present were again present. (The following members were also present ________.) The members were (not) present. The military judge and all parties previously present were again present, except ________, detailed defense counsel who had been excused by ________. ________, certified in accordance with Article 27(b) was present as individual military counsel, and was previously sworn.

INITIAL SESSION WITH MEMBERS

Note. Except in a special court-martial without a military judge, ordinarily members will be first present at this point. In a special court-martial without a military judge, ordinarily the members will he sworn and examined immediately after the accused has been afforded the opportunity to request enlisted members. In such cases, the following matters should be inserted at the appropriate point in the record.

Members sworn

The members of the court-martial were sworn in accordance with R.C.M. 807.

Note. If the military judge announced at this point that the court-martial was assembled, the record should so reflect. If assembly was announced at a different point, it should be so shown in the record.

Note. If the military judge gave preliminary instructions to members, this should be stated at the point at which they were given.

Preliminary instructions

The military judge instructed the members concerning their duties, the conduct of the proceedings, (________).

Note. If counsel examined the members concerning their qualifications, the record should so state. If any member was challenged for cause, the grounds for challenge should he summarized. In addition, when a challenge is denied, the challenged member's statements concerning the matter in question should be summarized in the record. For example:

Trial and defense counsel examined the members concerning their qualifications. ________, member was questioned concerning __________, and stated, under oath as follows:
The offense charged is, in my opinion, very serious, and worthy of a punitive discharge. My mind is not made up. I would consider all the evidence and the instructions of the military judge before deciding on an appropriate sentence.
The defense challenged ________ for cause. The challenge was denied. Neither side had any further challenges for cause. The trial counsel challenged-________ peremptorily.
The defense counsel challenged ________ peremptorily (and stated that it would have challenged another member had the challenge of ________ for cause been sustained).
________ and __________ were excused and withdrew from the courtroom.

Note. If any part of the examination of members is done outside the presence of other members, this should be stated in the record. If challenges are made at an Article 39(a) session this should be stated in the record.

Note. If the accused was arraigned at an Article 39(a) session, ordinarily the military judge will have announced at this point to the members how the accused pleaded to the charges and specifications, and the record should so state. If the pleas were mixed and the members were not made aware at this point of the offense(s) to which the accused pleaded guilty the record should so state.

Announcement of pleas

The military judge informed the members that the accused had entered pleas of (Not Guilty) (Guilty) to (the) (all) Charge(s) and Specification(s) (________).

PRESENTATION OF PROSECUTION CASE

Opening statement

The trial counsel made (an) (no) opening statement. The defense counsel made (an) (no) opening statement at this time.

Note. The record will contain a summary of the testimony presented. An example of the manner in which testimony may be summarized follows:

Testimony

The following witnesses for the prosecution were sworn and testified in substance as follows:
(name of witness, rank, and organization)

DIRECT EXAMINATION

I know the accused, ________, who is in the military service and a member of my company. We both sleep in the same barracks. When I went to bed on the night of October 7, 1984, I put my wallet under my pillow. The wallet had $7.00 in it; a $5.00 bill and two $1.00 bills. Sometime during the night something woke me up but I turned over and went to sleep again. When I woke up the next morning, my wallet was gone.

CROSS-EXAMINATION

I don't know the serial numbers on any of the bills. One of the $1.00 bills was patched together with scotch tape and one of the fellows told me that the accused had used a $1.00 bill just like that in a poker game the day after my wallet was missing.

Objection and ruling

Upon objection by the defense, so much of the answer of the witness as pertained to what he had been told was stricken.

Stipulation

The trial counsel offered in evidence a stipulation of fact entered into between the trial counsel, defense counsel, and the accused. The military judge ascertained that the accused understood and consented to the stipulation. It was admitted as Prosecution Exhibit 1.

PRESENTATION OF DEFENSE CASE

Opening statement

The defense counsel made (an) (no) opening statement. The following witnesses for the defense were sworn and testified in substance as follows:

EVIDENCE IN REBUTTAL, SURREBUTTAL
WITNESSES CALLED BY THE COURT-MARTIAL

Closing argument

The trial counsel made (an) (no) argument.
The defense counsel made (an) (no) argument.
The trial counsel made (an) (no) argument in rebuttal.

Instructions

The military judge instructed the members in accordance with R.C.M. 920, including the elements of each offense, (and of the lesser included offense(s) of ________) (the defense(s) of ________,) (the following evidentiary matters,) the presumption of innocence, reasonable doubt, and burden of proof as required by Article 51(c), and on the procedures for voting on the findings worksheet. (The members were given Appellate Exhibit ________, findings worksheet.) (The members were given Appellate Exhibit ________, a copy of the military judge's instructions.) (There were no objections to the instructions or requests for additional instructions.)

Note. If any party requested instructions which were not given, or objected to the instructions given, these matters should be summarized in the record.

Closing

The court-martial closed at ________ hours, ________.
The court-martial reopened at ________ hours, ________.

Note. If the military judge examined a findings worksheet and gave additional instructions, these should be summarized.

FINDINGS

Findings by members

The president announced that the accused was found:

Of all Charges and Specifications: (Not Guilty) (Guilty)
Of Specification 1 of Charge I: (Not Guilty) (Guilty)
Of Specification 2 of Charge I: (Not Guilty) (Guilty)
Of Charge I: (Not Guilty) (Guilty)
Of the Specification of Charge II: Not Guilty
Of Charge II: Not Guilty
etc.

Findings by military judge alone

Note. In trial by the military judge alone, there would be no instructions given, but the military judge may make general and special findings. Any request for special findings should be summarized, and if submitted in writing, the request should be attached as an Appellate Exhibit. The general findings must be announced in open session with all parties present and may be recorded in the record in the following form, together with any special findings announced at that time:

Announcement

The military judge announced the following general (and special) findings (and directed that ______ be appended to the record as Appellate Exhibit ______) (and stated that the special findings would be furnished to the reporter prior to authentication for insertion in the record as Appellate Exhibit ______):
Of all the Specifications and Charges: Guilty
or
Of the Specification of Charge I: Guilty.
Of Charge I: Guilty
Of the Specification of Charge II: Not Guilty.
Of Charge II: Not Guilty

Note. All general findings should be recorded as indicated above. Special findings delivered orally should be summarized. Any written findings, opinion or memorandum of decision should be appended to the record as an appellate exhibit and copies furnished to counsel for both sides.

Note. If the accused was acquitted of all charges and specifications, proceed to adjournment.

SENTENCING PROCEEDINGS

Data as to service

The trial counsel presented the data as to pay, service, and restraint of the accused as shown on the charge sheet. There were no objections to the data.

Introduction of exhibits

The trial counsel offered Prosecution Exhibits ______, ______, and ______ for identification, matters from the accused's personnel records. (The defense did not object.) (The defense objected to Prosecution Exhibit ______ for identification on grounds that it was not properly authenticated.) (The objection was (overruled) (sustained).) (Prosecution Exhibits ______, ______, and ______ were (not) received in evidence.)

Note. If the prosecution presented evidence in aggravation or of the accused's rehabilitative potential, this evidence should be summarized here, in the same way as evidence on the merits, above.

Inquiry of accused

The military judge informed the accused of the right to present matters in extenuation and mitigation, including the right to make a sworn or an unsworn statement or to remain silent. In response to the military judge the accused stated that he/she chose to (testify) (make an unsworn statement) (remain silent).

Note. If the defense calls witnesses in extenuation and mitigation, the testimony should be summarized in the record. If the accused makes an oral unsworn statement, personally or through counsel, this should be shown and the matters contained in the statement summarized.

Argument

The prosecution made (an) (no) argument on sentence. The defense made (an) (no) argument on sentence.

Instructions

The military judge instructed the members that the maximum punishment which could be adjudged for the offense(s) of which the accused had been found guilty was: ______ The military judge also instructed the members concerning the procedures for voting, the responsibility of the members, and the matters the members should consider in accordance with R.C.M. 1005(e). (The members were given Appellate Exhibit ______, a sentence worksheet.) (The members were given Appellate Exhibit ______, a copy of the military judge's instructions.) (There were no objections to the instructions or requests for additional instructions.)

Note. If any party requested instructions which were not given, or objected to the instructions given, these matters should be summarized in the record.

Note. If, in trial before military judge alone, the military judge announces what the military judge considers to be the maximum punishment, the stated maximum should be recorded.

Closing

The court-martial closed at ______ hours, ______ ______.

Reopening

The court-martial reopened at ______ hours, ______ ______.

Note. If the military judge examined a sentencing worksheet and gave additional instructions, these should be summarized.

Announcement

The (military judge) (president) announced the following sentence: ______.

Note. If trial was by military judge alone and there was a pretrial agreement, ordinarily the military judge will examine any sentence limitation after announcing the sentence. Any inquiry conducted at this point should be summarized.

Pretrial agreement

The military judge examined Appellate Exhibit ______. The military judge stated that, based on the sentence adjudged, the convening authority (was obligated, under the agreement to approve no sentence in excess of ______) (could approve the sentence adjudged if the convening authority so elected) (______).

Note. The military judge must inform the accused of the accused's post-trial and appellate rights. *See* R.C.M. 1010. The following is an example:

Advice concerning post-trial and appellate rights

The military judge informed the accused of: the right to submit matters to the convening authority to consider before taking action; (the right to have the case examined in the Office of The Judge Advocate General and the effect of waiver or withdrawal of such right;) the right to apply for relief from The Judge Advocate General; and the right to the advice and assistance of counsel in the exercise of the foregoing rights or any decision to waive them.

Adjournment

The court-martial adjourned at ______ hours, ______ ______.

b. *Examination of record by defense counsel*

Note. When the defense counsel has examined the record of trial before authentication the following form is appropriate:

______ ______

Form

"I have examined the record of trial in the foregoing case.
(Grade) (Name), Defense Counsel"

Note. If the defense counsel was not given the opportunity to examine the record before authentication, the reasons should be attached to the record. *See* R.C.M. 1103(i)(1)(B).

c. *Authentication of record of trial*

Military judge

(1) By general or special court-martial with members and a military judge
(Captain) (Colonel) ________, Military Judge [or (LTJG) (1LT)________, Trial Counsel, because of (death) (disability) (absence) of the military judge.] [(LCDR) (Major) or ________, a member in lieu of the military judge and the trial counsel because of (death) (disability) (absence) of the military judge and of (death) (disability) (absence) of the trial counsel.]
(2) By general or special court-martial consisting of only a military judge
(Captain) (Colonel) ________, Military Judge [or (LTJG) (1LT)________, Trial Counsel, because of (death) (disability) (absence) of the military judge.] [or the court reporter in lieu of the military judge and trial counsel because of (death) (disability) (absence) of the trial counsel.]

President

Note. If the rank of any person authenticating the record has changed since the court-martial, the current rank should be indicated, followed by "formerly________."

d. *Exhibits.*

See R.C.M. 1 103(b)(2)(D)

Note. Following the end of the transcript of the proceedings, insert any exhibits which were received in evidence, or, with the permission of the military judge, copies, photographs, or descriptions of any exhibits which were received in evidence and any appellate exhibits.

e. *Attachments*

Note. Attach to the record the matters listed in R.C.M. 1103(b)(3).

f. *Certificate of correction*

Note. *See* Appendix 14*f*

APPENDIX 14
GUIDE FOR PREPARATION OF RECORD OF TRIAL BY GENERAL COURT-MARTIAL AND BY SPECIAL COURT-MARTIAL WHEN A VERBATIM RECORD IS REQUIRED

a. *Record of trial.* The following guidelines apply to the preparation of all records of trial by general and special courts-martial when a verbatim record of trial is required by Rule for Courts-Martial 1103(b)(2)(B) and (c)(1).

1. *Paper.* All transcription will be completed only on one side of 8 1/2 x 11 inch paper. Use 15-pound or other high quality paper. Red-lined margins and other legal formats, such as numbered lines, are acceptable so long as they otherwise comport with the guidelines set forth herein.

2. *Margins.* A margin of 1 1/2 inches, or more as necessary, will be left at the top to permit binding. A one inch margin will be left on the bottom of the page and on the left side of each page. The left margin will be increased as necessary in the event that left hand binding is used rather than top binding. If left-hand binding is used, the top margin should be decreased to 1 inch.

3. *Font.* Use 10-pitch (pica) on typewriters and 12 point type on computers. Only Courier, Times-Roman, or Times-New Roman fonts may be used. Do not use cursive, script, or italic fonts, except when appropriate in specific situations (*e.g.*, citation). Use bold print for initial identification of the members, military judge, court reporter, and the parties to the trial. Certain standard stock entries (SSEs) will be in bold print within verbatim records of trial, as reflected in this appendix's Guide for Preparation of Trial (i.e., calling a witness, stage of examination, and questions by counsel, members or the military judge.

4. *Line Spacing.* Double-space text, returning to the left margin on second and subsequent lines, with the exception of pleas, findings, and sentence, which should be single spaced, indented, and in bold print. Indent the elements of separate offenses in guilty plea cases.

5. *Justification.* Use left justification only with the exception of pleas, findings, and sentence, which may be justified both left and right.

6. *Page Numbering.* All pages in the transcribed record of trial shall be numbered consecutively, beginning with "1". The page number shall be centered on the page 1/2 inch from the bottom.

7. *Additional/Inserted Pages.* Use preceding page number plus either an alphanumeric letter after the corresponding whole numbered page (*e.g.* "19a") or a decimal and an Arabic number after the corresponding whole numbered page (*e.g.* "19.1"). Annotate the bottom of the preceding page to reflect the following inserted page (*e.g.* "next page 19a" or "next page 19.1"). Be consistent throughout the record of trial using either the alphanumeric or decimal system. Annotate the return to consecutive numbering at the bottom of the last inserted page (*e.g.* "next page 20").

8. *Omitted Page Numbers.* If a page number is omitted, but no page is actually missing from the transcript, note the missing page at the bottom of the page preceding the missing page number (*e.g.* "there is no page 22; next page 23").

9. *Printing.* All records of trial forwarded for review under UCMJ Articles 66 and 69(a) shall be printed in such a manner as to produce a letter quality manuscript—a clear, solid, black imprint. All pen and ink changes to the transcribed record of trial shall be initialed.

10. *Organization of Contents of Record of Trial.* The contents of a record of trial, including allied papers accompanying the record, are set forth in R.C.M. 1103(b)(2)(B), (2)(D), and (3). To the extent applicable, the original record of trial shall contain signed originals of pertinent documents. Absence of an original document will be explained, and a certified true copy or signed duplicate original copy inserted in the record of trial. Arrangement of the contents of the record shall be as set forth on DD Form 490, with heavy stock dividers used to separate major components of the record as follows:

DD Form 490, Front Cover. The front cover will be followed by: (1) any orders transferring the accused to a confinement facility or paperwork pertaining to excess/appellate leave; (2) appellate rights statement and the accused's election as to appellate counsel or any waiver thereof; (3) DD Form 494, "Court-Martial Data Sheet", if any; (4) any briefs of counsel submitted after trial; (5) court-martial orders promulgating the result of trial; (6) proof of service on the defense counsel of the Staff Judge Advocate's recommendation and any response to the recommendation (if the defense response to the recommendation is combined into one document with the matters submitted by the accused pursuant to R.C.M. 1105, then the document should be placed in the record of trial as if it were solely matters submitted by the accused pursuant to R.C.M. 1105); (7) either proof of service on the accused of the Staff Judge Advocate's recommendation or a statement explaining why the accused was not served personally; (8) signed review of the Staff Judge Advocate including any addenda and attached clemency matters; (9) matters submitted by the accused pursuant to R.C.M. 1105; (10) any request for deferment of post-trial confinement and action thereon; (11) any request for deferment/waiver of automatic forfeitures and any action thereon; (12) any request for deferment of reduction in grade and any action thereon.

DD Form 457, "Investigating Officer's Report," pursuant to Article 32, if any, and all related exhibits and attachments. The original, signed investigation will be placed in the original copy of the record of trial.

Pretrial Allied Papers. These papers should include: (1) advice of the Staff Judge Advocate or legal officer; (2) requests by counsel and action of the convening authority taken thereon; (3) any other papers, endorsements, investigations which accompanied the charges when referred for trial; (4) record of any former trial.

Record of Proceedings of Court-Martial , in the following order: (1) errata sheet; (2) index sheet with reverse side containing receipt of accused or defense counsel for copy of record or certificate in lieu of receipt;

Note. The preprinted index may be inadequate to properly reflect the proceedings, witnesses, and exhibits. Court reporters should liberally expand the index and use additional sheets as necessary. Special attention should be paid to noting the pages at which exhibits are offered and accepted/rejected, to include annotating those page numbers on the bottom of an exhibit, as appropriate.

(3) convening and all amending orders; (4) any written orders detailing the military judge or counsel; (5) request for trial by military judge alone if not marked as an appellate exhibit; (6) any written request for enlisted members if not marked as an appellate exhibit; (7) verbatim transcript of the proceedings of the court, including all Article 39(a) sessions and original DD Form 458, "Charge Sheet"; (8) authentication sheet followed by Certificate of Correction, if any; (9) action of convening authority and, if appropriate, action of officer exercising general court-martial jurisdiction.

Note. Any necessary assumption of command orders should be included in the record of trial.

Post-trial sessions. Post-trial sessions will be authenticated and served in accordance with R.C.M. 1103, and are part of the record of trial. Page numbering should continue in sequence from the end of the transcript of the original proceedings, and will be separately authenticated if the initial proceedings have been previously authenticated. Additional exhibits should be lettered or numbered in sequence, following those already marked/admitted.

Prosecution Exhibits admitted into evidence. [The page(s) at which an exhibit is offered and admitted should be noted at the bottom of the exhibit, as appropriate, as well as noting those pages on the DD Form 490.]

Defense Exhibits admitted into evidence. [The page(s) at which an exhibit is offered and admitted should be noted at the bottom of the exhibit, as appropriate, as well as noting those pages on the DD Form 490.]

Prosecution Exhibits marked but not offered and/or admitted into evidence. [The page(s) at which an exhibit is offered and rejected should be noted at the bottom of the exhibit, as appropriate, as well as noting those pages on the DD Form 490.]

Defense Exhibits marked but not offered and/or admitted into evidence. [The page(s) at which an exhibit is offered and rejected should be noted at the bottom of the exhibit, as appropriate, as well as noting those pages on the DD Form 490.]

Appellate Exhibits. [The page(s) at which an exhibit is marked should be noted at the bottom of the exhibit, as appropriate, as well as noting those pages on the DD Form 490.]

Any records of proceedings in connection with vacation of suspension.

11. *Stock Dividers.* The foregoing bullets will be separated by the use of heavy stock dividers, colored, and labeled with gummed labels.

12. *Binding.* Volumes of the record will be bound at the top with metal or plastic fasteners. Top or left-side binding is acceptable with sufficient adjustment to the top or left margin. Volumes shall be bound to withstand repeated handling, utilizing DD Form 490. **Do not sew or stack fasteners together in gangs to bind thick volumes.**

13. *Dividing Records into Volumes.* Divide ROTs that are over 11/2 inches thick into separate volumes. Make the first volume of a multi-volume record an inch thick or smaller. This will allow for inclusion of the SJA recommendation, clemency matters, and other post-trial documents. Limit subsequent volumes to 11/2 inches thick, unless dividing them requires assembling an additional volume smaller than 1/2 inch thick. If the transcript is split into two or more volumes, indicate on the front cover which pages of the transcript are in which volume. (*e.g.* Volume 1 of 4, Transcript, pages 1-300). Number each volume of the ROT as follows: "Volume 1 of _____." In the upper right-hand corner of the DD Form 490, label the ROT to reflect which copy it is, i.e., "ORIGINAL," "ACCUSED," et cetera.

Words on the margins of this appendix are not part of the form of record.

As a general rule, all proceedings in the case should be recorded verbatim. *See* R.C.M. 1103.

Following this appendix does not necessarily produce a complete record of trial. It is to be used by the reporter and trial counsel as a guide in the preparation of the completed record of trial in all general and special court-martial cases in which a verbatim record is required.

RECORD OF TRIAL
of

(Name-last, first, middle initial) (SSN) (Rank or grade)

(Organization and armed force) (Station or ship)

by

____ COURT-MARTIAL

Convened by____

(Title of convening authority)

(Command of convening authority)

______________________ on ______________________

(Place or places of trial) (Date or dates of trial)

Note. The title should be followed by an index. The form and content of this index will be as prescribed in publications of the Secretary concerned.

However, it should cover important phases of the trial such as: introductory matters, arraignment, motions, pleas, providence inquiry, pretrial agreement inquiry, prosecution case-in-chief, defense case, prosecution case in rebuttal, trial counsel argument, defense counsel argument, instructions, findings, allocution rights, prosecution matters in aggravation, defense sentencing case, prosecution rebuttal, trial counsel argument, defense counsel argument, sentencing instructions, appellate rights, sentencing, and review of the sentencing terms of any pretrial agreement.

Moreover, the index should also reflect all exhibits (prosecution, defense, and appellate) whether offered/accepted into evidence or not.

COPIES OF RECORD

Copies of record

__________ copy of record furnished the accused as per attached certificate or receipt.

__________ copies of record forwarded herewith.

RECEIPT FOR COPY OF RECORD

Receipt for record

I hereby acknowledge receipt of a copy of the above-described record of trial, delivered to me at __________ this day of __________, __________.
(Signature of accused)
(Name of accused)

CERTIFICATE

__________, __________ __________
(Place) (Date)

Certificate in lieu of receipt

I certify that on this day delivery of a copy of the above-described record of trial was made to the accused, __________, at
(Name of accused)
__________, by __________ and that the receipt of the accused had
(Place of delivery) (Means of Delivery)
not been received on the date this record was forwarded to the convening authority. The receipt of the accused will be forwarded as soon as it is received.
(Signature of trial counsel)
(Name of trial counsel)

Note. If the accused's defense counsel receives the record, the trial counsel must attach an explanation to the record. *See* R.C.M. 1104(b)(1)(C). The following format may be used:

The accused's defense counsel was served the accused's copy of the record because (the accused so requested in a written request, which is attached) (the accused so requested on the record at the court-martial) (the accused was transferred to __________) (the accused is absent without authority) (__________).
(Signature of trial counsel)
(Name of trial counsel)

Note. If the accused cannot be served and has no counsel to receive the record, an explanation for failure to serve the record will be attached to the record. *See* R.C.M. 1104(b)(1)(C). The following format may be used:

The accused was not served a copy of this record because the accused (is absent without authority) (__________). Accused has no defense counsel to receive the record because (defense counsel has been excused under R.C.M. 505(d)(2)(B)) (__________).
(Signature of trial counsel)
(Name of trial counsel)

GUIDE FOR PREPARATION OF RECORD OF TRIAL

Note. While entries in this guide below are single-spaced, all records are to be double-spaced with the exception of the pleas, findings, and sentence.

PROCEEDINGS OF A SPECIAL/GENERAL COURT-MARTIAL

[The military judge called the Article 39(a) session to order at/on board __________ at, ________ hours, ________ __________,
pursuant to the following orders:]
[Court-Martial Convening Order Number ______, __________,
dated __________.] (command that issued the order)
[END OF PAGE]

Note. Here insert a copy of the orders convening the court-martial and copies of any amending orders. Copies of any written orders detailing the military judge and counsel will be inserted here. *See* R.C.M. 503(b) and (c). Any request of an enlisted accused for enlisted court members will be inserted immediately following the convening orders, together with any declaration of the nonavailability of such enlisted persons unless marked as an appellate exhibit. *See* R.C.M.503(a)(2), 903. Any written request for trial by military judge alone (R.C.M. 903) or statement that a military judge could not be obtained (R.C.M. 201(f)(2)(B)(ii)) will be inserted at this point unless marked as an appellate exhibit.

MJ: This Article 39(a) session is called to order.

TC: This court-martial is convened by ....

Note. The reporter records all the proceedings verbatim from the time the military judge calls the court to order. Thereafter, the reporter will use only standard stock entries, reporter's notes, or gestures.

SSEs, Reporter's Notes and Gestures

Note. SSEs, reporter's notes, and gestures (non-verbatim observations) will be placed in brackets, with the exception of SSEs identifying witnesses, stages of examination, and individual voir dire.

Paragraphing

Note. The court reporter shall utilize proper paragraphing techniques (i.e., a new line of thought starts a new paragraph) when typing long narratives, such as the military judge's instructions, counsel arguments, and lengthy "Q and A." Additionally, start a new paragraph for each separate element in a list; i.e., elements of an offense, legal definitions, accused's rights, and oral stipulations.

Punctuation Marks

Note. Do not use exclamation marks, capital letters, bolding, or italics to inject emphasis into the record of trial. Two hyphens (--) or a one em dash (—) may be used where the speaker changes thought or subject and four hyphens (----) or a two em dashes (— —) may be used where one participant interrupts another. Use periods at the end of complete thoughts to avoid lengthy sentences. Avoid phonetic spelling.

Prefixes

Note. Indent 5 spaces from the left margin and type the appropriate prefix to indicate identity of the speaker followed by a colon and two spaces.

Questions and Answer

Note. When typing "Q and A," ensure at least two lines, or the entire text of a question or answer appear at the bottom of a page. Page break in appropriate places where necessary. Do not repeat the "Q" or "A" prefix at the top of the next page. To the extent practicable, use page breaks so that the answer to a question does not appear on a page separate from the question.

Sessions of court

Note. Each session of court, as well as each Article 39(a) session or bench conference, shall commence on a new page, separate from the other transcribed proceedings. The reporter should note the time and date of the beginning and ending of each session of the court, including the opening and closing of the court-martial during trial. For example:

[The (court-martial) (session) was called to order at __________ hours, __________.]
[The (court-martial) (session) was (adjourned) (recessed) at ________ hours, __________.]
[The court-martial closed at ________ hours, __________.]

Administration of oaths

Note. It is not necessary to record verbatim the oath actually used, whether it be administered to a witness, the military judge, counsel, or the members. Regardless of the form of oath, affirmation, or ceremony by which the conscience of the witness is bound, R.C.M. 807, only the fact that a witness took an oath or affirmation is to be recorded. However, if preliminary qualifying questions are asked a witness prior to the administration of an oath, the questions and answers should be recorded verbatim. These preliminary questions and answers do not eliminate the requirement that an oath be administered. The following are examples of the recording of the administration of various oaths:

[The detailed reporter, ____________, was sworn.]
[The detailed interpreter, ______________, was sworn.]
[The military judge and the personnel of the prosecution and defense were sworn.]
[The members were sworn.]

Accounting for personnel during trial

Note. After the reporter is sworn, the reporter will record verbatim the statements, of the trial counsel with respect to the presence of personnel of the court-martial, counsel, and the accused. The reporter should note whether, when a witness is excused, the witness withdraws from the courtroom or, in the case of the accused, whether the accused resumes a seat at counsel table. Similarly, if the military judge excuses a member as a result of challenge and the member withdraws, the reporter should note this fact in the record. In a special court-martial without a military judge, if a challenged member withdraws from the court-martial while it votes on a challenge, and then is excused as a result of challenge or resumes a seat after the court-martial has voted on a challenge, the reporter should note this fact in the record. Examples of the manner in which such facts should be recorded are as follows:

[The (witness withdrew from the courtroom) (accused resumed his/her seat at the counsel table).]
[______________, the challenged member, withdrew from the courtroom.]
[______________, resumed his/her seat as a member of the court-martial.]

Arraignment

Note. The original charge sheet or a duplicate should be inserted here. If the charges are read, the charges should also be transcribed as read. *See* R.C.M. 1103(b)(2)(D)(i).

Recording testimony

Note. The testimony of a witness will be recorded verbatim in a form similar to that set forth below for a prosecution witness:

____________ was called as a witness for the prosecution, was sworn, and testified as follows:

DIRECT EXAMINATION

Questions by the (trial counsel) (assistant trial counsel):

Q. State your full name, (etc.) ______________________________.
A. ____.
Q. ____?
A. ____.

CROSS-EXAMINATION

Questions by the (defense counsel) (assistant defense counsel) (individual military counsel) (civilian defense counsel):

Q. ____?
A. ____.

REDIRECT EXAMINATION

Questions by the (trial counsel) (assistant trial counsel):

Q. ____?
A. ____.

RECROSS-EXAMINATION

Questions by the (defense counsel) (assistant defense counsel) (individual military counsel) (civilian defense counsel):

Q. ____?
A. ____.

EXAMINATION BY THE COURT-MARTIAL

Questions by (the military judge) (member's name):

Q. ____?
A. ____.

REDIRECT EXAMINATION

Questions by the (trial counsel) (assistant trial counsel):

Q. ____?
A. ____.

RECROSS-EXAMINATION

Questions by the (defense counsel) (assistant defense counsel) (individual military counsel) (civilian defense counsel):

Q. ____?
A. ____.

Bench conferences and Article 39(a) sessions

Note. Bench conferences and Article 39(a) sessions should be recorded and incorporated in the record of trial. *See* R.C.M. 803.

b. *Examination of record by defense counsel*

Note. When the defense counsel has examined the record of trial prior to its being forwarded to the convening authority, the following form is appropriate:

Form

"I have examined the record of trial in the foregoing case.
(Captain) (Lieutenant) __________, Defense Counsel."

Note. If defense counsel was not given the opportunity to examine the record before authentication, the reasons should be attached to the record. *See* R.C.M. 1103(i)(l)(B).

c. *Authentication of record of trial*

Note. The authentication should be dated.

(1) By general or special court-martial with members and a military judge.

Military Judge

__________(Captain) (Colonel) __________, Military Judge [or (LTJG) (1LT)__________, Trial Counsel, because of (death) (disability) (absence) of the military judge)] [or (LCDR) (Major)__________, a member in lieu of the military judge and the trial counsel because of (death) (disability) (absence) of the military judge, and of (death) (disability) (absence) of the trial counsel].

(2) By general court-martial consisting of only a military judge.

Military Judge

(Captain) (Colonel) , Military Judge [or (LTJG) (1LT) Trial Counsel, because of (death) (disability) (absence) of the military judge] [or the court reporter in lieu of the military judge and trial counsel because of (death) (disability) (absence) of the military judge, and of (death) (disability) (absence) of the trial counsel].

(3) By special court-martial without a military judge.

President

(CDR) (LTC) , President [or (LTJG) (lLT) , Trial Counsel, because of (death) (disability) (absence) of the president] [or (LT) (CPT) , a member in lieu of the president and the trial counsel because of (death) (disability) (absence) of the president, and of (death) (disability) (absence) of the trial counsel].

Note. If the rank of any person authenticating the record has changed since the court-martial, the current rank should he indicated, followed by "formerly (list the former rank)."

d. *Exhibits.See* R.C.M. 1103(b)(2)(D)

Note. Following the end of the transcript of the proceedings, insert any exhibits which were received in evidence, or, with the permission of the military judge, copies, photographs, or descriptions of any exhibits which were received in evidence, followed by exhibits marked/offered, but not admitted, and any appellate exhibits.

e. *Attachments*

Note. Attach to the record the matters listed in R.C.M. 1103(b)(3).

f. *Certificate of correction. See* R.C.M. 1104(d)

Note. The certificate should be dated.

United States
v.

The record of trial in the above case, which was tried by the court-martial convened by , dated , (at) (on board) , on , is corrected by the insertion on page , immediately following line , of the following:
"[The detailed reporter, was sworn.]"
This correction is made because the reporter was sworn at the time of trial but a statement of that effect was omitted, by error, from the record.
R.C.M. 1104(d) has been complied with.

Note. The certificate of correction is authenticated as indicated above for the record of trial in the case.

Copy of the certificate received by me this day of , .

(Signature of accused)
(Name of accused)

Note. The certificate of correction will be bound at the end of the original record immediately before the action of the convening authority.

g. *Additional copies of the record* An original and a minimum of four copies of the record will be prepared of a verbatim record. Individual services may require additional copies. In a joint or common trial, an additional copy of the record must be prepared for each accused. *See* R.C.M. 1103(g)(1)(A).

APPENDIX 15
Record of Trial by Summary Court-Martial (DD Form 2329)

RECORD OF TRIAL BY SUMMARY COURT—MARTIAL

1a. NAME OF ACCUSED *(Last, First, MI)*	b. GRADE OR RANK	c. UNIT OR ORGANIZATION OF ACCUSED	d. SSN
Arthur N. Sherry	PFC	Co A, 1st Battalion, 61st Inf	111-11-1111

2a. NAME OF CONVENING AUTHORITY *(Last, First, MI)*	b. RANK	c. POSITION	d. ORGANIZATION OF CONVENING AUTHORITY
Gail L. Busybody	COL	Commander	61st Infantry Brigade

3a. NAME OF SUMMARY COURT-MARTIAL *(If SCM was accuser, so state.)*	b. RANK	c. UNIT OR ORGANIZATION OF SUMMARY COURT-MARTIAL
Ron F. Andrews	MAJ	2d Battalion, 61st Inf

(Check appropriate answer)	YES	NO
4. At a preliminary proceeding held on 20 September 19 93, the summary court-martial gave the accused a copy of the charge sheet.	X	
5. At that preliminary proceeding the summary court-martial informed the accused of the following.		
a. The fact that the charge(s) had been referred to a summary court-martial for trial and the date of referral.	X	
b. The identity of the convening authority.	X	
c. The name(s) of the accuser(s).	X	
d. The general nature of the charge(s).	X	
e. The accused's right to object to trial by summary court-martial.	X	
f. The accused's right to inspect the allied papers and immediately available personnel records.	X	
g. The names of the witnesses who could be called to testify and any documents or physical evidence which the summary court-martial expected to introduce into evidence.	X	
h. The accused's right to cross-examine witnesses and have the summary court-martial cross-examine on behalf of the accused.	X	
i. The accused's right to call witnesses and produce evidence with the assistance of the summary court-martial if necessary.	X	
j. That during the trial the summary court-martial would not consider any matters, including statements previously made by the accused to the summary court-martial, unless admitted in accordance with the Military Rules of Evidence.	X	
k. The accused's right to testify on the merits or to remain silent, with the assurance that no adverse inference would be drawn by the summary court-martial from such silence.	X	
l. If any findings of guilty were announced, the accused's right to remain silent, to make an unsworn statement, oral or written or both, and to testify and to introduce evidence in extenuation or mitigation.	X	
m. The maximum sentence which could be adjudged if the accused was found guilty of the offense(s) alleged.	X	
n. The accused's right to plead guilty or not guilty	X	

6. At the trial proceeding held on 21 September 19 93, the accused, after being given a reasonable time to decide, ☐ did ☒ did not object to trial by summary court-martial.
(Note: The SCM may ask the accused to initial this entry at the time the election is made.) ANS *(Initial)*

7a. The accused ☐ was ☒ was not represented by counsel. *(If the accused was represented by counsel, complete b, c, and d below.)*

b. NAME OF COUNSEL *(Last, First, MI)*	c. RANK *(If any)*

d. COUNSEL QUALIFICATIONS

DD FORM 2329, 84 AUG

8. The accused was arraigned on the attached charge(s) and specification(s). The accused's pleas and the findings reached are shown below:

CHARGE(S) AND SPECIFICATION(S)	PLEA(S)	FINDINGS (including any exceptions and substitutions)
Ch. I	NG	G
Spec. 1	NG	NG
Spec. 2	NG	G except "$74.00" substituting "$25.00"
Ch. II	G	G
Spec.	G	G
Add'l Ch.	NG	NG
Spec.	NG	NG

9. The following sentence was adjudged:

Confinement for 15 days, forfeiture of $200.00 pay per month for 1 month, and reduction to grade of E-1.

10. The accused was advised of the right to request that confinement be deferred. (Note: When confinement is adjudged.)

☒ YES ☐ NO

11. The accused was advised of the right to submit written matters to the convening authority, including a request for clemency, and of the right to request review by the Judge Advocate General.

☒ YES ☐ NO

12. AUTHENTICATION

Ryan J. Andrews — Signature of Summary Court Martial

21 September 1993 — Date

13. ACTION BY CONVENING AUTHORITY

The sentence is approved and will be executed.

Gail L. Busybody — Typed Name of Convening Authority

Commander — Position of Convening Authority

Commander — Rank

Gail L. Busybody — Signature of Convening Authority

29 September 1993 — Date

☆ GPO : 1984 O - 421-645 (17049)

APPENDIX 16
FORMS FOR ACTION

The forms in this appendix are guides for preparation of the convening authority's initial action. Guidance is also provided for actions under R.C.M. 1112(f). Appendix 17 contains forms for later actions. The forms are guidance only, and are not mandatory. They do not provide for all cases. It may be necessary to combine parts of different forms to prepare an action appropriate to a specific case. Extreme care should be exercised in using these forms and in preparing actions. *See* R.C.M. 1107(f) concerning contents of the convening authority's action.

In addition to the matters contained in the forms below, the action should show the headquarters and place, or the ship, of the convening authority taking the action, and the date of the action. The signature of the convening authority is followed by the grade and unit of the convening authority, and "commander" or "commanding" as appropriate.

When the sentence includes confinement, the place of confinement is designated in the action unless the Secretary concerned prescribes otherwise. If the place of confinement is designated in the action, service regulations should be consulted first. *See* R.C.M. 1113(d)(2)(C).

In actions on a summary court-martial, when the action is written on the record of trial (*see* Appendix 15) the words "In the case of __________ " may be omitted.

INITIAL ACTION ON COURT-MARTIAL SENTENCE—FINDINGS NOT AFFECTED

Forms 1–10 are appropriate when the adjudged sentence does not include death, dismissal, or a dishonorable or bad-conduct discharge.

Adjudged sentence approved and ordered executed without modification. See R.C.M. 1107(f)(4).

1. In the case of __________, the sentence is approved and will be executed. (__________ is designated as the place of confinement.)

Adjudged sentence modified. See R.C.M. 1107(d)(1), (f)(4).

—Adjudged sentence approved in part and ordered executed.

2. In the case of __________, only so much of the sentence as provides for __________ is approved and will be executed. (__________ is designated as the place of confinement.)

— Adjudged sentence approved; part of confinement changed to forfeiture of pay.

3. In the case of __________, so much of the sentence extending to __________ months of confinement is changed to forfeiture of $ __________ pay per month for __________ months. The sentence as changed is approved and will be executed. (__________ is designated as the place of confinement.)

Credit for illegal pretrial confinement. See R.C.M. 305(k); 1107(f)(4)(F).

4. In the case of __________, the sentence is approved and will be executed. The accused will be credited with __________ days of confinement against the sentence to confinement. (__________ is designated as the place of confinement.)

Suspension of sentence. See R.C.M. 1107(f)(4)(B); 1108(d).

— Adjudged sentence approved and suspended.

5. In the case of __________, the sentence is approved. Execution of the sentence is suspended for __________ (months) (years) at which time, unless the suspension is sooner vacated, the sentence will be remitted without further action.

— Adjudged sentence approved; part of sentence suspended.

6. In the case of __________, the sentence is approved and will be executed but the execution of that part of the sentence extending to (confinement) (confinement in excess of __________ months) (forfeiture of pay) (__________) is suspended for __________ (months) (years), at which time, unless the suspension is sooner vacated, the suspended part of the sentence will be remitted without further action. (__________ is designated as the place of confinement.)

Deferment of confinement and termination of deferment. See R.C.M. 1101(c); 1107(f)(4)(E).

—Adjudged sentence approved; confinement deferred pending final review.

7. In the case of ________, the sentence is approved and, except for that portion extending to confinement, will be executed. Service of the sentence to confinement (is) (was) deferred effective ____________ ________, and will not begin until (the conviction is final) (________), unless sooner rescinded by competent authority.

—Adjudged sentence approved; deferment of confinement terminated.

8. In the case of ________, the sentence is approved and will be executed. The service of the sentence to confinement was deferred on ____________. (____________) is designated as the place of confinement.)

— Adjudged sentence approved; deferment of confinement terminated previously.

9. In the case of ________, the sentence is approved and will be executed. The service of the sentence to confinement was deferred on ____________ ____________, and the deferment ended on ____________ 20____________; (____________ is designated as the place of confinement.)

Disapproval of sentence; rehearing on sentence only ordered. See R.C.M. 1107(e), (f)(4)(A).

10. In the case of ________, it appears that the following error was committed: (evidence of a previous conviction of the accused was erroneously admitted) (________). This error was prejudicial as to the sentence. The sentence is disapproved. A rehearing is ordered before a (summary) (special) (general) court-martial to be designated.

When the adjudged sentence includes death, dismissal, or a dishonorable or a bad-conduct discharge, forms 1-10 are generally appropriate, but several will require modification depending on the action to be taken. This is because death, dismissal, or a dishonorable or bad-conduct discharge may not be ordered executed in the initial action. Therefore, unless an adjudged punishment of death, dismissal, or a dishonorable or bad-conduct discharge is disapproved, changed to another punishment, or (except in the case of death) suspended, the initial action must specifically except such punishments from the order of execution. This is done by adding the words "except for the (part of the sentence extending to death) (dismissal) (dishonorable discharge) (bad-conduct discharge)," after the words "is approved and" and before the words "will be executed" in the action. (A death sentence cannot be suspended. *See* R.C.M. 1108(b).)

Forms 11-14 provide examples of actions when the sentence includes death, dismissal, or a dishonorable or bad-conduct discharge.

Adjudged sentence approved and, except for death, dismissal, or discharge, ordered executed. See R.C.M. 1107(f)(4).

11. In the case of ________, the sentence is approved and, except for the (part of the sentence extending to death) (dismissal) (dishonorable discharge) (bad-conduct discharge), will be executed. (____________ is designated as the place of confinement.)

Adjudged sentence modified. See R.C.M. 1107(d)(1), (f)(4). Note if the part of the sentence providing for death, dismissal, or a dishonorable or a bad-conduct discharge is disapproved, *see* Form 2 above.

12. In the case of ________, only so much of the sentence as provides for (death) (dismissal) (a dishonorable discharge) (a bad-conduct discharge) (and____________) is approved and, except for the part of the sentence extending to (death) (dismissal) (dishonorable discharge) (bad-conduct discharge), will be executed. (____________ is designated as the place of confinement.)

— Adjudged sentence approved; discharge changed to confinement.

13. In the case of ________, so much of the sentence extending to a (dishonorable discharge) (bad conduct discharge) is changed to confinement for________ months (thereby making the period of confinement total ________ months). The sentence as changed is approved and will be executed. (________ is designated as the place of confinement.)

Suspension of sentence. See R.C.M. 1107(f)(4)(B); 1108(d). Note. If the portion of the sentence extending to dismissal or a dishonorable or a bad-conduct discharge is suspended, Form 5 or Form 6, as appropriate, may be used. If parts of the sentence other than an approved dismissal or discharge are suspended, the following form may be used:

— Adjudged sentence approved; part of sentence,

other than dismissal or dishonorable or bad-conduct discharge, suspended.

14. In the case of ________, the sentence is approved and, except for that part of the sentence extending to (dismissal) (a dishonorable discharge) (a bad-conduct discharge), will be executed, but the execution of that part of the sentence adjudging (confinement) (confinement in excess of ____________) (forfeiture of pay) (____________) is suspended for ____________ (months) (years) at which time, unless the suspension is sooner vacated, the suspended part of the sentence will be remitted without further action. (________ is designated as the place of confinement.)

INITIAL ACTION ON COURT-MARTIAL WHEN FINDINGS AFFECTED

Findings are addressed in the action only when any findings of guilty are disapproved, in whole or part. *See* R.C.M. 1107(c), (f)(3). The action must also indicate what action is being taken on the sentence. Appropriate parts of the foregoing forms for action on the sentence may be substituted in the following examples as necessary.

Some findings of guilty disapproved; adjudged sentence approved.

15. In the case of ________, the finding of guilty of Specification 2, Charge I is disapproved. Specification 2, Charge I is dismissed. The sentence is approved and (except for that part of the sentence extending to (dismissal) (a dishonorable discharge) (a bad-conduct discharge)) will be executed. (________ is designated as the place of confinement.)

Finding of guilty of lesser included offense approved; adjudged sentence modified.

16. In the case of ________, the finding of guilty of Specification 1, Charge II is changed to a finding of guilty of (assault with a means likely to produce grievous bodily harm, to wit: a knife) (absence without authority from the (unit) (ship) (________) alleged from ________ to ________ (in violation of Article 86)) (________). Only so much of the sentence as provides for ________ is approved and (, except for the (dismissal) (dishonorable discharge) (bad-conduct discharge)), will be executed. (________ is designated as the place of confinement.)

Some findings of guilty and sentence disapproved; combined rehearing ordered. See 1107(e). A rehearing may not be ordered if any sentence is approved. *See* R.C.M. 1107(c)(2)(B); (e)(1)(c)(i).

17. In the case of ________, it appears that the following error was committed: (Exhibit 1, a laboratory report, was not properly authenticated and was admitted over the objection of the defense) ________. This error was prejudicial as to Specifications 1 and 2 of Charge II. The findings of guilty as to Specifications 1 and 2 of Charge II and the sentence are disapproved. A combined rehearing is ordered before a court-martial to be designated.

All findings of guilty and sentence disapproved; rehearing ordered. See R.C.M. 1107(c)(2)(B).

18. In the case of ________, it appears that the following error was committed: (evidence offered by the defense to establish duress was improperly excluded) (________). This error was prejudicial to the rights of the accused as to all findings of guilty. The findings of guilty and the sentence are disapproved. A rehearing is ordered before a court-martial to be designated.

All findings of guilty and sentence disapproved based on jurisdictional error; another trial ordered. See R.C.M. 1107(e)(2). Note. This form may also be used when a specification fails to state an offense.

19. In the case of ________, it appears that (the members were not detailed to the court-martial by the convening authority) (________). The proceedings, findings, and sentence are invalid. Another trial is ordered before a court-martial to be designated.

All findings of guilty and sentence disapproved; charges dismissed. See R.C.M. 1107(c)(2)(B).

20. In the case of ________, the findings of guilty and the sentence are disapproved. The charges are dismissed.

ACTION ON A REHEARING

The action on a rehearing is the same as an action on an original court-martial in most respects. It differs first in that, as to any sentence approved following the rehearing, the accused must be credited with those parts of the sentence previously executed or otherwise served. Second, in certain cases the convening authority must provide for the restoration of certain rights, privileges, and property. *See* R.C.M. 1107(f)(5)(A).

Action on rehearing; granting credit for previously executed or served punishment.

21. In the case of ________, the sentence is approved and (except for the (dismissal) (dishonorable discharge) (bad-conduct discharge)), will be executed. The accused will be credited with any portion of the punishment served from ________ 20____ to ________ 20____ under the sentence adjudged at the former trial of this case.

Action on rehearing; restoration of rights.

22. In the case of ________, the findings of guilty and the sentence are disapproved and the charges are dismissed. All rights, privileges, and property of which the accused has been deprived by virtue of the execution of the sentence adjudged at the former trial of this case on ________ 20____ will be restored.

23. In the case of ________, the accused was found not guilty of all the charges and specifications which were tried at the former hearing. All rights, privileges, and property of which the accused has been deprived by virtue of the execution of the sentence adjudged at the former trial of this case on ________ will be restored.

WITHDRAWAL OF PREVIOUS ACTION

Form 24 is appropriate for withdrawal of an earlier action. *See* R.C.M. 1107(f)(2) concerning modification of an earlier action. Form 24a is appropriate for withdrawal of previous action pursuant to instructions from reviewing authority pursuant to R.C.M. 1107(f)(2) or (g). When the action of a predecessor in command is withdrawn due to ambiguity, *see United States v. Lower*, 10 M.J. 263 (C.M.A. 1981).

24. In the case of ________, the action taken by (me) (my predecessor in command) on ________ is withdrawn and the following substituted therefor: ________.

24a. In the case of ________, in accordance with instructions from (The Judge Advocate General) (the ________ Court of Criminal Appeals) pursuant to Rule for Courts-Martial [1107(f)(2)] [1107(g)], the action taken by (me) (my predecessor in command) is withdrawn. The following is substituted therefor: ________.

FORMS FOR ACTIONS APPROVING AND SUSPENDING PUNISHMENTS MENTIONED IN ARTICLE 58a AND RETAINING ACCUSED IN PRESENT OR INTERMEDIATE GRADE.

Under the authority of Article 58a, the Secretary concerned may, by regulation, limit or specifically preclude the reduction in grade which would otherwise be effected under that Article upon the approval of certain court-martial sentences by the convening authority. The Secretary concerned may provide in regulations that if the convening or higher authority taking action on the case suspends those elements of the sentence that are specified in Article 58a the accused may be retained in the grade held by the accused at the time of the sentence or in any intermediate grade. Forms 25-27 may be used by the convening or higher authority in effecting actions authorized by the Secretary concerned in regulations pursuant to the authority of Article 58a.

If the convening authority or higher authority when taking action on a case in which the sentence includes a punitive discharge, confinement, or hard labor without confinement elects to approve the sentence and to retain the enlisted member in the grade held by that member at the time of sentence or in any intermediate grade, that authority may do so if permitted by regulations of the Secretary concerned whether or not the sentence also includes a reduction to the lowest enlisted grade, by using one of the following forms of action. The first action, Form 25, is appropriate when the sentence does not specifically provide for reduction. The second and third actions, Forms 26 and 27, are appropriate when the sentence specifically provides for reduction to the grade of E-1. The action set forth in Form 26 is intended for a case in which the accused is to be probationally retained in the grade held by that accused at the time of sentence. The action set forth in Form 27 is for a case in which the accused is to serve probationally in an intermediate grade.

Automatic reduction suspended; sentence does not specifically include reduction.

25. In the case of ________, the sentence is approved and will be executed, but the execution of that part of the sentence extending to (a dishonorable discharge) (a bad-conduct discharge) (confinement) (hard labor without confinement)

(and ________) is suspended for ________ (months) (years) at which time, unless the suspension is sooner vacated, the suspended part of the sentence will be remitted without further action. The accused will (continue to) serve in the grade of ________ unless the suspension of (the dishonorable discharge) (the bad-conduct discharge) (confinement) (hard labor without confinement) is vacated, in which event the accused will be reduced to the grade of E-1 at that time.

Automatic reduction and adjudged reduction to E-l suspended; accused retained in grade previously held.

26. In the case of ________ , the sentence is approved and will be executed, but the execution of that part of the sentence extending to (a dishonorable discharge) (a bad-conduct discharge) (confinement) (hard labor without confinement) (________), and reduction to the grade of E-1 is suspended for ________ (months) (years), at which time, unless the suspension is sooner vacated, the suspended part of the sentence will be remitted without further action. The accused will continue to serve in the grade of ________ unless the suspension of (the dishonorable discharge) (the bad-conduct discharge) (confinement) (hard labor without confinement), or reduction to the grade of E-1 is vacated, in which event the accused will be reduced to the grade of E-1 at that time.

Automatic reduction and adjudged reduction to E-l suspended; accused retained in intermediate grade.

27. In the case of ________ , the sentence is approved and will be executed but the execution of that part of the sentence extending to (a dishonorable discharge) (a bad-conduct discharge) (confinement) (hard labor without confinement), and that part of the reduction which is in excess of reduction to the grade of ________ is suspended for- ________ (months) (years) at which time, unless the suspension is sooner vacated, the suspended part of the sentence will be remitted without further action. The accused will serve in the grade of ________ unless the suspension of (the dishonorable discharge) (bad-conduct discharge) (confinement) (hard labor without confinement), or reduction to the grade of E-1, is vacated, in which event the accused will be reduced to the grade of E-1 at that time.

ACTION UNDER R.C.M. 1112(f). The forms for action for the officer taking action under R.C.M. 1112(f) are generally similar to the foregoing actions. The officer taking action under R.C.M. 1112 (f) may order executed all parts of the approved sentence, including a dishonorable or bad-conduct discharge, except those parts which have been suspended without later vacation unless the record must be forwarded under R.C.M. 1112(g)(1). *See* R.C.M. 1113(c)(1)(A). The following are additional forms which may be appropriate:

Sentence approved when convening authority suspended all or part of it.

28. In the case of ________ , the sentence as approved and suspended by the convening authority is approved.

Sentence approved and, when confinement was deferred, ordered executed. See R.C.M. 1101(c)(6).

29. In the case of ________ , the sentence is approved and the confinement will be executed. The service of the sentence to confinement was deferred on ________ . (________ is designated as the place of confinement.)

Sentence includes unsuspended dishonorable or bad-conduct discharge; order of execution. See R.C.M. 1113(c)(1) and (2).

30. In the case of ________ , the sentence is approved. The (dishonorable discharge) (bad-conduct discharge) will be executed.

Findings and sentence disapproved; restoration as to parts ordered executed by convening authority. See R.C.M. 1208(b).

31. In the case of ________ , the findings of guilty and the sentence are disapproved. The charges are dismissed. (The accused will be released from the confinement adjudged by the sentence in this case and all) (All) rights, privileges, and property of which the accused has been deprived by virtue of the findings and sentence disapproved will be restored.

Findings and sentence disapproved; rehearing authorized. See R.C.M. 1112(f).

32. In the case of ________ , it appears that the following error was committed: (Exhibit 1, a statement of the accused, was not shown to have been preceded by Article 31 warnings as required and was admitted over the objection of the defense) (________). This error was prejudicial to the rights of the accused as to the findings and the sentence. The case is returned to the convening au-

thority who may order a rehearing or dismiss the charges.

Action taken is less favorable to the accused than that recommended by the judge advocate. See R.C.M. 1112(e), (f).

33. In the case of ________, the sentence is approved. As this action is less favorable to the accused than that recommended by the judge advocate, the record and this action shall be forwarded to the Judge Advocate General for review under Article 69(b).

Action when approved sentence includes dismissal. See R.C.M. 1113(c)(2).

34. In the case of ________, the sentence is approved. The record shall be forwarded to the Secretary of the ________.

APPENDIX 17
FORMS FOR COURT-MARTIAL ORDERS

a. *Forms for initial promulgating orders*

[Note. The following is a form applicable in promulgating the results of trial and the action of the convening authority in all general and special court-martial cases. Omit the marginal side notes in drafting orders. *See* R.C.M. 1114(c).]

Heading

(General) (Special) (Headquarters) (USS)
Court-Martial Order No. ______ ______

[Note. The date must be the same as the date of the convening authority's action, if any.]

(Grade) (Name) (SSN) (Armed Force)
(Unit)

Arraignment

was arraigned (at/on board ______) on the following offenses at a court-martial convened by (this command) (Commander, ______).

Offenses

CHARGE I. ARTICLE 86. Plea: G. Finding: G.

Specification 1: Unauthorized absence from unit from 1 April 1984 to 31 May 1984. Plea: G. Finding: G.

[Note. Specifications may be reproduced verbatim or may be summarized. Specific factors, such as value, amount, and other circumstances which affect the maximum punishment should be indicated in a summarized specification. Other significant matters contained in the specification may be included. If the specification is copied verbatim, include any amendment made during trial. Similarly, information included in a summarized specification should reflect any amendment to that information made during the trial.]

Specification 2: Failure to repair on 18 March 1984. Plea: None entered. Finding: Dismissed on motion of defense for failure to state an offense.

[Note. If a finding is not entered to a specification because, for example, a motion to dismiss was granted, this should be noted where the finding would otherwise appear.]

CHARGE II. ARTICLE 91. Plea: NG. Finding: NG, but G of a violation of ARTICLE 92.

Specification: Disobedience of superior noncommissioned officer on 30 March 1984 by refusing to inspect sentinels on perimeter of bivouac site. Plea: NG. Finding: G, except for disobedience of superior noncommissioned officer, substituting failure to obey a lawful order to inspect sentinels on perimeter of bivouac site.

CHARGE III. ARTICLE 112a. Plea: G. Finding: G.

Specification 1: Wrongful possession of 150 grams of marijuana on 24 March 1984. Plea: G. Finding: G.
Specification 2: Wrongful use of marijuana while on duty as a sentinel on 24 March 1984. Plea: G. Finding G.
Specification 3: Wrongful possession of heroin with intent to distribute on 24 March 1984. Plea: NG.Finding: G.

CHARGE IV. ARTICLE 121. Plea: NG. Finding: G.

Specification: Larceny of property of a value of $150.00 on 27 March 1984. Plea: NG. Finding: G, except the word "steal," substituting "wrongfully appropriate."

Acquittal

If the accused was acquitted of all charges and specifications, the date of the acquittal should be shown: "The findings were announced on ______________."

SENTENCE

Sentence adjudged on ______________: Dishonorable discharge, forfeiture of all pay and allowances, confinement for 2 years, and reduction to the lowest enlisted grade.

Action of convening authority

ACTION

[Note. Summarize or enter verbatim the action of the convening authority. Whether or not the action is recited verbatim, the heading, date, and signature block of the convening authority need not be copied from the action if the same heading and date appear at the top of this order and if the name and rank of the convening authority are shown in the authentication.]

Authentication

[Note. *See* R.C.M. 1114(e) concerning authentication of the order.]

Joint or common trial

[Note. In case of a joint or common trial, separate trial orders should be issued for each accused. The description of the offenses on which each accused was arraigned may, but need not, indicate that there was a co-accused.]

b. *Forms for supplementary orders promulgating results of affirming action*

[Note. Court-martial orders publishing the final results of cases in which the President or the Secretary concerned has taken final action are promulgated by departmental orders. In other cases the final action may be promulgated by an appropriate convening authority, or by an officer exercising general court-martial jurisdiction over the accused at the time of final action, or by the Secretary concerned. The following sample forms may be used where such a promulgating order is published in the field. These forms are guides. Extreme care should be exercised in using them. If a sentence as ordered into execution or suspended by the convening authority is affirmed without modifications and there has been no modification of the findings, no supplementary promulgating order is required.]

Heading
**See* above.

Sentence -Affirmed

In the (general) (special) court-martial case of *(name, grade or rank, branch of service, and SSN of accused,)* the sentence to bad-conduct discharge, forfeiture of ______, and confinement for ______, as promulgated in (General) (Special) Court-Martial Order No. ______, (Headquarters) (Commandant, ______ Naval District) dated ______________, has been finally affirmed. Article 71(c) having been complied with, the bad-conduct discharge will be executed.

or

-Affirmed in part

In the (general) (special) court-martial case of *(name, grade or rank, branch of service, and SSN of accused,)* only so much of the sentence promulgated in (General) (Special) Court-Martial Order No. ______, (Headquarters) (Commandant, ______ Naval District) ______, dated ______, as provides for ______, has been finally affirmed. Article 71(c) having been complied with, the bad-conduct discharge will be executed.

or

In the (general) (special) court-martial case of *(name, grade or rank, branch of service, and SSN of accused,)* the findings of guilty of Charge II and its specification have been set aside and only so much of the sentence promulgated in (General) (Special) Court-Martial Order No. ______, (Headquarters) (Commandant, ______, Naval District) ______, dated ______, as provides for ______, has been finally affirmed. Article 71(c) having been complied with, the bad-conduct discharge will be executed.

or

Affirmed in part; prior order of execution set aside in part

In the (general) (special) court-martial case of *(name, grade or rank, branch of service, and SSN of accused,)* the proceedings of which are promulgated in (General) (Special) Court-Martial Order No. ______, (Headquarters) (Commandant, ______ Naval District) ______, dated ______, the findings of guilty of Charge I and its specification, and so much of the sentence as in excess of ______ have been set aside and the sentence, as thus modified, has been finally affirmed. Article 71(c) having been complied with, all rights, privileges, and property of which the accused has been deprived by virtue of the findings of guilty and that portion of the sentence so set aside will be restored.

Finding and sentence set aside

In the (general)(special) court-martial case of *(name, grade or rank, branch of service, and SSN, of accused,)* the findings of guilty and the sentence promulgated by (General) (Special) Court-Martial Order No. ______, (Headquarters) (Commandant, ______ Naval District), ______, dated ______, were set aside on ______. (The charges are dismissed. All rights, privileges, and property of which the accused has been deprived by virtue of the findings of guilty and the sentence so set aside will be restored.) (A rehearing is ordered before another court-martial to be designated.)

Authentication

See R.C.M. 1114(e).

c. *Forms for orders remitting or suspending unexecuted portions of sentence*

Heading

See a above.

Remissions; suspension *See* R.C.M. 1108

The unexecuted portion of the sentence to __________, in the case of *(Name, grade or rank, branch of service and SSN of accused,)* promulgated in (General) (Special) Court-Martial Order No. __________, (this headquarters) (this ship) (Headquarters __________) (USS __________), __________, __________, is (remitted) (suspended for __________, months, at which time, unless the suspension is sooner vacated, the unexecuted portion of the sentence will be remitted without further action).

Authentication

See R.C.M. 1114(e).

d. *Forms for orders vacating suspension*

[Note. Orders promulgating the vacation of the suspension of a dismissal will be published by departmental orders of the Secretary concerned. Vacations of any other suspension of a general court-martial sentence, or of a special court-martial sentence that as approved and affirmed includes a bad-conduct discharge or confinement for one year, will be promulgated by the officer exercising general court-martial jurisdiction over the probationer (Article 72(b)). The vacation of suspension of any other sentence may be promulgated by an appropriate convening authority under Article 72(c). *See* R.C.M. 1109.]

Heading

See a above.

Vacation of Suspension

So much of the order published in (General) (Special) (Summary) (Court-Martial Order No. __________) (the record of summary court-martial), (this headquarters) (this ship) (Headquarters __________) (USS __________), __________. __________, in the case of *(name, grade or rank, branch of service, and SSN)*, as suspends, effective __________ __________, execution of the approved sentence to (a bad-conduct discharge) (confinement for- __________ (months) (years)) (forfeiture of __________), (and subsequently modified by (General) (Special) Court-Martial Order No. __________, (this headquarters) (this ship) (Headquarters __________) (USS __________), __________. __________, is vacated. (The unexecuted portion of the sentence to __________ will be executed.) (__________ is designated as the place of confinement.)

[Note. *See* R.C.M. 1113 concerning execution of the sentence.]

Authentication

See R.C.M.1114(e).

e. *Forms for orders terminating deferment*

[Note: When any deferment previously granted is rescinded after the convening authority has taken action in the case, such rescission will be promulgated in a supplementary order. *See* R.C.M. 1101(c)(7)(C).]

Heading

See a above.

Rescission of deferment

The deferment of that portion of the sentence that provides for confinement for ________ (months) (years) published in (General) (Special) Court-Martial Order ________ (this headquarters) (this ship) (Headquarters ________) (USS ________), ________ ________, in the case of *(name, grade or rank, branch of service, and SSN of accused)* (is rescinded) (was rescinded on ________ ________.) The portion of the sentence to confinement will be executed. (________ is designated as the place of confinement.)

Authentication

See R.C.M. 1114(e).

[Note. Deferment may be terminated by an appropriate authority once the conviction is final under Article 71(c) and R.C.M. 1208(a). *See* R.C.M. 1101(c)(7).]

Heading

See a above.

In the (general) (special) court-martial case of *(name, grade or rank, branch of service, and SSN of accused,)* the sentence to confinement (and ________), as promulgated in (General) (Special) Court-Martial Order No. ________, (Headquarters) (Commandant, ________ Naval District) ________, dated ________, has been finally affirmed. Service of confinement was deferred on ________ ________. Article 71(c) having been complied with, the (bad-conduct discharge and the) sentence to confinement will be executed. (________ is designated as the place of confinement.)

Authentication

See R.C.M. 1114(e).

APPENDIX 18

Report of Proceedings to Vacate Suspension of a General Court-Martial or of a Special Court-Martial Sentence Including a Bad-Conduct Discharge or Confinement for One Year Under Article 72, UCMJ, and R.C.M. 1109 (DD Form 455)

REPORT OF PROCEEDINGS TO VACATE SUSPENSION OF A GENERAL COURT- MARTIAL SENTENCE OR OF A SPECIAL COURT-MARTIAL SENTENCE INCLUDING A BAD—CONDUCT DISCHARGE UNDER ARTICLE 72, UCMJ, and R.C.M. 1109

1a. TO: *(Name of Officer exercising general court-martial jurisdiction — Last, First, MI)* Rabino, Arthur K.	2a. FROM: *(Name of Officer exercising special court-martial jurisdiction — Last, First, MI)* Roberts, Leonard E.
b. TITLE Commander	b. TITLE Commander
c. ORGANIZATION 5000th Support Wing APO AP 99999	c. ORGANIZATION 5001st Support Group APO AP 99999

3a. NAME OF PROBATIONER *(Last, First, MI)*	b. RANK	c. SSN	d. ORGANIZATION
Dice, Morris L.	Airman	000-00-0000	5001st Support Group

4. DATA AS TO TRIAL BY COURT-MARTIAL. ATTACH A COPY OF THE COURT-MARTIAL ORDER AND ANY SUPPLEMENTARY ORDERS OR, IF NO COURT-MARTIAL ORDER HAS BEEN PROMULGATED OR IS AVAILABLE, ATTACH A SUMMARY OF THE CHARGES AND SPECIFICATIONS, FINDINGS, SENTENCE, INITIAL ACTION, AND ANY SUPPLEMENTARY ACTIONS. ATTACH A COPY OF THE WRITTEN NOTICE OF SUSPENSION (see R.C.M. 1108(c)).

5. ALLEGED VIOLATION(S) OF THE CONDITIONS OF SUSPENSION. (BRIEF STATEMENT AND DATE. See R.C.M. 1108(c) AND 1109(a) CONCERNING THE CONDITIONS OF SUSPENSION.)

Assault on Master Sgt Vic Timm, while in the execution of duties on 15 September 1993, in violation of Article 91.

(Check appropriate answer)	YES	NO
6. PURSUANT TO THE PROVISIONS OF ARTICLE 72, UCMJ, AND R.C.M. 1109, A HEARING WAS HELD ON THE ALLEGED VIOLATION(S) OF THE CONDITIONS OF SUSPENSION.	X	
7. BEFORE THE HEARING THE AUTHORITY CONDUCTING THE HEARING CAUSED THE PROBATIONER TO BE NOTIFIED OF (see R.C.M. 1109(d)(1)(B)):		
a. THE TIME, PLACE, AND PURPOSE OF THE HEARING.	X	
b. THE RIGHT TO BE PRESENT AT THE HEARING.	X	
c. THE ALLEGED VIOLATION(S) OF THE CONDITIONS OF SUSPENSION AND THE EVIDENCE EXPECTED TO BE RELIED ON.	X	
d. THE RIGHT TO BE REPRESENTED AT THE HEARING BY CIVILIAN COUNSEL PROVIDED BY THE PROBATIONER OR, UPON REQUEST, BY MILITARY COUNSEL DETAILED FOR THIS PURPOSE.	X	
e. THE OPPORTUNITY TO BE HEARD, TO PRESENT WITNESSES AND OTHER EVIDENCE, AND THE RIGHT TO CONFRONT AND CROSS-EXAMINE ADVERSE WITNESSES UNLESS THE HEARING OFFICER DETERMINES THAT THERE IS GOOD CAUSE FOR NOT ALLOWING CONFRONTATION AND CROSS-EXAMINATION.	X	
8a. THE PROBATIONER REQUESTED DETAILED MILITARY COUNSEL.	X	

b. NAME OF DETAILED COUNSEL *(Last, First, MI)*	c. RANK	d. ORGANIZATION
Young, Louise	Captain	Area Defense Counsel, APO AP 99999

	YES	NO
e. DETAILED COUNSEL WAS QUALIFIED WITHIN THE MEANING OF ARTICLE 27(b), UCMJ, and R.C.M. 502(d).	X	

NOTE: If this form is used and additional space is required for any item, enter the additional material in Block 18 or on a separate sheet. Identify such material with the proper heading (*Example: "24"*). Securely attach any additional sheet(s) and add a note in the appropriate item: "See Block 18" or "See additional sheet." This form may be used to vacate a suspended special court-martial sentence not including a bad-conduct discharge or a suspended summary court-martial sentence under R.C.M. 1109(e) by lining through or altering the form, as appropriate.

DD FORM 455, 84 AUG — EDITION OF OCT 69 IS OBSOLETE.

(Check appropriate answer)	YES	NO
9a. THE PROBATIONER INDICATED THAT HE/SHE WOULD BE REPRESENTED BY CIVILIAN COUNSEL PROVIDED BY HIM/HER.		X
b. NAME OF CIVILIAN COUNSEL *(Last, First, MI)* — c. ADDRESS OF CIVILIAN COUNSEL		
d. ENTRY OF APPEARANCE BY PROBATIONER'S CIVILIAN COUNSEL. I HEREBY ENTER MY APPEARANCE FOR THE ABOVE NAMED PROBATIONER AND REPRESENT THAT I AM A MEMBER IN GOOD STANDING OF THE FOLLOWING BAR(S) (LIST) OR LICENSED OR OTHERWISE AUTHORIZED TO PRACTICE LAW (EXPLAIN) [see R.C.M. 502(d)(3) CONCERNING QUALIFICATIONS]:		
e. SIGNATURE OF COUNSEL — f. DATE		
10a. DETAILED COUNSEL OR CIVILIAN COUNSEL WAS PRESENT THROUGHOUT THE PROCEEDINGS. *(If probationer waives the right to have counsel present throughout part or all of the proceedings after requesting detailed counsel or employing civilian counsel, complete b below.)*	X	
b. STATE CIRCUMSTANCES AND SPECIFIC PROCEEDINGS CONDUCTED IN ABSENCE OF COUNSEL.		
11. *(To be signed by probationer if answer to items 9 or 9 was "No." If probationer fails to sign, the hearing officer shall explain in Item 18.)* I have been informed and understand my right under R.C.M. 1109(d) to representation at this hearing by civilian counsel provided by me or, upon request, by detailed military counsel. I hereby knowingly waive my right to such: a. ☐ Detailed Counsel b. ☒ Civilian Counsel		
c. SIGNATURE OF PROBATIONER [illegible] — d. DATE 1 October 1993		
12a. THE PROBATIONER WAS AFFORDED THE RIGHT TO OBTAIN WITNESSES AND PRODUCE EVIDENCE [see R.C.M. 405(g)].	X	
b. IN THE PRESENCE OF PROBATIONER I QUESTIONED UNDER OATH ALL AVAILABLE WITNESSES AND EXAMINED DOCUMENTARY AND REAL EVIDENCE FOR BOTH SIDES. ANY DOCUMENTS AND REAL EVIDENCE WERE SHOWN TO THE PROBATIONER.	X	
c. THE PROBATIONER WAS AFFORDED THE RIGHT TO CROSS-EXAMINE ALL AVAILABLE WITNESSES.	X	
d. I HAVE SUMMARIZED THE EVIDENCE CONSIDERED IN EXHIBIT 1	X	
e. THE FOLLOWING WITNESSES REQUESTED BY THE ACCUSED WERE NOT AVAILABLE UNDER R.C.M. 405(g) FOR THE REASONS INDICATED. *(Explain why requested witnesses were unavailable and any alternatives to testimony under R.C.M. 405(g)(4) used.)*		

NAME *(Last, First, MI)*	REASON UNAVAILABLE	ALTERNATIVES

13. AFTER HAVING BEEN INFORMED OF THE RIGHT TO REMAIN SILENT OR MAKE A STATEMENT, THE PROBATIONER	YES	NO
a. INDICATED THAT HE/SHE DID NOT WISH TO MAKE A STATEMENT		X
b. MADE A STATEMENT SUMMARIZED IN EXHIBIT 2	X	

2

(Check appropriate answer)	YES	NO
14a. THERE ARE REASONABLE GROUNDS TO BELIEVE THAT THE PROBATIONER NOW OR AT THE TIME OF THE ALLEGED VIOLATION WAS NOT MENTALLY RESPONSIBLE (see R.C.M. 916(k)) OR IS NOW INCOMPETENT TO PARTICIPATE IN THE VACATION PROCEEDING (see R.C.M. 909).		X
b. INDICATE THE GROUNDS FOR SUCH BELIEF AND THE ACTION TAKEN.		
c. A REPORT OF MEDICAL OFFICERS UNDER R.C.M. 706 IS ATTACHED IN EXHIBIT __________.		X
15. IF PROBATIONER WAS CONFINED PENDING VACATION PROCEEDINGS UNDER R.C.M. 1109(c):		
a. I FIND THAT THERE IS PROBABLE CAUSE TO BELIEVE THAT THE PROBATIONER VIOLATED THE CONDITIONS OF SUSPENSION.	X	
b. I DO NOT FIND THAT THERE IS PROBABLE CAUSE TO BELIEVE THAT THE PROBATIONER VIOLATED THE CONDITIONS OF SUSPENSION AND ORDER HIS/HER RELEASE UNDER R.C.M. 1109(c)(1)(E).		
16. RECOMMENDATION OF THE OFFICER EXERCISING SPECIAL COURT-MARTIAL JURISDICTION OVER THE PROBATIONER.		
a. I RECOMMEND THAT THE SUSPENSION OF THE SENTENCE BE VACATED. *(Indicate type and amount of punishment, if any, to be vacated.)* Bad-Conduct Discharge	X	
b. I RECOMMEND THAT THE PROCEEDINGS TO VACATE SUSPENSION BE DROPPED.		
c. I RECOMMEND *(state other recommendation)*:		

17a. NAME OF OFFICER EXERCISING SPECIAL COURT MARTIAL JURISDICTION OVER PROBATIONER	b. RANK	c. ORGANIZATION
Leonard E. Roberts	LTC	5001st Support Group

d. SIGNATURE	e. DATE
Leonard E. Roberts	1 October 1993

18. REMARKS

Airman Basic Dice struck Master Sgt Timm in the face twice with a closed fist after Timm directed Dice to clean up his living area. Although Airman Dice testified that Timm was prejudiced against him because he was a probationer, no evidence of such bias was offered. Dice offered no other extenuating or mitigating evidence and the record reveals none. Dice had served under the suspended sentence for 2 weeks before this offense without previous incident. Dice was previously convicted by a special court-martial of disrespect and disobedience toward superior NCOs on two different occasions. I am satisfied that Dice is guilty of the offense of assaulting a superior NCO in the execution of office. I recommend that the suspension of the bad-conduct discharge be vacated.

REMARKS (Continued)

(Check appropriate answer)	YES	NO
19. DECISION OF THE OFFICER EXERCISING GENERAL COURT-MARTIAL JURISDICTION OVER PROBATIONER.		
a. VACATE SUSPENSION OF THE SENTENCE TO (specify type/amount of punishment to be vacated): Suspension of bad-conduct discharge vacated.	X	
b. NOT TO VACATE.		

c. OTHER (specify):

d. IF DECISION IS TO VACATE, INDICATE EVIDENCE RELIED ON:
Testimony of Master Sgt Timm and Airman I.C. Nitt and Warren Teed established Airman Dice assaulted Timm, without provacation, while Timm was in the execution of his office. Medical report reflects Timm was bruised on check and forehead. Dice therefore violated conditions of suspension.

e. IF DECISION IS TO VACATE, INDICATE REASONS FOR VACATING:
Airman Dice's offense strikes at the heart of military discipline and reflects his failure to adapt despite second chance. Bad-conduct discharge is appropriate.

20a. NAME OF OFFICER EXERCISING GENERAL COURT-MARTIAL JURISDICTION OVER PROBATIONER	b. RANK	c. ORGANIZATION
Arthur K. Rubino	MC	Commander 5000th Support Wing APO AP 99999

d. SIGNATURE	e. DATE
Arthur K Rubino	30 October 1993

4

GPO : 1984 O - 421-646 (17346)

APPENDIX 19

Waiver/Withdrawal of Appellate Rights in General and Special Courts-Martial Subject to Review by a Court of Military Review (DD Form 2330)

WAIVER/WITHDRAWAL OF APPELLATE RIGHTS IN GENERAL AND SPECIAL COURTS–MARTIAL SUBJECT TO REVIEW BY A COURT OF MILITARY REVIEW

NOTE: See R.C.M. 1203(b) concerning which cases are subject to review by a Court of Military Review. See R.C.M. 1110 concerning waiver or withdrawal of appellate review.

I have read the attached action dated 1 November 1993.

I have consulted with Lieutenant Fender, my (associate) defense counsel concerning my appellate rights and I am satisfied with his/her advice.

I understand that:

1. If I do not waive or withdraw appellate review —

   a. My court-martial will be reviewed by the Navy-Marine Corps Court of Military Review.

   b. The Court of Military Review will review my case to determine whether the findings and sentence are correct in law and fact and whether the sentence is appropriate.

   c. After review by the Court of Military Review, my case could be reviewed for legal error by the United States Court of Military Appeals, on petition by me or on request of the Judge Advocate General.

   d. If the Court of Military Appeals reviews my case, my case could be reviewed for legal error by the United States Supreme Court on petition by me or the Government.

   e. I have the right to be represented by military counsel, at no cost to me, or by civilian counsel, at no expense to the United States, or both, before the Court of Military Review, the Court of Military Appeals, and the Supreme Court.

2. If I waive or withdraw appellate review —

   a. My case will not be reviewed by the Court of Military Review, or be subject to further review by the Court of Military Appeals, or by the Supreme Court under 28 U.S.C. 1259.

   b. My case will be reviewed by a judge advocate for legal error, and I may submit in writing allegations of legal error for consideration by the judge advocate.

   c. After review by the judge advocate and final action in my case, I may petition the Judge Advocate General for correction of legal errors under Article 69(b). Such a petition must be filed within 2 years of the convening authority's action, unless I can show good cause for filing later.

   d. A waiver or withdrawal, once filed, cannot be revoked, and bars further appellate review.

Understanding the foregoing, I (waive my rights to appellate review) [redacted]. I make this decision freely and voluntarily. No one has made any promises that I would receive any benefits from this waiver/[redacted], and no one has forced me to make it.

James R. Richards	PFC
TYPED NAME OF ACCUSED	RANK OF ACCUSED
James R Richards	5 November 1993
SIGNATURE OF ACCUSED	DATE

DD FORM 2330, 84 AUG

STATEMENT OF COUNSEL

(Check appropriate block)

[X] 1. I represented the accused at his/her court-martial.

[ ] 2. I am associate counsel detailed under R.C.M. 1110(b). I have communicated with the accused's (detailed) (individual military) (civilian) (appellate) defense counsel concerning the accused's waiver/withdrawal and discussed this communication with the accused.

[ ] 3. I am substitute counsel detailed under R.C.M. 1110(b).

[ ] 4. I am a civilian counsel whom the accused consulted concerning this matter. I am a member in good standing of the bar of ______________________________.

[ ] 5. I am appellate defense counsel for the accused.

I have advised the accused of his/her appellate rights and of the consequences of waiving or withdrawing appellate review. The accused has elected to (waive) ~~(withdraw)~~ appellate review.

Dudley D. Fender	
TYPED NAME OF COUNSEL	UNIT OF COUNSEL
Lieutenant, JAGC, USN	
RANK OF COUNSEL	BUSINESS ADDRESS *(If Civilian Counsel)*
Dudley D. Fender	5 November 1993
SIGNATURE OF COUNSEL	DATE

☆ GPO : 1984 O – 421-646 (17050)

APPENDIX 20

Waiver/Withdrawal of Appellate Rights in General Courts-Martial Subject to Examination in the Office of the Judge Advocate General (DD Form 2331)

WAIVER/WITHDRAWAL OF APPELLATE RIGHTS IN GENERAL COURTS—MARTIAL SUBJECT TO EXAMINATION IN THE OFFICE OF THE JUDGE ADVOCATE GENERAL

NOTE: See R.C.M. 1201(b)(1) concerning which cases are subject to examination in the Office of the Judge Advocate General. See R.C.M. 1110 concerning waiver or withdrawal of appellate review.

I have read the attached action, dated 1 November 1993.

I have consulted with Captain Rater, my (associate) defense counsel concerning my appellate rights and I am satisfied with his/her advice.

I understand that:

1. If I do not waive or withdraw appellate review —

   a. My case will be examined in the Office of the Judge Advocate General to determine whether the findings and sentence are legally correct and whether the sentence is appropriate.

   b. After examination in the Office of the Judge Advocate General and final action in my case, I may petition the Judge Advocate General for review under Article 69(b). Such a petition must be filed within 2 years after the convening authority took action in my case, unless I can show good cause for filing later.

2. If I waive or withdraw appellate review —

   a. My case will not be examined in the Office of the Judge Advocate General under Article 69(a), UCMJ.

   b. My case will be reviewed by a judge advocate for legal error, and I may submit in writing allegations of legal error for consideration by the judge advocate.

   c. After review by the judge advocate and final action in my case, I may petition the Judge Advocate General for review under Article 69(b). Such a petition must be filed within 2 years after the convening authority took action in my case, unless I can show good cause for filing later.

   d. A waiver or withdrawal, once filed, may not be revoked.

3. Understanding the above, I hereby (waive my rights to appellate review) [redacted] I make this decision freely and voluntarily. No one has made any promises that I would receive any benefits from this waiver/[redacted], and no one has forced me to make it.

Gregory C. Johns
TYPED NAME OF ACCUSED

LCPL, USMC
RANK OF ACCUSED

Gregory C. Johns
SIGNATURE OF ACCUSED

5 November 1993
DATE

DD FORM 2331
84 AUG

STATEMENT OF COUNSEL

(Check appropriate block)

[X] 1. I represented the accused at his/her court-martial.

[ ] 2. I am associate counsel detailed under R.C.M. 1110(b). I have communicated with the accused's (detailed) (individual military) (civilian) (appellate) defense counsel concerning the accused's waiver/withdrawal and discussed this communication with the accused.

[ ] 3. I am substitute counsel detailed under R.C.M. 1110(b).

[ ] 4. I am a civilian counsel whom the accused consulted concerning this matter. I am a member in good standing of the bar of ______________________________

[ ] 5. I am appellate defense counsel for the accused.

I have advised the accused of his/her appellate rights and of the consequences of waiving or withdrawing appellate review. The accused has elected to (waive) [redacted] appellate review.

Libby Rater	LSSS, Camp Blank, GA
TYPED NAME OF COUNSEL	UNIT OF COUNSEL
Captain, USMC	
RANK OF COUNSEL	BUSINESS ADDRESS *(If Civilian Counsel)*
Libby Rater	5 November 1993
SIGNATURE OF COUNSEL	DATE

☆ GPO : 1984 0 - 421-646 (1704)

Analysis of R.C.M.

Analysis of
R.C.M.

APPENDIX 21
ANALYSIS OF RULES FOR COURTS-MARTIAL

Introduction

The Manual for Courts-Martial, United States, 1984, includes Executive Order No. 12473 signed by President Reagan on 13 April 1984. This publication also contains various supplementary materials for the convenience of the user.

History of the Manual for Courts-Martial. The President traditionally has exercised the power to make rules for the government of the military establishment, including rules governing courts-martial. *See* W. Winthrop, *Military Law and Precedents* 27–28 (2d ed. 1920 reprint). Such rules have been promulgated under the President's authority as commander-in-chief, *see* U.S. Const., Art. II, sec. 2, cl.1., and, at least since 1813, such power also has been provided for in statutes. *See*W. Winthrop, *supra* at 26–27. In 1875 Congress specifically provided for the President to make rules for the government of courts-martial. Act of March 1, 1775, Ch. 115. 18 Stat. 337. Similar authority was included in later statutes (*see e.g.*, A.W. 38 (1916)), and continues in Article 36 of the Uniform Code of Military Justice. *See also* Articles 18 and 56. *See generally Hearings on H.R. 3804 Before the Military Personnel Subcom. of the House Comm. on Armed Services*, 96th Cong., 1st Sess. 5–6, 14, 17–18, 20–21, 52, 106 (1979). In 1979, Article 36 was amended to clarify the broad scope of the President's rulemaking authority for courts-martial. Act of November 9, 1979, Pub. L.No. 96–107, Section 801(b), 93 Stat. 810,811. *See generally Hearings on H.R. 3804, supra.*

In the nineteenth century the President promulgated, from time to time, regulations for the Army. Those regulations were published in various forms, including "Manuals". W. Winthrop, *supra* at 28. Such publications were not limited to court-martial procedures and related matters; however, they were more in the nature of compendiums of military law and regulations. The early manuals for courts-martial were informal guides and were not promulgated by the President. *See* MCM, 1895 at 1, 2; MCM, 1905 at 3; MCM, 1910 at 3; MCM, 1917 at III. *See also* MCM, 1921 at XIX.

The forerunner of the modern *Manual for Courts-Martial* was promulgated by the Secretary of War in 1895. *See* MCM, 1895 at 2. *See also* Hearings on H.R. 3805, *supra* at 5. (Earlier Manuals were prepared by individual authors. *See e.g.*, A. Murray, *A Manual for Courts-Martial* (3d ed. 1893); H. Coppee, *Field manual for Courts-Martial* (1863)). Subsequent Manuals through MCM, 1969 (Rev.) have had the same basic format, organization, and subject matter as MCM, 1895, although the contents have been modified and considerably expanded. *See e.g.*, MCM, 1921 at XIX–XX. The format has been a paragraph format, numbered consecutively and divided into chapters. The subject matter has included pretrial, trial, and post-trial procedure. In MCM, 1917, rules of evidence and explanatory materials on the punitive articles were included. *See*, MCM, 1917 at XIV. The President first promulgated the Manual for Courts-Martial as such in 1921. *See* MCM, 1921 at XXVI.

Background of this Manual. During the drafting of the Military Rules of Evidence (*see* Analysis, Part III, introduction, *infra*), the drafters identified several portions of MCM, 1969 (Rev.) in specific areas. However, the project to draft the Military Rules of Evidence had demonstrated the value of a more comprehensive examination of existing law. In addition, changing the format of the Manual for Courts-Martial was considered desirable. In this regard it should be noted that, as indicated above, the basic format and organization of the Manual for Courts-Martial had remained the same for over 80 years, although court-martial practice and procedure had changed substantially.

Upon completion of the Military Rules of Evidence in early 1980, the General Counsel, Department of Defense, with the concurrence of the Judge Advocates General, directed that the Manual for Courts-Martial be revised. There were four basic goals for the revision. First, the new Manual was to conform to federal practice to the extent possible, except where the Uniform Code of Military Justice requires otherwise or where specific military requirements render such conformity impracticable. *See* Article 36. Second, current court-martial practice and applicable judicial precedent was to be thoroughly examined and the Manual was to be brought up to date, by modifying such practice and precedent or conforming to it as appropriate. Third, the format of the Manual was to be modified to make it more useful to lawyers (both military and civilian) and nonlawyers. Specifically, a rule as opposed to paragraph format was to be used and prescriptive rules would be separated from nonbinding discussion. Fourth, the procedures in the new Manual had to be workable across the spectrum of circumstances in which courts-martial are conducted, including combat conditions.

These goals were intended to ensure that the Manual for Courts-Martial continues to fulfill its fundamental purpose as a comprehensive body of law governing the trial of courts-martial and as a guide for lawyers and nonlawyers in the operation and application of such law. It was recognized that no single source could resolve all issues or answer all questions in the criminal process. However, it was determined that the Manual for Courts-Martial should be sufficiently comprehensive, accessible, and understandable so it could be reliably used to dispose of matters in the military justice system properly, without the necessity to consult other sources, as much as reasonably possible.

The Joint-Service Committee on Military Justice was tasked with the project. The Joint-Service Committee consists of representatives from each of the armed forces, and a nonvoting representative from the Court of Military Appeals. Since 1980 the Joint-Service Committee has consisted of Colonel (later Brigadier General) Donald W. Hansen, USA, 1980-July 1981 (Chairman, October 1980–July 1981); Colonel Kenneth A. Raby, USA, July

1981–January 1984 (Chairman, July 1981–September 1982); Captain Edward M. Byrne, USN, 1980–July 1981 (Chairman through September 1980); Captain John J. Gregory, USN, July 1981–January 1984; Colonel Richard T. Yery USAF, 1980–March 1982; Colonel John E. Hilliard, USAF, March 1982–October 1983 (Chairman, October 1982–October 1983); Colonel Thomas L. Hemingway, USAF, October 1983-January 1984 (Chairman, October 1983–January 1984); Lieutenant Colonel A.F. Mielczarski, USMC, 1980–July 1982; Lieutenant Colonel G.W. Bond, USMC, July 1982–October 1982, Lieutenant Colonel Gary D. Solis, USMC, October 1982–March 1983; Lieutenant Colonel George Lange, III, USMC, June 1983–January 1984; Commander William H. Norris, USCG, 1980–August 1981; Commander Thomas B. Snook, USCG, August 1981–September 1983; Captain William B. Steinbach, USCG, October 1983–January 1984; and Mr. Robert H. Mueller of the Court of Military Appeals (1980–January 1984).

In the summer of 1980, Commander James E. Pinnell, USN, and Major Frederic I. Lederer, USA, prepared an initial outline of the new Manual.

Drafting was done by the Working Group of the Joint-Service Committee on Military Justice. Since September 1980, when the drafting process began, the Working Group consisted of: Major John S. Cooke, USA (Chairman); Commander James E. Pinnell, USN; Lieutenant Colonel Richard R. James, USAF (1980–December 1982); Lieutenant Colonel Robert Leonard, USAF (December 1982 to January 1984); Major Jonathan R. Rubens, USMC; and Mr. John Cutts, and Mr. Robert Mueller of the staff of the Court of Military Appeals. Mr. Francis X. Gindhart and Mr. Jack McKay of the staff of the Court of Military Appeals also participated early in the drafting process. Clerical support was provided by the Court of Military Appeals. In this regard, Mrs. Gail L. Bissi has been instrumental in the success of this project.

The Working Group drafted the Manual in fourteen increments. Each increment was circulated by each service to various field offices for comment. Following such comment, each increment was reviewed in the respective offices of the Judge Advocate General, the Director, Judge Advocate Division, Headquarters, USMC, and the Chief Counsel, USCG, and in the Court of Military Appeals. Following such review, the Joint-Service Committee met and took action on each increment. After all increments had been reviewed and approved, the Code Committee approved the draft. At this time the Code Committee consisted of Chief Judge Robinson O. Everett, Judge William H. Cook, and Judge Albert B. Fletcher, of the Court of Military Appeals; Rear Admiral James J. McHugh, the Judge Advocate General, USN; Major General Hugh J. Clausen, The Judge Advocate General, USA; Major General Thomas Bruton, The Judge Advocate General, USAF; and Rear Admiral Edward Daniels, Chief Counsel, USCG. Brigadier General William H. J. Tiernan, USMC, also sat as an *ex officio* member.

Following approval by the Code Committee, the draft was made available for comment by the public. 48 Fed. Reg. 23688 (May 26, 1983). In September and October 1983, the comments were reviewed. The Working Group prepared numerous modifications in the draft based on comments from the public and from within the Department of Defense, and on judicial decisions and other developments since completion of the draft. In October 1983, the Joint-Service Committee approved the draft for forwarding to the General Counsel, Department of Defense, for submission to the President after coordination by the Office of Management and Budget.

On November 18, 1983, Congress passed the Military Justice Act of 1983. This act was signed into law by the President on December 6, 1983, Pub. L. No. 98–209, 97 Stat. 1393 (1983). The Working Group had previously drafted proposed modifications to the May 1983 draft which would be necessary to implement the act. These proposed modifications were approved by the Joint-Service Committee in November 1983 and were made available to the public for comment in December 1983. 48 Fed. Reg. 54263 (December 1, 1983). These comments were reviewed and modifications made in the draft by the Working Group, and the Joint-Service Committee approved these changes in January 1984. The draft of the complete Manual and the proposed executive order were forwarded to the General Counsel, Department of Defense in January 1984. These were reviewed and forwarded to the Office of Management and Budget in January 1984. They were reviewed in the Departments of Justice and Transportation. The Executive Order was finally prepared for submission to the President, and the President signed it on 13 April 1984.

A note on citation form. The drafters generally have followed the*Uniform System of Citation* (13th ed. 1981), copyrighted by the *Columbia, Harvard, and University of Pennsylvania Law Reviews* and the *Yale Law Journal*, subject to the following.

This edition of the Manual for Courts-Martial is referred to generally as "this Manual." The Rules for Courts-Martial are cited, *e.g.*, as R.C.M. 101. The Military Rules of Evidence are cited, *e.g.*, as Mil. R. Evid. 101. Other provisions of this Manual are cited to the applicable part and paragraph, *e.g.*, MCM, Part V, paragraph 1a(1) (1984).

The previous edition of the Manual for Courts-Martial will be referred to as "MCM, 1969 (Rev.)." Except as otherwise noted, this includes Exec. Order No. 11476, 34 Fed. Reg. 10,502 (1969), as amended by Exec. Order No. 11835, 40 Fed. Reg. 4,247 (1975); Exec. Order No. 12018, 42 Fed. Reg. 57,943 (1977); Exec. Order No. 12198, 45 Fed. Reg.16,932 (1980); Exec. Order No. 12223, 45 Fed. Reg. 58,503 (1980); Exec. Order No. 12306, 46 Fed. Reg. 29,693 (1981); Exec. Order No. 12315, 46 Fed. Reg. 39,107 (1981); Exec. Order No. 12340, 47 Fed. Reg. 3,071 (1982); Exec. Order No. 12383, 47 Fed. Reg. 42,317 (1982), and Executive Order No. 12460, Fed. Reg. (1984). Earlier editions of the Manual for Courts-Martial, will be identified by a complete citation.

The Uniform Code of Military Justice, 10 U.S.C. Sections 801–940, as amended by the Military Justice Act of 1983, Pub. L. No. 98–209, 97 Stat. 1393 will be cited as follows:

Each individual section is denominated in the statute as an "Article" and will be cited to the corresponding Article. *E.g.*, 10 U.S.C. Section 801 will be cited as "Article 1"; 10 U.S.C. Section 802 will be cited as "Article 2"; 10 U.S.C. Section 940 will be cited as "Article 140". The entire legislation, Articles 1 through 140, will be referred to as "the Code" or "the UCMJ" without citation to the United States Code. When a change from MCM, 1969 (Rev.) is based on the Military Justice Act of 1983, Pub. L. No. 98–209, 97 Stat, 1393 (1983), this will be noted in the analysis, with citation to the appropriate section of the act. When this analysis was drafted, the specific page numbers in the statutes at large were not available.

Composition of the Manual for Courts-Martial (1984)

a. *Executive Order (1983).*

The Executive Order includes the Manual for Courts-Martial, which consists of the Preamble, Rules for Courts-Martial, Military Rules of Evidence, the Punitive Articles, and Nonjudicial Punishment Procedure. Each rule states binding requirements except when the text of the rule expressly provides otherwise. Normally, failure to comply with a rule constitutes error. *See* Article 59 concerning the effect of errors.

b. *Supplementary Materials*

As a supplement to the Manual, the Department of Defense, in conjunction with the Department of Homeland Security, has published a Discussion (accompanying the Preamble, the Rules for Courts-Martial, and the Punitive Articles), this Analysis, and various Appendices.

(1) *The Discussion*

The Discussion is intended by the drafters to serve as a treatise. To the extent that the Discussion uses terms such as "must" or "will", it is solely for the purpose of alerting the user to important legal consequences that may result from binding requirements in the Executive Order, judicial decisions, or other sources of binding law. The Discussion itself, however, does not have the force of law, even though it may describe legal requirements derived from other sources. It is in the nature of treatise, and may be used as secondary authority. The inclusion of both the President's rules and the drafters' informal discussion in the basic text of the Manual provides flexibility not available in previous editions of the Manual, and should eliminate questions as to whether an item is a requirement or only guidance. *See e.g., United States v. Baker*, 14 M.J. 361, 373 (C.M.A. 1973). In this Manual, if matter is included in a rule or paragraph, it is intended that the matter be binding, unless it is clearly expressed as precatory. A rule is binding even if the source of the requirement is a judicial decision or a statute not directly applicable to courts-martial. If the President had adopted a rule based on a judicial decision or a statute, subsequent repeal of the statute or reversal of the judicial decision does not repeal the rule. On the other hand, if the drafters did not choose to "codify" a principle or requirement derived from a judicial decision or other source of law, but considered it sufficiently significant that users should be aware of it in the Manual, such matter is addressed in the Discussion. The Discussion will be revised from time to time as warranted by changes in applicable law.

(2) *The Analysis*

The Analysis sets forth the nonbinding views of the drafters as to the basis for each rule or paragraph, as well as the intent of the drafters, particularly with respect to the purpose of substantial changes in present law. The Analysis is intended to be a guide in interpretation. In that regard, note that the Analysis accompanied the project from the initial drafting stage through submission to the President, and was continually revised to reflect changes prior to submission to the President. Users are reminded, however, that primary reliance should be placed on the plain words of the rules. In addition, it is important to remember that the Analysis solely represents the views of staff personnel who worked on the project, and does not necessarily reflect the views of the President in approving it, or of the officials who formally recommended approval to the President.

The Analysis frequently refers to judicial decisions and statutes from the civilian sector that are not applicable directly to courts-martial. Subsequent modification of such sources of law may provide useful guidance in interpreting rules, and the drafters do not intend that citation of a source in this Analysis should preclude reference to subsequent developments for purposes of interpretation. At the same time, the user is reminded that the amendment of the Manual is the province of the President. Developments in the civilian sector that affect the underlying rationale for a rule do not affect the validity of the rule except to the extent otherwise required as a matter of statutory or constitutional law. The same is true with respect to rules derived from the decisions of military tribunals. Once incorporated into the Executive Order, such matters have an independent source of authority and are not dependent upon continued support from the judiciary. Conversely, to the extent that judicial precedent is set forth only in the Discussion or is otherwise omitted from the Rules or the Discussion, the continuing validity of the precedent will depend on the force of its rationale, the doctrine of *stare decisis*, and similar jurisprudential considerations. Nothing in this Introduction should be interpreted to suggest that the placement of matter in the Discussion (or the Analysis), rather than the rule, is to be taken as disapproval of the precedent or as an invitation for a court to take a different approach; rather, the difficult drafting problem of choosing between a codification and common law approach to the law frequently resulted in noncodification of decisions which had the unanimous support of the drafters. To the extent that future changes are made in the Rules or Discussion, corresponding materials will be included in the Analysis.

The Appendices contain various nonbinding materials to assist users of this Manual. The Appendices also contain indent type='h' amt='10.'s from pertinent statutes. These indent type='h' amt='10.'s are appropriated for judicial notice of law, *see* Mil. R. Evid. 201A, but nothing herein precludes a party from proving a change in law through production of an official codification or other appropriate evidence.

PART I. PREAMBLE

Introduction.

The preamble is based on paragraphs 1 and 2 of MCM, 1969 (Rev.). *See generally Military Justice Jurisdiction of Courts-Martial* , DA PAM 27–174, chapter 1 (May 1980.)

1. Sources of military jurisdiction

This subsection is based on paragraph 1 of MCM, 1969 (Rev.). The provisions of the Constitution which are sources of jurisdiction of military courts or tribunals include: Art I, sec. 8, cl. 1, 9–16, 18; Art. II, sec. 2; Art. IV, sec. 4; and the fifth amendment. As to sources in international law, *see e.g., Ex Parte Quirin*, 317 U.S. 1 (1942); Geneva Convention Relative to the Treatment of Prisoners of War, Aug. 12, 1949, arts. 82–84, 6 U.S.T. 3316, 3382, T.I.A.S. No. 3365, 75 U.N.T.S. 287. *See generally* DA PAM 27–174, *supra* at paragraph 1–3.

2. Exercise of military jurisdiction

Subsection (a) is based on the first paragraph of paragraph 2 of MCM, 1969 (Rev.).

For additional materials on martial law, *see* W. Winthrop, *Military Law and Precedent* 817–30 (2d ed. 1920 reprint); *Ex parte Milligan, 71 U.S. (4 Wall.) 2 (1866). See also* paragraph 3, sec. 1 of MCM, 1910 (concerning the exercise of martial law over military affiliated persons).

For additional materials on military government, *see* W. Winthrop, *supra* at 798–817; *Madsen v. Kinsella*, 343 U.S. 341 (1952); *Mechanics' and Traders' Bank v. Union Bank*, 89 U.S. (22 Wall.) 276 (1875).

For additional materials on the exercise of military jurisdiction under the law of war,*see* W. Winthrop, *supra* at 831–46; *Trials of War Criminals Before the Nuremberg Tribunals* (U.S. Gov't Printing Off., 1950–51); *Trials of the Major War Criminals Before the International Military Tribunal* (International Military Tribunal, Nuremberg 1947);*In re Yamashita*, 327 U.S. 1 (1946);*Ex parte Quirin, supra; Ex parte Milligan, supra*; Articles 18 and 21.

Subsection (b) is based on the second paragraph of paragraph 2 of MCM, 1969 (Rev.). *See also* Article 21; DA PAM 27–174, *supra* at paragraph 1–5 *a*; W. Winthrop, *supra* at 802–05, 835–36. As to provost courts, *see also Hearings on H.R. 2498 Before a Subcomm. of the House Comm. on Armed Services*, 81st Cong., 1st Sess. 975, 1061 (1949). As to trial of prisoners of war, *see* Article 2(a)(9) and Article 102, 1949 Geneva Convention Relative to the Treatment of Prisoners of War, *supra*

3. Purpose of military law

See generally Chappel v. Wallace, 462 U.S. 296, 103 S.Ct. 2362 (1983); *Parker v. Levy*, 417 U.S. 733 (1974); S.Rep. No. 53, 98th Cong., 1st Sess. 2–3 (1983). For a discussion of the nature and purpose of military law, *see* R. Everett, *Military Justice in the Armed Forces of the United States* (1956); J. Bishop, *Justice Under Fire* (1974); Hodson, *Military Justice: Abolish or Change?*, 22 Kan. L. Rev. 31 (1975), *reprinted in* Mil. L. Rev. Bicent. Issue 579 (1976); Hansen,*Judicial Functions for the Commander*, 41 Mil.L.Rev. 1 (1968); *Hearings on H.R. 2498 Before a Subcomm. of the House Comm. on Armed Services*, 81st Cong., 1st Sess. 606, 778–86 (1949); H. Moyer, *Justice and the Military* 5–23 (1972).

4. Structure and application of the Manual for Courts-Martial

Self-explanatory. *See also* the *Introduction* of the Analysis.

PART II. RULES FOR COURTS-MARTIAL

CHAPTER I. GENERAL PROVISIONS

Rule 101 Scope

(a) *In general.* This subsection is patterned after Fed. R. Crim. P. 1. "Courts-martial" are classified by Article 16. Supplementary procedures include all procedures directly relating to the court-martial process, such as preparation and authentication of the record, vacation proceedings, preparation of orders, and professional supervision of counsel and military judges. The rules do not govern imposition of nonjudicial punishment (*see* Part V) or administrative actions.

(b) *Title.* This subsection is patterned after Fed.R..Crim.P. 60.

Rule 102 Purpose and construction

This rule restates Fed. R. Crim. P. 2 in terms strictly limiting the application of these rules to military justice. *Accord*, Mil. R. Evid. 102.

Rule 103 Definitions

The drafters have, whenever possible, followed the definitions used in the United States Code. *See* subsection (20). Some definitions have been made and followed for convenience, to avoid frequent repetition of complicated phases. Others have been made to address variations in the terminology used among the services. The drafters have attempted to minimize the number of definitions. It is the drafters' intent that the words of the Manual be construed in accordance with their plain meaning, with due deference to previous usage of terms in military law or custom.

(1) *"Article."* This definition was added to reduce repetitive citations to the Uniform Code of Military Justice. MCM, 1969 (Rev.) and its predecessors used the same convention.

(2) *"Capital case."* This definition is based on the first two sentences of paragraph 15 *a* (3) of MCM, 1969 (Rev.).

2005 Amendment: The definition was amended to provide consistently with the contemporaneous amendment to R.C.M. 201(f)(1)(A)(iii)(b), which altered the default referral position for capital cases.

(3) *"Capital offense."* This definition is based on the first sentence of paragraph 15 *a*(2) of MCM, 1969 (Rev).

(4) *"Code."* This definition was added to avoid frequent repetition of "Uniform Code of Military Justice."

(5) *"Commander."* This definition was added to avoid frequent repetition of the longer phrase, "commanding officer or officer in charge." *See* Articles 1(3) and (4).

(6) *"Convening authority."* This provision is based on paragraph 84*a* of MCM, 1969 (Rev.).

(7) *"Copy."* This definition was added to ensure that no construction of the Manual could result in delays of cases for the sake of unavailable specialized forms or office equipment.

(8) *"Court-martial."* Articles 16 and 39(a).

(9) *"Days."* This definition is added for clarity. *Cf. United States v. Manalo*, 1 M.J. 452 (C.M.A. 1976).

(10) *"Detail."* DoD Dir. 5550.7, Incl. 1, para. C.8 (Sep. 28, 1966).

(11) *"Explosive."* 18 U.S.C. §§ 232(5); 844(j).

(12) *"Firearm."* 18 U.S.C. § 232(4).

(13) *"Joint."* This definition is based on Joint Chiefs of Staff Publication 1, Dictionary of Military and Associated Terms 187 (1 Jun 79).

(14) *"Members."* This term is defined to avoid confusion about the membership of courts-martial.

(15) *"Military judge."* Article 1 (10). As to presidents of special courts-martial, *see* Mil. R. Evid. 101(c). The latter aspect was added for convenience and brevity in drafting.

(16) *"Party."* This definition was required by adoption of the

texts of federal civilian rules, which frequently use the term. The code uses the same term. *See e.g.*, Article 49. The Military Rules of Evidence also use the term.

(17) *"Staff judge advocate."* This term was not defined in the previous Manuals. It is defined to avoid variations in nomenclature among the services.

(18) *"sua sponte."* *"sua sponte"* has been used frequently to avoid gender-specific language ("on his or her own motion"). Its use has been limited to passages expected to be used mainly by lawyers or with their assistance. Nonetheless, a definition is necessary for the benefit of a president of a special court-martial without a military judge.

(19) *"War, time of."* This definition applies only to R.C.M.1004(c)(6) and to Parts IV and V of the Manual. Parts II (except for R.C.M. 1004(c)(6) and III do not use or refer to "time of war." The phrase appears in several articles of the code, other than punitive articles. *See* Articles 2(a)(10); 43(a), (e), and (f); 71(b). The discussions of several rules address "time of war" in relation to these articles. *See* R.C.M. 202(a) Discussion (4); 407(b) Discussion; 907(b)(2)(B) Discussion.

"Time of war" is used in six punitive articles. *See* Articles 101, 105, and 106 (which define offenses that can occur only in time of war—Articles 101 and 106 are capital offenses), and Articles 85, 90, and 113 (which are capital offenses in time of war). *See also* Article 82. In addition, three offenses in Part IV use time of war as an aggravating circumstance. *See* paragraphs 37, 40, and 104.

The code does not define "time of war," and Congress has not generally defined the term elsewhere, despite the appearance of "time of war" and similar language in many statutes. *See e.g.*, 18 U.S.C. § 3287; 37 U.S.C. §§ 301(d); 301a(c), 301(a). In at least one instance Congress has expressly qualified the phrase "time of war" by saying "time of war declared by Congress." 37 U.S.C. § 310(a). *Compare* 37 U.S.C. § 310(a) *with* 37 U.S.C. § 301(d); 301a(c). *See also* S.Rep. No. 544, 89th Cong., 1st Sess. 13 (1965) which equates "all out war" to a declared war.

The legislative history of the code contains few references to this matter. The only direct reference, relating to the deletion of the phrase from Article 102, indicates that the working group which initially drafted the code considered "time of war" to mean "a formal state of war." *Hearings on H.R. 2498 Before a Subcomm. of the House of Comm. on Armed Services*, 81st Cong., 1st Sess. 1228–29 (1949). This reference is not cited in any of the decisions of the Court of Military Appeals construing "time of war."

Judicial decisions before the code had long recognized that a state of war may exist without a declaration of war. *See Bas. v. Tingy*, 4 U.S. (4 Dall.) 37 (1800); *Hamilton v. M'Claughry*, 136 F. 445 (10th Cir. 1905). *See also United States v. Ayers*, 4 U.S.C.M.A. 220, 15 C.M.R. 220 (1954) and cases cited therein, W. Winthrop, *Military Law and Precedents* 668 (2d ed. 1920 reprint). *See generally* Carnahan, *The Law of War in the United States Court of Military Appeals*, 22 A.F.L. Rev. 120 (1980–81); Stevens, *Time of War and Vietnam*, 8 A.F.JAGL.Rev. 23 (May–June 1966).

The Court of Military Appeals has held that time of war, as used in several provisions of the code, does not necessarily mean declared war. Under the court's analysis, whether a time of war exists depends on the purpose of the specific article in which the phrase appears, and on the circumstances surrounding application of that article. *See United States v. Averette*, 19 U.S.C.M.A. 363, 41 C.M.R. 363 (1970) ("time of war" under Article 2(a)(10) means declared war; court-martial jurisdiction over civilians is to be construed narrowly); *United States v. Anderson*, 17 U.S.C.M.A. 558, 38 C.M.R. 386 (1968) (Vietnam war was time of war for purpose of suspension of statute of limitations under Article 43(a)); *accord Broussard v. Patton*, 466 F.2d 816 (9th Cir. 1972)); *United States v. Anderten*, 4 U.S.C.M.A. 354, 15 C.M.R. 354 (1954) (Korean war was time of war for purpose of Article 85); *United States v. Taylor*, 4 U.S.C.M.A. 232, 15 C.M.R. 232 (1954) (Korean war was time of war for purpose of suspension of statue of limitations under Article 43(f)); *United States v. Ayers, supra* (Korea war was time of war for purpose of suspension of statute of limitations under Article 43(a)); *United States v. Christensen*, 4 U.S.C.M.A. 22, 15 C.M.R. 22 (1954) (Korean war was time of war for purpose of Article 90); *United States v. Bancroft*, 3 U.S.C.M.A. 3. 11 C.M.R. 3 (1953) (Korean war was time of war for purpose of Article 113).

The circumstances the Court of Military Appeals has examined to determine whether time of war exists include: the nature of the conflict (generally, there must exist "armed hostilities against an organized enemy;" *United States v. Shell*, 7 U.S.C.M.A. 646, 650, 23 C.M.R. 110, 114 (1957)); the movement to and numbers of United States forces in, the combat area; the casualties involved and the sacrifices required; the maintenance of large numbers of active duty personnel; legislation by Congress recognizing or providing for the hostilities; executive orders and proclamations concerning the hostilities; and expenditures in the war effort. *See United States v. Bancroft, supra* at 5, 11 C.M.R. at 5. *See also United States v. Anderson, supra; United States v. Shell, supra; United States v. Sanders*, 7 U.S.C.M.A. 21, 21 C.M.R. 147 (1956);*United States v. Ayers, supra*.

During the Korean war it was suggested that "time of war" existed only in the Far Eastern theater. The court did not have to decide this issue with respect to whether the death penalty was authorized for Articles 85, 90, or 113 because the President suspended the Table of Maximum Punishments (paragraph 117c of MCM (Army), 1949; paragraph 127c of MCM, 1951), only in the Far Eastern command. *See* Exec. Order No. 10149, 3 C.F.R. 1949–53 Comp. 326 (1950); Exec. Order No. 10247, 3 C.F.R. 1949–53 Comp. 754 (1951). *See also United States v. Greco*, 36 C.M.R. 559 (A.B.R. 1965). The question as to Articles 85, 90, or 113 did not arise during the Vietnam war because the Table of Maximum Punishments was not suspended. There are no reported cases concerning Articles 101 and 106, and the only prosecutions under Article 105 were, of course, for offenses arising in the theater of operations. *See, e.g., United States v. Dickenson*, 6 U.S.C.M.A. 438, 20 C.M.R. 154 (1955); *United States v. Gallagher*, 23 C.M.R. 591 (A.B.R. 1957).

The Court of Military Appeals rejected the argument that "time of war" is geolineartally limited with respect to Article 43. *See United States v. Taylor, supra; United States v. Ayers, supra. See also United States v. Anderson, supra.* The court's analysis in *Taylor* and *Ayers* suggests, however, that for some purposes "time of war" may be geolineartally limited. For purposes of the death penalty, the prerequisite findings of aggravating circumstances under R.C.M. 1004 would screen out offenses which did not substantially affect the war effort. Therefore, possible geolineart limitations in "time of war" would be subsumed in the necessary findings under R.C.M. 1004.

Based on the foregoing, for at least some purposes of the punitive articles, "time of war" may exist without a declaration of war. The most obvious example would be a major attack on the United States and the following period during which Congress may be unable to meet. *Cf. New York Life Ins. Co. v. Bennion*, 158 F.2d 260 (10th Cir. 1946), *cert, denied*, 331 U.S. 811 (1947). Moreover, as both the Korean and Vietnam conflicts demonstrated, United States forces may be committed to combat of substantial proportions and for extended periods, while for many possible reasons (*see Bas v. Tingy, supra at 44*) war is not formally declared.

It should be noted that, under the article-by-article analysis used by the Court of Military Appeals to determine whether time of war exists, "time of war" as used in Article 106 may be narrower than in other punitive articles, at least in its application to civilians. *See United States v. Averette, supra. See also* Article 104.

The definition does not purport to give the President power to declare war. *See United States v. Ayers, supra* at 227, 15 C.M.R. at 227; *United States v. Bancroft, supra* at 5, 11 C.M.R. at 5. Instead, it provides a mechanism by which the President may recognize, for purposes of removing or specifically raising the maximum limits on punishments for certain offenses under Part IV, that a "time of war" exists. This determination would be based on the existing circumstances. For purposes of codal provisions triggered by "time of war," this determination would be subject to judicial review to ensure it is consistent with congressional intent. *Cf. United States v. Bancroft, supra.* Nevertheless, a determination by the President that time of war exists for these purposes would be entitled to great weight.

Paragraph 127c(5) of MCM, 1969 (Rev.) and the ninth paragraph 127c of MCM, 1951 provided for suspension of the Table of Maximum Punishments as to certain articles upon a declaration of war. The President could, and did in the Korean war, suspend the limits the President had established for those offenses. Thus, the effect of the definition of "time of war" in R.C.M. 103(19) is similar to the operation of those paragraphs. In either case, a declaration of war or specific action by the President affects the maximum punishments. The definition under R.C.M. 103(19) also provides guidance, subject to judicial review as noted above, on the application of codal provisions.

(20) "The definitions and rules of construction in 1 U.S.C. §§ 1 through 5 and in 10 U.S.C. §§ 101 and 801." Self-explanatory.

1990 Amendment: The change to the discussion corrects a previous typolineartal omission of clause (20) and misplacement of definitions of rank and rating. The note following clause (19) is not part of the definitions of 10 U.S.C. § 101 and was added to clarify usage of the terms "rank" and "grade" in this Manual.

1998 Amendment: The Discussion was amended to include new definitions of "classified information" in (14) and "national security" in (15). They are identical to those used in the Classified Information Procedures Act (18 U.S.C. App. III § 1, *et. seq.*). They were added in connection with the change to Article 62(a)(1) (Appeals Relating to Disclosure of Classified Information). *See* R.C.M. 908 (Appeal by the United States) and M.R.E. 505 (Classified Information).

Rule 104 Unlawful command influence

This rule based on Article 37 and paragraph 38 of MCM, 1969 (Rev.). *See also United States v. Charette*, 15 M.J. 197 (C.M.A. 1983); *United States v. Blaylock*, 15 M.J. 190 (C.M.A. 1983); *United States v. Ledbetter*, 2 M.J. 37 (C.M.A. 1976); *United States v. DuBay*, 17 U.S.C.M.A. 147, 37 C.M.R. 411 (1967); *United States v. Wright*, 17 U.S.M.A. 110, 37 C.M.R. 374 (1967); *United States v. Hawthorne*, 7 U.S.C.M.A. 293, 22 C.M.R. 83 (1956). The discussion is based on H.R. Rep. No. 491, 81st Cong., 1st Sess. 21 (1949). As to supervision of military judges and counsel,*see* Articles 6, 26, and 27. Subsection (b)(2)(B) is retained. It is rare that a military judge in a special court-martial is not assigned to the judicial agency or activity of the service concerned. *See e.g.*, AR 27–10, para. 8–6b (3) (Nov. 1982). Subsection (b)(2)(B) ensures that in the unusual situation that it is necessary to detail a military judge not so assigned, the military judge's performance of judicial duties will not be the subject of comment or evaluation in an efficiency or fitness report prepared or reviewed by the convening authority. The second sentence in subsection (b)(2)(B) clarifies that the convening authority may comment only on the military judge's nonjudicial duties in such a report. Subsection (D) is new and clarifies that the military judge, members, and counsel are not immune from action for any offense they might commit while in that capacity, e.g. failure to repair.

Rule 105 Direct communications: convening authorities and staff judge advocates; among staff judge advocates

This rule, while new to the Manual for Courts-Martial, is based on Article 6(b). Congress intended that Article 6(b) serve several purposes. First, by requiring convening authorities to communicate directly with their staff judge advocates on matters relating to the administration of military justice, it was intended that the position and effectiveness of the staff judge advocate be enhanced. Second, by providing for communications among judge advocates, it was intended to emphasize the independence of staff judge advocates, which in turn would ensure that staff judge advocates exercise their judicial functions in a fair and objective manner. Lastly, and most importantly, Article 6(b) was intended to help prevent interference with the due administration of military justice. *See* H.R. Rep. No. 491, 81st Cong., 1st Sess. 12–13 (1949); S.Rep. 486, 81st Cong., 1st Sess.9 (1949); 95 Cong. Rec.H. 5721 (1949); 96 Cong. Rec.S 1356 (1950). *See also Cooke v. Orser*, 12 M.J. 335 (C.M.A. 1982); *United States v. Davis*, 18 U.S.C.M.A. 170, 39 C.M.R. 170 (1969); *United States v. Walsh*, 11 M.J. 858 (N.M.C.M.R. 1981).

Rule 106 Delivery of military offenders to civilian authorities

This rule is based on Article 14(a) and on the second paragraph of paragraph 12 of MCM, 1969 (Rev.). *See also United States v. Reed*, 2 M.J. 64 (C.M.A. 1976) (delivery and speedy trial); 18 U.S.C. Appendix II. The second sentence is new. It provides express authority for restraining an offender to be delivered to civilian authorities, but only when such restraint is justified under the circumstances. Note that this rule does not apply to delivery to a foreign government; this situation ordinarily is governed by status of forces agreements. This rule applies to delivery to authorities of the United States or its political subdivisions. Occasionally when civilian authorities request delivery of a servicemember, the delivery cannot be effected immediately, e.g., when the offender is overseas. In such situations, reasonable restraint may be necessary to ensure that the delivery can be effected and to protect the community. The person responsible for deciding whether to relinquish the offender must decide whether there are adequate grounds for restraint in such cases. This rule is not intended to permit the military to restrain an offender on behalf of civilian authorities pending trial or other disposition. Restraint imposed under this rule is strictly limited to the time reasonably necessary to effect the delivery. Thus, if the civilian authorities are dilatory in taking custody, the restraint must cease.

The discussion is based on Article 14(b).

Rule 107 Dismissed officer's right to request trial by court-martial

This rule is based on Article 4 and paragraph 111 of MCM, 1969 (Rev.). *See also* H.R. Rep. No. 491, 81st Cong., 1st Sess. 12 (1949); W. Winthrop, *Military Law and Precedents* 64 (2d ed. 1920 reprint). The text of 10 U.S.C. § 1161(a) is as follows:

(a) No commissioned officer may be dismissed from any armed force except—

(1) by sentence of a general court-martial;

(2) in communication of a sentence of a general court-martial; or

(3) in time of war, by order of the President.

Rule 108 Rules of court

This rule is new and is based on Fed.R.Crim. P. 57(a) and Article 140. *Cf.* Article 66(f). *See also United States v. Kelson*, 3 M.J. 139 (C.M.A. 1977). Depending on the regulations, rules of court may be promulgated on a service-wide, judicial circuit, or trial judge level, or a combination thereof. The rule recognizes that differences in organization and operations of services and regional and local conditions may necessitate variations in practices and procedures to supplement those prescribed by the code and this Manual.

The manner in which rules of court are disseminated is within the sole discretion of the Judge Advocate General concerned. Service-wide rules, for example, may be published in the same manner as regulations or specialized pamphlets or journals. Local rules may be published in the same manner as local regulations or other publications, for example. Parties to any court-martial are entitled to a copy, without cost, of any rules pertaining thereto. Members of the public may obtain copies under rules of the military department concerned. The penultimate sentence ensures that failure to publish in accordance with the rules of the Judge Advocate General (or a delegate) will not affect the validity of a rule if a person has actual and timely notice or if there is no prejudice within the meaning of Article 59. *Cf.* 5 U.S.C. § 552(a)(1).

Rule 109 Professional supervision of military judges and counsel

This rule is based on paragraph 43 of MCM, 1969, (Rev.). *See also* Articles 1(13), 6(a), 26, and 27. The previous rule was limited to conduct of counsel in courts-martial. This rule also applies to military trial and appellate judges and to all judge advocates and other lawyers who practice in military justice, including the administration of nonjudicial punishment and pretrial and posttrial matters relating to courts-martial. The rule also applies to civilian lawyers so engaged, as did its predecessor. The rule does not apply to lay persons. Nothing in this rule is intended to prevent a military judge from excluding, in a particular case, a counsel from representing a party before the court-martial over which the military judge is presiding, on grounds of lack of qualifications under R.C.M. 502(d), or to otherwise exercise control over counsel in accordance with these rules. *See e.g.*, R.C.M. 801.

1993 Amendment: Subsection (a) was amended to conform with subsection (c). The amendment to subsection (a) clarifies that the Judge Advocates General are responsible for the supervision and discipline of judges and attorneys. The amendment to subsection (a) is not intended to limit the authority of a Judge Advocate General in any way.

New subsection (c) is based on Article 6a, Uniform Code of Military Justice. Article 6a, U.C.M.J. was enacted by the Defense Authorization Act for Fiscal Year 1990. "Military Appellate Procedures," Tit. XIII, § 1303, National Defense Authorization Act for Fiscal Year 1990, Pub. L. No. 101-189, 103 Stat. 1352, 1576 (1989). The legislative history reveals Congressional intent that, to the extent consistent with the Uniform Code of Military Justice, the procedures to investigate and dispose of allegations concerning judges in the military should emulate those procedures found in the civilian sector. *See* H.R. Conf. Rep. No. 331, 101st Cong., 1st Sess. 656 (1989) [hereinafter Conf. Rep. No. 331]. The procedures established by subsection (c) are largely patterned after the pertinent sections of the American Bar Association's Model Standards Relating to Judicial Discipline and Disability Retirement (1978) [hereinafter ABA Model Standard] and the procedures dealing with the investigation of complaints against federal judges in 28 U.S.C. § 372 (1988). The rule recognizes, however, the overall responsibility of the Judge Advocates General for the certification, assignment, professional supervision, and discipline of military trial and appellate military judges. *See* Articles 6, 26 & 66, Uniform Code of Military Justice.

Subsection (c)(2) is based on the committee report accompanying the FY 90 Defense Authorization Act. *See* Conf. Rep. No. 331 at 658. This subsection is designed to increase public confidence in the military justice system while contributing to the integrity of the system. *See, Landmark Communications v. Virginia*, 435 U.S. 829 (1978).

The first sentence of the Discussion to subsection (c)(2) is based on the committee report accompanying the Defense Authorization Act. Conf. Rep. No. 331 at 358. The second and third sentences of the discussion are based on the commentary to ABA Model Standard 3.4. *See also, Chandler v. Judicial Council*, 398 U.S. 74 (1970).

Subsection (c)(3), (c)(5), and (c)(7) reflect, and adapt to the conditions of military practice, the general principle that judges should investigate judges.

The first paragraph of the Discussion to subsection (c)(3) is based on the commentary to ABA Model Standard 4.1.

The discussion to subsection (c)(4) is based on the commentary to ABA Model Standard 4.6.

The clear and convincing standard found in subsection (c)(6)(c) is based on ABA Model Standard 7.10.

Under subsection (c)(7), the principle purpose of the commission is to advise the Judge Advocate General concerned as to whether the allegations contained in a complaint constitute a violation of applicable ethical standards. This subsection is not intended to preclude use of the commission for other functions such as rendering advisory opinions on ethical questions. *See,* ABA Model Standard 9 on the establishment and role of an advisory committee.

Subsection (c)(7)(a) is based on ABA Model Standard 2.3, which provides that one-third of the members of a commission should be active or retired judges.

CHAPTER II. JURISDICTION

Rule 201 Jurisdiction in general

Introduction. The primary source of court-martial jurisdiction is Art. I, sec. 8, cl. 14 of the Constitution, which empowers Congress to make rules for the government and regulation of the armed forces of the United States. Courts-martial are recognized in the provisions of the fifth amendment expressly exempting "cases arising in the land or naval forces" from the requirement of presentment and indictment by grand jury. *See also* Part I, Preamble, for a fuller discussion of the nature of courts-martial and the sources of their jurisdiction.

(a) *Nature of court-martial jurisdiction.* Subsection (1) reiterates the first sentence of the second paragraph of paragraph 8 of MCM, 1969 (Rev.). The discussion is based on paragraph 8 of MCM, 1969 (Rev.). *Cf.* Fed R. Crim. P.7(c)(2); 18 U.S.C. §§ 3611–20. Courts-martial generally have the power to resolve issues which arise in connection with litigating criminal liability and punishment for offenses, to the extent that such resolution is necessary to a disposition of the issue of criminal liability or punishment.

Subsection (2) restates the worldwide extent of court-martial jurisdiction. Article 5. *See Autry v. Hyde*, 19 U.S.C.M.A. 433, 42 C.M.R. 35 (1970). The discussion points out that, despite the worldwide applicability of the code, geolineartal considerations may affect court-martial jurisdiction. *See* R.C.M. 202 and 203.

Subsection (3) restates the third paragraph of paragraph 8 of MCM, 1969 (Rev.). *See also Chenoweth v. Van Arsdall*, 22 U.S.C.M.A. 183, 46 C.M.R. 183 (1973), which held that Art. III, sec, 2, cl. 3 of the Constitution (requiring crimes to be tried in the state in which committed) does not apply to courts-martial. The second sentence is based on Article 18. *See also Geneva Convention Relative to the Protection of Civilian Persons in Time of War*, August 12, 1949, 6 U.S.T. 3516, T.I.A.S. No. 3365.

(b) *Requisites of court-martial jurisdiction.* This rule is derived from the fourth paragraph of paragraph 8 of MCM, 1969 (Rev.). The first sentence in the rule is new. *See Rosado v. Wyman*, 397 U.S. 397, 404 n.3 (1970); *Wickham v. Hall*, 12 M.J. 145, 152 n.8 (C.M.A. 1981). *Cf. Ex parte Poresky*, 290 U.S. 30 (1933). The rule expands the list of requisites for court-martial jurisdiction to conform more accurately to practice and case law. Requisite (3) has been added to reflect the distinction, long recognized in military justice, between creating a court-martial by convening it, and extending to a court-martial the power to resolve certain issues by referring charges to it. Thus, a court-martial has power to dispose only of those offenses which a convening authority has referred to it. Not all defects in a referral are jurisdictional. *See United States v. Blaylock*, 15 M.J. 190 (C.M.A. 1983). Requisite (5) is listed separately for the first time. This requisite makes clear that courts-martial have the power to hear only those cases which they are authorized by the code to try (i.e., offenses made punishable by the code, and, in the case of general courts-martial, certain offenses under the law of war). Second, it recognizes the important effect of *O'Callahan v. Parker* , 395 U.S. 258 (1969), on courts-martial. Although nothing in this rule or R.C.M. 203 is intended to codify the service-connection requirement of *O'Callahan* or later decisions, the requirement cannot be ignored in the Manual for Courts-Martial.

Requisites (1) and (2) restate two requisites in paragraph 8 of MCM, 1969 (Rev.). *See Generally United States v. Ryan*, 5 M.J. 97 (C.M.A. 1978); *United States v. Newcomb*, 5 M.J. 4 (C.M.A. 1978). Contrary to the holdings in *Ryan* and *Newcomb*, "errors in the assignment or excusal of counsel, members, or a military judge that do not affect the required composition of a court-martial will be tested solely for prejudice under Article 59." S.Rep. No. 53, 98th Cong., 1st Sess. 12 (1983). The second sentence of subsection (2) makes this clear, and also emphasizes that counsel is not a jurisdictional component of a court-martial. *See Wright v. United States*, 2 M.J. 9 (C.M.A. 1976). Requisite (4) is somewhat broader than the statement in MCM, 1969 (Rev.), since jurisdiction over the person has been affected by judicial decisions. *See e.g., McElroy v. United States ex. rel. Guagliardo*, 361 U.S. 281 (1960); *Reid v. Covert*, 354 U.S. 1 (1957); *United States v. Averette*, 19 U.S.C.M.A. 363, 41 C.M.R. 363 (1970). Thus it is misleading to refer solely to the code as determining whether jurisdiction over the person exists. The discussion restates the basic principle that the judgment of a court-martial without jurisdiction is void.

(c) *Contempt.* This subsection restates Article 48, except for the deletion of military commissions and provost courts. These tribunals are also governed by Article 48, but need to be mentioned in rules pertaining to courts-martial.

(d) *Exclusive and nonexclusive jurisdiction.* Subsection (d) is based on paragraph 12 of MCM, 1969 (Rev.). Military offenses are those, such as unauthorized absence, disrespect, and disobedience, which have no analog in civilian criminal law. The second paragraph of paragraph 12 is omitted here, as the subject now appears at R.C.M. 106. Concurrent jurisdiction of courts-martial and domestic tribunals was formerly discussed separately from concurrent jurisdiction of courts-martial and foreign tribunals. The present rule treats both at once since, for purposes of the rule, each situation is treated the same. The differing considerations and legal implications in the domestic and foreign situations are treated in the discussion. *See* R.C.M. 907(b)(2)(c) for a discussion of the former jeopardy aspects of exercise of jurisdiction by more than one agency or tribunal. With respect to the exercise of jurisdiction by the United States or a foreign government. *Wilson v. Girard*, 354 U.S. 524 (1957), establishes that the determination of which nation will exercise jurisdiction is not a right of the accused.

The first paragraph in the discussion reaffirms the policy found in DOD Directive 5525.1, Jan. 22, 1966 (superceded by DOD Directive 5525.1, Aug. 7, 1979), which is implemented by a triservice regulation, AR 27–50/SECNAVINST 5820.4E/AFR

110–12, Dec. 1, 1978, that the United States seeks to maximize jurisdiction over its personnel.

The second paragraph in the discussion restates the third paragraph in paragraph 12 of MCM, 1969 (Rev.), which was based on *The Schooner Exchange v. McFaddon and Others*, 11 U.S. (7 Cranch) 116 (1812). *See also Wilson v. Girard, supra.*

(e) *Reciprocal jurisdiction.* This subsection is based on Article 17 and paragraph 13 of MCM, 1969 (Rev.). It continues the express presidential authorization for the exercise of reciprocal jurisdiction and the delegation of authority (Article 140) to the Secretary of Defense to empower commanders of joint commands or task forces to exercise such power. *See United States v. Hooper*, 5 U.S.C.M.A. 391, 18 C.M.R. 15 (1955). It also continues the guidance in MCM, 1969 (Rev.) concerning the exercise of reciprocal jurisdiction by commanders other than those empowered under R.C.M. 201(e)(2). The language is modified to clarify that manifest injury is not limited to a specific armed force. The subsection adds a clarification at the end of subsection (3) that a court-martial convened by a commander of a service different from the accused's is not jurisdictionally defective nor is the service of which the convening authority is a member an issue in which the accused has a recognized interest. The rule and its guidance effectuate the congressional intent that reciprocal jurisdiction ordinarily not be exercised outside of joint commands or task forces (*Hearings on H.R. 2498 Before a Subcommittee of the House Committee on Armed Services*, 81st Cong., 1st Sess. 612–615; 957–958 (1949)) and is designed to protect the integrity of intraservice lines of authority. *See United States v. Hooper, supra* (Brosman, J. and Latimer, J., concurring in the result).

1986 Amendment: Subsections (e)(2) and (e)(3) were revised to implement the Goldwater-Nichols Department of Defense Reorganization Act of 1986, Pub.L. No. 99 - 433, tit. II, § 211(b), 100 Stat. 992. Because commanders of unified and specified commands (the combatant commands) derive court-martial convening authority from Article 22(a)(3), as added by this legislation, they need not be established as convening authorities in the Manual.

Paragraph (2)(A), which sets forth the authority of the combatant commanders to convene courts-martial over members of any of the armed forces, is an exercise of the President's authority under Article 17(a). In paragraph (2)(B), the first clause is a delegation from the President to the Secretary of Defense of the President's authority to designate general court-martial convening authorities. This provision, which reflects the current Manual, may be used by the Secretary of Defense to grant general court-martial convening authority to commanders of joint commands or joint task forces who are not commanders of a unified or specified command. The second clause of paragraph 2(b) is an exercise of the President's authority under Article 17(a).

Nothing in this provision affects the authority of the President or Secretary of Defense, as superior authorities, to withhold court-martial convening authority from the combatant commanders in whole or in part.

2005 Amendment: This rule clarifies that when a service member is tried by a court-martial convened by a combatant or joint commander, the implementing regulations and procedures of the service to which the accused is a member shall apply.

2005 Amendment: Subsections (e)(2)(B) and (C) were revised to clarify that the reciprocal jurisdiction authority of joint commanders designated in either subsections (A), (B), or (C), is limited. This limitation is intended to preclude a joint commander from convening courts upon members who are not assigned or attached to a joint command.

Subsection (4) has been added to avoid possible questions concerning detailing military judges from different services.

2005 Amendment: Subsection (e)(4) was amended to clarify that members and counsel from different services may be detailed to a court-martial convened by a combatant or joint commander.

Subsection (5) restates Article 17(b).

1986 Amendment: Subsection (6) was inserted in the context of the Goldwater-Nichols Department of Defense Reorganization Act of 1986, Pub. L. No. 99-433, tit. II, 100 Stat. 992, to specify the process for resolving disagreements when two organizations, at the highest levels of each, assert competing claims for jurisdiction over an individual case or class of cases. Under this legislation, the commanders of unified and specified commands are authorized to convene courts-martial. At the same time, the military departments retain authority over all aspects of personnel administration, including administration of discipline, with respect to all persons assigned to joint duty or otherwise assigned to organizations within joint commands. In effect, the combatant commands and the military departments have concurrent jurisdiction over persons assigned to such commands. Under most circumstances, any issues as to jurisdiction will be resolved between the military department and the joint command. Paragraph (6) has been added to provide a means for resolving the matter when the Service Secretary and the commander of the joint organization cannot reach agreement. *See* H.R. Rep. No. 824, 99th Cong., 2d Sess. (1986), at 125. Paragraph (6) also requires use of the same procedure when there is a disagreement between two Service Secretaries as to the exercise of reciprocal jurisdiction.

Subsection (7) was added to ensure that the Secretaries of the military departments retain responsibility for the administration of discipline, including responsibility for all persons in their departments assigned to joint duty.

Paragraphs (6) and (7) apply only when the commander is acting solely in his joint capacity or when he is seeking to assert jurisdiction over a member of a different armed force. There are various provisions of the Manual addressing the duties or responsibilities of superior authorities, and it was considered more useful to establish who may act as a superior authority as a general proposition rather than to specify in great detail the relationship between joint commanders and Service Secretaries as to each such matter. Accordingly, when action is required to be taken by an authority superior to a combatant commander, the responsibility is given to the Secretary of the Military Department that includes the armed force of which the accused is a member. This includes responsibility for acting on matters such as a request for counsel of the accused's own selection. An exception is expressly set forth in paragraph (6), however, which specifically provides the procedure for resolving disagreements as to jurisdiction. The Service Secretary cannot withhold or limit the exercise of jurisdiction under R.C.M. 504(b) or under Part V (Nonjudicial Punishment Procedure) by a combatant commander over persons assigned to the joint command. Such action may be taken, however, by the Secretary of Defense, who may assign responsibility to the military department or the unified command for any case or class of cases as he deems appropriate.

The amendments to R.C.M. 201 are designed to govern organizational relationships between joint commands and military departments over a range of issues, and are not intended to confer rights on accused servicemembers. These provisions reflect the President's inherent authority as Commander-in-Chief to prescribe or modify the chain of command, his specific authority under Article 17 to regulate reciprocal jurisdiction, and his authority (and that of the Secretary of Defense) under 10 U.S.C. §§ 161-65 (as added by the 1986 legislation) to prescribe or modify the chain of command.

To the extent that a commander of a joint organization is "dual-hatted" (i.e., simultaneously serving as commander of a joint organization and a separate organization within a military department), subsections (6) and (7) apply only to the actions taken in a joint capacity.

(f) *Types of courts-martial.* The source for subsection (1) is Article 18. This subsection is substantially the same as paragraph 14 of MCM, 1969 (Rev.), although it has been reorganized for clarity. Several statements in MCM, 1969 (Rev.) concerning punishments by general courts-martial have been placed in the discussion. As to the second sentence in subsection (1)(A)(i), *see also Wickham v. Hall*, 12 M.J. 145 (C.M.A. 1983); *Wickham v. Hall*, 706 F.2d 713 (5th Cir. 1983).

The source for subsection (2) is Article 19. Subsection (2) is based on paragraph 15 of MCM, 1969 (Rev.), although it has been reorganized for clarity. Note that under subsection (2)(C)(ii) a general court-martial convening authority may permit a subordinate convening authority to refer a capital offense to a special court-martial. This is a modification of paragraph 15 *a*(1) of MCM, 1969 (Rev.), which said a general court-martial convening authority could "cause" a capital offense to be referred to a special court-martial without specifying whether the convening authority had to make the referral personally. Subsection (2)(C)(iii) permits the Secretary concerned to authorize special court-martial convening authorities to refer capital offense to special courts-martial without first getting authorization from a general court-martial convening authority. Several statements in MCM, 1969 (Rev.) have been placed in the discussion.

2002 Amendment: Subsections (f)(2)(B)(i) and (f)(2)(B)(ii) were amended to remove previous limitations and thereby implement the amendment to 10 U.S.C. Sec. 819 (Article 19, UCMJ) contained in section 577 of the National Defense Authorization Act for Fiscal Year 2000, P. L. No. 106-65, 113 Stat. 512 (1999). Subject to limitations prescribed by the President, the amendment increased the jurisdictional maximum punishment at special courts-martial to confinement for one year and forfeitures not exceeding two-thirds pay per month for one year, vice the previous six-month jurisdictional limitation.

As to subsection (3) summary courts-martial are treated separately in R.C.M. 1301–1306.

2005 Amendment: Subsection (1)(A)(iii)(b) was changed to reflect that a convening authority must affirmatively act to refer a capital punishment eligible offense for trial as a capital case. Changing the default referral position for capital cases is consistent with the federal criminal practice of requiring affirmative steps before a case can be referred as capital, see, e.g., United States Attorneys' Manual, Chapter 9-10.000, as well as the affirmative steps required of the government in order to refer a court-martial as capital. It also provides a default construct that is applicable to the vast majority of actual capital eligible cases.

(g) *Concurrent jurisdiction of other military tribunals.* This subsection is based on the last paragraph in paragraph 12 of MCM, 1969 (Rev.).

Rule 202 Persons subject to the jurisdiction of courts-martial

(a) *In general.* This subsection incorporates by reference the provisions of the code (*see* Articles 2,3,4, and 73) which provide jurisdiction over the person. *See also* Articles 83, 104, 106. The discussion under this subsection briefly described some of the more important requirements for court-martial jurisdiction over persons. Standards governing active duty servicemembers (Article 2(a)(1)) are emphasized, although subsection (4) brings attention to limitations on jurisdiction over civilians established by judicial decisions.

Subsection (2)(A) of the discussion dealing with inception of jurisdiction over commissioned officers, cadets, midshipmen, warrant officers, and enlisted persons is divided into three parts. The first part, enlistment, summarizes the area of the law in the wake of the amendment of Article 2 in 1979. Act of November 9, 1979, Pub.L. No. 96–107, § 801(a), 93 Stat. 810–11. In essence, the amendment eliminated recruiter misconduct as a factor of legal significance in matters involving jurisdiction, and reestablished and clarified the "constructive enlistment" doctrine. The statutory enlistment standards concerning capacity under 10 U.S.C. §§ 504 and 505 thus become critical, along with the issue of voluntariness. As to whether an enlistment is compelled or voluntary, *compare United States v. Catlow*, 23 U.S.C.M.A. 142, 48 C.M.R. 758 (1974)*with United States v. Wagner*, 5 M.J. 461 (C.M.A. 1978) *and United States v. Lightfoot*, 4 M.J. 262 (C.M.A. 1978). *See also United States v. McDonagh*, 14 M.J. 415 (C.M.A. 1983).

The second paragraph under (i) *Enlistment* is based on *United States v. Bean*, 13 U.S.C.M.A. 203, 32 C.M.R. 203 (1962); *United States v. Overton*, 9 U.S.C.M.A. 684, 26 C.M.R. 464 (1958); and 10 U.S.C. § 1170. The last sentence is based on Article 2(c) which provides that in case of constructive enlistment, jurisdiction continues until "terminated in accordance with law or regulations promulgated by the Secretary concerned."

The last paragraph restates Article 2(c). The last sentence of that paragraph takes account of the legislative history of Article 2(c). *See* S.Rep. No. 197, 96th Cong., 1st Sess. 122 (1979), which indicates that *United States v. King*, 11 U.S.C.M.A. 19, 28 C.M.R. 243 (1959) is overruled by the statute. This is also reflected in the first paragraph under (ii) *Induction.*

The first paragraph of (ii) *Induction* is (with the exception of the application of the constructive enlistment doctrine,*see* the immediately preceding paragraph) based on *United States v. Hall*, 17 C.M.A. 88, 37 C.M.R. 352 (1967); *United States v. Rodriguez*, 2 U.S.C.M.A. 101, 6 C.M.R. 101 (1952); *United States v. Ornelas*, 2 U.S.C.M.A. 96 C.M.R. 96 (1952). *See also Billings v. Truesdell*, 321 U.S. 542 (1944); *Mayborn v. Heflebower*, 145 F.2d 864 (5th Cir. 1944), *cert. denied*, 325 U.S. 854 (1945).

The second paragraph under (ii) *Induction* is based on *United States v. Scheunemann*, 14 U.S.C.M.A. 479, 34 C.M.R. 259 (1964). *See also United States v. Wilson*, 44 C.M.R. 891 (A.C.M.R. 1971). Although no military case has so held, *dicta* and *Scheunemann* supports the second sentence.

As to (iii) *Call to active duty, see* 10 U.S.C. §§ 672, 673 and 673(a), *See also United States v. Peel*, 4 M.J. 28 (C.M.A. 1977).

The second paragraph of this section reflects decisions in *United States v. Barraza*, 5 M.J. 230 (C.M.A. 1978); *United States v. Kilbreth*, 22 U.S.C.M.A. 390, 47 C.M.R. 327 (1973).

1986 Amendment: Paragraph (2)(A)(iii) of the Discussion was amended and paragraph (5) was added to reflect amendments to Articles 2 and 3 of the UCMJ contained in the "Military Justice Amendment of 1986," tit. VIII, § 804, National Defense Authorization Act for fiscal year 1987, Pub.L. No. 99–661, 100 Stat. 3905 (1986), which, among other things, preserves the exercise of jurisdiction over reservists for offenses committee in a duty status, notwithstanding their release from duty status, if they have time remaining on their military obligation. The legislation also provides express statutory authority to order reservists, including members of the National Guard of the United States and the Air National Guard of the United States who commit offenses while serving on duty under Title 10 of the United States Code, to active duty for disciplinary action, including the service of any punishment imposed.

The first paragraph under (B)*Termination of jurisdiction over active duty personnel* restates the basic rule. *See United States v. Brown*, 12 U.S.C.M.A. 693, 31 C.M.R. 297 (1962); *United States v. Scott*, 11 U.S.C.M.A. 646, 29 C.M.R. 462 (1960). *See also United States v. Griffin*, 13 U.S.C.M.A. 213, 32 C.M.R. 213 (1962).

Subsection (B)(i) is based on *United States v. Wheeley*, 6 M.J. 220 (C.M.A. 1979); *United States v. Smith*, 4 M.J. 265 (C.M.A. 1978); *United States v. Hutchins*, 4 M.J. 190 (C.M.A. 1978); *United States v. Hout*, 19 U.S.C.M.A. 299, 41 C.M.R. 299 (1970). *See also Dickenson v. Davis*, 245 F.2d 317 (10th Cir. 1957).

Subsection (B)(ii) describes what jurisdiction remains under Article 3(a) in light of *United States ex rel. Toth v. Quarles*, 350 U.S. 11 (1955). *See also United States v. Clardy*, 13 M.J. 308 (C.M.A. 1982).

The exceptions is subsection (B)(iii) are restated in slightly different language for clarity from paragraph 11 *b* of MCM, 1969 (Rev.). Exception (*b*) is based on *United States v. Clardy, supra. See also* 14 M.J. 123 (C.M.A. 1982). As to exception (c), jurisdiction over prisoners in the custody of the armed forces, *see Kahn v. Anderson*, 255 U.S. 1 (1921); *United States v. Nelson*, 14 U.S.C.M.A. 93, 33 C.M.R. 305 (1963). *See also Mosher v. Hunter*, 143 F.2d 745 (10th Cir. 1944), *cert. denied*, 323 U.S. 800 (1945). Although it has not been judicially interpreted, the sentence of paragraph 11*b* of MCM, 1969 (Rev.) has been included here. The principle it expressed has long been recognized. *See* the last sentence in paragraph 11*b* of MCM, 1951; the last sentence of the third paragraph of paragraph 10 of MCM (Army), 1949; and the last sentence of the fourth paragraph of paragraph 10 of MCM, 1928. As to jurisdiction under Article 3(b), see *Wickham v. Hall*, 12 M.J. 145 (C.M.A. 1981); *Wickham v. Hall*, 706 F.2d 713 (5th Cir. 1983).

Subsection (3) described the jurisdiction under Article 2(a)(8). *See also* 33 U.S.C. § 855; 42 U.S.C. § 217.

Subsection (4) of the discussion points out that jurisdiction over civilians has been restricted by judicial decisions. *See generally Reid v. Covert*, 354 U.S. 1 (1957); *Toth v. Quarles, supra.* The MCM 1969 (Rev.) referred to such limitations only in footnotes to Articles 2(a)(10) and (11) and 3(a). The discussion of R.C.M. 202 is a more appropriate place to bring attention to these matters. A brief reference in the discussion was considered sufficient, while the analysis provides primary sources of law in the area, should an issue arise on the subject.

The second sentence in the subsection (4) of discussion is based on *McElroy v. United States ex rel. Guagliardo*, 361 U.S. 281 (1960); *Grisham v. Hagan*, 361 U.S. 278 (1960); *Kinsella v. United States ex rel. Singleton*, 361 U.S. 234 (1960); *Reid v. Covert, supra*. It is not settled whether "peacetime" as used in these decisions means all times other than a period of declared war or whether "peacetime" ceases when armed forces are involved in undeclared wars or hostilities. There is some authority for the latter view. *See* W. Winthrop, *Military Law and Precedents,* 101 (2d ed. 1920 reprint).

With respect to Article 2(a)(10), the Court of Military Appeals has held that "time of war" means a formally declared war (based on U.S. Const., art. I, sec. 8, cl. 11). *United States v. Averette*, 19 U.S.C.M.A. 363, 41 C.M.R. 363 (1970). *But cf. Latney v. Ignatius*, 416 F.2d 821 (D.C. Cir. 1969) (assuming without deciding that Article 2(a)(10) could be invoked during period of undeclared war, no court-martial jurisdiction existed over civilian merchant seaman for murder in Vietnam because crime and accused were not sufficiently connected with the military). *See also* Analysis, R.C.M. 103(19).

The words "in the field" and "accompanying an armed force" have also been judicially construed. "In the field" implies military operations with a view to the enemy. 14 Ops. Atty Gen. 22 (1872). The question whether an armed force is "in the field" is not to be determined by the locality in which it is found, but rather by the activity in which it is engaged. *Hines v. Mikell*, 259 F.28, 34 (4th Cir. 1919). Thus, forces assembled in the United States for training preparatory for service in the actual theater of war were held to be "in the field." *Hines v. Mikell, supra.* A merchant ship and crew transporting troops and supplies to a battle zone constitute a military expedition "in the field." *In re Berue*, 54 F. Supp. 252 (S.D. Ohio 1944); *McCune v. Kilpatrick*, 53 F.Supp. 80 (E.D. Va. 1943). *See also Ex parte Gerlach*, 247 F.616 (S.D.N.Y. 1917); *United States v. Burney*, 6 U.S.C.M.A. 776, 21 C.M.R. 98 (1956); *Hearings on H.R. 2498 Before a Subcomm. of the House Comm. on Armed Services*, 81st Cong., 1st Sess. 872–3 (1949). *But see*, W. Winthrop, *supra* at 100–102; *Reid v. Covert, supra* at 34 n. 61.

One may be "accompanying an armed force" although not directly employed by it or the Government. For example, an employee of a contractor engaged on a military project or serving on a merchant ship carrying supplies or troops is "accompanying an armed force." *Perlstein v. United States*, 151 F.2d 167 (3d Cir. 1945), *cert. dism.*, 328 U.S. 822 (1946); *In re DiBartolo*, 50 F.Supp. 929 (S.D.N.Y. 1943); *In re Berue, supra; McCune v. Kilpatrick, supra.* To be "accompanying an armed force" one's presence within a military installation must be more than merely incidental; it must be connected with or dependent upon the activities of the armed forces or its personnel. Although a person "accompanying an armed force" may be "serving with" it as well, the distinction is important because even though a civilian's contract with the Government ended before the commission of an offense, and hence the person is no longer "serving with" an armed force, jurisdiction may remain on the ground that the person is "accompanying an armed force" because of continued connection with the military. *Perlstein v. United States, supra; Grewe v. France* , 75 F.Supp. 433 (E.D. Wis. 1948).

McElroy v. Guagliardo, supra at 285–87, discusses possible methods for extending court-martial jurisdiction over civilians in some circumstances. To date these methods remain undeveloped. *See also* Everett and Hourcle, *Crime Without Punishment—Ex-servicemen, Civilian Employees and Dependents*, 13 A.F.JAG L. Rev. 184 (1971). Civilians may be tried by general court-martial under Article 18 and the law of war. *See* R.C.M. 201(f)(1)(B); 202(b). *See also* Article 21. This includes trial by court-martial in places where the United States is an occupying power. *See e.g., Madsen v. Kinsella*, 343 U.S. 341 (1952) [upholding jurisdiction of military commission to try a dependent spouse in occupied Germany in 1950. Although a state of war with Germany still technically existed (*see* Proclamation No. 2950, 3 C.F.R. (1948–53 Comp.) 135 (1951)) hostilities were declared terminated on 31 December 1946 (*see* Proclamation No. 2714, 3 C.F.R. (1948–53 Comp.) 99 (1947)) and the United States Supreme Court observed in dicta that military courts might have jurisdiction in occupied territory even in peacetime, 343 U.S. at 360)]. *See also Wilson v. Bohlender*, 361 U.S. 281, 283 n. 2 (1960); *Kinsella v. Singleton, supra* at 244.

(b) *Offenses under the law of war.* This subsection is based on Article 18. *See also* Article 21. The phrase "offense subject to trial by court-martial" or "offense triable by court-martial" is used in the R.C.M. in recognition of the fact that the Manual for Courts-Martial governs courts-martial for offenses under the law of war as well as under the code. *See e.g.*, R.C.M. 301(b); 302(c); 304(c); 305(d). In such contexts, the phrase does not include a requirement for a jurisdictional determination.

(c) *Attachment of jurisdiction over the person.* This subsection is based on paragraph 11*d* of MCM, 1969 (Rev.), and states the basic principle that once the jurisdiction of a court-martial attaches, it continues until the process of trial, appeal, and punishment is complete. *See generally United States v. Douse*, 12 M.J. 473 (C.M.A. 1982); *United States v. Sippel*, 4 U.S.C.M.A. 50, 15 C.M.R. 50 (1954).

The discussion clarifies the distinction between the existence of personal jurisdiction and the attachment of jurisdiction.*Compare United States v. Douse, supra* at 479 (Everett, C.J., concurring in the result); *United States v. Wheeley*, 6 M.J. 220 (C.M.A. 1979); *United States v. Hutchins*, 4 M.J. 190 (C.M.A. 1978); and *United States v. Hout, supra* (opinion of Quinn, C.J.) *with United States v. Douse, supra* (opinion of Cook, J.); *United States v. Smith*, 4 M.J. 265 (C.M.A. 1978); *United States v. Hout, supra* at 302; 41 C.M.R. 299, 302 (1970) (Darden, J., concurring in the result); and *United States v. Rubenstein*, 7 U.S.C.M.A. 523, 22 C.M.R. 313 (1957). *See also* W. Winthrop, *supra* at 90–91.

Subsection (2) includes examples of means by which jurisdiction may attach. They are taken from paragraph 11 *d* of MCM, 1969 (Rev.) although "filing of charges" has been clarified to mean preferral of charges. *See United States v. Hout, supra.* This list is not exhaustive. *See United States v. Self*, 13 M.J. 132 (C.M.A. 1982); *United States v. Douse, supra; United States v. Smith, supra. See also United States v. Fitzpatrick*, 14 M.J. 394 (C.M.A. 1983); *United States v. Handy*, 14 M.J. 202 (C.M.A. 1982); *United States v. Wheeley, supra; United States v. Rubenstein, supra; United States v. Mansbarger*, 20 C.M.R. 449 (A.B.R. 1955).

Rule 203 Jurisdiction over the offense

This rule is intended to provide for the maximum possible court-martial jurisdiction over offenses. Since the constitutional limits of subject-matter jurisdiction are matters of judicial interpretation, specific rules are of limited value and may unnecessarily restrict jurisdiction more than is constitutionally required. Specific standards derived from current case law are treated in the discussion.

The discussion begins with a brief description of the rule under *O'Callahan v. Parker*, 395 U.S. 258 (1969). It also describes the requirements established in *United States v. Alef*, 3 M.J. 414 (C.M.A. 1977) to plead and prove jurisdiction. *See also* R.C.M. 907(b)(1)(A). The last three sentences in subsection (b) of the discussion are based on*United States v. Lockwood*, 15 M.J. 1 (C.M.A. 1983). The remainder of the discussion reflects the Working Group's analysis of the application of service-connection as currently construed in judicial decisions. It is not intended as endorsement or criticism of that construction.

Subsection (c) of the discussion lists the*Relford* factors, which are starting points in service-connection analysis, although the nine additional considerations in *Relford* are also significant. These factors are not exhaustive. *United States v. Lockwood, supra. See also United States v. Trottier*, 9 M.J. 337 (C.M.A. 1980). *Relford* itself establishes the basis for (c)(2) and (c)(3) of the discussion. It has never been seriously contended that purely military offenses are not service-connected per se. *See Relford* factor number 12. Decisions uniformly have held that offenses committed on a military installation are service-connected. *See, e.g., United States v. Hedlund, supra; United States v. Daniels*, 19 U.S.C.M.A. 529, 42 C.M.R. 131 (1970). *See Relford* factors 2, 3, 10, and 11. As to the third sentence in (c)(3), *see United States v. Seivers*, 8 M.J. 63 (C.M.A. 1979); *United States v. Escobar*, 7 M.J. 197 (C.M.A. 1979); *United States v. Crapo*, 18 U.S.C.M.A. 594, 40 C.M.R. 306 (1969); *Harkcom v. Parker*, 439 F.2d 265 (3d Cir. 1971). With respect to the fourth sentence of (c)(3), *see United States v. Hedlund, supra; United States v. Riehle*, 18 U.S.C.M.A. 603, 40 C.M.R. 315 (1969). *But cf. United States v. Lockwood, supra.* Although much of the reasoning in *United States v. McCarthy*, 2 M.J. 26 (C.M.A. 1976) has been repudiated by *United States v. Trottier, supra*, the holding of *McCarthy* still appears to support the penultimate sentence in (c)(3). *See also United States v. Lockwood, supra; United States v. Gladue*, 4 M.J. 1 (C.M.A. 1977). The last sentence is based on *United States v. Lockwood, supra.*

The discussion of drug offenses in (c)(4) is taken from *United States v. Trottier, supra.*

As to (c)(5), the first sentence is based on *United States v. Lockwood, supra.* Whether the military status of the victim or the accused's use of military identification card can independently support service-connection is not established by the holding in *Lockwood.* The second sentence is based on *United States v. Whatley*, 5 M.J. 39 (C.M.A. 1978); *United States v. Moore*, 1 M.J. 448 (C.M.A. 1976). The last sentence is based on *United States v. Conn, supra; United States v. Borys*, 18 U.S.C.M.A. 547, 40 C.M.R. 259 (1969) (officer status of accused does not establish service-connection under Article 134) (note: service-connection of Article 133 offenses has not been judicially determined); *United States v. Saulter*, 5 M.J. 281 (C.M.A. 1978); *United States v. Conn, supra* (fact that accused was military policeman did not establish service-connection); *United States v. Armes*, 19 U.S.C.M.A. 15, 41 C.M.R. 15 (1969) (wearing uniform during commission of offense does not establish service-connection).

Subsection (c)(6) of the discussion indicates that virtually all offenses by servicemembers in time of declared war are service-connected. There is little case authority on this point. The issue was apparently not addressed during the conflict in Vietnam; of course, the overseas exception provided jurisdiction over offenses committed in the theater of hostilities. The emphasis in *O'Callahan* on the fact that the offenses occurred in peacetime (*see Relford* factor number 5) strongly suggests a different balance in time of war. Furthermore, in *Warner v. Flemings*, a companion case decided with *Gosa v. Mayden*, 413 U.S. 665 (1973), Justices Douglas and Stewart concurred in the result in upholding Flemings' court-martial conviction for stealing an automobile while off post and absent without authority in 1944, on grounds that such an offense, during a congressionally declared war, is service-connected. The other Justices did not reach this question. Assigning *Relford* factor number 5 such extensive, indeed controlling, weight during time of declared war is appropriate in view of the need for broad and clear jurisdictional lines in such a period.

Subsection (d) of the discussion lists recognized exceptions to the service-connection requirement. The overseas exception was first recognized in *United States v. Weinstein*, 19 U.S.C.M.A. 29, 41 C.M.R. 29 (1969). *See also United States v. Keaton*, 19 U.S.C.M.A. 64, 41 C.M.R. 64 (1969). The overseas exception flows from *O'Callahan's* basic premise: that the service-connection requirement is necessary to protect the constitutional right of service members to indictment by grand jury and trial by jury. While this premise might not be evident from a reading of *O'Callahan* alone, the Supreme Court subsequently confirmed that this was the basis of the *O'Callahan* rule. *See Gosa v. Mayden, supra* at 677. Since normally no civilian court in which the accused would have those rights is available in the foreign setting, the service-connection limitation does not apply,

The situs of the offense, not the trial, determines whether the exception may apply. *United States v. Newvine*, 23 U.S.C.M.A. 208, 48 C.M.R. 960 (1974); *United States v. Bowers*, 47 C.M.R. 516 (A.C.M.R. 1973). The last sentence in the discussion of the overseas exception is based on *United States v. Black*, 1 M.J. 340 (C.M.A. 1976). *See also United States v. Gladue*, 4 M.J. 1(C.M.A. 1977); *United States v. Lazzaro*, 2 M.J. 76 (C.M.A. 1976). Some federal courts have suggested that the existence of court-martial jurisdiction over an overseas offense does not depend solely on the fact that the offense is not cognizable in the United States civilian courts. *See Hemphill v. Moseley*, 443 F.2d 322 (10th Cir. 1971). *See also United States v. King*, 6 M.J. 553 (A.C.M.R. 1978), *pet. denied*, 6 M.J. 290 (1979).

Several Federal courts which have addressed this issue have also held that the foreign situs of a trial is sufficient to support court-martial jurisdiction, although the rationale for this result has not been uniform. *See e.g., Williams v. Froehlke*, 490 F.2d 998 (2d Cir. 1974); *Wimberly v. Laird*, 472 F.2d 923 (7th Cir.), *cert. denied*, 413 U.S. 921 (1973); *Gallagher v. United States*, 423 F.2d 1371 (Ct. Cl.), *cert. denied*, 400 U.S. 849 (1970); *Bell v. Clark*, 308 F.Supp. 384(E.D. Va. 1970), *aff'd*, 437 F.2d 200 (4th Cir. 1971). As several of these decisions recognize, the foreign situs of an offense is a factor weighing heavily in favor of service-connection even without an exception for overseas offenses. *See Relford* factors 4 and 8. The logistical difficulties, the disruptive effect on military activities, the delays in disposing of offenses, and the need for an armed force in a foreign country to control its own members all militate toward service-connection for offenses committed abroad. Another consideration, often cited by the courts, is the likelihood that if the service-connection rule were applied overseas as it is in the United States, the practical effect would be far more frequent exercise of jurisdiction by host nations, thus depriving the individual of constitutional protections the rule is designed to protect.

The petty offenses exception rests on a similar doctrinal foundation as the overseas exception. Because there is no constitutional right to indictment by grand jury or trial by jury for petty offenses (*see Baldwin v. New York*, 399 U.S. 66 (1970);*Duncan v. Louisiana*, 391 U.S. 145 (1968); *Duke v. United States*, 301 U.S. 492 (1937)); the service-connection requirement does not apply to them. *United States v. Sharkey*, 19 U.S.C.M.A. 26, 41 C.M.R. 26 (1969). *Under Baldwin v. New York, supra*, a petty offense is one in which the maximum sentence is six months confinement or less. Any time a punitive discharge is included in the maximum punishment, the offense is not petty. *See United States v. Smith*, 9 M.J. 359, 360 n. 1 (C.M.A. 1980); *United States v. Brown*, 13 U.S.C.M.A. 333, 32 C.M.R. 333 (1962).

Sharkey relied on the maximum punishment under the table of maximum punishments in determining whether an offense is petty. It is the view of the Working Group that offenses tried by summary courts-martial and special courts-martial at which no punitive discharge may be adjudged are "petty offenses" for purposes of *O'Callahan,* in view of the jurisdictional limitations of such courts. Whether the jurisdictional limits of a summary of such special court-martial makes an offense referred to such a court-martial petty has not been judicially determined.

1995 Amendment : The discussion was amended in light of *Solorio v. United States,* 483 U.S. 435 (1987). *O'Callahan v. Parker,* 395 U.S. 258 (1969), held that an offense under the code could not be tried by court-martial unless the offense was "service connected." *Solorio* overruled *O'Callahan.*

Rule 204 Jurisdiction over certain reserve component personnel

1987 Amendment: R.C.M. 204 and its discussion were added to implement the amendments to Articles 2 and 3, UCMJ, contained in the "Military Justice Amendments of 1986," tit. VIII, § 804, National Defense Authorization Act for fiscal year 1987, Pub. L. No. 99-661, 100 Stat. 3905 (1986). Use of the term "member of a reserve component" in Article 3(d) means membership in the reserve component at the time disciplinary action is initiated. The limitation in subsection (b)(1) restricting general and special courts-martial to periods of active duty is based upon the practical problems associated with conducting a court-martial only during periods of scheduled inactive-duty training, and ensures that the exercise of court-martial jurisdiction is consistent with the policies set forth in Article 2(d). The last sentence of subsection (d) reflects legislative intent "not to disturb the jurisprudence of

United States ex rel. Hirshberg v. Cooke, 336 U.S. 210 (1949)" (H.R. Rep. No. 718, 99th Cong., 2d Sess. at 227 (1986)).

CHAPTER III. INITIATION OF CHARGES; APPREHENSION;PRETRIAL RESTRAINT; RELATED MATTERS

Rule 301 Report of offense

The primary sources of this rule are paragraphs 29 *a* and 31 of MCM, 1969 (Rev.). Those provisions were adopted in substance except that subsection (b) provides that reports be conveyed to the "immediate commander" of suspects, meaning the "commander exercising immediate jurisdiction. . . under Article 15." The language was changed because the previous language was cumbersome and legalistic. There is no corresponding provision in the Federal Rules of Criminal Procedure. the most closely analogous provision of the Federal Rules of Criminal Procedure is Rule 3 (complaints). However, "[w]ith respect to the complaint, in general, it should be noted that its principle purpose is to serve as the basis for an arrest warrant." J. Moore, *Moore's Federal Practice, Rules Pamphlet* (part 3) 10 (1982). That purpose is not the same as the purpose of R.C.M. 301. R.C.M. 301 is simply to assure that ordinarily information relating to offenses is conveyed promptly to the suspect's immediate commander.

Rule 302 Apprehension

(a) *Definition and scope.* The definition of "apprehension" in subsection (1) is taken from Article 7(a), as was its predecessor, paragraph 18 *a* of MCM, 1969 (Rev.).

The peculiar military term "apprehension" is statutory (Article 7(a)) and cannot be abandoned in favor of the more conventional civilian term, "arrest." *See generally United States v. Kinane,* 1 M.J. 309 (C.M.A. 1976). *See also United States v. Cordero,* 11 M.J. 210, 217, n.1 (C.M.A. 1981) (Everett, C.J., concurring).

The discussion of "apprehension" is also consistent with paragraphs 18 *a* and *b*(1) of MCM, 1969 (Rev.). The discussion draws a distinction between apprehensions and detentions. The distinction is based upon the duration of the status, the legal consequences of the impairment of liberty, and the circumstances under which the two forms are used. *Brown v. Texas,* 443 U.S. 47 (1979); *Dunaway v. New York,* 442 U.S. 200 (1979); *Terry v. Ohio,* 392 U.S. 1 (1968); *United States v. Schneider,* 14 M.J. 189 (C.M.A. 1982); *United States v. Texidor-Perez,* 7 M.J. 356 (C.M.A. 1979).

This rule conforms in intent with the substance of Fed. R. Crim. P. 3 through 5. However, the formal warrant application process and initial appearance requirement of those rules are impracticable, and, given the command control aspects of the military, unnecessary for military criminal practice. The purposes of Fed. R. Crim. P. 3 through 5 are achieved by later rules in this chapter.

Subsection (2) clarifies the scope of the rule. It does not affect apprehensions of persons not subject to trial by court-martial. Apprehension and detention of such persons by military law enforcement personnel is not part of the court-martial process; it is based on the commander's inherent authority to maintain law and order on the installation and on various state laws concerning citizen's arrest. *See United States v. Banks,* 539 F.2d 14 (9th Cir. 1976). The rule also does not affect the authority of persons not listed in subsection (b) to apprehend. The discussion gives some examples of such categories.

(b) *Who may apprehend.* This subsection restates the substance of Articles 7(b) and (c) and 8, and paragraphs 19a and 23 of MCM, 1969, (Rev.). Subsection (3), Federal civilian law enforcement officers, is the only new provision.

Subsection (1) is taken from paragraph 19 *a* of MCM, 1969 (Rev.). The phrase "whether subject to the code or not" is added to the present rule to make clear that contract civilian guards and police and similar civilian law enforcement agents of the military have the power to apprehend persons subject to the code.

The discussion of subsection (1) reflects the elimination of the previous restrictive policy against apprehensions of commissioned and warrant officers by enlisted and civilian law enforcement personnel. This recognizes the authority of such personnel commensurate with their law enforcement duties. The rule does not foreclose secretarial limitations on the discretion of such personnel.

1987 Amendment: The Discussion was amended to clarify that special agents of the Defense Criminal Investigative Service have the authority to apprehend persons subject to trial by courts-martial.

Subsection (2) restates the previous exercise of delegated authority under Article 7(b) to designate persons authorized to apprehend which appeared in the first clause in the first sentence of paragraph 19 *a* of MCM, 1969 (Rev.). The accompanying discussion is based on the second sentence of paragraph 19 *a* of MCM, 1969 (Rev.).

1990 Amendment: The words "or inactive-duty training" were added in conjunction with the enactment of the "Military Justice Amendments of 1986," tit. VIII, 804 National Defense Authorization for Fiscal Year 1987, Pub. L. No. 99–661, 100 Stat. 3905 (1986) expanding jurisdiction over reserve component personnel.

Subsection (3) restates Article 8. This seemingly duplicative statement is required because the codal provision as to deserters extends the Federal arrest power to state and local law enforcement agents who do not have the kind of Federal arrest power possessed by their colleagues listed in subsection (3). The fact that a person who apprehended a deserter was not authorized to do so is not a ground for discharging the deserter from military custody. *See* paragraph 23 of MCM, 1969 (Rev.).

(c) *Grounds of apprehension.* This subsection concerns apprehension of persons subject to the code or to trial by court-martial. Note that such persons may be apprehended under this rule only for offenses subject to trial by court-martial. *See also* the analysis of subsection (a)(2) of this rule. The power to apprehend under this rule lasts as long as the person to be apprehended is subject to the code or to trial by court-martial. This provision has no explicit parallel in MCM, 1969 (Rev.) but is consistent with the limitation of the apprehension power in both the code and that Manual to persons subject to the code. The Federal Rules of Criminal Procedure have no similar provision either, because the arrest power of civilian law enforcement officials is not similarly limited by the status of the suspect.

The subsection states alternative circumstances which must exist to permit apprehension during this period. The first two sentences restate the probable cause requirement for apprehension of suspects, the main use of the apprehension power of which Article 7(b) and paragraph 19 *a* of MCM, 1969 (Rev.) took note.

They are consistent with Fed. R. Crim. P. 4(a). No change to the substance of those provisions has been made, but the discussion provides that probable cause may be based on "the reports of others" to make clear that hearsay may be relied upon as well as personal knowledge. This addition is consistent with Fed.R. Crim. P. 4(b). The wording has been changed to eliminate the legal term, "hearsay."

The last sentence of the subsection restates the codal authority of commissioned, warrant, petty, and noncommissioned officers to use the apprehension power to quell disorders, and is based on Article 7(c) and paragraph 19 *b* of MCM, 1969 (Rev.), changed only as necessary to accommodate format. *Cf.* paragraph 19 *a* of MCM, 1951, and of MCM, 1969 (Rev.) (authority of military law enforcement official to apprehend on probable cause). *See also* Article of War 68 (1920). *Compare* paragraph 20*b* (authority of military police) *with* paragraph 20 *c* (quarrels and frays) of MCM (Army), 1949 and of MCM (AF), 1949. Article 7(b) expressly requires probable cause to believe an offense has been committed; Article 7(c) does not.

(d) *How an apprehension may be made.* In subsection (1) the general statement of procedure to make an apprehension is based on paragraph 19 *c*, MCM, 1969 (Rev.) but it has been amplified in accord with *United States v. Kinane,* 1 M.J. 309 (C.M.A. 1976). *See also United States v. Sanford,* 12 M.J. 170 (C.M.A. 1981).

Subsection (2) is consistent with military law. It is superficially inconsistent with Fed.R. Crim. P. 4, but the inconsistency is more apparent than real. Civilian law enforcement officials generally have power to arrest without warrant for offenses committed in their presence and for felonies upon probable cause. *See e.g.* 18 U.S.C. §§ 3052, 3053, and 3056. To restrict the military apprehension power by requiring warrants in all or most cases would actually be inconsistent with civilian practice. The problem of apprehensions in dwellings is addressed by cross-reference to subsection (e) (2).

Subsection (3) clarifies the power of military law enforcement officials to secure the custody of a person. There is no similar provision in the Federal Rules of Criminal Procedure. It is general, leaving to the services ample breadth in which to make more definitive regulations.

The discussion restates paragraph 19 *d* of MCM, 1969 (Rev.). There is no corollary provision in the Federal Rules of Criminal Procedure. The purpose of the notification is twofold. First, it ensures that the unit commander of the person in custody will know the status of that member of the command and can participate in later decision making that will affect the availability of the member apprehended. Second, it ensures that law enforcement officials will promptly bring the case and suspect before the commander, thus ensuring that later procedural requirements of the code and these rules will be considered and met if appropriate. This is parallel in intent to Fed. R. Crim. P. 5 and 5.1.

(e) *Where an apprehension may be made.* Subsection (1) is based on Article 5. It is similar to Fed. R. Crim. P. 4(d)(2) but broader because the code is not similarly limited by geography.

Subsection (2) adds the warrant requirement of *Payton v. New York,* 445 U.S. 573 (1980), conforming the procedure to military practice. *See also Steagald v. United States,* 451 U.S. 204 (1981); *United States v. Mitchell,* 12 M.J. 265 (C.M.A. 1982); *United States v. Davis,* 8 M.J. 79 (C.M.A. 1979); *United States v. Jamison,* 2 M.J. 906 (A.C.M.R. 1976). The first sentence clarifies the extent of Payton by citing examples of the kinds of dwellings in which one may and may not reasonably expect privacy to be protected to such a degree as to require application of *Payton* . Subsection (C) joins the warrant requirement to the traditional power of military commanders, and military judges when empowered, to authorize similar intrusions for searches generally and other kinds of seizures. The first sentence of the last paragraph in subsection (2) is based on *Steagald v. United States, supra* . The Working Group does not regard *Steagald* as requiring an exclusionary rule or supplying standing to an accused on behalf of a third party when the accused's right to privacy was not violated. *See Rakas v. Illinois,* 439 U.S. 128 (1978). Failure to secure authorization or warrant to enter a private dwelling not occupied by the person to be apprehended may violate the rights of residents of that private dwelling.

Rule 303 Investigation of charges

This rule is based on paragraph 32 of MCM, 1969 (Rev.). Much of the predecessor now appears in the accompanying discussion.

Rule 304 Pretrial restraint

(a) *Types of pretrial restraint.* Except for the "conditions on liberty" provision, which is new, this subsection is based on paragraphs 20 *a, b,* and *c* of MCM, 1969 (Rev.). Some of the former Manual which explained the distinction between arrest and restriction in lieu thereof and which described the consequences of breaking restrictions has been moved to the Discussion.

The "conditions on liberty" provision is set out separately in the Manual for the first time, although such conditions (several examples of which are included in the Discussion) have been in practice previously and have received judicial recognition. *See United States v. Heard,* 3 M.J. 14, 20 (C.M.A. 1977); *cf. Pearson v. Cox,* 10 M.J. 317, 321 n. 2 (C.M.A. 1981) (conditions during period of deferment of adjudged sentence). Such conditions also parallel the conditions on release described in 18 U.S.C. § 3146(a). *See also ABA Standards, Pretrial Release* § 10-5.2 (1979). The discussion notes that pretrial restraint, including conditions on liberty, may not improperly hinder trial preparation. *See United States v. Aycock,* 15 U.S.C.M.A. 158, 35 C.M.R. 130 (1964); *United States v. Wysong,* 9 U.S.C.M.A. 249, 26 C.M.R. 29 (1958).

The last sentence of the second paragraph of the discussion is based on *United States v. Weisenmuller*, 17 U.S.C.M.A. 636, 38 C.M.R. 434 (1968); *United States v. Smith*, 17 U.S.C.M.A. 427, 38 C.M.R. 225 (1968); *United States v. Williams,* 16 U.S.C.M.A. 589, 37 C.M.R. 209 (1967). *See also United States v. Nelson,* 5 M.J. 189 (C.M.A. 1978); *United States v. Powell,* 2 M.J. 6 (C.M.A. 1976).

1986 Amendment: A fourth paragraph was added to the Discussion to provide a cross-reference to the speedy trial rule in R.C.M. 707(a).

(b) *Who may order pretrial restraint.* This subsection restates, in a reorganized format, paragraph 21 *a* of MCM, 1969 (Rev.). It is based on Article 9(b) and (c). The code does not address forms of restraint less severe than arrest; there is no reason to permit a broader class of persons than those who may impose arrest or confinement to impose less severe forms of restraint. Subsection

(4) is based on *United States v. Gray,* 6 U.S.C.M.A. 615, 20 C.M.R. 331 (1956). A commander who, under subsection (4), has withheld authority to order pretrial restraint may, of course, later modify or rescind such withholding. Even if such modification or rescission is denominated a "delegation," it would be a rescission of the earlier withholding. The limits of subsection (3) would not apply.

(c) *When a person may be restrained.* This subsection is based on Articles 9(d) and 10. Although forms of restraint less severe than arrest are not addressed by these articles, it is appropriate to require probable cause and a need for restraint for all forms of pretrial restraint. An officer imposing restraint has considerable discretion in determining how much restraint is necessary (*cf.* 18 U.S.C. §§ 3146(a) and 3147), although a decision to confine is subject to thorough review under R.C.M. 305. The Discussion borrows from the language of Article 13 to admonish that the restraint must serve only the limited purpose of this rule. *See* subsection (f). *See also United States v. Haynes,* 15 U.S.C.M.A. 122, 35 C.M.R. 94 (1964).

(d) *Procedures for ordering pretrial restraint.* This subsection is based on Article 9(b) and (c) and on paragraph 20 *d*(2) and (3) of MCM, 1969 (Rev.). Since all forms of restraint other than confinement are moral rather than physical, they can be imposed only by notifying the person restrained.

(e) *Notice of basis for restraint.* This subsection is based on Article 10. Since all forms of restraint other than confinement involve some form of communication with the accused or suspect, this subsection will impose no undue burden on commanders. The Discussion refers to R.C.M. 305(e) which contains additional notice requirements for a person who is confined. Failure to comply with this subsection does not entitle the accused to specific relief in the absence of a showing of specific prejudice. *Cf. United States v. Jernigan,* 582 F. 2d 1211 (9th Cir.), *cert. denied*, 439 U.S. 991 (1978); *United States v. Grandi,* 424 F. 2d 399 (2d Cir. 1970); cert. denied, 409 U.S. 870 (1972).

Pretrial restraint other than pretrial confinement (*see* R.C.M. 305(e)(2) and (f)) does not alone require advice to the suspect of the right to detailed counsel or civilian counsel. Fed.R.Crim. P.5(c) is not analogous because the advice at the initial appearance serves multiple purposes other than for pretrial restraint short of confinement. The advice at the initial appearance is designed to protect the defendant not only when pretrial confinement is imposed, but for events in the criminal process which follow shortly thereafter. Thus, it is necessary under that provision to inform a defendant of the right to counsel immediately because the suspect or accused may shortly thereafter be called upon to make important decisions. In contrast, the Rules for Courts-Martial treat each step in the pretrial process separately and provide for advice of the right to counsel when counsel is necessary. R.C.M. 305(e)(2) and (f) (pretrial confinement); 406 (detailing counsel for an accused in an investigation under Article 32); 503 and 506 (detailing counsel for an accused in courts-martial); Mil.R. Evid. 305 (warnings to accompany interrogations). The difference is a result of the structural differences between these Rules and the Federal Rules of Criminal Procedure. The intent and result of both systems are the same.

(f) *Punishment prohibited.* This section is based on Article 13; paragraph 18 *b* (3) of MCM, 1969 (Rev.);*Hearings on H.R. 2498 Before a Subcomm. of the House Comm. on Armed Services*, 81st Cong., 1st Sess. 916 (1949). *See also United States v. Bruce,* 14 M.J. 254 (C.M.A. 1982); *United States v. Davidson,* 14 M.J. 81 (C.M.A. 1982); *United States v. Pringle,* 19 U.S.C.M.A. 324, 41 C.M.R. 324 (1970); *United States v. Bayhand,* 6 U.S.C.M.A. 762, 21 C.M.R. 84 (1956). *Cf. Bell v. Wolfish*, 441 U.S. 520 (1979). The remedy for a violation of this rule is meaningful sentence relief. *United States v. Pringle, supra; United States v. Nelson,* 18 U.S.C.M.A. 177, 39 C.M.R. 177 (1969).

(g) *Release.* This subsection is based on 21 *d* and on the second and third sentences of paragraph 22 of MCM, 1969 (Rev.).

1986 Amendment: The Discussion was amended to clarify that pretrial restraint may be imposed not only when charges are to be reinstated but also when a convening authority intends to order a rehearing or an "other" trial. *See* R.C.M. 1107(e). Restraint imposed during any of these situations is considered "imposed before and during disposition of offenses." *See* R.C.M. 304(a).

(h) *Administrative restraint.* This subsection clarifies the scope of this rule.

Rule 305 Pretrial confinement

Introduction. This rule clarifies the basis for pretrial confinement, and establishes procedures for the imposition and review of pretrial confinement. The rule conforms with requirements established by recent decisions. *See United States v. Lynch,* 13 M.J. 394 (C.M.A. 1982); *United States v. Malia,* 6 M.J. 65 (C.M.A. 1978); *United States v. Heard,* 3 M.J. 14 (C.M.A. 1977); *Cortney v. Williams,* 1 M.J. 267 (C.M.A. 1976). The most significant changes include: prevention of foreseeable serious misconduct as a basis for pretrial confinement; a system of review of pretrial confinement by neutral and detached officials; specific authority for a military judge to direct release of an accused from pretrial confinement; and a specific and meaningful remedy for violation of the rule.

The Working Group considered various procedural mechanisms for imposition and review of pretrial confinement. Numerous practical, as well as legal, concerns were analyzed and weighed in striking a balance between individual liberty and protection of society. The Working Group proceeded from the premise that no person should be confined unnecessarily. Neither the prisoner nor the government benefits from unnecessary confinement. On the other hand, in determining when confinement may be necessary, the nature of the military and its mission is an important consideration. Moreover, some of the collateral impact associated with pretrial confinement in civilian life (loss of job, income, and access to defense counsel) is normally absent in the military setting and pretrial confinement is seldom lengthy. *See* R.C.M. 707. Finally, the procedures for imposition and review of pretrial confinement had to be compatible with existing resources. More specific considerations are addressed below.

(a) *In general.* This subsection is based on the first sentence of paragraph 20 *c* of MCM, 1969 (Rev.). The second sentence of that paragraph is deleted here; the subject is treated at subsections (d) and (h)(2) of this rule. The first sentence of the discussion, with the addition of the words "of the United States," is Article 12. The second sentence is new, and restates current practice.

(b) *Who may be confined.* This subsection is new. It restates current law.

(c) *Who may order confinement. See* Analysis, R.C.M. 304(b).

(d) *When a person may be confined.* This subsection contains the two basic codal prerequisites for pretrial confinement: (1) probable cause to believe an offense has been committed by the person to be confined (Article 9(d)); and (2) circumstances require it (Article 10). This basic standard, which applies to all forms of pretrial restraint, was selected here in lieu of a more detailed formulation since the initial decision to confine often must be made under the pressure of events. The discussion encourages consideration of the factors discussed under (h)(2)(B) of this rule before confinement is ordered, and, as a practical matter, this will probably occur in many cases, since persons ordering confinement usually consider such matters in making their decision. An initial decision to confine is not illegal, however, merely because a detailed analysis of the necessity for confinement does not precede it. *Cf. Gerstein v. Pugh,* 420 U.S. 103, 113-14 (1975).

The discussion notes that confinement must be distinguished from custody incident to an apprehension. *See* R.C.M. 302. This paragraph is based on Article 9(e) and paragraphs 19 *d* and 174 *c* and *d* of MCM, 1969 (Rev.). Article 9(e) expressly distinguishes confinement from measures to "secure the custody of an alleged offender until proper authority may be notified". Such periods of custody are not confinement within the meaning of this rule. *See United States v. Ellsey,* 16 U.S.C.M.A. 455, 37 C.M.R. 75 (1966). Such custody may continue only for the period of time reasonably necessary for a proper authority under R.C.M. 304 to be notified and to act. *See* Article 9(e). *See also* paragraphs 21 and 22, Part IV.

(e) *Advice to the accused upon confinement.* Except for subsection (e)(1), which is based on Article 10 and appeared in subparagraph 20 *d* (4) of MCM, 1969 (Rev.) this subsection is new. It is similar to Fed.R.Crim. P.5(c) which requires the magistrate to give such advice to the defendant at the initial appearance. The rule does not specify who shall inform the accused. This affords considerable flexibility in implementing this provision.

Note that violation of this subsection does not trigger the remedy in subsection (k) of this rule. Consequently, a violation of this subsection must be tested for prejudice. *See* Article 59.

(f) *Military counsel.* This subsection is new. The primary purpose of the rule is to help protect the accused's interest in the pretrial confinement determinations. Secondarily, this requirement should enable the accused to avoid injury to the defense in subsequent proceedings, and, when necessary, to begin to marshal a defense. *See e.g.,* Article 49(a). The assignment of counsel at this stage is of central importance to ensuring the fairness of the pretrial confinement process. The requirement parallels similar requirements in federal practice (Fed.R.Crim. P.5(c) and 44(a)) and under the District of Columbia Code (D.C. Code § 23-1322(c)(4)). *See generally United States v. Jackson,* 5 M.J. 223 (C.M.A. 1978); *United States v. Mason,* 21 U.S.C.M.A. 389, 45 C.M.R. 163 (1972); *United States v. Przybycien,* 19 U.S.C.M.A. 120, 122n. 2, 41 C.M.R. 120, 122n. 2 (1969). Consequently, failure to do so triggers the remedy in subsection (k) of this rule.

The subsection does not require that counsel appointed at this stage will represent the prisoner throughout subsequent proceedings. Although this would be desirable, the mobility of the armed forces, the locations of confinement facilities, and the limits on legal resources render an inflexible requirement in this regard impracticable. Nothing in the code or the Constitution requires such early appointment of defense counsel for purposes of representation at trial. *Cf. Gerstein v. Pugh, supra* at 123; *Kirby v. Illinois,* 406 U.S. 682 (1972). *But see United States v. Jackson, supra.* Current case law permits assignment of counsel for a limited duration, at least if the limited nature of the relationship is made clear to the client at the outset. *See United States v. Timberlake,* 22 U.S.C.M.A. 117, 46 C.M.R. 117 (1973); *Stanten v. United States,* 21 U.S.C.M.A. 431, 45 C.M.R. 205 (1972); *United States v. Kelker,* 4 M.J. 323 (C.M.A. 1978); *cf. United States v. Booker,* 5 M.J. 238 (C.M.A. 1977). Where such a limited relationship is the practice, it should be included in the advice under subsection (e) of this rule to help prevent misunderstanding. If the limited nature of the relationship is not explained to the prisoner, it may not be possible, without the prisoner's consent, to terminate the relationship for the convenience of the government. *United States v. Catt,* 1 M.J. 41 (C.M.A. 1975); *United States v. Eason,* 21 U.S.C.M.A. 335, 45 C.M.R. 109 (1972); *United States v. Murray,* 20 U.S.C.M.A. 61, 42 C.M.R. 253 (1970).

Nothing in this rule requires that counsel assigned for pretrial confinement purposes be located near the prisoner. Once again, as desirable as this may be, such a requirement would be impracticable. It is not uncommon for a prisoner to be confined, at least initially, far from any available counsel. The rule is designed to afford the services considerable flexibility in dealing with such situations. The distance between the prisoner and defense counsel should not pose a serious problem for the defense. They can communicate by telephone, radio, or other means, and, under Mil. R. Evid. 502, such communications would be protected by the attorney-client privilege. Moreover, since the initial review may be accomplished without the presence of prisoner or defense counsel, the defense counsel may submit appropriate written matters without personal contact with either the prisoner or the reviewing officer.

1993 Amendment: The amendment to subsection (f) provides a specific time period by which to measure compliance. Because it is possible to obtain credit for violations of this section under subsection (k), a standard of compliance was thought necessary. *See e.g., United States v. Chapman,* 26 M.J. 515 (A.C.M.R. 1988), *pet. denied* 27 M.J. 404 (C.M.A. 1989). This amendment, while protecting the rights of the prisoner, also gives reasonable protection to the Government in those cases where the prisoner is confined in a civilian facility and the request is never, or is belatedly, communicated to military authorities. While it is expected that military authorities will have procedures whereby civilian confinement authorities communicate such requests in a timely fashion, the failure to communicate such a request, or the failure to notify military authorities in a timely manner should be tested for prejudice under Article 59 U.C.M.J., and should not be considered as invoking the credit provisions of subsection (k) of this rule.

(g) *Who may direct release from confinement.* This subsection is a substantial change from the following language from paragraph 22 of MCM, 1969 (Rev.): "The proper authority to release from confinement in a military confinement facility is the commanding officer to whose authority that facility is subject." Notwithstanding this provision, the authority of the commander to whose authority the confinement facility is subject was often treated as ministerial in nature, at least in some of the services. Authority to direct release was recognized to repose in a commander of the accused. *See generally* Boller, *Pretrial Restraint in the Military,* 50 Mil.L.Rev. 71, 96-99 (1970); *see also United States v. Pringle,*

19 U.S.C.M.A. 324, 41 C.M.R. 324 (1970). More recently, the authority of military judges (*see Porter v. Richardson,* 23 U.S.C.M.A. 704, 50 C.M.R. 910 (1975); *Courtney v. Williams, supra)* and officials appointed to do so under regulations (*see United States v. Malia, supra*) to order release from pretrial confinement has been recognized. The subsection expressly establishes the authority of such officials to direct release from pretrial confinement.

(h) *Notification and action by commander.* Subsection (1) is based on Article 11(b), although the terminology has been changed somewhat since the terms "commander of a guard" and "master at arms" no longer accurately describes the confinement personnel who are responsible for making the report. This subsection is also important in setting in motion the procedures for approval or disapproval of confinement. *See also,* Fed.R.Crim. P.5(a). The discussion is based on *Hearings on H.R. 2498 Before a Subcomm. of the Comm. on Armed Services of the House of Representatives*, 81st Cong., 1st Sess. 913 (1949).

Subsection (2)(A) places the real initial decision for pretrial confinement with the prisoner's commander. Although the immediate commander may not be a neutral and detached official for pretrial confinement purposes (*United States v. Stuckey,* 10 M.J. 347 (C.M.A. 1981); *but cf. United States v. Ezell,* 6 M.J. 307 (C.M.A. 1979); *Courtney v. Williams, supra*), it is appropriate to give this officer the initial decision on pretrial confinement, so that the command implications of this determination may be fully considered and developed for later review. *See* subsections (B) and (C). This will enable the commander, who is in the best position to assess the predictive elements of the pretrial confinement decision, including not only the prisoner's likely behavior, but also the impact of release or confinement on mission performance, to make a record of such factors for the initial review. Subsection (2)(B) provides additional guidance for the commander in making this decision.

The 72-hour requirement is intended to ensure reasonably prompt action by the commander, while at the same time allowing for situations in which the commander is not immediately available. If a commander were unavailable for a longer period, then some other official would normally qualify as acting commander (*see United States v. Kalscheuer,* 11 M.J. 373 (C.M.A. 1981); *United States v. Murray,* 12 U.S.C.M.A. 434, 31 C.M.R. 20 (1961); *United States v. Bunting,* 4 U.S.C.M.A. 84, 15 C.M.R. 84 (1954)) or the prisoner would be attached to another unit whose commander could act for these purposes.

1993 Amendment: The amendment to subsection (h)(2)(A) clarifies that the 72-hour period operates in two distinct situations: (a) if the commander orders the prisoner into pretrial confinement, the commander has 72 hours to decide whether pretrial confinement will continue; but (b) if someone other than the prisoner's commander orders the prisoner into pretrial confinement, the prisoner's commander has 72 hours from receipt of a report that the prisoner has been confined to decide whether pretrial confinement will continue.

Subsection (2)(B) sets forth the standards for pretrial confinement. Probable cause has long been recognized as a prerequisite to confinement in military law. *See* Article 9(d); paragraph 20 *d*(1) of MCM, 1969 (Rev.). Preventing flight is also well established as basis for confinement. *See* paragraph 20 *c* of MCM, 1969 (Rev.); *United States v. Bayhand,* 6 U.S.C.M.A. 762, 21 C.M.R. 84 (1956). Preventing foreseeable serious criminal misconduct has not been expressly recognized in the Manual before, although it was probably included in the "seriousness of the offense charged" language of paragraph 20 *c. See e.g., United States v. Nixon,* 21 U.S.C.M.A. 480, 45 C.M.R. 254 (1972). "Seriousness of the offense charged" was rejected as an independent justification for pretrial confinement in *United States v. Heard, supra,* at least insofar as it implied confinement may be ordered regardless of the need to prevent flight or serious criminal misconduct. *Cf. United States v. Nixon, supra; United States v. Jennings,* 19 U.S.C.M.A. 88, 41 C.M.R. 88 (1969).

Although prevention of serious misconduct is expressly authorized as a basis for pretrial confinement for the first time, it is, as the foregoing analysis indicates, not new to military practice. Indeed the phrase "foreseeable serious criminal misconduct" comes from *Heard. See also United States v. Nixon, supra; United States v. Gaskins,* 5 M.J. 772 (A.C.M.R. 1978); Dep't of Defense Directive 1325.4 (7 Oct 68). The need for confinement for such purposes has been recognized and sanctioned in civilian communities. *United States v. Edwards,* 430 A.2d 1321 (D.C. 1981), *cert. denied,*455 U.S. 1022 (1982). *See also* U.S. Dep't of Justice, *Attorney General's Task Force on Violent Crime, Final Report* 50-53 (August 1981); Burger, *Report of the Chief Justice to the American Bar Association*—1981, 67 A.B.A.J. 290, 292 (1981); Note, *Preventive Detention Before Trial,* 79 Harv.L.Rev. 1489 (1966). The need for confinement to prevent serious misconduct is particularly acute in the military. The business of military units and the interdependence of their members render the likelihood of serious criminal misconduct by a person awaiting trial of even graver concern than in civilian life. Moreover, as expressed in the last sentence of subsection (B), these concerns render a broader range or misconduct of a potentially serious nature. For example, the "quitter" who disobeys orders and refuses to perform duties, while others are expected to carry out unpleasant or dangerous tasks, has immensely adverse effect on morale and discipline which, while intangible, can be more dangerous to a military unit than physical violence. Thus, although the "pain in the neck" (*United States v. Heard, supra*) may not be confined before trial solely on that basis, the accused whose behavior is not merely an irritant to the commander, but is rather an infection in the unit may be so confined. Even constant supervision accomplishes little in such cases, and military resources do not permit, nor is it reasonable to require, the establishment of some holding facility other than a confinement facility for such persons.

The definition of national security is based on Exec. Order No. 12065 § 6-104 (June 28, 1978), 43 Fed.Reg. 28949, as amended by Exec. Order No. 12148 (July 1979), 44 Fed.Reg. 43239, and Exec. Order No. 12148 (July 19, 1979), 44 Fed.Reg. 56673, *reprinted at* 50 U.S.C.A. § 401 (West Supp. 1982). The second ("includes") phrase is taken from Joint Chiefs of Staff Publication 1, Dictionary of Military and Associated Terms 228 (1 July 79).

The factors for consideration in the discussion are taken from 18 U.S.C. § 3146(b), with minor modifications. *See also ABA Standards, Pretrial Release* §§ 10-3.2, 10-3.3, 10-4.4(d), 10-5.1(b) (1979), "embraced" in*United States v. Heard, supra* at 23-24. The discussion also notes that the Military Rules of Evidence do not apply to the information considered. Although the commander's decision is not directly analogous to a bail determination before a magistrate, this provision is consistent with 18 U.S.C. § 3146(f).

The last paragraph in the discussion is a reminder of the obligation to consider less severe forms of restraint before approving continued confinement. *United States v. Heard* and *United States v. Gaskins,* both *supra.*The alternatives, which are also referred to in R.C.M. 304, are derived from 18 U.S.C. § 3146(a).

The procedures in this rule are the same whether the basis of confinement is risk of flight or foreseeable serious misconduct. This is appropriate since bail is unavailable in the military. *United States v. Heard, supra;* 18 U.S.C. § 3156. *Cf. Levy v. Resor,* 17 U.S.C.M.A. 135, 37 C.M.R. 399 (1967). Since the decision is whether or not to confine, whether the basis is risk of flight or foreseeable misconduct, and since the factual, predictive, and discretionary determinations are qualitatively the same in either case, there is no reason for procedures to differ concerning them. Indeed, the District of Columbia Court of Appeals acknowledged that even where possibility of bail exists in potential flight cases, the two determinations involve the same fundamental considerations. *See United States v. Edwards, supra* at 1336-37.

The requirement for a memorandum in subsection (2)(C) is new although not to military practice. *See e.g.,* AR 27–10, para. 9-5 *b*(1), 16-5 *a* (1 September 1982); SECNAVINST 1640.10, para. 6 (16 August 1978). The memorandum is important to the remaining pretrial confinement procedures since it ordinarily provides the primary basis for subsequent decisions concerning pretrial confinement.

(i) *Procedures for review of pretrial confinement.* This subsection is new, although it roughly parallels current practice in the services. The requirement for review by an official, other than the commander ordering the confinement, who is neutral and detached, in subsection (2) is consistent with the requirement of- *Courtney v. Williams, supra.* Although in *United States v. Malia, supra,* the Court of Military Appeals identified the term "magistrate" with the term "judge," the Working Group did not construe this to require that a military judge must conduct the initial review. *Cf. United States v. Lynch, supra.* Judicial review is provided in subsection (j). Instead, the term as used in Malia appears to denote a neutral and detached official with independent power to review and order release from pretrial confinement. In any event, it is not practicable to require that the reviewing officer be a military judge, especially if the review is to occur promptly and if the accused is to be permitted to appear personally before the reviewing officer. There are not enough military judges available to accomplish this task. Moreover, a legally trained magistrate is not necessary since the pretrial confinement decision is essentially factual and predictive. *Cf. Shadwick v. City of Tampa,* 407 U.S. 345 (1972) (magistrate need not be a lawyer). Thus the rule leaves the selection of reviewing officers to service Secretaries.

The review must take place within 7 days of the imposition of confinement under R.C.M. 305. This is a more extended period than is the norm for an initial appearance in federal courts. *See* Fed.R.Crim. P.5(a); *Gerstein v. Pugh, supra.* However, Federal courts are willing to tolerate delays of several days, so long as the defendant does not suffer prejudice beyond the confinement itself during such periods. *See e.g., United States v. Motes-Zarate,* 552 F.2d 1330 (9th Cir. 1977), *cert. denied,* 435 U.S. 947 (1978); *see generally* 8 J. Moore, *Moore's Federal Practice,* ch. 5 (1982). The 7-day period is more closely analogous to the time periods authorized for the preventive detention hearing under D.C. Code § 23-1322(c)(3). The 7-day period, with a possible extension up to 10 days, is intended to accommodate a wide variety of circumstances. Because the review may be conducted entirely with written documents, without the prisoner's presence when circumstances so dictate, there should be no reason why a reviewing officer cannot conduct a review of the imposition of confinement within that time. Note that the 7-day period begins running from the time confinement is imposed by a person authorized to so under subsection (c) of this rule.

1993 Amendment: The amendment to subsection (i)(1) provides that the required review only becomes applicable whenever the accused is confined under military control. For example, if the prisoner was apprehended and is being held by civilian authorities as a military deserter in another state from where the prisoner's unit is located and it takes three days to transfer the prisoner to an appropriate confinement facility, the seven day period under this rule would not begin to run until the date of the prisoner's transfer to military authorities. Any unreasonable period of time that it may take to bring a prisoner under military control should be tested for prejudice under Article 59, U.C.M.J., and should not be considered as invoking the credit provisions of subsection (k) of this rule absent evidence of bad faith by military authorities in utilizing civilian custody. *But see United States v. Ballesteros,* 29 M.J. 14 (C.M.A. 1989). However, any time spent in civilian custody at the request of military authorities would be subject to pretrial confinement credit mandated by *United States v. Allen,* 17 M.J. 126 (C.M.A. 1984).

The amendment further clarifies the method of calculation to determine if the rule has been violated. *See United States v. DeLoatch,* 25 M.J. 718 (A.C.M.R. 1987); *contra, United States v. New,* 23 M.J. 889 (A.C.M.R. 1987).

The rule calls for a limited proceeding. Matters are to be presented in writing to facilitate the promptness of the proceeding and to ensure that a record is kept of the matters considered by the reviewing officer. Notwithstanding some authority to the contrary (*United States v. Heard, supra* at 25 (Fletcher, C.J., concurring); *ABA Standards, Pretrial Release* § 10-5.9 (1979)), an adversary hearing is not required. *Gerstein v. Pugh* and *United States v. Edwards,* both *supra.* Even if a more elaborate hearing might be called for in the civilian sphere (*ABA Standards, supra; cf. United States v. Wind,* 527 F.2d 672 (6th Cir. 1975)), it is appropriate to consider the institutional goals and needs of the military in measuring the due process requirements for pretrial confinement. *Cf. Wolff v. McDonnell,* 418 U.S. 539 (1974). *See Middendorf v. Henry,* 425 U.S. 25 (1976); *Parker v. Levy,* 417 U.S. 733 (1974). The procedures in the review include the opportunity for representation by counsel, access to all information presented to the reviewing officer, the right to present matters for the defense, and, ordinarily, the opportunity for the prisoner and defense counsel to personally address the reviewing officer. Measured against the military's mission, its structure and organization, and the resources available to it, these procedures, coupled with the opportunity for judicial review at an Article 39(a) session, adequately protect the liberty interests of the prisoner.

The review procedures are patterned after the procedures for parole revocation proceedings prescribed in *Morrissey v. Brewer,* 408 U.S. 471 (1972). There the Supreme Court required that an initial review of parole revocation must be conducted by a neutral person, who need not be a judge; the prisoner must receive notice and have an opportunity to be present and speak, and to present written matters; and the hearing officer must prepare an informal summary of the findings. (A later, more thorough hearing, to be held within approximately 2 months is required under *Morrissey*; judicial review under Article 39(a) coupled with the trial itself fulfills these purposes for pretrial confinement). These requirements are virtually identical to those in R.C.M. 305(i)(1). The only requirement in*Morrissey* not present in 305 is that the hearing officer have discretionary power to call witnesses for purposes of confrontation. On the other hand, R.C.M. 305 provides the prisoner with the opportunity to obtain counsel in all cases. This is not required for parole or probation revocation. *Gagnon v. Scarpelli,* 411 U.S. 778 (1973).

Although parole and probation revocations differ from pretrial confinement in that in the former there has already been an adjudication of guilt, the distinction cuts in the opposite direction insofar as (as was emphasized by the Supreme Court in *Morrissey v. Brewer, supra* at 482) the probationer or parolee typically faces a long period of confinement, unlike the pretrial confinee who, especially in the military, is not subjected to such a lengthy period. Moreover, in *Gerstein v. Pugh, supra,* the Supreme Court, noting the burden of adversary hearings at this pretrial stage (*id.*at 121 n. 23), distinguished *Morrissey* and *Gagnon* from pretrial probable cause hearings (*id.* at 121 n. 21) and did not require an adversary hearing at such pretrial proceedings. The District of Columbia Court of Appeals deciding that this holding in *Gerstein* applies to preventive detention hearings as well. *United States v. Edwards, supra.*

The provision that the Military Rules of Evidence do not apply at the initial review parallels federal civilian practice. *See* 18 U.S.C. § 3146(f). The burden of proof is on the government. A preponderance standard was selected because it strikes the best balance between the interests in the military setting of the prisoner and society and because it is easily understood. A higher standard is not constitutionally required. *Gerstein v. Pugh, supra* at 119-21. *See also Morrissey v. Brewer, supra* at 485-89. Federal civilian courts may deny bail in capital cases if "the court or judge has reason to believe that no one or more conditions of release will reasonably assure that the person will not flee or pose a risk of danger to the community." 18 U.S.C. § 3148. In non-capital cases, the judge "in the exercise of his discretion" decides whether and how much bail will be set and hence, in effect, whether the prisoner shall be released. 18 U.S.C. § 3146(a).

Subsection (7) specifically authorizes the presentation of additional matters to the reviewing officer, and thus makes clear the continuing authority and responsibility of that officer over pretrial confinement. This continuing authority is necessary, especially in the unusual case in which referral of charges is delayed.

(j) *Review by military judge.* This subsection is new. MCM, 1969 (Rev.) did not provide for review of pretrial confinement by the military judge, and it was only recently that the power of a military judge to order release from confinement was recognized, at least implicitly. *See Porter v. Richardson, supra; United States v. Lamb,* 6 M.J. 542 (N.C.M.R. 1978), *pet. denied,* 6 M.J. 162 (1979); *United States v. Otero,* 5 M.J. 781 (A.C.M.R.), *pet. denied,* 6 M.J. 121 (1978). *Contra,* paragraph 21*c* of MCM, 1969 (Rev.).

This subsection establishes that the military judge has the power after referral (*United States v. Newcomb,* 5 M.J. 4 (C.M.A. 1977)) to review pretrial confinement and to order release when appropriate. Two separate, but related, issues may be involved: (1) whether the prisoner should be released as of the time of the hearing; and (2) whether confinement already served was legal. The prisoner may raise either or both of these issues by motion for appropriate relief. All the procedures and protections normally attendant to an Article 39(a) session (*see* R.C.M. 803) apply. The rule does not specify when such a session would take place. As with other pretrial motions (*see* R.C.M. 905) and with scheduling proceedings generally (*see* R.C.M. 801), the determination when an Article 39(a) session will be conducted and when a motion will be litigated is a matter within the sound discretion of the military judge. Note also that the matter may be addressed in a conference under R.C.M. 802 and, if the parties agree, resolved without need for an Article 39(a) session. The standards for either decision posit that the reviewing officer's decision is entitled to substantial weight (*see United States v. Otero, supra*) and may not be overturned in the absence of an abuse of discretion, violation of subsections (i)(1)(B) and (C) of this rule, or information not presented to the reviewing officer. This procedure is analogous to the appeal provisions in 18 U.S.C. § 3147.

The rule is silent concerning the overlapping responsibilities of the military judge and the reviewing officer. Once charges are referred, the need for a reviewing officer diminishes, and it could be argued that the reviewing officer's role should terminate on referral. On the other hand, even after referral, the reviewing officer may be more accessible to the parties than the military judge, so that it was considered unwise to rule out further action by the reviewing officer.

The remedy for certain violations of the rule is prescribed in subsection (k) of this rule and is analyzed below. Note that the military judge must order the remedy when one or more of the identified violations occur.

(k) *Remedy.* The requirement for an administrative credit for violations in subsection (f), (h), (i), or (j) of this rule is based on *United States v. Larner,* 1 M.J. 371 (C.M.A. 1976). This credit is the sole remedy for violation of these provisions. *See United States v. Nelson,* 18 U.S.C.M.A.\177, 39 C.M.R. 177 (1969). Violations of other provisions would not render confinement illegal and hence would not trigger the sentence relief requirements. Such violations would be tested for specific prejudice, and, where such was found, would trigger a requirement to grant relief appropriate to cure the prejudice suffered. Note that if one of the required steps is omitted, but the next step occurs within the time period for the omitted step, and pretrial confinement is otherwise valid, no credit is required. For example, if the commander does not prepare a memorandum under subsection (h)(2)(C), but the review under subsection (i)(l) occurs within 72 hours of imposition of restraint, and the grounds for pretrial confinement are established, the accused is entitled to no credit. Similarly. if the military judge reviews pretrial confinement under subsection (j) within 7 days of the imposition of confinement and confinement is approved, the omission of the review under subsection (i)(l) would not entitle the accused to credit.

The one day credit is in addition to the day for day credit

provided by DOD Instruction 1325.4 as interpreted by *United States v. Allen,* 17 M.J. 126 (C.M.A. 1984) and is intended as an additional credit to deter violations of the rule. This remedy does not replace sanctions against persons who intentionally violate these rules. *See* Articles 97, and 98. The credit for illegal pretrial confinement (in addition to any other administrative credit) is provided as a matter of policy, and does not reflect a determination that such cumulative credit is otherwise required.

The credit applies against confinement, if adjusted, and then against several other specified penalties. Thus an accused entitled to sentence relief whose adjusted sentence includes no confinement usually will receive some form of sentence relief. Note, however, that the remedy does not apply to other forms of punishment including punitive discharges or reduction in grade. This is because these penalties are so qualitatively different from confinement that the fact that an accused has served confinement which was technically illegal should not automatically affect these forms of punishment.

The rule does not prescribe the mechanics for implementing the credit since this will depend on the stage at which the violation of the rule is discovered. *Cf. United States v. Larner, supra.* Usually the illegality will be determined by the trial judge, who shall also announce the remedy. After the sentence is announced, the military judge should announce on the record how the credit will apply to it. Where after application of this credit no confinement would remain to be served the accused should not be confined after trial. It is the responsibility of the convening authority to apply credit when action is taken on the sentence. *See* Article 57.

(l) *Confinement after release.* This subsection is new and is intended to prevent a "revolving door" situation by giving finality to the decision to release. *Cf. United States v. Malia, supra.*

(m) *Exceptions.* This subsection is new. Its purpose is to eliminate several procedural requirements in situations where military exigencies make then practically impossible to comply with. Subsection (1) would apply not only to combat situations, but also to circumstances in which a unit is deployed to a remote area or on a sensitive mission, albeit one not necessarily involving combat.

Subsection (2) recognizes the special problem of vessels at sea, and permits suspension of certain procedural requirements in such cases.

Rule 306 Initial disposition

Introduction. Rule 306 describes who may dispose of offenses and the options available to such authorities. Although these matters are covered more thoroughly elsewhere (*see* R.C.M. 401-407, and R.C.M. 601) they are included here to facilitate a chronological approach to disposition of offenses.

(a) *Who may dispose of offenses.* This rule and the first paragraph of the discussion are based on Articles 15, 22-24, and 30(b), and paragraphs 30-33, 35, and 128 of MCM, 1969 (Rev.). The second sentence of the rule and the discussion are also based on paragraphs 5 *b*(4) and 5*c* of MCM, 1969 (Rev.); *United States v. Charette,* 15 M.J. 197 (C.M.A. 1983); *United States v. Blaylock,* 15 M.J. 190 (C.M.A. 1983). *See also* Article 37; *United States v. Hawthorne,* 7 U.S.C.M.A. 293, 22 C.M.R. 83 (1956); *United States v. Rembert,* 47 C.M.R. 755 (A.C.M.R. 1973); *pet. denied,* 23 U.S.C.M.A. 598 (1974).

As noted in the second paragraph of the discussion a referral decision commits the disposition of an offense to the jurisdiction of a specific judicial forum, and thus bars other action on that offense until it is withdrawn from that court-martial by the convening authority or superior competent authority. *See United States v. Charette, United States v. Blaylock* both *supra. But see* Article 44; R.C.M. 97(b)(2)(C). Neither dismissal of charges nor nonjudicial punishment (for a serious offense) bars subsequent contrary action by the same or a different commander. Thus, a decision to dismiss charges does not bar a superior commander from acting on those charges if repreferred or from personally preferring charges relating to the same offenses, if no jeopardy attached to the earlier dismissal. *See Legal and Legislative Basis, Manual for Courts-Martial, United States, 1951,* 47. Cf. *United States v. Thompson,* 251 U.S. 407 (1920); Fed.R.Crim. P. 48; *United States v. Clay,* 481 F.2d 133 (7th Cir.), *cert, denied,* 414 U.S. 1009 (1973); *Mann v. United States,* 304 F.2d 394 (D.C.Cir.), *cert, denied,* 371 U.S. 896 (1962). *See also* Article 44, and R.C.M. 905(g) and Analysis, and R.C.M. 907(b)(3) and Analysis. Similarly, imposition of nonjudicial punishment does not bar a superior commander from referring the same offenses, if they are serious, to a court-martial (Article 15(f); *see also United States v. Fretwell,* 11 U.S.C.M.A. 377, 29 C.M.R. 193 (1960)), or from setting aside punishment already imposed. Article 15(e). *See generally* Part V.

(b) *Policy.* This subsection is based on paragraph 30 *g* of MCM, 1969 (Rev.). Although it is guidance only, it is sufficiently important to warrant inclusion in the rules as a presidential statement.

The second paragraph of the discussion provides guidelines for the exercise of the discretion to dispose of offenses. Guideline (A) is based on paragraph 33 *h* of MCM, 1969 (Rev.). Guidelines (B) through (G) are based on *ABA Standards, Prosecution Function* § 3-3.9(b) (1979). The other guidelines in § 3-3.9 are not needed here: § 3-3.9(a) (probable cause) is followed in the rule: § 3-3.9(b)(i) is inconsistent with the convening authority's judicial function; §§ 3-3.9(c) and (d) are unnecessary in military practice; and § 3-3.9(e) is implicit in § 3-3.9(a) and in the rule requiring probable cause. Guidelines (H), (I), and (J) were added to acknowledge other practical considerations.

(c) *How offenses may be disposed of.* This subsection is based generally on Articles 15, 22-24, and 30, and paragraphs 32-35, and 128 of MCM, 1969 (Rev.). The discussion provides additional guidance on the disposition options.

Rule 307 Preferral of Charges

(a) *Who may prefer charges.* This subsection is based on Article 30 and paragraph 29 *b* of MCM, 1969 (Rev.).

The first sentence of the first paragraph of the discussion is a new version of the former rule at paragraphs 5*a*(4) and 29 *c* of MCM, 1969 (Rev.), which provided that "A person subject to the code cannot be ordered to prefer charges to which he is unable truthfully to make the required oath on his own responsibility." This rule is subsumed in the oath requirement of Article 30 and subsection (b) of the rule. The discussion clarifies the circumstances under which an order to prefer charges may be given, but warns against such orders in some circumstances in which they may tend to encourage litigation or to invalidate an otherwise valid court-martial. The practice of ordering persons to prefer charges has a historical basis. W. Winthrop, *Military Law and Precedents* 154 (2d ed. 1920 reprint); *but cf. Hearings on H.R.*

2498 Before a Subcommittee of the House Committee on Armed Service, 81st Cong., 1st Sess. 850 (1949) (reflecting the fact that under the code a person who orders another to prefer charges is an accuser).

The second paragraph of the discussion is a simplified version of paragraph 25 of MCM, 1969 (Rev.). The discussion observes that charges may be preferred against a person subject to trial by court-martial at any time. *But see* Article 43. Thus, when charges may be preferred depends only on continued or renewed personal jurisdiction. The policy forbidding accumulation of charges in paragraph 25 of MCM, 1969 (Rev.) is now general guidance in the discussion. Furthermore, the "reasonable delay" aspects of the discussion are no longer contingent upon the absence of pretrial arrest and confinement, because delay for a reasonable period and good cause is always permitted. *See also* R.C.M. 707.

(b) *How charges are preferred; oath.* This subsection is taken from Article 30(a). This subsection is similar in purpose to Fed.R.Crim. P. 7(c)(1)'s requirement that the indictment or information "shall be signed by the attorney for the government." The same concept of requiring accountability for bringing allegations to trial appears again at R.C.M. 601 (referral).

The first paragraph of the discussion is based on Article 30 and paragraph 114*i* of MCM, 1969 (Rev.).

The last paragraph of the discussion is consistent with Fed.R.Crim. P. 4(b).

(c) *How to allege offenses.* Subsection (1) is based on paragraph 24a of MCM, 1969 (Rev.). The nomenclature of charge and specification is imbedded in the code. *Compare* Articles 30, 34(b), 43(b), 45(b), 54(a), 61, and 62 *with* Fed.R.Crim. P. 7(c)(1). Taking both the charge and specifications together, the practice is entirely consistent with Fed.R.Crim. P.7. There is no need in military practice for the differentiating nomenclature for indictments and informations (Fed.R.Crim P.7(a)); in military practice the same charges progress through the pretrial system without any change in nomenclature, regardless of the level of court-martial by which they are ultimately disposed. *See* U.S. Const, amend. V. That further permits military practice to disregard waiver of indictment (Fed.R.Crim. P.7(b)) insofar as the pleadings are concerned. Finally, military practice does not involve criminal forfeitures in the same sense as federal civilian practice. *Cf.* Fed.R.Crim. P.7(c)(2).

Subsection (2) is based on paragraph 24*a* and appendix 6*a* of MCM, 1969 (Rev.). The definition is consistent with that part of Fed.R.Crim. P.7(c)(1) which requires that "The indictment or information shall state for each count the official or customary citation of the statute, rule, regulation, or other provision of law which the defendant is alleged therein to have violated." The first paragraph of the accompanying discussion is based on paragraph 27 and appendix 6 *a* of MCM, 1969 (Rev.). The sources of the lettered subsections of the discussion are:

(A) *Numbering charges* —paragraph 24, and paragraph 3 of appendix 6*a* of MCM, 1969 (Rev.);

(B) *Additional charges* —id.

(C) *Preemption* —Article 134;

(D) *Charges under the law of war* —paragraph 12 of appendix 6*a* of MCM, 1969 (Rev.).

Subsection (3) restates Fed.R.Crim. P.7(c)(1) in military terms. That definition is consistent with paragraph 24 *a* and Chapter VI of MCM, 1969 (Rev.). The test of sufficiency of a specification follows *United States v. Sell,* 3 U.S.C.M.A. 202, 11 C.M.R. 202 (1953); paragraph 87 *a*(2) of MCM, 1969 (Rev.). Paragraph 29*d* of MCM, 1969 (Rev.) is deleted as unnecessary. A specific format for specifications is not prescribed. *See also* Introductory Discussion, Part IV.

2004 Amendment: The Rule was amended by modifying language in the Discussion at (H)(ix), and moving it in to the text of the Rule, to emphasize that facts that increase maximum authorized punishments must be alleged and proven beyond a reasonable doubt. *Jones v. United States,* 526 U.S. 227 (1999); *see also Apprendi v. New Jersey,* 530 U.S. 466 (2000). Prior convictions are not required to be alleged in a specification because *Apprendi* and *Jones* exempt prior convictions from those aggravating factors that must be included in charging documents and proven beyond a reasonable doubt. R.C.M. 1004 already establishes capital sentencing procedures that satisfy an accused's constitutional rights in this area. *See Ring v. Arizona,* 536 U.S. 584 (2002).

The sources of the lettered subsection of the accompanying discussion are:

(A) *Sample specifications* —paragraph 26 *a* of MCM, 1969 (Rev.);

(B) *Numbering specifications* —paragraph 3 of appendix 6 *a* of MCM, 1969 (Rev.);

(C) *Name and description of the accused;*

(i) *Name* —paragraphs 4 and 5 of appendix 6a of MCM, 1969 (Rev.);

(ii) *Military association* —paragraph 4 of appendix 6*a* of MCM, 1969 (Rev.);

(iii) *Social Security or service number* —paragraphs 4 and 6 of appendix 6 *a* of MCM, 1969 (Rev.) (note that the social security or service number ordinarily is entered in the data at the top of the charge sheet; *see* Appendix 4); and

(iv) *Basics of personal jurisdiction —United States v. Alef,* 3 M.J. 414 (C.M.A. 1977). *See also* Analysis, subsection (e)(3) Discussion (F) (Subject-matter jurisdiction) of this rule.

(D) *Date and time of offense* —paragraph 7 of appendix 6 *a* of MCM, 1969 (Rev.). As to "on or about," *see United States v. Heard,* 443 F.2d 856, 859 (6th Cir. 1971);

(E) *Place of offense* —paragraph 7 of appendix 6 *a* of MCM, 1969 (Rev.);

(F) *Subject-matter jurisdiction —United States v. Alef, supra.* As to subsection (iii), *United States v. Trottier,* 9 M.J. 337 (C.M.A. 1980) (jurisdiction over drug offenses). As to subsection (iv), *United States v. Newvine,* 23 U.S.C.M.A. 208, 48 C.M.R. 960 (1974); *United States v. Keaton,* 19 U.S.C.M.R. 64, 41 C.M.R. 64 (1969).

The guidance here is not prescriptive, just as the inclusion of subject-matter jurisdiction in the sample specifications (Part IV) is always parenthetical, a reminder and not as a requirement. The Working Group does not consider any particular format for such pleadings required by *Alef.*

Questions of jurisdiction are interlocutory questions to be decided by the military judge applying a preponderance standard. *See* R.C.M. 905(c); 907(b)(1)(A), and *United States v. Ruiz,* 4 M.J. 85 (C.M.A.1977); *United States v. Kuriger,* 4 M.J. 84 (C.M.A. 1977); *United States v. Cherry,* 4 M.J. 83 (C.M.A. 1977); *United States v. McCarthy,* 2 M.J. 26, 28n.1 (C.M.A.

1976); *United States v. Jessie,* 5 M.J. 573 (A.C.M.R.), *pet. denied,* 5 M.J. 300 (1978). *See also United States v. Laws,* 11 M.J. 475 (C.M.A. 1981). Ordinarily this finding will not be disturbed by findings by exceptions and substitutions on the general issue of guilt because of the higher standard of proof involved in such determinations. *See generally James, Pleadings and Practice under United States v. Alef,* 20 A.F.L. Rev. 22 (1978).

1995 Amendment: The discussion was amended in conformance with a concurrent change to R.C.M. 203, in light of *Solorio v. United States*, 483 U.S. 435 (1987). *O'Callahan v. Parker* , 395 U.S. 258 (1969), held that an offense under the code could not be tried by court-martial unless the offense was "service connected." *Solorio* overruled *O'Callahan.*

(G) *Description of offense.* —The sources of the section are:

(i) *Elements* —paragraph 28 *a*(3) of MCM, 1969 (Rev.);

(ii) *Words indicating criminality* — *id.*;

(iii) *Specificity* —paragraphs 28 *a*, 69 *b*, and 87 *a*(2) of MCM, 1969 (Rev.);

(iv) *Duplicity* —paragraph 28 *b* of MCM, 1969 (Rev.); accord, Fed.R.Crim. P.7,8.

(H) *Other considerations in drafting specifications.* —The sources of the sections are:

(i) *Principals* —paragraph 9 of appendix 6 *a* of MCM, 1969(Rev.);

(ii) *Victim* —paragraph 10 of appendix 6 *a* of MCM, 1969 (Rev.);

(iii) *Property* —paragraph 13 of appendix 6 *a* of MCM, 1969 (Rev.);

(iv) *Value* —paragraph 11 of appendix 6 *a* of MCM, 1969 (Rev.);

(v) *Documents* —paragraph 28 *c*, and paragraph 14 of appendix 6 *a* of MCM, 1969 (Rev.);

(vi) *Orders* —(a), (b)- *id.*; (c) *Negating exceptions- United States v. Cuffee*, 10 M.J. 381 (C.M.A. 1981); *United States v. Gohagen*, 2 U.S.C.M.A. 175, 7 C.M.R. 51 (1953);

(vii) *Oral Statements* —paragraph 28 *c* of MCM, 1969 (Rev.);

(viii) *Joint offenses* —paragraph 26 *d* and paragraph 8 of appendix 6 *a* of MCM, 1969 (Rev.);

(ix) *Matters in aggravation* —paragraph 127 *c* (Table of Maximum Punishments) of MCM, 1969 (Rev.); *United States v. Venerable*, 19 U.S.C.M.A. 174, 41 C.M.R. 174 (1970).

Subsection (4) is less restrictive than the former and traditional military practice reflected at paragraphs 25, 26 *b* and *c* of MCM, 1969 (Rev.) which favored trial of all known offenses at a single trial, but complicated that policy with policies against joining major and minor offenses and accumulating charges. The confusion is eliminated by leaving to the discretion of the convening authority which charges and specifications will be tried. *See* R.C.M. 601(d) and accompanying discussion. The rule in this subsection does not follow Fed.R.Crim. P.8(a), because that rule is entirely too unwieldy for a military criminal system, particularly in combat or deployment.

2005 Amendment: The first sentence of the non-binding discussion was moved to subsection (4) to reflect the decision of *United States v. Quiroz*, which identifies the prohibition against the unreasonable multiplication of charges as a 'a long-standing principle' of military law. *See United States v. Quiroz*, 55 M.J. 334, 337 (C.A.A.F. 2001).

Subsection (5) follows Fed.R.Crim. P.8(b). The civilian rule is consistent with the former approach of paragraph 26 *d* of MCM, 1969 (Rev.). The present rule goes even further by making it possible to allege related offenses against co-actors on a single charge sheet, but the rule does not require that approach. The rule is also consistent with the provision for common trials of paragraph 33 *l* of MCM, 1969 (Rev.).

(d) *Harmless error in citation.* The subsection restates in military nomenclature Fed.R.Crim. P.7(c)(3). The subsection is consistent with paragraphs 27 and 28 *c*, and paragraph 12 of appendix 6 *a* of MCM, 1969 (Rev.). It is not intended to provide a comprehensive rule on harmless error in drafting specifications.

Rule 308 Notification to accused of charges

(a) *Immediate commander.* This subsection paraphrases paragraphs 32 *f*(1) and 33 *c* of MCM, 1969 (Rev.). *See* Article 30. This subsection deletes the requirement for a report of the circumstances that make compliance impossible. The use of a certificate of notification is encouraged in the discussion. The identification of known accusers, including persons who ordered charges to be preferred, is new and protects the accused against unauthorized acts by such persons. *See* Article 1(9).

The certificate requirement is abandoned only as a requirement, and use of such certificates remains advisable, since they give evidence of compliance with Article 10. However, to require a certificate might risk an excessive remedy for a mere administrative failure to complete the certificate properly.

There is no precisely analogous rule in the federal civilian rules, though the federal civilian rules do reach the same end—to notify an accused of the pendency of the allegations. Fed.R.Crim. P.4 (arrest or summons upon complaint), 5 (initial appearance), 5.1 (preliminary examination), 6 (grand jury), 7 (indictment, information), and 9 (warrant or summons upon indictment or information) all provide a civilian defendant with notice of the impending prosecution.

The purpose of the subsection is to permit the accused to begin preparing a defense. *United States v. Stebbins*, 33 C.M.R. 677 (C.G.B.R. 1963). The subsection originates in Articles 10 and 30 and is one of the fundamental rights of an accused. *United States v. Clay*, 1 U.S.C.M.A. 74, 1 C.M.R. 74 (1951). It gains additional importance in this respect since the right of both the United States and the accused to take depositions arises upon preferral. Article 49(a).

(b) *Commanders at higher echelons.* This subsection reflects the same continuing duty to give notice of the preferred charges that appeared at paragraph 33 *c* of MCM, 1969 (Rev.).

(c) *Remedy.* This subsection is new and is based on the approach taken in *United States v. Stebbins, supra*, and consistent with paragraph 58 (continuances and postponements) of MCM, 1969 (Rev.).

CHAPTER IV. FORWARDING AND DISPOSITION OF CHARGES

Rule 401 Forwarding and disposition of charges in general

(a) *Who may dispose of charges.* This subsection is based on paragraphs 5, 32, 33, 35, and 128 *a* of MCM, 1969 (Rev.). *See* Articles 15, 22-24. The second sentence is based on *United States v. Hawthorne*, 7 U.S.C.M.A. 293, 22 C.M.R. 83 (1956); *United States v. Rembert*, 47 C.M.R. 755 (A.C.M.R. 1973), *pet. denied*, 23 U.S.C.M.A. 598 (1974). *See also United States v. Hardy*, 4 M.J. 20 (C.M.A. 1977). A superior authority who withholds from a subordinate the authority to dispose of offenses (*see* R.C.M. 306) or charges may later modify or rescind such withholding. Even if such modification or rescission is denominated a "delegation," it would be a rescission of the earlier withholding.

(b) *Prompt determination.* This subsection is based on Article 30(b) and the first sentence of paragraph 30 *i* of MCM, 1969 (Rev.). The discussion is also based on paragraphs 30 *f*, 32 *b, c, f*(1), 33 *a, d, m,* and 35 *a* of MCM, 1969 (Rev.).

(c) *How charges may be disposed of.* This subsection is based on paragraphs 32 and 33 of MCM, 1969 (Rev.). Most matters in those paragraphs, including the mechanics of forwarding charges, have been placed in the discussion as the practices of the services vary because of differing command structures. Specific requirements and additional details may be provided by service regulations.

(d) *National security matters.* This subsection is based on the first sentence in the second paragraph of paragraph 33 *f* of MCM, 1969 (Rev.). *See also* R.C.M. 407(b) and Article 43(e).

Rule 402 Action by commander not authorized to convene courts-martial

This rule is based on paragraph 32 of MCM, 1969 (Rev.). Paragraph 32 was written in terms of guidance. The structure of the paragraph and the descriptions of the alternatives available to an immediate commander indicated the powers of such commanders. R.C.M. 402 expresses these powers. The mechanics of forwarding charges, dismissal of charges, the requirement for prompt disposition, and guidance concerning these matters has been placed in R.C.M. 401 and its discussion because these matters apply to commanders at all levels. Other matters contained in paragraph 32 have been placed in other rules. *See* R.C.M. 303 (preliminary inquiry); 308 (notification of accused); 603 (amending charges). *See also* R.C.M. 306 which includes guidance on disposition determinations.

Rule 403 Action by commander exercising summary court-martial jurisdiction

This rule and the discussion are based on paragraph 33 of MCM, 1969 (Rev.). *See* Article 24. Paragraph 33 was written in terms of guidance. The structure of the paragraph and the descriptions of the alternatives available to the commander exercising summary court-martial jurisdiction indicated the powers of such commanders. R.C.M. 403 expresses these powers in clearer terms. Several matters covered in paragraph 33 are now covered in other rules. *See* R.C.M. 303 (preliminary inquiry); 308 (notification of accused); 401 (forwarding charges; discussion of suspected insanity, joint or common trials); 601 (instructions in referral order; common trials); 603 (amending charges). *See also* R.C.M. 306.

Rule 404 Action by commander exercising special court-martial jurisdiction

This rule is new. Paragraph 33 of MCM, 1969 (Rev.) treated both special and summary court-martial convening authorities. *See* paragraph 33 *j*(1) of MCM, 1969 (Rev.); Analysis, R.C.M. 403.

Rule 405 Pretrial investigation

(a) *In general.* This subsection is based on Article 32(a) and (d) and paragraph 34 *a* of MCM, 1969 (Rev.). Except insofar as the code requires otherwise, the rule is generally consistent with Fed.R.Crim. P.6 and 7. *See generally Johnson v. Sayre*, 158 U.S. 109 (1895); *Green v. Convening Authority*, 19 U.S.C.M.A. 576, 42 C.M.R. 178 (1970). The last sentence clarifies that the requirements for an Article 32 investigation apply only if charges are referred to a general court-martial. This sentence is not intended, however, to prevent the accused from challenging the fruits of a violation during a pretrial investigation of other rights the accused enjoys independent of the Article 32 investigation (e.g., moving to suppress a statement by the accused to the investigating officer because it was taken in violation of Article 31).

The first and third paragraphs of the discussion are based on paragraph 34 *a* of MCM, 1969 (Rev.). The second sentence has been added based on *Hutson v. United States*, 19 U.S.C.M.A. 437, 42 C.M.R. 39 (1970); *United States v. Samuels,* 10 U.S.C.M.A. 206, 27 C.M.R. 280 (1959); *Hearings on H.R. 2498 Before a Subcomm. of the House Comm. on Armed Services*, 81st Cong., 1st Sess. 997 (1949). *See also* Mil. R. Evid. 804(b) and Analysis. The second paragraph of the discussion is based on the third sentence of paragraph 33 *e*(2) of MCM, 1969(Rev.). The last paragraph in the discussion notes the possibility of waiver of the investigation. *See* subsection (k) of this rule and analysis. The Government is not required to accept waiver by the accused, and may conduct the investigation notwithstanding the accused's decision to waive it, since the investigation also serves the Government's interest.

(b) *Earlier investigation.* This subsection is based on Article 32(c) and paragraph 33 *e*(1) of MCM, 1969 (Rev.).

(c) *Who may direct investigation.* This subsection is new. There was previously no prescription of who had authority to direct an investigation under Article 32, although paragraph 33 *e* of MCM, 1969 (Rev.) suggested that the summary or special court-martial convening authority ordinarily would do so. The authority of convening authorities to direct an investigation is analogous to Fed.R.Crim. P.6(a) and the grand jury system generally.

(d) *Personnel.* This subsection follows Article 32 and paragraph 34 of MCM, 1969 (Rev.). It is consistent with Fed.R.Crim. P.6 in that witnesses, the investigating officer, and a representative of the prosecution may be present, but military practice extends further rights to presence and participation to the accused and defense counsel which are inconsistent with the grand jury system. *Compare* Article 32(B) *with* Fed.R.Crim. P.6(d) and (e)(2). Since the investigation under Article 32 is conducted by a single investigating officer, many of the provisions of the grand jury system are inconsistent, *e.g.,* Fed.R.Crim. P.6(b), (f), and (g).

Subsection (1) is based on Article 32 and paragraph 34a of MCM, 1969 (Rev.). *See also* Articles 25(d)(2), 26(d), 27(a). The discussion is also based on *United States v. Payne*, 3 M.J. 354 (C.M.A. 1977); *United States v. Grimm,* 6 M.J. 890 (A.C.M.R.), *pet. denied*, 7 M.J. 135 (1979). Subsection (2) is based on Articles 32(b) and 38(b) and paragraph 34 *c* of MCM, 1969 (Rev.). *See also* Article 27(a). Subsections (3)(B) and (C) are new to the Manual but conform to current practice. Fed.R.Crim. P.6(c) also provides for using reporters.

(e) *Scope of investigation.* This subsection and the discussion are based on Article 32(a) and paragraph 34 *a* of MCM, 1969 (Rev.).

1998 Amendment: This change is based on the amendments to Article 32 enacted by Congress in section 1131, National Defense Authorization Act for Fiscal Year 1996, Pub. L. No. 104-106, 110 Stat. 186, 464 (1996). It authorizes the Article 32 investigating officer to investigate uncharged offenses when, during the course of the Article 32 investigation, the evidence indicates that the accused may have committed such offenses. Permitting the investigating officer to investigate uncharged offenses and recommend an appropriate disposition benefits both the government and the accused. It promotes judicial economy while still affording the accused the same rights the accused would have in the investigation of preferred charges.

(f) *Rights of the accused.* This subsection is based on Article 32 and paragraph 34 *b*, *c*, and *d* of MCM, 1969 (Rev.). As to subsection (f)(3), *see also* R.C.M. 804(b)(2) and Analysis. The accused may waive the right to be present. *Cf.* R.C.M. 804(b) and Analysis. As to subsection (6), *see* Fed.R.Crim. P.5.

(g) *Production of witnesses and evidence; alternatives.* Subsection (1) is based on the third sentence of Article 32(b) and the first sentence in the first paragraph and the first sentence in the third paragraph of paragraph 34 *d* of MCM, 1969 (Rev.) as amplified in *United States v. Ledbetter*, 2 M.J. 37 (C.M.A. 1976). *See also* United States v. Roberts, 10 M.J. 308 (C.M.A. 1981); *United States v. Chestnut*, 2 M.J. 84 (C.M.A. 1976); *United States v. Webster,*, 1 M.J. 496 (A.F.C.M.R. 1975); *United States v. Houghton*, 31 C.M.R. 579 (A.F.B.R. 1961), *aff'd.*, 13 U.S.C.M.A. 3, 32 C.M.R. 3 (1962). Standards for production of evidence are also provided. These parallel the standards for the production of witnesses. Because of the absence of subpoena power at the Article 32 investigation, only evidence under the control of the Government is subject to production under this rule. The discussion amplifies the considerations in determining reasonable availability, and is based on the same sources.

1991 Amendment: Subsection (g)(1)(A) was amended by adding a requirement that a witness be located within 100 miles of the situs of the investigation to be "reasonably available." Given the alternatives to testimony available under subsection (g)(4), a bright-line rule of 100 statute miles simplifies the "reasonably available" determination and improves the efficiency of the investigation without diminishing the quality or fairness of the investigation. If a witness is located within 100 statute miles of the situs of the investigation, the investigating officer must consider the other factors in subsection (g)(1)(A) in determining availability. The remaining provisions of section (g) remain applicable. The production of witnesses located more than 100 statute miles from the situs of the investigation is within the discretion of the witness' commander (for military witnesses) or the commander ordering the investigation (for civilian witnesses).

1994 Amendment: Subparagraph (B)was amended to require the investigating officer to notify the appropriate authority of any requests by the accused for privileged information protected under Mil. R. Evid. 505 or 506. This puts the convening authority and other appropriate authorities on notice that a protective order, under subsection (g)(6) of this rule, may be necessary for the protection of any such privileged information that the government agrees to release to the accused. The Discussion was amended to reflect the purpose of the notice requirement.

2004 Amendment: The Discussion to subsection (g)(1)(A) is new. It was added in light of the decision in *United States v. Marrie*, 43 M.J. 35 (1995), that a witness beyond 100 miles from the site of the investigation is not *per se* unavailable.

Subsection (2) is new. The second sentence of the first paragraph of paragraph 34 *d* of MCM, 1969 (Rev.) recognized that the final decision on availability of a military witness is within the authority of that witness' commander. That paragraph did not elaborate on the reasonable availability determination. Subsection (2)(A) recognizes that a command determination of availability (which is essentially whether, and for how long, the witness can be spared without unduly impending the mission) is ordinarily only one of several factors to be weighed in determining reasonable availability. The investigating officer is in the best position to assess the potential significance of the witness and to weigh that against such factors as cost, difficulty, and delay. In many cases it will be clear that the witness need not be produced without formal application to the witness' commander. (The discussion notes, however, that advance communication with the commander will often be appropriate, as, for example, when the investigating officer needs to know how long a witness will be on leave.) Ultimately, the witness' importance to the witness' unit may outweigh all other factors; consequently, the commander of the witness may make a determination of nonavailability which is reviewable only at trial. Therefore, subsection (2)(A) allocates the responsibilities for determining reasonable availability in accordance with the practical considerations involved. *See generally United States v. Chestnut* and *United States v. Ledbetter,* both *supra; United States v. Cox*, 48 C.M.R. 723 (A.F.C.M.R.), *pet. denied*, 23 U.S.C.M.A. 616 (1974).

Subsection (2)(B) and the discussion are based on *United States v. Roberts, supra; United States v. Chuculate*, 5 M.J. 143 (C.M.A. 1978); *United States v. Chestnut, supra* and the first paragraph of paragraph 34 *d* of MCM, 1969 (Rev.).

Subsection (2)(C) applies a similar procedure for the production of evidence under the control of the Government. If the investigating officer questions the decision of the commander in subsection (2)(B) or the custodian in subsection (2)(C), the investigating officer may bring the matter to the attention of the commander who directed the investigation. When appropriate the matter can be pursued in command channels. It remains subject to judicial review on motion at trial.

Subsection (3) is based on paragraph 34*d* of MCM, 1969 (Rev.).

Subsection (4) is based on the third and fourth paragraphs of paragraph 34 *d* of MCM, 1969 (Rev.). *See also United States v. Samuels, supra.*

1991 Amendment: Subsection (4)(B) was amended by adding a new clause (v) which authorizes the investigating officer to consider, during time of war, unsworn statements of unavailable witnesses over objection of the accused. The burdens of wartime exigencies outweigh the benefits to be gained from requiring sworn statements when unsworn statements are available. Article 32, U.C.M.J., does not require the investigating officer to consider only sworn evidence or evidence admissible at courts-martial. The investigating officer should consider the lack of an oath in determining the credibility and weight to give an unsworn statement.

Subsection (5) is new. It parallels subsection (4).

1994 Amendment. Subsection (6) was added to allow the convening authority, or other person designated by service Secretary regulations, to attach conditions to the release of privileged information protected under Mil. R. Evid. 505 and 506 through the issuance of a protective order similar in nature to that which the military judge may issue under those rules. Though the prereferral authority to attach conditions already exists in Mil. R. Evid. 505(d)(4) and 506(d)(4), these rules did not specify who may take such action on behalf of the government or the manner in which the conditions may be imposed.

(h) *Procedure.* The second and fourth sentences in subsection (1) are based on Article 32(b). The first sentence is based on the first two sentences in the second paragraph of paragraph 34 *d* of MCM, 1969 (Rev.) and on *United States v. Samuels, supra.* The third sentence is based on the first sentence in the last paragraph of paragraph 34 *d* of MCM, 1969 (Rev.) except that now the investigating officer must allow the defense to examine all matters considered by the investigation officer, without exception. *See United States v. Craig*, 22 C.M.R. 466 (A.B.R. 1956), *aff'd*, 8 U.S.C.M.A. 218, 24 C.M.R. 28 (1957).

The first paragraph in the discussion is based on paragraph 114 *j* of MCM, 1969 (Rev.), except that the former oath has been divided into two oaths, one for the witness testifying at the investigation, the second to be given when the witness subscribes to a written summary after the hearing. The second oath is described in the second paragraph in the discussion. Note that instead of a second oath, the witness could be requested to sign a statement with the express proviso that the signature is made under penalty of perjury. *See* paragraph 57 of Part IV and Analysis. The second and third paragraph in the discussion are based on the second paragraph of paragraph 34 *d* of MCM, 1969 (Rev.). The admonition concerning the preservation of substantially verbatim notes and tapes of testimony at the end of the second paragraph has been added to avoid potential Jencks Act problems, 18 U.S.C. § 3500. *See* R.C.M. 914 Analysis.

The fourth paragraph in the discussion of subsection (1) is based on *United States v. Pruitt*, 48 C.M.R. 495 (A.F.C.M.R. 1974). *Cf. United States v. Washington*, 431 U.S. 181 (1977). Subsection (2) is new and is intended to promote the early identification of possible defects in the investigation so that they can be corrected promptly. *See also* subsection (k) of this rule. Subsection (2) clarifies the responsibility of the investigating officer as a judicial officer. *See generally United States v. Collins* , 6 M.J. 256 (C.M.A. 1979); *United States v. Payne, supra.* Requiring objections to be made to the investigating officer ensures that they will be placed in proper channels, so that they may be acted upon promptly. Many will concern matters which the investigating officer can rectify. *See generally United States v. Roberts*, and *United States v. Chestnut*, both *supra.* Other matters will fall within the province of the commander who directed the investigation, in whom most pretrial judicial authority reposes at this stage. *See generally United States v. Nix*, 15 U.S.C.M.A. 578, 36 C.M.R. 76 (1965). Nothing in R.C.M. 405 is intended to restrict the authority of the commander who directed the investigation to resolve issues involved in it, as long as that commander does not encroach upon the investigating officer's discretion and ability to personally make conclusions and recommendations.

Subsection (3) is new and is based on *MacDonald v. Hodson*, 19 U.S.C.M.A. 582, 42 C.M.R. 184 (1970). *See also* R.C.M. 806 for examples of some reasons why a pretrial investigation hearing might be closed. Fed.R.Crim. P.6 is generally inapplicable due to its different nature and purposes; it requires closed proceedings. Subsection (3) is not intended to express any preference for closed or open hearings.

(i) *Military Rules of Evidence.* This subsection is solely a cross-reference to the Military Rules of Evidence. Mil. R. Evid. 412, which concerns testimony of victims of sexual offenses at trial, does not apply at Article 32 hearings. However, there may be circumstances in which questioning should be limited by Mil. R. Evid. 303, which prohibits requiring degrading testimony in pretrial investigations and elsewhere. The privacy interests of the victim may also be protected by closure of the Article 32 hearings during appropriate periods. *See* subsection (h)(3) of this rule.

The first paragraph of the discussion is consistent with present practice. It is added to give additional guidance not included in paragraph 34 of MCM, 1969 (Rev.). It is also consistent with General civilian practice. *See* Office of the United States Attorney for the Southern District of Ohio, *Proving Federal Crimes* 3-3 (1980).

1993 Amendment: The amendment to R.C.M. 405(i) makes the provisions of Mil. R. Evid. 412 applicable at pretrial investigations.

(j) *Report of investigation.* This subsection is based on paragraphs 34 *d* and *e* of MCM, 1969 (Rev.). The provision for informal reports in paragraph 34 *f* of MCM, 1969 (Rev.) has been deleted. Because R.C.M. 405 applies only if charges are ultimately referred to a general court-martial, there is no need to describe informal reports. It if becomes apparent before completion of the investigation that charges will not be referred to a general court-martial, no report need be prepared unless the commander who directed the investigation requires it. In other cases a formal report will be necessary.

Subsection (1) is based on Article 32(a) and (b) and paragraph 34 *e* of MCM, 1969 (Rev.).

Subsections (2)(A) through (E) are based on Article 32(b) and paragraph 34 *e* of MCM, 1969 (Rev.). Subsection (2)(F) is new but is consistent with current practice and with the need to account for pretrial delays in relation to speedy trial issues. Subsections (2)(G) and (H) are based on Article 32(a) and paragraph 34 *a* of MCM, 1969 (Rev.). The probable cause standard is based on *United States v. Engle*, 1 M.J. 387, 389, n. 4 (C.M.A. 1976); *Hearings on H.R. 2498 Before a Subcomm. of the House Comm. on Armed Services*, 81st Sess. 997 (1949). Subsection (2)(I) is based on Article 32(a) and paragraph 34 *e*(6) of MCM, 1969 (Rev.).

Subsection (3) is based on the first sentence of paragraph 34 *e* of MCM, 1969 (Rev.) which implemented the requirement of the last sentence of Article 32(b). Subsection (3) leaves the mechanics of reproduction and distribution of the report to the Secretary concerned, or, in the absence of Secretarial regulations, to the commander concerned. Subsection (4) is new and is intended to encourage the early identification of possible defects in the report so that they can be corrected promptly when necessary. *See also* subsection (k) and Analysis.

(k) *Waiver.* The first sentence is based on Article 34(a), as amended. Military Justice Act of 1983, Pub.L.No. 98-209, § 4(a)(2), 97 Stat. 1393 (1983), which expressly permits waiver of the Article 32 investigation. This is consistent with previous practice. *See United States v. Schaffer*, 12 M.J. 425 (C.M.A. 1982). The remainder of this subsection is also new to the Manual for Courts-Martial. Along with subsections (h)(2) and (j)(4) of this rule, it is intended to promote efficiency in the pretrial process by placing the burden on the defense to raise objections when they can most easily be remedied, instead of waiting until trial. Recent decisions are consistent with this approach. *See United States v. Clark*, 11 M.J. 179 (C.M.A. 1981); *United States v. Cumberledge*, 6 M.J. 203 (C.M.A. 1979); *United States v. Cruz*, 5 M.J. 286 (C.M.A. 1978); *United States v. Chuculate, supra. See also* Article 34(d). Because the accused always has the right to be represented in the investigation by qualified counsel, this burden is appropriate. The amendment of Article 32(b) (Military Justice Amendments of 1981, Pub.L. No. 97-81, § 4, 95 Stat. 1085, 1088) guarantees that qualified counsel will be detailed to represent the accused for the investigation.

The defense may renew before the military judge any objection for which it has not received satisfactory relief. *See* R.C.M. 905(b)(2); R.C.M. 906(b)(3).

The last sentence in the discussion is based on *United States v. Cumberledge* and *United States v. Chuculate,* both*supra.*

Rule 406 Pretrial advice

(a) *In general.* This subsection is based on Article 34(a) as amended, Military Justice Act of 1983, Pub.L.No. 98–209, § 4, 97 Stat. 1393 (1983); and on paragraph 35 *b* of MCM, 1969 (Rev.).

(b) *Contents.* This subsection is based on Article 34(a). It is consistent with paragraph 35 *c* of MCM, 1969 (Rev.) (except insofar as Article 34 is modified). Matters which paragraph 35 *c* said "should" be included are not required, but are listed in the discussion. The rule states the minimum necessary to comply with Article 34(a). *Cf. United States v. Greenwalt*, 6 U.S.C.M.A. 569, 20 C.M.R. 285 (1955).

The first paragraph in the discussion is based on paragraph 35 *c* of MCM, 1969 (Rev.) and *United States v. Hardin*, 7 M.J. 399 (C.M.A. 1979); *United States v. Greenwalt, supra; United States v. Schuller*, 5 U.S.C.M.A. 101, 17 C.M.R. 101 (1954); *United States v. Pahl*, 50 C.M.R. 885 (C.G.C.M.R. 1975).

The second paragraph of the discussion is based on S.Rep. No. 53, 98th Cong., 1st Sess. 17 (1983), and on the second sentence in paragraph 35 *c* of MCM, 1969 (Rev.).

The last paragraph is based on *United States v. Greenwalt, supra. See also United States v. Rivera*, 20 U.S.C.M.A. 6, 42 C.M.R. 198 (1970); *United States v. Henry*, 50 C.M.R. 685 (A.F.C.M.R.), *pet. denied*, 23 U.S.C.M.A. 666, 50 C.M.R. 903 (1975); *United States v. Barton*, 41 C.M.R. 464 (A.C.M.R. 1969).

1991 Amendment: The Discussion to R.C.M. 406(b) was amended to state explicitly the applicable standard of proof. *See United States v. Engle*, 1 M.J. 387, 389 n.4 (C.M.A. 1976). The sentence concerning pretrial advice defects is based upon *United States v. Murray*, 25 M.J. 445 (C.M.A. 1988), in which the court reviewed the legislative history to the 1983 amendment to Article 34, U.C.M.J., and held that lack of a pretrial advice in violation of the article is neither jurisdictional nor *per se* prejudicial.

2004 Amendment: The Discussion to R.C.M. 406(b) was amended to add as additional, non-binding guidance that the SJA should include the recommendation of the Article 32 investigating officer.

(c) *Distribution.* This subsection is based on Article 34(b), as amended, Military Justice Act of 1983, Pub.L. No. 98–209, § 4(b), 97 Stat. 1393 (1983). Paragraph 35 *c* of MCM, 1969 (Rev.) also required that the staff judge advocate's recommendation be forwarded with the charges if referred to trial. This subsection makes clear that the entire advice is to be forwarded. This ensures that the advice can be subjected to judicial review when necessary. *See* R.C.M. 906(b)(3). *See also United States v. Collins*, 6 M.J. 256 (C.M.A. 1979); *United States v. Engle, supra.*

Rule 407 Action by commander exercising general court-martial jurisdiction

(a) *Disposition.* This subsection is based on Article 34(a) and paragraph 35 *a* of MCM, 1969 (Rev.). *See* Article 22.

(b) *National security matters.* This subsection is based on the second and third sentences of the second paragraph of paragraph 33 *f* of MCM, 1969 (Rev.) and Article 43(e). It has been broadened to expressly recognize the authority of service Secretaries to promulgate regulations governing disposition of sensitive cases. Note that the rule applies regardless of whether hostilities exist, although as the discussion notes the Article 43(e) procedure for suspending the statute of limitations could only be used in time of war.

CHAPTER V. COURT-MARTIAL COMPOSITION AND PERSONNEL; CONVENING COURT-MARTIAL

Rule 501 Composition and personnel of courts-martial

(a) *Composition of courts-martial.* This subsection is based on Article 16. Except for the change in the requirement as to the form of the request for trial by military judge alone, it is consistent with paragraph 4 *a* of MCM, 1969 (Rev.).

(b) *Counsel in general and special courts-martial.* This subsection is based on Article 27(a). Except for the change concerning who details counsel (*see* R.C.M. 503(c)), it is consistent with paragraph 6 *a* of MCM, 1969 (Rev.). This subsection includes reference to detailing associate defense counsel. This is based on Article 27(a), as amended Pub.L. No. 98 –209, § 3(c), (f), 97 Stat. 1393 (1983).

(c) *Other personnel.* This subsection is based on paragraph 7 of MCM, 1969 (Rev.).

Rule 502 Qualifications and duties of personnel of courts-martial

(a) *Members.* Subsection (1) is based on Article 25(a), (b) and (c) and on the first paragraph of paragraph 4 *b* and paragraph 4 *d* of MCM, 1969 (Rev.). Factors which disqualify a person from serving as a member are listed in R.C.M. 912(f)(1).

The discussion is based on the second paragraph of paragraph 4 *b* of MCM, 1969 (Rev.).

The references to use of members of the National Oceanic and Atmospheric Administration and of the Public Health Service carry forward the similar provision at paragraph 4 *b* of MCM, 1969 (Rev.). Similar provisions have been included in naval practice since at least 1937. *See, e.g., Naval Courts and Boards* § 347 (1937, 1945 reprint). The similar provision in MCM, 1951 was upheld in *United States v. Braud*, 11 U.S.C.M.A. 192, 29 C.M.R. 8 (1960) (Public Health Service commissioned officer served as member of Coast Guard court-martial), *decision below*, 28 C.M.R. 692 (C.G.B.R. 1959). *Braud* upheld the provision even though Article 25 is arguably ambiguous and the P.H.S. officer who served as a member had not been "militarized" and was not himself subject to the code. *Cf.* 42 U.S.C. § 217 (1976) (P.H.S. may be declared to be a military service in time of war; members become subject to personal jurisdiction of Code); 33 U.S.C. § 855 (NOAA may be transferred by President to military service in national emergency; members become subject to personal jurisdiction of Code); Art. 2(a)(8) (jurisdiction over members of Public Health Service and of Environmental Science Services Administration). The Environmental Science Services Administration, which succeeded the Coast and Geodetic Survey mentioned in some earlier Manuals, is now defunct. Its functions were transferred to the National Oceanic and Atmospheric Administration. Reorg. Plan No. 4 of 1970, 3 C.F.R. 1075 (1966–1970 Comp.), *reprinted in* 84 Stat. 2090. NOAA has only a commissioned officer corps. *Id.* § 2(f); 33 U.S.C.A. § 851 (Supp. 1981). P.H.S. has both commissioned and warrant officers. 42 § 204 (Supp. 1981).

Subsection (2) and the discussion are based on paragraph 41 *a* and *b* and the last paragraph of paragraph 53*d* of MCM, 1969 (Rev.). The admonition of MCM, 1969 (Rev.) that misconduct by members may constitute an offense and that members should be attentive and dignified has been deleted as unnecessary.

(b) *President.* Subsection (1) is based on paragraph 40 *a* of MCM, 1969 (Rev.). Subsections (2)(A) and (B) are based on paragraphs 40 *b*(1)(c) and (d) of MCM, 1969 (Rev.). Paragraphs 40 *b*(1) (a) and (b) are deleted. Paragraph 40 *b*(1)(a) conflicts with the authority of the military judge under R.C.M. 801(a)(1). Paragraph 40 *b*(1)(b) is unnecessary. Subsection (2)(c) is based on paragraph 40 *b*(2) of MCM, 1969 (Rev.). The general description of the duties of a president of a special court-martial without a military judge in paragraph 40*b*(2) is deleted here. Such a summarized description is an inadequate substitute for familiarity with the rules themselves.

(c) *Qualifications of military judge.* This subsection and the discussion are based on Article 26(b) and (c) and paragraph 4 *e* of MCM, 1969 (Rev.). Reasons for disqualification are described in R.C.M. 902.

1999 Amendment: R.C.M. 502(c) was amended to delete the requirement that military judges be "on active duty" to enable Reserve Component judges to conduct trials during periods of inactive duty for training (IDT) and inactive duty training travel (IATT). The active duty requirement does not appear in Article 26, UCMJ which prescribes the qualifications for military judges. It appears to be a vestigial requirement from paragraph 4 *e* of the 1951 and 1969 MCM. Neither the current MCM nor its predecessors provide an explanation for this additional requirement. It was deleted to enhance efficiency in the military justice system.

(d) *Counsel.* Subsection (1) is based on Article 27(b) and paragraph 6 of MCM, 1969 (Rev.). The possibility of detailing associate counsel has been added based on the amendment of Article 27(a) and 42(a). *See* Military Justice Act of 1983, Pub.L. No. 98–209, § 3(c), (f), 97 Stat. 1393 (1983). As the discussion indicates, "associate counsel" ordinarily refers to detailed counsel when the accused has military or civilian counsel. *See* Article 38(b)(6). An associate defense counsel must be qualified to act as defense counsel. An assistant defense counsel need not be. One other substantive change from MCM, 1969 (Rev.). has been made. Detailed defense counsel in special courts-martial must be certified by the Judge Advocate General concerned although this is not required by Article 27(c). Article 27(c) permits representation of an accused by a counsel not qualified and certified under Article 27(b) if the accused does not request qualified counsel, having been given the opportunity to do so, or when such counsel cannot be obtained on account of physical conditions or military exigencies. In the latter event, no bad-conduct discharge may be adjudged. Article 19. Currently, certified counsel is routinely provided in all special courts-martial, so the modification of the rule will not change existing practice. Moreover, the enforcement of waiver provisions in these rules and the Military Rules of Evidence necessitate, both for fairness and the orderly administration of justice, that the accused be represented by qualified counsel. *See also United States v. Rivas*, 3 M.J. 282 (C.M.A. 1977). Because of this rule, the rule of equivalency in Article 27(c) and (3) is not necessary.

Subsection (2) is based on the fifth sentence of the first paragraph of paragraph 6 *c* of MCM, 1969 (Rev.).

Subsection (3) is based on the first sentence of the second paragraph of paragraph 48 *a* of MCM, 1969 (Rev.) and on *Soriano v. Hosken*, 9 M.J. 221 (C.M.A. 1980); *United States v. Kraskouskas*, 9 U.S.C.M.A. 607, 26 C.M.R. 387 (1958). The discussion is taken from *Soriano v. Hosken, supra.*

Subsection (4) is based on Article 27(a) and on the fourth and fifth sentences of paragraph 6 *a* of MCM, 1969 (Rev.). *See also United States v. Catt*, 1 M.J. 41 (C.M.A. 1975). The accuser has been added to the list of disqualifications. *See ABA Standards, The Prosecution Function* , §§ 3–1(c); 3–3.9(c)(1979).

Subsection (5) is based on paragraph 44 *d* and 45 *a* of MCM, 1969 (Rev.) and on Article 38(d). The forum-based distinction as to the powers of an assistant trial counsel has been deleted. The trial counsel is responsible for the prosecution of the case. R.C.M. 805(c) requires the presence of a qualified trial counsel at general courts-martial. The discussion is based on paragraphs 44 *e, f, g,* and *h* of MCM, 1969 (Rev.). Some of the specific duties are now covered in other rules, *e.g.*, R.C.M. 701; 812, 813; 914; 919. Some examples and explanations have been deleted as unnecessary.

The first sentence of subsections (6) is new. *Cf.* paragraphs 46 *d* and 48 *c* of MCM, 1969 (Rev.). The second sentence of subsection (6) is based on Article 38(e). The rule does not require that defense counsel in the court-martial represent the accused in administrative or civil actions arising out of the same offenses. The discussion is based on paragraphs 46 *d*, 47, and 48 *c, d, e, f, g, h, j,* and *k* of MCM, 1969 (Rev.). The matters covered in paragraph 48 *k*(2) and (3) of MCM, 1969 (Rev.) are modified in the discussion based on the amendment of Articles 38(c) and 61. *See* Military Justice Act of 1983, Pub.L. No. 98–209, §§ 3(e)(3), 5(b)(1), 97 Stat. 1393 (1983). *See* R.C.M. 1105; 1110. As to associate counsel, *see* the Analysis subsection (d)(1) of this rule. *See also United States v. Breese*, 11 M.J. 17, 22 n. 13 (C.M.A. 1981); *United States v. Rivas, supra; United States v. Palenius*, 2

M.J. 86 (C.M.A. 1977); *United States v. Goode*, 1 M.J. 3 (C.M.A. 1975).

(e) *Interpreters, reporters, escorts, bailiffs, clerks, and guards.* This subsection is based on paragraphs 7, 49, 50, and 51 of MCM, 1969 (Rev.). The list of disqualifications, except for the accuser, is new and is intended to prevent circumstances which may detract from the integrity of the court-martial.

(f) *Action upon discovery of disqualification or lack of qualification.* This subsection is based on paragraphs 41 *c*, 44 *b*, 46 *b* of MCM, 1969 (Rev.).

Rule 503 Detailing members, military judge, and counsel

(a) *Members.* Subsection (1) is based on Article 25. Because of the amendment of Articles 26 and 27, the convening authority is no longer required to detail personally the military judge and counsel. Military Justice Act of 1983, Pub.L. No. 98–209, § 3(c), 97 Stat. 1393 (1983). The last sentence of paragraph 4 *b* of MCM, 1969 (Rev.) is deleted as unnecessary. The second paragraph in the discussion serves the same purpose as the third paragraph of paragraph 4 *b* of MCM, 1969 (Rev.): to alert the convening authority to avoid appointing people subject to removal for cause. Unlike that paragraph, however, no suggestion is now made that the convening authority commits error by appointing such persons, since the disqualifications are waivable. *See* Analysis, R.C.M. 912(f)(4).

Subsection (2) is based on Article 25(c) and the third paragraph of paragraph 4 *c* of MCM, 1969 (Rev.). The discussion is based on paragraph 36 *c*(2) of MCM, 1969 (Rev.).

1986 Amendment: Subsection (2) was amended to reflect an amendment to Article 25(c)(1), UCMJ, in the "Military Justice Amendments of 1986," tit. VIII, § 803, National Defense Authorization Act for fiscal year 1987, Pub. L. No. 99–661, 100 Stat. 3905, (1986) which authorizes enlisted accused to request orally on the record that at least one-third of the members of courts-martial be enlisted.

Subsection (3) is based on paragraphs 4 *f* and *g* of MCM, 1969 (Rev.). Subsection (3) combines treatment of members from a different command and those from a different armed force. The power of a commander to detail members not under the convening authority's command is the same whether the members are in the same or a different armed force. Therefore each situation can be covered in one rule. The discussion repeats the preference for members, or at least a majority thereof, to be of the same service as the accused which was found in paragraph 4 *g*(1) of MCM, 1969 (Rev.). Permission for the Judge Advocate General to detail members of another armed force is no longer required in the Manual. Detailing a military judge from a different command or armed force is now covered in subsection (d).

(b) *Military Judge.* Subsections (1) and (2) are based on Article 26(a), as amended, Military Justice Act of 1983, Pub. L. No. 98–209, § 3(c)(1), 97 Stat. 1393 (1983). The convening authority is no longer required to detail personally the military judge. *Id.* Subsection (1) requires that responsibility for detailing military judges will be in judicial channels. *See Hearings on S.2521 Before the Subcomm. on Manpower and Personnel of the Senate Comm. on Armed Services*, 97th Cong., 2nd Sess. 52 (1982). More specific requirements will be provided in service regulations. Subsection (2) is intended to make detailing the military judge administratively efficient. *See* S. Rep. No. 53, 98th Cong., 1st Sess. 3–5, 12 (1983), H.R. Rep. No. 549, 98th Cong., 1st Sess. 13–14 (1983). As long as a qualified military judge presides over the court-martial, any irregularity in detailing a military judge is not jurisdictional and would result in reversal only if specific prejudice were shown. *See* S. Rep. No. 53, 98th Cong., 1st Sess. 12 (1983).

Subsection (3) is based on Article 26. *See also* Article 6(a).

2005 Amendment: Subsection (b)(3) was amended to clarify that a military judge from any service may be detailed to a court-martial convened by a combatant or joint commander.

(c) *Counsel.* Subsections (1) and (2) are based on Article 27(a), as amended, Military Justice Act of 1983, Pub. L. No. 98–209, § 3(c)(2), 97 Stat. 1393 (1983). The convening authority is no longer required to detail personally the counsel. *Id.* Efficient allocation of authority for detailing counsel will depend on the organizational structure and operational requirements of each service. Therefore, specific requirements will be provided in service regulations. Subsection (2) is intended to make detailing counsel administratively efficient. *See* S. Rep. No. 53, 98th Cong., 1st Sess. 3–5, 12 (1983); H.R. Rep. No. 549, 98th Cong., 1st Sess. 13–14 (1983). Counsel are not a jurisdictional component of courts-martial. *Wright v. United States*, 2 M.J. 9 (C.M.A. 1976). Any irregularity in detailing counsel would result in reversal only if specific prejudice were shown. *See* S. Rep. No. 53, 98th Cong., 1st Sess. 12 (1983).

Subsection (3) is based on Article 27. *See also* Article 6(a).

2005 Amendment: Subsection (c)(3) was amended to clarify that counsel from any service may be detailed to a court-martial convened by a combatant or joint commander.

Rule 504 Convening courts-martial

(a) *In general.* This subsection substantially repeats the first sentence of paragraph 36 *b* of MCM, 1969 (Rev.).

(b) *Who may convene courts-martial.* Subsection (1) is based on Article 22 and paragraph 5 *a*(1) of MCM, 1969 (Rev.). The power of superiors to limit the authority of subordinate convening authorities is based on paragraph 5 *b*(4) of MCM, 1969 (Rev.). Although that paragraph applied only to special and summary courts-martial, the same principle applies to general courts-martial. *See* Article 22(b). *See generally United States v. Hardy*, 4 M.J. 20 (C.M.A. 1977); *United States v. Hawthorne*, 7 U.S.C.M.A. 293, 22 C.M.R. 83 (1956); *United States v., Rembert*, 47 C.M.R. 755 (A.C.M.R. 1973), *pet. denied*, 23 U.S.C.M.A. 598 (1974). The discussion is based on the second and third sentences of paragraph 5 *a*(5) of MCM, 1969 (Rev.).

Subsection (2) is based on Article 23 and paragraphs 5 *b*(1), (3), and (4) of MCM, 1969 (Rev.).

2005 Amendment: Subsection (b)(2)(B) was amended to clarify those authorized to determine when a unit is "separate or detached."

As to subsection (3), *see* Analysis, R.C.M. 1302(a).

Subsection (4) is based on the first sentence of paragraph 5 *a*(5) of MCM, 1969 (Rev.). *See also United States v. Greenwalt*, 6 U.S.C.M.A. 569, 20 C.M.R. 285 (1955); *United States v. Bunting*, 4 U.S.C.M.A. 84, 15 C.M.R. 84 (1954).

(c) *Disqualification.* This subsection is based on Articles 22(b) and 23(b) and on paragraph 5 *a*(3) of MCM, 1969 (Rev.). *See also* Article 1(5) and (9); *United States v. Haygood*, 12 U.S.C.M.A. 481, 31 C.M.R. 67 (1961); *United States v. LaGrange*, 1 U.S.C.M.A. 342,3 C.M.R. 76 (1952); *United States v. Kostes*, 38 C.M.R. 512 (A.B.R. 1967).

(d) *Convening orders.* This subsection is based on paragraph 36 *b* of MCM, 1969 (Rev.) with two substantive modifications. First, in conformity with the amendment of Articles 26(a) and 27(a), *see* Military Justice Act of 1983, Pub. L. No. 98–209, § 3(c) 97 Stat. 1393 (1983), the military judge and counsel are no longer included in the convening order. *See* R.C.M. 503(b) and (c) and Analysis. Second, several matters, such as the unit of any enlisted members, which were required by paragraph 36 *b* are not included here. These may be required by service regulations. Summary courts-martial are treated separately from general and special courts-martial because of their different composition.

(e) *Place.* This subsection is new. It derives from the convening authority's power to fix the place of trial (*see also* R.C.M. 906(b)(11)) and from the convening authority's control of the resources for the trial. It does not change current practice.

Rule 505 Changes in members, military judge, and counsel

(a) *In general.* This subsection is based on the first sentence of paragraph 37 *a* of MCM, 1969 (Rev.) except that it has been modified to conform to the amendment of Articles 26(a) and 27(a). *See* Military Justice Act of 1983, Pub. L. No. 98–209, § 3(c), 97 Stat. 1393 (1983). The discussion is based on the third and fourth sentences of paragraph 37 *c* of MCM, 1969 (Rev.).

(b) *Procedure.* This subsection is based on the first two sentences of paragraph 37 *c*(1) and on paragraph 37 *c*(2) of MCM, 1969 (Rev.). *See also United States v. Ware*, 5 M.J. 24 (C.M.A. 1978). It has been modified to reflect that military judges and counsel no longer must be detailed by the convening authority. The second paragraph in the discussion is based on *United States v. Herrington*, 8 M.J. 194 (C.M.A. 1980). References in paragraph 37 *b* to excusal as a result of challenges are deleted here as challenges are covered in R.C.M. 902 and 912.

(c) *Changes of members.* This subsection is based on Articles 25(e) and 29, and paragraphs 37 *b* and *c*, and 39 *e* of MCM, 1969 (Rev.). The limitation on the authority of the convening authority's delegate to excuse no more than one-third of the members is based on S. Rep. No. 53, 98th Cong., 1st Sess. 13 (1983).

(d) *Changes of detailed counsel.* Subsection (1) is based on that part of the second sentence of paragraph 37 *a* of MCM, 1969 (Rev.) which covered trial counsel.

Subsection (2) is new and conforms to the amendment of Article 27(a) concerning who details counsel. Subsection (2)(A) is consistent with that part of the second sentence of paragraph 37 *a* of MCM, 1969 (Rev.) which dealt with defense counsel. Subsection (2)(B) is based on Article 38(b)(5); *United States v. Catt*, 1 M.J. 41 (C.M.A. 1975); *United States v. Timberlake*, 22 U.S.C.M.A. 117, 46 C.M.R. 117 (1973); *United States v. Andrews*, 21 U.S.C.M.A. 165, 44 C.M.R. 219 (1972); *United States v. Massey*, 14 U.S.C.M.A. 486, 34 C.M.R. 266 (1964).

(e) *Change of military judge.* This subsection is based on Articles 26(a) and 29(d) and on paragraph 39 *e* of MCM, 1969 (Rev.). *See also United States v. Smith*, 3 M.J. 490 (C.M.A. 1975).

(f) *Good cause.* This subject is based on Article 29 and on *United States v. Greenwell*, 12 U.S.C.M.A. 560, 31 C.M.R. 146 (1961); *United States v. Boysen*, 11 U.S.C.M.A. 331, 29 C.M.R. 147 (1960); *Unites States v. Grow*, 3 U.S.C.M.A. 77, 11 C.M.R. 77 (1953). *See* S. Rep. No. 53, 98th Cong., 1st Sess. 13 (1983). As to defense counsel, *see also United States v. Catt, United States v. Timberlake, United States v. Andrews* , and *United States v. Massey*, all *supra*.

Rule 506 Accused's rights to counsel

(a) *In general.* This subsection is taken from the first two sentences of paragraph 48 *a* of MCM, 1969 (Rev.), which was based on Article 38(b) as amended. Act of November 20, 1981, Pub. L. No. 97–81; 95 Stat. 1085. Note that the amendment of Article 38(b) effectively overruled*United States v. Jordan*, 22 U.S.C.M.A. 164, 46 C.M.R. 164 (1973), which held that an accused who has civilian counsel is not entitled to individual military counsel. The amendment of Article 38(b) provides that the accused may be represented by civilian counsel "and" by detailed or requested military counsel instead of civilian counsel "or" requested military counsel as it formerly did. *See also* H.R. Rep. No. 306, 97th Cong., 1st Sess. 4–7 (1981).

Nothing in this rule is intended to limit the authority of the military judge to ensure that the accused exercises the rights to counsel in a timely fashion and that the progress of the trial is not unduly impeded. *See Morris v. Slappy*, 461 U.S. (1983), 33 Cr.L. Rptr. 3013 (1983); *United States v. Montoya*, 13 M.J. 268 (C.M.A. 1982); *United States v. Kinard*, 21 U.S.C.M.A. 300, 45 C.M.R. 74 (1972); *United States v. Brown*, 10 M.J. 635 (A.C.M.R. 1980); *United States v. Alicea-Baez*, 7 M.J. 989 (A.C.M.R. 1979); *United States v. Livingston*, 7 M.J. 638 (A.C.M.R. 1979), *aff'd* 8 M.J. 828 (C.M.A. 1980). *See also United States v. Johnson*, 12 M.J 670 (A.C.M.R. 1981); *United States v. Kilby*, 3 M.J. 938 (N.C.M.R.), *pet. denied*, 4 M.J. 139 (1977).

(b) *Individual military counsel.* Subsection (1) is based on paragraphs 48 *b*(1) and (2) of MCM, 1969 (Rev.). *See also* Article 38(b); H.R. Rep. No. 306, *supra* at 5–7; *United States v. Kelker*, 4 M.J. 323 (C.M.A. 1978); *United States v. Eason*, 21 U.S.C.M.A. 335, 45 C.M.R. 109 (1972); *United States v. Murray*, 20 U.S.C.M.A. 61, 42 C.M.R 253 (1970). The second sentence of the last paragraph of this subsection has been modified based on the amendment of Article 38(b)(7), Military Justice Act of 1983, Pub. L. No. 98–209, § 3(e)(2), 97 Stat. 1393 (1983).

Subsection (2) is taken from paragraph 48 *b*(3) of MCM, 1969 (Rev.). *See also* Article 38(b)(7). It ensures substantial uniformity in procedure among the services for handling requests for individual military counsel.

Subsection (3) is based on the fourth through eighth sentences in the second paragraph of paragraph 46 *d* of MCM, 1969 (Rev.) and on Article 38(b)(6). *See also* H.R. Rep. No. 306, *supra* at 4–7. Authority to excuse detailed counsel has been modified based on the amendment of Article 38(b)(6). *See* Military Justice Act of 1983, Pub. L. No. 98–209, § 3(e)(1), 97 Stat. 1393 (1983).

(c) *Excusal or withdrawal.* This subsection is based on *United States v. Iverson* , 5 M.J. 440 (C.M.A. 1978); *United States v. Palenius*, 2 M.J. 86 (C.M.A. 1977); *United States v. Eason, supra*; *United States v. Andrews*, 21 U.S.C.M.A. 165, 44 C.M.R. 219 (1972). *See* Analysis, R.C.M. 505(c)(2).

(d) *Waiver.* This subsection is based on the third sentence of the second paragraph of paragraph 48 *a* of MCM, 1969 (Rev.) and on *Faretta v. California*, 422 U.S. 806 (1975). As to the last two sentences, *see id.* at 834 n.46.

(e) *Nonlawyer present.* This subsection is based on the last sentence of the second paragraph of paragraph 48 *a* of MCM, 1969 (Rev.).

CHAPTER VI. REFERRAL, SERVICE, AMENDMENT, AND WITHDRAWAL OF CHARGES

Rule 601 Referral

(a) *In general.* This definition is new. MCM, 1969 (Rev.) did not define "referral."

(b) *Who may refer.* This section is also new, although MCM, 1969 (Rev) clearly implied that any convening authority could refer charges. *See also United States v. Hardy*, 4 M.J. 29 (C.M.A. 1977). Paragraphs 5 *b*(4) and 5 *c* of MCM, 1969 (Rev.) contained similar provisions.

(c) *Disqualification.* This section is added to the Manual to express the statutory disqualification of an accuser to convene a court-martial in parallel terms in relation to referral. *See* Articles 22(b), 23(b). *Cf.* Article 24(b). The discussion follows paragraph 33 *i* of MCM, 1969 (Rev.).

(d) *When charges may be referred.* Subsection (1) is new. Neither the code nor MCM, 1969 (Rev) have previously provided a standard for referral except in general courts-martial. *See* Article 34(a). Subsection (1) promotes efficiency by helping to prevent groundless charges from being referred for trial. This is consistent with Fed. R. Crim. P. 5.1(a). *Accord ABA Standards Prosecution Function* section 3–3.9(a) (1979). Consistent with the amendment of Article 34, subsection (1) does not require the convening authority to evaluate the legal sufficiency of the case personally. In general courts-martial the legal sufficiency determination must be made by the staff judge advocate. *See* Article 34(a) and subsection (3)(2) of this rule. Subsection (1) requires a similar determination in all courts-martial, including special and summary courts-martial. Because of the judicial limitations on the sentencing power of special and summary courts-martial, any judge advocate may make the determination or the convening authority may do so personally. (A special or summary court-martial convening authority does not always have access to a judge advocate before referring charges; moreover, this subsection does not require reference to a judge advocate, even if one is available, if the convening authority elects to make the determination personally.) A person who serves as a trial counsel is not disqualified from rendering this advice. *Cf. ABA Standards Prosecution Function* Section 3–3.9(a) (1979). Note that there is no requirement under this subsection that the judge advocate's advice be written or that the convening authority memorialize the basis of the referral in any way.

The "reasonable grounds" standard is based on Article 34's prerequisite to referral of charges to a general court-martial that the charges be warranted by the evidence in the report of the Article 32 investigation. Further, the legislative history of Article 32 strongly suggests that this is the intended standard of the investigation. *Hearings on H.R. 2498 Before a Subcomm, of the House Comm. on Armed Services*, 81st Cong., 1st Sess. 997 –98 (1949). Nothing suggests that the standard governing referral to inferior courts-martial should be different from that applicable to general courts-martial. It appears that the reasonable grounds standard has been in operation even without an explicit requirement. *See, e.g., United States v. Eagle*, 1 M.J. 387, 389 n.4 (C.M.A. 1976); *United States v. Kauffman*, 33 C.M.R. 748, 795 (A.F.B.R.), *rev'd on other grounds*, 14 U.S.C.M.A. 283, 34 C.M.R. 63 (1963). *Cf. Gerstein v. Pugh*, 420 U.S. 103 (1975).

Subsection (2) restates the prerequisites for referral to a general court-martial of Articles 32 and 34. It is consistent with paragraphs 30 *c* and *d*, 34 *a*, and 35 of MCM, 1969 (Rev.) except insofar as the amendment of Article 34 (*see* Military Justice Act of 1983, Pub. L. No. 98–209, § 4, 97 Stat. 1393 (1983)) requires otherwise. The function of this provision is the same as paragraph 30 of MCM, 1969 (Rev.) to serve as a reminder of procedural limitations on referral. The waiver provision is based on Article 32(d); S. Rep. No. 53, 98th Cong., 1st Sess. 17 (1983); *United States v. Schaffer*, 12 M.J. 425 (C.M.A. 1982); *United States v. Ragan*, 14 U.S.C.M.A. 119, 33 C.M.R. 331 (1963).

(e) *How changes shall be referred.* Subsection (1) is consistent with paragraph 33 *j*(1) of MCM, 1969 (Rev.). The personal responsibility of the convening authority to decide whether to refer and how to refer is emphasized, but the discussion makes clear that the administrative aspects of recording that decision may be delegated.

The discussion's instructions for subsequent referrals are based on paragraph 33 *j*(1) of MCM, 1969 (Rev.).

The special case of referrals to summary courts-martial by the only officer present in command follows paragraph 33 *j*(1) of MCM, 1969 (Rev.) and Article 24(b).

The discussion of limiting instructions follows paragraphs 33 *j*(1) and *k* of MCM, 1969 (Rev.). The advice that convening authorities be guided by the criteria for capital punishment found at R.C.M. 1004 is new. *See Gregg v. Georgia*, 428 U.S. 153, 225 (1976) (White, J., concurring in the judgment).

The last paragraph of the discussion on transmitting the referred charges and allied papers to the trial counsel is based on paragraph 33 *j*(2) of MCM, 1969 (Rev.).

Subsection (2) is less restrictive than the previous military rule found at paragraphs 26 *b* and *c* of MCM, 1969 (Rev.), which cautioned against joining major and minor offenses. This rule is inconsistent with Fed. R. Crim. P. 8(a), which requires (in general) separate trials for each offense. Such a requirement is too unwieldy to be effective, particularly in combat or deployment. Joinder is entirely within the discretion of the convening authority. The last two sentences of the rule dealing with additional charges are based on paragraph 65 *b* of MCM, 1969 (Rev.). The discussion encourages economy, following paragraph 33 *h* of MCM, 1969 (Rev.). The last sentence in subsection (2) is new and clarifies that the accused may consent to the referral of additional charges after arraignment. Since the prohibition of such referral is for the accused's benefit, the accused may forego it when it would be the accused's advantage. *See United States v. Lee*, 14 M.J. 983 (N.M.C.M.R. 1983).

The first two sentences of subsection (3) restate Fed. R. Crim. P. 8(b) in military nomenclature. They are consistent with the approach taken by paragraph 26 *d* of MCM, 1969 (Rev.). The last sentence is based on paragraph 33 *l* of MCM, 1969 (Rev.). There is no counterpart in federal civilian practice.

2005 Amendment: The Discussion section was amended to reflect the rule changes that require the convening authority to affirmatively refer a capital punishment eligible offense for trial as a capital case.

(f) *Referral by other convening authorities.* This new provision reflects the principle that a subordinate convening authority's decision does not preempt different dispositions by superior convening authorities. *See United States v. Charette*, 15 M.J. 197 (C.M.A. 1983); *United States v. Blaylock*, 15 M.J. 190 (C.M.A. 1983). *See also* Analysis, R.C.M. 306(a), Analysis, R.C.M. 905(g), and Analysis, R.C.M. 907(b)(2)(C).

Rule 602 Service of charges

This rule is based on Article 35 and paragraph 44 *h* of MCM, 1969 (Rev.). Fed. R. Crim. P. 9 is consistent in purpose with this rule, but not in structure. The warrant system of Fed. R. Crim. P. 9(a), (b)(1), and (c) (2) is unnecessary in military practice. The remand provision of Fed. R. Crim. P. 9(d) is inconsistent with the structure of military procedure but consistent with the convening authority's discretion to refer charges to a minor forum. *See* R.C.M. 306. The provision of Fed. R. Crim. P. 9(c) for service by mail or delivery to a residence is inconsistent with Article 35.

Rule 603 Changes to charges and specifications

(a) *Minor changes defined.* This definition and the discussion consolidate the tests and examples found at paragraphs 33 *d*, 44 *f*(1), and 69 *b*(1) of MCM, 1969 (Rev.). They are consistent with Fed. R. Crim. P. 7(e).

(b) *Minor changes before arraignment.* This provision is based on and consolidates the authority of various persons to make minor changes as stated at paragraphs 33 *d* and 44 *f*(1) of MCM, 1969 (Rev.). It is inappropriate for an Article 32 investigating officer to make changes, but an investigating officer may recommend changes. *See also* Article 34(b) which provides authority for the staff judge advocate or legal officer to amend charges or specifications for the reasons stated therein.

(c) *Minor changes after arraignment.* This provision is based on Fed. R. Crim. P. 7(e), which is generally consistent with military practice.

(d) *Major changes.* This subsection is based on paragraphs 33 *d* and 33 *e*(2) of MCM, 1969 (Rev.). *See also* Article 34(b) which provides authority for the staff judge advocate or legal officer to amend charges or specifications for the reasons stated therein.

Rule 604 Withdrawal of charges

(a) *Withdrawal.* This rule is based on paragraphs 5 *a*(6) and 56 *a* of MCM, 1969 (Rev.). The rule parallels Fed. R. Crim. P. 48(a), but leave of the court is not required for the convening authority to withdraw (or dismiss) charges and specifications. This would be inconsistent with the responsibilities of the convening authority under the Code. *See* Articles 34 and 60. The potential abuses which the leave-of-court requirement in the federal rule are designed to prevent are adequately prevented by the restraint on a later referral of withdrawn charges in the subsection (b).

The first paragraph in the discussion is new. It recognizes the distinction between withdrawal of charges, which extinguishes the jurisdiction of a court-martial over them, and dismissal of charges, which extinguishes the charges themselves. The discussion cautions that withdrawn charges, like any other unreferred charges, should be disposed of promptly. Dismissal of charges disposes of those charges; it does not necessarily bar subsequent disposition of the underlying offenses (*see* Analysis, R.C.M. 306(a)), although a later preferral and referral would raise the same issues as are discussed under subsection (b).

The second paragraph in the discussion is based on the last sentence of paragraph 56 *a* of MCM, 1969 (Rev.).

The third paragraph in the discussion is based on the second and fourth sentences in paragraph 56 *a* of MCM, 1969 (Rev.).

The first sentence of the fourth paragraph is based on the third sentence of paragraph 56 *a* of MCM, 1969 (Rev.) and *United States v. Charette*, 15 M.J. 197 (C.M.A. 1983); *United States v. Blaylock*, 15 M.J. 190 (C.M.A. 1983). The remainder of this paragraph is based on the second sentence of paragraph 56 *a* and paragraph 56 *d* of MCM, 1969 (Rev.).

(b) *Referral of withdrawn charges.* This rule is based on paragraphs 33 *j*(1) and 56 of MCM, 1969 (Rev.) and numerous decisions. *See, e.g., United States v. Charette, United States v. Blaylock*, and *United States v. Hardy*, all *supra; United States v. Jackson*, 1 M.J. 242 (C.M.A. 1976); *United States v. Walsh*, 22 U.S.C.M.A. 509, 47 C.M.R. 926 (1973); *Petty v. Convening Authority*, 20 U.S.C.M.A. 438, 43 C.M.R. 278 (1971). The second sentence in the rule is derived from portions of paragraphs 56 *b* and *c* of MCM, 1969 (Rev.) which were in turn based on *Wade v. Hunter*, 336 U.S. 684 (1949); *Legal and Legislative Basis, Manual for Courts-Martial, United States, 1951* at 64. *See* Article 44. The second sentence of paragraph 56 *b* of MCM, 1969 (Rev.) has been deleted. That sentence suggested that withdrawal after introduction of evidence on the merits for reasons other than urgent and unforeseen military necessity would not bar re-referral in some cases. If further prosecution is contemplated, such other possible grounds for terminating the trial after introduction of evidence has begun are more appropriately subject to a judicial determination whether to declare a mistrial under R.C.M. 915.

The first paragraph in the discussion contains a cross-reference to R.C.M. 915, Mistrial. Paragraph 56 of MCM, 1969 (Rev.) dealt with both withdrawal and mistrial. This was unnecessary and potentially confusing. Although the effect of a declaration of a mistrial may be similar to that of withdrawal, the narrow legal bases for a mistrial (*see United States v. Simonds*, 15 U.S.C.M.A. 641, 36 C.M.R. 139 (1966)) should be distinguished from withdrawal, which involves a far wider range of purposes and considerations. *See* Analysis, R.C.M. 915.

The second paragraph in the discussion is based on paragraph 56 *b* of MCM, 1969 (Rev.). Unlike paragraph 56 *b*, the current rules does not require a record in certain cases. Instead the discussion suggests that such a record is desirable if the later referral is more onerous to the accused. *See United States v. Blaylock, supra* at 192 n.1; *United States v. Hardy, supra.*

The third paragraph in the discussion is based on *United States v. Charette, United States v. Blaylock, United States v. Walsh*, and *Petty v. Convening Authority*, all *supra; United States v. Fleming*, 18 U.S.C.M.A. 524, 40 C.M.R. 236 (1969). *See* Article 37.

The fourth paragraph in the discussion is based generally on paragraphs 56 *b* and *c* of MCM, 1969 (Rev.), but more specificity is provided as to proper reasons for withdrawal and its effect at certain stages of the proceedings. The grounds for proper withdrawal and later referral are based on *United States v. Charette, United States v. Blaylock, United States v. Jackson*, all *supra*; *United States v. Lord*, 13 U.S.C.M.A. 78, 32 C.M.R. 78 (1962); and current practice. *United States v. Hardy* and *United*

States v. Walsh, both *supra*, indicate that the commencement of court-martial proceedings is, by itself, not important in analyzing the propriety of withdrawal. Arraignment is normally the first significant milestone for the same reasons that make it a cut-off point for other procedures. *See, e.g.*, R.C.M. 601; 603; 804. It should be noted that assembly of the court-martial, which could precede arraignment, could also have an effect on the propriety of a withdrawal, since this could raise questions about an improper intent to interfere with the exercise of codal rights or the impartiality of the court-martial. The importance of the introduction of evidence is based on Article 44. *See also* R.C.M. 907(b)(2)(C) and Analysis.

CHAPTER VII. PRETRIAL MATTERS

Rule 701 Discovery

Introduction. This rule is based on Article 46, as well as Article 36. The rule is intended to promote full discovery to the maximum extent possible consistent with legitimate needs for nondisclosure (*see e.g.*, Mil. R. Evid. 301; Section V) and to eliminate "gamesmanship" from the discovery process. *See generally ABA Standards, Discovery and Procedure Before Trial* (1978). For reasons stated below, the rule provides for broader discovery than is required in Federal practice. *See* Fed. R. Crim. P. 12.1; 12.2; 16. *See also* 18 U.S.C. § 3500.

Military discovery practice has been quite liberal, although the sources of this practice are somewhat scattered. *See* Articles 36 and 46; paragraphs 34, 44 *h*, and 115 *c* of MCM, 1969 (Rev.). *See also United States v. Killebrew*, 9 M.J. 154 (C.M.A. 1980); *United States v. Cumberledge* 6 M.J. 203, 204 n.4 (C.M.A. 1979). Providing broad discovery at an early stage reduces pretrial motions practice and surprise and delay at trial. It leads to better informed judgment about the merits of the case and encourages early decisions concerning withdrawal of charges, motions, pleas, and composition of court-martial. In short, experience has shown that broad discovery contributes substantially to the truth-finding process and to the efficiency with which it functions. It is essential to the administration of military justice; because assembling the military judge, counsel, members, accused, and witnesses is frequently costly and time-consuming, clarification or resolution of matters before trial is essential.

The rule clarifies and expands (at least formally) discovery by the defense. It also provides for the first time some discovery by the prosecution. *See* subsection (b) of the rule. Such discovery serves the same goal of efficiency.

Except for subsection (e), the rule deals with discovery in terms of disclosure of matters known to or in the possession of a party. Thus the defense is entitled to disclosure of matters known to the trial counsel or in the possession of military authorities. Except as provided in subsection (e), the defense is not entitled under this rule to disclosure of matters not possessed by military authorities or to have the trial counsel seek out and produce such matters for it. *But see* Mil. R. Evid. 506 concerning defense discovery of government information generally. Subsection (e) may accord the defense the right to have the Government assist the defense to secure evidence or information when not to do so would deny the defense similar access to what the prosecution would have if it were seeking the evidence or information. *See United States v. Killebrew, supra; Halfacre v. Chambers*, 5 M.J. 1099 (C.M.A. 1976).

(a) *Disclosure by the trial counsel.* This subsection is based in part on Fed. R. Crim. P. 16(a), but it provides for additional matters to be provided to the defense. *See ABA Standards, Discovery and Procedure Before Trial* § 11–2.1 (1978). Where a request is necessary, it is required to trigger the duty to disclose as a means of specifying what must be produced. Without the request, a trial counsel might be uncertain in many cases as to the extent of the duty to obtain matters not in the trial counsel's immediate possession. A request should indicate with reasonable specificity what materials are sought. When obviously discoverable materials are in the trial counsel's possession, trial counsel should provide them to the defense without a request. "Inspect" includes the right to copy. *See* subsection (h) of this rule.

Fed. R. Crim. P. 16(a)(1)(A) is not included here because the matter is covered in Mil. R. Evid. 304(d)(1). The discussion under subsection (a)(6) of this rule lists other discovery and notice provisions in the Military of Evidence.

Subsection (1) is based on paragraph 44 *h* of MCM, 1969 (Rev.). *See also* paragraph 33 *i*, *id.* 18 U.S.C. § 3500(a) is contra; the last sentence of Article 32(b) reflects Congressional intent that the accused receive witness statements before trial.

Subsection (2) is based on paragraph 115 *c* of MCM, 1969 (Rev.) and parallels Fed. R. Crim. P. 16(a)(1)(C) and (D).

Subsection (3)(A) is based on the last sentence in the second paragraph of paragraph 44 *h* of MCM, 1969 (Rev.). *See also* Appendix 5 at A5–1 of MCM, 1969 (Rev.); *United States v. Webster*, 1 M.J. 216 (C.M.A. 1975). Subsection (3)(B) is based on Fed. R. Crim. P. 12.1(b). Fed. R. Crim. P. 12.2 (notice based on mental condition) contains no parallel requirement for disclosure of rebuttal witnesses by the prosecution. The defense will ordinarily have such information because of the accused's participation in any court-ordered examination, so the distinction diminishes in practice. In the interest of full disclosure and fairness, subsection (3)(B) requires the prosecution to notify the defense of rebuttal witnesses on mental responsibility. *See also* R.C.M. 706.

1991 Amendment: Subsection (a)(3)(B) was amended to provide for prosecution disclosure of rebuttal witnesses to a defense of innocent ingestion. This conforms to the amendment to R.C.M. 701(b).

Subsection (4) is based on Fed. R. Crim. P. 16(a)(1)(B). The language is modified to make clear that the rule imposes no duty on the trial counsel to seek out prior convictions. (There is an ethical duty to exercise reasonable diligence in doing so, however. *See ABA Code of Professional Responsibility*, DR 6–101(A)(2); EC 6–4(1975).) The purpose of the rule is to put the defense on notice of prior convictions of the accused which may be used against the accused on the merits. Convictions for use on sentencing are covered under subsection (a)(5). Because of this distinction, under some circumstances the trial counsel may not be able to use a conviction on the merits because of lack of timely notice, but may be able to use it on sentencing.

Subsection (5) is based on paragraph 75 *b*(5) of MCM, 1969 (Rev.) *Cf.* Fed. R. Crim. P. 32(c)(3).

Subsection (6) is based on *ABA Standards, The Prosecution Function* § 3–3.11(a) (1979); *ABA Standards, Discovery and Pro-*

cedure Before Trial § 11–2.1(c) (1978). *See also United States v. Agurs*, 427 U.S. 97 (1976); *Brady v. Maryland*, 373 U.S. 83 (1963); *United States v. Brickey*, 16 M.J. 258 (C.M.A. 1983); *United States v. Horsey*, 6 M.J. 112 (C.M.A. 1979); *United States v. Lucas*, 5 M.J. 167 (C.M.A. 1978); *ABA Code of Professional Responsibility*, DR 7–103(B) (1975).

(b) *Disclosure by defense.* This subsection is based on Fed. R. Crim. P. 12.1, 12.2, and 16(b)(1)(A) and (B). *See generally Williams v. Florida*, 399 U.S. 78 (1970). The requirement in Fed. R. Crim. P. 12.1 for a written request by the prosecution for notice of an alibi defense was deleted because it would generate unnecessary paperwork. The accused is adequately protected by the opportunity to request a bill of particulars.

1986 Amendment. The phrase "a mental disease, defect, or other condition bearing upon the guilt of the accused" was deleted from this subsection, with other language substituted, in conjunction with the implementation of Article 50a, and the phrase "or partial mental responsibility" was deleted from the discussion to conform to the amendment to R.C.M. 916(k)(2).

1991 Amendment: Subsection (b)(1) has been revised to expand the open discovery that is characteristic of military practice. It provides the trial counsel with reciprocal discovery and equal opportunity to interview witnesses and inspect evidence as that available to the defense under subsection (a). *See* Article 46, U.C.M.J., and R.C.M. 701(e). Enhanced disclosure requirements for the defense are consistent with a growing number of state jurisdictions that give the prosecution an independent right to receive some discovery from the defense. *See* Mosteller, *Discovery Against the Defense: Tilting the Adversarial Balance*, 74 Calif. L. Rev. 1567, 1579–1583 (1986). Mandatory disclosure requirements by the defense will better serve to foster the truth-finding process.

1991 Amendment: Subsection (b)(2) was revised to add the requirement that the defense give notice of its intent to present the defense of innocent ingestion. The innocent ingestion defense, often raised during trials for wrongful use of a controlled substance, poses similar practical problems (*e.g.,* substantial delay in proceedings) as those generated by an alibi defense, and thus merits similar special treatment.

2002 Amendment: Subsection (b)(4) was amended to take into consideration the protections afforded by the new psychotherapist-patient privilege under Mil. R. Evid. 513.

1991 Amendment: Subsection (b)(5) was amended to clarify that when the defense withdraws notice of an intent to rely upon the alibi, innocent ingestion, or insanity defenses, or to introduce expert testimony of the accused's mental condition, neither evidence of such intention, nor statements made in connection therewith, are admissible against the servicemember who gave notice. This rule applies regardless of whether the person against whom the evidence is offered is an accused or a witness. *Fed. R. Crim.* P. 12.1 and 12.2, upon which the subsection is based, were similarly amended [*See* H.R. Doc. No. 64, 99th Cong., 1st Sess. 17–18 (1985)].

(c) *Failure to call witness.* This subsection is based on repealed subsection (a)(4) and (b)(3) of Fed. R. Crim. P. 16. Those subsections were inadvertently left in that rule after the notice of witnesses provisions were deleted by the conference committee. Act of December 12, 1975, Pub. L. No. 94–149, § 5, 89 Stat. 806. *But see* Fed. R. Crim. 12.1(f). Because notice of witnesses under R.C.M. 701 is required or otherwise encouraged (*see also* R.C.M. 703), such a provision is necessary in these rules.

(d) *Continuing duty to disclose.* This subsection is based on Fed. R. Crim. P. 16(c). *See also ABA Standards, Discovery and Procedure Before Trial* § 11–4.2 (1978).

(e) *Access to witnesses and other evidence.* This subsection is based on Article 46; paragraphs 42 *c* and 48 *h* of MCM, 1969 (Rev.); *United States v. Killebrew, supra; Halfacre, v. Chambers, supra; United States v. Enloe*, 15 U.S.C.M.A. 256, 35 C.M.R. 228 (1965); *United States v. Aycock*, 15 U.S.C.M.A. 158, 35 C.M.R. 130 (1964). The subsection permits witness (e.g., informant) protection programs and prevents improper interference with preparation of the case. *See United States v. Killebrew* and *United States v. Cumberledge, both supra. See also* subsection (f) of this rule; Mil. R. Evid. 507.

1986 Amendment. The discussion was added, based on *United States v. Treakle*, 18 M.J. 646 (A.C.M.R. 1984). *See also United States v. Tucker*, 17 M.J. 519 (A.F.C.M.R. 1984); *United States v. Lowery*, 18 M.J. 695 (A.F.C.M.R. 1984); *United States v. Charles*, 15 M.J. 509 (A.F.C.M.R. 1982); *United States v. Estes*, 28 C.M.R. 501 (A.B.R. 1959).

(f) *Information not subject to disclosure.* This subsection is based on the privileges and protections in other rules (*see, e.g.*, Mil. R. Evid. 301 and Section V). *See also Goldberg v. United States*, 425 U.S. 94 (1976); *United States v. Nobles*, 422 U.S. 225 (1975); *Hickman v. Taylor*, 329 U.S. 495 (1947). It differs from Fed. R. Crim. P. 16(a)(2) because of the broader discovery requirements under this rule. Production under the Jencks Act, 18 U.S.C. § 3500, is covered under R.C.M. 914.

(g) *Regulation of discovery.* Subsection (1) is based on the last sentence of Fed. R. Crim. P. 16(d)(2). It is a separate subsection to make clear that the military judge has authority to regulate discovery generally, in accordance with the rule. Local control of discovery is necessary because courts-martial are conducted in such a wide variety of locations and conditions. *See also* R.C.M. 108.

Subsection (g)(2) is based on Fed. R. Crim. P. 16(d)(1). *Cf.* Mil. R. Evid. 505; 506. *See also ABA Standards, Discovery and Procedures Before Trial* § 11–4.4 (1978).

Subsection (g)(3) is based on Fed. R. Crim. P. 16(d)(2), but it also incorporates the noncompliance provision of Fed. R. Crim. P.12.1(d) and 12.2(d). *But see Williams v. Florida, supra* at 83 n. 14; *Alicea v. Gagnon*, 675 F. 2d 913 (7th Cir. 1982). The discussion is based on *United States v. Myers*, 550 F.2d 1036 (5th Cir. 1977), *cert. denied*, 439 U.S. 847 (1978).

1993 Amendment. The amendment to R.C.M. 701(g)(3)(C), based on the decision of *Taylor v. Illinois*, 484 U.S. 400 (1988), recognizes that the Sixth Amendment compulsory process right does not preclude a discovery sanction that excludes the testimony of a material defense witness. This sanction, however, should be reserved to cases where the accused has willfully and blatantly violated applicable discovery rules, and alternative sanctions could not have minimized the prejudice to the Government. *See Chappee v. Commonwealth Massachusetts*, 659 F.Supp. 1220 (D. Mass. 1988). The Discussion to R.C.M. 701(g)(3)(C) adopts the test, along with factors the judge must consider, established by the *Taylor* decision.

(h) *Inspect.* This subsection is based on Fed. R. Crim. P. 16.

Rule 702 Depositions

(a) *In general.* This subsection is based on the first sentence in Fed. R. Crim. P. 15(a). The language concerning preferral of charges is added based on Article 49(a). The language concerning use at Article 32 investigations is also added because depositions may be used at such hearings.

"Exceptional" means out of the ordinary. Depositions are not taken routinely, but only when there is a specific need under the circumstances. As used in Fed. R. Crim. P. 15(a) "exceptional circumstances" is generally limited to preserving the testimony of a witness who is likely to be unavailable for trial. *See* 8 J. Moore, *Moore's Federal Practice* Para. 15.02[1]; 15.03 (1982 rev.ed.); *United States v. Singleton*, 460 F.2d 1148 (2d Cir. 1972). A deposition is not a discovery device under the Federal rule. 8.J. Moore, *supra* Para. 15.02[1]. *See also United States v. Rich*, 580 F.2d 929 (9th Cir.), *cert. denied*, 439 U.S. 935 (1978); *United States v. Adcock*, 558 F.2d. 397 (8th Cir.), *cert. denied*, 434 U.S. 921 (1977). The Court of Military Appeals has held that depositions may serve as a discovery device in certain unusual circumstances. *See* Analysis, subsection (c)(3)(A) *infra*. Consequently, "exceptional circumstances" may be somewhat broader in courts-martial. Nevertheless, the primary purpose of this rule is to preserve the testimony of unavailable witnesses for use at trial. *See* Article 49; *Hearings on H.R. 2498 Before a Subcomm. of the Comm. on Armed Services* 81st Cong. 1st Sess. 1064–1070 (1949).

The first paragraph in the discussion is based on Article 49(d) and (f) and on paragraph 117 *a* of MCM, 1969 (Rev.). The second and third paragraphs are based on Article 49(d), (e), and (f); paragraph 117 *b*(11) of MCM, 1969 (Rev.); Fed. R. Crim. P. 15(e). The admissibility of depositions is governed by Mil. R. Evid. 804 and by Article 49(d), (e), and (f) so it is unnecessary to prescribe further rules governing their use in R.C.M. 702. As to Article 49(d)(1), *see United States v. Davis*, 19 U.S.C.M.A. 217, 41 C.M.R. 217 (1970). *See also United States v. Bennett* , 12 M.J. 463, 471 (C.M.A. 1982); *United States v. Gaines*, 20 U.S.C.M.A. 557, 43 C.M.R. 397 (1971); *United States v. Bryson*, 3 U.S.C.M.A. 329, 12 C.M.R. 85 (1953). The fourth paragraph in the discussion is based on paragraphs 75 *b*(4) and 75 *e* of MCM, 1969 (Rev.).

(b) *Who may order.* This subsection is based on Article 49(a) and on the second and third sentences of paragraph 117 *b*(1) of MCM, 1969 (Rev.). As noted in subsection (i) the express approval of a competent authority is not required in order to take a deposition. *See also United States v. Ciarletta*, 7 U.S.C.M.A. 606, 23 C.M.R. 70 (1957). Express approval may be necessary in order to secure the necessary personnel or other resources for a deposition, when a subpoena will be necessary to compel the presence of a witness, or when the parties do not agree to the deposition.

(c) *Request to take deposition.* Subsection (1) is based on the first sentence in paragraph 117 *b*(1) of MCM, 1969 (Rev.). The discussion is based on the fourth sentence of that paragraph. Subsection (2) is based on the fifth and sixth sentences in paragraph 117 *b*(1).

Subsection (3)(A) is based on Article 49(a). The discussion provides guidance on what may be good cause for denial. The discussion indicates that ordinarily the purpose of a deposition is to preserve the testimony of a necessary witness when that witness is likely to be unavailable for trial. *See* Analysis, subsection (a) of this rule. The Court of Military Appeals has held that a deposition may be required in other circumstances described in the last sentence of the discussion. *See United States v. Killebrew*, 9 M.J. 154 (C.M.A. 1980); *United States v. Cumberledge*, 6 M.J. 203, 205, n. 3 (C.M.A. 1979) (deposition may be appropriate means to compel interview with witness when Government improperly impedes defense access to a witness); *United States v. Chuculate*, 5 M.J. 143, 145 (C.M.A. 1978) (deposition may be an appropriate means to allow sworn cross-examination of an essential witness who was unavailable at the Article 32 hearing); *United States v. Chestnut*, 2 M.J. 84 (C.M.A. 1976) (deposition may be an appropriate means to cure error where witness was improperly found unavailable at Article 32 hearing). *Chuculate* and *Chestnut* have construed Article 49 as means of satisfying the discovery purposes of Article 32 when the Article 32 proceeding fails to do so. *Killebrew* and *Cumberledge* have construed Article 49 as a means of permitting full investigation and preparation by the defense when the Government improperly interferes. Whether a deposition is an appropriate tool for the latter purpose may bear further consideration, especially since R.C.M. 701(e) makes clear that such interference is improper. *See also* R.C.M. 906(b)(7).

Subsection (3)(B) is based on the first sentence of paragraph 117 *b*(1) and on paragraphs 75 *b*(4) and *e* of MCM, 1969 (Rev.). *See also United States v. Jacoby*, 11 U.S.C.M.A. 428, 29 C.M.R. 244 (1960).

Subsection (3)(C) is new and is self-explanatory.

Subsection (3)(D) is based on *United States v. Cumberledge* and *United States v. Chuculate*, both*supra*.

(d) *Action when request is approved.* Subsection (1) and its discussion are new. *See* Article 49(c). Detailing the deposition officer is a ministerial act. When it is intended that the deposition officer issue a subpoena, it is important that the deposition officer be properly detailed. In other cases, proper detailing is not of critical importance so long as the deposition officer is qualified. *Cf. United States v. Ciarletta, supra.*

Subsection (2) is based on paragraph 117 *b* of MCM, 1969 (Rev.). That paragraph provided that the accused would have the same rights to counsel as that for the trial at which the deposition could be used. Under R.C.M. 502, the accused has the right to qualified counsel at both general and special courts-martial. If a summary court-martial is intended, ordinarily there is no need for an oral deposition; instead, the summary court-martial should be detailed and proceed to call the witness. Under subsection (g)(2)(A) the accused at a summary court-martial is not entitled to counsel for a written deposition. The first paragraph in the discussion is based on *United States v. Catt*, 1 M.J. 41 (C.M.A. 1975); *United States v. Timberlake*, 22 U.S.C.M.A. 117, 46 C.M.R. 117 (1973); *United States v. Gaines, supra. See also* R.C.M. 505(d)(2)(B) and analysis. The second paragraph in the discussion is based on the second sentence in paragraph 117 *b*(2) of MCM, 1969 (Rev.). The rule does not prohibit the accused from waiving the right to counsel at a deposition. *See* R.C.M. 506(d); *United States v. Howell*, 11 U.S.C.M.A. 712, 29 C.M.R. 528 (1960).

Subsection (3) is new and reflects the ministerial role of the deposition officer.

(e) *Notice.* This subsection is based on Article 49(b) and paragraph 117 *b*(4) of MCM, 1969 (Rev.). It is consistent with Fed.

R. Crim. P. 15(b). *See generally United States v. Donati*, 14 U.S.C.M.A. 235, 34 C.M.R. 15 (1963).

(f) *Duties of the deposition officer.* This subsection is based on paragraphs 117 *b*(5), (7), and (8) and *c*(3) and (4) of MCM, 1969 (Rev.). It is organized to provide a deposition officer a concise list of the duties of that office.

(g) *Procedure.* Subsection (1)(A) is based on paragraph 117 *b*(2) of MCM, 1969 (Rev.); Fed. R. Crim. P. 15(b). *See also United States v. Donati, supra.* Subsection (1)(B) is based on paragraph 117 *b* (6) and (7) of MCM, 1969 (Rev.). *See also* Fed. R. Crim. P. 15(d). Subsection (2) is based on the first sentence of paragraph 117 *b*(2) and paragraph 117 *c* of MCM, 1969 (Rev.). Subsection (2)(B) is based on paragraph 117 *c* of MCM, 1969 (Rev.). Note that if the accused and counsel can be present, it ordinarily is feasible to conduct an oral deposition. Written interrogatories are expressly provided for in Article 49.

Subsection (3) is new and is based on Article 49(d) and (f), as amended, Military Justice Act of 1983, Pub. L. No. 98–209, § 6(b), 97 Stat. 1393 (1983). The convening authority or military judge who orders the deposition has discretion to decide whether it will be recorded in a transcript or by videotape, audiotape, or similar material. Nothing in this rule is intended to require that a deposition be recorded by videotape, audiotape, or similar material. Factors the convening authority or military judge may consider include the availability of a qualified reporter and the availability of recording equipment. *See also United States v. Vietor*, 10 M.J. 69, 77 n.7 (C.M.A. 1980) (Everett, C.J., concurring in the result).

(h) *Objections.* This subsection is based on the second and third sentences of the penultimate paragraph of paragraph 117 *b* of MCM, 1969 (Rev.) and on Fed. R. Crim. P. 15(f). The waiver provisions are more specific than in paragraph 117 *b* in order to ensure that objections are made when the defect arises. This promotes efficiency by permitting prompt corrective action. *See* Fed. R. Crim. P.15(f). This requirement should not be applied so as to unduly impede the taking of a deposition, however. Only objections to matters which are correctable on the spot need be made. For example, an objection to opinion testimony should ordinarily be made at the deposition so that the necessary foundation may be laid, if possible. On the other hand, objections on grounds of relevance ordinarily are inappropriate at a deposition. Subsection (1) is also based on *United States v. Ciarletta supra. See also United States v. Gaines* and *United States v. Bryson*, both*supra.* Matters which ordinarily are waived if not raised include lack of timely notice and lack of qualifications of the deposition officer.

(i) *Deposition by agreement not precluded.* This subsection is based on Article 49(a) and on Fed. R. Crim. P. 15(g).

Rule 703 Production of witnesses and evidence

(a) *In general.* This subsection is based on Article 46.

(b) *Right to witnesses.* Subsections (1) and (2) are based on the fourth paragraph of paragraph 115 *a* of MCM, 1969 (Rev.). The second paragraph in the discussion is based on *United States v. Roberts*, 10 M.J. 308 (C.M.A. 1981). *See also United States v. Jefferson*, 13 M.J. 1 (C.M.A. 1982); *United States v. Bennett*, 12 M.J. 463 (C.M.A. 1982); *United States v. Credit*, 8 M.J. 190 (C.M.A. 1980) (Cook, J.); *United States v. Hampton*, 7 M.J. 284 (C.M.A. 1979); *United States v. Tangpuz*, 5 M.J. 426 (C.M.A. 1978) (Cook, J.); *United States v. Lucas*, 5 M.J. 167 (C.M.A. 1978); *United States v. Williams*, 3 M.J. 239 (C.M.A. 1977); *United States v. Carpenter*, 1 M.J. 384 (C.M.A. 1976); *United States v. Iturralde-Aponte*, 1 M.J. 196 (C.M.A. 1975). *Cf.* Fed. R. Crim. P. 17(b). *See generally* 8 J.Moore, *Moore's Federal Practice* Para. 17.05 (1982 rev.ed). Subsection (3) is based on *United States v. Bennett, supra; United States v. Daniels*, 23 U.S.C.M.A. 94, 48 C.M.R. 655 (1974). *See also United States v. Valenzuela-Bernal*, 458 U.S. 858, 102 S. Ct. 3440 (1982).

2007 Amendment: Subsection (b)(1) was amended to allow, under certain circumstances, the utilization of various types of remote testimony in lieu of the personal appearance of the witness.

(c) *Determining which witnesses will be produced.* This subsection is based generally on paragraph 115 *a* of MCM, 1969 (Rev.). The procedure for obtaining witnesses under Fed. R. Crim. P. 17 is not practicable in courts-martial. Under Fed. R. Crim. P. 17, witnesses are produced by process issued and administered by the court. In the military trial judiciary, no comparable administrative infrastructure capable of performing such a function exists, and it would be impracticable to create one solely for that purpose. The mechanics and costs of producing witnesses are the responsibility of the command which convened the court-martial. Moreover, military judges often do not sit at fixed locations and must be available for service in several commands or places. Note, however, that any dispute as to production of a witness is subject to a judicial determination. Experience has demonstrated that these administrative tasks should be the responsibility of trial counsel.

Subsection (1) is based on the first three sentences in the fourth paragraph of paragraph 115 *a* of MCM, 1969 (Rev.).

Subsection (2) is based generally on the remainder of paragraph 115 *a* of MCM, 1969 (Rev.). The procedure for production of defense witnesses prescribed in paragraph 115 *a* was questioned in several decisions. *See United States v. Arias*, 3 M.J. 436, 439 (C.M.A. 1977); *United States v. Williams, supra* at 240 n.2; *United States v. Carpenter, supra* at 386 n.8. The practical advantages of that procedure were recognized, however, in *United States v. Vietor*, 10 M.J. 69, 77 (C.M.A. 1980) (Everett, C.J., concurring in the result).

Subsection (2) modifies the former procedures to reduce the criticized aspects of the earlier practice while retaining its practical advantages. For reasons states above, the trial counsel is responsible for the administrative aspects of production of witnesses. Thus, under subsection (2)(A) the defense submits its list of witnesses to the trial counsel so that the latter can arrange for their production. The trial counsel stands in a position similar to a civilian clerk of court for this purpose. Because most defense requests for witnesses are uncontested, judicial economy is served by routing the list directly to the trial counsel, rather than to the military judge first. This also allows the trial counsel to consider such alternatives as offering to stipulate or take a deposition, or recommending to the convening authority that a charge be withdrawn. *See United States v. Vietor, supra.* Further, it allows arrangements to be made in a more timely manner, since the trial counsel is usually more readily available than the military judge. Only if there is a genuine dispute as to whether a witness must be produced is the issue presented to the military judge by way of a motion.

Subsections (2)(B) and (C) also further judicial economy and efficiency by facilitating early arrangements for the production of witnesses and by permitting the prompt identification and resolution of disputes. Subsection (2)(B) is based on the fifth and sixth sentences of the fourth paragraph of paragraph 115 *a* of MCM, 1969 (Rev.). *See also United States v. Valenzuela-Bernal, supra; United States v. Wagner*, 5 M.J. 461 (C.M.A. 1978); *United States v. Lucas*, 5 M.J. 167 (C.M.A. 1978). *Cf. United States v. Hedgwood*, 562 F.2d 946 (5th Cir. 1977), *cert, denied*, 434 U.S. 1079 (1978); *United States v. Barker*, 553 F.2d 1013 (6th Cir. 1977). Subsection (2)(C) is new. *See generally United States v. Menoken*, 14 M.J. 10 (C.M.A. 1982); and *United States v. Johnson*, 3 M.J. 772 (A.C.M.R.), *pet. denied*, 4 M.J. 50 (1977).

Subsection (2)(D) provides for resolution of disputes concerning witness production by the military judge. Application to the convening authority for relief is not required. It is permitted under R.C.M. 905(j). The last sentence in this subsection is based on *United States v. Carpenter, supra. See* subsection (b) of this rule as to the test to be applied.

(d) *Employment of expert witnesses.* This subsection is based on paragraph 116 of MCM, 1969 (Rev.). *See also United States v. Johnson*, 22 U.S.C.M.A. 424, 47 C.M.R. 402 (1973); *Hutson v. United States*, 19 U.S.C.M.A. 437, 42 C.M.R. 39 (1970). Because funding for such employment is the responsibility of the command, not the court-martial, and because alternatives to such employment may be available, application to the convening authority is appropriate. In most cases, the military's investigative, medical, or other agencies can provide the necessary service. Therefore the convening authority should have the opportunity to make available such services as an alternative. *Cf. United States v. Johnson, supra; United States v. Simmons* , 44 C.M.R. 804 (A.C.M.R. 1971), *pet. denied*, 21 U.S.C.M.A. 628, 44 C.M.R. 940 (1972). This subsection has no reference to ratification of employment of an expert already retained, unlike 18 U.S.C. § 3006A(e). *See also* Ms. Comp. Gen. B–49109 (June 25, 1949). This subsection does not apply to persons who are government employees or under contract to the Government to provide services which would otherwise fall within this subsection. The reference in paragraph 116 of MCM, 1969 (Rev.), to service regulations has been deleted as unnecessary.

(e) *Procedures for production.* Subsection (1) and the discussion are based on paragraph 115 *b* of MCM, 1969 (Rev.).

Subsection (2)(A) is consistent with current practice.

Subsection (2)(B) is based on Fed. R. Crim. P. 17(a) and (c) and on Appendix 17 of MCM, 1969 (Rev.). *See* Article 46. The discussion is taken from the second sentence of the second paragraph of paragraph 115 *a* of MCM, 1969 (Rev.). Note that the purpose of producing books, papers, documents, and other objects before a proceeding for inspection is to expedite the proceeding, not as a general discovery mechanism. *See Bowman Dairy Co. v. United States*, 341 U.S. 214 (1951). *See generally United States v. Nixon*, 418 683 (1974).

Subsection (2)(C) is based on paragraph 79 *b*, the third paragraph of paragraph 115 *a*, and the first sentence of paragraph 115 *d* (1) of MCM, 1969 (Rev.). Authority for the president of a court of inquiry and a deposition officer to issue a subpoena is expressly added to fill the gap left by MCM, 1969 (Rev). in regard to these procedures. *See* Article 47(a)(1), 135(f).

Subsection (2)(D) is based on Fed. R. Crim. P. 17(d) and on the second sentence of the fifth paragraph of paragraph 115 *d*(1) of MCM, 1969 (Rev.). *See also* 28 U.S.C. § 569(b). The discussion is based on paragraph 115 *d*(1) of MCM, 1969 (Rev.).

Subsection (2)(E) is based on Article 46 and the first sentence of paragraph 115 *d*(1) of MCM, 1969 (Rev.). It parallels Fed. R. Crim. P. 17(e)(1). Process in courts-martial does not extend abroad, except in occupied territory, nor may it be used to compel persons within the United States to attend courts-martial abroad. *See* Article 46; *United States v. Bennett, supra; United States v. Daniels, supra; United States v. Stringer*, 5 U.S.C.M.A. 122, 17 C.M.R. 122 (1954). *But see United States v. Daniels, supra* at 97, 48 C.M.R. at 658 (Quinn, J. concurring in the result) (suggesting possible use of 28 U.S.C. § 1783(a) to secure presence of witness overseas to testify in a court-martial). The discussion is based on the last paragraph of paragraph 115 *d*(1) of MCM, 1969 (Rev.). Note that under subsection (2)(E)(iii) any civilians in occupied territory are subject to compulsory process of the occupying force.

Subsection (2)(F) is based on Fed. R. Crim. P. 17(c), but is broader in that is not limited to a subpoena duces tecum. *Cf.* Fed. R. Crim. P. 17(f)(2).

Subsection (2)(G) and the discussion are based on paragraphs 115 *d*(2) and (3), MCM, 1969 (Rev.). The definition of "warrant of attachment" is based on 12 Op. Atty. Gen. 501, 502 (1868). The military power to use a warrant of attachment is inherent in the power to subpoena. 12 Op. Atty. Gen. 501 (1868) (construing Act of 3 March 1863, ch. 79, § 25, 12 Stat. 754, which became Article of War 22 of 1916 (39 Stat. 654), the predecessor of Article 46.). *See also* W. Winthrop, *Military Law and Precedents* 200–202, 202 n.46 (2d ed. 1920 reprint). The power of attachment has been included in the Manuals for Courts-Martial since 1895. Treatment of this enforcement provision in the Manual is in accord with the legislative intent to "leave mechanical details as to the issuance of process to regulation." H. R. Rep. No. 491, 81st Cong., 1st Sess. 24 (1949). The power has been used and sustained. *See, e.g., United States v. Shibley*, 112 F. Supp. 734 (S.D. Cal. 1953) (court of inquiry). Federal civilian courts have previously used the warrant of attachment but no longer do because the power to issue an arrest warrant is implied from Fed. R. Crim. P. 46(b) and 18 U.S.C. § 3149. *See Bacon v. United States*, 449 F.2d 933 (9th Cir. 1971) (arrest of material witness for testimony at grand jury before actual disobedience of subpoena). Warrants of attachment may be served in the same way and by the same officials as subpoenas. By their nature warrants of attachment have caused little litigation in military appellate courts. *See generally United States v. Sevaaetasi*, 48 C.M.R. 964 (A.C.M.R.), *pet. denied*, 23 U.S.C.M.A. 620, 49 C.M.R. 889 (1974); *United States v. Ercolin*, 46 C.M.R. 1259 (A.C.M.R. 1973); *United States v. Feeley*, 47 C.M.R. 581 (N.C.M.R.),*pet. denied*, 22 U.S.C.M.A. 635 (1973).

The procedure for issuing warrants of attachment is modified somewhat. The warrant must be authorized by the military judge, or, in special courts-martial without a military judge and summary courts-martial *(see* subsection (e)(2)(G)(v) of this rule), and for depositions and courts of inquiry, the convening authority. Paragraph 115 *d*(3) of MCM, 1969 (Rev.) required only that the trial counsel consult with the convening authority, or "after the court was convened" the military judge. Subsection (e)(2)(G) now requires written authorization from one of these persons. Second, subsection (e)(2)(G)(ii) incorporates as requirements the standards in the third paragraph 115 *d*(3) of MCM, 1969 (Rev.). That paragraph was seemingly advisory in nature. Subsection (e)(2)(G)(iv) is based on the second paragraph and the first sentence of the last paragraph of paragraph 115 *d*(3) of MCM, 1969 (Rev.). The last sentence of subsection (e)(2)(G)(iv) is new and is intended to ensure that any detention under this rule is limited to the minimum necessary to effect its purpose. These modifications provide additional safeguards to ensure that detention of witnesses is exercised only when necessary and appropriate. *See generally* Lederer, *Warrants of Attachment—Forcibly Compelling the Attendance of Witnesses*; 98 Mil. L. Rev. 1 (1982).

1998 Amendment. The Discussion was amended to reflect the amendment of Article 47, UCMJ, in section 1111 of the National Defense Authorization Act for Fiscal Year 1996, Pub. L. No. 104-106, 110 Stat. 186, 461 (1996). The amendment removes limitations on the punishment that a federal district court may impose for a civilian witness' refusal to honor a subpoena to appear or testify before a court-martial. Previously, the maximum sentence for a recalcitrant witness was "a fine of not more than $500.00, or imprisonment for not more than six months, or both." The law now leaves the amount of confinement or fine to the discretion of the federal district court.

(f) *Evidence.* This subsection is based generally on paragraph 115 *a* and *c* of MCM, 1969 (Rev.). *See also United States v. Toledo*, 15 M.J. 255 (C.M.A. 1983). It parallels the procedures for production of witnesses. Discovery and introduction of classified or other government information is covered by Mil. R. Evid. 505 and 506. Note that unlike the standards for production of witnesses, there is no difference in the standards for production of evidence on the merits and at sentencing. The relaxation of the rules of evidence at presentencing proceedings provides some flexibility as to what evidence must be produced at those proceedings.

Rule 704 Immunity

(a) *Types of immunity.* This subsection recognizes both transactional and testimonial or use immunity. *See Pillsbury Co. v. Conboy*, 459 U.S. 248 (1983); *Kastigar v. United States*, 406 U.S. 441 (1972); *Murphy v. Waterfront Commission*, 378 U.S. 52 (1964). *See also* 18 U.S.C. §§ 6001–6005; *United States v. Villines*, 13 M.J. 46 (C.M.A. 1982). *See generally* H. Moyer, *Justice and the Military* 376–381 (1972); Green, *Grants of Immunity and Military Law, 1971–1976*, 73 Mil. L. Rev. 1 (1976) (hereinafter cited as Green II); Green, *Grants of Immunity and Military Law*, 53 Mil. L. Rev. 1 (1971) (hereinafter cited as Green I).

Paragraph 68 *h* of MCM, 1969 (Rev.) expressly recognized transactional immunity. It did not address testimonial immunity. Nevertheless, testimonial immunity has been used in courts-martial. *See United States v. Villines, supra; United States v. Eastman*, 2 M.J. 417 (A.C.M.R. 1975); *United States v. Rivera*, 49 C.M.R. 259 (A.C.M.R.1974), *rev'd on other grounds*, 1 M.J. 107 (C.M.A. 1975). *See also* Mil. R. Evid. 301(c)(1).

Subsection (1) makes clear that transactional immunity extends only to trial by court-martial. *See* Dept. of Defense Dir. 1355.1 (July 21, 1981). Subsection (2) is written somewhat more broadly, however. Use immunity under R.C.M. 704 would extend to a State prosecution. *Cf. Murphy v. Waterfront Commission, supra.* Moreover, although a convening authority is not independently empowered to grant immunity extending to Federal civilian prosecutions, use immunity extending to such cases may be granted by a convening authority when specifically authorized under 18 U.S.C. §§ 6002 and 6004. *See* subsection (c) and Analysis.

The second paragraph in the discussion is based on 18 U.S.C. § 6004. The third paragraph in the discussion is based on *United States v. Rivera*, 1 M.J. 107 (C.M.A. 1975); *United States v. Eastman, supra.*

(b) *Scope.* This subsection clarifies the scope of R.C.M. 704. It is based on the last clause in 18 U.S.C. § 6002. Note that this rule relates only to criminal proceedings. A grant of immunity does not extend to administrative proceedings unless expressly covered by the grant.

(c) *Authority to grant immunity.* This subsection is based on paragraph 68 *h* of MCM, 1969 (Rev.) and on *United States v. Kirsch*, 15 U.S.C.M.A. 84, 35 C.M.R. 56 (1964). *See also United States v. Villines, supra. Kirsch* recognized codal authority for a convening authority to grant immunity (*see* Articles 30, 44, and 60) and found implementing Manual provisions to be a proper exercise of authority under Article 36. (At the time *Kirsch* was decided, the convening authority's powers now contained in Article 60 were in Article 64.) The enactment of 18 U.S.C. § § 6001–6005 did not remove this power. *See United States v. Villines, supra;* Department of Justice Memorandum, Subject: Grants of Immunity by Court-Martial Convening Authorities (Sept. 22, 1971) *discussed in Grants of Immunity*, The Army Lawyer 22 (Dec. 1973). *See also* Dept. of Defense Dir. 1355.1 (July 21, 1981). *See generally* Green I, *supra* at 27–35; H. Moyer, *supra* at 377–380. The rule recognizes, however, that the authority under the code of a general court-martial convening authority to grant immunity does not extend to federal prosecutions. *Id.* Consequently, the rule directs military authorities to 18 U.S.C. §§ 6001–6005 as a means by which such immunity can be granted when necessary. The discussion under subsection (1) offers additional guidance on this matter. *See* the penultimate paragraph of the Analysis of subsection (a) of this rule as to the effect of a grant of immunity to state prosecutions.

The rule makes clear that only a general court-martial convening authority may grant immunity. *See United States v. Joseph*, 11 M.J. 333 (C.M.A. 1981); *United States v. Caliendo*, 13 U.S.C.M.A. 405, 32 C.M.R. 405 (1962); *United States v. Thompson*, 11 U.S.C.M.A. 252, 29 C.M.R. 68 (1960); *United States v. Werthman*, 5 U.S.C.M.A. 440, 18 C.M.R. 64 (1955). *Cf. Pillsbury Co. v. Conboy, supra. Cooke v. Orser*, 12 M.J. 335 (C.M.A. 1982), is not to the contrary. In *Cooke* the majority found that due process required enforcement of promises of immunity under the facts of that case. One member of the majority also opined that the convening authority could be held, on the facts, to have authorized the grant of immunity. The limitations in subsection (c)(3) and the procedural requirements in subsection (d) are intended to reduce the potential for the kinds of problems which arose in *Cooke.*

The power to grant immunity and the power to enter into a pretrial agreement, while related, should be distinguished. R.C.M. 704 does not disturb the power of the convening authority, including a special or summary court-martial convening authority, to make a pretrial agreement with an accused under which the accused promises to testify in another court-martial, as long as the agreement does not purport to be a grant of immunity. Note that the accused-witness in such a case could not be ordered to testify pursuant to the pretrial agreement; instead, such an accused would lose the benefit of the bargained-for relief upon refusal to carry out the bargain. *See also* R.C.M. 705.

The first paragraph in the initial discussion under subsection (c) is based on *Cooke v. Orser* and *United States v. Caliendo,* both *supra.* As to the second paragraph in the discussion,*see United States v. Newman*, 14 M.J. 474 (C.M.A. 1983). The discussion under subsection (c)(1) is based on *Grants of Immunity*, The Army Lawyer 22 (Dec. 1973). *See also* Dept. of Defense Dir. 1355.1 (July 21, 1981); Memorandum of Understanding Between the Departments of Justice and Defense Relating to the Investigation and Prosecution of Crimes Over Which the Two Departments Have Concurrent Jurisdiction (1955).

As to whether the threat of a foreign prosecution is a sufficient basis to refuse to testify in a court-martial notwithstanding a grant of immunity, *see United States v. Murphy*, 7 U.S.C.M.A. 32, 21 C.M.R. 158 (1956). *See also United States v. Yanagita*, 552 F.2d 940 (2d Cir.1977); *In re Parker*, 411 F.2d 1067 (10th Cir. 1969), *vacated as moot*, 397 U.S. 96 (1970); Green II, *supra* at 12–14. *But see In re Cardassi*, 351 F. Supp. 1080 (D. Conn. 1972); *McCormick's Handbook of the Law of Evidence* 262–63 (E. Cleary ed. 1972). The Supreme Court has not decided the issue. *See Zicarelli v. New Jersey State Commission of Investigation* , 406 U.S. 472 (1974).

(d) *Procedure.* This subsection is new. It is intended to protect the parties to a grant of immunity by reducing the possibility of misunderstanding or disagreement over its existence or terms. *Cf. Cooke v. Orser, supra.*

The first paragraph in the discussion is based on *United States v. Kirsch, supra.*

The second paragraph in the discussion is based on *United States v. Conway*, 20 U.S.C.M.A. 99, 42 C.M.R. 291 (1970); *United States v. Stoltz*, 14 U.S.C.M.A. 461, 34 C.M.R. 241 (1964). *See also United States v. Scoles*, 14 U.S.C.M.A. 14, 33 C.M.R. 226 (1963); Green I, *supra* at 20–23.

The last paragraph in the discussion is based on Mil. R. Evid. 301(c)(2) and *United States v. Webster*, 1 M.J. 216 (C.M.A. 1975).

(e) *Decision to grant immunity.* This subsection is based on *United States v. Villines, supra.* Although there was no majority opinion in that case, each judge recognized the problem of the need to immunize defense witnesses under some circumstances, and each suggested different possible solutions. The rule addresses these concerns and provides a mechanism to deal with them. Note that the military judge is not empowered to immunize a witness. If the military judge finds that a grant of immunity is essential to a fair trial, the military judge will abate the proceedings unless immunity is granted by an appropriate convening authority.

1993 Amendment. Subsection (e) to R.C.M. 704 was amended to make the military practice for granting immunity for defense witnesses consistent with the majority rule within the Federal Courts. *United States v. Burns*, 684 F.2d 1066 (2d Cir. 1982), *cert. denied*, 459 U.S. 1174 (1983); *United States v. Shandell*, 800 F.2d 322 (2d Cir. 1986); *United States v. Turkish*, 623 F.2d 769 (2d Cir. 1980), *cert. denied*, 449 U.S. 1077 (1981); *United States v. Thevis*, 665 F.2d 616 (5th Cir. 1982), *cert. denied*, 459 U.S. 825 (1982); *United States v. Pennell*, 737 F.2d 521 (6th Cir. 1984); *United States v. Taylor*, 728 F.2d 930 (7th Cir. 1984); *United States v. Brutzman*, 731 F.2d 1449 (9th Cir. 1984); *McGee v. Crist*, 739 F.2d 505 (10th Cir. 1984); *United States v. Sawyer*, 799 F.2d 1494 (11th Cir. 1986). The amended rule conforms R.C.M. 704(e) with case law requiring the military judge to consider the Government's interest in not granting immunity to the defense witness. *See United States v. Smith*, 17 M.J. 994, 996 (A.C.M.R. 1984), *pet. denied*, 19 M.J. 71 (C.M.A. 1984); *United States v. O'Bryan*, 16 M.J. 775 (A.F.C.M.R. 1983), *pet. denied*, 218 M.J. 16 (C.M.A. 1984).

The majority rule recognizes that an accused has no Sixth Amendment right to immunized testimony of defense witnesses and, absent prosecutorial misconduct which is intended to disrupt the judicial fact-finding process, an accused is not denied Fifth Amendment due process by the Government's failure to immunize a witness. If the military judge finds that the witness is a target for prosecution, there can be no claim of Government overreaching or discrimination if the grant of immunity is denied. *United States v. Shandell, supra.*

The prior military rule was based on *United States v. Villines, supra*, which had adopted the minority view espoused in Government of Virgin Islands v. Smith, 615 F.2d 964 (3d Cir. 1980). This view permitted the court to immunize also a defense witness when the witness' testimony was clearly exculpatory, was essential to the defense case and there was no strong Government interest in withholding testimonial immunity. This rule has been sharply criticized. *See, e.g., United States v. Turkish, supra; United States v. Taylor, supra; United States v. Pennel, supra; United States v. Zayas*, 24 M.J. 132, 137 (C.M.A. 1987) (dissenting opinion by Judge Cox).

The current rule continues to recognize that a military judge is not empowered to immunize a witness. Upon a finding that all three prerequisites exist, a military judge may only abate the proceedings for the affected charges and specifications unless the convening authority grants immunity to the witness.

Rule 705 Pretrial agreements

Introduction. This rule is new. The code does not address pretrial agreements, and MCM, 1969 (Rev.) did not discuss them. Pretrial agreements have long existed and been sanctioned in courts-martial, however, *see United States v. Allen*, 8 U.S.C.M.A. 504, 25 C.M.R. 8 (1957). *See generally Gray, Pretrial Agreements*, 37 Fed. Bar. J. 49 (1978). The rule recognizes the utility of pretrial agreements. At the same time the rule, coupled with the requirement for judicial inquiry in R.C.M. 910, is intended to prevent informal agreements and protect the rights of the accused and the interests of the Government. *See also Santobello v. New York*, 404 U.S. 257 (1971); Fed. R. Crim. P. 11(e); *ABA Standards, Pleas of Guilty* (1979).

(a) *In general.* This subsection is based on *United States v. Allen, supra.* Only the convening authority may enter a pretrial agreement with an accused. *See United States v. Caruth*, 6 M.J. 184 (C.M.A. 1979); *United States v. Johnson*, 2 M.J. 541 (A.C.M.R. 1976); *United States v. Crawford*, 46 C.M.R. 1007 (A.C.M.R. 1972). *See also United States v. Troglin*, 21 U.S.C.M.A. 183, 44 C.M.R. 237 (1972). Pretrial agreements have long been subject to service regulations. *See, e.g.*, A.F.M. 111–1, para. 4–8 (May 13, 1980); JAGMAN Section 0114 (June 11, 1982). Subsection (a) expressly continues such authority. The discussion is based on Dept. of Defense Dir. 1355.1 (July 21, 1981).

(b) *Nature of agreement.* This subsection recognizes the matters contained in pretrial agreements. *See United States v. Cooke*, 12 M.J. 448 (C.M.A. 1982); *United States v. Schaffer*, 12 M.J. 425 (C.M.A. 1982); *United States v. Brown*, 12 M.J. 420 (C.M.A. 1982); *United States v. Bertelson*, 3 M.J. 314 (C.M.A. 1977); *United States v. Allen, supra.* As to prohibited and permitted terms and conditions, *see* subsection (c) of this rule. This discussion under subsection (2)(C) is based on *United States v. Cook, supra.*

1994 Amendment: The amendment to the Discussion accompanying R.C.M. 705(b)(2)(C), regarding reinstitution of offenses withdrawn or dismissed pursuant to a pretrial agreement and the standard of proof required of the government to withstand a defense motion to dismiss the reinstituted offenses, is based on *United States v. Verrusio*, 803 F.2d 885 (7th Cir. 1986). Alternative procedures available in Federal civilian practice, such as a motion by the government for relief from its obligation under the agreement before it proceeds to the indictment stage (*see United States v. Ataya*, 864 F.2d 1324, 1330 n.9 (7th Cir. 1988)), are inapposite in military practice and thus are not required. *See generally* R.C.M. 801(a).

(c) *Terms and conditions.* This subsection is intended to ensure that certain fundamental rights of the accused cannot be bargained away while permitting the accused substantial latitude to enter into terms or conditions as long as the accused does so freely and voluntarily. Subsection (1)(B) lists certain matters which cannot be bargained away. This is because to give up these matters would leave no substantial means to ensure judicially that the accused's plea was provident, that the accused entered the pretrial agreement voluntarily, and that the sentencing proceedings met acceptable standards. *See United States v. Mills*, 12 M.J. 1 (C.M.A. 1981); *United States v. Green*, 1 M.J. 453 (C.M.A. 1976); *United States v. Holland*, 1 M.J. 58 (C.M.A. 1975); *United States v. Care*, 18 U.S.C.M.A., 40 C.M.R. 247 (1969); *United States v. Cummings*, 17 U.S.C.M.A. 376, 38 C.M.R. 174 (1968); *United States v. Allen, supra.* The discussion under subsection (2) is based on *United States v. Holland, supra.* The rule is not intended to codify *Holland* to the extent that *Holland* may prevent the accused from giving up the right to make any motions before trial. *Cf. United States v. Schaffer, supra.* Subsection (1)(A) provides that any term or condition, even if not otherwise prohibited, must be agreed to by the accused freely and voluntarily. *Cf. United States v. Green, supra; United States v. Care, supra.*

Subsection (2) makes clear that certain terms or conditions are not included in subsection (1)(B) and are permissible so long as they are freely and voluntarily agreed to by the accused. Since the accused may waive many matters other than jurisdiction, in some cases by failure to object or raise a matter (*see* R.C.M. 905(e); Mil. R. Evid. 103(a)), or by a plea of guilty (*see* R.C.M. 910(j) and Analysis), there is no reason why the accused should not be able to seek a more favorable agreement by agreeing to waive such matters as part of a pretrial agreement. Indeed, authorization for such terms or conditions, coupled with the requirement that they be included in the written agreement (*see* subsection (d)(3) of this rule) prevents *sub rosa* agreements concerning such matters and ensures that a careful judicial inquiry into, and record of, the accused's understanding of such matters will be made. The matters listed in subsection (2) have been judicially sanctioned. As to subsection (2)(A), *see United States v. Thomas*, 6 M.J. 573 (A.C.M.R. 1978). *Cf. United States v. Bertelson, supra.* Subsection (2)(B) is based on *United States v. Reynolds*, 2 M.J. 887 (A.C.M.R. 1976); *United States v. Tyson*, 2 M.J. 583 (N.C.M.R. 1976). *See also United States v. Chavez-Rey*, 1 M.J. 34 (C.M.A. 1975); *United States v. Stoltz*, 14 U.S.C.M.A. 461, 34 C.M.R. 241 (1964).

Subsection (2)(C) is based on *United States v. Callahan*, 8 M.J. 804 (N.C.M.R. 1980); *United States v. Brown*, 4 M.J. 654 (A.C.M.R. 1977). Enforcement of a restitution clause may raise problems if the accused, despite good faith efforts, is unable to comply. *See United States v. Brown, supra.*

Subsection (2)(D) is based on *United States v. Dawson*, 10 M.J. 142 (C.M.A. 1982). Although the post-trial misconduct provision in *Dawson* was rejected, a majority of the court was apparently willing to permit such provisions if adequate protections against arbitrary revocation of the agreement are provided. However, *see United States v. Connell*, 13 M.J. 156 (C.M.A. 1982) in which a post-trial misconduct provision was held unenforceable without detailed analysis. Subsection (D) provides the same protections as revocation of a suspended sentence requires. *See* R.C.M. 1109 and Analysis. Given such protections, there is no reason why an accused who has bargained for sentence relief such as a suspended sentence should enjoy immunity from revocation of the agreement before action but not afterward. Other decisions have suggested the validity of post-trial misconduct provisions. *See United States v. Goode*, 1 M.J. 3 (C.M.A. 1975); *United States v. Thomas, supra; United States v. French*, 5 M.J. 655 (N.C.M.R. 1978). *Cf. United States v. Lallande*, 22 U.S.C.M.A. 170, 46 C.M.R. 170 (1973).

Subsection (2)(E) is based on *United States v. Schaffer, supra; United States v. Mills, supra; United States v. Schmeltz*, 1 M.J. 8 (C.M.A. 1975). Note that the list is not exhaustive. The right to enlisted members may be waived, for example.

1991 Amendment: Subsection (2) was amended to clarify that either side can propose the inclusion of the listed terms in a pretrial agreement. This conforms to the amendment to R.C.M. 705(d).

(d) *Procedure.* This subsection ensures that an offer to plead guilty pursuant to a pretrial agreement originates with the accused, and that the accused freely and voluntarily enters a pretrial agreement. At the same time it recognizes that a pretrial agreement is the product of negotiation and discussion on both sides, each of which is free to refuse to enter an agreement and go to trial. Subsection (1) is based on *United States v. Schaffer, supra.* This subsection, together with the prohibition against terms not freely and voluntarily agreed to by the accused and the requirement in R.C.M. 910 for an inquiry into the agreement, should prevent prosecutorial pressure or improper inducements to the accused to plead guilty or to waive rights against the accused's wishes or interest. *See United States v. Schaffer, supra* at 428–429.

Subsection (2) provides that once plea discussions are initiated by the defense the convening authority or a representative may negotiate with the defense. This recognizes that, while the offer must originate with the defense, the specific provisions in an agreement may be the product of discussions with the Government. *Schaffer, Mills, and Schmeltz* suggest that each term must originate with the defense. R.C.M. 705 is consistent with this insofar as it requires that the offer to plead guilty originate with the accused (subsection (d)(1)), that the written proposal be prepared by the defense (subsection (d)(3)), and that the accused enter or agree to each term freely and voluntarily (subsection (c)(1)(A)). It is of no legal consequence whether the accused's counsel or someone else conceived the idea for a specific provision so long as the accused, after thorough consultation with qualified counsel, can freely choose whether to submit a proposed agreement and what it will contain. *See United States v. Munt*, 3 M.J. 1082 (A.C.M.R. 1977), *pet. denied*, 4 M.J. 198 (C.M.A. 1978).

Subsection (3) ensures that all understandings be included in the agreement. This is in the interest of both parties. *See United States v. Cooke*, 11 M.J. 257 (C.M.A. 1981); *United States v. Lanzer*, 3 M.J. 60 (C.M.A. 1977);*United States v. Cox* , 22 U.S.C.M.A. 69, 46 C.M.R. 69 (1972). The last sentence is based on *United States v. Green, supra.* Note that the rule does not require the convening authority to sign the agreement. Although the convening authority must personally approve the agreement, (*see* subsection (a)) and has sole discretion whether to do so under subsection (4), the convening authority need not personally sign the agreement. In some circumstances, it may not be practicable or even physically possible to present the written agreement to the convening authority for approval. The rule allows flexibility in this regard. The staff judge advocate, trial counsel, or other person authorized by the convening authority to sign may do so. Authority to sign may by granted orally. Subsection (3) is not intended to preclude oral modifications in the agreement from being made on the record at trial with the consent of the parties.

Subsection (5) makes clear that neither party is bound by a pretrial agreement until performance begins. *See United States v. Kazena*, 11 M.J. 28 (C.M.A. 1981). In *Shepardson v. Roberts*, 14 M.J. 354 (C.M.A. 1983), the Court stated that the convening authority may be bound by a pretrial agreement before entry of a plea of guilty if the accused has detrimentally relied on the agreement. The Court indicated, however, that not all forms of reliance by the accused rise to the level of detrimental reliance as it used that term. Thus the Court held in *Shepardson* that exclusion of statements allegedly made by the accused as a result of the agreement (but not necessarily pursuant to it) was an adequate remedy, and enforcement of the agreement was not required when the convening authority withdrew from it before trial. Similarly, the Court opined that the fact that an accused made arrangements to secure employment or took similar actions in reliance on an agreement would not require enforcement of a pretrial agreement. Subsection (5) is consistent with this approach, but uses beginning of performance by the accused to provide a clearer point at which the right of the convening authority to withdraw terminates. Note that the beginning of performance is not limited to entry of a plea. It would also include testifying in a companion case, providing information to Government agents, or other actions pursuant to the terms of an agreement.

Note that the accused may withdraw from a pretrial agreement even after entering a guilty plea or a confessional stipulation, but, once the plea is accepted or the stipulation admitted, could not withdraw the plea or the stipulation except as provided under R.C.M. 910(h) or 811(d). The fact that the accused may withdraw at any time affords the accused an additional measure of protection against prosecutorial abuse. It also reflects the fact that the convening authority can retrieve any relief granted the accused. *See* Article 63; *United States v. Cook, supra.*

1991 Amendment: R.C.M. 705(d) was amended to authorize either party to initiate pretrial agreement negotiations and propose terms and conditions. The amendment does not change the general rule that all terms and conditions of a pretrial agreement proposed pursuant to this rule must not violate law, public policy, or regulation. Subparagraph (1) was eliminated and subparagraphs (2)–(5), as amended, were renumbered (1)–(4), respectively. This amendment is patterned after federal civilian practice [*see Fed. R. Crim. P.* 11(e)] where there is no requirement that negotiations for plea agreements originate with the defense. In courts-martial the military judge is required to conduct an exhaustive inquiry into the providence of an accused's guilty plea and the voluntariness of the pretrial agreement. R.C.M. 705(c) ensures that certain fundamental rights of the accused cannot be bargained away. Furthermore it can be difficult to determine which side originated negotiations or proposed a particular clause. *Cf. United States v. Jones*, 23 M.J. 305, 308–309 (C.M.A. 1987) (Cox, J., concurring).

(e) *Nondisclosure of existence of agreement.* This subsection is based on *United States v. Green, supra; United States v. Wood*, 23 U.S.C.M.A. 57, 48 C.M.R. 528 (1974). *See also* R.C.M. 910(f); Mil. R. Evid. 410.

Rule 706 Inquiry into the mental capacity or mental responsibility of the accused

This rule is taken from paragraph 121 of MCM, 1969 (Rev.). Minor changes were made in order to conform with the format and style of the Rules for Courts-Martial. *See also United States v. Cortes-Crespo*, 13 M.J. 420 (1982); *United States v. Frederick*, 3 M.J. 230 (C.M.A. 1977); Mil. R. Evid. 302 and Analysis. The rule is generally consistent with 18 U.S.C. § 4244. The penultimate paragraph in paragraph 121 is deleted as an unnecessary statement.

1987 Amendment: Subsection (c)(1) was modified, in light of changes to federal law, to allow the use of available clinical psychologists. *See* 18 U.S.C. §§ 4241, 4242, and 4247. Subsection (c)(2) was revised to implement Article 50a, which was added to the UCMJ in the [nb, N] "Military Justice Amendments of 1986," tit. [nb, A] VIII, § 802, National Defense Authorization Act for fiscal year 1987, Pub. L. No. 99–661, 100 Stat. 3905 (1986). Article 50a adopted some provisions of the Insanity Defense Reform Act, ch. IV, Pub. L. No. 98–473, 98 Stat. 2057 (1984). *See also* Analysis of R.C.M. 916(k). The subsection dealing with the volitional prong of the American Law Institute's Model Penal Code test was deleted. Subsection (A) was amended by adding and defining the word "severe." *See* R.C.M. 916(k)(1); S. Rep. No. 225, 98th Cong., 1st Sess. 229 (1983), *reprinted in* 1984 U.S. Code Cong. & Ad. News 1, 231. Subsection (C) was amended to state the cognitive test as now set out in R.C.M. 916(k)(1).

1998 Amendment. Subsection (c)(2)(D) was amended to reflect the standard for incompetence set forth in Article 76b, UCMJ.

Rule 707 Speedy trial

Introduction. This rule applies the accused's speedy trial rights under the 6th Amendment and Article 10, UCMJ, and protects the command and societal interest in the prompt administration of justice. *See generally Barker v. Wingo*, 407 U.S. 514 (1972); *United States v. Walls*, 9 M.J. 88 (C.M.A. 1980). The purpose of this rule is to provide guidance for granting pretrial delays and to eliminate after-the-fact determinations as to whether certain periods of delay are excludable. This rule amends the former rule, which excluded from accountable time periods covered by certain exceptions.

(a) *In general.* This subsection is based on *ABA Standards for Criminal Justice, Speedy Trial*, 12–2.1, 12–2.2 (1986). The ABA Standards set no time limit but leave the matter open depending on local conditions. The basic period from arrest or summons to trial under *The Federal Speedy Trial Act*, 18 U.S.C. § 3161, is 100 days. The period of 120 days was selected for courts-martial as a reasonable outside limit given the wide variety of locations and conditions in which courts-martial occur. The dates of the events which begin government accountability are easily ascertainable and will avoid the uncertainty involved in *Thomas v. Edington*, 26 M.J. 95 (C.M.A. 1988).

The 90-day rule previously established in R.C.M. 707(d) has been eliminated. As such, the 120-day rule established in subsection (a) of this rule applies to all cases, not just cases where the accused is in pretrial confinement. Judicial decisions have held, however, that when an accused has been held in pretrial confinement for more than 90 days, a presumption arises that the accused's right to a speedy trial under Article 10, UCMJ has been violated. In such cases, the government must demonstrate due diligence in bringing the case to trial. *United States v. Burton*, 44 C.M.R. 166 (C.M.A. 1971). Unless *Burton* and its progeny are reexamined, it would be possible to have a *Burton* violation despite compliance with this rule.

2002 Amendment: Burton and its progeny were re-examined in *United States v. Kossman*, 38 M.J. 258 (C.M.A. 1993), where the Court of Military Appeals specifically overruled Burton and reinstated the earlier rule from *United States v. Tibbs*, 15 C.M.A. 350, 353, 35 C.M.R. 322, 325 (1965). *See Kossman*, 38 M.J. at 262. In *Kossman*, the Court reinstated the "reasonable diligence" standard in determining whether the prosecution's progress toward trial for a confined accused was sufficient to satisfy the speedy trial requirement of Article 10, UCMJ.

The discussion is based on *United States v. McDonald*, 456 U.S. 1 (1982); *United States v. Marion*, 404 U.S. 307 (1971). *See also United States v. Lovasco*, 431 U.S. 783 (1977). Delay before restraint or referral of charges could raise due process issues. *See id.; United States v. McGraner*, 13 M.J. 408 (C.M.A. 1982). *See generally* Pearson and Bowen, *Unreasonable Pre-Preferral Delay*, 10 A.F. JAG Rptr. 73 (June 1981).

(b) *Accountability.* Subsection (1) is based on *United States v. Manalo*, 1 M.J. 452 (C.M.A. 1976). The reference to R.C.M. 304(a)(2)–(4) conforms to the language of R.C.M. 707(a)(2).

Subsection (2) is based on *ABA Standards, supra* at 12–2.2(a) (1986). *See also United States v. Talaveraz*, 8 M.J. 14 (C.M.A. 1979).

Subsection (3)(A) establishes that a mistrial or dismissal by any proper authority begins a new trial period. This subsection clarifies the date from which to begin measuring new time periods in cases involving rereferral, restraint, or no restraint.

Subsection (3)(B) clarifies the intent of this portion of the rule. The harm to be avoided is continuous pretrial restraint. *See United States v. Gray*, 21 M.J. 1020 (N.M.C.M.R. 1986). Where an accused is released from pretrial restraint for a substantial period, he will be treated the same as an accused who was not restrained. Therefore, unless the restraint is reimposed, the 120-day time period will run from the date of preferral or entry on active duty regardless of whether that event occurs before or after the accused was released from restraint.

Subsection (3)(C) clarifies the effect of government appeals on this rule. This subsection treats all government appeals the same. Once the parties are given notice of either the government's decision not to appeal under R.C.M. 908(b)(8) or the decision of the Court of Criminal Appeals under R.C.M. 908(c)(3), a new 120-day period begins.

This subsection clarifies how time should be counted for those charges not affected by the ruling that is subject to appeal. Under R.C.M. 908(b)(4), trial on such charges may in some circumstances proceed notwithstanding the appeal, or trial may await resolution of the appeal. Since the traditional policy of resolving all known charges at a single trial has not changed (*see* R.C.M. 906(b)(10), Discussion), charges not the subject of the appeal may be properly delayed without violating this rule. Accordingly where the trial is interrupted by a government appeal, all charges may be treated the same and proceeded upon at the same time once the appeal is resolved.

2004 Amendment: Subsection (3)(D) was amended in light of *United States v. Becker,* 53 M.J. 229 (2000), to clarify that the 120-day time period applies to sentence-only rehearings. The amendment also designates the first session under R.C.M. 803 as the point at which an accused is brought to trial in a sentence-only rehearing.

(c) *Excludable delays.* This subsection, based on *ABA Standards for Criminal Justice, Speedy Trial*, 12–1.3 (1986), follows the principle that the government is accountable for all time prior to trial unless a competent authority grants a delay. *See United States v. Longhofer*, 29 M.J. 22 (C.M.A. 1989). The rule of procedure established in subsection (1) is based on *United States v. Maresca*, 28 M.J. 328 (C.M.A. 1989). *See also United States v. Carlisle*, 25 M.J. 426, 428 (C.M.A. 1988).

The discussion to subsection (1) provides guidance for judges and convening authorities to ensure the full development of speedy trial issues at trial. *See United States v. Maresca, supra.* This amendment follows ABA guidance and places responsibility on a military judge or the convening authority to grant reasonable pretrial delays. Military judges and convening authorities are required, under this subsection, to make an independent determination as to whether there is in fact good cause for a pretrial delay, and to grant such delays for only so long as is necessary under the circumstances. *ABA Standards, supra* at 12 –1.3; *United States v. Longhofer, supra.* Decisions granting or denying pretrial delays will be subject to review for both abuse of discretion and the reasonableness of the period of delay granted. *Id.; United States v. Maresca, supra.*

1998 Amendment. In creating Article 76b, UCMJ, Congress mandated the commitment of an incompetent accused to the custody of the Attorney General. As an accused is not under military control during any such period of custody, the entire period is excludable delay under the 120-day speedy trial rule.

2004 Amendment: Subsection (c) was amended to treat periods of the accused's unauthorized absence as excludable delay for purposes of speedy trial. *See United States v. Dies,* 45 M.J. 376 (1996). The Discussion was deleted as superfluous.

(d) *Remedy.* This subsection is based on *The Federal Speedy Trial Act*, 18 U.S.C. § 3162. The Federal Rule provides dismissal as the sanction for speedy trial violations but permits the judge to dismiss with or without prejudice. Accordingly, this subsection permits the judge to dismiss charges without prejudice for non-constitutional violations of this rule. If, however, the accused has been denied his or her constitutional right to a speedy trial, the only available remedy is dismissal with prejudice. *Strunk v. United States*, 412 U.S. 434 (1973).

2004 Amendment: Subsection (d) was amended in light of *United States v. Becker,* 53 M.J. 229 (2000), to provide for sentence relief as a sanction for violation of the 120-day rule in sentence-only rehearings. The amendment sets forth factors for the court to consider to determine whether or to what extent sentence relief is appropriate and provides for the sentence credit to be applied to the sentence approved by the convening authority.

(e) *Waiver.* A lack of a demand for immediate trial will not constitute waiver and will not preclude an accused from raising speedy trial issues at trial. *See Barker v. Wingo, supra.*

CHAPTER VIII. TRIAL PROCEDURE GENERALLY

Rule 801 Military judge's responsibility; other matters

(a) *Responsibilities of military judge.* This subsection is based on paragraphs 39 *b* and 40 *b*(2) and the first sentence of paragraph 57 *a* of MCM, 1969 (Rev.). It is intended to provide the military judge or president of a special court-martial without a military judge broad authority to regulate the conduct of courts-martial within the framework of the code and the Manual, and to establish the outlines of their responsibilities. Much of the discussion is also derived from paragraphs 39 *b*, 40 *b*(2), and 53 *g* of MCM, 1969 (Rev.). A few minor changes have been made. For instance, the military judge, not the president, determines the uniform to be worn, and the military judge is not required to consult with the president, nor is the president of a special court-martial without a military judge required to consult with trial counsel, concerning scheduling. As a practical matter, consultation or coordination among the participants concerning scheduling or uniform may be appropriate, but the authority for these decisions should rest with the presiding officer of the court, either military judge or president of a special court-martial without a military judge, without being required to consult with others.

(b) *Obtaining evidence.* This subsection is taken from paragraph 54 *b* of the MCM, 1969 (Rev.). Some of the language in paragraph 54 *b* has been placed in the discussion.

(c) *Uncharged offenses.* This subsection is taken from paragraph 55 *a* of MCM, 1969 (Rev.). The discussion is designed to accomplish the same purpose as paragraph 55 *b* of MCM, 1969 (Rev.), although the language is no longer in terms which could be construed as jurisdictional.

(d) *Interlocutory questions and questions of law.* This subsection is similar in substance to paragraph 57 of MCM, 1969 (Rev.) and is based on Articles 51(b) and 52(c).

Subsections (1) and (2) are based on Articles 51(b) and 52(c). The provisions (R.C.M. 801(e)(1)(C); 801(e)(2)(C)) permitting a military judge or president of a special court-martial without a military judge to change a ruling previously made (Article 51(b)) have been modified to preclude changing a previously granted motion for finding of not guilty. *United States v. Hitchcock*, 6 M.J. 188 (C.M.A. 1979). Under R.C.M. 916(k) the military judge does not rule on the question of mental responsibility as an interlocutory matter. *See* Analysis, R.C.M. 916(k). Thus there are no rulings by the military judge which are subject to objection by a member.

Subsection (2)(D) makes clear that all members must be present at all times during special courts-martial without a military judge. The president of a special court-martial lacks authority to conduct the equivalent of an Article 39(a) session. *Cf. United States v. Muns*, 26 C.M.R. 835 (C.G.B.R. 1958).

Subsection (3) is based on Articles 51(b) and 52(c) and is derived from paragraph 57 *c, d, f,* and *g* of MCM, 1969 (Rev.). Some language from paragraph 57 *g* has been placed in the discussion.

Subsection (4) is taken from paragraph 57 *g*(1) of MCM, 1969 (Rev.). The rule recognizes, however, that a different standard of proof may apply to some interlocutory questions. *See, e.g.*, Mil. R. Evid. 314(e)(5). The assignments of the burden of persuasion are determined by specific rules or, in the absence of a rule, by the source of the motion. This represents a minor change from the language in paragraph 67 *e* of MCM, 1969 (Rev.), which placed the burden on the accused for most questions. This assignment was rejected by the Court of Military Appeals in several cases, *see, e.g., United States v. Graham*, 22 U.S.C.M.A. 75, 46 C.M.R. 75 (1972). Assignments of burdens of persuasion and, where appropriate, going forward are made in specific rules. "Burden of persuasion" is used instead of the more general "burden of proof" to distinguish the risk of non persuasion once an issue is raised from the burden of production necessary to raise it. *See McCormick's Handbook of the Law of Evidence* § 336 (E. Cleary ed. 1972). For example, although the defense may have the burden of raising an issue (e.g., statute of limitations), once it has done so the prosecution may bear the burden of persuasion.

The discussion under subsection (5) describes the differences between interlocutory questions and ultimate questions, and between questions of fact and questions of law. It is taken, substantially, from paragraph 57 *b* of MCM, 1969 (Rev.). As to the distinction between questions of fact and questions of law, *see United States v. Carson*, 15 U.S.C.M.A. 407, 35 C.M.R. 379 (1965). The discussion of issues which involve both interlocutory questions and questions determinative of guilt is based on *United States v. Bailey*, 6 M.J. 965 (N.C.M.R. 1979); *United States v. Jessie*, 5 M.J. 573 (A.C.M.R.), *pet, denied*, 5 M.J. 300 (1978). It is similar to language in the third paragraph of paragraph 57 *b* of MCM, 1969 (Rev.), which was based on *United States v. Ornelas*, 2 U.S.C.M.A. 96, 6 C.M.R. 96 (1952). *See Analysis of Contents, Manual for Courts-Martial, United States, 1969, Revised Edition*, DA PAM 27–2, 10–5 (July 1970). That example, and the decision in *United States v. Ornelas, supra* were questioned in *United States v. Laws*, 11 M.J. 475 (C.M.A. 1981). The discussion clarifies that when a military offense (i.e., one which requires that the accused be a "member of the armed forces," *see* Articles 85, 86, 99; *see also* Articles 88–91, 133) is charged and the defense contends that the accused is not a member of the armed forces, two separate questions are raised by that contention: first, whether the accused is subject to court-martial jurisdiction (*see* R.C.M. 202); and, second, whether, as an element of the offense, the accused had a military duty which the accused violated (e.g., was absent from the armed forces or a unit thereof without authority). The first question is decided by the military judge by a preponderance of the evidence. The second question, to the extent it involves a question of fact, must be decided by the factfinder applying a reasonable doubt standard. *United States v. Bailey, supra. See also United States v. McGinnis*, 15 M.J. 345 (C.M.A. 1983); *United States v. Marsh*, 15 M.J. 252 (C.M.A. 1983); *United States v. McDonagh*, 14 M.J. 415 (C.M.A. 1983). Thus it would be possible, in a case where larceny and desertion are charged, for the military judge to find by a preponderance of the evidence that the accused is subject to military jurisdiction and for the members to convict of larceny but acquit of desertion because they were not satisfied beyond reasonable doubt that the accused was a member of the armed forces.

Ornelas does not require a different result. The holding in *Ornelas* was that the law officer (military judge) erred in failing to permit the members to resolve a contested issue of the accused's status as a servicemember on a desertion charge. Language in the opinion to the effect that the "jurisdictional" issue should have been submitted to the members is attributable to language in paragraph 67 *e* of MCM, 1951, which suggested that "defenses," including "jurisdiction," were to be resolved by the members. Such a procedure for resolving motions to dismiss has been abolished. *See* R.C.M. 905; 907; and 916. Thus the procedure implied by a broad reading of *Ornelas* for resolving jurisdiction is not required by the Manual. *See generally United States v. Laws, supra. Cf. United States v. McDonagh, supra.* On the other hand, when military status is an element of the offense, the fact of such military status must be resolved by the factfinder. *Cf. United States v. McGinnis* and *United States v. Marsh*, both *supra.*

(f) *Rulings on record.* This subsection is based on paragraph 39 *c* of MCM, 1969 (Rev.). Paragraph 39 *c* did not include a reference to rulings and instructions by the president of a special court-martial without a military judge, nor was specific reference to them made elsewhere in the Manual. Since such rulings and instructions are subject to the same review as those of a military judge, the same standard should apply to both at this stage. The rule is based on Article 54. The discussion refers to R.C.M. 808 and 1103 to indicate what must be recorded at trial. Concerning requirements for verbatim records, *see United States v. Douglas*, 1 M.J. 354 (C.M.A. 1976); *United States v. Boxdale*, 22 U.S.C.M.A. 414, 47 C.M.R. 351 (1973); *United States v. Weber*, 20 U.S.C.M.A. 82, 42 C.M.R. 274 (1970).

(g) *Effect of failure to raise defenses or objections.* This subsection is based on Fed. R. Crim. P. 12(f), except for the addition of the term "motions" to make clear that motions may be covered by the rule and changes to conform to military terminology and procedure. Such waiver provisions are more specifically implemented as to many matters throughout the Rules. Several examples are listed in the discussion.

Rule 802 Conferences

Introduction. This rule is new. It is based on Fed. R. Crim. P. 17.1, but is somewhat broader and more detailed. Fed. R. Crim. P. 17.1 apparently authorizes, by its title, only pretrial conferences. Conferences other than pretrial conferences are also authorized in federal practice. *See* Fed. R. Crim. P. 43(c)(3); *Cox v. United States*, 309 F.2d 614 (8th Cir. 1962). R.C.M. 802 applies to all conferences. Nothing in this rule is intended to prohibit the military judge from communicating, even ex parte, with counsel concerning routine and undisputed administrative matters such as scheduling, uniform, and travel arrangements. Such authority was recognized in the fourth sentence of paragraph 39 *c* of MCM, 1969 (Rev.).

Like Fed. R. Crim. P. 17.1, this rule provides express authority for what is already common practice in many courts-martial, and regularizes the procedure for them. Fed. R. Crim. P. 17.1 is designed to be used in unusual cases, such as complicated trials. Conferences are needed more frequently in courts-martial because in many instances the situs of the trial and the home bases of the military judge, counsel, and the accused may be different. Even when all the participants are located at the same base, conferences may be necessary. *See ABA Standards, Discovery and Procedural Before Trial* § 11–5.4 (1978). After the trial has begun, there is often a need to discuss matters in chambers. *Cf.* Fed. R. Crim. P. 43(c); *United States v. Gregorio*, 497 F.2d 1253 (4th Cir.), *cert. denied*, 419 U.S. 1024 (1974).

(a) *In general.* This subsection is taken directly from the first sentence of Fed. R. Crim. P. 17.1, with modifications to accommodate military terminology. Subsection (c) provides that a conference may not proceed over the objection of a party and that, in effect, matters may be resolved at a conference only by agreement of the parties. Thus, the military judge can bring the parties together under subsection (a), but a conference could not proceed further without the voluntary participation of the parties. Nothing in this rule is intended to prohibit the military judge from communicating to counsel, orally or in writing, matters which may properly be the subject of rules of court. *See* R.C.M. 108; 801. This is also true under the federal rule. *See Committee on Pretrial Procedure of the Judicial Conference of the United States, Recommended Procedures in Criminal Trials*, 37 F.R.D. 95, 98 (1965); C. Wright, *Wright's Federal Practice and Procedure* Para. 292 (1969). *Cf. United States v. Westmoreland*, 41 F.R.D. 419 (S.D. Ind. 1967).

The discussion provides some examples of the potential uses of conferences. As noted, issues may be resolved only by agreement of the parties; they may not be litigated or decided at a conference. To do so would exceed, and hence be contrary to, the authority established under Article 39(a). The prohibition against judicial participation in plea bargaining is based on *United States v. Caruth*, 6 M.J. 184, 186 (C.M.A. 1979). *Cf. United States v. Allen*, 8 U.S.C.M.A. 504, 25 C.M.R. 8 (1957). *But, cf. ABA Standards, Pleas of Guilty* § 14–3.3(c) (1979).

(b) *Matters on record.* This subsection is based on the second sentence in Fed. R. Crim. P. 17.1. The federal rule requirement for a written memorandum was rejected as too inflexible and unwieldy for military practice. The interests of the parties can be adequately protected by placing matters on the record orally. If any party fears that such an oral statement will be inadequate, that party may insist on reducing agreed-upon matters to writing as a condition of consent. In any event, a party is not prohibited from raising the matters again at trial. *See* subsection (c) below.

The waiver provision has been added because the conference is not part of the record of trial under Article 54. The purpose of the requirement for inclusion in the record is to protect the parties, and therefore it may be waived. *United States v. Stapleton*, 600 F.2d 780 (9th Cir. 1979).

(c) *Rights of parties.* This subsection does not appear in the federal rule. It is intended to ensure that conferences do not become a substitute for Article 39(a) sessions. In this respect Fed. R. Crim. P. 17.1 is broader than R.C.M. 802, since the federal rule apparently includes "conferences" held on the record and permits the parties to be bound by matters resolved at the conference. *See* C. Wright, *supra* at Para. 292.

1991 Amendment: The prohibition against conferences proceeding over the objection of any party was eliminated as it conflicted with the military judge's specific authority to order conferences under section (a) of this rule and general authority to control the conduct of court-martial proceedings. While the military judge may compel the attendance of the parties, neither party may be compelled to resolve any issue or be pressured to make any concessions.

(d) *Accused's presence.* This subsection does not appear in Fed. R. Crim. P. 17.1. The silence of the federal rule on this matter has been controversial. *See* Douglas, J., dissenting from approval of Fed. R. Crim. P. 17.1 at 39 F.R.D. 276, 278 (1966). *See also* 8 J. Moore, *Moore's Federal Practice* Para. 17.1.02 [1]; 17.1.03 [3] (1982 rev. ed.); Rezneck, *The New Federal Rules of Criminal Procedure*, 54 Geo. L. J. 1276, 1294–99 (1966); *ABA Standards, Discovery and Procedure Before Trial* § 11–5.4(a) (1978). The presence of the accused is not necessary in most cases since most matters dealt with at conferences will not be substantive. The participation of the defense in conferences and whether the accused should attend are matters to be resolved between defense counsel and the accused.

Fed. R. Crim. P. 43(c)(2) authorizes conferences concerning questions of law to be held without the presence of the accused. The proceedings described in Fed. R. Crim. P. 43(c)(2) are analogous to those described in Article 39(a)(2), since the judge may make rulings at a 43(c)(2) conference and such a conference is "on the record." Article 39(a) expressly gives the accused the right to be present at similar proceedings in courts-martial. Because of this inconsistency, Fed. R. Crim. P. 43(c)(2) is not adopted. Questions of law may be discussed at a conference under R.C.M. 802, but the military judge may not decide them at such conferences.

(e) *Admission.* This subsection is taken from the third sentence of Fed. R. Crim. P. 17.1.

(f) *Limitations.* This subsection is based on the last sentence in Fed. R. Crim. P. 17.1, with the addition of the prohibition against conferences in special courts-martial without a military judge.

Rule 803 Court-martial sessions without members under Article 39(a)

Article 39(a) authorizes the military judge to call and conduct sessions outside the presence of members. The discussion contains a general description, based on paragraph 53 *d*(1) of MCM, 1969 (Rev.), of the types of matters which may be dealt with at Article 39(a) sessions. The quoted language in the first paragraph of the discussion is found in the legislative history of Article 39(a). *See* S. Rep. No. 1601, 90th Cong., 2nd Sess. 9–10 (1968).

The rule modifies the language concerning Article 39(a) sessions after sentence is announced. The former provision permitted such sessions only "when directed by the appropriate reviewing authority." Yet paragraphs 80 *b* and *c* of MCM, 1969 (Rev.) implied that a military judge could call such a session on the judge's own motion. R.C.M. 1102 also authorizes such action.

The first two paragraphs of the discussion are based on the second and third paragraphs of paragraph 53 *d*(1) of MCM, 1969 (Rev.), except that the present language omits "defenses" from the matters a military judge may hear at an Article 39(a) session. Clearly a military judge does not rule on the merits of a defense at an Article 39(a) session, and matters collateral to a defense which might be heard at an Article 39(a) session are adequately described elsewhere in the discussion.

As to the third paragraph of the discussion,*see* Articles 35 and 39. *See also United States v. Pergande*, 49 C.M.R. 28 (A.C.M.R. 1974).

Rule 804 Presence of the accused at trial proceedings

Introduction. Subsections (a) and (b) of this rule are very similar to Fed. R. Crim. P. 43(a) and (b). Subsection (c) is derived from paragraph 60 of MCM, 1969 (Rev.). Fed. R. Crim. P. 43(c) was not adopted since it is not compatible with military practice, as it concerns corporate defendants, misdemeanor proceedings, conferences or arguments upon questions of law, and sentence reduction proceedings. Of these, only presence of the accused at conferences or arguments upon questions of law has relation to military procedure. Article 39(b) would preclude absence by the accused from arguments, except as provided in subsection (b). Conferences are treated in R.C.M. 802.

Other differences between this rule and Fed. R. Crim. P. 43 and paragraphs 11 and 60 of the MCM, 1969 (Rev.) are discussed below.

(a) *Presence required.* Article 39 establishes the right of the accused to be present at all trial proceedings and Article 39(a) sessions. The right is grounded in the due process clause of the Fifth Amendment and the right to confrontation clause of the Sixth Amendment of the Constitution. This subsection is basically the same as Fed. R. Crim. P. 43(a) with modifications in language to conform to military procedures.

The requirement that the accused be present is not jurisdictional. While proceeding in the absence of the accused, without the express or implied consent of the accused, will normally require reversal, the harmless error rule may apply in some instances. *See United States v. Walls*, 577 F.2d 690 (9th Cir.) *cert. denied*, 439 U.S. 893 (1978); *United States v. Nelson*, 570 F.2d 258 (8th Cir. 1978); *United States v. Taylor*, 562 F.2d 1345 (2d Cir.), *cert. denied*, 434 U.S. 853 (1977).

(b) *2007 Amendment*: Subsection (b) *Presence by remote means*, is new and inserted to implement the amendment to 10 U.S.C. Sec. 839 (Article 39, UCMJ) contained in Section 556 of the National Defense Authorization Act for Fiscal Year 2006, P.L. 109-163, 6 January 2006. The amendment allows the presence of the accused at Article 39(a) sessions to be satisfied by the use of audiovisual technology, as prescribed by regulations of the Secretary concerned.

(c) *Continued presence not required.* This subsection is similar to Fed. R. Crim. P. 43(b). Aside from modifications in terminology, two minor substantive changes have been made. First, this subsection specifies that sentencing, as well as trial on the merits, may take place when the accused is absent under this rule. Such a construction is necessary in the military because delaying a sentence determination increases the expense and inconvenience of reassembling the court-martial and the risk that such reassembly will be impossible. Federal courts do not face a similar problem. *See United States v. Houghtaling*, 2 U.S.C.M.A. 230, 235, 8 C.M.R. 30, 35 (1953).

The second change substitutes the word "arraignment" for "the trial has commenced." This is a clearer demarcation of the point after which the accused's voluntary absence will not preclude continuation of the proceedings. Since there are several procedural steps, such as service of charges, which, while associated with the trial process, do not involve a session, the arraignment is a more appropriate point of reference. This is consistent with the previous military rule.

The discussion points out that, although not explicitly stated in this subsection (or Fed. R. Crim. P. 43(b)), the accused may expressly waive the right to be present at trial. Federal courts have so construed Rule 43. *See* 8 J. Moore, *Moore's Federal Practice*, § 43.02[2] (1982 rev. ed.):

[Rule 43] does not refer to express waiver of presence on the part of felony defendants, although it includes such a provision for misdemeanants. This omission was not intended to negate the right of felony defendants expressly to waive presence at the trial, for the *Diaz* case (*Diaz v. United States*, 223 U.S. 442 (1912)) cited as authority for the "voluntary absence" provision itself involved an express waiver. [Footnote omitted.]

See also Snyder v. Massachusetts, 291 U.S. 97, 106 (1934) (dicta); *In re United States*, 597 F.2d 27 (2d Cir. 1979); *United States v. Jones*, 514 F.2d 1331 (D.C. Cir. 1975); *United States v. Crutcher*, 405 F.2d 239 (2d Cir. 1968), *cert. denied*, 394 U.S. 908 (1969); *Pearson v. United States*, 325 F.2d 625 (D.C. Cir. 1963); *Cross v. United States*, 325 F.2d 629 (D.C. Cir. 1963). Such waiver should be made expressly by the accused in open court. *Compare Cross v. United States, supra, with Pearson v. United States, supra.* Federal cases also establish that there is no right to waive presence, *see, e.g., United States v. Durham*, 587 F.2d 799 (5th Cir. 1979); *United States v. Fitzpatrick*, 437 F.2d 19 (2d Cir. 1970). In*In re United States, supra*, the court stated that there is a duty on the part of a defendant in a felony trial to be present. 597 F.2d at 28.

Military cases also recognize that an accused may expressly waive the right to be present, *United States v. Blair*, 36 C.M.R. 750 (N.B.R. 1965), *rev'd on other grounds*, 16 U.S.C.M.A. 257, 36 C.M.R. 413 (1966). *See e.g., United States v. Holly*, 48 C.M.R. 990 (A.F.C.M.R. 1974). *Cf. United States v. Cook*, 20 U.S.C.M.A. 504, 43 C.M.R. 344 (1971). Some earlier military cases indicated that accused's counsel could waive the accused's right to be present. This is contrary to present authority. *See United States v. Holly, supra.*

Subsection (1) is similar to paragraph 11 *c* of MCM, 1969 (Rev.). The language in MCM, 1969 (Rev.), which indicated that an absence had to be unauthorized, has been omitted. The language now conforms to the federal rule in this respect. The term "unauthorized" has never been treated as significant. *See United States v. Peebles*, 3 M.J. 177 (C.M.A. 1977). As the discussion notes in the fourth paragraph, a person who is in custody or otherwise subject to military control cannot, while in such a status, voluntarily be absent from trial without expressly waiving the right on the record and receiving the permission of the military judge to be absent. *Cf. United States v. Crutcher, supra.* This appears to be the treatment that the term "unauthorized" was designed to effect. *See United States v. Peebles, supra* at 179 (Cook, J.).

Trial in absentia, when an accused voluntarily fails to appear at trial following arraignment, has long been permitted in the military. *United States v. Houghtaling, supra.* Authority for the third and fourth paragraphs of the discussion under *Voluntary absence* is found in *United States v. Peebles, supra. United States v. Cook, supra* requires that the voluntariness of an absence be established on the record before trial in absentia may proceed. Because the prosecution will be the party moving for trial in absentia, the discussion notes that the prosecution has the burden to prove voluntariness as well as absence. The example of an inference is taken from Judge Perry's separate opinion in *United States v. Peebles, supra. Compare United States v. Partlow*, 428 F.2d 814 (2d. Cir. 1970) *with Phillips v. United States*, 334 F.2d 589 (9th Cir. 1964), *cert, denied*, 379 U.S. 1002 (1965).

Subsection (2) is the same as Fed. R. Crim. P. 43(b)(2) except for changes in terminology. The rule and much of the discussion are based on *Illinois v. Allen*, 397 U.S. 337 (1970). The discussion also draws heavily on *ABA Standards, Special Functions of the Trial Judge* § 6–3.8 and Commentary (1978). With respect to binding an accused, *see United States v. Gentile*, 1 M.J. 69 (C.M.A. 1975). *See also United States v. Henderson*, 11 U.S.C.M.A. 556, 29 C.M.R. 372 (1960).

(d) *Voluntary absence for limited purpose of child testimony. 1999 Amendment:* The amendment provides for two-way closed circuit television to transmit a child's testimony from the courtroom to the accused's location. The use of two-way closed circuit television, to some degree, may defeat the purpose of these alternative procedures, which is to avoid trauma to children. In such cases, the judge has discretion to direct one-way television communication. The use of one-way closed circuit television was approved by the Supreme Court in *Maryland v. Craig*, 497 U.S. 836 (1990). This amendment also gives the accused the election to absent himself from the courtroom to prevent remote testimony. Such a provision gives the accused a greater role in determining how this issue will be resolved.

2007 Amendment: The specific terminology of the manner in which remote live testimony may be transmitted was deleted to allow for technological advances in the methods used to transmit audio and visual information.

(e) *Appearance and security of accused.* This subsection is similar to paragraph 60 of MCM, 1969 (Rev.).

In subsection (1), the last sentence represents a modification of previous practice by making the accused and defense counsel primarily responsible for the personal appearance of the accused. Because of difficulties the defense may face in meeting these responsibilities, the rule requires the commander to give reasonable assistance to the defense when needed. The discussion emphasizes the right (*see United States v. West*, 12 U.S.C.M.A. 670, 31

C.M.R. 256 (1962)) and the duty (*see United States v. Gentile, supra*) of the accused to appear in proper military uniform.

Subsection (2) reflects the changes since 1969 in rules governing pretrial restraint. These rules are now found in the sections referred to by R.C.M. 804(c)(2). Insofar as paragraph 60 of MCM, 1969 (Rev.) was a means of allocating responsibility for maintaining (as opposed to authorizing) custody over an accused until completion of trial, and insofar as this allocation is not mandated by other rules in this Manual, the service secretaries are authorized to prescribe rules to accomplish such allocation.

Subsection (3) is taken verbatim from paragraph 60 of MCM, 1969 (Rev.).

Rule 805 Presence of military judge, members, and counsel

(a) *Military judge.* This subsection is based on paragraph 39 *d* of MCM, 1969 (Rev.).

2007 Amendment: R.C.M. 805(a) was amended to implement the statutory change to 10 U.S.C. Sec 839 (Article 39, UCMJ) contained in Section 556 of the National Defense Authorization Act for Fiscal Year 2006, P.L. 109-163, 6 January 2006. The amendment allows the presence of the military judge at an Article 39(a) session to be satisfied by the use of audiovisual technology, as prescribed by regulations of the Secretary concerned.

(b) *Members.* This subsection is based on paragraphs 41 *c* and 41 *d*(1) and (2) and the first sentence of the second paragraph 62 *b* of MCM, 1969 (Rev.) and on Article 29(c). *See also United States v. Colon*, 6 M.J. 73 (C.M.A. 1978).

1986 Amendment: References to R.C.M. "911" were changed to R.C.M. "912" to correct an error in MCM, 1984.

(c) *Counsel.* This subsection modifies paragraphs 44 *c* and 46 *c* which required the express permission of the convening authority or the military judge for counsel to be absent. The rule now states only the minimum requirement to proceed. The discussion noted that proceedings ordinarily should not be conducted in the absence of any defense or assistant defense counsel unless the accused consents. The second sentence in the discussion is based on *Ungar v. Sarafite*, 376 U.S. 575 (1964); *United States v. Morris*, 23 U.S.C.M.A. 319, 49 C.M.R. 653 (1975); *United States v. Kinard*, 21 U.S.C.M.A. 300, 45 C.M.R. 74 (1972); *United States v. Hampton*, 50 C.M.R. 531 (N.C.M.R.), *pet. denied*, 23 U.S.C.M.A. 663 (1975); *United States v. Griffiths*, 18 C.M.R. 354 (A.B.R.), *pet. denied*, 6 U.S.C.M.A. 808, 19 C.M.R. 413 (1955). *See also Morris v. Slappy*, 461 U.S. 1 (1983); *Dennis v. United States*, 340 U.S. 887 (1950) (statement of Frankfurter, J.); *United States v. Batts*, 3 M.J. 440 (C.M.A. 1977); 17 AM. Jur. 2d §§ 34–37 (1964).

2007 Amendment: R.C.M. 805(c) was amended to implement the statutory change to 10 U.S.C. Sec. 839 (Article 39, UCMJ) contained in section 556 of the National Defense Authorization Act for Fiscal Year 2006, P.L. 109-163, 6 January 2006. The amendment allows the presence of counsel at an Article 39(a) session to be satisfied by the use of audiovisual technology, as prescribed by Regulations of the Secretary concerned.

(d) *Effect of replacement of member or military judge.* This subsection is based on Article 29(b), (c), and (d) and on paragraphs 39 *e* and 41 *e* and *f* of MCM, 1969 (Rev.). MCM, 1969 (Rev.) also provided a similar procedure when a member of a court-martial was temporarily excused from the trial. This rule does not authorize such a procedure. If a member must be temporarily absent, a continuance should be granted or the member should be permanently excused and the trial proceed as long as a quorum remains. Trial may not proceed with less than a quorum present in any event. This subsection provides a means to proceed with a case in the rare circumstance in which a court-martial is reduced below a quorum after trial on the merits has begun and a mistrial is inappropriate.

Rule 806 Public trial

Introduction. This rule recognizes and codifies the basic principle that, with limited exceptions, court-martial proceedings will be open to the public. The thrust of the rule is similar to paragraph 53 *e* of MCM, 1969 (Rev.), but the right to a public trial is more clearly expressed, and exceptions to it are more specifically and more narrowly drawn. This construction is necessary in light of recent decisions, particularly *United States v. Grunden*, 2 M.J. 116 (C.M.A. 1977).

(a) *In general.* This subsection reflects the holding in*United States v. Grunden, supra*, that the accused has a right to a public trial under the Sixth Amendment. *See also United States v. Brown*, 7 U.S.C.M.A. 251, 22 C.M.R. 41 (1956); *United States v. Zimmerman*, 19 C.M.R. 806 (A.F.B.R. 1955).

Although the Sixth Amendment right to a public trial is personal to the accused (*see Gannett Co., Inc. v. DePasquale*, 443 U.S. 368 (1979)), the public has a right under the First Amendment to attend criminal trials. *Richmond Newspapers, Inc. v. Virginia*, 448 U.S. 555 (1980). The applicability of these cases to courts-martial is not certain (*cf. Greer v. Spock*, 424 U.S. 828 (1976); *In re Oliver*, 333 U.S. 257, 26 n. 12 (1948); *but see United States v. Czarnecki*, 10 M.J. 570 (A.F.C.M.R. 1980) (dicta)), especially in view of the practical differences between civilian courts and courts-martial (i.e., courts-martial do not necessarily sit at a permanent or fixed site; they may sit overseas or at sea; and at remote or dangerous locations). Nevertheless the rule and the discussion are based on recognition of the value to the public of normally having courts-martial open to the public. This is particularly true since the public includes members of the military community.

(b) *Control of spectators.* Neither the accused nor the public has an absolute right to a public trial. This subsection recognizes the power of a military judge to regulate attendance at courts-martial to strike a balance between the requirement for a public trial and other important interests.

As the discussion notes, the right to public trial may be violated by less than total exclusion of the public. *See United States v. Brown, supra.* Whether exclusion of a segment of the public is proper depends on a number of factors including the breadth of the exclusion, the reasons for it, and the interest of the accused, as well as the spectators involved, in the presence of the excluded individuals. *See United States ex rel. Latimore v. Sielaff*, 561 F.2d 691 (7th Cir. 1977), *cert, denied*, 434 U.S. 1076 (1978); *United States ex rel. Lloyd v. Vincent*, 520 F.2d 1272 (2d Cir.), *cert. denied*, 423 U.S. 937 (1975). *See also Stamicarbon v. American Cyanamid Co.*, 506 F.2d 532 (2d Cir. 1974).

The third paragraph in the discussion of Rule 805(b) is based on *United States v. Grunden, supra.*

Judicial authority to regulate access to the courtroom to prevent overcrowding or other disturbances is clearly established and does not conflict with the right to a public trial. *See Richmond Newspapers, Inc. v. Virginia, supra* at 581 n. 18. *Cf. Illinois v. Allen*, 397 U.S. 337 (1970). In addition, there is substantial authority to support the example in the discussion concerning restricting access to protect certain witnesses. *See, e.g., United States v. Eisner*, 533 F.2d 987 (6th Cir.), *cert. denied*, 429 U.S. 919 (1976) (proper to exclude all spectators except press to avoid embarrassment of extremely timid witness); *United States ex rel. Orlando v. Fay*, 350 F.2d 967 (2d Cir. 1965), *cert. denied*, 384 U.S. 1008 (1966) (proper to exclude all spectators except press and bar to avoid intimidation of witnesses); *United States ex rel. Latimore v. Sielaff, supra* (proper to exclude all spectators except press, clergy, and others with specific interest in presence during testimony of alleged rape victim); *United States ex rel. Lloyd v. Vincent, supra* (proper to exclude spectators in order to preserve confidentiality of undercover agents' identity). *See also Gannett Co., Inc. v. DePasquale, supra* at 401–500 (Powell J., concurring); *United States v. Brown, supra; United States v. Kobli*, 172 F.2d 919 (3rd Cir. 1949).

Subsection (b) authorizes closure of court-martial proceedings over the accused's objection only when otherwise authorized in this Manual. Effectively, this means that the only time trial proceedings may be closed without the consent of the accused is when classified information is to be introduced. *See* Mil. R. Evid. 505(j). Article 39(a) sessions may also be closed under Mil. R. Evid. 505(i); 506(i); and 412(c). Some federal cases seem to suggest that criminal proceedings may be closed for other purposes. *See, e.g., United States ex rel. Lloyd v. Vincent, supra.* Selective exclusion of certain individuals or groups for good cause, under the first clause of this subsection, is a more appropriate and less constitutionally questionable method for dealing with the problems treated in such cases.

Court-martial proceedings may be closed when the accused does not object. As noted in the discussion, however, such closure should not automatically be granted merely because the defense requests or acquiesces in it. *See Richmond Newspapers, Inc., v. Virginia, supra. See also Gannett Co., Inc. v. DePasquale, supra.*

With respect to methods of dealing with the effect of publicity on criminal trials, as treated in the discussion, *see Nebraska Press Association v. Stuart*, 427 U.S. 539 (1976); *Sheppard v. Maxwell*, 384 U.S. 333 (1966); *Rideau v. Louisiana*, 373 U.S. 723 (1963); *Irvin v. Dowd*, 366 U.S. 717 (1961); *United States v. Calley*, 46 C.M.R. 1131 (A.C.M.R.), *aff'd*, 22 U.S.C.M.A. 534, 48 C.M.R. 19 (1973); *Caley v. Callaway*, 519 F.2d 184 (5th Cir. 1975), *cert. denied*, 425 U.S. 911 (1976). *See also ABA Standards, Fair Trial and Free Press* part III (1972).

2004 Amendment: Subsection (b) was divided to separate the provisions addressing control of spectators and closure and to clarify that exclusion of specific individuals is not a closure. The rules for control of spectators now in subsection (b)(1) were amended to require the military judge to articulate certain findings on the record prior to excluding specific spectators. *See United States v. Short,* 41 M.J. 42 (1994). The rules on closure now in subsection (b)(2) and the Discussion were amended in light of military case law that has applied the Supreme Court's constitutional test for closure to courts-martial. *See ABC, Inc. v. Powell,* 47 M.J. 363 (1997); *United States v. Hershey,* 20 M.J. 433 (C.M.A. 1985); *United States v. Grunden,* 2 M.J. 116 (C.M.A. 1977).

(c) *Photography and broadcasting prohibited.* This subsection is based on Fed. R. Crim. P. 53, and is consistent with paragraph 53 *e* of MCM, 1969 (Rev.) and practice thereunder. *See* C. Wright, *Wright's Federal Practice and Procedure* § 861 (1969); 8 *B* J. Moore, *Moore's Federal Practice* Para. 53.02 (1982 rev. ed.). The exception which authorizes contemporaneous transmission of the proceedings to another room (e.g., by closed circuit television) has been added to the language of the federal rule. Many military courtrooms have limited space, and such methods have been used to accommodate the accused's and the public's interest in attendance at courts-martial, as in the case of *United States v. Garwood*, NMC 81–1982 (1981). The Working Group considered the constitutional alternatives identified in *Chandler v. Florida*, 449 U.S. 560 (1981), but determined that Article 36 requires adherence to the federal rule except to the extent described. As to the matters in the discussion, *see Amsler v. United States*, 381 F.2d 37 (9th Cir. 1967).

2002 Amendment: Section (d) was added to codify the military judge's power to issue orders limiting trial participants' extrajudicial statements in appropriate cases. *See United States v. Garwood,* 16 M.J. 863, 868 (N.M.C.M.R. 1983) (finding military judge was justified in issuing restrictive order prohibiting extrajudicial statements by trial participants), *aff'd on other grounds*, 20 M.J. 148 (C.M.A. 1985), *cert. denied*, 474 U.S. 1005 (1985); *United States v. Clark*, 31 M.J. 721, 724 (A.F.C.M.R. 1990) (suggesting, but not deciding, that the military judge properly limited trial participants' extrajudicial statements).

The public has a legitimate interest in the conduct of military justice proceedings. Informing the public about the operations of the criminal justice system is one of the "core purposes" of the First Amendment. In the appropriate case where the military judge is considering issuing a protective order, absent exigent circumstances, the military judge must conduct a hearing prior to issuing such an order. Prior to such a hearing the parties will have been provided notice. At the hearing, all parties will be provided an opportunity to be heard. The opportunity to be heard may be extended to representatives of the media in the appropriate case.

Section (d) is based on the first Recommendation Relating to the Conduct of Judicial Proceedings in Criminal Cases, included in the Revised Report of the Judicial Conference Committee on the Operation of the Jury System on the "Free Press--Fair Trial" Issue, 87 F.R.D. 519, 529 (1980), which was approved by the Judicial Conference of the United States on September 25, 1980. The requirement that the protective order be issued in writing is based on Rule for Courts-Martial 405(g)(6). Section (d) adopts a "substantial likelihood of material prejudice" standard in place of the Judicial Conference recommendation of a "likely to interfere" standard. The Judicial Conference's recommendation was issued before the Supreme Court's decision in *Gentile v. State Bar of Nev.*, 501 U.S. 1030 (1991). *Gentile*, which dealt with a Rule of Professional Conduct governing extrajudicial statements, indicates that a lawyer may be disciplined for making statements that present a substantial likelihood of material prejudice to an accused's right to a fair trial. While the use of protective orders is distinguishable from limitations imposed by a bar's ethics rule, the *Gentile* decision expressly recognized that the "speech of lawyers representing clients in pending cases may be regulated under a less demanding standard than that established for regulation of the press in *Nebraska Press Ass'n v. Stuart*, 427 U.S. 539 (1976), and the cases which preceded it." 501 U.S. at 1074. The Court concluded that "the substantial likelihood of material prejudice' standard constitutes a constitutionally permissible balance between the First Amendment rights of attorneys in pending cases and the State's interest in fair trials." *Id.* at 1075. *Gentile* also supports the constitutionality of restricting communications of non-lawyer participants in a court case. *Id.* at 1072-73 (*citing Seattle Times Co. v. Rhinehart*, 467 U.S. 20, 32-33 (1984)). Accordingly, a protective order issued under the "substantial likelihood of material prejudice" standard is constitutionally permissible.

The first sentence of the discussion is based on the committee comment to the Recommendations Relating to the Conduct of Judicial Proceedings in Criminal Cases. *See* 87 F.R.D. at 530. For a definition of "party," *see* R.C.M. 103(16). The second sentence of the discussion is based on the first of the Judicial Conference's recommendations concerning special orders. *See* 87 F.R.D. at 529. The third sentence of the discussion is based on the second of the Judicial Conference's recommendations, *id.* at 532, and on *United States v. Salameh*, 992 F.2d 445, 447 (2d Cir. 1993) (*per curiam*), and *In re Application of Dow Jones & Co.*, 842 F.2d 603, 611 & n.1 (2d Cir.), *cert. denied*, 488 U.S. 946 (1988). The fourth sentence is based on *Salameh*, 992 F.2d at 447. The fifth sentence is based on Rule for Courts-Martial 905(d).

Rule 807 Oaths

(a) *Definition.* This rule and the discussion are taken from paragraph 112 *a* of MCM, 1969 (Rev.). *See also* Fed. R. Crim. P. 54(c).

(b) *Oaths in courts-martial.* Subsection (1) including the discussion is based on Article 42 and is based on paragraph 112 *b* and *c* of MCM, 1969 (Rev.). Subsection (2) is taken from paragraph 112 *d* of MCM, 1969 (Rev.). The discussion is taken in part from paragraph 112 *d* and in part from paragraph 114 of MCM, 1969 (Rev.). The oath for questioning members has been combined with the oath concerning performance of duties for administrative convenience and to impress upon the members the significance of voir dire. The reference in paragraph 112 *a* of MCM, 1969 (Rev.), to Article 135 has been deleted. The oaths for preferral of charges, and witnesses at Article 32 investigations and depositions are contained in the discussion of applicable rules.

Rule 808 Record of trial

The primary purpose of this rule is to highlight for participants at the trial stage the requirements for the record of trial. The discussion is based on paragraph 82 *a, b*, and *h*, of MCM, 1969 (Rev.). *See also United States v. Eichenlaub*, 11 M.J. 239 (C.M.A. 1981); *United States v. McCullah*, 11 M.J. 234 (C.M.A. 1981); *United States v. Boxdale*, 22 U.S.C.M.A. 414, 47 C.M.R. 351 (1973); *United States v. Bielecki*, 21 U.S.C.M.A. 450, 45 C.M.R. 224 (1972); *United States v. DeWayne*, 7 M.J. 755 (A.C.M.R.), *pet. denied*, 8 M.J. 25 (1979); *United States v. Hensley*, 7 M.J. 740 (A.F.C.M.R.), *pet. denied*, 8 M.J. 42 (1979); *United States v. Pearson*, 6 M.J. 953 (A.C.M.R.), *pet. denied*, 7 M.J. 164 (1979). The preparation, authentication, and disposition of records of trial is covered in Chapter XI. The administrative responsibility of trial counsel to prepare the record is codal. Article 38(a). *See also* R.C.M. 1103(b).

Rule 809 Contempt proceedings

(a) *In general.* This subsection restates codal authority. The discussion is based on paragraph 118 *a* of MCM 1969 (Rev.). The language of Article 48 applies only to "direct" contempts. *See* W. Winthrop, *Military Law and Precedents* 301–302 (2d ed. 1920 reprint); paragraph 101 of MCM, 1928; paragraph 109 of MCM (Army), 1949; paragraph 118 *a* of MCM, 1951; paragraph 118 *a* of MCM, 1969 (Rev.). The definition of a "direct" contempt is also based on these sources. *See also* 8B J. Moore, *Moore's Federal Practice* Para. 42.02[3] (1982 rev. ed); 18 U.S. § 401; *cf. Ex parte Savin*, 131 U.S. 267, witnessed by the court and other direct contempts is based on *Cooke v. United States*, 267 U.S. 517 (1925), and is important for procedural purposes. *See* subsection (b) below.

(b) *Method of disposition.* The subsection is based on Fed. R. Crim. P. 42. By its terms, Article 48 makes punishable contemptuous behavior which, while not directly witnessed by the court-martial, disturbs its proceedings (e.g., a disturbance in the waiting room). As Fed. R. Crim. P. 42(b) recognizes, this type of contempt may not be punished summarily. *See Johnson v. Mississippi*, 403 U.S. 212 (1971); *Cooke v. United States, supra.* Paragraph 118 of MCM, 1969 (Rev.) did not adequately distinguish these types of contempt. There may be technical and practical problems associated with proceeding under subsection (b)(2) but the power to do so appears to exist under Article 48.

(c) *Procedure; who may punish for contempt.* This subsection prescribes different procedures for punishment for contempt when members are or are not present. The Working Group examined the possibility of vesting contempt power solely in the military judge; but Article 48 provides that "court[s]-martial" may punish for contempt. When members are present, the military judge is not the court-martial. *See* Article 16. When trial by military judge alone is requested and approved, the military judge is the court-martial. Under Article 39(a) the military judge may "call the court into session without the presence of the members," and the military judge therefore acts as the court-martial within the meaning of Article 16 and 48. Since Article 48 authorizes summary punishment for contempt committed in the presence of the court-martial (*see Hearings of H. R. 2498 Before a Subcomm. of the House Comm. on Armed Services*, 81st Cong., 1st Sess. 1060 (1949)), its purpose would be destroyed by requiring members who were not present and did not observe the behavior to decide the matter. The second sentence in subsection (c)(1) parallels Fed. R. Crim. P. 42(a).

The procedure for contempt proceedings before members has been simplified to the extent possible consistent with the requirement for the members to decide the issue. The procedure for a preliminary ruling by the military judge to decide as a matter of law that no contempt has occurred is expressly recognized for the first time. *See* Article 51(b). The requirement for a two-thirds vote on findings and punishment is based on Article 52(a) and (b)(3).

(d) *Record; review.* This subsection is based on the eighth paragraph of paragraph 118 *b* of MCM, 1969 (Rev.) concerning the record and post-trial action. The requirement for approval and execution of the sentence by the convening authority is based on previous practice. *See* W. Winthrop, *supra* at 301–312; paragraph 101 of MCM, 1928, paragraph 109 of MCM (Army) and MCM (AF), 1949, paragraph 118 of MCM, 1951; paragraph 118 *b* of MCM, 1969 (Rev.). This requirement also reflects the need of the command to control its assets. The last sentence is also based on *Hearings on H. R. 2498 Before a Subcomm. of the House Comm. on Armed Services*, 81st Cong., 1st Sess. 1060 (1949).

(e) *Sentence.* This subsection is based on Article 57 and paragraph 118 *b* of MCM, 1969 (Rev.). It clarifies that the military judge may delay announcement of a sentence to permit participation of the contemnor when necessary. Paragraph 118 *b* of MCM, 1969 (Rev.) was ambiguous in this regard.

(f) *Informing person held in contempt.* This subsection and the discussion are based on paragraph 118 *b* of MCM, 1969 (Rev.); it has been modified for clarity.

1998 Amendment: R.C.M. 809 was amended to modernize military contempt procedures, as recommended in *United States v. Burnett*, 27 M.J. 99, 106 (C.M.A. 1988). Thus, the amendment simplifies the contempt procedure in trials by courts-martial by vesting contempt power in the military judge and eliminating the members' involvement in the process. The amendment also provides that the court-martial proceedings need not be suspended while the contempt proceedings are conducted. The proceedings will be conducted by the military judge in all cases, outside of the members' presence. The military judge also exercises discretion as to the timing of the proceedings and, therefore, may assure that the court-martial is not otherwise unnecessarily disrupted or the accused prejudiced by the contempt proceedings. See *Sacher v. United States*, 343 U.S. 1, 10, 72 S. Ct. 451, 455, 96 L. Ed. 717, 724 (1952). The amendment also brings court-martial contempt procedures into line with the procedure applicable in other courts.

Rule 810 Procedures for rehearings, new trials, and other trials

Introduction. This rule is based on Articles 63 and 73. It concerns only the procedures for rehearings, new trials, and other trials. Matters relating to ordering rehearings or new trials are covered in R.C.M. 1107 and 1210.

(a) *In general.* This subsection is based on paragraph 81 *b* of MCM, 1969 (Rev.).

(b) *Composition.* This subsection is based on Article 63(b) and the seventh paragraph of paragraph 92 *a* of MCM, 1969 (Rev.). As to subsection (3), *see also United States v. Staten*, 21 U.S.C.M.A. 493, 45 C.M.R. 267 (1972).

(c) *Examination of record of former proceedings.* This subsection is based on paragraph 81 *c* of MCM, 1969 (Rev.).

(d) *Sentence limitations.* Subsection (1) is based on the second sentence of Article 63 and its legislative history. *See* H. R. Rep. No. 491, 81st Cong., 1st Sess. 30 (1949) and paragraph 81 *d* of MCM, 1969 (Rev.). *See also United States v. Ball*, 163 U.S. 662 (1896); *United States v. Culver*, 22 U.S.C.M.A. 141, 46 C.M.R. 141 (1973); *United States v. Eschmann*, 11 U.S.C.M.A. 64, 28 C.M.R. 288 (1959); *United States v. Jones*, 10 U.S.C.M.A. 532, 28 C.M.R. 98 (1959); *United States v. Dean*, 7 U.S.C.M.A. 721, 23 C.M.R. 185 (1957). The provision (prohibiting advising members of the basis of the sentence limitation) in the third paragraph of paragraph 81 *d*(1) of MCM, 1969 (Rev.) has been placed, in precatory language, in the discussion. The prohibition was based on *United States v. Eschmann, supra. Analysis of Contents, Manual for Courts-Martial, United States, 1969, Revised edition*, DA PAM 27–2 at 15–2 (1970). The rationale of *Eschmann* is subject to reasonable challenge. *See United States v. Gutierrez*, 11 M.J. 122, 125 n.3 (C.M.A. 1981) (Everett, C. J., concurring in the result); *United States v. Eschmann, supra* at 67, 28 C.M.R. at 291 (Latimer, J., concurring in the result). By placing an admonition against such instructions in the discussion, rather than a prohibition in the rule, users are alerted to current decisional requirements while the issue is left open to future judicial development.

1995 Amendment: Subsection (d) was amended in light of the change to Article 63 effected by the National Defense Authorization Act for Fiscal Year 1993, Pub. L. No. 102–484, 106 Stat. 2315, 2506 (1992). The amendment reflects that subsection (d) sentencing limitations only affect the sentence that may be approved by the convening or higher authority following the rehearing, new trial, or other trial. Subsection (d) does not limit the maximum sentence that may be adjudged at the rehearing, new trial, or other trial.

Subsection (2) is based on the last sentence of Article 63, as amended, Military Justice Act of 1983, Pub. L. No. 98–209, § 5(d)(2)(C), 97 Stat. 1393 (1983).

(e) *Definition.* This definition is taken from paragraph 81 *d*(2) of MCM, 1969 (Rev.). *See also* paragraph 92 *b* of MCM, 1969 (Rev.).

Rule 811 Stipulations

(a) *In general.* This subsection restates the first sentence of paragraph 54 *f*(1) of MCM, 1969 (Rev.).

(b) *Authority to reject.* This subsection affirms the authority of the military judge to decline to accept a stipulation, as an exercise of discretion and in the interest of justice. This authority was implicit in paragraph 54 *f*(1) of MCM, 1969 (Rev.) which suggested that stipulations should not be accepted in certain circumstances. These examples are now included in the discussion. *See also United States v. Cambridge*, 3 U.S.C.M.A. 377, 12 C.M.R. 133 (1953); *United States v. Field*, 27 C.M.R. 863 (N.B.R. 1958).

(c) *Requirements.* This subsection makes clear that a stipulation can be received only with the consent of the parties. This consent must be manifested in some manner before the military judge may receive the stipulation, although the rule does not specify any particular form for the manifestation, as this rests within the discretion of the trial judge. *United States v. Cambridge, supra.* Although it is normally preferable to obtain it, the express consent of the accused on the record is not always necessary for admission of a stipulation. In the absence of circumstances indicating lack of consent by the accused (*see e.g., United States v. Williams*, 30 C.M.R. 650 (N.B.R. 1960)), the defense counsel's concurrence in the stipulation will bind the accused. *United States v. Cambridge, supra.* If there is any doubt, the accused should be personally questioned. *See United States v. Barbeau*, 9 M.J. 569 (A.F.C.M.R. 1980).

The last three paragraphs of the discussion deal with stipulation "which practically amount to a confession." Paragraph 54 *f*(1) of MCM, 1969 (Rev.), states that such a confession "should not be received in evidence." Despite this admonition, such stipulations were occasionally received in order to allow the defense to avoid waiving certain issues by pleading guilty while saving the parties the time and expense of a full trial when the accused's guilt, as a practical if not legal matter, was conceded. *See, e.g., United States v. Rempe*, 49 C.M.R. 367 (A.F.C.M.R. 1974). The Court of Military Appeals has approved this procedure, but only if an inquiry of the sort described in the discussion is conducted. *United States v. Bertelson*, 3 M.J. 314 (C.M.A. 1977). The definition of a stipulation which practically amounts to a confession in the discussion is based on *Bertelson*, along with*United States v. Schaffer*, 12 M.J. 425, 427–428 nn. 4.6 (C.M.A. 1982);; *United States v. Reagan*, 7 M.J. 490 (C.M.A. 1979); *United States v. Aiello*, 7 M.J. 99 (C.M.A. 1979); and *United States v. Long*, 3 M.J. 400 (C.M.A. 1977). These cases indicate that a stipulation practically amounts to a confession when it amounts to a *"de facto"* plea of guilty, rather than simply one which makes out a *prima facie* case. The example in the discussion is taken from *United States v. Long, supra.*

(d) *Withdrawal.* This subsection is taken, substantially verbatim, from paragraph 54 *f*(1) of MCM, 1969 (Rev.), and restates current law. *See also United States v. Daniels*, 11 U.S.C.M.A. 52, 28 C.M.R. 276 (1959).

(e) *Effect of stipulations.* This subsection modifies previous Manual rules in two respects. First, it states that a stipulation of fact is binding on the court-martial. This is consistent with federal practice, *see e.g., Jackson v. United States*, 330 F.2d 679 (8th Cir.), *cert. denied.* 379 U.S. 855 (1964), as well as the prevailing view in the vast majority of states. *See* 4 J. Wigmore, *Wigmore on Evidence* § 2590 (3d ed. 1940); 73 Am. Jur. 2d. *Stipulations*, § 8 (1974); 83 C.J.S. Stipulations, §§ 12–13 (1953). *See also H. Hackfield & Co. v. United States*, 197 U.S. 442 (1905). Paragraph 154 *b* of MCM, 1951, contained the following provision: "The court is not bound by a stipulation even if received. For instance its own inquiry may convince the court that the stipulated fact is not true." The provision was drawn verbatim from paragraph 140 *b* of MCM (Army), 1949, and of MCM(AF), 1949, and can be traced to paragraph 126 *b* of MCM, 1928. The Court of Military Appeals questioned the validity of this provision in *United States v. Gerlach*, 16 U.S.C.M.A. 383, 37 C.M.R. 3 (1966), but did not have to resolve whether the court-martial was bound by a stipulation of fact, since it held that the parties were. The above quoted language was omitted from MCM, 1969 (Rev.). The analysis to the Manual does not explain why. *See Analysis of Contents, Manual for Courts-Martial, 1969, Revised Edition*, DA PAM 27–2 at 27–49 (1970). Despite this omission, some courts-martial have apparently continued to apply the earlier rule. *See Military Criminal Law, Evidence* DA PAM 27–22, AFP 111–8 at paragraph 6–2 (1975). There is no reason not to follow federal practice on this matter. If the court-martial's "own inquiry" indicates that the stipulated facts may not be true, the parties should be afforded the opportunity to withdraw from the stipulation and to present evidence on the matter in question.

The second change is in the treatment of stipulations of a document's contents. MCM, 1969 (Rev.), applied the same "observations" it made concerning stipulations of facts to stipulations of documents' contents thus implying that, by stipulating to a documents' contents, the parties agreed that the contents are true. This may have been due to the treatment of admissions concerning documents' contents as a matter of civil procedure in Federal courts, *see* Fed. R. Civ. P. 36 (1948) (since replaced by Fed. R. Civ. P. 36 (1970)); *see also Wigmore, supra*, § 2596, and the fact that stipulations of a documents' contents, like stipulations of fact, are handed to the members of the court. Yet, it is clear that the parties may stipulate that a document contains certain text or other information, or that a given document is genuine, without necessarily agreeing that the text or other information in the document is true. In this sense, a stipulation as to a document's contents is like a stipulation of expected testimony, and the rule so treats it.

Otherwise, this subsection essentially restates paragraph 54 *f*(1) and (2) of MCM, 1969 (Rev.). *See also United States v. Bennett*, 18 U.S.C.M.A. 96, 39 C.M.R. 96 (1969) and *United States v. Gerlach, supra* for further discussion of the effects of stipulations. If the parties fail to object to inadmissible matters in a stipulation, this will normally constitute a waiver of such objection. Mil. R. Evid. 103. *Cf. United States v. Schell*, 18 U.S.C.M.A. 410, 40 C.M.R. 122 (1969). *See also Wigmore, supra* at § 2592.

(f) *Procedure.* This subsection is based on the second paragraph in paragraph 54 *f*(2) of MCM, 1969 (Rev.).

Rule 812 Joint and common trials

This rule is taken from paragraph 53 *c* of MCM, 1969 (Rev.). The rule itself substantially repeats the first sentence in paragraph 53 *c*. The discussion refers to other rules dealing with joint or common trials, and includes the examples discussed in paragraph 53 *c* of MCM, 1969 (Rev.). It also incorporates a statement on stipulations which appeared at paragraph 54 *f*(3) of MCM, 1969 (Rev.), and a statement concerning severances from paragraph 61 *h* of MCM, 1969 (Rev.). The rule does not change current law.

Rule 813 Announcing personnel of the court-martial and accused

This rule is based on paragraph 61 *c* of MCM, 1969 (Rev.) and is placed in Chapter 8 since the requirement for announcing the presence or absence of parties usually recurs several times during the trial. The rule has been rephrased to acknowledge the responsibility of the military judge to ensure that the matters covered are reflected in the record. Paragraph 61 *c* of MCM, 1969 (Rev.) required the trial counsel to make these announcements. This rule leaves to the discretion of the military judge who will make the announcements. The importance of requiring such announcements to be made on the record is emphasized in *United States v. Nichelson*, 18 U.S.C.M.A. 69, 39 C.M.R. 69 (1968).

CHAPTER IX. TRIAL PROCEDURE THROUGH FINDINGS

Rule 901 Opening session

Introduction. R.C.M. 901 through 903 set out in chronological order the procedures to be followed before arraignment. The order need not be followed rigidly.

(a) *Call to order.* This subsection is based on the first sentence in paragraph 61 *b* of MCM, 1969 (Rev.). The purpose of the subsection is to establish a definite point to indicate when a court-martial is in session. The first paragraph in the discussion is taken from paragraph 61 *a* of MCM, 1969 (Rev.), but the present provision has been expanded to include comparing the record of the referral on the charge sheet with the convening orders to ensure that they are consistent. The other matters in paragraphs

61 *a* and *b* of MCM, 1969 (Rev.), are omitted here as unnecessary.

The second paragraph in the discussion is based on paragraph 58 *c* of MCM, 1969 (Rev.) and serves as a reminder of the Article 35 requirements. *See United States v. Pergande*, 49 C.M.R. 28 (A.C.M.R. 1974). The failure to object is normally a waiver of the statutory right. *United States v. Lumbus*, 48 C.M.R. 613 (A.C.M.R. 1974). Because of the importance of the right, however, the military judge should secure an affirmative waiver. *See United States v. Perna*, 1 U.S.C.M.A. 438, 4 C.M.R. 30 (1952); *United States v. Pergande, supra.*

(b) *Announcement of parties.* This subsection is based on paragraph 61 *c* of MCM, 1969 (Rev.). Requiring an announcement is intended to guard against inadvertently proceeding in the absence of necessary personnel and to ensure that the record reflects the presence of required personnel. Failure to make the announcement is not error if it otherwise appears that no essential personnel were absent.

(c) *Swearing reporter and interpreter.* This subsection and its discussion are taken directly from paragraph 61 *d* of MCM, 1969 (Rev.).

(d) *Counsel.* This subsection, except for subsection (4)(A) and (D), is based on paragraphs 61 *e* and *f* of MCM, 1969 (Rev.). The qualifications of counsel and matters which disqualify counsel are treated at R.C.M. 502(d) and are not repeated here. The subsection makes clear that at trial the military judge is responsible for determining whether counsel is disqualified, *Soriano v. Hosken*, 9 M.J. 221 (C.M.A. 1980), and for seeing that appropriate action is taken. Of course, if a detailed counsel is disqualified the responsibility will fall upon the convening authority to rectify the problem. The discussion points out that defects in the qualification of counsel are not jurisdictional. *Wright v. United States*, 2 M.J. 9 (C.M.A. 1976). Subsection (4)(A) has been added to conform to the requirements of *United States v. Donohew*, 18 U.S.C.M.A. 149, 39 C.M.R. 149 (1969). *Cf.* Fed. R. Crim. P. 5(c). Subsection (4)(D) is based on Fed. R. Crim. P. 44(c) and *United States v. Breese*, 11 M.J. 17 (C.M.A. 1981). *See also United States v. Davis*, 3 M.J. 430 (C.M.A. 1977); *United States v. Blakey*, 1 M.J. 247 (C.M.A. 1976); *United States v. Evans*, 1 M.J. 206 (C.M.A. 1975).

(e) *Presence of members.* This subsection is new. Its purpose is to eliminate unnecessary attendance by members. *Accord* Article 39(a).

Rule 902 Disqualification of military judge

Introduction. This rule is based on 28 U.S.C. § 455, which is itself based on Canon III of the *ABA Code of Judicial Conduct*, and on paragraph 62 of MCM, 1969 (Rev.).

The procedures prescribed by 28 U.S.C. § 144 were not adopted. That statute provides that whenever a party "files a timely and sufficient affidavit that the judge before whom the matter is pending has a personal bias or prejudice either against him or in favor of any adverse party, such judge shall proceed no further therein." This section does not establish a different test from 28 U.S.C. § 455 for disqualification for prejudice or bias. Instead, 28 U.S.C. § 144 provides a procedure mechanism by which the disqualification determination may be made. *United States v. Sibla*, 624 F.2d 864 (9th Cir. 1980); *see also Parrish v. Board of Commissioners of Alabama State Bar*, 524 F.2d 98 (5th Cir. 1975) (*en banc*), *cert. denied*, 425 U.S. 944 (1976).

This procedure is not practicable for courts-martial because of the different structure of the military judiciary and the limited number of military judges.

(a) *In general.* This subsection is, except for changes in terminology, identical to 28 U.S.C. § 455(a). *See also* paragraph 62 *f*(13) of MCM, 1969 (Rev.); *United States v. Conley*, 4 M.J. 327 (C.M.A. 1978); *United States v. Head*, 2 M.J. 131 (C.M.A. 1977).

(b) *Specific grounds.* The stem and subsection (1) are, with changes in terminology, identical to the stem and subsection (1) of 28 U.S.C. § 455(b). *See also* paragraph 62 *f*(13) of MCM, 1969 (Rev.). Note that any interest or bias to be disqualifying must be personal, not judicial, in nature. *Berger v. United States*, 255 U.S. 22 (1921); *Azhocar v. United States*, 581 F.2d 735 (9th Cir. 1978), *cert. denied*, 440 U.S. 907 (1979); *United States v. Lewis*, 6 M.J. 43 (C.M.A. 1978); *United States v. Grance*, 2 M.J. 846 (A.C.M.R. 1976); *United States v. Stewart*, 2 M.J. 423 (A.C.M.R. 1975). *See also United States v. Lynch*, 13 M.J. 394, 398, n. 3 (C.M.A. 1982) (Everett, C.J. concurring).

Subsection (2) is based on paragraphs 62 *f*(5), (6), and (11) of MCM, 1969 (Rev.). *See United States v. Goodman*, 3 M.J. 1 (C.M.A. 1977). These grounds are analogous to the disqualifying activities in 28 U.S.C. § 455(b)(2).

Subsection (3) is based on paragraphs 62 *f*(3), (4), (9), (10), and (13) of MCM, 1969 (Rev.). *See also* Mil. R. Evid. 605; *United States v. Cooper*, 8 M.J. 5 (C.M.A 1979); *United States v. Bradley*, 7 M.J. 332 (C.M.A. 1979). The purpose of this section is analogous to that of 28 U.S.C. § 455(b)(3).

Subsection (4) is based on Article 26 and paragraph 62 *f*(1) and (2) and 62 *g* of MCM, 1969 (Rev). The matters in 28 U.S.C. § 455(b)(4) regarding financial interest in the proceedings are not of significance in courts-martial. The remote possibility that a judge or a member of the family might have a financial interest in the outcome of a court-martial is adequately covered in subsection (5) of this rule.

Subsection (5) is taken directly from 28 U.S.C. § 455(b)(5), with the added clarification that the interest in subsection (C) may be financial or otherwise.

The discussion is based on 28 U.S.C. § 455(c).

(c) *Definitions.* Subsections (1) and (2) are, with changes in terminology, identical to 28 U.S.C. § 455(d)(1) and (2). Subsection (3) has been added to clarify that the president of a special court-martial without a military judge is treated as any other member for purposes of qualifications and challenges. *See* R.C.M. 912. Subsection (3) of 28 U.S.C. § 455(d) is unnecessary.

(d) *Procedure.* This section including the discussion is based on Article 41 and paragraph 62 *d, g*, and *h* of MCM, 1969 (Rev.).

(e) *Waiver.* This section is, with changes in terminology, identical to 28 U.S.C. § 455(e).

Rule 903 Accused's elections on composition of court-martial

(a) *Time of elections.* This subsection is based on Articles 16, 18, 19, and 25. It is similar to paragraphs 53 *d*(2)(c) and 61 *g* and *h* of MCM, 1969 (Rev.) insofar as it concerns the timing of requests for enlisted members of trial by military judge alone. It parallels Fed. R. Crim. P. 23(a). Section (b) of Fed. R. Crim. P.

23 is inapplicable in the military, and the matters covered in Fed. R. Crim. P. 23(c) are covered in R.C.M. 918(b).

Article 25 states that a request for enlisted members must be made before the end of an Article 39(a) session, if any. The first Article 39(a) session is appropriate to consider these matters. Although the Court of Military Appeals has not decided the issue (*United States v. Morris*, 23 U.S.C.M.A. 319, 321, 49 C.M.R. 653, 655 n.2 (1975)), the Working Group concluded that this does not establish a jurisdictional deadline. *Cf. United States v. Bryant*, 23 U.S.C.M.A. 326, 49 C.M.R. 660 (1975); *United States v. Morris, supra* (Article 16 requirement that request be submitted before assembly is not jurisdictional). To permit greater flexibility, the military judge is authorized to permit the defense to defer a request for enlisted members until a later time. Such a request should be granted for good cause only, bearing in mind the burden which it may impose on the Government.

A request for trial by military judge alone should be made at the initial Article 39(a) session to simplify procedure and facilitate scheduling and preparation. However, since Article 16 gives the accused a statutory right to wait until assembly to request trial by military judge alone, subsection (2) allows automatic deferral of this request.

The discussion points out the statutory limits on requesting enlisted members or trial by military judge alone. *See* Articles 16, 18, and 25.

(b) *Form of election.* This subsection is based on Articles 16 and 25. The amendment of Article 16 permits a request for trial by military judge alone to be made orally on the record. Military Justice Act of 1983, Pub. L. No. 98–209, § 3(a), 97 Stat. 1393 (1983).

(c) *Action on request.* This subsection is based on Articles 16 and 25. Subsection (2)(A) is based on Article 16(1)(B) and on paragraph 53 *d*(2)(C) of MCM, 1969 (Rev.). It does not require an inquiry of the accused by the military judge, although, as the discussion points out, it is good practice to do so, and failure to do so could be error if the record otherwise left the accused's understanding of the rights in doubt. *See* S. Rep. No. 53, 98th Cong., 1st Sess. 12 (1983); *United States v. Parkes*, 5 M.J. 489 (C.M.A. 1978); *United States v. Turner*, 20 U.S.C.M.A. 167, 43 C.M.R. 7 (1970); *United States v. Jenkins*, 20 U.S.C.M.A. 112, 42 C.M.R. 304 (1970). This is consistent with prevailing federal civilian practice. *See, e.g., Estrada v. United States*, 457 F.2d 255 (7th Cir.), *cert. denied*, 409 U.S. 858 (1972); *United States v. Mitchell*, 427 F.2d 1280 (3d Cir. 1970); *United States v. Straite*, 425 F.2d 594 (D.C. Cir. 1970); *United States v. Hunt*, 413 F.2d 983 (4th Cir. 1969); *but see United States v. Scott*, 583 F.2d 362 (7th Cir. 1978) (establishing requirement for personal inquiry into jury waiver in Seventh Circuit). *See generally* 8AJ. Moore, *Moore's Federal Practice* Para. 23.03[2] (1982 rev. ed.).

Subsection (2)(B) is based on Article 16(1)(B) which makes trial by military judge alone contingent on approval by the military judge. *See United States v. Morris, supra* at 324, 49 C.M.R. at 658. The discussion is based on *United States v. Butler*, 14 M.J. 72 (C.M.A. 1982); *United States v. Ward*, 3 M.J. 365 (C.M.A. 1977); *United States v. Bryant, supra.*

1986 Amendment: Subsection (3) was amended to reflect clearly that requests for trial by military judge alone need not be in writing.

(d) *Right to withdraw request.* Subsection (1) is based on *United States v. Stipe*, 23 U.S.C.M.A. 11, 48 C.M.R. 267 (1974).

Subsection (2) is based on the fifth sentence of paragraph 39 *e* and on paragraph 53 *d* (2)(b) of MCM, 1969 (Rev.), and current practice.

(e) *Untimely requests.* This subsection is based on Articles 16 and 25, and *United States v. Jeanbaptiste*, 5 M.J. 374 (C.M.A. 1978); *United States v. Thorpe*, 5 M.J. 186 (C.M.A. 1978); *United States v. Wright*, 5 M.J. 106 (C.M.A. 1978); *United States v. Bryant, supra. See also United States v. Holmen*, 586 F.2d 322 (4th Cir. 1978).

Despite dicta in*United States v. Bryant, supra* at 328, 49 C.M.R. at 662 n. 2, that withdrawal must be in writing, the rule prescribes no format for withdrawal. *Cf.* Article 16(1)(B), as amended, *see* Military Justice Act of 1983, Pub. L. No. 98–209, § 3(a), 97 Stat. 1393 (1983).

1987 Amendment: Subsections (b)(1), (c)(1) and (c)(3) were amended to reflect an amendment to Article 25(c)(1) UCMJ, in the "Military Justice Amendments of 1986," tit. VIII, § 803, National Defense Authorization Act for fiscal year 1987, Pub. L. No. 99–661, 100 Stat. 3905 (1986). *See* Analysis R.C.M. 503.

Rule 904 Arraignment

This rule is based on Fed. R. Crim. P. 10 and paragraph 65 *a* of MCM, 1969 (Rev.). The second sentence of Fed. R. Crim. P. 10 has been deleted as unnecessary since in military practice the accused will have been served with charges before arraignment. Article 35; R.C.M. 602. the discussion is based on paragraph 65 of MCM, 1969 (Rev.).

Rule 905 Motions generally

Introduction. This rule is based generally on Fed. R. Crim. P. 12 and 47 and paragraphs 66 and 67 of MCM, 1969 (Rev.). Specific similarities and differences are discussed below.

(a) *Definitions and form.* The first sentence of this subsection is taken from the first sentence of paragraph 66 *b* of MCM, 1969 (Rev.). It is consistent with the first sentence of Fed. R. Crim. P. 47 and the second sentence of Fed. R. Crim. P. 12(a). The second sentence is based on the second sentence of paragraph 67 *c* of MCM, 1969 (Rev.), although to be consistent with Federal practice (*see* Fed. R. Crim. P. 12(b) (second sentence) and 47 (second sentence)) express authority for the military judge to exercise discretion over the form of motions has been added. The third sentence is based on the third sentence of Fed. R. Crim. P. 47 and is consistent with the first sentence of paragraph 67 *c* and the fourth sentence of paragraph 69 *a* of MCM, 1969 (Rev.). The last sentence in this subsection is based on the third sentence of paragraph 67 *c* of MCM, 1969 (Rev.). Although no parallel provision appears in the Federal Rules of Criminal Procedure, this standard is similar to federal practice. *See Marteney v. United States* , 216 F.2d 760 (10th Cir. 1954); *United States v. Rosenson*, 291 F. Supp. 867 (E.D. La. 1968), *affd*, 417 F.2d 629 (5th Cir. 1969); *cert. denied*, 397 U.S. 962 (1970). The last sentence in Fed. R. Crim. P. 47, allowing a motion to be supported by affidavit, is not included here. *See* subsection (h) of this rule and Mil. R. Evid. 104(a). *See generally* Fed. R. Crim. P. 47 *Notes Of Advisory Committee on Rules* n. 3.

(b) *Pretrial motions.* This subsection, except for subsection (6), is based on Fed. R. Crim. P. 12(b). Subsections (1) and (2) have been modified to conform to military practice and are consistent with the first two sentences of paragraph 67 *b* of MCM, 1969 (Rev.). Subsection (3) is consistent with Mil. R. Evid. 304(d)(2)(A); 311(d)(2)(A); 321(c)(2)(A). The discussion is based on paragraph 69A of MCM, 1969 (rev.). Subsection (4) is new. *See* R.C.M. 701; 703; 1001(e). Subsection (5) is also new. Subsection (6) is based on paragraphs 46 *d* and 48 *b*(4) of MCM, 1969 (Rev.) and*United States v. Redding*, 11 M.J. 100 (C.M.A. 1981).

(c) *Burden of proof.* This subsection is based on paragraphs 57 *g*(1) and 67 *e* of MCM, 1969 (Rev.). The assignment of the burden of persuasion to the moving party is a minor change from the language in paragraph 67 *e* of MCM, 1969 (Rev.), which placed the burden on the accused "generally." The effect is basically the same, however, since the former rule probably was intended to apply to motions made by the accused. *See also United States v. Graham*, 22 U.S.C.M.A. 75, 46 C.M.R. 75 (1972). The exceptions to this general rule in subsection (B) are based on paragraphs 68 *b* (1), 68 *c*, and 215 *e* of MCM, 1969 (Rev.). *See also United States v. McCarthy*, 2 M.J. 26, 28 n. 1 (C.M.A. 1976); *United States v. Graham, supra; United States v. Garcia*, 5 U.S.C.M.A. 88, 17 C.M.R. 88 (1954). The Federal Rules of Criminal Procedure are silent on burdens of proof.

Fed. R. Crim. P. 12(c) is not adopted. This is because in courts-martial, unlike civilian practice, arraignment does not necessarily, or even ordinarily, occur early in the criminal process. In courts-martial, arraignment usually occurs only a short time before trial and in many cases it occurs the same day as trial. Because of this, requiring a motions date after arraignment but before trial is not appropriate, at least as a routine matter. Instead, entry of pleas operates, in the absence of good cause, as the deadline for certain motions. A military judge could, subject to subsections (d) and (e), schedule an Article 39(a) session (*see* R.C.M. 803) for the period after pleas are entered but before trial to hear motions.

(d) *Ruling on motions.* This subsection is based on Fed. R. Crim. P. 12(e). It is consistent with the first sentence in paragraph 67 *e* of MCM, 1969 (Rev.). The admonition in the second sentence of that paragraph has been deleted as unnecessary. The discussion is based on the third paragraph of paragraph 67 *f* of MCM, 1969 (Rev.).

1991 Amendment: The discussion was amended to reflect the change to R.C.M. 908(b)(4).

(e) *Effect of failure to raise defenses or objections.* The first two sentences in the subsection are taken from Fed. R. Crim. P. 12(f) and are consistent with paragraph 67 *b* of MCM, 1969 (Rev.). The third sentence is based on paragraph 67 *a* of MCM, 1969 (Rev.). The Federal Rules of Criminal Procedure do not expressly provide for waiver of motions other than those listed in Fed. R. Crim. P. 12(b). (*But see* 18 U.S.C. § 3162(a)(2) which provides that failure by the accused to move for dismissal on grounds of denial of speedy trial before trial or plea of guilty constitutes waiver of the right to dismissal under that section.) Nevertheless, it has been contended that because Fed. R. Crim. P. 12(b)(2) provides that lack of jurisdiction or failure to allege an offense "shall be noticed by the court at any time during the pendency of the proceedings," "it may, by negative implications be interpreted as foreclosing the other defense if not raised during the trial itself." 8A J. Moore, *Moore's Federal Practice* Para. 12.03[1] (1982 rev. ed.). "Pendency of the proceedings" has been held to include the appellate process. *See United States v. Thomas*, 444 F.2d 919 (D.C. Cir. 1971). Fed. R. Crim. P. 34 tends to support this construction insofar as it permits a posttrial motion in arrest of judgment only for lack of jurisdiction over the offense or failure to charge an offense. There is no reason why other motions should not be waived if not raised at trial. *Moore's, supra* at Para. 12.03[1]; *accord* C. Wright, *Federal Practice and Procedure* §193 (1969). *See also United States v. Scott*, 464 F.2d 832 (D.C. Cir. 1972); *United States v. Friedland*, 391 F.2d 378 (2d Cir. 1968), *cert. denied*, 404 U.S. 867 (1969). *See generally United States ex rel. DiGiangiemo v. Regan*, 528 F.2d 1262 (2d Cir. 1975). Decisions of the United States Court of Military Appeals are generally consistent with this approach. *See United States v. Troxell*, 12 U.S.C.M.A. 6, 30 C.M.R. 6 (1960) (statute of limitations may be waived); *United States v. Schilling*, 7 U.S.C.M.A. 482, 22 C.M.R. 272 (1957) (former jeopardy may be waived). *Contra United States v. Johnson*, 2 M.J. 541 (A.C.M.R. 1976).

1990 Amendment: Subsection (e) was amended to clarify that "requests" and "objections" include "motions".

(f) *Reconsideration.* This subsection is new and makes clear that the military judge may reconsider rulings except as noted. The amendment of Article 62 (*see* Military Justice Act of 1983, Pub. L. No. 98–209, § 5(c), 97 Stat. 1393 (1983)), which deleted the requirement for reconsideration when directed by the convening authority' does not preclude this. *See* S. Rep. No. 53, 98th Cong., 1st Sess. 24 (1983).

1994 Amendment: The amendment to R.C.M. 905(f) clarifies that the military judge has the authority to take remedial action to correct any errors that have prejudiced the rights of an accused. *United States v. Griffith*, 27 M.J. 42, 47 (C.M.A. 1988). Such remedial action may be taken at a pre-trial session, during trial, or at a post-trial Article 39(a) session. *See also United States v. Scaff*, 29 M.J. 60, 65-66 (C.M.A. 1989). The amendment, consistent with R.C.M. 1102(d), clarifies that post-trial reconsideration is permitted until the record of trial is authenticated.

The amendment to the Discussion clarifies that the amendment to subsection (f) does not change the standard to be used to determine the legal sufficiency of evidence. R.C.M. 917(d); *see Griffith, supra; see also Scaff, supra.*

(g) *Effect of final determinations.* Except as noted below, this subsection is based on paragraph 71 *b* of MCM, 1969 (Rev.) and on *Ashe v. Swenson*, 397 U.S. 436 (1970); *Oppenheimer v. United States*, 242 U.S. 85 (1916); *United States v. Marks*, 21 U.S.C.M.A. 281, 45 C.M.R. 55 (1972); *Restatement of Judgements*, Chapter 3 (1942). *See also Commissioner of Internal Revenue v. Sunnen*, 333 U.S. 591 (1948); *United States v. Moser*, 266 U.S. 236 (1924); *United States v. Washington*, 7 M.J. 78 (C.M.A. 1979); *United States v. Hart*, 19 U.S.C.M.A. 438, 42 C.M.R. 40 (1970); *United States v. Smith*, 4 U.S.C.M.A. 369, 15 C.M.R. 369 (1954).

Subsection (g) differs from paragraph 71 *b* in two significant respects. First, the term, "res judicata" is not used in R.C.M. 905(g) because the term is legalistic and potentially confusing. "Res judicata" generally includes several distinct but related concepts: merger, bar, direct estoppel, and collateral estoppel. *Restatement of Judgments*, Chapter 3 Introductory Note at 160 (1942). *But see* 1B J. Moore, *Moore's Federal Practice*

Para. 0.441(1) (1980 rev. ed.) which distinguishes collateral estoppel from res judicata generally. Second, unique aspects of the doctrine of collateral estoppel are recognized in the "except" clause of the first sentence in the rule. Earlier Manuals included the concept of collateral estoppel within the general discussion of res judicata (*see* paragraph 72 *b* of MCM (Army), 1949; paragraph 71 *b* of MCM, 1951, paragraph 71 *b* of MCM, 1969 (Rev.); *see also United States v. Smith, supra*) without discussing its distinguishing characteristics. Unlike other forms of res judicata, collateral estoppel applies to determinations made in actions in which the causes of action were different. 1B J. Moore, *supra*, Para. 0.441[1]. Because of this, its application is somewhat narrower. Specifically, parties are not bound by determinations of law when the causes of action in the two suits arose out of different transactions. *Restatement of Judgments, supra*, §§ 68, 70. *See also Commissioner v. Sunnen, supra.* This distinction is now recognized in the rule.

The absence of such a clarifying provision in earlier Manuals apparently caused the majority, despite its misgivings and over the dissent of Judge Brosman, to reach the result it did in *United States v. Smith, supra.* When paragraph 71 *b* was rewritten in MCM, 1969 (Rev.), the result in *Smith* was incorporated into that paragraph, but neither the concerns of the Court of Military Appeals nor the distinguishing characteristics of collateral estoppel were addressed. *See Analysis of Contents of the Manual for Courts-Martial, United States, 1969, Revised Edition*, DA Pam 27–2 at 12–5 (July 1970). To the extent that *Smith* relied on the Manual, its result is no longer required. *But see United States V Martin*, 8 U.S.C.M.A. 346, 352, 24 C.M.R. 156, 162 (1957) (Quinn, C.J., joined by Ferguson, J. concurring in the result).

The discussion is based on the sources indicated above. *See also Restatement of Judgments, supra* § 49; *United States v. Guzman*, 4 M.J. 115 (C.M.A. 1977). As to the effect of pretrial determinations by a convening authority, *see* Analysis, R.C.M. 306(a).

(h) *Written motions.* This subsection is based on Fed. R. Crim. P. 47.

(i) *Service.* This subsection is based on Fed. R. Crim. P. 49(a) and (b), insofar as those provisions apply to motions.

(j) *Application to convening authority.* This subsection is taken from paragraph 66 *b* of MCM, 1969 (Rev.) although certain exceptions provided elsewhere in these rules (*e.g.*, R.C.M. 906(b)(1)) have been established for the first time. It is consistent with the judicial functions of the convening authority under Article 64. It also provides a forum for resolution of disputes before referral and in the absence of the military judge after referral. It has no counterpart in the Federal Rules of Criminal Procedure.

Fed. R. Crim. P. 12(g) and (h) are not included. Fed. R. Crim. P. 12(g) is covered at R.C.M. 803 and 808. The matters in Fed. R. Crim. P. 12(h) would fall under the procedures in R.C.M. 304 and 305.

(k) *Production of statements on motion to suppress.* This subsection is based on Fed. R. Crim. P. 12(i).

Rule 906 Motions for appropriate relief

(a) *In general.* This subsection is based on the first sentence of paragraph 69 *a* of MCM, 1969 (Rev.). The phrase concerning deprivation of rights is new; it applies to such pretrial matters as defects in the pretrial advice and the legality of pretrial confinement. Paragraph 69 *a* of MCM, 1969 (Rev.) provided only for the accused to make motions for appropriate relief This rule is not so restricted because the prosecution may also request appropriate relief. *See e.g., United States v. Nivens*, 21 U.S.C.M.A. 420, 45 C.M.R. 194 (1972). This change is not intended to modify or restrict the power of the convening authority or other officials to direct that action be taken notwithstanding the fact that such action might also be sought by the trial counsel by motion for appropriate relief before the military judge. Specific modifications of the powers of such officials are noted expressly in the rules or analysis.

(b) *Grounds for appropriate relief.* This subsection has the same general purpose as paragraph 69 of MCM, 1969 (Rev.). It identifies most of the grounds for motions for appropriate relief commonly raised in courts-martial, and provides certain rules for litigating and deciding such motions where these rules are not provided elsewhere in the Manual. Specific sources for the rules and discussion are described below.

Subsection (1) and the accompanying discussion are based on Article 40 and paragraphs 58 *b* and *c* of MCM, 1969 (Rev.). The rule provides that only a military judge may grant a continuance. Paragraph 58 *a* of MCM, 1969 (Rev.) which provided for "postponement" has been deleted. Reposing power to postpone proceedings in the convening authority is inconsistent with the authority of the military judge to schedule proceedings and control the docket. *See generally United States v. Wolzok*, 1 M.J. 125 (C.M.A. 1975). To the extent that paragraph 58 *a* extended to the military judge the power to direct postponement, it was duplicative of the power to grant a continuance and unnecessary.

Subsection (2) is based on paragraph 48 *b*(4) of MCM, 1969 (Rev.). *See also United States v. Redding*, 11 M.J. 100 (C.M.A. 1981).

Subsection (3) is based on paragraph 69 *c* of MCM, 1969 (Rev.). *See also* Articles 32(d) and 34; *United State v. Johnson*, 7 M.J. 396 (C.M.A. 1979); *United States v. Donaldson*, 23 U.S.C.M.A. 293, 49 C.M.R. 542 (1975); *United States v. Maness*, 23 U.S.C.M.A. 41, 48 C.M.R. 512 (1974).

Subsection (4) is based on paragraph 69 *b* of MCM, 1969 (Rev.). *See also* Article 30(a); paragraphs 29e and 33 *d* of MCM, 1969 (Rev.); Fed. R. Crim. P. 7(d). *See generally United States v. Arbic*, 16 U.S.C.M.A. 292, 36 C.M.R. 448 (1966); *United States v. Krutsinger*, 15 U.S.C.M.A. 235, 35 C.M.R. 207 (1965); *United States v. Johnson*, 12 U.S.C.M.A. 710, 31 C.M.R. 296 (1962).

Subsection (5) and its discussion are based on paragraph 28 *b* of MCM, 1969 (Rev.); *United States v. Collins*, 16 U.S.C.M.A. 167, 36 C.M.R. 323 (1966); *United States v. Means*, 12 U.S.C.M.A. 290, 30 C.M.R. 290 (1961); *United States v. Parker*, 3 U.S.C.M.A. 541, 13 C.M.R. 97 (1953); *United States v. Voudren*, 33 C.M.R. 722 (A.B.R. 1963). *See also* paragraphs 158 and 200 *a*(8) of MCM, 1969 (Rev). *But see United States v. Davis*, 16 U.S.C.M.A. 207, 36 C.M.R. 363 (1966) (thefts occurring at different places and times over four-month period were separate).

Subsection (6) is based on Fed. R. Crim. P. 7(f). Although not expressly provided for in the previous Manual, bills of particulars have been recognized in military practice. *See United States v. Alef*, 3 M.J. 414 (C.M.A. 1977); *United States v. Paulk*, 13 U.S.C.M.A. 456, 32 C.M.R. 456 (1963); *United States v. Calley*,

46 C.M.R. 1131, 1170 (A.C.M.R.), *aff'd*, 22 U.S.C.M.A 534, 48 C.M.R. 19 (1973); James, *Pleadings and Practice under United States v. Alef*, 20 A.F.L. Rev. 22 (1978); Dunn, *Military Pleadings*, 17 A.F.L. Rev. 17 (Fall, 1975). The discussion is based on *United States V. Mannino*, 480 F. Supp. 1182, 1185 (S.D. N.Y. 1979); *United States v. Deaton*, 448 F. Supp. 532 (N.D. Ohio 1978); *see also United States v. Harbin*, 601 F.2d 773, 779 (5th Cir. 1979); *United States v. Giese*, 597 F.2d 1170, 1180 (9th Cir. 1979); *United States v. Davis*, 582 F. 2d 947, 951 (5th Cir. 1978), *cert. denied*, 441 U.S. 962 (1979). Concerning the contents of a bill, *see United States v. Diecidue*, 603 F.2d 535, 563 (5th Cir. 1979); *United States v. Murray*, 527 F.2d 401, 411 (5th Cir. 1976); *United States v. Mannino, supra; United States v. Hubbard*, 474 F. Supp. 64, 80–81 (D. D.C. 1979).

Subsection (7) is based on paragraphs 75 *e* and 115 *a* of MCM, 1969 (Rev.). *See also* Fed. R. Crim. P. 12(b)(4); *United States v. Killebrew*, 9 M.J. 154 (C.M.A. 1980); *United States v. Chuculate*, 5 M.J. 143 (C.M.A. 1978).

Subsection (8) is new to the Manual although not to military practice. *See* Analysis, R.C.M. 305(j).

Subsection (9) is based on paragraph 69 *d* of MCM, 1969 (Rev.) and Fed. R. Crim. P. 14 to the extent that the latter applies to severance of codefendants. Note that the Government may also accomplish a severance by proper withdrawal of charges against one or more codefendants and rereferrals of these charges to another court-martial. *See* R.C.M. 604. The discussion is based on paragraph 69 *d* of MCM, 1969 (Rev.).

Subsection (10) is new. It roughly parallels Fed. R. Crim. P. 14, but is much narrower because of the general policy in the military favoring trial of all known charges at a single court-martial. *See* R.C.M. 601(e) and discussion; *United States v. Keith*, 1 U.S.C.M.A. 442, 4 C.M.R. 34 (1952). Motions to sever charges have, in effect, existed through the policy in paragraph 26c of MCM, 1969 (Rev.), against joining minor and major offenses. *See, e.g., United States v. Grant*, 26 C.M.R. 692 (A.B.R. 1958). Although that provision has been eliminated, severance of offenses may still be appropriate in unusual cases. *See generally United States v. Gettz*, 49 C.M.R. 79 (N.C.M.R. 1974).

Subsection (11) is based generally on paragraph 69 *e* of MCM, 1969 (Rev.) and on Fed. R. Crim. P. 21. *See United States v. Nivens, supra; United States v. Gravitt*, 5 U.S.C.M.A. 249, 17 C.M.R. 249 (1954). The constitutional requirement that the trial of a crime occur in the district in which the crime was committed (U.S. Const. Art. II, sec. 2, cl. 3; amend VI) does not apply in the military. *Chenoweth v. VanArsdall*, 22 U.S.C.M.A. 183, 46 C.M.R. 183 (1973). Therefore Fed. R. Crim. P. 21(b) is inapplicable. In recognition of this, and of the fact that the convening authority has an interest, both financial and operational, in fixing the place of the trial, the rule allows the situs of the trial to be set and changed for the convenience of the Government, subject to judicial protection of the accused's rights as they may be affected by that situs. *See United States v. Nivens, supra.*

Subsection (12) is based on paragraph 76 *a*(5) of MCM, 1969 (Rev.). *See also* Analysis, R.C.M. 907(b)(3)(B) and Analysis, R.C.M. 1003(c)(1)(C).

Subsection (13) is new to the Manual, although motions *in limine* have been recognized previously. *See* Mil. R. Evid. 104(c); *United States v. Cofield*, 11 M.J. 422 (C.M.A. 1981); Siano, *Motions in Limine*, The Army Lawyer, 17 (Jan. 1976).

1994 Amendment. The Discussion to subparagraph (13) was amended to reflect the holding in *United States v. Sutton*, 31 M.J. 11 (C.M.A. 1990). The Court of Military Appeals in *Sutton* held that its decision in*United States v. Cofield*, 11 M.J. 422 (C.M.A. 1981), should not be relied upon to determine reviewability of preliminary rulings in courts-martial. Instead, reviewability of preliminary rulings will be controlled by*Luce v. United States*, 469 U.S. 38 (1984).

Subsection (14) is based on paragraph 69 *f* of MCM, 1969 (Rev.). *See* Analysis, R.C.M. 706, R.C.M. 909, and Analysis, R.C.M. 916(k).

Rule 907 Motions to dismiss

(a) *In general.* This subsection is based on paragraphs 68 and 214 of MCM, 1969 (Rev.).

Fed. R. Crim. P. 48(a) is inapposite because the trial counsel may not independently request dismissal of charges, and unnecessary because the convening authority already has authority to withdraw and to dismiss charges. *See* R.C.M. 306(c)(1); 401(c)(1); 604. The matters contained in Fed. R. Crim. P. 48(b) are addressed by R.C.M. 707 and 907(b)(2)(A).

(b) *Grounds for dismissal.* This subsection lists common grounds for motions to dismiss. It is not intended to be exclusive. It is divided into three subsections. These correspond to nonwaivable (subsection (1)) and waivable (subsection (2) and (3)) motions to dismiss (*see* R.C.M. 905(e) and analysis), and to circumstances which require dismissal (subsections (1) and (2)) and those in which dismissal is only permissible (subsection (3).

Subsection (1) is based on paragraph 68 *b* of MCM, 1969 (Rev.). *See also* Fed. R. Crim. P. 12(b)(2) and 34.

Subsection (2)(A) is based on paragraph 68 *i* of MCM, 1969 (Rev.). *See also* 18 U.S.C. § 3162(a)(2). The rules for speedy trial are covered in R.C.M. 707.

2005 Amendment: The discussion was based upon the National Defense Authorization Act for Fiscal Year 2004, Pub. L. No. 108-136, § 551, 117 Stat. 1481 (2003). The amendment to Art. 43, UCMJ creates a statute of limitations period that extends until a child-victim attains the age of 25 years for certain specified UCMJ and federal offenses committed on or after 24 November 1998. Due to Ex Post Facto considerations, allowance is required for those child abuse cases in which the five-year statute of limitations was expired at the time the amendment to Article 43, UCMJ, became effective. *See generally Stogner v. California*, 539 U.S. 607, 609 (2003). All child abuse offenses committed prior to that date would be subject to the previous five-year statute of limitations that would expire on the day prior to the effective date of the amendment - November 24, 2003. The referenced case permits unexpired periods to be extended by the new statute, but does not allow the statute to renew an expired period.

2007 Amendment: The discussion was changed based upon the National Defense Authorization Act for Fiscal Year 2006, Pub. L. No. 109-163, § 553, 119 Stat. 3136 (2006). The amendment to Art. 43, UCMJ creates a statute of limitations period that extends through the life of a child-victim or for 5 years, whichever is longer, for certain specified UCMJ and federal offenses. At least one court has ruled that the new statute of limitations applied retrospectively to all offenses for which the original statute had not expired on the date when the extensions were enacted. *See United States v. Ratliff*, 65 M.J. 806 (N.M.C.C.A. 2007), *stay granted United States v. Ratliff*, 2007 CAAF LEXIS 1598 (C.A.A.F., Dec. 3, 2007).

Subsection (2)(B) is based on the first two paragraphs in paragraph 68 *c* of MCM, 1969 (Rev.); *United States v. Troxell*, 12 U.S.C.M.A. 6, 30 C.M.R. 6 (1960); *United States v. Rodgers*, 8 U.S.C.M.A. 226, 24 C.M.R. 36 (1957). The discussion is based on paragraphs 68 *c* and 215 *d* of MCM, 1969 (Rev.). *See also United States v. Arbic*, 16 U.S.C.M.A. 292, 36 C.M.R. 448 (1966); *United States v. Spain*, 10 U.S.C.M.A. 410, 27 C.M.R. 484 (1959); *United States v. Reeves*, 49 C.M.R. 841 (A.C.M.R. 1975).

1987 Amendment: The discussion under subsection (b)(2)(B) was revised to reflect several amendments to Article 43, UCMJ, contained in the "Military Justice Amendments of 1986," tit. VIII, § 805, National Defense Authorization Act for fiscal year 1987, Pub. L. No. 99–661, 100 Stat. 3905, (1986). These amendments were derived, in part, from Chapter 213 of Title 18, United States Code.

1990 Amendment: The fourth paragraph of the discussion under subsection (b)(2)(B) was amended to reflect the holding in *United States v. Tunnell*, 23 M.J. 110 (C.M.A. 1986).

Subsection (2)(C) is based on paragraph 215 *b* of MCM, 1969 (Rev.) and Article 44. *See also* paragraph 56 of MCM, 1969 (Rev.). Concerning the applicability to courts-martial of the double jeopardy clause (U.S. Const. Amend. V), *see Wade v. Hunter*, 336 U.S. 684 (1949); *United States v. Richardson*, 21 U.S.C.M.A. 54, 44 C.M.R. 108 (1971). *See also United States v. Francis*, 15 M.J. 424 (C.M.A. 1983).

Subsection (2)(C)(i) is based on Article 44(c). The applicability of *Crist v. Bretz*, 437 U.S. 28 (1978) was considered. *Crist* held that, in jury cases, jeopardy attaches when the jury is empanelled and sworn. For reasons stated below, the Working Group concluded that the beginning of the presentation of evidence on the merits, which is the constitutional standard for nonjury trial (*Crist v. Bretz, supra* at 37 n. 15; *Serfass v. United States*, 420 U.S. 377 (1975)) and is prescribed by Article 44(c), is the proper cutoff point.

There is no jury in courts-martial. *O'Callahan v. Parker*, 395 U.S. 258 (1969); *Ex parte Quirin*, 317 U.S. 1 (1942); *United States v. Crawford*, 15 U.S.C.M.A. 31, 35 C.M.R. 3, (1964). *See also United States v. McCarthy*, 2 M.J. 26, 29 n.3 (C.M.A. 1976). Members are an essential jurisdictional element of a court-martial. *United States v. Ryan*, 5 M.J. 97 (C.M.A. 1978). Historically the members, as an entity, served as jury *and* judge, or, in other words, as the "court." W. Winthrop, *Military Law and Precedents* 54–55, 173 (2d. ed., 1920 reprint). Assembling the court-martial has not been the last step before trial on the merits. *See* paragraph 61 *j* and appendix 8 *b* of MCM, 1969 (Rev.); paragraph 61 *h* and *i* and appendix 8 *a* of MCM, 1951; paragraph 61 of MCM, 1949 (Army); paragraph 61 of MCM, 1928; W. Winthrop,*supra* at 205–80. Congress clearly contemplated that the members may be sworn at an early point in the proceedings. *See* Article 42(a); H. Rep. No. 491, 81st Cong. 1st Sess. 22 (1949).

The role of members has become somewhat more analogous to that of a jury. *See, e.g.*, Article 39(a). Nevertheless, significant differences remain. When they are present, the members with the military judge constitute the court-martial and participate in the exercise of contempt power. Article 48. *See* R.C.M. 809 and analysis. Moreover members may sit as a special court-martial without a military judge, in which case they exercise all judicial functions. Articles 19; 26; 40; 41; 51; 52.

The holding in *Crist* would have adverse practical effect if applied in the military. In addition to being unworkable in special court-martial without a military judge, it would negate the utility of Article 29, which provides that the assembly of the court-martial does not wholly preclude later substitution of members. This provision recognizes that military exigencies or other unusual circumstances may cause a member to be unavailable at any stage in the court-martial. It also recognizes that the special need of the military to dispose of offenses swiftly, without necessary diversion of personnel and other resources, may justify continuing the trial with substituted members, rather that requiring a mistrial. This provision is squarely at odds with civilian practice with respect to juries and, therefore, with the rationale in *Crist*.

Subsection (2)(C)(ii) is based on paragraph 56 of MCM, 1969 (Rev). *See also Wade v. Hunter, supra; United States v. Perez*, 22 U.S. (9 Wheat.) 579 (1824). "Manifest necessity" is the traditional justification for a mistrial. *Id. See United States v. Richardson, supra. Cf.* Article 44(c), which does not prohibit retrial of a proceeding terminated on motion of the accused. *See also* Analysis, R.C.M. 915.

Subsection (2)(C)(ii) is taken from Article 44(b). *See United States v. Richardson, supra. See also* Article 63. *But see* R.C.M. 810(d).

Subsection(2)(C)(iv) is new. It is axiomatic that jeopardy does not attach in a proceeding which lacks jurisdiction. *Ball v. United States*, 163 U.S. 662 (1973). Therefore, if proceedings are terminated before findings because the court-martial lacks jurisdiction, retrial is not barred if the jurisdictional defect is corrected. For example, if during the course of trial it is discovered that the charges were not referred to the court-martial by a person empowered to do so, those proceedings would be terminated. This would not bar later referral of those charges by a proper official to a court-martial. *Cf. Lee v. United States*, 432 U.S. 23 (1977); *Illinois v. Somerville*, 410 U.S. 458 (1973). *See also United States v. Newcomb*, 5 M.J. 4 (C.M.A. 1977); *United States v. Hardy*, 4 M.J. 20 (C.M.A. 1977) authorizing re-referral of charges where earlier proceedings lacked jurisdiction because of defects in referral and composition. Res judicata would bar retrial by a court-martial for a jurisdictional defect which is not "correctable." *See, e.g.*, R.C.M. 202 and 203. *See also* R.C.M. 905(g).

By its terms, the rule permits a retrial of a person acquitted by a court-martial which lacks jurisdiction. The Court of Military Appeals decision in *United States v. Culver*, 22 U.S.C.M.A. 141, 46 C.M.R. 141 (1973) does not preclude this, although that decision raises questions concerning this result. There was no majority opinion in *Culver*. Judge Quinn held that the defect (absence of a written judge alone request) was not jurisdictional. In the alternative, Judge Quinn construed paragraph 81 *d* of MCM, 1969 (Rev.) and the automatic review structure in courts-martial as precluding retrial on an offense of which the accused had been acquitted. (Note that R.C.M. 810(d), using slightly different language, continues the same policy of limiting the maximum sentence for offenses tried at an "other trial" to that adjudged at the earlier defective trial.) Judge Duncan, concurring in the result in *Culver*, found that although the original trial was jurisdictionally defective, the defect was not so fundamental as to render the proceedings void. In Judge Duncan's view, the original court-martial had jurisdiction when it began, but "lost" it when the request for military judge alone was not reduced to writing. Therefore, the double jeopardy clause of the Fifth Amendment and Article 44 barred the second trial for an offense of which the accused had been acquitted at the first. Chief Judge Darden dissented. He held that because the earlier court-martial lacked jurisdiction, the proceedings were void and did not bar the second trial. Thus in *Culver*, two judges divided over whether the double jeopardy clause bars a second trial for an offense of which the accused was acquitted at a court-martial which lacked jurisdiction because of improper composition. The third judge held retrial was barred on non constitutional grounds.

Subsection (2)(D) is based on paragraph 68 *e f, g* , and *h* of MCM, 1969 (Rev.). As to subsection (iv) *see United States v. Williams.* 10 U.S.C.M.A. 615, 28 C.M.R. 181 (1959).

Subsection (3) sets out grounds which, unlike those in subsection (1) and (2), do not *require* dismissal when they exist. The military judge has discretion whether to dismiss or to apply another remedy (such as a continuance in the case of subsection (3)(A), or sentencing instructions in the case of subsection (3)(B)). *But see United States v. Sturdivant*, 13 M.J. 323 (C.M.A. 1982). *See also United States v. Baker*, 14 M.J. 361 (C.M.A. 1983).

Subsection (3)(A) and the discussion are based on paragraph 69 *b*(3) of MCM, 1969 (Rev.).

Subsection (3)(B) is based on paragraph 26 *b*, 74 *b*(4), and 76 *a*(5) of MCM, 1969 (Rev.); *United States v. Gibson*, 11 M.J. 435 (C.M.A. 1981); *United States v. Stegall*, 6 M.J. 176 (C.M.A. 1979); *United States v. Williams*, 18 U.S.C.M.A. 78, 39 C.M.R. 78 (1968).

Rule 908 Appeal by the United States

Introduction. This rule is based on Article 62, as amended, Military Justice Act of 1983, Pub. L. No. 98–209, § 5(c)(1), 97 Stat 1393 (1983). *See also* S. Rep. No. 53, 98th Cong., 1st. Sess. 23 (1983); 18 U.S.C. § 3731. Article 62 now provides the Government with a means to seek review of certain rulings or orders of the military judge. The need for such procedure has been recognized previously. *See United States v. Rowel*, 1 M.J. 289, 291 (C.M.A. 1976) (Fletcher, C.J., concurring). *See also Dettinger v. United States*, 7 M.J. 216 (C.M.A. 1978). It is not expected that every ruling or order which might be appealed by the Government will be appealed. Frequent appeals by the Government would disrupt trial dockets and could interfere with military operations and other activities, and would impose a heavy burden on appellate courts and counsel. Therefore this rule includes procedures to ensure that the Government's right to appeal is exercised carefully. *See* S. Rep. No. 53 *supra* at 23.

(a) *In general.* This subsection repeats the first sentence of Article 62(a).

1998 Amendment: The change to R.C.M. 908(a) resulted from the amendment to Article 62, UCMJ, in section 1141, National Defense Authorization Act for Fiscal Year 1996, Pub. L. No. 104–106, 110 Stat. 186, 466–67 (1996). It permits interlocutory appeal of rulings disclosing classified information.

(b) *Procedure.* Subsection (1) provides the trial counsel with a mechanism to ensure that further proceedings do not make an issue moot before the Government can file notice of appeal.

The first sentence in subsection (2) is based on the second sentence of Article 62(a). The second sentence in subsection(2) authorizes an initial measure to ensure that a decision to file notice of appeal is carefully considered. The Secretary concerned may require trial counsel to secure authorization from another person, such as the convening authority, the convening authority's designee, or the staff judge advocate. Because the decision whether to file the notice must be made within 72 hours, it probably will not be practicable in many cases to secure authorization from a more distant authority (*see* subsection (b)(5) and Analysis, below), but nothing in this subsection prohibits requiring this authorization to be secured from, for example, the chief of appellate Government counsel or a similar official in the office of the Judge Advocate General. Note that the Secretary concerned is not required to require authorization by anyone before notice of appeal is filed. The provision is intended solely for the benefit of the Government, to avoid disrupting trial dockets and the consequences this has on command activities, and to prevent overburdening appellate courts and counsel. The accused has no right to have the Government forego an appeal which it might take. *But see* R.C.M. 707(c)(1)(D). The authorization may be oral and no reason need be given.

Subsection (3) is based on the second and third sentences of Article 62(a). The second sentence is added to permit decisions by defense counsel and the military judge on how to proceed as to any unaffected charges and specifications under subsection (4).

Subsection (4) is necessary because, unlike in Federal civilian trials (*see Fed. R. Crim. P. 8(a)), unrelated offenses* may be and often are tried together in courts-martial. Consequently, a ruling or order which is appealable by the Government may affect only some charges and specifications. As to those offenses, the pendency of an appeal under this rule necessarily halts further proceedings. It does not necessarily have the same effect on other charges and specifications unaffected by the appeal. Subsection (4) provides several alternatives to halting the court-martial entirely, even as to charges and specifications unaffected by the appeal. Subsection (4)(A) permits motions to be litigated as to unaffected charges and specifications, regardless of the stage of the proceedings. Subsection (4)(B) permits unaffected charges and specifications to be served, but only before trial on the merits has begun, that is, before jeopardy has attached. *See* R.C.M. 907(b)(2)(C) and Analysis. Once jeopardy has attached, the accused is entitled to have all the charges and specification resolved by the same court-martial. *Cf. Crist v. Bretz*, 437 U.S. 28 (1978). It is expected that in most cases, rulings or orders subject to appeal by the Government will be made before trial on the merits has begun. *See* R.C.M. 905(b) and (e); Mil. R. Evid. 304(d), 311(d), and 321(c). Subsection (4)(C) provides a mechanism to alleviate the adverse effect an appeal by the Government may have on unaffected charges and specifications. Thus witnesses who are present but whom it may be difficult and expensive to recall at a later time may, at the request of the proponent party and in the discretion of the military judge, be called to testify during the pendency of any appeal. Such witnesses may be called out of order. *See also* R.C.M. 801(a); 914; Mil. R. Evid. 611. Note, however, that a party cannot be compelled to call such witnesses or present evidence until the appeal is resolved. This is because a party's tactics may be affected by the resolution of the appeal. Note also that if similar problems arise as to witnesses whose testimony relates to an affected specification, a deposition could be taken, but it could not be used at any later proceedings unless the witness was unavailable or the parties did not object.

Subsection (5) ensures that a record will be prepared promptly. Because the appeal ordinarily will involve only specific issues, the record need be complete only as to relevant matters. Defense counsel will ordinarily have the opportunity to object to any omissions. *See* R.C.M. 1103(i)(1)(B). Furthermore, the military judge and the Court of Criminal Appeals may direct preparation of additional portions of the record.

Subsection (6) provides for the matter to be forwarded promptly. No specific time limit is established, but ordinarily the matters specified should be forwarded within one working day. Note that the record need not be forwarded at this point as that might delay disposition. If the record is not ready, a summary may be forwarded for preliminary consideration before completion of the record. An appropriate authority will then decide whether to file the appeal, in accordance with procedures established by the Judge Advocate General. *See* S.Rep. No. 53, *supra* at 23. This is an administrative determination; a decision not to file the appeal has no effect as precedent. Again, no specific time limit is set for this decision, but it should be made promptly under the circumstances.

Subsection (7) is based on Article 62(b).

Subsection (8) ensures that trial participants are notified in the event no appeal is filed.

1991 Amendment: Subsection (4) was amended to state explicitly that, upon timely notice of appeal, the legal effect of an appealable ruling or order is stayed pending appellate resolution. Although most military practitioners understood this necessary effect of an appeal under the rule, some civilian practitioners were confused by the absence of an explicit statement in the rule.

New subsection (9) is based on 18 U.S.C. § 3143(c) governing the release of an accused pending appeal by the United States of an order of dismissal of an indictment or information, or an order suppressing evidence. Since appeals by the United States under Article 62, U.C.M.J., contemplate a situation in which the accused has not been convicted, a commander's decision whether to subject the individual to continued confinement after an appeal has been taken should be based on the same considerations which would authorize the imposition of pretrial confinement.

(c) *Appellate proceedings.* Subsection (1) is based on Article 70(b) and (c).

Subsection (2) is based on Article 62(b).

Subsection (3) is based on Article 67(b) and (h) and on 28 U.S.C. § 1259. Note that if the decision of the Court of Criminal Appeals permits it (i.e., is favorable to the Government) the court-martial may proceed as to the affected charges and specifications notwithstanding the possibility or pendency of review by the Court of Appeals for the Armed Forces or the Supreme Court. Those courts could stay the proceedings. The penultimate sentence is similar in purpose to Article 66(e) and 67(f).

(d) *Military judge.* This subsection is necessary because Article 62 authorizes appeals by the Government only when a military judge is detailed.

1998 Amendment: The change to R.C.M. 908(a) resulted from the amendment to Article 62, UCMJ, in section 1141, National Defense Authorization Act for Fiscal Year 1996, Pub. L. No. 104-106, 110 Stat. 186, 466-67 (1996). It permits interlocutory appeal of rulings disclosing classified information.

Rule 909 Capacity of the accused to stand trial by court-martial

This rule is based on paragraphs 120 *a* and *d*, and 122 of MCM, 1969 (Rev.). It has been reorganized and minor changes were made in some language in order to conform to the format and style of the Rules for Courts-Martial. The procedures for examining the mental capacity of the accused are covered in R.C.M. 706. Matters referring solely to the accused's sanity at the time of the offense are treated at R.C.M. 916(k). The rule is generally consistent with 18 U.S.C. § 4244. The standard of proof has been changed from beyond reasonable doubt to a preponderance of the evidence. This is consistent with the holdings of those federal courts which have addressed the issue. *United States v. Gilio* , 538 F.2d 972 (3d. Cir. 1976), *cert. denied*, 429 U.S. 1038 (1977); *United States v. Makris*, 535 F.2d 899 (5th Cir. 1976), *cert. denied*, 430 U.S. 954 (1977).

February 1986 Amendment: Following passage of the Insanity Defense Reform Act, ch. IV, Pub.L. No. 98–473, 98 Stat. 2058 (1984), the rule was changed pursuant to Article 36, to conform to 18 U.S.C. § 4241(d).

1998 Amendment: The rule was changed to provide for the hospitalization of an incompetent accused after the enactment of Article 76b, UCMJ, in section 1133 of the Nation Defense Authorization act for Fiscal Year 1996, Pub L. No. 104–106, 110 Stat. 464–66 (1996).

Rule 910 Pleas

Introduction. This rule is based generally on Article 45; paragraph 70 of MCM, 1969 (Rev.); and on Fed. R. Crim. P. 11. *See also* H.Rep. No. 491, 81st Cong., 1st Sess. 23–24 (1949); S.Rep. No. 486, 81st Cong., 1st Sess. 20–21 (1949). The format generally follows that of Fed. R. Crim. P. 11.

(a) *In general.* Subsection (1) is based on Article 45 and paragraph 70 *a* of MCM, 1969 (Rev.). The first sentence parallels the first sentence in Fed. R. Crim. P. 11(a)(1), except that no provision is made for pleas of nolo contendere. Such a plea is unnecessary in courts-martial. *Hearings on H. R. 4080 Before A Subcomm, of the Comm. on Armed Services of the House of Representatives*. 81st Cong., 1st Sess. 1054 (1949). *See* 8A.J. Moore, *Moore's Federal Practice* Para. 11.07(1) (1980 rev. ed) concerning the purpose of nolo pleas in civilian practice, and a discussion of the controversy about them. Furthermore, the practice connected with nolo pleas (*see* Fed. R. Crim. P. 11(f) which does not require that a factual basis be established in order to accept a plea of nolo contendere; *see also Moore's supra* at Para. 11.07(1) is inconsistent with Article 45. The second sentence on Fed. R. Crim. P. 11(a) is covered under subsection (b) of this rule insofar as it pertains to military practice.

1993 Amendment: The amendment to R.C.M. 910(a)(1) removed the necessity of pleading guilty to a lesser included offense by exceptions and substitutions. This parallels the amendment to R.C.M. 918(a)(1), allowing a finding of guilty to a named lesser included offense without mandating the use of exceptions and substitutions, made to correspond more closely to verdict practice in federal district courts. *See* Analysis comments for R.C.M. 918(a)(1).

Subsection (2) is based on Fed. R. Crim. P. 11(a)(2). Conditional guilty pleas can conserve judicial and governmental resources by dispensing with a full trial when the only real issue is determined in a pretrial motion. As in the federal courts, the absence of clear authority in courts-martial for such a procedure has resulted in some uncertainty as to whether an accused could preserve some issues for appellate review despite a plea of guilty. *See e.g., United States v. Schaffer*, 12 M.J. 425 (C.M.A. 1982); *United States v. Mallett*, 14 M.J. 631 (A.C.M.R. 1982). Now such issues may be preserved, but only in accordance with this subsection. *See* also subsection (j) of this rule.

There is no right to enter a conditional guilty plea. The military judge and the Government each have complete discretion whether to permit or consent to a conditional guilty plea. Because the purpose of a conditional guilty plea is to conserve judicial and government resources, this discretion is not subject to challenge by the accused. The rationale for this discretion is further explained in Fed. R. Crim. P. 11 advisory committee note:

(b) *Refusal to plead, irregular plea.* The subsection is based on Article 45(a) and paragraph 70 *a* of MCM, 1969 (Rev.). It parallels the second sentence of Fed. R. Crim. P. 11(a), but is broadened to conform to Article 45(a). The portion of Fed. R. Crim. P. 11(a) concerning corporate defendants does not apply in courts-martial. The discussion is based on the last sentence of the first paragraph of paragraph 70 *a* of MCM, 1969 (Rev.).

(c) *Advice of accused.* This subsection is taken from Fed. R. Crim. P. 11(c) and is consistent with paragraph 70 *b*(2) of MCM, 1969 (Rev.). *See also* H.R. Rep. No. 491, *supra* at 23–24; S.Rep. No. 486, *supra* at 20–21; *Boykin v. Alabama*, 395 U.S. 238 (1969); *McCarthy v. United States*, 394 U.S. 459 (1969); *United States v. Care*, 18 U.S.C.M.A. 535, 40 C.M.R. 247 (1969).

As to subsection (1), the requirement that the accused understand the elements of the offense is of constitutional dimensions. *Henderson v. Morgan*, 426 U.S. 637 (1976); *see also United States v. Care, supra*. The elements need not be listed as such, seriatim, if it clearly appears that the accused was apprised of them in some manner and understood them and admits (*see* subsection (e) of this rule) that each element is true. *See Henderson v. Morgan, supra; United States v. Grecco*, 5 M.J. 1018 (C.M.A. 1976); *United States v. Kilgore*, 21 U.S.C.M.A. 35, 44 C.M.R. 89 (1971). *But see United States v. Pretlow*, 13 M.J. 85 (C.M.A. 1982).

Advice concerning a mandatory minimum punishment would be required only when the accused pleads guilty to murder under clause (1) or (4) of Article 118. The accused could only do so if the case had been referred as not capital. As to advice concerning the maximum penalty, the adoption of the language of the federal rule is not intended to eliminate the requirement that the advice state the maximum including any applicable escalation provisions. As to misadvice concerning the maximum penalty *see United States v. Walls*, 9 M.J. 88 (C.M.A. 1981).

Subsection (2) of Fed. R. Crim. P. 11(c) has been modified because of the absence of a right to counsel in summary courts-martial. *See* R.C.M.1301(e) and Analysis. In other courts-martial, full advice concerning counsel would ordinarily have been given previously (*see* R.C.M.901(d)(4)) and need not be repeated here. The discussion is based on paragraph 70 *b*(1) of MCM, 1969 (Rev.) and H.Rep. 491, *supra* at 23–24, S.Rep. 486, *supra* at 20–21.

Subsections (3), (4), and (5) have been taken without substantial change from Fed. R. Crim. P. 11(c). Subsections (3) and (4) are consistent with the last paragraph and paragraph 70 *b* (2) of MCM, 1969 (Rev.). Subsection (5) corresponds to Mil. R. Evid. 410. As to the effect of failure to give the advice in subsection (5) *see United States v. Conrad* , 598 F.2d 506 (9th Cir. 1979).

(d) *Ensuring that the plea is voluntary.* This subsection is based on Fed. R. Crim. P. 11(d) and is consistent with paragraph 70 *b*(3) of MCM, 1969 (Rev.). As to the requirement to inquire concerning the existence of a plea agreement, *see United States v. Green*, 1 M.J. 453 (C.M.A. 1976).

(e) *Determining accuracy of plea.* This subsection is based on Fed. R. Crim. P. 11(f), except that "shall" replaces "should" and it is specified that the military judge must inquire of the accused concerning the factual basis of the plea. This is required under Article 45(b) and is consistent with paragraph 70 *b*(3) of MCM, 1969 (Rev.). *See also* H.R. Rep. 491, *supra* at 23–24; S.Rep. 486, *supra* at 20–21; *United States v. Davenport*, 9 M.J. 364 (C.M.A. 1980); *United States v. Johnson*, 1 M.J. 36 (C.M.A. 1975); *United States v. Logan*, 22 U.S.C.M.A. 349, 47 C.M.R. 1 (1973). Notwithstanding the precatory term "should," the factual basis inquiry in Fed. R. Crim. P. 11(f) is, in practice, mandatory, although the means for establishing it are broader. *See* J. Moore, *supra* at Para.11.02(2). *See also ABA Standards, Pleas of Guilty* §1.6 (1978). The last sentence requiring that the accused be placed under oath is designed to ensure compliance with Article 45 and to reduce the likelihood of later attacks on the providence of the plea. This is consistent with federal civilian practice. *See* Fed.R.Evid. 410.

The first paragraph in the discussion is also based on *United States v. Jemmings*, 1 M.J. 414 (C.M.A. 1976); *United States v. Kilgore, supra; United States v. Care, supra. See also United States v. Crouch*, 11 M.J. 128 (C.M.A. 1981).

The second paragraph in the discussion is new and is based on *United States v. Moglia*, 3 M.J. 216 (C.M.A. 1977); *United States v. Luebs*, 20 U.S.C.M.A. 475, 43 C.M.R. 315 (1971); *United States v. Butler*, 20 U.S.C.M.A. 247, 43 C.M.R. 87 (1971).

(f) *Plea agreement inquiry.* This subsection is based on Fed. R. Crim. P. 11(e), with substantial modifications to conform to plea agreement procedures in the military. *See* R.C.M. 705 and Analysis. The procedures here conform to those prescribed in *United States v. Green, supra. See also United States v. Passini*, 10 M.J. 109 (C.M.A. 1980).

It is not intended that failure to comply with this subsection will necessarily result in a improvement plea. *See United States v. Passini, supra; cf. United States v. Davenport, supra. Contra United States v. King*, 3 M.J. 458 (C.M.A. 1977). Proceedings in revision may be appropriate to correct a defect discovered after final adjournment. *United States v. Steck*, 10 M.J. 412 (C.M.A. 1981). Even if a prejudicial defect in the agreement is found, as a result of an inadequate inquiry or otherwise, allowing withdrawal of the plea is not necessarily the appropriate remedy. *See Santobello v. New York*, 404 U.S. 257 (1971); *United States v. Kraffa*, 11 M.J. 453 (C.M.A. 1981); *United States v. Cifuentes*, 11 M.J. 385 (C.M.A. 1981). If an adequate inquiry is conducted, however, the parties are normally bound by the terms described on the record. *Id,; United States v. Cooke* , 11 M.J. 257 (C.M.A. 1981). *But see United States v. Partin*, 7 M.J. 409 (C.M.A. 1979) (the parties were not bound by military judge's interpretation which had the effect of adding illegal terms to the agreement; the plea was held provident).

(g) *Findings.* This subsection is based on the last paragraph of paragraph 70 *b* of MCM, 1969 (Rev.). *See also* Articles 39(a)(3) and 52(a)(2). The discussion is new and recognizes that it may be unnecessary and inappropriate to bring to the member's attention the fact that the accused has pleaded guilty to some offenses before trial on the merits of others. *See United States v. Nixon*, 15 M.J. 1028 (A.C.M.R. 1983). *See also United States v. Wahnon*, 1 M.J. 144 (C.M.A. 1975).

1990 Amendment: The discussion to the subsection was changed in light of the decision in *United States v. Rivera*, 23 M.J. 89 (C.M.A.), *cert. denied*, 479 U.S. 1091 (1986).

(h) *Later action.* Subsection (1) is based on the fourth and fifth sentences of the penultimate paragraph of paragraph 70 *b* of MCM, 1969 (Rev.). Note that once a plea of guilty is accepted the accused may withdraw it only within the discretion of the military judge. Before the plea is accepted, the accused may withdraw it as a matter of right. *See United States v. Leonard*, 16 M.J. 984 (A.C.M.R. 1983); *United States v. Hayes*, 9 M.J. 825 (N.C.MR. 1980).

Subsection (2) is based on the first two sentences in the penultimate paragraph of paragraph 70 *b* of MCM, 1969 (Rev.) and on Article 45(a). *See also* Fed. R. Crim. P. 32(d). The discussion is based on *United States v. Cooper*, 8 M.J. 5 (C.M.A. 1979); *United States v. Bradley*, 7 M.J. 332 (C.M.A. 1979). Subsection (3) is based on *United States v. Green, supra. See also United States v. Kraffa, supra.*

(i) *Record of proceedings.* This subsection is based on subparagraph (4) of the first paragraph of paragraph 70 *b* of MCM, 1969. *See also* Article 54; H.R. Rep. No. 491, *supra* at 24; S. Rep. No. 486, *supra* at 21; *ABA Standards, Pleas of Guilty supra* at §1.7. This subsection parallels Fed. R. Crim. P. 11(g), except insofar as the former allows for nonverbatim records in inferior courts-martial. *See* Article 54(b).

(j) *Waiver.* This subsection replaces the third paragraph in paragraph 70 *a* of MCM, 1969 (Rev.) which listed some things a guilty plea did not waive, and which was somewhat misleading in the wake of the pleading standards under *United States v. Alef*, 3 M.J. 414 (C.M.A. 1977). This subsection is based on *Menna v. New York*, 423 U.S. 61 (1975); *Tollett v. Henderson*, 411 U.S. 258 (1973); *Parker v. North Carolina*, 397 U.S. 790 (1970); *McMann v. Richardson*, 397 U.S. 759 (1970); *Brady v. United States*, 397 U.S. 742 (1970); *United States v. Engle*, 1 M.J. 387 (C.M.A. 1976); *United States v. Dusenberry*, 23 U.S.C.M.A. 287, 49 C.M.R. 536 (1975); *United States v. Hamil*, 15 U.S.C.M.A. 110, 35 C.M.R. 82 (1964). *See also* subsection (a)(2) of this rule and its analysis.

Rule 911 Assembly of the court-martial

The code fixes no specific point in the court-martial for assembly although, as noted in the discussion, it establishes assembly as a point after which the opportunities to change the composition and membership of the court-martial are substantially circumscribed. *See United States v. Morris*, 23 U.S.C.M.A. 319, 49 C.M.R. 653 (1975); *United States v. Dean*, 20 U.S.C.M.A. 212, 43 C.M.R. 52 (1970).

The purpose of this rule is simply to require an overt manifestation of assembly in order to mark clearly for all participants the point at which the opportunities to elect freely as to composition or to substitute personnel has ended. Failure to make the announcement described in the rule has no substantive effect other than to leave open a dispute as to whether a change in composition or membership was timely.

The rule prescribes no specific point for assembly. The points noted in the discussion are based on paragraph 61 *j* of MCM, 1969 (Rev.). It is normally appropriate to assemble the court-martial at these points to protect the parties from untimely changes in membership or composition. In some circumstances flexibility is desirable, as when the military judge approves a request for trial by military judge alone, but recognizes that it may be necessary to substitute another judge because of impending delays. The discussion is also based on paragraphs 53 *d*(2)(c) and 61 *b* of MCM, 1969 (Rev.).

Rule 912 Challenge of selection of members; examination and challenges of members

(a) *Pretrial matters.* Subsection (1) recognizes the usefulness of questionnaires to expedite voir dire. Questionnaires are already used in some military jurisdictions. This procedure is analogous to the use of juror qualification forms under 28 U.S.C. § 1864(a). *See also* ABA Standards, Trial by Jury § 2.1(b) (1979). It is not intended that questionnaires will be used as a complete substitute for voir dire. As to investigations of members, *see also ABA Standards, The Prosecution Function* § 3-5.3(b) (1979); *The Defense Function* § 4-7.2(b) (1979).

Subsection (2) recognizes that in order to challenge the selection of the membership of the court-martial (*see* subsection (b) of this rule) discovery of the materials used to select them is necessary. Such discovery is already common. *See, e.g., United States v. Greene*, 20 U.S.C.M.A. 232, 43 C.M.R. 72 (1970); *United States v. Herndon*, 50 C.M.R. 166 (A.C.M.R. 1975); *United States v. Perry*, 47 C.M.R. 89 (A.C.M.R. 1973). The purpose of this procedure is analogous to that of 18 U.S.C. §§ 1867(f) and 1868. The rule is a discovery device; it is not intended to limit the types of evidence which may be admissible concerning the selection process.

(b) *Challenge of selection of members.* This subsection is based on 28 U.S.C. § 1867(a), (b) and (d). Other subsections in that section are inapposite to the military. No similar provision appeared in MCM, 1969 (Rev.). Nevertheless, a motion for appropriate relief challenging the selection of members and requesting a new one was recognized. *See United States v. Daigle*, 1 M.J. 139 (C.M.A. 1975); *United States v. Young*, 49 C.M.R. 133 (A.F.C.M.R. 1974). Except for matters affecting the composition of the court-martial (*see* Article 16 and 25(a), (b) and (c)), improper selection of members is not a jurisdictional defect. *United States v. Daigle, supra. See also* S. Rep. No. 53, 98th Cong., 18th Sess. 12 (1983). *Cf. United States v. Blaylock*, 15 M.J. 190 (C.M.A. 1983). The issue may be waived if not raised in a timely manner.

(c) *Stating of grounds for challenge.* This subsection is based on the second sentence of paragraph 62 *b* of MCM, 1969 (Rev.).

(d) *Examination of members.* This subsection is based on Fed. R. Crim. P. 24(a). Paragraph 62 *b* and *h* of MCM, 1969 (Rev.) discussed questioning members. Paragraph 62 *b* provided that "... the trial or defense counsel may question the court, or individual members thereof." *United States v. Slubowski*, 7 M.J. 461 (C.M.A. 1979), *reconsideration not granted by equally divided court*, 9 M.J. 264 (C.M.A. 1980), held that this provision did not establish a right of the parties to personally question members. Instead, the court recognized that the procedures in Fed. R. Crim. P. 24(a) are applicable to the military. *See also United States v. Parker*, 6 U.S.C.M.A. 274, 19 C.M.R. 400 (1955). Therefore, subsection (d) does not change current practice.

The discussion is based generally on paragraph 62*b* of MCM, 1969 (Rev.) and encourages permitting counsel to question personally the members. *See United States v. Slubowski, supra* at 463 n.4; ABA Standards, Trial by Jury § 2.4 (1979). As to the scope of voir dire generally, *see Ristaino v. Ross*, 424 U.S. 589 (1977); *United States v. Baldwin* , 607 F.2d 1295 (9th Cir. 1979); *United States v. Barnes*, 604 F.2d 121 (2d Cir. 1979); *United States v. Slubowski, supra; United States v. Parker, supra.* The second paragraph of the discussion is based on *ABA Standards, The Prosecution Function* § 3-5.3(c). (1979); *The Defense Function* § 4-7.2(c) (1979).

(e) *Evidence.* This subsection is based on the first sentence of paragraph 62 *h*(2) of MCM, 1969 (Rev.).

(f) *Challenges and removal for cause. See generally* Article 41(a). Subsection (1) is based on Article 25 and paragraph 62 *f* of MCM, 1969 (Rev.). The examples in the last paragraph of paragraph 62 *f* have been placed in the discussion.

Subsection (2) is based on paragraphs 62 *d* and *h*(1) of MCM, 1969 (Rev.).

Subsection (3) is based on Article 41(a) and paragraph 62 *h* of MCM, 1969 (Rev.). The first sentence is new. MCM, 1969 (Rev.) was silent on this matter. The procedure is intended to protect the parties from prejudicial disclosures before the members, and is in accord with practice in many courts-martial. Paragraph 62 *h*(2) of MCM, 1969 (Rev.) advised that the military judge "should be liberal in passing on challenges, but need not sustain a challenge upon the mere assertion of the challenger." The precatory language has been deleted from the rule as an unnecessary statement. This deletion is not intended to change the policy expressed in that statement.

The waiver rule in subsection (4) is based on *United States v. Beer*, 6 U.S.C.M.A. 180, 19 C.M.R. 306 (1955). *See also United States v. Dyche*, 8 U.S.C.M.A. 430, 24 C.M.R. 240 (1957); *United States v. Wolfe*, 8 U.S.C.M.A. 247, 24 C.M.R. 57 (1957). Grounds (A) and (B) in subsection (f)(1) may not be waived, except as noted. *See generally* H. R. Rep. No. 491, 81st Cong, 1st Sess. 17-18 (1949); *United States v. Newcomb*, 5 M.J. 4 (C.M.A. 1978). Membership of enlisted members of the enlisted members of the accused's unit has been held not to be jurisdictional, and, therefore, may be waived. *United States v. Wilson*, 16 M.J. 678 (A.C.M.R. 1983); *United States v. Kimball,* 13 M.J. 659 (N.M.C.M.R. 1982); *United States v. Tagert*, 11 M.J. 677 (N.M.C.M.R. 1981); *United States v. Scott*, 25 C.M.R. 636 (A.B.R. 1957). *Contra United States v. Anderson*, 10 M.J. 803 (A.F.C.M.R. 1981). The Court of Military Appeals has held that the presence of a statutorily ineligible member is not a jurisdictional defect. *United States v. Miller*, 3 M.J. 326 (C.M.A. 1977); *United States v. Beer, supra.* Ineligibility of enlisted members from the accused's unit is designed to protect the accused from prejudice and does not affect their competency. *See Hearings on H.R. 2498 Before a Subcomm. of the House Comm. on Armed Services*, 81st Cong. 1st Sess. 1140, 1150-52 (1949). *See also* S. Rep. No. 53, 98th Cong., 1st Sess. 12(1983).

The second sentence in subsection (4) is based on *United States v. Seabrooks*, 48 C.M.R. 471 (N.C.M.R. 1974). *See also United States v. Jones*, 7 U.S.C.M.A. 283, 22 C.M.R. 73 (1956). This is consistent with federal practice. *See, e.g., United States v. Richardson*, 582 F.2d 968 (5th Cir. 1978). The third sentence clarifies the effect of using or failing to use a peremptory challenge after a challenge for cause is denied. This has been a subject of some controversy. *See United States v. Harris*, 13 M.J. 288 (C.M.A. 1982); *United States v. Russell*, 43 C.M.R. 807 (A.C.M.R. 1971) and cases cited therein. Failure to use a peremptory challenge at all has been held to waive any issue as to denial of a challenge for cause. *United States v. Henderson*, 11 U.S.C.M.A. 556, 29 C.M.R. 372 (1960). Because the right to a peremptory challenge is independent to the right to challenge members for cause, *see* Article 41, that right should not be forfeited when a challenge for cause has been erroneously denied. *See United States v. Baker*, 2 M.J. 773 (A.C.M.R. 1976). *See also United States v. Rucker*, 557 F.2d 1046 (4th Cir. 1977); *United States v. Nell*, 526 F.2d 1223 (5th Cir. 1976). *See generally Swain v. Alabama*, 380 U.S. 202 (1965). The requirement that a party peremptorily challenging a member it has unsuccessfully challenged for cause state that it would have peremptorily challenged another member is designed to prevent a "windfall" to a party which had no intent to exercise its preemptory challenge against any other member. *See United States v. Harris, supra*; *United States v. Shaffer*, 2 U.S.C.M.A. 76, 6 C.M.R. 75 (1952); *United States v. Cooper*, 8 M.J. 538 (N.C.M.R. 1979).

2005 Amendment: This rule change is intended to conform military practice to federal practice and limit appellate litigation when the challenged panel member could have been peremptorily challenged or actually did not participate in the trial due to a peremptory challenge by either party. This amendment is consistent with the President's lawful authority to promulgate a rule that would result in placing before the accused the hard choice faced by defendants in federal district courts — to let the challenged juror sit on the case and challenge the ruling on appeal or to use a peremptory challenge to remove the juror and ensure an impartial jury. *See United States v. Miles*, 58 M.J. 192 (C.A.A.F. 2003); *United States v. Wiesen*, 56 M.J. 172 (C.A.A.F. 2001), *petition for reconsideration denied*, 57 M.J. 48 (C.A.A.F. 2002); *United States v. Armstrong*, 54 M.J. 51 (C.A.A.F. 2000).

(g) *Peremptory challenges.* Subsection (1) is based on Article 41(b). The second sentence is new. Paragraph 62 *e* of MCM, 1969 (Rev.) stated that a peremptory challenge "may be used before, during, or after challenges for cause." Subsection (1) does not prevent a party from exercising a peremptory challenge before challenges for cause, but it protects a party against being compelled to use a peremptory challenge before challenges for cause are made. Each party is entitled to one peremptory challenge. Article 41(b); *United States v. Calley*, 46 C.M.R. 1131, 1162 (A.C.M.R.), aff'd, 23 U.S.C.M.A. 534, 48 C.M.R. 19 (1973). *But see United States v. Harris, supra* at 294 n. 3 (C.M.A. 1982) (Everett, C.J., dissenting). Fed. R. Crim. P. 24(b) is inapplicable.

1994 Amendment. The Discussion for R.C.M. 912(g)(1) was amended to incorporate *Batson v. Kentucky*, 476 U.S. 79 (1986); *United States v. Curtis*, 33 M.J. 101 (C.M.A. 1991), *cert. denied*, 112 S.Ct. 1177 (1992); *United States v. Moore*, 28 M.J. 366 (C.M.A. 1989); and *United States v. Santiago-Davila*, 26 M.J. 380 (C.M.A. 1988).

Subsection (2) is based on *United States v. White* , 22 C.M.R. 892 (A.B.R. 1956); *United States v. Graham*, 14 C.M.R. 645 (A.F.B.R. 1954). *See also United States v. Fetch*, 17 C.M.R. 836 (A.F.B.R. 1954). The discussion is based on the last sentence of paragraph 62 *d* and the last sentence of paragraph 62 *h*(4) of MCM, 1969 (Rev.). The last sentence in the discussion is also based on*United States v. Lee*, 31 C.M.R. 743 (A.F.B.R. 1962).

(h) *Special courts-martial without a military judge.* This subsection is based on Articles 41, 51(a), and 52(c) and on paragraph 62 *h*(3) of MCM, 1969 (Rev.).

(i) *Definitions.* Subsection (2) is based on paragraph 63 of MCM, 1969 (Rev.). *See also United States v. Griffin*, 8 M.J. 66 (C.M.A. 1979); *United States v. Wilson*, 7 U.S.C.M.A. 656, 23 C.M.R. 120 (1957); *United States v. Moore*, 4 U.S.C.M.A. 675, 16 C.M.R. 249 (1954). The distinction between witnesses for the prosecution and witnesses for the defense has been eliminated for purpose of challenges, notwithstanding the statutory basis for the former (Article 25(d)(2)) but not the latter. Disqualification as a witness for the prosecution has been held to be waivable. *United States v. Beer*, 6 U.S.C.M.A. 180, 19 C.M.R. 306 (1955). Consequently, there is no substantive distinction between either ground.

Subsection (3) is taken from paragraph 64 of MCM, 1969 (Rev.). *Cf. United States v. Goodman*, 3 M.J. 1 (C.M.A. 1977) (military judge as investigator).

Rule 913 Presentation of the case on the merits

(a) *Preliminary instructions.* This subsection is based on Appendix 8 at 10-11 of MCM, 1969 (Rev.). *See also United States v. Waggoner*, 6 M.J. 77 (C.M.A. 1978).

1990 Amendment: The second sentence to the rule and the discussion which follows are based on the decision in *United States v. Rivera*, 23 M.J. 89 (C.M.A. 1986). *See also United States v. Wahnon*, 1 M.J. 144 (C.M.A. 1975).

(b) *Opening statement.* This subsection is based on the first of paragraph of paragraph 44 *g*(2) and the first paragraph of paragraph 48 *i* of MCM, 1969 (Rev.). The discussion is taken from*ABA Standards, The Prosecution Function* § 3-5.5 (1979); *The Defense Function* § 4-7.4 (1979).

(c) *Presentation of evidence.* Subsection (1) is based on paragraph 54a of MCM, 1969 (Rev.), except that (E), *Additional rebuttal evidence*, has been added to expressly note the occasional need for further rebuttal.

Subsection (2) is based on the first sentence of Fed. R. Crim. P. 26. The first paragraph of the discussion of subsection (2) is based on paragraphs 44 *g*(2), 48 *i*, and 54 *a* of MCM, 1969 (Rev.) and Mil. R. Evid. 611 and 614. The second paragraph of the discussion is based on paragraphs 54 *d* and *g* of MCM, 1969 (Rev.).

Subsection (3) and the discussion are based on paragraph 54 *e* of MCM, 1969 (Rev).

Subsection (4) is based on paragraph 54*c* of MCM, 1969 (Rev.).

Subsection (5) is based on the fourth sentence of the second paragraph of paragraph 71 *a* of MCM, 1969 (Rev.) and is consistent with current practice.

Rule 914 Production of statements of witnesses

Introduction. This rule is based on Fed. R. Crim. P. 26.2. Fed. R. Crim. P. 26.2 is based on the Jencks Act, 18 U.S.C. § 3500, which has long been applied in courts-martial. *United States v. Albo*, 22 U.S.C.M.A. 30, 46 C.M.R. 30 (1972); *United States v. Walbert*, 14 U.S.C.M.A. 34, 33 C.M.R. 246 (1963); *United States v. Heinel*, 9 U.S.C.M.A. 259, 26 C.M.R. 39 (1958). *See United States v. Jarrie*, 5 M.J. 193 (C.M.A. 1978); *United States v. Herndon*, 5 M.J. 175 (C.M.A. 1978); *United States v. Scott*, 6 M.J. 547 (A.F.C.M.R. 1978) (applied to statements made during Article 32 investigation and demand at trial); *United States v. Calley*, 46 C.M.R. 1131 (A.C.M.R.), *aff'd*, 22 U.S.C.M.A. 534, 48 C.M.R. 19 (1973); Kesler, *The Jencks Act: An Introductory Analysis*, 13 The Advocate 391 (Nov- Dec. 1981); Lynch, *Possession Under the Jencks Act*, 10 A.F.JAG Rptr 177 (Dec. 1981); O'Brien, *The Jencks Act- A Recognized Tool for Military Defense Counsel* , 11 The Advocate 20 (Jan- Fed 1979); Waldrop, *The Jencks Act*, 20 A.F.L. Rev. 93 (1978); Bogart, *Jencks Act*, 27 JAG J. 427 (1973); West, *Significance of the Jencks Act in Military Law*, 30 Mil. L. Rev. 83 (1965). Fed. R. Crim. P. 26.2 expands the Jencks Act by providing for disclosure by the defense as well as the prosecution, based on *United States v. Nobles*, 422 U.S. 225 (1975). Otherwise, it is not intended to change the requirements of the Jencks Act. Fed. R. Crim. P. 26.2 Advisory Committee Note (Supp. v. 1981). Prosecution compliance with R.C.M. 701 should make resort to this rule by the defense unnecessary in most cases.

This rule, like Fed. R. Crim. P. 26.2, applies at trial. It is not a discovery rule (*United States v. Ciesielski*, 39 C.M.R. 839 (N.M.C.R. 1968)), and it does not apply to Article 32 hearings (*contra, United States v. Jackson*, 33 C.M.R. 884, 890 nn.3, 4 (A.F.B.R. 1963)). It is a distinct rule from the rule requiring production for inspection by an opponent of memoranda used by a witness to refresh recollection. *United States v. Ellison*, 46 C.M.R. 839 (A.F.C.M.R. 1972); *cf.* Mil. R. Evid. 612 and accompanying Analysis. The rule is not intended to discourage voluntary disclosure before trial, even where R.C.M. 701 does not require disclosure, so as to avoid delays at trial. Further, this rule does not foreclose other avenues of discovery.

(a) *Motion for production.* This subsection is based on Fed. R. Crim. P. 26.2(a). It has been reworded to clarify what statements must be produced. "(I)n the possession of the United States," and "in the possession of the accused or defense counsel" are substituted for "in their possession" to make clear that the rule is not limited to statements in the personal possession of counsel. *See* 18 U.S.C. § 3500(a). As to the meaning of "in the possession of the United States," *see United States v. Calley, supra* (testimony at congressional hearing); *see also United States v. Ali*, 12 M.J. 1018 (A.C.M.R. 1982) (statements in possession of commander); *United States v. Boiser*, 12 M.J. 1010 (A.C.M.R. 1982) (notes of undercover informant); *United States v. Fountain*, 2 M.J. 1202 (N.C.M.R. 1976); *United States v. Brakefield*, 43 C.M.R. 828 (A.C.M.R. 1971) (notes taken by government psychiatrist).

(b) *Production of entire statement.* This subsection is taken from Fed. R. Crim. P. 26.2(b).

(c) *Production of excised statement.* This subsection is taken from Fed. R. Crim. P. 26.2(c). Failure of a judge to make the required examination on request is error. *United States v. White*, 37 C.M.R. 791 (A.F.B.R. 1966) (decision under Jencks Act). Failure to preserve the statement after denial or excision frustrates appellate review and is also error under decisions interpreting 18 U.S.C. § 3500. *United States v. Dixon*, 8 M.J. 149 (C.M.A. 1979); *United States v. Jarrie, supra.* However, the statement need not be appended to the record (where it would become public) because it is not error to consider the statement when forwarded separately as this rule provides. *United States v. Dixon, supra.*

(d) *Recess for examination of the statement.* This subsection is taken from Fed. R. Crim. P. 26.2(d).

(e) *Remedy for failure to produce statement.* This subsection is based on Fed. R. Crim. P. 26.2(e). Although not expressly mentioned there, the good faith loss and harmless error doctrines under the Jencks Act would apparently apply. *See United States v. Patterson*, 10 M.J. 599 (A.F.C.M.R. 1980); *United States v. Kilmon*, 10 M.J. 543 (N.C.M.R. 1980), *United States v. Dixon, United States v. Scott, United States v. Jarrie, and United States v. White, all supra.* Note, however, that under the Jencks Act decisions the accused need not demonstrate prejudice on appeal (*United States v. Albo, supra; but see United States v. Bryant*, 439 F.2d 642 (D.C. Cir. 1971); *United States v. Ali*, and *United States v. Boiser*, both *supra*) and that the military judge may not substitute the judge's assessment of the usefulness of the statement for the assessment of the accused and defense counsel (*United States v. Dixon and United States v. Kilmon*, both *supra).*

(f) *Definitions.* This subsection is taken from Fed. R. Crim. P. 26.6(f).

In subsection (1) the inclusion of statements approved or adopted by a witness is consistent with 18 U.S.C. § 3500(e)(1). *See United States v. Jarrie* and *United States v. Kilmon*, both *supra.*

In subsection (2) the inclusion of substantially verbatim recordings or transcriptions exceeds some interpretations under 18 U.S.C. § 3500. *See, e.g., United States v. Matfield*, 4 M.J. 843 (A.C.M.R.), *pet. denied.*, 5 M.J. 182 (1978) (testimony in a prior court-martial not accessible under 18 U.S.C. § 3500 but accessible under a general "military due process" right to discovery).

Rule 914A Use of remote live testimony of a child

1999 Amendment: This rule allows the military judge to determine what procedure to use when taking testimony under Mil. R. Evid. 611(d)(3). It states that normally such testimony should be taken via a two-way closed circuit television system. The rule further prescribes the procedures to be used if a television system is employed. The use of two-way closed circuit television, to some degree, may defeat the purpose of these alternative procedures, which is to avoid trauma to children. In such cases, the judge has discretion to direct one-way television communication. The use of one-way closed circuit television was approved by the Supreme Court in *Maryland v. Craig*, 497 U.S. 836 (1990). This amendment also gives the accused an election to absent himself from the courtroom to prevent remote testimony. Such a provision gives the accused a greater role in determining how this issue will be resolved.

2007 Amendment: The rule was amended to allow for technological advances in the methods used to transmit audio and visual information.

Rule 914B Use of remote testimony.

2007 Amendment: This rule describes the basic procedures that will be used when testimony of any witnesses, other than child witnesses pursuant to R.C.M. 914A, is received via remote means.

Rule 915 Mistrial

(a) *In general.* This subsection is based on the second and third sentences of paragraph 56 *e*(1) of MCM, 1969 (Rev.). *See generally Oregon v. Kennedy*, 456 U.S. 667 (1982); *Arizona v. Washington*, 434 U.S. 497 (1978); *Lee v. United States*, 432 U.S. 23 (1977); *United States v. Dinitz*, 424 U.S. 600 (1976); *Illinois v. Somerville* , 410 U.S. 458 (1973); *United States v. Jorn*, 400 U.S. 470 (1971); *United States v. Perez*, 22 U.S. (9 Wheat) 579 (1824); *United States v. Richardson*, 21 U.S.C.M.A. 54, 44 C.M.R. 108 (1971); *United States v. Schilling*, 7 U.S.C.M.A. 482, 22 C.M.R. 272 (1957).

(b) *Procedure.* This subsection is based on paragraph 56 *e*(2) of MCM, 1969 (Rev.). Because consent or lack thereof by the defense to a mistrial may be determinative of a former jeopardy motion at a second trial, the views of the defense must be sought.

(c) *Effect of a declaration of mistrial.* Subsection (1) is based on the first sentence of paragraph 56 *e*(1) of MCM, 1969 (Rev.). Note that dismissal of charges may have the same effect as declaring a mistrial, depending on the grounds for dismissal. *See Lee v. United States* and *Illinois v. Somerville,* both *supra.* Subsection (2) is based on the first two sentences of paragraph 56 *e*(3) of MCM, 1969 (Rev). *See also Oregon v. Kennedy, supra; United States v. Scott*, 437 U.S. 82 (1978); *Arizona v. Washington, United States v. Dinitz, Illinois v. Somerville*, and *United States v. Jorn, all supra; Gori v. United States*, 367 U.S. 364 (1961); *United States v. Richardson, supra.* Subsection (2) notes, as paragraph 56 *e* of MCM, 1969 (Rev.) did not, that a declaration of a mistrial after findings does not trigger double jeopardy protections. *See United States v. Richardson, supra.* Moreover subsection (2) notes that certain types of prosecutorial misconduct resulting in mistrial will trigger double jeopardy protections. *See United States v. Jorn*, and *United States v. Gori,* both *supra. See also United States v. Dinitz*, and *Illinois v. Sommerville,* both *supra.*

Rule 916 Defenses

(a) *In general.* This subsection and the discussion are based on the third paragraph of paragraph 214 of MCM, 1969 (Rev.).

Motions in bar of trial, which were also covered in paragraph 214, are now covered in R.C.M. 907 since they are procedurally and conceptually different from the defenses treated in R.C.M. 916.

(b) *Burden of proof.* This subsection is based on the fourth paragraph of paragraph 214 of MCM, 1969 (Rev.). *See also* paragraph 112 *a* of MCM, 1969 (Rev.). *See, e.g., United States v. Cuffee*, 10 M.J. 381 (C.M.A. 1981). The first paragraph in the discussion is based on the fifth paragraph of paragraph 214 of MCM, 1969 (Rev.). The second paragraph in the discussion is based on *United States v. Garcia*, 1 M.J. 26 (C.M.A. 1975); *United States v. Walker*, 21 U.S.C.M.A. 376, 45 C.M.R.150 (1972); *United States v. Ducksworth*, 13 U.S.C.M.A. 515, 33 C.M.R. 47 (1963); *United States v. Bellamy*, 47 C.M.R. 319 (A.C.M.R. 1973). It is unclear whether, under some circumstances, an accused's testimony may negate a defense which might otherwise have been raised by the evidence. *See United States v. Garcia, supra.*

1986 Amendment: The requirement that the accused prove lack of mental responsibility was added to implement Article 50 *a*, which was added to the UCMJ in the "Military Justice Amendments of 1986," Tit. VIII, § 802, National Defense Authorization Act for fiscal year 1987, Pub.L. No. 99-661, 100 Stat. 3905 (1986). Article 50a(b) adopted the provisions of 18 U.S.C. 20(b), created by the Insanity Defense Reform Act, ch. IV, Pub. L. No. 98-473, 98 Stat. 2057 (1984). *See generally Jones v. United States*, 463 U.S. 354, 103 S. Ct. 3043, 3051 n.17 (1983); *Leland v. Oregon*, 343 U.S. 790, 799 (1952); S.Rep. No. 225, 98th Cong., 1st Sess. 224-25 (1983), reprinted in 1984 U.S. Code Cong. & Ad. News 1, 226-27.

1998 Amendment: In enacting section 1113 of the National Defense Authorization Act for Fiscal Year 1996, Pub. L. No. 104-106, 110 Stat. 186, 462 (1996), Congress amended Article 120, UCMJ, to create a mistake of fact defense to a prosecution for carnal knowledge. The accused must prove by a preponderance of the evidence that the person with whom he or she had sexual intercourse was at least 12 years of age, and that the accused reasonably believed that this person was at least 16 years of age. The changes to R.C.M. 916(b) and (j) implement this amendment.

2007 Amendment: Changes to this paragraph, deleting "carnal knowledge", are based on section 552 of the National Defense Authorization Act for Fiscal Year 2006, P.L. 109-163, 6 January 2006, which supersedes the previous paragraph 45, Rape and Carnal Knowledge, in its entirety and replaces paragraph 45 with Rape, sexual assault and other sexual misconduct.

(c) *Justification.* This subsection and the discussion are based on paragraph 216 *a* of MCM, 1969 (Rev.). *See also United States v. Evans.* 17 U.S.C.M.A. 238, 38 C.M.R. 36 (1967); *United States v. Regalado*, 13 U.S.C.M.A. 480, 33 C.M.R. 12 (1963); *United States v. Hamilton*, 10 U.S.C.M.A. 130, 27 C.M.R. 204 (1959). The last sentence in the discussion is based on the second sentence of paragraph 195 *b* of MCM (1951).

(d) *Obedience to orders.* This subsection is based on paragraph 216*d* of MCM, 1969 (Rev.); *United States v. Calley*, 22 U.S.C.M.A. 534, 48 C.M.R. 19 (1973); *United States v. Cooley*, 16 U.S.C.M.A. 24, 36 C.M.R. 180 (1966). *See also United States v. Calley*, 46 C.M.R. 1131 (A.C.M.R. 1973).

(e) *Self-defense.* Subsection (1) is based on the first paragraph of paragraph 216 *c* of MCM, 1969 (Rev.). The discussion is based on the second paragraph of paragraph 216 *c* of MCM 1967 (Rev.). *See also United States v. Jackson*, 15 U.S.C.M.A. 603, 36 C.M.R. 101 (1966).

Subsection (2) is new and is based on *United States v. Acosta-Vergas*, 13 U.S.C.M.A. 388, 32 C.M.R. 388 (1962).

Subsection (3) is based on the fourth paragraph of paragraph 216 *c* of MCM, 1969 (Rev.). *See also United States v. Sawyer*, 4 M.J. 64 (C.M.A. 1977). The second paragraph in the discussion is based on *United States v. Jones*, 3 M.J. 279 (1977). *See also United States v. Thomas,* 11 M.J. 315 (C.M.A. 1981).

1986 Amendment: References to subsections "(c)(1) or (2)" was changed to "(e)(1) or (2)" to correct an error in MCM, 1984.

Subsection (4) is based on the third paragraph of paragraph 216 *c* of MCM, 1969 (Rev.). *See also United States v. Yabut*, 20 U.S.C.M.A. 393, 43 C.M.R. 233 (1971); *United States v. Green*, 13 U.S.C.M.A. 545, 33 C.M.R. 77 (1963); *United States v. Brown*, 13 U.S.C.M.A. 485, 33 C.M.R. 7 (1963). The second paragraph in the discussion is based on *United States v. Smith*, 13 U.S.C.M.A. 471, 33 C.M.R. 3 (1963).

Subsection (5) is based on paragraph 216c of MCM, 1969 (Rev.) which described self-defense in terms which also apply to defense of another. It is also based on *United States v. Styron*, 21 C.M.R. 579 (C.G.B.R. 1956); *United States v. Hernandez*, 19 C.M.R. 822 (A.F.B.R. 1955). *But see* R. Perkins, *Criminal Law* 1018-1022 (2d ed. 1969).

(f) *Accident.* This subsection and the discussion are based on paragraph 216 *b* of MCM, 1969 (Rev.). *See also United States v. Tucker*, 17 U.S.C.M.A. 551, 38 C.M.R. 349 (1968); *United States v. Redding*, 14 U.S.C.M.A. 242, 24 C.M.R. 22 (1963); *United States v. Sandoval*, 4 U.S.C.M.A. 61, 15 C.M.R. 61 (1954); *United States v. Small*, 45 C.M.R. 700 (A.C.M.R. 1972).

(g) *Entrapment.* This subsection and the discussions are based on paragraph 216 *e* of MCM, 1969 (Rev.). *See also United States v. Vanzandt*, 14 M.J. 332 (C.M.A. 1982).

(h) *Coercion or duress.* This subsection is based on paragraph 216 *f* of MCM, 1969 (Rev.). Paragraph 216 *f* required that the fear of the accused be that the accused would be harmed. This test was too narrow, as the fear of injury to relatives or others may be a basis for this defense. *United States v. Jemmings*, 1 M.J. 414 (C.M.A. 1976); *United States v. Pinkston*, 18 U.S.C.M.A. 261, 39 C.M.R. 261 (1969). The discussion is based on *United States v. Jemmings, supra.*

(i) *Inability.* This subsection is based on paragraph 216 *g* of MCM, 1969 (Rev.). *See United States v. Cooley, supra; United States v. Pinkston* , 6 U.S.C.M.A. 700, 21 C.M.R. 22 (1956); *United States v. Heims*, 3 U.S.C.M.A. 418, 12 C.M.R. 174 (1953).

(j) *Ignorance or mistake of fact.* This subsection is based on paragraph 216 *i* of MCM, 1969 (Rev.); *United States v. Jenkins*, 22 U.S.C.M.A. 365, 47 C.M.R. 120 (1973); *United States v. Hill*, 13 U.S.C.M.A. 158, 32 C.M.R. 158, (1962); *United States v. Greenwood*, 6 U.S.C.M.A. 209, 19 C.M.R. 335 (1955); *United States v. Graham*, 3 M.J. 962 (N.C.M.R.), *pet denied*, 4 M.J. 124 (1977); *United States v. Coker*, 2. M.J. 304 (A.F.C.M.R. 1976), rev'd on other grounds, 4 M.J. 93 (C.M.A. 1977). *See also United States v. Calley*, 46 C.M.R. 1131, 1179 (A.C.M.R. 1973), *aff'd*, 22 U.S.C.M.A. 534, 48 C.M.R. 19 (1973).

1998 Amendment: In enacting section 1113 of the National Defense Authorization Act for Fiscal Year 1996, Pub. L. No. 104-106, 110 Stat. 186, 462(1996), Congress amended Article 120, UCMJ to create a mistake of fact defense to a prosecution for carnal knowledge. The accused must prove by a preponderance of the evidence that the person with whom he or she had sexual intercourse was at least 12 years of age, and that the accused reasonably believed that this person was at least 12 years of age, and that the accused reasonably believed that this person was at least 16 years of age. The changes to R.C.M. 916(b) and (j) implement this amendment.

2007 Amendment: Changes to this paragraph, deleting "carnal knowledge" and consistent language, are based on section 552 of the National Defense Authorization Act for Fiscal Year 2006, P.L. 109-163, 6 January 2006, which supersedes the previous paragraph 45, Rape and Carnal Knowledge, in its entirety and replaces paragraph 45 with Rape, sexual assault and other sexual misconduct.

Paragraph (j)(3) is new and is based on the mistake of fact defense incorporated in section 552 of the National Defense Authorization Act for Fiscal Year 2006, P.L. 109-163, 6 January 2006, which supersedes the previous paragraph 45, Rape and Carnal Knowledge, in its entirety and replaces paragraph 45 with Rape, sexual assault and other sexual misconduct.

(k) *Lack of mental responsibility.* Subsection (1) is taken from paragraph 120 *b* of MCM, 1969 (Rev). *See also United States v. Frederick*, 3 M.J. 230 (C.M.A. 1977).

1986 Amendment: The test for lack of mental responsibility in subsection (1) was changed to implement Article 50a, which was added to the UCMJ in the "Military Justice Amendments of 1986, " tit. VIII, 802, National Defense Authorization Act for fiscal year 1987, Pub.L. No. 99-661, 100 stat. 3905 (1986). Article 50a is modeled on 18 U.S.C. 20. *See* Insanity Defense Reform Act, ch. IV, Pub. L. No. 98-473, 98 Stat. 2057 (1984). The new test deletes the volitional prong of the American Law Institute's Model Penal Code Standard (*see United States v. Lyons*, 731 F.2d 243 (5th Cir. 1984) (en banc), *cert. denied*, 105 S. Ct. 323 (1985)), which was applied to courts-martial in *United States v. Frederick*, 3 M.J. 230 (C.M.A. 1977). The new standard also changes the quantity of mental disability necessary to establish the defense from "lacks substantial capacity to appreciate" to being "unable to appreciate." The new test is very similar to the test in *M'Naghten's Case*, 10 Cl. & F. 200, 8 Eng. Rep. 718 (House of Lords. 1843). *See also* Carroll, *Insanity Defense Reform*, 114 Mil. L. Rev. 183 (1986).

2004 Amendment: The Discussion to R.C.M. 916(k)(1) was amended to add a cross-reference to R.C.M. 1102A.

Subsection (2) is taken from paragraph 120 *c* of MCM, 1969 (Rev.). *See also United States v. Higgins*, 4 U.S.C.M.A. 143, 15 C.M.R. 143 (1954).

1986 Amendment: Subsection (2) was amended to eliminate the defense of partial mental responsibility in conformance with Article 50a, which was added to the UCMJ in the "Military Justice Amendments of 1986," tit. VIII 802, National Defense Authorization Act for fiscal year 1987, Pub.L. No. 99-661, 100 Stat. 3905 (1986). Article 50a(a) is adopted from 18 U.S.C. § 20(a). Congress wrote the last sentence of 18 U.S.C. § 20(a) (now also the last sentence of Article 50(a)) "to insure that the insanity defense is not improperly resurrected in the guise of showing some other affirmative defense, such as that the defendant had has a ædiminished responsibilityÆ on some similarly asserted state of mind which would serve to excuse the offense and open the door, once again, to needlessly confusing psychiatric testimony." S.Rep. No. 225, 98th Cong. 1st Sess. 229(1983), *reprinted in* 1984 U.S.Code Cong. & Ad. News 1. 231. *See Muench v. Israel,* 715 F.2d 1124 (7th Cir. 1983), *cert. denied,* 104 S.Ct. 2682 (1984); *State v. Wilcox*, 436 N.E. 2d 523 (Ohio 1982).

Because the language of section 20(a) and its legislative history have been contended to be somewhat ambiguous regarding "diminished capacity" or "diminished responsibility," this aspect of the legislation has been litigated in Article III courts. *United States v. Pohlot*, Crim. No. 85-00354-01 (E.D. Pa. March 31, 1986) held that section 20(a) eliminated the defense of diminished capacity. *See also United States v. White*, 766 F.2d 22, 24-25 (1st Cir. 1985); U.S. DEPARTMENT OF JUSTICE, HANDBOOK ON THE COMPREHENSIVE CRIME CONTROL ACT OF 1984 AND OTHER CRIMINAL STATUTES ENACTED BY THE 98TH CONGRESS 58, 60 (December 1984). *Contra United States v. Frisbee*, 623 F. Supp. 1217 (N.D. Cal. 1985) (holding that Congress did not intend to eliminate the defense of diminished capacity). *See also* Carroll, *Insanity Defense Reform,* 114 Mil. L. Rev. 183, 196 (1986). The drafters concluded that Congress intended to eliminate this defense in section 20(a).

2004 Amendment: Subsection (k)(2) was modified to clarify that evidence of an accused's impaired mental state may be admissible. *See United States v. Schap,* 49 M.J. 317 (1998); *United States v. Berri,* 33 M.J. 337 (C.M.A. 1991); *Ellis v. Jacob,* 26 M.J. 90 (C.M.A. 1988).

Subsection (3)(A) and the discussion are based on paragraph 122 *a* of MCM, 1969 (Rev.). Several matters in paragraph 122a are covered in other parts of this subsection or in R.C.M. 909.

1986 Amendment: Subsection (3)(A) was amended to conform to article 50a(b) and R.C.M. 916(b).

Subsection (3)(B) and the discussion are based on paragraph 122 *b*(2) of MCM, 1969 (Rev.). The procedures for an inquiry into the mental responsibility of the accused are covered in R.C.M. 706.

Subsection (3)(C) is new. Article 51(b) prohibits a military judge from ruling finally on the factual question of mental responsibility. It does not, however, require that the question be treated as an interlocutory one, and there is no apparent reason for doing so. The import of Article 51(b) is that the issue of mental responsibility may not be removed from the factfinder. Moreover, to permit mental responsibility to be treated separately from other issues relating to the general issue could work to the detriment of the accused. *Cf. United States v. Laws*, 11 M.J. 475 (C.M.A. 1981).

(l) *Not defenses generally.*

Subsection (1) is based on the first sentence of paragraph 216 *j* of MCM, 1969 (Rev.). The discussion is based on the remainder of paragraph 216 *j* of MCM, 1969 (Rev.); R. Perkins, *supra* at 920-38. *See also United States v. Sicley*, 6 U.S.C.M.A. 402, 20 C.M.R. 118 (1955); *United States v. Bishop*, 2 M.J. 741 (A.F.C.M.R.), *pet, denied*, 3 M.J. 184 (1977).

Subsection (2) is based on paragraph 216h of MCM, 1969 (Rev.). *See also United States v. Hernandez*, 20 U.S.C.M.A. 219 43 C.M.R. 59 (2970); *United States v. Ferguson*, 17 U.S.C.M.A. 441, 38 C.M.R. 239 (1968); *United States v. Garcia*, 41 C.M.R. 638 (A.C.M.R. 1969). *See United States v. Santiago-Vargas*, 5 M.J. (C.M.A. 1978) (pathological intoxication).

Rule 917 Motion for a finding of not guilty

(a) *In general.* This subsection is based on Fed. R. Crim. P. 29(a) and on the first two sentences of paragraph 71 *a* of MCM, 1969 (Rev.). Paragraph 71 *a* did not expressly provide for a motion for a finding of not guilty to be made *sua sponte*, as does Fed. R. Crim. P. 29(a). Unlike Fed. R. Crim. P. 29, this rule requires the motion to be resolved before findings are entered. If the evidence is insufficient to support a rational finding of guilty, there is no reason to submit the issue to the members. That would be inefficient. Moreover, if a military judge set aside some but not all of the findings as "irrational," it would be awkward to proceed to sentencing before the same members. However, nothing in this rule is intended to limit the authority of a military judge to dismiss charges after findings on other grounds, such as multiplicity or improper findings (*e.g.,* conviction for both larceny as perpetrator and receiving stolen property, *see United States v. Cartwright*, 13 M.J. 174 (C.M.A. 1982); *United States v. Ford*, 12 U.S.C.M.A. 3, 30 C.M.R. 3 (1960);*cf. United States v. Clark*, 20 U.S.C.M.A. 140, 42 C.M.R. 332 (1970)).

(b) *Form of motion.* This subsection is based on the first sentence in the second paragraph of paragraph 71 *a* of MCM, 1969 (Rev.), except that now a statement of the deficiencies of proof is required. This will enable the trial counsel to respond to the motion.

(c) *Procedure.* This subsection is new, although it conforms to current practice. By ensuring that counsel may be heard on the motion, a precipitant ruling will be avoided. This is important since a ruling granting the motion may not be reconsidered. *See United States v. Hitchcock*, 6 M.J. 188 (C.M.A. 1979). The first paragraph in the discussion is based on the fifth sentence of the second paragraph of paragraph 71 *a* of MCM, 1969 (Rev.).

(d) *Standard.* This subsection is based on the fourth sentence of the second paragraph of paragraph 71 *a* of MCM, 1969 (Rev.). *See also Jackson v. Virginia*, 443 U.S. 307 (1979); *United States v. Varkonyi*, 645 F.2d 453 (5th Cir. 1981); *United States v. Beck*, 615 F.2d 441 (7th Cir. 1980).

(e) *Motion as to greater offense.* This subsection is new and is intended to resolve the problem noted in *United States v. Spearman*, 23 U.S.C.M.A. 31, 48 C.M.R. 405 (1974). *See Government of Virgin Islands v. Josiah*, 641 F.2d 1103, 1108 (3d Cir. 1981).

(f) *Effect of ruling.* This subsection is based on the third sentence of Article 51(a) and on *United States v. Hitchcock, supra.*

1994 Amendment. The amendment to subsection (f) clarifies that the military judge may reconsider a ruling denying a motion for a finding of not guilty at any time prior to authentication of the record of trial. This amendment is consistent with *United States v. Griffith*, 27 M.J. 42 (C.M.A. 1988). As stated by the court, the reconsideration is limited to a determination as to whether the evidence adduced is legally sufficient to establish guilt rather than a determination based on the weight of the evidence which remains the exclusive province of the finder of fact.

(g) *Effect of denial on review.* This subsection is based on the last sentence of the first paragraph of paragraph 71 *a* of MCM, 1969 (Rev.). *See also United States v. Bland*, 653 F.2d 989 (5th Cir.), *cert. denied*, 454 U.S. 1055 (1981).

Rule 918 Findings

(a) *General findings.* This subsection and the discussion are based on paragraphs 74 *b* and *c* of MCM, 1969 (Rev.). The discussion of lesser included offenses is also based on Article 80. *See also United States v. Scott*, 50 C.M.R. 630 (C.G.C.M.R. 1975).

Failure to reach findings as to the charge or the designation of a wrong article is not necessarily prejudicial. *United States v. Dilday*, 471 C.M.R. 172 (A.C.M.R. 1973).

1986 Amendment: The provisions allowing for findings of not guilty only by reason of lack of mental responsibility were added to subsections (a)(1) and (2) to implement Article 50a(c), which was added to the UCMJ in the "Military Justice Amendments of 1986," Tit. VIII, 802, National Defense Authorization Act for Fiscal Year 1987, Pub.L. No. 99-661, 100 Stat. 3905 (1986). This finding is modeled after 18 U.S.C. § 4242(b)(3), section 403 of the Insanity Defense Reform Act, ch. IV, Pub.L. No. 98-473, 98 Stat. 2057, 2059. The drafters intended that adoption of the finding of "not guilty only by reason of lack of mental responsibility" does not require conformance to the procedures that follow an insanity acquittal in federal courts (*see* U.S.C. § 4243 *et. seq.*). The Services are free to use available medical and administrative procedures which address disposition of servicemembers having psychiatric illnesses. The drafters further intended that, for purposes of subsequent appellate and other legal reviews under this Manual, a finding of "not guilty only by reason of lack of mental responsibility" shall be treated as any other acquittal.

1993 Amendment: The amendment to R.C.M. 918(a)(1) allows for a finding of guilty of a named lesser included offense of the charged offense, and eliminates the necessity of making findings by exceptions and substitutions. This serves to conform military practice to that used in criminal trials before federal district courts. *See* Fed. R. Crim. P. 31(c); E. Devitt and C. Blackman, *Federal Jury Practice and Instructions,* 18.07 (1977). The practice of using exceptions and substitutions is retained for those cases in which the military judge or court members must conform the findings to the evidence actually presented, *e.g.,* a larceny case in which the finding is that the accused stole several of the items alleged in the specification but not others.

(b) *Special findings.* This subsection is based on Article 51(d), paragraph 74 *i* of MCM, 1969 (Rev.); *United States v. Gerard*, 11 M.J. 440 (C.M.A. 1981). *See also United States v. Pratcher* 14 M.J. 819 (A.C.M.R. 1982); *United States v. Burke*, 4 M.J. 530 (N.C.M.R. 1977); *United States v. Hussey*, 1 M.J. 804 (A.F.C.M.R. 1976); *United States v. Baker*, 47 C.M.R. 506 (A.C.M.R. 1973); *United States v. Falin*, 43 C.M.R. 702 (A.C.M.R. 1971); *United States v. Robertson*, 41 C.M.R. 457 (A.C.M.R. 1969); Schinasi, *Special Findings: Their Use at Trial and on Appeal,* 87 Mil.L.Rev. (Winter 1980).

The requirement that a request for special findings be made before general findings are announced is based on the fifth sentence of paragraph 74 *i* of MCM, 1969 (Rev.), and on Fed. R. Crim. P.23(c). Article 51(d) is patterned after Fed. R. Crim. P. 23(c). *United States v. Gerard, supra.* The language in Article 51(d) is virtually identical to that in Fed. R. Crim. P. 23(c) as it existed when Article 51(d) was adopted in 1968. Fed. R. Crim. P. 23(c) was amended in 1977 to provide specifically that a request for special findings be made before general findings are entered. Pub. L. No. 95-78 § 2(b), 91 Stat. 320. This was done "to make clear that deadline for making a request for findings of fact and to provide that findings may be oral." *Id.,* Advisory Committee Note (Supp. v. 1981). Subsection (b), therefore, continues conformity with federal practice.

(c) *Basis of findings.* This subsection and the discussion are based on paragraph 74 *a* of MCM, 1969 (Rev.). The discussion of reasonable doubt has been modified based on *United States v.*

Cotten, 10 M.J. 260 (C.M.A. 1981); *United States v. Salley*, 9 M.J. 189 (C.M.A. 1980). *See also Holland v. United States*, 348 U.S. 121, 140-41 (1954); *United States v. Previte*, 648 F.2d 73 (1st Cir. 1981); *United States v. De Vincent*, 632 F.2d 147 (1st Cir.), *cert denied*, 449 U.S. 986 (1980); *United States v. Cortez*, 521 F.2d 1 (5th Cir. 1975); *United States v. Zeigler*, 14 M.J. 860 (A.C.M.R. 1982); *United States v. Sauer*, 11 M.J. 872 (N.C.M.R.), *pet. granted*, 12 M.J. 320 (1981); *United States v. Crumb*, 10 M.J. 520 (A.C.M.R. 1980); E. Devitt and C. Blackmar, *Federal Jury Practice Instructions*, § 11.14 (3d. ed. 1977). As to instructions concerning accomplice testimony, *see United States v. Lee*, 6 M.J. 96 (C.M.A. 1978); *United States v. Moore*, 8 M.J. 738 (A.F.C.M.R. 1980), *aff'd*, 10 M.J. 405 (C.M.A. 1981) (regarding corroboration).

Rule 919 Argument by counsel on findings

(a) *In general.* This subsection is based on Fed. R. Crim. P. 29.1. It has been reworded slightly to make clear that trial counsel may waive the opening and the closing argument. The rule is consistent with the first sentence of paragraph 72 *a* of MCM, 1969 (Rev.).

(b) *Contents.* This subsection is based on the first sentence of the second paragraph of paragraph 72 *b* of MCM, 1969 (Rev.). The discussion is based on paragraphs 72 *a* and *b* of MCM, 1969 (Rev.). *See also* paragraphs 44 *g* and 48 *c* of MCM, 1969 (Rev.); *Griffin v. California*, 380 U.S. 609 (1965) (comment on accused's failure to testify); *United States v. Saint John*, 23 U.S.C.M.A. 20, 48 C.M.R. 312 (1974) (comment on unrebutted nature of prosecution evidence); *United States v. Horn*, 9 M.J. 429 (C.M.A. 1980) (repeated use of "I think" improper but not prejudicial); *United States v. Knickerbocker*, 2 M.J. 128 (C.M.A. 1977) (personal opinion of counsel); *United States v. Shamberger*, 1 M.J. 377 (C.M.A. 1976) (inflammatory argument); *United States v. Nelson*, 1 M.J. 235 (C.M.A. 1975) (comment on Article 32 testimony of accused permitted; inflammatory argument; misleading argument); *United States v. Reiner*, 15 M.J. 38 (C.M.A. 1983); *United States v. Fields*, 15 M.J. 34 (C.M.A. 1983); *United States v. Fitzpatrick*, 14 M.J. 394 (C.M.A. 1983) (bringing to members' attention that accused had opportunity to hear the evidence at the Article 32 hearing is permissible); *United States v. Boberg*, 17 U.S.C.M.A. 401, 38 C.M.R. 199 (1968); *United States v. Cook*, 11 U.S.C.M.A. 99, 28 C.M.R. 323 (1959) (comment on community relations); *United States v. McCauley*, 9 U.S.C.M.A. 65, 25 C.M.R. 327 (1958) (citation of authority to members). *See generally* ABA Standards, *The Prosecution Function* § 3-5.8 (1979), *The Defense Function* § 4-7.8 (1979). *See also United States v. Clifton*, 15 M.J. 26 (C.M.A. 1983).

(c) *Waiver of objection to improper argument.* This subsection is based on Fed. R. Crim. P. 29.1 and is generally consistent with current practice. *See United States v. Grandy*, 11 M.J. 270 (C.M.A. 1981). *See also United States v. Doctor*, 7 U.S.C.M.A. 126, 21 C.M.R. 252 (1956). *But see United States v. Knickerbocker, United States v. Shamberger*, and *United States v. Nelson* all *supra; United States v. Ryan*, 21 U.S.C.M.A. 9, 44 C.M.R. 63 (1971); *United States v. Wood*, 18 U.S.C.M.A. 291, 40 C.M.R. 3 (1969) (military judge had duty to act on improper argument *sua sponte* where error was plain). As to the discussion, *see United States v. Knickerbocker*, and *United States v. Nelson*, both *supra; United States v. O'Neal*, 16 U.S.C.M.A. 33, 36 C.M.R. 189 (1966); *United States v. Carpenter*, 11 U.S.C.M.A. 418, 29 C.M.R. 234 (1960).

Rule 920 Instructions on findings

(a) *In general.* This subsection is based on the first sentence of paragraph 73 *a* of MCM, 1969 (Rev.). The discussion is based on the first paragraph of paragraph 73 *a* of MCM, 1969 (Rev.). *See United States v. Buchana*, 19 U.S.C.M.A. 394, 41 C.M.R. 394 (1970); *United States v. Harrison*, 19 U.S.C.M.A. 179, 41 C.M.R. 179 (1970); *United States v. Moore*, 16 U.S.C.M.A. 375, 36 C.M.R. 531 (1966); *United States v. Smith*, 13 U.S.C.M.A. 471, 33 C.M.R. 3(1963). *See also United States v. Gere*, 662 F.2d 1291 (9th Cir. 1981).

(b) *When given.* This subsection is based on the first sentence of paragraph 73 *a* and on paragraph 74 *e* of MCM, 1969 (Rev.), and is consistent with Fed. R. Crim. P. 30. This subsection expressly provides that additional instructions may be given after deliberations have begun without a request from the members. MCM, 1969 (Rev.) was silent on this point. The discussion is based on *United States v. Ricketts*, 1 M.J. 78 (C.M.A. 1975).

1993 Amendment: The amendment to R.C.M. 920(b) is based on the 1987 amendments to Federal Rule of Criminal Procedure 30. Federal Rule of Criminal Procedure 30 was amended to permit instructions either before or after arguments by counsel. The previous version of R.C.M. 920 was based on the now superseded version of the federal rule.

The purpose of this amendment is to give the court discretion to instruct the members before or after closing arguments or at both times. The amendment will permit courts to continue instructing the members after arguments as Rule 30 and R.C.M. 920(b) had previously required. It will also permit courts to instruct before arguments in order to give the parties an opportunity to argue to the jury in light of the exact language used by the court. *See United States v. Slubowski*, 7 M.J. 461 (C.M.A 1979); *United States v. Pendry*, 29 M.J. 694 (A.C.M.R. 1989).

(c) *Requests for instructions.* This subsection is based on the first three sentences in Fed. R. Crim. P. 30 and on the second and fourth sentences of paragraph 73 *d* of MCM, 1969 (Rev.). The discussion is based on the remainder of paragraph 73 *d*.

(d) *How given.* The first sentence of this subsection is based on the last paragraph of paragraph 73 *a* of MCM, 1969 (Rev.). The second sentence of this subsection permits the use of written copies of instructions without stating a preference for or against them. *See United States v. Slubowski*, 7 M.J. 461 (C.M.A. 1979); *United States v. Muir*, 20 U.S.C.M.A. 188, 43 C.M.R. 28 (1970); *United States v. Sampson*, 7 M.J. 513 (A.C.M.R. 1979); *United States v. Sanders*, 30 C.M.R. 521 (A.C.M.R. 1961). Only copies of instructions given orally may be provided, and delivery of only a portion of the oral instructions to the members in writing is prohibited when a party objects. This should eliminate the potential problems associated with written instructions. *See United States v. Slubowski, supra; United States v. Caldwell*, 11 U.S.C.M.A. 257, 29 C.M.R. 73 (1960); *United States v. Helm*, 21 C.M.R. 357 (A.B.R. 1956). Giving written instructions is never required. The discussion is based on the last paragraph of paragraph 73 *a* of MCM, 1969 (Rev.) and *United States v. Caldwell, supra.* As to the use of written instructions in federal district courts, *see generally United States v. Read*, 658 F.2d 1225 (7th

Cir. 1981); *United States v. Calabrase*, 645 F.2d 1379 (10th Cir.), *cert. denied*, 454 U.S. 831 (1981).

(e) *Required instructions.* This subsection is based on Article 51(c) and on the first paragraph of paragraph 73 *a* of MCM, 1969 (Rev.). *See also United States v. Steinruck*, 11 M.J. 322 (C.M.A. 1981); *United States v. Moore, supra; United States v. Clark*, 1 U.S.C.M.A. 201, 2 C.M.R. 107 (1952). As to whether the defense may affirmatively waive certain instructions (*e.g.,* lesser included offenses) which might otherwise be required, *see United States v. Johnson*, 1 M.J. 137 (C.M.A. 1975); *United States v. Mundy*, 2 U.S.C.M.A. 500, 9 C.M.R. 130 (1953). *See generally* Cooper, *The Military Judge: More Than a Mere Reference,* The Army Lawyer (Aug. 1976) 1; Hilliard, *The Waiver Doctrine: Is It Still Viable?,* 18 A.F.L. Rev. 45 (Spring 1976).

1986 Amendment: Subsection (2) was amended to require the accused to waive the bar of the statute of limitations if the accused desires instructions on any lesser included offense otherwise barred. *Spaziano v. Florida*, 468 U.S. 447 (1984). This overturns the holdings in *United States v. Wiedemann*, 16 U.S.C.M.A. 356, 36 C.M.R. 521 (1966) and *United States v. Cooper*, 16 U.S.C.M.A. 390, 37 C.M.R. 10 (1966). The same rule applies in trials by military judge alone. Article 51(d). This is consistent with Article 79 because an offense raised by the evidence but barred by the statute of limitations is "necessarily included in the offense charged," unless the accused waives the statute of limitations.

The first paragraph in the discussion is based on *United States v. Jackson*, 12 M.J. 163 (C.M.A. 1981); *United States v. Waldron*, 11 M.J. 36 (C.M.A. 19810; *United States v. Evans*, 17 U.S.C.M.A. 238, 38 C.M.R. 36 (1967); *United States v. Clark, supra. See United States v. Johnson*, 637 F.2d 1224 (9th Cir. 1980); *United States v. Burns*, 624 F.2d 95 (10th Cir), *cert. denied*, 449 U.S. 954 (1980).

The third paragraph in the discussion is based on paragraph 73 *a* of MCM, 1969 (Rev.) and on *Military Judges Benchbook,* DA Pam 27–9 Appendix A. (May 1982). *See also United States v. Thomas*, 11 M.J. 388 (C.M.A.1981); *United States v. Fowler*, 9 M.J. 149 (C.M.A. 1980); *United States v. James*, 5 M.J. 382 (C.M.A. 1978) (uncharged misconduct); *United States v. Robinson*, 11 M.J. 218 (C.M.A. 1981) (character evidence); *United States v. Wahnon*, 1 M.J. 144 (C.M.A. 1975) (effect of guilty plea on other charges); *United States v. Minter*, 8 M.J. 867 (N.C.M.R.), *aff'd,* 9 M.J. 397 (C.M.A. 1980); *United States v. Prowell*, 1 M.J. 612 (A.C.M.R. 1975) (effect of accused's absence from trial); *United States v. Jackson*, 6 M.J. 116 (C.M.A. 1979); *United States v. Farrington*, 14 U.S.C.M.A. 614, 34 C.M.R. 394 (1964) (accused's failure to testify). The list is not exhaustive.

The fourth paragraph in the discussion is based on paragraph 73 *c* of MCM, 1969 (Rev.). *See also United States v. Grandy*, 11 M.J. 270 (C.M.A. 1981).

1986 Amendment: Subsection (e)(5)(D) was amended to conform to amendments to R.C.M. 916(b).

1998 Amendment: This change to R.C.M. 920(e) implemented Congress' creation of a mistake of fact defense for carnal knowledge. Article 120(d), UCMJ, provides that the accused must prove by a preponderance of the evidence that the person with whom he or she had sexual intercourse was at least 12 years of age, and that the accused reasonably believed that this person was at least 16 years of age.

2007 Amendment: Changes to this paragraph, deleting "carnal knowledge" and consistent language, are based on section 552 of the National Defense Authorization Act for Fiscal Year 2006, P.L. 109-163, 6 January 2006, which supersedes the previous paragraph 45, Rape and Carnal Knowledge, in its entirety and replaces paragraph 45 with Rape, sexual assault and other sexual misconduct.

(f) *Waiver.* This subsection is based on the last two sentences in Fed. R. Crim. P. 30. *See also United States v. Grandy, supra; United States v. Salley*, 9 M.J. 189 (C.M.A. 1980).

Rule 921 Deliberations and voting on findings

(a) *In general.* This subsection is based on Article 39(b) and on the second, third, and fifth sentences of paragraph 74 *d*(1) of MCM, 1969 (Rev.). The first sentence of that paragraph is unnecessary and the fourth is covered in subsection (b) of this rule.

(b) *Deliberations.* The first sentence of this subsection is based on the fourth sentence of paragraph 74 *d*(1) of MCM, 1969 (Rev.). The second sentence is new but conforms to current practice. *See United States v. Hurt*, 9 U.S.C.M.A. 735, 27 C.M.R. 3 (1958); *United States v. Christensen*, 30 C.M.R. 959 (A.F.B.R. 1961). The third sentence is based on *United States v. Jackson*, 6 M.J. 116, 117 (C.M.A. 1979) (Cook, J., concurring in part and dissenting in part); *United States v. Smith*, 15 U.S.C.M.A. 416, 35 C.M.R. 388 (1965). *See also* paragraph 54 *b* of MCM, 1969 (Rev); *United States v. Ronder*, 639 F.2d 931 (2d Cir. 1981).

(c) *Voting.* Subsection (1) is based on the first sentence of Article 51(a) and on the first sentence of paragraph 73 *d*(2) of MCM, 1969 (Rev.).

Subsection (2) is based on Article 52(a) and on the first two sentences of paragraph 74 *d*(3) of MCM, 1969 (Rev.). *See also United States v. Guilford*, 8 M.J. 598 (A.C.M.R. 1979), *pet. denied*, 8 M.J. 242 (1980) (holding *Burch v. Louisiana*, 441 U.S. 130 (1979), does not apply to courts-martial.) The discussion is based on the third sentence of paragraph 74 *d*(3) of MCM, 1969 (Rev.).

Subsection (3) is based on the fourth sentence of paragraph 74 *d*(3) of MCM, 1969 (Rev.).

1986 Amendment: Subsections (4) and (5) were redesignated as subsections (5) and (6) and a new subsection (4) was inserted. New subsection (4) is based on Article 50a(e) and provides for bifurcated voting on the elements of the offense and on mental responsibility, and defines the procedures for arriving at a finding of not guilty only by reason of lack on mental responsibility. When the prosecution had the burden of proving mental responsibility beyond a reasonable doubt, the same as the burden regarding the elements of the offense, the members were unlikely to confuse the two general issues. Without any procedure for bifurcated voting under the 1984 amendment, substantial confusion might result if the members were required to vote simultaneously on whether the defense has proven lack of mental responsibility by clear and convincing evidence, and whether the prosecution has proven the elements of the offense beyond a reasonable doubt. Each issue might result in a different number of votes. Bifurcated voting is also necessary to provide the finding of "not guilty only by reason of lack of mental responsibility" provided for in R.C.M. 918(a). *But see* Carroll, *Insanity Defense Reform,* 114 Mil. L. Rev. 183, 216 (1986).

Subsection (4) is new to the Manual but it conforms to practice generally followed in courts-martial. Paragraph 74 *d*(2) of MCM, 1969 (Rev.) suggested that findings as to a specification and all lesser offenses included therein would be resolved by a single ballot. Such an approach is awkward, however, especially when there are multiple lesser included offenses. It is more appropriate to allow separate consideration of each included offense until a finding of guilty has been reached. *See Military Judges Benchbook,* DA Pam 27–9, para. 2.28 (May 1982).

Subsection (5) is based on the second sentence of Article 51(b) and on paragraph 74 *d*(2) of MCM, 1969 (Rev.). *See also United States v. Dilday*, 47 C.M.R. 172 (A.C.M.R. 1973).

(d) *Action after findings are reached.* This subsection and the discussion are based on paragraphs 74 *f*(1) and 74 *g* of MCM, 1969 (Rev.). *See United States v. Justice*, 3 M.J. 451 (C.M.A. 1977); *United States v. Ricketts*, 1 M.J. 78 (C.M.A. 1975); *United States v. McAllister*, 19 U.S.C.M.A. 420, 42 C.M.R. 22 (1970). The use of findings worksheets is encouraged. *See United States v. Henderson*, 11 M.J. 395 (C.M.A. 1981); *United States v. Barclay*, 6 M.J. 785 (A.C.M.R. 1978), *pet. denied,* 7 M.J. 71 (1979).

1986 Amendment: The word "sentence" was changed to "findings" to correct an error in MCM, 1984.

Rule 922 Announcement of findings

(a) *In general.* This subsection is based on Article 53 and on the first sentence of paragraph 74 *g* of MCM, 1969 (Rev.). *See also United States v. Dilday*, 47 C.M.R. 172 (A.C.M.R. 1973). The discussion is based on *United States v. Ricketts*, 1 M.J. 78 (C.M.A. 1975); *United States v. Stewart*, 48 C.M.R. 877 (A.C.M.R. 1974). The requirement for the announcement to include a statement of the percentage of members concurring in each finding of guilty and that the vote was by secret written ballot has been deleted. Article 53 does not require such an announcement and when instructions on such matters are given (*see* R.C.M. 920(e)(6)), the members are "presumed to have complied with the instructions given them by the judge," *United States v. Ricketts, supra* at 82. *See United States v. Jenkins*, 12 M.J. 222 (C.M.A. 1982). *Cf. United States v. Hendon*, 6 M.J. 171, 173-174 (C.M.A. 1979).

(b) *Findings by members.* This subsection is based on the second sentence of paragraph 74 *g* of MCM, 1969 (Rev.). The last sentence is based on the last sentence of paragraph 70 *b* of MCM, 1969 (Rev.).

1986 Amendment: R.C.M. 922(b) was amended by adding a new paragraph (2) as a conforming change to the amendment in R.C.M. 1004(a) making unanimity on findings a precondition to a capital sentencing proceeding. The Rule and the Discussion also preclude use of the reconsideration procedure in R.C.M. 924 to change a nonunanimous finding of guilty to a unanimous verdict for purposes of authorizing a capital sentencing proceeding. Thus, if a nonunanimous finding of guilty is reaffirmed on reconsideration and the vote happens to be unanimous, the president of the court-martial does not make a statement as to unanimity.

(c) *Findings by military judge.* This subsection is based on the second sentence of the last paragraph of paragraph 70 *b* and on the second paragraph of paragraph 74 *g* of MCM, 1969 (Rev.) *See also* Article 39(a).

(d) *Erroneous announcement.* This subsection is based on the third and fourth sentences of paragraph 74 *g* of MCM, 1969 (Rev.).

(e) *Polling prohibited.* This subsection is based on the requirement in Article 51(a) for voting by secret written ballot. This distinguishes military from civilian practice (*see*, Fed. R. Crim. P. 31(d)). Mil. R. Evid. 606(b) permits adequately broad questioning to ascertain whether a finding is subject to impeachment due to extraneous factors. To permit general inquiry into other matters, including actual votes of members, would be contrary to Article 51(a) and Article 39(b). *See United States v. Bishop*, 11 M.J. 7 (C.M.A. 1981); *United States v. West*, 23 U.S.C.M.A. 77, 48 C.M.R. 548 (1974) (Duncan, C.J.); *United States v. Nash*, 5 U.S.C.M.A. 550, 555, 18 C.M.R. 174, 179 (1955) (Brosman, J. concurring); *United States v. Connors*, 23 C.M.R. 636 (A.B.R. 1957); *United States v. Tolbert*, 14 C.M.R. 613 (A.F.B.R. 1953). *Contra* Caldwell, *Polling the Military Jury,* 11 The Advocate 53 (Mar- Apr, 1979); Feld, *A Manual for Courts-Martial Practice and Appeal* § 72 (1957). *See also United States v. Hendon, supra.*

Rule 923 Impeachment of findings

This rule is based on *United States v. Bishop*, 11 M.J. 7 (C.M.A. 1981); *United States v. West*, 23 U.S.C.M.A. 77, 48 C.M.R. 548 (1974). *See also United States v. Witherspoon*, 12 M.J. 588 (A.C.M.R. 1981), *pet. granted*, 13 M.J. 210 (C.M.A. 1982), *aff'd* 16 M.J. 252 (1983); *United States v. Hance*, 10 M.J. 622 (A.C.M.R. 1980); *United States v. Zinsmeister*, 48 C.M.R. 931, 935 (A.F.C.M.R.), *pet. denied*, 23 U.S.C.M.A. 620 (1974); *United States v. Perez-Pagan*, 47 C.M.R. 719 (A.C.M.R. 1973); *United States v. Connors*, 23 C.M.R. 636 (A.B.R. 1957); Mil. R. Evid. 606(b).

As to inconsistent findings, *see Harris v. Rivera* , 454 U.S. 339 (1981); *Dunn v. United States*, 284 U.S. 390 (1932); *United States v. Gaeta*, 14 M.J. 383, 391 n. 10 (C.M.A. 1983); *United States v. Ferguson*, 21 U.S.C.M.A. 200, 44 C.M.R. 254 (1972); *United States v. Jules*, 15 C.M.R. 517 (A.B.R. 1954). *But see United States v. Reid*, 12 U.S.C.M.A. 497, 31 C.M.R. 83 (1961); *United States v. Butler*, 41 C.M.R. 620 (A.C.M.R. 1969).

The rule is not intended to prevent a military judge from setting aside improper findings. This would include improper findings of guilty of "mutually exclusive" offenses, for example, larceny (as a perpetrator) of certain property and receiving the same stolen property. In such a case, the members should be instructed before they deliberate that they may convict of no more than one of the two offenses. *See Milanovich v. United States*, 365 U.S. 551 (1961); *United States v. Cartwright*, 13 M.J. 174 (C.M.A. 1982); *United States v. Clark*, U.S.C.M.A. 140, 42 C.M.R. 332 (1970); *United States v. Ford*, 12 U.S.C.M.A. 3, 30 C.M.R. 3 (1960).

Rule 924 Reconsideration of findings

(a) *Time for reconsideration.* This subsection is based on Article 52(c) and on the fourth and fifth sentences of paragraph 74 *d*(3) of MCM, 1969 (Rev.).

(b) *Procedure.* This subsection is based on Articles 52(a) and 53(c) and on the last three sentences of paragraph 74 *d*(3) of

MCM, 1969 (Rev.). *See also United States v. Boland*, 20 U.S.C.M.A. 83, 42 C.M.R. 275 (1970).

1987 Amendment: R.C.M. 924(b) was amended in conjunction with the adoption in R.C.M. 921(c)(4) of bifurcated voting on lack of mental responsibility. It is also necessary to bifurcate the vote on reconsideration to retain the relative burdens for reconsideration and to prevent prejudice to the accused.

(c) *Military judge sitting alone.* This subsection is new to the Manual, although the power of the military judge to reconsider findings of guilty has been recognized. *United States v. Chatman*, 49 C.M.R. 319 (N.C.M.R. 1974). It is also implicit in Article 16 which empowers the military judge sitting alone to perform the functions of the members. *See* Article 52(c).

1995 Amendment: The amendment limits reconsideration of findings by the members to findings reached in closed session but not yet announced in open court and provides for the military judge, in judge alone cases, to reconsider the "guilty finding" of a not guilty only by reason of lack of mental responsibility finding.

CHAPTER X. SENTENCING

Rule 1001 Presentencing procedure

Introduction. This rule is based on paragraph 75 of MCM, 1969 (Rev.). Additions, deletions, or modifications, other than format or style changes, are noted in specific subsections *infra.*

Sentencing procedures in Federal civilian courts can be followed in courts-martial only to a limited degree. Sentencing in courts-martial may be by the military judge or members. *See* Article 16 and 52(b). The military does not have—and it is not feasible to create—an independent, judicially supervised probation service to prepare presentence reports. *See* Fed. R. Crim. P. 32(c). This rule allows the presentation of much of the same information to the court-martial as would be contained in a presentence report, but it does so within the protections of an adversarial proceeding, to which rules of evidence apply (*but cf. Williams v. New York*, 337 U.S. 241 (1949)), although they may be relaxed for some purposes. *See* subsections (b)(4) and (5), (c)(3), (d), and (e) of this rule. The presentation of matters in the accused's service records (*see* subsection (b)(2) of this rule) provides much of the information which would be in a presentence report. Such records are not prepared for purposes of prosecution (*cf. United States v. Boles*, 11 M.J. 195 (C.M.A. 1981)) and are therefore impartial, like presentence reports. In addition, the clarification of the types of cases in which aggravation evidence may be introduced (*see* subsection (b)(4) of this rule) and authorization for the trial counsel to present opinion evidence about the accused's rehabilitative potential (*see* subsection (b)(5) of this rule) provide additional avenues for presenting relevant information to the court-martial. The accused retains the right to present matters in extenuation and mitigation (*see* subsection (c) of this rule).

In addition to Fed. R. Crim. P. 32(c), several other subsections in Fed. R. Crim. P. 32 are inapplicable to courts-martial or are covered in other rules. Fed. R. Crim. P. 32(a)(2) is covered in R.C.M. 1010. Fed. R. Crim. P. 32(b)(1) is inapposite; parallel matters are covered in R.C.M. 1114. Fed. R. Crim. P. 32(b)(2) is inapplicable as courts-martial lack power to adjudge criminal forfeiture of property. Fed. R. Crim. P. 32(d) is covered in R.C.M. 910(h). *See also* Article 45(a). As to Fed. R. Crim. P. 32(e), *see* R.C.M. 1108.

(a) *In general.* Subsection (a)(3) is based on the third sentence of paragraph 53 *h* of MCM, 1969 (Rev.) and on the second sentence of Fed. R. Crim. P. 32(a). *See alsoHill v. United States*, 368 U.S. 424 (1962); *Green v. United States*, 365 U.S. 301 (1961). Subsection (a)(3) of paragraph 75 of MCM, 1969 (Rev.) is deleted as the convening authority is no longer required to examine the findings for factual sufficiency. Subsection (a)(2) is consistent with the first sentence of Fed. R. Crim. P. 32(a). *See* Article 53. As to the last sentence of Fed. R. Crim. P. 32(a), *see* subsection (g) of this rule.

(b) *Matter to be presented by the prosecution.* Subsections (3) and (4) are modifications of paragraph 75 *b*(3) and (4) of MCM, 1969 (Rev.), and subsection (5) is new.

1986 Amendment: The word "age" in subsection (1) was deleted to correct error in MCM, 1984.

The fourth sentence of subsection (2) is modified by substituting "a particular document" for "the information." This is intended to avoid the result reached in *United States v. Morgan*, 15 M.J. 128 (C.M.A. 1983). For reasons discussed above, sentencing proceedings in courts-martial are adversarial. Within the limits prescribed in the Manual, each side should have the opportunity to present, or not present, evidence. *Morgan* encourages gamesmanship and may result in less information being presented in some case because of the lack of opportunity to rebut.

1987 Amendment: The words "all those records" were changed to "any records" to implement more clearly the drafters' original intent. According to the paragraph just above, the drafters "intended to avoid the result reached in *United States v. Morgan*," *supra,* by allowing the trial counsel to offer only such records as he or she desired to offer. In *Morgan*, the court held that, when the trial counsel offered adverse documents from the accused's service record, the "rule of completeness" under Mil. R. Evid. 106 required that all documents from that record be offered.

Subsection (3) deletes the exclusion of convictions more than 6 years old. No similar restriction applies to consideration of prior convictions at sentencing proceedings in Federal civilian courts. There is no reason to forbid their consideration by courts-martial, subject to Mil. R. Evid. 403.

Subsection (3) also eliminates the requirement that a conviction be final before it may be considered by the court-martial on sentencing. No similar restriction applies in Federal civilian courts. This subsection parallels Mil. R. Evid. 609. An exception is provided for summary courts-martial and special courts-martial without a military judge. *See* Analysis, Mil. R. Evid. 609. Whether the adjudication of guilt in a civilian forum is a conviction will depend on the law in that jurisdiction.

1986 Amendment: The reference to "Article 65(c)" was changed to "Article 64" to correct an error in MCM, 1984.

2002 Amendment: As previously written, R.C.M. 1001(b)(3)(A) offered little guidance about what it meant by "civilian convictions." *See, e.g., United States v. White*, 47 M.J. 139, 140 (C.A.A.F. 1997); *United States v. Barnes*, 33 M.J. 468, 472-73 (C.M.A. 1992); *United States v. Slovacek*, 24 M.J. 140, 141 (CMA), *cert. denied*, 484 U.S. 855 (1987). The present rule addresses this void and intends to give the sentencing authority as much information as the military judge determines is relevant in order to craft an appropriate sentence for the accused.

Unlike most civilian courts, this rule does not allow admission of more extensive criminal history information, such as arrests. Use of such additional information is not appropriate in the military setting where court-martial members, not a military judge, often decide the sentence. Such information risks unnecessarily confusing the members.

The present rule clarifies the term "conviction" in light of the complex and varying ways civilian jurisdictions treat the subject. The military judge may admit relevant evidence of civilian convictions without necessarily being bound by the action, procedure, or nomenclature of civilian jurisdictions. Examples of judicial determinations admissible as convictions under this rule include accepted pleas of *nolo contendere*, pleas accepted under *North Carolina v. Alford*, 400 U.S. 25 (1970), or deferred sentences. If relevant, evidence of forfeiture of bail that results in a judicial determination of guilt is also admissible, as recognized in *United States v. Eady*, 35 M.J. 15, 16 (C.M.A. 1992). While no time limit is placed upon the admissibility of prior convictions, the military judge should conduct a balancing test to determine whether convictions older than ten years should be admitted or excluded on the basis of relevance and fundamental fairness.

The two central factors in this rule are (1) judicial determination of guilt and (2) assumption of guilt. Assumption of guilt is an all-inclusive term meaning any act by the accused in a judicial proceeding accepting, acknowledging, or admitting guilt. As long as either factor is present, the "conviction" is admissible, if relevant. Consequently, this rule departs from the holding in *United States v. Hughes*, 26 M.J. 119, 120 (C.M.A. 1988), where the accused pleaded guilty in a Texas court, but the judge did not enter a finding of guilty under state law allowing "deferred adjudications." Under the present rule, the "conviction" would be admissible because the accused pleaded guilty in a judicial proceeding, notwithstanding the fact that the state judge did not enter a finding of guilty.

In contrast, "deferred prosecutions," where there is neither an admission of guilt in a judicial proceeding nor a finding of guilty, would be excluded. The rule also excludes expunged convictions, juvenile adjudications, minor traffic violations, foreign convictions, and tribal court convictions as matters inappropriate for or unnecessarily confusing to courts-martial members. What constitutes a æminor traffic violationÆ within the meaning of this rule is to be decided with reference only to federal law, and not to the laws of individual states. See U.S. Sentencing Guidelines Manual Sec. 4A1.2(c)(2); 'What ConstitutesÆ Minor Traffic Infraction' Excludable From Calculation of Defendant's Criminal History under United States Sentencing Guideline Sec. 4A1.2(c)(2),' 113 A.L.R. Fed. 561 (1993).

Additionally, because of the lack of clarity in the previous rule, courts sometimes turned to Mil. R. Evid. 609 for guidance. *See, e.g., Slovacek*, 24 M.J. at 141. We note that because the policies behind Mil. R. Evid. 609 and the present rule differ greatly, a conviction that may not be appropriate for impeachment purposes under Mil. R. Evid. 609, may nevertheless be admissible under the present rule.

The Federal Sentencing Guidelines were consulted when drafting the present rule. Although informed by those guidelines, the present rule departs from them in many respects because of the wide differences between the courts-martial process and practice in federal district court.

Subsection (4) makes clear that evidence in aggravation may be introduced whether the accused pleaded guilty or not guilty, and whether or not it would be admissible on the merits. This is consistent with the interpretation of paragraph 75 *b*(3) (later amended to be paragraph 75 *b*(4) of MCM, 1969 (Rev.) by Exec. Order No. 12315 (July 29, 1981)) in *United States v. Vickers*, 13 M.J. 403 (C.M.A. 1982). *See also* U.S. Dep't of Justice, Attorney General's Task Force on Violent Crime, Final Report Recommendation 14 (1981); Fed. R. Crim. P. 32(c)(2)(B) and (C). This subsection does not authorize introduction in general of evidence of bad character or uncharged misconduct. The evidence must be of circumstances directly relating to or resulting from an offense of which the accused has been found guilty. *See United States v. Rose*, 6 M.J. 754 (N.C.M.R. 1978), *pet. denied*, 7 M.J. 56 (C.M.A. 1979); *United States v. Taliaferro*, 2 M.J. 397 (A.C.M.R. 1975); *United States v. Peace*, 49 C.M.R. 172 (A.C.M.R. 1974).

1999 Amendment: R.C.M. 1001(b)(4) was amended by elevating to the Rule language that heretofore appeared in the Discussion to the Rule. The Rule was further amended to recognize that evidence that the offense was a *hate crime* may also be presented to the sentencing authority. The additional *hate crime* language was derived in part from section 3A1.1 of the Federal Sentencing Guidelines, in which hate crime motivation results in an upward adjustment in the level of the offense for which the defendant is sentenced. Courts-martial sentences are not awarded upon the basis of guidelines, such as the Federal Sentencing Guidelines, but rather upon broad considerations of the needs of the service and the accused and on the premise that each sentence is individually tailored to the offender and offense. The upward adjustment used in the Federal Sentencing Guidelines does not directly translate to the court-martial presentencing procedure. Therefore, in order to adapt this concept to the court-martial process, this amendment was made to recognize that ''hate crime'' motivation is admissible in the court-martial presentencing procedure. This amendment also differs from the Federal Sentencing Guideline in that the amendment does not specify the burden of proof required regarding evidence of ''hate crime'' motivation. No burden of proof is customarily specified regarding aggravating evidence admitted in the presentencing procedure, with the notable exception of aggravating factors under R.C.M. 1004 in capital cases.

Subsection (5) is new. (Paragraph 75b(5) of MCM, 1969 (Rev.) is deleted here, as it is now covered in R.C.M. 701(a)(5). *Cf.* Fed. R. Crim. P. 32(c)(3).) Subsection (5) authorizes the trial counsel to present, in the form of opinion testimony (*see* Mil. R. Evid., Section VII), evidence of the accused's character as a servicemember and rehabilitative potential. Note that inquiry into specific instances of conduct is not permitted on direct examination, but may be made on cross-examination. Subsection (5) will allow a more complete presentation of information about the accused to the court-martial. The accused's character is in issue as part of the sentencing decision, since the sentence must be tailored to the offender. *Cf. United States v. Lania*, 9 M.J. 100 (C.M.A. 1980). Therefore, introduction of evidence of this nature should not be contingent solely upon the election of the defense. Information of a similar nature, from the accused's employer or neighbors, is often included in civilian presentencing reports. *See, e.g.,* Fed. R. Crim. P. 32(c)(2). Subsection (5) guards against unreliable information by guaranteeing that the accused will have the right to confront and cross-examine such witnesses.

1994 Amendment: The amendment is based on decisional law interpreting subsection (b)(5), including *United States v. Pompey*, 33 M.J. 266 (C.M.A. 1991), *United States v. Claxton*, 32 M.J. 159 (C.M.A. 1991), *United States v. Aurich*, 31 M.J. 95 (C.M.A. 1990), *United States v. Ohrt*, 28 M.J. 301 (C.M.A. 1989), and *United States v. Horner*, 22 M.J. 294 (C.M.A. 1986).

(e) *Production of witnesses.* The language of subsection (2)(C) has been modified to clarify that only a stipulation of fact permits nonproduction. *See United States v. Gonzalez*, 16 M.J. 58 (C.M.A. 1983).

2007 Amendment: Subsection (e)(2)(D) was amended to allow the availability of various types of remote testimony to be a factor to consider in whether a pre-sentencing witness must be physically produced.

(f) *Additional matters to be considered.* This subsection is based on the third and fourth sentences of paragraph 76 *a*(2) of MCM, 1969 (Rev.) and on the first sentence of paragraph 123 of MCM 1969 (Rev.). The discussion is based on the last two sentences of paragraph 123 of MCM, 1969 (Rev.).

(g) *Argument.* The last paragraph is new. *See Analysis*, R.C.M. 919(c). As to the second sentence, *see United States v. Grady*, 15 M.J. 275 (C.M.A. 1983).

Rule 1002 Sentence determination

This rule is based on the first sentence in paragraph 76 *a*(1) of MCM, 1969 (Rev.).

Rule 1003 Punishments

Introduction. This rule lists the punishments a court-martial is authorized to impose, and presents general limitations on punishments not provided in specific rules elsewhere. Limitations based on jurisdiction (*see* R.C.M. 201(f)); rehearings, other and new trials (*see* R.C.M. 810(d)); and on referral instructions (*see* R.C.M. 601(e)(1)) are contained elsewhere, but are referred to this rule. *See* subsection (c)(3) and discussion. The maximum punishments for each offense are listed in Part IV. The automatic suspension of limitations at paragraph of paragraph 127 *c*(5) of MCM, 1969 (Rev.) is deleted since the maximum punishments now include appropriate adjustments in the maximum authorized punishment in time of war or under other circumstances.

(a) *In general.* This subsection provides express authority for adjudging any authorized punishment in the case of any person tried by court-martial, subject only to specific limitations prescribed elsewhere. It does not change current law.

(b) *Authorized punishments.* This subsection lists those punishments which are authorized, rather than some which are prohibited. This approach is simpler and should eliminate questions about what punishments a court-martial may adjudge.

Subsection (1) is based on paragraph 126 *f* of MCM, 1969 (Rev.). Admonition has been deleted as unnecessary.

Subsection (2) is based on paragraphs 126 *h*(1) and (2) of MCM, 1969 (Rev.).

1990 Amendment: Subsection (b)(2) was amended to incorporate the statutory expansion of jurisdiction over inactive-duty reserve component personnel provided in the Military Justice Amendments of 1986, tit. VIII, § 804, National Defense Authorization Act for Fiscal Year 1987, Pub. L. 99-661, 100 Stat. 3905 (1986).

1994 Amendment: The references to "retired" and "retainer" pay was added to make clear that those forms of pay are subject to computation of forfeiture in the same way as basic pay. Articles 17, 18, and 19, UCMJ, do not distinguish between these types of pay. Sentences including forfeiture of these types of pay were affirmed in *United States v. Hooper*, 9 U.S.C.M.A. 637, 26 C.M.R. 417 (1958) (retired pay), and *United States v. Overton*, 24 M.J. 309 (C.M.A. 1987) (retainer pay).

2005 Amendment: Hardship Duty Pay (HDP) superseded Foreign Duty Pay (FDP) on 3 February 1999. HDP is payable to members entitled to basic pay. The Secretary of Defense has established that HDP will be paid to members (a) for performing specific missions, or (b) when assigned to designated areas.

Subsection (3) is based on paragraph 126 *h*(3) of MCM, 1969 (Rev.). *See* R.C.M. 1113(d)(4) and Analysis concerning possible issues raised by enforcing a fine through confinement.

Detention of pay (paragraph 126 *h*(4) of MCM, 1969 (Rev.)) has been deleted. This punishment has been used very seldom and is administratively cumbersome.

2002 Amendment: The amendment clearly defines the authority of special and summary courts-martial to adjudge both fines and forfeitures. *See generally United States v. Tualla*, 52 M.J. 228 (2000).

Subsection (4) is based on paragraph 126 *i* of MCM, 1969 (Rev.).

Subsection (5) is based on the second paragraph of paragraph 126 *e* of MCM, 1969 (Rev.). The first sentence in the discussion is based on the same paragraph. The second sentence in the discussion is based on the last sentence in the first paragraph of paragraph 126 *e* of MCM, 1969 (Rev.).

Subsection (6) is based on paragraph 126 *g* and on the ninth sentence of the second paragraph 127 *c*(2) of MCM, 1969 (Rev.). The equivalency of restriction and confinement has been incorporated here and is based on the table of equivalencies at paragraph 127 *c* (2) of MCM, 1969 (rev.). *See also* Article 20.

Subsection (7) and the discussion are based on paragraph 126 *k* of MCM, 1969 (Rev.). The last sentence in the rule is new and is based on the table of equivalent punishments at paragraph 127 *c*(2) of MCM, 1969 (Rev.) *See also* Article 20.

2002 Amendment: This change resulted from the enactment of Article 56a, UCMJ, in section 581 of the National Defense Authorization Act for Fiscal Year 1998, Pub. L. No. 105-85, 111 Stat. 1629, 1759 (1997).

Subsection (8) is based on paragraph 126 *j* of MCM, 1969 (Rev.). Matters in the second paragraph of paragraph 126 *j* of MCM, 1969 (Rev.) are now covered in R.C.M. 1113(d)(2)(A).

Subsection (9) is based on the last paragraph of paragraph 125 of MCM, 1969 (Rev.). The last sentence is new and is based on the table of equivalent punishments at paragraph 127 *c*(2) of MCM, 1969 (Rev.).

Subsection (10)(A) is based on the second paragraph of paragraph 126 *d* of MCM, 1969 (Rev.). Subsections (10)(B) and (C) are based on paragraphs 76 *a*(3) and (4) and 127 *c* (4) of MCM, 1969 (Rev.).

1986 Amendment: Under R.C.M. 1003(c)(2)(A)(iv), a warrant officer who is not commissioned can be punished by a dishonorable discharge when convicted at general court-martial of any offense. This continued the rule of paragraph 126 *d* of MCM, 1969 (Rev.). The second sentence of subsection (10)(B), added in 1985, does not make any substantive change, but merely restates the provision in subsection (10)(B) to maintain the parallelism with subsection (10)(A), which governs dismissal of commissioned officers, commissioned warrant officers, cadets, and midshipmen.

As to subsection (11), *see* R.C.M. 1004.

Subsection (12) is based on Article 18.

Subsections (6), (7), and (9) incorporate equivalencies for restriction, hard labor without confinement, confinement, and confinement on bread and water or diminished rations. This makes the table of equivalent punishments at paragraph 127 *c*(2) of MCM, 1969 (Rev.) unnecessary and it had been deleted. That table was confusing and subject to different interpretations. For example, the table and the accompanying discussion suggested that if the maximum punishment for an offense was confinement for 3 months and forfeiture of two-thirds pay per month, for 3 months, a court-martial could elect to adjudge confinement for 6 months and no forfeitures. The deletion of the table and inclusion of specific equivalencies where they apply eliminates the possibility of such a result.

1999 Amendment: Loss of numbers, lineal position, or seniority has been deleted. Although loss of numbers had the effect of lowering precedence for some purposes, *e.g.*, quarters priority, board and court seniority, and actual date of promotion, loss of numbers did not affect the officer's original position for purposes of consideration for retention or promotion. Accordingly, this punishment was deleted because of its negligible consequences and the misconception that it was a meaningful punishment.

(c) *Limits on punishments.* Subsections (1)(A) and (B) are based on paragraph 127 *c*(1) of MCM, 1969 (Rev.). Subsection (1)(C) is based on the first 3 sentences and the last sentence of paragraph 76 *a*(5) of MCM, 1969 (Rev.). *See Blockburger v. United States*, 284 U.S. 299 (1932); *United States v. Washington*, 1 M.J. 473 (C.M.A. 1976). *See also Missouri v. Hunter*, 459 U.S. 359 (1983); *United States v. Baker*, 14 M.J. 361 (C.M.A. 1983). The discussion is based on paragraph 76 *a*(5) of MCM, 1969 (Rev.). As to the third paragraph in the discussion, *see e.g., United States v. Posnick*, 8 U.S.C.M.A. 201, 24 C.M.R. 11 (1957). *Cf. United States v. Stegall*, 6 M.J. 176 (C.M.A. 1979). As to the fourth paragraph in the discussion, *see United States v. Harrison*, 4 M.J. 332 (C.M.A. 1978); *United States v. Irving*, 3 M.J. 6 (C.M.A. 1977); *United States v. Hughes*, 1 M.J. 346 (C.M.A. 1976); *United States v. Burney*, 21 U.S.C.M.A. 71, 44 C.M.R. 125 (1971).

Subsection (2)(A) is based on paragraph 126 *d* of MCM, 1969 (Rev.). Paragraph 127 *a* of MCM, 1969 (Rev.) provided that the maximum punishments were "not binding" in cases of officers, but could "be used as a guide." Read in conjunction with paragraph 126 *d* of MCM, 1969 (Rev.) these provisions had the practical effect of prescribing no limits on forfeitures when the accused is an officer. This distinction has now been deleted. The maximum limits on forfeitures are the same for officers and enlisted persons.

Subsection (3) is based on paragraph 127 *b* of MCM, 1969 (Rev.). It serves as a reminder that the limits on punishments may be affected by other rules, which are referred to in the discussion.

The last sentence in subsections (1) and (2) is new. Under R.C.M. 1001(b)(3), a court-martial conviction may now be considered by the sentencing body whether or not it is final. Allowing such a conviction to affect the maximum punishment may cause later problems, however. The subsequent reversal of a conviction would seldom affect a sentence of another court-martial where that conviction was merely a factor which was considered, especially when the pendency of an appeal may also have been considered. However, reversal would always affect the validity of any later discharge or confinement for which it provided the basis.

1986 Amendment: Subsection (c)(3) was redesignated as subsection (c)(4) and new subsection (c)(3) was added to reflect the legislative restrictions placed upon punishment of reserve component personnel in certain circumstances in the amendment to Article 2, UCMJ, contained in the "Military Justice Amendments of 1986," tit. VIII, § 804, National Defense Authorization Act for Fiscal Year 1987, Pub.L. No. 99-661, 100 Stat. 3905 (1986).

(d) *Circumstances permitting increased punishments.* This subsection is based on Section B of the Table of Maximum Punishments, paragraph 127 *c* of MCM, 1969 (Rev.). *See also United States v. Timmons*, 13 M.J. 431 (C.M.A. 1982). The last two sentences in the discussion are based on *United States v. Mack*, 9 M.J. 300 (C.M.A. 1980); *United States v. Booker*, 5 M.J. 238 (C.M.A. 1977), *vacated in part,* 5 M.J. 246 (C.M.A. 1978). *Cf. United States v. Cofield*, 11 M.J. 422 (C.M.A. 1981).

1995 Amendment: Punishment of confinement on bread and water or diminished rations (R.C.M. 1003(d)(9)), as a punishment imposable by a court-martial, was deleted. Confinement on bread and water or diminished rations was originally intended as an immediate, remedial punishment. While this is still the case with nonjudicial punishment (Article 15), it is not effective as a court-martial punishment. Subsections (d)(10) through (d)(12) were redesignated (d)(9) through (d)(11), respectively.

Rule 1004 Capital cases

Introduction. This rule is new. It provides additional standards and procedures governing determination of a sentence in capital cases. It is based on the President's authority under Articles 18, 36, and 56. *See also* U.S. Const. Art. II, sec. 2, cl. 1.

This rule and the analysis were drafted before the Court of Military Appeals issued its decision in *United States v. Matthews*, 16 M.J. 354 (C.M.A. 1983) on October 11, 1983. There the court reversed the sentence of death because of the absence of a requirement for the members to specifically find aggravating circumstances on which the sentence was based. When this rule was drafted, the procedures for capital cases were the subject of litigation in *Matthews* and other cases. *See e.g., United States v. Matthews*, 13 M.J. 501 (A.C.M.R. 1982), *rev'd, United States v. Matthews, supra; United States v. Rojas*, 15 M.J. 902 (N.M.C.M.R. 1983). *See also United States v. Gay*, 16 M.J. 586 (A.F.C.M.R. 1982),*a'ffd* 18 M.J. 104 (1984) (decided after draft MCM was circulated for comment). The rule was drafted in recognition that, as a matter of policy, procedures for the sentence determination in capital cases should be revised, regardless of the outcome of such litigation, in order to better protect the rights of servicemembers.

While the draft Manual was under review following public comment on it (*see* 48 Fed. Reg. 23688 (1983)), the *Matthews* decision was issued. The holding in *Matthews* generated a necessity to revise procedures in capital cases. However, *Matthews* did not require substantive revision of the proposed R.C.M. 1004. The several modifications made in the rule since it was circulated for comment were based on suggestions from other sources. They are unrelated to any of the issues involved in *Matthews*.

Capital punishment is not unconstitutional *per se*. *Gregg v. Georgia*, 428 U.S. 153 (1976); *United States v. Matthews, supra.* Capital punishment does not violate Article 55. *Compare* Article 55 with Articles 85, 90, 94, 99-102, 104, 106, 110, 113, 118, and 120. *See United States v. Matthews, supra.* But *cf. Id.* at 382 (Fletcher, J., concurring in result) (absent additional procedural requirements, sentence of death violated Article 55). The Supreme Court has established that capital punishment does not violate the Eighth Amendment (U.S. Const. amend. VIII) unless it: "makes no measurable contribution to acceptable goals of punishment and hence is nothing more than a purposeless and needless imposition of pain and suffering"; "is grossly out of proportion to the crime" (*Coker v. Georgia,* 433 U.S. 584, 592 (1977)); or is adjudged under procedures which do not adequately protect against the arbitrary or capricious exercise of discretion in determining a sentence. *Furman v. Georgia*, 408 U.S. 238 (1972). *Cf. Barclay v. Florida*, 463 U.S. 939 (1983); *Zant v. Stephens,* 462 U.S. 862 (1983); *Godfrey v. Georgia,* 446 U.S. 420 (1980); *Jurek v. Texas,* 428 U.S. 262 (1976); *Proffitt v. Florida*, 428 U.S. 242 (1976); *Gregg v. Georgia, supra. See United States v. Matthews, supra.* Furthermore, while the procedures under which death may be adjudged must adequately protect against the unrestrained exercise of discretion, they may not completely foreclose discretion (at least in most cases, *see* subsection (e), *infra*) or the consideration of extenuating or mitigating circumstances. *See Eddings v. Oklahoma*, 455 U.S. 104 (1982); *Lockett v. Ohio*, 438 U.S. 586 (1978); *Roberts (Harry) v. Louisiana*, 431 U.S. 633 (1977); *Roberts (Stanislaus) v. Louisiana*, 428 U.S. 325 (1976); *Woodson v. North Carolina*, 428 U.S. 280 (1976). In *Matthews* the Court of Military Appeals suggested that similar considerations apply with respect to Article 55's prohibitions against cruel and unusual punishment. *United States v. Matthews, supra* at 368–69, 379–80.

The Court of Military Appeals listed several requirements for adjudication of the death penalty, based on Supreme Court decisions: (1) a separate sentencing procedure must follow the finding of guilt of a potential capital offense; (2) specific aggravating circumstances must be identified to the sentencing authority; (3) the sentencing authority must select and make findings on the particular aggravating circumstances used as a basis for imposing the death sentence; (4) the defendant must have an unrestricted opportunity to present mitigating and extenuating evidence; and (5) mandatory appellate review must be required to consider the propriety of the sentence as to the individual offense and individual defendant and to compare the sentence to similar cases within the jurisdiction. *See United States v. Matthews, supra* at 369–77 and cases cited therein.

The Supreme Court has not decided whether *Furman v. Georgia, supra,* and subsequent decisions concerning capital punishment apply to courts-martial. *See Schick v. Reed*, 419 U.S. 256 (1974). *But see Furman v. Georgia, supra* at 412 (Blackmun, J., dissenting); *id.* at 417–18 (Powell, J., dissenting). *See generally* Pfau and Milhizer, *The Military Death Penalty and the Constitution: There is Life After Furman,* 97 Mil.L.Rev. 35 (1982); Pavlick, *The Constitutionality of the UCMJ Death Penalty Provisions,* 97 Mil.L.Rev. 81 (1982); Comment, *The Death Penalty in Military Courts: Constitutionally Imposed?* 30 UCLA L. Rev. 366 (1982); Dawson, *Is the Death Penalty in the Military Cruel and Unusual?* 31 JAG J. (Navy) 53 (1980); English, *The Constitutionality of the Court-Martial Death Sentence,* 21 A.F.L. Rev. 552 (1979).

The Court of Military Appeals held in *United States v. Matthews, supra*, that the requirements established by the Supreme Court for civilian cases apply in courts-martial, at least in the absence of circumstances calling for different rules, such as combat conditions or wartime spying. *United States v. Matthews, supra* at 368. The court added that current military capital sentencing procedures are constitutionally adequate in the following respects: (1) there is a separate sentencing process in which the members are instructed by the military judge as to their duties; (2) certain aggravating factors (*e.g.*, premeditation) must be found by the members during findings, and evidence of other aggravating circumstances may be submitted during sentencing; (3) the accused has an unlimited opportunity to present relevant evidence in extenuation and mitigation; and (4) mandatory review is required by a Court of Military Review, and the Court of Military Appeals, with further consideration by the President. *United States v. Matthews, supra* at 377–78. The court held that the procedure is defective, however, in that the members are not required to "specifically identify the aggravating factors upon which they have relied in choosing to impose the death penalty," *id.* at 379, at least with respect to a peacetime murder case. *See id.* at 368.

The Court of Military Appeals stated in*Matthews* that constitutionally adequate procedures for capital cases may be promulgated by the President. *Id.* at 380–81. The President's unique authority over military justice, particularly its procedure and punishments is well established. *See* U.S. Const. Art. II, § 2, cl. 1; Articles 18, 36, and 56. Congress recently reaffirmed the broad scope of this Presidential authority. *See* Pub.L. No. 96-107, Title VIII, § 801(b), 93 Stat. 811 (Nov. 9, 1979); S.Rep. No. 107, 96th Cong., 1st Sess. 123–125 (1979); *Hearings on S.428 Before the Military Personnel Subcomm. of the House Comm. on Armed Services,* 96th Cong., 1st Sess. 5–6, 14, 17–18, 20–21, 52, 106 (1979). *See also United States v. Ezell*, 6 M.J. 307, 316–17 (C.M.A. 1978); W. Winthrop, *Military Law and Precedents* 27–33 (2d ed. 1920 reprint). *Cf. Jurek v. Texas, supra* (judicial construction may save an otherwise defective death penalty provision). The changes made in this rule are procedural. *See Dobbert v. Florida*, 432 U.S. 282 (1977).

R.C.M. 1004 is based on the recognition that, in courts-martial, as in civilian prosecution, death should be adjudged only under carefully tailored procedures designed to ensure that all relevant matters are thoroughly considered and that such punishment is appropriate.

At the same time, R.C.M. 1004 rests on the conclusion that the death penalty remains a necessary sanction in courts-martial and that it is an appropriate punishment under a broader range of circumstances than may be the case in civilian jurisdictions. This is because of the unique purpose and organization of the military, and its composition and the circumstances in which it operates. *Cf. Parker v. Levy*, 417 U.S. 733 (1974). *See also United States v. Matthews, supra* at 368.

1986 Amendment: The Rule was amended to substitute the

word "factor" for the word "circumstance" with respect to the aggravating factors under R.C.M. 1004(c). This will more clearly distinguish such factors from the aggravating circumstances applicable to any sentencing proceeding under R.C.M. 1001(b)(4), which may be considered in the balancing process in capital cases under R.C.M. 1004(b)(4)(B).

(a) *In general.* Subsection (1) is based on the code and reflects the first of two "thresholds" before death may be adjudged; the accused must have been found guilty of an offense for which death is authorized.

1986 Amendment: Subsection (2), referred to below in the original Analysis, was redesignated as subsection (3), and a new subsection (2) was added. The new subsection requires a unanimous verdict on findings before the death penalty may be considered. Nothing in this provision changes existing law under which a finding of guilty may be based upon a vote of two-thirds of the members, and a finding based upon a two-thirds vote will continue to provide the basis for sentencing proceedings in which any sentence other than death may be imposed. This is an exercise of the President's powers as commander-in-chief, and is not intended to cast doubt upon the validity of the sentence in any capital case tried before the effective date of the amendments.

Subsection (2) refers to the remaining tests in subsections (b) and (c) of the rule; the prosecution must prove, beyond a reasonable doubt, the existence of one or more aggravating circumstances listed in subsection (c) of the rule. Only if this second threshold is passed may the members consider death. If the members reach this point, their sentencing deliberations and procedures would be like those in any other case, except that the members must apply an additional specific standard before they may adjudge death. *See* subsection (b)(3) of this rule.

This rule thus combines two preliminary tests which must be met before death may be adjudged with a standard which must be applied before death may be adjudged. *Cf. Barclay v. Florida* and *Zant v. Stephens, both supra.* The Working Group considered the capital punishment provisions of those states which now authorize capital punishment, as well as the *ALI Model Penal Code* § 201.6(3), (4) (Tent. Draft No. 9, 1959) (quoted at *Gregg. v. Georgia, supra* at 193 n.44). The ABA Standards do not include specific provisions for capital punishment. *See ABA Standards, Sentencing Alternatives and Procedures* § 18–1.1 (1979). This rule is not based on any specific state statue. It should be noted, however, that this rule provides a greater measure of guidance for members than does the Georgia procedure which has been upheld by the Supreme Court. In Georgia, once a statutory aggravating factor has been proved, the statute leaves the decision whether to adjudge death entirely to the jury. *See* Ga. Code Ann. §§ 17–10–30, 17–10–31 (1982). (In Georgia, once an aggravating factor has been proved, the burden may effectively be on the defendant to show why death should not be adjudged. *See Coker v. Georgia, supra* at 590-91.) Subsection (b)(4)(B) of this rule supplies a standard for that decision. Many state statutes adopt a similar balancing test, although the specific standard to be applied varies. *See e.g.,* Ark. Stat. Ann. § 41–1302 (1977). *Cf. Barclay v. Florida, supra. See also* Analysis, subsection (b)(4)(B), *infra.*

(b) *Procedure.* Subsection (1) is intended to avoid surprise and trial delays. *Cf.* Ga. Code Ann. § 17–10 2(a)(1982). Consistent with R.C.M. 701, its purpose is to put the defense on notice of issues in the case. This permits thorough preparation, and makes possible early submission of requests to produce witnesses or evidence. At the same time, this subsection affords some latitude to the prosecution to provide later notice, recognizing that the exigencies of proof may prevent early notice in some cases. This is permissible as long as the defense is not harmed; ordinarily a continuance or recess will prevent such prejudice.

2005 Amendment: Subsection (1)(A) is intended to provide early and definitive notice that the case has been referred for trial as a capital case. Subsection (1)(B) is intended to provide the defense written notice of the aggravating factors it intends to prove, yet afford some latitude to the prosecution to provide later notice, recognizing that the exigencies of proof may prevent early notice in some cases.

Subsection (2) makes clear that the prosecution may introduce evidence in aggravation under R.C.M. 1001(b)(4). Note that depositions are not admissible for this purpose. *See* Article 49(d).

Subsection (3) is based on *Eddings v. Oklahoma* and *Lockett v. Ohio*, both *supra, Cf. Jurek v. Texas, supra.* The accused in courts-martial generally has broad latitude to introduce matters in extenuation and mitigation (*see* R.C.M. 1001(c)) although the form in which they are introduced may depend on several circumstances (*see* R.C.M. 1001(e)). This subsection reemphasizes that latitude. The rule is not intended to strip the military judge of authority to control the proceedings. *Eddings* and *Lockett* should not be read so broadly as to divest the military judge of the power to determine what is relevant (*see* Mil. R. Evid. 401, 403) or so decide when a witness must be produced (*see* R.C.M. 1001(e)). Those cases, and this subsection, stand for the proposition that the defense may not be prevented from presenting any relevant circumstances in extenuation or mitigation.

Subsection(4)(A) establishes the second "threshold" which must be passed before death may be adjudged. The requirement that at least one specific aggravating circumstance be found beyond a reasonable doubt is common to many state statutory schemes for capital punishment. *See, e.g.,* Del. Code Ann. tit. 11, § 4209(d)(1977); Ark. Stat. Ann. § 41–1302(1977); Ill. Ann. Stat. Ch. 38, § 9–1(f) (Smith-Hurd 1979), La. Code Crim. Proc. § 905.3 (West Supp 1982); Md. Ann. Code Art. 27 § 413(d)(1982); Ind. Code Ann. § 35–50–2–9(a)(Burns 1979). *See generally United States v. Matthews, supra.*

Subsection (4)(B) establishes guidance for the members in determining whether to adjudge death, once one or more aggravating factors have been found.

Note that under this subsection any aggravating matter may be considered in determining whether death or some other punishment is appropriate. Thus, while some factors may alone not be sufficient to authorize death they may be relevant considerations to weigh against extenuating or mitigating evidence. *See Barclay v. Florida* and *Zant v. Stephens, both supra. See generally* R.C.M. 1001(b)(4).

The rule does not list extenuating or mitigating circumstances as do some states. Some mitigating circumstances are listed in R.C.M. 1001(c)(1) and (f)(1). *See also* R.C.M. 1001(f)(2)(B). No list of extenuating or mitigating circumstances can safely be considered exhaustive. *See Eddings v. Oklahoma* and *Lockett v. Ohio, both supra;* cf.*Jurek v. Texas, supra.* Moreover, in many cases, whether a matter is either extenuating or mitigating depends on other factors. For example, the fact that the accused was under the influence of alcohol or drugs at the time of the offense could be viewed as an aggravating or an extenuating circumstance. Whether a matter is extenuating or mitigating is to be determined by each member, unless the military judge finds that a matter is extenuating or mitigating as a matter of law *(see e.g.,* R.C.M. 1001(c)(1) and (f)(1)) and so instructs the members. In contrast to subsection (b)(4)(A) there is no requirement that the members agree on all aggravating, extenuating, and mitigating circumstances under subsection (4)(B) in order to adjudge death. Each member must be satisfied that any aggravating circumstances, including those found under subsection (4)(A) substantially outweigh any extenuating or mitigating circumstances, before voting to adjudge death.

The test is not a mechanical one. *Cf. Zant v. Stephens, supra.* The latitude to introduce evidence in extenuation and mitigation, the requirement that the military judge direct the members' attention to evidence in extenuating and mitigation and instruct them that they must consider it, and the freedom of each member to independently find and weigh extenuating and mitigating circumstances all ensure that the members treat the accused "with that degree of uniqueness of the individual" necessary in a capital case. *See Lockett v. Ohio, supra* at 605. Thus each member may place on the scales any circumstance " [which in fairness and mercy, may be considered as extenuating or reducing the degree] of moral culpability or punishment." *Coker v. Georgia, supra* at 591 (1977) (quoting instructions by the trial judge). *See also Witherspoon v. Illinois*, 391 U.S. 510 (1968) (concerning disqualifications of jurors in capital cases based on attitude toward the death penalty).

1986 Amendment: The following stylistic changes were made in R.C.M. 1004(b)(4): first, subparagraph (a) was rewritten to provide that the members must find "at least" one factor under subsection (c); second, a new subparagraph (b) was added to underscore the notice and unanimity requirements with respect to the aggravating factors and to clarify that all members concur in the same factor or factors; and third, former subparagraph (B) was redesignated as subparagraph (C), with an express cross-reference to R.C.M. 1001(b)(4), the general rule governing aggravating circumstances in sentencing proceedings.

Subsection (5) makes clear the evidence introduced on the merits, as well as during sentencing proceedings, may be considered in determining the sentence.

Subsection (6) requires additional instructions in capital cases. *See also* R.C.M. 1005. In determining which aggravating circumstances on which to instruct, the military judge would refer to those of which the trial counsel provided notice. Even if such notice had been given, a failure to introduce some evidence from which the members could find an aggravating circumstance would result in no instruction being given on that circumstance. *Cf.* R.C.M. 917 The last sentence in this subsection is based on *Eddings v. Oklahoma* and *Lockett v. Ohio,* both*supra.*

Subsection (7) is based on Article 52(b)(1). The requirement for a separate specific finding of one or more aggravating circumstances is new, and is designed to help ensure that death will not be adjudged in an inappropriate case. Subsection (8) operates as a check on this procedure.

(c) *Aggravating circumstances.* The lists of aggravating circumstances under the laws of the states retaining capital punishment were examined and used as guidance for formulating the aggravating circumstances listed here. Those jurisdictions do not include certain military capital offenses, of course, such as desertion, mutiny, misbehavior as a guard, nor do they address some of the unique concerns or problems of military life. Therefore, several circumstances here are unique to the military. These circumstances, which apply to rape and murder, except as specifically noted, are based on the determination that death is not grossly disproportionate for a capital offense under the code when such circumstances exist, and that the death penalty contributes to accepted goals of punishment in such cases. As to proportionality, the aggravating circumstances together ensure that death will not be adjudged except in the most serious capital offenses against other individuals or against the nation or the military order which protects it. As to goals of punishment, in addition to specifically preventing the most dangerous offenders from posing a continuing danger to society, the aggravating circumstances recognize the role of general deterrence, especially in combat setting. *See United States v. Matthews, supra* at 368,; *United States v. Gay, supra* at 605–06 (Hodgson, C.J., concurring).

In a combat setting, the potentiality of the death penalty may be the only effective deterrent to offenses such as disobedience, desertion, or misbehavior. The threat of even very lengthy confinement may be insufficient to induce some persons to undergo the substantial risk of death in combat. At the same time, the rule ensures that even a servicemember convicted of such very serious offenses in wartime will not be sentenced to death in the absence of one or more of the aggravating circumstances.

In some cases proof of the offense will also prove an aggravating circumstance. *See e.g.,* Article 99 and subsection(c)(1) of this rule. Note, however, that the members would have to return a specific finding under this rule of such an aggravating circumstance before a sentence of death could be based on it. This ensures a unanimous finding as to that circumstance. A finding of not guilty does not ensure such unanimity. *See* Article 52(a)(2); *United States v. Matthews, supra* at 379–80; *United States v. Gay, supra* at 600. The prosecution is not precluded from presenting evidence of additional aggravating circumstances.

Subsection (1) reflects the serious effect of a capital offense committed before or in the presence of the enemy. "Before or in the presence of the enemy" is defined in paragraph 23, Part IV. Note that one may be "before or in the presence of the enemy" even when in friendly territory. This distinguishes this subsection from subsection (6).

Subsection (2) and (3) are based on the military's purpose: protection of national security. That this interest may be basis for the death penalty is well established. *See e.g., United States v. Rosenberg*, 195 F.2d 583 (2d Cir. 1952), *cert. denied*, 344 U.S. 838 (1952). The definition of national security, which appears at the end of subsection (c), is based on Exec. Order No. 12065 § 6–104 (June 28, 1978), 43 Fed.Reg. 28949, as amended by Exec. Order No. 12148 (July 19, 1979), 44 Fed.Reg. 43239, and Exec. Order No. 12163 (Sept. 29, 1979), 44 Fed.Reg. 56673, *reprinted at* 50 U.S.C.A. § 401 (West Supp 1982). The second ("includes") phrase is based on Joint Chiefs of Staff Publication 1. Dictionary of Military and Associated Terms 228 (1 July 79). Note that not all harm to national security will authorize death. Virtually all military activities affect national security in some way. *Cf. Cole v. Young*, 351 U.S. 536 (1956); *United States v. Trottier*, 9 M.J. 337 (C.M.A. 1980). Substantial damage is required to authorize death. The discussion provides examples of substantial damage.

Rape and murder may be aggravated under subsection (2) because the offender intended to harm national security or a mission, system, or function affecting national security, by the capital offense. Intent to harm the mission, system, or function will suffice. It must be shown, however, that regardless of whether the accused intended to affect national security, the mission, system, or function must have been such that had the intended damage been effected, substantial damage to national security would have resulted.

1986 Amendment: R.C.M. 1004(c)(2) was changed in conjunction with the enactment of the new Article 106 *a*.

Subsection (4) is similar to an aggravating circumstance in many states. *See, e.g.,* Neb. Rev. Stat. § 29-2523(1)(f)(1979); Miss. Code. Ann. § 99–19–101(5)(c)(1981 Supp.); Ga. Code Ann. § 17–10–30(b)(1982). This circumstance applies to all capital offenses (except rape) under the code; rape is excluded based on*Coker v. Georgia, supra.*

1986 Amendment: R.C.M. 1004(c)(4) was amended by adding a reference to Article 106a to distinguish this factor from the new aggravating factor in R.C.M. 1004(c)(12). It was also considered appropriate to exclude 104 from this aggravating factor. *See* R.C.M. 1004(c)(11).

1994 Amendment: R.C.M. 1004(c)(4) was amended to clarify that only one person other than the victim need be endangered by the inherently dangerous act to qualify as an aggravating factor. *See United States v. Berg*, 31 M.J. 38 (C.M.A. 1990); *United States v. McMonagle*, 38 M.J. 53 (C.M.A. 1993).

Subsection (5) reflects the special need to deter the offender who would desert or commit any other capital offense to avoid hazardous duty. Moreover, the effect such conduct has on the safety of others (including the offender's replacement) and the success of the mission justified authorizing death. Note that this circumstance applies to all capital offenses, including rape and murder. The person who murders or rapes in order to avoid hazardous duty is hardly less culpable than one who "only" runs away.

Subsection (6) is based on the special needs and unique difficulties for maintaining discipline in combat zones and occupied territories. History has demonstrated that in such an environment rape and murder become more tempting. At the same time the need for order in the force, in order not to encourage resistance by the enemy and to pacify the populace, dictates that the sanctions for such offenses be severe. Once again, in a combat environment, confinement, even of a prolonged nature, may be an inadequate deterrent.

Subsections (7) and (8) are based generally on examination of the aggravating circumstances for murder in various states. Subsection (7)(A) is intended to apply whether the sentence is adjudged, approved, or ordered executed, as long as, at the time of the offense, the term of confinement is at least 30 years or for life. The possibility of parole or early release because of "good time" or similar reasons does not affect the determination. Subsection (7)(F) is based on 18 U.S.C. §§ 351, 1114, and 11751. Subsection (7)(G) is modified to include certain categories of military persons. Subsection (7)(1) uses a more objective standard that the Georgia provision found wanting in *Godfrey v. Georgia, supra.*

1994 Amendment: Subsection (7)(B) was amended by adding an additional aggravating factor for premeditated murder--the fact that the murder was drug-related. This change reflects a growing awareness of the fact that the business of trafficking in controlled substances has become increasingly deadly in recent years. Current federal statutes provide for a maximum punishment including the death penalty for certain drug-related killings. *See* 21 U.S.C. § 848(e) (Pub. L. 100-690, §7001(a)(2)).

1986 Amendment: Three changes were made in R.C.M. 1004(c)(7)(F); first, the provision involving Members of Congress was expanded to include Delegates and Resident commissioners; second, the word "justice" was added to ensure that justices of the Supreme Court were covered; and third, the provision was extended to include foreign leaders in specified circumstances. These changes are similar to legislation approved by the Senate in S. 1765, 98th Cong., 1st Sess. (1983).

1994 Amendment: The amendment to subsection (c)(7)(I) of this rule defines "substantial physical harm" and was added to clarify the type of injury that would qualify as an aggravating factor under the subsection. The definition of "substantial physical harm" is synonymous with "great bodily harm" and "grievous bodily harm". *See* Part IV, paragraph 43(c). With respect to the term "substantial mental or physical pain and suffering", *see United States v. Murphy*, 30 M.J. 1040, 1056-1058 (ACMR 1990).

1999 Amendment: R.C.M. 1004(c)(7)(K) was added to afford greater protection to victims who are especially vulnerable due to their age.

1991 Amendment: Subsection (c)(8) was based on the Supreme Court's decision in *Enmund v. Florida*, 458 U.S. 782, 797 (1982), that the cruel and unusual punishment clause of the Eighth Amendment prohibits imposition of the death penalty on a defendant convicted of felony-murder [who] d[id] not himself kill, attempt to kill, or intend that a killing take place or that lethal force ... be employed. The amendment to subsection (c)(8) is based on the Supreme Court's decision in *Tison v. Arizona*, 481 U.S. 137 (1987) distinguishing *Enmund*. In *Tison,* the Court held that the *Enmund* culpability requirement is satisfied when a defendant convicted of felony-murder was a major participant in the felony committed and manifested a reckless indifference to human life.

Subsection (9) is based on the holding in *Coker v. Georgia, supra*, that the death penalty is unconstitutional for the rape of an adult woman, at least where she is not otherwise harmed.

Subsection (10) is based on Article 18. *See also Trial of the Major War Criminals Before the International Military Tribunal* (International Military Tribunal, Nurenberg, 1974); *Trials of War Criminals Before the Nurenberg Military Tribunals,* (U.S. Gov't Printing Off., 1950–51); *In re Yamashita,* 327 U.S. 1 (1946).

1986 Amendment: R.C.M. 1004(c)(11) was added to implement the statutory aggravating factors found in new Article 106 *a*. The aggravating factors in R.C.M. 1004(c)(11) were also considered appropriate for violations of Article 104. It is intended that the phrase "imprisonment for life was authorized by statute" in Article 106 *a*(c)(1) include offenses for which the President has authorized confinement for life in this Manual as authorized in Articles 18 and 55 (10 U.S.C. §§ 818 and 855).

2007 Amendment: Changes to this paragraph adding sexual offenses other than rape are based on subsection (d) of section 552 of the National Defense Authorization Act for Fiscal Year 2006, P.L. 109-163, 6 January 2006, which supersedes the previous paragraph 45, Rape and Carnal Knowledge, in its entirety and replaces paragraph 45 with Rape, sexual assault and other sexual misconduct.

(d) *Spying.* This subsection is based on Article 106. Congress recognized that in case of spying, no separate sentencing determination is required. *See* Article 52(a)(1). The rule provides for sentencing proceedings to take place, so that reviewing authorities will have the benefit of any additional relevant information.

The Supreme Court has held a mandatory death penalty to be unconstitutional for murder. *Woodson v. North Carolina, supra; Roberts (Stanislaus) v. Louisiana, supra.* It has not held that a mandatory death penalty is unconstitutional for any offense. *See Roberts (Harry) v. Louisiana, supra* at 637 n. 5.

In holding a mandatory death sentence for murder to be unconstitutional, the plurality in *Woodson* emphasized that the prevailing view before *Furman v. Georgia, supra,* was decidedly against mandatory death for murder. Contrarily, death has consistently been the sole penalty for spying in wartime since 1806. *See* W. Winthrop, *Military Law and Precedents* 765–66 (2d ed. 1920 reprint). Before 1920 the statue making spying in time of war triable by court-martial and punishable by death was not part of the Articles of War. *Id. See* A.W. 82 (Act of 4 June 1920, Ch. 227, 41 Stat. 804).

(e) *Other penalties.* The second sentence of this subsection is based on the second sentence of the third paragraph of paragraph 126 *a* of MCM, 1969 (Rev.), which was in turn based on JAGA 1946/10582; SPJGA 1945/9511; *United States v. Brewster*, CM 238138, 24 B.R. 173 (1943). As to the third sentence of this subsection,*see also United States v. Bigger*, 2 U.S.C.M.A. 297, 8 C.M.R. 97 (1953); W. Winthrop, *supra* at 428, 434.

2002 Amendment: This change resulted from the enactment of Article 56a, UCMJ, in section 581 of the National Defense Authorization Act for Fiscal Year 1998, Pub. L. No. 105-85, 111 Stat. 1629, 1759 (1997).

Rule 1005 Instructions on sentence

Introduction. Except as noted below, this rule and the discussion are taken from paragraph 76 *b*(1) of MCM, 1969 (Rev.).

(a) *In general.* Regarding the discussion *see generally United States v. Mamaluy*, 10 U.S.C.M.A. 102, 106-07, 27 C.M.R. 176, 180-81 (1959). *See also United States v. Lania*, 9 M.J. 100 (C.M.A. 1980)(use of general deterrence); *United States v. Smalls*, 6 M.J. 346 (C.M.A. 1979); *United States v. Slaton*, 6 M.J. 254 (C.M.A. 1979) (mental impairment as matter in mitigation); *United States v. Keith*, 22 U.S.C.M.A. 59, 46 C.M.R. 59 (1972) (recommendation for clemency); *United States v. Condon*, 42 C.M.R. 421 (A.C.M.R. 1970) (effect of accused's absence); *United States v. Larochelle*, 41 C.M.R. 915 A.F.C.M.R. 1969) (Vietnam service).

(b) *When given. See* Fed. R. Crim. P. 30 and paragraph 74 *e* of MCM, 1969 (Rev.).

(c) *Requests for instructions. See* Fed. R. Crim. P. 30 and*United States v. Neal*, 17 U.S.C.M.A. 363, 38 C.M.R. 161 (1968). The discussion is based on Fed. R. Crim. P. 30 and paragraph 73 *d* of MCM, 1969 (Rev.).

(d) *How given. See* Analysis, R.C.M. 921(d).

(e) *Required instructions.* The reference in the fourth sentence of the discussion of subsection (1) to rehearing or new or other trial is based on paragraph 81 *d*(1) of MCM, 1969 (Rev.). The second sentence of the first paragraph and the second paragraph of the discussion to (1) are based on *United States v. Henderson*, 11 M.J. 395 (C.M.A. 1981). The last clause of subsection (3) is based on *United States v. Givens*, 11 M.J. 694, 696 (N.M.C.M.R. 1981). The discussion under subsection (4) is based on the third sentence of paragraph 76 *b*(1) of MCM, 1969 (Rev.) and on*United States v. Davidson*, 14 M.J. 81 (C.M.A. 1982).

1998 Amendment: The requirement to instruct members on the effect a sentence including a punitive discharge and confinement, or confinement exceeding six months, may have on adjudged forfeitures was made necessary by the creation of Article 58b, UCMJ, in section 1122, National Defense Authorization Act for Fiscal Year 1996, Pub. L. No. 104-106, 110 Stat. 186, 463 (1996).

(f) *Waived.* This subsection is based on Fed. R. Crim. P. 30.

Rule 1006 Deliberations and voting on sentence

Introduction. Except as noted below, this rule and the discussion are based on Articles 51 and 52 and on paragraphs 76 *b*(2) and (3) of MCM, 1969 (Rev.).

(a) *In general.* The first sentence is based on the first sentence of paragraph 76 *b*(1) of MCM, 1969 (Rev.).

(b) *Deliberations. See* Analysis, R.C.M. 921(b) concerning the second, third, and fourth sentences of this subsection. *See also United States v. Lampani*, 14 M.J. 22 (C.M.A. 1982).

(c) *Proposal of sentences.* The second clause of the second sentence of this subsection is new and recognizes the unitary sentence concept. *See United States v. Gutierrez*, 11 M.J. 122, 123 (C.M.A.1981). *See generally Jackson v. Taylor*, 353 U.S. 569 (1957).

2002 Amendment: This change to the discussion resulted from the enactment of Article 56a, UCMJ, in section 581 of the National Defense Authorization Act for Fiscal Year 1998, Pub. L. No. 105-85, 111 Stat. 1629, 1759 (1997).

(d) *Voting.* As to subsection (3)(A) *see United States v. Hendon*, 6 M.J. 171, 172–73 (C.M.A. 1979); *United States v. Cates*, 39 C.M.R. 474 (A.B.R. 1968).

2002 Amendment: Subsection (d)(4)(B) was amended as a result of the enactment of Article 56a, UCMJ, in section 581 of the National Defense Authorization Act for Fiscal Year 1998, Pub. L. No. 105-85, 111 Stat. 1629, 1759 (1997).

As to subsection (d)(5), the second sentence of the third paragraph of paragraph 76 *b*(2) of MCM, 1969 (Rev.) has been limited to Article 118 offenses because, unlike Article 106, findings on an Article 118 offense do not automatically determine the sentence and do not require a unanimous vote. *See* Articles 52(a)(1) and (2). Thus a separate vote on sentence for an Article 105 offense is unnecessary.

As to subsection (d)(6) *see United States v. Jones* , 14 U.S.C.M.A. 177, 33 C.M.R. 389 (1963). The reference to no punishment was added to recognize this added alternative.

(e) *Action after sentence is reached. See United States v. Justice*, 3 M.J. 451, 453 (C.M.A. 1977). The second paragraph of the discussion is based on the second sentence of paragraph 76 *c*.

Rule 1007 Announcement of sentence

Introduction. Except as noted below, this rule and the discussion are based on paragraph 76 *c* of MCM, 1969 (Rev.).

(a) *In general.* The discussion is based on *United States v. Henderson* , 11 M.J. 395 (C.M.A. 1981); *United States v. Crawford,* 12 U.S.C.M.A. 203, 30 C.M.R. 203 (1961).

The requirement that the sentence announcement include a reference to the percentage of agreement or an affirmation that voting was by secret written ballot has been deleted. Article 53 does not require such an announcement, and when instructions incorporating such matters are given, the court-martial "is presumed to have complied with the instructions given them by the judge." *United States v. Ricketts*, 1 M.J.. 78, 82 (C.M.A. 1975). *See United States v. Jenkins*, 12 M.J. 222 (C.M.A. 1982). *Cf. United States v. Hendon*, 6 M.J. 171, 173–74 (C.M.A. 1979).

(c) *Polling prohibited. See* Analysis, Rule 923(e).

Rule 1008 Impeachment of sentence

This rule is based on Mil. R. Evid. 606(b) and *United States v. West*, 23 U.S.C.M.A. 77, 48 C.M.R. 548 (1974). *See United States v. Bishop*, 11 M.J. 7 (C.M.A. 1981).

Rule 1009 Reconsideration of sentence

Introduction. Except as noted below, this rule and discussion are based on Articles 52(c) and 62 and paragraphs 76 *c* and *d* of MCM, 1969 (Rev.).

(c) *Initiation of reconsideration.* Subsection (2)(A) was added to remedy the situation addressed in *United States v. Taylor*, 9 M.J. 848 (N.C.M.R. 1980). It is intended that the military judge have the authority to reduce a sentence imposed by that judge based on changed circumstances, as long as the case remained under that judge's jurisdiction. Since this action "undercuts the review powers" (*Id.* at 850) only to the extent that it reduces the upper limits available to reviewing authorities, there is no reason to prevent the military judge from considering additional matters before finalizing the sentence with authentication. Furthermore, granting the military judge power to reconsider an announced sentence recognizes that when sitting without members, the judge performs the same functions as the members. *See* Article 16.

The procedures in subsection (2)(B) are necessary corollaries of those set out in the fifth and sixth sentences of paragraph 76 *c*, MCM, 1969 (Rev.) adapted to the rules for reconsideration. This clarifies that a formal vote to reconsider is necessary when reconsideration is initiated by the military judge. MCM, 1969 (Rev.) was unclear in this regard. *See United States v. King,* 13 M.J. 838 (A.C.M.R.), *pet. denied,* 14 M.J. 232 (1982).

Subsection (3) is based on Article 62(b) and *United States v. Jones*, 3 M.J. 348 (C.M.A. 1977).

(d) *Procedure with members.* Subsection (1) is based on the general requirement for instructions on voting procedure. *See United States v. Johnson*, 18 U.S.C.M.A. 436, 40 C.M.R. 148 (1969). It applies whether reconsideration is initiated by the military judge or a member, since R.C.M. 1006(d)(3)(A) does not permit further voting after a sentence is adopted and there is no authority for the military judge to suspend that provision.

1995 Amendment: This rule was changed to prevent a sentencing authority from reconsidering a sentence announced in open session. Subsection (b) was amended to allow reconsideration if the sentence was less than the mandatory maximum prescribed for the offense or the sentence exceeds the maximum permissible punishment for the offense or the jurisdictional limitation of the court-martial. Subsection (c) is new and provides for the military judge to clarify an announced sentence that is ambiguous. Subsection (d) provides for the convening authority to exercise discretionary authority to return an ambiguous sentence for clarification, or take action consistent with R.C.M. 1107.

2002 Amendment: Subsection (e)(3)(B)(ii) was amended as a result of the enactment of Article 56a, UCMJ, in section 581 of the National Defense Authorization Act for Fiscal Year 1998, Pub. L. No. 105-85, 111 Stat. 1629, 1759 (1997).

Rule 1010 Advice concerning post-trial and appellate rights

This rule is based on S.Rep. No. 53, 98th Cong., 1st Sess. 18 (1983). *See also* Articles 60, 61, 64, 66, 67, and 69. It is similar to Fed.R.Crim. P. 32(a)(2), but is broader in that it applies whether or not the accused pleaded guilty. This is because the accused's post-trial and appellate rights are the same, regardless of the pleas, and because the powers of the convening authority and the Court of Criminal Appeals to reduce the sentence are important even if the accused has pleaded guilty.

1986 Amendment: This rule was changed to delete subsection-(b) which required an inquiry by the military judge. The Senate Report addresses only advice; inquiry to determine the accused's understanding is deemed unnecessary in view of the defense counsel's responsibility in this area.

1991 Amendment: This rule was changed to place the responsibility for informing the accused of post-trial and appellate rights on the defense counsel rather than the military judge. Counsel is better suited to give this advisement in an atmosphere in which the accused is more likely to comprehend the complexities of the rights.

Rule 1011 Adjournment

This rule is based on paragraph 77 *b* of MCM, 1969 (Rev.).

CHAPTER XI. POST-TRIAL PROCEDURE

Rule 1101 Report of result of trial; post-trial restraint; deferment of confinement

(A) *Report of the result of trial.* This subsection is based on the first two sentences of paragraph 44 *e* of MCM, 1969 (Rev.).

(B) *Post-trial confinement.* Subsection (1) is based on Article 57(b) and on the last sentence of paragraph 44 *e* of MCM, 1969 (Rev.). Subsection (1) makes clear that confinement is authorized when death is adjudged, even if confinement is not also adjudged. *See United States v. Matthews*, 13 M.J. 501 (A.C.M.R.), *rev'd on other grounds,* 16 M.J. 354 (C.M.A. 1983). *See also* R.C.M. 1004(e) and Analysis.

Subsection (2) is based on Article 57 and on paragraph 21 *d* of MCM, 1969 (Rev.). The person who orders the accused into confinement need not be the convening authority. *See Reed v. Ohman*, 19 U.S.C.M.A. 110, 41 C.M.R. 110 (1969); *Levy v. Resor*, 17 U.S.C.M.A. 135, 37 C.M.R. 399 (1967). The convening authority may withhold such authority from subordinates.

Article 57(b) provides that a sentence to confinement begins to run as soon as the sentence is adjudged. The mechanism for an accused to seek release from confinement pending appellate review is to request deferment of confinement under Article 57(d). *See* S.Rep. No. 1601, 90th Cong., 2d Sess. 13-14 (1968); *Pearson v. Cox,* 10 M.J. 317 (C.M.A. 1981). *See* subsection (c) of this rule.

The purpose of subsection (2) is to provide a prompt, convenient means for the command to exercise its prerogative whether to confine an accused when the sentence of the court-martial authorizes it. The commander may decide that, despite the sentence of the court-martial, the accused should not be immediately confined because of operational requirements or other reasons. A decision not to confine is for the convenience of the command and does not constitute deferment of confinement. *See* Article 57(d). An accused dissatisfied with the decision of the commander may request deferment in accordance with subsection (c) of this rule.

The first sentence of the second paragraph of paragraph 20 *d*(1) of MCM, 1969 (Rev.) has been deleted. That sentence provided for post-trial "arrest, restriction, or confinement to insure the presence of an accused for impending execution of a punitive discharge." The authority for such restraint was based on Article 13 which authorized arrest or confinement for persons awaiting the result of trial. *See Reed v. Ohman, supra; United States v. Teague,* 3 U.S.C.M.A. 317, 12 C.M.R. 73 (1953). The Military Justice Amendments of 1981 Pub. L. No. 97–81, § 3, 95 Stat. 1087 (1981), deleted the language concerning such detention pending the result of trial.

(C) *Deferment of confinement.* Subsection (1) is based on the first sentence of paragraph 88 *f* of MCM, 1969 (Rev.). The discussion is based on the second and third sentences of paragraph 88 *f* of MCM, 1969 (Rev.).

Subsection (2) is based on the first sentence in Article 57(d) and the third sentence of paragraph 88*f* of MCM, 1969 (Rev.). The requirement that the request be written is based on the third paragraph of paragraph 88 *f* of MCM, 1969 (Rev.).

Subsection (3) is based on Article 57(d) and *United States v. Brownd,* 6 M.J. 338 (C.M.A. 1978). *See also ABA Standards, Criminal Appeals,* § 21–2.5 (1978); *Trotman v. Haebel,* 12 M.J. 27 (C.M.A. 1981); *Pearson v. Cox, supra; Stokes v. United States,* 8 M.J. 819 (A.F.C.M.R. 1979), *pet. denied,* 9 M.J. 33 (1980). *See also* the first paragraph of paragraph 88 *f* of MCM, 1969 (Rev.). The penultimate sentence recognized the standard of review exercised by the Courts of Criminal Appeals, the Court of Appeals for the Armed Forces, and other reviewing authorities. *See United States v. Brownd, supra.* Because the decision to deny a request for deferment is subject to judicial review, the basis for denial should be included in the record.

Subsection (4) is based on the fourth paragraph of paragraph 88 *f* of MCM, 1969 (Rev.).

Subsection (5) is based on the fifth paragraph of paragraph 88 *f* of MCM, 1969 (Rev.) and on *Pearson v. Cox, supra.*

Subsection (6) modifies the last two paragraphs of paragraph 88 *f* of MCM, 1969 (Rev.) to conform to the amendment of Article 71(c), *see* Pub. L. No. 98–209, § 5(e), 97 Stat. 1393 (1983). The amendment of Article 71(c) permits confinement to be ordered executed in the convening authority's initial action in all cases. Article 57(d) is intended to permit deferment after this point, however. *See* S. Rep. No. 1601, 90th Cong., 2d Sess. 13–14 (1968). Therefore subsection (6) specifically describes four ways in which deferment may be terminated. The result is consistent with paragraph 88 *f* of MCM, 1969 (Rev.) and with *Collier v. United States,* 19 U.S.C.M.A. 511, 42 C.M.R. 113 (1970). Under subsection (A) the convening authority must specify in the initial action whether approved confinement is ordered executed, suspended, or deferred. *See* R.C.M. 1107(f)(4)(B), (E). Under subsection (B), deferment may be terminated at any time by suspending the confinement. This is because suspension is more favorable to the accused than deferment. Subsections (C) and (D) provide other specific points at which deferment may be terminated. Deferment may be granted for a specified period (e.g., to permit the accused to take care of personal matters), or for an indefinite period (e.g., completion of appellate review). Even if confinement is deferred for an indefinite period, it may be rescinded under subsection (D). When deferment is terminated after the initial action, it will be either suspended or executed. *See* subsection (7). The first sentence in the discussion is based on Article 57(d). The second, third, and fourth sentences are based on the last two paragraphs of paragraph 88 *f* of MCM, 1969 (Rev.).

Subsection (7) is based on the last sentence of Article 57(d) and on *Collier v. United States, supra.* Note that the information on which the rescission is based need not be new information, but only information which was not earlier presented to the authority granting deferment. *Cf. Collier v. United States, supra.* Note also that the deferment may be rescinded and the accused confined before the accused has an opportunity to submit matters to the rescinding authority. *See United States v. Daniels,* 19 U.S.C.M.A. 518, 42 C.M.R. 120 (1970).

Subsection (7)(C) is added based on the amendment of Article 71(c). Confinement after the initial action is not "served." It is deferred, suspended, or executed. Therefore, after deferment is rescinded, it is ordered executed (if not suspended). Subsection (7)(C) permits the accused an opportunity to submit matters before the order of execution, which precludes deferment under Article 57(d), is issued.

1991 Amendment: The Discussion accompanying this subsection was amended to provide for the inclusion of the written basis for any denial of deferment in the record of trial. Although written reasons for denials are not mandatory, and their absence from the record of trial will not per se invalidate a denial decision, their use is strongly encouraged. *See Longhofer v. Hilbert,* 23 M.J. 755 (A.C.M.R. 1986).

1998 Amendment: In enacting section 1121 of the National Defense Authorization Act for Fiscal Year 1996, Pub. L. No. 104-106, 110 Stat. 186, 462, 464 (1996), Congress amended Article 57(a) to make forfeitures of pay and allowances and reductions in grade effective either 14 days after being adjudged by a court-martial, or when the convening authority takes action in the case, whichever was earlier in time. Until this change, any forfeiture or reduction in grade adjudged by the court did not take effect until convening authority action, which meant the accused often retained the privileges of his or her rank and pay for up to several months. The intent of the amendment of Article 57(a) was to change this situation so that the desired punitive and rehabilitative impact on the accused occurred more quickly.

Congress, however, desired that a deserving accused be permitted to request a deferment of any adjudged forfeitures or reduction in grade, so that a convening authority, in appropriate situations, might mitigate the effect of Article 57(a).

This change to R.C.M. 1101 is in addition to the change to R.C.M. 1203. The latter implements Congress' creation of Article 57(a), giving the Service Secretary concerned the authority to defer a sentence to confinement pending review under Article 67(a)(2).

(d) *Waiving forfeitures resulting from a sentence to confinement to provide for dependent support.* *1998 Amendment:* This new subsection implements Article 58b, UCMJ, created by section 1122, National Defense Authorization Act for Fiscal Year 1996, Pub. L. No. 104-106, 110 Stat. 186, 463 (1996). This article permits the convening authority (or other person acting under Article 60) to waive any or all of the forfeiture of pay and allowances forfeited by operation of Article 58b(a) for a period not to exceed six months. The purpose of such waiver is to provide support to some or all of the accused's dependent(s) when circumstances warrant. The convening authority directs the waiver and identifies those dependent(s) who shall receive the payment(s).

Rule 1102

Introduction. This rule is based on Article 60(e) and on paragraphs 80 *c* and 86 *d* of MCM, 1969 (Rev.), all of which concern proceedings in revision. This rule also expressly authorizes post-trial Article 39(a) sessions to address matters not subject to proceedings in revision which may affect legality of findings of guilty or the sentence. *See United States v. Mead*, 16 M.J. 270 (C.M.A. 1983); *United States v. Brickey*, 16 M.J. 258 (C.M.A. 1983); *United States v. Witherspoon*, 16 M.J. 252 (C.M.A. 1983). *Cf. United States v. DuBay*, 17 U.S.C.M.A. 147, 37 C.M.R. 411 (1967).

(a) *In general.* This subsection is based on Article 60(e), on the first sentence of paragraph 80 *c* of MCM, 1969 (Rev.), which indicated that a court-martial could conduct proceedings in revision on its own motion, and on paragraph 86 *d* of MCM, 1969 (Rev.).

(b) *Purpose.* Subsection (1) is based on the second sentence of paragraph 86 *d* of MCM, 1969 (Rev.). The discussion of subsection (1) is based on the last paragraph of paragraph 80 *d* of MCM, 1969 (Rev.) and on *United States v. Steck*, 10 M.J. 412 (C.M.A. 1981); *United States v. Barnes*, 21 U.S.C.M.A. 169, 44 C.M.R. 223 (1972); *United States v. Hollis*, 11 U.S.C.M.A. 235, 29 C.M.R. 51 (1960). As to subsection (2), *see* the *Introduction,* Analysis, this rule. The discussion of subsection 21 is based on *United States v. Anderson, supra.*

1994 Amendment: The amendment to subsection (b)(2) of this rule clarifies that Article 39(a), UCMJ, authorizes the military judge to take such action after trial and before authenticating the record of trial as may be required in the interest of justice. *See United States v. Griffith*, 27 M.J. 42, 47 (C.M.A. 1988). The amendment to the Discussion clarifies that the military judge may take remedial action on behalf of an accused without waiting for an order from an appellate court. Under this subsection, the military judge may consider, among other things, misleading instructions, legal sufficiency of the evidence, or errors involving the misconduct of members, witnesses, or counsel. *Id.; See United States v. Scaff*, 29 M.J. 60, 65 (C.M.A. 1989).

(c) *Matters not subject to post-trial sessions.* This subsection is taken from Article 60(e)(2).

(d) *When directed.* This subsection is based on paragraph 86 *d* of MCM, 1969 (Rev.). *See also* Article 60(e); *United States v. Williamson*, 4 M.J. 708 (N.C.M.R. 1977), *pet. denied,* 5 M.J. 219 (1978). Paragraph 86 *d* indicated that a proceeding in revision could be used to "make the record show the true proceedings." A certificate of correction is the appropriate mechanism for this, so the former provision is deleted. Note that a trial session may be directed, when authorized by an appropriate reviewing authority (*e.g.*, the supervisory authority, or the Judge Advocate General), even if some or all of the sentence has been executed.

2007 Amendment: For purposes of this rule, the list of appropriate reviewing authorities included in the 1994 amendment includes any court authorized to review cases on appeal under the UCMJ.

(e) *Procedure.* Subsection (1) is based on paragraph 80 *b* of MCM, 1969 (Rev.). *See also* R.C.M. 505 and 805 and Analysis. Good cause for detailing a different military judge includes unavailability due to physical disability or transfer, and circumstances in which inquiry into misconduct by a military judge is necessary.

Subsection (2) is based on paragraph 80 *c* of MCM, 1969 (Rev.). Subsection (2) is more concise than its predecessor; it leaves to the military judge responsibility to determine what specific action to take.

Subsection (3) is based on paragraph 80 *d* of MCM, 1969 (Rev.).

Rule 1102A Post-trial hearing for person found not guilty only be reason of lack of mental responsibility.

1998 Amendment: This new Rule implements Article 76b(b), UCMJ. Created in section 1133 of the National Defense Authorization Act for Fiscal Year 1996, Pub. L. No. 104-106, 110 Stat. 186, 464-66 (1996), it provides for a post-trial hearing within forty days of the finding that the accused is not guilty only by reason of a lack of mental responsibility. Depending on the offense concerned, the accused has the burden of proving either by a preponderance of the evidence, or by clear and convincing evidence, that his or her release would not create a substantial risk of bodily injury to another person or serious damage to property of another due to a present mental disease or defect. The intent of the drafters is for R.C.M. 1102A to mirror the provisions of sections 4243 and 4247 of title 18, United States Code.

Rule 1103 Preparation of record of trial

(a) *In general.* This subsection is based on Article 54(c) and on the first sentence of paragraph 82 *a* of MCM, 1969 (Rev.).

(b) *General courts-martial.* Subsection (1)(A) is based on Article 38(a). In Federal civilian courts the reporter is responsible for preparing the record of trial. 28 U.S.C. § 753; Fed. R. App.P. 11 (b). The responsibility of the trial counsel for preparation of the record is established by Article 38(a), however. Subsection (1)(B) is based on the second paragraph of paragraph 82 *a* of MCM, 1969 (Rev.). *See also United States v. Anderson*, 12 M.J. 195 (C.M.A. 1982).

Subsection (2)(A) is based on Article 54(a) and the first sentence of paragraph 82 *b*(1) of MCM, 1969 (Rev.). *Cf.* Article 19.

Subsection (2)(B) is based on Article 54(c) and on the third sentence of paragraph 82 *b*(1) of MCM, 1969 (Rev.). *See* Rep. No. 53, 98th Cong., 1st Sess. 26 (1983); H.R. Rep. No.491, 81st Cong., 1st Sess. 27 (1949); S. Rep. No.486, 81st Cong., 1st Sess. 23–24 (1949). *See also* Articles 19 and 66; *United States v. Whitman*, 23 U.S.C.M.A. 48, 48 C.M.R. 519 (1974); *United States v. Thompson*, 22 U.S.C.M.A. 448, 47 C.M.R. 489 (1973); *United States v. Whitman*, 3 U.S.C.M.A. 179, 11 C.M.R. 179 (1953). The exception in the stem of subsection (2)(B) is based on Article 1(14). *See* Analysis, subsection (j) of this rule.

The first paragraph of the discussion under subsection (2)(B) is based on the third sentence of paragraph 82 *b*(1), and paragraphs 82 *b*(2) and (3) of MCM, 1969 (Rev.). *See* Analysis, R.C.M. 802 concerning the second paragraph in the discussion. The last paragraph in the discussion is based on the sixth sentence of paragraph 82 *b*(1) of MCM, 1969 (Rev.).

2002 Amendment: Subsection (b)(2)(B) was amended to implement the amendment to 10 U.S.C. Sec. 819 (Article 19, UCMJ) contained in section 577 of the National Defense Authorization Act for Fiscal Year 2000, P. L. No. 106-65, 113 Stat. 512 (1999) increasing the jurisdictional maximum punishment at special courts-martial. R.C.M. 1103(b)(2)(B) was amended to prevent an inconsistent requirement for a verbatim transcript between a general court-martial and a special court-martial when the adjudged sentence of a general court-martial does not include a punitive discharge or confinement greater than six months, but does include forfeiture of two-thirds pay per month for more than six months but not more than 12 months.

Subsection (2)(C) is based on the fourth sentence of paragraph 82 *b*(1) of MCM, 1969 (Rev.). *See* Article 54(c)(2). In Federal civilian courts a verbatim record is generally required in all cases (although not all portions of the record are necessarily transcribed). *See* 28 U.S.C. § 753(b); Fed. R. Crim. P. 11(g) and 12(g); and Fed. R. App. P. 10. *See also* Fed. R. Crim. P. 5.1(c). The Constitution requires a record of sufficient completeness to allow consideration of what occurred at trial, but not necessarily a verbatim transcript. *Mayer v. Chicago*, 404 U.S. 189 (1971); *Draper v. Washington*, 372 U.S. 487 (1963); *Coppedge v. United States*, 369 U.S. 438 (1962); *United States v. Thompson, supra.* A summarized record is adequate for the less severe sentences for which it is authorized.

Subsection (2)(D) is new. It lists items which are, in addition to a transcript of the proceedings, required for a complete record. *See United States v. McCullah*, 11 M.J. 234 (C.M.A. 1981).

Failure to comply with subsection (b)(2) does not necessarily require reversal. Rather, an incomplete or nonverbatim record (when required) raises a presumption of prejudice which the Government may rebut. *See United States v. Eichenlaub*, 11 M.J. 239 (C. M.A. 1981); *United States v. McCullah, supra; United States v. Boxdale*, 22 U. S.C.M.A. 414, 47 C. M.R. 35 (1973). As to whether an omission is sufficiently substantial to raise the presumption, *see United States v. Gray*, 7 M.J. 296 (C.M.A. 1979); *United States v. Sturdivant*, 1 M.J. 256 (C.M.A. 1976); *United States v. Webb*, 23 U.S.C.M.A. 333, 49 C.M.R. 667 (1975); *United States v. Boxdale, supra; United States v. Richardson*, 21 U.S.C.M.A. 383, 45 C.M.R. 157 (1972); *United States v. Weber*, 20 U.S.C.M.A. 82, 42 C.M.R. 274 (1970); *United States v. Donati*, 14 U.S.C.M.A. 235, 34 C.M.R. 15 (1963); *United States v. Nelson*, 3 U.S.C.M.A. 482, 13 C.M.R. 38 (1953).

1991 Amendment: Subsection (b)(2)(D)(iv) was redesignated as subsection (b)(2)(D)(v), and new subsection (b)(2)(D)(iv) was added. The 1984 rules omitted any requirement that the convening authority's action be included in the record of trial. This amendment corrects that omission.

Subsection (3) is based on paragraph 82 *b*(5), the last sentence of paragraph 84 *c*, paragraph 85 *d*, the third sentence of the third paragraph of paragraph 88 *f*, the penultimate sentence of paragraph 88 *g*, and the last sentence of paragraph 91 *c* of MCM, 1969 (Rev.). *See also* S. Rep. No. 53, 98th Cong., 1st Sess. 26 (1983); R.C.M. 1106(f) and Analysis; and *United States v. Lott*, 9 M.J. 70 (C.M.A. 1980).

1995 Amendment: Punishment of confinement on bread and water or diminished rations [R.C.M. 1003(d)(9)], as a punishment imposable by a court-martial, was deleted. Consequently, the requirement to attach a Medical Certificate to the record of trial [R.C.M. 1103(b)(3)(L)] was deleted. Subsections (3)(M) and (3)(N) were redesignated (3)(L) and (3)(M), respectively.

(c) *Special courts-martial.* This subsection is based on Articles 19 and 54(c) and paragraph 83 of MCM, 1969 (Rev.).

2002 Amendment: Subsection (c) was amended to implement the amendment to 10 U.S.C. Sec. 819 (Article 19, UCMJ) contained in section 577 of the National Defense Authorization Act for Fiscal Year 2000, P. L. No. 106-65, 113 Stat. 512 (1999) increasing the jurisdictional maximum punishment at special courts-martial. R.C.M. 1103(c) was amended to conform the requirements for a verbatim transcript with the requirements of Article 19 for a 'complete record' in cases where the adjudged sentence includes a bad-conduct discharge, confinement for more than six months, or forfeiture of pay for more than six months.

(e) *Acquittal; termination prior to findings.* This subsection is based on the fifth sentence of paragraph 82 *b*(1) and the third sentence of paragraph 83 *b* of MCM, 1969 (Rev.). The language of paragraph 82 *b*(1) which referred to termination "with prejudice to the Government" has been modified. If the court-martial terminates by reason of mistrial, withdrawal, or dismissal of charges, a limited record is authorized, whether or not the proceedings could be reinstituted at another court-martial.

(f) *Loss of notes or recordings of the proceedings.* This subsection is based on paragraph 82 *i* of MCM, 1969 (Rev.). *See also United States v. Lashley*, 14 M.J. 7 (C.M.A. 1982); *United States v. Boxdale. supra.*

2002 Amendment: Subsection (f)(1) was amended to implement the amendment to 10 U.S.C. Sec. 819 (Article 19, UCMJ) contained in section 577 of the National Defense Authorization Act for Fiscal Year 2000, P. L. No. 106Sec. 65, 113 Stat. 512 (1999) increasing the jurisdictional maximum punishment at special courts-martial. R.C.M. 1103(f)(1) was amended to include the additional limitations on sentence contained in Article 19, UCMJ.

2004 Amendment: Subsection (f)(2) was amended to reflect amendments to Article 63, UCMJ, in the National Defense Authorization Act for Fiscal Year 1993, Pub.L.No. 102-484, 106 Stat. 2315, 2506 (1992). The revisions provide that subsection (f)(2) sentencing limitations are properly applicable only to the sentence that may be approved by the convening authority following a rehearing. Subsection (f)(2) as revised does not limit the maximum sentence that may be adjudged at the rehearing. *See*

United States v. Gibson, 43 M.J. 343 (1995); *United States v. Lawson,* 34 M.J. 38 (C.M.A. 1992)(Cox, J., concurring); *United States v. Greaves,* 48 M.J. 885 (A.F.Ct.Crim.App. 1998), *rev. denied,* 51 M.J. 365 (1999).

(g) *Copies of the record of trial.* Subsection (1) is based on the first paragraph of paragraph 49 *b*(2) of MCM, 1969 (Rev.). The trial counsel is responsible for preparation of the record (*see* Article 38(a)), although, as paragraph 49 *b*(2) of MCM, 1969 (Rev.) indicated, ordinarily the court reporter actually prepares the record. In subsection (A), the number of copies required has been increased from two to four to conform to current practice.

1993 Amendment: Subsection (g)(1)(A) was amended by adding the phrase "and are subject to review by a Court of Criminal Appeals under Article 66" to eliminate the need to make four copies of verbatim records of trial for courts-martial which are not subject to review by a Court of Criminal Appeals. These cases are reviewed in the Office of the Judge Advocate General under Article 69 and four copies are not ordinarily necessary.

(h) *Security classification.* This subsection is based on the first sentence of paragraph 82 *d* of MCM, 1969 (Rev.). The remainder of that paragraph is deleted as unnecessary.

(i) *Examination of the record.* Subsection (1)(A) and the first paragraph of the discussion are based on the first paragraph of paragraph 82 *e* of MCM, 1969 (Rev.).

Subsection (1)(B) is based on the first sentence of the second paragraph of paragraph 82 *e* of MCM, 1969 (Rev.). The first paragraph of the discussion is based on *United States v. Anderson, supra* at 197. Examination before authentication will improve the accuracy of the record, reduce the possibility of the necessity for a certificate of correction, and obviate the problems discussed in *Anderson*. The first paragraph of the discussion is based on the fourth and fifth sentences of the second paragraph of paragraph 82 *e* of MCM, 1969 (Rev.). *See also United States v. Anderson, supra* at 197. The second paragraph of the discussion is based on*United v. Anderson, supra. See also United States v. Everett*, 3 M.J. 201, 202 (C.M.A. 1977). The third paragraph of the discussion is based on the second sentence of the second paragraph of paragraph 82 *e* of MCM, 1969 (Rev.).

(j) *Videotape and similar records.* This subsection is new and is based on Article 1(14), which is also new. *See* Military Justice Act of 1983, Pub.L. No. 98-209, § 6(a), 97 Stat. 1393 (1983). This subsection implements Article 1(14) in accordance with guidance in S.Rep. No. 53, 98th Cong., 1st Sess. 25-26 (1983). The concerns expressed in *United States v. Barton*, 6 M.J. 16 (C.M.A. 1978) were also considered.

Subsection (1) provides for recording courts-martial by videotape, audiotape, or similar means, if authorized by regulation of the Secretary concerned. Such Secretarial authorization is necessary to ensure that this procedure will be used only when appropriate equipment is available to permit its effective use, in accordance with the requirements for this rule. Such equipment includes not only devices capable of recording the proceedings accurately, but playback equipment adequate to permit transcription by trained personnel or examination by counsel and reviewing authorities. In addition, if transcription is not contemplated, the recording method used must be subject to production of duplicates for compliance with subsection (j)(5) of this rule.

Subsection (2) requires that, ordinarily, the record will be reduced to writing, even if recorded as described in subsection (1). This preference for a written record is based on the fact that such a record is easier to use by counsel, reviewing authorities, and the accused, and is often easier to produce in multiple copies. *Cf. United States v. Barton, supra.* Note, however, that the rule permits recording proceedings and transcribing them later without using a court reporter. This adds a measure of flexibility in the face of a possible shortage of court reporters. This subsection is consistent with the already common practice of using "back-up" recordings to prepare a record when the court reporter's equipment has failed.

Subsection (3) recognizes that military exigencies may prevent transcription of the record, especially at or near the situs of the trial. In such instances, where an accurate record already exists, the convening authority's action should not be postponed for lack of transcription, subject to the provisions in subsection (3). Thus, the convening authority may take action, and transcription for appellate or other reviewing authorities may occur later. *See* subsection (4). Note that additional copies of the record need not be prepared in such case, except as required in subsection (j)(5)(A). Note also, however, that facilities must be reasonably available for use by the defense counsel (and when appropriate the staff judge advocate or legal officer, *see* R.C.M. 1106) to listen to or view and listen to the recordings to use this subsection.

Subsection (4)(A) is based on the recognition that it is impracticable for appellate courts and counsel not to have a written record. *See* S.Rep. No. 53, *supra* at 26; *United States v. Barton, supra.* Note that the transcript need not be authenticated under R.C.M. 1104. Instead, under regulations of the Secretary concerned the accuracy of the transcript can be certified by a person who has viewed and/or heard the authenticated recording.

Subsection (4)(B) provides flexibility in cases not reviewed by the Court of Criminal Appeals. Depending on regulations of the Secretary, a written record may never be prepared in some cases. Many cases not reviewed by a Court of Criminal Appeals will be reviewed only locally. *See* R.C.M. 1112. The same exigencies which weigh against preparation of a written record may also exist before such review. If a written record in not prepared, the review will have to be conducted by listening to or viewing and listening to the authenticated recording.

Subsection (5) provides alternative means for the government to comply with the requirement to serve a copy of the record of trial on the accused. Article 54(d). Note that if a recording is used, the Government must ensure that it can provide the accused reasonable opportunity to listen to or view and listen to the recording.

Rule 1103A

2005 Amendment: The 1998 Amendments to the Manual for Courts-Martial introduced the requirement to seal M.R.E. 412 (rape shield) motions, related papers, and the records of the hearings, to "fully protect an alleged victim of 'sexual assault' against invasion of privacy and potential embarrassment." MCM Appendix 22, p. 36. As current Rule 412(c)(2) reads, it is unclear whether appellate courts are bound by orders sealing Rule 412 information issued by the military judge.

The effect and scope of a military judge's order to seal exhibits, proceedings, or materials is similarly unclear. Certain aspects of the military justice system, particularly during appellate review, seemingly mandate access to sealed materials. For example, appellate defense counsel have a need to examine an entire record of trial to advocate thoroughly and knowingly on behalf of a client. Yet there is some uncertainty about appellate defense counsel's authority to examine sealed materials in the absence of a court order. This authority applies to both military and civilian appellate defense counsel.

The rule is designed to respect the privacy and other interests that justified sealing the material in the first place, while at the same time recognizing the need for certain military justice functionaries to review that same information. The rule favors an approach relying on the integrity and professional responsibility of those functionaries, and assumes that they can review sealed materials and at the same time protect the interests that justified sealing the material in the first place. Should disclosure become necessary, then the party seeking disclosure is directed to an appropriate judicial or quasi-judicial official or tribunal to obtain a disclosure order.

Rule 1104 Records of trial: authentication; service; correction; forwarding

(a) *Authentication.* Subsection (1) is new and is self-explanatory.

Subsection (2) is based on Article 54(a) and (b) and paragraph 82 *f* of MCM, 1969 (Rev.). The former rule has been changed to require that the record, or even a portion of it, may be authenticated only be a person who was present at the proceedings the record of which that person is authenticating. This means that in some cases (*e.g.,* when more than one military judge presided in a case) the record may be authenticated by more than one person. *See United States v. Credit*, 4 M.J. 118 (C.M.A. 1977); S.Rep. No. 1601, 90th Cong., 2d Sess. 12-13 (1968); H.R. Rep. No. 1481, 90th Cong., 2d Sess. 10 (1968). *See also United States v. Galloway*, 2 U.S.C.M.A. 433, 9 C.M.R. 63 (1953). This subsection also changes the former rule in that it authorizes the Secretary concerned to prescribe who will authenticate the record in special courts-martial at which no bad-conduct discharge is adjudged. *See* Article 54(b). In some services, the travel schedules of military judges often result in delays in authenticating the record. Such delays are substantial, considering the relatively less severe nature of the sentences involved in such cases. This subsection allows greater flexibility to achieve prompt authentication and action in such cases. The second paragraph of the discussion is based on *United States v. Credit, supra; United States v. Cruz-Rijos*, 1 M.J. 429 (C.M.A. 1976). *See also United States v. Lott*, 9 M.J. 70 (C.M.A. 1980); *Unites States v. Green*, 7 M.J. 687 (N.C.M.R. 1979); *United States v. Lowery*, 1 M.J. 1165 (N.C.M.R. 1977). The third paragraph of the discussion is based on *United States v. Lott, supra; United States v.Credit, supra.*

2002 Amendment: Subsection (a)(2)(A) was amended to implement the amendment to 10 U.S.C. Sec. 819 (Article 19, UCMJ) contained in section 577 of the National Defense Authorization Act for Fiscal Year 2000, P. L. No. 106-65, 113 Stat. 512 (1999) increasing the jurisdictional maximum punishment at special courts-martial. R.C.M. 1104(a)(2)(A) was amended to ensure that the military judge authenticates all verbatim records of trial at special courts-martial.

(b) *Service.* Subsection (1)(A) is based on Article 54(d) and the first sentence of paragraph 82 *g*(1) of MCM, 1969 (Rev.) *See also* H.R. Rep. No. 2498, 81st Cong., 1st Sess. 1048 (1949).

Subsection (1)(B) is based on the third through fifth sentences of the first paragraph of paragraph 82 *g*(1) of MCM, 1969 (Rev.).

Subsection (1)(C) is based on H.R. Rep. No. 549, 98th Cong., 1st Sess. 15 (1983); *United States v. Cruz-Rijos, supra.* Service of the record of trial is now effectively a prerequisite to further disposition of the case. *See* Article 60(b) and (c)(2). As a result, inability to serve the accused could bring the proceeding to a halt. Such a result cannot have been intended by Congress. Article 60(b) and (c)(2) are intended to ensure that the accused and defense counsel have an adequate opportunity to present matters to the convening authority, and that they will have access to the record in order to do so. Cong. Rec. § 5612 (daily ed. April 28, 1983) (statement of Sen. Jepsen). As a practical matter, defense counsel, rather than the accused, will perform this function in most cases. *See* Article 38(c). Consequently, service of the record on defense counsel, as provided in this subsection, fulfills this purpose without unduly delaying further disposition. *See United States v. Cruz-Rijos, supra.* Note that if the accused had no counsel, or if the accused's counsel could not be served, the convening authority could take action without serving the accused only if the accused was absent without authority. *See* R.C.M. 1105(d)(4) and Analysis.

Subsection (1)(D) is based on the third and fourth paragraphs of paragraph 82 *g*(1) of MCM, 1969 (Rev.).

(c) *Loss of record.* This subsection is based on paragraph 82 *h* of MCM, 1969 (Rev.). Note that if more than one copy of the record is authenticated then each may serve as the record of trial, even if the original is lost.

(d) *Correction of record after authentication; certificate of correction.* Subsection (1) and the discussion are based on paragraph 86 *c* of MCM, 1969 (Rev.). *See also* the first paragraph of paragraph 95 of MCM, 1969 (Rev.). Subsection (2) is new and is based on *United States v. Anderson*, 12 M.J. 195 (C.M.A. 1982). *See also ABA Standards, Special Functions of the Trial Judge* § 6–1.6 (1978). The discussion is based on *United States v. Anderson, supra.* Subsection (3) is based on the second paragraph of paragraph 82 *g*(1) and paragraph 86 *c* of MCM, 1969 (Rev.).

(e) *Forwarding.* This subsection is based on Article 60. The code no longer requires the convening authority to review the record. However, a record of trial must be prepared before the convening authority takes action. *See* Article 60(b)(2) and (3), and (d). Therefore, it is appropriate to forward the record, along with other required matters, to the convening authority. This subsection is consistent with the first two sentences of paragraph 84 *a* of MCM, 1969 (Rev.).

2002 Amendment: Subsection (e) was amended to implement the amendment to 10 U.S.C. Sec. 819 (Article 19, UCMJ) contained in section 577 of the National Defense Authorization Act for Fiscal Year 2000, P. L. No. 106-65, 113 Stat. 512 (1999) increasing the jurisdictional maximum punishment at special courts-martial. This amendment reflects the change to R.C.M. 1106 for special court- martial with an adjudged sentence that includes confinement for one year.

Rule 1105 Matters submitted by the accused

(a) *In general.* This subsection is based on Articles 38(c) and 60(b). *See also* paragraphs 48 *k*(2) and 77 *a* of MCM, 1969 (Rev.).

(b) *Matters which may be submitted.* This subsection is based on Articles 38(c) and 60(b). The post-trial procedure as revised by the Military Justice Act of 1983, Pub.L. No. 98-209, 97 Stat.

1393 (1983) places a heavier responsibility on the defense to take steps to ensure that matters it wants considered are presented to the convening authority. Therefore this subsection provides guidance as to the types of matters which may be submitted. *See* Article 38(c). *See also* paragraph 48 *k*(3) and 77 *a* of MCM, 1969 (Rev.). Note that the matters the accused submits must be forwarded to the convening authority. *See United States v. Siders*, 15 M.J. 272 (C.M.A. 1983). As to the last paragraph in the discussion, *see also* Mil. R. Evid. 606(b) and Analysis; *United States Bishop*, 11 M.J. 7 (C.M.A. 1981); *United States v. West* , 23 U.S.C.M.A. 77, 48 C.M.R. 458 (1974); *United States v. Bourchier*, 5 U.S.C.M.A. 15, 17 C.M.R. 15 (1954).

1995 Amendment: The Discussion accompanying subsection (b)(4) was amended to reflect the new requirement, under R.C.M. 1106(d)(3)(B), that the staff judge advocate or legal advisor inform the convening authority of a recommendation for clemency by the sentencing authority, made in conjunction with the announced sentence.

(c) *Time periods.* This subsection is based on Article 60(b). Subsection (4) clarifies the effect of post-trial sessions. A re-announcement of the same sentence would not start the time period anew. Subsection (5) is based on H.R. Rep. No. 549, 98th Cong., 1st Sess. 15 (1983).

1986 Amendment: Subsection (c) was revised to reflect amendments to Article 60, UCMJ, in the "Military Justice Amendments of 1986," tit. VIII, § 806, National Defense Authorization Act for Fiscal Year 1987, Pub.L. No. 99–661, 100 Stat, 3905, (1986). These amendments simplify post-trial submissions by setting a simple baseline for calculating the time for submissions.

1994 Amendment: Subsection (c)(1) was amended to clarify that the accused has 10 days to respond to an addendum to a recommendation of the staff judge advocate or legal officer when the addendum contains new matter. *See United States v. Thompson*, 25 M.J. 662 (A.F.C.M.R. 1987). An additional amendment permits the staff judge advocate to grant an extension of the 10-day period.

(d) *Waiver.* Subsection (1) is based on Article 60(c)(2). Subsection (2) is based on Article 60(c)(2). This subsection clarifies that the defense may submit matters in increments by reserving in writing its right to submit additional matters within the time period. In certain cases this may be advantageous to the defense as well as the Government, by permitting early consideration of such matters. Otherwise, if the defense contemplated presenting additional matters, it would have to withhold all matters until the end of the period. Subsection (3) is based on Article 60(b)(4). Subsection (4) ensures that the accused cannot, by an unauthorized absence, prevent further disposition of the case. Cf. *United States v. Schreck*, 10 M.J. 226 (C.M.A. 1983). Note that if the accused has counsel, counsel must be served a copy of the record (*see* R.C.M. 1104(b)(1)(C)) and that the defense will have at least 7 days from such service to submit matters. Note also that the unauthorized absence of the accused has no effect on the 30, 20, or 7 day period from announcement of the sentence within which the accused may submit matters (except insofar as it may weigh against any request to extend such a period). The discussion notes that the accused is not required to raise matters, such as allegations of legal error, in order to preserve them for consideration on appellate review.

Rule 1106 Recommendation of the staff judge advocate or legal officer

(a) *In general.* This subsection is based on Article 60(d), *as amended, see* Military Justice Act of 1983, Pub.L. No. 98-209, § 5(a)(1), 97 Stat. 1393 (1983). The first paragraph of paragraph 85 *a* of MCM, 1969 (Rev.) was similar.

2002 Amendment: Subsection (a) was amended to implement the amendment to 10 U.S.C. Sec. 819 (Article 19, UCMJ) contained in section 577 of the National Defense Authorization Act for Fiscal Year 2000, P. L. No. 106-65, 113 Stat. 512 (1999) increasing the jurisdictional maximum punishment at special courts-martial. This amendment requires all special courts-martial cases subject to appellate review to comply with this rule.

(b) *Disqualification.* This subsection is based on Article 6(c) and on the second paragraph of paragraph 85 *a* of MCM, 1969 (Rev.). Legal officers have been included in its application based on Article 60(d). The discussion notes additional circumstances which have been held to disqualify a staff judge advocate. The first example is based on *United States v. Thompson*, 3 M.J. 966 (N.C.M.R. 1977), *rev'd on other grounds,* 6 M.J. 106 (C.M.A. 1978), *petition dismissed*, 7 M.J. 477 (C.M.A. 1979). The second example is based on *United States v. Choice*, 23 U.S.C.M.A. 329, 49 C.M.R. 663 (1975). *See also United States v. Cansdale*, 7 M.J. 143 (C.M.A. 1979); *United States v. Conn*, 6 M.J. 351 (C.M.A. 1979); *United States v. Reed*, 2 M.J. 64 (C.M.A. 1976). The third example is based on *United States v. Conn* and *United States v. Choice,* both *supra. Cf.* Articles 1(9); 6(c); 22(b); 23(b). The fourth example is based on *United States v. Collins*, 6 M.J. 256 (C.M.A. 1979); *United States v. Engle*, 1 M.J. 387 (C.M.A. 1976). *See also United States v. Newman*, 14 M.J. 474 (C.M.A. 1983) as to the disqualification of a staff judge advocate or convening authority when immunity has been granted to a witness in the case.

1986 Amendment: The phrase "or any reviewing officer" was changed to "to any reviewing officer" to correct an error in MCM, 1984.

(c) *When the convening authority does not have a staff judge advocate or legal officer or that person is disqualified.* Subsection (1) is based on the third paragraph of paragraph 85 *a* of MCM, 1969 (Rev.). Legal officers have been included in its application based on Article 60(d). Subsection (2) is new. It recognizes the advantages of having the recommendation prepared by a staff judge advocate. This flexibility should also permit more prompt disposition in some cases as well.

(d) *Form and content of recommendation.* This subsection is based on Article 60(d) and on S.Rep. No. 53, 98th Cong., 1st Sess. 20 (1983). As to the subsection (1), *see also* Article 60(c). Subsections (3), (4), and (5) conform to the specific guidance in S.Rep. No. 53, *supra.* Subsection (6) is based on S.Rep. No. 53, 98th Cong., 1st Sess. 21 (1983). The recommendation should be a concise statement of required and other matters. Summarization of the evidence and review for legal error is not required. Therefore paragraph 85 *b* of MCM, 1969 (Rev.) is deleted.

Paragraph 85 *c* of MCM, 1969 (Rev.) is also deleted. That paragraph stated that the convening authority should explain any decision not to follow the staff judge advocate's recommendation. *See also United States v. Harris*, 10 M.J. 276 (C.M.A. 1981); *United States v. Dixson*, 9 M.J. 72 (C.M.A. 1980); *United States v. Keller*, 1 M.J. 159 (C.M.A. 1976). The convening authority is no longer required to examine the record for legal or factual sufficiency. The convening authority's action is solely a matter of command prerogative. Article 60(c). Therefore the convening authority is not obligated to explain a decision not to follow the recommendation of the staff judge advocate or legal officer.

1995 Amendment: Subsection (d)(3)(B) is new. It requires that the staff judge advocate's or legal advisor's recommendation inform the convening authority of any clemency recommendation made by the sentencing authority in conjunction with the announced sentence, absent a written request by the defense to the contrary. Prior to this amendment, an accused was responsible for informing the convening authority of any such recommendation. The amendment recognizes that any clemency recommendation is so closely related to the sentence that staff judge advocates and legal advisors should be responsible for informing convening authorities of it. The accused remains responsible for informing the convening authority of other recommendations for clemency, including those made by the military judge in a trial with member sentencing and those made by individual members. *See United States v. Clear*, 34 M.J. 129 (C.M.A. 1992); R.C.M. 1105(b)(4). Subsections (d)(3)(B) - (d)(3)(E) are redesignated as (d)(3)(C) - (d)(3)(F), respectively.,

(e) *No findings of guilty.* This subsection is based on Article 60 and 63. When no findings of guilty are reached, no action by the convening authority is required. Consequently, no recommendation by the staff judge advocate or legal officer is necessary. The last paragraph of paragraph 85 *b* of MCM, 1969 (Rev.), which was based on Article 61 (before it was amended), was similar.

1990 Amendment: Subsection (e) was amended in conjunction with the implementation of findings of not guilty only by reason of lack of mental responsibility provided for in Article 50 *a*, UCMJ (Military Justice Amendments of 1986, tit. VIII, § 802, National Defense Authorization Act for Fiscal Year 1987, Pub. L. 99-661, 100 Stat. 3905 (1986)).

(f) *Service of recommendation on defense counsel; defense response.* This subsection is based on Article 60(d). *See also United States v. Goode*, 1 M.J. 3 (C.M.A. 1975). Subsection (1) is based on Article 60(d). *See also United States v. Hill*, M.J. 295 (C.M.A. 1977); *United States v. Goode, supra.*

1990 Amendment: Subsection (f)(1) was added to make clear that the accused should be provided with a personal copy of the recommendation.

1994 Amendment: The Discussion to subsection (f)(l) was amended to correct a grammatical error and to clarify that the method of service of the recommendation on the accused and the accused's counsel should be reflected in the attachments to the record of trial. If it is impractical to serve the accused, the record should contain a statement justifying substitute service. Subsection (f)(1) recognizes that Congress sanctions substitute service on the accused's counsel. H.R. Rep. No. 549, 98th Cong., 1st Sess. 15 (1983). *See also United States v. Roland*, 31 M.J. 747 (A.C.M.R. 1990).

Subsection (2) makes clear who is to be served with the post-trial review. *See United States v. Robinson*, 11 M.J. 218, 223 n.2 (C.M.A. 1981). This issue has been a source of appellate litigation. *See e.g., United States v. Kincheloe*, 14 M.J. 40 (C.M.A. 1982); *United States v. Babcock*, 14 M.J. 34 (C.M.A. 1982); *United States v. Robinson, supra; United States v. Clark*, 11 M.J. 70 (C.M.A. 1981); *United States v. Elliot*, 11 M.J. 1 (C.M.A. 1981); *United States v. Marcoux*, 8 M.J. 155 (C.M.A. 1980); *United States v. Brown*, 5 M.J. 454 (C.M.A. 1978); *United States v. Davis*, 5 M.J. 451 (C.M.A. 1978); *United States v. Iverson*, 5 M.J. 440 (C.M.A. 1978); *United States v. Annis*, 5 M.J. 351 (C.M.A. 1978). The last sentence in this subsection is based on *United States v. Robinson, United States v. Brown*, and *United States v. Iverson,* all *supra.* The discussion is based on *United States v. Robinson, supra.*

Subsection (3) is based on *United States v. Babcock, supra; United States v. Cruz*, 5 M.J. 286 (C.M.A. 1978); *United States v. Cruz-Rijos*, 1 M.J. 429 (C.M.A. 1976). Ordinarily the record will have been provided to the accused under R.C.M. 1104(b).

Subsections (4) and (5) are based on Article 60(d). *See also United States v. Goode, supra. See United States v. McAdoo*, 14 M.J. 60 (C.M.A. 1982).

1986 Amendment: Subsection (5) was amended to reflect amendments to Article 60, UCMJ, in the "Military Justice Amendments of 1986," tit. VIII, § 806, National Defense Authorization Act for Fiscal Year 1987, Pub.L. No. 99-661, 100 Stat. 3905 (1986). *See* Analysis to R.C.M. 1105(c).

Subsection (6) is based on Article 60(d). *See also* S. Rep. No. 53, 98th Cong., 1st Sess. 21 (1983); *United States v. Morrison, supra; United states v.Barnes*, 3 M.J. 406 (C.M.A. 1982); *United States v. Goode, supra. But see United States v. Burroughs, supra; United States v. Moles*, 10 M.J. 154 (C.M.A. 1981) (defects not waived by failure to comment).

Subsection (7) is based on*United States v. Narine* , 14 M.J. 55 (C.M.A. 1982).

1994 Amendment: Subsection (f)(7) was amended to clarify that when new matter is addressed in an addendum to a recommendation, the addendum should be served on the accused and the accused's counsel. The change also clarifies that the accused has 10 days from the date of service in which to respond to the new matter. The provision for substituted service was also added. Finally, the Discussion was amended to reflect that service of the addendum should be established by attachments to the record of trial.

Rule 1107 Action by convening authority

(a) *Who may take action.* This subsection is based on Article 60(c). It is similar to the first sentence of paragraph 84 *b* and the first sentence of paragraph 84 *c* of MCM, 1969 (Rev.) except insofar as the amendment of Article 60 provides otherwise. *See* Military Justice Act of 1983, Pub.L. No. 98-209, § 5(a)(1), 97 Stat. 1393 (1983). The first paragraph in the discussion is based on the last two sentences of paragraph 84 *a* of MCM, 1969 (Rev.). The second paragraph of the discussion is based on the second and third sentences of paragraph 84 *c* of MCM, 1969 (Rev.); *United States v. Conn*, 6 M.J. 351 (C.M.A. 1979); *United States v. Reed*, 2 M.J. 64 (C.M.A. 1976); *United States v. Choice*, 23 U.S.C.M.A. 329, 49 C.M.R. 663 (1975). *See also United States v. James*, 12 M.J. 944 (N.M.C.M.R.), *pet. granted*, 14 M.J. 235 (1982)*rev'd* 17 M.J. 51. The reference in the third sentence of paragraph 84 *c* of MCM, 1969 (Rev.) to disqualification of a convening authority because the convening authority granted immunity to a witness has been deleted. *See United States v. Newman*, 14 M.J. 474 (C.M.A. 1983). Note that although *Newman* held that a convening authority is not automatically disqualified from taking action by reason of having granted immunity, the Court indicated that a convening authority may be disqualified by granting immunity under some circumstances.

(b) *General considerations.* Subsection (1) and the discussion are based on Article 60(c). *See also* S.Rep. No. 53, 98th Cong., 1st Sess. 19 (1983).

Subsection (2) is based on Article 60(b) and (c).

Subsection (3)(A)(i) is based on Article 60(a). Subsection (3)(A)(ii) is based on Article 60(d). Subsection (3)(A)(iii) is based on Article 60(b) and (d). Subsection (3)(B) is based on Article 60 and on S.Rep. No. 53, 98th Cong., 1st Sess. 19–20 (1983). The second sentence in subsection (3)(B)(iii) is also based on the last sentence of paragraph 85 *b* of MCM, 1969 (Rev.). *See also United States v. Vara,* 8 U.S.C.M.A. 651, 25 C.M.R. 155 (1958); *United States v. Lanford,* 6 U.S.C.M.A. 371, 20 C.M.R. 87 (1955).

Subsection (4) is based on Article 60(c)(3). *See also* Article 60(e)(3). This subsection is consistent with paragraph 86 *b*(2) of MCM, 1969 (Rev.) except that it does not refer to examining the record for jurisdictional error.

1990 Amendment: Subsection (b)(4) was amended in conjunction with the implementation of findings of not guilty only by reason of lack of mental responsibility provided for in Article 50 *a*, UCMJ (Military Justice Amendments of 1986, tit. VIII, § 802, National Defense Authorization Act for Fiscal Year 1987, Pub. L. 99–661, 100 Stat. 3905 (1986)).

Subsection (5) is based on the second paragraph of paragraph 124 of MCM, 1969 (Rev.). *See also United States v. Korzeniewski,* 7 U.S.C.M.A. 314, 22 C.M.R. 104 (1956); *United States v. Washington,* 6 U.S.C.M.A.114, 19 C.M.R. 240 (1955); *United States v. Phillips,* 13 M.J. 858 (N.M.C.M.R. 1982).

1986 Amendment: The fourth sentence of subsection (b)(5) was amended to shift to the defense the burden of showing the accused's lack of mental capacity to cooperate in post-trial proceedings. This is consistent with amendments to R.C.M. 909(c)(2) and R.C.M. 916(k)(3)(A) which also shifted to the defense the burden of showing lack of mental capacity to stand trial and lack of mental responsibility. The second sentence was added to establish a presumption of capacity and the third sentence was amended to allow limitation of the scope of the sanity board's examination. The word "substantial" is used in the second and third sentences to indicate that considerable more credible evidence than merely an allegation of lack of capacity is required before further inquiry need be made. *Ford v. Wainwright,* 477 U.S. 399, 106 S.Ct. 2595, 2610 (1986) (Powell, J., concurring).

1998 Amendment: Congress created Article 76b, UCMJ in section 1133 of the National Defense Authorization Act for Fiscal Year 1996, Pub. L. No. 104-106, 110 Stat. 186, 464-66 (1996). It gives the convening authority discretion to commit an accused found not guilty only by reason of a lack of mental responsibility to the custody of the Attorney General.

(c) *Action of findings.* This subsection is based on Article 60(c)(2). Subsection (2)(B) is also based on Article 60(e)(1) and (3). The first sentence in the discussion is based on *Hearings on H.R. 2498 Before a Subcomm. of the House Comm. on Armed Services,* 81st Cong., 1st Sess. 1182–85 (1949). The second sentence in the discussion is based on Article 60(e)(3). The remainder of the discussion is based on S.Rep. No. 53, 98th Cong., 1st Sess. 21 (1983).

(d) *Action on the sentence.* Subsection (1) is based on Article 60(c) and is similar to the first paragraph of paragraph 88 *a* of MCM, 1969 (Rev.). The first paragraph of the discussion is based on paragraph 88 *a* of MCM, 1969 (Rev.). The second paragraph of the discussion is based on *Jones v. Ignatius,* 18 U.S.C.M.A. 7, 39 C.M.R. 7 (1968); *United States v. Brown,* 13 U.S.C.M.A. 333, 32 C.M.R. 333 (1962); *United States v. Prow,* 13 U.S.C.M.A. 63, 32 C.M.R. 63 (1962); *United States v. Johnson,* 12 U.S.C.M.A. 640, 31 C.M.R. 226 (1962); *United States v. Christenson,* 12 U.S.C.M.A. 393, 30 C.M.R. 393 (1961); *United States v. Williams,* 6 M.J. 803 (N.C.M.R.), *pet. dismissed,* 7 M.J. 68 (C.M.A. 1979); *United States v. Berg,* 34 C.M.R. 684 (N.B.R. 1963). *See also United States v. McKnight,* 20 C.M.R. 520 (N.B.R. 1955).

2002 Amendment: The Discussion accompanying subsection (d)(1) was amended to implement the amendment to 10 U.S.C. Sec. 819 (Article 19, UCMJ) contained in section 577 of the National Defense Authorization Act for Fiscal Year 2000, P. L. No. 106-65, 113 Stat. 512 (1999) increasing the jurisdictional maximum punishment at special courts-martial. R.C.M. 1107(d)(4) was amended to include the additional limitations on sentence contained in Article 19, UCMJ.

Subsection (2) is based on Article 60(c) and S. Rep. No. 53, 98th Cong., 1st Sess. 19 (1983). The second sentence is also based on *United States v. Russo,* 11 U.S.C.M.A. 352, 29 C.M.R. 168 (1960). The second paragraph of the discussion is based on the third paragraph of paragraph 88 *b* of MCM, 1969 (Rev.).

1995 Amendment: The last sentence in the Discussion accompanying subsection (d)(2) is new. It clarifies that forfeitures adjudged at courts-martial take precedence over all debts owed by the accused. Department of Defense Military Pay and Allowances Entitlement Manual, Volume 7, Part A, paragraph 70507a (12 December 1994).

Subsection (3) is based on Articles 19 and 54(c)(1) and on the third sentence of paragraph 82 *b*(1) of MCM, 1969 (Rev.).

1995 Amendment: Subsection (d)(3) is new. It is based on the recently enacted Article 57(e). National Defense Authorization Act for Fiscal Year 1993, Pub. L. No. 102–484, 106 Stat. 2315, 2505 (1992). *See generally* Interstate Agreement on Detainers Act, 18 U.S.C. App. III. It permits a military sentence to be served consecutively, rather than concurrently, with a civilian or foreign sentence. The prior subsection (d)(3) is redesignated (d)(4).

1998 Amendment: All references to "postponing" service of a sentence to confinement were changed to use the more appropriate term, "defer".

2002 Amendment: Subsection (d)(4) was amended as a result of the enactment of Article 56a, UCMJ, in section 581 of the National Defense Authorization Act for Fiscal Year 1998, Pub. L. No. 105-85, 111 Stat. 1629, 1759 (1997).

Subsection (d)(5) is new. The amendment addresses the impact of Article 58b, UCMJ. In special courts-martial, where the cumulative impact of a fine and forfeitures, whether adjudged or by operation of Article 58b, would otherwise exceed the total dollar amount of forfeitures that could be adjudged at the special court-martial, the fine and/or adjudged forfeitures should be disapproved or decreased accordingly. *See generally United States v. Tualla,* 52 M.J. 228, 231-32 (2000).

(e) *Ordering rehearing or other trial.* Subsection (1)(A) is based on Article 60(e), and on paragraph 92 *a* of MCM, 1969 (Rev.).

Note that the decision of the convening authority to order a rehearing is discretionary. The convening authority is not required to review the record for legal errors. Authority to order a rehearing is, therefore, "designed solely to provide an expeditious means to correct errors that are identified in the course of exercising discretion under Article 60(c)." S. Rep. No. 53, 98th Cong., 1st Sess. 21 (1983). Subsection (1)(B) is based on Article 60(e). As to subsection (1)(B)(ii), *see* S. Rep. No. 53, *supra* at 22. Subsection (1)(B)(ii) is based on the second sentence of the second paragraph of paragraph 92 *a* of MCM, 1969 (Rev.). The discussion is based on the second sentence of the fourth paragraph of paragraph 92 *a* of MCM, 1969 (Rev.). Subsection (1)(C)(i) is based on Article 62(e)(3) and on the first sentence of the third paragraph of paragraph 92 *a* of MCM, 1969 (Rev.). Subsection (1)(C)(ii) and the discussion are based on Article 60(e)(3) and on the first paragraph of paragraph 92 *a* of MCM, 1969 (Rev.). Subsection (1)(C)(ii) is based on the first sentence of the tenth paragraph of paragraph 92 *a* of MCM, 1969 (Rev.). Subsection (1)(D) is based on the sixth paragraph of paragraph 92 *a* of MCM, 1969 (Rev.). Subsection (1)(E) is based on the eighth paragraph of paragraph 92 *a* of MCM, 1969 (Rev.). Because of the modification of Article 71 (*see* R.C.M. 1113) and because the convening authority may direct a rehearing after action in some circumstances (*see* subsection (e)(1)(B)(ii) of this rule), the language is modified. The remaining parts of paragraph 92 *a*, concerning procedures for a rehearing, are now covered in R.C.M. 810.

1995 Amendment: The second sentence in R.C.M. 1107(e)(1)(C)(iii) is new. It expressly recognizes that the convening authority may approve a sentence of no punishment if the convening authority determines that a rehearing on sentence is impracticable. This authority has been recognized by the appellate courts. *See e.g., United States v. Monetesinos*, 28 M.J. 38 (C.M.A. 1989); *United States v. Sala*, 30 M.J. 813 (A.C.M.R. 1990).

2004 Amendment: The Discussion to R.C.M. 1107(e)(1)(B)(iii) was moved to new subsection (1)(B)(iv) to recognize expressly that, in cases where a superior authority has approved some findings of guilty and has authorized a rehearing as to other offenses, the convening authority may, unless otherwise directed, reassess a sentence based on approved findings of guilty under the criteria established by *United States v. Sales,* 22 M.J. 305 (C.M.A. 1986), and dismiss the remaining charges. *See United States v. Harris,* 53 M.J. 86 (2000). The power of convening authorities to reassess had been expressly authorized in paragraph 92a of MCM, 1969. The authorizing language was moved to the Discussion following R.C.M. 1107(e)(1)(B)(iii) in MCM, 1984. The Discussion was amended to advise practitioners to apply the criteria for sentence reassessment established by *United States v. Sales,* 22 M.J. 305 (C.M.A. 1986). *See also United States v. Harris,* 53 M.J. 86 (2000); *United States v. Eversole,* 53 M.J. 132 (2000). The Discussion was further amended to encourage practitioners to seek clarification from superior authority where the directive to the convening authority is unclear.

Subsection (2) is based on paragraph 92 *b* of MCM, 1969 (Rev.). *See also* paragraph 89 *c*(1) of MCM, 1969 (Rev.). If the accused was acquitted of a specification which is later determined to have failed to state an offense, another trial for the same offense would be barred. *United States v. Ball*, 163 U.S. 662 (1896). It is unclear whether an acquittal by a jurisdictionally defective court-martial bars retrial. *See United States v. Culver*, 22 U.S.C.M.A. 141, 46 C.M.R. 141 (1973).

(f) *Contents of action and related matters.* Subsection (1) is based on paragraph 89 *a* of MCM, 1969 (Rev.).

1991 Amendment: The 1984 rules omitted any requirement that the convening authority's action be included in the record of trial. This amendment corrects that omission.

Subsection (2) is based on paragraph 89 *b* of MCM, 1969 (Rev.). The second sentence is new. It is intended to simplify the procedure when a defect in the action is discovered in Article 65(c) review. There is no need for another authority to formally act in such cases if the convening authority can take corrective action. The accused cannot be harmed by such action. A convening authority may still be directed to take corrective action when necessary, under the third sentence. "Erroneous" means clerical error only. *See* subsection (g) of this rule. This new sentence is not intended to allow a convening authority to change a proper action because of a change of mind.

1995 Amendment: The amendment allows a convening authority to recall and modify any action after it has been published or after an accused has been officially notified, but before a record has been forwarded for review, as long as the new action is not less favorable to the accused than the prior action. A convening authority is not limited to taking only corrective action, but may also modify the approved findings or sentence provided the modification is not less favorable to the accused than the earlier action.

Subsection (3) is based on paragraph 89 *c*(2) of MCM, 1969 (Rev.). The provision in paragraph 89 *c*(2) of MCM, 1969 (Rev.) that disapproval of the sentence also constitutes disapproval of the findings unless otherwise stated is deleted. The convening authority must expressly indicate which findings, if any, are disapproved in any case. *See* Article 60(c)(3). The discussion is based on paragraph 89 *c*(2) of MCM, 1969 (Rev.). Subsection (4)(A) is based on paragraph 89 *c*(3) of MCM, 1969 (Rev.). The first sentence of paragraph 89 *c*(2)is no longer accurate. Since no action on the findings is required, any disapproval of findings must be expressed. Subsection (4)(B) is taken from paragraph 89 *c*(4) of MCM, 1969 (Rev.). Subsection (4)(D) is based on paragraph 89 *c*(6) of MCM, 1969 (Rev.). However, because that portion of the sentence which extends to confinement may now be ordered executed when the convening authority takes action (*see* Article 71(c)(2); R.C.M. 1113(b)), temporary custody is unnecessary in such cases. Therefore, this subsection applies only when death has been adjudged and approved. Subsection (4)(E) is taken from paragraph 89 *c*(7) of MCM, 1969 (Rev.). Subsection (4)(F) is new. *See* Analysis, R.C.M. 305(k). *See also United States v. Suzuki*, 14 M.J. 491 (C.M.A. 1983). Subsection (4)(G) is taken from paragraph 89 *c*(9) of MCM, 1969 (Rev.). Subsection (4)(H) is modified based on the amendment of Article 71 which permits a reprimand to be ordered executed from action, regardless of the other components of the sentence. Admonition has been deleted. *See* R.C.M. 1003(b)(1).

Subsection (5) is based on paragraph 89 *c*(8) of MCM, 1969 (Rev.). *See also* R.C.M. 810(d) and Analysis. The provision in paragraph 89 *c*(8) requiring that the accused be credited with time in confinement while awaiting a rehearing is deleted. Given the procedures for imposition and continuation of restraint while awaiting trial (*see* R.C.M. 304 and 305), there should not be a credit simply because the trial is a rehearing.

(g) *Incomplete, ambiguous, or erroneous action.* This subsection is based on paragraph 95 of MCM, 1969 (Rev.). *See generally United States v. Loft*, 10 J M.J. 266 (C.M.A. 1981); *United States v. Lower*, 10 M.J. 263 (C.M.A. 1981).

(h) *Service on accused.* This subsection is based on Article 61(a), *as amended, see* Military Justice Act of 1983, Pub.L. No. 98–209, § 5(b)(1), 97 Stat. 1393 (1983).

Rule 1108 Suspension of execution of sentence

This rule is based on Articles 71(d) and 74, and paragraphs 88 *e* and 97 *a* of MCM, 1969 (Rev.). *See also* Fed.R.Crim. P. 32(e). The second paragraph of the discussion to subsection (b) is based on *United States v. Stonesifer*, 2 M.J. 212 (C.M.A. 1977); *United States v. Williams*, 2 M.J. 74 (C.M.A. 1976); *United States v. Occhi*, 2 M.J. 60 (C.M.A. 1976). Subsection (c) is new and based on Article 71; *United States v. Lallande*, 22 U.S.C.M.A. 170, 46 C.M.R. 170 (1973); *United State v. May*, 10 U.S.C.M.A. 258, 27 C.M.R. 432 (1959). *Cf.* 18 U.S.C. § 3651 ("upon such terms and conditions as the court deems best"). The notice provisions are designed to facilitate vacation when that becomes necessary. *See* the Analysis, R.C.M. 1109. The language limiting the period of suspension to the accused's current enlistment has been deleted. *See United States v. Thomas*, 45 C.M.R. 908 (N.C.M.R. 1972). *Cf. United States v. Clardy*, 13 M.J. 308 (C.M.A. 1982). *See also* subsection (e) of this rule.

1990 Amendment: The third sentence was amended to delete the limitation of Secretarial designation to an "officer exercising general court-martial jurisdiction over the command to which the accused is assigned" and to permit such designation to any "commanding officer." This comports with the language of Article 74(a), UCMJ and paragraphs 97 *a* of MCM, 1951 and MCM, 1969. The specific designation of inferior courts-martial convening authorities to remit or suspend unexecuted portions was not intended to limit in any other respects the Secretarial designation power. Except for a sentence which has been approved by the President, remission or suspension authority is otherwise left entirely to departmental regulations.

The last sentence was added to clarify the authority of the officials named in section (b) to grant clemency or mitigating action on those parts of the sentence that have been approved and ordered executed but that have not actually been carried out. In the case of forfeiture the "carrying out " involves the actual collection after pay accrues on a daily basis. Thus, even when a sentence to total forfeiture has been approved and ordered executed, the named officials can still grant clemency or mitigating action. Although a prisoner may be administratively placed in a nonpay status when total forfeiture has been ordered executed, the total forfeiture is collected as it would otherwise accrue during the period that the prisoner is in a nonpay status. If clemency were granted, the prisoner could be returned administratively to a pay status, pay would accrue, and any resulting partial forfeiture would be collected as it accrues. Likewise, that portion of confinement which has not been served is "unexecuted".

2004 Amendment: Subsection (b) was amended to conform to the limitations on Secretarial authority to grant clemency for military prisoners serving a sentence of confinement for life without eligibility for parole contained in section 553 of the Floyd D. Spence National Defense Authorization Act for Fiscal Year 2001, Pub.L.No. 106-398, 114 Stat. 1654, Oct 30, 2000.

Rule 1109 Vacation of suspension of sentence

(a) *In general.* This subsection is based on Article 72 and paragraph 97 *b* of MCM, 1969 (Rev.).

(b) *Timeliness.* This subsection is based on the fourth paragraph of paragraph 97 *b* of MCM, 1969 (Rev.); *United States v. Pells* , 5 M.J. 380 (C.M.A. 1978); *United States v. Rozycki*, 3 M.J. 127, 129 (C.M.A. 1977).

(c) *Confinement of probationer pending vacation proceedings.* This subsection is new and based on*Gagnon v. Scarpelli*, 411 U.S. 778 (1973); *Morrissey v. Brewer*, 408 U.S. 471 (1972); *United States v. Bingham*, 3 M.J. 119 (C.M.A. 1977). It is consistent with Fed.R.Crim. P. 32.1(a)(1). Note that if the actual hearing on vacation under subsection (d)(1) or (e)(3) and (4) is completed within the specified time period, a separate probable cause hearing need not be held.

(d) *Violation of suspended general court-martial sentence or of a suspended court-martial sentence including a bad-conduct discharge.* This subsection is based on Article 72(a) and (b); the first two paragraphs of paragraph 97 *b* of MCM, 1969 (Rev.); *United States v. Bingham, supra; United States v. Rozycki*, supra. *See also* Fed.R.Crim. P. 32.1(a)(2).

(e) *Vacation of suspended special court-martial sentence not including a bad-conduct discharge or of a suspended summary court-martial sentence.* This subsection is based on Article 72(c); *United States v. Bingham, supra; United States v. Rozycki, supra.*

Fed.R.Crim. P. 32.1(b) is not adopted. That rule requires a hearing before conditions of probation may be modified. Modification is seldom used in the military. Because a probationer may be transferred or change duty assignments as a normal incident of military life, a commander should have the flexibility to make appropriate changes in conditions of probation without having to conduct a hearing. This is not intended to permit conditions of probation to be made substantially more severe without due process. At a minimum, the probationer must be notified of the changes.

1986 Amendment: Several amendments were made to R.C.M. 1109 to specify that the notice to the probationer concerning the vacation proceedings must be in writing, and to specify that the recommendations concerning vacation of the suspension provided by the hearing officer must also be in writing. *Black v. Romano*, 471 U.S. 606, 105 S.Ct. 2254 (1985). Several references to "conditions of probation" were changed to "conditions of suspension" for consistency of terminology.

1998 Amendment: The Rule is amended to clarify that "the suspension of a special court-martial sentence which as approved includes a bad-conduct discharge," permits the officer exercising special court-martial jurisdiction to vacate any suspended punishments other than an approved suspended bad-conduct discharge.

2002 Amendment: Subsection (e) was amended to implement the amendment to 10 U.S.C. Sec. 819 (Article 19, UCMJ) contained in section 577 of the National Defense Authorization Act for Fiscal Year 2000, P. L. No. 106-65, 113 Stat. 512 (1999) increasing the jurisdictional maximum punishment at special courts-martial.

(f) *Vacation of a suspended special court-martial sentence that includes a bad-conduct discharge or confinement for one year.*

Subsection (f) was amended to implement the amendment to 10 U.S.C. Sec. 819 (Article 19, UCMJ) contained in section 577 of the National Defense Authorization Act for Fiscal Year 2000, P. L. No. 106-65, 113 Stat. 512 (1999) increasing the jurisdictional maximum punishment at special courts-martial. This amendment reflects the decision to treat an approved sentence of confinement for one year, regardless of whether any period of confinement is suspended, as a serious offense, in the same manner as a suspended approved bad-conduct discharge at special courts-martial under Article 72, UCMJ, and R.C.M. 1109.

Rule 1110 Waiver or withdrawal of appellate review

Introduction. This rule is new and is based on Article 61, as amended, *see* Military Justice Act of 1983, Pub.L. No. 98–209, § 5(b)(1), 97 Stat. 1393 (1983). The rule provides procedures to ensure that a waiver or withdrawal of appellate review is a voluntary and informed choice. *See also* Appendices 19 and 20 for forms. *See* S. Rep. No. 53, 98th Cong., 1st Sess. 22-23 (1983).

(a) *In general.* This subsection is based on Article 61. The discussion is also based on Articles 64 and 69(b).

2002 Amendment: Subsection (a) was amended to implement the amendment to 10 U.S.C. Sec. 819 (Article 19, UCMJ) contained in section 577 of the National Defense Authorization Act for Fiscal Year 2000, P. L. No. 106-65, 113 Stat. 512 (1999) increasing the jurisdictional maximum punishment at special courts-martial.

(b) *Right to counsel.* This subsection is based on Article 61(a). Although Article 61(b) does not expressly require the signature of defense counsel as does Article 61(a), the same requirements should apply. Preferably counsel who represented the accused at trial will advise the accused concerning waiver, the appellate counsel (if one has been appointed) will do so concerning withdrawal. This subsection reflects this preference. It also recognizes, however, that this may not always be practicable; for example, the accused may be confined a substantial distance from counsel who represented the accused at trial when it is time to decide whether to waive or withdraw appeal. In such cases, associate counsel may be detailed upon request by the accused. *See* R.C.M. 502(d)(1) as to the qualification of defense counsel. Associate counsel is obligated to consult with at least one of the counsel who represented the accused at trial. In this way the accused can have the benefit of the opinion of the trial defense counsel even if the defense counsel is not immediately available. Subsection (2)(C) provides for the appointment of substitute counsel when, for the limited reasons in R.C.M. 505(d)(2)(B), the accused is no longer represented by any trial defense counsel. Subsection (3) contains similar provisions concerning withdrawal of an appeal. Note that if the case is reviewed by the Judge Advocate General, there would be no appellate counsel. In such cases, subsection (3)(C) would apply. Subsection (6) clarifies that here, as in other circumstances, a face-to-face meeting between the accused and counsel is not required. When necessary, such communication may be by telephone, radio, or similar means. *See also* Mil. R. Evid. 511(b). The rule, including the opportunity for appointment of associate counsel, is intended to permit face-to-face consultation with an attorney in all but the most unusual circumstances. Face-to-face consultation is strongly encouraged, especially if the accused wants to waive or withdraw appellate review.

(c) *Compulsion, coercion, inducement prohibited.* This subsection is intended to ensure that any waiver or withdrawal of appellate review is voluntary. *See* S. Rep. No. 53, *supra* at 22–23; *Hearings on S. 2521 Before the Subcomm. on Manpower and Personnel of the Senate Comm. on Armed Services,* 97th Cong., 1st Sess. 78, 128 (1982); *United States v. Mills*, 12 M.J. 1 (C.M.A. 1981). *See also* R.C.M. 705(c)(1)(B).

(d) *Form of waiver or withdrawal.* This subsection is based on Article 60(a) and on S. Rep. No. 53, *supra* at 23. Requiring not only the waiver but a statement, signed by the accused, that the accused has received essential advice concerning the waiver and that it is voluntary should protect the Government and the defense counsel against later attacks on the adequacy of counsel and the validity of the waiver or withdrawal.

(e) *To whom submitted.* Subsection (1) is based on Article 60(a). Article 60(b) does not establish where a withdrawal is filed. Subsection (2) establishes a procedure which should be easy for the accused to use and which ensures the withdrawal will be forwarded to the proper authority. A waiver or withdrawal of appeal is filed with the convening authority or authority exercising general court-martial jurisdiction for administrative convenience. *See* Hearings on S. 2521, *supra* at 31.

(f) *Time limit.* Subsection (1) is based on Article 60(a). Subsection (2) is based on Article 60(b). *See also* subsection (g)(3) and Analysis, below.

1991 Amendment: Language was added to clarify that, although the waiver must be filed within 10 days of receipt by the accused or defense counsel of the convening authority's action, it may be signed at any time after trial up to the filing deadline.

(g) *Effect of waiver of withdrawal, substantial compliance required.* Subsection (1) is based on Article 60(c). Subsections (2) and (3) are based on Article 64. Subsection (3) also recognizes that, once an appeal is filed (*i.e.,* not waived in a timely manner) there may be a point at which it may not be withdrawn as of right. *Cf.* Sup. Ct. R. 53; Fed.R.App. P.42; *Hammett v.Texas*, 448 U.S. 725 (1974); *Shellman v. U.S. Lines, Inc.*, 528 F. 2d 675 (9th Cir. 1975), *cert. denied*, 425 U.S. 936 (1976). Subsection (4) is intended to protect the integrity of the waiver or withdrawal procedure by ensuring compliance with this rule. The accused should be notified promptly if a purported waiver or withdrawal is defective.

Rule 1111 Disposition of the record of trial after action

This rule is based generally on paragraph 91 of MCM, 1969 (Rev.), but is modified to conform to the accused's right to waive or withdraw appellate review and to the elimination of supervisory review and of automatic review of cases affecting general and flag officers. *See* Articles 61, 64, 65, 66(b). Some matters in paragraph 91 of MCM, 1969 (Rev.) are covered in other rules. *See* R.C.M. 1103(b)(3)(F); 1104(b)(1)(B).

2002 Amendment: R.C.M. 1111(b) was amended to implement the amendment to 10 U.S.C. Sec. 819 (Article 19, UCMJ) contained in section 577 of the National Defense Authorization Act for Fiscal Year 2000, P. L. No. 106-65, 113 Stat. 512 (1999) increasing the jurisdictional maximum punishment at special courts-martial. The amendment ensures all special courts-martial not requiring appellate review are reviewed by a judge advocate under R.C.M. 1112.

Rule 1112 Review by a judge advocate

This rule is based on Articles 64 and 65(b), *as amended, see* Military Justice Act of 1983, Pub.L. No. 98-209, §§ 6(d)(1), (7)(a)(1), 97 Stat. 1393 (1983).

1986 Amendment: The last paragraph of R.C.M. 1112(d) was added to clarify the requirement that a copy of the judge advocate's review be attached to the original and each copy of the record of trial. The last paragraph of R.C.M. 1112(e), which previously contained an equivalent but ambiguous requirement, was deleted.

1990 Amendment: Subsection (b) was amended in conjunction with the implementation of findings of not guilty only by reason of lack of mental responsibility provided for in Article 50 *a*, UCMJ (Military Justice Amendments of 1986, tit. VIII, § 802, National Defense Authorization Act for Fiscal Year 1987, Pub. L. 99–661, 100 Stat. 3905 (1986)).

*2002 Amendment:*R.C.M. 1112(a)(2) was amended to implement the amendment to 10 U.S.C. Sec. 819 (Article 19, UCMJ) contained in section 577 of the National Defense Authorization Act for Fiscal Year 2000, P. L. No. 106-65, 113 Stat. 512 (1999) increasing the jurisdictional maximum punishment at special courts-martial. The amendment ensures all special courts-martial not requiring appellate review are reviewed by a judge advocate under R.C.M. 1112.

Rule 1113 Execution of sentences

Introduction. Fed.R.Crim. P. 38 is inapplicable. The execution of sentence in the military is governed by the code. *See* Articles 57 and 71. *See also* Articles 60, 61, 64, 65, 66, and 69.

(a) *In general.* This subsection is based on Article 71(c)(2) and the first paragraph of paragraph 98 of MCM, 1969 (Rev.). *See also* Articles 60, 61, 64, 65, 66, and 67.

1991 Amendment: The discussion was amended by adding a reference to subsection (5) of R.C.M. 1113(d). This brings the discussion into accord with the general rule of R.C.M. 1113(d)(2)(A) that any court-martial sentence to confinement begins to run from the date it is adjudged.

(b) *Punishments which the convening authority may order executed in the initial action.* This subsection is based on Article 71(d). *See also* the first paragraph of paragraph 88 *d*(1) of MCM, 1969 (Rev.). Note that under the amendment of Article 71 (*see* Pub. L. No. 98-209, § 5(e), 97 Stat. 1393 (1983)), the convening authority may order parts of a sentence executed in the initial action, even if the sentence includes other parts (*e.g.,* a punitive discharge) which cannot be ordered executed until the conviction is final.

(c) *Punishments which the convening authority may not order executed in the initial action.* This subsection is based on the sources noted below. The structure has been revised to provide clearer guidance as to who may order the various types of punishments executed. Applicable service regulations should be consulted, because the Secretary concerned may supplement this rule, and may under Article 74(a) designate certain officials who may remit unexecuted portions of sentences. *See also* R.C.M. 1206.

Subsection (1) is based on Article 71(c). *See also* Article 64(c)(3). The last two sentences of this subsection are based on S.Rep.No. 53, 98th Cong., 1st Sess. 25 (1983).

1991 Amendment: Language was added to the second sentence of the paragraph following subsection (c)(1)(B) to specify that a staff judge advocate's advice is required only when the servicemember is not on appellate leave on the date of final judgment and more than six months have elapsed since the convening authority's approval of the sentence. The third sentence was modified to reflect this change. The subsection was not intended to grant an additional clemency entitlement to a servicemember. Significant duty performance since the initial approval is relevant to the convening authority's determination of the best interest of the service. Since a member on appellate leave is performing no military duty, an additional staff judge advocate's advice would serve no useful purpose.

Subsection (2) is based on Article 71(b).

Subsection (3) is based on Articles 66(b), 67(b)(1), and 71(a).

(d) *Other considerations concerning execution of sentences.* Subsection (1) is based on the third paragraph of paragraph 126 *a* of MCM, 1969 (Rev.). The second paragraph of paragraph 88 *d*(1) of MCM, 1969 (Rev.) is deleted as unnecessary.

1986 Amendment: Subsection (d)(1)(B) was added to incorporate the holding in *Ford v. Wainwright*, 477 U.S. 399, 106 S.Ct. 2595 (1986). The plurality in *Ford* held that the Constitution precludes executing a person who lacks the mental capacity to understand either that he will be executed or why he will be executed. *See also United States v. Washington*, 6 U.S.C.M.A. 114, 119, 19 C.M.R. 240, 245 (1955). The Court also criticized the procedures specified by Florida law used to determine whether a person lacks such capacity because the accused was provided no opportunity to submit matters on the issue of capacity, but the case is unclear as to what procedures would suffice.

Because of this ambiguity, the drafters elected to provide for a judicial hearing, with representation for the government and the accused. This is more than adequate to meet the due process requirements of *Ford v. Wainwright.*

The word "substantial" is used in the third sentence to indicate that considerably more credible evidence than merely an allegation of lack of capacity is required before further inquiry need be made. *Ford v. Wainwright,* 447 U.S. 399, 426, 106 S.Ct. 2595, 2610 (1986) (Powell, J., concurring). The burden of showing the accused's lack of capacity is on the defense when the issue is before the court for adjudication. This is consistent with amendments to R.C.M. 909(c)(2) and R.C.M. 916(k)(3)(A) which shifted to the defense the burden of showing lack of mental capacity to stand trial and lack of mental responsibility. The rule also establishes a presumption of capacity and allows limits on the scope of the sanity board's examination.

Subsection (2)(A) is based on Articles 14 and 57(b) and paragraph 97 *c* of MCM, 1969 (Rev.). *See also* paragraph 126 *j* of MCM, 1969 (Rev.). Subsection (2)(B) is based on Article 58(b) and the third paragraph of paragraph 126 *j* of MCM, 1969 (Rev.). Subsection (2)(C) is based on Article 58(a) and paragraph 93 of MCM, 1969 (Rev.). Note that if the Secretary concerned so prescribes, the convening authority need not designate the place of confinement. Because the place of confinement is determined by regulations in some services, the convening authority's designation is a pro forma matter in such cases.The penultimate sentence in subsection (2)(C) is based on Article 12 and on paragraph 125 of MCM, 1969 (Rev.). The last sentence in subsection (2)(C) is based on 10 U.S.C. § 951. *See* the second paragraph of paragraph 18 *b*(3) of MCM, 1969 (Rev.).

1995 Amendment: Subsection (d)(2)(A)(iii) is new. It is based on the recently enacted Article 57(e). National Defense Authorization Act for Fiscal Year 1993, Pub. L. No. 102-484, 106 Stat. 2315,2505 (1992). *See generally* Interstate Agreement on Detainers Act, 18 U.S.C. App. III. It permits a military sentence to be served consecutively, rather than concurrently, with a civilian or foreign sentence.The prior subsections (d)(2)(A)(iii) - (iv) are redesignated (d)(2)(A)(iv) - (v), respectively.

Subsection (3) is based on paragraph 126 *h*(3) of MCM, 1969 (Rev.), but it is modified to avoid constitutional problems. *See Bearden v. Georgia*, 461 U.S. 660 (1983); *Tate v. Short*, 401 U.S. 395 (1971); *Williams v. Illinois*, 399 U.S. 235 (1970). *See also United States v. Slubowski*, 5 M.J. 882 (N.C.M.R. 1978), aff'd, 7 M.J. 461 (1979); *United States v. Vinyard*, 3 M.J. 551 (A.C.M.R.), *pet. denied*, 3 M.J. 207 (1977); *United States v. Donaldson*, 2 M.J. 605 (N.C.M.R. 1977), *aff'd* , 5 M.J. 212 (1978); *United States v. Martinez*, 2 M.J. 1123 (C.G. C.M.R. 1976); *United States v. Kehrli*, 44 C.M.R. 582 (A.F.C.M.R. 1971), *pet. denied*, 44 C.M.R. 940 (1972); ABA Standards, Sentencing Alternatives and Procedures § 18–2.7 (1979).

Subsection (4) is new. *See* Article 57(c).

Subsection (5) is based on the last paragraph of paragraph 125 MCM, 1969 (Rev.).

Paragraph 88 *d*(3) of MCM, 1969 (Rev.) is deleted based on the amendment of Articles 57(a) and 71(c)(2) which eliminated the necessity for application or deferment of forfeitures. Forfeitures always may be ordered executed in the initial action.

1995 Amendment: Subsection (5) was deleted when the punishment of confinement on bread and water or diminished rations [R.C.M. 1113(d)(9)], as a punishment imposable by a court-martial, was deleted. Subsection (6) was redesignated (5).

Rule 1114 Promulgating orders

(a) *In general.* Subsections (1) and (2) are based on the first paragraph of paragraph 90 *a* of MCM, 1969 (Rev.). Subsection (3) is based on paragraph 90 *e* of MCM, 1969 (Rev.). This rule is consistent in purpose with Fed.R.Crim. P. 32(b)(1).

(b) *By whom issued.* Subsection (1) is based on paragraph 90 *b*(1) of MCM, 1969 (Rev.) except that the requirement that the supervisory authority, rather than the convening authority, issue the promulgating order in certain special courts-martial has been deleted, since action by the supervisory authority is no longer required. *See* Article 65. The convening authority now issues the promulgating order in all cases. *See generally United States v. Schulthise*, 14 U.S.C.M.A. 31, 33 C.M.R. 243 (1963) (actions equivalent to publication). Subsection (2) is based on paragraphs 90 *b*(2) and 107 of MCM, 1969 (Rev.).

(c) *Contents.* Subsection (1) is based on Appendix 15 of MCM, 1969 (Rev.) but modifies it insofar as the only item which must be recited verbatim in the order is the convening authority's action. The charges and specifications should be summarized to adequately describe each offense, including allegations which affect the maximum authorized punishments. *Cf.* Fed. R. Crim. P. 32(b)(1). *See also* Form 25, Appendix of Forms, Fed.R.Crim. P. Subsection (2) is based on the third, fourth, and fifth paragraph of paragraph 90 *a* of MCM, 1969 (Rev.) except that reference is no longer made to action by the supervisory authority. *See* Article 65. *See United States v. Veilleux*, 1 M.J. 811, 815 (A.F.C.M.R. 1976); *United States v. Hurlburt*, 1 M.J. 742, 744 (A.F.C.M.R. 1975), rev'd on other grounds, 3 M.J. 387 (C.M.A. 1977).

Subsection (3) is based on the first sentence of the second paragraph of paragraph 90 *a* of MCM, 1969 (Rev.).

1986 Amendment: Reference to "subsequent actions" was changed to "subsequent orders" to correct an error in MCM, 1984.

1990 Amendment: Subsection (c)(2) was amended in conjunction with the implementation of findings of not guilty only by reason of lack of mental responsibility provided for in Article 50 *a*, UCMJ (Military Justice Amendments of 1986, tit. VIII, 802, National Defense Authorization Act for Fiscal Year 1987, Pub. L. 99-661, 100 Stat. 3905 (1986)).

(d) *Orders containing classified information.* This subsection is based on the first two paragraphs of paragraph 90 *c* of MCM, 1969 (Rev.). The second sentence of the first paragraph of paragraph 90 *c* is deleted as unnecessary.

(e) *Authentication.* This subsection is based on forms at Appendix 15 of MCM, 1969 (Rev.) and clarifies the authentication of promulgating orders. *See* Mil. R. Evid. 902(10). Note that this subsection addresses authentication of the order, not authentication of copies.

(f) *Distribution.* This subsection is based on paragraph 90 *d* of MCM, 1969 (Rev.). The matters in paragraph 96 of MCM, 1969 (Rev.) are deleted. These are administrative matters better left to service regulations.

1986 Amendment: Subsection (b)(2) was amended to clarify that actions taken subsequent to the initial action may also comprise the supplementary order. Section (c) was amended to simplify and shorten court-martial orders. *See* revisions to Appendix 17.

CHAPTER XII. APPEALS AND REVIEW

Rule 1201 Action by the Judge Advocate General

(a) *Cases required to be referred to a Court of Criminal Appeals.* This subsection is based on Article 66(b).

(b) *Cases reviewed by the Judge Advocate General.* Subsection (1) is based on Article 69(a). Subsection (2) is based on Article 64(b)(3) and Article 69(b). Subsection (3) is based on Article 69(b). Subsection (4) is based on Article 69(c). Subsection (b) is similar to paragraph 103 and the first two paragraphs of paragraph 110A of MCM, 1969 (Rev.) except insofar as the amendments of Articles 61, 64, and 69 dictate otherwise. *See* Military Justice Act of 1983, Pub.L. No. 98-209, §§ 4(b), 7(a), (e), 97 Stat. 1393 (1983). The last paragraph of paragraph 110A of MCM, 1969 (Rev.) was deleted as unnecessary.

1986 Amendment: Subsection (b)(3)(A) was changed to conform to the language of Article 69(b), as enacted by the Military Justice Act of 1983, which precludes review of cases previously reviewed under Article 69(a).

1990 Amendment: The discussion to subsection (b)(3)(A) was amended in conjunction with the implementation of Article 50 *a*,

UCMJ (Military Justice Amendments of 1986, tit. VIII, § 802, National Defense Authorization Act for Fiscal Year 1987, Pub. L. 99–661, 100 Stat. 3905 (1986)). To find an accused not guilty only by reason of lack of mental responsibility, the fact-finder made a determination that the accused was guilty of the elements of the offense charged or of a lesser included offense but also determined that, because he lacked mental responsibility at the time of the offense, he could not be punished for his actions. *See* R.C.M. 921(c)(4). Although the finding does not subject the accused to punishment by court-martial, the underlying finding of guilt is reviewable under this rule. Review, however, does not extend to the determination of lack of mental responsibility. Since the accused voluntarily raised the issue and has the burden of proving lack of mental responsibility by clear and convincing evidence, he has waived any later review of the propriety of that determination.

1990 Amendment: The date from which the two year period to file an application under R.C.M. 1201(b)(3) begins to run was amended to account for cases resulting in a finding of not guilty only by reason of lack of mental responsibility. Such cases would not proceed to sentencing but could be the subject of an application under this rule. As amended, the accused would have two years from the date findings were announced in which to file an application for review.

*1995 Amendment:*The Discussion accompanying subsection (1) was amended to conform with the language of Article 69(a), as enacted by the Military Justice Amendments of 1989, tit. XIII, sec. 1302(a)(2), National Defense Authorization Act for Fiscal Years 1990 and 1991, Pub. L. No. 101–189, 103 Stat. 1352, 1576 (1989).

(c) *Remission and suspension.* This subsection is based on Article 74. *See United States v. Russo,* 11 U.S.C.M.A. 352, 29 C.M.R. 168 (1960); *United States v. Sood,* 42 C.M.R. 635 (A.C.M.R.), *pet. denied,* 42 C.M.R. 356 (1970).

Rule 1202 Appellate counsel

(a) *In general.* This subsection is based on Article 70(a) and paragraph 102 *a* of MCM, 1969 (Rev.).

(b) *Duties.* This subsection is based on Article 70(b) and (c). *See also* the first two paragraphs of paragraph 102 *b* of MCM, 1969 (Rev.). The penultimate sentence in the rule is based on the penultimate sentence in the fourth paragraph of paragraph 102 *b* of MCM, 1969 (Rev.). The last sentence in the fourth paragraph of paragraph 102 *b* of MCM, 1969 (Rev.) is deleted as unnecessary. The last sentence in the rule is new. It is based on practice in Federal civilian courts. *See Rapp. v. Van Dusen,* 350 F. 2d 806 (3d Cir. 1965); Fed.R. App. P.21(b). *See also* Rule 27, Revised Rules of the Supreme Court of the United States (Supp. IV 1980); *United States v. Haldeman,* 599 F.2d 31 (D.C. Cir. 1976), *cert. denied,* 431 U.S. 933 (1977). *See generally* 9 J. Moore, B. Ward, and J. Lucas, Moore's Federal Practice Para. 221.03 (2d ed. 1982).

The first two paragraphs in the discussion modify the third and fourth paragraphs of paragraph 102 *b* of MCM, 1969 (Rev.). The Court of Appeals for the Armed Forces has held that appellate defense counsel is obligated to assign as error before the Court of Criminal Appeals all arguable issues unless such issues are, in counsel's professional opinion, clearly frivolous. In addition, appellate defense counsel must invite the attention of the court to issues specified by the accused, unless the accused expressly withdraws such issues, if these are not otherwise assigned as errors. Also, in a petition for review by the Court of Appeals for the Armed Forces, counsel must, in addition to errors counsel believes have merit, identify issues which the accused wants raised. *See United States v. Hullum,* 15 M.J. 261 (C.M.A. 1983); *United States v. Knight,* 15 M.J. 195 (C.M.A. 1982); *United States v. Grostefon,* 12 M.J. 431 (C.M.A. 1982). *See also United States v. Dupas,* 14 M.J. 28 (C.M.A. 1982); *United States v. Rainey,* 13 M.J. 462, 463 n. 1 (C.M.A. 1982) (Everett, C.J., dissenting). *But see Jones v. Barnes,* 463 U.S. 745 (1983) (no constitutional requirement for appointed counsel to raise every nonfrivolous issue requested by client). The third paragraph in the discussion is based on Article 70(d) and paragraph 102 of MCM, 1969 (Rev.). The fourth paragraph in the discussion is based on the establishment of review by the Supreme Court of certain decisions of the Court of Appeals for the Armed Forces. *See* Article 67(h) and 28 U.S.C. § 1259; Military Justice Act of 1983, Pub.L. No. 98–209, § 10, 97 Stat. 1393 (1983). The fifth paragraph in the discussion is based on *United States v. Patterson,* 22 U.S.C.M.A. 157, 46 C.M.R. 157 (1973). *See also United States v. Kelker,* 4 M.J. 323 (C.M.A. 1978); *United States v. Bell,* 11 U.S.C.M.A. 306, 29 C.M.R. 122 (1960).

Rule 1203 Review by a Court of Criminal Appeals

(a) *In general.* This subsection is based on Article 66(a). The discussion is based on Article 66(a), (f), (g), and (h). *See also* the first paragraph of paragraph 100 *a* and paragraph 100 *d* of MCM, 1969 (Rev.).

(b) *Cases reviewed by a Court of Criminal Appeals.* This subsection is based on Article 66(b) and the third sentence of Article 69(a). Interlocutory appeals by the Government are treated in R.C.M. 908. The third through the fifth paragraphs in the discussion are based on Articles 59 and 66(c) and (d) and are taken from the second and third paragraphs of paragraph 100 *a* and the first paragraph of paragraph 100 *b* of MCM, 1969 (Rev.). *See also United States v. Darville,* 5 M.J. 1 (C.M.A. 1978). The last sentence in the first paragraph is based on *United States v. Brownd,* 6 M.J. 338 (C.M.A. 1979); *United States v. Yoakum,* 8 M.J. 763 (A.C.M.R.), *aff'd,* 9 M.J. 417 (C.M.A. 1980). *See also Corley v. Thurman,* 3 M.J. 192 (C.M.A. 1977). The sixth paragraph in the discussion is based on *Dettinger v. United States,* 7 M.J. 216 (C.M.A. 1979); 28 U.S.C. § 1651(a). *See also United States v. LaBella,* 15 M.J. 228 (C.M.A. 1983); *United States v. Caprio,* 12 M.J. 30 (C.M.A. 1981); *United States v. Redding,* 11 M.J. 100 (C.M.A. 1981); *United States v. Bogan,* 13 M.J. 768 (A.C.M.R. 1982). The establishment of a statutory right of the Government to appeal certain rulings at trial might affect some of these precedents. *See United States v. Weinstein,* 411 F.2d 622 (2d. Cir. 1975), *cert. denied,* 422 U.S. 1042 (1976).

(c) *Action on cases reviewed by a Court of Criminal Appeals.* Subsection (1) is based on Article 67(b)(2). *See also* paragraph 100 *b*(2) and the first sentence of paragraph 100 *c*(1)(a) of MCM, 1969 (Rev.). *See also United States v. Leslie,* 11 M.J. 131 (C.M.A. 1981); *United States v. Clay,* 10 M.J. 269 (C.M.A. 1981).

Subsection (2) is based on Article 66(e). *See alsoUnited States v. Best*, 4 U.S.C.M.A. 581, 16 C.M.R. 155 (1954). The discussion is consistent with paragraph 100 *b*(3) of MCM, 1969 (Rev.).

Subsection (3) modifies paragraph 100 *c*(1)(a) of MCM, 1969 (Rev.). It allows each service to prescribe specific procedures for service of Court of Criminal Appeals decisions appropriate to its own organization and needs, in accordance with the increased flexibility allowed under the amendment of Article 67(c). *See* Military Justice Amendments of 1981, Pub.L. 97–81, 95 Stat. 1090.

Subsection (4) is based on the first paragraph of paragraph 105 *b* of MCM, 1969 (Rev.). *See also* Article 74.

Because R.C.M. 1203 is organized somewhat differently than paragraph 100 of MCM, 1969 (Rev.), the actions described in subsection (c) of this rule apply to cases referred by the Judge Advocate General to the Court of Criminal Appeals under Article 69 as well as Article 66. The actions described are appropriate for both types of cases, to the extent that they are applicable.

1986 Amendment: Subsection 5 is based on the second paragraph of paragraph 124 of MCM, 1969 (Rev.). The fourth sentence is based, in part, on *United States v. Williams*, 18 M.J. 533 (A.F.C.M.R. 1984). *See also United States v. Korzeniewski*, 7 U.S.C.M.A. 314, 22 C.M.R.104(1956); *United States v. Bledsoe*, 16 M.J. 977 (A.F.C.M.R. 1983). The provision assigning the burden of proof is consistent with amendments to R.C.M. 909(c)(2) and R.C.M. 916(k)(3)(A) which shifted to the defense the burden of showing lack of mental capacity to stand trial and lack of mental responsibility.

1998 Amendment: The change to the rule implements the creation of Article 57a, UCMJ, contained in section 1123 of the National Defense Authorization Act for Fiscal Year 1996, Pub. L. No. 104-106, 110 Stat. 186, 463-64 (1996). A sentence to confinement may be deferred by the Secretary concerned when it has been set aside by a Court of Criminal Appeals and a Judge Advocate General certifies the case to the Court of Appeals for the Armed Forces for further review under Article 67(a)(2). Unless it can be shown that the accused is a flight risk or a potential threat to the community, the accused should be released from confinement pending the appeal. *See Moore v. Akins*, 30 M.J. 249 (C.M.A. 1990).

(d) *Notification to accused.* This subsection is based on Article 67(c) (as amended, *see* Military Justice Amendments of 1981, Pub.L. 97–81, § 5, 95 Stat. 1088-89) and on the first paragraph of paragraph 100 *c* (1)(a) of MCM, 1969 (Rev.) (*see* Exec. Order No. 12340 (Jan. 20, 1982)). The discussion is based on Article 67(b) and on the second paragraph of paragraph 100 *c*(1)(a) of MCM, 1969 (Rev.).

(e) *Cases not reviewed by the Court of Appeals for the Armed Forces.* Subsection (1) is based on the first sentence of paragraph 100 *c*(1)(b) of MCM, 1969 (Rev.). *See* Article 71(b). Subsection (2) is based on the last sentence of paragraph 100c(1)(a) of MCM, 1969 Rev.). *See* Article 66(e).

(f) *Scope.* This subsection clarifies that the procedures for Government appeals of interlocutory rulings at trial are governed by R.C.M. 908.

Rule 1204 Review by the Court of Appeals for the Armed Forces

(a) *Cases reviewed by the Court of Appeals for the Armed Forces.* This subsection is based on the ninth sentence of Article 67(a)(1), on Article 67(b), and on the second sentence in Article 69. It generally repeats the first paragraph of paragraph 101 of MCM, 1969 (Rev.) except insofar as that paragraph provided for mandatory review by the Court of Appeals for the Armed Forces of cases affecting general and flag officers. *See* Article 67(b)(1), as amended by the Military Justice Act of 1983, Pub.L. No. 98–209, § 7(d), 97 Stat. 1393 (1983). The first paragraph in the discussion is based on Article 67(a), (d), and (e), which were repeated in the second and third paragraphs of paragraph 101 of MCM, 1969 (Rev.). The second paragraph in the discussion is based on *United States v. Frischholz*, 16 U.S.C.M.A. 150, 36 C.M.R. 306 (1966); 28 U.S.C. § 1651(a). *See also Noyd v. Bond*, 395 U.S. 683, 695 n. 7 (1969); *United States v. Augenblick*, 393 U.S. 348 (1969); *Dobzynski v. Green* 16 M.J. 84 (C.M.A. 1983); *Murray v. Haldeman*, 16 M.J. 74 (C.M.A. 1983); *United States v. Labella*, 15 M.J. 228 (C.M.A. 1983); *Cooke v. Orser*, 12 M.J. 335 (C.M.A. 1982); *Wickham v. Hall*, 12 M.J. 145 (C.M.A. 1981); *Cooke v. Ellis*, 12 M.J. 17 (C.M.A. 1981); *Vorbeck v. Commanding Officer*, 11 M.J. 480 (C.M.A. 1981); *United States v. Redding*, 11 M.J. 100 (C.M.A. 1981); *United States v. Strow*, 11 M.J. 75 (C.M.A. 1981); *Stewart v. Stevens*, 5 M.J. 220 (C.M.A. 1978); *Corley v. Thurman*, 3 M.J. 192 (C.M.A. 1977); *McPhail v. United States*, 1 M.J. 457 (C.M.A. 1976); *Brookins v. Cullins*, 23 U.S.C.M.A. 216, 49 C.M.R. 5 (1974); *Chenoweth v. Van Arsdall*, 22 U.S.C.M.A. 183, 46 C.M.R. 5 (1970); *United States v. Snyder*, 18 U.S.C.M.A. 480, 40 C.M.R. 192 (1969); *United States v. Bevilacqua*, 18 U.S.C.M.A. 10, 39 C.M.R. 10 (1968); *Gale v. United States*, 17 U.S.C.M.A. 40, 37 C.M.R. 304 (1967).

(b) *Petition by the accused for review by the Court of Appeals for the Armed Forces.* Subsection (1) is based on the last paragraph of paragraph 102 *b* of MCM, 1969 (Rev.). Note that if the case reached the Court of Criminal Appeals by an appeal by the Government under R.C.M. 908, the accused would already have detailed defense counsel. Subsection (2) is based on C.M.A.R. 19(a)(3).

(c) *Action on decision by the Court of Appeals for the Armed Forces.* Subsection (1) substantially repeats Article 67(f) as did its predecessor, the fourth paragraph of paragraph 101 of MCM, 1969 (Rev.) except that paragraph did not address possible review by the Supreme Court. *See* Article 67(h); 28 U.S.C. § 1259. Subsections (2) and (3) are based on Article 71(a) and (b) and on the last paragraph of paragraph 101 of MCM, 1969 (Rev.). Subsection (4) is new and reflects the possibility of review by the Supreme Court. *See* Article 67(h); 28 U.S.C. § 1259. *See also* Article 71.

Rule 1205 Review by the Supreme Court

This rule is new and is based on Article 67(h); 28 U.S.C. §§ 1259, 2101. *See* Military Justice Act of 1983, Pub.L. No. 98–209, § 10, 97 Stat. 1393 (1983).

Rule 1206 Powers and responsibilities of the Secretary

(a) *Sentences requiring approval by the Secretary.* This subsection is based on the first sentence of Article 71(b).

(b) *Remission and suspension.* Subsection (1) is based on Article 74(a). Subsection (2) is based on Article 74(b). Subsection (3) is based on the second paragraph of paragraph 105 *b* of MCM, 1969

(Rev.). *See* Exec. Order No. 10498 (Nov. 4, 1953), 18 Fed.Reg. 7003. The reference in paragraph 105 *a* of MCM, 1969 (Rev.) to Secretarial authority to commute sentences in deleted here as unnecessary. *See* Article 71(b).

Rule 1207 Sentences requiring approval by the President

This rule is based on the first sentence of Article 71(a). Paragraph 105 *a* of MCM, 1969 (Rev.), which stated the President's power to commute sentences, is deleted. Such a statement is unnecessary. *See also* U.S. Const. art. II, § 2, cl. 1; *Schick v. Reed*, 419 U.S. 256 (1974).

Rule 1208 Restoration

Introduction. This rule is based on Article 75.

(a) *New trial.* This subsection is based on paragraph 110 *d* of MCM, 1969 (Rev.). It has been modified based on the modification of the procedure for executing sentences in new trials. *See* Analysis, R.C.M. 1209. The last two paragraphs in paragraph 110 *d* are omitted here. They repeated Article 75(b) and (c), which are referred to in the discussion.

(b) *Other cases.* This subsection is based on paragraph 106 of MCM, 1969 (Rev.).

Rule 1209 Finality of courts-martial

(a) *When a conviction is final.* This subsection is based on Article 71(c), as amended, *see* Military Justice Act of 1983, Pub.L. No. 98–209, § 5(e)(1), 97 Stat. 1393 (1983). *See also* Article 64. Note that subsection (2)(B) qualifies (2)(A) even if the officer exercising general court-martial jurisdiction over the accused (or that officer's successor) approves the findings and sentence, the conviction is not final if review by the Judge Advocate General is required. *See* Article 64(c)(3); R.C.M. 1201(b)(2). As to the finality of an acquittal or disposition not amounting to findings of guilty, *see* Article 44; R.C.M. 905(g). *See also Grafton v. United States*, 206U.S. 333 (1907).

(b) *Effect of finality.* This subsection is taken from Article 76 and paragraph 108 of MCM, 1969 (Rev.). *See also* Article 69(b).

Rule 1210 New trial

This rule is based on Article 73 and is based on paragraphs 109 and 110 of MCM, 1969 (Rev.). Some matters in those paragraphs (*e.g.,* paragraphs 110 *a*(2) and 109 *d*) are covered in other rules. *See* R.C.M. 810; 1209. The second sentence of paragraph 109 *d*(1) has been deleted as unnecessary and potentially confusing. Subsections (f)(2) and (3) adequately describe the standards for a new trial. The rule is generally consistent with Fed.R.Crim. P. 33, except insofar as Article 73 provides otherwise. As to subsection (f), *see also United States v. Bacon*, 12 M.J. 489 (C.M.A. 1982); *United States v. Thomas*, 11 M.J. 135 (C.M.A. 1981). With respect to the second example under subsection (f)(3) of this rule, it should be noted that if the information concealed by the prosecution was specifically requested by the defense, a different standard may apply. *See United States v. Agurs*, 427 U.S. 97 (1976); *Brady v. Maryland*, 373 U.S. 83 (1963). *See also United States v. Horsey*, 6 M.J. 112 (C.M.A. 1979). The second sentence of paragraph 110 *f* of MCM, 1969 (Rev.) has been deleted. *See* Analysis, R.C.M. 1107(f)(3)(D)(i).

Subsections (h)(3), (4), and (5) have been modified to permit the convening authority of a new trial to take action in the same way as in a rehearing; i.e., the convening authority may, when otherwise authorized to do so (see R.C.M. 1113), order the sentence executed. Forwarding a new trial to the Judge Advocate General is not required just because the case was a new trial. The special circumstances of a new trial do not necessitate such different treatment in post-trial action.

1998 Amendment: R.C.M. 1210(a) was amended to clarify its application consistent with interpretations of Fed. R. Crim. P. 33 that newly discovered evidence is never a basis for a new trial of the facts when the accused has pled guilty. *See United States v. Lambert* , 603 F.2d 808, 809 (10th Cir. 1979); *see also United States v. Gordon*, 4 F.3d 1567, 1572 n.3 (10th Cir. 1993), *cert. denied*, 510 U.S. 1184 (1994); *United States v. Collins* , 898 F.2d 103 (9th Cir. 1990)(per curiam); *United States v. Prince*, 533 F.2d 205 (5th Cir. 1976); *Williams v. United States*, 290 F.2d 217 (5th Cir. 1961). *But see United States v. Brown*, 11 U.S.C.M.A. 207, 211, 29 C.M.R. 23, 27 (1960)(per Latimer, J.)(newly discovered evidence could be used to attack guilty plea on appeal in era prior to the guilty plea examination mandated by *United States v. Care*, 18 U.S.C.M.A. 535, 40 C.M.R. 247 (1969) and R.C.M. 910(e)). Article 73 authorizes a petition for a new trial of the facts when there has been a trial. When there is a guilty plea, there is no trial. See R.C.M. 910(j). The amendment is made in recognition of the fact that it is difficult, if not impossible, to determine whether newly discovered evidence would have an impact on the trier of fact when there has been no trier of fact and no previous trial of the facts at which other pertinent evidence has been adduced. Additionally, a new trial may not be granted on the basis of newly discovered evidence unless "[t]he newly discovered evidence, if considered by a court-martial in the light of all other pertinent evidence, would probably produce a substantially more favorable result for the accused." R.C.M. 1210(f)(2)(C).

CHAPTER XIII. SUMMARY COURTS-MARTIAL

Rule 1301 Summary courts-martial generally

(a) *Composition.* The first sentence is based on Article 16(3). In the second sentence the express authority for the Secretary concerned to provide for the summary court-martial to be from a different service than the accused is new. Paragraph 4 *g*(2) of MCM, 1969 (Rev.) included this statement: "However, a summary court-martial will be a member of the same armed force as the accused." The fact that this statement was included in a subparagraph entitled "Joint command or joint task force" left unclear what rule applied in other commands. The Working Group elected to clarify the situation by stating a general prohibition against detailing a summary court-martial from a service different from that of the accused, but allowing the service Secretaries to provide exceptions. This is based on the desirability of having the summary court-martial be from the same service as the accused, but recognizes that under some circumstances, as where a small unit of one service is collocated with another service, greater flexibility is needed, especially in order to comply with the policy in the third sentence of this subsection. The expression of policy in the third sentence is based on paragraph 4 *c* of MCM, 1969 (Rev.). The fourth sentence is based on Article 24(b) and the fifth sentence of the first paragraph of paragraph 5 *c* of MCM, 1969 (Rev.). The last sentence is based on the last sentence of the first paragraph of paragraph 5 *c* of MCM, 1969 (Rev.), but has been modified to clarify that the summary court-martial may be from outside the command of the summary court-martial convening authority.

2005 Amendment: Subsection (a) was amended to clarify that summary courts-martial convened by a combatant or joint commander are to be conducted in accordance with the implementing regulations and procedures of the service of which the accused is a member.

(b) *Function.* This subsection is based on paragraph 79 *a* of MCM, 1969 (Rev.). The rule does not restrict other lawful functions which a summary court-martial may perform under the Code. *See, e.g.,* Article 136. A summary court-martial appointed to dispose of decedent's effects under 10 U.S.C. § 4712 or 10 U.S.C. § 9712 is not affected by these rules. *See also* R.C.M. 101 and 201(a).

(c) *Jurisdiction.* This subsection is based on the first sentence of Article 20 and the first sentence of paragraph 16 *a* of MCM, 1969 (Rev.). The reference to Chapter II was added to bring attention to other jurisdictional standards which may apply to summary courts-martial.

(d) *Punishments.* This subsection is based on paragraph 16 *b* of MCM, 1969 (Rev.), and Article 20.

(e) *Counsel.* The code does not provide a right to counsel at a summary court-martial (Articles 27 and 38.). The Supreme Court of the United States held in *Middendorf v. Henry*, 425 U.S. 25 (1976), that an accused is not entitled to counsel in summary courts-martial, and that confinement may be adjudged notwithstanding the failure to provide the accused with counsel. In so holding, the Court distinguished summary courts-martial from civilian criminal proceedings at which counsel is required. *See Argersigner v. Hamlin*, 407 U.S. 25 (1972). Although the issue in *Middendorf v. Henry, supra*, was whether counsel must be provided to an accused at a summary court-martial, the Court's opinion clearly indicates that there is no right to any counsel (including retained counsel) at summary courts-martial. It is within the discretion of the convening authority to detail, or otherwise make available, a military attorney to represent the accused at a summary court-martial.

This rule does not provide a right to consult with counsel prior to a summary court-martial. There is no constitutional or statutory basis for such a right. *United States v. Mack*, 9 M.J. 300, 320-21 (C.M.A. 1980). A requirement for such consultation, although desirable under some circumstances, is unfeasible under others wherein it impedes the purposes of summary courts-martial by significantly delaying the proceedings. At present, the admissibility of a summary court-martial without a prior opportunity to consult with counsel in subsequent courts-martial has not been fully resolved. *United States v. Mack, supra; United States v. Booker*, 5 M.J. 238 (C.M.A. 1977). *See United States v. Kuehl*, 11 M.J. 126 (C.M.A. 1981).

(f) *Power to obtain witnesses and evidence.* This subsection is based on Article 46 and 47 and paragraphs 79 *b* and 115 of the MCM, 1969 (Rev.).

(g) *Secretarial limitations.* This subsection is new and recognizes the implicit authority of the service secretaries to provide additional rules, such as those governing the exercise of summary court-martial jurisdiction.

Rule 1302 Convening a summary court-martial

(a) *Who may convene summary courts-martial.* This subsection is based on Article 24(a) and paragraph 5 *c* of MCM, 1969 (Rev.).

(b) *When convening authority is the accuser.* This subsection is based on the second paragraph of paragraph 5 *c* of MCM, 1969 (Rev.).

(c) *Procedure.* This subsection clarifies that a separate written order is not necessary to convene a summary court-martial; this may be done directly on the charge sheet. Because there is little difference between summary, special, and general courts-martial with respect to the initiation and forwarding of charges, these procedures are simply referred to in the rule.

Rule 1303 Right to object to trial by summary court-martial

This rule is based on Article 20 and the second and third sentences of paragraph 16 *a* of MCM, 1969 (Rev.). Arraignment ends the right to object because arraignment is the point at which the accused is "brought to trial" within the meaning of Article 20.

Rule 1304 Trial procedure

(a) *Pretrial duties.* This subsection is based on paragraphs 79 *c* and 33 *d* of MCM, 1969 (Rev.).

(b) *Summary court-martial procedure.* Paragraph 79 *a* of MCM, 1969 (Rev.), suggested that the summary court-martial use the general court-martial trial guide. However, the general court-martial trial guide is inadequate for the person who ordinarily conducts the summary court-martial. The trial guide in Appendix 9 of this Manual was drafted to assist the lay presiding officer at summary courts-martial and incorporate the rules prescribed in this chapter.

Subsection (1) is based on paragraph 79 *d*(1) of MCM, 1969 (Rev.). The requirement to inform the accused of the date of referral was added to subsection (1)(B) to assist the accused in making motions to dismiss or for other relief. Subsection (1)(E) is intended to more fully inform the accused of the scope of the evidence (testimonial, documentary, and physical) expected to be introduced. Subsection (1)(F) is new and is designed to assist the accused in making motions and presenting evidence in defense and in extenuation and mitigation. Subsection (1)(G) is new and is designed to assure the accused that no evidence, including statements previously made to the officer detailed to conduct the summary court-martial, will be considered unless admitted in accordance with the Military Rules of Evidence. Subsection (1)(H) is new. Subsection (1)(L) is expanded to assure the accused that the exercise of rights guaranteed under the Fifth Amendment and Article 31 will not be held against the accused.

Subsection (2)(A) is based on Article 20 and the second paragraph of paragraph 79 *d*(1) of MCM, 1969 (Rev.).

Subsection (2)(B) is based on paragraph 79 *d*(2) of MCM, 1969 (Rev.).

Subsection (2)(C) is new. MCM, 1969 (Rev.) did not clarify the timing of motions in summary courts-martial.

Subsection (2)(D)(ii) is new and designed to standardize the guilty plea inquiry by referring the summary court-martial to

R.C.M. 909 which prescribed the inquiry for summary, special, and general courts-martial. Subsections (2)(D)(i) and (iii) through (v) are based on paragraph 79 *d*(2) of MCM, 1969 (Rev.). The provision in paragraph 79 *d*(2) which provided for hearing evidence on the offense(s) in a guilty plea case is omitted here because this procedure is covered in R.C.M. 1001(b)(4).

Subsection (2)(E)(i) is based on Mil. R. Evid. 101 and 1101. Subsections (2)(E)(ii) through (iv) are based on paragraph 79 *d* (3) of MCM, 1969 (Rev.).

Subsections (2)(F)(i) through (iii) are based on paragraph 79 *d*(4) of MCM, 1969 (Rev.). Note that the summary court-martial may consider otherwise admissible records from the accused's personnel file under R.C.M. 1001(b)(2). This was not permitted under MCM, 1969 (Rev.) before the amendment of paragraph 75 on 1 August 1981. *See* Exec. Order No. 12315 (July 29, 1981). Subsection (2)(F)(iv) is new and fulfills the summary court-martial's post-trial responsibility to protect the interests of the accused by informing the accused of post-trial rights.

Subsection (2)(F)(v) is new and designed to inform the convening authority of any suspension recommendation and deferment request before receipt of the record of trial. Subsection (2)(F)(vi) modifies paragraph 79 *d*(4) of MCM, 1969 (Rev.). It recognizes the custodial responsibility of the summary court-martial over an accused sentenced to confinement until the accused is delivered to the commander or the commander's designee. It does not address the subsequent disposition of the accused, as this is a prerogative of the commander.

Rule 1305 Record of trial

(a) *In general.* This rule is based on paragraphs 79 *e* and 91 *c* of MCM, 1969 (Rev.) insofar as they prescribed that the record of trial of a summary court-martial will consist of a notation of key events at trial and insofar as they permitted the convening or higher authority to require additional matters in the record. Additional requirements may be established by the Secretary concerned, the convening authority, or other competent authority. The modification of the format of the charge sheet (*see* Appendix 4) eliminated it as the form for the record of trial of a summary court-martial. A separate format is now provided at Appendix 15.

(b) *Contents.* This subsection is based on paragraphs 79 *e* and 91*c* of MCM, 1969 (Rev.).

1986 Amendment: R.C.M. 1305(b)(2) was amended to delete the requirement that the record of trial in summary courts-martial reflect the number of previous convictions considered. The Committee concluded that this requirement had only slight utility and also noted that DD Form 2329, which serves as the record of trial in summary courts-martial, has no entry for this information. The Committee also noted that the Services each have requirements for retaining documents introduced at summary courts-martial with the record of trial.

(c) *Authentication.* This subsection is based on paragraph 79 *e* of MCM, 1969 (Rev.).

2004 Amendment: This subsection was amended to require that summary courts-martial authenticate the original record of trial, as is currently the procedure for special and general courts-martial.

(d) *Forwarding copies of the record.* Subsection (1) is based on Article 60(b)(2). Subsection (2) is based on the third paragraph of paragraph 91*c* of MCM, 1969 (Rev.). Subsection (3) is self-explanatory.

2001 Amendment: Subsection (d)(2) was amended to strike the reference to "subsection (e)(1)" and insert a reference to "subsection (d)(1)" to reflect the 1995 amendment that redesignated R.C.M. 1305(e) as R.C.M. 1305(d).

Rule 1306 Post-trial procedure

(a) *Accused's post-trial petition.* This subsection is based on Article 60(b).*Cf.* Article 38(c).

(b) *Convening authority's action.* Subsection (1) refers to the detailed provisions concerning the convening authority's initial review and action in R.C.M. 1107. The time period is based on Article 60(b)(1). Subsections (2) through (4) are based on paragraph 90 *e* of the MCM, 1969 (Rev.). Subsection (2) is modified to reflect that the accused ordinarily will receive a copy of the record before action is taken. *See* Article 60(b)(2).

2004 Amendment: The cross-reference to subsection R.C.M. 1105(c)(3) is amended to R.C.M. 1105(c)(2) to conform to the 1987 Change 3 amendment that re-designated R.C.M. 1105(c)(3) as R.C.M. 1105(c)(2).

(c) *Review by a judge advocate.* This subsection is based on Article 64.

(d) *Review by the Judge Advocate General.* This subsection is based on Article 69 and refers to the detailed provisions governing such requests for review in R.C.M. 1201.

Analysis of
M.R.E.

Analysis of M.R.E.

APPENDIX 22
ANALYSIS OF THE MILITARY RULES OF EVIDENCE

SECTION I
General Provisions

The Military Rules of Evidence, promulgated in 1980 as Chapter XXVII of the Manual for Courts-Martial, United States, 1969 (Rev. ed.), were the product of a two year effort participated in by the General Counsel of the Department of Defense, the United States Court of Military Appeals, the Military Departments, and the Department of Transportation (the Department under which the Coast Guard was operating at that time). The Rules were drafted by the Evidence Working Group of the Joint Service Committee on Military Justice, which consisted of Commander James Pinnell, JAGC, U.S. Navy, then Major John Bozeman, JAGC, U.S. Army (from April 1978 until July 1978), Major Fredric Lederer, JAGC, U.S. Army (from August 1978), Major James Potuk, U.S. Air Force, Lieutenant Commander Tom Snook, U.S. Coast Guard, and Mr. Robert Mueller and Ms. Carol Wild Scott of the United States Court of Military Appeals. Mr. Andrew Effron represented the Office of the General Counsel of the Department of Defense on the Committee. The draft rules were reviewed and, as modified, approved by the Joint Service Committee on Military Justice. Aspects of the Rules were reviewed by the Code Committee as well. *See* Article 67(g). The Rules were approved by the General Counsel of the Department of Defense and forwarded to the White House via the Office of Management and Budget which circulated the Rules to the Departments of Justice and Transportation.

The original Analysis was prepared primarily by Major Fredric Lederer, U.S. Army, of the Evidence Working Group of the Joint Service Committee on Military Justice and was approved by the Joint Service Committee on Military Justice and reviewed in the Office of the General Counsel of the Department of Defense. The Analysis presents the intent of the drafting committee; seeks to indicate the source of the various changes to the Manual, and generally notes when substantial changes to military law result from the amendments. This Analysis is not, however, part of the Executive Order modifying the present Manual nor does it constitute the official views of the Department of Defense, the Department of Homeland Security, the Military Departments, or of the United States Court of Military Appeals.

The Analysis does not identify technical changes made to adapt the Federal Rules of Evidence to military use. Accordingly, the Analysis does not identify changes made to make the Rules gender neutral or to adapt the Federal Rules to military terminology by substituting, for example, "court members" for "jury" and "military judge" for "court". References within the Analysis to "the 1969 Manual" and "MCM, 1969 (Rev.)" refer to the Manual for Courts-Martial, 1969 (Rev. ed.) (Executive Order 11,476, as amended by Executive Order 11,835 and Executive Order 12,018) as it existed prior to the effective date of the 1980 amendments. References to "the prior law" and "the prior rule" refer to the state of the law as it existed prior to the effective date of the 1980 amendments. References to the "Federal Rules of Evidence Advisory Committee" refer to the Advisory Committee on the Rules of Evidence appointed by the Supreme Court, which prepared the original draft of the Federal Rules of Evidence.

During the Manual revision project that culminated in promulgation of the Manual for Courts-Martial, 1984 (Executive Order 12473), several changes were made in the Military Rules of Evidence, and the analysis of those changes was placed in Appendix 21. Thus, it was intended that this Appendix would remain static. In 1985, however, it was decided that changes in the analysis of the Military Rules of Evidence would be incorporated into this Appendix as those changes are made so that the reader need consult only one document to determine the drafters' intent regarding the current rules. Changes are made to the Analysis only when a rule is amended. Changes to the Analysis are clearly marked, but the original Analysis is not changed. Consequently, the Analysis of some rules contains analysis of language subsequently deleted or amended.

In addition, because this Analysis expresses the intent of the drafters, certain legal doctrines stated in this Analysis may have been overturned by subsequent case law. This Analysis does not substitute for research about current legal rules.

Several changes were made for uniformity of style with the remainder of the Manual. Only the first word in the title of a rule is capitalized. The word "rule" when used in text to refer to another rule, was changed to "Mil. R. Evid." to avoid confusion with the Rules for Courts-Martial. "Code" is used in place of Uniform Code of Military Justice. "Commander" is substituted for "commanding officer" and "officer in charge." *See* R.C.M. 103(5). Citations to the United States Code were changed to conform to the style used elsewhere. "Government" is capitalized when used as a noun to refer to the United States Government. In addition, several cross-references to paragraphs in MCM, 1969 (Rev.) were changed to indicate appropriate provisions in this Manual.

With these exceptions, however, the Military Rules of Evidence were not redrafted. Consequently, there are minor variations in style or terminology between the Military Rules of Evidence and other parts of the Manual. Where the same subject is treated in similar but not identical terms in the Military Rules of Evidence and elsewhere, a different meaning or purpose should not be inferred in the absence of a clear indication in the text or the analysis that this was intended.

Rule 101 Scope

(a) *Applicability.* Rule 101(a) is taken generally from Federal Rule of Evidence 101. It emphasizes that these Rules are applicable to summary as well as to special and general courts-martial. *See* "Rule of Construction." Rule 101(c), *infra.* Rule 1101 expressly indicates that the rules of evidence are inapplicable to investigative hearings under Article 32, proceedings for pretrial advice, search authorization proceedings, vacation proceedings, and certain other proceedings. Although the Rules apply to sentencing, they may be "relaxed" under Rule 1101(c) and R.C.M. 1001(c)(3).

The limitation in subdivision (a) applying the Rules to courts-martial is intended expressly to recognize that these Rules are not applicable to military commissions, provost courts, and courts of inquiry unless otherwise required by competent authority. *See* Part I, Para. 2 of the Manual. The Rules, however, serve as a "guide" for such tribunals. *Id.*

The Military Rules of Evidence are inapplicable to proceedings conducted pursuant to Article 15 of the Uniform Code of Military Justice.

The decisions of the United States Court of Appeals for the Armed Forces and of the Courts of Criminal Appeals must be utilized in interpreting these Rules. While specific decisions of the Article III courts involving rules which are common both to the Military Rules and the Federal Rules should be considered very persuasive, they are not binding; *see* Article 36 of the Uniform Code of Military Justice. It should be noted, however, that a significant policy consideration in adopting the Federal Rules of Evidence was to ensure, where possible, common evidentiary law.

(b) *Secondary sources.* Rule 101(b) is taken from Para. 137 of MCM, 1969 (Rev.) which had its origins in Article 36 of the Uniform Code of Military Justice. Rule 101(a) makes it clear that the Military Rules of Evidence are the primary source of evidentiary law for military practice. Notwithstanding their wide scope, however, Rule 101(b) recognizes that recourse to secondary sources may occasionally be necessary. Rule 101(b) prescribes the sequence in which such sources shall be utilized.

Rule 101(b)(1) requires that the first such source be the "rules of evidence generally recognized in the trial of criminal cases in the United States District courts." To the extent that a Military Rule of Evidence reflects an express modification of a Federal Rule of Evidence or a federal evidentiary procedure, the President has determined that the unmodified Federal Rule or procedure is, within the meaning of Article 36(a), either not "practicable" or is "contrary to or inconsistent with" the Uniform Code of Military Justice. Consequently, to the extent to which the Military Rules do not dispose of an issue, the Article III Federal practice when practicable and not inconsistent or contrary to the Military Rules shall be applied. In determining whether there is a rule of evidence "generally recognized", it is anticipated that ordinary legal research shall be involved with primary emphasis being placed upon the published decisions of the three levels of the Article III courts.

Under Rule 1102, which concerns amendments to the Federal Rules of Evidence, no amendment to the Federal Rules shall be applicable to courts-martial until 180 days after the amendment's effective date unless the President shall direct its earlier adoption. Thus, such an amendment cannot be utilized as a secondary source until 180 days has passed since its effective date or until the President had directed its adoption, whichever occurs first. An amendment will not be applicable at any time if the President so directs.

It is the intent of the Committee that the expression, "common law" found within Rule 101(b)(2) be construed in its broadest possible sense. It should include the federal common law and what may be denominated military common law. Prior military cases may be cited as authority under Rule 101(b)(2) to the extent that they are based upon a present Manual provision which has been retained in the Military Rules of Evidence or to the extent that they are not inconsistent with the "rules of evidence generally recognized in the trial of criminal cases in the United States District courts," deal with matters "not otherwise prescribed in this Manual or these rules," and are "practicable and not inconsistent with or contrary to the Uniform Code of Military justice or this Manual."

(c) *Rule of construction.* Rule 101(c) is intended to avoid unnecessary repetition of the expressions, "president of a special court-martial without a military judge" and "summary court-martial officer". "Summary court-martial officer" is used instead of "summary court-martial" for purposes of clarity. A summary court-martial is considered to function in the same role as a military judge notwithstanding possible lack of legal training. As previously noted in Para. 137, MCM, 1969 (Rev.), "a summary court-martial has the same discretionary power as a military judge concerning the reception of evidence." Where the application of these Rules in a summary court-martial or a special court-martial without a military judge is different from the application of the Rules in a court-martial with a military judge, specific reference has been made.

Disposition of present Manual. That part of Para. 137, MCM, 1969 (Rev.), not reflected in Rule 101 is found in other rules, *see, e.g.,* Rules 104, 401, 403. The reference in Para. 137 to privileges arising out of treaty or executive agreement was deleted as being unnecessary. *See generally* Rule 501.

Rule 102 Purpose and construction

Rule 102 is taken without change from Federal Rule of Evidence 102 and is without counterpart in MCM, 1969 (Rev.). It provides a set of general guidelines to be used in construing the Military Rules of Evidence. It is, however, only a rule of construction and not a license to disregard the Rules in order to reach a desired result.

Rule 103 Rulings on evidence

(a) *Effect of erroneous ruling.* Rule 103(a) is taken from the Federal Rule with a number of changes. The first, the use of the language, "the ruling materially prejudices a substantial right of a party" in place of the Federal Rule's "a substantial right of party is affected" is required by Article 59(a) of the Uniform Code of Military Justice. Rule 103(a) comports with present military practice.

The second significant change is the addition of material relating to constitutional requirements and explicitly states that errors of constitutional magnitude may require a higher standard than the general one required by Rule 103(a). For example, the harmless error rule, when applicable to an error of constitutional dimensions, prevails over the general rule of Rule 103(a). Because Section III of these Rules embodies constitutional rights, two standards of error may be at issue; one involving the Military Rules of Evidence, and one involving the underlying constitutional rule. In such a case, the standard of error more advantageous to the accused will apply.

Rule 103(a)(1) requires that a timely motion or objection generally be made in order to preserve a claim of error. This is similar to but more specific than prior practice. In making such a motion or objection, the party has a right to state the specific grounds of the objection to the evidence. Failure to make a timely and sufficiently specific objection may waive the objection for purposes of both trial and appeal. In applying Federal Rule 103(a), the Article III courts have interpreted the Rule strictly and held the defense to an extremely high level of specificity. *See, e.g., United States v. Rubin*, 609 F.2d 51, 61-63 (2d Cir. 1979) (objection to form of witness's testimony did not raise or preserve an appropriate hearsay objection); *United States v. O'Brien*, 601 F.2d 1067 (9th Cir. 1979) (objection that prosecution witness was testifying from material not in evidence held inadequate to raise or preserve an objection under Rule 1006). As indicated in the Analysis of Rule 802, Rule 103 significantly changed military law insofar as hearsay is concerned. Unlike present law under which hearsay is absolutely incompetent, the Military Rules of Evidence simply treat hearsay as being inadmissible upon adequate objection;*see* Rules 803, 103(a). Note in the context of Rule 103(a) that R.C.M. 801(a)(3) (Discussion) states: "The parties are entitled to reasonable opportunity to properly present and support their contentions on any relevant matter."

An "offer of proof" is a concise statement by counsel setting forth the substance of the expected testimony or other evidence.

Rule 103(a) prescribes a standard by which errors will be tested on appeal. Although counsel at trial need not indicate how an alleged error will "materially prejudice a substantial right" in order to preserve error, such a showing, during or after the objection or offer, may be advisable as a matter of trial practice to further illuminate the issue for both the trial and appellate bench.

2004 Amendment: Subdivision (a)(2) was modified based on the amendment to Fed. R. Evid. 103(a)(2), effective 1 December 2000, and is virtually identical to its Federal Rule counterpart. It is intended to provide that where an advance ruling is definitive, a party need not renew an objection or offer of proof at trial; otherwise, renewal is required.

(b) *Record of offer,* and (c) *Hearing of members—* Rule 103(b) and (c) are taken from the Federal Rules with minor changes in terminology to adapt them to military procedure.

(d) *Plain error—* Rule 103(d) is taken from the Federal Rule with a minor change of terminology to adapt it to military practice and the substitution of "materially prejudices" substantial rights of "affecting" substantial rights to conform it to Article 59(a) of the Uniform Code of Military Justice.

Rule 104 Preliminary questions

(a) *Questions of admissibility generally.* Rule 104(a) is taken generally from the Federal Rule. Language in the Federal Rule requiring that admissibility shall be determined by the "court, subject to the provisions of subdivision (b)" has been struck to ensure that, subject to Rule 1008, questions of admissibility are solely for the military judge and not for the court-members. The deletion of the language is not intended, however, to negate the general interrelationship between subdivisions (a) and (b). When relevancy is conditioned on the fulfillment of a condition of fact, the military judge shall "admit it upon, or subject to, the introduction of evidence sufficient to support a finding of the fulfillment of the condition."

Pursuant to language taken from Federal Rule of Evidence 104(a), the rules of evidence, other than those with respect to privileges, are inapplicable to "preliminary questions concerning the qualification of a person to be a witness, the existence of a privilege, the admissibility of evidence...." These exceptions are new to military law and may substantially change military practice. The Federal Rule has been modified, however, by inserting language relating to applications for continuances and determinations of witness availability. The change, taken from MCM, 1969 (Rev.), Para. 137, is required by the worldwide disposition of the armed forces which makes matters relating to continuances and witness availability particularly difficult, if not impossible, to resolve under the normal rules of evidence— particularly the hearsay rule.

A significant and unresolved issue stemming from the language of Rule 104(a) is whether the rules of evidence shall be applicable to evidentiary questions involving constitutional or statutory issues such as those arising under Article 31. Thus it is unclear, for example, whether the rules of evidence are applicable to a determination of the voluntariness of an accused's statement. While the Rule strongly suggests that rules of evidence are not applicable to admissibility determinations involving constitutional issues, the issue is unresolved at present.

(b) *Relevancy conditioned on fact.* Rule 104(b) is taken from the Federal Rule except that the following language had been added: "A ruling on the sufficiency of evidence to support a finding of fulfillment of a condition of fact is the sole responsibility of the military judge." This material was added in order to clarify the rule and to explicitly preserve contemporary military procedure, Para. 57, MCM, 1969 (Rev.). Under the Federal Rule, it is unclear whether and to what extent evidentiary questions are to be submitted to the jury as questions of admissibility. Rule 104(b) has thus been clarified to eliminate any possibility, except as required by Rule 1008, that the court members will make an admissibility determination. Failure to clarify the rule would produce unnecessary confusion in the minds of the court members and unnecessarily prolong trials. Accordingly, adoption of the language of the Federal Rules without modification is impracticable in the armed forces.

(c) *Hearing of members.* Rule 104(c) is taken generally from the Federal Rule. Introductory material has been added because of the impossibility of conducting a hearing out of the presence of the members in a special court-martial without a military judge. "Statements of an accused" has been used in lieu of "confessions" because of the phrasing of Article 31 of the Uniform Code of Military Justice, which has been followed in Rules 301–306.

(d) *Testimony by accused.* Rule 104(d) is taken without change from the Federal Rule. Application of this rule in specific circumstances is set forth in Rule 304(f), 311(f) and 321(e).

(e) *Weight and credibility.* Rule 104(e) is taken without change from the Federal Rule.

Rule 105 Limited admissibility

Rule 105 is taken without change from the Federal Rule. In view of its requirement that the military judge restrict evidence to its proper scope "upon request," it overrules *United States v. Grunden*, 2 M.J. 116 (C.M.A. 1977) (holding that the military judge must *sua sponte* instruct the members as to use of evidence of uncharged misconduct) and related cases insofar as they *require* the military judge to *sua sponte* instruct the members. *See e.g.*, S. SALTZBURG & K. REDDEN, *FEDERAL RULES OF EVIDENCE MANUAL* 50 (2d ed. 1977); *United States v. Sangrey*, 586 F.2d 1315 (9th Cir. 1978); *United States v. Barnes*, 586 F.2d 1052 (5th Cir. 1978); *United States v. Bridwell*, 583

F.2d 1135 (10th Cir. 1978); *but see United States v. Ragghianti*, 560 F.2d 1376 (9th Cir. 1977). This is compatible with the general intent of both the Federal and Military Rules in that they place primary if not full responsibility upon counsel for objecting to or limiting evidence. Note that the Rule 306, dealing with statements of co-accused, is more restrictive and protective than Rule 105. The military judge may, of course, choose to instruct *sua sponte* but need not do so. Failure to instruct *sua sponte* could potentially require a reversal only if such failure could be considered "plain error" within the meaning of Rule 103(d). Most failures to instruct *sua sponte,* or to instruct, cannot be so considered in light of current case law.

Rule 106 Remainder of or related writings or recorded statements

Rule 106 is taken from the Federal Rule without change. In view of the tendency of fact-finders to give considerable evidentiary weight to written matters, the Rule is intended to preclude the misleading situation that can occur if a party presents only part of a writing or recorded statement. In contrast to Para. 140 *a*, MCM, 1969 (Rev.), which applies only to statements by an accused, the new Rule is far more expansive and permits a party to require the opposing party to introduce evidence. That aspect of Para. 140 *a*(b) survives as Rule 304(h)(2) and allows the defense to complete an alleged confession or admission offered by the prosecution. When a confession or admission is involved, the defense may employ both Rules 106 and 304(h)(2), as appropriate.

SECTION II

Judicial Notice

Rule 201 Judicial notice of adjudicative facts

(a) *Scope of Rule.* Rule 201(a) provides that Rule 201 governs judicial notice of adjudicative facts. In so doing, the Rule replaced MCM, 1969 (Rev.), Para. 147 *a*. The Federal Rules of Evidence Advisory Committee defined adjudicative facts as "simply the facts of the particular case" and distinguished them from legislative facts which it defined as "those which have relevance to legal reasoning and the lawmaking process, whether in the formulation of a legal principle or ruling by a judge or court or in the enactment of a legislative body," reprinted in S. SALTZBURG & K. REDDEN, *FEDERAL RULES OF EVIDENCE MANUAL* 63 (2d ed. 1977). The distinction between the two types of facts, originated by Professor Kenneth Davis, can on occasion be highly confusing in practice and resort to any of the usual treatises may be helpful.

(b) *Kinds of facts.* Rule 201(b) was taken generally from the Federal Rule. The limitation with FED. R. EVID. 201(b)(1) to facts known "within the territorial jurisdiction of the trial court" was replaced, however, by the expression, "generally known universally, locally, or in the area, pertinent to the event." The worldwide disposition of the armed forces rendered the original language inapplicable and impracticable within the military environment. Notice of signatures, appropriate under Para. 147 *a*, MCM, 1969 (Rev.), will normally be inappropriate under this Rule. Rule 902(4) & (10) will, however, usually yield the same result as under Para. 147 *a.*

When they qualify as adjudicative facts under Rule 201, the following are examples of matters of which judicial notice may be taken:

The ordinary division of time into years, months, weeks and other periods; general facts and laws of nature, including their ordinary operations and effects; general facts of history; generally known geolineartal facts; such specific facts and propositions of generalized knowledge as are so universally known that they cannot reasonably be the subject of dispute; such facts as are so generally known or are of such common notoriety in the area in which the trial is held that they cannot reasonably be the subject of dispute; and specific facts and propositions of generalized knowledge which are capable of immediate and accurate determination by resort to easily accessible sources of reasonable indisputable accuracy.

(c) *When discretionary.* While the first sentence of the subdivision is taken from the Federal Rule, the second sentence is new and is included as a result of the clear implication of subdivision (e) and of the holding in *Garner v. Louisiana*, 368 U.S. 157, 173-74 (1961). In *Garner,* the Supreme Court rejected the contention of the State of Louisiana that the trial judge had taken judicial notice of certain evidence stating that:

There is nothing in the records to indicate that the trial judge did in fact take judicial notice of anything. To extend the doctrine of judicial notice ... would require us to allow the prosecution to do through argument to this Court what it is required by due process to do at the trial, and would be to turn the doctrine into a pretext for dispensing with a trial of the facts of which the court is taking judicial notice, not only does he not know upon what evidence he is being convicted, but, in addition, he is deprived of any opportunity to challenge the deductions drawn from such notice or to dispute the notoriety or truth of the facts allegedly relied upon. 368 U.S. at 173

(d) *When mandatory.* Rule 201(d) provides that the military judge shall take notice when requested to do so by a party who supplies the military judge with the necessary information. The military judge must take judicial notice only when the evidence is properly within this Rule, is relevant under Rule 401, and is not inadmissible under these Rules.

(e) *Opportunity to be heard; Time of taking notice; Instructing Members.* Subdivisions (e), (f) and (g) of Rule 201 are taken from the Federal Rule without change.

Rule 201A Judicial notice of law

In general. Rule 201A is new. Not addressed by the Federal Rules of Evidence, the subject matter of the Rule is treated as a procedural matter in the Article III courts; *see e.g.,* FED R. CRIM. P. 26.1. Adoption of a new evidentiary rule was thus required. Rule 201A is generally consistent in principle with Para. 147 *a*, MCM, 1969 (Rev.).

Domestic law. Rule 201A(a) recognizes that law may constitute the adjudicative fact within the meaning of Rule 201(a) and requires that when that is the case, *i.e.,* insofar as a domestic law is a fact that is of consequence to the determination of the action, the procedural requirements of Rule 201 must be applied. When domestic law constitutes only a legislative fact, *see* the Analysis to Rule 201(a), the procedural requirements of Rule 201 may be utilized as a matter of discretion. For purposes of this Rule, it is intended that "domestic law" include: treaties of the United States; executive agreements between the United States and any State thereof, foreign country or international organization or agency; the laws and regulations pursuant thereto of the United States, of the District of Columbia, and of a State, Commonwealth, or possession; international law, including the laws of war, general maritime law and the law of air and space; and the common law. This definition is taken without change from Para. 147 *a* except that references to the law of space have been added. "Regulations" of the United States include regulations of the armed forces.

When a party requests that domestic law be noticed, or when the military judge *sua sponte* takes such notice, a copy of the applicable law should be attached to the record of trial unless the law in question can reasonably be anticipated to be easily available to any possible reviewing authority.

1984 Amendment: Subsection (a) was modified in 1984 to clarify that the requirements of Mil. R. Evid. 201(g) do not apply when judicial notice of domestic law is taken. Without this clarification, Mil. R. Evid. 201A could be construed to require the military judge to instruct the members that they could disregard a law which had been judicially noticed. This problem was discussed in *United States v. Mead*, 16 M.J. 270 (C.M.A.1983).

Foreign law. Rule 201A(b) is taken without significant change from FED R. CRIM. P 26.1 and recognizes that notice of foreign law may require recourse to additional evidence including testimony of witnesses. For purposes of this Rule, it is intended that "foreign law" include the laws and regulations of foreign countries and their political subdivisions and of international organizations and agencies. Any material or source received by the military judge for use in determining foreign law, or pertinent extracts therefrom, should be included in the record of trial as an exhibit.

SECTION III

Exclusionary Rules and Related Matters Concerning Self-Incrimination, Search and Seizure, and Eyewitness Identification

Military Rules of Evidence 301–306, 311–317, and 321 were new in 1980 and have no equivalent in the Federal Rules of Evidence. They represent a partial codification of the law relating to self-incrimination, confessions and admissions, search and seizure, and eye-witness identification. They are often rules of criminal procedure as well as evidence and have been located in this section due to their evidentiary significance. They replace Federal Rules of Evidence 301 and 302 which deal with civil matters exclusively.

The Committee believed it imperative to codify the material treated in Section III because of the large numbers of lay personnel who hold important roles within the military criminal legal system. Non-lawyer legal officers aboard ship, for example, do not have access to attorneys and law libraries. In all cases, the Rules represent a judgement that it would be impracticable to operate without them. *See* Article 36. The Rules represent a compromise between specificity, intended to ensure stability and uniformity with the armed forces, and generality, intended usually to allow change via case law. In some instances they significantly change present procedure. *See, e.g.,* Rule 304(d) (procedure for suppression motions relating to confessions and admissions).

Rule 301 Privilege concerning compulsory self-incrimination

(a) *General rule.* Rule 301(a) is consistent with the rule expressed in the first paragraph, Para. 150 *b* of MCM, 1969 (Rev.), but omits the phrasing of the privileges and explicitly states that, as both variations apply, the accused or witness receives the protection of whichever privilege may be the more beneficial. The fact that the privilege extends to a witness as well as an accused is inherent within the new phrasing which does not distinguish between the two.

The Rule states that the privileges are applicable only "to evidence of a testimonial or communicative nature," *Schmerber v. California*, 384 U.S. 757, 761 (1966). The meaning of "testimonial or communicative" for the purpose of Article 31 of the Uniform Code of Military Justice is not fully settled. Past decisions of the Court of Military Appeals have extended the Article 31 privilege against self-incrimination to voice and handwriting exemplars and perhaps under certain conditions to bodily fluids. *United States v. Ruiz*, 23 U.S.C.M.A. 181, 48 C.M.R. 797 (1974). Because of the unsettled law in the area of bodily fluids, it is not the intent of the Committee to adopt any particular definition of "testimonial or communicative." It is believed, however, that the decisions of the United States Supreme Court construing the Fifth Amendment, *e.g., Schmerber v. California*, 384 U.S. 757 (1966), should be persuasive in this area. Although the right against self-incrimination has a number of varied justifications, its primary purposes are to shield the individual's thought processes from Government inquiry and to permit an individual to refuse to *create* evidence to be used against him. Taking a bodily fluid sample from the person of an individual fails to involve either concern. The fluid in question already exists; the individual's actions are irrelevant to its seizure except insofar as the health and privacy of the individual can be further protected through his or her cooperation. No persuasive reason exists for Article 31 to be extended to bodily fluids. To the extent that due process issues are involved in bodily fluid extractions, Rule 312 provides adequate protections.

The privilege against self-incrimination does not protect a person from being compelled by an order or forced to exhibit his or her body or other physical characteristics as evidence. Similarly, the privilege is not violated by taking the fingerprints of an individual, in exhibiting or requiring that a scar on the body be exhibited, in placing an individual's feet in tracks, or by trying shoes or clothing on a person or in requiring the person to do so, or by compelling a person to place a hand, arm, or other part of the body under the ultra-violet light for identification or other purposes.

The privilege is not violated by the use of compulsion in requiring a person to produce a record or writing under his or her control containing or disclosing incriminating matter when the record or writing is under control in a representative rather than a personal capacity as, for example, when it is in his or her control as the custodian for a non-appropriated fund. *See, e.g.,* Para. 150 *b* of MCM, 1969 (Rev.); *United States v. Sellers*, 12 U.S.C.M.A.

262, 30 C.M.R. 262 (1961); *United States v. Haskins*, 11 U.S.C.M.A. 365, 29 C.M.R. 181 (1960).

(b) *Standing.*

(1) *In general.* Rule 301(b)(1) recites the first part of the third paragraph of Para. 150 *b*, MCM, 1969 (Rev.) without change except that the present language indicating that neither counsel nor the court may object to a self-incriminating question put to the witness has been deleted as being unnecessary.

(2) *Judicial advice.* A clarified version of the military judge's responsibility under Para. 150 *b* of MCM, 1969 (Rev.) to warn an uninformed witness of the right against self-incrimination has been placed in Rule 301(b)(2). The revised procedure precludes counsel asking in open court that a witness be advised of his or her rights, a practice which the Committee deemed of doubtful propriety.

(c) *Exercise of the privilege.* The first sentence of Rule 301(c) restates generally the first sentence of the second paragraph of Para. 150 *b*, MCM, 1969 (Rev.). The language "unless it clearly appears to the military judge" was deleted. The test involved is purely objective.

The second sentence of Rule 301(c) is similar to the second and third sentences of the second paragraph of Para. 150 *b* but the language has been rephrased. The present Manual's language states that the witness can be required to answer if for "any other reason, he can successfully object to being tried for any offense as to which the answer may supply information to incriminate him..." Rule 301(c) provides: "A witness may not assert the privilege if the witness is not subject to criminal penalty as a result of an answer by reason of immunity, running of the statute of limitations, or similar reason." It is believed that the new language is simpler and more accurate as the privilege is properly defined in terms of consequence rather than in terms of "being tried." In the absence of a possible criminal penalty, to include the mere fact of conviction, there is no risk of self-incrimination. It is not the intent of the Committee to adopt any particular definition of "criminal penalty." It should be noted, however, that the courts have occasionally found that certain consequences that are technically non-criminal are so similar in effect that the privilege should be construed to apply. *See e.g., Spevack v. Klein*, 385 U.S. 511 (1967); *United States v. Ruiz*, 23 U.S.C.M.A. 181, 48 C.M.R. 797 (1974). Thus, the definition of "criminal penalty" may depend upon the facts of a given case as well as the applicable case law.

It should be emphasized that an accused, unlike a witness, need not take the stand to claim the privilege.

(1) *Immunity generally.* Rule 301(c)(1) recognizes that "testimonial" or "use plus fruits" immunity is sufficient to overcome the privilege against self-incrimination, *cf., United States v. Rivera*, 1 M.J. 107 (C.M.A. 1975), *reversing on other grounds,* 49 C.M.R. 259 (A.C.M.R. 1974), and declares that such immunity is adequate for purposes of the Manual. The Rule recognizes that immunity may be granted under federal statutes as well as under provisions of the Manual.

(2) *Notification of immunity or leniency.* The basic disclosure provision of Rule 301(c)(2) is taken from *United States v. Webster*, 1 M.J. 216 (C.M.A. 1975). Disclosure should take place prior to arraignment in order to conform with the timing requirements of Rule 304 and to ensure efficient trial procedure.

(d) *Waiver by a witness.* The first sentence of Rule 301(d) repeats without change the third sentence of the third paragraph of Para. 150 *b* of MCM, 1969 (Rev.).

The second sentence of the Rule restates the second section of the present rule.subparagraph but with a minor change of wording. The present text reads: "The witness may be considered to have waived the privilege to this extent by having made the answer, but such a waiver will not extend to a rehearing or new or other trial," while the new language is: "This limited waiver of the privilege applies only at the trial at which the answer is given, does not extend to a rehearing or new or other trial, and is subject to Rule 608(b)."

(e) *Waiver by the accused.* Except for the reference to Rule 608(b), Rule 301 (e) generally restates the fourth sentence of the third rule.subparagraph of Para. 149 *b*(1), MCM, 1969 (Rev.). "Matters" was substituted for "issues" for purposes of clarity.

The mere act of taking the stand does not waive the privilege. If an accused testifies on direct examination only as to matters not bearing upon the issue of guilt or innocence of any offense for which the accused is being tried, as in Rule 304 (f), the accused may not be cross-examined on the issue of guilt or innocence at all. *See* Para. 149 *b* (1), MCM, 1969 (Rev.) and Rule 608(b).

The last sentence of the third rule.subparagraph of Para. 149 *b*(1), MCM, 1969 (Rev.) has been deleted as unnecessary. The Analysis statement above, "The mere act of taking the stand does not waive the privilege," reinforces the fact that waiver depends upon the actual content of the accused's testimony.

The last sentence of Rule 301(e) restates without significant change the sixth sentence of the third rule.subparagraph of Para. 149 *b*(1), MCM, 1969 (Rev.).

(f) *Effect of claiming the privilege.*

(1) *Generally.* Rule 301(f)(1) is taken without change from the fourth rule.subparagraph of Para. 150 *b*, MCM, 1969 (Rev.). It should be noted that it is ethically improper to call a witness with the intent of having the witness claim a valid privilege against self-incrimination in open court, *see, e.g.,* ABA STANDARDS RELATING TO THE ADMINISTRATION OF CRIMINAL JUSTICE, STANDARDS RELATING TO THE PROSECUTION FUNCTION AND THE DEFENSE FUNCTION, Prosecution Standard 3–5.7(c); Defense Standard 4–7.6(c) (Approved draft 1979).

Whether and to what extent a military judge may permit comment on the refusal of a witness to testify after his or her claimed reliance on the privilege against self-incrimination has been determined by the judge to be invalid is a question not dealt with by the Rule and one which is left to future decisions for resolution.

(2) *On cross-examination.* This provision is new and is intended to clarify the situation in which a witness who has testified fully on direct examination asserts the privilege against self-incrimination on cross-examination. It incorporates the prevailing civilian rule, which has also been discussed in military cases. *See e.g., United States v. Colon-Atienza*, 22 U.S.C.M.A. 399, 47 C.M.R. 336 (1973); *United States v. Rivas*, 3 M.J. 282 (C.M.A. 1977). Where the assertion shields only "collateral" matters—*i.e.,* evidence of minimal importance (usually dealing with a rather distant fact solicited for impeachment purposes)—it is not appropriate to strike direct testimony. A matter is collateral when sheltering it would create little danger of prejudice to the accused.

Where the privilege reaches the core of the direct testimony or prevents a full inquiry into the credibility of the witness, however, striking of the direct testimony would appear mandated. Cross-examination includes for the purpose of Rule 301 the testimony of a hostile witness called as if on cross-examination. *See* Rule 607. Depending upon the circumstances of the case, a refusal to strike the testimony of a Government witness who refuses to answer defense questions calculated to impeach the credibility of the witness may constitute prejudicial limitation of the accused's right to cross-examine the witness.

(3) *Pretrial.* Rule 301(f)(3) is taken generally from Para. 140 *a* (4), MCM, 1969 (Rev.) and follows the decisions of the United States Supreme Court in *United States v. Hale*, 422 U.S. 171 (1975) and *Doyle v. Ohio*, 426 U.S. 610 (1976). *See also United States v. Brooks*, 12 U.S.C.M.A. 423, 31 C.M.R. 9 (1961); *United States v. McBride*, 50 C.M.R. 126 (A.F.C.M.R. 1975). The prior Manual provision has been expanded to include a request to terminate questioning.

(g) *Instructions.* Rule 301(g) has no counterpart in the 1969 Manual. It is designed to address the potential for prejudice that may occur when an accused exercises his or her right to remain silent. Traditionally, the court members have been instructed to disregard the accused's silence and not to draw any adverse inference from it. However, counsel for the accused may determine that this very instruction may emphasize the accused's silence, creating a prejudicial effect. Although the Supreme Court has held that it is not unconstitutional for a judge to instruct a jury over the objection of the accused to disregard the accused's silence, it has also stated: "It may be wise for a trial judge not to give such a cautionary instruction over a defendant's objection." *Lakeside v. Oregon*, 435 U.S. 333, 340-41 (1978). Rule 301(g) recognizes that the decision to ask for a cautionary instruction is one of great tactical importance for the defense and generally leaves that decision solely within the hands of the defense. Although the military judge may give the instruction when it is necessary in the interests of justice, the intent of the Committee is to leave the decision in the hands of the defense in all but the most unusual cases. *See also* Rule 105. The military judge may determine the content of any instruction that is requested to be given.

(h) *Miscellaneous.* The last portion of paragraph 150 *b*, MCM, 1969 (Rev.), dealing with exclusion of evidence obtained in violation of due process has been deleted and its content placed in the new Rules on search and seizure. *See e.g.,* Rule 312, Bodily Views and Intrusions. The exclusionary rule previously found in the last rule.subparagraph of Para. 150 *b* was deleted as being unnecessary in view of the general exclusionary rule in Rule 304.

Rule 302 Privilege concerning mental examination of an accused

Introduction. The difficulty giving rise to Rule 302 and its conforming changes is a natural consequence of the tension between the right against self-incrimination and the favored position occupied by the insanity defense. If an accused could place a defense expert on the stand to testify to his lack of mental responsibility and yet refuse to cooperate with a Government expert, it would place the prosecution in a disadvantageous position. The courts have attempted to balance the competing needs and have arrived at what is usually, although not always, an adequate compromise; when an accused has raised a defense of insanity through expert testimony, the prosecution may compel the accused to submit to Government psychiatric examination on pain of being prevented from presenting any defense expert testimony (or of striking what expert testimony has already presented). However, at trial the expert may testify *only* as to his or her conclusions and their basis and not as to the contents of any statements made by the accused during the examination. *See e.g., United States v. Albright*, 388 F.2d 719 (4th Cir. 1968); *United States v. Babbidge*, 18 U.S.C.M.A. 327, 40 C.M.R. 39 (1969). *See generally,* Lederer, *Rights Warnings in the Armed Services,* 72 Mil.L.Rev. 1 (1976); Holladay,*Pretrial Mental Examinations Under Military Law: A Re-Examination*, 16 A.F.L. Rev. 14 (1974). This compromise, which originally was a product of case law, is based on the premise that raising an insanity defense is an implied partial waiver of the privilege against self-incrimination and has since been codified in the Federal Rules of Criminal Procedure, FED. R. CRIM. P. 12-2, and MCM, 1969 (Rev.). Para. 140 *a*, 122 *b*, 150 *b*. The compromise, however, does not fully deal with the problem in the military.

In contrast to the civilian accused who is more likely to have access to a civilian doctor as an expert witness for the defense—a witness with no governmental status— the military accused normally must rely upon the military doctors assigned to the local installation. In the absence of a doctor-patient privilege, anything said can be expected to enter usual Government medical channels. Once in those channels there is nothing in the present Manual that prevents the actual psychiatric report from reaching the prosecution and release of such information appears to be common in contemporary practice. As a result, even when the actual communications made by the accused are not revealed by the expert witness in open court, under the 1969 Manual they may be studied by the prosecution and could be used to discover other evidence later admitted against the accused. This raises significant derivative evidence problems, *cf. United States v. Rivera*, 23 U.S.C.M.A. 430, 50 C.M.R. 389 (1975). One military judge's attempt to deal with this problem by issuing a protective order was commended by the Court of Military Appeals in an opinion that contained a caveat from Judge Duncan that the trial judge may have exceeded his authority in issuing the order, *United States v. Johnson*, 22 U.S.C.M.A. 424, 47 C.M.R. 401 (1973).

Further complicating this picture is the literal language of Article 31(b) which states, in part, that "No person subject to this chapter may ... request a statement from, an accused or a person suspected of an offense without first informing him ..." [of his rights].Accordingly, a psychiatrist who complies with the literal meaning of Article 31(b) may effectively and inappropriately destroy the very protections created by *Babbidge* and related cases, while hindering the examination itself. At the same time, the validity of warnings and any consequent "waiver" under such circumstances is most questionable because *Babbidge* never considered the case of an accused forced to choose between a waiver and a prohibited or limited insanity defense. Also left open by the present compromise is the question of what circumstances, if any, will permit a prosecutor to solicit the actual statements made by the suspect during the mental examination. In *United States v. Frederick*, 3 M.J. 230 (C.M.A. 1977), the Court of Military Appeals held that the defense counsel had opened the door via his questioning of the witness and thus allowed the prosecution a broader examination of the expert witness than would otherwise have been allowed. At present, what constitutes "opening the door" is unclear. An informed defense counsel must proceed with the greatest of caution being always concerned that what may be an innocent question may be considered to be an "open sesame."

Under the 1969 Manual interpretation of *Babbidge, supra,* the accused could refuse to submit to a Government examination until after the actual presentation of defense expert testimony on the insanity issue. Thus, trial might have to be adjourned for a substantial period in the midst of the defense case. This was conducive to neither justice nor efficiency.

A twofold solution to these problems was developed. Rule 302 provides a form of testimonial immunity intended to protect an accused from use of anything he might say during a mental examination ordered pursuant to Para. 121, MCM, 1969 (Rev.) (now R.C.M. 706, MCM, 1984). Paragraph 121 was modified to sharply limit actual disclosure of information obtained from the accused during the examination. Together, these provisions would adequately protect the accused from disclosure of any statements made during the examination. This would encourage the accused to cooperate fully in the examination while protecting the Fifth Amendment and Article 31 rights of the accused.

Paragraph 121 was retitled to eliminate "Before Trial" and was thus made applicable before and during trial. Pursuant to paragraph 121, an individual's belief or observations, reflecting possible need for a mental examination of the accused, should have been submitted to the convening authority with immediate responsibility for the disposition of the charges or, after referral, to the military judge or president of a special court-martial without a military judge. The submission could, but needed not, be accompanied by a formal application for a mental examination. While the convening authority could act on a submission under paragraph 121 after referral, he or she might do so only when a military judge was not reasonably available.

Paragraph 121 was revised to reflect the new test for insanity set forth in *United States v. Frederick*, 3 M.J. 230 (C.M.A. 1977), and to require sufficient information for the fact finder to be able to make an intelligent decision rather than necessarily relying solely upon an expert's conclusion. Further questions, tailored to the individual case, could also be propounded. Thus, in an appropriate case, the following might be asked:

Did the accused, at the time of the alleged offense and as a result of such mental disease or defect, lack substantial capacity to (possess actual knowledge), (entertain a specific intent), (premeditate a design to kill)?

What is the accused's intelligence level?

Was the accused under the influence of alcohol or other drugs at the time of the offense? If so, what was the degree of intoxication and was it voluntary? Does the diagnosis of alcoholism, alcohol or drug induced organic brain syndrome, or pathologic intoxication apply?

As the purpose of the revision of paragraph 121 and the creation of Rule 302 was purely to protect the privilege against self-incrimination of an accused undergoing a mental examination related to a criminal case, both paragraph 121 and Rule 302 were inapplicable to proceedings not involving criminal consequences.

The order to the sanity board required by paragraph 121 affects only members of the board and other medical personnel. Upon request by a commanding officer of the accused, that officer shall be furnished a copy of the board's full report. The commander may then make such use of the report as may be appropriate (including consultation with a judge advocate) subject only to the restriction on release to the trial counsel and to Rule 302. The restriction is fully applicable to all persons subject to the Uniform Code of Military Justice. Thus, it is intended that the trial counsel receive only the board's conclusions unless the defense should choose to disclose specific matter. The report itself shall be released to the trial counsel, minus any statements made by the accused, when the defense raises a sanity issue at trial and utilizes an expert witness in its presentation. Rule 302(c).

Although Rule 302(c) does not apply to determinations of the competency of the accused to stand trial, paragraph 121 did prohibit access to the sanity board report by the trial counsel except as specifically authorized. In the event that the competency of an accused to stand trial was at issue, the trial counsel could request, pursuant to paragraph 121, that the military judge disclose the sanity board report to the prosecution. In such a case, the trial counsel who had read the report would be disqualified from prosecuting the case in chief if Rule 302(a) were applicable.

As indicated above, paragraph 121 required that the sanity board report be kept within medical channels except insofar as it would be released to the defense and, upon request, to the commanding officer of the accused. The paragraph expressly prohibited any person from supplying the trial counsel with information relating to the contents of the report. Care should be taken not to misconstrue the intent of the provision. The trial counsel is dealt with specifically because in the normal case it is only the trial counsel who is involved in the preparation of the case at the stage at which a sanity inquiry is likely to take place. Exclusion of evidence will result, however, even if the information is provided to persons other than trial counsel if such information is the source of derivative evidence. Rule 302 explicitly allows suppression of any evidence resulting from the accused's statement to the sanity board, and evidence derivative thereof, with limited exceptions as found in Rule 302. This is consistent with the theory behind the revisions which treats the accused's communication to the sanity board as a form of coerced statement required under a form of testimonial immunity. For example, a commander who has obtained the sanity board's report may obtain legal advice from a judge advocate, including the staff judge advocate, concerning the content of the sanity board's report. If the judge advocate uses the information in order to obtain evidence against the accused or provides it to another person who used it to obtain evidence to be used in the case, Rule 302 authorizes exclusion. Commanders must take great care when discussing the sanity board report with others, and judge advocates exposed to the report must also take great care to operate within the Rule.

(a) *General Rule.* Rule 302(a) provides that, absent defense offer, neither a statement made by the accused at a mental examination ordered under paragraph 121 nor derivative evidence thereof shall be received into evidence against the accused at trial on the merits or during sentencing when the Rule is applicable. This should be treated as a question of testimonial immunity for the purpose of determining the applicability of the exclusionary rule in the area. The Committee does not express an opinion as to whether statements made at such a mental examination or derivative evidence thereof may be used in making an adverse determination as to the disposition of the charges against the accused.

Subject to Rule 302(b), Rule 302(a) makes statements made by an accused at a paragraph 121 examination (now in R.C.M. 706(c), MCM 1984) inadmissible even if Article 31 (b) and counsel warnings have been given. This is intended to resolve problems arising from the literal interpretation of Article 31 discussed above. It protects the accused and enhances the validity of the examination.

(b) *Exceptions.* Rule 301(b) is taken from prior law; *see* Para. 122 *b*, MCM 1969 (Rev.). The waiver provision of Rule 302(b)(1) applies only when the defense makes explicit use of statements made by the accused to a sanity board or derivative evidence thereof. The use of lay testimony to present an insanity defense is not derivative evidence when the witness has not read the report.

(c) *Release of evidence.* Rule 302(c) is new and is intended to provide the trial counsel with sufficient information to reply to an insanity defense raised via expert testimony. The Rule is so structured as to permit the defense to choose how much information will be available to the prosecution by determining the nature of the defense to be made. If the accused fails to present an insanity defense or does so only through lay testimony, for example, the trial counsel will not receive access to the report. If the accused presents a defense, however, which includes specific incriminating statements made by the accused to the sanity board, the military judge may order disclosure to the trial counsel of "such statement ... as may be necessary in the interest of justice."

Inasmuch as the revision of paragraph 121 and the creation of Rule 302 were intended primarily to deal with the situation in which the accused denies committing an offense and only raises an insanity defense as an alternative defense, the defense may consider that it is appropriate to disclose the entire sanity report to the trial counsel in a case in which the defense concedes the commission of the offense but is raising as its sole defense the mental state of the accused.

(d) *Non-compliance by the accused.* Rule 302(d) restates prior law and is in addition to any other lawful sanctions. As Rule 302 and the revised paragraph 121 adequately protect the accused's right against self-incrimination at a sanity board, sanctions other than that found in Rule 302(d) should be statutorily and constitutionally possible. In an unusual case these sanctions might include prosecution of an accused for disobedience of a lawful order to cooperate with the sanity board.

(e) *Procedure.* Rule 302(e) recognizes that a violation of paragraph 121 or Rule 302 is in effect a misuse of immunized testimony—the coerced testimony of the accused at the sanity board—and thus results in an involuntary statement which may be challenged under Rule 304.

Rule 303 Degrading questions

Rule 303 restates Article 31(c). The content of Para. 150 *a*, MCM, 1969 (Rev.) has been omitted.

A specific application of Rule 303 is in the area of sexual offenses. Under prior law, the victims of such offenses were often subjected to a probing and degrading cross-examination related to past sexual history— an examination usually of limited relevance at best. Rule 412 of the Military Rules of Evidence now prohibits such questioning, but Rule 412 is, however, not applicable to Article 32 hearings as it is only a rule of evidence; *see* Rule 1101. Rule 303 and Article 31(c) on the other hand, are rules of privilege applicable to all persons, military or civilian, and are thus fully applicable to Article 32 proceedings. Although Rule 303 (Article 31(c)) applies only to "military tribunals," it is apparent that Article 31(c) was intended to apply to courts-of-inquiry, and implicitly to Article 32 hearings. *The Uniform Code of Military Justice, Hearings on H.R. 2498 Before a Subcomm. of the House Comm. on Armed Services,* 81st Cong., 1st Sess. 975 (1949). The Committee intends that the expression "military tribunals" in Rule 303 includes Article 32 hearings.

Congress found the information now safeguarded by Rule 412 to be degrading. *See e.g.,* Cong. Rec. H11944-45 (Daily ed. Oct. 10, 1978) (Remarks of Rep. Mann). As the material within the constitutional scope of Rule 412 is inadmissible at trial, it is thus not relevant let alone "material." Consequently that data within the lawful coverage of Rule 412 is both immaterial and degrading and thus is within the ambit of Rule 303 (Article 31(c)).

Rule 303 is therefore the means by which the substance of Rule 412 applies to Article 32 proceedings, and no person may be compelled to answer a question that would be prohibited by Rule 412. As Rule 412 permits a victim to refuse to supply irrelevant and misleading sexual information at trial, so too does the substance of Rule 412 through Rule 303 permit the victim to refuse to supply such degrading information at an Article 32 for use by the defense or the convening authority. *See generally* Rule 412 and the Analysis thereto. It should also be noted that it would clearly be unreasonable to suggest that Congress in protecting the victims of sexual offenses from the degrading and irrelevant cross-examination formerly typical of sexual cases would have intended to permit the identical examination at a military preliminary hearing that is not even presided over by a legally trained individual. Thus public policy fully supports the application of Article 31(c) in this case.

1993 Amendment: R.C.M. 405(i) and Mil. R. Evid. 1101(d) were amended to make the provisions of Mil. R. Evid. 412 applicable at pretrial investigations. These changes ensure that the same protections afforded victims of nonconsensual sex offenses at trial are available at pretrial hearings. *See* Criminal Justice Subcommittee of House Judiciary Committee Report, 94th Cong., 2d Session, July 29, 1976. Pursuant to these amendments, Mil. R. Evid. 412 should be applied in conjunction with Mil. R. Evid. 303. As such, no witness may be compelled to answer a question calling for a personally degrading response prohibited by Rule 303. Mil. R. Evid. 412, however, protects the victim even if the victim does not testify. Accordingly, Rule 412 will prevent questioning of the victim or other witness if the questions call for responses prohibited by Rule 412.

Rule 304 Confessions and admissions

(a) *General rule.* The exclusionary rule found in Rule 304(a) is applicable to Rules 301–305, and basically restates prior law which appeared in paragraphs 140 *a*(6) and 150 *b*, MCM, 1969 (Rev.). Rule 304(b) does permit, however, limited impeachment use of evidence that is excludable on the merits. A statement that is not involuntary within the meaning of Rule 304(c)(3), Rule

305(a) or Rule 302(a) is voluntary and will not be excluded under this Rule.

The seventh paragraph of Para. 150 *b* of the 1969 Manual attempts to limit the derivative evidence rule to *statements* obtained through *compulsion* that is "applied by, or at the instigation or with the participation of, an *official or agent of the United States, or any State thereof or political subdivision of either, who was acting in a governmental capacity* ..." (emphasis added). Rule 304, however, makes all derivative evidence inadmissible. Although some support for the 1969 Manual limitations can be found in the literal phrasing of Article 31(d), the intent of the Article as indicated in the commentary presented during the House hearings, *The Uniform Code of Military Justice, Hearing on H.R. 2498 Before a Subcomm. of the House Comm. on Armed Services,*81st Cong., 1st Sess. 984 (1949), was to exclude "evidence" rather than just "statements." Attempting to allow admission of evidence obtained from statements which were the product of coercion, unlawful influence, or unlawful inducement would appear to be both against public policy and unnecessarily complicated. Similarly, the 1969 Manual's attempt to limit the exclusion of derivative evidence to that obtained through compulsion caused by "Government agents" has been deleted in favor of the simpler exclusion of all derivative evidence. This change, however, does not affect the limitation, as expressed in current case law, that the warning requirements apply only when the interrogating individual is either a civilian law enforcement officer or an individual subject to the Uniform Code of Military Justice acting in an official disciplinary capacity or in a position of authority over a suspect or accused. The House hearings indicate that all evidence obtained in violation of Article 31 was to be excluded and all persons subject to the Uniform Code of Military Justice may violate Article 31(a). Consequently, the attempted 1969 Manual restriction could affect at most only derivative evidence obtained from involuntary statements compelled by private citizens. Public policy demands that private citizens not be encouraged to take the law into their own hands and that law enforcement agents not be encouraged to attempt to circumvent an accused's rights via proxy interrogation.

It is clear that truly spontaneous statements are admissible as they are not "obtained" from an accused or suspect. An apparently volunteered statement which is actually the result of coercive circumstances intentionally created or used by interrogators will be involuntary. *Cf. Brewer v. Williams*, 430 U.S. 387 (1977), Rule 305(b)(2). Manual language dealing with this area has been deleted as being unnecessary.

(b) *Exceptions.* Rule 304(b)(1) adopts *Harris v. New York*, 401 U.S. 222 (1971) insofar as it would allow use for impeachment or at a later trial for perjury, false swearing, or the making of a false official statement, or statements taken in violation of the counsel warnings required under Rule 305(d)-(e). Under Paras. 140 *a*(2) and 153b, MCM, 1969 (Rev.), use of such statements was not permissible. *United States v. Girard*, 23 U.S.C.M.A. 263, 49 C.M.R. 438 (1975); *United States v. Jordan*, 20 U.S.C.M.A. 614, 44 C.M.R. 44 (1971). The Court of Military Appeals has recognized expressly the authority of the President to adopt the holding in *Harris* on impeachment. *Jordan, supra,* 20 U.S.C.M.A. 614, 617, 44 C.M.R. 44, 47, and Rule 304(b) adopts Harris to military law. A statement obtained in violation of Article 31(b), however, remains inadmissible for all purposes, as is a statement that is otherwise involuntary under Rules 302, 304(b)(3), or 305(a). It was the intent of the Committee to permit use of a statement which is involuntary because the*waiver of counsel* rights under Rule 305(g) was absent or improper which is implicit in Rule 304(b)'s reference to Rule 305(d).

1986 Amendment: Rule 304(b)(2) was added to incorporate the "inevitable discovery" exception to the exclusionary rule based on *Nix v. Williams,* 467 U.S. 431, 104 S.Ct. 2501 (1984); *see also United States v. Kozak*, 12 M.J. 389 (C.M.A. 1982); Analysis of Rule 311(b)(2).

1990 Amendment: Subsection (b)(1) was amended by adding "the requirements of Mil. R. Evid. 305(c) and 305(f), or." This language expands the scope of the exception and thereby permits statements obtained in violation of Article 31(b), UCMJ, and Mil. R. Evid. 305(c) and (f) to be used for impeachment purposes or at a later trial for perjury, false swearing, or the making of a false official statement. *See Harris v. New York*, 401 U.S. 222 (1971); *cf. United States v. Williams*, 23 M.J. 362 (C.M.A. 1987). An accused cannot pervert the procedural safeguards of Article 31(b) into a license to testify perjuriously in reliance on the Government's disability to challenge credibility utilizing the traditional truth-testing devices of the adversary process. *See Walder v. United States*, 347 U.S. 62 (1954); *United States v. Knox*, 396 U.S. 77 (1969). Similarly, when the procedural protections of Mil. R. Evid. 305(f) and *Edwards v. Arizona*, 451 U.S. 477 (1981), are violated, the deterrent effect of excluding the unlawfully obtained evidence is fully vindicated by preventing its use in the Government's case-in-chief, but permitting its collateral use to impeach an accused who testifies inconsistently or perjuriously. *See Oregon v. Hass*, 420 U.S. 714 (1975). Statements which are not the product of free and rational choice, *Greenwald v. Wisconsin* , 390 U.S. 519 (1968), or are the result of coercion, unlawful influence, or unlawful inducements are involuntary and thus inadmissible, because of their untrustworthiness, even as impeachment evidence. *See Mincey v. Arizona*, 437 U.S. 385 (1978).

1994 Amendment: Rule 304(b)(1) adopts *Harris v. New York*, 401 U.S. 222 (1971), insofar as it would allow use for impeachment or at a later trial for perjury, false swearing, or the making of a false official statement, statements taken in violation of the counsel warnings required under Mil R. Evid. 305(d)-(e). Under paragraphs 140a(2) and 153b, MCM, 1969 (Rev.), use of such statements was not permissible. *United States v. Girard*, 23 U.S.C.M.A. 263, 49 C.M.R. 438 (1975); *United States v. Jordan*, 20 U.S.C.M.A. 614, 44 C.M.R. 44 (1971). The Court of Military Appeals has recognized expressly the authority of the President to adopt the holding in *Harris* on impeachment. *Jordan*, 20 U.S.C.M.A. at 617, 44 C.M.R. at 47, and Mil R. Evid. 304(b) adopts *Harris* in military law. Subsequently, in *Michigan v. Harvey*, 494 U.S. 344 (1990), the Supreme Court held that statements taken in violation of *Michigan v. Jackson*, 475 U.S. 625 (1986), could also be used to impeach a defendant's false and inconsistent testimony. In so doing, the Court extended the Fifth Amendment rationale of *Harris* to Sixth Amendment violations of the right to counsel.

(c) *Definitions.*

(1) *Confession and admission.* Rules 304(c)(1) and (2) express without change the definitions found in Para. 140 *a*(1), MCM, 1969 (Rev.). Silence may constitute an admission when it does not involve a reliance on the privilege against self-incrimination

or related rights. Rule 301(f)(3). For example, if an imputation against a person comes to his or her attention under circumstances that would reasonably call for a denial of its accuracy if the imputation were not true, a failure to utter such a denial could possibly constitute an admission by silence. Note, however, in this regard, Rule 304(h)(3), and Rule 801(a)(2).

(2) *Involuntary.* The definition of "involuntary" in Rule 304(c)(3) summarizes the prior definition of "not voluntary" as found in Para. 140 *a*(2), MCM, 1969 (Rev.). The examples in Para. 140 *a*(2) are set forth in this paragraph. A statement obtained in violation of the warning and waiver requirements of Rule 305 is "involuntary." Rule 305(a).

The language governing statements obtained through the use of "coercion, unlawful influence, and unlawful inducement," found in Article 31(d) makes it clear that a statement obtained by any person, regardless of status, that is the product of such conduct is involuntary. Although it is unlikely that a private citizen may run afoul of the prohibition of unlawful influence or inducement, such a person clearly may coerce a statement and such coercion will yield an involuntary statement.

A statement made by the accused during a mental examination ordered under Para. 121, MCM, 1969 (Rev.) (now R.C.M. 706, MCM, 1984) is treated as an involuntary statement under Rule 304. *See* Rule 302(a). The basis for this rule is that Para. 121 and Rule 302 compel the accused to participate in the Government examination or face a judicial order prohibiting the accused from presenting any expert testimony on the issue of mental responsibility.

Insofar as Rule 304(c)(3) is concerned, some examples which may by themselves or in conjunction with others constitute coercion, unlawful influence, or unlawful inducement in obtaining a confession or admission are:

Infliction of bodily harm including questioning accompanied by deprivation of the necessities of life such as food, sleep, or adequate clothing;

Threats of bodily harm;

Imposition of confinement or deprivation of privileges or necessities because a statement was not made by the accused, or threats thereof if a statement is not made;

Promises of immunity or clemency as to any offense allegedly committed by the accused;

Promises of reward or benefit, or threats of disadvantage likely to induce the accused to make the confession or admission.

There is no change in the principle, set forth in the fifth paragraph of Para. 140 *a*(2), MCM, 1969 (Rev.), that a statement obtained "in an interrogation conducted in accordance with all applicable rules is not involuntary because the interrogation was preceded by one that was not so conducted, if it clearly appears that all improper influences of the preceding interrogations had ceased to operate on the mind of the accused or suspect at the time that he or she made the statement." In such a case, the effect of the involuntary statement is sufficiently attenuated to permit a determination that the latter statement was not " *obtained* in violation of" the rights and privileges found in Rule 304(c)(3) and 305(a) (emphasis added).

(d) *Procedure.* Rule 304(d) makes a significant change in prior procedure. Under Para. 140 *a*(2), MCM, 1969 (Rev.), the prosecution was required to prove a statement to be voluntary before it could be admitted in evidence absent explicit defense waiver. Rule 304(d) is intended to reduce the number of unnecessary objections to evidence on voluntariness grounds and to narrow what litigation remains by requiring the defense to move to suppress or to object to evidence covered by this Rule. Failure to so move or object constitutes a waiver of the motion or objection. This follows civilian procedure in which the accused is provided an opportunity to assert privilege against self-incrimination and related rights but may waive any objection to evidence obtained in violation of the privilege through failure to object.

(1) *Disclosure.* Prior procedure (Para. 121, MCM, 1969 (Rev.)) is changed to assist the defense in formulating its challenges. The prosecution is required to disclose prior to arraignment all statements by the accused known to the prosecution which are relevant to the case (including matters likely to be relevant in rebuttal and sentencing) and within military control. Disclosure should be made in writing in order to prove compliance with the Rule and to prevent misunderstandings. As a general matter, the trial counsel is not authorized to obtain statements made by the accused at a sanity board, with limited exceptions. If the trial counsel has knowledge of such statements, they must be disclosed. Regardless of trial counsel's knowledge, the defense is entitled to receive the full report of the sanity board.

(2) *Motions and objections.* The defense is required under Rule 304(d)(2) to challenge evidence disclosed prior to arraignment under Rule 304(d)(1) prior to submission of plea. In the absence of a motion or objection prior to plea, the defense may not raise the issue at a later time except as permitted by the military judge for good cause shown. Failure to challenge disclosed evidence waives the objection. This is a change from prior law under which objection traditionally has been made after plea but may be made, at the discretion of the military judge, prior to plea. This change brings military law into line with civilian federal procedure and resolves what is presently a variable and uncertain procedure.

Litigation of a defense motion to suppress or an objection to a statement made by the accused or to any derivative evidence should take place at a hearing held outside the presence of the court members. *See, e.g.,* Rule 104(c).

(3) *Specificity.* Rule 304(d)(3) permits the military judge to require the defense to specify the grounds for an objection under Rule 304, but if the defense has not had adequate opportunity to interview those persons present at the taking of a statement, the military judge may issue an appropriate order including granting a continuance for purposes of interview or permitting a general objection. In view of the waiver that results in the event of failure to object, defense counsel must have sufficient information in order to decide whether to object to the admissibility of a statement by the accused. Although telephone or other long distance communications may be sufficient to allow a counsel to make an informed decision, counsel may consider a personal interview to be essential in this area and in such a case counsel is entitled to personally interview the witnesses to the taking of a statement before specificity can be required. When such an interview is desired but despite due diligence counsel has been unable to interview adequately those persons included in the taking of a statement, the military judge has authority to resolve the situation. Normally this would include the granting of a continuance for interviews, or other appropriate relief. If an adequate opportunity to interview is absent, even if this results solely from the witness'

unwillingness to speak to the defense, then the specificity requirement does not apply. Lacking adequate opportunity to interview, the defense may be authorized to enter a general objection to the evidence. If a general objection has been authorized, the prosecution must present evidence to show affirmatively that the statement was voluntary in the same manner as it would be required to do under prior law. Defense counsel is not required to meet the requirements of Para. 115, MCM, 1969 (Rev.), in order to demonstrate "due diligence" under the Rule. Nor shall the defense be required to present evidence to raise a matter under the Rule. The defense shall present its motion by offer of proof, but it may be required to present evidence in support of the motion should the prosecution first present evidence in opposition to the motion.

If a general objection to the prosecution evidence is not authorized, the defense may be required by Rule 304(d)(3) to make specific objection to prosecution evidence. It is not the intent of the Committee to require extremely technical pleading, but enough specificity to reasonably narrow the issue is desirable. Examples of defense objections include but are not limited to one or more of the following non-exclusive examples:

That the accused was a suspect but not given Article 31(b) or Rule 305(c) warnings prior to interrogation.

That although 31(b) or Rule 305(c) warnings were given, counsel warnings under Rule 305(d) were necessary and not given (or given improperly). (Rule 305(d); *United States v. Tempia,* 16 U.S.C.M.A. 629, 37 C.M.R. 249 (1967).)

That despite the accused's express refusal to make a statement, she was questioned and made an admission. (*see e.g.,* Rule 305(f); *Michigan v. Mosely,* 423 U.S. 96 (1975); *United States v. Westmore,* 17 U.S.C.M.A. 406, 38 C.M.R. 204 (1968).)

That the accused requested counsel but was interrogated by the military police without having seen counsel. (*see e.g.,* Rule 305(a) and (d); *United States v. Gaines,* 21 U.S.C.M.A. 236, 45 C.M.R. 10 (1972).)

That the accused was induced to make a statement by a promise of leniency by his squadron commander. (*see e.g.,* Rule 304(b)(3), Manual for Courts-Martial, United States, 1969 (Rev. ed.), Para 140a(2); *People v. Pineda,* 182 Colo. 388, 513 P.2d 452 (1973).)

That an accused was threatened with prosecution of her husband if she failed to make a statement. (*see e.g.,* Rule 304(b)(3), *Jarriel v. State,* 317 So. 2d 141 (Fla. App. 1975).)

That the accused was held incommunicado and beaten until she confessed. (*see e.g.,* Rule 304(b)(3); *Payne v. Arkansas,* 356 U.S. 560 (1958).)

That the accused made the statement in question only because he had previously given a statement to his division officer which was involuntary because he was improperly warned. (*see e.g.,* Rule 304(b)(3); *United States v. Seay,* 1 M.J. 201 (C.M.A. 1978).)

Although the prosecution retains at all times the burden of proof in this area, a specific defense objection under this Rule must include enough facts to enable the military judge to determine whether the objection is appropriate. These facts will be brought before the court via recital by counsel; the defense will not be required to offer evidence in order to raise the issue. If the prosecution concurs with the defense recital, the facts involved will be taken as true for purposes of the motion and evidence need not be presented. If the prosecution does not concur and the defense facts would justify relief if taken as true, the prosecution will present its evidence and the defense will then present its evidence. The general intent of this provision is to narrow the litigation as much as may be possible without affecting the prosecution's burden.

In view of the Committee's intent to narrow litigation in this area, it has adopted a basic structure in which the defense, when required by the military judge to object with specificity, has total responsibility in terms of what objection, if any, to raise under this Rule.

(4) *Rulings.* Rule 304(d)(4) is taken without significant change from Federal Rule of Criminal Procedure 12(e). As a plea of guilty waives all self-incrimination or voluntariness objections, Rule 304(d)(5), it is contemplated that litigation of confession issues raised before the plea will be fully concluded prior to plea. Cases involving trials by military judge alone in which the accused will enter a plea of not guilty are likely to be the only ones in which deferral of ruling is even theoretically possible. If the prosecution does not intend to use against the accused a statement challenged by the accused under this Rule but is unwilling to abandon any potential use of such statement, two options exist. First, the matter can be litigated before plea, or second, if the accused clearly intends to plead not guilty regardless of the military judge's ruling as to the admissibility of the statements in question, the matter may be deferred until such time as the prosecution indicates a desire to use the statements.

(5) *Effect of guilty plea.* Rule 304(d)(5) restates prior law; *see, e.g., United States v. Dusenberry*, 23 U.S.C.M.A. 287, 49 C.M.R. 536 (1975).

(e) *Burden of proof.* Rule 304(e) substantially changes military law. Under the prior system, the armed forces did not follow the rule applied in the civilian federal courts. Instead, MCM, 1969 (Rev.) utilized the minority "Massachusetts Rule," sometimes known as the "Two Bite Rule." Under this procedure the defense first raises a confession or admission issue before the military judge who determines it on a preponderance basis: if the judge determines the issue adversely to the accused, the defense may raise the issue again before the members. In such a case, the members must be instructed not to consider the evidence in question unless they find it to have been voluntary beyond a reasonable doubt. The Committee determined that this bifurcated system unnecessarily complicated the final instructions to the members to such an extent as to substantially confuse the important matters before them. In view of the preference expressed in Article 36 for the procedure used in the trial of criminal cases in the United States district courts, the Committee adopted the majority "Orthodox Rule" as used in Article III courts. Pursuant to this procedure, the military judge determines the admissibility of confessions or admissions using a preponderance basis. No recourse exists to the court members on the question of admissibility. In the event of a ruling on admissibility adverse to the accused, the accused may present evidence to the members as to voluntariness for their consideration in determining what weight to give to the statements in question.

It should be noted that under the Rules the prosecution's burden extends only to the specific issue raised by the defense under Rule 304(d), should specificity have been required pursuant to Rule 304(d)(3).

(1) *In general.* Rule 304(e)(1) requires that the military judge

find by a preponderance that a statement challenged under this rule was made voluntarily. When a trial is before a special court-martial without a military judge, the ruling of the President of the court is subject to objection by any member. The President's decision may be overruled. The Committee authorized use of this procedure in view of the importance of the issue and the absence of a legally trained presiding officer.

(2) *Weight of the evidence.* Rule 304(e)(2) allows the defense to present evidence with respect to voluntariness to the members for the purpose of determining what weight to give the statement. When trial is by judge alone, the evidence received by the military judge on the question of admissibility also shall be considered by the military judge on the question of weight without the necessity of a formal request to do so by counsel. Additional evidence may, however, be presented to the military judge on the matter of weight if counsel chooses to do so.

(3) *Derivative evidence.* Rule 304(e)(3) recognizes that derivative evidence is distinct from the primary evidence dealt with by Rule 304, *i.e.,* statements. The prosecution may prove that notwithstanding an involuntary statement, the evidence in question was not "obtained by use of" it and is not derivative.

February 1986 Amendment: Because of the 1986 addition of Rule 304(b)(2), the prosecution may prove that, notwithstanding an involuntary statement, derivative evidence is admissible under the "inevitable discovery" exception. The standard of proof is a preponderance of the evidence (*Nix v. Williams*, 467 U.S. 431, 104 S.Ct. 2501 (1984)).

(f) *Defense evidence.* Rule 304(f) generally restates prior law as found in Para. 140 *a*(3) & (6), MCM, 1969 (Rev.). Under this Rule, the defense must specify that the accused plans to take the stand under this subdivision. This is already normal practice and is intended to prevent confusion. Testimony given under this subdivision may not be used at the same trial at which it is given for any other purpose to include impeachment. The language, "the accused may be cross-examined only as to matter on which he or she so testifies" permits otherwise proper and relevant impeachment of the accused. *See, e.g.,* Rule 607–609; 613.

(g) *Corroboration.* Rule 304(g) restates the prior law of corroboration with one major procedural change. Previously, no instruction on the requirement of corroboration was required unless the evidence was substantially conflicting, self-contradictory, uncertain, or improbable and there was a defense request for such an instruction. *United States v. Seigle,* 22 U.S.C.M.A. 403, 47 C.M.R. 340 (1973). The holding in *Seigle* in consistent with the 1969 Manual's view that the issue of admissibility may be decided by the members, but it is inconsistent with the position taken in Rule 304(d) that admissibility is the sole responsibility of the military judge. Inasmuch as the Rule requires corroborating evidence as a condition precedent to admission of the statement, submission of the issue to the members would seem to be both unnecessary and confusing. Consequently, the Rule does not follow *Seigle* insofar as the case allows the issue to be submitted to the members. The members must still weigh the evidence when determining the guilt or innocence of the accused, and the nature of any corroborating evidence is an appropriate matter for the members to consider when weighing the statement before them.

The corroboration rule requires only that evidence be admitted which would support an inference that the essential facts admitted in the statement are true. For example, presume that an accused charged with premeditated murder has voluntarily confessed that, intending to kill the alleged victim, she concealed herself so that she might surprise the victim at a certain place and that when the victim passed by, she plunged a knife in his back. At trial, the prosecution introduces independent evidence that the victim was found dead as a result of a knife wound in his back at the place where, according to the confession, the incident occurred. This fact would corroborate the confession because it would support an inference of the truth of the essential facts admitted in the confession.

(h) *Miscellaneous.*

(1) *Oral statements.* Rule 304(h)(1) is taken verbatim from 1969 Manual paragraph 140 *a*(6). It recognizes that although an oral statement may be transcribed, the oral statement is separate and distinct from the transcription and that accordingly the oral statement may be received into evidence without violation of the best evidence rule unless the specific writing is in question, *see* Rule 1002. So long as the oral statement is complete, no specific rule would require the prosecution to offer the transcription. The defense could of course offer the writing when it would constitute impeachment.

(2) *Completeness.* Rule 304(h)(2) is taken without significant change from 1969 Manual paragraph 140 *a*(6). Although Rule 106 allows a party to require an adverse party to complete an otherwise incomplete written statement in an appropriate case, Rule 304(h)(2) allows the defense to complete an incomplete statement regardless of whether the statement is oral or in writing. As Rule 304(h)(2) does not by its terms deal only with oral statements, it provides the defense in this area with the option of using Rule 106 or 304(h)(2) to complete a written statement.

(3) *Certain admission by silence.* Rule 304(h)(3) is taken from Para. 140 *a*(4) of the 1969 Manual. That part of the remainder of Para. 140 *a*(4) dealing with the existence of the privilege against self-incrimination is now set forth in Rule 301(f)(3). The remainder of Para. 140 *a*(4) has been set forth in the Analysis to subdivision (d)(2), dealing with an admission by silence, or has been omitted as being unnecessary.

1986 Amendment: Mil. R. Evid. 304(h)(4) was added to make clear that evidence of a refusal to obey a lawful order to submit to a chemical analysis of body substances is admissible evidence when relevant either to a violation of such order or an offense which the test results would have been offered to prove. The Supreme Court in *South Dakota v. Neville*, 459 U.S. 553 (1983) held that where the government may compel an individual to submit to a test of a body substance, evidence of a refusal to submit to the test is constitutionally admissible. Since the results of tests of body substances are non-testimonial, a servicemember has no Fifth Amendment or Article 31 right to refuse to submit to such a test. *United States v. Armstrong*, 9 M.J. 374 (C.M.A. 1980); *Schmerber v. State of California*, 384 U.S. 757 (1966). A test of body substances in various circumstances, such as search incident to arrest, probable cause and exigent circumstances, and inspection or random testing programs, among others, is a reasonable search and seizure in the military. *Murray v. Haldeman*, 16 M.J. 74 (C.M.A. 1983); Mil. R. Evid. 312; Mil. R. Evid. 313. Under the Uniform Code of Military Justice, a military order is a valid means to compel a servicemember to submit to a test of a body substance. *Murray v. Haldeman, supra.* Evidence of a refusal to obey such an order may be relevant as evidence of consciousness of guilt. *People v. Ellis*, 65 Cal.2d 529, 421 P.2d 393 (1966). *See also State v. Anderson*, Or.App., 631 P.2d 822 (1981); *Newhouse v. Misterly*, 415 F.2d 514 (9th Cir. 1969), *cert. denied* 397 U.S. 966 (1970).

This Rule creates no right to refuse a lawful order. A servicemember may still be compelled to submit to the test. *See, e.g.,* Mil. R. Evid. 312. Any such refusal may be prosecuted separately for violation of an order.

Rule 305 Warnings About Rights

(a) *General Rule.* Rule 305(a) makes statements obtained in violation of Rule 305, *e.g.,* statements obtained in violation of Article 31(b) and the right to counsel, involuntary within the meaning of Rule 304. This approach eliminates any distinction between statements obtained in violation of the common law voluntariness doctrine (which is, in any event, included within Article 31(d) and those statements obtained in violation, for example, of *Miranda* (*Miranda v. Arizona*, 384 U.S. 435 (1966) warning requirements. This is consistent with the approach taken in the 1969 Manual, *e.g.,* Para. 140 *a*(2).

(b) *Definitions.*

(1) *Persons subject to the Uniform Code of Military Justice.* Rule 305(b)(1) makes it clear that under certain conditions a civilian may be a "person subject to the Uniform Code of Military Justice" for purposes of warning requirements, and would be required to give Article 31(b) (Rule 305(c)) warnings. *See, generally, United States v. Penn*, 18 U.S.C.M.A. 194, 39 C.M.R. 194 (1969). Consequently civilian members of the law enforcement agencies of the Armed Forces, *e.g.,* the Naval Investigative Service and the Air Force Office of Special Investigations, will have to give Article 31 (Rule 305(c)) warnings. This provision is taken in substance from Para. 140 *a*(2) of the 1969 Manual.

(2) *Interrogation.* Rule 305(b)(2) defines interrogation to include the situation in which an incriminating response is either sought or is a reasonable consequence of such questioning. The definition is expressly not a limited one and interrogation thus includes more than the putting of questions to an individual. *See e.g., Brewer v. Williams*, 430 U.S. 387 (1977).

The Rule does not specifically deal with the situation in which an "innocent" question is addressed to a suspect and results unexpectedly in an incriminating response which could not have been foreseen. This legislative history and the cases are unclear as to whether Article 31 allows nonincriminating questioning. *See Lederer, Rights, Warnings in the Armed Services,* 72 Mil. L. Rev. 1, 32-33 (1976), and the issue is left open for further development.

(c) *Warnings concerning the accusation, right to remain silent, and use of statement.* Rule 305(c) basically requires that those persons who are required by statute to give Article 31(b) warnings give such warnings. The Rule refrains from specifying who must give such warnings in view of the unsettled nature of the case law in the area.

It was not the intent of the Committee to adopt any particular interpretation of Article 31(b) insofar as who must give warnings except as provided in Rule 305(b)(1) and the Rule explicitly defers to Article 31 for the purpose of determining who must give warnings. The Committee recognized that numerous decisions of the Court of Military Appeals and its subordinate courts have dealt with this issue. These courts have rejected literal application of Article 31(b), but have not arrived at a conclusive rule. *See e.g., United States v. Dohle*, 1 M.J. 223 (C.M.A. 1975). The Committee was of the opinion, however, that both Rule 305(c) and Article 31(b) should be construed at a minimum, and in compliance with numerous cases, as requiring warnings by those personnel acting in an official disciplinary or law enforcement capacity. Decisions such as *United States v. French*, 25 C.M.R. 851 (A.F.B.R. 1958), *aff'd in relevant part,* 10 U.S.C.M.A. 171, 27 C.M.R. 245 (1959) (undercover agent) are not affected by the Rule.

Spontaneous or volunteered statements do not require warnings under Rule 305. The fact that a person may have known of his or her rights under the Rule is of no importance if warnings were required but not given.

Normally, neither a witness nor an accused need to be warned under any part of this Rule when taking the stand to testify at a trial by court-martial. *See*, however, Rule 801(b)(2).

The Rule requires in Rule 305(c)(2) that the accused or suspect be advised that he or she has the "right to remain silent" rather than the statutory Article 31(b) warning which is limited to silence on matters relevant to the underlying offense. The new language was inserted upon the suggestion of the Department of Justice in order to provide clear advice to the accused as to the absolute right to remain silent. *See Miranda v. Arizona,* 384 U.S. 436 (1966).

(d) *Counsel rights and warnings.* Rule 305(d) provides the basic right to counsel at interrogations and requires that an accused or suspect entitled to counsel at an interrogation be warned of that fact. The Rule restates the basic counsel entitlement for custodial interrogations found in both Para. 140 *c*(2), MCM, 1969 (Rev.), and *United States v. Tempia*, 16 U.S.C.M.A. 629, 37 C.M.R. 249 (1967), and recognizes that the right to counsel attaches after certain procedural steps have taken place.

(1) *General rule.* Rule 305(d)(1) makes it clear that the right to counsel only attaches to an interrogation in which an individual's Fifth Amendment privilege against self-incrimination is involved. This is a direct result of the different coverages of the statutory and constitutional privileges. The Fifth Amendment to the Constitution of the United States is the underpinning of the Supreme Court's decision in *Miranda v. Arizona*, 384 U.S. 436 (1966) which is in turn the origin of the military right to counsel at an interrogation. *United States v. Tempia*, 16 U.S.C.M.A. 629, 37 C.M.R. 249 (1967). Article 31, on the other hand, does not provide any right to counsel at an interrogation; *but see United States v. McOmber*, 1 M.J. 380 (C.M.A. 1976). Consequently, interrogations which involve only the Article 31 privilege against self-incrimination do not include a right to counsel. Under present law such interrogations include requests for voice and handwriting samples and perhaps request for bodily fluids. *Compare United States v.Dionivio*, 410 U.S. 1 (1973); *United States v. Mara*, 410 U.S. 19 (1973); and *Schmerber v. California*, 384 U.S. 757 (1967) with *United States v. White*, 17 U.S.C.M.A. 211, 38 C.M.R. 9 (1967); *United States v. Greer*, 3 U.S.C.M.A. 576, 13 C.M.R. 132 (1953); and *United States v. Ruiz*, 23 U.S.C.M.A. 181, 48 C.M.R. 797 (1974). Rule 305(d)(1) requires that an individual who is entitled to counsel under the Rule be advised of the nature of that right before an interrogation involving evidence of a testimonial or communicative nature within the meaning of the

Fifth Amendment (an interrogation as defined in Rule 305(d)(2) and modified in this case by Rule 305(d)(1)) may lawfully proceed. Although the Rule does not specifically require any particular wording or format for the right to counsel warning, reasonable specificity is required. At a minimum, the right to counsel warning must include the following substantive matter:

(1) That the accused or suspect has the right to be represented by a lawyer at the interrogation if he or she so desires;

(2) That the right to have counsel at the interrogation includes the right to consult with counsel and to have counsel at the interrogation;

(3) That if the accused or suspect so desires, he or she will have a military lawyer appointed to represent the accused or suspect at the interrogation at no expense to the individual, and the accused or suspect may obtain civilian counsel at no expense to the Government in addition to or instead of free military counsel.

It is important to note that those warnings are in addition to such other warnings and waiver questions as may be required by Rule 305.

Rule 305(d)(1)(A) follows the plurality of civilian jurisdiction by utilizing an objective test in defining "custodial" interrogation. *See also United States v. Temperley*, 22 U.S.C.M.A. 383, 47 C.M.R. 235 (1978). Unfortunately, there is no national consensus as to the exact nature of the test that should be used. The language used in the Rule results from an analysis of *Miranda v. Arizona*, 384 U.S. 436 (1966) which leads to the conclusion that *Miranda* is predominately a voluntariness decision concerned with the effects of the psychological coercion inherent in official questioning. *See e.g., Lederer, Miranda v. Arizona—The Law Today,* 78 Mil. L. Rev. 107, 130 (1977).

The variant chosen adopts an objective test that complies with *Miranda's* intent by using the viewpoint of the suspect. The objective nature of the test, however, makes it improbable that a suspect would be able to claim a custodial status not recognized by the interrogator. The test makes the actual belief of the suspect irrelevant because of the belief that it adds nothing in practice and would unnecessarily lengthen trial.

Rule 305(d)(1)(B) codifies the Supreme Court's decisions in *Brewer v. Williams*, 480 U.S. 387 (1977) and *Massiah v. United States*, 377 U.S. 201 (1964). As modified by *Brewer, Massiah* requires that an accused or suspect be advised of his or her right to counsel prior to interrogation, whether open or surreptitious, if that interrogation takes place after either arraignment or indictment. As the Armed Forces lack any equivalent to those civilian procedural points, the initiation of the formal military criminal process has been utilized as the functional equivalent. Accordingly, the right to counsel attaches if an individual is interrogated after preferral of charges or imposition of pretrial arrest, restriction, or confinement. The right is not triggered by apprehension or temporary detention. Undercover investigation prior to the formal beginning of the criminal process will not be affected by this, but jailhouse interrogations will generally be prohibited. *Compare* Rule 305(d)(1)(B) with *United States v. Hinkson*, 17 U.S.C.M.A. 126, 37 C.M.R. 390 (1967) and *United States v. Gibson*, 3 U.S.C.M.A. 746, 14 C.M.R. 164 (1954).

1994 Amendment: Subdivision (d) was amended to conform military practice with the Supreme Court's decision in *McNeil v. Wisconsin*, 501 U.S. 171 (1991). In *McNeil*, the Court clarified the distinction between the Sixth Amendment right to counsel and the Fifth Amendment right to counsel. The court reiterated that the Sixth Amendment right to counsel does not attach until the initiation of adversary proceedings. In the military, the initiation of adversary proceedings normally occurs at preferral of charges. *See United States v. Jordan*, 29 M.J. 177, 187 (C.M.A. 1989); *See United States v. Wattenbarger*, 21 M.J. 41, 43 (C.M.A. 1985), *cert. denied*, 477 U.S. 904 (1986). However, it is possible that, under unusual circumstances, the courts may find that the Sixth Amendment right attaches prior to preferral. *See Wattenbarger*, 21 M.J. at 43-44. Since the imposition of conditions on liberty, restriction, arrest, or confinement does not trigger the Sixth Amendment right to counsel, references to these events were eliminated from the rule. These events may, however, be offered as evidence that the government has initiated adversary proceedings in a particular case.

(2) *Counsel.* Rule 305(d)(2) sets forth the basic right to counsel at interrogations required under 1969 Manual Para. 140 *a*(2). The Rule rejects the interpretation of Para. 140 *a*(2) set forth in *United States v. Hofbauer*, 5 M.J. 409 (C.M.A. 1978) and *United States v. Clark*, 22 U.S.C.M.A. 570, 48 C.M.R. 77 (1974) which held that the Manual only provided a right to military counsel at an interrogation in the event of financial indigency—minimum *Miranda* rule.

Rule 305(d)(2) clarifies prior practice insofar as it explicitly indicates that no right to individual military counsel of the suspect's or accused's choice exists. *See e.g., United States v. Wilcox*, 3 M.J. 803 (A.C.M.R. 1977).

(e) *Notice to Counsel.* Rule 305(e) is taken from *United States v. McOmber*, 1 M.J. 380 (C.M.A. 1976). The holding of that case bas been expanded slightly to clarify the situation in which an interrogator does not have actual knowledge that an attorney has been appointed for or retained by the accused or suspect with respect to the offenses, but reasonably should be so aware. In the absence of the expansion, present law places a premium on law enforcement ignorance and has the potential for encouraging perjury. The change rejects the view expressed in *United States v. Roy*, 4 M.J. 840 (A.C.M.R. 1978) which held that in the absence of bad faith a criminal investigator who interviewed the accused one day before the scheduled Article 32 investigation was not in violation of *McOmber* because he was unaware of the appointment of counsel.

Factors which may be considered in determining whether an interrogator should have reasonably known that an individual had counsel for purposes of this Rule include:

Whether the interrogator knew that the person to be questioned had requested counsel;

Whether the interrogator knew that the person to be questioned had already been involved in a pretrial proceeding at which he would ordinarily be represented by counsel;

Any regulations governing the appointment of counsel;

Local standard operating procedures;

The interrogator's military assignment and training; and

The interrogator's experience in the area of military criminal procedure.

The standard involved is purely an objective one.

1994 Amendment: Subdivision (e) was amended to conform military practice with the Supreme Court's decisions in *Minnick v. Mississippi*, 498 U.S. 146 (1990), and *McNeil v. Wisconsin*,

501 U.S. 171 (1991). Subdivision (e) was divided into two rule.subparagraphs to distinguish between the right to counsel rules under the Fifth and Sixth Amendments and to make reference to the new waiver provisions of subdivision (g)(2). Subdivision (e)(1) applies an accused's Fifth Amendment right to counsel to the military and conforms military practice with the Supreme Court's decision in *Minnick*. In that case, the Court determined that the Fifth Amendment right to counsel protected by *Miranda v. Arizona*, 384 U.S. 436 (1966), and *Edwards v. Arizona*, 451 U.S. 477 (1981), as interpreted in *Arizona v. Roberson*, 486 U.S. 675 (1988), requires that when a suspect in custody requests counsel, interrogation shall not proceed unless counsel is *present*. Government officials may not reinitiate custodial *interrogation* in the absence of counsel whether or not the accused has consulted with his attorney. *Minnick*, 498 U.S. at 150-152. This rule does not apply, however, when the accused or suspect initiates reinterrogation regardless of whether the accused is in custody. *Minnick*, 498 U.S. at 154-155; *Roberson*, 486 U.S. at 677. The impact of a waiver of counsel rights upon the *Minnick* rule is discussed in the analysis to subdivision (g)(2) of this rule. Subdivision (e)(2) follows *McNeil* and applies the Sixth Amendment right to counsel to military practice. Under the Sixth Amendment, an accused is entitled to representation at critical confrontations with the government after the initiation of adversary proceedings. In accordance with *McNeil*, the amendment recognizes that this right is offense-specific and, in the context of military law, that it normally attaches when charges are preferred. *See United States v. Jordan*, 29 M.J. 177, 187 (C.M.A. 1989); *United States v. Wattenbarger*, 21 M.J. 41 (C.M.A. 1985), *cert. denied*, 477 U.S. 904 (1986). Subdivision (e)(2) supersedes the prior notice to counsel rule. The prior rule, based on *United States v. McOmber*, 1 M.J. 380 (C.M.A. 1976), is not consistent with *Minnick* and *McNeil*. Despite the fact that *McOmber* was decided on the basis of Article 27, U.C.M.J., the case involved a Sixth Amendment claim by the defense, an analysis of the Fifth Amendment decisions of *Miranda v. Arizona*, 384 U.S. 436 (1966), and *United States v. Tempia*, 16 U.S.C.M.A. 629, 37 C.M.R. 249 (1967), and the Sixth Amendment decision of *Massiah v. United States*, 377 U.S. 201 (1964). Moreover, the *McOmber* rule has been applied to claims based on violations of both the Fifth and Sixth Amendments. *See, e.g. United States v. Fassler*, 29 M.J. 193 (C.M.A. 1989). *Minnick* and *McNeil* reexamine the Fifth and Sixth Amendment decisions central to the *McOmber* decision; the amendments to subdivision (e) are the result of that reexamination.

(f) *Exercise of rights.* Rule 305(f) restates prior law in that it requires all questioning to cease immediately upon the exercise of either the privilege against self-incrimination or the right to counsel. *See Michigan v. Mosely*, 423 U.S. 96 (1975). The Rule expressly does not deal with the question of whether or when questioning may be resumed following an exercise of a suspect's rights and does not necessarily prohibit it. The Committee notes that both the Supreme Court, *see e.g., Brewer v. Williams*, 480 U.S. 387 (1977); *Michigan v. Mosely*, 423 U.S. 96 (1975), and the Court of Military Appeals, *see, e.g., United States v. Hill*, 5 M.J. 114 (C.M.A. 1978); *United States v. Collier*, 1 M.J. 358 (C.M.A. 1976) have yet to fully resolve this matter.

1994 Amendment: The amendment to subdivision (f) clarifies the distinction between the rules applicable to the exercise of the privilege against self-incrimination and the right to counsel. *Michigan v. Mosley*, 423 U.S. 96 (1975). *See also United States v. Hsu*, 852 F.2d 407, 411, n.3 (9th Cir. 1988). The added language, contained in (f)(2), is based on *Minnick v. Mississippi*, 498 U.S. 146 (1990), and *McNeil v. Wisconsin*, 501 U.S. 171 (1991). Consequently, when a suspect or an accused undergoing interrogation exercises the right to counsel under circumstances provided for under subdivision (d)(l) of this rule, (f)(2) applies the rationale of *Minnick* and *McNeil* requiring that questioning must cease until counsel is present.

(g) *Waiver.* The waiver provision of Rule 305(g) restates current military practice and is taken in part from Para. 140 *a*(2) of the 1969 Manual.

Rule 305(g)(1) sets forth the general rule for waiver and follows *Miranda v. Arizona*, 384 U.S. 436, 475 (1966). The Rule requires that an affirmative acknowledgment of the right be made before an adequate waiver may be found. Thus, three waiver questions are required under Rule 305(g):

Do you understand your rights?
Do you want a lawyer?
Are you willing to make a statement?

(h) *Non-military interrogations.* Para. 140 *a*(2) of the 1969 Manual, which governed civilian interrogations of military personnel basically restated the holding of *Miranda v. Arizona*, 384 U.S. 436 (1966). Recognizing that the Supreme Court may modify the Miranda rule, the Committee has used the language in Rule 305(h)(1) to make practice in this area dependent upon the way the Federal district courts would handle such interrogations. *See* Article 36.

Rule 305(h)(2) clarifies the law of interrogations as it relates to interrogations conducted abroad by officials of a foreign government or their agents when the interrogation is not conducted, instigated, or participated in by military personnel or their agents. Such an interrogation does not require rights warnings under subdivisions (c) or (d) or notice to counsel under subdivision (e). The only test to be applied in such a case is that of common law voluntariness: whether a statement obtained during such an interrogation was obtained through the use of "coercion, unlawful influence, or unlawful inducement." Article 31(d).

Whether an interrogation has been "conducted, instigated, or participated in by military personnel or their agents" is a question of fact depending on the circumstances of the case. The Rule makes it clear that a United States personnel do not participate in an interrogation merely by being present at the scene of the interrogation, *see United States v. Jones*, 6 M.J. 226 (C.M.A. 1979) and the Analysis to Rule 311(c), or by taking steps which are in the best interests of the accused. Also, an interrogation is not "participated in" by military personnel or their agents who act as interpreters during the interrogation if there is no other participation. *See* Rule 311(c). The omission of express reference to interpreters in Rule 305(h)(2) was inadvertent.

Rule 306 Statements by one of several accused

Rule 306 is taken from the fifth rule.subparagraph Para. 140 *b* of the 1969 Manual and states the holding of *Bruton v. United States*, 391 U.S. 123 (1968). The remainder of the associated material in the Manual is primarily concerned with the co-conspirator's exception to the hearsay rule and has been superseded by adoption of the Federal Rules of Evidence. *See* Rule 801.

When it is impossible to effectively delete all references to a co-accused, alternative steps must be taken to protect the co-accused. This may include the granting of a severance.

The Committee was aware of the Supreme Court's decision in *Parker v. Randolph*, 442 U.S. 62 (1979) dealing with interlocking confessions. In view of the lack of a consensus in Parker, however, the Committee determined that the case did not provide a sufficiently precise basis for drafting a rule, and decided instead to apply Bruton to interlocking confessions.

Rule 311 Evidence obtained from unlawful searches and seizures

Rules 311–317 express the manner in which the Fourth Amendment to the Constitution of the United States applies to trials by court-martial, *Cf. Parker v. Levy*, 417 U.S. 733 (1974).

(a) *General rule.* Rule 311(a) restates the basic exclusionary rule for evidence obtained from an unlawful search or seizure and is taken generally from Para. 152 of the 1969 Manual although much of the language of Para. 152 has been deleted for purposes of both clarity and brevity. The Rule requires suppression of derivative as well as primary evidence and follows the 1969 Manual rule by expressly limiting exclusion of evidence to that resulting from unlawful searches and seizures involving governmental activity. Those persons whose actions may thus give rise to exclusion are listed in Rule 311(c) and are taken generally from Para. 152 with some expansion for purposes of clarity. Rule 311 recognizes that discovery of evidence may be so unrelated to an unlawful search or seizure as to escape exclusion because it was not "obtained as a result" of that search or seizure.

The Rule recognizes that searches and seizures are distinct acts the legality of which must be determined independently. Although a seizure will usually be unlawful if it follows an unlawful search, a seizure may be unlawful even if preceded by a lawful search. Thus, adequate cause to seize may be distinct from legality of the search or observations which preceded it. Note in this respect Rule 316(d)(4)(C), Plain View.

(1) *Objection.* Rule 311(a)(1) requires that a motion to suppress or, as appropriate, an objection be made before evidence can be suppressed. Absent such motion or objection, the issue is waived. Rule 311(i).

(2) *Adequate interest.* Rule 311(a)(2) represents a complete redrafting of the standing requirements found in Para. 152 of the 1969 Manual. The Committee viewed the Supreme Court decision in *Rakas v. Illinois*, 439 U.S. 128 (1978), as substantially modifying the Manual language. Indeed, the very use of the term "standing" was considered obsolete by a majority of the Committee. The Rule distinguishes between searches and seizure. To have sufficient interest to challenge a search, a person must have "a reasonable expectation of privacy in the person, place, or property searched." "Reasonable expectation of privacy" was used in lieu of "legitimate expectation of privacy," often used in *Rakas, supra*, as the Committee believed the two expressions to be identical. The Committee also considered that the expression "reasonable expectation" has a more settled meaning. Unlike the case of a search, an individual must have an interest distinct from an expectation of privacy to challenge a seizure. When a seizure is involved rather than a search the only invasion of one's rights is the removal of the property in question. Thus, there must be some recognizable right to the property seized. Consequently, the Rule requires a "legitimate interest in the property or evidence seized." This will normally mean some form of possessory interest. Adequate interest to challenge a seizure does not *per se* give adequate interest to challenge a prior search that may have resulted in the seizure.

The Rule also recognizes an accused's rights to challenge a search or seizure when the right to do so would exist under the Constitution. Among other reasons, this provision was included because of the Supreme Court's decision in *Jones v. United States*, 302 U.S. 257 (1960), which created what has been termed the "automatic standing rule." The viability of *Jones* after *Rakas* and other cases is unclear, and the Rule will apply *Jones* only to the extent that *Jones* is constitutionally mandated.

1986 Amendment: The words "including seizures of the person" were added to expressly apply the exclusionary rule to unlawful apprehensions and arrests, that is, seizures of the person. Procedures governing apprehensions and arrests are contained in R.C.M. 302. *See also* Mil. R. Evid. 316(c).

(b) *Exceptions:* Rule 311(b) states the holding of *Walder v. United States*, 347 U.S. 62 (1954), and restates with minor change the rule as found in Para. 152 of the 1969 Manual.

1986 Amendment: Rule 311(b)(2) was added to incorporate the "inevitable discovery" exception to the exclusionary rule of *Nix v. Williams*, 467 U.S. 431 (1984). There is authority for the proposition that this exception applies to the primary evidence tainted by an illegal search or seizure, as well as to evidence derived secondarily from a prior illegal search or seizure. *United States v. Romero*, 692 F.2d 699 (10th Cir. 1982), *cited with approval in Nix v. Williams, supra*, 467 U.S. 431, n.2. *See also United States v. Kozak*, 12 M.J. 389 (C.M.A. 1982); *United States v. Yandell*, 13 M.J. 616 (A.F.C.M.R. 1982). *Contra, United States v. Ward*, 19 M.J. 505 (A.F.C.M.R. 1984). There is also authority for the proposition that the prosecution must demonstrate that the lawful means which made discovery inevitable were possessed by the investigative authority and were being actively pursued prior to the occurrence of the illegal conduct which results in discovery of the evidence (*United States v. Satterfield*, 743 F.2d 827, 846 (11th Cir. 1984)).

As a logical extension of the holdings in*Nix* and *United States v. Kozak, supra*, the leading military case, the inevitable discovery exception should also apply to evidence derived from apprehensions and arrests determined to be illegal under R.C.M. 302 (*State v. Nagel*, 308 N.W.2d 539 (N.D. 1981) (alternative holding)). The prosecution may prove that, notwithstanding the illegality of the apprehension or arrest, evidence derived therefrom is admissible under the inevitable discovery exception.

Rule 311(b)(3) was added in 1986 to incorporate the "good faith" exception to the exclusionary rule based on *United States v. Leon*, 468 U.S. 897 (1984) and *Massachusetts v. Sheppard*, 468 U.S. 981 (1984). The exception applies to search warrants and authorizations to search or seize issued by competent civilian authority, military judges, military magistrates, and commanders. The test for determining whether the applicant acted in good faith is whether a reasonably well-trained law enforcement officer would have known the search or seizure was illegal despite the authorization. In *Leon* and *Sheppard*, the applicant's good faith was enhanced by their prior consultation with attorneys.

The rationale articulated in *Leon* and *Sheppard* that the deterrence basis of the exclusionary rule does not apply to magistrates extends with equal force to search or seizure authorizations issued by commanders who are neutral and detached, as defined in *United States v. Ezell*, 6 M.J. 307 (C.M.A. 1979). The United States Court of Military Appeals demonstrated in *United States v. Stuckey*, 10 M.J. 347 (C.M.A. 1981), that commanders cannot be equated constitutionally to magistrates. As a result, commanders' authorizations may be closely scrutinized for evidence of neutrality in deciding whether this exception will apply. In a particular case, evidence that the commander received the advice of a judge advocate prior to authorizing the search or seizure may be an important consideration. Other considerations may include those enumerated in *Ezell* and: the level of command of the authorizing commander; whether the commander had training in the rules relating to search and seizure; whether the rule governing the search or seizure being litigated was clear; whether the evidence supporting the authorization was given under oath; whether the authorization was reduced to writing; and whether the defect in the authorization was one of form or substance.

As a logical extension of the holdings in*Leon* and *Sheppard*, the good faith exception also applies to evidence derived from apprehensions and arrests which are effected pursuant to an authorization or warrant, but which are subsequently determined to have been defective under R.C.M. 302 (*United States v. Mahoney*, 712 F.2d 956 (5th Cir. 1983); *United States v. Beck*, 729 F.2d 1329 (11th Cir. 1984)). The authorization or warrant must, however, meet the conditions set forth in Rule 311(b)(3).

It is intended that the good faith exception will apply to both primary and derivative evidence.

(c) *Nature of search or seizure.* Rule 311(c) defines "unlawful" searches and seizures and makes it clear that the treatment of a search or seizure varies depending on the status of the individual or group conducting the search or seizure.

(1) *Military personnel.* Rule 311(c)(1) generally restates prior law. A violation of a military regulation alone will not require exclusion of any resulting evidence. However, a violation of such a regulation that gives rise to a reasonable expectation of privacy may require exclusion. *Compare United States v. Dillard*, 8 M.J. 213 (C.M.A. 1980), with *United States v. Caceres*, 440 U.S. 741 (1979).

(2) *Other officials.* Rule 311(c)(2) requires that the legality of a search or seizure performed by officials of the United States, of the District of Columbia, or of a state, commonwealth, or possession or political subdivision thereof, be determined by the principles of law applied by the United States district courts when resolving the legality of such a search or seizure.

(3) *Officials of a foreign government or their agents.* This provision is taken in part from *United States v. Jordan*, 1 M.J. 334 (C.M.A. 1976). After careful analysis, a majority of the Committee concluded that portion of the *Jordan* opinion which purported to require that such foreign searches be shown to have complied with foreign law is dicta and lacks any specific legal authority to support it. Further the Committee noted the fact that most foreign nations lack any law of search and seizure and that in some cases, *e.g.*, Germany, such law as may exist is purely theoretical and not subject to determination. The *Jordan* requirement thus unduly complicates trial without supplying any protection to the accused. Consequently, the Rule omits the requirement in favor of a basic due process test. In determining which version of the various due process phrasings to utilize, a majority of the Committee chose to use the language found in Para. 150 *b* of the 1969 Manual rather than the language found in *Jordan* (which requires that the evidence not shock the conscience of the court) believing the Manual language is more appropriate to the circumstances involved.

Rule 311(c) also indicates that persons who are present at a foreign search or seizure conducted in a foreign nation have "not participated in" that search or seizure due either to their mere presence or because of any actions taken to mitigate possible damage to property or person. The Rule thus clarifies *United States v. Jordan*, 1 M.J. 334 (C.M.A. 1976) which stated that the Fourth Amendment would be applicable to searches and seizures conducted abroad by foreign police when United States personnel participate in them. The Court's intent in *Jordan* was to prevent American authorities from sidestepping Constitutional protections by using foreign personnel to conduct a search or seizure that would have been unlawful if conducted by Americans. This intention is safeguarded by the Rule, which applies the Rules and the Fourth Amendment when military personnel or their agents conduct, instigate, or participate in a search or seizure. The Rule only clarifies the circumstances in which a United States official will be deemed to have participated in a foreign search or seizure. This follows dicta in *United States v. Jones*, 6 M.J. 226, 230 (C.M.A. 1979), which would require an "element of causation," rather than mere presence. It seems apparent that an American servicemember is far more likely to be well served by United States presence— which might mitigate foreign conduct— than by its absence. Further, international treaties frequently require United States cooperation with foreign law enforcement. Thus, the Rule serves all purposes by prohibiting conduct by United States officials which might improperly support a search or seizure which would be unlawful if conducted in the United States while protecting both the accused and international relations.

The Rule also permits use of United States personnel as interpreters viewing such action as a neutral activity normally of potential advantage to the accused. Similarly the Rule permits personnel to take steps to protect the person or property of the accused because such actions are clearly in the best interests of the accused.

(d) *Motion to suppress and objections.* Rule 311(d) provides for challenging evidence obtained as a result of an allegedly unlawful search or seizure. The procedure, normally that of a motion to suppress, is intended with a small difference in the disclosure requirements to duplicate that required by Rule 304(d) for confessions and admissions, the Analysis of which is equally applicable here.

Rule 311(d)(1) differs from Rule 304(c)(1) in that it is applicable only to evidence that the prosecution intends to offer against the accused. The broader disclosure provision for statements by the accused was considered unnecessary. Like Rule 304(d)(2)(C), Rule 311(d)(2)(C) provides expressly for derivative evidence disclosure of which is not mandatory as it may be unclear to the prosecution exactly what is derivative of a search or seizure. The Rule thus clarifies the situation.

(e) *Burden of proof.* Rule 311(e) requires that a preponderance of the evidence standard be used in determining search and seizure questions. *Lego v. Twomey*, 404 U.S. 477 (1972). Where the validity of a consent to search or seize is involved, a higher standard of "clear and convincing," is applied by Rule 314(e). This restates prior law.

February 1986 Amendment: rule.subparagraphs (e)(1) and (2) were amended to state the burden of proof for the inevitable discovery and good faith exceptions to the exclusionary rule, as prescribed in *Nix v. Williams*, 467 U.S. 431 (1984) and *United States v. Leon*, 468 U.S. 897 (1984), respectively.

1993 Amendment: The amendment to Mil. R. Evid. 311(e)(2) was made to conform Rule 311 to the rule of *New York v. Harris*, 495 U.S. 14 (1990). The purpose behind the exclusion of derivative evidence found during the course of an unlawful apprehension in a dwelling is to protect the physical integrity of the dwelling not to protect suspects from subsequent lawful police interrogation. *See id.* A suspect's subsequent statement made at another location that is the product of lawful police interrogation is not the fruit of the unlawful apprehension. The amendment also contains language added to reflect the "good faith" exception to the exclusionary role set forth in *United States v. Leon,* 468 U.S. 897 (1984), and the "inevitable discovery" exception set forth in *Nix v. Williams,* 467 U.S. 431 (1984).

(f) *Defense evidence.* Rule 311(f) restates prior law and makes it clear that although an accused is sheltered from any use at trial of a statement made while challenging a search or seizure, such statement may be used in a subsequent "prosecution for perjury, false swearing or the making of a false official statement."

(g) *Scope of motions and objections challenging probable cause.* Rule 311(g)(2) follows the Supreme Court decision in*Franks v. Delaware*, 422 U.S. 928 (1978), *see also United States v. Turck*, 49 C.M.R. 49, 53 (A.F.C.M.R. 1974), with minor modifications made to adopt the decision to military procedures. Although Franks involved perjured affidavits by police, Rule 311(a) is made applicable to information given by government agents because of the governmental status of members of the armed services. The Rule is not intended to reach misrepresentations made by informants without any official connection.

1995 Amendment: Subsection (g)(2) was amended to clarify that in order for the defense to prevail on an objection or motion under this rule, it must establish, *inter alia*, that the falsity of the evidence was "knowing and intentional" or in reckless disregard for the truth. *Accord Franks v. Delaware*, 438 U.S. 154 (1978).

(h) *Objections to evidence seized unlawfully.* Rule 311(h) is new and is included for reasons of clarity.

(i) *Effect of guilty plea.* Rule 311(i) restates prior law. *See, e.g., United States v. Hamil*, 15 U.S.C.M.A. 110, 35 C.M.R. 82 (1964).

Rule 312 Body views and intrusions

1984 Amendment: "Body" was substituted for "bodily" in the title and where appropriate in text. *See United States v. Armstrong*, 9 M.J. 374, 378 n.5 (C.M.A. 1980).

(a) *General rule.* Rule 312(a) limits all nonconsensual inspections, searches, or seizures by providing standards for examinations of the naked body and bodily intrusions. An inspection, search, or seizure that would be lawful but for noncompliance with this Rule is unlawful within the meaning of Rule 311.

(b) *Visual examination of the body.* Rule 312(b) governs searches and examinations of the naked body and thus controls what has often been loosely termed "strip searches." Rule 312(b) permits visual examination of the naked body in a wide but finite range of circumstances. In doing so, the Rule strictly distinguishes between visual examination of body cavities and actual intrusion into them. Intrusion is governed by Rule 312(c) and (e). Visual examination of the male genitals is permitted when a visual examination is permissible under this subdivision. Examination of cavities may include, when otherwise proper under the Rule, requiring the individual being viewed to assist in the examination.

Examination of body cavities within the prison setting has been vexatious. *See, e.g., Hanley v. Ward*, 584 F.2d 609 (2d Cir. 1978); *Wolfish v. Levi*, 573 F.2d 118, 131 (2d Cir. 1978), *reversed sub nom Bell v. Wolfish*, 441 U.S. 520 (1979); *Daughtry v. Harris*, 476 F.2d 292 (10th Cir. 1973), *cert. denied*, 414 U.S. 872 (1973); *Frazier v. Ward*, 426 F.Supp. 1354, 1362–67 (N.D.N.Y. 1977); *Hodges v. Klein*, 412 F.Supp. 896 (D.N.J. 1976). Institutional security must be protected while at the same time only privacy intrusions necessary should be imposed on the individual. The problem is particularly acute in this area of inspection of body cavities as such strong social taboos are involved. Rule 312(b)(2) allows examination of body cavities when reasonably necessary to maintain the security of the institution or its personnel. *See, Bell v. Wolfish*, 441 U.S. 520 (1979). Examinations likely to be reasonably necessary include examination upon entry or exit from the institution, examination subsequent to a personal visit, or examination pursuant to a reasonably clear indication that the individual is concealing property within a body cavity. *Frazier v. Ward*, 426 F.Supp. 1354 (N.D.N.Y. 1977); *Hodges v. Klein*, 412 F.Supp. 896 (D.N.J. 1976). Great deference should be given to the decisions of the commanders and staff of military confinement facilities. The concerns voiced by the Court of Appeals for the Tenth Circuit in *Daughtry v. Harris*, 476 F.2d 292 (10th Cir. 1973) about escape and related risks are likely to be particularly applicable to military prisoners because of their training in weapons and escape and evasion tactics.

As required throughout Rule 312, examination of body cavities must be accomplished in a reasonable fashion. This incorporates *Rochin v. California*, 342 U.S. 165 (1952), and recognizes society's particularly sensitive attitude in this area. Where possible, examination should be made in private and by members of the same sex as the person being examined.

1984 Amendment: In subsection (b)(2) and (c), "reasonable" replaced "real" before "suspicion." A majority of Circuit Courts of Appeal have adopted a "reasonable suspicion" test over a "real suspicion" test. *See United States v. Klein*, 592 F.2d 909 (5th Cir. 1979); *United States v. Asbury*, 586 F.2d 973 (2d Cir. 1978); *United States v. Wardlaw*, 576 F.2d 932 (1st Cir. 1978); *United States v. Himmelwright*, 551 F.2d 991 (5th Cir.), *cert. denied*, 434 U.S. 902 (1977). *But see United States v. Aman*, 624 F.2d 911 (9th Cir. 1980). In practice, the distinction may be minimal. *But see Perel v. Vanderford*, 547 F.2d 278, 280 n.1 (5th Cir. 1977). However, the real suspicion formulation has been criticized as potentially confusing. *United States v. Asbury, supra* at 976.

(c) *Intrusion into body cavities.* Actual intrusion into body cavities, *e.g.*, the anus and vagina, may represent both a significant invasion of the individual's privacy and a possible risk to the health of the individual. Rule 312(c) allows seizure of property discovered in accordance with Rules 312(b), 312(c)(2), or 316(d)(4)(C) but requires that intrusion into such cavities be accomplished by personnel with appropriate medical qualifications. The Rule thus does not specifically require that the intrusion be made by a doctor, nurse, or other similar medical personnel although Rule 312(g) allows the Secretary concerned to prescribe who may perform such procedures. It is presumed that an object easily located by sight can normally be easily extracted. The requirements for appropriate medical qualifications, however, recognize that circumstances may require more qualified personnel. This may be particularly true, for example, for extraction of foreign matter from a pregnant woman's vagina. Intrusion should normally be made either by medical personnel or by persons with appropriate medical qualifications who are members of the same sex as the person involved.

The Rule distinguishes between seizure of property previously located and intrusive searches of body cavities by requiring in Rule 312(c)(2) that such searches be made only pursuant to a search warrant or authorization, based upon probable cause, and conducted by persons with appropriate medical qualifications. Exigencies do not permit such searches without warrant or authorization unless Rule 312(f) is applicable. In the absence of express regulations issued by the Secretary concerned pursuant to Rule 312(g), the determination as to which personnel are qualified to conduct an intrusion should be made in accordance with normal procedures of the applicable medical facility.

Recognizing the peculiar needs of confinement facilities and related institutions, *see, e.g., Bell v. Wolfish*, 441 U.S. 520 (1979), Rule 312(c) authorizes body cavity searches without prior search warrant or authorization when there is a "real suspicion that the individual is concealing weapons, contraband, or evidence of crime."

(d) *Extraction of body fluids.* Seizure of fluids from the body may involve self-incrimination questions pursuant to Article 31 of the Uniform Code of Military Justice, and appropriate case law should be consulted prior to involuntary seizure. *See generally* Rule 301(a) and its Analysis. The Committee does not intend an individual's expelled breath to be within the definition of "body fluids."

The 1969 Manual Para. 152 authorization for seizure of bodily fluids when there has been inadequate time to obtain a warrant or authorization has been slightly modified. The prior language that there be "clear indication that evidence of crime will be found and that there is reason to believe that delay will threaten the destruction of evidence" has been modified to authorize such a seizure if there is reason to believe that the delay "could result in the destruction of the evidence." Personnel involuntarily extracting bodily fluids must have appropriate medical qualifications.

Rule 312 does not prohibit compulsory urinalysis, whether random or not, made for appropriate medical purposes, *see* Rule 312(f), and the product of such a procedure if otherwise admissible may be used in evidence at a court-martial.

1984 Amendment: The first word in the caption of subsection (d) was changed from "*Seizure*" to " *Extraction.*" This is consistent with the text of subsection (d) and should avoid possible confusion about the scope of the subsection. Subsection (d) does not apply to compulsory production of body fluids (*e.g.,* being ordered to void urine), but rather to physical extraction of body fluids (e.g., catheterization or withdrawal of blood). *See Murray v. Haldeman*, 16 M.J. 74 (C.M.A. 1983). *See also* Analysis, Mil. R. Evid. 313(b).

(e) *Other intrusive searches.* The intrusive searches governed by Rule 312(e) will normally involve significant medical procedures including surgery and include any intrusion into the body including x-rays. Applicable civilian cases lack a unified approach to surgical intrusions, *see, e.g., United States v. Crowder*, 513 F.2d 395 (D.C. Cir. 1976); *Adams v. State*, 299 N.E.2d 834 (Ind. 1973); *Creamer v. State*, 299 Ga. 511, 192 S.E.2d 350 (1972), Note, *Search and Seizure: Compelled Surgical Intrusion*, 27 Baylor L.Rev. 305 (1975), and cases cited therein, other than to rule out those intrusions which are clearly health threatening. Rule 312(e) balances the Government's need for evidence with the individual's privacy interest by allowing intrusion into the body of an accused or suspect upon search authorization or warrant when conducted by person with "appropriate medical qualification," and by prohibiting intrusion when it will endanger the health of the individual. This allows, however, considerable flexibility and leaves the ultimate issue to be determined under a due process standard of reasonableness. As the public's interest in obtaining evidence from an individual other than an accused or suspect is substantially less than the person's right to privacy in his or her body, the Rule prohibits the involuntary intrusion altogether if its purpose is to obtain evidence of crime.

(f) *Intrusions for valid medical purposes.* Rule 312(f) makes it clear that the Armed Forces retain their power to ensure the health of their members. A procedure conducted for valid medical purposes may yield admissible evidence. Similarly, Rule 312 does not affect in any way any procedure necessary for diagnostic or treatment purposes.

(g) *Medical qualifications.* Rule 312(g) permits but does not require the Secretaries concerned to prescribe the medical qualifications necessary for persons to conduct the procedures and examinations specified in the Rule.

Rule 313 Inspections and inventories in the armed forces

Although inspections have long been recognized as being necessary and legitimate exercises of a commander's powers and responsibilities, *see, e.g., United States v. Gebhart*, 10 U.S.C.M.A. 606, 610 .2, 28 C.M.R. 172, 176 n.2 (1959), the 1969 Manual for Courts-Martial omitted discussion of inspections except to note that the Para. 152 restrictions on seizures were not applicable to "administrative inspections." The reason for the omission is likely that military inspections *per se* have traditionally been considered administrative in nature and free of probable cause requirements. *Cf. Frank v. Maryland*, 359 .S. 360 (1959). Inspections that have been utilized as subterfuge searches have been condemned. *See, e.g., United States v. Lange*, 15 U.S.C.M.A. 486, 35C.M.R. 458 (1965). Recent decisions of the United States Court of Military Appeals have attempted, generally without success, to define "inspection" for Fourth Amendment evidentiary purposes, *see, e.g., United States v. Thomas*, 1 M.J. 397 (C.M.A. 1976) (*three separate opinions*), and have been concerned with the intent, scope, and method of conducting inspections. *See e.g., United States v. Harris*, 5 M.J. 44 (C.M.A. 1978).

(a) *General rule.*

Rule 313 codifies the law of military inspections and inventories. Traditional terms used to describe various inspections, *e.g.* "shakedown inspection" or "gate search," have been abandoned as being conducive to confusion.

Rule 313 does not govern inspections or inventories not conducted within the armed forces. These civilian procedures must be evaluated under Rule 311(c)(2). In general, this means that such inspections and inventories need only be permissible under the Fourth Amendment in order to yield evidence admissible at a court-martial.

Seizure of property located pursuant to a proper inspection or inventory must meet the requirements of Rule 316.

(b) *Inspections.* Rule 313(b) defines "inspection" as an "examination … conducted as an incident of command the primary purpose of which is to determine and to ensure the security, military fitness, or good order and discipline of the unit, organization, installation, vessel, aircraft, or vehicle." Thus, an inspection is conducted for the primary function of ensuring mission readiness, and is a function of the inherent duties and responsibilities of those in the military chain of command. Because inspections are intended to discover, correct, and deter conditions detrimental to military efficiency and safety, they must be considered as a condition precedent to the existence of any effective armed force and inherent in the very concept of a military unit. Inspections as a general legal concept have their constitutional origins in the very provisions of the Constitution which authorize the armed forces of the United States. Explicit authorization for inspections has thus been viewed in the past as unnecessary, but in light of the present ambiguous state of the law; *see, e.g. United States v. Thomas, supra; United States v. Roberts*, 2 M.J. 31 (C.M.A. 1976), such authorization appears desirable. Rule 313 is thus, in addition to its status as a rule of evidence authorized by Congress under Article 36, an express Presidential authorization for inspections with such authorization being grounded in the President's powers as Commander-in-Chief.

The interrelationship of inspections and the Fourth Amendment is complex. The constitutionality of inspections is apparent and has been well recognized; *see e.g., United States v. Gebhart*, 10 C.M.A. 606, 610 n.2, 28 C.M.R. 172, 176 n.2. (1959). There are three distinct rationales which support the constitutionality of inspections.

The first such rationale is that inspections are not technically "searches"within the meaning of the Fourth Amendment. *Cf. Air Pollution Variance Board v. Western Alfalfa Corps*, 416 U.S. 861 (1974); *Hester v. United States*, 265 U.S. 57 (1924). The intent of the framers, the language of the amendment itself, and the nature of military life render the application of the Fourth Amendment to a normal inspection questionable. As the Supreme Court has often recognized, the "Military is, [by necessity, a specialized society separate from civilian society.]" *Brown v. Glines*, 444 U.S. 348, 354 (1980) *citing Parker v. Levy*, 417 U.S. 733, 734 (1974). As the Supreme Court noted in *Glines, supra*, Military personnel must be ready to perform their duty whenever the occasion arises. To ensure that they always are capable of performing their mission promptly and reliably, the military services "must insist upon a respect for duty and a discipline without counterpart in civilian life." 444 U.S. at 354 (citations omitted). An effective armed force without inspections is impossible— a fact amply illustrated by the unfettered right to inspect vested in commanders throughout the armed forces of the world. As recognized in *Glines, supra*, and *Greer v. Spock*, 424 U.S. 828 (1976), the *way* that the Bill of Rights applies to military personnel may be different from the way it applies to civilians. Consequently, although the Fourth Amendment is applicable to members of the armed forces, inspections may well not be "searches" within the meaning of the Fourth Amendment by reason of history, necessity, and constitutional interpretation. If they are "searches," they are surely reasonable ones, and are constitutional on either or both of two rationales.

As recognized by the Supreme Court, highly regulated industries are subject to inspection without warrant, *United States v. Biswell*, 406 U.S. 311 (1972);*Colonnade Catering Corp. v. United States*, 397 U.S. 72 (1970), both because of the necessity for such inspections and because of the "limited threats to ... justifiable expectation of privacy." *United States v. Biswell, supra* , at 316. The court in *Biswell, supra*, found that regulations of firearms traffic involved "large interests," that "inspection is a crucial part of the regulatory scheme," and that when a firearms dealer enters the business "he does so with the knowledge that his business records, firearms, and ammunition will be subject to effective inspection," 406 U.S. 315, 316. It is clear that inspections within the armed forces are at least as important as regulation of firearms; that without such inspections effective regulation of the armed forces is impossible; and that all personnel entering the armed forces can be presumed to know that the reasonable expectation of privacy within the armed forces is exceedingly limited by comparison with civilian expectations. *See e.g., Committee for G.I. Rights v. Callaway*, 518 F.2d 466 (D.C. Cir. 1975). Under *Colonnade Catering, supra, and Bisell, supra*, inspections are thus reasonable searches and may be made without warrant.

An additional rationale for military inspection is found within the Supreme Court's other administrative inspection cases. *See Marshall v. Barlow's, Inc.*, 436 U.S. 397 (1978); *Camara v. Municipal Court*, 387 U.S. 523 (1967); *See City of Seattle*, 387 U.S. 541 (1967). Under these precedents an administrative inspection is constitutionally acceptable for health and safety purposes so long as such an inspection is first authorized by warrant. The warrant involved, however, need not be upon probable cause in the traditional sense, rather the warrant may be issued "if reasonable legislative or administrative standards for conducting an area inspection are satisfied …" *Camara, supra*, 387 U.S. at 538. Military inspections are intended for health and safety reasons in a twofold sense: they protect the health and safety of the personnel in peacetime in a fashion somewhat analogous to that which protects the health of those in a civilian environment, and, by ensuring the presence and proper condition of armed forces personnel, equipment, and environment, they protect those personnel from becoming unnecessary casualties in the event of combat. Although *Marshall v. Barlow's Inc., Camara*, and *See, supra*, require warrants, the intent behind the warrant requirement is to ensure that the person whose property is inspected is adequately notified that local law requires inspection, that the person is notified of the limits of the inspection, and that the person is adequately notified that the inspector is acting with proper authority. *Camara v. Municipal Court*, 387 U.S. 523, 532 (1967). Within the armed forces, the warrant requirement is met automatically if an inspection is ordered by a commander, as commanders are empowered to grant warrants. *United States v. Ezell*, 6 M.J. 307 (C.M.A. 1979). More importantly, the concerns voiced by the court are met automatically within the military environment in any event as the rank and assignment of those inspecting and their right to do so are known to all. To the extent that the search warrant requirements are intended to prohibit inspectors from utilizing inspections as subterfuge searches, a normal inspection fully meets the concern, and Rule 313(b) expressly prevents such subterfuges. The fact that an inspection that is primarily administrative in nature may result in a criminal prosecution is unimportant. *Camara v. Municipal Court*, 387 U.S. 523, 530–531 (1967). Indeed, administrative inspections may inherently result in prosecutions because such inspections are often intended to discover health and safety defects the presence of which are criminal offenses. *Id.* at 531. What is important, to the extent that the Fourth Amendment is applicable, is protection from unreasonable violations of privacy. Consequently, Rule 313(b) makes it clear that an otherwise valid inspection is not rendered invalid solely because the inspector has as his or her purpose a *secondary* "purpose of obtaining evidence for use in a trial by court-martial or in other disciplinary proceedings ..." An examination made, however, with a *primary* purpose of prosecution is no longer an administrative inspection. Inspections are, as has been previously discussed, lawful acceptable measures to ensure the survival of the American armed forces and the accomplishment of their mission. They do not infringe upon the limited reasonable expectation of privacy held by service personnel. It should be noted, however, that it is possible for military personnel to be granted a reasonable expectation of privacy greater than the minimum inherently recognized by the Constitution. An installation commander might, for example, declare a BOQ sacrosanct and off limits to inspections. In such a rare case the reasonable expectation of privacy held by the relevant personnel could prevent or substantially limit the power to inspect under the Rule. *See* Rule 311(c). Such extended expectations of privacy may, however, be negated with adequate notice.

An inspection "may be made 'of the whole or part' of a unit, organization, installation, vessel, aircraft, or vehicle ... (and is) conducted as an incident of command." Inspections are usually quantitative examinations insofar as they do not normally single out specific individuals or small groups of individuals. There is, however, no requirement that the entirety of a unit or organization be inspected. Unless authority to do so has been withheld by competent superior authority, any individual placed in a command or appropriate supervisory position may inspect the personnel and property within his or her control.

Inspections for contraband such as drugs have posed a major problem. Initially, such inspections were viewed simply as a form of health and welfare inspection, *see, e.g., United States v. Unrue*, 22 C.M.A. 466, 47 C.M.R. 556 (1973). More recently, however, the Court of Military Appeals has tended to view them solely as searches for evidence of crime. *See e.g. United States v. Roberts*, 2 M.J. 31 (C.M.A. 1976); *but see United States v. Harris*, 5 M.J. 44, 58 (C.M.A. 1978). Illicit drugs, like unlawful weapons, represent, however, a potential threat to military efficiency of disastrous proportions. Consequently, it is entirely appropriate to treat inspections intended to rid units of contraband that would adversely affect military fitness as being health and welfare inspections, *see, e.g., Committee for G.I. Rights v. Callaway*, 518 F.2d 466 (D.C. Cir. 1975), and the Rule does so.

A careful analysis of the applicable case law, military and civilian, easily supports this conclusion. Military cases have long recognized the legitimacy of "health and welfare" inspections and have defined those inspections as examinations intended to ascertain and ensure the readiness of personnel and equipment. *See, e.g., United States v. Gebhart*, 10 C.M.A. 606, 610 n.2, 28 C.M.R. 172, 176 n.2 (1959); "(these) types of searches are not to be confused with inspections of military personnel ... conducted by a commander in furtherance of the security of his command"; *United States v. Brashears*, 45 C.M.R. 438 (A.C.M.R. 1972), *rev'd on other grounds*, 21 C.M.A. 522, 45 C.M.R. 326 (1972). Among the legitimate intents of a proper inspection is the location and confiscation of unauthorized weapons. *See, e.g., United States v. Grace*, 19 C.M.A. 409, 410, 42 C.M.R. 11, 12 (1970). The justification for this conclusion is clear: unauthorized weapons are a serious danger to the health of military personnel and therefore to mission readiness. Contraband that "would affect adversely the security, military fitness, or good order and discipline" is thus identical with unauthorized weapons insofar as their effects can be predicted. Rule 313(b) authorizes inspections for contraband, and is expressly intended to authorize inspections for unlawful drugs. As recognized by the Court of Military Appeals in *United States v. Unrue*, 22 C.M.A. 466, 469–70, 47 C.M.R. 556, 559–60 (1973), unlawful drugs pose unique problems. If uncontrolled, they may create an "epidemic," 47 C.M.R. at 559. Their use is not only contagious as peer pressure in barracks, aboard ship, and in units, tends to impel the spread of improper drug use, but the effects are known to render units unfit to accomplish their missions. Viewed in this light, it is apparent that inspection for those drugs which would "affect adversely the security, military fitness, or good order and discipline of the command" is a proper administrative intent well within the decisions of the United States Supreme Court. *See, e.g., Camara v. Municipal Court*, 387 U.S. 523 (1967); *United States v. Unrue*, 22 C.M.A. 446, 471, 47 C.M.R. 556, 561 (1973) (Judge Duncan dissenting). This conclusion is buttressed by the fact that members of the military have a diminished expectation of privacy, and that inspections for such contraband are "reasonable" within the meaning of the Fourth Amendment. *See, e.g., Committee for G.I. Rights v. Callaway*, 518 F.2d 466 (D.C. Cir. 1975). Although there are a number of decisions of the Court of Military Appeals that have called the legality of inspections for unlawful drugs into question,*see United States v. Thomas, supra; United States v. Roberts*, 2 M.J. 31 (C.M.A. 1977), those decisions with their multiple opinions are not dispositive. Particularly important to this conclusion is the opinion of Judge Perry in *United States v. Roberts, supra.* Three significant themes are present in the opinion: lack of express authority for such inspections, the perception that unlawful drugs are merely evidence of crime, and the high risk that inspections may be used for subterfuge searches. The new Rule is intended to resolve these matters fully. The Rule, as part of an express Executive Order, supplies the explicit authorization for inspections then lacking. Secondly, the Rule is intended to make plain the fact that an inspection that has as its object the prevention and correction of conditions harmful to readiness is far more than a hunt for evidence. Indeed, it is the express judgment of the Committee that the uncontrolled use of unlawful drugs within the armed forces creates a readiness crisis and that continued use of such drugs is totally incompatible with the possibility of effectively fielding military forces capable of accomplishing their assigned mission. Thirdly, Rule 313(b) specifically deals with the subterfuge question in order to prevent improper use of inspections.

Rule 313(b) requires that before an inspection intended "to locate and confiscate unlawful weapons or other contraband, that would affect adversely the ... command" may take place, there must be either "a reasonable suspicion that such property is present in the command" or the inspection must be "a previously scheduled examination of the command." The former requirement requires that an inspection not previously scheduled be justified by "reasonable suspicion that such property is present in the command." This standard is intentionally minimal and requires only that the person ordering the inspection have a suspicion that is, under the circumstances, reasonable in nature. Probable cause is not required. Under the latter requirement, an inspection shall be scheduled sufficiently far enough in advance as to eliminate any reasonable probability that the inspection is being used as a subterfuge, *i.e.*, that it is being used to search a given individual for evidence of crime when probable cause is lacking. Such scheduling may be made as a matter of date or event. In other words, inspections may be scheduled to take place on any specific date, *e.g.*, a commander may decide on the first of a month to inspect on the 7th, 9th, and 21st, or on the occurrence of a specific event beyond the usual control of the commander, *e.g.*, whenever an alert is ordered, forces are deployed, a ship sails, the stock market reaches a certain level of activity, etc. It should be noted that "previously scheduled" inspections that vest discretion in the inspector are permissible when otherwise lawful. So long as the examination, *e.g.*, an entrance gate inspection, has been previously scheduled, the fact that reasonable exercise of discretion is involved in singling out individuals to be inspected is not improper; such inspection must not be in violation of the Equal Protection clause of the 5th Amendment or be used as a subterfuge intended to allow search of certain specific individuals.

The Rule applies special restrictions to contraband inspections because of the inherent possibility that such inspection may be used as subterfuge searches. Although a lawful inspection may be conducted with a secondary motive to prosecute those found in possession of contraband, the primary motive must be administrative in nature. The Rule recognizes the fact that commanders are ordinarily more concerned with removal of contraband from units— thereby eliminating its negative effects on unit readiness— than with prosecution of those found in possession of it. The fact that possession of contraband is itself unlawful renders the probability that an inspection may be a subterfuge somewhat higher than that for an inspection not intended to locate such material.

An inspection which has as its intent, or one of its intents, in whole or in part, the discovery of contraband, however slight, must comply with the specific requirements set out in the Rule for inspections for contraband. An inspection which does not have such an intent need not so comply and will yield admissible evidence if contraband is found incidentally by the inspection. Contraband is defined as material the possession of which is by its very nature unlawful. Material may be declared to be unlawful by appropriate statute, regulation, or order. For example, if liquor is prohibited aboard ship, a shipboard inspection for liquor must comply with the rules for inspections for contraband.

Before unlawful weapons or other contraband may be the subject of an inspection under Rule 313(b), there must be a determination that "such property would affect adversely the security, military fitness, or good order and discipline of the command." In the event of an adequate defense challenge under Rule 311 to an inspection for contraband, the prosecution must establish by a preponderance that such property would in fact so adversely affect the command. Although the question is an objective one, its resolution depends heavily on factors unique to the personnel or location inspected. If such contraband would adversely affect the ability of the command to complete its assigned mission in any significant way, the burden is met. The nature of the assigned mission is unimportant, for that is a matter within the prerogative of the chain of command only. The expert testimony of those within the chain of command of a given unit is worthy of great weight as the only purpose for permitting such an inspection is to ensure military readiness. The physiological or psychological effects of a given drug on an individual are normally irrelevant except insofar as such evidence is relevant to the question of the user's ability to perform duties without impaired efficiency. As inspections are generally quantitative examinations, the nature and amount of contraband sought is relevant to the question of the government's burden. The existence of five unlawful drug users in an Army division, for example, is unlikely to meet the Rule's test involving adverse effect, but five users in an Army platoon may well do so.

The Rule does not require that personnel to be inspected be given preliminary notice of the inspection although such advance notice may well be desirable as a matter of policy or in the interests, as perhaps in gate inspections, of establishing an alternative basis, such as consent, for the examination.

Rule 313(b) requires that inspections be conducted in a "reasonable fashion." The timing of an inspection and its nature may be of importance. Inspections conducted at a highly unusual time are not inherently unreasonable— especially when a legitimate reason of such timing is present. However, a 0200 inspection, for example, may be unreasonable depending upon the surrounding circumstances.

The Rule expressly permits the use of "any reasonable or natural technological aid." Thus, dogs may be used to detect contraband in an otherwise valid inspection for contraband. This conclusion follows directly from the fact that inspections for contraband conducted in compliance with Rule 313 are lawful. Consequently, the technique of inspection is generally unimportant under the new rules. The Committee did, however, as a matter of policy require that the natural or technological aid be "reasonable."

Rule 313(b) recognizes and affirms the commander's power to conduct administrative examinations which are primarily nonprosecutorial in purpose. Personnel directing inspections for contraband must take special care to ensure that such inspections comply with Rule 313(b) and thus do not constitute improper general searches or subterfuges.

1984 Amendment: Much of the foregoing Analysis was rendered obsolete by amendments made in 1984. The third sentence of Rule 313(b) was modified and the fourth and sixth sentences are new.

The fourth sentence is new. The Military Rule of Evidence did not previously expressly address *production* of body fluids, perhaps because of *United States v. Ruiz*, 23 U.S.C.M.A. 181, 48

C.M.R. 797 (1974). *Ruiz* was implicitly overruled in *United States v. Armstrong*, 9 M.J. 374 (C.M.A. 1980). Uncertainty concerning the course of the law of inspections may also have contributed to the drafter's silence on the matter. *See United States v. Roberts*, 2 M.J. 31 (C.M.A. 1976); *United States v. Thomas*, 1 M.J. 397 (C.M.A. 1976). Much of the uncertainty in this area was dispelled in *United States v. Middleton*, 10 M.J. 123 (C.M.A. 1981). *See also Murray v. Haldeman*, 16 M.J. 74 (C.M.A. 1983).

Despite the absence in the rules of express authority for compulsory production of body fluids, it apparently was the intent of the drafters to permit such production as part of inspections, relying at least in part on the medical purpose exception in Mil. R. Evid. 312(f). Mil. R. Evid. 312(d) applies only to nonconsensual extraction (*e.g.*, catheterization, drawing blood) of body fluids. This was noted in the Analysis, Mil. R. Evid. 312(d), which went on to state that "compulsory urinalysis, whether random or not, made for appropriate medical purposes, *see* Rule 312(f), and the product of such a procedure if otherwise admissible may be used at a court-martial."

There is considerable overlap between production of body fluid for a medical purpose under Mil. R. Evid. 312(f) and for determining and ensuring military fitness in a unit, organization, installation, vessel, aircraft, or vehicle. Frequently the two purposes are coterminous. Ultimately, the overall health of members of the organization is indivisible from the ability of the organization to perform the mission. To the extent that a "medical purpose" embraces anything relating to the physical or mental state of a person and that person's ability to perform assigned duties, then the two purposes may be identical. Such a construction of "medical purpose" would seem to swallow up the specific rules and limitations in Mil. R. Evid. 312(f), however. Therefore, a distinction may be drawn between a medical purpose— at least to the extent that term is construed to concern primarily the health of the individual— and the goal of ensuring the overall fitness of the organization. For example, it may be appropriate to test— by compulsory production of urine— persons whose duties entail highly dangerous or sensitive duties. The primary purpose of such tests is to ensure that the mission will be performed safely and properly. Preserving the health of the individual is an incident— albeit a very important one— of that purpose. A person whose urine is found to contain dangerous drugs is relieved from duty during gunnery practice, for example, not so much to preserve that person's health as to protect the safety of others. On the other hand, a soldier who is extremely ill may be compelled to produce urine (or even have it extracted) not so much so that soldier can return to duty— although the military has an interest in this— as for that soldier's immediate health needs.

Therefore, Mil. R. Evid. 313(b) provides an independent, although often closely related basis for compulsory production of body fluids, with Mil. R. Evid. 312(f). By expressly providing for both, possible confusion or an unnecessarily narrow construction under Mil. R. Evid. 312(f) will be avoided. Note that all of the requirements of Mil. R. Evid. 313(b) apply to an order to produce body fluids under that rule. This includes the requirement that the inspection be done in a reasonable fashion. This rule does not prohibit, as part of an otherwise lawful inspection, compelling a person to drink a reasonable amount of water in order to facilitate production of a urine sample. *See United States v. Mitchell*, 16 M.J. 654 (N.M.C.M.R. 1983).

The sixth sentence is based on*United States v. Middleton, supra. Middleton* was not decided on the basis of Mil.R. Evid. 313, as the inspection in *Middleton* occurred before the effective date of the Military Rules of Evidence. The Court discussed Mil. R. Evid. 313(b), but "did not now decide on the legality of this Rule (or) bless its application." *United States v. Middleton, supra* at 131. However, the reasoning and the holding in *Middleton* suggest that the former language in Mil. R. Evid. 313(b) may have established unnecessary burdens for the prosecution, yet still have been inadequate to protect against subterfuge inspections, under some circumstances.

The former language allowed an inspection for "unlawful weapons and other contraband when such property would affect adversely the security, military fitness, or good order and discipline of the command and when (1) there is a reasonable suspicion that such property is present in the command or (2) the examination is a previously scheduled examination of the command." This required a case-by-case showing of the adverse effects of the weapons or contraband (including controlled substances) in the particular unit, organization, installation, aircraft, or vehicle examined. *See* Analysis, Mil. R. Evid. 313(b). In addition, the examination had to be based on a reasonable suspicion such items were present, or be previously scheduled.

Middleton upheld an inspection which had as one of its purposes the discovery of contraband—i.e., drugs. Significantly, there is no indication in *Middleton* that a specific showing of the adverse effects of such contraband in the unit or organization is necessary. The court expressly recognized (*see United States v. Middleton, supra* at 129; *cf. United States v. Trottier* , 9 M.J. 337 (C.M.A. 1980)) the adverse effect of drugs on the ability of the armed services to perform the mission without requiring evidence on the point. Indeed, it may generally be assumed that if it is illegal to possess an item under a statute or lawful regulation, the adverse effect of such item on security, military fitness, or good order and discipline is established by such illegality, without requiring the commander to personally analyze its effects on a case-by-case basis and the submission of evidence at trial. The defense may challenge the constitutionality of the statute or the legality of the regulation (*cf. United States v. Wilson*, 12 U.S.C.M.A. 165, 30 C.M.R. 165 (1961); *United States v. Nation*, 9 U.S.C.M.A. 724, 26 C.M.R. 504 (1958)) but this burden falls on the defense. Thus, this part of the former test is deleted as unnecessary. Note, however, that it may be necessary to demonstrate a valid military purpose to inspect for some noncontraband items. *See United States v. Brown*, 12 M.J. 420 (C.M.A. 1982).

Middleton upheld broad authority in the commander to inspect for contraband, as well as other things, "when adequate safeguards are present which assure that the'inspection' was really intended to determine and assure the readiness of the unit inspected, rather than merely to provide a subterfuge for avoiding limitations that apply to a search and seizure in a criminal investigation." As noted above, the Court in *Middleton* expressly reserved judgment whether Mil. R. Evid. 313(b) as then written satisfied this test.

The two prongs of the second part of the former test were intended to prevent subterfuge. However, they did not necessarily do so. Indeed, the "reasonable suspicion" test could be read to expressly authorize a subterfuge search. *See, e.g., United States v. Lange*, 15 U.S.C.M.A. 486, 35 C.M.R. 458 (1965). The "previously scheduled" test is an excellent way to prove that an inspection was not directed as the result of a reported offense, and the new formulation so retains it. However, it alone does not ensure absence of prosecutorial motive when specific individuals are singled out, albeit well in advance, for special treatment.

At the same time, the former test could invalidate a genuine inspection which had no prosecutorial purpose. For example, a commander whose unit was suddenly alerted for a special mission might find it necessary, even though the commander had no actual suspicion contraband is present, to promptly inspect for contraband, just to be certain none was present. A commander in such a position should not be prohibited from inspecting.

The new language removes these problems and is more compatible with *Middleton*. It does not establish unnecessary hurdles for the prosecution. A commander may inspect for contraband just as for any other deficiencies, problems, or conditions, without having to show any particular justification for doing so. As the fifth sentence in the rule indicates, any examination made primarily for the purpose of prosecution is not a valid inspection under the rule. The sixth sentence identifies those situations which, objectively, raise a strong likelihood of subterfuge. These situations are based on *United States v. Lange, supra* and *United States v. Hay*, 3 M.J. 654, 655–56 (A.C.M.R. 1977) (*quoted in United States v. Middleton, supra* at 127–28 n.7; *see also United States v. Brown, supra*). "Specific individuals" means persons named or identified on the basis of individual characteristics, rather than by duty assignment or membership in a subdivision of the unit, organization, installation, vessel, aircraft, or vehicle, such as a platoon or squad, or on a random basis. *See United States v. Harris*, 5 M.J. 44 (C.M.A. 1978). The first sentence of subsection (b) makes clear that a part of one of the listed categories may be inspected. *Cf. United States v. King*, 2 M.J. 4 (C.M.A. 1976).

The existence of one or more of the three circumstances identified in the fifth sentence does not mean that the examination is, *per se,* not an inspection. The prosecution may still prove, by clear and convincing evidence, that the purpose of the examination was to determine and ensure security, military fitness, and good order and discipline, and not for the primary purpose of prosecution. For example, when an examination is ordered immediately following a report of a specific offense in the unit, the prosecution might prove the absence of subterfuge by showing that the evidence of the particular offense had already been recovered when the inspection was ordered and that general concern about the welfare of the unit was the motivation for the inspection. Also, if a commander received a report that a highly dangerous item (*e.g.,* an explosive) was present in the command, it might be proved that the commander's concern about safety was the primary purpose for the examination, not prosecution. In the case in which specific individuals are examined, or subjected to more intrusive examinations than others, these indicia of subterfuge might be overcome by proof that these persons were not chosen with a view of prosecution, but on neutral ground or for an independent purpose— *e.g.,* individuals were selected because they were new to the unit and had not been thoroughly examined previously. These examples are not exclusive.

The absence of any of the three circumstances in the fifth sentence, while indicative of a proper inspection, does not necessarily preclude a finding of subterfuge. However, the prosecution need not meet the higher burden of persuasion when the issue is whether the commander's purpose was prosecutorial, in the absence of these circumstances.

The new language provides objective criteria by which to measure a subjective standard, *i.e.,* the commander's purpose. Because the standard is ultimately subjective, however, the objective criteria are not conclusive. Rather they provide concrete and realistic guidance for commanders to use in the exercise of their inspection power, and for judicial authorities to apply in reviewing the exercise of that power.

(c) *Inventories.* Rule 313(c) codifies prior law by recognizing the admissibility of evidence seized via bona fide inventory. The rationale behind this exception to the usual probable cause requirement is that such an inventory is not prosecutorial in nature and is a reasonable intrusion. *See, e.g., South Dakota v. Opperman*, 428 U.S. 364 (1976).

An inventory may not be used as subterfuge search, *United States v. Mossbauer*, 20 C.M.A. 584, 44 C.M.R. 14 (1971), and the basis for an inventory and the procedure utilized may be subject to challenge in any specific case.Inventories of the property of detained individuals have usually been sustained. *See, e.g., United States v. Brashears*, 21 C.M.A. 552, 45 C.M.R. 326 (1972).

The committee does not, however, express an opinion as to the lawful scope of an inventory. *See, e.g., South Dakota v. Opperman*, 428 U.S. 364 (1976), in which the court did not determine the propriety of opening the locked trunk or glove box during the inventory of a properly impounded automobile.

Inventories will often be governed by regulation.

Rule 314 Searches not requiring probable cause

The list of non-probable cause searches contained within Rule 314 is intended to encompass most of the non-probable cause searches common in the military environment. The term "search" is used in Rule 314in its broadest non-technical sense. Consequently, a "search" for purposes of Rule 314 may include examinations that are not "searches" within the narrow technical sense of the Fourth Amendment. *See, e.g.*, Rule 314(j).

Insofar as Rule 314 expressly deals with a given type of search, the Rule preempts the area in that the Rule must be followed even should the Supreme Court issue a decision more favorable to the Government. If such a decision involves a non-probable cause search of a *type* not addressed in Rule 314, it will be fully applicable to the Armed Forces under Rule 314(k) unless other authority prohibits such application.

(a) *General Rule.* Rule 314(a) provides that evidence obtained from a search conducted pursuant to Rule 314 and not in violation of another Rule, *e.g.* , Rule 312, Bodily Views and Intrusions, is admissible when relevant and not otherwise inadmissible.

(b) *Border Searches.* Rule 314(b) recognizes that military personnel may perform border searches when authorized to do so by Congress.

(c) *Searches upon entry to United States installations, aircraft, and vessels abroad.* Rule 314(c) follows the opinion of Chief Judge Fletcher in *United States v. Rivera*, 4 M.J. 215 (C.M.A. 1978), in which he applied, 4 M.J. 215, 216 n.2, the border search doctrine, to entry searches of United States installations or enclaves on foreign soil. The search must be reasonable and its intent, in line with all border searches, must be primarily prophylactic. This authority is additional to any other powers to search or inspect that a commander may hold.

Although Rule 314(c) is similar to Rule 313(b), it is distinct in terms of its legal basis. Consequently, a search performed pursuant to Rule 314(c) need not comply with the burden of proof requirement found in Rule 313(b) for contraband inspections even though the purpose of the 314(c) examination is to prevent introduction of contraband into the installation, aircraft or vessel.

A Rule 314(c) examination must, however, be for a purpose denominated in the rule and must be rationally related to such purpose. A search pursuant to Rule 314(c) is possible only upon entry to the installation, aircraft, or vessel, and an individual who chooses not to enter removes any basis for search pursuant to Rule 314(c). The Rule does not indicate whether discretion may be vested in the person conducting a properly authorized Rule 314(c) search. It was the opinion of members of the Committee, however, that such discretion is proper considering the Rule's underlying basis.

1984 Amendment: Subsection (c) was amended by adding "or exit from" based on *United States v. Alleyne*, 13 M.J. 331 (C.M.A. 1982).

(d) *Searches of government property.* Rule 314(d) restates prior law, *see, e.g., United States v. Weshenfelder*, 20 C.M.A. 416, 43 C.M.R. 256 (1971), and recognizes that personnel normally do not have sufficient interest in government property to have a reasonable expectation of privacy in it. Although the rule could be equally well denominated as a lack of adequate interest, *see,* Rule 311(a)(2), it is more usually expressed as a non-probable cause search. The Rule recognizes that certain government property may take on aspects of private property allowing an individual to develop a reasonable expectation of privacy surrounding it. Wall or floor lockers in living quarters issued for the purpose of storing personal property will normally, although not necessarily, involve a reasonable expectation of privacy. It was the intent of the Committee that such lockers give rise to a rebuttable presumption that they do have an expectation of privacy, and that insofar as other government property is concerned such property gives rise to a rebuttable presumption that such an expectation is absent.

Public property, such as streets, parade grounds, parks, and office buildings rarely if ever involves any limitations upon the ability to search.

(e) *Consent Searches.*

(1) *General rule.* The rule in force before 1980 was found in Para. 152, MCM, 1969 (Rev.), the relevant sections of which state:

A search of one's person with his freely given consent, or of property with the freely given consent of a person entitled in the situation involved to waive the right to immunity from an unreasonable search, such as an owner, bailee, tenant, or occupant as the case may be under the circumstances [is lawful].

If the justification for using evidence obtained as a result of a search is that there was a freely given consent to the search, that consent must be shown by clear and positive evidence.

Although Rule 314(e) generally restates prior law without substantive change, the language has been recast. The basic rule for consent searches is taken from *Schneckloth v. Bustamonte*, 412 U.S. 218 (1973).

(2) *Who may consent.* The Manual language illustrating when third parties may consent to searches has been omitted as being insufficient and potentially misleading and has been replaced by Rule 314(e)(2). The Rule emphasizes the degree of control that an individual has over property and is intended to deal with circumstances in which third parties may be asked to grant consent. *See, e.g., Frazier v. Cupp*, 394 U.S. 731 (1969); *Stoner v. California*, 376 U.S. 483 (1964); *United States v. Mathis*, 16 C.M.A. 511, 37 C.M.R. 142 (1967). It was the Committee's intent to restate prior law in this provision and not to modify it in any degree. Consequently, whether an individual may grant consent to a search of property not his own is a matter to be determined on a case by case basis.

(3) *Scope of consent.* Rule 314(e)(3) restates prior law. *See, e.g., United States v. Castro*, 23 C.M.A. 166, 48 C.M.R. 782 (1974); *United States v. Cady*, 22 C.M.A. 408, 47 C.M.R. 345 (1973).

(4) *Voluntariness.* Rule 314(e)(3) requires that consent be voluntary to be valid. The second sentence is taken in substance from *Schneckloth v. Bustamonte*, 412 U.S. 218, 248–49 (1973).

The specific inapplicability of Article 31(b) warnings follows *Schneckloth* and complies with *United States v. Morris*, 1 M.J. 352 (C.M.A. 1976) (opinion by Chief Judge Fletcher with Judge Cook concurring in the result). Although not required, such warnings are, however, a valuable indication of a voluntary consent. The Committee does not express an opinion as to whether rights warnings are required prior to obtaining an admissible statement as to ownership or possession of property from a suspect when that admission is obtained via a request for consent to search.

(5) *Burden of proof.* Although not constitutionally required, the burden of proof in Para.152 of the 1969 Manual for consent searches has been retained in a slightly different form— "clear and convincing" in place of "clear and positive"— on the presumption that the basic nature of the military structure renders consent more suspect than in the civilian community. "Clear and convincing evidence" is intended to create a burden of proof between the preponderance and beyond a reasonable doubt standards. The Rule expressly rejects a different burden for custodial consents. The law is this area evidences substantial confusion stemming initially from language used in *United States v.Justice*, 13 C.M.A. 31, 34, 32 C.M.R. 31, 34 (1962): "It [the burden of proof] is an especially heavy obligation if the accused was in custody ...", which was taken in turn from a number of civilian federal court decisions. While custody should be a factor resulting in an especially careful scrutiny of the circumstances surrounding a possible consent, there appears to be no legal or policy reason to require a higher burden of proof.

(f) *Frisks incident to a lawful stop.* Rule 314(f) recognizes a frisk as a lawful search when performed pursuant to a lawful stop. The primary authority for the stop and frisk doctrine is *Terry v. Ohio*, 392 U.S. 1 (1968), and the present Manual lacks any reference to either stops or frisks. Hearsay may be used in deciding to stop and frisk. *See, e.g., Adams v. Williams*, 407 U.S. 143 (1972).

The Rule recognizes the necessity for assisting police or law enforcement personnel in their investigations but specifically does not address the issue of the lawful duration of a stop nor of the nature of the questioning, if any, that may be involuntarily addressed to the individual stopped. *See Brown v. Texas*, 440 U.S. 903 (1979), generally prohibiting such questioning in civilian life. Generally, it would appear that any individual who can be lawfully stopped is likely to be a suspect for the purposes of Article 31(b). Whether identification can be demanded of a military suspect without Article 31(b) warnings is an open question and may be dependent upon whether the identification of the suspect is relevant to the offense possibly involved. *See* Lederer, *Rights Warnings in the Armed Services*, 72 Mil.L.Rev. 1,40–41 (1976).

1984 Amendment: Subsection (f)(3) was added based on *Michigan v. Long*, 463 U.S. 1032 (1983).

(g) *Searches incident to a lawful apprehension.* The 1969 Manual rule was found in Para. 152 and stated:

A search conducted as an incident of lawfully apprehending a person, which may include a search of his person, of the clothing he is wearing, and of property which, at time of apprehension, is in his immediate possession or control, or of an area from within which he might gain possession of weapons or destructible evidence; and a search of the place where the apprehension is made [is lawful].

Rule 314(g) restates the principle found within the Manual text but utilizes new and clarifying language. The Rule expressly requires that an apprehension be lawful.

(1) *General Rule.* Rule 314(g)(1) expressly authorizes the search of a person of a lawfully apprehended individual without further justification.

(2) *Search for weapons and destructible evidence.* Rule 314(g)(2) delimits the area that can be searched pursuant to an apprehension and specifies that the purpose of the search is only to locate weapons and destructible evidence. This is a variation of the authority presently in the Manual and is based upon the Supreme Court's decision in *Chimel v. California*, 395 U.S. 752 (1969). It is clear from the Court's decision in *United States v. Chadwick*, 438 U.S. 1 (1977), that the scope of a search pursuant to a lawful apprehension must be limited to those areas which an individual could reasonably reach and utilize. The search of the area within the immediate control of the person apprehended is thus properly viewed as a search based upon necessity— whether one based upon the safety of those persons apprehending or upon the necessity to safeguard evidence. *Chadwick*, holding that police could not search a sealed footlocker pursuant to an arrest, stands for the proposition that the *Chimel* search must be limited by its rationale.

That portion of the 1969 Manual rule.subparagraph dealing with intrusive body searches has been incorporated into Rule 312. Similarly that portion of the Manual dealing with search incident to hot pursuit of a person has been incorporated into that portion of Rule 315 dealing with exceptions to the need for search warrants or authorizations.

1984 Amendment: Subsection (g)(2) was amended by adding language to clarify the permissible scope of a search incident to apprehension of the occupant of an automobile based on*New York v. Belton*, 453 U.S. 454 (1981). The holding of the Court used the term "automobile" so that word is used in the rule. It is intended that the term "automobile" have the broadest possible meaning.

(3) *Examination for other persons.* Rule 314(g)(3) is intended to protect personnel performing apprehensions. Consequently, it is extremely limited in scope and requires a good faith and reasonable belief that persons may be present who might interfere with the apprehension of individuals. Any search must be directed towards the finding of such persons and not evidence.

An unlawful apprehension of the accused may make any subsequent statement by the accused inadmissible, *Dunaway v. New York*, 442 U.S. 200 (1979).

1994 Amendment. The amendment to Mil. R. Evid. 314(g)(3), based on *Maryland v. Buie*, 494 U.S. 325 (1990), specifies the circumstances permitting the search for other persons and distinguishes between protective sweeps and searches of the attack area.

Subsection (A) permits protective sweeps in the military. The last sentence of this subsection clarifies that an examination under the rule need not be based on probable cause. Rather, this subsection adopts the standard articulated in *Terry v. Ohio*, 392 U.S. 1 (1968) and *Michigan v. Long*, 463 U.S. 1032 (1983). As such, there must be articulable facts that, taken together with the rational inferences from those facts, would warrant a reasonably prudent officer in believing the area harbors individuals posing a danger to those at the site of apprehension. The previous language referring to those "who might interfere" was deleted to conform to the standards set forth in *Buie*. An examination under this rule is limited to a cursory visual inspection of those places in which a person might be hiding.

A new subsection (B) was also added as a result of *Buie, supra*. The amendment clarifies that apprehending officials may examine the "attack area" for persons who might pose a danger to apprehending officials. *See Buie*, 494 U.S. at 334. The attack area is that area immediately adjoining the place of apprehension from which an attack could be immediately launched. This amendment makes it clear that apprehending officials do not need any suspicion to examine the attack area.

(h) *Searches within jails, confinement facilities, or similar facilities.* Personnel confined in a military confinement facility or housed in a facility serving a generally similar purpose will normally yield any normal Fourth Amendment protections to the reasonable needs of the facility. *See, United States v. Maglito*,20 C.M.A. 456, 43 C.M.R. 296 (1971). *See also* Rule 312.

(i) *Emergency searches to save life or for related purpose.* This type of search is not found within the 1969 Manual provision but is in accord with prevailing civilian and military case law. *See, United States v. Yarborough*, 50 C.M.R. 149, 155 (A.F.C.M.R. 1975). Such a search must be conducted in good faith and may not be a subterfuge in order to circumvent an individual's Fourth Amendment protections.

(j) *Searches of open fields or woodlands.* This type of search is taken from 1969 Manual paragraph 152. Originally recognized in *Hester v. United States*, 265 U.S. 57 (1924), this doctrine was revived by the Supreme Court in *Air Pollution Variance Board v. Western Alfalfa Corp.*, 416 U.S. 861 (1974). Arguably, such a search is not a search within the meaning of the Fourth Amendment. In *Hester*, Mr. Justice Holmes simply concluded that "the special protection accorded by the 4th Amendment to the people in their [persons, houses, papers, and effects] is not extended to the open fields." 265 U.S. at 59. In relying on *Hester*, the Court in *Air Pollution Variance Board* noted that it was "not advised that he [the air pollution investigator] was on premises from which the public was excluded." 416 U.S. at 865. This suggests that the doctrine of open fields is subject to the caveat that a reasonable expectation of privacy may result in application of the Fourth Amendment to open fields.

(k) *Other searches.* Rule 314(k) recognizes that searches of a *type* not specified within the Rule but proper under the Constitution are also lawful.

Rule 315 Probable cause searches

(a) *General Rule—* Rule 315 states that evidence obtained pursuant to the Rule is admissible when relevant and not otherwise admissible under the Rules.

(b) *Definitions.*

(1) *Authorization to search.* Rule 315(b)(1) defines an "authorization to search" as an express permission to search issued by proper military authority whether commander or judge. As such, it replaces the term "search warrant" which is used in the Rules only when referring to a permission to search given by proper civilian authority. The change in terminology reflects the unique nature of the armed forces and of the role played by commanders.

(2) *Search warrant.* The expression "search warrant" refers only to the authority to search issued by proper civilian authority.

(c) *Scope of authorization.—* Rule 315(c) is taken generally from Para. 152(1)–(3) of the 1969 Manual except that military jurisdiction to search upon military installations or in military aircraft, vessels, or vehicles has been clarified. Although civilians and civilian institutions on military installations are subject to search pursuant to a proper search authorization, the effect of any applicable federal statute or regulation must be considered. *E.g.*, the Right to Financial Privacy Act of 1978, 12 U.S.C. §§ 3401–3422, and DOD Directive 5400.12 (Obtaining Information From Financial Institutions).

Rule 315(c)(4) is a modification of prior law. Subdivision (c)(4)(A) is intended to ensure cooperation between Department of Defense agencies and other government agencies by requiring prior consent to DOD searches involving such other agencies. Although Rule 315(c)(4)(B) follows the 1969 Manual in permitting searches of "other property in a foreign country" to be authorized pursuant to subdivision (d), subdivision (c) requires that all applicable treaties be complied with or that prior concurrence with an appropriate representative of the foreign nation be obtained if no treaty or agreement exists. The Rule is intended to foster cooperation with host nations and compliance with all existing international agreements. The rule does not require specific approval by foreign authority of each search (unless, of course, applicable treaty requires such approval); rather the Rule permits prior blanket or categorical approvals. Because Rule 315(c)(4) is designed to govern intragovernmental and international relationships rather than relationships between the United States and its citizens, a violation of these provisions does not render a search unlawful.

(d) *Power to authorize* —Rule 315(d) grants power to authorize searches to impartial individuals of the included classifications. The closing portion of the subdivision clarifies the decision of the Court of Military Appeals in *United States v. Ezell*, 6 M.J. 307 (C.M.A. 1979), by stating that the mere presence of an authorizing officer at a search does not deprive the individual of an otherwise neutral character. This is in conformity with the decision of the United States Supreme Court in *Lo-Ji Sales v. New York*, 442 U.S. 319 (1979), from which the first portion of the language has been taken. The subdivision also recognizes the propriety of a commander granting a search authorization after taking a pretrial action equivalent to that which may be taken by a federal district judge. For example, a commander might authorize use of a drug detector dog, an action arguably similar to the granting of wiretap order by a federal judge, without necessarily depriving himself or herself of the ability to later issue a search authorization. The question would be whether the commander has acted in the first instance in an impartial judicial capacity.

(1) *Commander—* Rule 315(d)(1) restates the prior rule by recognizing the power of commanders to issue search authorizations upon probable cause. The Rule explicitly allows non-officers serving in a position designated by the Secretary concerned as a position of command to issue search authorizations. If a non-officer assumes command of a unit, vessel, or aircraft, and the command position is one recognized by regulations issued by the Secretary concerned, *e.g.*, command of a company, squadron, vessel, or aircraft, the non-officer commander is empowered to grant search authorizations under this subdivision whether the assumption of command is pursuant to express appointment or devolution of command. The power to do so is thus a function of position rather than rank.

The Rule also allows a person serving as officer-in-charge or in a position designated by the Secretary as a position analogous to an officer-in-charge to grant search authorizations. The term "officer-in-charge" is statutorily defined, Article 1(4), as pertaining only to the Navy, Coast Guard, and Marine Corps, and the change will allow the Army and Air Force to establish an analogous position should they desire to do so in which case the power to authorize searches would exist although such individuals would not be "officers-in-charge" as that term is used in the U.C.M.J.

(2) *Delegee—* Former subsection (2), which purported to allow delegation of the authority to authorize searches, was deleted in 1984, based on *United States v. Kalscheuer*, 11 M.J. 373 (C.M.A. 1981). Subsection (3) was renumbered as subsection (2).

(3) *Military judge—* Rule 315(d)(2) permits military judges to issue search authorizations when authorized to do so by the Secretary concerned. MILITARY MAGISTRATES MAY ALSO BE EMPOWERED TO GRANT SEARCH AUTHORIZATIONS. This recognizes the practice now in use in the Army but makes such practice discretionary with the specific Service involved.

(e) *Power to search.* Rule 315(e) specifically denominates those persons who may conduct or authorize a search upon probable cause either pursuant to a search authorization or when such an authorization is not required for reasons of exigencies. The Rule recognizes, for example, that all officers and non-commissioned officers have inherent power to perform a probable cause search without obtaining of a search authorization under the circumstances set forth in Rule 315(g). The expression "criminal investigator" within Rule 315(e) includes members of the Army Criminal Investigation Command, the Marine Corps Criminal Investigation Division, the Naval Criminal Investigative Service, the Air Force Office of Special Investigations, and Coast Guard special agents.

(f) *Basis for search authorizations.* Rule 315(f) requires that probable cause be present before a search can be conducted under the Rule and utilizes the basic definition of probable cause found in 1969 Manual Para. 152.

For reasons of clarity the Rule sets forth a simple and general test to be used in all probable cause determinations: probable cause can exist only if the authorizing individual has a "reasonable belief that the information giving rise to the intent to search is believable and has a factual basis." This test is taken from the "two prong test" of *Aguilar v. Texas*, 378 U.S. 108 (1964), which was incorporated in Para. 152 of the 1969 Manual. The Rule expands the test beyond the hearsay and informant area. The "factual basis" requirement is satisfied when an individual reasonably concludes that the information, if reliable, adequately apprises the individual that the property in question is what it is alleged to be and is where it is alleged to be. Information is "believable" when an individual reasonably concludes that it is sufficiently reliable to be believed.

The twin test of "believability" and "basis in fact" must be met in all probable cause situations. The method of application of the test will differ, however, depending upon circumstances. The following examples are illustrative:

(1) An individual making a probable cause determination who observes an incident first hand is only required to determine if the observation is reliable and that the property is likely to be what it appears to be.

For example, an officer who believes that she sees an individual in possession of heroin must first conclude that the observation was reliable (*i.e.*, if her eyesight was adequate—should glasses have been worn—and if there was sufficient time for adequate observation) and that she has sufficient knowledge and experience to be able to reasonably believe that the substance in question was in fact heroin.

(2) An individual making a probable cause determination who relies upon the in person report of an informant must determine both that the informant is believable and that the property observed is likely to be what the observer believes it to be. The determining individual may rely upon the demeanor of the informant in order to determine whether the observer is believable. An individual known to have a "clean record" and no bias against the individual to be affected by the search is likely to be credible.

(3) An individual making a probable cause determination who relies upon the report of an informant not present before the authorizing individual must determine both that the informant is credible and that the property observed is likely to be what the informant believed it to be. The determining individual may utilize one or more of the following factors, among others, in order to determine whether the informant is believable:

(A) *Prior record as a reliable informant*— Has the informant given information in the past which proved to be accurate?

(B) *Corroborating detail*— Has enough detail of the informant's information been verified to imply that the remainder can reasonably be presumed to be accurate?

(C) *Statement against interest*— Is the information given by the informant sufficiently adverse to the fiscal or penal interest of the informant to imply that the information may reasonably be presumed to be accurate?

(D) *Good citizen*— Is the character of the informant, as known by the individual making the probable cause determination, such as to make it reasonable to presume that the information is accurate?

Mere allegations may not be relied upon. For example, an individual may not reasonably conclude that an informant is reliable simply because the informant is so named by a law enforcement agent. The individual making the probable cause determination must be supplied with specific details of the informant's past actions to allow that individual to personally and reasonably conclude that the informant is reliable.

Information transmitted through law enforcement or command channels is presumed to have been reliably transmitted. This presumption may be rebutted by an affirmative showing that the information was transmitted with intentional error.

The Rule permits a search authorization to be issued based upon information transmitted by telephone or other means of communication.

The Rule also permits the Secretaries concerned to impose additional procedural requirements for the issuance of search authorizations.

1984 Amendment: The second sentence of subsection (f)(1) was deleted based on *Illinois v. Gates*, 462 U.S.213 (1983), which overturned the mandatory two-prong test of *Aguilar v. Texas, supra.* Although the second sentence may be technically compatible with *Gates*, it could be construed as requiring strict application of the standards of *Aguilar*. The former language remains good advice for those deciding the existence of probable cause, especially for uncorroborated tips, but is not an exclusive test. *See also Massachusetts v. Upton*, 466 U.S. 767 (1984).

(g) *Exigencies.* Rule 315(g) restates prior law and delimits those circumstances in which a search warrant or authorization is unnecessary despite the ordinary requirement for one. In all such cases probable cause is required.

Rule 315(g)(1) deals with the case in which the time necessary to obtain a proper authorization would threaten the destruction or concealment of the property or evidence sought.

Rule 315(g)(2) recognizes that military necessity may make it tactically impossible to attempt to communicate with a person who could grant a search authorization. Should a nuclear submarine on radio silence, for example, lack a proper authorizing individual, (perhaps for reasons of disqualification), no search could be conducted if the Rule were otherwise unless the ship broke radio silence and imperiled the vessel or its mission. Under the Rule this would constitute an "exigency." "Military operational necessity" includes similar necessity incident to the Coast Guard's performance of its maritime police mission.

The Rule also recognizes in subdivision (g)(3) the "automobile exception" created by the Supreme Court. *See, e.g., United States v. Chadwick*, 433 U.S. 1 (1977); *South Dakota v. Opperman*, 428 U.S. 364 (1976); *Texas v. White*, 423 U.S. 67 (1975), and, subject to the constraints of the Constitution, the Manual, or the Rules, applies it to all vehicles. While the exception will thus apply to vessels and aircraft as well as to automobiles, trucks,*et al,* it must be applied with great care. In view of the Supreme Court's reasoning that vehicles are both mobile and involve a diminished expectation of privacy, the larger a vehicle is, the more unlikely it is that the exception will apply. The exception has no application to government vehicles as they may be searched without formal warrant or authorization under Rule 314(d).

1984 Amendment: The last sentence of subsection (g) was amended by deleting "presumed to be." The former language could be construed to permit the accused to prove that the vehicle was in fact inoperable (that is, to rebut the presumption of operability) thereby negating the exception, even though a reasonable person would have believed the vehicle inoperable. The fact of inoperability is irrelevant; the test is whether the official(s) searching knew or should have known that the vehicle was inoperable.

(h) *Execution.* Rule 314(h)(1) provides for service of a search warrant or search authorization upon a person whose property is to be searched when possible. Noncompliance with the Rule does not, however, result in exclusion of the evidence. Similarly, Rule 314(h)(2) provides for the inventory of seized property and provisions of a copy of the inventory to the person from whom the property was seized. Noncompliance with the subdivision does not, however, make the search or seizure unlawful. Under Rule 315(h)(3) compliance with foreign law is required when executing a search authorization outside the United States, but noncompliance does not trigger the exclusionary rule.

Rule 316 Seizures

(a) *General Rule.* Rule 316(a) provides that evidence obtained pursuant to the Rule is admissible when relevant and not otherwise inadmissible under the Rules. Rule 316 recognizes that searches are distinct from seizures. Although rare, a seizure need not be proceeded by a search. Property may, for example, be seized after being located pursuant to plain view, *see* subdivision (d)(4)(C). Consequently, the propriety of a seizure must be considered independently of any preceding search.

(b) *Seizures of property.* Rule 316(b) defines probable cause in the same fashion as defined by Rule 315 for probable cause searches. *See* the Analysis of Rule 315(f)(2). The justifications for seizing property are taken from 1969 Manual Para. 152. Their number has, however, been reduced for reasons of brevity. No distinction is made between "evidence of crime" and "instrumentalities or fruits of crime." Similarly, the proceeds of crime are also "evidence of crime."

1984 Amendment: The second sentence of subsection (b) was deleted based on *Illinois v. Gates*, 462 U.S. 213 (1983). *See* Analysis, Mil. R. Evid. 315(f)(1), *supra.*

(c) *Apprehension.* Apprehensions are, of course, seizures of the person and unlawful apprehensions may be challenged as an unlawful seizure. *See, e.g., Dunaway v. New York*, 442 U.S. 200 (1979); *United States v. Texidor-Perez*, 7 M.J. 356 (C.M.A. 1979).

(d) *Seizure of property or evidence.*

(1) *Abandoned property.* Rule 316(d) restates prior law, not addressed specifically by the 1969 Manual chapter, by providing that abandoned property may be seized by anyone at any time.

(2) *Consent.* Rule 316(d)(2) permits seizure of property with appropriate consent pursuant to Rule 314(e). The prosecution must demonstrate a voluntary consent by clear and convincing evidence.

(3) *Government property.* Rule 316(d)(3) permits seizure of government property without probable cause unless the person to whom the property is issued or assigned has a reasonable expectation of privacy therein at the time of seizure. In this regard note Rule 314(d) and its analysis.

(4) *Other property.* Rule 316(d)(4) provides for seizure of property or evidence not otherwise addressed by the Rule. There must be justification to exercise control over the property. Although property may have been lawfully located, it may not be seized for use at trial unless there is a reasonable belief that the property is of a type discussed in Rule 316(b). Because the Rule is inapplicable to seizures unconnected with law enforcement, it does not limit the seizure of property for a valid administrative purpose such as safety.

Property or evidence may be seized upon probable cause when seizure is authorized or directed by a search warrant or authorization, Rule 316(d)(4)(A); when exigent circumstances pursuant to Rule 315(g) permit proceeding without such a warrant or authorization; or when the property or evidence is in plain view or smell, Rule 316(d)(4)(C).

Although most plain view seizures are inadvertent, there is no necessity that a plain view discovery be inadvertent— notwithstanding dicta, in some court cases; *see, Coolidge v. New Hampshire*, 403 U.S. 443 (1971). The Rule allows a seizure pursuant to probable cause when made as a result of plain view. The language used in Rule 316(d)(4)(C) is taken from the ALI MODEL CODE OF PREARRAIGNMENT PROCEDURES § 260.6 (1975). The Rule requires that the observation making up the alleged plain view be "reasonable." Whether intentional observation from outside a window, via flashlight or binocular, for example, is observation in a "reasonable fashion" is a question to be considered on a case by case basis. Whether a person may properly enter upon private property in order to effect a seizure of matter located via plain view is not resolved by the Rule and is left to future case development.

1984 Amendment: Subsection (d)(5) was added based on *United States v. Place*, 462 U.S. 696 (1983).

(e) *Power to seize.* Rule 316(e) conforms with Rule 315(e) and has its origin in Para. 19, MCM, 1969 (Rev.).

Rule 317 Interception of wire and oral communication

(a) *General Rule.* The area of interception of wire and oral communications is unusually complex and fluid. At present, the area is governed by the Fourth Amendment, applicable federal statute, DOD directive, and regulations prescribed by the Service Secretaries. In view of this situation, it is preferable to refrain from codification and to vest authority for the area primarily in the Department of Defense or Secretary concerned. Rule 317(c) thus prohibits interception of wire and oral communications for law enforcement purposes by members of the armed forces except as authorized by 18 U.S.C. § 2516, Rule 317(b), and when applicable, by regulations issued by the Secretary of Defense or the Secretary concerned. Rule 317(a), however, specifically requires exclusion of evidence resulting form noncompliance with Rule 317(c) only when exclusion is required by the Constitution or by an applicable statute. Insofar as a violation of a regulation is concerned, *compare United States v. Dillard*, 8 M.J. 213 (C.M.A. 1980) with *United States v. Caceres*, 440 U.S. 741 (1979).

(b) *Authorization for Judicial Applications in the United States.* Rule 317(b) is intended to clarify the scope of 18 U.S.C. § 2516 by expressly recognizing the Attorney General's authority to authorize applications to a federal court by the Department of Defense, Department of Homeland Security, or the military departments for authority to intercept wire or oral communications.

(c) *Regulations.* Rule 317(c) requires interception of wire or oral communications in the United States be first authorized by statute, *see* Rule 317(b), and interceptions abroad by appropriate regulations. *See* the Analysis to Rule 317(a), *supra*. The Committee intends 317(c) to limit only in interceptions that are non consensual under Chapter 119 of Title 18 of the United States Code.

Rule 321 Eyewitness identification

(a) *General Rule*

(1) *Admissibility.* The first sentence of Rule 321(a)(1) is the basic rule of admissibility of eyewitness identification and provides that evidence of a relevant out-of-court identification is admissible when otherwise admissible under the Rules. The intent of the provision is to allow any relevant out-of-court identification without any need to comply with the condition precedent such as in-court identification, significant change from the prior rule as found in Para. 153 *a*, MCM, 1969 (Rev.).

The language "if such testimony is otherwise admissible under these rules" is primarily intended to ensure compliance with the hearsay rule. Rule 802. It should be noted that Rule 801(d)(1)(C) states that a statement of "identification of a person made after perceiving the person" is not hearsay when "the declarant testifies at the trial or hearing and is subject to cross-examination concerning the statement." An eyewitness identification normally will be admissible if the declarant testifies. The Rule's statement, "the witness making the identification and any person who has observed the previous identification may testify concerning it," is not an express exception authorizing the witness to testify to an out-of-court identification notwithstanding the hearsay rule, rather it is simply an indication that in appropriate circumstances, *see* Rules 803 and 804, a witness to an out-of-court identification may testify concerning it.

The last sentence of subdivision (a)(1) is intended to clarify procedure by emphasizing that an in-court identification may be bolstered by an out-of-court identification notwithstanding the fact that the in-court identification has not been attacked.

(2) *Exclusionary rule.* Rule 321(a)(2) provides the basic exclusionary rule for eyewitness identification testimony. The substance of the Rule is taken from prior Manual paragraph 153 *a* as modified by the new procedure for suppression motions. *See* Rules 304 and 311. Subdivision (a)(2)(A) provides that evidence of an identification will be excluded if it was obtained as a result of an "unlawful identification process conducted by the United States or other domestic authorities" while subdivision (a)(2)(B) excludes evidence of an identification if exclusion would be required by the due process clause of the Fifth Amendment to the Constitution. Under the burden of proof, subdivision (d)(2), an identification is not inadmissible if the prosecution proves by a preponderance of the evidence that the identification process was not so unnecessarily suggestive, in light of the totality of the circumstances, as to create a very substantial likelihood of irreparable mistaken identity. It is the unreliability of the evidence which is determinative. *Manson v. Brathwaite*, 432 U.S. 98 (1977). "United States or other domestic authorities" includes military personnel.

Although it is clear that an unlawful identification may taint a later identification, it is unclear at present whether an unlawful identification requires suppression of evidence other than identification of the accused. Consequently, the Rule requires exclusion of nonidentification derivative evidence only when the Constitution would so require.

(b) *Definition of "unlawful."*

(1) *Lineups and other identification processes.* Rule 321(b) defines "unlawful lineup or other identification processes." When such a procedure is conducted by persons subject to the Uniform Code of Military Justice or their agents, it will be unlawful if it is "unnecessarily suggestive or otherwise in violation of the due process clause of the Fifth Amendment of the Constitution of the United States as applied to members of the armed forces." The expression, "unnecessarily suggestive" itself is a technical one and refers to an identification that is in violation of the due process clause because it is unreliable. *See Manson v. Brathwaite, supra; Stovall v. Denno*, 338 U.S. 292 (1967); *Neil v. Biggers*, 409 U.S. 188 (1972). *See also Foster v. California*, 394 U.S. 440 (1969). An identification is not unnecessarily suggestive in violation of the due process clause if the identification process was not so unnecessarily suggestive, in light of the totality of the circumstances, as to create a very substantial likelihood of irreparable mistaken identity. *See Manson v. Brathwaite, supra*, and subdivision (d)(2).

Subdivision (1)(A) differs from subdivision (1)(B) only in that it recognizes that the Constitution may apply differently to members of the armed forces than it does to civilians.

Rule 321(b)(1) is applicable to all forms of identification processes including showups and lineups.

1984 Amendment: Subsections (b)(1) and (d)(2) were modified to make clear that the test for admissibility of an out-of-court identification is reliability. *See Manson v. Brathwaite, supra.* This was apparently the intent of the drafters of the former rule. *See* Analysis, Mil. R. Evid. 321. The language actually used in subsection (b)(1) and (d)(2) was subject to a different interpretation, however. *See* S. Salzburg, L. Schinasi, and D. Schlueter, MILITARY RULES OF EVIDENCE MANUAL at 165–167 (1981); Gasperini, *Eyewitness Identification Under the Military Rules of Evidence*, The Army Lawyer at 42 (May 1980).

In determining whether an identification is reliable, the military judge should weigh all the circumstances, including: the opportunity of the witness to view the accused at the time of the offense; the degree of attention paid by the witness; the accuracy of any prior descriptions of the accused by the witness; the level of certainty shown by the witness in the identification; and the time between the crime and the confrontation. Against these factors should be weighed the corrupting effect of a suggestive and unnecessary identification. *See Manson v. Brathwaite, supra; Neil v. Biggers, supra.*

Note that the modification of subsection (b)(1) eliminates the distinction between identification processes conducted by persons subject to the code and other officials. Because the test is the reliability of the identification, and not a prophylactic standard, there is no basis to distinguish between identification processes conducted by each group. *See Manson v. Brathwaite, supra.*

(2) *Lineups: right to counsel.* Rule 321(b)(2) deals only with

lineups. The Rule does declare that a lineup is "unlawful" if it is conducted in violation of the right to counsel. Like Rule 305 and 311, Rule 321(b)(2) distinguishes between lineups conducted by persons subject to the Uniform Code of Military Justice or their agents and those conducted by others.

Subdivision (b)(2)(A) is the basic right to counsel for personnel participating in military lineups. A lineup participant is entitled to counsel only if that participant is in pretrial restraint (pretrial arrest, restriction, or confinement) under paragraph 20 of the Manual or has had charges preferred against him or her. Mere apprehension or temporary detention does not trigger the right to counsel under the Rule. This portion of the Rule substantially changes military law and adapts the Supreme Court's decision in *Kirby v. Illinois*, 406 U.S. 682, 689 (1972) (holding that the right to counsel attached only when "adversary judicial criminal proceedings" have been initiated or "the government has committed itself to prosecute") to unique military criminal procedure. *See also* Rule 305(d)(1)(B).

Note that *interrogation* of a suspect will require rights warnings, perhaps including a warning of a right to counsel, even if counsel is unnecessary under Rule 321. *See* Rule 305.

As previously noted, the Rule does not define "lineup" and recourse to case law is necessary. Intentional exposure of the suspect to one or more individuals for purpose of identification is likely to be a lineup. *Stovall v. Denno*, 388 U.S. 293, 297 (1967), although in rare cases of emergency (*e.g.,* a dying victim) such an identification may be considered a permissible "showup" rather than a "lineup." Truly accidental confrontations between victims and suspects leading to an identification by the victim are not generally considered "lineups"; *cf. United State ex rel Ragazzin v. Brierley*, 321 F.Supp. 440 (W.D. Pa. 1970). Photolineart identifications are not "lineups" for purposes of the right to counsel. *United States v. Ash*, 413 U.S. 300, 301 n.2 (1973). If a photolineart identification is used, however, the photographs employed should be preserved for use at trial in the event that the defense should claim that the identification was "unnecessarily suggestive." *See subdivision* (b)(1) *supra.*

A lineup participant who is entitled to counsel is entitled to only one lawyer under the Rule and is specifically entitled to free military counsel without regard to the indigency or lack thereof of the participant. No right to civilian counsel or military counsel of the participant's own selection exists under the Rule, *United States v. Wade*, 388 U.S. 218, n.27 (1967). A lineup participant may waive any applicable right to counsel so long as the participant is aware of the right to counsel and the waiver is made "freely, knowingly, and intelligently." Normally a warning of the right to counsel will be necessary for the prosecution to prove an adequate waiver should the defense adequately challenge the waiver. *See, e.g., United States v. Avers*, 426 F.2d 524 (2d Cir. 1970). *See also* Model Rules for Law Enforcement, Eye Witness Identification, Rule 404 (1974) cited in E. Imwinkelried, P. Giannelli, F. Gilligan, & F. Lederer, CRIMINAL EVIDENCE 366 (1979).

1984 Amendment: In subsection (b)(2)(A), the words "or law specialist within the meaning of Article 1" were deleted as unnecessary. *See* R.C.M. 103(26).

Subdivision (b)(2)(B) grants a right to counsel at non-military lineups within the United States only when such a right to counsel is recognized by "the principles of law generally recognized in the trial of criminal cases in the United States district courts involving similar lineups." The Rule presumes that an individual participating in a foreign lineup conducted by officials of a foreign nation without American participation has no right to counsel at such a lineup.

(c) *Motions to suppress and objections.* Rule 321(c) is identical in application to Rule 311(d). *See* the Analysis to Rules 304 and 311.

(d) *Burden of proof.* Rule 321(d) makes it clear that when an eyewitness identification is challenged by the defense, the prosecution need reply only to the specific cognizable defense complaint. *See also* Rules 304 and 311. The subdivision distinguishes between defense challenges involving alleged violation of the right to counsel and those involving the alleged unnecessarily suggestive identifications.

(1) *Right to counsel.* Subdivision (d)(1) requires that when an alleged violation of the right to counsel has been raised the prosecution must either demonstrate by preponderance of the evidence that counsel was present or that the right to counsel was waived voluntarily and intelligently. The Rule also declares that if the right to counsel is violated at a lineup that results in an identification of the accused any later identification is considered a result of the prior lineup as a matter of law unless the military judge determines by clear and convincing evidence that the latter identification is not the result of the first lineup. Subdivision (d)(1) is taken in substance from 1969 Manual Para. 153 *a.*

(2) *Unnecessarily suggestive identification.* Rule 321(d)(2) deals with an alleged unnecessarily suggestive identification or with any other alleged violation of due process. The subdivision makes it clear that the prosecution must show, when the defense has raised the issue, that the identification in question was not based upon a preponderance of the evidence, "so unnecessarily suggestive in light of the totality of the circumstances, as to create a very substantial likelihood of irreparable mistaken identity." This rule is taken from the Supreme Court's decisions of *Neil v. Biggers*, 409 U.S. 188 (1972) and *Stovall v. Denno,* 388 U.S. 293 (1967), and unlike subdivision (d)(1), applies to all identification processes whether lineups or not. The Rule recognizes that the nature of the identification process itself may well be critical to the reliability of the identification and provides for exclusion of unreliable evidence regardless of its source. If the prosecution meets its burden, the mere fact that the identification process was unnecessary or suggestive does not require exclusion of the evidence, *Manson v. Brathwaite, supra.*

If the identification in question is subsequent to an earlier, unnecessarily suggestive identification, the later identification is admissible if the prosecution can show by clear and convincing evidence that the later identification is not the result of the earlier improper examination. This portion of the Rule is consistent both with 1969 Manual Para. 153 *a* and *Kirby v. Illinois*, 406 U.S. 682 (1972).

(e) *Defense evidence.* Rule 321(e) is identical with the analogous provisions in Rules 304 and 311 and generally restates prior law.

(f) *Rulings.* Rule 321(f) is identical with the analogous provisions in Rules 304 and 321 and substantially changes prior law. *See* the Analysis to Rule 304(d)(4).

(g) *Effect of guilty plea.* Rule 321(g) is identical with the analogous provisions in Rules 304 and 311 and restates prior law.

SECTION IV

Relevancy and its Limits

Rule 401 Definition of "relevant evidence"

The definition of "relevant evidence" found within Rule 401 is taken without change from the Federal Rule and is substantially similar in effect to that used by Para. 137, MCM, 1969 (Rev.). The Rule's definition may be somewhat broader than the 1969 Manual's, as the Rule defines as relevant any evidence that has "any tendency to make the existence of any fact ... more probable or less probable than it would be without the evidence" while the 1969 Manual defines as "not relevant" evidence "too remote to have any appreciable probative value ..." To the extent that the 1969 Manual's definition includes considerations of "legal relevance," those considerations are adequately addressed by such other Rules as Rules 403 and 609. *See*, E. IMWINKELRIED, P. GIANNELLI, F. GILLIGAN & F. LEDERER, CRIMINAL EVIDENCE 62–65 (1979) (which, after defining "logical relevance" as involving only probative value, states at 63 that "under the rubric of [legal relevance,] the courts have imposed an additional requirement that the item's probative value outweighs any attendant probative dangers.") The Rule is similar to the 1969 Manual in that it abandons any reference to "materiality" in favor of a single standard of "relevance." Notwithstanding the specific terminology used, however, the concept of materiality survives in the Rule's condition that to be relevant evidence must involve a fact "which is of consequence to the determination of the action."

Rule 402 Relevant evidence generally admissible; irrelevant evidence inadmissible.

Rule 402 is taken without significant change from the Federal Rule. The Federal Rule's language relating to limitations imposed by "the Constitution of the United States, by Act of Congress, by these rules, or by other rules prescribed by the Supreme Court pursuant to statutory authority" has been replaced by material tailored to the unique nature of the Military Rules of Evidence. Rule 402 recognizes that the Constitution may apply somewhat differently to members of the armed forces than to civilians, and the Rule deletes the Federal Rule's reference to "other rules prescribed by the Supreme Court" because such Rules do not apply directly in courts-martial. *See* Rule 101(b)(2).

Rule 402 provides a general standard by which irrelevant evidence is always inadmissible and by which relevant evidence is generally admissible. Qualified admissibility of relevant evidence is required by the limitations in Sections III and V and by such other Rules as 403 and 609 which intentionally utilize matters such as degree of probative value and judicial efficiency in determining whether relevant evidence should be admitted.

Rule 402 is not significantly different in its effect from Para. 137 of the 1969 Manual which it replaces, and procedures used under the 1969 Manual in determining relevance generally remain valid. Offers of proof are encouraged when items of doubtful relevance are proffered, and it remains possible, subject to the discretion of the military judge, to offer evidence "subject to later connection." Use of the latter technique, however, must be made with great care to avoid the possibility of bringing inadmissible evidence before the members of the court.

It should be noted that Rule 402 is potentially the most important of the new rules. Neither the Federal Rules of Evidence nor the Military Rules of Evidence resolve all evidentiary matters; *see* Rule 101(b). When specific authority to resolve an evidentiary issue is absent, Rule 402's clear result is to make relevant evidence admissible.

Rule 403 Exclusion of relevant evidence on grounds of prejudice, confusion or waste of time

Rule 403 is taken without change from the Federal Rule of Evidence. The Rule incorporates the concept often known as "legal relevance", *see* the Analysis to Rule 401, and provides that evidence may be excluded for the reasons stated notwithstanding its character as relevant evidence. The Rule vests the military judge with wide discretion in determining the admissibility of evidence that comes within the Rule.

If a party views specific evidence as being highly prejudicial, it may be possible to stipulate to the evidence and thus avoid its presentation to the court members. *United States v. Grassi*, 602 F.2d 1192 (5th Cir. 1979), a prosecution for interstate transportation of obscene materials, illustrates this point. The defense offered to stipulate that certain films were obscene in order to prevent the jury from viewing the films, but the prosecution declined to join in the stipulation. The trial judge sustained the prosecution's rejection of the stipulation and the Fifth Circuit upheld the judge's decision. In its opinion, however, the Court of Appeals adopted a case by case balancing approach recognizing both the importance of allowing probative evidence to be presented and the use of stipulations as a tool to implement the policies inherent in Rule 403. Insofar as the latter is concerned, the court expressly recognized the power of a Federal district judge to compel the prosecution to accept a defense tendered stipulation.

Rule 404 Character evidence not admissible to prove conduct; exceptions; other crimes

(a) *Character evidence generally.* Rule 404(a) replaces 1969 Manual Para. 138 *f* and is taken without substantial change from the Federal Rule. Rule 404(a) provides, subject to three exceptions, that character evidence is not admissible to show that a person acted in conformity therewith.

Rule 404(a)(1) allows only evidence of a pertinent trait of character of the accused to be offered in evidence by the defense. This is a significant change from Para. 138 *f* of the 1969 Manual which also allows evidence of "general good character" of the accused to be received in order to demonstrate that the accused is less likely to have committed a criminal act. Under the new rule, evidence of general good character is inadmissible because only evidence of a specific trait is acceptable. It is the intention of the Committee, however, to allow the defense to introduce evidence of good military character when that specific trait is pertinent. Evidence of good military character would be admissible, for example, in a prosecution for disobedience of orders. The prosecution may present evidence of a character trait only in rebuttal to receipt in evidence of defense character evidence. This is consistent with prior military law.

Rule 404(a)(2) is taken from the Federal Rule with minor

changes. The Federal Rule allows the prosecution to present evidence of the character trait of peacefulness of the victim "in a homicide case to rebut evidence that the victim was the first aggressor." Thus, the Federal Rule allows prosecutorial use of character evidence in a homicide case in which self-defense has been raised. The limitation to homicide cases appeared to be inappropriate and impracticable in the military environment. All too often, assaults involving claims of self-defense take place in the densely populated living quarters common to military life. Whether aboard ship or within barracks, it is considered essential to allow evidence of the character trait of peacefulness of the victim. Otherwise, a substantial risk would exist of allowing unlawful assaults to go undeterred. The Federal Rule's use of the expression "first aggressor" was modified to read "an aggressor," as substantive military law recognizes that even an individual who is properly exercising the right of self-defense may overstep and become an aggressor. The remainder of Rule 404(a)(2) allows the defense to offer evidence of a pertinent trait of character of the victim of a crime and restricts the prosecution to rebuttal of that trait.

Rule 404(a)(3) allows character evidence to be used to impeach or support the credibility of a witness pursuant to Rules 607–609.

2004 Amendment: Subdivision (a) was modified based on the amendment to Fed. R. Evid. 404(a), effective 1 December 2000, and is virtually identical to its Federal Rule counterpart. It is intended to provide a more balanced presentation of character evidence when an accused attacks the victim's character. The accused opens the door to an attack on the same trait of his own character when he attacks an alleged victim's character, giving the members an opportunity to consider relevant evidence about the accused's propensity to act in a certain manner. The words "if relevant" are added to subdivision (a)(1) to clarify that evidence of an accused's character under this rule must meet the requirements of Mil. R. Evid. 401 and Mil. R. Evid. 403. The drafters believe this addition addresses the unique use of character evidence in courts-martial. The amendment does not permit proof of the accused's character when the accused attacks the alleged victim's character as a witness under Rule 608 or 609, nor does it affect the standards for proof of character by evidence of other sexual behavior or sexual offenses under Rules 412-415.

(b) *Other crimes, wrongs, or acts.* Rule 404(b) is taken without change from the Federal Rule, and is substantially similar to the 1969 Manual rule found in Para. 138 *g*. While providing that evidence of other crimes, wrongs, or acts is not admissible to prove a predisposition to commit a crime, the Rule expressly permits use of such evidence on the merits when relevant to another specific purpose. Rule 404(b) provides examples rather than a list of justifications for admission of evidence of other misconduct. Other justifications, such as the tendency of such evidence to show the accused's consciousness of guilt of the offense charged, expressly permitted in Manual Para. 138 *g*(4), remain effective. Such a purpose would, for example, be an acceptable one. Rule 404(b), like Manual Para. 138 *g*, expressly allows use of evidence of misconduct not amounting to conviction. Like Para. 138 *g*, the Rule does not, however, deal with use of evidence of other misconduct for purposes of impeachment. *See* Rules 608-609. Evidence offered under Rule 404(b) is subject to Rule 403.

1994 Amendment. The amendment to Mil. R. Evid. 404(b) was based on the 1991 amendment to Fed. R. Evid. 404(b). The previous version of Mil. R. Evid. 404(b) was based on the now superseded version of the Federal Rule. This amendment adds the requirement that the prosecution, upon request by the accused, provide reasonable notice in advance of trial, or during trial if the military judge excuses pretrial notice on good cause shown, of the general nature of any such evidence it intends to introduce at trial. Minor technical changes were made to the language of the Federal Rule so that it conforms to military practice.

Rule 405 Methods of proving character

(a) *Reputation or opinion.* Rule 405(a) is taken without change from the Federal Rule. The first portion of the Rule is identical in effect with the prior military rule found in Para. 138 *f*(1) of the 1969 Manual. An individual testifying under the Rule must have an adequate relationship with the community (*see* Rule 405(c)), in the case of reputation, or with the given individual in the case of opinion, in order to testify. The remainder of Rule 405(a) expressly permits inquiry or cross-examination "into relevant specific instances of conduct." This is at variance with prior military practice under which such an inquiry was prohibited. *See*, Para. 138 *f*(2), MCM, 1969 (Rev.) (character of the accused). Reputation evidence is exempted from the hearsay rule, Rule 803(21).

(b) *Specific instances of conduct.* Rule 405(b) is taken without significant change from the Federal Rule. Reference to "charge, claim, or defense" has been replaced with "offense or defense" in order to adapt the rule to military procedure and terminology.

(c) *Affidavits.* Rule 405(c) is not found within the Federal Rules and is taken verbatim from material found in Para. 146*b* of the 1969 Manual. Use of affidavits or other written statements is required due to the world wide disposition of the armed forces which makes it difficult if not impossible to obtain witnesses—particularly when the sole testimony of a witness is to be a brief statement relating to the character of the accused. This is particularly important for offenses committed abroad or in a combat zone, in which case the only witnesses likely to be necessary from the United States are those likely to be character witnesses. The Rule exempts statements used under it from the hearsay rule insofar as the mere use of an affidavit or other written statement is subject to that rule.

(d) *Definitions.* Rule 405(d) is not found within the Federal Rules of Evidence and has been included because of the unique nature of the armed forces. The definition of "reputation" is taken generally from 1969 Manual Para. 138 *f*(1) and the definition of "community" is an expansion of that now found in the same paragraph. The definition of "community" has been broadened to add "regardless of size" to indicate that a party may proffer evidence of reputation within any specific military organization, whether a squad, company, division, ship, fleet, group, or wing, branch, or staff corps, for example. Rule 405(d) makes it clear that evidence may be offered of an individual's reputation in either the civilian or military community or both.

Rule 406 Habit; routine practice

Rule 406 is taken without change from the Federal Rule. It is similar in effect to Para. 138*h* of the 1969 Manual. It is the intent of the Committee to include within Rule 406's use of the word, "organization," military organizations regardless of size. *See* Rule 405 and the Analysis to that Rule.

Rule 407 Subsequent remedial measures

Rule 407 is taken from the Federal Rules without change, and has no express equivalent in the 1969 Manual.

Rule 408 Compromise and offer to compromise

Rule 408 is taken from the Federal Rules without change, and has no express equivalent in the 1969 Manual.

Rule 409 Payment of medical and similar expenses

Rule 409 is taken from the Federal Rules without change. It has no present military equivalent and is intended to be applicable to courts-martial to the same extent that is applicable to civilian criminal cases. Unlike Rules 407 and 408 which although primarily applicable to civil cases are clearly applicable to criminal cases, it is arguable that Rule 409 may not apply to criminal cases as it deals only with questions of "liability"—normally only a civil matter. The Rule has been included in the Military Rules to ensure its availability should it, in fact, apply to criminal cases.

Rule 410 Inadmissibility of pleas, discussions, and related statements

Rule 410 as modified effective 1 August 1981 is generally taken from the Federal Rule as modified on 1 December 1980. It extends to plea bargaining as well as to statements made during a providency inquiry, civilian or military. *E.g., United States v. Care,* 18 C.M.A. 535 (1969). Subsection (b) was added to the Rule in recognition of the unique possibility of administrative disposition, usually separation, in lieu of court-martial. Denominated differently within the various armed forces, this administrative procedure often requires a confession as a prerequisite. As modified, Rule 410 protects an individual against later use of a statement submitted in furtherance of such a request for administrative disposition. The definition of "on the record" was required because no "record" in the judicial sense exists insofar as request for administrative disposition is concerned. It is the belief of the Committee that a copy of the written statement of the accused in such a case is, however, the functional equivalent of such a record.

Although the expression "false statement" was retained in the Rule, it is the Committee's intent that it be construed to include all related or similar military offenses.

Rule 411 Liability Insurance

Rule 411 is taken from the Federal Rule without change. Although it would appear to have potential impact upon some criminal cases, *e.g.,* some negligent homicide cases, its actual application to criminal cases is uncertain. It is the Committee's intent that Rule 411 be applicable to courts-martial only to the extent that it is applicable to criminal cases.

Rule 412 Nonconsensual sexual offenses; relevance of victim's past behavior

Rule 412 is taken from the Federal Rules. Although substantially similar in substantive scope to Federal Rule of Evidence 412, the application of the Rule has been somewhat broadened and the procedural aspects of the Federal Rule have been modified to adapt them to military practice.

Rule 412 is intended to shield victims of sexual assaults from the often embarrassing and degrading cross-examination and evidence presentations common to prosecutions of such offenses. In so doing, it recognizes that the prior rule, which it replaces, often yields evidence of at best minimal probative value with great potential for distraction and incidentally discourages both the reporting and prosecution of many sexual assaults. In replacing the unusually extensive rule found in Para. 153 *b* (2)(b), MCM, 1969 (Rev.), which permits evidence of the victim's "unchaste" character regardless of whether he or she has testified, the Rule will significantly change prior military practice and will restrict defense evidence. The Rule recognizes, however, in Rule 412(b)(1), the fundamental right of the defense under the Fifth Amendment of the Constitution of the United States to present relevant defense evidence by admitting evidence that is "constitutionally required to be admitted." Further, it is the Committee's intent that the Rule not be interpreted as a rule of absolute privilege. Evidence that is constitutionally required to be admitted on behalf of the defense remains admissible notwithstanding the absence of express authorization in Rule 412(a). It is unclear whether reputation or opinion evidence in this area will rise to a level of constitutional magnitude, and great care should be taken with respect to such evidence.

Rule 412 applies to a "nonconsensual sexual offense" rather than only to "rape or assault with intent to commit rape" as prescribed by the Federal Rule. The definition of "nonconsensual sexual offense" is set forth in Rule 412(e) and "includes rape, forcible sodomy, assault with intent to commit rape or forcible sodomy, indecent assault, and attempts to commit such offenses." This modification to the Federal Rule resulted from a desire to apply the social policies behind the Federal Rule to the unique military environment. Military life requires that large numbers of young men and women live and work together in close quarters which are often highly isolated. The deterrence of sexual offenses in such circumstances is critical to military efficiency. There is thus no justification for limiting the scope of the Rule, intended to protect human dignity and to ultimately encourage the reporting and prosecution of sexual offenses, only to rape and/or assault with intent to commit rape.

Rule 412(a) generally prohibits reputation or opinion evidence of an alleged victim of a nonconsensual sexual offense.

Rule 412(b)(1) recognizes that evidence of a victim's past sexual behavior may be constitutionally required to be admitted. Although there are a number of circumstances in which this language may be applicable, *see,* S. Saltzburg & K. Redden, FEDERAL RULES OF EVIDENCE MANUAL 92–93 (2d ed. Supp. 1979) (giving example of potential constitutional problems offered by the American Civil Liberties Union during the House hearings on Rule 412), one may be of particular interest. If an individual has contracted for the sexual services of a prostitute and subsequent to the performance of the act the prostitute demands increased payment on pain of claiming rape, for example, the past history of that person will likely be constitutionally required to be admitted in a subsequent prosecution in which the defense claims consent to the extent that such history is relevant and otherwise admissible to corroborate the defense position. Absent such peculiar circumstances, however, the past sexual behavior of the alleged victim, not within the scope of Rule 412(b)(2), is unlikely to be admissible regardless of the past sexual history. The mere fact that an individual is a prostitute is not normally admissible under Rule 412.

Evidence of past false complaints of sexual offenses by an alleged victim of a sexual offense is not within the scope of this rule and is not objectionable when otherwise admissible.

Rule 412(c) provides the procedural mechanism by which evidence of past sexual behavior of a victim may be offered. The Rule has been substantially modified from the Federal Rule in order to adapt it to military practice. The requirement that notice be given not later than fifteen days before trial has been deleted as being impracticable in view of the necessity for speedy disposition of military cases. For similar reasons, the requirement for a written motion has been omitted in favor of an offer of proof, which could, of course, be made in writing, at the discretion of the military judge. Reference to hearings in chambers has been deleted as inapplicable; a hearing under Article 39(a), which may be without spectators, has been substituted. The propriety of holding a hearing without spectators is dependent upon its constitutionality which is in turn dependent upon the facts of any specific case.

Although Rule 412 is not *per se* applicable to such pretrial procedures as Article 32 and Court of Inquiry hearings, it may be applicable via Rule 303 and Article 31(c). *See* the Analysis to Rule 303.

It should be noted as a matter related to Rule 412 that the 1969 Manual's prohibition in Para. 153 *a* of convictions for sexual offenses that rest on the uncorroborated testimony of the alleged victim has been deleted. Similarly, an express hearsay exception for fresh complaint has been deleted as being unnecessary. Consequently, evidence of fresh complaint will be admissible under the Military Rule only to the extent that it is either nonhearsay, *see*, Rule 801(d)(1)(B), or fits within an exception to the hearsay rule. *See*, subdivisions (1), (2), (3), (4), and (24) of Rule 803.

1993 Amendment. R.C.M. 405(i) and Mil. R. Evid. 1101(d) were amended to make the provisions of Rule 412 applicable at pretrial investigations. Congress intended to protect the victims of nonconsensual sex crimes at preliminary hearings as well as at trial when it passed Fed. R. Evid. 412. *See* Criminal Justice Subcommittee of the House Judiciary \ Committee Report, 94th Cong., 2d Session, July 1976.

1998 Amendment. The revisions to Rule 412 reflect changes made to Federal Rule of Evidence 412 by section 40141 of the Violent Crime Control and Law Enforcement Act of 1994, Pub L. No. 103-322, 108 Stat. 1796, 1918-19 (1994). The purpose of the amendments is to safeguard the alleged victim against the invasion of privacy and potential embarrassment that is associated with public disclosure of intimate sexual details and the infusion of sexual innuendo into the factfinding process.

The terminology "alleged victim" is used because there will frequently be a factual dispute as to whether the sexual misconduct occurred. Rule 412 does not, however, apply unless the person against whom the evidence is offered can reasonably be characterized as a "victim of alleged sexual misconduct."

The term "sexual predisposition" is added to Rule 412 to conform military practice to changes made to the Federal Rule. The purpose of this change is to exclude all other evidence relating to an alleged victim of sexual misconduct that is offered to prove a sexual predisposition. It is designed to exclude evidence that does not directly refer to sexual activities or thoughts but that the accused believes may have a sexual connotation for the factfinder. Admission of such evidence would contravene Rule 412's objectives of shielding the alleged victim from potential embarrassment and safeguarding the victim against stereotypical thinking. Consequently, unless an exception under (b)(1) is satisfied, evidence such as that relating to the alleged victim's mode of dress, speech, or lifestyle is inadmissible.

In drafting Rule 412, references to civil proceedings were deleted, as these are irrelevant to courts-martial practice. Otherwise, changes in procedure made to the Federal Rule were incorporated, but tailored to military practice. The Military Rule adopts a 5-day notice period, instead of the 14-day period specified in the Federal Rule. Additionally, the military judge, for good cause shown, may require a different time for such notice or permit notice during trial. The 5-day period preserves the intent of the Federal Rule that an alleged victim receive timely notice of any attempt to offer evidence protected by Rule 412, however, given the relatively short time period between referral and trial, the 5-day period is deemed more compatible with courts-martial practice.

Similarly, a closed hearing was substituted for the in camera hearing required by the Federal Rule. Given the nature of the in camera procedure used in Military Rule of Evidence 505(i)(4), and that an in camera hearing in the district courts more closely resembles a closed hearing conducted pursuant to Article 39(a), the latter was adopted as better suited to trial by courts-martial. Any alleged victim is afforded a reasonable opportunity to attend and be heard at the closed Article 39(a) hearing. The closed hearing, combined with the new requirement to seal the motion, related papers, and the record of the hearing, fully protects an alleged victim against invasion of privacy and potential embarrassment.

2007 Amendment: This amendment is intended to aid practitioners in applying the balancing test of MRE 412. Specifically, the amendment clarifies: (1) that under MRE 412, the evidence must be relevant for one of the purposes highlighted in subdivision (b); (2) that in conducting the balancing test, the inquiry is whether the probative value of the evidence outweighs the danger of unfair prejudice to the victim's privacy; and (3) that even if the evidence is admissible under MRE 412, it may still be excluded under MRE 403. The proposed changes highlight current practice. *See U.S. v. Banker*, 60 M.J. 216, 223 (2004) (Citing "It would be illogical if the judge were to evaluate evidence 'offered by the accused' for unfair prejudice to the accused. Rather, in the context of this rape shield statute, the prejudice in question is, in part, that to the privacy interests of the alleged victim. *Sanchez*, 44 M.J. at 178 ("[I]n determining admissibility there must be a weighing of the probative value of the evidence against the interest of shielding the victim's privacy.")."

Moreover, the amendment clarifies that MRE 412 applies in all cases involving a sexual offense wherein the person against whom the evidence is offered can reasonably be characterized as a "victim of the alleged sexual offense." Thus, the rule applies to: "consensual sexual offense", "nonconsensual sexual offenses"; sexual offenses specifically proscribed under the U.C.M.J., e.g., rape, aggravated sexual assault, etc.; those federal sexual offenses DoD is able to prosecute under clause 3 of Article 134, U.C.M.J., e.g., 18 U.S.C. § 2252A (possession of child pornography); and state sexual offenses DoD is able to assimilate under the Federal Assimilative Crimes Act (18 U.S.C. § 13).

Rule 413 Evidence of similar crimes in sexual assault cases

1998 Amendment. This amendment is intended to provide for more liberal admissibility of character evidence in criminal cases of sexual assault where the accused has committed a prior act of sexual assault.

Rule 413 is nearly identical to its Federal Rule counterpart. A number of changes were made, however, to tailor the Rule to military practice. First, all references to Federal Rule 415 were deleted, as it applies only to civil proceedings. Second, military justice terminology was substituted where appropriate (e.g. accused for defendant, court-martial for case). Third, the 5-day notice requirement in Rule 413(b) replaced a 15-day notice requirement in the Federal Rule. A 5-day requirement is better suited to military discovery practice. This 5-day notice requirement, however, is not intended to restrict a military judge's authority to grant a continuance under R.C.M. 906(b)(1). Fourth, Rule 413(d) has been modified to include violations of the Uniform Code of Military Justice. Also, the phrase "without consent" was added to Rule 413(d)(1) to specifically exclude the introduction of evidence concerning adultery or consensual sodomy. Last, all incorporation by way of reference was removed by adding subsections (e), (f), and (g). The definitions in those subsections were taken from title 18, United States Code §§ 2246(2), 2246(3), and 513(c)(5), respectively.

Although the Rule states that the evidence "is admissible," the drafters intend that the courts apply Rule 403 balancing to such evidence. Apparently, this also was the intent of Congress. The legislative history reveals that "the general standards of the rules of evidence will continue to apply, including the restrictions on hearsay evidence and the court's authority under evidence rule 403 to exclude evidence whose probative value is substantially outweighed by its prejudicial effect." 140 Cong. Rec. S12,990 (daily ed. Sept. 20, 1994) (Floor Statement of the Principal Senate Sponsor, Senator Bob Dole, Concerning the Prior Crimes Evidence Rules for Sexual Assault and Child Molestation Cases).

When "weighing the probative value of such evidence, the court may, as part of its rule 403 determination, consider proximity in time to the charged or predicate misconduct; similarity to the charged or predicate misconduct; frequency of the other acts; surrounding circumstances; relevant intervening events; and other relevant similarities or differences." (Report of the Judicial Conference of the United States on the Admission of Character Evidence in Certain Sexual Misconduct Cases).

2002 Amendment: Federal Rule of Evidence 415 which created a similar character evidence rule for civil cases, became applicable to the Military Rules of Evidence on January 6, 1996, pursuant to Rule 1102. Federal Rule 415, however, is no longer applicable to the Military Rules of Evidence, as stated in Section 1 of Executive Order, 2002 Amendments to the Manual for Court-Martial, United States, (2000) Rule 415 was deleted because it applies only to federal civil proceedings.

Rule 414 Evidence of similar crimes in child molestation cases

1998 Amendment. This amendment is intended to provide for more liberal admissibility of character evidence in criminal cases of child molestation where the accused has committed a prior act of sexual assault or child molestation.

Rule 414 is nearly identical to its Federal Rule counterpart. A number of changes were made, however, to tailor the Rule to military practice. First, all references to Federal Rule 415 were deleted, as it applies only to civil proceedings. Second, military justice terminology was substituted where appropriate (e.g. accused for defendant, court-martial for case). Third, the 5-day notice requirement in Rule 414(b) replaced a 15-day notice requirement in the Federal Rule. A 5-day requirement is better suited to military discovery practice. This 5-day notice requirement, however, is not intended to restrict a military judge's authority to grant a continuance under R.C.M. 906(b)(1). Fourth, Rule 414(d) has been modified to include violations of the Uniform Code of Military Justice. Last, all incorporation by way of reference was removed by adding subsections (e), (f), (g), and (h). The definitions in those subsections were taken from title 18, United States Code §§ 2246(2), 2246(3), 2256(2), and 513(c)(5), respectively.

Although the Rule states that the evidence "is admissible," the drafters intend that the courts apply Rule 403 balancing to such evidence. Apparently, this was also the intent of Congress. The legislative history reveals that "the general standards of the rules of evidence will continue to apply, including the restrictions on hearsay evidence and the court's authority under evidence rule 403 to exclude evidence whose probative value is substantially outweighed by its prejudicial effect." 140 Cong. Rec. S12,990 (daily ed. Sept. 20, 1994) (Floor Statement of the Principal Senate Sponsor, Senator Bob Dole, Concerning the Prior Crimes Evidence Rules for Sexual Assault and Child Molestation Cases).

When "weighing the probative value of such evidence, the court may, as part of its rule 403 determination, consider proximity in time to the charged or predicate misconduct; similarity to the charged or predicate misconduct; frequency of the other acts; surrounding circumstances; relevant intervening events; and other relevant similarities or differences." (Report of the Judicial Conference of the United States on the Admission of Character Evidence in Certain Sexual Misconduct Cases).

2002 Amendment: Federal Rule of Evidence 415 which created a similar character evidence rule for civil cases, became applicable to the Military Rules of Evidence on January 6, 1996, pursuant to Rule 1102. Federal Rule 415, however, is no longer applicable to the Military Rules of Evidence, as stated in Section 1 of Executive Order, 2002 Amendments to the Manual for Court-Martial, United States, (2000) Rule 415 was deleted because it applies only to federal civil proceedings.

SECTION V

PRIVILEGES

Rule 501 General rule

Section V contains all of the privileges applicable to military criminal law except for those privileges which are found within Rules 301, Privilege Concerning Compulsory Self-Incrimination;

Rule 302, Privilege Concerning Mental Examination of an Accused; and Rule 303, Degrading Questions. Privilege rules, unlike other Military Rules of Evidence, apply in "investigative hearings pursuant to Article 32; proceedings for vacation of suspension of sentence under Article 72; proceedings for search authorization; proceedings involving pretrial restraint; and in other proceedings authorized under the Uniform Code of Military Justice of this Manual and not listed in rule 1101(a)." *See* Rule 1101(c); *see also* Rule 1101(b).

In contrast to the general acceptance of the proposed Federal Rules of Evidence by Congress, Congress did not accept the proposed privilege rules because a consensus as to the desirability of a number of specific privileges could not be achieved. *See* generally, S. Saltzburg & K. Redden, FEDERAL RULES OF EVIDENCE MANUAL 200–201 (2d ed. 1977). In an effort to expedite the Federal Rules generally, Congress adopted a general rule, Rule 501, which basically provides for the continuation of common law in the privilege area. The Committee deemed the approach taken by Congress in the Federal Rules impracticable within the armed forces. Unlike the Article III court system, which is conducted almost entirely by attorneys functioning in conjunction with permanent courts in fixed locations, the military criminal legal system is characterized by its dependence upon large numbers of laymen, temporary courts, and inherent geolineartal and personnel instability due to the worldwide deployment of military personnel. Consequently, military law requires far more stability than civilian law. This is particularly true because of the significant number of non-lawyers involved in the military criminal legal system. Commanders, convening authorities, non-lawyer investigating officers, summary court-martial officers, or law enforcement personnel need specific guidance as to what material is privileged and what is not.

Section V combines the flexible approach taken by Congress with respect to privileges with that provided in the 1969 Manual. Rules 502–509 set forth specific rules of privilege to provide the certainty and stability necessary for military justice. Rule 501, on the other hand, adopts those privileges recognized in common law pursuant to Federal Rules of Evidence 501 with some limitations. Specific privileges are generally taken from those proposed Federal Rules of Evidence which although not adopted by Congress were non-controversial, or from the 1969 Manual.

Rule 501 is the basic rule of privilege. In addition to recognizing privileges required by or provided for in the Constitution, an applicable Act of Congress, the Military Rules of Evidence, and the Manual for Courts-Martial, Rule 501(a) also recognizes privileges "generally recognized in the trial of criminal cases in the United States district courts pursuant to Rule 501 of the Federal Rules of Evidence insofar as the application of such principles in trials by court-martial is practicable and not contrary to or inconsistent with the Uniform Code of Military Justice, these rules, or this Manual." The latter language is taken from 1969 Manual Para. 137. As a result of Rule 501(a)(4), the common law of privileges as recognized in the Article III courts will be applicable to the armed forces except as otherwise provided by the limitation indicated above. Rule 501(d) prevents the application of a doctor-patient privilege. Such a privilege was considered to be totally incompatible with the clear interest of the armed forces in ensuring the health and fitness for duty of personnel. *See* 1969 Manual Para. 151 *c*

It should be noted that the law of the forum determines the application of privilege. Consequently, even if a service member should consult with a doctor in a jurisdiction with a doctor-patient privilege for example, such a privilege is inapplicable should the doctor be called as a witness before the court-martial.

Subdivision (b) is a non-exhaustive list of actions which constitute an invocation of a privilege. The subdivision is derived from Federal Rule of Evidence 501 as originally proposed by the Supreme Court, and the four specific actions listed are also found in the Uniform Rules of Evidence. The list is intentionally non-exclusive as a privilege might be claimed in a fashion distinct from those listed.

Subdivision (c) is derived from Federal Rule of Evidence 501 and makes it clear that an appropriate representative of a political jurisdiction or other organizational entity may claim an applicable privilege. The definition is intentionally non-exhaustive.

1999 Amendment: The privileges expressed in Rule 513 and Rule 302 and the conforming Manual change in R.C.M. 706, are not physician-patient privileges and are not affected by Rule 501(d).

Rule 502 Lawyer-client privilege

(a) *General rule of privilege.* Rule 502(a) continues the substance of the attorney-client privilege found in Para. 151 *b*(2) of the 1969 Manual. The Rule does, however, provide additional detail. Subdivision (a) is taken verbatim from subdivision (a) of Federal Rule of Evidence 503 as proposed by the Supreme Court. The privilege is only applicable when there are "confidential communications made for the purpose of facilitating the rendition of professional legal services to the client." A mere discussion with an attorney does not invoke the privilege when the discussion is not made for the purpose of obtaining professional legal services.

(b) *Definitions—*

(1) *Client.* Rule 502(b)(1) defines a "client" as an individual or entity who receives professional legal services from a lawyer or consults a lawyer with a view to obtaining such services. The definition is taken from proposed Federal Rule 503(a)(1) as Para. 151*b*(2) of the 1969 Manual lacked any general definition of a client.

(2) *Lawyer.* Rule 502(b)(2) defines a "lawyer." The first portion of the paragraph is taken from proposed Federal Rule of Evidence 503(a)(2) and explicitly includes any person "reasonably believed by the client to be authorized" to practice law. The second clause is taken from 1969 Manual Para. 151 *b*(2) and recognizes that a "lawyer" includes "a member of the armed forces detailed, assigned, or otherwise provided to represent a person in a court-martial case or in any military investigation or proceeding" regardless of whether that person is in fact a lawyer. *See* Article 27. Thus an accused is fully protected by the privilege even if defense counsel is not an attorney.

The second sentence of the subdivision recognizes the fact, particularly true during times of mobilization, that attorneys may serve in the armed forces in a nonlegal capacity. In such a case, the individual is not treated as an attorney under the Rule unless the individual fits within one of the three specific categories recognized by the subdivision. Subdivision (b)(2)(B) recognizes that a servicemember who knows that an individual is a lawyer in civilian life may not know that the lawyer is not functioning as such in the armed forces and may seek professional legal assistance. In such a case the privilege will be applicable so long as the individual was "reasonably believed by the client to be authorized to render professional legal services to members of the armed forces."

(3) *Representative of a lawyer.* Rule 502(b)(3) is taken from proposed Federal Rule of Evidence 503(a)(3) but has been modified to recognize that personnel are "assigned" within the armed forces as well as employed. Depending upon the particular situation, a paraprofessional or secretary may be a "representative of a lawyer." *See* Para. 151 *b*(2) of the 1969 Manual.

(4) *Confidential communication.* Rule 502(b)(4) defines a "confidential" communication in terms of the intention of the party making the communication. The Rule is similar to the substance of 1969 Manual Para. 151 *b*(2) which omitted certain communications from privileged status. The new Rule is somewhat broader than the 1969 Manual's provision in that it protects information which is obtained by a third party through accident or design when the person claiming the privilege was not aware that a third party had access to the communication. Compare Rule Para. 151 *a* of the 1969 Manual. The broader rule has been adopted for the reasons set forth in the Advisory Committee's notes on proposed Federal Rule 504(a)(4). The provision permitting disclosure to persons in furtherance of legal services or reasonably necessary for the transmission of the communication is similar to the provision in the 1969 Manual for communications through agents.

Although Para. 151 *c* of the 1969 Manual precluded a claim of the privilege when there is transmission through wire or radio communications, the new Rules protect statements made via telephone, or, "if use of such means of communication is necessary and in furtherance of the communication," by other "electronic means of communication." Rule 511(b).

(c) *Who may claim the privilege.* Rule 502(c) is taken from proposed Federal Rule 503(b) and expresses who may claim the lawyer-client privilege. The Rule is similar to but slightly broader than Para. 151 *b*(2) of the 1969 Manual. The last sentence of the subdivision states that "the authority of the lawyer to claim the privilege is presumed in the absence of evidence to the contrary."

The lawyer may claim the privilege on behalf of the client unless authority to do so has been withheld from the lawyer or evidence otherwise exists to show that the lawyer lacks the authority to claim the privilege.

(d) *Exceptions.* Rule 502(d) sets forth the circumstances in which the lawyer-client privilege will not apply notwithstanding the general application of the privilege.

Subdivision (d)(1) excludes statements contemplating the future commission of crime or fraud and combines the substance of 1969 Manual Para. 151 *b*(2) with proposed Federal Rule of Evidence 503(d). Under the exception a lawyer may disclose information given by a client when it was part of a "communication (which) clearly contemplated the future commission of a crime of fraud," and a lawyer may also disclose information when it can be objectively said that the lawyer's services "were sought or obtained to commit or plan to commit what the client knew or reasonably should have known to be a crime or fraud." The latter portion of the exception is likely to be applicable only after the commission of the offense while the former is applicable when the communication is made.

Subdivisions (d)(2) through (d)(5) provide exceptions with respect to claims through the same deceased client, breach of duty by lawyer of client, documents attested by lawyers, and communications to an attorney in a matter of common interest among joint clients. There were no parallel provisions in the 1969 Manual for these rules which are taken from proposed Federal Rule 503(d). The provisions are included in the event that the circumstances described therein arise in the military practice.

Rule 503 Communications to clergy

(a) *General rule of privilege.* Rule 503(a) states the basic rule of privilege for communications to clergy and is taken from proposed Federal Rule of Evidence 506(b) and 1969 Manual Para. 151*b*(2). Like the 1969 Manual, the Rule protects communications to a clergyman's assistant in specific recognition of the nature of the military chaplaincy, and deals only with communications "made either as a formal act of religion or as a matter of conscience."

(b) *Definitions.*

(1) *Clergyman.* Rule 503(b)(1) is taken from proposed Federal Rule of Evidence 506(a)(1) but has been modified to include specific reference to a chaplain. The Rule does not define "a religious organization" and leaves resolution of that question to precedent and the circumstances of the case. "Clergyman" includes individuals of either sex.

(2) *Confidential.* Rule 503(b)(2) is taken generally from proposed Federal Rule of Evidence 506(a)(2) but has been expanded to include communications to a clergyman's assistant and to explicitly protect disclosure of a privileged communication when "disclosure is in furtherance of the purpose of the communication or to those reasonably necessary for the transmission of the communication." The Rule is thus consistent with the definition of "confidential" used in the lawyer-client privilege, Rule 502(b)(4), and recognizes that military life often requires transmission of communications through third parties. The proposed Federal Rule's limitation of the privilege to communications made "privately" was deleted in favor of the language used in the actual Military Rule for the reasons indicated. The Rule is somewhat more protective than the 1969 Manual because of its application to statements which although intended to be confidential are overheard by others. *See* Rule 502(b)(4) and 510(a) and the Analysis thereto.

2007 Amendment: The previous subsection (2) of MRE 503(b) was renumbered subsection (3) and the new subsection (2) was inserted to define the term "clergyman's assistant".

(c) *Who may claim the privilege.* Rule 503(c) is derived from proposed Federal Rule of Evidence 506(c) and includes the substance of 1969 Manual Para. 151 *b*(2) which provided that the privilege may be claimed by the "penitent." The Rule supplies additional guidance as to who may actually claim the privilege and is consistent with the other Military Rules of Evidence relating to privileges. *See* Rule 502(c); 504(b)(3); 505(c); 506(c).

Rule 504 Husband-wife privilege

(a) *Spousal incapacity.* Rule 504(a) is taken generally from *Trammel v. United States*, 445 U.S. 40 (1980) and significantly changes military law in this area. Under prior law, *see* 1969 Manual Para. 148 *e*, each spouse had a privilege to prevent the use of the other spouse as an adverse witness. Under the new rule, the *witness'* spouse is the holder of the privilege and may choose to testify or not to testify as the witness' spouse sees fit. *But see* Rule 504(c) (exceptions to the privilege). Implicit in the rule is the presumption that when a spouse chooses to testify against the other spouse the marriage no longer needs the protection of the privilege. Rule 504(a) must be distinguished from Rule 504(b), *Confidential communication made during marriage,* which deals with communications rather than the ability to testify generally at trial.

Although the witness' spouse ordinarily has a privilege to refuse to testify against the accused spouse, under certain circumstances no privilege may exists, and the spouse may be compelled to testify. *See* Rule 504(c).

(b) *Confidential communication made during marriage.* Rule 504(b) deals with communications made during a marriage and is distinct from a spouse's privilege to refuse to testify pursuant to Rule 504(a). *See* 1969 Manual Para. 151 *b*(2).

(1) *General rule of privilege.* Rule 504(b)(1) sets forth the general rule of privilege for confidential spousal communications and provides that a spouse may prevent disclosure of any confidential spousal communication made during marriage even though the parties are no longer married at the time that disclosure is desired. The accused may always require that the confidential spousal communication be disclosed. Rule 504(b)(3).

No privilege exists under subdivision (b) if the communication was made when the spouses were legally separated.

(2) *Definition.* Rule 504(b)(2) defines "confidential" in a fashion similar to the definition utilized in Rules 502(b)(4) and 503(b)(2). The word "privately" has been added to emphasize that the presence of third parties is not consistent with the spousal privilege, and the reference to third parties found in Rules 502 and 503 has been omitted for the same reason. Rule 504(b)(2) extends the definition of "confidential" to statements disclosed to third parties who are "reasonably necessary for transmission of the communication." This recognizes that circumstances may arise, especially in military life, where spouses may be separated by great distances or by operational activities, in which transmission of a communication via third parties may be reasonably necessary.

(3) *Who may claim the privilege.* Rule 504(b)(3) is consistent with 1969 Manual Para. 151 *b*(2) and gives the privilege to the spouse who made the communication. The accused may, however, disclose the communication even though the communication was made to the accused.

(c) *Exceptions.*

(1) *Spouse incapacity only.* Rule 504(c)(1) provides exceptions to the spousal incapacity rule of Rule 504(a). The rule is taken from 1969 Manual Para. 148 *e* and declares that a spouse may not refuse to testify against the other spouse when the marriage has been terminated by divorce or annulment. Annulment has been added to the present military rule as being consistent with its purpose. Separation of spouses via legal separation or otherwise does not affect the privilege of a spouse to refuse to testify against the other spouse. For other circumstances in which a spouse may be compelled to testify against the other spouse, *see* Rule 504(c)(2).

Confidential communications are not affected by the termination of a marriage.

(2) *Spousal incapacity and confidential communications.* Rule 504(c)(2) prohibits application of the spousal privilege, whether in the form of spousal incapacity or in the form of a confidential communication, when the circumstances specified in paragraph (2) are applicable. Subparagraphs (A) and (C) deal with anti-marital acts, *e.g.,* acts which are against the spouse and thus the marriage. The Rule expressly provides that when such an act is involved a spouse may not refuse to testify. This provision is taken from proposed Federal Rule 505(c)(1) and reflects in part the Supreme Court's decision in *Wyatt v. United States*, 362 U.S. 525 (1960). *See also Trammel v. United States*, 445 U.S. 40 at n.7 (1980). The Rule thus recognizes society's overriding interest in prosecution of anti-marital offenses and the probability that a spouse may exercise sufficient control, psychological or otherwise, to be able to prevent the other spouse from testifying voluntarily. The Rule is similar to 1969 Manual Para. 148 *e* but has deleted the Manual's limitation of the exceptions to the privilege to matters occurring after marriage or otherwise unknown to the spouse as being inconsistent with the intent of the exceptions.

Rule 504(c)(2)(B) is derived from Para. 148 *e* and 151 *b*(2) of the 1969 Manual. The provision prevents application of the privileges as to privileged communications if the marriage was a sham at the time of the communication, and prohibits application of the spousal incapacity privilege if the marriage was begun as a sham and is a sham at the time the testimony of the witness is to be offered. Consequently, the Rule recognizes for purposes of subdivision (a) that a marriage that began as a sham may have ripened into a valid marriage at a later time. The intent of the provision is to prevent individuals from marrying witnesses in order to effectively silence them.

2007 Amendment: (d) *Definition*. Rule 504(d) modifies the rule and is intended to afford additional protection to children. Previously, the term "a child of either," referenced in Rule 504(c)(2)(A), did not include a "de facto" child or a child who is under the physical custody of one of the spouses but lacks a formal legal parent-child relationship with at least one of the spouses. *See U.S. v. McCollum*, 58 M.J. 323 (C.A.A.F. 2003). Prior to this amendment, an accused could not invoke the spousal privilege to prevent disclosure of communications regarding crimes committed against a child with whom he or his spouse had a formal, legal parent-child relationship; however, the accused could invoke the privilege to prevent disclosure of communications where there was not a formal, legal parent-child relationship. This distinction between legal and "de facto" children resulted in unwarranted discrimination among child victims and ran counter to the public policy of protecting children. Rule 504(d) recognizes the public policy of protecting children by addressing disparate treatment among child victims entrusted to another. The "marital communications privilege should not prevent 'a properly outraged spouse with knowledge from testifying against a perpetrator' of child abuse within the home regardless of whether the child is part of that family." *U.S. v. McCollum*, 58 M.J. 323, 342, fn.6 (C.A.A.F. 2003) (citing *U.S. v. Bahe*, 128 F.3d 1440, 1446 (10th Cir. 1997)).

Rule 505 Classified information

Rule 505 is based upon H.R. 4745, 96th Cong., 1st Sess. (1979), which was proposed by the Executive Branch as a response to what is known as the "graymail" problem in which the defendant in a criminal case seeks disclosure of sensitive national security information, the release of which may force the government to discontinue the prosecution. The Rule is also based upon the Supreme Court's discussion of executive privilege in *United States v. Reynolds*, 345 U.S. 1 (1953), and *United States v. Nixon*, 418 U.S. 683 (1974). The rule attempts to balance the interests of an accused who desires classified information for his or her defense and the interests of the government in protecting that information.

(a) *General rule of privilege.* Rule 505(a) is derived from*United States v. Reynolds* , *supra* and 1969 Manual Para. 151. Classified information is only privileged when its "disclosure would be detrimental to the national security."

1993 Amendment: The second sentence was added to clarify that this rule, like other rules of privilege, applies at all stages of all actions and is not relaxed during the sentencing hearing under M.R.E. 1101(c).

(b) *Definitions.*

(1) *Classified information.* Rule 505(b)(1) is derived from section 2 of H.R. 4745. The definition of "classified information" is a limited one and includes only that information protected "pursuant to an executive order, statute, or regulation," and that material which constitutes restricted data pursuant to 42 U.S.C. 2014(y) (1976).

(2) *National security.* Rule 505(b)(2) is derived from section 2 of H.R. 4745.

(c) *Who may claim the privilege.* Rule 505(c) is derived from Para. 151 of the 1969 Manual and is consistent with similar provisions in the other privilege rules. *See* Rule 501(c). The privilege may be claimed only "by the head of the executive or military department or government agency concerned" and then only upon "a finding that the information is properly classified and that disclosure would be detrimental to the national security." Although the authority of a witness or trial counsel to claim the privilege is presumed in the absence of evidence to the contrary, neither a witness nor a trial counsel may claim the privilege without prior direction to do so by the appropriate department or agency head. Consequently, expedited coordination with senior headquarters is advised in any situation in which Rule 505 appears to be applicable.

(d) *Action prior to referral of charges.* Rule 505(d) is taken from section 4(b)(1) of H.R. 4745. The provision has been modified to reflect the fact that pretrial discovery in the armed forces, prior to referral, is officially conducted through the convening authority. The convening authority should disclose the maximum amount of requested information as appears reasonable under the circumstances.

(e) *Pretrial session.* Rule 505(e) is derived from section 3 of H.R. 4745.

(f) *Action after referral of charges.* Rule 505(f) provides the basic procedure under which the government should respond to a determination by the military judge that classified information "apparently contains evidence that is relevant and material to an element of the offense or a legally cognizable defense and is otherwise admissible in evidence." *See generally* the Analysis to Rule 507(d).

It should be noted that the government may submit information to the military judge for *in camera* inspection pursuant to subdivision (i). If the defense requests classified information that it alleges is "relevant and material ...," and the government refuses to disclose the information to the military judge for inspection, the military judge may presume that the information is in fact "relevant and material. ..."

(g) *Disclosure of classified information to the accused.* Paragraphs (1) and (2) of Rule 505(g) are derived from section 4 of H.R. 4745. Paragraph (3) is taken from section 10 of H.R. 4745 but has been modified in view of the different application of the Jencks Act, 18 U.S.C. § 3500 (1976) in the armed forces. Paragraph (4) is taken from sections 4(b)(2) and 10 of H.R. 4745. The reference in H.R. 4745 to a recess has been deleted as being unnecessary in view of the military judge's inherent authority to call a recess.

1993 Amendment: Subsection (g)(1)(D) was amended to make clear that the military judge's authority to require security clearances extends to persons involved in the conduct of the trial as well as pretrial preparation for it. The amendment requires persons needing security clearances to submit to investigations necessary to obtain the clearance.

(h) *Notice of the accused's intention to disclose classified information.* Rule 505(h) is derived from section 5 of H.R. 4745. The intent of the provision is to prevent disclosure of classified information by the defense until the government has had an opportunity to determine what position to take concerning the possible disclosure of that information. Pursuant to Rule 505(h)(5), failure to comply with subdivision (h) may result in a prohibition on the use of the information involved.

1993 Amendment: Subsection (h)(3) was amended to require specificity in detailing the items of classified information expected to be introduced. The amendment is based on *United States v. Collins* , 720 F.2d. 1195 (11th Cir. 1983).

(i) *In camera proceedings for cases involving classified information.* Rule 505(i) is derived generally from section 5 of H.R. 4745. The "*in camera*" procedure utilized in subdivision (i) is generally new to military law. Neither the accused nor defense counsel may be excluded from the *in camera* proceeding. However, nothing within the Rule requires that the defense be provided with a copy of the classified material in question when the government submits such information to the military judge pursuant to Rule 505(i)(3) in an effort to obtain an *in camera* proceeding under this Rule. If such information has not been disclosed previously, the government may describe the information by generic category, rather than by identifying the information. Such description is subject to approval by the military judge, and if not sufficiently specific to enable the defense to proceed during the *in camera* session, the military judge may order the government to release the information for use during the proceeding or face the sanctions under subdivision (i)(4)(E).

1993 Amendment: Subsection (i)(3) was amended to clarify that the classified material and the government's affidavit are submitted only to the military judge. The word "only" was placed at the end of the sentence to make it clear that it refers to "military judge" rather than to "examination." The military judge is to examine the affidavit and the classified information without disclosing it before determining to hold an *in camera* proceeding as defined in subsection(i)(1).

The second sentence of subsection (i)(4)(B) was added to provide a standard for admission of classified information in sentencing proceedings.

(j) *Introduction of classified information.* Rule 505(j) is derived from section 8 of H.R. 4745 and *United States v. Grunden*, 2 M.J. 116 (C.M.A. 1977).

1993 Amendment: Subsection (j)(5) was amended to provide that the military judge's authority to exclude the public extends to the presentation of any evidence that discloses classified information, and not merely to the testimony of witnesses. *See generally, United States v. Hershey*, 20 M.J. 433 (C.M.A. 1985), *cert. denied,* 474 U.S. 1062 (1986) (specifies factors to be considered in the trial judge's determination to close the proceedings).

(k) *Security procedures to safeguard against compromise of classified information disclosed to courts-martial.* Rule 505(k) is derived from section 9 of H.R. 4745.

Rule 506 Government information other than classified information

(a) *General rule of privilege.* Rule 506(a) states the general rule of privilege for nonclassified government information. The Rule recognizes that in certain extraordinary cases the government should be able to prohibit release of government information which is detrimental to the public interest. The Rule is modeled on Rule 505 but is more limited in its scope in view of the greater limitations applicable to nonclassified information. *Compare United States v. Nixon*, 418 U.S. 683 (1974) with *United States v. Reynolds*, 345 U.S. 1 (1953). Rule 506 addresses those similar matters found in 1969 Manual Para. 151 *b*(1) and 151 *b*(3). Under Rule 506(a) information is privileged only if its disclosure would be "detrimental to the public interest." It is important to note that pursuant to Rule 506(c) the privilege may be claimed only "by the head of the executive or military department or government agency concerned" unless investigations of the Inspectors General are concerned.

Under Rule 506(a) there is no privilege if disclosure of the information concerned is required by an Act of Congress such as the Freedom of Information Act, 5 U.S.C. § 552 (1976). Disclosure of information will thus be broader under the Rule than under the 1969 Manual. *See United States v. Nixon, supra.*

(b) *Scope.* Rule 506(b) defines "Government information" in a nonexclusive fashion, and expressly states that classified information and information relating to the identity of informants are solely within the scope of other Rules.

(c) *Who may claim the privilege.* Rule 506(c) distinguishes between government information in general and investigations of the Inspectors General. While the privilege for the latter may be claimed "by the authority ordering the investigation or any superior authority," the privilege for other government information may be claimed *only* "by the head of the executive or military department or government agency concerned." *See generally* the Analysis to Rule 505(c).

1990 Amendment: Subsection (c) was amended by substituting the words "records and information" for "investigations", which is a term of art vis-a-vis Inspector General functions. Inspectors General also conduct "inspections" and "inquiries," and use of the word "records and information" is intended to cover all documents and information generated by or related to the activities of Inspectors General. "Records" includes reports of inspection, inquiry, and investigation conducted by an Inspector General and extracts, summaries, exhibits, memoranda, notes, internal correspondence, handwritten working materials, untranscribed shorthand or stenotype notes of unrecorded testimony, tape recordings and other supportive records such as automated data extracts. In conjunction with this change, the language identifying the official entitled to claim the privilege for Inspector General records was changed to maintain the previous provision which allowed the superiors of Inspector General officers, rather than the officers themselves, to claim the privilege.

(d) *Action prior to referral of charges.* Rule 506(d) specifies action to be taken prior to referral of charges in the event of a claim of privilege under the Rule. *See generally* Rule 505(d) and its Analysis. Note that disclosures can be withheld only if action under paragraph (1)–(4) of subdivision (d) cannot be made "without causing identifiable damage to the public interest." (Emphasis added).

(e) *Action after referral of charges. See generally* Rule 505(f) and its Analysis. Note that unlike Rule 505(f), however, Rule 506(e) does not require a finding that failure to disclose the information in question "would materially prejudice a substantial right of the accused." Dismissal is required when the relevant information is not disclosed in a "reasonable period of time."

1995 Amendment: It is the intent of the Committee that if classified information arises during a proceeding under Rule 506, the procedures of Rule 505 will be used.

The new subsection (e) was formerly subsection (f). The matters in the former subsection (f) were adopted without change. The former subsection (e) was amended and redesignated as subsection (f) (see below).

(f) *Pretrial session.* Rule 506(f) is taken from Rule 505(e). It is the intent of the Committee that if classified information arises during a proceeding under Rule 506, the procedures of Rule 505 will be used.

1995 Amendment: See generally Rule 505(f) and its accompanying Analysis. Note that unlike Rule 505(f), however, Rule 506(f) does not require a finding that failure to disclose the information in question "would materially prejudice a substantial right of the accused." Dismissal is not required when the relevant information is not disclosed in a "reasonable period of time."

Subsection (f) was formerly subsection (e). The subsection was amended to cover action after a defense motion for discovery, rather than action after referral of charges. The qualification that the government claim of privilege pertains to information "that apparently contains evidence that is relevant and necessary to an element of the offense or a legally cognizable defense and is otherwise admissible in evidence in a court-martial proceeding" was deleted as unnecessary. Action by the convening authority is required if, after referral, the defense moves for disclosure and the Government claims the information is privileged from disclosure.

(g) *Disclosure of government information to the accused.* Rule 506(g) is taken from Rule 505(g) but deletes references to classified information and clearances due to their inapplicability.

(h) *Prohibition against disclosure.* Rule 506(h) is derived from Rule 505(h)(4). The remainder of Rule 505(h)(4) and Rule 505(h) generally has been omitted as being unnecessary. No sanction for violation of the requirement has been included.

1995 Amendment: Subsection (h) was amended to provide that government information may not be disclosed by the accused unless authorized by the military judge.

(i) *In camera proceedings.* Rule 506(i) is taken generally from Rule 505(i), but the standard involved reflects 1969 Manual Para. 151 and the Supreme Court's decision in *United States v. Nixon, supra.* In line with *Nixon*, the burden is on the party claiming the privilege to demonstrate why the information involved should not be disclosed. References to classified material have been deleted as being inapplicable.

1995 Amendment: Subsection (i) was amended to clarify the procedure for in camera proceedings. The definition in subsection (i)(1) was amended to conform to the definition of in camera proceedings in M.R.E. 505(i)(1). Subsections (i)(2) and (i)(3) were unchanged. Subsection (i)(4)(B), redesignated as (i)(4)(C), was amended to include admissible evidence relevant to punishment of the accused, consistent with *Brady v. Maryland*, 373 U.S. 83, 87 (1963). Subsection (i)(4)(C) was redesignated as (i)(4)(D), but was otherwise unchanged. The amended procedures provide for full disclosure of the government information in question to the accused for purposes of litigating the admissibility of the information in the protected environment of the in camera proceeding; *i.e.*, the Article 39(a) session is closed to the public and neither side may disclose the information outside the in camera proceeding until the military judge admits the information as evidence in the trial. Under subsection (i)(4)(E), the military judge may authorize alternatives to disclosure, consistent with a military judge's authority concerning classified information under M.R.E. 505. Subsection (i)(4)(F) allows the Government to determine whether the information ultimately will be disclosed to the accused. However, the Government's continued objection to disclosure may be at the price of letting the accused go free, in that subsection (i)(4)(F) adopts the sanctions available to the military judge under M.R.E. 505(i)(4)(E). *See United States v. Reynolds*, 345 U.S. 1, 12 (1953).

(k) *Introduction of government information subject to a claim of privilege.* Rule 506(k) is derived from Rule 505(j) with appropriate modifications being made to reflect the nonclassified nature of the information involved.

1995 Amendment: Subsection (j) was added to recognize the Government's right to appeal certain rulings and orders. *See* R.C.M. 908. The former subsection (j) was redesignated as subsection (k). The subsection speaks only to government appeals; the defense still may seek extraordinary relief through interlocutory appeal of the military judge's orders and rulings. *See generally*, 28 U.S.C. § 1651(a); *Waller v. Swift*, 30 M.J. 139 (C.M.A. 1990); *Dettinger v. United States*, 7 M.J. 216 (C.M.A. 1979).

(l) *Procedures to safeguard against compromise of government information disclosed to courts-martial.* Rule 506(k) is derived from Rule 505(k). Such procedures should reflect the fact that material privileged under Rule 506 is not classified.

Rule 507 Identity of informant

(a) *Rule of privilege.* Rule 507(a) sets forth the basic rule of privilege for informants and contains the substance of 1969 Manual Para. 151 *b*(1). The new Rule, however, provides greater detail as to the application of the privilege than did the 1969 manual.

The privilege is that of the United States or political subdivision thereof and applies only to information relevant to the identity of an informant. An "informant" is simply an individual who has supplied "information resulting in an investigation of a possible violation of law" to a proper person and thus includes good citizen reports to command or police as well as the traditional "confidential informants" who may be consistent sources of information.

(b) *Who may claim the privilege.* Rule 507(b) provides for claiming the privilege and distinguishes between representatives of the United States and representatives of a state or subdivision thereof. Although an appropriate representative of the United States may always claim the privilege when applicable, a representative of a state or subdivision may do so only if the information in question was supplied to an officer of the state or subdivision. The Rule is taken from proposed Federal Rule of Evidence 510(b), with appropriate modifications, and is similar in substances to Para. 151 *b*(1) of the 1969 Manual which permitted "appropriate governmental authorities" to claim the privilege.

The Rule does not specify who an "appropriate representative" is. Normally, the trial counsel is an appropriate representative of the United States. The Rule leaves the question open, however, for case by case resolution. Regulations could be promulgated which could specify who could be an appropriate representative.

(c) *Exceptions.* Rule 507(c) sets forth the circumstances in which the privilege is inapplicable.

(1) *Voluntary disclosures; informant as witness.* Rule 507(c)(1) makes it clear that the privilege is inapplicable if circumstances have nullified its justification for existence. Thus, there is no reason for the privilege, and the privilege is consequently inapplicable, if the individual who would have cause to resent the informant has been made aware of the informant's identity by a holder of the privilege or by the informant's own action or when the witness testifies for the prosecution thus allowing that person to ascertain the informant's identity. This is in accord with the intent of the privilege which is to protect informants from reprisals. The Rule is taken from Para. 151 *b*(1) of the 1969 Manual.

(2) *Testimony on the issue of guilt or innocence.* Rule 507(c)(2) is taken from 1969 Manual Para. 151 *b* (1) and recognizes that in certain circumstances the accused may have a due process right under the Fifth Amendment, as well as a similar right under the Uniform Code of Military Justice, to call the informant as a witness. The subdivision intentionally does not specify what circumstances would require calling the informant and leaves resolution of the issue to each individual case.

(3) *Legality of obtaining evidence.* Rule 507(c)(3) is new. The Rule recognizes that circumstances may exist in which the Constitution may require disclosure of the identity of an informant in the context of determining the legality of obtaining evidence under Rule 311; *see, e.g., Franks v. Delaware*, 438 U.S. 154, 170 (1978); *McCray v. Illinois*, 386 U.S. 300 (1976) (both cases indicate that disclosure may be required in certain unspecified circumstances but do not in fact require such disclosure). In view of the highly unsettled nature of the issue, the Rule does not specify whether or when such disclosure is mandated and leaves the determination to the military judge in light of prevailing case

law utilized in the trial of criminal cases in the Federal district courts.

(d) *Procedures.* Rule 507(d) sets forth the procedures to be followed in the event of a claim of privilege under Rule 507. If the prosecution elects not to disclose the identity of an informant when the judge has determined that disclosure is required, that matter shall be reported to the convening authority. Such a report is required so that the convening authority may determine what action, if any, should be taken. Such actions could include disclosure of the informant's identity, withdrawal of charges, or some appropriate appellate action.

Rule 508 Political vote

Rule 508 is taken from proposed Federal Rule of Evidence 507 and expresses the substance of 18 U.S.C. § 596 (1976) which is applicable to the armed forces. The privilege is considered essential for the armed forces because of the unique nature of military life.

Rule 509 Deliberation of courts and juries

Rule 509 is taken from 1969 Manual Para. 151 but has been modified to ensure conformity with Rule 606(b) which deals specifically with disclosure of deliberations in certain cases.

Rule 510 Waiver of privilege by voluntary disclosure

Rule 510 is derived from proposed Federal Rule of Evidence 511 and is similar in substance to 1969 Manual Para. 151 *a* which notes that privileges may be waived. Rule 510(a) simply provides that "disclosure of any significant part of the matter or communication under such circumstances that it would be inappropriate to claim the privilege" will defeat and waive the privilege. Disclosure of privileged matter may be, however, itself privileged; *see* Rules 502(b)(4); 503(b)(2); 504(b)(2). Information disclosed in the form of an otherwise privileged telephone call (*e.g.,* information overheard by an operator) is privileged, Rule 511(b), and information disclosed via transmission using other forms of communication may be privileged; Rule 511(b). Disclosure under certain circumstances may not be "inappropriate" and the information will retain its privileged character. Thus, disclosure of an informant's identity by one law enforcement agency to another may well be appropriate and not render Rule 507 inapplicable.

Rule 510(b) is taken from Para. 151 *b*(1) of the 1969 Manual and makes it clear that testimony pursuant to a grant of immunity does not waive the privilege. Similarly, an accused who testifies in his or her own behalf does not waive the privilege unless the accused testifies voluntarily to the privileged matter of communication.

Rule 511 Privileged matter disclosed under compulsion or without opportunity to claim privilege

Rule 511(a) is similar to proposed Federal Rule of Evidence 512. Placed in the context of the definition of "confidential" utilized in the privilege rules, *see,* Rule 502(b)(4), the Rule is substantially different from prior military law inasmuch as prior law permitted utilization of privileged information which had been gained by a third party through accident or design. *See* Para. 151 *b* (1), MCM, 1969 (Rev.). Such disclosures are generally safeguarded against via the definition "confidential" used in the new Rules. Generally, the Rules are more protective of privileged information than was the 1969 Manual.

Rule 511(b) is new and deals with electronic transmission of information. It recognizes that the nature of the armed forces today often requires such information transmission. Like 1969 Manual Para. 151 *b*(1), the new Rule does not make a non-privileged communication privileged; rather, it simply safeguards already privileged information under certain circumstances.

The first portion of subdivision (b) expressly provides that otherwise privileged information transmitted by telephone remains privileged. This is in recognition of the role played by the telephone in modern life and particularly in the armed forces where geolineartal separations are common. The Committee was of the opinion that legal business cannot be transacted in the 20th century without customary use of the telephone. Consequently, privileged communications transmitted by telephone are protected even though those telephone conversations are known to be monitored for whatever purpose.

Unlike telephonic communications, Rule 511(b) protects other forms of electronic communication only when such means "is necessary and in furtherance of the communication." It is irrelevant under the Rule as to whether the communication in question was in fact necessary. The only relevant question is whether, once the individual decided to communicate, the *means* of communication was necessary and in furtherance of the communication. Transmission of information by radio is a means of communication that must be tested under this standard.

Rule 512 Comment upon or inference from claim of privilege; instruction

(a) *Comment or inference not permitted.* Rule 512(a) is derived from proposed Federal Rule 513. The Rule is new to military law but is generally in accord with the Analysis of Contents of the 1969 Manual; United States Department of the Army, Pamphlet No. 27–2, Analysis of Contents, Manual for Courts-Martial 1969, *Revised Edition,* 27–33, 27–38 (1970).

Rule 512(a)(1) prohibits any inference or comment upon the exercise of a privilege by the accused and is taken generally from proposed Federal Rule of Evidence 513(a).

Rule 512(a)(2) creates a qualified prohibition with respect to any inference or comment upon the exercise of a privilege by a person not the accused. The Rule recognizes that in certain circumstances the interests of justice may require such an inference and comment. Such a situation could result, for example, when the government's exercise of a privilege has been sustained, and an inference adverse to the government is necessary to preserve the fairness of the proceeding.

(b) *Claiming privilege without knowledge of members.* Rule 512(b) is intended to implement subdivision (a). Where possible, claims of privilege should be raised at an Article 39(a) session or, if practicable, at sidebar.

(c) *Instruction.* Rule 512(c) requires that relevant instructions be given "upon request." *Cf.* Rule 105. The military judge does not have a duty to instruct *sua sponte.*

Rule 513 Psychotherapist-patient privilege

1999 Amendment: Military Rule of Evidence 513 establishes a psychotherapist-patient privilege for investigations or proceedings authorized under the Uniform Code of Military Justice. Rule 513 clarifies military law in light of the Supreme Court decision in *Jaffee v. Redmond*, 518 U.S. 1, 116 S. Ct. 1923, 135 L.Ed.2d 337 (1996). *Jaffee* interpreted Federal Rule of Evidence 501 to create a federal psychotherapist-patient privilege in civil proceedings and refers federal courts to state laws to determine the extent of privileges. In deciding to adopt this privilege for courts-martial, the committee balanced the policy of following federal law and rules, when practicable and not inconsistent with the UCMJ or MCM, with the needs of commanders for knowledge of certain types of information affecting the military. The exceptions to the rule have been developed to address the specialized society of the military and separate concerns that must be met to ensure military readiness and national security. *See Parker v. Levy*, 417 U.S. 733, 743 (1974); *U.S. ex rel. Toth v. Quarles*, 350 U.S. 11, 17 (1955); *Dept. of the Navy v. Egan*, 484 U.S. 518, 530 (1988). There is no intent to apply Rule 513 in any proceeding other than those authorized under the UCMJ. Rule 513 was based in part on proposed Fed. R. Evid. (not adopted) 504 and state rules of evidence. Rule 513 is not a physician-patient privilege. It is a separate rule based on the social benefit of confidential counseling recognized by Jaffee, and similar to the clergy-penitent privilege. In keeping with American military law since its inception, there is still no physician-patient privilege for members of the Armed Forces. *See* the analyses for Rule 302 and Rule 501.

(a) *General rule of privilege.* The words "under the UCMJ" in this rule mean Rule 513 applies only to UCMJ proceedings, and do not limit the availability of such information internally to the services, for appropriate purposes.

(d) *Exceptions* These exceptions are intended to emphasize that military commanders are to have access to all information that is necessary for the safety and security of military personnel, operations, installations, and equipment. Therefore, psychotherapists are to provide such information despite a claim of privilege.

SECTION VI

WITNESSES

Rule 601 General rule of competency

Rule 601 is taken without change from the first portion of Federal Rule of Evidence 601. The remainder of the Federal Rule was deleted due to its sole application to civil cases.

In declaring that subject to any other Rule, all persons are competent to be witnesses, Rule 601 supersedes Para. 148 of the 1969 Manual which required, among other factors, that an individual know the difference between truth and falsehood and understand the moral importance of telling the truth in order to testify. Under Rule 601 such matters will go only to the weight of the testimony and not to its competency. The Rule's reference to other rules includes Rules 603 (Oath or Affirmation), 605 (Competency of Military Judge as Witness), 606 (Competency of Court Member as Witness), and the rules of privilege.

The plain meaning of the Rule appears to deprive the trial judge of any discretion whatsoever to exclude testimony on grounds of competency unless the testimony is incompetent under those specific rules already cited *supra, see, United States v. Fowler*, 605 F.2d 181 (5th Cir. 1979), a conclusion bolstered by the Federal Rules of Evidence Advisory Committee's Note. S. Saltzburg & K. Redden, FEDERAL RULES OF EVIDENCE MANUAL 270 (2d ed. 1977). Whether this conclusion is accurate, especially in the light of Rule 403, is unclear. *Id.* at 269; *see also United States v. Calahan*, 442 F.Supp. 1213 (D. Minn. 1978).

Rule 602 Lack of personal knowledge

Rule 602 is taken without significant change from the Federal Rule and is similar in content to Para. 138 *d*, MCM, 1969 (Rev.). Although the 1969 Manual expressly allowed an individual to testify to his or her own age or date of birth, the Rule is silent of the issue.

Notwithstanding that silence, however, it appears that it is within the meaning of the Rule to allow such testimony. Rule 804(b)(4) (Hearsay Exceptions; Declarant Unavailable—Statement of Personal or Family History) expressly permits a hearsay statement "concerning the declarant's own birth ... or other similar fact of personal or family history, even though declarant had no means of acquiring personal knowledge of the matter stated." It seems evident that if such a hearsay statement is admissible, in-court testimony by the declarant should be no less admissible. It is probable that the expression "personal knowledge" in Rule 804(b)(4) is being used in the sense of "first hand knowledge" while the expression is being used in Rule 602 in a somewhat broader sense to include those matters which an individual could be considered to reliably know about his or her personal history.

Rule 603 Oath or affirmation

Rule 603 is taken from the Federal Rule without change. The oaths found within Chapter XXII of the Manual satisfy the requirements of Rule 603. Pursuant to Rule 1101(c), this Rule is inapplicable to the accused when he or she makes an unsworn statement.

Rule 604 Interpreters

Rule 604 is taken from the Federal Rule without change and is consistent with Para. 141, MCM, 1969 (Rev.). The oath found in Paras. 114 *e*, MCM, 1969 (Rev.) (now R.C.M. 807(b)(2) (Discussion), MCM, 1984), satisfies the oath requirements of Rule 604.

Rule 605 Competency of military judge as witness

Rule 605(a) restates the Federal Rule without significant change. Although Article 26(d) of the Uniform Code of Military Justice states in relevant part that "no person is eligible to act as a military judge if he is a witness for the prosecution ..." and is silent on whether a witness for the defense is eligible to sit, the Committee believes that the specific reference in the code was not intended to create a right and was the result only of an attempt to highlight the more grievous case. In any event, Rule 605, unlike Article 26(d), does not deal with the question of eligibility to sit as a military judge, but deals solely with the military judge's competency as a witness. The rule does not affect *voir dire.*

Rule 605(b) is new and is not found within the Federal Rules of Evidence. It was added because of the unique nature of the military judiciary in which military judges often control their own dockets without clerical assistance. In view of the military's stringent speedy trial roles, *see, United States v. Burton*, 21 U.S.C.M.A 112, 44 C.M.R. 166 (1971), it was necessary to preclude expressly any interpretation of Rule 605 that would prohibit the military judge from placing on the record details relating to docketing in order to avoid prejudice to a party. Rule 605(b) is consistent with present military law.

Rule 606 Competency of court member as witness

(a) *At the court-martial.* Rule 606(a) is taken from the Federal Rule without substantive change. The Rule alters prior military law only to the extent that a member of the court could testify as a defense witness under prior precedent. Rule 606(a) deals only with the competency of court members as witnesses and does not affect other Manual provisions governing the eligibility of the individuals to sit as members due to their potential status as witnesses. *See , e.g.,* Paras. 62 *f* and 63, MCM, 1969 (Rev.). The Rule does not affect *voir dire.*

(b) *Inquiry into validity of findings or sentence.* Rule 606(b) is taken from the Federal Rule with only one significant change. The rule, retitled to reflect the sentencing function of members, recognizes unlawful command influence as a legitimate subject of inquiry and permits testimony by a member on that subject. The addition is required by the need to keep proceedings free from any taint of unlawful command influence and further implements Article 37(a) of the Uniform Code of Military Justice. Use of superior rank or grade by one member of a court to sway other members would constitute unlawful command influence for purposes of this Rule under Para. 74 *d*(1), MCM, 1969 (Rev.). Rule 606 does not itself prevent otherwise lawful polling of members of the court, *see generally, United States v. Hendon*, 6 M.J. 171, 174 (C.M.A. 1979) and does not prohibit attempted lawful clarification of an ambiguous or inconsistent verdict. Rule 606(b) is in general accord with prior military law.

Rule 607 Who may impeach

Rule 607 is taken without significant change from the Federal Rule. It supersedes Para. 153 *b*(1), MCM, 1969 (Rev.), which restricted impeachment of one's own witness to those situations in which the witness is indispensable or the testimony of the witness proves to be unexpectedly adverse.

Rule 607 thus allows a party to impeach its own witness. Indeed, when relevant, it permits a party to call a witness for the sole purpose of impeachment. It should be noted, however, that an apparent inconsistency exists when Rule 607 is compared with Rules 608(b) and 609(a). Although Rule 607 allows impeachment on direct examination, Rules 608(b) and 609(a) would by their explicit language restrict the methods of impeachment to cross-examination. The use of the expression "cross-examination" in these rules appears to be accidental and to have been intended to be synonymous with impeachment while on direct examination. *See generally,* S. Saltzburg & K. Redden, FEDERAL RULES OF EVIDENCE MANUAL 298–99 (2d ed. 1977). It is the intent of the Committee that the Rules be so interpreted unless the Article III courts should interpret the Rules in a different fashion.

Rule 608 Evidence of character, conduct, and bias of witness

(a) *Opinion and reputation evidence of character.* Rule 608(a) is taken verbatim from the Federal Rule. The Rule, which is consistent with the philosophy behind Rule 404(a), limits use of character evidence in the form of opinion or reputation evidence on the issue of credibility by restricting such evidence to matters relating to the character for truthfulness or untruthfulness of the witness. General good character is not admissible under the Rule. Rule 608(a) prohibits presenting evidence of good character until the character of the witness for truthfulness has been attacked. The Rule is similar to Para. 153 *b* of the 1969 Manual except that the Rule, unlike Para. 153 *b*, applies to all witnesses and does not distinguish between the accused and other witnesses.

(b) *Specific instances of conduct.* Rule 608(b) is taken from the Federal Rule without significant change. The Rule is somewhat similar in effect to the military practice found in Para. 153 *b*(2) of the 1969 Manual in that it allows use of specific instances of conduct of a witness to be brought out on cross-examination but prohibits use of extrinsic evidence. Unlike Para. 153 *b*(2), Rule 608(b) does not distinguish between an accused and other witnesses.

The fact that the accused is subject to impeachment by prior acts of misconduct is a significant factor to be considered by the military judge when he or she is determining whether to exercise the discretion granted by the Rule. Although the Rule expressly limits this form of impeachment to inquiry on cross-examination, it is likely that the intent of the Federal Rule was to permit inquiry on direct as well, *see* Rule 607, and the use of the term "cross-examination" was an accidental substitute for "impeachment." *See* S. Saltzburg & K. Redden, FEDERAL RULES OF EVIDENCE MANUAL 312–13 (2d ed. 1977). It is the intent of the Committee to allow use of this form of evidence on direct examination to the same extent, if any, it is so permitted in the Article III courts.

The Rule does not prohibit receipt of extrinsic evidence in the form of prior convictions, Rule 609, or to show bias. Rule 608(c). *See also* Rule 613 (Prior statements of witnesses). When the witness has testified as to the character of another witness, the witness may be cross-examined as to the character of that witness. The remainder of Rule 608(b) indicates that testimony relating only to credibility does not waive the privilege against self-incrimination. *See generally* Rule 301.

Although 608(b) allows examination into specific acts, counsel should not, as a matter of ethics, attempt to elicit evidence of misconduct unless there is a reasonable basis for the question. *See generally* ABA PROJECT ON STANDARDS FOR CRIMINAL JUSTICE, STANDARDS RELATING TO THE PROSECUTION FUNCTION AND THE DEFENSE FUNCTION, Prosecution Function 5.7(d); Defense Functions 7.6(d) (Approved draft 1971).

(c) *Evidence of bias.* Rule 608(c) is taken from 1969 Manual Para. 153*d* and is not found within the Federal Rule. Impeachment by bias was apparently accidentally omitted from the Federal Rule, *see,* S. Saltzburg & K. Redden, FEDERAL RULES OF EVIDENCE MANUAL 313–14(2d ed. 1977), but is acceptable under the Federal Rules; *see, e.g., United States v. Leja*, 568 F.2d 493 (6th Cir. 1977); *United States v. Alvarez-Lopez,* 559 F.2d 1155 (9th Cir. 1977). Because of the critical nature of this form of impeachment and the fact that extrinsic evidence may be used to show it, the Committee believed that its omission would be impracticable.

It should be noted that the Federal Rules are not exhaustive, and that a number of different types of techniques of impeachment are not explicitly codified.

The failure to so codify them does not mean that they are no longer permissible. *See, e.g., United states v. Alvarez-Lopez,* supra 155; Rule 412. Thus, impeachment by contradiction, *see also* Rule 304(a)(2); 311(j), and impeachment via prior inconsistent statements, Rule 613, remain appropriate. To the extent that the Military Rules do not acknowledge a particular form of impeachment, it is the intent of the Committee to allow that method to the same extent it is permissible in the Article III courts. *See, e.g.,* Rules 402; 403.

Impeachment of an alleged victim of a sexual offense through evidence of the victim's past sexual history and character is dealt with in Rule 412, and evidence of fresh complaint is admissible to the extent permitted by Rules 801 and 803.

Rule 609 Impeachment by evidence of conviction of crime

(a) *General Rules.* Rule 609(a) is taken from the Federal Rule but has been slightly modified to adopt it to military law. For example, an offense for which a dishonorable discharge may be adjudged may be used for impeachment. This continues the rule as found in Para. 153 *b*(2)(b)(1) of the 1969 Manual. In determining whether a military offense may be used for purposes of impeachment under Rule 609(a)(1), recourse must be made to the maximum punishment imposable if the offense had been tried by general court-martial.

Rule 609(a) differs slightly from the prior military rule. Under Rule 609(a)(1), a civilian conviction's availability for impeachment is solely a function of its maximum punishment under "the law in which the witness was convicted." This is different from Para. 153 *b* (2)(b)(3) of the 1969 Manual which allowed use of a non-federal conviction analogous to a federal felony or characterized by the jurisdiction as a felony or "as an offense of comparable gravity." Under the new rule, comparisons and determinations of relative gravity will be unnecessary and improper.

Convictions that "involve moral turpitude or otherwise affect ... credibility" were admissible for impeachment under Para. 153 *b*(2)(b) of the 1969 Manual. The list of potential convictions expressed in Para. 153 *b*(2)(b) was illustrative only and non-exhaustive. Unlike the 1969 Manual rule, Rule 609(a) is exhaustive.

Although a conviction technically fits within Rule 609(a)(1), its admissibility remains subject to finding by the military judge that its probative value outweighs its prejudicial effect to the accused.

Rule 609(a)(2) makes admissible convictions involving "dishonesty or false statement, regardless of punishment." This is similar to intent in Para. 153*b*(2)(b)(4) of the 1969 Manual which makes admissible "a conviction of any offense involving fraud, deceit, larceny, wrongful appropriation, or the making of false statement." The exact meaning of "dishonesty" within the meaning of Rule 609 is unclear and has already been the subject of substantial litigation. The Congressional intent appears, however, to have been extremely restrictive with "dishonesty" being used in the sense of untruthfulness. *See generally* S. Saltzburg & K. Redden, FEDERAL RULES OF EVIDENCE MANUAL 336–45 (2d ed. 1977). Thus, a conviction for fraud, perjury, or embezzlement would come within the definition, but a conviction for simple larceny would not. Pending further case development in the Article III courts, caution would suggest close adherence to this highly limited definition.

It should be noted that admissibility of evidence within the scope of Rule 609(a)(2) is not explicitly subject to the discretion of the military judge. The application of Rule 403 is unclear.

While the language of Rule 609(a) refers only to cross-examination, it would appear that the Rule does refer to direct examination as well. *See* the Analysis to Rules 607 and 608(b).

As defined in Rule 609(f), a court-martial conviction occurs when a sentence has been adjudged.

1993 Amendment. The amendment to Mil. R. Evid. 609(a) is based on the 1990 amendment to Fed. R. Evid. 609(a). The previous version of Mil. R. Evid. 609(a) was based on the now superseded version of the Federal Rule. This amendment removes from the rule the limitation that the conviction may only be elicited during cross-examination. Additionally, the amendment clarifies the relationship between Rules 403 and 609. The amendment clarifies that the special balancing test found in Mil. R. Evid. 609(a)(1) applies to the accused's convictions. The convictions of all other witnesses are only subject to the Mil. R. Evid. 403 balancing test. *See Green v. Bock Laundry Machine Co.,* 490 U.S. 504 (1989).

(b) *Time limit.* Rule 609(b) is taken verbatim from the Federal Rule. As it has already been made applicable to the armed forces, *United States v. Weaver,* 1 M.J. 111 (C.M.A. 1975), it is consistent with the present military practice.

(c) *Effect of pardon, annulment, or certificate of rehabilitation.* Rule 609(c) is taken verbatim from the Federal Rule except that convictions punishable by dishonorable discharge have been added. Rule 609(c) has no equivalent in present military practice and represents a substantial change as it will prohibit use of convictions due to evidence of rehabilitation. In the absence of a certificate of rehabilitation, the extent to which the various Armed Forces post-conviction programs, such as the Air Force's 3320th Correction and Rehabilitation Squadron and the Army's Retraining Brigade, come within Rule 609(c) is unclear, although it is probable that successful completion of such a program is "an equivalent procedure based on the finding of the rehabilitation of the persons convicted" within the meaning of the Rule.

(d) *Juvenile adjudications.* Rule 609(d) is taken from the Federal Rule without significant change. The general prohibition in the Rule is substantially different from Para. 153*b*(2)(b) of the 1969 Manual which allowed use of juvenile adjudications other than those involving an accused. The discretionary authority vested in the military judge to admit such evidence comports with the accused's constitutional right to a fair trial,*Davis v. Alaska,* 415 U.S. 308 (1974).

(e) *Pendency of appeal.* The first portion of Rule 609(e) is taken from the Federal Rule and is substantially different from Para. 153 *b*(2)(b) of the 1969 Manual which prohibited use of convictions for impeachment purposes while they were undergoing appellate review. Under the Rule, the fact of review may be shown but does not affect admissibility. A different rule applies, however, for convictions by summary court-martial or by special court-martial without a military judge. The Committee believed that because a legally trained presiding officer is not required in these proceedings, a conviction should not be used for impeachment until review has been completed.

February 1986 Amendment: The reference in subsection (e) to "Article 65(c)" was changed to "Article 64" to correct an error in MCM, 1984.

(f) *Definition.* This definition of conviction has been added because of the unique nature of the court-martial. Because of its recognition that a conviction cannot result until at least sentencing, *cf. Lederer, Reappraising the Legality of Post-trial Interviews, The Army Lawyer,* July 1977, at 12, the Rule may modify *United States v. Mathews,* 6 M.J. 357 (C.M.A. 1979).

Rule 610 Religious beliefs or opinions

Rule 610 is taken without significant change from the Federal Rules and had no equivalent in the 1969 Manual for Courts-Martial. The Rule makes religious beliefs or opinions inadmissible for the purpose of impeaching or bolstering credibility. To the extent that such opinions may be critical to the defense of a case, however, there may be constitutional justification for overcoming the Rule's exclusion. *Cf. Davis v. Alaska*, 415 U.S. 308 (1974).

Rule 611 Mode and order of interrogation and presentation

(a) *Control by the military judge.* Rule 611(a) is taken from the Federal Rule without change. It is a basic source of the military judge's power to control proceedings and replaces 1969 Manual Para. 149 *a* and that part of Para. 137 dealing with cumulative evidence. It is within the military judge's discretion to control methods of interrogation of witnesses. The Rule does not change prior law. Although a witness may be required to limit an answer to the question asked, it will normally be improper to require that a "yes" or "no" answer be given unless it is clear that such an answer will be a complete response to the question. A witness will ordinarily be entitled to explain his or her testimony at some time before completing this testimony. The Manual requirement that questions be asked through the military judge is now found in Rule 614.

Although the military judge has the discretion to alter the sequence of proof to the extent that the burden of proof is not affected, the usual sequence for examination of witnesses is: prosecution witnesses, defense witnesses, prosecution rebuttal witnesses, defense rebuttal witnesses, and witnesses for the court. The usual order of examination of a witness is: direct examination, cross-examination, redirect examination, recross-examination, and examination by the court, Para. 54 *a*, MCM, 1969 (Rev.).

1995 Amendment: When a child witness is unable to testify due to intimidation by the proceedings, fear of the accused, emotional trauma, or mental or other infirmity, alternative to live in-court testimony may be appropriate. *See Maryland v. Craig*, 497 U.S. 836 (1990); *United States v. Romey*, 32 M.J. 180 (C.M.A.), *cert. denied*, 502 U.S. 924 (1991); *United States v. Batten*, 31 M.J. 205 (C.M.A. 1990); *United States v. Thompson*, 31 M.J. 168 (C.M.A. 1990), *cert. denied*, 498 U.S.C. § 1084 (1991). This is an evolving area of law with guidance available in case law. The drafters, after specifically considering adoption of 18 U.S.C. § 3509, determined it more appropriate to allow the case law evolutionary process to continue.

(b) *Scope of cross-examination.* Rule 611(b) is taken from the Federal Rule without change and replaces Para. 149 *b*(1) of the 1969 Manual which was similar in scope. Under the Rule the military judge may allow a party to adopt a witness and proceed as if on direct examination. *See* Rule 301(b)(2) (judicial advice as to the privilege against self-incrimination for an apparently uninformed witness); Rule 301(f)(2) (effect of claiming the privilege against self-incrimination on cross-examination); Rule 303 (Degrading Questions); and Rule 608(b) (Evidence of Character, Conduct, and Bias of Witness).

(c) *Leading questions.* Rule 611(c) is taken from the Federal Rule without significant change and is similar to Para. 149 *c* of the 1969 Manual. The reference in the third sentence of the Federal Rule to an "adverse party" has been deleted as being applicable to civil cases only.

A leading question is one which suggests the answer it is desired that the witness give. Generally, a question that is susceptible to being answered by "yes" or "no" is a leading question.

The use of leading questions is discretionary with the military judge. Use of leading questions may be appropriate with respect to the following witnesses, among others: children, persons with mental or physical disabilities, the extremely elderly, hostile witnesses, and witnesses identified with the adverse party.

It is also appropriate with the military judge's consent to utilize leading questions to direct a witness's attention to a relevant area of inquiry.

1999 Amendment: Rule 611(d) is new. This amendment to Rule 611 gives substantive guidance to military judges regarding the use of alternative examination methods for child victims and witnesses in light of the U.S. Supreme Court's decision in *Maryland v. Craig* , 497 U.S. 836 (1990) and the change in Federal law in 18 U.S.C. section 3509. Although *Maryland v. Craig* dealt with child witnesses who were themselves the victims of abuse, it should be noted that 18 U.S.C. section 3509, as construed by Federal courts, has been applied to allow non-victim child witnesses to testify remotely. *See, e.g., United States v. Moses*, 137 F.3d 894 (6th Cir. 1998) (applying section 3509 to a non-victim child witness, but reversing a child sexual assault conviction on other grounds) and *United States v. Quintero*, 21 F.3d 885 (9th Cir. 1994) (affirming conviction based on remote testimony of non-victim child witness, but remanding for resentencing). This amendment recognizes that child witnesses may be particularly traumatized, even if they are not themselves the direct victims, in cases involving the abuse of other children or domestic violence. This amendment also gives the accused an election to absent himself from the courtroom to prevent remote testimony. Such a provision gives the accused a greater role in determining how this issue will be resolved.

Rule 612 Writing used to refresh memory

Rule 612 is taken generally from the Federal Rule but a number of modifications have been made to adapt the Rule to military practice. Language in the Federal Rule relating to the Jencks Act, 18 U.S.C. § 3500, which would have shielded material from disclosure to the defense under Rule 612 was discarded. Such shielding was considered to be inappropriate in view of the general military practice and policy which utilizes and encourages broad discovery on behalf of the defense.

The decision of the president of a special court-martial without a military judge under this rule is an interlocutory ruling not subject to objection by the members, Para. 57 *a*, MCM, 1969 (Rev.).

Rule 612 codifies the doctrine of past recollection refreshed and replaces that portion of Para. 146 *a* of the 1969 Manual which dealt with the issue. Although the 1969 Manual rule was similar, in that it authorized inspection by the opposing party of a memorandum used to refresh recollection and permitted it to be offered into evidence by that party to show the improbability of it refreshing recollection, the Rule is somewhat more extensive as it also deals with writings used before testifying.

Rule 612 does not affect in any way information required to be disclosed under any other rule or portion of the Manual. *See*, Rule 304(c)(1).

Rule 613 Prior statements of witnesses

(a) *Examining witness concerning prior statement.* Rule 613(a) is taken from the Federal Rule without change. It alters military practice inasmuch as it eliminates the foundation requirements found in Para. 153 *b*(2)(c) of the 1969 Manual. While it will no longer be a condition precedent to admissibility to acquaint a witness with the prior statement and to give the witness an opportunity to either change his or her testimony or to reaffirm it, such a procedure may be appropriate as a matter of trial tactics.

It appears that the drafters of Federal Rule 613 may have inadvertently omitted the word "inconsistent" from both its caption and the text of Rule 613(a). The effect of that omission, if any, is unclear.

(b) *Extrinsic evidence of prior inconsistent statement of witness.* Rule 613(b) is taken from the Federal Rule without change. It requires that the witness be given an opportunity to explain or deny a prior inconsistent statement when the party proffers extrinsic evidence of the statement. Although this foundation is not required under Rule 613(a), it is required under Rule 613(b) if a party wishes to utilize more than the witness' own testimony as brought out on cross-examination. The Rule does not specify any particular timing for the opportunity for the witness to explain or deny the statement nor does it specify any particular method. The Rule is inapplicable to introduction of prior inconsistent statements on the merits under Rule 801.

Rule 614 Calling and interrogation of witnesses by the court-martial

(a) *Calling by the court-martial.* The first sentence of Rule 614(a) is taken from the Federal Rule but has been modified to recognize the power of the court members to call and examine witnesses. The second sentence of the subdivision is new and reflects the members' power to call or recall witnesses. Although recognizing that power, the Rule makes it clear that the calling of such witnesses is contingent upon compliance with these Rules and this Manual. Consequently, the testimony of such witnesses must be relevant and not barred by any Rule or Manual provision.

(b) *Interrogation by the court-martial.* The first sentence of Rule 614(b) is taken from the Federal Rule but modified to reflect the power under these Rules and Manual of the court-members to interrogate witnesses. The second sentence of the subdivision is new and modifies Para. 54 *a* and Para. 149*a* of the present manual by requiring that questions of members be submitted to the military judge in writing. This change in current practice was made in order to improve efficiency and to prevent prejudice to either party. Although the Rule states that its intent is to ensure that the questions will "be in a form acceptable to the military judge," it is not the intent of the Committee to grant carte blanche to the military judge in this matter. It is the Committee's intent that the president will utilize the same procedure.

(c) *Objections.* Rule 614(c) is taken from the Federal Rule but modified to reflect the powers of the members to call and interrogate witnesses. This provision generally restates prior law but recognizes counsel's right to request an Article 39(a) session to enter an objection.

Rule 615 Exclusion of witnesses

Rule 615 is taken from the Federal Rule with only minor changes of terminology. The first portion of the Rule is in conformity with prior practice, *e.g.,* Para. 53 *f*, MCM, 1969 (Rev.). The second portion, consisting of subdivisions (2) and (3), represents a substantial departure from prior practice and will authorize the prosecution to designate another individual to sit with the trial counsel. Rule 615 thus modifies Para. 53 *f*. Under the Rule, the military judge lacks any discretion to exclude potential witnesses who come within the scope of Rule 615(2) and (3) unless the accused's constitutional right to a fair trial would be violated. Developing Article III practice recognizes the defense right, upon request, to have a prosecution witness, not excluded because of Rule 615, testify before other prosecution witnesses.

Rule 615 does not prohibit exclusion of either accused or counsel due to misbehavior when such exclusion is not prohibited by the Constitution of the United States, the Uniform Code of Military Justice, this Manual, or these Rules.

2002 Amendment: These changes are intended to extend to victims at courts-martial the same rights granted to victims by the Victims' Rights and Restitution Act of 1990, 42 U.S.C. Sec. 10606(b)(4), giving crime victims '[t]he right to be present at all public court proceedings related to the offense, unless the court determines that testimony by the victim would be materially affected if the victim heard other testimony at trial,' and the Victim Rights Clarification Act of 1997, 18 U.S.C. Sec. 3510, which is restated in subsection (5). For the purposes of this rule, the term 'victim' includes all persons defined as victims in 42 U.S.C. Sec. 10607(e)(2), which means 'a person that has suffered direct physical, emotional, or pecuniary harm as a result of the commission of a crime, including'—(A) in the case of a victim that is an institutional entity, an authorized representative of the entity; and (B) in the case of a victim who is under 18 years of age, incompetent, incapacitated, or deceased, one of the following (in order of preference): (i) a spouse; (ii) a legal guardian; (iii) a parent; (iv) a child; (v) a sibling; (vi) another family member; or (vii) another person designated by the court. The victim's right to remain in the courtroom remains subject to other rules, such as those regarding classified information, witness deportment, and conduct in the courtroom. Subsection (4) is intended to capture only those statutes applicable to courts-martial.

SECTION VII
OPINIONS AND EXPERT TESTIMONY

Rule 701 Opinion testimony by lay witnesses

Rule 701 is taken from the Federal Rule without change and supersedes that portion of Para. 138 *e*, MCM, 1969 (Rev.), which dealt with opinion evidence by lay witnesses. Unlike the prior Manual rule which prohibited lay opinion testimony except when the opinion was of a "kind which is commonly drawn and which cannot, or ordinarily cannot, be conveyed to the court by a mere recitation of the observed facts," the Rule permits opinions or inferences whenever rationally based on the perception of the witness and helpful to either a clear understanding of the testimony or the determination of a fact in issue. Consequently, the Rule is broader in scope than the Manual provision it replaces. The specific examples listed in the Manual, "the speed of an automobile, whether a voice heard was that of a man, woman or child, and whether or not a person was drunk" are all within the potential scope of Rule 701.

2004 Amendment: Rule 701 was modified based on the amendment to Fed.R.Evid. 701, effective 1 December 2000, and is taken from the Federal Rule without change. It prevents parties from proffering an expert as a lay witness in an attempt to evade the gatekeeper and reliability requirements of Rule 702 by providing that testimony cannot qualify under Rule 701 if it is based on "scientific, technical, or other special knowledge within the scope of Rule 702."

Rule 702 Testimony by experts

Rule 702 is taken from the Federal Rule verbatim, and replaces that portion of Para. 138 *e*, MCM, 1969 (Rev.), dealing with expert testimony. Although the Rule is similar to the prior Manual rule, it may be broader and *may* supersede *Frye v. United States*, 293 F.1013 (C.D. Cir. 1923), an issue now being extensively litigated in the Article III courts. The Rule's sole explicit test is whether the evidence in question "will assist the trier of fact to understand the evidence or to determine a fact in issue." Whether any particular piece of evidence comes within the test is normally a matter within the military judge's discretion.

Under Rule 103(a) any objection to an expert on the basis that the individual is not in fact adequately qualified under the Rule will be waived by a failure to so object.

Para. 142 *e* of the 1969 Manual, "Polygraph tests and drug-induced or hypnosis-induced interviews," has been deleted as a result of the adoption of Rule 702. Para. 142 *e* states, "The conclusions based upon or lineartally represented by a polygraph test and conclusions based upon, and the statements of the person interviewed made during a drug-induced or hypnosis-induced interview are inadmissible in evidence." The deletion of the explicit prohibition on such evidence is not intended to make such evidence *per se* admissible, and is not an express authorization for such procedures. Clearly, such evidence must be approached with great care. Considerations surrounding the nature of such evidence, any possible prejudicial effect on a fact finder, and the degree of acceptance of such evidence in the Article III courts are factors to consider in determining whether it can in fact "assist the trier of fact." As of late 1979, the Committee was unaware of any significant decision by a United States Court of Appeals sustaining the admissibility of polygraph evidence in a criminal case, *see e.g., United States v. Masri*, 547 F.2d 932 (5th Cir. 1977); *United States v. Cardarella*, 570 F.2d 264 (8th Cir. 1978), although the Seventh Circuit, *see e.g., United States v. Bursten*, 560 F.2d 779 (7th Cir. 1977) (holding that polygraph admissibility is within the sound discretion of the trial judge) and perhaps the Ninth Circuit, *United States v. Benveniste*, 564 F.2d 335, 339 n.3 (9th Cir. 1977), at least recognize the possible admissibility of such evidence. There is reason to believe that evidence obtained via hypnosis may be treated somewhat more liberally than is polygraph evidence. *See, e.g., Kline v. Ford Motor Co.,* 523 F.2d 1067 (9th Cir. 1975).

2004 Amendment: Rule 702 was modified based on the amendment to Fed. R. Evid. 702, effective 1 December 2000, and is taken from the Federal Rule without change. It provides guidance for courts and parties as to the factors to consider in determining whether an expert's testimony is reliable in light of *Daubert v. Merrell Dow Pharmaceuticals, Inc.,* 509 U.S. 579 (1993), and *Kumho Tire Co. v. Carmichael,* 526 U.S. 137 (1999) (holding that gatekeeper function applies to all expert testimony, not just testimony based on science).

Rule 703 Bases of opinion testimony of experts

Rule 703 is taken from the Federal Rule without change. The Rule is similar in scope to Para. 138 *e* of the 1969 Manual, but is potentially broader as it allows reliance upon "facts or data" whereas the 1969 Manual's limitation was phrased in terms of the personal observation, personal examination or study, or examination or study "of reports of others of a kind customarily considered in the practice of the expert's specialty." Hypothetical questions of the expert are not required by the Rule.

A limiting instruction may be appropriate if the expert while expressing the basis for an opinion states facts or data that are not themselves admissible. *See* Rule 105.

Whether Rule 703 has modified or superseded the *Frye* test for scientific evidence, *Frye v. United States*, 293 F.1013 (D.C. Cir. 1923), is unclear and is now being litigated within the Article III courts.

2004 Amendment: Rule 703 was modified based on the amendment to Fed. R. Evid. 703, effective 1 December 2000, and is virtually identical to its Federal Rule counterpart. It limits the disclosure to the members of inadmissible information that is used as the basis of an expert's opinion. *Compare* Mil. R. Evid. 705.

Rule 704 Opinion on ultimate issue

Rule 704 is taken from the Federal Rule verbatim. The 1969 Manual for Courts-Martial was silent on the issue. The Rule does not permit the witness to testify as to his or her opinion as to the guilt or innocence of the accused or to state legal opinions. Rather it simply allows testimony involving an issue which must be decided by the trier of fact. Although the two may be closely related, they are distinct as a matter of law.

February 1986 Amendment: Fed. R. Evid. 704(b), by operation of Mil. R. Evid. 1102, became effective in the military as Mil. R. Evid. 704(b) on 10 April 1985. The Joint-Service Committee on Military Justice considers Fed. R. Evid. 704(b) an integral part of the Insanity Defense Reform Act, ch. IV, Pub.L. No. 98–473, 98 Stat. 2067–68 (1984), (hereafter the Act). Because proposed legislation to implement these provisions of the Act relating to insanity as an affirmative defense had not yet been enacted in the UCMJ by the date of this Executive Order, the Committee recommended that the President rescind the application of Fed. R. Evid. 704(b) to the military. Even though in effect since 10 April 1985, this change was never published in the Manual.

1986 Amendment: While writing the Manual provisions to implement the enactment of Article 50a, UCMJ ("Military Justice Amendments of 1986," National Defense Authorization Act for fiscal year 1987, Pub.L. No. 99–661, 100 Stat. 3905 (1986)), the drafters rejected adoption of Fed.R.Evid. 704(b). The statutory qualifications for military court members reduce the risk that military court members will be unduly influenced by the presentation of ultimate opinion testimony from psychiatric experts.

Rule 705 Disclosure of facts or data underlying expert opinion

Rule 705 is taken from the Federal Rule without change and is similar in result to the requirement in Para. 138 *e* of the 1969 Manual that the "expert may be required, on direct or cross-examination, to specify the data upon which his opinion was based and to relate the details of his observation, examination, or study." Unlike the 1969 Manual, Rule 705 requires disclosure on direct examination only when the military judge so requires.

Rule 706 Court appointed experts

(a) *Appointment and compensation.* Rule 706(a) is the result of a complete redraft of subdivision (a) of the Federal Rule that was required to be consistent with Article 46 of the Uniform Code of Military Justice which was implemented in Paras. 115 and 116, MCM, 1969 (Rev.). Rule 706(a) states the basic rule that prosecution, defense, military judge, and the court members all have equal opportunity under Article 46 to obtain expert witnesses. The second sentence of the subdivision replaces subdivision (b) of the Federal Rule which is inapplicable to the armed forces in light of Para. 116, MCM, 1969 (Rev.).

(b) *Disclosure of employment.* Rule 706(b) is taken from Fed.R.Evid. 706(c) without change. The 1969 Manual was silent on the issue, but the subdivision should not change military practice.

(c) *Accused's expert of own selection.* Rule 706(c) is similar in intent to subdivision (d) of the Federal Rule and adapts that Rule to military practice. The subdivision makes it clear that the defense may call its own expert witnesses at its own expense without the necessity of recourse to Para. 116.

Rule 707 Polygraph Examinations.

Rule 707 is new and is similar to Cal. Evid. Code 351.1 (West 1988 Supp.). The Rule prohibits the use of polygraph evidence in courts-martial and is based on several policy grounds. There is a real danger that court members will be misled by polygraph evidence that "is likely to be shrouded with an aura of near infallibility". *United States v. Alexander*, 526 F.2d 161, 168-169 (8th Cir. 1975). To the extent that the members accept polygraph evidence as unimpeachable or conclusive, despite cautionary instructions from the military judge, the members "traditional responsibility to collectively ascertain the facts and adjudge guilt or innocence is preempted". *Id.* There is also a danger of confusion of the issues, especially when conflicting polygraph evidence diverts the members' attention from a determination of guilt or innocence to a judgment of the validity and limitations of polygraphs. This could result in the court-martial degenerating into a trial of the polygraph machine. *State v. Grier*, 300 S.E.2d 351 (N.C. 1983). Polygraph evidence also can result in a substantial waste of time when the collateral issues regarding the reliability of the particular test and qualifications of the specific polygraph examiner must be litigated in every case. Polygraph evidence places a burden on the administration of justice that outweighs the probative value of the evidence. The reliability of polygraph evidence has not been sufficiently established and its use at trial impinges upon the integrity of the judicial system. *See People v. Kegler*, 242 Cal. Rptr. 897 (Cal. Ct. App. 1987). Thus, this amendment adopts a bright-line rule that polygraph evidence is not admissible by any party to a court-martial even if stipulated to by the parties. This amendment is not intended to accept or reject *United States v. Gipson*, 24 M.J. 343 (C.M.A. 1987), concerning the standard for admissibility of other scientific evidence under Mil. R. Evid. 702 or the continued vitality of *Frye v. United States*, 293 F. 1013 (D.C. Cir. 1923). Finally, subsection (b) of the rule ensures that any statements which are otherwise admissible are not rendered inadmissible solely because the statements were made during a polygraph examination.

SECTION VIII

HEARSAY

Rule 801 Definitions

(a) *Statement.* Rule 801(a) is taken from the Federal Rule without change and is similar to Para. 139 *a* of the 1969 Manual.

(b) *Declarant.* Rule 801(b) is taken from the Federal Rule verbatim and is the same definition used in prior military practice.

(c) *Hearsay.* Rule 801(c) is taken from the Federal Rule verbatim. It is similar to the 1969 Manual definition, found in Para. 139 *a*, which stated: "A statement which is offered in evidence to prove the truth of the matters stated therein, but which was not made by the author when a witness before the court at a hearing in which it is so offered, is hearsay." Although the two definitions are basically identical, they actually differ sharply as a result of the Rule's exceptions which are discussed *infra.*

(d) *Statements which are not hearsay.* Rule 801(d) is taken from the Federal Rule without change and removes certain categories of evidence from the definition of hearsay. In all cases, those categories represent hearsay within the meaning of the 1969 Manual definition.

(1) *Prior statement by witness.* Rule 801(d)(1) is taken from the Federal Rule without change and removes certain prior statements by the witness from the definition of hearsay. Under the 1969 Manual rule, an out-of-court statement not within an exception to the hearsay rule and unadopted by the testifying witness, is inadmissible hearsay notwithstanding the fact that the declarant is now on the stand and able to be cross-examined, Para. 139*a*; *United States v. Burge*, 1 M.J. 408 (C.M.A. 1976) (Cook, J., concurring). The justification for the 1969 Manual rule is presumably the traditional view that out-of-court statements cannot be adequately tested by cross-examination because of the time differential between the making of the statement and the giving of the in-court testimony. The Federal Rules of Evidence Advisory Committee rejected this view in part believing both that later

cross-examination is sufficient to ensure reliability and that earlier statements are usually preferable to later ones because of the possibility of memory loss. *See generally,* 4 J. Weinstein & M. Berger, WEINSTEIN'S EVIDENCE Para. 801(d)(1)(01)(1978). Rule 801(d)(1) thus not only makes an important shift in the military theory of hearsay, but also makes an important change in law by making admissible a number of types of statements that were either inadmissible or likely to be inadmissible under prior military law.

Rule 801(d)(1)(A) makes admissible on the merits a statement inconsistent with the in-court testimony of the witness when the prior statement "was given under oath subject to the penalty of perjury at a trial, hearing, or other proceeding, or in a deposition." The Rule does not require that the witness have been subject to cross-examination at the earlier proceeding, but requires that the witness must have been under oath and subject to penalty of perjury. Although the definition of "trial, hearing, or other proceeding" is uncertain, it is apparent that the Rule was intended to include grand jury testimony and may be extremely broad in scope. *See, United States v. Castro-Ayon*, 537 F.2d 1055 (9th Cir.), *cert. denied,* 429 U.S. 983 (1976) (tape recorded statements given under oath at a Border Patrol station found to be within the Rule). It should clearly apply to Article 32 hearings. The Rule does not require as a prerequisite a statement "given under oath subject to the penalty of perjury." The mere fact that a statement was given under oath may not be sufficient. No foundation other than that indicated as a condition precedent in the Rule is apparently necessary to admit the statement under the Rule. *But see* WEINSTEIN'S EVIDENCE 801–74 (1978).

Rule 801(d)(1)(B) makes admissible as substantive evidence on the merits a statement consistent with the in-court testimony of the witness and "offered to rebut an express or implied charge against the declarant of recent fabrication or improper influence or motive." Unlike Rule 801(d)(1)(A), the earlier consistent statement need not have been made under oath or at any type of proceeding. On its face, the Rule does not require that the consistent statement offered have been made prior to the time the improper influence or motive arose or prior to the alleged recent fabrication. Notwithstanding this, the Supreme Court has read such a requirement into the rule. *Tome v. United States*, 513 U.S. 150, 115 S.Ct. 696, 130 L.Ed. 2d 574 (1995); *see also United States v. Allison*, 49 M.J. 54 (C.A.A.F. 1998). The limitation does not, however, prevent admission of a consistent statement made after an inconsistent statement but before the improper influence or motive arose. *United States v. Scholle*, 553 F. 2d 1109 (8th Cir. 1977). Rule 801(d)(1)(B) provides a possible means to admit evidence of fresh complaint in prosecution of sexual offenses. Although limited to circumstances in which there is a charge, for example, of recent fabrication, the Rule, when applicable, would permit not only fact of fresh complaint, as is presently possible, but also the entire portion of the consistent statement.

Under Rule 801(d)(1)(C) a statement of identification is not hearsay. The content of the statement as well as the fact of identification is admissible. The Rule must be read in conjunction with Rule 321 which governs the admissibility of statements of pretrial identification.

(2) *Admission by party opponent.* Rule 801(d)(2) eliminates a number of categories of statements from the scope of the hearsay rule. Unlike those statements within the purview of Rule 802(d)(1), these statements would have come within the exceptions to the hearsay rule as recognized in the 1969 Manual. Consequently, their "reclassification" is a matter of academic interest only. No practical differences result. The reclassification results from a belief that the adversary system impels admissibility and that reliability is not a significant factor.

Rule 801(d)(2)(A) makes admissible against a party a statement made in either the party's individual or representative capacity. This was treated as an admission or confession under Para. 140 *a* of the 1969 Manual, and is an exception of the prior hearsay rule.

Rule 801(d)(2)(B) makes admissible "a statement of which the party has manifested the party's adoption or belief in its truth." This is an adoptive admission and was an exception to the prior hearsay rule. *Cf.* Para. 140 *a*(4) of the 1969 Manual. While silence may be treated as an admission on the facts of a given case, *see*, Rule 304(h)(3) and the analysis thereto, under Rule 801(d)(2) that silence must have been intended by the declarant to have been an assertion. Otherwise, the statement will not be hearsay within the meaning of Rule 801(d)(2) and will presumably be admissible, if at all, as circumstantial evidence.

Rule 801(d)(2)(C) makes admissible "a statement by a person authorized by the party to make a statement concerning the subject." While this was not expressly dealt with by the 1969 Manual, it would be admissible under prior law as an admission; *Cf.* Para. 140 *b*, utilizing agency theory.

Rule 801(d)(2)(D) makes admissible "a statement by the party's agent or servant concerning a matter within the scope of the agency or employment of the agent or servant, made during the existence of the relationship." These statements would appear to be admissible under prior law. Statements made by interpreters, as by an individual serving as a translator for a service member in a foreign nation who is, for example, attempting to consummate a drug transaction with a non-English speaking person, should be admissible under Rule 801(d)(2)(D) or Rule 801(d)(2)(C).

Rule 801(d)(2)(E) makes admissible "a statement by a co-conspirator of a party during the course and in furtherance of the conspiracy." This is similar to the military hearsay exception found in Para. 140 *b* of the 1969 Manual. Whether a conspiracy existed for purposes of this Rule is solely a matter for the military judge. Although this is the prevailing Article III rule, it is also the consequence of the Military Rules' modification to Federal Rule of Evidence 104(b). Rule 801(d)(2)(E) does not address many critical procedural matters associated with the use of co-conspirator evidence. *See* generally, Comment, Restructuring the Independent Evidence Requirement of the Coconspirator Hearsay Exception, 127 U.Pa.L.Rev. 1439 (1979). For example, the burden of proof placed on the proponent is unclear although a preponderance appears to be the developing Article III trend. Similarly, there is substantial confusion surrounding the question of whether statements of an alleged co-conspirator may themselves be considered by the military judge when determining whether the declarant was in fact a co-conspirator. This process, known as bootstrapping, was not permitted under prior military law. *See e.g., United States v. Duffy*, 49 C.M.R. 208, 210 (A.F.C.M.R. 1974); *United States v. LaBossiere*, 13 C.M.A. 337, 339, 32 C.M.R. 337, 339 (1962). A number of circuits have suggested that Rule 104(a) allows the use of such statements, but at least two circuits have held that other factors prohibit bootstrapping. *United States v. James*, 590 F.2d 575 (5th Cir.) (en banc), *cert. denied*, 442 U.S. 917 (1979); *United States v. Valencia*, 609 F.2d 603 (2d Cir. 1979). Until such time as the Article III practice is settled, discretion would dictate that prior military law be followed and that bootstrapping not be allowed. Other procedural factors may also prove troublesome although not to the same extent as bootstrapping. For example, it appears to be appropriate for the military judge to determine the co-conspirator question in a preliminary Article 39(a) session. Although receipt of evidence "subject to later connection" or proof is legally possible, the probability of serious error, likely requiring a mistrial, is apparent.

Rule 801(d)(2)(E) does not appear to change what may be termed the "substantive law" relating to statements made by co-conspirators. Thus, whether a statement was made by a co-conspirator in furtherance of a conspiracy is a question for the military judge, and a statement made by an individual after he or she was withdrawn from a conspiracy is not made "in furtherance of the conspiracy."

Official statements made by an officer—as by the commanding officer of a battalion, squadron, or ship, or by a staff officer, in an endorsement of other communication—are not excepted from the operation of the hearsay rule merely by reason of the official character of the communication or the rank or position of the officer making it.

The following examples of admissibility under this Rule may be helpful:

(1) *A is being tried for assaulting B.* The defense presents the testimony of C that just before the assault C heard B say to A that B was about to kill A with B's knife. The testimony of C is not hearsay, for it is offered to show that A acted in self-defense because B made the statement and not to prove the truth of B's statement.

(2) *A is being tried for rape of B.* If B testifies at trial, the testimony of B that she had previously identified A as her attacker at an identification lineup would be admissible under Rule 801(d)(1)(C) to prove that it was A who raped B.

(3) *Private A is being tried for disobedience of a certain order given him orally by Lieutenant B.* C is able to testify that he heard Lieutenant B give the order to A. This testimony, including testimony of C as to the terms of the order, would not be hearsay.

(4) *The accused is being tried for the larceny of clothes from a locker.* A is able to testify that B told A that B saw the accused leave the quarters in which the locker was located with a bundle resembling clothes about the same time the clothes were stolen. This testimony from A would not be admissible to prove that facts stated by B.

(5) *The accused is being tried for wrongfully selling government clothing.* A policeman is able to testify that while on duty he saw the accused go into a shop with a bundle under his arm; that he entered the shop and the accused ran away; that he was unable to catch the accused; and that thereafter the policeman asked the proprietor of the shop what the accused was doing there; and that the proprietor replied that the accused sold him some uniforms for which he paid the accused $30. Testimony by the policeman as to the reply of the proprietor would be hearsay if it was offered to prove the facts stated by the proprietor. The fact that the policeman was acting in the line of duty at the time the proprietor made the statement would not render the evidence admissible to prove the truth of the statement.

(6) *A defense witness in an assault case testifies on direct examination that the accused did not strike the alleged victim.* On cross-examination by the prosecution, the witness admits that at a preliminary investigation he stated that the accused had struck the alleged victim. The testimony of the witness as to this statement will be admissible if he was under oath at the time and subject to a prosecution for perjury.

Rule 802 Hearsay rule

Rule 802 is taken generally from the Federal Rule but has been modified to recognize the application of any applicable Act of Congress.

Although the basic rule of inadmissibility for hearsay is identical with that found in Para. 139*a* of the 1969 Manual, there is a substantial change in military practice as a result of Rule 103(a). Under the 1969 Manual, hearsay was incompetent evidence and did not require an objection to be inadmissible. Under the new Rules, however, admission of hearsay will not be error unless there is an objection to the hearsay. *See* Rule 103(a).

Rule 803 Hearsay exceptions; availability of declarant Immaterial

Rule 803 is taken generally from the Federal Rule with modifications as needed for adaptation to military practice. Overall, the Rule is similar to practice under Manual Paras. 142 and 144 of the 1969 Manual. The Rule is, however, substantially more detailed and broader in scope than the 1969 Manual.

(1) *Present sense impression.* Rule 803(1) is taken from the Federal Rule verbatim. The exception it establishes was not recognized in the 1969 Manual for Courts-Martial. It is somewhat similar to a spontaneous exclamation, but does not require a startling event. A fresh complaint by a victim of a sexual offense may come within this exception depending upon the circumstances.

(2) *Excited utterance.* Rule 803(2) is taken from the Federal Rule verbatim. Although similar to Para. 142 *b* of the 1969 Manual with respect to spontaneous exclamations, the Rule would appear to be more lenient as it does not seem to require independent evidence that the startling event occurred. An examination of the Federal Rules of Evidence Advisory Committee Note indicates some uncertainty, however. S. Saltzburg & K. Redden, FEDERAL RULES OF EVIDENCE MANUAL 540 (2d ed. 1977). A fresh complaint of a sexual offense may come within this exception depending on the circumstances.

(3) *Then existing mental, emotional, or physical condition.* Rule 803(3) is taken from the Federal Rule verbatim. The Rule is similar to that found in 1969 Manual Para. 142d but may be slightly more limited in that it may not permit statements by an individual to be offered to disclose the intent of another person. Fresh complaint by a victim of a sexual offense may come within this exception.

(4) *Statements for purposes of medical diagnosis or treatment.* Rule 803(4) is taken from the Federal Rule verbatim. It is substantially broader than the state of mind or body exception found in Para. 142 *d* of the 1969 Manual. It allows, among other matters, statements as to the cause of the medical problem pres-

ented for diagnosis or treatment. Potentially, the Rule is extremely broad and will permit statements made even to non-medical personnel (*e.g.*, members of one's family) and on behalf of others so long as the statements are made for the purpose of diagnosis or treatment. The basis for the exception is the presumption that an individual seeking relief from a medical problem has incentive to make accurate statements. *See generally*, 4 J. Weinstein & M. Berger, WEINSTEIN'S EVIDENCE Para. 804(4)(01) (1978). The admissibility under this exception of those portions of a statement not relevant to diagnosis or treatment is uncertain. Although statements made to a physician, for example, merely to enable the physician to testify, do not appear to come within the Rule, statements solicited in good faith by others in order to ensure the health of the declarant would appear to come within the Rule. Rule 803(4) may be used in an appropriate case to present evidence of fresh complaint in a sexual case.

(5) *Recorded recollection.* Rule 803(5) is taken from the Federal Rule without change, and is similar to the present exception for past recollection recorded found in Paras. 146 *a* and 149 *c*(1)(b) of the 1969 Manual except that under the Rule the memorandum may be read but not presented to the fact finder unless offered by the adverse party.

(6) *Record of regularly conducted activity.* Rule 803(6) is taken generally from the Federal Rule. Two modifications have been made, however, to adapt the rule to military practice. The definition of "business" has been expanded to explicitly include the armed forces to ensure the continued application of this hearsay exception, and a descriptive list of documents, taken generally from 1969 Manual Para. 144 *d*, has been included. Although the activities of the armed forces do not constitute a profit making business, they do constitute a business within the meaning of the hearsay exception, *see* Para. 144 *c*, of the 1969 Manual, as well as a "regularly conducted activity."

The specific types of records included within the Rule are those which are normally records of regularly conducted activity within the armed forces. They are included because of their importance and because their omission from the Rule would be impracticable. The fact that a record is of a type described within subdivision does not eliminate the need for its proponent to show that the *particular* record comes within the Rule when the record is challenged; the Rule does establish that the *types* of records listed are normally business records.

Chain of custody receipts or documents have been included to emphasize their administrative nature. Such documents perform the critical function of accounting for property obtained by the United States Government. Although they may be used as prosecution evidence, their primary purpose is simply one of property accountability. In view of the primary administrative purpose of these matters, it was necessary to provide expressly for their admissibility as an exception to the hearsay rule in order to clearly reject the interpretation of Para. 144 *d* of the 1969 Manual with respect to chain of custody forms as set forth in *United States v. Porter*, 7 M.J. 32 (C.M.A. 1979) and *United States v. Nault*, 4 M.J. 318 (C.M.A. 1978) insofar as they concerned chain of custody forms.

Laboratory reports have been included in recognition of the function of forensic laboratories as impartial examining centers. The report is simply a record of "regularly conducted" activity of the laboratory. *See, e.g., United States v. Strangstalien*, 7 M.J. 225 (C.M.A. 1979); *United States v. Evans*, 21 U.S.C.M.A. 579, 45 C.M.R. 353 (1972).

Paragraph 144 *d* prevented a record "made principally with a view to prosecution, or other disciplinary or legal action ..." from being admitted as a business record. The limitation has been deleted, *but see* Rule 803(8)(B) and its Analysis. It should be noted that a record of "regularly conducted activity" is unlikely to have a prosecutorial intent in any event.

The fact that a record may fit within another exception, *e.g.*, Rule 803(8), does not generally prevent it from being admissible under this subdivision although it would appear that the exclusion found in Rule 803(8)(B) for "matters observed by police officers and other personnel acting in a law enforcement capacity" prevent any such record from being admissible as a record of regularly conducted activity. Otherwise the limitation in subdivision (8) would serve no useful purpose. *See also* Analysis to Rule 803(8)(B).

Rule 803(6) is generally similar to the 1969 Manual rule but is potentially broader because of its use of the expression "regularly conducted" activity in addition to "business". It also permits records of opinion which were prohibited by Para. 144 *d* of the 1969 Manual. Offsetting these factors is the fact that the Rule requires that the memorandum was "made at or near the time by, or from information transmitted by a person with knowledge ...", but Para. 144 *c* of the 1969 Manual rule expressly did not require such knowledge as a condition of admissibility.

2004 Amendment: Rule 803(6) was modified based on the amendment to Fed. R. Evid. 803(6), effective 1 December 2000. It permits a foundation for business records to be made through certification to save the parties the expense and inconvenience of producing live witnesses for what is often perfunctory testimony. The Rule incorporates federal statutes that allow certification in a criminal proceeding in a court of the United States. (*See, e.g.*, 18 U.S.C. § 3505, Foreign records of regularly conducted activity.) The Rule does not include foreign records of regularly conducted business activity in civil cases as provided in its Federal Rule counterpart. This Rule works together with Mil. R. Evid. 902(11).

(7) *Absence of entry in records kept in accordance with the provisions of paragraph (6).* Rule 803(7) is taken verbatim from the Federal Rule. The Rule is similar to Paras. 143 *a*(2)(h) and 143 *b*(3) of the 1969 Manual.

(8) *Public records and reports.* Rule 803(8) has been taken generally from the Federal Rule but has been slightly modified to adapt it to the military environment. Rule 803(8)(B) has been redrafted to apply to "police officers and other personnel acting in a law enforcement capacity" rather the Federal Rule's "police officers and other law enforcement ersonnel". The change was necessitated by the fact that all military personnel may act in a disciplinary capacity. Any officer, for example, regardless of assignment, may potentially act as a military policeman. The capacity within which a member of the armed forces acts may be critical.

The Federal Rule was also modified to include a list of records that, when made pursuant to a duty required by law, will be admissible notwithstanding the fact that they may have been made as "matters observed by police officers and other personnel acting in a law enforcement capacity." Their inclusion is a direct result of the fact, discussed above, that military personnel may all function within a law enforcement capacity. The Committee determined it would be impracticable and contrary to the intent of the Rule to allow the admissibility of records which are truly administrative in nature and unrelated to the problems inherent in records prepared only for purposes of prosecution to depend upon whether the maker was at that given instant acting in a law enforcement capacity. The language involved is taken generally from Para. 144 *b* of the 1969 Manual. Admissibility depends upon whether the record is "a record of a fact or event if made by a person within the scope of his official duties and those duties included a duty to know or ascertain through appropriate and trustworthy channels of information the truth of the fact or event ..." Whether any given record was obtained in such a trustworthy fashion is a question for the military judge. The explicit limitation on admissibility of records made "principally with a view to prosecution" found in Para. 144 *d* has been deleted.

The fact that a document may be admissible under another exception to the hearsay rule, *e.g.*, Rule 803(6), does not make it inadmissible under this subdivision.

Military Rule of Evidence 803(8) raises numerous significant questions. Rule 803(8)(A) extends to "records, reports, statements, or data compilations" of public offices or agencies, setting forth (A) the activities of the office or agency." The term "public office or agency" within this subdivision is defined to include any government office or agency including those of the armed forces. Within the civilian context, the definition of "public offices or agencies" is fairly clear and the line of demarcation between governmental and private action can be clearly drawn in most cases. The same may not be true within the armed forces. It is unlikely that every action taken by a servicemember is an "activity" of the department of which he or she is a member. Presumably, Rule 803(8) should be restricted to activities of formally sanctioned instrumentalities roughly similar to civilian entities. For example, the activities of a squadron headquarters or a staff section would come within the definition of "office or agency." Pursuant to this rationale, there is no need to have a military regulation or directive to make a statement of a "public office or agency" under Rule 803(8)(A). However, such regulations or directives might well be highly useful in establishing that a given administrative mechanism was indeed an "office or agency" within the meaning of the Rule.

Rule 803(8)(B) encompasses "matters observed pursuant to duty imposed by law as to which matters there was a duty to report...." This portion of Rule 803(8) is broader than subdivision (8)(A) as it extends to far more than just the normal procedures of an office or agency. Perhaps because of this extent, it requires that there be a specific duty to observe and report. This duty could take the form of a statement, general order, regulation, or any competent order.

The exclusion in the Federal Rule for "matters observed by police officers" was intended to prevent use of the exception for evaluative reports as the House Committee believed them to be unreliable. Because of the explicit language of the exclusion, normal statutory construction leads to the conclusion that reports which would be within Federal or Military Rule 803(8) but for the exclusion in (8)(B) are not otherwise admissible under Rule 803(6). Otherwise the inclusion of the limitation would serve virtually no purpose whatsoever. There is no contradiction between the exclusion in Rule 803(8)(B) and the specific documents made admissible in Rule 803(8) (and Rule 803(6)) because those documents are not matters "observed by police officers and other personnel acting in a law enforcement capacity." To the extent that they might be so considered, the specific language included by the Committee is expressly intended to reject the subdivision (8)(B) limitation. Note, however, that all forms of evidence not within the specific item listing of the Rule but within the (8)(B) exclusion will be admissible insofar as Rule 803(8) is concerned, whether the evidence is military or civilian in origin.

A question not answered by Rule 803(8) is the extent to which a regulation or directive may circumscribe Rule 803(8). Thus, if a regulation establishes a given format or procedure for a report which is not followed, is an otherwise admissible piece of evidence inadmissible for lack of conformity with the regulation or directive? The Committee did not address this issue in the context of adopting the Rule. However, it would be at least logical to argue that a record not made in substantial conformity with an implementing directive is not sufficiently reliable to be admissible. *See*, Rule 403. Certainly, military case law predating the Military Rules may resolve this matter to the extent to which it is not based purely on now obsolete Manual provisions. As the modifications to subdivision (8) dealing with specific records retains the present Manual language, it is particularly likely that present case law will survive in this area.

Rule 803(8)(C) makes admissible, but only against the Government, "factual findings resulting from an investigation made pursuant to authority granted by law, unless the sources of information or other circumstances indicate lack of trustworthiness." This provision will make factual findings made, for example, by an Article 32 Investigating Officer or by a Court of Inquiry admissible on behalf of an accused. Because the provision applies only to "factual findings," great care must be taken to distinguish such factual determinations from opinions, recommendations, and incidental inferences.

(9) *Records of vital statistics.* Rule 803(9) is taken verbatim from the Federal Rule and had no express equivalent in the 1969 Manual.

(10) *Absence of public record or entry.* Rule 803(10) is taken verbatim from the Federal Rules and is similar to 1969 Manual Para. 143 *a*(2)(g).

(11-13) *Records of religious organizations: Marriage, baptismal, and similar certificates: Family records.* Rule 802(11)–(13) are all taken verbatim from the Federal Rules and had no express equivalents in the 1969 Manual.

(14-16) *Records of documents affecting an interest in property: Statements in documents affecting an interest in property; Statements in ancient documents.* Rules 803(14)–(16) are taken verbatim from the Federal Rules and had no express equivalents in the 1969 Manual. Although intended primarily for civil cases, they all have potential importance to courts-martial.

(17) *Market reports, commercial publications.* Rule 803(17) is taken generally from the Federal Rule. Government price lists have been added because of the degree of reliance placed upon them in military life. Although included within the general Rule, the Committee believed it inappropriate and impracticable not to clarify the matter by specific reference. The Rule is similar in scope and effect to the 1969 Manual Para. 144 *f* except that it lacks the Manual's specific reference to an absence of entries. The effect, if any, of the difference is unclear.

(18) *Learned treaties.* Rule 803(18) is taken from the Federal

Rule without change. Unlike Para. 138 *e* of the 1969 Manual, which allowed use of such statements only for impeachment, this Rule allows substantive use on the merits of statements within treaties if relied upon in direct testimony or called to the expert's attention on cross-examination. Such statements may not, however, be given to the fact finder as exhibits.

(19-20) *Reputation concerning personal or family history; reputation concerning boundaries or general history.* Rules 803(19)–(20) are taken without change from the Federal Rules and had no express equivalents in the 1969 Manual.

(21) *Reputation as to character.* Rule 803(21) is taken from the Federal Rule without change. It is similar to Para. 138 *f* of the 1969 Manual in that it creates an exception to the hearsay rule for reputation evidence. "Reputation" and "community" are defined in Rule 405(d), and "community" includes a "military organization regardless of size." Affidavits and other written statements are admissible to show character under Rule 405(c), and, when offered pursuant to that Rule, are an exception to the hearsay rule.

(22) *Judgment or previous conviction.* Rule 803(22) is taken from the Federal Rule but has been modified to recognize convictions of a crime punishable by a dishonorable discharge, a unique punishment not present in civilian life. *See also* Rule 609 and its Analysis.

There is no equivalent to this Rule in military law. Although the Federal Rule is clearly applicable to criminal cases, its original intent was to allow use of a prior criminal conviction in a subsequent civil action. To the extent that it is used for criminal cases, significant constitutional issues are raised, especially if the prior conviction is a foreign one, a question almost certainly not anticipated by the Federal Rules Advisory Committee.

(23) *Judgment as to personal, family or general history, or boundaries.* Rule 803(23) is taken verbatim from the Federal Rule, and had no express equivalent in the 1969 Manual. Although intended for civil cases, it clearly has potential use in courts-martial for such matters as proof of jurisdiction.

Rule 804 Hearsay exception; declarant unavailable

(a) *Definition of unavailability.* Subdivisions (a)(1)–(a)(5) of Rule 804 are taken from the Federal Rule without change and are generally similar to the relevant portions of Paras. 145 *a* and 145 *b* of the 1969 Manual, except that Rule 804(a)(3) provides that a witness who "testifies as to a lack of memory of the subject matter of the declarant's statement" is unavailable. The Rule also does not distinguish between capital and non-capital cases.

February 1986 Amendment: The phrase "claim or lack of memory" was changed to "claim of lack of memory" to correct an error in MCM, 1984.

Rule 804(a)(6) is new and has been added in recognition of certain problems, such as combat operations, that are unique to the armed forces. Thus, Rule 804(a)(6) will make unavailable a witness who is unable to appear and testify in person for reason of military necessity within the meaning of Article 49(d)(2). The meaning of "military necessity" must be determined by reference to the cases construing Article 49. The expression is not intended to be a general escape clause, but must be restricted to the limited circumstances that would permit use of a deposition.

(b) *Hearsay exceptions*

(1) *Former testimony.* The first portion of Rule 804(b)(1) is taken from the Federal Rule with omission of the language relating to civil cases. The second portion is new and has been included to clarify the extent to which those military tribunals in which a verbatim record normally is not kept come within the Rule.

The first portion of Rule 804(b)(1) makes admissible former testimony when "the party against whom the testimony is now offered had an opportunity and similar motive to develop the testimony by direct, cross, or redirect examination." Unlike Para. 145 *b* of the 1969 Manual, the Rule does not explicitly require that the accused, when the evidence is offered against him or her, have been "afforded at the former trial an opportunity, to be adequately represented by counsel." Such a requirement should be read into the Rule's condition that the party have had "opportunity and similar motive." In contrast to the 1969 Manual, the Rule does not distinguish between capital and non-capital cases.

The second portion of Rule 804(b)(1) has been included to ensure that testimony from military tribunals, many of which ordinarily do not have verbatim records, will not be admissible unless such testimony is presented in the form of a verbatim record. The Committee believed substantive use of former testimony to be too important to be presented in the form of an incomplete statement.

Investigations under Article 32 of the Uniform Code of Military Justice present a special problem. Rule 804(b)(1) requires that "the party against whom the testimony is now offered had an opportunity and similar motive to develop the testimony" at the first hearing. The "similar motive" requirement was intended primarily to ensure sufficient identity of issues between the two proceedings and thus to ensure an adequate interest in examination of the witness. *See, e.g.*, J. Weinstein & M. Berger, WEINSTEIN'S EVIDENCE Para. 804(b)(1)((04)) (1978). Because Article 32 hearings represent a unique hybrid of preliminary hearings and grand juries with features dissimilar to both, it was particularly difficult for the Committee to determine exactly how subdivision (b)(1) of the Federal Rule would apply to Article 32 hearings. The specific difficulty stems from the fact that Article 32 hearings were intended by Congress to function as discovery devices for the defense as well as to recommend an appropriate disposition of charges to the convening authority. *Hutson v. United States*, 19 U.S.C.M.A. 437, 42 C.M.R. 39 (1970); *United States v. Samuels*, 10 U.S.C.M.A. 206, 212, 27 C.M.R. 280, 286 (1959). *See generally, Hearing on H.R. 2498 Before a Subcomm. of the House Comm. on Armed Services*, 81st Cong., 1st Sess., 997 (1949). It is thus permissible, for example, for a defense counsel to limit cross-examination of an adverse witness at an Article 32 hearing using the opportunity for discovery alone, for example, rather than impeachment. In such a case, the defense would not have the requisite "similar motive" found within Rule 804(b)(1).

Notwithstanding the inherent difficulty of determining the defense counsel's motive at an Article 32 hearing, the Rule is explicitly intended to prohibit use of testimony given at an Article 32 hearing unless the requisite "similar motive" was present during that hearing. It is clear that some Article 32 testimony is admissible under the Rule notwithstanding the Congressionally sanctioned discovery purpose of the Article 32 hearing. Consequently, one is left with the question of the extent to which the

Rule actually does apply to Article 32 testimony. The only apparent practical solution to what is otherwise an irresolvable dilemma is to read the Rule as permitting only Article 32 testimony preserved via a verbatim record that is not objected to as having been obtained without the requisite "similar motive." While defense counsel's assertion of his or her intent in not examining one or more witnesses or in not fully examining a specific witness is not binding upon the military judge, clearly the burden of establishing admissibility under the Rule is on the prosecution and the burden so placed may be impossible to meet should the defense counsel adequately raise the issue. As a matter of good trial practice, a defense counsel who is limiting cross-examination at the Article 32 hearing because of discovery should announce that intent sometime during the Article 32 hearing so that the announcement may provide early notice to all concerned and hopefully avoid the necessity for counsel to testify at the later trial.

The Federal Rule was modified by the Committee to require that testimony offered under Rule 804(b)(1) which was originally "given before courts-martial, courts of inquiry, military commissions, other military tribunals, and before proceedings pursuant to or equivalent to those required by Article 32" and which is otherwise admissible under the Rule be offered in the form of a verbatim record. The modification was intended to ensure accuracy in view of the fact that only summarized or minimal records are required of some types of military proceedings.

An Article 32 hearing is a "military tribunal." The Rule distinguishes between Article 32 hearings and other military tribunals in order to recognize that there are other proceedings which are considered the equivalent of Article 32 hearings for purposes of former testimony under Rule 804(b)(1).

(2) *Statement under belief of impending death.* Rule 804(b)(2) is taken from the Federal Rule except that the language, "for any offense resulting in the death of the alleged victim," has been added and reference to civil proceedings has been omitted. The new language has been added because there is no justification for limiting the exception only to those cases in which a homicide charge has actually been preferred. Due to the violent nature of military operations, it may be appropriate to charge a lesser included offense rather than homicide. The same justifications for the exception are applicable to lesser included offenses which are also, of course, of lesser severity. The additional language, taken from Para. 142 *a*, thus retains the 1969 Manual rule, modification of which was viewed as being impracticable.

Rule 804(b)(2) is similar to the dying declaration exception found in Para. 142 *a* of the 1969 Manual, except that the Military Rule does not require that the declarant be dead. So long as the declarant is unavailable and the offense is one for homicide or other offense resulting in the death of the alleged victim, the hearsay exception may be applicable. This could, for example, result from a situation in which the accused, intending to shoot A, shoots both A and B; uttering the hearsay statement, under a belief of impending death, B dies, and although A recovers, A is unavailable to testify at trial. In a trial of the accused for killing B, A's statement will be admissible.

There is no requirement that death immediately follow the declaration, but the declaration is not admissible under this exception if the declarant had a hope of recovery. The declaration may be made by spoken words or intelligible signs or may be in writing. It may be spontaneous or in response to solicitation, including leading questions. The utmost care should be exercised in weighing statements offered under this exception since they are often made under circumstances of mental and physical debility and are not subject to the usual tests of veracity. The military judge may exclude those declarations which are viewed as being unreliable. *See*, Rule 403.

A dying declaration and its maker may be contradicted and impeached in the same manner as other testimony and witnesses. Under the prior law, the fact that the deceased did not believe in a deity or in future rewards or punishments may be offered to affect the weight of a declaration offered under this Rule but does not defeat admissibility. Whether such evidence is now admissible in the light of Rule 610 is unclear.

(3) *Statement against interest.* Rule 804(b) is taken from the Federal Rule without change, and has no express equivalent in the 1969 Manual. It has, however, been made applicable by case law, *United States v. Johnson*, 3 M.J. 143 (C.M.A. 1977). It makes admissible statements against a declarant's interest, whether pecuniary, proprietary, or penal when a reasonable person in the position of the declarant would not have made the statement unless such a person would have believed it to be true.

The Rule expressly recognizes the penal interest exception and permits a statement tending to expose the declarant to criminal liability. The penal interest exception is qualified, however, when the declaration is offered to exculpate the accused by requiring the "corroborating circumstances clearly indicate the trustworthiness of the statement." This requirement is applicable, for example, when a third party confesses to the offense the accused is being tried for and the accused offers the third party's statement in evidence to exculpate the accused. The basic penal interest exception is established as a matter of constitutional law by the Supreme Court's decision in *Chambers v. Mississippi*, 410 U.S. 284 (1973), which may be broader than the Rule as the case may not require either corroborating evidence or an unavailable declarant.

In its present form, the Rule fails to address a particularly vexing problem— that of the declaration against penal interest which implicates the accused as well as the declarant. On the face of the Rule, such a statement should be admissible, subject to the effects, if any, of *Bruton v. United States*, 391 U.S. 123 (1968) and Rule 306. Notwithstanding this, there is considerable doubt as to the applicability of the Rule to such a situation. *See generally,* 4 J. Weinstein & M. Berger, WEINSTEIN'S EVIDENCE 804–93, 804–16 (1978). Although the legislative history reflects an early desire on the part of the Federal Rules of Evidence Advisory Committee to prohibit such testimony, a provision doing so was not included in the material reviewed by Congress. Although the House included such a provision, it did so apparently in large part based upon a view that *Bruton, supra*, prohibited such statements— arguably an erroneous view of *Bruton, supra, see, Bruton, supra* n.3 at 128, *Dutton v. Evans*, 400 U.S. 74 (1970). The Conference Committee deleted the House provision, following the Senate's desires, because it believed it inappropriate to "codify constitutional evidentiary principles." WEINSTEIN'S EVIDENCE at 804–16 (1978) citing CONG.REC.H 11931–32 (daily ed. Dec. 14, 1974). Thus, applicability of the hearsay exception to individuals implicating the accused may well rest only on the extent to which *Bruton, supra* , governs such statement. The Committee intends that the Rule extend to such statements to the same extent that subdivision 804(b)(4) is held by the Article III courts to apply to such statements.

(4) *Statement of personal or family history.* Rule 804(b)(4) of the Federal Rule is taken verbatim from the Federal Rule, and had no express equivalent in the 1969 Manual. The primary feature of Rule 803(b)(4)(A) is its application even though the "declarant had no means of acquiring personal knowledge of the matter stated."

Rule 805 Hearsay within hearsay

Rule 805 is taken verbatim from the Federal Rule. Although the 1969 Manual did not exactly address the issue, the military rule is identical with the new rule.

Rule 806 Attacking and supporting credibility of declarant

Rule 806 is taken from the Federal Rule without change. It restates the prior military rule that a hearsay declarant or statement may always be contradicted or impeached. The Rule eliminates any requirement that the declarant be given "an opportunity to deny or explain" an inconsistent statement or inconsistent conduct when such statement or conduct is offered to attack the hearsay statement. As a result, Rule 806 supersedes Rule 613(b) which would require such an opportunity for a statement inconsistent with in-court testimony.

Rule 807 Residual exception

MRE 807 was adopted on 30 May 1998 without change from the Federal Rule and represents the residual exception to the hearsay rule formerly contained in MRE 803(24) and MRE 804(b)(5).

The Rule strikes a balance between the general policy behind the Rules of Evidence of permitting admission of probative and reliable evidence and the congressional intent "that the residual hearsay exceptions will be used very rarely, and only in exceptional circumstances." S. Rep. No. 93-1277, *reprinted* in 1974 U.S.C.C.A.N. 7051, 7066. MRE 807 represents the acceptance of the so-called "catch-all" or "residual" exception to the hearsay rule. Because of the constitutional concerns associated with hearsay statements, the courts have created specific foundational requirements in order for residual hearsay to be admitted. *See United States v. Haner*, 49 M.J. 72, 77-78 (C.A.A.F. 1998). These requirements are: necessity, materiality, reliability, and notice.

The necessity prong "'essentially creates a 'best evidence' requirement.'" *United States v. Kelley*, 45 M.J. 275, 280 (C.A.A.F. 1996) (quoting *Larez v. City of Los Angeles*, 946 F.2d 630, 644 (9th Cir. 1991)). Coupled with the rule's materiality requirement, necessity represents an important fact that is more than marginal or inconsequential and is in furtherance of the interests of justice and the general purposes of the rules of evidence.

There are two alternative tests in order to fulfill the reliability condition. If the residual hearsay is a "non-testimonial statement," the proponent of the statement must demonstrate that the statement has particularized guarantees of trustworthiness as shown from the totality of the circumstances. *Idaho v. Wright*, 497 U.S. 805 (1990). The factors surrounding the taking of the statement and corroboration by other evidence should be examined to test the statement for trustworthiness. The Court of Appeals for the Armed Forces has held that the Supreme Court's prohibition against bolstering the indicia of reliability under a Sixth Amendment analysis does not apply to a residual hearsay analysis. Therefore, in addition to evidence of the circumstances surrounding the taking of the statement, extrinsic evidence can be considered. *United States v. McGrath*, 39 M.J. 158, 167 (C.M.A. 1994)." However, if the residual hearsay is a "testimonial statement," e.g. "affidavits, custodial examinations, prior testimony that the [accused] was unable to cross-examine, or similar pretrial statements that declarants would reasonably expect to be used prosecutorially," the proponent of the statement must demonstrate that the declarant of the statement is unavailable and the accused had a prior opportunity to cross-examine the declarant on the statement. *Crawford v. Washington*, 541 U.S. 36 (2004).

SECTION IX
AUTHENTICATION AND INDENTIFICATION

Rule 901 Requirement of authentication or identification

(a) *General provision.* Rule 901(a) is taken verbatim from the Federal Rule, and is similar to Para. 143 *b* of the 1969 Manual, which stated in pertinent part that: "A writing may be authenticated by any competent proof that it is genuine— is in fact what it purports or is claimed to be." Unlike the 1969 Manual provision, however, Rule 901(a) is not limited to writings and consequently is broader in scope. The Rule supports the requirement for logical relevance. *See* Rule 401.

There is substantial question as to the proper interpretation of the Federal Rule equivalent of Rule 901(a). The Rule requires only "evidence sufficient to support a finding that the matter in question is what its proponent claims." It is possible that this phrasing supersedes any formulaic approach to authentication and that rigid rules such as those that have been devised to authenticate taped recordings, for example, are no longer valid. On the other hand, it appears fully appropriate for a trial judge to require such evidence as is needed "to support a finding that the matter in question is what its proponent claims," which evidence may echo in some cases the common law formulations. There appears to be no reason to believe that the Rule will change the present law as it affects chains of custody for real evidence— especially if fungible. Present case law would appear to be consistent with the new Rule because the chain of custody requirement has not been applied in a rigid fashion. A chain of custody will still be required when it is necessary to show that the evidence is what it is claimed to be and, when appropriate, that its condition is unchanged. Rule 901(a) may make authentication somewhat easier, but is unlikely to make a substantial change in most areas of military practice.

As is generally the case, failure to object to evidence on the grounds of lack of authentication will waive the objection. *See* Rule 103(a).

(b) *Illustration.* Rule 901(b) is taken verbatim from the Federal Rule with the exception of a modification to Rule 901(b)(10). Rule 901(b)(10) has been modified by the addition of "or by applicable regulations prescribed pursuant to statutory authority." The new language was added because it was viewed as impracticable in military practice to require statutory or Supreme Court action to add authentication methods. The world wide disposition of the armed forces with their frequent redeployments may require rapid adjustments in authentication procedures to preclude substantial interference with personnel practices needed to ensure operational efficiency. The new language does not require new statutory authority. Rather, the present authority that exists for the various Service and Departmental Secretaries to issue those regulations necessary for the day to day operations of their department is sufficient.

Rule 901(b) is a non-exhaustive list of illustrative examples of authentication techniques. None of the examples are inconsistent with prior military law and many are found within the 1969 Manual, *see*, Para. 143 *b*. Self-authentication is governed by Rule 902.

Rule 902 Self-authentication

Rule 902 has been taken from the Federal Rule without significant change except that a new subdivision, 4a, has been added and subdivisions (4) and (10) have been modified. The Rule prescribes forms of self-authentication.

(1) *Domestic public documents under seal.* Rule 902(1) is taken verbatim from the Federal Rule, and is similar to aspects of Paras. 143 *b*(2)(c) and (d) of the 1969 Manual. The Rule does not distinguish between original document and copies. A seal is self-authenticating and, in the absence of evidence to the contrary, is presumed genuine. Judicial notice is not required.

(2) *Domestic public documents not under seal.* Rule 902(2) is taken from the Federal Rule without change. It is similar in scope to aspects of Paras. 143 *b*(2)(c) and (d) of the 1969 Manual in that it authorizes use of a certification under seal to authenticate a public document not itself under seal. This provision is not the only means of authenticating a domestic public record under this Rule. *Compare* Rule 902(4); 902(4a).

(3) *Foreign public documents.* Rule 902(3) is taken without change from the Federal Rule. Although the Rule is similar to Paras. 143 *b*(2)(e) and (f) of the 1969 Manual, the Rule is potentially narrower than the prior military one as the Rule does not permit "final certification" to be made by military personnel as did the Manual rule nor does it permit authentication made by military personnel as did the Manual rule nor does it permit authentication made solely pursuant to the laws of the foreign nation. On the other hand, the Rule expressly permits the military judge to order foreign documents to "be treated as presumptively authentic without final certification or permit them to be evidenced by an attested summary with or without final certification."

(4) *Certified copies of public records.* Rule 902(4) is taken verbatim from the Federal Rule except that it has been modified by adding "or applicable regulations prescribed pursuant to statutory authority." The additional language is required by military necessity and includes the now existing statutory powers of the President and various Secretaries to promulgate regulations. *See, generally*, Analysis to Rule 901(b).

Rule 902(4) expands upon prior forms of self-authentication to acknowledge the propriety of certified public records or reports and related materials domestic or foreign, the certification of which complies with subdivisions (1), (2), or (3) of the Rule.

(4a) *Documents or records of the United States accompanied by attesting certificates.* This provision is new and is taken from the third rule.subparagraph of Para. 143 *b*(2)(c) of the 1969 Manual. It has been inserted due to the necessity to facilitate records of the United States in general and military records in particular. Military records do not have seals and it would not be practicable to either issue them or require submission of documents to those officials with them. In many cases, such a requirement would be impossible to comply with due to geolineartal isolation or the unwarranted time such a requirement could demand.

An "attesting certificate" is a certificate or statement, signed by the custodian of the record or the deputy or assistant of the custodian, which in any form indicates that the writing to which the certificate or statement refers is a true copy of the record or an accurate "translation" of a machine, electronic, or coded record, and the signer of the certificate or statement is acting in an official capacity as the person having custody of the record or as the deputy or assistant thereof. *See* Para. 143 *a*(2)(a) of the 1969 Manual. An attesting certificate does not require further authentication and, absent proof to the contrary, the signature of the custodian or deputy or assistant thereof on the certificate is presumed to be genuine.

(5-9) *Official publications; Newspapers and periodicals; Trade inscriptions and the like; Acknowledged documents; Commercial paper and related documents.* Rules 902(5)–(9) are taken verbatim from the Federal Rules and have no equivalents in the 1969 Manual or in military law.

(10) *Presumptions under Acts of Congress and Regulations.* Rule 902(10) was taken from the Federal Rule but was modified by adding "and Regulations" in the caption and "or by applicable regulation prescribed pursuant to statutory authority." *See generally* the Analysis to Rule 901(b)(10) for the reasons for the additional language. The statutory authority referred to includes the presently existing authority for the President and various Secretaries to prescribe regulations.

(11) *2004 Amendment:* Rule 902(11) was modified based on the amendment to Fed. R. Evid. 902(11), effective 1 December 2000, and is taken from the Federal Rule without change. It provides for self-authentication of domestic business records and sets forth procedures for preparing a declaration of a custodian or other qualified witness that will establish a sufficient foundation for the admissibility of domestic business records. This Rule works together with Mil. R. Evid. 803(6).

Rule 903 Subscribing witness' testimony unnecessary

Rule 903 is taken verbatim from the Federal Rule and has no express equivalent in the 1969 Manual.

SECTION X
CONTENTS OF WRITINGS, RECORDINGS, AND PHOTOGRAPHS

Rule 1001 Definitions

(1) *Writings and recordings.* Rule 1001(1) is taken verbatim from the Federal Rule and is similar in scope to Para. 143 *d* of the 1969 Manual. Although the 1969 Manual was somewhat more

detailed, the Manual was clearly intended to be expansive. The Rule adequately accomplishes the identical purpose through a more general reference.

(2) *Photographs.* Rule 1001(2) is taken verbatim from the Federal Rule and had no express equivalent in the 1969 Manual. It does, however, reflect current military law.

(3) *Original.* Rule 1001(3) is taken verbatim from the Federal Rule and is similar to Para. 143 *a*(1) of the 1969 Manual. The 1969 Manual, however, treated "duplicate originals,"*i.e.*, carbon and photolineart copies made for use as an original, as an "original" while Rule 1001(4) treats such a document as a "duplicate."

(4) *Duplicate.* Rule 1004(4) is taken from the Federal Rule verbatim and includes those documents Para. 143 *a*(1) of the 1969 Manual defined as "duplicate originals." In view of Rule 1003's rule of admissibility for "duplicate," no appreciable negative result stems from the reclassification.

Rule 1002 Requirement of the original

Rule 1002 is taken verbatim from the Federal Rule except that "this Manual" has been added in recognition of the efficacy of other Manual provisions. The Rule is similar in scope to the best evidence rule found in Para. 143 *a*(19) of the 1969 Manual except that specific reference is made in the rule to recordings and photographs. Unlike the 1969 Manual, the Rule does not contain the misleading reference to "best evidence" and is plainly applicable to writings, recordings, or photographs.

It should be noted that the various exceptions to Rule 1002 are similar to but not identical with those found in the 1969 Manual. *Compare* Rules 1005–1007 *with* Para. 143 *a*(2)(f) of the 1969 Manual. For example, Paras. 143 *a* (2)(e) and 144 *c* of the 1969 Manual excepted banking records and business records from the rule as categories while the Rule does not. The actual difference in practice, however, is not likely to be substantial as Rule 1003 allows admission of duplicates unless, for example, "a genuine question is raised as to the authenticity of the original." This is similar in result to the treatment of business records in Para. 144 *a* of the 1969 Manual. Omission of other 1969 Manual exceptions, *e.g.*, certificates of fingerprint comparison and identity, *see* Rule 703, 803, evidence of absence of official or business entries, and copies of telegrams and radiograms, do not appear substantial when viewed against the entirety of the Military Rules which are likely to allow admissibility in a number of ways.

The Rule's reference to "Act of Congress" will now incorporate those statutes that specifically direct that the best evidence rule be inapplicable in one form or another. *See, e.g.*, 1 U.S.C. §209 (copies of District of Columbia Codes of Laws). As a rule, such statutes permit a form of authentication as an adequate substitute for the original document.

Rule 1003 Admissibility of duplicates

Rule 1003 is taken verbatim from the Federal Rule. It is both similar to and distinct from the 1969 Manual. To the extent that the Rule deals with those copies which were intended at the time of their creation to be used as originals, it is similar to the 1969 Manual's treatment of "duplicate originals," Para. 143 *a*(1), except that under the 1969 Manual there was no distinction to be made between originals and "duplicate originals". Accordingly, in this case the Rule would be narrower than the 1969 Manual. To the extent that the Rule deals with copies not intended at their time of creation to serve as originals, however, *e.g.*, when copies are made of pre-existing documents for the purpose of litigation, the Rule is broader than the 1969 Manual because that Manual prohibited such evidence unless an adequate justification for the non-production of the original existed.

Rule 1004 Admissibility of other evidence of contents

Rule 1004 is taken from the Federal Rule without change, and is similar in scope to the 1969 Manual. Once evidence comes within the scope of Rule 1004, secondary evidence is admissible without regard to whether "better" forms of that evidence can be obtained. Thus, no priority is established once Rule 1002 is escaped. Although the 1969 Manual stated in Para. 143 *a*(2) that "the contents may be proved by an authenticated copy or by the testimony of a witness who has seen and can remember the substance of the writing" when the original need not be produced, that phrasing appears illustrative only and not exclusive. Accordingly, the Rule, the Manual, and common law are in agreement in not requiring categories of secondary evidence.

(1) *Originals lost or destroyed.* Rule 1004(1) is similar to the 1969 Manual except that the Rule explicitly exempts originals destroyed in "bad faith." Such an exemption was implicit in the 1969 Manual.

(2) *Original not obtained.* Rule 1004(2) is similar to the justification for nonproduction in Para. 143 *a*(2) of the 1969 Manual, "an admissible writing ... cannot feasibly be produced."

(3) *Original in possession of opponent.*

Rule 1004(3) is similar to the 1969 Manual provision in Para. 143 *a*(2) that when a document is in the possession of the accused the original need not be produced except that the 1969 Manual explicitly did not require notice to the accused, and the Rule may require such notice. Under the Rule, the accused must be "put on notice, by the pleadings or otherwise, that the contents would be subject of proof at the hearing." Thus, under certain circumstances, a formal notice to the accused may be required. Under no circumstances should such a request or notice be made in the presence of the court members. The only purpose of such notice is to justify use of secondary evidence and does not serve to compel the surrender of evidence from the accused. It should be noted that Rule 1004(3) acts in favor of the accused as well as the prosecution and allows notice to the prosecution to justify defense use of secondary evidence.

(4) *Collateral matters.* Rule 1004 is not found within the Manual but restates prior military law. The intent behind the Rule is to avoid unnecessary delays and expense. It is important to note that important matters which may appear collateral may not be so in fact due to their weight. *See, e.g., United States v. Parker*, 13 U.S.C.M.A. 579, 33 C.M.R. 111 (1963) (validity of divorce decree of critical prosecution witness not collateral when witness would be prevented from testifying due to spousal privilege if the divorce were not valid). The Rule incorporates this via its use of the expression "related to a controlling issue."

Rule 1005 Public records

Rule 1005 is taken verbatim from the Federal Rule except

that "or attested to" has been added to conform the Rule to the new Rule 902(4a). The Rule is generally similar to Para. 143 *a*(2)(c) of the 1969 Manual although some differences do exist. The Rule is somewhat broader in that it applies to more than just "official records." Further, although the 1969 Manual permitted "a properly authenticated" copy in lieu of the official record, the Rule allows secondary evidence of contents when a certified or attested copy cannot be obtained by the exercise of reasonable diligence. The Rule does, however, have a preference for a certified or attested copy.

Rule 1006 Summaries

Rule 1006 is taken from the Federal Rule without change, and is similar to the exception to the best evidence rule now found in Para. 143 *a*(2)(b) of the 1969 Manual. Some difference between the Rule and the 1969 Manual exists, however, because the Rule permits use of "a chart, summary, or calculation" while the Manual permitted only "a summarization." Additionally, the Rule does not include the 1969 Manual requirement that the summarization be made by a "qualified person or group of qualified persons," nor does the Rule require, as the Manual appeared to, that the preparer of the chart, summary, or calculation testify in order to authenticate the document. The nature of the authentication required is not clear although some form of authentication is required under Rule 901(a).

It is possible for a summary that is admissible under Rule 1006 to include information that would not itself be admissible if that information is reasonably relied upon by an expert preparing the summary. *See generally* Rule 703 and S. Saltzburg & K. Redden, FEDERAL RULES OF EVIDENCE MANUAL 694 (2d ed. 1977).

Rule 1007 Testimony or written admission of party

Rule 1007 is taken from the Federal Rule without change and had no express equivalent in the 1969 Manual. The Rule establishes an exception to Rule 1002 by allowing the contents of a writing, recording or photograph to be proven by the testimony or deposition of the party against whom offered or by the party's written admission.

Rule 1008 Functions of military judge and members

Rule 1008 is taken from the Federal Rule without change, and had no formal equivalent in prior military practice. The Rule specifies three situations in which members must determine issues which have been conditionally determined by the military judge. The members have been given this responsibility in this narrow range of issues because the issues that are involved go to the very heart of a case and may prove totally dispositive. Perhaps the best example stems from the civil practice. Should the trial judge in a contract action determine that an exhibit is in fact the original of a contested contract, that admissibility decision could determine the ultimate result of trial if the jury were not given the opportunity to be the final arbiter of the issue. A similar situation could result in a criminal case, for example, in which the substance of a contested written confession is determinative (this would be rare because in most cases the fact that a written confession was made is unimportant, and the only relevant matter is the content of the oral statement that was later transcribed) or in a case in which the accused is charged with communication of a written threat. A decision by the military judge that a given version is authentic could easily determine the trial. Rule 1008 would give the member the final decision as to accuracy. Although Rule 1008 will rarely be relevant to the usual court-martial, it will adequately protect the accused from having the case against him or her depend upon a single best evidence determination by the military judge.

SECTION XI MISCELLANEOUS RULES

Rule 1101 Applicability of rules

The Federal Rules have been revised extensively to adapt them to the military criminal legal system. Subdivision (a) of the Federal Rule specifies the types of courts to which the Federal Rules are applicable, and Subdivision (b) of the Federal Rule specifies the types of proceedings to be governed by the Federal Rules. These sections are inapplicable to the military criminal legal system and consequently were deleted. Similarly, most of Federal Rule of Evidence 1101(d) is inapplicable to military law due to the vastly different jurisdictions involved.

(a) *Rules applicable.* Rule 1101(a) specifies that the Military Rules are applicable to all courts-martial including summary courts-martial, to Article 39(a) proceedings, limited factfinding proceedings ordered on review, revision proceedings, and contempt proceedings. This limited application is a direct result of the limited jurisdiction available to courts-martial.

(b) *Rules of privilege.* Rule 1101(b) is taken from subdivision (c) of the Federal Rule and is similar to prior military law. Unlike the Federal Rules, the Military Rules contain detailed privileges rather than a general reference to common law. *Compare* Federal Rule of Evidence 501 with Military Rule of Evidence 501–512.

(c) *Rules relaxed.* Rule 1101(c) conforms the rules of evidence to military sentencing procedures as set forth in the 1969 Manual Para. 75 *c*. Courts-martial are bifurcated proceedings with sentencing being an adversarial proceeding. Partial application of the rules of evidence is thus appropriate. The Rule also recognizes the possibility that other Manual provisions may now or later affect the application of the rules of evidence.

(d) *Rules inapplicable.* Rule 1101(d) is taken in concept from subdivision (d) of the Federal Rule. As the content of the Federal Rule is, however, generally inapplicable to military law, the equivalents of the Article III proceedings listed in the Federal Rule have been listed here. They included Article 32 investigative hearings, the partial analog to grand jury proceedings, proceedings for search authorizations, and proceedings for pretrial release.

1993 Amendment. Mil. R. Evid. 1101(d) was amended to make the provisions of Mil. R. Evid. 412 applicable at pretrial investigations.

1998 Amendment. The Rule is amended to increase to 18 months the time period between changes to the Federal Rules of Evidence and automatic amendment of the Military Rules of

Evidence. This extension allows for timely submission of changes through the annual review process.

Rule 1102 Amendments.

Rule 1102 has been substantially revised from the original Federal Rule which sets forth a procedure by which the Supreme Court promulgates amendments to the Federal Rules subject to Congressional objection. Although it is the Committee's intent that the Federal Rules of Evidence apply to the armed forces to the extent practicable, *see* Article 36(a), the Federal Rules are often in need of modification to adapt them to military criminal legal system. Further, some rules may be impracticable. As Congress may make changes during the initial period following Supreme Court publication, some period of time after an amendment's effective date was considered essential for the armed forces to review the final form of amendments and to propose any necessary modifications to the President. Six months was considered the minimally appropriate time period.

Amendments to the Federal Rules are not applicable to the armed forces until 180 days after the effective date of such amendment, unless the President directs earlier application. In the absence of any Presidential action, however, an amendment to the Federal Rule of Evidence will be automatically applicable on the 180th day after its effective date. The President may, however, affirmatively direct that any such amendment may not apply, in whole or in part, to the armed forces and that direction shall be binding upon courts-martial.

1998 Amendment: The Rule is amended to increase to 18 months the time period between changes to the Federal Rules of Evidence and automatic amendment of the Military Rules of Evidence. This extension allows for the timely submission of changes through the annual review process.

2004 Amendment: See Executive Order 13365, dated 3 December 2004. The amendment to the Federal Rules of Evidence, effective in United States District Courts, 1 December 2000, creating Rule 902(12) is not adopted. Federal Rules 301, 302, and 415, were not adopted because they were applicable only to civil proceedings.

Rule 1103 Title

In choosing the title, Military Rules of Evidence, the Committee intends that it be clear that military evidentiary law should echo the civilian federal law to the extent practicable, but should also ensure that the unique and critical reasons behind the separate military criminal legal system be adequately served.

Analysis of
Punitive Articles

Analysis of
Punitive Articles

APPENDIX 23
ANALYSIS OF PUNITIVE ARTICLES

Introduction

Unless otherwise indicated, the elements, maximum punishments and sample specifications in paragraphs 3 through 113 are based on paragraphs 157 through 213, paragraph 127 *c* (Table of Maximum Punishments), and Appendix 6*c* of MCM, 1969 (Rev.).

1986 Amendment: The next to last paragraph of the introduction to Part IV was added to define the term "elements," as used in Part IV. In MCM, 1969 (Rev.), the equivalent term used was "proof." Both "proof" and "elements" referred to the statutory elements of the offense and to any additional aggravating factors prescribed by the President under Article 56, UCMJ, to increase the maximum permissible punishment above that allowed for the basic offense. These additional factors are commonly referred to as "elements," and judicial construction has approved this usage, as long as these "elements" are pled, proven, and instructed upon. *United States v. Flucas*, 23 U.S.C.M.A. 274, 49 C.M.R. 449 (1975); *United States v. Nickaboine*, 3 U.S.C.M.A. 152, 11 C.M.R. 152 (1953); *United States v. Bernard*, 10 C.M.R. 718 (AFBR 1953).

1. Article 77—Principals

b. *Explanation.*

(1) *Purpose.* Article 77 is based on 18 U.S.C. § 2. *Hearings on H. R. 2498 Before a Subcomm. of the House Comm. on Armed Services,* 81st Cong., 1st Sess. 1240-1244 (1949). The paragraph of subparagraph b(1) reflects the purpose of 18 U.S.C. § 2 (*see Standefer v. United States*, 447 U.S. 10 (1980)) and Article 77 (*see* Hearings, *supra* at 1240).

The common law definitions in the second paragraph of subparagraph b(1) are based on R. Perkins, *Criminal Law* 643–666 (2d ed. 1969); and 1 C. Torcia, *Wharton's Criminal Law and Procedure* §§ 29–38 (1978). Several common law terms such as "aider and abettor" are now used rather loosely and do not always retain their literal common law meanings, *See United States v. Burroughs*, 12 M.J. 380, 384 n.4. (C.M.A. 1982); *United States v. Molina*, 581 F.2d 56, 61 n.8 (2d Cir. 1978). To eliminate confusion, the explanation avoids the use of such terms where possible. *See United States v. Burroughs, supra* at 382 n.3.

(2) *Who may be liable for an offense.* Subparagraph (2)(a) is based on paragraph 156 of MCM, 1969 (Rev.). *See* 18 U.S.C.A. § 2 Historical and Revision Notes (West 1969). *See also United States v. Giles,* 300 U.S. 41 (1937); *Wharton's, supra* at §§ 30, 31, 35.

Subparagraph (2)(b) sets forth the basic formulation of the requirements for liability as a principal. An act (which may be passive, as discussed in this subparagraph) and intent are necessary to make one liable as a principal. *See United States v. Burroughs, supra; United States v. Jackson* , 6 U.S.C.M.A. 193, 19 C.M.R. 319 (1955); *United States v. Wooten*, 1 U.S.C.M.A. 358, 3 C.M.R. 92 (1952); *United States v. Jacobs*, 1 U.S.C.M.A. 209, 2 C.M.R. 115 (1952). *See also United States v. Walker*, 621 F.2d 163 (5th Cir. 1980), *cert. denied*, 450 U.S. 1000 (1981); *Morei v. United States*, 127 F.2d 827 (6th Cir. 1942); *United States v. Peoni*, 100 F.2d 401, 402 (2d Cir. 1938). The terms "assist" and "encourage, advise, and instigate" have been substituted for "aid" and "abet" respectively, since the latter terms are technical and may not be clear to the lay reader. *See Black's Law Dictionary* 5, 63 (5th ed., 1979). *See also Nye and Nissen v. United States*, 336 U.S. 613, 620 (1949); *Wharton's, supra* at 246-47.

The last two sentences in subparagraph (2)(b) are based on the third paragraph and paragraph 156 of MCM, 1969 (Rev.). *See United States v. Ford*, 12 U.S.C.M.A. 31, 30 C.M.R. 31 (1960); *United States v. McCarthy*, 11 U.S.C.M.A. 758, 29 C.M.R. 574 (1960); *United States v. Lyons*, 11 U.S.C.M.A. 68, 28 C.M.R. 292 (1959).

(3) *Presence.* This subparagraph clarifies, as paragraph 156 of MCM, 1969 (Rev.) did not, that presence at the scene is neither necessary nor sufficient to make one a principal. "Aid" and "abet" as used in 18 U.S.C. § 2, and in Article 77, are not used in the narrow common law sense of an "aider and abettor" who must be present at the scene to be guilty as such. *United States v. Burroughs, supra; United States v. Sampol*, 636 F.2d 621 (D.C. Cir. 1980); *United States v. Molina, supra; United States v. Carter*, 23 C.M.R. 872 (A.F.B.R. 1957). *Cf. Milanovich v. United States,* 365 U.S. 551 (1961). *See also Wharton's, supra* at 231. Subparagraph (b) continues the admonition, contained in the third paragraph of paragraph 156 of MCM, 1969 (Rev.), that presence at the scene of a crime is not sufficient to make one a principal. *See United State v. Waluski*, 6 U.S.C.M.A. 724, 21 C.M.R. 46 (1956); *United States v. Johnson*, 6 U.S.C.M.A. 20, 19 C.M.R. 146 (1955); *United States v. Guest*, 3 U.S.C.M.A. 147, 11 C.M.R. 147 (1953).

(4) *Parties whose intent differs from the perpetrators.* This subparagraph is based on the first paragraph in paragraph 156 of MCM, 1969 (Rev.). *See United States v. Jackson*, 6 U.S.C.M.A. 193, 19 C.M.R. 319 (1955); Wharton's, *supra* at § 35.

(5) *Responsibility for other crimes.* This paragraph is based on the first two paragraphs in paragraph 156 of MCM, 1969 (Rev.). *See United States v. Cowan*, 12 C.M.R. 374 (A.B.R. 1953); *United States v. Self*, 13 C.M.R. 227 (A.B.R. 1953).

Principals independently liable. This subparagraph is new and is based on Federal decisions. *See Standefer v. United States, supra; United States v. Chenaur* , 552 F.2d 294 (9th Cir. 1977); *United States v. Frye*, 548 F.2d 765 (8th Cir. 1977).

Withdrawal. This subparagraph is new and is based on*United States v. Williams*, 19 U.S.C.M.A. 334, 41 C.M.R. 334 (1970). *See also United States v. Miasel*, 8 U.S.C.M.A. 374, 24 C.M.R. 184, 188 (157); *United States v. Lowell*, 649 F.2d 950 (3d. Cir., 1981); *United States v. Killian*, 639 F. 2d 206 (5th Cir.), *cert. denied* 451 U.S. 1021 (1981).

2. Article 78—Accessory after the fact

c. *Explanation.*

(1) *In general.* This subparagraph is based on paragraph 157 of MCM, 1969 (Rev.). *See also United States v. Tamas*, 6 U.S.C.M.A. 502, 20 C.M.R. 218(1955).

(2) *Failure to report offense.* This subparagraph is based on paragraph 157 of MCM, 1969 (Rev.); *United States v. Smith*, 5 M.J. 129 (C.M.A. 1978).

(3) *Offense punishable by the code.* This subparagraph is based

on Article 78; *United States v. Michaels*, 3 M.J. 846 (A.C.M.R. 1977); *United States v. Blevins*, 34 C.M.R. 967 (A.F.B.R. 1964).

(4) *Status of principal.* This subparagraph is based on Article 78 and *United States v. Michaels*, 3 M.J. 846 (A.C.M.R. 1977); *United States v. Blevins*, 34 C.M.R. 967 (A.F.B.R. 1964).

(5) *Conviction or acquittal of principal.* The subparagraph is based on paragraph 157 of MCM, 1969 (Rev.); *United States v. Marsh*, 13 U.S.C.M.A. 252, 32 C.M.R. 252 (1962); and*United States v. Humble*, 11 U.S.C.M.A. 38, 28 C.M.R. 262 (1959). *See also United States v. McConnico*, 7 M.J. 302 (C.M.A. 1979).

(6) *Accessory after the fact not a lesser included offense.* This subparagraph is based on *United States v. McFarland*, 8 U.S.C.M.A. 42, 23 C.M.R. 266 (1957).

(7) *Actual Knowledge.* This paragraph is based on United States v. Marsh, supra. *See United States v. Foushee*, 13 M.J. 833 (A.C.M.R. 1982). MCM, 1984, APPENDIX 21, Part IV, ARTICLE 79

3. Article 79—Lesser included offenses

b. *Explanation.*

(1) *In general.* This subparagraph and the three subparagraphs are based on paragraph 158 of MCM, 1969 (Rev.). *See also United States v. Thacker*, 16 U.S.C.M.A. 408, 37 C.M.R. 28 (1966).

(2) *Multiple lesser included offenses.* This subparagraph is based on paragraph 158 of MCM, 1969 (Rev.). *See also United States v. Calhoun*, 5 U.S.C.M.A. 428, 18 C.M.R. 52 (1955).

(3) *Findings of guilty to a lesser included offense.* This subparagraph is taken from paragraph 158 of MCM, 1969 (Rev.).

4. Article 80—Attempts

c. *Explanation.*

(1) *In general.* This subparagraph is based on paragraph 159 of MCM, 1969 (Rev.).

(2) *More than preparation.* This subparagraph is based on paragraph 159 of MCM, 1969 (Rev.); *United States v. Johnson*, 7 U.S.C.M.A. 488, 22 C.M.R. 278 (1957); *United States v. Choat*, 7 U.S.C.M.A. 187, 21 C.M.R. 313 (1956); *United States v. Goff*, 5 M.J. 817 (A.C.M.R. 1978); *United States v. Emerson*, 16 C.M.R. 690 (A.F.B.R. 1954).

(3) *Factual impossibility.* This subparagraph is based on paragraph 159 of MCM, 1969 (Rev.); *United States v. Thomas*, 13 U.S.C.M.A. 278, 32 C.M.R. 278 (1962). *See United States v. Quijada*, 588 F.2d 1253 (9th Cir. 1978).

(4) *Voluntary abandonment.*

1995 Amendment: Subparagraph (4) is new. It recognizes voluntary abandonment as an affirmative defense as established by the case law. *See United States v. Byrd*, 24 M.J. 286 (C.M.A. 1987). *See also United States v. Schoof*, 37 M.J. 96, 103-04 (C.M.A. 1993); *United States v. Rios*, 33 M.J. 436, 440-41 (C.M.A. 1991); *United States v. Miller*, 30 M.J. 999 (N.M.C.M.R. 1990); *United States v. Walther*, 30 M.J. 829, 829-33 (N.M.C.M.R. 1990). The prior subparagraphs (4) - (6) have been redesignated (5) - (7), respectively.

(5) *Solicitation.* This subparagraph is based on paragraph 159 of MCM, 1969 (Rev.).

(6) *Attempts not under Article 80.* This subparagraph is based on paragraph 159 of MCM, 1969 (Rev.).

1986 Amendment: In 4 *c*(5), subparagraph (e) was redesignated as subparagraph (f), and a new subparagraph (e) was added to reflect the offense of attempted espionage as established by the Department of Defense Authorization Act, 1986, Pub.L. No. 99-145, § 534, 99 Stat. 583, 634-35 (1985) (art. 106a).

(7) *Regulations.* This subparagraph is new and is based on *United States v. Davis*, 16 M.J. 225 (C.M.A. 1983); *United States v. Foster*, 14 M.J. 246 (C.M.A. 1983).

e. *Maximum punishment*

1991 Amendment: This paragraph was revised to allow for the imposition of confinement in excess of 20 years for the offense of attempted murder. There are cases in which the aggravating factors surrounding commission of an attempted murder are so egregious that a 20 year limitation may be inappropriate. Although life imprisonment may be imposed by the sentencing authority, mandatory minimum punishment provisions do not apply in the case of convictions under Article 80.

5. Article 81—Conspiracy

c. *Explanation.*

(1) *Co-conspirators.* This subparagraph is based on paragraph 160 of MCM, 1969 (Rev.); *United States v. Kinder*, 14 C.M.R. 742 (A.F.B.R. 1953). The portion of paragraph 160 which provided that acquittal of all alleged co-conspirators precludes conviction of the accused has been deleted. *See United States v. Garcia* 16 M.J. 52 (C.M.A. 1983). *See also United States v. Standefer*, 447 U.S. 10 (1980).

(2) *Agreement.* This subparagraph is taken from paragraph 160 of MCM, 1969 (Rev.).

(3) *Object of the agreement.* This subparagraph is taken from paragraph 160 of MCM, 1969 (Rev.); *United States v. Kidd*, 13 U.S.C.M.A. 184, 32 C.M.R. 184 (1962). The last three sentences reflect "Wharton's Rule," 4 C. Torcia, Wharton's Criminal Law, § 731 (1981). *See Iannelli v. United States*, 420 U.S. 770 (1975); *United States v. Yarborough*, 1 U.S.C.M.A. 678, 5 C.M.R. 106 (1952); *United States v. Osthoff*, 8 M.J. 629 (A.C.M.R. 1979); *United States v. McClelland*, 49 C.M.R. 557 (A.C.M.R. 1974).

(4) *Overt act.* This subparagraph is taken from paragraph 160 of MCM, 1969 (Rev.); *United States v. Rhodes*, 11 U.S.C.M.A. 735, 29 C.M.R. 551 (1960); *United States v. Salisbury*, 14 U.S.C.M.A. 171, 33 C.M.R. 383 (1963); *United States v. Woodley*, 13 M.J. 984 (A.C.M.R. 1982).

(5) *Liability for offenses.* This subparagraph is taken from paragraph 160 of MCM, 1969 (Rev.). *See Pinkerton v. United States*, 328 U.S. 640 (1946); *United States v. Salisbury*, 14 U.S.C.M.A. 171, 33 C.M.R. 383 (1963); *United States v. Woodley*, 13 M.J. 984 (A.C.M.R. 1982).

(6) *Withdrawal.* This subparagraph is taken from paragraph 160 of MCM, 1969 (Rev.); *United States v. Miasel*, 8 U.S.C.M.A. 374, 24 C.M.R.184 (1957).

(7) *Factual impossibility.* This subparagraph is taken from paragraph 160 of MCM, 1969 (Rev.).

(8) *Conspiracy as a separate offense.* This subparagraph is taken from paragraph 160 of MCM, 1969 (Rev.). *See also United States v. Washington*, 1 M.J. 473 (C.M.A. 1976).

(9) *Special conspiracies under Article 134.* This subparagraph is taken from paragraph 160 of MCM, 1969 (Rev.); *United States v. Chapman*, 10 C.M.R. 306 (A.B.R. 1953).

6. Article 82—Solicitation

b. *Elements.* Solicitation under Article 82 has long been recognized as a specific intent offense. *See* paragraph 161 of MCM, 1969 (Rev.); paragraph 161 of MCM, 1951. *See generally United States v. Mitchell*, 15 M.J. 214 (C.M.A. 1983); *United States v. Benton*, 7 M.J. 606 (N.C.M.R. 1979). It has been added as an element for clarity.

c. *Explanation.* This paragraph is taken from paragraph 161 of MCM, 1969 (Rev.), *United States v. Wysong*, 9 U.S.C.M.A. 248, 26 C.M.R. 29 (1958); *United States v. Gentry*, 8 U.S.C.M.A. 14, 23 C.M.R. 238 (1957); *United States v. Benton*, 7 M.J. 606 (N.C.M.R. 1979).

7. Article 83—Fraudulent enlistment, appointment, or separation

c. *Explanation.* This paragraph is based on paragraph 162 of MCM, 1969 (Rev.); *United States v. Danley*, 21 U.S.C.M.A. 486, 45 C.M.R. 260 (1972). *See Wickham v. Hall*, 12 M.J. 145 (C.M.A. 1981).

e. *Maximum Punishment.* The reference to membership in, association with, or activities in connection with organizations, associations, etc., found in the Table of Maximum Punishments, paragraph 127 *c* of MCM, 1969 (Rev.), for Article 83, was deleted as unnecessary. The maximum punishment for all fraudulent enlistment cases was then standardized.

8. Article 84—Effecting unlawful enlistment, appointment, or separation

c. *Explanation.* This paragraph is taken from paragraph 163 of MCM, 1969 (Rev.). *See also United States v. Hightower*, 5 M.J. 717 (A.C.M.R. 1978).

e. *Maximum punishment.* The reference to membership in, with, or activities in connection with organizations, associations, etc., found in the Table of Maximum Punishments, paragraph 127*c* of MCM, 1969 (Rev.), or Article 84, was deleted as unnecessary. The maximum punishment for all cases was then standardized.

9. Article 85—Desertion

c. *Explanation.*

(1) Desertion with intent to remain away permanently.

(a) *In general.* This subparagraph is taken from paragraph 164a of MCM, 1969 (Rev.).

(b) *Absence without authority-inception, duration, termination. See* the Analysis, paragraph 10.

(c) *Intent to remain away permanently.* This subparagraph is taken from paragraph 164*a* of MCM, 1969 (Rev.). The last sentence is based on *United States v. Cothern*, 8 U.S.C.M.A. 158, 23 C.M.R. 382 (1957).

(d) *Effect of enlistment or appointment in the same or a different armed force.* This subparagraph is based on paragraph 164 *a* of MCM, 1969 (Rev.); *United States v. Huff*, 7 U.S.C.M.A. 247, 22 C.M.R. 37 (1956).

(2) *Quitting unit, organization, or place of duty with intent to avoid hazardous duty or to shirk important service.*

(a) *Hazardous duty or important service.* This subparagraph is taken from paragraph 164 *a* of MCM, 1969 (Rev.). *See also United States v. Smith*, 18 U.S.C.M.A. 46, 39 C.M.R. 46 (1968); *United States v. Deller*, 3 U.S.C.M.A. 409, 12 C.M.R. 165 (1953).

(b) *Quits.* This subparagraph is based on *United States v. Bondar* , 2 U.S.C.M.A. 357, 8 C.M.R. 157 (1953).

(c) *Actual Knowledge.* This subparagraph is based on *United States v. Stabler*, 4 U.S.C.M.A. 125, 15 C.M.R. 125 (1954) and rejects the view of paragraph 164 *a* of MCM, 1969 (Rev.) that constructive knowledge would suffice. To avoid confusion, the "constructive knowledge" language has been replaced with the statement that actual knowledge may be proved by circumstantial evidence. *See United States v. Curtin*, 9 U.S.C.M.A. 427, 26 C.M.R. 207 (1958).

(3) *Attempting to desert.* This subparagraph is taken from paragraph 164 *b* of MCM, 1969 (Rev.).

(4) *Prisoner with executed punitive discharge.* This subparagraph is taken from paragraphs 164 *a* and 165 of MCM, 1969 (Rev.).

e. *Maximum punishment.* As indicated in the Analysis, paragraph 4, attempts, the punishment for attempted desertion was made uniform. As a result, attempted desertion- "other cases of"- now conforms with the punishment for "desertion- other cases of." This amounts to an increase in the maximum punishment from confinement for one year to either two or three years, depending on the nature of termination.

10. Article 86—Absence without leave

c. *Explanation.*

(1) *In general.* This subparagraph is taken from paragraph 165 of MCM, 1969 (Rev.).

(2) *Actual knowledge.* This subparagraph clarifies that the accused must have in fact known of the time and place of duty to be guilty of a violation of Article 86(1) or (2). Cf. *United States v. Chandler*, 23 U.S.C.M.A. 193, 48 C.M.R. 945 (1974); *United States v. Stabler*, 4 U.S.C.M.A. 125, 15 C.M.R. 125 (1954). *See also United States v. Gilbert*, 23 C.M.R. 914 (A.F.B.R. 1957). The language in paragraph 165 of MCM, 1969 (Rev.) dealing with constructive knowledge has been eliminated. To avoid confusion, this language has been replaced with the statement that actual knowledge may be proved by circumstantial evidence. *See United States v. Curtin*, 9 U.S.C.M.A. 427, 26 C.M.R. 207 (1958).

(3) *Intent.* This subparagraph is based on paragraph 165 of MCM, 1969 (Rev.).

(4) *Aggravated forms of unauthorized absence.* This subparagraph is based on paragraphs 127 *c* and 165 of MCM, 1969 (Rev.).

(5) *Civil authorities.* This subparagraph is taken from paragraph 165 *f* MCM, 1969 (Rev.); *United States v. Myhre*, 9 U.S.C.M.A. 32, 25 C.M.R. 294 (1958); *United States v. Grover*, 10 U.S.C.M.A. 91, 27 C.M.R. 165 (1958). *See also United States v. Dubry*, 12 M.J. 36 (C.M.A. 1981).

(6) *Inability to return.* This subparagraph is taken from paragraph 165 of MCM, 1969 (Rev.).

(7) *Determining the unit or organization of an accused.* This subparagraph is based on *United States v. Pounds* , 23 U.S.C.M.A. 153, 48 C.M.R. 769 (1974); *United States v. Mitchell*, 7 U.S.C.M.A. 238, 22 C.M.R. 28 (1956).

(8) *Duration.* This subparagraph is taken from paragraphs 127 *c* and 165 of MCM, 1969 (Rev.); *United States v. Lovell*, 7 U.S.C.M.A. 445, 22 C.M.R. 235 (1956).

(9) *Computation of duration.* This subsection is based on paragraph 127 *c*(3) of MCM, 1969 (Rev.).

(10) *Termination—methods of return to military control.* This subparagraph is based on paragraph 165 of MCM, 1969 (Rev.); *United States v. Dubry, supra; United States v. Raymo*, 1 M.J. 31 (C.M.A. 1975); *United States v. Garner*, 7 U.S.C.M.A. 578, 23 C.M.R. 42 (1957); *United States v. Coates*, 2 U.S.C.M.A. 625, 10 C.M.R. 123 (1953); *United States v. Jackson*, 1 U.S.C.M.A. 190, 2 C.M.R. 96 (1952); *United States v. Petterson*, 14 M.J. 608 (A.F.C.M.R. 1982); *United States v. Coglin*, 10 M.J. 670 (A.F.C.M.R. 1981). *See also United States v. Zammit*, 14 M.J. 554 (N.M.C.M.R. 1982).

(11) *Findings of more than one absence under one specification.* This subsection is based on *United States v. Francis* , 15 M.J. 424 (C.M.A. 1983).

(e) *Maximum punishment.* The increased maximum punishment for unauthorized absence for more than 30 days terminated by apprehension has been added to parallel the effect of termination of desertion by apprehension and to encourage absent servicemembers to voluntarily return. A bad-conduct discharge was added to the permissible maximum punishment for unauthorized absence with intent to avoid maneuvers of field duty, because with sensitive, high value equipment used in exercises currently, the effect of such absence is more costly and, because of limited available training time, seriously disrupts training and combat readiness.

1990 Amendment: The Note in subsection b(4) was inserted and a conforming change was made in subsection f(4) to clarify the distinction between "unauthorized absence from a guard, watch, or duty section" and "unauthorized absence from guard, watch, or duty section with the intent to abandon it." *See* subsections c(4)(c) and c(4)(d).

11. Article 87—Missing movement

c. *Explanation.*

(1) *Movement.* This subparagraph is based on paragraph 166 of MCM, 1969 (Rev.); *United States v. Kimply*, 17 C.M.R. 469 (N.B.R. 1954).

(2) *Mode of movement.* This subparagraph is based on *United States v. Graham* , 16 M.J. 460 (C.M.A. 1983); *United States v. Johnson*, 3 U.S.C.M.A. 174, 11 C.M.R. 174 (1953); *United States v. Burke*, 6 C.M.R. 588 (A.B.R. 1952); *United States v. Jackson*, 5 C.M.R. 429 (A.B.R. 1952). *See also United States v. Graham*, 12 M.J. 1026 (A.C.M.R.), pet granted, 14 M.J. 223 (1982).

(3) *Design.* This subparagraph is based on *United States v. Clifton*, 5 C.M.R. 342 (N.B.R. 1952).

(4) *Neglect.* This subparagraph is taken from paragraph 166 of MCM, 1969 (Rev.).

(5) *Actual knowledge.* This subparagraph is based on *United States v. Chandler*, 23 U.S.C.M.A. 193, 48 C.M.R. 945 (1974); *United States v. Thompson*, 2 U.S.C.M.A. 460, 9 C.M.R. 90 (1953); and in part on paragraph 166 of MCM, 1969 (Rev.). This paragraph rejects the language of paragraph 166 of MCM, 1969 (Rev.), which has provided for "constructive knowledge," and adopts the "actual knowledge" requirement set forth in *Chandler*.

(6) *Proof of absence.* This subparagraph is taken from paragraph 166 of MCM, 1969 (Rev.).

e. *Maximum punishment.* The maximum punishment for missing movement was increased to make these punishments more equivalent to aggravated offenses of unauthorized absences and violations of orders. The major reliance of the armed forces on rapid deployment and expeditious movement of personnel and equipment to deter or prevent the escalation of hostilities dictates that these offenses be viewed more seriously.

12. Article 88—Contempt toward officials

c. *Explanation.* This paragraph is taken from paragraph 167 of MCM, 1969 (Rev.). For a discussion of the history of Article 88, *see United States v. Howe*, 17 U.S.C.M.A. 165, 37 C.M.R. 429 (1967).

e. *Maximum punishment.* This limitation is new and is based on the authority given the President in Article 56. Paragraph 127*c* of MCM, 1969 (Rev.) does not mention Article 88. The maximum punishment is based on the maximum punishment for Article of War 62, which was analogous to Article 88, as prescribed in paragraph 117 *c* of MCM (Army), 1949, and MCM (AF), 1949.

2007 Amendment. The analysis for paragraph 12a is amended by replacing the word "Transportation" with the words "Homeland Security" to reflect the reorganization of the United States Coast Guard under the Department of Homeland Security.

13. Article 89—Disrespect toward a superior commissioned officer

c. *Explanation.* This paragraph is taken from Article 1(5); paragraph 168 of MCM, 1969 (rev.); *United States v. Richardson*, 7 M.J. 320 (C.M.A. 1979); *United States v. Ferenczi*, 10 U.S.C.M.A. 3, 27 C.M.R. 77 (1958); *United States v. Sorrells*, 49 C.M.R. 44 (A.C.M.R. 1974); *United States v. Cheeks*, 43 C.M.R. 1013 (A.F.C.M.R. 1971); *United States v. Montgomery*, 11 C.M.R. 308 (A.B.R. 1953).

e. *Maximum punishment.* The maximum punishment was increased from confinement for 6 months to confinement for 1 year to more accurately reflect the serious nature of the offense and to distinguish it from disrespect toward warrant officers under Article 91. *See* paragraph 15 *c*.

14. Article 90—Assaulting or willfully disobeying superior commissioned officer

c. *Explanation.*

(1) *Striking or assaulting superior commissioned officer.* This subparagraph is based on paragraph 169 *a* of MCM, 1969 (Rev.) and other authorities as noted below.

(a) *Definitions.* "Strikes" is clarified to include any intentional offensive touching. Other batteries, such as by culpable negligence, are included in "offers violence." As to "superior commissioned officer," *see* Analysis, paragraph 13.

(d) *Defenses.* This subparagraph modifies the former discussion of self-defense since technically, because unlawfulness is not an element expressly, the officer must be acting illegally or otherwise outside the role of an officer before self-defense may be in issue. *See United States v. Struckman*, 20 U.S.C.M.A. 493, 43 C.M.R. 333 (1971).

(2) *Disobeying superior commissioned officer.* This subparagraph is based on paragraph 169 *b* of MCM, 1969 (Rev.) and other authorities as noted below.

(a) *Lawfulness of the order.*

(i) *Inference of lawfulness. See United States v. Keenan*, 18 U.S.C.M.A. 108, 39 C.M.R. 108 (1969); *United States v. Schultz*, 18 U.S.C.M.A. 133, 39 C.M.R. 133 (1969); *United States v. Kinder*, 14 C.M.R. 742 (A.B.R. 1954).

(ii) *2005 Amendment*: The Court of Appeals for the Armed Forces held that the lawfulness of an order is a question of law to be determined by the military judge, not the trier of fact. *See United States v. New*, 55 M.J. 95, 100-01 (C.A.A.F. 2001).

(iii) *Authority of issuing officer. See United States v. Marsh*, 3 U.S.C.M.A. 48, 11 C.M.R. 48 (1953).

(iv) *Relationship to military duty. See United States v. Martin*, 1 U.S.C.M.A. 674, 5 C.M.R. 102 (1952); *United States v. Wilson*, 12 U.S.C.M.A. 165, 30 C.M.R. 165 (1961) (restriction on drinking); *United States v. Nation*, 9 U.S.C.M.A. 724, 26 C.M.R. 504 (1958) (overseas marriage); *United States v. Lenox*, 21 U.S.C.M.A. 314, 45 C.M.R. 88 (1972); *United States v. Stewart*, 20 U.S.C.M.A. 272, 43 C.M.R. 112 (1971); *United States v. Wilson*, 19 U.S.C.M.A. 100, 41 C.M.R. 100 (1969); *United States v. Noyd*, 18 U.S.C.M.A. 483, 40 C.M.R. 195 (1969) (all dealing with matters that do not excuse the disobedience of an order).

(v) *Relationship to statutory or constitutional rights.* This subparagraph is based on Article 31; *United States v. McCoy*, 12 U.S.C.M.A. 68, 30 C.M.R. 68 (1960); *United States v. Aycock*, 15 U.S.C.M.A. 158, 35 C.M.R. 130 (1964).

(b) *Personal nature of the order. See United States v. Wartsbaugh*, 21 U.S.C.M.A. 535, 45 C.M.R. 309 (1972).

(d) *Specificity of the order. See United States v. Bratcher*, 18 U.S.C.M.A. 125, 38 C.M.R. 125 (1969).

(e) *Knowledge. See United States v. Pettigrew*, 19 U.S.C.M.A. 191, 41 C.M.R. 191 (1970); *United States v. Oisten*, 13 U.S.C.M.A. 656, 33 C.M.R. 188 (1963).

(g) *Time for compliance. See United States v. Stout*, 1 U.S.C.M.A. 639, 5 C.M.R. 67 (1952); *United States v. Squire*, 47 C.M.R. 214 (N.C.M.R. 1973); *United States v. Clowser*, 16 C.M.R. 543 (A.F.B.R. 1954).

15. Article 91— Insubordinate conduct toward warrant officer, noncommissioned officer, or petty officer

c. *Explanation.* (1) *In general.* This subparagraph is based on paragraph 170 of MCM, 1969 (Rev.) and paragraph 170 of MCM, 1951; a review of the legislative history of Article 91; *United States v. Ransom*, 1 M.J. 1005 (N.C.M.R. 1976); *United States v. Balsarini*, 36 C.M.R. 809 (C.G.B.R. 1965). Paragraph 170 of MCM, 1951 and MCM, 1969 (Rev.) discussed Article 91 as if Congress had required a superior-subordinate relationship in Article 91. *See Legal and Legislative Basis, Manual for Courts-Martial, United States, 1951, at 257. Analysis of Contents, Manual for Courts-Martial, United States, 1969 (Revised edition)*, DA PAM 27–2, at 28–6. This was in error and all references thereto have been removed. An amendment to Article 91 was suggested by The Judge Advocate General of the Army (*see Hearings on S.857 and H.R. 4080 Before a Subcommittee of the Senate Armed Service Committee*, 81st Cong., 1st Sess. 274 (1949)) to conform Article 91 to Articles 89 and 90, which explicitly require superiority, and was later offered, but it was not acted on. *See* Congressional Floor Debate on the Uniform Code of Military Justice (amendment M. p. 170). *See also Hearings Before a Subcommittee of the House Armed Services Committee on H.R. 2498*, 81st Cong. 1st Sess. 772, 814, 823 (1949). This present interpretation is consistent with the unambiguous language of Article 91 and its predecessors. *See* Articles of War 65 and 1(b) (1920); and paragraph 135, MCM, 1928; paragraph 153, MCM, (Army), 1949 and MCM (AF), 1949. *See also* Act of Aug. 10, 1956, Pub.L. No. 84–1028, §49(e), 70A Stat. 640 (catchlines in U.C.M.J. not relevant to congressional intent).

The remaining subparagraphs are all taken from paragraph 170 of MCM, 1969 (Rev.) and the discussion paragraphs of other articles.

e. *Maximum punishment.* Subparagraphs (2) and (7) are based on the aggravating circumstances that the victim is also superior to the accused. When this factor exists in a given case, the superiority of the victim must be alleged in the specification. The penalties for disobedience of noncommissioned and petty officers and for assault on and disrespect toward superior noncommissioned and petty officers were increased. In the case of the latter two offenses, this is done in part to distinguish assault on or disrespect toward a superior noncommissioned or petty officer from other assaults or disrespectful behavior, in light of the expansive coverage of the article. Moreover, increasing responsibility for training, complex and expensive equipment, and leadership in combat is placed on noncommissioned and petty officers in today's armed forces. The law should reinforce the respect and obedience which is due them with meaningful sanctions. The maximum punishment for disrespect toward warrant officers was adjusted to conform to these changes.

16. Article 92— Failure to obey order or regulation

c. *Explanation.* This paragraph is taken from paragraph 171 of MCM, 1969 (Rev.). The requirement that actual knowledge be an element of an Article 92(3) offense is based on *United States v. Curtin*, 9 U.S.C.M.A. 427, 26 C.M.R. 207 (1958).

As to publication under subparagraph c(1)(a), *see United States v. Tolkach*, 14 M.J. 239 (C.M.A. 1982).

Subparagraph (1)(e) *Enforceability* is new. This subparagraph is based on *United States v. Nardell*, 21 U.S.C.M.A. 327, 45 C.M.R. 101 (1972); *United States v. Hogsett* , 8 U.S.C.M.A. 681, 25 C.M.R. 185 (1958). The general order or regulation violated must, when examined as a whole, demonstrate that it is intended to regulate the conduct of individual servicemembers, and the direct application of sanctions for violations of the regulation must be self-evident. *United States v. Nardell, supra* at 329, 45

C.M.R. at 103. *See United States v. Wheeler*, 22 U.S.C.M.A. 149, 46 C.M.R. 149(1973); *United States v. Scott*, 22 U.S.C.M.A. 25, 46 C.M.R. 24 (1972); *United States v. Woodrum*, 20 U.S.C.M.A. 529, 43 C.M.R. 369 (1971); *United States v. Brooks*, 20 U.S.C.M.A. 42, 42 C.M.R. 220 (1970); *United States v. Baker*, 18 U.S.C.M.A. 504, 40 C.M.R. 216 (1969); *United States v. Tassos*, 18 U.S.C.M.A. 12, 39 C.M.R. 12 (1968); *United States v. Farley*, 11 U.S.C.M.A. 730, 29 C.M.R. 546 (1960); DiChiara, *Article 92; Judicial Guidelines for Identifying Punitive Orders and Regulations*, 17 A.F.L. Rev. Summer 1975 at 61.

e. *Maximum punishment.* The maximum punishment for willful dereliction of duty was increased from 3 months to 6 months confinement and to include a bad-conduct discharge because such offenses involve a flaunting of authority and are more closely analogous to disobedience offenses.

February 1986 Amendment: The rule was revised to add constructive knowledge as an alternative to the actual knowledge requirement in paragraph (*b*)(3)(*b*) and the related explanation in subparagraph c(3)(b). In reviewing these provisions, it was concluded that the reliance of the drafters of the 1984 revision on the *Curtin* case was misplaced because the portion of that case dealt with failure to obey under Article 92(2), not dereliction under Article 92(3). As revised, the elements and the explanation add an objective standard appropriate for military personnel.

17. Article 93— Cruelty and maltreatment

c. *Explanation.* This paragraph is based on paragraph 172 of MCM, 1969 (Rev.); *United States v. Dickey*, 20 C.M.R. 486 (A.B.R. 1956). The phrase "subject to the Code or not" was added to reflect the fact that the victim could be someone other than a member of the military. The example of sexual harassment was added because some forms of such conduct are nonphysical maltreatment.

18. Article 94— Mutiny and sedition

c. *Explanation.* This paragraph is taken from paragraph 173 of MCM, 1969 (Rev.). Subparagraph (1) is also based on *United States v. Woolbright*, 12 U.S.C.M.A. 450, 31 C.M.R. 36 (1961); *United States v. Duggan* , 4 U.S.C.M.A. 396, 15 C.M.R. 396 (1954). The reference in paragraph 173 of MCM, 1969 (Rev.) to charging failure to report an impending mutiny or sedition under Article 134 has been deleted in subparagraph (4). This is because such an offense was not listed in the Table of Maximum Punishments or elsewhere under Article 134 in that Manual. Article of War 67 included this offense, but Article 94 excludes it. The drafters of paragraph 173 of MCM, 1951 noted the change. To fill the gap they referred to Article 134. Instead, they should have referred to Article 92(3) because dereliction is the gravamen of the offense.

19. Article 95—Resistance, breach of arrest, and escape

b. *Elements.* The elements listed for breaking arrest and escape from custody or confinement have been modified. Paragraph 174 *b, c,* and *d* of MCM, 1969 (Rev.) provided that the accused by "duly" placed in arrest, custody, or confinement. "Duly" was deleted from the elements of these offenses. Instead, the elements specify that the restraint be imposed by one with authority to impose it. This was done to clarify the meaning of the word "duly" and the burden of going forward on the issues of authority to order restraint and the legal basis for the decision to order restraint.

"Duly" means "in due or proper form or manner, according to legal requirements." *Black's Law Dictionary* 450 (5th ed. 1979). *See also United States v. Carson*, 15 U.S.C.M.A. 407, 35 C.M.R. 379 (1965). Thus the term includes a requirement that restraint be imposed by one with authority to do so, and a requirement that such authority be exercised lawfully. Until 1969, the Manual also provided that arrest, confinement, or custody which is "officially imposed is presumed to be legal." Paragraph 174 of MCM, 1951. *See also* paragraph 157 of MCM, (Army), 1949, MCM (AF), 1949; paragraph 139 of MCM, 1928. In practical effect, therefore, the prosecution had only to present some evidence of the authority of the official imposing restraint to meet its burden of proof, unless the presumption of legality was rebutted by some evidence. *See United States v. Delagado*, 12 C.M.R. 651 (C.G.B.R. 1953). *Cf. United States v. Clansey*, 7 U.S.C.M.A. 230, 22 C.M.R. 20 (1956); *United States v. Gray*, 6 U.S.C.M.A. 615, 20 C.M.R. 331 (1956).

The drafters of MCM, 1969 (Rev.), deleted the presumption of legality. In their view the holding in *United States v. Carson, supra*, that this is a question of law to be decided by the military judge made such a presumption meaningless. *Analysis of Contents, Manual for Courts-Martial, United States, 1969 (Revised edition)*, DA PAM 27–2, at 28–8. The drafters considered deleting "duly" as an element but did not because the prosecution must show that restraint was "duly" imposed. *Id.* The result left the implication that the prosecution must produce evidence of both the authority of the person imposing or ordering restraint, and the legality of that official's decision in every case, whether or not the latter is contested. Given the dual meaning of the word "duly" and the reason for deleting the presumption of legality, it is unclear whether the drafters intended this result. *Cf. United States v. Stinson*, 43 C.M.R. 595 (A.C.M.R. 1970).

"Duly" is replaced with the requirement that the person ordering restraint be proved to have authority to do so. This clarifies that proof of arrest, custody, or confinement ordered by a person with authority to do so is sufficient without proof of the underlying basis for the restraint (e.g., probable cause, legally sufficient nonjudicial punishment, risk of flight), unless the latter is put in issue by the defense. This is consistent with Article 95 which on its face does not require the restraint to be lawful (*compare* Article 95 *with* Articles 90–92 which prohibit violations of "*lawful* orders"—which orders are presumed lawful in the absence of evidence to the contrary. *United States v. Smith*, 21 U.S.C.M.A. 231, 45 C.M.R. 5 (1972)). This construction is also supported by judicial decisions. *See United States v. Wilson*, 6 M.J. 214 (C.M.A. 1979); *United States v. Clansey, supra; United States v. Yerger*, 1 U.S.C.M.A. 288, 3 C.M.R. 22 (1952); *United States v. Delgado, supra. Cf. United States v. Mackie*, 16 U.S.C.M.A. 14, 36 C.M.R. 170 (1966); *United States v. Gray, supra. But see United States v. Rozier*, 1 M.J. 469 (C.M.A. 1976). This construction also avoids unnecessary litigation of a collateral issue and eliminates the necessity for the introduction of uncharged misconduct, except when the door is opened by the defense. *Cf. United States v. Yerger, supra; United States v. Mackie, supra.*

1991 Amendment: Subparagraph b(4) was amended by adding an aggravating element of post-trial confinement to invoke increased punishment for escapes from post-trial confinement.

c. *Explanation.*

(1) *Resisting apprehension.*

(a) *Apprehension.* This subparagraph is taken from Article 7.

(b) *Authority to apprehend. See* Analysis, R.C.M. 302(b). The last two sentences are based on paragraph 57 *a* of MCM, 1969 (Rev.); *United States v. Carson, supra.*

(c) *Nature of the resistance.* This subparagraph is taken from paragraph 174 *a* of MCM, 1969 (Rev.).

(d) *Mistake.* This subparagraph is taken from paragraph 174 *a* of MCM, 1969 (Rev.). *See also United States v. Nelson*, 17 U.S.C.M.A. 620, 38 C.M.R. 418 (1968).

(e) *Illegal apprehension.* The first sentence of this subparagraph is taken from paragraph 174*a* of MCM, 1969 (Rev.). Although such a rule is not without criticism, *see United States v. Lewis*, 7 M.J. 348 (C.M.A. 1979); *United States v. Moore*, 483 F.2d 1361, 1364 (9th Cir.1973), it has long been recognized in military and civilian courts. *John Bad Elk v. United States*, 177 U.S. 529 (1900); paragraph 174 *a* of MCM, 1951. *Cf.* paragraph 157 of MCM (Army), 1949; MCM (AF), 1949; paragraph 139 of MCM, 1928; W. Winthrop, *Military Law and Precedents* 122 (2d ed. 1920 reprint). (Before 1951 resisting apprehension was not specifically prohibited by the Articles of War. Earlier references are to breaking arrest or escape from confinement.)

The second sentence has been added to make clear that the issue of legality of an apprehension (e.g., whether based on probable cause or otherwise in accordance with requirements for legal sufficiency; *see* R.C.M. 302(e)) is not in issue until raised by the defense. *United States v. Wilson*, and *United States v. Clansey*, both *supra. Cf. United States v. Smith*, 21 U.S.C.M.A. 231, 45 C.M.R. 5 (1972). *See also* Analysis, paragraph 19 *b*. The presumption is a burden assigning device; it has no evidentiary weight once the issue is raised. Because the issue of legality is not an element, and because the prosecution bears the burden of establishing legality when the issue is raised, the problems of *Mullaney v. Wilbur*, 421 U.S. 684 (1975) and *Turner v. United States*, 396 U.S. 398 (1970) are not encountered. *Cf. Patterson v. New York*, 432 U.S. 197 (1977).

The third sentence is based on *United States v. Carson, supra.*

(2) *Breaking arrest.*

(a) *Arrest.* This subparagraph has been added for clarity.

(b) *Authority to order arrest. See* Analysis, R.C.M. 304(b); R.C.M. 1101; and paragraph 2, Part V.

(c) *Nature of restraint imposed by arrest.* This subparagraph is based on paragraph 174 *b* of MCM, 1969 (Rev.). *See also* Analysis, paragraph 19 *b*.

(d) *Breaking.* This subparagraph is based on paragraph 174 *b* of MCM, 1969 (Rev.).

(e) *Illegal arrest.* The first sentence in this subparagraph is based on paragraph 174 *b* of MCM, 1969 (Rev.). The second sentence has been added to clarify that legality of an arrest (e.g., whether based on probable cause or based on legally sufficient nonjudicial punishment or court-martial sentence) is not in issue until raised by the defense. *See* Analysis, paragraphs 19 *b* and 19 *c*(1)(e). The third sentence is based on*United States v. Carson, supra.*

(3) *Escape from custody.*

(a) *Custody.* This subparagraph is taken from paragraph 174*d* of MCM, 1969 (Rev.). As to the distinction between escape from custody and escape from confinement,*see United States v. Ellsey*, 16 U.S.C.M.A. 455, 37 C.M.R. 75 (1966). *But see United States v. Felty*, 12 M.J. 438 (C.M.A. 1982).

(b) *Authority to apprehend. See* Analysis, paragraph 19 *c*(1)(b).

(c) *Escape.* This cross-reference is based on paragraph 174 *c* of MCM, 1969 (rev.).

(d) *Illegal custody.* The first sentence in this subparagraph is based on paragraph 174 *b* of MCM, 1969 (Rev.). The second sentence has been added to clarify that legality of custody (e.g., whether based on probable cause) is not in issue until raised by the defense. *See* Analysis, paragraphs 19 *b* and 19 *c*(1)(*e*). The third sentence is based on *United States v. Carson, supra.*

(4) *Escape from confinement.*

(a) *Confinement. See* Article 9(a). *See also* Analysis, R.C.M. 305; R.C.M. 1101; and paragraph 5*c*, Part v.

1991 Amendment: Subparagraph c(4)(a) was amended to specify that escape from post-trial confinement is subject to increased punishment.

(b) *Authority to order confinement. See* Analysis, R.C.M. 304(b); R.C.M. 1101; and paragraph 2, Part V.

(c) *Escape.* This subparagraph is based on paragraph 174 *c* of MCM, 1969 (Rev.). *See also United States v. Maslanich*, 13 M.J. 611 (A.F.C.M.R. 1982).

(d) *Status when temporarily outside confinement facility.* This subparagraph is based on *United States v. Silk*, 37 C.M.R. 523 (A.B.r. 1966); *United States v. Sines*, 34 C.M.R. 716 (N.B.R. 1964).

(e) *Legality of confinement.* This subparagraph is based on 174 *a* of MCM, 1969 (Rev.). The second sentence has been added to clarify that legality of confinement (e.g., whether based on probable cause or otherwise in accordance with requirements for legal sufficiency) is not in issue until raised by the defense. *See* Analysis, paragraphs 19 *b* and 19 *c*(1)(e). The third sentence is based on *United States v. Carson, supra.*

1991 Amendment: Subparagraphs *e* and *f* were amended to provide increased punishment for escape from post-trial confinement. The increased punishment reflects the seriousness of the offense and is consistent with other federal law. *See* 18 U.S.C. 751(a).

1998 Amendment: Subparagraphs *a, b, c,* and *f* were amended to implement the amendment to 10 U.S.C. §895 (Article 95, UCMJ) contained in section 1112 of the National Defense Authorization Act for Fiscal Year 1996, Pub. L. No. 104-106, 110 Stat. 186, 461 (1996). The amendment proscribes fleeing from apprehension without regard to whether the accused otherwise resisted apprehension. The amendment responds to the U.S. Court of Appeals for the Armed Forces decisions in *United States v. Harris*, 29 M.J. 169 (C.M.A. 1989), and *United States v. Burgess*, 32 M.J. 446 (C.M.A. 1991). In both cases, the court held that resisting apprehension does not include fleeing from apprehension, contrary to the then-existing explanation in Part IV, paragraph 19c.(1)(c), MCM, of the nature of the resistance required for resisting apprehension. The 1951 and 1969 Manuals for Courts-Martial also explained that flight could constitute resisting apprehension under Article 95, an interpretation affirmed in the only early military case on point, *United States v. Mercer*, 11 C.M.R. 812 (A.F.B.R. 1953). Flight from apprehension should be expressly deterred and punished under military law. Military personnel are specially trained and routinely expected to submit to lawful authority. Rather than being a merely incidental or reflexive action, flight from apprehension in the context of the armed forces may have a distinct and cognizable impact on military discipline.

20. Article 96— Releasing prisoner without proper authority

c. *Explanation.* This paragraph is based on paragraph 175 of MCM, 1969 (Rev.); *United States v. Johnpier*, 12 U.S.C.M.A. 90, 30 C.M.R. 90 (1961). Subparagraphs (1)(c) and (d) have been modified to conform to rules elsewhere in this Manual and restated for clarity.

21. Article 97— Unlawful detention

c. *Explanation.* This paragraph is based on paragraph 176 of MCM, 1969 (Rev.); *United States v. Johnson*, 3 M.J. 361 (C.M.A. 1977). The explanation of the scope of Article 97 is new and results from *Johnson* and the legislative history of Article 97 cited therein. *Id.* at 363 n.6.

22. Article 98— Noncompliance with procedural rules

c. *Explanation.* This paragraph is taken from paragraph 177 of MCM, 1969 (Rev.).

e. *Maximum punishment.* The maximum punishment for intentional failure to enforce or comply with provisions of the Code has been increased from that specified in paragraph 127 *c* of MCM, 1969 (Rev.) to more accurately reflect the seriousness of this offense. *See generally* 18 U.S.C. § 1505, the second paragraph of which prohibits acts analogous to those prohibited in Article 98(2).

23. Article 99— Misbehavior before the enemy

c. *Explanation.* This paragraph is based on paragraphs 178 and 183*a* of MCM, 1969 (Rev.); *United States v. Sperland*, 1 U.S.C.M.A. 661, 5 C.M.R. 89 (1952) (discussion of "before or in the presence of the enemy"); *United States v. Parker*, 3 U.S.C.M.A. 541, 13 C.M.R. 97 (1953) (discussion of "running away"); *United States v. Monday*, 36 C.M.R. 711 (A.B.R. 1966), *pet. denied*, 16 U.S.C.M.A. 659, 37 C.M.R. 471 (1966) (discussion of "the enemy") (*see also United States v. Anderson*, 17 U.S.C.M.A. 588, 38 C.M.R. 386 (1968)); *United States v. Yarborough*, 1 U.S.C.M.A. 678, 5 C.M.R. 106 (1952) (discussion of "fear"); *United States v. Presley*, 18 U.S.C.M.A. 474, 40 C.M.R. 186 (1969); *United States v. King*, 5 U.S.C.M.A. 3, 17 C.M.R. 2 (1954) (discussion of illness as a defense to a charge of cowardice); *United States v. Terry*, 36 C.M.R. 756 (N.B.R. 1965), *aff'd* 16 U.S.C.M.A. 192, 36 C.M.R. 348 (1966) (discussion of "false alarm"); *United States v. Payne*, 40 C.M.R. 516 (A.B.R. 1969); *pet. denied*, 18 U.S.C.M.R. 327 (1969) (discussion of failure to do utmost).

24. Article 100— Subordinate compelling surrender

c. *Explanation.* This paragraph is taken from paragraph 179 of MCM, 1969 (Rev.).

25. Article 101— Improper use of countersign

c. *Explanation.* This paragraph is based on paragraph 180 of MCM, 1969 (Rev.).

26. Article 102— Forcing a safeguard

c. *Explanation.* This paragraph is taken from paragraph 181 of MCM, 1969 (Rev.). Note that a "time of war" need not exist for the commission of this offense. *See Hearings on H.R. 2498 Before a Subcomm. of the House Comm. on Armed Services*, 81st Cong., 1st Sess. 1229 (1949). *See also United States v. Anderson*, 17 U.S.C.M.A. 588, 38 C.M.R. 386 (1968) (concerning a state of belligerency short of formal war).

27. Article 103— Captured or abandoned property

c. *Explanation.* This paragraph is taken from paragraph 182 of MCM, 1969 (Rev.).

e. *Maximum punishment.* The maximum punishments based on value have been revised. Instead of three levels ($50 or less, $50 to $100, and over $100), only two are used. This is simpler and conforms more closely to the division between felony and misdemeanor penalties contingent on value in property offenses in civilian jurisdictions.

*2002 Amendment:*The monetary amount affecting the maximum punishments has been revised from $100 to $500 to account for inflation. The last change was in 1969 raising the amount to $100. The value has also been readjusted to realign it more closely with the division between felony and misdemeanor penalties in civilian jurisdictions. *See generally* American Law Institute, Model Penal Code and Commentaries Sec. 223.1 (1980) (suggesting $500 as the value). The amendment also adds the phrase 'or any firearm or explosive' as an additional criterion. This is because, regardless of the intrinsic value of such items, the threat to the community is substantial when such items are wrongfully bought, sold, traded, dealt in or disposed.

28. Article 104— Aiding the enemy

c. *Explanation.* This paragraph is based on paragraph 183 of MCM, 1969 (Rev.). *See also United States v. Olson*, 7 U.S.C.M.A. 460, 22 C.M.R. 250 (1957); *United States v. Batchelor*, 7 U.S.C.M.A. 354, 22 C.M.R. 144 (1956); *United States v. Dickenson*, 6 U.S.C.M.A. 438, 20 C.M.R. 154 (1955).

29. Article 105— Misconduct as a prisoner

c. *Explanation.* This paragraph is based on paragraph 184 of MCM, 1969 (Rev.). *See also United States v. Batchelor*, 7 U.S.C.M.A. 354, 22 C.M.R. 144 (1956); *United States v. Dickenson*, 7 U.S.C.M.A. 438, 20 C.M.R. 154 (1955).

30. Article 106— Spies

c. *Explanation.* This paragraph is taken from paragraph 185 of MCM, 1969 (Rev.). *See generally* W. Winthrop, *Military Law and Precedents* 766–771 (2d ed. 1920 reprint). Subparagraphs (4) and (6)(b) are also based on Annex to Hague Convention No. IV, Respecting the law and customs of war on land, Oct. 18, 1907, Arts. XXIX and XXXI, 36 Stat. 2303, T.S. No. 539, at 33.

30a. Article 106a— Espionage

Article 106a was added to the UCMJ in the Department of Defense Authorization Act, 1986, Pub.L. No. 99–145, § 534, 99 Stat. 583, 634–35 (1985).

c. *Explanation.* The explanation is based upon H.R. Rep. No. 235, 99th Cong., 1st Sess. (1985), containing the statement of conferees with respect to the legislation establishing Article 106a. *See also* 1985 U.S. Code Cong. & Ad. News 472, 577–79.

1995 Amendment: This subparagraph was amended to clarify that the intent element of espionage is not satisfied merely by proving that the accused acted without lawful authority. Article 106a, Uniform Code of Military Justice. The accused must have acted in bad faith. *United States v. Richardson*, 33 M.J. 127 (C.M.A. 1991); *see Gorin v. United States*, 312 U.S. 19, 21 n.1 (1941).

31. Article 107— False official statements

c. *Explanation.*

(1) *Official documents and statements.* This subparagraph is based on paragraph 186 of MCM, 1969 (Rev.); *United States v. Cummings*, 3 M.J. 246 (C.M.A. 1977). *See also United States v. Collier*, 23 U.S.C.M.A. 713, 48 C.M.R. 789 (1974) (regarding voluntary false statement to military police).

(2) *Status of victim.* The first sentence of this subparagraph is based on *United States v. Cummings, supra.* The second sentence is based on *United States v. Ragins*, 11 M.J. 42 (C.M.A. 1981).

(3) *Intent to deceive.* This subparagraph is based on paragraph 186 of MCM, 1969 (Rev.); *United States v. Hutchins*, 5 U.S.C.M.A. 422, 18 C.M.R. 46 (1955).

(4) *Material gain.* This subparagraph is based on paragraph 186 of MCM, 1969 (Rev.).

(5) *Knowledge that the document or statement was false.* This subparagraph is based on the language of Article 107 and on *United States v. Acosta*, 19 U.S.C.M.A. 341, 41 C.M.R. 341 (1970), and clarifies— as paragraph 186 of MCM, 1969 (Rev.), did not— that actual knowledge of the falsity is necessary. *See also United States v. DeWayne*, 7 M.J. 755 (A.C.M.R. 1979); *United States v. Wright*, 34 C.M.R. 518 (A.B.R. 1963); *United States v. Hughes*, 19 C.M.R. 631 (A.F.B.R. 1955).

2002 Amendment: Subparagraph c(6), 'Statements made during an interrogation,' was removed in light of questions raised by the Court of Appeals for the Armed Forces in *United States v. Solis*, 46 M.J. 31, 35 (C.A.A.F. 1997). In *Solis*, the court said subparagraph c(6) could be viewed as serving at least three different purposes. It could be (1) an expansive description of dicta with no intent to limit prosecutions; (2) protection for an accused against overcharging; or (3) guidance for the conduct of investigations. Subparagraph c(6) was never intended to establish either procedural rights for an accused or internal guidelines to regulate government conduct. Subparagraph (c)(6) was based upon *United States v. Aronson*, 8 U.S.C.M.A. 525, 25 C.M.R. 29 (1957); *United States v. Washington*, 9 U.S.C.M.A. 131, 25 C.M.R. 393 (1958) and *United States v. Davenport*, 9 M.J. 364 (C.M.A. 1980) and was intended merely to describe the rule developed in those cases that a false statement to a law enforcement agent, when made by a servicemember without an independent duty to speak, was not 'official' and therefore not within the purview of Article 107. The subparagraph is removed because the position of the Court of Military Appeals in the three decisions noted above was abandoned in *United States v. Jackson*, 26 M.J. 377 (C.M.A. 1988) and the deleted paragraph no longer accurately describes the current state of the law.

d. *Maximum punishment.* The maximum penalty for all offenses under Article 107 has been increased to include confinement for 5 years to correspond to 18 U.S.C. § 1001, the Federal civilian counterpart of Article 107. *See United States v. DeAngelo*, 15 U.S.C.M.A. 423, 35 C.M.R. 395 (1965).

32. Article 108— Military property of the United States— sale, loss, damage, destruction, or wrongful disposition

c. *Explanation.* This paragraph is based on paragraph 187 of MCM, 1969 (Rev.). *See also United States v. Bernacki*, 13 U.S.C.M.A. 641, 33 C.M.R. 173 (1963); *United States v. Harvey*, 6 M.J. 545 (N.C.M.R. 1978); *United States v. Geisler*, 37 C.M.R. 530 (A.B.R. 1966). The last sentence in subparagraph (c)(1) is based on *United States v. Schelin*, 15 M.J. 218 (C.M.A. 1983).

1986 Amendment: Subparagraph *c* (1) was amended to correct an ambiguity in the definition of military property. The previous language "military department" is specifically defined in 10 U.S.C. 101(7) as consisting of the Department of the Army, Navy and Air Force. Article 1(8), UCMJ, however, defines "military" when used in the Code as referring to all the armed forces. Use of the term "military department" inadvertently excluded property owned or used by the Coast Guard. The subparagraph has been changed to return to the state of the law prior to 1984, as including the property of all the armed forces. *See United States v. Geisler*, 37 C.M.R. 530 (A.B.R. 1966); *United States v. Schelin*, 15 M.J. 218, 220 n.6 (C.M.A. 1983).

d. *Lesser included offense. See United States v. Mizner*, 49 C.M.R. 26 (A.C.M.R. 1974).

1986 Amendment: Subparagraph *d* (1) was amended to include a lesser included offense previously omitted. *See United States v. Rivers*, 3 C.M.R. 564 (A.F.B.R. 1952) and 18 U.S.C. 641. Subparagraphs *d*(2) and (4) were amended to include lesser included offenses recognizing that destruction and damage of property which is not proved to be military may be a violation of Article 109. *See United States v. Suthers*, 22 C.M.R. 787 (A.F.B.R. 1956).

e. *Maximum punishment.* The maximum punishments have been revised. Instead of three levels ($50 or less, $50 to $100, and over $100) only two are used. This is simpler and conforms more closely to the division between felony and misdemeanor penalties contingent on value in property offenses in civilian jurisdictions. The punishments are based on 18 U.S.C. § 1361. The maximum punishment for selling or wrongfully disposing of a firearm or explosive and for willfully damaging, destroying, or losing such property or suffering it to be lost, damaged, destroyed, sold, or wrongfully disposed of includes 10 years confinement regardless of the value of the item. The harm to the military in such cases is not simply the intrinsic value of the item. Because of their nature, special accountability and protective measures are employed to protect firearms or explosives against loss, damage, destruction, sale, and wrongful disposition. Such property may be a target of theft or other offenses without regard to its value. Therefore, to protect the Government's special interest in such property, and the community against improper disposition, such property is treated the same as property of a higher value.

*2002 Amendment:*The monetary amount affecting the maximum punishments has been revised from $100 to $500 to account for inflation. The last change was in 1969 raising the amount to $100. The value has also been readjusted to realign it more closely with the division between felony and misdemeanor penalties in civilian jurisdictions. *See generally* American Law Institute, Model Penal Code and Commentaries Sec. 223.1 (1980) (suggesting $500 as the value). Although the monetary amount affecting punishment in 18 U.S.C. Sec. 1361, Government property or contracts, and 18 U.S.C. Sec. 641, Public money, property or records, was increased from $100 to $1000 pursuant to section 606 of the Economic Espionage Act of 1996, P. L. No. 104-294, 110 Stat. 3488 (1996), a value of $500 was chosen to maintain deterrence, simplicity, and uniformity for the Manual's property offenses.

33. Article 109— Property other than military property of the United States— waste, spoilage, or destruction

c. *Explanation.* This paragraph is based on paragraph 188 of MCM, 1969 (Rev.). *See also United States v. Bernacki*, 13 U.S.C.M.A. 641, 33 C.M.R. 173 (1963).

e. *Maximum punishment.* The maximum punishments have been revised. Instead of three levels ($50 or less, $50 to $100, and over $100), only two are used. This is simpler and conforms more closely to the division between felony and misdemeanor penalties contingent on value in property offenses in civilian jurisdictions.

*2002 Amendment:*The monetary amount affecting the maximum punishments has been revised from $100 to $500 to account for inflation. The last change was in 1969 raising the amount to $100. The value has also been readjusted to realign it more closely with the division between felony and misdemeanor penalties in civilian jurisdictions. *See generally* American Law Institute, Model Penal Code and Commentaries Sec. 223.1 (1980) (suggesting $500 as the value).

f. *Sample specification. See United States v. Collins*, 16 U.S.C.M.A. 167, 36 C.M.R. 323 (1966), concerning charging damage to different articles belonging to different owners, which occurred during a single transaction, as one offense.

34. Article 110— Improper hazarding of vessel

c. *Explanation.* This paragraph is based on paragraph 189 of MCM, 1969 (Rev.). *See also United States v. Adams*, 42 C.M.R. 911 (N.C.M.R. 1970), *pet. denied*, 20 U.S.C.M.A. 628 (1970); *United States v. MacLane*, 32 C.M.R. 732 (C.G.B.R. 1962); *United States v. Day*, 23 C.M.R. 651 (N.B.R. 1957).

35. Article 111— Drunken or reckless driving

a. *Text. 2002 Amendment*: Changes to this Article are contained in section 581 of the National Defense Authorization Act for Fiscal Year 2002, P.L. 107-107, 115 Stat. 1012 (2001).

Additionally, this change defines the offense in terms of what alcohol concentration level is prohibited by operation of State law or as otherwise provided. Also, the text reflects an amendment to section 911 of title 10, United States Code, in section 552 of the National Defense Authorization Act for Fiscal Year 2004 to restore the blood alcohol concentration limit that defines the offense of drunken operation of a vehicle, aircraft, or vessel in the United States to the limit that existed before the passage of section 581 of the National Defense Authorization Act for Fiscal Year 2002. Before passage of that Act, an alcohol concentration level in the person's blood or breath of 0.10 grams "or more" of alcohol per 100 milliliters of blood (or 210 liters of breath) was a punishable offense. By relying on the term "blood alcohol content limit," as defined to be the maximum permissible concentration to operate a vehicle, aircraft, or vessel, section 581 resulted in eliminating the level of 0.10 grams as a prohibited level of alcohol concentration and raised the definition of the offense to some level in excess of 0.10 grams.

2007 Amendment: Changes to this Article are contained in section 552 of the National Defense Authorization Act for Fiscal Year 2004, P.L. 108 136, 117 Stat.1392 (2003), and supersede any changes to Paragraph 35 by Executive Order 13387 (14 October 2005).

b. *Elements.* The aggravating element of injury is listed as suggested by sample specification number 75 and the Table of Maximum Punishments at 25–13 and A6–13 of MCM, 1969 (Rev.). The wording leaves it possible to plead and prove that the *accused* was injured as a result of the accused's drunken driving and so make available the higher maximum punishment. This result recognizes the interest of society in the accused's resulting unavailability or impairment for duty and the costs of medical treatment. Paragraph 190 (Proof, (c)) of MCM, 1969 (Rev.) used "victim," the ambiguity of which might have implied that injury to the accused would not aggravate the maximum punishment. *Analysis of Contents, Manual for Courts-Martial, United States, 1969 (Revised Edition)* DA PAM 27–2, at 28–10, does not suggest that the drafters intended such a result.

2007 Amendment: Paragraph b(2)(c) is amended for consistency with the changes in statutory text contained in section 552 of the National Defense Authorization Act for Fiscal Year 2004, P.L. 108 136, 117 Stat. 1392 (2003), and supersedes any changes to Paragraph 35 by Executive Order 13387 (14 October 2005).

c. *Explanation.* This paragraph is taken from paragraph 190 of MCM, 1969 (Rev.). *See also United States v. Bull*, 3 U.S.C.M.A. 635, 14 C.M.R. 53 (1954) (drunkenness); *United States v. Eagleson*, 3 U.S.C.M.A. 685, 14 C.M.R. 103 (1954) (reckless); *United States v. Grossman* , 2 U.S.C.M.A. 406, 9 C.M.R. 36 (1953) (separate offenses).

1991 Amendment: The order of the last and penultimate phrases was reversed to clarify that "so as to cause the particular vehicle to move" modifies only "the manipulation of its controls" and not the "setting of its motive power in action". This change makes clear that merely starting the engine, without movement of the vehicle, is included within the definition of "operating".

e. *Maximum Punishment.* The maximum authorized confinement for drunk driving resulting in injury was increased from 1 year to 18 months. This increase reflects the same concern for the seriousness of the misconduct as that which has, by current reports, motivated almost half the states to provide more stringent responses.

1986 Amendment: Subparagraphs b(2), c(3), and f were

amended to implement the amendment to Article 111 contained in the Anti-Drug Abuse Act of 1986, tit. III, § 3055, Pub.L. No. 99–570, enacted 27 October 1986, proscribing driving while impaired by a substance described in Article 112a(b). This amendment codifies prior interpretation of the scope of Article 111, as previously implemented in paragraph 35c(3).

1995 Amendment: This paragraph was amended pursuant to the changes to Article 111 included in the National Defense Authorization Act for Fiscal Year 1993, Pub. L. No. 102–484, 106 Stat. 2315, 2506 (1992). New subparagraphs c(2) and (3) were added to include vessels and aircraft, respectively. Paragraph 35 was also amended to make punishable actual physical control of a vehicle, aircraft, or vessel while drunk or impaired, or in a reckless fashion, or while one's blood or breath alcohol concentration is in violation of the described per se standard. A new subparagraph c(5) was added to define the concept of actual physical control. This change allows drunk or impaired individuals who demonstrate the capability and power to operate a vehicle, aircraft, or vessel to be apprehended if in the vehicle, aircraft, or vessel, but not actually operating it at the time.

The amendment also clarifies that culpability extends to the person operating or exercising actual physical control through the agency of another (*e.g.*, the captain of a ship giving orders to a helmsman). The amendment also provides a blood/alcohol blood/breath concentration of 0.10 or greater as a per se standard for illegal intoxication. The change will not, however, preclude prosecution where no chemical test is taken or even where the results of the chemical tests are below the statutory limits, where other evidence of intoxication is available. *See United States v. Gholson*, 319 F. Supp. 499 (E.D. Va. 1970).

A new paragraph c(9) was added to clarify that in order to show that the accused caused personal injury, the government must prove proximate causation and not merely cause–in–fact. *Accord United States v. Lingenfelter*, 30 M.J. 302 (C.M.A. 1990). The definition of "proximate cause" is based on *United States v. Romero*, 1 M.J. 227, 230 (C.M.A. 1975). Previous subparagraph c(2) is renumbered c(4). Previous subparagraphs c(3)–c(5) are renumbered c(6)–c(8), respectively, and previous subparagraph c(6) is renumbered c(10).

Subparagraphs d(1) and (2) are redesignated d(2)(b) and d(2)(c). The new d(2)(a) adds Article 110 (improper hazarding of a vessel) as a lesser included offense of drunken operation or actual physical control of a vessel.

The new d(1) adds Article 110 (improper hazarding of a vessel) as a lesser included offense of reckless or wanton or impaired operation or physical control of a vessel.

36. Article 112— Drunk on duty

c. *Explanation.* This paragraph is based on paragraph 191 of MCM, 1969 (Rev.). The discussion of defenses is based on *United States v. Gossett*, 14 U.S.C.M.A. 305, 34 C.M.R. 85 (1963); *United States v. Burroughs*, 37 C.M.R. 775 (C.G.B.R. 1966).

37. Article 112a— Wrongful use, possession, etc., of controlled substances

Introduction. This paragraph is based on Article 112a (*see* Military Justice Act of 1983, Pub.L. No. 98–209, § 8, 97 Stat. 1393 (1983)), and on paragraphs 127 and 213, and Appendix 6c of MCM, 1969 (Rev.), as amended by Exec. Order No. 12383 (Sep. 23, 1982). Paragraphs 127 and 213 and Appendix 6c of MCM, 1969 (Rev.) are consistent with Article 112a. *See* S.Rep. No. 53, 98th Cong., 1st Sess. 29 (1983).

The only changes made by Article 112a in the former Manual paragraphs are: elimination of the third element under Article 134; substitution of barbituric acid for phenobarbital and secobarbital (these are still specifically listed in subparagraph c), and inclusion of importation and exportation of controlled substances. The definition of "customs territory of the United States" is based on 21 U.S.C. § 951(a)(2) and on general headnote 2 to the Tariff Schedules of the United States. *See* 21 U.S.C. § 1202. *See also* H.R.Rep. No. 91–1444, 91st Cong., 2d Sess. 74 (1970). The maximum punishments for importing or exporting a controlled substance are based generally on 21 U.S.C. § 960. *See also* 21 U.S.C. §§ 951–53.

The definition of "missile launch facility" has been added to clarify that the term includes not only the actual situs of the missile, but those places directly integral to the launch of the missile.

The following is an analysis of Exec. Order No. 12383 (Sep. 23,1982):

Section 1 (now subparagraph e) amends paragraph 127 *c*, Section A of the MCM, 1969 (Rev.). This amendment of the Table of Maximum Punishments provides a completely revised system of punishments for contraband drug offenses under Article 134. The punishments under 21 U.S.C. §§ 841 and 844 were used as a benchmark for punishments in this paragraph. Thus, the maximum penalty for distribution or possession with intent to distribute certain Schedule I substances under 21 U.S.C. § 841—15 years imprisonment— is the same as the highest maximum punishment under paragraph 127 *c* (except when the escalator clause is triggered, *see* analysis of section 2 *infra.*)

Within the range under the 15 year maximum, the penalties under paragraph 127 *c* are generally somewhat more severe than those under 21 U.S.C. §§ 841 and 844. This is because in the military *any* drug offense is serious because of high potential for adversely affecting readiness and mission performance. *See generally Schlesinger v. Councilman*, 420 U.S. 738, 760 n.34 (1975); *United States v. Trottier*, 9 M.J. 337 (C.M.A. 1980). The availability of contraband drugs, especially in some overseas locations, the ambivalence toward and even acceptance of drug usage in some segments of society, especially among young people, and the insidious nature of drug offenses all require that deterrence play a substantial part in the effort to prevent drug abuse by servicemembers.

The following sentence enhancement provisions in the United States Code were not adopted: (1) the recidivism provisions in 21 U.S.C. §§ 841(b), 844(a), and 845(b), which either double or triple the otherwise prescribed maximum penalty; and (2) the provision in 21 U.S.C. § 845(a) which doubles the maximum penalty for distribution of a controlled substance to a person under the age of 21. (The latter provision would probably apply to a high percentage of distribution offenses in the armed forces, given the high proportion of persons in this age group in the armed forces.) These special provisions were not adopted in favor of a simpler, more uniform punishment system. The overall result is an absence of the higher punishment extremes of the Federal system, while some of the offenses treated more leniently in the lower end of the scale in the Federal system are subject to potentially higher punishments in the military, for the reasons stated in the preceding paragraph. There are no mandatory minimum sentences for any drug offense. *See* Article 56.

The expungement procedure in 21 U.S.C. § 844(b) and (c) is unnecessary and inappropriate for military practice. Alternatives to prosecution for drug offenses already exist. *See, e.g.*, Article 15. The use of such alternatives is properly a command prerogative.

Section 2 (now the last paragraph of subparagraph e) amends paragraph 127c Section B by adding an escalator clause to provide for certain special situations, unique to the military, in which drug involvement presents an even greater danger than normal. *See* 37 U.S.C. § 310 concerning hostile fire pay zones.

Section 3 (now subparagraphs b and c) amends paragraph 213, dealing with certain offenses under Article 134. Paragraph 213 *g* replaces the discussion of offenses involving some contraband drugs which was found in the last paragraph of paragraph 213 *b* of MCM, 1969 (Rev.). It was considered necessary to treat drug offenses more extensively in the Manual for Court-Martial because of the significant incidence of drug offenses in the military and because of the serious effect such offenses have in the military environment. It was also necessary to provide a comprehensive treatment of drugs, with a complete set of maximum punishments, in order to eliminate the confusion, disruption, and disparate treatment of some drug offenses among the services in the wake of *United States v. Courtney*, 1 M.J. 438 (C.M.A. 1976); *United States v. Jackson*, 3 M.J. 101 (C.M.A. 1977); *United States v. Hoesing*, 5 M.J. 355 (C.M.A. 1978); *United States v. Guilbault*, 6 M.J. 20 (C.M.A. 1978); *United States v. Thurman*, 7 M.J. 26 (C.M.A. 1979).

(1) *Controlled substance.* The list of drugs specifically punishable under Article 134 has been expanded to cover the substances which are, according to studies, most prevalent in the military community. *See, e.g.*, M. Burt, *et al. Highlights from the Worldwide Survey of Nonmedical Drug Use and Alcohol Use Among Military Personnel: 1980.* In addition, the controlled substances which are listed in Schedules I through V of the Comprehensive Drug Abuse Prevention and Control Act of 1970 (codified at 21 U.S.C. § 801 *et seq.*) as amended are incorporated. The most commonly abused drugs are listed separately so that it will be unnecessary to refer to the controlled substances list, as modified by the Attorney General in the Code of Federal Regulations, in most cases. Most commanders and some legal offices do not have ready access to such authorities.

(2) *Possess.* The definition of possession is based upon *United States v. Aloyian*, 16 U.S.C.M.A. 333, 36 C.M.R. 489 (1966) and paragraph 4–144, *Military Judges' Benchbook*, DA PAM 27–9 (May 1982). *See also United States v. Wilson*, 7 M.J. 290 (C.M.A. 1979) and cases cited therein concerning the concept of constructive possession. With respect to the inferences described in this subparagraph and subparagraph (5) *Wrongfulness, see United States v. Alvarez*, 10 U.S.C.M.A. 24, 27 C.M.R. 98 (1958); *United States v. Nabors*, 10 U.S.C.M.A. 27, 27 C.M.R. 101 (1958). It is important to bear in mind that distinction between inferences and presumptions. *See United States v. Mahan* , 1 M.J. 303 (C.M.R. 1976). *See also United States v. Baylor*, 16 U.S.C.M.A. 502, 37 C.M.R. 122 (1967).

(3) *Distribute.* This subparagraph is based on 21 U.S.C. § 802(8) and (11). *See also* E. Devitt and C. Blackmar, 2 *Federal Jury Practice and Instructions*, § 58.03 (3d ed. 1977).

"Distribution" replaces "sale" and "transfer." This conforms with Federal practice, *see* 21 U.S.C. § 841(a), and will simplify military practice by reducing pleading, proof, and associated multiplicity problems in drug offenses. *See, e.g., United States v. Long*, 7 M.J. 342 (C.M.A. 1979); *United States v. Maginley*, 13 U.S.C.M.A. 445, 32 C.M.R. 445 (1963). Evidence of sale is not necessary to prove the offense of distributing a controlled substance. *See United States v. Snow* , 537 F.2d 1166 (4th Cir. 1976); *United States v. Johnson*, 481 F.2d 645 (5th Cir. 1973). Thus, the defense of "agency" *see United States v. Fruscella*, 21 U.S.C.M.A. 26, 44 C.M.R. 80 (1971), no longer applies in the military. *Cf. United States v. Snow, supra; United States v. Pruitt*, 487 F.2d 1241 (8th Cir. 1973); *United States v. Johnson, supra* ("procuring agent" defense abolished under 21 U.S.C. § 801 *et seq.*). Evidence of sale is admissible, of course, on the merits as "part and parcel" of the criminal transaction (*see United States v. Stokes*, 12 M.J. 229 (C.M.A. 1982); *cf. United States v. Johnson, supra; see also* Mil. R. Evid. 404(b)), or in aggravation (*see* paragraph 75 *b* (4) of MCM, 1969 (Rev.); *see also United States v. Vickers*, 13 M.J. 403 (C.M.A. 1982)).

(4) *Manufacture.* This definition is taken from 21 U.S.C. § 802(14). The exception in 21 U.S.C. § 802(14) is covered in subparagraph (5).

(5) *Wrongfulness.* This subparagraph is based on the last paragraph of paragraph 213 *b* of MCM, 1969 (Rev.). *Cf.* 21 U.S.C. § 822(c). *See also United States v. West*, 15 U.S.C.M.A. 3, 34 C.M.R. 449 (1964); paragraphs 4–144 and 145, Military Judges' Benchbook, DA PAM 27–9 (May 1982). It is not intended to perpetuate the holding in *United States v. Rowe*, 11 M.J. 11 (C.M.A. 1981).

(6) *Intent to distribute.* This subparagraph parallels Federal law which allows for increased punishment for drug offenses with an intent to distribute. 21 U.S.C. §841(a)(1). The discussion of circumstances from which an inference of intent to distribute may be inferred is based on numerous Federal cases. *See, e.g., United States v. Grayson*, 625 F.2d 66 (5th Cir. 1980); *United States v. Hill*, 589 F.2d 1344 (8th Cir. 1979), *cert. denied*, 442 U.S. 919 (1979); *United States v. Ramirez-Rodriquez*, 552 F.2d 883 (9th Cir. 1977); *United States v. Blake*, 484 F.2d 50 (8th Cir. 1973); *cert. denied*, 417 U.S. 949 (1974). *Cf. United States v. Mather*, 465 F.2d 1035 (5th Cir.1972), *cert. denied*, 409 U.S. 1085 (1972). Possession of a large amount of drugs may permit an inference but does not create a presumption of intent to distribute. *See Turner v. United States*, 396 U.S. 398 (1970); *United States v. Mahan*, 1 M.J. 303 (C.M.A. 1976).

(7) *Certain amount.* This subparagraph is based on *United States v. Alvarez*, 10 U.S.C.M.A. 24, 27 C.M.R. 98 (1958); *United States v. Brown*, 45 C.M.R. 416 (A.C.M.R. 1972); *United States v. Burns*, 37 C.M.R. 942 (A.F.B.R. 1967); *United States v. Owens*, 36 C.M.R. 909 (A.B.R. 1966).

1993 Amendment. Paragraph *c* was amended by adding new paragraphs (10) and (11). Subparagraph (10) defines the term "use" and delineates knowledge of the presence of the controlled substance as a required component of the offense. *See United States v. Mance*, 26 M.J. 244 (C.M.A. 1988). The validity of a permissive inference of knowledge is recognized. *See United States v. Ford*, 23 M.J. 331 (C.M.A. 1987); *United States v.*

Harper, 22 M.J. 157 (C.M.A. 1986). Subparagraph (11) precludes an accused from relying upon lack of actual knowledge when such accused has purposefully avoided knowledge of the presence or identity of controlled substances. *See United States v. Mance, supra*, (Cox, J., concurring). When an accused deliberately avoids knowing the truth concerning a crucial fact (i.e. presence or identity) and there is a high probability that the crucial fact does exist, the accused is held accountable to the same extent as one who has actual knowledge. *See United States v. Newman*, 14 M.J. 474 (C.M.A. 1983). Subsection (11) follows federal authority which equates actual knowledge with deliberate ignorance. *See United States v. Ramsey*, 785 F.2d 184 (7th Cir. 1986), *cert. denied* , 476 U.S. 1186 (1986).

Section 4 (now subparagraph f) amends Appendix 6c. The new sample specifications are based on sample specifications 144 through 146 found in appendix 6c of the MCM, 1969 (Rev.), as modified to reflect the new comprehensive drug offense provision.

Section 5 provides an effective date for the new amendments.

Section 6 requires the Secretary of Defense to transmit these amendments to Congress.

38. Article 113— Misbehavior of sentinel or lookout

c. *Explanation.* Subparagraphs (1), (2), and (3) are based on paragraph 192 of MCM, 1969 (Rev.). Subparagraph (4) is based on *United States v. Seeser*, 5 U.S.C.M.A. 472, 18 C.M.R. 96 (1955); paragraph 192 of MCM, 1969 (Rev.); paragraph 174 of MCM (Army), 1949; paragraph 174 of MCM (AF), 1949. Subparagraph (6) is based on *United States v. Williams*, 4 U.S.C.M.A. 69, 15 C.M.R. 69 (1954); *United States v. Cook*, 31 C.M.R. 550 (A.F.B.R. 1961). *See also United States v. Getman*, 2 M.J. 279 (A.F.C.M.R. 1976).

39. Article 114— Duelling

c. *Explanation.* This paragraph is based on paragraph 193 of MCM, 1969 (Rev.). The explanation of conniving at fighting a duel was modified to reflect the requirement for actual knowledge and to more correctly reflect the term connive.

f. *Sample specification.* The sample specification for conniving at fighting a duel was redrafted to more accurately reflect the nature of the offense.

40. Article 115— Malingering

c. *Explanation.* This paragraph is based on paragraph 194 of MCM, 1969 (Rev.). *See also United States v. Kisner*, 15 U.S.C.M.A. 153, 35 C.M.R. 125 (1964); *United States v. Mamaluy*, 10 U.S.C.M.A. 102, 27 C.M.R. 176 (1959); *United States v. Kersten*, 4 M.J. 657 (A.C.M.R. 1977).

d. *Lesser included offenses. See United States v. Taylor*, 17 U.S.C.M.A. 595, 38 C.M.R. 393 (1968).

e. *Maximum punishment.* The maximum punishments were changed to reflect the greater seriousness of malingering in war or other combat situations and to add a greater measure of deterrence in such cases.

41. Article 116— Riot or breach of peace

c. *Explanation.* This paragraph is based on paragraph 195 of MCM, 1969 (Rev.) and *United States v. Metcalf*, 16 U.S.C.M.A. 153, 36 C.M.R. 309 (1966). The reference to "use of vile or abusive words to another in a public place" contained in paragraph 195 *b* of MCM, 1969 (Rev.) has been replaced by the language contained in the fourth sentence of subparagraph (2) since the former language was subject to an overly broad application. *See Gooding v. Wilson*, 405 U.S. 518 (1972).

f. *Sample specifications.* Riot— *see United States v. Randolf*, 49 C.M.R. 336 (N.C.M.R. 1974); *United States v. Brice*, 48 C.M.R. 368 (N.C.M.R. 1973).

42. Article 117— Provoking speeches or gestures

c. *Explanation.* Subparagraph (1) is based on paragraph 196 of MCM, 1969 (Rev.); *United States v. Thompson*, 22 U.S.C.M.A. 88, 46 C.M.R. 88 (1972). *See generally Gooding v. Wilson*, 405 U.S. 518 (1972); *United States v. Hughens*, 14 C.M.R. 509 (N.B.R. 1954). Subparagraph (2) is based on the language of Article 117 and *United States v. Bowden*, 24 C.M.R. 540 (A.F.B.R. 1957), *pet. denied*, 24 C.M.R. 311 (1957). *See also United States v. Lacy*, 10 U.S.C.M.A. 164, 27 C.M.R. 238 (1959).

1986 Amendment: The listing of "Article 134— indecent language" as a lesser included offense of provoking speeches was deleted. *United States v. Linyear*, 3 M.J. 1027 (N.M.C.M.R. 1977), held that provoking speeches is actually a lesser included offense of indecent language. Also, indecent language carries a greater maximum punishment than provoking speeches, which would be unusual for a lesser offense.

e. *Maximum punishment.* The maximum punishment was increased from that set forth in paragraph 127*c* of MCM, 1969 (Rev.) to more accurately reflect the seriousness of the offense.

43. Article 118— Murder

a. *Text.*

b. *Elements.* Element (b) in (3), *Act inherently dangerous to others*, has been modified based on *United States v. Hartley*, 16 U.S.C.M.A. 249, 36 C.M.R. 405 (1966).

2007 Amendment: Paragraph (4) of the text and elements has been amended for consistency with the changes to Article 118 under Section 552 of the National Defense Authorization Act for Fiscal Year 2006, P.L. 109-163, 6 January 2006. *See* subsection (d) of Section 552.

c. *Explanation.* This paragraph is based on paragraph 197 of MCM, 1969 (Rev.). Subparagraphs c(2)(b) is based on *United States v. Sechler*, 3 U.S.C.M.A. 363, 12 C.M.R. 119 (1953). As to subparagraph (c)(4)(A), *see United States v. Vandenack*, 15 M.J. 428 (C.M.A. 1983). Subparagraph c(4)(b) is based on *United States v. Stokes*, 6 U.S.C.M.A. 65, 19 C.M.R. 191 (1955).

d. *Lesser included offenses.* As to Article 118(3), *see United States v. Roa*, 12 M.J. 210 (C.M.A. 1982).

1993 Amendment: The listed lesser included offenses of murder under Article 118(3) were changed to conform to the rationale of *United States v. Roa*, 12 M.J. 210 (C.M.A. 1982). Inasmuch as Article 118(3) does not require specific intent, attempted murder, voluntary manslaughter, assault with intent to murder and assault with intent to commit voluntary manslaughter are not lesser included offenses of murder under Article 118(3).

1995 Amendment: The word "others" was replaced by the word "another" in Article 118(3) pursuant to the National Defense Authorization Act for Fiscal Year 1993, Pub. L. No. 102—484, 106 Stat. 2315, 2506 (1992). This change addresses the limited language previously used in Article 118(3) as identified in *United States v. Berg*, 30 M.J. 195 (C.M.A. 1990).

44. Article 119— Manslaughter

b. *Elements.*

2007 Amendment: Paragraph (4) of the elements has been amended for consistency with the changes to Article 118 under Section 552 of the National Defense Authorization Act for Fiscal Year 2006, P.L. 109-163, 6 January 2006. *See* subsection (d) of Section 552.

c. *Explanation.* This paragraph is based on paragraph 198 of MCM, 1969 (Rev.). *See also United States v. Moglia*, 3 M.J. 216 (C.M.A. 1977); *United States v. Harrison*, 16 U.S.C.M.A. 484, 37 C.M.R. 104 (1967); *United States v. Redding*, 14 U.S.C.M.A. 242, 34 C.M.R. 22 (1963); *United States v. Fox*, 2 U.S.C.M.A. 465, 9 C.M.R. 95 (1953).

e. *Maximum punishment.*

1994 Amendment. The amendment to paragraph 44e(1) increased the maximum period of confinement for voluntary manslaughter to 15 years. The 10-year maximum confinement period was unnecessarily restrictive; an egregious case of voluntary manslaughter may warrant confinement in excess of ten years.

1994 Amendment. The amendment to paragraph 44e(2) eliminated the anomaly created when the maximum authorized punishment for a lesser included offense of involuntary manslaughter was greater than the maximum authorized punishment for the offense of involuntary manslaughter. For example, prior to the amendment, the maximum authorized punishment for the offense of aggravated assault with a dangerous weapon was greater than that of involuntary manslaughter. This amendment also facilitates instructions on lesser included offenses of involuntary manslaughter. *See United States v. Emmons*, 31 M.J. 108 (C.M.A. 1990).

44a. Article 119a— Death or injury of an unborn child

c. *Explanation.* This paragraph is new and is based on Public Law 108-212, 18 U.S.C. Sec. 1841 and 10 U.S.C. Sec. 919a (Unborn Victims of Violence Act of 2004) enacted on 1 April 2004.

45. Article 120— Rape, sexual assault, and other sexual misconduct

b. *Elements. 2004 Amendment:* Paragraph 45(b)(2) was amended to add two distinct elements of age based upon the 1994 amendment to paragraph 45(e). See also concurrent change to R.C.M. 307(c)(3) and accompanying analysis.

c. *Explanation.* This paragraph is based on paragraph 199 of MCM, 1969 (Rev.). The third paragraph of paragraph 199(a) was deleted as unnecessary. The third paragraph of paragraph 199(b) was deleted based on the preemption doctrine. *See United States v. Wright*, 5 M.J. 106 (C.M.A. 1978); *United States v. Norris*, 2 U.S.C.M.A. 236, 8 C.M.R. 36 (1953). *Cf. Williams v. United States*, 327 U.S. 711 (1946) (scope of preemption doctrine). The Military Rules of Evidence deleted the requirement for corroboration of the victim's testimony in rape and similar cases under former paragraph 153 *a* of MCM, 1969. *See* Analysis, Mil. R. Evid. 412.

d. *Lesser included offenses.* Carnal knowledge was deleted as a lesser included offense of rape in view of the separate elements in each offense. Both should be separately pleaded in a proper case. *See generally United States v. Smith* , 7 M.J. 842 (A.C.M.R. 1979).

1993 Amendment. The amendment to para 45 *d*(1) represents an administrative change to conform the Manual with case authority. Carnal knowledge is a lesser included offense of rape where the pleading alleges that the victim has not attained the age of 16 years. *See United States v. Baker*, 28 M.J. 900 (A.C.M.R. 1989); *United States v. Stratton*, 12 M.J. 998 (A.F.C.M.R. 1982), *pet. denied*, 15 M.J. 107 (C.M.A. 1983); *United States v. Smith*, 7 M.J. 842 (A.C.M.R. 1979).

e. *Maximum punishment.*

1994 Amendment. Subparagraph *e* was amended by creating two distinct categories of carnal knowledge for sentencing purposes -- one involving children who had attained the age of 12 years at the time of the offense, now designated as subparagraph e(2), and the other for those who were younger than 12 years. The latter is now designated as subparagraph e(3). The punishment for the older children was increased from 15 to 20 years confinement. The maximum confinement for carnal knowledge of a child under 12 years was increased to life. The purpose for these changes is to bring the punishments more in line with those for sodomy of a child under paragraph 51e of this part and with the Sexual Abuse Act of 1986, 18 U.S.C. §§ 2241–2245. The alignment of the maximum punishments for carnal knowledge with those of sodomy is aimed at paralleling the concept of gender–neutrality incorporated into the Sexual Abuse Act.

1995 Amendment. The offense of rape was made gender neutral and the spousal exception was removed under Article 120(a). National Defense Authorization Act for Fiscal Year 1993, Pub. L. No. 102–484, 106 Stat. 2315, 2506 (1992).

Rape may "be punished by death" only if constitutionally permissible. In *Coker v. Georgia*, 433 U.S. 584 (1977), the Court held that the death penalty is "grossly disproportionate and excessive punishment for the rape of an adult woman," and is "therefore forbidden by the Eighth Amendment as cruel and unusual punishment." *Id.* at 592 (plurality opinion). *Coker*, however, leaves open the question of whether it is permissible to impose the death penalty for the rape of a minor by an adult. *See Coker*, 433 U.S. at 595. *See Leatherwood v. State*, 548 So.2d 389 (Miss. 1989) (death sentence for rape of minor by an adult is not cruel and unusual punishment prohibited by the Eighth Amendment). *But see Buford v. State*, 403 So.2d 943 (Fla. 1981) (sentence of death is grossly disproportionate for sexual assault of a minor by an adult and consequently is forbidden by Eighth Amendment as cruel and unusual punishment).

1998 Amendment: In enacting section 1113 of the National Defense Authorization Act for Fiscal Year 1996, Pub. L. No. 104-106, 110 Stat. 186, 462 (1996), Congress amended Article 120, UCMJ, to make the offense gender neutral and create a mistake of fact as to age defense to a prosecution for carnal knowledge.

The accused must prove by a preponderance of the evidence that the person with whom he or she had sexual intercourse was at least 12 years of age, and that the accused reasonably believed that this person was at least 16 years of age.

f. *Sample Specification. 2004 Amendment:* Paragraph 45(f)(2) was amended to aid practitioners in charging the two distinct categories of carnal knowledge created in 1994. For the same reason paragraph 45(f)(1) was amended to allow for contingencies of proof because carnal knowledge is a lesser-included offense of rape if properly pleaded. *See also* concurrent change to R.C.M.307(c)(3) and accompanying analysis.

2007 Amendment: Changes to this paragraph are contained in Div. A. Title V. Subtitle E, Section 552(a)(1) of the National Defense Authorization Act for Fiscal Year 2006, P.L. 109-163, 119 Stat. 3257 (6 January 2006), which supersedes the previous paragraph 45, Rape and Carnal Knowledge, in its entirety and replaces paragraph 45 with Rape, sexual assault and other sexual misconduct. In accordance with Section 552(c) of that Act, the amendment to the Article applies only with respect to offenses committed on or after 1 October 2007.

Nothing in these amendments invalidates any nonjudicial punishment proceeding, restraint, investigation, referral of charges, trial in which arraignment occurred, or other action begun prior to 1 October 2007. Any such nonjudical punishment proceeding, restraint, investigation, referral of charges, trial in which arraignment occurred, or other action may proceed in the same manner and with the same effect as if these amendments had not been prescribed.

This new Article 120 consolidates several sexual misconduct offenses and is generally based on the Sexual Abuse Act of 1986, 18 U.S.C. Sections 2241-2245. The following is a list of offenses that have been replaced by this new paragraph 45:

(1) Paragraph 63, 134 Assault - Indecent, has been replaced in its entirety by three new offenses under paragraph 45. *See* subsections (e) Aggravated Sexual Contact, (h) Abusive Sexual Contact, and (m) Wrongful Sexual Contact.

(2) Paragraph 87, 134 Indecent Acts or Liberties with a Child, has been replaced in its entirety by three new offenses under paragraph 45. *See* subsections (g) Aggravated Sexual Contact with a Child, (i) Abusive Sexual Contact with a Child, and (j) Indecent Liberty with a Child.

(3) Paragraph 88, Article 134 Indecent Exposure, has been replaced in its entirety by a new offense under paragraph 45. *See* subsection (n) Indecent Exposure.

(4) Paragraph 90, Article 134 Indecent Acts with Another, has been replaced in its entirety by a new offense under paragraph 45. *See* subsection (k) Indecent Act.

(5) Paragraph 97, Article 134 Pandering and Prostitution, has been amended. The act of compelling another person to engage in an act of prostitution with another person will no longer be an offense under paragraph 97 and has been replaced by a new offense under paragraph 45. *See* subsection (l), Forcible Pandering.

c. *Explanation.* Subparagraph (3), definition of "indecent," is taken from paragraphs 89.c and 90.c of the Manual (2005 ed.) and is intended to consolidate the definitions of "indecent," as used in the former offenses under Article 134 of "Indecent acts or liberties with a child," "Indecent exposure," and "Indecent acts with another," formerly at paragraphs 87, 88, and 90 of the 2005 Manual, and "Indecent language," at paragraph 89. The application of this single definition of "indecent" to the offenses of "Indecent liberty with a child," "Indecent act," and "Indecent exposure" under Article 120 is consistent with the construction given to the former Article 134 offenses in the 2005 Manual that were consolidated into Article 120. *See e.g. United States v. Negron*, 60 M.J. 136 (C.A.A.F. 2004).

d. *Additional Lesser Included Offenses.* The test to determine whether an offense is factually the same as another offense, and therefore lesser-included to that offense, is the "elements" test. *United States v. Foster*, 40 M.J. 140, 142 (C.M.A. 1994). Under this test, the court considers "whether each provision requires proof of a fact which the other does not." *Blockburger*, 284 U.S. 299 at 304 (1932). Rather than adopting a literal application of the elements test, the Court stated that resolution of lesser-included claims "can only be resolved by lining up elements realistically and determining whether each element of the supposed 'lesser' offense is rationally derivative of one or more elements of the other offense - and vice versa." *Foster*, 40 M.J. at 146. Whether an offense is a lesser-included offense is a matter of law that the Court will consider de novo. *United States v. Palagar*, 56 M.J. 294, 296 (C.A.A.F. 2002).

e. *Maximum punishment. See 1995 Amendment* regarding maximum punishment of death.

45a. Article 120a— Stalking

2007 Amendment. This paragraph is new and is based on section 551 of the National Defense Authorization Act for Fiscal Year 2006, P.L. 109-163, 6 January 2006.

46. Article 121— Larceny and wrongful appropriation

c. *Explanation.* This paragraph is based on paragraph 200 of MCM, 1969 (Rev.). The discussion in the fourth and fifth sentences of paragraph 200 *a* (4) was deleted as ambiguous and overbroad. The penultimate sentence in subparagraph c(1)(d) adequately covers the point. C. Torcia, *2 Wharton's Criminal Law and Procedure* § 393 (1980); *Hall v. United States*, 277 Fed. 19 (8th Cir. 1921). As to subparagraph c(1)(c) *see also United States v. Leslie*, 13 M.J. 170 (C.M.A. 1982). As to subparagraph c(1)(d) *see also United States v. Smith*, 14 M.J. 68 (C.M.A. 1982); *United States v. Cunningham*, 14 M.J. 539 (A.C.M.R. 1981). As to subparagraph c(1)(f), *see also United States v. Kastner*, 17 M.J. 11 (C.M.A. 1983); *United States v. Eggleton*, 22 U.S.C.M.A. 504, 47 C.M.R. 920 (1973); *United States v. O'Hara*, 14 U.S.C.M.A. 167, 33 C.M.R. 379 (1963); *United States v. Hayes*, 8 U.S.C.M.A. 627, 25 C.M.R. 131 (1958). As to subparagraph c(1)(h)(i) *see also United States v. Malone*, 14 M.J. 563 (N.M.C.M.R. 1982).

2002 Amendment: Subparagraph c(1)(h)(vi) is new. It was added to provide guidance on how unauthorized credit, debit, or electronic transactions should usually be charged. *See United States v. Duncan*, 30 M.J. 1284, 289 (N.M.C.M.R. 1990) (citing *United States v. Jones*, 29 C.M.R. 651 (A.B.R. 1960), petition denied, 30 C.M.R. 417 (C.M.A. 1960)) (regarding thefts from ATM machines). Alternative charging theories are also available, see *United States v. Leslie*, 13 M.J. 170 (C.M.A. 1982); *United States v. Ragins*, 11 M.J. 42 (C.M.A. 1981); *United States v.*

Schaper, 42 M.J. 737 (A.F. Ct. Crim. App. 1995); and *United States v. Christy*, 18 M.J. 688 (N.M.C.M.R. 1984). The key under Article 121 is that the accused wrongfully obtained goods or money from a person or entity with a superior possessory interest.

e. *Maximum punishment.* The maximum punishments have been revised. Instead of three levels ($50 or less, $50 to $100, and over $100) only two are used. This is simpler and conforms more closely to the division between felony and misdemeanor penalties contingent on value in property offenses in civilian jurisdictions. The maximum punishment for larceny or wrongful appropriation of a firearm or explosive includes 5 or 2 years' confinement respectively. This is because, regardless of the intrinsic value of such items, the threat to the community and disruption of military activities is substantial when such items are wrongfully taken. Special accountability and protective measures are taken with firearms and explosives, and they may be the target of theft regardless of value.

1986 Amendment: The maximum punishments for larceny were revised as they relate to larceny of military property to make them consistent with the punishments under Article 108 and paragraph 32e, Part IV, MCM, 1984. Before this amendment, a person who stole military property faced less punishment than a person who willfully damaged, destroyed, or disposed of military property. The revised punishments are also consistent with 18 U.S.C. § 641.

2002 Amendment: The monetary amount affecting the maximum punishments has been revised from $100 to $500 to account for inflation. The last change was in 1969 raising the amount to $100. The value has also been readjusted to realign it more closely with the division between felony and misdemeanor penalties in civilian jurisdictions. *See generally* American Law Institute, Model Penal Code and Commentaries Sec. 223.1 (1980) (suggesting $500 as the value). Although the monetary amount effecting punishment in 18 U.S.C. Sec. 1361, Government property or contracts, and 18 U.S.C. Sec. 641, Public money, property or records, was increased from $100 to $1000 pursuant to section 606 of the Economic Espionage Act of 1996, P. L. No. 104-294, 110 Stat. 3488 (1996), a value of $500 was chosen to maintain deterrence, simplicity, and uniformity for the Manual's property offenses.

47. Article 122— Robbery

c. *Explanation.* This paragraph is based on paragraph 201 of MCM, 1969 (Rev.). *See also United States v. Chambers*, 12 M.J. 443 (C.M.A. 1982); *United States v. Washington*, 12 M.J. 1036 (A.C.M.R. 1982), *pet. denied*, 14 M.J. 170 (1982). Subparagraph (5) is based on *United States v. Parker*, 17 U.S.C.M.A. 545, 38 C.M.R. 343 (1968).

d. *Lesser included offenses. See United States v. Calhoun*, 5 U.S.C.M.A. 428, 18 C.M.R. 52 (1955).

e. *Maximum punishment.* The aggravating factor of use of a firearm in the commission of a robbery, and a higher maximum punishment in such cases, have been added because of the increased danger when robbery is committed with a firearm whether or not loaded or operable. *Cf.* 18 U.S.C. §§ 2113 and 2114; *United States v. Shelton*, 465 F.2d 361 (4th Cir. 1972); *United States v. Thomas*, 455 F.2d 320 (6th Cir. 1972); *Baker v. United States*, 412 F.2d 1069 (5th Cir. 1969). *See also* U.S. Dep't of Justice, *Attorney General's Task Force on Violent Crime, Final Report* 29–33 (Aug. 17, 1981). The 15-year maximum is the same as that for robbery under 18 U.S.C. § 2111.

48. Article 123— Forgery

c. *Explanation.* This paragraph is based on paragraph 202 of MCM, 1969 (Rev.).

49. Article 123a— Making, drawing, or uttering check, draft, or order without sufficient funds

c. *Explanation.* This paragraph is based on paragraph 202A of MCM, 1969 (Rev.). The language in paragraph 202A using an illegal transaction such as an illegal gambling game as an example of "for any other purpose" was eliminated in subparagraph (7), based on *United States v. Wallace*, 15 U.S.C.M.A. 650, 36 C.M.R. 148 (1966). The statutory inference found in Article 123a and explained in subparagraph (17) was not meant to preempt the usual methods of proof of knowledge and intent. *See* S.Rep. No. 659, 87th Cong. 1st Sess. 2 (1961). Subparagraph (18) is based on *United States v. Callaghan*, 14 U.S.C.M.A. 231, 34 C.M.R. 11 (1963). *See also United States v. Webb*, 46 C.M.R. 1083 (A.C.M.R. 1972). As to share drafts *see also United States v. Palmer*, 14 M.J. 731 (A.F.C.M.R. 1982); *United States v. Grubbs*, 13 M.J. 594 (A.F.C.M.R. 1982).

e. *Maximum punishment.* The maximum punishment for subsection (1) has been revised. Instead of three levels ($50 or less, $50 to $100, and over $100) only two are used. This is simpler and conforms more closely to the division between felony and misdemeanor penalties contingent on value in property offenses in civilian jurisdiction.

2002 Amendment: The monetary amount affecting the maximum punishments has been revised from $100 to $500 to account for inflation. The last change was in 1969 raising the amount to $100. The value has also been readjusted to realign it more closely with the division between felony and misdemeanor penalties in civilian jurisdictions. *See generally* American Law Institute, Model Penal Code and Commentaries Sec. 223.1 (1980) (suggesting $500 as the value).

f. *Sample specification. See also United States v. Palmer* and *United States v. Grubbs*, both *supra* (pleading share drafts; pleading more than one check or draft).

50. Article 124— Maiming

c. *Explanation.* This paragraph is based on paragraph 203 of MCM, 1969 (Rev.). Subparagraph c(3) is based on *United States v. Hicks*, 6 U.S.C.M.A. 621, 20 C.M.R. 337 (1956). The discussion of intent has been modified to reflect that some specific intent to injure is necessary. *United States v. Hicks, supra.* The third sentence of the third paragraph of paragraph 203 of MCM, 1969 (Rev.), which was based on *Hicks (see Analysis of Contents, Manual for Courts-martial, United States, 1969 (Revised edition)*, DA PAM 27–2 at 28–15), was misleading in this regard. *Contra United States v. Tua*, 4 M.J. 761 (A.C.M.R. 1977), *pet. denied*, 5 M.J. 91 (1978).

e. *Maximum punishment. 2007 Amendment:* The maximum punishment for the offense of maiming was increased from 7 years confinement to 20 years confinement, consistent with the federal offense of maiming. 18 U.S.C. § 114.

51. Article 125— Sodomy

b. *Elements. 2004 Amendment:* Paragraph 51(b) was amended by adding two factors pertaining to age based upon the 1994 amendment to paragraph 51(e) that created two distinct categories of sodomy involving a child. *See also* concurrent change to R.C.M. 307(c)(3) and accompanying analysis.

c. *Explanation.* This paragraph is based on paragraph 204 of MCM, 1969 (Rev.). Fellatio and cunnilingus are within the scope of Article 125. *See United States v. Harris*, 8 M.J. 52 (C.M.A. 1979); *United States v. Scoby*, 5 M.J. 160 (C.M.A. 1978). For a discussion of the possible constitutional limitations on the application of Article 125 (for example, the sexual activity of a married couple), *see United States v. Scoby, supra.*

d. *Paragraph 51e.* The Analysis accompanying subparagraph 51e is amended by inserting the following at the end thereof:

1994 Amendment. One of the objectives of the Sexual Abuse Act of 1986, 18 U.S.C. §§ 2241–2245 was to define sexual abuse in gender-neutral terms. Since the scope of Article 125, U.C.M.J., accommodates those forms of sexual abuse other than the rape provided for in Article 120, U.C.M.J., the maximum punishments permitted under Article 125 were amended to bring them more in line with Article 120 and the Act, thus providing sanctions that are generally equivalent regardless of the victim's gender. Subparagraph e(1) was amended by increasing the maximum period of confinement from 20 years to life. Subparagraph e(2) was amended by creating two distinct categories of sodomy involving a child, one involving children who have attained the age of 12 but are not yet 16, and the other involving children under the age of 12. The latter is now designated as subparagraph e(3). The punishment for the former category remains the same as it was for the original category of children under the age of 16. This amendment, however, increases the maximum punishment to life when the victim is under the age of 12 years.

Lesser included offenses.

2007 Amendment. The former Paragraph 87 (1) (b), Article 134 Indecent Acts or Liberties with a Child, has been replaced in its entirety by paragraph 45. The former Paragraph 63 (2) (c), Article 134 Assault - Indecent, has been replaced in its entirety by paragraph 45. The former Paragraph 90 (3) (a), Article 134 Indecent Acts with Another, has been replaced in its entirety by paragraph 45. Lesser included offenses under Article 120 should be considered depending on the factual circumstances in each case.

e. *Maximum punishment.* The maximum punishment for forcible sodomy was raised in recognition of the severity of the offense which is similar to rape in its violation of personal privacy and dignity.

f. *Sample specifications. 2004 Amendment:* Paragraph 51(f) was amended to aid practitioners in charging the two distinct categories of sodomy involving a child created in 1994. *See also* concurrent change to R.C.M. 307(c)(3) and accompanying analysis.

52. Article 126— Arson

c. *Explanation.* This paragraph is based on paragraph 205 of MCM, 1969 (Rev.). *See United States v. Acevedo-Velez*, 17 M.J. 1 (C.M.A.1983); *United States v. Duke*, 16 U.S.C.M.A. 460, 37 C.M.R. 80 (1966); *United States v. Scott*, 8 M.J. 853 (N.C.M.R. 1980); *United States v. Jones*, 2 M.J. 785 (A.C.M.R. 1976).

e. *Maximum punishment.* The maximum period of confinement for simple arson of property of a value of more than $100 has been reduced from 10 to 5 years. This parallels 18 U.S.C. § 81. The separate punishment for simple arson of property of a value of $100 or less has been retained because 18 U.S.C. Sec. 81 does not cover most personal property.

2002 Amendment: The monetary amount affecting the maximum punishments has been revised from $100 to $500 to account for inflation. The last change was in 1969 raising the amount to $100. The value has also been readjusted to realign it more closely with the division between felony and misdemeanor penalties in civilian jurisdictions. *See generally* American Law Institute, Model Penal Code and Commentaries Sec. 223.1 (1980) (suggesting $500 as the value). A value of $500 was chosen to maintain deterrence, simplicity, and uniformity for the Manual's property offenses. 18 U.S.C. Sec. 81, Arson within special maritime and territorial jurisdiction, no longer grades the offense on the basis of value.

53. Article 127— Extortion

c. *Explanation.* This paragraph is based on paragraph 206 of MCM, 1969 (Rev.). *See also United States v. Schmidt*, 16 U.S.C.M.A. 57, 36 C.M.R. 213 (1966); R. Perkins, *Criminal Law* 373–74 (2d ed. 1969). Subparagraph (4) is based on *United States v. McCollum*, 13 M.J. 127 (C.M.A. 1982).

54. Article 128— Assault

c. *Explanation.* This paragraph is based on paragraph 207 of MCM, 1969 (Rev.). *See also United States v. Vigil*, 3 U.S.C.M.A. 474, 13 C.M.R. 30 (1953) (aggravated assault); *United States v. Spearman*, 23 U.S.C.M.A. 31, 48 C.M.R. 405 (1974) (grievous bodily harm).

e. *Maximum punishment.* The maximum punishment for (2) Assault consummated by a battery has been increased because of the range of types of harm which may be caused by a battery. These may include serious injury, even though unintended or not caused by a means or force likely to produce grievous bodily harm. The maximum punishment for (6) Assault upon a sentinel or lookout in the execution of duty, or upon any person who, in the execution of office, is performing security police, military police, shore patrol, master at arms, or other military or civilian law enforcement duties, has been increased based on 18 U.S.C. § 111 and 18 U.S.C. § 1114. The maximum punishment for aggravated assaults committed with firearms has been increased based on 18 U.S.C. § 924(c). *See also* U.S. Dep't of Justice, *Attorney General's Task Force on Violent Crime, Final Report* 29–33 (Aug. 17, 1981). Note that the higher maximum for assault with a dangerous weapon when the weapon is a firearm applies even if the firearm is used as a bludgeon. This is because the danger injected is significantly greater when a loaded firearm is used, even as a bludgeon.

In certain situations, this punishment scheme may have the effect of making intentional infliction of grievous bodily harm a lesser included offense of assault with a dangerous weapon. For example, if in the course of an assault with a loaded firearm the accused or a coactor stabs the victim with a knife, the assault with a dangerous weapon (the firearm) would carry an 8 year maximum penalty, as opposed to 5 years for the assault intentionally inflicting grievous bodily harm. In such a case, the specification should be carefully tailored to describe each facet of the assault.

1998 Amendment: A separate maximum punishment for assault with an unloaded firearm was created due to the serious nature of the offense. Threatening a person with an unloaded firearm places the victim of that assault in fear of losing his or her life. Such a traumatic experience is a far greater injury to the victim than that sustained in the course of a typical simple assault. Therefore, it calls for an increased punishment.

2007 Amendment: The maximum punishments for some aggravated assault offenses were established to recognize the increased severity of such offenses when children are the victims. These maximum punishments are consistent with the maximum punishments of the Article 134 offense of Child Endangerment, established in 2007.

55. Article 129— Burglary

c. *Explanation.* This paragraph is based on paragraph 208 of MCM, 1969 (Rev.). *See also United States v. Klutz*, 9 U.S.C.M.A. 20, 25 C.M.R. 282 (1958). Subparagraph c(2) and (3) have been revised based on R. Perkins, *Criminal Law* 192–193 and 199 (2d ed. 1969). As to subparagraph c(2), *see also* 13 AM.Jur. 2d *Burglary* § 18 (1964); Annot., 70 A.L.R. 3d 881 (1976).

f. *Sample specification. See United States v. Knight*, 15 M.J. 202 (C.M.A. 1983).

56. Article 130— Housebreaking

c. *Explanation.* This paragraph is based on paragraph 209 of MCM, 1969 (Rev.) and *United States v. Gillin*, 8 U.S.C.M.A. 669, 25 C.M.R. 173 (1958). *See also United States v. Breen*, 15 U.S.C.M.A. 658, 36 C.M.R. 156 (1966); *United States v. Hall*, 12 U.S.C.M.A. 374, 30 C.M.R. 374 (1961); *United States v. Taylor*, 12 U.S.C.M.A. 44, 3O C.M.R. 44 (1960) (all regarding "structure"); *United States v. Weaver*, 18 U.S.C.M.A. 173, 39 C.M.R. 173 (1969) ("separate offense"); *United States v. Williams*, 4 U.S.C.M.A. 241, 15 C.M.R. 241 (1954) ("entry").

57. Article 131— Perjury

c. *Explanation.* Subparagraph (1) and (2) are based on paragraph 210 of MCM, 1969 (Rev.). In the last sentence of subparagraph (2)(a), the phrase "unless the witness was forced to answer over a valid claim of privilege"which appeared at the end of the fourth paragraph of paragraph 210 of MCM, 1969 (Rev.) has been deleted based on*United States v. Mandujano*, 425 U.S. 564 (1976); *Harris v. New York*, 401 U.S. 222 (1971). *See also United States v. Armstrong*, 9 M.J. 374 (C.M.A. 1980). Subparagraph (3) is new and is based on Public Law 94–550 of 1976 which amended Article 131 by adding a second clause based on section 1746 of title 28 United States Code, which was also enacted as part of Pub.L. No. 94–550.

Text of section 1746 of title 28, United States Code

§ 1746. Unsworn declarations under penalty of perjury.

Whenever, under any law of the United States or under any rule, regulation, order, or requirement made pursuant to law, any matter is required or permitted to be supported, evidenced, established, or proved by the sworn declaration, verification, certificate, statement, oath, or affidavit, in writing of the person making the same (other than a deposition, or an oath of office, or an oath required to be taken before a specified official other than a notary public), such matter may, with like force and effect, be supported, evidenced, established, or proved by the unsworn declaration, certificate, verification, or statement, in writing of such person which is subscribed by him, as true under penalty of perjury, and dated, in substantially the following form:

(1) If executed without the United States: "I declare (or certify, verify, or state) under penalty of perjury under the laws of the United States of America that the foregoing is true and correct. Executed on (date).

(Signature)"

(2) If executed within the United States, its territories, possessions, or commonwealths: "I declare (or certify, verify, or state) under penalty of perjury that the foregoing is true and correct. Executed on (date).

(Signature)"

If someone signs a statement under penalty of perjury outside a judicial proceeding or course of justice, and Article 107 (false official statement) is not applicable, it may be possible to use Article 134 (clause 3) (*see* paragraph 60) to charge a violation of 18 U.S.C. § 1621.

Text of section 1621 of title 18, United States Code

§ 1621. Perjury generally

Whoever—

(1) having taken an oath before a competent tribunal, officer, or person, in any case in which a law of the United States authorizes an oath to be administered, that he will testify, declare, depose, or certify truly, or that any written testimony, declaration, deposition, or certificate by him subscribed, is true, willfully and contrary to such oath states or subscribes any material which he does not believe to be true; or

(2) in any declaration, certificate, verification, or statement under penalty of perjury as permitted under section 1746 of title 28, United States Code, willfully subscribes as true any material matter which he does not believe to be true; is guilty of perjury and shall, except or otherwise expressly provided by law, be fined not more than $2,000 or imprisoned not more than five years, or both. This section is applicable whether the statement or subscription is made within or without the United States.

2004 Amendment: Subsection (2)(b) was amended to comply with *United States v. Gaudin,* 515 U.S. 506 (1995), which held that when materiality is a statutory element of an offense, it must be submitted to the jury for decision. Materiality cannot be removed from the members' consideration by an interlocutory ruling that a statement is material. *See Gaudin,* 515 U.S. at 521 ("It is commonplace for the same mixed question of law and fact to be assigned to the court for one purpose, and to the jury for another."); and at 517 ("The prosecution's failure to provide minimal evidence of materiality, like its failure to provide minimal evidence of any other element, of course raises a question of 'law' that warrants dismissal.").

d. *Lesser included offenses.*

1991 Amendment: Subparagraph *d* was amended by deleting false swearing as a lesser included offense of perjury. *See United States v. Smith*, 26 C.M.R. 16 (C.M.A. 1958); MCM 1984, Part

IV, para. 79c(1). Although closely related to perjury, the offense of false swearing may be charged separately.

58. Article 132— Frauds against the United States

c. *Explanation.* This paragraph is based on paragraph 211 of MCM, 1969 (Rev.).

e. *Maximum punishment.* The maximum punishments have been revised. Instead of three levels ($50 or less, $50 to $100, and over $100) only two are used. This is simpler and conforms more closely to the division between felony and misdemeanor penalties contingent on value in property offenses in civilian jurisdictions.

2002 Amendment: The monetary amount affecting the maximum punishments has been revised from $100 to $500 to account for inflation. The last change was in 1969 raising the amount to $100. The value has also been readjusted to realign it more closely with the division between felony and misdemeanor penalties in civilian jurisdictions. *See generally* American Law Institute, Model Penal Code and Commentaries Sec. 223.1 (1980) (suggesting $500 as the value).

59. Article 133— Conduct unbecoming an officer and gentleman

c. *Explanation.* This paragraph is based on paragraph 212 of MCM, 1969 (Rev.). *See Parker v. Levy*, 417 U.S. 733 (1974) (constitutionality of Article 133). For a discussion of Article 133, *see United States v. Giordano*, 15 U.S.C.M.A. 163, 35 C.M.R. 135 (1964); Nelson, *Conduct Expected of an Officer and a Gentleman: Ambiguity*, 12 A.F.JAG L.Rev. 124 (Spring 1970). As to subparagraph (1), *see* 1 U.S.C. § 1; Pub.L. No. 94–106, § 803, 89 Stat. 537–38 (Oct. 7, 1975).

e. *Maximum punishment.* A maximum punishment is established for the first time in order to provide guidance and uniformity for Article 133 offenses.

f. *Sample specifications.* Some sample specifications for Article 133 in MCM, 1969 (Rev.) were deleted solely to economize on space.

60. Article 134— General article

Introduction. Paragraph 60 introduces the General Article. Paragraph 61–113 describe and list the maximum punishments for many offenses under Article 134. These paragraphs are not exclusive. *See generally Parker v. Levy*, 417 U.S. 733 (1974); *United States v. Sadinsky*, 14 U.S.C.M.A. 563, 34 C.M.R. 343 (1964).

Except as otherwise noted in the Analyses of paragraphs 61–113, the offenses listed below are based on paragraph 127 *c* (Table of Maximum Punishments), paragraph 213 *f*, and Appendix 6 (sample specifications 126–187) of MCM, 1969 (Rev.). Eight offenses previously listed (allowing prisoner to do unauthorized acts, criminal libel, criminal nuisance, parole violation, statutory perjury, transporting stolen vehicle in interstate commerce, unclean accoutrements, and unclean uniform) are not listed here because they occur so infrequently or because the gravamen of the misconduct is such that it is more appropriately charged under another provision.

c. *Explanation.* Except as noted below, this paragraph is based on paragraph 213 *a* through *e* of MCM, 1969 (Rev.).

(1) *In general. See Secretary of the Navy v. Avrech*, 418 U.S. 676 (1974); *Parker v. Levy, supra* (constitutionality of Article 134 upheld).

(4)(c)(ii)*Federal Assimilative Crimes Act. See United States v. Wright*, 5 M.J. 106 (C.M.A. 1978); *United States v. Rowe*, 13 U.S.C.M.A. 302, 32 C.M.R. 302 (1962).

(5)(a) *Preemption doctrine. See United States v. McCormick*, 12 U.S.C.M.A. 26, 30 C.M.R. 26 (1960) (assault on child under 16); *United States v. Hallet*, 4 U.S.C.M.A. 378, 15 C.M.R. 378 (1954) (misbehavior before the enemy); *United States v. Deller*, 3 U.S.C.M.A. 409, 12 C.M.R. 165 (1953) (absence offenses); *United States v. Norris*, 2 U.S.C.M.A. 236, 8 C.M.R. 36 (1953) (larceny). *But see* the following cases for examples of where offenses not preempted: *United States v. Wright, supra* (burglary of automobile); *United States v. Bonavita*, 21 U.S.C.M.A. 407, 45 C.M.R. 181 (1972) (concealing stolen property); *United States v. Maze*, 21 U.S.C.M.A. 260, 45 C.M.R. 34 (1972) (unlawfully altering public records); *United States v. Taylor*, 17 U.S.C.M.A. 595, 38 C.M.R. 393 (1968) (self-inflicted injury with no intent to avoid Service) *United States v. Gaudet*, 11 U.S.C.M.A. 672, 29 C.M.R. 488 (1960) (stealing from mail); *United States v. Fuller*, 9 U.S.C.M.A. 143, 25 C.M.R. 405 (1958) (fraudulent burning); *United States v. Holt*, 7 U.S.C.M.A. 617, 23 C.M.R. 81 (1957) (graft, fraudulent misrepresentation).

(5)(b) *Capital offense. See United States v. French*, 10 U.S.C.M.A. 171, 27 C.M.R. 245 (1959).

(6)(b) *Specifications under clause 3. See United States v. Mayo*, 12 M.J. 286 (C.M.A. 1982); *United States v. Perry*, 12 M.J. 112 (C.M.A. 1981); *United States v. Rowe, supra; United States v. Hogsett*, 8 U.S.C.M.A. 681, 25 C.M.R. 185 (1958).

(6)(c)*Specifications for clause 1 or 2 offenses not listed. See United States v. Sadinsky, supra; United States v. Mardis*, 6 U.S.C.M.A 624, 20 C.M.R. 340 (1956).

61. Article 134— (Abusing a public animal)

c. *Explanation.* This new paragraph defines "public animal."

62. Article 134— (Adultery)

c. *Explanation.*

(1) Subparagraph c(2) is based on *United States. v. Snyder*, 4 C.M.R. 15 (1952); *United States v. Ruiz*, 46 M.J. 503 (A. F. Ct. Crim. App. 1997); *United States v. Green*, 39 M.J. 606 (A.C.M.R. 1994); *United States v. Collier*, 36 M.J. 501 (A.F.C.M.R. 1992); *United States v. Perez*, 33 M.J. 1050 (A.C.M.R. 1991); *United States v. Linnear*, 16 M.J. 628 (A.F.C.M.R. 1983); Part IV, paragraph 60c(2)(a) of MCM. Subparagraph c(3) is based on *United States v. Poole*, 39 M.J. 819 (A.C.M.R. 1994). Subparagraph c(4) is based on *United States v. Fogarty*, 35 M.J. 885 (A.C.M.R. 1992); *Military Judges' Benchbook*, DA PAM 27-9, paragraph 3-62-1 and 5-11-2 (30 Sep. 1996). *See* R.C.M. 916(j) and (l)(1) for a general discussion of mistake of fact and ignorance, which cannot be based on a negligent failure to discover the true facts.

(2) When determining whether adulterous acts constitute the offense of adultery under Article 134, commanders should consider the listed factors. Each commander has discretion to dispose of offenses by members of the command. As with any alleged offense, however, under R.C.M. 306(b) commanders should dispose of an allegation of adultery at the lowest appropriate level. As the R.C.M. 306(b) discussion states, many factors must be taken into consideration and balanced, including, to the extent

practicable, the nature of the offense, any mitigating or extenuating circumstances, the character and military service of the military member, any recommendations made by subordinate commanders, the interests of justice, military exigencies, and the effect of the decision on the military member and the command. The goal should be a disposition that is warranted, appropriate, and fair. In the case of officers, also consult the explanation to paragraph 59 in deciding how to dispose of an allegation of adultery.

63. Article 134— (Assault— indecent)

c. *Explanation.* This paragraph is based on paragraph 213 *f*(2) of MCM, 1969 (Rev.). *See United States v. Caillouette*, 12 U.S.C.M.A. 149, 30 C.M.R. 149 (1961) regarding specific intent. *See also United States v. Headspeth*, 2 U.S.C.M.A. 635, 10 C.M.R. 133 (1953).

Gender-neutral language has been used in this paragraph, as well as throughout this Manual. This will eliminate any question about the intended scope of certain offenses, such as indecent assault such as may have been raised by the use of the masculine pronoun in MCM, 1969 (Rev.). It is, however, consistent with the construction given to the former Manual. *See, e.g., United States v. Respess*, 7 M.J. 566 (A.C.M.R. 1979). *See generally* 1 U.S.C. § 1 ("unless the context indicates otherwise ... words importing the masculine gender include the feminine as well ....").

d. *Lesser included offenses. See United States v. Thacker*, 16 U.S.C.M.A. 408, 37 C.M.R. 28 (1966); *United States v. Jackson*, 31 C.M.R. 738 (A.F.B.R. 1962).

2007 Amendment: This paragraph has been replaced in its entirety by paragraph 45. *See* Article 120 (e) Aggravated Sexual Contact, (h) Abusive Sexual Contact, and (m) Wrongful Sexual Contact.

64. Article 134— (Assault— with intent to commit murder, voluntary manslaughter, rape, robbery, sodomy, arson, burglary, or housebreaking)

c. *Explanation.* This paragraph is based on paragraph 213 *f*(1) of MCM, 1969 (Rev.).

2007 Amendment. This paragraph has been amended for consistency with the changes to Article 118 under Section 552 of the National Defense Authorization Act for Fiscal Year 2006, P.L. 109-163, 6 January 2006. *See* subsection (d) of Section 552.

65. Article 134— (Bigamy)

c. *Explanation.* This paragraph is based on paragraph 213 *f*(9) of MCM, 1969 (Rev.). *See also United States v. Pruitt*, 17 U.S.C.M.A. 438, 38 C.M.R. 236 (1968), concerning the defense of mistake.

66. Article 134— (Bribery and graft)

c. *Explanation.* This paragraph is new and is based on *United States v. Marshall*, 18 U.S.C.M.A. 426, 40 C.M.R. 138 (1969); *United States v. Alexander*, 3 U.S.C.M.A. 346, 12 C.M.R. 102 (1953). *See also United States v. Eslow*, 1 M.J. 620 (A.C.M.R. 1975).

d. *Lesser included offenses.* Graft is listed as a lesser included offense of bribery. *See United States v. Raborn*, 575 F.2d 688 (9th Cir. 1978); *United States v. Crutchfield*, 547 F.2d 496 (9th Cir. 1977).

e. *Maximum punishment.* The maximum punishment for bribery has been revised to reflect the greater seriousness of bribery, which requires a specific intent to influence. *See also* 18 U.S.C. § 201.

67. Article 134— (Burning with intent to defraud)

c. *Explanation.* This paragraph is new and is self-explanatory. For a discussion of this offense *see United States v. Fuller*, 9 U.S.C.M.A. 143, 25 C.M.R. 405 (1958).

68. Article 134— (Check, worthless, making and uttering— by dishonorably failing to maintain funds)

c. *Explanation.* This paragraph is based on paragraph 213 *f*(8) of MCM, 1969 (Rev.). *See also United States v. Groom*, 12 U.S.C.M.A. 11, 30 C.M.R. 11 (1960).

d. *Lesser included offense. See United States v. Downard*, 6 U.S.C.M.A. 538, 20 C.M.R. 254 (1955).

68a. Article 134— (Child Endangerment)

2007 Amendment. This offense is new to the Manual for Courts-Martial. Child neglect was recognized in *United States v. Vaughan*, 58 M.J. 29 (C.A.A.F. 2003). It is based on military custom and regulation as well as a majority of state statutes and captures the essence of child neglect, endangerment, and abuse.

69. Article 134— (Cohabitation, wrongful)

c. *Explanation.* This paragraph is new and is based on *United States v. Acosta*, 19 U.S.C.M.A. 341, 41 C.M.R. 341 (1970); *United States v. Melville*, 8 U.S.C.M.A. 597, 25 C.M.R. 101 (1958); *United States v. Leach*, 7 U.S.C.M.A. 388, 22 C.M.R. 178 (1956); and *United States v. Boswell*, 35 C.M.R. 491 (A.B.R. 1964), *pet. denied*, 35 C.M.R. 478 (1964).

70. Article 134— (Correctional custody— offenses against)

Introduction. The elements and sample specifications have been modified by replacing "duly" with "by a person authorized to do so." *See* Analysis, paragraph 19.

c. *Explanation.* This paragraph is taken from paragraph 213 *f*(13) of MCM, 1969 (Rev.). *See also United States v. Mackie*, 16 U.S.C.M.A. 14, 36 C.M.R. 170 (1966) (proof of the offense for which correctional custody imposed not required).

71. Article 134— (Debt, dishonorably failing to pay)

c. *Explanation.* This paragraph is based on paragraph 213 *f*(7) of MCM, 1969 (Rev.). *See also United States v. Kirksey*, 6 U.S.C.M.A. 556, 20 C.M.R. 272 (1955).

72. Article 134— (Disloyal statements)

c. *Explanation.* This paragraph is based on paragraph 213 *f*(5) of MCM, 1969 (Rev.); *Parker v. Levy*, 417 U.S. 733 (1974); *United States v. Priest*, 21 U.S.C.M.A. 564, 45 C.M.R. 338 (1972); *United States v. Gray*, 20 U.S.C.M.A. 63, 42 C.M.R. 255 (1970);

United States v. Harvey, 19 U.S.C.M.A. 539, 42 C.M.R. 141 (1970).

73. Article 134— (Disorderly conduct, drunkenness)

c. *Explanation.* (2) Disorderly. This subparagraph is based on *United States v. Manos*, 24 C.M.R. 626 (A.F.B.R. 1957). *See also United States v. Haywood*, 41 C.M.R. 939 (A.F.C.M.R. 1969) and*United States v. Burrow*, 26 C.M.R. 761 (N.B.R. 1958), for a discussion of disorderly conduct in relation to the offense of breach of the peace 40c).

74. Article 134— (Drinking liquor with prisoner)

c. *Explanation.* This paragraph is new.

75. Article 134— (Drunk Prisoner)

c. *Explanation. See* Analysis, paragraph 35.

76. Article 134— (Drunkenness— incapacitation for performance of duties through prior wrongful overindulgence in intoxicating liquor or drugs)

c. *Explanation.* This paragraph is based on *United States v. Roebuck*, 8 C.M.R. 786 (A.F.B.R. 1953); *United States v. Jones*, 7 C.M.R. 97 (A.B.R. 1952); *United States v. Nichols*, 6 C.M.R. 239 (A.B.R. 1952).

77. Article 134— (False or unauthorized pass offenses)

c. *Explanation.* This paragraph is based on paragraph 213 *f*(11) of MCM, 1969 (Rev.). *See also United States v. Burton*, 13 U.S.C.M.A. 645, 33 C.M.R. 177 (1963); *United States v. Warthen* , 11 U.S.C.M.A. 93, 28 C.M.R. 317 (1959).

78. Article 134— (False pretenses, obtaining services under)

c. *Explanation.* This paragraph is based on *United States v. Herndon*, 15 U.S.C.M.A. 510, 36 C.M.R. 8 (1965); *United States v. Abeyta*, 12 M.J. 507 (A.C.M.R. 1981); *United States v. Case*, 37 C.M.R. 606 (A.B.R. 1966).

e. *Maximum punishment.* The maximum punishments have been revised. Instead of three levels ($50 or less, $50 to $100, and over $100) only two are used. This is simpler and conforms more closely to the division between felony and misdemeanor penalties contingent on value in similar offenses in civilian jurisdictions.

2002 Amendment: The monetary amount affecting the maximum punishments has been revised from $100 to $500 to account for inflation. The last change was in 1969 raising the amount to $100. The value has also been readjusted to realign it more closely with the division between felony and misdemeanor penalties in civilian jurisdictions. *See generally* American Law Institute, Model Penal Code and Commentaries Sec. 223.1 (1980) (suggesting $500 as the value).

79. Article 134— (False swearing)

c. *Explanation.* This paragraph is based on paragraph 213 *f*(4) of MCM, 1969 (Rev.). *See also United States v. Whitaker*, 13 U.S.C.M.A. 341, 32 C.M.R. 341 (1962); *United States v. McCarthy* , 11 U.S.C.M.A. 758, 29 C.M.R. 574 (1960).

80. Article 134— (Firearm, discharging— through negligence)

c. *Explanation.* This paragraph is based on *United States v. Darisse*, 17 U.S.C.M.A. 29, 37 C.M.R. 293 (1967); *United States v. Barrientes*, 38 C.M.R. 612 (A.B.R. 1967). The term "carelessness" was changed to "negligence" because the latter is defined in paragraph 85c(2).

81. Article 134— (Firearm, discharging— willfully, under such circumstances as to endanger human life)

c. *Explanation.* This paragraph is based on *United States v. Potter*, 15 U.S.C.M.A. 271, 35 C.M.R. 243 (1965).

82. Article 134— (Fleeing scene of accident)

c. *Explanation.* (1) Nature or offense. This paragraph is based on *United States v. Seeger*, 2 M.J. 249 (A.F.C.M.R. 1976).

(2) *Knowledge.* This paragraph is based on *United States v. Eagleson* , 3 U.S.C.M.A. 685, 14 C.M.R. 103 (1954) (Latimer, J., concurring in the result). Actual knowledge is an essential element of the offense rather than an affirmative defense as is current practice. This is because actual knowledge that an accident has occurred is the point at which the driver's or passenger's responsibilities begin. *See United States v. Waluski*, 6 U.S.C.M.A. 724, 21 C.M.R. 46 (1956).

(3) *Passengers. See United States v. Waluski*, supra.

83. Article 134— (Fraternization)

Introduction. This paragraph is new to the Manual for Courts-Martial, although the offense of fraternization is based on longstanding custom of the services, as recognized in the sources below. Relationships between senior officers and junior officers and between noncommissioned or petty officers and their subordinates may, under some circumstances, be prejudicial to good order and discipline. This paragraph is not intended to preclude prosecution for such offenses.

c. *Explanation.* This paragraph is new and is based on *United States v. Pitasi*, 20 U.S.C.M.A. 601, 44 C.M.R. 31 (1971); *United States v. Free*, 14 C.M.R. 466 (N.B.R. 1953). *See also* W. Winthrop, *Military Law and Precedents* 41, 716 n.44 (2d ed. 1920 reprint); *Staton v. Froehlke*, 390 F.Supp. 503 (D.D.C. 1975); *United States v. Lovejoy*, 20 U.S.C.M.A. 18, 42 C.M.R. 210 (1970); *United States v. Rodriquez*, ACM 23545 (A.F.C.M.R. 1982); *United States v. Livingston*, 8 C.M.R. 206 (A.B.R. 1952). *See* Nelson, *Conduct Expected of an Officer and a Gentleman: Ambiguity*, 12 A.F. JAG. L.R. 124 (1970).

d. *Maximum punishment.* The maximum punishment for this offense is based on the maximum punishment for violation of general orders and regulations, since some forms of fraternization have also been punished under Article 92. As to dismissal, *see* Nelson, *supra* at 129–130.

f. *Sample specification. See United States v. Free, supra.*

84. Article 134— (Gambling with subordinate)

c. *Explanation.* This paragraph is new and is based on *United States v. Burgin*, 30 C.M.R. 525 (A.B.R. 1961).

d. *Maximum punishment.* The maximum punishment was increased from that provided in paragraph 127 *c* of MCM, 1969 (Rev.) to expressly authorize confinement. *Cf.* the second paragraph of paragraph 127 *c* (2) of MCM, 1969 (Rev.).

e. *Sample specification.* Sample specification 153 in Appendix 6c of MCM, 1969 (Rev.) was revised to more correctly reflect the elements of the offense.

85. Article 134— (Homicide, negligent)

c. *Explanation.* This paragraph is based on paragraph 213 *f*(12) of MCM, 1969 (Rev.); *United States v. Kick*, 7 M.J. 82 (C.M.A. 1979).

e. *Maximum punishment.*

1994 Amendment: Subparagraph e was amended to increase the maximum punishment from a bad conduct discharge, total forfeitures, and confinement for 1 year, to a dishonorable discharge, total forfeitures, and confinement for 3 years. This eliminated the incongruity created by having the maximum punishment for drunken driving resulting in injury that does not necessarily involve death exceed that of negligent homicide where the result must be the death of the victim.

86. Article 134— (Impersonating a commissioned, warrant, noncommissioned, or petty officer, or an agent or official)

b. *Elements.* The elements are based on *United States v. Yum*, 10 M.J. 1 (C.M.A. 1980).

c. *Explanation.* This paragraph is new and is based on *United States v. Demetris*, 9 U.S.C.M.A. 412, 26 C.M.R. 192 (1958); *United States v. Messenger*, 2 U.S.C.M.A. 21, 6 C.M.R. 21 (1952).

87. Article 134— (Indecent acts or liberties with a child)

c. *Explanation.* This paragraph is based on paragraph 213 *f*(3) of MCM, 1969 (Rev.). *See also United States v. Knowles*, 15 U.S.C.M.A. 404, 35 C.M.R. 376 (1965); *United States v. Brown*, 3 U.S.C.M.A. 454, 13 C.M.R. 454, 13 C.M.R. 10 (1953); *United States v. Riffe*, 25 C.M.R. 650 (A.B.R. 1957), *pet. denied*, 9 U.S.C.M.A. 813, 25 C.M.R. 486 (1958). "Lewd" and "lascivious" were deleted because they are synonymous with indecent. *See id. See also* paragraph 90c.

2007 Amendment. This paragraph has been replaced in its entirety by paragraph 45. *See* Article 120 (g) Aggravated Sexual Contact with a Child, (i) Abusive Sexual Contact with a Child, and (j) Indecent Liberty with Child.

88. Article 134— (Indecent exposure)

c. *Explanation.* This paragraph is new and is based on *United States v. Manos*, 8 U.S.C.M.A. 734, 25 C.M.R. 238 (1958). *See also United States v. Caune*, 22 U.S.C.M.A. 200, 46 C.M.R. 200 (1973); *United States v. Conrad*, 15 U.S.C.M.A. 439, 35 C.M.R. 411 (1965).

e. *Maximum punishment.* The maximum punishment has been increased to include a bad-conduct discharge. Indecent exposure in some circumstances (e.g., in front of children, but without the intent to incite lust or gratify sexual desires necessary for indecent acts or liberties) is sufficiently serious to authorize a punitive discharge.

2007 Amendment. This paragraph has been replaced in its entirety by paragraph 45. *See* Article 120 (n) Indecent Exposure.

89. Article 134— (Indecent language)

Introduction. "Obscene" was removed from the title because it is synonymous with "indecent." *See* paragraph 90c and Analysis. "Insulting" was removed from the title based on *United States v. Prince*, 14 M.J. 654 (A.C.M.R. 1982); *United States v. Linyear*, 3 M.J. 1027 (N.C.M.R. 1977).

Gender-neutral language has been used in this paragraph, as well as throughout this Manual. This will eliminate any question about the intended scope of certain offenses, such as indecent language, which may have been raised by the use of the masculine pronoun in MCM, 1969 (Rev.). It is, however, consistent with the construction given to the former Manual. *See e.g., United States v. Respess*, 7 M.J. 566 (A.C.M.R. 1979). *See generally* 1 U.S.C. §§ ("unless the context indicates otherwise … words importing the masculine gender include the feminine as well ….").

c. *Explanation.* This paragraph is new and is based on *United States v. Knowles*, 15 U.S.C.M.A. 404, 35 C.M.R. 376 (1965); *United States v. Wainwright*, 42 C.M.R. 997 (A.F.C.M.R. 1970). For a general discussion of this offense, *see United States v. Linyear supra.*

1986 Amendment: "Provoking speeches and gestures" was added as a lesser included offense. *United States v. Linyear*, 3 M.J. 1027 (N.M.C.M.R. 1977).

1995 Amendment: The second sentence is new. It incorporates a test for "indecent language" adopted by the Court of Military Appeals in *United States v. French*, 31 M.J. 57, 60 (C.M.A. 1990). The term "tends reasonably" is substituted for the term "calculated to" to avoid the misinterpretation that indecent language is a specific intent offense.

e. *Maximum punishment.* The maximum punishment in cases other than communication to a child under the age of 16 has been reduced. It now parallels that for indecent exposure.

90. Article 134— (Indecent acts with another)

c. *Explanation.* This paragraph is new and is based on *United States v. Holland*, 12 U.S.C.M.A. 444, 31 C.M.R. 30 (1961); *United States v. Gaskin*, 12 U.S.C.M.A. 419, 31 C.M.R. 5 (1962); *United States v. Sanchez*, 11 U.S.C.M.A. 216, 29 C.M.R. 32 (1960); *United States v. Johnson*, 4 M.J. 770 (A.C.M.R. 1978). "Lewd" and "lascivious" have been deleted as they are synonymous with "indecent." *See id.*

91. Article 134— (Jumping from vessel into the water)

Introduction. This offense is new to the Manual for Courts-Martial. It was added to the list of Article 134 offenses based on *United States v. Sadinsky*, 14 U.S.C.M.A. 563, 34 C.M.R. 343 (1964).

92. Article 134— (Kidnapping)

Introduction. This offense is new to the Manual for Courts-Martial. It is based generally on 18 U.S.C. § 1201. *See also Military Judges' Benchbook*, DA PAM 27–9, paragraph 3–190 (May 1982).

Kidnapping has been recognized as an offense under Article 134 under several different theories. Appellate courts in the military have affirmed convictions for kidnapping in violation of State law, as applied through the third clause of Article 134 and 18 U.S.C. § 13 (*see* paragraph 60), *e.g., United States v. Picotte*, 12 U.S.C.M.A. 196, 30 C.M.R. 196 (1961); in violation of Federal law (18 U.S.C. § 1201) as applied through the third clause of Article 134, *e.g., United States v. Perkins*, 6 M.J. 602 (A.C.M.R. 1978); and in violation of the first two clauses of Article 134, *e.g., United States v. Jackson*, 17 U.S.C.M.A. 580, 38 C.M.R. 378 (1968). As a result, there has been some confusion concerning pleading and proving kidnapping in courts-martial. *See, e.g., United States v. Smith*, 8 M.J. 522 (A.C.M.R. 1979); *United States v. DiGiulio*, 7 M.J. 848 (A.C.M.R. 1979); *United States v. Perkins, supra.*

After *United States v. Picotte, supra*, was decided, 18 U.S.C. § 1201 was amended to include kidnapping within the special maritime and territorial jurisdiction of the United States. Pub.L. 92–539, § 201, 86 Stat. 1072 (1972). Consequently, reference to state law through 18 U.S.C. § 13 is no longer necessary (or authorized) in most cases. *See United States v. Perkins, supra.* Nevertheless, there remains some uncertainty concerning kidnapping as an offense in the armed forces, as noted above. This paragraph should eliminate such uncertainty, as well as any different treatment of kidnapping in different places.

b. *Elements.* The elements are based on 18 U.S.C. § 1201. The language in that statute "for ransom or reward or otherwise" has been deleted. This language has been construed to mean that no specific purpose is required for kidnapping. *United States v. Healy*, 376 U.S. 75 (1964); *Gooch v. United States* 297 U.S. 124 (1936); *Gawne v. United States*, 409 F.2d 1399 (9th Cir. 1969), *cert. denied* 397 U.S. 943 (1970). Instead it is required that the holding be against the will of the victim. *See Chatwin v. United States*, 326 U.S. 455 (1946); 2 E. Devitt and C. Blackmar, *Federal Jury Practice and Instructions* § 43.09 (1977); *Military Judges' Benchbook, supra* at paragraph 3–190. *See also Amsler v. United States*, 381 F.2d 37 (9th Cir. 1967); *Davidson v. United States*, 312 F.2d 163 (8th Cir. 1963).

c. *Explanation.* Subparagraph (1) is based on *United States v. Hoog*, 504 F.2d 45 (8th Cir. 1974), *cert. denied*, 420 U.S. 961 (1975). *See also* 2 E. Devitt and C. Blackmar, *supra* at § 43.05.

Subparagraph (2) is based on *United States v. DeLaMotte*, 434 F.2d 289 (2d Cir. 1970), *cert. denied*, 401 U.S. 921 (1971); *United States v. Perkins, supra. See generally* 1 Am.Jur. 2d *Abduction and Kidnapping* § 2 (1962).

Subparagraph (3) is based on *Chatwin v. United States, supra*; 2 E. Devitt and C. Blackmar, *supra* at § 43.09. *See also Hall v. United States*, 587 F.2d 177 (5th Cir.), *cert. denied*, 441 U.S. 961 (1979); *Military Judges' Benchbook, supra*, paragraph 3–190.

Subparagraphs (4) and (5) are based on 18 U.S.C. § 1201; 2 E. Devitt and C. Blackmar, *supra* § § 43.05, 43.06, 43.10. *See also United States v. Hoog, supra.* The second sentence in subparagraph (4) is also based on *United States v. Healy, supra. See also United States v. Smith, supra.* The second sentence in subparagraph (5) is based on *United States v. Picotte, supra. See also United States v. Martin*, 4 M.J. 852 (A.C.M.R. 1978). The last sentence in subsection (5) is based on 18 U.S.C. § 1201. A parent taking a child in violation of a custody decree may violate state law or 18 U.S.C. § 1073. *See* 18 U.S.C.A. § 1073 Historical and Revision Note (West Supp. 1982). *See also* paragraph 60 *c*(4).

e. *Maximum punishment.* The maximum punishment is based on 18 U.S.C. § 1201. *See also United States v. Jackson, supra.*

93. Article 134— (Mail: taking, opening, secreting, destroying, or stealing)

c. *Explanation.* This paragraph is new and is based on *United States v. Gaudet*, 11 U.S.C.M.A. 672, 29 C.M.R. 488 (1960); *United States v. Manausa*, 12 U.S.C.M.A. 37, 30 C.M.R. 37 (1960). This offense is not preempted by Article 121. *See United States v. Gaudet, supra. See also* paragraph 60.

94. Article 134— (Mails: depositing or causing to be deposited obscene matters in)

c. *Explanation.* This paragraph is new and is based on *United States v. Holt*, 12 U.S.C.M.A. 471, 31 C.M.R. 57 (1961); *United States v. Linyear*, 3 M.J. 1027 (N.C.M.R. 1977). *See also Hamling v. United States*, 418 U.S. 87 (1974); *Miller v. California*, 413 U.S. 15 (1973).

f. *Sample specifications.* "Lewd" and "lascivious" were eliminated because they are synonymous with "obscene." *See* Analysis, paragraph 90 *c*.

95. Article 134— (Misprision of serious offense)

c. *Explanation.* This paragraph is based on paragraph 213 *f*(6) of MCM, 1969 (Rev.). The term "serious offense" is substituted for "felony" to make clear that concealment of serious military offenses, as well a serious civilian offenses, is an offense. Subsection (1) is based on *Black's Law Dictionary* 902 (5th ed. 1979). *See also United States v. Daddano*, 432 F.2d 1119 (7th Cir. 1970); *United States v. Perlstein*, 126 F.2d 789 (3d Cir.), *cert. denied*, 316 U.S. 678 (1942); 18 U.S.C. § 4.

96. Article 134— (Obstructing justice)

c. *Explanation.* This paragraph is new and is based on *United States v. Favors*, 48 C.M.R. 873 (A.C.M.R. 1974). *see also* 18 U.S.C. § § 1503, 1505, 1510, 1512, 1513; *United States v. Chodkowski*, 11 M.J. 605 (A.F.C.M.A. 1981).

f. *Sample specification.*

1991 Amendment: The form specification was amended by deleting the parentheses encompassing "wrongfully" as this language is not optional, but is a required component of a legally sufficient specification.

96a. Article 134— (Wrongful interference with an adverse administrative proceeding)

1993 Amendment. Paragraph 96 *a* is new and proscribes conduct that obstructs administrative proceedings. *See generally* 18 U.S.C. 1505, Obstruction of proceedings before departments, agencies, and committees. This paragraph, patterned after paragraph 96, covers obstruction of certain administrative proceedings not currently covered by the definition of criminal proceeding found in paragraph 96 *c*. This paragraph is necessary given the increased number of administrative actions initiated in each service.

97. Article 134— (Pandering and prostitution)

c. *Explanation.* This paragraph is new and is based on *United States v. Adams*, 18 U.S.C.M.A. 310, 40 C.M.R. 22 (1966); *United State v. Bohannon*, 20 C.M.R. 870 (A.F.B.R. 1955).

e. *Maximum punishment.* The maximum punishment for prostitution is based on 18 U.S.C. § 1384.

2007 Amendment: This paragraph has been amended. The act of compelling another person to engage in an act of prostitution with another person will no longer be punished under paragraph 97 and has been replaced by a new offense under paragraph 45. *See* Article 120 (l) Forcible Pandering.

2005 Amendment: b. Elements. Subparagraph (2) defines the elements of the offense of patronizing a prostitute. Old subparagraphs (2) and (3) are now (3) and (4) respectively.

97a. Article 134— (Parole, Violation of)

1998 Amendment. The addition of paragraph 97a to Part IV, Punitive Articles, makes clear that violation of parole is an offense under Article 134, UCMJ. Both the 1951 and 1969 Manuals for Courts-Martial listed the offense in their respective Table of Maximum Punishments. No explanatory guidance, however, was contained in the discussion of Article 134, UCMJ in the Manual for Courts-Martial. The drafters added paragraph 97a to ensure that an explanation of the offense, to include its elements and a sample specification, is contained in the Manual for Courts-Martial, Part IV, Punitive Articles. *See generally United States v. Faist,* 41 C.M.R. 720 (ACMR 1970); *United States v. Ford,* 43 C.M.R. 551 (ACMR 1970).

98. Article 134— (Perjury: subornation of)

c. *Explanation.* This paragraph is new. It is based on 18 U.S.C. § 1622 which applies to any perjury. *See* 18 U.S.C. § 1621. *See generally* R. Perkins, *Criminal Law* 466–67 (2d ed. 1969). *See also* the Analysis, paragraph 57; *United States v. Doughty*, 14 U.S.C.M.A. 540, 34 C.M.R. 320 (1964)(res judicata); *United States v. Smith*, 49 C.M.R. 325 (N.C.M.R. 1974) (pleading).

99. Article 134— (Public record: altering, concealing, removing mutilating, obliterating, or destroying)

c. *Explanation.* This paragraph is new and is based on Mil.-R.Evid. 803(8), but does not exclude certain types of records which are inadmissible under Mil. R. Evid. 803(8) for policy reasons. *See United States v. Maze*, 21 U.S.C.M.A. 260, 45 C.M.R. 34 (1972) for a discussion of one of these offenses in relation to the doctrine of preemption. *See generally* 18 U.S.C. § 2071.

f. *Sample specification.* The specification contained in Appendix 6c, no. 172, from MCM, 1969 (Rev.) was modified by deleting the word "steal" because this would be covered by "remove."

100. Article 134— (Quarantine: medical, breaking)

b. *Elements.* The word "duly" has been deleted from the elements of this offense for the same reasons explained in Analysis, paragraph 19.

c. *Explanation.* Putting a person "on quarters" or other otherwise excusing a person from duty because of illness does not of itself constitute a medical quarantine.

f. *Sample specification.* Sample specification no. 173, Appendix 6c of MCM, 1969 (Rev.) was modified based on the deletion of the word "duly," as explained in the analysis to paragraph 19. *See* subparagraph b, above.

100a. Article 134— (Reckless endangerment)

c. *Explanation.* This paragraph is new and is based on *United States v. Woods*, 28 M.J. 318 (C.M.A. 1989); *see also* Md. Ann. Code art. 27, § 120. The definitions of "reckless" and "wanton" have been taken from Article 111 (drunken or reckless driving). The definition of "likely to produce grievous bodily harm" has been taken from Article 128 (assault).

2004 Amendment: The sample specification was amended to add the word "wantonly" to make the sample specification consistent with the elements. The phrase "serious bodily harm" has been changed to read "grievous bodily harm" in the sample specification to parallel the language in the elements. Similarly, in the *Explanation,* the phrase "serious injury" was modified to read "grievous bodily harm." The format of the sample specification was also modified to follow the format of other sample specifications in the MCM.

101. Article 134— (Requesting commission of an offense)

Introduction. This offense is new to the Manual for Courts-Martial, and is based on *United States v. Benton*, 7 M.J. 606 (N.C.M.R. 1979), *pet. denied*, 8 M.J. 227 (1980).

c. *Explanation.* This paragraph is based on *United States v. Benton, supra. See also United States v. Oakley*, 7 U.S.C.M.A. 733, 23 C.M.R. 197 (1957).

e. *Maximum punishment.* The maximum punishment is based on *United States v. Oakley, supra.*

1990 Amendment: The offense of 'requesting the commission of an offense' was deleted. Solicitation of another to commit an offense, whether prosecuted under Article 82 or 134, UCMJ, is a specific intent offense. *See United States v. Mitchell*, 15 M.J. 214 (C.M.A. 1983). The preemption doctrine precludes the creation of a lesser included offense of solicitation which does not require specific intent. *See United States v. Taylor*, 23 M.J. 314 (C.M.A. 1987).

102. Article 134— (Restriction; breaking)

Elements. The word "duly" has been deleted from the elements of this offense, for the same reasons explained in Analysis, paragraph 19.

c. *Explanation.* This paragraph is new and is based on paragraph 20 *b* , 126 *g*, 131 *c*, and 174 *b* of MCM, 1969 (Rev.). *See also United States v. Haynes*, 15 U.S.C.M.A. 122, 35 C.M.R. 94 (1964).

f. *Sample specification.* Sample specification no. 175, appendix 6c of MCM, 1969 (Rev.) was modified based on the deletion of the word "duly," as explained in the analysis of paragraph 19. *See* subparagraph b, above.

103. Article 134— (Seizure: destruction, removal, or disposal of property to prevent)

Introduction. This offense is new. It is based on 18 U.S.C. § 2232. *See generally United States v. Gibbons*, 463 F.2d 1201 (3d Cir. 1972); *United States v. Bernstein*, 287 F.Supp. 84 (S.D. Fla. 1968); *United States v. Fishel*, 12 M.J. 602 (A.C.M.R. 1981), *pet denied*, 13 M.J. 20. *See also* the opinion in *United States v. Gibbons*, 331 F.Supp. 970 (D.Del. 1971).

c. *Explanation.* The second sentence is based on *United States v. Gibbons, supra. Cf. United States v. Ferrone*, 438 F.2d 381 (3d Cir.), *cert. denied*, 402 U.S. 1008 (1971).

e. *Maximum punishment.* The maximum punishment is based on 18 U.S.C. § 2232.

103a. Article 134— (Self-injury without intent to avoid service)

c. *Explanation. 1995 Amendment:* This offense is based on paragraph 183 *a* of MCM, U.S. Army, 1949; *United States v. Ramsey*, 35 M.J. 733 (A.C.M.R. 1992), *aff'd*, 40 M.J. 71 (C.M.A. 1994); *United States v. Taylor*, 38 C.M.R. 393 (C.M.A. 1968); *see generally* TJAGSA Practice Note, *Confusion About Malingering and Attempted Suicide*, The Army Lawyer, June 1992, at 38.

e. *Maximum punishment. 1995 Amendment:* The maximum punishment for subsection (1) reflects the serious effect that this offense may have on readiness and morale. The maximum punishment reflects the range of the effects of the injury, both in degree and duration, on the ability of the accused to perform work, duty, or service. The maximum punishment for subsection (1) is equivalent to that for offenses of desertion, missing movement through design, and certain violations of orders. The maximum punishment for subsection (2) is less than the maximum punishment for the offense of malingering under the same circumstances because of the absence of the specific intent to avoid work, duty, or service. The maximum punishment for subsection (2) is equivalent to that for nonaggravated offenses of desertion, willfully disobeying a superior commissioned officer, and nonaggravated malingering by intentional self-inflicted injury.

f. *Sample specification. 1995 Amendment: See* appendix 4, paragraph 177 of MCM, U.S. Army, 1949. Since incapacitation to perform duties is not an element of the offense, language relating to "unfitting himself for the full performance of military service" from the 1949 MCM has been omitted. The phrase "willfully injure" has been changed to read "intentionally injure" to parallel the language contained in the malingering specification under Article 115.

104. Article 134— (Sentinel or lookout: offenses against or by)

c. *Explanation.* This paragraph is new. *See* Analysis, paragraph 13 and Analysis, paragraph 38. The definition of "loiter" is taken from *United States v. Muldrow*, 48 C.M.R. 63, 65n. 1 (A.F.C.M.R. 1973).

e. *Maximum punishment.* The maximum punishment for loitering or wrongfully sitting on post by a sentinel or lookout was increased because of the potentially serious consequences of such misconduct. *Cf.* Article 113.

105. Article 134— (Soliciting another to commit an offense)

b. *Elements. See United States v. Mitchell*, 15 M.J. 214 (C.M.A. 1983); the Analysis, paragraph 6. *See also* paragraph 101.

c. *Explanation. See* the Analysis, paragraph 6.

d. *Lesser included offenses. See United States v. Benton*, 7 M.J. 606 (N.C.M.R. 1979), pet. denied, 8 M.J. 227 (1980).

1990 Amendment: Listing of "Article 134 — Requesting another to commit an offense, wrongful communication of language" as a lesser included offense of soliciting another to commit an offense was deleted in conjunction with the deletion of such a request as a substantive offense. *See United States v. Taylor*, 23 M.J. 314 (C.M.A. 1987); and, the Analysis, paragraph 101.

e. *Maximum punishment. See United States v. Benton, supra.*

February 1986 Amendment: The Committee considered maximum imprisonment for 5 years inappropriate for the offense of solicitation to commit espionage under new Article 106a. A maximum punishment authorizing imprisonment for life is more consistent with the serious nature of the offense of espionage.

106. Article 134— (Stolen property: knowingly receiving, buying, concealing)

c. *Explanation.* This paragraph is based on paragraph 213 *f*(14) of MCM, 1969 (Rev.). and *United States v. Cartwright*, 13 M.J. 174 (C.M.A. 1982); *United States v. Ford*, 12 U.S.C.M.A. 3, 30 C.M.R. 3 (1960). *See United States v. Rokoski*, 30 C.M.R. 433 (A.B.R. 1960) concerning knowledge. *See also United States v. Bonavita*, 21 U.S.C.M.A. 407, 45 C.M.R. 181 (1972), concerning this offense in general.

e. *Maximum punishment.* The maximum punishments have been revised. Instead of three levels (less than $50, $50 to $100, and over $100) only two are used. This is simpler and conforms more closely to the division between felony and misdemeanor penalties contingent on value in property offenses in civilian jurisdictions.

2002 Amendment: The monetary amount affecting the maximum punishments has been revised from $100 to $500 to account for inflation. The last change was in 1969 raising the amount to $100. The value has also been readjusted to realign it more closely with the division between felony and misdemeanor penalties in civilian jurisdictions. *See generally* American Law Institute, Model Penal Code and Commentaries Sec. 223.1 (1980) (suggesting $500 as the value).

107. Article 134— (Straggling)

c. *Explanation.* This paragraph is new and is based on *Military Judges' Benchbook*, DA PAM 27–9, paragraph 3–180 (May 1982).

108. Article 134— (Testify: wrongful refusal)

c. *Explanation.* This paragraph is new and is based on *United States v. Kirsch*, 15 U.S.C.M.A. 84, 35 C.M.R. 56 (1964). *See also United States v. Quarles*, 50 C.M.R. 514 (N.C.M.R. 1975).

f. *Sample specification.* "Duly appointed" which appeared in front of the words "board of officers" in sample specification no. 174, Appendix 6 of MCM, 1969 (Rev.) was deleted. This is because all of the bodies under this paragraph must be properly convened or appointed. Summary courts-martial were expressly added to the sample specification to make clear that this offense may occur before a summary court-martial.

109. Article 134— (Threat or hoax: bomb)

Introduction. This offense is new to the Manual for Courts-Martial. It is based generally on 18 U.S.C. § 844(e) and on *Military Judges' Benchbook*, DA PAM 27–9, paragraph 3–189 (May 1982). Bomb hoax has been recognized as an offense under clause 1 of Article 134. *United States v. Mayo* , 12 M.J. 286 (C.M.R. 1982).

c. *Explanation.* This paragraph is based on *Military Judges' Benchbook, supra* at paragraph 3–189.

2005 Amendment: This paragraph has been expanded to state the various means by which a threat or hoax is based. Whereas explosives were the instruments most commonly used in the past, new types of weapons have developed. Included in the new types of methods by which a threat or hoax is based are: weapons of mass destruction; chemical agents, substances, or weapons; biological agents, substances, or weapons; and hazardous materials. The definitions used in this amendment are based on the following U.S. Code provisions: 40 U.S.C. § 2302 (weapons of mass destruction); 22 U.S.C. § 6701 (chemical weapons); 50 U.S.C. § 1520a (biological agents); and 49 U.S.C. § 5301 (hazardous material).

e. *Maximum punishment.* The maximum punishment is based on 18 U.S.C. § 844(e).

2005 Amendment: This amendment increases the maximum punishment currently permitted under paragraph 109 from five years to ten years. Ten years is the maximum period of confinement permitted under 18 U.S.C. § 844(e), the U.S. Code section upon which the original paragraph 109 is based.

110. Article 134— (Threat, communicating)

c. *Explanation.* This paragraph is taken from paragraph 213 *f*(10) of MCM, 1969 (Rev.). *See also United States v. Gilluly*, 13 U.S.C.M.A. 458, 32 C.M.R. 458 (1963); *United States v. Frayer*, 11 U.S.C.M.A. 600, 29 C.M.R. 416 (1960).

111. Article 134— (Unlawful entry)

c. *Explanation.* This paragraph is new and is based on *United States v. Breen*, 15 U.S.C.M.A. 658, 36 C.M.R. 156 (1966); *United States v. Gillin*, 8 U.S.C.M.A. 669, 25 C.M.R. 173 (1958); *United States v. Love*, 4 U.S.C.M.A. 260, 15 C.M.R. 260 (1954). *See also United States v. Wickersham*, 14 M.J. 404 (C.M.A. 1983) (storage area); *United States v. Taylor*, 12 U.S.C.M.A. 44, 30 C.M.R. 44 (1960) (aircraft); *United States v. Sutton*, 21 U.S.C.M.A. 344, 45 C.M.R. 118 (1972) (tracked vehicle); *United States v. Selke*, 4 M.J. 293 (C.M.A. 1978) (summary disposition) (Cook, J., dissenting).

112. Article 134— (Weapon: concealed, carrying)

c. *Explanation.* This paragraph is new and is based on *United States v. Tobin*, 17 U.S.C.M.A. 625, 38 C.M.R. 423 (1968); *United States v. Bluel*, 10 U.S.C.M.A. 67, 27 C.M.R. 141 (1958); *United States v. Thompson*, 3 U.S.C.M.A. 620, 14 C.M.R. 38 (1954). Subsection (3) is based on *United States v. Bishop*, 2 M.J. 741 (A.F.C.M.R. 1977), *pet. denied*, 3 M.J. 184 (1977).

113. Article 134— (Wearing unauthorized insignia, decoration, badge, ribbon, device, or lapel button).

e. *Maximum punishment.* The maximum punishment has been increased to include a bad-conduct discharge because this offense often involves deception.

APPENDIX 24
ANALYSIS OF NONJUDICIAL PUNISHMENT PROCEDURE

1. General

c. *Purpose.* This paragraph is based on the legislative history of Article 15, both as initially enacted and as modified in 1962. *See generally* H.R.Rep. No. 491, 81st Cong., 1st Sess. 14–15 (1949); S.Rep. No. 1911, 87th Cong., 2d Sess. (1962).

d. *Policy.* Subparagraph (1) is based on paragraph 129*a* of MCM, 1969 (Rev.). Subparagraph (2) is based on the last sentence of paragraph 129*a* of MCM, 1969 (Rev.) and on service regulations. *See, e.g.*, AR 27–10, para. 3–4 *b* (1 Sep. 1982); JAGMAN sec. 0101. *Cf.* Article 37. Subparagraph (3) is based on the second paragraph 129*b* of MCM, 1969 (Rev.).

e. *Minor offenses.* This paragraph is derived from paragraph 128*b* of MCM, 1969 (Rev.), service regulations concerning "minor offenses" (*see, e.g.*, AR 27–10, para. 3–3*d* (1 Sep. 1982); AFR 111–9, para. 3*a*(3) (31 Aug. 1979)); *United States v. Fretwell,* 11 U.S.C.M.A. 377, 29 C.M.R. 193 (1960). The intent of the paragraph is to provide the commander with enough latitude to appropriately resolve a disciplinary problem. Thus, in some instances, the commander may decide that nonjudicial punishment may be appropriate for an offense that could result in a dishonorable discharge or confinement for more than 1 year if tried by general court-martial, e.g., failure to obey an order or regulation. On the other hand, the commander could refer a case to a court-martial that would ordinarily be considered at nonjudicial punishment, e.g., a short unauthorized absence, for a servicemember with a long history of short unauthorized absences, which nonjudicial punishment has not been successful in correcting.

f. *Limitations on nonjudicial punishment.*

(1) *Double punishment prohibited.* This subparagraph is taken from the first paragraph of paragraph 128*d* of MCM, 1969 (Rev.). Note that what is prohibited is the service of punishment twice. Where nonjudicial punishment is set aside, this does not necessarily prevent reimposition of punishment and service of punishment not previously served.

(2) *Increase in punishment prohibited.* This paragraph is taken from the second paragraph of paragraph 128 *d* of MCM, 1969 (Rev.).

(3) *Multiple punishment prohibited.* This paragraph is based on the guidance for court-martial offenses, found in paragraph 30g and 33 *h* of MCM, 1969 (Rev.).

(4) *Statute of limitations.* This paragraph restates the requirements of Article 43(c) regarding nonjudicial punishment.

(5) *Civilian courts.* This paragraph is derived from service regulations (*see, e.g.*, AR 27–10, chap. 4 (1 Sep. 1982)) and is intended to preclude the possibility of a servicemember being punished by separate jurisdictions for the same offense, except in unusual cases.

g. *Relationship of nonjudicial punishment to administrative corrective measures.* This paragraph is derived from paragraph 128*c* of MCM, 1969 (Rev.) and service regulations. *See e.g.*, AR 27–10, para. 3–4 (1 Sep. 1982).

h. *2005 Amendment*: Subsection (h) is new. This subsection was added to clarify that nonjudicial punishment proceedings conducted in a combatant or joint command are to be conducted in accordance with the implementing regulations and procedures of the service of which the accused is a member.

i. *Effect of errors.* This paragraph is taken from paragraph 130 of MCM, 1969 (Rev.).

2. Who may impose nonjudicial punishment

This paragraph is taken from paragraph 128*a* of MCM, 1969 (Rev.) and service regulations. *See, e.g.*, AR 27–10, para. 3–7 (1 Sep. 1982); JAGMAN sec. 0101; AFR 111–9, para. 3 (31 Aug. 1979). Additional guidance in this area is left to Secretarial regulation, in accordance with the provisions of Article 15(a).

2005 Amendment: Subsection (2) was amended to clarify the authority of the commander of a joint command to impose nonjudicial punishment upon service members of the joint command.

3. Right to demand trial

This paragraph is taken from Article 15(a) and paragraph 132 of MCM, 1969 (Rev.).

4. Procedure

This paragraph is based on paragraph 133 of MCM, 1969 (Rev.) and service regulations. It provides a uniform basic procedure for nonjudicial punishment for all the services. Consistent with the purposes of nonjudicial punishment (*see* S.Rep. No. 1911, 87th Cong. 2d Sess. 4 (1962)) it provides due process protections and is intended to meet the concerns expressed in the Memorandum of Secretary of Defense Laird, 11 January 1973. *See also United States v. Mack,* 9 M.J. 300, 320–21 (C.M.A. 1980). The Report of the Task Force on the Administration of Military Justice in the Armed Forces, 1972, and GAO Report to the Secretary of Defense, *Better Administration of Military Article 15 Punishments for Minor Offenses is Needed*, September 2, 1980, were also considered.

Note that there is no right to consult with counsel before deciding whether to demand trial by court-martial. Unless otherwise prescribed by the Secretary concerned, the decision whether to permit a member to consult with counsel is left to the commander. In *United States v. Mack, supra,* records of punishments where such opportunity was not afforded (except when the member was attached to or embarked in a vessel) were held inadmissible in courts-martial.

1986 Amendment: Subparagraph (c)(2) was amended to state clearly that a servicemember has no absolute right to refuse to appear personally before the person administering the nonjudicial punishment proceeding. In addition, Part V was amended throughout to use the term "nonjudicial punishment authority" in circumstances where the proceeding could be administered by a commander, officer in charge, or a principal assistant to a general court-martial convening authority or general or flag officer.

5. Punishments

This paragraph is taken from paragraph 131 of MCM, 1969 (Rev.). Subparagraph b(2)(b)4 is also based on S.Rep. 1911, 87th Cong., 1st Sess. 7 (1962). Subparagraph c(4) is also based on *id.* at 6–7 and *Hearings Before a Subcomm. of the House Comm. on Armed Services* , 87th Cong., 1st Sess. 33 (1962). Detention of pay was deleted as a punishment because under current centralized pay systems, detention of pay is cumbersome, ineffective, and seldom used. The concept of apportionment, authorized in Article 15(b) and set forth in paragraph 131 *d* of MCM, 1969 (Rev.), was eliminated as unnecessary and confusing. Accordingly, the Table of Equivalent Punishments is no longer necessary.

Subparagraph d, in concert with the elimination of the apportionment concept, will ease the commanders burden of determining an appropriate punishment and make the implementation of that punishment more efficient and understandable.

1987 Amendment: Subparagraph e was redesignated as subparagraph g and new subparagraphs e and f were added to implement the amendments to Articles 2 and 3, UCMJ, contained in the "Military Justice Amendments of 1986," tit. VIII, § 804, National Defense Authorization Act for fiscal year 1987, Pub. L. No. 99–661, 100 Stat. 3905 (1986).

1990 Amendment: Subsection (c)(8) was amended to incorporate the statutory expansion of jurisdiction over reserve component personnel provided in the Military Justice Amendments of 1990, tit. XIII, § 1303, National Defense Authorization Act of Fiscal Year 1990, Pub. L. 101–189, 103 Stat. 1352 (1989).

2007 Amendment: Paragraph 5.c.(8) was amended because Hardship Duty Pay (HDP) superseded Foreign Duty Pay (FDP) on 3 February 1999. HDP is payable to members entitled to basic pay. The Secretary of Defense has established that HDP will be paid to members (a) for performing specific missions, or (b) when assigned to designated areas.

6. Suspension, mitigation, remission, and setting aside

This paragraph is taken from Article 15, paragraph 134 of MCM 1969 (Rev.), and service regulations. *See e.g.*, AR 27–10, paras. 3–23 through 3–28 (1 Sep. 1982); JAGMAN sec. 0101; AFR 111–9, para 7 (31 Aug 1979). Subparagraph a dealing with suspension was expanded to: require a violation of the code during the period of suspension as a basis for vacation action, and to explain that vacation action is not in itself nonjudicial punishment and does not preclude the imposition of nonjudicial punishment for the offenses upon which the vacation action was based. Subparagraph a(4) provides a procedure for vacation of suspended nonjudicial punishment. This procedure parallels the procedure found sufficient to make admissible in courts-martial records of vacation of suspended nonjudicial punishment. *United States v. Covington*, 10 M.J. 64 (C.M.A. 1980).

1990 Amendment: A new subsection a(4) was added to permit punishment imposed under Article 15 to be suspended based on conditions in addition to violations of the UCMJ. This affords the same flexibility given to authorities who suspend punishment adjudged at court-martial under R.C.M. 1108(c). Experience has demonstrated the necessity and utility of such flexibility in the nonjudicial punishment context.

7. Appeals

This paragraph is taken from paragraph 135 of MCM, 1969 (Rev.) and service regulations dealing with appeals. *See* AR 27–10, paras. 3–29 through 3–35 (1 Sep. 1982); JAGMAN 0101; AFR 111–9, para. 8 (31 Aug. 1981). Subparagraph (d) requires an appeal to be filed within 5 days or the right to appeal will be waived, absent unusual circumstances. This is a reduction from the 15 days provided for in paragraph 135 and is intended to expedite the appeal process. Subparagraph f(2) is intended to promote sound practice, that is, the superior authority should consider many factors when reviewing an appeal, and not be limited to matters submitted by the appellant or the officer imposing the punishment. Subparagraph f(3) provides for "additional proceedings" should a punishment be set aside due to a procedural error. This is consistent with court-martial practice and intended to ensure that procedural errors do not prevent appropriate disposition of a disciplinary matter.

8. Records of nonjudicial punishment

This paragraph is taken from Article 15(g) and paragraph 133c of MCM, 1969 (Rev.).

APPENDIX 25
HISTORICAL EXECUTIVE ORDERS

EXECUTIVE ORDER 12473 AS AMENDED BY EXECUTIVE ORDER 12484, MANUAL FOR COURTS-MARTIAL, UNITED STATES, 1984

By virtue of the authority vested in me as President by the Constitution of the United States and by Chapter 47 of Title 10 of the United States (Uniform Code of Military Justice), I hereby prescribe the following Manual for Courts-Martial to be designated as "Manual for Courts-Martial, United States, 1984."

This Manual shall take effect on August 1, 1984, with respect to all court-martial processes taken on and after that date: *Provided*, That nothing contained in this Manual shall be construed to invalidate any restraint, investigation, referral of charges, designation or detail of a military judge or counsel, trial in which arraignment had been had, or other action begun prior to that date, and any such restraint, investigation, trial, or other action may be completed in accordance with applicable laws, Executive orders, and regulations in the same manner and with the same effect as if this Manual had not been prescribed; *Provided further*, That Rules for Courts-Martial 908, 1103(j), 1105-1107, 1110-1114, 1201, and 1203 shall not apply to any case in which the findings and sentence were adjudged by a court-martial before August 1, 1984, and the post-trial and appellate review of such cases shall be completed in accordance with applicable laws, Executive orders, and regulations in the same manner and with the same effect as if this Manual had not been prescribed; *Provided further*, That nothing contained in this Manual shall be construed to make punishable any act done or omitted prior to August 1, 1984, which was not punishable when done or omitted; *Provided further*, That nothing in part IV of this Manual shall be construed to invalidate the prosecution of any offense committed before the effective date of this Manual; *Provided further*, That the maximum punishment for an offense committed prior to August 1, 1984, shall not exceed the applicable limit in effect at the time of the commission of such offense; *Provided further*, That for offenses committed prior to August 1, 1984, for which a sentence is adjudged on or after August 1, 1984, if the maximum punishment authorized in this Manual is less than that previously authorized, the lesser maximum authorized punishment shall apply; *And provided further*, That Part V of this Manual shall not apply to nonjudicial punishment proceedings which were initiated before August 1, 1984, and nonjudicial punishment proceedings in such cases shall be completed in accordance with applicable laws, Executive orders, and regulations in the same manner and with the same effect as if this Manual had not been prescribed.

The Manual for Courts-Martial, 1969, United States (Revised edition), prescribed by Executive Order No. 11476, as amended by Executive Order Nos. 11835, 12018, 12198, 12233, 12306, 12315, 12340, 12383, and 12460 is hereby rescinded, effective August 1, 1984.

The Secretary of Defense shall cause this Manual to be reviewed annually and shall recommend to the President any appropriate amendments.

The Secretary of Defense, on behalf of the President, shall transmit a copy of this Order to the Congress of the United States in accord with Section 836 of Title 10 of the United States Code.

THE WHITE HOUSE
July 13, 1984

EXECUTIVE ORDER 12550 AMENDMENTS TO THE MANUAL FOR COURTS-MARTIAL, UNITED STATES, 1984

By the authority vested in me as President by the Constitution of the United States and by Chapter 47 of Title 10 of the United States Code (Uniform Code of Military Justice), in order to prescribe amendments to the Manual for Courts-Martial, United States, 1984, prescribed by Executive Order No. 12473, as amended by Executive Order No. 12484, it is hereby ordered as follows:

Section 1. Part II of the Manual for Courts-Martial, United States, 1984, is amended as follows:

a. R.C.M. 707(a) is amended to read as follows:

b. R.C.M. 805(b) is amended by

c. R.C.M. 903(c)(3) is amended by

d. R.C.M. 909 is amended

e. R.C.M. 916(e)(3) is amended by

f. R.C.M. 920(e)(2) is amended by

g. R.C.M. 921(d) is amended by

h. R.C.M. 922(b) is amended

i. R.C.M. 1001 is amended

j. R.C.M. 1003(b)(10)(B) is amended by

k. R.C.M. 1004 is amended

l. R.C.M. 1010 is amended

m. R.C.M. 1106(b) is amended by

n. R.C.M. 1114(c) is amended by

Section 2. Part III of the Manual for Courts-Martial, United States, 1984, is amended as follows:

a. Mil. R. Evid. 304 is amended as follows:

b. Mil. R. Evid. 311 is amended as follows:

c. Mil. R. Evid. 609(e) is amended by

d. Mil. R. Evid. 804(a) is amended by

Section 3. Part IV of the Manual for Courts-Martial, United States, 1984, is amended as follows:

a. Paragraph 16 is amended

b. Part IV is amended by inserting the following new paragraph after paragraph 30:

c. Part IV is amended by adding the following new sentence at the end of paragraph 105e:

Section 4. Part V of the Manual for Courts-Martial, United States, 1984, is amended as follows:

Section 5. The amendments to Mil. R. Evid. 704, which were implemented on 10 April 1985 pursuant to Mil. R. Evid. 1102, are hereby rescinded; *Provided*, That this rescission shall not apply in the trial of any case in which arraignment occurred while such amendments were in effect.

Section 6. These amendments shall take effect on 1 March 1986, with respect to all court-martial processes taken on and after that date: *Provided*, That nothing contained in these amendments shall be construed to invalidate any nonjudicial punishment proceeding, restraint, investigation, referral of charges, trial in which arraignment occurred, or other action begun prior to that date, and any such restraint, investigation, referral of charges, trial, or other action may proceed in the same manner and with the same effect as if these amendments had not been prescribed; *Provided further*, That the amendments made in Rule for Court-Martial 1004(c) shall apply in the trial of offenses committed on or after 1 March 1986; *Provided further*, That nothing contained in these amendments shall be construed to invalidate any capital sentencing proceeding conducted prior to 1 March 1986, and any such proceeding shall be completed and reviewed in the same manner and with the same effect as if these amendments had not been prescribed; *Provided further*, That amendments to Rule for Court-Martial 707(a) shall not apply to any condition on liberty imposed before 1 March 1986, and the effect of such a condition on liberty shall be considered under Rule for Court-Martial 707(a) as it existed before 1 March 1986; *Provided further*, That the amendments made in paragraph 16 of Part IV shall apply in trials of offenses committed on or after 1 March 1986; *Provided further*, That the amendments made in paragraph 30a of Part IV shall apply in the trials of offenses committed under Article 106a on or after 1 March 1986; *And provided further*, That the amendments made in paragraph 30a of Part IV authorizing capital punishment shall apply with respect to offenses under Article 106a committed on or after 1 March 1986.

Section 7. The Secretary of Defense, on behalf of the President, shall transmit a copy of this Order to the Congress of the United States in accord with Section 836 of Title 10 of the United States Code.

Ronald Reagan

THE WHITE HOUSE
February 19, 1986

EXECUTIVE ORDER 12586 AMENDMENTS TO THE MANUAL FOR COURTS-MARTIAL, UNITED STATES, 1984

By the authority vested in me as President by the Constitution of the United States and by Chapter 47 of title 10 of the United States Code (Uniform Code of Military Justice), in order to prescribe amendments to the Manual for Courts-Martial, United States, 1984, prescribed by Executive Order No. 12473, as amended by Executive Order Nos. 12484 and 12550, it is hereby ordered as follows:

Section 1. Part II of the Manual for Courts-Martial, United States, 1984, is amended as follows:

a. R.C.M. 201(e) is amended as follows:

b. Chapter II is amended by inserting the following new Rule following R.C.M. 203:

c. R.C.M. 503(a)(2) is amended by

d. R.C.M. 701(b)(2) is amended by

e. R.C.M. 706(c)(1) is amended to read as follows:

f. R.C.M. 706(c)(2) is amended as follows:

g. R.C.M. 707 is amended—

h. R.C.M. 903 is amended—

i. R.C.M. 916 is amended as follows:

j. R.C.M. 918(a) is amended—

k. R.C.M. 920(e)(5)(D) is amended by

l. R.C.M. 921(c) is amended—

m. R.C.M. 924(b) is amended by

n. R.C.M. 1001(b)(2) is amended by

o. R.C.M. 1003(c) is amended—

p. R.C.M. 1010(c) is amended to read as follows:

q. R.C.M. 1105(c) is amended by—

r. R.C.M. 1106(f)(5) is amended by

s. R.C.M. 1107(b)(5) is amended to read as follows:

t. R.C.M. 1109 is amended—

u. R.C.M. 1112 is amended—

v. R.C.M. 1113(d)(1) is amended to read as follows:

w. R.C.M. 1114 is amended as follows:

x. R.C.M. 1201(b)(3)(A) is amended by

y. R.C.M. 1203(c) is amended by

z. R.C.M. 1305(b)(2) is amended by

Section 2. Part III of the Manual for Courts-Martial, United States, 1984, is amended as follows:

a. Mil. R. Evid. 304(h) is amended by

b. Mil. R. Evid. 613(a) is amended by

c. Mil. R. Evid. 902(1) is amended by

Section 3. Part IV of the Manual for Courts-Martial, United States, 1984, is amended as follows:

a. Paragraph 4 is amended

b. Paragraph 10 is amended

c. Paragraph 32 is amended—

d. Paragraph 35 is amended—

e. Paragraph 42 is amended

f. Paragraph 46 is amended

g. Paragraph 89 is amended

Section 4. Part V of the Manual for Courts-Martial, United States, 1984, is amended by paragraph 5 by—

Section 5. These amendments shall take effect on 12 March 1987, subject to the following:

a. The addition of Rule for Courts-Martial 204, the amendments made to Rules for Courts-Martial 707 and 1003(c), and the amendments made to paragraph 5 of Part V, shall apply to any offense committed on or after 12 March 1987.

b. The amendments made to Rules for Courts-Martial 701(b), 706(c)(2), 916(b), 916(k), 918(a), 920(e), 921(c), and 924(b) shall apply to any offense committed on or after November 14, 1986, the date of enactment of the National Defense Authorization Act for fiscal year 1987, Pub. L. No. 99-661.

c. The amendments made to Rules for Courts-Martial 503 and 903 shall apply only in cases in which arraignment has been completed on or after 12 March 1987.

d. The amendments made to Rules for Courts-Martial 1105 and 1106 shall apply only in cases in which the sentence is adjudged on or after 12 March 1987.

e. Except as provided in section 5.b, nothing contained in these amendments shall be construed to make punishable any act done or omitted prior to 12 March 1987, which was not punishable when done or omitted.

f. The maximum punishment for an offense committed prior to 12 March 1987 shall not exceed the applicable maximum in effect at the time of the commission of such offense.

g. Nothing in these amendments shall be construed to invalidate any nonjudicial punishment proceeding, restraint, investigation, referral of charges, trial in which arraignment occurred, or other action begun prior to 12 March 1987, and any such restraint, investigation, referral of charges, trial, or other action may proceed in the same manner and with the same effect as if these amendments had not been prescribed.

Section 6. The Secretary of Defense, on behalf of the President, shall transmit a copy of this Order to the Congress of the United States in accord with Section 836 of title 10 of the United States Code.

THE WHITE HOUSE
March 3, 1987

EXECUTIVE ORDER 12708 AMENDMENTS TO THE MANUAL FOR COURTS-MARTIAL, UNITED STATES, 1984

By the authority vested in me as President by the Constitution of the United States and by chapter 47 of title 10 of the United States Code (Uniform Code of Military Justice), in order to prescribe amendments to the Manual for Courts-Martial, United States, 1984, prescribed by Executive Order No. 12473, as amended by Executive Order Nos. 12484, 12550 and 12586, it is hereby ordered as follows:

Section 1. Part II of the Manual for Courts-Martial, United States, 1984, is amended as follows:

a. R.C.M. 302(b)(2) is amended to read as follows:

b. R.C.M. 905(e) is amended to read as follows:

c. R.C.M. 913(a) is amended by

d. R.C.M. 1003(b)(2) is amended by

e. R.C.M. 1103(b)(2)(B)(i) is amended to read as follows:

f. R.C.M. 1103(e) is amended to read as follows:

g. R.C.M. 1106(c) is amended to read as follows:

h. R.C.M. 1106(f) is amended—

i. R.C.M. 1107(b)(4) is amended to read as follows:

j. R.C.M. 1108(b) is amended—

k. R.C.M. 1112(b) is amended to read as follows:

l. R.C.M. 1114(c)(2) is amended to read as follows:

m. R.C.M. 1201(b)(3)(C) is amended to read as follows:

Section 2. Part III of the Manual for Courts-Martial, United States, 1984, is amended as follows:

a. Mil. R. Evid. 304(b)(1) is amended to read as follows:

b. Mil. R. Evid. 506(c) is amended to read as follows:

Section 3. Part IV of the Manual for Courts-Martial, United States, 1984, is amended as follows:

a. Paragraph 10 is amended—

b. Paragraph 101 is deleted

c. Paragraph 105 is amended by—

Section 4. Part V of the Manual for Courts-Martial, United States, 1984, is amended as follows:

a. Paragraph 5 is amended by—

b. Paragraph 6a is amended by—

Section 5. These amendments shall take effect on 1 April 1990, subject to the following:

a. The amendment made to paragraph 10 of Part IV, shall apply to any offense committed on or after 1 April 1990.

b. The amendments made to Rule for Courts-Martial 905 and to Military Rule of Evidence 304 shall apply only in cases in which arraignment has been completed on or after 1 April 1990.

c. The amendment made to Rule for Courts-Martial 1106 shall apply only in cases in which the sentence is adjudged on or after 1 April 1990.

d. Nothing contained in these amendments shall be construed to make punishable any act done or omitted prior to 1 April 1990 which was not punishable when done or omitted.

e. The maximum punishment for an offense committed prior to 1 April 1990 shall not exceed the applicable maximum in effect at the time of the commission of such offense.

f. Nothing in these amendments shall be construed to invalidate any nonjudicial punishment proceeding, restraint, investigation, referral of charges, trial in which arraignment occurred, or other action begun prior to 1 April 1990, and any such restraint, investigation, referral of charges, trial, or other action may proceed in the same manner and with the same effect as if these amendments had not been prescribed.

Section 6. The Secretary of Defense, on behalf of the President, shall transmit a copy of this Order to the Congress of the United States in accord with Section 836 of title 10 of the United States Code.

George Bush

THE WHITE HOUSE
March 23, 1990

EXECUTIVE ORDER NO. 12767 AMENDMENTS TO THE MANUAL FOR COURTS-MARTIAL, UNITED STATES, 1984

By the authority vested in me as President by the Constitution of the United States of America, and by chapter 47 of title 10 of the United States Code (Uniform Code of Military Justice), in order to prescribe amendments to the Manual for Courts-Martial, United States, 1984, prescribed by Executive Order No. 12473, as amended by Executive Order No. 12484, Executive Order No. 12550, Executive Order No. 12586, Executive Order No. 12708, it is hereby ordered as follows:

Section 1. Part II of the Manual for Courts-Martial, United States, 1984, is amended as follows:

a. R.C.M. 405(g)(1)(A) is amended to read as follows:

b. R.C.M. 405(g)(4)(B) is amended—

c. R.C.M. 701(a)(3)(B) is amended to read as follows:

d. R.C.M. 701(b) is amended—

e. R.C.M. 705(c)(2) is amended by deleting the first sentence and substituting therefor the following sentence:

f. R.C.M. 705(d) is amended—

g. R.C.M. 707 is amended to read as follows:

h. R.C.M. 802(c) is amended to read as follows:

i. R.C.M. 908(b)(4) is amended to read as follows:

j. R.C.M. 908(b) is amended by inserting the following new sub-paragraph at the end thereof:

k. R.C.M. 1004(c)(8) is amended to read as follows:

l. R.C.M. 1010 is amended to read as follows:

m. R.C.M. 1103(b)(2)(D) is amended by—

n. R.C.M. 1107(f)(1) is amended to read as follows:

o. R.C.M. 1110(f)(1) is amended to read as follows:

p. R.C.M. 1113(c)(1) is amended in the first paragraph thereof to read as follows:

Section 2. Part III of the Manual for Courts-Martial, United States, 1984, is amended by adding the following new rule at the end of Section VII thereof: [M.R.E. Polygraph examinations]

Section 3. Part IV of the Manual for Courts-Martial, United States, 1984, is amended as follows:

a. Paragraph 4e is amended to read as follows:

b. Paragraph 19 is amended—

c. Paragraph 35c(2) is amended to read as follows:

d. Paragraph 57d is amended to read as follows:

e. Paragraph 96f is amended to read as follows:

Section 4. These amendments shall take effect on 6 July 1991, subject to the following:

a. The amendments made to Rule for Courts-Martial 1004(c)(8) and paragraphs 4c, 19, and 35c(2) of Part IV shall apply to any offense committed on or after 6 July 1991.

b. Military Rule of Evidence 707 shall apply only in cases in which arraignment has been completed on or after 6 July 1991.

c. The amendments made to Rules for Courts-Martial 701 and 705 shall apply only in cases in which charges are preferred on or after 6 July 1991.

d. The amendments made to Rules for Courts-Martial 707 and 1010 shall apply only to cases in which arraignment occurs on or after 6 July 1991.

e. The amendment made to Rule for Courts-Martial 908(b)(9) shall apply only to cases in which pretrial confinement is imposed on or after 6 July 1991.

f. The amendment made to Rule for Courts-Martial 1113(c)(1) shall apply only in cases in which the sentence is adjudged on or after 6 July 1991.

g. Nothing contained in these amendments shall be construed to make punishable any act done or omitted prior to 6 July 1991, which was not punishable when done or omitted.

h. The maximum punishment for an offense committed prior to 6 July 1991 shall not exceed the applicable maximum in effect at the time of the commission of such offense.

i. Nothing in these amendments shall be construed to invalidate any nonjudicial punishment proceeding, restraint, investigation, referral of charges, trial in which arraignment occurred, or other action begun prior to 6 July 1991, and any such restraint, investigation, referral of charges, trial, or other action may proceed in the same manner and with the same effect as if these amendments had not been prescribed.

Section 5. The Secretary of Defense, on behalf of the President, shall transmit a copy of this Order to the Congress of the United States in accord with section 836 of Title 10 of the United States Code.

THE WHITE HOUSE
June 27, 1991

EXECUTIVE ORDER 12888 AMENDMENTS TO THE MANUAL FOR COURTS-MARTIAL, UNITED STATES, 1984

By the authority vested in me as President by the Constitution and the laws of the United States of America, including chapter 47 of title 10, United States Code (Uniform Code of Military Justice, 10 U.S.C. 801–946), in order to prescribe amendments to the Manual for Courts-Martial, United States, 1984, prescribed by Executive Order No. 12473, as amended by Executive Order No. 12484, Executive Order No. 12550, Executive Order No. 12586, Executive Order No. 12708, and Executive Order No. 12767, it is hereby ordered as follows:

Section 1. Part II of the Manual for Courts-Martial, United States, 1984, is amended as follows:

a. R.C.M. 109 is amended as follows:

"(a) *In general.* Each Judge Advocate General is responsible for the professional supervision and discipline of military trial and appellate military judges, judge advocates, and other lawyers who practice in proceedings governed by the code and this Manual. To discharge this responsibility each Judge Advocate General may prescribe rules of professional conduct not inconsistent with this rule or this Manual. Rules of professional conduct promulgated pursuant to this rule may include sanctions for violations of such rules. Sanctions may include but are not limited to indefinite suspension from practice in courts-martial and in the Courts of Military Review. Such suspensions may only be imposed by the Judge Advocate General of the armed service of such courts. Prior to imposing any discipline under this rule, the subject of the proposed action must be provided notice and an opportunity to be heard. The Judge Advocate General concerned may upon good cause shown modify or revoke suspension. Procedures to investigate complaints against military trial judges and appellate military judges are contained in subsection (c) of this rule.

(b) *Action after suspension or disbarment.* When a Judge Advocate General suspends a person from practice or the Court of Military Appeals disbars a person, any Judge Advocate General may suspend that person from practice upon written notice and opportunity to be heard in writing.

(c) *Investigation of judges.*

(1) *In general.* These rules and procedures promulgated pursuant to Article 6a are established to investigate and dispose of charges, allegations, or information pertaining to the fitness of a military trial judge or appellate military judge to perform the duties of the judge's office.

(2) *Policy.* Allegations of judicial misconduct or unfitness shall be investigated pursuant to the procedures of this rule and appropriate action shall be taken. Judicial misconduct includes any act or omission that may serve to demonstrate unfitness for further duty as a judge, including but not limited to violations of applicable ethical standards.

(3) *Complaints.* Complaints concerning a military trial judge or appellate military judge will be forwarded to the Judge Advocate General of the service concerned or to a person designated by the Judge Advocate General concerned to receive such complaints.

(4) *Initial action upon receipt of a complaint.* Upon receipt, a complaint will be screened by the Judge Advocate General concerned or by the individual designated in subsection (c)(3) of this rule to receive complaints. An initial inquiry is necessary if the complaint, taken as true, would constitute judicial misconduct or unfitness for further service as a judge. Prior to the commencement of an initial inquiry, the Judge Advocate General concerned shall be notified that a complaint has been filed and that an initial inquiry will be conducted. The Judge Advocate General concerned may temporarily suspend the subject of a complaint from performing judicial duties pending the outcome of any inquiry or investigation conducted pursuant to this rule. Such inquiries or investigations shall be conducted with reasonable promptness.

(5) *Initial inquiry.*

(A) *In general.* An initial inquiry is necessary to determine if the complaint is substantiated. A complaint is substantiated upon finding that it is more likely than not that the subject judge has engaged in judicial misconduct or is otherwise unfit for further service as a judge.

(B) *Responsibility to conduct initial inquiry.* The Judge Advocate General concerned, or the person designated to receive complaints under subsection (c)(3) of this rule, will conduct or order an initial inquiry. The individual designated to conduct the inquiry should, if practicable, be senior to the subject of the complaint. If the subject of the complaint is a military trial judge, the individual designated to conduct the initial inquiry should, if practicable, be a military trial judge or an individual with experience as a military trial judge. If the subject of the complaint is an appellate military judge, the individual designated to conduct the inquiry should, if practicable, have experience as an appellate military judge.

(C) *Due process.* During the initial inquiry, the subject of the complaint will, at a minimum, be given notice and an opportunity to be heard.

(D) *Action following the initial inquiry.* If the complaint is not substantiated pursuant to subsection (c)(5)(A) of this rule, the complaint shall be dismissed as unfounded. If the complaint is substantiated, minor professional disciplinary action may be taken or the complaint may be forwarded, with findings and recommendations, to the Judge Advocate General concerned. Minor professional disciplinary action is defined as counseling or the issuance of an oral or written admonition or reprimand. The Judge Advocate General concerned will be notified prior to taking minor professional disciplinary action or dismissing a complaint as unfounded.

(6) *Action by the Judge Advocate General.*

(A) *In general.* The Judge Advocates General are responsible for the professional supervision and discipline of military trial and appellate military judges under their jurisdiction. Upon receipt of findings and recommendations required by subsection (c)(5)(D) of this rule the Judge Advocate General concerned will take appropriate action.

(B) *Appropriate Actions.* The Judge Advocate General concerned may dismiss the complaint, order an additional inquiry, appoint an ethics commission to consider the complaint, refer the matter to another appropriate investigative agency or take appropriate professional disciplinary action pursuant to the rules of professional conduct prescribed by the Judge Advocate General under subsection (a) of this rule. Any decision of a Judge Advocate General, under this rule, is final and is not subject to appeal.

(C) *Standard of Proof.* Prior to taking professional disciplinary action, other than minor disciplinary action is defined in subsection (c)(5)(D) of this rule, the Judge Advocate General concerned shall find, in writing, that the subject of the complaint engaged in judicial misconduct or is otherwise unfit for continued service as a military judge, and that such misconduct or unfitness is established by clear and convincing evidence.

(D) *Due process.* Prior to taking final action on the complaint, the Judge Advocate General concerned will ensure that the subject of the complaint is, at a minimum, given notice and an opportunity to be heard.

(7) *The Ethics Commission.*

(A) *Membership.* If appointed pursuant to subsection (c)(6)(B) of this rule, an ethics commission shall consist of at least three members. If the subject of the complaint is a military trial judge, the commission should include one or more military trial judges or individuals with experience as a military trial judge. If the subject of the complaint is an appellate military judge, the commission should include one or more individuals with experience as an appellate military judge. Members of the commission should, if practicable, be senior to the subject of the complaint.

(B) *Duties.* The commission will perform those duties assigned by the Judge Advocate General concerned. Normally, the commission will provide an opinion as to whether the subject's acts or omissions constitute judicial misconduct or unfitness. If the commission determines that the affected judge engaged in judicial misconduct or is unfit for continued judicial service, the commission may be required to recommend an appropriate disposition to the Judge Advocate General concerned.

(8) *Rules of procedure.* The Secretary of Defense or the Secretary of the service concerned may establish additional procedures consistent with this rule and Article 6A."

b. R.C.M. 305(f) is amended to read as follows:

" *Military Counsel.* If requested by the prisoner and such request is made known to military authorities, military counsel shall be provided to the prisoner before the initial review under subsection (i) of this rule or within 72 hours of such request being first communicated to military authorities, whichever occurs first. Counsel may be assigned for the limited purpose of representing the accused only during the pretrial confinement proceedings before charges are referred. If assignment is made for this limited purpose, the prisoner shall be so informed. Unless otherwise provided by regulations of the Secretary concerned, a prisoner does not have the right under this rule to have military counsel of the prisoner's own selection."

c. R.C.M. 305(h)(2)(A) is amended to read as follows:

"(A) *Decision.* Not later than 72 hours after the commander's ordering of a prisoner into pretrial confinement, or after receipt of a report that a member of the commander's unit or organization has been confined, whichever situation is applicable, the commander shall decide whether pretrial confinement will continue."

d. R.C.M. 305(i)(1) is amended to read as follows:

"(1) *In general.* A review of the adequacy of probable cause to believe the prisoner has committed an offense and of the necessity for continued pretrial confinement shall be made within 7 days of the imposition of confinement under military control. If the prisoner was apprehended by civilian authorities and remains in civilian custody at the request of military authorities, reasonable efforts will be made to bring the prisoner under military control in a timely fashion. In calculating the number of days of confinement for purposes of this rule, the initial date of confinement shall count as one day and the date of the review shall also count as one day."

e. R.C.M. 405(i) is amended to read as follows:

"(i) *Military Rules of Evidence.* The Military Rules of Evidence—other than Mil. R. Evid. 301, 302, 303, 305, 412, and Section V—shall not apply in pretrial investigations under this rule."

f. R.C.M. 701(g)(3)(C) is amended to read as follows:

"(C) Prohibit the party from introducing evidence, calling a witness, or raising a defense not disclosed; and".

g. R.C.M. 704(e) is amended to read as follows:

"(e) *Decision to grant immunity.* Unless limited by superior competent authority, the decision to grant immunity is a matter within the sole discretion of the appropriate general court-martial convening authority. However, if a defense request to immunize a witness has been denied, the military judge may, upon motion of the defense, grant appropriate relief directing that either an appropriate general court-martial convening authority grant testimonial immunity to a defense witness or, as to the affected charges and specifications, the proceedings against the accused be abated, upon findings that:

(1) The witness intends to invoke the right against self-incrimination to the extent permitted by law if called to testify; and

(2) The Government has engaged in discriminatory use of immunity to obtain a tactical advantage, or the Government, through its own overreaching, has forced the witness to invoke the privilege against self-incrimination; and

(3) The witness' testimony is material, clearly exculpatory, not cumulative, not obtainable from any other source and does more than merely affect the credibility of other witnesses."

h. R.C.M. 910(a)(1) is amended to read as follows:

"(1) *In general.* An accused may plead as follows: guilty; not guilty to an offense as charged, but guilty of a named lesser included offense; guilty with exceptions, with or without substitutions, not guilty of the exceptions, but guilty of the substitutions, if any; or, not guilty. A plea of guilty may not be received as to an offense for which the death penalty may be adjudged by the court-martial."

i. R.C.M. 918(a)(1) is amended to read as follows:

"(1) *As to a specification.* General findings as to a specification may be: guilty; not guilty of an offense as charged, but guilty of a named lesser included offense; guilty with exceptions, with or without substitutions, not guilty of the exceptions, but guilty of the substitutions, if any; not guilty only by reason of lack of mental responsibility; or, not guilty. Exceptions and substitutions may not be used to substantially change the nature of the offense or to increase the seriousness of the offense or the maximum punishment for it."

j. R.C.M. 920(b) is amended to read as follows:

"(b) *When given.* Instructions on findings shall be given before or after arguments by counsel, or at both times, and before the members close to deliberate on findings, but the military judge may, upon request of the members, any party, or *sua sponte*, give additional instructions at a later time."

k. R.C.M. 1103(g)(1)(A) is amended to read as follows:

" *In general.* In general and special courts-martial which require a verbatim transcript under subsections (b) or (c) of this rule and are subject to review by a Court of Military Review under Article 66, the trial counsel shall cause to be prepared an original and four copies of the record of trial. In all other general and special courts-martial the trial counsel shall cause to be prepared an original and one copy of the record of trial."

Section 2. Part III of the Manual for Courts-Martial, United States, 1984, is amended as follows:

a. Mil. R. Evid. 311(e)(2) is amended to read as follows:

"(2) *Derivative Evidence.* Evidence that is challenged under this rule as derivative evidence may be admitted against the accused if the military judge finds by a preponderance of the evidence that the evidence was not obtained as a result of an unlawful search or seizure, that the evidence ultimately would have been obtained by lawful means even if the unlawful search or seizure had not been made, or that the evidence was obtained by officials who reasonably and with good faith relied on the issuance of an authorization to search, seize, or apprehend or a search warrant or an arrest warrant. Notwithstanding other provisions of this Rule, an apprehension made in a dwelling in a manner that violates R.C.M. 302 (d)(2)&(e) does not preclude the admission into evidence of a statement of an individual apprehended provided (1) that the apprehension was based on probable cause, (2) that the statement was made subsequent to the apprehension at a location outside the dwelling, and (3) that the statement was otherwise in compliance with these rules."

b. Mil. R. Evid. 505(a) is amended to read as follows:

"(a) *General rule of privilege.* Classified information is privileged from disclosure if disclosure would be detrimental to the national security. As with other rules of privilege this rule applies to all stages of the proceedings."

c. Mil. R. Evid. 505(g)(1)(D) is amended by adding the following at the end:

"All persons requiring security clearance shall cooperate with investigatory personnel in any investigations which are necessary to obtain a security clearance."

d. Mil. R. Evid. 505(h)(3) is amended to read as follows:

"(3) *Content of notice.* The notice required by this subdivision shall include a brief description of the classified information. The description, to be sufficient, must be more than a mere general statement of the areas about which evidence may be introduced. The accused must state, with particularity, which items of classified information he reasonably expects will be revealed by his defense."

e. Mil. R. Evid. 505(i)(3) is amended to read as follows:

"(3) *Demonstration of national security nature of the information.* In order to obtain an in camera proceeding under this rule, the Government shall submit the classified information and an affidavit ex parte for examination by the military judge only. The affidavit shall demonstrate that disclosure of the information reasonably could be expected to cause damage to the national security in the degree required to warrant classification under the applicable executive order, statute, or regulation."

f. Mil. R. Evid. 505(i)(4)(B) is amended to read as follows:

"*Standard.* Classified information is not subject to disclosure under this subdivision unless the information is relevant and necessary to an element of the offense or a legally cognizable defense and is otherwise admissible in evidence. In presentencing proceedings, relevant and material classified information pertaining to the appropriateness of, or the appropriate degree of, punishment shall be admitted only if no unclassified version of such information is available."

g. Mil. R. Evid. 505(j)(5) is amended to read as follows:

"(5) *Closed session.* The military judge may exclude the public during that portion of the presentation of evidence that discloses classified information."

h. Mil. R. Evid. 609(a) is amended to read as follows:

"(a) *General rule.* For the purpose of attacking the credibility of a witness, (1) evidence that a witness other than the accused has been convicted of a crime shall be admitted, subject to Mil. R. Evid. 403, if the crime was punishable by death, dishonorable discharge, or imprisonment in excess of one year under the law under which the witness was convicted, and evidence that an accused has been convicted of such a crime shall be admitted if the military judge determines that the probative value of admitting this evidence outweighs its prejudicial effect to the accused; and (2) evidence that any witness has been convicted of a crime shall be admitted if it involved dishonesty or false statement, regardless of the punishment. In determining whether a crime tried by court-martial was punishable by death, dishonorable discharge, or imprisonment in excess of one year, the maximum punishment prescribed by the President under Article 56 at the time of the conviction applies without regard to whether the case was tried by general, special, or summary court-martial."

i. Mil. R. Evid. 1101(d) is amended to read as follows:

"(d) *Rules inapplicable.* These rules (other than with respect to privileges and Mil. R. Evid. 412) do not apply in investigative hearings pursuant to Article 32; proceedings for vacation of suspension of sentence pursuant to Article 72; proceedings for search authorizations; proceedings involving pretrial restraint; and in other proceedings authorized under the code or this Manual and not listed in subdivision (a)."

Section 3. Part IV of the Manual for Courts-Martial, United States, 1984, is amended as follows:

a. Paragraph 37c is amended by inserting the following new subparagraphs (10) and (11) at the end thereof:

"(10) *Use.* 'Use' means to inject, ingest, inhale, or otherwise introduce into the human body, any controlled substance. Knowledge of the presence of the controlled substance is a required component of use. Knowledge of the presence of the controlled substance may be inferred from the presence of the controlled substance in the accused's body or from other circumstantial evidence. This permissive inference may be legally sufficient to satisfy the government's burden of proof as to knowledge."

"(11) *Deliberate ignorance.* An accused who consciously avoids knowledge of the presence of a controlled substance or the contraband nature of the substance is subject to the same criminal liability as one who has actual knowledge."

b. The last paragraph of paragraph 37e is amended to read as follows:

"When an offense under paragraph 37 is committed: while the accused is on duty as a sentinel or lookout; on board a vessel or aircraft used by or under the control of the armed forces; in or at a missile launch facility used by or under the control of the armed forces; while receiving special pay under 37 U.S.C. Section 310; in time of war; or in a confinement facility used by or under the control of the armed forces, the maximum period of confinement authorized for such an offense shall be increased by 5 years."

c. Paragraph 43d is amended to read as follows:

"(d) *Lesser included offenses.*

(1) *Premeditated murder and murder during certain offenses.* Article 118(2) and (3)—murder

(2) *All murders under Article 118.*

(a) Article 119—involuntary manslaughter

(b) Article 128—assault; assault consummated by a battery; aggravated assault

(c) Article 134—negligent homicide

(3) *Murder as defined in Article 118(1), (2), and (4).*

(a) Article 80—attempts

(b) Article 119—voluntary manslaughter

(c) Article 134—assault with intent to commit murder

(d) Article 134—assault with intent to commit voluntary manslaughter".

d. Para 45d(1) is amended by adding the following at the end thereof:

"(e) Article 120(b)—carnal knowledge".

e. Para 45f(1) is amended to read as follows:

"(1) *Rape.*

In that ______ (personal jurisdiction data), did, (at/on board—location) (subject-matter jurisdiction data, if required) on or about ______ 19 ___, rape ______ (a person who had not attained the age of 16 years)."

f. The following new paragraph is inserted after paragraph 96:

96a. Article 134 (Wrongful interference with an adverse administrative proceeding)

a. *Text. See* paragraph 60.

b. *Elements.*

(1) That the accused wrongfully did a certain act;

(2) That the accused did so in the case of a certain person against whom the accused had reason to believe there were or would be adverse administrative proceedings pending;

(3) That the act was done with the intent to influence, impede, or obstruct the conduct of such adverse administrative proceeding, or otherwise obstruct the due administration of justice;

(4) That under the circumstances, the conduct of the accused was to the prejudice of good order

and discipline in the armed forces or was of a nature to bring discredit upon the armed forces.

c. *Explanation.* For purposes of this paragraph [adverse administrative proceeding] includes any administrative proceeding or action, initiated against a servicemember, that could lead to discharge, loss of special or incentive pay, administrative reduction in grade, loss of a security clearance, bar to reenlistment, or reclassification. Examples of wrongful interference include wrongfully influencing, intimidating, impeding, or injuring a witness, an investigator, or other person acting on an adverse administrative action; by means of bribery, intimidation, misrepresentation, or force or threat of force delaying or preventing communication of information relating to such administrative proceeding; and, the wrongful destruction or concealment of information relevant to such adverse administrative proceeding.

d. *Lesser included offenses.* None.

e. *Maximum punishment.* Dishonorable discharge, forfeiture of all pay and allowances, and confinement for 5 years.

f. *Sample specification.* In that ________ (personal jurisdiction data), did, (at/on board—location) (subject-matter jurisdiction data, if required), on or about ________ 19 ____, wrongfully (endeavor to) [impede (an adverse administrative proceeding) (an investigation) (________)] [influence the actions of ________, (an officer responsible for making a recommendation concerning the adverse administrative proceeding) (an individual responsible for making a decision concerning an adverse administrative proceeding) (an individual responsible for processing an adverse administrative proceeding) (________)] [(influence) (alter) the testimony of ________ a witness before (a board established to consider an adverse administrative proceeding or elimination) (an investigating officer) (________)] in the case of ________, by [(promising) (offering) (giving) to the said ________, (the sum of $ ________) (________, of a value of about $ ________)] [communicating to the said ________ a threat to ________] [________], (if) (unless) the said ________, would [recommend dismissal of the action against said ________] [(wrongfully refuse to testify) (testify falsely concerning ________) (________)] [(at such administrative proceeding) (before such investigating officer) (before such administrative board)] [________]].

Section 4. These amendments shall take effect on January 21, 1994, subject to the following:

a. The amendments made to paragraphs 37c, 37e, 43d(2), 45d(1), and 96a of Part IV shall apply to any offense committed on or after January 21, 1994.

b. The amendments made to Section III shall apply only in cases in which arraignment has been completed on or after January 21, 1994.

c. The amendment made to Rules for Courts-Martial 405(i), 701(g)(3)(C), and 704(e) shall apply only in cases in which charges are preferred on or after January 21, 1994.

d. The amendments made to Rules for Courts-Martial 910, 918, and 920 shall apply only to cases in which arraignment occurs on or after January 21, 1994.

e. The amendments made to Rule for Courts-Martial 305 shall apply only to cases in which pretrial confinement is imposed on or after January 21, 1994.

f. The amendment to Rule for Courts-Martial 1103(g)(1)(A) shall apply only in cases in which the sentence is adjudged on or after January 21, 1994.

g. Nothing contained in these amendments shall be construed to make punishable any act done or omitted prior to January 21, 1994, which was not punishable when done or omitted.

h. The maximum punishment for an offense prior to January 21, 1994, shall not exceed the applicable maximum in effect at the time of the commission of such offense.

i. Nothing in these amendments shall be construed to invalidate any nonjudicial punishment proceeding, restraint, investigation, referral of charges, trial in which arraignment occurred, or other action begun prior to January 21, 1994, and any such restraint, investigation, referral of charges, trial, or other action may proceed in the same manner and with the same effect as if these amendments had not been prescribed.

Section 5. The Secretary of Defense, on behalf of the President, shall transmit a copy of this order to the Congress of the United States in accord with section 836 of title 10 of the United States Code.

William J. Clinton

THE WHITE HOUSE
December 23, 1993.

EXECUTIVE ORDER 12936 AMENDMENTS TO THE MANUAL FOR COURTS-MARTIAL, UNITED STATES, 1984

By the authority vested in me as President by the Constitution and the laws of the United States of America, including chapter 47 of title 10, United States Code (Uniform Code of Military Justice, 10 U.S.C. 801–946), in order to prescribe amendments to the Manual for Courts-Martial, United States, 1984, prescribed by Executive Order No. 12473, as amended by Executive Order No. 12484, Executive Order No. 12550, Executive Order No. 12586, Executive Order No. 12708, Executive Order No. 12767, and Executive Order No. 12888, it is hereby ordered as follows:

Section 1. Part II of the Manual for Courts-Martial, United States, 1984, is amended as follows:

a. R.C.M. 405(g)(1)(B) is amended to read as follows:

"(B) *Evidence.* Subject to Mil. R. Evid., Section V, evidence, including documents or physical evidence, which is under the control of the Government and which is relevant to the investigation and not cumulative, shall be produced if reasonably available. Such evidence includes evidence requested by the accused, if the request is timely. As soon as practicable after receipt of a request by the accused for information which may be protected under Mil. R. Evid. 505 or 506, the investigating officer shall notify the person who is authorized to issue a protective order under subsection (g)(6) of this rule, and the convening authority, if different. Evidence is reasonably available if its significance outweighs the difficulty, expense, delay, and effect on military operations of obtaining the evidence."

b. R.C.M. 405(g) is amended by inserting the following new subparagraph (6) at the end thereof:

"(6) *Protective order for release of privileged information.* If, prior to referral, the Government agrees to disclose to the accused information to which the protections afforded by Mil. R. Evid. 505 or Mil. R. Evid. 506 may apply, the convening authority, or other person designated by regulations of the Secretary of the service concerned, may enter an appropriate protective order, in writing, to guard against the compromise of information disclosed to the accused. The terms of any such protective order may include prohibiting the disclosure of the information except as authorized by the authority issuing the protective order, as well as those terms specified in Mil. R. Evid. 505(g)(1)(B) through (F) or Mil. R. Evid. 506(g)(2) through (5)."

c. R.C.M. 905(f) is amended to read as follows:

"(f) *Reconsideration.* On request of any party or sua sponte, the military judge may, prior to authentication of the record of trial, reconsider any ruling, other than one amounting to a finding of not guilty, made by the military judge."

d. R.C.M. 917(f) is amended to read as follows:

"(f) *Effect of ruling.* A ruling granting a motion for a finding of not guilty is final when announced and may not be reconsidered. Such a ruling is a finding of not guilty of the affected specification, or affected portion thereof, and, when appropriate, of the corresponding charge. A ruling denying a motion for a finding of not guilty may be reconsidered at any time prior to authentication of the record of trial."

e. R.C.M. 1001(b)(5) is amended to read as follows:

"(5) *Evidence of rehabilitative potential.* Rehabilitative potential refers to the accused's potential to be restored, through vocational, correctional, or therapeutic training or other corrective measures to a useful and constructive place in ~society.~

(A) *In general.* The trial counsel may present, by testimony or oral deposition in accordance with R.C.M. 702(g)(1), evidence in the form of opinions concerning the accused's previous performance as a servicemember and potential for rehabilitation.

(B) *Foundation for opinion.* The witness or deponent providing opinion evidence regarding the accused's rehabilitative potential must possess sufficient information and knowledge about the accused to offer a rationally-based opinion that is helpful to the sentencing authority. Relevant information and knowledge include, but are not limited to, information and knowledge about the accused's character, performance of duty, moral fiber, determination to be rehabilitated, and nature and severity of the offense or offenses.

(C) *Bases for opinion.* An opinion regarding the accused's rehabilitative potential must be based upon relevant information and knowledge possessed by the witness or deponent, and must relate to the accused's personal circumstances. The opinion of the witness or deponent regarding the severity or nature of the accused's offense or offenses may not serve as the principal basis for an opinion of the accused's rehabilitative potential.

(D) *Scope of opinion.* An opinion offered under this rule is limited to whether the accused has rehabilitative potential and to the magnitude or quality of any such potential. A witness may not offer an opinion regarding the appropriateness of a punitive discharge or whether the accused should be returned to the accused's unit.

(E) *Cross-examination.* On cross-examination, inquiry is permitted into relevant and specific instances of conduct.

(F) *Redirect.* Notwithstanding any other provision in this rule, the scope of opinion testimony permitted on redirect may be expanded, depending upon the nature and scope of the cross-examination."

f. R.C.M. 1003(b)(2) is amended to read as follows:

"(2) *Forfeiture of pay and allowances.* Unless a total forfeiture is adjudged, a sentence to forfeiture shall state the exact amount in whole dollars to be forfeited each month and the number of months the forfeitures will last. Allowances shall be subject to forfeiture only when the sentence includes forfeiture of all pay and allowances. The maximum authorized amount of a partial forfeiture shall be determined by using the basic pay, retired pay, or retainer pay, as applicable, or, in the case of reserve component personnel on inactive-duty, compensation for periods of inactive-duty training, authorized by the cumulative years of service of the accused, and, if no confinement is adjudged, any sea or foreign duty pay. If the sentence also includes reduction in grade, expressly or by operation of law, the maximum forfeiture shall be based on the grade to which the accused is reduced."

g. R.C.M. 1004(c)(4) is amended to read as follows:

"(4) That the offense was committed in such a way or under circumstances that the life of one or more persons other than the victim was unlawfully and substantially endangered, except that this factor shall not apply to a violation of Articles 104, 106a, or 120."

h. R.C.M. 1004(c)(7)(B) is amended to read as follows:

"(B) The murder was committed: while the accused was engaged in the commission or attempted commission of any robbery, rape, aggravated arson, sodomy, burglary, kidnapping, mutiny, sedition, or piracy of an aircraft or vessel; or while the accused was engaged in the commission or attempted commission of any offense involving the wrongful distribution, manufacture, or introduction or possession, with intent to distribute, of a controlled substance; or, while the accused was engaged in flight or attempted flight after the commission or attempted commission of any such offense."

i. R.C.M. 1004(c)(7)(I) is amended to read as follows:

"(I) The murder was preceded by the intentional infliction of substantial physical harm or prolonged, substantial mental or physical pain and suffering to the victim." For purposes of this section, "substantial physical harm" means fractures or dislocated bones, deep cuts, torn members of the body, serious damage to internal organs or other serious bodily injuries.

The term "substantial physical harm" does not mean minor injuries, such as a black eye or a bloody nose. The term "substantial physical harm or physical pain and suffering" is accorded its common meaning and includes torture.

j. R.C.M. 1102(b)(2) is amended to read as follows:

"(2) *Article 39(a) sessions.* An Article 39(a) session under this rule may be called for the purpose of inquiring into, and, when appropriate, resolving any matter which arises after trial and which substantially affects the legal sufficiency of any findings of guilty or the sentence. The military judge may also call an Article 39(a) session, upon motion of either party or *sua sponte*, to reconsider any trial ruling that substantially affects the legal sufficiency of any findings of guilty or the sentence."

k. R.C.M. 1105(c)(1) is amended to read as follows:

"(1) *General and special courts-martial.* After a general or special court-martial, the accused may submit matters under this rule within the later of 10 days after a copy of the authenticated record of trial, or, if applicable, the recommendation of the staff judge advocate or legal officer, or an addendum to the recommendation containing new matter is served on the accused. If, within the 10-day period, the accused shows that additional time is required for the accused to submit such matters, the convening authority or that authority's staff judge advocate may, for good cause, extend the 10-day period for not more than 20 additional days; however, only the convening authority may deny a request for such an extension."

l. R.C.M. 1106(f)(7) is amended to read as follows:

"(7) *New matter in addendum to recommendation.* The staff judge advocate or legal officer may supplement the recommendation after the accused and counsel for the accused have been served with the recommendation and given an opportunity to comment. When new matter is introduced after the accused and counsel for the accused have examined the recommendation, however, the accused and counsel for the accused must be served with the new matter and given ten days from service of the addendum in which to submit comments. Substitute service of the accused's copy of the addendum upon counsel for the accused is permitted in accordance with the procedures outlined in subparagraph (f)(1) of this rule."

Section 2. Part III of the Manual for Courts-Martial, United States, 1984, is amended as follows:

a. Mil. R. Evid. 305(d)(1)(B) is amended to read as follows:

"(B) The interrogation is conducted by a person subject to the code acting in a law enforcement capacity or the agent of such a person, the interrogation is conducted subsequent to the preferral of charges, and the interrogation concerns the offenses or matters that were the subject of the preferral of charges."

b. Mil. R. Evid. 305(e) is amended to read as follows:

"(e) *Presence of counsel.*

(1) *Custodial interrogation.* Absent a valid waiver of counsel under subdivision (g)(2)(B), when an accused or person suspected of an offense is subjected to custodial interrogation under circumstances described under subdivision (d)(1)(A) of this rule, and the accused or suspect requests counsel, counsel must be present before any subsequent custodial interrogation may proceed.

(2) *Post-preferral interrogation.* Absent a valid waiver of counsel under subdivision (g)(2)(C), when an accused or person suspected of an offense is subjected to interrogation under circumstances described in subdivision (d)(1)(B) of this rule, and the accused or suspect either requests counsel or has an appointed or retained counsel, counsel must be present before any subsequent interrogation concerning that offense may proceed."

c. Mil. R. Evid. 305(f) is amended to read as follows:

"(f) *Exercise of rights.*

(1) *The privilege against self-incrimination.* If a person chooses to exercise the privilege against self-incrimination under this rule, questioning must cease immediately.

(2) *The right to counsel.* If a person subjected to interrogation under the circumstances described in subdivision (d)(1) of this rule chooses to exercise the right to counsel, questioning must cease until counsel is present."

d. Mil. R. Evid. 305(g)(2) is amended to read as follows:

"(2) *Counsel.*

(A) If the right to counsel in subdivision (d) is applicable and the accused or suspect does not decline affirmatively the right to counsel, the prosecution must demonstrate by a preponderance of the evidence that the individual waived the right to counsel.

(B) If an accused or suspect interrogated under circumstances described in subdivision (d)(1)(A) requests counsel, any subsequent waiver of the right to counsel obtained during a custodial interrogation concerning the same or different offenses is invalid unless the prosecution can demonstrate by a preponderance of the evidence that—

(i) the accused or suspect initiated the communication leading to the waiver; or

(ii) the accused or suspect has not continuously had his or her freedom restricted by confinement, or other means, during the period between the request for counsel and the subsequent waiver.

(C) If an accused or suspect interrogated under circumstances described in subdivision (d)(1)(B) requests counsel, any subsequent waiver of the right to counsel obtained during an interrogation concerning the same offenses is invalid unless the prosecution can demonstrate by a preponderance of the evidence that the accused or suspect initiated the communication leading to the waiver."

e. Mil. R. Evid. 314(g)(3) is amended to read as follows:

"(3) *Examination for other persons.*

(A) *Protective sweep.* When an apprehension takes place at a location in which other persons might be present who might endanger those conducting the apprehension and others in the area of the apprehension, a reasonable examination may be made of the general area in which such other persons might be located. A reasonable examination under this rule is permitted if the apprehending officials have a reasonable suspicion based on specific and articulable facts that the area to be examined harbors an individual posing a danger to those in the area of the apprehension.

(B) *Search of attack area.* Apprehending officials may, incident to apprehension, as a precautionary matter and without probable cause or reasonable suspicion, look in closets and other spaces immediately adjoining the place of apprehension from which an attack could be immediately launched."

f. Mil. R. Evid. 404(b) is amended to read as follows:

"(B) *Other crimes, wrongs, or acts.* Evidence of other crimes, wrongs, or acts is not admissible to prove the character of a person in order to show action in conformity therewith. It may, however, be admissible for other purposes, such as proof of motive, opportunity, intent, preparation, plan, knowledge, identity, or absence of mistake or accident, provided, that upon request by the accused, the prosecution shall provide reasonable notice in advance of trial, or during trial if the military judge excuses pretrial notice on good cause shown, of the general nature of any such evidence it intends to introduce at trial."

Section 3. Part IV of the Manual for Courts-Martial, United States, 1984, is amended as follows:

a. Paragraph 44e(1) is amended to read as follows:

"(1) *Voluntary manslaughter.* Dishonorable discharge, forfeiture of all pay and allowances, and confinement for 15 years."

b. Paragraph 44e(2) is amended to read as follows:

"(2) *Involuntary manslaughter.* Dishonorable discharge, forfeiture of all pay and allowances, and confinement for 10 years."

c. Paragraph 45e is amended to read as follows:

"(e) *Maximum punishment.*

(1) *Rape.* Death or such other punishment as a court-martial may direct.

(2) *Carnal knowledge with a child who, at the time of the offense, has attained the age of 12 years.* Dishonorable discharge, forfeiture of all pay and allowances, and confinement for 20 years.

(3) *Carnal knowledge with a child under the age of 12 years at the time of the offense.* Dishonorable discharge, forfeiture of all pay and allowances, and confinement for life."

d. Paragraph 51e is amended to read as follows:

"(e) *Maximum punishment.*

(1) *By force and without consent.* Dishonorable discharge, forfeiture of all pay and allowances, and confinement for life.

(2) *With a child who, at the time of the offense, has attained the age of 12 years, but is under the age of 16 years.* Dishonorable discharge, forfeiture of all pay and allowances, and confinement for 20 years.

(3) *With a child under the age of 12 years at the time of the offense.* Dishonorable discharge, forfeiture of all pay and allowances, and confinement for life.

(4) *Other cases.* Dishonorable discharge, forfeiture of all pay and allowances, and confinement for 5 years."

e. Paragraph 85e is amended to read as follows:

"(e) *Maximum punishment.*Dishonorable discharge, forfeiture of all pay and allowances, and confinement for 3 years."

Section 4. These amendments shall take effect on December 9, 1994, subject to the following:

a. The amendments made to Rule for Courts-Martial 1004(c)(4) shall only to offenses committed prior to December 9, 1994.

b. Nothing contained in these amendments shall be construed to make punishable any act done or omitted prior to December 9, 1994, which was not punishable when done or omitted.

c. The maximum punishment for an offense committed prior to December 9, 1994, shall no exceed the applicable maximum in effect at the time of the commission of such offense.

d. Nothing in these amendments shall be construed to invalidate any nonjudicial punishment proceeding, restraint, investigation, referral of charges, trial in which arraignment occurred, or other action begun prior to December 9, 1994, and any such restraint, investigation, referral of charges, trial, or other action may proceed in the same manner and with the same effect as if these amendments had not been prescribed.

Section 5. The Secretary of Defense, on behalf of the President, shall transmit a copy of this order to the Congress of the United States in accord with section 836 of title 10 of the United States Code.

THE WHITE HOUSE
November 10,1994.

EXECUTIVE ORDER 12960 AMENDMENTS TO THE MANUAL FOR COURTS-MARTIAL, UNITED STATES, 1984

By the authority vested in me as President by the Constitution and the laws of the United States of America, including chapter 47 of title 10, United States Code (Uniform Code of Military Justice, 10 U.S.C. 801–946), in order to prescribe amendments to the Manual for Courts-Martial, United States, 1984, prescribed by Executive Order No. 12473, as amended by Executive Order No. 12484, Executive Order No. 12550, Executive Order No. 12586, Executive Order No. 12708, Executive Order No. 12767, Executive Order No. 12888, and Executive Order No. 12936, it is hereby ordered as follows:

Section 1. Part I of the Manual for Courts-Martial, United States, 1984, is amended as follows:

Preamble, paragraph 4, is amended to read as follows:

4. Structure and application of the Manual for Courts-Martial.

The Manual for Courts-Martial shall consist of this Preamble, the Rules for Courts-Martial, the Military Rules of Evidence, the Punitive Articles, and the Nonjudicial Punishment Procedures (Parts I–V). The Manual shall be applied consistent with the purpose of military law.

The Manual shall be identified as "Manual for Courts-Marital, United States (19xx edition)." Any amendments to the Manual made by Executive Order shall be identified as "19xx Amendments to the Manual for Courts-Martial, United States."

Section 2 Part II of the Manual for Courts-Martial, United States, 1984, is amended as follows:

a. R.C.M. 810(d) is amended as follows:

"(d) *Sentence limitations.*

(1) *In general.* Sentences at rehearings, new trials, or other trials shall be adjudged within the limitations set forth in R.C.M. 1003. Except as otherwise provided in subsection (d)(2) of this rule, offenses on which a rehearing, new trial, or other trial has been ordered shall not be the basis for an approved sentence in excess of or more severe than the sentence ultimately approved by the convening or higher authority following the previous trial or hearing, unless the sentence prescribed for the offense is mandatory. When a rehearing or sentencing is combined with trial on new charges, the maximum punishment that may be approved by the convening authority shall be the maximum punishment under R.C.M. 1003 for the offenses being reheard as limited above, plus the total maximum punishment under R.C.M. 1003 for any new charges of which the accused has been found guilty. In the case of an "other trial" no sentence limitations apply if the original trial was invalid because a summary or special court-martial improperly tried an offense involving a mandatory punishment or one otherwise considered capital.

(2) *Pretrial agreement.* If, after the earlier court-martial, the sentence was approved in accordance with a pretrial agreement and at the rehearing the accused fails to comply with the pretrial agreement, by failing to enter a plea of guilty or otherwise, the approved sentence resulting at a rehearing of the affected charges and specifications may include any otherwise lawful punishment not in excess of or more serious than lawfully adjudged at the earlier court-martial".

b. R.C.M. 924(a) is amended as follows:

"(a) *Time for reconsideration.* Members may reconsider any finding reached by them before such finding is announced in open session".

c. R.C.M. 924(c) is amended as follows:

"(c) *Military judge sitting alone.* In a trial by military judge alone, the military judge may reconsider any finding of guilty at any time before announcement of sentence and may reconsider the issue of the finding of guilty of the elements in a finding of not guilty only by reason of lack of mental responsibility at any time before announcement of sentence or authentication of the record of trial in the case of a complete acquittal".

d. R.C.M. 1003(b)(9) is deleted.

e. R.C.M. 1003(b)(10), (11), and (12) are redesignated as subsections (9), (10), and (11) respectively.

f. R.C.M. 1009 is amended as follows:

"(a) *Reconsideration.* Subject to this rule, a sentence may be reconsidered at any time before such sentence is announced in open session of the court."

"(b) *Exceptions.*

(1) If the sentence announced in open session was less than the mandatory minimum prescribed for an offense of which the accused has been found guilty, the court that announced the sentence may reconsider such sentence after it has been announced, and may increase the sentence upon recon-

sideration in accordance with subsection (e) of this rule.

(2) If the sentence announced in open session exceeds the maximum permissible punishment for the offense or the jurisdictional limitation of the court-martial, the sentence may be reconsidered after announcement in accordance with subsection (e) of this rule."

(c) *Clarification of sentence.* A sentence may be clarified at any time prior to action of the convening authority on the case.

(1) *Sentence adjudged by the military judge.* When a sentence adjudged by the military judge is ambiguous, the military judge shall call a session for clarification as soon as practical after the ambiguity is discovered.

(2) *Sentence adjudged by members.* When a sentence adjudged by members is ambiguous, the military judge shall bring the matter to the attention of the members if the matter is discovered before the court-martial is adjourned. If the matter is discovered after adjournment, the military judge may call a session for clarification by the members who adjudged the sentence as soon as practical after the ambiguity is discovered.

(d) *Action by the convening authority.* When a sentence adjudged by the court-martial is ambiguous, the convening authority may return the matter to the court-martial for clarification. When a sentence adjudged by the court-martial is apparently illegal, the convening authority may return the matter to the court-martial for reconsideration or may approve a sentence no more severe than the legal, unambiguous portions of the adjudged sentence.

(e) *Reconsideration procedure.* Any member of the court-martial may propose that a sentence reached by the members be reconsidered.

(1) *Instructions.* When a sentence has been reached by members and reconsideration has been initiated, the military judge shall instruct the members on the procedure for reconsideration.

(2) *Voting.* The members shall vote by secret written ballot in closed session whether to reconsider a sentence already reached by them.

(3) *Number of votes required.*

(A) *With a view to increasing.* Subject to subsection (b) of this rule, members may reconsider a sentence with a view of increasing it only if at least a majority of the members vote for reconsideration.

(B) *With a view to decreasing.* Members may reconsider a sentence with a view to decreasing it only if:

(i) In the case of a sentence which includes death, at least one member votes to reconsider;

(ii) In the case of a sentence which includes confinement for life or more than 10 years, more than one-fourth of the members vote to reconsider; or

(iii) In the case of any other sentence, more than one-third of the members vote to reconsider.

(4) *Successful vote.* If a vote to reconsider a sentence succeeds, the procedures in R.C.M. 1006 shall apply".

g. R.C.M. 1103(b)(3)(L) is deleted.

h. R.C.M. 1103(b)(3)(M) and (N) are redesignated as subsections (L) and (M), respectively.

i. R.C.M. 1103(c)(2) is amended to read as follows:

"(2) *Not involving a bad-conduct discharge.* If the special court-martial resulted in findings of guilty but a bad-conduct discharge was not adjudged, the requirements of subsections (b)(1), (b)(2)(D), and (b)(3)(A) - (F) and (I) - (M) of this rule shall apply".

j. R.C.M. 1104(b)(2) is amended to read as follows:

"(2) *Summary courts-martial.* The summary court-martial record of trial shall be disposed of as provided in R.C.M. 1305(d). Subsection (b)(1)(D) of this rule shall apply if classified information is included in the record of trial of a summary court-martial".

k. R.C.M. 1106(d)(3) is amended, by adding a new subsection (B) as follows:

"(B) A recommendation for clemency by the sentencing authority, made in conjunction with the announced sentence";

l. R.C.M. 1106(d)(3)(B)-(E) are redesignated as subsections (C)-(F), respectively.

m. R.C.M. 1107(d) is amended by adding a new subparagraph (3) as follows:

"(3) *Postponing service of a sentence to confinement.*

(A) In a case in which a court-martial sentences an accused referred to in subsection (B), below, to confinement, the convening authority may postpone service of a sentence to confinement by a court-martial, without the consent of the accused, until after the accused has been permanently released to the armed forces by a state or foreign country.

(B) Subsection (A) applies to an accused who, while in custody of a state or foreign country, is temporarily returned by that state or foreign country to the armed forces for trial by court-martial; and after the court-martial, is returned to that state or foreign country under the authority of a mutual agreement or treaty, as the case may be.

(C) As used in subsection (d)(3), the term "state" means a state of the United States, the District of Columbia, a territory, and a possession of the United States."

n. R.C.M. 1107(d)(3) is redesignated R.C.M. 1107(d)(4).

o. R.C.M. 1107(e)(1)(C)(iii) is amended as follows:

"(iii) *Rehearing on sentence only.* A rehearing on sentence only shall not be referred to a different kind of court-martial from that which made the original findings. If the convening authority determines a rehearing on sentence is impracticable, the convening authority may approve a sentence of no punishment without conducting a rehearing".

p. R.C.M. 1107(f)(2) is amended to read as follows:

"(2) *Modification of initial action.* The convening authority may recall and modify any action taken by that convening authority at any time before it has been published or before the accused has been officially notified. The convening authority also may recall and modify any action at any time prior to forwarding the record for review, as long as the modification does not result in action less favorable to the accused than the earlier action. In addition, in any special court-martial not involving a bad conduct discharge or any summary court-martial, the convening authority may recall and correct an illegal, erroneous, incomplete, or ambiguous action at any time before completion of review under R.C.M. 1112, as long as the correction does not result in action less favorable to the accused than the earlier action. When so directed by a higher reviewing authority or the Judge Advocate General, the convening authority shall modify any incomplete, ambiguous, void, or inaccurate action noted in review of the record of trial under Article 64, 66, 67, or examination of the record of trial under Article 69. The convening authority shall personally sign any supplementary or corrective action".

q. R.C.M. 1108(b) is amended to read as follows:

"(b) *Who may suspend and remit.* The convening authority may, after approving the sentence, suspend the execution of all or any part of the sentence of a court-martial except for a sentence of death. The general court-martial convening authority over the accused at the time of the court-martial may, when taking the action under R.C.M. 1112(f), suspend or remit any part of the sentence. The Secretary concerned and, when designated by the Secretary concerned, any Under Secretary, Assistant Secretary, Judge Advocate General, or commanding officer may suspend or remit any part or amount of the unexecuted part of any sentence other than a sentence approved by the President. The commander of the accused who has the authority to convene a court-martial of the kind which adjudged the sentence may suspend or remit any part or amount of the unexecuted part of any sentence by summary court-martial or of any sentence by special court-martial which does not include a bad-conduct discharge regardless of whether the person acting has previously approved the sentence." The "unexecuted" part of any sentence includes that part which has been approved and ordered executed but which has not actually been "carried out".

r. R.C.M. 1113(d)(2)(A) is amended by adding a new subparagraph (iii) as follows:

"(iii) Periods during which the accused is in custody of civilian or foreign authorities after the convening authority, pursuant to Article 57(e), has postponed the service of a sentence to confinement";

s. R.C.M. 1113(d)(2)(A)(iii) - (iv) are redesignated 1113(d)(A)(iv) - (v), respectively.

t. R.C.M. 1113(d)(5) is deleted.

u. R.C.M. 1113(d)(6) is redesignated as subsection (5).

v. R.C.M. 1201(b)(3)(A) is amended to read as follows:

"(A) *In general.* Notwithstanding R.C.M. 1209, the Judge Advocate General may, *sua sponte* or, except when the accused has waived or withdrawn the right to appellate review under R.C.M. 1110, upon application of the accused or a person with authority to act for the accused, vacate or modify, in whole or in part, the findings, sentence, or both of a court-martial that has been finally reviewed, but has not been reviewed either by a Court of Military

Review or by the Judge Advocate General under subsection (b)(1) of this rule, on the ground of newly discovered evidence, fraud on the court-martial, lack of jurisdiction over the accused or the offense, error prejudicial to the substantial rights of the accused, or the appropriateness of the sentence".

w. R.C.M. 1305(d) is deleted.

x. R.C.M. 1305(e) is redesignated as subsection (d).

Section 3. Part III of the Manual for Courts-Martial, United States, 1984, is amended as follows:

a. M.R.E. 311(g)(2) is amended to read as follows:

"(2) *False statements.* If the defense makes a substantial preliminary showing that a government agent included a false statement knowingly and intentionally or with reckless disregard for the truth in the information presented to the authorizing officer, and if the allegedly false statement is necessary to the finding of probable cause, the defense, upon request, shall be entitled to a hearing. At the hearing, the defense has the burden of establishing by a preponderance of the evidence the allegation of knowing and intentional falsity or reckless disregard for the truth. If the defense meets its burden, the prosecution has the burden of proving by a preponderance of the evidence, with the false information set aside, that the remaining information presented to the authorizing officer is sufficient to establish probable cause. If the prosecution does not meet its burden, the objection or motion shall be granted unless the search is otherwise lawful under these rules".

b. M.R.E. 506(e) and (f) are amended to read as follows:

"(e) *Pretrial session.* At any time after referral of charges and prior to arraignment, any party may move for a session under Article 39(a) to consider matters relating to government information that may arise in connection with the trial. Following such motion, or *sua sponte*, the military judge promptly shall hold a pretrial session under Article 39(a) to establish the timing of requests for discovery, the provision of notice under subsection (h), and the initiation of the procedure under subsection (i). In addition, the military judge may consider any other matters that relate to government information or that may promote a fair and expeditious trial.

(f) *Action after motion for disclosure of information.* After referral of charges, if the defense moves for disclosure of government information for which a claim of privilege has been made under this rule, the matter shall be reported to the convening authority. The convening authority may:

(1) institute action to obtain the information for use by the military judge in making a determination under subdivision (i);

(2) dismiss the charges;

(3) dismiss the charges or specifications or both to which the information relates; or

(4) take other action as may be required in the interests of justice.

If, after a reasonable period of time, the information is not provided to the military judge, the military judge shall dismiss the charges or specifications or both to which the information relates".

M.R.E. 506(h) is amended to read as follows:

"(h) *Prohibition against disclosure.* The accused may not disclose any information known or believed to be subject to a claim of privilege under this rule unless the military judge authorizes such disclosure".

d. M.R.E. 506(i) is amended to read as follows:

(i) *In camera proceedings.*

(1) *Definition.* For purposes of this subsection, an "in camera proceeding" is a session under Article 39(a) from which the public is excluded.

(2) *Motion for in camera proceeding.* Within the time specified by the military judge for the filing of a motion under this rule, the Government may move for an in camera proceeding concerning the use at any proceeding of any government information that may be subject to a claim of privilege. Thereafter, either prior to or during trial, the military judge for good cause shown or otherwise upon a claim of privilege may grant the Government leave to move for an in camera proceeding concerning the use of additional government information.

(3) *Demonstration of public interest nature of the information.* In order to obtain an in camera proceeding under this rule, the Government shall demonstrate, through the submission of affidavits and information for examination only by the military judge, that disclosure of the information reasonably could be expected to cause identifiable damage to the public interest.

(4) *In camera proceeding.*

(A) *Finding of identifiable damage.* Upon finding that the disclosure of some or all of the information submitted by the Government under subsection (i)(3) reasonably could be expected to cause identifiable damage to the public interest, the military judge shall conduct an in camera proceeding."

(B) *Disclosure of the information to the defense.* Subject to subsection (F), below, the Government shall disclose government information for which a claim of privilege has been made to the accused, for the limited purpose of litigating, in camera, the admissibility of the information at trial. The military judge shall enter an appropriate protective order to the accused and all other appropriate trial participants concerning the disclosure of the information according to subsection (g), above. The accused shall not disclose any information provided under this subsection unless, and until, such information has been admitted into evidence by the military judge. In the in camera proceeding, both parties shall have the opportunity to brief and argue the admissibility of the government information at trial.

(C) *Standard.* Government information is subject to disclosure at the court-martial proceeding under this subsection if the party making the request demonstrates a specific need for information containing evidence that is relevant to the guilt or innocence or to punishment of the accused, and is otherwise admissible in the court-martial proceeding.

(D) *Ruling.* No information may be disclosed at the court-martial proceeding or otherwise unless the military judge makes a written determination that the information is subject to disclosure under the standard set forth in subsection (C), above. The military judge will specify in writing any information that he or she determines is subject to disclosure. The record of the in camera proceeding shall be sealed and attached to the record of trial as an appellate exhibit. The accused may seek reconsideration of the determination prior to or during trial.

(E) *Alternatives to full disclosure.* If the military judge makes a determination under this subsection that the information is subject to disclosure, or if the Government elects not to contest the relevance, necessity, and admissibility of the government information, the Government may proffer a statement admitting for purposes of the court-martial any relevant facts such information would tend to prove or may submit a portion or summary to be used in lieu of the information. The military judge shall order that such statement, portion, summary, or some other form of information which the military judge finds to be consistent with the interests of justice, be used by the accused in place of the government information, unless the military judge finds that use of the government information itself is necessary to afford the accused a fair trial.

(F) *Sanctions.* Government information may not be disclosed over the Government's objection. If the Government continues to object to disclosure of the information following rulings by the military judge, the military judge shall issue any order that the interests of justice require. Such an order may include:

(i) striking or precluding all or part of the testimony of a witness;

(ii) declaring a mistrial;

(iii) finding against the Government on any issue as to which the evidence is relevant and necessary to the defense;

(iv) dismissing the charges, with or without prejudice; or

(v) dismissing the charges or specifications or both to which the information relates.

e. A new M.R.E. 506(j) is added as follows:

"(j) *Appeals of orders and rulings.* In a court-martial in which a punitive discharge may be adjudged, the Government may appeal an order or ruling of the military judge that terminates the proceedings with respect to a charge or specification, directs the disclosure of government information, or imposes sanctions for nondisclosure of government information. The Government also may appeal an order or ruling in which the military judge refuses to issue a protective order sought by the United States to prevent the disclosure of government information, or to enforce such an order previously issued by appropriate authority. The Government may not appeal an order or ruling that is, or amounts to, a finding of not guilty with respect to the charge or specification".

f. M.R.E. 506(j) and (k) are redesignated as (k) and (l), respectively.

Section 4. Part IV of the Manual for Courts-Martial, United States, 1984, is amended as follows:

a. Paragraph 4.c. is amended by adding a new subparagraph (4) as follows:

"(4) *Voluntary abandonment.* It is a defense to an attempt offense that the person voluntarily and completely abandoned the intended crime, solely because of the person's own sense that it was wrong, prior to the completion of the crime. The voluntary abandonment defense is not allowed if the abandonment results, in whole or in part, from other reasons, such as, the person feared detection or apprehension, decided to await a better opportunity for success, was unable to complete the crime, or encountered unanticipated difficulties or unexpected resistance. A person who is entitled to the defense of voluntary abandonment may nonetheless be guilty of a lesser included, completed offense. For example, a person who voluntarily abandoned an attempted armed robbery may nonetheless be guilty of assault with a dangerous weapon".

b. Paragraph 4.c.(4), (5), and (6) are redesignated as subparagraphs (5), (6) and (7), respectively.

c. Paragraph 30a.c(1), is amended to read as follows:

"(1) *Intent.* "Intent or reason to believe" that the information "is to be used to the injury of the United States or to the advantage of a foreign nation" means that the accused acted in bad faith *and* without lawful authority with respect to information that is not lawfully accessible to the public."

d. Paragraph 35 is amended to read as follows:

"(35) *Article 111—Drunken or reckless operation of a vehicle, aircraft, or vessel*

(a) *Text.*

Any person subject to this chapter who-

(1) operates or physically controls any vehicle, aircraft, or vessel in a reckless or wanton manner or while impaired by a substance described in section 912a(b) of this title (Article 112a(b)), or

(2) operates or is in actual physical control of any vehicle, aircraft, or vessel while drunk or when the alcohol concentration in the person's blood or breath is 0.10 grams of alcohol per 100 milliliters of blood or 0.10 grams of alcohol per 210 liters of breath, as shown by chemical analysis, shall be punished as a court-martial may direct."

(b) *Elements.*

(1) That the accused was operating or in physical control of a vehicle, aircraft, or vessel; and

(2) That while operating or in physical control of a vehicle, aircraft, or vessel, the accused:

(a) did so in a wanton or reckless manner,

(b) was drunk or impaired, or

(c) the alcohol concentration in the accused's blood or breath was 0.10 grams of alcohol per 100 milliliters of blood or 0.10 grams of alcohol per 210 liters of breath, or greater, as shown by chemical analysis.

[Note: If injury resulted add the following element]

(3) That the accused thereby caused the vehicle, aircraft, or vessel to injure a person.

(c) *Explanation.*

(1) *Vehicle.* See 1 U.S.C. § 4.

(2) *Vessel.* See 1 U.S.C. § 3.

(3) *Aircraft.* Any contrivance used or designed for transportation in the air.

(4) *Operates.* Operating a vehicle, aircraft, or vessel includes not only driving or guiding a vehicle, aircraft, or vessel while it is in motion, either in person or through the agency of another, but also setting of its motive power in action or the manipulation of its controls so as to cause the particular vehicle, aircraft, or vessel to move.

(5) *Physical control and actual physical control.* These terms as used in the statute are synonymous. They describe the present capability and power to dominate, direct, or regulate the vehicle, vessel, or aircraft, either in person or through the agency of another, regardless of whether such vehicle, aircraft, or vessel is operated. For example, the intoxicated person seated behind the steering wheel of a vehicle with the keys of the vehicle in or near the ignition but with the engine not turned on could be deemed in actual physical control of that vehicle. However, the person asleep in the back seat with the keys in his or her pocket would not be deemed in actual physical control. Physical control necessarily encompasses operation.

(6) *Drunk or impaired.* "Drunk" and "impaired" mean any intoxication which is sufficient to impair the rational and full exercise of the mental or physical faculties. The term "drunk" is used in relation to intoxication by alcohol. The term "impaired" is used in relation to intoxication by a substance described in Article 112(a), Uniform Code of Military Justice.

(7) *Reckless.* The operation or physical control of a vehicle, vessel, or aircraft is "reckless" when it exhibits a culpable disregard of foreseeable consequences to others from the act or omission involved. Recklessness is not determined solely by reason of the happening of an injury, or the invasion of the rights of another, nor by proof alone of excessive

speed or erratic operation, but all these factors may be admissible and relevant as bearing upon the ultimate question: whether, under all the circumstances, the accused's manner of operation or physical control of the vehicle, vessel, or aircraft was of that heedless nature which made it actually or imminently dangerous to the occupants, or to the rights or safety of others. It is operating or physically controlling a vehicle, vessel, or aircraft with such a high degree of negligence that if death were caused, the accused would have committed involuntary manslaughter, at least. The nature of the conditions in which the vehicle, vessel, or aircraft is operated or controlled, the time of day or night, the proximity and number of other vehicles, vessels, or aircraft, and the condition of the vehicle, vessel, or aircraft, are often matters of importance in the proof of an offense charged under this article and, where they are of importance, may properly be alleged.

(8) *Wanton.* "Wanton" includes "reckless", but in describing the operation or physical control of a vehicle, vessel, or aircraft, "wanton" may, in a proper case, connote willfulness, or a disregard of probable consequences, and thus describe a more aggravated offense.

(9) *Causation.* The accused's drunken or reckless driving must be a proximate cause of injury for the accused to be guilty of drunken or reckless driving resulting in personal injury. To be proximate, the accused's actions need not be the sole cause of the injury, nor must they be the immediate cause of the injury; that is, the latest in time and space preceding the injury. A contributing cause is deemed proximate only if it plays a material role in the victim's injury.

(10) *Separate offenses.* While the same course of conduct may constitute violations of both subsections (1) and (2) of the Article, (*e.g.*, both drunken and reckless operation or physical control), this article proscribes the conduct described in both subsections as separate offenses, which may be charged separately. However, as recklessness is a relative matter, evidence of all the surrounding circumstances that made the operation dangerous, whether alleged or not, may be admissible. Thus, on a charge of reckless driving, for example, evidence of drunkenness might be admissible as establishing one aspect of the recklessness, and evidence that the vehicle exceeded a safe speed, at a relevant prior point and time, might be admissible as corroborating other evidence of the specific recklessness charged. Similarly, on a charge of drunken driving, relevant evidence of recklessness might have probative value as corroborating other proof of drunkenness.

(d) *Lesser included offense.*

(1) Reckless or wanton or impaired operation or physical control of a vessel. Article 110—improper hazarding of a vessel.

(2) Drunken operation of a vehicle, vessel, or aircraft while drunk or with a blood or breath alcohol concentration in violation of the described per se standard.

(a) Article 110—improper hazarding of a vessel

(a) Article 112—drunk on duty

(a) Article 134—drunk on station

(e) *Maximum punishment.*

(1) Resulting in personal injury. Dishonorable discharge, forfeiture of all pay and allowances, and confinement for 18 months.

(2) No personal injury involved. Bad-conduct discharge, forfeiture of all pay and allowances, and confinement for 6 months.

(f) *Sample specification.*

In that ________ (personal jurisdiction data), did (at/onboard—location) (subject-matter jurisdiction data, if required), on or about ________ 19 ___, (in the motor pool area) (near the Officer's Club) (at the intersection of ________ and ________) (while in the Gulf of Mexico) (while in flight over North America) physically control [a vehicle, to wit: (a truck) (a passenger car) (________)] [an aircraft, to wit: (an AH-64 helicopter) (an F-14A fighter) (a KC-135 tanker)(________)] [a vessel, to wit: (the aircraft carrier USS ________) (the Coast Guard Cutter) (________)], [while drunk] [while impaired by ________] [while the alcohol concentration in his (blood was 0.10 grams of alcohol per 100 milliliters of blood or greater) (breath was 0.10 grams of alcohol per 210 liters of breath or greater) as shown by chemical analysis] [in a (reckless) (wanton) manner by (attempting to pass another vehicle on a sharp curve) (by ordering that the aircraft be flown below the authorized altitude)] [and did thereby cause said (vehicle) (aircraft) (vessel) to (strike and) (injure ________)].

e. Paragraph 43.a.(3) is amended to read as follows:

"(3) is engaged in an act which is inherently dangerous to another and evinces a wanton disregard of human life; or";

f. Paragraph 43.b.(3)(c) is amended to read as follows:

"(c) That this act was inherently dangerous to another and showed a wanton disregard for human life";

g. Paragraph 43.c.(4)(a) is amended to read as follows:

"(a) *Wanton disregard for human life.* Intentionally engaging in an act inherently dangerous to another -- although without an intent to cause the death of or great bodily harm to any particular person, or even with a wish that death will not be caused -- may also constitute murder if the act shows wanton disregard of human life. Such disregard is characterized by heedlessness of the probable consequences of the act or omission, or indifference to the likelihood of death or great bodily harm. Examples include throwing a live grenade toward another or others in jest or flying an aircraft very low over one or more persons to cause alarm".

h. Paragraph 45.a.(a) is amended to read as follows:

"(a) Any person subject to this chapter who commits an act of sexual intercourse by force and without consent, is guilty of rape and shall be punished by death or such other punishment as a court-martial may direct".

i. Paragraph 45.b.(1) is amended to read as follows:

"(a) That the accused committed an act of sexual intercourse; and

(b) That the act of sexual intercourse was done by force and without consent".

j. Paragraph 45.c.(1)(a) and (b) are amended as follows:

"(a) *Nature of offense.* Rape is sexual intercourse by a person, executed by force and without consent of the victim. It may be committed on a victim of any age. Any penetration, however slight, is sufficient to complete the offense."

"(b) *Force and lack of consent.* Force and lack of consent are necessary to the offense. Thus, if the victim consents to the act, it is not rape. The lack of consent required, however, is more than mere lack of acquiescence. If a victim in possession of his or her mental faculties fails to make lack of consent reasonably manifest by taking such measures of resistance as are called for by the circumstances, the inference may be drawn that the victim did consent. Consent, however, may not be inferred if resistance would have been futile, where resistance is overcome by threats of death or great bodily harm, or where the victim is unable to resist because of the lack of mental or physical faculties. In such a case there is no consent and the force involved in penetration will suffice. All the surrounding circumstances are to be considered in determining whether a victim gave consent, or whether he or she failed or ceased to resist only because of a reasonable fear of death or grievous bodily harm. If there is actual consent, although obtained by fraud, the act is not rape, but if to the accused's knowledge the victim is of unsound mind or unconscious to an extent rendering him or her incapable of giving consent, the act is rape. Likewise, the acquiescence of a child of such tender years that he or she is incapable of understanding the nature of the act is not consent".

k. Paragraph 89.c. is amended to read as follows:

"(c) *Explanation.* "Indecent" language is that which is grossly offensive to modesty, decency, or propriety, or shocks the moral sense, because of its vulgar, filthy, or disgusting nature, or its tendency to incite lustful thought. Language is indecent if it tends reasonably to corrupt morals or incite libidinous thoughts. The language must violate community standards. See paragraph 87 if the communication was made in the physical presence of a child".

l. Paragraph 103. The following new paragraph is added after paragraph 103:

"(a) *Text.* See paragraph 60.

(b) *Elements.*

(1) That the accused intentionally inflicted injury upon himself or herself;

(2) That, under the circumstances, the conduct of the accused was to the prejudice of good order and discipline in the armed forces or was of a nature to bring discredit upon the armed forces.

[Note: If the offense was committed in time of war or in a hostile fire pay zone, add the following element]

(3) That the offense was committed (in time of war) (in a hostile fire pay zone).

(c) *Explanation.*

(1) *Nature of offense.* This offense differs from malingering (see paragraph 40) in that for this offense, the accused need not have harbored a design to avoid performance of any work, duty, or service

which may properly or normally be expected of one in the military service. This offense is characterized by intentional self-injury under such circumstances as prejudice good order and discipline or discredit the armed forces. It is not required that the accused be unable to perform duties, or that the accused actually be absent from his or her place of duty as a result of the injury. For example, the accused may inflict the injury while on leave or pass. The circumstances and extent of injury, however, are relevant to a determination that the accused's conduct was prejudicial to good order and discipline, or service-discrediting.

(2) *How injury inflicted.* The injury may be inflicted by nonviolent as well as by violent means and may be accomplished by any act or omission that produces, prolongs, or aggravates a sickness or disability. Thus, voluntary starvation that results in a debility is a self-inflicted injury. Similarly, the injury may be inflicted by another at the accused's request.

(d) *Lesser included offense.* Article 80—attempts

(e) *Maximum punishment.*

(1) *Intentional self-inflicted injury.* Dishonorable discharge, forfeiture of all pay and allowances, and confinement for 2 years.

(2) *Intentional self-inflicted injury in time of war or in a hostile fire pay zone.* Dishonorable discharge, forfeiture of all pay and allowances, and confinement for 5 years.

(f) *Sample specification.*

In that ________ (personal jurisdiction data), did, (at/on board--location) (in a hostile fire pay zone) on or about ________ 19 ____, (a time of war,) intentionally injure himself/herself by ________ (nature and circumstances of injury)".

Section 5. These amendments shall take effect on June 10, 1995, subject to the following:

a. Nothing in these amendments shall be construed to make punishable any act done or omitted prior to June 10, 1995.

b. The maximum punishment for an offense committed prior to June 10, 1995, shall not exceed the applicable maximum in effect at the time of the commission of such offense.

c. Nothing in these amendments shall be construed to invalidate any nonjudicial punishment proceeding, restraint, investigation, referral of charges, trial in which arraignment occurred, or other action begun prior to June 10, 1995, and any such restraint, investigation, referral of charges, trial, or other action may proceed in the same manner and with the same effect as if these amendments had not been prescribed.

THE WHITE HOUSE
May 12, 1995

EXECUTIVE ORDER 13086
1998 AMENDMENTS TO THE MANUAL FOR COURTS-MARTIAL, UNITED STATES

By the authority vested in me as President by the Constitution and the laws of the United States of America, including chapter 47 of title 10, United States Code (Uniform Code of Military Justice, 10 U.S.C. 801–946), in order to prescribe amendments to the Manual for Courts-Martial, United States, prescribed by Executive Order No. 12473, as amended by Executive Order No. 12484, Executive Order No. 12550, Executive Order No. 12586, Executive Order No. 12708, Executive Order No. 12767, Executive Order No. 12888, Executive Order No. 12936, and Executive Order No. 12960, it is hereby ordered as follows:

Section 1. Part II of the Manual for Courts-Martial, is amended as follows:

a. R.C.M. 305(g) through 305(k) are amended as follows:

"(g) *Who may direct release from confinement.* Any commander of a prisoner, an officer appointed under regulations of the Secretary concerned to conduct the review under subsections (i) and/or (j) of this rule or, once charges have been referred, a military judge detailed to the court-martial to which the charges against the accused have been referred, may direct release from pretrial confinement. For the purposes of this subsection, "any commander" includes the immediate or higher commander of the prisoner and the commander of the installation on which the confinement facility is located.

(h) *Notification and action by commander.*

(1) *Report.* Unless the commander of the prisoner ordered the pretrial confinement, the commissioned, warrant, noncommissioned, or petty officer into whose charge the prisoner was committed shall, within 24 hours after that commitment, cause a report to be made to the commander that shall contain the name of the prisoner, the offenses charged against the prisoner, and the name of the person who ordered or authorized confinement.

(2) *Action by commander.*

(A) *Decision.* Not later than 72 hours after the commander's ordering of a prisoner into pretrial confinement or, after receipt of a report that a member of the commander's unit or organization has been confined, whichever situation is applicable, the commander shall decide whether pretrial confinement will continue. A commander's compliance with this subsection may also satisfy the 48-hour probable cause determination of subsection R.C.M. 305(i)(1) below, provided the commander is a neutral and detached officer and acts within 48 hours of the imposition of confinement under military control. Nothing in subsections R.C.M. 305(d), R.C.M. 305(i)(1), or this subsection prevents a neutral and detached commander from completing the 48-hour probable cause determination and the 72-hour commander's decision immediately after an accused is ordered into pretrial confinement.

(B) *Requirements for confinement.* The commander shall direct the prisoner's release from pretrial confinement unless the commander believes upon probable cause, that is, upon reasonable grounds, that:

(i) An offense triable by a court-martial has been committed;

(ii) The prisoner committed it; and

(iii) Confinement is necessary because it is foreseeable that:

(a) The prisoner will not appear at trial, pretrial hearing, or investigation, or

(b) The prisoner will engage in serious criminal misconduct; and

(iv) Less severe forms of restraint are inadequate.

Serious criminal misconduct includes intimidation of witnesses or other obstruction of justice, serious injury to others, or other offenses that pose a serious threat to the safety of the community or to the effectiveness, morale, discipline, readiness, or safety of the command, or to the national security of the United States. As used in this rule, "national security" means the national defense and foreign relations of the United States and specifically includes: military or defense advantage over any foreign nation or group of nations; a favorable foreign relations position; or a defense posture capable of successfully resisting hostile or destructive action from within or without, overt or covert.

(C) *72-hour memorandum.* If continued pretrial confinement is approved, the commander shall prepare a written memorandum that states the reasons for the conclusion that the requirements for confinement in subsection (h)(2)(B) of this rule have been met. This memorandum may include hearsay and may incorporate by reference other documents, such as witness statements, investigative reports, or official records. This memorandum shall be forwarded to the 7-day reviewing officer under subsection (i)(2) of this rule. If such a memorandum was prepared by the commander before ordering confinement, a second memorandum need not be prepared; however, additional information may be added to the memorandum at any time.

(i) *Procedures for review of pretrial confinement.*

(1) *48-hour probable cause determination.* Review of the adequacy of probable cause to continue pretrial confinement shall be made by a neutral and detached officer within 48 hours of imposition of confinement under military control. If the prisoner is apprehended by civilian authorities and remains in civilian custody at the request of military authorities, reasonable efforts will be made to bring the prisoner under military control in a timely fashion.

(2) *7-day review of pretrial confinement.* Within 7 days of the imposition of confinement, a neutral and detached officer appointed in accordance with regulations prescribed by the Secretary concerned shall review the probable cause determination and necessity for continued pretrial confinement. In calculating the number of days of confinement for purposes of this rule, the initial date of confinement under military control shall count as one day and the date of the review shall also count as one day.

(A) *Nature of the 7-day review.*

(i) *Matters considered.* The review under this subsection shall include a review of the memorandum submitted by the prisoner's commander under subsection (h)(2)(C) of this rule. Additional written matters may be considered, including any submitted by the accused. The prisoner and the prisoner's counsel, if any, shall be allowed to appear before the 7-day reviewing officer and make a statement, if practicable. A representative of the command may also appear before the reviewing officer to make a statement.

(ii) *Rules of evidence.* Except for Mil. R. Evid., Section V (Privileges) and Mil. R. Evid. 302 and 305, the Military Rules of Evidence shall not apply to the matters considered.

(iii) *Standard of proof.* The requirements for confinement under subsection (h)(2)(B) of this rule must be proved by a preponderance of the evidence.

(B) *Extension of time limit.* The 7-day reviewing officer may, for good cause, extend the time limit for completion of the review to 10 days after the imposition of pretrial confinement.

(C) *Action by 7-day reviewing officer.* Upon completion of review, the reviewing officer shall approve continued confinement or order immediate release.

(D) *Memorandum.* The 7-day reviewing officer's conclusions, including the factual findings on which they are based, shall be set forth in a written memorandum. A copy of the memorandum and of all documents considered by the 7-day reviewing officer shall be maintained in accordance with regulations prescribed by the Secretary concerned and provided to the accused or the Government on request.

(E) *Reconsideration of approval of continued confinement.* The 7-day reviewing officer shall upon request, and after notice to the parties, reconsider the decision to confine the prisoner based upon any significant information not previously considered.

(j) *Review by military judge.* Once the charges for which the accused has been confined are referred to trial, the military judge shall review the propriety of the pretrial confinement upon motion for appropriate relief.

(1) *Release.* The military judge shall order release from pretrial confinement only if:

(A) The 7-day reviewing officer's decision was an abuse of discretion, and there is not sufficient information presented to the military judge justifying continuation of pretrial confinement under subsection (h)(2)(B) of this rule;

(B) Information not presented to the 7-day reviewing officer establishes that the prisoner should be released under subsection (h)(2)(B) of this rule; or

(C) The provisions of subsection (i)(1) or (2) of this rule have not been complied with and information presented to the military judge does not establish sufficient grounds for continued confinement under subsection (h)(2)(B) of this rule.

(2) *Credit.* The military judge shall order administrative credit under subsection (k) of this rule for any pretrial confinement served as a result of an abuse of discretion or failure to comply with the provisions of subsections (f), (h), or (i) of this rule.

(k) *Remedy.* The remedy for noncompliance with subsections (f), (h), (i), or (j) of this rule shall be an administrative credit against the sentence adjudged for any confinement served as the result of such noncompliance. Such credit shall be computed at the rate of 1 day credit for each day of confinement served as a result of such noncompliance. The military judge may order additional credit for each day of pretrial confinement that involves an abuse of discretion or unusually harsh circumstances. This credit is to be applied in addition to any other credit to which the accused may be entitled as a result of pretrial confinement served. This credit shall be applied first against any confinement adjudged. If no confinement is adjudged, or if the confinement adjudged is insufficient to offset all the credit to which the accused is entitled, the credit shall be applied against adjudged hard labor without confinement, restriction, fine, and forfeiture of pay, in that order, using the conversion formula under R.C.M. 1003(b)(6) and (7). For purposes of this subsection, 1 day of confinement shall be equal to 1 day of total forfeitures or a like amount of fine. The credit shall not be applied against any other form of punishment."

b. R.C.M. 405(e) is amended to read as follows:

"(e) *Scope of investigation.* The investigating officer shall inquire into the truth and form of the charges, and such other matters as may be necessary to make a recommendation as to the disposition of the charges. If evidence adduced during the investigation indicates that the accused committed an uncharged offense, the investigating officer may investigate the subject matter of such offense and make a recommendation as to its disposition, without the accused first having been charged with the offense. The accused's rights under subsection (f) are the same with regard to investigation of both charged and uncharged offenses."

c. R.C.M. 706(c)(2)(D) is amended to read as follows:

"(D) Is the accused presently suffering from a mental disease or defect rendering the accused unable to understand the nature of the proceedings against the accused or to conduct or cooperate intelligently in the defense of the case?"

d. R.C.M. 707(b)(3) is amended by adding subsection (E) which reads as follows:

"(E) *Commitment of the incompetent accused.* If the accused is committed to the custody of the Attorney General for hospitalization as provided in R.C.M. 909(f), all periods of such commitment shall be excluded when determining whether the period in subsection (a) of this rule has run. If, at the end of the period of commitment, the accused is returned to the custody of the general court-martial convening authority, a new 120-day time period under this rule shall begin on the date of such return to custody."

e. R.C.M. 707(c) is amended to read as follows:

"(c) *Excludable delay.* All periods of time during which appellate courts have issued stays in the proceedings, or the accused is hospitalized due to incompetence, or is otherwise in the custody of the Attorney General, shall be excluded when determining whether the period in subsection (a) of this rule has run. All other pretrial delays approved by a military judge or the convening authority shall be similarly excluded."

f. R.C.M. 809(b)(1) is amended by deleting the last sentence, which reads:

"In such cases, the regular proceedings shall be suspended while the contempt is disposed of."

g. R.C.M. 809(c) is amended to read as follows:

"(c) *Procedure.* The military judge shall in all cases determine whether to punish for contempt and, if so, what the punishment shall be. The military judge shall also determine when during the court-martial the contempt proceedings shall be conducted; however, if the court-martial is composed of members, the military judge shall conduct the contempt proceedings outside the members' presence. The military judge may punish summarily under subsection (b)(1) only if the military judge recites the facts for the record and states that they were directly witnessed by the military judge in the actual presence of the court-martial. Otherwise, the provisions of subsection (b)(2) shall apply."

h. R.C.M. 908(a) is amended to read as follows:

"(a) *In general.* In a trial by a court-martial over which a military judge presides and in which a punitive discharge may be adjudged, the United States may appeal an order or ruling that terminates the proceedings with respect to a charge or specification, or excludes evidence that is substantial proof of a fact material in the proceedings, or directs the disclosure of classified information, or that imposes sanctions for nondisclosure of classified information. The United States may also appeal a refusal by the military judge to issue a protective order sought by the United States to prevent the disclosure of classified information or to enforce such an order that has previously been issued by the appropriate authority.

However, the United States may not appeal an order or ruling that is, or amounts to, a finding of not guilty with respect to the charge or specification."

i. R.C.M. 909 is amended to read as follows:

"(a) *In general.* No person may be brought to trial by court-martial if that person is presently suffering from a mental disease or defect rendering him or her mentally incompetent to the extent that he or she is unable to understand the nature of the proceedings against them or to conduct or cooperate intelligently in the defense of the case.

(b) *Presumption of capacity.* A person is presumed to have the capacity to stand trial unless the contrary is established.

(c) *Determination before referral.* If an inquiry pursuant to R.C.M. 706 conducted before referral concludes that an accused is suffering from a mental disease or defect that renders him or her mentally incompetent to stand trial, the convening authority before whom the charges are pending for disposition may disagree with the conclusion and take any action authorized under R.C.M. 401, including referral of the charges to trial. If that convening authority concurs with the conclusion, he or she shall forward the charges to the general court-martial convening authority. If, upon receipt of the charges, the general court-martial convening authority similarly concurs, then he or she shall commit the accused to the custody of the Attorney General. If the general court-martial convening authority does not concur, that authority may take any action that he or she deems appropriate in accordance with R.C.M. 407, including referral of the charges to trial.

(d) *Determination after referral.* After referral, the military judge may conduct a hearing to determine the mental capacity of the accused, either *sua sponte* or upon request of either party. If an inquiry pursuant to R.C.M. 706 conducted before or after referral concludes that an accused is suffering from a mental disease or defect that renders him or her mentally incompetent to stand trial, the military judge shall conduct a hearing to determine the mental capacity of the accused. Any such hearing shall be conducted in accordance with paragraph (e) of this rule.

(e) *Incompetence determination hearing.*

(1) *Nature of issue.* The mental capacity of the accused is an interlocutory question of fact.

(2) *Standard.* Trial may proceed unless it is established by a preponderance of the evidence that the accused is presently suffering from a mental disease or defect rendering him or her mentally incompetent to the extent that he or she is unable to understand the nature of the proceedings or to conduct or cooperate intelligently in the defense of the case. In making this determination, the military judge is not bound by the rules of evidence except with respect to privileges.

(3) If the military judge finds the accused is incompetent to stand trial, the judge shall report this finding to the general court-martial convening authority, who shall commit the accused to the custody of the Attorney General.

(f) *Hospitalization of the accused.* An accused who is found incompetent to stand trial under this rule shall be hospitalized by the Attorney General as provided in section 4241(d) of title 18, United States Code. If notified that the accused has recovered to such an extent that he or she is able to understand the nature of the proceedings and to conduct or cooperate intelligently in the defense of the case, then the general court-martial convening authority shall promptly take custody of the accused. If, at the end of the period of hospitalization, the accused's mental condition has not so improved, action shall be taken in accordance with section 4246 of title 18, United States Code.

(g) *Excludable delay.* All periods of commitment shall be excluded as provided by R.C.M. 707(c). The 120-day time period under R.C.M. 707 shall begin anew on the date the general court-martial convening authority takes custody of the accused at the end of any period of commitment."

j. R.C.M. 916(b) is amended to read as follows:

"(b) *Burden of proof.* Except for the defense of lack of mental responsibility and the defense of mistake of fact as to age as described in Part IV, para. 45c.(2) in a prosecution for carnal knowledge, the prosecution shall have the burden of proving beyond a reasonable doubt that the defense did not exist. The accused has the burden of proving the defense of lack of mental responsibility by clear and convincing evidence, and has the burden of proving mistake of fact as to age in a carnal knowledge prosecution by a preponderance of the evidence."

k. R.C.M. 916(j) is amended to read as follows:

"(j) *Ignorance or mistake of fact.*

(1) *Generally.* Except as otherwise provided in

this subsection, it is a defense to an offense that the accused held, as a result of ignorance or mistake, an incorrect belief of the true circumstances such that, if the circumstances were as the accused believed them, the accused would not be guilty of the offense. If the ignorance or mistake goes to an element requiring premeditation, specific intent, willfulness, or knowledge of a particular fact, the ignorance or mistake need only have existed in the mind of the accused. If the ignorance or mistake goes to any other element requiring only general intent or knowledge, the ignorance or mistake must have existed in the mind of the accused and must have been reasonable under all the circumstances. However, if the accused's knowledge or intent is immaterial as to an element, then ignorance or mistake is not a defense.

(2) *Carnal knowledge.* It is a defense to a prosecution for carnal knowledge that, at the time of the sexual intercourse, the person with whom the accused had sexual intercourse was at least 12 years of age, and the accused reasonably believed the person was at least 16 years of age. The accused must prove this defense by a preponderance of the evidence."

l. R.C.M. 920(e)(5)(D) is amended to read as follows:

"(D) The burden of proof to establish the guilt of the accused is upon the Government. [When the issue of lack of mental responsibility is raised, add: The burden of proving the defense of lack of mental responsibility by clear and convincing evidence is upon the accused. When the issue of mistake of fact as to age in a carnal knowledge prosecution is raised, add: The burden of proving the defense of mistake of fact as to age in carnal knowledge by a preponderance of the evidence is upon the accused.]"

m. R.C.M. 1005(e) is amended to read as follows:

"(e) *Required Instructions.* Instructions on sentence shall include:

(1) A statement of the maximum authorized punishment that may be adjudged and of the mandatory minimum punishment, if any;

(2) A statement of the effect any sentence announced including a punitive discharge and confinement, or confinement in excess of six months will have on the accused's entitlement to pay and allowances;

(3) A statement of the procedures for deliberation and voting on the sentence set out in R.C.M. 1006;

(4) A statement informing the members that they are solely responsible for selecting an appropriate sentence and may not rely on the possibility of any mitigating action by the convening or higher authority; and

(5) A statement that the members should consider all matters in extenuation, mitigation, and aggravation, whether introduced before or after findings, and matters introduced under R.C.M. 1001(b)(1), (2), (3), and (5)."

n. The heading for R.C.M. 1101 is amended as follows:

"Rule 1101. Report of result of trial; post-trial restraint; deferment of confinement, forfeitures and reduction in grade; waiver of Article 58b forfeitures"

o. R.C.M. 1101(c) is amended as follows:

"(c) *Deferment of confinement, forfeitures or reduction in grade.*

(1) *In general.* Deferment of a sentence to confinement, forfeitures, or reduction in grade is a postponement of the running of a sentence.

(2) *Who may defer.* The convening authority or, if the accused is no longer in the convening authority's jurisdiction, the officer exercising general court-martial jurisdiction over the command to which the accused is assigned, may, upon written application of the accused at any time after the adjournment of the court-martial, defer the accused's service of a sentence to confinement, forfeitures, or reduction in grade that has not been ordered executed.

(3) *Action on deferment request.* The authority acting on the deferment request may, in that authority's discretion, defer service of a sentence to confinement, forfeitures, or reduction in grade. The accused shall have the burden of showing that the interests of the accused and the community in deferral outweigh the community's interest in imposition of the punishment on its effective date. Factors that the authority acting on a deferment request may consider in determining whether to grant the deferment request include, where applicable: the probability of the accused's flight; the probability of the accused's commission of other offenses, intimidation of witnesses, or interference with the administration of justice; the nature of the offenses (including the effect on the victim) of which the accused was convicted; the sentence adjudged; the command's

immediate need for the accused; the effect of deferment on good order and discipline in the command; the accused's character, mental condition, family situation, and service record. The decision of the authority acting on the deferment request shall be subject to judicial review only for abuse of discretion. The action of the authority acting on the deferment request shall be in writing and a copy shall be provided to the accused.

(4) *Orders.* The action granting deferment shall be reported in the convening authority's action under R.C.M. 1107(f)(4)(E) and shall include the date of the action on the request when it occurs prior to or concurrently with the action. Action granting deferment after the convening authority's action under R.C.M. 1107 shall be reported in orders under R.C.M. 1114 and included in the record of trial.

(5) *Restraint when deferment is granted.* When deferment of confinement is granted, no form of restraint or other limitation on the accused's liberty may be ordered as a substitute form of punishment. An accused may, however, be restricted to specified limits or conditions may be placed on the accused's liberty during the period of deferment for any other proper reason, including a ground for restraint under R.C.M. 304.

(6) *End of deferment.* Deferment of a sentence to confinement, forfeitures, or reduction in grade ends when:

(A) The convening authority takes action under R.C.M. 1107, unless the convening authority specifies in the action that service of confinement after the action is deferred;

(B) The confinement, forfeitures, or reduction in grade are suspended;

(C) The deferment expires by its own terms; or

(D) The deferment is otherwise rescinded in accordance with subsection (c)(7) of this rule. Deferment of confinement may not continue after the conviction is final under R.C.M. 1209.

(7) *Rescission of deferment.*

(A) *Who may rescind.* The authority who granted the deferment or, if the accused is no longer within that authority's jurisdiction, the officer exercising general court-martial jurisdiction over the command to which the accused is assigned, may rescind the deferment.

(B) *Action.* Deferment of confinement, forfeitures, or reduction in grade may be rescinded when additional information is presented to a proper authority which, when considered with all other information in the case, that authority finds, in that authority's discretion, is grounds for denial of deferment under subsection (c)(3) of this rule. The accused shall promptly be informed of the basis for the rescission and of the right to submit written matters on the accused's behalf and to request that the rescission be reconsidered. However, the accused may be required to serve the sentence to confinement, forfeitures, or reduction in grade pending this action.

(C) *Execution.* When deferment of confinement is rescinded after the convening authority's action under R.C.M. 1107, the confinement may be ordered executed. However, no such order to rescind a deferment of confinement may be issued within 7 days of notice of the rescission of a deferment of confinement to the accused under subsection (c)(7)(B) of this rule, to afford the accused an opportunity to respond. The authority rescinding the deferment may extend this period for good cause shown. The accused shall be credited with any confinement actually served during this period.

(D) *Orders.* Rescission of a deferment before or concurrently with the initial action in the case shall be reported in the action under R.C.M. 1107(f)(4)(E), which action shall include the dates of the granting of the deferment and the rescission. Rescission of a deferment of confinement after the convening authority's action shall be reported in supplementary orders in accordance with R.C.M. 1114 and shall state whether the approved period of confinement is to be executed or whether all or part of it is to be suspended."

p. R.C.M. 1101 is amended by adding the following new subparagraph (d):

"(d) *Waiving forfeitures resulting from a sentence to confinement to provide for dependent support.*

(1) With respect to forfeiture of pay and allowances resulting only by operation of law and not adjudged by the court, the convening authority may waive, for a period not to exceed six months, all or part of the forfeitures for the purpose of providing support to the accused's dependent(s). The convening authority may waive and direct payment of any such forfeitures when they become effective by operation of Article 57(a).

(2) Factors that may be considered by the convening authority in determining the amount of

forfeitures, if any, to be waived include, but are not limited to, the length of the accused's confinement, the number and age(s) of the accused's family members, whether the accused requested waiver, any debts owed by the accused, the ability of the accused's family members to find employment, and the availability of transitional compensation for abused dependents permitted under 10 U.S.C. 1059.

(3) For the purposes of this Rule, a "dependent" means any person qualifying as a "dependent" under 37 U.S.C. 401."

q. The following new rule is added after R.C.M. 1102:

"Rule 1102A. Post-trial hearing for person found not guilty only by reason of lack of mental responsibility

(a) *In general.* The military judge shall conduct a hearing not later than forty days following the finding that an accused is not guilty only by reason of a lack of mental responsibility.

(b) *Psychiatric or psychological examination and report.* Prior to the hearing, the military judge or convening authority shall order a psychiatric or psychological examination of the accused, with the resulting psychiatric or psychological report transmitted to the military judge for use in the post-trial hearing.

(c) *Post-trial hearing.*

(1) The accused shall be represented by defense counsel and shall have the opportunity to testify, present evidence, call witnesses on his or her behalf, and to confront and cross-examine witnesses who appear at the hearing.

(2) The military judge is not bound by the rules of evidence except with respect to privileges.

(3) An accused found not guilty only by reason of a lack of mental responsibility of an offense involving bodily injury to another, or serious damage to the property of another, or involving a substantial risk of such injury or damage, has the burden of proving by clear and convincing evidence that his or her release would not create a substantial risk of bodily injury to another person or serious damage to property of another due to a present mental disease or defect. With respect to any other offense, the accused has the burden of such proof by a preponderance of the evidence.

(4) If, after the hearing, the military judge finds the accused has satisfied the standard specified in subsection (3) of this section, the military judge shall inform the general court-martial convening authority of this result and the accused shall be released. If, however, the military judge finds after the hearing that the accused has not satisfied the standard specified in subsection (3) of this section, then the military judge shall inform the general court-martial convening authority of this result and that authority may commit the accused to the custody of the Attorney General."

r. R.C.M. 1105(b) is amended to read as follows:

"(b) *Matters that may be submitted.*

(1) The accused may submit to the convening authority any matters that may reasonably tend to affect the convening authority's decision whether to disapprove any findings of guilt or to approve the sentence. The convening authority is only required to consider written submissions.

(2) Submissions are not subject to the Military Rules of Evidence and may include:

(A) Allegations of errors affecting the legality of the findings or sentence;

(B) Portions or summaries of the record and copies of documentary evidence offered or introduced at trial;

(C) Matters in mitigation that were not available for consideration at the court-martial; and

(D) Clemency recommendations by any member, the military judge, or any other person. The defense may ask any person for such a recommendation."

s. R.C.M. 1107(b)(4) is amended to read as follows:

"(4) *When proceedings resulted in a finding of not guilty or not guilty only by reason of lack of mental responsibility, or there was a ruling amounting to a finding of not guilty.* The convening authority shall not take action disapproving a finding of not guilty, a finding of not guilty only by reason of lack of mental responsibility, or a ruling amounting to a finding of not guilty. When an accused is found not guilty only by reason of lack of mental responsibility, the convening authority, however, shall commit the accused to a suitable facility pending a hearing and disposition in accordance with R.C.M. 1102A."

t. The subheading for R.C.M. 1107(d)(3) is amended to read as follows:

"(3) *Deferring service of a sentence to confinement.*"

u. R.C.M. 1107(d)(3)(A) is amended to read as follows:

"(A) In a case in which a court-martial sentences an accused referred to in subsection (B), below, to confinement, the convening authority may defer service of a sentence to confinement by a court-martial, without the consent of the accused, until after the accused has been permanently released to the armed forces by a state or foreign country."

v. R.C.M. 1109 is amended to read as follows:

"Rule 1109. Vacation of suspension of sentence

(a) *In general.* Suspension of execution of the sentence of a court-martial may be vacated for violation of the conditions of the suspension as provided in this rule.

(b) *Timeliness.*

(1) *Violation of conditions.* Vacation shall be based on a violation of the conditions of suspension that occurs within the period of suspension.

(2) *Vacation proceedings.* Vacation proceedings under this rule shall be completed within a reasonable time.

(3) *Order vacating the suspension.* The order vacating the suspension shall be issued before the expiration of the period of suspension.

(4) *Interruptions to the period of suspension.* Unauthorized absence of the probationer or the commencement of proceedings under this rule to vacate suspension interrupts the running of the period of suspension.

(c) *Confinement of probationer pending vacation proceedings.*

(1) *In general.* A probationer under a suspended sentence to confinement may be confined pending action under subsection (d)(2) of this rule, in accordance with the procedures in this subsection.

(2) *Who may order confinement.* Any person who may order pretrial restraint under R.C.M. 304(b) may order confinement of a probationer under a suspended sentence to confinement.

(3) *Basis for confinement.* A probationer under a suspended sentence to confinement may be ordered into confinement upon probable cause to believe the probationer violated any conditions of the suspension.

(4) *Review of confinement.* Unless proceedings under subsection (d)(1), (e), (f), or (g) of this rule are completed within 7 days of imposition of confinement of the probationer (not including any delays requested by probationer), a preliminary hearing shall be conducted by a neutral and detached officer appointed in accordance with regulations of the Secretary concerned.

(A) *Rights of accused.* Before the preliminary hearing, the accused shall be notified in writing of:

(i) The time, place, and purpose of the hearing, including the alleged violation(s) of the conditions of suspension;

(ii) The right to be present at the hearing;

(iii) The right to be represented at the hearing by civilian counsel provided by the probationer or, upon request, by military counsel detailed for this purpose; and

(iv) The opportunity to be heard, to present witnesses who are reasonably available and other evidence, and the right to confront and cross-examine adverse witnesses unless the hearing officer determines that this would subject these witnesses to risk or harm. For purposes of this subsection, a witness is not reasonably available if the witness requires reimbursement by the United States for cost incurred in appearing, cannot appear without unduly delaying the proceedings or, if a military witness, cannot be excused from other important duties.

(B) *Rules of evidence.* Except for Mil. R. Evid. Section V (Privileges) and Mil. R. Evid. 302 and 305, the Military Rules of Evidence shall not apply to matters considered at the preliminary hearing under this rule.

(C) *Decision.* The hearing officer shall determine whether there is probable cause to believe that the probationer violated the conditions of the probationer's suspension. If the hearing officer determines that probable cause is lacking, the hearing officer shall issue a written order directing that the probationer be released from confinement. If the hearing officer determines that there is probable cause to believe that the probationer violated the conditions of suspension, the hearing officer shall set forth that decision in a written memorandum, detailing therein the evidence relied upon and reasons for making the decision. The hearing officer shall forward the original memorandum or release order to the probationer's commander and forward a copy to the probationer and the officer in charge of the confinement facility.

(d) *Vacation of suspended general court-martial sentence.*

(1) *Action by officer having special court-martial jurisdiction over probationer.*

(A) *In general.* Before vacation of the suspension of any general court-martial sentence, the officer having special court-martial jurisdiction over the probationer shall personally hold a hearing on the alleged violation of the conditions of suspension. If there is no officer having special court-martial jurisdiction over the probationer who is subordinate to the officer having general court-martial jurisdiction over the probationer, the officer exercising general court-martial jurisdiction over the probationer shall personally hold a hearing under subsection (d)(1) of this rule. In such cases, subsection (d)(1)(D) of this rule shall not apply.

(B) *Notice to probationer.* Before the hearing, the officer conducting the hearing shall cause the probationer to be notified in writing of:

(i) The time, place, and purpose of the hearing;

(ii) The right to be present at the hearing;

(iii) The alleged violation(s) of the conditions of suspension and the evidence expected to be relied on;

(iv) The right to be represented at the hearing by civilian counsel provided by the probationer or, upon request, by military counsel detailed for this purpose; and

(v) The opportunity to be heard, to present witnesses and other evidence, and the right to confront and cross-examine adverse witnesses, unless the hearing officer determines that there is good cause for not allowing confrontation and cross-examination.

(C) *Hearing.* The procedure for the vacation hearing shall follow that prescribed in R.C.M. 405(g), (h)(1), and (i).

(D) *Record and recommendation.* The officer who conducts the vacation proceeding shall make a summarized record of the proceeding and forward the record and that officer's written recommendation concerning vacation to the officer exercising general court-martial jurisdiction over the probationer.

(E) *Release from confinement.* If the special court-martial convening authority finds there is not probable cause to believe that the probationer violated the conditions of the suspension, the special court-martial convening authority shall order the release of the probationer from confinement ordered under subsection (c) of this rule. The special court-martial convening authority shall, in any event, forward the record and recommendation under subsection (d)(1)(D) of this rule.

(2) *Action by officer exercising general court-martial jurisdiction over probationer.*

(A) *In general.* The officer exercising general court-martial jurisdiction over the probationer shall review the record produced by and the recommendation of the officer exercising special court-martial jurisdiction over the probationer, decide whether the probationer violated a condition of suspension, and, if so, decide whether to vacate the suspended sentence. If the officer exercising general court-martial jurisdiction decides to vacate the suspended sentence, that officer shall prepare a written statement of the evidence relied on and the reasons for vacating the suspended sentence.

(B) *Execution.* Any unexecuted part of a suspended sentence ordered vacated under this subsection shall, subject to R.C.M. 1113(c), be ordered executed.

(e) *Vacation of a suspended special court-martial sentence wherein a bad-conduct discharge was not adjudged.*

(1) *In general.* Before vacating the suspension of a special court-martial punishment that does not include a bad-conduct discharge, the special court-martial convening authority for the command in which the probationer is serving or assigned shall cause a hearing to be held on the alleged violation(s) of the conditions of suspension.

(2) *Notice to probationer.* The person conducting the hearing shall notify the probationer, in writing, before the hearing of the rights specified in subsection (d)(1)(B) of this rule.

(3) *Hearing.* The procedure for the vacation hearing shall follow that prescribed in R.C.M. 405(g), (h)(1), and (i).

(4) *Authority to vacate suspension.* The special court-martial convening authority for the command in which the probationer is serving or assigned shall

have the authority to vacate any punishment that the officer has the authority to order executed.

(5) *Record and recommendation.* If the hearing is not held by the commander with authority to vacate the suspension, the person who conducts the hearing shall make a summarized record of the hearing and forward the record and that officer's written recommendation concerning vacation to the commander with authority to vacate the suspension.

(6) *Decision.* The special court-martial convening authority shall review the record produced by and the recommendation of the person who conducted the vacation proceeding, decide whether the probationer violated a condition of suspension, and, if so, decide whether to vacate the suspended sentence. If the officer exercising jurisdiction decides to vacate the suspended sentence, that officer shall prepare a written statement of the evidence relied on and the reasons for vacating the suspended sentence.

(7) *Execution.* Any unexecuted part of a suspended sentence ordered vacated under this subsection shall be ordered executed.

(f) *Vacation of a suspended special court-martial sentence that includes a bad-conduct discharge.*

(1) The procedure for the vacation of a suspended approved bad-conduct discharge shall follow that set forth in subsection (d) of this rule.

(2) The procedure for the vacation of the suspension of any lesser special court-martial punishment shall follow that set forth in subsection (e) of this rule.

(g) *Vacation of a suspended summary court-martial sentence.*

(1) Before vacation of the suspension of a summary court-martial sentence, the summary court-martial convening authority for the command in which the probationer is serving or assigned shall cause a hearing to be held on the alleged violation(s) of the conditions of suspension.

(2) *Notice to probationer.* The person conducting the hearing shall notify the probationer before the hearing of the rights specified in subsections (d)(1)(B)(i), (ii), (iii), and (v) of this rule.

(3) *Hearing.* The procedure for the vacation hearing shall follow that prescribed in R.C.M. 405(g), (h)(1), and (i).

(4) *Authority to vacate suspension.* The summary court-martial convening authority for the command in which the probationer is serving or assigned shall have the authority to vacate any punishment that the officer had the authority to order executed.

(5) *Record and recommendation.* If the hearing is not held by the commander with authority to vacate the suspension, the person who conducts the vacation proceeding shall make a summarized record of the proceeding and forward the record and that officer's written recommendation concerning vacation to the commander with authority to vacate the suspension.

(6) *Decision.* A commander with authority to vacate the suspension shall review the record produced by and the recommendation of the person who conducted the vacation proceeding, decide whether the probationer violated a condition of suspension, and, if so, decide whether to vacate the suspended sentence. If the officer exercising jurisdiction decides to vacate the suspended sentence, that officer shall prepare a written statement of the evidence relied on and the reasons for vacating the suspended sentence.

(7) *Execution.* Any unexecuted part of a suspended sentence ordered vacated under this subsection shall be ordered executed."

w. R.C.M. 1201(b)(3)(A) is amended to read as follows:

"(A) *In general.* Notwithstanding R.C.M. 1209, the Judge Advocate General may, *sua sponte* or upon application of the accused or a person with authority to act for the accused, vacate or modify, in whole or in part, the findings, sentence, or both of a court-martial that has been finally reviewed, but has not been reviewed either by a Court of Criminal Appeals or by the Judge Advocate General under subsection (b)(1) of this rule, on the ground of newly discovered evidence, fraud on the court-martial, lack of jurisdiction over the accused or the offense, error prejudicial to the substantial rights of the accused, or the appropriateness of the sentence."

x. R.C.M. 1203(c)(1) is amended to read as follows:

"(1) *Forwarding by the Judge Advocate General to the Court of Appeals for the Armed Forces.* The Judge Advocate General may forward the decision of the Court of Criminal Appeals to the Court of Appeals for the Armed Forces for review with respect to any matter of law. In such a case, the Judge Advocate General shall cause a copy of the decision of the Court of Criminal Appeals and the order forwarding the case to be served on the accused and on appellate defense counsel. While a review of a forwarded case is pending, the Secretary concerned may defer further service of a sentence to confinement that has been ordered executed in such a case."

y. R.C.M. 1210(a) is amended by adding at the end thereof the following sentence:

"A petition for a new trial of the facts may not be submitted on the basis of newly discovered evidence when the petitioner was found guilty of the relevant offense pursuant to a guilty plea."

Section 2. Part III of the Manual for Courts-Martial, United States, is amended as follows:

a. M.R.E. 412 is amended to read as follows:

"Rule 412. Nonconsensual sexual offenses; relevance of victim's behavior or sexual predisposition

(a) *Evidence generally inadmissible.* The following evidence is not admissible in any proceeding involving alleged sexual misconduct except as provided in subdivisions (b) and (c) of this rule:

(1) Evidence offered to prove that any alleged victim engaged in other sexual behavior; and

(2) Evidence offered to prove any alleged victim's sexual predisposition.

(b) *Exceptions.*

(1) In a proceeding, the following evidence is admissible, if otherwise admissible under these rules:

(A) Evidence of specific instances of sexual behavior by the alleged victim offered to prove that a person other than the accused was the source of semen, injury, or other physical evidence;

(B) Evidence of specific instances of sexual behavior by the alleged victim with respect to the person accused of the sexual misconduct offered by the accused to prove consent or by the prosecution; and

(C) Evidence the exclusion of which would violate the constitutional rights of the accused.

(c) *Procedure to determine admissibility.*

(1) A party intending to offer evidence under subdivision (b) of this rule must:

(A) file a written motion at least 5 days prior to entry of pleas specifically describing the evidence and stating the purpose for which it is offered unless the military judge, for good cause shown, requires a different time for filing or permits filing during trial; and

(B) serve the motion on the opposing party and the military judge and notify the alleged victim or, when appropriate, the alleged victim's guardian or representative.

(2) Before admitting evidence under this rule, the military judge must conduct a hearing, which shall be closed. At this hearing, the parties may call witnesses, including the alleged victim, and offer relevant evidence. The victim must be afforded a reasonable opportunity to attend and be heard. In a case before a court-martial composed of a military judge and members, the military judge shall conduct the hearing outside the presence of the members pursuant to Article 39(a). The motion, related papers, and the record of the hearing must be sealed and remain under seal unless the court orders otherwise.

(3) If the military judge determines on the basis of the hearing described in paragraph (2) of this subdivision that the evidence that the accused seeks to offer is relevant and that the probative value of such evidence outweighs the danger of unfair prejudice, such evidence shall be admissible in the trial to the extent an order made by the military judge specifies evidence that may be offered and areas with respect to which the alleged victim may be examined or cross-examined.

(d) For purposes of this rule, the term "sexual behavior" includes any sexual behavior not encompassed by the alleged offense. The term "sexual predisposition" refers to an alleged victim's mode of dress, speech, or lifestyle that does not directly refer to sexual activities or thoughts but that may have a sexual connotation for the factfinder.

(e) A "nonconsensual sexual offense" is a sexual offense in which consent by the victim is an affirmative defense or in which the lack of consent is an element of the offense. This term includes rape, forcible sodomy, assault with intent to commit rape or forcible sodomy, indecent assault, and attempts to commit such offenses."

b. M.R.E. 413 is added to read as follows:

Rule 413. Evidence of Similar Crimes in Sexual Assault Cases

(a) In a court-martial in which the accused is charged with an offense of sexual assault, evidence of the accused's commission of one or more offenses of sexual assault is admissible and may be considered for its bearing on any matter to which it is relevant.

(b) In a court-martial in which the Government intends to offer evidence under this rule, the Government shall disclose the evidence to the accused, including statements of witnesses or a summary of the substance of any testimony that is expected to be offered, at least 5 days before the scheduled date of trial, or at such later time as the military judge may allow for good cause.

(c) This rule shall not be construed to limit the admission or consideration of evidence under any other rule.

(d) For purposes of this rule, "offense of sexual assault" means an offense punishable under the Uniform Code of Military Justice, or a crime under Federal law or the law of a State that involved—

(1) any sexual act or sexual contact, without consent, proscribed by the Uniform Code of Military Justice, Federal law, or the law of a State;

(2) contact, without consent of the victim, between any part of the accused's body, or an object held or controlled by the accused, and the genitals or anus of another person;

(3) contact, without consent of the victim, between the genitals or anus of the accused and any part of another person's body;

(4) deriving sexual pleasure or gratification from the infliction of death, bodily injury, or physical pain on another person; or

(5) an attempt or conspiracy to engage in conduct described in paragraphs (1) through (4).

(e) For purposes of this rule, the term "sexual act" means:

(1) contact between the penis and the vulva or the penis and the anus, and for purposes of this rule, contact occurs upon penetration, however slight, of the penis into the vulva or anus;

(2) contact between the mouth and the penis, the mouth and the vulva, or the mouth and the anus;

(3) the penetration, however slight, of the anal or genital opening of another by a hand or finger or by any object, with an intent to abuse, humiliate, harass, degrade, or arouse or gratify the sexual desire of any person; or

(4) the intentional touching, not through the clothing, of the genitalia of another person who has not attained the age of 16 years, with an intent to abuse, humiliate, harass, degrade, or arouse or gratify the sexual desire of any person.

(f) For purposes of this rule, the term "sexual contact" means the intentional touching, either directly or through the clothing, of the genitalia, anus, groin, breast, inner thigh, or buttocks of any person with an intent to abuse, humiliate, harass, degrade, or arouse or gratify the sexual desire of any person.

(g) For purposes of this rule, the term "State" includes a State of the United States, the District of Columbia, Puerto Rico, Guam, the Virgin Islands, and any other territory or possession of the United States.'

c. M.R.E. 414 is added to read as follows:

"Rule 414. Evidence of Similar Crimes in Child Molestation Cases

(a) In a court-martial in which the accused is charged with an offense of child molestation, evidence of the accused's commission of one or more offenses of child molestation is admissible and may be considered for its bearing on any matter to which it is relevant.

(b) In a court-martial in which the Government intends to offer evidence under this rule, the Government shall disclose the evidence to the accused, including statements of witnesses or a summary of the substance of any testimony that is expected to be offered, at least 5 days before the scheduled date of trial or at such later time as the military judge may allow for good cause.

(c) This rule shall not be construed to limit the admission or consideration of evidence under any other rule.

(d) For purposes of this rule, "child" means a person below the age of sixteen, and "offense of child molestation" means an offense punishable under the Uniform Code of Military Justice, or a crime under Federal law or the law of a State that involved—

(1) any sexual act or sexual contact with a child proscribed by the Uniform Code of Military Justice, Federal law, or the law of a State;

(2) any sexually explicit conduct with children proscribed by the Uniform Code of Military Justice, Federal law, or the law of a State;

(3) contact between any part of the accused's body, or an object controlled or held by the accused, and the genitals or anus of a child;

(4) contact between the genitals or anus of the accused and any part of the body of a child;

(5) deriving sexual pleasure or gratification from the infliction of death, bodily injury, or physical pain on a child; or

(6) an attempt or conspiracy to engage in conduct described in paragraphs (1) through (5) of this subdivision.

(e) For purposes of this rule, the term "sexual act" means:

(1) contact between the penis and the vulva or the penis and the anus, and for purposes of this rule contact occurs upon penetration, however slight, of the penis into the vulva or anus;

(2) contact between the mouth and the penis, the mouth and the vulva, or the mouth and the anus;

(3) the penetration, however slight, of the anal or genital opening of another by a hand or finger or by any object, with an intent to abuse, humiliate, harass, degrade, or arouse or gratify the sexual desire of any person; or

(4) the intentional touching, not through the clothing, of the genitalia of another person who has not attained the age of 16 years, with an intent to abuse, humiliate, harass, degrade, or arouse or gratify the sexual desire of any person.

(f) For purposes of this rule, the term "sexual contact" means the intentional touching, either directly or through the clothing, of the genitalia, anus, groin, breast, inner thigh, or buttocks of any person with an intent to abuse, humiliate, harass, degrade, or arouse or gratify the sexual desire of any person.

(g) For purpose of this rule, the term "sexually explicit conduct" means actual or simulated:

(1) sexual intercourse, including genital-genital, oral-genital, anal-genital, or oral-anal, whether between persons of the same or opposite sex;

(2) bestiality;

(3) masturbation;

(4) sadistic or masochistic abuse; or

(5) lascivious exhibition of the genitals or pubic area of any person.

(h) For purposes of this rule, the term "State" includes a State of the United States, the District of Columbia, Puerto Rico, Guam, the Virgin Islands, and any other territory or possession of the United States."

d. M.R.E. 1102 is amended to read as follows:

"Amendments to the Federal Rules of Evidence shall apply to the Military Rules of Evidence 18 months after the effective date of such amendments, unless action to the contrary is taken by the President."

Section 3. Part IV of the Manual for Courts-Martial, United States, is amended as follows:

a. Paragraph 19 is amended to read as follows:

" **19. Article 95—Resistance, flight, breach of arrest, and escape**

a. *Text.*

"Any person subject to this chapter who-

(1) resists apprehension;

(2) flees from apprehension;

(3) breaks arrest; or

(4) escapes from custody or confinement shall be punished as a court-martial may direct."

b. *Elements.*

(1) *Resisting apprehension.*

(a) That a certain person attempted to apprehend the accused;

(b) That said person was authorized to apprehend the accused; and

(c) That the accused actively resisted the apprehension.

(2) *Flight from apprehension.*

(a) That a certain person attempted to apprehend the accused;

(b) That said person was authorized to apprehend the accused; and

(c) That the accused fled from the apprehension.

(3) *Breaking arrest.*

(a) That a certain person ordered the accused into arrest;

(b) That said person was authorized to order the accused into arrest; and

(c) That the accused went beyond the limits of arrest before being released from that arrest by proper authority.

(4) *Escape from custody.*

(a) That a certain person apprehended the accused;

(b) That said person was authorized to apprehend the accused; and

(c) That the accused freed himself or herself from custody before being released by proper authority.

(5) *Escape from confinement.*

(a) That a certain person ordered the accused into confinement;

(b) That said person was authorized to order the accused into confinement; and

(c) That the accused freed himself or herself from confinement before being released by proper authority. [Note: If the escape was from post-trial confinement, add the following element]

(d) That the confinement was the result of a court-martial conviction.

c. *Explanation.*

(1) *Resisting apprehension.*

(a) *Apprehension.* Apprehension is the taking of a person into custody. *See* R.C.M. 302.

(b) *Authority to apprehend. See* R.C.M. 302(b) concerning who may apprehend. Whether the status of a person authorized that person to apprehend the accused is a question of law to be decided by the military judge. Whether the person who attempted to make an apprehension had such a status is a question of fact to be decided by the factfinder.

(c) *Nature of the resistance.* The resistance must be active, such as assaulting the person attempting to apprehend. Mere words of opposition, argument, or abuse, and attempts to escape from custody after the apprehension is complete, do not constitute the offense of resisting apprehension although they may constitute other offenses.

(d) *Mistake.* It is a defense that the accused held a reasonable belief that the person attempting to apprehend did not have authority to do so. However, the accused's belief at the time that no basis existed for the apprehension is not a defense.

(e) *Illegal apprehension.* A person may not be convicted of resisting apprehension if the attempted apprehension is illegal, but may be convicted of other offenses, such as assault, depending on all the circumstances. An attempted apprehension by a person authorized to apprehend is presumed to be legal in the absence of evidence to the contrary. Ordinarily the legality of an apprehension is a question of law to be decided by the military judge.

(2) *Flight from apprehension.* The flight must be active, such as running or driving away.

(3) *Breaking arrest.*

(a) *Arrest.* There are two types of arrest: pretrial arrest under Article 9 (*see* R.C.M. 304), and arrest under Article 15 (*see* paragraph 5c.(3), Part V, MCM). This article prohibits breaking any arrest.

(b) *Authority to order arrest. See* R.C.M. 304(b) and paragraphs 2 and 5b, Part V, MCM, concerning authority to order arrest.

(c) *Nature of restraint imposed by arrest.* In arrest, the restraint is moral restraint imposed by orders fixing the limits of arrest.

(d) *Breaking.* Breaking arrest is committed when the person in arrest infringes the limits set by orders. The reason for the infringement is immaterial. For example, innocence of the offense with respect to which an arrest may have been imposed is not a defense.

(e) *Illegal arrest.* A person may not be convicted of breaking arrest if the arrest is illegal. An arrest ordered by one authorized to do so is presumed to be legal in the absence of some evidence to the contrary. Ordinarily, the legality of an arrest is a question of law to be decided by the military judge.

(4) *Escape from custody.*

(a) *Custody.* "Custody" is restraint of free locomotion imposed by lawful apprehension. The restraint may be physical or, once there has been a submission to apprehension or a forcible taking into custody, it may consist of control exercised in the presence of the prisoner by official acts or orders. Custody is temporary restraint intended to continue until other restraint (arrest, restriction, confinement) is imposed or the person is released.

(b) *Authority to apprehend. See* subparagraph (1)(b) above.

(c) *Escape.* For a discussion of escape, *see* subparagraph c(5)(c), below.

(d) *Illegal custody.* A person may not be convicted of this offense if the custody was illegal. An apprehension effected by one authorized to apprehend is presumed to be lawful in the absence of evidence to the contrary. Ordinarily, the legality of an apprehension is a question of law to be decided by the military judge.

(e) *Correctional custody. See* paragraph 70.

(5) *Escape from confinement.*

(a) *Confinement.* Confinement is physical restraint imposed under R.C.M. 305, 1101, or paragraph 5b, Part V, MCM. For purposes of the element of post-trial confinement (subparagraph b(5)(d), above) and increased punishment therefrom (subparagraph e (4), below), the confinement must have been imposed pursuant to an adjudged sentence of a court-martial, and not as a result of pretrial restraint or nonjudicial punishment.

(b) *Authority to order confinement. See* R.C.M. 304(b), 1101, and paragraphs 2 and 5b, Part V, MCM, concerning who may order confinement.

(c) *Escape.* An escape may be either with or without force or artifice, and either with or without the consent of the custodian. However, where a prisoner is released by one with apparent authority to do so, the prisoner may not be convicted of escape from confinement. *See also* paragraph 20c.(l)(b). Any completed casting off of the restraint of confinement, before release by proper authority, is an escape, and lack of effectiveness of the restraint imposed is immaterial. An escape is not complete until the prisoner is momentarily free from the restraint. If the movement toward escape is opposed, or before it is completed, an immediate pursuit follows, there is no escape until opposition is overcome or pursuit is eluded.

(d) *Status when temporarily outside confinement facility.* A prisoner who is temporarily escorted outside a confinement facility for a work detail or other reason by a guard, who has both the duty and means to prevent that prisoner from escaping, remains in confinement.

(e) *Legality of confinement.* A person may not be convicted of escape from confinement if the confinement is illegal. Confinement ordered by one authorized to do so is presumed to be lawful in the absence of evidence to the contrary. Ordinarily, the legality of confinement is a question of law to be decided by the military judge.

d. *Lesser included offenses.*

(1) *Resisting apprehension.* Article 128—assault; assault consummated by a battery

(2) *Breaking arrest.*

(a) Article 134—breaking restriction

(b) Article 80—attempts

(3) *Escape from custody.* Article 80—attempts

(4) *Escape from confinement.* Article 80—attempts

e. *Maximum punishment.*

(1) *Resisting apprehension.* Bad-conduct discharge, forfeiture of all pay and allowances, and confinement for 1 year.

(2) *Flight from apprehension.* Bad-conduct discharge, forfeiture of all pay and allowances, and confinement for 1 year.

(3) *Breaking arrest.* Bad-conduct discharge, forfeiture of all pay and allowances, and confinement for 6 months.

(4) *Escape from custody, pretrial confinement, or confinement on bread and water or diminished rations imposed pursuant to Article 15.* Dishonorable discharge, forfeiture of all pay and allowances, and confinement for 1 year.

(5) *Escape from post-trial confinement.* Dishonorable discharge, forfeiture of all pay and allowances, and confinement for 5 years.

f. *Sample specifications.*

(1) *Resisting apprehension.*

In that ________ (personal jurisdiction data), did (at/on board—location) (subject-matter jurisdiction data, if required), on or about ________ 19 ____, resist being apprehended by ________, (an armed force policeman) (________), a person authorized to apprehend the accused.

(2) *Flight from apprehension.*

In that ________ (personal jurisdiction data), did (at/on board—location) (subject-matter jurisdiction data, if required), on or about ________ 19 ____, flee apprehension by ________ (an armed force policeman) (________), a person authorized to apprehend the accused.

(3) *Breaking arrest.*

In that ________ (personal jurisdiction data), having been placed in arrest (in quarters) (in his/her company area) (________) by a person authorized to order the accused into arrest, did, (at/on board—location) on or about ________ 19 ____, break said arrest.

(4) *Escape from custody.*

In that ________ (personal jurisdiction data), did, (at/on board—location) (subject-matter jurisdiction data, if required), on or about ________ 19 ____, escape from the custody of ________, a person authorized to apprehend the accused.

(5) *Escape from confinement.*

In that ________ (personal jurisdiction data), having been placed in (post-trial) confinement in (place of confinement), by a person authorized to order said accused into confinement did, (at/on board—location) (subject-matter jurisdiction data, if required), on or about ______ 19 ___, escape from confinement."

b. The following new paragraph is added after paragraph 97:

"97a. Article 134—(Parole, Violation of)

a. *Text. See* paragraph 60.

b. *Elements.*

(1) That the accused was a prisoner as the result of a court-martial conviction or other criminal proceeding;

(2) That the accused was on parole;

(3) That there were certain conditions of parole that the parolee was bound to obey;

(4) That the accused violated the conditions of parole by doing an act or failing to do an act; and

(5) That, under the circumstances, the conduct of the accused was to the prejudice of good order and discipline in the armed forces or was of a nature to bring discredit upon the armed forces.

c. *Explanation.*

(1) "Prisoner" refers only to those in confinement resulting from conviction at a court-martial or other criminal proceeding.

(2) "Parole" is defined as "word of honor." A prisoner on parole, or parolee, has agreed to adhere to a parole plan and conditions of parole. A "parole plan" is a written or oral agreement made by the prisoner prior to parole to do or refrain from doing certain acts or activities. A parole plan may include a residence requirement stating where and with whom a parolee will live, and a requirement that the prisoner have an offer of guaranteed employment. "Conditions of parole" include the parole plan and other reasonable and appropriate conditions of parole, such as paying restitution, beginning or continuing treatment for alcohol or drug abuse, or paying a fine ordered executed as part of the prisoner's court-martial sentence. In return for giving his or her "word of honor" to abide by a parole plan and conditions of parole, the prisoner is granted parole.

d. *Lesser included offense.* Article 80—attempts.

e. *Maximum punishment.* Bad-conduct discharge, confinement for 6 months, and forfeiture of two-thirds pay per month for 6 months.

f. *Sample specification.*

In that ______ (personal jurisdiction data), a prisoner on parole, did, (at/on board—location), on or about ______ 20 ___, violate the conditions of his/her parole by ______."

c. Paragraph 45.a and b are amended to read as follows:

"45. Article 120—Rape and carnal knowledge

a. *Text.*

"(a) Any person subject to this chapter who commits an act of sexual intercourse by force and without consent, is guilty of rape and shall be punished by death or such other punishment as a court-martial may direct.

(b) Any person subject to this chapter who, under circumstances not amounting to rape, commits an act of sexual intercourse with a person—

(1) who is not his or her spouse; and

(2) who has not attained the age of sixteen years; is guilty of carnal knowledge and shall be punished as a court-martial may direct.

(c) Penetration, however slight, is sufficient to complete either of these offenses.

(d)(1) In a prosecution under subsection (b), it is an affirmative defense that—

(A) the person with whom the accused committed the act of sexual intercourse had at the time of the alleged offense attained the age of twelve years; and

(B) the accused reasonably believed that the person had at the time of the alleged offense attained the age of 16 years.

(2) The accused has the burden of proving a defense under subparagraph (d)(1) by a preponderance of the evidence."

b. *Elements.*

(1) *Rape.*

(a) That the accused committed an act of sexual intercourse; and

(b) That the act of sexual intercourse was done by force and without consent.

(2) *Carnal knowledge.*

(a) That the accused committed an act of sexual intercourse with a certain person;

(b) That the person was not the accused's spouse; and

(c) That at the time of the sexual intercourse the person was under 16 years of age."

d. Paragraph 45c.(2) is amended to read as follows:

"(2) *Carnal knowledge.* "Carnal knowledge" is sexual intercourse under circumstances not amounting to rape, with a person who is not the accused's spouse and who has not attained the age of 16 years. Any penetration, however slight, is sufficient to complete the offense. It is a defense, however, which the accused must prove by a preponderance of the evidence, that at the time of the act of sexual intercourse, the person with whom the accused committed the act of sexual intercourse was at least 12 years of age, and that the accused reasonably believed that this same person was at least 16 years of age."

e. Paragraph 54e.(l) is amended to read as follows:

"(1) *Simple Assault.*

(A) *Generally.* Confinement for 3 months and forfeiture of two-thirds pay per month for 3 months.

(B) *When committed with an unloaded firearm.* Dishonorable discharge, forfeiture of all pay and allowances, and confinement for 3 years."

Section 4. These amendments shall take effect on May 27, 1998, subject to the following:

(a) The amendments made to Military Rules of Evidence 412, 413, and 414 shall apply only to courts-martial in which arraignment has been completed on or after June 26, 1998.

(b) Nothing contained in these amendments shall be construed to make punishable any act done or omitted prior to June 26, 1998, which was not punishable when done or omitted.

(c) The amendment made to Part IV, para. 45c.(2), authorizing a mistake of fact defense as to age in carnal knowledge prosecutions is effective in all cases in which the accused was arraigned on the offense of carnal knowledge, or for a greater offense that is later reduced to the lesser included offense of carnal knowledge, on or after 10 February 1996.

(d) Nothing in these amendments shall be construed to invalidate any nonjudicial punishment proceeding, restraint, investigation, referral of charges, trial in which arraignment occurred, or other action begun prior to May 27, 1998, and any such nonjudicial punishment proceeding, restraint, investigation, referral of charges, trial or other action may proceed in the same manner and with the same effect as if these amendments had not been prescribed.

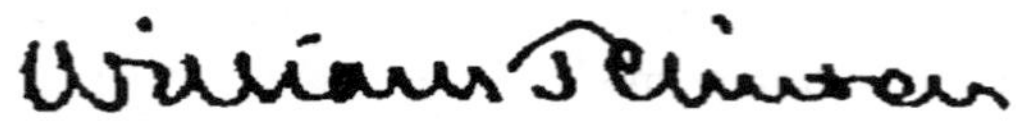

THE WHITE HOUSE

May 27, 1998

EXECUTIVE ORDER 13140
1999 AMENDMENTS TO THE MANUAL FOR COURTS-MARTIAL, UNITED STATES

By the authority vested in me as President by the Constitution and the laws of the United States of America, including chapter 47 of title 10, United States Code (Uniform Code of Military Justice, 10 U.S.C. 801-946), in order to prescribe amendments to the Manual for Courts-Martial, United States, prescribed by Executive Order 12473, as amended by Executive Order 12484, Executive Order 12550, Executive Order 12586, Executive Order 12708, Executive Order 12767, Executive Order 12888, Executive Order 12936, Executive Order 12960, and Executive Order 13086, it is hereby ordered as follows:

Section 1. Part II of the Manual for Courts-Martial, United States, is amended as follows:

a. R.C.M. 502(c) is amended to read as follows:

"(c) *Qualifications of military judge.* A military judge shall be a commissioned officer of the armed forces who is a member of the bar of a Federal court or a member of the bar of the highest court of a State and who is certified to be qualified for duty as a military judge by the Judge Advocate General of the armed force of which such military judge is a member. In addition, the military judge of a general court-martial shall be designated for such duties by the Judge Advocate General or the Judge Advocate General's designee, certified to be qualified for duty as a military judge of a general court-martial, and assigned and directly responsible to the Judge Advocate General or the Judge Advocate General's designee. The Secretary concerned may prescribe additional qualifications for military judges in special courts-martial. As used in this subsection "military judge" does not include the president of a special court-martial without a military judge."

b. R.C.M. 804 is amended by redesignating the current subsection (c) as subsection (d) and inserting after subsection (b) the following new subsection (c):

"(c) *Voluntary absence for limited purpose of child testimony.*

(1) *Election by accused.* Following a determination by the military judge that remote live testimony of a child is appropriate pursuant to Mil. R. Evid. 611(d)(3), the accused may elect to voluntarily absent himself from the courtroom in order to preclude the use of procedures described in R.C.M. 914A.

(2) *Procedure.* The accused's absence will be conditional upon his being able to view the witness' testimony from a remote location. Normally, a two-way closed circuit television system will be used to transmit the child's testimony from the courtroom to the accused's location. A one-way closed circuit television system may be used if deemed necessary by the military judge. The accused will also be provided private, contemporaneous communication with his counsel. The procedures described herein shall be employed unless the accused has made a knowing and affirmative waiver of these procedures.

(3) *Effect on accused's rights generally.* An election by the accused to be absent pursuant to subsection (c)(1) shall not otherwise affect the accused's right to be present at the remainder of the trial in accordance with this rule."

c. The following new rule is inserted after R.C.M. 914:

"Rule 914A. Use of remote live testimony of a child

(a) *General procedures.* A child shall be allowed to testify out of the presence of the accused after the military judge has determined that the requirements of Mil. R. Evid. 611(d)(3) have been satisfied. The procedure used to take such testimony will be determined by the military judge based upon the exigencies of the situation. However, such testimony should normally be taken via a two-way closed circuit television system. At a minimum, the following procedures shall be observed:

(1) The witness shall testify from a remote location outside the courtroom;

(2) Attendance at the remote location shall be limited to the child, counsel for each side (not including an accused pro se), equipment operators, and other persons, such as an attendant for the child, whose presence is deemed necessary by the military judge;

(3) Sufficient monitors shall be placed in the courtroom to allow viewing and hearing of the testimony by the military judge, the accused, the members, the court reporter and the public;

(4) The voice of the military judge shall be transmitted into the remote location to allow control of the proceedings; and

(5) The accused shall be permitted private, contemporaneous communication with his counsel.

(b) *Prohibitions.* The procedures described above shall not be used where the accused elects to absent himself from the courtroom pursuant to R.C.M. 804(c)."

d. R.C.M. 1001(b)(4) is amended by inserting the following sentences between the first and second sentences:

"Evidence in aggravation includes, but is not limited to, evidence of financial, social, psychological, and medical impact on or cost to any person or entity who was the victim of an offense committed by the accused and evidence of significant adverse impact on the mission, discipline, or efficiency of the command directly and immediately resulting from the accused's offense. In addition, evidence in aggravation may include evidence that the accused intentionally selected any victim or any property as the object of the offense because of the actual or perceived race, color, religion, national origin, ethnicity, gender, disability, or sexual orientation of any person."

e. R.C.M. 1003(b) is amended-

(1) by striking subsection (4) and

(2) by redesignating subsections (5), (6), (7), (8), (9), (10), and (11) as subsections (4), (5), (6), (7), (8), (9), and (10), respectively.

f. R.C.M. 1004(c)(7) is amended by adding at end the following new subsection:

"(K) The victim of the murder was under 15 years of age."

Sec. 2. Part III of the Manual for Courts-Martial, United States, is amended as follows:

a. Insert the following new rule after Mil. R. Evid. 512:

"Rule 513. Psychotherapist-patient privilege

(a) *General rule of privilege.* A patient has a privilege to refuse to disclose and to prevent any other person from disclosing a confidential communication made between the patient and a psychotherapist or an assistant to the psychotherapist, in a case arising under the UCMJ, if such communication was made for the purpose of facilitating diagnosis or treatment of the patient's mental or emotional condition.

(b) *Definitions.* As used in this rule of evidence:

(1) A "patient" is a person who consults with or is examined or interviewed by a psychotherapist for purposes of advice, diagnosis, or treatment of a mental or emotional condition.

(2) A "psychotherapist" is a psychiatrist, clinical psychologist, or clinical social worker who is licensed in any state, territory, possession, the District of Columbia or Puerto Rico to perform professional services as such, or who holds credentials to provide such services from any military health care facility, or is a person reasonably believed by the patient to have such license or credentials.

(3) An "assistant to a psychotherapist" is a person directed by or assigned to assist a psychotherapist in providing professional services, or is reasonably believed by the patient to be such.

(4) A communication is "confidential" if not intended to be disclosed to third persons other than those to whom disclosure is in furtherance of the rendition of professional services to the patient or those reasonably necessary for such transmission of the communication.

(5) "Evidence of a patient's records or communications" is testimony of a psychotherapist, or assistant to the same, or patient records that pertain to communications by a patient to a psychotherapist, or assistant to the same for the purposes of diagnosis or treatment of the patient's mental or emotional condition.

(c) *Who may claim the privilege.* The privilege may be claimed by the patient or the guardian or conservator of the patient. A person who may claim the privilege may authorize trial counsel or defense counsel to claim the privilege on his or her behalf. The psychotherapist or assistant to the psychotherapist who received the communication may claim the privilege on behalf of the patient. The authority of such a psychotherapist, assistant, guardian, or conservator to so assert the privilege is presumed in the absence of evidence to the contrary.

(d) *Exceptions.* There is no privilege under this rule:

(1) when the patient is dead;

(2) when the communication is evidence of spouse abuse, child abuse, or neglect or in a proceeding in which one spouse is charged with a crime against the person of the other spouse or a child of either spouse;

(3) when federal law, state law, or service regulation imposes a duty to report information contained in a communication;

(4) when a psychotherapist or assistant to a psychotherapist believes that a patient's mental or emotional condition makes the patient a danger to any person, including the patient;

(5) if the communication clearly contemplated the future commission of a fraud or crime or if the services of the psychotherapist are sought or obtained to enable or aid anyone to commit or plan to commit what the patient knew or reasonably should have known to be a crime or fraud;

(6) when necessary to ensure the safety and security of military personnel, military dependents, military property, classified information, or the accomplishment of a military mission;

(7) when an accused offers statements or other evidence concerning his mental condition in defense, extenuation, or mitigation, under circumstances not covered by R.C.M. 706 or Mil. R. Evid. 302. In such situations, the military judge may, upon motion, order disclosure of any statement made by the accused to a psychotherapist as may be necessary in the interests of justice; or

(8) when admission or disclosure of a communication is constitutionally required.

(e) *Procedure to determine admissibility of patient records or communications.*

(1) In any case in which the production or admission of records or communications of a patient other than the accused is a matter in dispute, a party may seek an interlocutory ruling by the military judge. In order to obtain such a ruling, the party shall:

(A) file a written motion at least 5 days prior to entry of pleas specifically describing the evidence and stating the purpose for which it is sought or offered, or objected to, unless the military judge, for good cause shown, requires a different time for filing or permits filing during trial; and

(B) serve the motion on the opposing party, the military judge and, if practical, notify the patient or the patient's guardian, conservator, or representative that the motion has been filed and that the patient has an opportunity to be heard as set forth in subparagraph (e)(2).

(2) Before ordering the production or admission of evidence of a patient's records or communication, the military judge shall conduct a hearing. Upon the motion of counsel for either party and upon good cause shown, the military judge may order the hearing closed. At the hearing, the parties may call witnesses, including the patient, and offer other relevant evidence. The patient shall be afforded a reasonable opportunity to attend the hearing and be heard at the patient's own expense unless the patient has been otherwise subpoenaed or ordered to appear at the hearing. However, the proceedings shall not be unduly delayed for this purpose. In a case before a court-martial composed of a military judge and members, the military judge shall conduct the hearing outside the presence of the members.

(3) The military judge shall examine the evidence or a proffer thereof in camera, if such examination is necessary to rule on the motion.

(4) To prevent unnecessary disclosure of evidence of a patient's records or communications, the military judge may issue protective orders or may admit only portions of the evidence.

(5) The motion, related papers, and the record of the hearing shall be sealed and shall remain under seal unless the military judge or an appellate court orders otherwise."

b. Mil. R. Evid. 611 is amended by inserting the following new subsection at the end:

"(d) *Remote live testimony of a child.*

(1) In a case involving abuse of a child or domestic violence, the military judge shall, subject to the requirements of subsection (3) of this rule, allow a child victim or witness to testify from an area outside the courtroom as prescribed in R.C.M. 914A.

(2) The term "child" means a person who is under the age of 16 at the time of his or her testimony. The term "abuse of a child" means the physical or mental injury, sexual abuse or exploitation, or negligent treatment of a child. The term "exploitation" means child pornography or child prostitution. The term "negligent treatment" means the failure to provide, for reasons other than poverty, adequate food, clothing, shelter, or medical care so as to endanger seriously the physical health of the child. The term "domestic violence" means an offense that has as an element the use, attempted use, or threatened use of physical force against a person and is committed by a current or former spouse, parent, or guardian of the victim; by a person with whom the victim shares a child in common; by a person who is cohabiting with or has cohabited with the victim as a spouse, parent, or guardian; or by a

person similarly situated to a spouse, parent, or guardian of the victim.

(3) Remote live testimony will be used only where the military judge makes a finding on the record that a child is unable to testify in open court in the presence of the accused, for any of the following reasons:

(A) The child is unable to testify because of fear;

(B) There is substantial likelihood, established by expert testimony, that the child would suffer emotional trauma from testifying;

(C) The child suffers from a mental or other infirmity; or

(D) Conduct by an accused or defense counsel causes the child to be unable to continue testifying.

(4) Remote live testimony of a child shall not be utilized where the accused elects to absent himself from the courtroom in accordance with R.C.M. 804(c)."

Sec. 3. Part IV of the Manual for Courts-Martial, United States, is amended as follows:

a. Insert the following new paragraph after paragraph 100:

"100a. Article 134—(Reckless endangerment)

a. *Text. See* paragraph 60.

b. *Elements.*

(1) That the accused did engage in conduct;

(2) That the conduct was wrongful and reckless or wanton;

(3) That the conduct was likely to produce death or grievous bodily harm to another person; and

(4) That, under the circumstances, the conduct of the accused was to the prejudice of good order and discipline in the armed forces or was of a nature to bring discredit upon the armed forces.

c. *Explanation.*

(1) *In general.* This offense is intended to prohibit and therefore deter reckless or wanton conduct that wrongfully creates a substantial risk of death or serious injury to others.

(2) *Wrongfulness.* Conduct is wrongful when it is without legal justification or excuse.

(3) *Recklessness.* "Reckless" conduct is conduct that exhibits a culpable disregard of foreseeable consequences to others from the act or omission involved. The accused need not intentionally cause a resulting harm or know that his conduct is substantially certain to cause that result. The ultimate question is whether, under all the circumstances, the accused's conduct was of that heedless nature that made it actually or imminently dangerous to the rights or safety of others.

(4) *Wantonness.* "Wanton" includes "reckless," but may connote willfulness, or a disregard of probable consequences, and thus describe a more aggravated offense.

(5) *Likely to produce* When the natural or probable consequence of particular conduct would be death or grievous bodily harm, it may be inferred that the conduct is "likely" to produce that result. *See* paragraph 54c(4)(a)(ii).

(6) *Grievous bodily harm.* "Grievous bodily harm" means serious bodily injury. It does not include minor injuries, such as a black eye or a bloody nose, but does include fractured or dislocated bones, deep cuts, torn members of the body, serious damage to internal organs, and other serious bodily injuries.

(7) *Death or injury not required.* It is not necessary that death or grievous bodily harm be actually inflicted to prove reckless endangerment.

d. *Lesser included offense.* None.

e. *Maximum punishment.* Bad-conduct discharge, forfeiture of all pay and allowances, and confinement for 1 year.

f. *Sample specification.*

In that ______ (personal jurisdiction data), did, (at/on board—location) (subject-matter jurisdiction data, if required), on or about ______ 20 ___, wrongfully and recklessly engage in conduct, to wit:(he/she)(describe conduct) and that the accused's conduct was likely to cause death or serious bodily harm to ______."

Sec. 4. These amendments shall take effect on 1 November 1999, subject to the following:

(a) The amendments made to Military Rule of Evidence 611, shall apply only in cases in which arraignment has been completed on or after 1 November 1999.

(b) Military Rule of Evidence 513 shall only apply to communications made after 1 November 1999.

(c) The amendments made to Rules for Courts-

Martial 502, 804, and 914A shall only apply in cases in which arraignment has been completed on or after 1 November 1999.

(d) The amendments made to Rules for Courts-Martial 1001(b)(4) and 1004(c)(7) shall only apply to offenses committed after 1 November 1999.

(e) Nothing in these amendments shall be construed to make punishable any act done or omitted prior to 1 November 1999, which was not punishable when done or omitted.

(f) The maximum punishment for an offense committed prior to 1 November 1999, shall not exceed the applicable maximum in effect at the time of the commission of such offense.

(g) Nothing in these amendments shall be construed to invalidate any nonjudicial punishment proceeding, restraint, investigation, referral of charges, trial in which arraignment occurred, or other action begun prior to 1 November 1999, and any such nonjudicial punishment, restraint, investigation, referral of charges, trial, or other action may proceed in the same manner and with the same effect as if these amendments had not been prescribed.

THE WHITE HOUSE
October 6, 1999.

18773

Federal Register

Vol. 67, No. 74

Wednesday, April 17, 2002

Presidential Documents

Title 3—

The President

Executive Order 13262 of April 11, 2002

2002 Amendments to the Manual for Courts-Martial, United States

By the authority vested in me as President by the Constitution and the laws of the United States of America, including chapter 47 of title 10, United States Code (Uniform Code of Military Justice, 10 U.S.C. 801–946), and in order to prescribe amendments to the Manual for Courts-Martial, United States, prescribed by Executive Order 12473, as amended, it is hereby ordered as follows:

Section 1. Thirty days after the date of this Executive Order, the provisions of Federal Rule of Evidence 415, adopted September 13, 1994, will no longer be applicable to the Military Rules of Evidence. This evidentiary rule became applicable to courts-martial on January 6, 1996, pursuant to Military Rule of Evidence 1102.

Sec. 2. The last subparagraph of paragraph 4, of Part I, of the Manual for Courts-Martial, United States, is amended as follows:

"The Manual shall be identified as "Manual for Courts-Martial, United States (2002 edition)." Any amendments to the Manual made by Executive Order shall be identified as "2002" Amendments to the Manual for Courts-Martial, United States" ; "2002" being the year the Executive Order was signed. If two or more Executive Orders amending the Manual are signed during the same year, then the second and any subsequent Executive Orders will be identified by placing a small case letter of the alphabet after the last digit of the year beginning with "a" for the second Executive Order and continuing in alphabetic order for subsequent Executive Orders.".

Sec. 3. Part II of the Manual for Courts-Martial, United States, is amended as follows:

a. R.C.M. 201(f)(2)(B) is amended to read as follows:

"(i) Upon a finding of guilty, special courts-martial may adjudge, under limitations prescribed by this Manual, any punishment authorized under R.C.M. 1003 except death, dishonorable discharge, dismissal, confinement for more than 1 year, hard labor without confinement for more than 3 months, forfeiture of pay exceeding two-thirds pay per month, or any forfeiture of pay for more than 1 year.

"(ii) A bad-conduct discharge, confinement for more than six months, or forfeiture of pay for more than six months, may not be adjudged by a special court-martial unless:

"(a) Counsel qualified under Article 27(b) is detailed to represent the accused; and

"(b) A military judge is detailed to the trial, except in a case in which a military judge could not be detailed because of physical conditions or military exigencies. Physical conditions or military exigencies, as the terms are here used, may exist under rare circumstances, such as on an isolated ship on the high seas or in a unit in an inaccessible area, provided compelling reasons exist why the trial must be held at that time and at that place. Mere inconvenience does not constitute a physical condition or military exigency and does not excuse a failure to detail a military judge. If a military judge cannot be detailed because of physical conditions or military exigencies, a bad-conduct discharge, confinement for more than six months, or forfeiture of pay for more than six months, may be adjudged provided the other conditions have been met. In that event, however, the convening authority shall, prior to trial, make a written statement explaining why a military judge could not be obtained. This statement shall be appended to the record of trial and shall set forth in detail the reasons why a military judge could not be detailed, and why the trial had to be held at that time and place."

b. R.C.M. 701(b)(4) is amended to read as follows:

"(4) Reports of examination and tests. If the defense requests disclosure under subsection (a)(2)(B) of this rule, upon compliance with such request by the Government, the defense, on request of trial counsel, shall (except as provided in R.C.M. 706, Mil. R. Evid. 302, and Mil. R. Evid. 513) permit the trial counsel to inspect any results or reports of physical or mental examinations and of scientific tests or experiments made in connection with the particular case, or copies thereof, that are within the possession, custody, or control of the defense that the defense intends to introduce as evidence in the defense case-in-chief at trial or that were prepared by a witness whom the defense intends to call at trial when the results or reports relate to that witness' testimony."

c. R.C.M. 806 is amended by adding at the end the following new subsection (d):

"(d) Protective orders. The military judge may, upon request of any party or sua sponte, issue an appropriate protective order, in writing, to prevent parties and witnesses from making extrajudicial statements that present a substantial likelihood of material prejudice to a fair trial by impartial members. For purposes of this subsection, "military judge" does not include the president of a special court-martial without a military judge.".

d. R.C.M. 1001(b)(3)(A) is amended to read as follows:

"(A) In general. The trial counsel may introduce evidence of military or civilian convictions of the accused. For purposes of this rule, there is a "conviction" in a court-martial case when a sentence has been adjudged. In a civilian case, a "conviction" includes any disposition following an initial judicial determination or assumption of guilt, such as when guilt has been established by guilty plea, trial, or plea of *nolo contendere*, regardless of the subsequent disposition, sentencing procedure, or final judgment. However, a "civilian conviction" does not include a diversion from the judicial process without a finding or admission of guilt; expunged convictions; juvenile adjudications; minor traffic violations; foreign convictions; tribal court convictions; or convictions reversed, vacated, invalidated or pardoned because of errors of law or because of subsequently discovered evidence exonerating the accused.".

e. R.C.M. 1003(b)(3) is amended to read as follows:

"(3) Fine. Any court-martial may adjudge a fine in lieu of or in addition to forfeitures. Special and summary courts-martial may not adjudge any fine or combination of fine and forfeitures in excess of the total amount of forfeitures that may be adjudged in that case. In order to enforce collection, a fine may be accompanied by a provision in the sentence that, in the event the fine is not paid, the person fined shall, in addition to any period of confinement adjudged, be further confined until a fixed period considered an equivalent punishment to the fine has expired. The total period of confinement so adjudged shall not exceed the jurisdictional limitations of the court- martial;"

f. R.C.M. 1003(b)(7) is amended to read as follows:

"(7) Confinement. The place of confinement shall not be designated by the court-martial. When confinement for life is authorized, it may be with or without eligibility for parole. A court-martial shall not adjudge a sentence to solitary confinement or to confinement without hard labor;".

g. R.C.M. 1004(e) is amended to read as follows:

"(e) Other penalties. Except for a violation of Article 106, when death is an authorized punishment for an offense, all other punishments authorized under R.C.M. 1003 are also authorized for that offense, including confinement for life, with or without eligibility for parole, and may be adjudged in lieu of the death penalty, subject to limitations specifically prescribed in this Manual. A sentence of death includes a dishonorable discharge or dismissal as appropriate. Confinement is a necessary incident of a sentence of death, but not a part of it."

h. R.C.M. 1006(d)(4)(B) is amended to read as follows:

"(B) Confinement for life, with or without eligibility for parole, or more than 10 years. A sentence that includes confinement for life, with or without eligibility for parole, or more than 10 years may be adjudged only if at least three-fourths of the members present vote for that sentence."

i. R.C.M. 1009(e)(3)(B)(ii) is amended to read as follows:

"(ii) In the case of a sentence which includes confinement for life, with or without eligibility for parole, or more than 10 years, more than one-fourth of the members vote to reconsider; or".

j. R.C.M. 1103(b)(2)(B)(i) is amended to read as follows:

"(i) Any part of the sentence adjudged exceeds six months confinement, forfeiture of pay greater than two-thirds pay per month, or any forfeiture of pay for more than six months or other punishments that may be adjudged by a special court-martial; or".

k. R.C.M. 1103(c) is amended to read as follows:

"(c) Special courts-martial.

"(1) Involving a bad-conduct discharge, confinement for more than six months, or forfeiture of pay for more than six months. The requirements of subsections (b)(1), (b)(2)(A), (b)(2)(B), (b)(2)(D), and (b)(3) of this rule shall apply in a special court-martial in which a bad-conduct discharge, confinement for more than six months, or forfeiture of pay for more than six months, has been adjudged.

"(2) All other special courts-martial. If the special court-martial resulted in findings of guilty but a bad-conduct discharge, confinement for more than six months, or forfeiture of pay for more than six months, was not adjudged, the requirements of subsections (b)(1), (b)(2)(D), and (b)(3)(A)–(F) and (I)–(M) of this rule shall apply.".

l. R.C.M. 1103(f)(1) is amended to read as follows:

"(1) Approve only so much of the sentence that could be adjudged by a special court-martial, except that a bad-conduct discharge, confinement for more than six months, or forfeiture of two-thirds pay per month for more than six months, may not be approved; or".

m. R.C.M. 1104(a)(2)(A) is amended to read as follows:

"(A) Authentication by the military judge. In special courts-martial in which a bad-conduct discharge, confinement for more than six months, or forfeiture of pay for more than six months, has been adjudged and in general courts-martial, except as provided in subsection (a)(2)(B) of this rule, the military judge present at the end of the proceedings shall authenticate the record of trial, or that portion over which the military judge presided. If more than one military judge presided over the proceedings, each military judge shall authenticate the record of the proceedings over which that military judge presided, except as provided in subsection (a)(2)(B) of this rule. The record of trial of special courts-martial in which a bad-conduct discharge, confinement for more than six months, or forfeiture of pay for more than six months, was not adjudged shall be authenticated in accordance with regulations of the Secretary concerned."

n. R.C.M. 1104(e) is amended to read as follows:

"(e) Forwarding. After every court-martial, including a rehearing and new and other trials, the authenticated record shall be forwarded to the convening authority for initial review and action, provided that in case of a special court-martial in which a bad-conduct discharge or confinement for one year was adjudged or a general court-martial, the convening authority shall refer the record to the staff judge advocate or legal officer for recommendation under R.C.M. 1106 before the convening authority takes action.".

o. R.C.M. 1106(a) is amended to read as follows:

"(a) In general. Before the convening authority takes action under R.C.M. 1107 on a record of trial by general court-martial or a record of trial by special court-martial that includes a sentence to a bad-conduct discharge or confinement for one year, that convening authority's staff judge advocate or legal officer shall, except as provided in subsection (c) of this rule, forward to the convening authority a recommendation under this rule.".

p. R.C.M. 1107(d)(4) is amended to read as follows:

"(4) Limitations on sentence based on record of trial. If the record of trial does not meet the requirements of R.C.M. 1103(b)(2)(B) or (c)(1), the convening authority may not approve a sentence in excess of that which may be adjudged by a special court-martial, or one that includes a bad-conduct discharge, confinement for more than six months, forfeiture of pay exceeding two-thirds pay per month, or any forfeiture of pay for more than six months.".

q. R.C.M. 1107(d) is amended by adding at the end the following new paragraph:

"(5) Limitations on sentence of a special court-martial where a fine has been adjudged. A convening authority may not approve in its entirety a sentence adjudged at a special court-martial when, if approved, the cumulative impact of the fine and forfeitures, whether adjudged or by operation of Article 58b, would exceed the jurisdictional maximum dollar amount of forfeitures that may be adjudged at that court-martial.".

r. R.C.M. 1109(e) and (e)(1) are amended to read as follows:

"(e) Vacation of a suspended special court-martial sentence wherein a bad-conduct discharge or confinement for one year was not adjudged.

"(1) In general. Before vacating the suspension of a special court-martial punishment that does not include a bad-conduct discharge or confinement for one year, the special court-martial convening authority for the command in which the probationer is serving or assigned shall cause a hearing to be held on the alleged violation(s) of the conditions of suspension.".

s. R.C.M. 1109(f) and (f)(1) are amended to read as follows:

"(f) Vacation of a suspended special court-martial sentence that includes a bad-conduct discharge or confinement for one year.

"(1) The procedure for the vacation of a suspended approved bad-conduct discharge or of any suspended portion of an approved sentence to confinement for one year, shall follow that set forth in subsection (d) of this rule.".

t. R.C.M. 1110(a) is amended to read as follows:

"(a) In general. After any general court-martial, except one in which the approved sentence includes death, and after any special court-martial in which the approved sentence includes a bad-conduct discharge or confinement for one year, the accused may waive or withdraw appellate review.".

u. R.C.M. 1111(b) is amended to read as follows:

"(1) Cases including an approved bad-conduct discharge or confinement for one year. If the approved sentence of a special court-martial includes a bad-conduct discharge or confinement for one year, the record shall be disposed of as provided in subsection (a) of this rule.

"(2) Other cases. The record of trial by a special court-martial in which the approved sentence does not include a bad-conduct discharge or confinement for one year shall be forwarded directly to a judge advocate for review under R.C.M. 1112. Four copies of the order promulgating the result of trial shall be forwarded with the record of trial, unless otherwise prescribed by regulations of the Secretary concerned.".

v. R.C.M. 1112(a)(2) is amended to read as follows:

"(2) Each special court-martial in which the accused has waived or withdrawn appellate review under R.C.M. 1110 or in which the approved sentence does not include a bad-conduct discharge or confinement for one year; and".

w. R.C.M 1305(d)(2) is amended to read as follows:

"(2) Forwarding to the convening authority. The original and one copy of the record of trial shall be forwarded to the convening authority after compliance with subsection (d)(1) of this rule.".

Sec. 4. Part III of the Manual for Courts-Martial, United States, is amended in Mil. R. Evid. 615 by striking the period at the end of the rule and adding ", or (4) a person authorized by statute to be present at courts-martial, or (5) any victim of an offense from the trial of an accused for that offense because such victim may testify or present any information in relation to the sentence or that offense during the presentencing proceedings.".

Sec. 5. Part IV of the Manual for Courts-Martial, United States, is amended as follows:

a. All "Sample specification(s)" subparagraphs in the Punitive Articles (Part IV, M.C.M.) are amended by striking "______ 19___" and inserting "______ 20___.".

b. Paragraph 27e(1)(a) is amended to read as follows:

"(a) of a value of $500.00 or less. Bad-conduct discharge, forfeiture of all pay and allowances, and confinement for 6 months.".

c. Paragraph 27e(1)(b) is amended to read as follows:

"(b) of a value of more than $500.00 or any firearm or explosive. Dishonorable discharge, forfeiture of all pay and allowances, and confinement for 5 years.".

d. Paragraph 27f(3) is amended to read as follows:

"(3) Dealing in captured or abandoned property. In that ______ (personal jurisdiction data), did, (at/on board - location), on or about ______ 20 ______, (buy) (sell) (trade) (deal in) (dispose of) (______) certain (captured) (abandoned) property, to wit: ______, (a firearm) (an explosive), of a value of (about) $______, thereby (receiving) (expecting) a (profit) (benefit) (advantage) to (himself/herself) (______, his/her accomplice) (______, his/her brother) (______).".

e. Strike paragraph 31c(6).

f. Paragraph 43e(1), is amended to read as follows:

"(1) Article 118(1) or (4)—death. Mandatory minimum—imprisonment for life with eligibility for parole.".

g. Paragraph 45e(3) is amended to read as follows:

"(3) Carnal knowledge with a child under the age of 12 years at the time of the offense. Dishonorable discharge, forfeiture of all pay and allowances, and confinement for life without eligibility for parole.".

h. Paragraph 46c(1)(h) is amended by adding at the end the following new clause:

"(vi) Credit, Debit, and Electronic Transactions. Wrongfully engaging in a credit, debit, or electronic transaction to obtain goods or money is an obtaining- type larceny by false pretense. Such use to obtain goods is usually a larceny of those goods from the merchant offering them. Such use to obtain money or a negotiable instrument (e.g., withdrawing cash from an automated teller or a cash advance from a bank) is usually a larceny of money from the entity presenting the money or a negotiable instrument. For the purpose of this section, the term 'credit, debit, or electronic transaction' includes the use of an instrument or device, whether known as a credit card, debit card, automated teller machine (ATM) card or by any other name, including access devices such as code, account number, electronic serial number or personal identification number, issued for the use in obtaining money, goods, or anything else of value.".

i. Paragraph 51e(1) is amended to read as follows:

"(1) By force and without consent. Dishonorable discharge, forfeiture of all pay and allowances, and confinement for life without eligibility for parole.".

j. Paragraph 51e(3) is amended to read as follows:

"(3) With a child under the age of 12 years at the time of the offense. Dishonorable discharge, forfeiture of all pay and allowances, and confinement for life without eligibility for parole."

k. Paragraph 62c is amended to read as follows:

"c. Explanation.

"(1) Nature of offense. Adultery is clearly unacceptable conduct, and it reflects adversely on the service record of the military member.

"(2) Conduct prejudicial to good order and discipline or of a nature to bring discredit upon the armed forces. To constitute an offense under the UCMJ, the adulterous conduct must either be directly prejudicial to good order and discipline or service discrediting. Adulterous conduct that is directly prejudicial includes conduct that has an obvious, and measurably divisive effect on unit or organization discipline, morale, or cohesion, or is clearly detrimental to the authority or stature of or respect toward a servicemember. Adultery may also be service discrediting, even though the conduct is only indirectly or remotely prejudicial to good order and discipline. Discredit means to injure the reputation of the armed forces and includes adulterous conduct that has a tendency, because of its open or notorious nature, to bring the service into disrepute, make it subject to public ridicule, or lower it in public esteem. While adulterous conduct that is private and discreet in nature may not be service discrediting by this standard, under the circumstances, it may be determined to be conduct prejudicial to good order and discipline. Commanders should consider all relevant circumstances, including but not limited to the following factors, when determining whether adulterous acts are prejudicial to good order and discipline or are of a nature to bring discredit upon the armed forces:

"(a) The accused's marital status, military rank, grade, or position;

"(b) The co-actor's marital status, military rank, grade, and position, or relationship to the armed forces;

"(c) The military status of the accused's spouse or the spouse of co-actor, or their relationship to the armed forces;

"(d) The impact, if any, of the adulterous relationship on the ability of the accused, the co-actor, or the spouse of either to perform their duties in support of the armed forces;

"(e) The misuse, if any, of government time and resources to facilitate the commission of the conduct;

"(f) Whether the conduct persisted despite counseling or orders to desist; the flagrancy of the conduct, such as whether any notoriety ensued; and whether the adulterous act was accompanied by other violations of the UCMJ;

"(g) The negative impact of the conduct on the units or organizations of the accused, the co-actor or the spouse of either of them, such as a detrimental effect on unit or organization morale, teamwork, and efficiency;

"(h) Whether the accused or co-actor was legally separated; and

"(i) Whether the adulterous misconduct involves an ongoing or recent relationship or is remote in time.

"(3) Marriage. A marriage exists until it is dissolved in accordance with the laws of a competent state or foreign jurisdiction.

Federal Register / Vol. 67, No. 74 / Wednesday, April 17, 2002 / Presidential Documents **18779**

"(4) Mistake of fact. A defense of mistake of fact exists if the accused had an honest and reasonable belief either that the accused and the co-actor were both unmarried, or that they were lawfully married to each other. If this defense is raised by the evidence, then the burden of proof is upon the United States to establish that the accused's belief was unreasonable or not honest.".

l. Paragraph 92e is amended to read as follows:

"e. Maximum punishment. Dishonorable discharge, forfeiture of all pay and allowances, and confinement for life without eligibility for parole.".

m. Paragraphs 32e, 33e, 46c(1)(g)(iii), 46e, 49e, 52e, 58e, 78c and 106e are amended by striking "$100.00" each place it appears and inserting "$500.00".

Sec. 6. These amendments shall take effect on May 15, 2002.

a. The amendments made to Rules for Courts-Martial 806(d) and 1001(b)(3)(A) shall only apply in cases in which arraignment has been completed on or after May 15, 2002.

b. The amendments made to Rules for Courts- Martial 1003(b)(7), 1004(e), 1006(d)(4)(B), and 1009(e)(3)(B)(ii) shall only apply to offenses committed after November 18, 1997. In cases not involving these amendments, the maximum punishment for an offense committed prior to May 15, 2002, shall not exceed the applicable maximum in effect at the time of the commission of such offense. Provided further, that for offenses committed prior to May 15, 2002, for which a sentence is adjudged on or after May 15, 2002, if the maximum punishment authorized in this Manual is less than that previously authorized, the lesser maximum authorized punishment shall apply.

c. The amendment made to Military Rules of Evidence 615 shall apply only in cases in which arraignment has been completed on or after May 15, 2002.

d. Nothing in these amendments shall be construed to make punishable any act done or omitted prior to May 15, 2002, that was not punishable when done or omitted.

e. Nothing in these amendments shall be construed to invalidate any nonjudicial punishment proceeding, restraint, investigation, referral of charges, trial in which arraignment occurred, or other action begun prior to May 15, 2002, and any such nonjudicial punishment, restraint, investigation, referral of charges, trial, or other action may proceed in the same manner and with the same effect as if these amendments had not been prescribed.

THE WHITE HOUSE,
April 11, 2002.

CHANGES TO THE DISCUSSION ACCOMPANYING THE MANUAL FOR COURTS-MARTIAL, UNITED STATES

a. The Discussion following the Preamble is amended by adding the following at the end of the Discussion:

"The amendment to paragraph 4 of the Preamble is intended to address the possibility of more frequent amendments to the Manual and the arrival of the 21st century. In the event that multiple editions of the Manual are published in the same year, the numbering and lettering of the edition should match that of the most recent Executive Order included in the publication."

b. The seventh paragraph of the Discussion following R.C.M. 601(e)(1) is amended to read as follows:

"The convening authority should acknowledge by an instruction that a bad-conduct discharge, confinement for more than six months, or forfeiture of pay for more than six months, may not be adjudged when the prerequisites under Article 19 will not be met. *See* R.C.M. 201(f)(2)(B)(ii). For example, this instruction should be given when a court reporter is not detailed.".

c. The Discussion following R.C.M. 701(a)(2)(B) is amended to read as follows:

"For specific rules concerning certain mental examinations of the accused or third party patients, *see* R.C.M. 701(f), R.C.M. 706, Mil. R. Evid. 302, and Mil. R. Evid. 513."

d. The ninth paragraph of the Discussion following R.C.M. 806(b) is amended to read as follows:

"There are other methods of protecting the proceedings from harmful effects of publicity, including a thorough *voir dire* (*see* R.C.M. 912), and, if necessary, a continuance to allow the harmful effects of publicity to dissipate. *See* R.C.M. 906(b)(1). Other methods that may occasionally be appropriate and which are usually preferable to closing a session include: directing members not to read, listen to, or watch any accounts concerning the case; issuing a protective order under R.C.M. 806(d); and selecting members from recent arrivals in the command, or from outside the immediate area. *See* R.C.M. 503(a)(3). In more extreme cases, the place of trial may be changed (*see* R.C.M. 906(b)(11), or members may be sequestered.

e. The following Discussion is added after R.C.M. 806(d):

"A protective order may proscribe extrajudicial statements by counsel, parties, and witnesses that might divulge prejudicial matter not of public record in the case. Other appropriate matters may also be addressed by such a protective order. Before issuing a protective order, the military judge must consider whether other available remedies would effectively mitigate the adverse effects that any publicity might create, and consider such an order's likely effectiveness in ensuring an impartial court-martial panel. A military judge should not issue a protective order without first providing notice to the parties and an opportunity to be heard. The military judge must state on the record the reasons for issuing the protective order. If the reasons for issuing the order change, the military judge may reconsider the continued necessity for a protective order."

f. The first paragraph of the Discussion following R.C.M. 808 is amended to read as follows:

"Except in a special court-martial not authorized to adjudge a bad-conduct discharge, confinement for more than six months, or forfeiture of pay for more than six months, the trial counsel should ensure that a qualified court reporter is detailed to the court-martial. Trial counsel should also ensure that all exhibits and other documents relating to the case are properly maintained for later inclusion in the record. *See also* R.C.M. 1103(j) as to the use of videotapes, audiotapes, and similar recordings for the record of trial. Because of the potential requirement for a verbatim transcript, all proceedings, including sidebar conferences, arguments, and rulings and instructions by the military judge, should be recorded."

Federal Register / Vol. 67, No. 74 / Wednesday, April 17, 2002 / Presidential Documents 18781

g. The Discussion following R.C.M. 1001(b)(3)(A) is amended by adding the following at the end of the Discussion:

"Whether a civilian conviction is admissible is left to the discretion of the military judge. As stated in the rule, a civilian "conviction" includes any disposition following an initial judicial determination or assumption of guilt regardless of the sentencing procedure and the final judgment following probation or other sentence. Therefore, convictions may be admissible regardless of whether a court ultimately suspended judgment upon discharge of the accused following probation, permitted withdrawal of the guilty plea, or applies some other form of alternative sentencing. Additionally, the term "conviction" need not be taken to mean a final judgment of conviction and sentence."

h. The sixth paragraph of the Discussion following R.C.M. 1003(b)(2) is amended to read as follows:

"At a special court-martial, if a bad-conduct discharge and confinement are adjudged, then the operation of Article 58b results in a forfeiture of two-thirds of pay only (not allowances) during that period of confinement. If only confinement is adjudged, and that confinement exceeds six months, then the operation of Article 58b results in a forfeiture of two-thirds of pay only (not allowances) during the period of confinement. If only a bad conduct discharge is adjudged, Article 58b has no effect on pay.".

i. The Discussion following R.C.M. 1003(b)(3) is amended by adding at the end the following paragraph:

"Where the sentence adjudged at a special court-martial includes a fine, *see* R.C.M. 1107(d)(5) for limitations on convening authority action on the sentence."

j. The Discussion following R.C.M. 1003(b)(8) is amended by adding the following at the end of the Discussion:

"See Article 56a."

k. The Discussion following R.C.M. 1003(c)(4) is amended by striking "R.C.M. 1107(d)(3)" and inserting "R.C.M. 1107(d)(4)."

l. The Discussion following R.C.M. 1006(c) is amended to read as follows:

"A proposal should state completely each kind and, where appropriate, amount of authorized punishment proposed by that member. For example, a proposal of confinement for life would state whether it is with or without eligibility for parole. See R.C.M. 1003(b)."

m. The second paragraph of the Discussion following R.C.M. 1107(d)(1) is amended to read as follows:

"When mitigating forfeitures, the duration and amounts of forfeiture may be changed as long as the total amount forfeited is not increased and neither the amount nor duration of the forfeitures exceeds the jurisdiction of the court-martial. When mitigating confinement or hard labor without confinement, the convening authority should use the equivalencies at R.C.M. 1003(b)(6) and (7), as appropriate. One form of punishment may be changed to a less severe punishment of a different nature, as long as the changed punishment is one that the court-martial could have adjudged. For example, a bad-conduct discharge adjudged by a special court-martial could be changed to confinement for up to one year (but not vice versa). A pretrial agreement may also affect what punishments may be changed by the convening authority.".

n. The Discussion following R.C.M. 1109(f) is amended to read as follows:

"An officer exercising special court-martial jurisdiction may vacate any suspended punishments other than an approved suspended bad-conduct discharge or any suspended portion of an approved sentence to confinement for one year, regardless of whether they are contained in the same sentence as the bad-conduct discharge or confinement for one year. See Appendix 18 for a sample of a Report of Proceedings to Vacate Suspension of a Special Court-Martial Sentence including a bad-conduct discharge or confinement for one year under Article 72, UCMJ, and R.C.M. 1109 (DD Form 455).".

o. The Discussion following R.C.M. 1110(a) is amended to read as follows:

"Appellate review is not available for special courts-martial in which a bad-conduct discharge or confinement for one year was not adjudged or approved or for summary courts-martial. Cases not subject to appellate review, or in which appellate review is waived or withdrawn, are reviewed by a judge advocate under R.C.M. 1112. Such cases may also be submitted to the Judge Advocate General for review. *See* R.C.M. 1201(b)(3). Appellate review is mandatory when the approved sentence includes death.".

CHANGES TO APPENDIX 8, GUIDE FOR GENERAL AND SPECIAL COURTS-MARTIAL, MANUAL FOR COURTS-MARTIAL, UNITED STATES

Appendix 8, is amended—

a. by amending the left margin entry to Note 100 to read as follows:

"Advice in GCMs and SPCMs in which BCD or confinement for one year is adjudged";

b. by amending Note 100 to read as follows:

"[Note 100. In cases subject to review by a Court of Criminal Appeals, the following advice should be given. In other cases proceed to Note 101 or 102 as appropriate.]";

c. by amending the left margin entry to Note 102 to read as follows:

"SPCM not involving a BCD or confinement for one year"; and

d. by amending Note 102 to read as follows:

[Note 102. In special courts-martial not involving BCD or confinement for one year, the following advice should be given.]".

CHANGES TO THE MAXIMUM PUNISHMENT CHART OF THE MANUAL FOR COURTS-MARTIAL, UNITED STATES

Appendix 12, the Maximum Punishment Chart, is amended—

a. by striking the item relating to Article 103 and inserting:

"103 Captured, abandoned property; failure to secure, etc. Of value of $500.00 or less . . . . . BCD 6 mos. Total

Of value of more than $500.00 . DD, BCD 5 yrs. Total

Any firearm or explosive . . . . . . DD, BCD 5 yrs. Total

Looting, pillaging . . . . DD, BCD Life4 Total"; and

b. in the items relating to Articles 108, 109, 121, 123a, 126, 132, and 134 (False Pretenses, obtaining services under; and Stolen Property, knowingly receiving, buying, concealing), by striking "100.00" each place it appears and inserting "$500.00".

CHANGES TO THE GUIDE FOR PREPARATION OF RECORD OF TRIAL WHEN A VERBATIM RECORD IS NOT REQUIRED, MANUAL FOR COURTS-MARTIAL, UNITED STATES

Appendix 13 is amended—

a. in the third subparagraph of paragraph a, by replacing "1-inch margin" with "one-inch margin" and replacing "left hand" with "left-hand".

CHANGES TO THE GUIDE FOR PREPARATION OF RECORD OF TRIAL WHEN A VERBATIM RECORD IS REQUIRED, MANUAL FOR COURTS-MARTIAL, UNITED STATES

Appendix 14, is amended—

a. at page A14–6, by amending the second bracketed format under the third note to read as follows:

"[The (court-martial) (session) was (adjourned) (recessed) at ________ hours, ________________.]".

CHANGES TO APPENDIX 17, FORMS FOR COURT-MARTIAL ORDERS, MANUAL FOR COURTS-MARTIAL, UNITED STATES

The first note to paragraph d of Appendix 17 is amended to read as follows:

"[Note. Orders promulgating the vacation of the suspension of a dismissal will be published by departmental orders of the Secretary concerned. Vacations of any other suspension of a general court-martial sentence, or of a special court-martial sentence that as approved and affirmed includes a bad-conduct discharge or confinement for one year, will be promulgated by the officer exercising general court-martial jurisdiction over the probationer (Article 72(b)). The vacation of suspension of any other sentence may be promulgated by an appropriate convening authority under Article 72(c). *See* R.C.M. 1109.]"

CHANGES TO APPENDIX 18, REPORT OF PROCEEDINGS TO VACATE SUSPENSION OF A GENERAL COURT-MARTIAL OR OF A SPECIAL COURT-MARTIAL SENTENCE INCLUDING A BAD-CONDUCT DISCHARGE UNDER ARTICLE 72, UCMJ, AND R.C.M. 1109 (DD FORM 455), MANUAL FOR COURTS-MARTIAL, UNITED STATES

The title to Appendix 18 is amended to read as follows:

"**Report of Proceedings to Vacate Suspension of a General Court-Martial or of a Special Court-Martial Sentence Including a Bad-Conduct Discharge or Confinement for One Year Under Article 72, UCMJ, and R.C.M. 1109 (DD Form 455).**".

CHANGES TO THE ANALYSIS ACCOMPANYING THE MANUAL FOR COURTS-MARTIAL, UNITED STATES.

1. *Changes to Appendix 21, the Analysis Accompanying the Rules for Courts-Martial, United States (Part II, MCM).*

a. The Analysis to R.C.M. 201(f) is amended by inserting after the second paragraph the following new paragraph:

"*2002 Amendment*: Subsections (f)(2)(B)(i) and (f)(2)(B)(ii) were amended to remove previous limitations and thereby implement the amendment to 10 U.S.C. § 819 (Article 19, UCMJ) contained in section 577 of the National Defense Authorization Act for Fiscal Year 2000, P. L. No. 106–65, 113 Stat. 512 (1999). Subject to limitations prescribed by the President, the amendment increased the jurisdictional maximum punishment at special courts-martial to confinement for one year and forfeitures not exceeding two-thirds pay per month for one year, vice the previous six-month jurisdictional limitation.".

b. The Analysis to R.C.M. 701(b) is amended by inserting after the discussion of the *1991 Amendment* to subsection (b)(2) the following new paragraph:

"*2002 Amendment*: Subsection (b)(4) was amended to take into consideration the protections afforded by the new psychotherapist-patient privilege under Mil. R. Evid. 513."

c. The Analysis to R.C.M. 707(a) is amended by inserting after the second paragraph the following new paragraph:

"*2002 Amendment*: *Burton* and its progeny were re-examined in *United States v. Kossman*, 38 M.J. 258 (C.M.A. 1993), where the Court of Military Appeals specifically overruled *Burton* and reinstated the earlier rule from *United States v. Tibbs*, 15 C.M.A. 350, 353, 35 C.M.R. 322, 325 (1965). *See Kossman*, 38 M.J. at 262. In *Kossman*, the Court reinstated the "reasonable diligence" standard in determining whether the prosecution's progress toward trial for a confined accused was sufficient to satisfy the speedy trial requirement of Article 10, UCMJ."

d. The Analysis accompanying R.C.M. 806 is amended by adding at the end the following new paragraphs:

"*2002 Amendment*: Section (d) was added to codify the military judge's power to issue orders limiting trial participants' extrajudicial statements in appropriate cases. *See United States v. Garwood*, 16 M.J. 863, 868 (N–M.C.M.R. 1983) (finding military judge was justified in issuing restrictive order prohibiting extrajudicial statements by trial participants), *aff'd on other grounds*, 20 M.J. 148 (C.M.A. 1985), *cert. denied*, 474 U.S. 1005 (1985);

United States v. Clark, 31 M.J. 721, 724 (A.F.C.M.R. 1990) (suggesting, but not deciding, that the military judge properly limited trial participants' extrajudicial statements).

"The public has a legitimate interest in the conduct of military justice proceedings. Informing the public about the operations of the criminal justice system is one of the "core purposes" of the First Amendment. In the appropriate case where the military judge is considering issuing a protective order, absent exigent circumstances, the military judge must conduct a hearing prior to issuing such an order. Prior to such a hearing the parties will have been provided notice. At the hearing, all parties will be provided an opportunity to be heard. The opportunity to be heard may be extended to representatives of the media in the appropriate case.

"Section (d) is based on the first Recommendation Relating to the Conduct of Judicial Proceedings in Criminal Cases, included in the Revised Report of the Judicial Conference Committee on the Operation of the Jury System on the "Free Press—Fair Trial" Issue, 87 F.R.D. 519, 529 (1980), which was approved by the Judicial Conference of the United States on September 25, 1980. The requirement that the protective order be issued in writing is based on Rule for Courts-Martial 405(g)(6). Section (d) adopts a "substantial likelihood of material prejudice" standard in place of the Judicial Conference recommendation of a "likely to interfere" standard. The Judicial Conference's recommendation was issued before the Supreme Court's decision in *Gentile v. State Bar of Nev.*, 501 U.S. 1030 (1991). *Gentile*, which dealt with a Rule of Professional Conduct governing extrajudicial statements, indicates that a lawyer may be disciplined for making statements that present a substantial likelihood of material prejudice to an accused's right to a fair trial. While the use of protective orders is distinguishable from limitations imposed by a bar's ethics rule, the *Gentile* decision expressly recognized that the "speech of lawyers representing clients in pending cases may be regulated under a less demanding standard than that established for regulation of the press in *Nebraska Press Ass'n v. Stuart*, 427 U.S. 539 (1976), and the cases which preceded it." 501 U.S. at 1074. The Court concluded that "the 'substantial likelihood of material prejudice' standard constitutes a constitutionally permissible balance between the First Amendment rights of attorneys in pending cases and the State's interest in fair trials." *Id.* at 1075. *Gentile* also supports the constitutionality of restricting communications of non-lawyer participants in a court case. *Id.* at 1072–73 (citing *Seattle Times Co. v. Rhinehart*, 467 U.S. 20, 32–33 (1984)). Accordingly, a protective order issued under the "substantial likelihood of material prejudice" standard is constitutionally permissible.

"The first sentence of the discussion is based on the committee comment to the Recommendations Relating to the Conduct of Judicial Proceedings in Criminal Cases. *See* 87 F.R.D. at 530. For a definition of "party," *see* R.C.M. 103(16). The second sentence of the discussion is based on the first of the Judicial Conference's recommendations concerning special orders. *See* 87 F.R.D. at 529. The third sentence of the discussion is based on the second of the Judicial Conference's recommendations, *id.* at 532, and on *United States v. Salameh*, 992 F.2d 445, 447 (2d Cir. 1993) (*per curiam*), and *In re Application of Dow Jones & Co.*, 842 F.2d 603, 611 & n.1 (2d Cir.), *cert. denied*, 488 U.S. 946 (1988). The fourth sentence is based on *Salameh*, 992 F.2d at 447. The fifth sentence is based on Rule for Courts-Martial 905(d).".

e. The Analysis accompanying R.C.M. 1001(b)(3)(A) is amended by inserting the following at the end thereof:

"*2002 Amendment*: As previously written, R.C.M. 1001(b)(3)(A) offered little guidance about what it meant by "civilian convictions." *See, e.g., United States v. White*, 47 M.J. 139, 140 (C.A.A.F. 1997); *United States v. Barnes*, 33 M.J. 468, 472–73 (C.M.A. 1992); *United States v. Slovacek*, 24 M.J. 140, 141 (CMA), *cert. denied*, 484 U.S. 855 (1987). The present rule addresses this void and intends to give the sentencing authority as much information as the military judge determines is relevant in order to craft an appropriate sentence for the accused.

"Unlike most civilian courts, this rule does not allow admission of more extensive criminal history information, such as arrests. Use of such additional information is not appropriate in the military setting where court-martial members, not a military judge, often decide the sentence. Such information risks unnecessarily confusing the members.

"The present rule clarifies the term "conviction" in light of the complex and varying ways civilian jurisdictions treat the subject. The military judge may admit relevant evidence of civilian convictions without necessarily being bound by the action, procedure, or nomenclature of civilian jurisdictions. Examples of judicial determinations admissible as convictions under this rule include accepted pleas of *nolo contendere*, pleas accepted under *North Carolina v. Alford*, 400 U.S. 25 (1970), or deferred sentences. If relevant, evidence of forfeiture of bail that results in a judicial determination of guilt is also admissible, as recognized in *United States v. Eady*, 35 M.J. 15, 16 (C.M.A. 1992). While no time limit is placed upon the admissibility of prior convictions, the military judge should conduct a balancing test to determine whether convictions older than ten years should be admitted or excluded on the basis of relevance and fundamental fairness.

"The two central factors in this rule are (1) judicial determination of guilt and (2) assumption of guilt. Assumption of guilt is an all-inclusive term meaning any act by the accused in a judicial proceeding accepting, acknowledging, or admitting guilt. As long as either factor is present, the "conviction" is admissible, if relevant. Consequently, this rule departs from the holding in *United States v. Hughes*, 26 M.J. 119, 120 (C.M.A. 1988), where the accused pleaded guilty in a Texas court, but the judge did not enter a finding of guilty under state law allowing "deferred adjudications." Under the present rule, the "conviction" would be admissible because the accused pleaded guilty in a judicial proceeding, notwithstanding the fact that the state judge did not enter a finding of guilty.

"In contrast, "deferred prosecutions," where there is neither an admission of guilt in a judicial proceeding nor a finding of guilty, would be excluded. The rule also excludes expunged convictions, juvenile adjudications, minor traffic violations, foreign convictions, and tribal court convictions as matters inappropriate for or unnecessarily confusing to courts-martial members. What constitutes a "minor traffic violation" within the meaning of this rule is to be decided with reference only to federal law, and not to the laws of individual states. *See* U.S. Sentencing Guidelines Manual § 4A1.2(c)(2); "What Constitutes 'Minor Traffic Infraction' Excludable From Calculation of Defendant's Criminal History under United States Sentencing Guideline § 4A1.2(c)(2)," 113 A.L.R. Fed. 561 (1993).

"Additionally, because of the lack of clarity in the previous rule, courts sometimes turned to Mil. R. Evid. 609 for guidance. *See, e.g., Slovacek*, 24 M.J. at 141. We note that because the policies behind Mil. R. Evid. 609 and the present rule differ greatly, a conviction that may not be appropriate for impeachment purposes under Mil. R. Evid. 609, may nevertheless be admissible under the present rule.

"The Federal Sentencing Guidelines were consulted when drafting the present rule. Although informed by those guidelines, the present rule departs from them in many respects because of the wide differences between the courts-martial process and practice in federal district court.".

f. The Analysis to R.C.M. 1003(b)(3) is amended by adding at the end the following new paragraph:

"*2002 Amendment*: The amendment clearly defines the authority of special and summary courts-martial to adjudge both fines and forfeitures. *See generally United States v. Tualla*, 52 M.J. 228 (2000)."

g. The Analysis accompanying R.C.M. 1003(b)(7) is amended by adding at the end the following new paragraph:

"*2002 Amendment*: This change resulted from the enactment of Article 56a, UCMJ, in section 581 of the National Defense Authorization Act for Fiscal Year 1998, Pub. L. No. 105–85, 111 Stat. 1629, 1759 (1997).".

h. The Analysis accompanying R.C.M. 1004(e) is amended by adding at the end the following new paragraph:

"*2002 Amendment*: This change resulted from the enactment of Article 56a, UCMJ, in section 581 of the National Defense Authorization Act for Fiscal Year 1998, Pub. L. No. 105–85, 111 Stat. 1629, 1759 (1997).".

i. The Analysis accompanying R.C.M. 1006(c) is amended by adding at the end the following new paragraph:

"*2002 Amendment*: This change to the discussion resulted from the enactment of Article 56a, UCMJ, in section 581 of the National Defense Authorization Act for Fiscal Year 1998, Pub. L. No. 105–85, 111 Stat. 1629, 1759 (1997).".

j. The Analysis accompanying R.C.M. 1006(d) is amended by inserting after the analysis of subsection 3(A) following paragraph:

"*2002 Amendment*: Subsection (d)(4)(B) was amended as a result of the enactment of Article 56a, UCMJ, in section 581 of the National Defense Authorization Act for Fiscal Year 1998, Pub. L. No. 105–85, 111 Stat. 1629, 1759 (1997).".

k. The Analysis accompanying R.C.M. 1009 is amended by adding at the end the following new paragraph:

"*2002 Amendment*: Subsection (e)(3)(B)(ii) was amended as a result of the enactment of Article 56a, UCMJ, in section 581 of the National Defense Authorization Act for Fiscal Year 1998, Pub. L. No. 105–85, 111 Stat. 1629, 1759 (1997).".

l. The Analysis to R.C.M. 1103 (b)(2) is amended by adding at the end the following new paragraph:

"*2002 Amendment*: Subsection (b)(2)(B) was amended to implement the amendment to 10 U.S.C. § 819 (Article 19, UCMJ) contained in section 577 of the National Defense Authorization Act for Fiscal Year 2000, P. L. No. 106–65, 113 Stat. 512 (1999) increasing the jurisdictional maximum punishment at special courts-martial. R.C.M. 1103(b)(2)(B) was amended to prevent an inconsistent requirement for a verbatim transcript between a general court-martial and a special court-martial when the adjudged sentence of a general court-martial does not include a punitive discharge or confinement greater than six months, but does include forfeiture of two-thirds pay per month for more than six months but not more than 12 months.".

m. The Analysis to R.C.M. 1103(c) is amended by adding at the end the following new paragraph:

"*2002 Amendment*: Subsection (c) was amended to implement the amendment to 10 U.S.C. § 819 (Article 19, UCMJ) contained in section 577 of the National Defense Authorization Act for Fiscal Year 2000, P. L. No. 106–65, 113 Stat. 512 (1999) increasing the jurisdictional maximum punishment at special courts-martial. R.C.M. 1103(c) was amended to conform the requirements for a verbatim transcript with the requirements of Article 19 for a 'complete record' in cases where the adjudged sentence includes a bad-conduct discharge, confinement for more than six months, or forfeiture of pay for more than six months.".

n. The Analysis to R.C.M. 1103(f) is amended by adding at the end the following new paragraph:

"*2002 Amendment*: Subsection (f)(1) was amended to implement the amendment to 10 U.S.C. § 819 (Article 19, UCMJ) contained in section 577 of the National Defense Authorization Act for Fiscal Year 2000, P. L. No. 106§65, 113 Stat. 512 (1999) increasing the jurisdictional maximum punishment at special courts-martial. R.C.M. 1103(f)(1) was amended to include the additional limitations on sentence contained in Article 19, UCMJ.".

o. The Analysis to R.C.M. 1104(a) is amended by adding at the end the following new paragraph:

"*2002 Amendment*: Subsection (a)(2)(A) was amended to implement the amendment to 10 U.S.C. § 819 (Article 19, UCMJ) contained in section 577 of the National Defense Authorization Act for Fiscal Year 2000, P. L. No. 106–65, 113 Stat. 512 (1999) increasing the jurisdictional maximum punishment at special courts-martial. R.C.M. 1104(a)(2)(A) was amended to ensure that the military judge authenticates all verbatim records of trial at special courts-martial.".

p. The Analysis to R.C.M. 1104(e) is amended by adding at the end the following new paragraph:

"*2002 Amendment*: Subsection (e) was amended to implement the amendment to 10 U.S.C. § 819 (Article 19, UCMJ) contained in section 577 of the National Defense Authorization Act for Fiscal Year 2000, P. L. No. 106–65, 113 Stat. 512 (1999) increasing the jurisdictional maximum punishment at special courts-martial. This amendment reflects the change to R.C.M. 1106 for special court- martial with an adjudged sentence that includes confinement for one year.".

q. The Analysis to R.C.M. 1106(a) is amended by adding at the end the following new paragraph:

"*2002 Amendment*: Subsection (a) was amended to implement the amendment to 10 U.S.C. § 819 (Article 19, UCMJ) contained in section 577 of the National Defense Authorization Act for Fiscal Year 2000, P. L. No. 106–65, 113 Stat. 512 (1999) increasing the jurisdictional maximum punishment at special courts-martial. This amendment requires all special courts-martial cases subject to appellate review to comply with this rule.".

r. The Analysis to R.C.M. 1107(d) is amended by inserting after the first paragraph the following new paragraph:

"*2002 Amendment*: The Discussion accompanying subsection (d)(1) was amended to implement the amendment to 10 U.S.C. § 819 (Article 19, UCMJ) contained in section 577 of the National Defense Authorization Act for Fiscal Year 2000, P. L. No. 106–65, 113 Stat. 512 (1999) increasing the jurisdictional maximum punishment at special courts-martial. R.C.M. 1107(d)(4) was amended to include the additional limitations on sentence contained in Article 19, UCMJ.".

s. The Analysis accompanying R.C.M. 1107(d) is amended by adding at the end the following new paragraphs:

"*2002 Amendment*: Subsection (d)(4) was amended as a result of the enactment of Article 56a, UCMJ, in section 581 of the National Defense Authorization Act for Fiscal Year 1998, Pub. L. No. 105–85, 111 Stat. 1629, 1759 (1997).

"Subsection (d)(5) is new. The amendment addresses the impact of Article 58b, UCMJ. In special courts-martial, where the cumulative impact of a fine and forfeitures, whether adjudged or by operation of Article 58b, would otherwise exceed the total dollar amount of forfeitures that could be adjudged at the special court-martial, the fine and/or adjudged forfeitures should be disapproved or decreased accordingly. *See generally United States v. Tualla*, 52 M.J. 228, 231–32 (2000)."

t. The Analysis to R.C.M. 1109 is amended by adding at the end the following new paragraphs:

"*2002 Amendment*: Subsection (e) was amended to implement the amendment to 10 U.S.C. § 819 (Article 19, UCMJ) contained in section 577 of the National Defense Authorization Act for Fiscal Year 2000, P. L. No. 106–65, 113 Stat. 512 (1999) increasing the jurisdictional maximum punishment at special courts-martial.

"(f) *Vacation of a suspended special court-martial sentence that includes a bad-conduct discharge or confinement for one year.* Subsection (f) was amended to implement the amendment to 10 U.S.C. § 819 (Article 19, UCMJ) contained in section 577 of the National Defense Authorization Act for Fiscal Year 2000, P. L. No. 106–65, 113 Stat. 512 (1999) increasing the jurisdictional maximum punishment at special courts-martial. This amendment reflects the decision to treat an approved sentence of confinement for one year, regardless of whether any period of confinement is suspended, as a serious offense, in the same manner as a suspended approved bad-conduct discharge at special courts-martial under Article 72, UCMJ, and R.C.M. 1109.".

u. The Analysis to R.C.M. 1110(a) is amended by adding at the end the following new paragraph:

"*2002 Amendment*: Subsection (a) was amended to implement the amendment to 10 U.S.C. § 819 (Article 19, UCMJ) contained in section 577 of the National Defense Authorization Act for Fiscal Year 2000, P. L. No. 106–65, 113 Stat. 512 (1999) increasing the jurisdictional maximum punishment at special courts-martial.".

v. The Analysis to R.C.M. 1111 is amended by adding at the end the following new paragraph:

"*2002 Amendment*: R.C.M. 1111(b) was amended to implement the amendment to 10 U.S.C. § 819 (Article 19, UCMJ) contained in section 577 of the National Defense Authorization Act for Fiscal Year 2000, P. L. No. 106–65, 113 Stat. 512 (1999) increasing the jurisdictional maximum punishment at special courts-martial. The amendment ensures all special courts-martial not requiring appellate review are reviewed by a judge advocate under R.C.M. 1112.".

w. The Analysis to R.C.M. 1112 is amended by adding at the end the following new paragraph:

"*2002 Amendment*: R.C.M. 1112(a)(2) was amended to implement the amendment to 10 U.S.C. § 819 (Article 19, UCMJ) contained in section 577 of the National Defense Authorization Act for Fiscal Year 2000, P. L. No. 106–65, 113 Stat. 512 (1999) increasing the jurisdictional maximum punishment at special courts-martial. The amendment ensures all special courts-martial not requiring appellate review are reviewed by a judge advocate under R.C.M. 1112.".

x. The Analysis to R.C.M. 1305 (d) is amended to read as follows:

"(d) *Forwarding copies of the record.* Subsection (1) is based on Article 60(b)(2). Subsection (2) is based on the third paragraph of paragraph 91c of MCM, 1969 (Rev.). Subsection (3) is self- explanatory.

"*2001 Amendment*: Subsection (d)(2) was amended to strike the reference to "subsection (e)(1)" and insert a reference to "subsection (d)(1)" to reflect the 1995 amendment that redesignated R.C.M. 1305(e) as R.C.M. 1305(d).".

2. *Changes to Appendix 22, the Analysis Accompanying the Military Rules of Evidence (Part III, MCM).*

a. The Analysis to Mil. R. Evid. 413 is amended by adding at the end the following new paragraph:

"*2002 Amendment*: Federal Rule of Evidence 415 which created a similar character evidence rule for civil cases, became applicable to the Military Rules of Evidence on January 6, 1996, pursuant to Rule 1102. Federal Rule 415, however, is no longer applicable to the Military Rules of Evidence, as stated in Section 1 of Executive Order , 2002 Amendments to the Manual for Court-Martial, United States, (date) Rule 415 was deleted because it applies only to federal civil proceedings.".

b. The Analysis to Mil. R. Evid. 414 is amended by adding at the end the following new paragraph:

"*2002 Amendment*: Federal Rule of Evidence 415 which created a similar character evidence rule for civil cases, became applicable to the Military Rules of Evidence on January 6, 1996, pursuant to Rule 1102. Federal Rule 415, however, is no longer applicable to the Military Rules of Evidence, as stated in Section 1 of Executive Order , 2002 Amendments to the Manual for Court-Martial, United States, (date) Rule 415 was deleted because it applies only to federal civil proceedings."

c. The analysis to Mil. R. Evid. 615 is amended by adding at the end the following new paragraph:

"*2002 Amendment*: These changes are intended to extend to victims at courts-martial the same rights granted to victims by the Victims' Rights and Restitution Act of 1990, 42 U.S.C. § 10606(b)(4), giving crime victims '[t]he right to be present at all public court proceedings related to the offense, unless the court determines that testimony by the victim would be materially affected if the victim heard other testimony at trial,' and the Victim Rights Clarification Act of 1997, 18 U.S.C. § 3510, which is restated in subsection (5). For the purposes of this rule, the term 'victim' includes all persons defined as victims in 42 U.S.C. § 10607(e)(2), which means 'a person that has suffered direct physical, emotional, or pecuniary harm as a result of the commission of a crime, including'—(A) in the case of a victim that is an institutional entity, an authorized representative of the entity; and (B) in the case of a victim who is under 18 years of age, incompetent, incapacitated, or deceased, one of the following (in order of preference): (i) a spouse; (ii) a legal guardian; (iii) a parent; (iv) a child; (v) a sibling; (vi) another family member; or (vii) another person designated by the court. 'The victim's right to remain in the courtroom remains subject to other rules, such as those regarding classified information, witness deportment, and conduct in the courtroom. Subsection (4) is intended to capture only those statutes applicable to courts-martial.".

3. *Changes to Appendix 23, the Analysis accompanying the Punitive Articles (Part IV, MCM).*

a. The Analysis to paragraph 27(e) is amended by adding at the end the following new paragraph:

"*2002 Amendment*: The monetary amount affecting the maximum punishments has been revised from $100 to $500 to account for inflation. The last change was in 1969 raising the amount to $100. The value has also been readjusted to realign it more closely with the division between felony and misdemeanor penalties in civilian jurisdictions. *See generally* American Law Institute, Model Penal Code and Commentaries § 223.1 (1980) (suggesting $500 as the value). The amendment also adds the phrase 'or any firearm or explosive' as an additional criterion. This is because, regardless of the intrinsic value of such items, the threat to the community is substantial when such items are wrongfully bought, sold, traded, dealt in or disposed.".

b. The Analysis to paragraph 31(c)(6) is amended to read as follows:

"*2002 Amendment*: Subparagraph c(6), 'Statements made during an interrogation,' was removed in light of questions raised by the Court of Appeals for the Armed Forces in *United States v. Solis*, 46 M.J. 31, 35 (C.A.A.F. 1997). In Solis, the court said subparagraph c(6) could be viewed as serving at least three different purposes. It could be (1) an expansive description of dicta with no intent to limit prosecutions; (2) protection for an accused against overcharging; or (3) guidance for the conduct of investigations. Subparagraph c(6) was never intended to establish either procedural rights for an accused or internal guidelines to regulate government conduct. Subparagraph (c)(6) was based upon *United States v. Aronson*, 8 U.S.C.M.A. 525, 25 C.M.R. 29 (1957); *United States v. Washington*, 9 U.S.C.M.A. 131, 25 C.M.R. 393 (1958) and *United States v. Davenport*, 9 M.J. 364 (C.M.A. 1980) and was intended merely to describe the rule developed in those cases that a false statement to a law enforcement agent, when made by a servicemember without an independent duty to speak, was not 'official' and therefore not within the purview of Article 107. The subparagraph is removed because the position of the Court of Military Appeals in the three decisions noted above was abandoned in *United States v. Jackson*, 26 M.J. 377 (C.M.A. 1988) and the deleted paragraph no longer accurately describes the current state of the law.".

c. The Analysis to paragraph 32(e) is amended by adding at the end the following new paragraph:

"*2002 Amendment*: The monetary amount affecting the maximum punishments has been revised from $100 to $500 to account for inflation. The last change was in 1969 raising the amount to $100. The value has also been readjusted to realign it more closely with the division between felony and misdemeanor penalties in civilian jurisdictions. *See generally* American Law Institute, Model Penal Code and Commentaries § 223.1 (1980) (suggesting $500 as the value). Although the monetary amount affecting punishment in 18 U.S.C. § 1361, *Government property or contracts*, and 18 U.S.C. § 641, *Public money, property or records*, was increased from $100 to $1000 pursuant to section 606 of the Economic Espionage Act of 1996, P. L. No. 104–294, 110 Stat. 3488 (1996), a value of $500 was chosen to maintain deterrence, simplicity, and uniformity for the Manual's property offenses.".

d. The Analysis to paragraph 33(e) is amended by adding at the end the following new paragraph:

"*2002 Amendment*: The monetary amount affecting the maximum punishments has been revised from $100 to $500 to account for inflation. The last change was in 1969 raising the amount to $100. The value has also been readjusted to realign it more closely with the division between felony and misdemeanor penalties in civilian jurisdictions. *See generally* American Law Institute, Model Penal Code and Commentaries § 223.1 (1980) (suggesting $500 as the value).".

e. The Analysis to paragraph 46(c) is amended by adding at the end the following new paragraph:

"*2002 Amendment*: Subparagraph c(1)(h)(vi) is new. It was added to provide guidance on how unauthorized credit, debit, or electronic transactions should usually be charged. *See United States v. Duncan*, 30 M.J. 1284, 289 (N.M.C.M.R. 1990) (citing *United States v. Jones*, 29 C.M.R. 651 (A.B.R. 1960), *petition denied*, 30 C.M.R. 417 (C.M.A. 1960)) (regarding thefts from ATM machines). Alternative charging theories are also available, *see United States v. Leslie*, 13 M.J. 170 (C.M.A. 1982); *United States v. Ragins*, 11 M.J. 42 (C.M.A. 1981); *United States v. Schaper*, 42 M.J. 737 (A.F. Ct. Crim. App. 1995); and *United States v. Christy*, 18 M.J. 688 (N.M.C.M.R. 1984). The key under Article 121 is that the accused wrongfully obtained goods or money from a person or entity with a superior possessory interest.".

f. The Analysis to paragraph 46(e) is amended by adding at the end the following new paragraph:

"*2002 Amendment*: The monetary amount affecting the maximum punishments has been revised from $100 to $500 to account for inflation. The last change was in 1969 raising the amount to $100. The value has also been readjusted to realign it more closely with the division between felony and misdemeanor penalties in civilian jurisdictions. *See generally* American Law Institute, Model Penal Code and Commentaries § 223.1 (1980) (suggesting $500 as the value). Although the monetary amount effecting punishment in 18 U.S.C. § 1361, *Government property or contracts*, and 18 U.S.C. § 641, *Public money, property or records*, was increased from $100 to $1000 pursuant to section 606 of the Economic Espionage Act of 1996, P. L. No. 104–294, 110 Stat. 3488 (1996), a value of $500 was chosen to maintain deterrence, simplicity, and uniformity for the Manual's property offenses.".

g. The Analysis to paragraph 49(e) is amended by adding at the end the following new paragraph:

"*2002 Amendment*: The monetary amount affecting the maximum punishments has been revised from $100 to $500 to account for inflation. The last change was in 1969 raising the amount to $100. The value has also been readjusted to realign it more closely with the division between felony and misdemeanor penalties in civilian jurisdictions. *See generally* American Law Institute, Model Penal Code and Commentaries § 223.1 (1980) (suggesting $500 as the value).".

h. The Analysis to paragraph 52(e) is amended by adding at the end the following new paragraph:

"*2002 Amendment*: The monetary amount affecting the maximum punishments has been revised from $100 to $500 to account for inflation. The last change was in 1969 raising the amount to $100. The value has also been readjusted to realign it more closely with the division between felony and misdemeanor penalties in civilian jurisdictions. *See generally* American

Law Institute, Model Penal Code and Commentaries § 223.1 (1980) (suggesting $500 as the value). A value of $500 was chosen to maintain deterrence, simplicity, and uniformity for the Manual's property offenses. 18 U.S.C. § 81, *Arson within special maritime and territorial jurisdiction*, no longer grades the offense on the basis of value.".

i. The Analysis to paragraph 58(e) is amended by adding at the end the following new paragraph:

"*2002 Amendment*: The monetary amount affecting the maximum punishments has been revised from $100 to $500 to account for inflation. The last change was in 1969 raising the amount to $100. The value has also been readjusted to realign it more closely with the division between felony and misdemeanor penalties in civilian jurisdictions. *See generally* American Law Institute, Model Penal Code and Commentaries § 223.1 (1980) (suggesting $500 as the value).".

j. The Analysis to paragraph 62. Article 134 ' (Adultery) is amended to read as follows:

"c. *Explanation.* (1) Subparagraph c(2) is based on *United States. v. Snyder*, 4 C.M.R. 15 (1952); *United States v. Ruiz*, 46 M.J. 503 (A. F. Ct. Crim. App. 1997); *United States v. Green*, 39 M.J. 606 (A.C.M.R. 1994); *United States v. Collier*, 36 M.J. 501 (A.F.C.M.R. 1992); *United States v. Perez*, 33 M.J. 1050 (A.C.M.R. 1991); *United States v. Linnear*, 16 M.J. 628 (A.F.C.M.R. 1983); Part IV, paragraph 60c(2)(a) of MCM. Subparagraph c(3) is based on *United States v. Poole*, 39 M.J. 819 (A.C.M.R. 1994). Subparagraph c(4) is based on *United States v. Fogarty*, 35 M.J. 885 (A.C.M.R. 1992); Military Judges' Benchbook, DA PAM 27–9, paragraph 3–62–1 and 5–11–2 (30 Sep. 1996). *See* R.C.M. 916(j) and (l)(1) for a general discussion of mistake of fact and ignorance, which cannot be based on a negligent failure to discover the true facts.

"(2) When determining whether adulterous acts constitute the offense of adultery under Article 134, commanders should consider the listed factors. Each commander has discretion to dispose of offenses by members of the command. As with any alleged offense, however, under R.C.M. 306(b) commanders should dispose of an allegation of adultery at the lowest appropriate level. As the R.C.M. 306(b) discussion states, many factors must be taken into consideration and balanced, including, to the extent practicable, the nature of the offense, any mitigating or extenuating circumstances, the character and military service of the military member, any recommendations made by subordinate commanders, the interests of justice, military exigencies, and the effect of the decision on the military member and the command. The goal should be a disposition that is warranted, appropriate, and fair. In the case of officers, also consult the explanation to paragraph 59 in deciding how to dispose of an allegation of adultery.".

k. The Analysis to paragraph 78(e) is amended by adding at the end the following new paragraph:

"*2002 Amendment*: The monetary amount affecting the maximum punishments has been revised from $100 to $500 to account for inflation. The last change was in 1969 raising the amount to $100. The value has also been readjusted to realign it more closely with the division between felony and misdemeanor penalties in civilian jurisdictions. *See generally* American Law Institute, Model Penal Code and Commentaries § 223.1 (1980) (suggesting $500 as the value).".

Law Institute, Model Penal Code and Commentaries § 223.1 (1980) (suggesting $500 as the value). A value of $500 was chosen to maintain deterrence, simplicity, and uniformity for the Manual's property offenses. 18 U.S.C. § 81, *Arson within special maritime and territorial jurisdiction*, no longer grades the offense on the basis of value.".

i. The Analysis to paragraph 58(e) is amended by adding at the end the following new paragraph:

"*2002 Amendment*: The monetary amount affecting the maximum punishments has been revised from $100 to $500 to account for inflation. The last change was in 1969 raising the amount to $100. The value has also been readjusted to realign it more closely with the division between felony and misdemeanor penalties in civilian jurisdictions. *See generally* American Law Institute, Model Penal Code and Commentaries § 223.1 (1980) (suggesting $500 as the value).".

j. The Analysis to paragraph 62. Article 134 ' (Adultery) is amended to read as follows:

"c. *Explanation.* (1) Subparagraph c(2) is based on *United States. v. Snyder*, 4 C.M.R. 15 (1952); *United States v. Ruiz*, 46 M.J. 503 (A. F. Ct. Crim. App. 1997); *United States v. Green*, 39 M.J. 606 (A.C.M.R. 1994); *United States v. Collier*, 36 M.J. 501 (A.F.C.M.R. 1992); *United States v. Perez*, 33 M.J. 1050 (A.C.M.R. 1991); *United States v. Linnear*, 16 M.J. 628 (A.F.C.M.R. 1983); Part IV, paragraph 60c(2)(a) of MCM. Subparagraph c(3) is based on *United States v. Poole*, 39 M.J. 819 (A.C.M.R. 1994). Subparagraph c(4) is based on *United States v. Fogarty*, 35 M.J. 885 (A.C.M.R. 1992); Military Judges' Benchbook, DA PAM 27–9, paragraph 3–62–1 and 5–11–2 (30 Sep. 1996). *See* R.C.M. 916(j) and (l)(1) for a general discussion of mistake of fact and ignorance, which cannot be based on a negligent failure to discover the true facts.

"(2) When determining whether adulterous acts constitute the offense of adultery under Article 134, commanders should consider the listed factors. Each commander has discretion to dispose of offenses by members of the command. As with any alleged offense, however, under R.C.M. 306(b) commanders should dispose of an allegation of adultery at the lowest appropriate level. As the R.C.M. 306(b) discussion states, many factors must be taken into consideration and balanced, including, to the extent practicable, the nature of the offense, any mitigating or extenuating circumstances, the character and military service of the military member, any recommendations made by subordinate commanders, the interests of justice, military exigencies, and the effect of the decision on the military member and the command. The goal should be a disposition that is warranted, appropriate, and fair. In the case of officers, also consult the explanation to paragraph 59 in deciding how to dispose of an allegation of adultery.".

k. The Analysis to paragraph 78(e) is amended by adding at the end the following new paragraph:

"*2002 Amendment*: The monetary amount affecting the maximum punishments has been revised from $100 to $500 to account for inflation. The last change was in 1969 raising the amount to $100. The value has also been readjusted to realign it more closely with the division between felony and misdemeanor penalties in civilian jurisdictions. *See generally* American Law Institute, Model Penal Code and Commentaries § 223.1 (1980) (suggesting $500 as the value).".

Executive Order 13365 of December 3, 2004 2004 Amendments to the Manual for Courts-Martial, United States

By the authority vested in me as President by the Constitution and the laws of the United States of America, including chapter 47 of title 10, United States Code (Uniform Code of Military Justice, 10 U.S.C. 801-946), and in order to prescribe amendments to the Manual for Courts-Martial, United States, prescribed by Executive Order 12473, as amended, it is hereby ordered as follows:

Section 1.

(a) Paragraph 4 of the Preamble to Part I of the Manual for Courts-Martial, United States, is amended by adding a third subparagraph to read as follows:

The Department of Defense Joint Service Committee (JSC) on Military Justice reviews the Manual for Courts-Martial and proposes amendments to the Department of Defense for con-sideration by the President on an annual basis. In conducting its annual review, the JSC is guided by DoD Directive 5500.17, "The Roles and Responsibilities of the Joint Service Committee (JSC) on Military Justice." DoD Directive 5500.17 includes provisions allowing public participation in the annual review process.

(b) Department of Defense Directive 5500.17 shall be included as Appendix 26 to the Manual for Courts-Martial, United States.

Part II of the Manual for Courts-Martial, United States, is amended as follows:

(a) R.C.M. 307(c)(3) is amended to read as follows: Specification. A specification is a plain, concise, and definite statement of the essential facts constituting the offense charged. A specification is sufficient if it alleges every element of the charged offense expressly or by necessary implication. Except for aggravating factors under R.C.M. 1003(d) and R.C.M. 1004, facts that increase the maximum authorized punishment must be alleged in order to permit the possible increased punishment. No particular format is required.

(b) R.C.M. 707(b)(3)(D) is amended to read as follows:

Rehearings. If a rehearing is ordered or authorized by an appellate court, a new 120-day time period under this rule shall begin on the date that the responsible convening authority receives the record of trial and the opinion authorizing or directing a rehearing. An accused is brought to trial within the meaning of this rule at the time of arraignment under R.C.M. 904 or, if arraignment is not required (such as in the case of a sentence-only rehearing), at the time of the first session under R.C.M. 803.

(c) R.C.M. 707(c) is amended to read as follows: Excludable delay. All periods of time during which appellate courts have issued stays in the proceedings, or the accused is absent without authority, or the accused is hospitalized due to incompetence, or is otherwise in the custody of the Attorney General, shall be excluded when determining whether the period in subsection (a) of this rule has run. All other pretrial delays approved by a military judge or the convening authority shall be similarly excluded.

(d) R.C.M. 707(d) is amended to read as follows: Remedy. A failure to comply with this rule will result in dismissal of the affected charges, or, in a sentence-only rehearing, sentence relief as appropriate.

(1) Dismissal. Dismissal will be with or without prejudice to the government's right to reinstitute court-martial pro-ceedings against the accused for the same offense at a later date. The charges must be dismissed with prejudice where the accused has been deprived of his or her constitutional right to a speedy trial. In determining whether to dismiss charges with or without prejudice, the court shall consider, among others, each of the following factors: the seriousness of the offense; the facts and circumstances of the case that lead to dismissal; the impact of a re-prosecution on the administration of justice; and any prejudice to the accused resulting from the denial of a speedy trial.

(2) Sentence relief. In determining whether or how much sentence relief is appropriate, the military judge shall consider, among others, each of the following factors: the length of the delay, the reasons for the delay, the accused's demand for speedy trial, and any prejudice to the accused from the delay. Any sentence relief granted will be applied against the sentence approved by the convening authority.

(e) R.C.M. 806(b) is amended to read as follows: (b) Control of spectators and closure.

(1) Control of spectators. In order to maintain the dignity and decorum of the proceedings or for other good cause, the military judge may reasonably limit the number of spectators in, and the means of access to, the courtroom, and exclude specific persons from the courtroom. When excluding specific persons, the

military judge must make findings on the record establishing the reason for the exclusion, the basis for the military judge's belief that exclusion is necessary, and that the exclusion is as narrowly tailored as possible.

(2) Closure. Courts-martial shall be open to the public unless (1) there is a substantial probability that an overriding interest will be prejudiced if the proceedings remain open; (2) closure is no broader than necessary to protect the over-riding interest; (3) reasonable alternatives to closure were considered and found inadequate; and (4) the military judge makes case-specific findings on the record justifying closure.

(f) R.C.M. 916(k)(2) is amended to read as follows:
(2) Partial mental responsibility. A mental condition not amounting to a lack of mental responsibility under subsection (k)(1) of this rule is not an affirmative defense.

(h) The following subsection (iv) is inserted after R.C.M. 1107(e)(1)(B)(iii) to read as follows:
(iv) Sentence reassessment. If a superior authority has approved some of the findings of guilty and has authorized a rehearing as to other offenses and the sentence, the convening authority may, unless otherwise directed, reassess the sentence based on the approved findings of guilty and dismiss the remaining charges. Reassessment is appropriate only where the convening authority determines that the accused's sentence would have been at least of a certain magnitude had the pre-judicial error not been committed and the reassessed sentence is appropriate in relation to the affirmed findings of guilty.

(i) R.C.M. 1108(b) is amended to read as follows:
(b) Who may suspend and remit. The convening authority may, after approving the sentence, suspend the execution of all or any part of the sentence of a court-martial, except for a sentence of death. The general court-martial convening authority over the accused at the time of the court-martial may, when taking the action under R.C.M. 1112(f), suspend or remit any part of the sentence. The Secretary concerned and, when designated by the Secretary concerned, any Under Secretary, Assistant Secretary, Judge Advocate General, or commanding officer may suspend or remit any part or amount of the unexecuted part of any sentence other than a sentence approved by the President or a sentence of confinement for life without eligi-bility for parole that has been ordered executed. The Secretary concerned may, however, suspend or remit the unexecuted part of a sentence of confinement for life without eligibility for parole only after the service of a period of confinement of not less than 20 years. The commander of the accused who has the authority to convene a court-martial of the kind that adjudged the sentence may suspend or remit any part of the unexecuted part of any sentence by summary court-martial or of any sentence by special court-martial that does not include a bad-conduct discharge regardless of whether the person acting has previously approved the sentence. The "unexecuted part of any sentence" is that part that has been approved and ordered executed but that has not actually been carried out.

(j) R.C.M. 1305(c) is amended to read as follows:
(1) Who shall act. Except as provided herein, the convening authority shall take action in accordance with R.C.M. 1107. The convening authority shall not take action before the period prescribed in R.C.M. 1105(c)(2) has expired, unless the right to submit matters has been waived under R.C.M. 1105(d).

Sec 3. Part III of the Manual for Courts-Martial, United States, is amended as follows:

(a) Mil. R. Evid. 103(a)(2) is amended to read as follows:
(2) Offer of proof. In case the ruling is one excluding evidence, the substance of the evidence was made known to the military judge by offer or was apparent from the context within which questions were asked. Once the military judge makes a definitive ruling on the record admitting or excluding evidence, either at or before trial, a party need not renew an objection or offer of proof to preserve a claim of error for appeal. The standard provided in this subdivision does not apply to errors involving requirements imposed by the Constitution of the United States as applied to members of the armed forces except insofar as the error arises under these rules and this subdivision provides a standard that is more advantageous to the accused than the constitutional standard.

(b) Mil. R. Evid. 404(a) is amended to read as follows:
(a) Character evidence generally. Evidence of a person's character or a trait of character is not admissible for the purpose of proving action in conformity therewith on a particular occasion, except:

(1) Character of accused. Evidence of a pertinent

trait of character offered by an accused, or by the prosecution to rebut the same, or if evidence of a pertinent trait of character of the alleged victim of the crime is offered by an accused and admitted under Mil. R. Evid. 404(a)(2), evidence of the same trait of character, if relevant, of the accused offered by the prosecution;

(2) Character of alleged victim. Evidence of a pertinent trait of character of the alleged victim of the crime offered by an accused, or by the prosecution to rebut the same, or evidence of a character trait of peacefulness of the alleged victim offered by the prosecution in a homicide or assault case to rebut evidence that the alleged victim was an aggressor;

(3) Character of witness. Evidence of the character of a witness, as provided in Mil. R. Evid. 607, 608, and 609.

(c) Mil. R. Evid. 701 is amended to read as follows: If the witness is not testifying as an expert, the witness' testimony in the form of opinions or inferences is limited to those opinions or inferences that are (a) rationally based on the perception of the witness, (b) helpful to a clear understanding of the witness' testimony or the determination of a fact in issue, and (c) not based in scientific, technical, or other specialized knowledge within the scope of Rule 702.

(d) Mil. R. Evid. 702 is amended to read as follows: If scientific, technical, or other specialized knowledge will assist the trier of fact to understand the evidence or to determine a fact in issue, a witness qualified as an expert by knowledge, skill, experience, training, or education may testify thereto in the form of an opinion or otherwise if (1) the testimony is based upon sufficient facts or data, (2) the testimony is the product of reliable principles and methods, and (3) the witness has applied the principles and methods reliably to the facts of the case.

(e) Mil. R. Evid. 703 is amended to read as follows: The facts or data in the particular case upon which an expert bases an opinion or inference may be those perceived by or made known to the expert, at or before the hearing. If of a type reasonably relied upon by experts in the particular field in forming opinions or inferences upon the subject, the facts or data need not be admissible in evidence in order for the opinion or inference to be admitted. Facts or data that are otherwise inadmissible shall not be disclosed to the members by the proponent of the opinion or inference unless the military judge determines that their probative value in assisting the members to evaluate the expert's opinion substantially outweighs their prejudicial effect.

(f) Mil. R. Evid. 803(6) is amended to read as follows:

Records of regularly conducted activity. A memorandum, report, record, or data compilation, in any form, of acts, events, conditions, opinions, or diagnoses, made at or near the time by, or from information transmitted by, a person with knowledge, if kept in the course of a regularly conducted business activity, and if it was the regular practice of that business activity to make the memorandum, report, record, or data compilation, all as shown by the testimony of the custodian or other qualified witness, or by certification that complies with Mil. R. Evid. 902(11) or any other statute permitting certification in a criminal proceeding in a court of the United States, unless the source of the information or the method or circumstances of preparation indicate a lack of trustworthiness. The term "business" as used in this paragraph includes the armed forces, a business, institution, association, profession, occupation, and calling of every kind, whether or not conducted for profit. Among those memoranda, reports, records, or data compilations normally admissible pursuant to this paragraph are enlistment papers, physical examination papers, outline-figure and fingerprint cards, forensic laboratory reports, chain of custody documents, morning reports and other personnel accountability documents, service records, officer and enlisted qualification records, logs, unit personnel diaries, individual equipment records, daily strength records of prisoners, and rosters of prisoners.

(g) The following subsection (11) is inserted after Mil. R. Evid. 902(10) to read as follows:

(11) Certified domestic records of regularly conducted activity. The original or a duplicate of a domestic record of regularly conducted activity that would be admissible under Mil. R. Evid. 803(6) if accompanied by a written declaration of its custodian or other qualified person, in a manner complying with any Act of Congress or rule prescribed by the Supreme Court pursuant to statutory authority, certifying that the record (A) was made at or near the time of the occurrence of the matters set forth by, or from information transmitted by, a person

with knowledge of those matters; (B) was kept in the course of the regularly conducted activity; and (C) was made by the regularly conducted activity as a regular practice. A party intending to offer a record into evidence under this paragraph must provide written notice of that intention to all adverse parties, and must make the record and declaration available for inspection sufficiently in advance of their offer into evidence to provide an adverse party with a fair opportunity to challenge them.

(h) Mil. R. Evid. 1102 is amended to read as follows:
(a) Amendments to the Federal Rules of Evidence shall apply to the Military Rules of Evidence 18 months after the effective date of such amendments, unless action to the contrary is taken by the President.
(b) Rules Determined Not To Apply. The President has determined that the following Federal Rules of Evidence do not apply to the Military Rules of Evidence: Rules 301, 302, 415, and 902(12).

Sec. 4. Part IV of the Manual for Courts-Martial, United States, is amended as follows:

(a) Paragraph 45(b)(2) is amended by deleting paragraph 45(b)(2)(c) and inserting the following after paragraph 45(b)(2)(b):
(c)(1) That at the time of the sexual intercourse the person was under the age of 12; or
(2) That at the time of the sexual intercourse the person had attained the age of 12 but was under the age of 16.

(b) Paragraph 45(f) is amended to read as follows:
f. Sample specifications.
(1) Rape.
In that (personal jurisdiction data), did, (at/on board--location) (subject-matter jurisdiction data, if required), on or about 20 , rape , (a person under the age of 12) (a person who had attained the age of 12 but was under the age of 16).
(2) Carnal Knowledge.
In that (personal jurisdiction data), did, (at/on board--location) (subject-matter jurisdiction data, if required), on or about 20 , commit the offense of carnal knowledge with , (a person under the age of 12) (a person who attained the age of 12 but was under the age of 16).

(c) Paragraph 51(b) is amended to read as follows:
(1) That the accused engaged in unnatural carnal copulation with a certain other person or with an animal.
(Note: Add any of the following as applicable)
(2) That the act was done with a child under the age of 12.
(3) That the act was done with a child who had attained the age of 12 but was under the age of 16.
(4) That the act was done by force and without the consent of the other person.

(d) Paragraph 51(f) is amended to read as follows:
f. Sample specification.
In that (personal jurisdiction data), did, (at/on boardlocation) (subject-matter jurisdiction data, if required), on or about _________ 20__, commit sodomy with
, (a child under the age of 12) (a child who had attained the age of 12 but was under the age of 16) (by force and without the consent of the said).

(e) Paragraph 57(c)(2)(b) is amended to read as follows:
(b) Material matter. The false testimony must be with respect to a material matter, but that matter need not be the main issue in the case. Thus, perjury may be committed by giving false testimony with respect to the credibility of a material witness or in an affidavit in support of a request for a continuance, as well as by giving false testimony with respect to a fact from which a legitimate inference may be drawn as to the existence or nonexistence of a fact in issue.

(f) Paragraph 100a(c)(1) is amended to read as follows:
(1) In general. This offense is intended to prohibit and therefore deter reckless or wanton conduct that wrongfully creates a substantial risk of death or grievous bodily harm to others.

(g) Paragraph 100a(f) is amended to read as follows:
f. Sample specification.
In that (personal jurisdiction data), did, (at/on boardlocation) (subject-matter jurisdiction data, if required), on or about 20 , wrongfully and (recklessly) (wantonly) engage in conduct, to wit: (describe conduct), conduct likely to cause death or grievous bodily harm to _________________.'

Sec. 5. These amendments shall take effect 30 days from the date of this order.

(a) Nothing in these amendments shall be construed to make punishable any act done or omitted prior to the effective date of this order that was not punishable when done or omitted.

(b) Nothing in these amendments shall be construed to invalidate any nonjudicial punishment proceeding, restraint, investigation, referral of charges, trial in which arraignment occurred, or other action begun prior to the effective date of this order, and any such nonjudicial proceeding, restraint, investigation, referral of charges, trial, or other action may proceed in the same manner and with the same effect as if these amendments had not been prescribed.

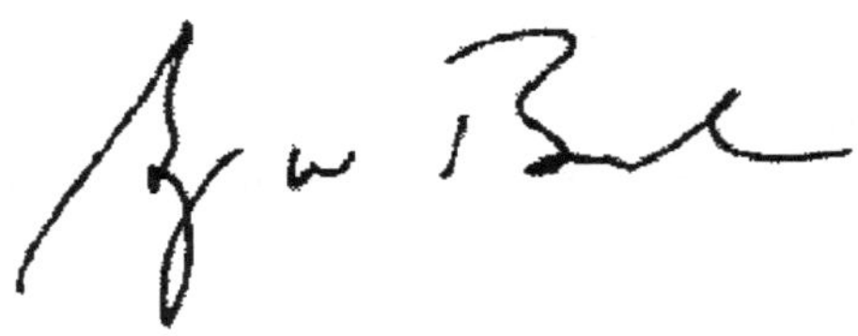

THE WHITE HOUSE
December 3, 2004.

Executive Order 13387: 2005 Amendments to the Manual for Courts-Martial, United States

By the authority vested in me as President by the Constitution and the laws of the United States of America, including chapter 47 of title 10, United States Code (Uniform Code of Military Justice, 10 U.S.C. 801-946), and in order to prescribe amendments to the Manual for Courts-Martial, United States, prescribed by Executive Order 12473, as amended, it is hereby ordered as follows:

Section 1. Part II of the Manual for Courts-Martial, United States, is amended as follows:

(a) R.C.M. 103(2) is amended by replacing the word "without" with the word "with" and by replacing the word "noncapital" with the word "capital".

(b) R.C.M. 201(e)(2)(B) is amended by adding the word "general" between the words "convene" and "courts-martial" and by inserting the following words after "armed forces":

"assigned or attached to a combatant command or joint command".

(c) R.C.M. 201(e)(2)(C) is amended by inserting the words "assigned or attached to a joint command or joint task force," immediately before the words "under regulations which the superior command may prescribe".

(d) R.C.M. 201(e)(3) is amended by inserting the following immediately after the words "armed force":

", using the implementing regulations and procedures prescribed by the Secretary concerned of the military service of the accused,".

(e) R.C.M. 201(e)(4) is amended by adding the words ", member, or counsel" after the words "military judge".

(f) R.C.M. 201(f)(1)(A)(iii)(b) is amended to read as follows:

"(b) The case has not been referred with a special instruction that the case is to be tried as capital."

(g) R.C.M. 307(c)(4) is amended by inserting the following at the end thereof:

"What is substantially one transaction should not be made the basis for an unreasonable multiplication of charges against one person."

(h) R.C.M. 501(a)(1) is amended to read as follows:

"(1) General courts-martial.

(A) Except in capital cases, general courts-martial shall consist of a military judge and not less than five members, or of the military judge alone if requested and approved under R.C.M. 903.

(B) In all capital cases, general courts-martial shall consist of a military judge and no fewer than 12 members, unless 12 members are not reasonably available because of physical conditions or military exigencies. If 12 members are not reasonably available, the convening authority shall detail the next lesser number of reasonably available members under 12, but in no event fewer than five. In such a case, the convening authority shall state in the convening order the reasons why 12 members are not reasonably available."

(i) R.C.M. 503(a)(3) is amended by deleting "court-martial" and inserting "courts-martial" in lieu thereof.

(j) R.C.M. 503(b)(3) is amended by inserting the words ", a combatant command or joint command" after the words "A military judge from one armed force may be detailed to a court-martial convened in a different armed force".

(k) R.C.M. 503(c)(3) is amended by inserting the words ", a combatant command or joint command" after the words "A person from one armed force may be detailed to serve as counsel in a court-martial in a different armed force".

(l) R.C.M. 504, (b)(2)(A) is amended by inserting the following at the end thereof:

"A subordinate joint command or joint task force is ordinarily considered to be "separate or detached.""

(m) R.C.M. 504, (b)(2)(B) is amended by deleting the word "or" at the end of the first element thereof, by deleting the period and adding "; or" at the end of the second element thereof, and by inserting the following as a third element:

"(iii) In a combatant command or joint command, by the officer exercising general court-martial jurisdiction over the command."

(n) R.C.M. 805(b) is amended by replacing the current second sentence with the following:

"No general court-martial proceeding requiring the presence of members may be conducted unless at least five members are present, or in capital cases, at least 12 members are present except as provided in R.C.M. 501(a)(1)(B), where 12 members are not reasonably available because of physical conditions or military exigencies. No special court-martial proceeding requiring the presence of members may be conducted unless at least three members are present except as provided in R.C.M. 912(h)."

(o) R.C.M. 912(f)(4) is amended by deleting the fifth sentence and by inserting the following words immediately after the words "When a challenge for cause has been denied" in the fourth sentence:

"the successful use of a peremptory challenge by either party, excusing the challenged member from further participation in the court-martial, shall preclude further consideration of the challenge of that excused member upon later review. Further,"

(p) R.C.M. 1003(b)(2) is amended by replacing the word "foreign" with the word "hardship."

(q) R.C.M. 1004(b) is amended by inserting the following after "(1) Notice." and before the word "Before":

"(A) Referral. The convening authority shall indicate that the case is to be tried as a capital case by including a special instruction in the referral block of the charge sheet. Failure to include this special instruction at the time of the referral shall not bar the convening authority from later adding the required special instruction, provided:

(i) that the convening authority has otherwise complied with the notice requirement of subsection (B); and

(ii) that if the accused demonstrates specific prejudice from such failure to include the special instruction, a continuance or a recess is an adequate remedy.

(B) Arraignment."

(r) Insert the following new R.C.M. 1103A after R.C.M. 1103:

"Rule 1103A. Sealed exhibits and proceedings.

(a) In general. If the record of trial contains exhibits, proceedings, or other matter ordered sealed by the military judge, the trial counsel shall cause such materials to be sealed so as to prevent indiscriminate viewing or disclosure. Trial counsel shall ensure that such materials are properly marked, including an annotation that the material was sealed by order of the military judge, and inserted at the appropriate place in the original record of trial. Copies of the record shall contain appropriate annotations that matters were sealed by order of the military judge and have been inserted in the original record of trial. This Rule shall be implemented in a manner consistent with Executive Order 12958, as amended, concerning classified national security information.

(b) Examination of sealed exhibits and proceedings. Except as provided in the following subsections to this rule, sealed exhibits may not be examined.

(1) Examination of sealed matters. For the purpose of this rule, "examination" includes reading, viewing, photocopying, photographing, disclosing, or manipulating the documents in any way.

(2) Prior to authentication. Prior to authentication of the record by the military judge, sealed materials may not be examined in the absence of an order from the military judge based on good cause shown.

(3) Authentication through action. After authentication and prior to disposition of the record of trial pursuant to Rule for Courts-Martial 1111, sealed materials may not be examined in the absence of an order from the military judge upon a showing of good cause at a post-trial Article 39a session directed by the Convening Authority.

(4) Reviewing and appellate authorities.

(A) Reviewing and appellate authorities may examine sealed matters when those authorities determine that such action is reasonably necessary to a proper fulfillment of their responsibilities under the Uniform Code of Military Justice, the Manual for Courts-Martial, governing directives, instructions, regulations, applicable rules for practice and procedure, or rules of professional responsibility.

(B) Reviewing and appellate authorities shall not, however, disclose sealed matter or information in the absence of:

(i) Prior authorization of the Judge Advocate General in the case of review under Rule for Courts-Martial 1201(b); or

(ii) Prior authorization of the appellate court before which a case is pending review under Rules for Courts-Martial 1203 and 1204.

(C) In those cases in which review is sought or pending before the United States Supreme Court, authorization to disclose sealed materials or information shall be obtained under that Court's rules of practice and procedure.

(D) The authorizing officials in paragraph (B)(ii) above may place conditions on authorized disclosures in order to minimize the disclosure.

(E) For purposes of this rule, reviewing and appellate authorities are limited to:

(i) Judge advocates reviewing records pursuant to Rule for Courts-Martial 1112;

(ii) Officers and attorneys in the office of the Judge Advocate General reviewing records pursuant to Rule for Courts-Martial 1201(b);

(iii) Appellate government counsel;

(iv) Appellate defense counsel;

(v) Appellate judges of the Courts of Criminal Appeals and their professional staffs;

(vi) The judges of the United States Court of Appeals for the Armed Forces and their professional staffs;

(vii) The Justices of the United States Supreme Court and their professional staffs; and

(viii) Any other court of competent jurisdiction."

(s) R.C.M. 1301(a) is amended by inserting the following after the second sentence:
"Summary courts-martial shall be conducted in accordance with the regulations of the military service to which the accused belongs."

Sec. 2. Part III of the Manual for Courts-Martial, United States, is amended as follows:
Mil. R. Evid. 317(b) is amended by replacing the word "Transportation" with the words "Homeland Security."

Sec. 3. Part IV of the Manual for Courts-Martial, United States, is amended as follows:

(a) Paragraph 14c(2)(a) is amended by inserting the following new subparagraph (ii) and renumbering existing subparagraphs (a)(ii) through (iv) as (a)(iii) through (v):
"(ii) Determination of lawfulness. The lawfulness of an order is a question of law to be determined by the military judge."

(b) Paragraph 16(c)(1)(a) is amended by replacing the word "Transportation" with the words "Homeland Security".

(c) Paragraph 35a is amended to read as follows:
"a. Text.

(a) Any person subject to this chapter who—

(1) operates or physically controls any vehicle, aircraft, or vessel in a reckless or wanton manner or while impaired by a substance described in section 912a(b) of this title (Article 112a(b)), or

(2) operates or is in actual physical control of any vehicle, aircraft, or vessel while drunk or when the alcohol concentration in the person's blood or breath is equal to or exceeds the level prohibited under subsection (b), as shown by chemical analysis, shall be punished as a court-martial may direct.

(b)(1) For purposes of subsection (a), the applicable level of the alcohol concentration in a person's blood or breath is as follows:

(A) In the case of the operation or control of a vehicle, aircraft, or vessel in the United States, the level is the blood alcohol concentration prohibited under the law of the State in which the conduct occurred, except as may be provided under paragraph (b)(2) for conduct on a military installation that is in more than one State, or the prohibited alcohol concentration level specified in paragraph (b)(3).

(B) In the case of the operation or control of a vehicle, aircraft, or vessel outside the United States, the level is the blood alcohol concentration specified in paragraph (b)(3) or such lower level as the Secretary of Defense may by regulation prescribe.

(2) In the case of a military installation that is in more than one State, if those States have different levels for defining their prohibited blood alcohol concentrations under their respective State laws, the Secretary concerned for the installation may select one such level to apply uniformly on that installation.

(3) For purposes of paragraph (b)(1), the level of alcohol concentration prohibited in a person's blood is 0.10 grams or more of alcohol per 100 milliliters of blood and with respect to alcohol concentration in a person's breath is 0.10 grams or more of alcohol per 210 liters of breath, as shown by chemical analysis."

(4) In this subsection, the term "United States" includes the District of Columbia, the Commonwealth of Puerto Rico, the Virgin Islands, Guam, and American Samoa, and the term "State" includes each of those jurisdictions."

(d) Paragraph 35b(2)(c) is amended to read as follows:
"(c) the alcohol concentration level in the accused's blood or breath, as shown by chemical analysis, was equal to or exceeded the applicable level provided in paragraph 35a above."

(e) Paragraph 35f is amended as follows:

"In that (personal jurisdiction data), did (at/on board required), on or about 20 , (in the motor pool area) (near the Officer's Club) (at the intersection of and) (while in the Gulf of Mexico) (while in flight over North America) physically control [a vehicle, to wit: (a truck) (a passenger car)( )] [an aircraft, to wit: (an AH-64 helicopter)(an F-14A fighter)(a KC-135 tanker)( )] [a vessel, to wit: (the aircraft carrier USS) (the Coast Guard Cutter)( )], [while drunk] [while impaired by] [while the alcohol concentration in his (blood)(breath) was, as shown by chemical analysis, equal to or exceeded (.10)( ) grams of alcohol per (100 milliliters of blood)(210 liters of breath), which is the limit under (cite applicable State law)(cite applicable statute or regulation)][in a (reckless) (wanton) manner by (attempting to pass another vehicle on a sharp curve)(by ordering that the aircraft be flown below the authorized altitude)] [and did thereby cause said (vehicle)(aircraft)(vessel) to (strike and)(injure)]."

(f) Paragraph 97 is amended by (1) inserting the following new subparagraph (b)(2) and renumbering the existing subparagraphs (b)(2) and (b)(3) as (b)(3) and (b)(4); (2) adding the words "and patronizing a prostitute" after the word "Prostitution" in subparagraph (e)(1); and (3) inserting the following new subparagraph (f)(2) and renumbering the existing subparagraphs (f)(2) and (f)(3) as (f)(3) and (f)(4):

"(b)(2) Patronizing a prostitute.

(a) That the accused had sexual intercourse with another person not the accused's spouse;

(b) That the accused compelled, induced, enticed, or procured such person to engage in an act of sexual intercourse in exchange for money or other compensation; and

(c) That this act was wrongful; and

(d) That, under the circumstances, the conduct of the accused was to the prejudice of good order and discipline in the armed forces or was of a nature to bring discredit upon the armed forces."

"(f)(2) Patronizing a prostitute.

In that (personal jurisdiction data), did, (at/on board location) (subject-matter jurisdiction data, if required), on or about 20 , wrongfully (compel) (induce) (entice) (procure) , a person not his/her spouse, to engage in (an act) (acts) of sexual intercourse with the accused in exchange for (money) ( )."

(g) Paragraph 109 is amended to read as follows:

"109. ARTICLE 134 B (Threat or hoax designed or intended to cause panic or public fear)

a. *Text. See* paragraph 60.

b. *Elements.*

(1) Threat.

(a) That the accused communicated certain language;

(b) That the information communicated amounted to a threat;

(c) That the harm threatened was to be done by means of an explosive; weapon of mass destruction; biological or chemical agent, substance, or weapon; or hazardous material;

(d) That the communication was wrongful; and

(e) That, under the circumstances, the conduct of the accused was to the prejudice of good order and discipline in the armed forces or was of a nature to bring discredit upon the armed forces.

(2) Hoax.

(a) That the accused communicated or conveyed certain information;

(b) That the information communicated or conveyed concerned an attempt being made or to be made by means of an explosive; weapon of mass destruction; biological or chemical agent, substance, or weapon; or hazardous material, to unlawfully kill, injure, or intimidate a person or to unlawfully damage or destroy certain property;

(c) That the information communicated or conveyed by the accused was false and that the accused then knew it to be false;

(d) That the communication of the information by the accused was malicious; and

(e) That, under the circumstances, the conduct of the accused was to the prejudice of good order and discipline in the armed forces or was of a nature to bring discredit upon the armed forces.

c. *Explanation.*

(1) *Threat.* A "threat" means an expressed present determination or intent to kill, injure, or intimidate a person or to damage or destroy certain property presently or in the future. Proof that the accused actually intended to kill, injure, intimidate, damage, or destroy is not required.

(2) *Explosive.* "Explosive" means gunpowder, powders used for blasting, all forms of high explosives, blasting materials, fuses (other than electrical circuit breakers), detonators, and other detonating agents, smokeless powders, any explosive bomb, grenade, missile, or similar device, and any incendiary bomb or grenade, fire bomb, or similar device, and any other explosive compound, mixture, or similar material.

(3) *Weapon of mass destruction.* A weapon of mass destruction means any device, explosive or otherwise, that is intended, or has the capability, to cause death or serious bodily injury to a significant number of people through the release, dissemination, or impact of: toxic or poisonous chemicals, or their precursors; a disease organism; or radiation or radioactivity.

(4) *Biological agent.* The term "biological agent" means any micro-organism (including bacteria, viruses, fungi, rickettsiac, or protozoa), pathogen, or infectious substance, and any naturally occurring, bioengineered, or synthesized component of any such micro-organism, pathogen, or infectious substance, whatever its origin or method of production, that is capable of causing—

(a) death, disease, or other biological malfunction in a human, an animal, a plant, or another living organism;

(b) deterioration of food, water, equipment, supplies, or materials of any kind; or

(c) deleterious alteration of the environment.

(5) *Chemical agent, substance, or weapon.* A chemical agent, substance, or weapon refers to a toxic chemical and its precursors or a munition or device, specifically designed to cause death or other harm through toxic properties of those chemicals that would be released as a result of the employment of such munition or device, and any equipment specifically designed for use directly in connection with the employment of such munitions or devices.

(6) *Hazardous material.* A substance or material (including explosive, radioactive material, etiologic agent, flammable or combustible liquid or solid, poison, oxidizing or corrosive material, and compressed gas, or mixture thereof) or a group or class of material designated as hazardous by the Secretary of Transportation.

(7) *Malicious.* A communication is "malicious" if the accused believed that the information would probably interfere with the peaceful use of the building, vehicle, aircraft, or other property concerned, or would cause fear or concern to one or more persons.

d. *Lesser included offenses.*

(1) *Threat.*

(a) Article 134 — communicating a threat

(b) Article 80 — attempts

(c) Article 128 — assault

(2) *Hoax.* Article 80 — attempts

e. *Maximum punishment.* Dishonorable discharge, forfeitures of all pay and allowances, and confinement for 10 years.

f. *Sample specifications.*

(1) *Threat.*

In that ________ (personal jurisdiction data) did, (at/on board—location) on or about ________ 20 ____, wrongfully communicate certain information, to wit: ________, which language constituted a threat to harm a person or property by means of a(n) [explosive; weapon of mass destruction; biological agent, substance, or weapon; chemical agent, substance, or weapon; and/or (a) hazardous material(s)].

(2) *Hoax.*

In that ________ (personal jurisdiction data) did, (at/on board—location), on or about ________ 20 ____, maliciously (communicate) (convey) certain information concerning an attempt being made or to be made to unlawfully [(kill) (injure) (intimidate) ________] [(damage) (destroy) ________] by means of a(n) [explosive; weapon of mass destruction; biological agent, substance, or weapon; chemical agent, substance, or weapon; and/or (a) hazardous material(s)], to wit: ________, which information was false and which the accused then knew to be false."

Sec. 4. Part V of the Manual for Courts-Martial, United States, is amended as follows:

(a) Paragraph 1(h) is amended by redesignating existing paragraph 1(h) as 1(i) and inserting the following new paragraph 1(h): "h. Applicable standards. Unless otherwise provided, the service regulations and procedures of the servicemember shall apply."

(b) Paragraph 2(a) is amended by replacing the words "Unless otherwise" with the word "As".

(c) Paragraph 2(a) is amended by inserting the following after the second sentence: "Commander includes a commander of a joint command."

(d) Paragraph 2(a) is amended by inserting the words "of a commander" in the third sentence after the words "the authority."

Sec. 5. These amendments shall take effect 30 days from the date of this order.

(a) Nothing in these amendments shall be construed to make punishable any act done or omitted prior to the effective date of this order that was not punishable when done or omitted.

(b) Nothing in these amendments shall be construed to invalidate any nonjudicial punishment proceeding, restraint, investigation, referral of charges, trial in which arraignment occurred, or other action begun prior to the effective date of this order, and any such nonjudicial punishment proceeding, restraint, investigation, referral of charges, trial, or other action may proceed in the same manner and with the same effect as if these amendments had not been prescribed.

GEORGE W. BUSH
THE WHITE HOUSE,
October 14, 2005.

Executive Order 13430: 2007 Amendments to the Manual for Courts-Martial, United States

By the authority vested in me as President by the Constitution and the laws of the United States of America, including chapter 47 of title 10, United States Code (Uniform Code of Military Justice, 10 U.S.C. 801-946), and in order to prescribe amendments to the Manual for Courts-Martial, United States, prescribed by Executive Order 12473 of April 13, 1984, as amended, it is hereby ordered as follows:

Section 1. Part II of the Manual for Courts-Martial, United States, is amended as follows:

(a) R.C.M. 703(b)(1) is amended by adding at the end the following new sentences:

"With the consent of both the accused and Government, the military judge may authorize any witness to testify via remote means. Over a party's objection, the military judge may authorize any witness to testify on interlocutory questions via remote means or similar technology if the practical difficulties of producing the witness outweigh the significance of the witness' personal appearance (although such testimony will not be admissible over the accused's objection as evidence on the ultimate issue of guilt). Factors to be considered include, but are not limited to, the costs of producing the witness; the timing of the request for production of the witness; the potential delay in the interlocutory proceeding that may be caused by the production of the witness; the willingness of the witness to testify in person; the likelihood of significant interference with military operational deployment, mission accomplishment, or essential training; and, for child witnesses, the traumatic effect of providing in-court testimony."

(b) R.C.M. 804 is amended by redesignating paragraphs (b), (c), and (d) as paragraphs (c), (d), and (e), respectively, and inserting the following new paragraph (b):

"(b) Presence by remote means. If authorized by the regulations of the Secretary concerned, the military judge may order the use of audiovisual technology, such as videoteleconferencing technology, between the parties and the military judge for purposes of Article 39(a) sessions. Use of such audiovisual technology will satisfy the "presence" requirement of the accused only when the accused has a defense counsel physically present at his location. Such technology may include two or more remote sites as long as all parties can see and hear each other."

(c) R.C.M. 804(c)(2) is redesignated as R.C.M. 804(d)(2) and amended to read as follows:

"(2) Procedure. The accused's absence will be conditional upon his being able to view the witness' testimony from a remote location. Normally, transmission of the testimony will include a system that will transmit the accused's image and voice into the courtroom from a remote location as well as transmission of the child's testimony from the courtroom to the accused's location. A one-way transmission may be used if deemed necessary by the military judge. The accused will also be provided private, contemporaneous communication with his counsel. The procedures described herein shall be employed unless the accused has made a knowing and affirmative waiver of these procedures."

(d) R.C.M. 805(a) is amended by adding at the end the following new sentence:

"If authorized by regulations of the Secretary concerned, for purposes of Article 39(a) sessions solely, the presence of the military judge at Article 39(a) sessions may be satisfied by the use of audiovisual technology, such as videoteleconferencing technology."

(e) R.C.M. 805(c) is amended by adding at the end the following new sentences:

"If authorized by regulations of the Secretary concerned, for purposes of Article 39(a) sessions solely, the presence of counsel at Article 39(a) sessions may be satisfied by the use of audiovisual technology, such as videoteleconferencing technology. At least one qualified defense counsel shall be physically present with the accused."

(f) R.C.M. 914A is amended by deleting the third sentence of paragraph (a).

(g) R.C.M. 914A is further amended by redesignating paragraph (b) as paragraph (c) and inserting the following new paragraph (b):

"(b) Definition. As used in this rule, "remote live testimony" includes, but is not limited to, testimony by videoteleconference, closed circuit television, or similar technology."

(h) New Rule R.C.M. 914B is inserted after R.C.M. 914A:

"Rule 914B. Use of remote testimony.

(a) *General procedures.* The military judge shall determine the procedures used to take testimony via remote means. At a minimum, all parties shall be able to hear each other, those in attendance at the remote site shall be identified, and the accused shall be permitted private, contemporaneous communication with his counsel.

(b) *Definition.* As used in this rule, testimony via "remote means" includes, but is not limited to, testimony by videoteleconference, closed circuit television, telephone, or similar technology."

(i) R.C.M. 1001(e)(2)(D) is amended by deleting the "or" before "former testimony" and inserting ", or testimony by remote means" after "former testimony."

Sec. 2. Part IV of the Manual for Courts-Martial, United States, is amended as follows:

(a) Paragraph 4.c.(6) is amended by redesignating paragraph (f) as paragraph (g) and inserting the following new paragraph (f):

"(f) Article 119a attempting to kill an unborn child"

(b) Paragraph 12a is amended by replacing the word "Transportation" with the words "Homeland Security".

(c) Paragraph 35a is amended to read as follows:

"(a) Any person subject to this chapter who —

(1) operates or physically controls any vehicle, aircraft, or vessel in a reckless or wanton manner or while impaired by a substance described in section 912a(b) of this title (Article 112a(b)); or

(2) operates or is in actual physical control of any vehicle, aircraft, or vessel while drunk or when the alcohol concentration in the person's blood or breath is equal to or exceeds the applicable limit under subsection (b), shall be punished as a court-martial may direct.

(b)(1) For purposes of subsection (a), the applicable limit on the alcohol concentration in a person's blood or breath is as follows:

(A) In the case of the operation or control of a vehicle, aircraft, or vessel in the United States, such limit is the lesser of —

(i) the blood alcohol content limit under the law of the State in which the conduct occurred, except as may be provided under paragraph (2) for conduct on a military installation that is in more than one State; or

(ii) the blood alcohol content limit specified in paragraph (3).

(B) In the case of the operation or control of a vehicle, aircraft, or vessel outside the United States, the applicable blood alcohol content limit is the blood alcohol content limit specified in paragraph (3) or such lower limit as the Secretary of Defense may by regulation prescribe.

(2) In the case of a military installation that is in more than one State, if those States have different blood alcohol content limits under their respective State laws, the Secretary may select one such blood alcohol content limit to apply uniformly on that installation.

(3) For purposes of paragraph (1), the blood alcohol content limit with respect to alcohol concentration in a person's blood is 0.10 grams of alcohol per 100 milliliters of blood and with respect to alcohol concentration in a person's breath is 0.10 grams of alcohol per 210 liters of breath, as shown by chemical analysis.

(4) In this subsection:

(A) The term "blood alcohol content limit" means the amount of alcohol concentration in a person's blood or breath at which operation or control of a vehicle, aircraft, or vessel is prohibited.

(B) The term "United States" includes the District of Columbia, the Commonwealth of Puerto Rico, the Virgin Islands, Guam, and American Samoa and the term "State" includes each of those jurisdictions.

(d) Paragraph 35b(2)(c) is amended to read as follows:

"(c) the alcohol concentration in the accused's blood or breath equaled to or exceeded the applicable limit under subparagraph (b) of paragraph 35a. [NOTE: If injury resulted add the following element]"

(e) Para 35f is amended to read as follows:

"In that ______ (personal jurisdiction data), did (at/onboard location)(subject matter jurisdiction data, if required), on or about ______ 20 ___, (in the motor pool area)(near the Officer's Club)(at the intersection of ______ and ______)(while in the Gulf of Mexico)(while in flight over North America) physically control [a vehicle, to wit: (a truck)(a passenger car)(______)] [an aircraft, to wit: (an AH 64 helicopter)(an F 14 A fighter)(a KC 135 tanker)(______)][a vessel, to wit: (the aircraft carrier USS)(the Coast Cutter)(______)], [while drunk] [while impaired by ______][while the alcohol concentration in his (blood or breath equaled or exceeded the applicable limit under subparagraph (b) of paragraph 35a) as shown by chemical analysis][in a (reckless)(wanton) manner by (attempting to pass another vehicle on a sharp curve)(by ordering that the aircraft be flown below the authorized altitude)] [and did thereby cause said (vehicle)(aircraft)-(vessel) to (strike and)(injure ______)]."

(f) By inserting the new paragraph 44a:

"44a. Article 119a — Death or injury of an unborn child

a. *Text.*

(a)(1) Any person subject to this chapter who engages in conduct that violates any of the provisions of law listed in subsection (b) and thereby causes the death of, or bodily injury (as defined in section 1365 of title 18 to, a child who is in utero at the time the conduct takes place, is guilty of a separate offense under this section and shall, upon conviction, be punished by such punishment, other than death, as a court-martial may direct, which shall be consistent with the punishments prescribed by the President for that conduct had that injury or death occurred to the unborn child's mother.

(2) An offense under this section does not require proof that —

(i) the person engaging in the conduct had knowledge or should have had knowledge that the victim of the underlying offense was pregnant; or

(ii) the accused intended to cause the death of, or bodily injury to, the unborn child.

(3) If the person engaging in the conduct thereby intentionally kills or attempts to kill the unborn child, that person shall, instead of being punished under paragraph (1), be punished as provided under sections 880, 918, and 919(a) of this title (articles 80, 118, and 119(a)) for intentionally killing or attempting to kill a human being.

(4) Notwithstanding any other provision of law, the death penalty shall not be imposed for an offense under this section.

(b) The provisions referred to in subsection (a) are sections 918, 919(a), 919(b)(2), 920(a), 922, 924, 926, and 928 of this title (articles 118, 119(a), 119(b)(2), 120(a), 122, 124, 126, and 128).

(c) Nothing in this section shall be construed to permit the prosecution

(1) of any person authorized by state or federal law to perform abortions for conduct relating to an abortion for which the consent of the pregnant woman, or a person authorized by law to act on her behalf, has been obtained or for which such consent is implied by law;

(2) of any person for any medical treatment of the pregnant woman or her unborn child; or

(3) of any woman with respect to her unborn child.

(d) As used in this section, the term "unborn child" means a child in utero, and the term "child in utero" or "child who is in utero" means a member of the species homo sapiens, at any stage of development, who is carried in the womb.

b. *Elements.*

(1) Injuring an unborn child.

(a) That the accused was engaged in the [(murder (article 118)), (voluntary manslaughter (article 119(a))), (involuntary manslaughter (article 119(b)(2))), (rape (article 120)), (robbery (article 122)), (maiming (article 124)), (assault (article 128)), of] or [burning or setting afire, as arson (article 126), of (a dwelling inhabited by) (a structure or property (known to be occupied by) (belonging to))] a woman;

(b) That the woman was then pregnant; and

(c) That the accused thereby caused bodily injury to the unborn child of that woman.

(2) Killing an unborn child.

(a) That the accused was engaged in the [(murder (article 118)), (voluntary manslaughter (article 119(a))), (involuntary manslaughter (article 119(b)(2))), (rape (article 120)), (robbery (article 122)), (maiming (article 124)), (assault (article 128)), of] or [burning or setting afire, as arson (article 126), of (a dwelling inhabited by) (a structure or property known to (be occupied by) (belong to))] a woman;

(b) That the woman was then pregnant; and

(c) That the accused thereby caused the death of the unborn child of that woman.

(3) Attempting to kill an unborn child.

(a) That the accused was engaged in the [(murder (article 118)), (voluntary manslaughter (article 119(a))), (involuntary manslaughter (article 119(b)(2))), (rape (article 120)), (robbery (article 122)), (maiming (article 124)), (assault (article 128)), of] or [burning or setting afire, as arson (article 126), of (a dwelling inhabited by) (a structure or property (known to be occupied by) (belonging to))] a woman;

(b) That the woman was then pregnant; and

(c) That the accused thereby intended and attempted to kill the unborn child of that woman.

(4) Intentionally killing an unborn child.

(a) That the accused was engaged in the [(murder (article 118)), (voluntary manslaughter (article 119(a))), (involuntary manslaughter (article 119(b)(2))), (rape (article 120)), (robbery (article 122)), (maiming (article 124)), (assault (article 128)), of] or [burning or setting afire, as arson (article 126), of (a dwelling inhabited by) (a structure or property (known to be occupied by) (belonging to))] a woman;

(b) That the woman was then pregnant; and

(c) That the accused thereby intentionally killed the unborn child of that woman.

c. *Explanation.*

(1) Nature of offense. This article makes it a separate, punishable crime to cause the death of or bodily injury to an unborn child while engaged in arson (article 126, UCMJ); murder (article 118, UCMJ); voluntary manslaughter (article 119(a), UCMJ); involuntary manslaughter (article 119(b)(2), UCMJ); rape (article 120(a), UCMJ); robbery (article 122, UCMJ); maiming (article 124, UCMJ); or assault (article 128, UCMJ) against a pregnant woman. For all underlying offenses, except arson, this article requires that the victim of the underlying offense be the pregnant mother. For purposes of arson, the pregnant mother must have some nexus to the arson such that she sustained some "bodily injury" due to the arson. For the purposes of this article the term "woman" means a female of any age. This article does not permit the prosecution of any —

(a) person for conduct relating to an abortion for which the consent of the pregnant woman, or a person authorized by law to act on her behalf, has been obtained or for which such consent is implied by law;

(b) person for any medical treatment of the pregnant woman or her unborn child; or

(c) woman with respect to her unborn child.

(2) The offenses of "injuring an unborn child" and "killing an unborn child" do not require proof that —

(a) the person engaging in the conduct (the accused) had knowledge or should have had knowledge that the victim of the underlying offense was pregnant; or

(b) the accused intended to cause the death of, or bodily injury to, the unborn child.

(3) The offense of "attempting to kill an unborn child" requires that the accused intended by his conduct to cause the death of the unborn child (*See* paragraph b(3)(c) above).

(4) Bodily injury. For the purpose of this offense, the term "bodily injury" is that which is provided by section 1365 of title 18, to wit: a cut, abrasion, bruise, burn, or disfigurement; physical pain; illness; impairment of the function of a bodily member, organ, or mental faculty; or any other injury to the body, no matter how temporary.

(5) Unborn child. "Unborn child" means a child in utero or a member of the species homo sapiens who is carried in the womb, at any stage of development, from conception to birth.

d. *Lesser included offenses.*

(1) Killing an unborn child. Article 119a — injuring an unborn child

(2) Intentionally killing an unborn child.

(a) Article 119a — killing an unborn child

(b) Article 119a — injuring an unborn child

(c) Article 119a — attempts (attempting to kill an unborn child)

e. *Maximum punishment.* The maximum punishment for (1) Injuring an unborn child; (2) Killing an unborn child; (3) Attempting to kill an unborn child; or (4) Intentionally killing an unborn child is such punishment, other than death, as a court-martial may direct, but shall be consistent with the punishment had the bodily injury, death, attempt to kill, or intentional killing occurred to the unborn child's mother.

f. *Sample specifications.*

(1) *Injuring an unborn child.* In that ________ (personal jurisdiction data), did (at/on board—location), (subject-matter jurisdiction data, if required), on or about ________ 20 ___, cause bodily injury to the unborn child of , a pregnant woman, by engaging in the [(murder) (voluntary manslaughter) (involuntary manslaughter) (rape) (robbery) (maiming) (assault) of] [(burning) (setting afire) of (a dwelling inhabited by) (a structure or property known to (be occupied by) (belong to))] that woman.

(2) *Killing an unborn child.* In that (personal jurisdiction data), did (at/on board—location), (subject-matter jurisdiction data, if required), on or about 20 , cause the death of the unborn child of , a pregnant woman, by engaging in the [(murder) (voluntary manslaughter) (involuntary manslaughter) (rape) (robbery) (maiming) (assault) of] [(burning) (setting afire) of (a dwelling inhabited by) (a structure or property known to (be occupied by) (belong to))] that woman.

(3) *Attempting to kill an unborn child.* In that (personal jurisdiction data), did (at/on board—location), (subject-matter jurisdiction data, if required), on or about 20 , attempt to kill the unborn child of , a pregnant woman, by engaging in the [(murder) (voluntary manslaughter) (involuntary manslaughter) (rape) (robbery) (maiming) (assault) of] [(burning) (setting afire) of (a dwelling inhabited by) (a structure or property known to (be occupied by) (belong to))] that woman.

(4) *Intentionally killing an unborn child.* In that (personal jurisdiction data), did (at/on board—location), (subject-matter jurisdiction data, if required), on or about 20 , intentionally kill the unborn child of , a pregnant woman, by engaging in the [(murder) (voluntary manslaughter) (involuntary manslaughter) (rape) (robbery) (maiming) (assault) of] [(burning) (setting afire) of (a dwelling inhabited by) (a structure or property known to (be occupied by) (belong to))] that woman."

(g) By inserting the new paragraph 45a to read:
"45a. Article 120a Stalking

Text.

(a) Any person subject to this section:

(1) who wrongfully engages in a course of conduct directed at a specific person that would cause a reasonable person to fear death or bodily harm, including sexual assault, to himself or herself or a member of his or her immediate family;

(2) who has knowledge, or should have knowledge, that the specific person will be placed in reasonable fear of death or bodily harm, including sexual assault, to himself or herself or a member of his or her immediate family; and

(3) whose acts induce reasonable fear in the specific person of death or bodily harm, including sexual assault, to himself or herself or to a member of his or her immediate family; is guilty of stalking and shall be punished as a court-martial may direct.

(b) In this section:

(1) The term "course of conduct" means:

(A) a repeated maintenance of visual or physical proximity to a specific person; or

(B) a repeated conveyance of verbal threat, written threats, or threats implied by conduct, or a combination of such threats, directed at or towards a specific person.

(2) The term "repeated," with respect to conduct, means two or more occasions of such conduct.

(3) The term "immediate family," in the case of a specific person, means a spouse, parent, child, or sibling of the person, or any other family member, relative, or intimate partner of the person who regularly resides in the household of the person or who within the six months preceding the commencement of the course of conduct regularly resided in the household of the person.

b. *Elements.*

(1) That the accused wrongfully engaged in a course of conduct directed at a specific person that would cause a reasonable person to fear death or bodily harm to himself or herself or a member of his or her immediate family;

(2) That the accused had knowledge, or should have had knowledge, that the specific person would be placed in reasonable fear of death or bodily harm to himself or herself or a member of his or her immediate family; and

(3) That the accused's acts induced reasonable fear in the specific person of death or bodily harm to himself or herself or to a member of his or her immediate family.

c. *Explanation. See* Paragraph 54.c(1)(a) for an explanation of "bodily harm".

d. *Lesser included offenses.* Article 80 — attempts.

e. *Maximum punishment.* Dishonorable discharge, forfeiture of all pay and allowances, and confinement for 3 years.

f. *Sample Specification.* In that (personal jurisdiction data), who (knew)(should have known) that would be placed in reasonable fear of (death)(bodily harm) to (himself) (herself) (, a member of his or her immediate family) did (at/on board — location), (subject-matter jurisdiction data, if required), (on or about ________ 20 ____)(from about ________ to about ________ 20 ____), wrongfully engage in a course of conduct directed at ________, to wit: ________________ thereby inducing in ________, a reasonable fear of (death)(bodily harm) to (himself)(herself) (____, a member of his or her immediate family)."

Sec. 3. Part V of the Manual for Courts-Martial, United States, is amended as follows:

(a) Paragraph 5.c.(8) is amended by replacing the word "foreign" with the word "hardship."

(b) Paragraph 7(e) is amended by replacing the word "Transportation" with the words "Homeland Security".

Sec. 4. Part IV of the Manual for Courts-Martial, United States, is amended by replacing the word "Transportation" with the words "Homeland Security."

Sec. 5. These amendments shall take effect 30 days from the date of this order.

(a) Nothing in these amendments shall be construed to make punishable any act done or omitted prior to the effective date of this order that was not punishable when done or omitted.

(b) Nothing in these amendments shall be construed to invalidate any nonjudicial punishment proceedings, restraint, investigation, referral of charges, trial in which arraignment occurred, or other action begun prior to the effective date of this order, and any such nonjudicial punishment, restraint, investigation, referral of charges, trial, or other action may proceed in the same manner and with the same effect as if these amendments had not been prescribed.

GEORGE W. BUSH
THE WHITE HOUSE,
April 18, 2007.

Executive Order 13447: Further 2007 Amendments to the Manual for Courts Martial, United States

By the authority vested in me as President by the Constitution and the laws of the United States of America, including chapter 47 of title 10, United States Code (Uniform Code of Military Justice, 10 U.S.C. 801-946), and in order to prescribe amendments to the Manual for Courts-Martial, United States, prescribed by Executive Order 12473, as amended, it is hereby ordered as follows:

Section 1. The second subparagraph of paragraph 4, of Part I, of the Manual for Courts-Martial, United States, as amended by section 2 of Executive Order 13262 of April 11, 2002, is amended by striking the third sentence.

Sec. 2. Parts II, III, and IV of the Manual for Courts-Martial, United States, are amended as described in the Annex attached and made a part of this order.

Sec. 3. These amendments shall take effect on October 1, 2007.

(a) Nothing in these amendments shall be construed to make punishable any act done or omitted prior to October 1, 2007, that was not punishable when done or omitted.

(b) Nothing in these amendments shall be construed to invalidate any nonjudicial punishment proceedings, restraint, investigation, referral of charges, trial in which arraignment occurred, or other action begun prior to October 1, 2007, and any such nonjudicial punishment, restraint, investigation, referral of charges, trial, or other action may proceed in the same manner and with the same effect as if these amendments had not been prescribed.

GEORGE W. BUSH
THE WHITE HOUSE,
September 28, 2007.

ANNEX

Section 1. Part II of the Manual for Courts-Martial, United States, is amended as follows:

(a) R.C.M. 916(b) is amended to read as follows:

"(b) Burden of proof.

(1) *General rule.* Except as listed below in paragraphs (2), (3), and (4), the prosecution shall have the burden of proving beyond a reasonable doubt that the defense did not exist.

(2) *Lack of mental responsibility.* The accused has the burden of proving the defense of lack of mental responsibility by clear and convincing evidence.

(3) *Mistake of fact as to age.* In the defense of mistake of fact as to age as described in Part IV, para. 45a(o)(2) in a prosecution of a sexual offense with a child under Article 120, the accused has the burden of proving mistake of fact as to age by a preponderance of the evidence. After the accused meets his or her burden, the prosecution shall have the burden of proving beyond a reasonable doubt that the defense did not exist.

(4) *Mistake of fact as to consent.* In the defense of mistake of fact as to consent in Article 120(a), rape, Article 120(c), aggravated sexual assault, Article 120(e), aggravated sexual contact, and Article 120(h), abusive sexual contact, the accused has the burden of proving mistake of fact as to consent by a preponderance of the evidence. After the defense meets its burden, the prosecution shall have the burden of proving beyond a reasonable doubt that the defense did not exist."

(b) R.C.M. 916(j)(2) is amended to read as follows:

"(2) Child Sexual Offenses. It is a defense to a prosecution for Article 120(d), aggravated sexual assault of a child, Article 120(f), aggravated sexual abuse of a child, Article 120(i), abusive sexual contact with a child, or Article 120(j), indecent liberty with a child that, at the time of the offense, the child was at least 12 years of age, and the accused reasonably believed the person was at least 16 years of age. The accused must prove this defense by a preponderance of the evidence."

(c) R.C.M. 916(j) is amended by inserting new paragraph R.C.M. 916(j)(3) after the Discussion section to R.C.M. 916(j)(2) as follows:

"(j)(3) Sexual offenses. It is an affirmative defense to a prosecution for Article 120(a), rape, Article 120(c), aggravated sexual assault, Article 120(e), aggravated sexual contact, and Article 120(h), abusive sexual contact that the accused held, as a result of ignorance or mistake, an incorrect belief that the other person engaging in the sexual conduct consented. The ignorance or mistake must have existed in the mind of the accused and must have been reasonable under all the circumstances. To be reasonable the ignorance or mistake must have been based on information, or lack of it, which would indicate to a reasonable person that the other person consented. Additionally, the ignorance or mistake cannot be based on the negligent failure to discover the true facts. Negligence is the absence of due care. Due care is what a reasonably careful person would do under the same or similar circumstances. The accused's state of intoxication, if any, at the time of the offense is not relevant to mistake of fact. A mistaken belief that the other person consented must be that which a reasonably careful, ordinary, prudent, sober adult would have had under the circumstances at the time of the offense."

(d) R.C.M. 920(e)(5)(D) is amended to read as follows:

"(D) The burden of proof to establish the guilt of the accused is upon the Government. [When the issue of lack of mental responsibility is raised, add: The burden of proving the defense of lack of mental responsibility by clear and convincing evidence is upon the accused. When the issue of mistake of fact under R.C.M. 916(j)(2) or (j)(3) is raised, add: The accused has the burden of proving the defense of mistake of fact as to consent or age by a preponderance of the evidence.]"

(e) R.C.M. 1004(c)(7)(B) is amended to read as follows:

"(B) The murder was committed: while the accused was engaged in the commission or attempted commission of any robbery, rape, rape of a child, aggravated sexual assault, aggravated sexual assault of a child, aggravated sexual contact, aggravated sexual abuse of a child, aggravated sexual contact with a child, aggravated arson, sodomy, burglary, kidnapping, mutiny, sedition, or piracy of an aircraft or vessel; or while the accused was engaged in the commission or attempted commission of any offense involving the wrongful distribution, manufacture, or introduction or possession, with intent to distribute, of a controlled substance; or, while the accused was engaged in flight or attempted flight after the commission or attempted commission of any such offense."

(f) R.C.M. 1004(c)(8) is amended to read as follows:

"(8) That only in the case of a violation of Article 118(4), the accused was the actual perpetrator of the killing or was a principal whose participation in the burglary, sodomy, rape, rape of a child, aggravated sexual assault, aggravated sexual assault of a child, aggravated sexual contact, aggravated sexual abuse of a child, aggravated sexual contact with a child, robbery, or aggravated arson was major and who manifested a reckless indifference for human life."

(g) R.C.M. 1102(b)(2) is amended to read as follows:

"(2) Article 39(a) sessions. An Article 39(a) session under this rule may be called, upon motion of either party or *sua sponte* by the military judge, for the purpose of inquiring into, and, when appropriate, resolving any matter that arises after trial and that substantially affects the legal sufficiency of any findings of guilty or the sentence. The military judge may also call an Article 39(a) session, upon motion of either party or *sua sponte*, to reconsider any trial ruling that substantially affects the legal sufficiency of any findings of guilty or the sentence. The military judge may, *sua sponte*, at any time prior to authentication of the record of trial, enter a finding of not guilty of one or more offenses charged, or may enter a finding of not guilty of a part of a specification as long as a lesser offense charged is alleged in the remaining portion of the specification. Prior to entering such a finding or findings, the military judge shall give each party an opportunity to be heard on the matter in a post-trial Article 39(a) session."

(h) R.C.M. 1102(d) is amended by deleting the last phrase of the second sentence, which reads:

", except that no proceeding in revision may be held when any part of the sentence has been ordered executed".

(i) R.C.M. 1102(e)(2) is amended by inserting the following sentence after the last sentence in R.C.M. 1102(e)(2):

"Prior to the military judge *sua sponte* entering a finding of not guilty of one or more offenses charged or entering a finding of not guilty of a part of a specification as long as a lesser offense charged is alleged in the remaining portion of the specification, the military judge shall give each party an opportunity to be heard on the matter."

(j) R.C.M. 1204(c)(2) is amended to read as follows:

"(2) Sentence requiring approval of the President. (A) If the Court of Appeals for the Armed Forces has affirmed a sentence that must be approved by the President before it may be executed, the Judge Advocate General shall transmit the record of trial, the decision of the Court of Criminal Appeals, the decision of the Court of Appeals for the Armed Forces, and the recommendation of the Judge Advocate General to the Secretary concerned.

(B) If the Secretary concerned is the Secretary of a military department, the Secretary concerned shall forward the material received under paragraph (A) to the Secretary of Defense, together with the recommendation of the Secretary concerned. The Secretary of Defense shall forward the material, with the recommendation of the Secretary concerned and the recommendation of the Secretary of Defense, to the President for the action of the President.

(C) If the Secretary concerned is the Secretary of Homeland Security, the Secretary concerned shall forward the material received under paragraph (A) to the President, together with the recommendation of the Secretary concerned, for the action of the President."

Sec. 2. Part III of the Manual for Courts-Martial, United States, is amended as follows:

(a) Mil. R. Evid. 412 is amended to read as follows:

"**Rule 412. Sex offense cases; relevance of alleged victim's sexual behavior or sexual predisposition**

(a) *Evidence generally inadmissible.* The following evidence is not admissible in any proceeding involving an alleged sexual offense except as provided in subdivisions (b) and (c):

(1) Evidence offered to prove that any alleged victim engaged in other sexual behavior.

(2) Evidence offered to prove any alleged victim's sexual predisposition.

(b) *Exceptions.*

(1) In a proceeding, the following evidence is admissible, if otherwise admissible under these rules:

(A) evidence of specific instances of sexual behavior by the alleged victim offered to prove that a person other than the accused was the source of semen, injury, or other physical evidence;

(B) evidence of specific instances of sexual behavior by the alleged victim with respect to the person accused of the sexual misconduct offered by the accused to prove consent or by the prosecution; and

(C) evidence the exclusion of which would violate the constitutional rights of the accused.

(c) *Procedure to determine admissibility.*

(1) A party intending to offer evidence under subsection (b) must —

(A) file a written motion at least 5 days prior to entry of pleas specifically describing the evidence and stating the purpose for which it is offered unless the military judge, for good cause shown, requires a different time for filing or permits filing during trial; and

(B) serve the motion on the opposing party and the military judge and notify the alleged victim or, when appropriate, the alleged victim's guardian or representative.

(2) Before admitting evidence under this rule, the military judge must conduct a hearing, which shall be closed. At this hearing, the parties may call witnesses, including the alleged victim, and offer relevant evidence. The alleged victim must be afforded a reasonable opportunity to attend and be heard. In a case before a court-martial composed of a military judge and members, the military judge shall conduct the hearing outside the presence of the members pursuant to Article 39(a). The motion, related papers, and the record of the hearing must be sealed and remain under seal unless the court orders otherwise.

(3) If the military judge determines on the basis of the hearing described in paragraph (2) of this subsection that the evidence that the accused seeks to offer is relevant for a purpose under subsection (b) and that the probative value of such evidence outweighs the danger of unfair prejudice to the alleged victim's privacy, such evidence shall be admissible under this rule to the extent an order made by the military judge specifies evidence that may be offered and areas with respect to which the alleged victim may be examined or cross-examined. Such evidence is still subject to challenge under Mil. R. Evid. 403.

(d) For purposes of this rule, the term "sexual offense" includes any sexual misconduct punishable under the Uniform Code of Military Justice, federal law, or state law. "Sexual behavior" includes any sexual behavior not encompassed by the alleged offense. The term "sexual predisposition" refers to an alleged victim's mode of dress, speech, or lifestyle that does not directly refer to sexual activities or thoughts but that may have a sexual connotation for the factfinder."

(b) Mil. R. Evid. 503(b) is amended by renumbering the existing subsection (2) as subsection (3) and inserting the following new subsection (2) after current Mil. R. Evid. 503(b)(1) to read as follows:

"(2) A "clergyman's assistant" is a person employed by or assigned to assist a clergyman in his capacity as a spiritual advisor."

(c) Mil. R. Evid. 504 is amended by inserting new subsection (d) after Mil. R. Evid. 504(c) to read as follows:

"(d) Definitions. As used in this rule:

(1) The term "a child of either" includes not only a biological child, adopted child, or ward of one of the spouses but also includes a child who is under the permanent or temporary physical custody of one of the spouses, regardless of the existence of a legal parent-child relationship. For purposes of this rule only, a child is: (i) an individual under the age of 18; or (ii) an individual with a mental handicap who functions under the age of 18.

(2) The term "temporary physical custody" includes instances where a parent entrusts his or her child with another. There is no minimum amount of time necessary to establish temporary physical custody nor must there be a written agreement. Rather, the focus is on the parent's agreement with another for assuming parental responsibility for the child. For example, temporary physical custody may include instances where a parent entrusts another with the care of their child for recurring care or during absences due to temporary duty or deployments."

Sec. 3. Part IV of the Manual for Courts-Martial, United States, is amended as follows:

(a) Paragraph 43, Article 118, Murder, paragraph a.(4) is amended to read as follows:

"(4) is engaged in the perpetration or attempted perpetration of burglary, sodomy, rape, rape of a child, aggravated sexual assault, aggravated sexual assault of a child, aggravated sexual contact, aggravated sexual abuse of a child, aggravated sexual contact with a child, robbery or aggravated arson; is guilty of murder, and shall suffer such punishment as a court-martial may direct, except that if found guilty under clause (1) or (4), he shall suffer death or imprisonment for life as a court-martial may direct."

(b) Paragraph 43, Article 118, Murder, paragraph b.(4)(d) is amended to read as follows:

"(d) That, at the time of the killing, the accused was engaged in the perpetration or attempted perpetration of burglary, sodomy, rape, rape of a child, aggravated sexual assault, aggravated sexual assault of a child, aggravated sexual contact, aggravated sexual abuse of a child, aggravated sexual contact with a child, robbery, or aggravated arson."

(c) Paragraph 44, Article 119, Manslaughter, paragraph b.(2)(d) is amended to read as follows:

"(d) That this act or omission of the accused constituted culpable negligence, or occurred while the accused was perpetrating or attempting to perpetrate an offense directly affecting the person other than burglary, sodomy, rape, rape of a child, aggravated sexual assault, aggravated sexual assault of a child, aggravated sexual contact, aggravated sexual abuse of a child, aggravated sexual contact with a child, robbery, or aggravated arson."

(d) Paragraph 45, Rape and Carnal Knowledge is amended to read as follows:

"45. Article 120 — Rape, sexual assault, and other sexual misconduct

a. *Text.*

"(a) *Rape.* Any person subject to this chapter who causes another person of any age to engage in a sexual act by —

(1) using force against that other person;

(2) causing grievous bodily harm to any person;

(3) threatening or placing that other person in fear that any person will be subjected to death, grievous bodily harm, or kidnapping;

(4) rendering another person unconscious; or

(5) administering to another person by force or threat of force, or without the knowledge or permission of that person, a drug, intoxicant, or other similar substance and thereby substantially impairs the ability of that other person to appraise or control conduct; is guilty of rape and shall be punished as a court-martial may direct.

(b) *Rape of a child.* Any person subject to this chapter who —

(1) engages in a sexual act with a child who has not attained the age of 12 years; or

(2) engages in a sexual act under the circumstances described in subsection (a) with a child who has attained the age of 12 years; is guilty of rape of a child and shall be punished as a court-martial may direct.

(c) *Aggravated sexual assault.* Any person subject to this chapter who —

(1) causes another person of any age to engage in a sexual act by —

(A) threatening or placing that other person in fear (other than by threatening or placing that other person in fear that any person will be subjected to death, grievous bodily harm, or kidnapping); or

(B) causing bodily harm; or

(2) engages in a sexual act with another person of any age if that other person is substantially incapacitated or substantially incapable of —

(A) appraising the nature of the sexual act;

(B) declining participation in the sexual act; or

(C) communicating unwillingness to engage in the sexual act; is guilty of aggravated sexual assault and shall be punished as a court-martial may direct.

(d) *Aggravated sexual assault of a child.* Any person subject to this chapter who engages in a sexual act with a child who has attained the age of 12 years is guilty of aggravated sexual assault of a child and shall be punished as a court-martial may direct.

(e) *Aggravated sexual contact.* Any person subject to this chapter who engages in or causes sexual contact with or by another person, if to do so would violate subsection (a) (rape) had the sexual contact been a sexual act, is guilty of aggravated sexual contact and shall be punished as a court-martial may direct.

(f) *Aggravated sexual abuse of a child.* Any person subject to this chapter who engages in a lewd act with a child is guilty of aggravated sexual abuse of a child and shall be punished as a court-martial may direct.

(g) *Aggravated sexual contact with a child.* Any

person subject to this chapter who engages in or causes sexual contact with or by another person, if to do so would violate subsection (b) (rape of a child) had the sexual contact been a sexual act, is guilty of aggravated sexual contact with a child and shall be punished as a court-martial may direct.

(h) *Abusive sexual contact.* Any person subject to this chapter who engages in or causes sexual contact with or by another person, if to do so would violate subsection (c) (aggravated sexual assault) had the sexual contact been a sexual act, is guilty of abusive sexual contact and shall be punished as a court-martial may direct.

(i) *Abusive sexual contact with a child.* Any person subject to this chapter who engages in or causes sexual contact with or by another person, if to do so would violate subsection (d) (aggravated sexual assault of a child) had the sexual contact been a sexual act, is guilty of abusive sexual contact with a child and shall be punished as a court-martial may direct.

(j) *Indecent liberty with a child.* Any person subject to this chapter who engages in indecent liberty in the physical presence of a child —

(1) with the intent to arouse, appeal to, or gratify the sexual desire of any person; or

(2) with the intent to abuse, humiliate, or degrade any person; is guilty of indecent liberty with a child and shall be punished as a court-martial may direct.

(k) *Indecent act.* Any person subject to this chapter who engages in indecent conduct is guilty of an indecent act and shall be punished as a court-martial may direct.

(l) *Forcible pandering.* Any person subject to this chapter who compels another person to engage in an act of prostitution with another person to be directed to said person is guilty of forcible pandering and shall be punished as a court-martial may direct.

(m) *Wrongful sexual contact.* Any person subject to this chapter who, without legal justification or lawful authorization, engages in sexual contact with another person without that other person's permission is guilty of wrongful sexual contact and shall be punished as a court-martial may direct.

(n) *Indecent exposure.* Any person subject to this chapter who intentionally exposes, in an indecent manner, in any place where the conduct involved may reasonably be expected to be viewed by people other than members of the actor's family or household, the genitalia, anus, buttocks, or female areola or nipple is guilty of indecent exposure and shall be punished as a court-martial may direct.

(o) *Age of child.*

(1) *Twelve years.* In a prosecution under subsection (b) (rape of a child), subsection (g) (aggravated sexual contact with a child), or subsection (j) (indecent liberty with a child), it need not be proven that the accused knew that the other person engaging in the sexual act, contact, or liberty had not attained the age of 12 years. It is not an affirmative defense that the accused reasonably believed that the child had attained the age of 12 years.

(2) *Sixteen years.* In a prosecution under subsection (d) (aggravated sexual assault of a child), subsection (f) (aggravated sexual abuse of a child), subsection (i) (abusive sexual contact with a child), or subsection (j) (indecent liberty with a child), it need not be proven that the accused knew that the other person engaging in the sexual act, contact, or liberty had not attained the age of 16 years. Unlike in paragraph (1), however, it is an affirmative defense that the accused reasonably believed that the child had attained the age of 16 years.

(p) *Proof of threat.* In a prosecution under this section, in proving that the accused made a threat, it need not be proven that the accused actually intended to carry out the threat.

(q) *Marriage.*

(1) *In general.* In a prosecution under paragraph (2) of subsection (c) (aggravated sexual assault), or under subsection (d) (aggravated sexual assault of a child), subsection (f) (aggravated sexual abuse of a child), subsection (i) (abusive sexual contact with a child), subsection (j) (indecent liberty with a child), subsection (m) (wrongful sexual contact), or subsection (n) (indecent exposure), it is an affirmative defense that the accused and the other person when they engaged in the sexual act, sexual contact, or sexual conduct were married to each other.

(2) *Definition.* For purposes of this subsection, a marriage is a relationship, recognized by the laws of a competent State or foreign jurisdiction, between the accused and the other person as spouses. A marriage exists until it is dissolved in accordance with the laws of a competent State or foreign jurisdiction.

(3) *Exception.* Paragraph (1) shall not apply if

the accused's intent at the time of the sexual conduct is to abuse, humiliate, or degrade any person.

(r) *Consent and mistake of fact as to consent.* Lack of permission is an element of the offense in subsection (m) (wrongful sexual contact). Consent and mistake of fact as to consent are not an issue, or an affirmative defense, in a prosecution under any other subsection, except they are an affirmative defense for the sexual conduct in issue in a prosecution under subsection (a) (rape), subsection (c) (aggravated sexual assault), subsection (e) (aggravated sexual contact), and subsection (h) (abusive sexual contact).

(s) *Other affirmative defenses not precluded.* The enumeration in this section of some affirmative defenses shall not be construed as excluding the existence of others.

(t) *Definitions.* In this section:

(1) *Sexual act.* The term "sexual act" means —

(A) contact between the penis and the vulva, and for purposes of this subparagraph contact involving the penis occurs upon penetration, however slight; or

(B) the penetration, however slight, of the genital opening of another by a hand or finger or by any object, with an intent to abuse, humiliate, harass, or degrade any person or to arouse or gratify the sexual desire of any person.

(2) *Sexual contact.* The term "sexual contact" means the intentional touching, either directly or through the clothing, of the genitalia, anus, groin, breast, inner thigh, or buttocks of another person, or intentionally causing another person to touch, either directly or through the clothing, the genitalia, anus, groin, breast, inner thigh, or buttocks of any person, with an intent to abuse, humiliate, or degrade any person or to arouse or gratify the sexual desire of any person.

(3) *Grievous bodily harm.* The term "grievous bodily harm" means serious bodily injury. It includes fractured or dislocated bones, deep cuts, torn members of the body, serious damage to internal organs, and other severe bodily injuries. It does not include minor injuries such as a black eye or a bloody nose. It is the same level of injury as in section 928 (article 128) of this chapter, and a lesser degree of injury than in section 2246(4) of title 18.

(4) *Dangerous weapon or object.* The term "dangerous weapon or object" means —

(A) any firearm, loaded or not, and whether operable or not;

(B) any other weapon, device, instrument, material, or substance, whether animate or inanimate, that in the manner it is used, or is intended to be used, is known to be capable of producing death or grievous bodily harm; or

(C) any object fashioned or utilized in such a manner as to lead the victim under the circumstances to reasonably believe it to be capable of producing death or grievous bodily harm.

(5) *Force.* The term "force" means action to compel submission of another or to overcome or prevent another's resistance by —

(A) the use or display of a dangerous weapon or object;

(B) the suggestion of possession of a dangerous weapon or object that is used in a manner to cause another to believe it is a dangerous weapon or object; or

(C) physical violence, strength, power, or restraint applied to another person, sufficient that the other person could not avoid or escape the sexual conduct.

(6) *Threatening or placing that other person in fear.* The term "threatening or placing that other person in fear" under paragraph (3) of subsection (a) (rape), or under subsection (e) (aggravated sexual contact), means a communication or action that is of sufficient consequence to cause a reasonable fear that non-compliance will result in the victim or another person being subjected to death, grievous bodily harm, or kidnapping.

(7) Threatening or placing that other person in fear.

(A) *In general.* The term "threatening or placing that other person in fear" under paragraph (1)(A) of subsection (c) (aggravated sexual assault), or under subsection (h) (abusive sexual contact), means a communication or action that is of sufficient consequence to cause a reasonable fear that non-compliance will result in the victim or another being subjected to a lesser degree of harm than death, grievous bodily harm, or kidnapping.

(B) *Inclusions.* Such lesser degree of harm includes —

(i) physical injury to another person or to another person's property; or

(ii) a threat —

(I) to accuse any person of a crime;

(II) to expose a secret or publicize an asserted fact, whether true or false, tending to subject some person to hatred, contempt, or ridicule; or

(III) through the use or abuse of military position, rank, or authority, to affect or threaten to affect, either positively or negatively, the military career of some person.

(8) *Bodily harm.* The term "bodily harm" means any offensive touching of another, however slight.

(9) *Child.* The term "child" means any person who has not attained the age of 16 years.

(10) *Lewd act.* The term "lewd act" means —

(A) the intentional touching, not through the clothing, of the genitalia of another person, with an intent to abuse, humiliate, or degrade any person, or to arouse or gratify the sexual desire of any person; or

(B) intentionally causing another person to touch, not through the clothing, the genitalia of any person with an intent to abuse, humiliate or degrade any person, or to arouse or gratify the sexual desire of any person.

(11) *Indecent liberty.* The term "indecent liberty" means indecent conduct, but physical contact is not required. It includes one who with the requisite intent exposes one's genitalia, anus, buttocks, or female areola or nipple to a child. An indecent liberty may consist of communication of indecent language as long as the communication is made in the physical presence of the child. If words designed to excite sexual desire are spoken to a child, or a child is exposed to or involved in sexual conduct, it is an indecent liberty; the child's consent is not relevant.

(12) *Indecent conduct.* The term "indecent conduct" means that form of immorality relating to sexual impurity that is grossly vulgar, obscene, and repugnant to common propriety, and tends to excite sexual desire or deprave morals with respect to sexual relations. Indecent conduct includes observing, or making a videotape, photograph, motion picture, print, negative, slide, or other mechanically, electronically, or chemically reproduced visual material, without another person's consent, and contrary to that other person's reasonable expectation of privacy, of —

(A) that other person's genitalia, anus, or buttocks, or (if that other person is female) that person's areola or nipple; or

(B) that other person while that other person is engaged in a sexual act, sodomy (under section 925 (article 125) of this chapter), or sexual contact.

(13) *Act of prostitution.* The term "act of prostitution" means a sexual act, sexual contact, or lewd act for the purpose of receiving money or other compensation.

(14) *Consent.* The term "consent" means words or overt acts indicating a freely given agreement to the sexual conduct at issue by a competent person. An expression of lack of consent through words or conduct means there is no consent. Lack of verbal or physical resistance or submission resulting from the accused's use of force, threat of force, or placing another person in fear does not constitute consent. A current or previous dating relationship by itself or the manner of dress of the person involved with the accused in the sexual conduct at issue shall not constitute consent. A person cannot consent to sexual activity if —

(A) under 16 years of age; or

(B) substantially incapable of —

(i) appraising the nature of the sexual conduct at issue due to —

(I) mental impairment or unconsciousness resulting from consumption of alcohol, drugs, a similar substance, or otherwise; or

(II) mental disease or defect that renders the person unable to understand the nature of the sexual conduct at issue;

(ii) physically declining participation in the sexual conduct at issue; or

(iii) physically communicating unwillingness to engage in the sexual conduct at issue.

(15) *Mistake of fact as to consent.* The term "mistake of fact as to consent" means the accused held, as a result of ignorance or mistake, an incorrect belief that the other person engaging in the sexual conduct consented. The ignorance or mistake must have existed in the mind of the accused and must have been reasonable under all the circumstances. To be reasonable, the ignorance or mistake must have been based on information, or lack of it, that would indicate to a reasonable person that the other person consented. Additionally, the ignorance or mistake cannot be based on the negligent failure

to discover the true facts. Negligence is the absence of due care. Due care is what a reasonably careful person would do under the same or similar circumstances. The accused's state of intoxication, if any, at the time of the offense is not relevant to mistake of fact. A mistaken belief that the other person consented must be that which a reasonably careful, ordinary, prudent, sober adult would have had under the circumstances at the time of the offense.

(16) *Affirmative defense.* The term "affirmative defense" means any special defense that, although not denying that the accused committed the objective acts constituting the offense charged, denies, wholly, or partially, criminal responsibility for those acts. The accused has the burden of proving the affirmative defense by a preponderance of evidence. After the defense meets this burden, the prosecution shall have the burden of proving beyond a reasonable doubt that the affirmative defense did not exist."

b *Elements.*

(1) *Rape.*

(a) Rape by using force.

(i) That the accused caused another person, who is of any age, to engage in a sexual act by using force against that other person.

(b) Rape by causing grievous bodily harm.

(i) That the accused caused another person, who is of any age, to engage in a sexual act by causing grievous bodily harm to any person.

(c) Rape by using threats or placing in fear.

(i) That the accused caused another person, who is of any age, to engage in a sexual act by threatening or placing that other person in fear that any person will be subjected to death, grievous bodily harm, or kidnapping.

(d) Rape by rendering another unconscious.

(i) That the accused caused another person, who is of any age, to engage in a sexual act by rendering that other person unconscious.

(e) Rape by administration of drug, intoxicant, or other similar substance.

(i) That the accused caused another person, who is of any age, to engage in a sexual act by administering to that other person a drug, intoxicant, or other similar substance;

(ii) That the accused administered the drug, intoxicant or other similar substance by force or threat of force or without the knowledge or permission of that other person; and

(iii) That, as a result, that other person's ability to appraise or control conduct was substantially impaired.

(2) *Rape of a child.*

(a) Rape of a child who has not attained the age of 12 years.

(i) That the accused engaged in a sexual act with a child; and

(ii) That at the time of the sexual act the child had not attained the age of 12 years.

(b) Rape of a child who has attained the age of 12 years but has not attained the age of 16 years by using force.

(i) That the accused engaged in a sexual act with a child;

(ii) That at the time of the sexual act the child had attained the age of 12 years but had not attained the age of 16 years; and

(iii) That the accused did so by using force against that child.

(c) Rape of a child who has attained the age of 12 years but has not attained the age of 16 years by causing grievous bodily harm.

(i) That the accused engaged in a sexual act with a child;

(ii) That at the time of the sexual act the child had attained the age of 12 years but had not attained the age of 16 years; and

(iii) That the accused did so by causing grievous bodily harm to any person.

(d) Rape of a child who has attained the age of 12 years but has not attained the age of 16 years by using threats or placing in fear.

(i) That the accused engaged in a sexual act with a child;

(ii) That at the time of the sexual act the child had attained the age of 12 years but had not attained the age of 16 years; and

(iii) That the accused did so by threatening or placing that child in fear that any person will be subjected to death, grievous bodily harm, or kidnapping.

(e) Rape of a child who has attained the age of 12 years but has not attained the age of 16 years by rendering that child unconscious.

(i) That the accused engaged in a sexual act with a child;

(ii) That at the time of the sexual act the child had attained the age of 12 years but had not attained the age of 16 years; and

(iii) That the accused did so by rendering that child unconscious.

(f) Rape of a child who has attained the age of 12 years but has not attained the age of 16 years by administration of drug, intoxicant, or other similar substance.

(i) That the accused engaged in a sexual act with a child;

(ii) That at the time of the sexual act the child had attained the age of 12 years but had not attained the age of 16 years; and

(iii)(a) That the accused did so by administering to that child a drug, intoxicant, or other similar substance;

(b) That the accused administered the drug, intoxicant, or other similar substance by force or threat of force or without the knowledge or permission of that child; and

(c) That, as a result, that child's ability to appraise or control conduct was substantially impaired.

(3) *Aggravated sexual assault.*

(a) Aggravated sexual assault by using threats or placing in fear.

(i) That the accused caused another person, who is of any age, to engage in a sexual act; and

(ii) That the accused did so by threatening or placing that other person in fear that any person would be subjected to bodily harm or other harm (other than by threatening or placing that other person in fear that any person would be subjected to death, grievous bodily harm, or kidnapping).

(b) Aggravated sexual assault by causing bodily harm.

(i) That the accused caused another person, who is of any age, to engage in a sexual act; and

(ii) That the accused did so by causing bodily harm to another person.

(c) Aggravated sexual assault upon a person substantially incapacitated or substantially incapable of appraising the act, declining participation, or communicating unwillingness.

(i) That the accused engaged in a sexual act with another person, who is of any age; and (Note: add one of the following elements)

(ii) That the other person was substantially incapacitated;

(iii) That the other person was substantially incapable of appraising the nature of the sexual act;

(iv) That the other person was substantially incapable of declining participation in the sexual act; or

(v) That the other person was substantially incapable of communicating unwillingness to engage in the sexual act.

(4) *Aggravated sexual assault of a child who has attained the age of 12 years but has not attained the age of 16 years.*

(a) That the accused engaged in a sexual act with a child; and

(b) That at the time of the sexual act the child had attained the age of 12 years but had not attained the age of 16 years.

(5) *Aggravated sexual contact.*

(a) Aggravated sexual contact by using force.

(i)(a) That the accused engaged in sexual contact with another person; or

(b) That the accused caused sexual contact with or by another person; and

(ii) That the accused did so by using force against that other person.

(b) Aggravated sexual contact by causing grievous bodily harm.

(i)(a) That the accused engaged in sexual contact with another person; or

(b) That the accused caused sexual contact with or by another person; and

(ii) That the accused did so by causing grievous bodily harm to any person.

(c) Aggravated sexual contact by using threats or placing in fear.

(i)(a) That the accused engaged in sexual contact with another person; or

(b) That the accused caused sexual contact with or by another person; and

(ii) That the accused did so by threatening or placing that other person in fear that any person will be subjected to death, grievous bodily harm, or kidnapping.

(d) Aggravated sexual contact by rendering another unconscious.

(i)(a) That the accused engaged in sexual contact with another person; or

(b) That the accused caused sexual contact with or by another person; and

(ii) That the accused did so by rendering that other person unconscious.

(e) Aggravated sexual contact by administration of drug, intoxicant, or other similar substance.

(i)(a) That the accused engaged in sexual contact with another person; or

(b) That the accused caused sexual contact with or by another person; and

(ii)(a) That the accused did so by administering to that other person a drug, intoxicant, or other similar substance;

(b) That the accused administered the drug, intoxicant, or other similar substance by force or threat of force or without the knowledge or permission of that other person; and

(c) That, as a result, that other person's ability to appraise or control conduct was substantially impaired.

(6) *Aggravated sexual abuse of a child.*

(a) That the accused engaged in a lewd act; and

(b) That the act was committed with a child who has not attained the age of 16 years.

(7) *Aggravated Sexual Contact with a Child.*

(a) Aggravated sexual contact with a child who has not attained the age of 12 years.

(i)(a) That the accused engaged in sexual contact with a child; or

(b) That the accused caused sexual contact with or by a child or by another person with a child; and

(ii) That at the time of the sexual contact the child had not attained the age of 12 years.

(b) Aggravated sexual contact with a child who has attained the age of 12 years but has not attained the age of 16 years by using force.

(i)(a) That the accused engaged in sexual contact with a child; or

(b) That the accused caused sexual contact with or by a child or by another person with a child; and

(ii) That at the time of the sexual contact the child had attained the age of 12 years but had not attained the age of 16 years; and

(iii) That the accused did so by using force against that child.

(c) Aggravated sexual contact with a child who has attained the age of 12 years but has not attained the age of 16 years by causing grievous bodily harm.

(i)(a) That the accused engaged in sexual contact with a child; or

(b) That the accused caused sexual contact with or by a child or by another person with a child; and

(ii) That at the time of the sexual contact the child had attained the age of 12 years but had not attained the age of 16 years; and

(iii) That the accused did so by causing grievous bodily harm to any person.

(d) Aggravated sexual contact with a child who has attained the age of 12 years but has not attained the age of 16 years by using threats or placing in fear.

(i)(a) That the accused engaged in sexual contact with a child; or

(b) That the accused caused sexual contact with or by a child or by another person with a child; and

(ii) That at the time of the sexual contact the child had attained the age of 12 years but had not attained the age of 16 years; and

(iii) That the accused did so by threatening or placing that child or that other person in fear that any person will be subjected to death, grievous bodily harm, or kidnapping.

(e) Aggravated sexual contact with a child who has attained the age of 12 years but has not attained the age of 16 years by rendering another or that child unconscious.

(i)(a) That the accused engaged in sexual contact with a child; or

(b) That the accused caused sexual contact

with or by a child or by another person with a child; and

(ii) That at the time of the sexual contact the child had attained the age of 12 years but had not attained the age of 16 years; and

(iii) That the accused did so by rendering that child or that other person unconscious.

(f) Aggravated sexual contact with a child who has attained the age of 12 years but has not attained the age of 16 years by administration of drug, intoxicant, or other similar substance.

(i)(a) That the accused engaged in sexual contact with a child; or

(b) That the accused caused sexual contact with or by a child or by another person with a child; and

(ii) That at the time of the sexual contact the child had attained the age of 12 years but had not attained the age of 16 years; and

(iii)(a) That the accused did so by administering to that child or that other person a drug, intoxicant, or other similar substance;

(b) That the accused administered the drug, intoxicant, or other similar substance by force or threat of force or without the knowledge or permission of that child or that other person; and

(c) That, as a result, that child's or that other person's ability to appraise or control conduct was substantially impaired.

(8) *Abusive sexual contact.*

(a) Abusive sexual contact by using threats or placing in fear.

(i)(a) That the accused engaged in sexual contact with another person; or

(b) That the accused caused sexual contact with or by another person; and

(ii) That the accused did so by threatening or placing that other person in fear that any person would be subjected to bodily harm or other harm (other than by threatening or placing that other person in fear that any person would be subjected to death, grievous bodily harm, or kidnapping).

(b) *Abusive sexual contact by causing bodily harm.*

(i)(a) That the accused engaged in sexual contact with another person; or

(b) That the accused caused sexual contact with or by another person; and

(ii) That the accused did so by causing bodily harm to another person.

(c) *Abusive sexual contact upon a person substantially incapacitated or substantially incapable of appraising the act, declining participation, or communicating unwillingness.*

(i)(a) That the accused engaged in sexual contact with another person; or

(b) That the accused caused sexual contact with or by another person; and (Note: add one of the following elements)

(ii) That the other person was substantially incapacitated;

(iii) That the other person was substantially incapable of appraising the nature of the sexual contact;

(iv) That the other person was substantially incapable of declining participation in the sexual contact; or

(v) That the other person was substantially incapable of communicating unwillingness to engage in the sexual contact.

(9) *Abusive sexual contact with a child.*

(i)(a) That the accused engaged in sexual contact with a child; or

(b) That the accused caused sexual contact with or by a child or by another person with a child; and

(ii) That at the time of the sexual contact the child had attained the age of 12 years but had not attained the age of 16 years.

(10) *Indecent liberty with a child.*

(a) That the accused committed a certain act or communication;

(b) That the act or communication was indecent;

(c) That the accused committed the act or communication in the physical presence of a certain child;

(d) That the child was under 16 years of age; and

(e) That the accused committed the act or communication with the intent to:

(i) arouse, appeal to, or gratify the sexual desires of any person; or

(ii) abuse, humiliate, or degrade any person.

(11) *Indecent act.*

(a) That the accused engaged in certain conduct; and

(b) That the conduct was indecent conduct.

(12) *Forcible pandering.*

(a) That the accused compelled a certain person to engage in an act of prostitution; and

(b) That the accused directed another person to said person, who then engaged in an act of prostitution.

(13) *Wrongful sexual contact.*

(a) That the accused had sexual contact with another person;

(b) That the accused did so without that other person's permission; and

(c) That the accused had no legal justification or lawful authorization for that sexual contact.

(14) *Indecent exposure.*

(a) That the accused exposed his or her genitalia, anus, buttocks, or female areola or nipple;

(b) That the accused's exposure was in an indecent manner;

(c) That the exposure occurred in a place where the conduct involved could reasonably be expected to be viewed by people other than the accused's family or household; and

(d) That the exposure was intentional.

c. *Explanation.*

(1) *Definitions.* The terms are defined in Paragraph 45a.(t), *supra.*

(2) *Character of victim. See* Mil. R. Evid. 412 concerning rules of evidence relating to the character of the victim of an alleged sexual offense.

(3) *Indecent.* In conduct cases, "indecent" generally signifies that form of immorality relating to sexual impurity that is not only grossly vulgar, obscene, and repugnant to common propriety, but also tends to excite lust and deprave the morals with respect to sexual relations. Language is indecent if it tends reasonably to corrupt morals or incite libidinous thoughts. The language must violate community standards.

d. *Lesser included offenses.* The following lesser included offenses are based on internal cross-references provided in the statutory text of Article 120. See subsection (e) for a further listing of possible lesser included offenses.

(1) *Rape.*

(a) Article 120 — Aggravated sexual contact

(b) Article 134 — Assault with intent to commit rape

(c) Article 128 — Aggravated assault; Assault; Assault consummated by a battery

(d) Article 80 — Attempts

(2) *Rape of a child.*

(a) Article 120 — Aggravated sexual contact with a child; Indecent act

(b) Article 134 — Assault with intent to commit rape

(c) Article 128 — Aggravated assault; Assault; Assault consummated by a battery; Assault consummated by a battery upon a child under 16

(d) Article 80 — Attempts

(3) *Aggravated sexual assault.*

(a) Article 120 — Abusive sexual contact

(b) Article 128 — Aggravated assault; Assault; Assault consummated by a battery

(c) Article 80 — Attempts

(4) *Aggravated sexual assault of a child.*

(a) Article 120 — Abusive sexual contact with a child; Indecent act

(b) Article 128 — Aggravated assault; Assault; Assault consummated by a battery; Assault consummated by a battery upon a child under 16

(c) Article 80 — Attempts

(5) *Aggravated sexual contact.*

(a) Article 128 — Aggravated assault; Assault; Assault consummated by a battery

(b) Article 80 — Attempts

(6) *Aggravated sexual abuse of a child.*

(a) Article 120 — Indecent act

(b) Article 128 — Assault; Assault consummated by a battery; Assault consummated by a battery upon a child under 16

(c) Article 80 — Attempts

(7) *Aggravated sexual contact with a child.*

(a) Article 120 — Indecent act

(b) Article 128 — Assault; Assault consummated by a battery; Assault consummated by a battery upon a child under 16

(c) Article 80 — Attempts

(8) *Abusive sexual contact.*

(a) Article 128 — Assault; Assault consummated by a battery

(b) Article 80 — Attempts

(9) *Abusive sexual contact with a child.*

(a) Article 120 — Indecent act

(b) Article 128 — Assault; Assault consummated by a battery; Assault consummated by a battery upon a child under 16

(c) Article 80 — Attempts

(10) *Indecent liberty with a child.*

(a) Article 120 — Indecent act

(b) Article 80 — Attempts

(11) *Indecent act.* Article 80 — Attempts

(12) *Forcible pandering.* Article 80 — Attempts

(13) *Wrongful sexual contact.* Article 80 — Attempts

(14) *Indecent exposure.* Article 80 — Attempts

e. *Additional lesser included offenses.* Depending on the factual circumstances in each case, to include the type of act and level of force involved, the following offenses may be considered lesser included in addition to those offenses listed in subsection d. (See subsection (d) for a listing of the offenses that are specifically cross-referenced within the statutory text of Article 120.) The elements of the proposed lesser included offense should be compared with the elements of the greater offense to determine if the elements of the lesser offense are derivative of the greater offense and vice versa. See Appendix 23 for further explanation of lesser included offenses.

(1)(a) *Rape by using force.* Article 120 — Indecent act; Wrongful sexual contact

(1)(b) *Rape by causing grievous bodily harm.* Article 120 — Aggravated sexual assault by causing bodily harm; Abusive sexual contact by causing bodily harm; Indecent act; Wrongful sexual contact

(1)(c) *Rape by using threats or placing in fear.* Article 120 — Aggravated sexual assault by using threats or placing in fear; Abusive sexual contact by using threats or placing in fear; Indecent act; Wrongful sexual contact

(1)(d) *Rape by rendering another unconscious.* Article 120 — Aggravated sexual assault upon a person substantially incapacitated; Abusive sexual contact upon a person substantially incapacitated; Indecent act; Wrongful sexual contact

(1)(e) *Rape by administration of drug, intoxicant, or other similar substance.* Article 120 — Aggravated sexual assault upon a person substantially incapacitated; Abusive sexual contact upon a person substantially incapacitated; Indecent act; Wrongful sexual contact

(2)(a)-(f) *Rape of a child who has not attained 12 years; Rape of a child who has attained the age of 12 years but has not attained the age of 16 years.* Article 120 — Aggravated sexual assault of a child; Aggravated sexual abuse of a child; Abusive sexual contact with a child; Indecent liberty with a child; Wrongful sexual contact

(3) *Aggravated sexual assault.* Article 120 — Wrongful sexual contact; Indecent act

(4) *Aggravated sexual assault of a child.* Article 120 — Aggravated sexual abuse of a child; Indecent liberty with a child; Wrongful sexual contact

(5)(a) *Aggravated sexual contact by force.* Article 120 — Indecent act; Wrongful sexual contact

(5)(b) *Aggravated sexual contact by causing grievous bodily harm.* Article 120 — Abusive sexual contact by causing bodily harm; Indecent act; Wrongful sexual contact

(5)(c) *Aggravated sexual contact by using threats or placing in fear.* Article 120 — Abusive sexual contact by using threats or placing in fear; Indecent act; Wrongful sexual contact

(5)(d) *Aggravated sexual contact by rendering another unconscious.* Article 120 — Abusive sexual contact upon a person substantially incapacitated; Indecent act; Wrongful sexual contact

(5)(e) *Aggravated sexual contact by administration of drug, intoxicant, or other similar substance.* Article 120 — Abusive sexual contact upon a person substantially incapacitated; Indecent act; Wrongful sexual contact

(6) *Aggravated sexual abuse of a child.* Article 120 — Aggravated sexual contact with a child; Aggravated sexual abuse of a child; Indecent liberty with a child; Wrongful sexual contact

(7) *Aggravated sexual contact with a child.* Article 120 — Abusive sexual contact with a child; Indecent liberty with a child; Wrongful sexual contact

(8) *Abusive sexual contact.* Article 120 — Wrongful sexual contact; Indecent act

(9) *Abusive sexual contact with a child.* Article 120 — Indecent liberty with a child; Wrongful sexual contact

(10) *Indecent liberty with a child.* Article 120 — Wrongful sexual contact

f. *Maximum punishment.*

(1) *Rape and rape of a child.* Death or such other punishment as a court martial may direct.

(2) *Aggravated sexual assault.* Dishonorable discharge, forfeiture of all pay and allowances, and confinement for 30 years.

(3) *Aggravated sexual assault of a child who has attained the age of 12 years but has not attained the age of 16 years, aggravated sexual abuse of a child, aggravated sexual contact, and aggravated sexual contact with a child.* Dishonorable discharge, forfeiture of all pay and allowances, and confinement for 20 years.

(4) *Abusive sexual contact with a child and indecent liberty with a child.* Dishonorable discharge, forfeiture of all pay and allowances, and confinement for 15 years.

(5) *Abusive sexual contact.* Dishonorable discharge, forfeiture of all pay and allowances, and confinement for 7 years.

(6) *Indecent act or forcible pandering.* Dishonorable discharge, forfeiture of all pay and allowances, and confinement for 5 years.

(7) *Wrongful sexual contact or indecent exposure.* Dishonorable discharge, forfeiture of all pay and allowances, and confinement for 1 year.

g. *Sample specifications.*

(1) *Rape.*

(a) *Rape by using force.*

(i) *Rape by use or display of dangerous weapon or object.*

In that _____ (personal jurisdiction data), did (at/on boardClocation) (subject-matter jurisdiction data, if required), on or about _____ 20 ___, cause _____ to engage in a sexual act, to wit: _____, by (using a dangerous weapon or object, to wit: _____ against (him)(her)) (displaying a dangerous weapon or object, to wit: _____ to (him)(her)).

(ii) *Rape by suggestion of possession of dangerous weapon or object.*

In that _____ (personal jurisdiction data), did (at/on boardClocation) (subject-matter jurisdiction data, if required), on or about _____ 20 ___, cause _____ to engage in a sexual act, to wit: _____, by the suggestion of possession of a dangerous weapon or an object that was used in a manner to cause (him)(her) to believe it was a dangerous weapon or object.

(iii) *Rape by using physical violence, strength, power, or restraint to any person.*

In that _____ (personal jurisdiction data), did (at/on boardClocation) (subject-matter jurisdiction data, if required), on or about _____ 20 ___, cause _____ to engage in a sexual act, to wit: _____, by using (physical violence) (strength) (power) (restraint applied to _____), sufficient that (he)(she) could not avoid or escape the sexual conduct.

(b) *Rape by causing grievous bodily harm.*

In that _____ (personal jurisdiction data), did (at/on boardClocation) (subject-matter jurisdiction data, if required), on or about _____ 20 ___, cause _____ to engage in a sexual act, to wit: _____, by causing grievous bodily harm upon (him)(her)(_____), to wit: a (broken leg)(deep cut)(fractured skull)(_____).

(c) *Rape by using threats or placing in fear.*

In that _____ (personal jurisdiction data), did (at/on boardClocation) (subject-matter jurisdiction data, if required), on or about _____ 20 ___, cause _____ to engage in a sexual act, to wit: _____, by [threatening] [placing (him)(her) in fear] that (he)(she)(_____) will be subjected to (death)(grievous bodily harm) (kidnapping) by _____.

(d) *Rape by rendering another unconscious.*

In that _____ (personal jurisdiction data), did (at/on boardClocation) (subject-matter jurisdiction data, if required), on or about _____ 20 ___, cause _____ to engage in a sexual act, to wit: _____, by rendering (him)(her) unconscious.

(e) *Rape by administration of drug, intoxicant, or other similar substance.*

In that _____ (personal jurisdiction data), did (at/on boardClocation) (subject-matter jurisdiction data, if required), on or about _____ 20 ___, cause _____ to engage in a sexual act, to wit: _____, by administering to (him)(her) a drug, intoxicant, or other similar substance, (by force) (by threat of force) (without (his)(her) knowledge or permission), and thereby substantially impaired (his)(her) ability to [(appraise) (control)][(his)(her)] conduct.

(2) *Rape of a child.*

(a) *Rape of a child who has not attained the age of 12 years.*

In that ______ (personal jurisdiction data), did (at/on boardClocation) (subject-matter jurisdiction data, if required), on or about ______ 20 ___, engage in a sexual act, to wit: ______ with ______, a child who had not attained the age of 12 years.

(b) *Rape of a child who has attained the age of 12 years but has not attained the age of 16 years by using force.*

(i) *Rape of a child who has attained the age of 12 years but has not attained the age of 16 years by use or display of dangerous weapon or object.*

In that ______ (personal jurisdiction data), did (at/on boardClocation) (subject-matter jurisdiction data, if required), on or about ______ 20 ___, engage in a sexual act, to wit: ______, with ______, a child who had attained the age of 12 years, but had not attained the age of 16 years, by (using a dangerous weapon or object, to wit: ______ against (him)(her)) (displaying a dangerous weapon or object, to wit: ______ to (him)(her)).

(ii) *Rape of a child who has attained the age of 12 years but has not attained the age of 16 years by suggestion of possession of dangerous weapon or object.*

In that ______ (personal jurisdiction data), did (at/on boardClocation) (subject-matter jurisdiction data, if required), on or about ______ 20 ___, engage in a sexual act, to wit: ______, with ______, a child who had attained the age of 12 years, but had not attained the age of 16 years, by the suggestion of possession of a dangerous weapon or an object that was used in a manner to cause (him)(her) to believe it was a dangerous weapon or object.

(iii) *Rape of a child who has attained the age of 12 years but has not attained the age of 16 years by using physical violence, strength, power, or restraint to any person.*

In that ______ (personal jurisdiction data), did (at/on boardClocation) (subject-matter jurisdiction data, if required), on or about ______ 20 ___, engage in a sexual act, to wit: ______ with ______, a child who had attained the age of 12 years, but had not attained the age of 16 years, by using (physical violence) (strength) (power) (restraint applied to ______) sufficient that (he)(she) could not avoid or escape the sexual conduct.

(c) *Rape of a child who has attained the age of 12 years but has not attained the age of 16 years by causing grievous bodily harm.*

In that ______ (personal jurisdiction data), did (at/on boardClocation) (subject-matter jurisdiction data, if required), on or about ______ 20 ___, engage in a sexual act, to wit: ______, with ______, a child who had attained the age of 12 years, but had not attained the age of 16 years, by causing grievous bodily harm upon (him-)(her)(______), to wit: a (broken leg)(deep cut)(fractured skull)(______).

(d) *Rape of a child who has attained the age of 12 years but has not attained the age of 16 years by using threats or placing in fear.*

In that ______ (personal jurisdiction data), did (at/on boardClocation) (subject-matter jurisdiction data, if required), on or about ______ 20 ___, engage in a sexual act, to wit: ______, with ______, a child who had attained the age of 12 years, but had not attained the age of 16 years, by [threatening] [placing (him)(her) in fear] that (he)(she)(______) would be subjected to (death)(grievous bodily harm) (kidnapping) by ______.

(e) *Rape of a child who has attained the age of 12 years but has not attained the age of 16 years by rendering that child unconscious.*

In that ______ (personal jurisdiction data), did (at/on boardClocation) (subject-matter jurisdiction data, if required), on or about ______ 20 ___, engage in a sexual act, to wit: ______, with ______, a child who had attained the age of 12 years, but had not attained the age of 16 years, by rendering (him)(her) unconscious.

(f) *Rape of a child who has attained the age of 12 years but has not attained the age of 16 years by administration of drug, intoxicant, or other similar substance.*

In that ______ (personal jurisdiction data), did (at/on boardClocation) (subject-matter jurisdiction data, if required), on or about ______ 20 ___, engage in a sexual act, to wit: ______, with ______, a child who had attained the age of 12 years, but had not attained the age of 16 years, by administering to (him)(her) a drug, intoxicant, or other similar substance (by force) (by threat of force) (without (his)(her) knowledge or permission), and thereby substantially impaired (his)(her) ability to [(appraise)(control)] (his)(her)] conduct.

(3) *Aggravated sexual assault.*

(a) *Aggravated sexual assault by using threats or placing in fear.*

In that ______ (personal jurisdiction data), did (at/on boardClocation) (subject-matter jurisdiction data, if required), on or about ______ 20 ___, cause ______ to engage in a sexual act, to wit: ______, by [threatening] [placing(him)(her) in fear of] [(physical injury to ______) (injury to ______'s property)(accusation of crime)(exposition of secret)(abuse of military position)(______)].

(b) *Aggravated sexual assault by causing bodily harm.*

In that ______ (personal jurisdiction data), did (at/on boardClocation) (subject-matter jurisdiction data, if required), on or about ______ 20 ___, cause ______ to engage in a sexual act, to wit: ______, by causing bodily harm upon (him-)(her)(______), to wit: ______.

(c) *Aggravated sexual assault upon a person substantially incapacitated or substantially incapable of appraising the act, declining participation, or communicating unwillingness.*

In that ______ (personal jurisdiction data), did (at/on boardClocation) (subject-matter jurisdiction data, if required), on or about ______ 20 ___, engage in a sexual act, to wit-: ______ with ______, who was (substantially incapacitated) [substantially incapable of (appraising the nature of the sexual act)(declining participation in the sexual act) (communicating unwillingness to engage in the sexual act)].

(4) *Aggravated sexual assault of a child who has attained the age of 12 years but has not attained the age of 16 years.*

In that ______ (personal jurisdiction data), did (at/on boardClocation) (subject-matter jurisdiction data, if required), on or about ______ 20 ___, engage in a sexual act, to wit: ______ with ______, who had attained the age of 12 years, but had not attained the age of 16 years.

(5) *Aggravated sexual contact.*

(a) *Aggravated sexual contact by using force.*

(i) *Aggravated sexual contact by use or display of dangerous weapon or object.*

In that ______ (personal jurisdiction data), did (at/on boardClocation) (subject-matter jurisdiction data, if required), on or about ______ 20 ___, [(engage in sexual contact, to wit-: ______ with ______) (cause ______ to engage in sexual contact, to wit: ______, with ______) (cause sexual contact with or by ______, to wit: ______)] by (using a dangerous weapon or object, to wit: ______ against (him)(her)) (displaying a dangerous weapon or object, to wit: ______ to (him)(her)).

(ii) *Aggravated sexual contact by suggestion of possession of dangerous weapon or object.*

In that ______ (personal jurisdiction data), did (at/on boardClocation) (subject-matter jurisdiction data, if required), on or about ______ 20 ___, [(engage in sexual contact, to wit: ______ with- ______)(cause ______ to engage in sexual contact, to wit: ______, with ______) (cause sexual contact with or by ______, to wit: ______)] by the suggestion of possession of a dangerous weapon or an object that was used in a manner to cause (him)(her)(______) to believe it was a dangerous weapon or object.

(iii) *Aggravated sexual contact by using physical violence, strength, power, or restraint to any person.*

In that ______ (personal jurisdiction data), did (at/on boardClocation) (subject-matter jurisdiction data, if required), on or about ______ 20 ___, [(engage in sexual contact, to wit: ______ w-ith ______)(cause ______ to engage in sexual contact, to wit: ______, with ______) (cause sexual contact with or by ______, to wit: ______)] by using (physical violence) (strength) (power) (restraint applied to ______), sufficient that (he)(she)(______) could not avoid or escape the sexual conduct.

(b) *Aggravated sexual contact by causing grievous bodily harm.*

In that ______ (personal jurisdiction data), did (at/on boardClocation) (subject-matter jurisdiction data, if required), on or about ______ 20 ___, [(engage in sexual contact, to wit: ______ with ______)(cause ______ to engage in sexual contact, to wit: ______, with ______) (cause sexual contact with or by ______, to wit: ______)] by causing grievous bodily harm upon (him)(her)(______), to wit: a (broken leg)(deep cut)(fractured skull)(______).

(c) *Aggravated sexual contact by using threats or placing in fear.*

In that ______ (personal jurisdiction data), did (at/on boardClocation) (subject-matter jurisdiction data, if required), on or about ______ 20 ___, [(engage in sexual contact, to wit: ______ with ______)(cause ______ to engage in sexual contact, to wit: ______, with ______) (cause sexual contact with or by ______, to wit: ______)] by [(threatening (him)(her)(______)] [(placing(him)(her)(______) in fear] that (he)(she)(______) will be subjected to (death)(grievous bodily harm)(kidnapping) by ______.

(d) *Aggravated sexual contact by rendering another unconscious.*

In that ______ (personal jurisdiction data), did (at/on boardClocation) (subject-matter jurisdiction data, if required), on or about ______ 20 ___, [(engage in sexual contact, to wit: ______ with ______)(cause ______ to engage in sexual contact, to wit: ______, with ______) (cause sexual contact with or by ______, to wit: ______)] by rendering (him)(her)(______) unconscious.

(e) *Aggravated sexual contact by administration of drug, intoxicant, or other similar substance.*

In that ______ (personal jurisdiction data), did (at/on boardClocation) (subject-matter jurisdiction data, if required), on or about ______ 20 ___, [(engage in sexual contact, to wit: ______ with ______)(cause ______ to engage in sexual contact, to wit: ______, with ______) (cause sexual contact with or by ______, to wit: (______)] by administering to (him)(her)(______) a drug, intoxicant, or other similar substance, (by force) (by threat of force) (without (his)(her)(______) knowledge or permission), and thereby substantially impaired (his)(her)(______) ability to [(appraise) (control)] [(his) (her)] conduct.

(6) *Aggravated sexual abuse of a child.*

In that ______ (personal jurisdiction data), did (at/on boardClocation) (subject-matter jurisdiction data, if required), on or about ______ 20 ___, engage in a lewd act, to wit: ______ with ______, a child who had not attained the age of 16 years.

(7) *Aggravated sexual contact with a child.*

(a) *Aggravated sexual contact with a child who has not attained the — age of 12 years.*

In that ______ (personal jurisdiction data), did (at/on boardClocation) (subject-matter jurisdiction data, if required), on or about ______ 20 ___, [(engage in sexual contact, to wit: ______ with ______, a child who had not attained the age of 12 years)(cause ______ to engage in sexual contact, to wit: ______, with ______, a child who had not attained the age of 12 years) (cause sexual contact with or by ______, a child who had not attained the age of 12 years, to wit: ______)].

(b) *Aggravated sexual contact with a child who has attained the age of 12 years but has not attained the age of 16 years by using force.*

(i) *Aggravated sexual contact with a child who has attained the age of 12 years but has not attained the age of 16 years by use or display of dangerous weapon or object.*

In that ______ (personal jurisdiction data), did (at/on board-location) (subject-matter jurisdiction data, if required), on or about ______ 20 ___, [(engage in sexual contact, to wit: ______ with ______, a child who had attained the age of 12 years, but had not attained the age of 16 years)(cause ______ to engage in sexual contact, to wit: ______, with ______, a child who had attained the age of 12 years, but had not attained the age of 16 years) (cause sexual contact with or by ______, a child who had attained the age of 12 years, but had not attained the age of 16 years, to wit: ______)] by (using a dangerous weapon or object, to wit: ______ against (him)(her)(______)) (displaying a dangerous weapon or object, to wit: ______ to (him)(her)(______)).

(ii) *Aggravated sexual contact with a child who has attained the age of 12 years but has not attained the age of 16 years by suggestion of possession of dangerous weapon or object.*

In that ______ (personal jurisdiction data), did (at/on boardClocation) (subject-matter jurisdiction data, if required), on or about ______ 20 ___, [(engage in sexual contact, to wit: ______ with ______, a child who had attained the age of 12 years, but had not attained the age of 16 years)(cause ______ to engage in sexual contact, to wit: ______, with ______, a child who had attained the age of 12 years, but had not attained the age of 16 years) (cause sexual contact with or by ______, a child who had attained the age of 12 years, but had not attained the age of 16 years, to wit: ______)] by the suggestion of possession of a dangerous weapon or an object that was used in a manner to cause (him)(her)(______) to believe it was a dangerous weapon or object.

(iii) *Aggravated sexual contact with a child who has attained the age of 12 years but has not attained the age of 16 years by using physical violence, strength, power, or restraint to any person.*

In that ______ (personal jurisdiction data), did (at/on boardClocation) (subject-matter jurisdiction data, if required), on or about ______ 20 ___, [(engage in sexual contact, to wit: ______ with ______, a child who had attained the age of 12 years, but had not attained the age of 16 years)(cause ______ to engage in sexual contact, to wit: ______, with ______, a child who had attained the age of 12 years, but had not attained the age of 16 years) (cause sexual contact with or by ______, a child who had attained the age of 12 years, but had not attained the age of 16 years, to wit: ______)] by using (physical violence) (strength) (power) (restraint applied to ______) sufficient that (he)(she)(______) could not avoid or escape the sexual conduct.

(c) *Aggravated sexual contact with a child who has attained the age of 12 years but has not attained the age of 16 years by causing grievous bodily harm.*

In that ______ (personal jurisdiction data), did (at/on boardClocation) (subject-matter jurisdiction data, if required), on or about ______ 20 ___, [(engage in sexual contact, to wit: ______ with ______, a child who had attained the age of 12 years, but had not attained the age of 16 years)(cause ______ to engage in sexual contact, to wit: ______, with ______, a child who had attained the age of 12 years, but had not attained the age of 16 years) (cause sexual contact with or by ______, a child who had attained the age of 12 years, but had not attained the age of 16 years, to wit: ______)] by causing grievous bodily harm upon (him)(her)(______), to wit: a (broken leg)(deep cut)(fractured skull)(______).

(d) *Aggravated sexual contact with a child who has attained the age of 12 years but has not attained the age of 16 years by using threats or placing in fear.*

In that ______ (personal jurisdiction data), did (at/on boardClocation) (subject-matter jurisdiction data, if required), on or about ______ 20 ___, [(engage in sexual contact, to wit: ______ with ______, a child who had attained the age of 12 years, but had not attained the age of 16 years)(cause ______ to engage in sexual contact, to wit: ______, with ______, a child who had attained the age of 12 years, but had not attained the age of 16 years) (cause sexual contact with or by ______, a child who had attained the age of 12 years, but had not attained the age of 16 years, to wit: ______)] by [threatening] [placing (him)(her)(______) in fear] that (he)(she)(______) will be subjected to (death) (grievous bodily harm)(kidnapping) by ______.

(e) *Aggravated sexual contact with a child who has attained the age of 12 years but has not attained the age of 16 years by rendering that child or another unconscious.*

(f) *Aggravated sexual contact with a child who has attained the age of 12 years but has not attained the age of 16 years by administration of drug, intoxicant, or other similar substance.*

In that ______ (personal jurisdiction data), did (at/on boardClocation) (subject-matter jurisdiction data, if required), on or about ______ 20 ___, [(engage in sexual contact, to wit: ______ with ______, a child who had attained the age of 12 years but had not attained the age of 16 years)(cause ______ to engage in sexual contact, to wit: ______, with ______, a child who had attained the age of 12 years but had not attained the age of 16 years) (cause sexual contact with or by ______, a child who had attained the age of 12 years but had not attained the age of 16 years, to wit: ______)] by administering to (him)(her)(______) a drug, intoxicant, or other similar substance (by force) (by threat of force) (without (his)(her)( ) knowledge or permission), and thereby substantially impaired (his)(her)( ) ability to [(appraise) (control)][(his) (her)] conduct.

(8) *Abusive sexual contact.*

(a) *Abusive sexual contact by using threats or placing in fear.*

In that (personal jurisdiction data), did (at/on boardClocation) (subject-matter jurisdiction data, if required), on or about 20 , [(engage in sexual contact, to wit: with) (cause to engage in sexual contact, to wit: , with) (cause sexual contact with or by , to wit:)] by [(threatening) (placing (him)(her)( ) in fear of)] [(physical injury to)(injury to 's property)(-accusation of crime)(exposition of secret)(abuse of military position)( )].

(b) *Abusive sexual contact by causing bodily harm.*

In that (personal jurisdiction data), did (at/on boardClocation) (subject-matter jurisdiction data, if required), on or about 20 , [(engage in sexual contact, to wit: with) (cause to engage in sexual contact, to wit: , with) (cause sexual contact with or by , to wit:)] by causing bodily harm upon (him)(her)( ), to wit: ( ).

(c) *Abusive sexual contact by engaging in a sexual act with a person substantially incapacitated or substantially incapable of appraising the act, declining participation, or substantially incapable of communicating unwillingness.*

In that (personal jurisdiction data), did (at/on boardClocation) (subject-matter jurisdiction data, if required), on or about 20 , [(engage in sexual contact, to wit: with) (cause to engage in sexual contact, to wit: , with) (cause sexual contact with or by , to wit:)] while (he)(she)( ) was [substantially incapacitated] [substantially incapable of (appraising the nature of the sexual contact) (declining participation in the sexual contact) (communicating unwillingness to engage in the sexual contact)].

(9) *Abusive sexual contact with a child.*

In that (personal jurisdiction data), did (at/on boardClocation) (subject-matter jurisdiction data, if required), on or about 20 , [(engage in sexual contact, to wit: with , a child who had attained the age of 12 years but had not attained the age of 16 years) (cause to engage in sexual contact, to wit: , with , a child who had attained the age of 12 years but had not attained the age of 16 years) (cause sexual contact with or by , a child who had attained the age of 12 years but had not attained the age of 16 years, to wit:)].

(10) *Indecent liberties with a child.*

In that (personal jurisdiction data), did, (at/on boardClocation) (subject-matter jurisdiction data, if required), on or about 20 , (take indecent liberties) (engage in indecent conduct) in the physical presence of , a (female) (male) under 16 years of age, by (communicating the words: to wit:) (exposing one's private parts, to wit:)( ), with the intent to [(arouse) (appeal to) (gratify) the (sexual desire) of the (or)] [(abuse)(humiliate)(degrade)].

(11) *Indecent act.*

In that (personal jurisdiction data), did (at/on boardClocation) (subject-matter jurisdiction data, if required), on or about 20 , wrongfully commit indecent conduct, to wit .

(12) *Forcible pandering.*

In that (personal jurisdiction data), did (at/on boardClocation), (subject-matter jurisdiction data, if required), on or about 20 , compel to engage in [(a sexual act)(sexual contact) (lewd act), to wit:] for the purpose of receiving money or other compensation with (a) person(s) to be directed to (him-)(her) by the said .

(13) *Wrongful sexual contact.*

In that (personal jurisdiction data), did (at/on board-location), (subject-matter jurisdiction data, if required), on or about 20 , engage in sexual contact with , to wit: , and such sexual contact was without legal justification or lawful authorization and without the permission of .

(14) *Indecent exposure.*

In that (personal jurisdiction data), did (at/on board-location), (subject-matter jurisdiction data, if required), on or about 20 , intentionally (expose in an indecent manner (his) (her)(________)(________) while (at the barracks window) (in a public place) (________).

(e) Paragraph 50, Article 124 — Maiming, paragraph e. is amended to read as follows:

"e. Maximum Punishment. Dishonorable discharge, forfeiture of all pay and allowances, and confinement for 20 years."

(f) Paragraph 51, Article 125 — Sodomy, paragraph d. is amended by deleting the following lesser included offenses under paragraphs d.(1)(b); d.(2)(c); and d.(3)(a), and replacing them, respectively, with the following:

"(b) Article 134 — indecent liberty with a child"

"(c) Article 134 — indecent assault"

"(a) Article 134 — indecent acts with another"

(g) Paragraph 51, Article 125 — Sodomy, paragraph d. is amended by adding at the end of paragraph d. the following note: "(Note: Consider lesser included offenses under Art. 120 depending on the factual circumstances in each case.)"

(h) Paragraph 54, Article 128 — Assault, paragraph b.(4)(a) is amended to read as follows:

"(a) Assault with a dangerous weapon or other means of force likely to produce death or grievous bodily harm.

(i) That the accused attempted to do, offered to do, or did bodily harm to a certain person;

(ii) That the accused did so with a certain weapon, means, or force;

(iii) That the attempt, offer, or bodily harm was done with unlawful force or violence; and

(iv) That the weapon, means, or force was used in a manner likely to produce death or grievous bodily harm. (Note: Add any of the following as applicable)

(v) That the weapon was a loaded firearm.

(vi) That the person was a child under the age of 16 years."

(i) Paragraph 54, Article 128 — Assault, paragraph b.(4)(b) is amended to read as follows:

"(b) Assault in which grievous bodily harm is intentionally inflicted.

(i) That the accused assaulted a certain person;

(ii) That grievous bodily harm was thereby inflicted upon such person;

(iii) That the grievous bodily harm was done with unlawful force or violence; and

(iv) That the accused, at the time, had the specific intent to inflict grievous bodily harm. (Note: Add any of the following as applicable)

(v) That the injury was inflicted with a loaded firearm.

(vi) That the person was a child under the age of 16 years."

(j) Paragraph 54, Article 128 — Assault, paragraph c.(4)(a) is amended by adding new paragraph c.(4)(a)(v) after c.(4)(a)(iv), to read as follows:

"(v) When committed upon a child under 16 years of age. The maximum punishment is increased when aggravated assault with a dangerous weapon or means likely to produce death or grievous bodily harm is inflicted upon a child under 16 years of age. Knowledge that the person assaulted was under the age of 16 years is not an element of the offense."

(k) Paragraph 54, Article 128 — Assault, paragraph c.(4)(b) is amended by adding new paragraph c.(4)(b)(iv), to read as follows:

"(iv) When committed upon a child under 16 years of age. The maximum punishment is increased when aggravated assault with intentional infliction of grievous bodily harm is inflicted upon a child under 16 years of age. Knowledge that the person assaulted was under the age of 16 years is not an element of the offense."

(l) Paragraph 54, Article 128 — Assault, paragraph (d)(6) is amended to read as follows:

"(6) Assault with a dangerous weapon or other means or force likely to produce death or grievous bodily harm. Article 128 — simple assault; assault consummated by a battery; (when committed upon a child under the age of 16 years; assault consummated by a battery upon a child under the age of 16 years)."

(m) Paragraph 54, Article 128 — Assault, paragraph d.(7) is amended to read as follows:

"(7) Assault in which grievous bodily harm is intentionally inflicted. Article 128 — simple assault; assault consummated by a battery; assault with a dangerous weapon; (when committed upon a child under the age of 16 years — assault consummated by a battery upon a child under the age of 16 years)."

(n) Paragraph 54, Article 128 — Assault, paragraph e.(8) is amended to read as follows:

"(8) Aggravated assault with a dangerous weapon or other means of force to produce death or grievous bodily harm." After current paragraph (a), insert paragraph (b) as follows below, and redesignate (b) as paragraph (c): "(b) Aggravated assault with a dangerous weapon or other means of force to produce death or grievous bodily harm when committed upon a child under the age of 16 years. Dishonorable discharge, total forfeitures, and confinement for 5 years."

(o) Paragraph 54, Article 128 — Assault, paragraph (e)(9) is amended to read as follows:

"(9) Aggravated assault in which grievous bodily harm is intentionally inflicted." After current paragraph (a), insert paragraph (b) as follows below, and redesignate paragraph (b) as paragraph (c): "(b) Aggravated assault in which grievous bodily harm is intentionally inflicted when committed upon a child under the age of 16 years. Dishonorable discharge, total forfeitures, and confinement for 8 years."

(p) Paragraph 54, Article 128 — Assault, paragraph (f)(8) is amended to read as follows:

"(8) *Assault, aggravated*—with a dangerous weapon, means or force.

In that ______ (personal jurisdiction data), did, (at/on boardClocation)(subject matter jurisdiction data, if required), on or about ______ 20 ____, commit an assault upon ______ (a child under the age of 16 years) by (shooting)(pointing)(striking)(cutting)(______) (at him/her)(him/her) (in-)(on)(the ______) with (a dangerous weapon)(a (means)(force) likely to produce death or grievous bodily harm), to wit: a (loaded firearm)(pickax)(bayonet)(club)(______)."

(q) Paragraph 54, Article 128 — Assault, paragraph (f)(9) is amended to read as follows:

"(9) *Assault, aggravated-inflicting grievous bodily harm.*

In that ______ (personal jurisdiction data), did, (at/on board-location)(subject matter jurisdiction data, if required), on or about ______ 20 ____, commit an assault upon ______ (a child under the age of 16 years) by (shooting)(striking)-(cutting)(______) (him/her)(on) the ______ with a (loaded firearm)(club)(rock) (brick)(______) and did thereby intentionally inflict grievous bodily harm upon him/her, to wit: a (broken leg)(deep cut)(fractured skull)(______)."

(r) Paragraph 64, Article 134 — (Assault — with intent to commit murder, voluntary manslaughter, rape, robbery, sodomy, arson, burglary, or housebreaking), paragraph c.(4), first sentence, is amended to read as follows:

"In assault with intent to commit rape, the accused must have intended to complete the offense."

(s) Paragraph 64, Article 134 — (Assault — with intent to commit murder, voluntary manslaughter, rape, robbery, sodomy, arson, burglary, or housebreaking), is amended by deleting the following lesser included offense under paragraph d.(3)(b): "(b) Article 134 — indecent assault"

(t) New paragraph 68a, Article 134 — (Child endangerment) is inserted:

"68a. Article 134 — (Child endangerment)

a. *Text. See* paragraph 60.

b. *Elements.*

(1) That the accused had a duty for the care of a certain child;

(2) That the child was under the age of 16 years;

(3) That the accused endangered the child's mental or physical health, safety, or welfare through design or culpable negligence; and

(4) That, under the circumstances, the conduct of the accused was to the prejudice of good order and discipline in the armed forces or was of a nature to bring discredit upon the armed forces.

c. *Explanation.*

(1) *In general.* This offense is intended to prohibit and therefore deter child endangerment through design or culpable negligence.

(2) *Design.* Design means on purpose, intentionally, or according to plan and requires specific intent to endanger the child.

(3) *Culpable negligence.* Culpable negligence is a degree of carelessness greater than simple negligence. It is a negligent act or omission accompanied by a culpable disregard for the foreseeable consequences to others of that act or omission. In the context of this offense, culpable negligence may include acts that, when viewed in the light of human experience, might foreseeably result in harm to a child, even though such harm would not necessarily be the natural and probable consequences of such acts. In this regard, the age and maturity of the child, the conditions surrounding the neglectful conduct, the proximity of assistance available, the na-

ture of the environment in which the child may have been left, the provisions made for care of the child, and the location of the parent or adult responsible for the child relative to the location of the child, among others, may be considered in determining whether the conduct constituted culpable negligence.

(4) *Harm.* Actual physical or mental harm to the child is not required. The offense requires that the accused's actions reasonably could have caused physical or mental harm or suffering. However, if the accused's conduct does cause actual physical or mental harm, the potential maximum punishment increases. *See* Paragraph 54(c)(4)(a)(iii) for an explanation of "grievous bodily harm".

(5) *Endanger.* "Endanger" means to subject one to a reasonable probability of harm.

(6) *Age of victim as a factor.* While this offense may be committed against any child under 16, the age of the victim is a factor in the culpable negligence determination. Leaving a teenager alone for an evening may not be culpable (or even simple) negligence; leaving an infant or toddler for the same period might constitute culpable negligence. On the other hand, leaving a teenager without supervision for an extended period while the accused was on temporary duty outside commuting distance might constitute culpable negligence.

(7) *Duty required.* The duty of care is determined by the totality of the circumstances and may be established by statute, regulation, legal parent-child relationship, mutual agreement, or assumption of control or custody by affirmative act. When there is no duty of care of a child, there is no offense under this paragraph. Thus, there is no offense when a stranger makes no effort to feed a starving child or an individual/neighbor not charged with the care of a child does not prevent the child from running and playing in the street.

d. *Lesser included offenses.*

(1) Child Endangerment by Design.

Article 134 — Child endangerment by culpable negligence

(2) Article 80 — Attempts

e. *Maximum punishment.*

(1) *Endangerment by design resulting in grievous bodily harm.* Dishonorable discharge, forfeiture of all pay and allowances, and confinement for 8 years.

(2) *Endangerment by design resulting in harm.* Dishonorable discharge, forfeiture of all pay and allowances, and confinement for 5 years.

(3) *Other cases by design.* Dishonorable discharge, forfeiture of all pay and allowances and confinement for 4 years.

(4) *Endangerment by culpable negligence resulting in grievous bodily harm.* Dishonorable discharge, forfeiture of all pay and allowances, and confinement for 3 years.

(5) *Endangerment by culpable negligence resulting in harm.* Bad-conduct discharge, forfeiture of all pay and allowances, and confinement for 2 years.

(6) *Other cases by culpable negligence.* Bad-conduct discharge, forfeiture of all pay and allowances, and confinement for 1 year.

f. *Sample specification.*

(1) *Resulting in grievous bodily harm.*

In that ______ (personal jurisdiction data),(at/on boardClocation) (subject matter jurisdiction data, if required) on or about ______, 20 ____, had a duty for the care of ______, a child under the age of 16 years and did endanger the (mental health) (physical health)(safety)(welfare) of said ______, by (leaving the said ______ unattended in his quarters for over ______ hours/days with no adult present in the home) (by failing to obtain medical care for the said ______'s diabetic condition)(______), and that such conduct (was by design)(constituted culpable negligence)(which resulted in grievous bodily harm, to wit:) (broken leg-)(deep cut)(fractured skull)(______).

(2) *Resulting in harm.*

In that ______ (personal jurisdiction data),(at/on boardClocation) (subject matter jurisdiction data, if required) on or about ______, 20 ____, had a duty for the care of ______, a child under the age of 16 years, and did endanger the (mental health) (physical health)(safety)(welfare) of said ______, by (leaving the said ______ unattended in his quarters for over ______ hours/days with no adult present in the home) (by failing to obtain medical care for the said ______'s diabetic condition)(______), and that such conduct (was by design)(constituted culpable negligence) (which resulted in (harm, to wit:) (a black eye)(bloody nose)(minor cut)(______).

(3) *Other cases.*

In that ______ (personal jurisdiction data),(at/on boardClocation) (subject matter jurisdiction data, if required) on or about ______, 20 ___, was responsible for the care of ______, a child under the age of 16 years, and did endanger the (mental health) (physical health)(safety)(welfare) of said ______, by (leaving the said ______ unattended in his quarters for over ______ hours/days with no adult present in the home) (by failing to obtain medical care for the said ______'s diabetic condition)(______), and that such conduct (was by design)(constituted culpable negligence)."

(u) Paragraph 63, Article 134 — (Assault-indecent) is deleted.

(v) Paragraph 87, Article 134 — (Indecent acts or liberties with a child) is deleted.

(w) Paragraph 88, Article 134 — (Indecent exposure) is deleted.

(x) Paragraph 90, Article 134 — (Indecent acts with another) is deleted.

(y) Paragraph 89, Article 134 — (Indecent language), paragraph c. is amended to read as follows:

"c. Explanation. "Indecent" language is that which is grossly offensive to modesty, decency, or propriety, or shocks the moral sense, because of its vulgar, filthy, or disgusting nature, or its tendency to incite lustful thought. Language is indecent if it tends reasonably to corrupt morals or incite libidinous thoughts. The language must violate community standards. *See* paragraph 45 if the communication was made in the physical presence of a child."

(z) Paragraph 97, Article 134 — (Pandering and prostitution) is amended to read as follows:

"(3) Pandering by inducing, enticing, or procuring act of prostitution.

(a) That the accused induced, enticed, or procured a certain person to engage in an act of sexual intercourse for hire and reward with a person to be directed to said person by the accused;

(b) That this inducing, enticing, or procuring was wrongful;

(c) That, under the circumstances, the conduct of the accused was to the prejudice of good order and discipline in the armed forces or was of a nature to bring discredit upon the armed forces."

(aa) Paragraph 97, Article 134 — (Pandering and prostitution), subsection (f)(3) is amended to read as follows:

"(3) *Inducing, enticing, or procuring act of prostitution.*

In that ______ (personal jurisdiction data), did (at/on boardClocation) (subject-matter jurisdiction data, if required), on or about ______ 20 ___, wrongfully (induce)(entice)(procure) ______ to engage in (an act)(acts) of (sexual intercourse for hire and reward) with persons to be directed to him/her by the said ______."

APPENDIX 26
THE JOINT SERVICE COMMITTEE ON MILITARY JUSTICE (JSC)

Department of Defense

DIRECTIVE

NUMBER 5500.17

May 3, 2003

GC, DoD

SUBJECT: Role and Responsibilities of the Joint Service Committee (JSC) on Military Justice

References: (a) DoD Directive 5500.17, "Role and Responsibilities of the Joint Service Committee (JSC) on Military Justice," May 8, 1996 (hereby canceled)
(b) Manual for Courts-Martial, United States
(c) Chapter 47 of title 10, United States Code (Uniform Code of Military Justice)
(d) Executive Order 12473, July 13, 1984
(e) through (g), see enclosure 1

1. REISSUANCE AND PURPOSE

This Directive:

1.1. Reissues reference (a).

1.2. Implements the requirement established by the President that reference (b) be reviewed annually.

1.3. Formalizes the Joint Service Committee (JSC) and defines the roles, responsibilities, and procedures of the JSC in reviewing and proposing changes to reference (b) and proposing legislation to amend reference (c).

1.4. Provides for the designation of a Secretary of a Military Department to serve as the Executive Agent for the JSC.

2. APPLICABILITY

This Directive applies to the Office of the Secretary of Defense, the Military Departments (including the Coast Guard by agreement with the Department of Homeland Security when it is not operating as a Service of the Department of the Navy), the Chairman of the Joint Chiefs of Staff, the Combatant Commands, the Inspector General of the Department of Defense, the Defense Agencies, the DoD Field Activities, and all other organizational entities in the Department of Defense (hereafter collectively referred to as "the DoD Components").

3. POLICY

To assist the President in fulfilling his responsibilities under the Uniform Code of Military Justice (UCMJ) (reference (c)), and to satisfy the requirements of Executive Order 12473 (reference (d)), the Department of Defense shall review the Manual for Courts-Martial (reference (b)) annually, and, as appropriate, propose legislation amending reference (c) to ensure that references (b) and (c) fulfill their fundamental purpose as a comprehensive body of military criminal law and procedure. The role of the JSC furthers these responsibilities. Under the direction of the General Counsel of the Department of Defense, the JSC is responsible for reviewing reference (b) and proposing amendments to it and, as necessary, to reference (c).

4. RESPONSIBILITIES

4.1. The General Counsel of the Department of Defense shall:

4.1.1. Administer this Directive, to include coordination on and approval of legislative proposals to amend reference (c), approval of the annual review of reference (b), and coordination of any proposed changes to reference (b) under OMB Circular A-19 (reference (e)).

4.1.2. Designate the Secretary of a Military Department to serve as the joint Service provider for the JSC. The joint Service provider shall act on behalf of the JSC for maintaining the JSC's files and historical records, and for publication of the updated editions of reference (b) to be distributed throughout the Department of Defense, as appropriate.

4.1.3. Invite the Secretary of Homeland Security to appoint representatives to the JSC.

4.1.4. Invite the Chief Judge of the United States Court of Appeals for the Armed Forces to provide a staff member to serve as an advisor to the JSC.

4.1.5. Invite the Chairman of the Joint Chiefs of Staff to provide a staff member from the Chairmans Office of Legal Counsel to serve as an advisor to the JSC.

4.1.6. Ensure that the Associate Deputy General Counsel (Military Justice and Personnel Policy), Office of the General Counsel, Department of Defense, shall serve as the General Counsel's representative to the JSC in a non-voting capacity. In addition, the United States Court of Appeals for the Armed Forces (USCAAF) and the Legal Counsel to the Chairman of the Joint Chiefs of Staff shall be invited to provide a staff member to serve as an advisor to the JSC in a non-voting capacity.

4.2. The Secretaries of the Military Departments shall ensure that the Judge Advocates General of the Military Departments and the Staff Judge Advocate to the Commandant of the Marine Corps appoint representatives to the JSC.

4.3. The Joint Service Committee (JSC) shall further the DoD policy established in section 3. of this Directive and perform additional studies or other duties related to the administration of military justice, as the General Counsel of the Department of Defense may direct. (See reference (f).) The membership of the JSC shall consist of one representative of each of the following, who shall comprise the JSC Voting Group:

4.3.1. The Judge Advocate General of the Army.

4.3.2. The Judge Advocate General of the Navy.

4.3.3. The Judge Advocate General of the Air Force.

4.3.4. The Staff Judge Advocate to the Commandant of the Marine Corps; and

4.3.5. By agreement with the Department of Homeland Security, the Chief Counsel, United States Coast Guard.

4.4. The JSC Working Group (WG) shall assist the JSC Voting Group in fulfilling its responsibilities under this Directive. The WG consists of non-voting representatives from each of the Services and may include the representatives from the USCAAF, and the Office of the Legal Counsel to the Chairman of the Joint Chiefs of Staff.

4.5. The JSC chairmanship rotates biennially among the Services in the following order: the Army, the Air Force, the Marine Corps, the Navy, and the Coast Guard. Due to its size and manning constraints, a Coast Guard's request not to be considered for JSC chairmanship shall be honored. The Military Service of the JSC Chairman shall provide an Executive Secretary for the JSC.

5. EFFECTIVE DATE AND IMPLEMENTATION

5.1. The foregoing policies and procedures providing guidelines for implementation of this Directive, as well as those contained in the enclosures, are intended exclusively for the guidance of military personnel and civilian employees of the Department of Defense, and the United States Coast Guard by agreement of the Department of Homeland Security. These guidelines are intended to improve the internal management of the Federal Government and are not intended to create any right, privilege, or benefit, substantive of procedural, to any person or enforceable at law by any party against the United States, its agencies, its officers, or any person.

5.2. This Directive is effective immediately.

Paul Wolfowitz
Deputy Secretary of Defense

Enclosures - 2
E1. References, continued
E2. Guidance to the JSC

E1. ENCLOSURE 1

REFERENCES, continued

(e) Office of Management and Budget Circular A-19, "Legislative Coordination and Clearance," September 20, 1979
(f) DoD Directive 5105.18, "DoD Committee Management Program," February 8, 1999
(g) DoD Directive 5500.1, "Preparation and Processing of Legislation, Executive Orders, Proclamations, and Reports and Comments Thereon," May 21, 1964

E2. ENCLOSURE 2

GUIDANCE TO THE JSC

E2.1. REVIEW OF THE MANUAL FOR COURTS-MARTIAL (REFERENCE (b))

E2.1.1. The JSC shall conduct an annual review of reference (b), in light of judicial and legislative developments in military and civilian practice, to ensure:

E2.1.1.1. Reference (b) implements reference (c) and reflects current military practice and judicial precedent.

E2.1.1.2. The rules and procedures of reference (b) are uniform insofar as practicable.

E2.1.1.3. Reference (b) applies, to the extent practicable, the principles of law and the rules of evidence generally recognized in the trial of criminal cases in United States district courts, but which are not contrary to or inconsistent with the UCMJ (reference (c)).

E2.1.1.4. Reference (b) is workable throughout the worldwide jurisdiction of the UCMJ; and,

E2.1.1.5. Reference (b) is workable across the spectrum of circumstances in which courts-martial are conducted, including combat conditions.

E2.1.2. During this review, any JSC voting member may propose for the Voting Group's consideration an amendment to reference (b). Proposed amendments to reference (b) shall ordinarily be referred to the JSC Working Group (WG) for study. The WG assists the JSC in staffing various proposals, conducting studies of proposals and other military justice related topics at the JSCs direction, and making reports to the JSC. Any proposed amendment to reference (b), if approved by a majority of the JSC voting members, becomes a part of the annual review.

E2.1.3. The JSC shall prepare a draft of the annual review of reference (b) and forward it to the General Counsel of the Department of Defense, on or about December 31st. The General Counsel of the Department of Defense may submit the draft of the annual review to the Code Committee established by Article 146 of reference (c), with an invitation to submit comments.

E2.1.4. The draft of the annual review shall set forth any specific recommendations for changes to reference (b), including, if not adequately addressed in the accompanying discussion or analysis, a concise statement of the basis and purpose of any proposed change. If no changes are recommended, the draft review shall so state. If the JSC recommends changes to reference (b), the draft review shall so state. If the JSC recommends changes to reference (b), the public notice procedures of paragraph E2.4.3., below, are applicable.

E2.2. CHANGES TO REFERENCE (b)

E2.2.1. By January 1st of each year, the JSC voting members shall ensure that a solicitation for proposed changes to reference (b) is sent to appropriate agencies within their respective Services that includes, but is not limited to, the judiciary, the trial counsel and defense counsel organizations, and the judge advocate general schools.

E2.2.2. The Federal Register announcement of each year's annual review of proposed changes to reference (b) shall also invite members of the public to submit any new proposals for JSC consideration during subsequent JSC annual reviews.

E2.2.3. When the JSC receives proposed changes to reference (b) either by solicitation or Federal Register notice, the JSC shall determine whether the proposal should be considered under paragraph E2.1.2. of this enclosure by determining if one or more of the JSC voting member(s) intends to sponsor the proposed change. The JSC shall determine when such sponsored proposals should be considered under the annual review process, taking into account any other proposals under consideration and any other reviews or studies directed by the General Counsel of the Department of Defense.

E2.2.4. Changes to reference (b) shall be proposed as part of the annual review conducted under section E2.1. of this enclosure, above. When earlier implementation is required, the JSC may send proposed changes to the General Counsel of the Department of Defense, for coordination under DoD Directive 5500.1 (reference (g)).

E2.3. PROPOSALS TO AMEND THE UCMJ (REFERENCE (c))

The JSC may determine that the efficient administration of military justice within the Armed Services requires amendments to reference (c), or that a desired amendment to the Manual for Courts-Martial (reference (b)) makes necessary an amendment to reference (c). In such cases, the JSC shall forward to the General Counsel of the Department of Defense, a legislative proposal to change reference (c). The General

Counsel of the Department of Defense may direct that the JSC forward any such legislative proposal to the Code Committee for its consideration under Article 146, UCMJ.

E2.4. PUBLIC NOTICE AND MEETING

E2.4.1. Proposals to amend reference (c) are not governed by the procedures set out in this section. (See reference (f). This section applies only to the JSC recommendations to amend reference (b).)

E2.4.2. It is DoD policy to encourage public participation in the JSC's review of reference (b). Notice that the Department of Defense, through the JSC, intends to propose changes to reference (b) normally shall be published in the Federal Register before submission of such changes to the President. This notice is not required when the Secretary of Defense in his sole and unreviewable discretion proposes that the President issue the change without such notice on the basis that public notice procedures, as set forth in this Directive, are unnecessary or contrary to the sound administration of military justice, or a Manual for Courts-Martial change corresponding to legislation is expeditiously required to keep reference (b) current and consistent with changes in applicable law.

E2.4.3. The Office of General Counsel of the Department of Defense shall facilitate publishing the Federal Register notice required under this section.

E2.4.4. The notice under this section shall consist of the publication of the full text of the proposed changes, including discussion and analysis, unless the General Counsel of the Department of Defense determines that such publication in full would unduly burden the Federal Register, the time and place where a copy of the proposed change may be examined, and the procedure for obtaining access to or a copy of the proposed change.

E2.4.5. A period of not fewer than 60 days after publication of notice normally shall be allowed for public comment, but a shorter period may be authorized when the General Counsel of the Department of Defense determines that a 60-day period is unnecessary or is contrary to the sound administration of military justice. The Federal Register notice shall normally indicate that public comments shall be submitted to the Executive Secretary of the JSC.

E2.4.6. The JSC shall provide notice in the Federal Register and hold a public meeting during the public comment period, where interested persons shall be given a reasonable opportunity to submit views on any of the proposed changes contained in the annual review. Public proposals and comments to the JSC should include a reference to the specific provision to be changed, a rational for the proposed change, and specific and detailed proposed language to replace the current language. Incomplete submissions might be insufficient to receive the consideration desired. The JSC shall seek to consider all views presented at the public meeting as well as any written comments submitted during the 60-day period when determining the final form of any proposed amendments to reference (b).

E2.5. INTERNAL RULES AND RECORD-KEEPING

E2.5.1. In furthering DoD policy, studying issues, or performing other duties relating to the administration of military justice, the JSC may establish internal rules governing its operation.

E2.5.2. The JSC shall create a file system and maintain appropriate JSC records.

APPENDIX 27
PUNITIVE ARTICLES APPLICABLE TO SEXUAL ASSAULT OFFENSES COMMITTED PRIOR TO 1 OCTOBER 2007

The punitive articles contained in this appendix were replaced or superseded by changes to Article 120, Uniform Code of Military Justice, contained in the National Defense Authorization Act for 2006. The effective date of the new Article 120 provision was 1 October 2007. Offenses occurring prior to this effective date must be charged under the former provisions of Article 120 or Article 134, which are listed below:

45. Article 120—Rape and carnal knowledge

a. *Text.*

(a) Any person subject to this chapter who commits an act of sexual intercourse by force and without consent, is guilty of rape and shall be punished by death or such other punishment as a court-martial may direct.

(b) Any person subject to this chapter who, under circumstances not amounting to rape, commits an act of sexual intercourse with a person—

(1) who is not his or her spouse; and

(2) who has not attained the age of sixteen years, is guilty of carnal knowledge and shall be punished as a court-martial may direct.

(c) Penetration, however slight, is sufficient to complete either of these offenses.

(d)(1) In a prosecution under subsection (b), it is an affirmative defense that—

(A) the person with whom the accused committed the act of sexual intercourse had at the time of the alleged offense attained the age of twelve years; and

(B) the accused reasonably believed that the person had at the time of the alleged offense attained the age of 16 years.

(2) The accused has the burden of proving a defense under subparagraph (d)(1) by a preponderance of the evidence.

b. *Elements.*

(1) *Rape.*

(a) That the accused committed an act of sexual intercourse; and

(b) That the act of sexual intercourse was done by force and without consent.

(2) *Carnal knowledge.*

(a) That the accused committed an act of sexual intercourse with a certain person;

(b) That the person was not the accused's spouse; and

(c)(1) That at the time of the sexual intercourse the person was under the age of 12; or

(2) That at the time of the sexual intercourse the person had attained the age of 12 but was under the age of 16.

c. *Explanation.*

(1) *Rape.*

(a) *Nature of offense.* Rape is sexual intercourse by a person, executed by force and without consent of the victim. It may be committed on a victim of any age. Any penetration, however slight, is sufficient to complete the offense.

(b) *Force and lack of consent.* Force and lack of consent are necessary to the offense. Thus, if the victim consents to the act, it is not rape. The lack of consent required, however, is more than mere lack of acquiescence. If a victim in possession of his or her mental faculties fails to make lack of consent reasonably manifest by taking such measures of resistance as are called for by the circumstances, the inference may be drawn that the victim did consent. Consent, however, may not be inferred if resistance would have been futile, where resistance is overcome by threats of death or great bodily harm, or where the victim is unable to resist because of the lack of mental or physical faculties. In such a case there is no consent and the force involved in penetration will suffice. All the surrounding circumstances are to be considered in determining whether a victim gave consent, or whether he or she failed or ceased to resist only because of a reasonable fear of death or grievous bodily harm. If there is actual consent, although obtained by fraud, the act is not rape, but if to the accused's knowledge the victim is of unsound mind or unconscious to an extent rendering him or her incapable of giving consent, the act is rape. Likewise, the acquiescence of a child of such tender years that he or she is incapable of understanding the nature of the act is not consent.

(c) *Character of victim. See* Mil. R. Evid. 412 concerning rules of evidence relating to an alleged rape victim's character.

(2) *Carnal knowledge.* "Carnal knowledge" is sexual intercourse under circumstances not amounting to rape, with a person who is not the accused's spouse and who has not attained the age of 16 years. Any penetration, however slight, is sufficient to complete the offense. It is a defense, however, which the accused must prove by a preponderance of the evidence, that at the time of the act of sexual intercourse, the person with whom the accused committed the act of sexual intercourse was at least 12 years of age, and that the accused reasonably believed that this same person was at least 16 years of age.

d. *Lesser included offenses.*

(1) *Rape.*

(a) Article 128—assault; assault consummated by a battery

(b) Article 134—assault with intent to commit rape

(c) Article 134—indecent assault

(d) Article 80—attempts

(e) Article 120(b)—carnal knowledge

(2) *Carnal knowledge.*

(a) Article 134—indecent acts or liberties with a person under 16

(b) Article 80—attempts

e. *Maximum punishment.*

(1) *Rape.* Death or such other punishment as a court-martial may direct.

(2) *Carnal knowledge with a child who, at the time of the offense, has attained the age of 12 years.* Dishonorable discharge, forfeiture of all pay and allowances, and confinement for 20 years.

(3) *Carnal knowledge with a child under the age of 12 years at the time of the offense.* Dishonorable discharge, forfeiture of all pay and allowances, and confinement for life without eligibility for parole.

f. *Sample specifications.*

(1) *Rape.* In that (personal jurisdiction data), did, (at/on board — location) (subject - matter jurisdiction data, if required), on or about ______, rape, ______ (a person under the age of 12) (a person who had attained the age of 12 but was under the age of 16).

(2) *Carnal knowledge.* In that (personal jurisdiction data), did, (at/on board — location) (subject - matter jurisdiction data, if required), on or about ______, commit the offense of carnal knowledge with ______, (a person under the age of 12) (a person who attained the age of 12 but was under the age of 16).

63. Article 134—(Assault—indecent)

a. *Text. See* paragraph 60.

b. *Elements.*

(1) That the accused assaulted a certain person not the spouse of the accused in a certain manner;

(2) That the acts were done with the intent to gratify the lust or sexual desires of the accused; and

(3) That, under the circumstances, the conduct of the accused was to the prejudice of good order and discipline in the armed forces or was of a nature to bring discredit upon the armed forces.

c. *Explanation.* See paragraph 54c for a discussion of assault. Specific intent is an element of this offense. For a definition of 'indecent', *see* paragraph 90*c*.

d. *Lesser included offenses.*

(1) Article 128—assault consummated by a battery; assault

(2) Article 134—indecent acts

(3) Article 80—attempts

e. *Maximum punishment.* Dishonorable discharge, forfeiture of all pay and allowances, and confinement for 5 years.

f. *Sample specification.* In that (personal jurisdiction data), did (at/on board—location), (subject-matter jurisdiction data, if required), on or about ______, commit an indecent assault upon a person not his/her wife/husband by ______, with intent to gratify his/her (lust) (sexual desires).

87. Article 134—(Indecent acts or liberties with a child)

a. *Text. See* paragraph 60.

b. *Elements.*

(1) *Physical contact.*

(a) That the accused committed a certain act upon or with the body of a certain person;

(b) That the person was under 16 years of age and not the spouse of the accused;

(c) That the act of the accused was indecent;

(d) That the accused committed the act with intent to arouse, appeal to, or gratify the lust, passions, or sexual desires of the accused, the victim, or both; and

(e) That, under the circumstances, the conduct of the accused was to the prejudice of good order and discipline in the armed forces or was of a nature to bring discredit upon the armed forces.

(2) *No physical contact.*

(a) That the accused committed a certain act;

(b) That the act amounted to the taking of indecent liberties with a certain person;

(c) That the accused committed the act in the presence of this person;

(d) That this person was under 16 years of age and not the spouse of the accused;

(e) That the accused committed the act with the intent to arouse, appeal to, or gratify the lust, passions, or sexual desires of the accused, the victim, or both; and

(f) That, under the circumstances, the conduct of the accused was to the prejudice of good order and discipline in the armed forces or was of a nature to bring discredit upon the armed forces.

c. *Explanation.*

(1) *Consent.* Lack of consent by the child to the act or conduct is not essential to this offense; consent is not a defense.

(2) *Indecent liberties.* When a person is charged with taking indecent liberties, the liberties must be taken in the physical presence of the child, but physical contact is not required. Thus, one who with the requisite intent exposes one's private parts to a child under 16 years of age may be found guilty of this offense. An indecent liberty may consist of communication of indecent language as long as the communication is made in the physical presence of the child.

(3) *Indecent. See* paragraph 89c and 90c.

d. *Lesser included offense.*

(1) Article 134—indecent acts with another

(2) Article 128—assault; assault consummated by a battery

(3) Article 80—attempts

e. *Maximum punishment.* Dishonorable discharge, forfeiture of all pay and allowances, and confinement for 7 years.

f. *Sample specification.* In that (personal jurisdiction data), did, (at/on board — location) (subject - matter jurisdiction data, if required), on or about ______, (take (indecent) liberties with) (commit an indecent act (upon) (with) the body of) ______, a (female) (male) under 16 years of age, not the (wife) (husband) of the said ______, by (fondling (her) (him) and placing his/her hands upon (her) (his) leg and private parts) (   ), with intent to (arouse) (appeal to) (gratify) the (lust) (passion) (sexual desires) of the said (   ).

88. Article 134—(Indecent exposure)

a. *Text. See* paragraph 60.

b. *Elements.*

(1) That the accused exposed a certain part of the accused's body to public view in an indecent manner;

(2) That the exposure was willful and wrongful; and

(3) That, under the circumstances, the accused's conduct was to the prejudice of good order and discipline in the armed forces or was of a nature to bring discredit upon the armed forces.

c. *Explanation.* "Willful" means an intentional exposure to public view. Negligent indecent exposure is not punishable as a violation of the code. See paragraph 90c concerning "indecent."

d. *Lesser included offense.* Article 80—attempts

e. *Maximum punishment.* Bad - conduct discharge, forfeiture of all pay and allowances, and confinement for 6 months.

f. *Sample specification.* In that (personal jurisdiction data), did (at/on board—location) (subject-matter jurisdiction data, if required), on or about ______, while (at a barracks window) (   ) willfully and wrongfully expose in an indecent manner to public view his or her ______.

90. Article 134—(Indecent acts with another)

a. *Text. See* paragraph 60.

b. *Elements.*

(1) That the accused committed a certain wrongful act with a certain person;

(2) That the act was indecent; and

(3) That, under the circumstances, the conduct of the accused was to the prejudice of good order and discipline in the armed forces or was of a nature to bring discredit upon the armed forces.

c. *Explanation.* "Indecent" signifies that form of immorality relating to sexual impurity which is not only grossly vulgar, obscene, and repugnant to common propriety, but tends to excite lust and deprave the morals with respect to sexual relations.

d. *Lesser included offense.* Article 80—attempts

e. *Maximum punishment.* Dishonorable discharge, forfeiture of all pay and allowances, and confinement for 5 years.

f. *Sample specification.* In that (personal jurisdiction data), did (at/on board—location) (subject-matter jurisdiction data, if required), on or about ______, wrongfully commit an indecent act with ______ by ______.

MCM INDEX